KT-430-046

READER'S DIGEST NEW ENCYCLOPEDIA *of* GARDEN PLANTS & FLOWERS

Published by The Reader's Digest Association Limited · London · New York · Sydney · Cape Town · Montreal

READER'S DIGEST NEW ENCYCLOPEDIA OF GARDEN PLANTS & FLOWERS was edited and designed by The Reader's Digest Association Limited, London.

Printed in France.
ISBN 0 276 42191 4

CONSULTANT EDITORS
Kenneth A. Beckett Barbara Haynes

CONTRIBUTORS
John Amand
Hugh Angus
Bill Ash
Helen L. Baldwin
Richard E. Baldwin
Peter Barnes
Trevor Bath
Kathryn Bradley-Hole
Denis Bradshaw
Ursula Buchan
Stephen Cafferty
Andi Clevely
Dilys Davies
Li De-Zhu
John A. Dyter
John Edgeley
Jack Elliott
Sue Fisher
Eileen Galbally
Jim Gardiner
Michael Gibson
Peter Gregory
Diana Grenfell
Christine Grey-Wilson
Christopher Grey-Wilson
Roger Grounds
John Howells
Alan Hulme
David Hunt
Graham Hutchins
Noel Kingsbury
Colin Lewis
Paul Lewis
Duncan Lowe
David McClintock
Graham Madill
Colin Morgan
John Bramwell Paton
Pauline Pears
Sue Phillips
Christine Skelmersdale
David Small
Anne Stevens
John Sutton
Philip Swindells
Alan Toogood
Timothy Walker
John Edward James White
Peter Wood
Will Giles
Mike Grey
Jack Hayward
Roy Knipe
Sandra Pond
Tamara Sternberg
Gill Tomblin

PLANT IDENTIFIER COMPILER
Charlie Butterworth

PHOTOGRAPHERS
Jonathan Buckley
Vernon Morgan
Emma Peios
Richard Surman
Pia Tryde
Juliet Wade
Jo Whitworth
Justyn Wilsmore

ILLUSTRATORS
Ian Atkinson
Peter Barrat
Wendy Bramall
Graham Byfield
Gavin Dunn

SPECIALIST ADVISERS
Peter Addington
Wendy Akers
James Allison
Sandra Bell
Peter Boyce
Madeleine Broome
David Lawrence Brown
Alan Cook
Anna Corbett
Ruth Davies
Peter Edwards
Barrie Frankland
Jack G. Grint
Peter William Harkness
Chris Lowe
Charles Miller
Steve Nickells
Andrew Norton
Paul Picton
Martin Raymond Puddle
David Pyecraft
Eric V. Rogers
Barbara Segall
Michael Upward
Christine Walkden

The publishers wish to thank the following organisations and their staff for help in compiling *New Encyclopedia of Garden Plants & Flowers*

Capel Manor Horticultural and Environmental Centre, Enfield, Middlesex
Chelsea Physic Garden, London
Sir Harold Hillier Gardens and Arboretum, Ampfield, Hampshire
Henry Doubleday Research Association, Ryton on Dunsmore, Warwickshire
Merrist Wood College, Worplesdon, Surrey
Pershore College, Pershore, Worcestershire
Royal Botanic Gardens, Kew, Surrey
Royal Horticultural Society Gardens, Wisley, Surrey
Royal Horticultural Society Lindley Library, London
Savill Gardens, Windsor, Berkshire

The following people, organisations and companies also assisted in the making of this book

a

Abbey Dore Court Gardens, Hereford & Worcester • Acton Beauchamp Roses, Acton Beauchamp, Hereford & Worcester • Agar's Nursery, Lymington, Hampshire • Alpine Garden Society • Anglia Alpines & Herbs Ltd, Huntingdon, Cambridgeshire • J.B. Angrave, Hadlow, Kent • Anthony Archer-Wills Ltd, West Chiltington, West Sussex • Apple Court, Lymington, Hampshire • Architectural Plants, Horsham, West Sussex • Arley House, Nr Bewdley, Hereford & Worcester • Arne Herbs, Chew Magna, Avon • Arrow Cottage, Ledgemoor, Hereford & Worcester • Avon Bulbs, South Petherton, Somerset • Axletree Nursery, Rye, East Sussex

b

Barncroft Nurseries, Stoke-on-Trent, Staffordshire • Barnhawk Nursery, Fordingbridge, Hampshire • Batsford Arboretum, Moreton-in-Marsh, Gloucestershire • Bayston Hill Nurseries, Bayley's Garden Centre, Shrewsbury, Shropshire • Beechcroft Nursery, Ewell, Surrey • Beeches Nursery, Saffron Walden, Essex • Beth Chatto Gardens Ltd, Elmstead Market, Colchester, Essex • Rn & R Bewley, Durham • The Birmingham Botanical Gardens • Bodenham Arboretum, Wolverley, Hereford & Worcester • The Botanic Nursery, Nr Melksham, Wiltshire • Bourton House Garden, Bourton-on-the-Hill, Gloucestershire • Bouts Cottage Nurseries, Inkberrow, Hereford & Worcester • Brackenbury Coombe, Gloucestershire • J Bradshaw & Son, Busheyfields Nursery, Herne Bay, Kent • Brandy Mount House, Hampshire • Brian and Heather Hiley Nursery, Wallington, Surrey • Brian Goodey Cacti, Southfield Nurseries, Bourne, Lincolnshire • Bridgemere Nurseries, Nr Nantwich, Cheshire • Broadleigh Gardens, Taunton, Somerset • Brockings Exotics, North Petherwin, Cornwall • Brodick Castle and Country Park, Isle of Arran, Scotland • Mrs P. J. Brown, Westlees Farm, Westcott, Surrey • Burncoose & Southdown Nurseries, Redruth, Cornwall

c

Cambridge University Botanic Garden • Camp Cottage, Highleadon, Nr Newent, Gloucestershire • Cannington College, Nr Bridgwater, Somerset • Caves Folly Nurseries, Hereford & Worcester • Cedarwood Lily Farm, Stoke on Trent, Staffordshire • Chennels Gate, Eardisley, Kington, Hereford & Worcester • Churchills Garden Nursery, Chudleigh, Devon • Churchtown Nurseries • The Citrus Centre, Pulborough, West Sussex • Clifton Nurseries, London • Colgrave Seeds Ltd, West Adderbury, Oxon • Collinwood Nurseries, Macclesfield, Cheshire • Conderton Manor, Tewkesbury, Hereford & Worcester • The Conservatory, Gomshall, Guildford, Surrey • Cotswold Garden Flowers, Evesham, Hereford & Worcester • County Park Nursery, Hornchurch, Essex • Craig House Cacti, Lancashire • J. Craven Garden Creation, Doncaster • Creative Landscapes, Hartlebury, Kidderminster

d

David Austin Roses Ltd, Albrighton, West Midlands • Delamare Street Nurseries, Winsford, Cheshire • D'Arcy & Everest, Huntingdon, Cambridgeshire • Dibley's Nurseries, Ruthin, Clwyd • Dobwalls, Higman Close, Cornwall • Drysdale Garden Exotics, Fordingbridge, Hampshire • Duchy of Cornwall, Lostwithiel, Cornwall • Dyffryn Botanical Garden, Cardiff

e-f

Eastgrove Cottage Garden Nursery, Little Witley, Hereford & Worcester • East Lambrook Manor Garden, Nr South Petherton, Somerset • Edrom Nurseries, Coldingham, Eyemouth, Berwick-on-Tweed • Fibrex Nurseries Ltd, Stratford-upon-Avon, Warwickshire • Fir Tree Farm Nursery, Falmouth, Cornwall • Kaytie Fisher, Ockham, Surrey • Floral Guernsey • Four Seasons, Norwich, Norfolk • Foxgrove Plants, Nr Newbury, Berkshire • Fuchsia Vale Nurseries, Kidderminster, Hereford & Worcester

g

The Gardens of the Rose, St Albans, Hertfordshire • Glebe Cottage Plants, Umberleigh, North Devon • Goldbrook Hostas, Eye, Suffolk • Goscote Nurseries Ltd, Cossington, Leicestershire • Grange Court • Grange Farm Nursery, Malvern, Hereford & Worcester • Great Campston, Llanushangel, Abergavenny • Greenacres Nursery, Bringsty, Bromyard, Hereford & Worcester • Greenholm Nurseries Ltd, Kingston Seymour Clevedon, Avon • Mr G.S. Greenway, Priorswood Clematis, Ware, Hertfordshire • Grove Cottage, Lower Lydbrook, Gloucestershire

h-i

Hadlow College of Agriculture and Horticulture • Hall Farm Nursery, Kinnerley, Shropshire • Hambrooks, Titchfield, Fareham, Hampshire • The Hannays of Bath, Bathwick, Bath, Avon • Hardy Exotics, Penzance, Cornwall • Hardy's Cottage Garden Plants, Whitchurch, Hampshire • Harlow Carr Botanical Gardens, Crag Lane, Harrogate • Hatsford Fuchsias, Aylton, Ledbury, Hereford & Worcester • Heldon Nursery, Uttoxeter, Staffordshire • Ivan Hicks • Hidcote Manor Garden, Hidcote Bartrim, Gloucestershire • Highgates Nursery, Belper, Derbyshire • Mr A. D. Hill, Umberleigh, Devon • The Hillier Garden, Nr Alcester, Warwickshire • Hillview Hardy Plants, Nr Bridgnorth, Shropshire • Hoecroft Plants, Dereham, Norfolk • Holehird, Windermere, Cumbria • Holly Gate Cactus Nursery, Ashington, West Sussex • Hoo House Nursery, Tewkesbury, Gloucestershire • Hopleys Plants Ltd, Much Hadham, Hertfordshire • Hunts Court Garden and Nursery, North Nibley, Gloucestershire • W.E. Th. Ingwerson Ltd, East Grinstead, West Sussex

j-k

Jacques Amand Ltd, Stanmore, Middlesex • Jasmine Cottage Gardens, Clevedon, North Somerset • Jeffs and Southorn • Jekkas Herb Farm, Alveston, Bristol • John Austen & Co, Covent Garden, London • Keepers Nursery, Maidstone, Kent • Kettlesing Nurseries • Kingsfield Conservation Nursery, Chard, Somerset • Kingston Maurward College, Dorchester, Dorset • Knap Hill and Slocock Nurseries, Woking, Surrey • Knoll Gardens, Nr Wimborne, Dorset

l

Lacham College, Lacock, Chippenham, Wiltshire • Langley Boxwood Nursery, Rake, Hampshire • Langthorns Plantery, Dunmow, Essex • Lingen Alpine Nursery, Nr Bucknell, Shropshire • Little Brook Fuchsia, Ash Green, Hampshire • Longstock Park Gardens, Nr Stockbridge, Hampshire • Lower Severalls Herb Nursery, Crewkerne, Somerset • Lydford Alpine Nursery, Okehampton, Devon

m

Macpennys Garden Nurseries, Christchurch, Dorset • Mallet Court Nursery • Malvern Flower Shows, Three Counties Showground, Great Malvern • Marston Exotics, Madley, Herefordshire • Marwood Hill Gardens, Barnstaple, Devon • Maureen Iddon Nursery • The Mead Nursery, Brokerswood, Nr Westbury, Wiltshire • Merriments Gardens, Hurst Green, East Sussex • Merton Nurseries, Shrewsbury, Shropshire • MJM Nursery, Sandiacre, Nottingham

n

Naked Cross Nurseries, Wimborne, Dorset • National Bamboo Collection, Drysdale Garden Exotics, Fordingbridge, Hampshire • Newby Hall Gardens, Ripon, Yorkshire • Nicky's Rock Garden Nursery, Honiton, Devon • Miss Sylvia Norton, Weavers Cottage, Wickham, Cambridge • Notcutts Nurseries

o

Oland Plants, Sawley • Old Court Nurseries, Nr Malvern, Worcestershire • Overcourt Garden Nursery, Sutton St Nicholas, Hereford & Worcester • Owen Bros Nursery, Bevere, Hereford & Worcester • Oxford Botanical Gardens, Oxford

p-q

Pantiles Nurseries Ltd, Chertsey, Surrey • Paradise Centre, Bures, Suffolk • Park Green Nurseries, Suffolk • Patio Clematis, Bransford Garden Plants, Bransford, Hereford & Worcester • Pear Tree Cottage, Stapely, Somerset • Penpregwm Plants, Abergevenny, Gwent • Pentwyn Cottage Garden, Bacton, Hereford & Worcester • Perryhill Nurseries, Hartfield, East Sussex • Peter Beales Roses, Attleborough, Norfolk • Philip Fivey & Sons, Leicester • Picton Garden, Colwall, Hereford & Worcester • Plantasia, Parc Tawe, West Glamorgan, Swansea • The Plant Lovers, Lincolnshire • The Plantsman Nursery, Okehampton, Devon • Plantworld Botanic Gardens, Newton Abbot, Devon • Plaxtol Nurseries, Sevenoaks, Kent • Mr Poulton and Mr Stenlake, St Johns, Hereford & Worcester • Potash Nurseries, Stowmarket, Suffolk • Potterton & Martin, Caistor, Lincolnshire • Preen Manor Church, Nr Church Stretton, Shropshire • The Priory, Tewkesbury, Gloucestershire • Queen Mary's Rose Garden, Regent's Park, London • Queenswood County Park, Hereford & Worcester

r

R.D. Plants, Axminster, Devon • Ravensthorpe Nursery, Ravensthorpe, Northamptonshire • Redwood House • Regent's Park, London • G. Reuthe Ltd, Crown Point Nursery, Nr Sevenoaks, Kent • Rhodes & Rockliffe, Nazeing, Essex • Roundhay Park, Leeds, Yorkshire • Rowden Gardens, Nr Tavistock, Devon • Royal Horticultural Society Chelsea Flower Show • Royal Horticultural Society Hampton Court Palace Flower Show • Royal Horticultural Society Hyde Hall • Royal Horticultural Society Rosemoor • Rumsey Gardens, Waterlooville, Hampshire • Rushfields of Ledbury, Ledbury, Hereford & Worcester

s

Jean Sambrook • Scotts Nurseries (Merriott) Ltd, Merriott, Somerset • Sherborne Garden, Litton, Avon • Shillinglee Nursery, Chiddingfold, Surrey • Snape Cottage, Chaffeymoor, Dorset • Southcombe Nurseries, Southcombe Gardens, Exeter, Devon • Southfield Nurseries, Lincolnshire • Southview Nurseries, Basingstoke, Hampshire • Springfields Gardens, Spalding, Lincolnshire • Springwood Pleione • Starborough Nursery, Edenbridge, Kent • Steven Bailey Ltd, Lymington, Hampshire • Richard Stockwell, Sherwood, Nottinghamshire • Stone House, Wellington, Hereford & Worcester • Stone House Cottage Nurseries, Stone, Nr Kidderminster, Hereford & Worcester • Stourton House & Nutkin Nursery, Ukfield, East Sussex • Strawberry Cottage, Leominster, Hereford & Worcester • Swallow Hayes, Albrighton, Shropshire • Swanland Nurseries, Hull, East Yorkshire • Swansea Botanic Gardens, Clyne Garden, Swansea

t

O.A. Taylor & Sons, Spalding, Lincolnshire • Taylor Service & Supplies, Cheshire • A. & A. Thorp, Theddingworth, Leicestershire • Three Counties Nurseries, Bridport, Dorset • Tin Penny Cottage, Nr Miserden, Stroud, Gloucestershire • Mrs S.M. Tracey, Shaugh Prior, Devon • Treasures of Tenbury Ltd, Burford House Gardens, Tenbury Wells, Hereford & Worcester • Trebah Garden, Falmouth, Cornwall • Trehane Camellia Nursery, Wimborne, Dorset • Tresco Abbey Gardens, Isles of Scilly • Trevi Garden, Hartpury, Gloucestershire • The Tropical Rainforest Nursery, Leeds

u-v

Ulverscroft Grange Nursery, Ulverscroft, Leicestershire • University of Bristol Botanical Garden • University of Exeter • University of Southampton • The Urn Cottage, Avon • Usual & Unusual Plants, Hailsham, East Sussex • Ventnor Botanic Garden, Isle of Wight

w-z

Wakehurst Place Garden, Ardingly, West Sussex • J. Walker's Bulbs, Spalding, Lincolnshire • Mr & Mrs Ward, 53 Ladywood, Eastleigh, Hampshire • Water Meadow Nursery, Cheriton, Hampshire • Waterperry Gardens, Wheatley, Oxfordshire • Webbs Garden Centres, Wychbold, Droitwich, Hereford & Worcester • Westonbirt Arboretum, Tetbury, Gloucestershire • The Wild Flower Centre, Loddon, Norfolk • Wilford Bulb Co. Ltd, East Leake, Leicestershire • Willow Cottage, Ross on Wye, Gloucestershire • Mr & Mrs J.H. Wood, Nr Mayhill, Gloucestershire • Woodfield Brothers, Stratford-upon-Avon, Warwickshire • Woodland Services and Supplies Ltd, Abergavenny, Gwent • Woodpeckers, Bidford-on-Avon, Warwickshire • Woodstock Orchids & Exotics, Milton Keynes • Writtle College, Chelmsford, Essex • Wychwood Waterlily and Carp Farm, Odiham, Hampshire

Contents of this book

Introduction

For more than two decades the Reader's Digest *Encyclopaedia of Garden Plants and Flowers* has been an acknowledged classic among gardening reference books. Now, after countless reprints and revisions, the time has come for a completely new book to meet the demands of a new era of gardening. The *New Encyclopedia of Garden Plants & Flowers* has been designed to preserve and build on the strengths of its predecessor while at the same time reflecting the profound changes that have occurred in gardening practice and the vast number of new plants available to modern gardeners. The consultants, writers, photographers and editors who worked on this book hope that it will prove both a worthy successor to the old encyclopedia and a source of untiring inspiration and delight to the new generation now discovering that fascinating and rewarding enthusiasm – a passion for plants.

How to use this book

If you know the name of a plant – either the common English name or the Latin botanical name – you can turn straight to the main section of the encyclopedia (pp. 10-718) which contains A-Z entries on hundreds of the most important genera, with thousands of synonyms and common names given as cross-references.

But gardeners do not always know the name of the plant they want to grow. To overcome this problem, an easy-to-use Plant Identifier chart has been specially devised for this book – see pp.750-95. Alternatively, if you are faced with a specific problem such as a damp, shady corner, or a requirement such as autumn colour, the place to start is with Plants for Special Purposes (pp.796-800).

Gardeners interested in particular types of plants, such as bamboos, ferns or orchids, or in using plants in a certain way, such as in a rock garden or for topiary, will find the 21 special features in the main section of the book helpful. At the back of the book are sections on fruit and vegetable gardening (ornamental varieties appear in the main A-Z section); cultivation, propagation and pruning techniques; and the diagnosis, prevention and treatment of pests and diseases. Finally, a Glossary has been included at the end of the book, which explains technical terms in layman's language.

Understanding plant names

For the gardener, the naming of a plant begins with its genus – roughly the equivalent of a surname. Each genus belongs to a larger group called a family, and above that to yet larger groupings, but these bear little practical relevance to gardening. Within a genus, plants are closely related and share important characteristics. They may, but need not, also look similar and have similar requirements. Genera are sub-divided into species, and the species name is written after the genus name. Thus the plant *Abutilon vitifolium* belongs to the genus *Abutilon* and is of the species *vitifolium*. Plants of the same species are very similar physically and genetically, and can interbreed. Even so, some wild species show enough variability to require further division into sub-species (ssp.), variety (var.) or forma (f.), the lowest level in plant classification. This nomenclature is international, and is presented with Latin names in italics (for example, *Abutilon vitifolium* var. *album*).

In cultivation, plants are frequently bred to enhance characteristics such as flower size, vigour, height or leaf variegation. This is known as hybridisation and the resulting plants are called cultivars (cultivated varieties) and given a cultivar name after the species name or, if the species is not known, after the genus name. The cultivar name is not italicised but appears in quotation marks (for example, *Abutilon vitifolium* 'Veronica Tennant', *Rosa* 'Masquerade').

Where variability exists among plants with the same parentage, they are described as groups, hybrids, series or selections (for example, *Anemone coronaria* De Caen Group, *Impatiens* New Guinea Hybrids). Hybrids between species of the same genus are indicated by a multiplication sign between the genus and the species name (for example, *Abutilon* × *suntense*). Hybrids bred from different genera take a multiplication sign before the genus name (for example, × *Fatshedera lizei*) while those created by grafting plants of different genera take a plus sign (for example, + *Laburnocytisus*).

Name changes & synonyms

The nomenclature followed in this book is based on that set out in *The International Code of Botanical Nomenclature* and *The International Code of Nomenclature for Cultivated Plants*. Plant classifications do change, however, as botanists acquire new information. Every attempt has been made to incorporate changes up to the time of going to press. However, many older synonyms and well-known common names have also been listed as cross-references.

Principles of selection

The plants recommended in this encyclopedia have been chosen by experts because they are easy to obtain and able to thrive in most gardens in Britain. Within these broad criteria a very wide range of plants is represented, both in terms of type (such as woody, perennial, annual or bulbous) and in the rewards they offer, whether of beauty, usefulness or reliability. The vast majority are suitable for gardeners of all levels, including complete beginners, but there are also plenty of suggestions for enthusiasts, and to encourage gardeners to branch out and explore the exciting ranges now available from specialist nurseries.

How entries are structured

The genus entries in this book have been designed for ease of use. Immediately beneath the genus name appear any common names applicable to the whole genus, and the family name. Then follows an overall description of the genus, the variety of plants it contains, and their main rewards and uses in the garden. To avoid repetition, any features common to all the plants

Order of plant names used in the encyclopedia

Abutilon	genus name
Flowering maple	common name(s) applying to whole genus
Malvaceae	family name
A. vitifolium	species
A. vitifolium var. *album*	natural variety
A. vitifolium 'Veronica Tennant'	cultivated variety (cultivar)
A. × *suntense*	natural hybrid
A. 'Ashford Red'	cultivated hybrid

Plant types

annual	Plant that completes its life cycle in a single year.
biennial	Plant that completes its life cycle in two years.
climber	Plant that has developed adaptations that enable it to climb, such as tendrils, stem roots, self-clinging pads or long flexible stems.
deciduous	Plant that sheds its foliage annually.
evergreen	Perennial plant that remains green throughout the year.
herbaceous	Any plant that does not form a persistent woody stem. Botanically, this includes annuals and bulbs, but in general usage the term commonly refers to perennial plants that die back in autumn and resprout again in spring.
perennial	Plant that lives for three years or more.
semi-evergreen	Plant that annually sheds some but not all of its leaves.
shrub	Woody plant that produces several stems from its base.
tree	Woody plant with a single stem supporting a branching head.

described in the entry are generally covered in the introduction. Any particular drawbacks such as toxicity and invasiveness are also mentioned.

Individually recommended plants are then listed alphabetically and described in detail. Where both a species and its varieties are mentioned, only the species receives a full description; the varieties are listed in an indented paragraph immediately after the species and only described in so far as they differ from it. Sometimes, however, varieties are not associated with a species, or the species is not described, in which case they are independently listed and fully described in their own right.

The symbol ♀ indicates that a plant holds the Royal Horticultural Society's Award of Garden Merit. Synonyms and common names that apply to a species or variety appear in brackets immediately after the botanical name. While every care has been taken to ensure that plant descriptions are as precise as possible, these are necessarily based on average specimens growing in average conditions, and a certain amount of variation will inevitably occur.

Hardiness

Plants described as hardy are capable of surviving most British winters out of doors, while half-hardy plants are less reliable and need protection. Plants referred to as tender usually originate from warmer or sub-tropical regions and, while they may flourish outside during summer, will be cut down by the first frost of autumn.

Height and spread

Plant size is a crucial factor in garden planning; spread in particular is useful as an indication of planting distance. The figures given in the book are for average specimens grown in appropriate conditions, and individual plants may vary slightly from the norm. In some cases it has been necessary to give a range rather than a single figure. For trees, interim measurements are given as appropriate – usually at ten, fifteen or twenty years – as well as at full mature size, and shrubs at five years and at maturity. The measurements given for perennials are for well-established plants, generally of about two or three years. For bulbous plants, only a height measurement is given, as the upright habit and brief period above ground make spread largely irrelevant. The height given for houseplants is what is normal for indoor cultivation in Britain, rather than the height that may be achieved in the natural habitat.

Cultivation, propagation, pruning, and pests and diseases

While specific advice appears in every genus entry, the basic techniques of good plant care are explained and illustrated in the reference sections on pp. 801-59.

Because of climatic variations across the British Isles, flowering periods and times for operations such as sowing seed are generally given as seasons rather than months.

For the purposes of this book greenhouses are described as 'cold' (completely unheated, with temperatures likely to drop below freezing in winter), 'cool' (heated to maintain a temperature above 4°C (39°F)) or 'warm' (heated to maintain a temperature above 10°C (50°F)).

Illustrations in this book

The many thousands of photographs in this book have been specially commissioned and selected to help gardeners to choose and plan planting schemes, and to aid in plant identification. While every attempt has been made to show representative specimens, factors such as soil type; a light, shady, protected or exposed site; and natural variation among plant populations, will inevitably affect the colour, size and habit of any individual example.

The small watercolour illustrations that appear in many entries are not intended to be accurate botanical representations, but rather to give a subjective impression of a plant's overall appearance and habit.

Helping with conservation

Across the world, natural habitats and flora are under threat, and unfortunately gardening practices are not always blameless. However, there are many steps that responsible gardeners can take to ensure that their hobby does not have a detrimental effect. Excellent peat substitutes are now available and should be used whenever possible to preserve threatened peat bogs. Limestone, which was once much used in landscaping and rockeries, is similarly irreplaceable and supports a unique flora. Most rock and alpine plants do just as well without it in carefully prepared raised beds, among artificial 'rocks' or on scree.

Before buying plants, bulbs or seeds, check that they have been raised in cultivation and not taken from the wild, particularly in the case of orchids, bulbs, alpines, palms, cacti and succulents. Many sellers declare the source of their stock; if not, it is wise to ask, both to set your own mind at ease and to raise awareness in the trade.

However tempting, resist the urge to collect plants from the wild when travelling. Although packets of seed are admitted from most countries, with more generous allowances within the European Union, other plant material is subject to many restrictions. These are set out in the *Traveller's guide to bringing plants back from abroad*, published by the Ministry of Agriculture, Fisheries and Food, and available from the Plant Health Division, MAFF, Whitehall Place (East Block), London SW1A 2HH.

Abbreviations and symbols

cv.	cultivar
f.	forma
hort.	hortulanorum ('of gardens') – term indicating a botanically incorrect but widely used name
ssp.	sub-species
spp.	'and its species' – used after a genus name to refer to all species within the genus
syn.	synonym
var.	variety
♀	Award of Garden Merit (AGM) – bestowed by the Royal Horticultural Society on the most rewarding and reliable plants for garden decoration, whether grown in the open or under glass.

Abelia

Caprifoliaceae

Abelia x grandiflora 'Francis Mason'

Abundant small clusters of white, pink or red funnel-shaped flowers are borne by these graceful shrubs or trees. They are deciduous or semi-evergreen and plants generally have slender, arching branches. Most species in cultivation need protection from cold, wind and frost in many areas and grow best against a warm south or west-facing wall. The sepals are 6-15mm (¼-½in) long and remain conspicuous and often colourful long after the flowers have fallen. The oval, pointed leaves are 1.5-4cm (½-1½in) long. Plants are native to China, Japan, the Himalayas and Mexico.

RECOMMENDED SPECIES AND VARIETIES

A. chinensis Fragrant white flowers, flushed pink outside, are borne in clusters from mid to late summer. Each flower is 1.5cm (½in) long and has 5 rose-pink sepals. A compact deciduous shrub with dark green leaves. HEIGHT & SPREAD 80×80cm (32×32in) after 5 years, ultimately 1.5m (5ft) tall.

***A.* 'Edward Goucher'**♀ Clusters of purplish pink flowers appear from mid to late summer. Each flower is 2cm (¾in) long with 2 reddish sepals. This deciduous or

▼ *Abelia* 'Edward Goucher'

▲ *Abelia floribunda*

semi-evergreen shrub has glossy, slightly toothed leaves, usually tinged bronze when young and bright green by summer. HEIGHT & SPREAD 80×80cm (32×32in) after 5 years, ultimately 1.5m (5ft) tall.

A. floribunda♀ Bright cherry-red flowers, 5cm (2in) long, are borne in drooping clusters in early summer. Each flower has 5 dull, reddish green sepals. This evergreen shrub with glossy, dark green, slightly toothed leaves is only hardy to about -10°C (14°F). HEIGHT & SPREAD 1×1m (3×3ft) after 5 years, ultimately 3m (10ft) tall.

▲ *Abelia* x *grandiflora*

A.* × *grandiflora♀ (syn. *A. rupestris* hort.) Slightly scented white flowers, tinged with pink, appear from mid summer to mid autumn. They are 2cm (¾in) long and have 2-5 pinkish sepals. This evergreen shrub has glossy, deep green, slightly toothed leaves. HEIGHT & SPREAD 1×1m (3×3ft) after 5 years, ultimately 1.8m (6ft) tall.

The leaves of **'Francis Mason'**♀ have a golden-yellow edge that is brighter on plants grown in a sunny position. It only reaches about 1.5m (5ft). **'Goldsport'** (syn. 'Aurea', 'Gold Strike') is the same height and has golden leaves.

A. rupestris hort. see *A.* ×*grandiflora*

A. schumannii Rosy pink outside and white with an orange blotch inside, the flowers appear from late summer to mid autumn. Each flower is 2.5cm (1in) long and has 2 reddish sepals. A deciduous shrub that has slender purple young shoots and glossy bright green leaves. HEIGHT & SPREAD 80×80cm (32×32in) after 5 years, ultimately 1.5m (5ft) tall.

A. triflora Clusters of fragrant white flowers, tinged pink outside and 2cm (¾in) long, appear in early summer. The slender flower tubes flare outwards, spreading to 1.5cm (½in) across. Each flower has 5 narrow red sepals. The deciduous leaves are up to 7.5cm (3in) long and sometimes have toothed edges. They are dull dark green above and paler and slightly hairy beneath. This large shrub or small spreading tree develops a ridged grey bark with age. HEIGHT & SPREAD 1.5×1m (5×3ft) after 5 years, ultimately 5m (16ft) tall.

CULTIVATION Plant in any well-drained, moderately fertile soil in full sun. All plants benefit from a sheltered position against a warm south or west-facing wall.

PRUNING None required but cut out any dead wood in spring. Trim or shape plants, if necessary, after flowering.

PROPAGATION Raise plants by taking softwood cuttings in summer.

PESTS AND DISEASES Usually trouble free.

Abies

Silver fir

Pinaceae

Abies koreana

Pyramids of long, graceful branches sweeping horizontally from a silvery grey trunk give these aromatic evergreen conifers their characteristic look. The glossy green, flat needles are between 1.5-7.5cm (½-3in) long and usually have two bold grey-green or white stripes on the lower surfaces.

Many species reach a majestic size at maturity: the rapid-growing *Abies grandis* eventually tops 100m (330ft) and *A. nordmanniana,* whose saplings are popular as Christmas trees, reaches 55m (180ft). Slow-growing and prostrate varieties are more suited for gardens but these can lack the strong shape of the tall species. The trees grow best in damp climates with cool winters, and prefer moist, acid soil. Most are hardy though some cultivated species need protection from late spring frosts.

Small male and large female cones are borne on the same tree in spring. The colour of the female cones varies according to variety from red through purple to blue

▲ *Abies balsamea* f. *hudsonia*

and even white or all green. All ripen to a dull brown when frost occurs and disintegrate in autumn winds. Male cones are usually carried in clusters on lower branches while female cones, borne singly and in clusters, are on upper branches. The female cones, 6-20cm (2½-8in) long, have scales spiralling around a central spike which is left on the tree after the scales and seeds have blown away. They are mostly cigar to barrel shaped and are held upright on the twigs. Silver firs generally bear cones after 20-25 years with the exception of *A. koreana,* which has blue cones after 5-10 years.

RECOMMENDED SPECIES AND VARIETIES

A. balsamea **f.** ***hudsonia*** ♀ The dwarf globular bush has short, aromatic glossy green needles. It does not bear cones but white resin-covered buds. The hardy native of the eastern United States is the most lime tolerant of the genus. HEIGHT & SPREAD 80×100cm (32×40in) after 20-30 years.

A. b. **'Nana'** is very similar to *hudsonia* but slower growing, forming a compact spherical bush. The glossy dark green needles are very densely arranged.

▲ *Abies concolor* 'Compacta'

A. concolor **'Compacta'** ♀ Stout, short stiff needles are a strong blue on the irregular-shaped dwarf plant. It has round, sticky resinous leaf buds. Cones are seldom produced. Annual growth is only about 3-5cm (1¼-2in). HEIGHT & SPREAD 50×75cm (20×30in) in 15-20 years.

A. koreana (Korean fir) The low, wide-spreading hardy tree forms a pyramid densely clothed with dark shiny needles that are a bright silver underneath. From an early age, 5-10 years old, it produces deep purplish blue, upright cylindrical cones with green inverted seed bracts in mid autumn, these turn brown as they mature. Rows of pink and green upright female flowers are borne in late spring. HEIGHT & SPREAD 2-3×1.2m (6½-10×4ft), but only after 30-40 years of very slow growth; ultimately 15m (50ft) in favourable conditions.

▲ *Abies koreana*

'Flava' has all the characteristics of the species but grows to just over half its size and the immature cones are pale green ripening to yellowish brown cones with the same inverted bracts. **'Silberlocke',** whose cones resemble those of 'Flava', has a silvery appearance because many of the needles display their pale grey underside. It is the smallest of the three, about half the size of the species, with the slowest growth.

A. lasiocarpa **'Arizonica Compacta'** ♀ The compact cone-shaped tree of deep silvery blue needles brightens up any garden corner that sees little sunshine as it does not tolerate high temperatures. It thrives in cool damp corners and is slow growing, making only 3-4cm (1¼-1½in) of growth a year. The cones are small and brown. HEIGHT & SPREAD 60-100×45cm (24-40×18in) after about 10 years, 2×1m (6½×3ft) when fully grown, after about 30 years.

A. nordmanniana **'Golden Spreader'** ♀ Light golden yellow needles with a yellowish white underside make a vivid, compact dwarf bush with wide-spreading branches. Cones are rarely produced. Protect the plant from frosts. Once established, annual growth is about 4-5cm (1½-2in). HEIGHT & SPREAD 1×1.5m (3×5ft) after 15 years.

▲ *Abies lasiocarpa* 'Arizonica Compacta'

A. procera **'Glauca Prostrata'** The pale, prostrate plant has bluish white needles. Some plants revert to having a leader which must be removed for the proper ground-hugging, broad shape to develop. HEIGHT & SPREAD 75cm×7m (2½×23ft).

CULTIVATION The plants grow well on most acid soils, including clays, but not on chalky soils. They are intolerant of atmospheric pollution. Late spring frosts can damage plants that receive early morning sun as new growth begins early in the year. The white and golden cultivars also require afternoon shade as strong sunlight can scorch the leaves. Plant in their permanent position when young.

PROPAGATION Grow plants from seed as cuttings will not root. Cultivars are best reproduced by grafting in early autumn.

PRUNING None required unless a length of clear stem is desired; remove any unwanted branches in winter.

PESTS AND DISEASES Aphids called adelgids can damage the plants but the chief threat to them is late spring frosts.

▼ *Abies koreana* 'Silberlocke'

a

Abutilon

Malvaceae

Abutilon 'Souvenir de Bonn'

Exotic flowers smother these fast-growing, soft-wooded shrubs for long periods. The flowers are generally bell or funnel-shaped, or they may be an open, saucer shape. Usually the flowers are borne singly, but some species produce flowers in small clusters. Colours include yellow, orange, red, pink, apricot, purple-red and white, and some flowers have conspicuous veins. The leaves are generally maple-like. Native to the tropics and subtropics, abutilons are generally short-lived but vary in hardiness. Species grown as small trees may be free-standing, but do best against a warm south or west-facing wall. Some abutilons make excellent conservatory plants. Others are good for summer bedding, providing dots of colour, while others do well in hanging baskets. The average height and spread measurements of the recommended plants are for specimens trained against a wall.

RECOMMENDED SPECIES AND VARIETIES

A. megapotamicum♀ (trailing abutilon) Orange-red and yellow lantern-like flowers make this a distinctive plant. The protective outer parts of the flower (calyxes) are orange-red and about 2.5 cm (1 in) long, while the yellow petals are about 4 cm (1½ in) long. This plant has dark evergreen leaves, 5-10 cm (2-4 in) long, which are ovate, slender and pointed, and a graceful habit. In flower from late spring to autumn, *A. megapotamicum* is fairly hardy but will grow best trained against a warm wall. HEIGHT & SPREAD 2×2 m (6½×6½ ft) after 5 years, ultimately 3 m (10 ft) tall.

'Variegatum' has mottled yellow leaves.

▼ *Abutilon megapotamicum* 'Variegatum'

A. × milleri♀ Orange bell-shaped flowers, about 4 cm (1½ in) long, with red veins and crimson stamens are borne continuously from summer through to late autumn. The dark green leaves are up to 10 cm (4 in) long. A tender plant, it can be grown successfully outdoors only in milder areas against a warm wall and is most commonly grown in a greenhouse or a conservatory, where it reaches about 1.8 m (6 ft) tall after 5 years. As a pot plant used as an outdoor annual, it reaches about 1 m (3 ft) tall. HEIGHT & SPREAD 1.8×1.8 m (6×6 ft) after 5 years, ultimately 3 m (10 ft) tall.

▲ *Abutilon × suntense*

A. × suntense Bowl-shaped flowers, about 4 cm (1½ in) across, in bright, bluish mauve with paler centres, bloom from late spring to mid summer. The leaves, to 12.5 cm (5 in) in length, are slightly grey, oval, lobed and toothed. This is a very fast-growing plant that particularly benefits from staking or being grown against a sunny wall. HEIGHT & SPREAD 3×1.8 m (10×6 ft) after 5 years, ultimately 4.5×3 m (15×10 ft).

'Jermyns'♀ has dark mauve flowers, while **'Violetta'** has deep violet flowers.

A. vitifolium Saucer-shaped, mauve or lavender flowers, up to 7.5 cm (3 in) across, open out flat when mature and are borne from mid spring to mid summer. The grey-green leaves, 10-15 cm (4-6 in) long, are sharply toothed, finely pointed and vine-like. The plant grows best given the protection of a warm wall, especially in cold areas. HEIGHT & SPREAD 1.5×1 m (5×3 ft) after 5 years, ultimately 3 m (10 ft) tall.

The snow white flowers of var. ***album*** are tinged pink when young. **'Tennant's White'**♀ has masses of pure white blooms, while **'Veronica Tennant'**♀ has large mauve flowers.

OTHER HYBRIDS

Many hybrids are available, offering a wide selection of flower colours. Most of the plants are half hardy and are best grown in a greenhouse or in a sheltered position against a warm wall. Alternatively, they may be used as summer bedding. They generally flower from early summer to late autumn outdoors and will flower all year round in a conservatory, with the best display in autumn. The flowers, unless stated otherwise, are open cups 5-7.5 cm (2-3 in) wide. The leaves are up to 12.5 cm (5 in) long. If treated as half-hardy annuals and grown as summer bedding, they will reach a height of 1 m (3 ft) and a spread of 60 cm (2 ft). Unless otherwise stated, plants trained against a wall reach a height and spread of about 1.8 m (6 ft) in 5 years and may ultimately grow to 3 m (10 ft) tall.

▲ *Abutilon* 'Ashford Red'

'Ashford Red'♀ has textured, bell-shaped flowers in salmon red. Appearing from spring to autumn, the flowers contrast with the pale green, evergreen leaves which are almost heart-shaped and serrated. The vigorous **'Boule de Neige'** has pure white flowers with orange stamens against dark green leaves. The primrose yellow, open bells of **'Canary Bird'**♀ appear against glossy leaves. This plant can be grown outdoors only in milder areas. The scarlet flowers, mottled yellow leaves and dwarf habit of **'Cannington Carol'**♀ make this plant ideal for hanging baskets, where it grows to a height and spread of 45 cm (18 in). **'Cannington Peter'**♀ has dark crimson

▲ *Abutilon* 'Canary Bird'

▼ *Abutilon* 'Cannington Peter'

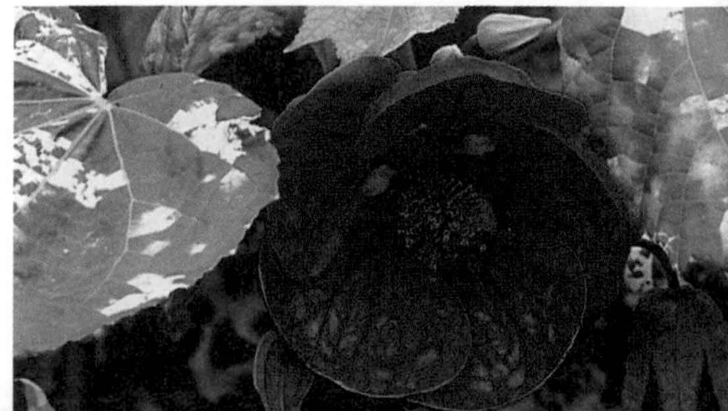

a

Abutilon 'Nabob'

flowers hanging among yellow mottled leaves. The flowers of **'Kentish Belle'**♀ are apricot coloured with faint red veins and are about 4cm (1½in) long. They hang all summer and autumn from this semi-evergreen, arching shrub which has purple shoots and deep green, deeply lobed leaves with purple veins. It thrives outdoors where it attains a height and spread of 1.2m (4ft). The dark purplish red flowers of **'Nabob'**♀ appear against dark green leaves on this plant, which can be grown outdoors in milder areas. **'Souvenir de Bonn'**♀ has long stalked, closed cups of deep orange-pink flowers with red veins. The leaves are edged with white. An erect plant, it grows to 3.5m (12ft) tall.

CULTIVATION Plant in spring in fertile, well-drained soil, avoiding heavy clays. For the best results outdoors, grow plants in a sheltered position against a warm south or west-facing wall, particularly in northern and eastern areas, in full or part sun. Tie the shoots of wall specimens close to the wall regularly. In winter, protect all species from cold with straw or bracken in all but the mildest areas. Repot greenhouse and conservatory specimens every spring, or discard plants every two years and replace with new. Water freely during the growing season, keeping the soil just moist for the rest of the year. Feed regularly from mid spring to early autumn.

PROPAGATION Take semi-ripe cuttings in late summer. Plants can be raised from seed but named varieties do not come true. Raise *A. vitifolium* from seed sown in spring, as rooting cuttings can be difficult.

PRUNING Cut out frost-damaged and dead wood in spring, and cut back the previous season's stems by two-thirds of their length. Cut back main stems of greenhouse plants by half and lateral shoots to about 10cm (4in) in early spring. Pinch out the tips of free-standing specimens in the growing season if necessary to encourage bushiness.

PESTS AND DISEASES Usually trouble free but greenhouse plants may need treatment against scale insects, greenhouse whitefly, mealy bugs and red spider mite.

Acacia

Wattle

Leguminosae

Acacia dealbata

The brilliant yellow flowers of these fast-growing, somewhat tender evergreen or semi-evergreen shrubs brighten the garden or conservatory in winter and spring and are often very fragrant. Native to Australia and Africa, acacia can be grown outdoors only in the milder regions of Britain, but if given the protection of a warm south or west-facing wall, plants can rapidly reach a large size. They are also particularly tolerant of drought conditions. In colder and exposed areas plants should be grown in large pots or specially prepared beds in a cool greenhouse or conservatory with plenty of space. Plants grown indoors will flower earlier than outdoor specimens.

Looking like a small fluffy pompom, each blossom is actually a tight ball of petalless flowers. Some acacias have modified leaf stalks, called phyllodes, that look like leaves. Others have bipinnate leaves, leaves made up of several stems which in turn carry many tiny leaflets.

RECOMMENDED SPECIES AND VARIETIES

A. baileyana♀ (Cootamundra wattle) Throughout late winter and spring this graceful, spreading shrub is profusely covered with bright yellow flowers in clusters up to 10cm (4in) long. The often pendulous branches carry fern-like bipinnate leaves, up to 5cm (2in) long with 10-20 pairs of narrow leaflets. The leaflets and young shoots are blue-green with a silvery bloom. HEIGHT & SPREAD 3.5×1.5m (12×5ft) after 5 years, ultimately 8m (26ft) tall.

'Purpurea'♀ has deep purple young foliage that creates an effective contrast with the blue green of older foliage.

A. dealbata♀ (mimosa, silver wattle) Clusters up to 15cm (6in) long of scented, fluffy, bright yellow flowers are borne throughout winter and spring, on plants that are grown outdoors usually in mid spring. Of an upright, open habit, these shrubs have bipinnate leaves, up to 12cm (4¾in) long, with 20-40 pairs of feathery, blue-green leaflets. HEIGHT & SPREAD 4×1.8m (13×6ft) after 5 years, ultimately 7.5m (25ft) tall.

Acacia dealbata

A. pravissima (Oven's wattle) The slender, angular branches of this graceful shrub are covered with clusters of rich yellow flowers throughout spring. Covered with a bluish grey bloom, the grey-green phyllodes are up to 2cm (¾in) long. HEIGHT & SPREAD 3×1.8m (10×6ft) after 5 years, ultimately 6m (20ft) tall.

A. retinodes♀ Large, loose flowerheads of pale yellow blossoms are produced freely, on and off, in spring and summer. The narrow, grey-green phyllodes are up to 18cm (7in) long and look like willow leaves. Forming a shrub or small tree, this species is more tolerant of limy soils. HEIGHT & SPREAD 4×2.4m (13×8ft) after 5 years, ultimately 6m (20ft) tall.

Acacia retinodes

CULTIVATION Plant in well-drained, fertile soil that is not too limy, although *A. retinodes* tolerates lime, against a south or west-facing wall. Protect plants in winter with a dry mulch. Where temperatures frequently fall below -5°C (23°F), grow under glass in pots or a greenhouse, maintaining a minimum winter temperature of 4°C (39°F). Plant in John Innes No.2 compost. Provide plenty of year-round light and ventilation and water moderately in autumn and winter, freely in spring and summer. Repot established specimens every other year in early spring. Feed fortnightly from late spring to late summer.

PROPAGATION Sow seed in mid spring or take heeled semi-ripe cuttings.

PRUNING Remove dead, diseased or crossing branches and restrict the size of large specimens by cutting plants back after flowering by up to two-thirds of their height.

PESTS AND DISEASES Root mealy bug, red spider mite and tortrix caterpillar can attack the plants.

Acacia, false see *Robinia pseudoacacia*

a

Acaena

New Zealand bur

Rosaceae

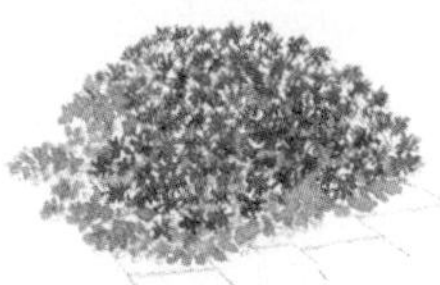

Acaena microphylla

The name of the genus is derived from the Greek *akaina*, 'thorn', and refers to the coloured burs (prickly seed vessels) which are the main attraction of the plants. Most species also have colourful leaves, 6-12cm (2½-4¾in) long and divided into 9-15 oval, toothed leaflets. The small greenish white to brown flowers are insignificant and are carried on erect stems above the ground-hugging foliage in late spring and summer. The tight balls of flowers are followed by spherical spiny burs, up to 4cm (1½in) across, in late summer and autumn which last throughout winter.

The creeping habit of these hardy evergreens makes them suitable for rock gardens although they can be very invasive. They can also be used to carpet the ground in which small early bulbs have been planted and, as they tolerate being trodden on, may be grown among paving stones.

Plants within this genus are vigorous and do best in well-drained soil and a sunny situation. They are native to the Southern Hemisphere, mostly from New Zealand.

RECOMMENDED SPECIES AND VARIETIES

A. adscendens see *A. magellanica* ssp. *laevigata*

***A.* 'Blue Haze'** (syn. *A.* 'Pewter') The pale blue foliage sets off the dark red burs. HEIGHT & SPREAD 10×75cm (4×30in).

A. buchananii Greenish yellow burs appear above the grey-green leaves in late summer. HEIGHT & SPREAD 2.5×75cm (1×30in).

A. caerulea see *A. caesiiglauca*

Acaena 'Blue Haze'

Acaena buchananii

Acaena caesiiglauca

A. caesiiglauca (syn. *A. caerulea*, *A. microphylla* 'Glauca') The mats of mid blue-green leaflets are covered in reddish brown burs in late summer. HEIGHT & SPREAD 5×75cm (2×30in).

***A.* 'Copper Carpet'** see *A. microphylla* 'Kupferteppich'

A. magellanica ssp. ***laevigata*** (syn. *A. adscendens*) The grey-green foliage is covered with dark red burs in summer. Native to southern South America. HEIGHT & SPREAD 15×15cm (6×6in).

Acaena microphylla

A. microphylla The bright crimson burs in late summer look stunning against the loose mats of rosy bronze tinted foliage. HEIGHT & SPREAD 5×15cm (2×6in).

'Kupferteppich' (syn. *A.* 'Copper Carpet', *A.* 'Purple Carpet') is a vigorous cultivar with coppery black foliage. Red burs appear in late summer.

***A. microphylla* 'Glauca'** see *A. caesiiglauca*

A. novae-zelandiae A shrubby perennial which produces red burs above bright grey-green leaves. This species is native to New Guinea as well as to New Zealand where it is known as bidgee-widgee and pirri-pirri bur. It is naturalised in sandy places near the coast in the British Isles. HEIGHT & SPREAD 15×90cm (6×36in).

A. ovalifolia Yellowish purple flowers in early summer appear above grey-green leaves, followed by white, globular burs. Native to South America and the Falkland Islands. HEIGHT & SPREAD 5×80cm (2×32in).

***A.* 'Pewter'** see *A.* 'Blue Haze'

***A.* 'Purple Carpet'** see *A. microphylla* 'Kupferteppich'

CULTIVATION Plant in well-drained sandy soil in full sun or partial shade. Most species tolerate poor soil. *A. microphylla* grows well in shade. Most species can be very invasive and smother less vigorous neighbouring plants. Excess growth should be cut back.

PROPAGATION In spring the plants can be increased by replanting self-rooting stolons or by division. Plants may also be raised from seed sown in autumn or early spring.

PESTS AND DISEASES Usually trouble free.

Acalypha

Euphorbiaceae

Of these tropical, evergreen shrubs there are two species in cultivation, one grown for its flowers, the other for its colourful foliage. The plants are very fast-growing and if the right conditions of warmth, humidity and strong light are met they make good indoor plants. The sap of the plants is toxic.

RECOMMENDED SPECIES

A. hispida (chenille plant, red-hot cat's tail) Tiny crimson flowers, packed in narrow, pendent spikes up to 40cm (16in) long, look like giant, fluffy catkins. The oval leaves are bright green and grow to 12cm (4¾in). Flowering is continuous when light levels are high. HEIGHT & SPREAD 1.5m×75cm (5×2½ft) after 5 years.

Acalypha hispida

A. wilkesiana (Jacob's coat, copperleaf) Coppery leaves, up to 12cm (4¾in) long, splashed with patches of red-brown are roughly triangular in shape. The flowers are carried in cream-coloured, narrow spikes and are quite inconspicuous. HEIGHT & SPREAD 1.2m×60cm (4×2ft) after 5 years.

CULTIVATION Site in direct sunlight or very good indirect light with a minimum temperature of 15°C (59°F) at night, and 17°C (63°F) in daytime. Keep humidity high and plants moist and well fed in the growing season. Plants survive temperatures as low as 7°C (45°F) in winter, but lose their leaves, and watering must be occasional. Propagate new plants every year or two.

PRUNING Cut down to within 30cm (12in) of the base in early spring.
PROPAGATION Take semi-ripe cuttings up to 10cm (4in) long. They root easily.
PESTS AND DISEASES Dry air encourages red spider mite and leaf-drop. Mealy bug can also be a problem.

Acanthocalycium see CACTI p.106

Acantholimon

Prickly heath
Plumbaginaceae

Spikes of long-lasting, delicate flowers are borne from early summer to early autumn on these low-growing, hardy evergreens. The plants form dense cushions of spiny foliage suitable for growing in rock gardens and on dry walls. The five-petalled flowers are about 1cm (⅜in) across, the needle-like leaves are up to 3cm (1¼in) long. Although plants are tolerant of low temperatures, they do not like excessive winter wet. They require sharp drainage, full sun and prefer limy soil. Plants are native throughout E Mediterranean to central Asia.

RECOMMENDED SPECIES

A. androsaceum see *A. ulicinum*

A. glumaceum White veined purple in bud, the flowers open to reveal bright pink petals. The flower spikes are about 10cm (4in) long. The leaves are deep green or grey-green. HEIGHT & SPREAD 15×30cm (6×12in).

Acantholimon glumaceum

A. ulicinum (syn. *A. androsaceum*) Bright pink flowers, white or purple in bud, are held in spikes about 8cm (3¼in) long above the dense cushions of blue-grey spines. HEIGHT & SPREAD 25×30cm (10×12in).

CULTIVATION Plant during spring in full sun in very well-drained, gritty, limy soil. Protect from winter wet with a cloche or pane of glass. The plants can also be grown in an alpine house.

PROPAGATION Sow ripe seed under glass in winter, although germination is unreliable, or take basal cuttings in summer.

PESTS AND DISEASES Usually trouble free.

Acanthus

Bear's breeches
Acanthaceae

Acanthus spinosus

These hardy perennials are grown for their handsome foliage and summer display of tall spikes of hooded flowers, which vary in colour from white to purple. Acanthus leaves are thought to have been the inspiration for the decoration on Corinthian columns in ancient Greece.

So that their striking basal leaves can be fully appreciated, the plants are often grown at the front of a border. The faded flower spikes may be dried for winter decoration.

RECOMMENDED SPECIES AND VARIETIES

A. balcanicus see *A. hungaricus*

A. hungaricus (syn. *A. balcanicus*, *A. longifolius*) The matt green, deeply lobed leaves are not as attractive as those of *A. mollis* and *A. spinosus*. They reach 60cm (2ft) in length and are not spiny. The pinkish white flowers, surrounded by purple bracts, are produced freely in summer. Native to the Balkans. HEIGHT & SPREAD 90×60cm (3×2ft).

A. longifolius see *A. hungaricus*

A. mollis Handsome, deeply cut green leaves, which grow to 60cm (2ft) long, are topped with spikes of mauve and white flowers in early summer. The leaves carry short, soft spines at the tips. Native to S Europe and NW Africa. HEIGHT & SPREAD 120×90cm (4×3ft).

The **Latifolius Group** of cultivars have particularly fine, shiny green leaves, but flowering is not as free as with the species.

A. spinosus ♀ Often considered to be the most striking acanthus because of its large leaves, up to 90cm (3ft) long, which are deeply toothed with long spines at their tips.

Acanthus mollis

It is also the hardiest species. The pale mauve and white flowers are freely produced in late summer. Native to S Europe. HEIGHT & SPREAD 120×60cm (4×2ft).

The **Spinosissimus Group** of cultivars display more finely divided and spiny leaves but need to be grown in hot, sunny positions to flower well.

CULTIVATION Plants of this genus are not fussy about soil, provided it is well drained. They need a sunny spot to flower well, although they will tolerate some shade. Their long, tough roots make the plants difficult to remove if wrongly positioned.

Plant them in spring and cut back the old flower stems in autumn. In cold areas, cover the crowns with straw for protection through winter as they will not tolerate wet, frozen soil.

PROPAGATION Lift and divide large clumps in spring. In winter use the thick roots as root cuttings – they will soon form new plants when placed in containers in a coldframe. Plants may also be raised from seed sown under glass in spring.

PESTS AND DISEASES Usually trouble free.

Acanthus hungaricus

Acanthus spinosus

a

Acer

Maple

Aceraceae

Finely cut, attractively coloured foliage, decorative bark and brilliant autumn tints make maples ideal as specimen plants, creating a highlight in the garden. The species listed here are all deciduous and range from large trees over 30m (100ft) to small shrubs just 1m (3ft) high.

Most grow throughout the temperate regions of the world and so are generally hardy in Britain, although some, particularly *Acer palmatum* and its cultivars, can be damaged by frost when they are small. They grow best in rich, moist but well-drained soil in a shady, sheltered spot.

Maples are easily recognised from their palmate leaves and the red and green winged seeds which appear in summer or autumn. Leaves generally have five rounded or pointed lobes. The Japanese maples, listed under *A. japonicum* and *A. palmatum*, are prized for their delicate appearance and spectacular red or yellow autumn colour. Many of the Japanese cultivars are particularly suitable for small gardens as they are slow-growing.

Ornamental bark gives several species interest in winter. The snake bark group of maples, including *A. capillipes*, *A. pensylvanicum* and *A. davidii*, has distinctively striped bark, while the new bark of *A. griseum* (the paper bark maple) is a rich cinnamon colour and the young stems of *A. palmatum* 'Sango-kaku' (coral bark maple) are a brilliant coral-red.

Pale yellow or green flower clusters, 2.5-15cm (1-6in) long, appear in spring on all maples, sometimes before the leaves, but in general these add little ornamental value.

RECOMMENDED SPECIES AND VARIETIES

A. capillipes ♀ (snake bark maple) This densely branched, domed tree has outstanding bark – white stripes run lengthways on a surface that is reddish green when young, aging to a more grey-green colour. Shiny leaves, 12cm (4¾in) long, with 3-5 lobes emerge with a reddish tint and turn a strong red or sometimes orange in autumn. The winged seeds are green. Native to Japan. HEIGHT & SPREAD 3x2m (10x6½ft) after 20 years, eventually 10m (33ft) tall.

A. circinatum ♀ (vine maple) The leaves, 12.5cm (5in) long, have 7-9 lobes and turn a bright reddish orange in autumn. This large shrub or small tree is upright and densely branched. Clusters of insignificant white flowers with purple sepals are borne in spring, followed by red, winged fruits during summer. Native to N America. HEIGHT & SPREAD 3x1m (10x3ft) in 20 years, ultimately 10m (33ft) tall.

***A. davidii* 'George Forrest'** ♀ This elegant small tree is of open, spreading, pendulous habit. It has striking striated bark and large rounded leaves, up to 18cm (7in) long, with pinkish red stems. In autumn, red, winged seed capsules hang among the reddish gold foliage. Although frost-hardy, this tree requires protection from harsh winds. HEIGHT & SPREAD 4x2m (13x6½ft) in 20 years, ultimately 10m (33ft) tall.

▲ *Acer japonicum* 'Aconitifolium'

***A. davidii* 'Serpentine'** ♀ The richly coloured bark is purplish red, heavily striped with white on a large erect shrub. The oval leaves, 10cm (4in) long, are dark green. Although it is frost-hardy, it requires protection from harsh winds. HEIGHT & SPREAD 5x3m (16x10ft) in 20 years, ultimately 6m (20ft) tall.

A. griseum ♀ (paper bark maple) One of the finest of all maples, this shapely tree has interest at every season and is tolerant of any soil. Its leaves, 10cm (4in) long and made up of 3 leaflets, colour a brilliant red in autumn and the cinnamon-coloured bark peels in tattered strips all year round revealing richer colouring beneath. It thrives best in a sheltered position with some shade from full sun. Native to China. HEIGHT & SPREAD 5x2m (16x6½ft) after 20 years, ultimately 12m (40ft) tall.

A. grosseri* var. *hersii ♀ Long, arching branches form an upright tree with a rounded crown. Its smooth green bark has white stripes that are tinged green. The shallowly lobed leaves, 12.5cm (5in) long, are a rich orange in autumn. Native to China. HEIGHT & SPREAD 4x2m (13x6½ft) after 20 years, ultimately 10m (33ft) tall.

A. japonicum (full moon maple, Japanese maple) This slow-growing, multistemmed tree of rounded habit has leaves, 15-20cm (6-8in) long with 7-9 lobes, which give brilliant crimson autumn colour. The winged seeds are red. Native to Japan. HEIGHT & SPREAD 5x3m (16x10ft) in 20 years, ultimately 15m (50ft) tall.

▲ *Acer griseum*

'Aconitifolium' ♀ has deeply cut, soft green leaves which give a lovely feathered appearance and turn a brilliant scarlet suffused with tints of gold and orange in autumn. This tree reaches 3m (10ft) high, has a spreading habit and is often as broad as it is tall. **'Aureum'** see *A. shirasawanum* 'Aureum'. **'Vitifolium'** ♀ the soft green, vine-shaped leaves, 5-25cm (2-10in) long,

Acer japonicum 'Vitifolium'

are flushed with yellow, crimson, gold and red in autumn. Often as broad as it is tall, this spreading tree reaches up to 12m (40ft) in height.

A. maximowiczianum (syn. *A. nikoense*) (Nikko maple) This pretty, slow-growing tree has a spreading habit and becomes rather flat-topped in old age. It is particularly lime-tolerant. The leaves, 10cm (4in) long, have 3 leaflets and turn rich reddish orange in late autumn. Native to Japan and China. HEIGHT & SPREAD 5x3m (16x10ft) after 20 years, ultimately 10m (33ft) tall.

A. micranthum♀ Dainty leaves, up to 7cm (2¾in) long, have 5-7 lobes and turn bright reddish orange in autumn. The seed wings are an attractive red throughout summer. This small graceful tree of upright habit prefers a sheltered position. Native to Japan. HEIGHT & SPREAD 3x1m (10x3ft) after 20 years, ultimately 7m (23ft) tall.

A. negundo (box elder) This rounded spreading tree has pinnate leaves, 10cm (4in) long, with up to 9 leaflets and winged green seeds. Native to N America. HEIGHT & SPREAD 6x4m (20x13ft) after 20 years, ultimately 15m (50ft) tall.

The varieties are prized for their variegation and shoot colour. **'Flamingo'**♀ has 5-7 lobed leaflets edged with white to pink. These colours fade with age but regular pruning each winter produces new leaves. This upright tree reaches 6m (20ft). For best results it requires shelter from wind. The young shoots of var. ***violaceum***♀ are blackish purple. This upright tree reaches a height of 12m (40ft) and a spread of 9m (30ft). It does best in a spot where some shelter is provided.

A. nikoense see *A. maximowiczianum*

A. palmatum (Japanese maple) This rounded multistemmed tree has red and green winged seeds. The delicately formed leaves, 5-12cm (2-4¾in) long, have 5-7 lobes and are bright green when they emerge. Autumn colour can be dazzling although variable from plant to plant and from year to year. Young specimens can be damaged by frosts. Native to E China, Japan and Korea. HEIGHT & SPREAD 4x3m (13x10ft) after 20 years, ultimately about 12m (40ft) tall.

▼ *Acer palmatum*

▲ *Acer palmatum* 'Crimson Queen'

▲ *Acer palmatum* var. *dissectum*

The huge diversity of this species has allowed for more than 600 varieties to be developed. Their autumn colour is more reliable than that of the species. Most of them are less hardy than the species, and in greater need of shelter. **'Aureum'** is a handsome, upright shrub with finely cut small leaves which emerge yellow with a touch of scarlet at the margins. They gradually show less scarlet as the season advances and finally turn golden yellow in autumn. It is fast-growing and reaches a height of 8m (26ft). **'Bloodgood'**♀ has foliage that is a very deep purple throughout the season. It is a narrow, upright tree that reaches 5m (16ft) in height. The seed capsules have decorative red wings in the autumn. **'Burgundy Lace'**♀ has deeply cut, purple serrated leaves, 8-10cm (3¼-4in) across. The colour can fade in dry conditions. This large, rounded shrub reaches a height of 5m (16ft). **'Butterfly'**♀ has grey-green leaves, 3-5cm (1¼-2in) long, irregularly lobed and with silvery white margins. The upright, densely branched shrub eventually grows to 3m (10ft), but so slowly that it is suitable for a small garden. **'Chitoseyama'**♀ is similar in height and slow growth but is spreading in habit. Its deep purple, 7-lobed, serrated leaves gradually turn a lighter red before turning scarlet in autumn. It will grow to 3m (10ft). **'Crimson Queen'**♀ is an outstanding weeping shrub, often wider than it is high and only slowly reaching its ultimate 2m (6½ft). The finely cut leaves emerge deep purple, gradually turning reddish purple by the end of summer.

▼ *Acer palmatum* 'Chitoseyama'

The cascading branches of var. ***dissectum***♀ form a large, spreading dome. Slow-growing, it reaches 4m (13ft) at most. The light green, deeply cut and lobed leaves give this shrub a delightful ferny appearance. In autumn its foliage can be brilliant red or yellow. Its cultivar, **'Dissectum Atropurpureum'** has deeply cut leaves that are a rich purple, turning crimson in autumn.

'Inaba-shidare'♀ has dark purple leaves and an open habit. It reaches only 2m (6½ft) in height. **'Linearilobum'**♀ gains a delicate look from its bright green, very narrowly lobed leaves. These colour to a warm yellow in autumn. This rounded shrub ultimately reaches 5m (16ft) in height. **'Osakazuki'**♀ forms a rounded tree with delicate 7-lobed leaves, up to 12cm (4¾in) long, that are a rich green during summer, turning to the most brilliant reds in autumn. It eventually reaches 8m (26ft) tall. **'Red Pygmy'**♀ makes a colourful, rounded mound that grows slowly to 2m (6½ft). Its narrow-lobed leaves emerge dark red, turning blue-green and eventually golden yellow in autumn. **'Sango-kaku'**♀ (syn. 'Senkaki') (coral bark maple) is a large upright shrub, eventually 7m (23ft) tall, whose young twigs of a brilliant coral-red retain their rich colour in winter. The leaves are a fresh green turning soft yellow in autumn and 3-7cm (1½-2¾in) long. **'Seiryû'**♀ grows into a wide rounded shrub, eventually 5m (16ft) tall, which is one of the very best for autumn colour. Its small delicate leaves are deeply dissected and

Acer palmatum 'Osakazuki'

▼ *Acer palmatum* 'Sango-kaku'

turn many shades of red, yellow and orange in autumn.

A. pensylvanicum (snake bark maple)🏆 White stripes mark the mature green bark while the young shoots are pink striped with white. This hardy tree is rounded with large 3-lobed leaves, up to 20cm (8in) long, that turn bright yellow in autumn. Native to eastern N America. HEIGHT & SPREAD 5×3m (16×10ft) after 20 years, ultimately 11m (36ft) tall.

'Erythrocladum'🏆 has even better bark colour, more striking in winter when it is brilliant pinky red. It reaches a height of 5-6m (16-20ft).

A. platanoides🏆 (Norway maple) This fast-growing, rounded tree tolerates chalky soil. Its shiny green leaves, 8-15cm (3¼-6in) long with 3-5 lobes, turn golden yellow in autumn. Bright, small green-yellow flowerheads 5-7.5cm (2-3in) across, appear before the leaves in spring. Native to Europe, the species is too tall for most gardens. HEIGHT & SPREAD 8×6m (26×20ft) after 20 years, ultimately 30m (100ft).

The cultivars are a more suitable size for the average garden. **'Crimson King'**🏆, which eventually reaches 15m (50ft), is one of the best purple-crimson leaved forms but lacks vivid autumn tints. It has pretty yellow flowers in spring. **'Drummondii'**🏆 reaches 10-12m (30-40ft) high and has small green

▲ *Acer platanoides* 'Drummondii'

Acer platanoides 'Schwedleri' ▲

leaves with white edges. **'Schwedleri'**🏆 is about 20m (66ft) tall when mature. The leaves are a lighter purple than 'Crimson King' and its autumn colour is brighter.

A. pseudoplatanus (Scottish maple, sycamore) These trees need to be planted at least 15m (50ft) from any building. The leaves are 10-15cm (4-6in) long, with 3-5 lobes. There are many plants bred from this native of central Europe that are more suitable with more colourful leaves. HEIGHT & SPREAD 9×6m (30×20ft) after 20 years, ultimately 30m (100ft).

'Brilliantissimum'🏆 has leaves that are pinky yellow when they emerge and which are an outstanding feature in spring. Slow-growing, it rarely exceeds 3m (10ft) tall. **'Leopoldii'**🏆 is a similar size with leaves that emerge pinkish but quickly become green, mottled with white and yellow. The 5-lobed leaves of **'Worley'**🏆 are a golden yellow when young, becoming pale green in summer. This tree reaches up to 15m (50ft) in height.

▼ *Acer pseudoplatanus* 'Brilliantissimum'

A. rubrum (red maple) Eye-catching small red flowers appear on the bare branches in spring. The 5-lobed leaves, 10cm (4in) long, are silvery grey on the underside, turning a brilliant red-orange in autumn. This rounded, open large tree is native to the USA. HEIGHT & SPREAD 6×4m (20×13ft) after 20 years, ultimately 20m (66ft) tall.

October Glory🏆 is smaller, more upright and less hardy, needing protection from strong winds. Autumn colour is a reliable brilliant crimson or dark orange-red. **Scanlon**🏆 has rich autumn colour and a very columnar form, growing to 15m (50ft) in height.

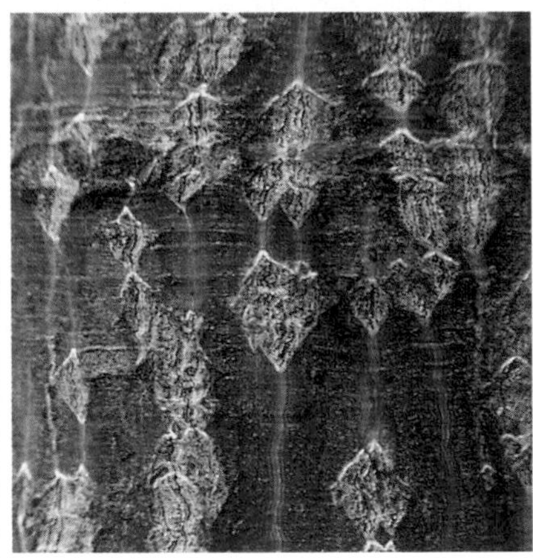

▲ *Acer rufinerve*

A. rufinerve (snake bark maple)🏆 Distinctive white stripes mark the green bark of this small tree. The 3 or 5-lobed leaves, 12.5cm (5in) long, are dark green above, light green beneath, turning bright red-orange in autumn. The tree is upright with slightly ascending branches. Native to Japan. HEIGHT & SPREAD 5×3m (16×10ft) after 20 years, ultimately 10m (33ft) tall.

A. shirasawanum **'Aureum'**🏆 (syn. *A. japonicum* 'Aureum') This slow-growing, compact, rounded shrub is excellent for a small garden. It has 7 or 9-lobed, golden yellow leaves, up to 10cm (4in) long, often with reddish edges. Winged seeds are red and green. Best grown in partial shade as hot sun can scorch the leaves; this maple also needs a site protected from wind. HEIGHT & SPREAD 3×2m (10×6½ft) after 20 years, ultimately 5m (16ft) tall.

A. tataricum ssp. *ginnala*🏆 (Amur maple) Small, dark green, 3-lobed leaves, 10cm (4in) long, turn scarlet in autumn. This rounded shrub becomes large but is slow-growing. HEIGHT & SPREAD 5×3m (16×10ft) after 20 years, eventually 10m (33ft).

CULTIVATION Plant in autumn or spring in any soil that is moisture retentive yet free-draining. Protect *A. palmatum* and other smaller species by providing shelter from strong winds and spring frosts; they also benefit from overhead shade.

PROPAGATION Maples can be raised from seed but the seedlings are then variable. Sow seed in late autumn in a coldframe. Some species, for example *A. griseum*, rarely produce viable seed and other species need cold stratification. Plants grown from seed are naturally variable so a grafted plant must be purchased if particular features are required. Most cultivars are grafted.

PRUNING None is required except to confine maples to a specific size, or to remove reverted branches on variegated plants.

PESTS AND DISEASES Generally free from pests, though squirrels can damage young trees. Maples are, on the whole, disease-free, but honey fungus is a problem in some areas, particularly if trees are already weakened by poor growing conditions.

Achillea

Milfoil, yarrow

Compositae

Achillea filipendulina 'Gold Plate'

Flowers in a wide range of colours make these hardy herbaceous and evergreen perennials a mainstay of a border for much of the summer and sometimes into autumn. The tiny blooms form flowerheads which are often closely massed into flat-topped clusters, although some are single. Upright leafy stems hold the flowers well above the foliage which, for all except *Achillea ptarmica* and *A. clavennae*, is soft and fern-like. Taller forms make good cut flowers and keep their colour well for dried display.

Smaller species, many with silvery foliage, are excellent rock-garden plants, adding colour at the height of summer when many alpines have finished flowering. These plants attract insects, especially bees and butterflies, into the garden. All are native to Europe and Asia.

RECOMMENDED SPECIES AND VARIETIES

A. ageratifolia🏆 White daisy-like flowerheads, 2-3cm (¾-1¼in) across, are carried

▲ *Achillea ageratifolia*

singly or in clusters. This evergreen forms whitish grey tufts of narrow, sometimes tapering, neatly toothed leaves, 4 cm (1½in) long. HEIGHT & SPREAD 20×30cm (8×12in).

A. ageratum (sweet nancy) Numerous yellow flowerheads form flat clusters up to 12.5cm (5in) wide. The grey-green, oblong, toothed leaves are 5cm (2in) long. This is a woody-based plant. HEIGHT & SPREAD 80×60cm (32×24in).

'W.B. Childs' has white flowers with a yellowish brown, central disk.

A. argentea hort. see *A. clavennae*

A. chrysocoma Sunny yellow flowerheads, 1cm (⅜in) across, open in broad clusters. Bright green, narrow leaves, 8cm (3¼in) long, form moss-like, spreading mats. A tuft of leaves remains in winter. HEIGHT & SPREAD 30×40cm (12×16in).

A. clavennae (syn. *A. argentea* hort.) Daisy-like white flowers, 1.5cm (½in) across, are borne in loose clusters. The white, hairy, oval leaves are lobed and up to 8cm (3¼in)

▲ *Achillea ageratum* 'W.B. Childs'

▲ *Achillea chrysocoma*

long They form mats on prostrate stems. This species dislikes winter wet. HEIGHT & SPREAD 15×25cm (6×10in).

A. erba-rotta ssp. ***rupestris*** The clusters of white, daisy-like flowers are about 1.5cm (½in) across. Spatula-like, 3cm (1¼in) long leaves have toothed tips. Tufts of leaves remain during winter. HEIGHT & SPREAD 15×20cm (6×8in).

A. filipendulina (syn. *A. eupatorium*) Deep gold flowerheads form flat clusters, 12.5cm (5in) wide. Mid green leaves, 20cm (8in) long, grow in clumps. HEIGHT & SPREAD 1.5×1m (5×3ft).

'Cloth of Gold' grows to 1m (3ft) tall, 60cm (2ft) wide, with flowerheads 15cm (6in) across. **'Gold Plate'**♀ is a vigorous form, 1.2m (4ft) tall and 60cm (2ft) wide.

A. grandifolia Creamy white flowers in heads, 6-10cm (2½-4in) wide, last into early autumn. Oval greyish leaves up to 12.5cm (5in) long form an evergreen clump. HEIGHT & SPREAD 1m×60cm (3×2ft).

A. × kolbiana White flowers, about 1.5cm (½in) across, form small, lax pompoms or can be solitary. Lobed, mostly basal, 6cm (2½in) long, whitish leaves, are narrow, oblong and hairy. A clump-forming hybrid. HEIGHT & SPREAD 25×25cm (10×10in).

***A. × lewisii* 'King Edward'**♀ Pale buff yellow flowers appear in clusters, 5cm (2in) wide. Softly hairy, grey-green leaves, up to 5cm (2in) long, form compact mats. HEIGHT & SPREAD 10×30cm (4×12in).

A. millefolium White or pink flowers last into early autumn, borne in dense flat heads up to 12.5cm (5in) wide. Green or greyish leaves, each up to 20cm (8in) long, form a wide mat. This common weed in lawns is the parent of many colourful varieties and hybrids. HEIGHT & SPREAD 60×60cm (2×2ft).

'Cerise Queen' is taller, to 1m (3ft), and has cerise or light crimson flowers with white centres. **'Lilac Beauty'** (syn. 'Lavender Beauty') has light lilac-mauve flowers with creamy white centres. **'Paprika'** has a mix of orange-red and yellow flowers. **'Sammetriese'** reaches 75cm (2½ft) tall and has bright crimson flowerheads. 'Paprika' has greyish green leaves; the other 3 have dark green foliage.

A. ptarmica (sneezewort) Flowers with short white petals and yellowish centres form lax clusters. The upright stems bear narrow,

▲ *Achillea* 'Huteri'

▲ *Achillea tomentosa*

dark green leaves, up to 8cm (3¼in) long. HEIGHT & SPREAD 75×60cm (2½×2ft).

'Perry's White' has pure white, rosette-like double flowers. **The Pearl Group** have many button-like flowerheads.

A. tomentosa♀ Numerous yellow flowerheads open in dense, 7.5cm (3in) wide clusters. Narrow, greyish or silvery 8cm (3¼in) long leaves, form hairy clumps. HEIGHT & SPREAD 30×40cm (12×16in).

'Aurea' (syn. 'Maynard's Gold') has bright yellow flowerheads.

OTHER HYBRIDS

There are many hybrid varieties available. Unless otherwise stated, they have a height of 60-75cm (2-2½ft) and a spread of 45-60cm (1½-2ft). Flowerheads are borne in clusters up to 12.5cm (5in) across.

'Apfelblüte' ('Appleblossom') has light pink flowers and mid green foliage. **'Coronation Gold'**♀ has rich golden flowerheads and grey-green leaves. A basal leaf rosette remains in winter. It reaches a height of 1m (3ft). The vigorous **'Fanal'** (syn. 'The Beacon') has darker leaves and rich red flowers. **'Hoffnung'** (syn. 'Great Expectations') bears unusual light yellow flowers and greyish green foliage. **'Huteri'** has white flowers and deep green oblong leaves in tufts that persist through winter. This plant has a height and spread of 30cm (1ft). **'Lachsschönheit'** ('Salmon Beauty') has salmon-pink blooms and greyish green leaves. **'Moonshine'**♀ has bright, light yellow flowerheads and grey-green leaves. **Summer Pastels Group** have cream, crimson, light buff yellow, pale purple, pink, salmon and white flowers. **'Taygetea'** has pale yellow blooms and grey-green leaves.

CULTIVATION Plant in early spring in well-drained soil in full sun, although *A. ptarmica* prefers damper conditions. Lift and divide every 3 years, after flowering or in early spring. Support taller types. Low-growing species, those less than 30cm (1ft) tall, will thrive in rock-garden pockets in gritty, preferably alkaline, soil. Protect these species from excessive winter wet.

PROPAGATION Sow seed under glass in late winter or early spring. Alternatively, divide in early spring.

PESTS AND DISEASES *A. ptarmica* is liable to powdery mildew in a dry situation.

Achimenes

Gesneriaceae

Achimenes longiflora

The trumpet-like flowers of these tropical houseplants provide a continuous display in summer and well into autumn. With their upright to trailing, wiry stems, they are ideal for hanging containers and, with some support, they can also grow into bushy plants in conventional pots. They die back during winter, coming back to life in late spring.

RECOMMENDED SPECIES AND VARIETIES

A. longiflora Abundant deep purple to mauve flowers appear from early summer to mid autumn. Each flower is up to 5cm (2in) long. The dark green, rather downy, oval leaves are reddish underneath and up to 5cm (2in) long. HEIGHT & SPREAD 25×45cm (10×18in).

'Alba' has white flowers spotted with yellow and faintly lined with purple. The white flowers of **'Ambroise Verschaffelt'** are heavily marked with purple. **'Paul Arnold'** has leaves strongly tinged with purple and dark purple flowers with a white throat and red dots.

OTHER HYBRIDS

There are many cultivated varieties available. The flowers are about 5cm (2in) long, the leaves are up to 7.5cm (3in) long and, unless otherwise stated, mid green. They reach 30-60cm (1-2ft) in height and spread.

'Admiration' has blue flowers and dark green foliage. **'Cattleya'** has light blue blooms. The flowers of **'Charm'** are coral-pink with a velvety crimson sheen. **'Little Beauty'** has deep pink flowers with a yellow eye. **'Old Rose Pink'** has deep pink blooms. **'Peach Blossom'** has soft peach-pink flowers. **'Purple King'** has deep purple flowers and dark green leaves with a purplish tinge. **'Vivid'** has crimson blooms.

▼ *Achimenes* 'Old Rose Pink'

Achimenes longiflora 'Ambroise Verschaffelt' ▲

CULTIVATION Plant rhizomes in spring in a peaty, soil-less compost in hanging baskets or pots; plants grown in an upright pot will need some staking. Grow in a well-lit place out of direct sun and keep at a minimum of 10°C (50°F). Water freely throughout the growing period, administering a liquid houseplant feed every 2-3 weeks once flower buds appear. When flowering has finished, stop watering and allow the plants to die back naturally. The rhizomes can remain in the compost until the spring or be removed and stored in a tray of peat kept in cool but frost-free conditions.

PROPAGATION Divide rhizomes in winter when dormant. Seed for mixed hybrids is often offered that will not come true to any named variety; this can be sown in spring.

PESTS AND DISEASES Greenfly can be a problem on achimenes.

Acidanthera see *Gladiolus*
Acinos see *Clinopodium*
Aconite, winter see *Eranthis*

Aconitum

Monkshood, wolf's bane

Ranunculaceae

Aconitum 'Bressingham Spire'

In late summer and autumn the typically blue or purple pyramids of aconitum flowers are a welcome foil to the predominant golds and russets of the border – but the genus does offer a few yellow, white or salmon-pink variants. The hooded flowers are up to 4cm (1½in) long and generally in loose spires up to 15cm (6in) long. Aconitums are hardy herbaceous perennials that generally form neat clumps about 50cm (20in) across and up to 1.2m (4ft) high. The stiff stalks are mostly self-supporting, but taller, branching varieties may need to be staked in exposed situations. The dark green, deeply divided, palmate leaves emerge in early spring and are beautiful throughout the growing season. Aconitums provide long-lasting flowers for indoor arrangements. Found throughout the Northern Hemisphere in lightly wooded mountain areas or alpine meadows, the plants are generally tuberous rooted so they tend to be drought resistant but prefer the moister parts of the garden and grow well in partial shade. *Aconitum lycoctonum* is fibrous rooted. All species and all parts of the plant are very poisonous, especially the root.

▲ *Aconitum* x *cammarum* 'Bicolor'

RECOMMENDED SPECIES AND VARIETIES

***A. × cammarum* 'Bicolor'**♀ Wide-branching stems bear spikes of violet-blue and white flowers arching forward from the stem in mid to late summer. The leaves are a glossy dark green. HEIGHT & SPREAD 1.2m×50cm (4ft×20in).

A. carmichaelii (syn. *A. fischeri* hort.) Stout flower stalks bear violet-blue flowers in profusion during late summer and early autumn. This species is native to central and W China and N America. HEIGHT & SPREAD 1.5m×50cm (5ft×20in).

'Arendsii' has very deep blue flowers. The larger, violet-blue flowers of **'Barker's Variety'** and the rich lavender-blue flowers of **'Kelmscott'**♀ appear in late summer and early autumn on stems up to 1.8m (6ft) tall.

A. cilicicum see *Eranthis hyemalis* Cilicica Group

A. fischeri hort. see *A. carmichaelii*

A. hemsleyanum This trailing plant has dark purple-blue to indigo flowers carried in loose racemes from mid to late summer. Plant it where it can scramble over shrubs rather than in a herbaceous border. The dark green leaves are paler on the undersides. Native to central and W China. HEIGHT & SPREAD 2×1m (6½×3ft).

A. hyemalis see *Eranthis hyemalis*

A. lycoctonum ssp. ***vulparia*** (syn. *A. vulparia*) These rather slender, upright plants need staking when the sparse yellowish green flowers appear in late summer above deeply incised leaves. It grows best in shady sites which do not dry out and flourishes at

▲ *Aconitum lycoctonum* ssp. *vulparia*

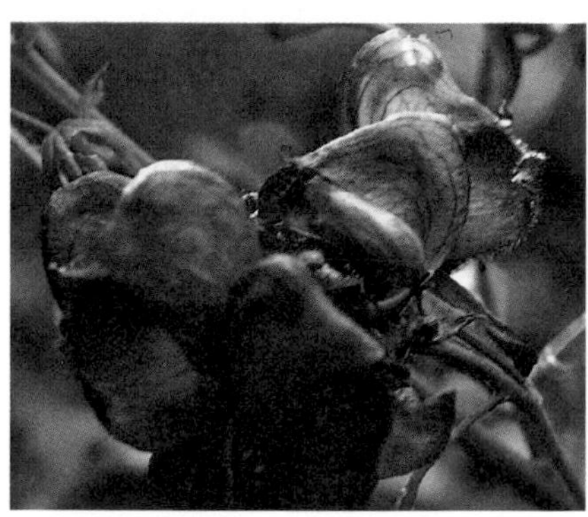

▲ *Aconitum napellus*

the edges of ponds. Native to Europe. HEIGHT & SPREAD 1.5m×30cm (5×1ft).

A. napellus (helmet flower, friar's cap) Deep pinkish violet flowers are borne from early to mid summer and if the spikes are cut back as soon as the flowers fade it is possible to obtain an autumn display. The glossy leaves are deeply divided. This perennial is a British native but is found also throughout Asia and Europe. HEIGHT & SPREAD 1.2m×30cm (4×1ft).

The flowers of ssp. ***vulgare*** **'Albidum'** are white. The blooms of ssp. ***v.*** **'Carneum'** are soft salmon-pink. It does best in northern gardens where the sun does not bleach colour from its flowers.

OTHER HYBRIDS

There are a variety of garden hybrids available, mostly derived from *A. napellus*.

From mid to late summer **'Blue Sceptre'** has deep violet-blue flowers with some white on the hoods. It reaches a height of 50cm (20in) and a spread of 15cm (6in). **'Bressingham Spire'**♀ is a slender plant with violet-blue hooded flowers, that reaches 1m (3ft) in height and 40cm (16in) in spread. **'Ivorine'** has pale yellow flowers from late spring onwards on strong stems which form neat bushy clumps, 50cm (20in) tall and 30cm (12in) wide. **'Newry Blue'** has deep blue flowers on upright stems from early to mid summer. It reaches a height of 1m (3ft) and a spread of 38cm (15in). **'Spark's Variety'**♀ has the darkest violet-blue flowers on open branching heads set against paler green leaves. It reaches a height of 1.5m (5ft) and a spread of 45cm (1½ft).

▲ *Aconitum* 'Spark's Variety'

CULTIVATION Plant in rich, cool, moisture-retentive soil, particularly in warmer southern gardens where it prefers semi-shade with a mulch in spring to keep the soil moist. Cut plants down in autumn.

PROPAGATION Divide roots between autumn and spring; take care when handling the poisonous root. Sow seed in early or mid spring.

PESTS AND DISEASES Usually trouble free.

Acorus

Araceae

The decorative foliage of these hardy marginal aquatics makes them striking plants for the edge of a pond or in a bog garden. In autumn, the leaves rarely die back completely, providing welcome interest throughout all but the most severe of winters. Freely growing, rhizomatous perennials, they do not become invasive like many reeds and rushes can. Plants occasionally produce small flower spikes – greenish, horn-like structures, about 5cm (2in) long – borne on the leaf blades during summer.

RECOMMENDED SPECIES AND VARIETIES

A. calamus (sweet flag) The bright green sword-like leaves are glossy and prominently ridged. Emitting a rich tangerine fragrance when bruised, the leaves were originally cultivated for strewing across floors. If grown in baskets, plants will achieve only about half the size of unrestricted plants. HEIGHT & SPREAD 1.5m×60cm (5×2ft).

'Variegatus' has cream and green variegated leaves. In early spring, the emerging shoots are heavily flushed with rose-pink which fades slowly as the foliage ages. The plants are no more than 1m (3ft) tall.

A. gramineus The narrowly tapering, grass-like leaves are a glossy dark green and mildly fragrant. This species is often planted in miniature water gardens or sink gardens. HEIGHT & SPREAD 30×30cm (1×1ft).

'Ogon' has bright greenish yellow leaves variegated with cream. **'Pusillus'** is a compact green-leaved plant, no more than 8cm (3¼in) high. **'Variegatus'** has mid green foliage striped creamy yellow.

▼ *Acorus gramineus* 'Variegatus'

CULTIVATION Plant in wet soil, directly in the pond or in aquatic planting baskets, choosing a position in full sun or partial shade. *A. calamus* and its cultivar will grow in up to 15cm (6in) of water while *A. gramineus* and its cultivars prefer no more than 5cm (2in).

PROPAGATION Raise new plants by dividing the rhizomes during spring.

PESTS AND DISEASES Usually trouble free.

Actaea

Baneberry

Ranunculaceae

These are hardy, clump-forming perennials grown for their attractive berries, which are highly poisonous. The berries of *Actaea spicata*, which is often found growing wild in northern Britain, are particularly toxic. The divided and toothed foliage reaches up to 80cm (32in) in length and is made up of two to three leaflets, 2.5-10cm (1-4in) long. Stems reaching 60cm-1m (2-3ft) are crowned with small, feathery flowers held on flower spikes in summer followed by colourful pea-sized berries throughout the autumn. The plants do well in woodland conditions and may also be grown in borders or beside a pool or stream.

RECOMMENDED SPECIES AND VARIETIES

A. alba♀ (syn. *A. pachypoda*) (doll's eyes, white baneberry) Elegant green foliage accompanies spikes of white, fluffy flowers in early summer. White berries, carried on fleshy red stalks, appear in late summer. Native to eastern N America. HEIGHT & SPREAD 1m×45cm (3×1½ft).

▼ *Actaea alba*

A. erythrocarpa (syn. *A. spicata* var. *rubra*) Creamy white flowers are framed by finely divided leaves. The deep red berries appear in late summer. Native to NE Europe, Siberia and Japan. HEIGHT & SPREAD 75×45 cm (2½×1½ ft).
A. pachypoda see *A. alba*
A. rubra♀ (red baneberry) The whitish flowers of this popular species are held above oval, divided, bright green leaves in summer. Shiny red berries follow in early autumn. Native to western N America. HEIGHT & SPREAD 45×30 cm (1½×1 ft).
A. spicata (herb Christopher) White flowers are followed by large black berries in late summer. The deeply toothed oval leaves are mid green. Native to Europe and W Asia. HEIGHT & SPREAD 45×45 cm (1½×1½ ft).
A. spicata var. *rubra* see *A. erythrocarpa*
CULTIVATION Plant in moist soil, well enriched with organic matter, in autumn or spring, preferably in partial shade.
PROPAGATION Lift and divide rhizomes in spring. Sow fresh seed in autumn in a coldframe or greenhouse.
PESTS AND DISEASES Usually trouble free.

Actinidia

Actinidiaceae

Actinidia kolomikta

Admired for their flowers, foliage and fruit, these hardy, deciduous, twining climbers are ideal for clothing walls and pergolas, while the taller varieties can ramble through trees. The fragrant, cup-shaped flowers are usually white and are carried in clusters along the branches among the toothed leaves. Apart from *Actinidia arguta*, the species below carry male and female flowers on separate plants – so to ensure an autumn crop of the gooseberry-like, edible fruit, both sexes must be grown in proximity. For more reliable fruiting, grow in a cool greenhouse. Native to E Asia.

RECOMMENDED SPECIES AND VARIETIES
A. arguta **'Issai'** White flowers, 2 cm (¾ in) across, with a pale green tint appear from early to mid summer. The bright, lustrous green, bristly leaves are broadly egg shaped and up to 12.5 cm (5 in) long. The greenish yellow, oblong fruits are edible but insipid. HEIGHT & SPREAD 6×3 m (20×10 ft) after 5 years, ultimately 15 m (50 ft) tall.
A. deliciosa (Chinese gooseberry, kiwi fruit) Creamy white flowers, 4 cm (1½ in) across, are borne from mid to late summer. The heart-shaped leaves, up to 20 cm (8 in) long, are covered with shaggy reddish hairs.

▲ *Actinidia kolomikta*

To encourage flowering and fruiting, pinch young shoots back to about 30 cm (1 ft) in summer. Further shorten the long spurs in winter. After harvesting, allow the fruit to develop in flavour for a month before using. HEIGHT & SPREAD 3×3 m (10×10 ft) after 5 years, ultimately 10 m (33 ft) tall.

'Hayward', a female clone, is one of the most reliable varieties for British gardens. **'Tomuri'** is the male counterpart.
A. kolomikta♀ Large, heart-shaped leaves, up to 15 cm (6 in) long, are green at first, then the upper sections of the leaves assume cream and pink variegations. The colour will not show on young plants nor on old plants grown in too much shade. Small white flowers, 1.5 cm (½ in) across, are borne in summer. The small, yellowish fruits are inconspicuous. HEIGHT & SPREAD 2.4×1.5 m (8×5 ft) after 5 years, ultimately 5 m (16 ft) tall.
CULTIVATION Plant in rich loam; avoid badly drained and chalky soils. Plant from mid autumn to early spring in a sunny or partially shaded site. The plants may require some initial training.
PROPAGATION Take semi-ripe cuttings in summer or sow seed of species in autumn.
PRUNING If space is restricted, thin out and cut back growth in late winter.
PESTS AND DISEASES Cats are attracted to some species, particularly *A. kolomikta*, and may damage the stems, occasionally killing the plants. Otherwise trouble free.

Adam's needle see *Yucca filamentosa*

Adenophora

Gland bellflower
Campanulaceae

Tall, slender spikes of blue or violet bell-shaped flowers hanging prettily on tiny stalks, lend a delicate beauty to a mixed herbaceous border in summer. Native to Europe and Asia, these herbaceous perennials are reliably hardy.

RECOMMENDED SPECIES
A. aurita Mauve-blue flowers, up to 4 cm (1½ in) long, are produced in spikes in mid or late summer. The coarse, silvery grey, leaves are up to 10 cm (4 in) long. HEIGHT & SPREAD 1 m×45 cm (3×1½ ft).
A. bulleyana Pale blue pendent blooms, up to 1 cm (⅜ in) long, are produced in branching clusters in late summer. The oval, downy green leaves are up to 7.5 cm (3 in) long. HEIGHT & SPREAD 1.2 m×60 cm (4×2 ft).
A. liliifolia Loose, spreading heads of fragrant blue or whitish blue flowers, each up to 2.5 cm (1 in) long, appear in late summer. The mid green leaves are rounded and tapering and up to 7.5 cm (3 in) long. HEIGHT & SPREAD 45×30 cm (1½×1 ft).
A. nikoensis Off-white flowers tinged with

▲ *Adenophora bulleyana*

▲ *Adenophora liliifolia*

blue and up to 2.5cm (1in) long are borne from mid to late summer. The mid green leaves are up to 10cm (4in) long. HEIGHT & SPREAD 45×45cm (1½×1½ft).

A. pereskiifolia Mid blue flowers, each 2.5cm (1in) long, appear in mid summer. The mid green, oval, toothed leaves, up to 15cm (6in) long, are arranged in whorls. HEIGHT & SPREAD 45×30cm (1½×1ft).

A. potaninii Bluish lavender flowers, each 2.5cm (1in) long, appear in arching sprays in late summer on this rosette-forming, woody-based plant. The mid green, oval or lance-shaped leaves are up to 10cm (4in) long. HEIGHT & SPREAD 45×60cm (1½×2ft).

A. tashiroi Sparse, pendent, violet blooms are produced on slender stems in late summer. The oval or lance-shaped mid green leaves are up to 7.5cm (3in) long. HEIGHT & SPREAD 45×45cm (1½×1½ft).

CULTIVATION Plant in moist but free-draining soil in full sun. Do not disturb established plants unnecessarily.

PROPAGATION Sow seed in spring or autumn, or take basal cuttings in spring.

PESTS AND DISEASES Froghoppers and downy mildew can damage plants.

Adiantum see FERNS p.262

Adonis

Pheasant's eye

Ranunculaceae

From late winter to early spring the brightly coloured flowers of hardy herbaceous perennials will enliven any rock garden or border front. The shiny, bowl-shaped flowers are composed of more petals and when fully open they are similar to daisies. The finely cut leaves are up to 10cm (4in) long.

▼ *Adonis amurensis* 'Flore Pleno'

RECOMMENDED SPECIES AND VARIETIES

A. amurensis Golden yellow flowers, up to 4cm (1½in) across, appear above ruffs of feathery foliage in late winter and early spring. Native to China and Japan. HEIGHT & SPREAD 30×23cm (12×9in).

'Flore Pleno', with double flowers, is more commonly grown than the species. **'Fukujukai'** has large, semidouble flowers.

CULTIVATION Plant in moist but well-drained soil. The plants are dormant in late summer and planting should be carried out between high summer and mid autumn. Grow in a sunny or partially shaded spot.

PROPAGATION Sow fresh seed in late summer in trays in a coldframe or unheated greenhouse, although germination may be slow. Alternatively, divide clumps of established plants in early autumn but do not allow the roots to dry out.

PESTS AND DISEASES The flower buds are particularly attractive to slugs.

Aechmea

Bromeliaceae

Bold foliage and showy flowers make these tropical evergreen perennials popular plants for the greenhouse or in the home. All have leaves that are sheathed at the base to form distinctive vase-shaped rosettes out of which rise striking, heavily bracted flower spikes which persist for several weeks. Native to S America.

RECOMMENDED SPECIES AND VARIETIES

A. chantinii♀ At the end of a 25cm (10in) stem, the bracted flower spike is crowded with red and white or pale blue tubular flowers. The dull green, toothed leaves are strap-shaped, up to 30cm (1ft) long and 5cm (2in) wide with 'blurred' greyish white stripes beneath. HEIGHT & SPREAD 30×30cm (1×1ft).

A. fasciata♀ (silver vase plant, urn plant) Dense, conical rose-pink and purple flowerheads are produced at almost any time of the year from the centre of the 'vase' of leaves. The grey-green leaves are up to 45cm (1½ft) long and 7.5cm (3in) wide. HEIGHT & SPREAD 45×60cm (1½×2ft).

***A.* Foster's Favorite Group**♀ (lacquered wine cup) Drooping spikes of 1cm (⅜in) long deep blue tubular flowers are produced from among the foliage throughout the summer. These are followed by tear-shaped red fruits up to 1cm (⅜in) long. The wine red leaves are strap-shaped, up to 30cm (1ft) long and 4cm (1½in) wide. HEIGHT & SPREAD 30×60cm (1½×2ft).

A. fulgens var. ***discolor***♀ During summer a stout flower stem emerges, densely clothed with tiny tubular violet blooms which turn red with age. These flowers are scarcely 1cm (⅜in) long, up to 50 being clustered together in a terminal spike. The glossy purple-green leaves are up to 45cm (1½ft) long and 5cm (2in) wide. HEIGHT & SPREAD 45×60cm (1½×2ft).

CULTIVATION Grow at a minimum temperature of 10°C (50°F) in plenty of light, but not in full sun. Plant in containers in a mixture of peat or coir, leaf mould and gritty sand and feed every 3 weeks from late spring to late summer. Water freely into the centre of the vase-shaped rosettes using soft, tepid water whenever possible. The plants benefit from occasional misting. Remove old flower spikes.

PROPAGATION Remove and plant off-sets during spring and early summer.

PESTS AND DISEASES Usually trouble free.

▲ *Aechmea fasciata*

Aechmea fulgens var. *discolor* ▲

a

Aegopodium

Ground elder
Umbelliferae

Of these invasive hardy perennials only *Aegopodium podagraria* 'Variegatum' is commonly cultivated for dense low ground cover in areas where little else will grow.

RECOMMENDED VARIETY

***A. podagraria* 'Variegatum'** This vigorous, spreading plant makes decorative ground cover for moist, shady or partially shady sites where it can be kept in control. The lobed leaves, up to 10 cm (4 in) across, are edged and splashed a pale creamy white. White flowers are carried in clusters in early summer. Native to Europe. HEIGHT & SPREAD 15×50 cm (6×20 in) after a year.

Aegopodium podagraria 'Variegatum'

CULTIVATION Grow in any moist soil in a shaded position. Dig up and discard any portions that revert to full green leaves.

PROPAGATION Divide the rhizomes in autumn or spring.

PESTS AND DISEASES Usually trouble free.

Aeonium

Crassulaceae

The fleshy leaves of these tender succulents are gathered in neat, symmetrical rosettes. Clusters of tiny star-shaped flowers appear early in the season. Mostly evergreen perennials, these plants are usually grown in a frost-free greenhouse or conservatory. However, in summer they can be planted outdoors as bedding or in containers placed in a warm sunny position, as long as they have gritty free-draining soil or compost.

RECOMMENDED SPECIES AND VARIETIES

A. arboreum♀ At the end of the branching stems of this succulent are leaf rosettes, each up to 15 cm (6 in) across. These are made up of narrow, glossy green leaves, up to 7.5 cm (3 in) long. Tiny yellow flowers, less than 1 cm (⅜ in) across, are produced in a dense oval flowerhead during spring and early summer. They are borne on stems that grow out of the older rosettes which then die back after flowering. HEIGHT & SPREAD 60 cm×1 m (2×3 ft) or more.

Aeonium 'Atropurpureum'

'Atropurpureum'♀ has foliage that is strongly flushed with dark purple-red and maroon. The leaves of **'Schwarzkopf'** are dark maroon and emerald green at the base. Both produce pyramidal clusters of yellow flowers during spring.

A. haworthii♀ (pinwheel) Neat green to blue-green leaf rosettes, up to 10 cm (4 in) across, are borne at the ends of the stems of this bushy plant. The leaves are roughly oval, up to 5 cm (2 in) long, and often have distinctive reddish edges. Spikes of small pale yellow flowers tinged with pink are produced during spring and early summer on stems that rise out of the leaf rosettes. HEIGHT & SPREAD 60×60 cm (2×2 ft).

A. tabuliforme♀ The flat, green leaf rosettes of this succulent hug the ground. The broadly triangular leaves are up to 10 cm (4 in) long. Tiny, pale yellow flowers are produced in loose spikes up to 30 cm (1 ft) tall that emerge from the centre of the leaf rosettes. After flowering, the main rosettes die. HEIGHT & SPREAD 30×45 cm (1×1½ ft).

CULTIVATION Outdoors, plant in an open position in full sun, in very well-drained soil, when all danger of frost has passed. Indoors, plant in pots of gritty compost and grow in a frost-free greenhouse. Feed sparingly during early autumn and early spring with a weak liquid houseplant feed.

PROPAGATION Sow seed under glass during summer. Raise shrubby species by taking cuttings of stems with small rosettes on them in late spring or early summer.

PESTS AND DISEASES Usually trouble free.

Aeschynanthus

Gesneriaceae

Brightly coloured flowers smother these tender, long-stemmed trailing plants throughout the summer and often well into autumn. Individual flowers last for two or three days. Plants of this genus are evergreen perennials that are usually grown in a greenhouse or conservatory, planted in hanging pots to make the most of their tumbling fleshy foliage and hooded, tubular, generally fragrant flowers. They can also be grown as houseplants. All prosper in any well-drained proprietary potting compost.

RECOMMENDED SPECIES AND VARIETIES

A. lobbianus (lipstick plant) (syn. *A. radicans* var. *lobbianus*) Bright red and purple flowers, up to 5 cm (2 in) long, are held in clusters at the ends of the stems. The grey-green fleshy leaves, up to 7 cm (2¾ in) long, are flushed with purple and carried densely on purple stems. If allowed to trail, the stems can reach up to 1 m (3 ft) in length. HEIGHT & SPREAD 15×30 cm (6×12 in).

A. longicaulis♀ (syn. *A. marmoratus*) Orange-red flowers, up to 2 cm (¾ in) long, are held singly in leaf axils and in small clusters at the ends of the stems. Each narrow, pointed, fleshy leaf is up to 7 cm (2¾ in) long. Trailing stems can reach 1 m (3 ft) long. HEIGHT & SPREAD 15×30 cm (6×12 in).

Aeschynanthus speciosus

A. speciosus♀ Orange-red flowers, up to 10 cm (4 in) long, are produced in upright clusters at the ends of the stems. The glossy leaves are narrowly oval and about 15 cm (6 in) long. Stems can trail up to 1 m (3 ft) long. HEIGHT & SPREAD 30×60 cm (1×2 ft).

CULTIVATION Plant in pots or hanging baskets in any well-drained proprietary potting compost. Line hanging baskets with traditional sphagnum moss. Keep plants in a greenhouse, conservatory or indoors, choosing a position shaded from full sun. Provide a minimum night-time temperature of 18°C (64°F). Water copiously during summer and feed regularly. Remove faded flowers or yellowing leaves.

PROPAGATION Take tip cuttings from non-flowering shoots in late spring and summer.

PESTS AND DISEASES Usually trouble free.

Aesculus

Horse chestnut, buckeye
Hippocastanaceae

Aesculus indica

Flowering deciduous trees and shrubs with spreading branches and colourful foliage, horse chestnuts grow vigorously and become quickly established, with strong, wide-spreading roots. Some species, such as

Aesculus hippocastanum (common horse chestnut), are far too big for most gardens and are best planted in parks and open spaces. There are smaller trees and shrubs to choose from within the genus, although they are really only suited to large gardens. Lifespan varies from 50-60 years for the more shrubby types to several hundred years for the larger trees.

Trees are generally hardy and mostly have rough flaky bark and thick, sweeping branches. Most have large, and often sticky, leaf buds. The palmate leaves, arranged in opposite pairs, are composed of 5-11 large toothed leaflets up to 25cm (10in) long. The prominent flowers are borne on large, erect, narrowly conical panicles, known as candles, and vary from 15-40cm (6-16in) tall. The fruit ripens in autumn; a leathery capsule that can be smooth, knobbly or spiny and contains up to three large, shiny brown seeds, called conkers, 2-6cm (¾-2½in) wide. The conkers, leaves, flowers and bark of all species are poisonous to humans and to animals. Trees in this genus are native to SE Europe, the Himalayas, E Asia and N America.

RECOMMENDED SPECIES AND VARIETIES

***A.* x *carnea* 'Briotii'**♀ Red flower candles appear in great profusion in late spring and are followed by knobbly round fruit. The dark green leaves turn golden in autumn. HEIGHT & SPREAD 10x6m (33x20ft) after 20 years, ultimately 25m (80ft) tall.

A. indica♀ (Indian horse chestnut) The yellow-green leaves are tinged with bronze or chocolate when they emerge in spring. In autumn, they turn pale yellow to orange. White or pink-flushed flower candles, 30-40cm (12-16in) long, appear in mid summer. The knobbly, pear-shaped fruit contains shiny, almost black conkers. HEIGHT & SPREAD 7x5m (23x16ft) after 20 years, ultimately 20m (66ft) tall.

Aesculus indica

'Sydney Pearce'♀ is very free-flowering with even denser flower candles.

***A.* x *neglecta* 'Erythroblastos'**♀ Bright pink as they emerge, the leaves become lighter pink and then pale yellow. They then turn green in early summer followed by gold and orange in autumn. This is a slow-growing tree which rarely flowers – when it does the flowers are yellowish tinged pink – and so rarely produces fruit. HEIGHT & SPREAD 6x4m (20x13ft) after 20 years, ultimately 15m (50ft) tall.

Aesculus parviflora ♀

A. parviflora♀ A very free-flowering, vigorous, open shrub that spreads via suckers. Bronzed at first, the mid green leaves often turn a glowing yellow in autumn. White flowers are borne in mid to late summer on candles, 30cm (12in) long, and are followed by smooth, pear-shaped fruit. HEIGHT & SPREAD 2x3m (6½x10ft) after 10 years, ultimately 4m (13ft) tall.

A. pavia♀ (syn. *A. splendens*) Bright red tubular flowers appear in early summer, followed in late summer by smooth, egg-shaped fruit. An attractive medium-sized shrub or small shrubby tree that has non-sticky winter buds and glossy green leaves that turn red in autumn. HEIGHT & SPREAD 2.1x2m (7x6½ft) after 10 years, ultimately 5m (16ft) tall.

A. splendens see *A. pavia*

CULTIVATION Plant in any fertile, well-drained, moist soil. Most species are hardy, except in very exposed conditions, and thrive in sun or semi-shade. *A. indica* and *A.* x *neglecta* 'Erythroblastos' do best in moist, semi-shade or woodland conditions which provide protection from late frosts.

PROPAGATION Raise species and natural varieties by sowing ripe seed in autumn. Hybrids and cultivars are propagated by budding or top-grafting.

PRUNING None normally needed, although older shrubby species may be thinned in late winter by cutting the oldest stems down to about 15cm (6in) from the ground.

PESTS AND DISEASES Occasionally, the leaves brown and wither and ugly eruptions may appear on some tree trunks; neither of these will affect the health of a plant. Scale insects may cause unsightly but harmless white patches. The genus is moderately susceptible to honey fungus and witches' broom are often seen on older trees.

a

Aethionema

Stonecress

Cruciferae

Small evergreens or semi-evergreens that thrive in a sunny rock garden or dry-stone wall. Their popularity is partly due to the masses of white or pink flowers carried above compact foliage. The flowers, which are around 1cm (⅜in) across, are made up of four rounded petals. The narrow leaves are 5-15mm (¼-½in) long. All species are hardy and easy to grow provided they are given well-drained soil.

RECOMMENDED SPECIES AND VARIETIES

A. armenum A dwarf, shrubby species with blue-green, lance-shaped leaves. Pale to dark pink flowers appear in profusion in summer. The plants are not long-lived. Native to Armenia and the Caucasus. HEIGHT & SPREAD 15x15cm (6x6in).

A. grandiflorum♀ (syn. *A. pulchellum*) (Persian stonecress) Large pink flowerheads appear above blue-green oblong-shaped leaves from early to mid summer. Native to Iran, Iraq and Turkey. HEIGHT & SPREAD 40x23cm (16x9in).

Aethionema grandiflorum

A. oppositifolium A tufted, cushion-forming species carrying a summer display of lilac-pink flowers above overlapping grey-green oval leaves. Native to the Lebanon, Caucasus and Turkey. HEIGHT & SPREAD 5x10cm (2x4in).

A. pulchellum see *A. grandiflorum*

***A.* 'Warley Rose'**♀ A low-growing plant with profuse dark pink flowers from late spring to mid summer and blue-grey leaves. HEIGHT & SPREAD 15x15cm (6x6in).

CULTIVATION Grow in a sunny position in well-drained, alkaline soil; growth will be more compact in poor soil.

PROPAGATION Sow seed in spring in a coldframe, or take cuttings of semi-ripe shoots in mid summer and root them in gritty soil in a coldframe or under a cloche.

PESTS AND DISEASES Usually trouble free.

Agapanthus

African lily

Liliaceae

Agapanthus africanus

Although the first plants to be introduced to this country from South Africa were tender and had to be kept in a frost-free conservatory over winter, there are now several compact, hardy forms available which can be grown in the open in most districts. All plants produce impressive blooms: the large umbels of tubular to trumpet-shaped flowers, 10-20cm (4-8in) across, are held on erect stems which can be up to 1.2m (4ft) tall. Flower colours vary from dark to light blue; white flowers are also available.

The leaves are strap-like and arching, up to 70cm (28in) long and 5cm (2in) wide. The deciduous species have narrower leaves and are more hardy than the evergreens.

Agapanthus thrives in a sunny position and fertile soil. Apart from garden decoration, the long-lived blooms make good cut flowers. Tender species in large containers look elegant on a sunny patio or terrace.

RECOMMENDED SPECIES AND VARIETIES
A. africanus♀ (African lily) As the original agapanthus to be introduced from South Africa, this remains a tender species with evergreen leaves and deep blue flowers in late summer. It is best grown in a large pot or tub that is kept almost dry in a frost-free greenhouse or conservatory over winter. HEIGHT & SPREAD up to 90×46cm (36×18½in).

'Albus'♀ has white flowers.

A. campanulatus Deciduous and hardy in most areas, this plant has flattish umbels of soft blue flowers in late summer above narrow, grey-green arching leaves. HEIGHT & SPREAD up to 120×46cm (48×18½in).

The flowers of var. ***albidus*** are white. **'Isis'** has deep blue flowers on stems up to 75cm (30in). The light blue flowers of ssp. ***patens***♀ (syn. *A. globosus*) are more open.

A. caulescens♀ Similar to *A. africanus*, this species is deciduous and hardier. Blue flowers are borne in late summer. HEIGHT & SPREAD up to 120 × 60cm (4 × 2ft).

A. globosus see *A. campanulatus* ssp. *patens*

A. orientalis see *A. praecox* ssp. *orientalis*

***A. praecox* 'Variegatus'**♀ Silvery white striped leaves are the most distinctive feature of this tender, blue-flowered cultivar. HEIGHT & SPREAD 90×60cm (3×2ft).

OTHER RECOMMENDED VARIETIES
Many cultivated forms exist where the parent species is unclear. Those recommended below flower in late summer.

'Bressingham White' is a pure white at 1m (3ft). The **Headbourne Hybrids** are a widely available race of hardy types that are also known as Palmer's Hybrids. Plants grow to 1m (3ft) tall with flowers in varying shades of blue. **'Lilliput'** is a dwarf plant, which reaches 45cm (18in) and has dark blue flowers. **'Peter Pan'** displays light blue flowers on stems up to 30cm (1ft) tall.

CULTIVATION Only the hardy hybrids survive outdoors during winter in most areas. Plant in mid spring in a sunny position in fertile, well-drained soil, with the crowns 5cm (2in) below soil level. In cold districts protect the plants in winter with a layer of bark fibre or bracken.

Grow more tender kinds in containers. Keep them in a frost-free conservatory or greenhouse for winter but stand them in a sunny position during summer. Feed plants in summer with liquid fertiliser.

PROPAGATION Lift and divide the rhizomatous rootstock of well-established plants in mid spring, replanting the divisions as soon as possible so that they do not dry out.

Plants are easily raised from seed sown under glass in spring. Grow the seedlings in small pots and plant in the open when good plants have been established. Seedlings take 2-3 years to flower. Seed collected from hybrid plants will not come true.

PESTS AND DISEASES Usually trouble free but slugs and snails may be a problem in mild, moist weather.

▼ *Agapanthus africanus* 'Albus'

▲ *Agapanthus campanulatus* 'Isis'

▲ *Agapanthus caulescens*

Agapetes

Ericaceae

Agapetes serpens

Agapetes serpens is the most commonly grown species in this genus of tender evergreen scrambling shrubs. Although it can be trained up a wall, it is more appealing when planted in a position where its long shoots bearing boldly coloured flowers are allowed to trail or hang down in graceful arches, such as in an old tree stump or hanging basket. Native to India and Nepal, it survives outside only in the mildest western gardens. Elsewhere it needs to be grown in a frost-free greenhouse or conservatory. The plant requires an acid soil.

RECOMMENDED SPECIES AND VARIETIES
A. serpens♀ Bright red tubular flowers, 2cm (¾in) long with v-shaped darker markings, hang in long rows beneath the arching branches from mid winter to mid spring. Green lance-shaped to oblong leaves are up to 2cm (¾in) long and sometimes flushed with purple above. HEIGHT & SPREAD 10×50cm (4×20in) after 5 years, ultimately 60cm (2ft) tall with stems climbing or trailing to 3m (10ft).

'Nepal Cream' has ivory flowers.

CULTIVATION Plants need to grow in well-drained, acid, humus-rich soil. In mild western gardens choose a shady, sheltered site, in cooler areas plant in a frost-free greenhouse or conservatory.

PROPAGATION Root semi-ripe cuttings in a peat compost under polythene with bottom heat or layer trailing shoots into pots.

PRUNING None normally required.

PESTS AND DISEASES The roots may be attacked by vine weevil larvae.

Agastache

Giant hyssop
Labiatae

Agastache foeniculum

Numerous spikes carry dense whorls of small flowers on these summer-flowering perennials. The oval, pointed, mid green leaves are serrated and resemble mint. They are aromatic and 3-8cm (1¼-3¼in) long. Most species are hardy, although *Agastache mexicana* should be treated as a half-hardy annual in cold areas. Most are native to the United States and Mexico, but *A. rugosa* is native to China and Japan.

RECOMMENDED SPECIES AND VARIETIES

A. anethiodora see *A. foeniculum*

A. anisata see *A. foeniculum*

***A. barberi* 'Firebird'** This cultivar produces coppery orange flowers in late summer. HEIGHT & SPREAD 60×30cm (2×1ft).

A. cana (syn. *A. mexicana* 'Rosea', *Cedronella cana*) Whitish, pink-tinged flowers are borne in mid summer. HEIGHT & SPREAD 60×30cm (2×1ft).

A. foeniculum (syn. *A. anethiodora*, *A. anisata*) Spikes of violet-blue flowers are borne on this hardy plant in late summer. HEIGHT & SPREAD 90×30cm (3×1ft).

'Alabaster' has white flowers.

A. mexicana (syn. *Cedronella mexicana*), (Mexican giant hyssop) A bushy plant with crimson-pink flower spikes from early summer to early autumn. It needs warm, dry conditions and is not long-lived. Grow as a half-hardy annual in cold areas. HEIGHT & SPREAD 60×30cm (2×1ft).

***A. mexicana* 'Rosea'** see *A. cana*

A. rugosa A hardy species with aniseed-flavoured leaves. The rose-purple flower spikes appear in late summer. HEIGHT & SPREAD 90-120×30cm (3-4×1ft) or more.

CULTIVATION Best grown in a warm, sunny position, ideally in front of a south-facing wall, and in fertile soil.

▼ *Agastache foeniculum*

▲ *Agastache mexicana*

PROPAGATION Sow seed under glass in spring. Alternatively, divide established clumps in spring. Root cuttings of young shoots in gritty soil during summer.

PESTS AND DISEASES Powdery mildew can be a problem, particularly in hot weather.

Agave

Agavaceae

These succulent tropical perennials are grown for their large, stiff, sword-shaped leaves arranged in rosettes. Flower spikes are rarely produced except on large, old plants. Native to Central and S America.

RECOMMENDED SPECIES AND VARIETIES

A. americana♀ (century plant) Curvy grey-green leaves, which are both toothed and armed with sharp spines, are arranged in bold rosettes. Leaves are up to 2m (6½ft) long. HEIGHT & SPREAD 2×2m (6½×6½ft).

'Mediopicta'♀ has grey-green leaves with a central pale yellow stripe.

A. filifera♀ Greyish green leaves, up to 30cm (12in) long, form neat rosettes. HEIGHT & SPREAD 45×60cm (18×24in).

CULTIVATION Under glass, grow in a free-draining gritty compost in a sunny position. Plants require a minimum temperature of 7°C (45°F) in winter.

PROPAGATION Sow seed under glass in spring or remove and plant the occasional suckers during spring or summer.

PESTS AND DISEASES Scale and mealy bug may cause problems.

▼ *Agave filifera*

Ageratum

Flossflower
Compositae

Small, powder-puff flowers in blue, lilac, pink or white cluster above the foliage of these half-hardy annuals. They are grown mainly for summer bedding displays, window boxes and containers, where they flower from early summer through to the first severe frosts. Although most are small plants, there are taller-growing varieties suitable for borders or to grow for cut blooms. Compact varieties are sometimes grown as greenhouse pot plants. Plants are native to the Americas.

RECOMMENDED SPECIES AND VARIETIES

A. houstonianum The mainly blue flowers are held in loose clusters of 5-15. The mid green leaves are 9cm (3½in) long, ovate, and serrated. HEIGHT & SPREAD 15-30×15-30cm (6-12×6-12in).

Flowers of hybrid plants are generally larger than the species. **'Adriatic'** grows to 20cm (8in) tall, with mid blue flowers early in the season. **'Bavaria'**, a 25cm (10in) bicolour, has blue flowers with white centres. **'Blue Horizon'**♀ reaches 75cm (30in) tall with clusters of purplish blue flowers. **'Blue Mink'** has powder-blue flowers and reaches to 23cm (9in). **'Pacific'**♀ has violet-blue flowers and reaches 20cm (8in) tall. **'Pink Powderpuffs'** is a compact plant to 15cm (6in) with masses of rose-pink flowers. **'White Hawaii'** is a compact variety with pure white flowers and a height of 15cm (6in).

▲ *Ageratum houstonianum* 'Pink Powderpuffs'

CULTIVATION Grow in full sun and a sheltered position. Plant outside in late spring or early summer, once there is no danger of frost. Plants will suffer in dry soil and should be watered in dry weather. Deadhead to prolong flowering.

PROPAGATION Sow shop-bought seed under glass at a temperature of 18°C (64°F) in early spring. Prick out the seedlings in boxes or trays and harden off before planting in the open. Sow seed in early autumn for early flowering in a greenhouse.

PESTS AND DISEASES Usually trouble free.

Aglaonema

Chinese evergreen

Araceae

Attractively marbled foliage and the ability to survive in most indoor situations are the main virtues of these evergreen perennials. The leaves, about 20cm (8in) long, are oblong to oval and have distinctly pointed tips. As the plant ages it develops a short trunk. The flowers, which are rarely produced, are arum-like with a cream or greenish spathe and creamy green spadix.

Aglaonemas come from the tropical forests of SE Asia, where they grow in poor light at ground level. They are compact, slow growing and relatively shade tolerant, all of which make them valuable houseplants, especially as they do not need quite such high humidity levels as many other tropical plants. Windowsills with indirect sunlight are best, but perhaps aglaonemas are more useful farther back in rooms. There is a good selection of varieties on the market and when several are grouped together they make an attractive display.

RECOMMENDED SPECIES AND VARIETIES

A. commutatum The original species has green leaves with occasional silver splashes. It is best appreciated when grown as a contrast to the more colourful varieties. HEIGHT 50cm (20in).

The leaves of var. ***maculatum* 'Pseudobracteatum'** are a complex pattern of gold, cream and several shades of green radiating out from the centre. The leaves are large, reaching 30cm (12in) in length.

***A.* 'Silver Queen'**♀ This is the most silvery variety that is commonly available, the green on the leaves being restricted to odd streaks against a background of silver-grey. HEIGHT 40cm (16in).

▼ *Aglaonema* 'Silver Queen'

▼ *Aglaonema commutatum* var. *maculatum* 'Pseudobracteatum'

CULTIVATION Pot in early spring in a rich, soil-less, well-drained compost. Plants do best in good but indirect sunlight, although largely green-leaved varieties will grow in poorer light. Do not allow the temperature to fall below 13°C (55°F) for long periods in winter and maintain local humidity by regularly misting plants. Keep compost just moist, and a little drier in winter. Feeding encourages steady growth but need not be generous. Repot in spring, but plants can go several years without repotting.

PROPAGATION Divide plants or take stem cuttings in spring.

PESTS AND DISEASES Red spider mite and mealy bug are the main pests.

Agrostemma

Corn cockle

Caryophyllaceae

The corn cockle used to be a common weed of cornfields, its poisonous seeds ripening with the crop and contaminating rye or wheat flour. Nowadays the corn cockle brings summer colour to cottage gardens, and is often included in wild flower seed mixtures. It is an easy-to-grow hardy annual. The flowers are good for cutting. They also attract bees. Plants may persist through mild winters. Native to the Mediterranean.

RECOMMENDED SPECIES AND VARIETIES

A. coronaria see *Lychnis coronaria*

A. githago Slender graceful stems carry magenta flowers, sometimes white-eyed, delicately veined. The flowers have 5 petals

▲ *Agrostemma githago*

and measure about 7.5cm (3in) across. The lance-shaped mid green leaves are as long as 12cm (4¾in) long. HEIGHT & SPREAD 60-90×25cm (2-3ft×10in).

'Milas' has deeper purplish red flowers.

CULTIVATION Grow in not too fertile, well-drained soil in full sun. Deadhead to prolong the flowering period.

PROPAGATION Sow seed in autumn or spring where the plants are to flower.

PESTS AND DISEASES Usually trouble free.

Ajuga

Bugle

Labiatae

Ajuga pyramidalis

Because of their creeping habit, these evergreens with colourful leaves and short flower spikes make excellent ground-cover plants. They are hardy perennials, thriving in sun or shade. Only two species (both from Europe) are widely cultivated. Both have rhizomatous roots, but *Ajuga repens* also produces stolons.

RECOMMENDED SPECIES AND VARIETIES

A. pyramidalis (syn. *A. metallica*) (pyramid bugle) The spoon-shaped leaves, up to 11cm (4¼in) long, are dark green. The creeping stems form a low carpet, through which small blue flower spikes protrude in spring. HEIGHT & SPREAD 15×45cm (6×18in).

'Metallica Crispa' is slightly smaller, reaching a height of 10cm (4in). It has dark blue flowers and bronze-tinted leaves that are crinkled at the edges.

A. reptans (common bugle) The glossy, paddle-shaped, dark green leaves are up to 9cm (3½in) long. Short blue flower spikes appear in spring to early summer. This species, a mat-forming creeper, puts out stolons carrying plantlets. HEIGHT & SPREAD 12.5×45cm (5×18in).

A. reptans has many cultivars. Some are grown for their flowers and others have colourful foliage. Those listed below all reach a height of 10-30cm (4-12in).

Cultivars grown for their flowers include the following: **'Alba'**, with white flowers and dark green leaves; the smaller **'Pink Elf'**, with pink flowers and dark green leaves; **'Pink Surprise'**, with deep pink flowers and dark purplish leaves; and **'Purple Torch'**, with pink flowers and dark green leaves.

Cultivars grown for their colourful foliage include: **'Atropurpurea'**♀ (syn. 'Purpurea'), with dark purple leaves, tinted with bronze; **'Braunherz'**♀, with dark purple shiny leaves; **'Burgundy Glow'**♀,

▼ *Ajuga reptans*

▲ *Ajuga reptans* 'Burgundy Glow'

▲ *Ajuga reptans* 'Delight'

with whitish green leaves variegated red; **'Catlin's Giant'**♀ (syn. 'Macrophylla'), a tall cultivar, reaching 30cm (1ft), with large bronze-coloured leaves; **'Delight'**, with bronze-coloured leaves marked yellow and pink; **'Jungle Beauty'** (syn. 'Jumbo'), with very large green leaves that turn brownish in winter; **'Multicolor'** (also sold as 'Rainbow' or 'Tricolor'), with dark brownish leaves marked with red, pink and gold; and **'Variegata'** (also sold as 'Argentea'), which has leaves marked with grey-green and cream, and a particularly neat habit of growth.

CULTIVATION Plant in autumn or spring in moisture-retentive soil. Plants will grow in sun or shade. The foliage of *A. reptans* 'Atropurpurea' colours best in a sunny position but *A. r.* 'Variegata' produces more colourful foliage in a shady spot.

PROPAGATION Divide clumps in the spring and, for *A. reptans*, lift the plantlets that form on the stolons.

PESTS AND DISEASES Usually trouble free.

Akebia

Lardizabalaceae

Vigorous, hardy climbing shrubs, akebia are grown for their unusually coloured spring flowers and shapely leaves. Fast-growing, deciduous or semi-evergreen plants, they climb by means of their twining stems and are excellent for growing over old stumps, through bushes or on wires to cover an unsightly wall.

The flowers have no petals but consist of large, slightly fleshy sepals and are borne in drooping flowerheads of both male and female blooms – the female flowers at the base, the male ones at the tip. The light green leaves are composed of 3-5 radiating rounded leaflets. In early autumn, if

▲ *Akebia x pentaphylla*

pollination has occurred, plants produce purplish sausage-shaped fruit, as long as 12.5cm (5in). The ripe fruit split lengthways to reveal black seeds embedded in a sticky, white pulp. The genus is native to China, Japan and Korea.

RECOMMENDED SPECIES

A.* x *pentaphylla The slightly scented blooms have maroon or deep purple female flowers, 3cm (1¼in) wide, and pale purple male flowers, up to 1cm (⅜in) wide. The deciduous leaves have 3-5 slightly lobed ovate leaflets, up to 10cm (4in) long. HEIGHT & SPREAD 4×4m (13×13ft) after 5 years, ultimately 10m (33ft) tall.

A. quinata Vanilla-scented flowerheads have maroon or deep purple female flowers, 3cm (1¼in) wide, and pale purple male flowers, up to 1cm (⅜in) wide. The semi-evergreen leaves usually have 5 oval or obovate leaflets, often notched at the tip, which are up to 7.5cm (3in) long. HEIGHT & SPREAD 4×4m (13×13ft) after 5 years, ultimately 6m (20ft) tall.

▲ *Akebia quinata*

A. trifoliata The deep purple, female flowers are 2cm (¾in) wide, the paler purple male flowers are 6mm (¼in) wide. The leaves are deciduous. They have 3 oval leaflets up to 10cm (4in) long, with scalloped or shallowly lobed edges. HEIGHT & SPREAD 4×4m (13×13ft) after 5 years, ultimately 10m (33ft) tall.

CULTIVATION Plant in a fertile, well-drained soil, in a sunny place. Provide some support for young twining stems. Young specimens will benefit from some protection in winter.

PROPAGATION Sow ripe seed in autumn or spring. Alternatively, take semi-ripe cuttings or layer in autumn.

PRUNING Not necessary but plants can be thinned in winter every 2-3 years.

PESTS AND DISEASES Usually trouble free.

Albizia

Leguminosae

Clusters of fluffy flowerheads cover these deciduous large shrubs or small trees late in the season. Mostly native to tropical or subtropical regions, only one species is reliably hardy in Britain. Quick-growing plants, they need well-drained soil and a sheltered position in full sun to bloom and prosper.

RECOMMENDED SPECIES AND VARIETIES

A. julibrissin (silk tree) White to pink flowers in fluffy clumps no more than 3.5cm (1⅜in) across, are freely produced during late summer and into autumn. The handsome ferny leaves are bipinnate; that is, they are leaves made up of several stems which are clothed in tiny oblong leaflets, 1.5cm (½in) long. Free-standing specimens have a dome-shaped canopy consisting of many branches. They are best grown against a south or west-facing aspect and adapt easily to being trained on a wall.

▲ *Albizia julibrissin f. rosea*

HEIGHT & SPREAD 6×6m (20×20ft) after 10 years, also its ultimate size.

The flowers of f. ***rosea*** are a much brighter pink. It is hardier than the species.

CULTIVATION Plant in a sheltered sunny spot in free-draining soil. Dress with a slow-release fertiliser in late spring. Purchase container-grown rather than bare-rooted plants as albizias resent their roots being disturbed. To train plants against a wall, tie in young shoots to wires or other supports.

PROPAGATION Sow seed in small pots under glass during early spring.

PRUNING Prune sparingly in late spring, removing any weak or crossing growths or stems damaged during winter. Cut back protruding branches of wall-trained plants to buds that face sideways.

PESTS AND DISEASES Usually trouble free.

Alcea

Hollyhock
Malvaceae

Alcea rosea

Tall spikes of open, funnel-shaped flowers, keep these old-fashioned cottage garden stalwarts firm favourites. Hollyhocks are hardy perennials but are best treated as biennials since the fungal disease known as rust, tends to spoil any plants allowed to grow for more than two years.

In the wild, hollyhocks grow in hot, sunny places in light, well-drained soil. Give them similar conditions in gardens, but improve the soil with organic matter for best results. They can reach a height of 3m (10ft) and the taller forms require staking as the stems develop.

RECOMMENDED SPECIES AND VARIETIES

A. rosea Long stems of single flowers, 5-10cm (2-4in) across, bloom throughout summer in a wide range of colours, including pink, white, purple, yellow and cream. The leaves, about 20cm (8in) long, are light green, slightly lobed and rough to the touch. The species is sometimes incorrectly called by its former name, *Althaea rosea*. It is native to Turkey. HEIGHT & SPREAD 3m×60cm (10×2ft).

Recommended forms include: **Chater's Double Group**, with fully double flowers in a variety of colours on spikes up to 2.4m (8ft) tall; the **Majorette Group,** containing dwarf forms that grow to 60cm (2ft), with semidouble flowers in pastel shades – usually grown as annuals; **'Nigra'**, which is impressive for its very dark, chocolate-maroon flowers; the **Powder Puff Group**, with fully double flowers in a good range of colours; and **'Summer Carnival'**, with fully double flowers in various hues, covering most of the stems.

▲ *Alcea rosea*

▲ *Alcea rosea* 'Nigra'

A. rugosa The pale yellow flowers are up to 12cm (4¾in) across. The foliage is coarse and hairy, with deeply lobed leaves growing to 20cm (8in) in length. It will hybridise freely with *A. rosea* to produce some interesting colours. The species is fairly resistant to rust. Native to the Ukraine. HEIGHT & SPREAD 2m×60cm (6½×2ft).

CULTIVATION To grow as biennials, sow seed in summer and plant out in early autumn. Plants in the Majorette Group and 'Summer Carnival' may be treated as half-hardy annuals: sow seed under glass in early spring and plant out when the seedlings are large enough to handle.

PESTS AND DISEASES Rust can be troublesome. To overcome it, raise new plants on a regular basis from clean seed. Cut back stems after flowering and burn them. Remove and burn the first leaves that appear in spring. *A. rugosa* has some resistance to the disease.

Alchemilla

Lady's mantle
Rosaceae

Alchemilla mollis

Plants form low mounds of silky green foliage. Masses of tiny star-shaped yellowish green flowers on short flower stalks make up many-branched inflorescences, held on long stems. These pretty sprays of flowers appear in summer, last for weeks, gradually turning brown, and are much sought after by flower arrangers.

Most alchemillas are hardy perennials and easy to grow in most soils. Taller plants, up to 50cm (20in) high when in flower, are useful for the front of a border while low-growing species, 10-20cm (4-8in) tall, can be used for ground cover. Dwarf plants, up to 15cm (6in) tall, are more suitable for a rock garden.

RECOMMENDED SPECIES

A. abyssinica (syn. *A. pedata*) The soft green, hairy leaves, up to 4cm (1½in) long, are kidney-shaped overall, with 7 serrated lobes. The plant creeps, with prostrate stems rooting at the leaf nodes. Native to E Africa. HEIGHT & SPREAD 5×60cm (2×24in).

A. alpina (alpine lady's mantle) The rounded, dark green leaves, up to 5cm (2in) wide, have 5-7 serrated lobes. They are smooth on the upper surface, but have silky hairs beneath. The flowers are held in upright clusters. Native to Europe. HEIGHT & SPREAD 15×45cm (6×18in).

A. conjuncta Clumps of relatively thick, star-shaped leaves, made up of 7-9 rounded lobes, are bluish green above with silvery hairs on the underside and up to 15cm (6in) across. A native of E France, the plant is naturalised in parts of northern Britain. HEIGHT & SPREAD 20×30cm (8×12in).

▲ *Alchemilla conjuncta*

▲ *Alchemilla elisabethae*

A. elisabethae This dwarf plant has blue-green, rounded leaves, up to 9cm (3½in) across, with 7 deep lobes. Native to the Caucasus. HEIGHT & SPREAD 15×30cm (6×12in).

A. ellenbeckii One of the smallest-leaved of the genus, this dwarf plant has red creeping stems, bearing soft green leaves, which are no more than 2cm (¾in) across, deeply cut with 5 square, serrated lobes. It likes damp soil but is not reliably hardy. Native to the mountains of E Africa. HEIGHT & SPREAD 5×60cm (2×24in).

A. erythropoda♀ The blue-green, rounded and serrated leaves of the small, hairy plants are slightly lobed and 3-5 cm (1¼-2 in) across. Native throughout the Balkans, Turkey and the Caucasus. HEIGHT & SPREAD 20×30 cm (8×12 in).
A. faeroensis The lobed, kidney-shaped leaves of this low-growing species are about 4 cm (1½ in) across and hairy beneath. As its name suggests, this plant is native to E Iceland and the Faeroe Islands. HEIGHT & SPREAD 15×25 cm (6×10 in).
A. mollis♀ (lady's mantle) The most widely grown species has sprays of fluffy, yellowy green flowers in early summer. The relatively large flowers, 5 mm (¼ in) across, are valued for cutting and suitable for drying. They are held above mounds of softly hairy, almost circular light green leaves with shallow lobes and serrated edges. Native to Turkey and the Caucasus. HEIGHT & SPREAD 50×75 cm (20×30 in).

▲ *Alchemilla mollis*

A. pedata see *A. abyssinica*
A. xanthochlora (syn. *A. vulgaris*) The yellowy green, rounded, lobed leaves reach 10 cm (4 in) across. They are smooth above but hairy beneath. A native to NW and central Europe, including Britain. HEIGHT & SPREAD 25-50×50 cm (10-20×20 in).
CULTIVATION Will grow in most soil provided it is not waterlogged. Plant in either autumn or spring in sun or shade.
PROPAGATION Divide established plants in autumn or spring or sow seed in spring. Some species, such as *A. mollis*, seed themselves freely in positions to their liking.
PESTS AND DISEASES Usually trouble free.

Alder see *Alnus*
Alecost see *Tanacetum balsamita*

Alisma

Water plantain

Alismataceae

Clouds of small flowers on large, branching sprays above neat clumps of greyish green leaves make water plantain particularly effective in a semi-wild setting. These plants are hardy herbaceous perennials that are easily grown in permanently wet ground or in shallow water at the edge of a pool. Native to temperate regions worldwide, including Britain.

RECOMMENDED SPECIES AND VARIETIES
A. plantago-aquatica Masses of white or pale lilac flowers open in the afternoon from mid to late summer. About 1 cm (⅜ in) across, the flowers have 3 petals that are sometimes tinged with pink or brown. Seedheads follow, about 6 mm (¼ in) wide. The oval leaves, up to 25 cm (10 in) long and held on long upright stalks, form a clump from which the tall flowering stems rise. HEIGHT & SPREAD 75×45 cm (30×18 in).

▲ *Alisma plantago-aquatica*

The flowers of var. *parviflorum* are smaller, measuring 4 mm (⅛ in) across, and the leaves are rounded rather than oval.
CULTIVATION Plant during mid or late spring in full sun in permanently wet soil or in water up to 25 cm (10 in) deep. In small ponds, deadhead flowers to prevent seed setting and the plants becoming invasive, and remove dead leaves in autumn so that rotting matter will not foul the water.
PROPAGATION Sow ripe seed or divide established plants in early spring.
PESTS AND DISEASES Usually trouble free.

Allamanda

Apocynaceae

Allamanda cathartica

Waxy, trumpet-shaped flowers produced freely among glossy, lance-shaped leaves offer a stunning display all summer long. These tropical shrubby or climbing plants are frost tender and are usually grown up into the roof of a conservatory or greenhouse, or twined around a cane or wire framework in large pots. Allamandas require copious amounts of water in summer. The genus is native to tropical N, Central and S America.

RECOMMENDED SPECIES AND VARIETIES
A. blanchetii (syn. *A. violacea*) Rose-purple blossoms, up to 6 cm (2½ in) across, appear in late summer and early autumn. The evergreen leaves, up to 12 cm (4¾ in) long, are almost oblong and are arranged in whorls. HEIGHT & SPREAD 3×1 m (10×3 ft).

▲ *Allamanda schottii*

▲ *Allamanda cathartica*

A. cathartica (golden trumpet) Striking yellow trumpet-like flowers, up to 10 cm (4 in) across, are borne in late summer and early autumn. The evergreen leaves of this strong and fast-growing climbing plant grow up to 15 cm (6 in) long and are arranged in whorls. HEIGHT & SPREAD 6×1 m (20×3 ft).
'Grandiflora' bears larger, more profuse flowers up to 10 cm (4 in) across.
A. schottii (syn. *A. neriifolia*) (bush allamanda) The yellow flowers, up to 6 cm (2½ in) across, each have a distinctive brown marking in the throat. The leaves are evergreen and up to 10 cm (4 in) long. They are produced on erect to clambering stems. Bushier than *A. cathartica*, this plant is excellent for training into the roof of a greenhouse. HEIGHT & SPREAD 6×1 m (20×3 ft).
A. violacea see *A. blanchetii*
CULTIVATION Grow in a greenhouse border or in large pots in any good proprietary potting compost. Tie in the twining stems as they develop. Avoid direct sunlight and water liberally in summer. The plants demand a minimum night temperature of 10°C (50°F).
PROPAGATION Take softwood cuttings in late spring and summer. Tie in the twining stems as they develop.
PRUNING In early spring cut stems back hard to 3 or 4 buds to encourage vigorous new growth.
PESTS AND DISEASES Red spider mite and whitefly can be a problem.

Take a closer look at the creatures in your garden – you may be surprised to see just how many act on your behalf

Every gardener is familiar with garden pests – the damage they cause is often apparent. Yet many creatures that inhabit flowerbeds, vegetable plots and other areas of the garden are our allies. They feed on pests and so help to keep them under control. These useful creatures come in all shapes and sizes, from tiny mites and insects to frogs and toads, hedgehogs, birds and bats (see guide overleaf).

The numbers of pests and thus their predators fluctuate from season to season and year to year. When conditions favour a particular pest, its numbers rise rapidly – and so do those of its predators and parasites. Eventually the pest's level falls dramatically and, with most of their prey consumed, the predators are left without food and subsequently die off. This enables any remaining pests to increase in number again, and so the cycle continues.

FRUITY FEAST *Pyracantha berries are irresistible to birds.*

To encourage garden allies, all that is needed is the provision of suitable food and shelter, and a minimal use of chemicals, as these may disrupt the natural cycle and destroy many beneficial creatures in addition to the target pests.

◀ NATURAL BEAUTY *A border filled with nectar-rich flowers is a charming way to support allies.*

Providing food for your allies

Many garden allies require food sources other than pests in order to complete their life cycle and to support them when their prey is not present. Having a range of nectar and pollen-rich plants in flower throughout most of the year is an effective way of attracting beneficial insects and keeping them in your garden.

Plants that have simple and open flowers or small flowers which provide easy access to their pollen and nectar are most useful because many predatory insects have short mouthparts and cannot reach into deep flowers.

Plants in the Umbelliferae family are particularly suitable. Their tiny flowers, which are carried in flat umbels, produce large amounts of nectar over short periods of time and are accessible to the smallest of parasitic wasps. For example, the golden flowers of *Foeniculum vulgare* (fennel), which appear in mid summer, attract almost 500 different types of insect.

Members of the Compositae family, such as *Helianthus annuus* (sunflower) which flowers in late summer and early autumn, are also popular with insects. They produce less nectar than umbellifers but over a longer period.

The list on the facing page gives a selection of the range of other plants that attract beneficial insects into the garden.

As so many plants flower over the summer, it is particularly important to provide nectar and pollen in spring and autumn when it is scarce. The catkins of *Corylus* (hazel) and *Salix* (willow) make good early food sources. In addition, most annuals, including *Limnanthes douglasii* (poached-egg flower) and *Phacelia tanacetifolia*, can be sown in autumn, or under glass in late winter for spring flowers.

Grow *Solidago* (golden rod) and *Aster novi-belgii* (Michaelmas daisy) to provide an autumn food supply. Alternatively, sow annuals in late spring for a late flowering.

▲ FLOWER POWER *Flat umbels of tiny flowers attract hundreds of beneficial insects.*

Do not confine flowering plants to flowerbeds and borders. For maximum effect, grow them among vegetables and fruit bushes, where pest control is often vital.

Include long-living plants, such as trees and shrubs, in the garden. Berry-bearing plants, which include *Cotoneaster* and *Pyracantha* (firethorn), are particularly useful as sources of food for birds.

Plants generally thought of as weeds – including *Achillea millefolium* (yarrow), *Anthriscus*

▼ RELAXED STYLE *Do not be too tidy; dead leaves provide shelter for spiders and beetles.*

sylvestris (cow parsley), *Carduus* and *Cirsium* (thistles) and *Urtica dioica* (stinging nettle) – attract a variety of beneficial creatures so it is worth allowing some to flourish in a corner.

As many as 100 species of insect may visit stinging nettles, for example. They include lacewings, hoverflies, anthocorid bugs, earwigs and a range of parasitic flies and wasps. In spring, nettle aphids are an important food source for the first generations of several species of ladybird, which then move on to feed on blackfly on garden plants. Cut the nettles down in summer to encourage predators to move out into the rest of your garden.

Giving shelter

Provide features and grow plants that offer shelter to your allies. Many of these can be incorporated into even the smallest garden. There is no need to create a specific wildlife area or for a garden to look wild or unkempt.

Encourage birds, bats and hedgehogs by installing nesting and hibernation boxes. The absence of cats will also help to encourage birds. Create a wildlife pond, which will serve as a breeding ground for frogs and toads, a bath for birds and provide drinking facilities for all manner of creatures. See WILDLIFE GARDENS (p.710).

A hedge or woodland area, makes a natural habitat for many beneficial creatures. Give preference to native species when choosing plants as they act as hosts to a more diverse range than imported species. *Fagus sylvatica* (beech), *Prunus spinosa* (blackthorn), *Corylus avellana* (hazel), *Carpinus betulus* (hornbeam), and *Crataegus monogyna* (hawthorn) are particularly good plants for garden allies. Leave the areas along the bottom of hedges undisturbed and let any autumn leaves that collect on the ground remain in place over winter.

Useful predators also make their homes among the plants that grow alongside hedges or underneath trees. For example, ground-cover plants provide protection for many creatures, including frogs, toads and insects. Bark, wood chip or compost mulches also act as safe cover for the smaller predators, such as centipedes, beetles and spiders.

▲ WILD WOOD *A woodland edge is home to bats, birds and all manner of helpful insects.*

A heap of logs or woody prunings – material that will not go through the compost heap – helps to support many small garden creatures. The insects and fungi that gradually consume the wood will, in their turn, feed other creatures.

Above all, do not be too tidy. Clearing up every corner is a sure way to discourage garden friends. Leave an area of grass in your garden uncut for overwintering insects. Hollow stems and fallen leaves in a herbaceous border are also favourite spots so allow the dead plants to remain in place until spring. However, you will still need to remove any diseased plant matter.

Living soil

The soil is full of living organisms: some are beneficial but there are pests and diseases too, just as there are above ground. Most of these organisms are microscopic, but despite their size they play an important role in soil and plant health. For example, tiny nematode worms infect slugs, helping to keep their numbers down. The more diverse and active the soil community, the less likely it is that any particular organism will get out of hand.

The key to creating a healthy community is to build up the soil's structure and fertility. This is achieved by digging in plenty of organic matter in the form of compost, leaf-mould and manure (see p.807).

The last resort

Garden allies can never completely eradicate pests and may also fail to keep pest numbers down to the levels the gardener would like. If necessary, use additional methods of pest and disease control, but whenever possible choose those which do not harm wildlife or valuable allies. These include netting and using traps and biological controls (see p.807).

Use pesticides only as a last resort. Young seedlings may need instant attention but most plants can tolerate low levels of infestations until the garden allies arrive to do their work.

If it is essential to spray, limit yourself to treating a specific pest or disease and spray only appropriate plants rather than the whole garden. Choose the least toxic product that is available.

PLANTS FOR BENEFICIAL INSECTS

- ***Anaphalis*** spp. (pearl everlasting) Erect perennials which bear flat-topped heads of fluffy white flowers in late summer to early autumn.
- ***Angelica archangelica*** Tall biennial bearing large rounded heads of greenish white flowers from early to late summer.
- ***Artemisia*** spp. (wormwood) Feathery-leaved perennials producing button-like flowerheads from summer to autumn.
- ***Convolvulus tricolor*** (annual convolvulus) Bushy annual with deep blue, funnel-shaped flowers from mid to late summer.
- ***Echium vulgare*** (viper's bugloss) Bushy annual with dense spikes of pink, blue or purple, tubular flowers in summer.
- ***Eryngium*** spp. Upright perennials bearing spiky thistle-like flowerheads from mid to late summer.
- ***Eschscholzia*** spp. (California poppy) Erect annuals bearing colourful poppy-like blooms from early to late summer.
- ***Iberis*** spp. (candytuft) Perennials and annuals with cross-shaped white or purple flowers in spring and summer.
- ***Leucanthemum* × *superbum*** (shasta daisy) Perennial bearing white-petalled flowers, with yellow centres, in early and mid summer.
- ***Limnanthes douglasii*** (poached-egg flower) Sprawling annual which bears many saucer-shaped white flowers, with yellow centres, from late spring to late summer.
- ***Nemophila menziesii*** (baby blue eyes) Spreading annual with saucer-shaped sky-blue flowers, with white centres, from early summer to mid autumn.
- ***Phacelia tanacetifolia*** Tall annual bearing dense spikes of fragrant blue or mauve flowers in summer.

KNOW YOUR FRIENDS

In the war against pests it pays to know which creatures are your enemies and which are your friends. Many insects look unpleasant but do no damage to your plants at all – they may even be helpful. If in doubt, leave them alone. The following guide will help you to recognise some of the more common garden allies and provide any particular conditions thev need to thrive in your garden.

1 Lacewings

Delicate-looking insects with green or brown bodies, large lacy wings and long antennae. The larvae are wingless with distinctive mouthparts and vary in colour. From late spring to mid autumn the adults and larvae feed on aphids, red spider and other mites, scale insects and caterpillars. Flowers provide adults with nectar and pollen.

2 Harvestmen

The eight very long legs of these arachnids make them look like spiders but they do not have a segmented body. Harvestmen are nocturnal hunters of aphids, caterpillars and other insects from spring to autumn. Give them undisturbed areas of vegetation in which to shelter and breed.

3 Earwigs

Dark brown shiny insects with horny pincers. From spring to autumn earwigs feed on aphids, mites and insect eggs, including those of the codling moth. Provide undisturbed sites, such as heaps of leaves and logs, for daytime shelter, breeding and overwintering.

4 Common wasps

Flying insects, with distinctive black and yellow stripes, active from spring to autumn. Wasps devour caterpillars, craneflies and other insect pests. Leave nests undisturbed.

5 Hoverflies

Black-and-gold flies that hover in the air making a high-pitched whine. From late spring to the end of summer the tiny pale green hoverfly larvae consume aphids, small caterpillars and fruit-tree red spider mites.

6 Capsids

Though most of these tiny, winged, beetle-like insects are sap-sucking pests, some are major predators of fruit-tree red spider mites, greenfly, thrips and caterpillars.

7 Spiders

Eight legs and a body divided into two parts characterise these arachnids. Spiders are voracious hunters of flies, woodlice, aphids and other flying insects. They are active from spring to autumn. Provide undisturbed vegetation, stones and logs for shelter and breeding.

8 Ladybirds

Small, rounded, red or yellow beetles with 2-14 black spots. The larvae are segmented and slate-blue with orange or yellow marks. From spring to autumn, adults and larvae feed on aphids, mealy bugs, mites, scale insects, caterpillars and plants affected by some diseases, such as mildew. Hollow stems provide overwintering sites.

9 Red velvet mites

Tiny velvety red mites that feed on aphids, caterpillars and other insects from spring to autumn. Provide undisturbed leaves for overwintering adults.

10 Anthocorid bugs

Small beetle-like insects with chequered bodies and long 'beaks' used to pierce prey. Adults are seen in late spring to early autumn, feeding on aphids, scale insects, midges, capsid bugs, caterpillars and mites.

11 Typhlodromid mites

Tiny narrow-bodied mites seen from spring to autumn. They feed on red spider mites. Adults overwinter under bark and in shrubs.

20 Toads

Small amphibians with dry, warty, greyish brown skin. Toads do not leap like frogs but crawl rather slowly. They eat slugs, snails, caterpillars, woodlice and other insects and, like frogs, require a pond in which to lay their eggs. Toads are active from spring to autumn and hibernate under stones, piles of logs and in other sheltered sites.

19 Birds

Vast quantities of garden pests, including caterpillars, snails, slugs, aphids and leatherjackets, are consumed by birds. One pair of blue tits, for example, needs 15 000 caterpillars to raise a single brood of young. In winter, birds will prey on surviving aphids and codling moths. Nesting sites and boxes, birdbaths and plants that produce edible berries will entice birds into your garden.

18 Bats

Small, night-flying mammals with an appetite for moths, aphids, gnats and other flying insects. One tiny pipistrelle, with a thumb-sized body, can eat 3000 insects in a night. Bats are active from spring to autumn, hibernating in cool caves, tunnels or similar hideaways. Bat boxes and a woodland edge encourage bats; ponds are also an attraction because bats feed on the insects that live and breed in or over them.

17 Slow-worms

Harmless smooth-skinned reptiles often mistaken for snakes. Slow-worms are legless lizards, grey-brown or fawn in colour and up to 25 cm (10 in) long. They can live for 20-30 years, clearing the garden of slugs, caterpillars and other small insects from spring to autumn. They hibernate deep in friable soil on a south-facing bank. Rock gardens, tall grass and other undisturbed sites encourage slow-worms. Do not disturb a compost heap during winter as slow-worms may be hibernating there.

16 Frogs

Smooth, slightly shiny amphibians with brown, green and yellow markings. Frogs move about by hopping or leaping. From spring to autumn they eat slugs, snails, caterpillars, woodlice and other insects. A pond encourages frogs into the garden as this is where they lay their eggs. Dense vegetation will give them cover while piles of stones and other secluded places will be used as hibernation sites. Many hibernate in the mud at the bottom of ponds, so always keep part of a pond clear of ice in winter.

13 Centipedes

Many-legged creatures, about 2.5 cm (1 in) long, with one pair of legs per segment. They feed on slugs, snails and cabbage and carrot rootfly larvae all year round. Mulches, ground-cover plants and piles of logs provide safe cover.

12 Ground and rove beetles

Shiny black beetles, up to 2.5 cm (1 in) long, which are active at night. They prey on slugs, root aphids, vine weevils, New Zealand flatworms and cabbage and carrot rootfly larvae all year round. Give them undisturbed soil for breeding, mulches, leaf litter, ground-cover plants and other shelter. Avoid using slug pellets that contain methiocarb as they poison beetles.

14 Parasitic wasps

These tiny wasps are harmless to people. They lay their eggs in the bodies of host creatures, including aphids, caterpillars and scale insects, which are then killed as the young wasps develop. Active in spring and summer, the wasps need flat-topped, open flowers for nectar and pollen.

15 Hedgehogs

Small, spiny mammals that are rarely seen because they are active at night. From spring to autumn they help to rid the garden of slugs, caterpillars, leatherjackets and other soil-inhabiting pests. Heaps of leaves, uncleared hedge bottoms and other undisturbed areas make good resting sites and will be useful when the hedgehogs need to hibernate. You could also provide a hedgehog box, covered with leaves to camouflage it.

Allium

Onion

Alliaceae

Allium giganteum

There are many highly ornamental allium species, which are grown for their large flowerheads held high on erect stems. They belong to the same genus as onions (*Allium cepa*) and garlic (*A. sativum*), and when their roots or leaves are bruised they give off a strong onion smell. The plants grow from bulbs or rhizomes, with flowers held on leafless stems rising above the leaves. While the larger ornamental species make excellent border plants, others are suited to raised beds or terraces, rock or sink gardens, or containers. Many make good cut flowers and the large, spherical flowerheads of *A. christophii* and several others can be dried for arrangements. Most are hardy in Britain, but a few need a cool greenhouse.

It is vital to give alliums well-drained soil, though species from the Far East must never be allowed to dry out. Most species bloom in early summer, but some have their flowers in spring and autumn.

Allium is a genus of great diversity. Fine grassy leaves give some species a delicate appearance, and fleshy strap-like leaves form sturdy clumps in others. There is even considerable variation within individual species in terms of height – as the list of recommended plants shows.

RECOMMENDED SPECIES AND VARIETIES

A. ***aflatunense*** see *A. hollandicum*

A. ***albopilosum*** see *A. christophii*

A. ***atropurpureum*** Reddish purple starry flowers are produced in handsome heads shaped like shuttlecocks in early to mid summer. An easy-to-grow plant, native to S Europe. HEIGHT 40cm-1m (16in-3ft).

A. ***bulgaricum*** see *Nectaroscordum siculum* ssp. *bulgaricum*

A. ***carinatum*** ssp. ***pulchellum***♀ (syn. *A. cirrhosum*, *A. pulchellum*) (keeled garlic) The flower stems, carrying loose heads of pendent, pinkish purple flowers, emerge from clumps of long narrow leaves in mid summer. The white f. ***album*** flowers at the same time, and the 2 make fine companions at the front of a border. Native to S Europe. HEIGHT 30-60cm (1-2ft).

A. ***cepa*** see onion p. 741

A. ***cernuum***♀ (lady's leek, nodding onion) The loose, drooping flowerheads consist of 30-40 pinkish purple, cup-shaped flowers. They appear from early to mid summer above clumps of narrow leaves. Native to

▲ *Allium karataviense*

▲ *Allium cyaneum*

▲ *Allium cyathophorum var. farreri*

N America. HEIGHT 30-70cm (12-28in).

A. ***christophii***♀ (syn. *A. albopilosum*) (star of Persia) Given a sunny, well-drained position, this outstanding plant is easy to establish. Its large spherical flowerheads in early summer are up to 20cm (8in) across, made up of 50 or more star-shaped, silvery lilac flowers. It has hairy, pale green, strap-shaped leaves. Native to Iran and Turkey. HEIGHT 1.2m (4ft).

A. ***cirrhosum*** see *A. carinatum*

A. ***cyaneum***♀ This easy-to-grow plant with fine grassy leaves produces brilliant violet-blue, pendent flower clusters in summer. Native to China. HEIGHT 10-30cm (4-12in).

A. ***cyathophorum*** var. ***farreri*** (syn. *A. farreri*) Given peaty well-drained soil that is kept moist in summer, this plant does well. It has grass-like leaves and loose heads of purplish flowers in late summer. Native to NW China. HEIGHT 15-30cm (6-12in).

A. ***fistulosum*** see Welsh onion p. 742

A. ***flavum***♀ The yellow flowers of this easily grown species appear in pendent clusters of up to 30 flowers in mid and late summer. Native to S Europe. HEIGHT 30-50cm (12-20in).

The dwarf varieties var. ***minus*** and var. ***nanum***, which are useful rock-garden plants, grow to 15cm (6in) in height.

A. ***giganteum***♀ Perhaps the most eye-catching species, this soaring plant has light violet flowers, carried in spherical heads 12cm (4¾in) in diameter on stout stems. They appear in early summer as the blue-green strap-shaped leaves wither, and last well as cut flowers. Native to central Asia and not fully hardy, so in cold areas apply a mulch in winter. HEIGHT 1-2m (3-6½ft).

A. ***glaucum*** see *A. senescens*

A. ***hollandicum***♀ (syn *A. aflatunense*) Appearing in spring and early summer, the spectacular hemispherical flowerheads consist of hundreds of pale violet flowers. The heads open on stout stems as the strap-like leaves wither. They are excellent cut flowers and their dried seed heads are used in floral arrangements. HEIGHT 75cm (2½ft).

'Purple Sensation'♀ has very dark purple flowers.

A. ***kansuense*** see *A. sikkimense*

A. ***karataviense***♀ Unusually, this species is grown for its broad, handsome leaves rather than its flowers. Each bulb produces 2 prostrate, grey-green leaves with reddish edges. The ball-shaped flowerheads are a dusky pink and appear in late spring or early summer. The plant is suitable for a rock garden or the front of a border. Native to Turkestan. HEIGHT 15-20cm (6-8in).

Allium moly

A. moly (golden garlic)♀ This well-known species produces clumps of glossy, bright yellow flowers in early to mid summer. Each stem carries up to 40 flowers in loose clusters 4-7 cm (1½-2¾ in) across. It spreads rapidly. Native to S Europe. HEIGHT 10-35 cm (4-14 in).

'Jeannine'♀ has larger flowerheads, about 9 cm (3½ in) across, and often produces 2 flower stems per bulb.

A. murrayanum see *A. unifolium*

A. neapolitanum (Naples garlic) As one of the earliest species to flower (from early spring), this allium is often grown to cut and enjoy indoors. Each flowerhead is made up of around 40 starry white flowers and is 5-8 cm (2-3¼ in) across. Originating in S Europe and N Africa, it is not fully hardy in Britain, but will succeed outside in a warm spot in southern Britain. It can also be grown as a pot plant in a cool greenhouse. HEIGHT 20-50 cm (8-20 in).

A. oreophilum♀ (syn. *A. ostrowskianum*) This colourful rock-garden plant bears loose clusters of pink to purple flowers in early and mid summer. Native to Turkestan. HEIGHT 5-10 cm (2-4 in).

▲ *Allium moly*

▲ *Allium moly* 'Jeannine'

'Zwanenburg'♀ is a particularly striking variety with carmine-pink flowers.

A. ostrowskianum see *A. oreophilum*

A. porrum see leeks p. 739

A. pulchellum see *A. carinatum*

A. sativum see garlic p. 742

A. schoenoprasum see chives p. 331

A. senescens (syn. *A. glaucum*, *A. spirale*) (German garlic, mountain garlic) This very variable species, useful in a rock garden or at the edge of a path, prefers well-drained soil. Lilac or pinkish purple, cup-shaped flowers are carried in hemispherical clusters up to 5 cm (2 in) across in mid summer to early autumn. HEIGHT 10-50 cm (4-20 in).

Many garden hybrids have developed from the 2 subspecies found in the wild. The European ssp. ***montanum*** has narrow grass-green leaves and grows to about 45 cm (1½ ft) tall. The Asian ssp. ***senescens*** has fleshy, green to grey-green leaves, sometimes attractively twisted, and grows from just a few to 60 cm (2 ft) tall. Plants bred to have grey or bluish green leaves are sometimes named *A. glaucum*, and those with twisted leaves *A. spirale*.

A. siculum see *Nectaroscordum siculum*

A. sikkimense (syn. *A. kansuense*, *A. tibeticum*) This clump-forming bulb has pretty, bell-shaped, blue flowers which hang in small clusters in summer among narrow leaves. Native to the Himalayas. HEIGHT 10-25 cm (4-10 in).

A. sphaerocephalon (round-headed leek) The flowers of this species are good for cutting and loved by bees. The pink to reddish purple, bell-shaped flowers are carried in dense heads in mid to late summer. Plant in tight clumps. Native to Europe, N Africa and W Asia. HEIGHT 50-60 cm (20-24 in).

A. spirale see *A. senescens*

A. tibeticum see *A. sikkimense*

A. triquetrum (three-cornered leek) Easily recognised by its 3-sided stems, this plant is pretty but invasive, and should be planted with caution. The white flowers, from early spring, have green stripes and hang in loose heads. Native to S Europe but naturalised in Britain. HEIGHT 15-30 cm (6-12 in).

A. tuberosum see Chinese chives p. 331

A. unifolium (syn. *A. murrayanum*) This plant does well in a hot and sunny position that recreates the conditions of its native habitat in western USA. In early summer it carries domed heads, consisting of up to 30 deep pink, bell-shaped flowers. HEIGHT 20-60 cm (8-24 in).

A. ursinum (ramson, wild garlic) The broad, bright green leaves grow in clumps round stems that bear loose heads of clear white starry flowers in late spring. The species is found throughout Europe and is often regarded as a weed in Britain. However, it is useful for growing in woodland conditions. The leaves give off a strong smell of garlic when crushed. HEIGHT 10-45 cm (4-18 in).

CULTIVATION Grow in fertile well-drained soil and a sunny sheltered position. Plant the bulbs in autumn, covering them to twice their diameter with soil. Leave them undisturbed for several years. Bulbs such as *A. cyaneum* and *A. oreophilum* may also be grown in pots in a cool greenhouse.

PROPAGATION Lift and divide old clumps of bulbs as soon as they have died down after flowering. Most can also be raised from seed sown in pots of gritty soil in late summer. If the old flowerheads are left on the plants, some species seed themselves.

PESTS AND DISEASES The bulbs may be damaged by the larvae of onion flies. Diseases such as white rot, fusarium and rust can also attack the plants. Aphids may be a problem for species grown under glass and can spread viruses.

Almond, ornamental see *Prunus*

▼ *Allium sikkimense*

Alnus

Alder

Betulaceae

Alnus glutinosa 'Imperialis'

Striking catkins, unusual cones and fine foliage are features of these splendid deciduous trees and shrubs. The bark splits into thick plates with age. Alders are hardy and fast-growing and thrive on poorer soils. They are also able to survive very wet conditions and often found growing by rivers and streams. *Alnus cordata* and *A. glutinosa* reach a height of 18m (60ft) or more.

Both male and female catkins are carried on the same plant and usually appear in clusters of between two and six from late winter to early spring – before the leaves. The male catkins are pendulous and can grow to about 10cm (4in) long; the females are shorter and develop into round, woody cones usually less than 2.5cm (1in) in diameter. The cones ripen in autumn and remain on the tree for several months. Alder is the only deciduous tree to produce a cone-like casing for its seeds. The leaves are alternate, grow up to 10cm (4in) long and often have a serrated edge.

RECOMMENDED SPECIES AND VARIETIES

A. cordata♀ (Italian alder) Heart-shaped finely toothed leaves, dark glossy green above and lighter beneath, are borne on an upright, rather conical tree. The yellow

▲ *Alnus cordata*

catkins grow to 7.5cm (3in) long. The tree grows well in all types of soil. Native to Italy. HEIGHT & SPREAD 8x3m (26x10ft) after 20 years, ultimately 18m (60ft) tall.

A. glutinosa (common alder) This conical tree is ideal for growing in very wet conditions and is often seen beside streams. The irregularly toothed leaves are generally pear-shaped and tapered at the base. They are dark green above and lighter beneath. The male catkins are dark yellow and can grow to 10cm (4in) long. Native to Britain. HEIGHT & SPREAD 8x3m (26x10ft) after 20 years, ultimately 18m (60ft) tall.

▲ *Alnus glutinosa* (bark)

'Imperialis'♀ is a beautiful conical tree with deeply cut leaves that give it a graceful feathery appearance. It is about half the size of the species. **'Laciniata'** is similar but has less deeply cut leaves.

A. incana (grey alder) An upright tree with dark green, serrated, oval leaves which are grey-hairy underneath. The yellow-brown catkins are 5-10cm (2-4in) long. Native to Europe and the Caucasus. HEIGHT & SPREAD 6x2m (20x6½ft) after 20 years, ultimately 15m (50ft) tall.

A. rugosa (speckled alder) This small tree of rounded habit has 10cm (4in) long, oval leaves that are dark green above and lighter beneath. The greenish yellow catkins grow to 10cm (4in) long. Native to N America. HEIGHT & SPREAD 2x2m (6½x6½ft) after 5 years, ultimately 5m (16ft) tall.

A. x spaethii♀ A fast-growing upright tree with large serrated leaves up to 15cm (6in) long. These are purplish at first, turning dark green above and lighter beneath with age. The catkins can grow to 15cm (6in) long. HEIGHT & SPREAD 7x3m (23x10ft) after 20 years, ultimately 15m (50ft) tall.

CULTIVATION Alders grow in a variety of soils. Most tolerate lime but *A. cordata* and *A. glutinosa* do not do well on shallow soils over chalk. *A. cordata* and *A. incana* prefer drier soil, and *A. glutinosa* tolerates very wet soils.

PROPAGATION Most alders are best grown from seed, but hardwood cuttings can also be successful. Cultivars need to be grafted.

PRUNING None is required.

PESTS AND DISEASES Phytophthora may affect alders on wet ground.

Aloe

Aloeaceae

Aloe variegata

Prominent rosettes of fleshy leaves give these perennial succulents and sub-shrubs an architectural character. The plants are also prized for their dense spikes of tubular flowers. Aloes require a minimum temperature of 7°C (45°F) and are suitable only as house or greenhouse plants.

RECOMMENDED SPECIES AND VARIETIES

A. aristata♀ Dark green, lance-shaped, leaves, 10cm (4in) long and 2cm (¾in) wide, form tight rosettes, up to 20cm (8in) across, which grow in dense clusters. The leaves are sparsely spined and have bands of white spots. Soft white teeth at the margins complete their unusual appearance. Red flowers, up to 4cm (1½in) long, are carried on branched spikes in early summer. HEIGHT & SPREAD 50x20cm (20x8in).

A. variegata (partridge breast aloe) The triangular dark green leaves, up to 15cm (6in) long and 5cm (2in) wide, are banded and blotched with white and form neat angular rosettes. An occasional spike of flesh-pink or dull scarlet flowers is produced in winter. HEIGHT & SPREAD 30x20cm (12x8in).

▲ *Aloe variegata*

CULTIVATION Grow in a very sunny spot in compost made up of equal parts of sharp grit and John Innes No.3. Water freely in spring and summer, sparingly in winter. Repot annually in spring and feed once or twice in summer with liquid houseplant fertiliser.

PROPAGATION Sow seeds under glass during spring, or divide the clusters of rosettes in spring or summer.

PESTS AND DISEASES Usually trouble free.

Alonsoa

Mask flower
Scrophulariaceae

Pink, orange and red are the predominant colours of the 2cm (¾in) wide flowers of these tropical American perennials, which are often grown as half-hardy annuals. Each flower resembles a tiny asymmetrical dish with a deeply scalloped edge, or possibly a theatrical mask. They are fairly easy summer-flowering bedding plants, though results can be disappointing in cool wet seasons. They may also be grown as conservatory and greenhouse plants. Those described are very free-flowering, much-branched species, which may bloom all summer.

RECOMMENDED SPECIES AND VARIETIES

A. meridionalis This good cut flower has pink, red and white blooms, available mixed and as the varieties **'Pink Beauty'** and **'Salmon Beauty'.** The toothed elongated oval leaves are up to 3.5cm (1⅜in) long. HEIGHT & SPREAD 60x30cm (2x1ft).

A. warscewiczii♀ Scarlet flowers adorn this popular species, which has toothed oval leaves, heart-shaped at the base. HEIGHT & SPREAD 60x30cm (2x1ft).

'Peachy-keen' has pale apricot flowers.

▲ *Alonsoa warscewiczii*

CULTIVATION Sow seed in heat – at least 18°C (64°F) – in early spring. Prick out 5cm (2in) apart, or into 8cm (3in) pots or cell trays. At 5cm (2in) high, pinch out the growing points to encourage branching. Harden off and plant out, 15-25cm (6-10in) apart, in a sunny, sheltered spot.

For greenhouse or conservatory plants, sow in late summer. During winter maintain a minimum temperature of 10°C (50°F). Use a 13cm (5in) diameter final pot and support the flowering stems.

PROPAGATION Sow seed, or take ripewood cuttings in late summer.

PESTS AND DISEASES Aphids may attack.

Aloysia

Verbenaceae

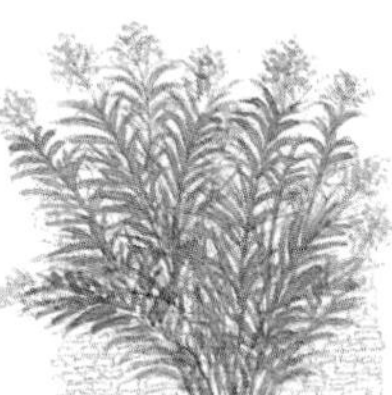

Aloysia triphylla

Handsome aromatic foliage and slender spikes of small tubular flowers characterise aloysias. *Aloysia triphylla*, a half-hardy deciduous shrub or sub-shrub, makes a splendid pot plant for a conservatory. It can also be grown outside in a sunny, sheltered spot. Its dried leaves are used for flavouring and potpourri.

RECOMMENDED SPECIES AND VARIETIES

A. triphylla (syn. *Lippia citriodora*) (lemon verbena) The coarse, lemon-scented leaves, up to 10cm (4in) long, are lance-shaped. Sprays of tiny white or purplish flowers are produced during summer on new terminal growths. Native to Argentina and Chile. HEIGHT & SPREAD 1.5x1.2m (5x4ft) tall.

▲ *Aloysia triphylla*

CULTIVATION Grow indoors in large pots in a soil-based compost such as John Innes No.3. Outside, plant in free-draining soil against a sunny south or west-facing wall. Give a protective mulch of composted bark or well-rotted garden compost in autumn.

PROPAGATION Take softwood cuttings in summer.

PRUNING Indoor plants retain their shrubby habit, but those grown outside usually suffer frost damage and may need to be pruned to the ground each spring.

PESTS AND DISEASES Greenfly can be a problem outside; whitefly and red spider mite may attack the plants under glass.

Alstroemeria

Peruvian lily, lily of the Incas
Alstroemeriaceae

Alstroemeria Ligtu Hybrids

Grown for their attractive, showy flowers, alstroemerias are colourful plants for garden borders and containers. Long-lasting when cut, the flowers are popular with both gardeners and commercial growers and, over the years, many hybrids have been bred to meet an increasing demand for new flower colours and a longer flowering period.

Herbaceous perennials, native to S America, alstroemerias have thick, rather brittle tubers, which spread to form colonies up to 1.2m (4ft) across. They are easily grown in fertile well-drained soil but do not like thin dry soils. The plants recommended below are hardy to -10°C (14°F).

Open, funnel-shaped flowers are borne in loose clusters at the ends of the stems. They are about 5cm (2in) long and have three narrow inner petals and three broader outer ones. The inner petals, two upper and one lower, are usually marked in a contrasting colour. Flower colours include shades of purple, pink, red, orange and yellow. The long stems bear many slightly twisted, lanceolate leaves, 5-10cm (2-4in) long.

RECOMMENDED SPECIES AND VARIETIES

A. aurea (syn. *A. aurantiaca*) Clusters of bright orange flowers, marked with deep red flecks, appear in summer. A vigorous plant, which often spreads to form large patches. HEIGHT 1m (3ft).

▲ *Alstroemeria aurea* 'Dover Orange'

'Dover Orange' is slightly taller and has deeper orange flowers.

A. psittacina (syn. *A. pulchella*) Stems, spotted with mauve, bear clusters of flowers from late summer to early autumn. The narrow flowers are green and deep wine-

a

red, spotted and streaked with maroon. HEIGHT 1m (3ft).

ALSTROEMERIA HYBRIDS

There are many hybrids that produce a wide range of different coloured flowers. Apart from the Ligtu Hybrids, which flower in early summer, all bloom from mid summer until the first frosts of autumn. Most grow to 1m (3ft) high, though there are dwarf hybrids that are excellent for pots. **'Apollo'**♀ has ivory-white flowers with a yellow spot and brown flecks on the inner petals. **'Charm'**♀ has pale pink blooms with creamy yellow inner petals, flecked with brown. The **Ligtu Hybrids**♀ produce flowers in a wide range of colours, from soft

▲ *Alstroemeria* 'Apollo'

▲ *Alstroemeria* Ligtu Hybrids

pink to orange and yellow. **'Marina'**♀ has dark pink flowers with a lemon-yellow centre and brown flecks. The brick-red petals of **'Mars'**♀ have a yellow flash; the inner petals are flecked brownish purple. **'Orange Glory'**♀ has deep orange-red flowers with a yellow mark and brown flecks on the inner petals. **'Princess Caroline'**♀ has soft apricot-orange flowers with a red blotch on the outer petals and a yellow throat. The flowers of **'Princess Elizabeth'**♀ are cream with a pink flush and a yellow throat. This hybrid only reaches 30cm (1ft). **'Princess Mira'**♀ has rich lilac-pink flowers with a white throat, and grows to 30cm (1ft). The flowers of **'Yellow Friendship'**♀ have lemon-yellow outer petals and deep yellow inner ones; the upper inner petals are flecked with brown.

CULTIVATION Outside, choose a sunny sheltered position with fertile, well-drained but moisture-retentive soil. Plant tubers 4-8cm (1½-3¼in) deep in early spring. Protect them from bright sun and water regularly until established. In winter, mulch young plants or plants growing in cold areas. Pot-grown alstroemerias are planted from spring to autumn, 3cm (1¼in) deep, in 30cm (12in) pots of loam-based compost. Overwinter in a light frost-free place, keeping the compost almost dry. Move pots outside once the danger of frost has passed. Deadhead for continuous flowering.

PROPAGATION Divide roots in early autumn or spring, replanting immediately.

PESTS AND DISEASES Young shoots can be damaged by slugs and snails, and swift moth caterpillars may feed on the roots. Red spider mite can be a problem under glass.

Althaea

Malvaceae

Pretty, pink to purple, cup-shaped flowers are carried on tall, erect stems in summer. Althaeas are closely related to the hollyhock, *Alcea rosea*, but have smaller flowers with five notched petals. The round, toothed leaves, up to 6cm (2½in) long, are pale green. Hardy plants, althaeas spread to form clumps and are suitable for a sunny spot at the back of a border.

RECOMMENDED SPECIES AND VARIETIES

A. officinalis (marsh mallow) The pale lilac-pink flowers, 3cm (1¼in) across, have a central boss of purplish red anthers and are borne singly or in small clusters at the leaf axils. The velvety ovate leaves have 3-5 lobes. A hardy perennial, native to grassy coastal areas or salt marshes in Europe. HEIGHT & SPREAD 2m×30cm (6½×1ft).

▲ *Althaea officinalis*

CULTIVATION Grow in any fertile soil in full sun. On windy sites stake taller plants.

PROPAGATION Divide in autumn or spring, or sow seed in open ground in spring and transplant to the final position in autumn.

PESTS AND DISEASES Capsid bugs, caterpillars and, in hot summers, red spider mites may be troublesome.

Aluminium plant see *Pilea cadierei*
Alum root see *Heuchera*

Alyogyne

Malvaceae

Though mostly confined to the greenhouse or conservatory, these hibiscus-like shrubs, with their large, purple hued, satiny flowers, can be moved outside in summer to bring colour to a patio or terrace. Native to Australia, they survive outside in Britain only when planted in a frost-free garden.

RECOMMENDED SPECIES AND VARIETIES

A. hakeifolia (satin hibiscus) Pale lilac or lilac-purple flowers are borne from early summer to mid autumn by this vigorous species. The finely cut, coarse green leaves are up to 7.5cm (3in) long. HEIGHT & SPREAD 3×1m (10×3ft) after 5 years and ultimately.

A. huegelii (lilac hibiscus) Saucer-shaped flowers, up to 10cm (4in) across, in lilac-purple or red with a darker spotted base, are carried from early summer to mid autumn. The deep green leaves are lobed and up to 8cm (3¼in) long. HEIGHT & SPREAD 3×1.2m (10×4ft) after 5 years and ultimately, half this size in smaller containers.

'Santa Cruz' has soft blue flowers tinged with pink, up to 10cm (4in) across.

▲ *Alyogyne huegelii*

CULTIVATION Grow in large pots in a frost-free conservatory or cool greenhouse. Bring outside during the summer and feed regularly. Water sparingly in winter.

PROPAGATION Take softwood cuttings in summer or sow seeds in warmth in spring.

PRUNING Trim off die-back in spring and reduce the main branches by two-thirds.

PESTS AND DISEASES Aphids, whitefly and red spider mites can trouble alyogynes, especially when they are under glass.

Alyssum

Cruciferae

Alyssum montanum

Dense clusters of tiny four-petalled flowers, usually yellow, occasionally white or pink, smother hummocks of grey or silver foliage from late spring to mid summer. Alyssums are hardy plants, but in the garden grow best in a well-drained, sunny position, edging borders, draping down walls or tucked into rock gardens. Most species are native to dry highlands in S Europe and W Asia. The hardy annual bedding plants known as alyssums have been reclassified as *Lobularia maritima*. The perennial once called *Alyssum saxatile* (yellow alyssum) is now *Aurinia saxatilis*. All the species listed below are low-growing evergreen perennials, except *A. spinosum*, which is a semi-deciduous shrub.

RECOMMENDED SPECIES AND VARIETIES

A. cuneifolium Buttercup-yellow flower clusters, 3.5 cm (1⅜ in) across, are borne on a compact plant. The silvery, hairy leaves form dense evergreen rosettes. HEIGHT & SPREAD 15×15 cm (6×6 in).

A dwarf variety is ssp. ***pirinicum***.

A. maritimum see *Lobularia maritima*

A. montanum Fragrant, deep yellow flowers are borne in clusters 5 cm (2 in) across. The leaves form dense, whitish rosettes. The plant has a spreading, mat-forming habit. It is easy to grow and often seeds around once established. HEIGHT & SPREAD 15×30 cm (6×12 in).

'Berggold' ('Mountain Gold') is lower growing with golden yellow flowers.

A. saxatile see *Aurinia saxatilis*

A. serpyllifolium This alyssum forms a sprawling mat of grey-green to silvery leaves. The bright yellow flower clusters measure 2.5 cm (1 in) across. HEIGHT & SPREAD 8×30 cm (3¼×12 in).

▼ *Alyssum cuneifolium*

▲ *Alyssum serpyllifolium*

A. spinosum (syn. *Ptilotrichum spinosum*) White to pink-purple flowers are borne in abundant rounded clusters 3.5 cm (1⅜ in) across. Colour varies considerably in plants raised from seed. This semi-deciduous, dense and rather prickly shrub forms rounded hummocks with silvery grey leaves. HEIGHT & SPREAD 60×30 cm (2×1 ft).

'Roseum'♀ has pale to deep pink-purple flowers. It is easy to grow and a reliable performer, especially in a raised bed or a scree, created by mixing coarse gravel or stone chippings with peat and soil.

▲ *Alyssum spinosum* 'Roseum'

A. wulfenianum Pale yellow flowers, in flat clusters up to 2.5 cm (1 in) across, appear in early to late summer above rosettes of silver-green foliage. This species does well in crevices in walls, paths and banks, being a tufted plant with spreading stems. HEIGHT & SPREAD 20×30 cm (8×12 in).

CULTIVATION Plant alyssums from spring to autumn on sunny well-drained sites. They especially like alkaline soils. In wetter areas protect them with a pane of glass or a cloche during winter.

PROPAGATION Take softwood cuttings in late spring or early summer, or sow seed from late summer to winter.

PRUNING Trim back lightly after flowering to encourage bushy growth.

PESTS AND DISEASES Usually trouble free.

Alyssum, sweet see *Lobularia maritima*

▼ *Alyssum wulfenianum*

Amaranthus

Amaranthaceae

Dangling flower tassels and varieties offering brilliantly coloured foliage earn these half-hardy annuals their place in borders and containers.

RECOMMENDED SPECIES AND VARIETIES

A. caudatus (love-lies-bleeding) Long drooping tassels, up to 45 cm (1½ ft) long, of tiny blood-red flowers, hang among pale green leaves in mid and late summer. HEIGHT & SPREAD 60×40 cm (24×16 in).

▲ *Amaranthus caudatus*

The tassels of **'Viridis'** are vivid green.

A. cruentus (syn. *A. paniculatus*) **'Foxtail'** Upright, deep blood-red flower spikes grow among bronze-red foliage on a plant 60 cm (2 ft) tall. **'Red Cathedral'**, with scarlet foliage and purple flowers, reaches 1 m (3 ft) or more tall. Both varieties have a spread of 40 cm (16 in).

A. hypochondriacus Deep crimson flowers are carried in densely packed, erect spikes among purple-tinted foliage from mid summer to mid autumn. HEIGHT & SPREAD 1.2 m×50 cm (4 ft×20 in).

'Green Thumb'♀ has green flowers and **'Pygmy Torch'**♀ has purple leaves and crimson flowers. They both grow to 60 cm (2 ft) high and 40 cm (16 in) wide.

A. paniculatus see *A. cruentus*

A. tricolor This tender species, grown for its striking foliage, makes a bright summer pot plant in a conservatory. The lower leaves of **'Illumination'** are green and chocolate-brown, the upper leaves bright rose-red and yellow. **'Joseph's Coat'** has chocolate-brown, yellow and green lower leaves and crimson, scarlet and gold upper leaves. HEIGHT & SPREAD 60×40 cm (2 ft×16 in).

CULTIVATION All, except the more tender *A. tricolor*, are easily grown in any soil. They do best in full sun. *A. tricolor* needs sheltered conditions in full sun. Support taller varieties and plants on exposed sites. Pinch out the growing points of *A. cruentus* while still small, to encourage branching.

PROPAGATION Sow seed in early spring in a heated greenhouse.

PESTS AND DISEASES Aphids can be troublesome to amaranthus.

Amaryllis

Amaryllidaceae

Large, pink or white, sweetly scented flowers are borne in late summer and early autumn by this not fully hardy, bulbous perennial. It should not be confused with the tender winter-flowering houseplant, native to S America, *Hippeastrum*, which is often mistakenly sold as *Amaryllis*. There is only one species in the genus.

Amaryllis belladonna (belladonna lily, Jersey lily) The trumpet-shaped blooms, 6-10 cm (2½-4 in) long, are borne in clusters of 6 on long purple stems. Dark green, strap-like leaves, 50 cm (20 in) long, appear in autumn after the flowers, and last through winter until the following summer. Native to South Africa, *A. belladonna* grows outdoors in Britain, and is also suitable for container planting, both indoors and out. HEIGHT 60 cm (2 ft).

▲ *Amaryllis belladonna*

'Johannesburg' has pale pink flowers with a lighter centre. **'Kimberley'** has deep crimson-pink flowers with a white centre.

CULTIVATION Plant amaryllis bulbs during late summer in mild areas and in spring elsewhere, choosing a sunny position in well-drained, humus-rich soil. The bulbs must receive direct sunlight in summer or they will not flower. Make sure that the top of the bulb is level with the soil surface; over time the bulb pulls itself down, sometimes as deep as 20 cm (8 in). In areas where winter temperatures often fall below -5°C (23°F), plants need the protection of a wall facing south or south-west and a winter mulch. Allow the leaves and flowers to die back before removing them.

PROPAGATION Lift mature plants between early and mid summer, remove large offsets and replant immediately. Plants propagated this way can take up to 3 years to flower. Sow seed when ripe, though plants may take up to 8 years to flower.

PESTS AND DISEASES Slugs, snails, narcissus flies, eelworm, bulb rot and narcissus leaf scorch may damage plants.

Amaryllis see also *Hippeastrum*

Amelanchier

Serviceberry, Snowy mespilus

Rosaceae

Amelanchier canadensis

White spring blossom and spectacular bright red and gold autumn foliage make this an outstanding plant at most times of the year. The star-shaped flowers, no more than 2.5 cm (1 in) in diameter, appear in a profusion of clusters. Most are pure white and are dazzling against the young coppery foliage. The simple, alternate leaves grow to 5 cm (2 in) long and are generally finely toothed. The summer berries are red at first, darkening to black. Most of the ten or so species of these hardy deciduous shrubs or small trees are native to N America.

▲ *Amelanchier* 'Ballerina'

RECOMMENDED SPECIES AND VARIETIES

***A.* 'Ballerina'**🏆 This large shrub or small tree of rounded habit bears 6 cm (2½ in) long clusters of white flowers in early spring. The finely toothed leaves are bronze when young and give good red and brown autumn colour. HEIGHT & SPREAD 1×1 m (3×3 ft) after 5 years, finally 3 m (10 ft) tall.

A. canadensis Small white flowers appear

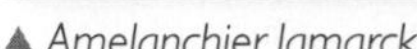

▲ *Amelanchier lamarckii*

in erect clusters, up to 6 cm (2½ in) long, in mid to late spring with the leaves. This erect, often multistemmed large shrub or small tree grows well in damp conditions. HEIGHT & SPREAD 1.2×1 m (4×3 ft) after 5 years, ultimately 7 m (23 ft) tall.

A. laevis Pendulous, 12 cm (4¾ in) long clusters of small white flowers appear in late spring and contrast with the young bronze foliage. The leaves turn dark green with age and give a display of orange and red autumn colour. The purple-black fruits are edible. This often multistemmed tree has a rather upright habit that becomes more spreading in old age. HEIGHT & SPREAD 1.5×1 m (5×3 ft) after 5 years, ultimately 8 m (26 ft) tall.

A. lamarckii🏆 Profuse clusters of small white flowers appear in mid to late spring and grow to 7.5 cm (3 in) long. The new, coppery bronze leaves emerge at the same time as the flowers and are covered in silky hairs which are eventually lost. The spectacular autumn colour normally combines brilliant yellows and reds. The plant has a multi-stemmed, rounded habit. HEIGHT & SPREAD 1.5×1.2 m (5×4 ft) after 5 years, ultimately 10 m (33 ft) tall.

CULTIVATION Plant in autumn and spring in any well-drained, moisture-retentive soil. Grow in full sun or partial shade. Amelanchiers prefer lime-free soil.

PROPAGATION This is normally from seed sown in autumn. But if a particular feature is required then grafting needs to be carried out. Layering and division are also success-

▼ *Amelanchier canadensis*

ful with the smaller, multistemmed shrubs.
PRUNING The multistemmed species may need thinning out from time to time.
PESTS AND DISEASES Usually trouble free, though fire blight is sometimes a problem.

Amicia

Leguminosae

Ramrod-straight, hollow, downy stems and eye-catching leaves distinguish this tall, semi-tender sub-shrub. Bamboo-like stems carry the leaves horizontally, giving the plants a layered appearance. Formed by four almost rectangular, notched leaflets, the leaves are bright green with prominent, paler midribs. Just beneath the flowers are pale green, almost circular leafy scales (stipules) which are streaked purplish brown with creamy beige edges. *Amicia zygomeris*, from the mountains of Mexico, is the only species generally grown in Britain. It needs a sheltered border or the protection of a wall in a warm, sunny garden.

RECOMMENDED SPECIES

A. zygomeris Yellow pea-like flowers, often flushed purple, appear in short axillary racemes from summer to autumn. The leaflets are about 7 cm (2¾ in) long. The narrow seedpods are jointed and flattened. HEIGHT & SPREAD 1-2 m x 1.2 m (3-6½ x 4 ft).

CULTIVATION Plant in spring in any fertile soil in a warm sunny position. Shelter from wind to avoid damage to the foliage. Protect the roots with a mulch in winter.

PROPAGATION Sow seed in spring or take semi-ripe cuttings in summer.

PESTS AND DISEASES Young plants are attacked by slugs and snails.

▲ *Amicia zygomeris*

Ammi

Umbelliferae

Frothy sprays of delicate white flowers distinguish these relatively tall, fast-growing, hardy annuals. They are closely related to the common native hedgerow plant known as cow parsley, though the foliage is more finely divided and therefore more appealing. The flowerheads last well when cut, and in arrangements provide a light-textured contrast to bolder, colourful blooms. Native to SW Asia, S Europe and N Africa.

▲ *Ammi majus*

RECOMMENDED SPECIES

A. majus Tiny white flowers are carried in compound umbels, up to 15 cm (6 in) across, on branching, upright stems from mid summer to early autumn. The leaves are mid to bluish green. The lower ones are pinnate with tooth-edged leaflets, the upper ones are still more divided, with a fern-like appearance. HEIGHT & SPREAD up to 1.2 m x 40 cm (4 ft x 16 in).

A. visnaga This species is very similar to *A. majus*, but has more finely divided foliage. HEIGHT & SPREAD 1.2 m x 40 cm (4 ft x 16 in).

CULTIVATION Ammis thrive even on poor, dry soils. Full-grown plants need staking against strong winds.

PROPAGATION Sow seed where the plants are to flower in mid to late spring.

PESTS AND DISEASES Aphids are an occasional nuisance.

Amorpha

Leguminosae

These fully hardy, free-flowering shrubs, many-branched and spreading, thrive in an open sunny position. The flowers have the characteristic pea-flower shape, with standard, wings and keel, constructed in this case from a single five-lobed petal. They appear in spiked clusters in summer. The deciduous leaves are pinnate, often fern-like in appearance, and sometimes strongly aromatic. The grey-green leaflets are downy and oval or elliptic in shape.

RECOMMENDED SPECIES

A. canescens (lead plant) This short, erect shrub has oval leaflets, no more than 2.5 cm (1 in) long, in a fern-like arrangement. The leaves are surmounted by terminal, upright, cylindrical heads of small violet flowers with orange anthers from mid to late summer. The flowerheads are as long as 15 cm (6 in). Native to eastern N America. HEIGHT & SPREAD 90 x 90 cm (3 x 3 ft) after 5 years and ultimately.

A. fruticosa (false indigo, bastard indigo) The leaflets on the divided foliage are oval and up to 5 cm (2 in) long. Tiny, purplish blue flowers with orange anthers, packed tightly into erect spikes up to 15 cm (6 in) tall, are produced in profusion in summer. A vigorous and fast-growing plant, native to southern USA. HEIGHT & SPREAD 4 x 3 m (13 x 10 ft) after 5 years and ultimately.

Amorpha fruticosa

CULTIVATION Grow amorphas in full sun in a very free-draining soil, not too rich in organic matter. Young plants should be pot grown if they are to establish quickly when planted outside in spring. Once established, plants benefit from regular feeding with a general liquid fertiliser in summer.

PROPAGATION Take softwood cuttings in summer or sow seed in a coldframe in autumn or early spring. *A. fruticosa* may also be propagated by removing rooted suckers in autumn.

PRUNING Remove damaged or badly placed branches and shoots in spring, bearing in mind that flowers are borne on the current season's growth.

PESTS AND DISEASES Usually trouble free.

▲ *Amorpha fruticosa*

Ampelopsis

Vitaceae

Ampelopsis glandulosa var. brevipedunculata

The handsome foliage of these vigorous, climbing deciduous shrubs provides dense cover for walls, pergolas or tree stumps. The oval leaves are lobed or divided. The plants cling by curling tendrils. Although easily cultivated and frost-hardy, they need plenty of room and a sheltered position.

RECOMMENDED SPECIES AND VARIETIES

A. glandulosa var. ***brevipedunculata*** (syn. *A. brevipedunculata*) This vigorous climber has dark green foliage. The leaves, up to 15 cm (6 in) long, are divided usually into 3 lobes, sometimes into 5. The small, late-summer clusters of tiny greenish flowers are followed in warm years by deep, greenish blue berries, 6 mm (¼ in) wide. Native to NE Asia. HEIGHT & SPREAD 3×1.8 m (10×6 ft) after 5 years, ultimately 5 m (16 ft) tall.

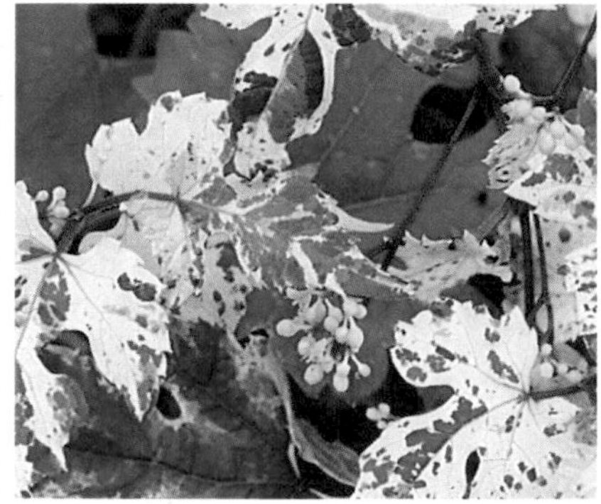

▲ *Ampelopsis glandulosa* var. *brevipedunculata* 'Elegans'

'Elegans' (syn. 'Tricolor') has smaller leaves, heavily splashed with pink and white. It reaches 3 m (10 ft) if given shelter.

A. henryana see *Parthenocissus henryana*

A. megalophylla Spectacularly large leaves, up to 60 cm (2 ft) long, are divided into 7 or more mid green, ovate leaflets which are whitish beneath. Tiny greenish flowers appear in clusters in late summer, sometimes followed by purple-black berries, 6 mm (¼ in) long. Native to W China. HEIGHT & SPREAD 6×3 m (20×10 ft) after 5 years, ultimately 10 m (33 ft).

A. sempervirens see *Cissus striata*

***A. tricuspidata* 'Veitchii'** see *Parthenocissus tricuspidata* 'Veitchii'

A. veitchii see *Parthenocissus tricuspidata* 'Veitchii'

CULTIVATION Plant in a sheltered position in any garden soil, in sun or partial shade. Provide adequate support while plants become established.

PROPAGATION Take semi-ripe cuttings during summer.

PRUNING None essential, but if the plant outgrows its space cut back in spring.

PESTS AND DISEASES Usually trouble free.

Amsonia

Blue star

Apocynaceae

In early summer, these slow-growing, hardy herbaceous perennials and sub-shrubs carry loose clusters of bright blue flowers. Suitable for the front of a border or in light shade, these plants form compact clumps of upright stems with abundant whorls of pointed, dark green leaves. The flowers are tubular, flaring open to star-shaped blooms with five petals.

RECOMMENDED SPECIES AND VARIETIES

A. ciliata Bright blue flowers, up to 2 cm (¾ in) across, are borne in clusters on slender upright stems. The long, narrow leaves, rolled under at the edges, are up to 5 cm (2 in) long. The least hardy of the species included here, it prefers a warm, sunny, sheltered site. Native to S United States. HEIGHT & SPREAD 1 m×50 cm (3 ft×20 in).

A. orientalis♀ The flowers are mostly blue, occasionally deep violet, and 1.5 cm (½ in) across. The narrow, pointed leaves, hairy along the edges, are up to 5 cm (2 in) long. Native to Greece and Turkey. HEIGHT & SPREAD 1 m×50 cm (3 ft×20 in).

A. tabernaemontana Pale sky-blue flowers, up to 2 cm (¾ in) across, are borne in short clusters. The smooth, dull green leaves are ovate or obovate and up to 6 cm (2½ in) long. This plant does best in a moist, shady position. Native to SE United States. HEIGHT & SPREAD 1 m×50 cm (3 ft×20 in).

The flower clusters of var. ***salicifolia*** are looser and smaller, the leaves are narrower and up to 9 cm (3½ in) long.

CULTIVATION Plant in autumn in fertile, moist but well-drained soil, placing in sun or light shade.

PROPAGATION Divide plants or sow seed in spring. Alternatively, take softwood cuttings in mid summer.

PESTS AND DISEASES Usually trouble free.

▲ *Amsonia tabernaemontana*

Anacyclus

Compositae

Forming small clumps of feathery foliage scattered with white daisies on arching stems, anacyclus are at their best in sheltered and sunny positions in rock gardens and raised beds. Native to the mountains of S Spain and N Africa, these plants are hardy if grown in freely draining soil.

RECOMMENDED SPECIES AND VARIETIES

A. pyrethrum (Mount Atlas daisy) This evergreen perennial has loose mats of tightly packed leaf rosettes, formed by ferny, grey-green leaves up to 4 cm (1½ in) long. The petals have a broad purple stripe underneath so that the flowers are purple in bud. They open out to white blooms, up to 5 cm (2 in) across. HEIGHT & SPREAD 7.5×30 cm (3×12 in).

The petals of var. ***depressus*** are deep crimson beneath and it reaches a height of 5 cm (2 in) and spread of 25 cm (10 in). **'Golden Gnome'** has yellow flowerheads.

CULTIVATION Plant during spring in full sun in very well-drained soil. Protect from wet weather in winter with a cloche or a pane of glass. Alternatively, grow in an unheated greenhouse or alpine house. Unless seed is wanted, deadhead regularly to prolong flowering.

PROPAGATION Sow seed in spring or take softwood cuttings in late summer.

PESTS AND DISEASES Aphids sometimes infest foliage, inviting sooty mould. Young plants are attractive to slugs.

▲ *Anacyclus pyrethrum* var. *depressus*

Anagallis

Pimpernel
Primulaceae

The vivid little flowers of this genus come in blues and reds, providing a splash of summer colour. The flowers, with five broad, rounded petals that open wide and flat or remain cupped, are borne singly. These annuals and evergreen perennials are suitable for a wild garden, a rock garden or the front of a border.

RECOMMENDED SPECIES AND VARIETIES

A. arvensis (common pimpernel, scarlet pimpernel) Wide open, scarlet, more rarely pink, flowers about 1cm (⅜in) across are borne in late spring and summer. The close-set pairs or whorls of light green ovate leaves are on sprawling stems that form a loose mat of growth. Because this annual or short-lived perennial seeds itself freely, it is best suited to a wild or informal garden. Native to Europe and W Asia. HEIGHT & SPREAD 10×50cm (4×20in).

The flowers produced by var. ***caerulea*** are bright blue.

A. monellii♀ (syn. *A. linifolia*) Profuse saucer-shaped flowers in brilliant blue, but occasionally red or pink, bloom from mid to late summer and are up to 1.5cm (½in) across. The pairs or whorls of narrow, pointed leaves are dark, glossy and evergreen. This short-lived perennial is not reliably hardy and should be treated as an annual. Native to SW Europe. HEIGHT & SPREAD 15×40cm (6×16in).

'Sunrise' has flowers of rich scarlet.

A. tenella (bog pimpernel) Bell-shaped pink flowers, up to 1cm (⅜in) across, appear in early to mid summer. The thread-like stems bear pairs of pale green oval to rounded leaves. Fairly hardy, this plant needs damp soil. A prostrate, evergreen perennial, native to W Europe. HEIGHT & SPREAD 4×40cm (1½×16in).

'Studland'♀ has deep pink, sweetly scented flowers.

CULTIVATION Plant *A. arvensis* and *A. monelli* in a sunny spot in gritty, well-drained soil. Grow *A. tenella* in moist soil and divide every 2 years to maintain vigour.

PROPAGATION Sow seed as soon as it is ripe. Take cuttings of *A. monelli* in summer. For *A. tenella,* pull off and pot up rooted shoots.

PESTS AND DISEASES Aphids, especially under glass, and slugs can cause damage.

▲ *Anagallis arvensis var. caerulea*

▲ *Anagallis monellii*

Ananas

Pineapple
Bromeliaceae

In tropical countries these evergreen perennials are grown for their fruit, but in the cooler climate of Britain they are valued more for their foliage. Rigid, strap-shaped leaves form rosettes out of which rise large, dense oblong heads of tiny tubular flowers, mainly in summer. The flowers are replaced by fleshy, succulent pineapples. All species need warm, humid conditions and make unusual houseplants or greenhouse specimens. Native to Brazil.

RECOMMENDED SPECIES AND VARIETIES

A. bracteatus (red pineapple, wild pineapple) Deep green leaves, up to about 1m (3ft) long and 2.5cm (1in) wide, have sharp red spines along the edges. The flowers are purplish blue to lilac surrounded by bracts. Keep at a minimum of 15°C (59°F). HEIGHT & SPREAD 1×1m (3×3ft).

The cultivar **'Striatus'** has variegated leaves that are striped with green and cream.

A. comosus (pineapple) Channelled, spiny-edged grey-green leaves, up to about 1m (3ft) long and 5cm (2in) wide, form rosettes. The tiny flowers, which are bluish, green or yellow and sometimes suffused with pink, are enclosed by bracts. Keep at a minimum of 10°C (50°F). HEIGHT & SPREAD 1m×60cm (3×2ft).

The leaves of var. ***variegatus*** are green and gold.

CULTIVATION Grow in pots of John Innes No.2 in a greenhouse or on a warm, well-lit windowsill. Keep out of draughts and water sparingly in winter. Feed when the fruit have set. Repot yearly in early spring.

PROPAGATION Remove sideshoots in spring or slice off the tuft of leaves on a healthy fruit and pot on.

PESTS AND DISEASES Red spider mite and mealy bug can be a nuisance.

▲ *Ananas comosus*

Anaphalis

Pearly everlasting
Compositae

Small, fluffy, pearly white flowers with yellow stamens glisten in summer on the hardy, easily grown perennials. They are borne in loose flat clusters, 10cm (4in) across. The undersides of the silver-grey, downy, narrow leaves, 6cm (2½in) long, are covered with fine hairs and look like white felt. The blooms often last until early autumn and are excellent for cutting and drying. To dry, cut stems soon after the flowers are fully open and hang upside down in small bunches in a light airy place. Plants are upright and clump-forming, standing up well at the front or middle of a herbaceous border. They are also generous contributors to a white border as both the foliage and flowers provide many months of silvery white colour.

RECOMMENDED SPECIES AND VARIETIES

A. cinnamomea see *A. margaritacea* var. *cinnamomea*

A. margaritacea Bushy clumps of silver-grey foliage form quickly and produce their loose heads of profuse white flowers in late summer and early autumn. This plant is found widely in the Northern Hemisphere, and is more drought tolerant than other

▲ *Anaphalis margaritacea*

species. HEIGHT & SPREAD 60×60cm (2×2ft).

Similar in growth and habit is var. ***cinnamomea*** (syn. *A. cinnamomea*) whose leaves are more densely covered with felt. **'Neuschnee'** ('New Snow') is a more compact variety, with a height and spread of 45cm (1½ft) and long grey-green leaves. The flowerheads of var. ***yedonensis***♀ (syn. *A. yedonensis*) are larger. It reaches up to 75cm (2½ft) in height.

A. nepalensis var. ***monocephala*** (syn. *A. nubigena*) These compact little plants are suitable for rock gardens, forming neat clumps of white woolly foliage with cream-white flowers in mid summer. Native to the Himalayas and W China. HEIGHT & SPREAD 15×15cm (6×6in).

A. nubigena see *A. nepalensis* var. *monocephala*

A. triplinervis♀ This serves as a ground-cover plant during mid summer and autumn, forming dense clumps of grey-green foliage with wide domed clusters of white flowers. Originating from the Himalayas and SW China. HEIGHT & SPREAD 60×60cm (2×2ft).

▲ *Anaphalis triplinervis*

▲ *Anaphalis triplinervis* 'Sommerschnee'

'Sommerschnee' ('Summer Snow') is a more compact variety with a height and spread of 45cm (1½ft).

A. yedonensis see *A. margaritacea* var. *yedonensis*

CULTIVATION Plant in a sunny position between autumn and early spring in soil that does not dry out too much in summer but is also free draining.

PROPAGATION Divide in autumn or spring or take basal cuttings in early spring.

PESTS AND DISEASES Usually trouble free.

Anchusa

Alkanet

Boraginaceae

Anchusa azurea 'Loddon Royalist'

Sprays of small, vivid blue flowers, carried on branching stems in early summer, provide a rare depth of colour especially when planted in groups. The foliage is bristly and somewhat coarse. Annuals, biennials and herbaceous perennials are included in the genus; the recommended plants are short-lived, hardy perennials. *Anchusa azurea* does well in the herbaceous border while *A. caespitosa* is more usually found in the rock garden; both are tolerant of drought.

RECOMMENDED SPECIES AND VARIETIES

A. azurea Tall spikes of tiny bright blue flowers, up to 2cm (¾in) across, sometimes with a white or yellow eye, are borne above coarse, mid green, lance-shaped leaves from late spring to early summer. Young plants give the best display. Native to Europe, N Africa and W Asia. HEIGHT & SPREAD 1.5m×60cm (5×2ft).

'Dropmore' has profuse deep blue, purple-tinted flowers. It reaches 1.8m (6ft) tall. **'Feltham Pride'** is shorter at 75cm (2½ft) and has true blue flowers. **'Little John'** has deep blue flowers and reaches 45cm (1½ft) tall. **'Loddon Royalist'**♀ grows to 1m (3ft) with a profusion of royal blue flowers on a bushy plant. **'Opal'**, at 1m (3ft), has light blue flowers set against dark green leaves.

▲ *Anchusa azurea* 'Loddon Royalist'

▼ *Anchusa azurea* 'Opal'

▲ *Anchusa caespitosa*

A. caespitosa♀ Deep blue, almost stemless flowers with a white eye are borne in mid summer in clusters above rough-haired rosettes of dark green strap leaves. This dwarf, Mediterranean plant is best suited to a rock garden. Native to Crete. HEIGHT & SPREAD 7.5×23cm (3×9in).

A. myosotidiflora see *Brunnera macrophylla*

CULTIVATION Plant in spring or autumn in full sun. *A. azurea* and its cultivars need fertile soil and *A. caespitosa* does best on sharply drained soil; protect it from winter rain with a pane of glass. Taller plants need staking. Cut back after flowering.

PROPAGATION Take root cuttings in late winter. Alternatively, raise *A. caespitosa* from seed sown in spring or from basal cuttings taken in mid summer.

PESTS AND DISEASES Usually trouble free but cucumber mosaic virus can cause mottling on the leaves.

Andromeda

Bog rosemary

Ericaceae

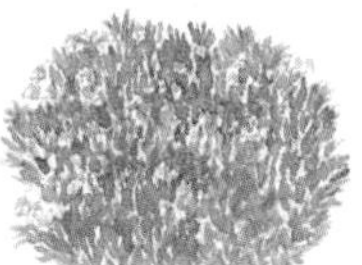

Andromeda polifolia

A heather bed, with its lime-free soil and open position, is particularly suitable for these dwarf shrubs bearing delightful, cluttered, bell-shaped flowers and evergreen foliage. These plants are equally at home in a rock garden, coldframe, alpine house or unheated greenhouse. They are extremely hardy plants, native to acid bogs and tundra in temperate and sub-Arctic regions of the Northern Hemisphere. Of the two species in this genus, *Andromeda polifolia* is the most widely available.

RECOMMENDED SPECIES AND VARIETIES
A. polifolia (marsh andromeda) The rounded bell-shaped flowers, about 6mm (¼in) long, are bright pink initially, gradually turning to white. They are borne in loose clusters from late spring to mid summer. The plant forms a low mound with shiny dark green, lanceolate to oval leaves, about 3cm (1¼in) long. HEIGHT & SPREAD 25×50cm (10×20in).

'Alba' bears white flowers. This cultivar forms a compact bush only 15cm (6in) tall.

Andromeda polifolia 'Kirigamine' ▲

▲ *Andromeda polifolia* 'Alba'

'Compacta'♀ has numerous white flowers and wide glaucous leaves up to 2.5cm (1in) long. **'Grandiflora'** has large clusters of pale to mid pink flowers and broad glaucous leaves on a plant just 15cm (6in) tall. **'Kirigamine'** can tolerate drier conditions than most varieties and has numerous mid pink flowers among narrow leaves. **'Macrophylla'**♀ has flowers which turn from dark pink to white set off against broad dark green leaves. **'Nana'** reaches just 15cm (6in) tall and is ideal for growing in troughs. **'Nikko'** has pale pink flowers on a compact plant with 2cm (¾in) long grey-green leaves. **'Shibutsu'** is free-flowering, with dense clusters of shiny pink flowers which gradually turn to white.

CULTIVATION Plant in lime-free, humus-rich soil in partial sun. Protect from strong summer sun.

Andromedas grow well in pots filled with a humus-rich compost in an unheated greenhouse or alpine house. Place under a partially shaded coldframe in the summer.

PROPAGATION Sow seed in autumn or early winter, or take greenwood cuttings in summer. Alternatively, lift and divide established plants in autumn.

PRUNING Trim back untidy growth after plants have flowered.

PESTS AND DISEASES Vine weevils can be a problem occasionally.

▲ *Andromeda polifolia* 'Macrophylla'

Androsace

Rock jasmine
Primulaceae

Androsace carnea

Dense cushions or loose mats of evergreen foliage, smothered in pink or white flowers, make these hardy evergreen perennials suitable for growing on rock gardens, in troughs and raised beds or in crevices in walls. They can also be grown in an unheated greenhouse or alpine house. The five-petalled flowers, about 1cm (⅜in) across, are borne singly or in clusters and have yellow eyes that turn red or pink after pollination. Most plants are made up of small leaf rosettes, composed of tiny leaves no more than 1.5cm (½in) in length. Androsaces need sharp drainage to thrive and do not tolerate excessive winter wet.

RECOMMENDED SPECIES AND VARIETIES
A. carnea Clusters of pink flowers on stalks 6cm (2½in) tall, are borne on this hairy plant from mid to late summer. The bright green, grass-like leaves form dense rosettes up to 2cm (¾in) across. HEIGHT & SPREAD 7.5×20cm (3×8in).

'Alba' has white flowers; **'Andorra'** is the most reliable cultivar to grow and has deep pink flowers; ssp. ***brigantiaca*** has larger rosettes and white flowers on stalks up to 15cm (6in) long; var. ***halleri*** see ssp. *rosea*; ssp. ***laggeri***♀ has rosettes about 1cm (⅜in) across and deep pink flowers; ssp. ***rosea***♀ (syn. var. *halleri*) is more vigorous with larger rosettes and larger, more open, pink flowers.

▲ *Androsace carnea* ssp. *brigantiaca*

▲ *Androsace cylindrica*

A. cylindrica White and yellow, early summer flowers on stalks 2cm (¾in) long, cover deep leaf cushions. Bristly, oblong, grey-green leaves form tiny rosettes, up to 2cm (¾in) across. Dead leaf rosettes persist on the plant; the new leaf rosettes grow on top of them, forming dense cylindrical masses. This plant should be grown in an alpine house or unheated greenhouse. HEIGHT & SPREAD 15×15cm (6×6in).

A. hirtella The white, spring flowers are borne singly or in pairs on short stems just above the leaf rosettes. Narrow, grey-green leaves covered with white hairs are grouped in tight rosettes, up to 1cm (⅜in) across, that form dense cushions. This species needs the protection of an alpine house or unheated greenhouse. HEIGHT & SPREAD 10×10cm (4×4in).

A. jacquemontii see *A. villosa* var. *jacquemontii*

▲ *Androsace lanuginosa*

A. lanuginosa♀ Clusters of flowers on stalks up to 10cm (4in) long, appear in late summer. Lilac with a greenish yellow eye at first, the flowers gradually turn pale pink with a darker pink eye. The grey-green, oval leaves, up to 2.5cm (1in) long, are not grouped in rosettes but form a loose mat, covered in silky hairs. This plant will grow on heavy clay soils provided that grit is added to improve drainage. HEIGHT & SPREAD 10×45cm (4×18in).

A. mollis see *A. sarmentosa* var. *yunnanensis*

A. mucronifolia hort. see *A. sempervivoides*

A. primuloides hort. see *A. sarmentosa*

***A. primuloides* 'Salmon's Variety'** see *A. sarmentosa* 'Salmon's Variety'

A. rotundifolia Clusters of pink, spring flowers surrounded by wide bracts are held on stems 15cm (6in) long. The rounded, lobed leaves are up to 6cm (2½in) in

a

Androsace sarmentosa

diameter. They are held on long stalks and form loose rosettes. HEIGHT & SPREAD 20×30cm (8×12in).

A. sarmentosa♀ (syn. *A. primuloides* hort.) Compact clusters of deep pink flowers surrounded by leafy bracts are borne on hairy stems, 4-10cm (1½-4in) long, from summer to autumn. The oval leaves are covered in silvery hairs. In winter, they make dense leaf rosettes about 1cm (⅜in) across; in spring these expand to 3cm (1¼in) across. This mat-forming plant spreads by reddish runners. HEIGHT & SPREAD 10×30cm (4×12in).

▲ *Androsace sarmentosa*

'Chumbyi' is hairier and forms denser mats than the species. **'Salmon's Variety'** has slightly larger flowers. **'Sherriff's'** has silvery leaves and pale pink flowers. The leaves of var. ***yunnanensis*** (syn. *A. mollis*) are very woolly.

A. sempervivoides♀ (syn. *A. mucronifolia* hort.) Clusters of bright pink flowers on stems up to 7.5cm (3in) long appear from late spring to mid summer. Long, smooth, symmetrical deep green leaves make rosettes, up to 2.5cm (1in) across, that form neat mats spread by short red runners. HEIGHT & SPREAD 7.5×30cm (3×12 in).

A. villosa var. ***jacquemontii*** Dense clusters of deep purple flowers on stems up to 4cm (1½in) long, appear in late spring to early summer. The oval leaves are covered in silvery hairs and sometimes have tiny red glands at the tips. The leaf rosettes are dense and 1cm (⅜in) across in winter, becoming looser and 1.5cm (½in) wide in summer. This mat-forming plant spreads by means of reddish runners. HEIGHT & SPREAD 4×30cm (1½×12in).

A. vitaliana see *Vitaliana primuliflora*

CULTIVATION Plant during spring or early summer in well-drained, gritty soil and add a top dressing of gravel. Choose a position in full sun or part shade. Protect plants from excessive winter wet with a pane of glass or cloche. *A. cylindrica* and *A. hirtella* should be grown in an unheated greenhouse or alpine house; the other species can also be grown indoors if wished.

PROPAGATION Sow seed as soon as it ripens or divide plants that spread by runners.

PESTS AND DISEASES Aphids, red spider mite and grey mould may be problems, especially in plants grown under glass.

Anemone

Windflower

Ranunculaceae

Anemone blanda

Whether it's in full sun or partial shade, in the herbaceous border or in light woodland, there is an anemone suitable for almost every garden situation. There are plants to provide flowers from early spring right through to late autumn, be they a delicate white, pink or blue, or a vibrant shade of red, yellow or violet.

Most anemones have deeply divided leaves with toothed edges that form a lush green foil to the delicate flowers. Each leaf usually has three to five main segments which again may be toothed or divided. The leaves generally grow in clumps at the base of the flowering stems and in whorls of three on the stems just below the flowers.

The rootstock of these hardy herbaceous perennials varies considerably. Some have a simple tuber, whereas others have a fibrous rootstock or a thick creeping rhizome.

RECOMMENDED SPECIES AND VARIETIES

EARLY-FLOWERING ANEMONES

These plants begin flowering in spring, early summer and mid summer and can be divided into two groups; those that prefer cool, semi-shaded spots and those that are best for hot, dry positions.

PLANTS FOR COOL, SEMI-SHADED SPOTS

These plants will grow in full sun but prefer dappled shade or shade for part of the day. They can be grown in the border, on the rock garden or in the woodland garden.

A. apennina♀ (blue anemone) Appearing in early spring, the starry flowers are bright blue, occasionally flushed with pink. Each flower is up to 3cm (1¼in) across and has 8-14 narrow oblong petals. The leaves are deep green and sometimes flushed purple. These plants grow from a thick rhizome. HEIGHT & SPREAD 15×30cm (6×12in).

The flowers of var. ***albiflora*** are white. **'Petrovac'** has deep blue flowers and more petals. **'Purpurea'** has rose-purple flowers.

A. baldensis (syn. *A. fragifera)* (Mt Baldo anemone) Slightly nodding, cup-shaped white flowers, sometimes flushed pink or purple outside, appear from early to mid summer. Each flower is up to 4cm (1½in) wide, with 8-10 oval petals. This clump-forming species has a fibrous rootstock. HEIGHT & SPREAD 12×30cm (4¾×12in).

A. fragifera see *A. baldensis*

A.* × *lesseri Rose-pink or sometimes yellowish, mauve or white, the upright flowers are borne from late spring to mid summer. The flowers are up to 3cm (1¼in) across and have from 5-8 broadly oval petals. This plant has a fibrous rootstock. HEIGHT & SPREAD 20×20cm (8×8in).

A.* × *lipsiensis Pale, sulphur-yellow, open flowers appear in spring. Each flower is up to 2cm (¾in) across and has 6-8 oval petals. This plant is grown from a rhizome. HEIGHT & SPREAD 15×15cm (6×6in).

A. multifida Cream, white, sometimes red or greenish cup-shaped flowers are seen from late spring through summer and, if the seed heads are removed, often into autumn. Borne in clusters of 1-8 upright flowers, each bloom is up to 2.5cm (1in) across with 5-10 elliptical petals. Grown from fibrous rootstock, this plant often seeds itself. HEIGHT & SPREAD 40×20cm (16×8in).

'Major' has creamy yellow flowers.

A. nemorosa (wood anemone) White, cup-shaped flowers, often flushed pink, purple or, occasionally, blue outside appear in spring. They are up to 4cm (1½in) across, with 6-8, sometimes more, oval petals. This woodland plant grows from a rhizome. HEIGHT & SPREAD 15×30cm (6×12in).

'Alba Plena' has white flowers with a pompom of pale yellow stamens. **'Allenii'**♀

▲ *Anemone nemorosa* 'Allenii'

has lavender flowers with a lilac or pale blue reverse and maroon leaf stalks. **'Blue Beauty'** has pale blue flowers and the foliage is often bronze-flushed. **'Bowles Purple'** has rich purple flowers. **'Grandiflora'** has large, white blooms, up to 5cm (2in) across. The white flowers of **'Leeds Variety'**♀ become flushed with pink. **'Lychette'** has white flowers. **'Robinsoniana'**♀ has lavender flowers, greyish on the outside, and maroon leaf stalks. The white flowers of **'Rosea'** turn pink. The flowers of **'Vestal'**♀ are white

▲ *Anemone nemorosa* 'Blue Beauty'

and have a pompom of white stamens. **'Viridiflora'** has green flowers.

A. ranunculoides♀ (yellow wood anemone) Cup-shaped yellow flowers, up to 2cm (¾in) across, with 5-7 oval petals are seen throughout spring. This patch-forming plant grows from a rhizome. HEIGHT & SPREAD 15×30cm (6×12in).

A. rivularis Blue or white flowers, flushed blue or pink on the outside, are borne in clusters of 3-5 from late spring to mid summer. Each flower is 1.5-3cm (½-1¼in) across, with 5-8 oval petals. This clump-forming plant grows from fibrous rootstock. HEIGHT & SPREAD 1m×45cm (3×1½ft).

A. sylvestris (snowdrop windflower) White, slightly nodding, cup-shaped flowers appear in early summer. Each flower, up to 6cm (2½in) across, has 5 oval petals. This patch-forming plant grows from a rhizome. HEIGHT & SPREAD 25×40cm (10×16in).

PLANTS FOR HOT, DRY POSITIONS

These plants need full sun and dry conditions, particularly during their summer dormancy, and can be planted anywhere in the garden that fulfils these requirements. They are also excellent plants for growing in pots.

A. blanda Starry flowers in blue, purple, pink or white, appear in early to mid spring. The flowers are up to 4cm (1½in) wide, with 12-18 narrow, oblong petals. This patch-forming plant grows from a tuber and it can be invasive. It will grow in dry woodland. HEIGHT & SPREAD 20×30cm (8×12in).

'Blue Mist' has pale blue flowers; **'Blue Pearl'**, mid blue flowers; **'Charmer'**, deep pink flowers; **'Fairy'**, snow-white flowers; **'Ingramii'**♀ (syn. 'Atrocaerulea'), dark sky-blue flowers and **'Pink Star'**, mid pink flowers. **'Radar'**♀ has deep magenta flowers with a white centre. The flowers of var. *rosea* are pale pink. **'Violet Star'** has amethyst flowers, whitish beneath. **'White Splendour'**♀ has glistening white flowers.

A. coronaria (crown anemone) The scarlet, pink, blue, mauve, white or bicoloured flowers have striking black stamens. Upright and cup-shaped, the flowers appear in spring and early summer. They have 5-8 oval, overlapping petals and measure 3-6cm (1¼-2½in) across. They grow from a thick, knobbly tuber and need to be fed regularly throughout the growing season. HEIGHT & SPREAD 60×15cm (24×6in).

This species has produced many popular cultivars. The **De Caen Group** has single flowers and includes different coloured varieties; **'Die Braut'** ('The Bride') has white flowers, **'Hollandia'** (syn. 'His Excellency') has large scarlet flowers with a white centre and **'Mister Fokker'** has violet-blue flowers. The **Saint Brigid Group** has semidouble flowers and includes **'The Admiral'** with bright pink flowers, **'Lord Lieutenant'**, with deep blue blooms and **'Mount Everest'**, with white flowers. The **Mona Lisa Group** includes F_1 hybrids, 10cm (4in) tall and with flowers up to 8cm (3¼in) across; **'Sylphide'** has single mauve flowers.

A. hortensis (syn. *A. stellata)* The pink, mauve or purple, upright starry flowers

▲ *Anemone nemorosa* 'Robinsoniana'

▲ *Anemone blanda* 'Radar'

▲ *Anemone blanda* var. *rosea*

▲ *Anemone nemorosa* 'Vestal'

▲ *Anemone blanda* 'Ingramii'

a

appear from mid to late spring. Each one is up to 4cm (1½in) wide and with 12-20 narrow oval petals. Plants grow from a thick tuber. HEIGHT & SPREAD 30x20cm (12x8in).

A. pavonina (peacock anemone) The flowers are scarlet, purple, deep blue, pink and, very rarely, white or yellowish with black stamens. The 8-12 oval petals are often white or creamish at the flower's centre. Upright, cupped up to 7.5cm (3in) across, and the blooms appear from mid to late spring. The stem leaves are bract-like and undivided. Grown from tubers, this is a patch-forming plant. HEIGHT & SPREAD 30x30cm (1x1ft).

A. pulsatilla see *Pulsatilla vulgaris*

A. vernalis see *Pulsatilla vernalis*

A. sulphurea see *Pulsatilla alpina* ssp. *apiifolia*

A. stellata see *A. hortensis*

LATE-FLOWERING ANEMONES

Tall plants with branching stems that flower from late summer to autumn, this group of anemones are particularly suitable for the herbaceous border. They prefer a partially shaded site but will grow in full sun in cooler, wetter regions. All are grown from creeping rhizomes.

A. hupehensis Clusters of white, pale pink or deep pink flowers, often tinged pink or mauve on the reverse, appear from late summer to mid autumn. Upright and cup-shaped, each flower is up to 6cm (2½in) in width, with 5-6 petals. HEIGHT & SPREAD 75x45cm (2½x1½ft).

'Bowles Pink' has deep purplish pink flowers and reaches up to 1m (3ft) in height. **'Hadspen Abundance'**♀ has very dark purplish pink flowers.

The flowers of var. ***japonica*** have up to 20 narrow, clear pink petals. Among its cultivars are **'Bressingham Glow'**, with semi-double flowers and up to 60cm (2ft) in height and **'Prinz Heinrich'**♀ ('Prince Henry'), with deep pink flowers.

The flowers of **'Praecox'** are more rosy pink than those of the species. **'September Charm'**♀ has silvery pink flowers, darker on the outside, and is about 1m (3ft) tall.

A. x hybrida (syn. *A. japonica* hort.) White, pink or mauve, shallow cup-shaped flowers appear from late summer to mid autumn. The flowers have 5-6 petals and are up to 6cm (2½in) wide. HEIGHT & SPREAD 1.5mx60cm (5x2ft).

'Geante des Blanches'♀ has white semidouble flowers with 15-20 petals. **'Honorine Jobert'**♀ has pure white, single flowers. **'Königin Charlotte'**♀ ('Queen Charlotte') has semidouble, pale purple flowers with frilly edges. **'Luise Uhink'** has white flowers, 4cm (1½in) wide with 8-10 petals. **'Margarete'** (syn. 'Lady Gilmour') has pale pink, double flowers. **'Monterosa'** has double, deep pink flowers. **'Richard Ahrens'** has rose-pink flowers up to 7cm (2¾in) wide. **'Whirlwind'** ('Wirbelwind') has semidouble white flowers with twisted petals and reaches a height of 1m (3ft).

▲ *Anemone tomentosa* 'Robustissima'

A. japonica hort. see *A. x hybrida*

A. tomentosa Clusters of up to 12 pale pink flowers appear from late summer to mid autumn. Each flower is up to 7.5cm (3in) in width and has 5-6 oval petals. HEIGHT & SPREAD 1mx40cm (3ftx16in).

'Robustissima' has darker pink flowers.

Anemone tomentosa

CULTIVATION

EARLY-FLOWERING ANEMONES

Plant the anemones grown from rhizomes during autumn in rich, moist but well-drained soil in sun or, preferably, partial shade. They will tolerate dry conditions during their summer dormancy.

Plants that grow from tubers should be planted in autumn in well-drained soil in a sunny position. Do not water during their summer dormancy. Alternatively, lift the tubers when the foliage has died back and store in sand. *A. coronaria* can be brought into flower throughout the year; grow under glass at a minimum of 10°C (50°F) and stagger planting over the year.

Plant the anemones with fibrous rootstock during spring and summer in well-drained soil in sun or semi-shade.

LATE-FLOWERING ANEMONES

Plant during spring or early summer in moist, yet well-drained soil, adding ample organic matter. Choose a position in sun or partial shade. Mulch during the hot, summer months. In cold areas protect the vulnerable crowns from frost damage with dry organic matter. Avoid disturbing plants except for purposes of propagation.

PROPAGATION

EARLY-FLOWERING ANEMONES

Divide plants grown from rhizomes in autumn or shortly after flowering.

Lift tubers and cut into pieces, ensuring each bit has at least one growing point. Leave the cut surfaces to dry before replanting, or treat with a suitable fungicide.

The plants with fibrous rootstock are best left undisturbed once planted; sow ripe seed in autumn or early winter.

LATE-FLOWERING ANEMONES

Divide plants in spring and replant straight away. Or take root cuttings in summer, choosing only thick healthy pieces.

PESTS AND DISEASES Pests include the eelworm and flea beetles. Slugs, snails and earwigs may also be a problem. Diseases include grey mould – especially on the flowerbuds – powdery and downy mildew, plum rust, anemone smut and cucumber mosaic viruses.

Anemonella

Ranunculaceae

Pretty, anemone-like white flowers nestle among delicate fern-like leaves on this hardy, tuberous perennial, the only species of its genus. This plant is fully frost hardy, but may succumb to excessive winter wet.

Anemonella thalictroides (rue anemone) Fine stems carry 2-5 cup-shaped flowers, up to 2cm (¾in) across, from mid spring to early summer. The pale olive green leaves have 5-9 rounded leaflets, each up to 2cm (¾in) long. Native to eastern N America. HEIGHT & SPREAD 25x30cm (10x12in).

'Flore Pleno' produces double white flowers. **'Rosea'** has single pink flowers and **'Rosea Plena'** has double pink flowers.

CULTIVATION Plant in rich, moist, but not wet, soil. In wet areas, grow in rich, gritty soil in an unheated greenhouse or conservatory, or grow in a coldframe.

PROPAGATION Sow fresh seed in summer, or divide established plants in autumn.

PESTS AND DISEASES Slugs can be a problem, especially with seedlings.

▼ *Anemonella thalictroides* 'Rosea Plena'

Anemonopsis

Ranunculaceae

This hardy herbaceous perennial, the sole species in the genus, forms large clumps of glossy dark green leaves that surround nodding, lavender-coloured flowers.

Anemonopsis macrophylla Loose clusters of waxy, drooping flowers, about 4 cm (1½ in) across and palest at the centre, are carried on slender, branching stems in mid summer. The 15-30 cm (6-12 in) long leaves have 9 or more rounded, toothed leaflets. The stems are blackish. Native to Japan. HEIGHT & SPREAD 80×80 cm (32×32 in).

CULTIVATION Plant in a moist, lime-free, leafy soil in partial shade – they will scorch badly in a sunny position. They do not thrive in dry conditions and do best in a cool situation.

PROPAGATION Sow seed in late summer, as soon as it ripens. Alternatively, divide established clumps in early spring.

PESTS AND DISEASES Slugs may be a particular problem.

Anethum

Dill

Umbelliferae

Popular for its herbal and medicinal properties, dill is also grown for its attractive feathery foliage with small greenish yellow, cartwheel-like flowers. There is only one species in the genus.

Anethum graveolens Finely divided aromatic fern-like leaflets are carried on this slender, easily grown annual. Tiny yellow blooms form plate-like flowerheads, about 10 cm (4 in) across, in summer. HEIGHT & SPREAD 60×25 cm (24×10 in).

CULTIVATION Plant in full sun in a free-draining, fertile soil.

PROPAGATION Sow seed in open ground between spring and late summer. Dill does not transplant well so seedlings should be thinned to about 10 cm (4 in) apart as soon as they are large enough to handle. A pinch of seed can be sown into a large pot and the seedlings thinned out if a suitable place is not available in the garden.

PESTS AND DISEASES Greenfly may invade the crowded flowerheads.

▲ *Anethum graveolens*

Angelica

Umbelliferae

Magnificent foliage and domed flowerheads make these biennial and short-lived, hardy, perennial herbs ideal ornamental plants. The flower clusters are borne on rigid and hollow branching stems from early to late summer above large, deeply divided leaves. Native to Europe and central Asia.

RECOMMENDED SPECIES AND VARIETIES

A. archangelica This tall biennial has thick, purple-tinged green stems and pale green, divided leaves, up to 60 cm (2 ft) long. Tiny greenish cream flowers are carried in clusters, 25 cm (10 in) across, from early to late summer. The plant has many culinary uses. HEIGHT & SPREAD 2 m×75 cm (6½×2½ ft).

A. sylvestris This bushy biennial has ridged, purple-tinged green stems and bright green, sharply toothed, divided leaves up to 60 cm (2 ft) long. The small white or pinkish blooms are carried in flat flowerheads, 15 cm (6 in) across, in summer. HEIGHT & SPREAD 2 m×60 cm (6½×2 ft).

CULTIVATION Plant in autumn in any moist, fertile soil in full sun or partial shade. Mulch in spring to conserve soil moisture. Plants need staking in windy positions.

PROPAGATION Sow seed in spring in the open ground. These plants will not flower the year they are sown but in the following year. Alternatively, transplant self-sown seedlings in autumn.

PESTS AND DISEASES Usually trouble free.

Angelica tree, Japanese see *Aralia elata*
Angel's trumpet see *Brugmansia arborea*
Angel's wings see *Caladium bicolor*

▲ *Angelica archangelica*

Anigozanthos

Kangaroo paw

Haemodoraceae

Upright flowering stems arise from fans of sword-shaped leaves on these half-hardy perennials. They are usually cultivated under glass, but where there is little or no frost they can be grown outside in a well-drained, sunny spot.

RECOMMENDED SPECIES AND VARIETIES

A. flavidus (yellow kangaroo paw) The 5 cm (2 in) long flowers are mostly yellow, sometimes flushed red and pink. The flowers are downy when they first appear in late spring. The narrow leaves of this bushy plant grow to 60 cm (2 ft) long. HEIGHT & SPREAD 1 m×45 cm (3×1½ ft).

▲ *Anigozanthos flavidus*

A. manglesii ♀ Green and red blooms are borne in clusters in late spring on this clump-forming plant. The narrow grey-green leaves, up to 60 cm (2 ft) long, are arranged in dense clumps. HEIGHT & SPREAD 1 m×60 cm (3×2 ft).

CULTIVATION In frost-free areas, plant outdoors in a very sheltered spot in free-draining soil. Elsewhere, grow in large pots of free-draining compost in a sunny position under glass. Pots can be moved outdoors during summer and then overwintered in a frost-free conservatory or greenhouse. Water freely in summer, incorporating a regular liquid feed. Water sparingly in winter. Remove old flowerheads from the base of the plant.

PROPAGATION Divide plants in early spring or sow ripe seed under glass in late summer.

PESTS AND DISEASES Greenfly may attack the plants.

Anise see *Pimpinella anisum*
Anise, Chinese see *Illicium anisatum*
Anise, purple see *Illicium floridanum*

Anomatheca

Iridaceae

The only anomatheca species suitable for planting in a British garden is *A. laxa*. Even then, the trumpet-shaped flowers that lend a delicate beauty to the front of a border or to a rockery can be enjoyed only in mild areas. In colder districts, this bulbous plant from S and E Africa is best kept under glass.

RECOMMENDED SPECIES AND VARIETIES

A. laxa (syn. *A. cruenta*, *Lapeirousia cruenta*) Clusters of pinkish red flowers open on arching wiry stems all summer. The flower tubes, each 2cm (¾in) long, flare out into 6-pointed flat-faced blooms,

▲ *Anomatheca laxa*

2.5cm (1in) across, all facing outwards. The lower 3 petals are marked with a darker colour at the centre of the flower. Egg-shaped seedpods follow the flowers and split to reveal bright red seeds. The sword-shaped basal leaves, up to 10cm (4in) long, form an upright fan. HEIGHT 20cm (8in).

The flowers of var. ***alba*** are pure white, **'Joan Evans'** has white petals with a bright red blotch in the centre of the flower.

CULTIVATION Plant 4cm (1½in) deep in spring in sun. In cold districts lift and store for winter or grow in pots in a greenhouse.

PROPAGATION Divide clumps of corms in autumn. Sow seed in spring in a coldframe or greenhouse. *A. laxa* self-sows freely.

PESTS AND DISEASES Usually trouble free.

Antennaria

Everlasting, pussy toes

Compositae

Antennaria dioica

Small clusters of white to cream, pink or red daisy-like flowers with papery bracts appear above mats of silvery leaves in late spring to early summer. The leaves of the hardy evergreen perennials, native to Europe, Asia and N America, are grey or whitish with hairs. They are well suited to path edges and patios and as ground cover for small bulbs, but can become invasive in a rock garden.

▲ *Antennaria parvifolia*

RECOMMENDED SPECIES AND VARIETIES

A. aprica see *A. parvifolia*

A. candida see *A. dioica* 'Minima'

A. dioica (syn. *Gnaphalium dioicum*, *Omalotheca dioica*) (catsfoot) Narrow oval leaves, up to 4cm (1½in) long, are densely woolly, especially underneath, and form silvery white mats. The flower bracts are white to pink-brown at the tips. HEIGHT & SPREAD 10×60cm (4×24in).

'Alex Duguid' has deep reddish pink flowers; **'Minima'** (syn. *A. candida*) is a dwarf form; **'Nyewoods Variety'** is compact, with deep rose-pink flowers; and **'Rubra'** has dark red flowers.

A. microphylla♀ (syn. *A. rosea*) The 2.5cm (1in) long leaves are woolly all over and form a spreading mat. The flowers are pink. HEIGHT & SPREAD 10×60cm (4×24in).

A. parvifolia (syn. *A. aprica*) Densely woolly leaves, 2-4cm (¾-1½in) long, form silvery grey mats. The brown-spotted flower bracts have white, sometimes pink, tips. HEIGHT & SPREAD 8×30cm (3¼×12in).

A. rosea see *A. microphylla*

CULTIVATION Plant from late autumn to spring in well-drained, gritty soil in full sun.

PROPAGATION Sow seed as soon as it is ripe in autumn or early winter. Divide in spring.

PESTS AND DISEASES Usually trouble free.

Anthemis

Compositae

Anthemis punctata ssp. cupaniana

The hardy annuals, herbaceous perennials and dwarf shrubs of this genus are grown for their daisy-like flowers and finely divided, occasionally aromatic, foliage. The perennials described offer the best garden value, with the low-growing *Anthemis punctata* ssp. *cupaniana* suitable for growing in large rock gardens and the others at their best in herbaceous borders. Native to Asia, Europe and N Africa.

RECOMMENDED SPECIES AND VARIETIES

A. nobilis see *Chamaemelum nobile*

A. punctata ssp. ***cupaniana***♀ Long-lasting, yellow-centred flowers, up to 6cm (2½in) across, with white 'petals' (ray florets) are carried above a mat of aromatic grey foliage in early summer. This woody-based perennial has finely divided pinnate leaves, up to 12.5cm (5in) long, covered in silky white hairs. HEIGHT & SPREAD 30×60cm (12×24in).

A. sancti-johannis (St.John's camomile) Daisy-like flowers, 5cm (2in) across, with yellow centres and orange 'petals' (ray florets) are carried individually at the ends of leafy stems from early to mid summer on this herbaceous perennial. The mid green feathery leaves are up to 5cm (2in) long. HEIGHT & SPREAD 60×60cm (24×24in).

A. tinctoria (golden marguerite) Golden yellow flowers, up to 4cm (1½in) across, are borne on branching stems from early to late summer. The flowering stems rise above a clump of ferny leaves that are mid green above and grey beneath. HEIGHT & SPREAD 60×60cm (24×24in).

'Alba' has white flowers. **'E.C. Buxton'** has pale lemon-yellow flowers and reaches 1m (3ft) tall. **'Grallach Gold'** bears large, vibrant flowers and attains a height and spread of up to 1m (3ft), but is not reliably perennial. **'Kelwayi'** is similar to 'Grallach

▲ *Anthemis tinctoria* 'Grallach Gold'

Gold', but has more finely divided leaves. **'Wargrave'** has very pale yellow flowers.

CULTIVATION Plant in an open, sunny site in well-drained soil in spring. Cut back the stems as soon as flowering is over.

PROPAGATION Divide in autumn or spring every 2 or 3 years. Alternatively, take basal cuttings in spring or late summer.

PESTS AND DISEASES Usually trouble free.

▼ *Anthemis punctata* ssp. *cupaniana*

Anthericum

St Bernard's lily

Anthericaceae

Loose spikes of starry, white flowers rise in summer from the compact tufts of shiny, grass-like leaves of these hardy herbaceous perennials. They are valuable for planting in a herbaceous border, in deep containers or in grass or light woodland. The plants are native to grassy plains and woodlands in Europe, Turkey and Africa.

RECOMMENDED SPECIES AND VARIETIES

A. algeriense see *A. liliago* var. *major*

A. liliago Each white flower on the spike is up to 4cm (1½in) across and has 6 pointed petals. At the centre is a cluster of stamens with prominent yellow anthers. The grey-green leaves are up to 40cm (16in) long. HEIGHT & SPREAD 1m×30cm (3×1ft).

The flowers of var. ***major***♀ (syn. *A. algeriense*) open out slightly flatter than those of the species.

A. ramosum The white flowers with 6 pointed petals and prominent yellow anthers are 1.5cm (½in) across and are borne on branched spikes. Up to 40cm (16in) long, the leaves are greyish green. HEIGHT & SPREAD 60×30cm (2×1ft).

CULTIVATION Plant in spring, in well-drained but moisture-retentive soil, choosing a position in sun or partial shade. Unless seed is wanted, cut back the stems after flowering to encourage foliage growth. Allow the leaves to die back naturally in autumn. Both species are hardy to -10°C (14°F) and *A. liliago* improves in flowering after a cold winter.

PROPAGATION Sow seed or divide plants in spring. Do not divide plants more frequently than every 5 years. Plants raised by division may not flower until the following year; those raised from seed may take 2-3 years to bloom.

PESTS AND DISEASES Usually trouble free.

▼ *Anthericum liliago*

Anthriscus

Umbelliferae

Anthriscus sylvestris 'Ravenswing'

Round, flattened domes of tiny white flowers rise above much divided, fern-like leaves on these easily cultivated, annual, biennial or sometimes perennial plants. *Anthriscus sylvestris*, commonly known as cow parsley or Queen Anne's lace, is a native British hedgerow plant that can be invasive in a garden. Cultivated varieties are grown for their ornamental foliage and flowers suitable for growing in a border, wild garden or among shrubs. Chervil (*A. cerefolium*) is a culinary herb with aniseed-flavoured leaves (see HERBS p.330).

RECOMMENDED SPECIES AND VARIETIES

A. cerefolium (chervil) see HERBS p.330.

***A. sylvestris* 'Ravenswing'** The finely divided, striking leaves of this biennial, sometimes perennial plant are brownish purple and fern-like, thin-textured and up to 30cm (12in) long. Small, 4-petalled creamy white flowers are borne in delicate clusters, up to 6cm (2½in) wide, from mid spring to early summer. These ripen into small, oval, green fruits which eventually become light brown. The furrowed stems are hollow and hairy towards the base. Native to Europe, N Asia, N Africa. HEIGHT & SPREAD Up to 1.5m×60cm (5×2ft).

CULTIVATION Best grown in a sunny or part-shaded border.

PROPAGATION Propagate *A. sylvestris* 'Ravenswing' by division.

PESTS AND DISEASES Usually trouble free.

Anthurium

Araceae

This eye-catching plant has exotic sail-like, red, pink or creamy white spathes with a central tail known as a spadix. The glossy leaves are oval or heart-shaped and sometimes strikingly marked. These tropical evergreen perennials, usually grown as greenhouse pot plants or houseplants, are very long-lived, making them one of the most popular pot plants where humidity and a minimum night temperature of 18°C (64°F) can be maintained.

A. andraeanum (tail flower) The leathery heart-shaped spathe, up to 12.5cm (5in) long, is bright red with a yellowish white central tail-like spike. The oval or arrow-like glossy green leaves grow up to 20cm (8in) long. HEIGHT & SPREAD 60×50cm (24×20in).

'Flamingo' has a bright pink spathe.

A.* × *ferrierense A fleshy, heart-shaped pink spathe, up to 15cm (6in) long, with a distinctive ivory-white, tail-like central spadix. The oval or heart-shaped glossy green leaves grow to 40cm (16in) long. This scrambling plant can be attached to a moss pole in the centre of the pot. HEIGHT & SPREAD 1m×45cm (3×1½ft).

'Roseum' has a large deep red spathe with a white spadix tipped with yellow.

A. scherzerianum (flamingo flower) Bright red oval spathes, up to 10cm (4in) long, have a distinctive twisted, pinkish spadix and are freely produced for much of the year. The erect, lance-shaped leaves, up to 20cm (8in) long, are dark green and leathery. This is one of the most widely grown houseplants. HEIGHT & SPREAD 30×30cm (12×12in).

CULTIVATION Grow in a free-draining compost with bark chippings or chopped sphagnum moss incorporated. Position away from direct sunlight and maintain a temperature of not less than 18°C (64°F) and humidity, even if this is just localised by regular spraying. Water freely throughout the growing season and administer a general liquid houseplant feed when the plants are flowering. Repot annually but keep the plants quite tight in their pots. Overpotting leads to excess foliage at the expense of the flowers. Clean the foliage regularly.

PROPAGATION Divide in spring or summer.

PESTS AND DISEASES Mealy bugs and scale insects can be a problem.

▲ *Anthurium andraeanum*

a

Anthyllis

Leguminosae

Anthyllis montana

Showy clusters of pea-like flowers crown finely divided leaves, up to 12cm (4¾in) long, on these hardy annual, biennial or perennial herbaceous or shrubby plants. *Anthyllis montana* thrives in a well-drained rock garden or wall crevice. *A. vulneraria* tolerates many soil types, provided they are well drained. It self-seeds and grows well in wild-flower gardens and rough grass, but is equally at home in a large rock garden.

RECOMMENDED SPECIES AND VARIETIES

A. montana Dense, clover-like heads of pink, red or purple pea flowers are carried above large clumps of foliage on this spreading perennial in summer. The hairy, greyish, pinnate leaves consist of 8-15, occasionally more, pairs of leaflets. Native to high, rocky areas of S Europe. HEIGHT & SPREAD 20×60cm (8×24in).

'Rubra'♀ has crimson flowers.

A. vulneraria (kidney vetch) Dense heads of yellow or cream pea flowers, often tinged with red, are borne on long stalks in summer on this short-lived perennial with erect to spreading stems. The lower leaves have up to 5 oval leaflets and the upper leaves have 11, sometimes more, smaller and narrower leaflets. Native to Europe, N Africa and W Asia. HEIGHT & SPREAD 20×60cm (8×24in).

The flowers of var. ***coccinea*** come in shades of red.

CULTIVATION Grow in well-drained soil and in full sun, preferably in a sheltered position away from cold winds.

PROPAGATION Sow seed in early spring.

PESTS AND DISEASES Slugs may attack seedlings.

▲ *Anthyllis vulneraria*

Antirrhinum

Snapdragon

Scrophulariaceae

The common snapdragon, *Antirrhinum majus,* with its familiar, sweetly scented flowers, has long been a favourite for cottage gardens and summer bedding schemes. Many modern varieties provide long-lasting flowers in a range of shapes and colours. These short-lived, half-hardy perennials are mostly grown as annuals and, in favourable areas, they may survive over winter to give an early display of flowers the following year. They can also be grown in pots under glass for the same purpose.

This genus also contains some delightful alpines that are ideal for raised beds, wall crevices or a rock garden. These species are evergreen perennials or sub-shrubs. They may be cut almost to ground level by frost but in spring they generally sprout again.

Most plants have the typical 'snapdragon' pouched, two-lipped flowers, 2.5-5cm (1-2in) long, with a closed mouth. The elliptic to lanceolate leaves are 2.5-7cm (1-2¾in) long. Antirrhinums are native to SW Europe and the Mediterranean region.

RECOMMENDED SPECIES AND VARIETIES

A. asarina see *Asarina procumbens*

A. majus (common snapdragon) A succession of pink or purple flowers appear from late spring to late summer. Dark green leaves are borne on branching, upright stems. HEIGHT & SPREAD 1.2×1m (4×3ft).

The cultivated varieties, bred for a more compact habit and resistance to rust are more commonly grown than the species. There are 4 flower types: irregular, with the typical, 2-lipped flowers; penstemon-flowered, with symmetrical, open 5-lobed trumpet-shaped flowers; peloric, with tubular flowers closed at the mouth; and double flowered forms. Unless otherwise stated, the flowers may be shades of pink, red, purple, yellow, bronze, orange or white. Plants vary in height and can be grouped into dwarf, intermediate and tall-growing varieties.

The dwarf plants are 15-30cm (6-12in) tall. **Floral Carpet Series**♀ are bushy F_1 hybrids with irregular flowers. **Kim Series**♀ have irregular flowers. **'Magic Carpet'** has irregular flowers and a spreading or trailing habit. **'Pixie'** is a stocky, penstemon-flowered, F_1 hybrid with blooms of crimson, pink, yellow, orange and white. **Royal Carpet Series** are small bushy plants with irregular flowers. **'Sweetheart'** is a bushy F_1 hybrid with double flowers in shades of red, bronze, pink, yellow and white. This variety is particularly resistant to rust. **'Tahiti'** has dense spikes of irregular flowers. It is a bushy, very rust-resistant, F_1 hybrid. **'Tom Thumb'** has dense spikes of irregular flowers. **'Trumpet Serenade'** is bushy and penstemon-flowered.

The intermediate varieties are 38-45cm (15-18in) tall. **'Cheerio'** is compact and bushy with irregular flowers. **Coronette Series**♀ are peloric-flowered, upright, F_1 hybrids. **Monarch Series** are compact, particularly rust-resistant plants with irregular flowers in various bright colours. **'Taff's White'** has white-edged foliage and is hardy enough to survive as a perennial. It has rosy purple irregular flowers.

The tall-growing varieties reach a height of 60cm-1m (2-3ft). **'Giant Forerunner'** has many branches rising from the base of the plant and dense spikes of irregular flowers. **'Madame Butterfly'** is a compact F_1 hybrid with double flowers.

A. molle Pale pink or white flowers, with yellow at the mouth, appear on leafy spikes throughout summer. A somewhat sticky alpine with spreading to trailing stems and grey-green leaves. HEIGHT & SPREAD 30×30cm (1×1ft).

A. pulverulentum Pale yellow flowers with deep yellow at the mouth appear in leafy spikes throughout summer. A hairy alpine with spreading to upright slender, branched stems clothed in grey-green leaves. HEIGHT & SPREAD 25×25cm (10×10in).

A. sempervirens Cream or white flowers with yellow and purple at the mouth and some violet veining are borne in loose, leafy spikes throughout summer. A somewhat sticky alpine with grey-green leaves. HEIGHT & SPREAD 25×25cm (10×10in).

▲ *Antirrhinum molle*

Antirrhinum majus Coronette Series ▲

CULTIVATION Plant in spring in well-drained, preferably neutral or limy soil. *A. majus* and its cultivars grow in sun or partial shade. The alpines prefer a sheltered site in full sun. Pinch out the tips of young plants to promote bushy growth. Deadhead flowers to encourage repeat flowering. Trim alpines after flowering or in early spring.

PROPAGATION Sow seed in a coldframe or cool greenhouse in late winter; sow thinly to avoid damping off. Take semi-ripe cuttings of alpines in mid or late summer.

PESTS AND DISEASES Seedlings are susceptible to damping-off and young plants may be affected by downy mildew. *A. majus* may be affected by rust.

Aphelandra

Acanthaceae

Evergreen shrubs native to the American tropics, aphelandras provide several species of houseplants grown for both their flowers and their foliage. The leaves are leathery and often variegated while the flowerhead is a squarish terminal spike, consisting of a tight cluster of geometrically arranged bracts with short-lived flowers emerging from the four corners of the head. The bracts themselves last for several months.

RECOMMENDED SPECIES AND VARIETIES

A. squarrosa (zebra plant) The glossy dark green leaves have very distinct cream-coloured veins, are pointed, oval to broadly lance-shaped and grow to 20cm (8in) long. The flowerheads, produced in late summer, are around 12.5cm (5in) long and have yellow bracts. The yellow flowers grow to 3cm (1¼in) in length. HEIGHT & SPREAD 1.2m×60cm (4×2ft).

'Dania' has golden bracts and silvery leaf veins and grows to 40cm (16in) tall. **'Louisae'** has red-tipped bracts and grows to 60cm (2ft).

CULTIVATION Aphelandras need warmth, humidity and indirect light. Give them a minimum winter temperature of 13°C (55°F). Keep the compost always slightly moist during the growing season, a little drier in winter. Feed regularly during the growing season.

PROPAGATION Take semi-ripe tip cuttings of shoots without flowers in late summer.

PESTS AND DISEASES Leaf drop and browning of leaf edges are caused by changes in conditions, draughts, dryness and direct sun.

▼ *Aphelandra squarrosa* 'Dania'

Aphyllanthes

Aphyllanthaceae

Aphyllanthes monspeliensis

There is only one species in this genus, an alpine, which grows happily in a sheltered, well-drained rock garden. The plant is hardy to -5°C (23°F).

Aphyllanthes monspeliensis A succession of starry blue flowers are produced from late spring to early summer. The flowers are up to 3cm (1¼in) across; each of the 6 petals has a darker central stripe. The blooms are borne singly or 2-3 together at the top of numerous short, wiry, rush-like stems. The plant appears to have no leaves because they are reduced to short reddish brown papery sheaths around the flat green stems. This herbaceous perennial is native to dry, sunny, rocky habitats in SW Europe. HEIGHT 40×15cm (16×6in).

▲ *Aphyllanthes monspeliensis*

CULTIVATION The plant is hardy enough for outdoor planting if it is sited in well-drained, gritty soil in full sun. It grows well in a coldframe or unheated greenhouse. In areas with excessive winter rain it is best kept under glass.

PROPAGATION Sow seed in autumn or early winter. Avoid lifting and dividing; established plants fail to thrive if disturbed.

PESTS AND DISEASES Usually trouble free.

Aponogeton

Aponogetonaceae

With handsome floating foliage and fragrant flowers, these perennial aquatics are widely used to add interest to ponds and aquaria. They grow from a rhizome or tuber and although they usually have floating foliage, some are noted for their underwater leaves. The genus is native to Africa, Asia and Australasia with the tuberous *Aponogeton distachyos* being the only species hardy enough to grow in Britain.

RECOMMENDED SPECIES

A. distachyos (pondweed, water hawthorn) Intriguing forked white flower spikes, up to 10cm (4in) long with distinctive purple-brown stamens, are borne just above the water surface from late spring until the first autumn frosts. The blooms have a strong vanilla fragrance and are often used in salads in their native South Africa. The dark green oblong or oval leaves, up to 15cm (6in) long, 5cm (2in) wide, are often splashed with maroon. SPREAD 1m (3ft).

▲ *Aponogeton distachyos*

CULTIVATION Plant the tubers at a depth of up to 75cm (30in) in aquatic compost or heavy loam in a planting basket top-dressed with pea gravel. Water hawthorns do best in a sunny spot and the tubers should be planted deep enough to be below the ice when it freezes in winter. Remove faded blossoms to prevent unwanted self-seeding.

PROPAGATION Divide crowns in spring.

PESTS AND DISEASES Water-lily aphids attack the flowers.

Aporocactus see CACTI p.106
Apple see p.723
Apple, crab see *Malus*
Apple, May see *Podophyllum peltatum*
Apricot, Japanese see *Prunus mume*

Aquilegia

Columbine

Ranunculaceae

Aquilegia vulgaris

Dainty, often nodding, spurred flowers are held on slender stems above lacy foliage in late spring to early summer on these easily grown plants. Blue, purple or white flowers are the most common, but yellow is also found, as well as bright red in some American species. The flowers have five petal-like sepals surrounding the five true

a

petals that form an inner funnel. Each petal extends backwards (usually upwards) into a prominent spur. The dissected and lobed leaves are green, grey-green or grey-and-blue-green and are decorative throughout the growing season. The plants are usually short-lived perennials but often seed themselves and hybridise freely if left to self-sow. More than 70 species are found across the Northern Hemisphere. Larger species suit a flower border or woodland garden, while smaller plants are excellent for a rock garden, raised bed, container or window box. Unless otherwise stated all those listed are hardy. All aquilegias are poisonous.

RECOMMENDED SPECIES AND VARIETIES

A. alpina (alpine columbine) Bright blue nodding flowers, up to 7.5cm (3in) across, bloom from late spring to early summer. They have straight or slightly curved spurs. HEIGHT & SPREAD 45-60×30cm (1½-2×1ft).

▲ *Aquilegia alpina*

A. bertolonii♀ Small violet-blue flowers with usually incurved spurs bloom in early to mid summer on these dwarf plants. HEIGHT & SPREAD 23×23cm (9×9in).

A. caerulea♀ Blue sepals contrast with the white of the petals and long spurs, making this one of the most elegant species. Flowers bloom from early to mid summer. HEIGHT & SPREAD 60×30cm (2×1ft).

A. canadensis♀ Sprays of small nodding flowers whose red sepals contrast with yellow petals bloom from late spring to mid summer. The leaves are dark green. HEIGHT & SPREAD 40× 30cm (16×12in).

'Nana' is a dwarf form, not more than 20cm (8in) tall.

A. flabellata♀ From mid spring to early summer the nodding flowerheads have blue or lavender sepals and short hooked spurs and white or cream-tipped petals. The foliage is rather fleshy and grey-green. HEIGHT & SPREAD 30×25cm (12×10in).

▼ *Aquilegia flabellata*

The flowers of var. ***pumila***♀ (syn. var. *nana*) are similar to those of the species but the plants are 10-20cm (4-8in) tall.

A. formosa This easily grown red-flowered species thrives in moist, partly shaded areas. The flowers, borne from late spring to mid summer, are usually red with inner yellow petals, but are sometimes all red. HEIGHT & SPREAD 90×45cm (3×1½ft).

▲ *Aquilegia formosa*

A. fragrans (fragrant columbine) The plant is grown for its strong fragrance and its large, nodding, pale flowers with their white or pale lilac sepals and contrasting pale yellow or cream petals. The flowers are borne from early to mid summer HEIGHT & SPREAD 30-75×30cm (1-2½×1ft).

A. longissima Extremely long curved slender spurs distinguish the half-nodding yellow flowers, whose surrounding sepals are often paler in colour than the petals. Branched stems bear the flowers in summer. HEIGHT & SPREAD 80×40cm (32×16in).

***A.* McKana** (McKenna) **Hybrids** The vigorous plants bear abundant large flowers of mixed bright colours with long spurs flared at the top. HEIGHT & SPREAD 85×60cm (34×24in).

***A.* Mrs Scott Elliot's Variety** The very long-spurred flowers in a range of pastel colours bloom in early summer amid blue-green leaves. HEIGHT & SPREAD 85×60cm (34in×24in).

A. viridiflora Unusual bicoloured flowers, with green sepals and chocolate-brown to chocolate-purple petals. The short-spurred fragrant flowers are borne from late spring to mid summer above deep green leaves. HEIGHT & SPREAD 20-30×30cm (8-12×12in).

A. vulgaris (columbine, granny's bonnet) This native British plant has blue, purple, reddish purple or occasionally pink or white flowers with hooked spurs. It is a free-flowering plant and generally seeds itself profusely. The nodding flowers are borne in early summer on branched stems above leaves that are deep green, bluish green, or sometimes flushed with pink or purple. HEIGHT & SPREAD 60×45cm (2×1½ft).

'Nivea'♀ ('Munstead White') has pure white flowers; the pompom-like double flowers of **'Nora Barlow'**♀ are pink with lime green and white; **'Red Star'** has red spurred flowers with white inner petals; the spurless flowers of var. ***stellata*** (*clematiflora*) come in various colours including white.

CULTIVATION Most aquilegias dislike heavy clay soils and prefer a well-drained yet moist soil rich in humus and a position in full sun or dappled shade. *A. vulgaris* tolerates dry situations. The small alpine species do best in a grittier mixture in full sun.

PROPAGATION Sow seed in autumn or early spring, sowing larger types where they are to flower, and smaller ones in pots. Alpine species may take 2 years to germinate. Plants generally flower in their second season from seed. Many species hybridise and produce unexpected colour combinations. Isolate species if pure seed is wanted.

Do not divide young plants. Choicer cultivars, which may not come true from seed, can be increased by careful division in early spring from their third year onwards, though this is a very tricky job usually as the plants have a simple branched taproot.

PESTS AND DISEASES Usually trouble free but leaf miners and aphids can affect plants.

Arabis

Rockcress

Cruciferae

Arabis alpina ssp. caucasica 'Flore Pleno'

The dense mats of foliage of these rock-garden plants are covered in spikes or clusters of small four-petalled flowers from spring to summer. In the wild they mostly grow in high rocky places in Europe, W Asia and N America. The plants are tough and reliable on low banks, walls and gaps in garden paths but can be invasive in gentler settings. Of the 120 species, the compact evergreen perennials are best in the garden.

RECOMMENDED SPECIES AND VARIETIES

A. alpina* ssp. *caucasica (syn. *A. albida*, *A. caucasica*) Loose rosettes of grey-green obovate, toothed leaves, up to 4cm (1½in) long, form a spreading mat. White or pale pink flowers, 1.5cm (½in) across, are borne in dense spikes that gradually elongate,

▲ *Arabis alpina* ssp. *caucasica* 'Variegata'
Arabis ferdinandi-coburgi 'Variegata' ▲

appearing in spring, occasionally summer. HEIGHT & SPREAD 25×60cm (10in×24in).

'Coccinea' has red flowers. **'Flore Pleno'** has double white flowers. **'Schneehaube'**♀ (also known as **'Snowcap'**), **'Snowdrop'** and **'Snow White'** are 3 fine white varieties, generally more compact growing than the species. **'Variegata'** has white edges to the leaves.

A. androsacea Spikes of small white flowers, each 1cm (⅜in) across, appear in spring on the dense, low hummocks of leaf rosettes. The silver-haired obovate leaves are about 1.5cm (½in) long. It is a good plant for troughs and raised beds. HEIGHT & SPREAD 8×30cm (3¼×12in).

'Rosabella' has soft pink flowers.

A. blepharophylla Deep pink flowers, up to 2cm (¾in) across, open throughout spring. The mid green obovate leaves are up to 3cm (1¼in) long with stiff hairs around the edges. HEIGHT & SPREAD 20×50cm (8×20in).

'Frühlingszauber'♀ (also known as **'Spring Charm'**) is more compact, only reaching 10cm (4in) tall with a spread of 30cm (12in). It has deep crimson flowers.

A. caucasica (see *A. alpina* ssp. *caucasica*)

A. ferdinandi-coburgi Dense, flat mats of leathery leaves in rosettes provide year-round ground cover in well-drained positions. The spring flowers are white, up to 1cm (⅜in) across, and held in spikes on 20cm (8in) stems. The deep green leaves are narrowly oblong, up to 3cm (1¼in)

▼ *Arabis ferdinandi-coburgi*

▲ *Arabis ferdinandi-coburgi* 'Aureovariegata'

long, long-stalked and hairy on both sides. HEIGHT & SPREAD 20×45cm (8×18in).

'Aureovariegata' has leaves with yellow edge variegations. **'Old Gold'** is smaller with shiny leaves covered in green and gold variegations. The flowers are white. **'Variegata'** has leaves with cream or yellow edges, often purple-tinged in winter.

CULTIVATION Plant in a sunny position in well-drained soil. Smaller species are suitable for troughs and raised beds while the larger species are useful for path edges and wall crevices. Trim lightly after flowering to encourage a bushier habit.

PROPAGATION Take softwood cuttings in summer or divide established plants after flowering. Alternatively for species, sow seed in spring or autumn. Variegated and double forms do not come true from seed.

PESTS AND DISEASES Caterpillars and aphids may attack new spring growth.

Aralia

Araliaceae

Aralia elata

Huge, elegant divided leaves, up to 1.2×1m (4×3ft), give these plants outstanding architectural interest. The leaves are doubly divided, with each main pinnate leaflet itself composed of numerous slender-tipped leaflets. Tiny white flowers are produced in large branched clusters in late summer. Thorns often cover the stems and leaves of the deciduous shrubs, small trees, perennial plants and climbers that make up the genus.

RECOMMENDED SPECIES AND VARIETIES

A. chinensis The large, doubly divided, deciduous leaves are finely toothed and slender tipped. Measuring 1m×60cm (3×2ft), they are quite glossy on their upper surface. Tiny creamy white flowers in small round clusters form an upright flowerhead up to 40cm (16in) tall on this frost-hardy tree. Native to China and Manchuria. HEIGHT & SPREAD 1.2×1m (4×3ft) after 5 years, ultimately 5m (16ft) tall.

▲ *Aralia chinensis*

A. elata♀ (Japanese angelica tree) The doubly divided leaves, up to 1.2m×60cm (4×2ft), have numerous dark green leaflets. The plant grows to a small, frost-hardy tree of upright habit or a shrub of rather spreading habit. Most parts are covered in prickles. Small creamy white flowers in round clusters form a flowerhead up to 60×30cm (2×1ft). Native to Korea, Japan and eastern Russia. HEIGHT & SPREAD 2.4×1m (8×3ft) after 10 years, ultimately 6m (20ft) tall.

'Aureovariegata' forms a shrub growing to about 3m (10ft). The margins of the leaflets are a golden yellow but become more silvery white as the season progresses. **'Variegata'**♀ has leaflets blotched and edged with a creamy white that becomes more silvery as the season progresses; it forms a wide-spreading shrub up to 3m (10ft) tall with branches arranged in tiers.

CULTIVATION Suitable for a wide range of conditions, the plants grow larger in mild areas. Shelter from cold winds is helpful and they grow best in moisture-retentive soil.

PROPAGATION Raise the species from seed or grow from root cuttings or suckers. For a variety with a particular feature, a grafted plant is needed.

PRUNING None is normally required.

PESTS AND DISEASES Usually trouble free.

Aralia, false see *Schefflera elegantissima*

a

Araucaria

Araucariaceae

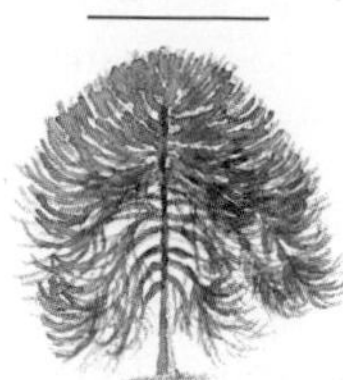

Araucaria araucana

Stiff, overlapping, scale-like leaves in spirals around sweeping, tiered branches give these conifers their distinctive appearance. Only one tree from this Chilean genus is hardy enough to be grown outdoors in Britain.

RECOMMENDED SPECIES

A. araucana (monkey puzzle, Chile pine) This statuesque evergreen tree is suitable for large gardens only. Individual leaves are oval with a narrowed, pointed end. Cones, up to 15cm (6in) across and either cylindrical or rounded, are sometimes produced on upper branches. Male and female cones are usually borne on different trees. The greyish brown trunk is straight and strongly ridged horizontally. HEIGHT & SPREAD 6x3m (20x10ft) after 10 years, ultimately 20m (66ft) tall.

CULTIVATION Plant in any well-drained soil in any position except full shade. Water well when the tree is young.

PRUNING None is required.

PROPAGATION Sow seed as soon as it is ripe in a propagator or in a greenhouse with a temperature of 20°C (68°F).

PESTS AND DISEASES Usually trouble free.

Arbutus

Strawberry tree

Ericaceae

Arbutus menziesii

Year round beauty is provided by these evergreen trees and shrubs with abundant, glossy, usually ovate leaves and round strawberry-like autumn fruits. Clusters of small, bell-shaped, white or pink flowers are borne in spring or autumn. Native to Europe, Asia Minor and NW America, the recommended plants are fairly hardy once they are established.

RECOMMENDED SPECIES AND VARIETIES

A.* x *andrachnoides ♀ Smooth, peeling, cinnamon bark contrasts with the ivory white flowers that hang in dense clusters in late autumn or early spring. Fruiting is not reliable. HEIGHT & SPREAD 5x3.5m (16x12ft) after 10-15 years, ultimately 9m (30ft) tall.

A. menziesii ♀ (madrona) This tree thrives only in acid soil in milder areas. In late spring fragrant white flowers open in large upright clusters among leaves that are whitish underneath. Fruits are red-orange. The bark is cinnamon-coloured. HEIGHT & SPREAD 7.5x5m (25x16ft) after 10-15 years, ultimately 10m (33ft) tall.

A. unedo ♀ (strawberry tree) Clusters of pendulous, small, honey-scented white or pink tinged flowers in late autumn are often accompanied by the previous year's orange-red fruit. This plant is not completely hardy in the coldest gardens. HEIGHT & SPREAD 4.5-6 x 3m (15-20x10ft) after 10-15 years, ultimately 10m (33ft) tall.

▲ *Arbutus unedo*

The form ***rubra*** ♀ has deep pink flowers.

CULTIVATION Plant in soil with good drainage with shelter from cold winds, especially when trees are young. *A. menziesii* requires acid soil but other plants tolerate limy soil and dry, poor soil. Strawberry trees do best in full sun.

PROPAGATION Sow seed in spring, except for *A. unedo* which should be raised from semi-ripe cuttings taken in mid summer.

PRUNING None is required.

PESTS AND DISEASES Leaf spot tends to occur if overwatered in summer.

Arctostaphylos

Bearberry

Ericaceae

Arctostaphylos uva-ursi

Clusters of tiny urn-shaped flowers followed by roundish fruits hang among the evergreen foliage of these acid-loving plants. The bearberries range from creeping shrubs to small trees, but from more than 50 mainly N American species, only a few are widely grown in Britain. They are chosen mainly for ground cover.

RECOMMENDED SPECIES AND VARIETIES

***A.* x *media* 'Woods Red'** This hybrid has obovate leaves, up to 2.5cm (1in) long, which are downy underneath. Clusters of white to pink flowers in mid spring are followed by red fruits. HEIGHT & SPREAD 25cmx1.5m (10inx5ft) after 5 years, ultimately spreading to 3m (10ft).

A. stanfordiana The smooth mahogany-coloured bark is most attractive as are the pale pink flowers in mid winter, which are followed by light red fruits. The ovate to lanceolate leaves are greyish blue, leathery and up to 6cm (2½in) long. This is the finest of the upright species although it is the least hardy of all the bearberries and requires a particularly warm and well-drained site if it is to survive the winter. HEIGHT & SPREAD 1mx60cm (3x2ft) after 5 years, ultimately 2m (6½ft) tall.

A. uva-ursi (common bearberry) Small white or pink flowers are produced in mid to late spring in drooping clusters above downy, greyish green foliage. They are followed by red berries. The alternate dark green glossy leaves, up to 3cm (1¼in) long, are obovate with pointed tips. The plant has a ranging and trailing habit. HEIGHT & SPREAD 20cmx1.5m (8inx5ft) after 5 years, ultimately spreading to 3m (10ft).

▲ *Arctostaphylos uva-ursi*

'Vancouver Jade' has pink flowers.

CULTIVATION Plant in any acid soil, including poor soil, on a warm dry site. *A. stanfordiana* requires a dry root run.

PROPAGATION Separate natural layers, or peg down shoots to promote layers, in spring. Alternatively take semi-ripe cuttings in summer.

PRUNING None is required, but cut back in spring to limit the spread if necessary.

PESTS AND DISEASES Usually trouble free.

Arctotis

African daisy

Compositae

Arctotis x hybrida

Brightly coloured daisy-like flowers appear from mid summer until early autumn, bringing long-lasting colour to a sunny border. The plants, which are half-hardy annuals and perennials, can also be grown in containers. The flowers generally have lighter coloured petals, properly called ray florets, surrounding darker central discs. They are borne one to a stem, usually leafless, rising from a tuft of coarse oval or lance-shaped leaves, often indented. Flowers tend to close in the afternoon and in dull weather. Native to South Africa.

RECOMMENDED SPECIES AND VARIETIES

A. acaulis Yellow flowers with coppery undersides and purple centres are carried on downy stems. Plants with orange or red flowers are also available. Flowers are up to 7.5cm (3in) wide. The plant, an easily grown perennial, has a thick, woody root system from which grow narrow, irregularly lobed, green leaves, up to 20cm (8in) long, with white woolly undersides. HEIGHT & SPREAD 25x45cm (10x18in).

A. fastuosa (Cape daisy) Flowers are orange, with purple-brown bases and maroon centres, and up to 5cm (2in) wide. The hoary leaves, up to 15cm (6in), are oblong and indented. This species is an annual. HEIGHT & SPREAD 60x60cm (2x2ft).

A. x hybrida Flowers are available in white, cream, yellow, peach, orange, pink or red. Many are attractively zoned with a contrasting colour. As wide as 7.5cm (3in), the flowers are borne on stems sometimes as long as 45cm (18in). The long, indented, lance-like leaves are felted or silvery and 15-30cm (6-12in) long. These strong-growing hybrids are treated as annuals, although they are short-lived perennials. HEIGHT & SPREAD 45x30cm (18x12in).

'Apricot' has flowers of a rich orange, while **'Flame'** is a brilliant orange-red.

A. venusta (blue-eyed African daisy) Purple-red flowers with blue centres are up to 10cm (4in) across. The indented, oval or lance-shaped leaves with grey undersides, are up to 20cm (8in) long. This perennial that flowers in late summer is usually treated as an annual. HEIGHT & SPREAD 30-60x30-40cm (12-24x12-16in).

'Grandis' has a height and spread of 45cm (18in), and larger, white to pale yellow flowers.

CULTIVATION Plant in an open, free-draining, sunny position, when all danger of frost has passed. Lift perennials for the winter and store in boxes of peat or a similar growing medium in a cool but frost-free place with good light.

PROPAGATION Sow annuals and perennials in a cool greenhouse or coldframe in spring. Grow on in small pots before planting out once there is no chance of frost. Alternatively, take stem cuttings of perennials at any time in the active growing season.

PESTS AND DISEASES Slugs may be a problem in damp weather.

▲ *Arctotis x hybrida* 'Apricot'

▲ *Arctotis x hybrida* 'Flame'

Arenaria

Sandwort

Caryophyllaceae

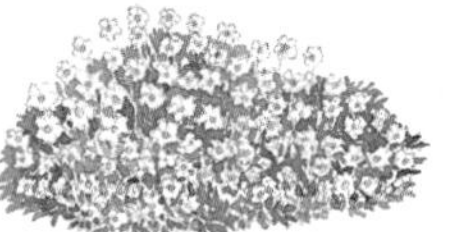

Arenaria montana

Spreading mats or tufts with small paired leaves support a mass of white or, rarely, pink flowers in spring or summer in a rock garden or raised bed. The flowers have four to five rounded petals and are held aloft on upright stems.

Most sandworts thrive in a sunny rock garden although *Arenaria balearica* does best on cool damp rocks beside a garden waterfall or pond, while *A. tetraquetra* is best grown in an alpine house or unheated greenhouse, or in an outdoor trough. These perennials, which are native to heathlands, woods and high rocky areas in temperate and Arctic regions of the Northern Hemisphere, come from a genus of some 150 species closely related to chickweeds.

RECOMMENDED SPECIES AND VARIETIES

A. balearica (mossy sandwort) White flowers, up to 1cm (3/8in) across, open above the

▲ *Arenaria balearica*

▲ *Arenaria montana*

bright green evergreen foliage in spring and summer, each on its own thread-like stem. The moss-like mats of foliage root down as they spread. The leaves are roundish, about 3mm (⅛in) long. HEIGHT & SPREAD 3×50cm (1¼×20in).

A. montana♀ Neat white flowers, about 2cm (¾in) across, appear on slender stems 10-20cm (4-8in) tall in early summer. The plant forms a loose, spreading mat of grey, narrowly oblong, hairy leaves, up to 2cm (¾in) long. HEIGHT & SPREAD 10-20×50cm (4-8×20in).

A. purpurascens (pink sandwort) This pretty sandwort has small clusters of pink, purplish or whitish flowers, up to 1cm (⅜in) across, on stems about 5cm (2in) tall in summer. Small rosettes of pointed evergreen leaves, up to 1cm (⅜in) long, form a loose, tufted cushion. HEIGHT & SPREAD 10×20cm (4×8in).

'Elliott's Variety' is more compact with an abundance of deep lilac-pink flowers.

A. tetraquetra White flowers, up to 1cm (⅜in) across, appear one to each very short stem in summer. The plant forms dense cushions of neatly packed, squarish rosettes of tiny evergreen leaves just 4mm (⅛in) long. HEIGHT & SPREAD 20×30cm (8×12in).

With grey-green foliage, ssp. ***amabilis*** is an even denser plant.

CULTIVATION Plant in a sunny, well-drained position. *A. purpurascens* grows best in a shady spot. *A. balearica* thrives in a damp, shady situation and must not dry out. This species may spread rampantly in mild, moist districts, but it tends to die off in a hard winter.

PROPAGATION Sow seed in pots in a cold-frame in autumn or early spring. Alternatively, lift and divide *A. balearica* and *A. montana* after flowering. Take semi-ripe cuttings of *A. purpurascens* and *A. tetraquetra* in spring or summer.

PESTS AND DISEASES Usually trouble free.

Argemone

Papaveraceae

Showy poppy-like blooms make these annuals or short-lived perennials popular for an open sunny border, although most have prickly or bristly stems and thistle-like leaves which could be a hazard near a path. Stems exude a yellowish sap if bruised. These rather untidy plants, which flower from mid to late summer, require free-draining soil. They are native to N, S and Central America, Hawaii and the W Indies.

RECOMMENDED SPECIES AND VARIETIES

A. grandiflora White or sometimes yellow flowers, up to 10cm (4in) wide, appear among the leafy stems of this perennial which is best treated as an annual. The prickly, lance-like leaves, up to 20cm (8in) long, are irregularly lobed and toothed. HEIGHT & SPREAD 75×75cm (30×30in).

▲ *Argemone grandiflora*

A. mexicana (Devil's fig, Mexican poppy) Papery, fragrant, bright yellow flowers, up to 7.5cm (3in) wide, appear among the foliage of this annual. The prickly leaves, up to 20cm (8in) long, have a grey waxy sheen and distinctive white markings over the veins. HEIGHT & SPREAD 90×45cm (3×1½ft).

▲ *Argemone mexicana*

CULTIVATION Plant in any gritty, free-draining soil in a sunny position. In exposed areas, grow the plants through thin supporting canes to keep them tidy. Remove dead flowerheads regularly to prolong the flowering season.

PROPAGATION Sow seed in the flowering position in spring. Thin when the seedlings are large enough to handle. They do not always transplant satisfactorily.

PESTS AND DISEASES Usually trouble free.

Argyranthemum

Marguerite, Paris daisy

Compositae

Argyranthemum frutescens

Abundant, daisy-like flowers, framed by attractive feathery foliage, have earned the marguerites a place among bedding plants since Victorian times. In S Europe they are widely grown as garden perennials but in Britain they are not quite hardy enough and must usually be grown afresh from cuttings each year, or overwintered in a frost-free greenhouse or conservatory.

In recent years the fashion for container gardening has boosted their popularity and they are particularly suitable for large patio tubs in sunny positions, flowering from early summer to mid autumn. Argyranthemums can also be trained as standard plants up to 1m (3ft) tall. They are useful for adding height to summer bedding schemes.

All the recommended plants have woody stem bases from which soft flowering shoots arise. The single flowers are generally about 5cm (2in) wide, made up of central yellow disc florets and radiating white ray florets. Most are native to the Canary Islands.

RECOMMENDED SPECIES AND VARIETIES

A. broussonetii The flowers of this species are larger than most, reaching up to 8cm (3¼in) across. The leaves are bright green. HEIGHT & SPREAD 30cm×1m (1×3ft).

▼ *Argyranthemum foeniculaceum*

▼ *Argyranthemum frutescens*

▼ *Argyranthemum* 'Jamaica Primrose'

▼ *Argyranthemum* 'Vancouver'

A. foeniculaceum Blue-green, finely cut foliage is seen on this species. HEIGHT & SPREAD 40cm×1m (16in×3ft).

'Royal Haze'♀ has blue-grey foliage.

A. frutescens This plant is similar to *A. foeniculaceum*, but has coarser bright green to greyish foliage and smaller flowers. HEIGHT & SPREAD 50cm×1m (20in×3ft).

A. gracile Especially finely divided greyish green leaves are carried on this upright species. HEIGHT & SPREAD 50cm×1m (20in×3ft).

'Chelsea Girl'♀ has even more finely divided foliage.

A. maderense♀ Small, 4cm (1½in) wide, yellow flowers and blue-grey lobed foliage distinguish this plant. HEIGHT & SPREAD 30cm×1m (1×3ft).

HYBRID VARIETIES

Most of the more widely grown argyranthemums are hybrids with at least two species as parents. They generally grow to 50cm (20in) tall and spread to 1m (3ft).

'Edelweiss' has semidouble white flowers. **'Jamaica Primrose'**♀ is vigorous, with dark green leaves and 6cm (2½in) wide, soft-yellow flowers. **'Mary Cheek'**♀ is compact with pale pink pompom flowers. **'Mary Wootton'** has pink, anemone-centred flowers with long outer florets. **'Peach Cheeks'** has pink blooms. **'Petite Pink'**♀ has a compact habit, silvery foliage and abundant small pink flowers. **'Powder Puff'** is compact with pale pink double flowers with quilled petals. **'Qinta White'**♀ (syn. 'Sark') has a slightly sprawling habit and anemone-centred flowers. **'Snowflake'** has semidouble flowers. **'Vancouver'**♀ is vigorous with deep pink anemone-centred flowers.

CULTIVATION Plant in a well-drained soil in a sunny position once the risk of frost has passed. Plants will survive outdoors in mild areas if covered with 10cm (4in) straw. Use a large tub or planter if growing as a container plant. Replace every 2 or 3 years. In a cool greenhouse or conservatory, plants need a winter temperature of about 10°C (50°F) to flower. Remove dead flowerheads to prolong the flowering season.

PROPAGATION Take cuttings in late summer and grow under glass.

PESTS AND DISEASES Aphids, capsid bugs and leaf miners may cause damage. Plants grown under glass may also suffer from red spider mite.

Arisaema

Araceae

Grown for their unusual blooms and glossy leaves, this genus of perennial tubers thrives in shady positions, and the plants do well under deciduous shrubs and trees. Each plant produces a leaf-like hood, called a spathe, in summer just before the true leaves unfurl. The spathe contains a prominent stalk, called a spadix. The tiny, true flowers cluster around its base. Orange-red berries, which are poisonous and can cause skin irritation, appear after the spathe dies.

RECOMMENDED SPECIES AND VARIETIES

A. candidissimum♀ White to greenish white with pale pink stripes at the top and with apple green white stripes at the base, the spathe contains a tapering, green spadix. The rose-scented flowers appear in early summer. Each plant has one leaf, made up of 3 broad leaflets, 10-20cm (4-8in) long. HEIGHT 30-40cm (12-16in).

▼ *Arisaema candidissimum*

A. consanguineum The spathe, which is usually white, striped in green, appears in mid to late summer. The leaf, made up of 10-20 slender leaflets, 20-40cm (8-16in) long, is held umbrella-like above the barely visible green spathe. HEIGHT 40-100cm (16-36in).

A. sikokianum The blackish to purple spathe appears in late spring and early summer. The white club-shaped spadix stands proud of the spathe. There are 2 leaves consisting of a total of 5 leaflets, each 15cm (6in) long. This plant is not hardy. HEIGHT 20-40cm (8-16in).

A. triphyllum (Jack-in-the-pulpit) A green or purple spathe with green or white stripes appears in late spring or early summer and encloses a green or purple spadix. The 2-3 leaves are made up of 3 leaflets about 8-15cm (3¼-6in) long. HEIGHT 20-60cm (8-24in).

CULTIVATION Plant tubers in late autumn or early spring in a moisture-retentive, humus-rich, well-drained soil. Protect with a mulch of leaves or bracken when temperatures fall below freezing for long periods.

PROPAGATION Remove offsets from mature plants in late autumn. Alternatively, sow ripe seed in late autumn.

PESTS AND DISEASES Usually trouble free.

Arisarum

Araceae

Unusual flowers peep out from the glossy, arrowhead-shaped foliage of these herbaceous perennials that thrive in woodland conditions. Native to Italy and Spain.

RECOMMENDED SPECIES

A. proboscideum (mouse plant) Sail-like, maroon and white, leaf-like spathes, up to 10cm (4in) long, have slender appendages curling outwards in late spring and early summer. At the base, they are wrapped round spikes of tiny petal-less flowers. The glossy leaves, up to 10cm (4in) long, half conceal these striking flowers. HEIGHT & SPREAD 15×30cm (6×12in).

CULTIVATION Plant in late summer or autumn in fertile, moist soil in partial shade. Mulch with leaf-mould in early spring.

PROPAGATION Divide in late summer or autumn.

PESTS AND DISEASES Usually trouble free.

▼ *Arisarum proboscideum*

a

Aristolochia

Dutchman's pipe
Aristolochiaceae

Aristolochia macrophylla

Unusual flowers, shaped like a curved smoker's pipe and often unpleasantly scented inspire the common name of this genus of tender and hardy perennials, shrubs and climbers. The leaves are heart or kidney-shaped, 10-25cm (4-10in) long. Native to moist woodlands and scrub, most of the plants prefer partial shade. They may take a couple of seasons to settle down into a flowering pattern.

RECOMMENDED SPECIES

A. clematitis (birthwort) With its creeping habit, this hardy herbaceous perennial will colonise semi-wild areas. The dull greeny yellow flowers, up to 2.5cm (1in) long, borne from late spring to mid summer are mostly hidden by the foliage. HEIGHT & SPREAD 60×60cm (2×2ft).

▲ *Aristolochia clematitis*

A. durior see *A. macrophylla*

A. littoralis♀ (syn. *A. elegans*) (calico flower) This tender, evergreen climber bears flowers, up to 10cm (4in) long, that are green-yellow to white, marbled with purple and maroon, with a darker throat. The flowers appear from mid summer to early autumn. The pale grey-green leaves are kidney or heart-shaped and smell unpleasant when crushed. HEIGHT & SPREAD 5m×60cm (16×2ft).

A. macrophylla (syn. *A. durior*, *A. sipho*) This hardy deciduous climber bears green flowers, up to 4cm (1½in) long, boldly marked with brown, yellow and purple. They appear in early summer. The dull green heart or kidney-shaped leaves have downy undersides. HEIGHT & SPREAD 10m×90cm (33×3ft).

CULTIVATION Grow *A. littoralis* in compost in a warm greenhouse or conservatory, with a minimum night time temperature of 13°C (55°F). Plant hardy plants in fertile, free-draining soil enriched with plenty of organic matter. Provide suitable support for the climbers. Give indoor and outdoor plants a balanced liquid feed monthly in summer.

PROPAGATION Take semi-ripe cuttings in summer or sow seed in spring.

PRUNING Remove weak shoots of climbers and train the developing main growths.

PESTS AND DISEASES Red spider mite may be troublesome under glass.

Armeria

Thrift, Sea pink
Plumbaginaceae

Armeria maritima

Dense, globular flowerheads, mainly pink in colour, are held on leafless stems above tufts or cushions of narrow, lance-shape or linear leaves in spring and summer. These hardy evergreen perennials are European natives, found on cliffs, seashores and on high mountains. They do well in rock gardens and make a neat, decorative edging along a garden path. The smaller species will thrive in a trough.

RECOMMENDED SPECIES AND VARIETIES

A. 'Bee's Ruby'♀ Ruby-red flowerheads, about 2.5cm (1in) across, stand over dark green leaves, up to 10cm (4in) long. HEIGHT & SPREAD 25×30cm (10×12in).

A. juniperifolia♀ (syn. *A. caespitosa*) Purple-pink flowers in dense heads, about 1.5cm (½in) across, are surrounded by papery bracts from late spring to mid summer. The green to greyish leaves, up to 1.5cm (½in) long, form dense clumps. HEIGHT & SPREAD 25×25cm (10×10in).

▲ *Armeria juniperifolia* 'Bevans Variety'

'Alba' has white flowers, while **'Beechwood'** has deep pink flowers. **'Bevan's Variety'**♀ forms dense foliage cushions with deep rose-pink flowers.

A. maritima (syn. *A. vulgaris*) (common thrift) White, pink or almost crimson flowerheads, about 2.5cm (1in) across, rise above spiky clumps of dark green leaves, about 10cm (4in) long. HEIGHT & SPREAD 20×50cm (8×20in).

'Alba' has large white flowerheads on short stalks. **'Bloodstone'** with its rich, dark red flowers reaches only 20cm (8in) tall. **'Corsica'** has very narrow leaves and salmon-pink flowers, while **'Düsseldorfer Stolz'** (syn. *A.* 'D. Pride') has rich crimson flowers. **'Laucheana'** has deep pink flowers, while those of **'Vindictive'**♀, which grows to 15cm (6in) tall, are deep rose-pink.

▲ *Armeria maritima* 'Düsseldorfer Stolz'

A. vulgaris see *A. maritima*

CULTIVATION Plant in spring to early summer in full sun in any well-drained soil.

PROPAGATION Take semi-ripe cuttings or divide established plants after flowering. Alternatively sow the seed of species in autumn or early winter.

PESTS AND DISEASES Usually trouble free.

Arnica

Compositae

Arnica montana

Yellow daisy-like flowers open in summer above a neat, tight crown of leaves. They bring glowing highlights to an open, well-drained, sunny border or a raised bed. The smaller species thrive in a rock garden. The recommended plants are hardy perennials.

RECOMMENDED SPECIES AND VARIETIES

A. chamissonis Clusters of flowers appear from mid to late summer above neat clumps of lance-shaped leaves, up to 15cm (6in) long. HEIGHT & SPREAD 90×45cm (36×18in).

A. montana (mountain tobacco) Groups of

flowers bloom on tall strong stems from mid to late summer. The oval or lance-shaped green leaves are up to 20cm (8in) long. HEIGHT & SPREAD 60×45cm (24×18in).

CULTIVATION Plant in spring in well-drained soil in an open sunny position where they can spread freely.

PROPAGATION Divide plants in spring. Sow seeds in a coldframe in spring or mid summer.

PESTS AND DISEASES Usually trouble free.

Arrhenatherum see GRASSES p.300
Arrowhead see *Sagittaria sagittifolia*

Artemisia

Wormwood

Compositae

Finely cut, feathery foliage in tones of silver and soft grey make these shrubs and perennials an asset. They look good in mixed borders and rock gardens, or as wall shrubs or ground cover. The leaves are often aromatic, silky in texture, and have long been grown in herb gardens. Clusters of tiny button-like yellow or whitish flowers from summer to autumn are not significant to the plant's appeal, except for *Artemisia lactiflora*. The genus is native to northern temperate regions, S America and South Africa. The recommended plants, which dislike winter wetness, vary in hardiness.

RECOMMENDED SPECIES AND VARIETIES

A. abrotanum♀ (southernwood, lad's love) The deciduous or semi-evergreen grey-green leaves of this hardy, compact shrub are very aromatic. Insignificant clusters of small yellow flowers appear in late summer. HEIGHT & SPREAD 70×50cm (28×20in).

A. absinthium (absinthe, wormwood) A rounded, woody-based perennial with aromatic, silver-green, evergreen leaves, this plant has clusters of small dull yellow flowers in summer. The plant is not fully hardy. HEIGHT & SPREAD 1m×50cm (3ft×20in).

'Lambrook Silver'♀ is smaller and the silver foliage is more finely cut.

A. alba (syn. *A. camphoreta*) This aromatic perennial with a lax, spreading habit has delicately cut, silver-grey filigree leaves. The insignificant yellow flowers appear in spring on silver stems. HEIGHT & SPREAD 45×45cm (18×18in).

'Canescens'♀ is a good ground-cover plant with narrow, curling silver leaves.

A. arborescens This showy woody-stemmed perennial with pale silver, finely divided leaves may not survive the hardest winters. HEIGHT & SPREAD 1m×50cm (3ft×20in).

'Faith Raven' is more hardy.

A. caucasica♀ (syn. *A. assoana, A. pedemontana* and *A. lanata*) This white, woolly perennial with a low spreading habit has dissected, glistening leaves. Ideal for a rock garden on limy soils, the plant is not fully

▲ *Artemisia arborescens*

hardy. HEIGHT & SPREAD 30×15cm (12×6in).

A. dracunculus see HERBS p.330

A. frigida♀ The spreading mats of this hardy, prostrate perennial form good ground cover. The plant runs along the earth and stems arise at intervals carrying tiny nodding flowers. The small, dissected leaves are silver grey and aromatic. HEIGHT & SPREAD 8×30cm (3¼×12in).

A. gnaphalodes see *A ludoviciana*

A. lactiflora♀ (white mugwort) Stiff stems carry conspicuous plumes of tiny, creamy-white flowers in late summer on this hardy perennial which needs staking. The large, jagged, deep green leaves are deeply cut. HEIGHT & SPREAD 1.8m×60cm (6×2ft).

A. lanata see *A. caucasica*

A. ludoviciana♀ (syn. *A. gnaphalodes, A. palmeri* and *A. pushiana)* A tall hardy perennial with silver-grey, aromatic, lance-shaped leaves, this plant can be invasive. Tiny grey-white flowers appear in mid summer in slender plumes. HEIGHT & SPREAD 1.2m×60cm (4×2ft).

▲ *Artemisia ludoviciana*

Pale silver leaves with jagged edges distinguish var. ***latiloba***, which is shorter than the species at 60cm (2ft).

'Silver Queen'♀ has a compact habit and grows to 75cm (30in). The leaves are dark yellow-grey above and pale green beneath. **'Valerie Finnis'** grows to 60cm (2ft) and has silver-grey leaves with jagged edges.

A. pedemontana see *A. caucasica*

A. pontica♀ Finely cut, feathery leaves form an aromatic, yellow-green hummock, making this a good ground-cover plant. However, it can be an invasive coloniser. The plant is not fully hardy. HEIGHT & SPREAD 40×40cm (16×16in).

***A.* 'Powis Castle'**♀ Silver-grey, filigree evergreen foliage forms a dense, bushy mound. The insignificant flowers rarely appear. The plant is not fully hardy in colder areas. HEIGHT & SPREAD 90cm×1.2m (3×4ft).

A. schmidtiana♀ Downy, silver semi-evergreen leaves are much divided on this plant which is best grown in a large rock garden. Tiny yellow flowers appear in early autumn. HEIGHT & SPREAD 30×30cm (12×12in).

▲ *Artemisia schmidtiana*

'Nana'♀ is smaller with neat evergreen mounds of intense silver-grey, silky leaves.

A. stelleriana White, felted, deeply cut leaves form loose mats on this hardy perennial. The yellow flowers are borne in slender sprays. HEIGHT & SPREAD 60×90cm (2×3ft).

▲ *Artemisia stelleriana*

'Mori' (syn. *A.* 'Boughton Silver') is more prostrate with silvery white leaves.

CULTIVATION Plant in spring in an open sunny spot with free-draining soil.

PROPAGATION Divide perennials in spring. Take softwood cuttings in early summer and grow on under glass until the following spring.

PRUNING Cut plants back in spring to keep their shape and produce good foliage. Treat *A. lactiflora, A. ludoviciana* and *A. vulgaris* as herbaceous border plants and cut down during the winter.

PESTS AND DISEASES Leaves can be infested by aphids and roots attacked by root aphids. Rust may cause brown pustules on the leaves.

a

Arthropodium

Anthericaceae

Dainty white or pale lilac drooping flowers are profusely borne in loose sprays on these perennial plants that are suitable for moist but well-drained borders or rock gardens. Native to New Guinea, Australia and New Zealand, they are hardy only in the southern counties and need shelter in colder areas. The flowers, borne above tufts of grass-like leaves, have petals that curve back, revealing hairy stamens. They are followed by seed capsules each of which holds a few black seeds.

RECOMMENDED SPECIES AND VARIETIES

A. candidum (grass lily) In mid summer, loose sprays of white flowers each about 1cm (⅜in) across droop from erect stems that hold them well above the leaves. The leaves are 20cm (8in) tall, soft and pale green; they die back in winter. HEIGHT & SPREAD 20x30cm (8x12in).

▲ *Arthropodium cirratum*

The leaves of f. ***purpureum*** are bronze.

A. cirratum (New Zealand rock lily) Broad sprays of numerous drooping flowers, each about 3cm (1¼in) across, are pale lilac in bud, opening to white with yellow and lilac stamens. They bloom in late spring or early summer on slender but stiff stems that hold them above pale green, arching, evergreen leaves about 40cm (16in) long. This plant is suitable for growing outside only where temperatures do not fall below -5°C (23°F). HEIGHT & SPREAD 55x60cm (22x24 in).

A. milleflorum (vanilla lily) Pale lilac flowers 1.5cm (½in) across hang in summer from the wiry, erect, branched stems. The flowers are carried well above the stiff, grassy, evergreen leaves about 20cm (8in) tall. HEIGHT & SPREAD 30x30cm (1x1ft).

CULTIVATION Plant in well-drained, fertile soil and keep it moist in summer. *A. candidum* prefers shade but *A. cirratum* thrives in sun or shade. *A milleflorum* does best on sandy or gravelly soil and in full sun. In cold areas grow the plants in containers and move them into a conservatory or greenhouse for winter.

PROPAGATION Raise from seed or divide established plants in late spring. *A. candidum* and *A. milleflorum* often self seed.

PESTS AND DISEASES Usually trouble free.

Arum

Araceae

The glossy, arrowhead-like leaves of the arum provide interest in the garden in late autumn and winter or emerge in spring. Most of these tuberous perennials flower in spring when the leaf-like spathe appears. Enclosed within the spathe is a prominent stalk called a spadix; the tiny petal-less true flowers cluster around its base. Most arums have an unpleasant odour of decay that attracts pollinating insects. The spadix bears bright red berries in late summer, after the leaves and spathe die back. The berries are poisonous if eaten and the plant sap and the juice of the berries can cause skin irritation.

RECOMMENDED SPECIES AND VARIETIES

A. creticum The cream or yellow showy spathe, 5-25cm (2-10in) long, turns back to reveal a yellow or dark purple spadix, sometimes longer than the spathe. This species is sweetly scented. The leaves, 8-25cm (3¼-10in) long, appear in late autumn. A Mediterranean plant for a rock garden. HEIGHT & SPREAD 40x20cm (16x8in).

A. italicum Dark green leaves, marked with white veins and up to 35cm (14in) long, emerge in late autumn or early winter. The greenish yellow spathe, 15-40cm (6-16in) long, encloses a yellow spadix up to half the length of the spathe. A Mediterranean plant for woodland gardens or for a shrub bed. HEIGHT & SPREAD 40x20cm (16x8in).

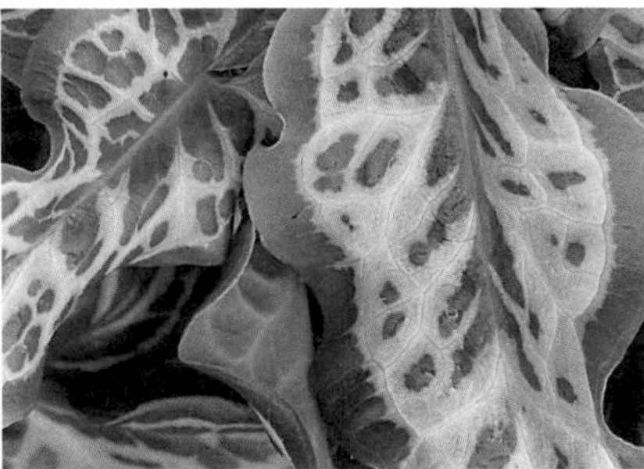

▲ *Arum italicum* 'Marmoratum'

'Marmoratum'♀ is grown for the pronounced marbling on its leaves.

A. maculatum (cuckoo pint, lords and ladies) A vigorous, spreading British native. Dark green leaves, sometimes spotted black and up to 20cm (8in) long, emerge in spring; so does the spathe, which is greenish white, sometimes edged with purple. Up to 25cm (10in) long, it encloses a purple or yellow spadix, half the length of the spathe. HEIGHT & SPREAD 30x30cm (12x12in).

CULTIVATION Plant tubers in summer, 10cm (4in) deep and 30cm (1ft) apart, in any soil that does not dry out too quickly and in partial shade. Top dress with well-rotted compost in late summer; keep moist in the growing season in winter and spring. Mulch *A. creticum* and *A. italicum* with dry organic matter in severe winters.

▲ *Arum creticum*

PROPAGATION Divide after flowering.

PESTS AND DISEASES Usually trouble free.

Arum, dragon see *Dracunculus vulgaris*
Arum lily see *Zantedeschia*

Aruncus

Goat's beard

Rosaceae

Elegant sprays of light green leaves make lush mounds from which feathery plumes of tiny cream flowers rise in mid summer. Female plants develop small, dull green seed pods that dry well for indoor arrangements. Male plants do not self seed. These hardy perennials thrive in moist soil round a pond.

RECOMMENDED SPECIES AND VARIETIES

A. aethusifolius Creamy white 20cm (8in) plumes of flowers are borne above deeply divided dark green leaves. Native to Korea. HEIGHT & SPREAD 23-30x30cm (9-12x12in).

A. dioicus♀ (syn. *A. plumosus*, *A. sylvestris*, *A. vulgaris*) Graceful, light green leaves, up

▼ *Aruncus dioicus*

to 30 cm (12 in) long, are enhanced by 20 cm (8 in) plumes of star-shaped, creamy white flowers, borne on tall stout stems in mid summer. Native to W and C Europe, S Russia and the Caucasus. HEIGHT & SPREAD 1.8×1.2 m (6×4 ft).

The variety **'Glasnevin'** reaches only 1.2 m×60 cm (4×2 ft), as does **'Kneiffii'**, which has dark, very finely cut, lacy leaves and thinner stems than those of the species.

A. plumosus see *A. dioicus*
A. sylvester see *A. dioicus*
A. vulgaris see *A. dioicus*

CULTIVATION Plant from autumn to early spring in rich, moist soil, ideally in partial shade, spacing the plants 60 cm (2 ft) apart.
PROPAGATION Lift and divide in autumn every 2 to 3 years.
PESTS AND DISEASES Usually trouble free.

Asarabacca see *Asarum europaeum*

Asarina
Creeping snapdragon
Scrophulariaceae

The trailing stems of this evergreen, short-lived perennial make year-round cover beneath trees, over rocks or down walls. A long flowering period increases its garden value. It is not fully hardy in Britain. There is only one species in the genus.

A. hispanica see *Antirrhinum hispanicum*

▼ *Asarina procumbens*

Asarina procumbens (syn. *Antirrhinum asarina, Antirrhinum procumbens, Maurandya asarina*) Snapdragon-like flowers, closed at the mouth by rounded upper and lower lips, are up to 4 cm (1½ in) long and borne from early summer to early autumn. They are creamy with faint purple veins. A softly hairy plant, sticky to the touch. The greyish green leaves, which grow in pairs along the stems are kidney-shaped and up to 6 cm (2½ in) wide. Native to the Pyrenees and N Spain. HEIGHT & SPREAD 10×60 cm (4×24 in).

'Nuria' is a more compact plant, suitable for small rock gardens and troughs.

CULTIVATION Plant in late spring after the last frosts in a well-drained soil, rich in humus, preferably alkaline, in partial shade. The species is hardy to -10°C (14°F); protect plants in winter with a cloche or overhead glass. In colder areas, grow the plants in pots and overwinter them under cover.
PROPAGATION Once established, the plant seeds itself freely each year. Alternatively, take cuttings in late spring or summer.
PESTS AND DISEASES Slugs may attack young plants.

Asarum
Wild ginger
Aristolochiaceae

Asarum europaeum

The glossy, deep green leaves of these low-growing, hardy herbaceous perennials provide luxuriant ground cover and are useful in shade. Curious, often sombre, urn-shaped flowers are held at ground level beneath the leaves. The insignificant, fleshy oval fruits break open and the seeds are dispersed by ants. They are mostly woodland plants in the wild and grow best in moist leafy soil but *Asarum caudatum* and *A. europaeum* are reasonably drought resistant. Plants form spreading evergreen or deciduous mats. Those described are evergreen.

RECOMMENDED SPECIES AND VARIETIES

A. caudatum Red-purple flowers appear below the leaves in spring, each one opening into a hairy urn from a folded bud. The heart-shaped, hairy leaves are up to 15 cm (6 in) long. Native to western N America. HEIGHT & SPREAD 15×40 cm (6×16 in).

A. europaeum (asarabacca) This hardy evergreen forms wide patches of shiny, kidney-shaped leaves, up to 12 cm (4¾ in) wide, usually plain green, sometimes with silver markings. Greeny purple, hairy, urn-shaped flowers appear in early spring. Best grown in deep shade. Native to W Europe. HEIGHT & SPREAD 10×50 cm (4×20 in).

A. hartwegii (syn. *A. marmoratum*) Purple-brown, hairy flowers appear in spring. The veins of the heart-shaped leaves are marked silver-grey. Native to SW North America. HEIGHT & SPREAD 10×30 cm (4×12 in).

'Silver Heart' is an especially well-marked leaf form.

CULTIVATION Plant in spring for ground cover in shade or as a specimen in a cool corner of a rock garden.
PROPAGATION Sow seed under glass or outdoors in autumn. Divide in early spring.
PESTS AND DISEASES The leaves are liable to slug and snail damage.

Asclepias
Silkweed, milkweed
Asclepiadaceae

Bright orange and red or pink flowers appear throughout summer or from late summer to autumn on these annuals, herbaceous perennials and shrubs. The fruits carry seeds with tufts of soft white hairs. The tops of the stems contain a milky sap, which can be a skin irritant. Asclepias have deep, fleshy tuberous roots which tend to spread. The plants listed are grown in sunny, protected borders or in a greenhouse or conservatory.

RECOMMENDED SPECIES AND VARIETIES

A. curassavica The flowers, 2 cm (¾ in) wide, are carried in clusters of 5 to 10. They are usually orange and red but from seed white and yellow forms can appear. The evergreen lance-shaped leaves, 5-15 cm (2-6 in) long, are carried in pairs on this sub-shrub. Native to Central America. HEIGHT & SPREAD 90×45 cm (36×18 in).

▲ *Asclepias curassavica*

A. incarnata (swamp milkweed) The pink, occasionally white, tubular flowers of this hardy perennial are carried in the leaf axils. The narrow leaves grow up to 15 cm (6 in) long. Native to NE and SE USA. HEIGHT & SPREAD 1.5 m×50 cm (5 ft×20 in).

A. tuberosa The orange and red flowers, 1 cm (⅜ in) across, are carried in tight clusters from late summer to early autumn. The lance-shaped leaves, 12 cm (4¾ in) long, spiral round the woody stem of this hardy herbaceous perennial. Native to S and E USA. HEIGHT & SPREAD 90×30 cm (3×1 ft).

CULTIVATION Grow in ordinary, well-drained soil in full sun. Plant after all danger of frost is over; protect with fleece initially.
PROPAGATION Sow seed under glass in late winter or divide in late spring.
PESTS AND DISEASES Whitefly can infest plants grown under glass.

Ash see *Fraxinus*
Ash, mountain see *Sorbus aucuparia*

▼ *Asclepias tuberosa*

Asparagus
Asparagaceae

Asparagus densiflorus Sprengeri Group

Fern-like foliage is the main appeal of these diverse perennials, which are native to Africa, Europe and Asia. With the exception of the culinary asparagus, *Asparagus officinalis*, they are evergreen indoor pot plants. *A. officinalis* is a hardy herbaceous perennial, commonly grown outdoors. Small white flowers appear amid the foliage of all species, sometimes followed by red, or more rarely black, berries.

RECOMMENDED SPECIES AND VARIETIES

***A. densiflorus* 'Myersii'**♀ (foxtail fern) Fine foliage in dense feathery spines adorns this half-hardy perennial which is popular for hanging pots or baskets. HEIGHT & SPREAD 90×50 cm (36×20 in).

Sprengeri Group♀ (emerald fern) has arching or scrambling wiry green stems densely clothed with bright green needle-like leaves up to 2.5 cm (1 in) long.

A. officinalis♀ Feathery, fine, green foliage is a feature of this hardy plant, the female forms of which have orange-red berries. Male plants, and all-male varieties, produce the strongest spears for culinary use. HEIGHT & SPREAD 1.2-1.5 m×60 cm (4-5×2 ft).

A. setaceus♀ A flat, fern-like triangular spray is formed by groups of up to 20 bright green needle-like leaflets which clothe the wiry stems of this twining plant. HEIGHT & SPREAD 1-2 m×50 cm (3-6½ ft×20 in).

'Pyramidalis' has a loose pyramidal non-twining habit.

A. verticillatus This prickly, scrambling, much-branched species for the greenhouse has fine green leaves in groups of up to 20. HEIGHT & SPREAD 4×1 m (13×3 ft).

CULTIVATION Grow indoor species in an open or partially shaded cool situation in a soil-based compost, such as John Innes No.3, which is moist but well drained. Give a liquid houseplant feed regularly in late spring and summer. Indoor species must be kept frost free. Cultivation details for culinary asparagus, *A. officinalis*, are given on p.732.

▼ *Asparagus densiflorus* 'Myersii'

PROPAGATION Sow seed in spring. Divide houseplant species in spring.

PESTS AND DISEASES Asparagus beetle may attack culinary asparagus; red spider mite affects indoor plants.

Asparagus see p.732

Asperula
Woodruff
Rubiaceae

Dainty tubular flowers flaring into four-pointed stars at the mouth bloom generously on these annual, perennial or shrubby plants. Those listed below are lime-tolerant evergreen perennials that flower in spring and early summer. They do well in an unheated greenhouse or conservatory or can be grown in troughs and raised beds, given protection from winter wet. Native mainly to the Mediterranean and SW Asia.

RECOMMENDED SPECIES AND VARIETIES

A. arcadiensis♀ (syn. *A. suberosa* hort.) Small clusters of pink flowers, each flower about 1 cm (⅜ in) long, cover pale grey-green mats of foliage in early summer. The spreading mats are formed by dense tufts of narrow elliptical, woolly leaves up to 1 cm (⅜ in) long, which grow in whorls up the stems. HEIGHT & SPREAD 5×30 cm (2×12 in).

▼ *Asperula arcadiensis*

A. gussonii Dense clusters of red flowers appear in late spring just above a mat of grey-green leaves. Each flower is up to 5 mm (¼ in) long. The leaves are elliptical and up to 1 cm (⅜ in) long. HEIGHT & SPREAD 2.5×30 cm (1×12 in).

A. odorata see *Galium odoratum*

A. sintenisii♀ Pink flowers, up to 1 cm (⅜ in) long, are held singly or in pairs smothering the dense tufts of foliage. The deep green elliptical to linear leaves are each up to about 1 cm (⅜ in) long, and pointed. HEIGHT & SPREAD 2×20 cm (¾×8 in).

▼ *Asperula sintenisii*

A. suberosa hort. see *A. arcadiensis*

CULTIVATION Plant in moist, well-drained soil in a sunny position. Protect from winter wet using overhead glass. Plants grow well on tufa. Otherwise grow in shallow pans in an unheated greenhouse or conservatory.

PROPAGATION Sow seed in winter or early spring or divide in spring or autumn.

PESTS AND DISEASES Occasionally troubled by aphids or slugs. In autumn and winter grey mould may be a problem.

Asphodeline
Jacob's rod
Asphodelaceae

Asphodeline lutea

Spires of yellow, star-like flowers rise in spring and summer above clumps of grassy leaves on these hardy herbaceous perennials. The plants, native to the Mediterranean area, have swollen rhizomatous roots that help them to withstand dry conditions.

RECOMMENDED SPECIES AND VARIETIES

A. liburnica Slender stems carry erect spikes, 20 cm (8 in) tall, of pale yellow flowers, sometimes striped with green, 3 cm (1¼ in) across, in early to mid summer. The narrow leaves are grey-green. HEIGHT & SPREAD 60×30 cm (2×1 ft).

A. lutea (syn. *Asphodelus luteus*) The linear, silver or dark green leaves form a tufted plant. Spikes of numerous, yellow fragrant flowers, each bloom 3 cm (1¼ in) across, appear from late spring to early summer and are followed by globular green seeds. HEIGHT & SPREAD 1.2 m×30 cm (4×1 ft).

CULTIVATION Plant out in early spring in free-draining soil that is fertile but not over-rich. If planted in autumn young plants may need some protection in a hard winter.

PROPAGATION Raise plants from seed sown when ripe in a coldframe. Grow on in open ground or in pots and plant out 30 cm (1 ft) apart early in the following spring.

PESTS AND DISEASES Usually trouble free.

Asphodelus
Asphodel
Asphodelaceae

With long, dense spikes of delicate white starry flowers that open in late spring or early summer above upright grassy foliage, these plants are excellent for the herbaceous border or in light shade among trees and shrubs. The plants included here are annuals

▲ *Asphodelus albus*

or herbaceous perennials with rhizomatous roots. Native to the Mediterranean, they need good drainage and some protection in winter where temperatures regularly fall below -5°C (23°F).

RECOMMENDED SPECIES AND VARIETIES

A. albus (white asphodel) The white or pink star-shaped flowers have long, fine prominent stamens. Each flower is about 4 cm (1½ in) across and has 6 petals, each with a pinkish brown central vein. The flowering stems rise out of dense clumps of narrow, grey-green, ridged leaves, up to 60 cm (2 ft) long. An herbaceous perennial. HEIGHT & SPREAD 1 m×30 cm (3×1 ft).

▲ *Asphodelus fistulosus*

A. fistulosus (hollow-leaved asphodel) The white or pink flowers are about 2.5 cm (1 in) wide and have prominent stamens. Each of the 6 petals has a light brown central vein. The stems and narrow mid green leaves, up to 35 cm (14 in) long, are hollow. This plant is an annual or short-lived perennial. HEIGHT & SPREAD 75×30 cm (2½×1 ft).

A. luteus see *Asphodeline lutea*

CULTIVATION Plant in early spring in free-draining soil in full sun or semi-shade. Unless seed is wanted, cut back the flowering stems when the blooms are over. Cut back the leaves in winter. Do not overwater or overfeed. Give plants protection during winter in colder areas of Britain.

PROPAGATION Sow seed or divide plants carefully in spring.

PESTS AND DISEASES Usually trouble free.

Aspidistra

Convallariaceae

Leathery, glossy, dark green foliage is the outstanding feature of these handsome evergreen perennials. The leaves are erect and lance-shaped and retain a healthy appearance in quite extreme conditions indoors. In the warmest parts of the country, areas in the south and west, given a moist, sheltered and shady position the plants can be grown outdoors, associating well with ferns.

A. elatior♀ (cast-iron plant) Most commonly grown as a houseplant, this slow-spreading plant has arching, long-stalked, tapering leaves, up to 60 cm (24 in) long. The leaves rise singly from a stout rhizome and it forms broad clumps. Insignificant urn-shaped flowers that are easily overlooked may be borne in spring or summer on a short stem at soil level. Fruits are dull brown berries in late summer but are rarely seen on a cultivated plant. Native to China. HEIGHT & SPREAD 60×60 cm (24×24 in).

▲ *Aspidistra elatior* 'Variegata'

The leaves of **'Variegata'**♀ are marked lengthways with irregular creamy stripes.

CULTIVATION Strong sunlight can scorch the foliage of an aspidistra though the colour of the variegated plant is more distinct given brighter light. Plant in well-drained, humus-rich soil in a sheltered, shady place not subject to frost.

PROPAGATION Divide established plants in spring.

PESTS AND DISEASES Usually trouble free, but slugs may damage the leaves. Scale insects and mealy bugs may infest pot plants.

Astelia

Asteliaceae

Bold sword-leaved clumps of silvery green are the outstanding plants in this genus, but it also includes small and unobtrusive green plants. These perennials from New Zealand, Tasmania and islands in the South Pacific need moist, acid soil and are not all hardy. In milder areas of Britain they make striking features in open borders, but in exposed gardens and colder areas they are generally best grown in tubs to be put outside in summer. The flowers and fruits are rarely seen in gardens, but if female plants are grown with a male nearby to fertilise them, the flower clusters develop into showy yellow, orange or red berries that are edible and sweet.

▲ *Astelia chathamica* 'Silver Spear'

RECOMMENDED SPECIES AND VARIETIES

***A. chathamica* 'Silver Spear'** Sword-like, evergreen leaves, 2 m (6½ ft) or more long and up to 10 cm (4 in) wide on established plants, curve outward. The upper surface is green with a silvery covering that eventually peels off. The underside is felted with white hairs. Sprays of greenish to maroon flowers are followed on fertilised plants by orange berries in summer. Give protection when temperatures drop below -5°C (23°F). HEIGHT & SPREAD 1.5×2.4 m (5×8 ft).

A. nervosa Silvery evergreen leaves 1 m (3 ft) and more long, arch stiffly outwards, hiding the flower clusters, which vary from green to dark maroon. The rarely seen summer fruits are orange to red. Tolerates temperatures down to -10°C (14°F). HEIGHT & SPREAD 60 cm×1.5 m (2×5 ft).

CULTIVATION Plant in moist, loamy, acid soil; make sure it stays moist in summer. In cold areas, grow the plants in tubs and overwinter in a conservatory or greenhouse.

PROPAGATION Raise from seed if it is available. Soak seed of *A. nervosa* overnight before sowing in late winter; germination is often very slow. Alternatively, divide a young plant carefully in summer, or lift and divide established clumps in spring.

PESTS AND DISEASES Usually trouble free.

▼ *Astelia nervosa*

Aster

Michaelmas daisy, starwort
Compositae

Aster alpinus

Daisy-like asters bring fresh colour to the garden in late summer and autumn or spring. Violet to lavender, white, pink, red or blue flowers with golden yellow centres are carried singly or in clusters. Asters are mostly herbaceous perennials – a few are annuals or biennials. The asters described are all hardy herbaceous perennials.

Autumn-flowering asters – known as Michaelmas daisies because they flower around Michaelmas, September 29 – make a fine show in a garden border, especially when planted in bold groups of one colour. They are excellent as cut flowers. Lower-growing asters, often spring-flowering, are suitable for rock gardens, raised beds, small borders and containers.

The petals are properly called ray florets and the central disc is made up of disc florets. Leaves are arranged alternately on the stems. All the recommended species and varieties flower between late summer and late autumn, except for *Aster alpinus* and *A. tongolensis* 'Napsbury', which bloom in late spring and early summer. The flowers attract butterflies and bees. Native to Europe, Asia, N America and South Africa.

RECOMMENDED SPECIES AND VARIETIES

A. acris see *A. sedifolius*

A. alpinus♀ (alpine aster) Flowers with violet, white or pink petals bloom from late spring to early summer on a small plant. Erect stems carry solitary flowers 3-5 cm (1¼-2 in) across. Spoon-shaped, grey-green leaves, 5-8 cm (2-3¼ in) long, form rosettes. HEIGHT & SPREAD 25×25 cm (10×10 in).

A. amellus (Italian starwort) Listed cultivars all have large flowers in loose, flat-topped clusters, about 15 cm (6 in) long and 25 cm (10 in) wide, on erect, woody stems. The grey-green leaves, 6 cm (2½ in) long, are oblong to lance-shaped. Mildew resistant.

The following grow 50 cm (20 in) tall and spread to 65 cm (26 in) unless stated otherwise. **'Framfieldii'**♀ is bushy, with violet-purple flowers; **'King George'**♀ has larger, rich violet-blue flowers; **'Nocturne'** produces large, deep lilac flowers and is 70 cm (28 in) tall; **'Pink Zenith'** ('Rosa Erfüllung') is sturdy and has bright pink flowers; the compact **'Veilchenkönigin'**♀ ('Violet Queen') has violet-purple blooms.

A. cordifolius Cultivars thrive in dappled shade as well as in sun. The small flowers are

▲ *Aster amellus* 'King George'

carried in graceful, open sprays about 60 cm (24 in) across. Erect wiry stems bear deep green, heart-shaped to broadly oval leaves, 8 cm (3¼ in) long. Resistant to mildew.

'Elegans', with white, lavender-tinted flowers, emerging in mid autumn, and **'Sweet Lavender'**♀, with pale violet-blue flowers, are both 1.2 m (4 ft) tall, spreading to 75 cm (30 in).

A. divaricatus This species is useful for shaded sites, where dark brown wiry stems, 60 cm (24 in) long, arch to the ground, creating effective cover when massed with white, starry flowers, 2.5 cm (1 in) wide, borne in clusters up to 20 cm (8 in) across. The broad, oval, pointed leaves are light green and up to 10 cm (4 in) long. HEIGHT & SPREAD 30 cm×1 m (1×3 ft).

A. ericoides Cultivars have elegant, spreading sprays, about 70 cm (28 in) long, carrying lots of small flowers. The mid green, narrow leaves are 1-7 cm (⅜-2¾ in) long. This is a very bushy plant. It survives drought better than many other autumn asters. Some resistance to mildew.

Listed plants reach heights and spreads of 1 m (3 ft), except the lavender-blue **'Blue Star'**♀, 80 cm (32 in) tall; **'Golden Spray'**♀ has white flowers; **'Pink Cloud'**♀ has mauve-pink flowers; **'White Heather'** bears upright sprays of white flowers.

A. × frikartii All cultivars are exceptionally free flowering and vigorous. Flowers are solitary. The dark green, oblong leaves, rough to the touch, are 8 cm (3¼ in) long on some plants. Resistant to mildew.

▼ *Aster ericoides* 'Golden Spray'

▼ *Aster ericoides* 'Pink Cloud'

'Flora's Delight', with rosy lilac flowers 4 cm (1½ in) across, is a compact plant, with a height and spread of about 45 cm (18 in). **'Wunder von Stäfa'**♀ has lavender-blue flowers up to 7 cm (2¾ in) across, and attains a height and spread of 1 m (3 ft).

***A.* 'Kylie'**♀ Small, pale rose-pink flowers are carried in elegant sprays 80 cm (32 in) long on tall, woody stems on this vigorous plant. The pale grey-green leaves are lance-shaped and up to 40 cm (16 in) long. Resistant to mildew. HEIGHT & SPREAD 1.4 m×80 cm (4½ ft×32 in).

A. lateriflorus Small, white-petalled flowers, with pale yellow discs that turn purple after the first few days, are produced in profusion within flat-topped clusters borne on the upper side of slender, spreading branches that extend almost at right angles from the main stem. Leaves are lance-shaped, as long as 15 cm (6 in), green often tinted purple, especially colourful in some cultivars. HEIGHT & SPREAD 1×1 m (3×3 ft).

'Coombe Fishacre' has flowers with pink petals encircling rosy purple central discs. **'Horizontalis'**♀, with purple-tinted leaves, is a compact plant that reaches a height of 60 cm (24 in) and spreads to 70 cm (28 in), flowering late, in mid autumn.

***A.* 'Little Carlow'**♀ Violet-blue flowers, 2.5 cm (1 in) wide, bloom abundantly in broad, branching clusters, 30 cm (12 in) across, on upright stems. The pointed, deep green leaves are about 12 cm (4¾ in) long. Some resistance to mildew. HEIGHT & SPREAD 1.4 m×80 cm (4½ ft×32 in).

A. novae-angliae (New England aster) Cultivars have flowers 3-5 cm (1¼-2 in) wide, appearing in open clusters, up to 18 cm (7 in) across, at the top of stout, woody stems covered with rough, lance-shaped, dull green leaves. Plants require very little staking. Resistant to mildew.

The following are 1 m (3 ft) tall and spread to 80-100 cm (32-40 in), unless stated otherwise. **'Andenken an Alma Pötschke'**♀, vivid cerise; **'Harrington's Pink'**♀, rose-pink, 1.2 m (4 ft) tall; **'Herbstschnee'**, ('Autumn Snow'), white; **'Lye End Beauty'** purple-pink, 1.2 m (4 ft) tall; **'Mrs S. T. Wright'**, rosy mauve, large

▼ *Aster novae-angliae* 'Mrs S. T. Wright'

▲ *Aster novae-angliae* 'Rosa Sieger'

flowers, 1.2m (4ft) tall; **'Purple Dome'**, blue-purple, compact, with a height and spread of 60cm (24in); **'Rosa Sieger'**, rose-pink, large flowers; **'Septemberrubin'** ('September Ruby'), red-purple flowers.

A. novi-belgii The selected cultivars bear flowers 3-5cm (1¼-2in) across, or more, in branched sprays, often pyramid-shaped, up to 30cm (12in) wide, on erect, branched stems. Leaves are narrow, mid to dark green and as long as 10cm (4in). Single offsets, taken in early spring and planted singly or in groups, produce the finest flowering stems.

TALL CULTIVARS

Plants listed here attain a height of about 1m (3ft) and a spread of 60cm (2ft), unless stated otherwise. **'Albanian'** white, double flowers; **'Anita Webb'**, pink flowers; **'Blue Eyes'**, deep lavender-pink, vigorous, 1.4m

▼ *Aster novi-belgii* 'Albanian'

▼ *Aster novi-belgii* 'Fellowship'

▲ *Aster novi-belgii* 'Helen Ballard'

▲ *Aster novi-belgii* 'Rufus'

(4½ft) tall; **'Coombe Rosemary'**, heather purple, double flowers; **'Fellowship'**, pale pink-mauve, large double flowers; **'Helen Ballard'**, purple-red, large double flowers; **'Marie Ballard'**, lavender-blue, large double flowers; **'Mistress Quickly'**, violet flowers with prominent yellow discs; **'Patricia Ballard'**, mauve-pink, large double flowers, grows quickly; **'Percy Thrower'**, lavender-blue, large double flowers; **'Rufus'**, purple-red, bushy habit; **'Sheena'**, pink, large double flowers; **'Winston S. Churchill'**, purple-red, bushy habit, 80cm (32in) tall.

DWARF CULTIVARS

These dense, bushy plants have short, stout branches, clothed to the ground with leaves. Those listed grow to a height of about 30cm (12in), and spread to about 45cm (18in), unless stated otherwise. **'Chatterbox'**, pale pink, double flowers; **'Chequers'**, bright violet flowers, 60cm (24in) tall; **'Jenny'**, purple-red, large double flowers; **'Kristina'**, white; **'Lady in Blue'**, lavender-blue; **'Remembrance'** lavender-blue, large, 50cm (20in) tall.

***A.* 'Ochtendgloren'**♀ Pink flowers up to 2.5cm (1in) wide are carried profusely in loose sprays, 80cm (32in) long, on erect stems. The long, narrow, mid green leaves are up to 10cm (4in) long. HEIGHT & SPREAD 1m×60cm (3×2ft).

***A.* 'Photograph'**♀ Open sprays, 50cm (20in) long, of small lavender-blue flowers are borne on slightly arching stems. Leaves are mid green, pointed and 7cm (2¾in) long. HEIGHT & SPREAD 1m×60cm (3×2ft).

***A. pringlei* 'Monte Cassino'**♀ Dainty white flowers are carried in 40cm (16in) sprays. The stems are wiry and erect, the bright green leaves narrow and up to 10cm (4in) long. HEIGHT & SPREAD 75×80cm (30×32in).

***A. pyrenaeus* 'Lutetia'** Large, lilac-blue flowers appear in branched clusters 35cm (14in) wide. Leaves are grey-green, pointed and 9cm (3½in) long. Resistant to mildew. HEIGHT & SPREAD 50cm×1.2m (20in×4ft).

A. sedifolius (syn. *A. acris*) Masses of small, starry, lavender-blue flowers are borne in flat-topped clusters, about 25cm (10in) across. Each flower has just 8-12 petals. The long, narrow leaves are grey-green and about 2cm (¾in) long. Mildew free. HEIGHT & SPREAD 75×80cm (30×32in).

***A. thomsonii* 'Nanus'** Large, lilac-blue flowers are held in numerous clusters, 10-15cm (4-6in) across. The grey-green leaves are ovate, toothed, hairy and 4cm (1½in) long. Mildew free. HEIGHT & SPREAD 40×55cm (16×22in).

***A. tongolensis* 'Napsbury'** This showy cultivar flowers from late spring to early summer. The large, solitary flowers are bright violet with prominent orange-yellow central discs. Leaves are grey-green, oval, slightly hairy and 5-10cm (2-4in) long. HEIGHT & SPREAD 40×20cm (16×8in).

A. umbellatus Masses of small flowers, each with 10-15 white petals, are carried in flat-topped clusters 40cm (16in) across on a vigorous plant. The light green, pointed, broad leaves are 12cm (4¾in) long. Mildew free. HEIGHT & SPREAD 1.5×1m (5×3ft).

CULTIVATION Plant in an open, sunny situation, in soil that is alkaline to slightly acid, fertile and retains moisture in spring and summer. *A. alpinus*, cultivars of *A. amellus* and *A.* × *frikartii*, plus *A. pyrenaeus* 'Lutetia' and *A. thomsonii* 'Nanus' require alkaline soils and good to sharp winter drainage. Plant out autumn-flowering asters in mid or late spring and spring-flowering asters in mid autumn or early spring. Many varieties over 60cm (24in) tall need staking with twiggy supports.

PROPAGATION Divide plants every 3-5 years, in early spring, to increase numbers and to maintain vigour. Divide cultivars of *A. novi-belgii* annually. Most species can be raised from seed. Sow seed of autumn-flowering asters between early spring and mid summer, and seed of spring-flowering asters in early spring, in a coldframe, to produce plants that flower the following year. Alternatively, take softwood cuttings in mid or late spring. *A. thomsonii* 'Nanus' is best propagated by this method.

PESTS AND DISEASES Spray plants against powdery mildew with a systemic fungicide. Destroy any plants affected by aster wilt.

Aster, China see *Callistephus*
Aster, Stokes' see *Stokesia*

a

Asteriscus

Compositae

An abundance of deep yellow, daisy-like flowers appears throughout summer on these herbaceous perennials with their soft, silky, greyish green foliage. *A. maritimus*, the only species commonly in cultivation, dislikes cold, wet conditions and requires a sunny sheltered spot in a rock garden or in the crevice of a stone wall. Asteriscus may be grown in containers as an annual and also does well in hanging baskets. Native to the Mediterranean coast and North Africa.

RECOMMENDED SPECIES AND VARIETIES

A. maritimus A dwarf, free-flowering, tufted plant. The deep yellow flowers, 4cm (1½in) across, have finely toothed petals. The silky greyish green leaves, 2cm (¾in) long, are wider near the tip than at the base. HEIGHT & SPREAD 25×30cm (10×12in).

▲ *Asteriscus maritimus*

CULTIVATION Plant in spring in a warm, sunny, sheltered spot in free-draining soil or grow in pots and place in a sunny, sheltered position outdoors or in a cold greenhouse.

PROPAGATION Take semi-ripe cuttings in summer, or sow seed in late winter in a warm greenhouse or frame. Keep young plants under glass for the first winter.

PESTS AND DISEASES Usually trouble free.

Astilbe

Saxifragaceae

Astilbe chinensis var. pumila

Fluffy-plumed astilbes are among the most rewarding summer-flowering hardy perennials when they are established in the rich, moist soil they need. They have handsome, fern-like leaves, up to 23cm (9in) long, and during mid to late summer produce spires, 15-20cm (6-8in) long, of tiny flowers on stiff stems that never require staking. The flowers are white, shades of pink, lilac or red. When the flowers have finished they leave a tracery of interesting seed heads which are a lovely shade of light brown; these remain intact throughout winter. The height of the different species and varieties ranges from dwarf astilbes of 30cm (1ft) to tall specimens of over 1.2m (4ft).

Astilbes are happiest in moist conditions near a pond or stream, in sun or half shade. They will never make a vigorous plant if allowed to dry out in summer. Where there is plenty of space in a garden, plant them in groups of three, five or more. They associate well with moisture-loving perennials including suitable shades of candelabra primulas, hostas, *Iris sibirica* and *Trollius*.

Nearly all astilbes sold are crosses from the following species: *A.* × *arendsii*, *A. chinensis*, *A. japonica*, *A.* × *rosea*, *A. simplicifolia* and *A. thunbergii*. To simplify the classification of cultivars they are listed in alphabetical order under HYBRIDS at the end of the recommended plants.

RECOMMENDED SPECIES AND VARIETIES

***A. chinensis* var. *pumila*♀** Narrow 15cm (6in) spikes of mauve-pink flowers are produced from mid summer to early autumn above fast-spreading, crowded rosettes of 15cm (6in) long leaves. Native to China. HEIGHT & SPREAD 30×40cm (12×16in).

***A. glaberrima* var. *saxatilis*♀** Finely cut, fern-like leaves are delicately edged with red. During mid summer the dwarf plant bears spikes of pink flowers, 10cm (4in) tall. Native to China and Japan. HEIGHT & SPREAD 23×23cm (9×9in).

***A. simplicifolia*♀** The rich green leaves are deeply cut and fern-like. Spikes of flowers, 15cm (6in) long, are a pretty, pale pink and are produced from mid summer onwards, sometimes still blooming in early autumn. The dwarf plant is excellent for pockets of moist soil at the edge of a small pond as it grows fairly slowly. Native to Japan. HEIGHT & SPREAD 23×23cm (9×9in).

HYBRIDS

The great range of named hybrids have ferny foliage and require moist soil at all times, especially when they are in bloom. They flower in mid summer unless otherwise indicated. The spread is generally equal to the height of the plants, which is given below. The list is grouped according to flower colour.

WHITE FLOWERS

'Brautschleier'♀ ('Bridal Veil'), flowers in early summer, 75cm (30in); **'Bridal Veil'** see 'Brautschleier'; **'Bumalda'**, dark green foliage, 75cm (30in); **'Deutschland'**, large lax spikes of flowers, 60cm (2ft); **'Irrlicht'**, deep green foliage, 45cm (18in); **'Praecox Alba'**, small bushy plant, 36cm (14in); **'Professor van der Wielen'**, 45cm (18in); **'Snowdrift'**, 60cm (2ft); **'W.E. Gladstone'**, 60cm (2ft); **'Weisse Gloria'** ('White Gloria'), creamy white flowers, early summer flowering, 60cm (2ft); **'White Gloria'** see 'Weisse Gloria'; **'William Buchanan'**, dwarf, compact plant, creamy white flowers, 23cm (9in).

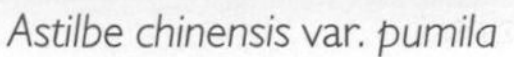

▲ *Astilbe chinensis* var. *pumila*

Astilbe 'Deutschland' ▲

PALE PINK FLOWERS

'Drayton Glory' see 'Peach Blossom'; **'Dunkellachs'**, thin spikes of pale salmon flowers, 60cm (2ft); **'Europa'**, 60cm (2ft); **'Peach Blossom'** ('Drayton Glory'), 60cm (2ft); **'Sprite'♀**, deep green foliage, graceful branching spikes of pale pink flowers, 30cm (1ft); **'Venus'**, pale salmon-pink, 1m (3ft).

MID PINK TO MAUVE FLOWERS

'Amethyst', deep pinky lilac flowers, 1m (3ft); **'Bressingham Beauty'**, pink spikes on strong stiff stems, 1m (3ft); **'Bronce Elegans'♀**, bronze-tinged foliage, pink flowers, 23cm (9in); **'Düsseldorf'**, bright pink, 50cm (20in); **'Federsee'**, dark stems, deep rose-pink, 60cm (2ft); **'Finale'**, dwarf plant, pink flowers, 40cm (16in); **'Granat'**, bright green foliage, dark stem, deep pink flowers, 80cm (32in); **'Hyacinth'** see 'Hyazinth'; **'Hyazinth'** ('Hyacinth'), deep mauve-pink flowers, 1m (3ft); **'Inshriach Pink'**, dwarf plant, pink, 36cm (14in); **'Jo Ophorst'**, upright habit, branched stems, bright lilac pink, late flowering, 75cm (30 in); **'Ostrich Plume'** see 'Straussenfeder'; **'Perkeo'♀**, dwarf compact plant, deep pink flowers, 23cm (9in); **'Purpurlanze'** ('Purple Lance'), mauve-pink flowers, 1m (3ft); **'Purple Lance'** see 'Purpurlanze'; **'Rheinland'♀**, compact, bright pink, 50cm (20in); **'Straussenfeder'** ('Ostrich Plume'), feathery plumes of salmon-pink, 1m (3ft); **'Superba'♀**, tall narrow spikes of mauve-pink flowers, 1m (3ft).

▼ *Astilbe* 'Amethyst'

▼ *Astilbe* 'Bressingham Beauty'

▲ *Astilbe* 'Hyazinth'

RED FLOWERS

'Aphrodite', carmine red, 40cm (16in); **'Cherry Ripe'** see 'Feuer'; **'Etna'**, deep red, 60cm (2ft); **'Fanal'**, light green foliage tinged with red, dark red stems and bright red flowers in early summer, 60cm (2ft); **'Feuer'** ('Fire'), deep salmon red, 60cm (2ft); **'Fire'** see 'Feuer'; **'Glow'** see 'Glut'; **'Glut'** ('Glow'), bright red flowers mid to late summer, 80cm (32in); **'Montgomery'**, bright orange-red, 60cm (2ft); **'Red Sentinel'**, dark foliage, deep red, 75cm (30in); **'Spartan'**, deep red, 60cm (2ft).

CULTIVATION Plant any time from autumn to early spring in rich, moist soil in a sunny or half-shady position. Space dwarf varieties

▲ *Astilbe* 'Feuer'

45cm (18in) apart and more vigorous varieties 60cm (2ft) apart. Apply a thick mulch of well-rotted manure or forest bark around the plants to retain soil moisture; manure also feeds the plants. Ensure that the plants do not dry out during summer.

Lift and divide established plants about every 4 years otherwise they can die in the centre.

Late frosts can scorch new spring leaves and kill the buds; foliage will be replaced but not the flowers. If frost is forecast, protect the plants at night with garden fleece.

PROPAGATION Species can be increased from seed but as germination is sometimes slow, it is easier to divide plants in autumn. Increase cultivars by division only. Seed-raised plants will not come true.

PESTS AND DISEASES Powdery mildew and leaf spot can be troublesome, especially in dry seasons. New foliage is sometimes nibbled by mice, voles and rabbits.

Astilboides

Saxifragaceae

The sole species of astilboides is a stunning hardy perennial foliage plant, prized for its large, round, pale green leaves. It needs a rich, moist soil and a sheltered spot in half-shade. It is native to China.

Astilboides tabularis Measuring up to 1m (3ft) across, the leaves are gently scalloped and held umbrella-like, on strong stems, 45cm (18 in) tall, that support the leaf in the middle. In mid summer, tiny, starry white flowers are carried well above the leaves, arranged in 15cm (6in) drooping panicles. HEIGHT & SPREAD 120×90cm (4×3ft).

▲ *Astilboides tabularis*

CULTIVATION Plant the rhizomes in spring in rich, damp soil that does not dry out in summer, choosing a sheltered spot in sun or half-shade. New growth may be damaged by late frosts.

PROPAGATION Divide and replant the rhizomes in spring.

PESTS AND DISEASES Usually trouble free.

Astrantia

Umbelliferae

The blooms of these herbaceous perennials are excellent for flower arrangements, both fresh and dried. The mid summer flowers are produced in star-like whorls of papery bracts, each flowerhead consisting of several flowers grouped together on short wiry stalks. All the species are very tolerant as to soil conditions, although they do prefer sun or partial shade. While they are often thought of as woodland plants, it is the richly organic nature of the soil rather than the canopy of shade that they appreciate. They are native to Europe and Asia.

RECOMMENDED SPECIES AND VARIETIES

A. carniolica Each silvery white flower is up to 2.5cm (1in) across, carried in clusters of 3-5 on upright stems. The coarse green leaves are irregularly toothed, with 5-7 roughly oval lobes up to 7.5cm (3in) long. HEIGHT & SPREAD 30-45×30cm (1-1½×1ft).

The flowers of var. ***rubra*** are silvery with a strong pink infusion.

A. major (greater masterwort) The handsome crispy flowers, held in groups of 5 or more, are up to 2.5cm (1in) across and whitish green and rose. They are borne just above coarse, toothed, mid green leaves, up to 10cm (4in) long, with 5-7 oval to lance-shaped lobes. The plant self-seeds easily. HEIGHT & SPREAD 60×45cm (2×1½ft).

There is a white-flowered form, var. ***alba***, while **'Hadspen Blood'** produces deep crimson blossoms. The flowers of ssp. ***involucrata*** are larger. Its cultivar **'Shaggy'**♀ is untidy, but with beautiful pinkish white blooms. The flowers of var. ***rosea*** and var. ***rubra*** are soft pink-white. **'Ruby Wedding'** has purplish red blooms. **'Sunningdale Variegated'**♀ has bold cream and green leaves and nondescript off-white flowers.

A. maxima♀ Pink flowers up to 2.5cm (1in) across bloom on branching stems. Shallowly toothed leaves, up to 10cm (4in) long, have 3-5 elliptical to oval lobes. HEIGHT & SPREAD 60×45cm (2×1½ft).

A. minor This neat compact plant has white, or occasionally pink-flushed flowers up to 2.5cm (1in) across, carried on stout branching stems. The leaves are finely toothed, with 7 lance-shaped lobes. HEIGHT & SPREAD 30×30cm (1×1ft).

CULTIVATION Plant from late autumn until spring in soil enriched with organic matter and in sun or semi-shade. Lift and divide every 3-4 years; deadhead after flowering.

PROPAGATION Sow seed in late summer or early spring in a coldframe. Increase named varieties by division in early spring as these do not come true from seed.

PESTS AND DISEASES Usually trouble free.

▼ *Astrantia major* ssp. *involucrata* 'Shaggy'

▼ *Astrantia major* var. *rosea*

▼ *Astrantia maxima*

a

Astrophytum see CACTI p. 106
Athyrium see FERNS p. 262

Atriplex

Chenopodiaceae

Grown for its silvery leaves, the shrubby *Atriplex halimus* resists the effects of salt-laden winds so is a valuable screen in seaside gardens. It is native to S Europe but fairly hardy. The half-hardy annual *A. hortensis* var. *rubra* is also salt-tolerant and grown for its decorative foliage. It is edible.

RECOMMENDED SPECIES AND VARIETIES
A. halimus (tree purslane) Silvery grey, 1.5-6 cm (½-2½ in) long, oval leaves cover this loosely branching, semi-evergreen shrub. The insignificant flowers and fruit are rarely seen. HEIGHT & SPREAD 1×1.2 m (3×4 ft) after 5 years, ultimately 2.4 m (8 ft) tall.

▲ *Atriplex hortensis* var. *rubra*

A. hortensis var. ***rubra*** (purple orache, red mountain spinach) Fast-growing, upright plants, these annuals can quickly form a temporary hedge. The triangular, deep purple leaves, 15 cm (6 in) long, can be used when young in salads or as a substitute for spinach. Spikes of insignificant flowers appear in summer. HEIGHT & SPREAD 1.2 m×30 cm (4×1 ft).

CULTIVATION Plant *A. halimus* in full sun in well-drained, not too fertile soil from mid autumn to early spring. *A. hortensis* var. *rubra* thrives in moisture-retentive, fertile soil in full sun. Water well during dry spells. Unless seed is required, pinch out the flowers as they appear.

PROPAGATION Raise *A. halimus* from semi-ripe or ripewood cuttings. Sow seed of *A. hortensis* var. *rubra* in the garden from late spring to early summer.

PRUNING To encourage more bushy growth, cut *A. halimus* back hard in spring to within 2 or 3 buds of old wood. Do the same with any loose sprays or frost-damaged shoots.

PESTS AND DISEASES Usually trouble free.

Aubrieta

Cruciferae

Aubrieta deltoidea

Forming low, compact cushions of grey-green foliage smothered in pink, purple or blue flowers throughout spring, these hardy evergreen perennials are ideally suited to rock gardens and for growing on dry sunny walls or in the cracks between paving. Native to dry rocky places in the mountain areas of SE Europe eastwards to the Lebanon and Iran, aubrietias thrive in neutral or limy soils. The colourful, cross-shaped flowers have four petals and are borne in elongating clusters.

RECOMMENDED SPECIES AND VARIETIES
A. deltoidea Violet to red-purple, sometimes white, flowers, each up to 2.5 cm (1 in) across, appear in spring. The grey-green oval leaves, up to 1 cm (⅜ in) long and with toothed edges, are borne on rather straggly stems that form a spreading mat. HEIGHT & SPREAD 15×60 cm (6×24 in).

'Nana Variegata' has leaves with cream markings. The plants of **Variegata Group** have pale blue flowers and leaves variegated with cream.

OTHER VARIETIES
There are many cultivated varieties available, most of which probably originate from *A. deltoidea*. Unless otherwise stated, the varieties included below have flowers up to 3 cm (1¼ in) across, held on stalks about 15 cm (6 in) tall, and toothed, grey-green, oval leaves, up to 1 cm (⅜ in) long, that form dense cushions. The plants, except where stated otherwise, grow to 15 cm (6 in) high and 60 cm (2 ft) wide.
'Alix Brett' has double, carmine flowers. **'April Joy'** has double, dark mauve blooms. The flowers of **'Argenteovariegata'** are purple and single and the leaves have silvery variegation. **'Astolat'** has single, purple blooms; its leaves are variegated. **'Aureovariegata'** has pale lavender-blue, single flowers and golden-green leaves.

▼ *Aubrieta* 'Astolat'

'Belisha Beacon' has bright rose-red, single flowers. **'Bob Saunders'** has double, red-purple flowers on stems up to 20 cm (8 in) long. **'Bressingham Pink'** has double, pink flowers. The single flowers of **'Doctor Mules'**♀ are rich violet. **'Greencourt Purple'** has semidouble, dark purple blooms. The single flowers of **'Gurgedyke'**

▲ *Aubrieta* 'Gurgedyke'

are deep purple. **'Mrs Rodewald'** has large, single, deep red blooms. The single flowers of **'Oakington Lavender'** are lavender-blue. **'Purple Cascade'** has single, deep purple flowers. **'Red Carpet'** has single, deep red flowers. **'Red Cascade'** and **'Royal Red'** both have single, red flowers. The single blooms of **'Triumphant'** are almost pure blue. **'Wanda'** has double, light red flowers.

CULTIVATION Plant aubrietias in free-draining, preferably limy, soil in full sun or partial shade. They can be planted in crevices in walls and paving, though they do not tolerate being walked upon. Trim back moderately after flowering to keep plants from becoming too straggly.

PROPAGATION Sow seed in early spring, take semi-ripe cuttings of named cultivars in summer or autumn, or divide plants in late summer and early autumn. Move self-sown seedlings and replant in autumn.

PESTS AND DISEASES Aubrietias can suffer from downy mildew and powdery mildew.

Aucuba

Cornaceae

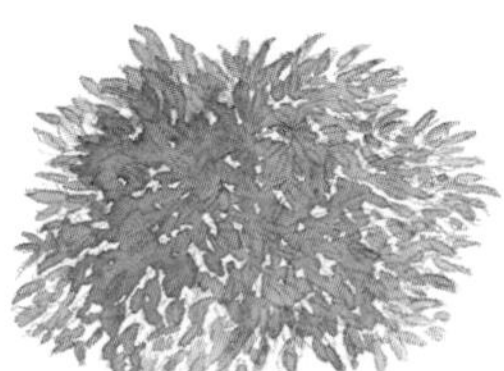

Aucuba japonica

Glossy, green, leathery leaves give permanent garden value to the sturdy evergreen shrub, aucuba – and in many varieties

golden yellow markings light up the foliage. The shrubs are easily grown, thrive in sun or shade, tolerate pollution and are good as background plants as well as more prominent features. They do well in containers, for placing in inhospitable corners or on paved areas. The pale purple flowers, which appear in early spring, are insignificant but quite decorative. Male and female flowers usually appear on different plants, so both sexes should be grown together to produce the vivid red, oval berries, which are borne in clusters and last for several months.

RECOMMENDED SPECIES AND VARIETIES

A. japonica (spotted laurel) Glossy, deep green, oval leaves, sometimes irregularly

▲ *Aucuba japonica* 'Crotonifolia'

finely toothed, grow up to 20cm (8in) long and 7.5cm (3in) wide. Male and female flowers appear on different plants during mid to late spring, and are followed on fertilised female plants by bright red berries in autumn. The small flowers are in short spikes, held upright. The bushy rounded shrub is frost hardy. Native to Japan. HEIGHT & SPREAD 1.5×1.2m (5×4ft) after 5 years, ultimately 3m (10ft) tall and wide.

Many of the cultivars are more decorative than the species, and they are generally smaller, reaching 2m (6½ft) in height. **'Crotonifolia'**♀, a female plant, is one of the brightest variegated forms with large, pale green, glossy leaves blotched with gold. **'Golden King'** is a male plant whose leaves have large splashes of gold. It does best in semi-shade. In the female plant f. ***longifolia***♀, the narrow lance-shaped leaves, up to 12.5cm (5in) long, have a slightly wavy margin and are pale glossy green. **'Nana Rotundifolia'** is a small round shrub reaching 1m (3ft) tall at best. It is a female selection, which fruits freely when grown near a

▲ *Aucuba japonica* f. *longifolia*

male bush. The small deep green leaves are sharply toothed near the tip. **'Rozannie'** is a compact shrub with bisexual flowers, which produces abundant berries without the assistance of another plant. The leaves are glossy dark green and toothed on the margin. **'Salicifolia'** is a female selection producing an abundance of bright red berries in autumn if a male aucuba is present. The leaves are narrow and willow-like. The leaves of **'Variegata'** (syn. 'Maculata') are densely spotted with gold. They are slightly wider and more toothed than the species. Both male and female plants are available.

CULTIVATION Aucubas grow under a very wide range of situations and conditions and are particularly good for areas of dense shade, though the variegated plants need to be planted in sun for good colour.

PROPAGATION To ensure plants with the characteristics of a particular cultivar, take semi-ripe cuttings in early to mid summer.

PRUNING Not normally required. Some of the variegated cultivars, however, may

▲ *Aucuba japonica* 'Variegata'

revert to plain green; cut out any green shoots as soon as they are noticed.

PESTS AND DISEASES Usually trouble free.

Aurinia

Cruciferae

There can be few more dazzling sights in spring than the brilliant yellow flowers of *Aurinia saxatilis*, long known as *Alyssum saxatile*. A hardy evergreen sub-shrub with soft stems and woody bases, it forms low hummocks smothered with flowers. Plant against a wall or bank, in a rock garden or a border in a sunny sheltered site.

RECOMMENDED SPECIES AND VARIETIES

A. saxatilis♀ (syn. *Alyssum saxatile*) (yellow alyssum, gold dust) Oval, silvery grey leaves, up to 15cm (6in) long, are a perfect contrast to the mass of small 4-petalled flowers borne in dense, flat-topped clusters, 12cm (4¾in) across, from mid spring to early summer. It is particularly

▼ *Aurinia saxatilis*

attractive with the lavender, pink. purple and red varieties of aubrietia. Native to the rocky highlands of central and SE Europe. HEIGHT & SPREAD 30×50cm (12×20in).

'Citrina'♀ has pale lemon-yellow flowers. **'Compacta'** is a compact dwarf cultivar, about 10cm (4in) high, with golden flowers. **'Dudley Nevill'** has flowers of an unusual biscuit-yellow colour and **'Dudley Nevill Variegated'** has variegated foliage; both grow to a height of 20cm (8in). **'Flore Pleno'** produces double, yellow flowers. **'Goldkugel'** ('Gold Ball') has a dense habit and bears masses of golden yellow flowers. **'Variegata'** has golden flowers and cream-splashed leaves.

CULTIVATION Plant in spring or summer in any well-drained soil, preferably in full sun.

PROPAGATION Sow seed in pots in a cold-frame in winter or early spring. Prick out the seedlings when they are large enough to handle. Plants often self-seed freely but cultivars may not come true to type.

PRUNING After flowering, cut the woody stems back lightly to encourage new growth and keep the plant compact.

PESTS AND DISEASES Usually trouble free.

Avens see *Geum*
Azalea see *Rhododendron*

Azara

Flacourtiaceae

Azara microphylla

Vigorous wall-trained shrubs with fragrant flowers, azaras quickly provide a thick covering of year-round foliage. The abundant clusters of tiny, petal-less flowers take their golden yellow colour from the long stamens. The shiny evergreen leaves are elliptic to ovate with toothed edges and appear to be arranged in pairs. The smaller of the pair, though, is not a true leaf but a stipule, or accessory leaf. Native to S America, azaras do best in milder areas of Britain, benefiting from the shelter of a wall.

RECOMMENDED SPECIES AND VARIETIES

A. dentata Borne in flattish clusters, 4cm (1½in) long, sweetly scented flowers appear in early summer. The leaves, 4cm (1½in) long, and accessory leaves, 2.5cm (1in) in length, are dark green and very downy underneath. The least hardy species, it is often confused with *A. serrata*. HEIGHT & SPREAD 1.5m×75cm (5×2½ft) after 5 years, ultimately 3m (10ft) tall.

▲ *Azara dentata*

A. lanceolata Mimosa-like clusters of flowers, 2.5cm (1in) wide and subtly scented, are borne in mid spring. The bright green, lanceolate leaves are up to 6cm (2½in) long and the accessory leaves are rounded and 1cm (⅜in) long. HEIGHT & SPREAD 1.5m×75cm (5×2½ft) after 5 years, ultimately 4m (13ft) tall.

▲ *Azara lanceolata*

A. microphylla♀ Small clusters of strongly vanilla-scented flowers are borne from late winter to early spring on the underside of the branches. The dark green leaves are 1cm (⅜in) long, the stipules 6mm (¼in) long. HEIGHT & SPREAD 2×1m (6½×3ft) after 5 years, ultimately 4m (13ft) tall.

▲ *Azara microphylla*

'Variegata' has leaves edged with pale yellow and is more slow-growing.

A. petiolaris The oval flower clusters appearing in early spring are banana-scented and up to 3cm (1¼in) long. The pendulous deep green leaves grow to 8cm (3¼in) in length and have 1 or 2 accessory leaves up to 1cm (⅜in) long. HEIGHT & SPREAD 1.5m×75cm (5×2½ft) after 5 years, ultimately 3m (10ft) tall.

▲ *Azara petiolaris*

A. serrata Rounded clusters of sweetly scented flowers, 6cm (2½in) long, appear in mid summer. The species has deep green leaves up to 5cm (2in) long, and stipules up to 2cm (¾in) that are smooth underneath. HEIGHT & SPREAD 2×1m (6½×3ft) after 5 years, ultimately 4m (13ft) tall.

CULTIVATION Plant in early to mid spring in fertile soil against a south or west-facing wall, tying plants to supports. If damaged in cold weather, cut plants down to ground level when the frosts have finished.

PROPAGATION Take semi-ripe cuttings in mid to late summer.

PRUNING Only necessary to restrict spread or remove overcrowded or dead branches.

PESTS AND DISEASES Usually trouble free.

Azorella

Umbelliferae

These hardy evergreen perennials make low cushions or mats of dense spreading foliage, covered in late spring and summer with clusters of tiny flowers. Azorellas are plants of year-round interest, suitable for very well-drained soils on a sunny site.

RECOMMENDED SPECIES AND VARIETIES

A. gummifera see *Bolax gummifera*

A. trifurcata (syn. *Bolax glebaria*) Leathery, pale green, shiny leaves, 1cm (⅜in) long with 3 pointed lobes, form densely packed rosettes. Sulphur-yellow, 5-petalled flowers, about 3mm (⅛in) wide, are borne in umbrella-like clusters, 2-3cm (¾-1¼in) wide, above the leaves. Native to S America HEIGHT & SPREAD 10×60cm (4in×2ft).

The compact **'Nana'** suits raised beds and large troughs, spreading to 15cm (6in).

CULTIVATION Azorellas thrive in a gritty mix of scree and humus, in full sun. They are hardy to -17°C (1°F) but intolerant of excessive winter wet. Give overhead protection in areas of high rainfall.

PROPAGATION Sow seed in pots in a cold-frame in autumn. Take semi-ripe or ripewood cuttings in late summer.

PESTS AND DISEASES Usually trouble free.

▼ *Azorella trifurcata*

b

Baby blue eyes see *Nemophila menziesii*
Baby's breath see *Gypsophila paniculata*
Bachelor's buttons see *Ranunculus acris* 'Flore Pleno'
Balloon flower see *Platycodon*

Ballota

Labiatae

Downy leaves, toothed or scalloped, characterise most of the hardy sub-shrubs or perennial plants in this genus. They are an excellent foil to more brightly coloured flowering plants in sunny beds or borders. Whorls of small tubular flowers, enclosed by prominent woolly calyxes, are borne from the leaf axils. The plants described here flower in summer.

RECOMMENDED SPECIES AND VARIETIES

B. acetabulosa Dense, greyish green, woolly, oval or heart-shaped leaves, up to 5cm (2in) long, cover this evergreen sub-shrub. It may not survive severe winters. The flowers are white or pink flushed with purple. Native to E Mediterranean. HEIGHT & SPREAD 60×75cm (2×2½ft).

▲ *Ballota* 'All Hallows Green'

***B.* 'All Hallows Green'** This hardy shrubby perennial has soft, lime-green leaves up to 5cm (2in) long and small, pale green flowers. HEIGHT & SPREAD 30×45cm (1×1½ft).

B. nigra (black horehound) Lilac or pink flowers cluster in the leaf axils of terminal shoots. The branched stems of this hardy herbaceous perennial carry coarse, green, malodorous leaves, up to 7.5cm (3in) long and 5cm (2in) wide. Native to Britain. HEIGHT & SPREAD 75×60cm (2½×2ft).

'Archer's Variegated' has strikingly spotted foliage, streaked with white, and pinkish flowers. It grows 45cm (1½ft) high.

B. pseudodictamnus♀ This plant has purple-spotted white flowers and greyish yellow-green, rounded, woolly leaves up to 2.5cm (1in) long. Native to the S Aegean. HEIGHT & SPREAD 45×60cm (1½×2ft).

CULTIVATION Plant in well-drained soil in a sunny position in spring. Keep well watered. Trim species with woolly leaves in spring. Cut down others when foliage has faded.

PROPAGATION Sow under cover in spring. Take short semi-ripe cuttings of sub-shrubs. Divide herbaceous perennials in spring.

PESTS AND DISEASES Usually trouble free.

Balm (culinary herb) see HERBS p.330
Balm, bastard see *Melittis*
Bamboo see p.76
Banana see *Musa*
Baneberry see *Actaea*

Baptisia

False indigo

Leguminosae

Clumps of blue-green foliage and loose spikes of lupin-like flowers distinguish these upright hardy herbaceous perennials. The leaves are alternate, up to 8cm (3¼in) long and divided into three leaflets. The flowers are up to 3cm (1¼in) long. Baptisias are native to E United States, where they grow in sandy or gravelly soil. They make fine additions to a herbaceous border.

▼ *Baptisia australis*

RECOMMENDED SPECIES

B. australis♀ Bright indigo flowers with orange anthers are borne in loose spikes in early summer. The striking black seed pods are sought after by flower arrangers. HEIGHT & SPREAD 1.2m×40cm (4ft×16in).

CULTIVATION These deeply rooted plants thrive in deep, well-drained, neutral to acid soil in full sun. On windy, exposed sites stake taller plants. They resent disturbance.

PROPAGATION Divide carefully in autumn. Alternatively, sow seed in late summer or spring in a coldframe or open ground and plant out in autumn.

PESTS AND DISEASES Usually trouble free.

Barberry see *Berberis*
Barrenwort see *Epimedium alpinum*
Bartlettina see *Eupatorium*
Basil (culinary herb) see HERBS p.330
Basil, wild see *Clinopodium vulgare*

Bassia

Chenopodiaceae

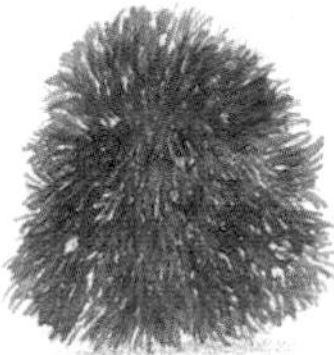

Bassia scoparia

With their neat shape and colourful foliage, bassias quickly provide height among low-growing summer bedding. Their dense upright growth also makes them suitable as temporary low hedging. A half-hardy annual, *B. scoparia*, is the only species to thrive in Britain. Bassias are native to warm temperate regions but usually survive the first frosts of autumn.

RECOMMENDED SPECIES

B. scoparia (syn. *Kochia scoparia*) (summer cypress) This dense shrub-like plant, shaped like a guardsman's busby, has abundant bright green, narrow, feathery leaves, up to 5cm (2in) long. Insignificant green flowers open from mid to late summer then turn to seed. HEIGHT & SPREAD 75×60cm (2½×2ft).

The leaves of f. ***trichophylla*** (syn. *Kochia trichophylla*) (burning bush) turn intense coppery red in late summer.

CULTIVATION Plant seedlings in late spring once the danger of frost has passed, in good soil, in full sun. Provide shelter or support.

PROPAGATION Sow seed on the surface of moist compost in early spring in a heated greenhouse. Prick out seedlings individually into pots and harden off in late spring.

PESTS AND DISEASES Usually trouble free.

BAMBOOS

AIRY FOLIAGE AND UPRIGHT SHAPES

DISTINCTIVE ARCHITECTURAL FORMS AND MASSES OF ORNAMENTAL FOLIAGE GIVE THESE PLANTS GREAT CREATIVE POTENTIAL

Dramatic plants that transform a garden, bamboos make excellent focal points and superb screens. They are essential for Japanese-style gardens and also make unusual container plants. Bamboos are usually hardy but benefit from shelter in cold, exposed or coastal areas. Most do best in full sun but a few tolerate shade.

Some of these evergreens form clumps and make excellent specimens. Others have running rhizomes and need to be confined unless grown in a wild garden or as ground cover. Both running and clumping bamboos make good hedging.

Bamboos belong to the grass family Gramineae. Most reach 1-6m (3-20ft) in height when grown in Britain, though there are also some dwarf species. The canes, which are known as culms, are usually hollow and green, but can be brown, black, yellow, pink or purple, or mottled or streaked. They range in diameter from 1mm-3cm (1/16-1¼in) and are usually erect; the culms of a few species, such as *Phyllostachys flexuosa,* may grow in a zigzag formation.

Bamboo culms are jointed, and branches, which carry the foliage, grow from the joints, or nodes. Protective sheaths surround new growth which appears in late spring or early summer. The sheaths of most bamboos are dull and short-lived, but in some species they may be an attractive feature and last for a year or more.

The plants bloom at irregular intervals, sometimes more than 100 years. Flowering may last a year or continue for decades. The flowerheads usually emerge in early summer, are brown and grass-like and can give the plant an untidy appearance. At flowering, the bamboo's foliage is reduced or dies, and the culms which have carried the flowers usually die. To encourage new growth, cut out these culms and feed and water the plant.

◀ ELEGANT GROVE *The slender culms of* Fargesia murieliae *arch gracefully over a stone ornament.*

RECOMMENDED PLANTS

Species that were formerly grouped under the genus *Arundinaria* have been reclassified to some of the genera listed below. Unless otherwise stated, the recommended plants have green culms that are hollow between the nodes. The leaves are narrow, lance-shaped and mid green with paler undersides, and the sheaths are short-lived, and almost colourless.

Chimonobambusa

The ornamental plants in this genus have running rhizomes and vary greatly in appearance.

C. marmorea (syn. *Arundinaria marmorea*) This colourful, slow-growing plant produces mottled brown and white, pink-tipped shoots that mature to thin, bronze-purple culms. Three or five branches grow from each node, carrying 10cm (4in) long leaves. The sheaths are marbled purple and brown and last a year. Native to Japan. HEIGHT & SPREAD 2.4×1m (8×3ft).

'Variegata' has pink culms and white-striped foliage.

C. quadrangularis (syn. *Arundinaria quadrangularis*) (square bamboo) The distinctive culms are stout and square-shaped with rounded edges. They have prominent nodes from which 3-8 branches grow with 15cm (6in) long leaves. The plant may be invasive in mild areas. Native to China. HEIGHT & SPREAD 4×1.8m (13×6ft).

▲ *Chimonobambusa quadrangularis*

C. tumidissinoda (syn. *Quiongzhuea tumidinoda*) The thick culms spread out elegantly and have markedly flared nodes. Between 3 and 8 branches grow from each of the nodes and the leaves reach 15cm (6in). Vigorous growth makes this shade-tolerant bamboo unsuitable for a small garden unless confined. Native to China. HEIGHT & SPREAD 3×3.5m (10×12ft).

Chusquea

These clump-forming plants have thick, pith-filled culms.

C. culeou♀ Tall, graceful culms have numerous short branches growing from the nodes and 8cm (3¼in) long leaves. The upper branches may weigh over the tops of the culms. Prominent sheaths are white and papery and last up to a year. Native to S America. HEIGHT & SPREAD 4×1m (13×3ft).

▲ *Chusquea culeou*

The thin culms of f. ***tenuis*** reach 2.1m (7ft) and grow outwards at a wide angle. It has longer leaves than the species.

Fargesia

Vigorous growers, these bamboos form clumps and make particularly elegant specimens.

F. murieliae♀ (syn. *Arundinaria murieliae, Sinarundinaria murieliae, Thamnocalamus spathaceus*) Narrow pale green culms have numerous slender branches growing from the nodes. The leaves are tapered and reach 6cm (2½in) in length. Native to China. HEIGHT & SPREAD 3×1m (10×3ft).

▲ *Fargesia murieliae*

'Simba' reaches only half the height or less.

F. nitida♀ (syn. *Arundinaria nitida, Sinarundinaria nitida*) Many branches grow from the nodes on the slender and often purple-tinged culms. The leaves are slightly tapered and 8cm (3¼in) long. Native to China. HEIGHT & SPREAD 4×1m (13×3ft).

× Hibanobambusa

There is only one plant in the genus, which is a hybrid of a *Phyllostachys* and a *Sasa*.

× ***H. tranquillans*** A single branch grows from each node on the thick culms. Broad leaves reach 15-25 cm (6-10 in)

▲ × ***Hibanobambusa tranquillans*** 'Shiroshima'

in length. The plant is moderately slow-running but vigorous. It is native to Japan. HEIGHT & SPREAD 3×1 m (10×3 ft).

The leaves of **'Shiroshima'** are striped with pale yellow which slowly turns to white.

Himalayacalamus

These elegant clump formers are native to the Himalayas.

H. falconeri (syn. *Arundinaria falconeri*) The thick culms have purple markings round their nodes and spread out at a wide

▲ ***Himalayacalamus falconeri*** 'Damarapa'

angle when mature. The plant has many branches which carry 6-10 cm (2½-4 in) long leaves. It is not fully hardy and grows best in mild areas. HEIGHT & SPREAD 5×1.8 m (16×6 ft).

The culms of **'Damarapa'** have purple mottling and pink and yellow streaks.

Indocalamus

Exceptionally long leaves are carried on the single branch that grows from each node. The sheaths persist for up to a year.

I. latifolius This short bamboo has thin, downy culms and leaves that grow up to 40 cm (16 in) long and 8 cm (3¼ in) wide. Native to China. HEIGHT & SPREAD 1.5 m×60 cm (5×2 ft).

▲ ***Indocalamus tessellatus***

I. tessellatus Slender culms are bent down by the weight of the large leaves to create a mound. The leaves reach 60 cm (2 ft) in length and 8 cm (3¼ in) in width, and the sheaths are longer than the internodes. Native to China. HEIGHT & SPREAD 1×1 m (3×3 ft).

Phyllostachys

The distinctive culms are stout and shallowly grooved on alternate sides. A waxy white powder appears beneath the nodes. At each node, there are two branches of unequal size and a third small one which often drops off. Numerous shoots grow from the branches. The leaves are 10 cm (4 in) long, and short-lived sheaths often have striking colouring. The plants, which are native to China, have running rhizomes but usually form clumps in Britain.

P. aurea♀ (fishpole bamboo) Graceful culms become yellow-brown with age. There are

▲ ***Phyllostachys aurea***

unusual cup-shaped swellings below the nodes which are especially noticeable at the base of the plant where they are close together and often asymmetrical. The sheaths have light brown streaks and spots. HEIGHT & SPREAD 4×1.5 m (13×5 ft).

'Holochrysa' has all-yellow culms; the leaves of **'Variegata'** are white striped.

P. aureosulcata (yellow-groove bamboo) The culms of this very hardy bamboo are yellow-green with dull yellow grooves. They can grow in a zigzag formation low down. The new growth is protected by white-striped sheaths. HEIGHT & SPREAD 4×1.5 m (13×5 ft).

The culms of **'Spectabilis'** are yellow with green grooves.

P. bambusoides (giant timber bamboo) Long leaves grow to 20 cm (8 in). The sheaths are heavily marked in brown and there is little or no waxy powder on the culms. HEIGHT & SPREAD 6×1.5 m (20×5 ft).

'Allgold' has all-yellow culms; **'Castillonis'**♀ has culms which are rich golden yellow with green grooves.

P. edulis (giant bamboo) This tall plant has culms that are grey and velvety when young. The thick hairy sheaths have brown

▲ ***Phyllostachys edulis***

mottling and the leaves are 7.5 cm (3 in) long. HEIGHT & SPREAD 6×1 m (20×3 ft).

P. flexuosa The slender culms of this bamboo can grow in a zigzag pattern low down and may turn almost black before dying. The sheaths have dark brown markings. HEIGHT & SPREAD 4×1.5 m (13×5 ft).

▲ ***Phyllostachys nigra***

P. nigra♀ (black bamboo) This attractive bamboo has slender culms which turn shiny black when mature. The tops of the sheaths are bristly. HEIGHT & SPREAD 3×1 m (10×3 ft).

▲ ***Phyllostachys nigra*** 'Boryana'

'Boryana' has taller, stouter culms that are blotched with brown; the all-green culms of var. ***henonis***♀ are also stouter and the plant has dense foliage. In f. ***punctata***, the stout culms have dark brown, sometimes almost black, markings.

P. sulphurea (syn. *P. viridis* 'Sulphurea') A curious pigskin-like texture distinguishes the culms of this bamboo. They become yellow with age and some have green stripes of varying widths. The thick sheaths are spotted and blotched with dark brown. HEIGHT & SPREAD 4×1 m (13×3 ft).

'Robert Young' has golden yellow culms, and the culms of var. ***viridis*** (syn. *P. viridis* 'Mitis') are mid green.
P. viridiglaucescens♀ This vigorous plant is one of the first to produce new shoots in spring. Its rough sheaths are marked with dark brown. HEIGHT & SPREAD 4×1m (13×3ft).

Pleioblastus

The plants in this genus have running rhizomes and sheaths that last for up to a year. They are native to Japan and China.
P. auricomus♀ (syn. *Arundinaria auricoma, A. viridistriata*) The broad leaves are pale green

▲ ***Pleioblastus auricomus***

with yellow stripes. Slender, often purple-tinged culms are downy when young and branch almost from the base with 1-2 branches at each node. The leaves are 3.5cm (1½in) wide and 20cm (8in) long and have downy undersides. This plant grows slowly and is an excellent choice for a small garden. Cut the culms to the ground at the end of winter. HEIGHT & SPREAD 1.2m×60cm (4×2ft).
P. chino (syn. *Arundinaria chino*) The leaves are green on both sides, 25cm (10in) long and vary in width. They are carried on the 3 or more branches that grow from each upper node. HEIGHT & SPREAD 3m×75cm (10×2½ft).
The leaves of f. ***elegantissimus*** have narrow white stripes.
P. gramineus Drooping grass-like leaves reach 28cm (11in) in length and 1cm (⅜in) in width. They are carried on the many branches that grow from each node. The culms may arch when mature. HEIGHT & SPREAD 4×1.5m (13×5ft).

▲ ***Pleioblastus humilis*** var. ***pumilus***

P. humilis var. ***pumilus*** (syn. *Arundinaria pumila*) Short culms branch from low down and have 1-3 branches growing from each markedly bristly node. The fresh green leaves are 15cm (6in) long. HEIGHT & SPREAD 1×1m (3×3ft).
P. pygmaeus (syn. *Arundinaria pygmaea*) (dwarf fern-leaved bamboo) Very slender, solid culms have 1-2 branches growing from each node. Pairs of leaves, which are 2-8cm (¾-3¼in) long, are arranged along the branches. The plant spreads to form short thickets and makes good ground cover. It also looks attractive grown in a shallow container. HEIGHT & SPREAD 25×12cm (10×4¾in).
The culms of var. ***distichus*** (syn. *Arundinaria disticha*) grow to 1m (3ft) and the leaves are longer and broader. It has a vigorous growth pattern.
P. simonii (syn. *Arundinaria simonii*) Very tall, stout culms have 3-7 branches from each

▲ ***Pleioblastus simonii*** f. ***variegatus***

upper node. The leaves are 20cm (8in) long. HEIGHT & SPREAD 5×1m (16×3ft).
Some of the narrow leaves of f. **variegatus** (syn. var. *heterophyllus*) are striped white.
P. variegatus♀ (syn. *Arundinaria variegata, A. fortunei*) White-striped and downy leaves

▲ ***Pleioblastus variegatus***

are 20cm (8in) long. One or two branches grow from nodes low down. The plant spreads slowly and is suitable for a small garden. Cut down culms in spring for fresh growth. HEIGHT & SPREAD 1×1.2m (3×4ft).

Pseudosasa

Plants in this genus have rhizomes that can run but usually form clumps in Britain.
P. japonica♀ (syn. *Arundinaria japonica*) A single branch grows

▲ ***Pseudosasa japonica***

from each upper node on the tall culms and the rough, dull brown sheaths are long-lived. The leaves are 25cm (10in) long. This bamboo is probably native to China. HEIGHT & SPREAD 4×1m (13×3ft).

Quiongzhuea see *Chimonobambusa*

Sasa

Sasas, which are native to Japan, are tolerant of shade and have running rhizomes. Their culms curve at the base and a single branch grows from each node. The leaves may wither at the edges in winter.
S. japonica see *Pseudosasa japonica*
S. palmata♀ (syn. *Arundinaria palmata*) Large, lustrous, rich green leaves have yellow midribs and look attractive all year round. They grow 40cm (16in)

▲ ***Sasa palmata***

long and 9cm (3½in) wide. The branches grow from the upper parts of the mottled brown culms. This rampant bamboo is very hardy. HEIGHT & SPREAD 3×1.5m (10×5ft).
S. tsuboiana This bamboo, which runs very slowly, has low-branching and erect culms. Its leaves reach 20cm (8in) in length. HEIGHT & SPREAD 1m×30cm (3×1ft).
S. veitchii The leaves develop strikingly decorative broad white stripes round their edges in early autumn. The leaves are 20cm (8in) long, have bluntly pointed tips and remain attractive all winter. The culms are purple-tinged. HEIGHT & SPREAD 1.5×1m (5×3ft).

Sasaealla

A single branch grows from each node of the erect culms. These plants have running rhizomes and are native to Japan.
S. masamuneana f. ***albostriata*** Grown for its attractive foliage, the leaves of this bamboo are 15cm (6in) long and have

▲ *Sasaella masamuneana* f. *albostriata*

white stripes that become yellow in maturity. HEIGHT & SPREAD 2×1 m (6½×3 ft).

S. ramosa (syn. *Arundinaria vagans*) This short bamboo branches horizontally from the middle of the culms, which are sometimes purple-tinged. It makes good ground cover in a wild garden but is very invasive. The leaves are 10-15 cm (4-6 in) long and have downy undersides. They may decay at the edges in winter. HEIGHT & SPREAD 1 m×45 cm (3×1½ ft).

Semiarundinaria

Plants in this genus have running rhizomes but are generally clump-forming in Britain.

S. fastuosa♀ (syn. *Arundinaria fastuosa*) This tall and stately bamboo has thick glossy culms, slightly grooved at the tops. Between 3 and 7 branches grow from each node. The attractive

▲ *Semiarundinaria fastuosa*

sheaths are shiny and wine-coloured inside and the thin leaves are 25 cm (10 in) long. The plant makes good hedging. Native to Japan. HEIGHT & SPREAD 5 m×60 cm (16×2 ft).

Sinarundinaria anceps see *Yushania anceps*
Sinarundinaria murieliae see *Fargesia murieliae*
Sinarundinaria nitida see *Fargesia nitida*

Shibataea

These bamboos have running rhizomes but tend to form clumps in Britain.

S. kumasasa The culms are slightly grooved and have short branches with 1 or 2 leaves,

▲ *Shibataea kumasasa*

which reach 8 cm (3¼ in) in length. The leaves are broad and may wither at the tips. The plant grows best in a moist soil. It is native to Japan. HEIGHT & SPREAD 1.5 m×30 cm (5×1 ft).

Thamnocalamus

These clump-forming plants produce numerous branches. Their sheaths last for up to a year and can be very decorative.

T. aristatus see *T. spathiflorus*

T. crassinodus The culms are grey when young and mature to yellowish green. They have prominent nodes and distinctive, white, tapered sheaths. The leaves are small and dainty-looking. This bamboo is native to the Himalayas. HEIGHT & SPREAD 5×1.5 m (16×5 ft).

'Kew Beauty' has purple-tinged leafstalks.

T. spathaceus see *Fargesia murieliae*

T. spathiflorus (syn. *Arundinaria spathiflora, T. aristatus*) This elegant, somewhat tender bamboo is best grown in milder areas. It has thin leaves, which are 10 cm (4 in) long, and tolerates a shady spot. Native to the Himalayas. HEIGHT & SPREAD 4×1 m (13×3 ft).

T. tessellatus Purple-tinged culms have numerous, rather

▲ *Thamnocalamus tessellatus*

short branches growing from each node, and sheaths that are noticeably white when young. The leaves are 10 cm (4 in) long. Native to South Africa. HEIGHT & SPREAD 4 m×60 cm (13×2 ft).

Yushania

Plants in this genus form tight clumps but their rhizomes run every few years.

Y. anceps♀ (syn. *Arundinaria anceps, A. jaunsarensis*) The culms arch at their tops and numerous branches grow from the nodes. The leaves are 10 cm (4 in) long. This bamboo is not

▲ *Yushania anceps*

fully hardy. It is native to the Himalayas. HEIGHT & SPREAD 4×1 m (13×3 ft).

'Pitt White' grows to twice the height.

Growing bamboos

CULTIVATION Most bamboos do well in well-drained soil in a sunny site but a few, including sasas, tolerate a shady spot. Prepare the ground well before planting in late spring, digging plenty of well-rotted organic matter and a general fertiliser into the soil.

Contain a species that has running rhizomes by digging a 23 cm (9 in) deep ditch round the plant and cutting off any rhizomes that appear in the ditch. Alternatively, surround the rhizome with a permanent underground barrier made from tough plastic or corrugated metal 30 cm (1 ft) deep.

Water a bamboo during the first summer, until it develops a good root system. Apply a general fertiliser in spring and summer and after flowering.

Once established, bamboos need little attention. Cut out any old culms in the centre of the plants in spring and remove dead culms after flowering. If bamboos spread beyond desirable limits, use a mattock or sharp spade to chop away any excess growth.

PROPAGATION Sever well-rooted sections of the running rhizomes in spring or early summer. Plant them in well-drained soil or a nursery bed and shelter from wind, then plant out the following summer. Divide large clumps in early spring. Chusqueas have solid rhizomes and culms and cannot easily be propagated.

PESTS AND DISEASES Bamboos are usually trouble free but rabbits, squirrels and deer may eat young shoots.

▶ RISING HIGH *The tall culms of* Phyllostachys sulphurea *create an imposing garden feature.*

Bastard indigo see *Amorpha fruticosa*
Bay (culinary herb) see HERBS p.330
Bay, bull see *Magnolia grandiflora*
Bay, sweet see *Laurus nobilis*
Beach wormwood see *Artemisia stelleriana*
Bead plant see *Nertera*
Bean, broad see p.733
Bean, buck see *Menyanthes trifoliata*
Bean, french see p.733
Bean, runner see p.734
Bearberry see *Arctostaphylos*
Beard-tongue see *Penstemon*
Bear's breeches see *Acanthus*
Beauty bush see *Kolkwitzia amabilis*
Bedstraw, lady's see *Galium verum*
Bedstraw, white see *Galium mollugo*
Bedstraw, yellow see *Galium veruni*
Beech see *Fagus*
Beech, southern see *Nothofagus*
Beefsteak plant see *Perilla frutescens*
Beetroot see p.734

Begonia

Begoniaceae

Begonia rex

Renowned for their generous displays of bright, colourful flowers – most notably in pink and red – and beautifully marked leaves, begonias thrive in a range of garden situations. Though only one species is hardy enough to be grown as a garden perennial, the genus contains some of the most widely grown bedding plants. There are pendulous varieties which make outstandingly showy plants for hanging baskets and window boxes, while other species and varieties are grown for the rich colours and exotic markings of their lop-sided leaves.

Begonias can thrive in shaded areas of the garden, where many other bedding plants cannot. This is in keeping with their native origins as part of the ground-level flora of tropical forests. Begonias also grow well in shaded conservatories and greenhouses. A few will also thrive in the relatively poor light conditions of the home.

RECOMMENDED SPECIES AND VARIETIES

Begonias can be divided into five groups: cane-stemmed, rhizomatous, semperflorens, shrub-like and tuberous. Plants within each group share similarities in terms of habit and/or cultivation techniques.

CANE-STEMMED BEGONIAS

These large, long-lived evergreens are often grown for many years as permanent features of a greenhouse or conservatory and their ability to withstand a little neglect makes them valuable houseplants. The taller varieties reach over 1m (3ft) in height and require staking, while the low-growing varieties are a good choice for hanging baskets. Height and spread details given below refer to plants grown in large pots.

B. albopicta White flowers appear on a freely branching species in summer. The spearhead-shaped, mid green leaves have white spots. HEIGHT & SPREAD 60×50cm (24×20in). **'Rosea'** bears pink flowers.

***B.* × *corallina* 'Lucerna'** This vigorous plant has large, bronze-green leaves with silver spots. It flowers all year round, producing large sprays of small pink blooms. HEIGHT & SPREAD 2m×60cm (6½×2ft).

***B.* 'Irene Nuss'** Pink flowers are borne in large clusters throughout the year. This vigorous plant has large velvety green leaves, serrated and speckled with silver. HEIGHT & SPREAD 1.2m×60cm (4×2ft).

▲ *Begonia* 'Irene Nuss'

***B.* 'Looking Glass'** Pink flowers are borne in early summer among the metallic-silver leaves with green veins and red undersides. HEIGHT & SPREAD 1m×60cm (3×2ft).

B. maculata This robust species bears long, tapered olive-green leaves with large silver spots. The small, pristine white flowers hang in clusters from mid to late summer. HEIGHT & SPREAD 2m×60cm (6½×2ft).

***B.* 'Orange Rubra'**♀ Orange-and-white flowers are freely produced throughout the year by this pendulous plant. The light green, lance-shaped leaves carry silver spots. It is an ideal plant for hanging baskets. HEIGHT & SPREAD 75cm×1m (2½×3ft).

▼ *Begonia* 'Orange Rubra'

RHIZOMATOUS BEGONIAS

These are characterised by a thickened stem – the rhizome – which develops on the surface of the soil, or in some cases just below it. Roots, leaf stalks and flowerheads all arise directly from the rhizome, which may be branched. Most are fine foliage plants.

B. bowerae (eyelash begonia) This dwarf, clump-forming species has oval leaves, up to 4cm (1½in) long. The waxy-looking, bright green leaves have brown stitch-like markings around the margins and are edged with fine, eyelash-like hairs. Delicate pale pink flowers are carried on long stems above the foliage in late winter and spring. This species and its varieties make fine houseplants, given a minimum temperature of 13°C (55°F). HEIGHT & SPREAD 15×25cm (6×10in).

Among the many hybrids are **'Beatrice Haddrell'**, **'Chantilly Lace'**, **'Norah Bedson'** and **'Red Planet'**. The last three reach just 10cm (4in) tall.

***B.* 'Cleopatra'**♀ (maple-leaf begonia) Maple-leaf shaped leaves, about 5cm (2in) across, are green and a rich bronze-brown, with long hairs around the edges. Clusters of small, pale pink flowers are sometimes carried well above the foliage, in spring. HEIGHT & SPREAD 20×25cm (8×10in).

▲ *Begonia* 'Cleopatra'

***B.* 'Little Brother Montgomery'** This upright begonia has large star-shaped leaves, heavily spotted with silver. HEIGHT & SPREAD 75×60cm (2½×2ft).

▲ *Begonia* 'Little Brother Montgomery'

▲ *Begonia masoniana*

B. masoniana♀ (Iron Cross begonia) Each green leaf bears a dark marking resembling the German medal. The plant is very like *B. rex* but slower growing. It requires a winter temperature of at least 13°C (55°F) and is sensitive to overwatering. HEIGHT & SPREAD 60×45cm (2×1½ft).
B. rex (king, painted leaf, fan begonia) This is one of the most striking of all ornamental foliage plants. The variously coloured, lop-sidedly heart-shaped leaves attain a width of up to 30cm (1ft). The surface is puckered and slightly hairy with a metallic sheen. The plant requires good humidity and a minimum temperature of 13°C (55°F). HEIGHT & SPREAD 40×50cm (16×20in).

▲ *Begonia rex* 'Fireworks'

'Fire Flush' has olive-green and red leaves. **'Fireworks'** has silver and raspberry-purple leaves. **'Princess of Hanover'** has velvety green leaves with white patches in a spiral pattern. **'Raspberry Swirl'** has red and silver leaves. **'Vesuvius'** has leaves in various shades of red.
B. 'Tiger Paws' Small white flowers are borne in spring. The small leaves have a

▲ *Begonia* 'Tiger Paws'

characteristic yellow-green and brown pattern. HEIGHT & SPREAD 25×25cm (10×10in).
SEMPERFLORENS GROUP
B. semperflorens (syn. *B.* × *carrierei*) (wax begonia) Numerous 3cm (1¼in) pink, red, white or bicoloured flowers are borne on

▲ *Begonia semperflorens*

these compact, bushy plants with fibrous roots. These popular bedding plants flower continuously from early summer until the first frosts. The rounded, shiny leaves are either dark green or bronze, contrasting attractively with the flowers. The height varies with the individual varieties and the spread is usually the same as the height.

The **Cocktail Series**, reaching 15cm (6in) tall, comprises only bronze-leaved varieties. Both green and bronze-leaved varieties are included in the **Excel, Olympia** and **Organdy Mixed Series**, which all reach 20cm (8in) tall.
SHRUB-LIKE BEGONIAS
Like the cane-stemmed begonias, these are also evergreen and long-lived, and best grown in a greenhouse, a conservatory or inside a house. Shrub-like begonias are fibrous rooted and most branch freely, producing basal shoots. Heights vary from 30cm (1ft) to 2m (6½ft) and their stems often need support.
B. foliosa White pendulous flowers appear along slender, arching stems in spring and autumn. The stems carry small leaves and may grow longer than 1m (3ft). This plant looks very attractive in a hanging basket. HEIGHT & SPREAD 30×80cm (1ft×2ft 8in).
B. fuchsioides♀ Fuchsia-like flowers are borne mainly during winter on freely branching stems with small leaves. Both a red and a pink variety are available. Keep this plant at or above 13°C (55°F). HEIGHT & SPREAD 75×60cm (2½×2ft).
B. haageana see *B. scharffii*
B. listada♀ White flowers are carried in autumn and winter against dark green, softly hairy leaves with red undersides. The plant is upright, branching and slow-growing. HEIGHT & SPREAD 30×30cm (1×1ft).
B. luxurians (palm leaf begonia) Large palmate leaves with up to 16 leaflets are borne by tall red stems. White flowers appear in winter or spring. HEIGHT & SPREAD 2m×60cm (6½×2ft).
B. metallica♀ White flowers are borne in large clusters in summer and autumn, contrasting attractively with the large, lustrous

▲ *Begonia metallica*

metallic green leaves. It is an easy-to-grow, vigorous and well-branched begonia that is safe at a winter minimum of 7°C (45°F). HEIGHT & SPREAD 1.5m×50cm (5ft×20in).
B. scharffii (syn. *B. haageana*) (elephant's ear) Pinkish white to pink flowers are produced all year round against heart-shaped leaves. The leaves, up to 25cm (10in) long, are bronze-green above and red beneath, and covered in red veins and fine hairs. HEIGHT & SPREAD 1.5m×75cm (5×2½ft).
B. serratipetala Striking serrated leaves distinguish this plant which bears its pink-and-white flowers intermittently throughout the year. It makes a good hanging-basket plant. HEIGHT & SPREAD 60×80cm (2×2ft 8in).
TUBEROUS BEGONIAS
B. grandis ssp. **evansiana** This is the only readily available begonia that is suitable for growing outdoors as a perennial in mild, sheltered regions of Britain. Sprays of pink flowers, each bloom up to 3cm (1¼in) across, are carried on fleshy stems above the handsome coppery foliage from late summer to mid autumn. The plants grow from tubers and produce bulbils in the leaf axils from which they can be propagated. HEIGHT & SPREAD 60×30cm (2×1ft).

'Alba' has white flowers.

b

B. × hiemalis These semi-tuberous begonias flower freely throughout the year and are widely available wherever pot plants are sold. Only the **Rieger** hybrids are commonly grown. Bushy plants bear single or double flowers up to 5cm (2in) across. They remain attractive for up to 3 months in a living room (for much longer in greenhouses) and are quite resistant to powdery mildew. Numerous varieties are grown commercially, but variety names are rarely shown on the labels. The **Charisma** hybrids (in orange and pink) come true from seed. HEIGHT & SPREAD 45×30cm (1½×1ft).

Begonia sutherlandii

B. sutherlandii ♀ Orange flowers are freely produced throughout summer among pointed, yellowish green leaves. Growth dies down in autumn, when watering should cease. This species has a weeping habit, making it good for hanging baskets. HEIGHT & SPREAD 30×45cm (1×1½ft).

▲ *Begonia sutherlandii*

Begonia × tuberhybrida Multiflora Group ▼

B. × tuberhybrida For outdoor garden cultivation as summer bedding plants, begonias in the **Multiflora Group** are usually chosen. These bushy plants attain a size of up to 30×30cm (1×1ft), with upright, succulent stems and leaves about 8cm (3in) long. The red, pink, orange, yellow or white flowers are 7.5cm (3in) across, and may be single, semi-double or double. They are freely produced throughout summer.

The **Non-Stop** hybrids and the **Prima Donna Series** are double-flowered. **'Pin-Up'** has double white flowers with bold pink edges to the petals.

Plants in the **Pendula Group** are very similar to those in the Multiflora Group, except that their stems are longer and thinner, giving plants a trailing habit suitable for hanging baskets and window boxes. These pendulous begonias have double flowers: the **Cascade Series** in orange, pink, red or yellow; **'Illumination'** in pink; **'Panorama Apricot'**; **'Panorama Orange'**; and the **Sensation Series** in a mix of colours.

Some tuberhybrida varieties produce enormous blooms. These are suitable only for growing in greenhouses. The flowers are double in most cases, and reach diameters of up to 25cm (10in). Plants are strong and upright, with leaves up to 25cm (10in) long. These hybrids reach a height and spread of 75cm (2½ft). **'Fairylight'** (white picotee), **'Majesty'** (yellow), **'Nell Gwynne'** (pale orange), **'Roy Hartley'** (pink), **'Sugar Candy'** (pink) and **'Tahiti'** (orange) are among the most worthwhile.

▲ *Begonia × tuberhybrida* 'Nell Gwynne'

CULTIVATION Begonias do best in neutral soils or compost and most prefer to be sited in partial shade. Whether in beds or in containers, it is worth removing any early flower buds to allow the plant to reach full size as quickly as possible. After the plant has flowered, deadheading improves its appearance and stimulates further flowers.

When growing begonias in a greenhouse, conservatory or home, they do best at 13°C (55°F) or more, although most will tolerate a minimum winter temperature of 10°C (50°F). In summer protect greenhouse plants from full sun. In the home, give the plants a position where they will receive good, indirect light. In a conservatory or greenhouse, maintain a humid atmosphere by frequent damping down, but do not spray plants directly. Water at the first sign of dryness in summer, but take care not to overwater in winter. Feed once a week in spring and summer.

Repot annually in early spring. For most begonias a 15cm (6in) pot is large enough. Tall plants are best kept in clay pots, to give more stability. Special cultivation requirements follow for each of the five groups.

CANE-STEMMED BEGONIAS
Light shading is required during the summer months – a north-facing conservatory gives ideal light conditions. Varieties with dark foliage can tolerate more sun than those with paler leaves. Cut back each spring, to just above the third or fourth leaf joint from the stem base.

RHIZOMATOUS BEGONIAS
These generally need quite high humidity and it is difficult to provide sufficiently humid conditions in a house. Do not place in direct sunlight – extra shading in mid summer improves leaf colouring. They grow best in a bathroom or kitchen.

SEMPERFLORENS GROUP
Plant out bedding plants when there is no risk of frost. They grow equally well in full sun or partial shade.

SHRUB-LIKE BEGONIAS
Houseplants do best in windows facing north or east. Light shading is required in the greenhouse for most varieties, but hairy-leaved varieties, such as *B. listada*, benefit from extra shading when the temperature exceeds 26°C (79°F).

TUBEROUS BEGONIAS
Plant out the perennial *B. grandis* ssp. *evansiana* in spring in a sheltered position, ideally near to a wall with a southerly aspect. A moisture-retentive, peaty soil helps to ensure flowering in dry weather.

Plant out bedding plants when all risk of frost has passed. They need a site which is sheltered from strong winds, and is not exposed to full sun during the middle of the day. The blooms and the foliage can otherwise scorch easily.

Rieger begonias are normally bought as plants in full flower. Repot about every 6 months, avoiding burying the exposed stem bases with fresh compost.

PROPAGATION

CANE-STEMMED BEGONIAS
Take stem cuttings in spring or summer, ensuring there are growth buds in the axils of the lower leaves. Root in a mix of half soilless compost and half coarse sand and keep at temperature of at least 18°C (65°F).

RHIZOMATOUS BEGONIAS
Divide or root pieces of the small rhizomatous types in spring. For larger plants use leaf cuttings.

SEMPERFLORENS GROUP
Sow seed in late winter in a propagator at 20-25°C (68-77°F). Do not cover the seed with compost. Maintain a high humidity. Protect the seedlings from full sunshine and

prick out after about 6 weeks. Begonias are among the more difficult plants to raise from seed. Even gardeners with well-heated greenhouses often resort to buying small young plants in early or mid spring to grow on to planting stage. Harden off before planting out.

SHRUB-LIKE BEGONIAS
Take stem cuttings in spring or summer. Root in a mixture of half soilless compost and either half perlite or half coarse sand and keep at a minimum temperature of 18°C (65°F).

TUBEROUS BEGONIAS
Divide *B. grandis* ssp. *evansiana* or remove and plant bulbils in early spring.

The tubers of the other species and varieties can be started into growth from early spring onwards in a heated greenhouse, or a month later in an unheated one. Harden off and plant out when there is no risk of frost. It is also possible to plant the tubers directly into their flowering positions in late spring. This results in a later start to flowering.

To save tubers for replanting the following year, move plants in autumn to frost-free conditions and allow them to die down and the soil to dry out. Then store tubers for the winter in almost dry sand, soil or soilless compost, in a cool, frost-free place.

Divide Rieger begonias in late spring or early summer, cutting back the older stems to allow young basal growths to form the new plant.

Some varieties of tuberous begonias can be raised from seed. Treatment is as for the Semperflorens Group, though even earlier sowing is advisable.

PESTS AND DISEASES Mealy bug and vine weevil can be troublesome. Most begonias are susceptible to powdery mildew.

Belladonna lily see *Amaryllis belladonna*
Bellflower see *Campanula*
Bellflower, gland see *Adenophora*
Bellflower, trailing see *Cyananthus*

Bellis
Daisy
Compositae

Bellis perennis 'Dresden China'

The most common species, *Bellis perennis*, a lawn weed, has given rise to many garden varieties, which make excellent plants for edging borders, carpet bedding or containers. Flowers with white, pink, red, purple or even blue petals – properly called ray florets – rise from mats or clumps of leaf rosettes. The flower centres, made up of disc florets, are usually yellow. These daisies are hardy perennials, but they are often grown in the garden as biennials, because flower size and quality declines with each flowering. Native to Europe and the Mediterranean.

RECOMMENDED SPECIES AND VARIETIES
B. perennis (common daisy) Flowers have white petals tinged pink encircling a yellow disc and measure up to 2.5cm (1in) across. The common daisy looks pretty on a lawn where wild flowers are encouraged. HEIGHT & SPREAD 13x20cm (5x8in).

Cultivars have single, semi-double or fully double flowers, up to 5cm (2in) wide and sometimes more, with white, pink, purple or red petals. All but the double forms have yellow centres. The bright green leaves, oblong or spatulate, grow in coarsely formed rosettes. Plants bloom from spring to early autumn. **'Alba Plena'** is a double white cultivar. **'Alice'** has large, semi-double, pink flowers. **'Aucubifolia'** has single white flowers and glossy gold-mottled foliage. **'Dresden China'**♀, a miniature pink form, has double flowers with quilled petals. **'Prolifera'** (Hen and Chickens) has double flowers, the petals white speckled pink, with smaller secondary flowers below the main bloom. **'Rob Roy'**♀ has large, double, crimson flowers.

▲ *Bellis rotundifolia* 'Caerulescens'

▲ *Bellis perennis* 'Alice'

▼ *Bellis perennis* 'Dresden China'

B. rotundifolia White petals flushed purple red surround a pale yellow centre, forming a flower up to 4cm (1½in) across. The grey-green leaves are rounded, toothed and shiny, 2.5-9cm (1-3½in) long. The flowers appear in spring. This plant needs a very sheltered site in the open garden or, better still, the protection of a coldframe or an unheated greenhouse in winter. HEIGHT & SPREAD 20x20cm (8x8in).

'Caerulescens' (syn. *B. perennis* 'Single Blue') is the most widely available form, with petals that are a soft pale blue.

CULTIVATION Grow in a well-drained yet moist soil that is rich with humus, in sun or partial shade. Regular deadheading prolongs flowering and prevents inferior seedlings sowing themselves.

PROPAGATION Divide at least every 2 years, in spring or autumn. This is the only way of propagating sterile cultivars. Sow seed of species in spring or early summer, or immediately after flowering, and plant out in late summer or early autumn.

PESTS AND DISEASES Aphids can get into the centre of the leaf rosettes, distorting and quickly weakening the plant.

Bells of Ireland see *Molucella laevis*
Bellwort see *Uvularia*
Beloperone see *Justicia*

Bedding Plants

Displays for just a season

These short-lived but valuable plants bring a mass of colourful flowers and foliage to beds and containers

While shrubs, trees and perennials provide the garden with a permanent framework, bedding plants offer temporary colour and interest. Moved into position at the young leafy or early flowering stage, they display their attractive flowers or foliage over several months. Most are at their best in summer but some bloom in spring and a few provide welcome colour during winter.

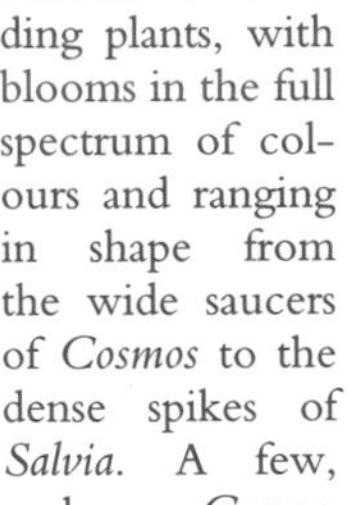

Spring interest *A carpet of polyanthus dispels the winter gloom.*

Many bedding plants are true annuals and die at the end of the season. Others are perennials which are treated as annuals because they produce their best displays in the first year or are not frost-hardy. Bulbs and evergreens can also be used as bedding and planted out for a single season.

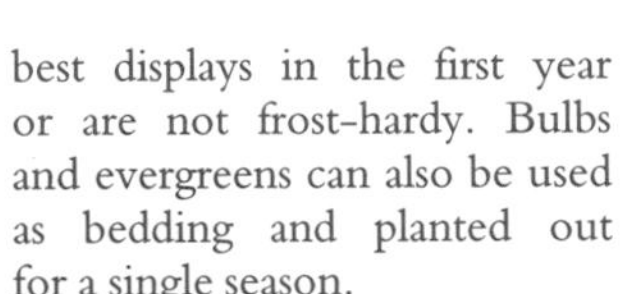

There are many hundreds of varieties of bedding plants, with blooms in the full spectrum of colours and ranging in shape from the wide saucers of *Cosmos* to the dense spikes of *Salvia*. A few, such as *Canna*, have architectural outlines. Bedding plants vary greatly in size, from neat, low-growing *Lobelia* to the tall *Helianthus* (sunflower).

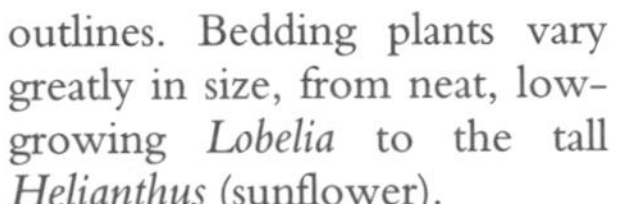

The tremendous wealth of plants that falls into the loose category of bedding means that there are plants for both formal and informal displays, for sub-tropical schemes and carpet bedding, and to provide instant interest in mixed borders or newly laid out beds. Bedding plants are also ideal for use in containers, bringing colour to balconies, windowsills, patios and small gardens.

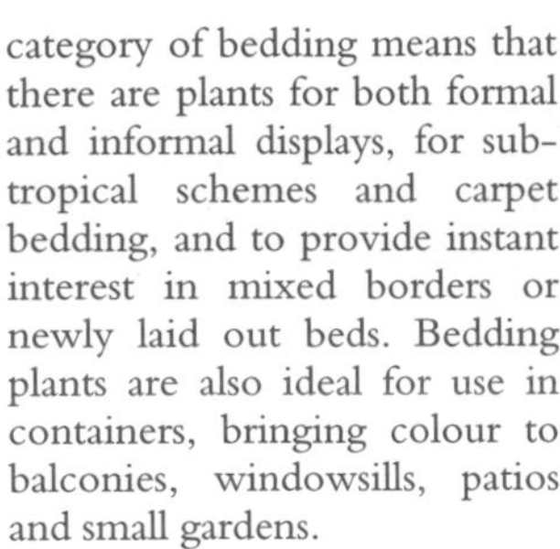

Annual beds

Flowerbeds and borders filled with solid blocks of colourful bedding plants are a traditional feature of summer. For the best effect, create informal clumps or drifts by grouping several plants of each species together. Use tall and striking plants, such as *Ricinus communis* (castor-oil plant), *Abutilon* or standard *Fuchsia*, to add height. Alternatively, grow climbing annuals like *Ipomoea* (morning glory) over a freestanding structure, such as a pyramid of canes, or up a trellis fixed to a wall at the back of a border.

Annual beds look attractive with a mixture of strong, bright colours, with toning shades of pastel colours, or with different shades of a single colour. The fewer colours used in a planting scheme, the more contrasts in habit, shape and texture are needed to create interest.

For a striking single-colour display, combine bright yellow-flowered varieties of *Dahlia*, which has an upright growth habit, with spreading *Gazania* (treasure flower) and bushy *Tagetes patula* (French marigold). Alternatively, pair pink-flowered varieties of *Cosmos*, which has bold single daisy-like flowers and feathery foliage, with the large spidery blooms of pink *Cleome* (spider flower).

Use exotic-looking plants to create an unusual sub-tropical scheme. Choose plants which have bold, dramatic shapes and strong colours. For example, *Tithonia rotundifolia* (Mexican sunflower), which has orange blooms, and the red-flowered *Amaranthus caudatus* (love-lies-bleeding) look very effective grouped with the bronze-leaved castor-oil plant.

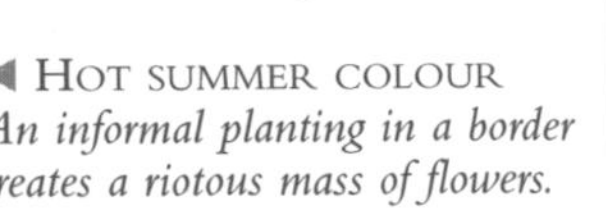

◀ Hot summer colour *An informal planting in a border creates a riotous mass of flowers.*

▲ Filling the gaps *Summer blooms enliven the permanent display of a mixed border.*

Formal schemes

For a formal flowerbed, plant rows of compact, low-growing plants, such as *Lobelia erinus* or *Lobularia maritima* (sweet alyssum), as edging round geometric rows or blocks of taller bedding. Bushy plants, which include French marigolds and *Pelargonium* (geranium), are suitable for this. Use tall specimens, such as *Cordyline* (cabbage tree), as dot plants at strictly regular intervals.

Low-growing foliage plants, including *Echeveria*, with its

▼ Perfect foil *Silver senecio and variegated pelargoniums contrast with purple heliotrope.*

A YEAR OF PLANTING

Bedding plants can be raised from seed in a warm greenhouse (see p.814) or are widely available as young plants or plugs (very young plants). Plugs should be grown on in a heated greenhouse or on a sunny indoor windowsill before being planted out.

A few of the hardier species, such as *Antirrhinum* (snapdragon) and pansies, can be planted out safely in early spring, as long as they have been hardened off. Plant out other bedding plants in late spring, when all danger of frost is past.

Most bedding plants grow best in well-drained soil in a sunny area of the garden. Remove any debris and weeds from the site, fork over the soil to loosen it and rake in a general fertiliser before planting.

Summer bedding plants flower from early or mid summer until the first frosts. At the end of the growing season, dig up and discard any annuals. Lift half-hardy perennials, such as fuchsias, osteospermums and pelargoniums, cut them back to a few centimetres from their bases and repot them. Keep the containers in a frost-free place throughout the winter. Alternatively, take cuttings in late summer – these will provide better specimens for the next year than plants that have been repotted.

After clearing away summer bedding, dig plenty of organic matter into the soil and plant out winter and spring bedding. Alternatively, wait until spring and plant out container-grown bedding plants that are coming into flower to create instant and colourful displays.

After spring bulbs have flowered, dig them up and replant elsewhere in the garden to allow their foliage to die down out of sight. Replace them with the summer bedding.

▲ IN FULL FLOWER *Pendulous fuchsia blooms hang above clumps of pelargonium and senecio, edged with ageratum.*

geometric rosettes of leaves tinged with grey, blue or green, and *Sempervivum* (houseleek), whose green rosettes are tipped with purple or brown, can be used to form complicated patterns. This kind of scheme, which is known as carpet bedding, is often found in parks and can be effective in the garden too, although it takes large numbers of plants and a considerable time to plant up.

FILLERS AND FOILS

Bedding plants are invaluable for filling spaces in mixed borders where early flowering plants have been cut back, or between new shrubs or perennials which have yet to grow and fill up their allocated spaces.

Use a mass of tall plants, such as stately cleomes and spider flowers, to create informal drifts. Alternatively, use plants which have many small flowers and spreading or bushy habits, such as *Diascia*, *Lobelia* or *Verbena*, to form low carpets. These can look particularly effective when they are planted beneath tall flowering plants, such as fuchsias.

Foliage bedding plants are excellent foils for flowering plants. For example, the handsome, lobed, silver-grey foliage of *Senecio cineraria* makes it an excellent choice for underplanting roses or as a contrast to the brightly coloured flowers of salvias and French marigolds.

Plants with silvery grey leaves, including *Echeveria elegans*, or attractive green foliage, such as *Bassia scoparia* var. *childsii* 'Evergreen', help to break up clashing colours by introducing a neutral background colour into the display.

Annual grasses, which have linear shapes and elegant seed heads, make striking textural contrasts when grouped informally among flowering plants.

AWKWARD SITES

Although most bedding plants require a well-drained soil and full sun, some tolerate less favourable conditions. In hot,

▼ IDEAL PARTNERS *Blood-red flowers of* Tulipa *'Cassini' rise from a sea of forget-me-nots.*

▲ FLORAL FRAME *Summer bedding and a clematis create a colourful setting for a window.*

▼ SITTING PRETTY *The foliage of helichrysum mingles with nicotiana and marigold flowers.*

dry areas, choose drought-tolerant plants, such as *Dorotheanthus* (Livingstone daisy), *Osteospermum* or *Portulaca*. Pelargoniums also thrive in these sites, making cheerful Mediterranean-style displays.

Begonia semperflorens, *Fuchsia* and *Impatiens* do well in shady sites, particularly when planted after they have started to bloom. *Tropaeolum majus* (nasturtium) actually prefers an impoverished soil; on rich soil it produces large, parasol-like leaves but very few flowers.

WINTER AND SPRING COLOUR

For early winter colour, plant *Brassica oleracea* var. *capitata* (ornamental cabbage), which has mauve or cream frilly leaves. Winter-flowering cultivars of *Viola* × *wittrockiana* (pansy) bloom until late spring in all but the worst weather and the tolerant winter-flowering heather *Erica* × *darleyensis* makes excellent bedding in cold or exposed sites.

Use massed plantings of *Erysimum* (wallflower), *Bellis* (daisy) and primrose or polyanthus cultivars of *Primula* to create spring interest. Bulbs also make good bedding and look most effective when they are planted in rows or blocks with other bedding plants. *Tulipa* (tulip) brings height to a carpet of daisies or *Myosotis* (forget-me-not); and *Narcissus* (daffodil) looks attractive in a bed of yellow primroses.

BEDDING PLANTS •FOR CONTAINERS•

Their long seasons make bedding plants ideal for growing in containers and bringing colour and interest to the smallest of areas. Use hanging baskets, troughs and tubs filled with flowers to decorate porches, entranceways and flights of steps; or patios and small town gardens where lack of space demands a concentrated effort. Create a welcoming floral display at the front of the house with several window boxes and hanging baskets.

▶ POT OF PLENTY *Pansies and brassica combine with perennials for a colourful autumn display.*

Where possible, match plants to the style of the container. For example, old-fashioned chimney pots are suited to cottage-style plants, such as nasturtiums, while a stately urn is appropriate for a tall specimen, such as *Datura* (thorn apple).

PLANTING DISPLAYS

Containers should be generously filled from the start. Pack in as many plants as possible – the adjacent rootballs of the plants can touch, provided that the container is sufficiently deep to allow at least a few centimetres of compost underneath. A simple display of a single species looks impressive. For

◀ COLOUR TRAIL *A mass of begonias, pelargoniums and petunias spill from hanging baskets and a window box.*

example, an annual climber, such as *Tropaeolum peregrinum* (canary creeper), makes an effective showing when trained over a trelliswork pergola or a wigwam of canes in a large tub.

Alternatively, create a varied display by grouping several different types of plants. Use an odd number for the strongest effect – three or five different types is sufficient for a medium-sized tub or hanging basket.

Choose plants of contrasting shape, texture and flower size, particularly if the display is based on a single colour, or use plants with small simple flowers, such as petunias, to surround a dominant larger plant, such as fuchsia. Modest-looking plants with scented flowers, such as *Matthiola longipetala* (night-scented stock), mixed in with more spectacular plants add perfume to a show of blooms and enhance the pleasure given, especially when the container is placed by a doorway or garden seat.

Choose trailing plants, such as verbenas and ivy-leaved pelargoniums, to cascade over the edges of window boxes. Team these with compact, upright plants, such as begonias, miniature pelargoniums and many ornamental herbs. Do not use very tall or climbing plants in a window box as they will obscure the window.

▼ BOLD BULBS *A terracotta container complements the spring colour of* Tulipa *'Prinses Irene'.*

Plant up hanging and wall baskets with compact plants and luxuriant climbers and trailers: climbers, such as *Lathyrus odoratus* (sweet pea), morning glory or *Thunbergia alata* (black-eyed Susan), will twine up the chains of a hanging basket, and trailers, including pendulous begonias, provide cascades of flowers.

Compact bushy plants, such as *Impatiens*, are good for cladding the sides of a wire hanging basket with a dense mass of blooms. Plants which have wiry stems, such as *Scaevola* (fan flower) or *Helichrysum petiolare*, are useful for supporting flowering plants with lax habits.

USING FOLIAGE

Foliage plants can transform the appearance of a container display. Silver-grey *Helichrysum petiolare* and cream or white-striped *Chlorophytum comosum* (spider plant) produce stunning foliage to contrast with the trailing flowers of many petunias, fuchsias and begonias.

Small evergreens provide excellent year-round backdrops to flowering displays. Use dwarf conifers for their crisp, textured foliage, ivies, such as the golden-leaved *Hedera helix* 'Midas Touch', for trails that tumble over the sides of containers, and small evergreen shrubs, such as *Santolina* or *Hebe*, for their green, purple, silver or variegated leaves. Plant up a large container with a permanent display of evergreens, leaving spaces for a few pots to be sunk between them. Use the pots to grow bedding plants for seasonal displays that can be replaced easily.

EARLY INTEREST

Fill containers with a selection of winter and spring bedding plants to introduce colour at colder times of year (see facing page). In hanging baskets try *Gaultheria procumbens* (wintergreen), whose red berries and evergreen foliage look attractive spilling out over the edges.

In the mild microclimates of some city gardens, hardier houseplants, such as *Cyclamen* and *Solanum pseudocapsicum* (Jerusalem cherry), can be moved into the garden to provide early winter colour.

LOOKING AFTER CONTAINERS

For flowers throughout the summer months, plant up containers in late spring – or in mid spring if they can be kept at first in a greenhouse or conservatory to protect them from frosts. For winter and spring flowers, plant up containers in early autumn, after the summer bedding has been cleared away.

Use a peat or soil-based potting compost or a specially formulated hanging-basket or container compost rather than garden soil for containers. Mix slow-release fertiliser and water-retaining gel granules into the compost. Plant up very large containers in place, as they will be too heavy to move once they are filled.

Line a wire hanging basket with moss or a fibrous liner to hold in the compost. To plant up the sides and the base, make holes in the liner with a sharp knife and push the roots of the plants through them. Then fill the container with the potting compost.

Keep containers in a sheltered position, where they receive full sun for at least part of the day. Regular care is necessary to keep displays looking their best. The soil in a pot dries out quickly so water plants frequently. If a hanging basket dries out, soak its base in a bucket of water for at least an hour. Feed flowering plants once or twice a week with a high-potash liquid feed, such as a tomato fertiliser, to encourage continuous flowering. Deadhead plants that have large flowers, such as fuchsias and pelargoniums, once a week.

In winter, keep containers in a very sheltered spot or plants will stop flowering. Water displays when the compost gets dry but prevent waterlogging by raising pots up on either bricks or pot feet (small ceramic angle-pieces).

SEASONS OF BEDDING PLANTS

Cultivated varieties of the following plants provide long-lasting colour.

SPRING

- ***Bellis perennis*** (daisy) White, pink, purple or red, single or double flowers and rosettes of leaves.
- ***Erysimum cheiri*** (wallflower) Spikes of fragrant colourful flowers and lance-shaped leaves.
- ***Primula*** (primrose and polyanthus) Small, flat-faced, colourful flowers and rosettes of leaves.
- ***Tulipa*** Colourful cup or goblet-shaped flowers and broad lance-shaped leaves.

SUMMER

- ***Begonia semperflorens*** Bright pink or red flowers and rounded, green or copper-coloured leaves.
- ***Cosmos bipinnatus*** Large, crimson, pink or white, saucer-shaped blooms and feathery foliage.
- ***Fuchsia*** Bell-like flowers, often in purples and pinks, and oval pointed leaves.
- ***Impatiens walleriana*** (busy lizzie) Masses of flat-faced colourful flowers and oval leaves.
- ***Lobelia erinus*** Small tubular flowers in blue, red or white, and tiny leaves.
- ***Pelargonium*** (geranium) Clusters of colourful flowers and rounded, sometimes marked, leaves.
- ***Petunia*** Trumpet-shaped flowers, in many colours, and oval leaves.
- ***Ricinus communis*** (castor-oil plant) Striking, lobed, bronze to green leaves.

WINTER

- ***Brassica oleracea*** var. ***capitata*** (ornamental cabbage) Green outer leaves and striking, red, white or pink inner foliage.
- ***Erica* × *darleyensis*** (winter-flowering heather) Tiny, white, pink or red, urn-shaped flowers and colourful foliage.
- ***Viola* × *wittrockiana*** (pansy) Colourful flat-faced flowers, with oval to heart-shaped leaves.

b

Berberis

Barberry

Berberidaceae

Berberis darwinii

Foliage, flowers and berries give good garden value in these versatile, easily grown shrubs. More than 450 species include evergreen and deciduous plants, from dwarf to large shrubs, for mixed borders, hedging, screening, rock gardens or specimen planting. Evergreen species have glossy dark green foliage and some, such as *Berberis darwinii* and *B. × stenophylla*, have abundant spring flowers and generally blue-black fruits. Deciduous shrubs can have brilliantly coloured autumn foliage and clusters of bright reddish berries which usually persist well into winter. The flowers of deciduous and evergreen species are yellow or orange, globular or cup-shaped, and up to 2cm (¾in) across. Flowers are most commonly borne in late spring, in small rounded clusters, or, occasionally, singly. Berberis plants mainly have small leaves 1 to 4cm (⅜ to 1½in) long, and spiny tough stems which make impenetrable barrier hedging. The recommended plants are all hardy.

RECOMMENDED SPECIES AND VARIETIES

DECIDUOUS SHRUBS

***B.* 'Little Favourite'** see *B. thunbergii* 'Atropurpurea Nana'.

***B.* x *ottawensis* 'Superba'**♀ (syn. *B. thunbergii* 'Atropurpurea Superba') The rounded to oval leaves are a rich wine purple on this vigorous shrub that complements or contrasts with many border plants. In spring upright branches, which arch at the top, bear hanging clusters of small, red-tinged yellow flowers; red fruits appear in autumn. HEIGHT & SPREAD 1.5x1.5m (5x5ft) after 5 years, 2.4x2.4m (8x8ft) after 10 years.

***B.* 'Rubrostilla'**♀ Small pale green leaves with silver undersides colour a brilliant red in autumn. Lax in habit with arching stems, the shrub bears large pale yellow flowers in early summer. Clusters of coral-red berries hang from the branches in autumn. HEIGHT & SPREAD 1.2x1.2m (4x4ft) after 5 years, 1.5x1.5m (5x5ft) after 10 years.

▼ *Berberis* 'Rubrostilla'

B. thunbergii♀ In spring, the neat compact shrub is covered in flowers of pale straw colour suffused with red on stiff, reddish brown thorny branches. Its small, broadly oval leaves are pale to mid green above, glaucous beneath. In autumn the small red ovoid berries harmonise with the brilliant red and orange foliage. Native to Japan. HEIGHT & SPREAD 1.5x1.5m (5x5ft) after 5 years, 1.8x2.4m (6x8ft) after 10 years.

▲ *Berberis thunbergii*

▲ *Berberis thunbergii* 'Atropurpurea Nana'

'Atropurpurea Nana'♀ (syn. 'Crimson Pygmy', 'Little Favourite') is an almost thornless dwarf shrub which, at 60x60cm (2x2ft), is suitable for a rock garden. The foliage is rich purple-red. Planted 38cm (15in) apart, the shrubs make a colourful low hedge. **'Atropurpurea Superba'** see *B. × ottawensis* 'Superba'. **'Aurea'** slowly makes a rounded bush, 1x1m (3x3ft) in 10 years, with stunning yellow leaves that fade to pale green by late summer. Yellow flowers bloom in mid spring; red berries appear in autumn. Plant in a sheltered and slightly shady position; in full sun the young leaves may scorch but the colour is best in good light. **'Bagatelle'**♀, with globular habit and bronze-purple foliage, is compact – 30x30cm (1x1ft) in 10 years. **'Crimson Pygmy'** see *B. thunbergii* 'Atropurpurea Nana'. **'Golden Ring'** has reddish purple leaves with a narrow gold margin, and reaches 1.5x1.5m (5x5ft) in 10 years. **'Helmond Pillar'** is a stiff erect shrub with large, rounded reddish bronze leaves. It reaches 1.5mx45cm (5x1½ft) after 10 years and makes an excellent hedge when plants are set 45cm (1½ft) apart. **'Red Chief'**♀ is also upright growing to about 1.8x1.5m (6x5ft) after 10 years, but with branches arching at the top. The stems are bright red with narrow, wine-red leaves. **'Red Pillar'** is an erect shrub to 1.5mx45cm (5x1½ft) after 10 years. Its reddish purple leaves turn scarlet in autumn. **'Rose Glow'**♀ has young leaves of purple marbled with silver and pink. It grows to 1.5x1.2m (5x4ft) after 10 years. **'Silver Beauty'** is a compact, slowly spreading bush to 1.2x1m (4x3ft) after 10 years, with white and bluish green variegated leaves, sometimes flushing through pink to crimson late in the season.

▲ *Berberis thunbergii* 'Bagatelle'

B. wilsoniae♀ Clusters of yellow flowers in early summer contrast with the small, lance-shaped, almost evergreen, grey-green leaves. These turn red and orange in autumn when large drooping clusters of berries ripen to orange-red. This low-growing, densely branched shrub is native to W China. HEIGHT & SPREAD 60cmx1m (2x3ft) after 5 years, 1x1.2m (3x4ft) after 10 years.

EVERGREEN SHRUBS

B. calliantha♀ Yellow flowers are borne in late spring on this dwarf shrub, followed in

▼ *Berberis wilsoniae*

▼ *Berberis calliantha*

autumn by blue-black berries with a white bloom. Its small holly-like leaves are waxy white beneath. Native to SE China. HEIGHT & SPREAD Up to 60×60cm (2×2ft) after 5 years, 1.5×1.5m (3×3ft) after 10 years.

▲ *Berberis darwinii*

B. darwinii Small, dark green, holly-like leaves provide a rich backdrop for the abundant clusters of crimson-tinted, golden yellow flowers that are borne in mid spring. Blue-purple berries ripen in early autumn. The dense shrubs make a good hedge when planted 60cm (2ft) apart. Native to Chile. HEIGHT & SPREAD 1.5×1.2m (5×4ft) after 5 years, 2×1.5m (6½×5ft) after 10 years.

***B. × frikartii* 'Amstelveen'** This dense, compact shrub has glossy, fresh green leaves with blue-white undersides. Yellow flowers in spring are followed by blue-black berries. HEIGHT & SPREAD 50×50cm (20×20in) in 5 years, 1×1m (3×3ft) in 10 years.

B. gagnepainii* var. *lanceifolia The dense growth of erect stems slowly forms an impenetrable hedge when plants are set 45-60cm (1½-2ft) apart. Clusters of bright yellow flowers in mid spring are followed in early autumn by black berries with a blue bloom. The narrow dark green leaves have a wavy margin. Native to China. HEIGHT & SPREAD 100×75cm (3×2½ft) in 5 years, 1.5×1.2m (5×4ft) after 10 years.

***B. glaucocarpa* 'Goldilocks'** Clusters of yellow flowers in spring, are followed by blackish purple berries. The spiny, holly-like leaves are a glossy dark green. HEIGHT & SPREAD 4×3m (13×10ft) after 10 years.

B. julianae Long sharp spines make the shrubs an excellent barrier hedge when planted 1m (3ft) apart. Narrow dark green leaves are copper-tinted when young. Yellow spring flowers in dense clusters are followed in autumn by black berries with a blue bloom. Native to central China. HEIGHT & SPREAD 1.5×1m (5×3ft) after 5 years, 3×2.4m (10×8ft) after 10 years.

***B. × lologensis* 'Apricot Queen'** Clusters of large orange flowers are massed on the stems in early to mid spring. Oval purple berries follow in autumn. The small holly-like leaves are glossy and dark green. HEIGHT & SPREAD 120×60cm (4×2ft) in 5 years, 2.4×1.2m (8×4ft) in 10 years.

***B. × media* 'Parkjuweel'** (Park Jewel) A low shrub forming a dense mound of oval, bright green glossy leaves that give good red autumn colour. Yellow flowers appear in late spring. HEIGHT & SPREAD 60×60cm (2×2ft) in 5 years, ultimately 1×1m (3×3ft).

▲ *Berberis × media* 'Parkjuweel' (Park Jewel)

B. × stenophylla From mid to late spring scented golden yellow flowers clothe the mass of long, thorny, arching branches on this graceful spreading shrub. Light crops of purple berries follow in autumn. The deep green narrow leaves are blue white beneath. The shrubs make an impenetrable hedge when planted 60cm (2ft) apart. HEIGHT & SPREAD 1.5×1.5m (5×5ft) in 5 years, 2.4×2.4m (8×8ft) in 10 years.

▲ *Berberis × stenophylla* 'Corallina Compacta'

'Corallina Compacta' is a slow growing dwarf shrub, reaching only 25×25cm (10×10in) in 10 years, with spiny stems and narrowly oval leaves. Coral buds open to small orange-yellow flowers in late spring.

B. verruculosa The neat, dense, slow-growing shrub has small, shiny, dark green, oval leaves that are white beneath. Golden yellow flowers appear singly or in pairs in early summer. Blue-black berries ripen in autumn. Set plants 60cm (2ft) apart for a compact hedge. Native to China. HEIGHT & SPREAD 75×75cm (2½×2½ft) in 5 years.

CULTIVATION Deciduous shrubs grown for autumn berries and colour are best in sunny positions. Evergreen plants thrive in sun or light shade. Berberis plants grow in a wide range of soils, but avoid waterlogged soil. Plant deciduous shrubs mid autumn to early spring and evergreen shrubs in early to mid autumn or early to mid spring. When planting a hedge cut off the upper quarter of all shoots to promote bushy growth.

PROPAGATION The species come true from seed; most of the cultivars come from cuttings. Take 8-12cm (3¼-4¾in) heeled cuttings in late summer from deciduous shrubs and in early autumn from evergreens. Root in a coldframe; transplant to a nursery bed the following spring; and, when shrubs are two years old, plant in their final positions.

PRUNING No regular pruning is required. Encourage fresh strong growth by cutting back a few of the oldest stems or removing them to ground level each year. Trim straggly shoots to maintain well-shaped plants. Cut deciduous species in late winter, evergreens after flowering. Trim hedges once a year – evergreens after flowering and deciduous hedges in late summer, or late autumn after the berries have fallen. Beware of thorns when pruning.

PESTS AND DISEASES Generally trouble free but honey fungus can kill quickly.

Bergamot see *Monarda*

Bergenia

Elephant's ear, pigsqueak

Saxifragaceae

Grown for their decorative foliage and early spring flowers, these hardy evergreen and semi-evergreen perennials make excellent ground cover and edging plants. The large handsome leaves are rounded or spoon-shaped and sometimes change to shades of red and purple in autumn and winter. Pink, mauve, red or white, the bell-shaped flowers grow in loose clusters among or above the foliage. Thick, crinkly, rhizome-like prostrate stems support flower stalks and leaf rosettes. Although plants are hardy, the early blooms can be damaged by hard frosts.

RECOMMENDED SPECIES AND VARIETIES

B. beesiana see *B. purpurascens*

B. ciliata White flowers, up to 5cm (2in) long, become tinged with rose. The round leaves are dark green, up to 30cm (1ft) long, and covered with short stubbly hairs. HEIGHT & SPREAD 30×45cm (1×1½ft).

B. cordifolia Pink flowers, 2.5cm (1in) long, rise above puckered, leathery round leaves up to 25cm (10in) wide. HEIGHT & SPREAD 45×60cm (1½×2ft).

'Purpurea' has dark purple flowers in spring and intermittently through summer. The leaves are bright purple in winter.

B. crassifolia Dark green, turning reddish

brown in winter, the coarse, fleshy leaves are oval or spoon-shaped and up to 20cm (8in) long. The flowers, up to 5cm (2in) long are in shades of purple and pink. HEIGHT & SPREAD 45×45cm (1½×1½ft).

B. delavayi see *B. purpurascens*

B. milesii see *B. stracheyi*

B. purpurascens ♀ (syn. *B. beesiana, B. delavayi*) Glossy green elliptic leaves, up to 25cm (10in) long, turn beetroot red above and mahogany beneath in autumn. Slender stems bear pink flowers, up to 5cm (2in) long. HEIGHT & SPREAD 45×60cm (1½×2ft).

B. stracheyi (syn. *B. milesii*) Spoon-shaped, semi-evergreen leaves, 20cm (8in) long turn reddish brown in winter. Nodding pale pink flowers are up to 5cm (2in) long. HEIGHT & SPREAD 20×30cm (8×12in).

OTHER RECOMMENDED VARIETIES

The many hybrids are more free-flowering than the species and, unless otherwise stated, those included here reach a height and spread of 30-45cm (1-1½ft).

'Abendglut' ('Evening Glow') has vivid rose-red flowers that are sometimes semi-double. Neat rosettes of crinkled leaves turn maroon in winter. **'Baby Doll'** has pale pink blooms. **Ballawley**, a semi-evergreen, has rose-pink flowers and can reach 60cm (2ft). **'Beethoven'** has white flowers and contrasting coral-red bracts. **'Bressingham Salmon'** has bright salmon-pink flowers and dark red winter leaves; **'Bressingham White'** has white flowers. In summer **'Morgenröte'** ♀ ('Morning Red') has a second flush of cherry-pink flowers. **'Silberlicht'** ♀ ('Silverlight') has large clusters of pure white flowers which turn pale pink. **'Sunningdale'** has rose-pink flowers on bright coral-red stems; its leaves are bronzed in winter. **'Wintermärchen'** ('Winter's Tale') has small, shiny, narrow leaves that turn bright scarlet in winter. The flowers are deep rose-red on red stems.

▼ *Bergenia* 'Baby Doll'

▼ *Bergenia* Ballawley

▲ *Bergenia* 'Bressingham White'

▲ *Bergenia* 'Wintermärchen'

CULTIVATION Plant from mid autumn to early spring in any soil in full sun or light shade. Leaf colour is improved by planting in poor soil in full sun.

PROPAGATION Divide plants in autumn or spring. Alternatively, raise species from seed sown in a coldframe in spring.

PESTS AND DISEASES Leaf spot fungus can cause brown patches on leaves.

Betony see *Stachys*

Betula

Birch

Betulaceae

Birches are graceful deciduous trees and shrubs noted for their glowing autumn colour and striking bark. Most of the 60 or so species are completely hardy in Britain. Some have attractive peeling bark, ranging in colour from silver to pale shades of gold, pink and brown. In some species, old trees eventually produce areas of fissured black bark starting at the base of the trunk.

The leaves are 6-10cm (2½-4in) long, mostly toothed, and more or less triangular. Arranged alternately on fine, sometimes pendulous, flexible twigs, they turn yellow and gold in autumn. Catkins, 3-10cm (1¼-4in) long, develop through the winter and then extend as the leaves unfold in the spring. Male and female catkins are borne on the same tree. Males are greenish yellow and usually hang like hazel catkins, but often appear in threes; females are greenish, shorter, and more upright. Autumn and winter winds scatter tiny, golden brown winged seeds and bits of catkin.

Most birches are unlikely to live for more than 60 years and are at their best when 10 to 25 years old. Established trees rarely blow down or become excessively large, and the roots are not widely spreading or invasive. Birches are effective planted in groups against an evergreen backdrop. Grass and many herbaceous plants will grow reasonably well beneath most species.

RECOMMENDED SPECIES AND VARIETIES

B. albo-sinensis* var. *septentrionalis ♀ This upright tree has the finest bark of all birches. It is pink, brown and copper coloured, often hanging in large, thin, peeling sheets after about 15 years. The matt green leaves are oval and toothed. Native to W China. HEIGHT & SPREAD 10 x 6m (33 x 20ft) after 20 years; to 25m (80ft) tall on a sheltered site.

B. costata Smooth, creamy white bark distinguishes this rounded graceful tree. It is quite tender and requires fairly sheltered conditions. The leaves are toothed, oval, pointed and downy when young. Native to NE Asia. HEIGHT & SPREAD 7×4m (23×13ft) after 20 years; ultimately 25m (80ft).

'Blush' has creamy white bark and is often sold as *B. costata*. It tends to grow more slowly than the species. **'Grayswood Hill'** ♀ is outstanding with a conical form when young and superb pale peeling bark.

B. medwedewii ♀ The broad elliptic leaves emerge from sticky winter buds and turn bright yellow in autumn on this stiff upright tree. Native to Asia Minor and hardy in Britain. HEIGHT & SPREAD 5×3m (16×10ft) after 20 years, ultimately 18m (60ft) tall.

B. nana (dwarf birch) This broad, knee-high birch, a British native, grows very slowly and thrives only in cold areas. The

▼ *Betula* 'Grayswood Hill'

small, shining, dark green leaves are almost round and seldom reach more than 1.5 cm (½ in) long. The oval catkins are also very small at 1 cm (⅜ in). HEIGHT & SPREAD 50 cm x 1 m (20 in x 3 ft) after 20 years, ultimately exceeding this only very slightly.

B. nigra♀ Wet ground suits this upright tree with distinctive dark brown and grey peeling bark. The diamond-shaped, glossy green leaves are double-toothed and turn golden yellow in autumn. It is native to E and central USA and is fairly hardy in Britain. HEIGHT & SPREAD On a riverside site it may grow to 10 x 5 m (33 x 16 ft) after 20 years, ultimately reaching 25 m (80 ft) tall.

▲ *Betula nigra*

B. pendula (silver birch)♀ The graceful common British native birch has weeping branch tips and is familiar throughout the country. In the garden it is hardy and reliable and displays peeling silver bark which becomes rough and blackened on older trees. Triangular, double-toothed leaves are 4-6 cm (1½-2½ in) long and turn yellow in autumn. HEIGHT & SPREAD 14 x 5 m (46 x 16 ft) after 20 years, ultimately 20 m (66 ft).

▲ *Betula pendula* (silver birch)

▲ *Betula pendula* 'Tristis'

Betula 'Trost's Dwarf' ▲

'Fastigiata' is slender and erect with droopy shoots. **'Laciniata'**♀ also has droopy shoots and pretty, deeply cut leaves. It grows more slowly than the species, reaching up to 10 m (33 ft) after 20 years. The leaves of **'Purpurea'** are flushed purple in early summer. **'Tristis'**♀ is tall with pendulous branches. **'Youngii'**♀ is dome-shaped and will weep to the ground like a weeping willow. It is useful for the smaller garden as it does not exceed 10 x 5 m (33 x 16 ft).

▲ *Betula pendula* 'Youngii'

***B.* 'Trost's Dwarf'** This slow-growing, small shrub has finely cut leaves and slender, arching branches, but is weak and susceptible to rust. HEIGHT & SPREAD 1 x 1 m (3 x 3 ft) after 10 years; ultimately 2 m (6½ ft).

The variety ***jacquemontii***♀ is a white stemmed tree and ***jacquemontii* 'Silver Shadow'**♀ has especially white bark. Fast-growing **'Jermyns'**♀ – 10 m (33 ft) in about 20 years – is distinguished by its creamy white, non-peeling bark and its long, hanging male catkins – up to 17 cm (6¾ in) long.

CULTIVATION Birches tolerate a wide range of soils, but most species prefer sandy, neutral or acid sites. Most require full sun. Wet, lime-rich clay soils may be debilitating except for wetland species such as *B. nigra*. Birches dislike root disturbance, so select container plants if available. Planting time is not critical if trees in containers are used, but roots of newly planted trees should not be allowed to dry out. Trees thrive planted singly or 2-3 m (6½-10 ft) apart in groups of up to 5 – if space permits – in the garden.

PROPAGATION Sow seed in early spring in containers, a coldframe or on open ground and cover with a thin layer of fine acid grit. Keep transplanting to a minimum.

▼ *Betula jacquemontii*

PRUNING Do any pruning that is required in summer, to prevent sap bleeding. Trees can be coppiced to rejuvenate them or to produce several stems instead of just one, thus increasing the impact of the bark.

PESTS AND DISEASES Aphids, caterpillars and weevils feed on the leaves, but infestations are rare. Insects, mites and fungi can cause witches' brooms among twigs; rust on the foliage may cause orange-yellow dots on the leaves in late summer; honey fungus can rot roots and cause trees to blow down.

Bidens

Compositae

Profuse bright yellow, dark-centred blooms through summer into autumn have made the two Central American species of this plant particularly popular for hanging baskets. The flowers, up to 5 cm (2 in) across, are borne in sprays of three or more among divided, ferny grey-green leaves. Their naturally spreading, thin-stemmed habit makes them ideal for containers and ground cover. The plants are true perennials which are almost always grown as half-hardy annuals.

RECOMMENDED SPECIES AND VARIETIES

***B. aurea* 'Sunshine'** Branching stems carry yellow flowers early summer to autumn. HEIGHT & SPREAD 50 x 40 cm (20 x 16 in).

B. ferulifolia (tickseed) Yellow flowers bloom in profusion from early summer to early autumn among fern-like leaves. HEIGHT & SPREAD 50 x 40 cm (20 x 16 in).

CULTIVATION This is an easily cultivated plant, tolerant of a wide range of summer conditions – including drying out. It does best in full sun but will accept light shade.

PROPAGATION Raise as half-hardy annuals, sowing seed in a heated greenhouse in early spring. Plant out when risk of hard frost has passed. Branching growth habit is encouraged if the growing points are pinched out when the young plants are 5 cm (2 in) tall. Plants can be overwintered in a frost-free greenhouse and divided in spring.

PESTS AND DISEASES Aphids, slugs and powdery mildew should be watched for.

▼ *Bidens ferulifolia*

b

Billardiera

Pittosporaceae

These evergreen, climbing plants are grown for their flowers and colourful fruits. Native to Australia, the plants are half hardy.

RECOMMENDED SPECIES

B. longiflora A freely flowering and fruiting evergreen perennial climber. It is slightly tender, suitable outside only in mild areas where it is best grown in half-shady sheltered situations, away from strong winds. Pale yellow-green, drooping, tubular flowers, 3cm (1¼in) long, are borne singly in early summer. In early autumn a showy, dangling display of rounded violet-blue berries is seen. The slender, twining branches are clothed with light green lance-shaped leaves, up to 4cm (1½in) long. White or red berried forms are also available. HEIGHT 3m (10ft) after 5 years.

▲ *Billardiera longiflora*

CULTIVATION Grow in a cool greenhouse or conservatory, either as a climber or in a hanging basket. Plant in loamy soil and do not allow it to dry out.

PROPAGATION Take semi-ripe cuttings in late summer. To grow from seed, sow seed when ripe in early spring. However, the seed can take a long time to germinate.

PRUNING None is needed, but occasionally cut out old and overcrowded branches.

PESTS AND DISEASES Sometimes attacked by greenfly.

Billbergia

Bromeliaceae

Brightly coloured tubular flowers embraced by a decorative rose-pink bract dangle over handsome rosettes of strap-shaped leaves. The flowers appear anytime between spring and autumn and last for three to four weeks. These tropical evergreen perennials prefer a semi-shaded position in the home or greenhouse, no cooler than 10°C (50°F) at night. Native to Central and S America.

RECOMMENDED SPECIES AND VARIETIES

B. nutans (Queen's tears, friendship plant) Small pale green flowers, edged with violet, are surrounded by slender bracts 2.5cm (1in) long and borne on simple arching stems. This suckering houseplant has narrow dull green leaves, up to 45cm (18in) long, that are occasionally toothed. HEIGHT & SPREAD 45×30cm (1½×1ft).

▲ *Billbergia nutans*

B. pyramidalis A strong-growing plant, it has erect, pyramidal flower spikes – massed ranks of small red or orange flowers often edged blue with bright rose-pink bracts up to 4cm (1½in) long. Lance-shaped green leaves, up to 60cm (2ft) long, are flushed purple and have white banding beneath. HEIGHT & SPREAD 60×45cm (2×1½ft).

B. x windii♀ (angel's tears) The pendulous flower stem consists of a wiry stalk with terminal bright pink or deep rose bracts. The emerging narrow green flowers, edged red with distinctive blue tips, are up to 7.5cm (3in) long. This erect, somewhat tubular-shaped plant has dull green leaves. HEIGHT & SPREAD 45×30cm (1½×1ft).

CULTIVATION Grow in pots in a well-lit position away from direct sunlight. The plants should be kept growing tightly in their pots and not overpotted. Do not let the compost dry out and add a liquid houseplant feed to the water in summer. Mist the foliage regularly with clear water. All billbergias thrive in a variety of potting composts, from peat to soil-based. Remove the flowers after they have faded.

PROPAGATION Remove suckering growths in spring and pot individually.

PESTS AND DISEASES Usually trouble free.

Bindweed see *Calystegia hederacea*
Biota see *Thuja*
Birch see *Betula*
Bird of Paradise see *Strelitzia Reginae*
Birthwort see *Aristolochia dematitis*
Bistort see *Persicaria bistorta*
Bitter root see *Lewisia rediviva*
Bittersweet, oriental see *Celastrus orbiculatus*
Blackberry see FRUIT p.729
Black cohosh see *Cimicifuga racemosa*
Black-eyed Susan see *Thunbergia alata*
Black horehound see *Ballota nigra*
Blackthorn see *Prunus spinosa*
Bladder nut see *Staphylea*
Bladder senna see *Colutea arborescens*
Blanket flower see *Gaillarda*
Blazing star see *Liatris*
Blechnum see FERNS p.263
Bleeding heart see *Dicentra spectabilis*
Bleeding heart vine see *Clerodendrum Thomsoniae*

Bletilla

Orchidaceae

The complex and intricate blooms produced by members of the orchid family give a tropical air to an outdoor garden. This is one of the terrestrial orchids – a fairly hardy plant from E Asia – whose corm-like pseudobulb survives to bloom year after year if given some winter protection. In colder areas grow the plants in pots indoors and move them outside for the summer, or keep them in a cool greenhouse (see ORCHIDS, p.464).

RECOMMENDED SPECIES

B. striata (syn. *B. hyacinthina)* Each flower has 5 narrow rose-purple petals radiating above a broad lower petal or lip with an outer lobe raised at either side of the centre lobe, crimped at the rim and marked with 5 shallow ribs. The flowers are about 2.5cm (1in) across and borne in early summer in sprays of 3-6 at the top of arching stems up to 40cm (16in) long. Slender, upright, pointed leaves of mid green are pleated and arch slightly at the tip. HEIGHT 45cm (18in).

▲ *Bletilla striata*

CULTIVATION Plant in early spring in moist but well-drained humus-rich soil, just covering the pseudobulb. Choose a shady or semi-shaded position sheltered from the north and east. In winter protect with a thick mulch of leaf-mould or other protective material such as conifer clippings.

PROPAGATION Divide the clustered pseudobulbs of established plants between autumn and early spring.

PESTS AND DISEASES Slugs may damage young shoots, but generally the plants are trouble free.

Bolax

Umbelliferae

Bolax gummifera

Rosettes of tiny overlapping leaves give this hardy, evergreen perennial the appearance of a neat, tight cushion. This is a slow-growing plant, best suited to the corner of a rock garden, a scree or raised bed, a pot or a trough. There is only one species.

Bolax glebaria see *Azorella trifurcata*

B. gummifera Blue-green leaves, thick and tough to the touch, each has 3 deep lobes and measures up to 6mm (¼in) in length. Greenish white or yellow flowers appear among the leaf rosettes in summer in miniature domed clusters about 2cm (¾in) across. The purple-brown fruits, 3.5mm (⅛in) long and clothed in minute star-shaped hairs, are more attractive. The species is native to the Falkland Islands, Patagonia and Tierra del Fuego. In the wild, bolax inhabits scrub, heaths and rocky places. HEIGHT & SPREAD 10×40cm (4×16in). Its ultimate spread, after about 8 years, is about 75cm (2½ft).

CULTIVATION Plant in a moist, humus-rich, well-drained soil, in full sunshine. Grow outdoors or in a coldframe or unheated greenhouse with plenty of ventilation.

PROPAGATION Sow the seeds when ripe in a coldframe, or take semi-ripe cuttings in late summer; alternatively, take offshoots in spring.

PESTS AND DISEASES Usually trouble free.

Boltonia

False camomile
Compositae

Boltonia asteroides

Loose clusters of daisy-like flowers bloom in late summer on these leafy-stemmed herbaceous perennials. They give height and airy blooms to a garden border, and make excellent cut flowers. Hardy and tolerant of light shade, boltonia grows in moist soils in the wild, in E Asia and the USA.

RECOMMENDED SPECIES AND VARIETIES

B. asteroides Flowers have white, sometimes purple, petals with prominent yellow central discs and measure 2cm (¾in) across. They are borne in clusters at the top of each stem. The glossy, grey-green, narrow and pointed leaves are up to 12cm (4¾in) long and 2cm (¾in) wide. HEIGHT & SPREAD 2.1×1.2m (7×4ft).

The slightly larger flowers of var. *latisquama* are a more definite lilac colour and the plant is shorter at 1.8m (6ft). This natural variety is the parent of **'Nana'**, suitable for smaller gardens at only 1m (3ft) tall. Its flowers are white. **'Snowbank'**, with snow-white flowers, is nearer the height of the species at 2m (6½ft).

CULTIVATION Grow in any reasonably fertile soil. Taller species or varieties need staking, preferably with twiggy sticks for the plant to grow through.

PROPAGATION Sow seed in spring. Divide the plant in autumn. Plant basal cuttings in late spring or early summer.

PESTS AND DISEASES Usually trouble free.

Bougainvillea

Nyctaginaceae

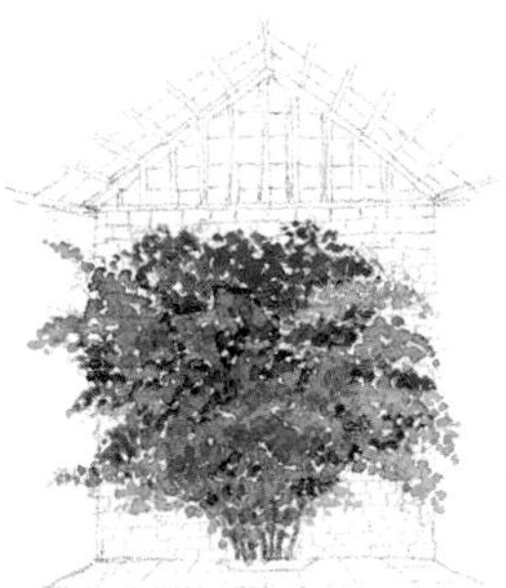

Bougainvillea glabra

Remarkable brilliantly coloured bracts decorate these tropical and sub-tropical flowering shrubs and scramblers. The flowers are generally insignificant. Bougainvilleas can be grown in a conservatory or greenhouse usually in large pots on a framework of wire or canes. Where space is available, however, the plants can be grown very successfully in a greenhouse border and trained up into the roof. All enjoy full sun and require a minimum night temperature of 10°C (50°F).

RECOMMENDED SPECIES AND VARIETIES

B. × buttiana A vigorous, scrambling, woody plant with dark green elliptical leaves up to 7.5cm (3in) long. The bright orange or purple papery bracts are about 3cm (1¼in) wide and slightly undulated. HEIGHT & SPREAD 5×1m (16×3ft).

'Golden Glow' has golden yellow bracts with a hint of pink. **'Killie Campbell'**♀ bears large bracts with ruffled edges that are copper through to red and magenta.

'Mrs Butt'♀ produces crimson-magenta bracts. **'Scarlet O'Hara'** sports orange to deep bright red bracts, which shade to orange.

▲ *Bougainvillea glabra*

Bougainvillea 'Mrs Butt' ▲

B. glabra♀ (paper flower) A vigorous, scrambling, shrubby plant with elliptical leaves that are 10cm (4in) long and pale green beneath. The white or magenta bracts, up to 3cm (1¼in) wide, persist long after the central tiny blossom has faded. The insignificant white flowers contrast well with the bold mauve to purple bracts. HEIGHT & SPREAD 5m×1m (16×3ft).

'Alexandra' has magenta bracts.

***B.* 'Poultonii Special'**♀ This moderately vigorous scrambling shrubby plant has elliptical leaves up to 7.5cm (3in) long. The striking rich rosy magenta bracts are 3cm (1¼in) wide. HEIGHT & SPREAD 3×1m (10×3ft).

***B.* 'Raspberry Ice'** This bushy, scrambling plant has elliptical leaves that are 7.5cm (3in) long, and creamy variegated with a pink flush. The bracts, up to 3cm (1in) long, are deep pink to red. HEIGHT & SPREAD 3×1m (10×3ft).

CULTIVATION All bougainvilleas thrive in full sun in a free-draining, soil-based compost. They require a night temperature that does not drop below a minimum of 10°C (50°F). For pot culture use John Innes No. 3 compost. Water freely during the summer months, but very sparingly in winter. Use a high-nitrogen liquid feed in spring and change to a high-potash one when flowering begins. Bougainvilleas are not self clinging and must be tied to their supports.

PROPAGATION Take semi-ripe cuttings of non-flowering wood in summer, or hardwood cuttings during winter.

PRUNING Cut back the previous season's lateral growths in spring; only spurs up to 3cm (1¼in) long should remain.

PESTS AND DISEASES Greenfly, whitefly, red spider and mealy bug are all common pest problems. Mildew, too, can sometimes cause trouble.

BONSAI

Miniature images of ancient trees

SEASONAL CHANGES ARE CAPTURED IN SPECTACULAR DETAIL BY BONSAI TREES, WHICH ARE STRAIGHTFORWARD TO CREATE

▲ GRACEFUL MAPLE *Slender branches and neat, elegant foliage give an acer bonsai its charm.*

▲ ROCKY CONTRAST *A stone forms the centrepiece to a display of spruce, elm and cotoneaster.*

▲ BONSAI WOODLAND *A group of hornbeams creates the impression of a leafy grove.*

Bonsai bring the pleasure and variety of trees to the smallest of areas. Once the basic techniques have been mastered, it is possible to create images of an ancient oak, a wind-blown mountain pine or a dense forest of beech within a few years.

Given the correct care, a bonsai can outlive a full-sized tree and will weather attractively throughout the years as pruning wounds heal, bark cracks and moss covers the surrounding soil. Pruning is necessary to simplify the branch structure and wire is used to shape branches and create a natural-looking growth pattern. New shoots are pinched out to keep the foliage neat.

Bonsai can be grown from seed or cuttings but most will take many years to develop; if you begin with an established plant, you should have a recognisable tree in four or five years.

Choose a hardy species that regenerates readily after pruning and has naturally small leaves, flowers and berries. *Carpinus* (hornbeam), *Pinus* (pine), *Picea* (spruce), *Juniperus* (juniper) *Ulmus* (elm) and *Crataegus* (hawthorn) are ideal. Look for a plant that is 30-50 cm (12-20 in) in height and has a well-shaped trunk that is flared at the base.

CREATING THE SHAPE

Specialist bonsai tools are available but all you need to begin with are sharp secateurs, wire cutters and a modelling knife. Aluminium wire for shaping can be bought from a garden centre or bonsai nursery. Make sure the wire is strong enough to keep a branch in place but not so heavy that it crushes the bark when it is applied.

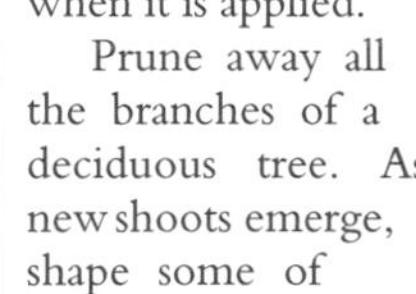

Prune away all the branches of a deciduous tree. As new shoots emerge, shape some of them with wire and remove the others. Do not remove all the branches of an evergreen at once as the plant will die. Instead, shorten them in stages, cutting back to healthy sideshoots in spring and again in summer. Once ample new shoots have appeared close to the trunk, prune the original branches hard and shape the new shoots to form new branches. The branches should be arranged evenly round the trunk with the bottom half of the front of the tree left clear.

Use wire to shape branches into the desired positions (see facing page). Keep the branches of a broad-leaved tree more or less horizontal and shape conifer branches into slightly downward sweeps. Sideshoots also need wiring in the same way. The trunk can be left to grow upright or, if it is supple enough, shaped with wire to lean as if wind-blown or to dip over the rim of the container.

Once they are wired, the branches and sideshoots should be left to grow freely until they have set in position. At this point, remove the wire before it begins to scar the bark. The branches can then be cut to the desired lengths.

Pinch out new growth throughout the growing season to keep foliage neat and bushy (see facing page). Once you are satisfied with the shape of your

•REMOVING A BRANCH•

Prune between autumn and spring, when the tree is dormant, or in mid summer, when the wounds heal rapidly.

1 To prune, cut the branch as close to the trunk as you can without damaging the bark. Then use a blade to hollow out the wound so it will heal flat.

2 Seal the wound with a non-drying modelling clay, such as Plasticine, mixed with a little olive oil. Bitumen stains the bark and is hard to remove.

▶ SEASONAL SHOW *The resilient hawthorn is most attractive in spring when it produces its blooms.*

bonsai, prune its roots and repot the tree in a shallow bonsai container (see below).

CARING FOR A BONSAI

Repot young trees every year and older trees or pines less often, but before the roots block the drainage holes.

Keep bonsai off the ground, ideally on slatted benches, in dappled shade. Bonsai need shelter from cold winds, severe frost and prolonged periods of rain. Place conifers against a south-facing wall, and broad-leaved trees in a shed or poly-tunnel during winter.

Water bonsai regularly and do not let the soil dry out. Water evaporates quickly from a bonsai's shallow pot, which can also become waterlogged, so use a compost that is moisture retentive but free draining and well aerated. Equal parts of sifted peat, sterilised loam and grit is a good mix.

When watering, soak the soil well until water runs freely from the container's drainage holes and immerse the pot in water periodically to ensure there are no dry spots.

Feed conifers once in mid winter and all trees from spring to late summer. A general fertiliser suits all except flowering bonsai, which need a tomato or rose fertiliser. Apply feed at half strength twice as often as recommended, to avoid 'burning' the roots. Add a nitrogen-free fertiliser in early autumn to harden growth and toughen the roots before winter.

•PINCHING OUT YOUNG GROWTH•

Finger-pinching encourages the growth of dense twigs and neat, bushy foliage. It also reduces the size of the leaves, which keeps them in proportion with the tree.

General techniques Remove the tips of young shoots of conifers as they grow. On broad-leaved trees, pinch out the growing tip once the shoot produces two or three leaves (left) or wait until six or seven leaves appear then cut back the shoot to the second leaf.

Chinese junipers *Juniperus chinensis* produces short, multi-branched shoots with scale-like foliage. To pinch out, grip a fan of shoots between your thumb and forefinger and break off the ends, leaving behind stubs of even length (right). Remove any vigorous shoots individually and continue the process throughout the growing season.

Pines In spring, *Pinus* buds develop into candle-like shoots, covered in needles. Break off half of each candle while the needles are pressed tight (left) or two-thirds when they start to open out. Begin at the bottom of the tree where shoots are weakest and work upwards over a week. Pull out some of the old needles in late summer to give new buds room to develop.

•SHAPING A BRANCH WITH WIRE•

Coil wire round a branch and bend to shape. Leave the wire in place until the branch sets in position. This can take weeks for a young deciduous branch or years for an older conifer.

1 Anchor the wire by coiling it round the trunk if shaping a branch or by pushing it into the soil if shaping a trunk. Coil the rest of the wire at a 45 degree angle round the branch or trunk and manipulate into position.

2 Leave the tree to rest in shade for a week, then check it regularly to see if the wire is cutting into the bark. When this happens, remove the wire and, if necessary, replace it coiled in the opposite direction.

▲ NATURAL SHAPE *The branches of this pine tree have been wired to slope downwards.*

•ROOT PRUNING AND REPOTTING•

Pruning roots and repotting is best done in early spring when the roots will heal rapidly. Do not feed for three weeks afterwards and delay wiring or pruning until growth restarts.

1 Lift the tree from its pot and gently tease out the roots with a stick until they hang loose. Then, cut back all of the thick roots as far as possible and the fine roots by about half.

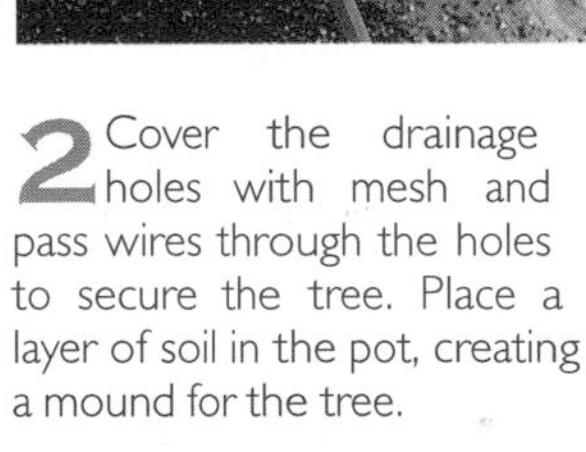

2 Cover the drainage holes with mesh and pass wires through the holes to secure the tree. Place a layer of soil in the pot, creating a mound for the tree.

3 Rotate the tree on the mound to settle it. Pull the wires over the roots. Twist them together and tighten to hold the tree steady. Work soil between the roots with a stick, making sure that there are no spaces. Water well and place the tree in a frost-free site until growth resumes.

b

Brachyglottis
Compositae

Silver-grey foliage and yellow daisy-like flowers in early to mid summer give lasting but unostentatious charm to these evergreen shrubs. The broadly oval leaves have dense white felt beneath and vary from olive to grey-green above. All these New Zealand natives are sun lovers, those listed here are reasonably hardy and tolerant of drought and strong winds.

RECOMMENDED SPECIES AND VARIETIES

B. compacta (syn. *Senecio compactus*) Small wavy-edged leaves clothe the close-set branches. Young branches and stems are densely felted. Flowers are borne in clusters or singly in mid summer. HEIGHT & SPREAD 1×2m (3×6½ft).

▲ *Brachyglottis compacta*

B. monroi♀ (syn. *Senecio monroi*) The small domed shrub bears large dense clusters of flowers in early to mid summer. The scalloped, wavy leaves are heavily felted on the underside. HEIGHT & SPREAD 1×1m (3×3ft).

***B.* Dunedin Group 'Sunshine'**♀ (syn. *Senecio greyi* hort., *S.* 'Sunshine') The leaves are silvery or grey-green above, white felted beneath. Flowers are borne in large clusters from mid to late summer. HEIGHT & SPREAD 1×2m (3×6½ft).

▼ *Brachyglottis* Dunedin Group 'Sunshine'

CULTIVATION Plant in spring in any well-drained soil in full sun.

PROPAGATION Take semi-ripe cuttings during summer or hardwood cuttings in mid to late autumn.

PRUNING Trim back after flowering to keep within bounds.

PESTS AND DISEASES Usually trouble free.

Brachyscome
Compositae

Grown for their white, blue or purple daisies, the brachyscome species recommended here are a half-hardy annual and an herbaceous perennial. The annual, *Brachyscome iberidifolia,* is suitable for summer bedding or in hanging baskets and other containers. It can also be grown as a winter-flowering indoor plant. The perennial, *B. rigidula,* is good for rock gardens but is only reliably hardy in milder regions. Native to Australasia and New Guinea.

RECOMMENDED SPECIES AND VARIETIES

B. iberidifolia (Swan River daisy) Usually blue, but sometimes violet or white, the abundant, fragrant flowers appear throughout summer. They measure up to 4cm (1½in) across. This bushy plant has pale green, deeply cut leaves, 10cm (4in) long. HEIGHT & SPREAD 30×45cm (12×18in).

▲ *Brachyscome iberidifolia*

Among the single-colour varieties available are **'Blue Star'**, **'Purple Splendour'** and **'White Splendour'**. **'Brachy Blue'** has blue flowers and reaches a height of 15cm (6in) and a spread of 20cm (8in).

B. rigidula Lavender-blue flowers, up to 2.5cm (1in) across, appear throughout summer on 8cm (3¼in) stems. Plants form dense low clumps of numerous leafy stems. The finely divided, dark green glossy leaves are 3cm (1¼in) long. HEIGHT & SPREAD 15×30cm (6×12in).

CULTIVATION Plant in late spring in well-drained soil, choosing a sheltered site in full sun. *B. iberidifolia* benefits from some support. Deadhead regularly.

PROPAGATION Raise *B. iberidifolia* from seed sown in a cool greenhouse in early spring. To grow indoor plants that flower in late winter, sow seed in early autumn, providing a minimum greenhouse temperature of 10°C (50°F). Propagate *B. rigidula* from seed, as for *B. iberidifolia,* or by division or by taking cuttings in spring or late summer.

PESTS AND DISEASES Usually trouble free.

Brassica
Cruciferae

Striking inner leaves that are partly or entirely red, white or pink are the most distinctive feature of these hardy annuals which, although they are the same species as broccoli, brussels sprouts and cauliflower, are unpleasant to eat. The outer leaves are green. The colours develop at night temperatures below 10°C (50°F) so they are at their most interesting in autumn. They thrive in almost any garden situation, including large containers. They have all arisen in cultivation.

RECOMMENDED SPECIES AND VARIETIES

B. oleracea* var. *acephala (ornamental kale) Fringed or deeply serrated foliage is loosely arranged and this plant has no recognisable heart. The varieties listed are F_1 hybrids. HEIGHT & SPREAD 45×45cm (18×18in).

'Nagoya' has heavily fringed red or white younger leaves. **'Peacock'** has white or red inner leaves and white or red veinal areas to outer leaves, all deeply toothed. Both these cultivars are up to 30cm (12in) tall and 30cm (12in) across. **'Feather'** is similar to 'Peacock' but taller, at 35cm (14in).

B. oleracea* var. *capitata (ornamental cabbage group) The fast-growing, uniform F_1 hybrids are more commonly grown. HEIGHT & SPREAD 45×45cm (18×18in).

▼ *Brassica oleracea* var. *capitata* 'Tokyo'

'Northern Lights' and **'Osaka'** are up to 50cm (20in) across and 25cm (10in) tall, with frilled leaf edges. **'Tokyo'** has smooth-edged leaves and reaches 25cm (10in) tall, with a spread of 30cm (12in).
CULTIVATION Plant in late summer or early autumn, in comparatively poor soil.
PROPAGATION Sow seed in a coldframe or unheated greenhouse in early to mid summer. Keep well watered, especially during the first week.
PESTS AND DISEASES Aphids and caterpillars attack plants. Pigeons may damage brassicas in autumn, especially in hard weather.

Brazilian plume see *Justicia carnea*
Bridal wreath see *Francoa*
Briza see GRASSES p.300
Broccoli see p.736
Brodiaea see *Triteleia*
Bromeliads see *Aechmea, Ananas, Billbergia, Cryptanthus, Guzmania, Neoregelia, Nidularium, Tillandsia, Vriesea*
Broom see *Cytisus*
Broom, Mt Etna see *Genista aetnensis*
Broom, Spanish see *Spartium*

Browallia

Bush violet
Solanaceae

Star-shaped, tubular flowers adorn these bushy evergreen perennials from early summer to early autumn. These free-flowering, frost-tender plants are grown indoors as pot plants or outdoors as summer bedding or in containers and hanging baskets. They are generally treated as half-hardy annuals and discarded after flowering.

The flowers have five rounded petals and white centres. The slightly sticky, mid green leaves are oval and pointed. Native to tropical S America.
RECOMMENDED SPECIES AND VARIETIES
B. speciosa Violet-blue flowers, about 5cm (2in) across, are borne singly on short stalks.

▼ *Browallia speciosa* 'Blue Troll'

The leaves are up to 9cm (3½in) long.
HEIGHT & SPREAD 45×45cm (18×18in).

'Blue Troll' has clear blue flowers and **'White Troll'** has white flowers; both grow to a height and spread of 25cm (10in).
B. viscosa This plant has violet-blue flowers 2.5cm (1in) across and smaller leaves.
HEIGHT & SPREAD 30×20cm (12×8in).

'Sapphire' has bright blue flowers.
CULTIVATION Plant outdoors in any soil, preferably moist but not wet, once all risk of frost has passed, choosing a sunny position. Alternatively grow in pots of John Innes No.2 indoors or in a well-ventilated greenhouse or conservatory, maintaining a minimum winter temperature of 13°C (55°F). Protect plants from direct sun. Pinch out growing points to ensure well-branched, bushy specimens.
PROPAGATION For outdoor plants, sow seed in early spring in a heated greenhouse. For indoor pot plants, sow seed in late winter to produce flowers in late spring and early summer. For flowers in late winter and early spring, sow seed under glass in mid to late summer, maintaining a minimum winter temperature of 13°C (55°F).
PESTS AND DISEASES Usually trouble free.

Bruckenthalia

Spike heath
Ericaceae

Bruckenthalia spiculifolia

This hardy evergreen shrub has a flowering period that falls between the winter-flowering and early summer-flowering heathers, ensuring that a small heather garden has continuity in its display of colour. It is also at home in peaty rock gardens or in pots and other containers. There is only one species in the genus; it is native to acid sub-alpine regions of SE Europe.
Bruckenthalia spiculifolia The neat plant bears short dense spikes, 2mm (⅛in) long, of bell-shaped flowers that are generally pink. The flowers are held above dark green whorls of up to 5 needle-like leaves, each up to 5mm (¼in) long. The flowers are usually in bloom from early to mid summer.
HEIGHT & SPREAD 25×50cm (10×20in).
CULTIVATION Plant in lime-free, moist but well-drained soil in full sun.
PROPAGATION Take semi-ripe heeled cuttings in mid summer.
PRUNING Trim lightly after flowering to remove dead flowerheads.
PESTS AND DISEASES Usually trouble free.

▲ *Bruckenthalia spiculifolia*

Brugmansia

Solanaceae

Brugmansia x candida 'Grand Marnier'

The large pendulous flowers of these tender shrubs and small trees are funnel-shaped and often strongly fragrant. They appear in summer and sometimes into autumn. The evergreen leaves, which are coarse and sometimes downy, may be lost in winter. All parts of these plants are poisonous. Native to central and S America, they need a minimum night temperature of 7°C (45°F) and are usually grown as greenhouse or conservatory plants. They can be moved outside in summer to a sheltered sunny position. All the plants recommended below are shrubs which attain their full size in five years. The heights and spreads given are for specimens planted out and either lightly pruned or not pruned at all. Pot-grown plants reach about half these sizes.
RECOMMENDED SPECIES AND VARIETIES
B. arborea (syn. *B. versicolor* hort., *Datura arborea*) (angel's trumpet) Strongly aromatic white flowers up to 20cm (8in) long appear from mid summer to autumn. The dull

green, narrowly oval leaves, 20 cm (8 in) long, are coarsely toothed. HEIGHT & SPREAD 4×2 m (13×6½ ft).

B.* × *candida Fragrant white, pink or yellow flowers up to 30 cm (12 in) long are borne from mid to late summer. Toothed, dull green, elliptic leaves are up to 20 cm (8 in) long. HEIGHT & SPREAD 5×3 m (16×10 ft).

'Grand Marnier'♀ has peach-pink flowers. **'Knightii'**♀ (syn. 'Plena') has double white flowers.

B. chlorantha see *B. sanguinea* ssp. *sanguinea* 'Flava'

B.* × *insignis (syn. *B. suaveolens* × *versicolor*) Pink to white flowers, up to 40 cm (16 in) long, appear from mid to late summer. Dull green, oval to elliptic leaves are 15 cm (6 in) long. HEIGHT & SPREAD 4×2 m (13×6½ ft).

'Orange' bears abundant orange-yellow flowers. There is a **pink** form (syn. *B. sanguinea* 'Rosea', *Datura rosea*) with salmon-pink blooms.

B. rosei see *B. sanguinea* ssp. *sanguinea* 'Flava'

B. sanguinea♀ (syn. *Datura rosei*, *D. sanguinea*) (red angel's trumpet) Yellow flowers, 25 cm (10 in) long, with a flared mouth that deepens to orange-red appear from mid to late summer. The large, dull green, rounded, lobed leaves are up to 15 cm (6 in) long. HEIGHT & SPREAD 5×4 m (16×13 ft).

▲ *Brugmansia sanguinea*

'Rosea' see *B.* × *insignis* pink. The fragrant flowers of ssp. ***sanguinea* 'Flava'** (syn. *B. chlorantha*, *B. rosei*) bloom all summer. They are up to 15 cm (6 in) long, with a larger flared mouth. The hairless leaves are oval or triangular and sharply toothed. It reaches a height and spread of 2 m (6½ ft).

B. suaveolens♀ (syn. *Datura suaveolens*) Night-scented white flowers, up to 30 cm (12 in) long, widening at the flare, are borne from mid to late summer. The oval or elliptic, dull green leaves are 15 cm (6 in) long. HEIGHT & SPREAD 4×3 m (13×10 ft).

B. suaveolens* × *versicolor see *B.* × *insignis*

B. versicolor hort. see *B. arborea*

B. versicolor (syn. *Datura versicolor*) White flowers, sometimes flushed pink or orange with age, up to 40 cm (16 in) long, appear from mid to late summer. Coarse, roughly oval, dull green leaves are 20 cm (8 in) long. HEIGHT & SPREAD 5×3 m (16×10 ft).

CULTIVATION Grow in pots of John Innes No.3. Place in a warm sunny spot in a greenhouse or conservatory or outside during summer. Water freely in spring and summer; sparingly in winter. Remove faded leaves and spent flowers.

PROPAGATION Sow seed under glass in spring. Take semi-ripe cuttings in summer.

PRUNING Cut back hard to the framework of branches during spring.

PESTS AND DISEASES Greenfly, whitefly and red spider mite attack regularly.

Brunfelsia

Solanaceae

Brunfelsia pauciflora 'Macrantha'

Large saucer-shaped flowers bedeck these tender evergreen shrubs. They make good indoor pot plants if pruned annually and are suitable for a heated greenhouse or conservatory. Natives of tropical America, brunfelsias require a minimum night-time temperature of 13°C (55°F).

RECOMMENDED SPECIES AND VARIETIES

B. americana (lady of the night) Flowers, up to 7.5 cm (3 in) across, appear in summer – often starting white but turning creamy yellow. They are fragrant, especially at night. The leaves are up to 10 cm (4 in) long, oval or elliptical in shape and with distinctive slender, pointed ends. HEIGHT & SPREAD 1.2×1 m (4×3 ft) after 5 years, ultimately 4 m (13 ft) tall.

B. pauciflora♀ (syn. *B. calycina*, *B. eximia*) (yesterday-today-and-tomorrow) A spreading shrub with clusters of white-eyed flowers, up to 7.5 cm (3 in) across, that start

▲ *Brunfelsia pauciflora*

purple and fade to almost white. They continue most of the year. The oval leaves, up to 7.5 cm (3 in) long, are dark green and glossy. HEIGHT & SPREAD 1×1 m (3×3 ft) after 5 years, ultimately 3 m (10 ft) tall.

'Macrantha' has larger flowers.

CULTIVATION Grow in soilless compost indoors or in a heated greenhouse or conservatory. Permit plenty of light, but not direct sun. Repot each spring. Water freely and feed regularly in spring and summer. Water sparingly in winter.

PROPAGATION Take semi-ripe cuttings in late summer of wood that has not flowered.

PRUNING Pinch out the growing points regularly to ensure a shapely bush.

PESTS AND DISEASES Mealy bug, whitefly and greenfly appear regularly.

Brunnera

Boraginaceae

Sprays of small blue or white flowers nestle among handsome coarse leaves in spring. These hardy herbaceous perennials make excellent ground cover. They prosper in most situations except dense shade.

RECOMMENDED SPECIES AND VARIETIES

B. macrophylla♀ (syn. *Anchusa myosotidiflora*) Tiny, star-shaped blue flowers are carried on wiry stems. The mid green leaves, up to 15 cm (6 in) long, are oval or roughly heart-shaped. Native to E Europe. HEIGHT & SPREAD 50×60 cm (20×24 in).

'Betty Bowring' has white flowers. **'Dawson's White'** carries white and green variegated foliage and bright blue flowers.

▲ *Brunnera macrophylla* 'Hadspen Cream'

'Hadspen Cream'♀ produces blue flowers and light green leaves splashed with cream. **'Langtrees'** has blue flowers and coarse green leaves, spotted silver at the edges.

CULTIVATION Plant in autumn or spring in any ordinary soil in light dappled shade, although brunneras will tolerate sun provided the soil does not dry out. Water well

▼ *Brunnera macrophylla* 'Langtrees'

in the first season. Remove faded flowerheads and foliage. Avoid disturbing the roots of the variegated plant, *B. macrophylla* 'Dawson's White', as this can encourage green shoots to appear.
PROPAGATION Divide in autumn or sow seed in a coldframe in spring.
PESTS AND DISEASES Usually trouble free.

Brussels sprouts see p. 736
Buckthorn see *Rhamnus*

Buddleja

Buddleiaceae

Buddleja 'Lochinch'

Tiny, profuse nectar-rich flowers, sometimes in globular clusters but mainly in long plumes, provide a long-lasting display in summer. The plumes reach 15-40 cm (6-16 in) long and range in colour through various shades of mauve, purple, white, orange and red. Some are sweetly scented and all attract butterflies. The often downy leaves taper to a point, and are generally 7.5-20 cm (3-8 in) long.

These large deciduous or semi-evergreen shrubs are fast-growing. Some are fully hardy, but there are more tender species that need the protection of a south or west-facing wall in mild areas and an unheated greenhouse in harsher climates. All like full sun and well-drained soil. Most species are native to E Asia.

RECOMMENDED SPECIES AND VARIETIES
B. alternifolia♀ Early summer is the best season for the fragrant, purple-lilac flowers which are borne in numerous small, bead-like bunches along the stem. Long, slightly upright young shoots quickly arch out and give the hardy shrub a graceful, rounded shape. The long, narrow leaves are dull green above with whitish down beneath. The fast-growing, deciduous shrub blooms when it is about 3 years old. It makes a fine weeping tree when trained. HEIGHT & SPREAD 2.4x2.4 m (8x8 ft) after 5 years, ultimately 4 m (13 ft) tall.
B. asiatica♀ Long, lax, slender spikes of very fragrant white flowers appear from late winter to mid spring. The young stems and the underside of the leaves are densely covered in silvery hairs. This semi-evergreen shrub is not hardy and needs a very sheltered position even in southern Britain. HEIGHT & SPREAD 2x2 m (6½x6½ ft) after 5 years, ultimately 3 m (10 ft) tall.
B. crispa The young stems and new leaves of this upright, deciduous shrub are covered in white hairs which give the pointed, pale grey-green leaves a silvery appearance. The terminal panicles of white-centred, lilac flowers that appear from mid to late summer are quite showy and have a pleasant fragrance. This tender plant needs the protection of a south-facing wall even in the south and a cold greenhouse elsewhere. HEIGHT & SPREAD 2x2 m (6½x6½ ft) after 5 years, ultimately 3 m (10 ft) tall.
B. davidii (butterfly bush) Fragrant, pale purple flower spikes are borne from mid summer to early autumn. The pale green leaves, up to 25 cm (10 in) long, are covered in fine hairs. This vigorous grower needs hard pruning if not to become straggly. Although frost hardy, the young shoots can be cut back by early frosts but without permanent harm being done. HEIGHT & SPREAD 3x3 m (10x10 ft) after 5 years, ultimately 5 m (16 ft) tall.

This species is the parent of many fine cultivars which do not usually grow as large, most averaging 2 m (6½ ft) in height and spread, although they can be kept smaller by pruning. **'Black Knight'**♀ has flower plumes of a deep violet. **'Dartmoor'**♀ has magenta flowers. **'Empire Blue'**♀ is a strong grower with orange-centred violet-blue flowers. The leaves of **'Harlequin'** are variegated creamy white, the flowers a deep reddish purple. **'Nanho Blue'** has pale blue flowers. The flowers of var. ***nanhoensis*** **'Alba'** are white. It is not a vigorous grower. One of the best red varieties is **'Royal Red'**♀ whose deep purple-red flowers are produced in plumes up to 50 cm (20 in) long. **'White Bouquet'** has white flowers with a yellow eye and a pleasant fragrance. The best white variety is **'White Profusion'**♀, whose yellow-eyed flowers are produced in abundance.

▲ *Buddleja davidii* 'Dartmoor'

B. fallowiana Long narrow plumes of richly fragrant, pale lavender-blue flowers are borne in late summer and early autumn. The leaves are dark green above with silvery hairs beneath. The stems are also covered in silvery hairs. The multistemmed, rounded, deciduous shrub is tender and needs the protection of a south-facing wall or a cold greenhouse. HEIGHT & SPREAD 2x2 m (6½x6½ ft) after 5 years, also the ultimate size.

▲ *Buddleja davidii* 'White Profusion'

▲ *Buddleja fallowiana* var. *alba*

Buddleja globosa ▲

The flowers of var. ***alba***♀ are pure white with an orange eye.
B. globosa♀ (orange ball tree) Globular clusters of small orange-yellow flowers up to 2 cm (¾ in) across appear in early summer. This rather open semi-evergreen shrub with dark green leaves is large but pruning restricts its size. It is frost hardy but benefits from the protection of a south-facing wall. HEIGHT & SPREAD 2x2 m (6½x6½ ft) after 5 years, ultimately 5 m (16 ft) tall.
B. lindleyana Purple-violet flowers are produced in slender, tapering, curved spikes during mid and late summer. The leaves are pale green and slightly hairy. This deciduous shrub needs protection from frost – the ends of the branches are sometimes cut back by winter frost but new spring growth replaces them. HEIGHT & SPREAD 2x2 m (6½x6½ ft) after 5 years, ultimately 5 m (16 ft) tall.
***B.* 'Lochinch'**♀ Scented spikes of violet-blue flowers with a deep orange centre are produced in late summer. The young leaves have a covering of grey hairs, which is later lost from the top of the matt green leaves. The deciduous shrub is not frost hardy.

▲ *Buddleja lindleyana*

HEIGHT & SPREAD 2x2m (6½x6½ft) after 5 years, also the ultimate size.

***B.* 'Pink Delight'**♀ Long narrow plumes of pink flowers are borne in late summer. Although frost hardy this deciduous plant may have the ends of the branches cut back by the first frosts, but spring growth replaces them. HEIGHT & SPREAD 2x2m (6½x6½ft) after 5 years, ultimately 4m (13ft) tall.

B.* x *weyeriana In mid to late summer grey-yellow or orange-yellow flowers open in globular clusters at the end of the branches on the rounded shrub. It is moderately frost hardy. HEIGHT & SPREAD 2x2m (6½x6½ft) after 5 years, ultimately 3m (10ft) tall.

'Golden Glow' makes a larger plant

▼ *Buddleja* x *weyeriana* 'Golden Glow'

◄ *Buddleja* 'Lochinch'

eventually and has yellow-orange flowers tinged with lilac. **'Sungold'**♀ has deep orange flowers.

CULTIVATION Plant in autumn or spring in any good well-drained garden soil, choosing a position in full sun. Grow less hardy species besides a south-facing wall or in a well-sheltered position. Alternatively, grow in pots of John Innes No.3 and overwinter in an unheated greenhouse or conservatory.

PROPAGATION Take semi-ripe cuttings in mid to late summer or hardwood cuttings from mid autumn to early spring.

PRUNING Prune *B. alternifolia* and *B. globosa* after flowering. Remove a third of the stems of *B. alternifolia*. Cut back the faded flowerheads plus 5-7.5cm (2-3in) of the flowering stems of *B. globosa*. Prune all other species and varieties hard in spring by cutting back all the previous year's growth to within 5-7.5cm (2-3in) of the old wood.

PESTS AND DISEASES Usually trouble free.

Bugbane see *Cimicifuga*
Bugle see *Ajuga*

Bulbocodium

Colchicaceae

Bulbocodium vernum

Starry, funnel-shaped flowers in shades of purple appear from these hardy corms early in the year, growing close to the ground. The leaves emerge with the flowers but only reach their full length after the blooms have finished. The genus consists of just two species, native to alpine meadows in the Pyrenees, Alps and Caucasus. Although fully hardy, plants do not like excessive wet and thrive in sunny rockeries, raised beds and well-drained borders. They also do well in an unheated greenhouse or alpine house.

RECOMMENDED SPECIES

B. vernum Virtually stemless, upright, pinky purple flowers, 4cm (1½in) tall and 2.5-4cm (1-1½in) wide, emerge as early as mid winter in mild regions or in early spring in colder areas. The dark green, arching, grass-like leaves are eventually up to 15cm (6in) long and die back in early or mid summer. HEIGHT 10cm (4in).

CULTIVATION Plant corms during autumn in any well-drained soil, setting them 10cm (4in) deep and 5cm (2in) apart. A sunny site is best but plants tolerate light shade.

PROPAGATION Separate offsets from the corms in summer after the foliage has died

▲ *Bulbocodium vernum*

down. Do this every 3-4 years to maintain vigorous flowering.

PESTS AND DISEASES Usually trouble free.

Buphthalmum

Oxeye

Compositae

Deep yellow, daisy-like flowers, borne on long, slender, upright stems against a mass of loose, dark green foliage appear throughout summer. These hardy herbaceous perennials are most effective in a herbaceous border or a wild garden.

RECOMMENDED SPECIES

B. salicifolium The flowers are solitary and up to 2cm (¾in) across. Both petals and central disc are yellow. The narrow, lance-shaped leaves are about 5cm (2in) long, smooth or slightly hairy. Native to Europe and Asia, where it is found in open wood-

▲ *Buphthalmum salicifolium*

land and the more stony grasslands. HEIGHT & SPREAD 75×45 cm (2½×1½ ft).
B. speciosum see *Telekia speciosa*
CULTIVATION Plant in autumn or spring in full sun or part shade, preferably in poor soil – in fertile soils, plants produce leaves at the expense of flowers and become invasive.
PROPAGATION Divide plants or sow seed in spring or autumn.
PESTS AND DISEASES Usually trouble free.

Burnet see *Sanguisorba*
Burning bush see *Bassia scoparia* f. *tricophylla, Dictamnus*
Bush violet see *Browallia*
Busy lizzie see *Impatiens walleriana*
Butcher's broom see *Ruscus*

Butomus

Flowering rush

Butomaceae

Grown for its twisted, rush-like leaves and loose clusters of pale pink flowers, this deciduous, hardy perennial aquatic is the only species in the genus. Native to temperate Europe and Asia.
Butomus umbellatus♀ The upright, narrow, twisted leaves, 1.5 m (5 ft) long, have tapering tips. Bronze-green when young, they turn mid green. Each upright stem ends with a loose head, pale pink cup-shaped flower, borne from mid summer to

▲ *Butomus umbellatus*

early autumn. Each 3 cm (1¼ in) wide flower has 6 petals around dark red stamens. The reddish fruit appears in autumn. HEIGHT & SPREAD 1.5×1 m (5×3 ft).
CULTIVATION Plant in full sun in any fertile soil in water up to 25 cm (10 in) deep. For strong flowering, divide or replant annually.
PROPAGATION Sow seed in spring in pots standing in 2.5-5 cm (1-2 in) of water. Divide established plants in spring.
PESTS AND DISEASES Aphids can be a problem.

Buttercup see *Ranunculus*
Butterfly bush see *Buddleja davidii*
Butterwort see *Pinguicula*

Buxus

Box

Buxaceae

Buxus sempervirens

Small evergreen leaves, dense growth and tolerance of frequent clipping make box ideal for hedging and topiary. Dwarf parterre hedges are traditionally composed of box. The leaves are 1-3 cm (⅜-1¼ in) long and are opposite, oval and leathery. The flowers are inconspicuous but, in some species, they are scented. In the wild, trees and shrubs usually grow in shady places in woods, but as garden plants they will also tolerate full sun. The deep green glossy foliage contrasts well with bright flowers and gravel paths. Very slow growth and a long lifespan are characteristics of all 70 shrubs and trees in the genus. Most are clipped so that height and spread are rigidly controlled. The smaller plants can be grown in pots and make strong neat features in a formal design.

RECOMMENDED SPECIES AND VARIETIES
B. microphylla A very hardy compact shrub with a dense rounded habit. It has narrow leaves and is widely used for miniature hedges. It may be native to Japan. HEIGHT & SPREAD 40×30 cm (16×12 in) after 5 years, ultimately 1 m (3 ft) tall.
'Compacta' has smaller leaves and grows only 30 cm (12 in) in 30 years.
B. sempervirens♀ (common box) The small, multistemmed tree, a native of Britain, has dark green glossy leaves, broadly oblong with a notch at the apex. It seeds itself freely. It can be clipped as a hedge or free grown. HEIGHT & SPREAD 1.2 m×75 cm (4×2½ ft) after 5 years, ultimately 4 m (13 ft) high.

▲ *Buxus sempervirens*

▲ *Buxus sempervirens* 'Suffruticosa'

▲ *Buxus sempervirens* 'Elegantissima'

'Elegantissima'♀ is a compact bush with variegated cream and green leaves. **'Latifolia Macrophylla'**♀ makes a large spreading bush whose small, broadly ovate leaves are dark green and shiny. **'Latifolia Maculata'** is a dense compact shrub. Its long leaves are blotched with yellow and are most colourful in full sun. **'Suffruticosa'**♀ is a small shrub traditionally used in formal gardens for edging flowerbeds. The ovate leaves are a bright shining green. It is very dense and can be clipped hard every year.
CULTIVATION Plant in autumn or spring in any garden soil in full sun or part shade. For hedges, space plants 25-30 cm (10-12 in) tall at intervals of 30-38 cm (12-15 in). Cut back the upper third of leading shoots after planting or in spring to promote bushy growth.
PROPAGATION Take semi-ripe cuttings in summer. These are usually a by-product of clipping back plants.
PRUNING Clip hedges and topiary 2 or 3 times a year.
PESTS AND DISEASES Leaf deformities caused by sucking insects and fungal brown spots may be a minor nuisance.

C

Cabbage see p. 736
Cabbage gum see *Eucalyptus pauciflora*
Cabbage tree see *Cordyline australis*
Cacti see p. 106

Caladium

Araceae

Brightly patterned foliage makes these tender herbaceous perennials from tropical S America rewarding greenhouse, conservatory or indoor plants. The insignificant white flowers are normally removed to retain high-quality foliage.

RECOMMENDED SPECIES AND VARIETIES

C. bicolor (syn. *C.* × *hortulanum*) (angel's wings) The roughly triangular or heart-shaped leaves are mid green, splashed with white, pink or red and may have coloured veins. The leaves are 15-45 cm (6-18 in) long. HEIGHT & SPREAD 90×75 cm (36×30 in).

'Mrs Arno Nehrling' has white leaves with dark green veins and red ribs. **'Pink Beauty'** has green leaves with pink marbled centres and prominent red ribs.

C.* × *hortulanum see *C. bicolor*

C. lindenii The arrow-shaped leaves are 15-45 cm (6-18 in) long and are dark green with white marked veins. HEIGHT & SPREAD 75×50 cm (30×20 in).

CULTIVATION Plant tubers in potting compost in early spring and keep indoors or under glass at a minimum of 18°C (64°F) and high humidity. Place in partial shade but with enough light to maintain leaf colour. Water regularly in the growing season and feed from mid summer to early autumn. Dry plants off in autumn and overwinter tubers at a minimum of 13°C (55°F).

PROPAGATION Separate small tubers before replanting in spring. Large tubers can be divided into sections during spring.

PESTS AND DISEASES Greenfly, whitefly, red spider mite and mealy bug can attack.

Caladium bicolor

Calamagrostis see GRASSES p. 300

Calamintha

Calamint

Labiatae

Calamintha nepeta

Profuse clusters of tiny flowers, attractive to bees and butterflies, provide a handsome display throughout summer on these aromatic, hardy herbaceous perennials. The two-lipped, tubular flowers are arranged in whorls on loose leafy spikes. The small, toothed mint-like leaves are oval or oblong. *Calamintha cretica* is a good choice for a rock garden and *C. nepeta* is suitable for planting in borders and herb gardens. *C. grandiflora* is best grown along pathways or in dappled shade.

RECOMMENDED SPECIES AND VARIETIES

C. cretica Small white flowers, about 1 cm (⅜ in) long, are carried from early to late summer. The roundish leaves, up to 1.5 cm (½ in) long, are covered with greyish hairs. Native to Crete, this woody-based plant forms a low symmetrical dome. HEIGHT & SPREAD 25×25 cm (10×10 in).

C. grandiflora Pink flowers, up to 4 cm (1½ in) long, appear from early summer to mid autumn. The deep green, aromatic leaves, up to 8 cm (3¼ in) long, are rounded. This woody-based plant forms spreading patches. Native to central and S Europe. HEIGHT & SPREAD 40×45 cm (16×18 in).

'Variegata' has cream-coloured leaves speckled with green.

C. nepeta (syn. *C. nepetoides*, *Satureja calamintha*) (lesser calamint) White, lilac or mauve flowers, 1.5 cm (½ in) long, appear on branching stems from mid summer to early autumn. The oval, greyish green leaves, up to 3 cm (1¼ in) long, are highly aromatic, especially when crushed. This bushy plant self-seeds freely. HEIGHT & SPREAD 50×45 cm (20×18 in).

The flowers of ssp. ***glandulosa* 'White Cloud'** are white and those of ssp. ***nepeta* 'Blue Cloud'** are bluish mauve.

C. nepetoides see *C. nepeta*

CULTIVATION Plant in spring in well-drained, preferably alkaline soil choosing a position in full sun, although *C. grandiflora* prefers dappled shade.

PROPAGATION Sow seed under glass or divide clumps in spring. Take basal cuttings in late spring to early summer.

PESTS AND DISEASES Usually trouble free.

Calamintha grandiflora 'Variegata'

Calamintha nepeta

Calamintha nepeta ssp. *glandulosa* 'White Cloud'

Calandrinia

Portulacaceae

These low-growing, fleshy-leaved plants are grown for their colourful, silky flowers in early and mid summer. These evergreen perennials are not frost hardy and in colder areas should be treated as half-hardy annuals or grown under glass. They also dislike excessive winter wet. The flowers have up to eight broad petals and a mass of stamens; they open in sunshine or bright light, but close in dull weather. The leaves form flat rosettes. Most species are from S America.

RECOMMENDED SPECIES AND VARIETIES

C. caespitosa Creamy flowers are borne singly on short stems, several flowers growing from the centre of each leaf rosette. Each flower is about 1.5 cm (½ in) across. Leaves are grey-green and narrow, broadest towards the tip, and 5 cm (2 in) long. This highly variable species also includes pink, red and orange-flowering varieties. HEIGHT & SPREAD 10×20 cm (4×8 in).

C. umbellata The cup-shaped flowers, 2 cm (¾ in) across, carried in short-stemmed clusters, are a satiny, rich dark red. Flowers bloom from mid to late summer. Each flower blooms for just 2 days. Leaves are grey-green, hairy, linear and up to 4 cm (1½ in) long. The plant's habit varies from sprawling to compact. It can be grown as a biennial outdoors in the warmer parts of Britain. HEIGHT & SPREAD 15×10 cm (6×4 in).

♥ *Calandrinia umbellata*

CULTIVATION Plant in spring in a light sandy soil, in a sunny, sheltered site. Protect plants from winter wet by covering them with a cloche or pane of glass. Alternatively, grow in pots of John Innes No. 1 in a greenhouse or conservatory with a minimum temperature of 5°C (41°F).

PROPAGATION Sow seed in spring under glass at a minimum of 18°C (64°F).

PESTS AND DISEASES Aphids attack emerging leaves in late winter and early spring.

Calathea

Marantaceae

The intricately marked leaves of these tropical evergreen perennials make them ideal houseplants. Their need for soft light, high temperatures and humidity can, however, limit suitable situations. A shaded, warm conservatory or greenhouse or a warm room that does not receive direct sunlight are probably best. Standing plants on gravel trays will improve humidity. Most calatheas have inconspicuous flowers. Native to rainforest floors in S America.

RECOMMENDED SPECIES AND VARIETIES

C. makoyana (peacock plant, cathedral windows) Light green leaves up to 25 cm (10 in) long with darker oval blotches have closely spaced, fine lines radiating from the midrib. Their purple-tinted underside is often visible because the paddle-shaped leaves are held upright on narrow stems. HEIGHT & SPREAD 60×30 cm (2×1 ft).

C. roseopicta Dark stripes stretch out from the midrib to a cream line just short of the edges of the light green leaves of this compact species. The highly patterned leaves are oval, up to 18 cm (7 in) long and carried on short stalks. They tend to lie horizontally. HEIGHT & SPREAD 25×30 cm (10×12 in).

C. zebrina (zebra plant) Vivid, fresh green leaves, up to 45 cm (18 in) long, have regular dark stripes spreading out from the midrib. Their surfaces have a velvety appearance and the underside, a purple hue. The height and spread given is for plants in a conservatory border; those in pots would probably be smaller. HEIGHT & SPREAD 60×30 cm (2×1 ft).

♥ *Calathea makoyana*

♥ *Calathea roseopicta*

CULTIVATION Grow in pots of John Innes No. 2 and keep indoors or under glass at a constant temperature of at least 20°C (68°F) and reasonable humidity during the growing season. Maintain a minimum temperature of 13°C (55°F) in winter. Ensure plants are grown in soft light; direct sun is harmful. Feed little and often. Keep compost moist but not wet and somewhat drier in cooler months. Avoid dry air, draughts and sudden temperature changes. Strongly growing plants form good-sized clumps, which may need annual repotting in spring.

PROPAGATION Divide in spring.

PESTS AND DISEASES Red spider mite can be troublesome.

Calceolaria

Slipper flower, slipperwort

Scrophulariaceae

Calceolaria uniflora

Vividly coloured and unusual pouched flowers are borne by these plants from Central and S America. This genus includes biennials and evergreen perennials and subshrubs that vary in hardiness. There are low-growing hardy perennials that are excellent plants for rock gardens or raised beds and troughs. There are also less hardy calceolarias that can be grown as summer bedding plants or in pots indoors or under glass.

RECOMMENDED SPECIES AND VARIETIES

C. biflora (syn. *C. plantaginea*) Small yellow flowers, up to 2 cm (¾ in) long, appear in clusters in summer. The softly hairy, oval leaves, up to 7.5 cm (3 in) long, are borne in neat basal rosettes. A hardy

♥ *Calceolaria biflora*

C

evergreen perennial. HEIGHT & SPREAD 25×20cm (10×8in).
C. falklandica Pale yellow flowers, speckled with purple in the throat and up to 1.5cm (½in) long, appear in summer. The mid green, oblong, hairy leaves grow to 10cm (4in) long. A hardy evergreen perennial. HEIGHT & SPREAD 25×20cm (10×8in).
C. **Herbeohybrida Group** Red, orange, yellow or white flowers often with darker spots or blotches and up to 8cm (3¼in) long are borne in spring and summer. The oval, mid green, softly hairy leaves are about 10cm (4in) long. A tender bushy biennial commonly grown as a pot plant or for summer bedding. HEIGHT & SPREAD 30×25cm (12×10in).

Anytime Series bears many 5cm (2in) long flowers that bloom at any time of the year just 4 months after sowing. It grows 20cm (8in) tall. **'Jewel Cluster'** has early, spotted flowers and grows to 28cm (11in).
C. integrifolia♀ (syn. *C. rugosa*) Clusters of rounded, bright yellow flowers, 1.5cm (½in) wide, are borne in late summer. The rough, grey-green leaves, up to 10cm (4in) long, are lance-shaped. A half-hardy evergreen sub-shrub, usually grown as annual. HEIGHT & SPREAD 1.2m×60cm (4×2ft).

▲ *Calceolaria integrifolia* var. *angustifolia*

The flower clusters of var. ***angustifolia***♀ are more elongated. **'Sunshine'**♀ bears dense clusters of bright yellow flowers, up to 2.5cm (1in) wide, in mid summer. It reaches a height of 25cm (10in).

▲ *Calceolaria integrifolia* 'Sunshine'

C. plantaginea see *C. biflora*
C. rugosa see *C. integrifolia*
C. tenella Clusters of bright yellow flowers, 1cm (⅜in) across, with a few red marks appearing in summer. This creeping evergreen perennial has oval, mid green, hairy leaves up to 1cm (⅜in) long. Will not withstand prolonged freezing weather. HEIGHT & SPREAD 8×30cm (3¼×12in).
C. uniflora The pendent summer flowers, up to 2.5cm (1in) long, are yellow with brown mottling and a white band on the large lower pouch. This mat-forming, often short-lived, hardy evergreen perennial has many deep green leaf rosettes made up of elliptical shiny leaves up to 4cm (1½in) long. HEIGHT & SPREAD 7.5×20cm (3×8in).
CULTIVATION Plant hardy evergreen perennials in a gritty, humus-rich soil and never allow to dry out. They require a bright position but dislike scorching sun. Plant *C. integrifolia* in a sheltered position in full sun; overwinter under glass and bed out in late spring. Grow *C.* Herbeohybrida Group in pots of John Innes No.2 and keep indoors or in a heated greenhouse or conservatory.
PROPAGATION Sow the seed of hardy evergreen perennials in a coldframe in autumn or early spring or take semi-ripe cuttings in summer. Take softwood cuttings of *C. integrifolia* in late spring or summer. Sow seed of *C. integrifolia* under glass in late winter. Sow seed of *C.* Herbeohybrida Group in gentle heat in spring or late summer; the seed of Anytime Series can be sown at any time except mid summer.
PESTS AND DISEASES Aphids and slugs can be a problem. Grey mould infects old flowers and leaves, especially of the hardy evergreen perennials.

Calendula

Marigold
Compositae

Calendula officinalis

These brightly coloured hardy annuals are easily cultivated, fast growing and long flowering, with blooms that last from late spring to late summer. Flower colours range through yellow, orange and apricot to cream. *Calendula officinalis* and the many varieties developed from it are the only plants of this genus usually grown.
RECOMMENDED SPECIES AND VARIETIES
C. officinalis (pot marigold) Branched stems carry single orange flowers, up to 7cm (2¾in) across, among thick aromatic leaves that are lance-shaped and pale green. HEIGHT & SPREAD 60×60cm (2×2ft).

The flowers of cultivated varieties are semidouble or double. **Art Shades Mixed** has semidouble flowers and reaches a height of 60cm (2ft). The densely branching

▲ *Calendula officinalis*

'Fiesta Gitana'♀ is a dwarf plant usually reaching less than 30cm (12in) tall. It is available in orange or yellow or in mixed colours. **Pacific Beauty Mixed** grows to a height of 60cm (2ft) and has fully double flowers in lemon and orange shades. **'Radio'** has double flowers with orange rolled petals. **'Touch of Red'** grows to a height of 45cm (18in) and is distinguished from other varieties by the red flushing of the oranges, creams and bright yellows contained in the mixture.

▲ *Calendula officinalis* 'Fiesta Gitana'

CULTIVATION Plant in spring in full sun or partial shade in any garden soil, although moist, fertile soil is not desirable since it encourages excessive leaf growth at the expense of flowering. Deadhead regularly.
PROPAGATION Sow seed in mid spring where the plant is to flower. Further sowing in late spring and early summer maintains a succession of flowers. Alternatively, sow seed in an unheated greenhouse from early spring onwards. Harden off and plant out from mid spring.

Calendulas can also be grown as greenhouse pot plants for early flowering. Sow seed in late summer and grow the plants on in 13-18cm (5-7in) pots. Given a minimum temperature of 7°C (45°F), they will flower by early spring.
PESTS AND DISEASES Plants are susceptible to powdery mildew and aphids.

Calico bush see *Kalmia latifolia*
Calico flower see *Aristolochia littoralis*
California lilac see *Ceanothus*

Calla

Bog arum
Araceae

Showy flowers and shiny heart-shaped leaves make this plant ideal for the edge of a pond or a bog garden. A hardy creeping perennial, deciduous or semi-evergreen, the plant grows in wet soil or water up to

15 cm (6 in) deep. There is only one species in the genus. Other plants called callas belong to the genus *Zantedeschia*. Native to N Europe and N America.
Calla palustris Each flower has a papery, white spathe, a leaf-like structure, and a spadix, an upright greenish spike that bears the insignificant true flowers and which emerges from the spathe. The spathe is up to 6 cm (2½ in) across and the spadix 2.5 cm (1 in) tall. They appear in late spring to early summer. The spathe has a greenish flush in spring. Red or deep orange poisonous berries are seen on the spadix in autumn. The dark green leaves are up to 8 cm (3¼ in) long. HEIGHT & SPREAD 25×30 cm (10×12 in).
CULTIVATION Plant in spring, at the edge of a pool in a basket filled with heavy, clay-loam soil or aquatic planting compost. Cover the compost with pea gravel. The plant prefers full sun, but will tolerate a little shade. Feed with aquatic fertiliser in spring.
PROPAGATION Divide adult plants every 2-3 years in spring. Take stem cuttings in spring and root in trays of mud. Sow seed in spring, in trays of mud in a coldframe.
PESTS AND DISEASES Usually trouble free.

Callicarpa

Beauty berry
Verbenaceae

Callicarpa bodinieri var. giraldii 'Profusion'

Eye-catching clusters of jewel-like fruit adorn these deciduous shrubs. Found in vivid shades of purple and white, the berries have a pearly lustre and combine with yellow to purple leaves to provide bold autumn colour. The fruit are just 3 mm (⅛ in) across, and appear in early autumn, often lasting well after leaf-fall. They are preceded by tiny, star-shaped flowers. The oval leaves have pointed tips and toothed edges. Plants need a sunny, sheltered position and may not survive outside where winters are prolonged or severe.
RECOMMENDED SPECIES AND VARIETIES
C. bodinieri Clusters of downy, lilac flowers appear in mid summer and are followed by dense clumps of violet fruit. Covered in fine hairs at first, the leaves become smooth and are 5-12 cm (2-4¾ in) long. HEIGHT & SPREAD 2×2 m (6½×6½ ft) after 5 years, ultimately 3 m (10 ft) tall.

The flowers of var. ***giraldii*** are less downy. **'Profusion'**♀ has pink flowers and bronzed, purple spring leaves that turn green in summer before turning purplish again in autumn. It reaches a height of 2 m (6½ ft) and a spread of 1.2 m (4 ft).

▲ *Callicarpa bodinieri* var. *giraldii*

C. japonica **'Leucocarpa'** The white, late-summer flowers are followed by white fruit. The hairless leaves are 7-12 cm (2¾-4¾ in) long. This species is slightly less hardy than *C. bodinieri*. HEIGHT & SPREAD 1.5×1.5 m (5×5 ft) after 5 years (also its ultimate size).
CULTIVATION Plant in autumn or spring in a sunny, sheltered spot in fertile, well-drained loam. Plant in groups to ensure cross-pollination and, therefore, numerous fruit. Mulch plants in late autumn.
PROPAGATION Take semi-ripe heeled cuttings or raise natural varieties from seed.
PRUNING Cut back old and damaged wood and straggly branches in spring, just after new growth commences.
PESTS AND DISEASES Usually trouble free.

Callistemon

Bottlebrush
Myrtaceae

Callistemon citrinus 'Splendens'

Minute flowers with long, colourful stamens form bold tufted spikes on these sun-loving, evergreen shrubs or small trees in summer. The cylindrical flowerheads are mostly in shades of yellow and red and measure 5-10 cm (2-4 in) long. The rather leathery leaves, up to 12 cm (4¾ in) long, are narrow and pointed. Of those recommended only *Callistemon salignus* is reasonably hardy and even this needs a sheltered site in colder areas. Others are suitable only for sheltered warm gardens or greenhouses and conservatories. Those grown outside need acid soil. Native to Australia.
RECOMMENDED SPECIES AND VARIETIES
C. citrinus Profuse flower spikes, usually with bright crimson stamens appear in early to mid summer. The grey-green leaves are hairy when young. This shrub is hardy only in mild areas and in a sheltered site. It makes an excellent greenhouse or conservatory plant. HEIGHT & SPREAD 2×2 m (6½×6½ ft) after 5 years, ultimately 5 m (16 ft) tall.

▲ *Callistemon citrinus*

'Splendens'♀ has scarlet flowers and grows to a height and spread of 2 m (6½ ft).
C. linearis♀ Red flower spikes appear from late spring to autumn. The linear leaves are dark green. This shrub is hardy only in mild, sheltered gardens. HEIGHT & SPREAD 1.8×1.8 m (6×6 ft) after 5 years, ultimately 3 m (10 ft) tall.
C. salignus♀ The willow-like leaves are reddish while young, becoming grey-green. Pale yellow flower spikes are carried in early summer. This fairly hardy shrub or small tree withstands all but the coldest winters. HEIGHT & SPREAD 3×2 m (10×6½ ft) after 5 years, ultimately 10 m (33 ft).
C. viminalis **'Captain Cook'**♀ A low-growing shrub with spreading to weeping branches. Large red flower spikes are produced abundantly from spring to summer. The leaves are mid green. It is suitable only for frost-free gardens or growing under glass. HEIGHT & SPREAD 1.2×1.2 m (4×4 ft) after 5 years, ultimately 2 m (6½ ft) tall.
CULTIVATION Outdoors, plant in spring in moist but well-drained, preferably acid, soil. Choose a sheltered position in full sun. Alternatively, grow in pots of John Innes No. 2 and keep in a frost-free greenhouse or conservatory in good light.
PROPAGATION Take semi-ripe cuttings in summer or sow seed under glass in early summer and keep the compost moist.
PRUNING None normally required but can be cut back in summer to produce more compact plants.
PESTS AND DISEASES Usually trouble free.

▼ *Callistemon viminalis* 'Captain Cook'

CACTI

Nature's tough survivors

UNUSUAL SHAPES AND OFTEN DAZZLING FLOWERS MAKE CACTI FASCINATING AND REWARDING PLANTS TO GROW INDOORS AND IN A GREENHOUSE

With forms that range from tall and statuesque columns to cushions or dangling tentacles, cacti make original sculptural plants for the house, conservatory or greenhouse.

Belonging to the Cactaceae family, cacti are succulents and have fleshy stems. They are distinguished from other succulents by their areoles, the pad-like shoots from which flowers, new growth, wool and spines develop.

Most cacti have spines, which can be straight, curved or hooked, long or short, stout and sharp or hair-like. The central spines emerge from the middle of the areole and are usually stronger and larger than the radial spines, which rise from the outer part.

▲ DESERT GARDEN Echinopsis *and* Echinocactus *make a fine display with other succulents.*

Although most cacti flower regularly, those that grow very large in the wild are unlikely to bloom when cultivated. The flowers are generally unstalked and funnel-shaped and may be any colour but blue. They are usually unscented but some of those that bloom at night emit a powerful scent to attract pollinating bats and moths. Small fleshy fruits develop after flowering; these appear on only a few cultivated species.

Cacti are native to the Americas, except for *Rhipsalis baccifera*, a species mainly from Sri Lanka and humid parts of Africa. None of the recommended plants are hardy. There are two distinct types of cacti: desert cacti and rain-forest cacti.

RECOMMENDED PLANTS

DESERT CACTI

Most cacti are desert plants and cope with extreme heat and drought by storing moisture in fleshy stems, roots or leaves. The stems are often globular or columnar and usually have vertical ribs, which enable the cactus to expand as it gains moisture and contract as it dries. The areoles may be mounted along the ribs, on conical or pyramidal protrusions, called tubercles, or over the surface of the stems.

Acanthocalycium

Closely related to *Echinopsis*, these plants are distinguished by the sharp scales that grow on the flower tubes.

A. spiniflorum (syn. *Echinopsis spiniflora*) This globular or cylindrical yellow-green cactus has sharp ribs and yellow or brown spines with dark tips. After 3-5 years, mauve, pink or white trumpet-shaped flowers, 4-5 cm (1½-2 in) across, appear in summer. HEIGHT & SPREAD 10×8 cm (4×3¼ in) in 5 years.

▲ *Acanthocalycium spiniflorum*

Aporocactus

Plants in this genus can be epiphytic, an unusual form for desert cacti.

A. flagelliformis The slender, bright green, pendulous stems are ribbed and covered with short yellow-brown spines. In spring, pink trumpet-shaped flowers, which are 5-8 cm (2-3¼ in) long, appear along the stems. They are followed by small red berries. The plant suits a hanging basket but its fast-growing stems may need cutting back regularly. HEIGHT & SPREAD 70×40 cm (28×16 in) after 5 years.

▲ *Aporocactus flagelliformis*

Astrophytum

The globular bodies of plants in this genus are divided by a small number of ribs into wide segments, rather like an orange. The cacti are slow-growing and become elongated with age.

A. myriostigma♀ (bishop's cap) The grey-green body of this cacti is covered with small woolly scales and has no spines. After 4 years, funnel-shaped bright yellow flowers are borne in spring and summer. They are 5 cm (2 in) across and grow close to the centre of the plant. HEIGHT & SPREAD 6×6 cm (2½×2½ in) after 5 years.

▲ *Astrophytum myriostigma*

Cephalocereus

Tall, and slow-growing, these columnar plants are hairy and rarely branch.

C. senilis (old man cactus) Long white hairs grow in tangles from the areoles, obscuring the ribs and spines. In cultivation, the plant is unlikely to bear flowers. To encourage a shaggy look, position the cactus in a window or greenhouse where it receives plenty of sunshine. To keep the hair white, clean occasionally with a warm detergent solution, using a soft

▼ *Cephalocereus senilis*

brush, and rinse with water. Keep the potting mixture covered to avoid soaking it with water. HEIGHT & SPREAD 10×5 cm (4×2 in) after 5 years.

Echinocactus

The spherical to shortly columnar plants of this genus have prominent ribs and attractive spines. Their crowns, sparsely covered in wool, bear rings of yellow or pink flowers when the plants are mature.

E. grusonii (golden barrel, mother-in-law's seat) The barrel-shaped, mid green body of this slow-growing cactus has

▲ *Echinocactus grusonii*

sharp ribs covered in distinctive golden spines. After 30 years, the diameter of the plant reaches 38 cm (15 in) and it produces small, golden, cup-shaped flowers in summer. HEIGHT & SPREAD 12×10 cm (4¾×4 in) after 5 years.

Echinopsis

After 3 years, these ribbed, globular to columnar plants, commonly known as sea-urchin cacti, produce beautiful flowers of various colours.

E. chamaecereus (peanut cactus) Branching readily, the plant forms a cluster of small,

▲ *Echinopsis chamaecereus*

slender, spreading stems that are pale green and have short white spines. During late spring and early summer, scarlet funnel-shaped flowers, 3 cm (1¼ in) long, appear along the sides of the stems. HEIGHT & SPREAD 10×20 cm (4×8 in) after 5 years.

E. oxygona Globular at first, this cactus becomes elongated with age and can form clusters.

▲ *Echinopsis oxygona*

Dark brown spines cover the mid green body. After 3-4 years, fragrant, pink, trumpet-shaped flowers, 17-25 cm (6¾×10 in) long, appear on the crown in summer. Opening at dusk, they wilt the next afternoon. To promote flowering, remove the offsets in the plant's early years. HEIGHT & SPREAD 10×8 cm (4×3¼ in) after 5 years.

E. spiniflora see *Acanthocalycium spiniflorum*

Espostoa

After 10 years, these cacti produce beards, called pseudocephalia. The beard grows on one side of the upper part of the ribbed columnar stem.

▲ *Espostoa lanata*

E. lanata (Peruvian old man cactus) Fine, radial spines clothe this cactus in a white wool, through which long red-tipped central spines protrude. At 10 years or more, plants may form side branches low down on the main stem. HEIGHT & SPREAD 10×5 cm (4×2 in) after 5 years.

Ferocactus

Commonly known as barrel cacti, plants in this genus have dramatic, curved spines and rounded shapes.

F. latispinus (crow's claw) Straw-coloured radial spines surround red central spines, the lowest of which is broad and fiercely hooked. The round or

▲ *Ferocactus latispinus*

barrel-shaped, grey-green body has prominent ribs. After 10-15 years, white, pink or purple, funnel-shaped flowers, 3 cm (1¼ in) long, appear close to the centre of the crown in spring or autumn. HEIGHT & SPREAD 5×10 cm (2×4 in) after 5 years.

Mammillaria

Plants of this genus, which is the largest in the cactus family, are known as pincushion cacti. They are mainly small, often clump-forming and flower reliably, producing small, funnel-shaped blooms. The areoles are mounted on tubercles.

M. bocasana♡ (snowball cactus) The blue-green globular body of this small, clump-forming cactus is covered in fine, white, radial spines which are clustered in groups on each tubercle. The central spines are red-brown and hooked at their tips. The flowers, which are 1.5 cm (½ in) long, are borne in a ring in late spring and summer. The petals are yellow to white, with a pink or brownish stripe running down the centre. They are followed by long red berries. HEIGHT & SPREAD 6×6 cm (2½×2½ in) in 5 years.

▲ *Mammillaria bombycina*

M. bombycina♡ The cylindrical green body of this clustering plant is swathed in fine, white down, through which yellow, red or brown hooked spines protrude. When the cactus is 4-5 years old, light carmine to pink flowers, up to 1.5 cm (½ in) in length, appear in a ring round the crown during late spring and summer. It has red or pink berries. HEIGHT & SPREAD 10×10 cm (4×4 in) in 5 years.

M. plumosa♡ This species forms a low cushion covered in fine and feathery, white radial spines. Off-white flowers, up to 1.5 cm (½ in) in length, are borne from mid autumn to

▲ *Mammillaria plumosa*

early spring, as long as the temperature remains above 5°C (41°F). If the temperature falls below this, the flowers will open in spring. HEIGHT & SPREAD 10×10 cm (4×4 in).

M. zeilmanniana♡ After 1 or 2 years, many pink to carmine blooms, which are up to 2 cm (¾ in) long, are borne in spring. This globular or oval, dark green plant may form clusters. White and frequently hair-like radial spines surround the

▲ *Mammillaria zeilmanniana*

stouter, brownish, hooked central spines. HEIGHT & SPREAD 10×17cm (4×6¾in) in 5 years.

Notocactus see *Parodia*

Opuntia

Plants in this large genus usually have jointed stems, comprising cylindrical or flattened pads. Areoles are scattered over the stem surfaces and have fine barbed bristles, called glochids. Most species also have spines.

O. basilaris The grey-green stems have egg-shaped to round segments, 10-20cm (4-8in) long. They may appear velvety and are often red around the areoles. The glochids are reddish-brown. Purple to red, bowl-shaped flowers, which are 5-8cm (2-3¼in) wide, appear from late spring to early autumn. HEIGHT & SPREAD 30×30cm (12×12in) in 5 years.

▲ *Opuntia basilaris*

O. cylindrica The bright green columnar stem has diamond-shaped tubercles, and white spines and glochids. The plant, which rarely flowers, will form branches if the top of a stem is cut off. Small cylindrical leaves appear briefly on the stem ends. HEIGHT & SPREAD 30×20cm (12×8in) in 5 years.

O. microdasys (teddy-bear cactus, bunny's ears) Velvety, pale yellow glochids, which are particularly fine and sharp, grow from the closely spaced areoles. Mid green pads are 8-15cm (3¼-6in) long and round to oval in outline. The pale yellow, bowl-shaped flowers are produced rarely. They are 4-5cm (1½-2in) wide and appear in spring and summer. HEIGHT & SPREAD 40×30cm (16×12in) in 5 years.

▲ *Opuntia microdasys*

Parodia

These low-growing, ribbed or tuberculate cacti have dense spines and many flower readily.

▲ *Parodia haselbergii*

P. haselbergii (syn. *Notocactus haselbergii*) This grey-green globular cactus has clusters of glossy white spines. In spring and summer, orange-red, funnel-shaped blooms, which are 1-1.5cm (⅜-½in) long, appear on the bristly crown. HEIGHT & SPREAD 6×6cm (2½×2½in) after 5 years.

P. leninghausii (syn. *Notocactus leninghausii*) (golden ball cactus, Goldfinger) The crown of this short pale green columnar plant slopes towards the sun. The bristly spines are golden yellow and up to 4cm (1½in) long. After 5-10 years, bright yellow, funnel-shaped flowers, which are up to 3cm (1¼in) long, are produced from the centre of the crown during the summer. HEIGHT & SPREAD 12×8cm (4¾×3¼in) in 5 years.

▲ *Parodia leninghausii*

P. mammulosa (syn. *Notocactus mammulosus*) The dark green globular body of this fast-growing cactus is often flat on top with a woolly crown. The radial spines are creamy white and the longer central spines are brown to grey. The yellow, funnel-shaped flowers, 4-6cm (1½-2½in) across, have eye-catching red stigmas and appear during spring and summer. HEIGHT & SPREAD 8×8cm (3¼×3¼in) in 5 years.

Rebutia

Cacti of this genus are usually the first to flower in spring.

▲ *Rebutia minuscula*

R. minuscula Orange or red, funnel-shaped blooms, 3cm (1¼in) long, are borne in spring and early summer. They grow from the lower parts of globular dark green, tuberculate stems, which form clusters. Short white radials surround brown-tipped central spines, 5mm (¼in) long. HEIGHT & SPREAD 4×4cm (1½×1½in) in 5 years.

Growing Desert Cacti

CULTIVATION Desert cacti need plenty of sunlight and some heat in winter. A well-ventilated cool greenhouse is an ideal site, but they can also be grown indoors on windowsills. If the light is one-sided, turn the cacti regularly to prevent distorted growth.

Use a good, well-drained compost, such as John Innes No.2. During growth, water plants generously, barely allowing the surface of the compost to dry out between waterings. Use rainwater if possible, or cooled boiled water, as hard tapwater can prevent nutrient uptake. Apply a cactus feed with every second watering. In early autumn, water less frequently until by mid autumn the compost is dry.

Allow cacti to become dormant by overwintering them in a cool greenhouse, an enclosed porch or unheated spare room, leaving them unwatered. If the temperature is above 10°C (50°F) they should be watered very sparingly. In spring, mist dormant plants and start light watering a week later.

Repot cacti in spring, at least every two years. Wear thick gloves or fold newspaper round the body to protect your hands from the spines. Sprinkle a layer of fine pea gravel or granite chippings on the top of the compost to help to distribute water evenly. Water plants lightly after potting.

PROPAGATION Take cuttings of branching or segmented cacti by removing a branch or segment at the joint with a sharp knife. On non-branching or columnar cacti, cut a section at least 5cm (2in) long cleanly from the top of the plant. Although this will spoil the plant's appearance, new shoots eventually sprout from the scar and may in turn be taken as cuttings. To propagate clustering cacti, such as *Echinopsis* and *Mammillaria*, cut off the offsets with a sharp knife.

Leave the fresh cuttings in a warm, dry place until the wounds harden. Then stand the cuttings upright in small pots, half-filled with compost and covered with a thin layer of fine grit. Top the pots up to the rim with grit. Large cuttings may need staking.

Offsets of some cacti, including *Echinopsis oxygona*, produce roots while still attached to the parent. These offsets are easily detached and the wounds tend to dry quickly.

All cacti can be propagated from seed. Fill pots that are at least 5cm (2in) in diameter with finely sieved John Innes seed compost. Scatter the seeds on top of the compost and stand the pot in water until the surface of the compost appears moist. Add a fungicide to the water to reduce the risk of damping-off. Then sprinkle a thin layer of fine grit over the compost. Place the pot in a propagator or cover it with a clear plastic bag and leave it in light shade, maintaining a temperature between 19°C (66°F) and 25°C (77°F) until the seeds germinate, usually within 2-3 weeks.

One year after germination, remove the pot from the propagator or plastic bag and place it in a bright position, such as a windowsill or greenhouse, but out of direct sunlight. Prick out seedlings when they become crowded, handling them carefully to avoid damage to roots.

PESTS AND DISEASES Desert cacti are prone to fungal diseases and rots caused by excessive watering, humidity or poorly drained compost. Prevention by good culture is important as these diseases are difficult to eradicate. If plants are affected, apply a systemic fungicide.

Mealy bugs may be a problem. Counter attacks by brushing adult insects with surgical spirit, using a small paint brush, or apply a systemic insecticide. Root mealy bugs and red spider mites can also affect cacti.

RAIN-FOREST CACTI

Most rain-forest cacti are epiphytes, living in pockets of leaf-mould in hollows of trees and other large plants. Their stems are designed to help the plant to absorb the maximum amount of light. They are jointed with flattened segments or are long, trailing growths that are flattened or cylindrical. The areoles are sited in notches along the edges of the stems and are naked or have small bristles. Some of the largest of all cactus flowers are produced by rain-forest cacti, some of which bloom in mid winter. They are good plants for hanging baskets.

Disocactus

Plants of this genus are known as orchid cacti because of their large, showy flowers. Their mid green main stems are cylindrical and the side stems are flattened.

D. nelsonii♀ This freely branching plant has pendent, slightly toothed side stems.

▲ *Disocactus nelsonii*

Its purple-pink, funnel-shaped flowers appear in spring and early summer. HEIGHT & SPREAD 60×30cm (2×1ft) in 5 years.

There are many disocactus hybrids, which are similar in appearance to *D. nelsonii.* **'Fortuna'** has salmon-pink flowers; those of **'Ignescens'** are fiery red; **'J.T. Barber'** has pale orange blooms; and **'Reward'** flowers have yellow-white inner petals and deeper yellow outer petals.

Epiphyllum

These cacti have luxuriant flowers, and flattened, leaf-like stems with a trailing habit. Spines are almost non-existent.

▲ *Epiphyllum anguliger*

E. anguliger (fishbone cactus) Scented, white or cream funnel-shaped flowers, which are 15cm (6in) long, are borne in late spring and summer on flattened, deeply notched, mid green stems. HEIGHT & SPREAD 70×45cm (28×18in)

Rhipsalis

The pendulous stems of these cacti can be rounded, thin and interlacing; rounded and segmented; or flat and strap-like.

R. pilocarpa Slender, rounded, segmented stems are dark green, tinged with purple and clothed in fine white spines. When the stems reach between 12cm (4¾in) and 15cm (6in) in length, they branch profusely. Small, pink-white or cream-coloured flowers are borne near the stem tips between autumn

▲ *Rhipsalis pilocarpa*

and spring. The bright red fruits are covered in pale bristles. HEIGHT & SPREAD 20×20cm (8×8in) after 5 years.

Schlumbergera

These reliably flowering, spineless cacti provide bright flushes of pink, red or orange flowers in winter, hence their common name of Christmas cacti. The mid to deep green stems are composed of short, leaf-like segments, which are up to 4cm (1½in) long and 3cm (1¼in) wide. The ruffled, trumpet-shaped flowers last for up to a week or more. Most cultivated schlumbergeras are hybrids or cultivars. The cacti grow to 15cm (6in) in 5 years.

'Firecracker' has bright red flowers; **'Gold Charm'** has pale orange blooms that are tinged maroon; and those of **'Lilac Beauty'** are pale lilac with deeper petal tips and edges.

▲ *Schlumbergera* **'Lilac Beauty'**

GROWING RAIN-FOREST CACTI

CULTIVATION Rain-forest cacti are best grown in a warm greenhouse but can also be grown on a sunny indoor windowsill. They require a well-aerated and moisture-retentive compost – an ericaceous compost is best. They need high humidity. Mist them daily, preferably with rainwater to avoid spotting the stems and damp down the floor of a warm greenhouse. In summer the plants benefit from being moved outside to a sheltered position in filtered sunlight. Water epiphytic cacti all year round, but allow the compost to dry out between waterings. In autumn, bring the plants back into the house and position them away from direct sunlight in a minimum temperature of 12°C (54°F). Water sparingly until mid winter to ensure flower buds develop.

PROPAGATION Rain-forest cacti are propagated by seed. Some, including all the recommended plants, can also be propagated from cuttings taken from segments or branches. (See facing page.)

PESTS AND DISEASES Mealy bugs are the main pest.

▲ JUNGLE FLOWERS *Epiphytic* Disocactus *hybrids produce a profusion of magnificent blooms.*

C

Callistephus

China aster
Compositae

Daisy-like flowers in bright colours, long-lasting when cut, have established this annual as a favourite. The single species flowers from late summer to early autumn, later than many other bedding plants. For cut flowers, grow taller varieties, in a mixed border. Smaller varieties make good bedding or container plants. Native to China.

Callistephus chinensis The varieties of this almost hardy annual have replaced the species in general cultivation. The species has single flowers, white to violet, with yellow centres. The flowers, very freely produced, are borne singly on branching, leafy stems. The leaves, arranged alternately on the stems, are dark green, oval, toothed, slightly hairy and up to 8 cm (3¼ in) long. HEIGHT & SPREAD 80×40 cm (32×16 in).

The listed varieties are in mixed colours and double-flowered, unless stated otherwise. Varieties sold as seed of mixed colours usually include the colours blue, purple, lavender, pink, red, cream and white. Flowers are 4-12 cm (1½-4¾ in) wide.

TALLER VARIETIES

'Andrella' has single flowers and reaches a height of 75 cm (30 in). **'Duchess'**, with large chrysanthemum-like flowers, the petals curving inwards, and **'Ostrich Plume'**, with long, feathery petals that curve backwards, are both 60 cm (24 in) tall. **'Matsumoto'** with many tightly formed flowers, grows to a height of 75 cm (30 in).

SHORTER VARIETIES

Plants 40-45cm (16-18 in) tall, spreading to 30 cm (12 in), are primarily valuable as garden plants, but still have stems long enough for cut flowers. **'All Change Blue'** has dark blue flowers and **'All Change Red'** has red flowers, both with white tips to the petals. The cultivar **'Pompon Mixed'** has button-like flowers.

DWARF VARIETIES

Choose these cultivars – which grow to no more than 40 cm (16 in) tall and spread to about 30 cm (12 in) – for beds, containers or the front of a border. **'Dwarf Comet'** is an upright plant, up to 20 cm (8 in) tall, which blooms a few weeks earlier than other cultivars. **'Lilliput'** has button-like pompon flowers and grows to 30-40 cm (12-16 in) tall. **'Milady'**, to 30 cm (12 in) tall, bears flowers with incurving petals. **'Pinocchio'**, up to 20 cm (8 in) tall, has a compact, round habit. **'Teisa Stars'** has quilled petals and an ultimate height of 25 cm (10 in).

▼ *Callistephus chinensis* 'Dwarf Comet'

▲ *Callistephus chinensis* 'Milady'

CULTIVATION Plant in reasonably fertile soil in a sheltered, sunny spot, as soon as all risk of hard frosts has passed. Deadhead regularly to maintain the production of new flowers. Support taller varieties.

PROPAGATION Sow seed in early spring at 10°C (50°F), hardening the plants off before planting out.

PESTS AND DISEASES Aphids attack young plants. The soil-borne disease callistephus wilt is a problem. Do not replant China asters on soil known to be infected for at least 8 years, except for resistant varieties such as *C. chinensis* 'Ostrich Plume'.

Calluna

Heather, Scots heather, ling
Ericaceae

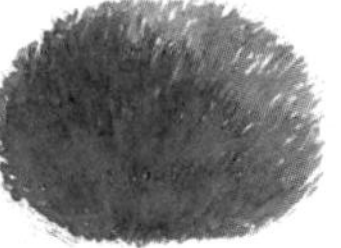

Calluna vulgaris 'Foxii Nana'

Their hardy, evergreen nature and ability to provide colour throughout the year have made the many varieties of *Calluna vulgaris*, the only species in the genus, important garden plants. They are particularly useful for gardens with acid soil, where they can be grown as specimen plants, as ground cover or, if small enough, in a rock garden. They can be difficult to establish in areas prone to drought, however, and will not tolerate limy soil.

Calluna vulgaris Varieties vary a great deal in habit of growth, ranging from prostrate plants only 5 cm (2 in) high to erect plants that grow as tall as 65 cm (26 in).

The tiny leaves, about 3 mm (⅛ in) long, are linear, slightly fleshy and closely overlapping. They range in colour from bright to dark green to grey, and are sometimes gold or red. The white to crimson flowers are usually held in crowded flower spikes up to 30 cm (12 in) long. Each flower is normally single with 4 oblong petals, 3 mm (⅛ in) long, concealed by 4 slightly larger, coloured sepals. There are some varieties with double flowers and some where the buds colour as in a normal plant but never open; these 2 kinds tend to flower late in the season.

Heather is widely distributed across W Europe, from Norway and Iceland to S Spain and Morocco. It has also become naturalised in E Canada, from seed contained in packing material used by early settlers. Varieties native to northern regions of Europe flower in Britain from early to late summer, while those from more southerly areas of Europe flower in Britain from late summer to late autumn.

RECOMMENDED VARIETIES

C. vulgaris has hundreds of named varieties. Those listed below are divided into 3 groups – low-growing, medium and tall. Unless stated otherwise, they are upright plants with dark green foliage and single mauve or lavender flowers that bloom between late summer and mid autumn. The heights and spreads given here are for 5 to 7-year-old plants that have been regularly trimmed after flowering.

LOW-GROWING VARIETIES

Unless stated otherwise, low-growing varieties grow to 15-25 cm (6-10 in) tall, with a spread of 30-50 cm (12-20 in).

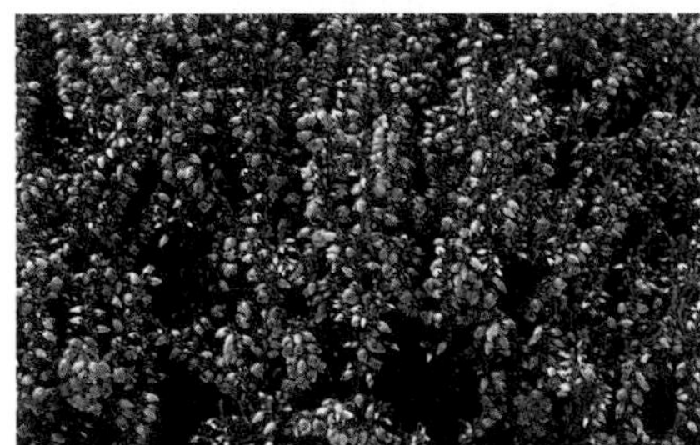

▲ *Calluna vulgaris* 'County Wicklow'

'County Wicklow'♀ has large double shell-pink flowers and mid green foliage with a compact, semi-prostrate habit. **'Cuprea'**, with distinctive copper-coloured foliage in summer, turns a warm bronze in winter. It spreads only to 25 cm (10 in).

Calluna vulgaris 'Dark Beauty'

'Dark Beauty' is a neat and compact plant, producing semidouble blood-red flowers turning purple-red with age. **'Darkness'**♀ is compact with masses of crimson flowers. **'Dark Star'**♀ bears bright, semidouble crimson flowers. **'Drum-ra'** produces white flowers in profusion and has light green foliage. **'Foxii Nana'**, with a poor show of flowers, is grown for its bright green dwarf 'pin-cushion' habit, making it very suitable for growing in troughs.

'Inshriach Bronze' has acid yellow foliage in spring, which turns a rich gold in summer and to bronze in winter. **'J.H. Hamilton'**♀ produces double deep pink flowers and its dwarf habit to just 10cm (4in) tall with a spread of 25cm (10in) makes it suitable for troughs. **'Jan Dekker'** has downy grey foliage and a semi-prostrate habit. **'Jimmy Dyce'**♀ bears double lilac-pink flowers from early to late autumn. It has a semi-prostrate habit. **'John F. Letts'** is a very low-growing form, to just 10cm (4in) tall with a spread of 25cm (10in). It has gold foliage in summer, which turns bronze in autumn and then red and orange in winter.

▲ *Calluna vulgaris* 'Inshriach Bronze'
Calluna vulgaris 'Kinlochruel' ▲

Kinlochruel'♀ carries pure white double flowers against bright green foliage which bronzes in winter. **'Mrs Pat'** produces pink new growth which persists for most of the year. **'Mullion'**♀, with lilac-pink flowers, is spreading and suitable for troughs. **'Multicolor'** has copper foliage frequently flecked with brilliant shades of orange and red for most of the year. Its dwarf habit to just 10cm (4in) tall with a spread of 25cm (10in) makes it ideal for troughs. **'Nana Compacta'** has bright green foliage forming a neat 'pincushion'.

'Radnor'♀ produces a neat hummock of double shell-pink flowers. **'Red Carpet'** is chiefly grown for its intense orange and red winter foliage which turns gold in summer. It has a semi-prostrate habit. **'Robert Chapman'**♀ spreads to 65cm (26in) and has gold foliage in summer, orange in autumn and red in winter and spring. **'Roland Haagen'**♀ is chiefly grown for its compact habit and golden yellow foliage which turns bright orange in winter.

'Sir John Charrington'♀ has deep lilac-pink flowers set against gold foliage which deepens to red in winter. **'Sister Anne'**♀ has grey-green summer foliage that

▲ *Calluna vulgaris* 'Sister Anne'

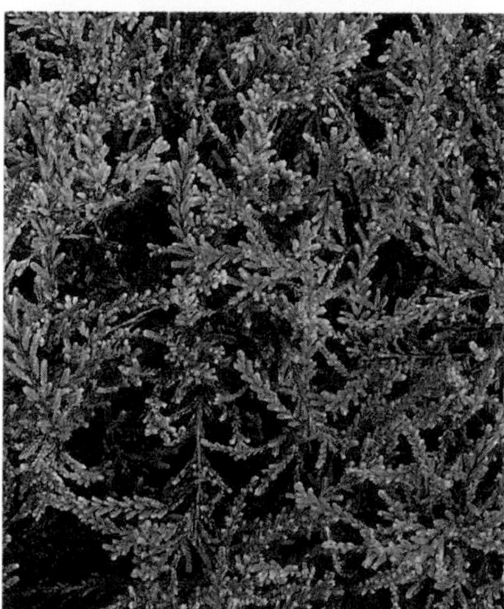

▲ *Calluna vulgaris* 'Sunset'

▲ *Calluna vulgaris* 'White Lawn'

turns a dull bronze in winter. It is just 10cm (4in) tall with a spread of 25cm (10in), making it suitable for troughs. **'Sunset'**♀ bears lilac-pink flowers against gold foliage that deepens to red in autumn and winter. It has a spreading habit. **'White Lawn'**♀, with its prostrate trailing habit, is ideal for rockeries and troughs. It has white flowers amid clear green foliage. It grows to just 5cm (2in) high. **'Winter Chocolate'** is broad and low with golden foliage whose pink summer tips turn bronze in winter. The new spring growth is salmon-pink.

MEDIUM-SIZED VARIETIES

Unless stated otherwise, medium-sized varieties reach 30-35cm (12-14in) tall with a spread of 40-50cm (16-20in).

'Alexandra' produces long spikes of magenta bud flowers from late summer to early winter; they are suitable for fresh or dried flower arrangements. **'Beoley Gold'**♀ has yellow foliage throughout the year and produces white flowers. **'Blazeaway'** spreads to 60cm (24in) and has gold foliage in summer which turns orange then fiery red in winter. **'Boskoop'** has rich gold foliage in summer turning orange with red tints in winter. **'Flamingo'** is chiefly grown for its pinkish red new growth in spring.

'Gold Haze'♀ has white flowers and pale yellow foliage throughout the year. **'H.E. Beale'** bears long spikes of double shell-pink flowers suitable for cutting. **'Hammondii Aureifolia'** produces white flowers against foliage that is light green tipped with yellow in spring and early summer. **'Joy Vanstone'**♀ has straw-coloured foliage in summer, which turns orange in winter.

'Kerstin' has downy, deep lilac-grey foliage in winter, colourfully tipped pale yellow and red in spring. **'Marleen'** carries white buds with purple tips which do not open but persist late into the season. **'Orange Queen'**♀ has orange winter foliage that turns gold in summer. **'Peter Sparkes'** spreads to 55cm (22in); it has long spikes of double rose-pink flowers, good as cut flowers, late in the season.

'Schurig's Sensation', with long spikes of dark pink double flowers, spreads to 55cm (22in). **'Serlei Aurea'**♀ bears white flowers on dense greenish yellow foliage tipped yellow in summer and autumn. **'Spring Cream'**♀ bears white flowers on mid green foliage, which has cream tips in spring, and makes a neat compact plant. **'Tib'**♀ has double mauve-pink flowers, from mid summer to mid autumn, but is a rather straggly plant. **'Underwoodii'**♀ produces lilac-pink buds, creating a late display of colour which turns silvery white and lasts well into winter. It spreads to 55cm (22in).

TALL VARIETIES

Unless stated otherwise, tall varieties reach 40-50cm (16-20in) tall with a spread of 50-70 (20-28in).

'Allegro'♀ has ruby flowers, and is vigorous but neat. **'Annemarie'**♀ bears outstanding double rose-pink flowers which are valued for cutting. **'Anthony Davis'**♀ produces long spikes of white flowers, suitable for cutting, against green-grey foliage. **'Battle of Arnhem'**♀ reaches 65cm (26in) tall. It has gunmetal-coloured buds opening to lilac-pink flowers composed of many bracts. It flowers from early to mid winter.

'Elsie Purnell'♀ carries long spikes of double lavender flowers, valuable for cutting, with grey-green foliage spreading to 75cm (30in). **'Finale'**♀ bears its amethyst

▲ *Calluna vulgaris* 'Elsie Purnell'
Calluna vulgaris 'Firefly' ▲

flowers from mid to late autumn. **'Firefly'**♀, with deep mauve flowers, has terracotta foliage in summer, turning brick red in winter. **'Glencoe'** has long spikes of double pink flowers suitable for cutting, on foliage that turns bronze in winter, and spreads to 75 cm (30 in). **'Mair's Variety'**♀ produces long spikes of white blooms, suitable as cut flowers, against mid green foliage. **'Melanie'** is a bud-flowering form with white buds persisting until mid winter. It only spreads to 40 cm (16 in). **'My Dream'** bears long spikes of double white flowers suitable for cutting. **'Red Star'**♀ bears double deep crimson flowers late in the season. **'Reini'** produces long spikes of white flowers and has brilliant yellow tips to the downy grey-green foliage in spring.

'Silver Knight' has downy grey foliage deepening to purplish grey in winter. **'Silver Queen'**♀ displays downy silver-grey foliage throughout the year and has a broad, spreading habit. **'Silver Rose'**♀ combines lilac-pink flowers with grey-green foliage. **'Spring Torch'** is chiefly grown for the cream, orange and red new growth that tips the mid green foliage in spring. **'Wickwar Flame'**♀, a broad grower, turns superb shades of orange then red in winter, from its gold summer foliage.

CULTIVATION Choose an open, sunny site for planting, away from deciduous trees. Cultivars are available as rooted cuttings or as 1 or 2-year-old plants. Plant deeply, with the lower leaves touching the soil, in lime-free soil that is well drained but not too dry. Keep well watered during the first spring and summer after planting.

PROPAGATION Take semi-ripe heel cuttings in mid summer.

PRUNING Clip back annually to the base of the dead flowers in mid spring to prevent the plants from becoming straggly.

PESTS AND DISEASES Pests rarely cause damage but fungal diseases, chiefly *Botrytis* and *Pythium*, may attack plants in warm, wet conditions.

Calocedrus

Incense cedar
Cupressaceae

Calocedrus decurrens

Although this genus contains three species of evergreen conifers, only one, *Calocedrus decurrens*, is hardy in Britain, where it is commonly found in parks and gardens.

RECOMMENDED SPECIES AND VARIETIES

C. decurrens♀ With branchlets arranged in broad sprays of flat, scale-like leaves, this elegant, bright green columnar tree adds grace to any large landscape. It makes an impressive lone specimen and can also be used for hedging in larger gardens, although it is rather slow-growing. The leaves are held in pairs and have sharp, pointed tips. The foliage always grows upwards, but not steeply, and is very aromatic when crushed.

▲ *Calocedrus decurrens*

The tiny male flowers colour the uppermost shoot tips in winter. The green female flowers are hardly noticed but develop into yellowish brown cones which ripen to a rusty brown colour. The 'cigar-shaped' cones are about 2.5 cm (1 in) long and are made up of 6 lax, overlapping scales. When open, a cone has the appearance of a duck's bill. Native to western N America. HEIGHT & SPREAD 4×1 m (13×3 ft) after 20 years, ultimately 40 m (130 ft) tall, after 60 years.

The cultivar **'Aureovariegata'** is slower growing, taking 100 years to reach its maximum height. Bold yellow variegations give it an attractive mottled appearance. HEIGHT & SPREAD 3 m×80 cm (10 ft×2 ft 8 in) after 20 years, ultimately 40 m (130 ft) tall.

CULTIVATION Plant away from extreme, drying winds, in a fertile, acid soil.

PROPAGATION Sow seed in late winter to early spring, or take hardwood cuttings in early autumn and root in a mixture of peat and sharp sand. Variegated forms must be raised from cuttings.

PRUNING Not advised, or necessary.

PESTS AND DISEASES A tree can be attacked by scale insects, giving the tree a sickly appearance and causing poor growth.

Caltha

Ranunculaceae

Caltha palustris

Spring and early summer finds these attractive plants displaying their buttercup-like flowers along the margins of garden ponds or streams. They thrive in very wet soil and usually form large leafy patches. The saucer or cup-shaped flowers are glossy white, yellow or golden, with conspicuous yellow stamens. They are followed by clusters of pod-like seed capsules. The genus contains about ten species of hardy herbaceous perennials, native to temperate regions worldwide.

RECOMMENDED SPECIES AND VARIETIES

C. leptosepala Solitary white flowers, tinged with green or blue, appear from spring to early summer above tufts of shiny light green leaves that darken with age. The flowers are up to 2 cm (¾ in) across with 9-15 oval petals. The oval leaves are about 5 cm (2 in) wide, but are only partly developed when the plant is in flower. HEIGHT & SPREAD 20×30 cm (8×12 in).

C. palustris♀ (kingcup, marsh marigold) Deep yellow cups are carried on branching stems above fleshy dark green leaves in spring. The flowers are up to 5 cm (2 in) across with 5-6 petals. The leaves, as wide as 15 cm (6 in), are rounded to kidney shaped. The species often grows too large for a rock

▼ *Caltha palustris* var. *palustris*

garden pool and is better suited to a bog garden or moist border. HEIGHT & SPREAD up to 50×60 cm (20×24 in).

White flowers appear on var. ***alba***, and are in bloom later than the flowers of the species. The flowers of var. ***minor*** are smaller, not more than 3 cm (1¼ in) across, while the stems are prostrate and rooting. Larger, solitary yellow flowers and lax to creeping leafy stems distinguish var. ***palustris***. Fully double 'button' flowers are produced by var. ***palustris*** **'Plena'**. All 4 varieties are smaller than the species and make fine plants for a rock garden.

The long, creeping stems of var. ***radicans*** root at the nodes and its cultivar, **'Flore Pleno'**♀, bears double flowers.

▲ *Caltha palustris* var. *radicans* 'Flore Pleno'

CULTIVATION Position where the flowers will be in the sun and the roots in constantly wet soil. The boggy soil at the edge of a large rock garden pool or stream is ideal. Alternatively, plant in the water itself – plants thrive in up to 15 cm (6 in) of water.
PROPAGATION Sow fresh seed in a cold-frame in autumn or winter. An easier method is to lift and divide established plants after flowering or in autumn.
PESTS AND DISEASES Usually trouble free.

Calystegia

Bindweed
Convolvulaceae

This rampant climber bears a profusion of showy, trumpet or funnel-shaped flowers and oval or heart-shaped leaves. Allow it to twine around trelliswork or fencing, or sprawl over a wall or old tree stump. Many species of the genus, a member of the bindweed family, are weeds. All are herbaceous perennials and hardy or half-hardy.

RECOMMENDED SPECIES AND VARIETIES
C. hederacea (syn. *C. japonica*) Rose-pink flowers, up to 3.5 cm (1⅜ in) across, are produced singly on winged flower stalks in mid and late summer. The leaves on this hardy scrambling or climbing plant are

▲ *Calystegia hederacea* 'Flore Pleno'

arrow or lance-shaped, hairy and up to 10 cm (4 in) long. HEIGHT & SPREAD 5×1 m (16×3 ft), with support.

'Flore Pleno' has semidouble flowers 5 cm (2 in) wide.
CULTIVATION Grow in a free-draining soil in a sunny place and leave undisturbed. The best time to plant is spring. As calystegia has a tendency to spread very quickly, it is a good idea to confine the roots by sinking upright tiles into the soil. To prevent a plant from becoming too untidy, cut it back to the ground once flowering has finished.
PROPAGATION Divide the creeping root-stock in spring.
PESTS AND DISEASES Greenfly may attack vigorous young shoots.

Camassia

Quamash
Liliaceae

Camassia leichtlinii

Tall spikes of slender-petalled, star-shaped flowers are borne from late spring to early summer above tufts of long, narrow, basal leaves. The flower colour of these hardy bulbs varies from blue to violet to white. Flowers open from the base of the flower spike upwards. In the wild, camassias usually grow beside streams or in damp meadows. They are native to N and S America. Plant them in borders or allow them to become naturalised in grass, where they will increase if left undisturbed. The leaves die down in late summer.

RECOMMENDED SPECIES AND VARIETIES
C. cusickii Pale blue flowers, each about 5 cm (2 in) across, open from late spring to early summer. The grey-green leaves are up to 50 cm (20 in) long. HEIGHT 1 m (3 ft).
C. esculenta see *C. quamash*
C. leichtlinii Flowers varying from white to purple, and each up to 7.5 cm (3 in) across, are borne on slender spikes from late spring. The narrow, erect leaves are bright green. HEIGHT 1 m (3 ft).

'Alba' has creamy white flowers; the

▲ *Camassia leichtlinii*

▲ *Camassia leichtlinii* 'Alba'

Caerulea Group have blue flowers; flowers of **'Blauwe Donau'** are lavender with lilac anthers, and **'Plena'** has translucent, greenish white, multipetalled flowers.
C. quamash (syn. *C. esculenta*) Short dense spikes bear pale blue to deep violet-blue or white flowers, each about 4 cm (1½ in) wide. The flowers bloom above a tuft of long, linear leaves. This is the best species for naturalising. HEIGHT 25–75 cm (10–30 in).
CULTIVATION Camassias can be grown in any good garden soil, but they do best in a soil that is rich in humus and retains moisture. Plant the bulbs in autumn 10 cm (4 in) deep in a sunny place. Leave them undisturbed for several years for good results. Cut the flower stems off after flowering unless seeds are required for increasing stock.
PROPAGATION Plants are easily grown from seed but will take 3–5 years to flower; sow immediately the flowers fade in soil that is moist but well drained. Cultivars will not come true from seed. Alternatively, lift and remove offsets from established clumps in late summer or early autumn and replant the offsets immediately.
PESTS AND DISEASES Usually trouble free.

C

Camellia

Chinese or Japanese rose
Theaceae

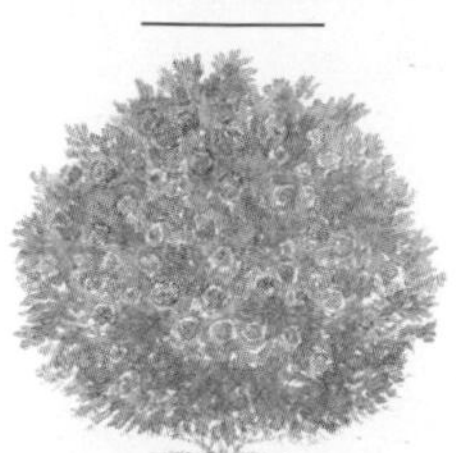

Camellia japonica 'Tricolor'

Conspicuous flowers and handsome evergreen foliage have made this genus of ornamental shrubs and trees deservedly popular. Native to India, China and Japan, there are over 200 species of camellia (about 45 in cultivation) and a staggering 20 000 different types have been grown and described over the years.

The abundant cup or bowl-shaped flowers range from 2.5-20 cm (1-8 in) across and are carried singly or in small bunches of 2-3. Each flower has 5-12 large, brightly coloured petals that are often fused together at the base. They may be white, pink, red or multicoloured and occasionally yellow. Numerous bright yellow stamens form a bold central mass and are sometimes petal-like. Some camellias with small flowers have a strong, sweet fragrance, which is missing in the large, showy varieties.

The mid to dark green, glossy leaves are narrow to broadly oval, almost stalkless and slightly toothed around the edges. They are arranged alternately on the shoots. The fruit, absent in many of the cultivated varieties, consists of a large round woody capsule, splitting from the top when ripe to reveal 5 chambers, each with one large oil-rich seed. Japanese ladies use this oil to dress their hair.

Because of their considerable differences in habit, hardiness, flower size, colour and form, flowering season (between late autumn and early summer) and ease of culture, there are suitable plants for many different garden situations throughout Britain. Most are suitable for borders and beds and there are camellias that make good hedging plants or are suitable for growing against walls. Some camellias make fine specimen plants for containers on patios and terraces, and the more tender varieties can be grown in a conservatory or unheated greenhouse.

When describing the flowers, the following categories are followed: 'single' denotes a flower with a single row of petals and a conspicuous centre of yellow stamens; 'semidouble' describes a flower with two or more rows of petals and a centre of yellow stamens; 'double' refers to a flower with numerous irregular rows of petals and virtually no stamens; 'formal double' describes a flower with numerous overlapping petals symmetrically arranged in spirals or tiers, and no stamens; 'anemone-like' denotes a flower with one or more rows of petals and a centre of petal-like and normal stamens; and 'peony-like' describes a flower with a rounded mass of petals, petal-like stamens and normal stamens.

All the heights and spreads given below are for 5-8-year-old plants. Camellias reach maturity at this age and thereafter growth is very slow.

RECOMMENDED SPECIES AND VARIETIES

C. **'Cornish Snow'**♀ Dainty, single white flowers, up to 7 cm (2¾ in) across, appear from early to late spring on this vigorous, spreading shrub. The young foliage is attractively bronzed. HEIGHT & SPREAD 2.4×2 m (8×6½ ft).

▲ *Camellia* 'Cornish Snow'

C. **'Freedom Bell'** Bright red, hose-in-hose, semidouble flowers, up to 10 cm (4 in) across, are produced from late winter to late spring. This plant has a dense, twiggy, upright growth. HEIGHT & SPREAD 3×2 m (10×6½ ft).

▲ *Camellia* 'Freedom Bell'

C. japonica Single red flowers, 5-10 cm (2-4 in) across, appear between late winter and early summer, depending on the variety. This compact shrub to small tree has broad oval glossy leaves, with pointed tips and shallowly toothed edges. The majority of cultivated varieties come from this species, a few of them scented, and it is by far the most popular camellia grown. It is also one of the hardiest of the evergreen shrubs, except in very exposed, windy conditions. HEIGHT & SPREAD 3-8×2-4 m (10-26×6½-13 ft).

The following cultivars are all vigorous, with compact, upright growth, unless stated otherwise.

'Adolphe Audusson'♀ bears large, deep red, semidouble flowers from mid to late spring. It is one of the most reliable cultivars. **'Akashigata'**♀ (syn. 'Lady Clare') is a spreading, pendulous shrub, ideal for growing against a wall. Large, peach-pink, semidouble flowers are carried from early to late spring. **'Alba Plena'** bears white, formal double flowers from early to mid spring. It is a slow-growing variety. **'Alba Simplex'** has large single white flowers from mid to late spring on a bushy, medium-sized shrub. **'Alexander Hunter'**♀ carries flattish, deep crimson, single flowers from early to late spring. **'Althaeiflora'** bears large, dark red, peony-like flowers from early to mid spring. It has very dark green leaves. **'Anemoniflora'** bears dark crimson, semidouble to anemone-like flowers in mid spring. **'Apollo'** is one of the hardiest of the *C. japonica* cultivars and will tolerate windier conditions than most of the others. The deep rose-pink, semidouble flowers are

▲ *Camellia japonica* 'Alba Simplex'

▼ *Camellia japonica* 'Alexander Hunter'

▲ *Camellia japonica* 'Apple Blossom'

occasionally marbled with white and appear in mid spring. The plant has a spreading habit, bearing leaves with characteristically twisted tips. **'Apple Blossom'**♀ (syn. 'Joy Sander') is a medium-sized, bushy shrub, bearing pale blush-pink, semidouble flowers from early to mid spring. **'Arajishi'** has large, narrow, coarsely toothed leaves. Large, blood-red, peony-like flowers with irregular wavy petals are produced from early to mid spring.

'Ballet Dancer'♀ bears cream (shading to coral-pink at the edges), peony-like flowers from early to late spring. **'Berenice Boddy'**♀ is a particularly hardy variety, tolerating windier conditions than most. It starts off with an upright habit, later becoming spreading, bearing light pink, semidouble flowers from early to mid spring. **'Betty Sheffield'** bears large, white, semidouble to loose peony-like flowers in mid spring. The petals are striped and blotched with red and pink. **'Betty Sheffield Supreme'** bears irregular double flowers in mid spring. The blooms are basically white with the petals edged in several shades of pink. **'Blood of China'** carries deep salmon-red, semidouble to peony-like, scented flowers from mid to late spring. **'Bob Hope'**♀ has large, dark red, semidouble to peony-like flowers from mid to late spring. It has dark green glossy leaves. The flower is the deepest red known in camellias and the plant is ideal for growing in containers. **'Bob's Tinsie'**♀ bears small, brilliant-red, anemone-like flowers in mid spring. **'Brushfield's Yellow'** bears

▼ *Camellia japonica* 'Bob's Tinsie'

creamy white (pale primrose in centre), anemone-like flowers from mid to late spring.

'C.M. Hovey'♀ bears carmine, formal double flowers from early to late spring. **'C.M. Wilson'**♀ is a slowly spreading variety with large, light pink, anemone-like flowers from early to mid spring. **'Carter's Sunburst'**♀ bears large, pale pink (marked with deeper pink flecks and stripes), semidouble to peony-like, scented flowers in mid spring. **'Chandleri Elegans'** see

▲ *Camellia japonica* 'Coquettii'

'Elegans'. **'Coquettii'**♀ (syn. 'Glen 40') is a slow-growing plant and carries bright red, semi to formal double flowers from mid to late spring.

'Debutante' carries light pink, peony-like flowers from early to mid spring. **'Dewatairin'** (syn. 'Hatsuzakura') bears large, light rose-pink, single flowers, with a mass of petal-like stamens in the centre, from mid to late spring. **'Doctor Tinsley'**♀ bears very pale pink (shading to deep pink at the edges), semidouble flowers in mid spring. It tolerates windier conditions than most of the other varieties. **'Donckelaeri'**

▲ *Camellia japonica* 'Drama Girl'

see 'Masayoshi'. **'Drama Girl'**♀ has an open, pendulous habit with large, deep rose-pink, semidouble flowers appearing from mid to late spring. **'Elegans'**♀ (syn. 'Chandleri Elegans') has a slowly spreading habit with large, deep rose-pink (often with white variegations) anemone-like flowers from early to mid spring.

'Glen 40' see 'Coquettii'. **'Gloire de Nantes'**♀ has large, bright rose-pink, flat to saucer-shaped, semidouble flowers from late winter to late spring. **'Grand Prix'**♀ develops a more open habit with age. Large, brilliant-red, flat semidouble flowers with irregular petals are borne from mid to late spring. **'Grand Slam'**♀ has deep green foliage and develops a more open habit with age. The large, semidouble to anemone-like, scented flowers are an unusually deep red for camellias, borne from mid to late spring. **'Guilio Nuccio'**♀ produces large, deep rose-pink, semidouble flowers with wavy petals in mid spring. It develops a spreading habit with age.

'Hagoromo'♀ (syn. 'Magnoliiflora') has cup-shaped, hose-in-hose, semidouble, blush-pink flowers in mid spring. **'Hakurakuten'**♀ bears large, white, semidouble to peony-like flowers with fluted petals from early to mid spring. **'Hatsuzakura'** see 'Dewatairin'. **'Hawaii'** is a slow-growing plant with pale pink, shading to a white edge, peony-like flowers from early to mid spring. **'Imbricata'** (syn. 'Imbricata Rubra') bears light red, formal double flowers from mid to late spring on a medium-sized plant. **'Joseph Pfingstl'** has an open habit and dark red, semidouble to peony-like flowers from early to mid spring. **'Joy Sander'** see 'Apple Blossom'. **'Jupiter'**♀ bears saucer-shaped, bright red, single to semidouble flowers in mid spring. The flowers are sometimes blotched with white. It is one of the best varieties for general planting and hardy in most areas. **'Konronkoku'**♀ (syn. 'Kouron-jura') carries an abundance of very dark red, semidouble to formal double flowers from early to late spring on a medium-sized plant. It is one of the darkest red camellias. **'Kramer's Supreme'** produces large, bright red, peony-like, scented flowers in mid spring. It is best grown under glass.

'Lady Clare' see 'Akashigata'. **'Lady de Saumarez'**♀ carries bright red, semidouble flowers blotched with white in mid spring. **'Lady Vansittart'** is slow-growing with unusual holly-like, twisted foliage. Saucer-shaped, white (flushed rose-pink), semidouble flowers appear from mid to late spring. **'Lady Vansittart Pink'** is a deep pink version of 'Lady Vansittart'. **'Lavinia Maggi'**♀ has an open habit and bears large, white to pale pink (with broad rose-cerise stripes), formal double flowers from early to late spring. **'Magnoliiflora'** see 'Hagoromo'. **'Margaret Davis Picotee'** bears white

▼ *Camellia japonica* 'Lady Vansittart Pink'

C

peony-like to double flowers with a narrow red border around the edges of the petals. **'Margherita Coleoni'** bears dark red, double to formal double flowers from mid to late spring. **'Mars'**♀ has an open, spreading habit with large, crimson, semidouble flowers from mid to late spring. Occasionally the flowers have white variegations. **'Masayoshi'**♀ (syn. 'Donckelaeri') is a slow-growing, bushy, pendulous plant with large, saucer-shaped, red (often marbled white), semidouble flowers from early to late spring. **'Mathotiana Alba'**♀ bears large, white (sometimes with pink spots), formal double flowers from mid to late spring. **'Mathotiana Rosea'** produces large, clear pink, formal double flowers from mid to late spring. **'Mercury'**♀ bears large, deep soft crimson (with slightly darker veins), semidouble flowers from early to late spring. **'Midnight'** carries dark red, semidouble to anemone-like flowers (with ruffled petals) in mid spring. **'Mikenjaku'** (syn. 'Nagasaki') is a slow-growing camellia with blotched red and white, semidouble flowers from mid to late spring. **'Miss Charleston'**♀ produces large, deep red, semidouble flowers that appear from mid to late spring. **'Mrs D.W. Davis'**♀ carries large, pendulous, cup-shaped flowers in mid spring. The semidouble blooms are blush-pink. The plant requires shelter from cold winds and frost or can be grown under glass.

'Nagasaki' see 'Mikenjaku'. **'Nobilissima'** bears white (with yellow shading), peony-like flowers from late winter to mid spring. **'Nuccio's Gem'**♀ produces white, formal double flowers from early to mid spring. **'Nuccio's Jewel'**♀ is slow-growing with white (flushed with pale pink), peony-like flowers from mid to late spring. It is an ideal choice for containers and tubs.

▲ *Camellia japonica* 'Preston Rose'

'Preston Rose' has an open habit with salmon-pink, peony-like flowers from mid to late spring. **'R.L. Wheeler'**♀ has large, rose-pink, semidouble to anemone-like flowers in mid spring. It has large, dark green leaves. **'Rubescens Major'**♀ bears large, carmine-red (with darker veins), semidouble to double flowers from early to mid spring. It has broad leaves. **'Scentsation'**♀ bears silvery pink, peony-like, scented flowers in mid spring. **'Silver Anniversary'** has white, semidouble flowers from early to mid spring. The petals are an irregular size and shape. **'Souvenir de Bahuaud-Litou'**♀ bears large, light pink, formal double flowers from mid to late spring. **'Spencer's Pink'**♀ has a low, spreading habit with large, light-pink, single flowers from early to mid spring.

▲ *Camellia japonica* 'Spencer's Pink'

'The Czar' bears large crimson semidouble flowers in mid spring. **'Tiffany'** bears very large peony-like flowers from mid to late spring. The blooms are pale pink, deepening around the edges. The plant becomes spreading with age and is best grown under glass. **'Tomorrow'** has an open, slightly pendulous habit with large, rose-red, semidouble to peony-like flowers from early to mid spring. It is best grown under glass. **'Tricolor'**♀ is one of the oldest cultivars. It is a dense, spreading plant bearing medium-sized white (streaked with carmine), semidouble flowers in mid spring. **'Yours Truly'** bears pale pink, semidouble flowers from mid to late spring. The petals have darker veining, and are streaked with deep pink and bordered with white. The plant is bushy with glossy dark green, holly-like leaves.

C. reticulata This is the most spectacular camellia of all, producing an abundance of 15-20 cm (6-8 in) wide blooms in vivid pinks and reds from late winter to mid spring. But it is also the most tender of the cultivated forms, only suitable for growing in a conservatory or unheated greenhouse, except in warmer sheltered gardens of southern Britain, where its open, spreading habit makes it ideal for training up walls and pergolas. The conspicuous net-like veining of the thick, narrow leaves gave rise to the name 'reticulata'. HEIGHT & SPREAD 3-4.5×2.4-3.5 m (10-15×8-12 ft).

Camellia reticulata 'Captain Rawes'

'Arch of Triumph'♀ is a vigorous, upright plant bearing large, deep rose-pink, peony-like flowers with an orange sheen from late winter to early spring. **'Captain Rawes'**♀ has a fairly open habit with large, carmine, semidouble flowers with irregular petals from early to late spring. **'Doctor Clifford Parks'**♀ bears large, flame-red, semidouble to loose peony-like flowers with wavy petals from early to late spring. It is hardier than most of the other *C. reticulata* cultivars and will survive outside farther north. **'Forty-Niner'**♀ has a dense, bushy growth with large, red, peony-like flowers from late winter to early spring. It is also fairly hardy, allowing it to be grown outdoors farther north than most of the other *C. reticulata* cultivars.

'Inspiration'♀ is another hardy hybrid with upright growth and light pink, semidouble, saucer-shaped flowers from early to late spring. **'Lasca Beauty'**♀ has an upright open habit, bearing large, soft pink, semidouble flowers with thick petals from early to late spring. The vigorous **'Leonard Messel'**♀ has an upright, slightly open habit and bears smaller than average, apricot-pink semidouble flowers with darker veining from early to late spring. **'Mandalay Queen'**♀ has an open, upright habit with large, deep rose, semidouble to peony-like flowers with fluted petals from early to mid spring.

'Salutation' is a medium-sized, open shrub with small, soft pink, semidouble flowers from late winter to mid spring. **'Satan's Robe'**♀ has wide, spreading growth, slender, arching shoots and large, brilliant-red, semidouble flowers from early to late spring. It is similar in hardiness to *C. japonicum* cultivars. **'Show Girl'** is a vigorous, upright, open shrub bearing large, pale pink, semidouble to peony-like flowers with irregular petals from late winter to mid spring.

C. sasanqua (mountain tea flower) Small, 2.5-5 cm (1-2 in) wide, white to rose-pink single flowers are produced freely from late autumn to late winter by this hardy, spreading shrub. The flowers have a sweet fragrance and the narrow oval leaves are dark green. HEIGHT & SPREAD 2.4-4×2-3 m (8-13×6½-10 ft).

'Crimson King'♀ bears deep mahogany-red single flowers with twisted petals. It has a low, spreading habit. **'Hugh Evans'** has a vigorous, tall habit with arching branches bearing rose-pink single flowers. It is ideal for growing on walls. **'Jean May'** has a dense, bushy growth making it suitable for hedging. The flowers are shell-pink, semidouble to double and up to 10 cm

▲ *Camellia sasanqua* 'Narumigata'

(4in) across. **'Narumigata'**♀ has a vigorous, upright growth with white pink-tinted, cup-shaped, single flowers up to 10cm (4in) across. It is best planted in a sheltered sunny spot against a wall.

C. sinensis (tea plant) Bushy shrub with long, narrow, wavy leaves and 2-3cm (¾-1¼in) waxy white, single, bell-shaped flowers from late autumn to mid winter. It is half hardy and can only be grown outside in the mildest parts of south-west. Britain. Elsewhere, grow it in an unheated conservatory or greenhouse. HEIGHT & SPREAD 2-3×1.5-2m (6½-10×5-6½ft).

'Spring Festival'♀ bears dainty, pink, semidouble to double flowers up to 7.5cm (3in) across from early to late spring. It has a narrow, upright habit and its small leaves are bronzed when young. It makes an excellent specimen tree in a small garden, but needs a sunny, sheltered position.

Camellia x williamsii 'Donation'

C.* x *williamsii These are the most easily grown and reliable for planting outdoors in Britain. They mostly form tall, dense shrubs with narrow oval leaves. The white to deep red flowers are 10-12cm (4-5in) across, mainly single or semidouble. HEIGHT & SPREAD 2-3×1.2-2m (6½-10×4-6½ft).

▼ *Camellia* x *williamsii* 'Anticipation'

▲ *Camellia* x *williamsii* 'Bow Bells'

'Anticipation'♀ is ideal for containers and small gardens. The deep rose-pink, peony-like flowers are produced from early to late spring. **'Ballet Queen'** bears an abundance of salmon-pink, peony-like blooms from early to late spring. **'Black Lace'** has a slow, fairly open growth with deep red, formal double flowers from early to late spring. **'Bow Bells'** bears mid pink, hose-in-hose, semidouble flowers from late winter to late spring. **'Bowen Bryant'**♀ has an upright, but open habit with rose-pink, bowl-shaped, semidouble flowers from early to late spring. **'Brigadoon'**♀ displays a small, dense upright habit with rose-pink, semidouble flowers from late winter to late spring.

'China Clay'♀ has an open habit bearing white, semidouble flowers from early to late spring. **'Citation'** is upright, bearing silvery blush-pink, semidouble flowers with irregular petals from early to mid spring. **'Cornish Spring'**♀ is a compact, bushy shrub, ideal for containers, with vivid pink, single to semidouble flowers, 5cm (2in) across, from early to late spring.

'Daintiness'♀ has an open habit with salmon-pink, semidouble flowers from mid to late spring. **'Debbie'**♀ has an upright growth with deep clear pink, semidouble to peony-like flowers from late winter to late spring. **'Donation'**♀ is upright with mid pink, semidouble flowers from late winter to early summer. It is one of the most versatile, robust and beautiful of the camellias. **'E.G. Waterhouse'** has a narrow, upright habit bearing light pink, formal double flowers from early to late spring. **'E.T.R. Carlyon'**♀ is upright with white, semidouble flowers from early to late spring. **'Elegant Beauty'** has an open habit with long, arching shoots and bronze foliage. It is ideal for training on walls. The deep rose-pink, anemone to peony-like flowers are freely produced from early to late spring. **'Elsie Jury'**♀ has a spreading habit and clear deep pink flowers, shaded with pale pink. The anemone to peony-like flowers appear from early to late spring.

'Francis Hanger' is small and upright with wavy-edged leaves and pure white, single flowers from early to late spring. **'Galaxie'**♀ is upright, bearing pink flowers with darker pink stripes and a rose-bud

▼ *Camellia* x *williamsii* 'Daintiness'

▼ *Camellia* x *williamsii* 'Debbie'

▲ *Camellia* x *williamsii* 'Donation'

▲ *Camellia* x *williamsii* 'E.G. Waterhouse'

▲ *Camellia* x *williamsii* 'Galaxie'

▲ *Camellia* x *williamsii* 'George Blandford'

▲ *Camellia* x *williamsii* 'Glenn's Orbit'

centre from early to late spring. The bowl-shaped blooms are semidouble to formal double with the petals rolling slightly inward. **'George Blandford'**♀ has a spreading habit with carmine, semidouble to anemone-like flowers from early to mid spring. **'Glenn's Orbit'**♀ has an upright habit with pink semidouble to loose peony-like flowers from early to mid spring. **'Golden Spangles'** has an upright, slightly open habit and dark green leaves with a pale yellow central band. The 7.5cm (3in) wide, deep rose-pink, hose-in-hose, semidouble flowers are seen from early to late spring.

'Hiraethlyn'♀ is upright with 7.5cm (3in) wide, very pale pink, funnel-shaped, hose-in-hose, semidouble flowers from early to late spring. **'Innovation'** is a very hardy, medium-spreading bush with wine-red, peony-like flowers from late winter to late spring. **'J.C. Williams'**♀ has a spreading, arching habit, bearing pale blush-pink, single flowers from late winter to late spring. **'Joan Trehane'**♀ has an upright, slightly open habit with clear rose-pink, formal double flowers from early to late spring. **'Julia Hamiter'**♀ has a medium-spreading habit with white, peony-like flowers tinged with pink, from early to late spring. **'Jury's Yellow'** forms a dense, upright, cone-shaped bush bearing creamy white, anemone-like flowers with wavy petals from early to late spring.

▲ *Camellia* x *williamsii* 'Mary Christian'

'Mary Christian'♀ has an upright habit bearing 7.5cm (3in) wide, clear deep pink single flowers from early to late spring. **'Mary Phoebe Taylor'** has an upright, slightly open habit with light rose-pink, semidouble to loose peony-like flowers from early to late spring. **'Muskoka'**♀ is upright with mid pink (veined with deeper pink), semidouble flowers from early to late spring.

▲ *Camellia* x *williamsii* 'Muskoka'

'Rose Parade'♀ forms a dense, upright shrub with deep rose-pink, formal double flowers from early to late spring. **'Saint Ewe'**♀ has a dense, upright habit with very glossy dark green leaves which contrast with its bright rose-pink flowers. The bell-shaped, single flowers are very freely produced from late winter to late spring. **'Tristrem Carlyon'** has an upright habit and rose-pink, peony-like flowers from early to late spring.

'Water Lily'♀ has an upright habit bearing lavender flowers flushed with bright pink. The formal double blooms have incurving petals and are seen from early to late spring. **'Wilber Foss'** has a dense, upright habit with brilliant pinkish red, peony-like flowers that appear from late winter to late spring.

CULTIVATION Plant between early spring and late summer in any reasonably well-drained, lime-free soil, in light shade or in a sheltered spot with a south-western to northern aspect. To protect the flowers from frost-thaw damage, position the plants away from full early morning sun and drying winds. *C. reticulata* and other early-flowering camellias are best grown in containers in a conservatory or unheated greenhouse, except in the mildest areas. They can be moved outside when the weather warms up.

Enrich non-peaty soils with leaf-mould or peaty compost. Feed annually in late spring or early summer with a general fertiliser, but do not apply fertiliser between late summer and early spring. Apply a mulch on planting and replenish when necessary. This helps to stop the plants drying out – especially important when they are flowering or coming into bud. Spray the foliage during prolonged dry spells.

PROPAGATION Cultivated varieties, except those of *C. reticulata,* are best propagated by inter-nodal or leaf-bud cuttings, taken in summer. Alternatively, use hardwood cuttings taken in mid autumn to early spring.

Propagate *C. reticulata* cultivars by layering in early autumn. The layers will be strong and well-rooted enough to separate after 18 months. Cleft or wedge grafting on *C. reticulata* rootstock is also used for these cultivated varieties. Natural species and forms are usually propagated by seed.

PRUNING Little pruning is needed other than cutting back straggly shoots, or to prevent plants encroaching on paths, lawns or other plants. Regular annual pruning and deadheading immediately after flowering are more advantageous than infrequent heavy pruning.

PESTS AND DISEASES Aphids may infest young shoots and scale insects suck sap from the undersides of leaves, especially under glass where mealy bugs often attack shoots

▼ *Camellia* x *williamsii* 'Rose Parade'

and buds, producing conspicuous tufts of white wool. Aphids and scale insects produce 'honeydew' which encourages sooty mould fungus. Bud drop occurs if soil conditions are too dry or if rapid thawing occurs after frost. The latter also damages camellia flowers. Where spring frosts occur, this damage can be avoided by providing light overhead shade or by siting the plants in south-west to north-facing positions. The leaves will turn yellow and die if the soil is alkaline or has too little humus.

Camomile see *Chamaemelum nobile*

Campanula

Bellflower, harebell

Campanulaceae

Bell or star-shaped flowers, usually in shades of blue, lavender, purple or white, characterise this group of summer-flowering plants. The flowers may be narrow or broad, pendent, half-nodding or upright. The genus includes large and imposing herbaceous perennials as well as small alpine species. Some are monocarpic, that is they take two or more years to reach flowering size then flower profusely and die. *Campanula portenschlagiana* and *C. poscharskyana* are good plants for rock crevices and gaps in paving and walls. Some high-alpine species, such as *C. cashmeriana* and *C. raineri,* perform best in troughs or raised beds where they can be shielded from winter wet, or in pots in an alpine house. *C. isophylla, C. carpatica* and *C. pyramidalis* all make fine pot plants for the conservatory or cool greenhouse. There are more than 300 species in the genus.

RECOMMENDED SPECIES AND VARIETIES

C. alliariifolia Erect spikes carry a series of pendent white or creamy white bells, 4cm (1½in) long, throughout summer. A clump-forming perennial, it has mounds of softly hairy, heart-shaped leaves. Native to Turkey and the Caucasus. HEIGHT & SPREAD 70×50cm (28×20in).

▼ *Campanula alliariifolia*

C. barbata (bearded bellflower) Hanging flowers, each up to 3cm (1¼in) long, range in colour from white to lavender-blue and are conspicuously bearded inside. They are borne on one-sided spikes during summer. This short-lived evergreen perennial or biennial forms a cluster of rosettes with grey-green, lance to oval-shaped leaves. Native to the Alps. HEIGHT & SPREAD 25×12.5cm (10×5in).

C. betulifolia♀ Loose clusters of white or pale pink broad bells, 3cm (1¼in) long, are borne on spreading stems. The plant forms a loose tuft of deep green, diamond to wedge-shaped leaves. Native to Turkey. HEIGHT & SPREAD 5×30cm (2×12in).

▲ *Campanula* 'Birch Hybrid'

***C.* 'Birch Hybrid'**♀ Deep violet or purple-blue open bells are borne in profusion throughout summer on this evergreen perennial. The plant forms dense mats of small, deep green, ivy-shaped leaves. HEIGHT & SPREAD 15×60cm (6×24in).

***C.* 'Burghaltii'**♀ (syn. *C.* × *burghaltii*) Upright to arching, leafy spikes of pale lavender hanging bells, 5cm (2in) long, appear in early and mid summer. A slightly spreading perennial with mid green, oval to lance-shaped leaves. The stems may need some support. HEIGHT & SPREAD 60×40cm (24×16in).

C. carpatica♀ Large upright blue, violet-purple or white bells, 3cm (1¼in) across, appear in mid to late summer. A clump or hummock-forming herbaceous perennial with smooth, rounded to oval leaves. A good pot plant, it can seed prolifically in a rock garden. Native to the Carpathians. HEIGHT & SPREAD 15×40cm (6×16in).

The flowers of f. ***alba*** are white. **'Blaeu Clips'** ('Blue Clips') has sky-blue flowers. The broader, saucer-shaped flowers of **'Blue Moonlight'** are grey-blue. **'Bressingham White'** has extra large, pure white flowers. **'Chewton Joy'** has pale blue flowers with a deeper blue rim. The pure white flowers of **'Weisse Clips'** ('White Clips') come true from seed.

Pale lavender flowers are often borne singly on each stem on var. ***turbinata*** (syn. 'Turbinata') which is not more than 10cm (4in) tall. **'Hannah'** has pure white, wide-spreading, bell-shaped flowers. The flowers of **'Isabel'** are wide-spreading bells of deep violet-blue. **'Karl Foerster'** has saucer-shaped flowers of deep sky-blue. The flowers of **'Wheatley Violet'** are a deep violet.

C. cashmeriana A mass of delicate, pale to bright blue nodding bells, 2cm (¾in) long, appear amid grey oval leaves in summer and early autumn on this short-lived perennial. This evergreen plant is best grown in a cool greenhouse as it does not tolerate winter wet. Native to W Himalayas. HEIGHT & SPREAD 15×30cm (6×12in).

Campanula cochleariifolia

C. cochleariifolia♀ (*C. pusilla*) Masses of small hanging or half-nodding pale blue or lavender bells, up to 1.5cm (½in) long, are borne in early to mid summer. This mat-forming herbaceous perennial bears numerous small, oval to rounded, bright glossy green leaves. Native to Europe. HEIGHT & SPREAD 10×60cm (4×24in) or more.

▲ *Campanula cochleariifolia*

The flowers of var. ***alba*** are white. **'Cambridge Blue'** has pale blue flowers. The double flowers of **'Elizabeth Oliver'**

▼ *Campanula cochleariifolia* 'Elizabeth Oliver'

C

are a very pale blue. **'Flore Pleno'** has rather small double flowers in pale blue. **'Tubby'** has china-blue rounded bells.
C. **'E.K. Toogood'** Bright blue, star-shaped flowers with a paler eye, up to 3cm (1¼in) across, appear throughout summer.

▲ *Campanula* 'E.K. Toogood'
Campanula fenestrellata ▲

This compact, clump-forming perennial has heart-shaped leaves. HEIGHT & SPREAD 70×50cm (28×20in).
C. fenestrellata (syn. *C. garganica* var. *fenestrellata*) Upright, star-shaped, mid blue flowers, 2.5cm (1in) across, appear throughout summer on this compact alpine. An evergreen perennial with rounded to heart-shaped leaves. Native to the Balkans. HEIGHT & SPREAD 3×20cm (1¼×8in).
C. formanekiana♀ Large white or bluish lilac bells, up to 6cm (2½in) long, are borne on this monocarpic perennial. Initially, plants form a large rosette of oval, grey, downy leaves. Native to the Balkans. HEIGHT & SPREAD 30×30cm (12×12in).
C. garganica♀ Starry, pale lavender flowers, 2cm (¾in) across, are borne in leafy spires during summer. A more or less evergreen perennial forming clumps of bright green, rounded to heart-shaped leaves. The plant flowers best in full sun and thrives in wall crevices. Native to Italy and W Greece. HEIGHT & SPREAD 5×30cm (2×12in).

'Dickson's Gold' has pale lavender flowers with yellow-flushed leaves.
C. glomerata Tight clusters of upright violet or purple flowers, 4cm (1½in) long, are borne in summer at the ends of leafy stems. This vigorous rhizomatous perennial, with deep green, lance to heart-shaped leaves, can be invasive. Native to Europe. HEIGHT & SPREAD 45×80cm (18×32in).

The flowers of var. ***acaulis*** are violet or blue on 15cm (6in) tall stems. The flowers of var. ***alba*** are white. **'Purple Pixie'** has small, deep violet-blue flowers. The flowers of **'Schneekrone'** ('Crown of Snow') are

▼ *Campanula glomerata* var. *acaulis*

▲ *Campanula glomerata* 'Superba'

white on a plant up to 30cm (12in) tall. **'Superba'**♀ grows to 75cm (30in) tall, with clusters of deep purple flowers.
C. × ***haylodgensis*** **'Plena'** A good rock-garden plant with bowl-shaped, double

▲ *Campanula* x *haylodgensis* 'Plena'

lavender-blue flowers in early to mid summer. The carpet-forming perennial has a mass of small, bright green, heart-shaped leaves. HEIGHT & SPREAD 5×20cm (2×8in).

'Warley White' has double white flowers and denser growth.
C. incurva Large, pale violet-blue bells, up to 5cm (2in) long, are borne in profusion in summer on this biennial or monocarpic evergreen perennial. Plants form large, softly hairy rosettes of heart-shaped, yellowish green leaves. Native to E Greece. HEIGHT & SPREAD 30×50cm (12×20in).
C. isophylla♀ (Italian bellflower) Masses of star-shaped, pale mauve-blue flowers, 2.5cm (1in) across, are borne throughout

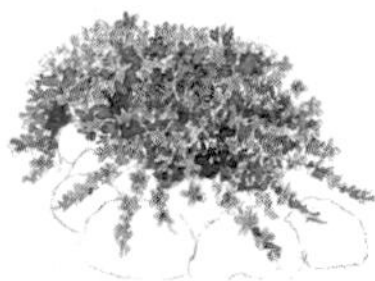

Campanula isophylla

summer on short stalks. Trailing stems, 20-30cm (8-12in) long, are densely covered with small, light green, heart-shaped leaves. The plant is not reliably hardy and is best grown indoors or in a greenhouse. HEIGHT & SPREAD 30×50cm (12×20in).

'Alba'♀ has pure white flowers.
C. **'Joe Elliott'**♀ Mid lavender-blue, funnel-shaped flowers, 3cm (1¼in) long, appear 2-3 to a stem throughout summer. The perennial plant forms mounds of small, heart-shaped, grey-green leaves. It dislikes winter wet and grows best in troughs or a cool greenhouse. HEIGHT & SPREAD 7.5×12.5cm (3×5in).
C. lactiflora Broad panicles of numerous, small upright bells, 2cm (¾in) long, in blue, milky blue or occasionally pink or white, are held on stiff leafy stems in summer and early autumn. This clump-forming herbaceous perennial has deep green, oval to oblong leaves. Native to the Caucasus. HEIGHT & SPREAD 120×70cm (48×28in).

C. l. **white**♀ has white flowers. **'Loddon Anna'**♀, up to 90cm (36in) tall, has soft lilac-pink flowers. **'Pouffe'** has mid blue flowers on stems up to 60cm (24in) tall. **'Prichard's Variety'**♀ has violet-blue flowers and grows to 1.5m (5ft)

▲ *Campanula lactiflora* 'Prichard's Variety'

tall so usually needs staking. **'White Pouffe'** has white flowers on stems up to 60cm (24in) tall.
C. latifolia (giant bellflower) Large, upright blue or lavender flowers, up to 5cm (2in) long, are borne in leafy spikes on stiff stems in mid summer. A clump-forming perennial with heart-shaped deep glossy green leaves. Native to Europe and Kashmir. HEIGHT & SPREAD 100×60cm (40×24in).

'Brantwood' has deep violet-blue flowers and oval leaves. The larger flowers of var. ***macrantha*** are violet-blue. The flowers of var. ***macrantha alba*** are white.
C. latiloba Deep blue, cup-shaped bell-flowers appear in summer on upright stems. A more or less evergreen perennial with lance-shaped leaves. Native to Siberia. HEIGHT & SPREAD 90×50cm (36×20in).

alba♀ has white flowers. **'Hidcote Amethyst'**♀ has amethyst-blue flowers. **'Highcliffe Variety'**♀ has violet-blue flowers. **'Percy Piper'**♀ has lavender flowers.

▼ *Campanula latiloba* 'Percy Piper'

C. medium (Canterbury bells) Imposing erect panicles of large blue, purple, mauve, pink or white bell-shaped flowers, 5cm (2in) long, are borne on thick stiff stems in late spring and early summer. This biennial has large basal rosettes of lance-shaped, fresh green leaves. Native to S Europe. HEIGHT & SPREAD 80x36cm (32x14in).

Various strains are offered as seed including tall and dwarf double-flowered types and the **cup & saucer** kinds with the calyx broad and saucer-shaped.

C. muralis see *C. portenschlagiana*

C. persicifolia Large, open, blue to violet-blue cup-shaped flowers, up to 5cm (2in)

Campanula persicifolia

long, are borne on loose slender wand-like spikes. This evergreen perennial has deep green, narrow, lance-shaped leaves. Native to Europe, W Asia and N Africa. HEIGHT & SPREAD 100x50cm (40x20in).

The flowers of ***alba*** are white, as are the semidouble flowers of **'Alba Coronata'**. **'Boule de Neige'** has large double white flowers. **'Fleur de Neige'**♀ has snowy white flowers. **'Pride of Exmouth'** has powder-blue flowers. **'Telham Beauty'** (syn. 'Maxima') has very large, pale blue flowers. **'White Queen'** has white flowers.

▲ *Campanula persicifolia* 'Boule de Neige'

Other kinds are listed as **cup & saucer white**♀, **double blue** (syn. 'Caerulea Flore Pleno'), **double white** (syn. 'Alba Flore Pleno') and var. **planiflora.**

C. portenschlagiana♀ (syn. *C. muralis*) Deep lavender-blue open bellflowers, up to 2cm (¾in) long, appear in summer in loose clusters on leafy stems. An evergreen spreading perennial that forms dense mats of deep green, heart-shaped to oval leaves. It is a good plant for rock and wall crevices. Native to S Europe. HEIGHT & SPREAD 15x50cm (6x20in).

'Resholdt's Variety' carries vivid deep blue flowers.

C. poscharskyana Starry violet-blue flowers, 2cm (¾in) long, appear in summer and early autumn in spreading clusters. This often rampant, spreading evergreen perennial has rounded, pale green leaves. It is a good plant for banks and old walls or the wild garden. Native to the Balkans. HEIGHT & SPREAD 10-15x60cm (4-6x24in).

'E.H. Frost' has milky-white flowers, **'Lisduggan'** has lavender-pink flowers and **'Stella'** has vivid violet-blue flowers.

C. pulla Dainty, solitary, deep violet bells, 2cm (¾in) long, appear in mid summer above a mat of oval to rounded leaves. This

▲ *Campanula pulla*

spreading perennial is an excellent rock-garden plant. Native to the NE Alps. HEIGHT & SPREAD 7.5x30cm (3x12in).

C. punctata Loose spires of rosy purple pendent bells, 5cm (2in) long and speckled inside with dark purple, appear in mid to late summer. This spreading semi-evergreen rhizomatous perennial has long-stalked oval to heart-shaped leaves. Native to Japan. HEIGHT & SPREAD 40x50cm (16x20in).

The creamy white flowers of f. ***albiflora*** (syn. 'Alba') are speckled with reddish purple inside. **'Rubriflora'** has creamy pink flowers flushed and speckled crimson-red.

▲ *Campanula punctata* 'Rubriflora'

C. pusilla see *C. cochleariifolia*

C. pyramidalis (chimney bellflower) Long narrow spires of star-shaped, blue, white, or bicoloured flowers, 4cm (1½in) across, appear from mid summer to early autumn on thick stems. This upright biennial or short-lived perennial has heart-shaped, deep green and rather glossy leaves. It can be grown in the open garden or in pots in a conservatory. Native to SE Europe. HEIGHT & SPREAD 70x50cm (28x20in).

The flowers of ***alba*** are white.

C. raineri♀ Solitary, upright broad bells of mid blue or lavender-blue flowers, 3cm (1¼in) across, are borne in summer on this perennial with grey-green oval leaves. This makes an excellent plant for an alpine house or a trough outside where it requires protection from winter wet. Native to SE Alps. HEIGHT & SPREAD 70x50cm (28x20in).

C. rapunculoides (creeping bellflower) Long leafy spikes of pendent, violet-blue flowers, 2-3cm (¾-1¼in) long, appear in summer. This rhizomatous perennial is a vigorous spreader and can be invasive. The long-stalked, deep green basal leaves are oblong or heart-shaped. Native to Europe. HEIGHT & SPREAD 75x75cm (30x30in).

C. rotundifolia (harebell) Several dainty, pendent blue bells, 2cm (¾in) long, appear in summer and early autumn on sparse, wiry stems. This rhizomatous perennial carries narrow stem leaves and contrasting rounded to heart-shaped basal leaves. It can be invasive. The plant is excellent for naturalising in grass. Native to the Northern Hemisphere. HEIGHT & SPREAD 45x45cm (18x18in).

'Olympica' has deep blue flowers on plants up to 25cm (10in) tall.

C. rupestris Narrow, upright lilac-blue flowers, 1.5-2cm (½-¾in) long, are carried above a rosette of soft hairy leaves. HEIGHT & SPREAD 15x40cm (6x16in).

C. takesimana Arching sprays of large, white bells, 5-6cm (2-2½in) long, are flushed with lilac and spotted maroon inside. They appear in summer on this spreading rhizomatous perennial with bright green, heart-shaped leaves mainly arranged in basal rosettes. Native to Japan and Korea. HEIGHT & SPREAD 60x50cm (24x20in).

C. thyrsoides (yellow bellflower) Soft yellow tubular bells, each 2cm (¾in) long

▼ *Campanula thyrsoides*

and arranged in dense crowded spikes, appear in summer. This biennial or monocarpic perennial initially has a rosette of rather pale green leaves. Native to the Alps and the Balkans. HEIGHT & SPREAD 25-40×20cm (10-16×8in).

C. trachelium Long violet-blue or purple upright bells, up to 5cm (2in) long, are borne in mid summer on long leafy spikes. This herbaceous perennial carries oval, pointed leaves. Native to Europe and Siberia. HEIGHT & SPREAD 80×40cm (32×16in).

The flowers of var. ***alba*** are white, as are the double flowers of **'Alba Flore Pleno'**. **'Bernice'** produces violet-purple double flowers and **'Puck'** has violet flowers.

C. zoysii Narrow lavender-blue crimped bells, up to 2cm (¾in) long, are borne in early to mid summer. This tufted perennial produces tiny glossy green leaves. The plant is best grown in an alpine house or trough as it tends to be susceptible to slug damage and winter wet. HEIGHT & SPREAD 5×10cm (2×4in).

CULTIVATION Campanulas are generally fairly easy to grow. Most require a fertile, moist yet well-drained soil and an open sunny position. However, some species – including *C. alliariifolia, C. glomerata, C. persicifolia, C. poscharskyana, C. rapunculoides* and *C. trachelium* – flower well in semi-shade. The taller plants need staking.

Many of the smaller campanulas are excellent for a rock garden, although some rhizomatous species, particularly *C. cochleariifolia* and *C. glomerata,* can be invasive. Lift and replant on a regular basis every 3-4 years. Some alpine species need protection from excessive winter wet – for example *C. betulifolia, C. cashmeriana* and *C. zoysii* – and need a grittier compost than the others.

PROPAGATION Divide the parent plants of perennial species after flowering or in autumn; those with long underground runners can be lifted around the margins and suitable rooted pieces removed, while the tighter clump formers will need to be lifted entirely and divided as stated. Remove cuttings of basal shoots and place in a propagating frame in spring or early summer.

Sow seed in autumn or late winter in pots in a coldframe.

Sow monocarpic species in spring, pricking out plants into individual pots. When the leaf-rosettes are large enough, generally by late summer, place young plants into their flowering positions.

Propagate alpine species from small summer cuttings or from offsets which may or may not be pre-rooted.

PESTS AND DISEASES Slugs and snails may prove a nuisance. Most species are also prone to rust infection.

Campion see *Silene*
Campion, rose see *Lychnis coronaria*

Campsis
Bignoniaceae

Campsis radicans

Vigorous woody climbers, these deciduous plants bloom from late summer to early autumn. The trumpet-shaped flowers, in shades of yellow, orange and red, are 5-7.5cm (2-3in) long. The tough stems are covered in dark green, pinnate leaves, with oval, toothed leaflets. Slender woody pods up to 12.5cm (5in) long may appear in late autumn. The plants cling to supports by aerial roots and are excellent for growing against a wall, although they do need plenty of space. They are fully hardy if planted in a sheltered, sunny position.

RECOMMENDED SPECIES AND VARIETIES

C. grandiflora Borne in drooping clusters of 6-12 blooms, each flower has a deep orange tapering tube, opening out to 5, spreading crimson lobes. The leaves have 7-9, smooth leaflets, each up to 6cm (2½in) long. HEIGHT & SPREAD 2×1m (6½×3ft) after 5 years, ultimately 6m (20ft) tall.

C. radicans (trumpet vine) The orange to red flowers are borne in clusters of 4-12 blossoms. The leaves have 7-11 leaflets, each 2-10cm (¾-4in) long, with fine hairs underneath. The brown pods may be produced in abundance after a hot summer. HEIGHT & SPREAD 2×1m (6½×3ft) after 5 years, ultimately 10m (33ft) tall.

The flowers of f. ***flava***♀ (syn. 'Yellow Trumpet') are a rich, clear yellow.

▲ *Campsis* x *tagliabuana* 'Madame Galen'

C. x *tagliabuana* **'Madame Galen'**♀ Flowers with yellow to orange tubes and 5 spreading, crimson to scarlet lobes are borne in large loose clusters of 6-12 blooms. The leaves have 7-11 leaflets, slightly hairy beneath and 8cm (3¼in) long. HEIGHT & SPREAD 2.4×1m (8×3ft) after 5 years, ultimately 10m (33ft) tall.

CULTIVATION Plant from late autumn to mid spring in any fertile, well-drained but moisture-retentive soil. Choose a sheltered sunny position, preferably with the protection of a wall. Tie plants to supports, especially young specimens of *C. grandiflora.*

PROPAGATION Take semi-ripe cuttings or layer long branches in winter.

PRUNING In late winter, prune back to within 2-4 buds.

PESTS AND DISEASES Powdery mildew, leaf spot and scale insects can be a problem.

Candytuft see *Iberis*

Canna
Cannaceae

The brilliant flowers and bold ornamental foliage of cannas always draw the eye in a garden display. Their exotic flowers appear in mid summer and last until the first frosts. These rhizomatous perennials are native to tropical regions of the Americas and are only half-hardy in Britain. As summer bedding plants, they give height in mixed borders and make a feature in a large container.

Most cannas are hybrids with trumpet-shaped blooms up to 15cm (6in) across held in abundance at the top of erect stems. The broadly ovate leaves, up to 60cm (24in) long, spiral up the stem.

RECOMMENDED SPECIES AND VARIETIES

C. edulis see *C. indica*

C. indica (Indian shot, arrowroot) The flowers are red, often spotted or edged with pink or yellow. The green leaves are up to 50cm (20in) long. HEIGHT 2m (6½ft).

C. x *generalis* (canna lily) This group of hybrids contains many interesting and varied plants. **'Black Knight'**, with rich red flowers and brown leaves, grows to 60cm (24in). Taller varieties reaching 80cm (32in) include **'Lucifer'** with scarlet flowers edged in golden yellow and green leaves;

▼ *Canna indica*

▲ *Canna* x *generalis* 'Rosemond Coles'

▲ *Canna* x *generalis* 'Wyoming'

'Rosemond Coles' with tomato-red flowers edged in canary-yellow above green leaves; and **'Wyoming'** with frilly, tangerine petals, darker at the edges and blotched with purple, above brown leaves.

CULTIVATION In late winter or early spring plant the rhizomes in a sandy peat mixture in pots and keep in a frost-free greenhouse until planting in a sunny spot outdoors when there is no danger of frosts. Lift the plants in late autumn, trim the rhizomes of dead growth and store in slightly moist peat in a frost-free conservatory or greenhouse.

PROPAGATION Divide the rhizomes before potting up in spring.

PESTS AND DISEASES Usually trouble free.

Canterbury bells see *Campanula medium*

Caper spurge see *Euphorbia lathyris*

Caragana

Pea tree

Leguminosae

Caragana arborescens 'Lorbergii'

With their small sweet-pea shaped flowers and delicate foliage, it is surprising that so few of these deciduous shrubs and small trees are to be found in British gardens. They are hardy and have decorative appeal with a good show of flowers, normally yellow, in early summer followed by dangling seedpods.

Most of the 80 species are native to central Asia and adapted to hot, dry summers and cold, dry winters. The mild, damp climate of Britain may mean a sparser show of leaves and flowers. The alternate leaves are pinnate and the terminal leaflet is often replaced by a sharp spine.

RECOMMENDED SPECIES AND VARIETIES

C. arborescens Yellow flowers, 1.5 cm (½ in) long, appear in a profusion of slightly drooping clusters during late spring and ripen to narrow cylindrical pods about 5 cm (2 in) long. The light green pinnate leaves, up to 7.5 cm (3 in) long, have 4-6 pairs of small leaflets, with a spine at the tip. The plant's rather upright habit becomes rounded with age. It grows in any soil and will survive the bleakest British winter. HEIGHT & SPREAD 1×1 m (3×3 ft) after 5 years, ultimately 5 m (16 ft) tall.

▲ *Caragana arborescens* 'Walker'

'Lorbergii'♀ has narrower, more feathery leaflets than the species and smaller flowers. It reaches an ultimate height of 3 m (10 ft). **'Pendula'** has a weeping habit and makes a small shrub, ultimately no more than 1.5 m (5 ft) tall. **'Walker'** has the weeping habit of 'Pendula' with the feathery foliage of 'Lorbergii'.

CULTIVATION Plant in full sun. The plants will tolerate most soils, doing best in a well-drained position.

PROPAGATION Sow seed in spring. Grafted plants are required for a specific feature.

PRUNING None required except to remove dead wood in spring.

PESTS AND DISEASES Usually trouble free.

▼ *Caragena arborescens* 'Pendula'

Cardamine

Cruciferae

Cardamine pratensis 'Flore Pleno'

Clusters of four-petalled flowers appear on erect stems in spring on these tuft or mat-forming hardy perennials. The genus includes some common weeds, but the plants listed are appropriate for a spring border combined with bulbs, a woodland garden or for a corner of a rock garden.

RECOMMENDED SPECIES AND VARIETIES

C. asarifolia see *Pachyphragma macrophyllum*

C. digitata see *C. pentaphyllos*

C. enneaphyllos Nodding clusters of flowers, each 1 cm (⅜ in) across, are pale yellow or cream. The leaves have 3, occasionally 4-5, toothed and pointed leaflets. Native to SE Europe. HEIGHT & SPREAD 20×30 cm (8×12 in).

C. heptaphylla White, pink or purplish flowers, 2 cm (¾ in) across, appear from spring to early summer. The leaves have 5-11 elliptical, toothed leaflets. Native to central and W Europe. HEIGHT & SPREAD 40×50 cm (16×20 in).

C. pentaphyllos (syn. *C. digitata*) The pale purple or white flowers are 2 cm (¾ in)

▼ *Cardamine pentaphyllos*

across. The leaves have 3-5 toothed leaflets. Native to mountain woods and rocky places in the Pyrenees and the Alps. HEIGHT & SPREAD 30×30cm (12×12in).

C. pratensis (cuckoo flower, lady's smock) The lilac to white flowers are 1.5cm (½in)

▲ Cardamine pratensis

across. The pinnate, rosette-forming leaves have up to 15 elliptical to rounded leaflets. Native to Europe, E Asia and N America. HEIGHT & SPREAD 50×30 m (20×12in).

'Edith' has double flowers that are pink in bud, fading to white. **'Flore Pleno'**♀ carries double pink to lilac flowers. **'William'** produces deep lilac flowers.

C. trifolia The white or pink flowers are 1cm (⅜in) across. The plant forms low hummocks or mats of small trifoliate leaves that are purplish below. It thrives in moist, shady places and nooks among rocks. Native to central and S Europe. HEIGHT & SPREAD 10×40cm (4×16in).

CULTIVATION Grow cardamines in partial shade in a moist, humus-rich soil. *C. pratensis* requires full sun.

PROPAGATION Divide established plants after flowering or in early autumn. Sow seed when ripe in early to mid summer before the seedpods explode open.

PESTS AND DISEASES Aphids and caterpillars attack the plants; slugs and snails can damage the seedlings.

Cardiocrinum

Liliaceae

Towering above the border, the large fragrant flower trumpets of these hardy, bulbous perennials make a dramatic display in summer. Cardiocrinum bulbs die after flowering but not before producing the bulblets and seed which can be used to replace the parent bulbs. These will take a few years to develop into flowering plants and so gardeners can guarantee flowers every year by planting mature bulbs for a few consecutive seasons. Native to woodland in the Himalayas, China and Japan.

RECOMMENDED SPECIES AND VARIETIES

C. giganteum♀ Richly scented white trumpets, tinged with green outside and striped with maroon inside, appear in mid to late

▲ Cardiocrinum giganteum

summer. There are up to 25 flowers, each about 20cm (8in) long, on the long stems. Dark green, heart-shaped leaves, some 30cm (12in) across, form a rosette at the base of the plant. Smaller leaves spiral up the stems. HEIGHT & SPREAD 1.8×1m (6×3ft).

The white flowers of var. ***yunnanense*** have red markings and the leaves are bronzed when young. The flower stems reach 2.1m (7ft).

CULTIVATION Plant bulbs in early autumn over several successive years, setting each with its tip level with the soil's surface. Grow in moist, but well-drained, very fertile soil in partial shade. Protect new growth with dry mulch in winter.

PROPAGATION In autumn, when the leaves have browned, dig up plants and remove the bulblets that have formed around the parent bulb; replant immediately. Plants raised this way will take some 3-5 years to flower. Alternatively, sow seed as soon as it ripens. The seed germinates readily but plants will take up to 7 years to flower.

PESTS AND DISEASES Aphids, botrytis and basal rot may be a problem. Slugs, mice and voles will eat the bulbs.

Carex see GRASSES p.302

Cardoon see *Cynara cardunculus*

Carlina

Carline thistle

Compositae

These eye-catching, thistle-like plants bear round flowerheads encircled by conspicuous coloured bracts, above rosettes of spiny-toothed leaves. Low-growing, carlinas are suitable for sunny banks, raised beds and larger rock gardens, and make attractive dried flowers. The flowerheads open out in dry weather and close up when it is damp. The plants listed are perennial and fully hardy. Native to S and E Europe.

RECOMMENDED SPECIES AND VARIETIES

C. acanthifolia Purple-brown flowerheads, 15cm (6in) wide and surrounded by pale yellow radiating bracts, appear on this stemless herbaceous perennial in summer, after 3 or 4 years. The broad, coarse leaves, up to 30cm (12in) long, are grey-green above, white-felted below, and very dissected and spiny. HEIGHT & SPREAD 15×60cm (6×24in).

C. acaulis From mid summer to early autumn this stemless or short-stemmed plant bears off-white or pale brown flowerheads 5-10cm (2-4in) across, with papery white or pink bracts. The spiny grey-green leaves grow up to 30cm (12in) long. Plants can live for 10 years. HEIGHT & SPREAD 20×40cm (8×16in).

ssp. ***simplex*** (syn. ssp. *caulescens*) has stems 30-60cm (12-24in) long, each with up to 6 flowerheads.

▲ Carlina acaulis

CULTIVATION Plant in any well-drained soil in a warm, sunny place.

PROPAGATION Sow seed in winter or early spring, under glass. Prick out seedlings the moment they are large enough to handle.

PESTS AND DISEASES Seeds are often parasitised by grubs.

Carnation see *Dianthus caryophyllus*

Carpenteria

Hydrangeaceae

Carpenteria californica

The single species in this genus produces a fine display of yellow-centred white flowers in summer. This evergreen shrub, native to California, does best against a sunny wall. After a cold spell it may look a little shabby, but soon regains its bushy appearance.

Carpenteria californica♀ The fragrant flowers, up to 6cm (2½in) across, have 5 rounded, often overlapping petals and a central boss of bright yellow stamens. These blooms are carried in clusters at the shoot tips from early to mid summer, and con-

▲ *Carpenteria californica*

tinue to appear more sporadically until early autumn. The lanceolate leaves, carried in pairs along the branches and growing up to 11cm (4¼in) long, are glossy dark green above and whitish beneath. HEIGHT & SPREAD 1×1m (3×3ft) after 5 years, ultimately 3m (10ft) tall.

'Ladhams' Variety' is more free-flowering with flowers up to 8cm (3¼in) across.
CULTIVATION Choose a compact, bushy specimen with pale young shoots and plant in a sheltered, sunny position, preferably against a wall facing south or west. Any garden soil will do as long as it is well-drained but not too dry.
PROPAGATION Layer in winter or take softwood cuttings in summer.
PRUNING In late winter prune lightly for compactness and to remove winter damage and spent old wood.
PESTS AND DISEASES Usually trouble free.

Carpinus
Hornbeam
Corylaceae

Carpinus betulus 'Fastigiata'

These hardy deciduous trees make graceful specimen plants and common hornbeam is a good hedging plant. Male and female flowers appear as green catkins hanging on the same tree in spring; the female catkins ripen in autumn to clusters of small winged seeds and make a decorative feature among the golden autumn foliage. The oval to ovate leaves, up to 7.5cm (3in) long, have a finely serrated edge.
RECOMMENDED SPECIES AND VARIETIES
C. ***betulus***♀ (common hornbeam) The dark green leaves of this medium to large tree have fine teeth and give a good display of yellow in autumn. The tree has a conical, upright habit when young, but becomes more rounded with age. The grey bark, although smooth, has an undulating surface. Seeds hang in tassels up to 15cm (6in) long in early autumn. It withstands severe clipping and the dense leaves stay on the shoots through winter. Native to Europe and Asia Minor. HEIGHT & SPREAD 6×3m (20×10ft) after 20 years, ultimately 20m (66ft) or more tall.

▲ *Carpinus betulus*

'Fastigiata'♀ (syn. 'Pyramidalis') has an erect conical habit and a broad base.

▲ *Carpinus betulus* 'Fastigiata'

CULTIVATION Plant in any soil, including clay, from mid autumn to early spring. Plant hedging plants 38-50cm (15-20in) apart and do not let them dry out.
PROPAGATION Species are easily grown from seed but cultivars must be grafted.
PRUNING Prune to keep in shape. Clip hedges in mid summer.
PESTS AND DISEASES Usually trouble free.

Carrot see p. 736

Carya
Hickory
Juglandaceae

These fast-growing deciduous specimen trees reach a great height and may live for over 100 years. They have slender, upright grey trunks with rounded to conical crowns. The pinnate leaves, up to 36cm (14in) long, produce reliable bright yellow autumn colour. Male and female flowers appear in spring on the same tree. Males are greenish yellow and catkin-like on second-year shoots, and females, on the new growth, are inconspicuous, erect, greenish spikes. The autumn nuts are seldom fertile or edible in Britain. The wide-spreading roots need considerable space.

▲ *Carya ovata*

RECOMMENDED SPECIES AND VARIETIES
C. ***ovata***♀ (shagbark hickory) The trunk of this narrow and upright tree has a flaky grey bark after about 20 years. The dark green leaves have 5 leaflets and change to rich yellow in autumn. Native to eastern USA. HEIGHT & SPREAD 8×5m (26×16ft) in 15-20 years, ultimately 20m (66ft) tall.
C. ***tomentosa*** (big-bud hickory) This round-headed tree has downy shoots with big, velvety winter leaf buds. The slightly aromatic dark green leaves, usually with 7 leaflets, turn a brilliant golden yellow in autumn. Native to USA. HEIGHT & SPREAD 8×6m (26×20ft) in 15-20 years, ultimately 18m (60ft) tall.
CULTIVATION Hickory trees prefer deep, moist, slightly acid soils.
PROPAGATION Raise from imported seed sown in spring after winter chilling. Plant out young seedlings as soon as possible.
PRUNING If necessary for shaping, prune in summer to avoid sap bleeding in spring.
PESTS AND DISEASES Usually trouble free.

Caryopteris
Verbenaceae

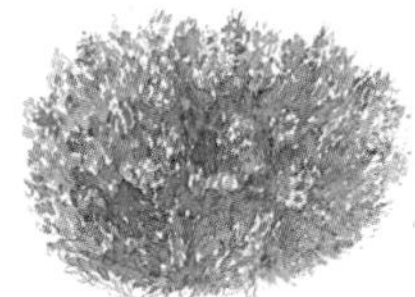
Caryopteris x clandonensis 'Heavenly Blue'

Compact clusters of tiny blue flowers make a stunning display on these deciduous shrubs late in the season. Covered in masses of aromatic leaves, they can look good with silvery leaved plants. The tubular flowers, 6mm (¼in) long, have prominent stamens and are held in clusters on the current season's growth. The pointed oval leaves are a dull green and often white or grey beneath. Native to E Asia.
RECOMMENDED SPECIES AND VARIETIES
C. × ***clandonensis*** Bright blue or violet-

C

▲ *Caryopteris* x *clandonensis* 'Heavenly Blue'

blue flowers appear in late summer and early autumn on this small, bushy shrub. The leaves, up to 5cm (2in) long, have impressed vein markings above and may have sparsely toothed edges. HEIGHT & SPREAD 60x100cm (2x3ft) after 5 years, ultimately 1m (3ft) tall.

'Arthur Simmonds' is 60cm (2ft) tall and more compact. **'Ferndown'** has deep violet-blue flowers from late summer to mid autumn. The more upright **'Heavenly Blue'**♀ has bright blue flowers. **'Kew Blue'** has deep blue flowers. **'Worcester Gold'**, 75cm (2½ft) tall, has golden yellow leaves.

▲ *Caryopteris* x *clandonensis* 'Worcester Gold'

C. incana (syn. *C. mastacanthus*) Violet-blue flowers appear in early and mid autumn. Up to 8cm (3¼in) long, the leaves may have coarsely toothed edges. The young shoots and flower stalks are covered in fine grey hairs. HEIGHT & SPREAD 70x100cm (28x40in) after 5 years, ultimately 1.5m (5ft) tall.

C. mastacanthus see *C. incana*

CULTIVATION Plant in autumn or spring in any well-drained soil, including chalk, in a sunny spot. *C. incana* may need the protection of a wall in positions where temperatures regularly fall below -5°C (23°F).

PROPAGATION Raise plants from semi-ripe or greenwood cuttings.

PRUNING In spring, cut the previous year's growth back hard to young healthy buds and cut weak stems down to ground level.

PESTS AND DISEASES Usually trouble free.

Cassia see *Senna*

Cassinia

Cottonwood

Compositae

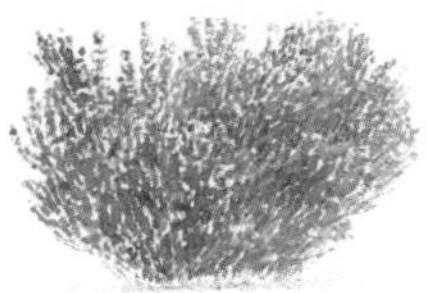

Cassinia 'Ward Silver'

Evergreen foliage and clusters of tiny flowers in summer are the chief virtues of these shrubs. The green, yellow or white ovate leaves grow to 1cm (⅜in) long. The species listed here, native to New Zealand, are hardy in all but the coldest of gardens. *Cassinia leptophylla* ssp. *fulvida*, the hardiest, is a suitable hedging plant for coastal gardens.

RECOMMENDED SPECIES AND VARIETIES

C. leptophylla The narrow, oblong leaves are yellowish or silver felted beneath on this shrub with slender, felted branches. The dense clusters of 100 or more white flowers are 2.5-5cm (1-2in) wide. HEIGHT & SPREAD 1x1m (3x3ft) after 5 years, ultimately up to 1.8m (6ft) tall.

The branchlets of ssp. ***fulvida*** (golden cottonwood) are covered with a golden felt. The young leaves are green above, yellow felted beneath and are sticky with a honey-like smell. In ssp. ***vauvilliersii*** the felted branches are greenish white.

***C.* 'Ward Silver'** The branches of this dense bush are white felted and the leaves are silver-grey. The dense clusters of about 100 white flowers are up to 6cm (2½in) across. HEIGHT & SPREAD 1x1m (3x3ft) after 5 years, ultimately 1.8m (6ft) tall.

CULTIVATION Grow in a well-drained soil in an open sunny position.

PROPAGATION Take cuttings from young branchlets at any time of the year.

PRUNING Prune to maintain a good shape.

PESTS AND DISEASES Usually trouble free.

▲ *Cassinia leptophylla* ssp. *fulvida*

Cassiope

Ericaceae

Pretty bell or goblet-shaped white flowers hang singly on delicate stalks in spring and early summer. The wiry stems of these tough, mat-forming evergreen shrubs are covered in overlapping, scale-like green or grey leaves up to 5mm (¼in) long. Each flower, up to 1cm (⅜in) long, has a pink or red calyx. Cassiopes are slow-growing and will reach their ultimate size in about five to eight years. Native to alpine areas and tundra of the Northern Hemisphere, cassiopes thrive in cool, moist, acid conditions.

RECOMMENDED SPECIES AND VARIETIES

***C.* 'Badenoch'** A profusion of white flowers are borne on slender, many-branched stems in mid spring. HEIGHT & SPREAD 15x30cm (6x12in).

***C.* 'Edinburgh'**♀ Slender, dark green stems carry many pure white flowers. The green calyxes are edged red. The plant will tolerate warm, dry conditions. HEIGHT & SPREAD 30x40cm (12x16in).

C. lycopodioides♀ The flowers of this prostrate, wiry shrub are white or cream. The stems are covered in dark green, scaly leaves and form a dense, interwoven mat. HEIGHT & SPREAD 10x30cm (4x12in).

'Beatrice Lilley' has abundant white flowers and is shorter and more compact.

***C.* 'Medusa'** Profuse white flowers on slender, wiry stalks are borne on this much-branched plant. HEIGHT & SPREAD 20x40cm (8x16in).

▲ *Cassiope* 'Edinburgh'

▲ *Cassiope lycopodioides*

C. mertensiana The white or pink flowers have a red or green calyx. The dark green leaves are pressed close to the stem. The spreading branches of this clump-forming plant are upright at the tips. HEIGHT & SPREAD 25×50cm (10×20in).

ssp. ***gracilis*** is free-flowering with white flowers and rather hairy leaves.

C. **'Muirhead'**♀ Profuse, nodding white flowers are carried on pinkish stalks. The leaves are grey-green. HEIGHT & SPREAD 15×30cm (6×12in).

C. **'Randle Cooke'**♀ A profusion of white flowers are borne on the strong, branched stems of this vigorous, easy-to-grow plant. HEIGHT & SPREAD 15×30cm (6×12in).

CULTIVATION Cassiopes thrive in a moist, well-drained acid soil that is rich in humus. They do best in an open cool position away from hot sun, but with good light. They make excellent pan plants for a cool, airy greenhouse or shaded coldframe.

PROPAGATION Take semi-ripe cuttings in late summer or early autumn. Alternatively, layer in spring.

PRUNING Remove any brown or straggly bits in early spring.

PESTS AND DISEASES Vine weevils occasionally attack the plants. Glasshouse specimens may be susceptible to red spider mite.

Castanea

Fagaceae

Castanea sativa

An old sweet chestnut tree in a garden provides a bold landscape feature, and it might even bear edible nuts. However, a castanea tree will take up a great deal of space and could shed branches from time to time. Chestnuts live from 100 to 1000 years. They do not mix well with other plants and can cast a heavy shadow. In the British Isles, *Castanea sativa* is the most widely grown of the 12 species of deciduous trees and shrubs. All have ridged bark, toothed leaves and bear catkins in summer. Newly planted trees may take a few years to establish, but then annual growth in excess of 30cm (1ft) may be expected for 50-100 years, though growth is faster in southern Britain.

▼ *Castanea sativa*

RECOMMENDED SPECIES AND VARIETIES

C. sativa (sweet chestnut)♀ The huge rounded crown consists of tough, glossy, narrowly oval leaves that are 18cm (7in) long and have coarsely toothed edges. Lax, greenish white scented catkins, 15cm (6in) long, appear in mid summer. Male flowers are spaced along the upper part of the catkin, female flowers are spaced along the lower part and develop into red-brown nuts in bristly husks. The broad trunk becomes ridged, often spirally, when mature. The large, shade-tolerant tree, originally native to S Europe, Asia Minor and N Africa, has been naturalised in Britain for many centuries. HEIGHT & SPREAD 9×5m (30×16ft) in 15-20 years, ultimately 30m (100ft) tall.

▲ *Castanea sativa* 'Albomarginata'

The smaller cream variegated forms, **'Albomarginata'** and **'Variegata'**, need full light to develop strong leaf colouring.

CULTIVATION Grow in light, well-drained acid soils. The trees are intolerant of lime.

PROPAGATION Easy to grow from seed and seedlings. Young plants transplant well.

PRUNING None is required.

PESTS AND DISEASES Usually trouble free.

Castor-oil plant see *Ricinus*

Catalpa

Bignoniaceae

Catalpa bignonioides

Unmistakable huge leaves and a shapely rounded head make a catalpa an eye-catching specimen tree. There are spectacular late-summer flowers too, but only on mature trees, often after 25 years or more. Catalpas, although hardy, grow best in warm situations and away from strong winds. They tolerate harsh city conditions. There are about 12 species in the genus.

RECOMMENDED SPECIES AND VARIETIES

C. ***bignonioides***♀ (Indian bean tree) The ornamental, rich green, aromatic leaves are heart-shaped and opposite, and do not appear until early summer on this broad-headed, spreading tree from N America. The leaves grow up to 30cm (12in) long and 20cm (8in) wide. They weigh down the branches so cultivated trees often have to be pollarded, pruned or braced to prevent the branches from snapping. Panicles of upright, white, frilly, foxglove-like flowers with yellow and purple markings appear in mid to late summer on mature trees. These are followed by bunches of drooping, thin, green bean pods that are 36cm (14in) long. The pods blacken but remain on the tree throughout winter. HEIGHT & SPREAD 10×8m (33×26ft) after 25 years, ultimately 15m (50ft) tall.

▲ *Catalpa bignonioides*

'Aurea'♀ is a velvety, pale yellow-leaved form. It is slightly more tender than the species and does not grow so fast or so large, ultimately reaching up to 10m (33ft) tall.

C. × ***erubescens*** **'Purpurea'**♀ The new leaves that emerge in early summer are almost black, changing to dark green as they mature. The tree can grow as broad as it is tall. HEIGHT & SPREAD 4.5×3m (15×10ft) after 20 years in sheltered conditions, ultimately 15m (50ft) tall.

CULTIVATION Catalpas tolerate every kind of soil, even heavy clay, but prefer one that is deep, fertile and moisture-retentive. They do best in hot sunshine and full light. Protect young plants from late frosts.

PROPAGATION Grow from seed sown outside in autumn or take semi-ripe softwood cuttings in mid summer.

PRUNING None required unless the weight of the leaves is cracking branches.

PESTS AND DISEASES Usually trouble free.

C

Catananche

Cupid's dart

Compositae

Dark-eyed, blue or white flowerheads are held on wiry stems in summer (and can be dried for winter decoration). With their narrow, greyish leaves, the catananches are best sited among other grey-foliaged plants at the front or middle of a border. Of the five species of annuals and perennials in the genus, only the hardy perennial, *Catananche caerulea*, is generally grown.

RECOMMENDED SPECIES AND VARIETIES

C. caerulea Shiny, purplish blue flowerheads, about 4cm (1½in) across, are made up of strap-shaped ray florets with serrated edges. The surrounding papery bracts each have a central silver stripe. The toothed, linear greyish leaves grow to 30cm (1ft) long. On heavier clays the plant may be short-lived. Native to SW Europe. HEIGHT & SPREAD 1m×45cm (3×1½ft).

▲ *Catananche caerulea* 'Alba'

▲ *Catananche caerulea*

'Alba' has white flowers. **'Major'**♀ has deep lavender-blue flowers.

CULTIVATION Plant in spring or autumn in well-drained soil in full sun. Cut the stems back after flowering.

PROPAGATION Divide or take root cuttings in winter. Seed sown in a warm greenhouse in early spring usually produces plants flowering in a range of shades that summer.

PESTS AND DISEASES Usually trouble free.

Catchfly see *Lychnis, Silene*

Catharanthus

Apocynaceae

Catharanthus roseus

With their brightly coloured flowers carried above soft green oval leaves for most of the year, these bushy plants look attractive in a well-lit window, conservatory or greenhouse. Keep them at a temperature of at least 7°C (45°F).

RECOMMENDED SPECIES AND VARIETIES

C. roseus♀ (Madagascar periwinkle) Rose-pink to red flowers, with mauve throats, up to 4cm (1½in) wide, put on a good show from spring until autumn, with a few blooms in winter. Each flower is made up of 5 broadly triangular, satiny petals. The soft, glossy evergreen leaves are up to 5cm (2in) long, with prominent midribs. Although a perennial, the plant is often treated as an annual, because young plants look and grow better. Growth can be controlled by pinching back vigorous shoots. Native to tropical and sub-tropical Madagascar. HEIGHT & SPREAD 60×45cm (2×1½ft).

The **Ocellatus Group** produces flowers that are red, pink, white or a mixture of these colours. This group includes the **Bright Eyes** series and other coloured forms. Some colour selections are shorter-growing than the species.

▼ *Catharanthus roseus*

▲ *Catharanthus roseus* Ocellatus Group

CULTIVATION Use a soil-based compost such as John Innes No. 2. Keep soil damp by watering regularly in summer; less so in winter. Prune straggly growth in spring.

PROPAGATION Sow seed in a propagator in spring, or raise from softwood cuttings.

PESTS AND DISEASES Greenfly, whitefly and mealy bug can be troublesome.

Cathcartia

Papaveraceae

Nodding, pale yellow poppy-like flowers appear in summer over the clumps of leaf rosettes. These hardy perennials thrive in dappled shade and are an excellent choice for a woodland garden.

RECOMMENDED SPECIES

C. villosa (syn. *Meconopsis villosa*) (woodland poppy) Branched stems carry the 5cm (2in) wide flowers made up of 4 rounded, slightly overlapping petals. Rosettes are formed from bristly, oval to round leaves, about 12cm (4¾in) long, with 3-5 deep lobes. Smooth, cylindrical seed capsules, about 8cm (3¼in) long, follow the flowers. HEIGHT & SPREAD 60×30cm (2×1ft).

CULTIVATION Plant in spring or summer in moist but well-drained, humus-rich, slightly acid to neutral soil in a cool, partially shaded site. Protect from excessive winter wet.

PROPAGATION Sow seed in early spring or divide after flowering or in early spring.

PESTS AND DISEASES Crown rot can kill plants in waterlogged soils and seedlings are prone to damping-off disease.

Catmint see *Nepeta cataria*
Cattleya see ORCHIDS p. 465
Cauliflower see p. 737

Cautleya

Zingiberaceae

Brightly coloured flowers carried in erect spikes and large, glossy lance-shaped leaves are the main features of these exotic-looking plants, which make a distinctive addition to herbaceous and mixed borders. Upright in habit with luxuriant foliage and fleshy stems, these medium-sized herbaceous perennials grow from creeping rhizomes. Plants will tolerate a touch of frost, but must be grown in a free-draining, sheltered position. Native to the Himalayas.

RECOMMENDED SPECIES AND VARIETIES

C. spicata (syn. *C. spicata* 'Robusta') Light orange or soft yellow flowers partly enclosed by maroon-red bracts are borne in large spikes, up to 25cm (10in) long and 7.5cm (3in) across, during late summer and early autumn. The glossy green leaves are up to 30cm (12in) long and 7.5cm (3in) wide. HEIGHT & SPREAD 60cm×1m (2×3ft).

CULTIVATION Plant in spring, in a sunny, sheltered corner of the garden, in fertile free-draining soil. Moisture is essential but do not allow the soil to become waterlogged. Scatter a balanced, slow-release fertiliser around the plants in early spring, but do not feed in summer as this may promote soft growth that will not survive winter. Remove faded flowers.

PROPAGATION Divide and replant the rhizomes or sow seed under glass in spring.

PESTS AND DISEASES Usually trouble free.

▼ *Cautleya spicata*

Ceanothus

California lilac

Rhamnaceae

Ceanothus impressus

These sun-loving shrubs are unrivalled for their dense and often showy clusters of blue flowers, ranging in colour from powder blue to deep indigo. Rose-pink and white flowers are also available. In most species the blooms appear in late spring, but some varieties flower through late summer and early autumn. The individual flowers are quite small but they are grouped together in clusters 5-12.5cm (2-5in) long.

The genus includes both deciduous and evergreen species. Generally smooth and even glossy, the leaves of most ceanothus are dark green in colour, 2-5cm (¾-2in) long and oval, egg-shaped or oblong.

Plants range in habit from ground-coverers to small trees; *Ceanothus prostratus* grows to only 7.5cm (3in) in height, while *C. arboreus* 'Trewithen Blue' can reach up to 6m (20ft). Most are grown as freestanding shrubs, although some varieties can easily be trained against walls by tying branches to supports. Generally fast growing, most ceanothus species flower abundantly in their second season, particularly if planted in full sun. They are not, however, long-lived in cultivation and it is rare to find specimens more than 20 years old.

Hardiness varies, although healthy plants can survive limited periods of -15°C (5°F). They are ideal for gardens in coastal regions. Native to Central and N America.

RECOMMENDED SPECIES AND VARIETIES

C. arboreus **'Trewithen Blue'**♀ Large conical clusters of deep blue flowers are seen during mid to late spring. The mid green leaves have fine, soft grey hairs beneath and can grow up to 8cm (3¼in) long. A round-headed evergreen shrub or small tree, this plant benefits from being trained against a wall. HEIGHT & SPREAD 3.5×3.5m (12×12ft) after 5 years, ultimately 6m (20ft) tall.

C. **'Autumnal Blue'**♀ This late-flowering variety produces loose clusters of powder-blue flowers in late summer and autumn. An evergreen shrub with large, glossy, mid green leaves, it is one of the hardiest and one of the best for wall-training. HEIGHT & SPREAD 1.5×1.5m (5×5ft) after 5 years, ultimately 2.1m (7ft) tall.

C. **'Blue Mound'**♀ Dense, rounded clusters of bright blue flowers are seen in late spring and early summer on this thick, clump-forming evergreen shrub. HEIGHT & SPREAD 1.5×1.8m (5×6ft) after 5 years, ultimately 2.1m (7ft) tall.

▲ *Ceanothus* 'Blue Mound'

C. **'Burkwoodii'**♀ Lavender-blue flowers are borne in clusters from mid summer to early autumn. One of the hardier evergreens, this dense shrub has glossy serrated leaves that are grey and hairy beneath. HEIGHT & SPREAD 1.5×1.5m (5×5ft) after 5 years, ultimately 2.1m (7ft) tall.

C. **'Cascade'**♀ This evergreen variety has arching stems that make it suitable for training against a wall, where it can reach a height and spread of 3.5m (12ft). Clusters of powder-blue flowers appear in late spring. HEIGHT & SPREAD 1.8×1.8m (6×6ft) after 5 years, ultimately 5m (16ft) tall.

▲ *Ceanothus* 'Cascade'

C. **'Concha'** Reliably producing an abundance of flowers, this evergreen shrub has a compact habit and narrow glossy leaves. Reddish in bud, the indigo flowers put on a dazzling display in late spring. HEIGHT & SPREAD 1.8×1.8m (6×6ft) after 5 years, ultimately 2.4m (8ft) tall.

C. **'Dark Star'** resembles *C.* 'Concha', differing only in its darker flowers and tiny leaves, just 1cm (⅜in) in length. It also has a more spreading habit. HEIGHT & SPREAD 1.8×2.4m (6×8ft) after 5 years, ultimately 2.4m (8ft) tall.

C. **'Delight'**♀ Abundant clusters of rich blue flowers appear in late spring. A large, thick evergreen shrub with glossy, light green leaves, this is a good choice for training against a wall. HEIGHT & SPREAD 3×3m (10×10ft) after 5 years and ultimately.

▲ *Ceanothus* 'Delight'

***C.* × *delileanus* 'Gloire de Versailles'** ♀ Large clusters of powder-blue flowers, 8cm (3¼in) long, are seen from mid summer to early autumn. An upright-growing, deciduous shrub of open habit, it has large leaves, 8cm (3¼in) long, that are downy underneath. HEIGHT & SPREAD 1.5×1m (5×3ft) after 5 years, ultimately 1.8m (6ft) tall.

***C.* × *delileanus* 'Topaze'** ♀ Darker blue flowers than 'Gloire de Versailles' and a more compact habit distinguishes this variety. HEIGHT & SPREAD 1.2m×75cm (4 × 2½ft) after 5 years, ultimately 1.5m (5ft) tall.

***C.* 'Edinburgh'** ♀ Violet-blue flowers appear during late spring on this dense evergreen shrub with olive-green leaves. HEIGHT & SPREAD 2.1×2.1m (7×7ft) after 5 years, ultimately 2.7m (9ft).

▲ *Ceanothus* 'Edinburgh'

***C. griseus* var. *horizontalis* 'Yankee Point'** Abundant clusters of bright blue flowers are borne by this fast-growing evergreen shrub in late spring or early summer. The very dark green, toothed leaves are hairy and greyish green beneath and leathery in texture. A nearly prostrate, spreading plant, this variety forms neat, compact clumps. HEIGHT & SPREAD 60cm×2.1m (2×7ft) after 5 years and ultimately.

C. impressus Clusters of deep lavender-blue flowers appear in profusion during late spring on this densely branched, broad-spreading evergreen shrub. The very small, crinkled leaves are less than 1.5cm (½in) long. HEIGHT & SPREAD 1.5×1.5m (5×5ft) after 5 years, ultimately 2.1m (7ft) tall.

***C.* 'Italian Skies'** ♀ This wide-spreading, thick evergreen shrub bears dense clusters of brilliant, deep blue flowers in late spring. The small mid green leaves are about 1.5cm (½in) long. HEIGHT & SPREAD 1.5×2.4m (5×8ft) after 5 years and ultimately.

***C.* × *pallidus* 'Marie Simon'** Pale pink flowers are borne in dense, conical clusters from mid summer to early autumn on this bushy deciduous shrub. This and *C.* × *p.* 'Perle Rose', are among the hardiest shrubs of the genus. HEIGHT & SPREAD 1.5×1.5m (5×5ft) after 5 years and ultimately.

▲ *Ceanothus* × *pallidus* 'Marie Simon'

▲ *Ceanothus* × *pallidus* 'Perle Rose'

***C.* × *pallidus* 'Perle Rose'** A deciduous shrub with strawberry-pink flowers that otherwise resembles *C.* × *p.* 'Marie Simon'. HEIGHT & SPREAD 1.5×1.5m (5×5ft) after 5 years and ultimately.

C. prostratus This prostrate evergreen is one of the hardiest species. The flowers vary in shade but are generally lavender-blue and are seen during late spring and early summer. The leathery, holly-like leaves are small, measuring less than 2.5cm (1in) in length. HEIGHT & SPREAD 7.5cm×2.1m (3in×7ft) after 5 years and ultimately.

***C.* 'Puget Blue'** ♀ Bright, cornflower-blue flowers appear in profusion during early summer on this dense evergreen shrub. HEIGHT & SPREAD 2.1×2.1m (7×7ft) after 5 years, ultimately 3m (10ft) tall.

C. repens see *C. thyrsiflorus* var. *repens*

***C.* 'Southmead'** ♀ Abundant clusters of rich blue flowers are seen during late spring and early summer on this dense evergreen shrub. It is excellent for training against a wall. HEIGHT & SPREAD 1.5×1.5m (5×5ft) after 5 years, ultimately 2.4m (8ft) tall.

C. thyrsiflorus Pale to deep blue flowers are seen in great profusion during late spring and early summer. A large broad-spreading evergreen shrub or small tree, this is one of the hardiest species. HEIGHT & SPREAD 1.8×1.8m (6×6ft) after 5 years, ultimately 2.4m (8ft) tall.

The prostrate variety, var. ***repens*** ♀ (syn. *C. repens*), forms a dense carpet, covered with a mass of lilac-blue flowers in late spring. HEIGHT & SPREAD 45cm×2.7m (1½×9ft) after 5 years and ultimately.

▲ *Ceanothus* × *veitchianus*

C.* × *veitchianus Dense clusters of vivid, deep blue flowers are borne in abundance during late spring and early summer. The small, evergreen leaves are less than 2cm (¾in) long. This shrub is often seen trained against a wall. HEIGHT & SPREAD 2.1×2.1m (7×7ft) after 5 years and ultimately.

CULTIVATION Plant in fertile, free-draining soil in full sun; shallow, chalky soils are unsuitable. Ceanothus tolerate light shade but do not flower well in deep shade. In known frost pockets or areas where the winters are prolonged, use a south or south-west facing wall for shelter. Protect newly planted specimens from cold winds.

Evergreen varieties are best planted when young since established plants do not like their roots being disturbed. The deciduous species, however, will bear some transplanting in spring.

PROPAGATION Raise evergreen species from semi-ripe cuttings; deciduous species from greenwood cuttings.

PRUNING Prune evergreen varieties that flower in late spring and early summer just after flowering by trimming the current season's growth to within 2.5cm (1in) of the previous season's growth. Prune late summer and autumn-flowering evergreens in spring before growth commences. Cut back to half of the previous season's growth.

Deciduous species are also pruned in spring. Once a height of 1–1.2m (3–4ft) has been established (after 3 or 4 years), they can be cut back annually to within 2 or 3 buds of the previous season's growth.

PESTS AND DISEASES Usually trouble free, although some plants can suffer from chlorosis if the soil is too limy.

Cedar see *Cedrus*
Cedar, Japanese
see *Cryptomeria japonica*
Cedar, western red see *Thuja plicata*
Cedar, white see *Thuja occidentalis*

Cedrus

Cedar
Pinaceae

Cedrus libani ssp. atlantica Glauca Group

Sweeping lawns round grand houses are the only fit setting for the largest cedars, but there are several smaller varieties for displaying some of the virtues of this noble genus in more modest gardens. Cedars are evergreen, and mainly conical when young but irregular and broad when old. They need moist, fertile soil and do equally well in sun and half shade. The trees are hardy, but late spring frosts may damage new growth on young plants. The smooth, dark grey bark flakes and develops vertical fissures with maturity.

Thin needles, varying from dark green to silver-blue or golden yellow, grow in dense rosettes on the sideshoots and stalks. Male flowers are held in upright clusters 7.5cm (3in) long and resemble catkins. On trees 30 or 40 years old female flowers, which are borne on the same tree as male flowers, change from green globes about 1cm (⅜in) across into barrel-shaped cones up to 12.5cm (5in) long. These are held upright and ripen from greenish purple to brown.

RECOMMENDED SPECIES AND VARIETIES
C. atlantica see *C. libani* ssp. *atlantica*

▲ *Cedrus libani* ssp. *atlantica* Glauca Group

C. deodara Giant proportions put this striking tree from the Himalayas beyond consideration for most gardens. Its growth is fast and takes it above 50m (165ft) in height. Plants bred from it share its conical shape and densely packed needles, up to 4cm (1½in) long, on shoots that droop at the tip.

'Aurea' rarely exceeds 5m (16ft) tall. It takes 20-30 years to reach full size and its spread is about half its height. The needles are golden yellow when new, maturing to

▲ *Cedrus deodara* 'Feelin' Blue'

greenish yellow. **'Feelin' Blue'** is a little more spreading in habit, eventually reaching some 5×3m (16×10ft), and its needles are blue-grey. **'Golden Horizon'**, which has yellow needles, is low with spreading layers of branches, but conical overall. It reaches 75cm×1.5m (2½×5ft), growing about 15cm (6in) a year upwards and outwards. **'Pendula'** makes very slow growth and has greyish green to blue foliage on markedly drooping branches that are easily trained to an umbrella shape. It reaches 1.5×1m (5×3ft) after 20 years.

C. libani ssp. ***atlantica*** (Atlantic cedar) This sub-species of cedar of Lebanon (*C. libani*) makes a magestic lawn specimen but requires enormous space. HEIGHT & SPREAD 3×2m (10×6½ft) after 10 years, ultimately over 25m (80ft) tall and wide.

Glauca Group has blue-grey foliage, but otherwise resembles *C. l.* ssp. *atlantica.* **'Glauca Pendula'** has pendulous branches cascading to the ground. When supported by stakes, the branches, clothed with 2cm (¾in) long needles, create a grey-blue canopy. The tree reaches 2×3m (6½×10ft) after 10 years, ultimately 4×6m (13×20ft).

C. libani ssp. ***libani*** **'Sargentii'** is a low, broad tree useful for rock gardens and ground cover. Its short, sturdy trunk bears numerous weeping branches clothed with dense, blue needles 3cm (1¼in) long. The wide growth is easily kept within bounds by pruning. After 10 years it is just 50cm (20in) tall with a spread of 2.4m (8ft), ultimately reaching 1.5×10m (5×33ft).

CULTIVATION Plant cedars in spring or autumn. They tolerate most conditions but do best in moist, fertile, acid soil.

PROPAGATION Although cedar species come true from seed, the recommended cultivars can be raised only by grafting and are best bought as young specimens.

PRUNING Cedars cannot be pruned to restrict their size except for the prostrate branches of *C. libani* ssp. *libani* 'Sargentii', which tolerate trimming. Lower branches on the larger cultivars and on the species tend to die back; cut off dead wood.

PESTS AND DISEASES Generally trouble free although damage caused by mowing may lead to root rot or stem rot. Honey fungus occasionally strikes.

Celandine, greater
see *Chelidonium majus*
Celandine, lesser
see *Ranunculus ficaria*

Celastrus

Bittersweet
Celastraceae

Celastrus orbiculatus

Colourful autumn fruits bedeck these mostly deciduous scrambling shrubs or twining climbers. The pea-sized, round or three-lobed fruit split when ripe to reveal brightly coloured seeds and hang on the branches, ignored by birds, well into the winter. Hardy, vigorous and easily grown, the plants are best seen cascading from a deciduous tree or climbing up a wall.

RECOMMENDED SPECIES AND VARIETIES
C. orbiculatus (oriental bittersweet, staff vine) Dull yellow fruits cover this fast-growing, twining climber in autumn and, when ripe, reveal a bright yellow inner surface and scarlet seeds. In summer, starry, greenish flowers appear in small clusters in the leaf axils. The leaves are short-stalked, rounded, shallow-toothed, abruptly pointed and up to 12.5cm (5in) long. Both male and female plants are necessary to ensure pollination and fruiting. Native to NE Asia. HEIGHT & SPREAD 3×3m (10×10ft) after 5 years, ultimately climbing to 12m (40ft).

Plants in the **Hermaphrodite Group**♀ are self-fertile and only one plant is needed for a fine show of fruit in the garden.

CULTIVATION Plant in deep, fertile, loamy soil in full or partial shade. Support by tying to wires on a wall. Alternatively, plant beside an established deciduous tree and tie shoots to one or more stakes, until the shoots reach the tree's branches.

PROPAGATION Take semi-ripe cuttings in summer or sow seed in autumn. Seedlings from the hermaphrodite forms do not inherit the self-fertile characteristic.

PRUNING If it is necessary to restrict spread, prune in winter after the fruits have fallen.

PESTS AND DISEASES Usually trouble free.

Celery see p.737

▼ *Celastrus orbiculatus*

C

Celmisia

Compositae

Handsome leaves and white daisy flowerheads, each with a yellow centre, make a striking display. The flowerheads are borne mainly in summer, with a few in late spring. The genus includes evergreen perennials and small shrubs which thrive in rock gardens or raised beds. Larger varieties are valuable in winter for their architectural foliage which may be hairy. The plants listed are hardy but dislike intense cold and need shelter from icy winds.

RECOMMENDED SPECIES AND VARIETIES

C. argentea Dense silvery cushions are formed by tiny narrow leaves, up to 1.5cm (½in) long. This perennial bears stemless 3cm (1¼in) flowerheads in mid summer. HEIGHT & SPREAD 10×25cm (4×10in).

▲ *Celmisia argentea*

C. bellidioides Flowerheads appear in profusion in early summer, about 2cm (¾in) across on short stalks. This reliable perennial has 1cm (⅜in) long, dark green shiny leaves which form an attractive mat. HEIGHT & SPREAD 5×60cm (2×24in).

C. ramulosa Sticky 4cm (1½in) stalks carry this small shrub's 2.5cm (1in) wide solitary flowerheads in mid summer. The pleated leaves have a white woolly underside and are about 1cm (⅜in) long. HEIGHT & SPREAD 20×20cm (8×8in).

The dark grey leaves of var. ***tuberculata*** are covered in silvery knobs.

C. semicordata Erect sword-like leaves up to 40cm (16in) long reveal a satiny, silvery underside, making this an eye-catching perennial. It is clump-forming and flowers in early to mid summer with heads about 6cm (2½in) across. HEIGHT & SPREAD 40×40cm (16×16in).

CULTIVATION Grow in a moist but well-drained soil in a sunny position. Never let it dry out. In too rich a soil plants are more likely to rot or be killed by frost.

PROPAGATION Take greenwood cuttings and keep well watered and well aired until rooted. Seed is fertile only if more than one plant of the same species is grown. Sow it in late summer, as soon as it is ripe.

PESTS AND DISEASES Aphids may attack.

Celosia

Cockscomb, Prince of Wales' feather

Amaranthaceae

Celosia argentea var. plumosa

Tiny brightly coloured flowers borne in feathery plumes from mid summer to early autumn characterise these tropical plants. Only varieties of the annual species *Celosia argentea* are cultivated in Britain. Some can be grown outdoors as exotic summer bedding, given a warm, sheltered position, while others need to be grown as pot plants in a warm greenhouse or conservatory.

RECOMMENDED VARIETIES

C. argentea Feathery plumes of whitish flowers are seen on this rarely cultivated species. Its varieties are much more garden worthy. HEIGHT & SPREAD 60×30cm (2×1ft).

▲ *Celosia argentea*

The crested flowerheads of var. ***cristata*** look like velvety cockscombs. The pointed leaves are narrow, oval to lance-shaped, and up to 15cm (6in) long. This variety should be grown under glass and reaches a height and spread of 30×25cm (12×10in).

'Coral Garden' and **'Jewel Box'** are dwarf plants available in a mixture of orange, pink, purple, red and yellow.

▼ *Celosia argentea* var. *plumosa* 'Century' (rose)

▲ *Celosia argentea* var. *plumosa* 'Century' (yellow)

The feathery flowerheads of var. ***plumosa*** are not usually long-lasting. This plant can be grown outdoors in summer, but only in a warm, sheltered site. It reaches a height and spread of 45×30cm (1½×1ft).

'Century', at 50-70cm (20-28in), is suitable as a cut flower, both fresh and dried. **'Kimono'** is a dwarf strain at 20cm (8in) tall. Both 'Century' and 'Kimono' are available in a mixture of purple, pink, orange, red and yellow. **'New Look'** has dark red foliage and deep red plumes and reaches 40cm (16in) high.

The tall, slender var. ***spicata*** has plumed flowerheads, like large, coloured ears of wheat, that are suitable as cut flowers. It can be grown as a half-hardy annual outdoors in warm, sheltered spots, reaching a height and spread of 1m×25cm (3ft×10in).

The flowerheads of **'Flamingo Feather'** are deep pink at the top, fading to a paler

▼ *C. argentea* var. *spicata* 'Flamingo Feather'

colour at the base, and are freely produced over a long period.
CULTIVATION Plant outdoors when all risk of frost has passed, in fertile, moisture-retentive soil, choosing a sheltered site in full sun. Pinch out the growing points of *C. argentea* var. *spicata* when the plants are 10 cm (4 in) tall to promote branching.

Alternatively, grow var. *cristata* and var. *plumosa* in pots in the greenhouse. No artificial heating is needed after mid spring. Grow in good light, but shade from direct midday sun. Feed weekly and water generously, maintaining a humid atmosphere.
PROPAGATION Sow seed in a greenhouse in early spring, providing a minimum temperature of 15°C (59°F).
PESTS AND DISEASES Red spider mite can be troublesome under glass. Leaf-spotting and root rot may also occur.

Celtis

Nettle tree, hackberry
Ulmaceae

Celtis australis

Rough-textured, nettle-shaped leaves clothe the broad dome of these deciduous trees which prefers limy soil and warm weather. In some species the foliage may turn yellow in autumn. The small purplish black or red berries that follow the tiny greenish flowers are edible, but they are seldom profuse in Britain. The genus is native to S Europe, SE Asia and N America and the trees tend to be slow-growing in Britain. The American species, such as *Celtis occidentalis*, grow and fruit best.
RECOMMENDED SPECIES
C. australis (European nettle tree) The bark of this round-headed tree is smooth and grey. The leaves are up to 15 cm (6 in) long and 7 cm (2¾ in) wide. They have a rough, dark green upper surface and are greyish beneath. HEIGHT & SPREAD 4×2 m (13×6½ ft) after 10 years, ultimately 12 m (40 ft) tall.
C. occidentalis (hackberry) A broad crown develops above a trunk covered with rough, warty, grey bark. The leaves are slightly smaller than those of *C. australis*. HEIGHT & SPREAD 4×2 m (13×6½ ft) after 10 years, ultimately 18 m (60 ft) tall.
CULTIVATION The trees grow in most soils, but do best in limy conditions. Give them a sunny site. Mature trees tolerate dryness.
PROPAGATION Sow seed in spring.
PRUNING Seldom necessary.
PESTS AND DISEASES Usually trouble free.

Centaurea

Knapweed, cornflower
Compositae

Centaurea montana

Bright summer flowers that attract bees and butterflies into the garden are a valued feature of these popular annuals and perennials. The large flowerheads, some of which are good for drying, have neatly overlapping bracts and a central, thistle-like boss of florets, surrounded by colourful, spreading, rather spidery, ray florets. Stiff upright stems make the larger perennials bold plants for beds and borders. They do well on poor soils, particularly chalky sites in full sun, and survive anywhere with good drainage.

The familiar and colourful annual *Centaurea cyanus* is an important feature of annual wild-flower meadows, mixing well with poppies and corn marigolds. It makes a fine cut flower and its cultivars come in a good range of colours, including blue, pink and red. The genus is native to Europe, W and central Asia and N Africa. All are hardy in Britain except *C. cineraria*.
RECOMMENDED SPECIES AND VARIETIES
C. bella Pink to pale purple flowerheads, up to 4 cm (1½ in) across, appear on this low mound-forming herbaceous perennial from late spring to mid summer. Silvery grey leaves, basically lyre-shaped but with lobes, are 12 cm (4¾ in) long, white with woolly hairs beneath. The plant is sometimes found in nursery catalogues under *C. simplicicaulis*. HEIGHT & SPREAD 40×40 cm (16×16 in).

▲ *Centaurea bella*

C. cineraria♀ (syn. *C. gymnocarpa)* White-felted foliage makes this evergreen perennial useful as a dot or edging plant. The leaves are up to 20 cm (8 in) long and deeply divided with lyre-shaped lobes. Purple flowers, up to 3 cm (1¼ in) across with dark brown pointed bracts beneath, open in small clusters during mid summer but are secondary to the foliage. This plant dislikes winter wet and is not reliably hardy below -15°C (5°F) in most regions, so is often grown each year from seed. HEIGHT & SPREAD 1 m×45 cm (3×1½ ft).
C. cyanus (cornflower) Blue, pink, purple, red or white flowers 2.5-5 cm (1-2 in) across appear on these annual plants in branching sprays from early summer to early autumn. The narrow, tapering leaves are grey-green and up to 15 cm (6 in) long. HEIGHT & SPREAD up to 1 m×30 cm (3×1 ft).

'Blue Diadem' is a tall variety, 60 cm-1 m (2-3 ft) high, with large, deep blue flowers 7.5 cm (3 in) across. Compact forms to 30 cm (1 ft) tall are suited to bedding and growing in pots. They include **'Dwarf Rose Gem'** with rose-red flowers, **'Jubilee Gem'** with blue flowers, and **'Polka Dot'** available in mixed colours.
C. dealbata Bright pink flowers, about 6 cm (2½ in) across, are freely borne from mid to late summer, nestling among the upper leaves on stiff erect stems. This clump-forming herbaceous perennial has finely cut, light green leaves up to 45 cm (18 in) long, grey with woolly hairs beneath. HEIGHT & SPREAD up to 1 m×60 cm (3×2 ft).

'Steenbergii' has carmine-lilac flowers and is just 60 cm (2 ft) tall.
C. gymnocarpa see *C. cineraria*♀
C. hypoleuca Bright pink flowers, 4 cm (1½ in) across, are freely borne in mid summer by this upright herbaceous perennial. Finely cut mid green leaves have a white underside with woolly hairs and are 25 cm (10 in) long, basically lyre-shaped but with up to 9 lobes. HEIGHT & SPREAD 60×45 cm (2×1½ ft).

'John Coutts' has deep rose flowers up to 7.5 cm (3 in) wide, and is more spreading than the species; to 60 cm (2 ft).
C. macrocephala Large yellow flowers, about 5 cm (2 in) across and surrounded by papery, silvery brown bracts, distinguish this vigorous, clump-forming herbaceous perennial. Narrowly oval mid green leaves are 30 cm (12 in) long and 6 cm (2½ in) wide. The flowers, which appear in mid summer, dry well for display. HEIGHT & SPREAD 1 m×60 cm (3×2 ft).
C. montana (mountain or perennial cornflower) Purple to violet-blue flowers, up to 7.5 cm (3 in) across, appear in profusion during late spring and early summer on this vigorous spreading, herbaceous to partly

▼ *Centaurea montana*

evergreen perennial. This popular old cottage garden flower is patch-forming with a dense mass of roots that produce a number of stems carrying one or more flowers. The grey-green leaves, up to 18cm (7in) long, are narrow to elliptical and tapering. The undersides of the leaves are woolly. HEIGHT & SPREAD 50×60cm (20×24in).

▲ *Centaurea montana* 'Alba'

▲ *Centaurea montana* 'Carnea'

'Alba' has white flowers and paler leaves than the species. **'Carnea'** (syn. 'Rosea') bears bright pink flowers. **'Parham'** has deep amethyst blooms.
C. ruthenica This imposing herbaceous perennial has solitary sulphur-yellow flowers, about 5cm (2in) across, borne in mid summer on stiffly erect stems. The deep green, dissected leaves are oblong and hairless, up to 25cm (10in) long at the base of the plant and shorter on the stems. The base of the plant gradually becomes woody as it matures. HEIGHT & SPREAD 1.5m×80cm (60×32in).
C. simplicicaulis Numerous rose-pink flowers, up to 5cm (2in) across, appear from late spring to mid summer on this mound-forming herbaceous perennial with stiff erect stems. Lobed, oblong to lyre-shaped leaves are deep green above and grey with hairs beneath. HEIGHT & SPREAD 40×40cm (16×16in).

▼ *Centaurea simplicicaulis*

C. triumfettii Blue or lilac flowers, up to 7.5cm (3in) across with paler or whitish centres, are produced in early and mid summer. This fairly robust, partly evergreen perennial has short rhizomes and grey-green oblong to elliptical leaves covered at first in whitish cobweb-like hairs. HEIGHT & SPREAD up to 70×50cm (28×20in).

White flowers distinguish ssp. ***cana*** which has woolly leaves and flower bracts and grows up to 20cm (8in) tall; **'Rosea'** bears rose-pink flowers. The flowers of ssp. ***stricta*** are blue and the plant grows up to 50cm (20in) tall.
CULTIVATION Plant perennials from autumn to spring in any free-draining soil in a sunny spot. *C. montana* tolerates a range of conditions, from moist to dryish sites in sun or semi-shade. Stake taller plants.
PROPAGATION Divide when replanting after flowering or in early spring. Sow seed of perennials in pots in a coldframe in late winter or early spring and plant out as soon as large enough. Examine home-grown seed carefully for maggots. Take cuttings of *C. cineraria* in mid summer, root under glass and plant out in spring. Sow seed of annuals in their flowering position in spring.
PESTS AND DISEASES Powdery mildew may attack foliage and stems of many species, especially in mid to late summer.

Centradenia

Melastomataceae

Centradenia inaequilateralis 'Cascade'

Grown mainly as indoor pot plants or in a greenhouse, these tropical evergreen plants provide beautiful year-round foliage and winter floral colour. They need a minimum temperature of 13°C (55°F) to thrive.
RECOMMENDED SPECIES AND VARIETIES
C. inaequilateralis (syn. *C. rosea*) Small, pink, 4-petalled flowers in clusters about 10cm (4in) across, appear at the ends of the branches during winter. The soft, oval to lance-shaped leaves are up to 10cm (4in) long. Mid green in colour, they are strongly suffused with red. This species forms a small sub-shrub. Native to Mexico. HEIGHT & SPREAD 30×30cm (1×1ft).

▲ *Centradenia inaequilateralis* 'Cascade'

'Cascade' has a pendulous habit and is ideal for a permanent hanging basket.
C. rosea see *C. inaequilateralis*
CULTIVATION Grow in pots or hanging baskets in good-quality, general-purpose compost. Choose a lightly shaded position in a warm greenhouse or indoors. Repot annually in spring. Feed plants freely and water well in summer; feed and water more moderately in winter.
PROPAGATION Sow seed in spring or summer or take softwood cuttings in summer.
PRUNING Pinch out the tips of young plants to promote a bushy habit and cut back old plants each spring to ensure a leafy, well-clothed plant.
PESTS AND DISEASES Whitefly, red spider mite and mealy bug may attack the plants.

Centranthus

Valerianaceae

The long flowering season, from early summer to early autumn, is a valued feature of these annuals and hardy perennials.
RECOMMENDED SPECIES AND VARIETIES
C. ruber (red valerian) Panicles of 6mm (¼in) crimson to pale red, star-shaped flowers are borne above grey-green fleshy oval leaves, up to 10cm (4in) long. Native to Europe and the Mediterranean, this species is an easily grown, striking perennial for a sunny dry spot on chalk, where it forms an erect, bushy, compact plant. On richer soils it tends to be more lax and possibly not so long-lived. Its nectar attracts butterflies and hawkmoths into the garden. HEIGHT & SPREAD 60×60cm (2×2ft) or more.

▼ *Centranthus ruber*

▲ *Centranthus ruber coccineus*

White flowers are seen on ***albus***, while ***coccineus*** has deep red flowers.

CULTIVATION Grow *C. ruber* in the herbaceous border, on dry slopes or in crevices in walls. It does best in poor, particularly chalky soil. In a herbaceous border replant it every 3 or 4 years as it becomes leggy in rich soil, but elsewhere it can be left. Trimming after the first flowering helps to preserve the shape and encourage a second crop of new leaves and flowers.

PROPAGATION Divide or sow seed in spring. The young seedlings should be grown in pots so that the taproot is not damaged in transplanting. In suitable conditions the plant self-seeds.

PESTS AND DISEASES Usually trouble free.

Cephalaria

Giant scabious

Dipsacaceae

Dense, rounded heads of numerous small tubular flowers, resembling pin cushions, appear above the dark green foliage in early summer. The flowers, in buttery-yellow, ivory or white, are long-lasting.

The two hardy perennials listed below make imposing plants in a large border or woodland garden. They need plenty of room to develop and are therefore not suitable for a small garden. The genus contains annuals and perennials – all widely distributed through Europe, Asia and N Africa.

RECOMMENDED SPECIES

C. alpina The yellow flowerheads, 3 cm (1¼ in) across, are carried at the top of thin, hairy stems. The basal leaves are up to 10 cm (4 in) long made up of 9-15 paired leaflets. Each leaflet is 3 cm (1¼ in) long, oval with pointed tips and slightly toothed edges. The stem leaves are smaller. HEIGHT & SPREAD 1.2×1 m (4×3 ft).

▼ *Cephalaria gigantea*

C. gigantea (syn. *C. tatarica*) Ridged stems carry the ivory to pale yellow flowerheads, up to 5 cm (2 in) across. The 40 cm (16 in) long basal leaves are composed of up to 15 leaflets, each up to 10 cm (4 in) long with coarsely toothed edges. The stem leaves are smaller. HEIGHT & SPREAD 1.8×1.2 m (6×4 ft).

C. tatarica see *C. gigantea*

CULTIVATION Plant in autumn or spring in any soil in full sun. In sheltered gardens the plants can be grown without staking.

PROPAGATION Sow seed in autumn in open ground or divide in spring.

PESTS AND DISEASES Usually trouble free.

Cephalocereus see CACTI p. 106

Cephalotaxus

Plum yew

Cephalotaxaceae

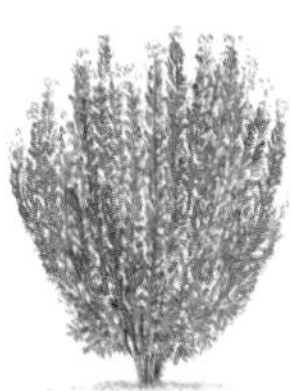

Cephalotaxus harringtonia 'Fastigiata'

Glossy, dark green leaves, straight-sided and very narrow, are lined up in rows on either side of the shoots, luxuriantly clothing these slow-growing evergreen conifers. The plants make handsome, spreading specimens, or can be clipped into a hedge, while *Cephalotaxus fortunei* 'Prostrate Spreader' is useful as ground cover. Native to E Asia and the Himalayas, the species listed below are generally hardy and do best in a shaded part of the garden with cool, moist soil.

Tiny cream flowers open in early spring, or sometimes in late winter, along the underside of the shoot at the base of each leaf on male trees, and on females at the tips of shoots before the flush of new growth. The brown cones borne on female trees (if fertilised by a nearby male) resemble olives or small plums.

RECOMMENDED SPECIES AND VARIETIES

C. fortunei The tree forms a shapely, low umbrella of growth and tolerates constant shade. The soft leaves grow to 10 cm (4 in) long and curve down at the tip. New spring growth suffers damage from late spring frosts. HEIGHT & SPREAD 1×2 m (3×6½ ft) after 10 years, ultimately 10 m (33 ft) tall.

'Prostrate Spreader' is very similar to the species, but much lower and more spreading, always being wider than it is tall. It reaches 1×5 m (3×16 ft) in 30 years and makes an excellent ground-cover plant for dark, damp positions. Its bark is reddish brown and flaking.

C. harringtonia Dark, shiny leaves, 5 cm (2 in) long with 2 faint silvery, parallel bands underneath, are aligned in rows. The plant is rounded and shrubby with flaky brown bark. HEIGHT & SPREAD 1×1 m (3×3 ft) after 10 years, ultimately 6 m (20 ft) tall.

▲ *Cephalotaxus harringtonia* var. *drupacea*

▲ *Cephalotaxus harringtonia* 'Fastigiata'

The smaller var. ***drupacea*** has shorter needles than the species. **'Fastigiata'** has a nearly columnar habit, with steeply upright branches. The needles are spirally arranged rather than ranked.

CULTIVATION Although acid soils suit cephalotaxus plants best, they are among the few conifers that also do well in chalky soils. They thrive in cool, damp sites, including heavy clay, and revel in shade whether dappled or deep.

PROPAGATION Take semi-ripe or hardwood cuttings from terminal shoots; side-shoot cuttings do not produce leaders.

PRUNING None is necessary except for removing any badly shaped branches in mid to late spring. New shoots may appear at wounds exposed to light – a response that makes the plants (except for 'Prostrate Spreader') suitable for clipping as a hedge.

PESTS AND DISEASES Usually trouble free.

Cerastium

Mouse-ear chickweed

Caryophyllaceae

C

Mounds of attractive grey-green or white foliage are decorated in summer with small white flowers with five deeply notched petals and ten yellowish stamens. There are at least 60 species around the world – hardy annuals and herbaceous perennials. All but a few are too invasive and weedy for the garden. Those that are cultivated are suitable for rock gardens or raised beds or for covering banks or walls.

RECOMMENDED SPECIES AND VARIETIES
*C. **alpinum*** (alpine chickweed) Compact and mat-forming, this hardy evergreen perennial is covered with soft greyish hairs. The grey-green leaves are oval and 1 cm (⅜ in) long. White flowers 1.5 cm (½ in) across are borne singly or in loose clusters of up to 5 flowers on short stalks. Flowers appear in late spring and early summer. Some leaves wither in cold winters. Grow in a sunny niche in a rock garden or in a gap between paving. Native to grassy and rocky uplands across Europe. HEIGHT & SPREAD 10×30 cm (4×12 in).

White hairs cover var. ***lanatum***. Protect it from damp winter conditions.

▲ *Cerastium tomentosum*

*C. **tomentosum*** (snow-in-summer) This popular plant, a hardy evergreen perennial, forms a greyish white spreading mat made up of narrow white-felted leaves, 2 cm (¾ in) long. A profusion of starry white flowers, 2 cm (¾ in) across, are borne in lax clusters throughout summer. This is a very vigorous plant, providing effective cover for banks, walls and dry path edges. It is too invasive for a rock garden or raised bed. Native to the Apennines and Sicily. HEIGHT & SPREAD 20 cm×1 m (8 in×3 ft).

Var. ***columnae*** is a more compact form.

CULTIVATION Plant in gritty, well-drained soil in a sunny site, in spring or early summer. Protect *C. alpinum* in winter with a pane of glass. Grow *C. alpinum* var. *lanatum* in pans in an unheated greenhouse.

PROPAGATION Divide plants in spring or late summer. Sow seed when ripe or in spring in a coldframe.

PESTS AND DISEASES Usually trouble free.

Ceratostigma

Plumbaginaceae

Ceratostigma willmottianum

Bright blue flowers and fine reddish bronze autumn foliage provide a wonderful display on these low-growing shrubs. Rounded, five-lobed flowers, borne in clusters, last from summer into autumn and make an impact at the front of a border or in a rock garden. The shrubs may be deciduous or evergreen and have small oval to obovate leaves. Ceratostigmas, native to China and the Himalayas, are not fully hardy and are treated as herbaceous perennials and cut back to ground level in winter in cold areas.

RECOMMENDED SPECIES AND VARIETIES
*C. **griffithii*** The deep blue flowers, up to 1 cm (⅜ in) across, appear from late summer to mid autumn, but can be rather sparse. The dull green leaves, 3 cm (1¼ in) long, turn bright red in autumn. The multi-stemmed, evergreen shrub has a rounded habit. HEIGHT & SPREAD 80×80 cm (32×32 in).

▲ *Ceratostigma griffithii*

*C. **plumbaginoides***♀ (syn. *C. larpentae*) The brilliant blue flowers, about 1.5 cm (½ in) across, are borne on this plant from early to mid autumn. The deep green, deciduous leaves, up to 4 cm (1½ in) long, produce rich red tints in autumn. The plant is multi-stemmed and spreading. HEIGHT & SPREAD 40×50 cm (16×20 in).

*C. **willmottianum***♀ (Chinese plumbago) Rich blue flowers, 1.5 cm (½ in) across, are carried in profusion from mid summer to mid autumn on this slender, multistemmed, deciduous shrub with a rounded habit. The light green leaves, up to 5 cm (2 in) long, are hairy on both sides and tinted red in autumn. HEIGHT & SPREAD 60×60 cm (2×2 ft).

CULTIVATION Grow in a dry, well-drained soil in full sun. The plant requires protection and does best against a south-facing wall.

PROPAGATION Take semi-ripe cuttings in mid to late summer. Divide in winter.

PRUNING Cut back to ground level any shoots that have been killed by frost.

PESTS AND DISEASES Usually trouble free.

Cercidiphyllum

Cercidiphyllaceae

Cercidiphyllum japonicum

The foliage of this upright, sometimes multistemmed, tree, the sole species of its genus, takes on subtle autumn colours – pale yellows, purple and pink – that light up the garden. It is frost-hardy in all situations and is native to Japan and China.

Cercidiphyllum japonicum♀ (Katsura tree) The deciduous leaves are a rounded heart shape, 5 cm (2 in) across. New spring leaves are often a glowing bronze colour, then become bluish green above and bluish green-white beneath. There are separate male and female trees; both bear small, insignificant red flowers on bare branches in mid spring. Female flowers develop into bunches of small pods, up to 1 cm (⅜ in) long, containing seeds which are fertile only if a male tree grows nearby.

An autumn bonus is the smell of caramel or candyfloss that the tree gives off and that often carries 70 m (75 yd). HEIGHT & SPREAD 6×3 m (20×10 ft) after 20 years, ultimately more than 20 m (66 ft) tall.

The leaves of var. ***magnificum***♀ are larger and turn a golden yellow in autumn. It is a rarer and smaller tree reaching 10 m (33 ft) eventually. The leaf size and colour of f. ***pendulum*** is as the species but the tree has long pendulous branches.

CULTIVATION The trees do best on a fairly deep, rich, moist soil. In times of little rain they sometimes shed their leaves before the autumn display of colour. Plant trees from late autumn to early spring; container-

▼ *Cercidiphyllum japonicum pendulum*

grown trees can be planted out at any time.
PROPAGATION Readily propagated from seed or hardwood cuttings.
PRUNING None required other than to remove dead branches.
PESTS AND DISEASES Usually trouble free.

Cercis
Leguminosae

Cercis siliquastrum

Clusters of small pinkish purple flowers cover the bare branches of these small, spreading deciduous trees in late spring. They remain on the tree for two to three weeks as the foliage unfolds. The distinctive, broad alternate leaves, 5-15 cm (2-6 in) long, are paper-thin, bright green and shaped like a rounded heart. If conditions are favourable, they turn a warm yellow colour in autumn. The fruits contain a line of hard-coated seeds in flat, green pods. Plants are slow-growing in Britain. They need a sheltered, sunny position.
RECOMMENDED SPECIES AND VARIETIES
***C. canadensis* 'Forest Pansy'**♀ The tree or large shrub has distinctive bronze, reddish purple foliage all season. It does not reliably flower in Britain. HEIGHT & SPREAD 4.5 x 3 m (15×10 ft) after 15-20 years, ultimately 12 m (40 ft) high. Native to southern USA.

▲ *Cercis siliquastrum*

C. siliquastrum (Judas tree)♀ A spectacular display of rose-purple flowers is borne in late spring on the rounded tree. The plant grows best in hot, dry stony places and is most suited to southern Britain. The pods become rosy coloured in late summer. Native to SE Europe and W Asia. HEIGHT & SPREAD 6×3.5 m (20×12 ft) in 15-20 years, ultimately 10 m (33 ft) tall and can be equally as wide.

The flowers of f. *albida* are white; the leaves are pale green.
CULTIVATION Trees do well on both acid and lime-rich soils. They prefer dry conditions and good drainage and do not thrive in heavy, wet soils. Shelter from late frosts.
PROPAGATION Sow seed under glass in early spring. Plant into the permanent growing position when 2 years old as these trees do not transplant well. Trees take 5-6 years to bear flowers.
PRUNING None necessary, but trees can be cut back hard in winter or pruned lightly after flowering to keep them small.
PESTS AND DISEASES Coral spot can be a problem. Canker occurs in wild stands of *C. canadensis* in N America, and cultivated specimens could possibly be affected.

Ceropegia
Asclepiadaceae

A fine trailing habit makes this versatile succulent an ideal houseplant. It can be grown in troughs to tumble down as a 'living curtain' and makes a good companion for other succulents and desert plants, like cacti. The recommended species originates in dry regions of E South Africa. Simple cultivation makes it easy for children to grow.
RECOMMENDED SPECIES AND VARIETIES
C. linearis ssp. ***woodii***♀ (rosary vine, string of hearts) Curious flowers produced in late summer are up to 2.5 cm (1 in) long and curve upwards, resembling pink pipes. Small potato-like tubers produce long thin stems with, at intervals, heart-shaped leaves up to 2 cm (¾ in) long, attractively marked with shades of grey. These tubers allow easy

▲ *Ceropegia linearis ssp. woodii*

propagation of the plant. It spreads to the width of the container. HEIGHT 2 m (6½ ft).
CULTIVATION Grow where the plant will receive several hours of direct sunlight a day to encourage the leaves to colour, although it tolerates poor light. High temperatures are not necessary; it survives cold conditions, to freezing point if kept dry. Water sparingly, letting the compost dry out first. In winter, water very occasionally; not at all if temperatures fall below 7°C (45°F). Feed little and often if growth is desired. Repot annually only if large plants are wanted. Cut the plant back if it trails too far or is untidy.

PROPAGATION Take cuttings or detach tubers from the stems in spring and pot them up into a very gritty compost. Put additional grit, sharp sand or perlite around the base of the cutting or tuber to prevent rotting. Water sparingly until plants start active growth, which may not happen for several months.
PESTS AND DISEASES Plants may suffer from infestations of mealy bug.

Cestrum
Solanaceae

Cestrum parqui

Clusters of small, tubular flowers in shades of red, yellow and purple appear in late spring and summer on these tender evergreen or deciduous shrubs. They can be grown outdoors in mild areas, given a warm sheltered position, but elsewhere they require a conservatory or unheated greenhouse. The plants originate in S America. All parts may be poisonous if eaten.
RECOMMENDED SPECIES AND VARIETIES
C. elegans♀ (syn. *C. purpureum*) An upright evergreen shrub with slender, arching branches that bear clusters of reddish purple flowers throughout summer. The narrow, pitcher-shaped flowers are 2.5 cm (1 in) long. The downy, slender pointed leaves are a dull green and up to 12.5 cm (5 in) long. Shiny, deep purple berries, 2 cm (¾ in) long may form in late summer and autumn. HEIGHT & SPREAD 1.2×1 m (4×3 ft) after 5 years, ultimately 3 m (10 ft) tall.
***C.* 'Newellii'**♀ Clusters of red, pitcher-shaped flowers, each 2.5 cm (1 in) long, are borne from late spring to mid summer on this evergreen shrub. The narrow, oval, dull green leaves are up to 15 cm (6 in) long. HEIGHT & SPREAD 1.2×1 m (4×3 ft) after 5 years, ultimately 3 m (10 ft) tall.
C. parqui♀ Large drooping clusters of night-scented flowers appear from mid summer to early autumn on this deciduous

▼ *Cestrum* 'Newellii'

C

▲ *Cestrum parqui*

shrub. Greenish yellow and tubular, the flowers are 2cm (¾in) long with spreading, pointed lobes. The bright green willow-like leaves are up to 12.5cm (5in) long. Purplish brown to black fruits, 1cm (⅜in) long, are rare. HEIGHT & SPREAD 1.2×1m (4×3ft) after 5 years, ultimately 2.4m (8ft) tall.
C. purpureum see *C. elegans*
CULTIVATION Outdoors, plant in well-drained, preferably rich, loamy soil against a sheltered, south or west-facing wall. Under glass, plant in well-drained potting compost and place in a sunny or partially shaded spot.
PROPAGATION Raise plants from seed or semi-ripe cuttings.
PRUNING Not necessary but plants can be cut back in early spring to restrict size.
PESTS AND DISEASES Usually trouble free.

Chaenomeles

Flowering quince, japonica
Rosaceae

Chaenomeles japonica

Early spring flowers bloom on the bare branches of these easily grown, hardy deciduous shrubs. The bowl-shaped flowers, up to 5cm (2in) across, are borne singly or in clusters. Usually five petalled, there are shades of pink, red, orange and white. Flowers are often followed in autumn by large – up to 7.5cm (3in) long – fragrant, yellow-green fruits. The dense branches are thorny. Flowering quinces do well trained against a sunny wall; they may also be grown in a border and used for low ornamental hedging. The three species in the genus are native to China and Japan.

RECOMMENDED SPECIES AND VARIETIES
C. japonica Clusters of flowers are mostly red with prominent golden anthers but colour on different plants can vary. For reliability of colour, cultivars of *C.* × *superba* are more commonly grown. Flowers are followed by apple-shaped fruits, up to 4cm (1½in) across. The rounded, oval leaves are toothed and up to 5cm (2in) long. The low-growing, spreading shrub has a rounded habit. HEIGHT & SPREAD 60cm×1m (2×3ft) after 5 years, ultimately 1m (3ft) high and twice as broad.
C. speciosa Clusters of flowers on the multistemmed shrub appear in profusion in early spring and can be a range of colours but are predominantly red with attractive pale to bright yellow anthers. The inconsistency in flower colour makes the range of cultivars a more reliable buy. Fragrant fruits, up to 6cm (2½in) across, follow the flowers. These are green speckled with white and tend to be apple or pear-shaped. The oval, glossy green leaves reach 7.5 cm (3in) long. HEIGHT & SPREAD 1×1.2m (3×4ft) after 5 years, ultimately 3×5m (10×16ft).

'Geisha Girl'♀ is a smaller, low-growing plant with double, deep apricot-coloured flowers. **'Moerloosei'** ('Apple Blossom')

▲ *Chaenomeles speciosa* 'Geisha Girl'

▲ *Chaenomeles speciosa* 'Nivalis'

bears a profusion of white flowers with tinges of pink. **'Nivalis'** reaches 2×3m (6½×10ft) and has large pure white flowers. **'Rosea Plena'** has a semidouble pink to coral pink flower. The fruits are more ovate in shape and are quite often ribbed. **'Rubra Grandiflora'** has large crimson flowers and is of a low spreading habit, rarely more than 1m (3ft) high. The low-growing **'Simonii'** normally reaches no more than 1m (3ft) in height but spreads much wider. It has blood red, semidouble flowers produced in profusion. The large single white flowers of **'Snow'** are rather sparsely produced.
C.* × *superba It is best to select a named cultivar if a particular colour is required. The flowers of the dense, rounded shrub appear in early spring through to early summer and most have decorative yellow anthers. The apple-shaped fruits ripen in autumn. Leaves are up to 5cm (2in) long and are rather rounded with small teeth. HEIGHT & SPREAD 1×1.2m (3×4ft) after 5 years, ultimately 1.5m (5ft) tall and about twice as wide.

▲ *Chaenomeles speciosa* 'Simonii'

'Crimson and Gold'♀ is a handsome shrub with deep crimson flowers with a mass of golden anthers. **'Jet Trail'** has pure white flowers borne in profusion. The abundant flowers of **'Knap Hill Scarlet'**♀ are long lasting and are a bright orange-

▲ *Chaenomeles* × *superba* 'Crimson and Gold'

scarlet. **'Nicoline'**♀ has scarlet red flowers. **'Pink Lady'**♀ is dark pink in bud opening to rose pink. The flowers of **'Rowallane'**♀ are a bright crimson.
CULTIVATION Chaenomeles are adaptable shrubs and grow under a wide range of conditions but they grow best in well-drained soil and flower better in full sun. Plant them from late autumn to early spring.
PROPAGATION Grow from seed but if a particular flower colour is needed a specific cultivar is required and a grafted plant must be purchased.
PRUNING None normally required unless it is to thin out the often numerous branches or to keep a plant to a certain size. Train plants grown against a wall by cutting back the previous season's growth to two or three buds after flowering.
PESTS AND DISEASES Usually trouble free.

Chaenorhinum

Scrophulariaceae

A mass of small, snapdragon-like flowers are produced throughout summer in shades of lilac, violet, blue and yellow by these sun-loving hardy annuals and perennials, suited to raised beds and rock gardens.

RECOMMENDED SPECIES AND VARIETIES
C. glareosum Violet and yellow flowers, about 8mm (⅜in) long, are borne in showy spikes by this handsome perennial which has arching stems and spreads to form tufts. Its light blue-green roundish leaves are up to 1.5cm (½in) long. Native to S Spain. HEIGHT & SPREAD 15×35cm (6×14in).
C. origanifolium (syn. *Linaria origanifolia*) Lilac-blue flowers 1-2cm (⅜-¾in) long with darker stripes and a pale yellow or

▲ *Chaenorhinum origanifolium*

white patch on the lip appear in late spring and all summer. This tufted perennial has lax stems up to 35cm (14in) long and 1-2cm (3/8-3/4in) long oval leaves. Some forms spread, while others are more upright. Native to the Pyrenees. HEIGHT & SPREAD 10-20×25-30cm (4-8×10-12in).
CULTIVATION Grow in a sunny open site in gritty, well-drained, preferably limy, soil.
PROPAGATION Sow seed in pots in a cold-frame during autumn and winter.
PESTS AND DISEASES Usually trouble free.

Chaerophyllum

Hairy chervil
Umbelliferae

Fern-like foliage sets off the billowing, flattish lilac-pink or white flowerheads of the annuals, biennials and perennials in this genus to perfection. Brighten a late spring border with the hardy herbaceous perennial described; do not confuse it with chervil, the culinary herb, *Anthriscus cerefolium* (see HERBS, p. 330), and do not use for cooking.

RECOMMENDED SPECIES AND VARIETIES

***C. hirsutum* 'Roseum'** Numerous tiny lilac-pink flowers grouped in small rosettes are borne in rounded clusters 7.5-12.5cm (3-4in) across on erect, branching stems. Each cluster carries as many as 30 rosettes. The broadly incised, dark green leaves, 15×15cm (6×6in), are arranged alternately on 25-30cm (9-12in) long stalks. Both leaves and stalks are covered with soft hairs. Clusters of flattened, ovoid seeds follow the flowers. Native to Europe. HEIGHT & SPREAD 30-60×30-60cm (1-2×1-2ft).
CULTIVATION Plant in dampish ground, wooded areas, or the usual garden soils, in spring or autumn. Position in sun or partial shade. Split clumps every 2-3 years.
PROPAGATION Divide in spring or autumn. Sow seed as soon as it ripens.
PESTS AND DISEASES Slugs and snails attack young plants.

▼ *Chaerophyllum hirsutum* 'Roseum'

Chamaecyparis

False cypress
Cupressaceae

Chamaecyparis lawsoniana 'Lutea'

Exceptionally varied evergreen conifers – dwarf, tall, round, shrubby, conical and columnar – make up this genus. Foliage colour ranges through green, blue, grey and golden; often the coldest winters bring out the best colour. The scale-like, overlapping leaves form flattened sprays that are held in pairs on either side of the shoots.

The trees are planted in groups for screening and formal schemes, and individually for accent plants in borders, rock gardens, patios and tubs. Growth rates vary with conditions but many of the numerous varieties are too large for most gardens and cannot be kept small by pruning. The plants are hardy but easily damaged by any weight of snow. These natives of eastern N America, Japan and Taiwan prefer acid, clay soils but do well on most fertile garden soils.

RECOMMENDED SPECIES AND VARIETIES

C. lawsoniana (Lawson cypress) This narrow, conical tree gains up to 60cm (2ft) of height a year and is far too large for most gardens. There is a great choice of varieties that make more suitable garden plants; all have the drooping leading shoots characteristic of the species. Tiny red male flowers open in spring at the new branchlet tips; blue female flowers appear on the same tree, borne on the previous year's growth tips and sideshoots. The female flowers mature into globular cones almost 1cm (3/8in) across. HEIGHT & SPREAD 6×2.4m (20×8ft) after 10 years, ultimately 50m (165ft) tall.

The recommended varieties are grouped below as broad, narrow and dwarf.

BROAD VARIETIES

'Albospica' has green foliage sprays splashed with creamy white, giving it a speckled appearance. It makes very slow growth, reaching only about 1.5m×75cm (5×2½ft) after 10 years. **'Alumigold'** is compact, upright and slow growing, reaching only 2m×50cm (6½ft×20in) in 10 years; it has yellow, soft-textured new

▲ *Chamaecyparis lawsoniana* 'Golden Wonder'

spring foliage that matures to blue-green on the ascending branches. **'Erecta Viridis'** ('Erecta') forms a flame-shaped silhouette, ultimately growing to about 25×6m (80×20ft), and has bright green sprays of foliage held upright on erect branches. **'Golden Wonder'** bears bright golden foliage all year round, particularly if sited in the sun. It is fast growing, reaching 20×4m (66×13ft) or more in just 30 years. **'Green Hedger'**♀ is an erect grower with dense, fresh green foliage. If unchecked, it becomes a towering 25×4m (80×13ft), but it can be controlled to form a dense hedge with regular clipping in spring and autumn. **'Nana Albospica'** is a short and slow grower that reaches only 2×1.5m (6½×5ft) after 40 years. The dark blue-green foliage is flecked with creamy white.

NARROW VARIETIES

'Ellwoodii'♀ has dense sprays of grey-green leaves on a bushy, multistemmed tree 10m (33ft) high. In winter the foliage turns steel

▼ *Chamaecyparis lawsoniana* 'Ellwoodii'

C

blue. **'Ellwood's Gold'**♀ has dense, yellowish green foliage tipped with gold all year round. It has a compact habit and grows slowly to about 5m (16ft). **'Fletcheri'**♀ is a dense, upright grower suitable for planting in a row to make a screen up to 6m (20ft) high. The feathery sprays of foliage are greyish green. **'Grayswood Pillar'**♀ develops quickly to 9×1m (30×3ft). Its steeply ascending branches bear dense, grey foliage. **'Kilmacurragh'**♀ has short, steeply upright branches bearing dense sprays of dark, grey-green foliage. It reaches about 25×2m (80×6½ft) in 40 years. **'Lane'**♀ makes a golden column about 6×1.5m (20×5ft) high. It is clothed right to its base with drooping, feathery sprays of foliage. **'Lutea'**♀ reaches 25×3m (80×10ft) and has luxuriant, feathery golden foliage. **'Pelt's Blue'**♀ is 4×2m (13×6½ft) with silvery blue foliage. **'Pembury Blue'**♀, with striking silver-blue, dense foliage, grows to 4×1.2m (13×4ft) in 10 years and eventually to twice this size. It needs a warm spot.

▲ *Chamaecyparis lawsoniana* 'Aurea Densa'

▲ *Chamaecyparis obtusa* 'Kosteri'

▲ *Chamaecyparis lawsoniana* 'Pembury Blue'

▲ *Chamaecyparis lawsoniana* 'Minima Glauca'

▲ *Chamaecyparis obtusa* 'Tetragona Aurea'

'Wisselii'♀ is particularly striking in spring when all its branch tips are laden with tiny, red male flowers. Sprays of dark green leaves are packed on the branches of a tree that reaches 10×2m (33×6½ft) in 40 years.

DWARF VARIETIES

'Aurea Densa'♀ develops into a rounded, conical shape with dense, overlapping sprays of golden foliage all year round. It grows only 1cm (⅜in) a year, eventually reaching 2m×75cm (6½ft×30in). **'Chilworth Silver'**♀ produces dense, blue-grey, needle-like foliage on upright branches. It grows slowly to 3×1.5m (10×5ft), broadening towards the top. **'Forsteckensis'** forms a globular bush only 1.5×2m (5×6½ft) after 60 years. The foliage, so close-packed that it resembles moss, appears grey-blue from a distance but greener close up. **'Gimbornii'**♀ makes a neat globe of dense, bluish green foliage, tipped with mauve in winter. It barely reaches 2×1.8m (6½×6ft) after 40 years. **'Lutea Nana'**♀ is slow-growing with quite openly arranged golden foliage. It reaches 2×2m (6½×6½ft) after 60 years. **'Minima Aurea'**♀ makes a compact egg shape whose foliage sprays are golden on the upper surface and bright yellow underneath. The extremely hardy plant reaches just 80cm (32in) after 40 years. **'Minima Glauca'**♀ forms a 2m (6½ft) globe with sea-green foliage in short vertical sprays. **'Pygmaea Argentea'**♀ slowly develops into a rounded bush whose erect branches bear dark, bluish green foliage tipped with silvery white. Strong sunlight scorches this plant. Because it grows to only about 2m×75cm (6½×2½ft), it is suitable for a tub or planter.

C. obtusa (Hinoki cypress) This tall, fast-growing species forms a dense cone with a wide spread at the base. The shiny, deep green, scale-like leaves are borne in flattened sprays and have bright, white 'x' marks on the underside. Small orange male and pale brown female flowers occur on the same tree in clusters at the shoot tips in spring, males on the new leading tips and females on the previous year's shoots and sideshoots. Round, scaly cones ripen from green to brown and grow to 1.5cm (½in) across. HEIGHT & SPREAD 5.5×2.4m (18×8ft) after 10 years, ultimately 30m (100ft) tall.

The varieties listed are smaller than the species and more suitable for gardens. **'Crippsii'**♀ reaches approximately 10×3m (33×10ft). The new foliage each year is bright golden yellow, fading rather in its second year, and the inner foliage is green. **'Kosteri'**♀ grows extremely slowly into a densely packed, conical bush about 1.2m (4ft) high. The flattened, dense, moss-like sprays of foliage are bright green. **'Nana'**♀ grows very slowly, taking 40 years to make a neat dome only 75×100cm (30×40in). Tight, rounded sprays of foliage are held in dense tiers and are a very dark, almost black, green. This is an extremely hardy plant. **'Nana Aurea'**♀ has the same shape as 'Nana' but is slightly taller and has more loosely arranged, golden foliage. **'Nana Gracilis'**♀ is more conical in shape and eventually reaches about 2m (6½ft) after some 40 years. Its flat fans of foliage are held erect and are dark, glossy green. **'Tetragona Aurea'**♀ is sparsely branched when young but becomes a bushy, upright plant 5×2.4m (16×8ft) after 50 years. Its dense foliage, in compact sprays, is a strong yellow and needs full sun to bring out the best colour.

C. pisifera (Sawara cypress) The broadly conical tree reaches a majestic height. Its ferny foliage sprays are held at a slight angle

C

to the shoots and consist of pointed, overlapping scale-like leaves that are bright green with a conspicuous white line on the underside. Male and female flowers are almost identical but the females are a paler brown. The cones look like peas. The varieties listed are smaller than the species and include plants to suit most gardens. HEIGHT & SPREAD 6×2.4m (20×8ft) after 10 years, ultimately 35m (115ft) tall.

'Boulevard'♀ is 6×3m (20×10ft) after 40 years and a dense grower. Upturned needles, borne on ascending branches, are steel-blue with white stripes on the underside. **'Filifera Aurea'**♀, although an untidy plant, makes a 2.4m (8ft) cascade of golden foliage, spreading to 4.5m (15ft) at ground level after 30 years. The foliage scorches in full sun, but the very similar 'Sungold' raised from this plant is resistant to scorching. **'Golden Mop'** reaches only 45×30cm (18×12in), and is a small, densely clothed form of 'Filifera Nana'. The foliage is a richer gold and does not scorch in bright sun. **'Nana Aureovariegata'** is also a slow-grower; it forms a tight cushion only 60cm×1.2m (2×4ft) in 40 years. Golden-tinged foliage is held in tightly packed sprays shaped like cockleshells. Splashes of gold variegation occur on some plants. **'Plumosa Compressa'** produces yellow, green, grey and blue foliage on the same plant. It can scorch to a dull brown in sun and winter winds and become unsightly. If sheltered and healthy, it reaches 1×1.5m (3×5ft) after 40 years. **'Snow'** is a compact, dense-leaved dome with blue-grey foliage flecked white at the tips. It needs protection

▼*Chamaecyparis pisifera* 'Snow'

from strong sun and easterly winds, often doing best in a well-placed container since it reaches only 2×2m (6½×6½ft) in 20 years. **'Sungold'** see 'Filifera Aurea' above.
C. thyoides **'Andelyensis'**♀ Tiny, abundant, red male flowers clothe this tree in spring, followed by pea-size cones. The plant forms a dark bluish green column. HEIGHT & SPREAD 1.2m×75cm (4×2½ft) after 10 years, ultimately 10m (33ft) tall.

'Andelyensis Nana'♀ is a dwarf form of 'Andelyensis' and reaches 1×1.5m (3×5ft). **'Ericoides'**♀ has soft-textured, sea-green foliage that turns a striking purplish brown in cold weather. It is conical and grows to about 1.5m×80cm (5ft×32in) in 60 years. **'Rubicon'** is upright and its dense foliage is blue-green when new, turning deep plum-purple in winter. It reaches 2×1m (6½×3ft).
CULTIVATION Plant in fertile soil. Acid soils give the best results. Feed plants often.
PROPAGATION Take heeled softwood or hardwood cuttings in spring or autumn; those taken in autumn need bottom heat.
PRUNING None required, except to remove any diseased branches. To raise the canopy, clear the trunk of all branches to the desired height. Make any cuts in spring or autumn.
PESTS AND DISEASES Phytophthora, honey fungus, root rot and butt rot may affect plants. Aphids may be troublesome.

Chamaedorea

Palmae

These palms originate in the shade of Central and S American rain forests and are excellent houseplants for poorly lit rooms. Most types are slow-growing and compact.
RECOMMENDED SPECIES
C. elegans♀ (parlour palm) This neat plant usually grows as a small clump of stems, with the leaves arching attractively away from them. On mature plants the fresh green leaves are around 50-60cm (20-24in) long, less on young plants, with leaflets just over 1cm (⅜in) wide spreading out from a

▼ *Chamaedorea elegans*

central midrib. Older specimens flower occasionally, producing pale yellow stems with almost berry-like orange blooms. HEIGHT & SPREAD 100×50cm (40×20in), usually only after many years.
CULTIVATION Grow in soft, indirect light for best results, although they tolerate quite poor light, especially in winter. Avoid long periods of direct sun. Humidity is preferred, but dry air at room temperature is acceptable. Very dry air, particularly at high temperatures, can cause dry brown leaf tips. In winter, plants require slightly dry compost and a minimum of 5°C (41°F). A temperature of up to 25°C (77°F), frequent watering and weekly feeding are required during the growing season. Repot every other year if strong growth is desired.
PROPAGATION At home, possible only with seed from a specialist dealer. Sow absolutely fresh seed immediately at 25°C (77°F).
PESTS AND DISEASES Red spider mite.

Chamaemelum

Compositae

The strongly aromatic herb, *Chamaemelum nobile*, or camomile, is the most commonly grown species of this genus. This hardy evergreen perennial forms a dense mat of feathery leaves, sprinkled with white and yellow flowers during summer. It is the flowers which are dried and used to make camomile tea. This is an ideal plant for an open sunny spot on a rock garden or in paving. The foliage smells particularly strong if crushed or stepped upon and *C. nobile* 'Treneague' can be grown into a lush, low-maintenance lawn.
RECOMMENDED SPECIES AND VARIETIES
C. nobile (syn. *Anthemis nobilis*) (camomile) Daisy-like white flowers with yellow centres cover this plant; each flower is 1cm (⅜in) across. The bright green, aromatic leaves are very finely divided and up to 5cm (2in) long. Native to W Europe. HEIGHT & SPREAD 25×45cm (10×18in).

▼ *Chamaemelum nobile* 'Flore Pleno'

'Flore Pleno' has double flowers and reaches up to 15cm (6in) high and 30cm (12in) across. **'Treneague'** is a non-flowering variety that can be used to make a camomile lawn. Its height is up to 12.5cm (5in), spreading to 30cm (12in) across.
CULTIVATION Plant during autumn or spring in very free-draining soil, choosing a warm sunny spot. If drying the flowers, cut them at their peak. Otherwise, unless seed is

required, deadhead plants once flowering is over. Clip the foliage often to ensure compact bushy growth. To make a camomile lawn, plant groups of *C. nobile* 'Treneague', placing plants 10cm (4in) apart. Clip or mow regularly in summer.
PROPAGATION Divide established plants in spring or sow seed of the species in summer or early autumn. Take cuttings of *C. nobile* 'Treneague' in late spring or late summer.
PESTS AND DISEASES Usually trouble free.

Chamaerops
European fan palm
Palmae

This modest palm tree is popular as a pot plant in a conservatory or greenhouse, or as a summer focal plant in elaborate bedding schemes. It is native to the Mediterranean and there is only one species. It should be kept frost-free throughout winter.
Chamaerops humilis♀ Broad green fans of lance-shaped leaflets 45cm (18in) long and as much as 60cm (24in) wide, are carried on prickly stalks up to 90cm (36in) long. They usually resemble a crown of leaves emerging almost from ground level and only rarely, in ideal conditions, form a proper trunk. Bunches of greenish yellow flowers are occasionally produced. The plant achieves full height after about 10 years. HEIGHT & SPREAD 4×1m (13×3ft).
CULTIVATION Grow in a conservatory or greenhouse, in John Innes No.2 potting compost and water well. Liquid feed regularly during spring and summer. Stand the plant outside in a sunny spot in summer. Cut fading leaves off at the base and remove flowers as they appear or as soon as they finish. Keep frost-free in winter, at no less than 7°C (45°F), and reduce watering to a minimum. For summer bedding, plunge the whole pot into the ground. Lift in early autumn and put under glass for winter.
PROPAGATION Sow seed in a heated propagator in spring. Remove suckers in spring and summer and insert in compost.

▼ *Chamaerops humilis*

PESTS AND DISEASES Glasshouse red spider mite, scale insects, mealy bug and root mealy bug can attack plants.

Chamomile
see *Chamaemelum nobile*
Chaste tree see *Vitex agnus-castus*
Cheiranthus see *Erysimum*

Chelidonium
Greater celandine
Papaveraceae

The single species in the genus is a cheerful yellow spring and summer-flowering perennial. Chelidonium takes its name from the Greek for a swallow, *chelidon*, as it is supposed to start flowering when these birds arrive, and to wither as they leave. It is not related to the lesser celandine. This erect branching plant with leafy stems is hardy, easy to grow in any soil that is not waterlogged and freely self-seeding, making it excellent for a wild-flower garden.
C. japonicum see *Hylomecon japonicum*
Chelidonium majus The short-lived flowers are up to 2.5cm (1in) wide, made up of 4 rounded, deep yellow, well-spaced petals and are borne in loose clusters. They open in late spring and early summer and are followed by erect narrow seed capsules, up to 5cm (2in) long, enclosing black seeds. The fresh green leaves, 10-15cm (4-6in) long, are composed of 5-7 oblong, toothed leaflets, whitish beneath with bright orange sap. Native to Britain and much of Europe, N Africa and Asia. HEIGHT & SPREAD 60×30cm (2×1ft).
'Flore Pleno' has longer-lasting double flowers.
CULTIVATION Plant in any soil that is not waterlogged, in sun or shade.
PROPAGATION Sow seed in the flowering position in spring or when ripe.
PESTS AND DISEASES Usually trouble free.

▲ *Chelidonium majus*

▼ *Chelidonium majus* 'Flore Pleno'

Chelone
Turtle head
Scrophulariaceae

When other border plants are beginning to succumb to end-of-season raggedness, the new white or pink flowers of these hardy herbaceous perennials are most welcome. They appear at the end of tall, sturdy, leafy stems from late summer to mid autumn. The curiously shaped flowers, up to 3.5cm (1⅜in) long, resemble the head of a turtle or tortoise with its mouth open. The interior of the flower is bearded. Chelones spread by underground runners and need plenty of room to expand. A patch of chelones makes good ground cover and suppresses weeds. Natives of marshy places in N America, chelones are at home in waterlogged soils but will also do well on better drained ground.
RECOMMENDED SPECIES AND VARIETIES
C. glabra (syn. *C. obliqua* var. *alba*) (balmony) The flowers are white flushed with pale or deep pink; the beard is white. The mid green leaves are almost stalkless, broadly or narrowly lance-shaped, with toothed edges, up to 7.5cm (3in) long. HEIGHT & SPREAD 75×100cm (30×40in).
C. lyonii The flowers are pink with a yellow beard. The oval, stalked mid green

▼ *Chelone obliqua*

C

leaves grow up to 15cm (6in) long. HEIGHT & SPREAD 70×100cm (28×40in).

C. obliqua The flowers are deep rose-purple with a yellow beard. The stems, maroon-tinged in early growth, are thickly clad with oval or narrow pointed, mid green leaves, to 12cm (4¾in) long, on short stalks. The margins are sharply toothed and the veins well marked. Globular seed heads, 1cm (⅜in) across, are closely pressed to the stem to form an interesting spike in mid autumn. HEIGHT & SPREAD 1×1 m (3×3ft).

C. obliqua var. *alba* see *C. glabra*

CULTIVATION Plant at any time of year in any garden soil, in sun or part shade. Divide chelones occasionally to maintain vigour and to prevent them choking other plants.

PROPAGATION Divide roots in spring or after flowering, or sow seeds in spring.

PESTS AND DISEASES Usually trouble free.

Cherry, bladder see *Physalis alkekengi*
Cherry, Cornelian see *Cornus mas*
Cherry, edible see p.724
Cherry, Jerusalem see *Solanum pseudocapsicum*
Cherry, ornamental see *Prunus*
Cherry, winter see *Solanum pseudocapsicum*
Cherry laurel see *Prunus laurocerasus*
Cherry pie see *Heliotropium arborescens*
Chervil see *Anthriscus cerefolium*
Chervil (culinary herb) see HERBS, p.330
Chestnut, golden see *Chrysolepis chrysophylla*
Chestnut, horse see *Aesculus*
Chestnut, sweet see *Castanea sativa*

Chiastophyllum

Lamb's tail
Crassulaceae

This genus contains only one species, native to the steep, rocky woodlands of the Caucasus. It is a hardy and reliable alpine, suitable for growing in a rock garden or in the crevices of a stone wall and looks very attractive cascading over rocky ledges. A horizontal planting in a wall or ledge also ensures that its roots are well drained.

Chiastophyllum oppositifolium♀ (syn. *C. simplicifolium)* Tiny bright yellow bell-shaped flowers are carried in arching sprays from late spring to early summer. The flower sprays stand well above the creeping foliage, with the drooping tips appearing like golden chains or, indeed, lambs' tails. It is an evergreen, and is grown as much for its fleshy leaves as for its flowers. The bright green oval and toothed leaves, 5cm (2in) long, may redden with age. A loose clump of leaf rosettes is formed as the plant spreads. HEIGHT & SPREAD 14×30cm (5½×12in).

▼ *Chiastophyllum oppositifolium*

▲ *Chiastophyllum oppositifolium* 'Jim's Pride'

'Jim's Pride' (also known as **'Frosted Jade'**) has cream-variegated foliage and brighter yellow flowers.

CULTIVATION Plant in most soils in a well-drained position in sun or partial shade. The plant does best if its roots are in the shade and its branches are in the sun.

PROPAGATION Take cuttings or divide well-established plants after flowering.

PESTS AND DISEASES Usually trouble free.

Chimonanthus

Winter sweet
Calycanthaceae

Chimonanthus praecox

Lemon yellow flowers with a delightful spicy fragrance are the glory of this moderately sized, hardy Chinese shrub. It is compact and bushy in habit. Chimonanthus is best mixed with summer-flowering plants – climbers make good companions – because it is not spectacular itself in summer. The shrub also benefits from the shelter provided by neighbouring plants. The flowers are borne on willowy stems before the leaves appear, and superficially resemble pale forsythia. It can take five to six years for plants to flower. There are three species in the genus, only one of which is suitable for cultivation in the British Isles.

RECOMMENDED SPECIES AND VARIETIES

C. praecox Waxy, bell-shaped yellow flowers, 2.5cm (1in) across, open in mid winter. They have narrow forward-pointing petals, purple at the centre. The glossy, deciduous, lanceolate leaves, 5-12.5cm (2-5in) long, are mid green and willow-like. HEIGHT & SPREAD 1.5×1m (5×3ft) in 5 years, ultimately 3×2m (10×6½ft).

▲ *Chimonanthus praecox*

▲ *Chimonanthus praecox*

'Grandiflorus' has showier, larger, deeper yellow flowers, 2.5cm (1in) wide, with purplish red centres that sometimes extend as thin lines up the petals. **'Luteus'** has clear yellow flowers that appear a little later in the season than those of the species, usually in early spring. Both cultivars are less strongly scented than the species.

CULTIVATION Well-drained, lime-rich soil and a sunny, sheltered position are best. Protect from north and east winds.

PROPAGATION Layering in mid summer is the most reliable way of raising plants. Sow seed under glass in late winter.

PRUNING Cut out weak or overcrowded stems after flowering.

PESTS AND DISEASES Usually trouble free.

Chimonobambusa see BAMBOOS, p.76

Chionanthus

Fringe tree
Oleaceae

Chionanthus virginicus

Abundant white flowers with unusual, thin narrow petals, produce a decorative show throughout summer on these deciduous trees and shrubs. The leaves are often covered with down when young and turn yellowish in autumn. Small plum-like fruits are occasionally produced after the flowers. The species listed here are both hardy. Native to Asia and eastern USA.

RECOMMENDED SPECIES AND VARIETIES

C. retusus A large shrub with light green leaves about 10cm (4in) long with downy white undersides. Erect sprays of snow white flowers, up to 10cm (4in) long, appear in mid summer. Dark purple oval fruits may follow in autumn. HEIGHT & SPREAD 2×1m (6½×3ft) after 5 years, ultimately 4m (13ft) tall.

▲ *Chionanthus virginicus*

C. virginicus An attractive large bush or small tree with glossy green leaves, up to 20cm (8in) long, that turn yellow in autumn. Drooping sprays of slender, fragrant white flowers, 10cm (4in) long, are borne in early summer. Dark blue, egg-shaped single fruits, up to 1cm (⅜in) long, sometimes appear in autumn. HEIGHT & SPREAD 3×2m (10×6½ft) after 5 years, ultimately 5m (16ft) tall.

CULTIVATION Plant during autumn or spring in a free-draining, rich moist soil in a hot, sunny position. Do not allow to dry out at any time.

PROPAGATION Sow seed in autumn in a coldframe.

PRUNING Prune in spring to maintain a good shape. Remove any weak, crossing or damaged shoots at the same time.

PESTS AND DISEASES Usually trouble free.

Chionodoxa

Hyacinthaceae

Chionodoxa sardensis

Starry blue, occasionally pink or white flowers emerge just before the glossy, grass-like foliage appears. These hardy, early spring-flowering bulbs are suitable for a rock garden, the front of a border or for naturalising among shrubs where they will self-seed easily.

RECOMMENDED SPECIES AND VARIETIES

C. forbesii (glory of the snow) This freely spreading dwarf bulb has green grassy leaves up to 25cm (10in) long. Deep blue flowers with a white centre are borne in groups of between 4 and 12 on a leafless flower stem. Each blossom is 1cm (⅜in) across. HEIGHT & SPREAD 25×10cm (10×4in).

'Pink Giant' has soft pink flowers with a white centre. **Siehei Group**♀ has deep blue to lilac-blue flowers with white centres.

C. gigantea see *C. lucilliae* Gigantea Group

C. luciliae♀ A free-flowering dwarf bulb with a pair of broad grass-like basal leaves up to 10cm (4in) long. The leafless stem produces 1-3 upward-facing blue flowers, each 1cm (⅜in) across, with white centres. HEIGHT & SPREAD 10×8cm (4×3¼in).

Gigantea Group (syn. *C. gigantea*) has blue to violet-blue flowers.

▲ *Chionodoxa forbesii* 'Pink Giant'

Chionodoxa luciliae ▼

▲ *Chionodoxa sardensis*

C. sardensis♀ The leafless flower stems carry 5-10 flat, outward-facing or pendent, deep blue flowers up to 2cm (¾in) across. These dwarf bulbous plants bear a pair of narrow, lance-shaped, semi-erect basal leaves up to 20cm (8in) long. HEIGHT & SPREAD 20×8cm (8×3¼in).

CULTIVATION Plant in autumn in a moist, free-draining soil in sun or partial shade.

PROPAGATION Sow seed as soon as it is ripe in a coldframe or greenhouse. Lift and divide bulbs after the foliage has faded and plant immediately.

PESTS AND DISEASES Usually trouble free.

Chionohebe

Scrophulariaceae

A plant for the alpine enthusiast, chionohebe grows into a cushion or mat of tiny overlapping green leaves. Plants are usually grown in pans in a well-ventilated, unheated greenhouse. Outside, they are best grown with other alpine plants in a rock garden or raised or scree bed. Chionohebe is a hardy, slow-growing, evergreen subshrub. Small white or purple flowers appear in spring. Stemless and with five petals, they are borne singly, rather than in clusters, unlike hebe and parahebe. Native to the mountains of Australia and New Zealand.

RECOMMENDED SPECIES AND VARIETIES

C. pulvinaris (syn. *Pygmaea pulvinaris*)

▼ *Chionohebe pulvinaris*

(snow hebe) This plant has a dense cushion-like habit. The greyish green, hairy leaves, about 3mm (⅛in) long, are arranged in small rosettes. White flowers, 4mm (⅛in) across, appear from mid to late spring. HEIGHT & SPREAD 4×15cm (1½×6in).
CULTIVATION Plant at any time of year in gritty, well-drained soil. Position plants where they will get plenty of light, whether in a greenhouse or the garden. Water all year round.
PROPAGATION Divide plants after flowering or in summer.
PESTS AND DISEASES Downy mildew may affect plants forced on under glass.

Chives (culinary herb)
see HERBS p.331

Chlorophytum

Spider plant
Anthericaceae

This popular, easy-to-grow houseplant has distinctive arching, lance-shaped leaves arising from a dense crown. These tropical and sub-tropical evergreen perennials are frost-tender and require a minimum temperature of 5°C (41°F), but given the right conditions they can be used for summer bedding. Tiny plantlets hang from long, slender stems, mainly in spring and summer. The lily-like blooms, when produced, are insignificant.
RECOMMENDED SPECIES AND VARIETIES
C. comosum Narrow green leaves, up to 45cm (1½ft) long, are arranged in a strong tufted rosette and are often striped with white. HEIGHT & SPREAD 60cm×1m (2×3ft).
'Variegatum'♀ has leaves with white or cream edges. **'Vittatum'**♀ carries curved leaves with a bold white central stripe.
CULTIVATION Grow indoors in any good

▲ *Chlorophytum comosum* 'Variegatum'

▲ *Chlorophytum comosum* 'Vittatum'

potting compost. Feed regularly in spring and summer with a liquid houseplant feed. Remove flower stems as they appear, unless plantlets are to be encouraged. Plants tolerate most light levels but should not be placed in direct sunlight. Outdoors, position in a sunny spot in well-drained soil.
PROPAGATION Remove and pot the plantlets in spring and summer. Divide plants in spring or summer.

Choisya

Rutaceae

Choisya 'Aztec Pearl'

Profuse clusters of sweetly scented white flowers are set against the glossy evergreen foliage of this shrub. The opposite leaves are composed of three, occasionally two or four, bright green, slender leaflets that are highly aromatic when crushed. The small starry flowers usually have five petals. Native to Mexico and SW United States, this neat, rounded bush is frost resistant.
RECOMMENDED SPECIES AND VARIETIES
***C.* 'Aztec Pearl'**♀ The small white flowers are flushed pink when in bud and have a pleasant almond scent when they open in mid summer. There are 3-5 flowers, each 2.5cm (1in) across, in each cluster. The leaves grow to 10cm (4in) long. HEIGHT & SPREAD 60×60cm (2×2ft) after 5 years, ultimately 2m (6½ft) tall.

▲ *Choisya* 'Aztec Pearl'

C. ternata♀ (Mexican orange blossom) Abundant small, citrus-scented white flowers, each 1.5-2.5cm (½-1in) across, are produced in clusters of up to 6 from mid spring onwards. The leaves grow to 10cm (4in) long. HEIGHT & SPREAD 1×1m (3×3ft) after 5 years, ultimately 3m (10ft) tall.

▲ *Choisya ternata* 'Sundance'

'Sundance'♀ has bright yellow foliage that fades as the season progresses and which is at its most striking in full sun. It reaches an ultimate height of 1.8m (6ft). It is also more susceptible to frost damage.
CULTIVATION Plant in spring in any well-drained soil in a sunny, sheltered position. In northern gardens they usually require the protection of a south or west-facing wall.
PROPAGATION Raise from softwood or semi-ripe cuttings.

PRUNING None is required.
PESTS AND DISEASES Usually trouble free.

Christmas tree see *Picea abies*
Chrysanthemum For plants known by the common name, chrysanthemum, see *Dendranthema.* For other plants previously included in the genus *Chrysanthemum* see *Argyranthemum*, *Leucanthemopsis*, *Leucanthemum* and *Tanacetum*

Chrysogonum

Golden star, green-and-gold
Compositae

The yellow daisy-like blooms, long flowering period and the neat size and habit of this semi-evergreen perennial make it an attractive plant for the front of a border. These plants make good ground cover in sun or shade but they require winter protection in very cold gardens. There is only one species in the genus.

Chrysogonum virginianum Each flower has 5 broad, yellow petals up to 3cm (1¼in) long, surrounding a small, yellow, central disc, with leafy bracts. They bloom from late spring to early autumn. The hairy, bright green, oval, scalloped leaves are up to 7cm (2¾in) long. Stems are also hairy. Native to eastern N America. HEIGHT & SPREAD 20×30cm (8×12in).

▲ *Chrysogonum virginianum*

CULTIVATION Plant in spring or autumn in moist but well-drained, humus-rich soil that is not too limy. Choose a position in sun or partial shade.
PROPAGATION Divide plants in spring or sow seed under glass when fresh.
PESTS AND DISEASES Usually trouble free.

Chrysolepis

Fagaceae

Chrysolepis chrysophylla

These half-hardy, shrubby evergreen trees have lustrous deep green leaves that are densely covered underneath with fine, golden yellow hairs. Creamy white, fragrant catkins appear in mid summer and are sometimes followed in autumn by spiky fruit, similar to sweet chestnuts. Slow-growing, these are good trees for small gardens. Native to California and Nevada, these trees will grow only in the milder areas of Britain and should be sheltered from icy winds, especially when young.

RECOMMENDED SPECIES

C. chrysophylla (golden chestnut) The slender pointed leaves are 5-14cm (2-5½in) long. Held in rigid clusters, the catkins are 4cm (1½in) long and consist of male and female flowers. Fruits appear in Britain, but when seen they have green, spiny husks that contain 1-3, chestnut-brown, edible nuts. The rough, grey bark is hard and deeply ridged. When shoots are young they are covered with brownish green felt. HEIGHT & SPREAD 3.5×3m (12×10ft) after 15 years, ultimately 10m (33ft) tall.

▲ *Chrysolepsis chrysophylla*

CULTIVATION Plant in spring in a sheltered site in fertile, well-drained soil that is not too limy. Pinch out the tips of shoots in spring to encourage bushy growth. Do not transplant established specimens.
PROPAGATION Sow seed under glass in late winter, keeping seedlings in the shade.
PRUNING Thin in spring by cutting back branches to the stem or a main branch.
PESTS AND DISEASES Usually trouble free.

Chusquea see BAMBOOS p.76

Cicerbita

Sow thistle
Compositae

Cicerbita plumieri

Tall panicles of blue thistle-like flowerheads appear on these hardy herbaceous perennials in mid summer. These robust plants are best used in a wild or woodland garden and are not really suitable for a herbaceous border. The genus is related to the lettuce, and this is evident in the plants' rosettes of basal leaves.

RECOMMENDED SPECIES

C. plumieri (syn. *Lactuca plumieri*) Pale blue flowers appear in branched spikes on smooth, stout stems in mid summer. Each flower is up to 2cm (¾in) across. The lobed leaves are up to 25cm (10in) long and 12cm (4¾in) wide with a large, rounded terminal lobe. Native to mountainous regions of S Europe. HEIGHT & SPREAD 1.5m×50cm (5ft×20in).

CULTIVATION Plant in autumn or spring in a moist but well-drained, humus-rich, acid-to-neutral soil in partial shade. Staking may be necessary. Remove seed heads before they open to stop plants becoming invasive.
PROPAGATION Sow seed in trays in spring.
PESTS AND DISEASES Usually trouble free.

Cider gum see *Eucalyptus gunnii*

Cimicifuga

Bugbane, rattletop
Ranunculaceae

Long spires of tiny white flowers on tall stems rise above compact clumps of fresh green, deeply divided leaves that often change colour in autumn. These tall, hardy herbaceous perennials are excellent plants for the back of the border. Most grow best on damper soils with some shade to protect the leaves from being scorched by the sun. The individual flowers are star-shaped, 1 cm (⅜ in) across and have an unusual, slightly unpleasant smell. Both flowers and leaves are good for cutting.

RECOMMENDED SPECIES AND VARIETIES

C. japonica Tall, leafless stems carry a mass of white flowers in late summer. The glossy leaves have up to 3-9 oval, lobed leaflets, about 10 cm (4 in) long. This species needs a more protected position. HEIGHT & SPREAD 1.5 m×30 cm (5×1 ft).

C. racemosa♀ (black cohosh, black snake-root) Long spikes of white flowers appear throughout summer. The delicate leaves have oval, deeply toothed leaflets, up to 10 cm (4 in) long. HEIGHT & SPREAD 2.1 m×50 cm (7 ft×20 in).

▼ *Cimicifuga racemosa*

C. ramosa see *C. simplex* 'Pritchard's Giant'

C. simplex Mainly unbranched, drooping flower spikes of pure white starry flowers appear in late summer. The glossy leaves have about 20 deeply divided leaflets, up to 8 cm (3¼ in) long. HEIGHT & SPREAD 1.2 m×60 cm (4×2 ft).

Plants in the **Atropurpurea Group** have purple leaves but the colour can vary considerably. **'Elstead'**♀ has purplish stems with brown buds opening to creamy white flowers. **'Prichard's Giant'** (syn. *C. ramosa*) is a taller plant at 1.5 m (5 ft). **'White Pearl'** has pure white flowers, pale green leaves and pale lime-green seed heads.

▲ *Cimicifuga simplex* 'Elstead'

CULTIVATION Plant from autumn to spring in moist soil in partial shade. Plants may need some staking. Unless seed is required, deadhead the flowers. Cut back plants to ground level in late autumn or early winter.

PROPAGATION Raise plants from ripe seed sown in autumn or by division from autumn to spring; divide plants no more than every 5 years.

PESTS AND DISEASES Usually trouble free.

Cineraria see *Pericallis* × *hybrida*
Cinquefoil see *Potentilla*

Cirsium

Compositae

Striking pincushion-like flowerheads are carried on erect stems in summer. As with most thistles the hairy, deeply lobed leaves have bristly margins. Some of the 200 species of biennials and herbaceous perennials are pernicious weeds best left to grow in the wild, but the two hardy species listed here can make colourful additions to the herbaceous border.

RECOMMENDED SPECIES AND VARIETIES

C. japonicum The rose-pink to lilac flowerheads, up to 5 cm (2 in) across, are borne singly or in clusters. The shiny dark green leaves of this short-lived herbaceous perennial are 30 cm (12 in) long. Native to Japan. HEIGHT & SPREAD 1.5 m×50 cm (5 ft×20 in).

▲ *Cirsium japonicum* 'Rose Beauty'

'Pink Beauty' has soft pink flowers. **'Rose Beauty'** has deep carmine flowers. **'Snow Beauty'** and **'White Victory'** both have white flowers.

C. rivulare **'Atropurpureum'** The deep crimson flowerheads, carried singly or in clusters, are 3 cm (1¼ in) across. The shiny dark green leaves of this herbaceous perennial grow up to 45 cm (1½ ft) long. HEIGHT & SPREAD 1.2 m×60 cm (4×2 ft).

CULTIVATION Plant in autumn or spring in full sun in any soil. *C. japonicum* will also do well in moister spots. Deadhead before the seed is dispersed.

PROPAGATION Sow seed of the species under glass in spring. Divide cultivars in autumn or spring.

PESTS AND DISEASES Usually trouble free.

▲ *Cirsium rivulare* 'Atropurpureum'

C

Cissus

Vitaceae

Cissus antarctica

Too tender to grow reliably outside, these evergreen, woody-stemmed climbers make fine houseplants with decorative foliage. Most have tendrils and are easy to train over a lightweight cane framework. The tiny summer flowers are greenish and insignificant. Height and spread details given below are the natural height of the plants after about five years. However, growth is usually restricted by pinching back the young shoots to whatever size is required. Native to Africa, S America, Asia and Australasia.

RECOMMENDED SPECIES AND VARIETIES

C. antarctica ♀ (kangaroo vine) Glossy, leathery green, oval, pointed leaves densely clothe the woody stems of this vine. The leaves have serrated edges and are up to 10cm (4in) long and 5cm (2in) wide. HEIGHT & SPREAD 5×1m (16×3ft).

▲ *Cissus antarctica*

C. discolor (rex begonia vine) Deep velvety green leaves with prominent silver bands cover the slender woody stems of this climber. The oval, pointed leaves are up to 15cm (6in) long and 5cm (2in) wide and deep plum, purple or maroon underneath. HEIGHT & SPREAD 3m×60cm (10×2ft).

C. rhombifolia ♀ (grape ivy) Coarsely toothed, glossy green leaves cover this moderately vigorous climber. Each leaf is divided into 3 leaflets each up to 8cm (3¼in) long and 5cm (2in) wide. HEIGHT & SPREAD 3×1m (10×3ft).

The widely available **'Ellen Danica'** ♀ has a more vigorous, bushier growth and slightly larger, rich green glossy leaves.

C. striata (syn. *Ampelopsis sempervirens*) (ivy of Paraguay, miniature grape ivy) This vigorous woody-stemmed climber bears dull green leaves that are 8cm (3¼in) long and across, made up of 3-5 serrated oval

▲ *Cissus rhombifolia*

leaflets. Small, glossy black fruits appear in late summer, after the insignificant flowers. The plant is reasonably hardy outdoors if grown on a warm, sheltered wall. HEIGHT & SPREAD 10×1m (33×3ft).

CULTIVATION Position in good light but not full sun. Feed in spring and summer. Most species require a minimum temperature of 7°C (45°F), except *C. discolor* which must be kept above 18°C (64°F). Provide the plants with a framework support and regularly pinch young shoots back to keep them in the desired shape.

PROPAGATION Take semi-ripe stem cuttings in summer.

PESTS AND DISEASES Scale insects and mealy bugs can be troublesome.

Cistus

Sun rose

Cistaceae

Cistus x aguilarii

Evergreen hardy and half-hardy shrubs, native to the Mediterranean and the Iberian peninsula, that are excellent for sunny positions in light, poor soil, particularly in coastal areas. Showy, saucer-shaped papery flowers, 2.5-10cm (1-4in) across, are borne in early to mid summer. Leaves are oval or lance-shaped and 2.5-10cm (1-4in) long.

RECOMMENDED SPECIES AND VARIETIES

The ultimate size of the plants given below is attained within 5 years.

C.* × *aguilarii The yellow-centred small white flowers of this hardy shrub are profusely borne. The large leaves are bright green. HEIGHT & SPREAD 1×1.5m (3×5ft).

The flowers of **'Maculatus'** have a ring of crimson blotches around yellow centres.

C. algarvensis see *Halimium ocymoides*

C.* × *corbariensis see *C.* × *hybridus*

C. crispus Large, purple-red to cerise flowers are borne on this hardy rounded shrub with small, hoary, grey-green leaves. HEIGHT & SPREAD 60×60cm (2×2ft).

▲ *Cistus* x *hybridus*

C.* × *cyprius ♀ Large white flowers with carmine basal spots are produced in crowded clusters by this hardy vigorous hybrid. The large, bright green leaves emit a strong aroma. HEIGHT & SPREAD 2×2m (6½×6½ft).

C.* × *dansereaui This small hardy shrub bears large white flowers with crimson basal spots and has large dull green leaves. HEIGHT & SPREAD 60×75cm (2×2½ft).

'Decumbens' ♀ has white flowers and a more spreading habit, to 45cm (1½ft) high.

***C.* 'Elma'** ♀ A hardy hybrid of sturdy, bushy habit, this shrub has large, glossy, deep green leaves and large, pure white flowers. HEIGHT & SPREAD 2×2m (6½×6½ft).

C.* × *florentinus The medium-sized white flowers have yellow basal spots. Small dull green leaves of this multi-branched, compact, hardy shrub are often downy when young. HEIGHT & SPREAD 1×1m (3×3ft).

C. formosus see *Halimium lasianthum*

***C.* 'Grayswood Pink'** A low-growing hardy shrub with medium-sized pale pink flowers and small grey-green leaves. HEIGHT & SPREAD 60×60cm (2×2ft).

C.* × *hybridus ♀ (syn. *C.* × *corbariensis*) The white flowers of this dense, hardy shrub have yellow basal spots and are heavily infused with red in bud. Coarse, wrinkled, small leaves are dark green above and paler beneath. HEIGHT & SPREAD 1×1m (3×3ft).

C. ingwerseniana see × *Halimiocistus* 'Ingerwersenii'

C. ladanifer ♀ (gum cistus) Large white flowers with maroon markings around the yellow stamens are borne on an upright, half-hardy shrub with large dark green leaves. HEIGHT & SPREAD 2.4×1m (8×3ft).

The **Palhinhae Group** ♀ includes very hardy, low-growing compact plants, rarely

▼ *Cistus ladanifer*

exceeding 1m (3ft) in height and spread. The large flowers are pure white.
C. lasianthus see *Halimium lasianthum*
C. laurifolius♀ A hardy, upright plant bearing large white flowers with yellow basal spots. The leaves are dark glaucous green. HEIGHT & SPREAD 1.5x1.5m (5x5ft).
C. x *loretii* Small white flowers with crimson basal blotches are borne on an upright, dwarf, hardy shrub with medium leaves that are dark green above and greyish beneath. HEIGHT & SPREAD 1x1m (3x3ft).
C. **'Merrist Wood Cream'** see X *Halimiocistus wintonensis* 'Merrist Wood Cream'
C. x *obtusifolius* A small, rounded, hardy shrub bearing small white flowers with a yellow basal mark and small grey-green leaves. HEIGHT & SPREAD 60x60cm (2x2ft).

▲ *Cistus* 'Peggy Sammons'

C. **'Peggy Sammons'**♀ Pale pink blossoms on downy stems adorn a bushy, hardy shrub with small grey-green downy leaves. HEIGHT & SPREAD 1x1m (3x3ft).
C. x *pulverulentus*♀ A half-hardy shrub with medium-sized, purple-pink to cerise-rose flowers and sage green leaves with grey down. HEIGHT & SPREAD 60x60cm (2x2ft).
'Sunset' and **'Warley Rose'** have vivid magenta and cerise flowers respectively.
C. x *purpureus*♀ Medium-sized pink flowers with dark red basal spots are borne on a bushy half-hardy shrub. Small leaves are grey-green. HEIGHT & SPREAD 1x1m (3x3ft).
C. ocymoides see *Halimium ocymoides*
C. sahucii see X *Halimiocistus sahucii*
C. salviifolius Medium-sized white flowers with yellow basal spots are borne on this spreading half-hardy shrub. The small, oval, grey-green leaves have a rough, wrinkled surface. HEIGHT & SPREAD 60cmx1m (2x3ft).

▼ *Cistus* x *pulverulentus* 'Sunset'

C. **'Silver Pink'** A hardy and widely planted hybrid with pale, silvery pink medium-sized flowers and leaves, pale green above and greyish beneath. HEIGHT & SPREAD 60x60cm (2x2ft).
C. x *skanbergii*♀ Pale pink flowers are set off by small green leaves on this hardy shrub. HEIGHT & SPREAD 1x1m (3x3ft).
C. wintonensis see X *Halimiocistus wintonensis*

CULTIVATION Plant in spring in a sunny, well-drained spot. Deadhead regularly.
PROPAGATION Take softwood cuttings in summer or sow seed of the species in spring.
PRUNING Prune out all dead or damaged stems in spring.
PESTS AND DISEASES Aphids can be a problem.

Citron see *Citrus medica*

Citrus

Rutaceae

Citrus aurantium

With their lustrous dark foliage and waxy white flowers these tender evergreen shrubs and trees, native to E Asia, are handsome conservatory plants. This group includes all the popular citrus fruits – orange, lemon, lime and grapefruit. Plants need a minimum winter temperature of 5-10°C (41-50°F). The fragrant flowers have five oblong petals that curve outwards and prominent stamens; these generally appear in summer in a cool conservatory, but in ideal conditions flowers are produced at intervals throughout much of the year. The height and spread of plants given below are for planted out specimens. Plants in large pots will reach only half these sizes.

RECOMMENDED SPECIES AND VARIETIES
C. aurantiifolia (lime) Glossy oval leaves, 8cm (3¼in) long, are carried on spiny branches. The waxy white flowers are followed by green fruits 3-6cm (1¼-2½in) across. HEIGHT & SPREAD 5x2m (16x6½ft).
'Tahiti' bears large seedless fruits.
C. aurantium (Seville orange, bitter orange) This tree with a rounded crown has spiny branches and oval leaves up to 10cm (4in) long. The fragrant, waxy, white flowers are followed by bright orange spherical fruits 8cm (3¼in) across. HEIGHT & SPREAD 10x3m (33x10ft).

▲ *Citrus aurantiifolia* 'Tahiti'

The heavily scented flowers of the dwarf tree **'Bouquet de Fleurs'** are used in perfume. It grows to 3m (10ft) high and 1.5m (5ft) wide. **'Seville'** has slightly larger flowers and has the best fruit for preserves.
C. limon (lemon) A small tree with glossy oval leaves up to 8cm (3¼in) long. The flowers are white with a purplish tinge and the oval yellow fruits are 5-10cm (2-4in) long. HEIGHT & SPREAD 5x2m (16x6½ft).
'Garey's Eureka' (syn. 'Quatre Saisons') has a continuous flowering and fruiting cycle. **'Variegata'** produces striking green and cream variegated glossy foliage. The fruits eventually ripen to clear yellow.

▲ *Citrus limon* 'Variegata'

C. maxima (shaddock) A vigorous tree with a rounded crown. White fragrant flowers are followed by round yellow fruits up to 15cm (6in) across. The oval or elliptical glossy leaves are up to 10cm (4in) long. HEIGHT & SPREAD 5x3m (16x10ft).
C. medica (citron) A shrubby tree with branches that may be flushed purple when young. White flowers with a pink blush are followed by fragrant, oval, yellow fruits, up to 20cm (8in) long. Dark green leaves are oval or elliptical and up to 15cm (6in) long. HEIGHT & SPREAD 3x2m (10x6½ft).
'Ethrog' has lemon-sized fragrant fruits.
C. x *meyeri* **'Meyer'** (Meyer's lemon) A small tree with oval glossy leaves up to 8cm (3¼in) long. The white flowers are waxy and the oval yellow fruits are 8cm (3¼in) wide. This is the hardiest lemon and the best to grow indoors for good-quality fruit. HEIGHT & SPREAD 3x1.5m (10x5ft).

▲ *Citrus* × *paradisi* 'Golden Special'

C.* × *paradisi (grapefruit) A large tree with a rounded crown and dense foliage of dark green oval leaves 8cm (3¼in) long. The waxy white flowers are followed by large, yellow, globular fruits up to 15cm (6in) across. HEIGHT & SPREAD 5×3m (16×10ft).

'Golden Special' is a commercial variety and the fruits have white flesh.

C. reticulata (mandarin, clementine, satsuma, tangerine) A shrub or small tree with spiny branches and glossy, oval, dark green leaves up to 8cm (3¼in) long. Waxy white flowers are followed by yellow-orange to orange-red globular fruits 8cm (3¼in) across. HEIGHT & SPREAD 4×2m (13×6½ft).

'Clementine' has bright orange-red fruits and a more upright bushy habit. **'Satsuma'** is a compact shrub, up to 3m (10ft) tall, with a rather pendulous habit and bright orange fruits. **'Variegata'** has cream and green variegated foliage.

C. sinensis (sweet orange) A tree with spiny branches bearing glossy oval leaves 8cm (3¼in) long. The waxy white flowers are fragrant and the orange or yellow fruits, up to 10cm (4in) across, are oval or globe-shaped. HEIGHT & SPREAD 10×4m (33×13ft).

'Valencia' has bright orange fruits, up to 10cm (4in) across, with thinner skins. **'Valencia Late'** is the same as 'Valencia', but retains its crop much longer. **'Washington Navel'** is a virtually seedless orange with fruits up to 10cm (4in) across.

***C.* × *tangelo* 'Seminole'** (tangelo) A hybrid between a grapefruit and a mandarin with leaves up to 8cm (3¼in) long. Waxy white flowers are followed by yellow or reddish orange fruit up to 12.5cm (5in) across. HEIGHT & SPREAD 5×2m (16×6½ft).

▲ *Citrus sinensis* 'Washington Navel'

CULTIVATION Grow as conservatory plants, and stand pots outside in a sunny place in summer. Rapid changes in light or temperature can result in defoliation. Water freely in spring and summer, sparingly in winter.

PROPAGATION Sow pips from fruits in a propagator, but resulting plants are variable. Most modern varieties are grafted on to a citrus rootstock, but for an amateur semi-ripe cuttings in summer is the best method.

PRUNING During spring prune out any weak wood or any wood that has died back over winter. Shorten long lateral shoots by at least a third.

PESTS AND DISEASES Scale insects and mealy bugs may infest the plants.

Clarkia

Onagraceae

Clarkia unguiculata

Free-flowering, easily grown hardy annuals with spikes or clusters of flowers from mid summer to early autumn. They are erect bushy plants with branched stems and green to grey-green leaves, usually lance-shaped. Native to N America.

Varieties bred from specific species are listed separately in catalogues as godetia, but are now included in clarkia.

RECOMMENDED SPECIES AND VARIETIES

C. bottae Cup-shaped flowers, 3cm (1¼in) across, have 4 lavender-blue petals, each with a white base, and are borne in loose spikes. A slender-stemmed plant with 4cm (1½in) long narrow leaves. HEIGHT & SPREAD 25×40cm (10×16in).

'Pink Joy' has pink flowers.

C. elegans see *C. unguiculata*

C. pulchella Leafy spikes of 4-petalled, cup-shaped lilac flowers are borne near the end of slender stems on this graceful plant. Narrow pointed leaves are 6cm (2½in) long. HEIGHT & SPREAD 40×20cm (16×8in).

'Filigree' has pink, purple and white semidouble or double flowers. **'Lace Mixed'** bears pink, purple and white semidouble flowers. **'Snowflake'** has double white flowers.

C. unguiculata (syn. *C. elegans*) Tall plants with upright stems that become long spikes bearing cup-shaped, 4cm (1½in) wide, pink, mauve or red 4-petalled flowers. Short-stalked leaves are up to 6cm (2½in) long. HEIGHT & SPREAD 120×40cm (48×16in).

▲ *Clarkia* 'Salmon Princess'

'Apple Blossom' is pink, 1-1.2m (3-4ft) tall, **'Asterix'** is a dwarf mixture to 30cm (12in) tall with a 25cm (10in) spread, **'Love Affair'** is a colour mixture to 60-75cm (24-30in) high with a spread of 30cm (12in). All bear double flowers.

Godetia varieties produce their showy, funnel-shaped flowers, up to 10cm (4in) across, in clusters at the ends of stems. They range from white to pink, orange and red.

The following have mixed-colour single flowers with 4 petals unless otherwise described, and a spread up to 30cm (12in). **'Azalea-Flowered'** is 40-50cm (16-20in) tall with white to pink semidouble flowers. **'Bonita Mixed'** is 25cm (10in) tall. **'Cherie'** reaches 40-50cm (16-20in) with pink double blooms, **'F_1 Grace Mixed'** is 75cm (30in) tall and especially suitable for cutting. **'Salmon Princess'** is 30cm (12in) high with pink flowers, **'F_1 Satin Mixed'** is 30cm (12in) tall, **'Sybil Sherwood'** reaches 35cm (14in) high and has salmon-pink flowers with a white edge.

CULTIVATION Grow in light shade in any soil. When 7-10cm (2¾-4in) high, pinch out growing tips to enhance bushiness.

PROPAGATION Sow seed where required in mid spring. Thin out in stages when they begin to crowd each other, to 25cm (10in). For early cut flowers, sow where required in early autumn and cover with cloches, or sow in individual pots under glass in early spring. For spring-flowering pot plants in heated greenhouses, sow in early autumn.

PESTS AND DISEASES Aphids may cause problems.

Clary see *Salvia sclarea* var. *turkestanica*

▼ *Clarkia unguiculata*

Clematis

Virgin's bower

Ranunculaceae

With its beauty of form, subtleties of colouring and generous display, clematis is widely revered as the queen of climbers. There are plants flowering in every season, even winter. So with careful selection, it is possible to enjoy the delightful blooms of clematis all year round

Twisting through trees or scrambling over hedges, clematis brightens up drab greenery with sumptuous colour. Trellis-work, arbours and walls are fitting locations, and the use of these versatile climbers is limited only by your imagination.

The genus consists of a large number of woody climbing and scrambling plants as well as a few herbaceous perennials. Most plants are deciduous, though there is a small evergreen group.

Most clematis blooms are single, some are double and a few are multiple like a peony. Flowers usually open out flat or saucer-like, but there are also stars, single and double bells, lanterns and tulip-shaped blooms. The largest blooms reach 25cm (10in) in diameter, the smallest less than 1cm ($\frac{3}{8}$in). In general the larger the flowers, the smaller the number produced.

Some flowers are heavily scented – all of them in the 10 small-flowered groups, with the exception of the early large-flowered 'Fair Rosamond'. When the flowers have

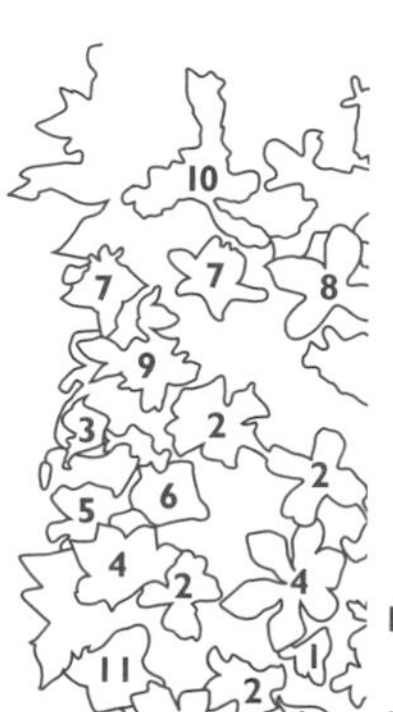

1 'Duchess of Albany'
2 'Comtesse de Bouchaud'
3 'Etoile Rose'
4 'Andromeda'
5 'Minuet'
6 'Royal Velours'
7 'Multi Blue'
8 'Warszawska Nike'
9 'Bill Mackenzie'
10 'Purpurea Plena Elegans'
11 'Madame Julia Correvon'

C

INDEX OF SPECIES AND VARIETIES

The species and varieties of clematis can be divided into 12 groups which loosely follow the order of flowering:

(1) The Evergreen Group
(2) The Alpina Group
(3) The Macropetala Group
(4) The Montana Group
(5) The Rockery Group
(6) The Early Large-flowered Group
(7) The Late Large-flowered Group
(8) The Herbaceous Group
(9) The Viticella Group
(10) The Texensis Group
(11) The Orientalis Group
(12) The Late Species Group

A list of plants covered follows in alphabetical order with the relevant group number in brackets.

'Abundance' (9)
addisonii (5)
aethusifolia (11)
akebioides (11)
'Alba' (8)
'Alba Plena' (6)
'Alba Luxurians' (9)
'Allanah' (7)
alpina (2)
ssp. *sibirica* (2)
'Andromeda' (7)
'Apple Blossom' (1)
'Arabella' (8)
'Arctic Queen' (6)
armandii (1)
'Asao' (6)
'Ascotiensis' (9)
'Aureolin' (11)
'Barbara Dibley' (6)
'Barbara Jackman' (6)
'Beauty of Worcester' (6)
'Bees' Jubilee' (6)
'Belle of Woking' (6)
'Betty Corning' (9)
'Bicolour' (6)
'Bill Mackenzie' (11)
'Blue Belle' (9)
'Blue Lagoon' (3)
'Broughton Star' (4)
'Burford' (11)
campaniflora (9)
'Campanile' (8)
'Cardinal Wyszynski' (7)
× *cartmanii* (5)
cirrhosa (1)
'Columbine' (2)
'Comtesse de Bouchaud' (7)
'Continuity' (4)
'Corry' (11)
'Côte d'Azur' (8)
'Countess of Lovelace' (6)
'Daniel Deronda' (6)
'Dawn' (6)
'Doctor Ruppel' (6)
'Duchess of Albany' (10)
'Duchess of Edinburgh' (6)
× *durandii* (8)
'Edward Prichard' (8)
'Elizabeth' (4)
'Elsa Späth' (6)
× *eriostemon* 'Hendersonii' (9)
'Ernest Markham' (9)
'Etoile Rose' (10)
'Etoile Violette' (9)
'Fair Rosamond' (6)
fargesii (12)
'Fireworks' (6)
flammula (12)
florida (6)
forrestii (1)
forsteri (1)
'Frances Rivis' (2)
'Frankie' (2)
'Freckles' (1)
'Freda' (4)
'Général Sikorski' (6)
'Gillian Blades' (6)
'Gipsy Queen' (7)
'Golden Harvest' (11)
'Gravetye' (11)
'Gravetye Beauty' (10)
'H.F. Young' (6)
'Hagley Hybrid' (7)
'Haku-ôkan' (6)
'Helios' (11)
'Henryi' (6)
heracleifolia (8)
var. *davidiana* (8)
'Horn of Plenty' (6)
'Huldine' (9)
indivisa (1)
'Jackmanii Alba' (6)
'Jackmanii Rubra' (6)
'Jackmanii Superba' (7)
'Jacqueline Du Pré' (2)
'Jan Lindmark' (3)
'Jan Pawel II' (7)
'Joanna' (5)
'Joe' (5)
'John Huxtable' (7)
'John Paul II' (7)
'John Warren' (6)
× *jouiniana* 'Praecox' (8)
'Kakio' (6)
'Kardynal Wyszynski' (7)
'Kathleen Dunford' (6)
'Kathleen Wheeler' (6)
'Kermesina' (9)
ladakhiana (11)
'Lady Betty Balfour' (9)
'Ladybird Johnson' (10)
'Lady Caroline Nevill' (6)
'Lady Northcliffe' (6)
'Lambton Park' (11)
'Lasurstern' (6)
'Lawsoniana' (6)
'Liberation' (6)
'Lilacina Floribunda' (7)
'Lincoln Star' (6)
'Little Nell' (9)
'Lord Nevill' (6)
'Louise Rowe' (6)
'Ludlow & Sherrif' (11)
macropetala (3)
'Madame Baron Veillard' (7)
'Madame Edouard André' (7)
'Madame Grangé' (9)
'Madame Julia Correvon' (9)
'Madame Le Coultre' (6)
'Maidwell Hall' (3)
'Margaret Hunt' (9)
'Margot Koster' (9)
'Marie Boisselot' (6)
'Marjorie' (4)
'Markham's Pink' (3)
marmoraria (5)
'Maureen' (6)
'Mayleen' (4)
'Minuet' (9)
'Miss Bateman' (6)
montana (4)
f. *grandiflora* (4)
var. *rubens* (4)
var. *wilsonii* (4)
'Moonlight' (6)
'Mrs Cholmondeley' (6)
'Mrs N. Thompson' (6)
'Mrs Robert Brydon' (8)
'Mrs Spencer Castle' (9)
'Multi Blue' (6)
napaulensis (1)
'Nelly Moser' (6)
'Niobe' (6)
'Norfolk Lady' (6)
'Odorata' (4)
'Olgae' (8)
'Pagoda' (9)
'Pamela Jackman' (2)
'Pangbourne Pink' (8)
paniculata (1)
'Pastel Blue' (8)
'Pastel Pink' (8)
patens (6)
'Perle d'Azur' (7)
'Petit Faucon' (8)
'Picton's Variety' (4)
'Pink Champagne' (6)
'Pink Fantasy' (7)
'Pink Perfection' (4)
'Polish Spirit' (9)
'Prince Charles' (9)
'Proteus' (6)
'Purpurea' (9)
'Purpurea Plena Elegans' (9)
recta 'Purpurea' (8)
rehderiana (11)
'Richard Pennell' (6)
'Rosea' (8)
'Rosy O'Grady' (3)
'Rosy Pagoda' (2)
'Rouge Cardinal' (7)
'Royalty' (6)
'Royal Velours' (9)
'Ruby' (2)
'Sealand Gem' (6)
serratifolia (11)
'Sieboldii' (6)
'Silver Moon' (6)
'Sir Trevor Lawrence' (10)
'Snowbird' (3)
'Snowdrift' (1)
'Snow Queen' (6)
'Star of India' (7)
'Sylvia Denny' (6)
tangutica (11)
'Tapestry' (8)
'Tetrarose' (4)
'The President' (6)
'The Princess Of Wales' (10)
tibetana ssp. *vernayi* (11)
× *triternata* 'Rubromarginata' (9)
'Twilight' (7)
'Venosa Violacea' (9)
'Veronica's Choice' (6)
'Victoria' (7)
'Ville de Lyon' (9)
viticella (9)
'Voluceau' (9)
'Vyvyan Pennell' (6)
'W.E. Gladstone' (6)
'Wada's Primrose' (6)
'Warszawska Nike' (7)
'White Columbine' (2)
'White Moth' (2)
'Will Goodwin' (6)
'William (6)
'Willy' (2)
'Wisley Cream' (1)
'Wyevale' (8)

faded, many clematis go on to create a dramatic effect with their large, fluffy seed heads. Especially fine heads are displayed by plants in the macropetala, orientalis and late species groups.

Though it is not apparent at first glance, clematis flowers do not have petals. Instead, the sepals take on the appearance of petals and are known as 'tepals'. Their colour varies from white through pinks, mauves and purples to dark red, and fades as the flower ages. The stamens are often conspicuous in colour also, while the alpina and macropetala groups have the added interest of colourful petal-like 'staminodes' (infertile stamens situated between the fertile stamens and the tepals). Yellow flowers are found mainly in the orientalis group.

Most clematis climb by twisting the stalks (petioles) of their leaves round a support, but the herbaceous and texensis groups clamber and scramble. The leaves of the large-flowered clematis are usually ternate (made up of 3 leaflets) and opposite (2 leaves face one another at each node along the stem). In the 10 small-flowered groups the leaves may be made up of 5-9 leaflets. Leaf colour varies from dark or grey-green to bright green, but most clematis plants have mid green leaves.

There is an enormous variation in the height of clematis: the shortest species, *C. marmoraria*, is just 4cm (1½in) tall, while plants in the montana group can soar to 12m (40ft) or more. The measurements given below refer to mature plants.

Clematis plants grow in any soil as long as there is no extreme of acidity or alkalinity and they are given plenty of water. Most are hardy throughout Britain, although a few imported varieties need the shelter of a conservatory. All the climbing species and varieties benefit from a sheltered position as strong winds can tear the petioles away from their supports.

▲ *Clematis armandii*

(1) THE EVERGREEN GROUP

These plants provide welcome colour and scent throughout the winter months (and into early summer with the blooms of *C. forsteri*). Because they have been introduced from countries warmer than Britain, they need to be planted in the shelter of a wall facing south or south-west.

C. armandii Clusters of creamy white, vanilla-scented flowers appear in early spring. They are bell-shaped at first and then open almost flat to 4cm (1½in) across, displaying 4-7 tepals and yellow stamens. The plant has large, leathery, ternate leaves, up to 15cm (6in) long. It can be rather large, but is an exceptional and most desirable plant when there is room for it. HEIGHT & SPREAD 9×4.5m (30×15ft).

'Apple Blossom' has pale pink flowers and bronze-tinted young leaves. **'Snowdrift'** bears pure white flowers that open out before the new leaves which carry an attractive coppery tint.

C. cirrhosa♀ Citrus-scented, yellow-white hanging bells, 4cm (1½in) across, can be seen from early winter to spring. The 4 tepals may be freckled inside with red, contrasting with the cream anthers held on green filaments. The fern-like foliage sometimes turns bronze in winter. HEIGHT & SPREAD 6×2m (20×6½ft).

'Freckles'♀ is heavily speckled with red-purple inside. **'Wisley Cream'** has cream flowers and a few faint red markings.

C. forrestii see *C. napaulensis*

C. napaulensis (syn. *C. forrestii*) Light green leaves surround clusters of creamy yellow bell flowers which are rather sparsely produced. Each flower is 2.5cm (1in) long, made up of 4 tepals and protruding purple stamens. For most of the year this plant appears to be lifeless but its flowers bring an instant revival in a conservatory or on a sheltered warm wall in early winter. HEIGHT & SPREAD 7×3m (23×10ft).

New Zealand species

All New Zealand species have separate male and female plants with the male plants having slightly larger blooms. The leaves are ternate unless stated otherwise. For dwarf New Zealand species see the Rockery Group (p.154).

C. forsteri Lemon-scented, pale greenish yellow flowers appear among a mass of tangled, scrambling stems in early summer. The star-like blooms are about 2cm (¾in) across, made up of 5-8 tepals, with golden stamens. The pale green leaves are made up of 3 lobed leaflets up to 5cm (2in) long. HEIGHT & SPREAD 3.5×2.4m (12×8ft).

C. indivisa see *C. paniculata*

C. paniculata (syn. *C. indivisa*) Pure white flowers with yellow stamens appear in clusters in late spring. Each flower has 6-8 tepals and reaches up to 8cm (3¼in) across. The large ovate leaves are leathery. HEIGHT & SPREAD 4.5×1.5m (15×5ft).

(2) THE ALPINA GROUP

The alpinas are more robust than Group 1 and provide a display of dainty colourful flowers from mid to late spring, even on a north-facing wall. The parent species, *C. alpina*, originated in the mountains of Europe and Asia, and as a result all its descendants are hardy and will grow happily in poor soil.

The pendent blooms are single and bell-shaped, 4-5cm (1½-2in) long, made up of 4 tepals which taper to a point; in some varieties the flowers open flat to about 5cm (2in) across as they mature. Inside the flowers are petal-like infertile stamens, known as staminodes, which are usually a different colour from the main bloom. The stamens themselves cannot be seen. The flowers are followed by pretty, fluffy seed heads.

The soft green leaves are up to 15cm (6in) long and 7.5cm (3in) wide, made up of 9 ovate to lance-shaped leaflets. The alpinas are climbers, reaching a height of 1.8-2.7m (6-9ft) and a spread of 1.5m (5ft).

'Columbine' has elegant flowers made up of pale lavender tepals and creamy white staminodes. **'Frances Rivis'**♀ bears flowers up to 6cm (2½in) long, made up of rich blue tepals and white staminodes lightly suffused with violet. **'Frankie'** has mauve-blue tepals and cream staminodes. **'Jacqueline Du Pré'** has rosy mauve tepals and pink staminodes. **'Pamela Jackman'** has purple-blue tepals and white staminodes. **'Rosy Pagoda'** has red tepals edged with white and creamy white staminodes. **'Ruby'** has purple-pink tepals and cream staminodes tinged with red. Creamy white, semi-double flowers are produced by ssp. ***sibirica*** **'White Moth'**. **'White Columbine'**♀ has cream tepals and white staminodes. **'Willy'** flowers earlier than most, displaying its pale pink tepals, which darken to the base, and cream staminodes in early spring.

(3) THE MACROPETALA GROUP

These plants bloom in mid to late spring, coming into flower just after the alpinas so the two flowering periods overlap. They are similar to the alpinas in many respects, but have larger staminodes which are sometimes longer than the 4 tepals so that they protrude from the bell-shaped bloom and make it look double. The flowers are up to 10cm (4in) across and are followed by seed heads that are among the best of all clematis.

The light green leaves are up to 10cm (4in) long and 5cm (2in) wide, made up of 9 toothed ovate to lance-shaped leaflets. The plants are medium sized and hardy enough to grow on north-facing walls. They climb up to 2.4×2.4m (8×8ft).

C. macropetala The parent species is as showy as any in the group. The tepals are dark violet-blue and the staminodes are the same colour flecked with white.

'Blue Lagoon' see 'Maidwell Hall'. **'Jan Lindmark'** has mauve tepals and twisted pale purple staminodes. **'Maidwell Hall'**♀ (syn. 'Blue Lagoon') has dark mauve tepals and staminodes. **'Markham's Pink'**♀ has dark pinky mauve tepals and pink staminodes. **'Rosy O' Grady'** has rosy lilac tepals and pink staminodes. **'Snowbird'** has white tepals and staminodes tinged with green.

(4) THE MONTANA GROUP

Late spring sees the giants of the clematis world, the montanas, open their abundant, showy blooms. The vigorous, easy-to-grow montanas have some disadvantages, however. They flower for only 3-4 weeks and in a hard winter the leafless twigs are an unappealing sight, although the brief show of glorious colour is worth waiting for. A hard frost may damage or even destroy the flower buds, though not usually the plants.

The parent species, *C. montana*, is native to the mountains of India and China.

▲ *Clematis montana* 'Elizabeth'

Clematis montana

The flowers, many of them scented, vary from 5-9 cm (2-3½ in) across, unless stated otherwise, and consist of 4 tepals. The leaves are ternate and up to 25 cm (10 in) long. Sometimes the foliage is bronzed – notably that of 'Elizabeth', 'Freda', 'Odorata' and 'Tetrarose'. The most vigorous varieties can climb to 9 m (30 ft) and beyond with a spread of 3 m (10 ft) or more.

C. montana (syn. *C. montana alba*) A profusion of short-lived white blooms, up to 4 cm (1½ in) across with cream stamens, are produced by this, the parent species.

'Broughton Star' is free-flowering with deep pink double blooms and golden stamens. The inner tepals are a stronger colour than the outer ones, making an unusual two-tone flower. **'Continuity'** bears pink flowers with yellow stamens, held on long stalks. **'Elizabeth'**♀ bears pale pink blooms with yellow stamens and a strong vanilla fragrance. **'Freda'**♀ displays its cherry-pink flowers against fine coppery foliage. The blooms, only 4 cm (1½ in) across, have deeper pink on the margins and golden stamens. The plant is less vigorous than most montanas and suitable for a small garden.

The vigorous f. ***grandiflora***♀ produces an abundance of large, unscented, white blooms with yellow stamens. **'Marjorie'** bears a smattering of semidouble, creamy pink flowers with salmon-pink stamens. **'Mayleen'** has richly scented pinky mauve blooms, 5 cm (2 in) across, with a prominent boss of golden stamens. **'Odorata'** produces its creamy pink, heavily scented flowers with yellow stamens in early summer. **'Picton's Variety'** is not vigorous, making it suitable for a small garden. The pink blooms with cream stamens have a spicy fragrance. **'Pink Perfection'** produces a profusion of pale pink flowers with cream stamens. Usually, though not always, a vigorous plant, var. ***rubens***♀ has pale violet-pink flowers with yellow stamens. The blooms are scented.

▼ *Clematis montana* 'Mayleen'

▲ *Clematis montana* 'Tetrarose'

'Tetrarose'♀ produces deep pink short-lived blooms with straw-coloured stamens and a spicy scent. It is not a large plant, making it suitable for a small garden. The vigorous var. ***wilsonii*** bears white flowers with prominent yellow stamens and a chocolate fragrance. The flowers appear a month later than most montanas.

(5) THE ROCKERY GROUP

Most plants within the rockery group are in flower from mid spring to mid summer. There are two sub-sections: New Zealand and American. The plants are short, from about ankle height to 60 cm (2 ft). Ideally suited to rockeries, these plants also grow well in an alpine house.

New Zealand species

The dwarf New Zealand species bear male and female flowers on separate plants. Larger New Zealand species are found in the Evergreen Group (p. 152).

C. marmoraria♀ It may take 3 or 4 years before this, the smallest clematis, flowers, but when it does you will know it has been worth the wait. In spring its cushion of evergreen parsley-like leaves are covered in creamy white, green-tinged blooms shaped like upright buttercups. The blooms have 5-8 tepals and are about 2 cm (¾ in) across. They give way to spectacular downy yellow-tinged seedheads. Protect from winter wet. In very cold areas the plant is best grown in pots which are put into the ground for the flowering period and moved to a conservatory or porch in the winter. It thrives in an alpine house. HEIGHT & SPREAD 6×25 cm (2½×10 in).

***C. × cartmanii* 'Joe'** At flowering, in mid spring, this plant is covered with pure white or creamy white male flowers, often tinged with green. The saucer-shaped flowers are up to 4 cm (1½ in) across made up of 4 tepals, borne on trailing growth with evergreen, leathery, finely divided leaves. HEIGHT & SPREAD 30×60 cm (1×2 ft).

The female equivalent, **'Joanna'**, has smaller flowers with a boss of green carpels.

American species

C. addisonii Although it is a slow grower, this species is admired for its attractive hanging bells, just 2.5 cm (1 in) long. The flowers are reddish purple on the outside and cream on the inside. The plant has wide, heart-shaped leaves. HEIGHT & SPREAD 30×30 cm (1×1 ft).

(6) THE EARLY LARGE-FLOWERED GROUP

As their name suggests, these plants produce the largest blooms. They all give a spectacular show from late spring to mid summer, often followed by another display in late summer or early autumn. Plants that have double flowers usually produce these in the first flush, with single blooms appearing in the second flush.

The flowers come in a wide range of colours, including whites, pinks, reds, purples, blues and a few yellows. Some have a broad central stripe down each tepal. Blooms vary in size from 10-25 cm (4-10 in) across and can be single, semidouble,

▲ *Clematis* 'Bees' Jubilee'

double or multitepalled. The leaves are opposite on the stem and invariably ternate.

Plants in this group are the most susceptible to wilt of all clematis and require special care. A few cultivars have been bred to have some (though not complete) resistance to wilt, including 'Barbara Jackman', 'Doctor Ruppel', 'Lasurstern' and 'Nelly Moser'.

The young growths need to be fanned out and tied in carefully as they are very brittle. The ultimate spread of plants in this group is highly dependent on the gardener's fanning out and can vary from 50cm to 1.8m (1½-6ft). The height varies from 1.5-5m (5-16ft). The following varieties are medium sized unless stated otherwise.

▲ *Clematis* 'Elsa Späth'

'Arctic Queen' has fine double white flowers in its first flowering and, unusually, also in its second flush. The flowers have 6-7 tiers of tepals and cream stamens. **'Asao'** bears flowers composed of 6-7 large rosy-carmine tepals with a white stripe and brown stamens. **'Barbara Dibley'** has flowers made up of 8 deep red tepals with wavy edges and a central red stripe. The stamens are dark red. The vigorous **'Barbara Jackman'** bears flowers composed of 8 deep purple tepals with a broad crimson stripe and cream stamens. **'Beauty of Worcester'** produces large double flowers in the first

▲ *Clematis florida* 'Sieboldii'

▲ *Clematis* 'Général Sikorski'

flush followed by a late flush of single blooms. They have deep blue tepals, 6 on the single blooms, and white stamens. **'Bees' Jubilee'**♀ has mauve-pink tepals with broad carmine stripes and maroon stamens. The flowers are larger than those of 'Nelly Moser'. **'Belle of Woking'** bears large multitepalled silvery mauve flowers with yellow stamens. **'Countess of Lovelace'** produces large double lilac-blue flowers with pale cream stamens. **'Daniel Deronda'**♀ has multitepalled violet-blue flowers with cream stamens, followed by a second flush of single flowers. **'Dawn'** carries flowers made up of 8 pinky white tepals edged in pinky violet and carmine stamens. The compact plant is just 1.5m (5ft) tall. **'Doctor Ruppel'**♀ bears flowers composed of 8 bright red tepals with a brilliant carmine stripe and golden stamens. The plant is reliably profuse with its flowers and makes vigorous growth. **'Elsa Späth'**♀ bears flowers with 6-8 lavender tepals and reddish purple stamens on a reliably vigorous plant. **'Fair Rosamond'** has flowers made up of 8 white tepals tinged with violet, and purple stamens. It is violet-scented, the only large-flowered clematis with pronounced perfume. **'Fireworks'**♀ produces large light purple blooms with a broad maroon stripe on the 6-8 tepals. Dark red stamens open to reveal white filaments.

C. florida **'Alba Plena'** has striking, long-lasting flowers, up to 10cm (4in) across with 6 creamy white tepals and a boss of greenish white staminodes that open to make the flower appear double. It requires winter protection by a sheltered wall. *C. florida* **'Bicolour'** (see *C. f.* 'Sieboldii'). *C. florida* **'Sieboldii'** has the same features as *C. f.* 'Alba Plena', except that the staminodes are maroon-purple.

'Général Sikorski'♀ has blooms with 6 mid blue wavy edged tepals and golden stamens. The plant is vigorous. **'Gillian Blades'**♀ produces a flower of delicate beauty with 8 pure white tepals, suffused with purple at the wavy edges, and golden stamens. **'H.F. Young'**♀ has blooms composed of 8 Wedgwood blue tepals with creamy white stamens. It is one of the best blues and makes vigorous growth. **'Haku-ôkan'** carries a first flush of large, semi-double violet flowers with white stamens and a second flush of single blooms with 7-8 tepals. The vigorous **'Henryi'**♀ has flowers composed of 6-8 creamy white tepals with brown stamens. **'Horn of Plenty'**♀ bears flowers made up of 8 rosy purple tepals and purple stamens. **'Jackmanii Alba'** has a first flush of semidouble flowers with white tepals and brown stamens and a second crop of single blooms with 5-6 tepals. **'Jackmanii Rubra'** has flowers with velvety crimson tepals and cream stamens. Semidouble flowers are borne first, followed by a later flush of single blooms with 4-6 tepals. **'John Warren'** has flowers with 6-8 rich cerise-pink pointed tepals and brown stamens on a low-growing plant. **'Kakio'** (syn. 'Pink Champagne') has rather small, deep pink flowers. Each of the 8 tepals bears a white stripe. **'Kathleen Dunford'** bears large rosy purple flowers with yellow stamens. The blooms are semi-double in the first flowering and single with 8 tepals in the later flush. **'Kathleen Wheeler'** has flowers with 6-8 large plum-mauve tepals and yellow stamens. **'Lady Caroline Nevill'** produces large lavender-blue flowers made up of 8 tepals and beige stamens. **'Lady Northcliffe'** has flowers with 6 deep purple-blue tepals and white stamens. **'Lasurstern'**♀ is outstanding for its generous display of single blooms and its later second crop. The flowers are a rich

▼ *Clematis* 'Fireworks'

▼ *Clematis* 'Gillian Blades'

▼ *Clematis* 'Horn of Plenty'

▼ *Clematis* 'Henryi'

mauve-blue with 7-8 wavy edged tepals and white stamens. The vigorous **'Lawsoniana'** carries massive blooms with 6-8 lavender-blue, rosy tinged tepals and beige stamens. **'Liberation'** has magenta flowers. Each of the 8 tepals carries a deeper magenta stripe and the stamens are golden. **'Lincoln Star'** has large pink flowers made up of 8 tepals, each with a bright pink central stripe. Its growth is moderate. **'Lord Nevill'**♀ has large deep blue flowers composed of 6-8 tepals and dark maroon stamens. **'Louise Rowe'** is unusual in that it sometimes carries single, semidouble and double flowers at the same time. The white tepals have a violet tinge and the stamens are golden. The plant flowers in early summer and again in early autumn. It is not vigorous and is susceptible to wilt, but is

▼ *Clematis* 'Marie Boisselot'

Clematis 'Silver Moon' ▼

▲ *Clematis* 'Mrs N. Thompson'

Clematis 'Proteus' ▲

worth growing for the mixed blooms. **'Madame Le Coultre'** see *C.* 'Marie Boisselot'. **'Marie Boisselot'**♀ has flowers with 6-8 pure white tepals and pale yellow stamens. It is tall and one of the best white clematis, continuously flowering from mid spring to early autumn. **'Maureen'** bears large velvety purple flowers with 6 tepals and creamy stamens. **'Miss Bateman'**♀ produces dramatic white blooms of 6-8 tepals with a conspicuous boss of brownish red stamens. The first flowers are sometimes attractively tinged with green. A second crop is produced in early autumn. **'Moonlight'** has flowers with 8 pale creamy yellow tepals and creamy yellow stamens on a short plant reaching only 1.8m (6ft). It flowers in late spring and early autumn. **'Mrs Cholmondeley'**♀ bears large blooms with 6-8 lavender-blue tepals and brown stamens on a tall plant. It has a rather gappy flower, but it is valued for its reliability and continuous flowering from late spring to early autumn. **'Mrs N. Thompson'** has flowers composed of 4-6 deep violet-blue tepals with a vivid scarlet stripe and deep red stamens. The plant is a weak grower, reaching a maximum of 1.5m (5ft) and suits a small garden. **'Multi Blue'** has blooms with numerous tepals in varying shades of blue-purple with blue tips. The flower opens up layer by layer – about a layer a day. **'Nelly Moser'**♀ produces blooms made up of 8 pale mauve-pink tepals striped with carmine and maroon stamens. The colours last longer when the plant is grown in semi-shade. There are two crops of flowers. **'Niobe'**♀ has blooms with 6 velvety ruby-red tepals and golden stamens. The flowers appear almost black when they first open. The plant is vigorous and flowers continuously from mid spring to early autumn. **'Norfolk Lady'** has delicate pearly white blooms made up of 6-8 tepals and yellow stamens.

Clematis 'Nelly Moser'

C. patens An attractive curiosity, this is one of the original parents of many of the large-flowered clematis. It bears flowers with 8 mauve tepals and purple-red stamens. **'Pink Champagne'** see *C.* 'Kakio'. **'Proteus'** bears flowers with many rose-lilac tepals and yellow stamens in a peony-like flower. **'Richard Pennell'**♀ has flowers with 8 rosy purple tepals and golden stamens. It is a reliable flowerer from late spring to early autumn. **'Royalty'**♀ has blooms with rich purple-mauve tepals and yellow stamens. It is moderately vigorous. **'Sealand Gem'** bears flowers with 6 or 7 pale lavender-blue tepals carrying a carmine stripe and mauve stamens. **'Silver Moon'**♀ has large blooms composed of 6-8 lilac tepals and yellow stamens. The vigorous **'Snow Queen'** has flowers made up of 6 white tepals with wavy violet edges and deep burgundy stamens. **'Sylvia Denny'** bears flowers with white tepals and yellow stamens – semidouble at first and single in the second flush.

'The President'♀ produces blooms with 8 deep purple tepals and reddish purple stamens. The plant is vigorous and flowers continuously from early summer to early autumn. **'Veronica's Choice'** has lavender wavy-edged tepals and yellow sta-

▲ *Clematis* 'Sealand Gem'

mens. It is moderately vigorous, producing double blooms in the first flush followed by single flowers. **'Vyvyan Pennell'** is one of the most beautiful of the genus. The flowers are a kaleidoscope of blue, violet and purple in peony-like blooms, multitepalled in the first flush and single (shown) with 6-8 tepals in the second. Unfortunately, the plant is particularly susceptible to wilt.

'Wada's Primrose' has flowers with 8 soft primrose tepals and creamy yellow stamens. Early flowers are sometimes tinged with green. It is a low-growing variety. **'W.E. Gladstone'** produces the largest flowers of the group with 6 or 7 lilac-blue tepals and purple stamens. It often dies right back in winter only to reappear in spring with a profuse show of blooms. **'Will Goodwin'**♀ has large lavender-blue flowers composed of 6-10 tepals and yellow stamens. **'William Kennett'** has large flowers with 8 deep lavender-blue wavy-edged tepals and purple stamens. It is a vigorous plant, flowering continuously from early summer to early autumn.

(7) THE LATE LARGE-FLOWERED GROUP

These strong-growing clematis varieties flower from late summer to early autumn. The flowers are usually 6-15cm (2½-6in) across, either flat or saucer shaped, there are no double or yellow flowers and they are not scented. The leaves are usually ternate but this sometimes extends to 5 leaflets.

Many of the plants, which are often known as the jackmanii group, have *C. viticella* in their parentage and benefit from its resistance to wilt. They may suffer from mildew but this is easily cured.

The spread, 1-2.4m (3-8ft), depends on the available support and careful training of the stems. The height ranges from 1.8-6m (6-20ft). Smaller plants do well in a tub or a pot if given support. The following varieties are medium sized unless stated otherwise.

▼ *Clematis* 'The President'

C

▲ *Clematis* 'Gipsy Queen'

'Allanah' bears large flowers, up to 20 cm (8 in) across, with 8 bright red tepals and dark brown stamens. It thrives in a sunny spot. **'Andromeda'** bears white flowers with a pink stripe along each tepal. **'Cardinal Wyszynski'** see *C.* 'Kardynal Wyszynski'. **'Comtesse de Bouchaud'**♀ is one of the finest varieties and is easy to grow. The freely produced satiny pink blooms have 6 tepals and yellow stamens. **'Gipsy Queen'**♀ has flowers composed of 6 bluish purple tepals with dark, reddish purple stamens. This very vigorous plant is often misnamed 'Jackmanii' or 'Jackmanii Superba' but can be distinguished by its stamen colour. **'Hagley Hybrid'** is probably the most reliable of all the large-flowered clematis in terms of habit and disease resistance. The freely produced flowers have 6 or 7 shell-pink tepals and brown stamens. **'Jackmanii Superba'** has flowers with 4-6 velvety deep purple tepals and green stamens. **'John Huxtable'** bears large

▼ *Clematis* 'Vyvyan Pennell'

Clematis 'Hagley Hybrid' ▼

▲ *Clematis* 'John Huxtable'

Clematis 'Perle d'Azur' ▲

flowers with 6 pure white tepals and creamy yellow stamens. **'John Paul II'** (also sold as **'Jan Pawel II'**) produces 6-tepalled large white flowers with pink shading and brown stamens. **'Kardynal Wyszynski'** has large flowers with crimson tepals and brown stamens. **'Lilacina Floribunda'** bears large blooms with 6-8 rich purple tepals and dark brown stamens. **'Madame Baron Veillard'** flowers from mid to late autumn. It is a tall plant bearing abundant blooms with 6 rosy

▲ *Clematis* 'Rouge Cardinal'

pink tepals and white stamens. It needs a sunny position. **'Madame Edouard André'**♀ has flowers with 6 wine-red tepals and cream stamens. The flowers are borne

▲ *Clematis* 'Star of India'

from early summer to early autumn on a short plant, reaching only 2.1 m (7 ft). **'Perle d'Azur'**♀ is prized for its profuse and vivid flowers. The large flowers that appear from early summer to early autumn are made up of 5 or 6 deep violet tepals and pale green stamens. **'Pink Fantasy'**, only 1.8 m (6 ft) tall, produces large pinky violet flowers. Each of the 6 tepals has a brown stripe and the stamens are purple. The low-growing **'Rouge Cardinal'** carries flowers with 4-6 velvety purple-red tepals and magenta stamens from early summer to early autumn. **'Star of India'**♀ has large velvety flowers composed of 6 plummy red tepals with a distinct red stripe, surrounding yellow stamens. This free-flowering plant is vigorous and among the tallest of the group.

'Twilight' has slightly iridescent flowers, up to 15 cm (6 in) across, with 6 mauve tepals and yellow stamens. It is moderately vigorous and flowers from mid summer to

▲ *Clematis* 'Warszawska Nike'

mid autumn. **'Victoria'** is an often neglected yet worthwhile clematis. It is very reliable and is a good choice for a cold climate, where it remains vigorous and free flowering. Its flowers have 4-6 rosy-purple tepals and yellow-green stamens and appear from early summer to early autumn on a fairly tall plant. **'Warszawska Nike'** (also sold as **'Warsaw Nike'**) has large rich purple flowers, up to 25 cm (10 in) across, with 6 tepals and yellow stamens.

(8) THE HERBACEOUS GROUP

From early summer into, or through, autumn is the flowering time for this group. The plants do not use petioles for climbing, but scramble instead. The stems die down in winter and so do not need pruning; just clear away any dead matter.

The plants are divided into two subsections: the tidy integrifolias and the larger, coarser heracleifolias.

Integrifolias

The cultivars in this section have been developed from *C. integrifolia.* The nodding bell-like flowers are up to 5 cm (2 in) long and borne singly or in loose clusters. The stems carry pairs of lance-shaped leaves, up to 10 cm (4 in) long. The plants scramble over low shrubs in a border, or make a clump about 1 m (3 ft) high and 3 m (10 ft) across if given artificial support.

'Alba' has scented white flowers. **'Arabella'** has large blue-purple flowers on a plant that scrambles up to 1.8 m (6 ft). It blooms in early summer to mid autumn. ***C.* x *durandii***♀ is long-flowering species, from early summer to mid autumn, with indigo-blue flowers. The firm stems of the flowers make them excellent for cutting. The plant

▼ *Clematis* x *durandii*

Clematis integrifolia

can clamber up to 1.8m (6ft). **'Olgae'** has mid blue, scented blooms. **'Pangbourne Pink'** has reddish pink flowers. **'Pastel Blue'** has light blue, scented flowers. **'Pastel Pink'** has light pink flowers. **'Petit Faucon'** has deep indigo flowers with unusual twisting tepals. **'Rosea'**♀ has deep pink scented flowers. **'Tapestry'** has mauvy red blooms.

Heracleifolias

Most of the plants in this section are developments from *C. heracleifolia*. The small scented blooms are held in dense clusters. Slightly downy ternate leaves, up to 15cm (6in) long, almost hide the flowers. The plants grow to 1m (3ft) tall, but can scramble up to 3m (10ft) over nearby shrubs.

'Campanile' has mid blue flowers. **'Côte d'Azur'** has pale blue flowers. Indigo-blue flowers are carried by var. ***davidiana***. Pale blue flowers are seen on var. ***davidiana*** **'Wyevale'**♀. **'Edward Prichard'** is not as robust as the others but its deep blue flowers are strongly perfumed.

C* ×*jouiniana **'Praecox'**♀ is the finest scrambling clematis and since it can extend over a large area it is useful for ground cover. White flowers with violet margins are produced in profusion, obscuring the coarse leaves. **'Mrs Robert Brydon'** has blue-and-white unscented flowers and is vigorous. ***C. recta*** **'Purpurea'** is a bushy plant, bearing scented clusters of many small, starry white flowers. The dark, pinnate leaves are purplish bronze when young. It reaches a height of 1.2m (4ft), spreading widely as a bush.

▲ *Clematis recta* 'Purpurea'

(9) THE VITICELLA GROUP

Masses of medium-sized flowers appear from mid summer to mid autumn on these vigorous climbers. They are all hardy and disease resistant, offering a trouble-free alternative to the large-flowered clematis. The flowers are in a wide range of colours but not yellow. They are often saucer shaped, though some open as bells at first. The flowers are up to 6cm (2½in) across and have 4 tepals.

The plants reach 6m (20ft) in height with a spread of up to 3m (10ft), depending on the support and training given. Only *C. viticella*, *C.* 'Betty Corning' and *C.* × *triternata* 'Rubromarginata' are scented. Most have leaves of 3-9 leaflets. They are excellent among shrubs, roses and small trees.

C. viticella The parent species from S Europe has small, deep purple nodding bells with green stamens.

'Abundance' has vivid pink-red flowers with creamy green stamens. **'Alba Luxurians'**♀ produces green-tipped creamy white blooms with creamy green stamens. It is unusual because the leaves and tepals merge. **'Ascotiensis'**♀ bears azure-blue flowers up to 12cm (4¾in) across with creamy green stamens in late summer. **'Betty Corning'** bears its scented pale lavender-blue bells over a long period. **'Blue Belle'** is very vigorous with tepals more mauve than blue and yellow stamens. ***C. campaniflora*** has small nodding white bells tinged with violet. ***C.*** × ***eriostemon*** **'Hendersonii'** makes a shrub-like plant to 3m (10ft) tall, with broad, bell-shaped deep blue flowers with yellow stamens. **'Ernest Markham'**♀ has large red blooms, up to 15cm (6in) across, with beige stamens.

▲ *Clematis* 'Abundance'

▲ *Clematis* 'Little Nell'

▲ *Clematis* 'Ascotiensis'

▲ *Clematis* 'Madame Grangé'

▼ *Clematis* 'Ernest Markham'

▲ *Clematis* 'Margaret Hunt'

▲ *Clematis* 'Prince Charles'

'Etoile Violette'♀ has large purple blooms with creamy yellow stamens.

'Huldine' bears large flowers, about 10cm (4in) across, with 6 silvery white tepals and greenish white stamens. **'Kermesina'** has deep wine-red flowers and red-brown stamens. **'Lady Betty Balfour'** blooms in early to mid autumn. The flowers are up to 12.5cm (5in) across with violet-blue tepals and yellow stamens. **'Little Nell'** has creamy white flowers edged with violet and green stamens. **'Madame Grangé'**♀ produces crimson-violet blooms, up to 12.5cm (5in) across, with broad red stripes on the tepals and off-white stamens. **'Madame Julia Correvon'**♀ has wine-red flowers with golden stamens. **'Margaret Hunt'** carries its mauve-pink flowers with brown stamens from early summer to mid autumn. **'Margot Koster'** has mauve-pink flowers with white stamens. **'Minuet'**♀ has white flowers edged with pinky mauve. The stamens are green. **'Mrs Spencer Castle'** bears mauve-pink, semidouble flowers up to 12.5cm (5in) across. **'Pagoda'** has wide purple-and-white bells with yellow-green stamens. **'Polish Spirit'**♀ bears rich purple-blue flowers with rosy purple stamens. **'Prince Charles'** produces an abundance of light violet flowers with green stamens. **'Purpurea Plena Elegans'**♀ has violet-purple double blooms. **'Royal Velours'**♀ bears reddish purple blooms with reddish stamens. The flowers have a velvety sheen. **'Rubra'** (see 'Kermesina'). *C.* x *triternata* **'Rubromarginata'**♀ produces masses of heavily scented, tiny white star-shaped flowers edged in red with pale yellow stamens. **'Venosa Violacea'** bears large white flowers veined and edged with purple. **'Ville de Lyon'** blooms in late summer producing carmine flowers with darker edges and creamy stamens. **'Voluceau'** has red flowers, up to 14cm (5½in) across, with yellow stamens and blooms from early summer to early autumn.

▲ *Clematis* 'Ville de Lyon'

▲ *Clematis* 'Duchess of Albany'

▲ *Clematis* 'Gravetye Beauty'

(10) THE TEXENSIS GROUP

This group flowers from mid summer to mid autumn and contains plants with tulip-shaped blooms of different shades up to 6cm (2½in) long. The plants make a bush up to 1.8m (6ft) tall and about 1m (3ft) wide. The small leaves are glaucous and made up of 5-9 leaflets. Plants within the texensis group have weak petioles for climbing and thus scramble and clamber over shrubs or artificial supports.

'Duchess of Albany'♀ has clear pink flowers with broad, rose-pink stripes and cream stamens. **'Etoile Rose'** bears hanging tubular flowers of vivid cherry-purple edged in silver with greeny yellow stamens. **'Gravetye Beauty'** produces rich ruby-red flowers with red stamens. **'Ladybird Johnson'** has dusky red flowers with cream stamens. The flowers of **'Sir Trevor Lawrence'** are crimson inside with cream-coloured stamens. On the outside they are a satiny cream-and-red mixture. **'The Princess Of Wales'** is vivid pink with creamy yellow stamens.

(11) THE ORIENTALIS GROUP

The plants in this group of yellow clematis flower in late summer and early autumn. All have yellow, hanging lanterns or bells up to 7.5cm (3in) across. The plants have fine foliage, many have spectacular seed heads, and they are easy to grow. They are hardy throughout Britain, reaching about 3.5m (12ft) tall with a spread of up to 1.8m (6ft).

'Bill Mackenzie'♀ has large open bells with beige stamens, borne from mid summer to late autumn. It often bears flowers and seed heads together. **'Helios'** is a shorter plant than most in this group, reaching only 1.2m (4ft), which makes it suitable for a small garden. It starts flowering early – in late spring – and continues until mid summer. The large pale yellow flowers are produced in profusion.

C. tangutica Characterised by 5cm (2in) lantern-shaped, lemon-yellow flowers, this plant also has attractive, large seed heads. HEIGHT & SPREAD 4.5x1.8m (15x6ft)

Reliable varieties include **'Aureolin'**♀, **'Burford'**, **'Corry'**, **'Gravetye'** and **'Lambton Park'**.

C. tibetana ssp. ***vernayi*** **LS&E 13342** (also known as **'Ludlow & Sherrif'**) This plant is generally known as 'orange peel' clematis because of the thick, yellow tepals that make up the flowers. The blooms are downward-facing open bowls which can be seen in mid autumn. They have slaty purple stamens. HEIGHT & SPREAD 3.5x1.8m (12x6ft).

Related plants

Several species resemble the orientalis group in their flowers and flowering time.

C. aethusifolia has pale primrose bell-shaped flowers and lacy foliage. It can be shy to flower, but when it does so it is from late summer to mid autumn. HEIGHT & SPREAD 1.8x1.2m (6x4ft).

C. akebioides has glaucous leaves and dark yellowish green bell-shaped flowers. HEIGHT & SPREAD 1.2x1.2m (4x4ft).

C. ladakhiana has ferny foliage that tends to hide the yellow star-shaped flowers that appear in late summer. HEIGHT & SPREAD 1.8x1.2m (6x4ft).

C. rehderiana♀ is a giant of a plant, reaching 6m (20ft) tall. In late summer it is covered with clusters of small straw-yellow tubular flowers with recurving tips and a strong cowslip scent. HEIGHT & SPREAD 6x1.8m (20x6ft).

C. serratifolia bears pale yellow, star-shaped flowers with purple stamens for a few weeks in late summer. The leaves are sharply toothed. HEIGHT & SPREAD 2.4x1.2m (8x4ft).

(12) THE LATE SPECIES GROUP
The plants within this group flower in late summer and autumn. Most are outstanding for their generous displays of blooms while some are also highly fragrant. As sunlight is limited in autumn the plants benefit from being positioned in the sunniest places.

C. fargesii The flowers have 6 white tepals with greenish white stamens. With no pruning, the plant can start flowering in early summer and goes on to late autumn. With pruning, it starts flowering in mid summer. HEIGHT & SPREAD 7.5×3m (25×10ft).

C. flammula A cloud of tiny star-shaped white flowers covers the plant. The 1cm (⅜in) wide blooms are held in clusters, have white stamens and a strong, sweet scent. HEIGHT & SPREAD 6×3m (20×10ft).

CULTIVATION Spring planting is best because the plants are ready to make growth as the soil warms. Ten groups – all but the two large-flowered groups – are planted just like any other shrubs. The large-flowered clematis, especially the early large-flowered group, need special treatment due to their susceptibility to wilt: work a general-purpose fertiliser into the planting area and set the plants with the junction of roots and shoots 10cm (4in) below the soil surface. They then make several shoots under the ground – if a shoot is killed by wilt another will replace it. In the first year after planting prune all plants hard to within 23cm (9in) of the ground to promote the production of several strong shoots.

Soil can be alkaline or acid as long as it is not extreme. It is more important to provide plenty of water – a minimum of 4 litres (7 pints) a week for one plant, with 4 times as much needed in hot weather. A mulch spread around the base of the plant helps to retain moisture. Clematis plants like a rich soil and a rich feeding programme as they make a great deal of growth in the course of the year. Work manure and compost into the soil around established plants each year in spring, and in autumn apply bone meal at the rate of 100g per m^2 (3oz per sq yd).

The large-flowered clematis have extra feeding requirements. In spring add a handful of artificial fertiliser rich in potash plus additional liquid fertiliser rich in potash once a week during the growing period. Then in mid summer give the plants another handful of fertiliser rich in potash.

The ideal position for a clematis is against a south-facing wall sheltered from strong winds. However, many clematis do well enough in less than ideal surroundings, even on a north-facing wall. They can be used in a number of ways. Walls provide excellent support as do fences, trellises, screens, poles, pyramids, tripods, umbrellas and arches. When using physical structures make sure that you supply wires, struts or netting for the clematis to cling on to. Some gardeners prefer natural supports, such as shrubs, small trees and climbing roses.

Clematis are unlikely to need winter protection apart from an extra mulch in a very cold winter and a layer of garden fleece for tender plants.

▲ *Clematis rehderiana*

PROPAGATION Layering is the best method for producing a small number of plants. Lift and divide herbaceous plants in winter. Raise from stem cuttings if a large number of plants is required.

Only seed of the species will come true unless they have been hybridised.

PRUNING The earlier a clematis flowers, the less pruning it needs. This is because the flowers are borne on growth made during the previous year, and if this is cut off the next crop of flowers, goes with it. The later a clematis flowers, the more pruning it needs. This is because the flowers are on new growth made in spring. Cutting back hard in winter encourages a lot of growth and thus a lot of flowers later in the year. If you do not know which group a plant belongs to, let it grow for a year and it will become apparent.

The first five groups of clematis – the evergreen, alpina, macropetala, montana and rockery groups – do not need pruning. If the plant has extended outside its allotted space cut it back when flowering ends to just below its allotted space. New growth that year will just fill the space given to it.

Just one group, the early large-flowered group, needs light pruning. In late winter or early spring examine each stem from the **top** down until you reach an outpointing healthy pair of buds. Prune off the growth above them. Fan out the remaining stems.

Five groups need severe pruning – the late large-flowered, herbaceous, viticella, texensis and late species. In late winter or early spring examine each stem from the **bottom** up until you find a strong pair of outward pointing buds. Cut above the buds. No harm will come to the plant even if the cut is virtually at ground level. If the plants look untidy in autumn you can do a preliminary pruning down to about 1m (3ft). Tie the shoots together and then complete the pruning in early spring.

In the orientalis group there is a choice; light pruning promotes early blooming and severe pruning stimulates more and larger flowers, but later.

In all pruning take care not to cut into strong woody stems. Rather, prune the green stems above them. When a plant has been neglected and has become a tangled mass, cut below the mass avoiding the brown woody stems.

PESTS AND DISEASES Clematis plants are remarkably healthy apart from clematis wilt (or 'stem rot'), a serious fungal disease that causes the stems to rot. Wilt strikes before a plant has developed thick brown stems, which are resistant to it. The greatest danger is in the first 2 years. Plants are particularly susceptible in humid conditions at a temperature of about 23°C (73°F), or if their stems are damaged. Plants in the early large-flowered group are the most vulnerable, late large-flowered clematis are less so. The other groups are free of wilt.

Remove any infected stems from below the wilting leaves and burn them. Wilt does not necessarily kill the plant; the roots are alive, so keep watering and fertilising the plant to bring on new growth. Water a fungicide into the ground around large-flowered plants once a month from mid spring until early autumn.

Powdery mildew affects the late large-flowered clematis and the texensis group. As soon as the mildew appears apply systemic fungicides and in the case of the texensis group an appropriate fungicide should be routinely employed once a week when the plants are in flower.

Cleome

Spider flower

Capparaceae

Although always attracting interest wherever it is grown, this free-flowering, half-hardy annual of exotic appearance remains an unusual plant in British gardens. Owners of small gardens may find its size discouraging, as it usually reaches about 1.2m (4ft) in height. It does, however, have a long flowering period and its blooms last well in water when cut. Cleomes can also be grown in pots or other containers as large summer-flowering greenhouse plants.

RECOMMENDED SPECIES AND VARIETIES

C. hassleriana (syn *C. spinosa* hort.) Dense clusters of white, pink, violet or purple scented flowers are borne at the end of each stem from early summer to early autumn. Each flower has 4 narrow petals, up to 3cm (1¼in) long, and long protruding stamens and styles which give the flowers a spidery appearance. The long-stalked, palmate leaves have spines at the base of their stalks. The narrow pointed leaflets are up to 12cm (4¾in) long. Native to S America. HEIGHT & SPREAD 1.2m×45cm (4×1½ft).

▲ *Cleome hassleriana*

'Cherry Queen' has cherry-pink flowers. The seed mixture **'Colour Fountain'** offers pink, violet, purple and white flowers. **'Helen Campbell'** produces white flowers, **'Pink Queen'** has pink blooms and **'Violet Queen'** produces violet flowers.

C. spinosa hort. see *C. hassleriana*

CULTIVATION Plant in sandy soil after the risk of frost has passed, choosing a position in full sun. Alternatively, grow in 15cm (6in) pots of multipurpose compost and keep in a greenhouse, in a brightly lit position, shaded from the midday sun. No artificial heating is required after mid spring. Deadhead plants to prolong flowering.

PROPAGATION Sow seed in a heated greenhouse in early spring. Pot on seedlings into 9cm (3½in) pots and harden off before planting out.

PESTS AND DISEASES Aphids may damage young plants.

Clerodendrum

Verbenaceae

Clerodendrum bungei

Showy, fragrant flower clusters of these shrubs and climbers provide late summer and early autumn interest. Most of the 400 species are not hardy in Britain, but given a sheltered position, *Clerodendrum bungei* and *C. trichotomum* survive outdoors. *C. splendens* and *C. thomsoniae* can be grown in tubs in heated conservatories or greenhouses and moved outside in summer.

RECOMMENDED SPECIES AND VARIETIES

C bungei♀ Deep pink, highly scented flowers bloom in large clusters, 10cm (4in) across. The heart-shaped, mid green leaves grow to 20cm (8in) long and emit an unpleasant smell. This multistemmed, suckering shrub may die back to ground level in a severe winter, but will grow again from the base in spring. Native to China. HEIGHT & SPREAD 80×80cm (2ft8in × 2ft8in) after 5 years, ultimately 1.8m (6ft) tall.

C. splendens♀ Scarlet flowers are carried in clusters 12.5cm (5in) across on this evergreen climber. The dark green ovate leaves grow to 12.5cm (5in) long. The plant is tender and requires the protection of a heated conservatory or greenhouse. Native to Sierra Leone. HEIGHT & SPREAD Up to 2×2m (6½×6½ft) after 5 years, ultimately 3m (10ft) tall.

▼ *Clerodendrum bungei*

C. thomsoniae♀ Each flower in the hanging clusters, 10cm (4in) across, has a bell-shaped pure white calyx and crimson petals. The ovate leaves grow to 17cm (6¾in) long. This tender evergreen climber needs the protection of a heated conservatory or greenhouse. Native to W Africa. HEIGHT & SPREAD Up to 2×2m (6½×6½ft) after 5 years, ultimately 4m (13ft) tall.

C. trichotomum Small, fragrant white flowers are held in drooping clusters up to 15cm (6in) across. Bright blue berries enclosed in lobed, reddish calyxes follow the flowers and eventually turn black. The leaves, up to 20cm (8in) long, have an unpleasant smell. This rounded deciduous shrub is one of the hardiest species. Native to Japan and China. HEIGHT & SPREAD 1×1m (3×3ft) after 5 years, ultimately 6m (20ft) tall.

▲ *Clerodendrum trichotomum*

The very similar var. ***fargesii***♀ has slightly paler berries and calyxes. The leaves are sometimes red when they emerge, developing a purple hue.

CULTIVATION Plant in a well-drained, humus-rich soil in a sunny, sheltered position. *C. splendens* and *C. thomsoniae* need a minimum temperature of 15°C (59°F).

PROPAGATION Sow seed in spring, take root cuttings in early winter or separate suckers from the parent plant in spring and pot up or replant immediately.

PRUNING Not normally required, but remove any dead wood in early spring.

PESTS AND DISEASES Usually trouble free.

▼ *Clerodendrum trichotomum* var. *fargesii*

Climbers

Versatile plants for vertical sites

A MANTLE OF FLOWERS OR LUXURIANT FOLIAGE BRIGHTENS UP DULL WALLS AND ADDS BEAUTY TO MANY OTHER GARDEN STRUCTURES

Practical and ornamental, climbing plants bring a pleasurable extra dimension to gardens, clothing walls, arches, pergolas, screens and even trees and shrubs with their flowers and foliage. They can be used to conceal unattractive features, provide privacy and help to integrate house and garden.

Many climbers produce spectacular blooms, including *Clematis* and *Rosa.* Others are grown for their attractive foliage, such as *Parthenocissus quinquefolia* (Virginia creeper), or for their colourful fruits, such as *Celastrus orbiculatus.*

SCENT LADEN *The delicate flowers of honeysuckle will fill the air with sweet fragrance.*

Some climbing plants will cling unaided to a support: *Hedera* (ivy) uses aerial roots and *Parthenocissus* has sucker pads. However, most ascend by tendrils, like *Lathyrus,* by curling leafstalks, like *Clematis,* by twining stems, like *Lonicera* (honeysuckle), or by hooked thorns, like roses. All these plants will climb unaided through the branches of trees or shrubs but need training on wires or up a trellis if grown against a wall (see p. 809). Although they are not true climbers, some shrubs, including *Ceanothus* (California lilac) and *Jasminum nudiflorum* (winter jasmine), can also be trained against a support.

The extensive range of climbers means there is a choice of plants for most garden situations. *Passiflora* (passion flower) and *Trachelospermum* require a sunny and sheltered site but *Jasminum officinale* (summer jasmine) and *Clematis montana* thrive in shady or sunny areas. Ivy or *Hydrangea anomala* ssp. *petiolaris* (climbing hydrangea) are tough enough to cope with an exposed, shady position.

Walls and fences

Climbing plants relieve the starkness of bare brickwork or fencing. They look particularly effective when their flowers or foliage contrast with the background. For example, golden or variegated foliage stands out against red-brick walls and dark fences. Try the golden-leaved hop, *Humulus lupulus* 'Aureus', or an ivy with white or cream-splashed foliage, such as *Hedera colchica* 'Dentata Variegata'. Alternatively, choose plants with pale blooms, such as the white-flowered *Clematis* 'Jackmanii Alba' or *C. montana.*

A light-coloured wall or fence makes an effective background for richly coloured blooms, such as the wine-red flowers of *C.* 'Madame Julia Correvon' or the vivid purple of *C.* 'Etoile Violette'. Dark green ivy or the striking *Actinidia kolomikta,* which has pink, cream and green leaves, also look attractive here.

As the soil by a wall is often poorer than elsewhere in the garden and receives less rain, it needs careful preparation before planting (see p. 809).

Vertical features

Freestanding structures, such as pergolas or arches, are attractive focal points. They make excellent supports for climbing plants. *Aristolochia macrophylla, Parthenocissus henryana, Vitis* (grapevine) or *Wisteria* are all good choices. On a smaller scale, an arbour or gazebo makes a secluded retreat, and an archway or short pergola enhances a path or entranceway. *Humulus* (hop) and other foliage plants grown over them provide leafy shade and some climbers, including *Lonicera caprifolium,* have the added appeal of scent.

A freestanding tripod or obelisk creates height in a border, and is a suitable support for less vigorous climbers, such as the clematis 'H.F. Young', which has Wedgwood blue

◀ IN UNION *A combination of climbing rose and clematis makes a stunning display.*

▲ WALL HANGING *Green ivy complements the warm autumn tones of parthenocissus foliage.*

▼ SHADED SPOT *Climbing hydrangea brings floral interest to inhospitable and sunless sites.*

flowers, or the small-leaved ivy *Hedera helix* 'Glacier', with its variegated, grey-green leaves.

Climbing partners

Grow two climbers together to create an impressive display. Combine plants that bloom at the same time but have flowers of contrasting colours or shapes. The violet flowers of *Clematis* 'Perle d'Azur' look attractive with the pale pink climbing rose 'New Dawn', for example.

Alternatively, grow climbers that have different flowering times, to create a longer season of interest. Plant early flowering *Lonicera periclymenum* 'Belgica' with the later flowering 'Serotina' or with *C. florida* which bears large creamy white flowers in late summer and early autumn.

A flowering climber, such as *C. alpina* 'Pamela Jackman', looks good against a backdrop of leaves provided by a foliage plant, such as the gold-splashed *Hedera helix* 'Oro di Bogliasco'.

Trees and shrubs make natural supports for less vigorous climbers. Do not use a rampant plant, such as *C. montana* or *Fallopia baldschuanica* (Russian vine), which may overpower and strangle its host. Choose flower colours that contrast with the supporting plant's foliage. For example, pale-flowered *Lathyrus latifolius* 'White Pearl' looks attractive when grown through dark-leaved shrubs, such as *Garrya elliptica*, *Pyracantha* (firethorn) or *Ceanothus*, and bright *Tropaeolum speciosum* combines well with an evergreen hedge, shrub or dark green conifer.

To partner large shrubs or small trees, choose climbers that die back to the ground in autumn, such as *Lathyrus latifolius* (perennial pea), or that can be hard pruned annually, such as *Humulus lupulus* 'Aureus' and *Clematis viticella.* Annual climbers are suitable choices for growing through other plants as they die off in autumn, so there is no danger of them taking over.

▶ Added cheer *Fast-growing* Thunbergia alata *softens stark lines at the corner of a house.*

Fast cover

A climber can be trained up a trellis to screen a dustbin, compost heap or unsightly area. Ivies, including *Hedera helix* 'Buttercup' which has bright yellow foliage, are particularly useful as they provide year-round cover and thrive in almost any site.

For quick or temporary cover, use an annual climber which grows rapidly. The morning glory *Ipomoea tricolor* 'Heavenly Blue', which has large saucer-shaped blue flowers, and *Thunbergia alata* (black-eyed Susan), which has vivid orange-yellow flowers with black centres, provide effective and colourful cover and are easily raised from seed.

▼ Focal point *The cascading flowers of* Clematis montana *var.* rubens *make a floral frame.*

Some perennials can be treated as annuals because they grow quickly and flower well in the first year. They include the purple bell vine *Rhodochiton atrosanguineus*, which has dark purple tubular blooms.

Small gardens

In small gardens or on patios, choose climbers with compact habits. These can be grown in containers and used to lend height to a group of pot plants. Support the climber with a tripod of bamboo canes, secured with wire mesh, or buy a ready-made support.

Many large-flowered clematis, including 'Arctic Queen' with its ice-white flowers and 'Fireworks', which has red-striped blue flowers, make excellent pot plants, as do many of the annual climbers.

Miniature climbing roses, which reach up to 1.8 m (6 ft) in height, are valuable plants to train against walls and trellises or over tripods in confined areas. *Rosa* Laura Ford has rich yellow flowers and Warm Welcome has bright orange blooms.

Fragrant flowers

For an effect that is more than purely visual, plant climbers that have fragrant blooms. 'Gloire de Dijon', which has yellow flowers, and 'Climbing Etoile de Hollande', with its crimson-red blooms, are magnificently scented climbing roses. Wisteria, summer jasmine and the honeysuckles *Lonicera periclymenum* 'Graham Thomas', 'Belgica' and 'Serotina' also have sweet fragrances. Plant scented climbers near garden seats or round windows for maximum effect.

Climbers for sun and shade

Full Sun

- ***Actinidia kolomikta*** Heart-shaped green leaves with pink and cream tips; small white, cup-shaped flowers in early summer.
- ***Passiflora caerulea*** Pink or purple-flushed, white flowers in late summer and autumn.
- ***Rosa* 'Gloire de Dijon'** Buff-yellow double or quartered fragrant flowers from summer to autumn.
- ***Vitis* 'Brant'** Green leaves turning red in autumn, and clusters of black fruit.
- ***Wisteria floribunda* 'Alba'** Trails of small white fragrant flowers in late spring and early summer.

Partial Shade

- ***Aristolochia macrophylla*** Green flowers, marbled with purple, yellow and brown, in summer.
- ***Celastrus orbiculatus*** Yellow fruits, which have scarlet-coated seeds, and yellow leaves in autumn.
- ***Lathyrus latifolius*** Purple pea flowers from early summer to early autumn.
- ***Lonicera periclymenum* 'Belgica'** Fragrant, pink and red tubular flowers in mid summer, followed by orange to red berries.
- ***Parthenocissus henryana*** Large, dark green leaves, marked silver white, turning red in autumn.

Shade

- ***Clematis* 'Nelly Moser'** Large, open mauve-pink flowers, striped with carmine, in early summer.
- ***Hedera helix* 'Glacier'** Green and silvery grey evergreen leaves with narrow white margins.
- ***Hydrangea anomala* ssp. *petiolaris*** Large, flat, cream and white lace-cap flowers in early and mid summer.
- ***Jasminum nudiflorum*** Small, yellow, tubular flowers from late winter to early spring.
- ***Lonicera* × *tellmanniana*** Large clusters of red-flushed yellow flowers in late spring and early summer.

Clethra

Clethraceae

Clethra alnifolia

Beautiful spires of small, white or pink-tinged flowers, often fragrant, appear from mid summer to mid autumn on these shrubs and trees. Since evergreen species are generally suitable for only the mildest of British gardens, the plants recommended below are deciduous and need acid soil.

RECOMMENDED SPECIES AND VARIETIES
C. alnifolia (sweet pepper bush) White fragrant flowers are held erect in spires up to 15cm (6in) long from late summer to mid autumn. The toothed obovate leaves on upright shoots are 10cm (4in) long. They are downy when young and turn yellow in autumn. Native to eastern N America. HEIGHT & SPREAD 1m×60cm (3×2ft) after 5 years, ultimately up to 4m (13ft) tall.

▲ *Clethra alnifolia*

'Paniculata'♀ has arching branches and larger flowers than the species. **'Pink Spire'** and **'Rosea'** have pink-tinged flowers.
C. barbinervis♀ Fragrant white flowers, in spires up to 15cm (6in) long, appear from early summer to early autumn. The sharply toothed obovate leaves, 5-15cm (2-6in) long, provide red and yellow autumn colour. The flaking bark is grey-green with fawn patches. In colder, inland gardens this large bushy shrub needs a sheltered site. Native to Japan. HEIGHT & SPREAD 1m×50cm (36×20in) after 5 years, ultimately up to 10m (33ft) tall.
C. delavayi♀ From mid to late summer pink buds open into a profusion of scented yellow-tinged white flowers held in spikes up to 15cm (6in) long. The deep green, toothed leaves grow up to 15cm (6in) long. This upright shrub or small tree requires a sheltered site except in very mild districts. Native to W China. HEIGHT & SPREAD 1.2m×30cm (4×1ft) after 5 years, ultimately up to 10m (33ft) tall.

CULTIVATION Grow in an acid, humus-rich soil in a lightly shaded, moist but well-drained site sheltered from the wind.
PROPAGATION Sow seed in spring or take greenwood cuttings in early summer. Low arching branches can be layered. *C. alnifolia* produces suckers which can be removed from the parent plant.
PRUNING Not necessary, but cut back hard any straggly plants in winter or early spring.
PESTS AND DISEASES Usually trouble free.

Clianthus

Leguminosae

Clianthus puniceus

Only *Clianthus puniceus* is commonly grown, mainly for its crimson flowers, grouped in graceful pendent clusters, and its attractive, trailing foliage. This evergreen shrub is best suited to a cold greenhouse or conservatory, although it will grow outdoors in a warm garden trained against a wall facing south or west. The plant will tolerate temperatures as low as -5°C (23°F).

RECOMMENDED SPECIES AND VARIETIES
C. puniceus♀ (parrot's bill, kaka beak, lobster claw) Pendulous clusters of up to 20 flowers appear in spring and early summer. Each beak-like flower is about 6cm (2½in) long. The mid green leaves are up to 10cm (4in) long and pinnate, made up of 20-30 narrow leaflets about 2cm (¾in) long. The shrub is open branched, the stems forming a fan. When grown unsupported, it tends to spread sideways rather than upwards; when trained against a wall, the drooping flowers are seen more easily. Native to New Zealand. HEIGHT & SPREAD 1.2×1.2m (4×4ft) after 5 years, ultimately 3.5m (12ft) tall.

'Albus'♀ bears white flowers, subtly tinged with green.

▼ *Clianthus puniceus*

▲ *Clianthus puniceus* 'Albus'

CULTIVATION Plant in well-drained soil in full sun or light shade. Young plants can grow fast and might flower at one year old.
PROPAGATION Sow seed under glass in early spring. Colour forms usually come true. Take semi-ripe cuttings from young, woody growth and root in summer, growing on in well-drained soil.
PRUNING Cut back after flowering to promote bushiness.
PESTS AND DISEASES Red spider mite, slugs and snails cause problems.

Clinopodium

Labiatae

These attractive plants are grown for their long display of small flowers in summer. Excellent for attracting bees and butterflies, they make useful, easy-to-grow plants for a rock garden or the front of a flower border. Plants of the genus are hardy or half-hardy annuals or perennials. They resemble thyme or mint in appearance, but are not used in the kitchen. The two-lipped flowers are borne in crowded whorls at intervals along the stems. The mid green, oval leaves, carried in pairs, are aromatic when crushed. Native to Europe and W Asia.

RECOMMENDED SPECIES AND VARIETIES
C. acinos (syn. *Acinos arvensis*) (basil thyme) Violet flowers with white markings appear in mid and late summer. Each flower is about 1cm (⅜in) long. This tufted plant

▼ *Clinopodium vulgare*

has evergreen leaves, rather fleshy, up to 1.5 cm (½ in) long, on erect, hairy stems. Although hardy, the plant is short-lived, lasting 2-3 years, but will often self-seed. HEIGHT & SPREAD 30×20 cm (12×8 in).

C. vulgare (syn. *Calamintha vulgaris*) (wild basil) Pinkish purple flowers, 2 cm (¾ in) long, bloom from mid summer to early autumn. This softly hairy, hardy herbaceous perennial, has erect, mostly unbranched stems and leaves up to 6 cm (2½ in) long. HEIGHT & SPREAD 50×30 cm (20×12 in).

CULTIVATION Plant out in late winter or early spring in a light, well-drained soil, choosing a warm, sunny site.

PROPAGATION Sow seed in autumn or early spring in pots in a coldframe. *C. vulgare* can be divided after flowering or in early spring.

PESTS AND DISEASES Usually trouble free.

Clintonia

Convallariaceae

Starry flowers with six white, yellowish green or dull red petals are borne on erect stems, either singly or in clusters. Slender, creeping rhizomes form rosettes of mid to light green, slightly fleshy, oblong or elliptic leaves. These small woodland perennials are native to N America and Asia and require a neutral or acid soil in a shady position. Flowers in late spring or summer are followed in late summer or early autumn by fleshy black or bluish berries. The species listed below are hardy.

RECOMMENDED SPECIES AND VARIETIES

C. andrewsiana Clusters of bell-shaped, deep reddish purple flowers open in early summer at the end of a slender stem and often in one or two clusters along it. The flower stem rises out of a rosette of oval or tongue-shaped leaves up to 25 cm (10 in) long. Each flower has narrow 1.5 cm (½ in) long petals and a slender hairy stalk. The deep blue-black berries that come after the flowers are about 1 cm (⅜ in) across. Native to south-western regions of the USA. HEIGHT & SPREAD 50×30 cm (20×12 in).

▲ *Clintonia andrewsiana*

C. borealis A single stem ends with a cluster of nodding greenish yellow flowers with narrow petals 2 cm (¾ in) long. Vigorous plants may have a second and third flower cluster below the first. Clumps of ovate or tongue-shaped light green leaves, up to 20 cm (8 in) long with slightly hairy margins, are thrown up by the underground stems. Deep blue berries are seen after the flowers. Native to eastern N America. HEIGHT & SPREAD 30×25 cm (12×10 in).

CULTIVATION Plant in spring in moist but well-drained, lime-free soil rich in leaf-mould. Mulch annually with leaf-mould.

PROPAGATION Sow seed in autumn in a coldframe or carefully lift and divide established plants in early spring.

PESTS AND DISEASES Usually trouble free but may need protection from slugs.

Clivia

Amaryllidaceae

With their brightly coloured, trumpet-shaped flowers and gracefully arching long, fleshy leaves, these tender evergreen perennials make striking pot plants. Native to the sunny eastern coasts of South Africa, they must be grown under cover in Britain and will thrive in a warm greenhouse, conservatory or a well-lit window in the home.

RECOMMENDED SPECIES AND VARIETIES

C. miniata♀ Bold scarlet or deep orange trumpets with bright yellow throats appear in late winter or early spring. Up to 20 of the 5 cm (2 in) long flowers are carried at the top of a strong, erect stem. The leathery, strap-like leaves are dark green, and grow to 60 cm (2 ft) long and 5 cm (2 in) wide, splaying out from around the base of the flower stem. Small orange fruits may be produced. HEIGHT & SPREAD 75×60 cm (2½×2 ft).

There are several **Miniata** hybrids available producing flowers in a range of colours from red through to yellow.

CULTIVATION Grow in pots of John Innes No. 3 compost in a sunny spot with a minimum temperature of 10°C (50°F). Water freely in spring and summer and sparingly in winter although the plants must be kept moist as this is when they flower. Feed every 3 weeks in spring and summer. Wait until the plants are bursting from their pots and then move only one size up.

PROPAGATION Divide after flowering and plant crowns singly in 13 cm (5 in) pots. Sow seed in spring and raise in a propagator.

PESTS AND DISEASES Mealy bugs are a nuisance, but generally free of diseases.

▼ *Clivia miniata*

Clover see *Trifolium*

Cobaea

Cup-and-saucer vine
Polemoniaceae

Large, bell-shaped flowers are carried from mid summer to the first frosts on this climber. *Cobaea scandens* is the only species grown in Britain. It is a perennial which is almost always grown as a half-hardy annual. A rapid grower, it is ideal for covering a sunny trellis or a wall. It can also be grown in containers in a conservatory.

▲ *Cobaea scandens*

RECOMMENDED SPECIES AND VARIETIES

C. scandens♀ Scented flowers, up to 7.5 cm (3 in) long, are borne singly on long stems. The flowers are greenish cream as they open but change to violet and finally to purple. Plants grown in the open flower from mid summer to mid autumn. The grey-green leaves are divided into 3 pairs of oval leaflets, the end leaflet being replaced by a tendril. In greenhouse conditions the plant can produce stems up to 8 m (26 ft) in length in its first year. Native to Mexico. HEIGHT & SPREAD 3×1.5 m (10×5 ft) when grown outdoors.

The flowers of ***alba***♀ are white.

CULTIVATION Plant in a sheltered, sunny spot, allowing 60 cm (2 ft) between plants. Use support wires or netting to train them against a wall. Indoors, grow in a large pot of soil-based compost. Water and feed regularly through the summer months.

PROPAGATION Sow large seeds individually in pots in a warm greenhouse in early spring. Plant out after the risk of frost has passed. Softwood cuttings can be taken.

PESTS AND DISEASES Aphids and red spider mites may be troublesome.

Cobnut see *Corylus avellana*
Cockscomb see *Celosia*

C

Codiaeum

Euphorbiaceae

Codiaeum variegatum var. pictum

This ornamental foliage plant with brightly coloured leathery leaves is widely grown as a pot plant for the home or heated greenhouse. The flowers are small and insignificant. *Codiaeum* is a tropical evergreen shrub native to Malaysia and the Pacific Islands, and is therefore tender in Britain.

RECOMMENDED SPECIES AND VARIETIES

C. variegatum Oval or lobed leathery leaves, up to 15cm (6in) long, are variegated with gold, green, red, pink or orange. The white flowers have no decorative merit. HEIGHT & SPREAD 2×1.5m (6½×5ft).

The species is never grown and it is var. ***pictum*** that is usually offered to gardeners. It is similar to the species, but the leaves have more pronounced veining and stronger colours. **'Mrs Iceton'** has black-green oval leaves heavily overlaid with red and pink. The young leaves carry a splash of cream. **'Reidii'** has large, broadly oval deep red leaves with prominent black veins, overlaid with green and gold.

CULTIVATION Grow in John Innes No.3 compost out of full sunlight. Ensure a minimum temperature of 13°C (55°F). Variable light levels and temperature results in leaf drop. Water freely in spring and summer, sparingly in winter. Apply tomato feed in summer to enhance leaf colour.

PROPAGATION Take stem cuttings in spring and summer.

PRUNING Cut back leggy plants in spring.

PESTS AND DISEASES Scale insects and mealy bugs are a regular nuisance.

▲ *Codiaeum variegatum* var. *pictum*

Codonopsis

Campanulaceae

Codonopsis ovata

Brilliant colours and fascinating forms characterise these twining, erect or sprawling herbaceous perennials which bloom in summer or autumn. Most flowers are bell-shaped while some resemble open saucers.

These tuberous-rooted hardy plants are native to the Himalayas and Japan and thrive in a sunny rock garden. A raised bed is particularly suitable, allowing the inner flower detail to be appreciated. Wasps adore the blooms, undeterred by the unpleasant musky smell that is a feature of many, as it is of some foliage. Plants are best chosen in flower as species are often confused.

RECOMMENDED SPECIES AND VARIETIES

C. clematidea Startling orange markings adorn the insides of distinctive blue-grey hanging bells up to 2.5cm (1in) long. Lax stems make this early-summer flowering plant rather untidy. Its oval grey-green leaves are up to 3cm (1¼in) long. HEIGHT & SPREAD 60×40cm (24×16in).

▲ *Codonopsis clematidea*

C. forrestii This robust twining climber has deep lavender-blue saucer-shaped flowers up to 9cm (3½in) across from late summer to early autumn. The bright mid green leaves are narrow-oval or lance-shaped and up to 10cm (4in) long. HEIGHT & SPREAD 3×1m (10×3ft).

C. grey-wilsonii (syn. C. *nepalensis* hort.) Blue saucer-shaped flowers, about 4cm (1½in) across with a red central ring, are carried from late summer to early autumn. Thin, twining stems carry this vigorous plant up supports and over nearby shrubs. Its plain mid green leaves are up to 7cm (2¾in) long and range from oval to lance-shaped and toothed. HEIGHT & SPREAD 1.5m×50cm (5ft×20in).

'Himal Snow' (syn. **'Alba'**) has pure white flowers and pale green leaves.

C. meleagris Grey-blue to pale jade, bell-shaped flowers about 3cm (1¼in) long with striking dark veins appear at the end of erect stems in mid summer, usually singly. The deep green elliptical leaves are up to 8cm (3¼in) long and grow mostly at the base of the stems in a lax rosette. HEIGHT & SPREAD 40×15cm (16×6in).

C. nepalensis hort. see *C. grey-wilsonii*

C. ovata Solitary pale blue flared bells, 2cm (¾in) long with purple veins and orange markings inside, are borne on slender stems during early summer. This neat erect plant has grey-green oval hairy leaves, up to 2cm (¾in) long, near the base of the stems. HEIGHT & SPREAD 40×20cm (16×8in).

▲ *Codonopsis ovata*

C. tangshen Hanging yellowy green bell-shaped flowers, up to 6cm (2½in) long with purple flecks and an orange ring inside, appear on this rampant, twining species from mid summer to early autumn. The almost hairless deep grey-green rounded leaves are up to 5cm (2in) long. HEIGHT & SPREAD 2×1m (6½×3ft).

C. vinciflora Mauve-blue, saucer-shaped flowers, up to 4.5cm (1¾in) across, bloom from mid summer to early autumn. This sprawling or climbing plant has delicate, twining, thread-like stems and 2cm (¾in)

▼ *Codonopsis tangshen*

long mid green, neatly toothed, oval leaves. This species needs sheltered, moist conditions. HEIGHT & SPREAD 40×40cm (16×16in).
CULTIVATION Grow in a cool, moist humus-rich soil in dappled shade, except *C. clematidea* and *C. ovata* which need full sun.
PROPAGATION Sow seed thinly in pots in a coldframe in autumn or winter. Leave for a year then pot on the tubers. With *C. forrestii*, *C. grey-wilsonii* and *C. vinciflora*, separate small tubers in late winter.
PESTS AND DISEASES Vulnerable to slugs, aphids indoors and out, and red spider mite under glass. Systemic pesticides often cause yellowing of the foliage.

Coelogyne see ORCHIDS p. 464

Colchicum

Autumn crocus, meadow saffron
Colchicaceae

Colchicum speciosum 'Album'

Upright, goblet-shaped flowers are produced from corms mainly in autumn, mostly before the leaves appear. Although the flowers are reminiscent of those of the crocus, colchicums are more closely related to lilies. Plants range in size from large hardy species that make excellent, trouble-free garden plants to tiny alpines. Despite their friendly common name of meadow saffron, however, all colchicums contain the poisonous alkaloid colchicene.

Flowers of the recommended plants are in shades of lilac-pink or white and may be attractively chequered with a darker shade. Some species produce several flowers from the corm, others produce a single bloom. The flowers rise directly from the corm as the flower stalk is a tubular extension of the petals. The plants with weaker tubes need careful placing to give them shelter and support, as do those with very large leaves, which can swamp smaller plants in spring and make mowing a problem when naturalised in grass. There are varieties suitable for growing in grass, planting under shrubs and growing in rock gardens.

The broad ovate to lance-shaped leaves are in general taller than the flowers. Most colchicum leaves appear after flowering and gradually elongate through the spring. They die back in summer for a dormant period.

Colchicums are native to Europe, the Mediterranean, N India and W China. Not all of the 45 species are available but there are plenty of cultivars to choose from. The plants do best in a fertile yet free-draining soil in sun or partial shade. All plants listed are hardy unless stated otherwise.

RECOMMENDED SPECIES AND VARIETIES

C. agrippinum ♀ The numerous small pale lilac flowers, produced in early autumn, have pointed petals and are heavily chequered with deep purple. The leaves, with wavy margins, up to 15cm (6in) tall, appear after the flowers and are among the smallest in the species so are not too intrusive. Easily grown, this species increases freely in the garden, preferring a well-drained, sunny situation. HEIGHT 10cm (4in).

▲ Colchicum agrippinum

C. autumnale (meadow saffron) Up to 6 small lilac flowers are produced in succession in early autumn. The lance-shaped leaves, up to 30cm (12in) high, appear later in the year. HEIGHT 15cm (6in).

The flowers of ***album*** are white.

C. bivonae (syn. *C. bowlesianum)* The bold flowers of this autumn-flowering corm are chequered with rosy purple. Each corm produces up to 6 flowers up to 8cm (3¼in) long. HEIGHT 20cm (8in).

C. bowlesianum see *C. bivonae*

C. byzantinum ♀ (syn. *C. autumnale* var. *major*) One of the easiest to grow of the smaller-flowered colchicums, this corm bears up to 20 rounded, lilac-pink blooms from late summer to early autumn. The tips of the petals are deep purple. The pleated leaves appear in spring and are up to 30cm (12in) high. No seed is set by this species. HEIGHT 15cm (6in).

▼ Colchicum byzantinum

C. speciosum ♀ This robust, vigorous corm produces 1-3 showy flowers in autumn, varying in colour from pale to deep rose-pink (most have a white throat). Erect, glossy leaves, 25cm (10in) long, develop after flowering. HEIGHT 23cm (9in).

'Album' ♀ bears large white flowers.

▲ Colchicum speciosum 'Album'

GARDEN CULTIVARS

Most cultivars produce a succession of large showy flowers on tall tubes. **'Autumn Queen'** ♀ (syn. 'Queen Astrid') reaches 20cm (8in) and has rounded, mid lilac-pink flowers that are lightly chequered. **'Lilac Wonder'** bears lilac flowers with narrow segments and faint white lines. The plant grows to 20cm (8in) high. **'The Giant'** bears a succession of rather tall, lightly chequered pale lilac flowers with white bases. One of the easiest corms to grow, it reaches 23cm (9in) and increases rapidly. The large, fully double flowers of **'Waterlily'** are rosy purple. Growing to 15cm (6in) tall, they tend to collapse and should be planted near other small plants to provide support.
CULTIVATION The large colchicums are easily grown in any well-drained fertile soil that does not become too dry in summer as the leaves must be allowed to mature. An ideal situation is in semi-shade, among shrubs. The most vigorous can be grown in grass but they will not increase as well. Plant in small clumps 10cm (4in) deep in late summer or early autumn.
PROPAGATION Remove offsets when plants are dormant in mid summer. Sow seed of species in late summer as soon as the seed is ripe. Keep seed trays outside in shade and do not allow them to dry out. Seedlings can take up to 6 years to reach flowering size.
PESTS AND DISEASES Prone to attack by slugs which can destroy entire colonies.

Coleus see *Solenostemon*

Colletia

Rhamnaceae

Colletia hystrix

The spiny deciduous shrubs within this genus, a member of the buckthorn family, resemble cacti. Colletia produces very few, inconspicuous leaves; instead the fleshy stem divides into rigid, upright branches, covered with deep green, thick, pointed spines. Profuse little bell-shaped flowers, sometimes scented, nestle among the spines in late summer.

Even in winter the plants add architectural interest to a garden. They are moderately hardy natives of southern regions of S America, suited to open borders in milder areas of Britain. In colder areas they must be grown in a sheltered corner.

RECOMMENDED SPECIES AND VARIETIES

C. armata see *C. hystrix*

C. hystrix (syn. *C. armata*) Abundant and richly fragrant tiny white flowers bloom in late summer and early autumn on this spreading shrub. The plant does best when planted in a position where it is given a little protection from the cold by nearby plants. HEIGHT & SPREAD 60×60cm (2×2ft) after 5 years, ultimately 2.4m (8ft) tall.

Colletia hystrix

Colletia hystrix (in bloom)

The flower buds of **'Rosea'** are flushed pink before opening.

CULTIVATION Plant in well-drained soil in an open, sunny position. The plants tolerate poor soils well.

PROPAGATION Take semi-ripe heel cuttings in mid summer and give them some bottom heat while rooting.

PRUNING None required.

PESTS AND DISEASES Usually trouble free.

Collinsia

Scrophulariaceae

Collinsia heterophylla

Loose clusters of showy bicoloured flowers provide a long-lasting summer display. These easy-to-grow hardy annuals thrive in partly shaded areas and are suitable for bedding, borders and woodland gardens. Collinsias can also be grown as spring and summer-flowering pot plants in an alpine house or unheated greenhouse and make good cut flowers. Only *Collinsia heterophylla* is widely grown in Britain.

RECOMMENDED SPECIES AND VARIETIES

C. heterophylla (syn. *C. bicolor*) Slender stems carry the bicoloured flowers, about 2.5cm (1in) long, that have a white upper lip and a rose-purple lower one. These are freely produced throughout summer. The lance-shaped, mid green leaves are about 8cm (3¼in) long. Native to California. HEIGHT & SPREAD 50×20cm (20×8in).

The flowers of **'Blushing Rose'** are white and shell pink.

CULTIVATION Grow in moisture-retentive soil in the shade of trees or shrubs. Some support is required unless the plants are in an informal situation where their stems can be left to sprawl. Water in prolonged dry weather. Collinsias self-seed readily.

PROPAGATION Sow seed where it is to flower in early to mid spring, or in autumn for an earlier flowering the following summer. For raising a batch of greenhouse pot plants, sow seed in early autumn, overwinter at 5°C (41°F) and pot up the seedlings in spring in 13cm (5in) pots.

PESTS AND DISEASES Usually trouble free.

Colobanthus

Caryophyllaceae

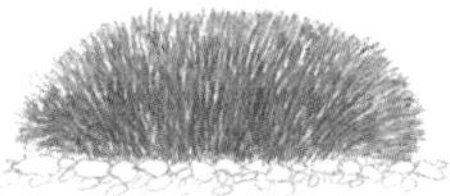

Colobanthus canaliculatus

Masses of tiny bright green leaves clothe these tufted or cushion-forming evergreen perennials. In early summer small greenish flowers appear in tight clusters. The flowers are rather unspectacular and these plants are grown more for their attractive symmetrical cushion-forming habit. They are best grown in a sunny spot in a raised bed, trough or rock garden and will thrive in an alpine house or unheated greenhouse.

The genus is native to Australasia and the Pacific side of S America. Of the 20 species in the genus, *Colobanthus canaliculatus* is the most widely grown.

RECOMMENDED SPECIES

C. canaliculatus Dense, symmetrical cushions are formed of tiny pointed leaves, each up to 4mm (⅛in) long. The cushions become covered in clusters of small, greenish flowers in early summer. HEIGHT & SPREAD 3×15cm (1¼×6in).

CULTIVATION Plant in gritty, well-drained soil in a sunny position, or in moist, free-draining compost in an alpine house or unheated greenhouse.

PROPAGATION Sow seed into pots in a coldframe when they ripen or in spring and plant out when large enough to handle. Otherwise take short, leafy cuttings in spring or late summer.

PESTS AND DISEASES Usually trouble free.

Columbine see *Aquilegia*

Columnea

Gesneriaceae

Columnea microphylla

Hanging baskets and planters burst into life when these eye-catching evergreen perennials come into bloom. Hooded tubular flowers, often in vivid shades of red, are carried in profusion along trailing stems crowded with velvety dark green leaves. Since these plants are adapted to the tropical regions of Central and S America and the West Indies, they must be grown indoors or in a warm greenhouse in Britain.

RECOMMENDED SPECIES AND VARIETIES

C.* x *banksii Scarlet flowers, up to 7.5cm (3in) long, are freely produced throughout winter and spring. The fleshy, dull green, oval leaves, up to 2.5cm (1in) long, cover the stems which trail to 1m (3ft).

Columnea banksii

***C.* 'Chanticleer'**♀ Pale orange flowers, about 4cm (1½in) long, appear intermittently throughout the year on this bushy, easy-to-grow plant. The stems bear light green leaves and are quite short, growing upwards before trailing to 30cm (1ft).

C. gloriosa (goldfish plant) Scarlet flowers, up to 7.5cm (3in) long with yellow throats, appear from autumn to spring. The dull green, oval leaves are 2.5cm (1in) long and covered with reddish hairs. The plant trails to 1m (3ft).

'Purpurea' has leaves with a deep purple cast and red flowers.

C. hirta♀ Orange-scarlet flowers, up to 7.5cm (3in) long, are produced freely during spring. The irregularly oval, dull green leaves, up to 5cm (2in) long, clothe the stems that trail to 60cm (2ft).

C. microphylla Scarlet flowers, up to 7.5cm (3in) long, are produced during winter and spring. The rounded dull green leaves, 1cm (⅜in) long and covered in brownish hairs, clothe the stems which trail to 60cm (2ft).

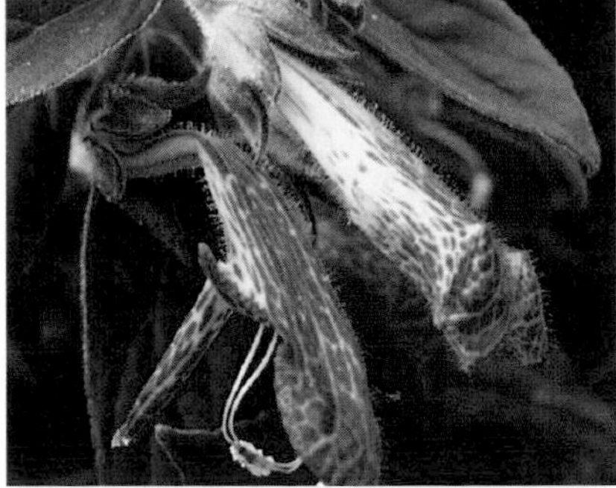

Columnea schiedeana

Columnea 'Stavanger'

C. schiedeana Marbled yellow-brown and red flowers, 5cm (2in) long, are produced during summer on this scrambling perennial with hairy, purple stems. The lance-shaped leaves, up to 10cm (4in) long, lightly cover the stems which trail to 1m (3ft).

***C.* 'Stavanger'**♀ (Norse fire plant) This reliable variety bears scarlet flowers, up to 7.5cm (3in) long, on and off throughout the year. The stems trail to 60cm (2ft) and are lined with tiny dark green glossy leaves.

CULTIVATION Grow in bright but indirect sunlight in a warm, humid atmosphere kept above 15°C (59°F). Water freely during spring and summer but sparingly in autumn and winter. Feed during the summer. Pinch back shoots to maintain a bushy plant.

PROPAGATION Take softwood cuttings after flowering and grow in a propagator.

PESTS AND DISEASES Aphids and mealy bugs may attack the plants.

Colutea

Leguminosae

Colutea arborescens

Clusters of small sweetpea-like flowers appear from early summer to mid autumn and are followed by bladder-like pods enclosing poisonous seeds. The leaves of these fast-growing, hardy deciduous shrubs have many leaflets. Native to S Europe, NW Africa and SW China.

RECOMMENDED SPECIES AND VARIETIES

C. arborescens (bladder senna) Yellow flowers, 2cm (¾in) wide, are carried in clusters from early summer onwards. The decorative 7.5cm (3in) pods are flushed red. The pinnate leaves have 9-13 small leaflets and grow to about 12.5cm (5in) long. Pruning may be required to keep the plant in good shape. HEIGHT & SPREAD 1.2 × 1.2m (4×4ft) after 5 years, ultimately 4m (13ft) tall.

Colutea arborescens

Colutea x *media*

C.* x *media The coppery flowers are 1.5cm (½in) across and are followed by red-tinged seedpods up to 7.5cm (3in) long. The greyish pinnate leaves grow to 12.5cm (5in) long and have 11-13 leaflets. HEIGHT & SPREAD 1.2×1.2m (4×4ft) after 5 years, ultimately 4m (13ft) tall.

'Copper Beauty' has bright orange flowers and blue-green leaves.

CULTIVATION Plant in any well-drained soil in full sun. Coluteas will thrive even in poor soils and do not like too much shade.

PROPAGATION Sow seed in early to mid spring. Alternatively take semi-ripe cuttings in mid summer.

PRUNING Hard prune in early spring to give plants a better shape or to keep them under control.

PESTS AND DISEASES Usually trouble free.

Comfrey see *Symphytum*

Commelina

Commelinaceae

These half-hardy perennials, often grown as annuals, are useful fillers for established borders. The three-petalled flowers, each lasting one day, are freely produced through the summer months.

RECOMMENDED SPECIES AND VARIETIES

C. coelestis Flowers are bright blue and 2-3cm (¾-1¼in) across. The bright green lance-shaped leaves grow up to 15cm (6in) long. This fleshy-rooted perennial is often treated as an annual, although it can be successfully lifted and overwintered. HEIGHT & SPREAD 45×30cm (18×12in).

C. dianthifolia The blue flowers are up to 3cm (1¼in) across. A fleshy-rooted, tender perennial with narrow, grass-like leaves up to 15cm (6in) long. HEIGHT & SPREAD 30×25cm (12×10in).

C. tuberosa This is a sprawling, tuberous-rooted perennial with blue flowers about 3cm (1¼in) across. The narrow, lance-shaped leaves, up to 10cm (4in) long, are often hairy towards the margins. HEIGHT & SPREAD 30×30cm (12×12in).

'Alba' has white flowers.

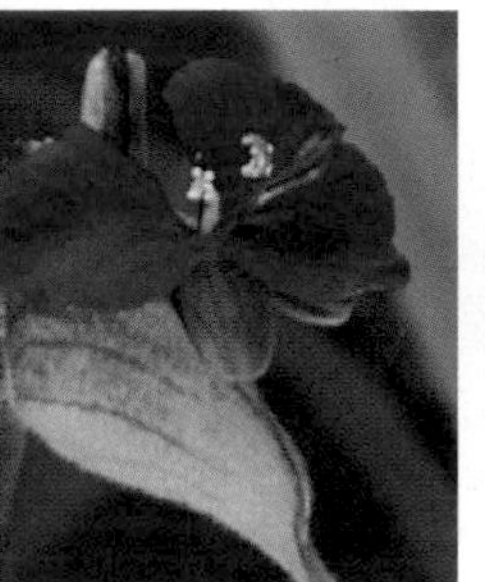

▲ *Commelina coelestis*

Commelina tuberosa 'Alba' ▲

CULTIVATION Grow in a sunny position with shelter from wind. Plant out when all danger of frost has passed and treat as a bedding plant. Alternatively, grow as a half-hardy perennial and lift in autumn and store in a cool, dry, frost-free place over winter.

PROPAGATION Sow seed in spring. Divide overwintered plants and replant in spring.

PESTS AND DISEASES Usually trouble free.

Coneflower see *Echinacea, Rudbeckia*

Consolida

Larkspur

Ranunculaceae

Spires of brightly coloured flowers bring height to a border in summer and make good cut flowers. These annuals tolerate most soils and situations. All cultivated species are hardy. Each rounded flower, to 2cm (¾in) across, has two satiny petals, each with 3-5 lobes, giving the appearance of at least 6 petals, and a single spur. Finely divided bright green leaves, 2-10cm (¾-4in) long, grow alternately on the stems below the upright flower spike. Flowers bloom all through summer. Native to the Mediterranean and W and central Asia.

RECOMMENDED SPECIES

C. ajacis (syn. *C. ambigua*) Spikes of blue or purple spurred flowers, occasionally pink or white, up to 45cm (18in) tall, appear above the feathery foliage on erect stems. HEIGHT & SPREAD 90×30cm (36×12in).

▲ *Consolida ajacis*

C. regalis Deep blue, pink or white flowers are carried in spikes up to 30cm (12in) tall. The stems are covered with short hairs. HEIGHT & SPREAD 60×30cm (24×12in).

CULTIVATION Sow seed in any good garden soil, in a position where the plants will get plenty of sun. Water plants in dry weather.

PROPAGATION In mild areas, sow seed in autumn, in a sheltered spot or a coldframe. Elsewhere, sow seed in the garden in spring. Support seedlings when they are over 8cm (3¼in) tall with twigs or short stakes and continue support as the plant grows.

PESTS AND DISEASES Greenfly, slugs and snails regularly attack young plants.

Convallaria

Lily of the valley

Liliaceae

Convallaria majalis

Moist, shady places become colonised by this hardy perennial with its sprays of dainty, sweet-smelling flowers in mid and late spring. The genus has one species.

Convallaria majalis♀ Up to 10 white or pinkish, waxy, bell-shaped flowers, 6mm (¼in) long, hang from thread-like stalks on each gently arching stem. The elliptic mid green leaves, about 20cm (8in) long, grow in pairs. The plant forms vigorous, branching rhizomes. It is native to woodlands in Asia, Europe and N America. HEIGHT 15-20cm (6-8in).

The leaves of **'Albostriata'** are striped pale creamy white. **'Fortin's Giant'**, with larger flowers and broader foliage, is late flowering. **'Prolificans'** carries many double flowers on a tightly branched spike. The flowers of var. ***rosea*** are pale pink.

▲ *Convallaria majalis*

▲ *Convallaria* 'Fortin's Giant'

▲ *Convallaria* var. *rosea*

CULTIVATION Plants thrive in sun or partial shade in a deep, damp soil containing plenty of compost or leaf-mould. Plant between autumn and early spring with the crowns just below the soil surface. Top dress with leaf-mould each winter.

To force plants for an early display of flowers, lift and pot the crowns in mid winter. Keep the plants indoors at room temperature and water them frequently.

PROPAGATION Lift and divide the clumps during winter. Alternatively, sow freshly ripe seed and let the seedlings grow for 3 years before planting them out.

PESTS AND DISEASES Usually trouble free.

Convolvulus

Bindweed
Convolvulaceae

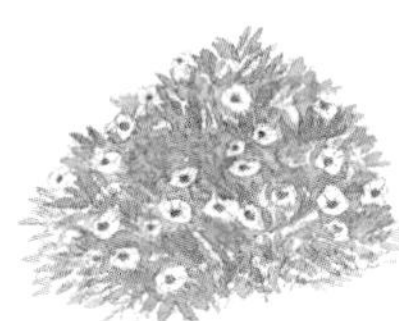

Pleated funnel-shaped flowers that open in sunlight characterise this diverse genus, which includes climbers, trailers, shrubs and annuals – as well as pernicious weeds such as *Convolvulus arvensis*, common bindweed. The listed species are undemanding plants, flowering in summer. Native to Europe and N Africa, they are hardy to -5°C (23°F). Trailing growth makes *C. sabatius* ideal for large containers and hanging baskets or for banks and walls. It will also trail over rocks or gravel, as does *C. athaeoides*. Leaves are 2.5-6cm (1-2½in) long.

RECOMMENDED SPECIES AND VARIETIES

C. ***althaeoides*** (mallow-leaved bindweed) Pink flowers up to 5cm (2in) across appear throughout summer along slender, climbing or trailing stems. The grey-green, oval to heart-shaped leaves are often deeply lobed. This vigorous clump-forming perennial can be invasive in warm mild gardens. HEIGHT & SPREAD 1x2m (3x6½ft).

Silvery leaves with slender lobes are seen on ssp. ***tenuissimus*** (syn. *C. elegantissimus*).

C. ***cneorum***♀ (silverbush) Pink-flushed buds open into white flowers 2.5cm (1in) across that bloom in clusters at the stem ends from late spring to late summer. This low, rounded evergreen shrub is also valued for its silvery, oval to lance shaped leaves. HEIGHT & SPREAD 60x60cm (24x24in).

C. ***lineatus*** Pink flowers 1.5-2.5cm (½-1in) across appear throughout summer on this evergreen woody-based perennial. The elliptical leaves are silvery and silky and the stems are trailing to ascending. HEIGHT & SPREAD 20x50cm (8x20in).

C. ***sabatius***♀ (syn. *C. mauritanicus*) Bright blue flowers up to 4cm (1½in) across are borne all through summer (earlier in a conservatory) by this vigorous, woody-based spreading or trailing evergreen perennial. The slender stems are thickly clothed in small, oval, deep green leaves. HEIGHT & SPREAD 20x50cm-2m (8x20in-6½ft).

Dark blue flowered forms are available, but they do not have formal cultivar names.

C. ***tricolor*** Deep blue flowers up to 5cm (2in) across with white and yellow centres open from mid to late summer on this upright bushy annual. Dark green oval leaves clothe slender hairy stems. HEIGHT & SPREAD 60x40cm (24x16in).

'Blue Flash' only reaches a height of up to 30cm (12in). **'Royal Ensign'** grows up to 50cm (20in) tall.

CULTIVATION Plant perennials in spring after the last frosts. Choose a warm, sheltered, sunny site; borders under south or west-facing walls are ideal. In cooler districts grow in containers and place outdoors in summer and in a frost-free site for winter.

PROPAGATION Sow seeds of perennials in late winter to early spring in pots in a cold-frame at 15-18°C (59-64°F). Take heel cuttings in summer in a propagating frame. Overwinter under glass for planting out the following year. Sow annuals thinly in spring where required or, in mild areas, sow in autumn and overwinter under a cloche.

PRUNING Trim dead or weak growths of evergreen perennials in spring.

PESTS & DISEASES Slugs attack seedlings. Susceptible to red spider mite under glass.

▼ *Convolvulus sabatius*

Copperleaf see *Acalypha wilkesiana*

▼ *Convolvulus althaeoides ssp. tenuissimus*

▼ *Convolvulus cneorum*

Coprosma

Rubiaceae

Evergreen foliage and yellow, orange, red, white, blue, purple or black berries give these shrubs prolonged garden value. Plants range from compact mat-forming shrubs to large shrubs and small trees. A female plant bears berries in late summer and autumn if grown beside a male plant. Leaves are linear, oval, oblong or rounded. There are small greenish flowers in late spring and summer. Some species are fully hardy. Others will survive outside in protected sites or where winters are mild; in exposed areas grow in an unheated greenhouse, standing plants outside in summer. Mainly native to Australia and New Zealand.

RECOMMENDED SPECIES AND VARIETIES

C. **'Beatson's Gold'** A sprawling shrub, not reliably hardy, with oval, bright green leaves, variegated yellow, and red, currant-like fruit. HEIGHT & SPREAD 1x1.8m (3x6ft).

▲ *Coprosma x kirkii* 'Kirkii Variegata'

C. x ***kirkii*** **'Kirkii Variegata'** This low spreading shrub has fine deep green leaves, edged white, but no berries. Grow outside in a sheltered spot or in an unheated greenhouse. HEIGHT & SPREAD 60x100cm (2x3ft).

C. ***repens*** (mirror plant) Leaves are glossy and thick, and berries are orange to yellow. These shrubs or small trees are not reliably hardy. HEIGHT & SPREAD 2x2m (6½x6½ft) after 8-10 years, ultimately 8m (26ft) tall.

These varieties, which can be planted out only in mild gardens, make good summer window-box and tub plants. **'Exotica'**, with dark green leaves with a central yellow splash, is female, bearing orange berries in autumn. **'Marble Queen'**, male, without berries, has cream leaves blotched green. **'Pink Splendour'**, male, without berries, has green leaves edged in cream and pink.

CULTIVATION Plant in well-drained soil in full sun. Water pot plants well in summer.

PROPAGATION Sow seed in early spring or take semi-ripe cuttings in mid summer.

PRUNING Not necessary except to keep shrubs within bounds.

PESTS AND DISEASES Usually trouble free.

Coral plant see *Russelia equisetiformis*

Cordyline
Cabbage tree
Agavaceae

These palm-like trees, grown for their evergreen architectural form, are attractive plants for gardens where winters are mild. Elsewhere they can be grown in large tubs and containers in a cool greenhouse or conservatory and brought into the garden for summer bedding displays. *Cordyline fruticosa* is a popular houseplant. Native to India, the Pacific Islands and New Zealand.

RECOMMENDED SPECIES AND VARIETIES

C. australis (cabbage tree) The erect rough grey-brown trunk usually grows several feet tall before it branches. Each upright branch culminates in a spiky mass of stiff, sword-like, green leaves that often reach 1m (3ft) in length, but are only 6cm (2½in) wide. The leaves arch outwards with age. Large dense plumes of starry, white, sweet-scented flowers are produced in summer, followed by small, round, greenish-white berries in autumn. HEIGHT & SPREAD 2.4×2m (8×6½ft) after 10 years, ultimately 5m (16ft) tall.

Trees with purple or bronze leaves are collectively known as the **Purpurea Group.** **'Pink Stripe'** has leaves with purplish edges and a rich pink central stripe. **'Sundance'** has dark green leaves, sunset-red at the base and with a pinkish midrib. **'Torbay Red'** has plum-red leaves.

There are also a few variegated varieties, such as **'Albertii'** with cream edges to the mid green leaves and a pinkish purple midrib, and **'Torbay Dazzler'** which has bright green leaves with white stripes and creamy yellow edges.

C. fruticosa (goodluck plant, Ti plant) (syn. *Cordyline terminus*) In Britain this species is grown as a houseplant. The broadly lance-shaped leaves, 30-50cm (12-20in) long and 6-15cm (2½-6in) wide, sprout sideways from an upright trunk. Glossy reddish young growth matures to shiny dark green. In many varieties both young and mature leaves have a coloured banding or edging. Older plants occasionally branch. Plants

▼ *Cordyline australis*

▲ *Cordyline australis* 'Albertii'

raised indoors rarely flower. When they do, they produce white blooms in long dense clusters followed by red berries. HEIGHT & SPREAD 1m×40cm (3ft×16in).

The leaves of **'Kiwi'** are streaked with pink, cream and green. **'Red Edge'** has green leaves with red streaks and margins.

C. indivisa Broad sword-shaped leaves form a large tuft at the top of a stout trunk. Leaves are 1m (3ft) or more long and up to 15cm (6in) wide, drooping only as they age. Greenish white flowers in dense clusters, in summer, are followed by dark blue berries. HEIGHT & SPREAD 2×2m (6½×6½ft) after 10 years and ultimately.

CULTIVATION Plant in a moist, rich soil. *C. indivisa*, best grown in shade, will not tolerate a dry atmosphere. For overwintering in cold areas tie leaves together to protect the crowns and wrap trunks in fleece or straw.

Grow the houseplant *C. fruticosa* in a pot of free-draining, medium-fertility compost and site in bright, indirect light. Maintain a minimum temperature of 15°C (59°F). Water freely and feed weekly in summer, water sparingly in winter.

PROPAGATION Sow seed in early spring. Take cuttings of young branches in spring or summer. Seed is best for *C. australis*.

PESTS AND DISEASES Usually trouble free. Red spider mite and mealy bug may be troublesome indoors.

Coreopsis
Tickseed
Compositae

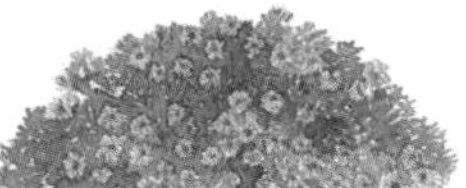

Coreopsis verticillata 'Grandiflora'

Bright yellow and, occasionally, red or pink blooms are borne on the fine, wiry, upright stems of these hardy annuals and herbaceous perennials. They form compact plants with bright green foliage that produce masses of single or double flowers in summer. These plants are particularly suitable for a herbaceous border. The taller species provide excellent cut flowers.

RECOMMENDED SPECIES AND VARIETIES

The listed plants are all perennials. Most of them are fast growing but they can be short-lived and it is therefore advisable to raise new plants each year to replace any losses. They all bloom throughout summer, unless stated otherwise.

C. auriculata Single yellow flowers with ragged-edged petals are borne in early summer on this low, bushy plant. The oval or narrow, pointed leaves are light green and often lobed; they measure up to 12cm (4¾in) long. HEIGHT & SPREAD 50×45cm (20×18in).

'Schnittgold' ('Cutting Gold') has vivid golden petals. **'Superba'** has bright yellow petals, blotched with purple at the base.

C. grandiflora This perennial, often grown as an annual, bears single yellow flowers, 6cm (2½in) across, with ragged-edged petals. The bright green leaves are strap-shaped, about 10cm (4in) long and often divided. They form a compact clump at the base of the plant. HEIGHT & SPREAD 60×45cm (2×1½ft).

▲ *Coreopsis grandiflora* 'Early Sunrise'

▲ *Coreopsis grandiflora* 'Mayfield Giant'

▼ *Coreopsis rosea* 'American Dream'

▲ *Coreopsis verticillata* 'Zagreb'

'Early Sunrise' has golden semidouble flowers. **'Mayfield Giant'** has bright yellow single flowers. **'Sunray'** has deep yellow double flowers.

C. lanceolata The bright yellow single flowers are up to 6 cm (2½ in) across and have ragged-edged petals. Bright green leaves, up to 15 cm (6 in) long, form a clump at the plant base. Trim back flowering stems occasionally in summer to strengthen the plant. HEIGHT & SPREAD 55×40 cm (22×16 in).

'Goldfinck' bears golden, single flowers and reaches a height of 25 cm (10 in). **'Sonnenkind'** ('Baby Sun') produces gold single flowers and grows to 40 cm (16 in) tall. **'Sunburst'**, taller at 75 cm (2½ ft), has yellow double flowers.

C. rosea The single flowers are deep to light pink, occasionally white, up to 2.5 cm (1 in) wide, with ragged edges to the petals. Leaves are up to 5 cm (2 in) long, sometimes with 2-3 lobes. This is a compact plant for a border front. It spreads by runners. HEIGHT & SPREAD 30-60×30-45 cm (12-24×12-18 in).

'American Dream' has rosy pink, starry, single flowers.

C. verticillata When in bloom, this bushy plant is covered with starry, yellow, single flowers, up to 6 cm (2½in) across. The finely divided, fern-like, bright green leaves are about 6 cm (2½in) long. HEIGHT & SPREAD 60×45 cm (2×1½ ft).

'Golden Shower' has yellow flowers. The golden flowers of **'Grandiflora'**♀ are 8 cm (3¼ in) across. **'Moonbeam'**, with pale lemon-yellow blooms, is less robust than the other cultivars. **'Zagreb'** has golden yellow flowers.

CULTIVATION Plant in late spring in fertile, well-drained garden soil, choosing a position in full sun. Overfeeding will encourage leaf growth at the expense of the flowers. Stake tall plants. Cut shoots of perennials down to soil level in late autumn.

PROPAGATION Raise annuals from seed sown under glass in early spring. Propagate perennials by division in spring or by taking stem cuttings in summer.

PESTS AND DISEASES Usually trouble free.

Coriander (culinary herb)
see HERBS p. 331
Corn cockle see *Agrosstemma*
Cornflower see *Centaurea*

Cornus
Cornel, dogwood
Cornaceae

Cornus kousa var. chinensis

The dogwoods, mainly deciduous small trees or shrubs, are grown for their show of flowers, their brilliant winter stem colour or their foliage. Summer-blooming species have small, button-like clusters of insignificant green-yellow flowers surrounded by larger, petal-like bracts, which may be white, creamy white, pink or red. Many summer-flowering shrubs produce strawberry-like fruits in autumn, while others produce black, red or blue-white berries.

Stem colour, at its most vibrant in winter, ranges from coral-pink to dark red and purple to yellow-green. Some of the best dogwoods combine attractive flaking bark and good autumn leaf colour. Some plants have variegated foliage. All the plants listed below have opposite leaves, except *Cornus alternifolia* and *C. controversa*. In general leaves are oval with a tapered point and not more than 12.5 cm (5 in) long, often with a slightly curled appearance.

Dogwoods are on the whole fairly hardy. The genus is native to northern temperate zones throughout the world.

RECOMMENDED SPECIES AND VARIETIES

C. alba (red-barked dogwood) This hardy shrub, with crimson-red stems, is best grown as a multistemmed plant. It is a vigorous plant, spreading by suckers. The ovate leaves are dark green above and glaucous beneath, turning crimson and purple in autumn. Flattened clusters of small yellow-white flowers in early summer are followed by pale blue-white berries. HEIGHT & SPREAD Up to 2×2 m (6½×6½ ft) after 2 years, when pruned regularly; ultimately 3 m (10 ft) tall, if left unpruned.

'Aurea', with pale yellow leaves, rarely grows more than 2 m (6½ ft) tall. **'Sibirica'**♀ ('Westonbirt') has brilliant coral-pink to crimson stems. It is less vigorous than the species, rarely growing taller than 1.5 m (5 ft). **'Sibirica Variegata'** has green and creamy white leaves, carried on deep red stems. **'Spaethii'**♀ has oval leaves with golden yellow margins, deep red stems in winter and round black berries in autumn.

▼ *Cornus alba* 'Aurea'

▲ *Cornus alba* 'Sibirica Variegata'

C. alternifolia A hardy tall shrub to small tree of spreading habit with branches gracefully arranged in horizontal tiers. The alternate, pointed, oval leaves are dark green above, bluish beneath. Clusters of small white flowers borne from late spring to early summer are followed by black berries. HEIGHT & SPREAD 2×1.2 m (6½×4 ft) after 5 years, ultimately up to 8×3 m (26×10 ft).

'Argentea'♀ has small bright green leaves variegated with white and grows to 6 m (20 ft) tall. Place in a sheltered spot.

▲ *Cornus canadensis*

C. canadensis♀ This hardy, creeping herbaceous perennial spreads by underground shoots to form a low carpet. A good ground-cover plant, it does best on an acid soil, in partial shade. Clusters of tiny greenish red flowers, each surrounded by 4 large white bracts, appear in early summer. Bright red fruits follow. Shiny mid green oval leaves change to deep red in autumn. HEIGHT & SPREAD 15×60 cm (6×24 in).

C. controversa (table dogwood) This is a hardy, medium-sized tree of upright habit

▼ *Cornus controversa*

C

C

with horizontal tiered branches. The alternate, oval leaves, up to 15 cm (6 in) long, are glossy green above and glaucous beneath. They turn purple-red in autumn. Tiny creamy white flowers appear in large, broad, flat clusters in early summer. There are round blue-black fruits in autumn. HEIGHT & SPREAD 6×3 m (20×10 ft) after 20 years, ultimately up to 15 m (50 ft) tall.

'Variegata'♀ is a conical tree, up to 6 m (20 ft) tall, with horizontal branches that bear attractive foliage all year round. It is slower growing than the species. Long, narrow, mid green leaves have margins variegated with cream. Creamy white flowers are borne in large flat clusters.

***C.* 'Eddies White Wonder'**♀ One of the best flowering dogwoods, this small, hardy tree or tall shrub of upright habit is a cross between *C. florida* and *C. nuttallii*. In early summer it produces a mass of large white bracts, which are nearly circular and overlap. The leaves are slightly glossy green above, grey beneath. They turn red and orange in autumn. HEIGHT & SPREAD 2.4×1.5 m (8×5 ft) after 10 years, ultimately 10 m (33 ft) tall.

Cornus florida

C. florida (flowering dogwood) This tall, hardy, slow-growing shrub to small tree is the summer-flowering dogwood most likely to grow well in Britain. Small clusters of green flowers surrounded by white bracts are borne in late spring and early summer. Red strawberry-like fruits add decorative interest in autumn. The dark green oval leaves go on to give rich autumn colour. The bark flakes attractively with age. Flowering, which starts when a plant is about 7 years old, is most impressive in mild areas, where summers are hot and autumns are warm. The plant grows best in neutral to acid soil. Avoid shallow chalky soils. HEIGHT & SPREAD 2.4×1.2 m (8×4 ft) after 10 years, ultimately 6 m (20 ft) tall.

The cultivar **'Cherokee Chief'**♀ has deep red bracts in late spring.

C. kousa A tall hardy shrub or small tree with spreading horizontal branches. Numerous pointed creamy white bracts, sometimes later flushed with pink, surround small, purple-green flower clusters, borne on slender stalks in late spring and early summer. Strawberry-like red fruits appear in autumn. The ovate leaves, with wavy margins, are dark green above and blue-green beneath; they give good orange-red autumn colour. The bark flakes with age, giving an attractive mottled appearance. The plant is best grown on neutral to acid soil. It does not like shallow chalk. HEIGHT & SPREAD 2.4×1.8 m (8×6 ft) after 10 years, ultimately 7×4 m (23×13 ft).

Among the best of the flowering dogwoods, var. ***chinensis***♀ bears creamy yellow bracts that are larger than those of the species. There are red fruits and red tinted foliage in autumn. **'Satomi'**♀ has deep pink bracts, and the leaves give a good display of purple and red autumn colour.

▲ *Cornus kousa* var. *chinensis*

C. mas (Cornelian cherry)♀ A large hardy shrub or small tree of spreading habit that grows well on limestone soil. Rounded clusters of tiny golden yellow flowers appear in late winter and early spring on the bare branches. The small oval leaves are dark green and glossy. The bright red fruits, up to 1 cm (⅜ in) long, are not reliably produced in Britain. HEIGHT & SPREAD 2×1.2 m (6½×4 ft) after 5-10 years, ultimately 5×4.5 m (16×15 ft).

Some good cultivars are available, which are less vigorous and smaller than the species, rarely attaining a height of more than 3 m (10 ft). **'Aurea'**, with pale yellow leaves that become more green in colour as summer progresses, tends not to flower or fruit as well as the species. Some shelter from the wind is beneficial. **'Variegata'**♀ is an outstanding cultivar with a broad white margin to its grey-green leaves. At its best it can be a good fruiter. It is slow-growing and prefers a shady spot.

***C.* 'Norman Hadden'**♀ This small tree has a graceful, open, spreading habit of growth. Four white bracts, later deep pink, surround each cluster of small green flowers in early summer. The bark peels attractively with age. In milder regions some of the oval, pale green leaves are retained throughout winter. Red strawberry-like fruits are normally abundantly produced in autumn. Though hardy, the tree grows best when protected from strong winds. HEIGHT & SPREAD 2.4×1.8 m (8×6 ft) after 10 years, ultimately 6×4 m (20×13 ft).

▲ *Cornus kousa*

***C. stolonifera* 'Flaviramea'**♀ The bright yellow-green stems of this vigorous, multi-stemmed shrub are very striking when bare in winter, especially when grown in a group with a red-stemmed dogwood. The leaves, dark green above and blue-green beneath, give a good display of autumn colour. Off-white flowers are borne in late spring and clusters of blue-white berries follow in autumn. The plant is best grown in moist acid soil. It should be cut back every 2-3 years to maintain good colour. HEIGHT & SPREAD 1.5×1.5 m (5×5 ft) after 5 years, ultimately 2.4 m (8 ft) tall.

Cornus stolonifera 'Flaviramea'

The cultivar **'Kelsey'** rarely grows taller than 75 cm (2½ ft) and is sometimes called 'Kelseyi Dwarf'. It has yellow-green shoots which are red towards the tips.

▼ *Cornus stolonifera* 'Flaviramea'

CULTIVATION Plant shrubs with coloured stems in any garden soil, preferably in a position with plenty of sun. They give their best displays when planted in large groups, because this adds to the depth of colour. Summer-flowering dogwoods need fertile, neutral to acid soil, in sun or light shade, and shelter from spring frosts. *Cornus mas* prefers neutral to acid, fertile soils in sun or light shade. *Cornus canadensis* needs acid soil and partial shade.
PROPAGATION Mainly from hardwood cuttings, taken in late winter for the winter stem colour species. Other species can be grown from seed but as this can give variable results, grafted plants are needed if specific features are required. Suckering species can be propagated by replanting suckers in early winter. Semi-ripe cuttings can be taken in late summer for tree species only.
PRUNING To maintain good colour, shrubs grown for winter stem colour need to be pruned back to nearly ground level every 2-3 years in late spring before the leaves appear, depending on how vigorously the plants are growing.
PESTS AND DISEASES Usually trouble free.

Corokia

Escalloniaceae

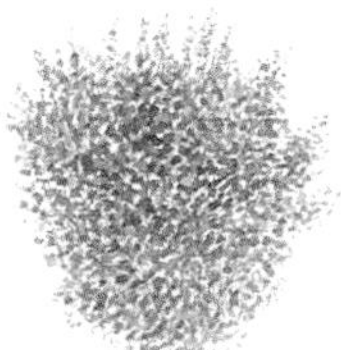

Corokia x virgata

Many small, starry, yellow flowers enliven these evergreen shrubs in late spring. They are followed in autumn by yellow, orange, red or black berry-like fruits. The species and hybrids cultivated in Britain are all native to New Zealand.

RECOMMENDED SPECIES AND VARIETIES
C. buddlejoides This erect shrub has narrow shiny leaves that are white felted beneath. The berries, usually dark red, often stay on the plant all winter. The species is only suitable for a very sheltered position in a warm garden. HEIGHT & SPREAD 2×1m (6½×3ft) after 5 years, ultimately 3m (10ft) tall.
C. cotoneaster (wire netting bush) Stiff, wiry, dark branches zig-zag and interlace, earning the shrub its common name. They are sparsely clothed with tiny spoon-shaped leaves of variable colour, from green to dark purple. The long-lasting berries are orange-red. This is the hardiest corokia, but even so needs a warm sheltered spot in the garden. HEIGHT & SPREAD 1-2×1-2m (3-6½×3-6½ft) after 10 years.
C. × virgata This is a variable hybrid. Shrubs, usually erect, may have bronze, apple-green or grey-green leaves and felted

▲ *Corokia buddlejoides*

▲ *Corokia x virgata*

stems. It needs a sheltered position. Yellow, orange or red fruits follow the flowers. HEIGHT & SPREAD 2.4×1.8m (8×6ft).
CULTIVATION Good drainage and open situations are essential for *C. cotoneaster*. Plant *C. buddlejoides* and *C. × virgata* and in a sunny sheltered site with well-drained soil.
PROPAGATION Semi-ripe cuttings taken in autumn root well if kept on a heated bench over winter.
PRUNING Seldom necessary.
PESTS AND DISEASES Usually trouble free.

Coronilla

Leguminosae

Coronilla valentina ssp. glauca

Circular clusters of yellow flowers, resembling a small crown, decorate these annuals, perennials and shrubs in spring or summer. The greyish foliage has small, pinnate leaves and the seedpods have a beaded appearance. Species vary in hardiness.

The most suitable plants for a British garden are the evergreen shrubs listed below, although in most areas they require the protection of a sunny wall. Native to Europe, W Asia and the Canary Islands.

RECOMMENDED SPECIES AND VARIETIES
C. comosa see *Hippocrepis comosa*
C. emerus see *Hippocrepis emerus*
C. glauca see *C. valentina* ssp. *glauca*
C. minima Fragrant bright yellow flowers, up to 8mm (⅜in) long, are borne in clusters of up to 15 from early to mid summer. This sprawling plant has grey-green leaves 2.5-7.5cm (1-3in) long, with 2-6 pairs of rounded leaflets. HEIGHT & SPREAD 15×20cm (6×8in) after 5 years, ultimately 45cm (18in) tall.
C. valentina Scented bright yellow flowers, about 1cm (⅜in) long, are carried in clusters of up to 14 from late spring to mid summer on a bushy plant. The leaves are about 4cm (1½in) long, with 7-11 rounded to wedge-shaped leaflets, are dark green above and grey-green beneath. HEIGHT & SPREAD 45×45cm (18×18in) after 5 years, ultimately 1.2m (4ft) tall.

The compact ssp. ***glauca***♀ (syn. *C. glauca*) bears fragrant bright yellow flowers, 1.5cm (½in) long, in clusters of up to 10 per slender stalk from mid spring to early summer. The blue-grey leaves are as long as 4cm (1½in), each with 5-7 rounded

▲ *Coronilla valentina*

▲ *Coronilla valentina ssp. glauca*

leaflets. The plant reaches a height and spread of 60cm (2ft) after 5 years, ultimately growing to 3m (10ft) tall.

'Citrina'♀ has pale lemon-yellow flowers. **'Variegata'** has typical yellow flowers, but the leaflets have creamy white edges.
CULTIVATION Plant in a sheltered position in a well-drained soil and full sun. *C. valentina* and its varieties are best grown against a wall facing south or west.
PROPAGATION Sow seeds in early spring or take softwood cuttings in summer.
PESTS AND DISEASES Usually trouble free.

C

Correa

Australian fuchsia
Rutaceae

Correa 'Mannii'

Striking tubular or bell-shaped flowers adorn these half-hardy evergreen shrubs from early winter to spring. Native to Australia, the plants need a warm sheltered garden in southern or south-west Britain. The flowers have four thick petals with outward curving tips and protruding stamens. The undersides of the small oval leaves are usually covered with thick down.

RECOMMENDED SPECIES AND VARIETIES

C. backhousiana♀ Drooping greenish yellow flowers, up to 2.5 cm (1 in) long, are borne on this densely branched shrub. The greyish green leaves have downy brown undersides. One of the hardiest of the genus, this plant can flower all winter in a mild climate on a sheltered site. HEIGHT & SPREAD 90×60 cm (3×2 ft) after 5 years, ultimately 1 m (3 ft) tall.

▲ *Correa backhousiana*

Correa 'Dusky Bells' ▲

C. **'Dusky Bells'** Clusters of pinky red flowers hang from reddish stems. HEIGHT & SPREAD 1×1.5 m (3×5 ft) after 5 years, ultimately 1 m (3 ft) tall.

C. **'Mannii'**♀ (syn. *C.* 'Harrisii') Red flowers, up to 3 cm (1¼ in) long, hang from erect branches, sometimes throughout winter. However, this is a plant for warm gardens only. HEIGHT & SPREAD 90×50 cm (35×20 in) after 5 years, ultimately 2 m (6½ ft) tall.

CULTIVATION Plant in spring in well-drained, neutral to acid soil on a sheltered site. Protect from cold winds if necessary.

PROPAGATION Sow seed under glass in spring. Alternatively, in late summer take semi-ripe cuttings. Pot them up and keep under glass for the first winter.

PRUNING Trim back in summer to make these naturally leggy plants more compact.

PESTS AND DISEASES Usually trouble free.

Cortaderia see GRASSES p. 300

Cortusa

Primulaceae

Delicately formed bell-shaped flowers hang down in one-sided clusters on these clump-forming hardy herbaceous perennials that are closely related to primulas. The broad, lobed leaves are arranged in rosettes. The plants are easy to grow, thriving in moist, shady spots. Native to central and SE Europe, central Russia and Japan.

RECOMMENDED SPECIES AND VARIETIES

C. matthioli (alpine bells) Deep purple flowers, about 1 cm (⅜ in) long, hang in loose clusters of up to 20 in late spring and early summer. The rounded or kidney-shaped leaves, up to 12.5 cm (5 in) wide, are deeply lobed and irregularly toothed at the edge. The leaves and stem of this variable species are often covered in reddish brown hairs. HEIGHT & SPREAD 35×35 cm (14×14 in).

▲ *Cortusa matthioli*

'Alba' has white flowers. The leaves of ssp. ***pekinensis*** are very hairy and the flowers are often deeper purple than the species.

CULTIVATION Plant in spring or early summer in a moist but well-drained, humus-rich soil in a shady part of a rock garden or beneath trees.

PROPAGATION Divide and replant established plants after flowering. Sow fresh seed when ripe, or sow saved seed in early spring.

PESTS AND DISEASES Usually trouble free.

▼ *Cortusa* ssp. *pekinensis*

Corydalis

Papaveraceae

Corydalis solida

Spikes of tubular, spurred flowers appear above delicate, often ferny leaves between late spring and autumn. These perennials and annuals grow in shaded spots in borders, rock gardens or under shrubs, and are also suitable for an alpine house. Some species self-seed easily and thrive in cracks in old walls and brickwork. The plants have tuberous, fibrous or rhizomatous roots. Native to the temperate zones of the Northern Hemisphere, all the plants are fully hardy, but *Corydalis tomentella* and *C. wilsonii* dislike winter wet.

RECOMMENDED SPECIES AND VARIETIES

C. ambigua (of gardens) see *C. fumariifolia*

C. cashmeriana Vivid sky blue flowers 2 cm (¾ in) long with down-curved spurs are carried in dense spikes throughout summer. The pale blue-green leaves of this rhizamatous plant have narrow leaflets. HEIGHT & SPREAD 15×25 cm (6×10 in).

C. caucasica var. *alba* see *C. malkensis*

C. cava♀ A tuberous perennial with pink to purple flowers, up to 3 cm (1¼ in) long. The flowers are borne in spikes above pale green leaves from early to late spring. HEIGHT & SPREAD 20×10 cm (8×4 in).

C. cheilanthifolia Bright yellow flowers, about 1.5 cm (½ in) long, appear in dense spikes from mid spring to mid summer. The mid green leaves are carried in rosettes and often have attractive bronze tints in autumn. This fibrous-rooted evergreen perennial, suitable for shady places, grows best in deep, well-drained, humus-rich soil. HEIGHT & SPREAD 25×40 cm (10×16 in).

C. flexuosa Pale to deep blue or blue-purple flowers, about 2 cm (¾ in) long, are carried in loose clusters from late spring to mid summer. The leaves are usually deep green with a touch of bronze. This perennial produces numerous small, scaly rhizomes both at and above ground level. HEIGHT & SPREAD 30×30 cm (12×12 in).

'Blue Panda' is very vigorous with bright sky blue flowers. **'China Blue'** has pale blue flowers and rather bright green foliage. **'Père David'**, a shorter plant, has mid blue flowers and grey-green foliage. **'Purple Leaf'** has purple-blue flowers and bronze-purple leaves.

C. fumariifolia (syn. *C. ambigua* of gardens) Blue, mauve or pink flowers, up to 2 cm (¾ in) long, are carried in dense oblong clusters from mid to late spring on this tuberous plant. The leaves have rounded,

▲ *Corydalis flexuosa* 'China Blue'
Corydalis flexuosa 'Purple Leaf' ▲

glaucous leaflets. HEIGHT & SPREAD 15×10cm (6×4in).

C. lutea (syn. *Pseudofumaria lutea*) Yellow flowers, 2cm (¾in) long, appear in oblong clusters from late spring to autumn. The leaves are soft green above, glaucous below. This tap-rooted perennial, often seen on old walls, self-seeds in profusion and makes good ground cover for shaded areas. HEIGHT & SPREAD 20×50cm (8×20in).

C. malkensis ♀ (syn. *C. caucasica* var. *alba*) Erect spikes of white flowers, up to 3cm (1¼in) long, appear in early to mid spring. The leaves of this tuberous perennial are pale green. HEIGHT & SPREAD 12.5×7.5cm (5×3in).

▲ *Corydalis malkensis*

C. ophiocarpa A vigorous tap-rooted annual with yellow flowers 1.5cm (½in) long that are carried in loose spikes in late spring to mid summer. The grey-green leaves are arranged in neat rosettes. HEIGHT & SPREAD 60×50cm (24×20in).

C. sempervirens The pink flowers, up to 1.5cm (½in) long, have yellow tips and are borne from early to late spring. The blue-green leaves have many leaflets. This generously self-seeding, tap-rooted biennial or short-lived perennial can be invasive. HEIGHT & SPREAD 60×50cm (24×20in).

C. solida ♀ The flowers, up to 2.5cm (1in) long and borne in oblong spikes from early to late spring, can be pink, red, purple or

▲ *Corydalis solida* 'George Baker'

occasionally white. The leaves of this tuberous perennial are grey-green. HEIGHT & SPREAD 20×20cm (8×8in).

'Beth Evans' ♀ has pale pink flowers with whitish spurs. **'George Baker'** ♀ has deep terracotta flowers. **'Highland Mist'** carries dense racemes of deep smoky pink flowers.

C. wilsonii Yellow flowers, up to 2cm (¾in) long, have a greenish tinge and are borne in short sturdy spikes. The fern-like, rather fleshy leaves are blue-green. The tap-rooted perennial, less hardy than other species, may survive a mild winter in a sheltered spot, but is usually grown under glass. HEIGHT & SPREAD 20×20cm (8×8in).

CULTIVATION Plant in a well-drained, humus-rich soil in semi-shade. Tuberous plants require more moisture in winter and partial drying out in summer. The tubers generally double or treble each year so colonies can soon be built up. Plant those with tuberous roots in autumn, the others in spring, at a depth of 5cm (2in). In an alpine house, plant in a mix of equal parts John Innes No.3 compost, moss peat and coarse grit. Plunge the pots up to their necks in a damp sand bed to prevent drying out. Repot annually.

PROPAGATION Divide carefully in autumn or early spring. All species can be propagated from freshly ripe seed, but seedlings of tuberous plants may take several years to flower.

PESTS AND DISEASES All species are susceptible to slug damage. *C. wilsonii* is prone to grey mould.

Corylopsis

Hamamelidaceae

Corylopsis glabrescens

Dense clusters of bell-shaped yellow flowers appear in pendulous racemes on slender bare shoots before the leaves of this deciduous shrub emerge in early spring. The blooms, which are sometimes fragrant, are held in racemes 2.5-15cm (1-6in) long. The leaves, up to 10cm (4in) long, are roughly oval with bristly edges and heart-shaped bases. Native to China amd Japan, most plants are hardy but, as they flower in early spring, they need protection from cold winds and early frosts. They generally dislike alkaline soil.

RECOMMENDED SPECIES AND VARIETIES

C. glabrescens This large, spreading, open shrub of rounded habit often grows as broad as it is tall. The flowers are pale yellow. Leaves are dark green above and blue green beneath. Native to Japan. HEIGHT & SPREAD 1.2×1m (4×3ft), ultimately 2m (6½ft) tall.

▲ *Corylopsis glabrescens*

C. pauciflora ♀ Abundant primrose-yellow, slightly scented flowers appear in short racemes on this multistemmed, spreading shrub of rounded habit. Each raceme has 2–3 open flowers, which are larger than those of other plants in the genus. The small bright green leaves often have a pink flush when they first appear. This plant prefers a cool moist position and needs shelter from spring frosts, cold winds and excessive sun. HEIGHT & SPREAD 1×1m (3×3ft), ultimately 2m (6½ft) tall.

C. sinensis var. ***sinensis*** ♀ Bright yellow, slightly scented flowers appear in mid spring thickly clustered in small tassels. The leaves of this rounded, spreading shrub are blue-green beneath. Although hardy, this plant grows best with protection from frosts. HEIGHT & SPREAD 1.2×1m (4×3ft), ultimately 4m (13ft) tall.

'Spring Purple' has striking purple-green leaves.

C. spicata Racemes of narrow, slightly scented flowers in early to mid spring are pale greenish yellow. The leaves are blue-green beneath and up to 10cm (4in) long. This is an open shrub with a spreading habit. HEIGHT & SPREAD 1×1m (3×3ft), ultimately 2m (6½ft) tall.

C. veitchiana ♀ Prominent red anthers distinguish the small yellow flowers of this erect, bushy shrub, while the bright green leaves have a purplish tinge when young. This plant is not reliably hardy. HEIGHT & SPREAD 1.2×1m (4×3ft), ultimately 2m (6½ft) tall.

▲ *Corylopsis veitchiana*

CULTIVATION Plant in moist but well-drained acid to neutral soil in a slightly shaded position. Protect from cold winds, early frosts and early morning sun.
PROPAGATION Sow the seed of species in mid autumn, or layer plants using 2-3 year old shoots in mid autumn. Cultivars are usually grown from grafted plants.
PRUNING No pruning is necessary except to remove dead or diseased wood.
PESTS AND DISEASES Usually trouble free.

Corylus
Hazel
Betulaceae

Corylus avellana 'Contorta'

Easily grown, these hardy deciduous shrubs and small trees are valued for their early spring catkins, leaf shape and colour, and edible nuts. The clusters of pendulous, yellow male catkins, 4-7.5cm (1½-3in) long, develop during winter. They expand to shed their pollen in late winter or early spring. The female flowers, which grow alongside the males, are tiny swollen buds with red tassels. Pollinated female flowers develop into ovoid nuts enclosed in leafy bracts in autumn. The serrated leaves, up to 12.5cm (5in) long, are alternate and broadly oval with heart-shaped bases. Only three species and their cultivars are generally found in the garden. These are easy to grow, particularly on chalk, and tolerate a wide range of conditions including shade.
RECOMMENDED SPECIES AND VARIETIES
C. avellana (common hazel, cobnut) The male catkins of this plant hang in clusters from late winter to early spring before the mid green leaves appear. Edible nuts surrounded by green bracts form in autumn if pollination has been good. Native to Europe, this multi-stemmed shrub has a rounded, spreading habit. It is useful for hedging. HEIGHT & SPREAD 3×2.4m (10×8ft) after 5 years, ultimately 6m (20ft) tall.

▼ *Corylus avellana*

The recommended cultivars of *C. avellana* reach about half the size of the species. **'Aurea'** has leaves that flush pale yellow, gradually becoming more green towards the end of summer. **'Contorta'**♀ (corkscrew hazel) is grown mainly for fascinating corkscrew-like growth of its stems and branches. Although slow growing, it can eventually grow 3m (10ft) tall. **'Cosford Cob'** produces attractive edible nuts in autumn.

▲ *Corylus avellana* 'Contorta'

C. colurna♀ This elegant, ornamental tree is grown for its pyramid shape above a single trunk. Shining dark green leaves turn yellow in autumn. The clusters of autumn nuts are almost completely enclosed in bracts. Native to SE Europe and Asia Minor. HEIGHT & SPREAD 6×2m (20×6½ft) after 20 years, ultimately 15m (50ft) tall.
C. maxima (filbert) Grown mainly for its nuts, this hazel is most attractive when grown as a multistemmed shrub, although it can grow as a small tree. HEIGHT & SPREAD 1.5×1m (5×3ft), ultimately 6m (20ft) tall.

▼ *Corylus maxima* 'Purpurea'

'Kentish Cob' gives a good crop of nuts. **'Purpurea'**♀ has purple catkins and fruit husks as well as purple leaves.
CULTIVATION Plant in any soil in any position.
PROPAGATION Sow seed or layer plants in late summer. Grafted plants are best when specific features are required.
PRUNING Not normally required but if desired prune between late autumn and early spring to control the size of the plant.
PESTS AND DISEASES Relatively trouble free, but honey fungus can be a problem and squirrels often steal the nuts.

Cosmos
Compositae

Brightly coloured saucer-shaped flowers are carried on tall slender stems. Although they look delicate, these hardy and half-hardy annuals and perennials are easy to grow and are excellent on poor, well-drained soil in a sunny position. They are free-flowering from mid summer to early autumn. All the recommended plants, except *Cosmos atrosanguineus*, have deeply cut, fern-like foliage. All are native to sub-tropical N America.
RECOMMENDED SPECIES AND VARIETIES
C. atrosanguineus (chocolate cosmos) Deep velvety black-red or maroon flowers, up to 5cm (2in) across, appear one to a stem from mid summer to early autumn. They have a strong chocolate-like scent.

▼ *Cosmos atrosanguineus*

▲ *Cosmos bipinnatus*

The oval dark green leaves, up to 15 cm (6 in) long, are finely divided into segments. The plant is a half-hardy tuberous perennial. HEIGHT & SPREAD 60×45 cm (24×18 in).

C. bipinnatus Saucer-shaped flowers, up to 8 cm (3¼ in) wide, with yellow centres have petals in rose, crimson, pink or sometimes white from mid summer to autumn. This plant is a half-hardy, bushy annual. HEIGHT & SPREAD 1.5 m×60 cm (5×2 ft).

'Sea shells' has unusual fluted petals in shades of pink, red and white, and mixtures of these colours. **'Sensation'** has saucer-shaped flowers, up to 10 cm (4 in) across, in red, pink or white. **'Sonata'** has shorter stems with white petals surrounding the yellow centre.

▲ *Cosmos bipinnatus* 'Sensation'

C. sulphureus Yellow or orange flowers, 5 cm (2 in) across, are borne from mid summer to early autumn on this annual plant. The divided foliage is more coarsely cut and less feathery than other species. HEIGHT & SPREAD 60×30 cm (2×1 ft).

CULTIVATION Plant in spring in any free-draining soil, ideally in a sunny position. Plant *C. atrosanguineus* when all danger of frost has passed. Support tall annuals and deadhead all plants regularly. Lift *C. atrosanguineus* tubers once the first frost has cut back its foliage and store in a cool, dry, frost-free place over winter.

PROPAGATION Sow annuals in their flowering position in spring. Take basal stem cuttings of half-hardy perennials in spring.

PESTS AND DISEASES Greenfly, slugs and snails are frequently a problem.

Costmary see *Tanacetum balsamita*

Cotinus

Anacardiaceae

Cotinus coggygria 'Royal Purple'

Brilliant yellow, red, orange and purple autumn colours, a choice of purple summer foliage and plumes of tiny summer flowers make these hardy deciduous trees or shrubs especially valuable for contrast among green plants. They are also striking freestanding specimens. Native to N America, S Europe and Asia, cotinus is easy to grow.

RECOMMENDED SPECIES AND VARIETIES

C. coggygria♀ (smoke bush, smoke tree) The bright green obovate leaves, 7.5 cm (3 in) long, of this rounded, spreading shrub turn red and yellow in autumn. Profuse fawn flower plumes, up to 20 cm (8 in) long, appear in mid summer and turn grey later. HEIGHT & SPREAD 1.2×1.2 m (4×4 ft) after 5 years, ultimately 4 m (13 ft) tall.

'Royal Purple'♀ has purple leaves that turn bright red in autumn. The flowers are purple. The plant is slightly smaller than the species. The **Rubrifolius Group** includes a wide range of striking purple and red leaved plants. The leaves show a green tinge as the season progresses. **'Velvet Cloak'** bears dark purple leaves, sometimes almost black, until they turn red in autumn. The flowers have a pink tinge.

▲ *Cotinus coggygria* Rubrifolius Group

***C.* 'Flame'**♀ The dark green rounded leaves, up to 12.5 cm (5 in) long, of this vigorous, bushy shrub provide a fiery display of reds and oranges in autumn. The flower plumes, up to 20 cm (8 in) long, have a pink tinge. HEIGHT & SPREAD 1.2×1 m (4×3 ft) after 5 years, ultimately 4 m (13 ft) tall.

▼ *Cotinus* 'Flame'

***C.* 'Grace'**♀ The obovate leaves of this plant show off the purplish pink flower plumes, which are up to 20 cm (8 in) long. The purple leaves, which are up to 7.5 cm (3 in) long, turn scarlet in autumn. HEIGHT & SPREAD 1.2×1 m (4×3 ft) after 5 years, ultimately 4 m (13 ft) tall.

▲ *Cotinus obovatus*

C. obovatus♀ This large shrub or small tree produces one of the most brilliant displays of autumn colour. The obovate leaves, up to 12.5 cm (5 in) long, turn purple, red and orange. The flower plumes, up to 30 cm (12 in) long, are pale green. HEIGHT & SPREAD 1.5×1 m (5×3 ft) after 5 years, ultimately 9 m (30 ft) tall.

CULTIVATION Plant in any free-draining soil, preferably in a sunny position. The leaves do not colour as well on rich, manured soils.

PROPAGATION Take semi-ripe cuttings in early to mid summer or use low shoots for layering in early to mid autumn.

PRUNING None is necessary, but remove any dead wood in spring and cut back to maintain the desired size.

PESTS AND DISEASES Usually trouble free.

Cotoneaster

Rosaceae

Cotoneaster horizontalis

These evergreen or deciduous shrubs, mostly hardy, range from prostrate mat-forming types and hummocks to large bushes and trees. Brilliantly coloured berries, about 6 mm (¼ in) wide, appear in autumn, preceded by less significant flowers, white tinged with pink, in late spring and early summer. Many deciduous species

bring rich autumn tints to the garden. Some plants are semi-evergreen, losing their leaves in severe winters. The evergreen species and hybrids are useful for hedging and screening, while creeping plants make good ground cover. There are also varieties suitable for a rock garden, covering a wall or as a specimen shrub in a border.

The flowers, mostly in clusters, have five petals and are flattened or cup-shaped. Some are very attractive to bees. Leaves are generally oval and smooth-edged. The berries are bright red and spherical unless stated otherwise.

Although tolerant of most soils and situations, deciduous plants prefer full sun, while evergreens do well in sun or partial shade. The genus is native to China, Burma, Tibet and the Himalayas as far west as Kashmir.

RECOMMENDED SPECIES AND VARIETIES

The recommended plants are divided into two groups:

(1) Deciduous plants

(2) Evergreens and semi-evergreens

DECIDUOUS PLANTS

C. ***adpressus***♀ Leaves, shoots and branches form a dense, low, spreading shrub. The dullish green, wavy-edged leaves, up to 1cm (⅜in) long, turn scarlet in autumn. The flowers attract bees. HEIGHT & SPREAD 7.5×40cm (3×16in) after 5 years, ultimately 40cm (16in) tall.

▲ *Cotoneaster adpressus*

C. ***atropurpureus*** **'Variegatus'**♀ (syn. *C. horizontalis* 'Variegatus') Fan-like branches carry numerous leaves, up to 1.5cm (½in) long. Edged with white, the leaves are suffused with pink in winter. HEIGHT & SPREAD 20×40cm (8×16in) after 5 years, ultimately 60cm (2ft) tall.

Cotoneaster atropurpureus 'Variegatus' ▼

▼ *Cotoneaster cochleatus*

C. ***bullatus***♀ Conspicuously corrugated, glossy, dark green leaves, up to 7.5cm (3in) long, turn rich colours in autumn. This plant is sparsely branched with a strong, upright, arching habit. The berries are egg-shaped to globular. HEIGHT & SPREAD 1.5×1.2m (5×4ft) after 5 years, ultimately 3.5m (12ft) tall.

C. ***horizontalis***♀ (fish bone cotoneaster) The branches of this shrub are arranged in herringbone fashion. Glossy green leaves, up to 1.5cm (½in) long, turn red in autumn when thick clusters of berries appear. This plant is valuable for covering unsightly banks or for clothing north or east-facing walls. HEIGHT & SPREAD 30×60cm (1×2ft) after 5 years, ultimately 60cm×1.8m (2×6ft) tall.

▲ *Cotoneaster horizontalis*

C. ***simonsii***♀ This deciduous or semi-evergreen shrub is best grown in groups or for hedging. It has an upright habit with dark green glossy leaves, up to 2.5cm (1in) long. The berries are orange-red. HEIGHT & SPREAD 1.5×1m (5×3ft) after 5 years, ultimately 2.7m (9ft) tall.

C. ***splendens***♀ Slender, arching shoots are covered with bright green leaves and egg-shaped orange berries in autumn. HEIGHT & SPREAD 1.5×1.2m (5×4ft) after 5 years, ultimately 2.4m (8ft) tall.

EVERGREENS AND SEMI-EVERGREENS

C. ***cochleatus***♀ This is a prostrate, mound forming, slow-growing evergreen. The glossy dark green leaves, about 1cm (⅜in) long, are egg-shaped, rounded and notched at the apex. HEIGHT & SPREAD 10×70cm (4×28in) after 5 years, ultimately 20cm (8in) tall.

C. ***congestus*** This creeping shrub of congested habit forms a carpet of tightly packed branches covered with dull green leaves about 1cm (⅜in) long. HEIGHT & SPREAD 10×80cm (4×32in) after 5 years, ultimately 15cm (6in) tall.

'Nanus' is especially suitable for a rock garden. It grows to only 5×50cm (2×20in) after 5 years and has a maximum spread of about 60cm (2ft).

C. ***conspicuus*** **'Decorus'**♀ This prostrate evergreen or semi-evergreen forms a dense mound of arching stems. The plant is upright when young. The dark green, glossy, oblong leaves are greyish beneath, and up to 6mm (¼in) long. HEIGHT & SPREAD 20cm×1.2m (8in×4ft) after 5 years, ultimately 30cm (12in) tall.

C. ***dammeri***♀ Ideal for carpeting banks and bare ground beneath taller trees and shrubs, this prostrate shrub has ground-hugging stems that root where they touch the soil. The plant spreads at about 60cm (2ft) a year. The downy, prominently veined leaves are up to 4cm (1½in) long. HEIGHT & SPREAD 5cm×1.2m (2in×4ft) after 5 years, ultimately 7.5cm (3in) tall.

C. ***franchetii*** Pinkish white flowers appear in mid summer, followed by a splendid display of orange-red, egg-shaped berries in autumn. This graceful semi-evergreen makes a good hedge or screen. The sage-green leaves are about 3cm (1¼in) long.

▲ *Cotoneaster franchetii*

HEIGHT & SPREAD 1.2×1.2m (4×4ft) after 5 years, ultimately 2.7m (9ft) tall.

C. ***frigidus*** **'Cornubia'**♀ Large pendeant clusters of berries, up to 10cm (4in) across, weigh down the long branches of this vigorous, semi-evergreen in autumn and winter. The lance-shaped leaves are about 12cm (4¾in) long. HEIGHT & SPREAD 1.5×1.5m (5×5ft) after 5 years, ultimately 6m (20ft) tall.

C. ***integrifolius*** Large, deep pink berries appear on this dwarf shrub in autumn. The glossy leaves are about 1cm (⅜in) long. The plant is useful for draping banks and walls. It is widely grown as *C. microphyllus*. HEIGHT & SPREAD 20cm×1m (8in×3ft) after 5 years, ultimately 45cm (18in) tall.

C. ***lacteus***♀ Milky white flowers appear in flat-topped clusters in early summer, followed by abundant orange-red berries. The shrub has a dense habit, with pendulous twigs and broad leaves about 5cm (2in) long. They are dark olive to greyish green above and grey and hairy underneath. Particularly wind hardy, this plant is grown as a specimen, against north or east-facing walls or as a hedge. See HEDGES p.318. HEIGHT & SPREAD 1.5×1.5m (5×5ft) after 5 years, ultimately 3m (10ft) tall.

C. ***microphyllus***♀ This hummock-forming shrub with slender, rigid shoots running along the soil is clothed in tiny leaves up to 1.5cm (½in) long. HEIGHT & SPREAD 30cm×1m (1×3ft) after 5 years, ultimately 75cm (2½ft) tall.

▲ *Cotoneaster microphyllus*

C. salicifolius This evergreen or semi-evergreen shrub is a parent of many cultivars and hybrids.

'Exburyensis' is an arching shrub with a low, broad habit. Leaves are bright green, lance-shaped and up to 12.5cm (5in) long. Pale yellow fruits are sometimes tinged apricot pink. The height and spread are 1.2×1.2m (4×4ft) after 5 years, ultimately reaching 3m (10ft) tall. **'Gnom'** forms a

▲ *Cotoneaster* 'Gnom'

shallow mound, made up of slender, purplish, arching shoots – splendid for ground cover or trained up a north or east facing wall. Lance-shaped leaves up to 3cm (1¼in) long are tinged bronze in winter. Small berries ripen late. The plant grows to 10×85cm (4×34in) after 5 years, ultimately 20cm (8in) tall. **'Pendulus'** ('Hybridus Pendulus') is often a weeping standard with

Cotoneaster salicifolius 'Pendulus'

glossy ovate leaves up to 7.5cm long. It may also be grown as a groundcover plant, with a height and spread of 60×180 cm (2×6ft). **'Rothschildianus'**♀ has willow-like semi-evergreen leaves, up to 12.5cm (5in) long. They are light green, as is the wood. Clusters of creamy yellow fruits ripen late, remaining well into winter. This plant reaches 1.5×1.2cm (5×4ft) after 5 years, ultimately 4.5m (15ft) tall.

▲ *Cotoneaster Salicifolius* 'Exburyensis'

C. serotinus♀ An arching shrub, *C. serotinus* flowers profusely in mid and late summer. The berries ripen in early winter and last until spring. Leaves are blue-green above, sometimes downy beneath, and up to 7.5cm (3in) long. HEIGHT & SPREAD 1.5×1.5cm (5×5ft) after 5 years, ultimately 6m (20ft) tall.

***C.* x *suecicus* 'Coral Beauty'** Arching branches are densely covered with glossy dark green leaves 2cm (¾in) long. Berries are a bright coral red. Best used as ground cover or for climbing north or east-facing walls. It will grow against a wall or fence with the minimum of support. HEIGHT & SPREAD 25cm×1.2m (10in×4ft) after 5 years, ultimately 60cm (2ft) tall.

CULTIVATION Plant, preferably in spring or autumn, in full sun or partial shade in dry soil. Avoid waterlogged soils.

PROPAGATION Take cuttings in summer or layer the plant in mid or late autumn. Sow seed of species, such as *C. lacteus* and *C. simonsii*, in autumn.

PRUNING No regular pruning is required, but, if desired to restrict the size, cut ever-

▲ *Cotoneaster* x *suecicus* 'Coral Beauty'

greens back hard in early spring and prune deciduous plants in late winter. Prune overgrown specimens hard into the old wood. See HEDGES p.318.

PESTS AND DISEASES Generally trouble free. However, aphids and scale insects may cause problems. Fireblight may damage flowers and leaves in central and southern Britain. Silverleaf may damage foliage and kill shoots.

Cotton lavender
see *Santolina chamaecyparissus*

Cotula

Brass buttons
Compositae

C

Quaint, button-like flowerheads, borne singly, appear above finely divided foliage from late spring to summer. *Cotula hispida* and *C. lineariloba* require well-drained soil and are suitable for a rock garden, gaps in paving or raised beds. *C. coronopifolia* thrives in moist situations and is a useful marginal water plant. The tufted or mat-forming perennials listed here are native to South Africa.

RECOMMENDED SPECIES AND VARIETIES

C. coronopifolia Yellow flowerheads, up to 1cm (⅜in) across, have purple-tinged bracts. The oval mid green leaves of this hardy perennial grow to 12cm (4¾in) long and are divided into narrow lobes. HEIGHT & SPREAD 40×30cm (16×12in).

▲ *Cotula coronopifolia*

'Cream Button' has cream flowerheads.

C. hispida The bright yellow flowerheads, 1.5cm (½in) wide, of this mat-forming perennial often redden with age. The silvery grey, hairy leaves grow up to 3cm (1¼in) long and are divided into numerous slender segments. HEIGHT & SPREAD 7.5×30cm (3×12in).

C. lineariloba This tufted, often mat-forming perennial has bright yellow to red flowerheads up to 2cm (¾in) across. The hairy, silver leaves, 3cm (1¼in) long, are finely divided into numerous linear segments. HEIGHT & SPREAD 15×40cm (6×16in).

CULTIVATION Plant *C. hispida* and *C. lineariloba* in well-drained gritty soil in a sunny position. Plant *C. coronopifolia* on a moist site in sun or partial shade. *C. hispida* and *C. lineariloba* are hardy only to -5°C (23°F) and require winter protection.

PROPAGATION Take cuttings or rooted pieces pulled from the parent plant in summer. Alternatively, sow seed in late winter or early spring.

PESTS AND DISEASES Usually trouble free.

Courgette see p.740
Cowberry see *Vaccinium vitis-idaea*
Cowslip see *Primula veris*

Crambe

Cruciferae

Clouds of tiny white flowers among thick leaves provide a magnificent display. The starry flowers, each about 1 cm (⅜ in) across, are sweetly scented. Native to Europe, parts of Asia and tropical Africa, crambes do well in seaside gardens and will tolerate fairly poor soil. The recommended plants are hardy perennials.

RECOMMENDED SPECIES AND VARIETIES

*C. **cordifolia***♀ The flowers of this decorative plant appear on widely branching stems in early summer. The ovate, dark green, glossy leaves, up to 30 cm (12 in) long, are coarsely toothed. HEIGHT & SPREAD 2.4 × 1.5 m (8 × 5 ft).

▲ *Crambe cordifolia*

▲ *Crambe maritima*

*C. **maritima*** (seakale) Often grown as a vegetable for its edible stems and leaves, seakale also makes a good ornamental plant. The sculptural, fleshy, blue-green leaves, up to 60 cm (2 ft) long, are glaucous, notched and lobed. The flowers are carried in large panicles in early summer. HEIGHT & SPREAD 75 cm × 1 m (2½ × 3 ft).

CULTIVATION Plant about 1 m (3 ft) apart in ordinary, well-drained soil in a sunny position. As the foliage and flowers of *C. cordifolia* die back, use late-flowering annuals to fill the gap that is left.

PROPAGATION Sow seed under glass in spring, pot the seedlings on and plant outside when they are large enough. Alternatively, divide plants in late spring.

PESTS AND DISEASES Slugs may be a nuisance in early spring.

Cranberry see *Vaccinium*
Cranesbill see *Geranium*

Crassula

Crassulaceae

Fleshy leaves and clusters of starry or tubular flowers are the main features of this genus. Most species are tender succulents native to South Africa, and make excellent pot plants that flourish on a warm sunny windowsill. The dimensions given below are for pot plants grown in the home, although greenhouse specimens may well grow larger.

RECOMMENDED SPECIES AND VARIETIES

*C. **arborescens*** (silver jade plant, silver dollar) Stout, branching stems are clothed with rounded or oval, blue-green leaves up to 5 cm (2 in) across with a greyish bloom and purple edges. Short sprays of small tubular flowers in cream tinged with red may appear in summer, although they are rarely produced in Britain. HEIGHT & SPREAD 60 × 60 cm (2 × 2 ft).

*C. **falcata***♀ (airplane plant) The fleshy grey-green leaves, up to 10 cm (4 in) long, of this branching shrubby plant are lance-shaped and twisted like a propeller. Small, bright red, fragrant flowers are carried in large flattened or rounded heads, up to 15 cm (6 in) across, during summer. HEIGHT & SPREAD 50 × 45 cm (20 × 18 in).

*C. **ovata***♀ (dollar plant, jade plant) The stems of this multibranched plant have a thin peeling skin or bark and are clothed with rounded, shiny, dark green leaves. The leaves are up to 4 cm (1½ in) across and often edged with red or pale green. Clusters of small white flowers tinged with pink are produced in autumn. HEIGHT & SPREAD 1 × 1 m (3 × 3 ft).

*C. **rupestris***♀ (bead vine, necklace vine) Blue-green leaves, flushed with brown-red especially at the edges, cover the flaking stems. These rounded, fleshy leaves are rarely more than 1 cm (⅜ in) across. Clusters of tiny white flowers tinged with red are borne for much of the year. HEIGHT & SPREAD 50 × 50 cm (20 × 20 in).

CULTIVATION Grow in pots in a free-draining compost. Place in a sunny position in the home or in a cool greenhouse at a temperature of no less than 5°C (41°F). Water freely during summer, but sparingly in winter. Remove faded flowerheads. Feed monthly throughout summer. Repot each spring.

PROPAGATION Take stem or leaf cuttings and root under glass in spring and summer. Alternatively, sow seed under glass at 15-18°C (59-64°F) in early spring.

PESTS AND DISEASES Usually trouble free.

▼ *Crassula ovata*

▼ *Crassula arborescens*

Crataegus

Rosaceae

Crataegus laevigata 'Paul's Scarlet'

Spring flowers in profusion, bright berries and good autumn colour are provided by these deciduous shrubs and small trees. Some of the best plants combine all these elements and are also frost hardy and easy to grow. Most species are well armed with thorns and make impenetrable hedging plants. Birds are drawn by the bunches of round berries (haws) in winter and by the chance of safe nesting sites in spring.

The oval, toothed leaves are sometimes lobed and tend to be small, less than 10 cm (4 in) long. The scented flowers, most commonly creamy white, are small but grouped in numerous flat clusters up to 10 cm (4 in)

▲ *Crataegus laevigata* 'Paul's Scarlet'

▲ *Crataegus laevigata* 'Rosea Flore Pleno'

across. Most of the hundreds of species are native to eastern and central N America.

RECOMMENDED SPECIES AND VARIETIES

C. laevigata (syn. *C. oxyacantha*) (Midland hawthorn, may) Showy white flowers, sometimes flushed with pink, appear on this British native in late spring. Red haws follow. This plant has a rounded, spreading habit and glossy dark green leaves that have 3–5 lobes. HEIGHT & SPREAD 1.2×1m (4×3ft) after 5 years, ultimately 5m (16ft) tall.

'Paul's Scarlet'♀ (syn. 'Coccinea Plena') has double red flowers in spring, but does not reliably produce berries. **'Plena'** has double white flowers fading to pale pink before they fall. The pink flowers of **'Rosea Flore Pleno'**♀ are double.

C.* x *lavallei The glossy dark green leaves clothing this densely branched, rounded tree give good red-orange autumn colour. Clusters of white flowers in early summer are followed by orange-red fruits that remain on the tree until early winter. HEIGHT & SPREAD 1.5×1.2m (5×4ft) after 5 years, ultimately 5m (16ft) tall.

'Carrierei'♀ has longer glossy green leaves that turn bright red-orange in autumn and has larger orange-red fruits.

C. monogyna (common hawthorn, may) Hedging is the traditional main use for this British native hawthorn, which has an array of thorns and is densely branched. It forms a small tree with a rounded top. The strong-smelling, late spring flowers are short lived. Glossy leaves with 5–7 lobes usually turn

▲ *Crataegus lavallei* 'Carrierei'

red and orange in autumn. The berries are shiny red. HEIGHT & SPREAD 4×3m (13×10ft) after 20 years, ultimately 8m (26ft) tall.

'Biflora' (Glastonberry thorn) occasionally produces an extra crop of flowers in winter and normally comes into leaf early in the year. **'Stricta'** (syn. 'Fastigiata') has a very upright columnar habit.

▲ *Crataegus persimilis* 'Prunifolia'

***C. persimilis* 'Prunifolia'**♀ (syn. *C. prunifolia*) The glossy dark green leaves of this small, spreading tree take on orange and scarlet tints in autumn. Rounded clusters of white flowers in early summer are followed by dark red fruits produced in profusion. HEIGHT & SPREAD 1×1m (3×3ft) in 5 years, ultimately 3m (10ft) tall.

C. prunifolia see *C. persimilis* 'Prunifolia'♀

CULTIVATION Plant in winter in any garden soil in a position that receives full sun. For hedging, use a double row of 30-45cm (12-18in) high plants of *C. monogyna*, spacing them at intervals of 30-38cm (12-15in).

PROPAGATION Sow seed in early spring or sow immediately after collection and overwinter plants outside. Germination is slow and can be up to 18 months. Only grafted plants are sure to produce the features of the named varieties.

PRUNING None is generally required but if necessary trim after flowering. Trim hedges of *C. monogyna* once the leaves have fallen.

PESTS AND DISEASES Usually trouble free.

Creeping Jenny
see *Lysimachia nummularia*

Crepis
Hawksbeard
Compositae

These dandelion-like flowers, borne in summer, look pretty in rock gardens or along the front of a flower border. Each flowerhead is formed entirely of narrow, petal-like ray florets. Plants grow in tufts or clumps, with leaves often forming rosettes. The hardy plants include annuals, biennials and perennials. Many crepis species are weeds, but the recommended plants are well worth growing. They are native to S Europe .

RECOMMENDED SPECIES AND VARIETIES

C. aurea (golden hawksbeard) Coppery orange or bright yellow flowers, often with a reddish reverse, 3cm (1¼in) across, bloom from mid summer to early autumn on slender stems that are generally unbranched. The light green, dandelion-like leaves, up to 10cm (4in) long, form a lax basal rosette. The plant is a perennial. HEIGHT & SPREAD 30×30cm (12×12in).

C. incana♀ (pink dandelion) Pink or purplish flowers, 3-5cm (1¼-2in) wide, grow on branching stems in mid and late summer. This perennial plant forms clumps of grey-green hairy leaf rosettes, each leaf lance-shaped but broadest towards the tip, up to 12.5cm (5in) long, with large teeth. HEIGHT & SPREAD 20×20cm (8×8in).

C. rubra (pink hawksbeard) Pink or white flowers, 3-5cm (1¼-2in) across, are carried on upright stems rising from leaf rosettes in summer. The flowers are usually one to a stem. The leaves of this annual are pale green, lance-shaped, deeply toothed, and up to 15cm (6in) long. HEIGHT & SPREAD 40×30cm (16×12in).

CULTIVATION Plant in any well-drained garden soil, including poor soil, in a sunny position. Plant perennial species in late summer or early autumn.

PROPAGATION Sow seeds of perennial

▼ *Crepis incana*

species in winter or early spring in a coldframe. Prick out into pots when large enough to handle and plant out in permanent positions in mid summer. Sow seeds of *C. rubra* in the flowering site in early autumn or early to mid spring. Divide older plants in mid spring.
PESTS AND DISEASES Usually trouble free.

Cress, violet see *Ionopsidium*

Crinodendron

Lantern tree
Elaeocarpaceae

Crinodendron hookerianum

Grown for their dark, shiny foliage and lantern-like flowers, this genus consists of two species of small evergreen trees or large shrubs.

The plants prefer cool root conditions and benefit from the shade of lower growing shrubs. Both species prefer a sheltered site because the leaves scorch if exposed to full sun and cold winds. They do best in the milder south and west, although *Crinodendron hookerianum* can survive temperatures as low as -10°C (14°F) given a sheltered position. *C. patagua* is more tender and can be grown outdoors only in mild areas: it should be grown in a cool conservatory elsewhere. *C. hookerianum* can also be grown as a conservatory plant if so wished. Growing crinodendron in containers will effectively restrict their size.

▼ *Crinodendron hookerianum*

RECOMMENDED SPECIES AND VARIETIES
C. hookerianum ♀ (syn. *Tricuspidaria lanceolata*) (Chilean lantern tree) This vigorous plant forms a small, dense, bushy tree or large shrub. Many long-stalked buds appear in autumn but it is not until late spring and early summer the following year that they flower. Then the buds swell until the flowers resemble partly opened tulips hanging upside down from the branches. The waxy crimson flowers, about 3cm (1¼in) long, are borne from the base of the leaves on downy, reddish stalks up to 7.5cm (3in) long. The leathery, narrowly elliptic leaves are up to 12cm (4¾in) long with coarsely toothed margins and downy stalks. This species looks good planted among low-growing ericaceous shrubs such as azaleas and gaultherias. HEIGHT & SPREAD 3-4×2m (10-13×6½ft) after 10 years, ultimately 9m (30ft) tall.
C. patagua (syn. *Tricuspidaria dependens*) Similar in size and habit to *C. hookerianum*, this plant has broader, more finely toothed leaves. Its buds also apppear in autumn. They open to fragrant white flowers in mid to late summer. The flowers are more open and bell-like than those of *C. hookerianum*, and the tips of the petals turn outwards, giving the flowers a fringed appearance. HEIGHT & SPREAD 3×2m (10×6½ft) after 10 years, ultimately 10m (33ft) tall.
CULTIVATION Plant at any time – although mid to late spring is probably best – in fertile, moist, well-drained soil that is free of lime. Choose a position with partial shade.
PROPAGATION Take semi-ripe heel cuttings or sow seed in autumn.
PRUNING No pruning is necessary, but dead or damaged stems can be removed at any time of year.
PESTS AND DISEASES Usually trouble free.

Crinum

Amaryllidaceae

Glorious trumpet blooms bring a touch of the exotic to the garden in late summer. These are hardy and half-hardy bulbous plants. Flowers have six satiny petals and six prominent stamens. They are borne on tall, erect stalks above a shock of long, narrow, glossy leaves that generally only partially die back in winter. In the garden, plants are best grown at the base of a warm wall. They can be grown in a cool, frost-free greenhouse or conservatory, but not in the house. In summer, move plants outdoors, or keep them under glass that is shaded.
RECOMMENDED SPECIES AND VARIETIES
C. × powellii ♀ Large, fragrant, funnel-shaped pink flowers are produced during late summer and early autumn on a strong leafless stem. Several plants together look particularly stunning. Each plant has 3-4 stems and as many as 10 flowers grouped together on each stem. The flowers are up to 15cm (6in) long and almost as wide at the flared opening. The bright green strap-shaped leaves are as long as 60cm (2ft). Plants will tolerate temperatures as low as -5°C (23°F). HEIGHT & SPREAD 90×60cm (3×2ft).
'Album' has pure white flowers.

▲ *Crinum × powellii* 'Album'

CULTIVATION Plant bulbs in spring, in a sheltered, sunny position in free-draining but moisture-retaining soil. In severe winters, cover the bulbs with horticultural fleece or straw to protect their exposed necks. In summer, water freely and apply tomato feed every 3 weeks. Remove faded blossoms.
PROPAGATION Divide clumps of bulbs in spring. Sow seed in spring, ideally in a propagator if one is available.
PESTS AND DISEASES Usually trouble free.

Crocosmia

Montbretia
Iridaceae

Crocosmia 'Lucifer'

With striking yellow, orange or red flowers and abundant bright green, sword-like foliage, crocosmias create a splash of colour from late summer to early autumn. They grow quickly and soon form large clumps that are ideal among shrubs. There are seven species in this genus of perennial corms and many hybrid cultivars. They all have slightly hooded, funnel-shaped flowers with prominent stamens carried above the leaves on tall, arching stems. Each flower has six petals, a yellow throat and some also have darker marks at the base of each petal.

Native to South Africa, crocosmias prefer a rich, moist but well-drained soil in sun or light shade. Although drought tolerant, they benefit from generous watering in hot, dry periods. The well-known montbretia, *Crocosmia* × *crocosmiiflora,* can be invasive and has become naturalised in mild and wet regions in Britain. Although crocosmias are hardy they do not like long periods of hard frost and a winter mulch is advisable in cold areas. The large-flowered cultivars are less hardy than the smaller-flowered varieties.

RECOMMENDED SPECIES AND VARIETIES

C.* × *crocosmiiflora (syn. *Montbretia crocosmiiflora*) Small orange or orange-red flowers are borne in short spikes amid broad, grass-like leaves with a papery texture. HEIGHT 1 m (3 ft).

C. masoniorum ♀ Orange flowers are carried along the top of arching stems above large, ribbed leaves. HEIGHT 1 m (3 ft).

C. paniculata (syn. *Antholyza coccinea*, *A. paniculata*, *Curtonus paniculatus*) Curved orange-red flowers alternate along the branched reddish brown stems giving a zigzag appearance. Wide, ribbed leaves and tall, flowering stems make this an ideal architectural plant. HEIGHT 1.2 m (4 ft).

C. rosea see *Tritonia disticha* ssp. *rubrolucens*

OTHER VARIETIES

There are many cultivars available with flowers in a wide range of reds, oranges and yellows. They vary in height from 45 cm (1½ ft) to 1 m (3 ft). Small flowered varieties produce a large number of slender blooms, 3-4 cm (1¼-1½ in) across. These plants are very vigorous and increase rapidly. Cultivars with large flowers bear a succession of broad-petalled, wide-open blooms, 6-8 cm (2½-3¼ in) across. Individually, they are very showy but they are less vigorous, less hardy and slower to increase than the small-flowered cultivars.

'Canary Bird' has small, golden yellow flowers with unmarked petals. **'Carmin Brilliant'** has small pinkish red flowers on dark stems. **'Citronella'** has small, pale lemon-yellow blooms. **'Emberglow'** has small, nodding, dark red flowers on deep reddish brown stems. It is one of the earliest to flower. The large, clear orange flowers of **'Emily McKenzie'** have prominent mahogany-red marks in the throat.

▲ *Crocosmia* 'Canary Bird'

▲ *Crocosmia* 'Lucifer'

'Jackanapes' has small flowers with alternating yellow and dark orange petals. **'James Coey'** has small, deep orange-red flowers. **'Lady Hamilton'** has small yellow flowers with a pale apricot ring inside. The large flowers of **'Lucifer'** ♀ are flame red: this plant is 1.1 m (3½ ft) in height. **'Norwich Canary'** has small golden yellow flowers. **'Queen of Spain'** has large orange-red flowers with a yellow centre and contrasting maroon mark at the base of each petal. The flowers of **'Severn Sunrise'** are pinkish orange. **'Solfaterre'** ♀ has small apricot-yellow flowers and bronze-green, grass-like foliage. **'Spitfire'** has small, fiery orange flowers. **'Star of the East'** has large, clear orange flowers.

CULTIVATION Plant in moist but well-drained soil, choosing a site in sun or part shade. Put pot-grown crocosmias in during autumn or spring or plant dormant corms in late winter. Plant them 7.5-10 cm (3-4 in) deep and 10-15 cm (4-6 in) apart, in clumps. Remove flowerheads when faded but let the leaves die naturally. Cover plants with a mulch in winter. Divide overcrowded clumps every 3-4 years but do not separate individual strings of corms.

▼ *Crocosmia* 'Severn Sunrise'

▲ *Crocosmia* 'Spitfire'

▲ *Crocosmia* 'Jakanapes'

PROPAGATION Divide plants in spring before growth starts. This can be done every 2-3 years for cultivars, every 4-5 years for the species. Alternatively, sow the ripe seed of species under glass: seedlings take 2 or more years to flower.

PESTS AND DISEASES Red spider mite may be troublesome in hot summers.

Crocus, autumn see *Colchicum*

C

Crocus

Iridaceae

Growing wild in a broad band stretching from Portugal to central Asia, crocuses are well loved in British gardens as bright heralds of spring. In fact these cormous perennials, in their different species, offer a flowering season spanning more than half the year, from late summer to mid spring.

Each crocus corm produces between one and five honey-scented flowers, which vary in length from 2-8cm (¾-3¼in). The funnel-shaped, six-petalled flowers (strictly speaking their 'petals' are tepals or perianth segments) are borne at the end of a narrow perianth tube. The flowers, which open and close with sunlight, are coloured in yellows and browns, blues and purples, as well as white, often with a colour contrast between outer and inner petals. In some species the flowers open out widely, in others the petals are rounded, curving inwards at the top to create a goblet shape.

The narrow, grass-like leaves of crocuses have a silver-grey to white central stripe and lengthen as the flowers fade. Several autumn species flower before the leaves appear. In all spring-flowering crocuses, flowers and leaves appear together.

The sex organs of the flowers may be conspicuously coloured, and it is from the stigmas of some species of autumn-flowering crocus that the spice saffron is produced.

Crocuses are suitable for planting in groups in borders or in a rock garden. Some species naturalise in grass. All the species included here are hardy to -20°C (-4°F), but some need a dry summer dormant period and are best grown in an alpine house. Cultivars of *Crocus vernus* and *C. chrysanthus* can be forced for indoor display.

RECOMMENDED SPECIES AND VARIETIES

These are divided into winter and spring-flowering and autumn-flowering crocuses.

WINTER AND SPRING-FLOWERING CROCUSES

C. ancyrensis In late winter up to 3 golden yellow flowers, 2cm (¾in) long, appear on comparatively long perianth tubes. Native to Turkey, it requires a sunny well-drained position. HEIGHT 7cm (2¾in).

'Golden Bunch' is more robust with up to 5 flowers.

C. angustifolius♀ (syn. *C. susianus*) Slightly pointed, deep yellow flowers, with a dark bronze mark on the outer petals,

Crocus angustifolius

▲ *Crocus chrysanthus* 'Blue Bird'

appear in late winter or early spring. The outer petals arch back in the sun. Native to the Ukraine. HEIGHT 7cm (2¾in).

C. aureus see *C. flavus* ssp. *flavus*

C. biflorus ssp. ***alexandri*** White flowers with a large dark purple mark on the outer petals appear in early spring. Native to the Balkans. HEIGHT 11cm (4¼in).

C. chrysanthus Cultivars of this species, native to Turkey, and hybrids of it and *C. biflorus*, produce up to 5 compact and rounded flowers in late winter. Frequently the outer petals are flushed or striped with brown. HEIGHT 10cm (4in).

'Advance' is yellow with violet outer petals. **'Blue Bird'** is white with grey-blue outer petals. **'Blue Pearl'**♀ is silvery blue with a pale brown base to the outer petals. **'Cream Beauty'**♀ has rounded flowers of rich cream. **'E.P. Bowles'** has lemon-yellow flowers, suffused with brown on the exterior. **'Gipsy Girl'** bears large flowers of deep yellow, heavily striped with brown on the outside. **'Ladykiller'**♀ has slender flowers of pure white with a large deep purple mark on the outer petals. **'Snow Bunting'**♀ is white with a light brown mark at the base of the outer petals. **'Zwanenburg Bronze'**♀ has golden yellow flowers with purple-bronze marking on the outer petals.

▼ *Crocus chrysanthus* 'Cream Beauty'

▼ *Crocus chrysanthus* 'Ladykiller'

C. corsicus♀ This early spring-flowering species has slender flowers, the inner petals of which are pale lilac. The buff-coloured outer petals are striped with purple. Native to Corsica, this species does best in a sunny, well-drained position. HEIGHT 8cm (3¼in).

C. etruscus♀ Flowering in early spring, the corm produces 1 or 2 lilac flowers lightly striped with purple. Native to NW Italy. HEIGHT 10cm (4in).

'Zwanenburg', a vigorous cultivar, is the one most widely grown.

C. flavus ssp. ***flavus***♀ (syn. *C. aureus*) This vigorous and freely seeding, early spring-flowering corm has up to 4 orange-yellow flowers. Native to the Balkans and Turkey. HEIGHT 12cm (4¾in).

C. imperati♀ One of the earliest crocuses, flowering in mid and late winter, this species has large flowers 5cm (2in) long. The biscuit-coloured outer petals are strongly marked with violet feathering. They open in the sun to reveal intensely lilac inner petals. An easily grown crocus, native to Italy. HEIGHT 8cm (3¼in).

C. korolkowii Intense yellow flowers, suffused with brown on the outside, are borne in late winter by this very hardy crocus, native to central Asia. It is easily grown in a gritty soil in full sun. HEIGHT 8cm (3¼in).

***C.* x *luteus* 'Golden Yellow'**♀ This vigorous late winter or early spring-flowering hybrid bears flowers of an intense golden yellow. It is sterile but easily increased by dividing the clumps. HEIGHT 12cm (4¾in).

C. malyi♀ The slender white flowers, appearing in late winter, have a yellow throat and a conspicuous orange stigma. A crocus for a sheltered site in full sun. Native to the Balkans. HEIGHT 10cm (4in).

C. minimus This delicate, late winter-flowering crocus has small, 3cm (1¼in) long, flowers on relatively long perianth tubes. The pale biscuit-coloured outer petals have dark purple veins, contrasting with the bright purple inner petals. It needs a well-drained soil in full sun. Native to Corsica and Sardinia. HEIGHT 8cm (3¼in).

***C.* 'Purpureus'** see *C. vernus* 'Purpureus Grandiflorus'

C. sieberi♀ (syn. *C. sibiricus*) This very variable but easily grown crocus has well-rounded flowers and is one of the best for late winter or early spring display. Native to SW Balkans and Crete. HEIGHT 10cm (4in).

'Albus'♀ (syn. 'Bowles White') has pure white flowers and is early flowering. **'Hubert Edelsten'**♀ is a large-flowered hybrid. Its purple outer petals each have a diagonal white mark, while the inner petals are white. A striking crocus, ssp. ***sublimis* 'Tricolor'**♀ has petals divided into three bands of colour – deep purple at the petal tips, white, and yellow in the throat. It is best grown in a sheltered position or in an alpine house. **'Violet Queen'** is a vigorous

▲ *Crocus malyi*

▲ *Crocus sieberi* ssp. *sublimis* 'Tricolor'

Crocus boryi ▲

Crocus tommasinianus ▲

Crocus tommasinianus

crocus with intensely blue-violet flowers.

C. susianus see *C. angustifolius*

C. tommasinianus ♀ This early spring-flowering crocus increases rapidly and is good for naturalising in grass. The slender flowers, on 5 cm (2 in) long perianth tubes, are very variable in colour. Most commonly they have silvery lilac outer petals and pale lilac inner petals, which are revealed when the flowers open in the sun. Native to Bulgaria, Hungary and Serbia. HEIGHT 8-10 cm (3¼-4 in).

Pure white flowers are borne by f. ***albus.***

▲ *Crocus tommasinianus* 'Ruby Giant'

'Ruby Giant' has larger, more rounded flowers of rich purple. It flowers slightly later and is sterile. **'Whitewell Purple'** has typical slender flowers of deep purple.

C. vernus The species, native to Italy, Austria and E Europe, is the parent of the well-known Dutch crocuses and rarely cultivated. Its cultivars are much larger and more vigorous. They produce large, 8 cm (3¼ in) long, rounded flowers in late winter or early spring, being among the last crocuses to bloom. They are excellent garden plants and can be naturalised in grass. They grow 15-20 cm (6-8 in) tall.

'Jeanne d'Arc' has pure white flowers with a deep purple base. **'Pickwick'** has grey-white flowers striped with violet and with a deep violet base. **'Purpureus Grandiflorus'** (syn. *C.* 'Purpureus') has slightly smaller flowers of intense violet-purple and is very free-flowering. **'Remembrance'** has rounded violet flowers with a silvery sheen above a dark base.

AUTUMN-FLOWERING CROCUSES

C. asturicus see *C. serotinus* ssp. *salzmannii*

C. banaticus ♀ Flowering in early autumn, this unusual crocus has lilac flowers whose inner petals are considerably smaller and paler than the outer ones. It needs a humus-rich soil that does not completely dry out in summer. The leaves are broader than normal, 6 mm (¼ in) wide, and appear after the flowers. Native to Romania, Ukraine and Serbia. HEIGHT 12 cm (4¾ in).

C. boryi ♀ The large flowers of this mid autumn-flowering corm are usually white, occasionally lightly veined with purple. The leaves appear at the same time as the flowers. Native to Greece, it should be kept dry in summer, so is best grown in an alpine house. HEIGHT 11 cm (4¼ in).

C. cartwrightianus ♀ Widely opening lilac flowers are heavily veined with purple and have long, branching, bright red stigmas. They appear in mid to late autumn. The leaves appear at the same time as the flowers. Native to Greece, it can be grown in a sunny position in the garden, though it flowers best in an alpine house. HEIGHT 8-10 cm (3¼-4 in).

'Albus' ♀ has pure white flowers.

C. clusii see *C. serotinus* ssp. *clusii*

C. goulimyi ♀ This delicate crocus bears 4 cm (1½ in) long, pale lilac flowers on tall perianth tubes in mid autumn. The leaves are present at flowering time. Easily grown in well-drained gritty soil in full sun, or an attractive crocus for an alpine house. Native to S Greece. HEIGHT 18 cm (7 in).

C. hadriaticus ♀ This vigorous crocus, native to Greece, is easily grown outside in a well-drained soil in full sun. However, the white flowers, with their striking scarlet stigmas, are easily damaged by bad weather. The leaves are present at flowering time, mid to late autumn. HEIGHT 9 cm (3½ in).

C. kotschyanus ssp. ***kotschyanus*** ♀ (syn. *C. zonatus*) The flowers have cream stamens and pale lilac petals, which are lightly veined with purple and have a central yellow ring inside. They appear in mid autumn before the leaves. An easily grown crocus with distinctive irregular corms, it only flowers well after a hot dry summer, and does best in a gritty soil in full sun. Native to Turkey. HEIGHT 8 cm (3¼ in).

C. laevigatus **'Fontenayi'** Small fragrant flowers, 3 cm (1¼ in) long, appear in early winter at the same time as the leaves. The outer petals of the lilac flowers have heavy dark purple stripes. An easily grown crocus, it can be naturalised, but flowers best in a sunny spot in a rock garden. Native to Greece. HEIGHT 7.5 cm (3 in).

C. longiflorus ♀ The 1 or 2 scented flowers, which appear with the leaves in mid autumn, are lilac, often veined with purple. Best in an alpine house. Native to S Italy, Malta and Sicily. HEIGHT 10 cm (4 in).

▼ *Crocus vernus* cultivars

C

▲ *Crocus kotschyanus* ssp. *kotschyanus*

*C. **medius***♀ This striking crocus has rounded flowers, usually of deep purple, with a scarlet stigma, in mid autumn. Leaves emerge as the flowers fade and may be damaged in a hard winter. Native to S France and NW Italy. HEIGHT 10cm (4in).

▲ *Crocus medius*

*C. **niveus*** This is one of the largest autumn-flowering crocuses, bearing flowers up to 5cm (2in) long in mid autumn. They are white or pale lilac with a deep yellow throat. The leaves are present at flowering time. Native to S Greece, it is best grown in an alpine house. HEIGHT 15cm (6in).

*C. **nudiflorus*** The pale to deep purple, solitary, slender flower of this crocus appears in early to mid autumn before the leaves. The corms are stoloniferous and should be planted in a well-drained position where they may spread if left undisturbed. They can be grown in light grass. Native to NE Spain and SW France, and naturalised in parts of Britain where it was grown as a source of saffron. HEIGHT 10-15cm (4-6in).

*C. **ochroleucus***♀ Creamy white, slender flowers with yellow throats, just 2cm (¾in) long, are borne in late autumn. The leaves of this small crocus have usually just emerged at flowering time. Native to Israel, Lebanon and Syria, it is easily grown in well-drained soil. HEIGHT 5-8cm (2-3¼in).

*C. **pulchellus***♀ The open, goblet-shaped flowers are pale lilac-blue with faint darker veining and a yellow throat. With cream anthers, they appear in mid autumn before the leaves. A vigorous crocus, preferring a drier position and best in a sunny border, where it may freely seed. Native to the Balkans and Turkey. HEIGHT 18cm (7in).

'Zephyr'♀ has very large flowers of pale lilac, grows to 20cm (8in) and is sterile.

▲ *Crocus pulchellus*

*C. **sativus*** (saffron crocus) The large, 3cm (1¼in) long, widely opening flowers are a rich purple with darker veins. The striking scarlet stigma is the source of the saffron for which this species has long been cultivated. The leaves are present in mid autumn at flowering time. This sterile crocus, not in fact a wild species, requires deep, 15cm (6in), planting in rich soil in full sun to encourage it to flower. Origin unknown but naturalised in the Mediterranean area and N India. HEIGHT 10cm (4in).

*C. **serotinus*** ssp. ***clusii***♀ (syn. *C. clusii*) Rich purple, rounded flowers appear in mid and late autumn with the leaves. The earlier flowering ssp. ***salzmannii*** (syn. *C. asturicus*) has pale lilac flowers. Both subspecies are easily grown in any well-drained soil in full sun. Native to Portugal, Spain and N Africa. HEIGHT 12cm (4¾in).

*C. **speciosus***♀ This very vigorous crocus has an exceptionally long flowering period – from early to late autumn. The flowers vary in colour from blue-purple to lilac-blue or white and appear before the leaves. Increasing rapidly by both offsets and seedlings, it is a crocus that naturalises easily in grass. Native to N Turkey and N Iran. HEIGHT 15-20cm (6-8in).

'Aitchisonii' has very large lavender-violet flowers. **'Albus'**♀ has pure white blooms. **'Conqueror'** is very vigorous with lavender-blue flowers.

*C. **tournefortii***♀ Pale lilac flowers, occasionally lightly veined with purple, come out in late autumn after the leaves have appeared. They have white anthers and a multibranched, scarlet stigma. Once open the flowers do not close again. Best in an alpine house. Native to S Greece and Crete. HEIGHT 7-10cm (2¾-4in).

*C. **zonatus***
see *C. kotschyanus* ssp. *kotschyanus*

CULTIVATION Plant crocus corms in well-drained soil in full sun, 7-12cm (3-5in) deep and 5-8cm (2-3in) apart. Plant them in clumps at the front of a sunny border or in a rock garden – in late summer for autumn-flowering species and in autumn for spring-flowering species. Some of the smaller species with their delicate flowers are best grown in a gritty compost in pans in an alpine house, or in a bulb frame where they can also be kept dry during their

▲ *Crocus tournefortii*

summer dormancy. The most vigorous species, such as *C. speciosus*, *C. tommasinianus* and *C. vernus*, are suitable for naturalising in grass under trees. *C. banaticus* requires a humus-rich soil. To force cultivars of *C. chrysanthus* and *C. vernus* for indoor decoration, fill a container with corms in autumn. Plant them just below the surface of the potting compost – use bulb fibre if your container has no drainage holes. Place the pots in a cold dark place, or plunge outside, until the shoots are well grown, then bring them indoors.

PROPAGATION Remove offsets from the corms when the leaves wither, or sow freshly gathered ripe seed.

PESTS AND DISEASES Mice and voles eat crocus corms, especially newly planted ones. Birds may damage the flowers.

Crossandra

Acanthaceae

High temperatures and humidity are essential for these free-flowering perennials from the rain forests of E Africa, S India and Sri Lanka. They have glossy leaves and large flowers emerging from tight heads of bracts, and are happiest in a warm conservatory.

RECOMMENDED SPECIES AND VARIETIES

*C. **infundibuliformis*** (firecracker plant) Salmon-orange flowers, 3cm (1¼in) wide and roughly tubular, are produced in succession from spring to autumn from a 4cm (1½in) tall tight green spike on the tips of leafy shoots. The dark green, oval to lance-shaped leaves are up to 12cm (4¾in) long and pointed with slightly wavy margins. The plant is fairly slow growing. HEIGHT & SPREAD 45×30cm (18×12in).

'Mona Walhead' is a relatively reliable dwarf form to 30cm (12in) high. The flowers are more salmon-pink than orange.

CULTIVATION Grow in good light but out of direct sun. Maintain humidity by placing the pots on trays of gravel or pebbles and growing with other plants. During the growing season feed regularly, maintain

▲ *Crossandra infundibuliformis* 'Mona Walhead'

22-25°C (72-77°F) and keep moist but not wet. Deadhead to encourage more blooms and repot annually. In winter, ensure a minimum of 13°C (55°F) and water only enough to stop the compost drying out.
PROPAGATION Take 5-8 cm (2-3 in) long softwood cuttings in spring or early summer. Dip in rooting powder and root over bottom heat; flowering plants should be produced within months.
PESTS AND DISEASES Red spider mite, whitefly and mealy bug may attack.

Crowfoot see *Ranunculus*
Crown imperial see *Fritillaria imperialis*

Cryptanthus
Earth star
Bromeliaceae

Cryptanthus zonatus

Striking foliage is the main attraction of these evergreen, rosette-forming, tropical perennials from Brazil. If grown under the right conditions, small clusters of tubular white flowers appear from the centre of each rosette during summer. They require good but indirect light, some humidity and a minimum temperature of 13°C (55°F).
RECOMMENDED SPECIES AND VARIETIES
C. acaulis (green earth star) Lance-shaped leaves up to 15 cm (6 in) long are arranged in a neat rosette. They are bright green above and grey and scaly beneath, with toothed edges. The flowers are fragrant. HEIGHT & SPREAD 10×20 cm (4×8 in).

The foliage of var. ***ruber*** is flushed red.
C. bivittatus♀ Broad lance-shaped, wavy leaves, up to 20 cm (8 in) long with toothed margins, form loose, flat rosettes. The leaves are green, banded lengthways with coppery buff stripes. Can be grown as a houseplant. HEIGHT & SPREAD 15×30 cm (6×12 in).

'Pink Starlight'♀ has mid green leaves with a strong deep pink suffusion. It is less likely to flower than the species.
C. bromelioides (rainbow star) The strap-shaped, finely toothed, wavy leaves are olive-green banded with grey and buff above, greyish and scaly beneath. They grow to 20 cm (8 in) long. HEIGHT & SPREAD 20×45 cm (8×18 in).

▼ *Cryptanthus bivittatus* 'Pink Starlight'

▲ *Cryptanthus bromelioides* var. *tricolor*

The leaves of var. ***tricolor*** are striped cream and green with a rose-pink flush.
C. zonatus (zebra plant) This houseplant species has loose rosettes of strap-shaped, wavy, finely toothed leaves up to 20 cm (8 in) long. They are dark green and brown, banded irregularly with silver-grey or cream, flushed with pinkish brown. HEIGHT & SPREAD 15×40 cm (6×16 in).

The leaves of var. ***argyraeus*** are strongly marked with silver.
CULTIVATION Grow indoors or in a greenhouse in a well-lit position out of direct sunlight. Plant in pots of free-draining compost mixed with equal parts of coir or composted bark. Water freely during spring and summer and feed with a general liquid fertiliser. Water sparingly during winter.
PROPAGATION Detach young suckering rosettes with a piece of root in the spring and pot up.
PESTS AND DISEASES Mealy bug and scale insect can be major problems.

Cryptomeria
Japanese cedar
Taxodiaceae

Cryptomeria japonica 'Elegans'

The branches of this graceful evergreen conifer are densely covered in tiny needle-like leaves. Striking reddish brown bark peels from mature trees in long strips. The Japanese cedar is hardy and grows best in a moist, acid soil. It is fast growing and rather too tall for most gardens, but there are a number of elegant smaller cultivars available. There is just one species.
Cryptomeria japonica♀ A broadly columnar tree with sweeping branches. The pointed, needle-like leaves are bright green, sometimes grey-green, and may have a bronzy tint in winter. Mature trees bear rusty brown cones 2 cm (¾ in) across. The green female flowers appear in small tight clusters at the tips of the new shoots in spring. Yellow-brown male flowers are hidden in the leaf axils. HEIGHT & SPREAD 10×2.4 m (33×8 ft) after 20 years, ultimately 30 m (100 ft) tall.

'Bandai-sugi'♀ is a slow-growing dwarf tree, rounded when young but maturing into an irregularly shaped bush reaching 2 m (6½ ft) tall. The dense blue-green foliage bronzes well in cold winters. **'Cristata'** forms a conical tree, growing to 15 m (50 ft) tall. Many of the branchlets and shoot tips are twisted into cockscomb-like crests. **'Elegans'** forms a beautiful rounded tree with soft feathery foliage that is blue-green in summer, bronze-red or purple in winter and pale silvery green in spring. The weeping lower branches layer freely. Reaches a height of 10 m (33 ft). **'Elegans Aurea'**, growing to 5 m (16 ft) tall, has yellow-green foliage that turns bronze in winter. **'Elegans Compacta'**♀, a dwarf up to 2 m (6½ ft) tall, has extremely soft and feathery foliage that turns deep purple in winter. **'Sekkan-sugi'**, a slow-grower up to 10 m (33 ft) tall, has creamy yellow new shoots. **'Spiralis'**, also known as 'granny's ringlets', is a slow-growing shrub which eventually makes a dense, broadly conical bush 2 m (6½ ft) high. Bright green leaves are twisted spirally around the shoots. **'Vilmoriniana'**♀ is a

▲ *Cryptomeria japonica* 'Cristata'

▼ *Cryptomeria japonica* 'Sekkan-sugi'

C

slow-growing dwarf conifer, reaching only 80cm (32in) tall and suitable for a rock garden. The dense, light green foliage is tinged reddish brown in winter.

CULTIVATION Plant in moist acid soil. Japanese cedars withstand cold, but may need shelter when young.

PROPAGATION Raise the species from seed. Take cuttings of the cultivars in spring or autumn.

PRUNING Not usually required.

PESTS AND DISEASES Honey fungus can be a problem.

Ctenanthe

Marantaceae

Often brightly coloured leaves with a distinct pointed tip distinguish these elegant and fairly robust houseplants, native to the Brazilian rain forest. They enjoy the soft light and temperate conditions of a sunless warm room and combine well with other leafy tropicals and orchids. The species described is one of the most graceful foliage houseplants and fairly easy to care for.

RECOMMENDED SPECIES AND VARIETIES

C. oppenheimiana Tall purple-brown stems up to 1m (3ft) long carry silver-grey leaves with neat, dark green curving stripes running from the midrib to the margins. The leaves are 30cm (1ft) long, 10cm (4in) wide and shaped rather like a paddle. They have a red-purple-brown underside which is attractive when backlit. Inconspicuous purple-brown flowers are occasionally produced. In warm conditions the leaves move to face the light, and growth can be rapid. HEIGHT & SPREAD 150×30cm (5×1ft).

'Tricolor'♀ (never-never plant) Much shorter leaf stalks produce a smaller plant 70cm (28in) high. The leaves are strongly marked with cream, light green and dark green and the back of the leaf is dark red.

▼ *Ctenanthe oppenheimiana* 'Tricolor'

CULTIVATION Place in good indirect light if possible. Lower light is tolerated, however, especially if plants can be given brighter conditions for several months a year. Humidity is required in a warm room but unnecessary at normal indoor temperatures. Avoid direct sunlight and hot dry air which rapidly cause leaf scorching. A minimum of 20°C (68°F) is needed for growth. Ctenanthes remain in good condition for years at lower temperatures, but growth is minimal. In the growing season, keep the compost just moist and feed frequently. In winter, maintain at least 13°C (55°F), though *C. oppenheimiana* can survive to 10°C (50°F), and let the compost dry out slightly between waterings. Repot when new shoots press against the edge of the pot.

PROPAGATION Divide clumps of mature plants in spring.

PESTS AND DISEASES Red spider mite is the main problem.

Cuckoo flower see *Cardamine pratensis*
Cuckoopint see *Arum maculatum*
Cucumber see VEGETABLES p.738
Cup and saucer vine see *Cobaea*

Cuphea

Lythraceae

A free-flowering habit and neat foliage make these small shrubby perennials valuable conservatory plants. Native to tropical and sub-tropical Central and S America, they are not frost-hardy, though in summer they can be moved outdoors to a sunny sheltered spot in their containers. The plants described below are all evergreen and have an upright branching habit. They are often short-lived plants, but replacements are easily raised from cuttings.

RECOMMENDED SPECIES AND VARIETIES

C. cyanaea Orange-red tubular flowers, up to 2.5cm (1in) long, are borne from early summer to late autumn among mid green, oval, pointed leaves. HEIGHT & SPREAD 60×60cm (2×2ft).

C. hyssopifolia♀ (false heather) Small star-like flowers, pale purple, pink or white, are freely produced over a long period in summer and autumn. The glossy dark green leaves are small and very narrow. HEIGHT & SPREAD 60×75cm (2×2½ft).

▼ *Cuphea hyssopifolia*

▲ *Cuphea ignea*

C. ignea♀ (cigar plant) Flowering from seed in its first year, the plant has tubular scarlet flowers about 2.5cm (1in) long, each with a black tip edged white. These are very freely produced from spring to autumn. If grown on as a conservatory or greenhouse plant it eventually makes a small bushy shrub. It is hardy enough to be used as a summer bedding plant in sheltered conditions. HEIGHT & SPREAD 30×30cm (1×1ft), 60-90cm (2-3ft) tall if grown on.

CULTIVATION In a greenhouse or conservatory, a minimum winter temperature of 7°C (45°F) is adequate. Prune in late winter, cutting the stems back by about two-thirds. Move outside only when all risk of frost has passed. Space bedding plants of *C. ignea* about 20cm (8in) apart.

PROPAGATION Take softwood cuttings in late spring. Sow seed in a heated greenhouse in late winter or early spring with a bottom heat of 20-23°C (68-73°F).

PESTS AND DISEASES Whitefly may trouble plants grown under glass. Cupheas are also susceptible to powdery mildew.

Cupid's dart see *Catananche*

x Cupressocyparis

Cupressaceae

x *Cupressocyparis leylandii*

These tall columnar conifers make magnificent specimen trees. They are hardy and fast growing, so be careful when choosing a variety for hedging as many are too vigorous for this purpose.

RECOMMENDED SPECIES AND VARIETIES

x *C. leylandii* (syn. 'Leighton Green') (Leyland cypress) The fastest-growing conifer in Britain, this tree forms a dense upright column, tapering gently to a fine point. The scale-like leaves are borne in flattened, drooping sprays, dark green above

▲ x *Cupressocyparis leylandii* 'Castlewellan'

and paler green below. Very small flowers appear in tiny clusters at the tips of the shoots in mid to late spring. Small round cones are occasionally produced.

Trees of 35m (115ft) tall and up to 10m (33ft) wide have been recorded after only 60 years – making this tree suitable for only the largest of gardens.

'Castlewellan' (syn. 'Castlewellan Gold', 'Galway Gold') is slower growing, forming a more regular column with a flattened top. The foliage is coarser and starts golden yellow, maturing to greenish yellow with bronzing tips. Trees of 30 years are 15m (50ft) high and 3m (10ft) wide all the way up. **'Gold Rider'**♀ is a stronger yellow than 'Castlewellan' with finer foliage which does not turn brown at the tips in full sun. It reaches 3m (10ft) tall and 1m (3ft) wide after 10 years. **'Robinson's Gold'**♀ is similar to 'Castlewellan', with old-gold foliage.

▲ x *Cupressocyparis leylandii* 'Robinson's Gold'

CULTIVATION Plant in acid to neutral soils. Be warned that the trees will steal all nutrients, moisture, and eventually light from any plants in their vicinity. Never buy a tree from a nursery that is taller than 45cm (1½ft) as it is likely to be pot-bound and will die when planted out.
PROPAGATION Take semi-ripe cuttings in spring or autumn. Rooting takes about 12 weeks if bottom heat and a 50/50 peat and sharp sand mixture are used.
PRUNING Choose 'Castlewellan' or 'Robinson's Gold' for hedging as they are slower growing. They will need clipping four times a year in spring and autumn.
PESTS AND DISEASES Canker and honey fungus can kill the trees. Drought is also a major threat to the thirsty Leyland cypress.

Cupressus
Cypress
Cupressaceae

Plumes of green, blue or gold foliage give a feathered outline to these slender evergreen conifers. The plumes consist of dense sprigs of tiny, scale-like, aromatic leaves. Clusters of small yellow flowers are borne from late winter to early spring. Round cones, up to 4cm (1½ in) across, are borne in profusion. They are green at first, becoming brown and woody in the second year and may remain on the tree for several years. The flaking bark is red to brown. The plants recommended are among the hardiest of a genus that prefers milder climates. *Cupressus torulosa* 'Cashmeriana', with long pendulous branches and blue-grey foliage, is a handsome conifer, but is not reliably hardy in this country.

RECOMMENDED SPECIES AND VARIETIES
C. arizonica var. *glabra* (smooth Arizona cypress) The blue-grey foliage of this narrowly conical tree has white resin flecks on the undersides. HEIGHT & SPREAD 3×1m (10×3ft) after 10 years, ultimately 20m (66ft) tall.

'Blue Ice' has silvery blue foliage. **'Conica'** has glaucous blue foliage carried on plentiful, but loosely arranged, branchlets. **'Pyramidalis'**♀ has blue-grey foliage borne on dense branches. This narrow conical tree comes into its own in mid to late winter, when it is covered in a profusion of bright yellow male flowers.

▲ *Cupressus arizonica* var. *glabra* 'Pyramidalis'

C. macrocarpa (Monterey cypress) Vigorous growth and a marked broadening with age makes the species too large for most gardens, but excellent cultivars have been developed from it. HEIGHT & SPREAD 15×3m (50×10ft) after 10 years, ultimately 25m (80ft) tall.

'Donard Gold'♀ is a columnar tree with deep yellow foliage. Mature trees reach a height of 15m (50ft) and tend to lean.

▲ *Cupressus macrocarpa* 'Donard Gold'

'Gold Spread'♀, up to 1m (3ft) tall, is a wide-spreading ground-cover plant forming a superb golden carpet. It is not suitable for cold gardens. **'Goldcrest'**♀ is a narrow, conical tree growing to 15m (50ft) tall with rich golden yellow foliage.
C. sempervirens (Italian cypress) The narrow, upright tree carries erect sprays of dark green leaves. HEIGHT & SPREAD 2m×50cm (6½ft×20in) after 10 years, ultimately 30m (100ft) tall.

'Green Spire' (**'Green Pencil'**) has bright green foliage. It is a hardy tree, very slender and tapering to a sharp point. **'Swane's Gold'**♀ has golden foliage. It is a compact columnar tree, up to 4m (13ft) tall, better suited to small gardens and containers. It is tender, however, so avoid cold, windy and frosty sites.
CULTIVATION Plant in mid to late autumn or early to mid spring in any well-drained soil in a sunny position away from cold, drying, easterly winds. The yellow-leaved varieties require an open position. Stake young trees for the first few years.
PROPAGATION Take cuttings in spring or autumn and place in a coldframe or on a bench with bottom heat.
PRUNING None required except to remove diseased branches.
PESTS AND DISEASES Phytophthora and canker may cause problems.

Currant, edible see FRUIT p.725
Currant, ornamental see *Ribes*

▼ *Cupressus sempervirens* 'Swane's Gold'

C

Cyananthus

Trailing bellflower

Campanulaceae

Cyananthus lobatus

Generous displays of blue, violet, white or yellow flowers appear in early autumn on these low-growing, spreading herbaceous perennials. The tubular flowers splay out into five large petals and are carried at the tips of stems bearing small alternate leaves. Native to the Himalayas, cyananthus plants are hardy in Britain and suitable for rock gardens and troughs. They only do well in cooler, northern regions

RECOMMENDED SPECIES AND CULTIVARS

C. lobatus♀ Bright blue flowers, up to 4 cm (1½ in) across with very hairy dark calyxes, are borne from late summer to early autumn. The stems carry pale green, deeply lobed, rounded leaves up to 1.5 cm (½ in) long. HEIGHT & SPREAD 10×40 cm (4×16 in).

The flowers of **'Albus'** are almost white. **'Dark Beauty'** has dark blue flowers. **'Sherriff's Variety'**, the most beautiful of all, has very large pale azure flowers.

C. microphyllus♀ Violet-blue flowers, up to 2.5cm (1 in) across with dark-hairy calyxes, appear in late summer and early autumn. The thyme-like leaves are no more than 5 mm (¼ in) long. HEIGHT & SPREAD 5×20 cm (2×8 in).

▲ *Cyananthus microphyllus*

CULTIVATION Plant in well-drained but moist, humus-rich, lime-free soil. Avoid siting the plants in full sun.

PROPAGATION Sow seed when ripe or in winter in pots in a coldframe. Take late summer cuttings, overwinter the plantlets in a coldframe and plant out in late spring.

PESTS AND DISEASES Slugs may attack emerging shoots and flowers.

Cyathodes

Epacridaceae

Cyathodes colensoi

Their colourful new growth earns the heath-like cyathodes a place in the garden. The genus ranges from prostrate shrubs to small trees, all native to Australasia and Polynesia. Only one species is much grown in Britain, *Cyathodes colensoi*, a low-growing evergreen shrub. It is ideal for a rock garden or peat border, thriving in acid soil and hardy in all but the severest gardens, down to a temperature of -5°C (23°F).

RECOMMENDED SPECIES

C. colensoi Narrow oblong leaves, about 8 mm (⅜ in) long, clothe the erect stems. New leaves have pinkish tips; mature leaves are bluish green. Erect clusters of between 3 and 5 small, white, tubular flowers are carried at the tips of the new growth in spring. Male and female flowers occur on separate plants, and fruit sets on females only if plants of both sexes are grown. The berries, rarely produced in cultivation, are white to deep pink or red, round and up to 5 mm (¼ in) in diameter. Native to New Zealand. HEIGHT & SPREAD 20×30 cm (8×12 in) after 5 years, ultimately 45 cm (18 in) tall.

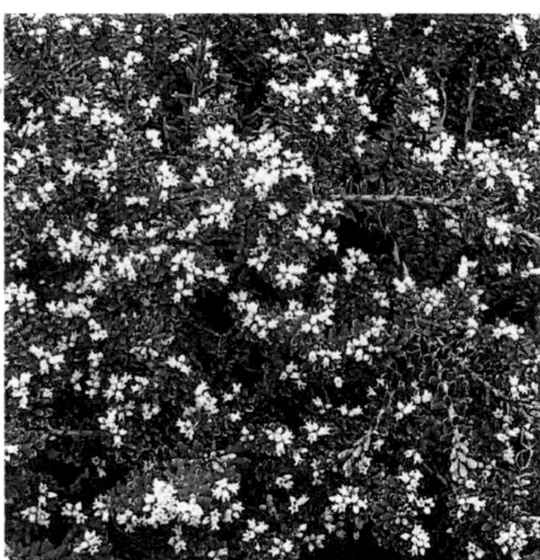

▲ *Cyathodes colensoi*

CULTIVATION Plant *C. colensoi* in moist, humus-rich, well-drained and acid soil. Choose a sheltered position in partial shade, though full sun is tolerated in cooler areas where the soil remains moist in summer.

PROPAGATION Take semi-ripe cuttings in mid to late summer and root in a peat and sand mixture or in a gritty compost, with bottom heat.

PRUNING Not necessary except to tidy straggly shoots. This is best carried out immediately after flowering.

PESTS AND DISEASES Usually trouble free.

Cyclamen

Primulaceae

Elegant flowers in shades of pink, mauve, crimson or white rise above rounded or heart-shaped leaves, often finely marbled with silver or white. The flowers have reflexed petals, gracefully curved backwards, and many are fragrant. By carefully selecting species according to flowering period, these beautiful, low-growing plants can be in bloom during most months of the year, and their patterned foliage sustains a long period of interest. Not all are hardy but several of the finest are fully hardy, flowering even in the depths of winter.

The hardy cyclamen are excellent for naturalising in groups among trees and shrubs. They thrive in sun or part shade. A border devoted to one species can be an interesting and colourful feature in the garden. Cyclamen are also good for pockets in a rock garden or for growing in troughs and containers. The less hardy types are perfect for pot culture in an unheated greenhouse. The florist's cyclamen, *Cyclamen persicum*, is an outstanding pot plant.

The rootstock of the cyclamen plant is a tuber, with leaves and flowers borne from the upper surface. Dried tubers are often sold, but planting is more successful from plants 'in the green' – growing in pots – as the tubers can dry out too much.

There are 20 species, which are mainly native to central and S Europe, the Mediterranean and Turkey eastwards to the Caucasus and N Iran.

RECOMMENDED SPECIES AND VARIETIES

C. africanum The flowers of this autumn-blooming cyclamen are pale to deep pink, with a magenta-purple, V-shaped mark at the base of each petal. The flowers usually appear before the leaves. These are heart-shaped and dark green or grey-green on the upper surface, patterned with silvery grey or cream. Not frost-hardy. HEIGHT & SPREAD 12.5×15 cm (5×6 in).

C. cilicium♀ Flowering in late summer and autumn, the plant is hardy in most winters and can be grown outside in mild areas. Flowers are pale to mid pink, with a magenta or purple blotch at the base of each

▲ *Cyclamen cilicium*

petal. The unlobed oval leaves have a heart-shaped base and are deep green, patterned with grey or creamy white above. HEIGHT & SPREAD 7×12.5cm (2¾×5in).

The flowers of f. ***album*** are pure white. It is a plant that comes true from seed.

C. coum♀ One of the finest species for the open garden, this hardy plant flowers from mid winter to early spring. The flowers are pale pink to rose or magenta, with an M-shaped purple or magenta mark at the base of each rounded petal. The rounded to kidney-shaped, unlobed leaves have a heart-shaped base and vary in colour. They can be deep green, either plain or with a well-marked pattern in paler green, grey or silver, or they may be silver or pewter overall. HEIGHT & SPREAD 6×15cm (2½×6in).

▲ *Cyclamen coum* 'Album'

'Album' has white flowers with a purple or magenta blotch at the base of each petal. The leaves are plain deep green. **Pewter Group**♀ has leaves that are pewter above, often with a green midrib or margin. The flowers are in shades of pink or magenta.

C. cyprium Sweetly scented flowers appear from autumn to early winter – white or very pale pink with a small M-shaped magenta blotch at the base of each petal. The leaves are broadly heart-shaped and deep grey-green with grey, silver or cream patterning. The plant needs frost protection and should be grown in a cold greenhouse. HEIGHT & SPREAD 7.5×12.5cm (3×5in).

C. europaeum see *C. purpurascens*

C. graecum Flowering in late summer and autumn, this cyclamen is an excellent plant for a deep pot. The flowers are pale to deep pink, or reddish purple, with purple or magenta line markings at the base of each petal. The heart-shaped leaves are a deep velvety green, but are very variable in coloration and patterning, often beautifully marked with grey or silver above. The plant needs a really dry summer dormancy to flower, and thrives outside only in mild areas at the base of a sunny wall. Plant the tubers 10-15cm (4-6in) deep. HEIGHT & SPREAD 12.5×15cm (5×6in).

▲ *Cyclamen graecum*

The flowers of f. ***album*** are pure white and it comes true from seed.

C. hederifolium♀ (syn. *C. neapolitanum*) This hardy cyclamen, flowering in late summer and autumn, has pale to deep pink

▲ *Cyclamen hederifolium*

▲ *Cyclamen hederifolium* 'Album'

flowers, up to 2cm (¾in) long. The leaves are deep grey-green above with a well marked pattern in grey, cream or silver. They are generally heart shaped but vary. HEIGHT & SPREAD 15×23cm (6×9in).

The flowers of **'Album'** are pure white.

C. intaminatum A delightful small species for troughs and raised beds, where it seeds itself once it is established. The tiny flowers, borne in late summer and autumn, are white or very pale pink, with pale grey veins. The rounded leaves are plain green or attractively patterned with silvery white. HEIGHT & SPREAD 6×9cm (2½×3½in).

C. latifolium see *C. persicum*

C. libanoticum♀ The flowers of this cyclamen bloom from late winter to early spring. They are white or very pale pink with a

▲ *Cyclamen intaminatum*

▲ *Cyclamen libanoticum*

magenta or crimson mark at the base of each broad petal, and have a peppery scent. The broadly heart-shaped leaves are deep grey-green mottled with grey or white. In mild areas it may be grown outside in a sheltered spot. HEIGHT & SPREAD 7.5×15cm (3×6in).

C. mirabile♀ Appearing from late summer to autumn, the pale pink flowers of this hardy cyclamen have toothed petals. The rounded leaves have a scalloped margin, often with a deep pink flush on the upper surface when young. The plant is generally grown in pots in a cold greenhouse. HEIGHT & SPREAD 6×12.5cm (2½×5in).

C. neapolitanum see *C. hederifolium*

C. persicum (florist's cyclamen) (syn. *C. latifolium*) The many varieties developed from this species are most commonly grown as houseplants, flowering from late winter to spring. The scented flowers may be white, pink, mauve, purple or red. The paler ones usually have a rose-pink nose. The heart-shaped leaves are deep green or grey-green, and plain or patterned in grey, cream or silver. The wild form makes an excellent pot plant for a cold greenhouse or conservatory. Some varieties are hardier than others but few are frost-hardy and a minimum temperature of 5°C (41°F) is recommended. The numerous large-flowered

C

▲ *Cyclamen pseudibericum*

florist's types appear in a great variety of colours, some with frilled or bearded petals; most require higher temperatures. Modern selections include miniature varieties in a full range of colours – white, pink, mauve, lavender, purple, rose, red, carmine, crimson and scarlet – as well as bicolours and feathered colours. HEIGHT & SPREAD 15-30×15-30cm (6-12×6-12in).

*C. **pseudibericum***♀ Fragrant pink flowers appear in early spring. There is a white ring around the mouth of each bloom and the petals have a dark purple mark at the base. The leaves are heart-shaped and dark green with attractive silver-green markings. Moderately hardy, this species thrives in a dry position in a rock garden, and is also suitable for growing in a cold greenhouse. HEIGHT & SPREAD 12×10cm (4¾×4in).

▲ *Cyclamen purpurascens*

*C. **purpurascens***♀ (syn. *C. europaeum*) A hardy cyclamen, this plant bears very fragrant, rich carmine flowers from mid summer to early autumn. The rounded leaves are mid green with faint silvery green markings. Thrives in alkaline soil. HEIGHT & SPREAD 10×10cm (4×4in).

*C. **repandum*** ssp. ***repandum***♀ Scented, deep carmine-magenta flowers are borne in mid to late spring by this frost-hardy cyclamen, which grows outside in most areas of Britain. The heart-shaped leaves have scalloped edges and are deep green with a well-marked pattern in grey-green or silver. HEIGHT & SPREAD 12.5×15cm (5×6in).

'Album' has pure white flowers.

*C. **trochopteranthum*** Primrose-scented, propeller-shaped flowers, borne from late winter to spring, vary in colour from pale to deep pink or magenta pink. The leaves have a scalloped margin and are very variable in markings. Although hardy, this cyclamen is more often grown in pots than in the open. HEIGHT & SPREAD 6×15cm (2½×6in).

CULTIVATION The hardy cyclamen, mainly *C. cilicium*, *C. coum*, *C. hederifolium*, *C. intaminatum*, *C. purpurascens* and *C. repandum*, do well in a variety of soils so long as they are well drained. The ideal soil is moist and humus-rich. Annual top dressings of leaf-mould or garden compost, as well as bone meal, are beneficial. Plant tubers 2.5-5cm (1-2in) deep, except those of *C. repandum*, which should be buried at twice this depth, and *C. graecum* at 10-15cm (4-6in) deep. Plant cyclamen tubers at any time, though the best time is just before they start into growth in late summer and early autumn. Do not disturb the plants for several years after they have been planted, but seedlings can be removed.

Species grown in pots need well-drained humus-rich compost. The tuber should be planted close to the surface, except for *C. repandum*, which should be halfway down the pot. Increase watering as plants come into growth in late summer and autumn. As the leaves begin to yellow and die down in spring, watering should be gradually withheld. Water cyclamen in pots from the base. Few species (except *C. cyprium*, *C. graecum* and *C. persicum*) benefit from a complete summer bake; aim to give a little water through the summer months but never soak the compost during this period.

PROPAGATION Sow seed as soon as it is ripe – in mid to late summer. Older, dried seed germinates eventually, particularly if given a soak in warm water for 12 hours before sowing. Place the sown pots in complete darkness to speed germination and move them into the light as soon as germination has occurred. Prick out the seedlings when the first true leaf appears. Alternatively, leave the pots for a year, then prise the small tubers apart and pot them up individually.

Aim to keep the seedlings growing right through their first year if possible. Weak liquid feeds through the growing season benefit both seedlings and mature plants.

PESTS AND DISEASES The prime pests of cyclamen are aphids, vine weevils and root eelworms. Diseases include bacterial rot of the tubers and virus diseases; in these cases infected plants should be destroyed. Grey mould may attack fading flowers or leaves, especially during autumn and winter. Any portion infected should be removed to prevent the spread of the disease to other parts of the plant, especially the tuber.

Cydonia

Quince

Rosaceae

Cydonia oblonga

White or pale pink spring flowers, yellow autumn foliage and golden aromatic fruit are among the chief attributes of these handsome deciduous trees with crooked branches. In colder regions, quince trees require the protection of a wall for the fruit to ripen. The flowers, up to 5cm (2in) across, appear in late spring and have five rounded petals surrounding a mass of yellow stamens. The fruit is edible with firm but rather gritty flesh, and only palatable when cooked. There is only one species, native to W Asia.

Cydonia oblonga (common quince) This spreading tree bears ovate to elliptic leaves up to 7.5cm (3in) long, which are dark green above, greyish and hairy beneath; they turn rich yellow in autumn. White to pale pink flowers appear in spring. The pear-shaped fruits, up to 10cm (4in) long, are golden yellow when ripe and strongly aromatic. HEIGHT & SPREAD 4×3m (13×10ft) after 10 years, ultimately 6m (20ft) tall.

'Meech's Prolific' bears bright golden fruit of excellent flavour, which ripen in mid autumn. **'Vranja'**♀ has strongly fragrant golden yellow fruit. Both these cultivars reach a mature height of 5m (16ft).

▲ *Cydonia oblonga* 'Meech's Prolific' (flower)

CULTIVATION Plant from mid autumn to early spring in a sunny spot in any fertile soil, preferably one that is rich and loamy. In cooler regions, provide the shelter of a south or west-facing fence or wall. Harvest fruit in mid autumn and store in a cool but frost-free place.

PROPAGATION Bud graft onto quince 'A' rootstock in summer.

PRUNING In winter, cut out any dead, diseased or crossing shoots.

PESTS AND DISEASES Brown rot, mildew and honey fungus can all be a problem.

Cymbalaria
Scrophulariaceae

Cymbalaria muralis

Small white, violet or purple flowers are borne all summer long on thread-like stems. The flowers are around 1.5cm (½in) long and flare out at the mouth into two rounded lips. These creeping, evergreen to herbaceous, hardy perennials, suitable for rock gardens, are native to S and W Europe.

RECOMMENDED SPECIES AND VARIETIES

C. hepaticifolia (syn. *Linaria hepaticifolia*) The lilac or violet flowers have darker markings in the throat. The hairless leaves, about 2.5cm (1in) long, have pale veins and are mostly rounded, occasionally lobed. HEIGHT & SPREAD 2×40cm (¾×16in).

C. muralis (syn. *Linaria cymbalaria*) (ivy-leaved toadflax) Long trailing stems bear lilac or violet flowers with a yellow patch on the lower lip and darker markings. The 1.5cm (½in) long leaves, usually have 3-5 lobes. HEIGHT & SPREAD 2×60cm (¾×24in).

'Nana Alba' is more compact and produces numerous white flowers. **'Pallidior'** has white flowers with a yellow throat.

C. pallida (syn. *Linaria pallida*) Large pale mauve, sometimes white, flowers are about 2.5cm (1in) long. The rounded or lobed leaves, 2.5cm (1in) long, are prettily veined. HEIGHT & SPREAD 2×20cm (¾×8in).

▲ *Cymbalaria muralis* 'Nana Alba'

Cymbalaria pilosa ▲

C. pilosa (syn. *Linaria pilosa*) The pale lilac flowers have yellow markings on the lower lip. The kidney-shaped leaves, to 1cm (⅜in) long, have 5-11 lobes and are covered with soft hairs. The plant forms a spreading carpet. HEIGHT & SPREAD 2×35cm (¾×14in).

CULTIVATION Plant in shade or partial shade in moist but well-drained soil.

PROPAGATION Sow seed in winter or transplant rooted stems. Cymbalaria self-seeds prolifically and can be invasive

PESTS AND DISEASES Usually trouble free.

Cymbidium see ORCHIDS p.466

Cynara
Compositae

The large, arching leaves of cynaras are of great architectural value to a border, and from late summer to mid autumn the plants produce large thistle-like flowers. The species described below is a herbaceous perennial, native to the Mediterranean and N Africa, and is not completely hardy in colder parts of Britain

RECOMMENDED SPECIES

C. cardunculus♀ (cardoon) Solitary flowerheads are carried on branching stems above large, divided leaves. Each flowerhead consists of numerous slender florets protruding from spiny bracts and is up to 5cm (2in) across. The flowers may be blue or purple, occasionally white. The leaves are bright green above and downy white beneath, thick lobed, spiny and toothed, growing to about 50cm (20in) long and 35cm (14in) wide. Also grown as a vegetable. HEIGHT & SPREAD 1.5m×60cm (5×2ft).

▲ *Cynara cardunculus*

CULTIVATION Plant in well-drained soil in spring, preferably in a sunny position.

PROPAGATION Sow seed in spring and plant out as soon as the plants are large enough to handle.

PESTS AND DISEASES Aphids can infest the young flowerheads. Slugs may attack young shoots in late winter or early spring.

Cynoglossum
Hound's tongue
Boraginaceae

Cynoglossum nervosum

Sprays of forget-me-not-like flowers, usually blue but sometimes white, pink or purple, are borne from late spring to early autumn by these hardy biennials and herbaceous perennials. Cynoglossums often have hairy or bristly leaves and stems.

▲ *Cynoglossum amabile*

RECOMMENDED SPECIES

C. amabile♀ (Chinese forget-me-not) A biennial flowering in mid summer, it is usually treated as an annual to fill gaps in the herbaceous border. Seed sown under glass in autumn will provide plants to decorate conservatories in the early part of the year. The flowers can be white, pink or blue. The coarse leaves are grey-green. Native to E Asia. HEIGHT & SPREAD 60×30cm (2×1ft).

C. nervosum A succession of intense blue flowers, 1cm (⅜in) across, appears in open sprays from early to late summer on a compact, clump-forming perennial. The narrow leaves are mid green and hairy. Native to NW India and Pakistan. HEIGHT & SPREAD 1m×30cm (3×1ft).

C. officinale In the garden this biennial British native can be naturalised on the margins of wooded areas or on gravelly soil; it also grows well near the sea. Sprays of dark purple flowers are borne from late spring to late summer. HEIGHT & SPREAD 1m×38cm (3×1¼ft).

CULTIVATION Cynoglossums grow best in moderately fertile, well-drained but moist soil in a sunny spot. Perennial species such as *C. nervosum* tolerate some shade. Plants may need supporting. Cut down dead stems in mid autumn.

PROPAGATION Sow biennials for the open border in late summer and plant them out in spring. Divide *C. nervosum* in spring.

PESTS AND DISEASES Usually trouble free.

Cypress, Hinoki
see *Chamaecyparis obtusa*
Cypress, Italian
see *Cupressus sempervirens*

Cypress, Lawson
see *Chamaecyparis lawsoniana*
Cypress, Leyland
see × *Cupressocyparis leylandii*
Cypress, Patagonian
see *Fitzroya cupressoides*
Cypress, Sawara
see *Chamaecyparis pisifera*
Cypress, smooth Arizona
see *Cupressus arizonica* var. *glabra*
Cypress, swamp
see *Taxodium distichum*
Cypripedium see ORCHIDS p. 464

Cyrtanthus
Fire lily
Amaryllidaceae

Large funnel-shaped flowers, colourful and often scented, appear from spring to autumn. Including both deciduous and evergreen bulbous perennials, the fire lilies, native mainly to South Africa, vary in hardiness. *Cyrtanthus elatus* is evergreen and hardy enough for a warm sheltered garden in Britain. Elsewhere it is best grown in pots in a cool greenhouse. As a houseplant, it thrives on a windowsill in indirect sunlight.

RECOMMENDED SPECIES

C. elatus (syn. *C. purpureus*, *C. speciosus*, *Vallota speciosa*) (Scarborough lily, George lily) Slightly fragrant, scarlet flowers, 10 cm (4 in) across, appear from mid summer to early autumn in a cluster of 6-9 at the top of a thick stem. Each flower has whitish markings in the throat. Bright green, strap-shaped basal leaves, up to 45 cm (1½ ft) long, surround the flowering stem. The bulb is poisonous. HEIGHT 30-60 cm (1-2 ft).

▲ *Cyrtanthus elatus*

CULTIVATION Plant in a loam-based compost with added sharp sand and leaf-mould, in a sheltered and well-drained position in the garden, or in a similar mixture in pots. Pot-bound plants flower best.

PROPAGATION Sow seed in spring or divide bulbs in late autumn after flowering.

PESTS AND DISEASES Mealy bugs sometimes infest cyrtanthus plants.

Cyrtomium see FERNS p. 262

Cytisus
Broom
Leguminosae

Small pea-like flowers swathe brooms in sheets of yellow, cream, orange or red, between late spring and early summer. Brooms range from prostrate shrubs to small trees, and many have a graceful spreading form, with slender branches and delicate green leaves.

Each flower has five petals: an upper petal known as the standard, two narrow lateral petals called the wings and two lower petals termed the keel. The flowers, usually 1-2 cm (⅜-¾ in) long, are borne singly or in clusters. The leaves are tiny, generally about 5 mm (¼ in) long and 2 mm (⅛ in) wide.

All plants described here are deciduous and in many species new leaves remain on the plant for only a few months. They are mostly hardy, preferring sandy soils and plenty of sun. Brooms are short-lived, however, lasting ten years or so before they die or become unattractively leggy, especially on heavy or poorly drained soils. Native to Europe, Asia Minor and N Africa.

RECOMMENDED SPECIES AND VARIETIES

Listed plants are divided into two groups: low-growing shrubs and larger shrubs.

LOW-GROWING SHRUBS

C. ardoinii Bright yellow flowers smother this dense semi-prostrate shrub. The tiny grey-green leaves are trifoliate and hairy. HEIGHT & SPREAD 10×30 cm (4×12 in) after 3 or 4 years, ultimately 20 cm (8 in) tall.

C. × beanii Deep golden yellow flowers are borne in arching sprays singly or in clusters of up to 3. This is a semi-prostrate plant with mid green, hairy, linear leaves. HEIGHT & SPREAD 30×60 cm (1×2 ft) after 3 or 4 years, ultimately 40 cm (16 in) tall.

C. 'Cottage' A profusion of creamy yellow flowers and trifoliate mid green leaves are borne by this low-growing, upright broom. HEIGHT & SPREAD 30×40 cm (12×16 in) after 3 or 4 years, ultimately 40 cm (16 in) tall.

▲ *Cytisus × beanii*

C. × kewensis Masses of pale sulphur-yellow flowers are borne on a low spreading shrub. Trifoliate mid green leaves grow along the downy stems. HEIGHT & SPREAD 30 cm×1 m (12×36 in) after 3 or 4 years, ultimately 40 cm (16 in) tall.

LARGER SHRUBS

C. battandieri (Moroccan broom, pineapple broom) Pineapple-scented, golden yellow flowers are carried in conical clusters, up to 10 cm (4 in) tall, from late spring to mid summer. Silky white hairs cover the young shoots and large trifoliate leaves, giving the plant a silvery appearance. This is a broom of upright, almost tree-like habit, growing best against a south-facing wall. Plant it as a freestanding shrub only in southern Britain, in full sun. HEIGHT & SPREAD 3×3 m (10×10 ft) after 3 or 4 years, ultimately 4 m (13 ft) tall.

C. 'Burkwoodii' This vigorous, upright broom bears numerous flowers with cerise standards and deep crimson wings edged with yellow. The lance-shaped, silvery grey leaves grow only sparsely. Do not plant in

▲ *Cytisus* 'Cottage'

very acid or very alkaline soils. HEIGHT & SPREAD 1.8×1.5m (6×5ft) after 3 or 4 years, ultimately 3m (10ft) tall.

C. **'Fulgens'** Orange-yellow and crimson flowers, 2cm (¾in) long, cover a dense, compact plant. The insignificant leaves, usually trifoliate, are 6-15mm (¼-½in) long. HEIGHT & SPREAD 1.2×1.2m (4×4ft) after 3 or 4 years, ultimately 1.8m (6ft) tall.

C. **'Golden Cascade'** This broom has golden yellow flowers 3cm (1¼in) long, a graceful, semi-weeping habit of growth and small, mostly trifoliate leaves. HEIGHT & SPREAD 1.5×1.4m (5×4½ft) after 3 or 4 years, ultimately 1.8m (6ft) tall.

C. **'Hollandia'**♡ Pale cream and cerise standards contrast with darker cerise wings on small flowers up to 12mm (½in) long. The plant has a lax habit of growth and mainly trifoliate leaves. HEIGHT & SPREAD 1.5×1.5m (5×5ft) after 3 or 4 years, ultimately 2.4m (8ft) tall.

C. **'Killiney Salmon'** Salmon-red flowers with orange wings are borne on a compact upright plant. The leaves are usually trifoliate. HEIGHT & SPREAD 1.2×1.2m (4×4ft) after 3 or 4 years, ultimately 1.5×1.5m (5×5ft).

▲ *Cytisus* 'Killiney Salmon'

C. **'Lena'**♡ Red and yellow flowers are freely produced on an upright compact plant. The leaves are dark green and trifoliate. HEIGHT & SPREAD 1.2×1.2m (4×4ft) after 3 or 4 years, ultimately 1.8m (6ft) tall.

C. **'Minstead'**♡ Slender arching branches are covered with clouds of small ivory-white flowers with purple wings. The insignificant leaves are mostly trifoliate. HEIGHT & SPREAD 1.2×1.2m (4×4ft) after 3 or 4 years, ultimately 1.8m (6ft) tall.

C. ***multiflorus***♡ (white Spanish broom) Graceful arching branches carry cascades of white flowers in feathery sprays. The grey-green leaves are up to 1.5cm (½in) long, the upper leaves simple and the lower ones trifoliate. A bushy species of upright habit. HEIGHT & SPREAD 1.6×1.5m (5¼×5ft) after 3 or 4 years, ultimately 2.4m (8ft) tall.

C. ***nigricans*** This broad, rounded broom bears bright yellow flowers from mid summer to early autumn. Sweetly scented, helmet-shaped flowers, 2.5cm (1in) long, are carried in slender erect spikes. The leaves are small, mid green and trifoliate. HEIGHT & SPREAD 1×1m (3×3ft) after 3 or 4 years, ultimately 1.5m (5ft) tall.

C. **'Porlock'**♡ Fragrant, butter-yellow flowers appear as early as mid winter when this hybrid is grown against a warm wall in southern Britain or in a conservatory. The plant is hardy in mild areas: in cold gardens it requires wall protection. The flowers are borne singly or in clusters of up to 4. The light green, trifoliate leaves are semi-evergreen and about 1.5cm (½in) long. HEIGHT & SPREAD 1.8×1.4m (6×4½ft) after 3 or 4 years, ultimately 3m (10ft) tall.

C. × ***praecox*** Pale yellow flowers are profusely borne in mid and late spring along the length of the arching stems of this compact shrub. They appear before the silky, grey-green, short-lived leaves. HEIGHT & SPREAD 1×1m (3×3ft) after 3 or 4 years, ultimately 1.2 (4ft) tall.

'Albus' has white flowers. **'Allgold'**♡ bears deep yellow flowers on arching sprays and is slightly taller. **'Warminster'**♡ has long-lasting, sulphur-yellow flowers with an acrid smell.

▲ *Cytisus* × *praecox* 'Allgold'

C. ***scoparius*** (common broom) Rich yellow, 2.5cm (1in) long flowers are freely produced, singly or in pairs, by this upright, rounded broom. Bright green branches give an evergreen effect in winter. The tiny mid green leaves are trifoliate at the base of the shoots, but simple above. Native to Britain. HEIGHT & SPREAD 1.5×1.5m (5×5ft) after 3 or 4 years, ultimately 1.8m (6ft) tall.

An arching shrub, f. ***andreanus***♡ has bright yellow and rich crimson flowers, which grow along elegant green branchlets.

C. **'Windlesham Ruby'** Large ruby-red flowers, 2.5cm (1in) long, grow singly or in pairs on slender arching stems. The mainly trifoliate leaves grow to 1.5cm (½in) long. HEIGHT & SPREAD 1.5×1.2m (5×4ft) after 3 or 4 years, ultimately 1.6m (5¼ft) tall.

C. **'Zeelandia'**♡ Flowers about 7mm (¼in) across, with lilac and cream standard petals, pink wings and cream keels, are carried in long, lax, arching sprays. The leaves are mostly trifoliate. HEIGHT & SPREAD 1.2×1.2m (4×4ft) after 3 or 4 years, ultimately 1.5m (5ft) tall.

CULTIVATION Plant brooms in autumn or spring, in any well-drained, ordinary but not too rich soil, in full sun. Most brooms, though not *C. scoparius*, tolerate lime.

PROPAGATION Raise species from seed sown in spring. The cultivars do not come true from seed, so take semi-ripe cuttings with a heel in late summer. Pot up cuttings and seedlings as soon as possible, and pinch out at 25cm (10in) high for bushy plants.

PRUNING Brooms that flower in spring on the previous year's wood may be cut back hard immediately after flowering. Take care not to cut into old wood. *C. nigricans*, which flowers later in the year on growth of the current season, may be pruned hard in spring before growth begins. Again, take care not to cut into old wood. After flowering, cut off the flowered portions of the stems. Pruning is only necessary, though, to keep plants within bounds. They are more elegant in habit, and flower more profusely, if left unpruned. The low-growing brooms just want light trimming to keep in shape.

PESTS AND DISEASES Usually trouble free.

▲ *Cytisus* × *praecox* 'Warminster'

d

Daboecia

St Dabeoc's heath
Ericaceae

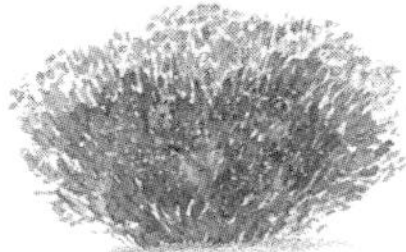

Daboecia cantabrica

A long flowering period and evergreen foliage earn this heath a place in any garden with a neutral to acid soil. The first flush of flowers, in early summer, is followed by a second in early autumn, which lasts until the first frosts. The pendent urn-shaped flowers range in colour from white through lavender to deep purple. Plants are useful for ground cover and for growing with other dwarf shrubs, such as *Genista hispanica*, in a mixed border or traditional heather bed. The listed plants are hardy, but may suffer winter damage if they are planted in clay soils or frost pockets. The sizes given are for five to seven-year-old plants that have been regularly pruned after flowering.

RECOMMENDED SPECIES AND VARIETIES

D. cantabrica Lavender flowers, 1 cm (⅜in) long, appear on one-sided spikes from early summer to mid autumn. The alternate leaves are glossy dark green above and white beneath. They are lance shaped and about 1.5cm (½in) long. This sprawling sub-shrub is improved by annual pruning. HEIGHT & SPREAD 40×70cm (16×28in).

Flowers of plants grouped under f. ***alba*** are white. **'Atropurpurea'** has deep purple flowers. **'Bicolor'**♀ bears combinations of white, pink, dark red or striped flowers. **'David Moss'**♀ is a free-flowering white. **'Hookstone Purple'** has large amethyst flowers, lasting until late autumn. **'Polifolia'** has pale mauve flowers and greyish green foliage. **'Praegerae'**, with cerise flowers, often sheds its leaves in winter. Compact **'Waley's Red'**♀ has magenta flowers.

D. x scotica Many flowers appear from early summer to late autumn on this hybrid. The glossy dark green leaves are smaller than those of *D. cantabrica*. HEIGHT & SPREAD 20×45cm (8×18in).

'Jack Drake'♀ produces ruby flowers. **'Silverwells'**♀ has white flowers. **'William Buchanan'**♀ carries deep crimson flowers.

CULTIVATION Plant deeply in autumn so that the lower leaves touch the soil surface in well-drained neutral to acid soil that is not too dry. Choose an open, sunny site away from deciduous trees. Keep well watered during the first spring and summer.

PROPAGATION Take semi-ripe heel cuttings in mid summer.

PRUNING Deadheading is beneficial, otherwise prune annually to the base of the dead flowers in late spring.

PESTS AND DISEASES Usually trouble free.

▲ *Daboecia cantabrica*

Daboecia cantabrica 'Praegerae' ▲

Dactylorhiza

Marsh orchid
Orchidaceae

Dactylorhiza foliosa

Dense, erect cylindrical spikes of flowers, mainly in shades of pink and purple, brighten a woodland border or damp meadow area between late spring and mid summer. Dactylorhizas are among the easiest of hardy orchids to grow. Each hooded flower, up to 2cm (¾in) long, has a three-lobed lip patterned with darker dots and streaks. The stiff stems also carry spiralled leaves, often narrow, which are 10-25cm (4-10in) long and sometimes marked with dark spots or dashes. Native to Europe, Asia, N America and N Africa.

RECOMMENDED SPECIES AND VARIETIES

D. elata♀ Deep purple-magenta flowers appear in early summer. The plain mid to deep green leaves are lance-shaped. HEIGHT & SPREAD 75×30cm (2½×1ft).

D. foliosa♀ (syn. *D. maderensis*) Deep maroon-purple flowers are produced in early summer. The deep green lance-shaped leaves are unspotted. HEIGHT & SPREAD 60×30cm (2×1ft).

▲ *Dactylorhiza elata*

▲ *Dactylorhiza foliosa*

D. fuchsii (common spotted orchid) Flowers, in white, pinks and mauves, are borne from late spring to mid summer. The mid green leaves are linear to linear-lanceolate and spotted with purple. This species will clump up well in gardens and often self seeds. HEIGHT & SPREAD 60×30cm (2×1ft).

D. latifolia see *D. majalis*

D. maculata (heath spotted orchid) White to pink, mauve or red flowers are carried from late spring to early summer. The ovate to linear-lanceolate leaves may be plain bright green or coarsely spotted with purple. HEIGHT & SPREAD 50×20cm (20×8in).

D. maderensis see *D. foliosa*

D. majalis (syn. *D. latifolia*) (marsh orchid) Pink to lilac or magenta flowers are held in egg-shaped to cylindrical spikes from late spring to early summer. The ovate to ovate-lanceolate leaves are mid to dark green in colour, plain or spotted. HEIGHT & SPREAD 45×30cm (1½×1ft).

CULTIVATION Plant in any moist, humus-rich soil in an open yet fairly sheltered site, in full sun or partial shade.

PROPAGATION Lift and carefully prise apart the clusters of tubers in autumn, after the plants have died down. Pull the tubers into one-shoot pieces.

PESTS AND DISEASES Vine weevils and eelworm may attack the tubers. Slugs, snails and rabbits may eat emerging shoots. The plants may suffer from various viral diseases.

Daffodil see *Narcissus*

Dahlia

Compositae

The dazzling choice offered by dahlias in the way of flower shape, size and colour makes them outstanding both in the garden and as cut flowers. They are easy to grow and flower long and late, from mid summer to the first autumn frosts

Some of these frost-tender herbaceous perennials have flowers with a single row of petals around a central disc; there are also the popular ball and pompon varieties with spherical flowerheads, the star-like flowerheads of the cactus dahlias, the collerette dahlias with inner rings of contrasting petals, and even plants with blooms resembling anemones, water lilies or orchids.

Almost all dahlias currently grown are hybrids originally derived from cross-breeding wild species. There are now over 20000 hybrid varieties, available in many different shades of white, yellow, orange, pink, red and purple – but never blue. The dahlia is native to Central and S America, as far south as Colombia. It was the Spanish who brought the first specimens to Europe, to the botanic gardens of Madrid.

Flowers vary in size from the 30cm (12in) wide blooms of giant decorative dahlias to 2.5cm (1in) wide pompons. In single-flowered varieties, the petals, more correctly called ray florets, surround a central disc made up of disc florets. In double varieties, the petals completely cover the central disc. The flowers generally grow in

1 *D.* 'Hillcrest Royal'
2 *D.* 'Superfine'
3 *D.* 'Kathleen's Alliance'
4 *D.* 'Barbarry Snowball'
5 *D.* 'Wootton Cupid'
6 *D.* 'Jeanette Carter'
7 *D.* 'Jescot Julie'
8 *D.* 'Fashion Monger'
9 *D.* 'Chimborazo'
10 *D.* 'Small World'
11 *D. coccinea* 'Bishop of Llandaff'
12 *D.* 'Trengrove Jill'
13 *D.* 'Pearl of Heemstede'

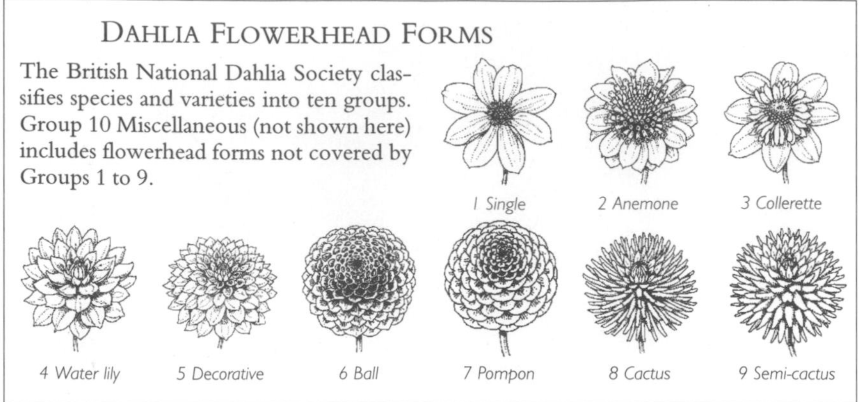

clusters, most often of three blooms, but they are sometimes borne singly. There is a flowerbud at the end of each stem, and side buds on very short stalks just below.

Plants are erect and bushy, with leaves as long as 40cm (16in), which are divided into several pairs of oppositely arranged ovate leaflets, up to 15cm (6in) long. The foliage is mostly mid to dark green, but a few varieties have bronze, copper or purple leaves.

Varieties of all kinds can be planted in beds and borders, with dwarf varieties primarily used as bedding plants and sometimes planted in pots or tubs. The dark foliage adds depth and body to planting schemes and the flowers themselves provide concentrated colour at a time when many other plants are past their best. Group dahlias together or intersperse them with other plants – but take care that they do not overwhelm more modest neighbours.

Dahlias will tolerate almost any soil and a certain amount of shade. To give of their best, however, they need a site in full sun, with a soil that is free-draining but at the same time retains moisture.

In Britain the clusters of tuberous roots attached to the bases of the old stems are normally lifted in autumn and stored in frost-free conditions until the following spring. Only in the mildest areas is it reasonably safe to leave the root system where it is, and treat the plant as a hardy perennial. The shoot growth of the following season arises from buds around the bases of the old stems. Some dwarf varieties can be grown annually from seed.

RECOMMENDED SPECIES AND VARIETIES

The genus can be divided into two groups:

- Species
- Hybrid varieties

SPECIES

D. coccinea Eight red petals are arranged in a single row around a central yellow disc on the 8cm (3¼in) wide flowers of this freely branching plant. Each petal is narrowly oval, tapering to a blunt tip. There are also varieties with yellow or orange petals. HEIGHT & SPREAD 120×60cm (4×2ft).

'Bishop of Llandaff'♀ differs chiefly in the colour of its foliage, a very deep red.

D. merckii Small lilac-petalled flowers with maroon central discs grow on slender stems. The single flowers are about 5cm (2in) across. This plant has a tendency to spread. HEIGHT & SPREAD 90×60cm (3×2ft).

The variety **'Alba'** bears white flowers.

HYBRID VARIETIES

The British National Dahlia Society classifies varieties into ten groups. This system of classification is used by all nurseries in Britain and in many other countries too. Within these ten groups, varieties are divided according to flower size, from giant-flowered to miniature-flowered.

Plant heights and spreads are within the range 90-140×60-100cm (36-56×24-40in), except where stated otherwise.

▲ *Dahlia* 'Bishop of Llandaff'

▲ *Dahlia* 'Preston Park'

▲ *Dahlia* 'Yellow Hammer'

Group 1 Single flowered

A single row of broad petals, or 2 rows, surround a central disc, on a flower about 8cm (3¼in) across. Plants in this group are mostly dwarf varieties, suitable for bedding.

'Coltness Gem Hybrids' have a wide colour range, reach heights of 45-60cm (18-24in), and can be grown from seed.

Dahlia 'Coltness Gem Hybrids'

'Preston Park'♀ has flowers with scarlet petals and golden discs. The flowers of **'Yellow Hammer'**♀ are a rich yellow, with orange discs. Both have dark purple leaves and reach a height of 45cm (18in) or so.

Group 2 Anemone flowered

One or more rows of broad petals surround a tuft of smaller, closely packed florets, presenting a pincushion-like appearance. Flowers are about 8cm (3¼in) wide.

'Lemon Puff' has white and yellow flowers and grows to 75cm (30in).

Group 3 Collerette dahlias

A single row of broad petals encircles an inner 'collar' of shorter florets, usually in a contrasting colour, which surrounds a central disc. Flowers are 10-15cm (4-6in) across. Collerette varieties are among the best for cutting.

The first colour given is for the outer ring of petals, the second for the inner ring. **'Chimborazo'** has dark maroon and yellow flowers; **'Christmas Carol'** has red and cream flowers; **'Clair de Lune'**♀ has yellow and cream flowers; **'Dandy'**, a mixture raised from seed, produces flowers of various colours and grows to only 50-60cm (20-24in) tall; **'Elizabeth Snowdon'** has pink and white flowers; **'Fashion Monger'** has flowers with outer petals striped red and yellow, and cream centres; **'La Cierva'** has purple and white flowers.

Group 4 Water lily flowered

These dahlias have fully double flowers with broad, almost flat, petals and a strong similarity to water lilies. The stems are long and stiff, and varieties within the group are among the most popular for cutting.

Varieties, all with small flowers 10-15cm (4-6in) wide, include: **'Gerrie Hoek'** (pink), **'Glorie van Heemstede'**♀ (yellow), **'John Street'**♀ (red), **'Kyoto'** (red and white), **'Pearl of Heemstede'**♀ (pink) and **'Yelno Harmony'**♀ (apricot-orange).

Group 5 Decorative flowered

Flowers are fully double, with broad, flattish petals usually bluntly pointed.

Giant-flowered varieties, with flowers 25cm (10in) wide and over, include: **'Almand's Climax'**♀ (lilac and white) and **'Hamari Gold'**♀ (bronze).

▲ *Dahlia* 'Glorie van Heemstede'

▲ *Dahlia* 'Hamari Gold'

Large-flowered varieties, with flowers 20-25 cm (8-10 in) wide, include **'Elma E'** with pink flowers.

Medium-flowered varieties, with flowers 15-20 cm (6-8 in) wide, include **'Keith's Choice'** (red), **'Neal Gillson'** (bronze), **'Thomas Edison'** (purple) and **'Trengrove Jill'** (bronze).

Small-flowered varieties, with flowers 10-15 cm (4-6 in) wide, include: **'Arabian Night'** with dark reddish purple flowers; **'Edinburgh'** with purple flowers tipped white, and **'Hamari Fiesta'** with yellow flowers tipped red.

Miniature-flowered varieties, flowers under 10 cm (4 in) wide, include: **'Abridge Bertie'** with purple flowers; **'Berliner Kleene'** with pink blooms, only 40 cm (16 in) tall; **'David Howard'**♀ with orange-yellow flowers and darker green foliage than is usual; **'Jeanette Carter'**♀ (yellow) and **'Karenglen'**♀ (red).

Group 6 Ball flowered

Flowers are ball-shaped, fully double and 5-15 cm (2-6 in) across. The sides of the ray florets curve inwards for more than half their length, have blunt tips and are arranged spirally.

Small-flowered varieties, with flowers 10-15 cm (4-6 in) wide, include **'Jessie G'** with red flowers.

▲ *Dahlia* 'David Howard'

▲ *Dahlia* 'Pearl of Heemstede'

▲ *Dahlia* 'Hillcrest Royal'

Miniature-flowered varieties, with flowers that are under 10 cm (4 in) wide, include: **'Barbarry Snowball'** with white flowers; **'Periton'** with red flowers, and **'Wootton Cupid'**♀ with pink flowers marked with cream.

Group 7 Pompon dahlias

These plants have flowers that are also ball-shaped, but smaller – no more than 5 cm (2 in) across. The tightly packed florets curve inwards along their whole length. Plants flower profusely. Although the flowers are so small, plant heights and spreads are within the usual range.

Recommended varieties include: **'Brilliant Eye'** (bright red), **'Moor Place'** (purple), **'Wendy's Place'** (light purple), **'Johann'** (red), **'Minley Linda'** (orange-red), **'Pomponette'** (pink), **'Pop Willo'** (apricot), **'Pride of Berlin'** ('Stolze von Berlin') with pink flowers suffused with lilic, and **'Small World'** (white).

Group 8 Cactus flowered

Varieties in this group have fully double flowers with the petal margins rolled back, or quilled, for over half their length. The petal tips are pointed, giving the flowers a spiky appearance.

Medium-flowered varieties, with flowers that are 15-20 cm (6-8 in) wide, include **'Banker'** (orange-red) and **'Hillcrest Royal'**♀ (purple-red).

Small-flowered varieties, with flowers 10-15 cm (4-6 in) wide, include: **'Dana Iris'**♀ (red), **'Kathleen's Alliance'**♀ (purplish pink), **'Pink Paul Chester'**♀ (pink), **'Doris Day'** (red) and **'Superfine'** (yellow).

▼ *Dahlia* 'Jeanette Carter'

▲ *Dahlia* 'Pink Paul Chester'

Group 9 Semi-cactus flowered

Flowers are intermediate in form between those of true cactus-flowered varieties and the flat-petalled decorative varieties. The petals are broader than those of cactus flowered varieties and quilled for half their length or less.

Giant-flowered varieties, with flowers over 25 cm (10 in) wide, include **'Evening Mail'**♀ (yellow) and **'Rose Jupiter'** (pink).

Dahlia 'Hamari Accord'

Large-flowered varieties, with flowers 20-25 cm (8-10 in) wide, include: **'Hamari Accord'**♀ (yellow), **'Kenora Challenger'**, (white) and **'Show and Tell'** (red).

Medium-flowered varieties, with flowers 15-20 cm (8-10 in) wide, include: **'Hillcrest Albino'**♀ (white), **'Hit Parade'** (red), **'Pink Pastelle'**♀ (pink) and **'Wootton Impact'**♀ (bronze).

Small-flowered varieties, with flowers 10-15 cm (4-6 in) wide, include: **'My Love'** (creamy white), **'Scottish Relation'**♀ (dark pink) and **'Star's Favourite'** (pale pink).

Miniature-flowered varieties, with flowers that are less than 10 cm (4 in) wide,

▲ *Dahlia* 'Wootton Impact'

▲ *Dahlia* 'Hillcrest Albino'

▲ *Dahlia* 'Hamari Accord'

include: **'Andries' Amber'** (orange-bronze flowers), **'Andries' Orange'** (orange) and **'Kenora Petite'** (pink).

Group 10 Miscellaneous

The most notable dahlias in this category are *D. coccinea* and *D. merckii* (described above), the dwarf miniature-flowered Lilliput Group, dwarf bedding dahlias with semidouble or double flowers, and orchid flowered varieties.

Lilliput (syn. Baby) dahlias are no more than 40cm (16in) tall and produce tiny flowers up to 3cm (1¼in) wide in abundance. They can be grown outside in pots and tubs. **'Inflammation'** (orange) and **'Omo'** (white) are good examples.

Dwarf bedding dahlias include: **'Bednall Beauty'** with dark red double flowers and deep bronze-purple foliage; **'Ellen Houston'**♀ with double scarlet flowers and purple foliage, and **'Longwood Dainty'** with apricot flowers. 'Bednall Beauty' grows to 60cm (24in) tall and 'Ellen Houston' and 'Longwood Dainty' both reach 40cm (16in). All three are propagated from cuttings. Normally raised from seed are **'Diablo'** and **'Redskin'**, both bronze-foliaged mixtures around 40cm (16in) tall, as is **'Figaro'**, only 30cm (12in) tall. All have semidouble and double blooms.

Orchid flowered varieties have fewer petals than others, and the petal margins are rolled back, like the petals of cactus flowered dahlias. The flowers are less regular than in other variety groups, giving them a distinctive, somewhat orchid-like appearance. The variety **'Jescot Julie'** is orange with the reverse side of the petals purple.

CULTIVATION Dahlias need well-drained rich soil and full sun to achieve their potential. They will withstand poorer soils, however, so long as they are not badly drained. Avoid sites in shadow for much of the day.

Before planting, fork a general-purpose fertiliser into the top 15cm (6in) of the soil, at the rate of 140-200g per m^2 (4-6oz per sqyd). As the shoots grow, tie them to a cane or stake. Only dwarf bedding dahlias do not need support.

Dahlias may be planted as unsprouted tubers, tubers with established shoot growths present, or young plants raised from cuttings or seed. Plant unsprouted tubers in mid or late spring, 8-10cm (3¼-4in) below the soil surface. Keep all other dahlia planting material in pots in a greenhouse or a coldframe, or in a sheltered spot outdoors,

▼ *Dahlia* 'Ellen Houston'

protecting overnight with a covering such as newspaper or horticultural fleece. Only plant out when all risk of frost has passed.

CARE AFTER PLANTING

Shortly after planting, 'stop' the plant by removing the stem growing point, snapping the young stem just above the fifth pair of leaves. Shoots will then grow from each point on the stem to which a leaf is attached, and a bushy plant should develop.

Water heavily in dry weather, and mulch around plants, to prevent moisture evaporating from the soil surface. Feed plants in summer, especially if they are on light soils. The ideal method is a weekly liquid feed. Alternatively, apply a general-purpose garden fertiliser in mid summer, at the rate of 100g per m^2 (3oz per sqyd), and water in.

For larger-flowered dahlias and varieties grown for cutting, disbudding is worthwhile. Flower buds usually develop in threes at the stem ends. Retain the central bud, the largest, and snap off the two just below it. The remaining flower will grow to a larger size, and bloom unchallenged on its own stem. For a longer clear stem, also remove the two sideshoots that arise from the first leaf joint below the flower stalk.

Remove dying flowers to enhance the plant's appearance and encourage it to produce more shoots and flowers. Deadhead bedding dahlias by simply plucking off the flowers, but remove flower stalks as well from larger varieties, using a knife.

STORING TUBERS OVER WINTER

Once autumn frost has blackened plants, cut through the stems about 15cm (6in) above soil level. Only in the mildest areas of

Britain and on freely drained soil can dahlias be left in the ground over winter. In which case, apply a thick mulch after cutting back.

In other conditions, the tuberous roots must be dug up and stored every autumn. Gently lift the tuber clusters, removing as much soil as possible. Place these clusters upside down in a frostproof greenhouse or shed and allow the hollow stem bases to drain and any soil to dry out. Shake off the soil, then dip the tuber clusters in a fungicide solution as a protection against botrytis (grey mould). Dry the clusters again. Next, arrange them in single layers, close together and the right way up, in boxes or trays, surrounded with peat, sand or almost dry soil, leaving the crowns exposed. (The crown is where the tubers arise from the base of the previous season's stem.)

Keep the open containers in a cool, frostproof shed, loft, garage or greenhouse. If temperatures fall below freezing, place them inside larger boxes, packing the space between with newspaper or straw, and loosely covering the whole. Inspect the tubers from time to time – cut away any portions infected with fungus and treat the exposed surfaces with fungicide.

PROPAGATION With hybrid dahlia varieties, take cuttings or replant the divided tuber sections, because they do not come true from seed. The seed of pompon, cactus and large-flowered dahlias is available, but results are varied, generally including a proportion of single and semidouble flowers.

Dwarf bedding dahlias come sufficiently true for raising from seed to be the usual method, but not always. Of the listed dwarf bedding dahlias, 'Bednall Beauty', 'Ellen Houston', 'Longwood Dainty', 'Preston Park' and 'Yellow Hammer' can only be perpetuated by means of cuttings or tubers.

Dahlia species are raised from seed, from replanted tuber sections or from cuttings.

PROPAGATION BY SEED
Sow seed in a heated greenhouse in early spring, ensuring a temperature of at least 15°C (60°F) in the seed compost. Alternatively, germinate seeds in a suitable place in the home, such as an airing cupboard, moving the seedlings to a greenhouse, with better light, as soon as they emerge. When raising plants in an unheated greenhouse or coldframe, proceed in the same way but put off sowing until mid spring.

Prick out the seedlings at least 8cm (3¼in) apart in a box, or singly into 9cm (3½in) pots. Harden off in readiness for planting out as soon as the risk of frost has ended.

PROPAGATION BY DIVISION OF TUBERS
Plants grown from tubers bloom earlier than those grown from cuttings, especially if the tubers are sprouted in a greenhouse before being planted out. These flower about 6 weeks after planting, depending on the variety and the early summer weather.

Unsprouted tubers may be planted in their final flowering positions in mid or late spring. Cut each tuber crown into at least two portions, each with one or more shoot buds. If the shoot buds cannot be identified, start the tubers into growth first. A temperature of 13°C (55°F) is warm enough to bring them into growth, with a thorough watering. If necessary, tubers can be kept in a poorly lit, even dark place, but divide and plant out before the shoot buds elongate and become spindly.

For sprouted tubers, start the tubers into growth by moving them into a frost-free greenhouse or coldframe in mid spring. Keep home-grown tubers in the containers in which they spent the winter. Keep purchased tubers in trays or pots, in potting compost. Take care that the crowns are left exposed. Water thoroughly and ensure there is plenty of light. When shoots are clearly visible, divide the tuber clusters as described above. Plant each division in its own pot, to grow on in readiness for planting. Once there is no risk of frost, plant out in the flowering positions

PROPAGATION BY CUTTINGS
The largest flowers are produced on plants grown from cuttings. It is on these plants that flowering into autumn is best sustained. Use this method to multiply stock, since every tuber produces a number of shoots, each of which can be used as a cutting.

Treat tubers to be used for cuttings in the same way as those that are to be divided. Take cuttings once shoots have reached a length of about 7.5cm (3in) from base to growing point. Cut just above the point at which the shoot arises from the crown of the tuber cluster. Then cut through the stem of the shoot just below the lowest leaf joint, where a pair of small leaflets arises. Dip the cutting base in a rooting hormone powder, and insert it 2.5cm (1in) deep into a pot of rooting compost.

Water in and, in the absence of special propagation facilities, place the pots on a sunny windowsill. Once the pots are filled with roots, move young plants to larger containers and eventually harden off for planting out after the last spring frost.

PESTS AND DISEASES Dahlias are generally trouble free, but the following problems may arise. Botrytis (grey mould) can cause tubers in storage to decay. In a greenhouse, aphids and red spider mites may infest young plants. Slugs attack dahlias that have recently been planted out. Later in the summer aphids, capsid bugs and earwigs may give trouble. Flowers that become diseased in a wet summer should be removed without delay. Destroy plants infected with viruses such as dahlia mosaic, causing stunted growth, and cucumber mosaic, causing yellow mottled foliage, both of which are carried by aphids.

Daisy see *Bellis*
Daisy, African see *Arctotis*
Daisy, barberton see *Gerbera*
Daisy, globe see *Globularia*
Daisy, Livingstone see *Dorotheanthus*
Daisy, Michaelmas see *Aster*
Daisy, oxeye see *Leucanthemum vulgare*
Daisy, shasta see *Leucanthemum × superbum*
Daisy bush see *Olearia*

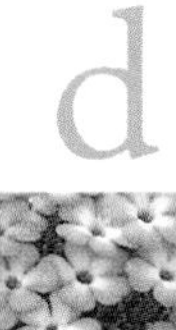

Danae

Alexandrian laurel
Ruscaceae

Danae racemosa

This is a slow-growing, hardy evergreen shrub for a shady moist place, where few other plants will grow. The plant forms a compact clump of arching green stems and elegant lance-shaped cladodes (flattened stems that function as leaves). The foliage is excellent for cutting, lasting well in water. The single species is closely related to *Ruscus aculeatus* (butcher's broom) and similar in appearance, but not prickly.

▲ *Danae racemosa*

Danae racemosa ♀ (syn. *Ruscus racemosus*) The glossy, dark green, leathery cladodes are 3-7cm (1¼-2¾in) long. Tiny, spherical, cream flowers, 3mm (⅛in) wide, with 6 petals, are borne in small terminal clusters of 5-8 flowers in early summer. Glossy orange-red berries 6mm (¼in) wide sometimes follow in autumn. Native to SW Asia. HEIGHT & SPREAD 40×50cm (16×20in) after 5 years, ultimately 1.2×1.5m (4×5ft).

CULTIVATION Plant in any soil that is fairly moist, but well-drained, in sun or partial shade. Foliage in sun becomes paler.

PROPAGATION Divide plants in winter or early spring. Alternatively, sow seed in autumn, but growth from seed is slow.

PRUNING No pruning required.

PESTS AND DISEASES Usually trouble free.

Daphne

Thymelaeaceae

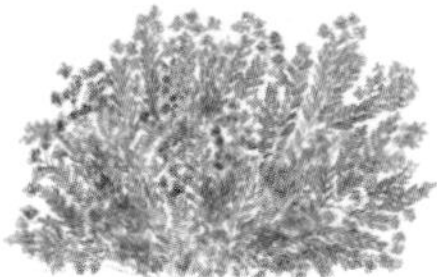

Daphne cneorum

Daphnes are grown for their abundant clusters of fragrant, pink, white or yellow flowers, which appear between late winter and early summer, depending on the species. The flowers, basically tubular, 1-2cm (⅜-¾in) across, open out into four spreading petals. Some species bloom when in full leaf, others on bare branches. Several species put on a bold display of berries in late summer. The berries of all species are poisonous. Taller daphnes enhance a border or make fine specimen plants, while smaller plants are suitable for a rock garden, raised bed or trough. Most species grow best in sunny positions but some prefer the cool dappled shade of a woodland environment. Daphnes are native to Europe and Asia.

Unless stated otherwise, the listed species are evergreen shrubs, hardy in Britain, and tend not to be long-lived. The flowers are generally borne in dense terminal clusters.

RECOMMENDED SPECIES AND VARIETIES

D. acutiloba Small clusters of white flowers, sometimes flushed with purple, produced in

▲ *Daphne acutiloba*

▲ *Daphne arbuscula*

▲ *Daphne cneorum* 'Eximia'

early and mid summer, precede an impressive display of bright red berries in late summer. Bright green leaves, lanceolate to oblong, are up to 10cm (4in) long. The species grows best in woodland conditions. HEIGHT & SPREAD 1m×30cm (3×1ft) after 5 years, ultimately 1.5m (5ft) tall.

D. arbuscula♀ Pink to deep rose, occasionally white, flowers appear from mid spring to early summer. The plant, very slow-growing, forms a low mound. The deep green, leathery, linear leaves are up to 2cm (¾in) long, with edges rolled under. The fruits, if produced, are not showy. HEIGHT & SPREAD 10×25cm (4×10in) after 5 years, ultimately 20cm (8in) tall.

D. bholua Sweetly fragrant pink flowers are produced in late winter. The black berries are rarely seen. Leaves are semi-evergreen, deep dull green, elliptical to oblanceolate, and up to 10cm (4in) long. HEIGHT & SPREAD 1.5m×60cm (5×2ft) after 5 years, ultimately 3m (10ft) tall.

'Gurkha'♀, the hardiest variety, is deciduous, with mid pink flowers. **'Jacqueline Postill'**♀ has large deeper pink flowers.

D. blagayana Large clusters of sweetly fragrant creamy white flowers are carried on a lax, spreading, mat-forming shrub in early to mid spring. Dull grey-green oval leaves, up to 5cm (2in) long, are grouped at the stem tips, leaving branches bare below. Plant in woodland conditions or on a peat bed. HEIGHT & SPREAD 10×30cm (4×12in) after 5 years, ultimately 30cm (1ft) tall.

D. × burkwoodii♀ A profusion of scented, purplish pink-and-white flowers appear from late spring to early summer, sometimes later, on a semi-evergreen, densely branched, rounded plant. Scattered elliptical leaves are up to 4cm (1½in) long. HEIGHT & SPREAD 85cm×1m (2ft 9in×3ft) after 5 years, ultimately 1.5m (5ft) tall.

'Carol Mackie' is vigorous with gold-edged leaves. **'Somerset'** has pale pink to white flowers among pale green foliage.

D. cneorum This low spreading plant bears scented, pale to deep rose-pink flowers with deep carmine-pink tubes from mid spring to early summer. Crowded oblong leaves, deep green above, greyish beneath, are to 2cm (¾in) long. HEIGHT & SPREAD 20×75cm (8×30in) after 5 years and ultimately.

'Eximia' is vigorous with deep crimson buds. The leaves of **'Variegata'** have yellow edges; the flowers are pale to mid pink.

D. laureola (spurge laurel) This rather upright plant is chiefly grown for its deep glossy green, oblanceolate leaves, up to 7.5cm (3in) long. Clusters of small, honey-scented, yellowish green flowers, held among the leaves close to the shoot tips in late winter, are followed by black berries. Plant in dry woodland conditions, especially on heavier soils. It often self-sows. HEIGHT & SPREAD 60×40cm (24×16in) after 5 years, ultimately 1.5m (5ft) tall.

Flowers of ssp. ***philippi*** are often tinged purple; 20×30cm (8in×1ft) after 5 years, the plant finally grows to 30cm (1ft).

▲ *Daphne laureola*

D. mezereum (mezereon) Pink or reddish purple flowers, very fragrant, are borne singly or in small clusters along bare stems in late winter. A sumptuous display of shiny red berries follows in mid summer. Rather upright branches bear deciduous, pale green, oblanceolate leaves up to 10cm (4in) long. The plant often self seeds. Grow in woodland conditions or a more open spot. HEIGHT & SPREAD 60×30cm (2×1ft) after 5 years, ultimately 1.2m (4ft) tall.

Daphne mezereum

Small white flowers are borne by f. ***alba***, followed by yellow fruits, while deep reddish purple flowers distinguish var. ***rubra***.

D. × napolitana♀ Fragrant pink flowers, open from rosy purple buds on a bushy plant from late winter to mid spring. The deep green leathery leaves are up to 4cm (1½in) long. Fruit is never set. This is one of the easiest and most reliable daphnes. HEIGHT & SPREAD 40×30cm (16×12in) after 5 years, ultimately 60cm (2ft) tall.

D. pontica♀ Yellowish green honey-scented flowers with narrow, pointed petals are carried in spidery clusters in spring

▲ *Daphne* × *napolitana*

among the upper leaves of greenish young shoots. Deep shiny green obovate leaves are to 10cm (4in) long. Black berries follow. The plant grows well in woodland conditions or close to a partially shaded wall. HEIGHT & SPREAD 1m×25cm (3ft×10in) after 5 years, ultimately 1.5m (5ft) tall.

▲ *Daphne pontica*

D. retusa see *D. tangutica* Retusa Group

D. tangutica♀ Pale pink flowers appear in late spring and early summer, sometimes in autumn, on an upright shrub. Deep green, elliptical, leathery leaves are to 3cm (1¼in) long. HEIGHT & SPREAD 60×45cm (24×18in) after 5 years, ultimately 80cm (2ft 8in) tall.

The small rounded shrubs belonging to the **Retusa Group**♀ (syn. *D. retusa*) are particularly recommended for a rock garden. Rose-red buds open into rose-purple flowers, white or pale pink inside, borne from mid to late spring and occasionally in autumn. Glossy deep green leaves, leathery, elliptical and up to 4cm (1½in) long, are usually crowded towards the shoot tips, especially in older plants. Berries are shiny red. HEIGHT & SPREAD 30×30cm (1×1ft) after 5 years, ultimately 60cm (2ft) tall.

CULTIVATION Plant in late winter or early spring in any type of soil as long as it is well-drained yet moist. All except woodland species grow best in a sunny position. Avoid moving established plants.

▲ *Daphne tangutica* Retusa Group

PROPAGATION Take semi-ripe cuttings in summer. Use layering with species that have a prostrate or semi-prostrate habit.

PRUNING None usually required. Remove straggly growths in early spring.

PESTS AND DISEASES Aphids, red spider mites (especially under glass), various caterpillars and leaf miners may attack plants. Plants can suffer from viral diseases causing leaf mottling and the fungal disease grey mould. Daphnes are not usually long-lived and tend to suffer from progressive die-back after a few years.

Darmera

Umbrella plant
Saxifragaceae

Enormous umbrella-like leaves create a magnificent mound of dark green foliage that turns bronze-pink in autumn. Rounded clusters of white or pale pink flowers precede the leaves in early spring, topping a mass of naked stalks. The single species, a hardy, herbaceous, rhizomatous perennial, thrives in damp or boggy soil and comes into its own when planted alongside a large garden pond or a stream.

Darmera peltata♀ (syn. *Peltiphyllum peltatum, Saxifraga peltata*) Five-petalled flowers, to 1.5cm (¾in) wide, with prominent dark pink stamens, appear in early spring. They are carried in dense clusters 12cm (4¾in) wide, each cluster supported by an erect, thick, hairy stem 30-100cm (12-36in) long. As the flowers fade in early summer, so the leaves grow upwards and open out. Each large leaf, rounded with 6-10 lobes, grows as wide as 45cm (18in). Native to the forests of N California and S Oregon in the USA. HEIGHT & SPREAD 90-180×60-90cm (3-6×2-3ft).

'Nana' has stems up to 30cm (1ft) long and leaves up to 25cm (10in) across.

CULTIVATION Plant in autumn or spring, in deep, moist soil or marshy ground alongside ponds or streams, in sun or light shade. Flowers may require protection from frost, because they bloom so early in the year.

PROPAGATION Divide rhizomes in autumn or spring and replant directly or lay horizontally in pots or wide, deep pans. Sow seed in spring, in a greenhouse preferably heated to 16-21°C (61-70°F).

▲ *Darmera peltata*

PESTS AND DISEASES Protect seedlings from slugs. Vine weevil is sometimes a problem, especially for pot grown plants.

Date plum see *Diospyros lotus*

Datura

Thorn apple
Solanaceae

Striking trumpet-shaped flowers and coarse downy leaves are borne in mid to late summer by these vigorous, bushy, half-hardy annuals. Large spiny fruit follow. All parts of daturas are poisonous, particularly the fruit. Native to southern N America.

RECOMMENDED SPECIES

D. arborea see *Brugmansia arborea*

D. inoxia (syn. *D. meteloides*) (angel's trumpet) The fragrant flowers, pink or lavender, veined with green, are as long as 20cm (8in). The green oval fruits are up to 5cm (2in) long. Broadly oval greyish green leaves grow to 25cm (10in) long. HEIGHT & SPREAD 90×45cm (3×1½ft).

D. meteloides see *D. inoxia*

D. rosea see *Brugmansia* × *insignis* pink

D. rosei see *Brugmansia sanguinea*

D. sanguinea see *Brugmansia sanguinea*

D. sauveolens see *Brugmansia sauveolens*

D. stramonium (common thorn apple) Erect white or purplish flowers, up to 10cm (4in) long, are followed by green rounded to oval fruits, to 10cm (4in) long, with very prominent spines. The elliptical or oval, greyish green leaves are up to 10cm (4in) long. HEIGHT & SPREAD 1m×60cm (3×2ft).

D. versicolor see *Brugmansia versicolor*

CULTIVATION Grow in free-draining soil in a sunny position. Deadhead after flowering to prevent the poisonous fruit forming.

PROPAGATION Sow seed either outside when all danger of frost is over, or under glass in early spring.

PESTS AND DISEASES Aphids are the only likely problem.

Davallia see FERNS p.263

▼ *Datura stramonium*

Davidia

Chinese dove tree, handkerchief tree
Cornaceae

Davidia involucrata

Fluttering pale handkerchief-like bracts, arranged in unequal-sized pairs, hang on the tree among handsome rich green foliage, shielding the true flowers. These appear in late spring and are tight, rounded clusters of dull greenish brown. A fairly hardy deciduous tree, it is native to W China. There is only one species.

▲ *Davidia involucrata*

Davidia involucrata ♀ Spreading branches and a domed crown make a stately, medium to large tree. The alternate, toothed, deep green leaves are ovate with a pointed tip. Prominently veined, they are 15 cm (6 in) long and have fine hairs on the underside. The unequal creamy bracts are 15 cm and 7.5 cm (6 in and 3 in) long, tapering to a point. Single egg-shaped green fruits take on a purple tinge in autumn. HEIGHT & SPREAD 10×6 m (33×20 ft) after 20 years, ultimately about 20 m (66 ft) tall.

The leaves of var. ***vilmoriniana*** ♀ are smoother and paler.

CULTIVATION Plant from autumn to spring. Davidia thrives in a sheltered position in sun or partial shade on moist fertile soils. Severe drought causes some die-back.

PROPAGATION Seeds are generally sown in late winter, but plants raised from softwood cuttings in mid to late summer will flower more quickly. Seedlings can take 10-20 years to flower. Alternatively, raise new plants by layering low branches or basal shoots. Protect young trees from frost in winter and late spring.

PRUNING None required.

PESTS AND DISEASES Usually trouble free.

Decaisnea

Lardizabalaceae

Decaisnea fargesii

Autumn shows these deciduous shrubs at their best, with huge divided leaves and colourful fleshy seedpods. In late spring and early summer the leaves are the background for unusual drooping spikes of trumpet-shaped flowers. These pale green and yellow striped flowers, up to 2.5 cm (1 in) long, have six petals, and are held on spikes up to 30 cm (12 in) long. The genus contains just two species, *Decaisnea fargesii* and *D. insignis*. *D. fargesii* is frost-hardy and the hardier of the two and hence more widely grown. It is native to W China and the Himalayas and hardy throughout Britain.

RECOMMENDED SPECIES

D. fargesii The pale green, pinnate leaves are up to 1 m (3 ft) long with 13-25 ovate leaflets. The yellow-green flowers, which hang in loose clusters, look like pixie hats with narrow, pointed petals. These give way to bright blue, finger-sized pods, which hang from the plant as the leaves turn an attractive butter-yellow in autumn. The shrub has quite an upright habit when young, becoming more rounded and spreading in maturity. HEIGHT & SPREAD 1.2 m×50 cm (4 ft×20 in) after 5 years, ultimately 3 m (10 ft) tall.

▲ *Decaisnea fargesii*

CULTIVATION The shrub grows well in moist but well-drained soil. It is suited to either sun or shade but late spring frosts may damage the flowers.

PROPAGATION Sow seed in spring.

PRUNING Not normally necessary unless it is to remove dead wood.

PESTS AND DISEASES Usually trouble free.

Delphinium

Ranunculaceae

Delphinium 'Loch Leven'

Prized for their majestic spires of intense blue flowers, these sun-loving herbaceous plants have been popular in borders and cottage gardens for centuries. The delphiniums described here fall broadly into two categories: garden varieties which have been developed from taller-growing species (mainly *Delphinium elatum*), and the shorter species delphiniums which are sometimes suitable for rock gardens. The annual larkspurs now belong to the genus *Consolida*.

Delphiniums come in shades of blue from soft azure to purple, and also in white, yellow, pink and red. Each flower is 5-7.5 cm (2-3 in) wide and consists of colourful hooded or spreading sepals which form a nectar-containing spur behind the true petals. The petals are small, forming a conspicuous eye which is often referred to as the 'bee' since it resembles a small bumble bee. Delphiniums are important as a cut flower. Most delphiniums are native to northern temperate regions of the world.

RECOMMENDED SPECIES AND VARIETIES

GARDEN VARIETIES

Because of their height, garden hybrids are ideal for the back of a herbaceous border or the middle of island beds. The divided leaves provide lush growth early in the year, hiding any supports that may be used with some plants before the dense flower spires develop in early to mid summer.

The plants below are perennials but tend to be short-lived and should be propagated regularly from cuttings. The cultivar groups are usually raised from seed and grown as annuals to give a reliable display of flowers.

***D.* Astolat Group** The flowers are in shades of pink and lilac with black eyes. HEIGHT & SPREAD 1.5 m×60 cm (5×2 ft).

***D.* Belladonna Group 'Cliveden Beauty'** This compact variety produces spikes of sky-blue flowers. It will continue to flower until autumn if the old spikes are removed. HEIGHT & SPREAD 1.2 m×60 cm (4×2 ft).

***D.* Black Knight Group** The deep violet-purple flowers with black eyes are borne in dense tall spikes. HEIGHT & SPREAD 1.5 m×60 cm (5×2 ft).

***D.* Blue Bird Group** Clear blue flowers with white eyes are carried in dense spikes. HEIGHT & SPREAD 1.5 m×60 cm (5×2 ft).

▲ *Delphinium* Blue Fountains Group

D. **Blue Fountains Group** These compact plants produce dense spikes of blue to near white flowers, usually with dark eyes. HEIGHT & SPREAD 75×30cm (2½×1ft).

D. **'Blue Nile'**♀ Clear blue flowers, the white eyes streaked with light blue, are borne in close spikes about 60cm (2ft) long. HEIGHT & SPREAD 1.5m×75cm (5×2½ft).

D. **Cameliard Group** The flowers are lavender-blue to lavender-pink with white eyes. HEIGHT & SPREAD 1.5m×60cm (5×2ft).

D. **'Conspicuous'**♀ Lavender-blue flowers with brown eyes are carried in long spikes. HEIGHT & SPREAD 1.5m×60cm (5×2ft).

D. **'Fanfare'**♀ Light blue-mauve, white-eyed flowers are carried on spikes to 75cm (2½ft). HEIGHT & SPREAD 2×1m (6½×3ft).

D. **'Faust'**♀ A tall variety with ultramarine-blue flowers, shaded with purple, with dark eyes. HEIGHT & SPREAD 1.8m×60cm (6×2ft).

D. **'Fenella'**♀ Rich, deep blue flowers with a violet flush and black eyes, are borne in dense spikes up to 1m (3ft) long. HEIGHT & SPREAD 1.5×1m (5×3ft).

D. **Galahad Group** Pure white flowers are borne in generous spikes. HEIGHT & SPREAD 1.5m×60cm (5×2ft).

D. **'Gillian Dallas'**♀ Pale lilac, white-eyed flowers are borne in dense spikes to 75cm (2½ft). HEIGHT & SPREAD 1.8×1m (6×3ft).

D. **Guinevere Group** Rosy lavender, white-eyed flowers are borne in dense spikes. HEIGHT & SPREAD 1.5m×60cm (5×2ft).

D. **King Arthur Group** The flowers in shades of violet have white eyes. HEIGHT & SPREAD 1.5m×60cm (5×2ft).

D. **'Loch Leven'**♀ White-eyed, blue flowers are borne in dense spikes to 1m (3ft). HEIGHT & SPREAD 1.5m×75cm (5×2½ft).

D. **'Mighty Atom'**♀ Solid spikes, up to 75cm (2½ft) long, are composed of lavender-blue flowers with brown eyes. HEIGHT & SPREAD 2×1m (6½×3ft).

D. **'Rosemary Brock'**♀ The soft pink flowers have dark brown eyes. HEIGHT & SPREAD 1.5m×60cm (5×2ft).

D. **'Royal Flush'**♀ The deep pink flowers have contrasting white eyes. HEIGHT & SPREAD 1.5m×60cm (5×2ft).

D. **'Sandpiper'**♀ This compact plant bears 75cm (2½ft) long spikes of striking pure white flowers with dark brown eyes. HEIGHT & SPREAD 1.2m×45cm (4×1½ft).

D. **'Spindrift'**♀ White-eyed flowers with lilac petals, tinged pale blue or green, are held in dense, 1m (3ft) long, spikes. HEIGHT & SPREAD 1.5m×60cm (5×2ft).

D. **Summer Skies Group** The light blue, white-eyed flowers are held in dense spikes. HEIGHT & SPREAD 1.5m×60cm (5×2ft).

D. **'Summerfield Miranda'**♀ Dark-eyed, pale lilac flowers are borne in dense spikes to 70cm (2½ft), with several side branches. HEIGHT & SPREAD 1.8m×75cm (6×2½ft).

D. **'Sungleam'**♀ White flowers with a distinct yellow tinge and yellow eyes are borne in 60cm (2ft) long spikes. HEIGHT & SPREAD 2×1m (6½×3ft).

SPECIES

The recommended species tend to be small plants. They are short-lived perennials and should be regularly propagated from seed, which is usually set in abundance.

D. ***ajacis*** see *Consolida ajacis*

D. ***ambiguum*** see *Consolida ajacis*

D. ***brunonianum*** Pouched, hairy, purplish blue flowers, up to 5cm (2in), with a dark centre, are borne in lax clusters in early to mid summer. This part-evergreen perennial has shiny rounded and lobed leaves, mostly held near the plant's base. HEIGHT & SPREAD 20–40×30cm (8–16×12in).

D. ***cardinale*** Scarlet flowers, 4cm (1½in) long with a yellow centre, are carried in tall spikes in summer. The hand-like leaves are deeply lobed. HEIGHT & SPREAD 60–90×40cm (24–36×16in).

D. ***cashmerianum*** Pouched purple-blue flowers, 4cm (1½in) long, with a dark centre, are borne in short spikes in early to mid summer. The rounded grey-green, hairy leaves have 5–7 lobes. HEIGHT & SPREAD 25×20cm (10×8in) or more.

D. ***chinense*** see *D. grandiflorum*

D. ***consolida*** see *Consolida ajacis*

D. ***grandiflorum*** (syn. *D. chinense*) Blue, violet or white flowers, 4cm (1½in) across, with a long, slender spur are borne in short, branched spikes in summer. Deep green leaves are narrowly divided. This perennial is often grown as an annual. HEIGHT & SPREAD 25–60×30cm (10–24×12in).

'Blue Butterfly' has vivid blue flowers.

D. ***nudicaule*** Slender stems bear spikes of orange-red flowers, 3cm (1¼in) long, in late spring and summer. Leaves are deeply lobed and divided. The plant is more reliable in an alpine house, and is sometimes grown outside as an annual. HEIGHT & SPREAD 30–45×20cm (12–18×8in).

'Luteum' has bright yellow flowers.

D. ***tatsienense*** A much-branched plant with deeply lobed, rounded leaves. Bright blue, spurred flowers have orange eyes and are borne in loose spikes to 15cm (6in). HEIGHT & SPREAD 25–45×25cm (10–18×10in).

CULTIVATION Plant perennial species and hybrids in early autumn or early spring, in freely drained, fertile soil, preferably somewhat limy. Choose a sunny site sheltered from strong wind. Stake taller hybrids. Remove faded flower spikes promptly. Plant out species and hybrids grown as annuals in mid spring. *D. brunonianum* and *D. cashmerianum* need very well-drained yet moist soil. *D. tatsienense* does best in a moist, humus-rich soil. *D. nudicaule* and *D. cardinale* thrive in sunny conditions.

PROPAGATION Take basal cuttings of hybrids in early spring (or earlier, from roots started under glass). Raise cultivars from seed sown in pots in a cool greenhouse in mid winter, or in flowering position in early autumn or early spring. Sow seed of species in winter or early spring in a coldframe. Plant out in spring or early summer. Root cuttings of young shoots in a sandy medium under glass in spring and early summer then plant out the following spring.

PESTS AND DISEASES Slugs and snails harm new growth. Aphids infest young leaves and flower buds. Earwigs can damage the flowers. Fungal diseases attack the roots. Powdery mildew can affect the leaves.

▼ *Delphinium grandiflorum*

Delphinium nudicaule 'Luteum' ▶

d

Dendranthema

Chrysanthemum

Compositae

Chrysanthemums offer an extensive range of flower forms from delicate sprays of daisy-like flowers to large showy blooms, across a wide palette of colours. As well as giving long-lasting colour to the late summer garden, the plants are ideal as cut flowers and are prized as exhibition blooms

This genus includes many of the plants previously classified under *Chrysanthemum*, the name by which they are still commonly known. The flowerheads come in a wide range of shapes, sizes and colours. There are chrysanthemums to bring colour to the border late in the season and varieties – both for outdoors and for the greenhouse – whose showy blooms are superb as cut flowers. There are also chrysanthemums suitable for growing in pots as houseplants.

Dendranthemas are herbaceous perennials, mostly half-hardy, and their blooms are composed of many tiny individual florets. The flowers are classified according to type (see panel, p. 209).

The size and number of flowers a chrysanthemum produces can be controlled by cultivation techniques. They can be grown to have either a large individual bloom at the end of each stem, or sprays of smaller flowers on each stem. Florists' varieties in particular are treated this way.

All chrysanthemums have dark green leaves, up to 15 cm (6 in) long, that are lobed and often deeply toothed.

RECOMMENDED SPECIES AND VARIETIES

The genus can be divided into three groups: (1) Garden varieties – hardy plants that can be grown outdoors throughout Britain. (2) Florists' varieties – plants cultivated for cut flowers or for shows, mostly grown in a greenhouse. (3) Pot plants.

The name of a variety often indicates its flower colour. Where this is not the case, the colour has been given in brackets.

GARDEN VARIETIES

Many chrysanthemums are hardy enough to survive permanently in the open in British gardens with minimal protection against winter weather. They flower in late summer and early autumn. Unlike the florists' varieties, these plants still look attractive when not in flower.

Garden (or Cushion) chrysanthemums These densely branched, mound-forming plants reach about 45 cm (1½ ft) in height and 30 cm (1 ft) in spread.

Varieties include **'Barbara'** (pink, pompon), **'Bravo'**♀ (red, intermediate), **'Debonair'**♀ (lavender, intermediate), **'Holly'**♀ (yellow, pompon), **'Nicole'** (white, pompon), **'Robin'** (orange-bronze, pompon) and **'Sunny Linda'** (yellow, intermediate).

Korean Hybrids Flowering freely from late summer until the first hard frosts, these hybrids have a multi-branched habit, reaching 75 cm (2½ ft) in height and 45 cm (1½ ft) in spread.

Good varieties include **'Brightness'** (red, semidouble), **'Raquel'** (pink, single), **'Ruby Mound'** (red, double) and **'Starlet'** (bronze, double).

Rubellum Hybrids These plants have a multibranched habit and reach a height of 1 m (3 ft) and a spread of 45 cm (1½ ft).

Good varieties include: **'Clara Curtis'** (pink, single), **'Duchess of Edinburgh'** (red, single), **'Emperor of China'** (syn. 'Cottage Pink') (rose-pink,

1 *D.* 'Raquel'
2 *D.* 'Bronze Margaret'
3 *D.* 'Mary Stoker'
4 *D.* 'Duchess of Edinburgh'
5 *D.* 'Ruby Mound'
6 *D.* 'Mei-kyo'
7 *D.* 'Starlet'
8 *D. yezoense*

▲ *Dendranthema* 'Debonair'

▲ *Dendranthema* 'Clara Curtis'

▲ *Dendranthema* 'Max Riley'

▲ *Dendranthema* 'Crimson Yvonne Arnaud'

double), **'Innocence'** (very pale pink, single), **'Mary Stoker'** (yellow, single) and **'Paul Boissier'** (bronze, double).

D. weyrichii This mat-forming species flowers freely in late summer and early autumn, producing white or pink single flowers up to 4 cm (1½ in) across. It makes a useful plant for the rock garden. HEIGHT & SPREAD 20×25 cm (8×10 in).

D. yezoense♀ (syn. *Chrysanthemum arcticum*) Masses of white, single flowers appear in mid autumn against the dark green foliage. The flowers are up to 5 cm (2 in) wide. This is a good plant for ground cover and does best in full sun. HEIGHT & SPREAD 30×45 cm (1×1½ ft).

'Roseum' has pink flowers.

FLORISTS' VARIETIES

Chrysanthemums are among the longest lasting of all cut flowers and a dozen plants could provide as many as a hundred large blooms from late summer to the New Year.

▲ *Dendranthema weyrichii*

They are popular plants to grow for exhibition and gardeners can use cultivation methods to develop the flowers to a particular standard. The florists' varieties can be subdivided into 2 further groups: early-flowering outdoor varieties and late-flowering indoor varieties.

Dendranthema Flower Forms

Within the three main groups of dendranthema – garden varieties, florists' varieties and pot plants – plants are further divided into different classifications according to their flower type. These nine different flower forms are best demonstrated by the illustrations opposite.

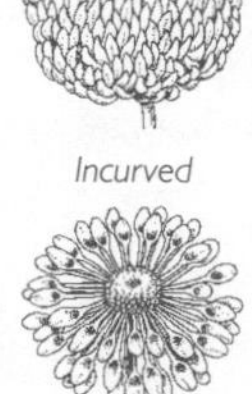

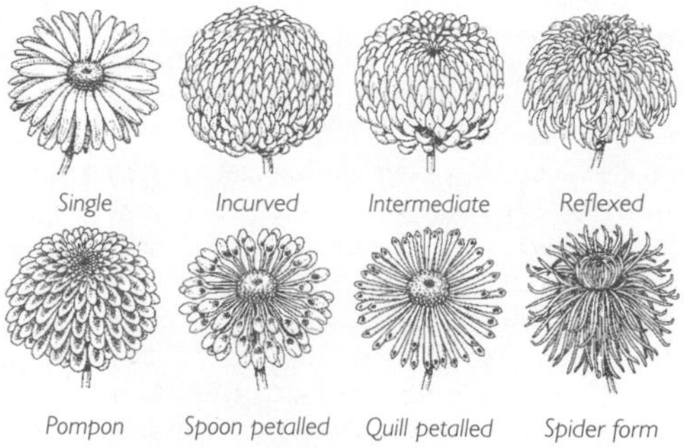

Single · Incurved · Intermediate · Reflexed

Anemone-centred · Pompon · Spoon petalled · Quill petalled · Spider form

Dendranthema 'Wendy'

d

Early-flowering outdoor varieties

These flower outdoors in late summer and early autumn, with most varieties continuing to bloom until the first frosts. Unfortunately, with very few exceptions, they are not reliably hardy and cannot safely be left outdoors over winter. They should be brought into an unheated or cool greenhouse in mid autumn. Even those plants hardy enough to survive the winter will not flower as well if treated as herbaceous perennials by being grown outdoors all year round. Although excellent for cut flowers, they have long, leggy stems and are not ideal garden plants. The following varieties have a height of about 1 m (3 ft) and a spread of about 30 cm (1 ft). The letter S after a variety name means that the plant is normally grown as a spray.

Among those varieties with incurved blooms are: **'Gazelle'** (white), **'Max Riley'**🏆 (yellow) and **'Winnie Bramley'** (yellow). Among those with reflexed blooms are: **'Crimson Yvonne Arnaud'** (red), **'Dorridge Beauty'** (red), **'Gambit'** (purple), **'George Griffiths'**🏆 (red) and **'Pearl Celebration'** (pink). The following varieties have intermediate blooms: **'Allouise'**🏆 (pink), **'Anna Marie'**🏆 (white), **'Bronze Margaret'**🏆S, **'Fleet Margaret'**🏆S (syn. 'Orange Margaret') (orange), **'Gingernut'** (bronze), **'Heide'**🏆S (white), **'Orange Allouise'**, **'Pink Margaret'**🏆S, **'Red Margaret'**S, **'Red Wendy'**🏆S, **'Salmon Allouise'**, **'Wendy'**🏆S (bronze), **'White Allouise'**🏆, **'White Margaret'**🏆S, **'Yellow Gingernut'**, **'Yellow Heide'**🏆S and **'Yellow Margaret'**🏆S. Single-flowered varieties include: **'Enbee Wedding'**🏆S (pink), **'Pennine Jade'**🏆S (bronze), **'Pennine Soldier'**🏆S (red), **'Red Enbee Wedding'**🏆S, **'White Enbee Wedding'**🏆S and **'Yellow Enbee Wedding'**🏆S. **'Pennine Marie'**S (pink) has anemone-centred flowers. The pompon-flowered varieties include: **'Anastasia'**S (pink), **'Bronze Elegance'**S and **'Mei-kyo'**S (pink). These last 3 are hardy.

▲ *Dendranthema* 'Wendy'

▲ *Dendranthema* 'Yellow Heide'

▲ *Dendranthema* 'Enbee Wedding'

▲ *Dendranthema* 'Mei-kyo'

Late-flowering indoor varieties

These chrysanthemums flower under glass between mid autumn and early winter. They are usually grown in the open in large pots during the summer and moved into a greenhouse in early autumn. These late-flowering varieties are also classified according to time of flowering – those that flower in mid autumn and those that flower in late autumn and early winter. They are about 1.2 m (4 ft) tall, with a spread of about 45 cm (1½ ft) and their blooms are up to 20 cm (8 in) across – even larger if grown by exhibitors' techniques.

The following varieties bloom in mid autumn. Among those with reflexed blooms are: **'Bronze John Wingfield'**, **'Cream West Bromwich'**, **'John Wingfield'** (white), **'Pink John Wingfield'**, **'Riley's Dynasty'** (pink), **'West Bromwich'** (white) and **'Yellow John Wingfield'**. These have intermediate blooms: **'Bronze Fairway'**, **'Bronze Pauline White'**, **'Cream Pauline White'**, **'Pauline White'** (pink) and **'Pink Fairway'**.

The following bloom in late autumn and early winter. Among those with incurved blooms are: **'Cream John Hughes'**, **'John Hughes'** (white), **'Polar Gem'** (white) and **'Yellow John Hughes'**. With reflexed flowers are: **'Bryan Kirk'** (purple), **'Dorridge King'** (crimson), **'Red Shoesmith Salmon'**, **'Roblaze'**S (red) and **'Shoesmith Salmon'**🏆 (pink). Among those with intermediate blooms are: **'Balcombe Perfection'** (bronze), **'Bronze Mayford Perfection'**🏆, **'Fred Shoesmith'** (white), **'Gold Foil'** (yellow), **'Green Satin'**, **'Ivy Garland'** (cream), **'Mayford Perfection'**🏆 (pink), **'Red Balcombe Perfection'**, **'Red Mayford Perfection'**, **'Yellow Balcombe Perfection'**, **'Yellow Fred Shoesmith'**, **'Yellow Ivy Garland'** and **'Yellow Mayford Perfection'**🏆. Among those with single flowers are: **'Galaxy'**🏆S (bronze), **'My Love'** (pink), **'Purple Nu Rosemary'**🏆S, **'Rynoon'** (pink), **'Salmon Nu Rosemary'**🏆S, **'White Nu Rosemary'**S and **'Yellow Galaxy'**🏆S. **'Long Island Beauty'**🏆S has white, anemone-centred flowers and **'White Spider'**S has white, spider flowers.

POT PLANTS

Nearly all chrysanthemums sold as pot plants have been treated with height-reducing chemicals which are not available to amateur gardeners. However, there are varieties that the amateur can cultivate as pot plants. Garden (Cushion) chrysanthemums can be grown in this way – see varieties section above and the cultivation section below. They will flower in summer and early autumn either indoors in a greenhouse, or outdoors.

Charm chrysanthemums

Spectacular pot plants that flower from mid autumn to early winter, each plant producing hundreds of scented blooms in the full range of chrysanthemum colours. HEIGHT & SPREAD 60 cm × 1 m (2×3 ft).

'Bullfinch' has red flowers, **'Morning Star'** has yellow blooms.

CULTIVATION

GARDEN VARIETIES

Plant in late spring or when all risk of hard frost has passed, in any fertile, well-drained garden soil, choosing a position in full sun. Provide taller plants with some support. Two weeks after planting, snap off or pinch out the end 1.5 cm (½ in) of the stem tips to

▲ *Dendranthema* 'Cream John Hughes'

▲ *Dendranthema* 'Dorridge King'

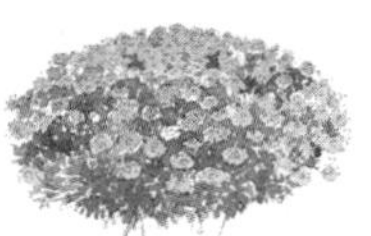
Dendranthema 'Morning Star'

encourage branching. This is referred to as 'stopping'. For Garden (Cushion) chrysanthemums, continue to stop the resulting lateral and side shoots when they reach 10 cm (4 in) in length, until mid summer.

When the first hard frosts kill the flowers, cut stems back to about 10 cm (4 in). Protect plants with a 10 cm (4 in) layer of mulch in winter. In wet soils, lift plants after cutting back and transfer them to a coldframe or unheated greenhouse for winter. Thin out shoots of each clump in spring to encourage stronger stems and a better appearance.

FLORISTS' VARIETIES

Early-flowering outdoor varieties Plant rooted cuttings 13 cm (5¼ in) apart in potting compost in a 10 cm (4 in) deep box. Move the box to a coldframe in mid spring

▲ *Dendranthema* 'Roblaze'

▲ *Dendranthema* 'Green Satin'

▲ *Dendranthema* 'Salmon Nu Rosemary'

▲ *Dendranthema* 'Morning Star'

and harden the cuttings off. Plant out in late spring, once the risk of any late hard frost has passed, in any fertile, well-drained soil, choosing a position in full sun, and water in thoroughly.

Support the plants with canes at least 1.2 m (4 ft) long, tying stems loosely to the supports. Alternatively, enclose plants within 13-15 cm (5¼-6 in) mesh netting, stretched around 4 corner posts. Pinch out, or 'stop', the growing points a week after planting. For the largest flowers, reduce the number of lateral shoots to a maximum of 3 per plant. To control the size and number of flowers, disbud plants as soon as the buds appear. To ensure large individual blooms, carefully remove all buds except the one at the very end of each sideshoot. For sprays, reverse the procedure and remove the bud at the end of the sideshoot, retaining all the other buds.

Top dress with fertiliser in mid summer and water it in thoroughly. Water plants frequently in dry weather. After they have flowered, cut the stems back to a height of 20 cm (8 in). Lift the plants and overwinter them in an unheated or cool greenhouse in pots or trays of multipurpose compost.

Late-flowering indoor varieties Cultivation for these varieties depends on when cuttings were rooted. For exhibition blooms treat plants as follows. Pot cuttings rooted by mid spring into 8 cm (3 in) or 9 cm (3½ in) pots. Transfer to 13 cm (5 in) pots 3-4 weeks later. Alternatively, set rooted cuttings 13 cm (5¼ in) apart in a 10 cm (4 in) deep layer of compost in a box. In mid spring, move plants to a coldframe and harden off. Pot cuttings rooted in late spring into 8 cm (3 in) or 9 cm (3½ in) pots; do not transfer these into 13 cm (5 in) pots.

Transfer cuttings into their final pots, 25 cm (10 in) across, in late spring or early summer. Cuttings rooted by late spring can be planted 2 to a pot. Put pots outside in late spring or early summer. Insert a stout, 1.2 m (4 ft) cane into each pot and tie stems loosely. To ensure that plants do not fall over in high winds, tie tops of canes to a horizontal wire, strung between posts. Water during summer. Feed weekly with a general-purpose fertiliser from early summer until the buds begin to open.

In mid spring, when plants are 20-25 cm (8-10 in) tall, pinch out the growing point of plants raised from cuttings taken in mid or late winter. As lateral shoots develop, remove all but 3 of them. Pinch out the growing points of these in early summer. Remove all but 3 of the sideshoots that develop from each of these shoots, so that plants have up to 9 shoots each.

Stop plants raised from cuttings taken in early or mid spring about 10 days after the final potting; allow up to 9 shoots per plant to grow. Plants grown from cuttings taken in late spring and grown 2 per pot, should be stopped and up to 5 of the resulting sideshoots retained per plant. Chrysanthemums grown for exhibition should have fewer sideshoots per plant; consult specialist publications for more detailed guidance.

Two alternative methods of growing are less time-consuming and troublesome but are also less likely to produce blooms of prize-winning quality. Start with rooted cuttings taken in early spring. Four weeks after rooting, pinch out the growing points; the lateral shoots that then develop are taken as cuttings for both of these methods.

In the first method, take cuttings in early summer and, when rooted, plant 3 in a 25 cm (10 in) pot. Stop the growing points 2 weeks after potting and allow just 3 of the lateral shoots that develop to grow on. Do not stop the growing points of these shoots.

The second and easier method is to take the cuttings in mid summer and, when rooted, plant them straight into prepared soil in the greenhouse 20 cm (8 in) apart. Stop the growing point 2 weeks later, and retain just 2 evenly matched lateral shoots on each plant. Again, do not stop the growing points of these lateral shoots.

Disbud all late-flowering indoor vari-

d

eties in the same way as given for early-flowering outdoor varieties. Do this when flower buds appear in the late summer.

Move plants back into a well-ventilated greenhouse in early autumn, before the first frosts. Maintain a minimum temperature of 4°C (39°F) for plants that flower in mid autumn and a minimum temperature of 8°C (46°F) for those that flower in late autumn and early winter. Ventilate when the temperature reaches 20°C (68°F), or less in dull weather. Never close ventilators completely once flower buds begin to open.

After flowering, keep the best plants to produce cuttings for the following season. Cut back the main stems to 20cm (8in) above their base and overwinter, in their pots, in a cool greenhouse.

POT PLANTS
Once cuttings of Charm chrysanthemums have rooted, pot on in the same way as late-flowering indoor florists' varieties. Final pot size should be 20-25cm (8-10in) across.

Move pots outdoors in early summer. Pinch or 'stop' each plant once it reaches 15cm (6in) high. Put plants in a well-ventilated, cool greenhouse in early autumn, before risk of night frosts. After flowering, discard plants or keep them to produce cuttings in late winter. Cut back stems to 20cm (8in) and keep in a frost-free greenhouse.

Garden (Cushion) chrysanthemums can be used to produce pot plants that flower in summer. When cuttings have rooted, pot up one cutting in a 13cm (5in) pot or 3 in an 18cm (7in) pot. Stop plants 2 weeks after potting. Keep them in a well-ventilated, cold greenhouse or a sheltered site outdoors and feed the plants weekly.

PROPAGATION All chrysanthemums can be propagated by cuttings taken from the stool – the cluster of shoots that arise from the rootstock at the base of a plant. Take cuttings 5-6cm (2-2½in) long. (The time of year cuttings are taken depends on the type of chrysanthemum – see below.) Dip the bottom 1cm (½in) of the cutting in rooting hormone powder and insert in pots containing a mixture of half peat and half sand. Water in very thoroughly and provide a bottom temperature of at least 15°C (59°F). Prevent cuttings drying out by placing them in a propagating case or by covering with polythene until they have rooted; this will take up to 3 weeks.

GARDEN VARIETIES
Take cuttings in spring, preferably early spring, and when rooted harden off and plant out in late spring. Alternatively, sow seed in late winter in a heated greenhouse, providing a bottom temperature of 16-20°C (61-68°F) to ensure germination. Prick out into boxes with at least 5cm (2in) depth of compost, planting seedlings 8cm (3¼in) apart. Once seedlings reach at least 5cm (2in) in height, harden off and plant out in late spring. It is also possible to lift and divide plants every 2-3 years, as new growth starts in spring. Replant vigorous shoots from the edge of the old clump and discard the congested central portion.

FLORISTS' VARIETIES
Take cuttings of early-flowering outdoor varieties in early or mid spring. Take cuttings of late-flowering indoor varieties from mid winter to mid summer, according to the method of growing to be adopted.

POT PLANTS
Take cuttings from Charm chrysanthemums in late winter or early spring, or sow seed in late winter in a heated greenhouse. Take cuttings of Garden chrysanthemums from mid spring to early summer.

Cuttings can be taken from shop-bought pot plants once flowering is over – the new plants will no longer be dwarf and will flower in mid or late autumn in a frost-proof greenhouse. Take cuttings from the shoots that arise from the base of the plant.

PESTS AND DISEASES Capsid bugs, red spider mites and thrips can harm both flowers and foliage. Aphids and chrysanthemum leaf miners may seriously damage leaves. Chrysanthemum eelworms can seriously affect growth by destroying leaf tissue. Chrysanthemum stool miners damage roots and stems. Western flower thrips can transmit the virus disease, tomato spotted wilt. White rust, grey mould and chrysanthemum virus diseases can also be a problem.

Dendrobium see ORCHIDS p.466
Deschampsia see GRASSES p.300

Desfontainia

Desfontainiaceae

Desfontainia spinosa

Bright tubular flowers contrast with glossy, holly-like leaves on these evergreen shrubs whose native habitat is damp cool regions in the mountains of S America. The waxy single flowers, borne in mid to late summer, are pendulous and tubular.

RECOMMENDED SPECIES AND VARIETIES
D. spinosa♀ Yellow-tipped scarlet blooms, up to 4cm (1½in) long and very narrow hang from the shoots in profusion, making a dazzling sight in mid to late summer. The small evergreen shrub is slow growing. As it is not frost-hardy, it needs the protection of a south-facing wall. Small leaves, to 4cm (1½in) long, are dark green with spiny edges. Native to S America. HEIGHT & SPREAD 1m×50cm (3ft×20in) after 5 years, ultimately 1.5m (5ft) tall and nearly as broad.

▲ *Desfontainia spinosa*

'Harold Comber' has flowers, up to 5cm (2in), which are vermilion-red.

CULTIVATION Plant in late spring. *D. spinosa* needs a cool, lime-free soil, dappled shade, moist air and a sheltered position even in mild areas.

PROPAGATION Take basal cuttings in mid autumn, overwinter in a coldframe and pot up in spring when rooted.

PRUNING Seldom required except to keep the shrub shapely.

PESTS AND DISEASES Usually trouble free.

Deutzia

Hydrangeaceae

Deutzia x elegantissima 'Rosealind'

These free-flowering, easily grown deciduous shrubs bear white, pink or purple flowers from late spring to early summer, when the long stems are studded with clusters of five-petalled, star-shaped or cupped flowers, 1.5-2.5cm (½-1in) wide. Opposite leaves are fairly narrow, 5-10cm (2-4in) long, and mid green to grey. The plants have an upright, somtimes arching, habit. Almost all are fully hardy, but young growth may be damaged by late frost. Native to the Himalayas, China, Japan and Central America.

RECOMMENDED SPECIES AND VARIETIES
***D. compacta* 'Lavender Time'** Sweet-smelling, cup-shaped lilac flowers, later pale lavender, are held in heads 7.5cm (3in) wide. HEIGHT & SPREAD 1.2×1.2m (4×4ft) after 5 years, ultimately 1.5m (5ft) tall.
***D. crenata* 'Flore Pleno'** see *D. scabra* 'Plena'

A dwarf, compact shrub, var. ***nakaiana*** **'Nikko'** has small white flowers. Leaves are narrow, pointed and up to 6 cm (2½ in) long. HEIGHT & SPREAD 80×80 cm (32×32 in) after 5 years, ultimately 1 m (3 ft) tall.

D.* × *elegantissima Scented, pink star-shaped flowers in clusters 6 cm (2½ in) wide, cover the arching branches of this upright, bushy plant. Matt green leaves are lance-shaped. HEIGHT & SPREAD 1×1 m (3×3 ft) after 5 years, ultimately 1.5 m (5 ft) tall.

▲ *Deutzia* × *elegantissima* 'Rosealind'

'Rosealind'♀ is an erect branched bush with deep carmine flowers in upright heads.

D. gracilis A multitude of pure white star-shaped flowers is held in erect heads 7.5 cm (3 in) tall. Leaves are lance-shaped, toothed and pointed at the end. Protect from late frosts. HEIGHT & SPREAD 1×1 m (3×3 ft) after 5 years, ultimately 1.2 m (4 ft) tall.

D.* × *hybrida A group of free-flowering, bushy shrubs. The star-shaped flowers grow in clusters, 5-7.5 cm (2-3 in) across, and the leaves are pale to mid green and lance-shaped. HEIGHT & SPREAD 1.2×1 m (4×3 ft) after 5 years, ultimately 1.8 m (6 ft) tall.

'Magicien' has mauve-pink petals edged in white. **'Mont Rose'**♀ is vigorous and erect with arching stems, deep pink flowers with golden anthers, and dark green, toothed leaves. **'Rosea Plena'** has dense heads of pink double flowers that turn white.

D.* × *kalmiiflora Graceful, arching branches carry clusters of 5-12 flowers, white inside and deep rose on the reverse, 2.5 cm (1 in) across. Leaves are mid to deep green. HEIGHT & SPREAD 1×1 m (3×3 ft) after 5 years, ultimately 1.5 m (5 ft) tall.

D.* × *magnifica White double flowers appear in broad, erect heads 7.5 cm (3 in) tall. An elegant, arching shrub with narrow, oval leaves. HEIGHT & SPREAD 1.8×1.5 m (6×5 ft) after 5 years, ultimately 2.4 m (8 ft) tall.

D. ningpoensis Starry white flowers with yellow anthers are arranged in pyramidal heads, 10 cm (4 in) long, on lateral branches. The habit is pendulous. Leaves are willow-like. HEIGHT & SPREAD 1×1 m (3×3 ft) after 5 years, ultimately 1.8 m (6 ft) tall.

D. pulchra Pink-tinged, white cupped flowers appear in drooping sprays. Dark leathery leaves last into winter when the bark peels. The plant is less hardy than most. HEIGHT & SPREAD 1.5×1.2 m (5×4 ft) after 5 years, ultimately 2.4 m (8 ft) tall.

D.* × *rosea Open bell-shaped, soft rose-pink flowers grow in rounded clusters, 5-7.5 cm (2-3 in) wide, amid oval leaves on this compact plant with arching branches. HEIGHT & SPREAD 75×75 cm (30×30 in) after 5 years, ultimately 1 m (3 ft) tall.

'Carminea'♀ has petals with outer surfaces deep pink and spreads to 90 cm (3 ft) or so after 5 years, ultimately to 1.2 m (4 ft).

▲ *Deutzia* × *rosea*

▲ *Deutzia scabra*

D. scabra Cup-shaped white flowers, sometimes flushed pink, appear in erect, branched clusters up to 15 cm (6 in) high. The brown bark peels in winter. HEIGHT & SPREAD 1.5×1.2 m (5×4 ft) after 5 years, ultimately 3×1.8 m (10×6 ft).

'Candidissima' has large clusters of double white flowers and grows ultimately to 3.5 m (12 ft). **'Plena'** (syn. *D. crenata* 'Flore Pleno') has double flowers suffused with rose-purple on the outside. **'Pride of Rochester'** has pink tinted double flowers.

CULTIVATION Plant bare-rooted shrubs in well-drained garden soil, between mid autumn and early spring; at any time for container-grown plants. Position in full sun or partial shade, avoiding open positions with northerly aspects. Mulch in spring.

PROPAGATION Take semi-ripe cuttings in late summer or take hardwood cuttings in autumn.

PRUNING Encourage new stems by cutting back old flowering stems to a strong new shoot low down on the stem. Prune once flowering is over, in mid summer.

PESTS AND DISEASES Usually trouble free, but snails can eat new shoots.

Dianella

Flax lily

Phormiaceae

Clumps of sword-like evergreen leaves give constant garden value to these rhizomatous perennials. Erect sprays of small, nodding flowers are borne on long stems in summer. Flowers have six tepals, usually turned back to reveal erect yellow stamens. After flowering, generally shiny berries appear. Native to S America, Asia, Australia and New Zealand, flax lilies are reasonably hardy in southern Britain, but elsewhere need a cold greenhouse or conservatory.

RECOMMENDED SPECIES AND VARIETIES

D. nigra Greenish white flowers, in sprays 30 cm (12 in) wide and up to 1.2 m (4 ft) long, rise out of tufts of grassy leaves 50 cm (20 in) long. The 6 mm (¼ in) wide flowers are followed by shiny violet-blue or sometimes greyish berries. HEIGHT 50 cm (20 in).

D. tasmanica Violet-blue flowers 1.5 cm (½ in) long appear in early to mid summer, followed by violet-blue berries. Flower sprays are branched to 8 cm (3¼ in) wide. Greyish leaves are 60 cm (2 ft) or more long and 2 cm (¾ in) wide. HEIGHT 1 m (3 ft).

'Variegata' has white-striped leaves.

CULTIVATION Plant in well-drained soil and half shade in spring or summer.

PROPAGATION Lift and divide rhizomes in spring or summer, or sow seed in pots in late summer and keep in an unheated greenhouse. Germination may take 2 years.

PESTS AND DISEASES Usually trouble free.

▲ *Dianella tasmanica* 'Variegata'

Dianthus

Carnations, pinks

Caryophyllaceae

Few flowers are more evocative of the simple charm of the cottage garden than pinks. Their close relative, the carnation, is a symbol of elegance. Both have a delightful and distinctive perfume

The beautiful clove-scented flowers of carnations, pinks and sweet williams vary widely in size, from five-petalled singles, just 1.5cm (½in) across, to doubles with up to 60 petals, about 10cm (4in) across. The petals, which emerge from a tubular five-toothed calyx, may be smooth-edged, as in most border carnations, or slightly toothed or deeply fringed, as in many pinks and perpetual-flowering carnations. The main colour groups are: selfs, bicolours, laced pinks, fancies and picotees (see diagram opposite).

The evergreen leaves of carnations and pinks are smooth and linear or lance-shaped, usually with pointed tips. The stalks have swollen nodes, from which the leaves grow in opposite pairs. Most are glaucous blue-grey to grey-green, associating well with many colour schemes in the garden and brightening up the dull days of winter. The leaves of sweet williams are usually matt green.

Perennial border carnations, pinks and dianthus species are fully hardy. They prefer neutral or slightly alkaline soil and an open sunny situation, not overshadowed by trees or taller-growing plants. They are tolerant of salt-laden winds and smoke-polluted air.

The more tender perpetual-flowering carnations may be grown in pots outdoors in summer, but require greenhouse protection with a minimum temperature of 7°C (45°F) if they are to bloom in winter.

RECOMMENDED SPECIES AND VARIETIES

The plants are divided into:

- Dianthus species and varieties
- Alpine hybrids
- Garden pinks
- Border carnations
- Annual carnations
- Perpetual-flowering carnations

Dianthus Flower-Colour Groups

The flowers of carnations and pinks are broadly divided into five colour groups. Selfs are of a single uniform colour. Bicolours have an outer zone of one colour and a central eye or zone of another. Laced pinks are of white or pink ground with a contrasting central zone which extends to form an edging round each petal. Fancies have contrasting irregular markings of another colour. Picotees have an edging of contrasting colour round each petal.

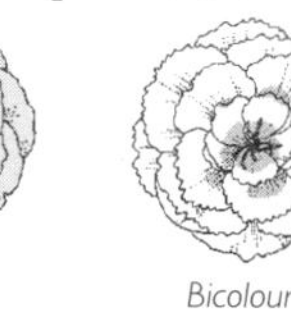
Self

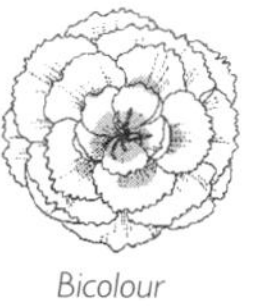
Bicolour

Laced

Fancy

Picotee

DIANTHUS SPECIES AND VARIETIES

These hardy perennials, with single flowers, are suitable for growing in rock gardens or at the front of herbaceous borders.

D. alpinus♀ (Alpine pink) Solitary rose-pink to crimson flowers, up to 4cm (1½in) across and speckled with tiny white spots, appear in early and mid summer. This perennial forms a close mat of deep green, blunt-tipped foliage. The plant thrives in a humus-rich, gritty compost in a rock garden or trough. Native to the E Alps. HEIGHT & SPREAD 5×20cm (2×8in).

Dianthus alpinus

'Joan's Blood'♀ has rich crimson blooms.

D. anatolicus Small white flowers, 6mm (¼in) across, appear in mid summer on tall slender stems well above a dense hummock of narrow, pointed, deep green leaves. The plant dislikes excessive winter wet. Native to Turkey and Iran. HEIGHT & SPREAD 20-30×20-40cm (8-12×8-16in).

D. arenarius The fragrant white flowers, 2cm (¾in) across and carried in sprays, have deeply cut petals that are often stained with purple at the base. This sub-shrub forms lax hummocks of grassy, dark green leaves. Native to parts of central, N and E Europe. HEIGHT & SPREAD 30×50cm (12×20in).

D. armeria♀ (Deptford pink) Tall, wiry stems carry clusters of small, bright cerise-pink flowers, about 1.5cm (½in) across, in summer. This biennial or short-lived, tuft-forming perennial, with narrow, lance-shaped, deep green leaves, is suitable for rock gardens and the front of sunny borders or banks. Native to S Europe and W Asia. HEIGHT & SPREAD 30×45cm (12×18in).

D. × arvernensis♀ (syn. *D.* 'Arvernensis') Rich pink flowers, up to 3cm (1¼in) across, appear in summer on rather short stems. A good rock garden plant, this mat-forming perennial has grey-green linear leaves. A hybrid found naturally in France. HEIGHT & SPREAD 15×30cm (6×12in).

'Albus' bears white flowers.

D. barbatus (sweet william) This garden plant, although a short-lived perennial, is usually grown as a biennial. Small, occasionally double, flowers form densely packed, sweetly scented flat clusters up to 12.5cm (5in) across. The flowers are white, pink or red, selfs or bicolours. The leaves

1 *D.* 'Marg's Choice'
2 *D.* 'Dunkirk Spirit'
3 *D.* 'Fragrant Ann'
4 *D.* 'Betty Norton'
5 *D.* 'Devon Maid'
6 *D.* 'Monica Wyatt'
7 *D.* 'Joe Vernon'
8 *D.* 'Audrey Robinson'
9 *D.* 'Crompton Princess'
10 *D.* 'Joanne's Highlight'
11 *D.* 'Joanne'
12 *D.* 'Whitesmith'
13 *D.* 'Salamanca'
14 *D. barbatus*
15 *D.* 'Doris'
16 *D.* 'Kesteven Kirkstead'
17 *D.* 'Clara's Lass'
18 *D.* 'Becky Robinson'
19 *D.* 'Peter Wood'
20 *D.* 'Ann Franklin'

▼ *Dianthus arenarius*

▲ *Dianthus barbatus*

d

are matt green. Native to E Europe. HEIGHT & SPREAD 30-60×20-25cm (12-24×8-10in).

'Auricula-eyed'♀ has flowers of various colours with white central eyes and edging. **Nigrescens Group**♀ has deep crimson-maroon flowers.

D. caesius see *D. gratianopolitanus*

D. callizonus Solitary pink or carmine flowers, about 3cm (1¼in) across and with a central zone of darker dots, appear in summer. A flattish, mat-forming perennial with linear, deep green and rather glossy leaves, suitable for a rock garden or raised bed. Native to the Carpathians. HEIGHT & SPREAD 10-15×15-25cm (4-6×6-10in).

▲ *Dianthus callizonus*

D. carthusianorum (Carthusian pink) Tall wiry stems bear a tight cluster of deep pink to purple or red flowers in summer. The flowers, about 2cm (¾in) across, have contrasting purple-brown calyxes and bracts. A lax tufted perennial with long, grass-like, rather bright green leaves, this rock or wild garden plant naturalises in dry grassy places. Native to central and S Europe. HEIGHT & SPREAD 20-50×10-30cm (8-20×4-12in).

D. caryophyllus (carnation, clove-pink, gilliflower) The single, pinkish purple flowers, up to 4cm (1½in) across, are scented and borne in mid summer. The leaves are grey-green. Native to W and S France. HEIGHT & SPREAD 60×45cm (2×1½ft).

D. chinensis (syn. *D. sinensis*) (Indian pink) The individual flowers may be single or double, selfs or bicolours. They have fringed petals and grow to 4cm (1½in) across. In shades of red, pink and white, they bloom from early summer until the first frosts. The leaves are pale to mid green. The species has a number of cultivars, annuals and short-lived perennials which make attractive patio container plants if deadheaded regularly. Native to E Asia. HEIGHT & SPREAD 15-20×15cm (6-8×6in).

'Baby Doll' comes in shades of red, rose, white and some bicolours. **'Magic Charms'** are coral, pink and crimson selfs. **'Snowfire'** has pure white flowers with scarlet centres. **'Raspberry Parfait'** has deep pink flowers with large crimson eyes and dark green leaves. **'Strawberry Parfait'** has light rose-pink flowers with scarlet eyes and dark green leaves.

D. deltoides♀ (maiden pink) Cerise-pink flowers, about 1.5cm (½in) across, appear in lax clusters in summer on this spreading, mat-forming perennial. It has narrow lance-shaped, deep green leaves and is suitable for rock gardens and the front of dry sunny borders or banks. Native to Britain. HEIGHT & SPREAD 15×30cm (6×12in).

'Albus' has white flowers. **'Brilliant'** has bright carmine flowers. **'Leuchtfunk'** ('Flashing Light') has brilliant cerise flowers. **'Microchip'** is an annual with pink to red flowers.

D. erinaceus (hedgehog pink) Solitary, purplish pink flowers, about 1.5cm (½in) across, appear in mid to late summer. This dense, hummock-forming perennial has stiff, pointed, grey-green leaves. The plant is excellent for a raised bed or a rock garden in a warm, sunny position, but dislikes too much winter wet. Native to Turkey. HEIGHT & SPREAD 20×50cm (8×20in).

D. freynii The solitary pink flowers, about 1.5cm (½in) across, are borne in early to mid summer on this grey-green, tufted perennial with stiff, very narrow leaves. Native to the Balkans. HEIGHT & SPREAD 5-10×10-15cm (2-4×4-6in).

D. glacialis (glacier pink) Solitary pale to deep pink flowers, up to 1.5cm (½in) across, are borne on short stems in early and mid summer. A tufted to hummock-forming perennial with linear, deep green leaves. Native to E Alps and Carpathians. HEIGHT & SPREAD 5-10×10-20cm (2-4×4-8in).

D. gratianopolitanus♀ (syn. *D. caesius*) (Cheddar pink) Intensely fragrant, solitary, pale pink flowers, up to 3cm (1¼in) across, appear on long slender stems in summer. The lax tufted or mat-forming perennial has narrow grey-green leaves and is an excellent rock garden plant. Native to Britain. HEIGHT & SPREAD 15×30cm (6×12in).

▲ *Dianthus deltoides* 'Brilliant'

▲ *Dianthus chinensis* 'Raspberry Parfait'

'Flore Pleno' has semidouble flowers.

D. haematocalyx The solitary deep pink flowers, up to 3cm (1¼in) across and slightly spotted, have a beige reverse and a red calyx. This cushion-forming plant, with grey or blue-green, narrow, sharply pointed leaves, makes a good rock garden or trough plant. Native to the central Balkans. HEIGHT & SPREAD 10-20×10-20cm (4-8×4-8in).

D. knappii Sulphur-yellow flowers, 1.5cm (½in) across, are borne in clustered heads in summer on this tufted, rather lax perennial. The narrow lance-shaped leaves are pale grey-green. Native to the Balkans. HEIGHT & SPREAD 30-40×10-20cm (12-16×4-8in).

D. microlepis Small, solitary, pink to purple flowers, up to 1.5cm (½in) across, appear in early to mid summer. Each petal is toothed on the margin, not fringed as in most other pinks. Forming a dense cushion of silvery grey or grey-green leaves, it is best suited to a trough in lime-free soil. Native to Bulgaria. HEIGHT & SPREAD 5×15cm (2×6in).

D. myrtinervius Bright pink flowers with darker spotting or markings in the centre appear in summer. They are rather rounded, almost stemless and up to 1.5cm (½in) across. Forming low, moss-like cush-

▲ *Dianthus erinaceus*

ions of tiny bright green leaves, this perennial requires full sun and a gritty soil to flower well, and tends to be rather short-lived. Native to mountains of N Greece. HEIGHT & SPREAD 5×20 cm (2×8 in).

D. pavonius♀ (syn. *D. neglectus*) (three-veined pink) The rather flat flowers, borne singly or in clusters, are pale to deep purplish pink or pink, with a contrasting buff reverse. They appear in early to mid summer and grow to 2.5 cm (1 in) across. The neat, cushion-forming plant with spiky grey-green leaves makes a good rock garden or trough plant. Native to the Alps. HEIGHT & SPREAD 5–10×20 cm (2–4×8 in).

D. petraeus Solitary, pale pink flowers, about 1 cm (⅜ in) across, appear in mid to late summer on short leafless stems. A cushion-forming or matted perennial with stiff, sharply pointed, green or grey-green leaves, the plant is suitable for a rock garden or a raised bed. Native to the Balkans. HEIGHT & SPREAD 10–15×15–25 cm (4–6×6–10 in).

White flowers are borne by ssp. ***noeanus.***

D. plumarius (common pink) Intensely fragrant solitary flowers, about 3 cm (1¼ in) across, appear in summer and vary in colour from white to bright pink. This lax hummock to mat-forming perennial with narrow, pointed, grey-green leaves is ideal for a rock garden or for dry sunny places. Native to central Europe. HEIGHT & SPREAD 30–40×30–40 cm (12–16×12–16 in).

Dianthus plumarius

D. sinensis see *D. chinensis*

D. squarrosus Fragrant, pure white, deeply fringed flowers, about 1.5 cm (½ in) across, appear in summer. This mat or hummock-forming perennial with sharply pointed, grey-green leaves is good for a rock garden or trough. Native to Ukraine and Kazakhstan. HEIGHT & SPREAD 20×20 cm (8×8 in).

D. subacaulis (short pink) Solitary carmine-pink flowers, rarely more than 1.5 cm (½ in) across, appear in summer on this mat-forming perennial suitable for a raised bed or a trough. The tufted, blunt-tipped leaves are deep green. Native to SW Europe. HEIGHT & SPREAD 10–15×10–15 cm (4–6×4–6 in).

D. superbus Beautifully fragrant, deeply fringed pale pink to purple flowers, up to 5 cm (2 in) across, with darker veins, appear in mid to late summer. A rather sprawling perennial with broadly linear, pale to mid green leaves. Native to Europe. HEIGHT & SPREAD 15–20×20–30 cm (6–8×8–12 in).

ALPINE HYBRIDS

Most of the species hybridise easily, producing numerous cultivated varieties suitable for a rock garden, raised bed, trough or alpine house. The plants form tufted or bushy clumps of narrow grey or grey-green foliage and most have fragrant flowers up to 3 cm (1¼ in) across, with fringed or serrated petals and stems 7.5–15 cm (3–6 in) high.

'Betty Norton' rose with a maroon centre; single. **'Dewdrop'** white with a yellowish green edge; single. **'Dubarry'** rose-lilac flowers with a crimson centre; double.

▲ *Dianthus* 'Dewdrop'

'Fanal' reddish purple flowers with a deeper crimson centre; single. **'Fusilier'** rose-red, zoned crimson; single. **'Hidcote'** rose-red; single. **'Highland Fraser'** pale pink laced and zoned maroon; single. **'Inshriach Dazzler'**♀ carmine pink with buff reverse on the petals; single. **'La Bourboule'**♀ solitary pink flowers; single. **'La Bourboule Albus'** white; single. **'Lemsii'** pink flushed with purple; single to semidouble. **'Little Jock'** mauve-pink with a crimson eye; semidouble. **'Mars'** bright crimson; semidouble. **'Nyewood's Cream'** cream or ivory-white flowers, 1.5 cm (½ in) across, with smooth-edged petals; single. **'Oakington'** solitary, rich purple-pink flowers; semidouble or double. **'Pike's Pink'**♀ pale pink with a cerise eye; double. **'Pink Jewel'** light purple, semidouble flowers 1.5 cm (½ in) across; stems 5–10 cm (2–4 in). **'Prince Charming'** pink flowers that are paler in the centre; single. **'Waithman's Beauty'** ruby splashed pink with clock-face markings; single. **'Whatfield Gem'** pink flowers laced maroon; double. **'Whatfield Joy'** lilac-pink with a darker eye and petals that are smooth-edged; single. **'Whatfield Magenta'** magenta; single. **'Whatfield Wisp'** very pale pink; single. **'Whitehills'**♀ pink with a central crimson zone; single.

▲ *Dianthus* 'Little Jock'

GARDEN PINKS

Old-fashioned and modern pinks are hybrids derived from cross-breeding various species. The leaves, stems and nodes of the pink are identical to those of the carnation, but on a smaller scale. The flowers, 4–6 cm (1½–2½ in) across and single, semidouble or double, have fringed or deeply serrated, occasionally smooth, petal edges. The main colour groups are selfs, bicolours, laced pinks and fancies. Most are scented, some with a heavy clove scent. The plants may be low-spreading or bushy. HEIGHT & SPREAD 25–38×23–30 cm (10–15×9–12 in).

Old-fashioned pinks

This group includes older varieties – some claimed to date from the 17th century – and newer ones having the same low-spreading or bushy habit of growth. All have one flush of bloom for 2 or 3 weeks in early summer and, except where stated, all the pinks listed have double flowers.

'Allspice' magenta, edged and lightly splashed white; single. **'Brympton Red'** deep rose with a darker zone and edging; single. **'Dad's Favourite'** white ground laced ruby-red. **'Inchmery'** pale pink self. **'Mrs Sinkins'** white, splits its calyx. **'Musgrave's Pink'** (syn. 'Charles Musgrave') white with pale green eye; single. **'Sam Barlow'** white, zoned deep maroon-purple. **'Sops-in-Wine'** white, zoned deep crimson-purple.

▲ *Dianthus* 'Inchmery'

▲ *Dianthus* 'Mrs Sinkins'

d

d

Modern pinks
Old-fashioned pinks were crossed with perpetual-flowering carnations, and resulted in the hybrid group known as *D.* × *allwoodii*, from which most modern pinks derive. These are more vigorous than old-fashioned pinks, producing many more blooms. Flowering is mainly in early to mid summer, and all have double flowers unless otherwise stated. Young plants should have their growing tips pinched out in spring to promote bushy growth.

'Becky Robinson'♀ rose-pink, laced with ruby-red. **'Claret Joy'**♀ crimson. **'Cranmere Pool'**♀ creamy white with a magenta centre. **'Devon Cream'** pale yellow with light magenta flecks. **'Devon Dove'**♀ white with a green eye. **'Devon General'**♀ deep red. **'Devon Glow'**♀ magenta. **'Devon Maid'**♀ white with a magenta eye. **'Devon Wizard'**♀ cyclamen-purple with a ruby-red centre. **'Diane'**♀ salmon-pink. **'Doris'**♀ salmon-pink with a scarlet eye. **'Gran's Favourite'**♀ white with cerise-pink lacing. **'Haytor White'**♀ white. **'Houndspool Cheryl'**♀ light crimson. **'Houndspool Ruby'**♀ rose-pink with a reddish centre. **'Joy'**♀ salmon-pink. **'Kesteven Kirkstead'**♀ white with a red-

▲ *Dianthus* 'Becky Robinson'
Dianthus 'Devon Cream' ▲

▲ *Dianthus* 'Cranmere Pool'
Dianthus 'Diane' ▲

▲ *Dianthus* 'Claret Joy'

▲ *Dianthus* 'Gran's Favourite'
Dianthus 'Haytor White' ▲

purple eye; single. **'Laced Monarch'** pink laced with maroon-purple. **'Lincolnshire Poacher'**♀ lavender-pink with a maroon eye; single. **'Marg's Choice'**♀ light salmon-pink. **'Monica Wyatt'**♀ cyclamen-pink with a magenta eye. **'Old Mother Hubbard'**♀ pink flecked with deeper pink. **'Strawberries and Cream'** creamy white, splashed with two shades of pink. **'Valda Wyatt'**♀ lavender-pink with a deeper centre. **'Widecombe Fair'**♀ pastel pink.

BORDER CARNATIONS
Border carnations have evolved through 4 centuries of selective breeding from *D. caryophyllus*. These hardy perennial plants have grey-green or grey-blue leaves and double flowers that are 6-8 cm (2½-3¼ in) across with smooth-edged petals. They can be selfs, fancies or picotees. They flower only once in the season – in mid to late summer in the south, starting and finishing a little later in the north. Each stem can bear 5 or more flowers. HEIGHT & SPREAD 50-80×45 cm (20-32×18 in).

'Angelo' yellow, edged and marked deep purple. **'Bryony Lisa'**♀ white, edged and marked rosy-carmine. **'Catherine Glover'** bright yellow, edged and barred scarlet. **'Chris Crew'**♀ deep apricot, edged red. **'Eileen O'Connor'**♀ golden apricot. **'Flanders'**♀ deep scarlet. **'Golden Cross'**♀ yellow. **'Hannah Louise'**♀ yellow, heavily edged scarlet. **'Hazel Ruth'**♀ white, boldly striped blood-red. **'Howard Hitchcock'**♀ yellow, edged and evenly striped rosy red.

▲ *Dianthus* 'Devon Dove'

▲ *Dianthus* 'Laced Monarch'

'Irene Della-Torré'♀ white, evenly marked fuchsia-pink, with a scent of cloves. **'Lavender Clove'** lavender, clove-scented. **'Merlin Clove'** white, heavily edged and striped purple, clove-scented. **'Peter Wood'**♀ light pink, flaked bright red. **'Portsdown Clove'** shell-pink, clove-scented. **'Sandra Neal'**♀ apricot with broad flakes of deep pink. **'Uncle Teddy'**♀ white, edged and boldly striped purple. **'Whitesmith'**♀ white, sweetly scented.

ANNUAL CARNATIONS
These half-hardy perennials, evolved from *D. caryophyllus*, have double flowers 5 cm (2 in) across. Usually grown from seed as annuals, occasionally as biennials, they flower from mid summer until the first frosts, and are excellent bedding plants. Sometimes sold as border carnations, they should not be confused with the hardy border carnations previously described.

Floristan Series, usually grown as biennials, produce flowers in most carnation self colours, some with picotee markings. They grow to a height of 75 cm (30 in). **Knight Series**, 30 cm (12 in) tall with flowers in a range of colours – orange picotees, rose, crimson, scarlet and white self colours or a mixture of these. **Lillipot Series** are dwarf bushy plants 23 cm (9 in) tall, with double flowers, mostly selfs but some bicolours.

PERPETUAL-FLOWERING CARNATIONS
These carnations, grown under glass for cutting, have double flowers up to 10 cm (4 in) across. They are available as selfs, fancies and picotees. Given a temperature of 10°C (50°F), they bloom all year round. At 7°C (45°F) they still provide a fair number of winter flowers, and at 5°C (41°F) a few

blooms may be produced. Plants grown in a cold greenhouse will often survive a few degrees of frost, but growth will be checked and slow to start in spring.

'Ann Franklin' pale yellow, edged and flecked maroon. **'Audrey Robinson'** white, heavily edged and marked deep purple. **'Clara'** yellow, edged and flecked red; scented. **'Clara's Lass'** white, edged and ticked red; scented. **'Cream Sue'** cream. **'Crompton Princess'** pure white. **'Dunkirk Spirit'** orange-apricot, lightly flecked red. **'Fragrant Ann'**♀ white, heavily clove-scented. **'Jacqueline Ann'**♀ white, flecked rose-pink; scented. **'Joanne'** cerise-pink; scented. **'Joanne's Highlight'** light pink. **'Joe Vernon'** deep purple. **'Raggio di Sole'** orange-apricot, marked deeper orange. **'Ron's Joanne'** light cerise with light pink markings. **'Salamanca'** bright yellow. **'Scarlet Joanne'** scarlet, scented. **'Valencia'** bronze-yellow.

Malmaison carnations

These old-fashioned carnations, widely grown in Victorian and Edwardian times, produce large, self-coloured blooms with a heavy clove scent. The flowers, up to 12.5cm (5in) across, have so many petals that the calyxes invariably split. They are cultivated and propagated in the same way as perpetual-flowering carnations.

'Duchess of Westminster' bright rose-pink. **'Princess of Wales'** rose-pink. **'Souvenir de la Malmaison'** ('Old Blush') blush-pink flowers. **'Tayside Red'** brick-red. **'Thora'** pale blush.

CULTIVATION

SPECIES AND ALPINE HYBRIDS Most of the alpine species and their hybrids thrive in full sun in a well-drained rock garden or raised bed in alkaline soil, though most tolerate neutral to slightly acid conditions. The smaller and tighter cushion-forming species are also excellent for troughs or for growing in pots in an alpine house. *D. glacialis* and *D. microlepis* prefer acid soil. *D. callizonus* and *D. glacialis* require a dry atmosphere but also plenty of moisture at the roots, which can be provided by digging a lot of organic matter into the soil. *D. deltoides* and its cultivars tolerate partial shade, but will not flower as profusely.

GARDEN PINKS AND BORDER CARNATIONS Plant out in early to mid autumn. Incorporate well-rotted manure or garden compost into the ground and rake in bonemeal or blood, fish and bone before planting. Do not bury the lower leaves when planting, and after frosty weather check that plants have not been lifted out of the ground. In very exposed areas plants may be overwintered in a coldframe in 8cm (3in) pots, and planted out in early spring.

Pinks generally do not require staking, but border carnations should be supported when they start to spindle in late spring.

Border carnations are disbudded to secure larger flowers. With first-year plants remove the small bud below the crown bud; second-year plants may have some of the smaller axillary buds removed as well; and a plant in its third season should be allowed only 2 or 3 flowers a stem.

Pinks are never disbudded, but regular removal of dead flowers from modern pinks and the application of a balanced fertiliser in mid summer encourages further flowering. In their second and third season, carnations and pinks benefit from the application of a balanced fertiliser in spring.

After 3 years, plants become rather lanky and woody, and are best replaced with fresh young plants.

ANNUAL CARNATIONS Before planting, prepare soil as for cultivation of garden pinks and border carnations. Regular deadheading encourages a longer flowering period. Do not disbud.

PERPETUAL-FLOWERING CARNATIONS Plants require full light and plenty of ventilation, and the greenhouse should ideally have glass down to ground level. Move rooted cuttings into 6cm (2½in) pots in late winter or early spring, in John Innes No. 1 compost or a soil-less equivalent.

When 8 or 9 pairs of leaves have developed, stop the plant by snapping out the growing tip cleanly at a joint, leaving 5 or 6 joints or pairs of leaves. Sideshoots will then grow from every leaf axil. Before the plant becomes potbound pot on into a 15cm (6in) pot, using either John Innes No. 2 compost or a soil-less equivalent, and support with a 1m (3ft) cane and rings. Stopping for a second time – when each sideshoot has developed 8 or 9 pairs of leaves – will result in many more side growths, all of which will eventually flower. However, it is more usual to stop only half of the shoots, leaving the remainder to bloom in summer and autumn. These flowers are followed in winter by flowers from the stopped growths. Do not stop all the shoots at once, and all stopping should cease by mid summer. As well as stopping, perpetual-flowering carnations also need disbudding. All sidebuds are removed to leave only the top, or crown, bud on each stem. This disbudding should be a gradual process as removing all the buds at once would result in split calyxes.

Do not allow the plants to dry out, but avoid overwatering. Apply shading to the glass in early summer, and in hot weather damp down the greenhouse path and the area around the pots.

Feed plants grown in soil-less compost 6 weeks after repotting, but for soil-grown plants this is not necessary until the first flower buds develop. Apply a balanced liquid fertiliser every 7–10 days during summer and autumn. In winter, give a monthly feed only when a temperature of 7°C (45°F) is maintained.

In their second year, plants are repotted into 20–23cm (8–9in) pots, and supported with a 1.2m (4ft) cane. At the end of the second year, plants are best discarded and replaced with fresh young stock.

PROPAGATION

SPECIES AND ALPINE HYBRIDS Take cuttings of non-flowering shoots of species and hybrids in summer. Pot them on as soon as they have rooted adequately, generally after 4–6 weeks. Sow seed of the species in autumn or early winter in pots in a coldframe. Some of the tufted types can be divided in spring or straight after flowering.

Sow seed of sweet williams under glass in late winter or early spring at a temperature of 13°C (55°F). Prick out seedlings and plant in late spring to flower during summer. Alternatively, sow seed in open ground in mid spring and transplant to the flowering site in mid autumn, where the plants will bloom early the following year.

GARDEN PINKS AND BORDER CARNATIONS Layer border carnations in mid summer in the following manner. Strip non-flowering sideshoots of all but the top 5 or 6 pairs of leaves. Insert a sharp-pointed penknife through the middle of the stem immediately below the node or joint with the lowest leaves, and cut downwards through the next joint bringing the blade out just below it. The cut should form a tongue that is held open and pegged down with a wire hoop into a fresh mixture of soil, peat and sand. If the plants are kept just damp, new roots should form in about 6 weeks. Sever the layer from the parent plant and replant elsewhere.

For garden pinks, take cuttings of non-flowering sideshoots in early summer.

ANNUAL CARNATIONS Sow under glass from mid winter to early spring, and either plant out in late spring or grow on as container plants. Floristan Series is raised from seed sown from mid spring to mid summer, and planted out in autumn to flower the following summer.

PERPETUAL-FLOWERING CARNATIONS Take close-jointed, non-flowering shoots, with about 6 pairs of leaves, and cut just below the lowest joint, removing the bottom pair of leaves. Dip the base of the cutting in hormone rooting powder and insert into sharp sand with a bottom heat of 18–24°C (64–75°F). Rooting should take place in about 3 weeks.

PESTS AND DISEASES Root aphids and other types of aphid can infest most pinks and introduce harmful viruses into plants. Carnation fly maggots and tortrix caterpillars feed on leaves and stems. Thrips infest flowers under glass and outdoors, and red spider mites attack greenhouse carnations.

Carnation stem-rot occurs on some plants under glass after the stems have been cut. Basal rot of cuttings is caused by the same fungus. Rust attacks the leaves and stems and leaf spot can be a problem. Fusarium and verticillium wilt can attack perpetual-flowering carnations under glass.

Diascia

Scrophulariaceae

A profusion of shell-like, two-spurred flowers in shades of pink are borne throughout the summer on these South African perennials and annuals. They form compact clumps of matted sprawling growth or more extensive upright plants with loose spikes of flowers, each flower up to 2cm (¾in) across. The leaves are often heart shaped and up to 3.5cm (1¼in) long.

The first flush of bloom is in early summer and if the plant is trimmed back new shoots with a second flush of bloom appear later in the season. The plants are not reliably hardy but are easily propagated by division, cuttings and seed, and young plants are more free-flowering. Although they grow best in a sunny position they do not flourish in soil that dries out. Suitable for the front of a border and the rock garden, they also do well in containers. The recommended plants are all perennials.

RECOMMENDED SPECIES AND VARIETIES

D. anastrepta Tangled stems rise from the crown of the plant carrying rich pink flowers in long, lax sprays. The ovate leaves are dark green. It needs a moist site to grow well. HEIGHT & SPREAD 30×50cm (12×20in).

D. barberae A dense mass of slender stems bears sprays of deep rose-pink flowers over a long period in summer. The glossy leaves are ovate and dark green. HEIGHT & SPREAD 30×40cm (12×16in).

D. cordata A mat-forming plant with sprawling spikes bearing clusters of bright pink flowers. The small rounded leaves are deep green. HEIGHT & SPREAD 30×50cm (12×20in).

D. fetcaniensis A very free-flowering plant with a mass of rosy pink flowers from late spring onwards. An upright bushy plant, it has deep green leaves. HEIGHT & SPREAD 25×40cm (10×16in).

D. integerrima♀ A good border plant with slender erect spikes of rose-pink flowers and narrow lance-shaped leaves. HEIGHT & SPREAD 40×40cm (16×16in).

D. lilacina A mat-forming plant with solitary lilac-pink flowers, usually in the axils of the pale green leaves, in early summer. HEIGHT & SPREAD 20×40cm (8×16in).

D. rigescens♀ A bushy plant with strong stems carrying long spikes of profuse, dusky crimson-pink flowers from late spring until early autumn. The leaves are pale green ageing to a reddy brown. HEIGHT & SPREAD 50×40cm (20×16in).

D. stachyoides A mat-forming plant with stems bearing deep rose-pink flowers in the axils of the round leaf-like bracts. It does not always flower regularly. HEIGHT & SPREAD 40×40cm (16×16in).

D. vigilis♀ The plant spreads over a wide area so space plants 50cm (20in) apart. It is usually regarded as the hardiest species. The flowers are a soft clear pink. HEIGHT & SPREAD 50×50cm (20×20in).

GARDEN VARIETIES

These plants are usually up to 45cm (18in) high with a spread of 40cm (16in) or more.

SALMON-APRICOT SHADES

'Blackthorn Apricot'♀, **'Hopley's Apricot'**♀, **'Joyce's Choice'**♀, **'Lady Valerie'**♀ and **'Salmon Supreme'**.

PINK SHADES

'Elizabeth'♀, **'Fisher's Flora'**♀, **'Frilly'**♀, **'Ruby Field'**♀ and **'Rupert Lambert'**♀.

PURPLY PINK SHADES

'Lilac Belle'♀, **'Lilac Mist'**♀ and **'Twinkle'**♀.

DARK PINK SHADES

'Dark Eyes'♀ and **'Hector's Hardy'**♀.

CULTIVATION Plant in late spring in any fertile soil. Trimming off old flowerheads as they fade will encourage a further flush of late-season flowers.

PROPAGATION Sow seed in late winter under glass. Semi-ripe cuttings of cultivars taken from actively growing plants in summer or early autumn root readily under glass. Pot on the resulting plants and keep frost-free until spring planting. Established plants can also be divided in spring.

PESTS AND DISEASES Usually trouble free.

▲ *Diascia integerrima*

▼ *Diascia cordata*

▼ *Diascia* 'Hopley's Apricot'

Dicentra

Bleeding hearts

Papaveraceae

Heart-shaped flowers dangle like rows of lockets below the arching stems of these hardy herbaceous perennials. The blooms range from red, purple and deep pink to white or yellow and are borne from early spring to early summer with some species flowering intermittently throughout the summer. The recommended plants form compact clumps, 25-30cm (10-12in) across, of finely divided, often glaucous leaves, apart from *Dicentra scandens* which is a climber. In general, they do best in bright semi-shade and moist soils. They also flourish in a woodland setting and are best planted where they are protected from cold spring winds as the early shoots and flowers are rather delicate and easily frost-damaged.

RECOMMENDED SPECIES AND VARIETIES

D. cucullaria (Dutchman's breeches) A woodland plant bearing yellow-tipped, cream white flowers in spring; pink varieties are also known. Blue-green leaves, roughly triangular in outline, are composed of up to 23 segments. Native to N America. HEIGHT & SPREAD 25×25cm (10×10in).

D. formosa The plant bears pendent flowers from late spring to early summer, coloured variously from rose-purple to yellow to white. The fern-like, basal leaves are glaucous beneath and often so on the upper surfaces. Native to western N America. HEIGHT & SPREAD 50×50cm (20×20in).

D. macrantha The long pale yellow flowers dangle from the stems in late spring. This plant is suitable for cooler conditions in the garden if it is shielded from cold winds. Native to China. HEIGHT & SPREAD 45×25-30cm (18×10-12in).

D. scandens (syn. *D. thalictrifolia*) The divided leaves of this climber have the end leaflet modified into a tendril which allows the plant to cling to shrubs or to training wires. Yellow or white flowers have flared tips coloured pink or purple and are borne from late summer to early autumn. Native to SE Asia. HEIGHT Up to 4m (13ft).

D. spectabilis♀ (Dutchman's breeches, bleeding heart) The most widely grown of the species, this plant makes a compact clump of fern-like leaves with a mass of arching stems on which the graceful flowers are borne from early spring to early summer. Each flower is a rich rose red with white protruding inner petals. Even though native to shady woodland in China, Korea and Siberia, it needs protection from cold winds and late spring frosts. HEIGHT & SPREAD 60×45cm (24×18in).

'Alba'♀ is a beautiful form with pure white flowers.

D. thalictrifolia see *D. scandens*

GARDEN VARIETIES

These plants flower in late spring and early summer and spread 15-20cm (6-8in).

'Adrian Bloom' is a large-flowered deep red, 30cm (12in) high. **'Bacchanal'** has soft crimson-red flowers on arching stems 30cm (12in) high. **'Bountiful'**♀, 30cm (12in) high, has glaucous leaves and deep rosy red flowers. **'Langtrees'**♀, 30cm (12in) high, is a pale pink with glaucous blue leaves and can be a rampant grower on light soils in shady sites. **'Luxuriant'**♀, 30cm (12in) high, has mounds of fresh green, fern-like foliage and large bright pink flowers. **'Pearl Drops'** has glaucous leaves and dangling pink-tinged white flowers on stems about 30cm (12in) high. **'Snowflakes'** has white flowers amid finely cut fresh green foliage and grows up to 25cm (10in) high. **'Spring Morning'**, 30cm (12in) high, has palest pink flowers. **'Stuart Boothman'**♀, 25cm (10in) high, has finely cut, steel blue leaves with dusty pink flowers through summer.

▲ *Dicentra spectabilis* 'Alba'

▲ *Dicentra* 'Bountiful'

CULTIVATION The plants grow best in a humus-rich moist soil, in sheltered sunny places or in dappled shade.

PROPAGATION Established plants can grow for many years without replanting but when clumps need dividing do this from autumn to late winter, taking care not to damage the central crown. Replant in well-drained soil to which plenty of well-rotted compost has been added. Sow seed in early spring and plant seedlings out in autumn; on heavy soils leave the new plants in pots until early spring. Alternatively, for brittle rooted species such as *D. spectabilis*, take root cuttings, 10cm (4in) long, from established plants. Root in early spring in peat and sand compost in a coldframe.

PESTS AND DISEASES Slugs and snails can be troublesome in spring.

Dicksonia see FERNS p.263

Dictamnus

Burning bush, dittany

Rutaceae

Dictamnus albus

The common name of this plant derives from the volatile lemon-scented oil given off by its flowers, which has been known to ignite spontaneously on still, dry summer evenings. People with sensitive skin can suffer a rash from the oil. There is only one species in the genus, a long-lived herbaceous perennial found throughout SW Europe and across into Asia. It is hardy in Britain and makes a good plant for a sunny border, thriving in alkaline soil.

Dictamnus albus♀ Impressive spikes of white star-shaped flowers are produced in early summer on a bushy plant. The flowers, which are sometimes streaked and spotted with purple, are 3cm (1¼in) across with protruding stamens. The star-shaped seed capsules that come after the flowers are valued by flower arrangers. Dark green leathery leaves, up to 7.5cm (3in) long, consist of 9-11 leaflets. HEIGHT & SPREAD 60×25cm (24×10in).

The plant var. ***purpureus*** (syn. *D. fraxinella*) is as the species but the flowers are pale mauve-pink, streaked with purple.

D. fraxinella see *D. albus* var. *purpureus*

CULTIVATION Plant in well-drained fertile soil – preferably alkaline – in a sunny or partially shaded site. Avoid moving plants, particularly the large ones, once they have become established.

PROPAGATION Sow seed in late summer into open ground and transplant the seedlings into their final positions as soon as they are large enough to handle, either that autumn or the following spring. It may be several years before these plants flower.

PESTS AND DISEASES Usually trouble free.

▲ *Dictamnus albus*

▲ *Dictamnus albus* var. *purpureus*

d

Dieffenbachia

Dumb cane
Araceae

Very large, oval or broadly lance-shaped green leaves, often splashed with cream or white, are the main feature of these evergreen perennials. The leathery leaves grow alternately from an upright, fleshy, cane-like stem as tall as 2m (6½ft). Greenish cream to white flowers, 2.5cm (1in) long, bloom intermittently, and not at all when the plant is raised indoors. Dieffenbachias are usually grown as houseplants in Britain, in a temperature of at least 15°C (59°F). The sap is poisonous and a skin irritant. Plants are native to tropical Central and S America. The leaves of recommended plants are up to 25cm (10in) long and 10cm (4in) wide, unless stated otherwise.

RECOMMENDED SPECIES AND VARIETIES

D.* x *bausei Yellowish green leaves have several large green blotches and a number of prominent small white spots. HEIGHT & SPREAD 90×90cm (36×36in).

▲ *Dieffenbachia* 'Camille'

***D.* 'Camille'** Striking greenish cream leaves are edged with green. HEIGHT & SPREAD 80×60cm (32×24in).

D. maculata The leaves, as long as 45cm (18in) and 10cm (4in) wide, are mid green heavily spotted with white. HEIGHT & SPREAD 90×75cm (36×30in).

'Roehrsii' has yellowish green leaves faintly spotted white, with green midribs and margins.

D. oerstedi The velvety, dark green leaves are often slightly asymmetrical. HEIGHT & SPREAD 1m×60cm (3×2ft).

On **'Variegata'**, the midribs form a bold cream line down the centre of each leaf.

D. seguine Glossy, dark green leaves, often with tiny white spots, grow to 45cm (18in) long and 15cm (6in) wide. HEIGHT & SPREAD 1m×60cm (3×2ft).

'Amoena' has dark green leaves with creamy white markings along the veins. This plant grows to 1.5m (5ft) or more and spreads to 75cm (30in). **'Exotica'** is a slow-growing, relatively small variety, with leaves to 25cm (10in) long, dark green splashed greenish white. The plant reaches a height of 45cm (18in) and spreads to 50cm (20in). **'Rudolph Rhoers'** has creamy green leaves that develop darker green spots, edges and veins as they age. The leaves on **'Tropic Snow'** are a creamy green with paler markings towards the centre, green midribs and darker edges.

CULTIVATION Grow in a warm well-lit room out of direct sunlight and draughts. Use John Innes No.3 compost and keep constantly damp. Twice a week, syringe the foliage with clean tepid water. Remove any faded leaves immediately.

PROPAGATION Take stem cuttings or air layer in summer. Place pieces of leafless stem horizontally in trays of good rooting medium during spring or summer.

PESTS AND DISEASES Mealy bug and vine weevil are sometimes a nuisance.

Dierama

Angel's fishing rods
Iridaceae

With their arching stems of pendent, bell-like summer flowers and long, sword-like leaves these perennials are ideal for a damp, sunny spot beside a pool or arching across a path. The evergreen, clump-forming plants grow from corms. Recommended species are native to South Africa.

RECOMMENDED SPECIES AND VARIETIES

D. dracomontanum (syn. *D. pumilum*) The nodding pink or purplish, bell or funnel-shaped flowers, 2.5cm (1in) long, are borne in mid to late summer. A hardy plant with slender mid green leaves up to 45cm (18in) tall. HEIGHT & SPREAD 75×30cm (30×12in).

D. pendulum (syn. *D. ensifolium*) Arching sprays of deep pinkish purple, funnel-shaped flowers, up to 2.5cm (1in) long, are carried in profusion on tall wiry stems in late summer. These elegant and hardy plants have narrow strap-like leaves that can grow up to 1.5m (5ft) in length. HEIGHT & SPREAD 1.5m×20cm (5ft×8in).

var. ***pumilum*** see *D. dracomontanum*

▼ *Dierama dracomontanum*

▲ *Dierama pulcherrimum*

D. pulcherrimum Wiry stems carry graceful, arching sprays of deep pink, funnel-shaped flowers up to 5cm (2in) long. A hardy, upright plant with broad grass-like leaves up to 1.5m (5ft) long. Native to South Africa. HEIGHT & SPREAD 1.5m×30cm (5×1ft).

CULTIVATION Grow in a richly organic but free-draining soil in a very sunny spot. The plants dislike disturbance so divide the clumps only when there is a noticeable deterioration in flower quality and quantity – usually only after many years. Plant corms in mid autumn or mid spring. Remove old flower stems and faded foliage.

PROPAGATION Divide and replant corms in spring. Sow seed in a coldframe in spring.

PESTS AND DISEASES Thrips are the only persistent problem.

Diervilla

Bush honeysuckle
Caprifoliaceae

Diervilla sessilifolia

Clusters of small yellow flowers are borne on the new season's growth of these easily grown, summer-flowering small shrubs. They are deciduous, multistemmed and of rounded habit. The individual flowers, only 1.5cm (½in) long, are tubular and grow from the base of the leaves. The leaves, up to 18cm (7in) long, are opposite on the stem. Natives of N America, all diervillas are frost-hardy.

▲ *Diervilla sessilifolia*

▲ *Diervilla x splendens*

RECOMMENDED SPECIES

D. sessilifolia Flower clusters, up to 7.5cm (3in) across, appear in early summer and last through to late summer. HEIGHT & SPREAD 80×80cm (32×32in) after 5 years, ultimately 1.2m (4ft) tall.

D. × splendens Flower clusters in mid summer last through to early autumn. HEIGHT & SPREAD 80×80cm (32×32in) after 5 years, ultimately 1.2m (4ft) tall.

CULTIVATION Plant in any well-drained soil in full sun or partial shade.

PROPAGATION Take semi-ripe cuttings from mid to late summer, or sow seed in a coldframe in autumn or winter.

PRUNING None usually necessary except to shape plants or to remove dead wood. Prune before growth begins in spring.

PESTS AND DISEASES Usually trouble free.

Digitalis

Foxglove

Scrophulariaceae

Digitalis purpurea

Tall spires of colourful, tubular flowers are borne in summer above glossy or downy foliage. These biennial and perennial border plants, ranging in height from 45cm (1½ft) to 2m (6½ft), enjoy moist, humus-rich soil and benefit from a little shade. The mainly lance-shaped leaves grow as a basal rosette or clump with smaller leaves growing up the stem. Most foxgloves carry their flowers on one side of the stem. Some perennial species deteriorate after their first flowering and are best treated as biennials. *Digitalis purpurea* and *D. lutea* spread freely by self-seeding. All parts of the plant are poisonous. Native throughout Europe to central Asia.

RECOMMENDED SPECIES AND VARIETIES

D. ambigua see *D. grandiflora*

***D.* Apricot hybrids** see *D. purpurea* 'Sutton's Apricot'

D. ciliata Small, cream tubular flowers are borne on the stout stem of this perennial. Very hairy leaves grow to 15cm (6in) long. HEIGHT & SPREAD 60×45cm (2×1½ft).

D. davisiana Sparse, pale yellow blooms, 2.5cm (1in) long, with distinctive orange veining, are borne in summer. This perennial has smooth, narrow, dark green leaves to 12cm (4¾in) long. HEIGHT & SPREAD 75×30cm (2½×1ft).

D. dubia Purplish flowers with darker internal spotting, up to 5cm (2in) long, are sparsely produced in summer on a short flower stem. The coarse, matt green leaves of this short-lived and half-hardy perennial grow to 20cm (8in) and lie in flat rosettes. HEIGHT & SPREAD 45×30cm (1½×1ft).

D. eriostachya see *D. lutea*

D. ferruginea (rusty foxglove) Pale orange-brown to off-white flowers, each 3.5cm (1½in) long, are borne in summer on tall spikes above rosettes of soft, downy, broad leaves up to 25cm (10in) long. A perennial that behaves as a biennial in the garden. HEIGHT & SPREAD 1.2m×60cm (4×2ft).

▼ *Digitalis ferruginea*

D. grandiflora♀ (syn. *D. ambigua*, *D. orientalis*) (large yellow foxglove) Stout, upright flower spikes are clothed in mid to late summer with pale yellow flowers with brown veins inside, like pendent tubular bells, each flower up to 5cm (2in) long. Finely toothed, mid green leaves are lance-shaped while basal leaves are oval. Leaves are up to 25cm (10in) long. This is a perennial plant that is best treated as a biennial. HEIGHT & SPREAD 1m×45cm (3×1½ft).

The flowers of **'Temple Bells'** are slightly larger.

D. heywoodii see *D. purpurea* ssp. *heywoodii*

D. kishinskyi see *D. parviflora*.

D. laevigata Small pendent flowers are produced in summer on stiff, upright stems. Each bloom is no more than 3cm (1¼in) long and brownish white with internal brown-purple veining and a distinctive white lip. This perennial produces rosettes of dark green, smooth, slightly toothed leaves up to 25cm (10in) long. HEIGHT & SPREAD 1m×60cm (3×2ft).

D. lanata♀ (syn. *D. lamarckii* hort.) (Grecian foxglove) The off-white to pale caramel-coloured flowers, 2.5cm (1in) long, are marked with brown veining and appear from mid to late summer. The narrow, grey-green, downy leaves grow to 20cm (8in). A short-lived perennial usually treated as an biennial. HEIGHT & SPREAD 75×45cm (2½×1½ft).

D. lutea (syn. *D. eriostachya*) (straw foxglove) From mid to late summer the dark green, smooth flower spike is densely covered with pale yellow, pendent flowers, up to 2.5cm (1in) long. The glossy, dark green leaves of this reliably perennial foxglove are up to 25cm (10in) long. HEIGHT & SPREAD 60-90cm×45cm (2-3×1½ft).

D. × mertonensis♀ The pendent flowers are crushed strawberry pink and up to 5cm (2in) long. Flowers are borne from mid to late summer above neat rosettes of greyish green, soft, downy leaves that are broad lance-shaped and grow to 25cm (10in) long. This is a perennial hybrid which is best treated as a biennial. HEIGHT & SPREAD 75×45cm (2½×1½ft).

D. obscura (willow-leaved foxglove) A shrubby half-hardy perennial with yellow flowers marked red inside, up to 4cm (1½in) long, from mid to late summer. The narrow, shiny, dark green leaves grow to 10cm (4in) long. Protect the plant from cold and winter wet. HEIGHT & SPREAD 60×60cm (2×2ft).

D. orientalis see *D. grandiflora*

D. parviflora (syn. *D. kishinskyi*) The tiny, reddish brown and white flowers, up to 1.25cm (½in) long, are densely borne all round the flowering stem of this plant in summer. The mid green leaves grow up to 10cm (4in) long and have slightly toothed edges. Though reasonably reliable as a perennial, the plant is best replaced after 3-4 years. HEIGHT & SPREAD 60×45cm (2×1½ft).

▲ *Digitalis purpurea*

D. purpurea (common foxglove) In summer this biennial species bears flowers up to 5cm (2in) long, ranging in colour from pink to purple with deep purple internal spotting. The soft, greyish green, oval or lance-shaped leaves grow up to 25cm (10in) long in neat basal clumps. This foxglove is an extremely variable species both in stature and in behaviour. HEIGHT & SPREAD 1.5m×60cm (5×2ft).

▲ *Digitalis purpurea* Excelsior Group

Digitalis purpurea f. *albiflora* ▲

The flowers of f. ***albiflora***♀ are white. It reaches a height of 1-1.5m (3-5ft). **Excelsior Group**♀ bears flowers in a wide range of pastel colours, from creamy white to purple-pink, all with purple internal spotting. They are borne more evenly round the stem than in the common species. Plants reach a height of 2m (6½ft) or more. **Foxy Group** has red, pink, cream and white flowers, all heavily spotted with maroon. Plants reach a height of 75cm (2½ft). **Giant Spotted Group** has red, pink, cream and white flowers, all heavily spotted with maroon. The foliage of ssp. ***heywoodii*** is silvery grey and the flowers are white to pale purple. It reaches a height of 1m (3ft). **'The Shirley'**♀ in Gloxinioides Group bears funnel-shaped flowers, up to 5cm (2in) long and 5cm (2in) wide at the opening, in colours ranging from white through cream and pink to purple, all heavily spotted with maroon. **'Sutton's Apricot'** has apricot-coloured flowers and comes true from seed. It reaches a height of 2m (6½ft).

D. viridiflora A perennial with small, green-yellow flowers, up to 1cm (⅜in) long, with prominent greenish veins on a slender spike in summer. Lance-shaped, plain green leaves grow up to 15cm (6in) long. HEIGHT & SPREAD 60×30cm (2×1ft).

CULTIVATION Plant in sun or partial shade in humus-rich, moist but free-draining soil.

PROPAGATION Sow seed from spring until late summer either in a frame or in the open ground. Divide the dependable perennial species in early spring.

PESTS AND DISEASES Usually trouble free.

Dill see *Anethum graveolens*
Dill (culinary herb) see HERBS p.331

Dimorphotheca

Star of the veldt, Cape marigold

Compositae

These colourful South African daisies are among the easiest and most free-flowering of half-hardy annuals for a well-drained soil. A sunny site is best as the flowers close up in shade and in dull weather. They are fairly drought-tolerant and thrive on rockeries and at the foot of south-facing walls, where they make a quick temporary ground cover. Both species readily available make rather spreading plants with the abundant flowers displayed well above dark green, aromatic, narrow leaves. Leaves are deeply toothed and up to 10cm (4in) long.

RECOMMENDED SPECIES AND VARIETIES

D. aurantiaca see *D. sinuata*

D. ecklonis see *Osteospermum ecklonis*

***D. pluvialis* 'Glistening White'** The scented white flowers, borne from mid summer to early autumn, are about 5cm (2in) across with a dark brownish purple central disc. The slight violet tinge of the flower arises from the purple underside of the petals. HEIGHT & SPREAD 25-40×15-30cm (10-16×6-12in).

D. sinuata (syn. *D. aurantiaca*) The most widely grown species has unscented flowers up to 8cm (3¼in) across from mid summer to early autumn. They have a dark golden-brown central disc and are generally available in a mixed colour range, dominated by salmon, orange and pink but also including some whites and creams. HEIGHT & SPREAD 30×30cm (12×12in).

'Salmon Queen' is a mixture of apricot and salmon shades. **'Tetra Pole Star'** has white flowers with a purple eye.

▲ *Dimorphotheca pluvialis* 'Glistening White'

CULTIVATION Plant in late spring after the risk of frost has passed in well-drained, preferably sandy, soil, in a sunny spot. Deadhead regularly to prolong flowering. Alternatively, grow in pots and keep in a greenhouse or conservatory at a minimum temperature of 7°C (45°F). Choose a sunny position and water sparingly.

PROPAGATION Sow seed in mid or late spring where the plants are to grow. For earlier flowers, sow the seed in a heated greenhouse in early spring and plant out seedlings in late spring.

PESTS AND DISEASES Grey mould may affect flowers in prolonged wet weather.

Dionysia

Primulaceae

Dionysia aretioides

A multitude of pink, violet or yellow, five-petalled primrose-like flowers cover these compact, cushion-forming alpines in late winter and spring. The cushions of foliage can be loose or dense and are made up of a mass of small leaf-rosettes with the dead leaves of previous years clothing the stems below.

Dionysias are native to the mountains of the Middle East, growing on shaded or partially shaded cliffs, and require the shelter of an alpine house in the relatively cold, damp climate of Britain.

RECOMMENDED SPECIES AND VARIETIES

D. aretioides Solitary yellow flowers cover the hummocks of grey-green leaves from late winter to spring, although some flowers may appear in autumn. The flowers are 1cm (⅜in) across. The oblong leaves, up to 1.5cm (½in) long, are hairy with their toothed edges rolled under. HEIGHT & SPREAD 20×50cm (8×20in).

'Paul Furse' has large flowers, up to 1.5cm (½in) across, with rather rounded petals. **'Phyllis Carter'** has an abundance of flowers with narrower petals.

▲ *Dionysia aretioides* 'Paul Furse'

▲ *Dionysia involucrata*

D. curviflora Solitary pink flowers with yellow eyes clothe the dense, greyish cushions of foliage from late winter to spring. Each flower is 6mm (¼in) across. The tiny leaves are up to 6mm (¼in) long. HEIGHT & SPREAD 8×40cm (3¼×16in).
D. involucrata Violet-purple flower clusters cover the sticky, deep green cushions of foliage in spring. The clusters are composed generally of 2-3 tightly packed tiers of flowers up to 5cm (2in) long. Each bloom is about 1cm (⅜in) across, with a white eye that gradually turns deep crimson-purple. The leaves are 1cm (⅜in) wide, and toothed in the upper half. HEIGHT & SPREAD 15×20cm (6×8in).
CULTIVATION Plants of this species must be grown in an alpine house. Plant them in well-drained gritty compost with a layer of grit around the collar of the plant. Water with care always making sure that the cushions of foliage are not left with water lying on them. Water sparingly in winter, and more frequently in summer.
PROPAGATION Sow seed in pots when ripe or in winter.
PESTS AND DISEASES Aphids can be a problem in spring. The fungal disease botrytis can infect the cushions.

Diospyros
Persimmon
Ebenaceae

Diospyros kaki

Colourful autumn foliage is the chief garden value of these trees or large shrubs, though dainty flowers and glossy leaves give interest in summer. On mature plants there may be the bonus of fruits, if male and female plants are grown. Fruits are edible and juicy but full of seeds. Most species in the genus are tropical plants, the two deciduous Asiatic species listed below are most suitable for British gardens and eventually produce fruits, given the right conditions.
RECOMMENDED SPECIES
D. kaki (persimmon) Small yellowish white, bell-shaped flowers appear in mid summer. Male trees carry flowers in clusters while females carry single blooms. Glossy leaves are 15cm (6in) long and turn orange, red and purple in autumn, when the fruits are borne. Fruits are orange when ripe, round and 7.5cm (3in) in diameter. The greyish brown bark is scaly and furrowed beneath a rounded dome of foliage. HEIGHT & SPREAD 6×4m (20×13ft) after 20 years, ultimately 12m (40ft) tall.
D. lotus (date plum) The tiny flowers in mid summer are like translucent pale pink porcelain bells carried in clusters (males) or singly (females). Small brown fruits are 3cm (1¼in) across. The dark brown bark beneath the rounded crown becomes fissured with age. The tree shape and its growth rate are variable. HEIGHT & SPREAD 5×3m (16×10ft) after 20 years, ultimately 20m (66ft) tall.
CULTIVATION Plant in a sheltered sunny position when the soil is warm. If fruit is desired, male and female plants need to be grown together. The recommended species grow best on dry fertile sites among other trees to give them shelter.

▼ *Diospyros kaki*

PROPAGATION Sow seed in spring. Alternatively take semi-ripe cuttings in summer or layer in winter. When grown from a seedling, it is 20 years before the tree flowers and its sex can be determined. The waiting time is reduced if the tree is grown from a cutting or a graft (as often sold in garden nurseries).
PRUNING Not usually necessary.
PESTS AND DISEASES Usually trouble free.

Dipelta
Caprifoliaceae

Dipelta floribunda

Small, fragrant flowers are borne in profusion from late spring to early summer on the tall, deciduous shrubs. This genus has only four species, all of them native to China.
RECOMMENDED SPECIES
D. floribunda Fragrant, pinky white flowers, 3cm (1¼in) long, with orange markings in the throat are produced in clusters of up to 6. The bark is creamy and flaking.

▲ *Dipelta floribunda*

Oval leaves, up to 10cm (4in) long, are light green and hairy. The shrub is fully hardy. HEIGHT & SPREAD 1.5m (5ft) tall after 5 years, ultimately 5×2m (16×6½ft).
D. ventricosa Pale to deep pink flowers with an orange throat, up to 2.5cm (1in) long, are borne in groups on this multi-stemmed shrub. Narrow, pointed, light green leaves are up to 12.5cm (5in) long. Grow in a sheltered position as the plant is only moderately frost-hardy. HEIGHT & SPREAD 100×60cm (3×2ft) after 5 years, ultimately up to 2m (6½ft) tall.

D. yunnanensis A frost-hardy multi-stemmed shrub with clusters of orange-throated, cream flowers up to 2.5cm (1in) long. Narrow leaves, up to 12.5cm (5in) long, are dark green above, hairy and paler beneath. The creamy white bark flakes with age. HEIGHT & SPREAD 1.5×1m (5×3ft) after 5 years, ultimately 3×1.5m (10×5ft) tall.
CULTIVATION Best grown in fairly rich soil but can survive quite happily on fairly shallow limy soils. It prefers a position in full sun and stands exposure well, though *D. ventricosa* needs a sheltered position.
PROPAGATION Sow seed in spring or take semi-ripe cuttings from early to mid summer. Plant out from autumn to early spring but if container grown, plant at any time and water in dry periods.
PRUNING None required but thin out after flowering if stems become too crowded.
PESTS AND DISEASES Usually trouble free.

Diphylleia
Umbrella leaf
Berberidaceae

Huge leaves on tall stems are embellished with small clusters of white flowers from late spring to early summer followed by indigo-blue berries in late summer and early autumn. These hardy, herbaceous perennials grow best in open or shady moist borders or woodland gardens. *Diphylleia cymosa* is the species most commonly seen in Britain.
RECOMMENDED SPECIES
D. cymosa Dark green, 2-lobed and toothed leaves up to 40cm (16in) across grow in pairs over a dense mass of stout stems. The leaves have well-marked veining. Rounded clusters of about 10 small, white flowers appear above the leaves, each star-like flower is up to 1.5cm (½in) across and has 6 oval petals. The blue, spherical berries, 1cm (⅜in) wide, also stand clear of the leaves on red stalks. An erect plant with leaves that tend to overlap when mature. The plant only becomes untidy on open sites subject to strong winds. Native to the Appalachian mountains of N America, the species grows on the banks of streams. HEIGHT & SPREAD 60×120cm (2×4ft).

▼ *Diphylleia cymosa*

CULTIVATION Plant in autumn to spring, in moist, humus-rich soil in full or partial shade. Protect the plant against wind by placing it next to a tree, larger shrub or wall that will act as a windbreak.
PROPAGATION Divide the rootstock in spring. Sow seeds when ripe or in spring. Seedlings grow slowly.
PESTS AND DISEASES Usually trouble free but slugs and snails attack seedlings.

Diplacus see *Mimulus*

Diplarrhena
Butterfly iris
Iridaceae

Clusters of iris-like flowers stand on wiry stems amid fans of long, strap-like leaves in summer. The flowers of this perennial though short-lived plant have a sweet fragrance and lend elegance to herbaceous borders in warm, southern gardens. In colder areas they can be grown in containers in a greenhouse or conservatory.
RECOMMENDED SPECIES
D. moraea Clusters of white flowers are held on erect stalks up to 1m (3ft) tall. The flowers open in succession and are about 5cm (2in) across, composed of 3 rounded outer petals and 3 smaller inner petals suffused with yellow or purple. The stiff, grass-like leaves are evergreen and grow to 15–60cm (6–24in) long and about 1cm (⅜in) wide, arising from short rhizomes. Native to forest margins of E Australia including Tasmania. HEIGHT & SPREAD 1m×40cm (36×16in).

▲ *Diplarrhena moraea*

CULTIVATION Plant in any well-drained soil in full sun or in a pot of sandy compost in a greenhouse.
PROPAGATION Divide the fans after flowering or sow seeds in early spring under glass.
PESTS AND DISEASES Usually trouble free.

Dipsacus
Teasel
Dipsacaceae

The large, egg-shaped spiny flowerheads of teasels make a striking feature in an informal border. The tall, straight stems are often branched near the top and in mid summer each branch carries a single flowerhead, densely packed with tiny papery flowers that are very attractive to bees. In autumn the large seed heads encourage goldfinches and other seed-eating birds into the garden.

The slender stems carry pairs of narrow, pointed leaves, 10cm (4in) long and often united to form a cup at the stem. Stems and leaves are usually armed with spines. Teasels occur widely throughout Europe and Asia. The recommended plants are biennials.
RECOMMENDED SPECIES
D. fullonum (common teasel) The large flowerheads, up to 8cm (3¼in) long, are tightly packed with numerous tiny purple flowers. A ruff of bracts encircles the base of each flowerhead. HEIGHT & SPREAD 2m×60cm (6½×2ft).

▲ *Dipsacus fullonum*

D. sativus Large, pale purple flowerheads, up to 11cm (4¼in) long, carry prominent, rigid and sharply hooked bracts. HEIGHT & SPREAD 2m×60cm (6½×2ft).
CULTIVATION Plant in full sun in any soil, though heavier soils suit teasels best.
PROPAGATION Sow ripe seed into garden position either as soon as gathered or in spring. Plants often self seed.
PESTS AND DISEASES Usually trouble free.

Dipteronia

Aceraceae

Forming a small, bushy deciduous tree or large shrub, *Dipteronia sinensis* is fully hardy and is grown for its colourful autumn leaves and striking, red, winged fruits. Native to central and SW China.

RECOMMENDED SPECIES

D. sinensis As the small greenish white flowers fade in summer, winged fruits appear which turn red by early autumn. The fruits are composed of a small central nutlet, surrounded by a circular wing, and they are joined in pairs. Fruits first appear when plants are more than 6 years old. The pinnate leaves are mid green and slightly bronzed, turning yellow in autumn. They have 7-13 oval, pointed leaflets, up to 10cm (4in) long. HEIGHT & SPREAD 4.5×1.8m (15×6ft) after 10 years, ultimate height up to 10m (33ft).

▲ *Dipteronia sinensis*

CULTIVATION Plant in any fertile, moist but well-drained soil, in full sun or light shade.

PROPAGATION Sow ripe seed in autumn or take softwood cuttings.

PRUNING Rarely necessary.

PESTS AND DISEASES Usually trouble free.

Disa see ORCHIDS p.464

Disanthus

Hamamelidaceae

Disanthus cercidifolius

The chief beauty of this medium-sized shrub is its varied autumn colour. It is a sprawling deciduous plant, and there is only one species. Native to SE China and Japan.

Disanthus cercidifolius ♀ Blue-green in summer, the rounded to heart-shaped foliage ranges from gold to orange and eventually purplish red in autumn. The undersides of the leaves are a more muted shade of the upper side. The insignificant pairs of purple flowers are star-like and are borne in autumn. Though a hardy plant it should be protected from cold winds and frost. HEIGHT & SPREAD 1.5×1m (5×3ft) after 5 years, ultimately 1.8×3m (6×10ft).

CULTIVATION This shrub thrives only on moist, acid soils. Its native habitat is moist woodland and it requires dappled shade to produce its best colour as the thin leaves burn easily in strong sunlight. Young plants should be protected from frost in winter.

PROPAGATION It is relatively easy to layer lower branches in autumn and winter.

PRUNING Carry out sparingly as growth is not particularly strong and hard pruning does not stimulate growth.

PESTS AND DISEASES Usually trouble free.

Disporum

Fairy bells

Convallariaceae

Small, narrowly bell-shaped flowers bloom on the tips of erect or arching leafy stems in late spring or early summer. The drooping flowers of these easily grown, sometimes spreading, perennials are solitary or in clusters – creamy white, yellowish or green and sometimes spotted or tinged with purple. Colourful berries, which can be orange, red or black, may follow the flowers in autumn.

The more vigorous of these clump-forming plants are best when left to colonise beneath small shrubs. More compact species make attractive dot plants in woodland conditions. Mostly hardy, the plants are easily grown in light shade, in a well-drained soil rich in leaf-mould or peat. Native to E Asia and western N America.

RECOMMENDED SPECIES AND VARIETIES

D. sessile Creamy white flowers, each segment tipped with green, are borne in late spring in clusters of 1-3 on arching stems clothed with lance-shaped, mid green leaves up to 15cm (6in) in length. Blue-black berries ripen in early autumn. The plant is vigorous and may eventually form an extensive colony. HEIGHT & SPREAD 30-60×20-40cm (12-24×8-16in).

'Variegatum' is the most commonly grown variety, and has leaves handsomely striped with white.

D. smithii (fairy lantern) Clusters of up to 6 creamy white flowers, each 2.5cm (1in) long, are borne in spring on the clump-forming plant. The leaves, up to 12cm (5in) long, are ovate, mid green, often wavy-edged. Bright orange oval berries follow in late summer to autumn. The branching stems are erect to arching. HEIGHT & SPREAD 40-90×30-60cm (16-36×12-24in).

▲ *Disporum sessile* 'Variegatum'

CULTIVATION Easily grown in a fairly moist but well-drained soil rich in humus. The plants do best in a partially shaded position and are excellent for woodland sites.

PROPAGATION Sow seed in autumn or divide established clumps in early spring.

PESTS AND DISEASES Usually trouble free but may be damaged by slugs.

Dodecatheon

Shooting star

Primulaceae

Dodecatheon meadia

Elegant flowers in white and shades of pink, purple, lavender and magenta make an impressive spring and summer display in moist, but not waterlogged, spots in the garden. These herbaceous perennials thrive alongside ponds, at the edges of bog gardens and in rock gardens. They also look well in mixed borders in dappled shade, providing the soil is moist and humus-rich. The plants listed are fully hardy to -25°C (-13°F).

The nodding, pointed flowers are borne in clusters on long stalks. The flowers have four or five petals that are swept backwards and upwards leaving the stamens protruding as a distinctive cone below. After a flower is fertilised it points up to the sky as the fruit develops. The leaves form basal tufts or rosettes similar to those of a primula.

RECOMMENDED SPECIES AND VARIETIES

D. alpinum Magenta to lavender-pink, 4-petalled flowers, up to 2.5cm (1in) long, are borne in small clusters from mid spring to mid summer. The tufts of mid green, linear to oval, leaves are smooth, hairless and untoothed. Native to western USA. HEIGHT & SPREAD 30×20cm (12×8in).

d

D. dentatum ♀ White, usually 5-petalled flowers, 2.5 cm (1 in) long, have a yellowish band at the base of the petals and a reddish purple cone of stamens. They are carried in clusters of 3-7 in late spring to summer. The pale green leaves are oblong to ovate with a toothed margin. A good woodland border plant, it is native to SW Canada and western USA, except California. HEIGHT & SPREAD 40×20 cm (16×8 in).
D. hendersonii ♀ Magenta to lavender or white flowers, about 2.5 cm (1in) long, are borne in stout clusters of up to 17 in mid spring to summer. The flowers have 5 petals and a maroon and yellow cone of stamens. The ovate to spoon-shaped leaves are rather fleshy and slightly toothed. Native to western N America. HEIGHT & SPREAD 45×30 cm (18×12 in).
D. jeffreyi Lavender to magenta, rarely white, flowers are carried in clusters of up to 18. The flowers are about 2.5 cm (1 in) long with 4-5 petals and a maroon and yellow cone of stamens. The oval, pale to mid green leaves are sticky and somewhat fleshy. Native to western N America. HEIGHT & SPREAD 60×30 cm (24×12 in).
D. meadia ♀ (syn. *D. pauciflorum*) (shooting star, American cowslip) Stout clusters of about 50 rose to rose-purple or lilac flowers appear from late spring to mid summer. The flowers, up to 2 cm (¾ in) long, are usually 5-petalled with a yellow, maroon-striped cone of stamens. The leaves are ovate to spoon shaped and entire to markedly toothed. Native to eastern USA. HEIGHT & SPREAD 50×25 cm (20×10 in).

The flowers on f. *album* ♀ (syn. 'Album') are white with yellow anthers. **'Pulchellum'** has deep crimson flowers.
D. pauciflorum see *D. meadia*
D. pulchellum ♀ (syn. *D. radicatum*) Pink to lavender, purple and magenta flowers are borne in clusters of up to 25 in late spring to summer. The 5-petalled flowers, about 2 cm (¾ in) long, have a yellow or a yellow and maroon cone of stamens. The oval to spoon-shaped leaves are entire to slightly toothed, and can be sticky. Native to damp grassland and scrub of central and eastern USA. HEIGHT & SPREAD 50×25 cm (20×10 in).

'Red Wings' has deep crimson flowers. **'Sooke's Variety'** is neater, up to 30 cm (12 in) tall, with pink or purple flowers.
D. radicatum see *D. pulchellum*

CULTIVATION Grow in a moist, humus-rich soil in sun or part-shade. The plants grow best in cool places.

PROPAGATION Sow seed when ripe in pots in a shaded coldframe. Prick out seedlings in spring. Divide parent clumps after flowering or in early spring. Several species produce tiny grain-like bulbils at the base of the plant and these can be detached and grown on in autumn; put in pots and grow on until large enough to plant out.

PESTS AND DISEASES Aphids and slugs may attack young shoots in spring. Root aphids can be a problem after a mild winter.

♥ *Dodecatheon meadia f. album*

♥ *Dodecatheon pulchellum*

Dodonaea

Sapindaceae

Dodonaea viscosa 'Purpurea'

The only species widely available in Britain is *D. viscosa,* a neat, large conical evergreen shrub or tree, grown for its foliage. It is the hardiest of the genus, most of which are native to Australia. Even so, it is only suitable for warmer regions of Britain as it suffers badly or will even die from prolonged frosts of -5°C (23°F) or below. It is ideal for southern coastal gardens as it withstands strong winds and salty spray. Elsewhere it may be safer to grow it in a pot so that it can be brought under shelter during cold snaps.

RECOMMENDED SPECIES AND VARIETIES
D. viscosa The evergreen, rather leathery oblong leaves, about 8×2 cm (3¼×¾ in), are carried alternately. Tiny green to reddish flowers are borne in terminal clusters in spring, male and female flowers on separate plants. Female plants, if pollinated, produce purple-red, winged seed capsules in summer. HEIGHT & SPREAD 3×2 m (10×6½ ft) after 5 years, ultimately up to 6 m (20 ft) tall.

'Purpurea' has reddish purple leaves.

CULTIVATION Plant in well-drained soil in full sun.

PROPAGATION Sow fresh seed or take semi-ripe cuttings in early autumn.

PRUNING None normally necessary.

PESTS AND DISEASES Usually trouble free.

♥ *Dodonaea viscosa*

Dogwood see *Cornus*
Dondia see *Hacquetia*

Doronicum

Leopard's bane
Compositae

Golden yellow, daisy-like flowers, 5-10 cm (2-4 in) across, are generally carried in spring on slender stems above low clusters of bright green, heart-shaped, hairy leaves. These easily grown, hardy herbaceous perennials are native to Europe and W Asia.

RECOMMENDED SPECIES AND VARIETIES
D. caucasicum see *D. orientale*
D. x *excelsum* **'Harpur Crewe'** A hybrid with large golden yellow flowerheads on stems 60 cm (2 ft) high.
D. **'Frühlingspracht'** ('Spring Beauty') has double, golden yellow flowerheads and grows to 40 cm (16 in) tall.
D. **'Miss Mason'** ♀ has bright yellow flowerheads and grows to 45 cm (18 in) high.
D. orientale The yellow flowerheads are

♥ *Doronicum x excelsum 'Harpur Crewe'*

▲ *Doronicum* 'Frühlingspracht'

borne singly well above the leaves which have scalloped margins. HEIGHT & SPREAD 30-60×15 cm (12-24×6 in).

'Magnificum' has large yellow flowerheads on stems up to 50 cm (20 in) high.

D. pardalianches (great leopard's bane) From late spring to mid summer each stem has 3-5 yellow flowerheads above a clump of hairy, ovate leaves. All parts of this plant are reputed to be poisonous. HEIGHT & SPREAD 90×60 cm (3×2 ft).

CULTIVATION Easy plants to grow in a wide range of soils. To maintain vigour divide and replant every 3-4 years, between autumn and early spring, spacing plants 38-45 cm (15-18 in) apart. The taller varieties need some support when in flower. Deadhead regularly.

PROPAGATION Divide immediately after flowering or while dormant, or sow in spring. *D. orientale* 'Magnificum' comes true from seed.

PESTS AND DISEASES Powdery mildew can be a problem.

Dorotheanthus

Livingstone daisy
Aizoaceae

These low-growing succulent annuals, with daisy-like flowers, produce a carpet of brilliant colour from early summer to early autumn. Grow them in poor, dry soils, in a sunny position as the flowers close up in shade or dull weather. The flowers, borne singly, are up to 4 cm (1½ in) across. Succulent, glistening, pale green leaves, 5-7.5 cm (2-3 in) long, clothe fleshy stems. Livingstone daisies were previously called mesembryanthemums. Native to S Africa.

RECOMMENDED SPECIES AND VARIETIES

D. bellidiformis (syn. *Mesembryanthemum criniflorum*) Crimson, orange, pink, red or white flowers sometimes have petal bases of a contrasting, paler colour, forming an inner zone around the darker central disc. The fleshy, prostrate stems form a mat. Seed is usually available only in mixed colours. HEIGHT & SPREAD 10×30 cm (4×12 in).

D. gramineus This species bears flowers of the same colours as *D. bellidiformis.* However, it has a tufted rather than mat-forming habit of growth. HEIGHT & SPREAD 10×20 cm (4×8 in).

▲ *Dorotheanthus bellidiformis*

D. oculatus **'Lunette'** (syn.'Yellow Ice') Flowers are a soft yellow with a russet-coloured central disc. They are less inclined to close in dull weather than the flowers of other plants. This is a mat-forming plant. HEIGHT & SPREAD 10×30 cm (4×12 in).

CULTIVATION Grow in sun, in dry soil, planting in late spring, or mid spring in milder areas. Where garden soil is not free-draining, plants do best in a raised bed or in pockets of soil in the crevices of a south-facing dry wall. Deadhead regularly.

PROPAGATION Sow seed where plants are to grow. Flowering begins about 3 months after sowing. For flowering in early summer sow seed under glass in early spring and plant out in late spring.

PESTS AND DISEASES Slugs may attack seedlings and young plants. In wet conditions, roots may rot.

Douglasia see *Vitaliana*
Dove Tree see *Davidia*

Draba

Whitlow grasses
Cruciferae

Draba aizoides

Neat cushions or tufts of foliage bearing masses of small yellow flowers in spring and early summer earn these delicate alpines a place in a raised bed, trough or rock garden. Although hardy in Britain, most drabas suffer from excessively damp conditions and outdoor plants need winter protection with a pane of glass. It is safer to grow them in an alpine house or unheated greenhouse.

All the recommended plants are cushion-forming evergreen perennials producing clusters of 4-petalled flowers, less than 1 cm (⅜ in) across, in shades of yellow. The individual leaves are usually less than 1 cm (⅜ in) long and form densely packed rosettes. Native to mountainous regions of the Northern Hemisphere and S America.

RECOMMENDED SPECIES AND VARIETIES

D. aizoides (yellow whitlow grass) A hardy plant with lemon-yellow flowers above dense tufts of deep green, rigid, linear leaves. HEIGHT & SPREAD 10×15 cm (4×6 in).

D. bruniifolia Golden yellow flowers appear above a mat or cushion of bristly, deep green, rigid, linear leaves. HEIGHT & SPREAD 7.5×30 cm (3×12 in).

D. longisiliqua♀ Pale yellow flowers appear in clusters on long slender stalks above the domed, downy, dense grey cushions of tiny leaves. HEIGHT & SPREAD 15×20 cm (6×8 in).

▲ *Draba longisiliqua*

D. mollisima Pale yellow flowers appear in heads above the grey-white, dense, domed hummocks of tiny oblong leaves. HEIGHT & SPREAD 15×20 cm (6×8 in).

D. polytricha Bright yellow flowers appear in heads just above the cushions of small leaves covered in white hairs. HEIGHT & SPREAD 7.5×7.5 cm (3×3 in).

▼ *Draba polytricha*

▼ *Draba rigida*

D. rigida A hardy plant with deep yellow flowers above cushions of spreading, linear leaves. HEIGHT & SPREAD 10×10cm (4×4in).

The leaf tips are inflexed in var. *bryoides*. The smaller var. *imbricata* reaches only 3cm (1¼in) across.

CULTIVATION Plant in well-drained gritty soil and full sun. Protect from winter wetness. In the alpine house ensure good ventilation at all times.

PROPAGATION Sow seed in autumn or late winter in pots in a coldframe and prick out in spring when large enough to handle into small pots. Alternatively take cuttings of single rosette pieces in late summer and place them in pots of fine sharp sand in a propagating frame to be planted out in spring or early summer.

PESTS AND DISEASES Plants grown under glass may be invaded by red spider mite, especially during hot sunny weather. The softer cushion types can be infected with downy mildew, particularly in damp weather during autumn and winter months.

Dracaena

Dracaenaceae

Dracaena deremensis 'Bausei'

Brightly coloured sword-like foliage makes these tender evergreen perennials a popular choice for the home or conservatory. Plants develop a palm-like habit and may eventually bear small lily-like flowers. When grown indoors, dracaenas rarely reach more than 2m (6½ft) tall, but in a warm greenhouse or conservatory they may reach the sizes described below. Native to tropical Africa and the Canary Islands.

RECOMMENDED SPECIES AND VARIETIES

D. australis see *Cordyline australis*

D. deremensis Sword-like green leaves, up to 45cm (18in) long, arch outwards. The leaves have 2 longitudinal white stripes. HEIGHT & SPREAD 1.8–3×1m (6–10×3ft).

'Bausei' bears leaves with 2 white bands down the middle. **'Lemon Lime'** has pale green leaves with a pale yellow central stripe and edges. **'Warneckei'**♀ has grey-green leaves with a white stripe along each edge. The leaves of **'Yellow Stripe'** have a yellow central stripe and edges. The last three cultivars are shorter than the species.

D. fragrans Pale green, sword-like leaves, up to 1m (3ft) long and 10cm (4in) wide, sprout from the top of a sturdy trunk. HEIGHT & SPREAD 3×1.2m (10×4ft).

The varieties are smaller. **'Lindenii'** has green leaves with creamy white edges. **'Messangeana'**♀ has glossy, lime-green leaves with a central stripe of yellowy green.

The **Compacta** group has denser growth with leaves no more than 60cm (2ft) long and 5cm (2in) wide. The foliage of **'Compacta Purpurea'** has a purple caste while **'Compacta Variegata'** is green striped with creamy-white.

D. marginata♀ (Madagascan dragon tree) The easiest species to grow indoors. A slender trunk bears a crown of strap-like leaves, up to 45cm (18in) long. The green leaves have red or brownish edges. HEIGHT & SPREAD 3–5×2m (10–16×6½ft).

▲ *Dracaena marginata*

The leaves of the smaller **'Colorama'** have cream centres and red edges. **'Tricolor'** resembles 'Colorama' but the red edges are less prominent.

D. sanderiana♀ (ribbon plant) Lance-shaped leaves, up to 25cm (10in) long, are glossy green with silvery white stripes. HEIGHT & SPREAD 1.5m×60cm (5×2ft).

D. surculosa (spotted dracaena) Narrow dark green leaves, up to 20cm (8in) long, are smothered with tiny gold and white dots. HEIGHT & SPREAD 1–2×1m (3–6½×3ft).

The smaller **'Florida Beauty'** has dark green leaves blotched with off-white.

CULTIVATION Use John Innes No.2 compost and keep plants damp and humid during summer. Keep at 18°C (64°F). Cut leggy plants to the base in spring and let them resprout. Repot every other spring.

PROPAGATION Sow seed in a heated propagator during spring for the species. Air layer or take stem cuttings in summer for named varieties.

PESTS AND DISEASES Usually trouble free.

Dracocephalum

Labiatae

Grown for the beauty of their tubular, two-lipped flowers, mostly in white or shades of blue, these hardy herbaceous perennials will brighten a sunny border in early to mid summer. They also grow in dappled shade. The flowers are borne in whorls of 2–4 on short spikes. Like other members of the mint family, the plants carry their lance-shaped leaves in pairs.

RECOMMENDED SPECIES

D. argunense Blue or white flowers, 4cm (1½in) long, are borne in leafy spikes. The deep green leaves are up to 5cm (2in) long. HEIGHT & SPREAD 75×40cm (30×16in).

▲ *Dracocephalum ruyschianum*

D. ruyschianum Dense clusters of violet-blue, sometimes pink or white, flowers appear in summer. Each flower is up to 3cm (1¼in) long. The mid green leaves are up to 7.5cm (3in) long. HEIGHT & SPREAD 45×30cm (18×12in).

CULTIVATION Plant in dry, well-drained soil in sun or partial shade.

PROPAGATION Sow seed in autumn or late winter, or divide established plants in early spring or autumn.

PESTS AND DISEASES Usually trouble free.

Dracunculus

Dragon arum

Araceae

Exotic-looking purple flowers and large palmate leaves lend a tropical look to sunny, sheltered areas of the garden. Of the 3 tuberous perennials in the genus, *D. vulgaris,* from the Mediterranean, is the most widely available. It grows well in sun but tolerates some shade in southern gardens.

RECOMMENDED SPECIES

D. vulgaris (dragon arum) Large purple flowers, up to 40cm (16in) long, appear in early summer on 1m (3ft) high stalks. The striking flowers have a deep velvety purple spathe and an almost black spadix and an odour of rotting meat which usually lasts for just a few days. The leaves are palmate with

▼ *Dracunculus vulgaris*

an overall kidney shape, 20cm (8in) long and 35cm (14in) wide. Both leaves and stems are deep green with white spots or stripes. The plant is not entirely hardy in exposed gardens. HEIGHT & SPREAD 1m×60cm (3×2ft).

CULTIVATION Plant in spring in well-drained soil with a sunny aspect. In colder gardens protect the plant in winter with a cloche, dead bracken or branches.

PROPAGATION Remove young offsets in late summer or sow seed under glass in autumn and plant out the following spring.

PESTS AND DISEASES Usually trouble free.

Drimys

Winteraceae

Drimys winteri

Although these evergreen trees and shrubs grow fairly well in Britain, they need a sheltered spot. Only two species *D. lanceolata* and *D. winteri* are widely cultivated. Native to S America, Malaysia and Australasia.

RECOMMENDED SPECIES

D. lanceolata (mountain pepper, pepper tree) (syn. *Tasmannia lanceolata*) A dense shrub with aromatic leaves and crimson young branches. Shiny, light green leaves are rather leathery, usually about 5cm (2in) long and 2cm (¾in) wide. Clusters of white or cream flowers, 1.5cm (½in) wide appear in mid to late spring. The flowers have 2-8 linear, curled-back petals. Pollinated female plants produce small red to black berries. The plant is hardy in warmer areas. HEIGHT & SPREAD 2×2m (6½×6½ft) after 10 years, ultimately 3m (10ft) tall.

▲ *Drimys lanceolata*

D. winteri (winter's bark) A sometimes shrubby tree with a conical habit and grey, aromatic bark. The leaves are similar to those of *D. lanceolata,* but glaucous beneath, about 15cm (6in) long and 6cm (2½in) wide. The white flowers reach 3cm (1¼in) across and are solitary or in small groups. This species can grow to a large size and is suitable only for gardens with little or no frost. HEIGHT & SPREAD 3×2.4m (10×8ft) after 10 years, ultimately 10m (33ft) tall.

CULTIVATION Both species do best in light shade on any well-drained soil.

PROPAGATION Take semi-ripe cuttings or sow seed in early autumn.

PRUNING Seldom necessary.

PESTS AND DISEASES Usually trouble free.

Dropwort see *Filipendula vulgaris*

Dryas

Mountain avens

Rosaceae

Dryas octopetala

From late spring to early summer these hardy, prostrate woody-based perennials are brought to life by large white or yellowish flowers held just above the mat of glossy evergreen foliage. By autumn the flowers have been replaced by decorative feathery seed heads. A sunny site in a rock garden is the ideal setting for these plants, and they will spread across bare rock. Smaller varieties are suitable for growing in troughs.

The flowers are carried singly at the top of erect slender stalks and may be erect or nodding, with 7-10 petals surrounding a boss of golden stamens. The dark green leaves are generally oak-like with a whitish coating beneath. Native to N America, Europe and NE Asia.

RECOMMENDED SPECIES AND VARIETIES

D. integrifolia (syn. *D. tenella*) The flowers open wide to 2.5cm (1in) across among glossy leaves, up to 2.5cm (1in) long, which may be toothed near the base. Pinkish seed heads are globular and feathery. HEIGHT & SPREAD 10×20cm (4×8in).

D. octopetala♀ (mountain avens) The white flowers, about 4cm (1½in) wide, are followed by fluffy silvery or pink-tinged seed heads in autumn. The glossy, mid to dark green, leaves are up to 3cm (1¼in) long with scalloped edges. HEIGHT & SPREAD 20×60cm (8×24in).

'Minor'♀ is a dwarf, compact variety with smaller flowers, reaching 8cm (3¼in) high and spreading to 20cm (8in).

D. x suendermannii♀ Yellowish buds open widely to cream, slightly nodding flowers. The scalloped leaves are up to 3cm (1¼in) long. HEIGHT & SPREAD 18×60cm (7×24in).

D. tenella see *D. integrifolia*

CULTIVATION Plant in a well-drained, peaty soil in full sun.

PROPAGATION Sow seed in late summer or autumn, alternatively take semi-ripe cuttings in summer.

PESTS AND DISEASES Usually trouble free.

▼ *Dryas octopetala*

Dryopteris see FERNS p.263

Duchesnea

Rosaceae

These low-growing herbaceous perennials resemble strawberry plants in fruit, leaf and habit, and are good plants for a hanging basket and ground cover, sending out spreading runners to form extensive mats of foliage from spring to autumn. They are too vigorous to put near choice small plants.

The small flowers have five yellow petals and open from mid spring to autumn. Each flower has a conspicuous green ruff of sepals and broad, toothed bracts as long as the petals. The leaves, up to 4cm (1½in) long, are composed of three mid green, oval leaflets. The fruits are edible, but rather bland. Native to India, China and Japan.

RECOMMENDED SPECIES AND VARIETIES

D. indica (syn. *Fragaria indica*) (Indian strawberry) The flowers are up to 2cm (¾in) across, followed by glossy bright red fruits, about 1.5cm (½in) long. HEIGHT & SPREAD 10cm (4in) tall, spreading about 15-30cm (6-12in) a year.

'Harlequin' (syn. 'Variegata') has cream-edged leaves and is free flowering.

CULTIVATION Plant in any well-drained soil in sun or light shade. Cut back excess growth in autumn or early spring.

PROPAGATION Divide in autumn or spring or detach rooted plantlets from the runners.

PESTS AND DISEASES Usually trouble free.

Dumb cane see *Dieffenbachia*
Dyer's greenweed see *Genista tinctoria*

▼ *Duchesnea indica*

d

Eccremocarpus

Chilean glory vine

Bignoniaceae

Brightly coloured flowers adorn these half-hardy, fast-growing climbers. Their leaf tendrils cling to walls, fences, trellis or other plants with ease, making them ideal for climbing through hedges or up trees. Only in the mildest areas will plants survive the winter unscathed. Frost destroys most or all of the stem system, but regrowth occurs in spring, both from below ground and from surviving seed. Easily grown from seed and climbing up to 3m (10ft) in their first year, eccremocarpus are often treated as half-hardy annuals. They may also be grown in pots under glass.

▲ *Eccremocarpus scaber*

RECOMMENDED SPECIES AND VARIETIES

E. scaber♀ Orange, tubular flowers appear in clusters, about 12.5cm (5in) long, in summer and early autumn. The dark green, often toothed leaves are bipinnate with a branched tendril at the tip of each stalk. HEIGHT & SPREAD 3×1m (10×3ft).

Anglia Hybrids, **'Fireworks'** and **Tresco Hybrids** provide flowers in a mixture of cream, yellow, red, pink and mauve.

CULTIVATION Plant in spring in a sunny, sheltered spot on light, well-drained soil. Mulch plants in autumn. Alternatively, grow in pots of general-purpose or potting compost in a cool greenhouse or conservatory, choosing a position in full sun.

PROPAGATION Sow seed in early spring, transplant self-sown seedlings in spring or take softwood cuttings in early summer.

PESTS AND DISEASES Usually trouble free.

Echeveria

Crassulaceae

Echeveria derenbergii

Rosettes of fleshy leaves, often grey and brightly coloured at the tips, and cup-shaped or tubular waxy blooms distinguish these popular houseplants. The rosettes are sometimes held on short stems and the flower stalks are often pendent. These tender perennial succulents can be used in summer bedding. Native to Central and S America. The heights given below are the height of leaf rosettes rather than the height of the plant during flowering.

RECOMMENDED SPECIES AND VARIETIES

E. derenbergii♀ Handsome rosettes of small grey-white leaves, up to 2.5cm (1in) long, form a clump. In spring a flower stem, up to 7.5cm (3in) tall, rises out of the leaf rosettes, bearing small, cup-shaped, yellow-and-red or orange blossoms. HEIGHT & SPREAD 5×30cm (2×12in).

▲ *Echeveria derenbergii*

▲ *Echeveria elegans*

E. elegans♀ (Mexican snowball) Small alabaster white rosettes with greenish edges, and up to 2.5cm (1in) long, form dense rosettes. If grown in full sun, the foliage often takes on a pinkish tinge. Pink tubular flowers, each tipped with orange-yellow and up to 1.5cm (½in) long, are produced on stems up to 15cm (6in) high during spring and summer. HEIGHT & SPREAD 15×30cm (6×12in).

E. gibbiflora Pointed greyish leaves, 20cm (8in) long and 5cm (2in) wide and more, form rosettes at the end of short stems. The leaves are tinged with purple and have distinctive wavy margins. In autumn this shrubby succulent produces a large flowering stem which may be as much as 1m (3ft) tall. The stem is greatly branched and bears greyish green waxy tubular blossoms strongly flushed with red. HEIGHT & SPREAD 30×25cm (12×10in).

The leaves of var. ***carunculata*** are covered with blister-like growths, while the leaves of var. ***metallica***♀ have a bronzy sheen and fine red edges.

E. harmsii♀ Upright, branching stems, up to 30cm (12in) long, terminate in 10cm (4in) wide rosettes of short, narrow, spear-shaped, pale green leaves. The leaves have red tips and edges and are covered in fine hairs. Cup-shaped red flowers have orange-tipped petals that are yellow on the inside. Up to 3cm (1¼in) long, they are produced on stems up to 20cm (8in) high in summer. HEIGHT & SPREAD 25×30cm (10×12in).

▲ *Echeveria harmsii*

E. secunda Short stems terminate in rosettes of fleshy, light greyish green leaves that are reddish at the tips. The individual leaves are up to 5cm (2in) long and 2.5cm (1in) wide. Cup-shaped blooms, with petals that are red outside and yellow on the inside, are held in groups of 5 or more on flowering stems up to 30cm (12in) tall. HEIGHT & SPREAD 4×30cm (1½×12in).

Often seen in gardens, var. ***glauca*** has a much bluer colour to the foliage.

E. setosa♀ (Mexican firecracker) Small green hairy leaves, convex on both sides and no more than 2.5cm (1in) long, form tight stemless rosettes. In summer tubular red flowers with yellow tips and interiors are freely produced on stems up to 25cm (10in) high. This is one of the few echeverias that benefit from a little light shade. HEIGHT & SPREAD 4×25cm (1½×10in).

CULTIVATION Plant outdoors in free-draining soil in a sunny position. Bring indoors before the first frosts and pot individually for overwintering. Keep houseplants tightly potted in gritty cactus compost or John Innes No.1 compost mixed with up to a quarter by volume of sharp sand or grit.

PROPAGATION Separate offsets and pot in-

dividually during spring or summer. Alternatively, sow seed under glass during spring or take stem or leaf cuttings in summer.
PESTS AND DISEASES Mealy bug can be a nuisance under glass.

Echinacea
Coneflower
Compositae

Large daisy-like flowers, in purple, rose-pink or white, make a striking display in a late summer herbaceous border. The flowers are up to 15cm (6in) across, composed of petals (strictly speaking, ray florets) radiating from a cone-shaped centre. Each flower is held on a tall stem which also carries alternate, lance-shaped, mid green leaves, up to 20cm (8in) long. The flowers can continue to appear for over two months and last well when cut. They are often used in dried arrangements. Native to eastern USA, these rhizomatous perennials are completely hardy in Britain.
RECOMMENDED SPECIES AND VARIETIES
E. pallida The flowers are made up of drooping, pale purple petals around a purple-brown cone. HEIGHT & SPREAD 1m×45cm (3×1½ft).
E. purpurea (syn. *Rudbeckia echinacea* var. *purpurea*, *R. purpurea*) The flowers have white to purple petals and an orange-brown centre. Because of variation that can occur in seed-raised plants it is more usual to grow one of the cultivars. HEIGHT & SPREAD 1.5m×50cm (5ft×20in).

▲ *Echinacea purpurea* 'Magnus'

'Magnus' has deep purple petals around a deep orange boss. **'White Lustre'** is a warm white with a green-flushed cone and **'White Swan'** is a pale greenish white with a golden central cone. Both of the white varieties are only 75cm (2½ft) tall.
CULTIVATION Plant in any fertile soil in full sun. Deadhead to prolong flowering.
PROPAGATION Divide from autumn to spring or take root cuttings in early spring and root in peat and sand mixture in a coldframe to plant out later in the year. Sow seed in early spring under glass or outside in late spring. The resulting plants can be set out in the border during autumn.
PESTS AND DISEASES Usually trouble free.

Echinocactus see CACTI p. 107

Echinops
Globe thistle
Compositae

Echinops bannaticus 'Taplow Blue'

Globular flower clusters are borne from mid summer to early autumn on these stately, erect plants. The flowerheads, up to 4cm (1½in) across, are mostly blue or white and carried on stout stems. Thistle-like, spiky leaves, are divided, greyish to deep green and up to 20cm (8in) long. The flowerheads can be cut before they open fully and dried. These plants tolerate poor soil and drought and grow best in warm sunny spots. This large genus consists of hardy herbaceous perennials, biennials and annuals and is native to Europe, Asia and Africa.
RECOMMENDED SPECIES AND VARIETIES
E. albus see *E.* 'Nivalis'
E. bannaticus Grey-blue flowerheads are carried on branching stems amid the dark green slender leaves. HEIGHT & SPREAD 1.2m×38cm (4ft×15in).

'Blue Globe' has rounder flowerheads and grows to a height of 1m (3ft). **'Taplow Blue'**♀ is a tall plant, at a height of 1.5m (5ft), with powder-blue flowers.

▼ *Echinops* 'Nivalis'

***E.* 'Nivalis'** (syn. *E. albus*) Greyish white globular flowerheads are carried on grey stems on this hybrid with greyer leaves. HEIGHT & SPREAD 1.2m×50cm (4ft×20in).
E. ritro♀ The dark steel blue flowerheads of this compact plant colour well in the early stages of growth. HEIGHT & SPREAD 75×30cm (2½×1ft).

▲ *Echinops ritro* 'Veitch's Blue'

The flowers of ssp. ***ruthenicus*** are a bright blue. It has dark green shiny leaves that are covered on the underside with a white sheen. This subspecies reaches a height of 1m (3ft) and a spread of 50cm (20in). **'Veitch's Blue'** produces flowers that are a deeper shade of blue.
E. sphaerocephalus This plant forms a grand clump when allowed to develop to its full majesty. It is larger in all its parts than the others listed here. Flowerheads are 6cm (2½in) across and greyish white. HEIGHT & SPREAD 2.1×1m (7×3ft).
CULTIVATION Plant at any time from autumn to spring in any well-drained soil, choosing a site in full sun.
PROPAGATION Divide established plants in spring or autumn or take root cuttings in late autumn and root in a coldframe over winter. Seeds of species only can be sown in spring outdoors and grown on for planting out in the autumn.
PESTS AND DISEASES Usually trouble free.

Echinopsis see CACTI p. 107

e

Echium

Boraginaceae

Echium plantagineum

Upward-facing, bell-shaped flowers in blue, pink, purple or white add colour to a mixed herbaceous border from early to late summer. The flowers, carried in large impressive spikes, also entice bees and butterflies into the garden.

The oblong or lance-shaped leaves, up to 15 cm (6 in) long and 2 cm (¾ in) wide, are usually hairy and can cause an allergic reaction in some people. The genus contains a mix of annuals, biennials and short-lived perennials native to Europe, the Canary Islands, Africa and W Asia, most doing best in a frost-free garden. In colder regions grow the perennials in a cool greenhouse.

RECOMMENDED SPECIES AND VARIETIES

E. candicans (syn. *E. fastuosum)* (pride of Madeira) Blue or white funnel-shaped flowers with protruding pink stamens open from pink buds. This perennial has a woody base and whitish hairy lance-shaped leaves. HEIGHT & SPREAD 2.4×1.5 m (8×5 ft).

E. fastuosum see *E. candicans*

E. lycopsis see *E. plantagineum*

E. pininana (syn. *E. pinnifolium)* This half-hardy, short-lived, perennial bears lance-shaped deep green hairy leaves. After about 3 years it bears rose or mauve tubular flowers, held in spikes on side stems. It dies after flowering. HEIGHT & SPREAD 4×1 m (13×3 ft).

▼ *Echium pininana*

E. pinnifolium see *E. pininana*

E. plantagineum (syn. *E. lycopsis*) (purple viper's bugloss) The bell-shaped flowers of this annual or biennial undergo a change in colour from blue to red over the summer. The mid green basal leaves are lance-shaped, up to 15 cm (6 in) long. HEIGHT & SPREAD 60×25 cm (24×10 in).

E. vulgare (viper's bugloss) Spikes of 1 cm (⅜ in) long, tubular flowers come in white and shades of pink, blue or purple on this erect bushy plant. The mid green hairy leaves are oblong to lance-shaped. It is a long-flowering annual or biennial. HEIGHT & SPREAD 60×30 cm (2×1 ft).

The cultivars reach only 30 cm (1 ft) tall. **'Blue Bedder'** has blue flowers and the **Dwarf Hybrids** are a mixture of colours.

CULTIVATION Plant during spring in any fertile soil in full sun.

PROPAGATION Sow the annuals where they are to flower in spring, or under glass in late winter. Raise the perennials from seed sown in a heated propagator in late winter and planted out in late spring after the danger of frost is over. Take softwood cuttings of perennials in summer.

PESTS AND DISEASES Whitefly can be troublesome, especially in a greenhouse.

Edelweiss see *Leontopodium*

Edelweiss, New Zealand see *Leucogenes leontopodium*

Edraianthus

Campanulaceae

Edraianthus pumilio

These low-growing, cushion or mat-forming herbaceous perennials, grown for their bright, bell-shaped flowers and neat habit, make first-class plants for troughs and raised beds or rock gardens. The summer flowers, borne singly or in clusters, generally nestle on short stems amid the grass-like foliage. Plants are hardy but susceptible to winter wet. Native chiefly to the mountains of central and S Europe.

RECOMMENDED SPECIES AND VARIETIES

E. graminifolius♀ Blue to deep violet flowers, up to 3 cm (1¼ in) long, appear in terminal clusters on slender, wiry, stems in mid and late summer. This is a tufted plant with linear, deep green leaves up to 15 cm (6 in) long. HEIGHT & SPREAD 15×15 cm (6×6 in).

E. pumilio♀ (syn. *Wahlenbergia pumilio*) Deep lavender or violet-blue flowers, about 2 cm (¾ in) long, appear from early to mid summer. They are carried singly on short, leafy, upright stalks. The deep green linear leaves are not more than 2 cm (¾ in) long. This plant forms a dense tuft or low hummock. HEIGHT & SPREAD 5×15 cm (2×6 in).

▲ *Edraianthus graminifolius*

▲ *Edraianthus pumilio*

E. serpyllifolius (syn. *Wahlenbergia serpyllifolia*) Dark violet flowers, about 2 cm (¾ in) long, bloom in mid summer. The semi-evergreen leaves are narrow, spoon-shaped and up to 3 cm (1¼ in) long on a tufted plant. HEIGHT & SPREAD 5×25 cm (2×10 in).

CULTIVATION Plant in spring or early summer in gritty well-drained soil, choosing a site in full sun. Avoid excessive wet around the collar of the plant during winter – protect plants in wet areas by covering them with a sheet of glass, or a cloche. Alternatively, grow in pots of well-drained gritty compost in an unheated greenhouse or alpine house.

PROPAGATION Sow seed in autumn or early spring in a coldframe, although seed sown fresh gives the best results.

PESTS AND DISEASES Slugs may attack the crown of plants, especially when new growth appears in spring.

Eichhornia

Pontederiaceae

Eichhornia crassipes

Spikes of orchid-like blossoms and interesting buoyant foliage are the distinguishing features of these tropical floating aquatic plants. *Eichhornia crassipes* can be grown in outdoor pools in summer, but should be taken indoors before the first frosts.

RECOMMENDED SPECIES AND VARIETIES
E. crassipes (water hyacinth) This free-floating perennial has glossy bright green leaves with inflated stalks. The oval to rounded leaves, up to 15cm (6in) long and 10cm (4in) across, are arranged in neat rosettes. The blue to lilac flowers, up to 3cm (1¼in) across, are flat with a prominent yellow eye and are carried in erect spikes in summer. Purple-green roots, about 25cm (10in) long, hang down in the water. This tender evergreen or semi-evergreen produces plants from runners and can soon form an extensive floating group. Native to S America. HEIGHT & SPREAD 20×30cm (8×12in).

'Major', the most commonly grown selection, is a little larger.

CULTIVATION Float in a sunny spot when all danger of frost has passed. Eichhornia, as a free-floating plant, obtains its nourishment directly from the water. Remove dead flower spikes. Take plants indoors before the first frosts and place in a pan of very wet mud and keep in a light, frost-free greenhouse at around 15°C (59°F).

PROPAGATION Detach young plants from runners for overwintering.

PESTS AND DISEASES Usually trouble free.

Elaeagnus

Elaeagnaceae

Elaeagnus pungens 'Maculata'

Attractive glossy foliage is the chief value of these easily grown, hardy evergreen and deciduous trees and shrubs. The leaves are usually pointed, up to 7.5cm (3in) long, and can be bright green, silvery or variegated with gold. Small, fragrant, bell-shaped flowers, less than 1.5cm (½in) across, are produced in profusion in the leaf axils and may be followed by ornamental, sometimes colourful berries. The stems can be spiny. The plants tolerate wind and the evergreens are useful for hedging and windbreaks in coastal gardens. Elaeagnus are not exacting plants in their soil requirements though they do not grow as well on thin chalk. The plants recommended below are native to S Europe and Asia.

RECOMMENDED SPECIES AND VARIETIES
E. angustifolia♀ Narrow deciduous leaves, up to 7.5cm (3in) long, are pale green above and silvery beneath. Small, fragrant, yellow-green flowers are produced in profusion from early summer onwards followed by small silvery orange fruits in autumn. The shoots of this rounded, spreading tree can be quite spiny. HEIGHT & SPREAD 3×3m (10×10ft) after 10 years, ultimately 9m (30ft) tall.

Elaeagnus angustifolia

***E. angustifolia* Caspica Group** see *E.* 'Quicksilver'

E.* x *ebbingei The semi-evergreen leaves are a glossy dark green above and silver beneath. Small, very fragrant flowers are produced from mid autumn through till spring. Fruits appear in autumn and they are orange speckled with silver. The young, gingery brown shoots are also speckled with silver scales. This vigorous shrub is fast-growing once established and is an excellent shelter plant, even in coastal regions. It can be pruned if necessary. HEIGHT & SPREAD 1×1m (3×3ft) after 5 years, ultimately 3m (10ft) tall.

▲ *Elaeagnus* x *ebbingei* 'Gilt Edge'

'Gilt Edge'♀ has a striking yellow-gold margin to the leaf. **'Limelight'** has a golden yellow blotch of variable size in the leaf centre. This cultivar frequently reverts to plain green and any reversion must be pruned out.

E. parvifolia♀ Arching branches are covered in deciduous silvery leaves that become glossy bright green as the season progresses. Small, fragrant, cream-white flowers appear in spring and are followed in autumn by red fruits. A large rounded shrub. HEIGHT & SPREAD 1×1m (3×3ft) in 5 years, ultimately 3m (10ft) tall.

E. pungens The dark green, upper surface of the leaves has silver scales while the underside is more of a dull silver. The margins have a crinkled edge. Clusters of small, fragrant, white flowers appear during mid and late autumn. A large evergreen shrub. HEIGHT & SPREAD 1.5×1.2m (5×4ft) after 5 years, ultimately 4.5m (15ft) tall.

The narrow leaves of **'Frederici'** are a pale creamy yellow with a green margin. It is slower growing than the species and eventually makes a medium-sized shrub to 3m (10ft) tall. **'Goldrim'** has glossy dark green leaves with attractive gold margins. It makes a large shrub of similar size to the species. The glossy green leaves of **'Maculata'**♀ have a decorative central gold blotch though it is prone to revert. It is a rounded, spreading shrub to 3m (10ft) tall.

▲ *Elaeagnus pungens* 'Frederici'

▲ *Elaeagnus pungens* 'Goldrim'

E. **'Quicksilver'**♀ (syn. *E. angustifolia* Caspica Group) Striking, silvery, narrow leaves, at their best when young, clothe this deciduous small tree or large shrub. HEIGHT & SPREAD 1×1m (3×3ft) after 5 years, ultimately 3m (10ft) tall.

CULTIVATION Plant deciduous species from mid autumn to early winter, evergreen species in mid spring or early autumn. Grow in any fertile well-drained soil, except shallow chalk. Deciduous species need to be grown in full sun, evergreen species will tolerate partial shade.

PROPAGATION Sow seed under glass in autumn. Take greenwood cuttings or semi-ripe cuttings of deciduous species and semi-ripe cuttings of evergreens. Alternatively, remove rooted suckers in autumn.

PRUNING Not normally required, except to control the shape or size by pruning after flowering. Remove shoots on variegated plants that revert to green.

PESTS AND DISEASES Usually trouble free.

Elder see *Sambucus*
Elecampane see *Inula helenium*
Elm see *Ulmus*
Elymus see GRASSES p.301

Embothrium

Proteaceae

Embothrium coccineum

Fiery red flowers set alight these shrubs and small trees in summer. The plants, natives of S America, are not fully hardy and need lime-free soil in a sheltered sunny position if they are to succeed in Britain. But where they do thrive, they draw every eye when the clusters of spidery blooms emerge to stand out against the evergreen leaves. Only one species and its cultivars is available for British gardens.

RECOMMENDED SPECIES AND VARIETIES

E. coccineum (Chilean fire bush) Brilliant scarlet, tubular flowers, very narrow and 5 cm (2 in) long, appear in tight clusters from late spring to early summer. The leathery, dark green, oblong leaves are up to 12 cm (4¾ in) long on a rounded head of slender branches. This plant is suitable for growing outdoors in only the milder parts of Britain. HEIGHT & SPREAD 1.2×1 m (4×3 ft) after 5 years, ultimately 9 m (30 ft) tall.

▲ *Embothrium coccineum*

Plants in the **Lanceolatum Group** are hardier than the species and form more slender plants. Among them, **'Inca Flame'** displays fine orange-red flowers and **'Ñorquinco Form'**♀ bears profuse flowers that are distinctly more orange in colour, but it is semi-evergreen.

CULTIVATION Plant in a sunny position against a south or south-west facing wall or in woodland, in moist but well-drained, lime-free soil. Provide some protection from frost.

PROPAGATION Raise from seed, separate suckers from the parent plant or take semi-ripe cuttings.

PRUNING None is necessary except for removing any dead wood or frost-damaged shoots after flowering.

PESTS AND DISEASES Usually trouble free.

Enkianthus

Ericaceae

Enkianthus campanulatus

Flaming shades of red and yellow mark the autumn foliage of these shrubs and small trees. Dainty cup or bell-shaped flowers, borne in drooping clusters during late spring and early summer, are also a feature. Native to E Asia, they require acid or neutral soil. They make a good specimen plant or can be massed in a woodland garden. All except *Enkianthus chinensis* are hardy. Those listed are deciduous.

RECOMMENDED SPECIES AND VARIETIES

E. campanulatus♀ Pale cream to pink or red cup-shaped flowers, each about 1 cm (⅜ in) long, often with deeper-coloured veins, are borne in abundant clusters of up to 15. The dull green oval leaves are about 5 cm (2 in) long. This shrub is the hardiest species. It spreads less in a shaded site. HEIGHT & SPREAD 2.4×1.2 m (8×4 ft) in 10 years, ultimately 5 m (16 ft) tall.

The flowers of f. ***albiflorus*** are white or greenish white and those of var. ***palibinii*** smaller and a deep red.

E. cernuus* f. *rubens♀ Rich red, fringed flowers, each 6 mm (¼ in) long, are borne in nodding clusters of 10-12. This shrub has roundish leaves 2.5 cm (1 in) long. HEIGHT & SPREAD 1 m×60 cm (3×2 ft) in 5 years, ultimately 3 m (10 ft).

E. chinensis Some of the largest flowerheads of the genus adorn this shrub but, unfortunately, it is less hardy than the other species. Bell-shaped cream blooms, 1 cm (⅜ in) long, with thin pink stripes, are borne in hanging clusters of 12-24 during late spring and early summer. The oblong leaves are up to 7.5 cm (3 in) long. HEIGHT & SPREAD 1.5×1 m (5×3 ft) after 5 years, ultimately 3.5 m (12 ft) tall.

▼ *Enkianthus cernuus f. rubens*

▲ *Enkianthus perulatus*

E. perulatus♀ Groups of 3-10, white pitcher-shaped flowers, about 1 cm (⅜ in) long, are carried on the slender, drooping stalks of this compact shrub. The 2.5-5 cm (1-2 in) long, fine-pointed, narrowly oval leaves are exceptionally blazing in autumn. HEIGHT & SPREAD 60×40 cm (2 ft×16 in) after 5 years, ultimately 1.8 m (6 ft) tall.

CULTIVATION Plant in autumn or early spring in acid to neutral soil, enriched with leaf-mould. Choose a site in sun or part shade and sheltered from wind.

PROPAGATION Sow seed under glass in late winter or early spring or take semi-ripe heeled cuttings in summer.

PRUNING Not normally required but older, straggly specimens can be cut back hard if necessary in spring.

PESTS AND DISEASES Usually trouble free.

Eomecon

Snow poppy, dawn poppy

Papaveraceae

The single species of this genus is a vigorously spreading herbaceous perennial, most valued for its attractive foliage, which makes an interesting carpet under large, established shrubs. The flowers are only sparsely produced for a brief period in early summer. The plant is not completely hardy in colder districts and may be short lived.

▲ *Eomecon chionantha*

Eomecon chionantha The scalloped, heart-shaped, pale to mid green leaves, up to 10 cm (4 in) across, are borne on fleshy beige-green stalks. The erect, branching stems bear loose clusters of pure white flowers up to 4 cm (1½ in) across, composed of 4 oval petals and a mass of deep yellow stamens. Native to E China. HEIGHT & SPREAD 45×60 cm (1½×2 ft).

CULTIVATION Plant in spring or summer in acid, humus-rich soil, preferably in full sun, although partial shade is tolerated.
PROPAGATION Lift and divide established plants in spring or summer.
PESTS AND DISEASES Usually trouble free.

Epilobium

Willowherb
Onagraceae

Epilobium glabellum

The willowherbs include tall herbaceous perennials as well as several smaller alpine species, some of them evergreen. All have four-petalled flowers and slender seedpods, which burst to release many fluffy seeds.

RECOMMENDED SPECIES AND VARIETIES

E. angustifolium (rosebay willowherb) Tapered spikes of deep rose-pink flowers are borne on erect leafy stems from mid to late summer. This robust, strongly rhizomatous herbaceous perennial is aggressively invasive and best confined to a wild garden. HEIGHT & SPREAD 1.5×1m (5×3ft).

'Album' has pure white flowers and is less rampant than the species.

E. californicum hort. see *Zauschneria californica*

E. canum see *Zauschneria californica* ssp. *cana*

▲ *Epilobium dodonaei*

E. dodonaei Spikes of deep rose-purple flowers appear in mid to late summer on this hardy herbaceous perennial. The slender, erect stems are densely clothed in narrow leaves. HEIGHT & SPREAD 80×60cm (32×24in).

E. fleischeri Abundant purple-pink flowers appear from mid to late summer. A spreading, hardy herbaceous perennial. HEIGHT & SPREAD 30×30cm (1×1ft).

E. glabellum Small, white to pale rose-violet flowers appear in short, leafy, erect spikes from late spring to early autumn, on this low-growing, hardy evergreen perennial alpine. The leaves are deep glossy green, often flushed red. An excellent plant for a cool and moist place in a rock garden. HEIGHT & SPREAD 20×40cm (8×16in).

'Sulphureum' has yellow blooms.

E. microphyllum see *Zauschneria californica* ssp. *cana*

E. obcordatum Rose-purple flowers arise in clusters in late summer on this low-growing, evergreen alpine. Slender stems bear grey-green leaves. It requires a moist, sheltered site and will not withstand prolonged frost. HEIGHT & SPREAD 7.5×30cm (3×12in).

E. villosum see *Zauschneria californica* ssp. *mexicana*

CULTIVATION Plant in full sun in soil of average fertility; in rich soils they tend to become vigorous and too leafy. The alpine species tolerate partial shade.
PROPAGATION Sow ripe seed in a cold-frame. Divide plants after flowering or in the early spring. Take softwood cuttings of alpines in summer.
PESTS AND DISEASES Usually trouble free.

Epimedium

Berberidaceae

Epimedium x youngianum 'Niveum'

The various epimediums available are valued for their fine foliage. In spring, the fresh green of the emerging leaves is often tinted with shades of copper, pink or red. The leaves become a deeper green during summer, and many turn to yellow, red or bronze in autumn. Airy sprays of dainty flowers bloom through spring, varying in colour from deep coral-red through orange and yellow to pure white.

Epimediums are clump-forming, herbaceous and evergreen perennials. Many species and varieties retain their leaves throughout winter. Most epimediums are fully hardy, including all the plants recommended below. Larger, more vigorous plants make splendid ground cover, especially in dappled shade, in a border or woodland garden. Grow smaller plants in a rock garden or in pots in an unheated, well-ventilated greenhouse.

The leaves are generally divided into leaflets, often with sharply serrated edges. The pendulous flowers, usually about 1.5cm (½in) across, are mostly star-shaped and often spurred. They are borne in lax sprays, that are simple or branched, on wiry stems above or among the leaves. Native to Europe and Asia.

RECOMMENDED SPECIES AND VARIETIES

E. alpinum (barrenwort) Glossy, oval, angled leaves, up to 12.5cm (5in) long, with 5-9 leaflets, are bronze when young and bronze or red in autumn. The flowers are yellow with red spurs. This herbaceous plant often has a carpeting growth habit. HEIGHT & SPREAD 25×30cm (10×12in).

E. x cantabrigiense This evergreen plant has a clump-forming to carpeting habit of growth. The leaves have oval to heart-shaped, pointed leaflets up to 15cm (6in) long, 7-17 to a leaf. They are bronze or tipped with red in spring. The flowers are dull red and pale yellow. HEIGHT & SPREAD 50×60cm (20×24in).

E. diphyllum Each leathery, deep green leaf has 2 heart-shaped leaflets, 2-5cm (¾-2in) long, flushed purple when young. White flowers, 1cm (⅜in) across, are borne in mid and late spring on this herbaceous perennial. HEIGHT & SPREAD 25×30cm (10×12in).

E. grandiflorum ♀ (syn. *E. macranthum*) A herbaceous plant with narrow, oval, apple-green leaflets, up to 12.5cm (5in) long, generally 9 to a leaf, that flush bronze in spring, and again in autumn. Long-spurred flowers, up to 4cm (1½in) across, white, pink, violet or rose-red, bloom in spring and early summer. HEIGHT & SPREAD 25×30cm (10×12in).

'Nanum' ♀ has pale purple flowers on a plant not more than 20cm (8in) tall. **'Rose Queen'** ♀ has deep pink flowers that contrast well with dark, copper-tinged young leaves. **'White Queen'** ♀ has bronze-tinged young leaves and pure white flowers.

▲ *Epimedium grandiflorum* 'Rose Queen'

E. macranthum see *E. grandiflorum*

E. x perralchicum ♀ The leaflets are rounded to oval and up to 10cm (4in) long on this tufted evergreen plant. There are 9, sometimes 3, leaflets to a leaf. They start off red or bronze in spring, before turning green. The flowers are yellow, with short spurs. HEIGHT & SPREAD 40×30cm (16×12in).

▲ *Epimedium perralchicum* 'Fröhnleiten'

'Fröhnleiten' has golden yellow flowers and attractively marbled young foliage.
E. perralderianum Glossy, rounded to oval leaflets, to 10cm (4in) long, on a semi-evergreen plant, are bright green, marked bronze-red when young, deep green in summer and copper-bronze in winter. Flowers are yellow and short-spurred. HEIGHT & SPREAD 30×45cm (1×1½ft).
E. pinnatum* ssp. *colchicum♀ (syn. *E. p.* ssp. *elegans*) Oval to rounded, downy leaflets, up to 7.5cm (3in) long and 5 to a leaf, are flushed red when young and again in autumn. Bright yellow flowers with short spurs are carried on slender, arching stems. This evergreen has a carpeting habit. HEIGHT & SPREAD 25×25cm (10×10in).
E. × rubrum♀ This is a deciduous plant with clump to carpeting habit of growth and heart-shaped leaflets, to 12.5cm (5in) long, which flush brownish red in spring and turn orange and yellow in autumn. The crimson flowers have yellowish white spurs. HEIGHT & SPREAD 30×40cm (12×16in).
***E. × versicolor* 'Sulphureum'**♀ This herbaceous perennial, clump-forming or carpeting, has 5-15 fresh green, heart-shaped leaflets, 6cm (2½in) long and with prickly edges, that flush reddish purple in spring and bronze in autumn. The yellow flowers have long reddish spurs. HEIGHT & SPREAD 30×50cm (12×20in).

▲ *Epimedium × warleyense*

E. × warleyense Prickly, heart-shaped leaves, to 10cm (4in) long, divided into 5-9 leaflets, flush reddish purple in spring and autumn on a semi-evergreen plant. Flowers are bright orange. HEIGHT & SPREAD 30×40cm (12×16in).
***E. × youngianum* 'Niveum'**♀ This semi-evergreen with white flowers has 2-9, prickly, heart-shaped leaflets up to 10cm (4in) long, flushed bronze in spring and orange-red in autumn. HEIGHT & SPREAD 25×30cm (10×12in).
'Roseum' (syn. 'Lilacinum') has mauve-purple flowers and reaches 30cm (1ft) tall.
CULTIVATION Plant in early spring or autumn in preferably moist and leafy but well-drained soil. Choose a site in full or partial shade; in a sunny position, the foliage may be scorched in hot weather. Place plants prone to frost damage in sheltered positions or protect in winter with a cloche or fleece. To make flower displays more noticeable, shear off evergreen leaves from the previous year in late winter or early spring, before the flower stems emerge.
PROPAGATION Divide plants in autumn or early spring. Sow seed as soon as it ripens, in early or mid summer, into pots kept in a coldframe. Prick out seedlings the moment they are large enough to handle and keep them shaded until they are well-established.
PESTS AND DISEASES Vine weevil may attack the rootstock and aphids and slugs can attack young leaves and flowers.

Epipactis
Helleborine
Orchidaceae

These striking orchids bear yellowish green or white flowers in profusion on erect spikes. Hardy deciduous perennials, they are ideal in damp, partially shady spots that resemble the boggy riversides, marshes and moorlands that are their natural habitat. The plant forms an attractive clump with lance-shaped leaves arranged spirally up stems culminating in flower spikes that bear many loose, spreading flowers in late summer and early autumn.
RECOMMENDED SPECIES AND VARIETIES
E. gigantea (giant helleborine) Spikes up to 25cm (10in) long bear flowers, 4cm (1½in) across with greenish yellow, purple-veined outer petals and inner petals strongly flushed purple with darker purple veining. The lowermost petal is yellow and fleshy. The leaves are up to 20cm (8in) long. This plant is native to N America. HEIGHT & SPREAD 1m×50cm (3ft×20in).

▼ *Epipactis palustris*

▲ *Epipactis gigantea*

E. palustris (marsh helleborine) Flowers, 3cm (1¼in) wide, held on 20cm (8in) long spikes, have green to brown outer petals, striped with violet, and white and pink inner petals. The wide lower petal is fleshy and slightly frilled. The leaves are up to 15cm (6in) long. This species is native to Europe and temperate Asia. HEIGHT & SPREAD 70×30cm (28×12in).
CULTIVATION Plant in partial shade in damp soil that has not been treated with any soil improver. Leave undisturbed. Water occasionally in hot, dry weather, if the soil becomes dry.
PROPAGATION Divide plants in winter.
PESTS AND DISEASES Slugs and snails can be a problem.

Epiphyllum see CACTI p.109

Epipremnum
Devil's ivy
Araceae

These climbers from tropical Asia can create a leafy tropical effect indoors or in a greenhouse, if provided with a steady warm temperature and reasonable humidity. They can be trained as climbers or allowed to trail from their pots, forming a curtain of foliage.
RECOMMENDED SPECIES AND VARIETIES
E. aureum♀ (syn. *Scindapsus aureus*) The dark green leaves are heart-shaped and glossy, with golden cream streaks and spots that spread outwards from the midrib. The leaves can grow up to 15cm (6in) long in a room indoors or up to 60cm (2ft) in a greenhouse. The stems produce masses of small aerial roots which the plant uses to cling onto damp surfaces. HEIGHT & SPREAD 1.8m×30cm (6×1ft).
'Marble Queen' has white-cream variegation covering much of the leaf, with streaks of different shades of green spreading from the centre. It is less vigorous than the species, and less tolerant of shade, which may cause it to produce plain green leaves. It will reach a height of 2m (6½ft) and a spread of 50cm (20in).

▲ *Epipremnum aureum* 'Marble Queen'

CULTIVATION Grow in pots of well-drained, soil-less compost and keep warm and humid. Allow to dry out slightly between waterings. Water sparingly in winter. Repot to encourage growth or feed occasionally to maintain healthy foliage. Plants can be grown as freestanding against a moss pole – mist poles regularly. In a conservatory or greenhouse where damp surfaces can be maintained, encourage plants to climb up moss poles, cork bark or rough brickwork. Alternatively, train plants by tying to supports.
PROPAGATION Root shoot tips or semi-ripe stem cuttings with at least 2 leaf nodes in spring or summer or layer by bending a shoot into a compost-filled pot.
PRUNING Cut back to just above the last healthy leaf at the start of the growing season. Encourage plants to branch more by pinching out the growing tip.
PESTS AND DISEASES Usually trouble free.

Episcia

Gesneriaceae

Episcia dianthiflora

Warm, humid conditions are ideal for these low-growing, tropical evergreens. Episcias can be raised in pots and hanging baskets or as ground cover in greenhouse beds.
RECOMMENDED SPECIES AND VARIETIES
E. cupreata (flame violet) The marbled dark green or bronze-green leaves with silver veins are oval, puckered and 8cm (3¼in) long. Tubular flowers, 2.5cm (1in) wide, open in spring and summer and are scarlet or orange-red, with a yellow throat. The plant's stems spread to the edge of the pot and its leaves completely cover the soil. HEIGHT 15cm (6in).
E. dianthiflora (lace flower) White tubular flowers, up to 3cm (1¼in) across, with fringed petals appear in summer. The bright green, velvety leaves are up to 3cm (1¼in) long. Stems trail to about 50cm (20in) over the edge of the pot. HEIGHT 6cm (2½in).
CULTIVATION Plant in a warm, humid greenhouse out of direct light, in potting compost kept constantly moist but not wet. Water a little less in winter. Feed throughout the growing season, using half normal-strength solution. Repot annually in spring.
PROPAGATION In spring, cut off and pot up the stems that have roots, as required.
PESTS AND DISEASES Usually trouble free.

Eranthis

Winter aconite
Ranunculaceae

Brightly coloured, cup-shaped yellow or white flowers make a charming floral carpet beneath trees. These winter and spring-flowering perennials are hardy and grow from tubers that need a dry summer dormancy. The leaves are deeply dissected and form a ruff around the solitary flowers. Native to S Europe and Asia.
RECOMMENDED SPECIES AND VARIETIES
E. hyemalis ♀ (syn. *Aconitum hyemalis*) The shiny lemon-yellow flowers, up to 2.5cm (1in) across, appear from late winter onwards. The finely cut, bright green leaves are about 5cm (2in) across. HEIGHT & SPREAD 15×15cm (6×6in).

▲ *Eranthis hyemalis*

Cilicica Group (syn. *Aconitum cilicicum*) have yellow flowers in early spring. The leaves are tinged bronze when they emerge. Plants reach 10cm (4in) in height.
CULTIVATION Plant in any well-drained soil that is dry in summer. Dormant tubers can be difficult to establish and so growing plants are often planted in early spring. Rake off faded leaves when they turn brown.
PROPAGATION Sow ripe seed in early summer in a coldframe. The plants self-seed easily. Lift and plant tubers immediately after flowering and when in full leaf. Bought tubers benefit from soaking in water overnight before planting.
PESTS AND DISEASES Usually trouble free.

Eremurus

Foxtail lily
Liliaceae

Towering spires of small, star-shaped blossoms create a majestic display in late spring and early summer. These hardy, occasionally tender, herbaceous perennials have long, fleshy, strap-shaped leaves that deteriorate rapidly and are best planted among shrubs in a mixed border where the fading foliage is hidden. Native to central and W Asia, foxtail lilies make good cut flowers.
RECOMMENDED SPECIES AND VARIETIES
E. bungei see *E. stenophyllus* ssp. *stenophyllus*
E. himalaicus The tiny white flowers have prominent orange stamens and are carried in tall spikes in late spring. The bright green leaves grow to 1m (3ft) long. HEIGHT & SPREAD 2×1m (6½×3ft).
E. × ***isabellinus*** **Ruiter Hybrids** Spikes of small starry blooms, ranging from rusty red and orange to yellow and bright pink, appear in late spring and early summer. The leaves grow to 1m (3ft) long. HEIGHT & SPREAD 2×1m (6½×3ft).
E. × ***isabellinus*** **Shelford Hybrids** Yellow, orange, pink or white flowers are carried in spikes in late spring and early summer. The narrow leaves are 60cm (2ft) long. HEIGHT & SPREAD 1.2×1m (4×3ft).
E. robustus Dense spires of bright pink flowers appear in early summer. The leaves, up to 1m (3ft) long, are glaucous and start to die back as the flowers emerge. A vigorous plant. HEIGHT & SPREAD 2.4×1m (8×3ft).
E. stenophyllus ssp. ***stenophyllus*** (syn. *E. bungei*) Crowded spikes of bright yellow flowers, each up to 2cm (¾in) across, appear in early summer. The smooth, narrow leaves grow to 60cm (2ft) long. HEIGHT & SPREAD 1m×60cm (3×2ft).
CULTIVATION Plant in autumn in full sun in free-draining soil. Mulch the emerging crowns to protect from sharp frosts. Stake tall species and remove old flower spikes when the blooms fade.
PROPAGATION Sow seed in spring. Divide in spring or early autumn.
PESTS AND DISEASES Usually trouble free.

▼ *Eremurus* x *isabellinus* 'Shelford Hybrid'

Erica

Heath, heather

Ericaceae

Erica cinerea 'Pink Ice'

e

Year-round displays in sparkling white and every shade of pink are easily created with heaths and heathers in any garden that has acid soil and plenty of light. For alkaline soil the choice is more limited but there are enough lime-tolerant varieties to contribute to the garden in every season – especially all forms of *Erica carnea* and *E.* × *darleyenis*.

Traditionally, heaths and heathers are grown in their own heather bed, but they work equally well in a mixed border and some are useful ground-cover plants, crowding out weeds. The more compact varieties flourish in large pots and tubs – which also give the opportunity to grow acid-loving species in a limy garden.

Heaths and heathers are evergreen shrubs with narrow, folded leaves in various greens and golds, and tubular flowers. The genus contains over 750 diverse species with a wide distribution in the wild, from the temperate conditions of western Europe to the dry, hot climate of South Africa; it has naturalised in Australia.

More than 700 species are from the more southerly regions and suitable only for conservatories or greenhouses in Britain. The European species, however, are hardy in Britain, but they can be difficult to establish in areas prone to drought. The sizes given are for five to seven-year-old plants that have been regularly clipped back following flowering.

RECOMMENDED SPECIES AND VARIETIES

E. arborea (tree heath) Tall, upright branches are covered with whorls of 3 or 4 bright green needles, smooth above and grooved beneath. The 3mm (⅛in) bell-shaped flowers, borne in clusters near the ends of the branches in early to late spring, are greyish white and honey scented.

The species is native to S Europe and N Africa and can vary in hardiness, but in general, only hardy strains are sold in Britain. Heavy snow may break the branches, but new growth will come from the root stock. It is not as tolerant of lime as commonly supposed and is best grown in acid soil. Trim young plants to shape in the early years to avoid untidy growth. HEIGHT & SPREAD 6×3m (20×10ft).

The following cultivars are all hardy. **'Albert's Gold'**♀ has golden foliage with a few white flowers. It reaches 1.8m (6ft) tall and spreads to 80cm (32in). The variety ***alpina***♀, with the same height and spread, produces white flowers in dense cylindrical clusters. **'Estrella Gold'**♀ bears white flowers in profusion on compact, lime-green foliage, tipped bright yellow in spring and summer. It grows to 120cm (4ft) with a spread of 75cm (2½ft).

E. australis♀ (Spanish heath) Showy purplish pink tubular flowers, 8mm (⅜in) long, are produced from mid spring to early summer on a tall, open plant. Its dark green, linear leaves, grooved underneath, are in whorls of 4. The plant is hardy but does not tolerate lime and is prone to damage by wind or snow. It requires acid soil conditions. Prune young plants heavily after flowering to avoid straggly growth. Native to W Spain and Portugal. HEIGHT & SPREAD 1.8×1m (6×3ft).

'Mr. Robert'♀ produces masses of white flowers. It is 1.8m (6ft) tall and 90cm (3ft) wide. **'Riverslea'**♀ has the same spread, but is only 1.2m (4ft) tall. It has lilac-pink flowers.

E. carnea (syn. *E. herbacea*) (alpine heath, winter heath) This hardy, lime-tolerant species flowers in late spring or early summer, bearing urn-shaped, usually pink, 6mm (¼in) flowers. The mid to dark green linear leaves are held in whorls of 4.

It forms a low maintenance ground-cover plant, in sun or light shade, needing only an occasional trim round the edges immediately after flowering. Native to the alpine regions of Europe. HEIGHT & SPREAD 15×40cm (6×16in).

Unless stated otherwise, the listed cultivars have mid to dark green foliage with a neat compact habit, 15×45cm (6×18in). The mauve-pink flowers last for 6 to 8 weeks and open between mid winter and mid spring; plants in milder areas can be as much as 2 months earlier than those in colder spots.

'Adrienne Duncan'♀ has bronze-tinged foliage and a long flowering period. **'Ann Sparkes'**♀ has distinctive old gold foliage with bright bronze tips in spring. The flowers open rose-pink, darkening to mauve-pink. It is less spreading than most cultivars – to 25cm (10in). **'Challenger'**♀ bears striking magenta flowers. **'Foxhollow'**♀ has yellow foliage tipped bronze which deepens to reddish orange in very cold weather. **'Foxhollow Fairy'**, with a trailing habit, produces pale shell-pink flowers which deepen with age. It reaches 20cm (8in) in height. **'Golden Starlet'**♀ bears white flowers against lime-green foliage which turns a glowing yellow in summer. **'Ice Princess'** is perhaps the best white-flowering *E. carnea*, holding its flowers in semi-erect spikes on compact bright green foliage. **'Loughrigg'**♀ is a vigorous cultivar with flowers that open pink and deepen through rose-pink to mauve-pink during the season. **'Myretoun Ruby'**♀, whose flowers deepen to crimson as the season progresses, is one of the best red forms. **'Nathalie'** has the deepest flower colour of all – a glowing deep crimson. **'Pink Spangles'**♀, whose shell-pink flowers deepen with age, has a vigorous, trailing habit. It spreads to 30cm (1ft). **'Praecox Rubra'**♀ is one of the earliest to flower. **'R.B. Cooke'**♀ is covered with pink flowers which age to mauve. **'Springwood White'**♀ has a vigorous trailing habit and masses of white flowers among bright green foliage. It spreads to 60cm (2ft). **'Sunshine**

▼ *Erica carnea* 'Challenger'

▲ *Erica carnea* 'Foxhollow Fairy'

▲ *Erica carnea* 'Golden Starlet'

▲ *Erica carnea* 'Loughrigg'

▲ *Erica carnea* 'Praecox Rubra'

Rambler'♀ is grown mainly for its bright yellow foliage which is tinged with red in winter. **'Vivellii'**♀ has a bronze hue to the foliage and the flowers darken to magenta during the season. **'Westwood Yellow'**♀ has a more upright habit than other yellow-leaved cultivars and shell-pink flowers.

E. ciliaris (Dorset heath) Long spikes of flowers, usually lilac-pink, bloom from mid summer to mid autumn on an erect, open shrub. The flowers – the largest of any European species – are 1 cm (⅜ in) long, tubular and sharply contracted at the mouth. The ovate leaves are grey-green or dark green above, white beneath and borne in whorls of 3. Severe winters can damage the plants, so leave the dead flowers on during the winter to provide protection and trim them off by mid spring. Native to W Spain, Portugal, NW France and southern Britain. HEIGHT & SPREAD 36×45 cm (14×18 in).

The cultivars typically reach 25 × 45 cm (10×18 in). **'Corfe Castle'**♀ has rose-pink flowers and mid green foliage. **'David McClintock'**♀ produces bicolour flowers, white at the base, pink at the mouth, set against grey-green leaves. **'Mrs C.H. Gill'**♀ has crimson flowers and dark green foliage. **'Stoborough'**♀ has white flowers and bright green foliage.

▼ *Erica carnea* 'Westwood Yellow'

E. cinerea (bell heather) White, pink or purple bell-shaped flowers, 6 mm (¼ in) long, are borne in profusion from early summer to early autumn. The leaves are usually bottle green, linear and strongly curled under along the edges. This much underrated species is hardy throughout Britain but does not tolerate lime. HEIGHT & SPREAD 30×50 cm (12×20 in).

There is a multitude of cultivars available. Those listed have dark green foliage and erect growth to 25 × 50 cm (10 × 20 in), unless stated otherwise.

'Alba Minor'♀, with white flowers and mid green foliage, makes a good ground-cover plant and is compact enough for growing in tubs. **'C.D. Eason'**♀ displays bright magenta flowers and makes a good ground-cover plant. **'C.G. Best'**♀ is larger than most, reaching 30 cm (1 ft) tall with a spread of 70 cm (2 ft 4 in). It produces a graceful display of rose-pink flowers. **'Cevennes'**♀ has similar dimensions to 'C.G. Best'. It bears abundant mauve flowers against mid green foliage.

'Cindy'♀, with a semi-prostrate habit, carries its purple flowers from early summer to late autumn. **'Eden Valley'**♀ has lavender flowers shading to white at their base and mid green foliage. **'Fiddler's Gold'**♀, with yellow-gold foliage deepening to red in winter, has lilac-pink flowers and a semi-prostrate habit. **'Golden Hue'**♀ has amethyst flowers and pale yellow foliage tipped with orange in winter. It grows to 35 cm (14 in) tall and 70 cm (28 in) wide. **'Hookstone White'**♀ has similar dimensions to 'Golden Hue'. It produces long spikes of white flowers among mid green foliage. **'P.S. Patrick'**♀ bears long spikes of purple flowers. **'Pentreath'**♀ makes a neat carpet of beetroot-coloured flowers. Its height is 20 cm (8 in) and its spread is 30 cm (12 in). **'Pink Ice'**♀ has clear, rose-pink flowers and a dwarf habit, growing to just 15 cm (6 in) tall with a spread of 35 cm (14 in). **'Stephen Davis'**♀, with a neat erect dwarf habit, produces masses of glowing magenta flowers. **'Velvet Night'**♀ has deep purple flowers. **'Windlebrooke'**♀ has a few mauve flowers and is chiefly grown for its foliage, which is golden in summer, turning orange-red in winter. It has a prostrate habit, 15 cm (6 in) in height and spreading to 45 cm (1½ ft).

▼ *Erica cinerea* 'Stephen Davis'

E. × darleyensis This bushy, hardy plant is one of the easiest heathers to grow and is suitable for all soils. It has needle-like leaves and pink urn-shaped flowers, 5 mm (¼ in) long, usually between mid winter and mid spring; it can start flowering as early as mid autumn in mild conditions. It is particularly effective at smothering weeds. HEIGHT & SPREAD 45×60 cm (1½×2 ft).

Unless stated otherwise, the cultivars listed have pink flowers, mid-green leaves and upright growth to 45×60 cm (1½×2 ft).

'Arthur Johnson'♀ produces 20 cm (8 in) long spikes of slightly scented flowers on foliage which is tipped cream in spring. It grows to 60 cm (2 ft) and has a spread of 75 cm (2½ ft). **'Furzey'**♀ bears lilac-pink flowers deepening to mauve-pink during the season. The leaves are tipped with pink in spring. **'Ghost Hills'**♀ has light green foliage which is tipped cream in spring. **'J.W. Porter'**♀ bears mauve-pink flowers against dark green foliage which is tipped red and cream in spring.

'Jack H. Brummage' has mauve-pink flowers; its foliage is yellow-orange throughout the year. **'Kramer's Rote'** (also sold as **'Kramer's Red'**)♀ has vivid magenta flowers, bronze-green foliage and a spreading habit. **'White Perfection'**♀ has white flowers and bright green foliage.

E. erigena (syn. *E. hibernica*, *E. mediterranea*) (Irish heath) Deep lilac, urn-shaped blooms, 5 mm (¼ in) long, are honey-scented and much loved by bees. They are borne between mid spring and early winter among linear leaves on an upright plant. The plant is hardy and can be grown in most soils. It is suitable for informal hedging but the brittle stems will break under heavy snow. Native to western Ireland and northern Spain. HEIGHT & SPREAD 2.4 m×60 cm (8×2 ft).

'Golden Lady'♀ produces sparse white

▼ *Erica erigena* 'Golden Lady'

flowers but bright golden-yellow foliage. It can be burnt by cold winds. It reaches a height of 30cm (1ft) and spreads to 40cm (1ft 4in). **'Irish Dusk'**♀ has clear rose-pink flowers, sometimes from mid autumn, against dark grey-green foliage. It reaches a height of 60cm (2ft) and spreads to 45cm (1½ft). **'W.T. Rackliff'**♀ has masses of white flowers on rich green foliage and a neat, compact habit. It reaches a height of 75cm (2½ft) and spreads to 60cm (2ft).

E. herbacea see *E. carnea*

E. hibernica see *E. erigena*

E. lusitanica♀ (Portuguese heath) Pink buds on an elegant, erect plant open to white tubular or sometimes cup-shaped flowers, 3mm (⅛in) long, between early winter and late spring. The leaves are smooth and linear. The plant will grow in most soils but can be considered hardy only in southern and western Britain. Native to W Spain, Portugal and S France. HEIGHT & SPREAD 3m×75cm (10×1½ft).

E. manipuliflora Lime-tolerant and hardy, this plant has 3mm (⅛in) long rose-pink cup-shaped flowers during autumn. The mid green narrow leaves are 6mm (¼in) long held in whorls of 3 or 4. HEIGHT & SPREAD 1×1m (3×3ft).

E. m. ssp. ***anthura* 'Heaven Scent'**♀ is hardy and bears long sprays of strongly scented lilac-pink flowers and only spreads to 60cm (2ft).

▲ *Erica manipuliflora* ssp. *anthura* 'Heaven Scent'

E. manipuliflora* x *vagans Lime-tolerant and hardy, this hybrid's most popular cultivar is **'Valerie Griffiths'**. It has a few pale pink cup-shaped 3mm (⅛in) flowers in mid summer to mid autumn and yellow foliage deepening to golden yellow in winter. HEIGHT & SPREAD 40×60cm (1ft 4in×2ft).

E. mediterranea see *E. erigena*

E. x praegeri see *E. × stuartii*

E. stricta see *E. terminalis*

E. x stuartii (syn. *E.* × *praegeri*) Acid soil is needed for this hardy hybrid. The lilac-pink flower clusters are borne on the tips of shoots clothed in grey-green foliage. Native to W Ireland. HEIGHT & SPREAD 25×45cm (10×18in).

'Irish Lemon'♀ takes its name from the brilliant lemon new growth in spring. The

▲ *Erica stuartii* 'Irish Lemon'

▲ *Erica terminalis*

8mm (⅜in) long mauve flowers appear between late spring and early autumn.

E. terminalis♀ (syn. *E. stricta*) (Corsican heath) The lime-tolerant, erect plant bears lilac-pink, urn-like flowers, 5mm (¼in) long, in clusters at the tips of shoots. The flowers appear from mid summer to mid autumn and, when faded, provide an attractive russet hue all winter. Kept well pruned when young, it makes a good specimen plant or it can be used for hedging. Native to S Spain, S Italy and Corsica. HEIGHT & SPREAD 1.5×1m (5×3ft).

E. tetralix (cross-leaved heath) From early summer to mid autumn, pale pink urn-like flowers, 6mm (¼in) long and contracted at the mouth, are borne in clusters at the tips of shoots. The hardy plant has narrow grey-green leaves, white beneath, arranged in whorls of 4 to form a cross. Native to boggy areas of W Europe, it requires acid, preferably moist, soil. HEIGHT & SPREAD 30×35cm (1ft × 1ft 2in).

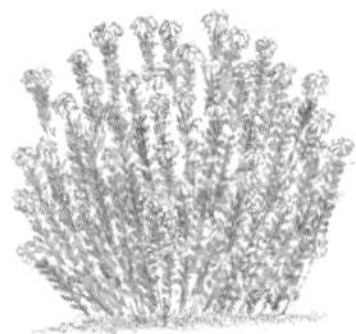

'Alba Mollis'♀ is shorter than the species, 20cm (8in), and has pure white flowers and silver-grey foliage. **'Con**

▼ *Erica tetralix* 'Pink Star'

▲ *Erica tetralix* 'Alba Mollis'

Underwood'♀ is more spreading, to 50cm (20in), and bears magenta flowers. **'Pink Star'**♀ is shorter than the species, 20cm (8in), and produces lilac-pink star-like flowers held horizontally.

E. vagans (Cornish heath) A hardy plant, with linear dark green leaves, this species produces small cup-like pink, mauve or white flowers, held in cylindrical flower spikes from mid summer to mid autumn. The blooms attract many species of brown butterfly and hoverfly. The plant grows successfully on any magnesium-rich soil and is made more vigorous with hard pruning. Native to the Lizard Peninsula in Cornwall, S France and N Spain. HEIGHT & SPREAD 50×80cm (1ft 8in×2ft 8in).

The cultivars listed have dark green leaves unless stated otherwise. They generally reach a height of 20-30cm (8-12in) with a spread of 45-60cm (1½-2ft).

▲ *Erica vagans* 'Birch Glow'

'Birch Glow'♀ produces rose-pink flowers. **'Cornish Cream'**♀ has off-white flowers in long spikes and bright green foliage. It is larger than most, reaching 35cm (14in) tall with a spread of 65cm (26in). **'Fiddlestone'**♀ bears deep cerise flowers. **'Kevernensis Alba'**♀ has clear white flowers enhanced by bright green foliage. **'Lyonesse'**♀ has pure white flowers with bright green foliage.

'Mrs D.F. Maxwell'♀ bears light rose-pink flowers. **'Valerie Proudley'**♀ is smaller than the rest, 15×30cm (6×12in). It produces only a few white flowers but has bright yellow foliage throughout the year. It can be badly damaged by cold winds.

E.* x *veitchii The plant grows in most alkaline soil but varies from half-hardy to hardy. Half-hardy plants can only be grown outdoors in southern and western Britain. White cup-shaped flowers, 3 mm (⅛ in) long, appear in early spring to early summer, among the linear, mid green leaves. HEIGHT & SPREAD 80×65 cm (2 ft 8 in×2 ft 2 in).

'Gold Tips'♀ is hardier than most varieties and grows in most parts of the country. The new growth in spring is tipped yellow. It has a height of 65 cm (2 ft 2 in) and spreads to 60 cm (2 ft).

E.* x *watsonii Pink urn-shaped flowers are borne in clusters at the tips of the shoots from mid to late summer. The grey-green foliage is tipped red or yellow in spring. It is a hardy plant requiring acid soil. HEIGHT & SPREAD 20×35 cm (8×14 in).

'Dawn'♀ bears deep pink flowers between mid summer and mid autumn among grey-green foliage. The new spring growth is red turning golden later.

E.* x *williamsii This lime-tolerant plant produces spikes of pink, mauve or white cup-shaped flowers from mid summer to mid autumn. The new spring growth is bright yellow in colour. HEIGHT & SPREAD 25×45 cm (10×18 in).

'P.D. Williams'♀ displays lilac-pink flowers between mid summer and late autumn, with the yellow-tipped spring growth persisting well into summer.

CULTIVATION All heaths and heathers require acid soil except the European species flowering in winter and spring, which are lime tolerant. Of the summer-flowering species, *E. manipuliflora*, *E. terminalis*, *E. vagans* and *E.* x *williamsii* will grow on most soils.

Grow the plants in an open, sunny site away from deciduous trees, which cast more shade than conifers and whose fallen leaves can cause a variety of fungal problems if left on top of the plants.

Cultivars can be bought as rooted cuttings or as one or two-year-old plants. Plant deeply, so that the lower leaves touch the soil surface.

In the case of *E. carnea* cultivars that have a loose habit, bunch the trailing stems together before planting and plant deeply, covering some of the leaves. This ensures that the plants do not go bare in the centre in later years. Keep well watered during the first spring and summer after planting.

PROPAGATION Take semi-ripe heel cuttings in mid summer.

PRUNING Cut back summer-flowering species annually to the base of the dead flowers in mid spring. Winter-flowering species need only be pruned to retain shape. If done, it must be immediately after flowering and never later than mid spring.

PESTS AND DISEASES Usually trouble free.

Erigeron

Fleabane

Compositae

A generous display of colourful daisies, from early to late summer, earns fleabanes a place in a sunny border or rock garden. Although the genus contains annuals, it is mainly the perennials that are grown and it is these that are listed below. The mid or greyish green leaves are spatulate to lance-shaped. The flowerheads are generally 5 to 7.5 cm (2 to 3 in) across with yellow centres and colourful ray florets, and are held at the top of more or less leafy stems.

RECOMMENDED SPECIES AND VARIETIES

E. alpinus (alpine fleabane) The plant has lilac-pink to reddish purple flowers held on leafy stems. HEIGHT & SPREAD 25×25 cm (10×10 in).

E. aurantiacus Bright orange flowers appear on the sturdy erect stems of this partly evergreen plant. HEIGHT & SPREAD 25×30 cm (10×12 in).

'Sulphureus' has yellow flowers.

E. aureus Small, bright-yellow flowers appear from late spring to late summer. This evergreen clump-former dislikes winter wet and is best grown in an alpine house. HEIGHT & SPREAD 10×15 cm (4×6 in).

'Canary Bird'♀ has creamy yellow blooms.

***E. chrysopsidis* 'Grand Ridge'**♀ Bright yellow flowers are carried by this clump or tuft-forming evergreen with arching, mostly basal, linear leaves. HEIGHT & SPREAD 7.5×15 cm (3×6 in).

E. compositus Small white, pinkish or bluish flowers are borne by this tufted or cushion-forming plant with crowded fan-shaped, dissected leaves. HEIGHT & SPREAD 10×20 cm (4×8 in).

E. glaucus Pale violet flowers appear above a mound of grey-green foliage. The plant is part evergreen with oval leaves. HEIGHT & SPREAD 50×75 cm (1 ft 8 in×2 ft 6 in).

▼ *Erigeron chrysopsidis* 'Grand Ridge'

'Albus' bears white flowers. **'Elstead Pink'** bears lilac-pink flowers.

E. karvinskianus♀ (syn. *E. mucronatus*) (wall daisy) Dainty white flowers, appearing in late spring, gradually change to pink then purple and last into early autumn. This is a spreading plant with slender, much-branched stems and greyish green lance-shaped leaves. It will die right down in a severe winter, but normally sprouts anew in spring. It is an excellent plant for wall or paving crevices, but it can become invasive in mild areas, and self-sows in many gardens. HEIGHT & SPREAD 15×40 cm (6×16 in).

▲ *Erigeron karvinskianus*

GARDEN HYBRIDS

These plants provide colour from early to late summer and sometimes beyond. They are good for the border, forming compact clumps. The heights are given for each cultivar and the spread varies from 30 to 50 cm (1 ft to 1 ft 8 in).

'Azurfee' (also sold as **'Azure Fairy'**) blue flowers; 30 cm (1 ft) tall. **'Charity'** pale pink flowers with greenish centres; 60 cm (2 ft) tall. **'Dignity'** violet-mauve flowers; 60 cm (2 ft) tall. **'Dimity'** bright pink flowers (orange-tinted in bud); 25 cm (10 in) tall. **'Dunkelste Aller'**♀ (**'Darkest of All'**) masses of deep purple flowers; 80 cm (2 ft 8 in) tall.

'Foersters Liebling'♀ semidouble pale pink flowers; 80 cm (2 ft 8 in) tall. **'Four Winds'** pale pink flowers; 30 cm (1 ft) tall. It is a good ground-cover plant. **'Gaiety'** bright pink flowers; 60 cm (2 ft) tall. **'Quakeress'** delicate lilac-pink flowers; 80 cm (2 ft 8 in) tall.

'Rosa Juwel' (**'Pink Jewel'**) pale lilac flowers; 60 cm (2 ft) tall. **'Schneewittchen'** (**'Snow White'**) pure white flowers; 60 cm (2 ft) tall.

CULTIVATION Plant in a well-drained, but moist, fertile soil in a sunny position in autumn or spring. Give annual top dressings of fertiliser or well-rotted compost in autumn or spring. Some twiggy staking may be necessary to support the stems. Deadheading prolongs flowering.

PROPAGATION Divide clumps every 3 or 4 years after flowering or in early spring. Take basal softwood cuttings in spring, root in a coldframe and plant out in early summer.

PESTS AND DISEASES Usually trouble free.

e

Erinus

Scrophulariaceae

Erinus alpinus

A spring and summer display of numerous dainty, bright flowers characterises this delightful small plant. The species most commonly grown is a hardy evergreen – though shortlived – perennial. It flourishes on very little soil, such as on a rock garden or in wall crevices, and will do well in sun or partial shade. It self-sows freely.

RECOMMENDED SPECIES AND VARIETIES

E. alpinus ♀ (fairy foxglove) Small pink or purple 5-petalled flowers, up to 1 cm (⅜ in) across, are borne in spikes from late spring to mid summer, appearing intermittently into autumn – especially if old spikes are deadheaded. The deep green leaves are mostly arranged in basal rosettes, and the tufted plant mounds with age. Native to the mountains of central and S Europe. HEIGHT & SPREAD 6×12.5 cm (2½×5 in).

The flowers of var. *albus* are pure white. **'Dr Hähnle'** has deep pink flowers. **'Mrs Charles Boyle'** ♀ has soft pale pink flowers.

▲ *Erinus alpinus*

Erinus alpinus var. albus ▼

CULTIVATION Plant in autumn or early spring in any well-drained soil in sun or partial shade. Encourage a second flowering by deadheading, unless seed is required.

PROPAGATION Sow seed under glass in autumn or early spring.

PESTS AND DISEASES Usually trouble free.

Eriobotrya

Rosaceae

Eriobotrya japonica

Large ornamental shrubs or small trees, eriobotryas are grown for their handsome evergreen leaves. In their native habitat, they bear fragrant, creamy white flowers and delicious edible fruit but neither is produced freely in Britain. Carried in upright, branched clusters, the open flowers have five petals and measure up to 2 cm (¾ in) across. The soft orange fruits have velvety skins and contain a few large chestnut-brown seeds; *Eriobotrya japonica* produces the fruit called loquat. Native to the Himalayas and much of E Asia, eriobotryas are fairly hardy, grown against a warm wall.

RECOMMENDED SPECIES AND VARIETIES

E. deflexa The leathery, oblong leaves are up to 25 cm (10 in) long and have strongly impressed veins and toothed edges. Young leaves are sometimes bronze-coloured, becoming mid green above and lighter green beneath. The flowers appear from late spring to mid summer. The sharp but sweet orange oval fruits, about 2.5 cm (1 in) long, may be seen in late autumn, but rarely. HEIGHT & SPREAD 1.5×1 m (5×3 ft) after 5 years, ultimately 9 m (30 ft) tall.

E. japonica ♀ (loquat, Japanese medlar) The glossy, dark green, corrugated leaves are covered underneath with rust brown hairs. Oblong or pointed, with sharply toothed edges they measure up to 30 cm (1 ft) long. The flowers have rust-brown stalks and appear intermittently from late autumn to mid spring, being produced in any abundance only after hot summers. When fruit does appear, it ripens in spring and may, therefore, be damaged by late frosts. Rounded or egg-shaped and orange-yellow with a soft downy skin, the juicy fruits have a tart flavour and are up to 4 cm (1½ in) long. HEIGHT & SPREAD 1.5×1 m (5×3 ft) after 5 years, ultimately 8 m (26 ft) tall.

▼ *Eriobotrya japonica*

CULTIVATION Plant during early autumn in any fertile, well-drained soil in a sunny, sheltered position, preferably against a south or west-facing wall.

PROPAGATION Sow seed in spring or summer.

PRUNING Not required, although plants can be shaped by cutting back in winter.

PESTS AND DISEASES Usually trouble free.

Eriogonum

Wild buckwheat

Polygonaceae

Rounded clusters of small, cup-shaped flowers adorn these evergreen perennials or sub-shrubs in summer. The plants have a neat habit which fits them perfectly for display in a rock garden or alpine house. Warmly tinted fruits often follow the flowers. Well-drained soil and a position in the sun are vital. The genus is native to mountains of N America.

RECOMMENDED SPECIES AND VARIETIES

E. umbellatum (sulphur flower) Tiny yellow flowers in dense, long-stalked clusters – up to 7.5 cm (3 in) across – appear in mid summer on this matted perennial. The flowers are soon followed by coppery fruits. The elliptical 2 cm (¾ in) leaves are deep

▲ *Eriogonum umbellatum*

Eriogonum umbellatum var. torreyanum ▼

green with white hairy undersides. HEIGHT & SPREAD 30×40cm (12×16in).

The flowers of var. *torreyanum* are bright yellow; the deep green leaves are hairless on the undersides.

CULTIVATION Plant in a sunny site in spring in well-drained yet moisture-retentive soil.

PROPAGATION Sow seed when ripe in autumn or early spring in pots and place in a coldframe. Alternatively, take semi-ripe cuttings in mid to late summer.

PESTS AND DISEASES Usually trouble free.

Eriophyllum

Compositae

Eriophyllum lanatum

Showy yellow summer flowerheads embellish the only plant in the genus to be grown in Britain. Because both the centres and surrounding ray florets are yellow, the flowers stand out boldly at the front of a mixed border. Distinctive silvery white foliage adds to the effect. The smaller variety makes more impact in a rock garden. This hardy perennial plant requires well-drained soil and full sun to thrive. The genus is native to N America.

RECOMMENDED SPECIES AND VARIETY

E. lanatum (woolly sunflower) Masses of bright yellow flowerheads, up to 5cm (2in) across, bloom from early to mid summer. Woolly grey or silvery leaves, up to 7.5cm (3in) long, offset them. This clump-forming to spreading hardy perennial is herbaceous or semi-evergreen. HEIGHT & SPREAD 30×40 cm (12×16in).

'Nanum' reaches just 20cm (8in) tall.

CULTIVATION Plant in early spring or early autumn in well-drained soil and in full sun.

PROPAGATION Divide plants after flowering or in early spring as growth commences.

PESTS AND DISEASES Slugs or birds may attack young shoots in spring.

▼ *Eriophyllum lanatum*

Erodium

Stork's bill

Geraniaceae

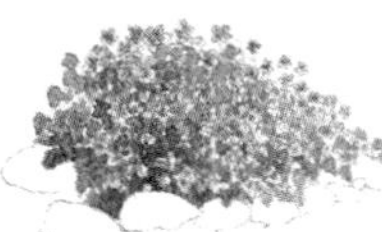

Erodium reichardii

A long summer show of cheerful cup-shaped flowers earns the stork's bills a place in the garden. The fruits that follow the flowers are like long, pointed beaks – giving rise to the common name. The genus mostly contains evergreen or semi-evergreen perennials, although there are some sub-shrubs and annuals. Many of the perennials are neat enough for the rock garden – the smaller ones particularly suited to raised beds, troughs or paving – and these are described below. Native to Europe, W and central Asia, they are generally hardy.

RECOMMENDED SPECIES AND VARIETIES

E. castellanum Rose-pink flowers, 2.5cm (1in) across with darker veins on the 3 upper petals, appear throughout summer. This compact, stemless species bears dissected grey-green leaves up to 15cm (6in) long with alternate large and small lobes. HEIGHT & SPREAD 20×30cm (8×12in).

E. chamaedryoides see *E. reichardii*

E. chrysanthum Pale sulphur-yellow flowers, 2cm (¾in) across, are borne in small sprays from late spring to early summer and occasionally later. This mound-forming plant has neatly dissected, silvery grey silky leaves, up to 15cm (6in) long. HEIGHT & SPREAD 20×30cm (8×12in).

▲ *Erodium chrysanthum*

E. corsicum Small pink flowers, 2cm (¾in) across, with dark veins are held singly or in small clusters from late spring to early summer. Small, downy, grey-green oval leaves, just 1.5cm (½in) long with crumpled edges, crowd the branches. This compact, mound-forming plant suffers from excess wet but is excellent for a trough, if protected in winter. It thrives in an alpine house. HEIGHT & SPREAD 7.5×20cm (3×8in).

E. foetidum see *E. petraeum*

E. glandulosum♀ (syn. *E. macradenum*, *E. petraeum* ssp. *glandulosum*) Pale lilac flowers, 2.5cm (1in) across, have violet-purple blotches on the 2 upper petals. They are borne in small clusters in summer. The leaves of this aromatic plant are deeply divided, grey-green and up to 15cm (6in) long. HEIGHT & SPREAD 20×20cm (8×8in).

▲ *Erodium glandulosum*

E. guttatum Pale pink flowers are borne in small clusters during the summer. The flowers are 2.5cm (1in) across with deep-pink veins and a deep-pink blotch on the two upper petals. This woody-based, clump-former bears numerous heart-shaped leaves, neatly toothed along the edges and up to 2.5cm (1in) long. HEIGHT & SPREAD 15×20cm (6×8in).

***E. × kolbianum* 'Natasha'** Pale rose-pink flowers, 2cm (¾in) across, appear in small clusters during the summer on this small plant. The silvery grey leaves are finely dissected, giving the foliage a ferny appearance. HEIGHT & SPREAD 15×15cm (6×6in).

E. macradenum see *E. glandulosum*

E. manescavi Pinkish purple flowers, 3cm (1¼in) across, with darker blotches on the 2 upper petals, appear intermittently from late spring until early autumn. The plant forms mounds of dissected, ferny, blue-green leaves, each up to 30cm (1ft) long. HEIGHT & SPREAD 40×60cm (16in×2ft).

E. petraeum (syn. *E. foetidum)* Small pink flowers, 2cm (¾in) across with red veins, appear throughout the summer. This compact mound-former has softly hairy, grey-green, deeply cut leaves up to 10cm (4in) long. HEIGHT & SPREAD 20×20cm (8×8in).

For ssp. *glandulosum* see *E. glandulosum*.

'Roseum' has rose-pink flowers with darker veins.

E. reichardii (syn. *E. chamaedryoides*) (alpine geranium) Small, solitary white

▲ *Erodium petraeum*

▲ *Erodium reichardii*

flowers, 1cm (⅜in) across with shell-pink veins, appear throughout the summer. The deep green, heart-shaped leaves have finely toothed edges and are 1.5cm (½in) long. This mound-forming perennial suits raised beds and troughs; it dislikes excessive winter wet. HEIGHT & SPREAD 5×20cm (2×8in).

E. rupestre Plain white flowers, 1.5cm (½in) across, are borne in small clusters in summer. This species bears silvery grey dissected leaves, up to 7.5cm (3in) long. HEIGHT & SPREAD 10×20cm (4×8in).

▲ *Erodium trifolium*

E. trifolium Pink flowers are borne in loose sprays in late spring and early summer. The 2.5cm (1in) blooms have brown blotches on the two upper petals. Grey-green, 3-lobed leaves, about 5cm (2in) long, cover the stems of this short-lived evergreen, which often self-sows in the garden. HEIGHT & SPREAD 35×35cm (14×14in).

E. × variabile Small white to bright pink flowers, 1.5cm (½in) across, appear during the summer and early autumn. This is a cushion to mound-forming plant bearing deep green to grey-green, oval leaves with scalloped edges, up to 2.5cm (1in) long. HEIGHT & SPREAD 20×40cm (8×16in).

'Album' has pure white flowers. **'Bishop's Form'** has brighter pink flowers and a looser habit. **'Flore Pleno'** bears double pink flowers, like tiny rosettes, with darker veins. **'Roseum'**♀ has pink flowers with crimson veins.

CULTIVATION Plant in spring, choosing a well-drained, sunny site and preferably a neutral-to-alkaline soil.

PROPAGATION Sow seed in autumn or early spring in pots in a coldframe. The species tend to hybridise in the garden so that seedlings cannot be guaranteed to be pure if two or more species or cultivars are grown side by side. An alternative is to take basal cuttings of leafy shoots from late spring through the summer.

E. glandulosum, *E.* × *kolbianum* 'Natasha', *E. rupestre* and *E. trifolium* can be divided carefully in autumn or early spring, ensuring that each portion has an ample amount of root attached.

PESTS AND DISEASES Grey rot may infect the crown of cushion-forming plants if they become too wet in winter outdoors. Overhead protection, such as a cloche or pane of glass, may help to prevent this.

Eryngium

Eryngo

Umbelliferae

Eryngium bourgatii 'Oxford Blue'

The bold flowerheads of these majestic plants give interest and add stature to the flower border during summer. The thistle-like flowerheads – which attract butterflies and bees – are adorned by more spectacular, often spiny bracts, which, like the upper stems, are usually highly coloured. Most of the eryngiums listed here are perennial, half of them are evergreen and only two are not fully hardy. They all flower from mid to late summer and make excellent dried flowers for decorative winter arrangements.

▼ *Eryngium × giganteum*

RECOMMENDED SPECIES AND VARIETIES

E. agavifolium This clump-forming, half-hardy, evergreen perennial produces greenish white flowerheads, up to 5cm (2in) across. The deep green, stiff, sword-shaped leaves have sharp saw-toothed margins, and mostly grow in basal rosettes. HEIGHT & SPREAD 1.5m×75cm (5×2½ft).

E. alpinum♀ (Alpine eryngo) Purplish blue, teasel-like flowerheads, to 5cm (2in) long, are surrounded by similarly coloured, feathery bracts. This clump-forming, hardy herbaceous perennial, has glossy, deep green basal leaves which are heart-shaped with a toothed margin. HEIGHT & SPREAD 1m×70cm (3ft×2ft4in).

'Blue Star' has deep blue flowerheads and bracts.

E. amethystinum Small blue flowerheads, 2cm (¾in) across, are surrounded by spiky darker blue bracts. This evergreen hardy perennial has very spiny, dissected basal leaves. HEIGHT & SPREAD 60×60cm (2×2ft).

E. bourgatii Rounded flowerheads, 2.5cm (1in) across, which change from steely blue and green to lilac-blue, are borne on similarly coloured stems. The deeply cut, grey-green basal leaves of this hardy herbaceous perennial bear striking silver veining. HEIGHT & SPREAD 60×50cm (24×20in).

'Oxford Blue'♀ has flowerheads of dark silvery blue.

E. × giganteum♀ (Miss Willmott's ghost) This stiff, robust and statuesque biennial has blue flowerheads, 4cm (1½in) long, surrounded by handsome, broad, silvery spiny bracts. The basal leaves are oval and deep

▼ *Eryngium bourgatii*

green. It spreads itself freely by seed. HEIGHT & SPREAD 1.2m×75cm (4×2½ft).
E. maritimum (sea holly) Small pale blue flowerheads, 2.5cm (1in) across, are surrounded by spiny blue-grey bracts on short stiff stems. This tufted, short-lived, evergreen perennial has spiny, leathery, blue-grey basal leaves. Ideal for the rock garden. HEIGHT & SPREAD 50×50cm (20×20in).
E. x oliverianum♀ Upright stems of lavender-blue flowerheads, about 4cm (1½in) long, are surrounded by narrow, spreading, spiny bracts. This hardy herbaceous perennial has mid green oval basal leaves with saw-tooth margins. HEIGHT & SPREAD 1m×60cm (3×2ft).
E. pandanifolium Clusters of small, rounded, purplish flowerheads, to 1cm (⅜in) across, are carried on tall, stiff stems. This robust, half-hardy perennial has basal tufts of very long, strap-like, mid green leaves with soft, spiny margins. HEIGHT & SPREAD 2.4×1.2m (8×4ft).
E. planum Numerous, small, deep blue flowerheads, 1.5cm (½in) across, are surrounded by similarly coloured, spreading, spine-tipped bracts. This partly evergreen hardy perennial has dark green, leathery basal leaves which contrast with the blue-flushed, spiny upper stem leaves. HEIGHT & SPREAD 75×40cm (2ft6in×1ft4in).
E. x tripartitum♀ Airy sprays of small blue flowerheads, 1cm (⅜in) long, are surrounded by spreading, spine-tipped bracts. This partly evergreen hardy perennial has wiry stems and basal rosettes of deep grey-green, coarsely toothed leaves. HEIGHT & SPREAD 1m×50cm (3ft×1ft 8in).
E. variifolium The branched clusters of small silver-blue flowerheads, up to 2cm (¾in) across, have narrow, spreading, silvery white or silvery blue spine-tipped bracts. This evergreen hardy perennial has rosettes of oval, jagged-toothed, deep green basal leaves, marbled with white which contrast with the spiny divided stem leaves. HEIGHT & SPREAD 50×25cm (20×10in).
E. x zabelii This hybrid bears deep purple-blue flowerheads, up to 2.5cm (1in) long, surrounded by rigid, spine-toothed bracts of silvery blue. A hardy herbaceous perennial, it has rounded, three-part basal leaves with spine-toothed margins. HEIGHT & SPREAD 50×30cm (20×12in).
'Violetta' has larger violet-blue flowerheads and grows to 75cm (2½ft) tall.
CULTIVATION Plant eryngiums on a sunny well-drained site in most garden soils.
PROPAGATION Sow seed in autumn or winter in pots in a coldframe. Alternatively, take root cuttings of perennial species in winter or carefully divide plants in early spring.
PESTS AND DISEASES Crown rot may affect plants in colder and wetter regions. To help to prevent this, particularly in rock gardens, clear the plants of dead leaves and give some protection from winter wet.

Erysimum
Wallflower
Cruciferae

Erysimum cheiri 'Harpur Crewe'

The common wallflower, *Erysimum cheiri*, has long been associated with cottage gardens, admired for its early, fragrant blooms. It is often used in spring bedding schemes, mixing effectively with bulbs, especially tulips. If the plants are cut back they will continue to flower intermittently through the summer.

Most wallflowers can be used at the front of a border for colour in spring and early summer, while *E. helveticum*, *E. hieraciifolium* and *E. pulchellum* make freely flowering rock-garden plants. The plants described below have four-petalled flowers, which are generally about 2cm (¾in) across and borne in spikes. Native across the Northern Hemisphere, particularly Europe and Asia. Many of the species were formerly included in the genus *Cheiranthus*.

RECOMMENDED SPECIES AND VARIETIES
E. x allionii (hort.) see *E. hieraciifolium*
E. 'Bowles Mauve'♀ Spikes of deep mauve flowers are borne by this evergreen perennial with a bushy habit. It is hardy to -15°C (5°F). The stiff, branched stems carry dark grey-green, narrow to lance-shaped leaves. HEIGHT & SPREAD 75×60cm (2½×2ft).
E. 'Bredon'♀ Dense spikes of bright, rich yellow flowers are carried by this partly evergreen bushy perennial. The stems are rather crowded with dark green, narrowly elliptical leaves with a bluish tint. HEIGHT & SPREAD 45×45cm (1½×1½ft).
E. 'Butterscotch' Spikes of toffee-yellow flowers are carried by this low-growing perennial which has mid green oval leaves. HEIGHT & SPREAD 25×25cm (10×10in).

▼ *Erysimum* 'Butterscotch'

E. capitatum Flowers, varying in colour from yellow to orange-brown and maroon-purple, are borne in clusters. This biennial has erect, somewhat branched stems and deep green, lance-shaped, toothed leaves. HEIGHT & SPREAD 45×25cm (18×10in).
E. cheiri (common wallflower) Spikes of large, intensely fragrant flowers are produced in a wide range of colours, particularly yellow, cream, orange, bronze and red. This bushy evergreen is hardy with mid to deep green lanceolate leaves. It is often grown as a biennial for bedding purposes. HEIGHT & SPREAD Seed merchants sell different strains: tall, up to 60×45cm (2×1½ft); intermediate, up to 45×30cm (1½×1ft); and dwarf, up to 20×20cm (8×8in).

'Harpur Crewe' has double yellow flowers, opening in succession from late spring to mid summer. It grows up to 45cm (1½ft) tall.
E. 'Chelsea Jacket'♀ Large, rich magenta, scented flowers are borne by this compact evergreen perennial. The lanceolate leaves are deep green. HEIGHT & SPREAD 1m×50cm (3ft×20in).
E. 'Constant Cheer'♀ Spikes of violet-mauve flowers flushed with amber are borne by this rather upright evergreen perennial. It also bears deep green lanceolate leaves. HEIGHT & SPREAD 60×40cm (24×16in).

▲ *Erysimum helveticum*

E. helveticum (syn. *E. pumilum*) Fragrant bright yellow flowers appear in broad clusters from late spring to mid summer. This clump-forming, partly evergreen perennial bears deep green or grey-green, crowded narrow-lanceolate leaves. HEIGHT & SPREAD 15×20cm (6×8in).
E. hieraciifolium♀ (syn. *E. × allionii* [hort.]) (Siberian wallflower) Orange flowers with hairs on the reverse of the petals are carried by this compact, bushy perennial. The deep green leaves are oblong to lance-shaped, and often wavy and toothed. HEIGHT & SPREAD 1m×50cm (36×20in).
E. 'Moonlight' Pale yellow flowers are borne in spikes from late spring to mid summer and occasionally later. This mat-

forming, evergreen perennial has mid green, narrow oval leaves. HEIGHT & SPREAD 10×30cm (4×12in).

E. pulchellum Golden-yellow flowers are borne in spikes from early to mid summer. This tufted evergreen perennial has rather dense lance-shaped to oblong, mid to deep green leaves which are coarsely toothed. HEIGHT & SPREAD 40×30cm (1ft 4in× 1ft).

E. pumilum see *E. helveticum*

E. **'Wenlock Beauty'**♀ Spikes of somewhat fragrant yellow flowers, attractively flushed with bronze, are carried by this bushy evergreen perennial. The elliptical to lance-shaped leaves are deep green. HEIGHT & SPREAD 25×25cm (10×10in).

CULTIVATION Erysimums will grow in any well-drained soil in sunny but sheltered positions. Rich or moist soil leads to reduced flowering. Plant bedding types in late summer or early autumn; plant out perennials in spring. Trim after flowering to encourage further blooms. As the plants are short-lived, regular propagation is advisable.

PROPAGATION Take 6cm (2½in) semi-ripe cuttings with a heel of the perennial species and cultivars in summer, overwinter under glass and plant out the following spring. Seed of the species may be sown in spring under glass and then treated as cuttings. Seed of *E. cheiri* is best sown in early summer and the seedlings planted in their flowering positions in autumn.

PESTS AND DISEASES Cabbage root fly, flea beetles, slugs, snails and caterpillars attack the plants. Various leaf and stem spots and rots, and root rots affect erysimums, as does infection from turnip mosaic virus.

Erythrina

Coral tree

Leguminosae

Spectacular brilliant red flowers characterise this genus of deciduous or semi-evergreen perennials, shrubs and trees. The leaves are composed of three broad leaflets and the branches of some species are spiny. Of the 100 species, only one may be grown in Britain and then only in milder areas.

RECOMMENDED SPECIES

E. crista-galli Scarlet beak-like flowers, up to 5cm (2in) long, are borne in late summer and autumn in long spikes. The oval, leathery, sea-green leaflets, up to 12cm (4¾in) long, have a spiny stalk. This deciduous shrub will grow outdoors in sheltered spots in mild areas. In harsh winters, stems that have not been pruned may be killed back to ground level but new shoots will emerge the following year. This plant can also be grown in a container under glass. Native to S America. HEIGHT & SPREAD 1×1m (3×3ft) after 5 years, ultimately 3m (10ft) tall.

CULTIVATION Plant in spring in a fertile, well-drained soil in full sun, ideally against a south or west-facing wall. In winter, protect the rootstock with a dry mulch. Alternatively, grow in a container of well-drained potting compost, such as John Innes No 2, and place in a cool greenhouse or conservatory. Plants can be moved outside after the danger of frost has passed. When the leaves fall, keep the compost almost dry.

▲ *Erythrina crista-galli*

PROPAGATION Take semi-ripe cuttings in summer or sow seed under glass in early spring.

PRUNING Cut plants growing outdoors to ground level in late autumn, and cut back those under glass every second year.

PESTS AND DISEASES Plants grown under glass are susceptible to red spider mite.

Erythronium

Dog's tooth violet

Liliaceae

Erythronium revolutum

Grown for their pendent blossoms and attractively mottled foliage, these tuberous perennials are a delight to behold in spring. The flowers, with their prominent stamens and reflexed petals, nod gracefully at the top of smooth slender stems rising above the oval to lance-shaped leaves. All species are hardy and benefit from a little shade, doing best in the dappled sunlight of a woodland environment. Native to northern USA, except *Erythronium dens-canis*, which comes from Europe and Asia.

RECOMMENDED SPECIES AND VARIETIES

E. americanum (trout lily) Shy to flower, when solitary bright yellow flowers, 4cm (1½in) wide, are carried at the top of beige stems up to 20cm (8in) high. The semi-erect green leaves are mottled with brown and up to 15cm (6in) long and 4cm (1½in) wide. HEIGHT & SPREAD 20×20cm (8×8in).

E. californicum♀ In spring pinkish brown buds open into creamy white flowers with a yellow eye. Up to three 5cm (2in) wide blooms are carried on each purple stem. Lance-shaped leaves, 15cm (6in) long and 6cm (2½in) wide, are mid green mottled white. HEIGHT & SPREAD 30×30cm (1×1ft).

'White Beauty'♀, a vigorous plant, has white starry flowers, up to 6cm (2½in) across, and more heavily marbled leaves than those of the species.

E. **'Citronella'** up to 3 lemon-yellow flowers hang together in a loose spike. The semi-erect leaves, heavily mottled with brown, are 10cm (4in) long and 5cm (2in) wide. HEIGHT & SPREAD 25×20cm (10×8in).

E. dens-canis♀ (dog's tooth violet) Solitary starry flowers, 4cm (1½in) wide, with swept-back petals in pink, purple or white are carried on 20cm (8in) stems. The leaves of this free-flowering species are mottled brown, 15cm (6in) long and 5cm (2in) wide. HEIGHT & SPREAD 20×15cm (8×6in).

E. japonicum Purple funnel-shaped flowers, 3.5cm (1⅜in) across, are borne singly, in spring, on dark green stems with a purplish flush. The lance-shaped leaves are up to 15cm (6in) long and dark green mottled purple. HEIGHT & SPREAD 15×15cm (6×6in).

E. **'Pagoda'**♀ Up to 10 pale yellow blossoms, 6cm (2½in) wide, are carried on stems up to 25cm (10in) high. At the base of the stems this robust, vigorous plant bears glossy green leaves up to 15cm (6in) long and 5cm (2in) wide, mottled with brown. HEIGHT & SPREAD 25×20cm (10×8in).

▲ *Erythronium californicum*

▲ *Erythronium dens-canis*

Erythronium revolutum ▲

E. revolutum♀ A loose spike of up to 4 pink 7.5 cm (3 in) wide blossoms rises out of the attractive, brown-dappled foliage. The semi-erect, wavy edged green leaves are up to 20 cm (8 in) long and 5 cm (2 in) wide. HEIGHT & SPREAD 25×20 cm (10×8 in).

E. tuolumnense♀ Heads of up to 10 bright yellow flowers, 5 cm (2 in) across, are borne on green stems. This quickly spreading plant bears pairs of semi-erect glossy green leaves up to 15 cm (6 in) long and 5 cm (2 in) wide. HEIGHT & SPREAD 30×20 cm (12×8 in).

CULTIVATION Erythroniums prefer cool conditions. Plant in a richly organic, moist soil in partial shade in autumn, and ensure that the tubers are not baked by the sun during the dormant period in summer.

PROPAGATION Divide the tubers in late summer or early autumn. Replant immediately so that the tubers do not dry out.

PESTS AND DISEASES Usually trouble free.

Escallonia

Escalloniaceae

Escallonia 'C.F. Ball'

Brilliant pink or red flower clusters are set off magnificently by the dark, glossy leaves of this shrub. Escallonias give year-round interest to the garden, with flowers in bloom from early summer to early autumn and gleaming, deep green leaves through winter. These mostly evergreen shrubs and small trees grow well in southern and western Britain, including western Scotland, particularly by the sea, where they withstand salt-laden sea breezes and are much used for hedging and as windbreaks. Elsewhere, most species do best if they have a sheltered position, such as against a wall. Cultivars tend to be hardy, but sometimes lose leaves in periods of prolonged frost.

The small flowers have five rounded petals and are generally cup or bell-shaped. They measure up to 1.5 cm (½ in) across and are borne in clusters 5 to 10 cm (2 to 4 in) long. The flowers appear in abundance in early summer, and then bloom intermittently until early autumn. The leaves, arranged alternately on the stem, are up to 5 cm (2 in) long and fairly narrow, often oval. Plants have a rounded habit, with stems upright or arching downwards. The genus is native to South America.

The varieties listed below are evergreen, with glossy dark green leaves that have finely serrated edges. They are all frost-hardy, except for *E.* 'Iveyi', which is only moderately so.

RECOMMENDED SPECIES AND VARIETIES

E. **'Apple Blossom'**♀ Flowers are cup-shaped and pink or white or a combination of the two. This shrub grows into a good hedge, with pruning. HEIGHT & SPREAD 1×1 m (3×3 ft) after 5 years, ultimate height 1.5 m (5 ft).

E. **'C.F. Ball'** Crimson flowers, tubular in shape, appear from late spring to late summer. This vigorous plant is particularly suited to gardens close to the seashore. The leaves are fragrant when crushed. HEIGHT & SPREAD 1.5×1.5 m (5×5 ft) after 5 years, ultimately 3 m (10 ft) tall.

▲ *Escallonia* 'C.F. Ball'

E. **'Donard Beauty'** Decorative pinkish red flowers first appear in early spring. HEIGHT & SPREAD 1×1 m (3×3 ft) after 5 years, ultimately 1.8 m (6 ft) tall.

E. **'Donard Brilliance'** Flowers are carmine red with golden anthers. HEIGHT & SPREAD 1×1 m (3×3 ft) after 5 years, ultimately 1.8 m (6 ft) tall.

E. **'Donard Radiance'**♀ Flowers are deep pink. HEIGHT & SPREAD 1×1 m (3×3 ft) after 5 years, ultimately 1.8 m (6 ft) tall.

E. **'Donard Seedling'** A vigorous plant whose white flowers are tinged with pink, and about 2 cm (¾ in) across. HEIGHT & SPREAD 1.2×1.2 m (4×4 ft) after 5 years, ultimately 3 m (10 ft) tall.

E. **'Edinensis'**♀ A compact shrub with pale pink flowers that are a deeper pink when in bud. HEIGHT & SPREAD 1.2×1.2 m (4×4 ft) after 5 years, ultimately 2.4 m (8 ft) tall.

E. **'Gwendolyn Anley'** This is a fine, spreading shrub. The pale pink flowers can be as much as 2 cm (¾ in) across. HEIGHT & SPREAD 60 cm×1 m (2×3 ft) after 5 years, ultimately 1×2 m (3×6½ ft).

▼ *Escallonia* 'Edinensis'

▲ *Escallonia* 'Iveyi'

E. **'Iveyi'**♀ White flowers grow in branched clusters up to 10 cm (4 in) long, in mid and late summer. The flowers are pale pink in bud. They are slightly fragrant, as are the leaves when crushed. This fine plant is a strong grower, but only moderately frost-hardy and so is best grown against a wall. HEIGHT & SPREAD 1.5×1.5 m (5×5 ft) after 5 years, ultimately 2.7 m (9 ft) tall.

E. **'Langleyensis'**♀ Rose-pink flowers cover the arching branches. The leaves grow to only 2.5 cm (1 in) long. HEIGHT & SPREAD 1.2×1.2 m (4×4 ft) after 5 years, ultimately 2.4 m (8 ft).

E. **'Peach Blossom'**♀ Flowers are a pale pink. HEIGHT & SPREAD 1.2×1.2 m (4×4 ft) after 5 years, ultimately 2.4 m (8 ft).

E. **'Pride of Donard'**♀ The bright red flowers on this outstanding plant, some as wide as 2 cm (¾ in), are among the largest borne by any escallonia. HEIGHT & SPREAD 1.2×1.2 m (4×4 ft) after 5 years, ultimately 2 m (6½ ft) tall.

E. **'Red Elf'** The flowers are a deep crimson. HEIGHT & SPREAD 1.5×1.5 m (5×5 ft) after 5 years, ultimately 2 m (6½ ft) tall.

▼ *Escallonia* 'Peach Blossom'

▲ *Escallonia* 'Pride of Donard'

e

E. rubra Cultivars of this evergreen shrub are hardier and less variable in flower colour than the species. Deep pink to crimson flowers grow in clusters up to 10cm (4in) long. The leaves are up to 5cm (2in) long. HEIGHT & SPREAD 1.5×1.5m (5×5ft) after 5 years, ultimately 4m (13ft) tall.

'Crimson Spire'♀, a good hedging plant, has bright crimson flowers. It grows to 1.2×1.2m (4×4ft) in 5 years, and ultimately to 2m (6½ft). **'Ingramii'** has an upright habit and grows to over 3.5×2.5m (12×8ft). A strong-growing plant with bright rosy red flowers, var. *macrantha* should measure about 1.5×1.5m (5×5ft) after 5 years. It eventually reaches a height of 4m (13ft). The leaves are aromatic when crushed. This is another cultivar that makes a good hedge, particularly in areas close to the sea. **'Woodside',** also known as 'Pygmaea', produces crimson flowers. With its compact habit, it is small enough for a rock garden, growing to 50cm (20in) tall at most and spreading a little wider.

E. **'Slieve Donard'** The flowers are pale pink and the leaves only about 1.5cm (½in) long on this neat, compact plant. HEIGHT & SPREAD 1×1m (3×3ft) after 5 years, ultimately 1.5m (5ft) tall.

CULTIVATION Escallonias thrive in any well-drained soil, in sun or shade. Shelter the more tender species and varieties from frost and cold winds, by growing them against a south-facing wall, for instance.

PROPAGATION Take semi-ripe cuttings in early or mid summer.

PRUNING Prune straggly plants immediately after flowering, to keep them in shape. Otherwise, pruning is not required.

PESTS AND DISEASES Usually trouble free.

▼ *Escallonia* 'Red Elf'

Eschscholzia

California poppy
Papaveraceae

Bright poppy-like flowers with silky petals are carried on slender stems well above finely divided, blue-green leaves on this free-flowering, hardy annual. This easily grown plant flourishes in poor, dry soil and needs full sun as the flowers close in shade. Only two species are widely grown, both native to W America. Flowering begins in early summer and continues until the end of summer. Plants commonly self-seed.

RECOMMENDED SPECIES AND VARIETIES

E. caespitosa♀ A dwarf plant with bright yellow flowers, 2.5cm (1in) across, and finely divided leaves. HEIGHT & SPREAD 15×15cm (6×6in).

'Sundew' has pale yellow, scented flowers up to 5 cm (2 in) across.

E. californica♀ Profuse yellow and orange flowers, up to 7cm (2¾in) across, are carried on erect, slender stems above finely divided blue-grey foliage from early summer to mid autumn. Garden seed strains are offered in a wide range of colours. HEIGHT & SPREAD 35×20cm (14×8in).

'Dali' has single red flowers with a yellow eye. **'Mission Bells'** is a mixture of double varieties with a wide colour range from cream to pink, orange, white and yellow. **'Monarch Art Shades'** comprises semi-double and double varieties. The petals are frilled and colours range from cream to pink, orange, red and yellow.

CULTIVATION Grow in a sunny position in poor, fast-draining soil. Moist, rich soils are undesirable, as they encourage lush foliage at the expense of flowers. Deadhead plants regularly to prolong flowering.

PROPAGATION Sow seed in flowering position as the plants resent root disturbance. Sow in early to mid spring or in early autumn and thin seedlings to 15cm (6in) apart. Once introduced to a garden, plants generally self-seed in subsequent years.

PESTS AND DISEASES Usually trouble free.

▲ *Eschscholzia californica*

Eschscholzia californica 'Dali' ▼

Espostoa see CACTI p.107

Eucalyptus

Gum tree
Myrtaceae

Eucalyptus pauciflora ssp. niphophila

A light, open head of grey-green leaves hanging from sinuous pale branches gives the fast-growing eucalyptus its unmistakable appearance. Unlike the leaves, the bark is deciduous, peeling off each year once the tree is four or five years old to reveal startling creamy patches against the browner mature bark.

The leaves of young plants are quite different from the lance-shaped or sickle-shaped foliage on mature plants. The juvenile leaves are oval or round, about 4cm (1½in) long, opposite and generally a silvery blue-green colour. They are much used in flower arrangements. If cut in winter they remain fresh in water for two to three weeks. Mature leaves are generally alternate, pendulous and less grey. They turn edgeways to bright sunlight to reduce moisture loss and overheating. Clusters of tiny cream flowers, each about 1cm (⅜in) long with prominent tufts of stamens, are borne in summer on trees past the age of 10 to 15 years. These are followed by bunches of urn-shaped, hard-shelled seed capsules, 5 to 10mm (¼ to ⅜in) long, which are usually green, maturing to brown.

Most species of these native Australian trees are tender in Britain, though some are suitable for growing in milder parts of the country if sheltered from strong cold winds. Never plant them in confined spaces, near buildings or on shrinkable clays: their roots, running wide to satisfy the need for plenty of water, can easily damage walls.

RECOMMENDED SPECIES AND VARIETIES

E. coccifera (Mount Wellington peppermint, Tasmanian snow gum)♀ Smooth, brilliant white bark clothes the shrubby, open-crowned tree. The adult leaves are thick, greyish and smell of peppermint. Creamy white flowers are produced in clusters in late spring. HEIGHT & SPREAD 8×4m (26×13ft) after about 20 years, ultimately 18m (60ft), but variable according to provenance. The hardiest, most vigorous plants come from exposed high altitudes.

E. dalrympleana♀ One of the hardier species, the large slender tree has an open crown of orange-red twigs emerging from pink, white and grey branches. Unless the tree is chosen for its ornamental peeling bark, it can be pruned annually for a constant display of young blue-grey foliage. Clusters of white flowers are produced between late summer and autumn. HEIGHT & SPREAD 20×8m (66×26ft) in 20 years with a continued growth rate of 1m (3ft) a year, ultimately about 30m (100ft).

▲ *Eucalyptus gunnii*

▲ *Eucalyptus pauciflora* ssp. *niphophila*

E. globulus (Tasmanian blue gum)♀ Unusual in its dense crown of heavy branches, the tree grows large and fast. On mature trees the bark peels and white flowers bloom from late summer to autumn. It is widely available as a 1-year-old seedling to grow in a border for its silvery blue-green foliage. The 1-year-old plants reach about 1m×50cm (3ft×1ft8in) and are pulled out at the end of the season. Mature trees are often killed by extremely severe winters. HEIGHT & SPREAD 15×6m (50×20ft) after 15–20 years, ultimately 40m (130ft) in warm locations.

E. gunnii (cider gum)♀ One of the hardiest of the genus, the leggy, slender tree has grey and pale green bark and an open crown. It lacks the scent of other species. It is often grown as a shrub, cut back to produce its round-leaved juvenile foliage, which is pale blue-grey, usually tinged pink when young. HEIGHT & SPREAD Trees grow to 15×6m (50×20ft) in 20 years and up to 35m (115ft) in height. Plants grown for juvenile foliage, and cut back, reach up to 1m (3ft) each year.

E. parvifolia (small-leaved gum)♀ Slow-growing, so ideal for garden use, this elegant tree has grey bark, which flakes off in plates, and narrow blue-green leaves. It tolerates annual pruning to a height of 2m (6½ft) for some 20 years, but then the cream flowers, seen simply as clusters of stamens in late summer, will be lost. HEIGHT & SPREAD if left unpruned, 12×4m (40×13ft) after 10 years, ultimately 20m (66ft) tall.

E. pauciflora (cabbage gum) Reddish twigs bearing grey-green leaves make an open crown on this hardy, slender, upright tree with chalky white bark. Cream flowers may appear in early summer. HEIGHT & SPREAD 15×6m (50×20ft) in 15 years, ultimately 20m (66ft) tall.

The subspecies ***niphophila*** (snow gum)♀ is more hardy and has brilliant white bark. It is often grown as a prostrate or leaning tree. Its size is not predictable though the largest specimen known is 25×10m (80×33ft).

▲▼ *Eucalyptus perriniana*

▲ *Eucalyptus pauciflora*

E. perriniana (spinning gum) The slow growth and upright slender crown make this tree suitable for smaller gardens. It is similar to *E. gunnii* but has noticeable ring scars encircling the young stems where the juvenile leaves have spun round in the wind before falling off. Juvenile foliage is purple-blue with paired leaves joining to encircle the stem. Adult leaves are long and narrow and are complemented in mid summer by white flowers that grow in clusters. HEIGHT & SPREAD 10×5m (33×16ft) in 20years, ultimately 20m (66ft) tall.

CULTIVATION Full sun is essential and moist, but well-drained, soil is preferable. Choose a sheltered situation, out of cold winds, for young plants. A deep mulch helps to stop soil freezing.

PROPAGATION Unusual hybrids often result from seed collected from cultivated plants and kept for a year to mature before sowing. The best plants are obtained from seeds of hardy strains originating from areas where frosts are more severe than at the intended planting site.

Sow seeds in containers in early spring and, with as little root disturbance as possible, plant out seedlings in mid summer. Eucalyptus cuttings do not strike.

PRUNING With correct pruning, a eucalyptus can be kept to any desired size. A small tree with a short trunk, and slender shoots with juvenile leaves, is created by cutting off a 1-year-old plant about 80cm (2ft 8in) from the ground and then cutting it back each year in early spring before growth starts. Trees pollarded for juvenile foliage still develop a peeling bark after 4 or 5 years.

For a constant supply of juvenile foliage, cut back all shoots to ground level or close to it in early spring after the severest frosts but before new growth begins.

PESTS AND DISEASES *E. gunnii* is grazed by rabbits because it is not aromatic. Silver leaf disease can be a problem. In very wet conditions, oedema causes warty patches to appear on the foliage; ensure free drainage and prune to improve air circulation.

Eucomis

Pineapple flower, pineapple lily
Hyacinthaceae

Numerous small, starry flowers appear in late summer, packed densely around a thick stem and topped with a tuft of leafy bracts to form a flowerhead in the shape of a pineapple – hence the common name. On fading the flowers form long-lasting seedpods. Dark green strap-shaped leaves come up straight from the bulb to form a rosette around the erect flower stem.

The plants are native to South Africa and suit a sunny border, but in most areas the bulbs need to be brought indoors over winter. They can be grown in pots for the patio in summer and greenhouse in winter.

RECOMMENDED SPECIES AND VARIETIES

E. autumnalis (syn. *E. undulata*) A sturdy flower stalk carries up to 45 whitish green flowers in a compact flowerhead, up to 15 cm (6 in) long. The dark green lanceolate leaves have wavy edges and up to 45 cm (18 in) long. HEIGHT 40cm (16 in).

E. bicolor Oblong, bright green leaves with purple edges fan out from a thick purple-flecked stem with up to 40 tightly packed, greenish, purple-tinged flowers in a 25 cm (10 in) long head. HEIGHT 50 cm (20 in).

▲ *Eucomis comosa*

Eucomis bicolor ▲

E. comosa (syn. *E. punctata*) A stately spike of up to 30 flowers rises out of a basal rosette of strap-shaped, purple-spotted leaves up to 50 cm (20 in) long. The flowers vary in colour from white to shades of pink, each centred by a violet-purple ovary and carried on a purple-spotted stem. HEIGHT 60 cm (2 ft).

E. punctata see *E. comosa*

E. undulata see *E. autumnalis*

CULTIVATION Plant in early spring, setting the bulbs 10 cm (4 in) deep and 25 cm (10 in) apart. Choose a sunny, well-drained spot in a rich soil. In all but the mildest, southernmost regions of Britain, lift and store the bulbs indoors through winter.

PROPAGATION Divide clumps in autumn or spring. Alternatively, sow seed in trays in spring and autumn. Seed-raised plants produce flowers after 5-6 years.

PESTS AND DISEASES Usually trouble free.

Eucryphia

Eucryphiaceae

Eucryphia x nymansensis 'Nymansay'

Abundant white flowers are borne in late summer on these large shrubs or small trees. The flowers, sometimes scented, are usually four-petalled, up to 6 cm (2½ in) across, and cupped round an array of numerous golden tipped stamens which gives them a feathery appearance. Flowers are generally produced on trees 10-15 years old. All the plants are evergreen in their native Australia and S America but some shed most of their leaves in colder climates. The leaves, less than 7.5 cm (3 in) long, generally have a serrated or wavy edge and are variable, mostly divided into three or more leaflets. Most shrubs are not fully hardy in cold northern areas of Britain. They grow best in the south and west and even there need a sheltered site. With the exception of *Eucryphia* x *nymansensis* and, to a lesser degree, *E. cordifolia* they do not tolerate lime.

RECOMMENDED SPECIES AND VARIETIES

E. cordifolia* x *lucida Only warm southern gardens suit this small, evergreen tree. The leaves are glossy dark green above and glaucous beneath. Large, scented white flowers, up to 6 cm (2½ in) across, with numerous stamens appear in late summer. HEIGHT & SPREAD 2 m×75 cm (6½×2½ ft) after 10 years, ultimately 8 m (26 ft) tall.

E. glutinosa♀ Masses of large, unscented white flowers cover this large, spreading shrub or small tree in mid to late summer. The dark green shiny leaves have 3 or 5 leaflets and they take on a rich orange-red autumn colour. Semi-evergreen in milder regions, this species is usually deciduous in most of the country. Though not truly frost-hardy it is one of the hardiest eucryphias. It does not tolerate lime and is a slow-growing plant. HEIGHT & SPREAD 1.5×1 m (5×3 ft) after 5 years, ultimately 6×2 m (20×6½ ft).

E. x intermedia This small evergreen tree flowers profusely, bearing numerous yellow-centred white flowers in late summer to early autumn. The leaves are sometimes divided into 3 leaflets. This species will withstand some frost. HEIGHT & SPREAD 5×2 m (16×6½ ft) after 20 years, ultimately 6 m (20 ft) tall.

'Rostrevor'♀ is a very free-flowering, fast-growing variety.

E. lucida Fragrant white flowers, slightly smaller than in other species, appear in profusion from early to mid summer on this slender evergreen tree. The glossy dark green leaves are slightly glaucous beneath. This species is moderately frost-hardy. HEIGHT & SPREAD 2 m×75 cm (6½×2½ ft) after 10 years, ultimately 6 m (20 ft) tall.

E. milliganii This slow-growing, upright, evergreen tree bears its small white flowers, 2 cm (¾ in) wide, in mid summer. It blooms

▲ *Eucryphia x intermedia*

from a very early age – between 7-10 years old. The leaves are shiny dark green above and blue-green beneath. It will stand some degree of frost but is not perfectly hardy. HEIGHT & SPREAD 2 m×60 cm (6½×2 ft) after 10 years, ultimately 6×2 m (20×6½ ft).

E. x nymansensis This small columnar tree is the most frost-hardy and the most tolerant of limy soils. Masses of white flowers are produced, singly or in clusters, in mid to late summer. The evergreen leaves are pinnate, divided into 3 or 5 leaflets, or undivided. HEIGHT & SPREAD 5×1.8 m (16×6 ft) after 20 years, ultimately 12 m (40 ft) tall.

The white flowers of the fast-growing **'Nymansay'**♀ are large, as much as 6 cm (2½ in) across, and are generally more numerous than the species.

▼ *Eucryphia x nymansensis* 'Nymansay'

CULTIVATION Plant in late spring after the threat of frosts has passed. Most species do best in an acid soil. All must have protection from cold spring winds and from winter frosts. They grow best in warm, moist climates. A favourable site promotes vigorous growth and as the plants get larger they become less susceptible to wind and frost damage. They do best with their roots in cool soil that is moist.
PROPAGATION Plants are easy to raise from seed, from semi-ripe cuttings taken in late summer or by layering. Those grown from seed do not always come true.
PRUNING None is required.
PESTS AND DISEASES Usually trouble free.

Euonymus

Spindle trees
Celastraceae

Euonymus alatus

Both deciduous and evergreen shrubs and trees belong to this genus. The deciduous species, grown for their eye-catching, yellow to deep scarlet autumn leaves and distinctive lobed fruit, are valued as border plants and freestanding specimens. The evergreen species provide dense, year-round foliage often marked with white, yellow or pink and are grown as climbers, for ground cover and as hedging plants that can be clipped into shape.

The leaves are mostly oval, 2.5-7.5 cm (1-3 in) long, and have serrated edges. Insignificant white, brown or greenish flowers appear in late spring and early summer. The red or pink, lobed or winged fruit, about 1 cm (⅜ in) across, become noticeable in early autumn. They often split to reveal bright orange seeds. All parts of the plants are harmful if eaten.

Most of the species are native to woods and scrubland throughout Europe and Asia. They grow well in any soil and are especially useful on chalky ground. Most species are hardy, although some evergreens are suitable only for milder, sheltered areas.

RECOMMENDED SPECIES AND VARIETIES

E. alatus♀ (winged spindle tree) In mid autumn the deciduous leaves turn a fiery red. The reddish purple, 4-lobed fruits open partially and often look lopsided because some of the 4 orange seeds may fail to develop. Four distinct corky wings run intermittently along the stems of this densely branched, spreading shrub. HEIGHT & SPREAD 1.2×1.5 m (4×5 ft) after 5 years, ultimately 2.4 m (8 ft) tall.

'Compactus'♀ (syn. 'Cliodentatus') is a dense plant, reaching only 1 m (3 ft) tall and is often used for low hedging.

▲ *Euonymus alatus*

***E. europaeus* 'Red Cascade'**♀ Long slender leaves turn bright red or purple in early autumn. At the same time abundant clusters of ripe, reddish pink, 4-lobed fruit, about 2 cm (¾ in) wide, open to reveal the white and orange seeds. This deciduous bushy shrub or small tree has green angular stems. HEIGHT & SPREAD 2×1.2 m (6½×4 ft) after 5 years, ultimately 5 m (16 ft) tall.

▲ *Euonymus europaeus* 'Red Cascade'

E. fortunei This hardy evergreen shrub and its many cultivated varieties provide ground cover plants, hedging and climbers. The pink fruit are rarely produced in Britain. HEIGHT & SPREAD 3×2 m (10×6½ ft) after 5 years (also its ultimate size).

The leaves of **'Emerald Gaiety'**♀ have a narrow, creamy white edge that turn bronze in the winter. This shrub reaches a height of 1 m (3 ft) and a spread of 1.5 m (5 ft). The leaves of the climber **'Emerald 'n' Gold'**♀ have bright green centres and wide, irregular, golden yellow edges that become tinged with pink in winter. **'Golden Prince'** (syn. 'Gold Tip') has yellow-tinged leaves and its branches are golden yellow at the tip. Unlike the other *E. fortunei* cultivars with yellow leaf markings, this plant retains its yellow colouring when grown in full sun. **'Harlequin'** has mottled white and green leaves in spring that become whiter in summer and then suffused with pink in winter. A low-growing, mounded shrub, it reaches a height and spread of 1 m (3 ft). **'Kewensis'** is only 5 cm (2 in) high with tiny leaves, 6 mm (¼ in) long. Spreading to form small hummocks or creeping over stones, it is good for rock gardens. **'Minimus'** is similar in habit but more vigorous and with larger 1.5 cm (½ in) mid green leaves. **'Sheridan Gold'** makes an erect, compact shrub up to 50 cm (20 in) in height. The young leaves are tinged yellow at first, turning green later. **'Silver Queen'**♀ has leaves with broad white edges that are tinted rose in winter. The deep green leaves of **'Sunspot'** (syn. 'Gold Spot') have a long, golden spot at the centre and are tinged red beneath in winter. **'Variegatus'** (syn. 'Gracilis', 'Silver Gem') has grey-green leaves with white edges, although the leaves tend to revert to grey-green as the plant ages. It is more tolerant of shade and a coastal climate.

▼ *Euonymus fortunei* 'Emerald Gaiety'

▲ *Euonymus fortunei* 'Emerald 'n' Gold'
Euonymus fortunei 'Golden Prince' ▲

▲ *Euonymus fortunei* 'Harlequin'
Euonymus fortunei 'Sunspot' ▲

E. hamiltonianus* ssp. *sieboldianus♀ (syn. *E. h.* ssp. *hians*, *E. h.* ssp. *yedoensis*, *E. yedoensis*) This upright deciduous shrub or small tree has large leaves, 12 cm (4¾ in) long, that change to pastel shades of yellow and pink in autumn. The abundant 4-lobed, claw-like fruit ripen in early autumn when a few may open slightly to reveal the orange-red seeds. The fruit persist on the tree long after leaf fall. HEIGHT & SPREAD

▲ *Euonymus fortunei* 'Silver Queen'

▲ *Euonymus oxyphyllus*

1.2×1m (4×3ft) after 5 years, ultimately 4.5m (15ft) tall.

E. ***hamiltonianus*** var. ***yedoensis*** see
*E. h.*ssp. *sieboldianus*

E. ***hamiltonianus*** ssp. ***hians*** see
E. h. ssp. *sieboldianus*

E. ***japonicus*** These evergreen shrubs or small trees have glossy green leaves. The pale pink fruit are rarely produced in Britain. Both the species and its cultivars grow best in mild and coastal areas and need protection from late spring frosts. HEIGHT & SPREAD 1.2×1m (4×3ft) after 5 years, ultimately 5m (16ft) tall.

The many cultivars provide a wide range of different coloured leaves and their upright bushy habit makes them suitable for planting as hedging. **'Aureus'** (syn. 'Aureopictus', 'Luna') has leaves with golden yellow centres and dark green edges. The leaves of **'Duc d'Anjou'** are grey-green with pale yellow centres. **'Latifolius Albomarginatus'**♀ (syn. 'Macrophyllus Albus') has grey-green leaves with conspicuous creamy white edges. The dense compact form **'Microphyllus'** reaches a height and spread of 1.5m (5ft) and has small, dark green leaves, 1cm (⅜in) long. The leaves of **'Microphyllus Albovariegatus'** (syn. 'Microphyllus Variegatus') have white edges whereas those of **'Microphyllus Pulchellus'** (syn. 'Microphyllus Aureus') are tinged with yellow. **'Ovatus Aureus'**♀ (syn. 'Aureovariegatus', 'Marieke') is a dense, compact plant reaching a height of 2m (6½ft) and a spread of 1.5m (5ft) that has 2 kinds of foliage; yellow leaves tinged with green and green leaves with yellow stripes and edges.

E. ***oxyphyllus*** In early autumn, the deciduous leaves of this large rounded shrub or small tree turn a rich plum red. At the same time, the deep red, 4-5 ribbed, round fruit open to reveal bright orange seeds hanging on fine short threads. HEIGHT & SPREAD 2×1.5m (6½×5ft) after 5 years, ultimately 5m (16ft) tall.

E. ***phellomanus*** This large deciduous shrub is grown for its abundant autumn fruit. Pink to rose-red, the fruit have 4 prominent lobes and open partially to reveal dark brown to deep red seeds. The leaves turn red in early autumn and have slender pointed tips and strong veining. There are 4 corky wings running intermittently along the length of the stems. HEIGHT & SPREAD 2×1.5m (6½×5ft) after 5 years, ultimately 5m (16ft) tall.

E. ***planipes***♀ (syn. *E. sachalinensis*) In early autumn, the leaves of this large deciduous shrub turn a bright red and the abundant scarlet fruit open to expose the 4-5 orange seeds held on short threads. The fruit have 4-5 ridges and measure 1.5cm (½in) across. HEIGHT & SPREAD 2×1.5m (6½×5ft) after 5 years, ultimately 5m (16ft) tall.

E. ***sachalinensis*** see *E. planipes*

E. ***yedoensis*** see *E. hamiltonianus*
ssp. *sieboldianus*

CULTIVATION Plant autumn or spring in any well-drained garden soil in sun or semi-shade. Evergreens grow well in full shade if it is not too dense. Most species are hardy although evergreens do best when sheltered from prolonged cold winds. Where possible, plant the deciduous varieties grown for ornamental fruit in small groups to ensure cross-pollination and, therefore, increase the fruit produced.

PROPAGATION Take heeled, semi-ripe cuttings or sow the seed of species and natural varieties in autumn. Seed may take 18 months to germinate. Layer evergreen creepers and climbers or cut off shoots that have rooted themselves.

PRUNING Regular pruning is not necessary although plants can be cut back hard to encourage new growth or to prevent them encroaching on other plants. This can be done at any time except spring. Pinch out the tips of evergreen shoots to encourage bushy growth and clip hedges in late spring and late summer. Trim back the shoots of deciduous plants and straggly creepers and climbers to maintain shape. Cut out shoots of variegated varieties that revert to green.

PESTS AND DISEASES Usually trouble free but occasionally infested with blackfly or caterpillars, such as those of the tortrix moth. Powdery mildew may occur on some evergreens.

Eupatorium

Compositae

Eupatorium purpureum

Fluffy clusters of tiny tubular flowers top the upright stems of these tall leafy plants that look good in wild gardens or among more informal borders. Most eupatoriums are either hardy herbaceous perennials or tender evergreen shrubs. The hardy species thrive in an open sunny position in moist but well-drained soil and the tender species make excellent large plants for the warm greenhouse or conservatory. This genus is native to E United States and Eurasia.

RECOMMENDED SPECIES AND VARIETIES

E. ***altissimum*** Dense clusters, 10cm (4in) across, of small white flowers appear on tall, upright stems in late summer. The very downy, mid green lance-shaped leaves are up to 15cm (6in) long. This is a hardy herbaceous perennial. HEIGHT & SPREAD 2×1m (6½×3ft).

'Braunlaub' has brownish leaves.

E. ***aromaticum*** (syn. *Ageratina aromatica*) Dense white flowerheads, 10cm (4in) across, are produced on this hardy herbaceous perennial during late summer. The oval leaves, up to 10cm (4in) long, often have crinkled or serrated edges. HEIGHT & SPREAD 1.5×1m (5×3ft).

E. ***cannabinum*** (hemp agrimony) Dense flowerheads, 7.5cm (3in) across, of white, pink or purple blooms appear during late summer and early autumn. The divided green leaves have serrated edges and are up to 10cm (4in) long. This species is a hardy herbaceous perennial. HEIGHT & SPREAD 2×1m (6½×3ft).

'Flore Pleno' has rosy double flowers.

E. ***ligustrinum*** (syn. *Ageratina ligustrina, E. micranthum, E. weinmannianum*) This

▲ *Eupatorium ligustrinum*

tender evergreen shrub with crowded branches bears creamy white or rose-tinted fragrant flowerheads, 20 cm (8 in) across, in autumn. The mid green elliptic leaves are up to 10 cm (4 in) long. HEIGHT & SPREAD 5×3 m (16×10 ft). This is the ultimate size, reached after 5 years.

E. micranthum see *E. ligustrinum*

E. purpureum (Joe Pye weed) Dense clusters, up to 25 cm (10 in) across, of pinkish purple flowers appear on strong purple stems during late summer. The oval leaves are up to 10 cm (4 in) long and have a coarse surface. A hardy herbaceous perennial. HEIGHT & SPREAD 2×1 m (6½×3 ft).

The stems of ssp. ***maculatum*** are blotched or mottled. Its cultivar,

▲ *Eupatorium purpureum* ssp. *maculatum*

'Atropurpureum', has deep purple-red flowerheads, 30 cm (12 in) across.

E. sordidum (syn. *Bartlettina sordida*) Neat heads, up to 10 cm (4 in) across, of tiny violet flowers cover these tender evergreen shrubs in autumn and winter. Its oval, toothed leaves, up to 10 cm (4 in) long, are dull green and rather hairy. HEIGHT & SPREAD 1.5×2 m (5×6½ ft). This is the ultimate size, reached after 5 years.

E. weinmannianum see *E. ligustrinum*

CULTIVATION Plant the hardy herbaceous species from autumn to spring in moist but well-drained soil, choosing a position in full sun. Grow the tender species in a greenhouse or conservatory in pots of good-quality potting compost. Keep at a minimum temperature of 7°C (45°F), out of direct sunlight. Deadhead when the flowers fade and cut herbaceous varieties back to the ground each autumn.

PROPAGATION Divide herbaceous perennials in autumn or take stem cuttings from the tender evergreen shrubs in summer. Sow the seed of species and natural varieties under glass in spring.

PRUNING Trim the shrubby species as required throughout the year. If any major pruning is necessary, cut back in spring.

PESTS AND DISEASES Usually trouble free.

Euphorbia

Spurge

Euphorbiaceae

Euphorbia polychroma

With their unusual blooms and fine foliage, euphorbias can create a dramatic effect in the garden. This one genus contains nearly 2000 different species, ranging from tiny annuals to large succulent trees. Euphorbias are found in almost every part of the globe and there must be a species available for almost every garden situation. Their blooms are unique and what appears to be flowers are, in fact, cyathia. Each cyathium has two bracts forming a cup that contains the tiny petal-less male and female flowers. In most species these bracts are a striking yellowy green that is peculiar to euphorbias. Around the true flowers is a ring of small nectar-secreting glands that vary in shape and colour and which can be a noticeable feature of the blooms. After the true flowers fade, the bracts usually persist. All euphorbias contain a milky white sap that is toxic and irritates the skin. Fish are sensitive to this sap and euphorbias should not be planted hanging over a fishpond.

RECOMMENDED SPECIES AND VARIETIES

The species included here are divided into 4 groups; evergreen perennials, herbaceous perennials, annuals and biennials, and greenhouse plants. Unless otherwise stated, all the plants, with the exception of the greenhouse varieties, are fully hardy and have narrow, pointed leaves.

EVERGREEN PERENNIALS

E. amygdaloides (wood spurge) Pale lime-green flower spikes, up to 15 cm (6 in) long, appear from mid spring to early summer. The narrow, obovate leaves, 10 cm (4 in) long, are grey-green. The stems and underside of the leaves are often a reddish purple. This woodland native prefers a shady spot. HEIGHT & SPREAD 45×45 cm (1½×1½ ft).

'Purpurea' (syn. 'Rubra') has purple leaves and stems and pale yellow flowers. The bracts and leaves may fade to mid green after flowering. This cultivar will grow in a well-drained sunny site. One of the best ground-cover plants for growing beneath trees, var. ***robbiae***🏆 (syn. *E. robbiae*) has 20 cm (8 in) long flower spikes. Its dark green leaves are paler beneath and unfurl in much the same way as a fern does.

E. biglandulosa see *E. rigida*

E. characias🏆 This large shrubby plant forms a loose dome with large, dull green flowerheads, 20 cm (8 in) long, that appear from mid to late spring. Each individual bloom has dark purple glands. Plants have biennial stems and flower on the previous season's growth. The pale grey-green leaves are about 11 cm (4¼ cm) long and sometimes covered with hairs. This plant is hardy except where winters are persistently wet and cold. It prefers full sun, although it will tolerate dappled shade. HEIGHT & SPREAD 1.5×1.8 m (5×6 ft).

The flowers of ssp. ***characias***🏆 have brown to black glands and pale green bracts. The oval flowerheads are up to 30 cm (1 ft) long. **'Blue Hills'** forms a compact dome with a height and spread of 1 m (3 ft) and has blue-green leaves. **'Humpty Dumpty'** has dark brown glossy bracts and velvety, blue-green leaves. It reaches a height and spread of 1.2 m (4 ft).

e

The flowers of ssp. ***wulfenii***🏆 (syn. *E. veneta*, *E. wulfenii*) have yellow glands and clear yellow bracts and are held in spherical flowerheads, up to 30 cm (1 ft) across. The blue-green leaves are up to 15 cm (6 in) long. Plants grow to a height and spread of 2 m (6½ ft). **'John Tomlinson'**🏆 (syn. Kew form) is a slightly smaller plant with oval flowerheads. **'Lambrook Gold'**🏆 has rich, golden khaki bracts. The young leaves of **'Purple and Gold'** (syn. 'Purpurea') are deep purple and covered in fine hairs, contrasting with the 20 cm (8 in) long, golden yellow flowerheads – the purple fades over summer. This variety reaches a height of 1.2 m (4 ft) and a spread of 1.5 m (5 ft).

E. longifolia see *E. mellifera*

E. × martinii🏆 Flowers with bright red glands appear in early summer in flowerheads 25 cm (10 in) long, borne on the previous year's shoots. Narrow, grey-green leaves, 10 cm (4 in) long, are held on reddish stems. Forming a dome-shaped clump, this is a good plant in both sun and partial shade. HEIGHT & SPREAD 60×60 cm (2×2 ft).

'Red Dwarf' has dusty red bracts.

E. mellifera (syn. *E. longifolia*) Clusters of honey-scented flowers, 12 cm (4¾ in) across, appear in mid spring. The yellowy green bracts enclose golden to red glands. The light green leaves, up to 15 cm (6 in) long, have pink edges and yellow central veins. This species is hardy only in milder regions but it can be grown in a pot and overwintered in a frost-free greenhouse. HEIGHT & SPREAD 1.2×1.2 m (4×4 ft).

E. myrsinites🏆 Flowerheads, up to 10 cm

▼ *Euphorbia myrsinites*

(4 in) across, appear from late winter to mid spring. The yellowy green bracts may fade to orange during summer. This low-growing plant has prostrate biennial stems – flowers are borne on the previous season's shoots. The thick, obovate, blue-grey leaves, about 3 cm (1¼ in) long, are arranged on the stems in spirals. HEIGHT & SPREAD 15×60 cm (6×24 in).

E. nicaeensis Clusters of flowers appear in late spring; they are 6 cm (2½ in) wide at first but have doubled in size by mid summer. Blue-green leaves, up to 5 cm (2 in) long, are borne on stems that are often tinted red. The plants form hemispherical clumps. HEIGHT & SPREAD 60 cm×1 m (2×3 ft).

E. pithyusa Clusters of flowers, about 10 cm (4 in) across, appear from late spring to early summer. The narrow, pointed blue-green leaves, 1.5 cm (½ in) long, are densely packed. This low, branching species makes a good rock-garden plant. HEIGHT & SPREAD 30 cm×1 m (1×3 ft).

E. rigida (syn. *E. biglandulosa*) Flower clusters appear in early spring on the previous season's shoots. They turn red in summer. The blue-green leaves are up to 5 cm (2 in) long. This plant has prostrate stems that do not like to lie across wet soil. It needs a sunny position and regular feeding if it is to flower every year. HEIGHT & SPREAD 60 cm×1.2 m (2×4 ft).

E. robbiae see *E. amygdaloides* var. *robbiae*

E. seguieriana ssp. ***niciciana*** Clear yellow flowerheads, up to 14 cm (5½ in) across, appear in late summer. The grey-green leaves are about 3 cm (1¼ in) long. This plant forms a loose clump. HEIGHT & SPREAD 60×60 cm (2×2 ft).

▲ *Euphorbia characias* ssp. *wulfenii*

E. veneta see *E. characias* ssp. *wulfenii*

E. wulfenii see *E. characias* ssp. *wulfenii*

HERBACEOUS PERENNIALS

E. cornigera (syn. *E. longifolia* hort.) Borne on red-tinged stems, the dark green leaves, 7.5 cm (3 in) long, have a cream stripe down the middle. The flower clusters, 10 cm (4 in) across, appear in mid summer. HEIGHT & SPREAD 30×75 cm (1×2½ ft).

E. cyparissias Profuse flower clusters, 8 cm (3¼ in) across, appear in mid spring. The bracts turn orange in summer. The light green, needle-like leaves are up to 4 cm (1½ in) long and turn clear yellow in autumn. This low-growing plant tolerates some shade and is good as ground cover. However, it can be invasive. HEIGHT & SPREAD 40 cm×1.2 m (16 in×4 ft).

E. donii (syn. *E. longifolia*) The dark green leaves, 13 cm (5¼ in) long. have a distinct white stripe down the centre and a faint pink edge. The stems are sometimes reddish. Lime-green flowers are produced from mid to late summer. This clump-forming plant prefers a sunny site on moist but well-drained soil. HEIGHT & SPREAD 30 cm×1 m (1×3 ft).

***E. dulcis* 'Chameleon'** This plant flowers in mid spring and has dark purple leaves and bracts. The oblanceolate leaves are up to 7 cm (2¾ in) long. This plant will do well in sun and shade. If cut down to ground level after flowering and fed and watered it will produce a second flush of foliage. HEIGHT & SPREAD 60×60 cm (2×2 ft).

▲ *Euphorbia dulcis* 'Chameleon'

E. epithymoides see *E. polychroma*

E. griffithii Orange or bright red flower clusters, 10 cm (4 in) across, appear in late spring. The emerging leaves are flushed with red before fading to dark green. They are 11 cm (4¼ in) long. This species prefers a semi-shady, moist site and is a good plant for the bog garden. HEIGHT & SPREAD 75×75 cm (2½×2½ ft).

▲ *Euphorbia griffithii*

'Dixter'♀ has deep orange flowerheads and reaches a height of 45 cm (1½ ft). **'Fireglow'** bears bright red flower clusters.

E. longifolia see *E. donii*

E. longifolia hort. see *E. cornigera*

E. oblongata Bright yellow flowerheads appear in late spring. The narrow pointed dark green leaves, 6 cm (2½ in) long, have a cream stripe down the middle. This clump-forming plant has warty seed capsules. It can be cut down in mid summer to stimulate new growth later in the year. This is a good plant for the dry garden. HEIGHT & SPREAD 30×60 cm (1×2 ft).

E. palustris♀ Clusters of flowers, up to 12.5 cm (5 in) across, with bright yellow glands appear from late spring to early summer. The 10 cm (4 in) long leaves may become tinged with orange in autumn. Plants form leafy clumps that will require some support. This plant prefers shady, moist sites but will still grow in dry, sunny places. HEIGHT & SPREAD 1×1 m (3×3 ft).

E. polychroma♀ (syn. *E. epithymoides*) Clusters of flowers with bright yellow bracts appear in mid spring. The dark green, pointed, oval leaves are up to 6 cm (2½ in) long and in some plants become tinged with shades of red and purple in autumn. This plant forms a dome that requires some support. HEIGHT & SPREAD 60×60 cm (2×2 ft).

The young shoots and leaves of **'Candy'** (syn. 'Purpurea') are tinged with purple during the spring.

E. schillingii♀ The dark green leaves, up to 10 cm (4 in) long, have a distinct white stripe down the centre. The flowers appear during late summer and the bracts retain their yellow colour well into autumn. These plants form a neat clump and prefer a moist soil in full sun. HEIGHT & SPREAD 60×75 cm (2×2½ ft).

E. sikkimensis Bright pink shoots first appear in late winter but do not grow until the temperature rises in spring. The bright green leaves, up to 12.5 cm (5 in) long, retain some of this pink along their edges and midribs. The flowers appear in early summer. This plant forms a dense, spreading clump and prefers moist soil. HEIGHT & SPREAD 1×1 m (3×3 ft).

E. villosa Flowering in early summer, this plant has mid green leaves up to 7.5 cm (3 in) long, which may be tinged bright red and orange in autumn. It forms a large clump that needs some support. HEIGHT & SPREAD 1×1.2 m (3×4 ft).

E. wallichii Yellow flower clusters, up to 10 cm (4 in) across, appear in early summer. The dark green leaves, up to 8 cm (3¼ in) long, have a white stripe down their centres. The stout stems form a clump which may need some support. HEIGHT & SPREAD 60 cm×1 m (2×3 ft).

ANNUALS AND BIENNIALS

E. lathyris (caper spurge, molewort) This biennial blooms in its second year, producing huge flowerheads, up to 1 m (3 ft) across. The bracts and leaves are deep blue-green, mottled with white veins. The leaves are in opposite pairs, held at right angles to the stem. On a sunny day, the capsules may explode, scattering the seeds widely. HEIGHT & SPREAD 60 cm×1.8 m (2×6 ft).

E. marginata This half-hardy annual has variegated leaves and bracts with bright

▲ *Euphorbia lathyris*

white edges. The leaves are narrow and pointed and measure up to 7 cm (2¾ in) long. An upright, branching plant. HEIGHT & SPREAD 60 cm x 1.2 m (2x4ft).

GREENHOUSE PLANTS

E. fulgens Bright scarlet flowers, up to 1.5 cm (½ in) across, are borne in clusters at the end of the slender, arching stems, usually in winter. The fresh green, elliptical leaves are up to 10 cm (4 in) long. HEIGHT & SPREAD 1 m x 75 cm (3 x 2½ ft).

E. milii♀ (crown of thorns) This sprawling succulent shrub has very thorny hexagonal stems. The bright green, obovate leaves, about 3 cm (1¼ in) long, sometimes drop off in winter but new ones appear in spring. Clusters of flowers with bright red bracts appear throughout the year. HEIGHT & SPREAD 1 m x 60 cm (3 x 2 ft).

'Splendens' (syn. *E. splendens*) is a larger plant with leaves up to 6 cm (2½ in) long.

E. obesa This ball-shaped succulent bears a circle of small yellow flowers at the top of a dark green, spherical, ridged stem in summer. The stem is often marked with a light green, chequered pattern. Male and female flowers are produced on separate plants. HEIGHT & SPREAD 5 x 5 cm (2 x 2 in).

E. pulcherrima (poinsettia) This popular houseplant has large blood-red, pink or cream bracts, that look like brightly coloured leaves, at the top of upright stems. They surround a cluster of very small yellow flowers and appear when light levels fall to less than 12 hours each day. The true leaves are dark green, oval and sometimes shallowly lobed. Plants are usually discarded when the leaves and bracts have fallen. HEIGHT & SPREAD 75 x 45 cm (2½ x 1½ ft).

E. splendens see *E. milii* 'Splendens'

CULTIVATION Plant outdoor species during spring, in any fertile soil. Unless otherwise specified above, most euphorbias prefer well-drained soil in full sun. *E. myrsinites*, *E. × martinii*, *E. nicaeensis*, *E. rigida* and *E. characias* and its sub species and varieties, all produce biennial stems from a woody crown. This means that plants have 2 types of shoot; the previous season's shoots, on which the flowers are borne, and the current season's growth. Cut back the flowering shoots to ground level in late summer or autumn so that the current season's shoots can flower the following year.

Plant *E. obesa* in a freely draining compost with added grit or sharp sand. Plant the remaining greenhouse species in pots of loam-based compost with added organic matter. Place in a position in direct light but shade from the midday sun during the hottest months. Provide a minimum temperature of 15°C (59°F). Water moderately from spring to autumn and sparingly in winter, ensuring that the compost is dry before each watering. Keep the compost of *E. obesa* completely dry in winter. Mist *E. pulcherrima* frequently during the growing season. Repot *E. fulgens* and *E. milii* regularly in spring.

PROPAGATION Divide the herbaceous species in spring or autumn. *E. polychroma*, *E. palustris*, *E. villosa* and *E. wallichii* have a thick woody stem below the crown; to divide these species, lift the whole crown and cut cleanly in half with a knife, dusting the cut surfaces with a suitable fungicide. Alternatively, sow seed of all species, except most of the greenhouse plants, in spring in a coldframe. Raise *E. obesa* by sowing fresh seed under glass. The evergreen perennials and greenhouse species can be propagated by softwood cuttings taken in late spring or early summer. The young plants should be overwintered in a coldframe.

PESTS AND DISEASES Usually trouble free, although *E. amygdaloides* and *E. × martinii* may suffer from powdery mildew. Plants grown under glass can have problems with mealy bug and whitefly.

Euryops

Compositae

Euryops acraeus

Large, generally yellow or orange, daisy-like flowerheads contrast delightfully with the grey or silvery foliage of these handsome evergreen shrubs. They are bold bushes for formal bedding schemes, or tubs and conservatories where they will flower through much of the summer. They are native to South Africa and only one species, *Euryops acraeus*, is hardy. It makes an unusual small shrub for a sheltered corner of a rock garden. The other species listed require a minimum of 5°C (41°F) and are best grown in a cool greenhouse. Outside, they need a warm sheltered site in free-draining soil. All are vigorous and reach their full size within five years.

RECOMMENDED SPECIES AND VARIETIES

E. acraeus♀ (syn. *E. evansii* hort.) Numerous small, lemon-yellow flowerheads, 2-3 cm (¾-1¼ in) across and borne in a cluster or singly, are produced on this distinguished shrub from late spring to early summer. This species is silvery white, densely branched and hardy to -15°C (5°F). The plant, which sometimes has a suckering habit, has rather leathery and fleshy linear leaves with a 3-toothed tip. HEIGHT & SPREAD 60 x 50 cm (24 x 20 in).

▲ *Euryops acraeus*

E. chrysanthemoides Solitary or clustered yellow flowerheads, each up to 5.5 cm (2¼ in) across, appear on this plant throughout the summer. The deeply lobed, oval grey-green leaves are up to 10 cm (4 in) long and have narrow, tapering to egg-shaped pointed segments. HEIGHT & SPREAD 1.8 x 1.5 m (6 x 5 ft).

E. evansii hort. see *E. acraeus*

E. pectinatus♀ Yellow flowerheads 5-6 cm (2-2½ in) across are carried often singly, sometimes 2 or 3 together. The lobed, deep grey-green rather downy leaves measure up to 10cm (4in) long. HEIGHT & SPREAD 1.8×1.5m (6×5ft).

E. virgineus Leafy clusters of yellow flowerheads, each about 1.5cm (½in) across, appear from spring to early summer on this densely branched species. The closely overlapping leathery leaves are egg-shaped, up to 12.5cm (5in) long and have few lobes. HEIGHT & SPREAD 1.8×1.8m (6×6ft).

CULTIVATION Plant outdoors in a sheltered, sunny site in well-drained soil. Only *E. acraeus* is hardy enough to be grown outside throughout Britain. Alternatively, plant in pots of loam-based compost with additional grit or sharp sand. Move pots to a frost-free place over winter and keep almost dry but do not let the plants wilt. Deadhead to prolong flowering.

PROPAGATION Sow seed in spring or take greenwood or semi-ripe cuttings anytime during summer.

PESTS AND DISEASES Aphids may attack, especially new shoots in spring.

Everlasting see *Antennaria*

Exacum

Gentianaceae

The one species of this genus commonly grown is *Exacum affine*, a tender biennial usually grown as an annual. These compact evergreens with their prolific mauve or white, sweetly scented flowers make ideal container plants for a warm greenhouse or conservatory, or for a light windowsill.

RECOMMENDED SPECIES

E. affine (German, Persian, Arabian or gentian violet) Abundant flowers with distinctive yellow stamens are borne from mid summer to mid autumn, although plants can be raised from seed to flower in spring. The flowers are 1.5cm (½in) wide and have 5 petals. The glossy green, pointed, oval leaves are up to 4cm (1½in) long. HEIGHT & SPREAD 20×30cm (8×12in).

▲ *Exacum affine*

CULTIVATION Plant in containers of compost composed of 2 parts loam to 1 part mixture of peat and sand. Keep in a greenhouse or conservatory or on a windowsill at a minimum temperature of 10°C (50°F) and out of draughts. Choose a position in good light but out of direct summer sun. Mist plants daily during periods of warm weather. Keep the compost moist and feed weekly. Deadhead regularly to prolong the flowering period.

PROPAGATION Sow seed under glass in spring. To grow spring-flowering plants, sow seed under glass in autumn, ensuring a minimum daytime temperature of 15°C (59°F) and keep in a spot in good light throughout winter.

PESTS AND DISEASES Usually trouble free.

Exochorda

Rosaceae

Exochorda giraldii var. wilsonii

Showy white flowers similar to wild roses bloom in clusters on long, arching branches in early summer, making a dazzling show on these elegant deciduous shrubs. The display is brief, however, so the plants are best placed in a mixed border which offers a succession of interest. Planting in partial shade extends the flowering period. Sprays of pale green, soft, oval leaves, up to 7.5cm (3in) long and arranged alternately, intermingle with the flowers. The plants, native to N Asia, are hardy and generally tolerate a wide range of soils.

RECOMMENDED SPECIES AND VARIETIES

E. giraldii* var. *wilsonii The abundant flowers are the largest in the genus, reaching 5cm (2in) across, and are held upright in airy, 15cm (6in) long clusters on pink stalks. This mature shrub is large and handsome. HEIGHT & SPREAD 1×1m (3×3ft) after 5 years, ultimately 3m (10ft) tall.

***E. × macrantha* 'The Bride'**♀ A dense array of flowers, each one up to 3cm (1¼in) across, is carried in drooping clusters up to 10cm (4in) long. This shrub, with typical arching branches, is slow-growing. HEIGHT & SPREAD 1×1m (3×3ft) after 5 years, ultimately 2m (6½ft) tall.

E. racemosa Profuse flowers up to 4cm (1½in) across are held erect in loose clusters up to 10cm (4in) long and set off by bluish green leaves. This slow-growing, large, rounded species does not thrive on chalky soils. HEIGHT & SPREAD 1.2×1m (4×3ft) after 5 years, ultimately 3m (10ft) tall.

▲ *Exochorda × macrantha* 'The Bride'

CULTIVATION Plant in a well-drained position. The shrubs do best in full sun but tolerate light shade. Most soils are suitable except thin, chalky soils.

PROPAGATION Sow seed in autumn or, to ensure a new plant comes true, separate a sucker from the parent plant. Softwood cuttings come true but are difficult to root.

PRUNING Prune only to keep the shrubs shapely by cutting back straggly growth after flowering.

PESTS AND DISEASES Usually trouble free.

▲ *Exochorda racemosa*

Fabiana
Solanaceae

Fabiana imbricata

Tubular white or purplish flowers and a mass of tiny, narrowly triangular, mid green leaves distinguish these small evergreen shrubs. The flowers are borne in profusion during early summer, followed in autumn by small light green pods, which turn light brown and split in two. Native to S America, the plants tolerate little if any frost.

RECOMMENDED SPECIES AND VARIETIES

F. imbricata Abundant dull white flowers, 1.5cm (½in) long, are borne in early and mid summer along the plume-like branches of this erect species. HEIGHT & SPREAD 80×60cm (32×24in) after 5 years, ultimately 2.4×2.4m (8×8ft).

'Prostrata', considered to be the hardiest form, has lilac-tinted white flowers and is compact and bushy, growing to 1m (3ft) high with a spread of 1.8m (6ft).

The flowers of f. ***violacea***♀ are mauve or pinkish violet. It is more compact than the species, spreading to just 1.8m (6ft).

▼ *Fabiana imbricata f. violacea*

CULTIVATION Plant in fertile, well-drained soil in a sunny, sheltered position, such as the foot of a south or west-facing wall.
PROPAGATION Take semi-ripe cuttings.
PRUNING Seldom necessary.
PESTS AND DISEASES Usually trouble free.

Fagus
Beech
Fagaceae

Fagus sylvatica 'Dawyck'

Majestic size, elegant form and attractive foliage are the most valued features of beech trees. Some take on outstanding gold and bronze tints before the autumn leaf-fall. The common beech, a native British tree, needs a lot of space, but it is the parent of many weeping, columnar and coloured varieties suitable for a more moderately sized garden. The common beech can be grown as a hedging plant since clipping does not cause any damage and if it is done in mid summer the leaves stay on the branches, giving them a russet covering through winter.

Beech leaves are smooth and glossy with wavy edges. They are a pointed oval shape, up to about 10cm (4in) long and arranged alternately on the stem. Insignificant green male and female flowers are borne in late spring on the same tree. Female flowers mature in autumn to dark brown triangular nuts enclosed in a hard prickly husk.

RECOMMENDED SPECIES AND VARIETIES

F. sylvatica (common beech)♀ This large hardy tree has a rather upright appearance when young but develops a rounded habit as it matures, often becoming as broad as it is tall. The smooth bark is light brown, turning silvery grey in maturity. The leaves open as delicate green which darkens as the season progresses. At its best this species produces a stunning display of yellows, golds, coppers, greens and browns in autumn but this varies depending on the season or the particular tree. It makes a good hedging plant and is one of the best large trees for chalky soils. HEIGHT & SPREAD 6×3m (20×10ft) after 20 years, ultimately 30m (100ft) or more tall.

'Dawyck'♀ has ascending branches which give it a very narrow, conical, upright habit. The green leaves often turn coppery gold in autumn. It is sometimes named 'Fastigiata'. The leaves of **'Dawyck Gold'**♀ are particularly vivid, opening bright yellow and gradually changing to pale yellow by summer. **'Dawyck Purple'** is similar to 'Dawyck' but the leaves are a rich deep purple throughout the season. All 3 cultivars reach 6×1.8m (20×6ft) after 20 years, ultimately making slightly smaller trees than the species.

A wide range of leaf shapes is seen on var. ***heterophylla*** but one of the best cultivars is **'Aspleniifolia'**. It has narrow, deeply

▲ *Fagus sylvatica var. heterophylla* 'Aspleniifolia'

cut pale green leaves that give variable autumn colour depending on the individual tree and the particular season. It produces a smaller tree than the species, with an eventual height of 20m (66ft), but has the same spreading, rounded habit.

'Pendula' is a weeping form of the common green-leaved beech and makes an outstanding tree when mature, with curtains of hanging branches. It may eventually reach 18m (60ft) tall by 10m (33ft) wide. **'Purple Fountain'** is a narrow tree with drooping branches and purple leaves. After 5 years it grows to 5×2.4m (16×8ft) and eventually reaches 20m (66ft) tall. The

Fagus sylvatica 'Pendula'

small, elegant **'Purpurea Pendula'** is a purple-leaved variety. It has a weeping habit with a rounded crown and is suitable for a small garden since it rarely reaches more than 5m (16ft) tall. **'Rohanii'** is the purple form of the cut-leaved beech, 'Aspleniifolia', although it is slower growing. It can, however, make a rounded tree ultimately reaching 20m (66ft) tall with a spread of 10m (33ft). The leaves develop a green tinge later in the season. **'Zlatia'** looks at its best on a sunny day in mid summer when the pale yellow leaves are at their most dazzling; they darken to pale green by the end of summer. The mature tree is smaller than the species, with a height of 20m (66ft), and is slower growing, but of similar habit.

CULTIVATION Beeches tolerate a wide range of conditions but do not thrive in wet, heavy clay soils. They grow particularly well in the thin chalky soils of southern

Britain. Examine purple-leaved cultivars before buying, looking for leaves free of green tinges. Plant out young trees from mid autumn to early spring.

For hedging, plant in double rows 45×45 cm (18×18 in) apart. Take out the leading shoot when the required height is reached and trim every year to maintain the shape. Trim in late summer if you wish the leaves to stay on through winter.

PROPAGATION Beech trees can be grown from seed but use grafted plants when a particular feature is required.

PRUNING Not normally necessary except for hedging plants.

PESTS AND DISEASES Usually trouble free, though honey fungus can be a problem in times of stress. Beech bark disease may affect older specimens.

Fallopia

Polygonaceae

Known for their rampant and invasive nature these hardy herbaceous perennials and woody climbers, formerly part of the genus *Polygonum*, are best suited to wild or informal gardens. Although they must be positioned carefully so as not to overwhelm neighbouring plants, they are useful for filling spaces or disguising unsightly buildings.

RECOMMENDED SPECIES AND VARIETIES

F. aubertii see *F. baldschuanica*

F. baldschuanica ♀ (syn. *F. aubertii*, *Polygonum aubertii*, *P. baldschuanicum*) (Russian vine, mile-a-minute plant) This rampant, deciduous twining climber has heart-shaped bright green leaves, up to 10 cm (4 in) long. Loose sprays of tiny white flowers with a pinkish tinge appear during late summer. HEIGHT & SPREAD 15×15 m (50×50 ft) after 5 years (also its ultimate size).

▲ *Fallopia baldschuanica*

F. japonica (syn. *Polygonum cuspidatum*, *P. japonica*) (Japanese knotweed) Owing to its very invasive nature, this herbaceous perennial is suitable only for isolated situations, where there is plenty of room. Cane-like stems bear bold shovel-shaped leaves, up to 15 cm (6 in) long, that are dull green with a strong reddish brown tinge. Tiny creamy flowers in upright sprays, up to 20 cm (8 in) long, appear in late summer and early autumn. HEIGHT & SPREAD 2×1 m (6½×3 ft).

Growing to a height and spread of only 75 cm (2½ ft), var. ***compacta*** (syn. *Polygonum reynoutria*) has circular leaves almost 15 cm (6 in) across. The upright sprays of creamy blossoms are up to 7.5 cm (3 in) long. **'Spectabilis'** has leaves which start reddish green, but are later marbled with yellow. It has sprays of creamy flowers 10 cm (4 in) long and reaches a height of 1.5 m (5 ft). **'Variegata'** has green leaves variegated with cream and short sprays of creamy flowers. It reaches a height of 1.5 m (5 ft).

CULTIVATION Plant in spring or autumn in any garden soil in sun or shade.

PROPAGATION Take semi-ripe cuttings in summer from *F. baldschuanica* and divide *F. japonica* in autumn or spring.

PRUNING No pruning is necessary but cut back invasive plants in spring.

PESTS AND DISEASES Usually trouble free.

Fargesia see BAMBOOS p. 76

Fascicularia

Bromeliaceae

Evergreen foliage arranged in a crowded rosette becomes flushed red in summer on these half-hardy perennials. In addition, small, dense clusters of tiny, blue or white stalkless flowers are borne at the centre of the rosette in summer. Fascicularias are generally grown in the house or conservatory. Native to central and S Chile.

RECOMMENDED SPECIES AND VARIETIES

F. bicolor A densely packed rosette of narrow dark green leaves 60 cm (2 ft) long but only 2.5 cm (1 in) wide forms a hummock-shaped plant. The toothed leaves are rough to the touch. Those at the centre of the rosette turn red when the flowers – pale blue surrounded by bright red bracts – appear. It is best to keep this plant indoors, although it will tolerate a very sheltered corner of a garden in mild areas. Keep the plant at a minimum temperature of 2°C (36°F). HEIGHT & SPREAD 60×60 cm (2×2 ft).

F. pitcairniifolia Rich green leaves up to 1 m (3 ft) long and 5 cm (2 in) wide grow in a bold rosette. The leathery toothed leaves have short brown spines and a scaly underside. At the centre of the rosette are blue or violet flowers with white bracts surrounded by bright red leaves. Grow the plant in a temperature of at least 6°C (43°F). HEIGHT & SPREAD 60 cm×1 m (2×3 ft).

▲ *Fascicularia bicolor*

CULTIVATION Grow plants, indoors or out, in a free-draining soil-based compost, such as John Innes No. 2, with sand or perlite making up as much as a third of the whole. Keep houseplants in partial shade and away from draughts, watering freely during spring and summer, and sparingly in winter. Feed occasionally in summer. Plant outdoor specimens in spring and protect from winter frost with fleece and from wet with a pane of glass.

PROPAGATION Separate well-grown offsets in late spring.

PESTS AND DISEASES Mealy bug is sometimes troublesome.

× Fatshedera

Araliaceae

x Fatshedera lizei

This exotic-looking, sprawling shrub is grown for its striking evergreen leaves. It is a hybrid plant, resulting from the union of *Fatsia japonica* 'Moseri' and *Hedera helix* 'Hibernica'. Although hardy, the plant benefits from being grown within the shelter of a wall. It is also a useful plant for cool, unheated, shady rooms in the house.

▲ × *Fatshedera lizei*

× ***F. lizei*** ♀ The deeply lobed, glossy dark green leaves are up to 15 cm (6 in) across held on stout shoots which tend to grow erect and then flop. Small, greenish white, starry flowers, in 20 cm (8 in) long terminal clusters, appear in late summer. HEIGHT &

SPREAD 2×2m (6½×6½ft) after 5 years and ultimately up to twice as large.

There are several varieties with colourful leaves, which are grown in conservatories as well as in the garden. The foliage of **'Annemieke'**♀ is variegated with yellow. Golden-green leaves are seen on **'Aurea'**. **'Variegata'**♀ has green leaves with yellow veins and narrowly edged with white. All the varieties are slightly less vigorous than × *F. lizei* and have an ultimate height and spread of 1.5×1.5m (5×5ft).

CULTIVATION Grow in free-draining soil in a sheltered position, ideally in partial shade. The best time for planting in the garden is spring. Protect leaves from freezing winds. It is possible to train plants as wall shrubs, tying them to wires on a wall or fastening them around pillars. Alternatively, train plants up free-standing canes, pinching out shoot tips to encourage bushiness.

Pot houseplants in John Innes No.2 compost and water freely, except in mid winter. Keep in indirect light to prevent foliage from scorching, but note that too much shade will lead to pale, feeble growth.

PROPAGATION Take semi-ripe stem cuttings in summer or autumn.

PRUNING No pruning required, except the removal of untidy side branches on plants trained up a wall or other support.

PESTS AND DISEASES Usually trouble free.

Fatsia

Araliaceae

Fatsia japonica

Large, glossy palmate leaves give a year-round display and provide an exotic backdrop for the clusters of white flowers that appear in late summer. The single species of this genus makes an excellent conservatory plant, but given the right conditions it can be grown outside in a herbaceous border.

F. ***japonica***♀ Mid to dark green glossy leaves, about 30cm (12in) across, have up to 9 pointed lobes and are carried on long stalks. Sprays of creamy white globular flower clusters appear at the end of the stalks in autumn. This slow-growing, rounded evergreen shrub thrives in coastal gardens. It is hardy, but does better if given shelter in colder regions. Native to Japan. HEIGHT & SPREAD 75×75cm (2½×2½ft) after 5 years, ultimately 4.5m (15ft) tall.

'Variegata'♀ bears leaves which have white tips to the pointed lobes. The plant is less hardy than the species and smaller, reaching an ultimate height of 3m (10ft).

▲ *Fatsia japonica* 'Variegata'

CULTIVATION Grow in well-drained soil in a sheltered position out of the wind in sun or partial shade.

PROPAGATION Sow seed in early to mid spring, or take cuttings in mid to late summer after the wood has become firmer.

PRUNING Not normally required.

PESTS AND DISEASES Usually trouble free.

Felicia

Compositae

Masses of small blue daisies characterise this genus of South African perennials, sub-shrubs and half-hardy annuals. The perennials and sub-shrubs, with the exception of *Felicia petiolata*, are not hardy, so should be grown permanently or overwintered under glass. Felicias look their best in a sunny spot, since their flowers close when in shade.

RECOMMENDED SPECIES AND VARIETIES

F. ***amelloides*** (syn. *F. capensis*, *F. coelestis*) (blue marguerite) This evergreen sub-shrub bears yellow-centred, light blue flowers, 4cm (1½in) across, from summer to early autumn. It flowers freely in its first year. Its bright green leaves are oval and stalkless. HEIGHT & SPREAD 30×30cm (12×12in).

'Read's Blue' and **'Read's White'** have blue and white flowers, respectively, that are 5cm (2in) across. **'Santa Anita'**♀ has blue flowers 5cm (2in) across. **'Santa Anita Variegated'**♀ bears leaves stippled white.

F. ***amoena*** (syn. *F. pappei*) This herbaceous perennial has yellow-eyed blue flowers up to 4cm (1½in) across and elliptical, greyish green hairy leaves. It flowers from late spring in a greenhouse and from mid summer to mid autumn outdoors. HEIGHT & SPREAD 50×40cm (20×16in).

▼ *Felicia amelloides* 'Read's White'

▲ *Felicia amelloides* 'Santa Anita'

F. ***bergeriana*** (kingfisher daisy) This mat-forming annual bears bright blue, yellow-eyed flowers, 3cm (1¼in) across, from mid summer to mid autumn. It has downy, lance-shaped leaves up to 4cm (1½in) long. HEIGHT & SPREAD 15×15cm (6×6in).

F. ***capensis*** see *F. amelloides*

F. ***coelestis*** see *F. amelloides*

F. ***heterophylla*** All-blue flowers on 20cm (8in) stems are borne above low-growing foliage throughout summer by this annual. HEIGHT & SPREAD 25×25cm (10×10in).

F. ***natalensis*** see *F. rosulata*

F. ***pappei*** see *F. amoena*

F. ***petiolata*** This sub-shrub is hardy in sheltered positions in southern Britain. It is low-growing and looks good in hanging baskets and other containers. Its small pink flowers, 2cm (¾in) across, are produced from late spring to mid summer. Its leaves are lance-shaped, about 2.5cm (1in) long. HEIGHT & SPREAD 80cm×1.2m (32in×48in).

F. ***rosulata*** (syn. *F. natalensis*) Blue 4cm (1½in) wide flowers appear in early summer on this hairy-leaved herbaceous perennial. HEIGHT & SPREAD 25×25cm (10×10in).

CULTIVATION Plant in a sunny, sheltered position when the risk of hard frosts has passed. Deadhead in summer to prolong flowering. The sub-shrubs can be cut back by about a third as flowering ends to stimulate a second, late-summer flush.

In autumn move perennials and sub-shrubs to a cool, dry greenhouse or sunny conservatory.

PROPAGATION Sow seed of *F. amelloides* and *F. bergeriana* under glass in early spring. Take semi-ripe cuttings of *F. amelloides* and *F. petiolata* in late summer. Divide the herbaceous perennials in early spring.

PESTS AND DISEASES Powdery mildew may be troublesome.

Fennel see *Foeniculum*
Fennel (culinary) see HERBS p.331
Fennel, giant see *Ferula*
Fennel flower see *Nigella hispanica*
Ferns see pp.262-5
Ferocactus see CACTI p.107

ELEGANT, TEXTURED FOLIAGE AND A TOLERANCE FOR SHADE MAKE FERNS VALUABLE PLANTS FOR THE GARDEN AND THE HOME

Diverse in shape and size, ferns can provide architectural interest, act as foils for flowering plants and form drifts of ground cover. They relieve the gloom of sunless paths, create oases of life in rocky clefts and walls and provide stunning complements to water plants when sited round a pond. Many ferns also make excellent container plants, in hanging baskets and pots.

Terrestrial ferns, which grow in the ground, thrive in soil enriched by leaf-mould in a shady, humid site – the base of a tree is often ideal. Most terrestrial ferns prefer an acid or neutral soil but a few tolerate limy soil. Epiphytic ferns grow on trees, rocks and walls, drawing nutrients from rotting vegetation which collects in crevices.

▼ GREEN HARMONY *Feathery* Matteuccia struthiopteris *looks good with broad-leaved plants such as* Hosta *and* Rodgersia.

Ferns can be evergreen or deciduous and have leaf-like fronds, which usually emerge in spring. The young fronds, which are known as crosiers, are tightly curled.

The fronds may be triangular, such as those of *Adiantum pedatum*; lance-shaped, as in *Matteuccia struthiopteris*; simple and strap-like, as in *Asplenium scolopendrium*; or antler-like as in *Platycerium bifurcatum*.

Once-divided fronds, such as those of *Asplenium trichomanes*, are known as once-pinnate or pinnate. If the segments or pinnae are further divided, the fronds are described as bipinnate or tripinnate.

The fronds of most ferns grow from rhizomes. These are coated in a furry, scaly covering that is black, brown or silver-white. Most fern rhizomes extend both above and below ground, and may extend over a long distance, as in *Matteuccia struthiopteris* which produces crowns of fronds at intervals. Some rhizomes are distinctly upright, as in *Dicksonia antarctica*, and may have the appearance of thick tree trunks.

Ferns do not produce flowers or seeds. Instead, tiny spores are released from capsules on the undersides of their fertile fronds and, in the right conditions, these will germinate.

Some ferns, including *Asplenium bulbiferum*, reproduce not only through spores but also by means of little plantlets or bulbils which are produced on their fronds.

RECOMMENDED PLANTS

Adiantum

Adiantaceae

Delicate, black-stemmed fronds distinguish these plants, which are commonly known as maidenhair ferns. Most are native to tropical and subtropical regions of N and S America.

A. pedatum♀ (five-fingered maidenhair fern) The upright, deciduous, triangular fronds are

▲ *Adiantum pedatum*

lime green and bipinnate. This hardy fern makes a good houseplant or looks attractive grown with other ferns in a border. Grow it in full or partial shade, and apply a mulch to outdoor plants. Plants develop fairly quickly from spores or can be propagated by division. HEIGHT & SPREAD 30×30cm (12×12in).

Asplenium

Aspleniaceae

This genus includes terrestrial and epiphytic ferns, which are commonly known as spleenworts. They grow throughout the world in a range of habitats.

A. bulbiferum♀ Finely dissected, lance-shaped fronds are dark green and bear many small bulbils. This evergreen fern needs a very sheltered position that is out of direct sunlight. In winter, protect the crown with a covering of straw or old fronds. The fern makes an excellent houseplant in indirect light. Propagate from spores or bulbils. HEIGHT & SPREAD 50×30cm (20×12in).

A. scolopendrium♀ (hart's tongue fern) This evergreen is very hardy and has a crown of simple, mid green, strap-like fronds. The crosiers look like small green cobras and are shown to best effect when the old fronds are removed from the centre of the plant in spring.

The plant grows best in a deep, fertile, free-draining soil which is rich in lime. It is drought tolerant and can be grown in crevices among alkaline rocks or in a prepared planting hole in a wall. It is propagated from spores, by division or from cuttings taken of the frond bases. HEIGHT & SPREAD 55×35cm (22×14in).

A. trichomanes (maidenhair spleenwort) The evergreen, pinnate, linear fronds are bright green and have glossy black

▲ *Asplenium trichomanes*

midribs. Often seen growing in sunny dry-stone walls along country lanes, this hardy and drought-tolerant fern thrives in lime-rich conditions but is adaptable to most soils. It is propagated from spores. HEIGHT & SPREAD 25×20cm (10×8in).

Athyrium

Woodsiaceae

Moisture loving and hardy, these deciduous terrestrial ferns are found in temperate and tropical woodlands. They generally spread freely but are intolerant of dry conditions.

A. filix-femina♀ (lady fern) The pale green, lance-shaped fronds are bipinnate or tripinnate. In winter the fronds die down leaving a central scaly crown. The fern is suitable for a variety of situations, from exposed walls to shady riverbanks. It grows best in an acid soil but will also tolerate some lime. Propagate either by spores or by division. HEIGHT & SPREAD 50x30cm (20x12in).

▲ *Athyrium filix-femina*

A. niponicum var. ***pictum***♀ Metallic silver-grey in colour, this Japanese fern has striking, lance-shaped fronds which are bipinnate or tripinnate with purple midribs. The plant grows best on a moist and fertile soil and prefers a sheltered position. Propagate from spores or by division. HEIGHT & SPREAD 30x30cm (12x12in).

Blechnum

Blechnaceae

Leathery, usually once-pinnate or deeply lobed, ladder-like fronds are the distinguishing characteristic of these mainly evergreen, acid-loving ferns from moist, temperate and tropical regions. They grow well in shady borders and woodland areas.

B. spicant♀ (hard fern) The linear to lance-shaped fertile fronds, which are held erect in neat rosettes, are dark green and grow to 30cm (12in) in length. The glossy sterile fronds, which are also dark green, grow up to 20cm (8in) long. They are lax and deeply lobed. This species is easy to grow, particularly on moist, acid soil. It is propagated by spores. HEIGHT & SPREAD 30x30cm (12x12in).

▲ *Blechnum spicant*

Cyrtomium

Dryopteridaceae

These upright and tough ferns from China and Japan make striking architectural plants.

C. fortunei (holly fern) The dark green, pinnate fronds have oval to broadly lance-shaped pinnae. They are evergreen and grow erect from short, scaly, dark brown rhizomes, becoming lax with age. A woodland plant, this fern prefers a moist soil in full or partial shade in a sheltered spot. It is propagated from spores. HEIGHT & SPREAD 60x30cm (2x1ft).

▲ *Cyrtomium fortunei*

Davallia

Davalliaceae

Twining rhizomes are a decorative feature of these mostly epiphytic, tropical ferns, which thrive in warm, damp sites. The triangular fronds are usually finely dissected.

D. mariesii♀ (squirrel's foot fern) Very thick, scaly rhizomes give rise to the common name of this epiphytic fern. The deciduous mid green fronds have fertile and sterile segments, the fertile ones being narrower than the sterile. The plant thrives in acid, moisture-retentive and free-draining compost, in filtered sunlight and high humidity. It is a good choice for a container in a greenhouse or a bathroom. Propagate from spores or by division. HEIGHT & SPREAD 60x60cm (2x2ft) in 5 years.

▲ *Davallia mariesii*

Dicksonia

Dicksoniaceae

The upright rhizomes of these ferns, from the temperate and tropical highland forests of Australasia and S America, have the appearance of tree trunks and become covered with the old frond bases and roots.

D. antarctica♀ (soft tree fern) Impressive, mid green, bipinnate or tripinnate fronds grow up to 2m (6½ft) long. The new fronds, which are broad and lance-shaped, are generally produced in early to mid summer. The trunk-like rhizome is covered in dark brown matted roots and occasionally forks. The fern tolerates some direct sunlight and prefers moist soil. In winter protect the growing point with straw or old fronds, and wrap an insulating material, such as hessian, round the trunk of a young plant. Alternatively, overwinter the fern in a cool greenhouse. Propagate by spores, but plants take a long time to reach maturity. HEIGHT & SPREAD 6x2.5m (20x8ft).

▲ *Dicksonia antarctica*

Dryopteris

Dryopteridaceae

From temperate regions of the Northern Hemisphere, these easy-to-grow woodland ferns are found by streams and lakes.

D. affinis♀ (scaly male fern) In spring, the crowns of golden crosiers unfurl to display dark green, lance-shaped bipinnate fronds with golden scales on the midribs. This native, semi-evergreen fern prefers to grow in shade but tolerates sun. Planted near a pond, it makes a good backdrop to water plants. It is propagated from spores or by division. HEIGHT & SPREAD 1m x40cm (3ft x16in).

▲ *Dryopteris affinis*

D. erythrosora♀ (copper shield fern) This evergreen has a neat crown of glossy triangular fronds, which are bipinnate or tripinnate. Pink to red when young, they turn copper and then dark green as they mature. The compact plant is useful for the front of a border. It prefers moist, humus-rich soil in a partially shaded, sheltered spot; the fronds turn yellowish if they are given too much light. To achieve the best colour, remove untidy fronds before growth starts in spring. Propagate from spores or by division. HEIGHT & SPREAD 40x30cm (16x12in).

D. filix-mas♀ (male fern) Thriving in shade, this native, semi-evergreen fern tolerates full sun. It is similar in appearance and uses to *D. affinis* but there are fewer scales on the midribs. Propagate from spores or by division. HEIGHT & SPREAD 1m x40cm (3ft x16in).

Matteuccia
Woodsiaceae

Graceful and moisture-loving, these ferns are native to the deciduous woodlands of N America, E Asia and Europe. They grow well beside ponds and in damp woodland.
M. struthiopteris ♀ (ostrich fern, shuttlecock fern) This elegant deciduous fern resembles a large shuttlecock and has lance-shaped, pinnate fronds. The rich green, sterile fronds may reach 1.5m (5ft) in length. They surround the light to mid green fertile fronds, which grow only 50cm (20in) long. The fertile fronds turn brown in late summer and persist for over a year, creating a striking sculptural display. The plant thrives in full or partial shade, in a moist, humus-rich soil. It spreads rapidly, sending up new crowns from invasive rhizomes. Propagate from spores or by severing new crowns. HEIGHT & SPREAD 1.5×1m (5×3ft).

▲ *Matteuccia struthiopteris*

Nephrolepis
Nephrolepidaceae

Grown as houseplants, these tropical ferns are fast-growing in warm, humid conditions.
***N. exaltata* 'Bostoniensis'** (Boston fern) Graceful, arching, rich green fronds, which are linear to lance-shaped and pinnate, make this an attractive evergreen for a hanging basket or pot. It requires an open, free-draining compost and filtered light. Maintain a humid atmosphere by misting the fronds with soft water. This fern spreads by long stolons, which root at their tips forming new plantlets. Propagate from spores or by pegging down the plantlets into a pot of moist compost. Sever them when they are well rooted. HEIGHT & SPREAD 60×60cm (2×2ft).

▲ *Nephrolepis exaltata* 'Bostoniensis'

Onoclea
Woodsiaceae

These lush deciduous ferns are found in moist sites in N Asia and N America. Some species may become invasive.
O. sensibilis ♀ (sensitive fern) This attractive moisture-loving fern produces triangular, pink-bronze erect fronds that later become mid green and arching. The pinnate sterile fronds, which grow to 1m (3ft), die back with the first frost. The more persistent bipinnate fertile fronds, which reach up to 60cm (24in), become dark brown. When massed together, they produce a striking winter display. Propagate from spores or by division. HEIGHT & SPREAD 60×60cm (2×2ft).

▲ *Onoclea sensibilis*

Osmunda
Osmundaceae

These large, imposing, deciduous ferns have upright fronds. They grow throughout the world, except for Australasia.
O. regalis ♀ (royal fern) The erect, lance-shaped, bipinnate fronds of this large, stately fern emerge brown, turn green then fade to yellowish hues in autumn. They grow up to 1.5m (5ft) tall. Many develop distinctive, upright, rust-brown fertile pinnae in summer. The plant thrives in a moist soil in sun or shade, and is particularly suited to waterside locations. Mulching with a well-rotted manure in the spring, before new growth starts, is beneficial. The royal fern also makes an excellent container plant, provided that it is regularly watered. Propagate by spores, which should be sown when green and fresh. They require light to germinate. HEIGHT & SPREAD 1.5×1m (5×3ft).

▲ *Osmunda regalis*

Phegopteris
Thelypteridaceae

From damp woodland sites in the Northern Hemisphere and SE Asia, these deciduous, terrestrial ferns have a spreading habit which makes them excellent plants for ground cover.
P. connectilis (syn. *Thelypteris phegopteris*) (beech fern) This graceful fern has triangular, pinnate, lime green fronds, which are up to 30cm (12in) long. The newly emerging crosiers are a bright yellowish green. This plant is very hardy and will tolerate a site with some direct sunlight. It is propagated either from spores or by division. HEIGHT & SPREAD 30×30cm (12×12in) after 5 years.

▲ *Phegopteris connectilis*

Platycerium
Polypodiaceae

Commonly known as staghorn ferns, these epiphytic evergreen plants are notable for the nests of brown fronds at their bases. They are native to the temperate and tropical rain forests of Africa, Asia and Australia.
P. bifurcatum ♀ (elkhorn fern) The kidney-shaped basal fronds reach up to 60cm (2ft) and turn brown on maturity. They form a shield round the base of antler-like fronds which grow up to 80cm (32in) long and remain mid green. Keep the plant in a humid place indoors that has filtered sunlight, such as a bathroom. Mist it daily and feed every month during active growth. When the green fronds

▲ *Platycerium bifurcatum*

show signs of wilting, immerse the whole plant in water for an hour and then suspend it to allow excess water to drain. It is propagated by division or from spores, but plants obtained by this method can be difficult to establish. HEIGHT & SPREAD 60×60cm (2×2ft).

Polypodium

Polypodiaceae

Drought tolerant and adaptable, these spreading ferns come mainly from the tropical regions of the Americas.

P. interjectum (intermediate polypody) Tolerant of full sun, this hardy evergreen fern makes

▲ *Polypodium interjectum*

excellent ground cover. It has dark green, lance-shaped and deeply lobed fronds and spreads by green rhizomes which eventually form mats. It prefers an alkaline soil, though it tolerates other types. Propagate from spores or by division. HEIGHT & SPREAD 40×60cm (16×24in) after 5 years.

P. vulgare (common polypody) This hardy fern thrives in acid soils and grows well on rocks and trees. It is similar in appearance to *P. interjectum* but has narrower fronds. HEIGHT & SPREAD 40×60cm (16×24in) after 5 years.

Polystichum

Dryopteridaceae

These ferns produce handsome fronds with golden scales. They prefer acid soils and grow in a wide range of habitats.

P. aculeatum♀ (hard shield fern) This evergreen fern has elegant crowns of lance-shaped, pinnate or bipinnate fronds, which are glossy, dark green and leathery. The plant requires a moist, open soil in a fully or partially

▲ *Polystichum aculeatum*

shaded area. The rhizome is short and thick, and covered in large brown scales. The plant is propagated either by division or from spores. HEIGHT & SPREAD 50×30cm (20×12in).

P. setiferum♀ (soft shield fern) Intricately dissected, bipinnate dark green fronds and densely scaled crosiers are produced by this graceful evergreen. It tolerates direct sunlight, provided that the soil does not dry out. New crowns are sometimes sent up by the rhizome, which is covered in papery orange-brown scales. Propagate from spores or by division. HEIGHT & SPREAD 1.2×1m (4×3ft).

Thelypteris see *Phegopteris*

Woodwardia

Blechnaceae

These ferns of warm temperate regions favour damp sites and have bold, arching fronds.

W. unigemmata Stout, scaly rhizomes bear leathery, triangular, bipinnate evergreen fronds,

▲ *Woodwardia unigemmata*

up to 1.2m (4ft) long. New fronds are scarlet as they unfurl and expand, gradually turning green as they arch. Layers of fronds form thick mats. Grow the fern in a moist soil in full or partial shade, and apply a heavy top dressing of well-rotted manure in spring. Propagate by spores or by the bulbils which are produced on the tips of some fronds. HEIGHT & SPREAD 1×2m (3×6½ft).

Growing ferns

CULTIVATION Most ferns thrive in moist, humus-rich, free-draining soil in full or partial shade, although some, like *Dicksonia antarctica*, will tolerate full sun for part of the day. Others, including *Polypodium* species, are drought tolerant and are suitable for cultivation in walls and rocks. They require gritty, free-draining compost. Some ferns, such as *Asplenium scolopendrium*, thrive in or are tolerant of a limy soil.

Plant ferns in spring and water them well in the first growing season, soaking the soil to a depth of about 10cm (4in). Dig plenty of leaf-mould or well-rotted manure into the soil to add humus and apply a mulch of the same material round terrestrial ferns in spring.

PROPAGATION All ferns can be propagated from spores, but in most cases there are alternative methods that are simpler and produce quicker results. Most ferns can be divided and this is best done in spring.

Some ferns, such as *Asplenium bulbiferum*, produce bulbils or plantlets. Use bent wire to peg the parent frond to the ground and sever new plants once they are well rooted.

Take a cutting of the base of the frond stalk from *Asplenium scolopendrium*. Lay the frond base on a mixture of three parts sand to one part peat. Sever and pot on the small plantlets that develop, in the same mixture.

Propagating from spores is a time-consuming process but yields high numbers of plants. Remove a portion of spore-bearing frond when the capsules are brown. Place it in a paper envelope and leave to dry in a well-ventilated place. The spores are ready for sowing when they start to be released as a yellow-brown dust. They are usually viable for several years.

In spring, sterilise a container and an equal parts mixture of coir and sand with boiling water. Level the surface of the potting compost with the sterilised base of another pot. Cover the mixture with cling film until cool. Use the point of a knife to collect a small amount of spores. Then, sow them very thinly and re-cover the pot to retain moisture and humidity. Place newspaper over the cling film until germination occurs, to cut down the light and prevent algal and moss growth.

In the case of *Osmunda regalis*, the spores should be scraped off the frond with a sharp knife or razor blade while they are still green. Sow in the same mixture as described above but do not cover the pot with newspaper – the spores need light to germinate.

It can take several weeks before germination occurs and several months before small heart-shaped growths, known as prothalli, appear. Keep the soil moist by standing the container in water regularly. Once the prothalli develop into small plants, carefully prick them out into pans filled with the compost mixture. When they are large enough to handle, harden them off and pot singly.

PESTS AND DISEASES Ferns are usually pest and disease free, but mealy bugs can be a problem with indoor plants.

▲ SHADE LOVER *Ferns, such as this* Dryopteris filix-mas, *make lively features for sunless corners.*

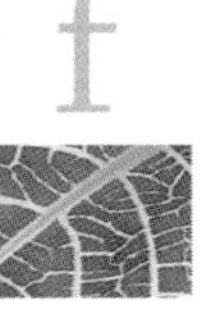

Ferula

Giant fennel
Umbelliferae

A massive mound of feathery leaves is adorned in early summer with globe-shaped clusters of bright yellow blooms carried on tall flower stems. Grow this towering, hardy herbaceous perennial at the back of a border, or by itself, perhaps beside water. The vegetable and culinary herb called fennel are found in the genus *Foeniculum*.

RECOMMENDED SPECIES AND VARIETIES

F. communis A mass of shiny, bright green foliage arises from the base of the main stem. Each finely dissected leaf is up to 45cm (1½ft) long. The small yellow-green flowers are borne in clusters 7.5-15cm (3-6in) across. The stem is supported by one or more long taproots. In late summer seed heads appear, made up of a mass of small, brown seeds. There are also bronze and purple-leaved forms. An herbaceous perennial, native to the Mediterranean. HEIGHT & SPREAD 3×1m (10×3ft).

▲ *Ferula communis*

CULTIVATION Plant in any fertile well-drained soil, choosing a position in full sun. Cut back the foliage and seed heads in autumn. The taproots make it difficult to move plants from one position to another in the garden.

PROPAGATION Sow seed in a coldframe, grow on in pots and then plant out in spring in the final position.

PESTS AND DISEASES Usually trouble free.

Festuca see GRASSES p.301
Feverfew see *Tanacetum parthenium* 'Aureum'

Ficus

Moraceae

Ficus benjamina

Most of the cultivated plants in this genus are tender in Britain and are commonly grown as pot plants. However, the common fig tree, *Ficus carica,* is hardy and, given the right conditions, can produce abundant fruit. The indoor species are grown for their foliage, although some also produce fruit. They are either upright and tree-like or trailing in habit. All bear insignificant flowers.

RECOMMENDED SPECIES AND VARIETIES

F. benjamina♀ (weeping fig) Dark green glossy leaves cover the weeping branches of this evergreen houseplant. The oval leaves are about 8cm (3¼in) long. Tiny orange-red fruits that turn black may appear in summer. It requires a minimum of 10°C (50°F). HEIGHT & SPREAD 3×2m (10×6½ft).

'Exotica' has green leaves with extended, twisted tips. **'Starlight'** has golden variegated leaves.

F. carica♀ (common fig) In a good summer green pear-shaped fruits with a strong purple or brown flush and pink flesh grow up to 5cm (2in) long on this hardy tree. For a more regular supply of fruit grow this species in a cool greenhouse. A spreading tree, it is usually trained against a wall. It has large green, rather rough leaves, deeply indented and up to 15cm (6in) across. The branches and trunk are greyish in colour. HEIGHT & SPREAD 4.5×4.5m (15×15ft) after 10 years, ultimately 10m (33ft) tall.

'Brown Turkey'♀ produces greenish brown pear-shaped fruit with red flesh.

F. deltoidea var. ***diversifolia*** (mistletoe fig) This slow-growing shrub, requiring a minimum of 18°C (64°F), is grown as a houseplant either indoors or under glass. The bright green, rounded leaves, 5cm (2in) long, are often flushed reddish brown beneath. Small, pea-like, dull yellow fruits appear in summer and turn orange or red. HEIGHT & SPREAD 2.4×2.4m (8×8ft).

***F. elastica* 'Robusta'** (rubber plant) This popular pot plant has glossy green, leathery oval leaves up to 20cm (8in) long. Prominent spear-like orange or red shoots are found at the tips of its stems. The minimum temperature required is 10°C (50°F). HEIGHT & SPREAD 1.5m×60cm (5×2ft).

'Doescheri' has leaves variegated green, grey-green and creamy yellow or white. The leaf stems and midribs are pink.

F. pumila♀ (creeping fig) This climber does well as a trailing houseplant or as a creeper on walls in greenhouses and conservatories. It requires a minimum of 5°C (41°F). The bright green leaves are heart-shaped at first, becoming more oval and up to 8cm (3¼in) long. Green fruits, up to 6cm (2½in) long, are flushed purple as they ripen in late summer. HEIGHT & SPREAD 3×1m (10×3ft).

▲ *Ficus carica* 'Brown Turkey'

'Minima' is tiny and slow growing. It can be grown in bottle gardens. **'Sonny'** has tiny wavy leaves with irregular cream edges.

▼ *Ficus pumila* 'Sonny'

'Variegata' is a moderate growing variety with cream, white and green variegation.

CULTIVATION Plant *F. carica* in spring in any free-draining garden soil in full sun. Train against a wall by tying branches to supports. Water copiously while the trees are in fruit. Alternatively, grow under glass in pots of John Innes No.3 compost. Plants can be moved outside in summer.

Grow indoor plants in free-draining organic-rich compost. Position in full light and ensure the minimum temperature as indicated in the plant descriptions above. Water well in summer. Clean leaves regularly with a little warm milk on a piece of cotton wool. Use a liquid houseplant feed regularly during spring and summer.

PROPAGATION Remove large suckers from *F. carica* in spring and pot them up. Take stem or leaf-bud cuttings, or air-layer indoor plants in spring and summer.

PRUNING Cut back *F. carica* hard during the dormant season. Trim houseplants as required during the growing season, pinching back unwanted growths.

PESTS AND DISEASES Mealy bug, scale insects and red spider mite are major pests of indoor plants.

Fig see *Ficus*
Figwort, water see *Scrophularia auriculata*
Filbert see *Corylus maxima*

Filipendula

Rosaceae

Filipendula purpurea

Foaming heads of white, cream, pink or red flowers appear in summer. Most of these hardy herbaceous perennials have divided mid green or golden leaves and the majority have flowers with a musky fragrance. Filipendulas generally thrive in moist soil and are ideal for growing in damper and wilder parts of the garden.

RECOMMENDED SPECIES AND VARIETIES

F. camtschatica Flat, frothy flowerheads, up to 25cm (10in) across, of tiny pink or white fragrant flowers, appear in late summer. The palmate leaves are up to 25cm (10in) long. HEIGHT & SPREAD 3×1m (10×3ft).

The flowers of var. ***rosea*** are rose-pink.

***F. digitata* 'Nana'** see *F. palmata* 'Nana'

F. hexapetala see *F. vulgaris*

***F.* 'Kahome'** Deep rose-pink flowerheads, up to 15cm (6in) across, appear in mid summer. The dark green, deeply cut leaves are coarse-textured and up to 20cm (8in) long. HEIGHT & SPREAD 60×45cm (2×1½ft).

▲ *Filipendula* 'Kahome'

F. palmata Massed sprays, up to 10cm (4in) across, of small white flowers are produced at the tops of shoots during summer. The deeply divided leaves, up to 15cm (6in) long, are green with a pink tinge beneath. HEIGHT & SPREAD 1m×60cm (3×2ft).

The cultivar **'Alba'** has white flowers; **'Elegantissima'** (syn. *Spiraea palmata* ssp. *elegans*) has dark rose-pink blooms, followed by bronze seed heads; **'Nana'** (syn. 'Digitata Nana', *F. digitata* 'Nana') is a dwarf variety with deep rose-pink flowers, which grows to only about half the height and spread of the species; ssp. *purpurea* see *F. purpurea*; **'Rosea'** produces pink flowers.

F. purpurea ♀ (syn. *F. palmata* ssp. *purpurea*) Spreading frothy heads, up to 20cm (8in) across, of tiny purple-red flowers appear in mid to late summer. The deeply divided, bright green leaves are up to 25cm (10in) long. HEIGHT & SPREAD 1.2m×60cm (4×2ft).

The flowers of f. ***albiflora*** are white.

F. rubra (queen of the prairie) Massed heads of tiny pink flowers, up to 25cm (10in) across, crowd the plant in summer. The 3-lobed leaves are up to 20cm (8in) long. HEIGHT & SPREAD 2m×60cm (6½×2ft).

'Venusta' ♀ (syn. 'Venusta Magnifica', *Spiraea venusta* 'Magnifica') is an outstanding variety with consistently deep rose-pink flowers.

F. ulmaria (syn. *Spiraea ulmaria*) (meadowsweet) Frothy heads, up to 25cm (10in) across, of innumerable tiny creamy white,

▲ *Filipendula ulmaria* 'Aurea'

sweetly scented flowers appear in mid summer. The leaves have 7-15 leaflets carried on contrasting reddish stalks, and may grow to 30cm (12in) long. HEIGHT & SPREAD 1.5m×60cm (5×2ft).

The leaves of **'Aurea'** are golden. The blooms of **'Flore Pleno'** are creamy white and fully double. It is slightly less tall.

▲ *Filipendula ulmaria* 'Variegata'

'Rosea' has soft pink flowers. The green leaflets of **'Variegata'** have a central yellow stripe or patch. The creamy flowers are not especially attractive and can be removed to maintain the quality of the foliage. A plant so treated reaches about 1m (3ft).

F. vulgaris (syn. *F. hexapetala*) (dropwort) Dense heads, up to 10cm (4in) across, of tiny white flowers, often tinged pink in bud, appear in early to mid summer. The finely divided, dark green, ferny leaves are up to 25cm (10in) long. HEIGHT & SPREAD 75×45cm (2½×1½ft).

'Multiplex' (syn. 'Plena') has fully double flowers. This is the most showy cultivar available.

CULTIVATION Plant from autumn to spring in sun or semi-shade in moist soil, including the boggy margins of ponds, with the exception of *F. vulgaris* which needs well-drained limy soil in full sun. Remove faded flowerheads. Fertilise sparingly in early spring with a slow-release, high-potash feed. Cut back withered foliage in autumn.

PROPAGATION Divide established plants from mid autumn to early spring or sow seed under glass in spring.

PESTS AND DISEASES Usually trouble free.

Fir, Douglas see *Pseudotsuga menziesii*
Fir, silver see *Abies*
Firebush, Chilean see *Embothrium coccineum*
Firecracker plant see *Crossandra infundibuliformis*
Firecracker vine see *Manettia luteorubra*
Firethorn see *Pyracantha*

Fittonia

Acanthaceae

These evergreen perennials from S America have distinctively marked leaves with slightly textured surfaces. Because they need high humidity, fittonias are perfect for bottle gardens, terrariums and plant cases. They will grow in a warm shaded conservatory and may flourish indoors if grown among other tropical houseplants that together can create the humid microclimate that they require. Old plants often become bare in the middle, but fittonias have trailing, rooting stems and new plants are easily raised. The insignificant flowers, occasionally produced, are yellow and emerge from a spike of tight little green bracts.

RECOMMENDED SPECIES AND VARIETIES

***F. verschaffeltii* 'Argyroneura'** (net plant, snakeskin plant, lace leaf) Dark green oval leaves, up to 5cm (2in) long, are marked with a network of white veins and have a

▼ *Fittonia verschaffeltii* 'Argyroneura'

slightly quilted surface. HEIGHT 15cm (6in).
F. verschaffeltii **'Argyroneura Nana'** The white-veined leaves, up to 3.5cm (1¾in) long, have a quilted texture. Tolerant of average humidity, this plant is more suitable for indoor cultivation. HEIGHT 10cm (4in).
CULTIVATION Plant in pots of houseplant compost, providing a minimum of 13°C (55°F) and high humidity. Place in good light but out of direct sun. Water regularly, keeping compost slightly damp. Give a half normal strength feed weekly in the growing season. Repot plants when they spread beyond their pots.
PROPAGATION Layer in spring or take softwood cuttings in early summer.
PESTS AND DISEASES Usually trouble free.

Five spot see *Nemophila maculata*
Flaming Katy see *Kalanchoë blossfeldiana*
Flaming sword see *Vriesa splendens*
Flax see *Linum*
Flax, mountain see *Phormium cookianum*
Flax lily see *Phormium*
Fleabane see *Erigeron*
Foam flower see *Tiarella*

Fitzroya

Patagonian cypress
Cupressaceae

Fitzroya cupressoides

This hardy, slow-growing, S American tree, the sole species of its genus, makes a broadly conical tree, rounded at the top and with branch tips that droop with age. Trees in the wild can live for over 2000 years and grow to 50m (165ft). Native to Chile and Argentina.
Fitzroya cupressoides Glossy, dark green, bluntly tipped needles, 6mm (¼in) long, grow in whorls of 3 from the same point. Distinctively each needle has twin white bands on the top and bottom. Female and male flowers can be borne on the same or on separate trees. Female flowers appear in mid spring and are tiny, yellowish green and insignificant; male flowers, borne at the same time, are yellow and practically invisible to the naked eye. Occasional small, brown, 9-scaled cones, 1cm (⅜in) across, matured from female flowers, are carried on the tips of some shoots. The bark is browny red and peels in long vertical strips. Female trees are more common in Britain. These trees take about 100 years to reach their ultimate height. HEIGHT & SPREAD 2.4×1m (8×3ft) after 20 years, ultimately 10m (33ft) tall.
CULTIVATION Plant in moist but well-drained, slightly acid soil in full sun. Provide some shelter from cold winds.
PROPAGATION Take semi-ripe cuttings in late summer. Seed produced in Britain is not generally fertile.
PRUNING Do not clip trees to keep them small as this will destroy their shape. The tree has a tendency to fork when young and grow multistemmed. Select the best stem and remove the others while young.
PESTS AND DISEASES Usually trouble free.

Foeniculum

Fennel
Umbelliferae

The feathery, bright green foliage of common fennel makes a decorative contrast to other plants in a herbaceous or mixed border. This hardy herbaceous perennial is also grown as a culinary herb (see p.331). There is also a variety grown as a garden vegetable, Florence fennel.
RECOMMENDED SPECIES AND VARIETIES
F. vulgare (common fennel) The fine feathery leaves are about 30cm (1ft) long. Flattened clusters of flowerheads, 10cm (4in) wide, have masses of tiny, bright

▲ *Foeniculum vulgare*

yellow flowers in mid summer. The stems, leaves and tiny seeds have a strong, slightly sweet, aniseed flavour. This plant seeds itself easily and can become invasive in light soils. HEIGHT & SPREAD 2m×60cm (6½×2ft).
'Purpureum' (syn. 'Bronze') a bronze or purple-leaved plant. This cultivar is best propagated by division.
CULTIVATION Plant in late spring in full sun, ideally in light, sandy soil although fennel will grow on other well-drained soils. Staking is not normally necessary. Cut off flowerheads as soon as they fade if you wish to restrict self-seeding.
PROPAGATION On light soil, sow seed in its growing position in late spring. Otherwise, sow seed in early spring under glass and plant out as soon as the seedlings are large enough to handle. Alternatively, divide and replant in spring.
PESTS AND DISEASES Usually trouble free.

Forget-me-not see *Myosotis*
Forget-me-not, Chinese see *Cynoglossum amabile*

Forsythia

Oleaceae

Forsythia x intermedia

A forsythia ablaze with golden flowers is one of the glories of the garden in spring. Hardy and easily grown, forsythias include large and small shrubs, plants for creating an informal hedge and for training up a wall. The flowers, in shades of yellow, generally appear before the leaves emerge. Individual flowers are tubular at the base with four expanding oblong lobes. They appear on the previous year's wood either singly or in clusters of up to five.
RECOMMENDED SPECIES AND VARIETIES
F. **'Arnold Dwarf'** This low, self-layering shrub has dense interlacing branches bearing bright green oval leaves 2.5-5cm (1-2in) long. Alone among forsythias, its flowers are comparatively insignificant – they are pale yellow and rarely produced. The plant makes useful ground cover. HEIGHT & SPREAD 30×75cm (1×2½ft) after 5 years, ultimately 1m (3ft) tall.
F. **'Beatrix Farrand'** Large, deep canary-yellow flowers with orange markings in the throat, 4cm (1½in) across, are borne in early and mid spring by this shrub of upright, dense habit. HEIGHT & SPREAD 1.8×1.8m (6×6ft) after 5 years, ultimately 2.4m (8ft) tall.
F. **'Fiesta'** Rich green leaves with bright cream and gold variegation are borne on a compact and bushy plant. Its golden yellow flowers, 2.5cm (1in) across, appear from early to mid spring. HEIGHT & SPREAD 1.5×1.5m (5×5ft) after 5 years, ultimately 1.8m (6ft) tall.
F. giraldiana A large shrub of graceful habit, this is the first forsythia to flower, bearing pale yellow flowers, 2cm (¾in) across, in late winter. The blooms are followed by the leaves – elliptical to lance-shaped or oblong and up to 12cm (4¾in) in length. HEIGHT &

SPREAD 2.4×2.4m (8×8ft) after 5 years, ultimately 4m (13ft) tall.
F. **'Golden Nugget'** Large golden yellow flowers, up to 5cm (2in) across, are borne in mid spring. The narrow, oval, toothed leaves are 10cm (4in) long. A vigorous, compact and densely branched shrub. HEIGHT & SPREAD 1.8×1.8m (6×6ft) after 5 years, also its ultimate size.
F.* × *intermedia Upright, arching stems carry golden yellow flowers, up to 3cm (1¼in) across, from early to mid spring. Its dark green leaves are oval to lance-shaped, sometimes 3-lobed. A vigorous hybrid. HEIGHT & SPREAD 1.8×1.5m (6×5ft) after 5 years, ultimately 2.7m (9ft) tall.

'Lynwood'♡ has broad-petalled, rich yellow flowers up to 4cm (1½in) across.

▼ *Forsythia* x *intermedia* 'Lynwood'

This free-flowering variety is often used to make informal hedges. It may reach a height of 3m (10ft). **'Minigold'** carries a mass of small, deep yellow flowers with broad lobes in early and mid spring. They are followed by oblong, mid green leaves. Its full-grown height is 1.8m (6ft). **'Spectabilis'** carries a profusion of deep yellow flowers, up to 3cm (1¼in) across, in early and mid spring, succeeded by dark green, sharply toothed leaves. Fully grown it will reach 2.4m (8ft). **'Spring Glory'** bears masses of bright sulphur-yellow

▼ *Forsythia* x *intermedia* 'Spring Glory'

flowers, followed by oblong, bright green leaves. It will make a plant 1.8m (6ft) high. **'Variegata'** has toothed leaves with yellow edges and bears medium yellow flowers in mid spring. It may reach 2.4m (8ft) high.

F. ovata This species of domed habit bears primrose-yellow flowers, 2cm (¾in) across, in early and mid spring. The dark green, broadly oval leaves, up to 7.5cm (3in) long, may turn yellow in autumn. HEIGHT & SPREAD 1m×75cm (3×2½ft) after 5 years, ultimately 1.5m (5ft) tall.

'Tetragold' is smaller growing than the species. Its flowers are larger and more richly coloured, and appear earlier.
F. suspensa♡ This arching to pendent-stemmed shrub has interlacing branches studded with bright yellow, pendulous flowers, 2.5cm (1in) across, in early and mid spring. Its mid green leaves are broadly oval and sometimes 3-lobed. HEIGHT & SPREAD 1.8×1.8m (6×6ft) after 5 years, ultimately 3m (10ft) tall.

The upright stems of f. ***atrocaulis*** are black-purple when young. The pale yellow flowers, about 3cm (1¼in) across, appear in late spring. **'Nymans'** has erect, bronze-purple branches carrying primrose-yellow, nodding flowers, up to 5cm (2in) across, in late spring.
F. **'Tremonia'** has incised, bottle-green, serrated leaves up to 7.5cm (3in) long. Medium yellow flowers are sparsely produced in mid spring. HEIGHT & SPREAD 1m×75cm (3×2½ft) after 5 years, ultimately 1.5m (5ft) tall.
F. viridissima Erect, square-stemmed, green branches carry, bright yellow flowers in late spring. The dark green, lance-shaped leaves flush maroon in autumn. HEIGHT & SPREAD 1.8×1.5m (6×5ft) after 5 years, ultimately 2.4m (8ft) tall.

'Bronxensis' is a dense, compact variety whose twiggy branchlets bear primrose-yellow flowers, 1.5cm (½in) across, in mid spring, followed by oval leaves 4cm (1½in) long. It reaches a final height of 60cm (2ft).
CULTIVATION Plant in any garden soil in full sun or partial shade. *F. suspensa* can be grown against walls, even north facing, but must be tied into supports. To create informal hedges of *F.* × *intermedia* 'Lynwood', plant 60cm (2ft) apart; prune by a third on planting; when shoots are 15cm (6in) long, pinch back to encourage bushiness.
PROPAGATION Take semi-ripe cuttings in summer or hardwood cuttings in autumn. *F. suspensa* can be layered.
PRUNING After flowering, prune flowered shoots to within 1 or 2 buds of the old wood, and tip vigorous young shoots to encourage branching; every few years cut out old flowering wood to the base in well-established bushes. Neglected specimens can be cut down almost to ground level but a flowering season will be missed. *F. suspensa* grown against walls should have lateral growths cut back immediately after flowering to within 1 or 2 buds of the old wood. Established hedges should be lightly cut back after flowering.
PESTS AND DISEASES Birds may destroy flower buds.

Fothergilla

Hamamelidaceae

Fothergilla major

Outstanding autumn foliage and unusual late-spring flowers make these small deciduous shrubs stand out. The flowers have no petals but consist of close-set, long, creamy white stamens. The broad oval leaves are dark green above, paler and hairy below and toothed towards the tip. Although hardy, these natives of south-eastern USA need a sunny position to give the best autumn colour. They require lime-free soil.

RECOMMENDED SPECIES AND VARIETIES
F. gardenii Lightly scented flower clusters up to 4cm (1½in) long are carried on this multistemmed, erect shrub that broadens with age. The leaves, 6cm (2½in) long, turn brilliant red and crimson in autumn. HEIGHT & SPREAD 50×50cm (20×20in) after 5 years, ultimately 1m (3ft) tall.

▲ *Fothergilla gardenii*

'Blue Mist' has blue-green summer foliage before its autumn colour.
F. major♡ The sweetly fragrant flowerheads are up to 5cm (2in) long. The 10cm (4in) long leaves turn scarlet, orange and yellow in autumn. A rounded, multistemmed shrub. HEIGHT & SPREAD 1×1m (3×3ft) after 5 years, ultimately 3m (10ft) tall.

The **Monticola Group** are more spreading and the leaves, which are not paler underneath, are especially bright in autumn.
CULTIVATION Plant in lime-free soil in full sun, although plants thrive in partial shade.
PROPAGATION Take semi-ripe cuttings or layer in early autumn.
PRUNING None is required.
PESTS AND DISEASES Usually trouble free.

Foxglove see *Digitalis*
Foxglove, fairy see *Erinus alpinus*
Frageria see *Duchesnea*

Francoa

Bridal wreath, maiden's wreath

Saxifragaceae

Attractive low-growing evergreen perennials from Chile, francoas have long, pretty flower stems that give an airy effect when they bloom in summer. The flowers make a long-lasting border display and they may bloom again in autumn. Francoas can also be grown as pot plants. They are moderately hardy, preferring warm, well-drained soil where they will happily self-seed without becoming a nuisance.

RECOMMENDED SPECIES AND VARIETIES

F. ramosa White flowers, often spotted with pink, carried in upright branched sprays, appear in early and mid summer. Each flower has 5 petals and is about 1.5 cm (½ in) across. Softly hairy leaves, 15 cm (6 in) long, form small clumps. HEIGHT & SPREAD 75×38 cm (30×15 in).

F. sonchifolia Open, bell-shaped flowers appear from early to mid summer. They are white or, more commonly, pink with darker spots at the base. Each flower has 5 petals and is about 1.5 cm (½ in) across. Dark green, softly hairy and deeply lobed leaves, up to 20 cm (8 in) long, form rosettes. This is the hardiest francoa. HEIGHT & SPREAD 75×45 cm (30×18 in).

CULTIVATION Plant in spring in sun or light shade in well-drained, moisture-retentive soil. In cold areas, lift and overwinter in a frost-free greenhouse. Alternativly, grow in pots outdoors or in a cold greenhouse and overwinter in frost-free conditions.

PROPAGATION Sow seed in spring, take softwood cuttings in late spring or divide between early spring and early summer.

PESTS AND DISEASES Vine weevil may attack pot plants.

▼ *Francoa sonchifolia*

Fraxinus

Ash

Oleaceae

Fraxinus angustifolia 'Raywood'

The common ash has been grown in Europe throughout history for its strong, flexible wood. Given plenty of room, it makes a magnificent specimen tree or a tough component of a shelterbelt. Most species rapidly become large trees, requiring full light and plenty of space and are not suitable for small gardens.

The genus contains about 60 species of mainly hardy deciduous trees from all round the temperate world. They tolerate exposed sites and urban pollution, but are hungry for moisture and nutrients and nothing will grow under them. The opposite leaves are usually pinnate, 20-30 cm (8-12 in) long and composed of about 5-13 leaflets that are 7-11 cm (2¾-4¼ in) long. Seeds have a single wing and hang in bunches, known as ash keys, often until the end of winter. Trees are known to live for 300 years, but most ash reach their mature height and crown spread in just 80 years.

RECOMMENDED SPECIES AND VARIETIES

***F. angustifolia* 'Raywood'**♀ (syn. 'Flame') This elegant, rounded tree is the best narrow-leaved ash. It came originally from the western Mediterranean and N Africa, but it is hardy in lowland Britain. The narrow, pointed leaves are glossy dark green and turn a reddish purple in autumn. The large winter buds are velvety and brown. HEIGHT & SPREAD 8×5 m (26×16 ft) after 20 years, ultimately 21 m (69 ft) tall.

F. excelsior♀ (common ash) This fast-growing British native has wide-spreading surface roots and should not be planted close to walls, paths or buildings, or allowed to hang over flowerbeds. Tiny flowers with crimson anthers appear in mid spring and the dark green leaves turn briefly yellow in autumn. The winter buds are black. HEIGHT & SPREAD 9×6 m (30×20 ft) after 20 years, and ultimately 38 m (125 ft) tall.

'Jaspidea'♀ has golden yellow winter twigs and yellow leaves in spring and autumn. **'Pendula'**♀ (weeping ash) has strongly weeping branches. **'Westhof's Glorie'**♀ starts off vigorously but soon slows down and is eventually rather smaller than the species with a rounded habit.

F. ornus (manna ash)♀ The round-headed tree is grown primarily for its dense panicles of fluffy, scented, creamy white flowers that are produced in early summer. It originates from S Europe and W Asia but is hardy throughout lowland Britain. HEIGHT & SPREAD 8×6 m (26×20 ft) after 20 years, ultimately 18 m (60 ft) tall.

▼ *Fraxinus excelsior* 'Pendula'

▲ *Fraxinus ornus*

CULTIVATION Plant in late spring in a sunny position in moist, rich clay loams which are neutral to alkaline. Avoid root disturbance.

PROPAGATION Species can be raised from seed, but it may take 18 months to germinate. The cultivars should be grafted in late winter. Ash trees are very easy to graft but they may produce unsightly lumps at the point of grafting.

PRUNING Not generally necessary.

PESTS AND DISEASES Ash bud moth can delay leaf production until mid summer. Ash canker and honey fungus cause disfiguration and may eventually kill trees.

Freesia

Iridaceae

Delicate funnel-shaped flowers in shades of pink, red, yellow, violet and white stand on erect, wiry stems in spring and summer, surrounded by a fan of light green, sword-shaped leaves. Apart from their colourful blooms, most freesias are admired for their sweet fragrance – the perfume of just a few cut flowers can quickly fill a room.

Freesias grow from corms, each corm producing one, sometimes more, branched flowering stems. The funnel-shaped, 4 cm (1½ in) long flowers are irregularly spaced along one side of the inflorescence which is held horizontally to the main stem.

Freesias are native to South Africa and are generally too tender to survive a British winter. In autumn the corms must be lifted and stored until the following spring. They can be left in the ground in only the mildest, southernmost parts of Britain. For a supply of cut flowers and more reliable or early flowering, grow freesias in containers in a cool greenhouse or conservatory.

RECOMMENDED VARIETIES
Garden centres supply a range of colourful varieties, usually in mixed batches. They reach a height of about 30cm (1ft). Species are seldom offered.

The variety **'Ballerina'** has white flowers. **'Corona'** has yellow blooms. **'Oberon'** has scarlet flowers. **'Royal Blue'** bears lilac-blue flowers. **'Winter Gold'** has golden yellow blooms.

CULTIVATION For summer flowers, plant corms outdoors in mid spring in a sunny, well-drained spot. Place them 5cm (2in) apart and 3cm (1¼in) deep. Provide twigs for support unless the site is sheltered. Lift corms in autumn and store in a dry, cool but frost-free place for winter. In mild areas, for perennial flowering, plant the corms in late summer. They will flower the following spring and each spring thereafter.

For containers under glass use the same spacing of bulbs in a loam-based compost with a third of sharp sand. Plant in late summer to early winter for flowers from mid winter to mid spring. Keep at 5°C (41°F) and water sparingly until growth begins. When plants have 7 or 8 leaves showing, bring them into a warmer position, 10°C (50°F), and feed every 2 weeks.

PROPAGATION Remove offsets when corms are lifted or sow seed in late summer.

PEST AND DISEASES Aphids, red spider mite, gladiolus dry rot and fusarium wilt affect plants grown under glass.

▼ *Freesia* 'Royal Blue'

Fremontodendron

Sterculiaceae

Fremontodendron californicum

Masses of bright yellow flowers appear during summer on these deciduous or semi-evergreen shrubs from the USA. What appear to be yellow petals are in fact five coloured calyxes (modified leaves fused together). Pointed oval leaves are borne alternately on the stem and are deciduous or semi-evergreen depending on how sheltered the plant is. Fremontodendrons are not fully hardy and in Britain they need the protection of a south-facing wall in all but the mildest locations. Good drainage is also required. They are relatively easy to train against a wall and do well on limy soils. Rich soils may produce excessive growth at the expense of flowers. The hairs on these plants can irritate the eyes and skin.

RECOMMENDED SPECIES AND VARIETIES

F. **'California Glory'**♀ Yellow flowers, up to 6cm (2½in) across, appear from summer through to autumn. The leaves, up to 10cm (4in) long, are often roughly 3-lobed, with a crinkled appearance. The upper surface is dull green, sprinkled with hairs, the underside covered with pale brown hairs. HEIGHT & SPREAD 3x2m (10x6½ft) after 10 years, ultimately 5m (16ft) tall.

▲ *Fremontodendron* 'California Glory'

F. californicum Yellow flowers, up to 5cm (2in) across, are produced from summer through to autumn. The leaves are crinkled, dull dark green above with tufts of hair, and covered underneath in dense pale brown hairs. Often bluntly 3-lobed, the leaves are up to 10cm (4in) long. HEIGHT & SPREAD 3x2m (10x6½ft) after 10 years, ultimately 5m (16ft) tall.

F. **'Pacific Sunset'** Orange-yellow flowers, 6cm (2½in) across, appear from summer to autumn, fading to paler yellow as the season progresses. The leaves are dark green above, felted with pale brown hairs below, and grow to 8cm (3¼in) long, with 3 or 5 blunt lobes. HEIGHT & SPREAD 3x2m (10x6½ft) after 10 years, ultimately 5m (16ft) tall.

CULTIVATION Plant in autumn to spring, in well-drained, preferably limy soil, choosing a position in full sun.

PROPAGATION Take semi-ripe cuttings in mid to late summer.

PRUNING None is required, unless to train plants into a particular shape. Prune after the first flowers.

PESTS AND DISEASES Usually trouble free.

Friendship plant see *Billbergia nutans, Pilea involucrata*
Fringe cup see *Tellima*
Fringe tree see *Chionanthus*

f

Fritillaria

Fritillary
Liliaceae

Fritillaria imperialis

Their bell-shaped flowers in unusual colours, often mottled or chequered, give the fritillaries a subtle charm in spring. The shorter species are best grown in clumps at the front of a border or raised in a rockery so that their delicate stems and nodding blooms can be fully appreciated. A dense planting of the large *Fritillaria imperialis* makes a dramatic display as the massive orange heads are raised far above a sea of green foliage on stout stems.

All the plants in the genus are bulbous and generally produce pendent, bell-shaped flowers, 1.5-5cm (½-2in) long, near the top of erect leafy stems. The flowers are made up of six petals and are held singly or in clusters, usually in mid to late spring. The leaves are usually narrow, from 5-15cm (2-6in) long, carried in whorls or scattered up the stems.

The 100 or so species of fritillary are widely distributed through temperate regions of the Northern Hemisphere. They are generally hardy.

RECOMMENDED SPECIES AND VARIETIES

F. acmopetala♀ The large bell-shaped flowers have 3 pale green outer petals and 3 inner purplish brown petals; the bells narrow above the tips which then flare out. They hang singly, or occasionally in groups of 2-3, on stems bearing narrow, grey-green lanceolate leaves. This is one of the easiest species to grow and increases by numerous small bulbils. HEIGHT 30cm (1ft).

F. arabica see *F. persica*

F. camschatcensis (black sarana) The large flowers are almost black (occasionally yellowish green), carried in clusters of up to 5, making a striking display against the glossy pale green leaves in early summer. The leaves are up to 5cm (2in). This woodland plant thrives in moist conditions, increasing by bulbils. HEIGHT 30cm (1ft).

F. imperialis (crown imperial) The regal flowerheads, at the top of tall, stout stems, consist of a ring of large bell-shaped flowers, typically bright orange, crowned by a conspicuous tuft of leaf-like bracts (resembling a pineapple top). Most people find the scent unpleasant. Glossy pale green leaves are carried in numerous whorls on the lower half of the stems. This is the largest of the fritillaries and grows best in rich, heavy loams. HEIGHT 1.5m (5ft).

'Aurora' has bright reddish orange flowers. **'Maxima Lutea'**♀ is a robust variety with large lemon-yellow flowers. **'Rubra'** has the deepest orange-red flowers.

▲ *Fritillaria imperialis* 'Maxima Lutea'

▲ *Fritillaria imperialis* 'Rubra'

F. involucrata Large pale green blooms, sometimes covered with a faint to dark red chequering, are borne singly. Slender lanceolate leaves are scattered up the stem and held in a group of 3 above each flower. The plant is slow to increase in the garden. HEIGHT 30cm (12in).

▼ *Fritillaria meleagris*

F. meleagris♀ (snake's head fritillary) Each slender stem carries 1 (rarely 2) pendent bells, typically pinkish purple, heavily chequered with dark purple, though the flower colour is variable. The narrow lanceolate leaves are grey-green. HEIGHT 25cm (10in).

Two pure white varieties are available: ssp. ***alba***♀ and **'Aphrodite'**, the latter often a little larger and with a greenish tinge. These are easy to grow in a border or in grass, in sun or partial shade; they spread by bulb increase and by self-sowing.

F. messanensis The large flowers, generally up to 3 to a stem, are reddish brown with green towards the centre of each petal and a variable amount of darker mottling. The narrow leaves are usually glaucous and scattered up the stem with a cluster of 2-3 above the flowers. The plant increases slowly but is easily raised from seed. Its persistence makes it a good species for the garden. HEIGHT 25cm (10in).

▲ *Fritillaria michailovskyi*

F. michailovskyi♀ The striking two-tone flowers are dark purplish brown with deep yellow towards their tips. Short stems carry 1-3 of these blooms and broadly lanceolate, glaucous leaves. This plant needs well-drained soil in full sun. HEIGHT 15cm (6in).

F. pallidiflora♀ Flowering later than most (in early summer), this plant produces large, cream-coloured, square-shouldered bells. Each stem bears 1-4 flowers and broad oval bluish green leaves about 4cm (1½in) wide. The plant has an unpleasant odour. Since it is a woodland species, give it rich soil in semi-shade. It is easily raised from seed. HEIGHT 45cm (1½ft).

▼ *Fritillaria persica*

F. persica (syn. *F. arabica*) Abundant whorls of narrow, highly glaucous leaves anchor tall spires of up to 20 blackish purple, though sometimes greenish, conical flowers. The flowers are 2cm (¾in) long, held on long flower stalks. The plant flowers best after a hot summer the previous year. HEIGHT 1m (3ft).

'Adiyaman' is a robust variety with many very dark flowers to a stem.

F. pontica The flowers are large, solitary pale green bells. They have no chequering but usually have some reddish brown along the petal edges. Broadly lanceolate bluish leaves are scattered up the stem and held in a group of 3 around the flowers. The plant is best grown from seed, since bulb increase is slow. HEIGHT 30cm (1ft).

F. pyrenaica♀ One of the easiest fritillaries to grow, in grass or a border, in full sun or light shade, this plant bears single large bells that vary in colour, but which are green within and mostly dark chocolate-brown outside, usually with some darker mottling. The blue-green leaves are narrow. The plant increases slowly by bulb splitting and by self-sowing. HEIGHT 30cm (1ft).

F. uva-vulpis Chocolate-brown, narrow bells with yellow tips are borne 1-3 together on a slender plant with glossy, lanceolate leaves. It is very easy to grow and increases freely from bulbils in well-drained soil in the garden or in an unheated greenhouse. HEIGHT 25cm (10in).

F. verticillata Loose spikes of up to 6 creamy, nodding, broad bells appear in early summer. The glossy grey-green tendril-like leaves are carried in whorls up the stem. The plant is easily grown in sun or partial shade, but it takes a year or two to flower freely and increase. HEIGHT 45cm (1½ft).

CULTIVATION Plant most species in very well-drained soil in an open sunny spot. Alternatively, grow in well-drained gritty compost in pots or a bulb frame. *F. persica* and *F. michailovskyi* benefit from being kept almost dry from the time the leaves die down until early autumn and in wet areas are best grown in pots. Grow the woodland species in partial shade in moist soil.

PROPAGATION Some species increase rapidly by forming small bulbils around the parent bulb. These can be left on the plants or removed and treated like young bulbs when lifting and dividing in autumn.

Seed is the best method of propagation, producing flowering plants in 3-5 years. Sow seed in autumn and keep the pots cold until germination in spring, or occasionally the following spring. Keep the seedlings well watered (except when dormant) for 2 years, and then separate and repot annually until they reach adult size and are large enough to plant in permanent positions.

PESTS AND DISEASES Slugs may be a problem outdoors and grey mould may affect plants under glass.

Fuchsia

Ladies' eardrops

Onagraceae

Abundant, jewel-like blooms hang from the branches of these deciduous shrubs for many months. These exquisite flowers have justly earned fuchsias a place among the most popular plants for both garden and greenhouse

Hanging flowers, often in shades of the most vivid pink and purple, grace these free-flowering deciduous shrubs from early summer to mid autumn, when grown outdoors. This long flowering period and the ease of care and great versatility of fuchsias have long made them favourites.

Flower colour ranges from the gaudy to pure white, with most possible shades and combinations in between. The pendulous blooms are formed by a tube that opens out into four spreading waxy sepals. Emerging from the sepals are four overlapping petals, forming a bell, that are often a contrasting colour to the sepals. Flowers can be single, double, or semi-double. All have prominent stamens, usually eight, very rarely four, which can also be highly coloured, often complementing the most flamboyant part of the flower. If grown in a conservatory or greenhouse, fuchsias can flower for eight months of the year. Usually inconspicuous, small purple berries are produced from mid summer onwards.

Fuchsias differ widely in hardiness and

1 *F.* Nellie Nuttal
2 *F. × bacillaris*
3 *F. procumbens*
4 *F.* Madam Cornelissen
5 *F.* Heidi Ann
6 *F.* Tennessee Waltz
7 *F.* Garden News
8 *F.* Mary
9 *F.* Coralle
10 *F.* Abb Farges
11 *F.* Billy Green
12 *F.* Mrs Popple
13 *F.* Margaret Brown

habit. There are trailing types, well suited to growing in containers and hanging baskets. The upright, bushy fuchsias brighten up a border, make excellent focal plants and, in mild areas, can even be grown as hedging. They also make good standard shrubs (see p. 277). Some hybrids grow to no more than 50 cm (20 in) tall, while others can exceed 2 m (6½ ft). Fuchsias tend to make rather larger plants when set out in beds and borders than when grown in pots or other containers, because the unrestricted rooting range enables them to do better for water and nutrients.

There are hardy fuchsias that will survive outdoors all year round and half-hardy varieties, generally used as summer bedding or greenhouse and conservatory plants, that need to be overwintered in a frost-free environment. Fuchsias are, fortunately, among the easiest plants to propagate from cuttings and so raising replacement plants is not a problem.

Fuchsias are native to Central and S America and New Zealand.

RECOMMENDED SPECIES AND VARIETIES

Fuchsias are hardy or half-hardy and can be divided into groups accordingly.

HARDY SPECIES AND VARIETIES

The following fuchsias will survive winters in most parts of Britain if they have well-drained soil and an unexposed site. In milder areas they may remain green all winter and often grow as an ordinary shrub or an informal hedge. In colder sites they may behave like herbaceous perennials, with any growth above ground level being killed by frost and new growth sprouting from the base in spring.

F. magellanica Deep crimson sepals, purple petals and protruding stamens characterise this bushy species, which is the hardiest of the genus. In very mild areas, it can reach a height of 3 m (10 ft). The flowers are small, about 4 cm (1½ in) long and 2 cm (¾ in) across. Mid green, pointed leaves arise from the stems in pairs and are elongated, oval and up to 7 cm (2¾ in) long. HEIGHT & SPREAD 1.2 m×50 cm (4 ft×20 in).

Fuchsia magellanica

The scarlet sepals and violet petals of var. *gracilis* **'Aurea'** are dramatic against its narrow, golden leaves. It has a more slender habit than the species, and arching stems. The same colour flowers appear on var. *gracilis* **'Variegata'**♀ which is less vigorous. It reaches a height of 60 cm (2 ft) and spreads to 60 cm (2 ft). The leaves are edged with creamy yellow.

The leaves of var. ***molinae*** (syn. 'Alba') are light green. It has white sepals and pale lavender petals. The flowers of its cultivar, **'Sharpitor'** (syn. *F.* 'Overbecks', *F.* 'Sharpitor') are the same colour but its grey-green leaves are edged with white. 'Sharpitor' reaches a height of 75 cm (2½ ft) and a spread of 60 cm (2 ft).

'Riccartonii' see *F.* **'Riccartonii'**. **'Versicolor'**♀ (syn. *F.* 'Versicolor') has flowers similar to the species which contrast well with its grey-green leaves.

HARDY HYBRIDS

Larger flowers and a wider colour range distinguish these erect, bushy hybrids from the hardy species. They are single-flowered unless otherwise indicated. The oval, pointed leaves are mid green and up to 7 cm (2¾ in) long. Most of these hybrids are slightly less hardy than *F. magellanica*, which is one of the parent species. They flower from mid summer to mid autumn.

'Abbé Farges' has very freely produced small semidouble flowers with cherry-red sepals and rosy lilac petals. **'Alice Hoffman'** has freely produced, small semidouble flowers with pink sepals and white petals. **'Eva Boerg'** has pink-white sepals with greenish tips and purplish pink petals, which pale towards the base and are marked with pink. It has an arching habit and reaches a height and spread of up to 75 cm (2½ ft). **'Garden News'**♀ has medium to large double flowers with pink sepals and cerise petals. **'Lady Thumb'**♀ has semidouble flowers with white petals showing pale pink veins and vivid pink sepals with a purplish hue. It grows to a height of 60 cm (2 ft) and a spread of 40 cm (16 in). **'Lena'**♀ has semidouble flowers with pale pink sepals and purple petals. It has a compact, arching habit and is up to 60 cm (2 ft) tall and wide. **'Madame Cornelissen'**♀ bears semidouble flowers with deep crimson sepals and white petals. It reaches a height of 1.2 m (4 ft) and a spread of 80 cm (32 in). **'Margaret'**♀ has abundant flowers with crimson sepals and scarlet-streaked, bluish purple petals that are paler at the base. It reaches a height of 1.2 m (4 ft) and a spread of 80 cm (32 in). **'Margaret Brown'** has pink sepals and petals and is vigorous, growing to 1 m (3 ft) tall and spreading to 65 cm (26 in). **'Mrs Popple'**♀ blooms for several weeks longer than most other hardy hybrids. The abundant flowers have scarlet sepals and rich purple petals. It is a vigorous plant with a spreading and trailing habit, reaching a height and spread of up to 1.2 m (4 ft). **'Riccartonii'** (syn. *F. magellanica* 'Riccartonii') is a robust, hardy plant with broad, dark crimson sepals. It reaches a height of 2 m (6½ ft) and a spread of 1.2 m (4 ft). **'Rufus'** (syn. *F.* 'Rufus the Red') has dark red sepals and dark red petals with a vivid pink hue. It is a robust grower up to 50 cm (20 in) tall and 33 cm (13 in) wide.

▲ *Fuchsia* 'Lady Thumb'

▲ *Fuchsia* 'Lena'

▲ *Fuchsia* 'Mrs Popple'

'Snowcap'♀ (syn. *F.* 'Wendy') has semi-double flowers with red sepals and white petals with cherry-pink veins. **'Tennessee Waltz'**♀ is fast-growing and very free-flowering with double blooms, rose to reddish orange sepals, and mauve to rose petals.

HALF-HARDY SPECIES

Half-hardy species are mainly grown in large pots or planted into beds as long-term greenhouse or conservatory plants. They will also thrive outdoors in summer either in pots or planted out in beds, although they are less popular than the half-hardy hybrids: these tend to be larger plants with more brightly coloured flowers. Most half-hardy fuchsias can be overwintered successfully in a greenhouse or conservatory given only enough artificial heating to exclude frost. Half-hardy fuchsias usually bear larger flowers than fully hardy plants.

F.* × *bacillaris (syn. *F. aprica* hort., *F. parviflora* hort.) Tiny pink-to-red flowers less than 1 cm (⅜ in) long and across open on this small-leaved, spreading shrub. The narrowly oval, mid green leaves are up to 2.5 cm (1 in) long. HEIGHT & SPREAD 2×2 m (6½×6½ ft).

F. denticulata (syn. *F. serratifolia*) Long, tubular flowers with red sepals and bright orange petals grace this large, erect shrub. The dark green leaves are narrow, up to 15 cm (6 in) long and arise in threes or fours from the stems. HEIGHT & SPREAD 4×1.5 m (13×5 ft).

F. microphylla Small purple-red flowers characterise this dwarf, small-leaved, bushy shrub. They are 1.5 cm (½ in) long, with petals slightly paler than the sepals. Dark green, narrow leaves are up to 4 cm (1½ in) long. HEIGHT & SPREAD 60×60 cm (2×2 ft).

F. procumbens Distinctive pale orange flowers about 1.5 cm (½ in) across are held erect. The dark green, heart-shaped leaves are up to 1.5 cm (½ in) long. Bright red, long-lasting fruit about 1.5 cm (½ in) across are a conspicuous attraction. Its prostrate habit makes it a good rockery plant that is wide-spreading in very mild areas. HEIGHT & SPREAD 10 cm×1 m (4 in×3 ft).

Fuchsia procumbens

HALF-HARDY HYBRIDS

A very much wider range of flower colour and form distinguishes this most popular group from other fuchsias. Many also have much larger flowers. They are not hardy enough to grow outdoors all year round but make excellent summer bedding and container plants. They can be kept over winter in a greenhouse but are more often grown just for the one season. The most important distinction in habit is between the erect bushy and trailing varieties, although some are intermediate between the two. Trailing varieties are most often chosen for hanging baskets and window boxes. There are 2 other half-hardy hybrid groups, the Triphylla and Encliandra hybrids, that are distinguished by their unusual flowers.

▲ *Fuchsia* 'Dancing Flame'

▲ *Fuchsia* 'Heidi Ann'

Erect bushy varieties

The plants included here are all single-flowered unless otherwise indicated. They have oval, pointed foliage that is mid green and up to 7 cm (2¾ in) long. They reach a height of 30-60 cm (1-2 ft) and a spread of 30-45 cm (1-1½ ft).

'Checkerboard'♀ is upright and very free-flowering. The slender blooms have dark red petals and red, changing to white, upward curving sepals. **'Coachman'** bears salmon-pink sepals, orange-vermilion petals and is free flowering. **'Dancing Flame'** is double-flowered with orange sepals and carmine petals. **'Heidi Ann'**♀ has a neat, very bushy, habit. The double flowers have crimson sepals and lilac-pink petals that are less vivid near the base, and streaked with bright pink veins. **'Nellie Nuttall'** is free-flowering with crimson sepals and white petals. **'Royal Velvet'**♀ is very free-flowering. Its double blooms have crimson sepals and rich purple petals, marked with crimson. **'Swingtime'**♀ has large double flowers with deep red sepals and white petals with pale streaks of red. **'Winston Churchill'**♀ has a small, bushy habit and is very free-flowering. The pink sepals are greenish at the tip and vivid pink underneath. The lavender-blue petals gradually turn to pale purple and are veined with pink.

▲ *Fuchsia* 'Royal Velvet'

▲ *Fuchsia* 'Nellie Nuttall'

Fuchsia 'Swingtime'

Trailing varieties

Trailing forms are often catalogued as basket or cascading varieties. All are single-

▲ *Fuchsia* 'Cascade'

▲ *Fuchsia* 'Red Spider'

▲ *Fuchsia* 'Trumpeter'

flowered unless otherwise indicated. The mid green leaves are oval, pointed and up to 7cm (2¾in) long. They reach a height of 10-20cm (4-8in) and a spread of 30-40cm (12-16in).

'Cascade' is very free-flowering with long flowers. The white sepals are flushed pink and backward-curving; the petals are a rich crimson. **'Florabelle'** has small but abundant red and purple semidouble flowers and comes true from seed. **'Golden Marinka'**♀ has red sepals, deep red petals and variegated green and gold foliage, streaked with red.

▼ *Fuchsia* 'Mantilla'

'Mantilla' see Triphylla hybrids below. **'Pink Galore'** is very free-flowering and has double blooms with pink sepals and pale rose-pink petals. **'Pink Marshmallow'** is easy to grow with very large double flowers. The white sepals are pinkish underneath with a green hue to the tips; the white petals have a hint of light pink and pale pink veins. **'Red Spider'** has freely produced long flowers with intense crimson sepals and red petals. **'Trumpeter'** see Triphylla hybrids below.

Triphylla hybrids

The triphyllas differ from other hybrid varieties in that the flowers have very short sepals and very long tubes, formed by the bottom of the petals fusing, and the flowers are borne in clusters rather than singly. They are sometimes called clustered fuchsias. Those plants included here have single-colour flowers. The pointed, oval leaves are up to 7cm (2¾in) long and arise from the stems in threes. There are upright bushy varieties that reach 30-60cm (1-2ft) in height and 30-45cm (1-1½ft) in spread. There are also trailing varieties that reach 10-20cm (4-8in) tall with a spread of 30-40cm (12-16in).

'Billy Green'♀ is very free-flowering with deep pink flowers, olive-green leaves and a vigorous upright habit. **'Coralle'**♀ has abundant orange flowers, blue-green leaves and is for use only as a bush plant. **'Gartenmeister Bonstedt'**♀ is free-flowering with deep orange flowers, bronze-red leaves and an upright habit. **'Mantilla'** has crimson flowers with a purple hue produced very freely, bronze-green narrow leaves and a vigorous, cascading habit. **'Mary'**♀ has scarlet flowers, bronze-purple narrow leaves and an upright habit. **'Thalia'**♀ bears orange-red flowers, red to bronze leaves. It has a vigorous, upright habit and is very free-flowering. This is the most widely grown Triphylla hybrid. **'Trumpeter'** has freely borne candyfloss-pink flowers, blue-green leaves and a bushy, trailing habit.

Encliandra hybrids

This group is the least often seen, and plants can be purchased only from specialist fuchsia nurseries. They have abundant, very small flowers and a fern-like appearance. Most have a spreading habit which is well adapted to their use in hanging baskets and near the edge of tubs and patio containers.

'Fuksie Foetsie', which has pale pink flowers, is the most widely available.

CULTIVATION

HARDY FUCHSIAS

Plant outdoors from mid spring onwards in any soil, choosing a site in full sun or partial shade. Water new plants to establish them. Apply a protective mulch in autumn around the base of each plant, using bark chips, bracken or straw. Cut all top growth back in autumn to about 30cm (1ft) above the ground. This helps to prevent strong winds rocking the roots in wet soil during winter and causing damage. Apply a general-purpose fertiliser in late winter. In spring, when shoot buds appear, cut each branch back hard, leaving 1 or 2 buds to grow from the base of the branch.

▲ *Fuchsia* 'Gartenmeister Bonstedt'

▲ *Fuchsia* 'Mary'

▲ *Fuchsia* 'Coachman'

▲ *Fuchsia* 'Garden News'

HALF-HARDY FUCHSIAS
If growing as half-hardy fuchsias outdoors as summer bedding, plant them out in any soil after all risk of hard late frosts has passed. Choose a position in full sun or partial shade. Water during dry weather. Apply a potash-rich fertiliser in mid summer and water this in thoroughly.

Fuchsias can also be grown outdoors in pots or hanging baskets containing multi-purpose compost. Containers should be at least 30cm (1ft) in diameter. Water pot-grown plants frequently and give a weekly potash-rich liquid feed.

Fork up plants from their beds or remove them from their containers in autumn and move to a cool, dry frost-free environment. This can be either a greenhouse or conservatory with enough heating for frost protection, or a shed or garage. Water just often enough to prevent the roots drying out. In late winter or early spring, restart the plants into growth by watering them and putting them into a greenhouse with a minimum temperature of 5°C (41°F), or placing them on a sunny windowsill. Once the growth of new shoots begins, cut back the previous season's leafless woody shoots to within 1 or 2 buds.

If growing fuchsias indoors, plant at anytime and maintain a minimum temperature of 7°C (45°F) to ensure that plants retain their foliage. In spring and summer, provide shade to protect plants from the full force of the sun, water freely and give regular liquid food. Remove dying flowers to promote the production of more blooms and to improve the plants' appearance. Water much less frequently once growth slows or ceases after summer, but never let the compost dry out.

Avoid a dry atmosphere, which can cause dropping flower buds and leaf-fall. Fuchsias appreciate higher humidity than is normally found in living rooms or even kitchens. To create a more humid microclimate, grow them among plenty of other plants, stand pots on a tray of gravel that is kept permanently wet, plunge the pots in moist peat in a windowsill plant trough, or syringe with a fine spray. *F.* 'Golden Marinka' needs good light conditions.

PROPAGATION Take softwood cuttings any time from late winter to mid autumn. Cuttings taken in late spring or summer are very easily rooted in an unheated greenhouse or on a sunny windowsill. Bottom heat may be needed to ensure rooting at other times.

Maintain high humidity round the cuttings until roots begin to form. Use a propagator, or insert 3 very short lengths of cane round the rim of the pots in which the cuttings are to be rooted and put a polythene bag over the top.

PESTS AND DISEASES Fuchsias are vulnerable to red spider mite and greenfly, rust and bud-drop, although the latter are usually short-lived. Whitefly and grey mould are problems in a greenhouse.

Fuchsia, Australian see *Correa*
Fuchsia, Cape see *Phygelius capensis*
Furze see *Ulex europaeus*

Standard Fuchsias

A standard fuchsia makes an impressive individual specimen or centrepiece in a large container. It is also traditionally used as a 'dot' plant in large beds. With a single woody stem anything up to 1.2m (4ft) tall, the naturally pendent flowers are raised and so are seen to their best advantage.

They are expensive, but gardeners with a greenhouse in which a minimum winter temperature of 10°C (50°F) can be maintained, can produce their own. They are usually saved over winter.

Erect bushy fuchsias are used to make standards. The following varieties are particularly good: *F.* 'Checkerboard', *F.* 'Coachman', *F.* 'Garden News', *F.* 'Royal Velvet', *F.* 'Snowcap', *F.* 'Swingtime' and *F.* 'Tennessee Waltz'.

The process of forming a standard is best carried out entirely in a greenhouse, and takes around a year before the well-grown young standard is ready for planting out in the garden or large container. It will require a final position reasonably sheltered from wind.

Take cuttings in late spring or early summer. The taller the stem required, the earlier cuttings should be taken. Insert in a mixture of half sand, half peat or peat-based compost and water thoroughly. Maintain high humidity until the roots form, either by placing the cuttings in a propagator or by putting 3 short canes round the rim of the pot in which the cuttings are to be rooted and placing a polythene bag over them.

Once rooted, after about 3 weeks, put each cutting into a 9cm (3½in) pot and insert a thin cane, 50cm (20in) long. Tie the shoot to the cane but do not pinch out the growing point. The ties should be about 8cm (3¼in) apart.

When the cutting reaches the top of the cane, pot on into a 13cm (5in) pot, and insert a cane at least 1.2m (4ft) tall. Canes can be longer but they must be at least 30cm (1ft) taller than the intended height of the stem. Continue to support the stem by tying it to the new cane. Remove any sideshoots that develop, but let the leaves remain.

When the stem reaches the height required, pinch out the growing point. Vigorous sideshoots usually develop from the 3 uppermost leaf joints. Remove any sideshoots which develop below these. Pinch out the growing point of each of the retained sideshoots just beyond their second pair of leaves.

As the resulting shoots grow, pinch these out too, just beyond the third pair of leaves. Continue in this manner until a good round head is achieved.

g

Gaillardia

Blanket flower
Compositae

Gaillardia 'Dazzler'

Fiery red or yellow daisies bring colour to the garden through summer and into early autumn. Large flowers, about 8-12.5 cm (3¼-5 in) wide, and straight stems make these excellent plants for cutting. They are most commonly available in hybrid form, as hardy, short-lived herbaceous perennials, living three to five years if the soil is not too damp and poorly drained. Annuals are also available. Native to N and S America.

RECOMMENDED SPECIES AND VARIETIES

G. x ***grandiflora*** Yellow petals (properly called ray florets) encircle a central red disc (made up of disc florets). The soft, hairy, grey-green leaves are lance-shaped, alternate and up to 15 cm (6 in) long. The whole plant is sticky and aromatic. HEIGHT & SPREAD 60-90×45 cm (2-3×1½ ft).

'Burgunder' has deep wine-red petals with a dark red centre. **'Dazzler'**♀ has orange-red petals with yellow tips. An annual, it reaches 60 cm (2 ft) tall. **'Kobold'**, with red and gold petals and a red centre, is a dwarf, growing only 25 cm (10 in) high.

▼ *Gaillardia* 'Dazzler'

▲ *Gaillardia* 'Kobold'

CULTIVATION Plants grow best in a sunny position, in light, well-drained soil. Plant out in spring. Taller plants need twiggy supports. Deadhead fading flowers.

PROPAGATION Sow seeds of perennial species in a row in open ground in spring, then transfer them to their final position in early autumn or the following spring. Divide named cultivars in spring. Take root cuttings in winter and grow on in a coldframe before planting in spring. For annuals, sow seed either in the flowering site in late spring, or under glass in winter at 16°C (61°F). Prick out in boxes, harden off and plant out in late spring.

PESTS AND DISEASES Downy mildew may attack the underside of leaves, causing them to turn yellow.

Galanthus

Snowdrop
Amaryllidaceae

Galanthus nivalis

The common snowdrop, *Galanthus nivalis*, is one of the most widely grown winter-flowering bulbs and it naturalises readily in grass. Most snowdrops flower early in the year, though there are some that flower in autumn. With few exceptions they are very hardy bulbs, being native throughout Europe and into Turkey and Iran.

All snowdrops have hanging flowers, about 6-20 mm (¼-¾ in) long at maturity, with six unequal petals. The longer, outer petals are usually plain white, whereas the shorter, inner ones form a cup with each petal carrying distinctive green markings. The plants normally have two narrow basal leaves, usually 2 cm (¾ in) wide and 15-30 cm (6-12 in) long. The leaves are short at flowering time, extending considerably afterwards.

RECOMMENDED SPECIES AND VARIETIES

G. ***allenii*** Almond-scented flowers appear in mid winter and carry a single green mark on each inner petal. The matt green leaves are relatively broad, up to 2.5 cm (1 in) wide. HEIGHT 12 cm (4¾ in).

G. **'Arnott's Seedling'** see *G.* 'S. Arnott'

G. **'Atkinsii'**♀ A vigorous plant that flowers in mid winter, with flowers up to 4 cm (1½ in) long. One outer petal is sometimes deformed so that it is twisted and longer than the others. Inner petals each carry a single green mark. The leaves have a silver central stripe. HEIGHT 25 cm (10 in).

G. ***caucasicus***♀ The rounded flowers carry a single green mark on each inner petal. This variable species can bloom in late autumn or winter. It has 2.5 cm (1 in) wide grey leaves. HEIGHT 15 cm (6 in).

▲ *Galanthus caucasicus*

G. ***elwesii***♀ The very variable flowers, borne in mid to late winter, have an elongated appearance, to 3 cm (1¼ in), and display 2 green marks on the inner petals. The plant has broad, 3 cm (1¼ in) wide, grey-green leaves, up to 30 cm (12 in) long. It grows best in a dry, limy soil and can be difficult to establish in some gardens. HEIGHT 10-20 cm (4-8 in).

G. ***gracilis*** (syn. *G. graecus*) A delicate-looking snowdrop with grey-green leaves, 6 mm (¼ in) wide and 5-15 cm (2-6 in) long, in some forms spirally twisted. The flowers appear in late winter with each inner petal carrying a pair of green marks. It prefers a dry situation. HEIGHT 10 cm (4 in).

G. ***ikariae*** ssp. ***ikariae***♀ The 2.5 cm (1 in) long, claw-shaped flowers carry a single large green mark on each inner petal. HEIGHT Variable up to 15 cm (6 in).

The **Latifolius Group** has broad green

▼ *Galanthus ikariae* ssp. *ikariae*

leaves and the flowers have a V-shaped mark on each inner petal.

G. 'Lady Beatrix Stanley' Double flowers are borne by this snowdrop early in the year. HEIGHT 12cm (4¾in).

G. 'Magnet'♀ The large flowers, 3cm (1¼in) long, of this vigorous variety appear to float on the exceptionally long flower stalks. HEIGHT 23cm (9in).

G. 'Merlin' The distinctive flowers have inner petals that are almost entirely green. HEIGHT 20cm (8in).

G. nivalis♀ (common snowdrop) The inner petals of the 1.5-2.5cm (½-1in) long flowers each have a single green mark. Grey-green leaves are up to 1cm (⅜in) wide and up to 20cm (8in) long. The plant can be naturalised in light grass. HEIGHT Variable, from 7.5-20cm (3-8in).

▲ *Galanthus nivalis*

▲ *Galanthus nivalis* 'Pusey Green Tip'

'Flore Pleno'♀ is a vigorous plant with fully double flowers. **'Lady Elphinstone'** has double flowers which in some soils have yellow rather than green markings. **'Pusey Green Tip'** is a double form with green marks on the tips of the outer petals rather than the inner ones. **'Sandersii'** (syn. 'Lutescens') is slow to increase and has small flowers with yellow ovaries and inner markings. **'Scharlockii'** is a delicate plant with small flowers and light green marks on the outer petals. **'Viridapicis'** is a robust snowdrop with bold green marks on the outer petals.

G. 'Ophelia' The double flowers of this tall, imposing snowdrop are up to 3cm (1¼in) long. The inner petals each carry a single green mark. HEIGHT 20cm (8in).

G. plicatus♀ The flowers are 1.5-3cm (½-1¼in) long and each inner petal has a single green mark. Leaves are dull green with a grey-green central stripe and margins folded back. The species seeds freely in some gardens. HEIGHT 20cm (8in).

ssp. ***byzantinus***♀ has 2 green markings on each inner petal; **'Warham'** has broad leaves and large flowers bearing a large U-shaped green mark on each inner petal.

G. reginae-olgae An autumn-flowering species very similar to *G. nivalis* but with a silvery central stripe on its narrow leaves. The leaves may be absent or only just showing when the plant is flowering. It requires a dry, sunny position. HEIGHT 10cm (4in).

G. 'S. Arnott'♀ (syn. 'Sam Arnott', 'Arnott's Seedling') This robust variety grows well and multiplies rapidly. It has large, well rounded, almond-scented flowers in late winter and 3cm (1¼in) wide leaves. HEIGHT 23cm (9in).

G. 'Straffan' Waxy flowers are borne in late winter, often 2 from one bulb. HEIGHT 18cm (7in).

CULTIVATION Apart from the exceptions given under individual entries, snowdrops are easily grown in a well-drained, humus-rich soil where there is plenty of moisture available when they are growing. They prefer dappled shade during summer when dormant and can be grown under deciduous trees and shrubs. Plant in small groups.

PROPAGATION Plant the bulbs 10cm (4in) deep in early autumn if freshly dug bulbs are available, or after flowering. Divide and replant clumps after flowering, making sure that the bulbs do not dry out. Water well after transplanting.

To increase cultivars remove offsets after flowering and replant immediately. Some species increase naturally by seeding if conditions suit them.

PESTS AND DISEASES Stem eelworm, large narcissus fly, grey mould and various rots attack snowdrops.

Galax

Wandflower

Diapensiaceae

The only species in the genus is a hardy, slowly spreading, evergreen perennial useful for year-round ground cover in shady situations and lime-free soil. Native to mountain woods of eastern N America.

Galax urceolata (syn. *G. aphylla*) Erect, wiry stems bear slender spikes, up to 25cm (10in) tall, carrying many tiny creamy white flowers from late spring to early summer above a dense mat of foliage. The long-stalked, shiny, rounded to heart-shaped leaves are up to 12.5cm (5in) wide. They are tinted with bronze or purple in winter. The plant withstands considerable frosts without damage to its foliage. HEIGHT & SPREAD 30-60cm×1m (1-2×3ft).

CULTIVATION Plant in a shaded or partially shaded position in a cool, humus-rich, acid or neutral soil.

PROPAGATION Divide in spring. Sow seed in spring, although it is rarely available.

PESTS AND DISEASES Usually trouble free.

Galega

Goat's rue, French lilac

Leguminosae

Graceful spikes of small pea-shaped flowers adorn this tall, hardy herbaceous perennial in summer. Position at the back of a large border, or in a wild or herb garden. Plants are floppy, and can be grown through open shrubs rather than being staked. White, blue or violet flowers are carried in loose spikes about 15cm (6in) long on erect stems, each flower being up to 1.5cm (½in) across. The plentiful foliage is made up of soft green leaves, on short stalks, divided into four to eight pairs of oppositely arranged, oval to oblong leaflets, each leaflet about 5cm (2in) long and 1.5cm (½in) wide. Native to S Europe, Asia Minor and E Africa.

RECOMMENDED SPECIES AND VARIETIES

***G. × hartlandii* 'Alba'**♀ Pure white flowers are borne in summer on this erect, clump-forming plant with dark green divided leaves. HEIGHT & SPREAD 1.5×1m (5×3ft).

G. officinalis (syn. G. *bicolor*) Flowers vary in colour from white to purple, occasionally blue, and appear in mid and late summer. HEIGHT & SPREAD 1.5×1m (5×3ft).

The flowers of **'Alba'** are pure white.

▼ *Galega × hartlandii* 'Alba'

▼ *Galega officinalis*

G. orientalis Blue to violet flowers are borne from early to late summer on a plant that can become invasive when grown in more fertile soils. HEIGHT & SPREAD 1.2m×60cm (4×2ft).
CULTIVATION Plant between mid autumn and early spring, in sun or light shade in moist but well-drained soil. In richer soil plants may sprawl and need staking.
PROPAGATION Raise plants from seed sown in open ground in spring, transplant seedlings into a nursery plot and plant in final positions in autumn. Divide existing plants when replanting, between mid autumn and early spring.
PESTS AND DISEASES Usually trouble free.

Galeobdolon see *Lamium*

Galium

Rubiaceae

A large group of annuals, biennials and herbaceous perennials grown for their flowers. The plants may be upright, scrambling or climbing. The genus also contains troublesome weeds. Plants are best suited to a wild garden or to informal situations. Most grow best in an open sunny position, but *Galium odoratum* also enjoys partial shade. They all need soil with good drainage.
RECOMMENDED SPECIES
G. mollugo (hedge bedstraw) Loose clusters of very small, star-like white flowers, flecked with purple, adorn the erect scrambling stems of this hardy perennial species in summer. Flowers are seen to best advantage if the plant is allowed to scramble through a large shrub, wander among other plants or across open ground. The tough, wiry stems are clothed with very small lance-shaped leaves. Native to Europe and N America. HEIGHT & SPREAD 1.5×1m (5×3ft).

▼ *Galium mollugo*

▲ *Galium odoratum*

G. odoratum (syn. *Asperula odorata*) (sweet woodruff) A hardy plant that can spread rapidly, producing a carpet of bright green umbrella-shaped leaves in early spring. Masses of tiny, white, star-like flowers cover the plants in late spring and early summer. Native to N Africa and Europe. HEIGHT & SPREAD 15×30cm (6×12in).
CULTIVATION Plant in spring in full sun or light shade in well-drained soil. Apply a slow-release fertiliser sparingly in spring.
PROPAGATION Divide established plants. Alternatively sow seed in early spring in their flowering position.
PESTS AND DISEASES Usually trouble free.

Galtonia

Summer hyacinth
Hyacinthaceae

Tall spires of nodding, bell-shaped white flowers rise out of a clump of stiff, glossy, strap-like leaves in late summer. These free-flowering bulbous perennials can remain outdoors in most areas, if given a thick mulch of leaf-mould, but in very cold or wet areas it is safer to lift bulbs in autumn and store them throughout winter. Plants are native to South Africa.
RECOMMENDED SPECIES
G. candicans (summer hyacinth) Fleshy, leafless flower spikes carry up to 30 white flowers, each up to 2.5cm (1in) long. The bright green, strap-shaped leaves reach a length of 60cm (2ft). HEIGHT 1m (3ft).
G. princeps A similar plant to *G. candicans*, but the leaves are rarely more than 45cm (1½ft) long and the flower stem is shorter with fewer flowers. The white petals are tinged with green. HEIGHT 75cm (2½ft).
G. viridiflora Leafless flower stems bear up to 30 bell-like, pale green flowers about 2.5 (1in) long. The grey-green, strap-like leaves are up to 60cm (2ft) long. HEIGHT & SPREAD 60cm (2ft).
CULTIVATION Plant in spring in a soil which does not readily dry out, although it must be free-draining. Cut back flower stems when they have faded. In very cold or wet areas, lift the bulbs in autumn and store in a frost-free place in a tray of peat until replanting in the following spring.
PROPAGATION Lift established clumps in spring and separate out young bulbs for growing on. Sow seed in a coldframe immediately after it ripens. Keep seedlings frost free for the first 2 years, seedlings will flower after 2 or 3 years.
PESTS AND DISEASES Usually trouble free.

▲ *Galtonia candicans*

Galtonia viridiflora ▲

Gardenia

Rubiaceae

Deliciously scented flowers are a major attraction of these lime-hating evergreen shrubs, which have very dark green, glossy foliage. They thrive in pots in cool, well-lit rooms and conservatories, and also do well in a conservatory border with acid soil. Gardenias usually flower in summer, although with warmth and good light they can bloom into winter. If their needs are met they can be long-lived, rewarding plants. The genus is native to S China.
RECOMMENDED SPECIES
G. augusta (syn. *G. jasminoides*) (opera flower) Creamy white, usually semidouble flowers 5–7cm (2–2¾in) across produce a strong scent throughout summer. Leaves up to 10cm (4in) long are broadly lance-shaped. This dense, twiggy shrub is usually compact, but can be trained as a standard. HEIGHT & SPREAD 120×70cm (48×28in).

▼ *Gardenia augusta*

CULTIVATION Grow in a lime-free proprietary compost and feed weekly or fortnightly during the growing season. Place in good indirect light in summer and keep the compost slightly moist. Never let gardenias dry out or become waterlogged. Use soft water or coffee grounds, which are quite acid. In winter, ensure plants receive some direct sunlight and let the compost dry out a little before watering. Maintain a night-time temperature of at least 16°C (61°F), and 21°C (70°F) during the day to encourage flowering. Stand pots on trays of wet gravel to increase humidity. Repot in spring but only when roots fill the pot, as gardenias flower better when slightly pot-bound.
PROPAGATION Take cuttings of tips of shoots around 7 cm (2¾ in) long in spring. Use a rooting compound and bottom heat. Rooting takes about a month.
PRUNING Cut long shoots back in spring if the plant is becoming too large. Cutting back hard into old wood has no ill effect. Remove shoots from the trunk or base. Also prune once flowering is over. Take care with standards to maintain the overall shape.
PESTS AND DISEASES Bud-drop is a problem. Red spider mite can attack in dry air and whitefly and mealy bug can also be tiresome.

Garland flower
see *Hedychium coronarium*
Garlic, edible see p. 742

Garrya
Silk tassel bush
Garryaceae

Garrya elliptica

Festoons of long, silky catkins from mid winter to early spring are an outstanding feature on these evergreen shrubs or trees. Male and female flowers are produced on separate trees. Male trees have showier catkins and are more widely available. The opposite leaves are glossy and leathery. Plants tolerate salt air and pollution and do well in coastal areas and in town gardens.
RECOMMENDED SPECIES AND VARIETIES
G. elliptica Silver-green catkins, composed of tiny flowers, grow to 15 cm (6 in) long on male plants. Female plants produce long clusters of purple-brown fruits in autumn. The rounded, frost-hardy plant has oval leaves, 7.5 cm (3 in) long, dark green above and grey beneath. Native to California and Oregon. HEIGHT & SPREAD 1×1 m (3×3 ft) after 5 years, ultimately 5 m (16 ft) tall.

▲ *Garrya elliptica* 'James Roof'

'James Roof'♀ is a vigorous male plant with catkins up to 20 cm (8 in) long.
CULTIVATION Grow in any well-drained soil in a sheltered position. Plants tolerate shade, but produce the best catkins when grown in sun. Protect from cold winter winds in northern gardens and ideally plant the shrubs against a wall.
PROPAGATION Take semi-ripe cuttings in summer.
PRUNING None usually necessary, but remove any dead wood or trim to keep a neat shape. Make any cuts immediately after flowering as catkins are borne on the previous season's wood.
PESTS AND DISEASES Usually trouble free.

x *Gaulnettya* see *Gaultheria*

Gaultheria
Ericaceae

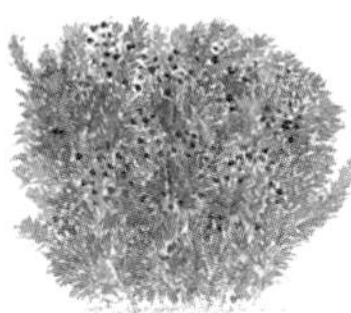
Gaultheria mucronata

Showy berries, shapely blooms and evergreen foliage give these small shrubs year-round appeal. Pitcher or bell-shaped white flowers during late spring and summer are followed by autumn and winter berries in shades of white, pink, red, blue or purple. Creeping species make excellent ground cover; more erect types are suited to a woodland or peat garden. The plants are fully to half hardy and require acid, moist soil. Native to the Americas, Asia and Australasia. The previously separate genera *Pernettya* and × *Gaulnettya* are now included in *gaultheria*.
RECOMMENDED SPECIES AND VARIETIES
G. cuneata♀ Nodding clusters of white, 6 mm (¼ in) long, urn-shaped flowers appear from late summer to early autumn on this compact, ground-covering species. The plant bears spherical white fruit in late summer. Glossy, leathery leaves up to 3 cm (1¼ in) long are of varied shape. HEIGHT & SPREAD 20-30 cm×1.8 m (8-12 in×6 ft).
G. miqueliana White or pink berries, 1 cm (⅜ in) across, appear on this ground-covering species in late summer following clusters of 6 mm (¼ in) long, urn-shaped white flowers during late spring and early summer. The rounded glossy leaves are 2-4 cm (¾-1½ in) long. HEIGHT & SPREAD 30×30 cm (12×12 in).
G. mucronata♀ (syn. *Pernettya mucronata*) White, pink, lilac, purple or red globular berries, 1 cm (⅜ in) across, appear on the female forms of this stiff, thickly branched shrub during late summer and autumn. Planting a male plant (which does not berry) with each female or group of females ensures a good crop of fruit. Oval to urn-shaped white flowers, around 6 mm (¼ in) long, appear in late spring and early summer and the shrub, which spreads by suckers to form a tight, prickly bush, is densely clothed with glossy, sharply pointed, dark green leaves up to 2 cm (¾ in) long. HEIGHT & SPREAD 45-150×150 cm (1½-5×5 ft).

▲ *Gaultheria mucronata* 'Bell's Seedling'

▲ *Gaultheria mucronata* 'Pink Pearl'

'Bell's Seedling'♀ self-fertile with deep red fruits, **'Crimsonia'**♀ carmine-red fruits, **'Mulberry Wine'**♀ maroon turning dark purple fruits, **'Pink Pearl'** lilac pink fruits, **'Sea Shell'**♀ light pink fruits turning clear pink, and **'Wintertime'**♀ pure white fruits.
G. procumbens♀ (wintergreen) This creeping species forms a glossy mat of broadly oval, leathery dark-green leaves that grow to 4 cm (1½ in) long. It has pinkish or white, 6 mm (¼ in) long, conical to urn-shaped flowers in mid to late summer followed by dark red fruit. HEIGHT & SPREAD 7.5-15 cm×1 m (3-6 in×3 ft).
G. shallon (salal) Deep shade does not deter this vigorous species which bears 6 mm (¼ in) long, pink-tinged white flowers in late spring and early summer. These broadly urn-shaped blooms are followed by rounded, red to dark purple berries in autumn. The oval to rounded, leathery, dark

g

green leaves are 5-10 cm (2-4 in) long. HEIGHT & SPREAD 1×1.5 m (3×5 ft).

G.* x *wisleyensis (syn. × *Gaulnettya wisleyensis*) Clusters of up to 15 pearl-white flowers open in late spring and early summer, followed by red fruits in autumn. This bushy species has pointed, oval to oblong dark green leaves up to 4 cm (1½ in) long. HEIGHT & SPREAD 1×1.5 m (3×5 ft).

▲ *Gaultheria* x *wisleyensis* 'Pink Pixie'

'Wisley Pearl' has crowded bunches of deep red fruits, **'Pink Pixie' has** pink-tinged flowers.

CULTIVATION Grow in moist, but not boggy, humus-rich soil. *G. shallon* excepted, the plants require a site with plenty of light and must not dry out in summer. Dwarf species prefer a peat bed but can be grown in containers if the roots are kept moist and cool in summer.

PROPAGATION Root from semi-ripe or ripe cuttings in a peat and grit or perlite medium with bottom heat if possible, or in a coldframe. Divide spreading species in autumn or early spring and grow in pots for the first season or two. Extract seed from the dried-out fruit and sow on peat in a coldframe. Prick out seedlings when they are large enough to handle. Cultivars will not come true from seed and bear berries of various colours.

PRUNING None usually required except to curb vigorous shoots in winter. Dig or pull out suckers.

PESTS AND DISEASES Usually trouble free.

Gaura

Onagraceae

Slender spikes of white flowers rise above lance-shaped leaves and make this graceful, late-flowering plant useful for a border or the sunny edges of a woodland garden. Flowers are sometimes pink or red. Of this genus of hardy annuals, biennials and herbaceous perennials, only one species, *Gaura lindheimeri*, is commonly grown.

RECOMMENDED SPECIES

G. lindheimeri ♀ White flowers suffused with pink, up to 2.5 cm (1 in) wide, bloom

▲ *Gaura lindheimeri*

in mid summer to mid autumn. Each flower lasts only a day. Flowers are carried in lax, open clusters on branched stems. Mid green, lance-shaped leaves are up to 7.5 cm (3 in) long. In Britain this plant is a short-lived perennial. Native to southern USA. HEIGHT & SPREAD 1.5 m×50 cm (5 ft×20 in).

CULTIVATION Plant in light, well-drained soil. Gauras prefer sun, but tolerate light shade. Some light staking may be necessary.

PROPAGATION Sow seed in a cool greenhouse or coldframe in early spring and put young plants out in flowering positions as soon as they are large enough, usually in late spring. The plants can seed freely.

PESTS AND DISEASES Usually trouble free.

Gay feather see *Liatris*

Gazania

Treasure flower

Compositae

Gazania rigens var. uniflora

Easily grown and very showy, daisy-flowered plants native to South Africa. Gazania flowers are mostly brown, orange, red and yellow and are very freely produced from mid summer to mid autumn. Their colours are enhanced by the foliage, which in many varieties is grey or silvery. The recommended plants are all tender herbaceous perennials, and will only survive outdoors in sheltered positions in milder areas of Britain. Elsewhere they can be lifted and overwintered in a cool greenhouse or raised annually from seed or cuttings. Gazanias close up in dull weather or in shade, a sunny position is therefore needed. The plants are fairly drought-tolerant and suitable for rockeries, banks and dry-stone walls, as well as for seaside gardens. They make good container plants.

RECOMMENDED SPECIES AND VARIETIES

G. rigens (syn. *G. splendens*) Orange flowers, 7 cm (2¾ in) across, are borne on stems up to 30 cm (1 ft) long from mid summer to mid autumn. The petals each have a black spot at the base forming a dark ring round the flower's yellow centre. The foliage clusters at ground level around the base of the flower stems. The narrow, dark green, oblong leaves are up to 12 cm (4¾ in) long with a silver underside. HEIGHT & SPREAD 30×30 cm (12×12 in).

The flowers of var. ***uniflora*** are yellow and it has felted silver foliage. **'Variegata'** ♀ has gold-and-cream variegated leaves.

GARDEN VARIETIES

Plant height is about 30 cm (1 ft), except where shown otherwise.

'Aztec' ♀ has cream flowers with a maroon ring round a yellow centre. It is silver foliaged. **'Chansonette' Series** ♀ produces flowers up to 8 cm (3¼ in) across, which are mainly bronze, orange and yellow; many have dark basal rings and dark

▲ *Gazania* 'Aztec'

Gazania 'Cookei' ▲

centres. Plants grow to 25 cm (10 in) tall and come true from seed. The flowers of **'Christopher'** are dark pink with a green centre. **'Cookei'** ♀ has grey foliage and orange flowers with an olive-green ring around a yellow centre. **'Cream Beauty'** has cream flowers and grey-green foliage. **'Daybreak Bright Orange'** has orange flowers with a darker basal ring, and silvery leaves. Plants grow to 20 cm (8 in) and come true from seed. The flowers of **'Mini-Star' Series** are up to 8 cm (3¼ in) across, white, pink, orange, yellow and bronze; many have dark rings around dark centres. Plants have deeply toothed silvery green leaves, grow to 20 cm (8 in) tall and come true from seed. **'Silver Beauty'** has yellow flowers with a black centre and deeply cut silver foliage. **'Sundance' Series** has very large flowers 10 cm (4 in) and more across, mainly in shades of bronze, orange and red. It grows to 30 cm (12 in) tall and comes true from seed. The flowers of the **'Talent' Series** ♀ have a very wide colour range – bronze, cream, pink, white and yellow. With silver-grey leaves, it grows to 20 cm (8 in) tall and comes true from seed.

▲ *Gazania* 'Talent' Series

▲ *Gazania* 'Talent' Series

CULTIVATION Plant in free-draining soil in a sunny site. Do not add nitrogen-rich fertiliser or manure. Plant when risk of hard frost has gone; if hardened-off, gazanias survive slight frosts undamaged. Deadhead regularly. To overwinter plants, lift in mid autumn, plant in 15 cm (6 in) deep boxes and place in a frost-free greenhouse.

PROPAGATION Sow seed under glass in early spring or take semi-ripe cuttings in late summer.

PESTS AND DISEASES Usually trouble free.

Genista

Papilionaceae

Showy bright yellow flowers bloom in spring or summer in racemes or clusters at the ends of rich green or grey-green shoots on these broom-like, hardy and half-hardy shrubs and small trees. In shape, the flowers are typical of the pea family and they are succeeded by small pods. Although most plants are deciduous, including those described, the shoots give them an evergreen appearance. The small leaves are simple or divided into three leaflets. Low-growing and prostrate shrubs may be planted to cascade over a dry-stone wall, clothe a sunny bank or adorn a rock garden, while larger shrubs and small trees make fine specimen plants. All species require a sunny position and well-drained soil; poor, sandy soil is most suitable for the larger shrubs and trees. The recommended plants are hardy, apart from *Genista* × *spachiana*, which is hardy only in mild areas. About 90 species are known, growing wild in much of Europe and W Asia.

RECOMMENDED SPECIES AND VARIETIES

G. aetnensis♀ (Mount Etna broom) From mid to late summer, the slender, arching branches of this elegant small tree are wreathed in small bright yellow flowers, followed by pods containing 2-3 seeds. The tiny narrow leaves are sparse or even absent from most of the broom-like shoots. The graceful habit of the tree enhances its value as a specimen plant. Native to Sicily. HEIGHT & SPREAD 1 m×45 cm (3×1½ ft) after 5 years, ultimately 8 m (26 ft) tall.

G. hispanica (Spanish gorse) Small golden yellow flowers are borne profusely in dense upright racemes, up to 4 cm (1½ in) long, on this low, rounded, softly spiny bush in early summer. It is especially tolerant of dry, sunny sites and poor soil. The small oval leaves are present only on the flowering shoots. Native to SW Europe. HEIGHT & SPREAD 30×30 cm (1×1 ft) after 5 years, ultimately 60×90 cm (2×3 ft).

G. lydia♀ Clusters, 5 cm (2 in) long, of deep yellow flowers are freely borne on much-branched prostrate green stems in late spring and early summer. The narrow, dark green leaves, 1 cm (⅜ in) long, are deciduous. Native to the Balkans. HEIGHT & SPREAD 10×30 cm (4×12 in) after 5 years, ultimately 30 cm (12 in) tall.

▲ *Genista hispanica*

▼ *Genista lydia*

G. pilosa (hairy greenweed) Solitary or paired, golden yellow flowers, 1 cm (⅜ in) long, are carried in great abundance along leafy stems. This shrub has small, ovate dark green leaves. Dwarf or prostrate forms are the most successful in the garden. Native to W and central Europe. HEIGHT & SPREAD 10-30×60 cm (4-12×24 in) after 5 years, ultimately 20-40 cm×1 m (8-16 in×3 ft).

'Goldilocks' is a low-spreading, bushy shrub that reaches 60 cm×1 m (2×3 ft). **'Procumbens'** forms prostrate mats up to 60 cm (2 ft) wide. **'Vancouver Gold'** is a compact dwarf form making a mound up to 45 cm (1½ ft) tall. **'Yellow Spreader'** has lemon-yellow flowers and spreads in low mats, reaching 30×90 cm (1×3 ft).

G. sagittalis Racemes, 5 cm (2 in) long, of deep yellow flowers are borne in late spring and early summer on the erect, broadly winged, dark green shoots of this mat-forming plant. The shoots also bear scattered, small elliptic leaves. Native to S and central Europe. HEIGHT & SPREAD 15×30 cm (6×12 in) after 5 years, ultimately 20×60 cm (8×24 in).

The shoots of ssp. ***delphinensis***♀ are silky hairy. It reaches 15×60 cm (6×24 in).

G. × spachiana Fragrant, rich yellow flowers bloom on slender racemes, up to 10 cm (4 in) long, from late winter to early spring. Three small oval leaflets, covered with silky hairs on the underside, make up the dark

▲ *Genista sagittalis*

▼ *Genista* × *spachiana*

green leaves. The plant is hardy only in very mild areas. HEIGHT & SPREAD 1×1m (3×3ft) after 5 years, ultimately 5×2m (16×6½ft).

G. ***tinctoria*** (dyer's greenweed) Golden yellow flowers are borne in profuse racemes, 6cm (2½in) long, at the ends of the branches throughout summer. Habit varies from prostrate to erect. Bright green deciduous leaves are divided into 3 narrow leaflets, up to 4cm (1½in) long. Native to much of Europe. HEIGHT & SPREAD 30cm-2m×45cm-1m (1-6½×1½-3ft).

'Flore Pleno'🏆 has long-lasting double flowers and is a low, sprawling shrub. It reaches just 30×45cm (12×18in). **'Royal Gold'**🏆 is erect but compact, and has showy, branched racemes of flowers. It reaches 60×60cm (2×2ft).

CULTIVATION Plant out in early autumn in any moderately fertile, well-drained soil in full sun. The larger shrubs and trees thrive on poor, sandy soils.

PROPAGATION Sow seeds of the species in a coldframe in early spring. Take cuttings of cultivars in late summer. Grow on singly in pots before planting out as they dislike root disturbance.

PRUNING Prune lightly in late winter but do not cut into old wood.

PESTS AND DISEASES Usually trouble free but plants may be affected by gall mites.

Gentiana

Gentian

Gentianaceae

Gentiana lutea

Valued for the vivid blues of their flowers, these hardy perennial plants range from small tufted or carpeting evergreens for the rock garden to large and imposing herbaceous border plants or woodlanders.

Although gentian flowers are known as being blue, they may also be white, yellow, purple or red. The flowers are trumpet, tubular or salver-shaped with four to seven lobes, usually five, and are borne singly or in clusters. The leaves are arranged in pairs or whorls along the stems.

The plants have exacting soil requirements which need to be satisfied if they are to grow well. Most spring and summer-flowering gentians are sun-loving and flourish in neutral to limy soils. They thrive in the well-drained conditions found in rock gardens, troughs, raised beds and in pots in an alpine house. However, *Gentiana asclepiadea* needs moister, leafy, woodland conditions and will grow among shrubs or other herbaceous perennials in partial shade. The stately *G. lutea* is a good border plant for a sunny position.

Most of the autumn-flowering types need an acid, moisture-retaining soil, rich in leaf-mould, and prefer a position in the rock garden out of the midday sun. *G. sino-ornata* is suitable for the front of the border and will also make an outstanding container plant. In warmer, drier parts of the country these autumn-flowering gentians benefit from dappled shade, but in cooler, more northerly regions they will flourish in more open situations. All the plants listed are hardy to at least -20°C (-4°F). Most gentians are poisonous.

RECOMMENDED SPECIES AND VARIETIES

G. ***acaulis***🏆 (syn. *G. kochiana*) (trumpet gentian) Erect trumpets of vivid blue flowers, up to 7cm (2¾in) long, are borne in spring. The flowers, with 5 triangular petal-lobes, have green markings on the outside and in the throat. These mat or low hummock-forming plants have deep green, rather leathery, oval or elliptical evergreen leaves up to 5cm (2in) long. Native to central and S Europe. Long-lived in the garden, this is one of the easiest and most reliable species. HEIGHT & SPREAD 12.5×50cm (5×20in).

'Krumrey' has deep kingfisher-blue flowers. **'Rannoch'**, only 5cm (2in) tall, has deep blue flowers that are striped with green and white.

G. ***angustifolia*** Sky-blue flowers appear in summer and are 5cm (2in) long, with some green markings in the throat. The lance-shaped leaves, up to 5cm (2in) long, are dull green. Native to the Pyrenees and SW Alps. HEIGHT & SPREAD 10×30cm (4×12in).

G. ***asclepiadea***🏆 (willow gentian) Trumpet-shaped azure-blue flowers, up to 4cm (1½in) long, have varying amounts of green spotting and white striping in the throat; they appear in summer, sometimes lasting into early autumn. The bright green, oval, unstalked leaves, 3-4cm (1¼-1½in) long, have a heart-shaped base and a pointed apex. Native to central Europe to Turkey and the Caucasus. HEIGHT & SPREAD 90×60cm (36×24in).

The flowers of var. ***alba*** are pure white. **'Knightshayes'** grows to 50cm (20in) and has deep blue flowers with a white throat.

G. ***clusii*** The trumpet-shaped, deep azure-blue flowers, up to 6cm (2½in) long, are borne in spring. The mats of deep green elliptical leaves, up to 5cm (2in) long, are leathery and very glossy. Native to the mountains of central and SE Europe where it grows on limestone. HEIGHT & SPREAD 14×50cm (5½×20in).

G. ***cruciata*** (cross gentian) Erect, bell-shaped azure-blue flowers, 2.5cm (1in) long, are carried in dense clusters and whorls in summer. The glossy, deep green leaves of this tufted herbaceous perennial are oval to lance-shaped. Basal rosette leaves grow to 20cm (8in) long. Native to mountain meadows and open woodland from central and S Europe to the Caucasus. HEIGHT & SPREAD 40×40cm (16×16in).

G. ***gracilipes*** (syn. *G. purdomii*) Solitary, narrow, bell-shaped flowers, 4cm (1½in) long, are deep purple-blue with a distinctive greenish tube and are borne in summer. The slender stems are branched and somewhat spreading at the base with up to 4 pairs of deep green, lance-shaped leaves 8-15cm (3¼-6in) long. Basal leaves grow to 15cm (6in) long. Native to NW China. HEIGHT & SPREAD 20×30cm (8×12in).

G. **'Inverleith'**🏆 Rich sky-blue, solitary, trumpet-shaped flowers, borne in autumn, have darker striping on the outside and are 7cm (2¾in) long. Thin, trailing stems bear linear mid green leaves up to 15cm (6in) long. HEIGHT & SPREAD 9×30cm (3½×12in).

G. ***kochiana*** see *G. acaulis*

G. ***lagodechiana*** see *G. septemfida* var. *lagodechiana*

▲ *Gentiana asclepiadea* var. *alba*

▼ *Gentiana asclepiadea*

Gentiana asclepiadea 'Knightshayes' ▼

▲ Gentiana lutea

▲ Gentiana septemfida

G. lutea (great yellow gentian) Tight whorls of yellow flowers, each 3cm (1¼in) long, appear in summer in leafy spikes. The rather fleshy, glaucous leaves are broadly elliptical and strongly ribbed with 3-7 main veins. The basal rosette leaves grow to 30cm (12in) long, the upper leaves are cupped in pairs below each flower cluster. Plants are slow to establish and may take 5 or more years to reach flowering size. Native to the mountains of central and S Europe. HEIGHT & SPREAD 120×80cm (4ft×32in).

G. × macaulayi♀ Deep blue, trumpet-shaped flowers, 6cm (2½in) long, with deeper stripes on the outside are borne in autumn. Mid green leaves are paired and linear. A free-flowering plant with a neat, compact habit. HEIGHT & SPREAD 8×20cm (3¼×8in).

'Kidbrooke Seedling' bears large deep blue flowers up to 7cm (2¾in) long. **'Kingfisher'** has large deep blue flowers, 7cm (2¾in) long. **'Praecox'** produces mid blue flowers from late summer onwards. **'Well's Variety'** (syn. *G. wellsii*) carries rather pale to mid blue flowers from late summer onwards.

G. purdomii see *G. gracilipes*

G. saxosa White bell-shaped flowers, up to 2cm (¾in) long, in summer and early autumn are either solitary or borne in small clusters. This short-lived plant forms a low evergreen mat or tuft of deep green, leathery spoon-shaped to lance-shaped leaves, 1-2cm (⅜-¾in) long, and often flushed purplish brown. Native to New Zealand where it grows in sand dunes and coastal rocks. HEIGHT & SPREAD 7×25cm (2¾×10in).

G. septemfida♀ Deep blue or purplish blue bell-shaped flowers with green spots in the throat are borne in clusters in summer and early autumn. The flowers, up to 4cm (1½in) long, often have 6 or 7 lobes. This easy-to-grow, long-lasting plant forms tufts of pointed, mid green leaves 2-4cm (¾-1½in) long. Native to the mountains of central and W Asia. HEIGHT & SPREAD 30×40cm (12×16in).

▼ Gentiana saxosa

The flowers of var. ***lagodechiana***♀ (syn. *G. lagodechiana*) are either solitary or in groups of 2-3. The plant will only reach a height of 10cm (4in). Usually borne in small groups, the flowers of var. ***lagodechiana* 'Hascombensis'** are rather larger and deeply coloured.

G. sino-ornata♀ (autumn gentian) Rich blue, trumpet-shaped flowers, 6cm (2½in) long, appear in autumn and are striped with darker blue and greenish yellow bands on the outside. The tufted plant is a herbaceous perennial with slender prostrate to trailing stems arising from a small crown. Rather pale to mid green leaves, 2-5cm (¾-2in) long, are paired, linear and pointed. Native to wet mountain meadows in SW China. HEIGHT & SPREAD 8×40cm (3¼×16in).

Gentiana sino-ornata

'Alba' has white flowers flushed green on the tube. **'Angel's Wings'** has white flowers with a flush of blue along the folds and deep green foliage. **'Edith Sarah'** deep blue flowers with neat white stripes. **'Mary Lyle'** white flowers with a flush of blue along the folds and deep green leaves.

G. × stevenagensis♀ Deep blue, funnel-shaped flowers, up to 7cm (2¾in) long, are spotted and striped greenish yellow within and appear in autumn. A free-flowering plant with mid green, lance-shaped leaves. HEIGHT & SPREAD 8×30cm (3¼×12in).

G. 'Strathmore'♀ Sky-blue, trumpet-shaped flowers borne in autumn are up to 7cm (2¾in) long and have silvery white stripes on the outside. The prostrate stems carry paired, linear mid green leaves. HEIGHT & SPREAD 7.5×25cm (3×10in).

G. ternifolia Pale to mid blue trumpet-shaped flowers, in late summer and autumn, are 5cm (2in) long. The prostrate stems form a small mat of grey-green linear leaves, up to 3cm (1¼in) long, usually in groups of 3. Native to the mountains of SW China. HEIGHT & SPREAD 6×20cm (2½×8in).

The flowers of **'Dali'** are mid sky-blue.

G. verna (spring gentian) Rich vivid blue, salver-shaped flowers, are about 2.5cm (1in) long and have a white centre. The flowers are borne in spring. The grey-green, lance-shaped to elliptical leaves, 2-3cm (¾-1¼in) long, are arranged in rosettes and form small mats or low hummocks. Native to Britain and mountain meadows and rocks of central and S Europe. HEIGHT & SPREAD 8×20cm (3¼×8in).

The flowers of ssp. ***angulosa*** are a deep sky-blue.

G. wellsii see *G. × macaulayi* 'Well's Variety'

CULTIVATION Spring and summer flowerers need a sunny position in well-drained, neutral to limy soil. However, *G. asclepiadea* needs dappled shade and a moister soil. Autumn flowerers need moisture-retaining, humus-rich acid soil; some shade is necessary in warmer, drier parts of the country.

PROPAGATION Sow seed the moment it is ripe or in autumn or winter. Overwinter in the open or in a coldframe. Alternatively, take semi-ripe cuttings any time after flowering to late summer. Divide spring-flowering gentians immediately after flowering. Divide autumn-flowering species in early spring. This is best done every 2 or 3 years as plants often begin to lose vigour.

PESTS AND DISEASES Gentians may be attacked by slugs, snails, aphids and thrips. Rust and stem rot may also infest the plants.

▲ Gentiana verna

▼ Gentiana sino-ornata

Geranium

Cranesbill
Geraniaceae

Geranium maderense

Easily grown free-flowering geraniums are outstanding garden plants that fit a whole range of diverse conditions and situations. Hardy and mainly perennial, they can transform problem places such as dry shade, hot sunny banks or moist shade and also provide dense ground cover.

Flower shapes are basically rounded, usually 2-4cm (¾-1½in) across, with five petals, varying from small and demure to large and eye-catching. Colours range through purple, pink, blue, mauve and white, with many intermediate shades, distinctive veining and contrasting centres.

The leaves have a long season of interest; many are evergreen and some have the bonus of autumn colour. They are basically circular, generally 2.5-12.5cm (1-5in) across, and divided into five or seven lobes which are intricately cut and subdivided.

Recommended plants are hardy unless stated otherwise. They are listed below by size: large geraniums 1.2m (4ft) and over; medium geraniums up to 1m (3ft); low-growing plants with trailing top growth up to 30cm (1ft) and low-growing plants with compact growth up to 30cm (1ft).

True geraniums should not be confused with the bedding and pot plants listed under the botanical name, *Pelargonium*.

RECOMMENDED SPECIES AND VARIETIES

LARGE GERANIUMS OVER 1M (3FT)

G. ***anemonifolium*** see *G. palmatum*

G. ***armenum*** see *G. psilostemon*

G. ***maderense***♀ Multibranched stems carry numerous round, purplish pink flowers with dark crimson centres and a network of pale veins. Shiny green leaves, up to 60cm (2ft) across, are divided and subdivided to give a stiff ferny appearance. Under glass it can flower from early spring to early summer. Native to Madeira, the plant needs to be grown in a warm greenhouse. HEIGHT & SPREAD 1.5×1.5m (5×5ft).

G. ***palmatum***♀ (syn. *G. anemonifolium*) The lavish flowers, borne from late spring to late summer, are rosy purple and dark throated. The large leaves are evergreen and are carried in rosettes on a short stem. Native to Madeira, it survives as a short-lived perennial in sheltered places, but otherwise needs a frost-free greenhouse. HEIGHT & SPREAD 1.2×1m (4×3ft).

▲ *Geranium psilostemon*

G. ***psilostemon***♀ (syn. *G. armenum*) Brilliant rounded flowers of bright magenta, strikingly black-eyed and veined, bloom from early summer to early autumn. The large, deeply cut leaves, over 20cm (8in) across at the base, give good autumn colour. Native to Turkey and the Caucasus. HEIGHT & SPREAD 1.2×1.05m (4×3½ft).

MEDIUM GERANIUMS UP TO 1M (3FT)

G. **'Brookside'** Bowl-shaped flowers, in early to late summer, are clear blue with a white centre. The large leaves are divided. HEIGHT & SPREAD 38×30cm (15×12in).

G. ***clarkei*** The large, upward-looking flowers bloom all summer and are variable in colour. The finely divided leaves form attractive low clumps. Native to Kashmir. HEIGHT & SPREAD 30×45cm (12×18in).

'Kashmir Pink' has clear pink flowers. **'Kashmir Purple'** has deep purple flowers. The warm white flowers of **'Kashmir White'** have deep pink veining.

G. ***endressii***♀ An indispensable ground-cover plant with jaggedly divided leaves, usually evergreen, that form a close mat. Bright pink flowers are borne from late spring to autumn. Cut back in mid summer for a longer season. Native to S Europe. HEIGHT & SPREAD 45×45cm (18×18in).

G. ***eriostemon*** see *G. platyanthum*

G. ***gracile*** Pale pink, upward-looking, funnel-shaped flowers with delicate dark veining bloom from late spring onwards. The 5-lobed leaves are light green. It grows best in cool, not too dry, shaded conditions. Native to Turkey and the Caucasus. HEIGHT & SPREAD 50×20cm (20×8in).

▼ *Geranium gracile*

▲ *Geranium himalayense* 'Gravetye'

G. ***himalayense*** A compact plant with big flowers and a long season. The deep violet-blue flowers have a central reddish flush. Dark green leaves are large and roundish with many subdivisions. The main flowering season is summer but can continue into autumn. Native to the Himalayas. HEIGHT & SPREAD 43×45cm (17×18in).

'Gravetye'♀ is a slightly smaller plant with a more pronounced red centre to the larger flowers. The fully double flowers of **'Plenum'** (syn. 'Birch Double') are rich lilac-blue shading to purple at the centre. The plant has a more compact habit.

G. **'Johnson's Blue'**♀ Flat, open flowers of clear blue with a paler centre bloom from late spring to autumn. An ideal edging plant with low mounds of finely cut leaves. HEIGHT & SPREAD 30×30cm (12×12in).

G. ***maculatum*** Many round flowers, pale purplish pink with a white centre, are carried in late spring to mid summer above distinctive leaves widely divided into 5 or 7 sections. The plant grows best in soil that does not dry out. Native to N America. HEIGHT & SPREAD 60×45cm (24×18in).

Growing to 45cm (18in), f. ***albiflorum*** is smaller with pure white flowers and golden stamens. The paler green leaves emphasise the two-tone green mottling.

G. x ***magnificum***♀ Rich violet-blue flowers in early summer have broad notched petals and a red suffusion in the centre. Dark green matt leaves colour in autumn and provide good ground cover. HEIGHT & SPREAD 60×60cm (24×24in).

G. **'Nimbus'** Violet-blue flowers with widely spaced petals give the effect of stars floating over clouds of very finely cut, light green leaves. The plant flowers from late spring to mid summer. It increases gradually at the base, but is balanced by quite voluminous top growth. HEIGHT & SPREAD 60cm×1m (2×3ft).

G. x ***oxonianum*** Funnel-shaped flowers in shades of pink, often strongly veined, are borne for a long season, usually from spring to autumn if trimmed back at mid summer. Unless otherwise stated the cultivars listed below make good clumps of dark green leaves. The varieties are all hybrids between *G. endressii* and *G. versicolor*. HEIGHT & SPREAD 75×75cm (2½×2½ft).

'A.T. Johnson'🏆 has light pink flowers, becoming darker at maturity. It grows up to 30cm (12in) tall. The large flowers of **'Claridge Druce'** are deep pink with darker veins. A strong growing plant, up to 1m (3ft) high, its clumps of dark green leaves stay evergreen in winter and are quite a feature. **'Rose Clair'** has clear pink, faintly veined flowers. **'Thurstonianum'** is a large plant, up to 1m (3ft) tall. The distinctive flowers have very narrow petals set wide apart, rich purple in the best forms. Flowers bloom from early summer until early autumn. **'Walter's Gift'** has shiny green leaves with a reddish brown central area and is useful for foliage effect. The flowers are mid pink with intricate darker veining. The round flowers of **'Wargrave Pink'**🏆 are a rich creamy pink. **'Winscombe'** has flowers that open white and age to shades of pink.

G. phaeum (dusky cranesbill) Small, very dark purplish red flowers are slightly reflexed with a silky texture and are borne from late spring into autumn above broad dark leaves which are evergreen. The plant is tolerant of dry shade. Native to Europe. HEIGHT & SPREAD 60×45cm (24×18in).

'Album' has pure white flowers with golden anthers. **'Lily Lovell'** has large, rich violet-blue flowers with a paler centre. The leaves are paler green. **'Samobor'** is an outstanding foliage plant with large, round, bright green leaves with a distinct chocolate-brown ring. The small dark flowers bloom for a shorter season. The leaves of **'Variegatum'** are wide and dark green with areas of paler green and cream, and red spots between the divisions.

G. platyanthum (syn. *G. eriostemon*) Rather flat, pale violet-blue flowers are borne from spring and early summer. Large, dark green leaves with shallow lobes take on autumn colour. Native to Asia. HEIGHT & SPREAD 45-60×45cm (18-24×18in).

G. pogonanthum From mid to late summer this graceful plant bears mid purplish pink reflexed flowers. The leaves, marbled in light and dark green, are sharply toothed and lobed. The plant prefers some shade. Native to the Far East. HEIGHT & SPREAD 45-60×15cm (18-24×6in).

G. pratense (meadow cranesbill) A native plant that bears a succession of large, round flowers in clear mid blue. Dark green leaves with jagged divisions are cut into 7 or 9 and then subdivided. HEIGHT & SPREAD 60-100×100cm (24-36×36in).

The flowers of f. ***albiflorum*** are pure white. **'Mrs Kendall Clark'**🏆 has big flat flowers in pale lavender-blue with raised white veining. **'Plenum Caeruleum'** has many small, loosely petalled double flowers. They are soft lavender-blue with a reddish centre and appear in late summer. **'Plenum Violaceum'**🏆 is more compact and flowers a little later. The petals of the double flowers are more symmetrically arranged in a tight rosette that is rich violet shading to mauve at the centre. **'Striatum'** (syn. 'Bicolor') can have blue or white flowers. Some forms are mainly white with random streaks and spots of blue. Others are either blue or white with one or more petals of the alternative colour.

▲ *Geranium sylvaticum* 'Album'

***G. psilostemon* 'Bressingham Flair'** Soft purple flowers with dark brown centres appear from early to late summer on this compact plant with deeply cut leaves. HEIGHT & SPREAD 80×50cm (32×20in).

G. reflexum Small, dull rose-pink flowers with a white centre, borne in late spring to early summer, are distinctively reflexed. Native to Italy, Croatia and N Greece. HEIGHT & SPREAD 60×45cm (24×18in).

G. robustum Purplish pink flowers with pale centres bloom through summer amid very finely cut, greyish green leaves. Native to South Africa, it is best planted in sun and overwinters and seeds in most areas. HEIGHT & SPREAD 60×45cm (24×18in).

G. sinense Each flower has a small flat ring of very dark purple, almost black, velvety petals, long reddish pink filaments and black anthers. Downward-facing, reflexed flowers in late summer are best viewed in a raised position. The leaves are mottled in two shades of green. Native to China. HEIGHT & SPREAD 60×40cm (24×16in).

***G.* 'Spinners'** From late spring onwards a long succession of bowl-shaped flowers in rich bluish purple are borne above big clumps of well cut, dark green leaves. HEIGHT & SPREAD 1m×75cm (3ft×30in).

G. sylvaticum The main flush of upward-facing flowers, violet-blue with a white centre, occurs in early summer. The plant can then be cut back to produce a fresh crop of leaves and later flowers. The large, fresh green leaves are deeply divided with the divisions profusely lobed and toothed nearly to the base. Native to Europe. HEIGHT & SPREAD 30-70×38cm (12-28×15in).

'Album'🏆 has pure white flowers with green centres. The more compact **'Amy Doncaster'** has round blue flowers with a white eye. **'Mayflower'**🏆 has bright violet-blue flowers with a small white eye.

G. versicolor White trumpet-shaped flowers, intricately veined with magenta, are borne from late spring to early autumn on this bushy plant. The clumps of evergreen leaves are shiny green with reddish brown markings. Native to Europe. HEIGHT & SPREAD 30×30cm (12×12in).

G. wlassovianum Young leaves in spring are bright shiny green with a chocolate-brown suffusion spreading from the centre. The late summer flowers are dark violet-purple with darker veins and continue into autumn to contrast with the oldest leaves which turn red. Native to Siberia. HEIGHT & SPREAD 30×30cm (12×12in).

LOW-GROWING PLANTS WITH TRAILING TOP GROWTH UP TO 30CM (1FT)

***G.* 'Ann Folkard'** Large bright purple flowers, black-centred and veined, bloom from mid summer until the first frosts. The young leaves are flushed with bright gold. HEIGHT & SPREAD 30×90cm (1×3ft).

G. asphodeloides Elongated flowering stems above mounds of mid green leaves weave through neighbouring plants and carry star-shaped flowers in pale purple, pink or white, sometimes with darker veining from mid to late summer. Trim back top growth after the first flush of flowers. Native to S Europe. HEIGHT & SPREAD 30×38cm (12×15in).

G. macrorrhizum Broadly lobed, evergreen leaves are strongly aromatic and take on autumn and winter colour. A drought-resistant plant, it is ideal for ground cover and forms a close mat. Small magenta flowers are borne from late spring to early summer. Native to Europe. HEIGHT & SPREAD 25×60cm (10×24in).

Geranium macrorrhizum

The flowers of **'Album'**🏆 are a very pale pink although late flowers are more truly white. **'Ingwersen's Variety'**🏆 has clear

▲ *Geranium macrorrhizum* 'Ingwersen's Variety'

pink flowers. **'Variegatum'** produces pink flowers and makes a splendid foliage plant with grey-green leaves that have strong cream markings.

G. procurrens Subdued purple flowers with a dark eye are carried from mid summer to autumn. The long, prostrate, flowering stems root at the nodes to form new plants which repeat the process. It can be diverted by training it up or through small shrubs. The toothed leaves have 5 large divisions. Native to the Himalayas. HEIGHT & SPREAD 15 cm × 1 m (6×36 in).

***G. × riversleaianum* 'Russell Prichard'**♀ has neat mats of small, greyish green leaves with bright rosy magenta flowers from mid summer onwards. HEIGHT & SPREAD 23×45 cm (9×18 in).

'Mavis Simpson' also makes neat mats with soft pink flowers, flecked with white.

***G.* 'Salome'** A trailing plant whose rounded flowers in summer are pale violet-purple with dark centres and veining. Young leaves are blotched with yellow. HEIGHT & SPREAD 30 cm × 1 m (12×36 in).

G. wallichianum Mauve-blue, star-shaped flowers, borne from late summer into autumn, have very striking black stamens, stigma and veining. The leaves are mottled. Native to the Himalayas. HEIGHT & SPREAD 25 cm × 1 m (10×36 in).

'Buxton's Variety'♀ (syn. 'Buxton's Blue') The round, cupped flowers of clear blue have a white zone at the centre and are often at their best at the end of the season when the leaves take on autumn colour. It is best grown in cool semi-shade.

LOW-GROWING PLANTS WITH COMPACT GROWTH UP TO 30 CM (1 FT)

***G. × cantabrigiense* 'Cambridge'** Small, bright pink flowers bloom in abundance from late spring into summer on this compact, mat-forming plant. The small, neat, aromatic leaves are usually evergreen. HEIGHT & SPREAD 25×30 cm (10×12 in).

The flowers of **'Biokovo'** are white tinged with pink.

G. cinereum Round, pale pink flowers with darker veins bloom from late spring to early summer above dainty tufts of grey-green, deeply divided leaves. Grows best in well-drained soil in sun. HEIGHT & SPREAD 15×23 cm (6×9 in).

'Ballerina'♀ The pale purplish pink flowers of this small alpine geranium have dark brown centres and feathered veins and bloom from early to late summer. Small, grey-green leaves form mats. The small but showy rockery plant var. *subcaulescens*♀ carries crimson-magenta flowers with a black eye in early summer. The leaves are scalloped and grey-green. **'Splendens'**♀ has round, bright magenta-pink flowers with a small white area at the base of the petals and a dark centre.

G. dalmaticum♀ An alpine species best grown in a raised or scree bed that has clear rose-pink flowers all summer. The small, shiny green, red-edged leaves take on autumn colour before dying back. HEIGHT & SPREAD 10×25 cm (4×10 in).

'Album' has pure white flowers.

G. farreri♀ A dwarf alpine plant with pale pink flowers borne in late spring to early summer and small, delicately cut leaves. Native to W China. HEIGHT & SPREAD 12.5×10 cm (5×4 in).

G. malviflorum Eye-catching flowers in mid to late spring are clear violet-blue with strongly marked veins. The plant dies back after flowering. Finely cut leaves appear in autumn, persisting through the winter. A hot dry site is essential for a good show of flowers. Native to Spain and N Africa. HEIGHT & SPREAD 30×25 cm (12×10 in).

G. nodosum Small, light purplish pink flowers bloom through summer to autumn. The leaves are shiny green. It is a good shade plant. Native to central Europe. HEIGHT & SPREAD 30×40 cm (12×16 in).

G. pylzowianum Deep pink flowers bloom in early summer among plain green finely cut leaves which last through winter. Too invasive for the rockery, it is best in poor soil in paving or beside a path. Native to China. HEIGHT & SPREAD 10×20 cm (4×8 in).

G. renardii♀ A low, clump-forming alpine with rounded, grey-green leaves, scalloped in appearance with a soft texture. Off-white flowers with violet veins bloom in mid summer. Best grown in well-drained soil in a sunny spot. Native to the Caucasus. HEIGHT & SPREAD 30×25 cm (12×10 in).

Geranium sanguineum

G. sanguineum (bloody cranesbill) Round, bright purple flowers bloom in late spring to late summer on this low-growing alpine. Deeply divided leaves form solid mats of dark green, which colour well in autumn. HEIGHT & SPREAD 25×40 cm (10×16 in).

▲ *Geranium sanguineum*

'Album'♀ has pure white, star-shaped flowers. The large, bright magenta-pink flowers of **'Cedric Morris'** are crumpled-looking. **'Glenluce'** has large, soft pink flowers. **'Shepherd's Warning'**♀ is a good wall plant with clear shocking-pink flowers. The flowers of var. ***striatum***♀ (syn. var. *lancastriense*) are palest pink with crimson centres and veining.

Geranium sanguineum 'Glenluce' ▼

▼ *Geranium sanguineum* 'Album'

▲ *Geranium sanguineum* var. *striatum*

Geranium sessiliflorum ssp. *novae-zelandiae* 'Nigricans' ▲

***G. sessiliflorum* ssp. *novae-zelandiae* 'Nigricans'** A very small, mat-forming plant which requires careful placing to show off the miniature clumps of small, very dark brown to bottle-green leaves with minute white flowers almost obscured among them. The plant is native to New Zealand.

▼ *Geranium cinereum* 'Ballerina'

▼ *Geranium renardii*

▼ *Geranium sanguineum* 'Shepherd's Warning'

HEIGHT & SPREAD 10×12.5 cm (4×5 in).

'Porter's Pass' has dark red leaves.

G. traversii var. ***elegans*** Small, mid to pale pink flowers with paler edges are borne in early summer to early autumn above rounded greyish green leaves. Native to the Chatham Islands, this alpine-type plant is not entirely hardy in Britain. It does best in sun in well-drained soil. HEIGHT & SPREAD 15-20×20 cm (6-8×8 in).

CULTIVATION Geraniums adapt to any type of soil, even chalk. Larger varieties tolerate shade, and often prefer it. True alpines or alpine types require a sunny, well-drained position. Cut back larger, clump-forming plants after flowering, to prevent overseeding and to produce new growth.

PROPAGATION Division is easy with most of the medium-sized, clump-forming plants, usually at the end of summer, but also in spring. Most species come true from seed, but not hybrids and named cultivars, which should be propagated by division. Species which form thick roots, such as *G. pratense* and *G. sanguineum,* can be propagated by root division and root cuttings.

Take softwood cuttings of new growth early in the year for alpines such as *G. cinereum* which make plants too small for easy division. Root cuttings may also be taken in late autumn.

PESTS AND DISEASES Rabbits may feast on young leaves. Vine weevil may attack plants with thick rootstocks. *G. pratense* is susceptible to mildew in hot dry weather.

Geranium see also *Pelargonium*

Gerbera

Barbeton daisy
Compositae

Valued for their brightly coloured daisy-like flowers, these half-hardy and tender perennials are mostly grown indoors in Britain, although they may survive outdoors in mild, sheltered areas of the south and west.

Flowers are available in a wide range of colours, including yellow, orange, cream, pink, crimson and purple. The lance-shaped, hairy, mid green leaves are prominently lobed and arranged in rosettes. They will flower for much of the year, if well cared for, and keep some leaves all year round. Gerberas make excellent, long-lasting cut flowers.

RECOMMENDED SPECIES

G. jamesonii Numerous solitary yellow, orange or bright red flowers, 7.5-13 cm (3-5 in) across, are borne from late spring to late summer. Single and double-flowered hybrids and varieties are available. The plant forms an upright clump with leaves, generally evergreen, up to 40 cm (16 in) long. Native to South Africa. HEIGHT & SPREAD 60×45 cm (24×18 in).

▲ *Gerbera jamesonii*

CULTIVATION Grow in deep pots or a permanent position in a border, in a bright, well-lit, frost-free greenhouse or conservatory. Plant in spring, preferably in a richly organic, but free-draining soil. It can be up to 2 years before seed-raised specimens flower freely, although occasional blossoms appear in the first year. Feed plants liberally with a liquid houseplant fertiliser when they are in flower. Water well in spring and summer, sparingly in autumn and winter. Remove faded flowerheads and leaves.

Outdoors, grow in ordinary, well-drained garden soil, in a sunny, sheltered position at the foot of a wall. Cut faded flower stems down to ground level.

PROPAGATION Sow seed under glasss or divide established plants into single crowns in early spring.

PESTS AND DISEASES Red spider mites, mealy bugs and vine weevils may all be troublesome.

Germander see *Teucrium*

Geum

Avens
Rosaceae

Geum chiloense 'Dolly North'

Vibrant globular or cup-shaped blooms in shades of white, yellow, red and orange add impact to the front of a herbaceous border or a large rock garden. The flowers are produced throughout summer, and can be single, semidouble or double. These hardy evergreen or deciduous perennials are best-suited to soil that is moist but well-drained.

▼ *Geum chiloense* 'Fire Opal'

RECOMMENDED SPECIES AND VARIETIES

G. chiloense Bright, single scarlet flowers, up to 5 cm (2 in) across, are carried in erect, laxly branched clusters in summer. This clump-forming plant has rather woolly, 3-lobed leaves. The stem leaves are smaller and more deeply cut or toothed than the basal ones. Native to Chile. HEIGHT & SPREAD 80×50 cm (32×20 in).

'Dolly North' grows to 50 cm (20 in) tall and bears single yellow flowers flushed orange. **'Fire Opal'**♀ grows to 75 cm (30 in) tall and has semidouble orange flowers, flushed scarlet, on purple stems. **'Georgenberg'** is a compact plant, 25 cm (10 in) tall, with single orange flowers flushed gold. **'Lady Stratheden'**♀ grows to 60 cm (24 in) tall and carries bright yellow semidouble flowers with green stamens. **'Mrs J. Bradshaw'**♀ is 60 cm (24 in) tall and has bright brick-red flowers that are semi-double and rounded. **'Mrs J. Bradshaw Improved'** has flowers twice the size.

▲ *Geum chiloense* 'Mrs J. Bradshaw'

G. coccineum Bright red single flowers, up to 4 cm (1½ in) across, are borne in erect, lax clusters in summer and early autumn. The deep green, kidney-shaped basal leaves have 5-7 toothed segments and are rather hairy. Native to the Balkans. HEIGHT & SPREAD 45×40 cm (18×16 in).

▲ *Geum coccineum* 'Borisii'

'Borisii', up to 30 cm (12 in) tall, is compact and has single orange-red flowers with prominent yellow stamens. **'Coppertone'** is an early-flowering plant that grows up to 25 cm (10 in) tall and bears single apricot

flowers against clumps of fresh green leaves.

G. 'Coppertone' see *G. coccineum* 'Coppertone'

G. x *intermedium* The semi-nodding flowers, 2.5cm (1in) across, can be cream, cream flushed with pink, or pale to mid yellow flushed with pink or copper. It is useful for moist places or for a wild garden. HEIGHT & SPREAD 50x40cm (20x16in).

G. *montanum* ♀ (alpine or mountain avens) Bright yellow cupped or wide-spreading flowers, up to 4cm (1½in) across, appear in late spring and early summer, occasionally later. Borne singly or in groups of 2-3 on short, branched stems these flowers are followed by fluffy seedheads that are reddish at first, turning pale brown. The deep green, mostly basal leaves are pinnately lobed with a large end leaflet. This clump-forming plant has thick, slowly creeping rhizomes. Native to the mountains of central and S Europe, this is a good rock-garden plant. HEIGHT & SPREAD 15x30cm (6x12in).

G. 'Mrs Bradshaw' see *G. chiloense* 'Mrs J. Bradshaw'

G. *rivale* (water avens, Indian chocolate) The bell-shaped, nodding single flowers, up to 3cm (1¼in) across, have pink or cream petals and a contrasting brownish purple calyx. Borne in airy sprays in late spring and summer the flowers are followed by fluffy seedheads. The mid to deep green basal leaves of these clump-forming, rhizomatous plants have up to 13 leaflets, the stem leaves have 3 leaflets. Native to wet places in many parts of Europe and W Asia. HEIGHT & SPREAD 50x70cm (20x28in).

'Album' grows to 30cm (12in) tall and has white flowers with paler green leaves. **'Leonard's Variety'** grows to 30cm (12in) tall and has broad, bell-shaped coppery pink flowers flushed orange against deep green foliage. **'Lionel Cox'** grows to 30cm (12in) tall and has primrose-yellow flowers flushed apricot against pale green foliage.

G. *urbanum* Erect, saucer-shaped pale yellow flowers, 1.5cm (½in) across, are borne singly on slender, branched stems in summer and early autumn. The leaves have 3-11 dark green toothed leaflets. This clump-forming rhizomatous plant can become a weed and is best left to naturalise in a wild garden. Native to much of Europe and W Asia. HEIGHT & SPREAD 60x40cm (24x16in).

▼ *Geum rivale* 'Album'

CULTIVATION Grow in any moist but well-drained soil in a sunny position. *G. rivale* also thrives in damp, cool and shady spots.

PROPAGATION Divide in autumn or early spring. Alternatively, sow seed in a cold-frame in winter.

PESTS AND DISEASES Usually trouble free.

Gilia

Birds' eyes
Polemoniaceae

Feathery foliage on slender stems and charming clusters of flowers from mid summer to early autumn earn these plants a place in the border. The genus contains annuals, biennials and perennials although the latter two are not widely grown. The hardy annuals described below are native to dry regions of W United States.

RECOMMENDED SPECIES AND VARIETIES

G. *achilleifolia* Violet-blue funnel-shaped flowers, 2.5cm (1in) across, appear in dense, fan-shaped clusters on a bushy, branching plant. The mid green leaves are slightly sticky. HEIGHT & SPREAD 60x20cm (24x8in).

G. *aggregata* see *Ipomopsis aggregata*

G. *capitata* This plant is similar to *G. achilleifolia* in habit and foliage. The tiny lavender-blue tubular flowers, however, are carried in dense rounded heads, up to 4cm (1½in) across. The flowers are good for cutting. HEIGHT & SPREAD 60x20cm (24x8in).

▲ *Gilia capitata*

G. *rubra* see *Ipomopsis rubra*

G. *tricolor* (birds' eyes) Small clusters of 2cm (¾in) wide bell-shaped flowers are borne by this plant. The flowers are blue or violet with a darker ring at the centre. HEIGHT & SPREAD 40x25cm (16x10in).

'Snow Queen' has white flowers with golden throats.

CULTIVATION Grow in light, well-drained soil in a sunny situation. On heavier soils the plants do best in a raised bed. The slender stems may need some twiggy supports. Deadhead frequently to prolong flowering.

PROPAGATION Sow seed in spring where the plants are to grow. In particularly sheltered positions early-autumn sowing is often successful, too. Gilias can be grown as pot plants to flower in late winter and spring in cool or unheated greenhouses by sowing seed directly into 13cm (5in) pots in early autumn. Thin to 3 or 4 plants per pot and keep the seedlings dry in winter.

PESTS AND DISEASES Powdery mildew may require control.

Gilia, scarlet see *Ipomopsis aggregata*

Gillenia

Bowman's root, Indian physic
Rosaceae

Dainty white flowers show to advantage against dark green foliage in mid summer on this hardy herbaceous perennial. The plant recommended here, *Gillenia trifoliata*, is best suited to a herbaceous or mixed border or woodland margin. Native to the woods of eastern and central N America.

RECOMMENDED SPECIES AND VARIETIES

G. *trifoliata* ♀ White flowers 1cm (⅜in) across, with red calyxes, appear in loose clusters on tall, branched, red-green stems up to 5cm (2in) long. Each flower has 5 lance-shaped petals. The plant forms a rounded clump with tough, wiry stems. The lance-shaped leaflets, up to 7cm (2¾in) long, are arranged in groups of 3. HEIGHT & SPREAD 1.2mx60cm (4x2ft).

▲ *Gillenia trifoliata*

CULTIVATION Plant in any fertile soil, preferably neutral to acid, in spring. This woodland plant prefers partial shade, but tolerates a sunny site if the soil is moist. Support stems by staking with twigs.

PROPAGATION Sow seed in a greenhouse or coldframe in late winter and plant out in spring or early summer. Seed-raised plants not ready for planting out until early summer will flower in late summer and early autumn. Divide established plants in spring or autumn.

PESTS AND DISEASES Usually trouble free.

Ginger, kahili see *Ipomopsis aggregata*

Ginkgo

Ginkgoaceae

Ginkgo biloba

The brilliant golden autumn foliage and distinctive leaves are the main features of this remarkable deciduous conifer. *Ginkgo biloba* is the sole species of the genus and is thought to be the only survivor from a group of trees that died out millions of years ago. The bark is dark grey, and becomes fissured on mature trees. Ginkgos tolerate urban pollution.

Ginkgo biloba ♡ (maidenhair tree) This hardy, slow-growing tree is conical at first, spreading as it matures. The beautiful leathery leaves, the only tree leaves with a fan shape, are often 7.5 cm (3 in) across and have a notch in the outer edge. Pale green

▲ *Ginkgo biloba*

Ginkgo biloba 'Variegata' ▲

in spring, they darken with age and turn a wonderful butter yellow in autumn. The male and female flowers, appearing with the leaves, are carried on separate trees but are insignificant. The female flowers go on to develop foul-smelling, olive-like fruits so it is advisable to plant male ginkgo trees. Native to China. HEIGHT & SPREAD 5×2 m (16×6½ ft) after 20 years, ultimately 18 m (60 ft) tall.

'Pendula' is smaller than the species and has weeping branches. **'Variegata'** has creamy white variegated leaves.

CULTIVATION Plant in spring or autumn in any well-drained soil in sun or partial shade.
PROPAGATION Raise from seed in spring. Alternatively take semi-ripe cuttings in summer.
PRUNING None is required.
PESTS AND DISEASES Usually trouble free.

Gladiolus

Sword lily
Iridaceae

Gladiolus carneus

Spectacular spikes of vibrant funnel-shaped flowers make gladioli ideal flowers for cutting. The large-flowered hybrids have huge, showy blooms in nearly every colour except blue. The flowers are made up of 6 petals and are arranged on a thick stem, more or less facing in the same direction, above the ribbed, basal, sword-like leaves.

In many, each flower has the upper central petal extended forward, like a hood, with the side petals slightly reflexed. The blooms are often attractively shaded, flecked or streaked with another hue and the petal edges may be plain, frilled or fluted. For the longest vase-life, water the plants before cutting the flower stems just as the first two or three flowers have opened.

Although these gaudy and striking hybrids can be grown in a border, the smaller hybrids and more modest species are easier to associate with other plants. The species, in particular, make dainty punctuation marks when planted in irregular clumps in a mixed border.

All gladioli are cormous perennials and most of those grown in gardens are not completely hardy, originating as they do from southern and central Africa. The corms need lifting in autumn.

Gladioli have been extensively hybridised which accounts for the large number available in all their glorious colour variations. The hybrids are grouped according to their common origins, although it is not possible to attach individual hybrids to specific parent species.

▼ *Gladiolus callianthus*

▲ *Gladiolus carneus*

▲ *Gladiolus papilio*

RECOMMENDED SPECIES AND VARIETIES

G. callianthus ♡ (syn. *Acidanthera bicolor* var. *murieliae)*. Tall spikes of white flowers with dark red or purplish throats appear from late summer to early autumn. The flowers are highly scented, up to 5 cm (2 in) across, with 2-10 displayed on each stem. HEIGHT 70 cm-1 m (2 ft 4 in-3 ft).

'Murieliae' is slightly more robust, with flowers up to 7.5 cm (3 in) across.

G. carneus (painted lady) Loose spikes of 3-12 funnel-shaped flowers are displayed from late spring to summer. The blooms, up to 5 cm (2 in) across, can be cream, white, mauve or pink with a red or purple marking on the lower petals and dark blotches in the throats. HEIGHT 30 cm-1 m (1-3 ft).

G. communis ssp. ***byzantinus*** ♡ Dense spikes of deep purple-red flowers, 5 cm (2 in) long with narrow pale marks outlined in dark purple on the lower lobes, appear from late spring to summer. This species, hardier than most, is widely grown in southern Britain as a flower for cutting. It self-seeds readily. HEIGHT 60 cm-1 m (2-3 ft).

G. papilio Bell-shaped, nodding greenish yellow flowers, 4 cm (1½ in) across and flushed purple, are displayed 3-10 per stem from mid summer to early autumn. The plant spreads by rhizomes. HEIGHT 1 m (3 ft).

G. tristis ♀ (marsh Africaner) Loose spikes of 1-13 scented flowers appear in mid to late summer. The flowers are 5cm (2in) across in white, cream or pale yellow tinged with green and flushed reddish brown. HEIGHT 30cm-1.5m (1-5ft).

LARGE-FLOWERED HYBRIDS

The large-flowered hybrids produce magnificent spikes of flowers, each bloom reaching an impressive 18cm (7in) across, from mid summer to early autumn. These vigorous plants may need staking as they reach a height of 1-1.2m (3-4ft).

▲ *Gladiolus* 'Nova Lux'

▲ *Gladiolus* 'Wind Song'

Gladiolus 'The Bride'▲

'Nova Lux' is golden yellow. **'Peter Pears'** is orange. **'Trader Horn'** is bright scarlet. **'Fidelio'** has purple flowers with a white blotch. **'Wind Song'** has pinkish mauve blooms with a white blotch.

▼ *Gladiolus* 'Seraphin'

BUTTERFLY HYBRIDS

Appearing from mid to late summer, the flowers of these hybrids grow to 10cm (4in) across and are closely packed on the flower spikes. Many cultivars bear flowers with contrasting colours in the throat and some have ruffled petals. They grow to 1-1.2m (3-4ft) tall.

'Jupiter' has golden yellow flowers with red throats. **'Seraphin'** has delicately ruffled pink flowers with white throats. **'Pop Art'** is light cerise, with the lower petals flushed white. **'Green Woodpecker'** ♀ bears greenish yellow flowers with a reddish blotch at the centre of the throat. **'Tinkerbelle'** has orange flowers with yellow throats.

PRIMULINUS HYBRIDS

The flowers of the primulinus hybrids are up to 9cm (3½in) across with the top petal markedly hooded. They appear in loose spikes from mid to late summer. The plants reach a height of 60cm-1m (2-3ft).

'Columbine' has pastel-pink blooms with white throats and a darker marking at the base of the petals. **'Leonore'** has lemon-yellow flowers. **'Robin'** is a light purplish red. **'White City'** has pure white flowers.

MINIATURE HYBRIDS

Also know as Nanus hybrids, these are grown in clumps in borders. Flowers up to 5cm (2in) across are carried in densely packed spikes from early to mid summer. The plants grow to 60cm-1m (2-3ft) tall.

'Amanda Mahy' has bright salmon-red flowers with pale mauve blotches in the centre of the petals. **'Charm'** has purplish pink flowers with a creamy blotch in the centre of the petals. **'Guernsey Glory'** has deep rose pink flowers with red edges and creamy blotches in the centre of the petals. **'Perky'** has deep pink blooms with white centres. **'Robinetta'** ♀ has deep purplish red blooms with a creamy blotch on the lower petal. **'The Bride'** ♀ has pure white flowers.

CULTIVATION Plant in a well-manured, well-drained soil that is neutral to slightly acidic. Choose a sunny site and plant the corms 10-15cm (4-6in) deep and 15-20cm (6-8in) apart on a layer of sand in spring. Use a fungicidal dip before planting.

Only the very large hybrids need staking. Put the stakes in on the opposite side to the flower buds and secure with wire rings.

Lift the corms in mid autumn. When they have dried, discard the old corm which is beneath the new one. Clean and remove the many small cormlets formed during the summer. Store in a cool but frost-free place until the following spring.

PROPAGATION Gladioli are easily increased from cormlets formed during the growing season, but these can take 1-3 years to flower. Plant in rows about 5cm (2in) deep and 1cm (⅜in) apart with a layer of sharp sand above and below the cormlet. Keep the young plants weed free and well watered, lifting and treating the cormlets in the same manner as for adult corms.

Alternatively sow seed in early spring into a sandy soil mix. The seedlings take 2-3 years to flower and will not be true to type.

PESTS AND DISEASES Thrips, aphids, leatherjackets and eelworms may attack the plants. Blue mould may cause corms to rot and gladiolus scab and gladiolus yellows may damage foliage.

▼ *Gladiolus* 'Green Woodpecker'

Glaucidium

Glaucidiaceae

Poppy-like flowers that are delicate yet showy combine with handsome foliage on this imposing herbaceous perennial. The solitary cup-shaped blooms, each with four petal-like sepals, open in spring and early summer. The genus contains a single species which is suited to a cool, sheltered north-facing border in dappled shade because, although hardy, its large-lobed leaves are easily scorched or bruised by buffeting winds. It is an excellent woodland plant. Although slow to establish, with the right conditions it will eventually spread by rhizomes to form large multiflowered clumps. It is native to Japan.

Glaucidium palmatum ♀ Erect flowers in lilac or mauve and about 8cm (3¼in) across appear above 2-5 pairs of soft green, hand-like leaves 20cm (8in) long, deeply lobed and toothed and borne towards the top of stiff, upright, unbranched stems. HEIGHT & SPREAD 40-50×30-50cm (16-20×12-20in).

The flowers of var. ***leucanthum*** (syn. 'Album') are pure white.

CULTIVATION Plant in a sheltered position out of full sun in fertile, moisture-retentive soil with added leaf-mould. Moist, acidic humus is ideal.

PROPAGATION Sow seed in winter or early spring in pots using a gritty medium with plenty of well-sieved garden compost. Place pots in a coldframe and prick seedlings off

▼ *Glaucidium palmatum*

when large enough to handle, being careful not to damage the fragile root system. Plant out in spring.

Divide after flowering with great care as established plants dislike disturbance. Leave the root as intact as possible and replant immediately. Pot on small pieces until large enough to plant outside.

PESTS AND DISEASES Slugs and snails can quickly devour young foliage.

Glaucium

Horned poppy

Papaveraceae

Thriving in dry spots between paving and in low-maintenance areas, the recommended plants have cup-shaped flowers and slender seedpods which are curved like a horn. Native to Europe, SW Asia and N Africa.

RECOMMENDED SPECIES AND VARIETIES

G. corniculatum (syn. *G. phoenicium)* Loose clusters of flowers, each about 5cm (2in) wide, appear in early summer. A succession of flowers, varying from orange to red, often with darker spots in the centre open and fade each day. This annual has pinnate, grey-green leaves, 25cm (10in) long, with a blue-grey, waxy bloom. HEIGHT & SPREAD 45×30cm (18×12in).

▲ *Glaucium flavum*

Glaucium corniculatum ▲

G. flavum (yellow horned poppy) Yellow flowers, up to 5cm (2in) wide, appear singly on hairy stems in mid summer. This biennial or short-lived perennial has deeply divided, bristly, blue-green leaves, up to 25cm (10in) long, with lobed and toothed edges. HEIGHT & SPREAD 60×30cm (2×1ft).

G. phoenicium see *G. corniculatum*

CULTIVATION Plant between autumn and spring in well-drained, sandy soil without added manure. Choose a sunny position.

PROPAGATION Sow seed in a coldframe in spring. Transfer to individual pots when the seedlings are about 3cm (1¼in) high, because they will not transplant easily from a tray without their roots breaking. Plant outdoors when about 10cm (4in) tall. Alternatively, sow seed in the growing position in early spring.

PESTS AND DISEASES Usually trouble free.

Glechoma

Labiatae

Throughout summer, small clusters of flowers in shades of purple-blue enliven vigorous, mat-forming and hardy perennial plants. The genus of 12 species is native to Europe. Only one species is commonly grown in British gardens. Its tendency to spread is not always welcome in a border, but makes the plant well suited as ground cover beneath trees and shrubs. It also trails prettily from hanging baskets and troughs or softens the transition from a border edge to a lawn, where it spreads freely and can withstand limited mowing. The form with variegated leaves is especially decorative in a window box.

RECOMMENDED SPECIES AND VARIETIES

G. hederacea (ground ivy, alehoof, field balm) From mid to late summer lavender to purple-blue tubular flowers highlight rounded dark green leaves that are up to 3cm (1¼in) across. HEIGHT & SPREAD 15×90cm (6×36in).

'Variegata' is less invasive than the species. Its matt green leaves are irregularly bordered with white.

▲ *Glechoma hederacea*

▲ *Glechoma hederacea* 'Variegata'

CULTIVATION Plant in a sunny or shaded position in any garden soil from autumn to spring.

PROPAGATION Divide plants in autumn or spring and replant in open ground. For use in hanging baskets or troughs, divide plants in autumn and pot up to grow on in a cool greenhouse until spring.

PESTS AND DISEASES Usually trouble free.

Gleditsia

Leguminosae

Gleditsia triacanthos 'Sunburst'

Delicate feathery foliage offers an impressive display of colour in autumn on this hardy, deciduous tree. Its branches and trunk are usually well armed with spines. Long brown seedpods, up to 30cm (12in) long, appear in autumn and remain on the tree well into winter.

RECOMMENDED SPECIES AND VARIETIES

G. triacanthos (honey locust) Frond-like, pale green leaves up to 20cm (8in) long and divided into 20-32 leaflets, turn clear yellow in autumn. The trunk and branches bear simple or branched thorns up to 10cm (4in) long. Native to central and eastern N America. HEIGHT & SPREAD 5×1.8m (16×6ft) after 20 years, ultimately 18m (60ft) tall.

▲ *Gleditsia triacanthos*

Gleditsia triacanthos 'Sunburst' ▲

'Rubylace' has new foliage in a deep bronze-red which fades as the season progresses. This is a smaller tree, reaching an ultimate height of about 10m (33ft).

'Sunburst'♀ has leaves that are bright yellow at first, fading to pale green. The stem and branches are thornless. This tree ultimately reaches about 12m (40ft).

CULTIVATION Plant in spring or autumn in any good soil in sun or partial shade. Gleditsia tolerates polluted town air.

PROPAGATION The trees grow readily from seed, but only grafted plants reliably reproduce the features of the varieties.

PRUNING None is necessary except to remove any dead wood in spring.

PESTS AND DISEASES Usually trouble free.

Globeflower see *Trollius*
Globe thistle see *Echinops*

GARDENING UNDER GLASS

A GREENHOUSE, CONSERVATORY OR COLDFRAME PROVIDES AN IDEAL YEAR-ROUND SPACE FOR GROWING CROPS OR ORNAMENTAL PLANTS

Gardening under glass lessens the gardener's dependence on the weather and extends the growing season. Many plants will start into growth several weeks before those grown outdoors and may continue well into the autumn. The warm, protective conditions enable the gardener to propagate a range of plants. In addition, a greenhouse or conservatory can be used throughout the year to house an exotic display of ornamentals.

EXTENDED SEASON *Many plants flower for longer under glass.*

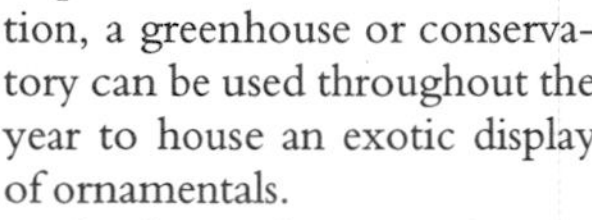

As the environment is controlled by the gardener, growing under glass is more time-consuming and labour-intensive than most forms of outdoor gardening. Plants must be fed and watered, protected from the hot sun and given warmth, ventilation and humidity. The structure will need regular cleaning, particularly the glass, and the frame may require repairing or painting.

All glass structures will aid the gardener but a heated greenhouse offers the greatest versatility. Throughout the year a minimum temperature is maintained, enabling a wide range of plants to be grown. A cool greenhouse has a minimum temperature of 4°C (39°F) and a warm greenhouse has a temperature of at least 10°C (50°F). Hot, or tropical, greenhouses have a minimum temperature of at least 15°C (59°F) but the cost of heating them makes these greenhouses rare among amateur gardeners. If a greenhouse is divided into compartments, two temperatures, such as cool and warm, can be maintained.

RAISING PLANTS

Raising plants from seed or cuttings under glass is cheaper than buying them from garden centres or nurseries; it also allows the gardener to cultivate less common varieties.

Alpines, shrubs and hardy bulbs, perennials and vegetables can all be propagated in an unheated greenhouse or a coldframe. Hardy annuals, such as *Lathyrus odoratus* (sweet pea), can be raised in a cold greenhouse for earlier flowering than those sown outdoors.

A heated greenhouse allows more plants to be propagated, including tender crops, such as aubergines, cucumbers and tomatoes, and greenhouse pot plants, including *Calceolaria* and *Solenostemon* (coleus).

Most half-hardy annuals and half-hardy perennials for summer bedding can also only be raised in a warm greenhouse. However, a temporary heater can be used in spring to increase the temperature of a cold or cool greenhouse and provide the right conditions. A few bedding plants, including *Alyssum*, *Antirrhinum* (snapdragon) and *Tagetes* species, can be raised in an unheated or cool greenhouse if sown in mid or late spring. However, they will flower a few weeks later than plants raised in a warm greenhouse.

A heated propagating unit with soil-warming cables will provide the optimum germination or rooting temperatures for many plants, including summer bedding. Keep the unit and trays or pots of seeds and cuttings on the staging, which is easily accessible. The young seedlings will need plenty of light to develop; shelves in the roof space are ideal places to keep them as they receive maximum light there – although shade from the sun is vital. Harden off young plants in a coldframe, cloche or polythene tunnel before planting out. See PROPAGATION (p. 814).

◀ PRACTICAL PURPOSE *A heated greenhouse provides good conditions for propagation.*

▲ LAYERS OF PLANTS *Tiered staging makes the most of a range of flowering plants.*

CROPS UNDER GLASS

Tender vegetables that have a short season outdoors, such as tomatoes, peppers, cucumbers and aubergines, ripen faster and produce crops for a longer period and often of better quality under glass. Many hardy vegetables, including french beans and lettuces, also grow well and produce early or late crops in a greenhouse.

Use a coldframe for cultivating low-growing vegetables, such as lettuces and chilli peppers. In a greenhouse that has glass to the ground, use soil borders, containers or growing bags for vegetables. Make maximum

GLASS FOR ALL PURPOSES

The traditional greenhouse is free-standing and square or rectangular but other types may be more suitable, depending on the purpose of the greenhouse. Rounded or sloping-sided structures, such as a Dutch light greenhouse, capture more light and warmth; and circular or dome-shaped structures make good features and display ornamental plants well. A lean-to, which is constructed against a wall, takes up less space and can be cheaper to heat. Alpine houses have plenty of vents and provide the cool and airy conditions in which alpine plants thrive.

Glass-to-ground models are the most versatile types; plants can be grown on and under fitted staging and indoor borders can be used for tall-growing plants like tomatoes. A greenhouse which has a solid wall to the height of the staging is more substantial and loses heat less rapidly, so may be a better choice if the structure is to be heated.

A conservatory is integral to the house, providing an extra room. Its main use is to display ornamental plants. A coldframe or walk-in polytunnel is an economical alternative to a cold greenhouse. They are used for the same purposes though coldframes do not have room for tall plants. Cloches, which are made from glass, rigid plastic or polythene sheeting, are used outdoors to warm up the soil before planting and protect plants in cold months. They are light and easily moved

A free-standing greenhouse or a coldframe is best sited in an open but sheltered situation. The ridge of a greenhouse should run from east to west so maximum benefit is derived from the sun in winter and spring. A lean-to should be located on a south or west-facing wall for extra warmth.

use of space by interspersing tall plants, such as tomatoes, with smaller ones, like lettuces.

Some fruits, such as figs, grapes, peaches and nectarines, thrive under glass. They do not need high light intensity at ground level so can be cultivated in greenhouses that have solid sides up to the staging. Shade is essential for these plants so apply shading paint in spring. Grow them in containers and train a peach or nectarine tree or a grapevine onto the back wall of a lean-to.

Strawberry plants also do well under glass and give early fruits when forced in a cool or warm greenhouse.

ORNAMENTAL DISPLAYS

Use a conservatory or greenhouse to display plants in bloom all year round. Alpines and hardy bulbs make attractive winter and spring shows in a cold greenhouse or conservatory, while *Camellia* produces unblemished flowers under glass. Bedding plants add colour in summer and late-flowering indoor chrysanthemums (*Dendranthema*) and *Fuchsia* provide autumn colour. In a heated greenhouse or conservatory, the display may include a year-round show of perpetual-flowering carnations (*Dianthus*), a wide range of pot plants, such as *Hippeastrum* (amaryllis) and *Strelitzia*, and tender climbers like *Passiflora* (passion flower).

Tiered staging is particularly good for displaying ornamental plants in the greenhouse but any shelving can be used. Move bulbous plants under the staging when they are dormant to make room for plants in flower or active growth. Trailing plants look attractive in hanging baskets suspended from the roof. Climbers and wall shrubs can be grown in a border and trained up the back wall of a lean-to greenhouse or conservatory, or grown in containers.

WATERING AND FEEDING

Plants in a greenhouse need frequent watering and feeding. An automatic watering system can be useful, particularly if you spend a lot of time away. In a capillary watering system, pots stand on water-retentive fibre matting and take up moisture continuously. With trickle irrigation, each pot is supplied with a thin tube which delivers water from a main supply pipe.

Watering by hand is time-consuming but enables you to water each plant according to its needs. In general, water greenhouse plants when the surface of the compost is becoming dry. All plants need less water during their dormant periods, usually in autumn and winter. Use rainwater, collected in a butt, for any lime-hating greenhouse plants, such as camellias.

Feed plants only during the growing season. Most plants benefit from a feed every seven to fourteen days but newly potted plants should not be fed for several weeks as the compost will contain sufficient nutrients.

Do not apply fertiliser when the compost is dry, when plants are wilting due to lack of water, or in very cold weather. Some fertilisers, such as a tomato feed, are specially formulated to encourage fruit or flower production. However, a general-purpose liquid fertiliser is suitable for most plants in a greenhouse. Alternatively, insert fertiliser pellets into the compost. These release a steady supply of nutrients throughout the growing season.

▲ TEMPORARY PROTECTION *A cloche provides shelter for young plants, improving growth.*

▼ USING A FRAME *Save space in the greenhouse by using a coldframe to raise hardy plants.*

USING SPACE

This greenhouse has been organised to provide room for plant raising, growing crops and displaying ornamentals.

1 Shading blind
2 Display shelf
3 Maximum and minimum thermometer
4 Greenhouse border
5 Temporary heater
6 Staging
7 Seed trays
8 Water supply
9 Propagating unit
10 Vent

Temperature and Humidity

You can install permanent heating but a cheaper option is to use a small gas, electric or paraffin heater. Also available are thermostatically controlled fan heaters, which come on automatically when needed.

Most greenhouses have roof and side ventilators. When they are open, cool air is sucked in through the side vents and warm air escapes through the roof vents. Vents can be fitted with automatic openers, and electric extractor fans can also be used to improve ventilation.

Ventilating the greenhouse when the sun shines will prevent the temperature reaching a damagingly high level and keep the air fresh. It will also reduce humidity, which is vital on cold sunny days when the air should be kept dry to help to prevent disease.

In spring and summer, shading protects plants from scorching and helps to prevent excessively high temperatures. Ideally, a greenhouse or conservatory should be fitted with internal or external blinds, which allow you to shade as necessary. An alternative is to paint a liquid shading material onto the outside of the greenhouse glass in spring. Use white rather than green paint, to create more natural conditions inside. Unless it wears off naturally, remove the shading paint in autumn when plants need the maximum amount of light.

When the temperature rises above 15°C (59°F), damp down the floor and staging, using a watering can with a rose, or a hosepipe or sprayer. As the water evaporates, it lowers the temperature and creates humidity, which helps plants to retain water. In very warm conditions, mist plants with water. Damp down early in the morning, and several times during the day in very hot weather, if possible. Give plants time to dry off before nightfall if wetted.

Start heating the greenhouse when the weather turns cold in autumn and line the glass with clear bubble polythene to reduce heat loss. Fittings are available to hold the polythene in place, 12-25 mm (½-1 in) from the glass. Insulate ventilators with pieces of polythene cut to size so that they can still be opened. Remove insulating material in spring.

Pests and Diseases

Prevent pests and diseases by maintaining hygiene. Use fresh compost and clean containers. Clean the greenhouse thoroughly once a year and keep it well-ventilated. When pests or diseases occur, act quickly as they can spread rapidly. See PESTS AND DISEASES (p. 824). Biological control – the use of predatory or parasitic insects or mites to control pests – is particularly effective under glass.

A SEASON-BY-SEASON GUIDE TO GROWING UNDER GLASS

Unheated and heated greenhouses can be used throughout the year for propagation and cultivation. This guide gives you the basic seasonal tasks necessary to grow a range of crops and ornamentals, and many of the tasks can also be carried out in a coldframe or conservatory.

SPRING

Ventilate freely, use shading and increase watering. Start feeding from mid spring. Damp down on hot days. Remove insulation and turn off heating in late spring.

COLD

- Sow seed of lettuces and hardy annuals.
- Take cuttings of greenhouse and outdoor plants.
- Plant aubergines, cucumbers, peppers and tomatoes.
- Start chrysanthemums into growth.
- Harden off seedlings for transplanting outdoors.
- Pot rooted cuttings.
- Pot on perennial pot plants, including chrysanthemums.
- Pot summer-flowering bulbs, such as crinums.
- Move camellias in containers outdoors.
- Display alpines, hardy annuals, bulbs and camellias.

COOL

- Sow french beans, lettuces, calceolarias, freesias, gerberas, pericallis, primulas and sweet peas.
- Plant aubergines, cucumbers, peppers and tomatoes.
- Take cuttings of greenhouse and outdoor plants.
- Harden off seedlings.
- Pot rooted cuttings.
- Pot on perennial pot plants, including chrysanthemums.
- Pot summer bulbs.
- Display hardy annuals, calceolarias, camellias, perpetual-flowering carnations, clivias, crocuses, freesias, gerberas, hyacinths, narcissi, pericallis, primulas and tulips.

WARM

- Sow aubergines, cucumbers, french beans, peppers, summer bedding and pot plants, such as coleus and streptocarpus.
- Take cuttings of greenhouse and outdoor plants.
- Pot rooted cuttings.
- Pot begonia tubers, rhizomes of achimenes and summer bulbs.
- Pot on and pinch out fuchsias.
- Pot on other perennial container plants.
- Take cuttings of greenhouse and outdoor plants.
- Prune bougainvilleas and passion flowers.
- Move dahlias to a coldframe.
- Display amaryllis, fuchsias, regal pelargoniums and strelitzias.

SUMMER

Ventilate the greenhouse freely, keep plants adequately shaded and damp down liberally in hot weather. Feed and water growing plants.

COLD

- Take cuttings of greenhouse and outdoor plants.
- Pot on rooted cuttings.
- Stand chrysanthemums outdoors.
- Thin bunches of grapes, cut back new shoots on figs and move outdoors.
- Display bedding plants, coleus, fuchsias and regal pelargoniums.

COOL

- Sow calceolarias, pericallis, primulas and schizanthus.
- Take cuttings of greenhouse and outdoor plants.
- Pot on rooted cuttings.
- Move chrysanthemums outdoors.
- Thin bunches of grapes, cut back new shoots on figs and move outdoors.
- Pot strawberry runners and stand outdoors.
- Pot up freesia corms.
- Display perpetual-flowering carnations, coleus, fuchsias, gerberas, neriums and regal pelargoniums.

WARM

- Pot on rooted cuttings.
- Cut back new shoots on figs and move outdoors.
- Move regal pelargoniums outdoors.
- Display achimenes, tuberous begonias, celosias, coleus, fuchsias, hibiscus, neriums, passion flowers and regal pelargoniums.

AUTUMN

Reduce watering and stop feeding. Remove shading, reduce ventilation, insulate and start heating. Clean and repair the greenhouse.

COLD

- Sow lettuces and hardy annuals for early display.
- Take cuttings of greenhouse and outdoor plants.
- Pot alpines for early display; pot hardy bulbs for spring and move outdoors.
- Bring in chrysanthemums.
- Bring in bulbs for forcing, camellias and tender plants.
- Pot young figs.
- Display chrysanthemums and fuchsias.

COOL

- Sow lettuces and hardy annuals for early display.
- Take cuttings of greenhouse and outdoor plants.
- Pot hardy bulbs for spring and move outdoors.
- Bring in chrysanthemums.
- Pot young figs.
- Pot seedlings of calceolaria, pericallis and schizanthus.
- Dry off amaryllis bulbs.
- Bring in fuchsias and dry off, bring in other tender plants, bulbs for forcing, camellias and figs.
- Display perpetual-flowering carnations, chrysanthemums, primulas, fuchsias and lapagerias.

WARM

- Sow lettuces.
- Take cuttings of outdoor and greenhouse plants.
- Dry off begonia tubers and rhizomes of achimenes.
- Bring in tender plants.
- Pot young fig trees.
- Display bougainvilleas, fuchsias, passion flowers and streptocarpus.

WINTER

Keep heating, ventilate when necessary and water plants sparingly.

COLD

- Sow lettuces.
- Repot figs, repot and prune grapevines.
- Cut chrysanthemums down.
- Bring in bulbs for forcing.
- Display alpines, hardy bulbs, camellias and chrysanthemums.

COOL

- Sow lettuces.
- Repot figs, repot and prune grapevines.
- Cut chrysanthemums down and start into growth.
- Bring in strawberries and bulbs for forcing.
- Display bulbs, camellias, perpetual-flowering carnations, chrysanthemums, freesias and pericallis.

WARM

- Sow lettuces, tomatoes and some summer bedding plants, including antirrhinums, begonias, lobelias and salvias.
- Take cuttings, cut back and repot fuchsias.
- Repot figs, repot and prune grapevines.
- Pot rooted cuttings.
- Pot amaryllis bulbs.
- Cut chrysanthemums down and start into growth.
- Start dahlias into growth and take cuttings.
- Bring in strawberries for forcing.
- Display amaryllis, winter-flowering begonias and perpetual-flowering carnations.

Globularia

Globe daisy

Globulariaceae

Globularia nudicaulis

Masses of blue or pink, fluffy, pompom flowerheads cover this charming alpine plant in early to mid summer. Low-growing, herbaceous and shrubby, globularias are often found in exposed rocky places, forming mats or tufts of rather leathery evergreen leaves. The plants are excellent for the sunny parts of a rock garden and the smaller ones are ideal for troughs and raised beds. Dwarf shrublet types will cling to the surface of rock or compost and in time will grow down over the edge of containers.

RECOMMENDED SPECIES AND VARIETIES

G. aphyllanthes *see G. punctata*

G. bellidifolia see *G. meridionalis*

G. cordifolia♀ The mid lavender-blue or mauve-blue, usually solitary flowerheads are up to 2cm (¾in) across. This mat-forming shrublet has low-spreading stems and deep green, rather lustrous spoon-shaped leaves mainly in basal rosettes. Native to the mountains of central and S Europe. HEIGHT & SPREAD 5×20cm (2×8in).

▲ *Globularia cordifolia*

'Alba' has white flowers; **'Rosea'** has pink flowers.

G. incanescens Solitary, powder-blue flowerheads, up to 2cm (¾in) across, are carried on thin erect stems. This tufted herbaceous perennial has grey-green, rounded to oval leaves. Native to the mountains of N Italy. HEIGHT & SPREAD 10×10cm (4×4in).

G. meridionalis (syn. *G. bellidifolia*, *G. pygmaea*) Solitary, lavender-purple flowerheads, up to 2cm (¾in) across, are held just above the leaves. The broadly lance-shaped, shiny leaves form a dense domed mat. Native to Italy and SE Europe. HEIGHT & SPREAD 10×25cm (4×10in).

G. nudicaulis Mauve-blue flowerheads, up to 3cm (1¼in) across, are carried on stiff stems on this tufted semi-evergreen perennial. The obovate deep green leaves, up to 12.5cm (5in) long, are more or less erect and clustered at the base of the plant. Native of the Pyrenees and Alps. HEIGHT & SPREAD 30×20cm (12×8in).

▲ *Globularia trichosantha*

G. punctata (syn. *G. aphyllanthes*) The blue or mauve-blue flowerheads, about 1.5cm (½in) across, appear in summer. This tufted semi-evergreen perennial has deep green leathery leaves. The lower leaves are obovate to spoon-shaped and arranged in basal rosettes, the upper leaves smaller and narrower. Native to many parts of W and S Europe where it grows on dry hills. HEIGHT & SPREAD 30×20cm (12×8in).

G. pygmaea see *G. meridionalis*

G. trichosantha Pale blue flowerheads, about 2.5cm (1in) across are borne on this tufted perennial. The basal leaves, arranged in distinct rosettes, are horizontal and obovate and often notched at the apex. Native to the dry hills of the eastern Balkans. HEIGHT & SPREAD 20×50cm (8×20in).

CULTIVATION Plant in full sun in a well-drained loamy soil and surround with coarse grit or gravel. In wet winters protect with an open-ended cloche or pane of glass. Use a soil-based compost with added grit or sharp sand for plants grown in containers.

PROPAGATION Sow seed in winter and place in a coldframe. Divide the perennial types in spring or after flowering. Take soft or semi-ripe cuttings of the woody types in mid to late summer.

PESTS AND DISEASES Red spider mite may be a problem under glass.

Gloriosa

Glory lily

Colchicaceae

Six, thin, crinkled petals on each brilliant yellow, orange or red flower fold back fully to reveal six prominent stamens. This tender, deciduous climber is native to tropical Africa and Asia and must be grown in a pot in a conservatory or cool greenhouse. It can, however, be placed outside in a warm, sheltered, sunny position in summer. It has long fleshy tubers and requires free-draining soil. All parts of this perennial plant are poisonous. There is only one species.

Gloriosa superba♀ Showy yellow or red blooms with petals up to 8cm (3¼in) long appear in abundance from early to late summer. Tendrils up to 5cm (2in) long at the tips of glossy bright green leaves allow this plant, which is often grown on a circular frame, to climb to 2.4m (8ft). Its tapering oval to oblong leaves are about 6cm (2½in) long, borne on light green stems. HEIGHT & SPREAD 2-2.4m×30cm (6½-8×1ft).

▲ *Gloriosa superba* 'Rothschildiana'

'Rothschildiana' produces red-edged yellow flowers in late summer.

CULTIVATION During mid to late winter plant the tubers horizontally just below the surface in a 15-20cm (6-8in) pot in the greenhouse, with compost rich in organic matter and gritty sand and loam. Give support with a frame. Liquid feed plants while in active growth. Stop watering and feeding in autumn and keep the tubers dry until the following spring. Place outdoors in the sun during warm summers.

PROPAGATION Divide the tubers in late autumn or winter. Alternatively, sow seed as soon as it ripens.

PESTS AND DISEASES Usually trouble free.

Glory bush see *Tibouchina urvilleana*
Glory of the snow see *Chionodoxa forbesii*
Glory vine, Chilean see *Eccremocarpus*
Glory vine, crimson see *Vitis coignetiae*
Gloxinia see *Sinningia speciosa*
Glyceria see GRASSES p.301
Gold dust see *Aurinia saxatilis*
Golden club see *Orontium*
Golden-rain tree see *Koelreuteria paniculata*
Goldenrod see *Solidago*

Gomphrena

Amaranthaceae

Gomphrena globosa

The clover-like flowerheads on these half-hardy annuals and herbaceous perennials can be dried for winter decoration. The rounded to ovoid, rather hairy flowerheads appear all summer on these low-growing plants with stalkless, lance-shaped leaves. Perennials are usually treated as annuals.

RECOMMENDED SPECIES AND VARIETIES

G. globosa Purple or white flowerheads,

▲ *Gomphrena globosa*

sometimes pink, yellow or orange, up to 5 cm (2 in) long, are borne in loose terminal clusters on erect stems. The plant, a fast-growing, bushy annual, has plain green, oval, hairy leaves, each up to 12.5 cm (5 in) long. HEIGHT & SPREAD 30×20 cm (12×8 in).

'Buddy' has purple flowers and a more compact habit of growth.

CULTIVATION Plants must have a sheltered sunny spot in a free-draining, gritty soil that has had plenty of organic matter added over the previous winter. Thin out seedlings as soon as they are large enough to handle. Water freely when conditions are dry and do not feed on a well-prepared soil.

PROPAGATION Sow seed under glasss in spring, or directly into open ground once the danger of frost has passed.

PESTS AND DISEASES Usually trouble free.

Good-luck plant see *Oxalis tetraphylla*
Gooseberry, Chinese see *Actinidia deliciosa*
Gooseberry, edible see p. 725
Gorse, European see *Ulex europaeus*
Gorse, Spanish see *Genista hispanica*
Granadilla, giant see *Passiflora quadrangularis*
Grape, edible see p. 726
Grape, Oregon see *Mahonia aquifolium*
Grapefruit see *Citrus paradisi*
Grape vine see *Vitis*
Grasses see p. 300

Grevillea

Proteaceae

Grevillea juniperina f. sulphurea

These evergreen trees and shrubs are grown for their deeply cut or finely divided leaves and, with the exception of *Grevillea robusta*, for their tubular flowers, often bright yellow. Their habit of growth varies from upright to scrambling. Half-hardy or tender, they are best grown in Britain in a conservatory or a very sheltered part of the garden. Plants are fully grown at five years old. Native to Australia.

▲ *Grevillea juniperina* f. *sulphurea*

RECOMMENDED SPECIES AND VARIETIES

G. juniperina* f. *sulphurea♀ The plant bears masses of bright green, needle-like leaves and terminal clusters of yellow flowers on multibranched, arching stems, in late spring and early summer. Both flowers and leaves are about 2.5 cm (1 in) long. This bushy shrub is not reliably hardy but will grow in the garden at the base of a protecting wall. HEIGHT & SPREAD 1×1 m (3×3 ft).

G. robusta♀ (silky oak) This pot plant will grow from seed to 30 cm (12 in) in less than a year. Olive-green, fern-like leaves, up to 30 cm (12 in) long, grow symmetrically on a woody upright stem. Although useful as a dot plant in summer bedding schemes, it must be overwintered indoors. The plant requires a minimum temperature of 5°C (41°F), whether indoors or in a garden. The species seldom flowers in cultivation. HEIGHT & SPREAD 2×1 m (6½×3 ft).

G. rosmarinifolia♀ Dense clusters of tubular red or pink, occasionally white, flowers, 2.5 cm (1 in) long, are carried on many-branched stems from late spring to early autumn on this half-hardy, rounded shrub. The needle-like leaves, up to 5 cm (2 in) long, are dark green with a silvery cast. HEIGHT & SPREAD 2×2 m (6½×6½ ft).

▲ *Grevillea rosmarinifolia* 'Canberra Gem'

'Canberra Gem'♀ bears red flowers all through spring and summer.

CULTIVATION Establish plants in the garden in spring, in a sheltered, sunny place in free-draining acid or neutral soil. Grow pot plants in a soil-based compost such as John Innes No. 3, adding peat or peat substitute to make up to a quarter of the volume. Water freely, except during winter. Feed regularly in summer with a liquid houseplant fertiliser.

PROPAGATION Sow seed under glass during spring or take semi-ripe cuttings in summer.

PRUNING Shape plants after flowering.

PESTS AND DISEASES Mealy bug and red spider mite attack plants grown indoors.

Griselinia

Griseliniaceae

Decorative, bright, glossy green leaves and a rounded habit of growth make this evergreen shrub or small tree a handsome addition to a garden. The two species listed will grow outdoors in milder areas, ideally in a sheltered position among other shrubs and trees. The oval to oblong leaves grow alternately on the smooth, erect stems. The flowers, which appear in late spring, are small, green and insignificant. They are carried in unbranched flower clusters up to 15 cm (6 in) long. Native to New Zealand, Chile and SE Brazil.

RECOMMENDED SPECIES AND VARIETIES

G. littoralis♀ The attractive oval leaves are glossy green and will grow up to 11 cm (4¼ in) long and about half as wide. The plant is only moderately frost hardy, but makes a good hedging plant in coastal areas. HEIGHT & SPREAD 1.5×1.2 m (5×4 ft) after 5 years, ultimately 3 m (10 ft) tall, 10 m (33 ft) in a mild climate.

'Dixon's Cream' is a fine cultivar, the leaves splashed with white and green markings. It grows to about 2.4 m (8 ft) tall. **'Variegata'** also has decorative variegated leaves. The white markings are restricted more to the margins of each leaf.

▲ *Griselinia littoralis* 'Variegata'

G. lucida The thick glossy-green leaves are as long as 18 cm (7 in) and 12.5 cm (5 in) wide. This plant is not frost hardy and will survive only in the mildest areas. HEIGHT & SPREAD 1×1 m (3×3 ft) after 5 years, ultimately 2.4 m (8 ft) tall.

CULTIVATION Griselinias do well on most soils. Plant out between late autumn and mid spring. Position plants where they will be sheltered from the cold, in sun or shade. They withstand exposure to sea breezes.

PROPAGATION Take semi-ripe cuttings in early or mid summer.

PRUNING No pruning is normally required, unless it is needed to keep the plant in shape. Variegated cultivars are prone to reversion, however. Cut out any branches bearing leaves that have reverted to plain green as soon as they are spotted.

PESTS AND DISEASES Usually trouble free.

Gum tree see *Eucalyptus*

VERSATILE AND EASY TO GROW, THESE TALL AND STATELY PLANTS MAKE A VALUABLE CONTRIBUTION TO ANY GARDEN

Prized for their shapes, leaves and flowerheads, grasses have long seasons and most need little attention once established. They bring movement into the garden, as they sway in the wind and the flowers fluff out in sun and close up in wet weather.

Grasses make effective specimen plants and also look attractive in borders where their fine foliage complements the bolder and broader leaves and brightly coloured flowers of many shrubs and perennials.

The term grasses embraces sedges, rushes and cat's-tails as well as the true grass family, Gramineae, which includes bamboos (see BAMBOOS p.76). True grasses usually have rounded, hollow stems with regularly spaced swellings, or nodes, from which the leaves emerge. Sedges, rushes and cat's-tails have solid stems, which do not have nodes; the stems of sedges are three-sided.

Grass leaves are long and narrow. Their colours include shades of green, blue, grey and yellow. A few are boldly variegated, as in the green, red and white-striped *Zea mays* 'Harlequin'. In some grasses, the leaves change colour through the seasons, and are attractively tinted in autumn and winter.

The flowers of grasses are small but may be held in large, showy panicles, spikes or plumes, as in many true grasses, or form stiff poker-like heads, as in the cat's-tails. They are often borne well above the mounds of leaves. Sedges and rushes are usually grown for their foliage rather than their flowers.

Most grasses have fibrous roots and are clump-forming, increasing in girth slowly. A few have rhizomes and a spreading habit. The heights and spreads given for the plants below refer to the dimensions of the leaf mounds.

RECOMMENDED PLANTS

TRUE GRASSES

True grasses include annuals and perennials, and evergreen and deciduous species.

Perennials from warmer climates, which include *Cortaderia* and *Miscanthus*, grow vigorously in summer, flowering towards the end of the season. Grasses from cooler, temperate regions, such as *Festuca* and *Milium*, produce new growth in late winter and flower in spring or early to mid summer; they may become dormant after flowering. The annual grasses generally have poor foliage but flower profusely in summer.

The flowers of true grasses are grouped in spikelets and borne in panicles, spikes or plumes, many of which are popular in dried flower arrangements. Most true grasses flower best when they receive sun for at least two-thirds of the day. Without sufficient sun, they are likely to become drawn and lax, and flower poorly, if at all.

◀ SHOW STEALER *The striking* Cortaderia selloana *makes a superb feature in a flower border.*

Avena see *Helictotrichon*

Briza

B. media (perennial quaking grass) In early summer, pale green, heart-shaped spikelets hang in loose panicles from 60cm (2ft) tall stems. They rattle in a breeze and turn straw coloured by late summer. This tufted perennial grass has mid green leaves. It is tolerant of heavy and poorly drained soils. Native to N and W Europe and W Asia. HEIGHT & SPREAD 38×30cm (15×12in).

▲ ***Briza media***

'Limouzi' has larger flowerheads and grey-green leaves.

Calamagrostis

C. × acutiflora (feather reed grass) The narrow, long-living plumes are purple-green and turn brown. They are borne on 1.3m (4½ft) tall stems in early summer and last until late winter. This rhizomatous perennial has mid green leaves which form tufts. It is native to Europe and Russia. HEIGHT & SPREAD 2m×60cm (6½×2ft).

'Karl Foerster' bears red-bronze flower panicles which become buff; **'Overdam'** has white-edged leaves.

▲ ***Calamagrostis × acutiflora*** 'Karl Foerster'

Cortaderia

C. selloana (pampas grass) The showy silvery plumes are 45cm (18in) long. They are borne in late summer, on 2.4m (8ft) tall stems, and last into winter. Arching, mid green, evergreen leaves form dense clumps. Leave dead foliage on the plant over winter to protect it from frost. Native to S America. HEIGHT & SPREAD 1×1m (3×3ft).

'Albolineata' has 1.2m (4ft) tall stems and white-edged leaves; **'Aureolineata'**♀ has yellow-edged leaves; **'Pumila'**♀ (dwarf pampas grass) bears many plumes on 1.5m (5ft) tall stems; and **'Sunningdale Silver'**♀ has 3m (10ft) tall stems which bear plumes in mid autumn.

Deschampsia

D. cespitosa (tufted hair grass, tussock grass) In early summer, silvery purple flower panicles are borne on 1m (3ft) tall stems above tussocks of dark evergreen leaves. Native to Europe, Asia and Africa. HEIGHT & SPREAD 45×60cm (1½×2ft).

'Bronzeschleier' has light bronze panicles; **'Goldgehänge'** has golden yellow panicles.

▲ ***Deschampsia cespitosa*** 'Bronzeschleier'

D. flexuosa Open brown panicles are borne in early to mid summer on 38cm (15in) tall stems. The thread-like blue-green leaves form tufts. This evergreen prefers an acid soil in shade. Native to Asia, Europe, S America and USA. HEIGHT & SPREAD 20×20cm (8×8in).

'Tatra Gold' has bright, yellowish leaves.

Elymus

E. hispidus Intensely blue leaves form loose tufts. The narrow silvery blue flowerheads appear in early summer on

▲ *Elymus hispidus*

60cm (2ft) tall stems. This perennial grass is native to Europe and Asia. HEIGHT & SPREAD 30×45cm (12×18in).

E. magellanicus This grass is similar to *E. hispidus* but has lax flower stems. It is native to S America. HEIGHT & SPREAD 15×45cm (6×18in).

Festuca

F. amethystina Steel-blue, needle-like, evergreen leaves form dense tufts. Narrow blue flowerheads turn brown and are borne on 45cm (18in) tall stems in early summer. Clip in late summer to remove stems and in spring to remove damaged leaf tips. Native to Europe. HEIGHT & SPREAD 23×30cm (9×12in).

F. glauca Blue-grey needle-like leaves are evergreen and form dense tufts. Blue-grey plumes are borne on 30cm (12in) tall stems in early summer. Native to temperate regions. HEIGHT & SPREAD 20×23cm (8×9in).

▼ *Festuca glauca*

'Elijah Blue' has vivid blue leaves; those of **'Golden Toupee'** are bright yellow in spring.

Glyceria

***G. maxima* 'Variegata'** Arching, cream-striped, green leaves are tinged pink in spring. This rhizomatous perennial thrives in moist soil or pond margins and spreads vigorously. Its green panicles are borne on 1.2m (4ft) stems in mid summer. Native to Europe and Asia. HEIGHT & SPREAD 50cm×1.8m (20in×6ft).

Hakonechloa

H. macra (hakone grass) Deep green arching leaves form dense mounds. Red panicles appear in late summer on 30cm (12in) tall stems. The rhizomatous grass spreads slowly and tolerates shade. Native to Japan. HEIGHT & SPREAD 30×60cm (1×2ft).

'Alboaurea' has green, white and yellow leaves; the green-striped yellow leaves of **'Aureola'**♀ flush red in summer.

Helictotrichon

H. sempervirens♀ (syn. *Avena candida*) The slender, steely blue, evergreen leaves form

▲ *Helictotrichon sempervirens*

tufts. Arching stems, 1m (3ft) tall, bear pale straw-coloured panicles in summer. The plant is native to Europe. HEIGHT & SPREAD 38×45cm (15×18in).

Holcus

***H. mollis* 'Albovariegatus'** (velvet grass) This rhizomatous grass has white-striped green

▲ *Holcus mollis* 'Albovariegatus'

leaves which form loose tufts. It bears open whitish panicles in early summer on stems 30cm (12in) tall. The plant prefers a moist, semi-shaded site. It is native to Europe. HEIGHT & SPREAD 15×45cm (6×18in).

Hordeum

H. jubatum (fox-tail barley) Dense panicles of light green spikelets, with long, showy bristles, are tinted red or purple and become beige. They are borne in summer on 50cm

▲ *Hordeum jubatum*

(20in) tall, upright stems. The leaves of this ornamental annual are light green. Native to NE Asia and N America. HEIGHT & SPREAD 30×30cm (12×12in).

Imperata

***I. cylindrica* 'Rubra'** (Japanese blood grass) Erect narrow leaves are red tipped and become blood-red. This rhizomatous, warm-climate grass rarely flowers. It spreads slowly and prefers a humus-rich soil. The species is native to Japan. HEIGHT & SPREAD 30×30cm (12×12in).

Lagurus

L. ovatus (hare's tail grass) Arching, lance-shaped, green leaves form tufts. Fluffy, green, oval plumes which turn beige are borne throughout summer on 60cm (2ft) tall stems. This annual grass is native to the Mediterranean. HEIGHT & SPREAD 23×23cm (9×9in).

Milium

***M. effusum* 'Aureum'** (Bowles' golden grass) The flat, golden, arching leaves of this tufted perennial are brightest in the spring. In early summer, tiny yellow spikelets are borne in

▲ *Milium effusum* 'Aureum'

open panicles on 60cm (2ft) tall stems. This self-seeding grass grows best in woodland sites and moist soil. The species is native to Europe, Asia and N America. HEIGHT & SPREAD 30×20cm (12×8in).

Miscanthus

M. floridulus♀ Narrow, arching, pale green leaves with white midribs form clumps. This perennial has upright 3m (10ft) tall stems. It rarely flowers. Native to SE Asia. HEIGHT & SPREAD 3×1.5m (10×5ft).

M. sinensis♀ The purple-silver, feathery panicles are borne on

▲ *Miscanthus sinensis*

2.4 m (8 ft) tall stems from mid summer to early winter. Erect or arching, slender, bluish green leaves have silver midribs. This clump-forming perennial is native to SE Asia. HEIGHT & SPREAD 2×1.2 m (6½×4 ft).

There are more than 140 named cultivars of *M. sinensis*.

▲ *Miscanthus sinensis* 'Zebrinus'

They include **'Ferne Osten'**, which bears red panicles, turning silver, from mid summer to late winter on 1.2 m (4 ft) tall stems; and **'Zebrinus'**, whose broad and arching leaves have golden-yellow crossbanding.

Molinia

M. caerulea (purple moor grass) Slender, green, upright leaves form mounds. Open panicles of purple flowers appear in mid summer on stems up to 1 m (3 ft) tall. This perennial tolerates boggy, acidic soils. Native to Europe and Asia. HEIGHT & SPREAD 30×15 cm (12×6 in).

'Variegata'♀ has strikingly decorative cream and green variegated leaves.

Panicum

P. virgatum (switch grass) Large multibranched panicles of tiny green spikelets grow on thread-like stems, 1 m (3 ft) tall, in late summer. The slender, mid green leaves form clumps. This perennial is native to N and Central America. HEIGHT & SPREAD 1×1.2 m (3×4 ft).

▲ *Panicum virgatum* 'Rubrum'

'Rubrum' is slightly taller and has leaves that are tinged red in autumn; **'Warrior'** is taller and has large clusters of purple spikelets.

Pennisetum

P. alopecuroides (fountain grass) This perennial produces brown bottlebrush-like flower spikes in late summer on stems 1.2 m (4 ft) tall. The green leaves form dense tufts. Native to E Asia and Australia. HEIGHT & SPREAD 75 cm×1.5 m (2½×5 ft).

'Hameln' has reddish brown spikelets and is shorter.

P. villosum (Abyssinian fountain grass) The mid green leaves form loose tufts. Upright or arching 60 cm (2 ft) tall stems bear bristly, white, bottlebrush-like plumes in mid summer. The plant is grown as an annual. Native to NE Africa. HEIGHT & SPREAD 60×45 cm (2×1½ ft).

▲ *Pennisetum villosum*

Phalaris

P. arundinacea var. ***picta***♀ (gardener's garters) This invasive rhizomatous grass has striking green and white-striped leaves and makes good ground cover. Narrow white flower panicles are carried in early summer on 1.2 m (4 ft) tall stems. The species is native to Europe, Asia, southern Africa and N America. HEIGHT & SPREAD 1 m (3 ft) with indefinite spread.

Stipa

S. calamagrostis The greenish white, feathery plumes become buff. They are borne from mid summer to autumn on arching 1.2 m (4 ft) stems. This perennial has thin green leaves which form rounded mounds. Native to S Europe. HEIGHT & SPREAD 60 cm×1.2 m (2×4 ft).

▲ *Stipa gigantea*

S. gigantea♀ (Spanish oats, golden oats) The large, golden, oat-like plumes appear in early summer. They are carried on stems 1.8 m (6 ft) tall, and shimmer above dense clumps of dark green evergreen leaves. The plant is native to Spain and Portugal. HEIGHT & SPREAD 60 cm×1.2 m (2×4 ft).

Zea

Z. mays♀ (maize, sweetcorn) This annual grass has broad arching leaves. In mid summer, the purplish green male flowers are held in tassel-like panicles at the top of 1.5 m (5 ft) tall stems.

▲ *Zea mays*

The female flowers appear in the leaf axils and are followed by cobs, which have large edible grains that are usually yellow. The plant is native to Mexico. HEIGHT & SPREAD 1.5 m×60 cm (5×2 ft).

'Harlequin' has green, red and white-striped leaves and its cobs have deep red grains; the leaves of **'Gracillima Variegata'** are boldly striped cream and green, and its cobs have bright yellow grains. Both cultivars are shorter than the species.

Growing True Grasses

CULTIVATION Grow true grasses in any well-drained soil in a sunny site, unless otherwise stated in the plant's description. Plant warm-climate grasses in spring and cool-climate grasses at any time. The fibrous root systems of perennial grasses make most tolerant of drought and few will need watering once they are established. However, an annual mulch of organic matter is beneficial.

If a clump-former grows too large, split it with a spade or two forks and replant a small section. Rhizomatous plants may need trimming back two or three times a season, to contain their growth.

Cut back deciduous grasses to 5-10 cm (2-4 in) above ground level in late winter or early spring, while they are still dormant. Lightly trim evergreens in late spring.

PROPAGATION Divide warm-climate perennial grasses in late spring or early summer, before flowering. Perennials that are native to temperate regions can be divided at any time of the year except mid summer.

Sow seed of annual grasses under glass in early spring and plant out in late spring.

PESTS AND DISEASES True grasses are usually free from pests or diseases.

Sedges

Grown for their attractive foliage, plants in the sedge family, Cyperaceae, thrive in moist soils and make excellent additions to a bog garden. Their flowers are grouped into spikelets which, although often richly coloured, never open out like those of true grasses.

Carex

C. comans The drooping, greenish white and hair-like leaves form dense mounds. In summer, the greenish brown flower spikes are carried on 1 m (3 ft) long, lax stems. This evergreen grass is native to New Zealand. HEIGHT & SPREAD 30 cm×1 m (1×3 ft).

'Bronze Form' has matt brown leaves.

***C. elata* 'Aurea'**♀ The leaves of this colourful perennial are bright yellow and narrowly edged with green. They form dense mounds. The dark brown flower spikes are carried in early summer, on stems which are 60cm (2ft) tall. The species is native to Europe. HEIGHT & SPREAD 60cm×1m (2×3ft).

▲ *Carex elata* 'Aurea'

C. hachijoensis **'Evergold'**♀ (syn. *C. oshimensis* 'Evergold') The narrow, arching, cream leaves, which are edged with green, form tufts. Brown flower spikes, on 30cm (12in) stems, are borne in summer. The plant is an evergreen, and the species is native to Japan. HEIGHT & SPREAD 30×45cm (12×18in).

C. pendula (pendulous sedge) This robust evergreen grass has broad, arching and mid green leaves. Its upright stems, which reach 1.2m (4ft) in height, bear green catkin-like spikes in summer. The plant is native to Europe. HEIGHT & SPREAD 1×1.5m (3×5ft).

C. riparia **'Variegata'** This upright sedge has arching white leaves which become green by mid summer. The dark brown flower spikes, which are carried

▲ *Carex riparia* 'Variegata'

on 60cm (2ft) tall stems, appear in spring. This rhizomatous plant is very invasive and is best grown in a container in moist soil. The species is native to the Northern Hemisphere. HEIGHT & SPREAD 30cm (12in) with indefinite spread.

C. siderosticha **'Variegata'** The broad leaves are light green and white-striped, and tinged with pink in spring. They form tufts above which dark brown flower spikes are held in late spring on stems that are 25cm (10in) tall. This rhizomatous sedge spreads slowly. The species is native to Japan. HEIGHT & SPREAD 25×45cm (10×18in).

GROWING SEDGES

CULTIVATION Sedges grow well in sun or shade but require a moist soil. In spring, cut back deciduous sedges almost to the ground and trim off any split ends of evergreen stems.

PROPAGATION Divide in spring or early summer.

PESTS AND DISEASES Sedges are usually trouble free.

RUSHES

The rush family Juncaceae includes the true rush *Juncus* and the woodrush *Luzula*, both of which are prized for their attractive foliage.

True rushes have flattened or cylindrical leaves. They thrive in the moist soil of a bog garden. Woodrushes have flattened leaves with hairy edges. They grow well in damp and shady places and make excellent ground-cover plants. The flowers of rushes are borne in flat-topped clusters.

Juncus

J. effusus **'Spiralis'** (curly rush) Growing in a tangled mass, the green cylindrical stems of this rush are twisted into spirals. The tiny brown flowers are held in loose clusters at the sides of the stems, and appear in summer. The evergreen plant has no leaves, and the species is native to Europe, Asia and N America. HEIGHT & SPREAD 30×60cm (1×2ft).

Luzula

L. nivea (snowy woodrush) The light green leaves form loose tufts. White flower clusters are borne in summer on slender 50cm (20in) tall stems. This evergreen grass is native to

▲ *Luzula nivea*

central Europe. HEIGHT & SPREAD 30×30cm (12×12in).

L. sylvatica (common woodrush) Glossy, dark green, evergreen leaves form low tufts. Chestnut-brown flower clusters are borne from mid spring to early summer on stems which are 30cm (12in) tall. Native to Europe. HEIGHT & SPREAD 38×60cm (15×24in).

'Aurea' has leaves which are bright yellow in winter and turn

▲ *Luzula sylvatica* 'Aurea'

green by mid summer; **'Marginata'** has green leaves with narrow white margins.

GROWING RUSHES

CULTIVATION Grow *Juncus* in moist soil, such as a bog garden or the margins of a pond. Plant *Luzula* in moist woodland or shaded areas.

PROPAGATION Divide clumps of both rushes in spring.

PESTS AND DISEASES Rushes are usually trouble free.

CAT'S-TAILS

These deciduous marginals have invasive rhizomes and belong to the Typhaceae family. The flowerheads are poker-shaped, and topped with a thin spike.

▶ BORDER LINE Miscanthus, Cortaderia *and* Calamagrostis *add flowing form to a flowerbed.*

Typha

T. angustifolia Brown spikes, on 1.5m (5ft) tall stems, appear in summer above clumps of arching mid green leaves. Native to Europe, Asia, N Africa and N and S America. HEIGHT & SPREAD 1m (3ft) with indefinite spread.

T. latifolia (bulrush or reed mace) Stout upright stems, 2.4m (8ft) tall, bear dark brown flower spikes in summer. The leaves are arching and mid green. Native to Europe, Asia, N Africa and N America. HEIGHT & SPREAD 2.4m (8ft) with indefinite spread.

▲ *Typha latifolia*

T. minima (dwarf reedmace) This plant is less invasive than *T. latifolia* and bears dark brown flower spikes in summer on 1m (3ft) tall stems. Its leaves are light green. Native to Europe and Asia. HEIGHT & SPREAD 60cm (2ft) with indefinite spread.

GROWING CAT'S-TAILS

CULTIVATION Grow cat's-tails in containers, in moist soil or the margins of a pond. Remove flowerheads in winter to prevent self-seeding.

PROPAGATION Propagate by division in spring.

PESTS AND DISEASES Cat's-tails are usually trouble free.

Gunnera

Gunneraceae

Gunnera manicata

Giant, waterside perennials as well as ground-hugging rock plants are included in this genus. *Gunnera manicata* and *G. tinctoria* – which have large prickly, leathery leaves – are suitable for planting on a grand scale beside water, while the other species suit a moist patch in a rock garden. The plants thrive in soils with plenty of organic matter and generous watering in dry spells.

All gunneras produce flowers in early summer, although they are not particularly decorative. Some species are not fully hardy – their crowns need winter protection and early shoots may be damaged by frost.

RECOMMENDED SPECIES

G. chilensis see *G. tinctoria*

G. hamiltonii This spreading, slow-growing evergreen has flat rosettes of grey-green leaves. The oval to triangular leaves are each up to 3cm (1¼in) long, with finely toothed margins. Inconspicuous greenish yellow flowers are carried on short spikes. HEIGHT & SPREAD 5×30cm (2×12in).

▲ *Gunnera magellanica*

G. magellanica The glossy, bright green, kidney-shaped leaves, about 10cm (4in) wide, have ruffled and toothed margins. Clusters of greenish yellow flowers are followed by red or orange fruits. Although this plant is fairly hardy, its young leaves may be damaged by frosts in late spring. It is often grown as a pot plant for its brightly coloured fruits. HEIGHT & SPREAD 20cm×1m (8in×3ft).

G. manicata🏆 (giant rhubarb) Prickly stems emerge in early spring from brown furry root crowns. The lobed leaves, about 1.8m (6ft) wide, start brownish and turn green as summer progresses. Small, greenish red flowers are crammed into cone-shaped

▲ *Gunnera prorepens*

flowerheads about 2m (6½ft) long. The tiny green fruits turn red as they ripen. HEIGHT & SPREAD 1.8×2.4m (6×8ft).

G. prorepens Purplish green, oval leaves, about 3cm (1¼in) long, have finely toothed margins. The dense, blunt flower spikes are up to 5cm (2in) long and are followed by red or purple fruits. HEIGHT & SPREAD 6×45cm (2½×18in).

G. scabra see *G. tinctoria*

G. tinctoria (syn. *G. chilensis*, *G. scabra*) Leaves up to 1.5m (5ft) wide grow from a furry root crown in early spring. The spikes of greenish red flowers are followed by red fruits. HEIGHT & SPREAD 1.5×2m (5×6½ft).

CULTIVATION Plant *G. manicata* and *G. tinctoria* in spring in moist soil with a good dressing of manure or bulky compost. In winter, protect the plants by folding the leaves around the crown and covering with bracken, old branches, straw or fleece. Apply a top dressing of compost or manure in early spring. Grow the other species in moist, humus-rich soil. If growing *G. magellanica* as a pot plant, use humus-rich compost with one third sharp sand.

PROPAGATION Sow seed in sandy compost under glass in autumn and plant out seedlings in spring. Alternatively, divide in spring. Remove self-rooted pieces of the rock garden plants in summer.

PESTS AND DISEASES Usually trouble free.

Guzmania

Bromeliaceae

These evergreen, epiphytic perennials are valued for their showy flowerheads and vase-like rosettes of long, glossy leaves. Small tubular flowers bloom in a rounded cluster from the middle of the leaf rosette at almost any time of year, but most often in summer. Surrounding the flowers are large, brightly coloured, pointed bracts. Native to tropical Central and S America, guzmanias must be grown at a minimum temperature of 15°C (59°F) in the greenhouse or home and positioned out of direct sunlight.

RECOMMENDED SPECIES

G. lingulata🏆 Shiny, bright green leaves, narrow and ridged, grow as long as 45cm (1½ft). The 6cm (2½in) long crimson bracts, triangular and outstretched, encircle a cluster of yellow-white flowers. Bracts and flowers together surmount a 30cm (1ft) high stem at the centre of the leaf rosette. HEIGHT & SPREAD 30×45cm (1×1½ft).

G. monostachya🏆 Leaves up to 45cm (1½ft) long and 2.5cm (1in) wide form a green, brown and white vase of foliage. A short stem, 15cm (6in) long, carries scarlet and brownish purple bracts and white flowers. HEIGHT & SPREAD 45×45cm (1½×1½ft).

G. sanguinea🏆 Broad strap-like leaves up to 30cm (1ft) long and 5cm (2in) wide form a flattened green rosette. A short stem in the centre of the rosette carries a neat cluster of 5cm (2in) long yellow flowers surrounded by red bracts. HEIGHT & SPREAD 20×30cm (8×12in).

CULTIVATION Plant in spring or summer in free-draining, richly organic compost. John Innes No.1 compost mixed with equal amounts of chopped green sphagnum moss is ideal. Use 7.5-10cm (3-4in) pots and place in a partially shaded position.

Plants benefit from high humidity and regular watering in spring and summer, along with an occasional liquid houseplant feed. If possible use soft water, such as rainwater, keeping the vases full. Water sparingly in winter.

PROPAGATION Leave offshoots until they are rooted then remove in spring.

PESTS AND DISEASES Mealy bugs, and to a lesser extent scale insects, attack the plants.

Gymnocladus

Leguminosae

Gymnocladus dioica

With its large, handsome leaves and open, upright habit, gymnocladus makes an excellent specimen tree, especially when planted against a dark background of conifers. The deciduous leaves are bipinnate (each leaf has one main stem with several smaller stems branching off, each bearing many leaflets). Gymnocladus is hardy in Britain, although the tiny spring flowers are rarely seen.

RECOMMENDED SPECIES

G. dioica (Kentucky coffee tree) Leaves open in late spring, flushed a delicate pink. They turn pale green in summer and clear yellow in autumn. Each leaf is about 75cm (2½ft) long with numerous oval leaflets. In later life the tree develops a rounded crown. HEIGHT & SPREAD 4×1.5m (13×5ft) after 20 years, ultimately 12m (40ft) tall.

CULTIVATION Plant from late autumn to mid spring in well-drained soil in full sun.

PROPAGATION Raise plants from seed.

PRUNING Not normally necessary.

PESTS AND DISEASES Usually trouble free.

Gynura
Compositae

A dense coating of purple hairs on dark green leaves distinguishes this unusual houseplant. It is easy to grow but needs good light to flourish and to develop the leaf colour. A fast-grower, it becomes leggy and unattractive with age, even if cut back. However, because it is so easy to propagate, any old, unsightly plants can be readily replaced with younger, more shapely specimens. Native to Java.

RECOMMENDED SPECIES AND VARIETIES

***G. aurantiaca* 'Purple Passion'**♀ (velvet plant) Orange dandelion-like flowers appear in winter but many people remove them, feeling that they clash with the leaves and have an unpleasant smell. The deeply toothed leaves are 10-15 cm (4-6 in) long. HEIGHT & SPREAD 30×40 cm (12×16 in).

CULTIVATION Grow at a minimum temperature of 10°C (50°F) in good light, with direct sun for at least a few hours each day. Let the compost dry out somewhat before watering and do not wet the leaves, which are easily scorched. Feed every 2 weeks in summer. In winter ensure the plant receives as much direct sun as possible and water only enough to stop the compost drying out completely. Repot in spring, but it is better to replace the plant.

PROPAGATION Take 7 cm (2¾ in) long tip cuttings in spring and root in compost with grit or perlite added. Water carefully until well rooted, which usually takes 6 weeks.

PESTS AND DISEASES Aphids may attack. Deal with them quickly.

Gypsophila
Caryophyllaceae

The dainty flowers and soft outlines of the gypsophilas make them an ideal foil for bolder flowers in a border. They are also popular as a cut flower. This genus of hardy annuals and perennials also includes small alpine species that thrive in rock gardens, troughs and raised beds. All species have small, five-petalled saucer or cup-shaped flowers in shades of white, pink or mauve.

▲ *Gypsophila cerastioides*

▲ *Gypsophila repens* 'Rosea'

▲ *Gypsophila tenuifolia*

RECOMMENDED SPECIES AND VARIETIES

G. cerastioides White flowers with purple veins, 1 cm (⅜ in) across, appear in clusters from late spring to mid summer. This evergreen perennial has small, oval, hairy leaves. HEIGHT & SPREAD 10×25 cm (4×10 in).

G. dubia see *G. repens* 'Dubia'

G. elegans Masses of small white flowers, 2 cm (¾ in) across, sometimes with pink or purple veins, are borne in summer. The upright, thin stems of this annual branch in the upper half. The fleshy, grey-green, lance-shaped leaves are 4 cm (1½ in) long. HEIGHT & SPREAD 60×25 cm (2 ft×10 in).

G. paniculata (baby's breath) Flowering from mid summer to early autumn, this robust herbaceous perennial produces large airy sprays of small white, pink-veined flowers only 5 mm (¼ in) across, on erect, branched stems. The grey-green leaves, up to 7 cm (2¾ in) long, are fleshy and lance-shaped. HEIGHT & SPREAD 1.2×1 m (4×3 ft).

'Bristol Fairy'♀ has tiny double white flowers and dark green foliage. **'Compacta Plena'** is a compact plant growing to about 60 cm (2 ft) tall. It has double white flowers. The flowers of **'Flamingo'** are double and pale pink. This plant tends to be short-lived. **'Schneeflocke'** ('Snowflake') has double white flowers on a plant not more than 60 cm (2 ft) tall.

G. repens♀ Broad airy sprays of white, pink or lilac flowers, up to 1 cm (⅜ in) across, appear in summer on this mat-forming, semi-evergreen perennial. The grey-green leaves are lance-shaped and 3 cm (1¼ in) long. HEIGHT & SPREAD 10×50 cm (4×20 in).

'Dorothy Teacher'♀ has white flowers ageing to deep pink. **'Dubia'** (syn. *G. dubia*) has white flowers flushed with pink, on a compact red-stemmed plant. It has a spread of up to 30 cm (1 ft). **'Fratensis'** grows up to 30 cm (1 ft) across and has pink flowers. **'Rosea'** has dark rose-pink buds opening to bright pink flowers.

G. tenuifolia Sprays of white or pale pink flowers, up to 1.5 cm (½ in) across, appear in mid summer on erect wiry stems. A cushion-forming evergreen perennial with pale green, needle-like leaves up to 1 cm (⅜ in) long. HEIGHT & SPREAD 10×25 cm (4×10 in).

CULTIVATION Plant herbaceous perennials in early spring in well-drained, neutral to alkaline soils in an open sunny position. Support tall plants with twiggy sticks or wires. Cut back after flowering to encourage a second flush of blooms.

Plant alpine species from early spring to early summer in well-drained gritty compost, except for *G. cerastioides* which does better in humus-rich soil.

PROPAGATION Sow seed of herbaceous and evergreen perennials in pots in a coldframe in winter or early spring. Alternatively, take softwood cuttings in summer. Sow seed of annuals in spring where they are to flower.

PESTS AND DISEASES Slugs and snails attack the young shoots of perennials.

PRACTICAL GROUND-COVER PLANTS BRING COLOUR AND INTEREST TO MANY OF THE MOST AWKWARD SITES IN THE GARDEN

Any plant that forms a thick mat of leaves can be used as ground cover, to suppress weeds and hide the soil from view. Low-growing shrubs, conifers and other evergreens, which offer interest throughout the year, and herbaceous perennials, which create drifts of seasonal colour, are all suitable. Dense plantings of bulbs also make attractive flowering carpets but appear too early in the year to suppress weeds.

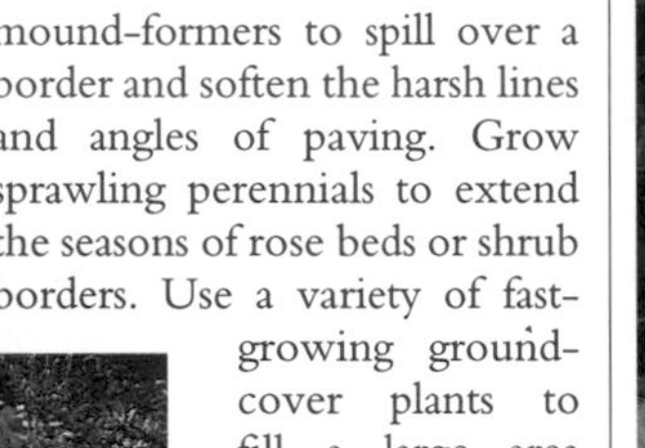

MAT OF GREEN Trillium, Pachysandra *and* Tanacetum *clothe the ground with foliage.*

Many ground-cover plants are easy to grow and are tolerant of difficult conditions or poor light. Use spreading shrubs to cover steep slopes which are awkward to mow. Allow mound-formers to spill over a border and soften the harsh lines and angles of paving. Grow sprawling perennials to extend the seasons of rose beds or shrub borders. Use a variety of fast-growing ground-cover plants to fill a large area quickly. Combine them with taller shrubs and other plants to create a textured effect.

Ground-cover plants will knit together to form an effective carpet in one to three years, depending on the species and the planting distance used. Once they are established, they will smother annual weeds and require little maintenance. Evergreen plants, such as *Erica* (heather), are particularly effective at weed control but herbaceous perennials will also work well if, like hardy *Geranium* (cranesbill), they produce their new growth early in the year.

▲ SUMMER SETTING *Densely planted campanulas form low carpets of blue in a rose border.*

BETTER BORDERS

In mixed borders, low-growing plants, such as *Alchemilla* (lady's mantle) and *Persicaria* (knotweed), provide an extra tier of interest and, often, a longer season. The shade-tolerant *Geranium* 'Ann Folkard' and *Vinca minor* 'Argenteovariegata' (lesser periwinkle) are particularly good choices because they scramble up through the lower branches of shrubs as well as covering the soil. Early flowering dwarf bulbs, including *Anemone blanda* and *Galanthus* (snowdrop), are also useful, providing flower-covered mats in the spring.

A single-colour carpet provides a setting for flowering shrubs which does not distract the eye. *Campanula carpatica*, with its blue, purple or white bell-shaped flowers, or silver-leaved *Stachys byzantina* 'Silver Carpet' are ideal.

COVER FOR SLOPES

Ground cover provides an alternative to grass on steep slopes. Sunny slopes often have dry, poor soil so use tough plants that establish easily. *Hypericum*

◀ COLOUR IN SHADE *A mass of Spanish bluebells brings life to the area beneath a tree's canopy.*

▶ FLORAL MOUND *Tolerant* Hypericum calycinum *spills out onto a gravel pathway.*

▲ LEAFY TAPESTRY *Spikes of* Dactylorhiza *emerge from a mat of* Epimedium, *flanked by ferns.*

calycinum (rose of Sharon), whose yellow flowers appear in summer and autumn, is a suitable choice and complements *Cotoneaster horizontalis*, with its glossy dark green leaves and brilliant red autumn berries. Add clumps of *Narcissi* (daffodil) to bring splashes of yellow to the site in spring.

Shady banks tend to be cool with moister soil. *Vinca minor* and *Arum italicum* 'Marmoratum' grow well here, and look good with the bugles *Ajuga reptans* 'Atropurpurea' or 'Burgundy Glow'.

SHADY PLACES

Deep shade and dry impoverished soil can make a site beneath large trees unwelcoming for plants. *Hedera helix* (ivy) and the wood spurge *Euphorbia amygdaloides* var. *robbiae* cope with the conditions, providing year-long interest and some seasonal blooms. Plant them with shade-tolerant shrubs, such as *Buxus sempervirens* (box), and use *Phalaris arundinacea* var. *picta* (gardener's garters), which has white-splashed leaves, to bring flashes of light to the area.

Trillium grandiflorum (wake robin), spotty-leaved *Pulmonaria officinalis* and the spreading *Pachysandra terminalis* make an attractive show in damp woodland and other moist, shady sites. In an informal garden, *Hyacinthoides hispanica* (Spanish bluebell) creates a stunning carpet in late spring under a canopy of dense shrubs or trees. It looks attractive planted with other flowering plants that tolerate shade, including *Geranium phaeum* and *Brunnera macrophylla*. Bluebells are invasive, however, so plant them only where there is plenty of room for them to spread.

BOGGY SITES

Even among versatile groundcover plants, there is a limited choice for wet, boggy soil. However, the red, cream and green foliage of *Houttuynia cordata* 'Chameleon' livens up boggy areas in sun or light shade. It does not produce new growth until early summer but combines well with *Mimulus guttatus* (monkey flower) and large-leaved hostas, such as *Hosta sieboldiana*, which offer spring and summer interest.

HOT, DRY AREAS

Raised beds, hollow walls and planting areas in gravel or paving are hot and dry sites in which only a few plants thrive. Low-growing species of *Juniperus* (juniper) are particularly reliable and spread out to blur hard edges of brick or stonework. *J. communis* 'Green Carpet' and *J. horizontalis* 'Prince of Wales' are good choices and go well with *Euphorbia cyparissias* with its spiky needle-like leaves and architectural flowerheads.

Silver-leaved plants, such as flowering *Anthemis punctata* ssp. *cupaniana*, thrive in these sites. To add aroma, plant ornamental herbs, including *Origanum vulgare* 'Aureum', *Salvia officinalis* 'Tricolor' and creeping *Thymus serpyllum*.

PLANTING FOR GOOD COVER

Prepare the ground well, using a glyphosate weedkiller to clear the site of perennial weeds and digging plenty of organic matter into the soil.

Planting distances vary according to the plant's habit and spread. As a general rule, leave a distance two-thirds the ultimate spread between each plant but place mound-formers more closely together to ensure they form a dense carpet.

After planting, spread a thick mulch of well-rotted garden compost or manure to encourage plants to establish quickly, and keep moisture in the soil.

Use short lengths of bent wire to peg down stems into the mulch. This will help the plants to spread faster and cover the ground more evenly. The area will need regular weeding for at least a year, until the covering is deep enough to smother any germinating weeds. To avoid weeding, cover the area with either landscape fabric or a continuous sheet of perforated or slitted black polythene before planting. Make x-shaped cuts in the material with a sharp knife, and insert plants through the cuts. Camouflage the fabric or plastic with chipped bark.

Each spring, apply a general fertiliser, and clip unruly growth in autumn.

CARPETS FOR SUN AND SHADE

FULL SUN

- ***Acaena microphylla*** Rosy bronze, oval, evergreen leaves, and red burs in late summer to late winter.
- ***Juniperus horizontalis* 'Prince of Wales'** Bright green evergreen needles.
- ***Persicaria affinis*** Pink or red flower spikes in late summer and narrow oval leaves with autumn tints.
- ***Stachys byzantina* 'Silver Carpet'** Silvery, pointed oval, evergreen leaves with a velvety texture.
- ***Thymus serpyllum*** Small mauve, purple or white flowers in summer and dark green, lance-shaped, evergreen leaves.

PARTIAL SHADE

- ***Alchemilla mollis*** Fluffy yellow-green flowers in early summer, and light green, fan-shaped leaves.
- ***Arum italicum* 'Marmoratum'** Arrowhead-shaped leaves from autumn to spring, with greenish flower spathes and red fruit.
- ***Brunnera macrophylla*** Sprays of pale blue flowers in spring and oval or heart-shaped mid green leaves.
- ***Geranium* 'Ann Folkard'** Saucer-shaped purple flowers in summer and autumn and gold-flushed, rounded foliage.
- ***Vinca minor* 'Argenteo-variegata'** Violet spikes in spring and summer, and narrow, yellow-striped, evergreen leaves.

SHADE

- ***Ajuga reptans*** Blue flower spikes in spring and summer and glossy, paddle-shaped, evergreen leaves.
- ***Epimedium* × *rubrum*** Star-shaped crimson flowers in spring and heart-shaped, evergreen leaves, tinted in spring and autumn.
- ***Euphorbia amygdaloides* var. *robbiae*** Spikes of green flowers in early summer and dense evergreen leaves.
- ***Hedera helix* 'Oro di Bogliasco'** Lobed evergreen leaves marked with golden-yellow patches.

h

Haberlea

Gesneriaceae

Haberlea rhodopensis

This shade-loving, hardy herbaceous rock plant can bring interest to cool corners of a rock garden or to north-facing crevices but will also thrive in troughs. Open clusters of funnel-shaped, two-lipped flowers, ranging from violet-blue to white, appear on short stems above foliage rosettes in late spring and summer. The dust-like seeds are held in narrow seed capsules. There is one species of this drought-resistant genus which is native to the Balkans.

Haberlea rhodopensis ♀ Violet-blue flowers, up to 2.5 cm (1 in) long, have white throats. The scallop-edged, grey-green leaves are up to 8 cm (3¼ in) long and hairy on both surfaces. HEIGHT & SPREAD 12×40 cm (4¾×16 in).

Smooth hairless leaves distinguish var. *ferdinandi-coburgii* (syn. *H. ferdinandi-coburgii*) which has larger flowers and leaves than the species.

▼ *Haberlea rhodopensis* 'Virginalis'

'Virginalis' bears white flowers with a yellowish throat.

CULTIVATION Plant in early autumn or early spring in fertile, moist but well-drained soil enriched with leaf-mould on a site where rain will not fill the leaf rosettes. Transplant with care once the plant is established.

PROPAGATION Take leaf cuttings in summer or divide mature plants in spring or immediately after flowering. Pot in moist, humus-rich compost and place in a shady coldframe until established. Sow seed in a propagating frame immediately it is ripe or in autumn. Prick out the seedlings when large enough to handle and keep in a humid environment for about a year, then move them to a shaded cool greenhouse or frame. It takes 3-4 years to flower from seed.

PESTS AND DISEASES Slugs may attack young plants and aphids occasionally harm developing flowers.

Hackberry see *Celtis occidentalis*

Hacquetia

Umbelliferae

Thriving in moist shady borders or shaded parts of a rock garden, this low-growing woodland plant looks especially good set against dark-leaved plants. It is easy to grow and, once established, will often self-seed around the garden. Although hacquetia tolerates sun, it dislikes dry, light soils and hot, dry conditions. This hardy herbaceous perennial, native to central Europe, has just one species.

▲ *Hacquetia epipactis*

Hacquetia epipactis ♀ (syn. *Dondia epipactis*) Small clusters, 1 cm (⅜ in) across, of tiny yellow flowers appear from early to late spring, surrounded by conspicuous ruffs of brighter, glossy, leaf-like bracts. These gradually change colour over the months, turning from yellow to apple green. The flowers are followed by clumps of bright green, 3-lobed leaves. HEIGHT & SPREAD 6×20 cm (2½×8 in).

CULTIVATION Plant in early spring or autumn in any moisture-retentive soil in dappled or partial shade.

PROPAGATION Sow seed in pots during autumn or winter and overwinter outdoors or in a coldframe. Alternatively, divide the plants after flowering.

PESTS AND DISEASES Usually trouble free.

Haemanthus

Amaryllidaceae

Exotic flowerheads in white, pink or red grace these tender evergreen or deciduous bulbous plants in early summer and early winter. The flowerheads have a conspicuous central boss of stamens surrounded by petal-like bracts. Clusters of white oval berries follow.

Native to S Africa, the plants should be grown in a heated greenhouse or conservatory or, in the case of *Haemanthus coccineus,* as a houseplant.

RECOMMENDED SPECIES AND VARIETIES

H. albiflos Yellow-tipped white stamens and white bracts give the flowerhead the appearance of a shaving brush. The head, up to 3 cm (1¼ in) wide, is carried on a leafless stem above leathery, evergreen leaves, which are oblong or elliptical, up to 40 cm (16 in) long. HEIGHT 35 cm (14 in).

▲ *Haemanthus coccineus*

H. coccineus (blood lily) Red stamens with yellow tips are packed into 6 cm (2½ in) wide flowerheads, enclosed by red bracts. The robust green stems are spotted red. Two or three strap-shaped leaves, up to 60 cm (2 ft) long, appear after flowering. HEIGHT 35 cm (14 in).

CULTIVATION Plant one to a pot in a gritty, humus-rich, well-drained compost in spring. Use a pot twice as wide as the bulb and keep the top of the bulb level with, or just above, the soil surface. Stand in a well-lit position with a minimum temperature of 10°C (50°F). Water copiously and feed regularly during the growing season but keep them dry at other times.

PROPAGATION Separate and replant bulbs in late spring. Sow seed immediately it ripens.

PESTS AND DISEASES Mealy bug may cause problems.

Hakonechloa see GRASSES p. 301

Halesia

Styracaceae

Halesia monticola

In late spring, the bare branches of these large deciduous shrubs or small trees are covered in clusters of nodding, white, bell-shaped flowers. The blooms are up to 2.5cm (1in) across and appear in profusion once the plant is about ten years old. Unusual egg-shaped fruit with four wings, about 5cm (2in) long, appear in autumn. The oval or oblong leaves, up to 16cm (6¼in) long, are sometimes hairy. Native to SE USA, halesia is hardy but does not tolerate limy soils.

The chief difference between the recommended plants is their size.

RECOMMENDED SPECIES AND VARIETIES

H. carolina see *H. tetraptera*

H. monticola (mountain snowdrop tree) Upright when young, this plant spreads with age. HEIGHT & SPREAD 3.5×2.4m (12×8ft) after 20 years, ultimately 9m (30ft) tall.

The flowers of var. ***vestita***🏆, up to 4cm (1½in) across, are slightly larger than the species and are sometimes flushed pink. The leaves are more hairy.

H. parviflora see *H. tetraptera*

H. tetraptera (syn. *H. carolina, H. parviflora*) (snowdrop tree) This is a large shrubby species with wide-spreading branches. HEIGHT & SPREAD 1×1m (3×3ft) after 5 years, ultimately 3m (10ft) tall.

CULTIVATION Plant from late autumn to early spring in moist but well-drained, lime-free soil, in either full sun or partial shade.

PROPAGATION Sow seed in early or mid spring or layer in spring.

PRUNING Not usually necessary.

PESTS AND DISEASES Usually trouble free.

▼ *Halesia monticola*

▼ *Halesia tetraptera*

× Halimiocistus

Cistaceae

× Halimiocistus wintonensis 'Merrist Wood Cream'

From early to mid summer, saucer-shaped papery blossoms cover these evergreen shrubs, which are hardy in all but the coldest winters. All the recommended species are dwarf shrubs, reaching their mature size within five years. They are good plants for poor, dry soils.

RECOMMENDED SPECIES AND VARIETIES

× ***H.* 'Ingwersenii'** (syn. *Cistus ingwerseniana*) This easy-to-grow spreading shrub bears pure white flowers, up to 2.5cm (1in) across. The slender, downy shoots bear narrow dark green, downy leaves. HEIGHT & SPREAD 45cm×1m (1½×3ft).

× ***H. revolii*** hort. see × *H. sahucii*

× ***H. sahucii***🏆 (syn. × *H. revolii* hort., *Cistus sahucii*) Pure white flowers, up to 4cm (1½in) across, are borne on this spreading shrub. Flowering sometimes continues into autumn. The plant has narrow, rather downy, dark green leaves. HEIGHT & SPREAD 45cm×1m (1½×3ft).

× ***H. wintonensis***🏆 (syn. *Cistus wintonensis, Halimium wintonense*) This compact shrub produces flowers up to 5cm (2in) across. The flowers are white with a yellow centre and bands of crimson-maroon markings at the base of the petals. The leaves are grey-green. HEIGHT & SPREAD 60×90cm (2×3ft).

'Merrist Wood Cream'🏆 (syn. *Cistus* 'Merrist Wood Cream') has flowers in shades of deep cream to soft yellow with dark maroon centres.

CULTIVATION Plant in spring in a sunny, sheltered spot in any well-drained soil, preferably light and gritty. Apply a slow-release general fertiliser in spring.

PRUNING Trim to shape in late spring and remove any shoots that have died back.

PROPAGATION Take semi-ripe cuttings during summer and root in a coldframe.

PESTS AND DISEASES Usually trouble free.

Halimium

Cistaceae

Showy, saucer-shaped flowers, about 4 or 5cm (1½ or 2in) wide, appear on these dwarf evergreen shrubs in early and mid summer. The small leaves are green or grey-green. Halimiums reach full size after five years and are good plants for coastal gardens. They may be injured by severe frost.

RECOMMENDED SPECIES AND VARIETIES

H. commutatum (syn. *H. libanotis*) Yellow flowers appear on this semi-upright plant. HEIGHT & SPREAD 60×60cm (2×2ft).

H. lasianthum🏆 (syn. *H. formosum, Cistus formosus, C. lasianthus*) Golden flowers with crimson blotches cover this spreading shrub. HEIGHT & SPREAD 1×1.5m (3×5ft).

The flowers of f. *concolor* are yellow. The blooms of ssp. *formosum* have crimson spots on a yellow background. **'Sandling'** has yellow petals blotched with maroon.

H. libanotis see *H. commutatum*

H. ocymoides🏆 (syn. *Cistus algarvensis, C. ocymoides*) The golden yellow flowers of this dense upright shrub have black or brown spots at the base of the petals. HEIGHT & SPREAD 60×90cm (2×3ft).

▲ *Halimium ocymoides*

***H.* 'Susan'**🏆 Abundant bright yellow flowers are borne on this dense spreading shrub. HEIGHT & SPREAD 45×60cm (1½×2ft).

H. umbellatum (syn. *Helianthemum umbellatum*) Red buds open to white flowers on this upright plant. HEIGHT & SPREAD 45×60cm (1½×2ft).

H. wintonense see × *Halimiocistus wintonensis*

CULTIVATION Plant in spring in any well-drained soil in a sunny sheltered position. Apply a slow-release fertiliser in mid spring.

PRUNING Trim dead shoots in spring.

PROPAGATION Take semi-ripe cuttings in summer and root in a coldframe.

PESTS AND DISEASES Usually trouble free.

▼ *Halimium umbellatum*

Heaths & Heathers

Colour for every season

LONG-LASTING ORNAMENTAL APPEAL MAKES THESE COLOURFUL AND VERSATILE SHRUBS POPULAR IN CONTAINERS AND GARDENS

Heaths and heathers offer great diversity of size, flower and foliage colour and flowering season. Most of these evergreen shrubs can be grown only in an acid soil, but the winter-flowering species – *Erica carnea*, *E.* × *darleyensis* and *E. erigena* – will tolerate a soil that contains some lime.

BRIGHT BED *Heathers bring year-round colour and interest to a border.*

Strictly speaking, the term heath refers to the genus *Erica*, and heather is used for the genus *Calluna*. In practice the terms, particularly heather, are used loosely for both genera and for *Daboecia*.

Heathers vary in habit from upright to prostrate. The smallest are no more than a few centimetres tall, while the tree heath *Erica arborea* can reach a height of up to six metres. The flowers are shaped like small urns or bells and range in their colour from white through pink and lilac to crimson and deep purple. The foliage includes bright greens, yellows and oranges and dull reds.

Heathers need an open position in full sun and thrive in exposed gardens. Many are natural carpeters and make excellent ground-cover plants. They are also splendid additions to beds and borders and useful container plants, particularly those that bloom in winter when few other pot plants provide colour. Heathers are ideal for a low-maintenance garden because they require little care once established.

Using heathers

For an effective display, use groups of three or five of the same species or cultivar. In a large area, blend heathers with different colours, heights and flowering times to create a patchwork effect.

Plants with strong features, such as berries, striking stems, catkins or leathery leaves, combine particularly well with heathers. For example, a covering of the gold to red-toned *Calluna vulgaris* 'Sir John Charrington' complements the autumn tints and berries of *Cotoneaster*, *Pyracantha* (firethorn) and *Euonymus europaeus*.

Use heathers to extend the season of spring or summer-flowering shrub borders. The acid-loving *Camellia*, *Magnolia*,

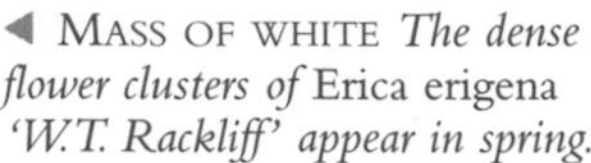

◀ MASS OF WHITE *The dense flower clusters of* Erica erigena *'W.T. Rackliff' appear in spring.*

Rhododendron and *Pieris* team well with a carpet of autumn or winter-flowering heathers such as *Calluna vulgaris* 'Allegro' and *Erica carnea* 'Springwood White'. Keep the heathers in a sunny position at the front of the bed where they provide a green foreground when the shrubs bloom, and give a second flowering season of their own later in the year.

Use compact and prostrate heathers as low ground cover between medium-sized shrubs, such as *Gaultheria* or *Skimmia*. *C. v.* 'Kinlochruel' or 'Sister Anne' or *E. c.* 'Foxhollow' are excellent choices. Include some other ground-cover plants, for example *Bergenia*, to provide contrasts in texture.

A combination of these plants and taller heathers, such as *C. v.* 'My Dream' and 'Silver Rose', provide good cover on the sunny side of trees and larger shrubs.

In wild gardens with acid soils, heathers can form an important part of the scenery. Team them with *Betula* (birch), *Cytisus* (broom) and *Myrica gale* (bog myrtle) to create an open heath-style landscape.

Conifers are classic companions to heathers. Choose plants that offer architectural interest, such as weeping *Cedrus* (cedar),

◀ LEAFY CONTRAST *Ivy and bergenia mingle with* Erica × darleyensis *'Arthur Johnson'.*

▶ HIGH AND LOW *Conifers provide tall contrasts to a multi-coloured blanket of heathers.*

▲ COLOURFUL CARPET *Varieties of winter-flowering* Erica × darleyensis *create undulating swathes of pinks, purples and whites.*

pencil-slim *Taxus* (yew) and prostrate *Juniperus* (juniper) species. Include summer and winter-flowering heathers for a changing display. *Daboecia cantabrica* 'Bicolor' and 'Atropurpurea', which provide a summer-long season of flowers, and the winter-flowering *Erica × darleyensis* 'J.W. Porter' make a good combination. Add variety with deciduous shrubs, such as red or gold-leaved *Berberis* (barberry) and *Cotinus* species, and some strongly featured perennials, including *Crambe cordifolia* and the grasses *Miscanthus* and *Cortaderia selloana* (pampas grass).

EXPOSED SITES

Naturally plants of wide, open spaces, heathers are invaluable in exposed areas, including roof gardens and banks.

In a level garden, create an undulating effect by alternating groups of compact varieties with taller, more upright heathers planted at irregular intervals. A low, continuous carpet of mixed purple, pink and mauve heathers, such as *Erica carnea* 'Vivellii' and *E. × darleyensis* 'Furzey', combines well with rolling mounds of *E. × d.* 'Arthur Johnson' and 'Ghost Hills'.

Choose the tall and shrubby tree heath *E. australis* 'Riverslea' to create raised points of interest without changing the basic theme, and add other plants that are tolerant of wind, such as junipers.

On windy banks, a combination of heathers, for example *Calluna vulgaris* 'White Lawn' and *E. carnea* 'Westwood Yellow', and low-growing species of the broom-like *Genista* provide an effective covering.

Use the shrubs *Tamarix* and *Hippophae rhamnoides* (sea buckthorn) in coastal gardens. These have stark architectural features which contrast well with a soft carpet of heathers.

WINTER GARDEN

Heathers provide excellent winter colour because they bloom reliably and continuously over a long period. Some cultivars flower for two or three months in late autumn and early winter, or winter and spring, while others, including *Erica carnea* 'Springwood White' and *E. × darleyensis* 'Arthur Johnson', can flower for up to four or five months.

Create a striking display in a border or open area of the garden by using a massed planting under winter-flowering shrubs or trees, including *Garrya elliptica*, *Hamamelis* (witch hazel) and *Chimonanthus* (winter sweet).

You can also use winter-flowering heathers to bring colour to a container garden. They look good planted singly in small pots or grouped round taller plants. Heathers are also useful in hanging baskets, where they combine well with trailing plants like *Hedera* (ivy).

HARD LANDSCAPING

Their soft mounds of foliage and colourful flowers make heathers the perfect foils for severe hard landscape features. Grow them in planting sites made by removing slabs from an expanse of paving, and add variety by including spreading plants, such as *Genista sagittalis*. Low-growing heathers, such as *Erica cinerea* 'Cindy' and 'Pink Ice', look attractive interspersed with cobblestones or small slabs.

Use heathers to help to create a low-maintenance, minimalist garden along Japanese lines. Use carpeting species or cultivars to make effective contrasts to groups of starkly outlined trees, such as junipers and birches, and stones of different shapes and sizes.

▼ CONTAINER GARDEN *Their long flowering seasons make heathers valuable plants for pots.*

HEATHERS FOR ACID AND LIMY SOILS

ACID SOIL

- ***Calluna vulgaris* 'Beoley Gold'** White flowers in late summer and autumn, and yellow foliage.
- ***Calluna vulgaris* 'Dark Beauty'** Red flowers in late summer and autumn, and dark green foliage.
- ***Calluna vulgaris* 'Robert Chapman'** Purple flowers in late summer and autumn, and orange foliage with tints of red and gold.
- ***Calluna vulgaris* 'Sir John Charrington'** Pink flowers in late summer and autumn and gold to red foliage.
- ***Daboecia cantabrica* 'Atropurpurea'** Purple flowers in summer and autumn, and green leaves.
- ***Erica arborea* var. *alpina*** Dense clusters of white flowers in spring, and bright green foliage.
- ***Erica cinerea* 'Pink Ice'** Pink flowers throughout summer and green foliage tinted bronze in winter.
- ***Erica vagans* 'Mrs D.F. Maxwell'** Pink blooms in late summer and autumn, and dark green leaves.

ACID OR LIMY SOIL

- ***Erica carnea* 'Ann Sparkes'** Rose-pink flowers in spring, and gold foliage with darker tips.
- ***Erica carnea* 'Foxhollow'** Pink flowers from winter to mid spring, and yellow foliage tipped with bronze.
- ***Erica carnea* 'Springwood White'** White flowers from winter to spring and bright green foliage.
- ***Erica × darleyensis* 'J.W. Porter'** Pink flowers in winter and spring, and green leaves tipped red in spring.
- ***Erica × darleyensis* 'Kramer's Rote'** Magenta flowers in winter and spring, and bronze-green foliage.
- ***Erica erigena* 'Irish Dusk'** Rose-pink flowers from mid autumn to summer, and grey-green foliage.
- ***Erica erigena* 'W.T. Rackliff'** White flowers from spring to early winter, and rich green foliage.

Hamamelis

Witch hazel

Hamamelidaceae

The distinctive spidery flowers of the witch hazels, in glowing shades of yellow, red and orange, bring colour to the garden when it is badly needed from early winter to late spring. The flowers are usually about 3cm (1¼in) across, made up of strap-shaped crinkly petals about 1.5cm (½in) long. Appearing in clusters on leafless branches, these unusual flowers survive the harshest frosts. Most have at least a slight fragrance.

The witch hazels are also worth growing for their colourful autumn foliage in fiery hues. The shallow-toothed, hairy leaves are usually egg-shaped to almost circular, up to 10cm (4in) long and nearly as broad.

Although they are slow-growing, these multistemmed, medium-to-large deciduous shrubs often become as broad as they are tall. They deserve to be given an ample amount of space and prominence in the garden, doing best in a shady spot. Native to eastern N America and Asia.

RECOMMENDED SPECIES AND VARIETIES

H.* x *intermedia The flowers appear on bare branches from mid to late winter. The plant is rather variable and is rarely grown, being superseded by its many cultivars. HEIGHT & SPREAD 1x1m (3x3ft) after 5 years, ultimately 4m (13ft) tall.

The following cultivars are reliable in terms of flower colour and tend to make slightly smaller plants than the parent. **'Arnold Promise'**♀ has numerous bright yellow flowers and yellow autumn foliage. **'Diane'**♀ is the best red-flowering variety. The leaves turn bright red in the autumn. **'Jelena'**♀ has yellow flowers tinted with a coppery red, giving them an orange appearance. The leaves in autumn are a burning display of reds, oranges and scarlets. **'Pallida'**♀ see *H. mollis* 'Pallida'. **'Ruby Glow'** has coppery red flowers and reddish autumn foliage (although 'Diane'♀ is a better red variety with more flowers).

H. japonica (Japanese witch hazel) The crinkled yellow flowers appear in mid or late winter. The leaves are oval. HEIGHT & SPREAD 1x1m (3x3ft) after 5 years, ultimately 3m (10ft) tall.

▼ *Hamamelis* x *intermedia* 'Jelena'

The flowers of **'Zuccariniana'** are a paler yellow than the parent species. They are produced later than normal, usually around early spring. The plant is vigorous, reaching 1.2x1.2m (4x4ft) in 5 years, ultimately 4m (13ft) or more tall and often nearly as broad. The oval leaves turn yellow in the autumn.

H. mollis♀ (Chinese witch hazel) This plant is probably the finest of all the species. The clusters of small golden yellow flowers appear in profusion during mid winter. They have quite a strong, sweet scent. The roundish leaves, up to 12.5cm (5in) long and nearly as broad, turn pure yellow in the autumn. HEIGHT & SPREAD 1.2x1.2m (4x4ft) after 5 years, ultimately 4m (13ft) tall.

'Pallida'♀ (syn. *H.* x *intermedia* 'Pallida') produces an abundance of strongly scented, pale sulphur-yellow flowers in mid winter. The leaves turn a deep yellow in autumn.

***H. vernalis* 'Sandra'**♀ The pale yellow flowers appear from mid winter to early spring. The leaves when they emerge are tinted a purplish plum colour but this is lost from the upper surface as the season progresses. They give an attractive display of oranges, purples and reds in the autumn. HEIGHT & SPREAD 80x80cm (2ft 8in x 2ft 8in) after 5 years, ultimately 2m (6½ft) tall.

▲ *Hamamelis vernalis* 'Sandra'

CULTIVATION Plant in neutral to acid soil that is free draining.

PROPAGATION Sow the hard shiny black seeds in early to mid spring. They may take two years to germinate. Grafting will be necessary if a particular feature is required, although layering can be successful.

PRUNING Not normally required except to remove dead wood in autumn and winter.

PESTS AND DISEASES Usually trouble free.

Harebell see *Campanula rotundifolia*
Hawk's-beard see *Crepis*
Hawkweed see *Hieracium*
Hawthorn see *Crataegus monogyna*
Hazel see *Corylus*
Heartsease see *Viola tricolor*
Heath see *Erica*
Heather see *Calluna, Erica*

Hebe

Shrubby veronica

Scrophulariaceae

Hebe 'Midsummer Beauty'

Versatile evergreen shrubs, hebes are popular for their fine blooms and neat foliage. They range considerably in habit, from low-growing, ground-cover plants to taller shrubs for mixed borders, shrubberies or low hedges. Small individual blooms in white and shades of purple, red and blue are grouped together in showy flowerheads.

Leaves vary in shape and size; mostly they are oval, oblong or obovate, often pointed at the tip. Some hebes have tiny overlapping leaves, pressed closely against the stems so that plants look like cypress – these are known as whipcord hebes.

Hebes are tolerant of salt-laden wind, and so are ideal for seaside gardens, but they vary in hardiness. Some are half hardy and in cooler regions they are grown in pots in a cool greenhouse or conservatory, or treated as bedding plants and planted outside in summer – hebes can be happily transplanted. Others are moderately hardy and tolerate short periods at temperatures as low as -10°C (14°F), while the rest are fully hardy. Hebes grow on most soils, even chalk, as long as it is not too wet and not too dry – although the whipcord species tolerate drought. All the species and hybrids included here are native to New Zealand.

RECOMMENDED SPECIES AND VARIETIES

Hebes reach mature size within a few years. Unless otherwise indicated, the heights and spreads given below are the ultimate size of the plants, attained within 5 years.

H. albicans♀ White flowers in dense racemes, up to 6cm (2½in) long, appear in mid summer. The thick, grey-green leaves are up to 3cm (1¼in) long. This species is hardy. HEIGHT & SPREAD 60cm x 1.5m (2x5ft) after 5 years, ultimately 1m (3ft) tall.

▲ *Hebe albicans*

H. 'Alicia Amherst'♀ (syn. *H.* 'Royal Purple', *H.* 'Veitchii') Racemes, up to 15 cm (6 in) long, of rich violet-blue flowers appear in abundance during late summer and autumn. The glossy, dark green leaves are about 9 cm (3½ in) long. This erect shrub is one of the least hardy hebes. HEIGHT & SPREAD 1×1.2 m (3×4 ft).

H. x *andersonii* 'Variegata' (syn. *H.* x *andersonii* 'Argenteovariegata') The narrow leaves, about 10 cm (4 in) long, are pale greyish green with darker green markings and white to cream edges. Lilac flower spikes up to 12 cm (4¾ in) long are borne abundantly from mid summer to late autumn. A fairly hardy erect to bushy shrub. HEIGHT & SPREAD 2×1.5 m (6½×5 ft).

H. 'Autumn Glory' Violet flowers in 5 cm (2 in) long racemes are freely produced from mid summer to late autumn. The mid-green leaves are 5 cm (2 in) long and have reddish edges. This bushy shrub is hardy. HEIGHT & SPREAD 60×75 cm (2×2½ ft).

▲ *Hebe* 'Autumn Glory'

H. 'Baby Marie' In late spring or early summer the very pale lilac blooms are carried in showy flowerheads, 3 cm (1¼ in) long. The mid green leaves are about 1 cm (⅜ in) long. This compact shrub is moderately hardy. HEIGHT & SPREAD 40×40 cm (16×16 in).

H. 'Blue Clouds'♀ Bluish mauve flowers, in spikes up to 10 cm (4 in) long, appear from early summer to early winter. Green in summer, the 4 cm (1½ in) long leaves turn purple in winter. A hardy, bushy shrub. HEIGHT & SPREAD 1×1.2 m (3×4 ft).

H. buchananii♀ White flowers in racemes up to 2 cm (¾ in) long, appear in late spring and early summer. The thick, slightly concave, greyish green leaves are about 6 mm (¼ in) long. This dense, small shrub is hardy. HEIGHT & SPREAD 30×30 cm (1×1 ft).

'Minor' (syn. 'Nana') is a tiny hebe, up to 4 cm (1½ in) tall, that seldom flowers.

H. 'Caledonia' (syn. *H.* 'E.B. Anderson', *H.* 'Knightshayes') Violet flower spikes, about 6 cm (2½ in) long, are produced in abundance from mid summer to late autumn. The long, pointed leaves have purplish red edges and midribs and measure up to 3 cm (1¼ in) long. This erect shrub is hardy. HEIGHT & SPREAD 60×60 cm (2×2 ft).

H. cupressoides This whipcord hebe has grey-green leaves and branches that generally emit a resinous scent. Pale lilac-blue flower spikes, up to 2.5 cm (1 in) long, appear in early summer. A hardy species. HEIGHT & SPREAD 1.5×2 m (5×6½ ft) after 5 years, ultimately 1.8 m (6 ft) tall.

Hebe cupressoides

▲ *Hebe cupressoides* 'Boughton Dome'

'Boughton Dome'♀ forms a dense grey-green dome about 60 cm (2 ft) high and 1 m (3 ft) wide. It rarely flowers.

H. 'E.B. Anderson' see *H.* 'Caledonia'

H. 'Emerald Green'♀ (syn. *H.* 'Green Globe') This compact, rounded, hardy bush has bright green, 3 mm (⅛ in) long leaves and bright green stems. Flowers are rare, but if seen are white and appear in summer. HEIGHT & SPREAD 35×50 cm (14×20 in).

H. 'Eveline' (syn. *H.* 'Gauntlettii') Showy spikes, 8 cm (3¼ in) long, of pink flowers appear from late summer to late autumn. The mid-green leaves are 6–10 cm (2½–4 in) long. A moderately hardy, bushy shrub. HEIGHT & SPREAD 1×1 m (3×3 ft).

H. x franciscana Large white, lilac, violet or magenta flowers in broad clusters up to 6 cm (2½ in) long appear from early summer to mid autumn. The thick, light green leaves are 3–7 cm (1¼–2¾ in) long. These bushy shrubs are half hardy. HEIGHT & SPREAD 1.5×1.5 m (5×5 ft).

▲ *Hebe* x *franciscana* 'Variegata'

'Blue Gem'♀ has lilac or deep violet flowers. **'Variegata'**♀ has shiny, dark green leaves shaded pale green with a broad, irregular creamy yellow edge. The pretty lilac flowers are on display from mid summer to mid autumn.

H. 'Gauntlettii' see *H.* 'Eveline'

▲ *Hebe* 'Great Orme'

H. 'Great Orme'♀ The narrow, pointed leaves are up to 9 cm (3½ in) long. Clear pink flowers that gradually turn white are borne in abundant spikes up to 10 cm (4 in) long from mid summer to late autumn. This erect shrub is moderately hardy. HEIGHT & SPREAD 1.5×1 m (5×3 ft).

H. 'Green Globe' see *H.* 'Emerald Green'

H. hulkeana♀ Large sprays, up to 40 cm (16 in) long, of delicate white, blue or lilac flowers appear from mid to late spring. The shiny leaves, 3–10 cm (1¼–4 in) long, have toothed edges that are often red. This hardy shrub of loose habit is susceptible to downy mildew and so requires an open, sunny site. HEIGHT & SPREAD 60×60 cm (2×2 ft).

H. 'James Stirling' see *H. ochracea* 'James Stirling'

H. 'Knightshayes' see *H.* 'Caledonia'

H. 'La Séduisante'♀ Large, purplish crimson racemes, up to 10 cm (4 in) long, appear from mid summer to late autumn. Stems and leaf buds are purplish red. The leaves

▼ *Hebe* 'La Séduisante'

are 8 cm (3¼ in) long and tinged with purple. A small, moderately hardy, bushy shrub. HEIGHT & SPREAD 60×60 cm (2×2 ft).

H. macrantha ♀ Large, pure white flowers, up to 3 cm (1¼ in) across, are borne in short racemes of about 10 flowers in early summer. The thick leaves, up to 2 cm (¾ in) long, have toothed edges. A moderately hardy upright shrub which tends to become leggy. HEIGHT & SPREAD 60×60 cm (2×2 ft).

Hebe macrantha

***H.* 'Midsummer Beauty'** ♀ Pale violet flowers appear in spikes up to 30 cm (1 ft) long from mid summer to late autumn. The 10 cm (4 in) long leaves are purplish when young. A moderately hardy, bushy to erect shrub. HEIGHT & SPREAD 1.5×1 m (5×3 ft).

***H.* 'Mrs Winder'** ♀ (syn. *H.* 'Waikiki') Flower spikes, up to 10 cm (4 in) long, of violet-blue blooms are sparsely produced in autumn. The leaves are up to 4 cm (1½ in) long with reddish purple edges and midrib; younger leaves turn dark purple in winter. The young branches are also dark purple. A compact, hardy shrub. HEIGHT & SPREAD 1×1 m (3×3 ft).

▲ *Hebe* 'Nicola's Blush'

***H.* 'Nicola's Blush'** Pink flowers, fading to white, in broad clusters up to 8 cm (3¼ in) long are very freely produced from late spring to mid summer and again in autumn, often continuing through into mid winter. The leaves are tinged with purple and about 3 cm (1¼ in) long. A hardy, bushy shrub. HEIGHT & SPREAD 75×75 cm (2½×2½ ft).

H. ochracea This whipcord species has ochre, scale-like leaves and branches. Small white flower spikes, up to 2 cm (¾ in) long, appear in late spring and early summer. A slow-growing, hardy shrub. HEIGHT & SPREAD 60×45 cm (2×1½ ft) after 5 years, ultimately 1 m (3 ft) tall.

▲ *Hebe ochracea* 'James Stirling'

'James Stirling' ♀ is a compact, spreading form reaching about 40 cm (16 in) tall and spreading to 60 cm (2 ft).

***H. odora* 'New Zealand Gold'** Small, rigid bright green leaves, about 1.5 cm (1½ in) long, are closely set on the upright branches. White flowers, in 3 cm (1¼ in) long spikes, appear in early to mid summer. A hardy, strong growing, erect shrub. HEIGHT & SPREAD 1×1 m (3×3 ft).

H. parviflora* var. *angustifolia ♀ Small white flowers in dense clusters, 7 cm (2¾ in) long, appear from late summer to early autumn. Light green, linear leaves, about 3 cm (1¼ in) long, are borne on the erect, slender, brown branchlets of this hardy shrub. HEIGHT & SPREAD 1×1 m (3×3 ft).

***H.* 'Pewter Dome'** ♀ White flowers, in broad clusters up to 4 cm (1½ in) long, appear from mid to late summer. The grey-green leaves are 2 cm (¾ in) long. A hardy rounded bush. HEIGHT & SPREAD 60×60 cm (2×2 ft) after 5 years, finally 1 m (3 ft) tall.

***H. pimeleoides* 'Quicksilver'** ♀ Violet-blue flowers, in spikes up to 4 cm (1½ in) long, appear in mid and late summer. Stiff, silver-

▲ *Hebe pimeleoides* 'Quicksilver'

grey leaves, up to about 1 cm (⅜ in) long, are borne on wiry dark branches. An open, sprawling, hardy shrub. HEIGHT & SPREAD 60 cm×1 m (2×3 ft).

***H. pinguifolia* 'Pagei'** ♀ White flower spikes, 3 cm (1¼ in) long, appear in mid and late spring. The thick greyish leaves are about 1 cm (⅜ in) long. A hardy, prostrate shrub that is an excellent ground cover plant. HEIGHT & SPREAD 20×60 cm (8 in×2 ft).

***H. pinguifolia* 'Sutherlandii'** Abundant white flower spikes, 3 cm (1¼ in) long, are produced in late spring and early summer. The thick, grey-green, concave leaves are up to 1.5 cm (½ in) long. A hardy bushy shrub, upright at first but spreading later. HEIGHT & SPREAD 45×60 cm (1½×2 ft).

***H.* 'Purple Tips'** see *H. speciosa* 'Tricolor'

H. rakaiensis ♀ Short clusters of white flowers are produced in summer. The slightly glossy leaves are about 2 cm (¾ in) long. A hardy, spreading, fairly dense, bushy shrub. HEIGHT & SPREAD 60 cm×1 m (2×3 ft).

H. recurva ♀ Slender white flower spikes, 4 cm (1½ in) long, appear in late summer. The narrow pointed leaves, 4 cm (1½ in) long, are grey-green. A hardy spreading shrub. HEIGHT & SPREAD 60×75 cm (2×2½ ft).

▲ *Hebe rakaiensis*

▲ *Hebe* 'Red Edge'

***H.* 'Red Edge'** ♀ Pale violet-blue flower spikes, up to 3 cm (1¼ in) long, appear in summer. The grey-green leaves, about 2 cm (¾ in) long, have red edges. Leaf buds and young leaves become pinkish in winter. This hardy hebe forms a neat rounded bush. HEIGHT & SPREAD 60×60 cm (2×2 ft).

***H.* 'Royal Purple'** see *H.* 'Alicia Amherst'

***H.* 'Simon Delaux'** ♀ Showy crimson flower spikes, up to 10 cm (4 in) long, appear from mid summer to early autumn and sometimes until late autumn. The thick shiny leaves, up to 10 cm (4 in) long, are purplish in bud. A half-hardy, upright shrub. HEIGHT & SPREAD 1 m×60 cm (3×2 ft) after 5 years, ultimately 1.5 m (5 ft) tall.

***H.* 'Spender's Seedling'** ♀ Slender, white flower spikes, up to 10 cm (4 in) long, are seen in profusion from mid summer to early autumn. The mid to dark green linear leaves are about 6 cm (2½ in) long. A hardy shrub with erect branches. HEIGHT & SPREAD 1 m×60 cm (3×2 ft).

▲ *Hebe topiaria*

H. topiaria White flower spikes up to 3 cm (1¼ in) long appear from early to mid summer. The thick, grey-green leaves, about 1 cm (⅜ in) long, are slightly concave. A neat, slow-growing, hardy shrub that forms a dense dome. HEIGHT & SPREAD 45×75 m (1½×2½ ft) after 5 years, ultimately 1 m (3 ft) tall.

***H.* 'Veitchii'** see *H.* 'Alicia Amherst'

H. vernicosa White flower spikes, up to 5 cm (2 in) long, bloom from mid spring to early summer. The glossy, bright green leaves are about 1.5 cm (½ in) long. A low-growing, spreading hardy hebe. HEIGHT & SPREAD 30×45 m (1×1½ ft) after 5 years, ultimately 60 cm (2 ft) tall.

***H.* 'Waikiki'** see *H.* 'Mrs Winder'

***H.* 'Wingletye'** Lilac-blue flowers in clusters 5 cm (2 in) long, appear all summer. The grey-green leaves are about 1 cm (⅜ in) long. A low-growing, hardy shrub. HEIGHT & SPREAD 20 cm×1 m (8 in×3 ft).

▼ *Hebe* 'Youngii'

***H.* 'Youngii'** (syn. *H.* 'Carl Teschner') Loose violet-blue flower clusters, fading to white and about 3.5 cm (1⅜ in) long, appear in summer. Shiny, red-edged leaves, about 1 cm (⅜ in) long, are borne on near-black branches. A moderately hardy hebe. HEIGHT & SPREAD 20×60 cm (8 in×2 ft).

CULTIVATION Plant hebes during autumn or spring in any well-drained soil, choosing a site in full sun.

PROPAGATION Raise plants from semi-ripe cuttings in late summer.

PRUNING Not usually necessary, but if plants become leggy or too large cut back some branches hard in spring. Cut back the remaining old growth, the following year.

PESTS AND DISEASES Downy mildew, particularly in damp autumn weather, and leaf spot can be problems.

Hedera

Ivy

Araliaceae

Hedera hibernica

The evergreen foliage of these hardy self-clinging climbers makes a splendid sight growing against walls, fences and pergolas. Some varieties can also be encouraged to grow as ground-cover plants, and are especially useful in shady places. Ivies are popular houseplants and can be grown trailing or scrambling from pots. All have insignificant yellowish green clusters of flowers when mature and often produce black, cream, red, orange or yellow fruits.

RECOMMENDED SPECIES AND VARIETIES

H. algeriensis (syn. *H. canariensis* hort.) (Algerian ivy) The mid to dark green leaves, up to 15 cm (6 in) long, have 3-5 lobes when young, but become more heart-shaped as they mature. They often have reddish hairs on the undersides and leaf stalks. The plant is not reliably evergreen and may lose its foliage in very cold winters. Commonly grown as a houseplant. HEIGHT & SPREAD 6×5 m (20×16 ft) after 5 years.

'Gloire de Marengo'♀ has light green leaves that are heavily variegated with yellow and cream. **'Marginomaculata'**♀ produces leaves with dark and pale green irregular zones with or without cream or white margins. **'Ravensholst'**♀, often used for ground cover, has glossy green leaves.

H. canariensis hort. see *H. algeriensis*

▲ *Hedera algeriensis* 'Marginomaculata'

H. colchica♀ (Persian ivy) A vigorous plant with lobed oval, elliptical or heart-shaped leaves up to 20 cm (8 in) long. The dark green foliage is thick and leathery and emits a strong smell of celery if bruised. The undersides of the young leaves are covered with reddish down. HEIGHT & SPREAD 10×5 m (33×16 ft) after 5 years.

'Dentata'♀ has slightly larger soft green leaves with occasional teeth along the margins. **'Dentata Variegata'**♀ (syn. 'Dentata Aurea') is a striking plant with bright green leaves shaded with grey. The leaf margins are creamy yellow when young, turning creamy white with age. **'Sulphur Heart'**♀ (syn. 'Paddy's Pride') bears foliage that is boldly splashed with yellow and pale green. Some leaves are almost entirely yellow.

▲ *Hedera colchica* 'Dentata Variegata'

Hedera colchica 'Dentata Variegata'

H. helix (common ivy) The dark to mid-green leaves, up to 15 cm (6 in) long, have 3-5 lobes. This is one of the most adaptable garden plants, widely used as a climber or for ground cover outdoors. The variegated varieties are suitable for pot culture. HEIGHT & SPREAD 10×5 m (33×16 ft) after 5 years.

'Adam' has small light green leaves, no more than 5 cm (2 in) long, with silvery margins. It is slightly less hardy than most varieties and loses its foliage during severe winters, but rapidly recovers. It grows to 1.2m (4ft) tall. **'Angularis Aurea'**♀ has glossy, light green leaves, up to 7.5cm (3in) long, with strong yellow variegation. It is not suitable for ground cover. Grows to 4m (13ft) tall. **'Atropurpurea'**♀ has leaves, up to 7.5cm (3in) long, entire or with 2 small lobes, that are dark purple-green in winter with bright green veins. Grows to 4m (13ft) tall. In full sun, **'Buttercup'**♀ has bright yellow leaves about 4cm (1½in) long. Grows to 2m (6½ft) tall.

'Caecilia' has creamy yellow and green leaves up to 5cm (2in) long. Grows to 1.2m (4ft) tall. **'Cavendishii'**♀ produces mid-green, 3-lobed leaves, up to 7.5cm (3in) long, mottled with grey and with creamy white margins. Grows to 1.2m (4ft) tall. **'Chicago'** has mid-green leaves, up to 3cm (1¼in) long, with paler veins. Grows to 3m (10ft) tall. **'Congesta'**♀ is a slow-growing, stiff, upright plant with small, dark green, arrow-shaped leaves up to 2.5cm (1in) long. Although non-climbing it benefits from being grown near a wall, fence or large stone in a rock garden. Grows to 1m (3ft) tall. **'Conglomerata'** (clustered ivy) is a hummock-forming plant, ideal for a rock garden. Its stiff upright stems bear dark green wavy leaves up to 2.5cm (1in) long. Grows to 1m (3ft) tall. **'Dragon Claw'** has grey-green, wavy-edged leaves up to 7.5cm (3in) long. Best used as a ground-cover plant. Grows to 2m (6½ft). **'Duckfoot'**, an excellent ground-cover plant, has pea-green, 3-lobed leaves up to 2cm (¾in) long. Grows to 1m (3ft).

'Erecta'♀ is slow-growing with stiff erect branches and 3-lobed, arrow-shaped leaves up to 2.5cm (1in) long. Grows to 1m (3ft) tall. **'Eva'**♀ is a small-leafed variety with grey-green and cream leaves. The leaves may fall in severe winters. Grows to 1.2m (4ft) tall. **'Glacier'**♀ has silvery grey and green leaves, about 4cm (1½in) long, with narrow white margins. Grows to 3m (10ft) tall. **'Goldchild'**♀, a popular houseplant, has young bright green leaves, up to 7.5cm (3in) long, with a pale green centre and a broad golden yellow margin. As they mature the leaves become blue-green and grey-green with creamy yellow margins. Grows to 1.2m (4ft) tall. **'Goldheart'** see

▼ *Hedera helix* 'Eva'

▲ *Hedera helix* 'Glacier'

'Oro di Bogliasco'. **'Goldstern'** produces lime-green lobed leaves up to 5cm (2in) long with a dark green central splash. Grows to 1.2m (4ft) tall. **'Green Ripple'** has mid-green leaves up to 7.5cm (3in) long with prominent veins and wavy,

▲ *Hedera helix* 'Green Ripple'

undulating margins. A scrambling plant rather than a climber and excellent for ground cover. Grows to 1.2m (4ft) tall. **'Harald'** displays green and grey-green, 5-lobed leaves, up to 5cm (2in) long, with creamy white margins. Grows to 1.2m (4ft) tall. ***H. helix*** ssp. ***hibernica*** see *H. hibernica*. **'Ivalace'**♀, a very good ground-cover plant, has 5-lobed, wavy, glossy green leaves up to 7.5cm (3in) long. Grows to 1.2m (4ft) tall. **'Jubilee'** is a bushy plant with grey-green and white variegated leaves up to 4cm (1½in) long. Grows to 1m (3ft) tall. **'Kolibri'**♀ carries mid green leaves, up to 5cm (2in) long, that are heavily speckled and variegated white. Grows to 1m (3ft) tall. **'Königers Auslese'** has arrow-like mid green leaves up to 7.5cm (3in) long. Grows to 1.5m (5ft) tall. **'Little Diamond'**♀, a very bushy plant, has roughly diamond-shaped silvery and grey variegated leaves up to 5cm (2in) long. It eventually reaches a height of about 60cm (2ft).

'Manda's Crested'♀ bears wavy-edged mid-green leaves, up to 7.5cm (3in) long, that turn coppery in autumn. Grows to 2m (6½ft) tall. **'Melanie'** has mid-green crinkled leaves with a reddish tinge. Grows to 2m (6½ft) tall. **'Midas Touch'**♀ is a very slow-growing golden variety with heart-shaped leaves up to 5cm (2in) long. Grows to 1m (3ft) tall. **'Minor Marmorata'** has small 5-lobed leaves, rarely more than 4cm (1½in) long, that are dark green with grey and white spotting and blotching. In cold weather the foliage is often tinged pink. Grows to 2m (6½ft) tall. Grows to 1m (3ft) tall. **'Oro di Bogliasco'** (syn. 'Goldheart') carries green leaves up to 5cm (2in) long with yellow patches. Grows to 1.2m (4ft) tall. **'Parsley Crested'** has light green leaves, up to 7.5cm (3in) long, that are crimped and crested at the margins. Not suitable for ground cover. Grows to 2m (6½ft) tall. **'Pedata'**♀ (bird's foot ivy) carries deeply lobed grey-green leaves, up to 5cm (2in) long, with a longer central lobe. Grows to 4m (13ft) tall.

'Sagittifolia' bears deeply cut dark green leaves up to 5cm (2in) long. Grows to 1.2m (4ft) tall. **'Sagittifolia Variegata'** has deeply cut creamy white and green variegated leaves up to 4cm (1½in) long. Grows to 1m (3ft) tall. **'Shamrock'**♀ is popularly used for ground cover and has dark green leaves up to 2.5cm (1in) long borne on short-jointed stems. Grows to 60cm (2ft) tall. **'Spetchley'**, a miniature ivy, has tiny, dark green, arrow-shaped leaves up to 2.5cm (1in) long and is suitable

▲ *Hedera helix* 'Sagittifolia Variegata'

▲ *Hedera helix* 'Spetchley'

for a rock garden. Grows to 30cm (1ft) tall. **'Très Coupé'** has broadly arrow-shaped deep green leaves that are deeply cut and up to 4cm (1½in) long. Grows to 1m (3ft) tall. **'Tricolor'** produces roughly triangular, greyish green leaves, about 5cm (2in) long, that have pale grey-green or creamy veins and are edged with white and pink in winter. It makes a handsome climber, reaching up to 2m (6½ft). **'Triton'** is a sprawling ground-cover plant with deeply cut dark green leaves up to 7.5cm (3in) long. Grows to 45cm (1½ft) tall.

H. hibernica♀ (syn. *H. helix* ssp. *hibernica*) (Atlantic ivy, Irish ivy) A vigorous climbing ivy that is good for ground cover. The mid-green leaves, up to 15cm (6in) long, are roughly heart-shaped. HEIGHT & SPREAD 7×5m (23×16ft).

'Anne Marie' has golden cream and bright green leaves up to 12.5cm (5in) long. Grows to 5m (16ft) tall. **'Deltoidea'** (shield ivy) is a compact plant with broadly heart-shaped, dark green leaves, up to 10cm (4in) long, which turn purplish in winter. Eventually grows to 5m (16ft) tall.

CULTIVATION Plant ivy from early autumn to early spring in heavy, humus-rich soil, or indoors in pots in John Innes No.3 compost. Ivies tolerate shade, but this often pales the colours of variegated varieties, as does excessively rich compost or soil. Indoors, position away from direct sunlight.

PROPAGATION Cuttings taken in spring and summer root easily in a coldframe.

PRUNING Trim to keep under control. Undertake any major pruning in spring.

PESTS AND DISEASES Indoors ivy is susceptible to mealy bugs and red spider mite.

Hedychium

Ginger lily, garland flower
Zingiberaceae

Tender or half-hardy herbaceous perennials with exotic fragrant flowers, hedychiums are generally grown as large pot plants in Britain. They can be kept under glass all year round or overwintered in a greenhouse and moved to a sunny spot outside in summer. They can also be treated like annuals and planted out as part of tropical bedding schemes. However, in sheltered gardens in milder areas *Hedychium coccineum*, *H. densiflorum* and *H. gardnerianum* will survive outdoors all year round if planted against a sunny wall.

Hedychiums have erect, cane-like stems that bear dense spikes of tubular flowers. These appear in late summer or autumn on plants grown outdoors and between spring and autumn on indoor specimens. The tapering pointed leaves are mid green and carried in two alternate ranks.

RECOMMENDED SPECIES AND VARIETIES

H. coccineum ♀ (red ginger lily) Bright scarlet flowers about 5cm (2in) long are held in 25cm (10in) long spikes. The leaves are 50cm (20in) long. When planted outdoors, this species reaches up to 2m (6½ft) in height. Native to the Himalayas. HEIGHT & SPREAD 2×1m (6½×3ft) or more.

'Tara' ♀ has orange flowers with protruding orange styles.

H. coronarium (garland flower, butterfly ginger lily) White flowers, 8cm (3¼in) long, are carried in spikes 30cm (1ft) long. The leaves, which are often downy underneath, grow to 60cm (2ft) long. Native to India. HEIGHT & SPREAD 2.4×1m (8×3ft).

H. densiflorum Orange or coral-red flowers, up to 8cm (3¼in) long, are borne on 20cm (8in) long spikes. The leaves are 35cm (14in) long. Outdoors, it may reach 2.4m (8ft) high. Native to the Himalayas. HEIGHT & SPREAD 3×1m (10×3ft) or more.

'Assam Orange' has vivid orange blooms.

H. gardnerianum (Kahili ginger) The flowers, 5cm (2in) long, are pale yellow with bright red protruding stamens. They are carried in spikes up to 35cm (14in) long. The leaves are 40cm (16in) long. In hot summers, specimens planted outdoors may reach the same height as those grown under glass. Native to the Himalayas. HEIGHT & SPREAD 1.5×1m (5×3ft).

▲ *Hedychium spicatum*

H. spicatum White flowers with orange bases and reddish stamens, up to 8cm (3¼in) long, are held in spikes up to 20cm (8in) long. The leaves are 60cm (24in) long. Native to the Himalayas. HEIGHT & SPREAD 1.5m×60cm (5×2ft).

CULTIVATION Plant in pots of fertile, soil-based compost in late winter in a warm greenhouse in full sun. Once established, water well. *H. coccineum*, *H. densiflorum*, *H. gardnerianum* and *H. spicatum* can be moved to a cool greenhouse.

H. coronarium will grow in a cool greenhouse, but does much better in a warm one. All species can be moved outside once the danger of frost has passed and returned to the greenhouse in autumn.

Alternatively, plant established specimens of *H. coccineum*, *H. densiflorum*, *H. gardnerianum* and *H. spicatum* outdoors in late spring in moist, but well-drained soil against a south or west-facing wall, and in as much light as possible. Keep covered with mulch and well watered. Mulch again in autumn to protect plants over winter.

PROPAGATION Divide plants in spring and pot on to grow to flowering size.

PESTS AND DISEASES Usually trouble free.

Hedyotis see *Houstonia*

Hedysarum

Leguminosae

These hardy, deciduous perennials and shrubs are grown for their slender spikes of long-lasting, richly coloured sweetpea-like flowers and attractive leaves. Both plants recommended below are easy to grow in a mixed border in full sun. The shrub, *Hedysarum multijugum*, will also do well in sandy soil on a sunny bank.

RECOMMENDED SPECIES

H. coronarium (French honeysuckle) Intensely fragrant, bright purple to red flowers, 2cm (¾in) long, are carried on elegant spikes all summer by these shrubby perennials. The leaves are composed of 7-15 opposite-growing pairs of mid green, elliptical to oval leaflets up to 3cm (1¼in) long. HEIGHT & SPREAD 1×1m (3×3ft).

H. multijugum Erect spikes of vivid magenta flowers, each 2cm (¾in) long, are borne from early summer to early autumn by these deciduous shrubs. Zig-zag branchlets carry sea-green leaves with up to 20 pairs of oval to oblong leaflets 1.5cm (½in) long. HEIGHT & SPREAD 1×1m (3×3ft) after 5 years, ultimately 1.5m (5ft) tall.

CULTIVATION Plant in full sun in fertile, well-drained soil, preferably in spring. Once established the plants should not be disturbed. *H. coronarium* may be planted in late summer, then cut back to just above ground level in late autumn.

PROPAGATION Sow seed of both species outdoors when ripe or in spring or take semi-ripe cuttings of both species in mid summer. Layer long shoots of *H. multijugum* in early autumn and sever from the parent plant one year later.

PRUNING In mid spring thin out any old and weak wood of *H. multijugum* and shorten straggly shoots of the previous year.

PESTS AND DISEASES Usually trouble free.

▼ *Hedysarum coronarium*

HEDGES

Practical and decorative boundaries

FOR LIVING SHAPE AND STRUCTURE, PLANT A HEDGE THAT CHANGES WITH THE SEASONS OR BRINGS YEAR-ROUND COLOUR TO THE GARDEN

Hedges are ornamental and functional features which define boundaries and provide privacy; they offer shelter from wind and noise, and screen unsightly views.

The best plants for hedging are bushy trees and shrubs that produce plenty of sideshoots when trimmed. Evergreen plants stay a welcome green throughout the year and often tolerate shady sites; deciduous plants may withstand a cold or exposed site well and, as they change with the seasons, are often more decorative than evergreens.

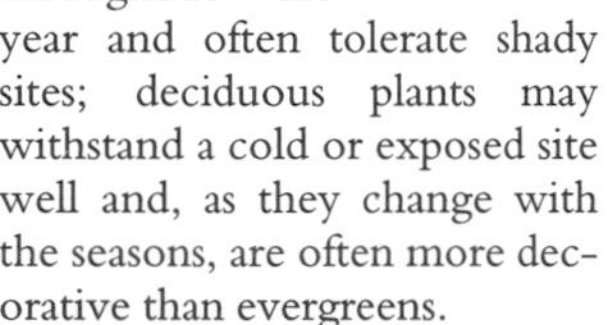

EVERGREEN FRAME *Amid winter's skeletons holly proves its value.*

Hedges can set or complement the garden style. Clipped to strict, geometrical outlines, *Fagus* (beech) or *Taxus* (yew) hedges suit formal areas; a more informal garden is enhanced by a colourful and unrestrained hedge of *Rosa* or *Pyracantha* (firethorn).

For wildlife, hedges can provide shelter and valuable feeding and nesting sites. A combination of native trees and shrubs, such as species of beech, *Ilex* (holly), *Corylus* (hazel) and *Crataegus* (hawthorn), supports a wide range of species. See WILDLIFE GARDENS (p. 710).

SELECTING A STYLE

A formal hedge imposes a linear structure on a garden and provides a solid backdrop for shrubs and borders. It is most effective when planted with a single species, such as *Aucuba* or *Ligustrum* (privet), and trimmed to a smooth, neat outline. Formal hedges may need clipping several times a year, and can be scalloped or castellated for additional interest. See TOPIARY (p. 670).

Some evergreens, such as yew and *Thuja plicata* (western red cedar), the semi-evergreen privet and a number of deciduous species, including beech, have coloured or variegated varieties. These make attractive formal hedges with less uniform appearances. Plant differently coloured varieties of the same species alternately to create an impressive tapestry of green and gold or purple.

An informal hedge blends harmoniously with the rest of the garden. It can be planted with a combination of plants, as in a wildlife hedge, or with a single species, such as *Elaeagnus* or *Spiraea*. For an unusual and distinctive screen, try a graceful bamboo or the striking tall grass, *Miscanthus*. *Rosa rugosa*, which flowers throughout summer and sometimes also produces red hips, and *Choisya ternata* (Mexican orange blossom), with its mass of scented white flowers in spring, are also attractive choices.

Many hedging plants are particularly suited to either an informal or a formal style, but some adapt well to both. For example, clip the glossy-leaved *Osmanthus delavayi* regularly to create a formal hedge or leave it to form a soft, rounded shape and produce white, fragrant flowers in spring.

PRACTICAL CHOICES

Boundary hedges need to be clipped into formal contours that mark the precise area which they enclose. Choose beech, yew or hawthorn to create a tall screen which provides sheltered seclusion and reduces noise. These plants are best used in large gardens as a tall hedge makes the enclosed area appear smaller. In smaller gardens, *Ligustrum ovalifolium* (oval-leaved privet) and *Berberis* (barberry) are good alternatives. Hedging plants with spines, which include hawthorn and berberis, help to keep out animals or intruders.

Use an evergreen plant, especially a conifer which has dense foliage, to create an effective screen that hides eyesores throughout the year. *Chamaecyparis lawsoniana* (Lawson's cypress) or *Thuja plicata* make

◀ CLASSICALLY CLIPPED *A formal yew hedge is the ideal foil for a summer herbaceous border.*

▲ SUMMER BLOOMING *Rosa 'Grootendorst Supreme' and 'Pink Grootendorst' as hedging.*

▶ SQUARE SYMMETRY *Low box hedging forms a centrepiece in a small courtyard garden.*

excellent screens and both are relatively fast growing.

Hedges filter strong winds without creating turbulence and provide protective conditions for other plants. Good plants for windbreaks include *Larix* (larch), *Picea* (spruce) and *Alnus* (alder). In coastal areas, choose trees or shrubs that tolerate salt as well as wind. *Elaeagnus pungens*, *Quercus ilex* (holm oak) or *Hippophae rhamnoides* (sea buckthorn) are ideal.

LOW HEDGES

A low hedge makes a decorative border to contain a herb and vegetable garden. Low hedges can also be used round flowerbeds or to separate different areas of the garden.

In formal gardens, use the glossy-leaved *Buxus sempervirens* (box) or *Lonicera nitida* (box-leaved honeysuckle) kept closely clipped. They make neat surrounds for knot gardens and parterres. *Santolina*, *Lavandula* (lavender) or *Rosmarinus* (rosemary) are excellent plants for informal low hedges. These bushy flowering shrubs are sweetly scented and spill attractively over pathways.

▼ AUTUMN RIPENING *Dense clusters of pyracantha berries make a solid wall of colour.*

ESTABLISHING A HEDGE

Mark out the run of the hedge, making sure that the site for a boundary hedge lies entirely inside your property. For a tall vigorous hedge that may bush out to 60cm (2ft) or more at the base, dig a strip 90cm (3ft) wide, extending a further 60-90cm beyond each end. For a low-growing hedge, that will reach 30cm (1ft) wide at the base, prepare a strip 45cm (18in) wide, extending a further 45cm (18in) at each end.

Dig over and weed the site, then add plenty of organic material. Allow several weeks for the disturbed soil to settle, and apply general fertiliser before planting.

Choose bushy plants, one to three years old. Plant bare-rooted deciduous species in autumn and evergreens in early to mid autumn on light soils or early to mid spring on clay. Plant container-grown plants whenever the soil is workable. Apply a mulch and stake plants that grow tall.

To encourage dense lateral growth, cut back most hedging plants to half their height after planting or towards the end of their first summer. Leave conifers to grow unchecked until they reach two-thirds of their final height. Then remove the tip of the main leader.

Water well during the first two seasons of growth. Do not feed in the first year, but thereafter apply a mulch or top dressing of general fertiliser in early spring.

Clip only when the hedge is well established. An annual trim is usually sufficient for informal hedges. If they are grown for fruit, cut them back in spring. Otherwise, cut back straggly shoots after flowering. Trim formal evergreen hedges during the growing season and deciduous plants at any time. Use canes and string as a guide, at least for the first cut of the season. Shape a tall evergreen hedge to be slightly narrower at the top, so light reaches the lower branches.

To rejuvenate a neglected hedge, hard prune deciduous species while dormant, and evergreens in late spring, when all danger of frost is past. Cut one side each year a little short of the final dimensions, to allow room for new growth. Feed generously afterwards.

PLANTS FOR DIFFERENT STYLES

FORMAL HEDGES

- ***Aucuba japonica*** Evergreen with glossy, deep green, oval leaves.
- ***Buxus sempervirens*** Evergreen with small, oval, dark green, polished leaves.
- ***Chamaecyparis lawsoniana* 'Pembury Blue'** Evergreen conifer with silver-blue foliage.
- ***Crataegus laevigata*** Thorny deciduous shrub which has polished, dark green, oval leaves.
- ***Fagus sylvatica*** Deciduous tree with glossy, pointed leaves that have colourful tints in autumn.
- ***Ilex aquifolium*** Evergreen with glossy, wavy-edged, spiny foliage.
- ***Taxus baccata*** Evergreen conifer which has dense, dark green needles.
- ***Thuja plicata* 'Atrovirens'** Evergreen conifer with glossy, dark green, scale-like foliage.

INFORMAL HEDGES

- ***Elaeagnus pungens*** Evergreen with dark green, glossy, pointed leaves and clusters of fragrant white flowers in autumn.
- ***Hippophae rhamnoides*** Spiny deciduous shrub with narrow silver-green leaves, and bright yellow-orange berries in autumn.
- ***Osmanthus delavayi*** Evergreen with dark green, rounded leaves, clusters of white flowers in spring and blue-black fruits in summer.
- ***Pyracantha* 'Mohave'** Spiny evergreen with dark green, oval leaves, white clusters in summer and red-orange autumn berries.
- ***Rosa rugosa* 'Scabrosa'** Spiny deciduous shrub with bright green, oval leaves, purple-pink, open flowers in summer and red hips.
- ***Santolina chamaecyparissus*** Evergreen with silvery leaves and rounded yellow blooms in summer.
- ***Spiraea* 'Arguta'** Deciduous shrub with bright green, tapered leaves and white clusters in spring.

Helenium

Sneezeweed

Compositae

Helenium autumnale

From late summer into autumn the daisy-like blooms of helenium bring yellow, orange and bronze hues to a sunny herbaceous border. The flowers, with their silky, fringed petals and central velvety boss of brown or yellow, smother the branching stems of the hardy perennials listed below.

Native to N America, heleniums earned their common name of sneezeweed after being used by early American colonists to make snuff. They are hardy throughout Britain but do not do well in very dry soils.

RECOMMENDED SPECIES AND VARIETIES

H. autumnale Clusters of yellow flowers, up to 5 cm (2 in) across, are borne freely from late summer to mid autumn. This species has winged stems and mid green lance-shaped leaves up to 15 cm (6 in) long. HEIGHT & SPREAD 1.5 m×45 cm (5×1½ ft).

H. bigelovii Orange-yellow flowers, up to 6 cm (2½ in) across with a brownish yellow central disc, are borne from mid to late summer. The lance-shaped, shiny leaves are up to 25 cm (10 in) long. HEIGHT & SPREAD 60×45 cm (2×1½ ft).

H. hoopesii Yellow or orange flowers, up to 8 cm (3¼in) across, open in early summer. The lance-shaped basal leaves, up to 30 cm (1 ft) long, form a rosette. HEIGHT & SPREAD 1 m×45 cm (3×1½ ft).

GARDEN HYBRIDS

Many hybrid heleniums are available to gardeners – all crosses between *H. autumnale*, *H. bigelovii* and other species, though they are usually listed under their hybrid names.

▲ *Helenium* 'Golden Youth'

▲ *Helenium* 'Bruno'

Unless stated otherwise the following types produce 5 cm (2 in) diameter flowers from late summer to mid autumn and grow to 1 m (3 ft) tall with a spread of 30 cm (1 ft).

'Bruno' is up to 1.2 m (4 ft) tall and has crimson-mahogany flowers. **'Butterpat'** has rich yellow flowers. **'Chipperfield Orange'** has orange flowers. **'Coppelia'** bears rich orange and copper red flowers. **'Crimson Beauty'** has soft mahogany-red flowers from early summer onwards. **'Golden Youth'** ('Goldene Jugend') has pure yellow flowers from early to mid summer. **'Moerheim Beauty'** is a sturdy plant, bearing bronze to crimson flowers from mid summer. **'Pumilum Magnificum'** has pale yellow flowers. **'Red and Gold'** ('Rotgold') grows to 1.2 m (4 ft) tall and has two-tone flowers in brick-red and yellow. **'The Bishop'** has clear yellow flowers in late summer. **'Waldtraut'** reaches 1.2 m (4 ft) tall and has large orange-brown flowers. **'Wyndley'** grows to a height of 75 cm (30 in) and has yellow and copper flowers from early to late summer.

CULTIVATION Plant in any fertile soil that is not too dry. Support the taller varieties. Remove stem tips immediately after the first flowering of early varieties to encourage a second flush.

PROPAGATION Lift and divide clumps every 2-3 years when dormant. Otherwise take basal cuttings in spring.

PESTS AND DISEASES Slugs may attack the stems, leaves and flowers, and tortrix moth caterpillars may eat the leaves. The plants may suffer from viral diseases and leaf spot.

Helianthemum

Rock rose

Cistaceae

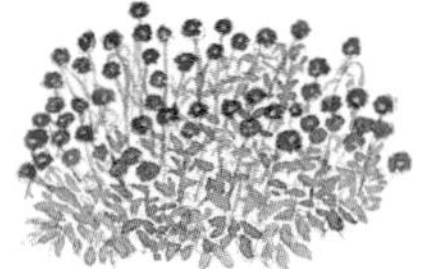

Helianthemum nummularium

These bright, sun-loving evergreen shrubs or sub-shrubs produce a succession of colourful flowers from late spring through the summer months. Rock roses thrive in warm, sunny sites and make excellent rock garden plants, but they are equally useful for lining path edges or for the margin of terraces. These low, often spreading plants are also important elements of a Mediterranean garden where they combine well with plants such as cistus. Some of the more vibrant cultivars need to be placed with care, especially in a rock garden, as they can clash and detract from other plants. However, a sunny, gritty bed devoted to a selection of carefully contrasting rock roses can make an interesting feature.

The flowers, borne in one-sided clusters, are available in a range of clear, bright colours including pinks, reds, rusts and yellows, as well as white and more pastel shades. The four or five thin, rather crumpled petals surround a central mass of stamens. The small oval leaves are arranged in pairs, and often have the untoothed margin folded neatly under.

RECOMMENDED SPECIES AND VARIETIES

H. lunulatum Yellow flowers, about 1.5 cm (½ in) across, are borne in early to mid summer. Each petal has a neat crescent-shaped orange mark towards the base. The lance-shaped leaves, up to 1 cm (⅜ in) long, are grey-green. This small, partly deciduous sub-shrub has a rather upright habit, spreading more with age. Native to dry rocky places in the Maritime Alps. HEIGHT & SPREAD 25×30 cm (10×12 in).

H. nummularium (common rock rose) The yellow, pink or white flowers grow up to 2 cm (¾ in) across and are borne in one-sided clusters of up to 12 during the summer. Plants form low, rather dense flattish or domed sub-shrubs, often mat-forming, with oval to lance-shaped green or grey-green leaves, up to 5 cm (2 in) long. This variable plant is native to many parts of Europe, including Britain. HEIGHT & SPREAD 50×60 cm (20×24 in).

ssp. ***glabrum*** has orange-yellow flowers.

RECOMMENDED HYBRIDS

The colourful rock roses most commonly seen in gardens are hybrids. Plants vary in habit, but most are low-spreading sub-shrubs, 20-40 cm (8-16 in) tall, that form a dense, interlaced hummock or mat. The flowers are single and the leaves are mid green unless otherwise stated.

'Amy Baring'♀ has deep yellow flowers with orange centres and grey-green leaves. **'Annabel'** has soft pink double flowers. **'Beech Park Red'** carries crimson-pink flowers and grey-green leaves. **'Ben Afflick'** produces deep orange buff-flushed flowers with an orange centre. **'Ben Dearg'** has vivid orange-red flowers. **'Ben Fhada'** carries golden flowers with an orange centre and grey-green leaves. **'Ben Heckla'** displays bronzy gold flowers. **'Ben Hope'** has carmine-red flowers with an orange centre and pale grey-green leaves. **'Ben Ledi'** produces deep bright rose flowers and dark green leaves. **'Ben More'** carries bright orange flowers with a deeper centre and deep green leaves. **'Ben Nevis'** has rich yellow flowers with a crimson-bronze

▲ *Helianthemum* 'Ben More'

centre and deep green leaves. **'Boughton Double Primrose'** carries double primrose-yellow flowers and dark green leaves.

'Cerise Queen' produces intense cerise-red double flowers and dark green leaves. **'Chocolate Blotch'** has buff and chocolate flowers. **'Double Cream'** has double cream flowers. **'Fire Dragon'**♀ has bright orange-scarlet flowers and grey-green leaves. **'Georgeham'** bears pink and yellow flowers. **'Golden Queen'** has bright yellow flowers and deep green leaves. **'Henfield Brilliant'**♀ has brick-red flowers

▲ *Helianthemum* 'Henfield Brilliant'

and grey-green leaves. **'Jubilee'**♀ has double primrose-yellow flowers. **'Mrs C.W. Earle'**♀ bears double red flowers with dark green leaves. **'Old Gold'** has soft rich yellow flowers.

'Praecox' produces lemon-yellow flowers and silvery grey leaves. It flowers earlier

▼ *Helianthemum* 'Mrs C.W. Earle'

than most of the other cultivars. **'Raspberry Ripple'** bears rich reddish pink flowers edged with white and dark green leaves. **'Red Orient'** see 'Supreme'. **'Rhodanthe Carneum'**♀ carries carmine-pink flowers with an orange centre and silvery grey foliage. **'Rose of Leeswood'** has

▲ *Helianthemum* 'Rhodanthe Carneum'

double pink flowers and deep green leaves. **'Salmon Queen'** displays bright salmon-pink flowers. **'Sudbury Gem'** produces deep pink flowers with a bright red centre and grey-green leaves. **'Supreme'** (syn. 'Red Orient') carries dark red flowers and grey-green leaves. **'The Bride'**♀ bears cream flowers with a bright yellow centre and silvery grey leaves. **'Wisley Primrose'**♀ produces primrose-yellow

▲ *Helianthemum* 'Wisley Primrose'

flowers and pale grey-green leaves. **'Wisley White'** displays pure white flowers with yellow stamens and grey leaves.

CULTIVATION Plant in any well-drained soil in a warm, sunny position. On heavy soils add sharp grit to assist drainage. Although fully hardy, rock roses may need protection from cold, desiccating winds.

PROPAGATION Sow seed of the species in pots in autumn or winter and overwinter in a coldframe. Prick out seedlings as soon as they are large enough to handle. Raise selected forms and hybrids from semi-ripe cuttings in mid summer.

PRUNING Trim lightly to moderately in early spring or immediately after flowering to keep in shape.

PESTS AND DISEASES Usually trouble free.

Helianthus

Sunflower
Compositae

Helianthus annuus

With their large, brilliant yellow daisy flowers on strong, leafy stems, sunflowers are unmistakable. They are well known as being easy to grow and hardy, but the larger varieties are considered by some to be rather too obtrusive. Indeed, these varieties may look out of place in a small garden, but when there is room for them they make a bold and impressive display clumped together at the back of a border. There are also much smaller-flowered and shorter varieties available which can be used elsewhere, even in window boxes.

All species flower from late summer to early autumn, except *Helianthus salicifolius* which commences flowering in early autumn. The flowers attract bees, and the large edible seeds that follow encourage finches into the garden. The genus includes *H. tuberosus*, the Jerusalem artichoke, grown for its knobbly edible tubers.

RECOMMENDED SPECIES AND VARIETIES

H. annuus (common sunflower) A solitary flower, up to 30cm (1ft) across and usually with a brown or purple centre, stands at the top of this annual's stout stem. The stem also bears heart-shaped leaves 20-40cm (8-16in) long. HEIGHT & SPREAD 2.4m×60cm (8×2ft).

'Tall Single' (also known as 'Giant Single' or 'Russian Giant') is single stemmed and very widely grown. It is the classic sunflower of childhood memory.

Shorter, branching varieties are listed below, all bearing flowers up to 15cm (6in) across. They spread to about 50cm (20in).

'Moonwalker' has pale yellow flowers and reaches a height of up to 1.5m (5ft).

▼ *Helianthus* 'Moonwalker'

▲ *Helianthus annuus* 'Velvet Queen'

'Music Box Mixed' is a dwarf variety, reaching about 60cm (2ft) tall. It has cream, yellow and red flowers. **'Pacino'**, up to 60cm (2ft) tall, has single golden yellow flowers. **'Prado Red'** and **'Prado Yellow'** have red and deep yellow flowers respectively, and grow to 1.5m (5ft) tall. The flowers produce little pollen, making them useful for cutting.

'Sunburst' grows to 1.2m (4ft) tall and bears 10cm (4in) flowers in a mixture of colours from pale yellow to maroon. Some of them have two-toned 'petals' (ray florets) – red at the base and yellow beyond, for example. **'Teddy Bear'** has fully double yellow flowers and grows up to 60cm (2ft) tall. **'Velvet Queen'** grows up to 1.5m (5ft) tall and bears deep velvety red flowers.

H. atrorubens (dark-eyed sunflower) The orange-yellow flowers grow up to 9cm (3½in) across and have maroon centres. The leaves of this rather invasive perennial are oval to lance-shaped. They grow to a length of 30cm (1ft) long and are crowded towards the stem bases. HEIGHT & SPREAD 2m×60cm (6½×2ft).

▼ *Helianthus atrorubens* 'Gullick's Variety'

▲ *Helianthus* x 'Loddon Gold'

The vigorous **'Gullick's Variety'** has smaller flowers. **'Monarch'**♀ has golden semi-double flowers up to 15cm (6in) across with quilled petals.

H.* x *multiflorus Golden yellow flowers, up to 12.5cm (5in) across, are borne on this bushy, rapidly spreading perennial. The leaves are lance-shaped to broadly oval and up to 20cm (8in) long. HEIGHT & SPREAD 1.5m×75cm (5ft×30in).

'Capenoch Star'♀ has lemon-yellow flowers. **'Loddon Gold'**♀ has golden yellow double flowers.

H. salicifolius (willow-leaved sunflower) Loose clusters of golden yellow flowers, 7.5cm (3in) across, appear in early autumn. The stout, branching stems are smooth, bearing numerous drooping, shiny, narrow leaves, about 20cm (8in) long. This perennial species is valued for its foliage. HEIGHT & SPREAD 2.4m×60cm (8×2ft).

'Lemon Queen' is smaller, reaching a height of 1.5m (5ft).

CULTIVATION Plant in any soil, but preferably a clay loam. Despite their name, sunflowers do well in partial shade as well as full sun. Bear in mind that the flowerheads will turn to the sun. In a windy site, all but the shortest varieties require support.

Plant perennials in early spring. Yearly lifting and replanting of *H. atrorubens* and *H. multiflorus* helps to curtail their spread.

Sow *H. annuus* and its varieties straight into their flowering positions and thin out the seedlings when large enough to handle.

PROPAGATION Sow seed of *H. annuus* and varieties in mid spring. Divide perennials in early spring, though late autumn is also satisfactory if the soil is not too wet.

PESTS AND DISEASES Aphids and powdery mildew can be a problem, and slugs are a danger to young seedlings.

Helichrysum

Compositae

Helichrysum italicum

Daisy-like flowers, whose 'petals' are, in fact, dry, papery bracts, are the common feature of helichrysums. In some species these are cut and dried as 'everlasting flowers'. Many plants, though, are more prized for their silvery grey foliage. Only one species included here is an annual – *Helichrysum bracteatum* – whose cultivars have everlasting flowers of many colours. The rest are mostly low-growing, evergreen perennials or sub-shrubs, and all are fully hardy, except *H. arwae*. The perennials *H. italicum*, *H. petiolare* and *H. splendidum* reach a height of 45cm (1½ft) tall or above and are grown chiefly for their foliage effect. All helichrysums require free-draining soil and full sun, and the smaller plants demand dry winter conditions.

RECOMMENDED SPECIES AND VARIETIES

H. angustifolium see *H. italicum*

H. arwae This dense, evergreen sub-shrub forms a compact mat of prostrate stems clothed with narrow, 1cm (⅜in) long leaves, covered with silky, white hairs. White flowers, 2cm (¾in) across and flushed with crimson on the back, appear in summer. Native to the Yemen. HEIGHT & SPREAD 5×30cm (2×12in).

H. bellidioides In late spring and summer, brilliant white flowers, 2-3cm (¾-1¼in) across, rise on 8cm (3¼in) stalks above a dense carpet of short oval or rounded leaves, which are dark green above, silvery white beneath. This evergreen sub-shrub is native to New Zealand. HEIGHT & SPREAD 10×30cm (4×12in).

H. bracteatum (syn. *Bracteantha bracteatum*) (strawflower) This annual or short-lived deciduous perennial bears solitary, lemon-yellow to golden flowers on upright, branching, slightly bristly stems. The plant is native to Australia. HEIGHT & SPREAD 30cm-1.5m×20-40cm (1-5ft×8-16in).

From this species we get the brightly coloured everlasting strawflowers, much used in dried arrangements. The blooms, 5-7.5cm (2-3in) across, are borne from mid summer to mid autumn. There are short varieties for the front of a border or containers, taller varieties for mid border. The double flowers of **'Bright Bikini Mixed'**♀ come in 8 colours ('Hot Bikini'♀ is a striking scarlet and gold). These reach a height of 30cm (12in). **'Dargan Hill Monarch'**

▲ *Helichrysum frigidum*

▲ *Helichrysum orientale*

has golden yellow, single flowers. It grows to 1 m (3 ft) in height, and is hardier, surviving the winter on sheltered sites. **Drakkar Pastel Mixed** has flowers in pale shades of salmon, pink and yellow. It grows to a height of 1 m (3 ft). **Dwarf Spangle Mixed** grows to 30 cm (1 ft) tall and bears double flowers in a wide range of colours.

H. coralloides see *Ozothamnus coralloides*

H. frigidum This evergreen sub-shrub forms a close mat of slender stems, densely covered with white hairs. The narrow, silvery leaves are about 5 mm (¼ in) long. White daisies about 1.5 cm (½ in) across appear singly at the tips of the branches in summer. Native to Corsica and Sardinia. HEIGHT & SPREAD 10×20 cm (4×8 in).

H. italicum♀ (syn. *H. angustifolium*) (curry plant) This hardy, evergreen sub-shrub from S Europe is admired for its mass of narrow, aromatic grey leaves, 3 cm (1¼ in) long. Clusters 8 cm (3¼ in) across carry numerous small, mustard-yellow flowers on erect white stems in mid summer. HEIGHT & SPREAD 60 cm×1 m (2×3 ft).

▼ *Helichrysum italicum*

H. ledifolium see *Ozothamnus ledifolius*

H. milfordiae♀ This evergreen perennial forms a low mat of closely packed silvery rosettes with oval leaves, 1.5 cm (½ in) long. Short-stalked, white flowers, 2.5 cm (1 in) across, open from crimson buds in early summer and retain this colour on the undersides. Native to South Africa. HEIGHT & SPREAD 10×20 cm (4×8 in).

H. orientale Large, branched clusters of round, bright lemon-yellow flowers, 1 cm (⅜ in) wide, are borne at the ends of the stems of this loosely branched, hardy evergreen sub-shrub. The stems and narrow tongue-shaped leaves, up to 6 cm (2½ in) long, are covered with dense, white, woolly hairs. Native to Greece. HEIGHT & SPREAD 30×30 cm (1×1 ft).

H. petiolare♀ (syn. *H. petiolatum*) This half-hardy, evergreen sub-shrub, grown mainly for its foliage effect in borders and containers, makes a mound of silver-grey trailing stems. The woolly, grey, broadly oval leaves are 4 cm (1½ in) across. Creamy white flowers appear from mid summer to late autumn, carried in loose terminal clusters up to 5 cm (2 in) across. Native to South Africa. HEIGHT & SPREAD 50 cm×1 m (20 in×3 ft).

▼ *Helichrysum petiolare* 'Variegatum'

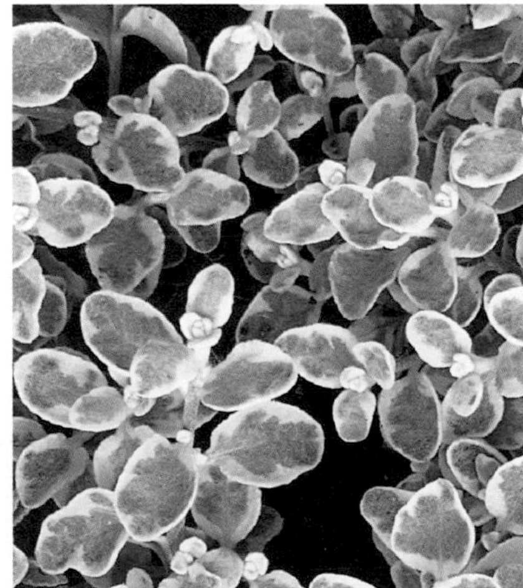

'Limelight' has lime-green leaves. **'Variegatum'**♀ has leaves variegated cream and grey-green.

H. plicatum In mid summer shiny, round, bright yellow flowers are held in branched clusters up to 6 cm (2½ in) across, above the foliage of this hardy evergreen perennial. The narrow, oblong, green leaves are 4 cm (1½ in) long and have woolly hairs on the edges. Native to the Balkans. HEIGHT & SPREAD 45×30 cm (1½×1 ft).

H. rosmarinifolium see *Ozothamnus rosmarinifolius*

H. selago see *Ozothamnus selago*

H. sessilioides (syn. *H. sessile*) In late summer, solitary, yellow-centred white flowers, sometimes tinged with red and 1 cm (⅜ in) across, spangle mats of small, oval, dark green leaves covered with white, silky hairs. This creeping evergreen sub-shrub is native to South Africa. HEIGHT & SPREAD 5×30 cm (2×12 in).

***H.* 'Schwefellicht'** ('Sulphur Light') Masses of small, fluffy, sulphur-yellow flowers are borne throughout the summer in clusters, 5 cm (2 in) across. The lance-shaped leaves of this hardy herbaceous perennial are silver-grey, woolly and 4 cm (1½ in) long. The flowers can be dried for winter arrangements. HEIGHT & SPREAD 60×30 cm (2×1 ft).

H. splendidum♀ This bushy, evergreen sub-shrub, grown mainly for its foliage, has woolly, white shoots clothed in grey, oblong leaves, 6 cm (2½ in) long. Rounded clusters, 4 cm (1½ in) across and composed of a mass of tiny, yellow flowers, appear in mid summer. Native to South Africa. The plant is fairly hardy. HEIGHT & SPREAD 1.2×1.2 m (4×4 ft).

CULTIVATION Plant helichrysums in spring in any free-draining soil in full sun. Grow the smaller alpine species in an alpine house or protect them from excessive winter wet on the foliage; they are also well suited to cultivation in troughs. The larger sub-shrubs should have frost-damaged growth cut back hard in spring.

PROPAGATION Divide herbaceous perennials in spring. Take semi-ripe cuttings of sub-shrubs and alpines in summer and grow on in a coldframe until the following spring. Sow seed of the annual varieties outside in mid spring, or in gentle heat in early spring for planting out in late spring.

PESTS AND DISEASES Usually trouble free.

Helictotrichon see GRASSES p. 301

h

Heliophila
Cruciferae

The half-hardy annuals, perennials and sub-shrubs of this genus are characterised by dainty, cross-shaped, four-petalled flowers. A sunny border is brightened by the only species that is commonly grown.

RECOMMENDED SPECIES

H. coronopifolia (syn. *H. longifolia*) Papery blue flowers, up to 1cm (⅜in) across, with white or yellowish centres, appear in clusters in mid to late summer on this showy annual. They are followed in autumn by narrow green pod-like fruits. Lance-shaped smooth green leaves grow up to 15cm (6in) long. Native to southern Africa. HEIGHT & SPREAD 25x30cm (10x12in).

CULTIVATION Plant in an open sunny position in a free-draining soil once the danger of frost has passed.

PROPAGATION Sow seed under glass in mid spring, or where plants are to flower in late spring.

PESTS AND DISEASES Usually trouble free.

h

Heliopsis
Compositae

Only one species of this genus of hardy and half-hardy annuals and perennials is commonly grown. *Heliopsis helianthoides* has showy flowers that stand out in a border from mid summer to early autumn.

RECOMMENDED SPECIES AND VARIETIES

H. helianthoides Upright yellow, daisy-like flowers, up to 7.5cm (3in) across, rise above coarse, spear-shaped green leaves, each up to 15cm (6in) long. The plant is a free-flowering, hardy herbaceous perennial, native to N America. HEIGHT & SPREAD 1.5x1m (5x3ft).

'Hohlspiegel' has semidouble, orange-yellow flowers and dark green leaves. It reaches a height of 1.2m (4ft) and a spread of 60cm (2ft). The flowers of var. ***scabra*** are less numerous and the leaves are coarser than those of the species. Its cultivar, **'Goldgrünherz',** has semidouble flowers with lime-green centres. It reaches a height of 1m (3ft). **'Sommersonne'** ('Summer Sun') has single yellow flowers, up to 10cm (4in) across, on a compact plant no more than 1m (3ft) high.

▲ *Heliopsis helianthoides* 'Hohlspiegel'

▲ *Heliopsis helianthoides* var. *scabra* 'Sommersonne'

CULTIVATION Plant between late autumn and spring in a sunny position in well-drained, medium to heavy, loamy soil. Deadhead regularly and provide plants with some support.

PROPAGATION Divide dormant crowns between late autumn and early spring.

PESTS AND DISEASES Usually trouble free.

Heliotrope see *Heliotropium*

Heliotropium
Heliotrope
Boraginaceae

Dense heads of blue, purple or white, sometimes richly fragrant, flowers throughout summer are complemented by wrinkled leaves. The half-hardy annuals, evergreen shrubs and sub-shrubs in this genus bring height and drama to bedding schemes and flourish in outdoor containers and in conservatories. Native to tropical areas the plants described are hardy to 2°C (36°F).

RECOMMENDED SPECIES AND VARIETIES

H. arborescens (cherry pie) Sweet-smelling dense heads of tiny tubular violet, purple or white flowers adorn this evergreen shrub all summer. The leathery oval or elliptical green leaves are up to 10cm (4in) long and 5cm (2in) wide. The plant may be kept compact by light pruning in spring. If raised annually it will reach about 45cm (18in). HEIGHT & SPREAD 2mx90cm (6½x3ft).

'Chatsworth'♀ is strong-growing and suitable for training as a standard. Highly scented purple flowers are borne in dense clusters among mid to dark green leaves.

▲ *Heliotropium arborescens* 'Gatton Park'

'Gatton Park' has sweetly scented pale blue flowers and crinkled mid green leaves. It reaches 60cm (24in) in height and spread. **'Marine'** has large clusters, up to 10cm (4in) across, of richly fragrant, deep purple flowers. Very wrinkled dark green leaves add to its character. This compact and bushy plant reaches 45cm (18in) in height and spread. **'Dwarf Marine'** reaches just 30cm (12in). **'P.K. Lowther'** bears fragrant pale to lavender blue flowers in dense clusters and has a height of 60cm (24in) and a spread of 45cm (18in). **'Princess Marina'**♀ has clusters of sweetly scented rich purple flowers offset by violet-green crinkly foliage. Its height is 60cm (24in) and spread 45cm (18in). **'White Lady'** has silvery mauve, sweetly scented flowers that are

▲ *Heliotropium arborescens* 'Princess Marina'

▲ *Heliotropium arborescens* 'White Lady'

pink in bud, ageing to white, and mid green foliage. It grows to 60cm (24in) with a spread of 45cm (18in).

CULTIVATION For conservatory decoration, plant in pots in spring, using John Innes No.3 soil-based compost. Plants will grow in full sun but require plenty of ventilation. Outdoors, plant after the danger of frost has passed. Lift plants grown outside before any danger of frost, pot and keep in a light but cool frost-free place over winter. Tip-prune plants in early spring and cut back any that are leggy.

PROPAGATION Sow seed of the species and 'Marine' in heat in a greenhouse in early spring. Take softwood cuttings of other recommended cultivars in summer.

PESTS AND DISEASES Greenfly and whitefly may infest plants grown indoors and overwintered plants in early spring.

Helipterum

Strawflower

Compositae

Charming flowers with a straw-like texture that create a decorative display in herbaceous borders and bedding schemes. They also make excellent dried flowers and can be grown in pots under glass. Strawflowers thrive in full sun in poor, dry soils. The flowers close in shade, in dull weather and at night so they should be positioned away from shadows cast by buildings or larger plants. The two species of the genus are annuals and native to Australia.

RECOMMENDED SPECIES AND VARIETIES

H. humboldtianum (syn. *Pteropogon humboldtianum)* Small golden yellow flowers are borne in tight, flat-topped clusters, about 8cm (3¼in) across, from mid to late summer. The flowers dry very well, but turn green. The linear leaves, about 3cm (1¼in) long, are hairy and appear almost white. This small, neat plant makes a fine addition to the front of a bed or along a path edge. HEIGHT & SPREAD 40×20cm (16×8in).

H. roseum (syn. *Acrolinium roseum)* The semidouble, daisy-like flowers, 5cm (2in)

▲ *Helipterum roseum*

across, are borne in mid to late summer and are various shades of pink or white, all with a yellow central disc. The petals are papery in texture. The narrow, pointed grey-green leaves are smooth and about 4cm (1½in) long. HEIGHT & SPREAD 45×25cm (18×10in).

'Goliath' has cerise flowers offset by a dark amber central disc. The flowers dry very well.

CULTIVATION Grow on fast-draining, poor, dry soil in a sunny, open position. On moisture-retentive soil with a good nutrient supply, leaf growth will be favoured and flowering reduced. Cut *H. humboldtianum* for drying when all flowers on the cluster have opened; cut *H. roseum* before the flowers are fully expanded. Hang the flowers upside down to dry in bunches in a cool, airy place.

PROPAGATION Sow seed in the flowering site in mid spring. Alternatively, start in a greenhouse as a half-hardy annual, with young plants grown in small pots or a cell tray so that root disturbance is kept to a minimum. Plant out when the risk of hard, late frosts has passed.

PESTS AND DISEASES Aphids may be troublesome.

Hellebore, stinking see *Helleborus foetidus*
Helleborine see *Epipactis*

Helleborus

Hellebore

Ranunculaceae

These hardy evergreen and deciduous perennials bring colour and interest to the garden from mid winter to late spring. The cup or saucer-shaped flowers borne on strong, upright stems, come in white and various unusual shades of green and purple. The divided leaves have three to seven or more oval or lance-shaped leaflets, 10-20cm (4-8in) long. Hellebores grow well in shade or semi-shade, provided the soil is moist, and are native to Europe and Asia.

RECOMMENDED SPECIES AND VARIETIES

H. argutifolius♀ (syn. *H. corsicus*) Apple-green, cup-shaped flowers, up to 4cm (1½in) across, are borne in terminal clusters on thick, cane-like stems. The flowers last from mid winter well into spring. The dark evergreen leaves are slightly prickly. HEIGHT & SPREAD 1m×60cm (3×2ft).

▲ *Helleborus argutifolius*

H. cyclophyllus Scented, yellow-green, cup-shaped flowers, 5-7.5cm (2-3in) across, with prominent yellowish stamens appear in spring. The deeply divided dark green leaves are up to 20cm (8in) long. HEIGHT & SPREAD 45×45cm (1½×1½ft).

H. foetidus♀ (stinking hellebore) Nodding, green cup-shaped flowers, flushed or edged with purple and up to 2.5cm (1in) across, are borne in clusters from late winter to early spring. The leaves are dark green or grey-green. This evergreen, almost shrubby perennial has an unpleasant scent and can cause skin irritation. HEIGHT & SPREAD 75×60cm (2½×2ft).

Plants sold under the name **Wester Flisk Group** have stems, leaf and flower stalks suffused with red.

H. lividus♀ Clusters of cup-shaped yellow-green flowers, tinged with purple and up to 5cm (2in) across, appear in late winter. The mid green leaves are marbled with pale green and have purplish undersides. A half-hardy evergreen perennial requiring a warm sheltered site in the garden. HEIGHT & SPREAD 45×45cm (1½×1½ft).

H. niger♀ (Christmas rose) This evergreen perennial bears saucer-shaped, nodding flowers on short stout stems in mid winter. Up to 7.5cm (3in) across, the flowers have white petals, which may turn pinkish with age, and protruding golden stamens. The leaves have 7 to 9 dark green leaflets. HEIGHT & SPREAD 30×45cm (1×1½ft).

'Potter's Wheel' has larger flowers, up to 10cm (4in) across, with a greenish centre. **'White Magic'** produces consistently white flowers.

H. odorus Cup-shaped, scented, yellowish green flowers, 5-7.5cm (2-3in) across, droop in small clusters on strong upright stems during winter and early spring. This usually evergreen perennial has large, dull green, leathery leaves. HEIGHT & SPREAD up to 45×45cm (1½×1½ft).

H. orientalis hort. (Lenten rose) Saucer-shaped flowers, up to 7.5cm (3in) across, appear singly or in clusters in late winter and early spring. Colours range from white through pink to purple. This semi-evergreen has deep green divided leaves, up to 25cm (10in) long. A very variable plant. HEIGHT & SPREAD 45×45cm (1½×1½ft).

▲ *Helleborus orientalis* 'Ballard's Group'

h

▲ *Helleborus orientalis* ssp. *guttatus*

'Ballard's Group' has dark purply black flowers. Commercial strains known as black seedlings are usually the same colour but can be variable. The flowers of ssp. ***guttatus*** are white or cream, spotted red-purple. The **Kochii Group** has nodding yellow-green flowers that open to primrose yellow and large, coarsely toothed leaves. There is a selection of named colour forms within the group. Also, a number of selected seedling strains are available known as *H. o.* pink, *H. o.* purple and *H. o.* white.

H. purpurascens Deep purple flowers, purple-green within and with yellowish green stamens, are produced in early spring

▲ *Helleborus purpurascens*

by this neat, deciduous plant. The nodding, cup-shaped blooms are up to 5cm (2in) across. The dark green leaves, up to 30cm (12in) long, have lobed and toothed leaflets. HEIGHT & SPREAD up to 30×30cm (1×1ft).

H. × sternii Dense clusters of cup-shaped pale green flowers tinged with pink appear in winter and early spring. The grey-green divided leaves are up to 25cm (10in) long. HEIGHT & SPREAD 45×50cm (18×20in).

The compact plants of the **Blackthorn Group**♀, up to 60cm (2ft) high and 45cm (1½ft) wide, bear green flowers distinctly flushed with pink and have noticeably veined grey-green foliage. **'Boughton Beauty'** has flowers suffused with rose and leaves marked and tinted with pinky purple. Plants in the **Boughton Group** are of neat habit and have green, pink-flushed flowers and foliage.

▲ *Helleborus × sternii* 'Boughton Beauty'

H. torquatus Nodding, cup or saucer-shaped flowers, up to 6cm (2½in) across, are borne in clusters in winter and early spring. Violet-purple, often blue-green within, they appear before the erect, dark green, toothed leaves. A deciduous perennial. HEIGHT & SPREAD 40×30cm (16×12in).

H. viridis (green hellebore) Green, nodding, saucer-shaped flowers, up to 5cm (2in) across, appear in clusters in mid winter. This deciduous plant has mid green leaves with 7 to 11 leaflets. HEIGHT & SPREAD up to 30×30cm (1×1ft).

The leaves of ssp. ***occidentalis*** have broad leaflets with toothed edges.

CULTIVATION Plant in autumn or winter in deep, richly organic, moist soil, preferably in shade or partial shade. Remove the fading foliage of deciduous hellebores as the flowers appear. After flowering, mulch plants with well-rotted compost or leaf-mould. Hellebores take 12-18 months to become established and resent disturbance.

PROPAGATION Divide clumps in autumn. Sow the ripe seed of species in mid to late summer in a coldframe.

PESTS AND DISEASES Greenfly can be a nuisance in late spring and early summer.

Hemerocallis

Day lily
Hemerocallidaceae

Brilliantly coloured exotic flowers, in almost every shade from white to deepest red-black, create a majestic summer display against a backdrop of strap-shaped, arching leaves. Although each flower lasts for one day only, these easy-to-grow hardy perennials produce a profusion of new blooms day after day, once established.

Some day lilies open in the early morning, others open late in the afternoon, remain open all night and close the following day. The flowers are composed of three petals above and three sepals underneath. The species and early cultivars have tapered lily-like or open star-like flowers; the modern hybrids tend to have full, round and ruffled flowers. There are also spider-shaped varieties. Some day lilies have a band of colour, known as the eyezone, above the throat. The flower texture can be shiny, satiny or creped.

These herbaceous, semi-evergreen or evergreen clump-forming plants have mid to dark green – occasionally yellowish or bluish green – strap-shaped leaves, 23cm-1.2m (9in-4ft) long. The selected plants are herbaceous unless otherwise stated. The evergreen varieties are slightly tender and should be planted in spring rather than autumn.

Tall day lilies associate well with grasses and other plants with architectural foliage, while the medium and smaller flowered varieties make ideal border plants. The compact, colourful dwarf varieties, many of which are re-blooming, are suitable for smaller gardens and containers. Some of the newer varieties are often most effective when massed in borders with other day lilies, or planted alongside a path or a driveway. Day lilies tolerate windy sites and are suitable for growing in coastal gardens. The flowers also look magnificent when planted along a stream side or river bank. Place dark coloured flowers against a lighter coloured background for emphasis.

This genus of 13 species is native to China, Japan and Korea where it grows in mountainous terrains, marshy river valleys, meadows and at forest margins. There are now well over 30 000 hemerocallis hybrids in cultivation.

RECOMMENDED SPECIES AND VARIETIES

'American Revolution' Velvety black to wine-red, tapered lily-like flowers, 14 cm (5½ in) across, with green throats. HEIGHT 70 cm (28 in).

▲ *Hemerocallis* 'Ann Kelley'

'Ann Kelley' Semi-evergreen with deep rose-pink ruffled flowers, 14 cm (5½ in) across, of triangular to full form, with lighter midribs and black anthers. HEIGHT 65 cm (26 in).

'Beauty to Behold' Semi-evergreen with ruffled, green-throated lemon flowers 14 cm (5½ in) across. HEIGHT 60 cm (24 in).

'Berlin Red'♀ Bright red, yellow-throated open flowers, 15 cm (6 in) across, with yellow midribs. HEIGHT 75 cm (30 in).

'Bertie Ferris' Persimmon-orange ruffled flowers 6 cm (2½ in) across. HEIGHT 50 cm (20 in).

'Betty Woods' Evergreen; fragrant double, ruffled yellow flowers, 14 cm (5½ in) across, with green throats. HEIGHT 65 cm (26 in).

'Black Magic' Star-shaped, deep mahogany-red flowers that are 9 cm (3½ in) across. HEIGHT 1 m (3 ft).

▼ *Hemerocallis* 'Betty Woods'

▲ *Hemerocallis* 'Bonanza'

'Bonanza' Trumpet-shaped, pale orange-yellow flowers, 7.5 cm (3 in) across, with a brownish centre. HEIGHT 85 cm (34 in).

'Burning Daylight'♀ Flaring, ruffled rich orange flowers, 15 cm (6 in) across, with a hint of crimson. HEIGHT 75 cm (30 in).

'Cartwheels'♀ Wide-open, flat orange-gold flowers 15 cm (6 in) across. HEIGHT 75 cm (30 in).

'Catherine Woodbery' Wide-petalled, lightly ruffled, light lavender-pink flowers, 15 cm (6 in) across, with chartreuse throats. Very fragrant. HEIGHT 75 cm (30 in).

'Cherry Cheeks' The flowers are bright cherry-red, 15 cm (6 in) across, and have creamy pink midribs, contrasting black anthers and a small chartreuse throat. HEIGHT 70 cm (28 in).

'Chicago Apache' Open, roundish and velvety scarlet flowers, 12 cm (4¾ in) across, with deeper red, ruffled edges and white midribs. The flowers have green throats. HEIGHT 70 cm (28 in).

'Chicago Sunrise' Semi-evergreen with deep yellow to golden orange, round, ruffled flowers, 12 cm (4¾ in) across. They are green-throated. HEIGHT 65 cm (26 in).

'Children's Festival' Heavily ruffled, trumpet-shaped, soft peach-apricot flowers, 10 cm (4 in) across, tinted rose-pink. HEIGHT 60 cm (24 in).

'Corky'♀ Pale yellow, tapered lily-shaped flowers, 6 cm (2½ in) across, with mahogany brown-backed sepals bloom for 2 days. HEIGHT 85 cm (34 in).

'Cream Drop' Ruffled, trumpet-shaped, creamy yellow flowers, 7.5 cm (3 in) across, with chartreuse throat. HEIGHT 43 cm (17 in).

H. dumortieri The deep yellow, bell-shaped flowers are 6 cm (2½ in) across. HEIGHT 50 cm (20 in).

'Edna Spalding' Semi-evergreen with tapered, lily-shaped, pure mid pink flowers, 11 cm (4¼ in) across, with a yellow-green throat. HEIGHT 60 cm (24 in).

'Fairy Tale Pink' Semi-evergreen with round, very ruffled pale melon to beige-pink flowers 14 cm (5½ in) across. Semi-double flowers may be produced in very hot summers. HEIGHT 60 cm (24 in).

▲ *Hemerocallis* 'Fairy Tale Pink'

▲ *Hemerocallis* 'Frans Hals'

H. flava see ***H. lilioasphodelus***

'Frans Hals' Rust-red flowers, 13 cm (5 in) across, with orange sepals and creamy orange midribs. HEIGHT 60 cm (24 in).

***H. fulva* 'Green Kwanso'** (syn. f. 'Kwanso Flore Pleno') Semi-evergreen with double tawny-orange flowers, 10 cm (4 in) across, and dark red eyezone. HEIGHT 75 cm (30 in).

***H. fulva* 'Kwanso Variegata'** Semi-evergreen with double tawny-orange flowers, 12 cm (5 in) across, and white-margined leaves. HEIGHT 75 cm (30 in).

'Gentle Shepherd' This slightly tender semi-evergreen has oval, ruffled flowers, 14 cm (5½ in) across, that are near white with green throats. HEIGHT 72.5 cm (29 in).

'George Cunningham' Trumpet-shaped, ruffled flowers, 12.5 cm (5 in) across, are melon-apricot with a faint lavender midrib and a tangerine throat. HEIGHT 1 m (3 ft).

'Golden Chimes'♀ Deep yellow bell-shaped flowers, 5 cm (2 in) across, with brown-backed sepals. HEIGHT 70 cm (28 in).

'Green Flutter'♀ Semi-evergreen. Canary yellow, green-throated, ruffled flowers 9 cm (3½ in) across. HEIGHT 50 cm (20 in).

'Helle Berlinerin'♀ The wide open, roundish flowers are near-white and

▲ *Hemerocallis* 'Helle Berlinerin'

12.5 cm (5 in) across, with orange-yellow throats. HEIGHT 70 cm (28 in).

'Hyperion' The narrow, tapered lily-shaped lemon-yellow flowers, 10 cm (4 in) across, are very fragrant and occasionally double. HEIGHT 90 cm (36 in).

'Joan Senior' This evergreen has an abundance of lightly ruffled, near-white flowers, 15 cm (6 in) across, with yellowish green throats. HEIGHT 63 cm (25 in).

'Judah' Deep gold, bronze-edged rounded flowers, 15 cm (6 in) across, with yellow throats. HEIGHT 75 cm (30 in).

'Kindly Light' Spider-shaped with slender, bright yellow flowers, 22 cm (8¾ in) across, and a faint salmon-pink eyezone on cool evenings. Evergreen. HEIGHT 68 cm (27 in).

H. lilioasphodelus ♀ (syn. *H. flava*) Fragrant semi-evergreen with tapered lily-shaped lemon-yellow flowers 9 cm (3½ in) across. HEIGHT 1 m (3 ft).

'Little Gypsy Vagabond' Evergreen with round, flat, light yellow flowers, 9 cm (3½ in) across, bold black-purple eyezone and green throat. HEIGHT 45 cm (18 in).

'Little Wine Cup' Trumpet-shaped wine-red flowers, 5 cm (2 in) across, with tiny chartreuse throats. HEIGHT 50 cm (20 in).

▼ *Hemerocallis* 'Luxury Lace'

'Luxury Lace' Frilly, star-shaped pinkish lavender flowers, 10 cm (4 in) across, with green throats. HEIGHT 80 cm (32 in).

'Marion Vaughn' ♀ Very fragrant, tapered lily-shaped, pale lemon-yellow flowers, 10 cm (4 in) across. HEIGHT 84 cm (33 in).

'Millie Schlumpf' Round, ruffled, pure pale pink flowers, 12.5 cm (5 in) across, with a light green throat. HEIGHT 50 cm (20 in).

'Mini Pearl' Round, ruffled, blush-pink flowers, 7.5 cm (3 in) across, with a green-lemon throat. HEIGHT 40 cm (16 in).

'Moonlight Mist' Evergreen with pale ivory to cream-pink round and ruffled flowers, 7.5 cm (3 in) across, with chartreuse throats. HEIGHT 45 cm (18 in).

'Night Raider' Fragrant, round, very dark red flowers, 14 cm (5½ in) across, with small green throats. HEIGHT 70 cm (28 in).

'Nova' ♀ Fragrant, star-shaped, satiny lemon-yellow flowers, 14 cm (5½ in) across, with green throats. HEIGHT 60 cm (24 in).

'Olive Bailey Langdon' This evergreen has rounded, rich violet-purple flowers, 12.5 cm (5 in) across, with yellow-green throats. HEIGHT 70 cm (28 in).

'Pandora's Box' Evergreen with fragrant pale cream flowers, 7.5 cm (3 in) across, with a vivid burgundy eyezone and a green throat. HEIGHT 48 cm (19 in).

'Pardon Me' Fragrant, round, cranberry-red flowers, 7.5 cm (3 in) across, with chartreuse throats. HEIGHT 45 cm (18 in).

▲ *Hemerocallis* 'Pandora's Box'

▲ *Hemerocallis* 'Pardon Me'

'Pink Damask' ♀ Star-shaped, buff-tinged rose-pink flowers, 12.5 cm (5 in) across, with yellow throats and distinctive cream-pink midribs. HEIGHT 95 cm (38 in).

'Prairie Blue Eyes' This semi-evergreen has trumpet-shaped lavender flowers, 12 cm (4¾ in) across, with a chartreuse throat and a near-blue eyezone. HEIGHT 70 cm (28 in).

'Purple Rain' Evergreen with round, ruffled grape-purple flowers, 7.5 cm (3 in) across, with a prominent deep purple to near black eyezone. HEIGHT 38 cm (15 in).

'Real Wind' Round salmon-peach flowers, 16.5 cm (6½ in) across. A rose pink eyezone and a gold throat. HEIGHT 65 cm (26 in).

'Sammy Russell' Trumpet-shaped dark red flowers 10 cm (4 in) across. HEIGHT 70 cm (28 in).

'Siloam Fairy Tale' Round, ruffled, frosted pale pink flowers, 7.5 cm (3 in) across. Deep orchid-pink eyezone. HEIGHT 45 cm (18 in).

'Siloam Little Girl' Round, ruffled shrimp-pink flowers, 9 cm (3½ in) across. with a rose-red eyezone and green-gold throat. HEIGHT 45 cm (18 in).

'Siloam Tiny Mite' Round, golden-yellow flowers, 6 cm (2½ in) across, with a gold throat and maroon eyezone. HEIGHT 50 cm (20 in).

'Siloam Virginia Henson' Round, ruffled, pink-tinted cream flowers, 10 cm (4 in) across, with a ruby-red eyezone and green throat. HEIGHT 45 cm (18 in).

'Stafford' Scarlet, tapered lily-shaped flowers, 10 cm (4 in) across, with green-yellow throats. HEIGHT 70 cm (28 in).

'Stella de Oro' ♀ Fragrant bell-shaped, brassy yellow flowers 7 cm (2¾ in) across. HEIGHT 28 cm (11 in).

▲ *Hemerocallis* 'Summer Wine'

'Summer Wine' Trumpet-shaped, light wine-red flowers, 14 cm (5½ in) across, with a chartreuse throat. HEIGHT 60 cm (24 in).

'Tonia Gay' Evergreen with round, ruffled, baby-pink flowers, 14 cm (5½ in) across, with green throats. HEIGHT 40 cm (16 in).

'Varsity' Trumpet-shaped, ivory flowers,

10 cm (4 in) across, with a maroon eyezone and a green throat. HEIGHT 75 cm (30 in).
'Whichford'♀ Trumpet-shaped, fragrant, delicate lemon flowers, 10 cm (4 in) across, with green throats. HEIGHT 70 cm (28 in).
CULTIVATION Grow in fertile, moisture-retentive soil in full sun. Generally, adequate flowering cannot be expected if grown in dry conditions or in shade, but red and purple-flowered varieties can be intolerant of heavy rainfall and very hot sun. Plant the more tender evergreen varieties in spring rather than in autumn. Divide every 3 or 4 years to maintain vigour.
PROPAGATION Divide in late summer or early spring.
PESTS AND DISEASES Usually trouble free. Foliage is sometimes disfigured by rust and flower buds may be infected by gall midge. Slugs and snails damage young foliage in late winter and early spring. Crown rot can be a problem in hot and humid situations.

Hemlock see *Tsuga*
Hemp agrimony see *Eupatorium cannabinum*

Hepatica

Ranunculaceae

Bright pink, blue or white flowers add a splash of colour to the garden from late winter to early spring. These hardy herbaceous or evergreen perennials are ideal for semi-shaded positions but dislike exposed dry or windy sites. They are fully hardy but take a while to establish and do not like to be disturbed. They make good plants for a woodland garden or for a semi-shaded trough and can also be grown in pots in an unheated greenhouse or conservatory. Each flower has six to ten oval petals with a small ruff of three bracts immediately underneath. The leaves, which are 4-12.5 cm (1½-5 in) across, form a lax basal rosette and last all summer, long after the flowers have faded. They are long-stalked with three lobes and are often attractively mottled or marbled.
RECOMMENDED SPECIES AND VARIETIES
H. acutiloba Lavender-blue, occasionally pink or white, flowers up to 2 cm (¾ in) across appear in late winter and spring. The deep green evergreen leaves have distinctively pointed lobes. Native to calcareous woodland in eastern N America. HEIGHT & SPREAD 15-25×15-25 cm (6-10×6-10 in).
H. americana Bluish lavender flowers up to 2.5 cm (1 in) across appear in spring. The evergreen leaves have broad, blunt, rounded lobes. Native to dry acid woodlands of eastern N America. HEIGHT & SPREAD 10-15×10-15 cm (4-6×4-6 in).
H. angulosa see *H. transsilvanica*
***H. × media* 'Ballardii'**♀ Masses of vivid, rich blue, semidouble flowers, 3 cm (1¼ in) across, appear in early spring. Soft green, scalloped leaves are semi-evergreen. HEIGHT & SPREAD 10×20 cm (4×8 in).
H. nobilis♀ (syn. *H. triloba*) Blue, purple, pink or white flowers, 2 cm (¾ in) across, are borne in late winter and early spring. Double-flowered forms are occasionally seen. The kidney-shaped evergreen leaves are sometimes marbled with pale or dark green or grey and are often purple beneath. Native to mountains of continental Europe. HEIGHT & SPREAD 7.5×15 cm (3×6 in).

▲ *Hepatica nobilis*

▲ *Hepatica nobilis* var. *japonica*

Selected forms are listed as **blue** (blue shades), **pink** (pink shades) and **white** (pure white); the flowers of var. ***japonica*** are usually white, sometimes with a hint of pink, and the leaves have more pointed lobes.

▲ *Hepatica transsilvanica*

H. transsilvanica♀ (syn. *H. angulosa*) Pink, purple or lavender-blue flowers, 3 cm (1¼ in) across, appear in spring on this robust and reliably long-lived herbaceous species. The large mid green leaves, which occasionally have 5 lobes, are markedly round-toothed. Native to mountain woods in Romania. HEIGHT & SPREAD 10×20 cm (4×8 in).
H. triloba see *H. nobilis*
CULTIVATION Plant in early spring or autumn in moist, humus-rich soil in partial shade and sheltered from the wind. Those grown in pots should be plunged in a sandy medium to keep roots cool during summer.
PROPAGATION Sow seed when ripe in pots in a cool, partially shaded coldframe. Prick out seedlings in autumn or the following spring and pot individually. Divide in late spring or early autumn, taking care not to damage the roots.
PESTS AND DISEASES Vine weevil and aphids can attack those in pots.

Heracleum

Umbelliferae

The giant hogweed *Heracleum mantegazzianum* is a massive, architectural plant that looks spectacular in an informal or wild garden. However, all parts of the plant are poisonous and contact with the skin can cause severe irritation and even permanent scarring, and it is not recommended for areas where children are unsupervised. The plant self-seeds easily, especially on moist ground, and it is considered a widespread nuisance in parts of the country.
RECOMMENDED SPECIES
Heracleum mantegazzianum (giant hogweed) Branched stems carry flat heads, each about 30 cm (1 ft) wide, of white or pink-tinged flowers in mid summer, followed by massive seed heads. The stout stems of this biennial or hardy short-lived perennial are ridged and purple-blotched. The pinnate, lobed leaves are about 3 m (10 ft) long. HEIGHT & SPREAD 3×2.8 m (10×9 ft).

▲ *Heracleum mantegazzianum*

CULTIVATION Plant in spring or autumn in any soil in woodland conditions. Staking is only necessary in windy locations. Remove seed heads to prevent the plant spreading. It is an offence to cause it to grow in the wild, by seeding over a boundary, for example.
PROPAGATION Sow seed in spring in nursery rows and transplant when the seedlings are about 15 cm (6 in) tall, or sow in the final position on well-cultivated open ground.
PESTS AND DISEASES Usually trouble free.

Herb Christopher see *Actaea spicata*
Herb Paris see *Paris*
Herbs see p. 330

AROMATIC FOLIAGE, DECORATIVE FLOWERS AND SPICY SEEDS MAKE HERBS A COMBINATION OF VISUAL AND CULINARY DELIGHTS

These annual, perennial and shrubby plants are cultivated for culinary purposes but many are attractive enough to be included in ornamental borders. Most have flavoursome leaves but some are grown for their roots and seeds. Flavours vary from the refreshing taste of spearmint to the warm spiciness of coriander seeds and hot pungency of horseradish roots.

Many herbs produce attractive flowers in spring or summer, which may tempt bees and other insects. To concentrate the plant's energy on leaf production, remove the flowers as soon as they appear. If the seeds are edible or you wish the plant to self-sow, let some of the flowers develop.

Herbs are easy to grow and rarely suffer from pests or diseases. A herb garden in a sunny site is a good place to display them, but they also go well in flowerbeds and vegetable plots. Many thrive in containers, or under glass where they have a longer season.

▲ KITCHEN GARDEN *Herbs grouped with flowering plants make an attractive edible display.*

Harvest early in the morning before the sun becomes too hot. The flavours and aromas of herbs are usually strongest when they are fresh but many freeze or dry well. Pick leaves for preserving before the plant flowers.

To freeze herbs, wash sprigs or individual leaves. Pat them dry, place small amounts in freezer bags and freeze immediately. Alternatively, chop the leaves finely and freeze with a little water in ice-cube trays.

Dry herbs in a dark, dry, warm place, such as an airing cupboard. Place leaves flat on drying racks or sheets of kitchen paper, or tie sprigs into bunches and hang them upside down. Pick flowerheads in full bloom and spread to dry on kitchen paper. Harvest seeds once pods ripen and begin to turn brown, and dry in paper bags. Store dried herbs in airtight jars.

Balm
Melissa officinalis
Labiatae

Balm or lemon balm has serrated oval leaves which are mid green and downy. They have a distinctive lemon scent and flavour. Use them fresh in fruit salads, cold drinks or sweet or savoury dishes. This bushy perennial bears small, white flowers in summer. HEIGHT & SPREAD 1m×45cm (3×1½ft).

CULTIVATION Grow balm in any soil, in full sun or partial shade.
PROPAGATION Sow seed outdoors in spring or leave the plant to self-seed. Divide in spring or autumn.
PESTS AND DISEASES Mildew may affect mature plants.

Basil
Ocimum basilicum
Labiatae

The bright green, oval leaves of basil, or sweet basil, have a warm, pungent and slightly spicy flavour. They lose much of their flavour when frozen and are best used fresh. Use them in tomato and garlic-based dishes and sauces, and salads, omelettes and olive oil. Basil is an annual and produces its small white flowers in late summer. HEIGHT & SPREAD 45×15cm (18×6in).
Bush or **Greek basil** (var. *minimum*) This compact plant has small pointed leaves, with a mild flavour and scent. HEIGHT & SPREAD 30×15cm (12×6in).
Lettuce-leaf basil ('Napolitano') The leaves are large and crinkled and have a particularly fine flavour. HEIGHT & SPREAD 45×15cm (18×6in).
Purple basil (var. *purpurascens*) The dark purple leaves are ruffled and the plant bears pink-purple flowers. HEIGHT & SPREAD 45×15cm (18×6in).

CULTIVATION Grow in light, well-drained soil in full sun. Cut back before flowering to promote leaf growth.
PROPAGATION Sow seed indoors in early spring, or outside in late spring, once all danger of frost has passed and the soil is warm.
PESTS AND DISEASES Greenfly and whitefly may be a problem.

Bay
Laurus nobilis
Lauraceae

The dark green, lance-shaped leaves of this moderately hardy, evergreen shrub or tree are leathery, glossy and sweetly aromatic. Use them in bouquet garni, and fresh or dried in casseroles, stocks and soups. Small, yellow-green flowers appear in spring. HEIGHT & SPREAD 2.4×1.2m (8×4ft) or more after 10 years.
CULTIVATION Grow in rich, well-drained soil in a sunny, sheltered site. Bay does well in a container but protect roots from frost by wrapping the pot in hessian in winter.

PROPAGATION Sow seed under glass in autumn or take 10cm (4in) semi-ripe stem cuttings in early or mid summer.
PESTS AND DISEASES Scale insects may attack the leaves.

Chervil
Anthriscus cerefolium
Umbelliferae

The delicate, finely cut, mid green leaves of this small biennial have a subtle aniseed flavour. They are produced through most of the year. Use fresh leaves in omelettes, sauces, soups, and vegetable or fish dishes. Umbels of white flowers appear in the summer. HEIGHT & SPREAD 38×30cm (15×12in).

CULTIVATION Chervil thrives in moist but well-drained soil. Keep summer crops in a shady site as chervil has a tendency to bolt in hot weather; other crops prefer shade but tolerate sun.
PROPAGATION Sow seed outdoors at monthly intervals from spring to autumn, or allow plants to self-sow.
PESTS AND DISEASES Chervil is usually trouble free.

Chives
Allium **spp.**
Alliaceae

Chives produce clumps of mid green, grass-like leaves. Use fresh leaves to flavour soft cheese or butter, or in salads, soups or stir-fries. These perennials are related to onions (see p.741) and garlic (see p.742).

Chives (*A. schoenoprasum*) The hollow cylindrical leaves of chives have a mild onion flavour. The plant produces globular mauve-pink blooms in summer. HEIGHT & SPREAD 30×20cm (12×8in).
Garlic chives (*A. tuberosum*) A mild garlic flavour characterises the long flat leaves. Small white flowers are borne in late summer. HEIGHT & SPREAD 30×20cm (12×8in).
CULTIVATION Grow in moist, fertile soil, in sun or light shade.
PROPAGATION Sow seed outdoors in spring. Divide plants every 3-4 years in autumn.
PESTS AND DISEASES Chives may be affected by rust or mildew in damp conditions.

Coriander
Coriandrum sativum
Umbelliferae

The feathery, mid green, upper leaves are spicy and pungent; the flat lower leaves have a slightly unpleasant smell. Coriander leaves can be frozen but are best used fresh in curries, stews and salads. The lower leaves make decorative garnishes. Sprays of white flowers

produce seeds that have a sweet, spicy, orangey flavour when ripe. Add them to sweet and savoury dishes, including chutneys. HEIGHT & SPREAD 45×25cm (18×10in).
CULTIVATION Plant in rich, light soil, in sun or partial shade and away from fennel.
PROPAGATION Sow seed outdoors in spring.
PESTS AND DISEASES Coriander is usually trouble free.

Dill
Anethum graveolens
Umbelliferae

This annual has fine, feathery, blue-green leaves, which have a distinctive aniseed flavour. Use

them fresh to garnish salads and flavour fish dishes, sauces, marinades and stews. The flat yellow flowerheads, which appear in mid summer, have a stronger flavour than the leaves and are used in dill pickles. Add the seeds whole to chutneys or use them crushed to flavour bread dough. HEIGHT & SPREAD 60×25cm (24×10in).
CULTIVATION Grow in well-drained, fertile soil, in full sun. Do not plant near fennel.
PROPAGATION Sow seed outdoors from early spring to late summer or leave to self-seed.
PESTS AND DISEASES Slugs may be a problem.

Fennel
Foeniculum vulgare
Umbelliferae

The blue-green, thread-like fragrant foliage has a slightly sweet, strongly aniseed flavour. Use it fresh in salads or as an accompaniment to fish, cheese or vegetable dishes. The seeds also have an aniseed flavour and are good in curries, sauces and bread. This perennial bears umbels of tiny yellow flowers in

mid summer. HEIGHT & SPREAD 2m×60cm (6½×2ft).
CULTIVATION Plant in a well-drained soil in full sun, away from dill and coriander to prevent cross-pollination. Cut a few stems to the ground in early summer to promote leaf growth.
PROPAGATION Sow seed outdoors or divide in spring or leave the plant to self-seed, which it does prolifically.
PESTS AND DISEASES Fennel is usually trouble free.

Horseradish
Armoracia rusticana
Cruciferae

This tough hardy perennial is prized for its edible roots, which have a hot pungent flavour. Harvest them from late summer to autumn and grate fresh or store in a cool dark place. Use in salads or to make horseradish sauce. Pick the dark green, dock-like leaves when they are young and use them in salads. HEIGHT & SPREAD 1m×60cm (3×2ft).

CULTIVATION Plant in well-drained soil, in sun or partial shade. The long roots of horseradish are difficult to eradicate, so grow it in a large, deep container, sunk to the rim.
PROPAGATION Sow seed outdoors in spring or divide the roots in autumn.
PESTS AND DISEASES Cabbage white caterpillars may eat leaves.

Lovage
Levisticum officinale
Umbelliferae

The large, mid green, divided leaves and hollow stems have a celery-like flavour. Add them fresh to stews, stocks and soups and use young leaves in salads. Add the seeds to bread dough. This tall perennial bears greenish yellow flowers from early to mid summer. HEIGHT & SPREAD 2m×75cm (6½×2½ft).
CULTIVATION Plant in any ordinary, well-drained soil, in sun or partial shade.
PROPAGATION Sow seed outdoors in autumn, allow to self-seed or divide in autumn.
PESTS AND DISEASES Lovage is usually trouble free.

Marjoram
Origanum spp.
Labiatae

The small, oval, slightly downy leaves are aromatic and have a sweet, fresh, spicy flavour. Use them fresh or dried in pizzas, pasta dishes or meat and tomato dishes and sauces.

Common marjoram or **oregano** (*O. vulgare*) This tall hardy perennial has apple-green leaves and small rose-purple blooms during summer. HEIGHT & SPREAD 30 cm × 1 m (1×3 ft).

French or **pot marjoram** (*O. onites*) This dwarf shrub is hardy and produces a year-round supply of bright green leaves when grown indoors. It produces mauve to white flowers in summer. HEIGHT & SPREAD 60×60 cm (2×2 ft).

Sweet marjoram (*O. majorana*) The grey-green leaves of this half-hardy perennial have the finest flavour. Best grown as an annual, the plant produces clusters of small white flowers during summer. HEIGHT & SPREAD 60×30 cm (2×1 ft).

CULTIVATION Plant marjoram in any ordinary, well-drained soil in full sun. In autumn cut back common marjoram to keep the plant neat.

PROPAGATION Sow seed under glass in autumn or spring. Take softwood cuttings in late spring or divide in early spring.

PESTS AND DISEASES Marjoram is usually trouble free.

Mint
Mentha spp.
Labiatae

The common mint (*M. spicata*) is the most widely grown of the culinary mints. All have clean, fresh flavours and can be dried or frozen. Mint leaves make good garnishes for vegetables, fruit salads and summer drinks. They are also used to make mint sauce or jelly. These invasive hardy perennials have long growing seasons and bear small purple flowers in summer.

Apple mint (*M. suaveolens*) The rounded, hairy, grey-green leaves have a strong fragrance and aroma, and are particularly good in mint sauce. HEIGHT & SPREAD 1×1.2 m (3×4 ft).

Bowles' mint (*M.* × *villosa* var. *alopecuroides*) The large and rounded leaves are light green and downy. HEIGHT & SPREAD 1×1.2 m (3×4 ft).

Common mint, garden mint or **spearmint** (*M. spicata*) This robust mint has mauve stems and dark green, pointed leaves with a strong flavour. HEIGHT & SPREAD 1×1.2 m (3×4 ft).

Peppermint (*M.* × *piperita*) This compact mint has dark green, lance-shaped, pungent leaves. The stems are reddish. HEIGHT & SPREAD 50 cm × 1 m (20×36 in).

CULTIVATION Mint thrives in any ordinary, moist soil, in sun or partial shade. Grow it in a container sunk to the rim to confine the roots. Cut the stems back in summer to promote new leaf growth.

PROPAGATION Sow seed outdoors or take root cuttings in spring; divide plants at any time.

PESTS AND DISEASES Mint rust and mildew may affect plants.

Parsley
Petroselinum crispum
Umbelliferae

The dark green, intricately cut or densely curled leaves of parsley have a clean, refreshing and mildly spicy flavour. Use the fresh leaves in salads, as a garnish or in bouquet garni, and either fresh or dried in herb butter, soups, sauces, egg and fish dishes. The plant is a hardy biennial. Its tiny yellow flowers appear in the summer of the plant's second year. However, because the leaves have a better flavour in the first year, the plant is often grown as an annual. HEIGHT & SPREAD 30×20 cm (12×8 in).

French parsley (var. *neapolitanum*) This tall upright variety of parsley has flattened, dark green leaves which have a more pronounced flavour.

CULTIVATION Plant in moist, fertile soil, in sun or partial shade. Protect plants with cloches during winter.

PROPAGATION Sow seed outdoors in spring and summer for a year-round supply. To aid germination, soak the seeds overnight in warm water before sowing or sow in a seed tray at 21°C (70°F). Alternatively, leave the plant to self-seed.

PESTS AND DISEASES Aphids, slugs, leaf miner and virus diseases may affect plants.

Rosemary
Rosmarinus officinalis
Labiatae

The needle-shaped leaves of this hardy or half-hardy evergreen shrub are mid to dark green with pale silvery undersides. They are strongly aromatic and can be dried. Add sprigs or chopped leaves sparingly to lamb, pork or oily fish. The plant bears clusters of small, pale mauve-blue flowers from spring to late summer. HEIGHT & SPREAD 1.2×1 m (4×3 ft).

CULTIVATION Grow in well-drained soil in a sheltered, sunny position. Cut back straggling or frost-damaged stems in spring. Bring plants grown in containers indoors or under glass for protection in winter.

PROPAGATION Sow seed under glass in spring or take semi-ripe cuttings in mid to late summer.

PESTS AND DISEASES Rosemary is usually trouble free.

Sage
Salvia officinalis
Labiatae

This hardy evergreen shrub has rough, grey-green, oval leaves which have a strong aroma and a slightly bitter taste. Use them fresh or dried to complement rich meats and cheese, or in tomato-based sauces and stuffings. The dried leaves have a stronger flavour than fresh so use them sparingly. Purple-blue flower spikes appear in early to

mid summer. HEIGHT & SPREAD 60 cm × 1 m (2×3 ft).

CULTIVATION Grow in well-drained soil in full sun. Trim in spring and after flowering.

PROPAGATION Sow seed under glass in early spring or outdoors in mid to late spring. Alternatively, layer a long branch by pegging to the soil surface or take semi-ripe cuttings in early autumn. Renew plants every 3 or 4 years.

PESTS AND DISEASES Capsid bugs and powdery mildew may attack the leaves.

Savory
Satureja spp.
Labiatae

Strongly aromatic leaves have a peppery, slightly bitter flavour. Use them in salads or fresh, dried or frozen in bean dishes.

Summer savory (*S. hortensis*) The narrow, dark green leaves

of this bushy annual have a slightly spicy flavour, which is especially pronounced before flowering. Tiny lilac blooms are borne from mid summer to early autumn. HEIGHT & SPREAD 45×30 cm (1½×1 ft).

Winter savory (*S. montana*) This hardy evergreen has grey-green leaves which have a coarser flavour than those of summer savory. Small pale rose flowers are borne from mid summer to mid autumn. Winter savory usually gives a year-round supply of leaves although some may drop after hard frosts. HEIGHT & SPREAD 45×30 cm (1½×1 ft).

CULTIVATION Grow in well-drained soil in full sun. Prune winter savory in spring and replace plants every 2 or 3 years.

PROPAGATION Sow summer savory outdoors in either spring or autumn. Sow winter savory under glass in spring or take semi-ripe cuttings in summer.

PESTS AND DISEASES Savory is usually trouble free.

Sorrel

***Rumex* spp.**
Polygonaceae

The leaves of these hardy perennials have an acidic sourness, which counters the richness of meats. Use them fresh, dried or frozen. Sorrel leaves are good as flavourings for soups, added to salads or cooked like spinach.

Buckler-leaf or **French sorrel** (*R. scutatus*). The greyish green, triangular leaves have a mild lemony flavour. Small, reddish green flowers are borne in mid summer. HEIGHT & SPREAD 15×60 cm (6×24 in).

Common sorrel (*R. acetosa*) Spear-shaped leaves are fleshy and mid green. The plant produces spikes of tiny reddish flowers from early to mid summer. HEIGHT & SPREAD 60×30 cm (2×1 ft).

CULTIVATION Grow in well-drained, fertile soil, in full sun or partial shade.

PROPAGATION Sow seed outdoors in spring, or divide plants in spring or early autumn.

PESTS AND DISEASES Leaf-eating insects and slugs may affect plants.

Sweet cicely

Myrrhis odorata
Umbelliferae

The fragrant fern-like leaves of this perennial have a sweet aniseed taste. Use them fresh or dried in omelettes and salad dressings, or with stewed fruit. Cut back some of the clusters of tiny white flowers, which appear in early summer, to prolong leaf harvest. Leave some flowers to produce their sweet, nutty-flavoured seeds. Add these, green or ripe, to fruit salads or pies and ice cream. Lift roots in autumn and use in salads or as a vegetable. HEIGHT & SPREAD 1 m×60 cm (3×2 ft).

CULTIVATION Grow in any moist soil, in sun or light shade .

PROPAGATION Sow seed outside in early to mid spring, leave to self-seed or divide in autumn.

PESTS AND DISEASES Mildew can be troublesome.

Tarragon

***Artemisia* spp.**
Compositae

The needle-shaped leaves of this perennial herb have a peppery-anise flavour. Use them fresh or dried in béarnaise sauce or vinegar and as flavourings in fish, chicken and vegetable dishes.

French tarragon (*A. dracunculus*) This tarragon is the best for culinary purposes. Its dark green foliage has a warm aroma and subtle taste. French tarragon is not fully hardy and needs protection from winter wet. Small yellow flowers appear in late summer. HEIGHT & SPREAD 1 m×45 cm (3×1½ ft).

Russian tarragon (*A. dracunculoides*) The leaves have a slightly bitter and less distinctive flavour

than French tarragon and are narrower and paler. The plant is fully hardy and vigorous. It can be grown from seed. HEIGHT & SPREAD 1.2 m×45 cm (4×1½ ft).

CULTIVATION Tarragon grows best in a sunny, sheltered position in very well-drained soil. Cut back French tarragon in autumn and lay a mulch over the base to protect it from frost or grow it in a pot and bring indoors for winter use.

PROPAGATION Divide French tarragon in spring or take softwood cuttings in late spring to early summer. Replace plants every 2-3 years. Sow Russian tarragon outdoors in spring.

PESTS AND DISEASES Rust may be a problem for both French and Russian tarragon.

Thyme

***Thymus* spp.**
Labiatae

The dark green, aromatic leaves have a pungent flavour. Use fresh sprigs in bouquet garni and fresh or dried leaves or sprigs in stuffings, sauces, stocks, stews or marinades. These dwarf hardy evergreen shrubs have upright habits and produce small mauve or pink flowers in early summer.

Broad-leaved thyme (*T. pulegioides*) The leaves are large and rounded and are strongly flavoured. HEIGHT & SPREAD 8×30 cm (3×12 in).

Common thyme (*T. vulgaris*) Small leaves are oval and pointed. They have a slightly peppery flavour. HEIGHT & SPREAD 15×30 cm (6×12 in).

Lemon thyme (*T.* × *citriodorus*) The leaves are larger than those of common thyme and have a strong lemon scent. HEIGHT & SPREAD 15×15 cm (6×6 in).

CULTIVATION Grow in well-drained soil, in full sun. Trim regularly in the growing season to encourage new growth. Renew plants every 2-3 years.

PROPAGATION Sow seed under glass in early or mid spring or divide at this time. Layer in summer or take semi-ripe cuttings in early summer.

PESTS AND DISEASES Thyme is usually trouble free.

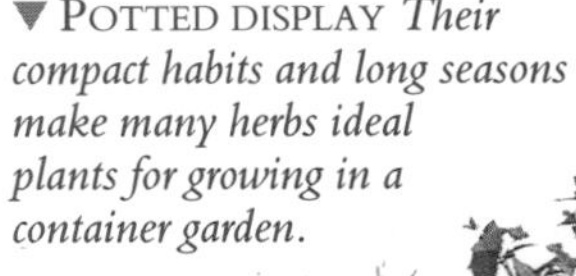

▼ POTTED DISPLAY *Their compact habits and long seasons make many herbs ideal plants for growing in a container garden.*

h

Hermodactylus

Iridaceae

Fragrant, yellowish green and dark brown or blackish flowers in early and mid spring lend distinction to this tuberous hardy perennial. It tolerates any type of well-drained soil but a sunny position in the garden is essential. A border edge is a good spot to display the plant. The single species in the genus is native to S Europe.

▲ *Hermodactylus tuberosus*

Hermodactylus tuberosus (widow iris, snake's head iris) Scented flowers, up to 5 cm (2 in) long and 4 cm (1½ in) across, emerge from slender, grass-like leaves, up to 45 cm (18 in) long. HEIGHT 25 cm (10 in).

CULTIVATION Plant the finger-like tubers 7.5 cm (3 in) deep in well-drained garden soil, in late summer or autumn. Choose as warm a spot as possible – the dormant plants require plenty of sun in summer in order to flower well the following year. Remove faded flowerheads.

PROPAGATION Divide and replant the tubers in late summer.

PESTS AND DISEASES Greenfly may infest the plants in late spring and early summer.

Hesperis

Sweet rocket, dame's violet

Cruciferae

Fragrant flowers in white and shades of pink to purple are borne in long spikes in early summer. Their scent is stronger in the evening. The four-petal blooms are carried on tall, branching stems bearing narrow mid green leaves which are up to 10 cm (4 in) long but shorter near the top of the stem. These annuals and short-lived herbaceous perennials are hardy and suit a border or woodland garden. They tolerate poor soil, doing best in a shaded site. Double-flowered specimens make good cut flowers. Native to Europe and Asia.

RECOMMENDED SPECIES AND VARIETIES

H. matronalis Butterflies are drawn to the lilac or white flowers which are 2 cm (¾ in) across and borne in lax spires. HEIGHT & SPREAD 1 m x 30 cm (3 x 1 ft).

▲ *Hesperis matronalis* var. *albiflora* 'Lilacina Flore Pleno'

Pure white flowers adorn var. ***albiflora***, while **'Lilacina Flore Pleno'**, which is seen less often, has a profusion of double lilac flowers.

CULTIVATION Plant in well-drained soil 30 cm (12 in) apart. Add leaf-mould or compost before planting 'Lilacina Flore Pleno'.

PROPAGATION Divide cultivars in spring. Take basal cuttings in early summer, rooting them in a coldframe. Sow seed of the species where required in spring, thinning out as necessary. Plants become woody with age so raise new stock every 2-3 years. White-flowered forms usually come true from seed, although there may be some with pink tints.

PESTS AND DISEASES Usually trouble free.

Heuchera

Alum root, coral bells

Saxifragaceae

Heuchera micrantha var. diversifolia 'Palace Purple'

The shallowly lobed or scalloped leaves of the plants in this genus may be strikingly coloured or marbled with silver. Hardy perennials, they provide effective evergreen ground cover. In some species, including those described here, the foliage is enhanced by airy sprays of small creamy white, greenish, yellowish green, pink or red flowers, usually about 1 cm (⅜ in) long, opening in early and mid summer. There may be a second flush in late summer. Plants with colourful foliage tend to have smaller flowers. All plants have slowly spreading woody rhizomes. Native to woodlands in N America.

RECOMMENDED SPECIES AND VARIETIES

H. americana Small greenish flowers, about 5 mm (¼ in) long, appear in sprays to 30 cm (12 in) long. The broad, lobed leaves, up to 10 cm (4 in) wide, form a handsome clump. They open with a bronze flush and veining, later becoming a satiny dark green, and make a greater visual impact than the flowers. HEIGHT & SPREAD 45 x 30 cm (18 x 12 in).

***H.* Bressingham Hybrids** Bell-shaped white, pink or red flowers form elegant sprays, about 15 cm (6 in) long. The rounded leaves, up to 10 cm (4 in) long, are often slightly mottled with silver and may be purple-tinged when young. HEIGHT & SPREAD 45 x 30 cm (18 x 12 in).

***H. cylindrica* 'Greenfinch'** The yellowish green flowers are held in narrow spikes, up to 15 cm (6 in) long. Dense clumps of dark green heart-shaped leaves, about 5 cm (2 in) across, offset them. HEIGHT & SPREAD 1 m x 30 cm (3 x 1 ft).

***H.* 'Green Ivory'** Green-tipped yellowish white, bell-shaped flowers are borne in open sprays, up to 20 cm (8 in) long, above neat clumps of rounded, slightly lobed, mid green leaves, up to 10 cm (4 in) long. HEIGHT & SPREAD 60 x 30 cm (2 x 1 ft).

***H.* 'Leuchtkäfer'** ('Firefly') Fragrant, light scarlet flowers are carried in narrow, erect spikes, up to 15 cm (6 in) long, well above compact mats of rounded, mid green leaves. HEIGHT & SPREAD 60 x 30 cm (2 x 1 ft).

***H. micrantha* var. *diversifolia* 'Palace Purple'**♀ The clumps of broad, coppery purple leaves, up to 10 cm (4 in) wide, have a metallic sheen. Tiny creamy white

▲ *Heuchera micrantha* var. *diversifolia* 'Palace Purple'

flowers, borne in open sprays up to 20 cm (8 in) long, contrast well with them. The foliage is variable when raised from seed. HEIGHT & SPREAD 60 x 30 cm (24 x 12 in).

***H.* 'Pewter Moon'** Shallowly lobed, purplish leaves are heavily marbled with silvery grey and grow in compact clumps. Bell-shaped, pale pink flowers 5 mm (¼ in) wide,

▲ *Heuchera* 'Pewter Moon'

are borne in open sprays, up to 15cm (6in) long. HEIGHT & SPREAD 30×30cm (12×12in).

***H.* 'Rachel'** Coral-pink bells are carried in sprays, up to 15cm (6in) long, well above clumps of broad, purple-flushed leaves. HEIGHT & SPREAD 30×20cm (12×8in).

▲ *Heuchera* 'Rachel'

***H.* 'Red Spangles'**♀ Bell-shaped scarlet flowers are borne in open sprays, up to 15cm (6in) long, well above clumps of rounded, lobed, mid green leaves. The plant often flowers a second time in late summer. HEIGHT & SPREAD 60×30cm (24×12in).

H. sanguinea Rounded, dark green leaves with scalloped margins, marbled with silver, often purple-flushed, form compact clumps. Bell-shaped red flowers bloom in sprays to 15cm (6in) long. HEIGHT & SPREAD 60×30cm (24×12in). The many hybrids derived from this species are listed under their cultivar names.

***H.* 'Scintillation'**♀ Silvery marbled leaves, up to 7.5cm (3in) long, grow in compact clumps. The bell-shaped flowers are tipped with intense deep pink and borne in sprays up to 15cm (6in) long. HEIGHT & SPREAD 45×30cm (18×12in).

***H.* 'Snow Storm'** Rounded, shallowly lobed, white, variegated leaves flushed pink in winter, to 10cm (4in) long, form compact clumps. Cerise bells are borne in sprays 10cm (4in) long. Grow in partial shade. HEIGHT & SPREAD 45×30cm (18×12in).

CULTIVATION Plant in early autumn, in any fertile, fairly moist soil, in sun or light shade. Every 2 or 3 years, divide in early autumn and give the soil a good feed, or replant in fresh soil. Mulch annually in autumn.

PROPAGATION Divide in early autumn.

PESTS AND DISEASES Plants are occasionally infected by leafy gall.

x Heucherella

Saxifragaceae

Sprays of tiny, bell-shaped pink flowers rise above the handsome foliage of these hardy, evergreen perennials throughout summer. The green leaves, rounded and lobed, up to 12cm (4¾in) across, are mottled brown when young, then turn bronze in autumn. Plants have a neat spreading habit of growth. This genus is a hybrid between heuchera and tiarella.

RECOMMENDED SPECIES AND VARIETIES

x *H. alba* 'Bridget Bloom' The flowers are shell pink. Bright green leaves form a clump at the base of the plant. HEIGHT & SPREAD 40×30cm (16×12in).

▲ x *Heucherella alba* 'Bridget Bloom'

'Rosalie' has deeper pink flowers.

x *H. tiarelloides*♀ Bright pink flowers are borne on reddish brown stems. The soft green leaves form bold clumps. The plant spreads by sending out runners. HEIGHT & SPREAD 40×50cm (16×20in).

CULTIVATION Plant in autumn or spring in any well-drained but moisture-retentive soil, preferably in sun or partial shade. Full shade is tolerated. Water well in dry weather to maintain foliage, but if this is not done, plants will recover after the next heavy rain. Top dress with well-rotted compost in spring to ensure strong growth.

PROPAGATION Divide and replant in autumn or spring.

PESTS AND DISEASES Usually trouble free.

x ***Hibanobambusa*** see BAMBOOS p.77

▼ x *Heucherella alba* 'Rosalie'

Hibiscus

Rose mallow

Malvaceae

Hibiscus rosa-sinensis

Showy, colourful flowers produced in abundance over a long period add an exotic touch to many garden situations. The flowers come in many colours including pink, orange, red, yellow, purple and white, frequently with dark centres. The petals form a flared, sometimes frilly edged trumpet, surrounding a prominent column of stamens. The flowers tend to be short-lived and in most species are borne singly. The leaves, are generally dark green and vary in size. This large genus, found in warmer climates throughout the world, includes hardy and half-hardy annuals, hardy flowering shrubs and conservatory or greenhouse plants.

RECOMMENDED SPECIES AND VARIETIES

***H. acetosella* 'Coppertone'** This bedding plant, treated as a half-hardy annual, is grown for its handsome foliage. The large maple-shaped leaves, up to 30cm (12in) long, are a deep copper-bronze. The flowers are yellow or purple. HEIGHT & SPREAD 75×40cm (30×16in).

H. manihot (syn. *Abelmoschus manihot)* A short-lived, hairy, bushy perennial, the plant flowers freely in its first season from seed and is usually grown as a half-hardy annual. The flowers, up to 15cm (6in) across, pale yellow or white, with a purple centre, are borne from late summer until the first frosts. The narrow-lobed leaves are coarsely toothed. HEIGHT & SPREAD 1.5m×40cm (5ft×16in).

'Cream Cup' has cream flowers with a dark maroon centre.

H. moscheutos A half-hardy, woody-based herbaceous perennial usually grown as a half-hardy annual. Flowers are white to pink, 15cm (6in) across, from mid summer to early autumn. The leaves are ovate and toothed. HEIGHT & SPREAD 1.5×1m (5×3ft).

'Disco Belle Mixed' is a dwarf plant, growing to a height of 50cm (20in). It has pink, red and white flowers, which measure 20cm (8in) across.

H. rosa-sinensis (rose of China) The red flowers, 10cm (4in) across, have a striking central column, which carries the stamens. They are borne from spring to autumn. The glossy leaves are oval with serrated edges. Usually grown as a pot plant, this half-hardy evergreen shrub can also be planted out in summer as a special feature in a bed or large

▲ *Hibiscus rosa-sinensis*

container and brought indoors before frosts occur. HEIGHT & SPREAD 2.4×2.4m (8×8ft).

'Cooperi', with scarlet flowers and leaves variegated red, pink and white, grows as tall as 1.5m (5ft). **'La France'** has pink flowers. The vigorous **'Lemon Chiffon'** has lemon-yellow flowers. **'Weekend'** produces rich orange flowers.

H. schizopetalus ♀ (Japanese lantern) Grow this evergreen shrub indoors. Pendent pink flowers, 6cm (2½in) across, with fringed, reflexed petals and a conspicuous central stamen column 8cm (3¼in) long, are borne in summer on long stalks. The plant has a spreading habit and can be trained as a climber. The leaves are ovate and toothed. HEIGHT & SPREAD 3×1.8m (10×6ft).

Hibiscus syriacus

H. syriacus A hardy deciduous shrub with an upright habit. Lilac-bue flowers, 8cm (3¼in) across, are freely produced in late summer and early autumn. The leaves are lobed. HEIGHT & SPREAD 2.4×1.8m (8×6ft).

'Diana' has white flowers and petals with crinkled edges. **'Hamabo'** ♀ bears pink flowers with a crimson eye and reaches a height and spread of 1.5m (5ft). **'Meehanii'** carries magenta flowers with a crimson eye and has variegated foliage. **'Oiseau Bleu'** ♀ ('Blue Bird') has lilac-blue flowers with a deep red eye. **'Pink Giant'** ♀ bears pink flowers and grows to a height of 3m (10ft), spreading to 1.8m (6ft). **'Red Heart'** ♀ produces white flowers with conspicuous red centres. **'Woodbridge'** ♀ has large rich pink flowers with dark centres.

▼ *Hibiscus syriacus*

▲ *Hibiscus syriacus* 'Diana'

▲ *Hibiscus syriacus* 'Pink Giant'

▲ *Hibiscus syriacus* 'Red Heart'

▲ *Hibiscus syriacus* 'Woodbridge'

H. trionum (flower-of-an-hour) This erect plant, grown as an annual, is hardy enough to be sown in the open to flower the same season. Many short-lived flowers, 5cm (2in) across, creamy white or pale yellow with purple centres, are produced in late summer and early autumn. The leaves are deeply divided and coarsely toothed. HEIGHT & SPREAD 60×30cm (24×12in).

'Sunny Day' is a dwarf, with lemon-yellow flowers with dark purple centres.

CULTIVATION *H. acetosella*, *H. manihot* and *H. moscheutos*, although perennials, are usually treated like other frost-tender bedding plants. They need a sunny, sheltered position and well-drained soil. Plant out young plants after the risk of frost has passed. *H. trionum* is hardy and does best in full sun.

H. rosa-sinensis is generally grown in large pots in a greenhouse or conservatory, with full exposure to sun. When still small the plant will thrive on a sunny windowsill. Keep plants quite dry in winter, in a minimum temperature of 7°C (45°F). In spring, cut plants back hard. Water liberally in summer. Treat *H. schizopetalus* similarly, but keep plants in a temperature of at least 10°C (50°F) in winter.

The shrub *H. syriacus*, although hardy, requires a sunny, sheltered situation. In cold areas, plant near a south-facing wall. Plant container-grown specimens in early spring in a well-drained soil; in lighter soils incorporate organic matter before planting. Deadheading, where practicable, will prolong the flowering display of all species.

PROPAGATION Sow seed of *H. acetosella* 'Coppertone', *H. manihot* and *H. moscheutos* under glass in winter. From sowings in mid to late spring, plants may be grown in pots in their first season and overwintered in a cool greenhouse in at least 5°C (41°F); they will then do very well outdoors in their second season. Sow seed of *H. trionum* where it is to flower in mid spring; it does not transplant well.

Take semi-ripe cuttings of perennial species. Bottom heat is needed to ensure successful rooting. *H. syriacus* cultivars will also come from semi-ripe cuttings in late summer, but are slow.

PESTS AND DISEASES Aphids may infest all species. Plants that are grown under glass are susceptible to whitefly, mealy bugs and fungal root rot.

Hieracium

Hawkweed

Compositae

These hardy herbaceous or evergreen perennials bear rosettes of leaves, generally silvery grey, to 15cm (6in) long, and yellow flowers. The flowers – strictly 'flowerheads' made up of ray and disc florets – are borne all summer through. Remove the fluffy seed-heads that follow, or the plants will become weeds. The listed species are attractive to insects and so are good for a wildflower garden. *Hieracium lanatum* and *H. villosum* are also suitable for a rock garden, but *H. maculatum* self-seeds too freely. The featured species are all native to Europe.

RECOMMENDED SPECIES

H. lanatum Mounds of downy grey elliptical leaves retain their beauty into winter. Flowers are small, about 2.5cm (1in) wide. HEIGHT & SPREAD 30×45cm (12×18in).

▲ *Hieracium maculatum*

H. maculatum The flowers, about 2.5 cm (1 in) across, are borne in lax clusters, in late spring and summer. The oblong, sharply toothed, evergreen leaves, up to 10 cm (4 in) long, are deep green blotched with purple. HEIGHT & SPREAD 40×30 cm (16×12 in).

▲ *Hieracium villosum*

H. villosum There are 2-4 sulphur-yellow flowers, about 5 cm (2 in) across, on each downy stem. The woolly, silvery white, oblong leaves are borne in rosettes at the base of the plant – generally several rosettes are grouped together, occasionally there is a single large rosette. This is an evergreen plant. HEIGHT & SPREAD 30×20 cm (12×8 in).

CULTIVATION *H. lanatum* and *H. villosum* thrive in well-drained gritty soil, in a sunny spot. In wet areas, protect leaves during winter by placing a pane of glass or a cloche overhead. *H. maculatum* will thrive in most garden soils and often self-sows freely.

PROPAGATION Sow seed in pots, in winter, and prick out seedlings as soon as they are large enough to handle. Plant out in early to mid summer in the garden.

PESTS AND DISEASES Powdery mildew may appear on the foliage late in the season.

Himalayacalamus see BAMBOOS p.77

Hippeastrum

Amaryllis

Amaryllidaceae

Large funnel-shaped flowers are carried on strong, leafless hollow stems above at least four mid to deep green strap-shaped leaves, about 60 cm (24 in) long. These are among the boldest flowering greenhouse or pot plants. Modern hybrids produce up to six blooms, 20-25 cm (8-10 in) across, each with six petals. They bloom between early autumn and early winter, if heat treated to induce early bud formation, or from mid winter to mid or late spring, if untreated.

These tropical or sub-tropical bulbs are native to S America and not hardy. They are sold before Christmas as 'Amaryllis' for flowering indoors in spring. However, the true *Amaryllis,* which is similar in appearance, is hardier and can be grown outdoors.

RECOMMENDED SPECIES AND VARIETIES

H. papillo (butterfly amaryllis) Pale green flowers streaked and stained dark red appear in spring. This is one of the few species produced commercially. Feed all year round to maintain growth. HEIGHT 60 cm (24 in).

Among the hybrids, of uncertain parentage, are **'Apple Blossom'**, white flushed

▲ *Hippeastrum* 'Apple Blossom'

and speckled pink; **'Bestseller'**♀, deep cerise, short-stemmed; **'Orange Sovereign'**♀, pure orange; **'Star of Holland'**, scarlet with a white throat and **'White Dazzler'**, white.

CULTIVATION Buy bulbs, up to 15 cm (6 in) wide, from early autumn to early spring for growing in a greenhouse or indoors. Plant at once in a pot 5 cm (2 in) wider than the bulb, half in and half out of an equal mix of well-rotted manure, coarse sand and John Innes compost. Water sparingly, increasing as growth begins. Feed with a liquid fertiliser every 7-10 days. Flowers appear 1-3 months after planting, depending how warm plants are kept. Planting at intervals ensures a succession of blooms, if the temperature is constant, although the later they are planted, the quicker they grow. Remove the flower stem immediately after flowering and keep the plant in a greenhouse. Stop watering in early autumn and let the foliage die down. In mid to late autumn cut back the old foliage and leave the bulb dormant. Top dress before growth begins and, once it has started, begin watering again. Maintain 12°C (54°F) minimum.

PROPAGATION Sow seed as soon as it is ripe, in summer, in a sand and John Innes mix. Keep a minimum temperature of 16°C (61°F) and transplant into a 10 cm (4 in) pot when the seedlings reach 10-13 cm (4-5¼ in) high, which takes 9-18 months. Water the seedlings all year to sustain growth until mature. Repot annually in autumn, taking care not to damage the roots. When repotting large bulbs, remove offsets and pot on.

PESTS AND DISEASES Mealy bug, red spider mite, thrips and tomato spotted wilt virus can all be problems.

Hippocrepis

Leguminosae

Bright yellow heads of small, sweet-pea shaped flowers add colour to a sunny rock garden or border, generally from late spring into summer. The flowers are followed by curious curved, segmented pods. There are annuals, perennials and shrubs, all hardy, varying in habit from prostrate to upright. Native to Europe, N Africa and W Asia.

RECOMMENDED SPECIES

H. comosa (syn. *Coronilla comosa*) (horseshoe vetch) Whorls of 4-10 flowers are carried on erect stems above a spreading, leafy mat. The mid green leaves are made up of oblong leaflets. Pods are reddish brown and 2.5 cm (1 in) long. This prostrate perennial may overwhelm smaller, less vigorous plants. HEIGHT & SPREAD 10×60 cm (4×24 in).

H. emerus (syn. *Coronilla emerus*) (scorpion senna) Small clusters of fragrant flowers, yellow marked with brown, appear in early and mid summer on slender stalks. Leaves, to 6 cm (2½ in) long, are divided into small, rounded, bright green leaflets, on a robust deciduous shrub. Brown pods as long as 10 cm (4 in) resemble scorpions' tails. HEIGHT & SPREAD 80 cm×1 m (32×36 in) after 5 years, ultimately 2.4 m (8 ft) tall.

CULTIVATION Plant in early spring, in full sun in any well-drained soil. Plants are especially happy on chalk soils.

PROPAGATION Sow seed in early spring. Take softwood cuttings from *H. comosa* at some point during summer.

PRUNING Not normally necessary.

PESTS AND DISEASES Usually trouble free.

▼ *Hippocrepis comosa*

Hippophaë

Elaeagnaceae

Bright berries and silvery or sage-green foliage are the principal features of these hardy deciduous shrubs. There are three species, the most commonly grown being *Hippophaë rhamnoides*.

RECOMMENDED SPECIES

H. rhamnoides ♀ (sea buckthorn) Tough, salt-tolerant, linear leaves, grey-green above and silver haired below, cover the great tangles of sharp spiny branches. Thick clusters of golden orange berries are borne in autumn and winter. Plants form an impenetrable screen, making excellent windbreaks in exposed areas, both on the coast and inland. There are inconspicuous yellow-green flowers in early spring. Grow a male sea buckthorn with several female shrubs, to allow for pollination by wind. Native to Europe, including coastal areas of Britain, and temperate Asia. HEIGHT & SPREAD 1.8×3m (6×10ft) after 5 years, ultimately 4m (13ft) tall, spread indefinite.

▲ *Hippophaë rhamnoides*

CULTIVATION Grow in any ordinary, well-drained garden soil.

PROPAGATION Easy to raise from seed, or dig up and transplant root suckers in winter.

PRUNING Trim in mid or late summer.

PESTS AND DISEASES Usually trouble free.

Hoheria

Lacebark, ribbon wood

Malvaceae

Masses of delicate white flowers cover small, graceful trees, hardy in southern Britain, in mid to late summer. Trees first flower at about five years old. The five-petalled flowers, up to 4cm (1½in) across, resemble cherry blossom. The smooth bark easily peels off in long strips, revealing several inner layers of lacy fibres. Species may be evergreen or deciduous. The alternate leaves vary in shape according to the tree's age. They are normally smaller and more deeply lobed and toothed on young plants, though adult trees often carry 'juvenile' leaves. Native to New Zealand.

RECOMMENDED SPECIES AND VARIETIES

H. angustifolia This evergreen tree, slender and sparsely leaved, has mid green lance-shaped leaves, to 5cm (2in) long. Young branchlets are often tangled and drooping. HEIGHT & SPREAD 2×1m (6½×3ft) after 10 years, ultimately 8m (26ft) tall.

H. glabrata ♀ (mountain ribbonwood) An open, deciduous tree, closely resembling *H. lyallii*. The leaves are much less hairy, with scalloped edges and drip tips.

▲ *Hoheria glabrata*

H. 'Glory of Amlwch' ♀ Larger flowers are borne by an untidy tree with pale green, saw-edged leaves, 9cm (3½in) long, that remain through mild winters. HEIGHT & SPREAD 2×2m (6½×6½ft) after 10 years, ultimately 6m (20ft) tall.

H. lyallii ♀ This deciduous tree has distinctive white hairy leaves up to 10cm (4in) long and 5cm (2in) wide in various shapes, often toothed. HEIGHT & SPREAD 4×4m (13×13ft) after 10 years, ultimately 6m (20ft) tall.

H. sexstylosa ♀ Rich green leaves, acutely toothed, about 10cm (4in) long and 3cm (1¼in) wide, clothe an upright evergreen tree. HEIGHT & SPREAD 4×3m (13×10ft) after 10 years, ultimately 6m (20ft) tall.

CULTIVATION Plant in a well-drained soil in a site that is sheltered from cold winds. All hoherias thrive on chalk.

PROPAGATION Sow seed in spring or take semi-ripe heel cuttings in early autumn.

PRUNING Tidy and thin out in spring.

PESTS AND DISEASES Usually trouble free.

Holcus see GRASSES p.301
Holly see *Ilex*
Hollyhock see *Alcea*

▼ *Hoheria sexstylosa*

Holodiscus

Rosaceae

Feathery plumes of small creamy white flowers tumble down this large deciduous shrub from mid to late summer. This is a graceful spreading plant, particularly suited to a bank, where its arching habit can be fully enjoyed. Native to N and S America.

RECOMMENDED SPECIES

H. discolor (ocean spray) Tiny rounded flowers, white, cream and light brown, are borne in large branched clusters, up to 30cm (12in) long, which hang at the end of long strong shoots. The dark green leaves, with undersides covered in grey hairs, have 4 or 8 lobes and are sharply toothed. The leaves are as long as 9cm (3½in) and sometimes almost as wide. HEIGHT & SPREAD 1.5×1.2m. (5×4ft) after 5 years, ultimately 3.5×3m (12×10ft).

▲ *Holodiscus discolor*

CULTIVATION Grow in sun or shade in any soil. Do not let plants dry out.

PROPAGATION Take semi-ripe cuttings, or sow seed in early or mid spring.

PRUNING Not normally required. Thin out stems, if necessary, in spring.

PESTS AND DISEASES Usually trouble free.

Honesty see *Lunaria*
Honeysuckle see *Lonicera*
Honeysuckle, French see *Hedysarum coronarium*
Hop, common see *Humulus lupulus*
Hop tree see *Ptelea trifoliata*
Hordeum see GRASSES p.301

Horminum

Dragonmouth

Labiatae

Dense one-sided spikes of richly coloured flowers rise from lustrous leaf rosettes in summer on this hardy evergreen perennial, native to the Alps and Pyrenees. There is only one species in the genus. The plant is best grown in a rock garden, sandwiched between two rocks, or in a crack in a wall.

Horminum pyrenaicum Nodding, violet-blue, funnel-shaped flowers, about 2cm

▲ *Horminum pyrenaicum*

(¾ in) long, borne on short stalks, appear in early and mid summer, occasionally later. The deep green, stalked leaves, about 7.5 cm (3 in) long, rounded or oval, are shiny, crinkled and leathery. HEIGHT & SPREAD 25×40 cm (10×16 in).

CULTIVATION Grow plants in moist, well-drained soil, in sun or partial shade. They dislike acid soil.

PROPAGATION Sow seed in pots in winter in a coldframe and prick out seedlings when they are large enough to handle. Divide in early spring or immediately after flowering. They will often self-sow.

PESTS AND DISEASES Usually trouble free.

Hornbeam see *Carpinus*
Hornbeam, hop see *Ostrya*
Horseradish (culinary herb)
see HERBS p. 331

Hosta

Plantain lily
Hostaceae

Hosta fortunei var. albopicta

Most hostas are grown for the architectural qualities of their sumptuous foliage. The sculptured leaves vary from lance-shaped to almost round, and from a few inches to more than a foot long. Leaf colour varies through cool blue-greens, silver-blues, darkest greens and yellow to variegations of gold and cream in splashes and outlined margins. Often richly textured with prominent veins, the leaves can be heavily corrugated and puckered and matt or glossy. They provide interest from spring to first frosts, dying down in late autumn.

Trumpet or bell-shaped flowers, in shades of purple, mauve and white, bloom in summer, usually well above the mound of leaves. They are borne on stems that are bare or have leaf-like bracts.

Hardy and adaptable perennials, hostas provide excellent ground cover and several varieties have a creeping root system that fills a big area, making them attractive and useful plants for mass planting. Once established, they can be left undisturbed for years. Most are suitable for shady borders and woodland gardens and many are ideally suited to container growing. Deeply cupped varieties collect debris from trees in their leaves and are best planted in shade from buildings. Dwarf and miniature varieties are excellent in shaded rock gardens.

All hostas require a moist soil and grow best in light to full shade, unless stated otherwise. They all need to be sheltered from wind, as otherwise their leaves can split or scorch at the edges. Natives of Japan, China and Korea, the genus has 25 or more species and over 1500 registered cultivars.

RECOMMENDED SPECIES AND VARIETIES

The hostas listed below are divided into 3 groups:

(1) Very large to large
(2) Large to medium
(3) Medium to small

VERY LARGE TO LARGE HOSTAS

***H.* 'Big Daddy'** The rounded, cupped leaves are intensely blue and heavily furrowed and puckered. Pale lavender to nearly white flowers bloom from early to mid summer. It is quite slow to establish. HEIGHT & SPREAD 60×90 cm (24×36 in).

***H.* 'Blue Angel'**♀ Smooth, arching, blue-grey leaves are nearly heart-shaped and pointed with gently wavy edges. The plant has a lush, tropical appearance. Flowers, from mid to late summer, are near white. HEIGHT & SPREAD 1×1.2 m (3×4 ft).

***H. fluctuans* 'Sagae'** (syn. *H. fluctuans* 'Variegated'♀) Soft sage-green leaves with bold cream to yellow margins are held horizontally on upright leaf stalks. Broadly wedge-shaped and gracefully pointed, they emerge twisted but become gently wavy. Flowers from early to mid summer are pale lavender suffused with purple. Slow to establish, the plant eventually forms a huge clump. HEIGHT & SPREAD 1×1.2 m (3×4 ft).

***H.* 'Frances Williams'**♀ A handsome plant with thick, puckered, heart-shaped leaves that are deep blue-green with wide, irregular cream to yellow margins. The pale lavender to near white flowers are borne in dense heads from early to mid summer. Best grown in full shade, as the leaf edges may scorch. HEIGHT & SPREAD 60 cm×1 m (2×3 ft).

***H. montana* 'Aureomarginata'** Upright and arching, oval to heart-shaped leaves have broad golden yellow margins. This is usually the first hosta to emerge in spring, but the plant is prone to frost damage. If damaged leaves are removed, the next flush may escape the frosts. Flowers from early to mid summer are near-white suffused with lavender. The plant grows best in full shade. HEIGHT & SPREAD 75 cm×1 m (2½×3 ft).

▼ *Hosta montana* 'Aureomarginata'

H. nigrescens The ashy grey-green leaves are puckered and cupped. Oval to almost heart-shaped, they are carried on long leaf stems. The flowers are pale lavender to nearly white, from mid to late summer. HEIGHT & SPREAD 65×70 cm (26×28 in).

H. sieboldiana The large, thick, heart-shaped to almost round leaves are very puckered and bluish grey-green. The flowers, from early to mid summer, are pale lavender to nearly white on stems about the same height as the leaf mound. HEIGHT & SPREAD 60 cm×1 m (2×3 ft).

'Elegans'♀ is a superb variety with intense blue-green leaves.

▲ *Hosta sieboldiana* 'Elegans'

***H.* 'Sum and Substance'**♀ The slightly heart-shaped leaves, satiny yellowish green to golden yellow, are very thick and puckered when mature. Flowers are pale lavender to nearly white, from mid summer to early autumn. Leaves assume a better colour in full sun. Requires plenty of moisture. HEIGHT & SPREAD 75 cm×1.5 m (2½×5 ft).

***H.* 'Zounds'** Heart-shaped leaves, puckered and somewhat twisted, satiny yellow-green to rich yellow-gold, sometimes with green streaks, hold their colour even in the shade. Pale lavender to nearly white flowers are borne from early to mid summer. HEIGHT & SPREAD 40×75 cm (16×30 in).

LARGE TO MEDIUM HOSTAS

***H.* 'August Moon'** The oval to heart-shaped leaves, slightly puckered, are pale

▼ *Hosta* 'Zounds'

green at first, becoming soft yellow. Pale lavender to near white flowers bloom from mid to late summer. This is a vigorous plant that is easy to grow. It colours better in sun than in shade. HEIGHT & SPREAD 75×75 cm (30×30 in).

H. fortunei* var. *albopicta In spring the heart-shaped leaves are a soft yellow streaked with green, with dark green margins. The leaves fade to a faintly variegated green by flowering time. Blooms are lavender, from early to mid summer. HEIGHT & SPREAD 60 cm×1 m (2×3 ft).

▲ *Hosta fortunei* var. *albopicta*

The leaves of var. ***aureomarginata*** have an irregular yellow to cream margin and the grey-green leaves of var. ***hyacinthina*** have a faint pencil-line margin.

***H.* 'Francee'** One of the best of the white-margined hostas. The flat, narrowly heart-shaped leaves are dark olive-green, with a narrow, irregular, white margin. The lavender flowers bloom from mid to late

▲ *Hosta fortunei* var. *aureomarginata*

Hosta fortunei var. *hyacinthina* ▼

▲ *Hosta* 'Francee'

summer. The plant increases rapidly. It is best grown in light shade. HEIGHT & SPREAD 60 cm×1 m (2×3 ft).

***H.* 'Patriot'** is similar, but with much wider margins to the leaves.

***H.* 'Gold Standard'** The oval to heart-shaped leaves are first dark green with yellow-green margins, then golden yellow, fading to beige, with a deep green margin. In too much sun leaves turn white and can burn; in too little sun they remain green. Lavender flowers are borne from mid to late summer. Adequate moisture is essential. HEIGHT & SPREAD 50 cm×1 m (20 in×3 ft).

***H.* 'Invincible'** Thick, glossy, olive-green leaves are wedge-shaped tapering to a long point and very wavy. Many lightly fragrant, lavender to near white flowers are borne from late summer to early autumn. Best grown in light shade to sun. Less attractive to slugs and snails than many other hostas. HEIGHT & SPREAD 40 cm ×1 m (16 in×3 ft).

H. lancifolia The shiny mid green leaves are oval to lance-shaped with a pointed tip and slightly wavy margins. Intense purple-violet flowers are borne from late summer to early autumn. The plant provides useful ground cover. If left undisturbed it forms large colonies. The flowers can be attacked by blackfly. It flourishes in light shade. HEIGHT & SPREAD 30×60 cm (1×2 ft).

***H.* 'Midas Touch'** The cupped and deeply puckered heart-shaped leaves are a rich golden yellow with a bronze-metallic caste. Pale lavender to near white flowers bloom from mid to late summer. Leaves colour best in direct sunlight. HEIGHT & SPREAD 30×75 cm (12×30 in).

***H.* 'Patriot'** see *H.* 'Francee'

***H.* 'Paul's Glory'** The puckered, heart-shaped leaves are first bright yellow, then creamy white, with an irregular, broad blue-green margin. Flowers are pale lavender to near white, from early to mid summer. Grows best in light shade or some sun. HEIGHT & SPREAD 45×65 cm (18×26 in).

H. plantaginea Glossy light to mid green leaves are heart-shaped with deeply impressed veins and lightly wavy edges. The plant rarely flowers. Large, fragrant, white blooms are sometimes produced in late summer and early autumn in warm sheltered areas. Best grown in a large tub, against a south-facing wall or in a conservatory. HEIGHT & SPREAD 45 cm×1 m (1½×3 ft).

'Grandiflora' (syn *H. p.* var. *japonica*) has laxer and longer leaves and flowers with longer tubes.

***H.* 'Royal Standard'** Narrowly heart-shaped, glossy, light green leaves become puckered when mature. Fragrant white flowers bloom from mid summer to early autumn. The plant does best in sun. HEIGHT & SPREAD 45 cm ×1 m (1½×3 ft).

▲ *Hosta* 'Royal Standard'

***H.* 'Shade Fanfare'** Heart-shaped leaves are a soft sage green, irregularly margined with cream. Lavender flowers are borne from early to mid summer. HEIGHT & SPREAD 40×60 cm (16×24 in).

***H.* 'So Sweet'** The glossy, deep green, oval leaves, somewhat puckered, with wide creamy white margins, carried on very long stems, form an upright clump. Lightly fragrant white flowers open from mauve buds in mid and late summer. The plant flowers best in more sun than most hostas require. HEIGHT & SPREAD 35×60 cm (14×24 in).

***H.* 'Thomas Hogg'** see *H. undulata* var. *albomarginata*

H. undulata* var. *undulata Twisted leaves, broadly oval to lance shaped, are creamy white with irregular green margins. Lavender flowers appear from early to mid summer. The plant is best grown in full shade because leaves may scorch in the sun. It is prone to damage from pests. HEIGHT & SPREAD 35×45 cm (14×18 in).

▼ *Hosta undulata* var. *undulata*

H. undulata* var. *albomarginata (syn. 'Thomas Hogg') has larger, less wavy edged, matt green leaves with irregular white margins. ***H. undulata* var. *univittata*** has a larger, flatter, matt green leaf with a narrow, white, central variegation.

H. ventricosa One of the best green-leaved hostas. Glossy, heart-shaped, spinach green leaves have rippled margins and widely spaced veins. Rich bluish purple flowers are borne from mid summer to early

▲ *Hosta ventricosa*

autumn. Best grown in shade as the leaves are somewhat thin and scorch at the edges. HEIGHT & SPREAD 50cm×1m (20in×3ft).

MEDIUM TO SMALL HOSTAS

H. albomarginata see *H. sieboldii* 'Paxton's Original'

***H.* 'Blue Moon'** The blue-grey leaves are rounded to heart-shaped, cupped and puckered. Many pale lavender-grey to white flowers, in early and mid summer. Slow to increase, the plant does best in dappled shade. HEIGHT & SPREAD 20×25cm (8×10in).

***H.* 'Blue Wedgwood'** Wedge-shaped blue-green leaves have wavy margins and taper to a point. The flowers are pale lavender to white, in early and mid summer. HEIGHT & SPREAD 25×60cm (10×24in).

***H.* 'Gold Edger'** The thick, heart-shaped leaves are at first greenish yellow, then a rich soft yellow. Many pale lavender to near white flowers bloom in early and mid summer. Plants increase rapidly, making good ground cover. Best in light shade to sun. HEIGHT & SPREAD 30×70cm (12×28in).

***H.* 'Golden Prayers'** Leaves are deep yellow, oval to heart-shaped and upright. Thick in texture, they become puckered when mature. The flowers are palest lavender to near white, in early and mid summer. The plant is best in light shade. HEIGHT & SPREAD 30×50cm (12×20in).

***H.* 'Golden Tiara'**♀ A neat, compact plant that increases rapidly. The oval to heart-shaped, matt green leaves are irregularly

▲ *Hosta* 'Golden Tiara'

margined with creamy yellow. Showy, deep lavender flowers striped with purple bloom from mid to late summer. HEIGHT & SPREAD 36×60cm (14×24in).

***H.* 'Hadspen Blue'** The thick, heart-shaped leaves, an intense grey-blue, form neat, dense mounds. Lavender flowers bloom in early and mid summer. The plant grows best in dappled shade. HEIGHT & SPREAD 25×45cm (10×18in).

***H.* 'Halcyon'**♀ The smooth, heart-shaped

▲ *Hosta* 'Halcyon'

leaves are silver-blue. Flowers are greyish lavender to near white, in early and mid summer. Best in dappled shade. HEIGHT & SPREAD 50cm×1m (20in×3ft).

***H.* 'June'** is similar, but with yellow leaves with striking, irregular blue-green margins.

***H.* 'Devon Green'** is again similar, with glossy mid green leaves.

***H.* 'Lemon Lime'** Bright greenish yellow leaves are lance-shaped with wavy edges. The flowers, lavender striped with purple, are borne from mid to late summer. Good for a shaded rock garden or peat bed. HEIGHT & SPREAD 10×45cm (4×18in).

***H.* 'Love Pat'**♀ see *H. tokudama*

***H. sieboldii* 'Paxton's Original'** (syn. *H. albomarginata*) Narrowish leaves are a dull dark green, edged with white. Lavender flowers with dark purple stripes are borne from mid to late summer. The plant needs a damp situation. It tolerates more sun than many other hostas. It spreads slowly into extensive clumps. HEIGHT & SPREAD 20×25cm (8×10in).

H. s.* var. *alba has mid green leaves and white flowers.

H. tokudama The thick, rounded, strongly cupped, deeply puckered leaves are greyish dark blue. Flowers are palest lavender to nearly white, from early to mid summer. This beautiful hosta is slow to increase. HEIGHT & SPREAD 30×60cm (1×2ft).

The superb variety ***H.* 'Love Pat'**♀ is larger and more vigorous.

H. venusta♀ The satiny green leaves are variable on shape, but usually oval to heart-shaped. Flowers are a deep lavender. HEIGHT & SPREAD 8×10cm (3¼×4in).

***H.* 'Wide Brim'**♀ The heart-shaped, slightly cupped and puckered leaves are a satiny rich, mid green with a wide irregular cream margin. The flowers are pale lavender to nearly white. This plant increases rapidly. It grows best in light shade. HEIGHT & SPREAD 60cm×1m (2×3ft).

CULTIVATION Plant hostas in spring or autumn. They thrive best in rich, friable loam just the acid side of neutral. Although they grow well in alkaline soils, they seldom flourish on shallow, chalky soils, which cause leaves to assume a yellowish tinge. Large hostas will grow well on heavy clay soils rich in plant nutrients, but can be slower to become established. They will grow more quickly if, before planting, the soil is lightened by working in copious and equal quantities of coarse grit and garden compost or well-rotted manure. Mulch regularly in autumn and keep well watered. Smaller and dwarf hostas need a more friable mixture of peat and garden compost, regularly mulched with leaf-mould and coarse grit. Feed all hostas with a balanced plant food in spring and early summer.

PROPAGATION Divide clumps in late summer or early spring. Hostas are easily grown from seed but do not usually come true, other than *H. ventricosa*.

PESTS AND DISEASES Slugs and snails can do considerable damage especially when new shoots first appear above the ground, and again 2 weeks later as leaves unfurl. For container-grown hostas vine weevil larvae can be a problem – renew soil annually. In addition, virus damage can affect hostas, and leaf spot is occasionally a problem.

Hottonia

Primulaceae

Whorls of pale mauve or white flowers up to 2.5cm (1in) wide distinguish these submerged or floating aquatic perennials. They are hardy, easily grown herbaceous plants for a sunny pond or slowly running stream. The finely segmented light green leaves, up to 10cm (4in) long, are mostly under water. The flowers, borne in early and mid summer, are carried well above the surface. Tiny, rounded, light green fruit pods containing numerous seeds appear in late summer. Native to Europe, W Asia and eastern N America.

RECOMMENDED SPECIES

H. palustris (water violet) Flowers are pale mauve or lilac. Each has a short tube and 5 spreading lobes, which are notched at the tips. Both free-floating and rooted stems bear feathery submerged leaves. HEIGHT & SPREAD 15–25cm (6–10in) above water, spread indefinite.

CULTIVATION Plant in spring, in an aquatic plant basket containing a fertile soil-based compost, in 15cm (6in) of water, near the edge of a pond or stream, in full sun.

PROPAGATION Take greenwood cuttings in early summer. Established plants may naturalise by self-sown seeds.

PESTS AND DISEASES Usually trouble free.

Hound's tongue see *Cynoglossum*
Houseleek see *Sempervivum*

▼ *Hottonia palustris*

BRING THE OUTSIDE WORLD INTO THE HOME AND TRANSFORM INTERIORS WITH LIVING DISPLAYS OF COLOUR AND FORM

Ranging from tiny cacti to tall stately palms, houseplants offer the gardener a vast array of shapes, textures, colours and markings to enjoy. Exotic foliage, showy flowers and colourful ornamental fruits combine to create a diverse indoor garden that provides interest throughout the year.

Choose species that will tolerate the conditions in different areas of your home. Many houseplants prefer a site in bright indirect light but some, such as *Tolmiea menziesii* (pick-aback plant) thrive in cool and shady rooms. A few, including tough succulents, will flourish in brightly lit, warm areas. Only very dark sites are unsuitable for all houseplants.

As well as bringing a living dimension to a room, indoor plants can add charm and elegance and help to set the room's style. A shapely palm, such as a *Howea*, for example, is ideally suited to a formal setting; a spiky-leaved *Dracaena* or *Yucca* sets off an interior that is starkly architectural; while a row of *Pelargonium* (geranium) cultivars in containers looks bright and cheerful on the windowsill of a country cottage.

BRILLIANT RED *Bright poinsettias are at their best in deepest winter.*

◄ LUXURIANT FRUITS *Jerusalem cherry adds colour to a grouping of lush foliage plants.*

RICH FOLIAGE

Houseplants that have attractive foliage create long-lived displays that look good all year round. The range of leaf shapes is huge, from the large, luxuriant, deeply cut foliage of *Monstera deliciosa* (Swiss cheese plant) to the sharp-edged geometric leaves of *Sansevieria trifasciata* (mother-in-law's tongue). There are plants with delicately divided fronds, such as *Adiantum* (maidenhair fern), and with palmate leaves, such as *Schefflera elegantissima* (false aralia). There are also rounded shapes, such as the leaves of *Maranta*, or arrow shapes, such as the leaves of *Syngonium podophyllum* (goosefoot plant).

Leaf texture is varied, from the smooth, glossy shininess of *Philodendron* to the intricate, rippled surfaces of the leaves of some species of *Begonia* and *Pilea*. Interest is also provided by variations in shades of green, such as the dark green of *Aspidistra elatior* (cast-iron plant) and the fresh green of *Chamaedorea elegans* (parlour palm), and by richly coloured markings in purples, reds, greens and yellows, such as those of *Solenostemon* (coleus). Other houseplants, including the weeping fig *Ficus benjamina* 'Starlight', display variegated leaves which are marked with silver, gold or cream.

BRIGHT COLOUR

If given the correct conditions, some houseplants will flower regularly and make colourful shows. *Saintpaulia* (African violet) and *Streptocarpus* (Cape primrose) are among the best for length of flowering season. When kept in a warm and well-lit room, *Pelargonium* also provides blooms throughout much of the year.

Schlumbergera (Christmas cactus) flowers reliably and provides a welcome splash of colour in winter. Exotic plants, such as *Anthurium scherzerianum* (flamingo flower) with its large, waxy red flowers, *Phalaenopsis amabilis* (moth orchid) and the scented climber *Stephanotis floribunda,* will produce flowers as long as their needs for warmth, humidity and good indirect light are met.

Some flowering plants can be treated as temporary residents, brought into the house for a display of blooms and removed after flowering. Short-lived flowering plants, such as

▲ STRIKING FOLIAGE *The bold, glossy leaves of a variegated schefflera gleam in sunlight.*

▼ LONG-LASTING DISPLAY *Cape primroses provide colourful blooms over several months.*

▶ CENTRAL FOCUS *Bright pelargoniums attract attention in a setting of dark green foliage.*

Exacum affine (Persian violet) and *Primula*, are a source of instant colour. Other plants for temporary displays include *Cyclamen*, *Pericallis* and *Euphorbia pulcherrima* (poinsettia), with its brilliant red, pink or cream bracts.

Bright colour is also contributed by plants with ornamental fruits. Chilli peppers and *Solanum pseudocapsicum* (Jerusalem cherry), which has orange-red berries that last through much of autumn and winter, make good houseplants.

SHAPELY FORMS

Houseplants vary dramatically in their size and form. Tall erect plants may have a tree-like appearance, for example *Ficus elastica* 'Robusta' (rubber plant) or false aralia with its attractive whorls of glossy leaves. Tall houseplants can be displayed anywhere with suitable conditions where there is room, and are useful for areas with high ceilings, such as halls.

Plants may be upright, for example columnar cacti, form rosettes like the succulent *Echeveria* or be spreading or bushy like *Pilea*. Bushy species look particularly effective when displayed in fireplaces, or on side tables and plant stands. Low-growing plants which have spreading habits, such as *Begonia*, are useful for windowsills or shelves, where there is little vertical space.

Some houseplants have a climbing or trailing habit, such as *Cissus rhombifolia* (grape ivy), *Hedera helix* (ivy) and *Philodendron scandens* (sweetheart plant). Grow a climber up a moss pole or train it up wires or a wall-mounted trellis. A trailing plant looks particularly attractive when its leaves and stems are left to cascade from a hanging basket, a container placed on a high shelf or a pot that has been fixed to a wall.

STRIKING DISPLAYS

Tall houseplants can make good focal points when they are displayed as specimens. A *Howea*, or other large palm, set singly in a high-ceilinged room makes a graceful feature, for example, while a large climber trained up a moss pole in a stairwell commands attention.

Most indoor plants, however, are best displayed in a group, where they create a slightly humid microclimate. Place tall plants with more compact ones for a balanced display. Use climbers as backdrops and upright plants as centrepieces. Create interest and variety by combining houseplants that have differently shaped, coloured or textured leaves.

Plants which have plain green leaves provide simple contrasts to the strong colour of *Codiaeum* foliage, and accentuate the decorative patterns of *Maranta* leaves. Similarly, the corrugated foliage of some *Peperomia* is highlighted when set against the smooth-surfaced leaves of the peace lily *Spathiphyllum wallisii*. A plant with large, striking foliage, such as the Swiss cheese plant or a big-leaf philodendron, go well with delicate-looking plants, such as *Mimosa pudica* (sensitive plant) which has light green divided leaves.

Flowering plants look good among foliage plants, whose leaves provide an attractive backdrop. The feathery maidenhair fern and *Asparagus setaceus*, for example, combine well with cyclamen in winter, bulbs in spring and pelargoniums in summer. Another colourful combination is the variegated spider plant *Chlorophytum comosum* 'Vittatum' and the dark-leaved *Begonia* 'Cleopatra'. Add Cape primroses to provide extra colour from mid spring right through to early autumn.

LIGHT CONDITIONS

Many houseplants grow best in bright filtered light. Site them on a sunny windowsill and screen the window with a translucent curtain, or place plants a short way back from the window. Houseplants also grow well in areas that receive direct light for only part of the day.

Positioned in a site with too little light, many houseplants produce weak growth and their leaves turn paler. In excess light, foliage becomes scorched. As plants grow towards the light, they benefit from regular turning to prevent lopsided growth.

In very sunny areas in front of south-facing windows, display shrubby flowering conservatory plants, such as *Abutilon*, *Bougainvillea* and *Hibiscus*. The plants will thrive here provided that they have enough space.

In poorly lit areas, use houseplants that are shade tolerant, such as *Aglaonema* (Chinese evergreen), *Ficus deltoidea* var. *diversifolia* (mistletoe fig) and × *Fatshedera lizei*. Even shade-tolerant plants may deteriorate if light levels are very low. Rotate them every few weeks, moving the plants to an area with better light so that they produce healthy growth.

Many other houseplants, especially flowering ones, will benefit from being moved to positions where they can get as much sunlight as possible during the winter months.

▲ LEAFY VARIATION *Differing shapes and textures of foliage make an eye-catching show.*

Temperature zones

Houseplants need higher temperatures during the day and throughout the growing season than at night and in winter. Many houseplants grow well in centrally heated rooms, in a daytime temperature range of 18–23°C (64–73°F) and a minimum night-time temperature of 13°C (55°F).

Hardy plants, such as ivy and *Fatsia japonica*, thrive in unheated rooms. Provided there is sufficient light and a minimum temperature of 10°C (50°F), *Citrus, Bougainvillea* and other half-hardy shrubs that enjoy cool, airy conditions will also do well here.

In rooms that are kept very warm – at temperatures of 23°C (74°F) or above – dry air may cause damage, including brown leaf edges. To combat this, use a humidifier to create a moist atmosphere or group plants on trays of wet gravel. This is particularly important for those that have delicate leaves, such as *Calathea*. Misting the plants also increases humidity and is of particular benefit to those that absorb water through their foliage, such as the bromeliad *Tillandsia*, or through their aerial roots, such as the epiphytic orchids.

Most houseplants react badly to extreme fluctuations in temperature. Do not site them in areas where this is likely to occur – above a radiator or near a badly fitted window or door, for example. A plant on a windowsill that is curtained off from the warmth of the room may also suffer damage on a cold night.

◀ Foliage frame *A weeping fig at a doorway guides the eye towards the garden beyond.*

◀ Natural harmony *A simple grouping of plants is enhanced by the timber setting.*

Watering amounts

Both overwatering and underwatering plants causes poor growth as well as making the plant more vulnerable to pests and diseases.

Except for moisture-lovers, such as *Spathiphyllum*, most houseplants should be watered once the surface 2.5 cm (1 in) of compost has dried out. Use your finger or a stick to test the soil, which will tend to cling if it is moist. Alternatively, lift up the pot to check its weight – it will feel lighter when the soil is dry than when it is wet.

When watering during the growing season, flood the soil until water leaks out of the drainage holes in the bottom of the pot, then drain thoroughly. Water a delicate plant by standing the container in a saucer of water, to avoid splashing and marking the foliage.

During winter, reduce the watering to encourage plants to rest while light levels are low. Drought-tolerant plants, such as *Crassula, Aloe* and other succulents, should be kept unwatered in a cool room. If the room is warm, water these plants very sparingly to prevent shrivelling.

Tap water is suitable for many houseplants, but check the individual requirements. Lime haters, such as orchids, and bromeliads, should be watered with rainwater.

Feeding and potting

A plant growing in a container has a limited supply of nutrients and will cease growth almost entirely when these are exhausted. Feeding and occasional repotting are essential to maintain healthy growth.

Slow-release pellets or sticks save effort as only one application a year is needed. Alternatively, use a general-purpose fertiliser during the growing season; flowering plants benefit from a high-potash feed, such as a tomato fertiliser, which stimulates flowering.

Apply feed at half strength to slow-growing plants, such as succulents and bromeliads. Do not feed plants when growth has slowed or ceased in winter.

If a plant begins to look starved, with little new growth and yellowing leaves, and its soil dries out quickly, it probably needs repotting. When it is tipped from its pot, the plant will reveal a mass of roots round its soil ball.

Young plants benefit from repotting each spring. Move those growing in pots less than 10 cm (4 in) wide into pots that

▲ SHAPELY LEAVES *A Swiss cheese plant and parlour palm bring elegance to a living room.*

are 2-4 cm (¾-1½ in) wider. Repot plants growing in larger containers into pots 4-6 cm (1½-2½ in) wider.

Use a compost that is specifically designed for houseplants, preferably a soil-based compost like John Innes No. 2 or No. 3. This provides better stability than a soil-less mixture. Add one part perlite or grit to ten parts compost for plants that are moisture-sensitive, such as African violets and peperomias. For succulents, add one part grit to three parts compost.

Slow-growing species and mature specimens do not need annual repotting; very fast-growing species are also best repotted less frequently or they will soon become too large for their space. Top dress these plants by removing the top layer of compost, to a depth of around 2-5 cm (¾-2 in) depending on pot size, and replacing it with fresh compost.

Training and pruning

Tie tall plants to a cane to keep them straight and upright. Climbers also need some support. Slower-growing species that have thick shoots, such as philodendrons, are best trained up a trellis. Lighter, faster-growing plants, including *Cissus*, climb easily up a network of wires.

Many houseplants can be pruned in spring, at the beginning of active growth. This keeps the plants manageable, encourages strong new growth and promotes branching. Pinch out growing tips on fast-growing plants to encourage dense and bushy growth.

Preventing problems

Meeting the individual needs of houseplants will help to prevent disease. In addition, keep plants free of dust and dirt. Wipe smooth-surfaced leaves with a damp cloth and brush hairy or textured leaves gently with an old toothbrush. If pests or diseases occur, act quickly to prevent spreading. (See PESTS AND DISEASES p. 823.)

▼ SCRAMBLING STEMS Syngonium podophyllum *tumbles over a side table.*

HOUSEPLANTS FOR FLOWERS AND YEAR-ROUND INTEREST

Plants for flowers

- ***Cyclamen persicum*** (florist's cyclamen) Scented colourful flowers from winter to spring, above green or grey-green, sometimes patterned, heart-shaped leaves.
- ***Phalaenopsis amabilis*** (moth orchid) Slender spikes of white moth-like flowers all winter and leathery, oblong, mid green leaves.
- ***Saintpaulia* hybrids** (African violet) Colourful starry flowers through most of the year above rosettes of rounded, dark or bright green, velvet-textured foliage.
- ***Schlumbergera* hybrids** (Christmas cactus) Pink, red or orange, trumpet-shaped flowers in winter and fleshy, flattened green stems.
- ***Streptocarpus* hybrids** (Cape primrose) Clusters of white, pink or purple flowers from spring to autumn and wrinkled, strap-like, mid to dark green leaves.

Plants for foliage

- ***Aglaonema* 'Silver Queen'** Silvery grey, pointed, oval leaves with green streaks.
- ***Begonia bowerae*** (eyelash plant) Bright green, oval leaves with black stitch-like markings and very small pink flowers on stems from late winter to spring.
- ***Maranta leuconeura* var. *kerchoveana*** (rabbit's foot) Greyish green, oval leaves patterned with purple-brown or olive-green markings.
- ***Nephrolepis exaltata* 'Bostoniensis'** (Boston fern) Rich green, feathery fronds with an arching habit.
- ***Pelargonium crispum*** (lemon geranium) Mid green, lobed leaves with a strong lemon scent and pale pink flower clusters in summer.

Tolerant plants

- ***Asparagus setaceus*** Fern-like foliage with bright green, needle-like leaflets. Tolerates low temperatures and poor light.
- ***Aspidistra elatior*** (cast-iron plant) Dark green, leathery, arching leaves. Tolerates poor light levels.
- ***Chlorophytum comosum* 'Vittatum'** White-striped, lance-shaped arching leaves. Tolerates cool temperatures and poor light.
- **× *Fatshedera lizei*** Large and glossy, dark green, deeply lobed leaves and clusters of small greenish white flowers in late summer. Tolerates cool temperatures and poor light.
- ***Ficus elastica* 'Robusta'** (rubber plant) Large, leathery, glossy green, oval leaves. Tolerates poor light.

Specimen plants

- ***Chamaedorea elegans*** (parlour palm) Light green divided leaves which arch from a short woody trunk.
- ***Ctenanthe oppenheimiana*** Silver-grey, paddle-shaped leaves with dark green stripes on purplish stems.
- ***Dracaena marginata* 'Tricolor'** Green, red and cream-striped, narrow, strap-like leaves above a slender woody trunk.
- ***Ficus benjamina*** (weeping fig) Leathery, glossy, dark green, oval leaves held on weeping branches.
- ***Schefflera elegantissima*** (false aralia) Glossy, bronze, evenly toothed, narrow leaves on slender stalks.
- ***Yucca aloifolia*** (Spanish bayonet) Dark green, rigid, sword-shaped leaves with finely toothed edges, crowning a woody stem.

Trailers and climbers

- ***Cissus rhombifolia*** (grape ivy) Climber with coarsely toothed, dark green, diamond-shaped leaves.
- ***Ficus pumila*** (creeping fig) Climber or trailer with small, heart-shaped to oval, bright green leaves and red-flushed orange fruits in late summer.
- ***Philodendron scandens*** (sweetheart plant) Climber with large, glossy, rich green, heart-shaped leaves.
- ***Tradescantia fluminensis* 'Quicksilver'** (inch plant) Trailer with pointed oval leaves, striped green and silver, and clusters of white flowers in summer.

h

Houstonia

Bluet
Rubiaceae

Solitary white, blue or blue-violet flowers sprinkle these low-growing hardy perennials throughout the summer. The dainty four-petalled flowers are held on thread-like stems just above spreading evergreen mats of small shining leaves, ideal for a rock garden. Native to eastern N America.

RECOMMENDED SPECIES AND VARIETIES

H. michauxii (syn. *H. caerulea* hort., *Hedyotis michauxii*) Star-shaped clear blue flowers, 1cm (⅜in) across, appear from late spring to early autumn, on a carpet of 1cm (⅜in) long, oval bright green leaves. HEIGHT & SPREAD 7.5×40cm (3×16in).

▲ *Houstonia michauxii*

The flowers of var. ***alba*** are white. **'Fred Mullard'** has deep blue flowers and a dense mat of foliage.

CULTIVATION Plant in spring in a shaded or semi-shaded moist site, ideally lime-free, such as a leafy woodland area or cool corner of a rock garden.

PROPAGATION Divide in spring and replant at once; keep moist until established.

PESTS AND DISEASES Slugs may attack very young plants.

Houttuynia

Saururaceae

Evergreen heart-shaped leaves borne on erect stems, flowers that bloom from early to mid summer, a neat habit and tolerance of different soils make this hardy herbaceous perennial a distinctive ground-cover plant. It flourishes in moist soil, where it may become invasive, but also grows on pond margins or in dry soil. Replant frequently if it outgrows its allotted space, re-using only a small portion of the plant. Some forms have brightly coloured foliage. A delicate citrus fragrance is emitted when the leaves are crushed. The genus consists of a single species, which is native to E Asia.

▲ *Houttuynia cordata*

Houttuynia cordata The flowerhead is a short spike, about 2.5cm (1in) long, carried on a leafy stem, 50cm (20in) tall. The flowers themselves are inconspicuous – the pure white bracts more striking. The heart-shaped bluish green leaves, up to 9cm (3½in) long, have rust-coloured margins. HEIGHT & SPREAD 45×45cm (1½×1½ft).

▲ *Houttuynia cordata* 'Chameleon'

'Chameleon' has decorative leaves marked with vivid red, dark green and cream. **'Flore Pleno'** bears crowded flower spikes consisting of numerous petal-like bracts decreasing in size upwards. The leaves are marked red and cream. **Variegata Group** has leaves patterned red and cream.

CULTIVATION Plant in moist soil in autumn in sun or partial shade.

PROPAGATION Divide plants in autumn and plant pieces of underground stem, each with a growing point or developed shoot.

PESTS AND DISEASES Usually trouble free.

Howea

Kentia palm, sentry palm
Palmae

These statuesque and elegant palms from Lord Howe Island in the S Pacific are among the best for indoor cultivation. Growing from a single stem, the leaves are up to 40cm (16in) long and divided to the midrib, each dark green leaflet being around 2.5cm (1in) wide. In a greenhouse or conservatory they grow well with the other Edwardian favourites, chamaedorea palms and aspidistras, and also group successfully with other, more modern foliage exotics, such as monsteras and philodendrons. Tolerating a wide range of light levels and dry air, they make excellent large houseplants. There are two species.

RECOMMENDED SPECIES

H. belmoreana The leaves initially grow upright but then arch gracefully outwards, a habit shared by the leaflets. HEIGHT & SPREAD 2×2m (6½×6½ft) after 5 years, ultimately 2.5m (8ft) tall.

▲ *Howea forsteriana* (Kentia palm)

H. forsteriana♀ (Kentia palm) The leaves of this faster-growing species tend to grow horizontally. The leaflets grow straight at first, then droop. HEIGHT & SPREAD 2×2m (6½×6½ft) after 5 years, ultimately 2.5m (8ft) tall.

CULTIVATION Pot Kentia palms in soil-based compost or a compost containing grit, to counterbalance the top-heaviness of the plants. They prefer a well-lit position and a temperature that does not fall below 10°C (50°F). In summer, keep slightly moist and feed regularly; allow to dry out between waterings in winter.

PROPAGATION Germinate fresh seed at 25°C (77°F). The seedlings grow slowly.

PRUNING Not normally required.

PESTS AND DISEASES Usually trouble free.

Hoya

Wax flower

Asclepiadaceae

Attractive foliage and waxy flowers make hoyas rewarding indoor plants. Most are climbers, and can be trained round wire hoops or up trelliswork. They do best in good light, and make flamboyant plants in a conservatory, where they are also more likely to produce clusters of star-shaped, 1 cm (⅜ in) wide flowers. Native to SE Asia.

RECOMMENDED SPECIES

H. australis (wax flower) Admired for its fresh green leaves on climbing stems, this plant also bears fragrant white flowers with reddish spots in late summer. The glossy leaves are up to 8 cm (3¼ in) long and rounded with a sharp tip. HEIGHT 3 m (10 ft).

H. carnosa♀ (wax plant) Fleshy mid green oval leaves, up to 8 cm (3¼ in) long, have pointed tips. The fragrant flowers are borne in late summer and vary in colour from white to pale pink, with red spots in the centre. HEIGHT 3 m (10 ft).

▲ *Hoya carnosa*

H. lanceolata ssp. ***bella***♀ (miniature wax plant) Much smaller than most hoyas, this plant has a trailing habit, to about 40 cm (16 in). The mid green leaves are up to 3 cm (1¼ in) long, oval to lance-shaped with a distinctive dark midrib. The branches begin with an upright habit and then start to trail. The fragrant flowers are white with a red centre and appear in late summer. It is ideal for hanging baskets. HEIGHT 30 cm (1 ft).

CULTIVATION Hoyas need moderate sunlight and can survive temperatures of 7°C (45°F) but ideally keep above 13°C (55°F). Water when the top of the compost is beginning to dry out, allowing more pronounced drying in winter. Keep slightly pot bound for a good show of flowers and feed regularly. Use neutral or slightly acid compost mixed with grit or perlite.

PROPAGATION Take cuttings in spring or summer or use layering in late spring.

PRUNING Tidy up older plants in spring or after flowering. Leave old flower stalks as new bunches often grow from them.

PESTS AND DISEASES Mealy bug (rarely).

Humulus

Hop

Cannabaceae

Bold, large-lobed leaves and decorative flowers (hops) on the female plant in autumn earn these herbaceous perennial climbers a place in the garden. Rapid, freely twining growth makes them useful as temporary screening plants for a wall or wire-netting fence. Bright summer foliage can adorn an arch or arbour, or enliven dull hedging. Each plant bears either male or female flowers from mid to late summer.

▲ *Humulus lupulus*

Humulus lupulus 'Aureus' ▼

RECOMMENDED SPECIES AND VARIETIES

H. lupulus (common hop) On female plants aromatic bracts hide pale green, drooping cone-like flower clusters, 2 cm (¾ in) long. The bracts enlarge to form 5 cm (2 in) long pale green fruits. On the males, tiny yellow flowers grow in clusters up to 10 cm (4 in) long. HEIGHT 3-6 m (10-20 ft).

'Aureus'♀ has golden leaves.

CULTIVATION Plant in fertile, well-drained soil. 'Aureus' needs full sun to colour well.

PROPAGATION Propagate by greenwood cuttings in early summer.

PESTS AND DISEASES Usually trouble free.

Hyacinth, grape see *Muscari armeniacum*

Hyacinth, summer see *Galtonia candicans*

Hyacinth, tassel see *Muscari comosum*

Hyacinth, water see *Eichornia crassipes*

Hyacinthoides

Bluebell

Hyacinthaceae

Carpets of intense blue spreading through light woodland are one of the delights of the British countryside in late spring. And, on some soils, bluebells are just as eager to carpet a garden; they are easy to grow and spread vigorously, but can be invasive. Bell-shaped violet-blue, white or pink flowers are borne in loose spikes in late spring. An oval seed pod containing several black seeds follows. These hardy bulbous perennials have slightly fleshy green leaves. Massing bluebells beneath trees intensifies the vivid colour of the flowers, and a border is transformed by bluebells growing beneath deciduous shrubs. The sweetly scented native British bluebell, *Hyacinthoides non-scripta* is especially suitable for a wild-flower garden. *H. hispanica*, with larger flowers, but unscented, is common in British gardens and the two species hybridise readily.

RECOMMENDED SPECIES

H. hispanica (syn. *Scilla campanulata*) (Spanish bluebell) Wide bells, about 2 cm (¾ in) long, hang round an erect stem in a conical cluster. There are from 12-20 flowers on a stem. The most common colour is violet-blue, lightening towards the tips, but flowers are sometimes pink or white. Arching, narrow bright green leaves, up to 30 cm (12 in) long, are produced by fleshy white bulbs. Native to S Europe and N Africa, *H. hispanica* seeds readily and spreads easily. HEIGHT 40cm (16 in).

▲ *Hyacinthoides hispanica*

H. non-scripta (syn. *Scilla non-scripta, S. nutans*) (bluebell) Rich violet-blue, fragrant narrow bells, up to 2 cm (¾ in) long and curving out markedly at the tips, hang at the arched top of an upright stem, in a loose one-sided spike of up to 16 flowers. White flowers are sometimes seen. The narrow green glossy leaves grow from white bulbs. Bluebells are native to western Europe.

HEIGHT & SPREAD 40×30cm (16×12in).
CULTIVATION Plant bulbs in autumn, in any fairly moist soil in partial shade.
PROPAGATION Sow seeds in autumn (it may be 4-5 years before flowers are produced), or divide established clumps of bulbs in late summer.
PESTS AND DISEASES Usually trouble free.

Hyacinthus

Hyacinthaceae

Hyacinthus orientalis 'L'Innocence'

The sweetly perfumed, colourful flowers of hyacinths appear in mid spring. The plants, with their erect, cylindrical flowerheads and fleshy, strap-like leaves, retain their perfection for two or three weeks. The flower stems may be densely packed – carrying up to 60 individual bell-shaped florets – or more loosely spaced as in the 'fairy' types. Multiflora hyacinths are grown from bulbs that have been specially treated to produce several smaller flower spikes instead of one dense spike. They are sold by colour only. There are also double-flowered varieties. Hyacinths are fully hardy and ideal for planting in containers, as well as in informal borders and formal bedding schemes. For text book results, buy new bulbs every year. The once-used bulbs produce fewer flowers per stem and can be replanted in less formal areas of the garden. To flower indoors in mid winter, bulbs specially prepared for forcing can be bought in autumn. Dust from the skins of hyacinth bulbs may irritate the skin.

RECOMMENDED SPECIES AND VARIETIES
H. orientalis This parent of all the modern hyacinth cultivars produces sparsely flowered stems, up to 20cm (8in) tall, bearing blue, violet, pink or white flowers. Indoors, prepared bulbs will flower from Christmas to late winter; non-prepared bulbs bloom from late winter to early spring. Outdoors, hyacinths flower during early spring. There are earlier and later varieties – but all flower within about a month of one another.

▼ *Hyacinthus orientalis* 'Anna Marie'

▲ *Hyacinthus orientalis* 'L'Innocence'

Early flowering varieties include **'Anna Marie'**♀, light rosy pink flowers; **'Ben Nevis'**, ivory-white double flowers; **'Bismarck'**, methyl-violet blooms; **'Blue Magic'**, purple-violet flowers; **'Borah'**♀, a fairy type with porcelain-blue flowers; **'Delft Blue'**♀, blooms of soft lilac-blue; **'Jan Bos'**, red blooms; **'L'Innocence'**♀, ivory-white flowers; **'Lady Derby'**, rose-pink flowers; **'Ostara'**♀, deep blue flowers; **'Pink Pearl'**♀, deep pink blooms; and **'Violet Pearl'**, mallow-purple flowers.

▼ *Hyacinthus* 'Pink Pearl'

▲ *Hyacinthus* 'Carnegie'

Mid-season-flowering varieties include **'Blue Jacket'**♀, dark blue flowers with a purple stripe; and **'Gipsy Queen'**♀, dark salmon and apricot flowers.

Late-flowering varieties include **'Amethyst'**, lilac-violet flowers; **'Carnegie'**, a dense spike of white flowers; **'City of Haarlem'**♀, primrose-yellow blooms; **'Distinction'**, slightly smaller than other cultivars with beetroot-purple flowers; **'Hollyhock'**, slender stems of double crimson flowers; and **'Peter Stuyvesant'**, dark violet blooms.

CULTIVATION Plant bulbs outside from late summer to late autumn in a sunny position in fairly fertile, well-drained soil. Set 15-24cm (6-9½in) apart and 10cm (4in) deep. (They will not be fully hardy if grown in containers that become frosted right through.) Plant bulbs for forcing indoors before mid autumn in bulb-forcing compost. Then keep in a cool, dark place for 8-10 weeks, ideally at 7-10°C (45-50°F): a shed or garage is ideal. Bring into a light, warm room, where they will flower 3 or 4 weeks later. Bulbs can also be grown in hyacinth vases. Keep the bulb in its vase in a cool, dark place until its roots have developed, making sure that the bulb itself does not touch the water, or it may rot.
PROPAGATION Producing fresh hyacinth bulbs involves specialist techniques: buy new bulbs. Hyacinths take 6 years or more to flower if grown from seed.
PESTS AND DISEASES Hyacinths may be affected by grey bulb rot, grey mould, soft rot and yellow disease (*Xanthomonas hyacinthi*) – which is similar to soft rot and should be treated similarly. They may also be attacked by aphids, bulb mites, narcissus flies, slugs and stem eelworms.

Hydrangea

Hydrangeaceae

Delicate lacecap or robust mop-head, sturdy shrub or delicate climber, hydrangeas are suitable for all but the coldest areas. Used to frame a low window or decorate a plain wall, they add grace and charm to cottage gardens and urban settings alike

This genus of shrubs and climbers contains plants in a wide variety of sizes and flower form. Some hydrangeas reach a final height of just 60 cm (2 ft) while others will grow to 6 m (20 ft). The flowers are borne in rounded, flat or conical heads of varying size. The foliage of several species gives good autumn colour. Some varieties are variegated. The climbers, *Hydrangea anomala* and *H. serratifolia*, the latter being the only evergreen included here, are self-clinging: they attach to a support by means of aerial roots and do not need tying in.

The flowers of hydrangeas are of two types: the fertile flowers are very small and, apart from their colour, insignificant; the sterile flowers – known as ray florets, with three to five coloured sepals, are usually 2-3 cm (¾-1¼ in) across. In most species the flowerhead is flat, composed of a large number of fertile flowers surrounded by a few ray florets; this is the 'lacecap'. The mop-headed, 'hortensia' hydrangeas have domed flowerheads, composed mainly or entirely of large ray florets. *H. paniculata, H. quercifolia* and *H. serratifolia* have conical flowerheads, some consisting entirely of fertile flowers, some entirely of ray florets, and some a mixture of the two.

In many species and cultivars, flower colour is determined by the acidity of the soil. Hydrangeas that have intensely blue flowers on acid soil may have pink flowers on neutral and alkaline soils. Hydrangeas that produce red blooms on alkaline soil may be pale blue on acid soil.

Hydrangeas are ideal for town gardens and for tub planting. North of the Midlands the shelter of walls will help, but greenhouse growing will be more successful. Some species are fully hardy, notably *H. arborescens*, *H. aspera*, *H. macrophylla* and *H. paniculata*. Tolerant of salt-laden winds, hybrids and cultivars of *H. macrophylla* and *H. serrata* will grow happily near the sea. *H. arborescens* and *H. quercifolia* are native to N America and *H. serratifolia* to S America, all the rest are native to E Asia.

1 *H. paniculata* 'Everest'
2 *H. macrophylla* 'Libelle'
3 *H.* 'Blue Deckle'
4 *H. arborescens* 'Annabelle'
5 *H. macrophylla* 'Veitchii'
6 *H. macrophylla* 'Amethyst'
7 *H. quercifolia* 'Snow Flake'
8 *H. macrophylla* 'Nigra'
9 *H. macrophylla* 'Blue Wave'
10 *H. macrophylla* 'Mme Emile Mouillère'
11 *H. paniculata* 'Grandiflora'
12 *H. macrophylla* 'Geoffrey Chadbund'
13 *H. macrophylla* 'Ayesha'

▲ *Hydrangea anomala* ssp. *petiolaris*

Hydrangea anomala ssp. petiolaris

RECOMMENDED SPECIES AND VARIETIES

H. anomala ssp. ***petiolaris***♀ (syn. *H. petiolaris*) These vigorous hardy climbers bear flat, cream and white, lacecap flowerheads, up to 25cm (10in), across in early and mid summer. Their oval serrated leaves are dark green above, pale green and downy on the underside, and grow to 10cm (4in) in length. Avoid planting against a south-facing wall or fence. HEIGHT & SPREAD 2×1m (6½×3ft) after 5 years, ultimately 3.5m (12ft) tall on walls or 5m (16ft) growing up a tree.

H. arborescens From mid summer to early autumn this fully hardy, loosely growing shrub carries rounded flowerheads, up to 15cm (6in) across, of crowded tiny, matt white, fertile flowers and an outer ring of large, showy ray florets. It has bright green oval leaves up to 18cm (7in) long. HEIGHT & SPREAD 1×1m (3×3ft) after 5 years, ultimately 1.8m (6ft) tall.

▲ *Hydrangea arborescens* 'Annabelle'

'Annabelle'♀ puts out strong straight stems bearing large rounded flowerheads, up to 30cm (12in) across, of pure white ray florets from early summer to the first frosts. More compact growing than the species, it may reach a height of 1.5m (5ft) at maturity. **'Grandiflora'**♀ bears large heads of pure white ray florets, up to 25cm (10in) across. They are sometimes so heavy that the stems droop. The lightly scented white heads of ssp. ***radiata***, 15-18cm (6-7in) across, are fringed with ray florets. Its leaves have dense white hair on their undersides.

H. aspera This species will grow on chalk and also tolerates dryish soil. Its fertile flowers are white to porcelain-blue, ringed with lilac-pink (purple on acid soil) or white ray florets, each up to 2.5cm (1in) across. Flat-topped heads, up to 25cm (10in) wide, appear from early to mid summer. Velvety oval leaves grow up to 25cm (10in) long. HEIGHT & SPREAD 1.5×1.5m (5×5ft) after 5 years, ultimately 3m (10ft) tall.

Hydrangea macrophylla

'Macrophylla'♀ bears 25cm (10in) wide lacecap heads of dark purple fertile flowers, with pure white ray florets forming a coronet around them, from mid to late summer. The dark bluish green leaves have a thick down on both surfaces. 'Macrophylla' will grow to 3m (10ft) tall. The flowerheads of ssp. ***sargentiana***♀ (syn *H. sargentiana*) are flat, 15-25cm (6-10in) across, with rose-lilac fertile flowers, surrounded by pink, shading to white, ray florets. They appear from mid to late summer. The narrow oval leaves, dull green and velvety on top and bristly beneath, are up to 25cm (10in) long on sterile shoots and 12.5cm (5in) on flowering shoots. Grows to 3.5m (12ft). The **Villosa Group**♀ (syn. *H. villosa*) are rounded shrubs with flattened rather than round shoots. They have lacecap flowerheads of pale purple (pale mauve even on alkaline soil) up to 15cm (6in) across, borne mid summer to early autumn. The dull green, lance-shaped leaves, 15cm (6in) long, are bristly on top. Final height 2.4m (8ft).

***H.* 'Blue Deckle'** The matt green leaves of this lacecap turn deep violet in autumn. Flowerheads, up to 14cm (5½in) across, and produced from tips and sideshoots mid to late summer, are electric blue on acid soil, and on neutral and alkaline soil, luminous pink. Flower buds appear early on the current year's wood, so may be damaged by late frosts. HEIGHT & SPREAD 1.2×1m (4×3ft) after 5 years, ultimately 1.8m (6ft) tall.

H. heteromalla **Bretschneideri Group**♀ Sturdy bushes with chestnut-brown peeling bark bear broad, greenish white lacecap flowerheads, up to 15cm (6in) across, from mid to late summer. The outer ring of sterile flowers turns deep pink with age. Leaves grow to 12cm (4¾in) long. HEIGHT & SPREAD 1.8×1.2m (6×4ft) after 5 years, ultimately 3m (10ft) tall.

▲ *Hydrangea heteromalla* Bretschneideri Group

H. integerrima see *H. serratifolia*

H. involucrata This small shrub bears broadly dome-shaped, lacecap flowerheads, 7.5-12.5cm (3-5in) across, late summer to early autumn. The fertile flowers are blue or pink, the ray florets white or pale blue. The oval, rough textured leaves grow to 15cm (6in). HEIGHT & SPREAD 60×60cm (2×2ft) after 5 years, ultimately 1m (3ft) tall.

'Hortensis'♀ has salmon-pink double ray florets, resembling tiny roses. Smaller than the species, up to 75cm (2½ft) tall, this cultivar is also less hardy.

H. macrophylla This is the species from which many of the best-known cultivars have been developed. They form rounded shrubs and bear broadly oval, coarsely toothed leaves, shiny and light to mid green, up to 13cm (5¼in) long. There are two types, differing according to the form of the flowerhead. The mop-headed 'hortensia' types form rounded flowerheads made mainly of sterile ray florets. The 'lacecaps' bear flattened heads of fertile flowers surrounded by a ring of coloured ray florets. The varieties flower from mid to late summer, except where stated otherwise.

HORTENSIA VARIETIES

'Alpenglühen' ('Alpen Glow') has crimson heads (purple on acid soil), up to 23cm (9in) across, and dark green oval leaves. It reaches a height of 1.5m (5ft). **'Altona'**♀ has cherry-pink (mid blue on acid soils)

▲ *Hydrangea aspera* 'Macrophylla'

▲ *Hydrangea aspera* ssp. *sargentiana*

Hydrangea aspera Villosa Group ▲

▲ *Hydrangea macrophylla* 'Alpenglühen'

▲ *Hydrangea macrophylla* 'Ami Pasquier'

flowerheads, 18 cm (7 in) across, from late summer onwards, turning crimson (or purple) with age. A shrub of stiff, erect habit, it grows to 1 m (3 ft) high and does best in shade. **'Amethyst'** has double, frilled, pale pink flowerheads (mauve on acid soil). It produces its best blooms in early autumn, so needs protection from early frosts. A vigorous grower. **'Ami Pasquier'**♀ bears numerous vivid crimson (light blue on acid soil) flowerheads, 11 cm (4¼ in) across, and has characteristic shiny, rounded leaves. It is a slow-grower and reaches an ultimate height of 1 m (3 ft). **'Ayesha'**♀ has rather flattened, dense heads, composed of slightly scented, pale mauve or light blue flowers which are cup-shaped and thick-petalled. Its foliage is glossy and it grows to 1.5 m (5 ft) on sheltered sites. **'Blauer Prinz'** ('Blue Prince') bears 18 cm (7 in) wide flowerheads, cornflower-blue on acid soil, otherwise rosy red, freely produced in late summer and early autumn. It reaches an ultimate height of 1.5 m (5 ft).

▲ *Hydrangea macrophylla* 'Europa'

▲ *Hydrangea macrophylla* 'Parzifal'

'Europa'♀ carries heads, up to 28 cm (11 in) across, of deep pink flowers (purplish blue on acid soil) from late summer onwards. On just slightly acid soil of pH 6 the colour will be dull. It can reach an ultimate height of 1.8 m (6 ft). **'Générale Vicomtesse de Vibraye'**♀ is a free-flowering variety, bearing heads 15-20 cm (6-8 in) across, of bright pink flowers, tinged crimson in autumn (sky-blue flowers on acid soil). It has matt pale green leaves, thrives among trees and can grow to 1.5 m (5 ft) tall. **'King George'** has rosy red blooms and good autumn leaf colour. **'Kluis Superba'** is free-flowering, early and mid summer only, with 15 cm (6 in) heads of light rose-red flowers (violet-blue on acid soil). May reach a height of 2.4 m (8 ft). **'Madame Emile Mouillère'**♀ has white flowerheads, later pink-tinted if grown in full sun, 10-15 cm (4-6 in) across, from mid summer until the first frosts. Its tough, luxuriant foliage becomes tinged with russet and crimson in autumn. Reaches an ultimate height of 1.8 m (6 ft). The dark purplish brown stems of **'Nigra'**♀ contrast with its rose-pink (or blue on acid soil) flowerheads 10-15 cm (4-6 in) wide. Ultimate height 1.8 m (6 ft). **'Parzifal'**♀, a shrub reaching 1.2 m (4 ft) tall when mature, bears dark pink flowerheads (deep blue on acid soil), 15 cm (6 in) wide. **'Pia'** carries irregular-shaped, slightly flattened hemispheres, to 12.5 cm (5 in) across, of bright carmine-red flowers from mid to late summer. It grows to 60 cm (2 ft) high. **'Soeur Thérèse'** ('Sister Therese') has white flowers shading blue towards the centre on a flattened, 18 cm (7 in) wide, flowerhead, from mid summer to mid autumn. The pointed leaves are dark bluish green and it grows to a height of 1.5 m (5 ft).

LACECAP VARIETIES

'Blue Wave' see 'Mariesii Perfecta'. **'Geoffrey Chadbund'**♀ has small light red fertile flowers surrounded by brick-red ray florets. They remain these colours even on acid soil and are carried on a 15 cm (6 in) wide head. Grows well in full sun and reaches a height of 1.5 m (5 ft). **'Lanarth White'**♀ is very free flowering, and has blue or pink fertile flowers ringed by white ray florets, carried on 15 cm (6 in) diameter heads in mid summer. Its leaves are often narrow and sharply pointed. Best in partial shade, it grows to a height of 1.5 m (5 ft). **'Libelle'** flowers prolifically from late summer until frosts. White ray florets, up to 6 cm (2½ in) across, surround small, deep blue fertile flowers on a head 12.5 cm (5 in) across. Grows to 1.5 m (5 ft). **'Lilacina'** has flowerheads up to 12.5 cm (5 in) across from mid summer to late autumn. Mauve to blue ray florets surround the darker blue fertile flowers. Of upright habit it will grow to 1.8 m (6 ft). **'Maculata'** (syn. 'Variegata') has slightly wrinkled leaves with a creamy white border. The flowerheads, with few ray florets, are up to 18 cm (7 in) across and pinkish white, darkening with age. It grows to 1.8 m (6 ft) tall. **'Mariesii'** has wide, flat flowerheads, to 15 cm (6 in) across, with rosy pink ray florets surrounding blue-tinted fertile flowers, rich blue on very acid soils. The leaves are intensely green, shiny and pointed. Flowering in mid and late summer, it has a mature height of 1.8 m (6 ft). **'Mariesii Perfecta'**♀ (syn. 'Blue Wave') bears rich blue flowerheads, 12.5 cm (5 in) across, on acid soil, otherwise pink or mauve. The fertile flowers are darker than the surrounding ray florets. It grows to 1.8 m (6 ft) tall. **'Quadricolor'** has handsome variegated foliage, with light and dark green, cream and bright yellow mottling. The flowerheads, borne in late summer, are white or mauvish pink and up to 20 cm (8 in) across. It has a mature height of 1.8 m (6 ft). **'Tricolor'**♀ has three-way variegated

▲ *Hydrangea macrophylla* 'Ayesha'

Hydrangea macrophylla 'Générale ▲ Vicomtesse de Vibraye' (on acid soil)

▲ *Hydrangea macrophylla* 'Générale Vicomtesse de Vibraye'

h

▲ *Hydrangea macrophylla* 'Quadricolor'

leaves of sea-green, greenish white and yellow. The lacecap heads, up to 20cm (8in) across, are mauve-pink to white and appear in late summer. It may grow to 2.4m (8ft) tall. **'Veitchii'**♀ has pure white flowerheads, up to 20cm (8in) across, which turn crimson-pink in autumn. Its broad leaves grow up to 20cm (8in) long. It is a very lime-tolerant hydrangea, growing to a height of 1.8m (6ft) and spreading to 2.4m (8ft). **'White Wave'**♀ bears flattened flowerheads, 15cm (6in) across, in late summer and early autumn. The bluish or pinkish fertile flowers are surrounded by pearl-white ray florets with a toothed edge. Grows to 1.5m (5ft).

H. paniculata Conical, creamy white flowerheads, 15-20 cm (6-8in) long, made up of both fertile and sterile flowers are borne in late summer and early autumn. The leaves, up to 15cm (6in) long, often appear in threes. HEIGHT & SPREAD 1.8×1.5m (6×5ft) after 5 years, ultimately 2.4m (8ft) tall.

'Brussels Lace' has yellowish beige fertile flowers with off-white, pink-spotted, very small ray florets, producing the effect of openwork lace. Flowering from mid summer until the frosts, it reaches a height of 1.8m (6ft). **'Everest'** has large flowerheads of densely packed, creamy white ray florets, which turn pink with age. A splendid hydrangea with handsome deep green foliage. **'Grandiflora'**♀ bears conical heads, up to 30cm (12in) long and 10cm (4in) wide at the base, from late summer to early autumn. The flowers, densely packed sterile florets, turn from white to purplish pink. The plant has dark green tapering leaves and may grow to 3m (10ft) tall and half as wide. **'Kyushu'**♀ is a fine white variety, freely flowering from late summer to mid

▲ *Hydrangea paniculata* 'Grandiflora'

autumn. The flowerheads are liberally sprinkled with ray florets. Of upright habit, it may grow to an ultimate height of 2.4m (8ft), twice as tall as wide. **'Pink Diamond'** has conical heads up to 30cm (1ft) long and 20cm (8in) at the base. The white fertile flowers, which are tinged pink before the buds open, turn bright pink in full sun. The sterile flowers, up to 4cm (1½in) wide, open white with a pink centre but rapidly turn all pink. Ultimately 1.8m (6ft) tall. **'Praecox'**♀, flowering in early and mid summer, produces abundant, rounded as well as conical, pure white heads, with fertile flowers at the centre or top and sterile flowers on the outside or below. Will grow to 1.8m (6ft). **'Tardiva'** bears large conical flowerheads covered with small white ray florets from late summer to mid autumn. Of upright habit, it may grow to an ultimate height of 2.4m (8ft), twice as tall as wide. **'Unique'**♀ has conical flowerheads, up to 38cm (15in) long, of densely packed sterile florets about 5cm (2in) across. Appearing from mid summer to mid autumn, the flowers turn from white to purplish pink. The shrub may reach a height of 4m (13ft).

H. petiolaris see *H. anomala* ssp. *petiolaris*

***H.* 'Preziosa'**♀ Mop-heads, up to 15cm (6in) wide, of glistening, salmon-pink, sterile flowers, which turn warm red, are borne in mid summer and early autumn. The young leaves and stems are reddish brown on rather slender woody parts. HEIGHT & SPREAD 1m×75cm (3×2½ft) after 5 years, ultimately 1.5m (5ft) tall.

H. quercifolia♀ Conical flowerheads 10-30cm (4-12in) long are borne in late summer and mid autumn. The creamy white sterile and fertile flowers turn purplish or orange-pink with age. The dark green, strongly lobed leaves, wrinkled and tough in texture, grow to 20cm (8in) in length and change colour in autumn, turning vivid shades of orange, crimson and purple. HEIGHT & SPREAD 1.8×1.5m (6×5ft) after 5 years, ultimately 4m (13ft) tall.

'Snow Flake' (syn. 'Flore Pleno') has double ray florets which give an unusual appearance to its conical heads; it may reach 3m (10ft) tall. **'Snow Queen'** bears erect, conical flowerheads, in mid summer and early autumn, of numerous greenish white fertile florets, which soon tinge with pink.

H. sargentiana see *H. aspera* ssp. *sargentiana*

H. serrata This species bears flattened lacecap heads of blue or white fertile flowers circled by pink, bluish or white ray florets, turning a deeper colour in autumn. HEIGHT & SPREAD 60×60cm (2×2ft) after 5 years, ultimately 1m (3ft) tall.

'Bluebird'♀ flowers from early summer to mid autumn. The flowerheads, 15-20cm (6-8in) across, have mid blue fertile flowers at the centre, surrounded by light blue ray florets. The flowers are reddish purple on chalk soil and deep blue on acid soil. The narrow pointed leaves are about 5cm (2in) long and turn coppery red in the autumn. It reaches a final height of 1.2m (4ft). **'Diadem'** has small dome-shaped flowerheads, 10cm (4in) across. The scented flowers are vivid blue or pink (redder in full sun), and appear from early summer onwards, rather sparsely at first but with a copious second flush of blooms in early autumn. The flowerheads are borne on sideshoots up the stems. The foliage is purple on plants grown in an open position. Reaches an ultimate height of 1m (3ft).

▲ *Hydrangea serrata* 'Grayswood'

'Grayswood'♀ has well-spaced heads, 15cm (6in) across, composed of layers of ray florets, which change from white to orange-pink to translucent burgundy-red. They appear early summer to mid autumn. It has lance-shaped leaves up to 10cm (4in) long and reaches an ultimate height of 2m (6½ft). **'Miranda'**, a dense bush growing to a height of 75cm (2½ft), has pale blue or pink lacecap flowerheads, 10cm (4in) across. Leaves have a clearly defined network of veins and give good autumn colour. Reddish fertile flowers, surrounded by a lower layer of white outer florets and an upper layer of rose-pink, form the 15cm (6in) flowerheads of **'Rosalba'**♀. Light green leaves grow to 15cm (6in) long, and the plant to a final height of 1.2m (4ft).

H. serratifolia (syn. *H. integerrima*) This evergreen hydrangea of creeping or climbing habit has off-white flowerheads up to 15cm (6in) across, usually made entirely of

fertile flowers and appearing mid to late summer. The oval leaves, 5-15 cm (2-6 in) long, are light to mid green when young, dark green and leathery when older. HEIGHT & SPREAD 1.8×1.5 m (6×5 ft) after 5 years, ultimately 3 m (10 ft) tall on walls or 4.5 m (15 ft) growing up a tree.
H. villosa see *H. aspera* Villosa Group
CULTIVATION Plant in moisture-retentive soil, which has had well-rotted manure or compost dug in. Some hydrangeas thrive in full sun but most prefer partial shade, so choose a sheltered site against a wall, under high trees or in the lee of, but away from, a hedge. Avoid east-facing sites as tender young growths are damaged by late spring frost. In early spring feed established plants with a balanced fertiliser and apply a 10 cm (4 in) thick mulch.

The blue varieties of *H. macrophylla* are blue only on acid soil. On neutral or slightly alkaline soil, apply an annual dressing of well-decayed compost or manure in the spring; during the growing season apply aluminium sulphate to induce blueing, and sequestrene to combat chlorosis. Pink or red varieties of *H. macrophylla* may be less clear or turn shades of blue on acid soil: apply a 75 g per m^2 (2 oz per sq yd) dressing of ground limestone annually in winter to preserve the pink colouring.
PROPAGATION Take semi-ripe cuttings of shrubby hydrangeas in late summer and of the climbers in early summer.
PRUNING Leave the faded flowerheads of hydrangeas on as protection against frost until spring. Then cut back weak, old or diseased shoots to the lowest bud. Shorten remaining stems to a strong bud. If extra large flowers are wanted on *H. arborescens* and *H. paniculata*, species that flower on the new season's wood, prune the previous season's growth in late winter or early spring to 2 or 3 pairs of buds. Otherwise, to produce larger shrubs with smaller flowers – often the preferred option – shorten the previous year's flowering shoots by half to two-thirds in late winter or early spring. *H. aspera* and its cultivars need minimal pruning in spring, but be sure to cut out weak or diseased wood. Prune climbers only to keep them close to the wall, not at all if grown on trees. With all species, cut out old, exhausted stems at ground level.
PESTS AND DISEASES. Aphids may attack foliage. Very alkaline soils cause chlorosis.

Hylomecon

Papaveraceae

This woodland poppy is grown for its early display of rich yellow flowers and carpet-like habit. A hardy herbaceous perennial, it is valued for its tolerance of shade. It mixes well with many other woodland species, flowering at the same time as trilliums and wood anemones (*Anemone nemorosa*). It also shows to advantage in a larger rock garden. It is a single species genus.
Hylomecon japonica Yellow poppy-like flowers appear in spring and early summer. Each flower, up to 5 cm (2 in) across, has 4 petals and a dense cluster of yellow stamens. A vigorous, spreading mat of leaves lasts through summer, dying away in autumn. Each leaf, up to 25 cm (10 in) long, divides into 5-7 toothed, oval leaflets. Native to the forests of Japan, NE China and Korea. HEIGHT & SPREAD 30×40 cm (12×16 in).

▲ *Hylomecon japonica*

CULTIVATION Plant in humus-rich, fairly moist soil in full or partial shade.
PROPAGATION Divide plants in autumn or early spring. Water newly planted portions well until they have become established. Hylomecon is easily grown from seed, sown in autumn or winter in pots in a cold frame, or in the open in spring.
PESTS AND DISEASES Slugs attack young plants, otherwise generally trouble free.

Hymenocallis

Spider lily
Amaryllidaceae

Spectacular, funnel-shaped flowers, usually white or yellow, are borne by these tender bulbous plants. Native to the tropical regions of the Americas, they require a minimum temperature of 15°C (59°F), so are only suitable for growing under glass or as houseplants.
RECOMMENDED SPECIES AND VARIETIES
H. ×festalis White, heavily fragrant flowers, up to 15 cm (6 in) across, are produced in mid and late summer. The flower is a long, flared trumpet, surrounded at the base by 6 narrow petals. As many as 6 are carried at the end of a strong, single stem. The leaves, up to 45 cm (18 in) long, are narrow, dark green and strap-like. HEIGHT 60 cm (2 ft).
H. 'Sulphur Queen' Fragrant, sulphurous

▲ *Hymenocallis × festalis*

yellow flowers with greenish veins, up to 20 cm (8 in) across, formed of a frilly-edged trumpet with 6 large petals, are borne from mid to late summer. Between 2 and 5 flowers are carried on the stem. The strap-like, semi-erect, dark green leaves grow to 30 cm (1 ft) long. HEIGHT 60 cm (2 ft).
CULTIVATION Plant the bulbs in John Innes No. 3 potting compost in early spring – one bulb per 10 cm (4 in) pot or 3 bulbs per 25 cm (10 in) pot – with the tip of the bulb just showing. Water sparingly until the young shoots appear, and then freely. Use a houseplant feed when the flower buds appear. Cease watering when the leaves start to wither in autumn. Dry off the bulbs and store in a cool, frost-free place.
PROPAGATION Remove any offsets when repotting.
PESTS AND DISEASES Greenfly can be troublesome.

Hypericum

Saint John's wort
Guttiferae

Hypericum androsaemum

Sparkling yellow flowers, with prominent golden stamens and often borne in abundance, characterise these shrubs, sub-shrubs and herbaceous perennials. The leaves of some hypericums turn an attractive rusty pink in autumn. Some of the low-growing species are ideal as ground cover.

Many of the shrubby hypericums have evergreen or semi-evergreen foliage. Those described as semi-evergreen are only reliably evergreen in milder areas. Although most shrubby hypericums are reasonably hardy, a few are only reliably so in milder districts and need protection elsewhere, or may be grown under glass. Those with coloured leaves and the dwarf forms – those below 30cm (12in) tall – tend to be short-lived in colder areas. A few of the dwarf species, such as *Hypericum coris* and *H. olympicum*, are excellent plants in a cold greenhouse, conservatory or alpine house.

RECOMMENDED SPECIES AND VARIETIES

Hypericums are fast-growing and, unless otherwise stated the heights and spreads given below are the ultimate size of the plant, achieved within 5 years.

H. aegypticum Pale yellow flowers, up to 2.5cm (1in) across, appear in late summer. The buds are tinged with red. The grey-green, oval leaves are up to 2.5cm (1in) long. Both flowers and foliage are carried on upright stems. This semi-evergreen shrub is hardy only in the mildest areas. HEIGHT & SPREAD 50×50cm (20×20in).

▲ *Hypericum aegypticum*

H. androsaemum (tutsan) Clusters of clear, golden blooms, 2cm (¾in) across, are produced from early summer onwards. Purple berries, which later turn black, appear after flowering. The rich green, oval leaves are 10cm (4in) long. This semi-evergreen plant forms a rounded shrub. It tolerates deep shade. HEIGHT & SPREAD 1×1m (3×3ft).

H. calycinum (rose of Sharon) Bright yellow flowers, up to 6cm (2½in) across, are borne from early summer to early autumn. The bright green, oval leaves are up to 7.5cm (3in) long. This semi-evergreen shrub has a tough, creeping rootstock. It is a good hypericum for ground cover in dry, shady areas. HEIGHT & SPREAD 25×75cm (10in×2½ft) after 5 years, ultimately 30cm (12in) tall.

▲ *Hypericum calycinum*

H. coris Clear golden flowers, up to 2cm (¾in) across, with faintly red-streaked petals, appear mid summer. The oval, evergreen grey-green leaves are up to 1.5cm (½in) long. This sub-shrub forms a neat dome. HEIGHT & SPREAD 25×25cm (10×10in).

H. forrestii♀ (syn. *H. patulum* var. *forrestii*) Golden flowers, up to 6cm (2½in) across, appear from mid summer to early autumn. The mid-green leaves grow to 4cm (1½in) long. In autumn these turn to orange and red and in a mild season they may remain on the plant well into winter. Bronze seed pods appear after flowering. This deciduous species forms a rounded shrub. HEIGHT & SPREAD 75cm×1m (2½×3ft) after 5 years, ultimately 1.5m (5ft) tall.

H. fragile hort. see *H. olympicum* f. *minus*

H. grandiflorum see *H. kouytchense*

▲ *Hypericum* 'Hidcote'

***H.* 'Hidcote'**♀ Large golden flowers, up to 7cm (2¾in) across, appear in profusion from mid summer to mid autumn. The dark green, pointed leaves are up to 4cm (1½in) long. A semi-evergreen rounded shrub. HEIGHT & SPREAD 1.2×1m (4×3ft) after 5 years, ultimately 1.5m (5ft) tall.

H. kouytchense♀ (syn. *H. grandiflorum*, *H.* 'Sungold') Light golden yellow flowers, up to 6cm (2½in) across, appear from mid summer to early autumn. They have petals that curve backwards. The dark green leaves grow to 4cm (1½in) in length. Bronze-red berries are produced after the flowers. A semi-evergreen, rounded shrub. HEIGHT & SPREAD 60×75cm (2×2½ft) after 5 years, ultimately 1.8m (6ft) tall.

▲ *Hypericum forrestii*

▲ *Hypericum kouytchense*

H. × moserianum♀ Golden yellow blossoms with reddish anthers and up to 6cm (2½in) across, are carried at the tips of reddish, arching stems, from mid summer to mid autumn. The deep green, semi-evergreen, oval leaves grow to 5cm (2in) long. The plant forms a broad, rounded shrub. HEIGHT & SPREAD 40×75cm (16×30in) after 5 years, ultimately 75cm (30in) tall.

The flowers of **'Tricolor'** (syn. 'Variegatum') are 2.5cm (1in) across. The leaves have pink and white edges and the stems are flushed with red. It reaches a height of 38cm (15in). It is slightly tender and needs shelter if grown outdoors.

H. olympicum♀ Clusters of golden flowers

▲ *Hypericum × moserianum*

▲ *Hypericum × moserianum* 'Tricolor'

with extended stamens are borne mid to late summer. Each flower is up to 5 cm (2 in) across. The oval grey-green leaves grow to 3 cm (1¼ in) long. A semi-evergreen sub-shrub, it forms a loose, sprawling mound. HEIGHT & SPREAD 20×20 cm (8×8 in).

The pointed leaves of f. ***minus*** (syn. *H. fragile* hort., *H. polyphyllum, H. reptans*

▲ *Hypericum olympicum f. minus*

hort.) are carried on prostrate or upright stems. The pale yellow flowers of its cultivar, **'Sulphureum'** (syn. *H. polyphyllum* 'Citrinum', *H. p.* 'Sulphureum'), are 2.5 cm (1 in) across. The yellow flowers of f. ***uniflorum*** (syn. 'Grandiflorum', *H. polyphyllum* 'Grandiflorum') contrast with grey-blue foliage. Its cultivar, **'Citrinum'**♀, has pale lemon flowers, 3 cm (1¼ in) across.

H. orientale Lemon-yellow starry flowers, up to 3 cm (1¼ in) across, are produced in clusters at the tips of the stems during mid summer. The sticky, mid to dark green leaves are narrow with toothed edges, and reach a length of 4 cm (1½ in). This evergreen species forms an upright shrub. HEIGHT & SPREAD 15×15 cm (6×6 in).

H. patulum var. ***forrestii*** see *H. forrestii*

H. perforatum Bright yellow, starry flowers, up to 3 cm (1¼ in) across, appear in mid summer. The narrow mid green leaves, up to 2.5 cm (1 in) long, have a thick, papery texture. A spreading herbaceous perennial. HEIGHT & SPREAD 45×45 cm (18×18 in).

H. polyphyllum see *H. olympicum* f. *minus*

***H. polyphyllum* 'Grandiflorum'** see *H. olympicum* f. *uniflorum*

H. reptans hort. see *H. olympicum* f. *minus*

***H.* 'Rowallane'**♀ Bright golden yellow flowers, up to 7.5 cm (3 in) across, are produced from late spring to mid autumn. The pointed oval leaves, up to 6 cm (2½ in) long, are a rich green above and greenish grey underneath. It may be cut back by a hard winter but new growth usually appears in spring. A graceful, arching, semi-evergreen shrub. HEIGHT & SPREAD 1.2×1 m (4×3 ft) after 5 years, ultimately 1.5 m (5 ft) tall.

***H.* 'Sungold'** see *H. kouytchense*

H. trichocaulon Golden flowers, to 2.5 cm (1 in) across, emerge from crimson buds in late spring and mid summer on a neat prostrate sub-shrub. The narrow, bluish green, evergreen leaves grow to 7 cm (2¾ in) long. HEIGHT & SPREAD 5×45 cm (2×18 in).

CULTIVATION Plant in well-drained fertile soil, preferably in full sun. Most hypericums tolerate some shade and *H. androsaemum* and *H. calycinum* grow well even in deep shade. Plant *H. aegypticum* and *H.* 'Rowallane' against a south-facing wall, and in colder areas protect the base of the plant with mulch in winter. Alternatively, grow them under glass in 15-20 cm (6-8 in) pots. Repot annually in early spring.

PROPAGATION Take softwood cuttings of smaller hypericums and semi-ripe cuttings of the larger kinds. *H. calycinum* can also be increased by root division in winter. Divide *H. perforatum* in spring or autumn.

PRUNING Prune in early spring. Cut *H. calycinum* back to within 5 cm (2 in) of the base every 3 years and in intervening years trim as necessary to maintain a compact shape. Shorten the previous year's shoots of other species and varieties to within a few buds of the old wood.

PESTS AND DISEASES Powdery mildew and rust affect hypericums.

Hypoestes

Acanthaceae

Grown mainly for their decorative foliage, hypoestes are a genus of tender, mainly evergreen perennials and shrubs, requiring a minimum temperature of 10°C (50°F).

RECOMMENDED SPECIES AND VARIETIES

H. phyllostachya♀ (syn. *H. sanguinolenta*) (polka dot plant) The dark green stems of this sub-shrub from Madagascar are densely clothed with soft oval leaves up to 5 cm (1 in) long. The dark green leaves carry bold spots of pink through to purple-red. HEIGHT & SPREAD 45×30 cm (1½×1 ft).

The variety **'Carmina'** has bright red leaves. The foliage of **'Purpuriana'** is deep plum purple; the leaves of **'Wit'** have white marbling; and **'Splash'** has large pink spots.

▼ *Hypoestes phyllostachya*

H. sanguinolenta see *H. phyllostachya.*

CULTIVATION Grow in 10-15 cm (4-6 in) pots of soil-less compost in full light. Give liquid feed once a month in summer. Mist foliage daily from spring to early autumn and occasionally in winter, using soft or distilled water. Pinch out frequently to encourage bushy growth and remove flowerheads as they appear. Cut back plants hard in spring to encourage vigorous growth. Repot from time to time as the plants develop. Discard plants that have reached full height and replace with younger ones, since young plants have better foliage.

PROPAGATION Root short stem cuttings in a propagator during spring and summer.

PESTS AND DISEASES Greenfly and whitefly may be troublesome.

Hypsela

Campanulaceae

This low, spreading herbaceous perennial produces mats of shiny leaves. These are adorned with solitary erect flowers, which appear dotted above the patches of leaves continuously throughout summer. The plants are ideal for the rock garden and as ground cover.

RECOMMENDED SPECIES

H. reniformis (syn. *H. longiflora*) The pale pinkish mauve flowers, with a central splash of deep reddish purple, are 1.5 cm (½ in) across and have spreading petals unevenly spaced and of unequal size. The flowers are followed in the autumn by erect green berries. The rounded 1.5 cm (½ in) long leaves form dense patches. A hardy, vigorous plant, native to S America, it spreads 30-60 cm (1-2 ft) in a year. HEIGHT 5 cm (2 in). The spread is indefinite.

▲ *Hypsela reniformis*

CULTIVATION Plant in partial shade in loamy soil that does not readily dry out.

PROPAGATION Divide in summer or sow seed in spring.

PESTS AND DISEASES Slugs and snails can be troublesome.

Hyssop, giant see *Agastache*

Iberis
Candytuft
Cruciferae

Iberis amara

Masses of small cross-shaped flowers appear in spring and summer on these annuals, perennials and sub-shrubs, that are suitable for a number of garden situations. The flowers have two long and two short petals and are borne in dense clusters. They are often scented and attract various insects, particularly butterflies. The smaller candytufts are excellent for a rock garden and for raised beds, while the larger ones, especially *Iberis sempervirens*, are appropriate for the front of a flower border, for path and patio edges or for the top of a retaining wall. The only annuals, *I. amara* and *I. umbellata*, are colourful space-fillers for a flower border and make good cut flowers. The genus is native to S Europe and W Asia.

RECOMMENDED SPECIES AND VARIETIES

I. amara (common candytuft) Fragrant small white, pink or lilac flowers are borne in dense clusters, up to 4 cm (1½ in) across, in summer. This erect, bushy annual is fast-growing and has mid green lance-shaped leaves that are toothed towards the apex. HEIGHT & SPREAD 30×15 cm (12 × 6 in).

Hyacinth Flowered Series These strong vigorous plants grow to 40 cm (16 in) tall and have white to pink, lilac or purple flowers.

▼ *Iberis amara*

▲ *Iberis sempervirens*

▲ *Iberis sempervirens* 'Weisser Zwerg'

▲ *Iberis sempervirens* 'Schneeflocke'

I. candolleana see *I. pruitii*

I. gibraltarica The white to reddish lilac flowers are carried in late spring and early summer in dense clusters about 5 cm (2 in) across. The oblong leaves, with or without a few marginal teeth, are deep green and fleshy. This evergreen sub-shrub, with a somewhat woody base, is hardy only to -15°C (5°F). HEIGHT & SPREAD 25×20 cm (10×8 in).

I. pruitii (syn. *I. candolleana, I. spruneri*) White to lilac summer flowers are borne in clusters up to 4 cm (1½ in) across. The fleshy deep green leaves are narrowly oblong or spoon-shaped. The lower leaves are arranged in a lax rosette. This sub-shrub, occasionally behaving as an annual, is hardy only to -15°C (5°F). HEIGHT & SPREAD 15×15 cm (6×6 in).

I. saxatilis The white summer flowers, carried in oblong clusters about 3 cm (1¼ in) across, often become purplish as they age. This small evergreen sub-shrub has fleshy, almost cylindrical leaves. HEIGHT & SPREAD 15×15 cm (6×6 in).

Iberis sempervirens

I. sempervirens♀ The pure white flowers are carried in broad clusters, up to 5 cm (2 in) across, and appear in mid spring and early summer. This spreading evergreen sub-shrub has numerous branches and leaves that are pointed and spoon-shaped to oblong. HEIGHT & SPREAD 30×60 cm (1×2 ft).

'Little Gem' see 'Weisser Zwerg'. **'Pygmaea'** (including 'Minima') This mound-forming dwarf plant grows to 15 cm (6 in) tall and has white flowers. **'Schneeflocke'** ('Snowflake')♀ A mat-forming plant 25 cm (10 in) tall with deep green leaves and glistening white flowers in spring. **'Weisser Zwerg'** (syn. 'Little Gem') White flowers are borne in profusion in spring on this compact, mound-forming plant, 15 cm (6 in) tall.

I. spruneri see *I. pruitii*

I. umbellata Pink or purple flowers in dense clusters, up to 5 cm (2 in) across, appear in late spring and summer. This fast-growing annual has narrow, lance-shaped leaves and is usually branched in the upper half. HEIGHT & SPREAD 30×20 cm (12×8 in).

'Dwarf Fairy' (Fairy Series) grows to 20 cm (8 in) tall and bears flowers in shades of pink, red, purple or white. **'Pink Queen'** has rose-pink flowers. **'Red Flash'** bears vivid carmine flowers. **'Rose Cardinal'** has rose-scarlet flowers.

CULTIVATION Candytufts thrive on most well-drained soils in full sun, and are especially suitable for rather dry soils. *I. gibraltarica* and *I. pruitii* can be grown in pots in a well-ventilated greenhouse. Severe pruning is undesirable, but clip back the larger sub-shrubs after flowering to encourage bushy growth.

PROPAGATION Sow seed in spring or autumn – the annuals in their flowering position, the others in pots in a coldframe. Take semi-ripe cuttings of the sub-shrubs in early summer.

PESTS AND DISEASES Slugs and snails occasionally attack the young plants, especially the annuals.

Ice plant see *Sedum spectabile*

Ilex

Holly

Aquifoliaceae

Ilex altaclerensis 'Lawsoniana'

The hollies range from small shrubs to medium-sized trees. They can be planted as specimen trees, clipped to shape as topiary or, because they tolerate pollution and wind, used as hedging or windbreaks. Easy to care for, although slow to establish, hollies are generally slow growing. There are several deciduous species but all the recommended plants are evergreen.

Glossy leaves, often armed with sharp spines, provide interest throughout the year alongside the colourful berries of the female plants. The leaves are usually dark green but some plants have a definite blue tinge. There are also many variegated varieties, with margins or splashes of cream, gold or silver – excellent for brightening a drab corner. The leaves range in length from a few millimetres to 15 cm (6 in) long.

Insignificant male and female flowers in late spring usually grow on separate plants. Male plants must be grown among the female plants to produce a good crop of berries. The exceptions are 'J.C. van Tol'♀ and 'Pyramidalis' which are self-pollinating. Berries vary from black to yellow but various shades of red are the most common. All holly berries are attractive to birds.

There are over 400 species, varying in hardiness. They grow in every part of the world except NW America and Australasia.

RECOMMENDED SPECIES AND VARIETIES

I.* × *altaclerensis (Highclere holly) An upright tree with large, glossy, spiny leaves, up to 10 cm (4 in) long. Frost-hardy and pollution-tolerant, this plant is faster growing than most other hollies and makes good hedging. HEIGHT & SPREAD 2.4×1 m (8×3 ft) after 10 years, ultimately 8 m (26 ft) or more tall.

'Belgica Aurea'♀ is a female variegated plant with irregular, creamy yellow leaf margins, sparsely spined. The centres of the leaves are deep green with pale green or grey-green mottling. The plant eventually makes a shrub about 3 m (10 ft) tall. **'Camelliifolia'**♀ has the largest leaves of any holly, growing up to 15 cm (6 in) long. They are a glossy deep green and almost spineless. The fruits are large and deep red. Conical in shape, it reaches 5 m (16 ft). The leaves of **'Golden King'**♀, a female plant, have striking gold margins. The large red fruits are often abundant. **'Hodginsii'**♀ is a male plant with shiny rounded leaves with large triangular spines. The slightly spiny leaves of **'Lawsoniana'**♀ have a dark green margin while the centre is variegated paler green and gold-yellow. Any plain green leaves must be pruned to retain the variegation. It bears dull red berries. **'Wilsonii'**♀ makes a handsome tree to 9 m (30 ft) or more tall. The glossy dark green leaves have numerous stout spines. The plant bears large red fruits.

I. aquifolium♀ (common holly) An evergreen, frost-hardy plant which normally makes a small conical tree. A good hedging plant, it is useful as a screen from wind and grows well in a shady position. The dark green leaves are paler beneath and grow up to 7.5 cm (3 in) long. The wavy edge is well armed with stiff spines up to 1 cm (⅜ in) long. The berries are bright red. HEIGHT & SPREAD 3×1.2 m (10×4 ft) after 10 years, ultimately 20 m (66 ft) or more tall.

'Alaska' is a frost-hardy, narrow, upright tree, smaller than the common holly. **'Angustifolia'** is a slow-growing, very erect tree eventually reaching 6 m (20 ft) or more. Female plants bear tiny red berries. The dark green leaves are very narrow and have 5-7 small spines on each side. **'Argentea Marginata'**♀ is a conical plant, to 5 m (16 ft) tall with attractive silver-edged leaves. The red berries are plentiful. The weeping shrub **'Argentea Marginata Pendula'** has a rounded habit. The leaves have a silver margin. It normally makes a large shrub no more than 3 m (10 ft) tall. It bears abundant red berries.

'Bacciflava' (syn. 'Fructu Luteo') has yellow berries and dark green leaves. It eventually makes an upright tree 9 m (30 ft) or more in height. The male variety **'Ferox'** (hedgehog holly) has many spines both on the margin and upper surface of the small contorted leaves. **'Ferox Argentea'**♀ (silver hedgehog holly) is a male plant that has attractive dark green leaves with white margins and spines. The upper surface of the leaf is also dotted with spines. Young shoots are a rich purple. **'Ferox Aurea'** has a dark green leaf with a central gold-yellow blotch. It is a male plant.

The male variety **'Golden Milkboy'**♀ has large, 10 cm (4 in) long, flattened leaves with spines along the edges. They are dark green with a large central blotch of gold. **'Golden Queen'**♀ (syn. 'Aurea Regina') is, despite its name, a male plant that does not bear berries. It has dark green leaves with a gold margin and plenty of spines. Some leaves can be wholly or partly gold. The young shoots are pale green. The dark green leaves of **'Golden van Tol'** have a gold-yellow margin and few spines. A female plant, it is of spreading habit and

▲ *Ilex altaclerensis* 'Golden King'

▲ *Ilex aquifolium* 'Bacciflava'

▲ *Ilex aquifolium* 'Ferox Argentea'

▼ *Ilex* x *altaclerensis* 'Belgica Aurea'

▼ *Ilex aquifolium* 'Argentea Marginata'

▼ *Ilex aquifolium* 'Golden van Tol'

makes a small shrub. **'Green Pillar'**♀ has an upright, narrow habit and dark green spiny leaves. A female plant with red berries, it makes a good screening plant or can be grown happily in a container. **'Handsworth New Silver'**♀ is a handsome upright female holly with striking purple new shoots. The leaves are dark green, streaked pale green-grey, with a heavily spined white margin.

▲ *Ilex aquifolium* 'Handsworth New Silver'

'Hascombensis' is a small holly which eventually grows to 1.2m (4ft) high and is often broader than it is tall. It is slow growing, in 10 years it reaches 60×60cm (2×2ft) and this slow growth rate plus its very dense habit makes it a good plant for a low hedge. The small, narrow dark green leaves are sharply spined.

'J.C. van Tol'♀ is a self-pollinating plant that produces abundant bright red berries in winter. The dark green leaves have few spines. **'Madame Briot'**♀ is a female plant whose mottled green leaves have a gold-yellow margin with numerous spines. At times the whole leaf may be gold-yellow. The young shoots are purple. It has deep red berries.

'Myrtifolia' has small, glossy dark green leaves with fine spines along their edges It is a compact male shrub with purple shoots when young. **'Myrtifolia Aurea Maculata'**♀ is a small, compact male holly. The dark green leaves have an irregular splash of gold down the centre. The bark on young shoots is purple.

▼ *Ilex aquifolium* 'J.C. van Tol'

'Pyramidalis' is self-pollinating and bears quantities of red berries among glossy dark green leaves. It is a conical tree but broadens out in old age. **'Pyramidalis Fructu Luteo'**♀ has a narrow conical habit eventually reaching 5m (16ft) or more tall. The glossy dark green leaves with varying numbers of spines complement the abundant yellow fruits. The leaves of the female variety **'Silver Milkmaid'**♀ have a central creamy-white blotch and numerous spines along their margin. The shoots are prone to revert and must be pruned out. **'Silver Queen'**♀ (syn. 'Argentea Regina') is a slow-growing male plant with a conical upright habit, eventually reaching 5m (16ft) or more tall. The dark green leaves are faintly marbled grey with a white margin. Emerging young leaves are a striking salmon pink in colour.

▲ *Ilex aquifolium* 'Silver Milkmaid'

I. crenata (Japanese holly) The small, glossy green leaves of this frost-hardy, slow-growing plant are oblong, rarely more than 1.5cm (½in) long, and have few, very fine teeth. HEIGHT & SPREAD 1×1m (3×3ft) after 5 years, ultimately 3m (10ft) tall.

'Convexa'♀ bears large quantities of small black berries and makes good low hedging as it reaches only 30-60cm (1-2ft) high and grows broader than it is tall. The upper surfaces of the leaves are convex. **'Golden Gem'**♀ is a low-growing, spreading shrub, to 1.8×1.8m (6×6ft), with green leaves flecked with yellow-gold. These look at their best in a sunny position during the early part of the year. It does not fruit well.

▼ *Ilex aquifolium* 'Silver Queen'

I. × koehneana **'Chestnut Leaf'**♀ The thick, leathery pale green leaves, up to 15cm (6in) long, have many stout spines along their edges and resemble the sweet chestnut leaf. The female form bears large red berries. This upright and conical tree is frost-hardy. HEIGHT & SPREAD 3×1.5m (10×5ft) after 10 years, ultimately 7m (23ft) or more tall.

I. × meserveae (blue holly) The leaves of this frost-hardy bushy shrub have a delightful blue tinge to them and although they are well-spined along their margins, they are soft to touch. The shoots are a deep purple. HEIGHT & SPREAD 1.8×1m (6×3ft) after 10 years, ultimately 2m (6½ft) or more tall.

'Blue Angel'♀ has glossy blue-green leaves that turn a rich purple-green in winter. Although well spined they are soft to touch. A slow-growing female plant, it produces a profusion of bright red berries in winter. **'Blue Prince'** is a male plant with deep bluish green leaves and purple-tinged stems. **'Blue Princess'**♀ is a female plant with glossy, spined blue-green leaves. It produces numerous red berries in winter.

▲ *Ilex × meserveae* 'Blue Angel'

CULTIVATION Plant in any soil from autumn to mid spring avoiding frosty conditions.

PROPAGATION Take heeled cuttings in early autumn. Alternatively, species and their forms can be layered in October and cut from the parent after 2 years. The variegated forms are mostly grafted, particularly if they are of the weeping form.

PRUNING None normally required or necessary unless a particular shape is required, or to retain variegated forms that will revert to plain green unless pruned. Nonetheless, holly responds well to pruning in mid summer or during the dormant season.

PESTS AND DISEASES Usually trouble free.

Illicium

Illiciaceae

These hardy and half-hardy shrubs are grown for their decorative and aromatic evergreen foliage and unusual star-shaped flowers. The flowers have numerous narrow petals, and the leaves are narrow oval to lance-shaped. Native to SE Asia, SE United States and the West Indies.

RECOMMENDED SPECIES

I. anisatum (Chinese anise) The flowers of this slow-growing, hardy shrub of conical habit are 2.5 cm (1 in) across with greenish yellow petals; they appear in clusters from early to late spring. The dark green, glossy leaves grow up to 12.5 cm (5 in) long. HEIGHT & SPREAD 2×1.5 m (6½×5 ft) after 5 years, ultimately 6 m (20 ft) tall.

▼ *Illicium anisatum*

I. floridanum (purple anise) The flowers of this half-hardy bushy shrub are produced singly on nodding stems in late spring and early summer. They grow up to 5 cm (2 in) across and have dark red, purple or maroon petals. The leathery leaves grow to 10 cm (4 in) long. HEIGHT & SPREAD 1.5×1.5 m (5×5 ft) after 5 years, ultimately 6 m (20 ft).

CULTIVATION Plant in sheltered, moist, neutral-to-acid soil in partial shade. *I. floridanum* does best against a sunny wall: protect it from frost with fleece or hessian.

PROPAGATION Take semi-ripe cuttings in mid to late summer.

PRUNING Remove any winter-damaged shoots in spring and trim to shape.

PESTS AND DISEASES Usually trouble free.

▼ *Illicium floridanum*

Impatiens

Busy lizzie

Balsaminaceae

Impatiens walleriana

A profusion of colourful flowers enlivens beds and borders, window boxes, hanging baskets and tubs through summer and into early autumn. With the exception of *Impatiens tinctoria*, all the recommended plants can also be grown indoors, where some will flower all year round.

The five-petalled flowers, usually about 6 cm (2½ in) wide, are cup-shaped or open flat. The uppermost petal is often hooded, while the other four are fused into two lobed pairs. The lowest sepal may extend backwards into a tubular spur. Flowers are one to a stem or in clusters. The bushy plants have undivided leaves and succulent stems. The genus grows wild in most warm areas of the world, and includes annuals and evergreen perennials and sub-shrubs.

RECOMMENDED SPECIES AND VARIETIES

I. balsamina (balsam) A compact, half-hardy annual, best grown as an indoor pot plant, it can also be used as bedding in sheltered positions. The double flowers are pink, purple, red or white open and flat. The pale green, lance-shaped leaves are up to 9 cm (3½ in) long. HEIGHT & SPREAD 70×45 cm (28×18 in).

I. holstii see *I. walleriana*

▼ *Impatiens* New Guinea Group 'Tonga'

***I.* New Guinea Group** Hybrids are grown indoors or as summer bedding on a sheltered site, when the tender perennials flower from late spring to early autumn. Flowers may be red, orange, pink, purple or white. Erect bushy plants produce a dense growth of lance-shaped leaves, up to 20 cm (8 in) long and red or bronze or a mixture of colours. Variegated leaves are often yellow with a dark green rim and a pink midrib. HEIGHT & SPREAD 60×40 cm (24×16 in).

'Aruba' has purple flowers and dark bronze foliage, **'Eurema'** orange-red flowers and variegated leaves, **'Papete'** purple flowers, and **'Spectra'** mixed colours. **'Tahiti'** has pink flowers, **'Tango'**, has orange flowers and dark bronze-green foliage, and **'Tonga'** is lilac with deep bronze leaves.

I. niamniamensis This bushy perennial is generally grown in a conservatory or greenhouse. Its 3 cm (1¼ in) long flowers are shaped like a parrot's bill, with an upright white or yellow-green petal and a prominent, red – sometimes with white, pink or yellow – pouch-like spur. The oval, toothed, dark green leaves grow to 20 cm (8 in). HEIGHT & SPREAD 1 m×40 cm (36×16 in).

'Congo Cockatoo' has larger flowers, each with a pale green standard and yellow and red spur.

I. sultani see *I. walleriana*

I. tinctoria This tall half-hardy perennial is the only species with fragrant flowers. These are white or pink, hooded, with purple markings in the throat and long spurs and stalks. They bloom in late summer and early autumn in spike-like clusters on long stems. The dark green leaves are oblong, toothed and up to 20 cm (8 in) long. This is a tuberous-rooted plant, of erect, bushy habit. Lift tubers after the first frost and store over winter in almost dry peat or sand in a frost-proof place. HEIGHT & SPREAD 1.5 m×80 cm (5 ft×2 ft 8 in).

I. walleriana (syn. *I. holstii*, *I. sultani*) (busy lizzie) Among the most free-flowering of bedding plants in shady conditions, the hybrids of this species are easily grown in beds, borders and containers, indoors and out. They are perennials, but are usually treated as half-hardy annuals. Varieties have lilac, pink, red or white flowers; some are striped with two colours. The open flat flowers are 2.5-5 cm (1-2 in) wide, each with a slender 5 cm (2 in) long spur. The pale green, succulent leaves are oval with scalloped edges and about 5 cm (2 in) long. They are quite brittle and easily broken. Plants are naturally bushy, but in shade can become leggy. HEIGHT & SPREAD 30×30 cm (1×1 ft), unless stated otherwise.

The **Accent** and **Super Elfin Series** are available in mixed and separate colours and

▼ *Impatiens walleriana* (busy lizzie)

are both 15-25 cm (6-10 in) tall. **'Mega Orange Star'** is 15-20 cm (6-8 in) tall and has salmon-orange flowers with white radial markings. **'Novette Star'** is equally dwarf, and available only in mixed colours – lilac, pink and red; each flower has white, radial markings, giving the effect of a star.

▲ *Impatiens* 'Mega Orange Star'

Double-flowered varieties do not come true from seed: the **Enchantment** and **Super Enchantment Series**, both 30 cm (1 ft) tall, are propagated from cuttings. The latter, with green and cream variegated foliage, includes **'Blackberry Ice'**, which has purple flowers, and **'Peach Ice'** with salmon-coloured flowers.

CULTIVATION

AS BEDDING PLANTS

Grow in any well-drained fertile garden soil that retains some moisture. Impatiens will thrive in shade or sun. Plant out in spring when all risk of frost has passed. Water regularly through spring and summer.

AS POT PLANTS

Keep plants above a minimum temperature of 10°C (50°F) in autumn and winter. For continuous flowering, a temperature above about 15°C (60°F) is needed. Avoid direct sunlight in summer, but expose plants to full sunlight in winter to keep them in flower. Feed weekly from late winter to early autumn. Reduce watering in winter, especially in cool temperatures. Pinch out shoot tips to promote bushiness. All impatiens flower best when pot-bound.

PROPAGATION Take stem cuttings of species grown in pots at any time in spring and summer. Impatiens root easily, but are among the most difficult bedding plants to raise from seed. An easier method is to buy seedlings or plug plants. Prick out into seed trays and grow on in a greenhouse before hardening off and planting out.

PESTS AND DISEASES Aphids are common pests. Plants under glass may suffer from red spider mite and whitefly. In cool damp conditions grey mould may infect flower buds.

Imperata see GRASSES p. 301

Incarvillea

Bignoniaceae

Incarvillea delavayi

Bold foliage and large trumpet-shaped flowers characterise these exotic-looking summer-flowering plants. The larger ones are ideal for the flower border; the smaller ones best restricted to a rock garden or raised bed. Their boldness and bright colours do not generally mix easily with other plants but look excellent close to herbaceous perennials that are grown primarily for their foliage, such as hostas. All species can be grown in containers and *I. delavayi* makes a splendid patio plant.

Those listed are all herbaceous perennials. Their deep green leaves vary from 10 to 30 cm (4 to 12 in) long and 2 to 15 cm (¾ to 6 in) wide and are divided into pairs of leaflets. Long, narrow and often bean-like green fruit contains numerous seeds and appears after the flowers, turning brown as it ripens, from mid to late summer. Native to the Himalayas, central and E Asia, all the plants described are hardy.

RECOMMENDED SPECIES AND VARIETIES

I. delavayi Rich purple trumpets 6-8 cm (2½-3¼ in) across with yellow throat markings appear, erectly held, in stout clusters in early summer. This herbaceous perennial has tuberous rootstock and large, mostly basal leaves with 6-12 pairs of toothed, oval leaflets. Woody beaked fruit are up to 12 cm (4¾ in) long. HEIGHT & SPREAD 70×30 cm (2 ft 4 in × 1 ft).

'Bees Pink' has large flesh-pink blooms; the flowers of **'Snowtop'** (**'Alba'**) are pure white with a greenish centre.

▼ *Incarvillea mairei*

I. mairei Erect clusters of up to 5 purple or crimson flowers 5-7.5 cm (2-3 in) across with yellow throats appear in early summer. The plant has a tuberous rootstock and basal leaves up to 30 cm (1 ft) long with up to 7 pairs of small leaflets and a large end leaflet. HEIGHT & SPREAD 30×20 cm (12×8 in).

'Frank Ludlow' is 10 cm (4 in) tall, with large crimson flowers flushed pink.

I. olgae Lax clusters of 7 or more mid pink flowers 5 cm (2 in) across with a pale throat appear on this tall, elegant plant. It has a fleshy rootstock and 10 cm (4 in) long leaves divided into narrow, oblong leaflets. HEIGHT & SPREAD 1 m×45 cm (3×1½ ft).

CULTIVATION Plant the tuberous species (*I. delavayi* and *I. mairei*) in groups just below the surface of well-drained ordinary soil in early spring, in full sun. Protect the crown of hardy species in winter with bark chippings, fern fronds or horticultural fleece.

PROPAGATION Sow seed in autumn or winter in pots in a coldframe. Prick out seedlings into individual pots once they have made their first true leaf. Feed regularly through summer until autumn. Plant out in the spring of the second year. Most take 2 or 3 years to flower from seed. Established plants resent root disturbance so division is rarely practical.

PESTS AND DISEASES Young plants may be attacked by slugs or snails.

Indian bean tree see *Catalpa bignoniodes*
Indian shot see *Canna inica*
Indigo, false see *Baptisia*

Indigofera

Leguminosae

Indigofera heterantha

Densely packed clusters of pink, 1.5 cm (½ in) flowers appear from early summer to autumn among the elegant, fern-like leaves of these tropical and sub-tropical shrubs. The pinnate, oval to oblong leaves, 10 to 15 cm (4 to 6 in) long, are formed by 5 to 20 leaflets. All the recommended plants are fairly frost-hardy, but do best in a sheltered, sunny position. They are deciduous and the stems may die back to ground level in hard frost, though new shoots will appear from the base in early to mid spring, creating a

▲ *Indigofera amblyantha*

rounded shrub. While indigoferas grow on most soils, they prefer a well-drained site.

RECOMMENDED SPECIES AND VARIETIES

I. amblyantha ♀ Pale pink flowers grow in clusters up to 11cm (4¼in) long, and each leaf stem bears up to 11 grey-green hairy leaflets. HEIGHT & SPREAD 1m×60cm (3×2ft) after 5 years, ultimately 1.5m (5ft) tall.

▲ *Indigofera heterantha*

I. heterantha ♀ (syn. *I. gerardiana*) Purple-pink flowers in clusters up to 12.5cm (5in) long distinguish this plant. The 13-20 leaflets are covered in short grey hairs. HEIGHT & SPREAD 1m×60cm (3×2ft) after 5 years, ultimately 2.4m (8ft) tall.

I. potaninii Clusters of pale pink flowers are up to 7.5cm (3in) long. The leaves are made up of 5-9 leaflets. HEIGHT & SPREAD 1m×30cm (3×1ft) after 5 years, ultimately 1.8m (6ft) tall.

CULTIVATION Plant from early autumn to spring, avoiding frosty or dry periods, in any soil, preferably well drained, in a sheltered, sunny position.

PROPAGATION Sow seed in early spring; take semi-ripe cuttings early or mid summer.

PRUNING None necessary in mild areas. In cold areas, cut back almost to ground level in spring to remove any dead wood.

PESTS AND DISEASES Usually trouble free.

Indocalamus see BAMBOOS p.77

Inula

Compositae

Inula royleana

A mass of yellow daisy-like flowers with long, narrow ray florets embellish this robust plant in summer. The flowers are either solitary or in loose, flat-topped clusters, and have a yellow or orange centre. Taller species add colour to a border, shorter ones brighten a rock garden. Most of those cultivated are hardy herbaceous perennials. Inulas are native to Asia, Caucasia and Europe.

RECOMMENDED SPECIES AND VARIETIES

I. ensifolia Solitary flowers 3cm (1¼in) across with silky bracts appear in mid summer. Erect wiry stems are loosely clasped by narrow, 5cm (2in) long leaves, each with 3-7 prominent parallel veins. HEIGHT & SPREAD 45×30cm (1½×1ft).

'Gold Star' is 30cm (1ft) tall.

▲ *Inula ensifolia*

▲ *Inula ensifolia* 'Gold Star'

I. glandulosa see *I. orientalis*

I. helenium (elecampane) Lax clusters of 2-3 large flowerheads up to 8cm (3¼in) across open in late summer. Toothed leaves with a hairy underside are 70cm (28in) long. This tall species is rather a coarse plant, suited to wilder parts of the garden. It has long been cultivated as a medicinal plant. HEIGHT & SPREAD 2.5×1m (8×3ft).

I. hookeri Bright, pale yellow ray florets open in late summer on this rapid spreader which bears solitary blooms. Stiff stems carry oval hairy leaves, up to 13cm (5in) long and 3cm (1¼in) wide. Clumps can increase rapidly, so choose the position with care. HEIGHT & SPREAD 75×60cm (2½×2ft).

I. macrocephala see *I. royleana*

I. magnifica Vivid deep yellow flowers up to 15cm (6in) across open in clusters in late summer, from brownish buds on top of stout brownish stems. The stems also bear 25cm (10in) long, broad oval leaves which are rough textured and dark green. The clumps increase rapidly in size, so the plant is not suitable for a small garden. HEIGHT & SPREAD 1.8×1m (6×3ft).

I. orientalis (syn. *I. glandulosa*) Woolly buds open into solitary orange-yellow blooms up to 3cm (1¼in) across. Oval hairy leaves are 12cm (4¾in) long and serrated. HEIGHT & SPREAD 60×45cm (2×1½ft).

▲ *Inula magnifica*

▲ *Inula royleana*

I. royleana (syn. *I. macrocephala*) Orange-bronze tinted florets distinguish this smaller species which may take a year or two to become established. Solitary flowers 5cm (2in) across appear in late summer to early autumn. Oval leaves are 25cm (10in) long. HEIGHT & SPREAD 60×45cm (2×1½ft).

CULTIVATION Plant during autumn through to spring in full sun in any reasonable soil, 45-60 cm (1½-2ft) apart, depending on the plant's ultimate size. Stake taller species, especially if exposed to the wind. Ensure that rampant forms do not engulf their neighbours.

PROPAGATION Sow seed in a nursery bed in spring and plant out between summer and autumn. Divide and replant established plants between autumn and spring.

PESTS AND DISEASES Usually trouble free.

Ionopsidium

Violet cress
Cruciferae

Ionopsidium acaule

Small fragrant flowers adorn this low-growing annual from summer to early autumn. It is a fast-growing single species with a tufted habit and is one of the few small annuals suitable for a rock garden, edging paths or naturalising in gravel areas.

This useful filler for pockets in a rock garden, or at the front of a flower border, is especially valuable for those gaps left where early spring bulbs, such as crocuses, have died down. Ionopsidiums are native to Portugal and hardy to -20°C (-4°F). They can also be grown in pots under glass in early autumn for a display of flowers in late winter and spring.

Ionopsidium acaule Clusters of 4-petalled lilac or violet flowers, up to 1cm (⅜in) across, are borne by this stemless plant which has rosettes 3-7.5cm (1¼-3in) across

▲ *Ionopsidium acaule*

of bright green oval or rounded leaves. HEIGHT & SPREAD 7.5×10 cm (3×4in).

CULTIVATION Plant in well-drained soil in a sunny position. If growing under glass in autumn, plant in a sunny site with a temperature between 5-15°C (41-59°F).

PROPAGATION Sow seed in early spring, or in autumn for an early display. The plants dislike disturbance, so sow in their flowering position, thinning the seedlings if necessary. Established plants often self-sow.

PESTS AND DISEASES Slugs and snails may attack young seedlings.

Ipheion

Alliaceae

Ipheion uniflorum 'Wisley Blue'

Star-shaped flowers shoot from the leaves of these perennial bulbs in spring. The plants are mostly hardy. For maximum effect, mass them in a sunny spot at the edge of a well-drained border, in a rock garden, or at the dryish base of a wall. They form clumps which can be left undisturbed for many years. The genus is native to S America.

RECOMMENDED SPECIES AND VARIETIES

***I.* 'Rolf Fiedler'**♀ In spring, startling electric blue, fragrant flowers appear above tufts of greyish green strap-like leaves, up to 15cm (6in) long. It is not completely hardy in cold conditions combined with wet soil, so a well-drained spot is essential; it will also grow in an unheated greenhouse or conservatory. HEIGHT & SPREAD 15×10cm (6×4in).

▲ *Ipheion uniflorum*

▲ *Ipheion uniflorum* 'Froyle Mill'

I. uniflorum (syn. *Triteleia uniflora*) (spring starflower) Fragrant white star-like flowers, tinged blue to violet, 2.5cm (1in) across, appear from early to late spring. They open from dense clumps of narrow, grassy, rather untidy leaves that are up to 25cm (10in) long. Bruised foliage smells a little like

▲ *Ipheion* 'Rolf Fiedler'

garlic. HEIGHT & SPREAD 15×10cm (6×4in).

'Album' has large white flowers, up to 3cm (1¼in) across. **'Froyle Mill'**♀ is striking for its violet flowers. **'Wisley Blue'**♀ has violet-blue blossoms.

CULTIVATION Plant bulbs in autumn in a sunny position in well-drained soil. Plants like being crowded and flower best if left alone. Remove faded blossoms after flowering and once old foliage has died back.

PROPAGATION In autumn lift and divide clumps and replant the bulbs immediately.

PESTS AND DISEASES Usually trouble free.

Ipomoea

Morning glory
Convolvulaceae

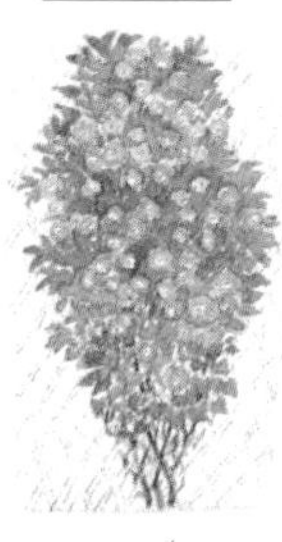

Ipomoea tricolor 'Heavenly Blue'

The morning glories grown in Britain are half-hardy annual and herbaceous perennial twining climbers. Their abundantly produced, cheerful trumpet-shaped flowers are very short-lived, usually opening in the morning and fading in the early afternoon. Morning glories flower during summer and early autumn, beginning to bloom according to sowing date and conditions.

Grow them in a sunny, sheltered position outdoors or in a greenhouse or conservatory. In poor summers *Ipomoea indica* and *I. nil* may not succeed at all outdoors. The hardiest species, *I. purpurea*, will tolerate more exposed situations. The seeds of many species are poisonous.

RECOMMENDED SPECIES AND VARIETIES

I. acuminata see *I. indica*

I. coccinea (red morning glory) This half-hardy annual has small scarlet flowers with a yellow throat, up to 2cm (¾in) across. The fragrant blooms are carried in clusters of up to 8. The heart-shaped leaves are sometimes

▲ *Ipomoea indica*

toothed. HEIGHT & SPREAD 3×1m (10×3ft).
I. indica♀ (syn. *I. acuminata*, *I. learii*) (blue dawn flower) Blue or purple flowers, up to 7cm (2¾in) across and either solitary or held in small clusters, are borne by this very

▲ *Ipomoea purpurea*

vigorous, half-hardy herbaceous perennial. The heart-shaped leaves are sometimes 3-lobed. HEIGHT & SPREAD 6×1.5m (20×5ft).
I. nil This short-lived, half-hardy herbaceous perennial bears blue flowers, 5cm (2in) across. The leaves on its hairy stems are oval to round, sometimes 3-lobed. HEIGHT & SPREAD 5×1m (16×3ft).

'Early Call' flowers 1 or 2 weeks earlier than the species. Its flowers, up to 10cm (4in) across, come in a range of colours including blues, pinks and reds.
I. purpurea (common morning glory).The flowers of this half-hardy annual are up to 6cm (2½in) across and may be white, pink, purple or red, or striped with those colours on a white background. The leaves are oval to round in shape, and hairy. HEIGHT & SPREAD 2.5m×60cm (8×2ft).
I. tricolor (syn. *I. rubro-caerulea*, *I. violacea* hort.) This half-hardy annual bears bright sky-blue flowers, with a white tube, up to 8cm (3in) across. The plant's growth is not dense enough to screen completely the support that it is given to climb. The plant has smooth heart-shaped leaves. HEIGHT & SPREAD 4×1m (13×3ft).

'Heavenly Blue', with intense sky-blue flowers, is the most widely grown variety. **'Flying Saucers'** has blue-and-white marbled flowers.
CULTIVATION Plant outdoors 40cm (16in) apart in a sunny, sheltered spot after risk of frost has passed. Under glass, the perennial species can be overwintered if frost is excluded, but these plants are often very rampant in their second year. Plant 3 or 4 seeds in a 20cm (8in) or larger pot. Support on wires, trellis or canes.
PROPAGATION Sow seed of all species under glass in early spring. Soak the seeds for 24 hours in tepid water before sowing to soften their hard coats. Sow 2 seeds to a 10cm (4in) pot. In warmer parts of the country, *I. purpurea* can be sown in mid spring directly where it is to grow.
PESTS AND DISEASES Red spider mite and whitefly can be troublesome in greenhouses and against south-facing walls.

Ipomopsis
Polemoniaceae

These striking plants offer finely divided foliage and colourful spikes of tubular flowers with a star-like appearance. Suitable for a conservatory or cool greenhouse, these perennials and biennials may be grown as half-hardy annuals in a border. The flowers appear from mid summer to early autumn.
RECOMMENDED SPECIES AND VARIETIES
I. aggregata (syn. *Gilia aggregata*) (scarlet gilia) The stems of this biennial may branch from the base; scarlet to pink flowers are up to 4cm (1½in) across, and pinnate leaves, about 20cm (8in) long, form a basal rosette. HEIGHT & SPREAD 75×40cm (30×16in).
I. rubra (syn. *Gilia rubra)* (standing Cypress) This erect perennial, more vigorous than *I. aggregata*, has unbranched stems, spikes of scarlet flowers, 2.5cm (1in) across, and pinnate leaves arranged in a basal rosette. HEIGHT & SPREAD 2m×40cm (6½ft×16in).

▲ *Ipomopsis aggregata*

CULTIVATION Grow in well-drained soil in a sunny position or in pots in general-purpose compost in a greenhouse.
PROPAGATION As half-hardy annuals, sow seed in late winter or early spring in a warm greenhouse. Plant out in late spring. As biennials, sow in early summer and overwinter in a coldframe. Keep the plants dry in winter and plant out in spring.
PESTS AND DISEASES Usually trouble free.

Iresine
Amaranthaceae

These tender S American perennials are valued for their brightly coloured foliage. In Britain they should be grown in a greenhouse or conservatory or planted out as part of summer bedding displays. The species described can also be grown as houseplants. All have insignificant flowers.
RECOMMENDED SPECIES AND VARIETIES
I. herbstii This has bright carmine, translucent stems. The maroon oval leaves are up to 10cm (4in) long and are distinctively veined in a lighter shade of red. HEIGHT & SPREAD 60×45cm (2×1½ft) or more.

The variety **'Aureoreticulata'** has

▲ *Iresine herbstii* 'Aureoreticulata'

▲ *Iresine lindenii*

reddish stems and deep green leaves with yellow veins and blotches. **'Brilliantissima'** produces rich crimson foliage.
I. lindenii♀ The deep blood-red leaves have a central band of lighter or darker red. They are oval to lance-shaped and very glossy. They grow to 10cm (4in) in length. HEIGHT & SPREAD 1m×45cm (3×1½ft).
CULTIVATION Grow in pots of soil-based compost in full sun at a minimum temperature of 10°C (50°F). Encourage leaf colour with a high-potash fertiliser in summer. Remove flowerheads as they appear. Bring bedding plants indoors before the first frost. Cut back overwintered plants hard in spring.
PROPAGATION Take soft stem cuttings in spring and root in a propagator; or take cuttings in summer.
PESTS AND DISEASES Greenfly may infest overwintered stock in spring.

Iris, snakeshead
see *Hermodactylus tuberosus*

Iris

Iridaceae

Named for the Greek goddess of the rainbow, iris flowers combine an exquisite architectural flower form with a huge range of rich and delicate colours and their beauty has been celebrated since earliest times

Irises are prized for the beauty of their flower form and the richness and diversity of their colour range. They comprise a very large genus consisting of some 300 species varying from tiny rockery flowers to giant water irises. There are varieties suitable for many different areas of the garden, in particular alongside ponds, in borders and in rockery beds. The flowering season varies from mid winter to mid summer and with careful selection it is possible to have irises in bloom for nine months of the year. Given the right conditions irises are generally easy to grow and long-lasting, requiring only periodic division.

The typical iris has flower parts in groups of three. The three inner petals, or 'standards', normally stand up while the three outer petals, or 'falls', tend to droop. Within the flower structure are three style branches which can be highly ornamental.

•RHIZOMATOUS IRISES•

Irises that grow from fleshy, creeping stems, or rhizomes, are classified into three groups: bearded irises have a central line of hairs on the falls, beardless irises have no hairs on the falls while those known as crested irises have a fleshy crest on the falls.

BEARDED IRISES

All bearded irises prefer a neutral or slightly alkaline soil. There are two distinct groups, the Arillate Group and the Eupogon Group. The Arillate Group are so called because each seed has attached to it a fleshy outgrowth, or aril. They are very difficult to grow and greenhouse or cloche cultivation is necessary. The Eupogon Group do not have arillate seeds, and provide the most impressive irises of the spring and early

INDEX OF SPECIES AND VARIETIES

Irises can be either rhizomatous or bulbous. Rhizomatous irises are divided into three groups: bearded, beardless and crested. The bearded irises may be miniature dwarf bearded (MDB), standard dwarf bearded (SDB), intermediate bearded (IB), border bearded (BB), miniature tall bearded (MTB) or tall bearded (TB). The beardless irises are sub-divided into Californicae, Hexagonae, Laevigatae, Sibiricae, Spuriae or Miscellaneous.

Bulbous irises are divided into three groups: Reticulata, Juno and Xiphium. A list of plants covered in this book follows in alphabetical order with the relevant divisions in parentheses.

'Adobe Sunset' (Beardless/Spuriae)
'Anniversary' (Beardless/Sibiricae)
aphylla (Bearded/SDB)
'Arnold Sunrise' (Beardless/Californicae)
attica (Bearded/MDB)
'Banbury Beauty' (Beardless/Californicae)
'Banbury Melody' (Beardless/Californicae)
'Beverly Sills' (Bearded/TB)
'Bibury' (Bearded/SDB)
'Black Swan' (Bearded/TB)
'Blue Ballerina' (Beardless/Californicae)
'Blue Eyed Brunette' (Bearded/TB)
'Blue Pools' (Bearded/SDB)
'Blue Rhythm' (Bearded/TB)
'Broadleigh Carolyn' (Beardless/Californicae)
'Bronzaire' (Bearded/IB)
bucharica (Bulbous/Juno)
'Butter & Sugar' (Beardless/Sibiricae)
'Cambridge' (Beardless/Sibiricae)
'Cantab' (Bulbous/Reticulata)
'Champagne Elegance' (Bearded/TB)
chrysographes (Beardless/Sibiricae)
'Cliffs of Dover' (Bearded/TB)
confusa (Crested)
cristata (Crested)
cristata 'Alba' (Crested)
'Curlew' (Bearded/IB)
'Dancer's Veil' (Bearded/TB)
danfordiae (Bulbous/Reticulata)
douglasiana (Beardless/Californicae)
'Dovedale' (Bearded/TB)
'Dreaming Yellow' (Beardless/Sibiricae)
'Dusky Challenger' (Bearded/TB)
Dutch (Bulbous/Xiphium)
'Early Light' (Bearded/TB)
'Edale' (Bearded/TB)
'Edith Wolford' (Bearded/TB)
English (Bulbous/Xiphium)
ensata (Beardless/Laevigatae)
ensata 'Rose Queen' (Beardless/Laevigatae)
ensata 'Variegata' (Beardless/Laevigatae)
'Florentina' (Bearded/IB)
foetidissima (Beardless/Miscellaneous)
foetidissima citrina (Beardless/Miscellaneous)
forrestii (Beardless/Sibiricae)
fulva (Beardless/Hexagonae)
× *fulvala* (Beardless/Hexagonae)
'Gay Parasol' (Bearded/TB)
'George' (Bulbous/Reticulata)
'Gerald Darby' (Beardless/Laevigatae)
germanica (Bearded/IB)
'Going My Way' (Bearded/TB)
graminea (Beardless/Spuriae)
'Harmony' (Bulbous/Reticulata)
'Holden Clough' (Beardless/Laevigatae)
'Honey Glazed' (Bearded/IB)
innominata (Beardless/Californicae)
'J.S. Dijt' (Bulbous/Reticulata)

◀ *Iris* 'Curlew'

summer garden. All are hardy and easy to grow given sunshine and good drainage.

The sword-shaped leaves grow in fans from the tip of the rhizome. Most are grey-green. The flowering stems rise from the centre of the fan of leaves and once flowering is over the leaves generally die back.

The flowering season of bearded irises tends to be related to height, with shorter plants flowering earlier than taller ones. Bearded irises are classified into six groups, depending on height and flowering time.

Miniature dwarf bearded (MDB)
The flowers, borne from mid to late spring, are usually 5-7.5 cm (2-3 in) across. These irises are less than 20 cm (8 in) tall. All plants are hardy but most prefer a well-drained sunny position in a rock garden or well-ventilated, unheated greenhouse.

I. attica Yellow flowers are tinged with green on this plant which is not reliably hardy in cold wet winters. Native to Greece and Turkey. HEIGHT 5-10 cm (2-4 in).

I. lutescens (syn. *I. chamaeiris*) Flowers, up to 10 cm (4 in) wide, are white, purple or yellow. Native to SE France and NW Italy. HEIGHT 15-25 cm (6-10 in).

I. pumila The first bearded iris to flower in mid spring, the flowers are up to 7.5 cm (3 in) across with downward-curving falls, in shades of purple, white, yellow or yellow with brown tints. Most forms are stemless, with the flower itself giving height. The plant is best grown in a well-ventilated, unheated greenhouse or a rockery. Native to SE Europe. HEIGHT up to 10 cm (4 in).

▲ *Iris attica*

Standard dwarf bearded (SDB)
These irises flower in late spring and are 20-38 cm (8-15 in) high. The flowers are up

'Jane Philips' (Bearded/TB)
japonica (Crested)
japonica 'Ledger's Variety' (Crested)
'Jeremy Brian' (Bearded/SDB)
'Joyce' (Bulbous/Reticulata)
'Joyce Terry' (Bearded/TB)
'Katharine Hodgkin' (Bulbous/Reticulata)
'Kent Pride' (Bearded/TB)
'Kentucky Bluegrass' (Bearded/SDB)
kerneriana (Beardless/Spuriae)
laevigata (Beardless/Laevigatae)
laevigata 'Alba' (Beardless/Laevigatae)
latifolia (Bulbous/Xiphium)
'Lavender Royal' (Beardless/Californicae)
'Limeheart' (Beardless/Sibiricae)
lutescens (Bearded/MDB)
magnifica (Bulbous/Juno)
'Mary Frances' (Bearded/TB)
'Maui Moonlight' (Bearded/IB)
'Melon Honey' (Bearded/SDB)
milesii (Crested)
'Miss Carla' (Bearded/IB)
'Mystique' (Bearded/TB)
'Natascha' (Bulbous/Reticulata)
'No-name' (Beardless/Californicae)
'Orange Dawn' (Bearded/TB)
orientalis (Beardless/Spuriae)
'Orville Fay' (Beardless/Sibiricae)
pallida (Bearded/TB)
pallida 'Argentea Variegata' (Bearded/TB)
pallida 'Aurea Variegata' (Bearded/TB)
pallida ssp. *cengialtii* (Bearded/MTB)
pallida ssp. *pallida* (Bearded/TB)
'Paradise' (Bearded/TB)
'Paradise Bird' (Bearded/TB)
'Pascoe' (Bearded/TB)
'Pauline' (Bulbous/Reticulata)
'Professor Blaauw' (Bulbous/Xiphium)
pseudacorus (Beardless/Laevigatae)
pseudacorus 'Variegata' (Beardless/Laevigatae)
pumila (Bearded/MDB)
'Rare Edition' (Bearded/IB)
'Raspberry Blush' (Bearded/IB)
reticulata (Bulbous/Reticulata)
'Roman Emperor' (Bearded/TB)
'Ruffled Velvet' (Beardless/Sibiricae)
sanguinea (Beardless/Sibiricae)
'Sarah Taylor' (Bearded/SDB)
setosa (Beardless/Miscellaneous)
'Shelford Giant' (Beardless/Spuriae)
'Shirley Pope' (Beardless/Sibiricae)
sibirica (Beardless/Sibiricae)
'Silver Edge' (Beardless/Sibiricae)
'Snowy Owl' (Bearded/TB)
'Soft Blue' (Beardless/Sibiricae)
'Song of Norway' (Bearded/TB)
spuria (Beardless/Spuriae)
'Stepping Out' (Bearded/TB)
'Sun Dappled' (Bearded/TB)
'Superstition' (Bearded/TB)
'Tangerine Sunrise' (Bearded/TB)
tectorum (Crested)
'Titan's Glory' (Bearded/TB)
unguicularis (Beardless/Miscellaneous)
unguicularis 'Alba' (Beardless/Miscellaneous)
unguicularis 'Mary Barnard' (Beardless/Miscellaneous)
unguicularis 'Walter Butt' (Beardless/Miscellaneous)
'Vanity' (Bearded/TB)
versicolor (Beardless/Laevigatae)
virginica (Beardless/Laevigatae)
'Warleggan' (Bearded/TB)
'Wedgwood' (Bulbous/Xiphium)
'White Excelsior' (Bulbous/Xiphium)
'White Swirl' (Beardless/Sibiricae)
winogradowii (Bulbous/Reticulata)
'Wisley White' (Beardless/Sibiricae)
xiphium (Bulbous/Xiphium)

▲ *Iris pumila*

to 10cm (4in) across. All are hardy and excellent for the border or rock garden.

I. aphylla Each branched stem bears 3-5 blue-purple flowers with a white or bluish beard. The plant sometimes blooms again in autumn. Native to the Caucasus, Ukraine and parts of Turkey. HEIGHT 15-45cm (6-18in), but usually 30-38cm (12-15in).

Extensive hybridising between *I. aphylla* and *I. lutescens* has produced plants with scented flowers on branched stems which often flower twice in the season.

The many standard dwarf bearded hybrids include **'Bibury'** which has creamy white flowers and blue beards and reaches a height of 30cm (12in). The white flowers of **'Blue Pools'** have a dark blue spot with a bluish white beard. The plant grows to 25cm (10in). **'Jeremy Brian'**♀ has light blue flowers with a white flash and cream beard and grows to 25cm (10in). **'Kentucky Bluegrass'** has creamy lime-green flowers with a dark blue beard and reaches 36cm (14in). The flowers of **'Melon Honey'**♀ are melon and pale orange with a cream beard. The plant grows to 30cm (12in). **'Sarah Taylor'**♀ has primrose-yellow flowers with a blue beard and reaches 30cm (12in).

▲ *Iris* 'Bronzaire'

▲ *Iris* 'Maui Moonlight'

Intermediate bearded (IB)

The intermediate bearded irises bloom between mid and late spring. The flowers are up to 10cm (4in) across. The plants reach 40-70cm (16-28in) in height. They are mostly derived from crossing dwarf bearded irises with tall bearded irises.

***I.* 'Florentina'**♀ The white flowers are flushed bluish and are borne 4 or 5 to a well-branched stem. Native to central Italy. HEIGHT 45cm (18in).

I. germanica♀ (purple flag) A freely flowering iris that bears 4 or 5 blue-purple to violet flowers with a whitish beard. Parent of many garden hybrids. Native to S Europe. HEIGHT 70cm (28in).

Iris germanica

Intermediate bearded hybrids include **'Bronzaire'**♀ which has golden bronze flowers with brown beards and grows to 50cm (20in). **'Curlew'** has clear yellow flowers with white-streaked falls and reaches 48cm (19in) high. **'Honey Glazed'** has white and amber-brown flowers with orange-yellow beards and grows to 70cm (28in). **'Maui Moonlight'**♀ has bright lemon flowers with a paler flash and lemon yellow beards and grows to 65cm (26in). Flowers of **'Miss Carla'**♀ are cream infused with blue and blue beards. The plant reaches 55cm (22in). **'Rare Edition'** has rosy purple and white flowers rimmed with violet-purple and grows to 60cm (24in). Flowers of **'Raspberry Blush'**♀ are lilac pink with a raspberry pink spot and pinkish red beard. The plant reaches 50cm (20in).

Border bearded (BB)

These are shorter types of tall bearded irises which flower in late spring. The plants are not commonly available and must be sought from specialist suppliers.

Miniature tall bearded (MTB)

These are miniature versions of tall bearded irises producing flowers, 5-6cm (2-2½in) across, in mid spring. They have slender stems and short foliage. Plants reach 38-63cm (15-25in) in height.

I. pallida* ssp. *cengialtii♀ Up to 6 scented, blue-violet flowers are borne on branched stems. Native to N Italy to the Balkans. HEIGHT 45cm (18in).

Tall bearded (TB)

Flowers, 10-15cm (4-6in) across, bloom in late spring through to early summer. Most plants are about 1m (3ft) tall but different varieties may be anything from 70cm-1.5m (28in-5ft) tall.

▲ *Iris pallida*

I. pallida Six scented, pale lavender-blue flowers are carried on each branched stalk among blue-green leaves. A good plant for the border and for cutting. Native to the Adriatic coast. HEIGHT up to 1m (3ft).

'Argentea Variegata' has white-striped leaves and is somewhat slow-growing. **'Aurea Variegata'** has golden yellow to cream stripes and is a strong-growing vigorous plant which flowers well.

I. pallida* ssp. *pallida (syn. *I. pallida* var. *dalmatica*) is similar to the species but is stronger with better weather resistance.

There are thousands of garden varieties to choose from in all colours of the rainbow except pure spectrum red. It is important to know the expected height before buying a plant as the number of flowers on the stem may vary from 6-15 according to height. The more flowers the longer the flowering season. However, one of the main attractions of irises is the elegance and grace of individual flowers and too many blooms on a stalk can look crowded while too few can look sparse and be over too quickly. Generally, 8-9 blooms to a stalk is considered ideal, giving a good blooming season while showing each flower to good effect. All the varieties listed usually have 7-9

▲ *Iris* 'Dusky Challenger'

▲ *Iris* 'Jane Phillips'

▲ *Iris* 'Snowy Owl'

▲ *Iris* 'Early Light'

▲ *Iris* 'Tangerine Sunrise'

▲ *Iris* 'Blue Eyed Brunette'

flowers, and more if the previous summer was hot and dry when flower buds were being laid down in the rhizome.

Modern hybrids have large ruffled blooms and clear colours on elegant stems.

Light blue varieties include **'Jane Phillips'**♀ and **'Song of Norway'**♀. A mid blue variety is **'Blue Rhythm'**. Lavender hybrids include **'Mary Frances'**♀ and **'Roman Emperor'**♀. Deep purple varieties are **'Dusky Challenger'** and **'Titan's Glory'**♀. Black varieties are **'Black Swan'** and **'Superstition'**♀. White varieties are **'Cliffs of Dover'**♀ and **'Snowy Owl'**♀. A cream variety is **'Edale'**♀. Yellow varieties are **'Early Light'**♀ and **'Joyce Terry'**. Orange varieties are **'Orange Dawn'**♀ and **'Tangerine Sunrise'**♀. A brown-red variety is **'Blue Eyed Brunette'**♀. Pink varieties are **'Beverly Sills'**, **'Paradise'**♀ and **'Vanity'**♀. Raspberry varieties include **'Dovedale'**♀ and **'Paradise Bird'**♀.

Hybrids of mixed colour have terms to describe colour combinations. Amoena is used for irises with white standards and coloured falls. **'Sun Dappled'** has white standards with yellow falls. **'Champagne Elegance'** has white standards and pink-peach falls. Bitone describes flowers that are 2 shades of the same colour. Blue-violet bitones are known as neglecta. Varieties include **'Gay Parasol'**♀ with mauve-tinged white standards and rosy purple falls, and **'Mystique'** with light blue standards and deep purple falls. **'Pascoe'**♀ has pale lavender standards and very dark purple falls and **'Warleggan'**♀ has bluish white standards and mid blue falls. Bicolour describes irises

▼ *Iris* 'Stepping Out'

of 2 different colours. **'Edith Wolford'** has buff-yellow standards and violet falls. Plicata (cool) describes flowers with a white ground stippled with blue, purple or wine. Hybrids include **'Dancer's Veil'**♀, **'Going My Way'** and **'Stepping Out'**♀. Plicata (hot) describes flowers with a yellow to pink ground stippled wine, brown or pink. **'Kent Pride'** is included in this group.

BEARDLESS IRISES

Beardless irises are so named because they have no hairs or crests on the falls. The falls are smooth and insects are attracted to the heart of the flower by a 'signal' (a patch of different colour on the top parts of the falls) which may be more or less developed. The rhizomes of beardless irises are usually more slender than those of the bearded kind and are mostly buried under the soil rather than exposed on the surface.

There are numerous types of beardless iris, for convenience they are divided into 5 sections plus a miscellaneous section containing species which do not fit into any of the 5 main groups. The 5 sections are Californicae, Hexagonae, Laevigatae, Sibiricae and Spuriae.

Californicae

Commonly known as Pacific Coast Irises (PCI), the 11 species originate from the west coast of N America. They grow best in acid soil in dappled shade with a cool root run and should not be allowed to dry out. Plants do well under trees. The height varies from 15-60 cm (6-24 in). One or two species are not reliably hardy but most hybrids will withstand British winters. Plants flower in late spring.

I. douglasiana♀ Each branched stem carries 4 or 5 flowers that are 7.5 cm (3 in) across. The colour is variable, but is usually in shades of blue-purple and lavender with veining on the falls. A lime-tolerant species. Native to California. Plant 60 cm (24 in) apart. HEIGHT 30-45 cm (12-18 in).

I. innominata Each stem carries a single flower, or occasionally 2. Flowers, up to 6 cm (2½ in) wide, have broad segments that are cream, buff, yellow or orange, with rich brown veins. The narrow leaves are evergreen in very mild areas. The species is variable. Native to Oregon. Plant 23 cm (9 in) apart. HEIGHT up to 15 cm (6 in).

Hybrids available within the Californicae Group include **'Banbury Beauty'**♀ with lavender flowers marked bright violet, and **'Banbury Melody'**♀ with deep pink flowers with cream flecks. **'Broadleigh Carolyn'**♀ has clear blue flowers on very strong stems. **'No-name'**♀ is a yellow-flowered variety and **'Lavender Royal'**♀ has pale purple flowers with darker markings centrally along the standards and the falls. White flowers with yellow markings are found on **'Arnold Sunrise'**♀. White flowers with blue markings are characteristic of **'Blue Ballerina'**♀.

▲ *Iris fulva*

▲ *Iris ensata* 'Rose Queen'

Hexagonae
These beautiful plants, commonly called Louisiana irises, are generally not sufficiently hardy in Britain to grow and flower well outdoors. They originate from the Mississippi delta and need copious moisture and high summer temperatures. They tolerate cold winters but do not flower well and in Britain are best grown in a cool greenhouse, where they flower from early to mid summer. They are called hexagonae because the seedpods have 6 sides.

I. fulva Terracotta blooms, 7.5-10 cm (3-4 in) across, are borne in leaf axils in early summer. The plant only flowers reliably if the conditions suit. Native to New Orleans. HEIGHT 45 cm (18 in).

I* x *fulvala♀ flowers more reliably than *I. fulva* with red-purple or blue-purple flowers, 10 cm (4 in) across, in mid summer. HEIGHT 60 cm (24 in).

Laevigatae
Irises which flourish in or near water are included within this sub-section. There are five common species which have been hybridised to produce a considerable number of varieties. In particular, many originate from the Japanese water iris, *Iris ensata*. Only *I. laevigata* must be grown in water – all the other 'water' irises may be grown in ordinary garden soil provided it does not dry out.

I. ensata♀ (syn. *I. kaempferi*) (Japanese water iris) Deep purple flowers from early to mid summer, borne 2 or 3 to a stem, have short standards and broad falls with a yellow streak or blaze. The plant differs from other species in the Laevigatae group by having no black watermarks in the foliage, which is heavily ribbed. It is a waterside rather than a water iris and is a lime-hater. HEIGHT 60 cm-1 m (24-36 in).

From this species a huge number of 'Japanese irises' have been developed in many colours, from blue to red-purple, pink, lavender and white. They may be self-coloured or blends of colours and may be dotted and striped with coloured veins. Flowers are from 10-20 cm (4-8 in) across, and may be single, semidouble or double.

A white and grey-green variegated form **'Variegata'**♀ is available which contrasts well with the wine-purple flowers. **'Rose Queen'**♀ has rosy lavender-pink flowers.

I. laevigata♀ In early to mid summer mid blue flowers are borne 4 to a stem, occasionally more. The leaves are pale green with black watermarks in the veins. A vigorous plant, it will stand some lime. Native to Manchuria, Korea and Japan. HEIGHT 45-60 cm (18-24 in) when planted in water which is 15 cm (6 in) deep.

A white form **'Alba'** is equally good.

I. pseudacorus♀ (yellow water flag) The common native plant with yellow flowers, up to 12 cm (4¾ in) across, in late spring is a very vigorous plant, perhaps too vigorous for smaller gardens. Native to Europe, Asia Minor and N Africa. HEIGHT Variable, from 60 cm (24 in) for the dwarf form to 2 m (6½ ft) for the full-sized plant.

▲ *Iris pseudacorus*

Spring foliage of **'Variegata'**♀ is striped green and cream, but the variegation fades to fresh green by early summer when the plants bear yellow flowers. The plant grows to 1 m (3 ft). Cream, primrose, white and golden yellow varieties exist. All have black watermarks in the foliage.

'Holden Clough'♀ resembles a small *I. pseudacorus* but the yellow flowers are veined maroon giving an overall brown appearance to the flowers which are good for cutting. To 60-75 cm (24-30 in) high.

I. versicolor♀ Up to 9 flowers in blue or red-purple are borne on a branched stem. The standards are shorter than the falls. The plant has shiny seeds and black watermarks in the foliage. It is happy in water or moist soil and tolerates a little lime. Native to N America. HEIGHT 60 cm (24 in).

I. virginica Flower colour varies from deep blue to wine with standards the same length as the falls. Up to 9 flowers are borne on each branched stem. It grows best in water or moist soil and tolerates some lime. The foliage displays black watermarks. Native to N America. HEIGHT 50-75 cm (20-30 in).

▲ *Iris versicolor*

Iris 'Gerald Darby' ▲

'Gerald Darby'♀ has bright mid blue flowers and black-purple stems which may reach 90 cm (36 in).

Sibiricae
These hardy irises do well in herbaceous borders provided the soil is not excessively dry. They can also be grown as marginal plants at the edges of pools or in water meadows, but they resent waterlogging. Foliage is grassy, slender and elegant. Stems, which should rise above the foliage, vary from very short forms suitable for a rock garden to 1.2 m (4 ft) specimens which can be grown anywhere in the garden if they have a reasonable amount of sunshine.

I. sanguinea♀ Unbranched stems carry 2 blue-purple flowers, up to 7.5 cm (3 in) across in early summer. Native to Siberia, Manchuria and Japan. HEIGHT 1 m (3 ft).

▲ *Iris sibirica*

Iris sibirica 'Anniversary' ▲

I. sibirica Up to 5 flowers, 5-6 cm (2-2½ in) across, which vary from white to blue, are borne in early summer on stems with 1 or 2 branches. Native to Europe, including Russia and Turkey. HEIGHT 1 m (3 ft).

From these 2 species modern Siberian irises have been developed. The colour range is wide and flowers, up to 10 cm (4 in) across, are more robust, flaring and ruffled.

The following plants are 60 cm-1 m (24-36 in) tall with 2-5 flowers per stalk: **'Anniversary'**♀ (white), **'Butter & Sugar'**♀ (white and yellow), **Cambridge'**♀

▲ *Iris* 'Wisley White'

▲ *Iris* 'Butter & Sugar'

(light blue), **'Dreaming Yellow'** (white and pale lemon), **'Limeheart'** (greenish white centre), **'Orville Fay'**♀ (different tones of blue), **'Ruffled Velvet'**♀ (ruffled deep violet), **'Shirley Pope'**♀ (deep violet with white markings in flower's throat), **'Silver Edge'**♀ (deep blue edged in white), **'Soft Blue'**♀ (light blue, early), **'White Swirl'**♀ (white), **'Wisley White'**♀ (white).

Chrysographes The sibirica section also includes species which require more moisture and are termed chrysographes.

I. chrysographes♀ Deep wine-red to purple-black flowers with gold markings on the falls are up to 6 cm (2½ in) across. Flowers are borne 2 on a stem in early summer. Native to Sichuan, Yunnan and Burma. HEIGHT 36 cm (14 in).

I. forrestii♀ Yellow flowers, 5 cm (2 in) across, have black lines on the falls in early summer. The standards are erect over drooping falls. Native to Yunnan. HEIGHT 20-45 cm (8-18 in).

Spuriae

The flowers, 6-10 cm (2½-4 in) across, have narrow, upright standards and oval falls. These hardy plants are tolerant and will grow in sun or semi-shade, lime or lime-free soil, wet or dry conditions. Height varies from 15 cm (6 in) to 1.8 m (6 ft) with most 40 cm-1 m (16-36 in). Foliage is usually a glossy mid green, slender and reedy.

I. graminea♀ Blue-purple flowers over-topped by grassy leaves are borne 2 to a stem in early summer. Native to Europe. HEIGHT 25-38 cm (10-15 in).

I. kerneriana♀ Pale creamy lemon flowers, 5-7.5 cm (2-3 in) across, in late spring to early summer, have intensely recurved falls which commonly curl right back to touch the stem. HEIGHT 30-38 cm (12-15 in).

I. orientalis♀ (syn *I. ochroleuca*) Large white flowers have a yellow patch on falls that tuck under. The flowers are borne in early to mid summer, 4-9 on a stem which rises above the shorter leaves. Native to Turkey. HEIGHT 1-1.2 m (3-4 ft).

'Shelford Giant'♀ has yellow flowers and reaches 1.8 m (6 ft) in height.

I. spuria Up to 10 violet-blue, yellow or white flowers are borne on each stem of this easy-going plant in mid summer. Native to Europe and the Middle East. HEIGHT 50-75 cm (20-30 in).

Garden hybrids of spuria irises are available in a wide range of colours and colour combinations. Most are 1-1.2 m (3-4 ft) in height but shorter ones of 60 cm (2 ft) are available. **'Adobe Sunset'** has deep orangey yellow flowers with margins and veins coloured dark brown. It reaches 1.8 m (6 ft).

Miscellaneous

There are a number of other beardless iris species not classified in the categories above. Some are very difficult to grow but those below make excellent garden plants.

I. foetidissima♀ (stinking iris, gladdon iris) This species is grown mainly for the seed-pods that develop after flowering and open in autumn and winter to display orange-scarlet seeds. The flowers themselves are insignificant, up to 7.5 cm (3 in) across, slate-grey flushed with pink and brown and

▲ *Iris chrysographes*

▲ *Iris* 'Soft Blue'

Iris 'White Swirl' ▲

Iris foetidissima

are borne 2–9 to the stem in early summer. Evergreen foliage is dark green and glossy, and gives off an unpleasant odour when crushed. Native to Britain and other parts of Europe. HEIGHT 50 cm (20 in).

I. f. citrina has creamy yellow flowers.

I. setosa♀ Slate-blue to deep violet flowers are borne in early summer. The standards are reduced to bristles and the falls are broad. The plant is among the hardiest of all irises and thrives in moist soil, ideally on the margins of a pool or stream. Lift and divide in early autumn. Native to Siberia and Alaska. HEIGHT 15-75 cm (6-30 in).

I. unguicularis♀ (winter-flowering iris, Algerian iris) The lilac-mauve flowers, up to 7.5 cm (3 in) across, have a yellow blaze on the falls. Flowering begins in autumn and continues during mild periods through winter until March. The foliage can be untidy and may be trimmed back in autumn before flowering starts. The plant requires a good baking in the summer and should be given the hottest and driest situation in the garden with some shelter from cold winds in winter. The foot of a south-facing wall is an ideal position. Native to the Mediterranean. HEIGHT 23 cm (9 in).

A white form **'Alba'** is available, **'Mary Barnard'** is a fine deep violet. **'Walter Butt'** is a free-flowering variety with scented, very pale lavender flowers.

▲ *Iris forrestii*

CRESTED IRISES

Crested irises bear a superficial resemblance to bearded ones but the marking that looks like a beard is in fact a raised band of tissue running along the midrib of the falls. The plants are evergreen with slender rhizomes and do best in moist, organic soil and in a sheltered position with dappled shade. Several of the more showy species are not reliably hardy in Britain and even when plants survive flowers can be badly damaged by late spring frosts. They are suitable for a cool greenhouse or conservatory. The flowers are 4-7.5cm (1½-3in) across and are delicately coloured with dainty petals. The shiny leaves are evergreen. Crested irises resent being moved and are extremely susceptible to slugs and snails.

I. confusa♀ White flowers, 5cm (2in) across, have a yellow crest and bloom from early to mid summer. This evergreen plant should be grown in a cool greenhouse or conservatory. HEIGHT 1m (3ft).

I. cristata♀ Pale lavender flowers, about 5cm (2in) across with an orange crest, appear in mid to late spring. One of the more hardy species, it will grow in a sheltered rock garden. Native to N America. HEIGHT 10cm (4in).

'Alba' has white flowers.

I. japonica♀ Dozens of small pale lavender flowers marked violet and orange are carried on well-branched stalks in mid to late spring. Glossy green leaves are up to 45cm (18in) long. Native to China and Korea. HEIGHT up to 1m (36in).

'Ledger's Variety' is slightly hardier than the type.

I. milesii♀ Flowers in shades of pink mottled with violet are borne in profusion for several weeks in early summer. Grow in a sheltered spot. HEIGHT 30-75cm (12-30in).

I. tectorum Each flower stem bears 2 lilac-violet flowers with a jagged crest, 7.5cm (3in) across, in late spring or early summer. Plants are susceptible to a virus that causes dark flecking on flowers. Leaves are a light apple-green. The plant is reasonably hardy if grown against a warm sunny wall. Native to China. HEIGHT up to 45cm (18in).

•BULBOUS IRISES•

Bulbous irises are divided into three groups – Reticulata, Juno and Xiphium. The smallest, Reticulata, flower earliest, beginning in winter and going on to early spring. The Juno Group follows in spring and the Xiphium Group in early summer.

RETICULATA GROUP

Ideal bulbous plants for rockeries, fronts of borders and pots in early spring. They need sunny well-drained soil and a sheltered position in full sun. Plant bulbs 20cm (8in) deep. Flowers grow to about 15cm (6in) tall and open from winter into spring. The outer layer of the bulb is strongly netted (reticulated). After the flowers have faded, the narrow leaves, usually 2 to a stem, extend to 30-45cm (12-18in).

▲ *Iris danfordiae*

***I.* 'Cantab'** Pale blue flowers, lighter at the tip, have a yellow crest with a white rim. HEIGHT 15cm (6in).

I. danfordiae Scented, bright yellow flowers are borne in mid to late winter. The falls have a deep yellow or orange central ridge which is surrounded by sparse green spots. Native to Turkey. HEIGHT 10cm (4in).

***I.* 'George'** Large flowers have plum-purple standards and slightly darker falls with a yellow crest on a whitish ground striped with purple. HEIGHT 15cm (6in).

▲ *Iris* 'George'

▲ *Iris* 'Harmony'

***I.* 'Harmony'** The flowers have deep blue standards and royal blue falls with a yellow blotch rimmed in white. Flowers are carried well above the leaves. HEIGHT 15cm (6in).

***I.* 'J.S.Dijt'** Purple flowers have marked reddish purple falls. HEIGHT 15cm (6in).

***I.* 'Joyce'** Sky-blue flowers with an orange crest on the falls. HEIGHT 12cm (4¾in).

***I.* 'Katharine Hodgkin'** The large flowers have bluish green standards and yellowish green falls with a yellow blotch veined slate-blue. An easy and reliably perennial plant. HEIGHT 12cm (4¾in).

▲ *Iris* 'J.S.Dijt'

***I.* 'Natascha'** The flowers have ivory-white standards and ivory-white falls with a golden yellow crest. HEIGHT 15cm (6in).

***I.* 'Pauline'** Violet flowers have dark purple falls with a white-variegated blue blotch. HEIGHT 12cm (4¾in).

Iris reticulata

I. reticulata♀ Violet-blue or purple flowers have a buttercup-yellow central crest. Native to Turkey, NW Iran and NE Iraq. HEIGHT 15cm (6in).

I. winogradowii♀ Yellow flowers are borne in early spring. The blade of the falls has a central ridge surrounded by green spots. The plant needs a peaty soil and does best when grown in a pot. Native to Transcaucasus. HEIGHT 15cm (6in).

JUNO GROUP

This large group flowers in early to mid spring and generally needs to be grown in a well-ventilated, unheated greenhouse. However, recommended plants can also be grown in a sunny rock garden in warmer parts of Britain.

The flowers, 6-7.5cm (2½-3in) wide, have standards that are little more than bristles, and large falls. All plants have alternating stem-clasping leaves.

I. magnifica♀ Large, pale lilac flowers are borne several to a stem in mid spring above glossy green leaves. The falls have a yellow patch in the centre. HEIGHT up to 60cm (24in). Native to central Asia.

I. bucharica♀ Golden yellow to almost white flowers have blotches of either green, brown or pale violet on either side of a yellow ridge on the blades of the falls. Scented flowers are borne 2-6 on a stem in mid to late spring. Bright green leaves have a whitish margin. Native to central Asia. HEIGHT 45cm (18in).

Iris bucharica

XIPHIUM GROUP

This is the most easily grown group of bulbous irises and includes Dutch, Spanish and English irises. Plants flower in early summer with a strong stem bearing 1 or 2 large flowers among slender leaves.

Dutch irises As well as being good border plants, these irises are bred from *I. xiphium* and *I. tingitana* for forcing at any time of year for florist's cut flower trade. Flower colour ranges through white, yellow, blue and purple, and the blooms are 10-15cm (4-6in) across with narrow, upright standards. These hardy plants need a sunny position in well-drained soil and reach a height of 38-60cm (15-24in). **'Professor Blaauw'**♀ has dark blue flowers with a narrow yellow stripe. **'Wedgwood'** has lavender-blue flowers with a yellow blotch on pale blue falls. The large white flowers of **'White Excelsior'** have a yellow zone on the falls.

I. latifolia♀ (syn. *I. xiphioides*) (English iris) Large flowers, 12.5cm (5in) across, are borne on stiff stems amid narrow silver-green leaves. Colours range through white, blue, pink and purple, with distinctively marked. HEIGHT up to 65cm (26in).

I. xiphium (Spanish iris) These graceful flowers, 10cm (4in) across, are blue-violet or occasionally white or bicoloured, with a yellow or orange blotch on the falls. Flowers are borne amid narrow leaves. The plants are usually sold as mixed collections. The colour range includes blues, purples, mauves, whites, yellows and browns. HEIGHT 60cm (24in).

CULTIVATION

The cultivation requirements of irises varies according to their classification – refer to the relevant group.

BEARDED IRISES

Plant rhizomes in an open sunny position with good drainage in mid summer or early autumn. Plant tall bearded irises 45cm (18in) apart, intermediate bearded irises 30-38cm (12-15in) apart and dwarf bearded irises 15-23cm (6-9in) apart. Position the rhizomes so that they are pointing towards the sun. The rhizomes should lie half exposed on the surface of the soil. Keep them well watered for the first 2 or 3 weeks after planting. Raised beds a few inches above soil level may be necessary on heavy soils or in wet areas. Plants do well in either heavy or light soil provided drainage is good, and tolerate a wide variation in pH. Neutral to slightly alkaline is generally considered best and bearded irises are a good choice for chalk or limestone-based soils.

BEARDLESS IRISES

Plant the slender rhizomes of the beardless irises 3-5cm (1¼-2in) deep.

Californicae Plant in acid soil with dressings of leaf-mould. *I. innominata* needs full sun, all other plants in this category like a cool root run and light or dappled shade.

Hexagonae Transplant seed-raised plants into small pots when large enough to handle, and plant in the final position with minimal root disturbance. Plant rhizomes singly in mid summer, just below the surface. A moist but not wet site, sheltered from winds, and a humus-rich soil is ideal.

Laevigatae Plant rhizomes 5cm (2in) deep in autumn or spring. Position in full sun in neutral to acid soil with plenty of moisture. *I. laevigata* and *I pseudacorus* are true water irises, suitable for planting 5-25cm (2-10in) deep in a pool. *I. ensata* does not tolerate lime and requires humus-rich soil.

Sibericae Plant rhizomes in full sun in moist, but not waterlogged, neutral to acid soil about 2.5cm (1in) deep and 45-60cm (18-24in) apart. Mid summer to early autumn is the best time. The plants are heavy feeders and top-dressing with manure or compost is beneficial. Avoid surface cultivation to prevent damage to surface roots.

The chrysographes group require more moisture and neutral to acid soil.

Spuriae Plant rhizomes in rich, neutral to alkaline soil in late summer or early autumn. Position them 2.5cm (1in) deep in a sunny or dappled shade position.

Miscellaneous *I. setosa* grows best in moist soil on the margins of a pool. *I. unguicularis* requires the hottest, driest and most sheltered situation in the garden. *I. foetidissima* and *I. f. citrina* grow best in moist shade but will also tolerate dry shade.

CRESTED IRISES

Plant rhizomes in groups in early autumn or spring just below the soil level. These irises prefer dappled shade and a sheltered position in rich soil.

BULBOUS IRISES

Juno Group bulbs need protection from wet and must be grown in an unheated, well-ventilated greenhouse. Water on the flowers can cause fungal attacks. Hardier plants can be grown in a sunny rock garden in warmer areas. Bulb roots should not be damaged during planting. Plant bulbs in early autumn in a light, well-drained preferably alkaline soil, not more than 7.5cm (3in) deep in a sunny position.

Plant Reticulata bulbs in early to mid autumn in a sunny well-drained, preferably alkaline, soil in clumps 5-8cm (2-3¼in) apart and at least 20cm (8in) deep. Add a little lime to the soil. After flowering, feed every 2 weeks with a liquid low-nitrogen tomato fertiliser until the foliage dies down.

Plant Xiphium bulbs in early to mid autumn, 10-15cm (4-6in) deep and 15cm (6in) apart, in a well-drained sunny position.

PROPAGATION

Bearded irises Divide rhizomes about every third year, preferably shortly after flowering but between the end of flowering and early autumn. Discard the centre and cut off pieces from the outer part of the clump, making sure each has 1 or 2 strong fans. Replant miniature tall bearded irises immediately after lifting and dividing. Other bearded irises can be left for a week or two before replanting if necessary.

Beardless irises Divide Pacific Coast Irises in early autumn into fairly large portions rather than individual rhizomes, and plant in slightly acidic soil with plentiful organic matter. Keep well-watered until the plants are established. Divide again only when clumps have outgrown their space or are beginning to die back in the centre.

Divide water-iris rhizomes after they have finished flowering – generally every 3 years or so. Replant immediately.

Siberian irises benefit from being lifted and divided every 4-5 years. If necessary, trim foliage to 25cm (10in) to avoid water-loss and wind damage. Divide into clumps with at least 5 or 6 growing points a few weeks after flowering or in early autumn. Plant rhizomes about 2.5cm (1in) deep.

Lift and divide *I. foetidissima* and *I. f. citrina* in autumn or sow seeds where they are to flower.

Bulbous irises Increase by the removal of offsets when the plant is dormant.

PESTS AND DISEASES

Leaves and flowers of all irises may be eaten by caterpillars.

Rhizomatous irises Most rhizomatous irises are vulnerable to slugs and snails. Aphids also cause damage and may transmit virus diseases. The most pernicious is a grey mealy aphid which settles in the axils between the leaf and the stem, and a dark aphid which infests the base of the stem, particularly on Siberian and Spuriae irises.

The following diseases may damage all rhizomatous irises.

Arabis mosaic virus and cucumber mosaic virus cause yellow streaks and spots on the leaves and flowers. Leaf spot due to a fungus may appear in spring or autumn, particularly in wet weather. Brown oval spots develop on the leaves and fuse together until the whole leaf is killed.

Rhizome rot causes rhizomes to decay into an evil-smelling, slimy mass.

Rust occasionally occurs on *I. foetidissima*, *I. pseudacorus*, all bearded iris forms and on some other cultivated species. Small red-brown pustules show on the leaves.

Scorch shows as a reddish flush on the leaves. Young leaves become affected first and gradually the whole plant dies.

Bulbous irises The Reticulata Group are susceptible to ink disease, which shows as deep black scales and is caused by the fungus *Drecholes iridis*. Plants can also be attacked by aphids and slugs.

Isatis

Woad

Cruciferae

Loosely clustered flowers, followed by winged or wingless seedpods, characterise the genus. The species in cultivation, both as an ornamental plant and for use by craft dyers, is a hardy biennial or short-lived perennial. Woad was used for dyeing the skins of ancient Britons as well as cloth. The plant adds height to an informal border, thriving in a sunny position, and is also at home in a semi-wild setting in the garden. Showy yellow flower clusters in summer contrast with blue-green leaves and are followed by decorative seed heads in autumn. The 30 species in the genus are found in central and S Europe, the Mediterranean and W Asia.

RECOMMENDED SPECIES AND VARIETIES

I. tinctoria (dyer's woad) Tiny, 4-petalled, bright yellow flowers are carried in a loose, domed cluster, up to 23 cm (9 in) wide, at the top of an erect stem from mid to late summer. Narrow and tapering, the blue-green leaves, up to 15 cm (6 in) long, are the source of blue pigment used in dyeing. The upper leaves clasp the stem. Clusters of drooping, dark brown, oblong, winged seed-pods hold the small seeds in early autumn. Native to central and S Europe. HEIGHT & SPREAD 120×60 cm (4×2 ft).

CULTIVATION Plant in spring or autumn in any well-drained soil and in a position that is in full sun.

PROPAGATION Sow seeds in autumn or early spring. Once established, the plant often seeds itself.

PESTS AND DISEASES Usually trouble free.

Isotoma see *Laurentia*

▲ *Isatis tinctoria*

Itea

Escalloniaceae

These deciduous and evergreen shrubs produce graceful, narrow, loose spikes of fragrant flowers in summer. The foliage is either handsomely glossy or offers autumn colour. The plants are easily grown in a fertile, acid-to-neutral soil and enjoy damp conditions, but some species require a sheltered position in sun or light shade.

RECOMMENDED SPECIES AND VARIETIES

I. ilicifolia♀ Tiny, honey-scented, greenish white flowers are borne in slender, pendulous spikes, up to 30 cm (1 ft) long in late summer. The glossy evergreen alternate leaves, 5-10 cm (2-4 in) long, are reminiscent of holly but thinner in texture and with softer spines. Requiring some shelter, this bushy shrub grows well against a wall but the soil must be kept moist. Native to W China. HEIGHT & SPREAD 1×1 m (3×3 ft) after 5 years, ultimately 3 m (10 ft) tall.

I. virginica This deciduous shrub forms an erect mass of slender stems, branched near the tips, which bear spikes of small, fragrant, white flowers in mid summer. Bright green, narrowly oval leaves, up to 9 cm (3½ in) long, turn shades of orange and red in late autumn. Native to the eastern USA. HEIGHT & SPREAD 1 m×60cm (3×2 ft) after 5 years, ultimately 1.5 m (5 ft) tall.

CULTIVATION Plant in autumn in a fertile, moist but well-drained, lime-free soil and in a part-shaded or sunny site. *I. ilicifolia* needs the shelter of a wall in most parts of Britain.

PROPAGATION *I. virginica* is best increased by division in early autumn, but semi-ripe cuttings may be tried in late summer. Take semi-ripe cuttings of *I. ilicifolia* in mid to late summer.

PRUNING The older stems of *I. virginica* should be thinned out every 2-3 years. *I. ilicifolia* needs no pruning.

PESTS AND DISEASES Usually trouble free.

▲ *Itea ilicifolia*

Ivy see *Hedera*

Ivy, Boston
see *Parthenocissus tricuspidata*

Ivy, devil's see *Epipremnum*

Ivy, grape, see *Cissus rhombifolia*

Ivy, ground see *Glechoma hederacea*

Ixia

Corn lily, wand flower

Iridaceae

These spring and summer-flowering, half-hardy cormous perennials, native to southern Africa, have thin, wiry stems bearing dense clusters of 20 or more flattish to bowl-shaped, six-petalled flowers. The basal leaves are narrow and sword-shaped.

RECOMMENDED VARIETIES

***I.* Mixed Hybrids** The species are seldom offered, but these brightly coloured flowers with dark centres are widely available. HEIGHT 60 cm (2 ft).

CULTIVATION Plant the corms in a sunny, south-facing position in well-drained soil, 8 cm (3¼ in) apart and 5 cm (2 in) deep. Bulbs planted in mid autumn flower in late spring and early summer, and need protection from frost. Those planted in early or mid spring flower in mid and late summer. To maintain late summer flowering, lift the bulbs in autumn and store till spring. For growing in pots, plant 8-10 corms in autumn, 5 cm (2 in) deep in a 13 cm (5 in) pot in a soil or peat-based compost. Plunge the pots in a coldframe. Water sparingly during winter and keep from severe frost. When the flower spikes show, bring the pots into the light and warmth, and water until they have finished flowering.

PROPAGATION Remove offsets in autumn when the foliage has died down and store till spring.

PESTS AND DISEASES Protect from slugs and snails.

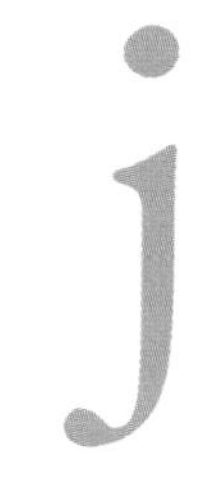

Jack-in-the-pulpit see *Arisaema triphyllum*
Jacob's ladder see *Polemonium*
Japanese maple see *Acer japonicum, A. palmatum*
Japonica see *Chaenomeles*

Jasione

Sheep's bit
Campanulaceae

Jasione laevis

Flowerheads like small pompoms attract butterflies to these pretty European annual and perennial meadow plants. The flowers, with protruding stamens, are surrounded by ruffs of green bracts. They bloom above clumps of mid to deep green leaves, up to 2.5cm (1in) long, and bring summer colour to rock gardens and the front of borders.

RECOMMENDED SPECIES AND VARIETIES

J. heldreichii (syn. *J. jankae*) Blue flowerheads, 3cm (1¼in) across, borne throughout summer complement narrow, pointed leaves. A herbaceous perennial or biennial. HEIGHT & SPREAD 10-20×15cm (4-8×6in).

J. laevis (syn. *J. perennis*) (shepherd's scabious, sheep's bit) Blue flowerheads, about 3cm (1¼in) wide, appear in summer. This perennial has narrow, oval, slightly toothed leaves. HEIGHT & SPREAD 15×15cm (6×6in).

'Blaulicht' ('Blue Light') has brilliant blue flowers, and is larger at 20cm (8in) tall.

J. montana (mountain sheep's bit) Blue, or occasionally white, pink or purple flowerheads appear throughout summer. This annual or biennial has narrow, oval leaves. HEIGHT & SPREAD 15-30×20cm (6-12×8in).

CULTIVATION Plant in any well-drained soil in full sun. In rich soil flowers are fewer.

PROPAGATION Sow seed in a coldframe in winter. In spring transplant self-sown seedlings. Divide perennials in spring.

PESTS AND DISEASES Usually trouble free.

Jasmine, Madagascar see *Stephanotis floribunda*

Jasminum

Jasmine
Oleaceae

Jasminum officinale

These deciduous and evergreen shrubs and climbers are grown for their decorative foliage and often fragrant flowers which are tubular, flaring open and lobed at the mouth. They are usually borne either singly or in clusters on the tips of the branches or in the fork between leaf and stem. Most have leaves with three to seven oval leaflets, 2-5cm (¾-2in) long.

RECOMMENDED SPECIES AND VARIETIES

J. beesianum Scented, pink to rose-red blossoms, up to 1cm (⅜in) wide, cover this deciduous or evergreen scrambler in late spring and early summer. The lance-shaped, dark green leaves are about 5cm (2in) long. HEIGHT & SPREAD 1.5-2.4×2.4m (5-8×8ft) after 5 years, ultimately 4.5m (15ft) tall.

***J. humile* 'Revolutum'**♀ (syn. *J. reevesii*) Fragrant, deep yellow flowers are borne from early spring to late autumn among glossy bright green evergreen leaflets. The plant is best grown against a warm wall. HEIGHT & SPREAD 1.8×1.5m (6×5ft) after 5 years, ultimately 2.4m (8ft) tall.

J. mesnyi♀ (syn. *J. primulinum*) (primrose jasmine) Mid yellow, semidouble flowers, up to 5cm (2in) wide, appear from mid spring to mid summer. This half-hardy scrambling evergreen with mid green leaves does best in a greenhouse or conservatory at a minimum temperature of 7°C (45°F), tied to a support. It can be grown outdoors only in frost-free districts, trained against a warm wall. HEIGHT & SPREAD 1.8×1.5m (6×5ft) after 5 years, ultimately 3m (10ft) tall.

J. nudiflorum♀ (winter jasmine) Bright yellow flowers, up to 2.5cm (1in) across, appear on bare, slender stems from late autumn to early spring. Dark green leaves appear in early spring. A deciduous scrambler commonly trained against a wall. HEIGHT & SPREAD 2.4×1.8m (8×6ft) after 5 years, ultimately 4.5m (15ft) tall.

'Aureum' has yellow-blotched leaves.

J. officinale♀ (common white jasmine) Fragrant white flowers, up to 2.5cm (1in) wide, cluster from mid summer to early autumn on this deciduous twining climber. The mid green leaves are up to 7.5cm (3in) long. HEIGHT & SPREAD 3.5×3m (12×10ft) after 5 years, ultimately 9m (30ft) tall.

The flowers of f. ***affine*** (syn. 'Grandiflorum') are pink outside. **'Argenteovariegatum'**♀ (syn. 'Variegatum') has grey-green leaves with creamy white edges. **'Aureum'** (syn. 'Aureovariegatum') has yellow-blotched leaves.

J. parkeri Masses of yellow flowers, 1.5cm (½in) across, appear in early summer. An evergreen shrub with mid green leaves. HEIGHT & SPREAD 15×15cm (6×6in) after 5 years, ultimately 30cm (1ft) tall.

J. primulinum see *J. mesnyi*

J. reevesii see *J. humile* 'Revolutum'

J. × stephanense♀ Pale pink scented flowers, up to 1.5cm (½in) across, bloom from early to mid summer on this semi-evergreen climber. The leaves are olive-green. HEIGHT & SPREAD 3×3m (10×10ft) after 5 years, ultimately 4.5m (15ft) tall.

CULTIVATION Plant hardy and half-hardy species in any well-drained soil, in a warm sheltered site, except for *J. nudiflorum* and *J. officinale* which can be planted in any position. Plant at any time except for *J. mesnyi*

▲ *Jasminum officinale*

▼ *Jasione* 'Blaulicht'

▼ *Jasminum nudiflorum*

▼ *Jasminum officinale* 'Argenteovariegatum'

Jasminum parkeri ▼

which is best planted in spring. Protect half-hardy species in winter.
PROPAGATION Take semi-ripe cuttings in summer or layer branches during autumn.
PRUNING After flowering, thin out *J. officinale* and *J.* × *stephanense* and cut back the flowering shoots of *J. mesnyi* and *J. nudiflorum* to within 5-7.5 cm (2-3 in) of the base. Remove dead or diseased wood and tie in new growths. If *J. officinale* is cut back hard regularly it will form a self-supporting bush. Other species require only the occasional thinning out of overgrown plants.
PESTS AND DISEASES Aphids may attack young shoots. Under glass, mealy bug may attack stems and leaves.

Jeffersonia

Berberidaceae

Jeffersonia dubia

Masses of springtime flowers and handsome leaves, often flushed pink or purple when young, provide valuable colour and interest in dappled shade. The clump-forming, herbaceous perennials are originally woodland plants and need deep, humus-rich soil.
RECOMMENDED SPECIES AND VARIETIES
J. diphylla White, cup-shaped flowers, up to 3 cm (1¼ in) across, borne on long stalks appear in mid spring. The pale green to mid green leaves, up to 20 cm (8 in) across, are divided into 2 distinct kidney shapes. Native to eastern N America. HEIGHT & SPREAD 20×20 cm (8×8 in).
J. dubia The pale lilac to purple cup-shaped flowers, up to 3 cm (1¼ in) across, appear in mid to late spring with the emerging leaves. Almost round young leaves, up to 25 cm (10 in) across, are flushed pink or purple and turn blue-green later. Native to NE Asia. HEIGHT & SPREAD 15×20 cm (6×8 in).

▼ *Jeffersonia dubia*

'**Alba**' has pure white flowers.
CULTIVATION Plant in deep, moist, humus-rich soil in dappled shade in early spring or autumn. Do not disturb once established.
PROPAGATION Sow seed in pots in a cold-frame during winter. Plant out young plants in the spring of their second season. Transplant self-sown seedlings in autumn.
PESTS AND DISEASES Usually trouble free.

Jewel of the Veldt see *Ursinia*
Joe Pye weed see *Eupatorium purpureum*
Jonquil see *Narcissus* (Jonquilla daffodils)
Judas tree see *Cercis siliquastrum*

Juglans

Walnut
Juglandaceae

Juglans nigra

Large elegant leaves, a domed crown and spreading branches make a walnut an ornamental specimen tree. Once established, the hardy deciduous trees are fast-growing and need a lot of space. In early summer greenish yellow male flowers are borne in catkins with small female flowers in clusters on the same plant. In ideal conditions, green fruits containing the nut develop after pollination when trees are about ten years old.
J. nigra (black walnut)♀ A big tree grown for its appearance rather than the nuts, which, although edible, are difficult to extract. It has rugged grey-brown bark and glorious golden autumn colour. Lustrous aromatic foliage, 30-60 cm (1-2 ft) long, consists of pinnate leaves with up to 23 oval leaflets. Native of E and central N America. HEIGHT & SPREAD 10×6 m (33×20 ft) after 20 years, ultimately 30×18 m (100×60 ft) tall.
J. regia (common walnut) Edible nuts are borne singly, in ovoid green fruits on the smooth silvery barked tree. Trees are wind pollinated but are not always self fertile because male and female flowers can occur at different times. Each pinnate mid green leaf, about 30 cm (12 in) long, has 7-9 oval leaflets; there is usually no autumn colour. HEIGHT & SPREAD 8×5 m (26×16 ft) after 20 years, ultimately 25×15 m (80×50 ft).

'**Laciniata**' has deeply cut leaflets and slightly weeping branches.
CULTIVATION Plant in late spring in warm, well-drained but moisture-retentive neutral soil; some lime is tolerated but wet, heavy clay is not. Frosty sites are a problem, especially for young plants, though long cold

▲ *Juglans nigra*

Juglans regia ▲

winters are vital for good nut production.
PROPAGATION Sow seed in autumn in a coldframe. Fruiting cultivars are grafted on to common walnut seedlings.
PRUNING Trim for shape in mid summer or early autumn to avoid sap bleeding.
PESTS AND DISEASES Gall mite cause leaf yellowing and abnormal growth.

Juncus see GRASSES p. 303
Juniper see *Juniperus*

Juniperus

Juniper
Cupressaceae

Juniperus virginiana 'Grey Owl'

Versatile in shape and colour, hardy, evergreen and tolerant of most soils, the juniper is a conifer that is welcome in any garden. Among the species and the hundreds of plants bred from them there are plants for lawn specimens, for troughs and rock gardens, and for clothing slopes and hollows.

Foliage may be green, yellow, grey or bluish, and has juvenile and adult stages. Young leaves are usually sharp needles, which may cause skin irritation, but when mature they are like fleshy scales pressed against the stems. Tiny flowers are borne in tight clusters at branchlet tips. The berry-like cones ripen to blue or black. Both male and female trees are usually needed for the female to produce berries. Long-lived junipers are native across the Northern Hemisphere. Except for *Juniperus* × *media* and its descendants, most are slow-growing.
RECOMMENDED SPECIES AND VARIETIES
J. chinensis The narrow conical tree has about 75 cm (2½ ft) of clear stem below dense foliage in which a blue-white band marks each leaf. The berries are blue. This

▼ *Juniperus chinensis* 'Aurea'

▲ *Juniperus chinensis* 'Plumosa Aurea'

tree reaches 25 m (80 ft) tall but is the parent of many more suitable garden plants.

'Aurea'♀ makes a gently tapering column of growth, 12×1 m (40×3 ft) and rounded at the top. The dense foliage is golden when new, turning blue-grey after the first year; the gold scorches in strong sun. **'Blaauw'**♀ resembles 'Aurea' but is slightly wider and has rich, blue-grey foliage. **'Blue Alps'** is a striking grey-blue and vigorous but of modest size, reaching only 3×2m (10×6½ft) in 40 years. **'Kaizuka'**♀ has plenty of blue berries in autumn and bright green foliage all year. The small, broad tree makes slow growth, taking 60 years or more to reach 6×4m (20×13 ft). **'Obelisk'**♀ is multistemmed but narrow, forming a blue-green to grey-green column 5×1m (16×3 ft) after 30 years. It is easily damaged by snow. **'Plumosa Aurea'**♀ has yellow-green foliage that turns purple-brown in winter. The growth sprays out widely from the base, forming a flattened shuttlecock shape that reaches about 1×3m (3×10 ft) in 20 years. **'Pyramidalis'**♀ slowly makes a pillar, 60×30 cm (2×1 ft). The dense growth is smothered with prickly blue-grey needles.

J. communis (common juniper) This small tree has ferociously prickly, glossy green needles marked with a broad white lengthways stripe. The berries ripen to black. The species grows so slowly that ultimate size is only 6×2m (20×6½ft). The tree's habit varies from conical to creeping and its variability is reflected in the range of garden plants bred from it.

'Compressa'♀ is one of the slowest growing miniature plants available, eventually forming a column 1 m×30 cm (3×1 ft). It thrives in rockeries and containers provided they are not exposed to easterly or salt-laden winds. The densely packed, greyish, sharply pointed leaves tend to revert to green. **'Green Carpet'**♀ forms a dense, ground-hugging mass of dark green foliage that reaches only 30×100 cm (12×40 in) in 15 years. **'Hibernica'**♀ (Irish juniper) must have acid soil. It forms a narrow column with a long, drooping leader and bears crowded silver-blue needles. The exceptionally slow-growing plant takes some 100 years or more to reach 6 m×60 cm (20×2 ft). **'Hornibrookii'**♀ creates an undulating carpet of loosely spreading branches with blue-green needles that are silver-white on the underside. After 10 years it is only 30 cm (12 in) high but 2 m (6½ ft) across. **'Repanda'**♀ is a dwarf creeper that forms a carpet of densely arranged branches bearing open grey-green foliage. The leaves are not scorched by full sun, but may bronze over in winter. After 10 years it is 30 cm (12 in) high and 2 m (6½ ft) across. **'Sentinel'** forms a narrow column of erect branches, tapering to a point. The deep blue-green needles are borne on reddish purple shoots. In 30 years it reaches 4 m×50 cm (13 ft×20 in).

J. conferta (shore juniper) Dense, creeping branches that turn upright at the tip create a carpet of apple-green foliage. Each needle is sharply pointed, has a central groove and bears a white stripe. There are male and female flowers on one plant, followed by purplish black berries. HEIGHT & SPREAD 30 cm×1 m (1×3 ft) and growing 10 cm (4 in) along the ground each year but never growing much higher than 30 cm (1 ft).

J. horizontalis There is a pronounced steely blue or grey hue in the short, sharp needles that cover the very long branches. These can reach 2-3 m (6½-10 ft) after 40 years and spread quite loosely from a centre about 30 cm (12 in) high, so that other, more upright plants can grow between them.

Juniperus horizontalis 'Bar Harbor'

'Bar Harbor' makes a spread of some 8 m (26 ft) across in about 30 years, but keeps to a height of only 30 cm (12 in). The bluish green foliage turns purple in winter and is scale-like, not prickly. **'Blue Chip'** has foliage of a brilliant, distinctive blue all year round. After about 20 years its branches are spreading out from a centre 50 cm (20 in) high to form a tidy carpet some 3 m (10 ft) across. **'Emerald Spreader'** has bright green foliage and reaches 30 cm×3 m (1×10 ft) in 20 years. Plants of the **Glauca Group** produce dense, blue carpets with slightly raised centres and long, trailing fringes to 3 m (10 ft) across. **'Hughes'** has silvery blue foliage, perhaps the bluest of all trailing junipers. It makes a flat mat some 2 m (6½ ft) across after 10 years, with a neatly radiating branch pattern. **'Plumosa'**♀ bears gently ascending branches densely covered with grey-green foliage. It spreads quite vigorously to 8 m

▲ *Juniperus horizontalis* 'Blue Chip'

(26 ft) and reaches a height of 60 cm (2 ft) in 30 years. **'Prince of Wales'** slowly forms a mat, 15 cm (6 in) high, and continues spreading at a rate of 10-18 cm (4-7 in) a year with dense, trailing growths whose bright green foliage is tinged blue and takes on a purple flush in winter. **'Wiltonii'**♀ is one of the bluest carpeting plants with long, ground-hugging branches covering an area 3 m (10 ft) wide after 10 years.

J. × media This group of variable, often extremely vigorous plants includes some that are large, spreading and unmanageable. The varieties listed are more suitable garden plants but are faster-growing than plants bred from other juniper species.

'Carbery Gold' has pale golden foliage and matures into a bowl shape about 1.5 m×75 cm (5×2½ft), formed by strong, gently rising branches. **'Gold Coast'** forms a yellow, flat-topped spreading plant. It exceeds 1.5 m (5 ft) in about 25 years and continues to grow vigorously, making it unsuitable for small gardens. **'Old Gold'**♀ is more slow-growing than others in this group, reaching 1×2m (3×6½ft) in 40 years. Its dense branches are tight-packed with bronze-gold foliage whose colour does not fade in sun and is enhanced in winter. **'Pfitzeriana'**♀ has long branches, slanting upwards from a short trunk, drooping at the tips and bearing scale-like, green leaves with a slight blue tinge. The plant easily reaches

▼ *Juniperus × media* 'Carbery Gold'

▼ *Juniperus x media* 'Pfitzeriana'

▲ *Juniperus procumbens* 'Nana'
Juniperus sabina 'Tamariscifolia' ▲

3×5 m (10×16 ft) in 40 years and cannot be kept smaller by pruning. **'Pfitzeriana Aurea'** is identical to 'Pfitzeriana' except for having golden yellow terminal shoots that mature to yellowy green. **'Pfitzeriana Compacta**♀**'**, which reaches about two-thirds the size of 'Pfitzeriana', has very prickly blue foliage.

***J. procumbens* 'Nana'**♀ This tiny tree, which prefers dry, sandy soil and spreads by only 1.5 cm (½ in) a year, is well suited to a rockery, and its toleration of salty breezes lets it thrive in coastal gardens. Its stiff branches, clothed with bright green, prickly foliage, form a cushion shape reaching barely 30×60 cm (1×2 ft) after 50 years.

J. recurva (drooping juniper) From an early age, this tidy tree has an almost perfectly conical form. Its drooping branches bear sharply pointed, grey-green needles just 6 mm (¼ in) long and marked on the under side by 2 white stripes. The species is self-fertile, bearing blue-black berries just under 1 cm (⅜ in) across. The bark peels off in strips. HEIGHT & SPREAD 2 m×40 cm (6½ ft×16 in) after 10 years, ultimately 15×3 m (50×10 ft).

***J. sabina* 'Tamariscifolia'** Flat-topped in shape and low initially, this plant covers a dry bank or spreads between rocks or boulders. The dense growth, whose dark green needles release an acrid smell when crushed, dies back at the tips in frosty weather. HEIGHT & SPREAD 20×30 cm (8×12 in) after 10 years, ultimately 1×2 m (3×6½ ft).

J. scopulorum (Rocky Mountain juniper) Foliage that varies from green to grey-blue and consists of fleshy scales clothes this narrow, conical plant. Dark blue pea-sized berries succeed flowers in alternate years. Plant size rarely exceeds 12×2.4 m (40×8 ft).

'Blue Heaven'♀ makes a neat narrow pyramid, seldom more than 5 m (16 ft) tall, with very blue foliage and an abundant crop of berries every year. **'Skyrocket'** is taller and slender, reaching 7 m (23 ft) or more in a blue-grey column tapering to a fine tip while only 30 cm (1 ft) across at the base.

J. squamata Short needles are carried in whorls of 3 on branchlets that nod at the tip. Cold conditions are best for this variable plant, which sometimes makes a ground-hugging shrub, sometimes a small tree with a height and spread of 2×4 m (6½×13 ft).

'Blue Carpet'♀ is a slow-growing, ground-cover plant that makes a blue-grey carpet of sharp, pointed needles 30 cm×1.2 m (1×4 ft) after 10 years. **'Blue Star'**♀ takes 30 years to form a tight, silvery blue mound 60 cm×1 m (2×3 ft). **'Holger'**♀ is often tricoloured, with new, butter-yellow foliage mingled with older grey-green and blue foliage. It grows slowly into a stocky cube shape, eventually reaching 2×2 m (6½×6½ ft).

▲ *Juniperus squamata* 'Holger'

J. virginiana Sharply ascending branches rise from the thick trunk and form a tall, tapering column not more than 2 m (6½ ft) wide at the base but eventually more than 30 m (100 ft) tall. It is clothed with fleshy scale-like green foliage with a blue tinge. The berries are blue with a white bloom.

'Grey Owl'♀ is a flat-topped, fast-grower that stands regular pruning – but the clusters of purple berries may then be sacrificed. This shrub reaches 2×4 m (6½×13 ft) in 30 years, and has branches ascending from a central point and bearing nodding sprays of grey foliage. **'Sulphur Spray'**♀ takes 30 years to grow to 2×2 m (6½×6½ ft). It makes a bright splash of pale, sulphur yellow that is sometimes mottled.

CULTIVATION Plant between autumn and spring in sun or light shade. Soil that is dry and shaly suits junipers best but they are tolerant of many soils, including chalky ones.
PROPAGATION Root from hardwood cuttings taken in autumn and given some bottom heat. Species are best grown from seed sown in a coldframe in late winter.
PRUNING None is needed but most plants can be pruned in spring and autumn.
PESTS AND DISEASES Fungal root and butt diseases, especially phytophthora, afflict junipers. Foliage may be attacked by aphids.

Justicia
Acanthaceae

Beautiful and unusually shaped flowers are freely borne by these tender evergreen shrubs. Being rapid growers, they do best in good light, so are ideal conservatory plants.

RECOMMENDED SPECIES

J. brandegeeana♀ (syn. *J. guttata, Beloperone guttata*) (shrimp plant) Given good light and temperatures above 15°C (59°F), this plant blooms almost all year round. The pale lilac flowers are small but emerge from highly distinctive heads composed of overlapping bracts, pinky brown at the base, becoming paler towards the tip. The flowerheads are about 6 cm (2½ in) long and curve gently downwards. The leaves of this densely branching shrub are 5-8 cm (2-3¼ in) long, dark green, roughly diamond-shaped and covered with soft hairs. HEIGHT & SPREAD 80×80 cm (32×32 in) after 5 years.

CULTIVATION Grow in full sun or good indirect light in summer and full sun in winter. 10°C (50°F) is an acceptable winter minimum temperature. (*J. brandegeeana* can survive a winter temperature as low as 3°C (37°F) but will shed its leaves.) Hot dry air should be avoided. Keep the compost constantly moist when in active growth. Apply potash-rich feed regularly to encourage flowering. Repot plants annually. Top-dress old, large plants each year instead.
PROPAGATION Take cuttings in spring or summer.
PRUNING Pinch out tips for bushy growth. Rejuvenate leggy plants by cutting back hard at the end of the growing season.
PESTS AND DISEASES Whitefly.

▼ *Justicia brandegeeana*

Kalanchoë

Crassulaceae

Kalanchoë blossfeldiana

These tender, succulent perennials from southern Africa and Madagascar are grown as houseplants for their foliage and tubular flowers. Most are compact enough to make ideal subjects for a sunny windowsill.

RECOMMENDED SPECIES AND VARIETIES

K. blossfeldiana (flaming Katy) Scarlet flowers, up to 2.5 cm (1 in) long, are borne in flattish heads on this erect, compact plant. The dark green oval leaves are up to 4 cm (1½ in) long with scalloped edges. Short day lengths stimulate the plant into producing flowers. For year-round flowering, keep it in the dark for a few hours every day in late spring and summer, prolonging its night to more than 12 hours. Varieties are available with pink, yellow or white flowers. HEIGHT 35 cm (14 in).

K. pumila ♀ Pale pink flowers, just 1 cm (⅜ in) long, are produced in late winter in small clusters. The 3 cm (1¼ in) long oval leaves are coated with a layer of white powder, as are the stems, which are rather weak and thus tend to trail making it good for hanging baskets. HEIGHT 20 cm (8 in).

CULTIVATION Plant in a soil-based compost with added grit or perlite and keep at a minimum temperature of 21°C (70°F) in full sun. Water whenever the compost starts to dry out. *K. pumila* needs a dormant period in winter with temperatures down to 10°C (50°F) and minimal watering. Feed weekly during active growth. Repot yearly.

PROPAGATION Take softwood cuttings in spring. A well-drained open compost and cautious watering are important for success.

PESTS AND DISEASES Mealy bug.

▼ *Kalanchoë blossfeldiana*

Kalmia

Ericaceae

Kalmia latifolia

Exquisite flowers resembling miniature parasols characterise these hardy, lime-hating shrubs, most of which are evergreen. The blooms, in shades of pink, red, purple, lilac and white, are borne at the end of stems in rounded dense clusters during spring and summer. The conspicuous shape reflects the pollination mechanism – the stamens jerk upright when touched by visiting insects, showering them with pollen. The plants require acid soil. They add colour to a shrub border and are native to N America and Cuba. All are poisonous to livestock.

RECOMMENDED SPECIES AND VARIETIES

K. angustifolia ♀ (sheep laurel) Rosy red flowers in 5 cm (2 in) groups appear in early summer. This species spreads rapidly by underground suckers and has oval to egg-shaped leaves up to 5 cm (2 in) long. HEIGHT & SPREAD 60×60 cm (2×2 ft) after 5 years, ultimately 1.2×1.2m (4×4ft).

The flowers of f. ***rubra*** are red-purple.

K. latifolia ♀ (mountain laurel, calico bush) White, pink, purple or red flowers 2.5 cm (1 in) across, sometimes with a deeper band round the outside, open over several days in early to mid summer from ribbed, cone-shaped buds that are often deeper in colour than the opened petals. Glossy leaves up to 12.5 cm (5 in) long and 4 cm (1½ in) wide are yellowish and leathery. The plant often looks sparse because of a small root system. It may take several years to flower. HEIGHT & SPREAD 60×60 cm (2×2 ft) after 5 years, ultimately 3×4.5 m (10×15 ft).

'Carousel' white with a deep band of dark red, **'Minuet'** smaller leaves and more compact, relatively large light pink flowers with a cinnamon-maroon band, **'Olympic Fire'** red buds opening to pink flowers, quite easy and vigorous, **'Ostbo Red'** ♀ the most widely grown, red buds opening to pink, **'Pink Frost'** light to deeper pink.

K. polifolia (eastern bog laurel) Pink-purple flowers, about 1.5 cm (½ in) across, open in mid to late spring on this straggly species which is best grown through other plants for support. It has narrow leaves up to 4 cm (1½ in) long. Supported, it can reach 50 cm (20 in) high; otherwise it is low ground cover which spreads infinitely in the right conditions. It is the easiest kalmia to grow. HEIGHT & SPREAD 10–20×60 cm (4–8×24 in) after 5 years, ultimately 10–20 cm×1m (4–8 in×3 ft).

▼ *Kalmia angustifolia* f. *rubra*

▲ *Kalmia latifolia*

▲ *Kalmia latifolia* 'Pink Frost'

CULTIVATION Plant in moisture-retentive soil in full sun or light shade. *K. latifolia* needs full sun and well-mulched peaty soil. *K. polifolia* will grow in boggy places.

PROPAGATION Root 2–3 cm (¾–1¼ in) ripewood cuttings of all except *K. latifolia* from August to October in a peat and grit or peat and perlite mixture. Bottom heat is not vital but speeds up rooting. Layer *K. angustifolia* and *K. polifolia* in late summer or in spring. They often layer themselves.

PRUNING Trim *K. angustifolia* and *K. polifolia* every few years after flowering to encourage bushiness. Regeneration can be slow after pruning. Deadhead *K. latifolia*.

PESTS AND DISEASES Usually trouble free.

Kalmiopsis

Ericaceae

Kalmiopsis leachiana

Purple-tinged, rose-pink, bell-shaped flowers feature on this dwarf evergreen shrub which usually forms a neat, compact mound. It requires acid soil and is suited to a rock garden, or to growing in a container in an alpine house. The genus is native to western N America and is hardy, but it is difficult to grow well, seldom being long-lived. There is only one species.

Kalmiopsis leachiana♀ Flowers, 2cm (¾in) across, open in 2.5-5cm (1-2in) long clusters of 6-9 blooms over a long period throughout spring and into early summer. The numerous bright green leaves, which have a sticky underside, are pointed, oval, sometimes broader towards the tip, and up to 2cm (¾in) long. HEIGHT & SPREAD 30×30cm (1×1ft) after 5 years, ultimately 30×60-90cm (1×2-3ft).

k

▲ *Kalmiopsis leachiana*

Low-growing, compact **'Umpqua'** is sometimes sold as **'Le Piniec'** after its discoverer; the reliable and free-flowering **'Glendoick'** is more vigorous and easier to please.

CULTIVATION Grow in well-drained acid soil. Choose a sunny site in cool areas, otherwise semi-shade. Keep the roots fairly cool and do not let them dry out in summer.

PROPAGATION Root semi-ripe cuttings in peat, or a peat and grit/perlite mixture.

PRUNING None is required.

PESTS AND DISEASES An as-yet-unknown fungal disease attacks. Treat with a general fungicide.

Kangaroo paw see *Anigozanthos*
Kangaroo vine see *Cissus antarctica*
Katsura tree see *Cercidiphyllum japonica*
Kentia see *Howea*

Kerria

Rosaceae

Kerria japonica 'Picta'

Slender, arching stems carry abundant yellow flowers in spring on this easily grown, deciduous shrub. Suitable for sun or part shade and tolerant of most soils, it can be grown either freestanding or against a wall. A member of the rose family with five-petalled flowers, kerria is native to central and western China, and Japan. It is a genus of a single species.

Kerria japonica An abundance of small, solitary, yellow flowers, like single roses, up to 5cm (2in) across, are borne during mid to late spring on this dense, suckering shrub. Narrow oval leaves, up to 7.5cm (3in) long, are a dull green with finely toothed margins and the whole leaf has a ridged appearance. The green stems in winter are a bonus. It is frost-hardy. HEIGHT & SPREAD 1×1m (3×3ft) after 5 years, ultimately 1.8m (6ft) tall.

'Golden Guinea'♀ is a single-flowering variety with larger flowers than the species. The main garden value of **'Picta'** (syn. 'Variegata') is its creamy white variegated foliage as it does not flower prolifically. It tends to be a lower-growing, more spreading plant, reaching a height and spread of 60cm (2ft) in 5 years, and rarely growing to more than 1.2m (4ft) high and eventually wider than it is tall. **'Pleniflora'**♀ is the most common form grown in gardens with a profusion of double golden yellow flowers in mid or late spring. A more vigorous plant than the species, it has a more upright habit growing to a height of 1.2m (4ft) and spreading to 1m (3ft) in 5 years, and eventually to 3m (10ft) tall. **'Variegata'** see 'Picta'.

▲ *Kerria japonica* 'Picta'

▲ *Kerria japonica* 'Golden Guinea'

▲ *Kerria japonica* 'Pleniflora'

CULTIVATION Kerria grows in all soils but does best in a well-drained soil. Plant in the spring or autumn in a sunny or semi-shaded position but avoid a site that is very open and exposed. In cold areas, protect kerrias by siting plants against walls or fences; the variegated forms do best on a south or west-facing wall.

PROPAGATION This plant is easily raised from semi-ripe cuttings taken in early to mid summer and can also be layered in autumn to be dug up when rooted after 1 or 2 years. Alternatively, plants composed of many stems may be divided and replanted in autumn or spring.

PRUNING None is normally required but may be needed to maintain a particular size. If the plant becomes old and woody, prune older stems from the base. Any pruning should be done after flowering.

PESTS AND DISEASES Usually trouble free.

Kingcup see *Caltha palustris*

Kirengeshoma

Hydrangeaceae

For late-summer flowers in moist shady places kirengeshoma, which is native to Japan and Korea, makes an elegant feature plant. Tall groups of dark, arching, leafy stems are slowly formed, bent by the weight of loose sprays of creamy yellow, shuttlecock flowers that are the epitome of Oriental grace. The large, maple-like leaves are clear, bright green. This perennial, which prefers acid soil, is hardy to -20°C (-4°F) and deserves a choice place in cool dappled shade recalling the mountain woods of its homeland.

RECOMMENDED SPECIES AND VARIETIES

K. palmata♀ A prominent calyx and 5 fleshy, 3cm (1¼in) petals hang on branching, dark brown stems from terminal leaves. Stout rhizomes produce erect stems carrying hand-shaped leaves, 12-20cm (4¾-8in) long, with 7-10 shallow, toothed lobes. HEIGHT & SPREAD 1.2×1m (4×3ft).

▲ *Kirengeshoma palmata*

Koreana Group are more erect and taller, reaching 1.8m (6ft). Paler, upright flowers, 4cm (1½in) long, open more widely, and the leaves are slightly egg-shaped.

CULTIVATION Plant in spring or autumn. Although the plant prefers acid soil, it will grow well in any soil provided that it is moist and humus-rich. Choose a site in partial shade. Give ample summer water and mulch well: plants will quickly flag if allowed to become dry in sunshine.

PROPAGATION Divide in spring or autumn when stems die down. Sow seed in spring.

PESTS AND DISEASES Slugs may attack young plants.

Kiwi fruit see *Actinidia deliciosa*
Knapweed see *Centaurea*

Knautia

Dipsacaceae

Knautia macedonica

Flowers packed with prominent stamens and resembling small pincushions, dance on the loose, wiry, thin stems of these hardy perennials in summer and early autumn. Their exuberant habit is especially suited to the informality of cottage and wild-flower gardens. The plants thrive towards the front of a sunny, well-drained border. Plants flowering heavily may exhaust themselves in two or three years.

RECOMMENDED SPECIES AND VARIETIES

K. arvensis (field scabious) Bluish violet pincushion-like flowers, up to 4cm (1½in) across, are carried on tall, loose, hairy stems above a base of toothed or tapering pale green, hairy leaves, up to 10cm (4in) long, from mid summer to early autumn. Deeply cut leaves grow up the hairy stems. The plant is native to Europe. HEIGHT & SPREAD 80×60cm (32×24in).

K. macedonica Crimson, occasionally lilac, pincushion-like flowers, 5cm (2in) across, are made up of many small flowers, with an outer basal ring of the most mature. They grow on curving, branched stems, up to 50cm (20in) tall, from mid to late summer. The first leaves are basal and wither away before flowering time. The pinnate leaves, about 10cm (4in) long, are mid green and have an oval lobe at the top. The plant is native to the Balkans. HEIGHT & SPREAD 50×45cm (20×18in).

The flowers of the pink form have a pretty, deep rose hue.

CULTIVATION Plant in spring in any well-drained soil in a sunny site. Plants flourish in chalky or limy soil.

PROPAGATION Sow seeds in spring or take cuttings with a basal heel.

PESTS AND DISEASES Plants rot in wet soils; otherwise trouble free.

Kniphofia

Red-hot poker, torch lily

Asphodelaceae

Tall spikes of flowers in glowing shades of red, orange and yellow do indeed resemble red-hot pokers. Numerous pendent, tubular flowers, up to 4cm (1½in) long, are densely packed together to form a tapering head at the top of a strong stem which rises out of a clump of grass-like leaves.

Kniphofia 'Royal Standard'

There are about 70 species of herbaceous perennials in this genus, mostly native to eastern and southern Africa. Though many of the species are unreliably hardy in all but the mildest of British gardens, their survival in cold regions can be helped by siting the plants in a warm spot and using a protective mulch in winter. Most of the garden varieties will grow well in all but the coldest gardens. The roots are rhizomatous but generally do not spread so much as to become a nuisance.

The plants can be used to colour a herbaceous border and, since there is a wide choice of hybrids on the market, careful selection ensures a display of yellow, orange and red flowers throughout the summer.

▼ *Kniphofia caulescens*

▲ *Kniphofia triangularis*

▲ *Kniphofia* 'Buttercup'

▲ *Kniphofia thomsonii* var. *snowdenii*

▲ *Kniphofia* 'Ice Queen'

▲ *Kniphofia* 'Brimstone'

k

RECOMMENDED SPECIES AND VARIETIES

K. caulescens♀ Soft coral-red flowers turn lemonish white as they develop in mid summer. This is the only truly hardy kniphofia, with a mass of long grey leaves, broad at the base, arising from stems which lie on the ground and root into it. HEIGHT & SPREAD 1.2m×60cm (4×2ft).

K. citrina Light yellow flowers appear in late summer. HEIGHT & SPREAD 1m×50cm (3ft×1ft 8in).

K. galpinii♀ Dense heads of small, red-orange flowers are carried on slender stems in late summer. Several other plants are often (wrongly) sold under this name. HEIGHT & SPREAD 60×30cm (2×1ft).

K. thomsonii* var. *snowdenii Coral-red trumpets are rather sparsely spaced on the stems of this decidedly tender plant in early autumn. HEIGHT & SPREAD 1m×30cm (3×1ft).

K. triangularis♀ Typically, this species bears flame-coloured flowers in late summer, though it is very variable. HEIGHT & SPREAD 60×50cm (2ft×1ft 8in).

K. uvaria Bold red flowers are carried above a mass of rather untidy strap-shaped leaves in autumn. HEIGHT & SPREAD 1.2m×60cm (4×2ft).

'Nobilis'♀ has deep orange flowers.

GARDEN VARIETIES

There are several garden varieties which generally flower in mid summer. The colours and heights are listed, and the spread is up to 50cm (1ft 8in).

'Alcazar' has bright red flowers and is 1.5m (5ft) tall. **'Bees' Sunset'**♀ bears soft orange blooms and is 80cm (2ft 8in) tall. **'Border Ballet'** is in various shades from cream to pink and reaches 60cm (2ft) tall. **'Brimstone'**♀ bears green buds which open into yellow flowers, though the blooms are later than most. It is 60cm (2ft) tall. **'Buttercup'**♀ also carries green buds which open into yellow flowers, earlier than most. The plant grows to 1m (3ft) tall.

'Early Buttercup' has large early spikes of bright yellow flowers and is 1m (3ft) tall. **'Fiery Fred'** bears orange-red flowers and is 1.1m (3½ft) tall.

'Green Jade' has bright green late flowers in spikes up to 1.1m (3½ft) tall. **'Ice Queen'** bears cream flowers tinged with green. It is also 1.1m (3½ft) tall. **'Jenny Bloom'** bears late cream and coral-pink flowers and grows up to 1m (3ft) in height. **'Little Maid'**♀ has ivory blooms tipped with soft yellow. Smaller than most, it reaches a height of up to 55cm (22in) tall.

'Percy's Pride' has green flowers suffused with yellow and is up to 80cm (2ft 8in) tall. **'Royal Standard'**♀ has bright yellow and vermilion flowers and is 1m (3ft) tall. **'Samuel's Sensation'**♀ is a striking plant with long spikes of late yellow flowers changing to red at the tips. It grows to 1.5m (5ft) tall. **'Shining Sceptre'** has bright yellow spikes of flowers and grows to 1.1m (3½ft) tall. **'Sunningdale Yellow'**♀ bears yellow flowers over a long period, and grows to 75cm (2½ft) tall.

'Toffee Nosed'♀ bears cream flowers tipped with brown and is 1m (3ft) tall. **'Yellow Hammer'** has flowers of a very pure yellow and is up to 60cm (2ft) tall.

CULTIVATION Plant in early autumn or spring in a well-drained but not too rich soil and in a sunny situation.

PROPAGATION Divide in autumn or sow seed of species in late winter under glass and grow in a coldframe until large enough to plant out the following spring.

PESTS AND DISEASES The flowers and the leaves can be mottled and distorted by thrips, especially in hot, dry summers.

Knotweed see *Persicaria*
Kochia see *Bassia*

Koelreuteria

Sapindaceae

Deciduous flowering trees or shrubs are grown for their elegant foliage and golden summer flowers. They are sun-loving plants and only one species is readily available in Britain. Native to China and Taiwan.

RECOMMENDED SPECIES

K. paniculata♀ (golden rain tree, pride of India) Large pinnate leaves emerge in spring flushed with red, are mid green in summer and turn red and yellow in autumn with a more spectacular display if grown in poor, dryish soil. The graceful leaves are up to 45cm (18in) long with 9-15 toothed leaflets. The tiny, golden yellow flowers, 1.5cm (½in) across, are borne in mid to late summer in airy, erect sprays up to 30cm (1ft) long. Flowers only appear in great numbers in a hot, dry summer and may be followed in late autumn by trailing, red-flushed, green seedpods up to 5cm (2in)

▲ *Koelreuteria paniculata*

long. A medium-sized upright tree, it has a spreading crown and is hardy. It is native to China. HEIGHT & SPREAD 4x2m (13x6½ft) after 20 years, ultimately 10m (33ft) tall.
CULTIVATION Plant from mid autumn to mid spring in any well-drained soil in a sunny site; the trees flower most profusely during hot, dry summers.
PROPAGATION Seed is the commonest form of propagation, sown under glass in autumn, but seed is rarely set in this country. Root cuttings taken in autumn can be successful but are more difficult.
PRUNING None is required, but if dead wood needs cutting out, this should be done in winter.
PESTS AND DISEASES Usually trouble free but coral spot can be a problem at times. This needs to be cut out and the diseased wood burnt.

Kohleria

Gesneriaceae

Tubular foxglove-like flowers and hairy foliage make these tender herbaceous perennials from Central America unusual and worthwhile houseplants. They are compact enough for windowsills, or shelves if there is enough light.

They combine well with African violets, streptocarpus, achimenes and the smaller begonias. Kohlerias die down in winter to small, scaly tubers.

RECOMMENDED SPECIES
K. amabilis (syn. *Isoloma amabilis*) This summer-flowering species bears deep pink, broadly tubular flowers, 2.5cm (1in) long, flaring out to display lobes that are covered in red speckles. The oval leaves are up to 10cm (4in) long, dark green with purple and silvery markings. There are various hybrids with red, yellow or white flowers. HEIGHT 60cm (2ft).
CULTIVATION Plant in a standard houseplant compost in spring and keep reasonably humid, at a minimum temperature of 21°C (70°F) in summer and 10°C (50°F) in winter. Position in good indirect light, or limited direct sun. Water sparingly during active growth when the compost starts to dry out; when top growth dies down, keep almost dry until spring. Feed every 2 weeks in summer. Pot on annually in spring.
PROPAGATION Divide the tubers when repotting in spring. Alternatively, take softwood cuttings in spring or summer.
PESTS AND DISEASES Aphids may be a problem.

Kolkwitzia

Beauty bush
Caprifoliaceae

Kolkwitzia amabilis

Abundant pink flowers festoon the long, arching branches of this hardy deciduous shrub in late spring and early summer.

Kolkwitzias can grow as wide as they are tall and so need to be positioned carefully. A member of the honeysuckle family, there is only one species in the genus.
Kolkwitzia amabilis A profusion of small flowers, up to 2cm (¾in) long, appear in dense clusters along the branches of this hardy rounded shrub in early summer. The flowers resemble small foxgloves with a wide, 5-lobed mouth, and are a delicate pink with an orange speckled throat. The small dark green leaves, up to 7.5cm (3in) long, are ovate and pointed. Native to W China. HEIGHT & SPREAD 1x1m (3x3ft) after 5 years, ultimately 3m (10ft) tall.

▲ *Kolkwitzia amabilis*

▲ *Kolkwitzia amabilis* 'Pink Cloud'

'Pink Cloud'♀ blooms more reliably than the species. It makes a smaller plant, growing to 80cm (32in) in height and spread after 5 years, ultimately reaching 2m (6½ft) in height, and often the same in breadth.
CULTIVATION Kolkwitzias grow well on any soil but do best in sunny positions.
PROPAGATION Take semi-ripe cuttings in early to mid summer. Alternatively, plant the freely produced rooted suckers at any time, though spring is ideal.
PRUNING None is normally required unless it is to thin out the number of stems.
PESTS AND DISEASES Usually trouble free.

+Laburnocytisus

Leguminosae

+ Laburnocytisus 'Adamii'

Two different coloured flowers bloom at the same time on this hardy deciduous tree, a graft hybrid between *Laburnum anagyroides* and *Cytisus purpureus*. There is only one plant in the genus.

***+Laburnocytisus* 'Adamii'** Flowers in long sprays, up to 18cm (7in), appear in late spring or early summer. A mixture of yellow laburnum and pink-purple cytisus flowers are borne, normally appearing on different branches. Small and upright when young, this tree becomes more rounded and broad in old age. HEIGHT & SPREAD 1.5m×75cm (5×2½ft) after 5 years, ultimately 7m (23ft) tall.

▲ + *Laburnocytisus* 'Adamii'

CULTIVATION Plant in any well-drained, good garden soil, choosing a position in full sun or partial shade.

PROPAGATION New plants can be raised only by grafting laburnum onto cytisus.

PRUNING None is normally required but dead wood should be removed.

PESTS AND DISEASES Usually trouble free.

Laburnum

Leguminosae

Laburnum x watereri 'Vossii'

Long, pendulous clusters of golden yellow flowers cover these fast-growing, hardy deciduous trees. Excellent specimen trees, the long, trailing flowers are also shown to great advantage when grown over arches and pergolas. Plants grown from seed will take five to eight years to flower but most purchased plants will flower immediately. The small leaves are made up of three leaflets, the airy foliage casting dappled shade. All parts of the tree are poisonous but the small seeds in flattened pods, up to 5cm (2in) long, are particularly so.

RECOMMENDED SPECIES AND VARIETIES

***L. alpinum* 'Pendulum'** Slightly fragrant, golden yellow flowers appear in clusters, about 25cm (10in) long, in early summer. The shiny green leaves are paler beneath. A domed tree with stiff, pendulous branches. HEIGHT & SPREAD 1m×60cm (3×2ft) after 5 years, ultimately 3m (10ft) tall.

▼ *Laburnum alpinum* 'Pendulum'

***L. × watereri* 'Vossii'** ♀ Profuse trailing clusters, up to 38cm (15in) long, of golden yellow flowers appear in late spring or early summer. The individual flowers are 2cm (¾in) long. Leaves are a glossy pale green. Seed is sparsely produced. A small upright tree when young, it becomes more rounded. HEIGHT & SPREAD 1.5×1m (5×3ft) after 5 years, ultimately 6m (20ft) tall.

CULTIVATION Plant in any well-drained soil

▲ *Laburnum* × *watereri* 'Vossii'

in full sun. Young trees may need staking.

PROPAGATION Raise from seed. This gives some variation in the amount of flowers, so it is better to buy a grafted plant.

PRUNING None is normally required but if any weak or misplaced branches need to be cut out this should be done in late summer.

PESTS AND DISEASES Usually trouble free.

Lacebark see *Hoheria*
Lactuca see *Cicerbita*
Lady's mantle see *Alchemilla*
Lady's smock see *Cardamine pratensis*
Laelia see ORCHIDS p.466
Lagurus see GRASSES p.301
Lamb's ears see *Stachys byzantina*
Lamb's tongue see *Stachys byzantina*
Lamiastrum see *Lamium*

Lamium

Dead nettle

Labiatae

Easy-to-grow ground-cover plants, some with mottled or tinted foliage, make lamium a popular garden choice. This genus also includes plants for the herbaceous border and the alpine *Lamium armenum* which is normally grown under glass but will survive outdoors in a raised bed if protected from winter wet.

Unless stated otherwise, the recommended plants are hardy herbaceous perennials with ovate leaves and early summer flowers, sometimes with intermittent flowers later. They thrive on alkaline to neutral soil and may become invasive. Dead nettles will grow in full sun but most plants prefer some shade. Some species do not like excessively damp soil in winter.

RECOMMENDED SPECIES AND VARIETIES

L. armenum Pale pink to white flowers, about 5cm (2in) long, with prominent, hairy, hood-like upper lips, appear in whorls in late spring and early summer. This mat-forming, evergreen perennial has pairs of diamond-shaped to oval, rather coarsely toothed, leaves up to 2.5cm (1in) long. It is short lived. HEIGHT & SPREAD 10×20cm (4×8in).

L. galeobdolon (syn. *Galeobdolon luteum, Lamiastrum galeobdolon)* (yellow archangel) Tubular, yellow flowers often flecked with brown, up to 2cm (¾in) long, appear in mid summer on this evergreen. The leaves, 6cm (2½in) long, have heart-shaped bases. HEIGHT & SPREAD 60cm×1m (2×3ft).

▲ *Lamium galeobdolon* 'Florentinum'

'Florentinum' has silver-splashed leaves that turn purple in winter. **'Hermann's Pride'** has narrow, toothed leaves streaked with silver, while **'Silberteppich'** ('Silver Carpet'), which tends to form clumps, is heavily spotted with silver.

L. garganicum ssp. ***garganicum*** Pink tubular flowers, up to 3cm (1¼in) long, appear above mats of leaves, each 7cm (2¾in) long. HEIGHT & SPREAD 45×80cm (18×32in).

L. maculatum A central white stripe usually runs along the leaves which are up to 5cm (2in) long. The tubular flowers are red, purple or occasionally white, about 2cm (¾in) long. HEIGHT & SPREAD 40cm×1m (16in×3ft).

The flowers of var. ***album*** are white. The leaves of **'Aureum'** are gold with white centres, while **'Beacon Silver'** is a dwarf plant with entirely silver leaves. **'Canon's Gold'** has golden leaves and **'Chequers'** has broad leaves with thin, silver stripes. **'Pink Pewter'** has leaves tinted with silver and rich, pink flowers, while ssp. ***roseum*** (syn. 'Shell Pink') has pink flowers. **'White Nancy'**♀ has silver leaves with green edges and white flowers.

L. orvala The red or purple tubular flowers are 4cm (1½in) long. The toothed leaves are up to 15cm (6in) long. A compact plant. HEIGHT & SPREAD 1m×60cm (3×2ft).

▼ *Lamium orvala*

CULTIVATION Plant from autumn to spring in any well-drained soil in sun or partial shade. Cut back after flowering to encourage good foliage growth. Plant *L. armenum* in a gritty compost in a cold greenhouse or in a scree or raised bed outside. Provide plenty of ventilation and ample water during the growing season, but restrict watering in winter.

PROPAGATION Divide plants between autumn and spring or take cuttings of non-flowering shoots in summer. Alternatively, sow the seed of species in a coldframe during winter.

PESTS AND DISEASES Usually trouble free.

Lampranthus

Aizoaceae

Lampranthus spectabilis

These tender succulents carry a succession of vivid daisy-like flowers in summer, that open in full sun but close on dull days. Native to South Africa and Australia, these plants are best grown under glass in Britain.

RECOMMENDED SPECIES AND VARIETIES

L. aurantiacus Bright orange flowers up to 5cm (2in) across appear in summer. Dark green cylindrical leaves, up to 2.5cm (1in) long, densely clothe the ground-hugging stems. HEIGHT & SPREAD 30×60cm (1×2ft).

L. blandus Pink flowers up to 6cm (2½in) across appear in summer. The light green leaves are triangular in cross-section and grow to 4cm (1½in) in length. HEIGHT & SPREAD 45×45cm (1½×1½ft).

L. spectabilis Magenta blooms, 7.5cm (3in) across with yellow centres, appear in summer. Completely yellow blooms may appear. The mid green leaves are triangular in cross-section and up to 2.5cm (1in) long. HEIGHT & SPREAD 30×45cm (1×1½ft).

▼ *Lampranthus aurantiacus*

▲ *Lampranthus blandus*

'Tresco Red' has fiery red flowers.

CULTIVATION Grow in pots of well-drained soil-based compost. Place in full sun in a greenhouse or conservatory or on a windowsill and provide a winter minimum of 5°C (41°F). Pots can be moved outside to a sheltered sunny spot in summer.

PROPAGATION Take stem cuttings in spring or late summer or sow seed in a greenhouse or coldframe in spring.

PESTS AND DISEASES Usually trouble free.

Lantana

Shrub verbena

Verbenaceae

Lantana montevidensis

These evergreen shrubs from S America are grown for their colourful flowers. Masses of flowerheads in a range of bright colours appear throughout summer. All the plants are tender but can be grown in a greenhouse or conservatory. They also make a valuable addition to summer bedding schemes and look decorative in tubs and planters for summer display. Lantanas are particularly attractive to butterflies.

▲ *Lantana camara*

RECOMMENDED SPECIES AND VARIETIES
L. camara Rounded heads, up to 7.5cm (3in) across, of tiny flowers are produced in summer. The yellow, orange or red flowers often have darker contrasting centres. Blooms of different colours often appear on the same plant. The oval, mid green leaves, up to 12.5cm (5in) long, are coarsely textured and wrinkled and often have a pungent aroma. This shrub has more or less spiny stems. HEIGHT & SPREAD 2×2m (6½×6½ft).

'Brasier' has bright red flowers. **'Drap d'or'** is golden yellow. **'Feston Rose'** has deep pink blooms. The flowers of **'Snow White'** are creamy white.

1

L. montevidensis Dense clusters, up to 10cm (4in) across, of small, deep pinkish purple flowers are freely produced in summer. The oval or lance-shaped mid green leaves, up to 4cm (1½in) long, have coarsely toothed margins. This shrub has a somewhat sprawling habit. HEIGHT & SPREAD 60cm×1m (2×3ft).

▼ *Lantana montevidensis*

CULTIVATION Grow in pots of free-draining soil-based compost and keep at a minimum temperature of 5°C (41°F). Water freely during summer and sparingly at other times. Use a high-potash feed in late spring and again in mid summer. Pinch back straggling shoots regularly during the growing season to keep the shrubs neat. Trim back any dead or weak shoots in spring. Overwinter outdoor specimens in a cool, light, frost-free place.
PROPAGATION Take semi-ripe cuttings in summer and root under glass or sow seed in a propagator during spring.
PESTS AND DISEASES Red spider mite and whitefly may attack plants under glass.

Lantern tree see *Crinodendron*

Lapageria
Philesiaceae

Lapageria rosea

This evergreen twining climber, grown for its large, waxy flowers, is the only species in this genus. It dislikes both cold and heat and is best grown in a cool conservatory or greenhouse. It can be grown as a freestanding specimen in a pot if given some support to climb on. These plants can then be moved into the house in autumn for the flowering season.
***Lapageria rosea*♀** Dark red, thick, waxy flowers, up to 7cm (2¾in) long, appear in autumn and early winter. The flowers are bell-shaped and hang gracefully from wiry, twining stems. The arrow-shaped leaves are up to 15cm (6in) long, dark green and glossy. Pink berries sometimes follow the flowers. Native to Chile. HEIGHT & SPREAD 3×3m (10×10ft) after 5 years, ultimately 6m (20ft) tall.
CULTIVATION Grow in pots of lime-free compost in a cool conservatory or greenhouse. Place in a cool position with soft indirect light and good ventilation. Do not allow plants to dry out but do not overwater; they like soft water. Feed fortnightly during the growing season. Large pots, up to 30cm (12in) across, are needed for a mature plant. Train plants up wooden or plastic trellis as wire can scorch the stems.
PROPAGATION Sow seed under glass in autumn after soaking in water for 2 days or take semi-ripe cuttings in early summer. Layering is the most reliable method of propagation, although plants raised this way take 2 years to root.
PESTS AND DISEASES Usually trouble free but aphids, slugs and snails can attack the young growth.

Lapeirousia see *Anomatheca*
Larch, Chinese golden see *Pseudolarix*

Larix
Larch
Pinaceae

Larix decidua

Long-lasting pale green or blue-green foliage with stunning autumn tints and pretty pink, red or purple thimble-shaped flowers grace these statuesque coniferous trees. Larches are conical when young, maturing into fine broad trees with slightly flattened crowns and weeping young shoots. They are unusual in being deciduous when most conifers are evergreen. They make very hardy specimen trees, but are extremely fast-growing and may reach a height of 40m (130ft) in 70 years.

The soft, flat, needle-like leaves, 4cm (1½in) long, turn yellow to gold or orange in autumn and remain on the tree until early winter, even after the first frosts. Oval, scaly cones, 2.5-4cm (1-1½in) long, develop in spring and last until the following winter.

RECOMMENDED SPECIES AND VARIETIES
***L. decidua*♀** (European larch) Pale green needles are borne singly on new growing tips, but on older twigs and branches they are arranged in rosettes up to 6cm (2½in) across. The flowers are brilliant red, turning purple later. This larch has wide-spreading roots and branches. It has a conical crown at first that broadens with age. Native to the mountains of N Europe. HEIGHT & SPREAD 15×4m (50×13ft) after 20 years, ultimately 40m (130ft).

▲ *Larix decidua*

L. kaempferi♀ (Japanese larch) The needles, arranged in rosettes up to 7cm (2¾in) across, are grey-green. The flowers are pink, occasionally pale lime green, and the shoots are orange-red. Native to Japan. HEIGHT & SPREAD 12x3.5m (40x12ft) after 20 years, ultimately 30m (100ft).

A shrubby bush, **'Blue Dwarf'** is slow-growing, reaching a height of 1m (3ft) and a spread of 1.5m (5ft) after 20 years. It has blue-green leaves. **'Pendula'** is a slender, columnar tree with very pendulous branches. It has fine orange and yellow autumn tints and beautiful deep red flowers.

CULTIVATION Plant in late autumn or early spring in well-drained soil in a sunny position. Larches do not grow well in wet or alkaline soils but will grow happily on most other soils.

PROPAGATION Sow seed from late winter to mid spring. Raise cultivars by grafting.

PRUNING Remove dead branches in autumn. On larger specimens the crown can be lifted by pruning the lower branches back to the trunk.

PESTS AND DISEASES Larches are prone to attack by woolly aphid and honey fungus. European larches are particularly susceptible to stem canker.

Larkspur see *Consolida*

Lathyrus

Leguminosae

Lathyrus odoratus

Lathyrus bring a mass of delicate colour to the garden all summer long and sometimes in spring or early autumn as well. Most are climbing plants that cling with twining leaf tendrils. They look splendid covering a wigwam of sticks in a border or a wall or fence, or when growing up through an established shrub. The flowers are excellent for cutting. There are bushy, non-climbing, self-supporting species suitable for beds and mixed borders, including dwarf varieties of the sweet pea, *Lathyrus odoratus*, that can be successfully grown in containers.

The genus includes annuals and herbaceous perennials. Almost all the cultivated lathyrus species are hardy and easy to grow. Only poorly drained soils and heavily shaded sites pose problems.

Flowers have the characteristic pea-flower shape, with one upstanding petal (the standard), two side petals (the wings) and two lower petals fused together to make a keel. They are carried on stalks from the leaf axils. *L. nervosus* and *L. odoratus* are the highly scented species.

Every leaf is made up of one or more pairs of leaflets. Leaves and stems are generally mid green and, occasionally, hairy. The leaves of climbers each have a branched tendril. Leaflets mostly range between 4cm (1½in) and 10cm (4in) in length.

RECOMMENDED SPECIES AND VARIETIES

The species and varieties described here are divided into 2 groups:

(1) Annual species and varieties.

(2) Perennial species and varieties.

ANNUAL SPECIES AND VARIETIES

L. odoratus♀ (sweet pea) This climber has fragrant flowers, pink, white or purple, up to 4cm (1½in) across, arranged in clusters of 1-3 flowers, amid single pairs of ovate leaflets. Flowers bloom between early and late summer. Native to Italy and Crete. HEIGHT & SPREAD 2m x 30cm (6½x1ft).

▲ *Lathyrus odoratus*

There are 3 principal groups of *L. odoratus* cultivars – tall, intermediate and dwarf varieties. They have standard petals with wavy or frilled edges and often have little scent to speak of.

Tall varieties of *L. odoratus* grow to heights of 1.8-3m (6-10ft) and bear flowers up to 5cm (2in) across. Of these, cultivars of the **Spencer Type**, with 4-5 blooms on each long flower stalk, are by far the most popular. They include: **'Beaujolais'** and **'Midnight'**, both with maroon flowers; **'Mrs Bernard Jones'**, with rose-pink flowers on a white ground; **'Noel Sutton'**, with blue flowers; **'Royal Wedding'**, with white flowers; **'Southbourne'**, with pink flowers on a white ground; **'White Leamington'**, with white flowers; **'Winston Churchill'**, with crimson flowers; **'W.J. Unwin'**, with flowers orange pink. All but the last 2 are highly fragrant.

Other tall varieties have a larger number of blooms carried on each flowering stalk. The **Early Multiflora Gigantea Type**, **Galaxy Type** and **Royal Type**, with up to 8 flowers a stalk, are usually only available in a mixture of colours – white, cream and all shades of pink, red and blue. The Early Multiflora Gigantea and Galaxy types come into flower 7-10 days earlier than the Spencer varieties.

Intermediate varieties reach a height of 60cm-1m (2-3ft) and spread to 15-20cm (6-8in). They include **'Continental'** and **'Jet Set'**, both 1m (3ft) tall and both needing support. **'Snoopea'** and **'Supersnoop'**, 60-75cm (2-2½ft) tall, are erect plants with no tendrils and do not need support. 'Supersnoop' flowers slightly earlier than 'Snoopea'. Seed of all 4 is available only in mixed colours.

▲ *Lathyrus odoratus* 'Jet Set'

Dwarf varieties are 15-40cm (6-16in) tall and spread to 15cm (6in). They are upright, self-supporting plants that do not climb. They look good if allowed to flow freely over the edges of containers or raised beds. Those included here are only generally available in mixed colours. **'Bijou'** is up to 40cm (16in) tall. **'Cupid'**, 15cm (6in) tall and also well-scented, has a spreading habit. **'Patio'** is 30cm (12in) tall and particularly well-scented.

L. sativus (chickling pea) A climber with blue, white, or white-flushed blue flowers, 2cm (¾in) wide, carried singly on short stalks. Each leaf has 1-2 pairs of long, narrow leaflets. Native to Europe. HEIGHT & SPREAD 1m x 20cm (3ft x 8in).

PERENNIAL SPECIES AND VARIETIES

L. aureus hort. Flowers are golden yellow at first, later turning dark amber. Each 2cm (¾in) wide, they are borne 12 or more to a stalk at the shoot tips in late spring and early summer. The yellowish green leaves each have 3-6 pairs of ovate leaflets. A bushy plant, forming a dense clump that does not need support. Native to the Balkans. HEIGHT & SPREAD 60x30cm (2x1ft).

L. grandiflorus (everlasting pea) This vigorous, spreading climber has flowers, 3cm (1¼in) across, with deep blue standards and purple wing petals. There are 2-3 blooms on each flowering stalk. Leaves have single pairs of ovate, blue-green leaflets. The plant is hairy. Native to Italy and S Balkans. HEIGHT & SPREAD 1.8 x 1 m (6 x 3 ft).

L. latifolius ♀ (perennial pea) As many as 15 purple flowers, up to 3cm (1¼in) across, are carried closely on each stalk from early summer to early autumn. This rampant climber also makes good ground cover with or without support. Each leaf has a single pair of narrowly ovate, dull green leaflets. Native to central and S Europe. HEIGHT & SPREAD 3 x 1 m (10 x 3 ft).

▲ *Lathyrus latifolius*

▲ *Lathyrus latifolius* 'Albus'

▲ *Lathyrus latifolius* 'Red Pearl'

The flowers of **'Albus'** are white to creamy white, sometimes with a hint of green. **'Red Pearl'** has flowers of a deep, vivid red. **'Rosa Perle'** ('Pink Pearl') bears pink flowers that are particularly long-

▲ *Lathyrus latifolius* 'White Pearl'

lasting. **'White Pearl'** ♀ (syn. 'Weisse Perle') has pure white flowers.

L. nervosus (Lord Anson's blue pea) Sweetly scented, blue flowers, 2cm (¾in) across, are borne on long stalks, each with 3-7 blooms, on a climber with grey-green leaves made up of single pairs of oval leaflets. It can be grown as an annual, since if seed is sown in early spring it will flower in summer. Native to S America. HEIGHT & SPREAD 1.5 x 1 m (5 x 3 ft).

L. rotundifolius (Persian everlasting pea) Deep pink flowers, 2cm (¾in) across, bloom in crowded terminal clusters on 20cm (8in) stalks in early summer. This vigorous climber, has single pairs of rounded, dark green leaflets. Native to E Europe and W Asia. HEIGHT & SPREAD 1 x 1 m (3 x 3 ft).

L vernus ♀ (spring vetch) Purple flowers, fading to blue, 1.5cm (½in) across, are freely produced in 5cm (2in) long clusters in mid and late spring. This bushy, erect-stemmed plant is not a climber. Leaves consist of 2-4 pairs of ovate leaflets. The plant dies back in summer once flowering has ended. Native to Europe. HEIGHT & SPREAD 40 x 30cm (16 x 12in).

'Alboroseus', less vigorous, has flowers that are pink and white.

▲ *Lathyrus vernus* 'Alboroseus'

CULTIVATION Plant annuals in any well-drained, but moisture-retentive, soil. Avoid heavily shaded sites. If grown on south-facing walls and fences, blooming will come to an early end. Provide some support for

▲ *Lathyrus vernus*

climbers and tie in shoots as necessary. Encourage vigorous growth by removing the growing tip of the first shoot beyond the third pair of leaves from the bottom when about 15cm (6in) long. Deadhead frequently to encourage continuous flowering through summer. Water plants in dry weather. Plant perennials in any good garden soil. *L. grandiflorus*, *L. latifolius* and *L. vernus* thrive in dappled shade or in places that are in shadow through part of the day. *L. rotundifolius* does best in shady conditions. Provide some support for climbers or allow a plant to ramble through hedges or shrubs. Deadhead to prolong flower display. Watering is not normally needed, except to establish newly planted specimens. Cut stems down to ground level in autumn. Mulch *L. nervosus* in mid autumn and protect from winter rain with a pane of glass or a cloche.

PROPAGATION Sow the seed of annuals where the plants are to grow, in early or mid spring for early summer flowering. For flowering 3 weeks earlier, sow seed in early spring in a coldframe or unheated greenhouse or in late winter in a warm greenhouse. For an earlier flowering still – of 1½-2 weeks – and the highest quality blooms, sow seed in mid autumn in a coldframe or unheated greenhouse.

Soak the seed of dwarf *L. odoratus* varieties and any other varieties with hard-coated seed, in water overnight before sowing. Nick the coat of any seeds that have not swollen.

Sow the seed of perennials in early spring in pots or directly in the flowering site. Alternatively, divide in early spring, taking particular care with climbing species, as they dislike disturbance.

PESTS AND DISEASES Mice eat seed and birds, slugs and snails eat seedlings. Aphids and thrips can be troublesome. Fungal root rot and foot rots sometimes attack young plants, especially in wet conditions.

Laurel, bay see *Laurus nobilis*
Laurel, mountain see *Kalmia latifolia*
Laurel, Portugal see *Prunus lusitanica*
Laurel, sheep see *Kalmia angustifolia*
Laurel, spotted see *Aucuba japonica*

1

Laurentia

Campanulaceae

Starry, fragrant flowers cover the fine foliage of *Laurentia axillaris* from early summer until early autumn. They look particularly attractive when allowed to cascade over the edge of a hanging basket or other container, outdoors or in a conservatory or greenhouse. The plant also does well in garden beds and borders. It is a half-hardy herbaceous perennial, almost always grown as an annual. The sap of these plants is an eye-irritant.

RECOMMENDED SPECIES AND VARIETIES
L. axillaris (syn. *Isotoma axillaris, Solenopsis axillaris*) Long-tubed flowers, lavender blue, about 2.5cm (1in) across, with 5 narrow petal lobes, are borne singly on slender stems. This many-branched, dome-shaped plant has narrow dark green leaves, as long as 10cm (4in), with slender teeth-like lobes. Native to Australia. HEIGHT & SPREAD 30×25cm (12×10in).

▲ *Laurentia axillaris.*

The flowers of **'Blue Stars'** are sky blue, and **'Shooting Stars'** has white flowers. Lilac-pink flowers are available in colour mixtures.

CULTIVATION Plant in full sun or in a position that is in shade for part of the day only. There are no special soil requirements. Plant out in spring, after the danger of frost has passed.

PROPAGATION Sow seed in a propagator or equivalent at a temperature of 18-20°C (64-68°F). If seed is sown in mid winter, flowering will begin in early summer. Sow seed in early autumn and overwinter in a cool greenhouse, for flowers from late spring onwards. Alternatively, take semi-ripe stem cuttings in late summer and overwinter in a cool greenhouse, for flowers from late spring.

PESTS AND DISEASES Usually trouble free.

Laurus

Bay

Lauraceae

Laurus nobilis

This beautiful shrub is grown for its aromatic, dark evergreen leaves. The bay is generally too tender to attain tree size in much of Britain, and damage from frost and winter wind is a problem. Place in sheltered spots, against a wall or beside other shrubs and sturdy plants. Bays are grown as hedging in areas where the climate is very mild. The leaves are used in cooking.

RECOMMENDED SPECIES AND VARIETIES
L. nobilis♀ (bay laurel, bay tree, sweet bay) The glossy dark green leaves are lance-shaped, with wavy edges. They are up to 10cm (4in) long and 4cm (1½in) wide, and produced alternately. Small yellow-green flowers with inconspicuous petals and prominent pale yellow stamens appear from mid spring to early summer. The flowers are carried in rounded clusters up to 2cm (¾in) wide, each holding 3-5 blooms. Plants are male or female – the latter bears 1.5cm (½in) long shiny black berries. If left unpruned, the plant develops a conical shape. It is moderately frost hardy. This species is often grown in a tub, and kept outdoors in summer, and under glass, in cool, light, well-ventilated conditions, in winter. Native to the Mediterranean. HEIGHT & SPREAD 2.4×1.2m (8×4ft) after 10 years, ultimately 6m (20ft) tall.

The narrow leaves of f. ***angustifolia*** resemble those of some willow trees, and so this form of the species is often called the willow-leaved bay. **'Aurea'**♀ has golden

▲ *Laurus nobilis* 'Aurea'

yellow leaves that are at their best in late winter and early spring.

CULTIVATION Plant preferably in fertile soil in full sun, although bays can stand poorer soils and shade. Plant out in late spring, when all danger of frost has passed.

PROPAGATION Take semi-ripe cuttings in early or mid summer. Sow the seed of species in autumn.

PRUNING Not essential but plants can be clipped to size or shape in summer.

PESTS AND DISEASES Usually trouble free.

Laurustinus see *Viburnum tinus*

Lavandula

Lavender

Labiatae

Lavandula angustifolia

An ornamental appearance complements the delightfully fragrant flowers, in bloom from summer to autumn, and aromatic foliage of these evergreen shrubs and sub-shrubs. As hedges or specimens they create soft misty outlines billowing over paths and lawn edges. They require well-drained, preferably limy, soil, flowering best in poor, stony but sunny sites and are successful seaside plants. The plants recommended here are hardy or half-hardy. Half-hardy lavenders need to be planted in a warm sheltered site, especially in areas prone to frost. They may also be grown in pots outside in summer and overwintered in a frost-free greenhouse. The flowers may be dried for use in sachets and potpourris. Plants grow leggy with age unless pruned quite severely and need to be replaced every six to eight years, so ultimate heights of the recommended species and varieties have been omitted. The plants are native to the Mediterranean and S Europe.

RECOMMENDED SPECIES AND VARIETIES
L. angustifolia♀ (syn. *L. officinalis, L. spica*) (old English lavender) Pale grey-blue, fragrant flower spikes, up to 6cm (2½in) long, appear from late spring to late summer. The

▼ *Lavandula angustifolia* 'Alba'

1

linear, oblong leaves, up to 4cm (1½in) long, are greyish turning greener in mid to late summer. This plant is hardy. HEIGHT & SPREAD 60×60cm (2×2ft) after 5 years.

'Alba' has almost white flower spikes, up to 7.5cm (3in) long, on erect stems, 50cm (20in) tall, from mid to late summer. The leaves are grey-green. **'Bowles' Early'** (syn. 'Bowles Grey', 'Bowles Variety') is pale purple and has very fresh green foliage that becomes greyish. It reaches up to 45cm (18in) in spread. **'Folgate'** has rather open

▲ *Lavandula angustifolia* 'Folgate'

▲ *Lavandula angustifolia* 'Hidcote'

purple-blue flower spikes, up to 10cm (4in) long, which bloom in mid summer above narrow grey-green leaves. **'Hidcote'**♀ (syn. *L.* 'Hidcote Blue') displays a striking contrast in early to mid summer, when flower spikes of deepest blue, up to 5cm (2in) long, bloom above the silvery foliage. It reaches a height and spread of 45cm (1½ft). **'Hidcote Pink'** has pale lilac pink flowers and silvery foliage. It reaches the same height and spread as 'Hidcote'. **'Imperial Gem'** produces dark purple flowers. Its leaves are greyish. It reaches a height and spread of 45cm (1½ft). **'Loddon Blue'** has blue-purple flowers in mid summer. The foliage is grey-green. This plant reaches up to 45cm (1½ft) in height and spread. **'Loddon Pink'** (syn. *L.* 'Loddon Pink') carries soft pink flowers in mid summer on a compact shrub with narrow grey-green leaves. It reaches a height and spread of 45cm (1½ft). **'Munstead'** bears short open spikes of lilac blue flowers from mid to late summer and narrowly oblong, greyish green leaves. **'Nana Alba'** has dense spikes of white flowers, up to 2.5cm (1in) long, in mid summer and grey-green leaves. It reaches 23cm (9in) in height and spread. **'Princess Blue'** bears pale lavender-blue flower spikes, up to 5cm (2in) long, from early to late summer on a compact shrub. It has grey-green leaves and reaches a height of 50cm (20in) and spread of 45cm (1½ft). **'Rosea'** (syn. *L.* 'Jean Davis', *L.* 'Rosea') carries dusty pink flowers from early to mid summer on stems up to 75cm (2½ft) tall. **'Royal Purple'** has long heads of mid purple flowers and large green-grey leaves. **'Twickel Purple'**♀ has slender, purple, mid summer flower spikes, up to 10cm (4in) long. The leaves are grey-green. This plant has a rounded habit and reaches a height of 60cm (2ft) and spread of 45cm (1½ft).

***L.* 'Cornard Blue'** see *L.* 'Sawyers'

L. dentata Densely packed spikes, up to 6cm (2½in) long, of soft blue and purple flowers with remarkable lilac bracts at the top are borne in late summer on stems up to 1m (3ft) tall. The deeply toothed leaves are dark green. A half-hardy plant. HEIGHT & SPREAD 45×45cm (1½×1½ft).

The flowers and bracts of var. ***candicans* silver form** are pale purple and the leaves, up to 4cm (1½in) long, are covered with white hairs. It reaches a height and spread of 60cm (2ft).

***L.* 'Hidcote Blue'** see *L. angustifolia* 'Hidcote'

***L.* x *intermedia* Dutch Group**♀ Soft blue flower spikes, up to 6cm (2½in) long, are carried on stems, up to 75cm (2½ft) tall, from mid summer to early autumn. The plants have grey-green, linear-oblong leaves and a dense habit. They are hardy. HEIGHT & SPREAD 75×75cm (2½×2½ft) after 5 years.

▼ *Lavandula angustifolia* 'Hidcote Pink'

'Grappenhall' has faintly fragrant, small pale purple flowers, on strong stems, up to 1.2m (4ft) tall, from mid to late summer. The grey-green leaves are narrowly oblong. It reaches a height of 50cm (20in) and a spread of 80cm (32in). **'Seal'** has pale lavender, pointed flower spikes, up to 8cm (3¼in) long, from summer to early autumn. It reaches a height and spread of 1m (3ft).

***L.* 'Jean Davis'** see *L. angustifolia* 'Rosea'

L. lanata♀ Fragrant, bright violet flower spikes, up to 7.5cm (3in) long, are borne from mid summer to early autumn on stems up to 60cm (2ft) long, above white, woolly, linear leaves up to 5cm (2in) long. This plant is half-hardy. HEIGHT & SPREAD 75×75cm (2½×2½ft) after 5 years.

***L.* 'Loddon Pink'** see *L. angustifolia* 'Loddon Pink'

L. officinalis see *L. angustifolia*

L. pinnata (syn. *L. pterostoechas* ssp. *pinnata*) Purple flower spikes, up to 9cm (3½in) long, are borne on stems up to 30cm (1ft) long from late spring until the first frost. The finely divided leaves have many leaflets covered in short, grey hairs. This half-hardy plant dies after the first frosts but not before setting seed. The seed can be collected and the plant grown as an annual. HEIGHT & SPREAD 60×60cm (2×2ft) after 5 years.

L. pterostoechas ssp. ***pinnata*** see *L. pinnata*

***L.* 'Rosea'** see *L. angustifolia* 'Rosea'

***L.* 'Sawyers'** (syn. 'Cornard Blue') Pale purple flowers bloom from early to late summer above velvety, pale grey-green foliage. The plant is hardy. HEIGHT & SPREAD 60×60cm (2×2ft) after 5 years.

L. spica see *L. angustifolia*

L. stoechas♀ (French lavender) Dark purple fragrant flowers in dense heads, up to 4cm (1½in) long, bloom from late spring to early summer with a second flowering in early autumn. Rose-purple bracts grow in tufts from the tops and persist after the flowers have faded. The linear leaves, up to 3cm (1¼in) long, are silver-grey. Although hardy, this plant needs sharp drainage to ensure its survival through winter. HEIGHT & SPREAD 45×45cm (1½×1½ft) after 5 years.

The flowers and bracts of f. ***leucantha*** (syn. var. *albiflora*) are white. The dark purple flowers and bright purple bracts of ssp. ***pedunculata***♀ (syn. 'Papillon') are borne on stems up to 15cm (6in) long. Its cultivar, **'James Compton'**, carries deep purple flower spikes and graceful bracts, up to 4cm (1½in) long, above scented grey-tinted divided leaves.

L. viridis Small white flowers are carried from late spring to mid autumn. They are enclosed by bracts, which give the plant an overall effect of lime green. The pale green leaves are lemon-scented. This plant is half-hardy. HEIGHT & SPREAD 60×60cm (2×2ft) after 5 years.

CULTIVATION Plant in spring in any ordinary, well-drained soil in a sunny position. If growing as hedging, plant *L. angustifolia* 45cm (1½ft) apart, *L. a.* 'Hidcote' 30cm (1ft) apart, *L. a.* 'Munstead' 38cm (15in) apart. Remove flower stems as blooms fade.
PROPAGATION Take softwood cuttings in late spring and grow under glass. Take semi-ripe cuttings in late summer. Take ripewood cuttings in early autumn and insert in their flowering positions outdoors. Sow the seed of *L. pinnata* under glass from early to mid spring.
PRUNING Trim lightly in autumn. Cut back straggly plants in mid spring to promote bushy new growth from the base. Clip established hedges to shape in mid spring.
PESTS AND DISEASES Froghopper and leaf spot can be a problem.

Lavatera

Tree mallow
Malvaceae

Lavatera 'Burgundy Wine'

Saucer-shaped, five-petalled flowers in shades of pink and white are borne freely over a long season, from mid summer until the first frosts. These showy annuals, biennials, perennials and semi-evergreen subshrubs are hardy and are easily grown in free-draining soil in any sunny position, sheltered from the wind. Lavateras are rapid growers and new shrubs and perennials will often provide a display of flowers within a season. The heart-shaped to triangular leaves are generally 7.5-10cm (3-4in) long with three to five lobes.

▼ *Lavatera arborea* 'Variegata'

RECOMMENDED SPECIES AND VARIETIES
L. arborea **'Variegata'** A vigorous, large leaved, shrubby plant grown for its mid green leaves heavily marbled with white. The leaves are roughly heart-shaped and up to 20cm (8in) long. The lilac or rose flowers, up to 5cm (2in) across, and any stray green shoots are normally removed, to maintain the variegation. The plant is best grown in a sheltered position. HEIGHT & SPREAD 3×2m (10×6½ft).
L. bicolor see *L. maritima*
L. cachemiriana Deep pink flowers, up to 4cm (1½in) across, with a paler centre are borne in mid to late summer. The mid green leaves are smooth above and downy beneath. A hardy annual or short-lived perennial. Native to Kashmir. HEIGHT & SPREAD 2×1m (6½×3ft).
L. maritima♀ (syn. *L. bicolor*) The white, rose or pink flowers, 2.5cm (1in) across, of

▲ *Lavatera maritima*

this small shrub, are conspicuously marked with purple veins. The leaves are grey-green and downy. This lavatera is best grown in a sheltered well-drained site. Native to the Mediterranean. HEIGHT & SPREAD 1m×30cm (3×1ft).
L. thuringiaca Large pink or reddish pink flowers are borne in profusion on this shrubby perennial from mid summer to late autumn. The grey-green leaves are downy. Native to central and SE Europe. HEIGHT & SPREAD 2×1.5m (6½×5ft).

The cultivar **'Ice Cool'** has pure white flowers. This variety reaches a height of up to 1.5m (5ft).
L. trimestris Large rose-pink flowers, 7.5-10cm (3-4in) across, are borne from mid summer to early autumn on this bushy hardy annual. The glossy leaves are dark green. Native to the Mediterranean. HEIGHT & SPREAD 1m×45cm (3ft×18in).

'Mont Blanc' is a white flowered variety. **'Pink Beauty'** has very pale pink flowers with darker veins. **'Silver Cup'** has silvery pink flowers with darker veins. They reach a height of 60cm (2ft) while **'Loveliness'**, which bears deep rose-pink flowers, grows to 1m (3ft).

OTHER CULTIVARS
There are a variety of cultivated varieties available. Unless otherwise stated, they reach a height and spread of 2m (6½ft) and have grey-green leaves, up to 12.5cm (5in) long.

'Barnsley'♀ has white flowers with a conspicuous red eye fading to delicate pink. **'Bredon Springs'** has pink flowers flushed with mauve. **'Burgundy Wine'** has dark pink flowers with darker veins. **'Candy Floss'** bears pale pink flowers. **'Kew Rose'** has dark pink flowers and purplish stems.

▲ *Lavatera* 'Candy Floss'

▲ *Lavatera* 'Pink Frills'

'Pink Frills' has pale pink, crinkled flowers and reaches a height of 1m (3ft) and a spread of 75cm (2½ft).
CULTIVATION Plant in spring in full sun in well-drained soil, sheltered from wind. Provide some support for shrubby varieties early in the season. Remove faded blooms.
PROPAGATION Take softwood cuttings in late spring or summer Sow the seed of *L. trimestris* in situ mid spring.
PRUNING Shorten excessive growth in autumn and prune hard in spring.
PESTS AND DISEASES Aphids can be a nuisance during spring and summer.

Lavender see *Lavandula*
Leadwort see *Plumbago*
Leeks see p.739

1

Grassy areas for leisure and style

WHETHER PAMPERED SWARD OR HARD-WEARING TURF, A WELL-TREATED LAWN CAN BE THE FOCAL POINT OF ANY GARDEN

A lawn provides a pleasant outdoor living area and is usually the central feature of a garden. Its smooth, close-cropped surface creates a restful atmosphere and forms an attractive contrast to the many textures, colours and shapes of plants in beds and borders.

Most lawns consist of a mixture of grasses, which are available as seed or turf. Fine-leaved *Festuca* (fescue) and *Agrostis* (bent) species make up ornamental lawns, which have lush appearances and stand some use. For lawns in frequent use, hard-wearing utility mixtures are better choices. They comprise coarse-leaved grasses, such as *Lolium perenne* (perennial rye grass), *Cynosurus cristatus* (crested dog's tail) and *Poa* species (meadow grass). Some ornamental mixtures include rye grass and will take a reasonable amount of wear. There are also mixtures that contain slow-growing varieties of grass and require less frequent mowing.

Some low-growing fragrant plants, including *Chamaemelum nobile* 'Treneague' (camomile) or *Thymus serpyllum* (thyme), can be used instead of grass for ornamental lawns.

Generally, a lawn can be made on any well-drained soil in an open sunny position. However, a utility lawn can be created in a shady site if a mixture of meadow grasses and fescues is used.

Steep banks, which are difficult to mow, and areas with waterlogged soil are unsuitable places for lawns and are better planted with other kinds of ground cover (see p. 306). In very small gardens, where the grass can soon become worn through overuse, timber decking, gravel or paving may be better alternatives.

Making a lawn

Seed is cheaper and easier to handle than turf but takes longer to establish. Field-grown turf is usually supplied in 90×30 cm (3×1 ft) pieces and, unless of the best quality, may contain some weeds and unsuitable grasses. Lightweight rolls of seeded turf are more expensive but are easier to lay and composed entirely of lawn grasses.

Mark out and start preparing the lawn site at least two months before sowing seed or laying turf. Use wooden pegs and string to lay out a geometric shape for a formal lawn, and a hosepipe or rope to create an informal shape. Then mark the outline with sand.

Use a glyphosate weedkiller to eradicate perennial weeds. Level the site if necessary, then dig it over, incorporating plenty of bulky organic matter. Leave the soil to settle for several weeks, then break it down with a fork, firm and rake it level. Apply a lawn-site fertiliser ten days before sowing or turfing and rake it in well.

Laying turf

Lay field-grown turf in autumn, winter or early spring, and seeded turf in autumn or early spring. Start laying turf on the side closest to where it is stacked. Do not walk over the prepared ground but work on boards placed over the laid turf.

Lay field-grown turfs in rows, staggering the joints as in a brick wall. Butt the turfs up close together. Lay rolls of seeded turf in strips, as advised by the supplier.

After laying, fill any gaps with fine soil and firm the new lawn with a light garden roller. Do not allow it to dry out or the turfs will shrink. Mark out the site of the lawn again and trim the edges with a half-moon edging tool.

Sowing seed

Sow grass seed in spring or early autumn at a rate of 50 g per m^2 (1½ oz per sq yd) or as specified by the supplier. Rake the site in

▲ Green formality *A geometric lawn surrounded by brick paving is an ordered space amid densely planted borders.*

DESIGNING A LAWN

A lawn that takes up a quarter to a third of the garden provides a good balance between grass and flowerbeds. For a formal effect, use a geometric shape such as a rectangle, hexagon or circle. As angles make a small garden look smaller, use a circle in the centre or a semicircle set into a corner. An informal lawn with a gently curving outline looks attractive in any garden. Use an S shape to make a long, narrow garden appear wider.

Small circular lawn

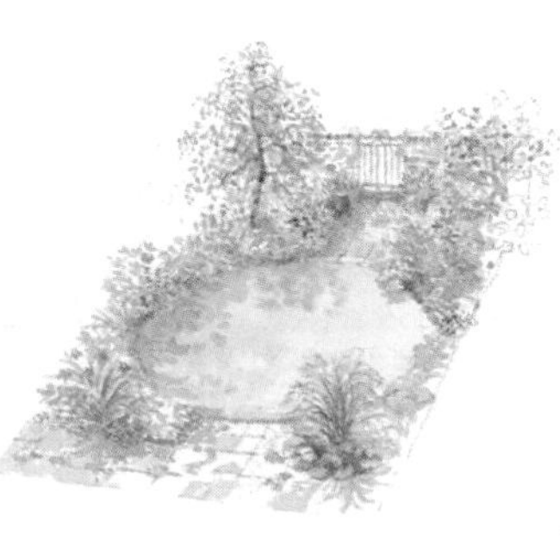

A circular lawn provides the maximum width in a small, formal garden.

Serpentine lawn

A serpentine shape makes a long, narrow space seem wider and unifies different areas.

Informal paths

Flowing grassy paths that create irregular shapes bring informality to a large garden.

straight lines to create shallow drills. For accurate sowing, mark out the site into square metres using string. In each square, scatter half the seed in one direction and the other half at right angles to the first.

Lightly rake soil across the drills, then cover with horticultural fleece to protect the seed from birds and help to retain moisture in the soil. Alternatively, keep birds away by stretching black thread, supported on short sticks, across the site or by laying twiggy branches on it. Do not allow the soil to dry out.

When the seedlings are 5-8 cm (2-3¼ in) high, leave the surface of the soil to dry then lightly roll the lawn. Mow for the first time when the grass is about 8 cm (3¼ in) high, removing only the top 2.5 cm (1 in). After the first mowing, mark out the site again and cut a clean edge with a half-moon edging tool. Thereafter, mow regularly, gradually lowering the mower blades with each cut. Do not mow closer than 1.5 cm (½ in) in the first year.

▶ SPRING HALO *Daffodils in the turf produce a golden halo around an apple tree in spring.*

WHEN TO MOW

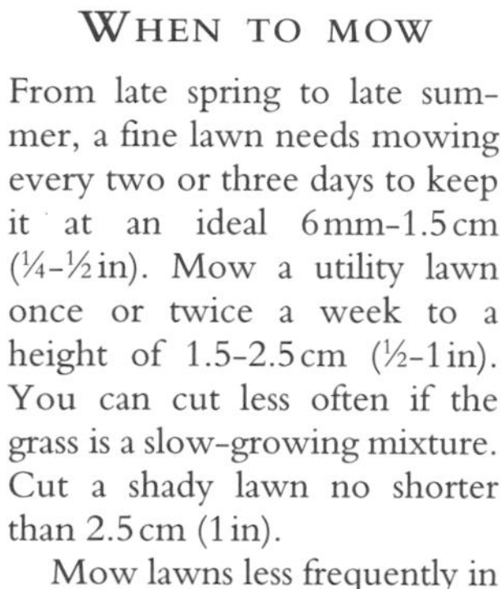

From late spring to late summer, a fine lawn needs mowing every two or three days to keep it at an ideal 6 mm-1.5 cm (¼-½ in). Mow a utility lawn once or twice a week to a height of 1.5-2.5 cm (½-1 in). You can cut less often if the grass is a slow-growing mixture. Cut a shady lawn no shorter than 2.5 cm (1 in).

Mow lawns less frequently in early spring and autumn, when grass grows slowly, and rarely, if at all, in winter. At these times, cut an ornamental lawn to 2 cm (¾ in) and a utility lawn to 2.5-4 cm (1-1½ in).

Mow in straight lines, each slightly overlapping the next. Change the direction each time you mow to correct any faults. Do not mow wet or frozen grass, or during a drought.

▼ BORDER LINES *Irregular shapes in the lawn give an impression of paths leading off into other parts of the garden.*

▲ WHEN TO CUT *Allow the leaves of crocuses and other bulbs to die down before mowing.*

LOOKING AFTER YOUR LAWN

Apply lawn fertiliser in spring, and an autumn lawn feed to toughen up grass for winter. Water the lawn in dry weather. It needs about 20 litres per m^2 (4 gallons per sq yd) a week. Use a sprinkler and place a small vessel beside it to measure the amount of water given. Move the sprinkler when the vessel collects 2 cm (¾ in) of water.

Lawns benefit from regular light raking to remove surface debris, such as leaves, and vigorous raking in early autumn to remove dead grass and moss.

In autumn, aerate the lawn to improve drainage and fertility. Use a garden fork or aerating machine to make holes or slits, a few centimetres deep, in the lawn. Every second year, apply top dressing to the aerated area at 1.8 kg per m^2 (4 lb per sq yd) and work in with a stiff brush or the back of a rake. A good general mix is 6 parts sand, 3 parts loam and 1 part coconut fibre.

Repair any bare or damaged areas during the growing season. Lightly fork over the soil to a depth of about 1.5 cm (½ in) and rake it to a fine tilth. Then sow with the same grass mixture as the rest of the lawn.

WEEDS, PESTS AND DISEASES

Spot-treat any isolated weeds, and apply a lawn weedkiller for large numbers of weeds in spring or early summer. Control moss with lawn moss-killer in spring or early autumn, or use an all-in-one fertiliser, weedkiller and moss-killer.

Patches of yellow or dead grass may signify chafer beetles or leatherjackets. Fungal diseases, such as dollar spot, fusarium wilt and red thread, may also affect lawns (see p. 824).

Lemon see *Citrus limon*
Lemon verbena see *Aloysia triphylla*
Lemonwood
see *Pittosporum eugenioides*

Leontopodium
Edelweiss
Compositae

Leontopodium alpinum

Small, tight clusters of brownish button flowerheads with a collar of large oblong white furry bracts appear from late spring to mid summer. Native to the Alps and mountains of Asia, these hardy herbaceous perennials need alkaline soil and are suited to rock gardens, troughs and raised beds. They are often short-lived but are easily propagated.

RECOMMENDED SPECIES AND VARIETIES

L. alpinum Rounded flowerheads without obvious petals are carried on thin, erect woolly stems and surrounded by broad bracts, 10cm (4in) long, which gradually turn from silvery to grey. The narrow oblong leaves are about 4cm (1½in) long, grey and hairy with a densely woolly underside. HEIGHT & SPREAD 15×15cm (6×6in).

1

▲ *Leontopodium alpinum*

▲ *Leontopodium alpinum* 'Mignon'

The mat-forming **'Mignon'** has deep green leaves with grey undersides and many smaller flowerheads. It reaches 10cm (4in) high and spreads to 30cm (12in).

CULTIVATION Plant in moist but well-drained gritty compost in a sunny position. Cover with glass to protect from excessive winter wet. Divide 'Mignon' regularly to produce a vigorous, free-flowering plant.

PROPAGATION Divide in early spring or just after flowering. Sow seed as soon as it is ripe in summer, in pots in a coldframe.

PESTS AND DISEASES Slugs may attack young plants.

Leopard's bane see *Doronicum*

Leptospermum
Tea tree
Myrtaceae

Leptospermum scoparium

Aromatic leaves and a profusion of small, rose-like flowers adorn these evergreen shrubs from late spring to early summer. Small, woody seed capsules succeed the flowers and persist for many months. The plants vary widely from prostrate to erect or weeping, and from small shrubs to trees.

Leptospermum thrives in mild, sheltered districts and prefers acid or neutral soil. Most of these Australian and New Zealand natives are not reliably hardy in cold areas, where they need the shelter of a conservatory or unheated greenhouse.

RECOMMENDED SPECIES AND VARIETIES

L. lanigerum♀ The leaves are hairy and variable in colour from green to silvery green. The white flowers are borne in early summer. The plant is hardy and fairly fast-growing, especially in a mild garden. HEIGHT & SPREAD 1.5×1m (5×3ft) after 5 years, ultimately 3×1–3m (10×3–10ft).

L. humifusum see *L. rupestre*

L. prostratum see *L. rupestre*

L. rupestre♀ (syn. *L. humifusum*, *L. prostratum*) Small white flowers are borne by this usually prostrate but sometimes bushy shrub. The smooth, blunt, hairless leaves are dark green. This is the hardiest plant of the genus. HEIGHT & SPREAD 30×80cm (1ft×2ft 8in) after 5 years, ultimately up to 1×1.5m (3×5ft).

L. scoparium This variable species has white flowers and long narrow leaves.

▲ *Leptospermum rupestre*

There is considerable choice among the 50 or more varieties, with flowers in white, pink or red and sometimes double. The pink and red forms are showier but less hardy. HEIGHT & SPREAD 1.5×1m (5×3ft) after 5 years, ultimately 3×2m (10×6½ft). **'Kiwi'**♀ is a dwarf form, ultimately only 1×1m (3×3ft) with red flowers and reddish purple foliage. **'Nichollsii'**♀ grows to 2×1m (6½×3ft) and has small bronze-purple leaves and crimson flowers. **'Nichollsii Nanum'**♀ is a compact dwarf form, reaching 30×30cm (1×1ft), with purplish leaves and red flowers. **'Red Damask'**♀ is lax, growing to about 2×1m (6½×3ft), with purplish foliage and deep red, fully double flowers.

CULTIVATION All require a warm, sunny situation in soil that is preferably on the acid side and never dries out completely.

PROPAGATION Seed sown in spring germinates freely. Cultivars do not come true to type so take semi-ripe cuttings in summer.

PRUNING Seldom necessary.

PESTS AND DISEASES Usually trouble free.

Lettuce see p. 739

Leucanthemopsis
Moon daisy
Compositae

Cheerful displays of daisies cover patches of feathery foliage during most of the summer. The hardy evergreen dwarf perennial described is a reliable choice for rock, scree and gravel gardens.

RECOMMENDED SPECIES

L. alpina (syn. *Chrysanthemum alpinum*, *Leucanthemum alpinum*) (alpine moon

▼ *Leucanthemopsis alpina*

daisy) White petals encircle a golden yellow central disc. The 4cm (1½in) wide flowerheads are carried on slender, upright stems above tufts of deeply cut, grey-green leaves. The plant's natural habitats are high rocky or grassy areas of European mountains. HEIGHT & SPREAD 15×25cm (6×10in).
CULTIVATION Plant in well-drained, gritty soil in full sun.
PROPAGATION Lift and divide every few years in spring, or sow ripe seed in spring in a coldframe and plant out in summer.
PESTS AND DISEASES Aphids can cause the shoots to become distorted.

Leucanthemum

Compositae

Leucanthemum vulgare

These easily grown summer daisies perform well in almost all garden conditions. The cheerful blooms, with white petals and yellow centres, make long-lasting cut flowers. Semidouble and double flowers are available on some of the shasta-daisy cultivars. Leaves are arranged alternately along the stems and in a rosette at the base of the plant. The genus, which includes both annuals and herbaceous perennials, is native to temperate Europe and Asia.

RECOMMENDED SPECIES AND VARIETIES
L. alpinum see *Leucanthemopsis alpina*
L. paludosum (syn. *Chrysanthemum paludosum*) This dwarf half-hardy perennial, of bushy habit, is usually grown as an annual. The grey-green leaves are narrow, deeply toothed and 5cm (2in) long. Solitary flowers, 3cm (1¼in) across, are produced freely from mid summer to early autumn. HEIGHT & SPREAD 15×20cm (6×8in).
L. × superbum (syn. *Chrysanthemum maximum*) (shasta daisy) Flowers up to 10cm (4in) wide appear in early and mid summer borne singly on erect stems. The dark green shiny leaves, narrow with toothed edges, are up to 20cm (8in) long. The shasta daisy is a fully hardy perennial. HEIGHT & SPREAD 1m×60cm (3×2ft).

'Aglaia'♀ has semidouble flowers and is just under 1m (3ft) tall. **'Bishopstone'** has single flowers with fringed petals and grows to about 75cm (2½ft) tall. **'Esther Read'**, with semidouble flowers, grows up to 60cm (2ft). **'Horace Read'** has double flowers and reaches up to 60cm (2ft) tall. **'Phyllis Smith'** has single flowers with particularly finely cut petals and an ultimate height of 75cm (2½ft). Single flowers are seen on **'Silberprinzesschen'** (syn. 'Little Silver Princess') which only reaches 45cm (1½ft) tall. **'Snow Lady'** has single flowers about 7.5cm (3in) wide, and reaches 25cm (10in). **'Sonnenschein'** (syn. 'Sunshine') has flowers with creamy yellow petals and grows to 80cm (32in) high. **'Starburst'**, with single flowers as wide as 12.5cm (5in), reaches 70cm (28in) in height.

▲ *Leucanthemum × superbum* 'Starburst'

'T.E. Killin'♀ and **'Wirral Supreme'**♀ both have flowers in which the usual central disc is replaced by more or less upright to spreading tubular florets, creating a boss at the centre of the flower, and grow to a height of 1m (3ft). 'Wirral Supreme' has larger central florets and hence looks more like a double-flowered variety.
L. vulgare (syn. *Chrysanthemum leucanthemum*) (marguerite, oxeye daisy) On this hardy plant the solitary flowers are 8cm (3¼in) wide, on upright stems, and the spoon-shaped, long-stalked leaves are up to 10cm (4in) long. The flowering season extends from late spring to mid summer. HEIGHT & SPREAD 60×30cm (2×1ft).
CULTIVATION Plant in almost any soil, in full sun or partial shade. However, moisture-retaining alkaline soils give best results, so it is a good idea to lime acid soils.

Young plants of *L. × superbum* and *L. vulgare* that have been bought in can be planted out in early spring, but wait until late spring before moving plants raised under glass from seed into the garden. Plant out *L. paludosum* in late spring, after the risk of frost has passed. The taller varieties will need support.

Remove fading flowers, cutting stems well below the flowerheads. Cut old stems down to ground level in autumn. Apply a general-purpose fertiliser to poorer soils after the first winter, in early spring. Divide after the second winter, in early spring.
PROPAGATION Divide clumps just before growth recommences in early spring. When cutting up a large clump, retain the outer shoots for replanting and discard the centre.

Flowers can be achieved in the first year from seed, if seed is sown in late winter. Germinate seed at a temperature of 15-20°C (59-68°F), in a propagator, then keep in a cool greenhouse. Do not plant out until late spring, after the last frosts. Once established, *L. × superbum* and *L. vulgare* will tolerate normal British winter weather.

Alternatively, for flowers in the year following sowing, sow seed outdoors in late spring in a seedbed, moving them to their final quarters early the following spring. Of the *L. × superbum* cultivars, only 'Silberprinzesschen', 'Snow Lady' and 'Starburst' come true from seed.
PESTS AND DISEASES Usually trouble free.

Leucogenes

Compositae

These evergreen woody-based perennials have striking silvery or greyish leaves with short woolly hairs and make excellent rock garden plants. They also thrive in a trough or raised bed. The small button-like flowerheads are enhanced conspicuous white woolly bracts. Native to New Zealand, the plants are hardy to -5°C (23°F).

RECOMMENDED SPECIES AND VARIETIES
L. grandiceps Clusters of yellowish or brownish flowerheads enclosed by neat ruffs of rounded, whitish bracts, about 2.5cm (1in) across, bloom from early to late summer on this mat-forming, hairy plant. The silvery rounded or oval leaves are closely overlapping and grow up to 1cm (⅜in) long. HEIGHT & SPREAD 15×30cm (6×12in).
L. leontopodium (New Zealand edelweiss) Silvery white oval leaves, about 2cm (¾in) long and closely overlapping, embellish stout clusters of stiff erect shoots. The flowerheads, borne in clusters in early summer, are about 2.5cm (1in) across and are made up of ruffs of white, woolly bracts surrounding small silvery white flowerheads. HEIGHT & SPREAD 15×20cm (6×8in).

▼ *Leucogenes leontopodium*

1

CULTIVATION Plant in sun or partial shade in a well-drained, humus-rich, gritty soil. Do not disturb established plants.
PROPAGATION Take semi-ripe cuttings in summer or sow seed as soon as it is ripe.
PESTS AND DISEASES Usually trouble free.

Leucojum
Snowflake
Amaryllidaceae

Delicate sprays of bell-like white flowers characterise these hardy bulbous plants. There are species suitable for growing in borders, rockeries, damp soil by the side of a pond and rough grass. Once established, the bulbs are best left undisturbed.

RECOMMENDED SPECIES AND VARIETIES

L. aestivum (summer snowflake) Flowering in late spring, this bulb produces dainty, waxy white flowers, 2.5 cm (1 in) long, with green edges. There are up to 7 flowers on each slender stem. Strap-like, bright green upright leaves arrive with the flowers. Plant 15 cm (6 in) apart. Native to Europe. HEIGHT 75 cm (2½ ft).

'Gravetye Giant' is a larger plant reaching 1 m (3 ft) high with larger flowers up to 4 cm (1½ in) long.

L. autumnale♀ (autumn snowflake) Slender wand-like stems carry several white bell-like flowers which are flushed with pink in early to mid autumn. The delicate-looking plant needs a sunny, well-drained position and is suitable for a rock garden or a well-drained border. The narrow, thread-like leaves are mid green and up to 15 cm (6 in) long. Plant 5 cm (2 in) apart. Native to the Mediterranean. HEIGHT 15 cm (6 in).

1

L. nicaeense♀ This small bulb is suitable for the rock garden and needs a sunny, well-drained position. White bell-like flowers, up to 1.5 cm (½ in) long, are usually carried singly or in pairs on short stems up to 15 cm (6 in) high. The narrow, grassy leaves, up to 20 cm (8 in) long, are produced at the same time as the flowers in spring and early summer. Plant 5 cm (2 in) apart. In colder regions it may be better off in pots in an alpine house or unheated greenhouse. Native to S France. HEIGHT 15 cm (6 in).

▲ *Leucojum aestivum* 'Gravetye Giant'

L. vernum♀ (spring snowflake) Cup-shaped flowers carried on short stout stems are waxy white with conspicuous green spots on the tips of each petal. Borne in late winter to early spring, they are 1.5 cm (½ in) deep and up to 2 cm (¾ in) across. The stout, upright, strap-like leaves are bright green and up to 20 cm (8 in) high. Plant 5 cm (2 in) apart in a cool spot with soil that is not too dry. Native to E and Central Europe. HEIGHT 20 cm (8 in).

▲ *Leucojum vernum*

CULTIVATION Plant dormant bulbs at a depth of 5-10 cm (2-4 in) in autumn, except for *L. autumnale* which should be planted in late summer. *L. aestivum* and *L. vernum* grow best in humus-rich soil. Remove faded flowerheads and allow the foliage to die back naturally before removing.
PROPAGATION Divide bulbs in spring or early autumn. Freshly sown seed usually germinates freely, stored seed rarely.
PESTS AND DISEASES Usually trouble free.

Leucothoë
Ericaceae

Leucothoë 'Scarletta'

Tiny, urn-shaped flowers massed on upright or hanging stalks appear in summer on these shrubs. The species included here are hardy evergreens with narrow, pointed, leathery leaves.

RECOMMENDED SPECIES AND VARIETIES

L. davisiae Nodding, white flowers cluster on erect stalks in early summer. The leaves of this erect, stiff shrub are up to 5 cm (2 in) long. HEIGHT & SPREAD 45×30 cm (1½×1 ft) after 5 years, ultimately 1 m (3 ft) tall.

L. fontanesiana♀ (syn. *L. walteri*) The white flowers are crowded on hanging stalks in early summer. The lance-shaped leaves, 5-15 cm (2-6 in) long, taper to a long pointed tip and are borne on arching branches. New growth is reddish in colour. HEIGHT & SPREAD 60×60 cm (2×2 ft) after 5 years, ultimately 1.8×3 m (6×10 ft).

▲ *Leucothoë fontanesiana*

'Rainbow' has leaves that are irregularly flashed with pink when young, turning to white variegation later. **'Rollissonii'**♀ has smaller, narrower leaves than the species. **'Scarletta'** has leaves that are rich scarlet when young, turning to green and shaded red in winter. Smaller than the species, it reaches a final height of 60 cm (2 ft).

L. walteri see *L. fontanesiana*

▲ *Leucothoë* 'Scarletta'

CULTIVATION Plant in moist, humus-rich, acid soil, preferably in partial shade. Apply general-purpose fertiliser to *L. walteri* if a vigorous plant is required.
PROPAGATION Take semi-ripe cuttings of species and cultivars in late summer, or sow seed of species in early to mid spring. Sever and pot up the suckers and layers that usually develop on mature plants.
PRUNING Not usually necessary. Preserve the habit of *L. walteri* by thinning out older branches at ground level after flowering.
PESTS AND DISEASES Usually trouble free.

Lewisia

Portulacaceae

These popular, N American, hardy alpines are grown for the shot-silk colours of their sumptuous flowers, which open on a bright spring or summer day to a broad bowl or saucer shape. They include both evergreen and herbaceous plants. All species can be grown in the open garden if placed in semi-shaded rock or wall crevices or troughs, in positions where they will stay reasonably dry. Lewisias, particularly *Lewisia rediviva* and *L. tweedyi*, dislike excessively wet conditions and can be grown under glass.

RECOMMENDED SPECIES AND VARIETIES

L. brachycalyx♀ Posies of white to pale pink flowers emerge from leaf rosettes in early to mid spring. Each flower is about 4cm (1½in) across. The narrow, grey-green, inward-pointing leaves are up to 7.5cm (3in) long. In summer this herbaceous species dies down to a small crown of leaves. HEIGHT & SPREAD 7.5x15cm (3x6in).

▲ *Lewisia columbiana* ssp. *wallowensis*

L. columbiana Small pink or magenta blooms, each up to 2cm (¾in) across, are borne in airy clusters well above the leaf rosettes in late spring and summer. This is an evergreen species with loose leaf rosettes composed of deep green, strap or spoon-shaped leaves, up to 10cm (4in) long. HEIGHT & SPREAD 25x15cm (10x6in).

The flowers of ssp. ***rupicola*** are slightly larger and deep magenta or rose-pink. The leaves are up to 3cm (1¼in) long and held in flattish, compact rosettes. Plants reach about 20cm (8in) tall. In ssp. ***wallowensis*** the flowers are white with pink veins and no more than 1.5cm (½in) across. The leaves, up to 4cm (1½in) long, form lax rosettes. The plant is up to 15cm (6in) tall.

L. cotyledon♀ Flowers vary from pink with deep pink or purple stripes to white or cream with yellow or orange stripes. They are borne from late spring to late summer in stout compact clusters well above the spreading leaf rosettes. Each flower is up to 4cm (1½in) across. The thick and rather leathery leaves, about 6-10cm (2½-4in)

Lewisia cotyledon

long, are dark green, strap-shaped, and often rather wavy edged. HEIGHT & SPREAD 30x30cm (1x1ft).

'Alba' carries pure white flowers. **Ashwood strain** bears clear yellow blooms. The flowers of var. ***heckneri***♀ are smaller and the leaves have small, fleshy teeth. **Sunset Group**♀ flowers in a range of colours from yellow to orange-red.

***L.* 'George Henley'** Profuse sprays of wine-red flowers about 2cm (¾in) across, appear in early and mid summer. Narrow, strap-shaped evergreen leaves, each up to 8cm (3¼in) long, form compact rosettes. HEIGHT & SPREAD 15x15cm (6x6in).

L. longipetala This plant has fragrant, pale to rose-pink flowers, up to 3.5cm (1⅜in) across, carried in short spikes of 2 or 3 blooms. They appear in late spring to early summer. This is a herbaceous plant with bright green rosettes of thick, strap-shaped leaves up to 5cm (2in) long. HEIGHT & SPREAD 5x10cm (2x4in).

L. nevadensis White flowers, or white flushed with pink, about 3cm (1¼in) across, are borne in tight posies in the centre of the leaf rosettes in late spring and early summer. The mid green, strap-shaped or narrowly oblong leaves are up to 10cm (4in) long. This species is herbaceous. HEIGHT & SPREAD 7.5x10cm (3x4in).

L. pygmaea Small white, pink or carmine flowers, up to 1.5cm (½in) across, are borne in spreading, often prostrate, spikes in late spring or early summer. This herbaceous species has deep green tufts of spreading to upright, strap-shaped or narrow-oval leaves, each about 9cm (3½in) long. HEIGHT & SPREAD 7.5x12.5cm (3x5in).

L. rediviva (bitter root) White to deep pink or occasionally carmine flowers, up to 6cm (2½in) across, appear in clusters in late spring and early summer. The strap-shaped deep green leaves, up to 5cm (2in) long, are often borne in cylindrical tufts. This species is best grown in pots in an alpine house. HEIGHT & SPREAD 5x7.5cm (2x3in).

L. tweedyi♀ Large satiny blooms, up to 7.5cm (3in) across, in pink, peach or soft yellow appear in mid spring to early summer in stout spikes. This evergreen has deep green, leathery, obovate leaves, up to 8cm (3¼in) long, often flushed with purple, that form symmetrical rosettes. This species is best grown in pots in an alpine house. HEIGHT & SPREAD 20x20cm (8x8in).

CULTIVATION Plant during spring in a well-drained, gritty but humus-rich, acid or neutral soil. Choose a site out of direct sun. Water herbaceous species in late autumn and early winter, and then only sparingly. Water evergreens throughout the year, but sparingly in summer. Surround plants with gravel to keep their necks dry. Feed plants regularly throughout the growing season.

All species grow well in pots in an alpine house, cool conservatory or unheated greenhouse. Repot every year or two – the evergreens after flowering and the herbaceous species in autumn.

PROPAGATION Sow seed in pots in autumn or winter and keep in a coldframe. Alternatively, divide leaf rosettes or remove offsets in spring and establish in a shaded coldframe before potting on.

PESTS AND DISEASES Aphids and dianthus fly larvae may attack. Scale insects may trouble evergreens. A virus-like malaise sometimes occurs, mottling the leaves with yellow and orange.

Leycesteria

Caprifoliaceae

Leycesteria formosa

Unusual and attractive flowers are borne in mid summer by these tall, deciduous, hollow-stemmed shrubs. The flowers are produced in long dangling tassels. This small genus contains six species native to China and the Himalayas. Only one species survives outside in Britain.

RECOMMENDED SPECIES AND VARIETIES

L. formosa (Himalayan honeysuckle, pheasant berry) Dense spikes of flowers dangle from this erect, hardy shrub from early summer to early autumn. The small flowers are actually white, up to 2cm (¾in) long, and complemented by the large claret-coloured bracts which grow among them. The heart-shaped leaves taper to a long point and grow up to 18cm (7in) long. Glossy purple berries ripen in late autumn. The stems with arching tips are an attractive green and covered in a bluish bloom at first

▼ *Leycesteria formosa*

which is lost as the season advances. In colder regions the plant is often killed to ground level in winter, but if established will sprout from the base in spring and can reach its full height in 2 growing seasons. HEIGHT & SPREAD 1.8×1m (6×3ft).
CULTIVATION Plant from mid autumn to early spring in a rich soil and in full sun.
PROPAGATION Sow seed, which is freely produced, in autumn. A more difficult method is to take hardwood cuttings in late autumn to early winter.
PRUNING None required, although cutting down half of the stems to ground level in spring stimulates a flush of new growth.
PESTS AND DISEASES Usually trouble free.

Liatris

Gay feather, blazing star
Compositae

Flower spikes like stiff bottlebrushes are borne by these hardy herbaceous perennials from N America. The individual flowers are tubular, up to 2cm (¾in) long, and open from the top of the spike downwards. The grass-like leaves on the stems are often dotted with resin, and the lower leaves, which form a rosette at the base of the plant, may reach 40cm (16in) in length.
RECOMMENDED SPECIES AND VARIETIES
L. aspera Up to 20 rose-pink or purple flowers are borne on loose terminal spikes throughout summer. HEIGHT & SPREAD 1m×30cm (3×1ft).
L. callilepis see *L. spicata*
L. spicata (syn. *L. callilepis*) (Kansas gay feather, button snakewort) Long spikes of 10-18 tightly packed, mauve florets appear on robust stems throughout summer. A favourite flower with many florists. HEIGHT & SPREAD 1m×30cm (3×1ft).
'Alba' has white flowers. **'Floristan Violett'** has purple flowers. **'Floristan Weiss'** has pure white flowers. **'Kobold'** (also sold as **'Goblin'**) has mauve-pink flowers. These varieties are shorter than the species at 45-60cm (1½-2ft) tall.
CULTIVATION Plant in full sun in any well-drained soil at 30cm (1ft) apart. Deadhead to prolong flowering.

▼ *Liatris spicata*

PROPAGATION Sow the seed of species in spring in a coldframe. Divide both species and cultivated varieties in spring.
PESTS AND DISEASES Slugs may be troublesome in early spring.

Libertia

Iridaceae

Sprays of small white or blue flattish flowers with six spreading petals give interest to a border between late spring and late summer. Seed capsules follow, usually ripening in late summer or autumn. These clump-forming evergreen perennials have fans of grass-like or sword-shaped, stiff leaves. They are native to S America, Australia and New Zealand and suited to sun or shade but require frost protection at the roots.
RECOMMENDED SPECIES AND VARIETIES
L. caerulescens Closely packed sky-blue flowers in late spring are followed by 3-celled seed capsules. The 1cm (⅜in) wide erect green leaves are about 30cm (12in) long. HEIGHT & SPREAD 60×50cm (24×20in).
L. formosa White flowers in dense clusters are borne from early to mid summer, followed by brown 3-celled seed capsules. The leaves are 20cm (8in) long. HEIGHT & SPREAD 40×50cm (16×20in).
L. grandiflora Broad open sprays of white flowers are carried high above the leaves between early and mid summer. The 2cm (⅜in) wide leaves are 50cm (20in) long. Brown to reddish seeds carried in dark brown capsules follow the flowers. HEIGHT & SPREAD 80×50cm (32×20in).
L. ixioides White flowers bloom in loose sprays during early to mid summer, followed by yellow seed capsules. The leaves are 50cm (20in) long, often with a prominent yellowish central vein. HEIGHT & SPREAD 50×50cm (20×20in).
'Nelson Dwarf' reaches 20cm (8in) high and wide, and has tufted leaves about 15cm (6in) long.
L. peregrinans White flowers bloom in early to mid summer followed by yellow to orange seed capsules. Its spreading rhizomes produce fans of leaves, which are often orange, up to 15cm (6in) away from the parent plant. HEIGHT & SPREAD 50cm×1m (20in×3ft).
CULTIVATION Plant in early autumn in light, well-drained soil in sun or half shade.
PROPAGATION Divide in spring or sow seed as soon as it is ripe.
PESTS AND DISEASES Usually trouble free.

▼ *Libertia formosa*

Ligularia

Leopard plant
Compositae

Ligularia 'Gregynog Gold'

The yellow or orange daisy-like flowers of these hardy perennials appear in tall, eye-catching spikes, or in rounded clusters, depending on the species. Some ligularia have coloured foliage. The plants do best on moist soils by the side of water or in dappled shade. They will survive in a mixed border but species with larger leaves may wilt if exposed to strong winds in the hot midday sun. The flowers of the recommended plants appear in mid summer unless stated otherwise.
RECOMMENDED SPECIES AND VARIETIES
L. clivorum see *L. dentata*
L. dentata (syn. *L. clivorum*) This compact, clump-forming plant has dark green, heart-shaped, leathery leaves, up to 30cm (1ft) wide. The vivid orange flowers, 12cm (4¾in) wide, appear in clusters. HEIGHT & SPREAD 1.2m×60cm (4×2ft).
'Desdemona'🏆 has brownish green leaves with dark mahogany undersides while **'Othello'** has purplish green leaves.
***L.* 'Gregynog Gold'**🏆 Bright orange flowers grow in conical spires over the rounded saw-toothed leaves, up to 30cm (1ft) wide. This plant can withstand full sun. HEIGHT & SPREAD 1.8m×60cm (6×2ft).
L. macrophylla Dense spikes of bright yellow flowers, each 5cm (2in) wide, appear in late summer. This striking plant has greyish green, elliptic-ovate leaves up to 60cm (2ft) long. HEIGHT & SPREAD 1.5m×60cm (5×2ft).
L. przewalskii Masses of small, yellow flowers are highlighted against the black stems of this species. The deeply cut, fan-

▼ *Ligularia dentata* 'Othello'

▲ *Ligularia przewalskii*

shaped leaves are dark green. HEIGHT & SPREAD 1.8×1m (6×3ft).

***L.* 'The Rocket'**♀ This plant resembles *L. przewalskii*, but its flowers are a brighter yellow and it is stronger growing. HEIGHT & SPREAD 1.8×1m (6×3ft).

L. veitchiana Slender spikes carry a mass of golden yellow daisies, each about 6cm (2½in) wide, set above broad bracts. Fluffy seed heads follow in autumn. The bright green, toothed, circular basal leaves, up to 30cm (1ft) across, make a handsome clump. HEIGHT & SPREAD 1.5m×60cm (5×2ft).

CULTIVATION Plant from autumn to spring in humus-rich, moist soil. Mulch each year with bulky compost. Stake tall plants that are exposed to wind.

PROPAGATION Divide from autumn to spring. Sow seed for species under glass in early spring and plant the seedlings outside when they are 10-15cm (4-6in) tall.

PESTS AND DISEASES Slugs and snails may damage new leaves in early spring.

Ligustrum

Privet

Oleaceae

Best known as hedging plants, privets also make fine single specimens. These deciduous or evergreen shrubs and small trees are shade-tolerant and grow well in any soil.

RECOMMENDED SPECIES AND VARIETIES

L. japonicum (Japanese privet) These evergreen shrubs, with glossy, deep green, oval leaves up to 10cm (4in) long, bear upright, conical flower clusters, 10-20cm (4-8in) long, in mid summer and early autumn. HEIGHT & SPREAD 1.2m×75cm (4×2½ft) after 5 years, ultimately 3.5m (12ft) tall.

'Rotundifolium' (syn. 'Coriaceum') has dense masses of broadly oval to round leaves

Ligustrum lucidum

up to 6 cm (2½in) long and flowerheads to 7.5cm (3in) long. It is a slow-grower and reaches an ultimate height of 1.8m (6ft).

L. lucidum♀ Narrow, oval, glossy leaves, up to 15cm (6in) long, are borne by this evergreen shrub or tree. Creamy white flowerheads, 20cm (8in) long, appear in late summer and early autumn. HEIGHT & SPREAD 1.5×1.2m (5×4ft) after 5 years, ultimately 9m (30ft) tall.

'Excelsum Superbum'♀ has bright green leaves marked with pale green and bearing yellow margins. The leaves of **'Tricolor'** have an irregular white border that is pinkish when young.

L. ovalifolium (oval-leafed privet) The traditional hedging privet has glossy, mid green, oval leaves 2.5-6cm (1-2½in) long, evergreen except in the severest winters. If left untrimmed it produces unpleasantly scented, white flower clusters up to 7.5cm (3in) long in mid summer, followed by black berries. HEIGHT & SPREAD 1.5×1.2m (5×4ft) after 5 years, ultimately, if unpruned, 4.5m (15ft) tall.

'Argenteum' (syn. 'Variegatum') has green leaves with creamy white borders. **'Aureum'**♀ (syn. 'Aureomarginatum') (golden privet) has green leaves with broad, bright yellow borders. Both cultivars are slightly less vigorous than the species.

▲ *Ligustrum ovalifolium* 'Aureum'

L. quihoui♀ This deciduous shrub of rounded habit bears slender sprays of fragrant flowers from early to mid autumn, followed by purplish fruits. The narrowly oval leaves are up to 5cm (2in) long. HEIGHT & SPREAD 1.5×1.2m (5×4ft) after 5 years, ultimately 3m (10ft) tall.

L. sinense This deciduous shrub (evergreen in mild winters) bears masses of fragrant flowers in sprays up to 10cm (4in) long in mid summer, followed by small, black-purple berries. The pale green leaves are elliptical to oblong and up to 7.5cm (3in) in length. HEIGHT & SPREAD 1.5×1m (5×3ft) after 5 years, ultimately 4.5m (15ft) tall.

The leaves of **'Variegatum'** are grey-green and white. **'Wimbei'**, with very dark green 6mm (¼in) long leaves, is of upright, columnar habit, reaching 50cm (20in) tall after 5 years and 1m (3ft) at maturity.

***L.* 'Vicaryi'** Broad, oval, bright golden leaves, up to 6cm (2½in) long, turn bronze-purple in winter on this dense, semi-evergreen bush. In mid summer crowded clusters of small, white flowers appear. HEIGHT & SPREAD 1.2×1m (4×3ft) after 5 years, ultimately 3m (10ft) tall.

▲ *Ligustrum* 'Vicaryi'

L. vulgare (common privet) Britain's native privet is a semi-evergreen shrub, shedding its lance-shaped leaves, 2.5-6cm (1-2½in) long, only in the harshest winters. Dull white flower clusters, up to 5cm (2in) long, appear from early to mid summer. The shiny black autumn fruits are attractive to birds. HEIGHT & SPREAD 1.5×1.2m (5×4ft) after 5 years, ultimately 3m (10ft) tall.

CULTIVATION Plant in any garden soil, in sun or shade, from mid autumn to early spring. For hedging, plant *L. ovalifolium* or *L. vulgare* 30-45cm (1-1½ft) apart. If the soil is poor, work in manure or garden compost and add a slow-release fertiliser.

PROPAGATION Take hardwood cuttings of *L. ovalifolium* and *L. vulgare* in early winter. Take semi-ripe cuttings of the other species and cultivars in late summer.

PRUNING No regular pruning is needed for privets grown as shrubs. To make a hedge, cut back all shoots by a half to two-thirds in mid spring after planting. A year later cut back all growths by half again. Keep cutting all new growth by half its length in late summer each successive year, until the desired height is reached. Then clip to shape twice a year, in late spring and early autumn, or once a year, in mid summer. To renovate thin, straggly hedges, cut back hard in late winter to within 30cm (1ft) of the ground and apply slow-release fertiliser.

PESTS AND DISEASES Leaf miners, thrips and leaf spot damage leaves. Honey fungus can be a problem.

Lilac see *Syringa*

Lilium

Lily

Liliaceae

With their exquisite blooms, lilies command a position of honour in mixed borders, woodland gardens and in containers. The flowers, often fragrant and available in a wide palette of colours, are also excellent for cutting

The strikingly beautiful and often richly scented flowers of lilies appear from early summer to early autumn. The flowers of these hardy, occasionally half-hardy, bulbous perennials come in all colours except blue, and many species and cultivars have flowers splashed or spotted with a different colour. In addition, the conspicuous, pollen-bearing anthers of the flowers are frequently of a contrasting colour. Lilies range in height from 30 cm (1 ft) to 2 m (6½ ft). Many lilies are well suited to growing in pots and containers, either outside or under glass.

The flowers of lilies, ranging in size from 5 cm (2 in) to 25 cm (10 in) across, are produced towards the top of the stem, either singly, or in flowerheads that may carry up to 50 blooms, according to species. The shape of the flowers is determined by the degree to which the six petals (correctly speaking tepals) spread out and bend back (or recurve). The appearance of the flowers is also affected by the stalks. These vary greatly in length and may be straight or curved, and this, together with the angle at which the flower grows from the stalk, determines whether the flowers are upward, outward or downward-facing. The upward-facing flowers are cup or star-shaped with spreading petals, which may be straight or recurved at the tips. Outward-facing flowers are either bowl-shaped, with spreading petals that recurve about halfway along their length, or trumpet or funnel-shaped, with petals that overlap for most of their length and recurve at the tips. Downward-facing, or pendulous, flowers may be either bell-shaped, with petals that are not widely spreading and either straight or gently recurved, or of the Turk's-cap type with petals that recurve tightly.

The leaves of lilies are mostly stalkless, varying in length from 5 cm (2 in) to 15 cm (6 in), and in shape from very narrow to broadly oval. They are borne on the stem in two main ways: either scattered up and around the stem (densely or sparsely), or in whorls, like the spokes of a wheel, at intervals up the stem.

Most lilies enjoy partial shade and a cool, deep root run in a humus-rich, well-drained, fertile soil. In many species and cultivars, the stem, put out by the bulb, itself makes roots. Such 'stem-rooting' lilies need to be planted deeply, so it is important to know in advance if the lily you are planting is of this type.

RECOMMENDED SPECIES AND VARIETIES

African Queen Group Large yellow or orange fragrant, trumpet-shaped flowers, up to 15 cm (6 in) long and as much across, are carried in pyramidal heads in mid to late summer. HEIGHT 1.5 m (5 ft).

▲ *Lilium* African Queen Group

L. auratum (golden-rayed lily) The magnificent, outward-facing, bowl-shaped flowers, up to 25 cm (10 in) across, are white with prominent golden bands down the centre of each petal. The inside of the flower is heavily sprinkled with maroon or brown spots. A highly fragrant lily, up to 10 blooms are carried on the single stem in late summer. *L. auratum* is stem-rooting and is often grown as a container plant in a conservatory. HEIGHT 1.5 m (5 ft).

Lilium auratum

The flowers of var. ***platyphyllum***♀ (syn. 'Gold Band') have fewer spots and the plant has slightly broader lance-shaped leaves.

***L.* Bellingham Hybrids**♀ Turk's-cap lilies in a wide range of both pastel and warm colours, from soft pink to orange, appear from early to mid summer. The individual flowers, most with internal spotting, grow to 15 cm (6 in) across and are borne in groups of up to 15 on a stem. They increase freely. HEIGHT 2 m (6½ ft).

***L.* 'Black Dragon'**♀ Outward-facing, scented, trumpet-shaped flowers with dark purplish red exteriors and white interiors are produced from mid to late summer.

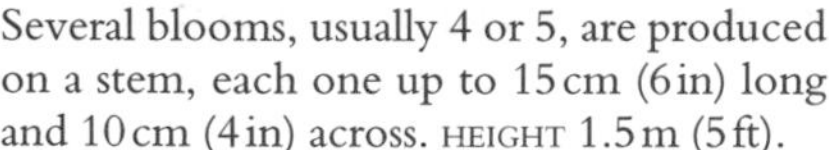

Several blooms, usually 4 or 5, are produced on a stem, each one up to 15cm (6in) long and 10cm (4in) across. HEIGHT 1.5m (5ft).

***L.* 'Bright Star'** The flattish, outward-facing flowers are white with orange internal streaking and distinctly recurved tepals. As many as 8 blooms, up to 15cm (6in) across, are produced on the single stem in mid to late summer. HEIGHT 1.5m (5ft).

***L. bulbiferum* var. *croceum*♀** This attractive short-growing lily produces up to 5 upward-facing, bright orange, bowl-shaped flowers, 7.5cm (3in) long and 10cm (4in) across, in early to mid summer. Stem-rooting. HEIGHT 90cm (3ft).

L. canadense (Canada lily) As many as 12 pendulous, yellow or orange-red, bell-shaped flowers, up to 10cm (4in) across and with distinctive recurved tips to the petals, are borne on very long stalks in late summer. This is a beautiful lily for dappled shade, but it must have plenty of moisture and is also a lime-hater. Stem-rooting. HEIGHT 1.5m (5ft).

▲ *Lilium* Bellingham Hybrids

Lilium canadense

***L. candidum*♀** (Madonna lily) This is the typical white-flowered lily of the cottage garden, bearing between 5 and 20 outward-facing, broadly funnel-shaped, fragrant blooms, up to 7.5cm (3in) long, in early to mid summer. Plant bulbs in late summer in order to establish a root system and a rosette of foliage before winter. HEIGHT 1.5m (5ft).

***L.* 'Casa Blanca'♀** This heavily scented hybrid bears outward-facing, waxy, widely bowl-shaped white flowers up to 25cm (10in) across, with conspicuous, orange-brown pollen on the anthers, in mid to late summer. It is a popular pot plant. HEIGHT 1.2m (4ft).

***L. chalcedonicum*♀** (scarlet Turk's-cap lily) Nodding red or reddish orange Turk's-cap flowers, slightly scented and up to 7.5cm (3in) long and 12.5cm (5in) across are produced in mid summer. Up to 12 blooms are carried on strong stems. Stem-rooting. HEIGHT 90cm (3ft).

▲ *Lilium candidum*

▲ *Lilium* Citronella Group

▲ *Lilium* 'Connecticut King'

L. Citronella Group Up to 30 pendulous, lemon-yellow, Turk's-cap flowers, 7.5cm (3in) across, with small, faint black spots are carried in mid summer. HEIGHT 1.5m (5ft).

L. 'Connecticut King' As many as 15 bright yellow, upward-facing, star-like flowers, 15cm (6in) across, are produced in terminal groups on very leafy stems in early summer. A vigorous variety well suited to the open garden and containers. HEIGHT 90cm (3ft).

▲ *Lilium* 'Côte d' Azur'

L. 'Côte d' Azur' The bowl-shaped, upward-facing blooms of this hybrid are deep rose-pink with darker spotted throats and up to 10cm (4in) across. The flowers are produced in terminal groups from early to mid summer. An excellent variety for container cultivation. HEIGHT 60cm (2ft).

***L.* x *dalhansonii* 'Marhan'**♀ (syn. *L.* Marhan) This hybrid has orange-yellow, thick-petalled, Turk's-cap flowers, mostly spotted internally with reddish brown. As many as 13 flowers, 7.5cm (3in) across, are borne in extended groups up the slender stems in early summer. A lily of strong constitution which naturalises freely. Stem-rooting. HEIGHT 1.5m (5ft).

▲ *Lilium davidii*

L. davidii♀ This Turk's-cap lily bears up to 20 pendulous, red or orange flowers with conspicuous, dark internal spots in mid to late summer. The petals are recurved and up to 7.5cm (3in) long. Stem-rooting. HEIGHT 90cm (3ft).

Lilium 'Enchantment'

L. 'Enchantment'♀ Up to 12 bright orange-red, upward-facing, star-shaped flowers, 10cm (4in) across and with black-spotted throats, are produced in large terminal groups on strong stems in early and mid summer. The most popular modern hybrid, widely used for general garden decoration, naturalising, pot and container cultivation, as well as cutting. HEIGHT 90cm (3ft).

L. 'Fire King' Widely trumpet-shaped, bright orange-red flowers with purple spots, outward-facing and up to 10cm (4in) across, are borne in terminal groups in mid to late summer. Excellent variety for container growing. HEIGHT 90cm (3ft).

L. formosanum From 3-5 large, outward-facing, trumpet-shaped, fragrant white flowers, up to 15cm (6in) long and often flushed on the exterior with crimson-purple, are borne in late summer. This is a tender lily for growing in a conservatory or a greenhouse and, unlike most other lilies, is commonly raised from seed, flowering just 9 months after sowing. Stem-rooting. HEIGHT 1.5m (5ft).

The variety *pricei*♀ is much shorter, rarely growing more than 60cm (2ft) tall, making it ideal for pot culture.

L. 'Green Dragon'♀ The large, outward-facing, trumpet-shaped flowers of this hybrid have a deep purplish brown and green exterior and a pure white interior. As many as 8 blooms, up to 15cm (6in) long and 10cm (4in) across, are borne in terminal heads on strong flower stems in mid to late summer. HEIGHT 1.2m (4ft).

L. hansonii♀ The 12.5cm (5in) wide flowers of this scented, Turk's-cap lily are orange-yellow with thick petals. Each bulb produces up to 12 blooms in mid summer. The leaves are dark green, up to 20cm (8in) long and borne in distinctive whorls. Stem-rooting. HEIGHT 1.2m (4ft).

L. henryi♀ Between 20 and 50 nodding, Turk's-cap flowers are borne in late summer on a vigorous stem. The blooms are bright orange, conspicuously spotted with black. Up to 10cm (4in) across, they have distinctive warty growths (papillae) at the base of each petal. Preferring an alkaline soil, this plant is ideal for naturalising among shrubs or in grass. Stem-rooting. HEIGHT 3m (10ft).

▲ *Lilium henryi*

L. 'Karen North'♀ The Turk's-cap flowers of this hybrid are orange-pink, spotted with deep pink inside. They grow to 10cm (4in) across, and 8 or more appear in groups along the upper part of the flower stem in mid to late summer. HEIGHT 1.2m (4ft).

L. lancifolium (syn. *L. tigrinum*) (tiger lily) The flowers of this Turk's-cap lily are bright orange spotted with purple. They grow to 10cm (4in) across and are borne in late summer and early autumn in spires of up to 40. This stem-rooting lily often carries tiny, black bulbils in the leaf axils. Stem-rooting. HEIGHT 90cm (3ft).

The flowers of var. ***flaviflorum*** are yellow.

L. 'Limelight'♀ Large, trumpet-shaped, soft greenish yellow fragrant flowers, up to 15cm (6in) long and 10cm (4in) across, are borne in terminal heads on a strong flower

▲ *Lilium longiflorum*

▲ *Lilium* 'Mont Blanc'

▲ *Lilium* Pink Perfection Group

stem in mid to late summer. The individual flowers, although outward-facing, tend to be a little pendent. HEIGHT 1.2m (4ft).

L. longiflorum ♀ (Easter lily) Between 1 and 6 large, fragrant, pure white trumpet-shaped flowers, up to 20cm (8in) long, are produced by this half-hardy lily in mid to late summer. Widely grown for cut flowers, it is an excellent lily for containers. Stem-rooting. HEIGHT 90cm (3ft).

L. mackliniae ♀ (Manipur lily) Up to 6 bell-shaped, slightly pendent, rose-pink to purple-pink flowers, 7.5cm (3in) across, are borne in early summer. The small, oval or lance-shaped leaves, up to 5cm (2in) in length, are scattered around the lower stem but grow in whorls beneath the flowerhead. Stem-rooting. HEIGHT 45cm (1½ft).

***L.* 'Marhan'** see *L.* × *dalhansonii* 'Marhan'

L. martagon (martagon lily, Turk's cap lily) The scented, waxy flowers of this species are 7.5cm (3in) across, mauve-pink and darkly spotted. Up to 50 are produced on a stem clothed with whorls of dark green lance-shaped leaves, growing to 15cm (6in) long. This is one of the easiest lilies to naturalise in grass and is very tolerant of lime. Stem-rooting. HEIGHT 1.2m (4ft).

Pure white, unspotted flowers are borne by var. ***album*** ♀, while var. ***cattaniae*** ♀ has unspotted, maroon flowers.

L. monadelphum ♀ (syn. *L. szovitsianum*) The fragrant, yellow, Turk's-cap flowers are usually strongly marked on the inside with dark red or purple spots. The blooms are up to 15cm (6in) across and the individual recurved petals as long as 10cm (4in). As many as 20 flowers per stem are produced in mid summer. This is a good all-round garden lily, which, if left undisturbed, spreads freely. Stem-rooting. HEIGHT 1.2m (4ft).

***L.* 'Mont Blanc'** Creamy white, upward-facing, star-shaped flowers, up to 15cm (6in) across, are produced in terminal groups from early to mid summer. A popular variety for both border decoration and pot cultivation. HEIGHT 60cm (2ft).

***L.* 'Mrs R.O. Backhouse'** ♀ Tawny gold, purple-spotted, Turk's-cap flowers, 10cm (4in) across with thick waxy petals, are borne on slender stems from early to mid

▲ *Lilium nepalense*

summer. An excellent lily for naturalising among shrubs in the open border or in grass. HEIGHT 1.5m (5ft).

L. nepalense Pendulous, bell-shaped flowers with recurved, greenish yellow and purple petals, up to 15cm (6in) long, appear in late summer. It needs a sheltered position and should not be allowed to become too wet. Stem-rooting. HEIGHT 1m (3ft).

L. pardalinum var. ***giganteum*** ♀ (panther lily) As many as 30 often scented Turk's-cap flowers, with recurved densely spotted crimson and yellow petals up to 10cm (4in) long, are borne in mid summer. An excellent lily for a damp, semi-shady position. HEIGHT 3m (10ft).

***L.* Pink Perfection Group** ♀ The beautiful, highly scented flowers are trumpet-shaped and rich fuchsia-pink, growing to 15cm (6in) long and 10cm (4in) across. Up to 15 drooping blooms are produced in mid to late summer. Ideal for containers and borders. Stem-rooting. HEIGHT 1.2m (4ft).

L. pumilum ♀ (syn. *L. tenuifolium*) This short-growing, Turk's-cap lily has slightly scented, bright red flowers, spotted with black. Between 5 and 20 blooms, just 5cm (2in) across, are produced in mid summer. It requires a well-drained position in full sun. Stem-rooting. HEIGHT 30cm (1ft).

L. pyrenaicum ♀ (yellow Turk's-cap lily)

▲ *Lilium pyrenaicum*

Bright yellow, purple-spotted, Turk's-cap flowers appear in early summer. Up to 12 blooms, 10cm (4in) across, are produced on the stem. The flowers are strangely malodorous. This stem-rooting lily is easy to grow and naturalises freely in moist soil. HEIGHT 1.2m (4ft).

L. regale ♀ (regal lily) Huge, heavily fragrant and outward-facing funnel-shaped

▼ *Lilium regale*

1

▲ *Lilium regale* Album Group

blooms, up to 15cm (6in) long and 12.5cm (5in) across, appear in mid and late summer. As many as 20 are produced on a single stem. The petals have pinkish purple exteriors but are white inside and have a distinctive yellow base. Magnificent in the garden border or in large pots in the conservatory. Stem-rooting. HEIGHT 1.2m (4ft).

Album Group has almost pure white flowers with an occasional blush of pink on the outside of the petals.

L. **'Rosemary North'**♀ This graceful lily has slightly fragrant, rich orange flowers, sometimes with darker spots. The Turk's-cap blooms, appearing from mid to late summer, grow to 10cm (4in) across and are borne on slender stems in a terminal group of up to 12. HEIGHT 90cm (3ft).

L. speciosum♀ This very distinctive, late summer and early autumn-flowering lily has open, richly scented Turk's-cap flowers of waxy, satiny texture up to 10cm (4in) across. The petals are white or pink, spotted with pink or crimson. Up to 4 flowers are carried on a stem. This stem-rooting lily is not fully hardy and makes a popular conservatory plant. HEIGHT 1.2m (4ft).

Pure white flowers with a faint, greenish band in the centre of each petal are borne on purple stems by var. ***album***, while var. ***rubrum*** has purple or brownish stems and blooms suffused and spotted with carmine.

L. **'Star Gazer'** Open, funnel to star-shaped blooms of rich carmine spotted with crimson are produced in late summer. The upward-facing, richly fragrant flowers are up to 12.5cm (5in) across and produced in a cluster of 5-8. HEIGHT 90cm (3ft).

L. **'Sterling Star'** Open, upward-facing star-shaped white flowers, up to 12.5cm (5in) across, with tiny brown spots on the inside of the petals, are produced in groups of 5-8 in early and mid summer. Excellent for growing in the open ground as well as in pots. HEIGHT 1.2m (4ft).

L. superbum♀ (swamp lily) An elegant stem carries up to 40 nodding, Turk's-cap flowers in late summer and early autumn. The blooms, growing to 10cm (4in) across, are orange flushed with red and have maroon internal spotting. It revels in moist, acid soil. Stem-rooting. HEIGHT 2m (6½ft).

L. szovitsianum see *L. monadelphum*

L. tenuifolium see *L. pumilum*

L. × ***testaceum***♀ (Nankeen lily) This Turk's-cap lily produces 6 to 12 fragrant, light orange to brownish yellow flowers, 10cm (4in) across and often spotted with red on the inside, in early to mid summer. The narrow, lance-shaped dark green leaves, up to 7.5cm (3in) long, tend to be curved and twisted. Grow this lily in a sunny spot with shelter from cold winds. HEIGHT 1.2m (4ft).

L. tigrinum see *L. lancifolium*

CULTIVATION

BEDS AND BORDERS

Plant lily bulbs as soon as purchased in well-drained, humus-rich soil at any time from late autumn to early spring. The majority grow best in shade or partial shade, although a number of the Turk's-cap types are quite happy naturalised in the open. Plant stem-rooting lilies at a depth of 15-20cm (6-8in). *L. candidum* and *L.* × *testaceum* should be covered by a depth of soil no more than the height of the bulb. Cover the others by a depth of soil twice the height of the bulb. Apply a mulch of well-rotted garden compost or leaf-mould after planting. Scatter slug pellets near the plants in early spring, at the same time making preparations for staking any varieties that require support. Wire ring supports are the easiest to use and the least obtrusive. Remove the faded flowers, but leave as much foliage as possible in order to build up the bulbs for the following year. Each spring apply slow-release fertiliser and mulch. Lift and replant every 3 years to maintain vigour.

POTS AND CONTAINERS

Plant 2 or 3 bulbs in a 25cm (10in) pot in John Innes No. 2 compost with a good layer of crocks at the base of the pot. Plant the stem-rooting varieties low down in the container with at least 7.5cm (3in) of compost beneath them, gradually filling it as the shoots of the bulbs extend. Plant the others at a depth three times their own height, except *L. candidum* and *L.* × *testaceum,* which should be planted at a depth twice their height. Water freely during the growing period, and give a high-potash liquid feed once a month. Store the bulbs over winter in their pots, or place them in boxes of damp peat in a cool, dry place. Repot every autumn.

PROPAGATION Lift and separate clumps of bulbs in autumn or spring. Remove the outer scales of bulbs in autumn or spring and plant them in trays of moist compost, placed upright with the tip just visible. Some varieties produce bulbils in the leaf axils, where the leaves join the stems. Plant these miniature bulbs as soon as they ripen in late summer or autumn, or store them in damp peat in a cool place for planting in spring. Seed of species may be sown in deep trays or pots in a coldframe in spring. Most lilies take 3-6 years to flower from seed. The exceptions to this are *L. formosanum* and *L. longiflorum,* which may flower 9 months after sowing

PESTS AND DISEASES Aphids are a constant nuisance and spread virus diseases. Slugs, lily beetles, grey mould, basal rot and lily disease (leaf blight) are common problems.

Lily see *Lilium*
Lily, African see *Agapanthus*
Lily, arum see *Zantedeschia aethiopica*
Lily, belladonna see *Amaryllis belladonna*
Lily, corn see *Ixia*
Lily, day see *Hemerocallis*
Lily, flax see *Phormium*
Lily, foxtail see *Eremurus*
Lily, ginger see *Hedychium*
Lily, glory see *Gloriosa*
Lily, kaffir see *Schizostylis*
Lily, Lent see *Narcissus pseudonarcissus*
Lily, May see *Maianthemum*
Lily, Peruvian see *Alstroemeria*
Lily, pineapple see *Eucomis*
Lily, plantain see *Hosta*
Lily, St Bernard's see *Anthericum*
Lily, St Bruno's see *Paradisea liliastrum*
Lily, toad see *Tricyrtis*
Lily, trout see *Erythronium americanum*
Lily, water see *Nymphaea*
Lily-of-the-valley see *Convallaria majalis*
Lily-of-the-valley bush see *Pieris japonica*
Lily tree see *Ophiopogon*
Lime see *Citrus aurantiifolia*
Lime tree see *Tilia*

Limnanthes

Meadow foam

Limnanthaceae

This fast-growing annual with its buttercup-like flowers makes a cheerful display from late spring to late summer. The profuse blooms look best at the front of a border or in large pockets on a rock garden. Limnanthes seeds easily and often colonises gravel paths and driveways.

RECOMMENDED SPECIES

L. douglasii♀ (poached egg flower) Saucer-shaped flowers with deep golden yellow centres and conspicuous white petal tips give this plant its popular name. Borne on sprawling stems, the flowers, which are up to 3cm (1¼in) across, are lightly scented and irresistible to bees. The rather succulent leaves are yellow-green, smooth and shiny with slender segments. The plant's natural habitat is moist grassland and open woods in W America. HEIGHT & SPREAD 15×20cm (6×8in).

CULTIVATION Grow on any moist soil, except poorly drained.

▲ Limnanthes douglasii

PROPAGATION Sow seed in autumn or early spring where the plants are required to flower. Transplant self-sown seedlings that appear the following year.
PESTS AND DISEASES Usually trouble free.

Limonium
Sea lavender, statice
Plumbaginaceae

Limonium platyphyllum

Tiny, funnel-shaped flowers carried for the most part in spreading clusters provide a pleasing contrast with the bolder growth and flowers of other border plants. Smaller species do well in a sunny position in a rock garden. The flowers are in bloom from mid or late summer to early autumn. They are often grown for cutting or drying. *L. dumosum* and *L. sinuatum* make particularly good dried flowers. This genus was known in the past as *Statice.*

All the species commonly grown in Britain are herbaceous perennials. The plants described below are all hardy except *L. sinuatum*, which is grown as a half-hardy annual. The listed species, once again with the exception of *L. sinuatum,* have dark green, often leathery, spoon-shaped leaves arranged in basal rosettes – one rosette in the first year of the plant's life, subsequently more – and leafless flower stems.

RECOMMENDED SPECIES AND VARIETIES
L. bellidifolium Blue to pinkish blue trumpet-shaped flowers are prolifically borne in short, loose sprays on delicate, many-branched stems in late summer and early autumn. The deep green leathery leaves are about 5 cm (2 in) long and clumped at the base of the plant. This is a good plant for a rock garden. It requires especially well-drained soil. Native to Europe. HEIGHT & SPREAD 20×10 cm (8×4 in).

▲ Limonium bellidifolium

L. cosyrense Short, upright clusters of mauve flowers bloom from mid summer onwards. The leaves are about 2.5 cm (1 in) long. This small plant is sometimes grown in pots in a conservatory or greenhouse. Native to SE Europe. HEIGHT & SPREAD 10×10 cm (4×4 in).
L. dumosum (syn. *Goniolimon tataricum*) Red and white flowers are produced in spreading clusters from mid summer to early autumn. The leaves are fleshy and leathery, and up to 15 cm (6 in) long. Native to SE Europe. HEIGHT & SPREAD 30×30 cm (12×12 in).
L. platyphyllum (syn. *L. latifolium*) Masses of tiny pale lavender-blue flowers are carried on wiry stems in diffuse clusters up to 25 cm (10 in) long in mid and late summer and early autumn. The leaves are downy, wavy-edged and few in number, but may grow as long as 60 cm (24 in). Native to SE Europe. HEIGHT & SPREAD 60×45 cm (24×18 in).

The flowers of **'Violetta'** are a darker violet colour.

▲ Limonium platyphyllum 'Violetta'

L. sinuatum This is a perennial usually treated as a half-hardy annual. It produces blue, pink, red, white or yellow flowers from mid summer to early autumn. Seed is available in single colours and in mixtures. The branched stems, upright and winged, carry flowers in clusters about 10 cm (4 in) long. Leaves clothe the stems as well as forming basal rosettes. They are deep green, lance-shaped with deeply lobed and waved margins, hairy and up to 10 cm (4 in) long. Native to the Mediterranean region. HEIGHT & SPREAD 45×30 cm (18×12 in).
L. suworowii see *Psylliostachys suworowii*
CULTIVATION Plant out in spring, in full sun, in any well-drained soil. Apply lime if the soil is acid. *L. dumosum* and *L. platyphyllum* both do well on naturally dry soils. Deadhead to maintain the display of flowers. Cut out the stems of perennials that have finished flowering.
PROPAGATION Sow seed of species raised as half-hardy annuals in early spring, in a warm greenhouse. A minimum temperature of 15°C (59°F) is needed for swift germination, but subsequently 10°C (50°F) is warm enough. Plant out when all risk of frost has passed. It is possible to sow seed out of doors later on in mid spring, where the plants are to grow, but flowering will not then begin until late summer.

Sow seed of perennials in late spring, or take root cuttings in late winter.
PESTS AND DISEASES Fungal root rot can cause losses in wet soil.

Linanthus
Mountain phlox
Polemoniaceae

Clusters of funnel-shaped flowers and finely divided foliage are the main features of the two linanthus species described below, both of them erect, hardy annuals. They flower from mid summer to early autumn. These species will appeal to gardeners who like to include some unfamiliar plants among better-known ones in mixed beds and borders. They also make unusual pot plants for cool greenhouses or conservatories, where they flower in spring. The flowers are 2-3 cm (¾-1¼ in) wide, with 5 broad spreading lobes. The genus, which includes hardy herbaceous perennials as well as annuals, is mostly native to western N America. It is closely related to gilia.

RECOMMENDED SPECIES AND VARIETIES
L. grandiflorus Lilac or pink flowers, about 3 cm (1¼ in) across, are borne in dense heads. The leaves have 5-11 linear lobes, each up to 3 cm (1¼ in) long. HEIGHT &

▲ Linanthus grandiflorus

SPREAD up to 50×20cm (20×8in).

L. liniflorus This plant has branched clusters of slender-stalked, lavender-blue flowers, about 2cm (¾in) wide. Leaves divide into 3-9 needle-like segments, up to 1.5cm (½in) long. HEIGHT & SPREAD up to 50×20cm (20×8in).

CULTIVATION Choose a site fully exposed to sun, with light, well-drained soil. The only attention normally needed is weeding and deadheading.

PROPAGATION Sow seed in mid spring, where the plants are to be grown. Once well-established, thin seedlings to 15cm (6in) apart.

For pot plants kept in a cool greenhouse or conservatory, sow seed in early autumn in 13cm (5in) pots. Thin young plants to 4 per pot in mid autumn. During winter, only water enough to prevent wilting. Provide support with short brushwood in late winter.

PESTS AND DISEASES Usually trouble free.

Linaria

Toadflax

Scrophulariaceae

Linaria alpina

1

With their clusters or spikes of flowers in a wide range of colours, toadflaxes are popular plants for borders and rock gardens. Among this genus of annuals, biennials and herbaceous perennials are plants that flower over long periods, often from mid summer into autumn. The perennial species tend to be short-lived but they often self-seed.

The flowers are spurred with two lips, often with distinctive markings on the lower lip. The narrow often fleshy leaves are paired or in small whorls along the stem. Native to the northern temperate zone, most species are hardy, but *Linaria genistifolia* ssp. *dalmatica* and *L. triornithophora* will not withstand long periods below freezing.

RECOMMENDED SPECIES AND VARIETIES

L. alpina (alpine toadflax) Purple or violet flowers, about 2cm (¾in) long, with yellow or orange markings at the mouth are borne in dense clusters in late spring and summer. The blue or grey-green, lance-like leaves are up to 1cm (⅜in) long. A clump-forming alpine, evergreen perennial or biennial. HEIGHT & SPREAD 10×25cm (4×10in).

'Purpurea' has deeper purple flowers. The flowers of **'Rosea'** are rose-pink.

L. genistifolia ssp. *dalmatica* Spikes of lemon or canary-yellow flowers, with orange at the mouth and about 2-4cm (¾-1½in) long, are carried from mid summer to early autumn by this statuesque semi-evergreen perennial. The upright stems have upward-pointing, lance-like, mid green glossy leaves, up to 12.5cm (5in) long. HEIGHT & SPREAD 1m×60cm (3×2ft).

▲ *Linaria alpina*

▲ *Linaria alpina* 'Rosea'

L. maroccana Violet-purple flowers, up to 1.5cm (½in) long, with yellow or orange in the throat are borne on spikes during the summer. The narrow leaves are up to 4cm (1½in) long. A slender, upright annual. HEIGHT & SPREAD 30×15cm (12×6in).

'Carminea' has rose-carmine flowers. The flowers of **Excelsior Hybrids** vary from white to yellow and from pink to red. **'Fairy Bride'** has white flowers and **'Fairy Bridesmaid'** has lemon-yellow flowers. **'Ruby King'** has deep blood-red blooms.

L. purpurea (purple toadflax) Violet flowers, up to 1.5cm (½in) long, appear in long slender spikes throughout the summer and early autumn on this graceful semi-evergreen perennial. The narrow mid to grey-green leaves are 6cm (2½in) long. HEIGHT & SPREAD 1m×60cm (3×2ft).

'Canon Went' has pink flowers with orange in the mouth and grey-green leaves. **'Springside White'** (syn. 'Alba') has white flowers and grey-green leaves.

L. triornithophora Purple and yellow flowers, up to 5cm (2in) long, are borne in summer. This short-lived, upright semi-evergreen perennial has grey-green, oval or lance-like leaves, 2.5-7cm (1-2¾in) long. HEIGHT & SPREAD 1m×50cm (3ft×20in).

L. vulgaris (common toadflax) Bright yellow flowers, up to 3cm (1¼in) long, in short or long spikes, are produced from mid summer to mid autumn by this invasive herbaceous perennial. Upright stems, often branched near the base, are crowded with elliptical pale to grey-green leaves 2.5-6cm (1-2½in) long. HEIGHT & SPREAD 30-45×60cm (1-1½×2ft).

▲ *Linaria alpina* 'Purpurea'

CULTIVATION Plant in spring in well-drained soil in an open, sunny position. *L. alpina* prefers gritty soil in a raised bed or in a pocket in a rock garden.

PROPAGATION Sow the seed of annual species in spring, thinly where the plants are to flower. Sow the seed of perennial species in winter or early spring in a coldframe. Alternatively, divide perennials in spring or take softwood cuttings in spring or early summer. Move self-sown seedlings to new positions in late winter or early spring.

PESTS AND DISEASES Usually trouble free.

Lindera

Lauraceae

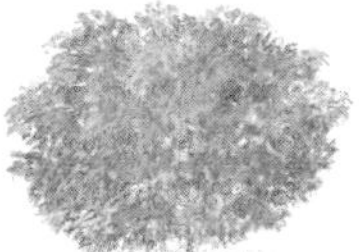

Lindera obtusiloba

Golden autumn foliage illuminates the lindera plants that are grown in British gardens. Some 80 species of hardy deciduous and evergreen trees and shrubs make up this genus of the laurel family. The few linderas that are readily available in Britain prefer lime-free soil. They are deciduous with unobtrusive tight clusters of small, late spring flowers. On female plants grown close to a male to fertilise them, the flowers are followed in summer by red berries up to 1cm (⅜in) long. Leaves, generally less than 10cm (4in) long and half as wide, are alternate on the shoots.

RECOMMENDED SPECIES AND VARIETIES

L. benzoin (spice bush) Bright green oval leaves about 10cm (4in) long and gently pointed at the top release a pleasant aroma when crushed. They cover a large rounded

▲ Lindera obtusiloba

▲ Lindera benzoin

shrub with vibrant yellow in autumn. Native to E United States. HEIGHT & SPREAD 80×80cm (32×32in) after 5 years, ultimately 3.5m (12ft) tall.

L. obtusiloba♀ Bright green leaves clothe this small tree in summer and turn butter-yellow in autumn. Tiny bright yellow flowers, covered in fine, silky hairs, appear in clusters in late spring before the leaves emerge. Growing up to 12cm (4¾in) long, the leaves are heart-shaped at the base and usually rounded at the tip, but often plants also carry a few 3-lobed leaves. Native to China, Korea and Japan. HEIGHT & SPREAD 1.2×1m (4×3ft) after 5 years, ultimately 8m (26ft) tall.

CULTIVATION Linderas do best in lime-free soil with some shade from the sun.

PROPAGATION Buy young plants or seed. There is no fertile seed to collect from a single plant in a garden and cuttings are difficult to root.

PRUNING None is required.

PESTS AND DISEASES Usually trouble free.

Lindheimera

Star daisy

Compositae

Yellow flowers bloom from mid summer to mid autumn on this free-flowering hardy annual from Texas, USA. Grow in a mixed bed or border, in a sunny situation. There is only one species in the genus.

Lindheimera texana The flowers, about 2.5cm (1in) across, are produced in loose, branched clusters. Each flower has 5, occasionally 4, broad, petal-like ray florets and a green and yellow centre. Pale green, pointed oval leaves up to 4cm (1in) long grow from the reddish, branched stems. Both stems and leaves are hairy. The plant has an erect habit of growth. Flowers do not last well in water. HEIGHT & SPREAD 60×30cm (24×12in).

▲ Lindheimera texana

CULTIVATION The plant, although hardy, needs full exposure to the sun. Then it will thrive on any well-drained soil. On heavy clay soils it would do best in a raised bed. When it has reached a height of about 10cm (4in), pinch out the growing point to encourage a branching habit of growth. Deadhead regularly.

PROPAGATION Sow seed outdoors in mid spring. Alternatively, sow seed under glass in early spring and plant out in late spring, for an earlier start to flowering.

PESTS AND DISEASES Usually trouble free.

Ling see *Calluna*

Linnaea

Twin-flower

Caprifoliaceae

Linnaea borealis

Pink or white flowers like tiny pendent bells nod above the evergreen carpet of this creeping sub-shrub. This woodland plant forms a loose mat of glossy foliage and makes excellent ground cover for a peat bed or rock garden, or under trees. Native to cool moist forests and tundra, twin-flowers dislike hot, dry conditions, especially when young, and may be difficult to establish. They do best in acid or neutral soil and dappled shade.

▲ Linnaea borealis

RECOMMENDED SPECIES AND VARIETIES

L. borealis Fragrant, pale pink or white flowers, patterned deep rose inside, and about 8mm (⅜in) long, appear in pairs on slender stems from early to mid summer. The creeping mats have small, oval, deep green leaves and spread by runners. HEIGHT & SPREAD 5×60cm (2in×2ft).

The flowers of var. *americana* are a deep rose pink. They are slightly longer and more tubular.

CULTIVATION Plant during spring in cool, moist, humus-rich acid or neutral soil. Water well, especially in warm, dry weather.

PROPAGATION Tease rooted runners away from the parent plant in spring and plant in a shaded coldframe. Once established, plant out in autumn or early spring. Alternatively, take semi-ripe cuttings from late summer to early autumn.

PESTS AND DISEASES Usually trouble free.

Linum

Flax

Linaceae

Linum flavum 'Compactum'

Brightly coloured cup or saucer-shaped flowers are carried on delicate leafy stems. Individual flowers are short-lived and may stay closed in dull or wet weather, but new ones quickly take their place, giving many weeks of colour. The leaves are usually narrow and rarely more than 3cm (1¼in) long. Linum may be annuals, biennials, perennials, or short-lived dwarf shrubs. They are popular in borders, and the smaller plants are ideal for a rock garden. Although fully hardy, some of the rock plants dislike prolonged freezing weather or excessive winter wet. Most flaxes prefer an alkaline soil, but will grow in any soil.

RECOMMENDED SPECIES AND VARIETIES

L. arboreum♀ (shrubby flax) Bright yellow flowers, up to 3cm (1¼in) wide, appear in early summer. This compact evergreen shrub, which thrives in a rock garden, has crowded, dark bluish green, elliptical to spoon-shaped leaves. HEIGHT & SPREAD 30×30cm (12×12in).

L. flavum (golden flax, yellow flax) Bright yellow flowers, up to 4cm (1½in) across, appear from mid summer. This bushy, evergreen perennial has elliptical, deep green leaves. HEIGHT & SPREAD 25×25cm (10×10in).

'Compactum', a dwarf plant about 15cm (6in) high with pale yellow flowers, is ideal in a trough but dislikes winter wet. **'Gemmell's Hybrid'**♀ has rich yellow flowers, 3cm (1¼in) wide, in early to mid summer above domes of oval grey-green leaves. It does well in a trough or raised bed. HEIGHT & SPREAD 15×20cm (6×8in).

L. monogynum White flowers, 2.5cm (1in) wide, appear from early to mid summer on this short-lived perennial with linear to lance-shaped pointed leaves. HEIGHT & SPREAD 60×40cm (24×16in).

▲ *Linum flavum* 'Gemmell's Hybrid'

▲ *Linum monogynum*

L. narbonense (beautiful flax) Pale to deep azure blue flowers, about 3cm (1¼in) wide, appear from late spring to mid summer. This herbaceous or semi-evergreen perennial has grey-green, narrow to lance-shaped leaves. It often seeds itself around the garden. HEIGHT & SPREAD 50×30cm (20×12in).

'Heavenly Blue'♀ has a profusion of vivid blue flowers.

L. perenne (syn. *L. sibiricum*) (perennial flax) Masses of pale blue flowers, each up to 2.5cm (1in) wide, appear throughout summer and early autumn. This herbaceous perennial has grass-like, deep green leaves. HEIGHT & SPREAD 40×25cm (16×10in).

White flowers grace f. *album* (syn. *L. perenne* 'Alba'), while **'Blau Saphir'** ('Blue Sapphire') has deep, sapphire-blue flowers.

L. sibiricum see *L. perenne*

L. suffruticosum ssp. *salsoloides* The pearly white flowers, flushed and veined in pink with deep violet-pink centres, are about 3cm (1¼in) wide. They appear in early to mid summer. This semi-evergreen perennial has numerous short, linear, grey-green leaves. HEIGHT & SPREAD 20×15cm (8×6in).

▲ *Linum narbonense* 'Heavenly Blue'

▲ *Linum perenne* f. *album*

'Nanum' is a semi-prostrate dwarf plant that is ideal for a raised bed or trough.

CULTIVATION Plant in spring or early summer in any well-drained soil in an open sunny position.

PROPAGATION Sow the seeds of perennials under glass in autumn or late winter, or take cuttings from mid to late summer. Sow the seed of annuals thinly in their growing position in spring.

PESTS AND DISEASES Aphids may infest the young shoots and flower buds.

Lippia see *Aloysia*

Liquidambar

Hamamelidaceae

Liquidambar styraciflua

A kaleidoscope of colour transforms these deciduous trees in autumn. The leaves are purple-hued in spring, but in autumn the colours range from pale yellow to dark crimson. The leaves have pointed lobes with serrated edges. Inconspicuous green or yellow flowers are followed by oval fruits.

RECOMMENDED SPECIES AND VARIETIES

L. formosana This tree, with leaves about 12.5cm (5in) wide, becomes roughly conical. Not always frost tolerant, it usually does well in southern Britain. HEIGHT & SPREAD 5×2.4m (16×8ft) after 20 years, ultimately 10m (33ft) tall.

▼ *Liquidambar styraciflua*

L. styraciflua (sweet gum) One of the best trees for autumn colour, this frost-hardy species has leaves up to 15cm (6in) across. HEIGHT & SPREAD 6×4m (20×13ft) after 20 years, ultimately 20m (66ft) tall.

'Lane Roberts'🏆 has rich crimson leaves in autumn, while the leaves of **'Worplesdon'**🏆 turn bright yellow and orange.

CULTIVATION For the best show of colour, plant in an acid soil in a sheltered position protected from frost. Even mature trees can be killed by prolonged frost.

PROPAGATION Grow the species from seed. Raise cultivars by grafting.

PRUNING None is necessary.

PESTS AND DISEASES Usually trouble free.

Liriodendron

Tulip tree

Magnoliaceae

Liriodendron tulipifera

Curious 'squared off' leaves, which turn a soft yellow in autumn, and remarkable flowers distinguish this monumental deciduous tree. Tulip-like, pale green flowers appear in early to mid summer on trees that are over 15 years old. The flowers mature to cone-shaped fruits which disperse winged seeds in autumn. These trees have a graceful, upswept branch system and need a lot of space. They are also hungry feeders and grow rapidly in deep, fertile soil. There are two species, one native to N America and one to China. They are similar to one another, but the Chinese tulip tree is smaller with slightly smaller flowers.

RECOMMENDED SPECIES AND VARIETIES

L. chinensis (Chinese tulip tree) The pale greenish flowers measure 6cm (2½in) across. HEIGHT & SPREAD 7×5m (23×16ft) after 20 years, ultimately 22m (72ft) tall.

L. tulipifera (tulip tree)🏆 This N American tree can grow into a huge specimen – trunks have been recorded at over 2.4m (8ft) across, and the crown spread may exceed 20m (66ft). The yellowish green cup-shaped flowers, 7.5cm (3in) across, have orange markings and prominent stamens. The bark is silvery grey and smooth for 20 years before an intricate lattice of vertical ridges develops, adding interesting textures to its great size. HEIGHT & SPREAD 10×6m (33×20ft) in 15-20 years, up to 35m (115ft) tall on rich moist sites.

'Aureomarginatum' is a slower growing form with variagated yellowish green leaf margins, while **'Fastigiatum'** is columnar.

▲ *Liriodendron tulipifera*

▲ *Liriodendron tulipifera*

▲ *Liriodendron tulipifera* 'Aureomarginatum'

Both trees are smaller than the species, reaching 22×12m (72×40ft) and 24×8m (79×26ft) respectively.

CULTIVATION For best results, plant in fertile, well-drained, warm soil.

PROPAGATION Plant pot-grown specimens in early autumn or late spring. Growing seed is not usually worth the trouble but if doing so, use only imported seed. Cultivars must be grown from grafts.

PRUNING None usually necessary, but essential cutting or training is best done after flowering.

PESTS AND DISEASES Usually trouble free if planted on a good, fertile, sheltered site.

Liriope

Liliaceae

Upright spikes of dense lavender, mauve or white flowers appear on these evergreen hardy perennials from late summer to late autumn. Glossy, strap-like or grass-like leaves are usually attractively coloured, while the small flowers are bell-like or tubular. The plants, which form clumps, are fairly drought tolerant and make valuable ground cover. The genus is native to China, Taiwan, Vietnam and Japan.

RECOMMENDED SPECIES AND VARIETIES

L. exiliflora **'Ariaka-janshige'** Strongly variegated leaves, up to 45cm (18in) long, in white and gold are produced in heavy clumps. The bell-like flowers are mauve. HEIGHT & SPREAD 20×30cm (8×12in).

L. muscari🏆 Dense clusters of small, dark mauve, bell-like flowers appear densely clustered on stiff spikes in late summer to late autumn. The dark green leaves, up to 45cm (18in) long, are strap-like. HEIGHT & SPREAD 30×45cm (12×18in).

'Gold-banded' has arching leaves edged with gold. It is a very compact plant, up to 35cm (14in) tall and spreading to about 30cm (12in). **'Majestic'** has handsome green foliage with stems of rich violet flowers. **'Monroe White'** is similar but has spikes of pure white flowers. **'Variegata'** has green leaves striped with gold at the margins. It spreads only about 30cm (12in).

L. spicata Small, bell-like flowers in pale mauve to white are carried in dense spikes in late summer. The grassy dark green leaves are glossy and up to 30cm (12in) long. HEIGHT & SPREAD 45×30cm (18×12in).

▲ *Liriope muscari* 'Majestic'

1

▲ *Liriope spicata* 'Alba'

'Alba' has small, tubular, white flowers amid narrow, grass-like, dark green leaves. It grows about 20cm (8in) tall and about 25cm (10in) wide.

CULTIVATION Grow liriope in any good well-drained soil, ideally with plenty of well-rotted organic matter incorporated into it. Choose a warm site in full sun if possible. Plant in spring, ideally using pot-grown plants. Remove faded blossoms and old leaves regularly when new foliage appears.

PROPAGATION Lift, divide and replant established crowns in spring.

PESTS AND DISEASES Usually trouble free, but slugs may damage young growth.

Lithodora

Boraginaceae

Lithodora diffusa 'Heavenly Blue'

Masses of tubular or funnel-shaped flowers decorate these small, long-flowering, evergreen shrubs or sub-shrubs. The plants, which form low, bristly mats, are good as specimen plants, or in a rock garden or raised bed. They can also be grown in patio containers. Although hardy, lithodora can be damaged by strong, cold wind. Different species have different soil requirements, but they all favour a well-drained soil.

▲ *Lithodora diffusa*

RECOMMENDED SPECIES AND VARIETIES

L. diffusa (syn. *Lithospermum diffusum*, *Lithospermum prostratum*) Bright blue flowers, each up to 2cm (¾in) long, appear in clusters at the shoot tips in early summer. This sub-shrub creates an intricately branched mat of rather crowded, bristly, narrow, elliptical leaves. It prefers moist but well-drained, acid soil, otherwise the flowers become more purple than blue and the leaves become more yellow than deep green. The plant is native to woodlands and coastal sands of SW Europe. HEIGHT & SPREAD 30×50cm (12×20in).

▲ *Lithodora diffusa* 'Grace Ward'

'Alba' has white flowers. **'Grace Ward'**♀ has deep blue flowers. **'Heavenly Blue'**♀ aptly describes the azure flowers of this plant with a trailing habit.

L. oleifolia♀ (syn. *Lithospermum oleifolium*) Pale pink flowers that age to blue, about 1cm (⅜in) long, appear in curved clusters in early and mid summer, occasionally later. The oblong-oval leaves are grey-green with silky hairs underneath. This plant, which comes from rocky parts of the eastern Pyrenees, prefers alkaline soil and forms a neat hummock. HEIGHT & SPREAD 20×80cm (8×32in).

L. zahnii (syn. *Lithospermum zahnii*) Azure flowers, about 1cm (⅜in) long, appear from late spring to mid summer. There are many branches with rather upright growth. The bristly greyish green leaves are roughly linear. Originally from the cliffs of southern Greece, this sub-shrub prefers an alkaline soil. It is usually grown in a greenhouse. HEIGHT & SPREAD 30×30cm (1×1ft).

▲ *Lithodora zahnii*

CULTIVATION Plant in spring or early summer in a sheltered, sunny position. Avoid disturbing the roots once the plant is established.

PROPAGATION Sow seed under glass in winter or early spring, or take semi-ripe cuttings in late summer and keep them in a frostproof frame during winter. Plant out the following spring or early summer.

PESTS AND DISEASES Usually trouble free, although red spider mite can cause problems under glass in hot, dry weather.

Lithops

(Living stone, pebble plant)

Aizoaceae

These curious perennial succulents are desert plants from southern Africa. Two swollen elliptical leaves are separated by a narrow slit from which a solitary flower, 4-5cm (1½-2in) across, emerges in late summer or early autumn. The upper surfaces of the leaves are opaque or semi-translucent, and are usually marked and coloured rather like a pebble.

RECOMMENDED SPECIES

L. erniana (syn. *L. karasmontana* ssp. *eberlanzii*) A dense network of red-brown lines and spots covers this grey plant with a deeply fissured surface. The white flower opens in early autumn. HEIGHT & SPREAD 3×3cm (1¼×1¼in).

L. hookeri see *L. turbiniformis*

L. karasmontana ssp. *eberlanzii* see *L. erniana*

L. lesliei The plants are grey-green to pale brown. Their flat to convex upper surface is olive-green with beige marbling. The yellow flower opens in autumn. HEIGHT & SPREAD 3×5cm (1¼×2in).

▲ *Lithops lesliei*

L. salicola Convex, olive-green to grey upper surfaces are irregularly edged with reddish beige. The rest of the plant is greyish green. The white flower appears in late summer or early autumn. HEIGHT & SPREAD 5×3cm (2×1¼in).

L. turbiniformis (syn. *L. hookeri*) The flat upper surfaces are rich brown with many darker brown fissures. The yellow flower appears in early autumn. HEIGHT & SPREAD 3×4cm (1¼×1½in).

CULTIVATION Plant in an equal mixture of compost and grit or sharp sand in late spring. Place in good light and water lightly at first. Increase watering until late summer, then stop all together until mid spring. Keep at a minimum of 5°C (41°F).
PROPAGATION Surface-sow seeds on a compost such as John Innes No.2 in mid spring. Maintain a temperature of 21°C (70°F). Alternatively, divide clumps in early summer, leave them to dry for 3-4 days then pot them separately.
PESTS AND DISEASES Mealy bugs and root mealy bugs may be troublesome.

Lithospermum see *Lithodora*
Living stone see *Lithops*

Lobelia

Campanulaceae

Lobelia x speciosa 'Queen Victoria'

Valued for their small flowers in glowing colours, borne profusely over several months, lobelias are available in a wide range of heights and habits of growth, fitting them for a variety of uses in the garden. The genus includes annuals, herbaceous perennials and sub-shrubs. Plants may be hardy, half-hardy or tender. Annuals and those perennials that are grown as half-hardy annuals are often used in containers, especially hanging baskets, as well as for edging and summer bedding plants. The hardy perennials make fine border plants and also do well along the edges of pools and streams. They are among the most dramatic of all herbaceous garden plants – many of them having dark foliage and red flowers. The flowers are tubular and have five lobes with the lower three lobes much larger than the two upper ones and flattening into a characteristic fan-like 'lip'. Some lobelias are poisonous.

RECOMMENDED SPECIES AND VARIETIES

L. cardinalis ♀ (cardinal flower) Scarlet flowers, up to 5cm (2in) across, are borne in long spikes from mid summer until autumn on this hardy, clump-forming perennial plant. Narrow, toothed, mid green leaves, up to 10cm (4in) long, form rosettes at the base of the stems. Both leaves and stems are heavily tinged in purple-bronze. The plant tends to be short-lived, lasting 2-3 years. Native to N America. HEIGHT & SPREAD 1m×25cm (36×10in).

L. erinus (edging and trailing lobelia) Violet-blue and white flowers, each 5mm (¼in) across, appear in profusion from late spring until the first autumn frosts. Numerous slender, sprawling branches carry flowers about 10 weeks after sowing. Although a short-lived perennial, *L. erinus* and its varieties are almost all treated as half-hardy annuals. The light green leaves, up to 2cm (¾in) long, are ovate at the base of the plant, longer and narrower on the stems. Native to South Africa. HEIGHT & SPREAD 15×15cm (6×6in).

Compact varieties make neat domes suitable for edging borders and for containers. **'Crystal Palace'** has deep blue flowers and dark bronze-green leaves. **'Mrs Clibran'** produces dark blue flowers, each with a conspicuous white eye. **'Cambridge Blue'** carries light blue flowers. **'Kathleen Mallard'**,

Lobelia erinus 'Cambridge Blue'

bearing blue double flowers, does not come true from seed, so must be propagated from cuttings. The flowers of **'Rosamund'** are deep cherry-red with white eyes. **'White Lady'** has white flowers, while **'Riviera Lilac'** has lilac-blue flowers, and those of **'Riviera Blue Splash'** are pale blue, marked darker blue.

Varieties with a trailing habit, spreading to 30cm (12in) or more, are ideal for hanging baskets and other containers. They include the **'Cascade'**, **'Fountain'** and **'Regatta'** series, which are available in single and mixed colours, including white, blue, lilac, mauve and purple-red. The cultivar **'Sapphire'** has deep blue flowers with white eyes.

L. x gerardii Pinkish violet to purple flowers, marked with white, up to 5cm (2in) across, form dense spikes from mid summer to early autumn. The leaves are dark green, ovate and 4cm (1½in) long. The plant is quite hardy but in colder areas it might not survive winter without a protective mulch. HEIGHT & SPREAD 1m×25cm (36×10in).

'Vedrariensis' has dark violet flowers and dark green leaves tinged with red.

▼ *Lobelia x gerardii* 'Vedrariensis'

▲ *Lobelia x gerardii* 'Tania'

'Tania' has crimson-purple flowers.

L. laxiflora (syn. *L. cavanillesii*) A branching sub-shrub, hardy only in milder areas, the plant has pendulous red-and-yellow flowers, 4cm (1½in) long, in late summer and early autumn. Leaves are narrow, dark green and up to 8cm (3¼in) long. Native to Arizona, Mexico and Colombia. HEIGHT & SPREAD 60×30cm (24×12in).

▲ *Lobelia laxiflora*

The narrower-leaved var. ***angustifolia*** is more commonly grown.

L. linnaeoides Each white and purple flower is about 1cm (⅜in) across on this perennial which flowers in short spikes from early to mid summer. It has widely spread, slender, prostrate stems. The rounded dark green leaves, up to 1cm (⅜in) long, have toothed margins. Native to New Zealand, this moisture-loving plant is for a rock garden in milder areas or an unheated greenhouse. HEIGHT & SPREAD 5×20cm (2×8in).

L. siphilitica (blue cardinal flower) Spikes up to 60cm (24in) long of blue flowers, 2.5cm (1in) wide, appear from mid summer to early autumn. Leaves are light green. lance-shaped and up to 10 cm (4 in) long. This hardy perennial can be short-lived, unless divided every other year. Native to E United States. HEIGHT & SPREAD 60×30 cm (24×12 in).

There is a white variety, **'Alba'**.

L.* x *speciosa This herbaceous perennial has red or violet flowers, 3 cm (1¼ in) wide, in loose spikes from late summer to mid autumn. Leaves are oblong to ovate and about 10 cm (4 in) long. HEIGHT & SPREAD 90×50 cm (36×20 in).

Most varieties are fully hardy. Those listed below grow to a height of 90 cm (36 in) unless stated otherwise. None can be grown from seed except **'Queen Victoria'** and **'Pink Flamingo'**.

'Cherry Ripe' has cerise-scarlet flowers with leaves often tinged reddish bronze. **'Dark Crusader'**, with red flowers and copper tinted leaves, reaches an ultimate height of 75 cm (30 in). **'Eulalia Berridge'** bears bright raspberry-coloured flowers. **'Pink Flamingo'** has rosy-pink flowers and grows to 120 cm (48 in) high. **'Queen Victoria'**♀ has red flowers with dark red foliage. **'Russian Princess'** has purple flowers and dark leaves. It grows up to 75 cm (30 in) tall.

The **'Compliment'** and **'Fan'** series of F_1 hybrids come true from seed. Both are available in a range of colours. Plants of the **'Compliment'** series grow to 75 cm (30 in) tall and have unbranched stems. Plants belonging to the **'Fan'** series branch at the base and reach a height of 60 cm (24 in). Particularly notable are ***L.* 'Compliment Scarlet'**♀ and ***L.* 'Fan Deep Red'**.

L. tenuior Erect slender stems carry an abundance of bright blue flowers, 2.5 cm (1 in) across, in loose clusters from mid summer to mid autumn. Leaves are ovate, light green and up to 3 cm (1¼ in) long.

▲ *Lobelia* 'Compliment Scarlet'

This plant resembles *L. erinus* in habit and is also a tender perennial generally treated as a half-hardy annual when grown in the garden. It is also grown as a pot plant. Native to W Australia. HEIGHT & SPREAD 30×25 cm (12×10 in).

The cultivar **'Blue Wings'** has cobalt-blue flowers.

L. tupa This large clump-forming perennial has brick-red flowers, 5 cm (2 in) wide, in spikes that bloom from late summer to mid autumn. Pale green, lance-shaped, downy leaves, 15-30 cm (6-12 in) long, grow on the stout stems. The plant particularly suits a waterside site. Native to Chile, *L. tupa* is hardy, except in severe winters. HEIGHT & SPREAD 1.8 m×1 m (6×3 ft).

L. valida Sky-blue flowers with white centres are freely produced from early summer to mid autumn on a bushy plant of upright habit with fleshy, branched stems and dark green leaves. This is a tender perennial, ordinarily treated as a half-hardy annual. Native to South Africa. HEIGHT & SPREAD 1 m×75 cm (3 ft×30 in).

CULTIVATION Plant in a rich, moisture-retaining but well-drained soil in full sun or partial shade, with some shelter from wind. Water generously in summer. Protect half-hardy plants, and those treated as half-hardy, from frost with a dry mulch.

BEDDING AND CONTAINER PLANTS

L. erinus, *L. tenuior* and *L. valida* are usually treated as half-hardy summer bedding plants. Plant out in spring when the risk of hard frosts has passed. They will tolerate slight frosts if properly hardened off before planting out. Position plants in containers out of full sun. Water to keep soil moist – especially those in containers. Feed container-grown plants with a low-nitrogen liquid fertiliser. Cut back straggly growth and older stems that no longer produce many flowers.

L. erinus and *L. tenuior* also make fine pot plants for a cool greenhouse or conservatory. They cannot be kept in a house for any length of time because there is not enough light. Water sparingly in winter.

HERBACEOUS PERENNIALS

Planting is best done in mid spring. Mulch after planting and every spring to reduce loss of moisture from the soil surface. Apply a top dressing of a general-purpose fertiliser to established plants. Support tall plants, such as *L. tupa*.

Cut down stems to ground level after they have been destroyed by frost and apply a thick mulch to protect the plants from frost damage. Bracken or leaves held in place by netting are ideal. If a plant is unlikely to survive the winter, lift it after the first frost and overwinter it in a deep box inside a coldframe.

PROPAGATION

BEDDING AND CONTAINER PLANTS

Sow seed uncovered on the compost surface in late winter if a minimum temperature of 13°C (55°F) can be maintained after germination. If this minimum temperature cannot be guaranteed, sow later. Prick out the seedlings in groups of 5 or so. Sow seed of *L. erinus* and *L. tenuior* in late winter for summer flowering, or in late summer for flowering in spring. Treat plants as half-hardy annuals.

HERBACEOUS PERENNIALS

Divide in spring and, if possible, grow on the divided shoots in pots in a coldframe for about a month before planting out. Alternatively, sow seed in summer for spring flowers or sow seed in late winter for summer flowers. If possible, keep the young plants in a cool or unheated greenhouse during winter.

PESTS AND DISEASES Slugs can be a menace and leaf spot may affect some plants. In wet winters on soil with poor drainage, plants may be lost because of crown rot.

Lobster claw see *Clianthus*

Lobularia

Cruciferae

Masses of colourful summer flowers earn this group of southern European hardy annuals and perennials its place in gardens. The plant most widely cultivated is the easy-to-grow annual, *Lobularia maritima*.

RECOMMENDED SPECIES AND VARIETIES

L. maritima (sweet alyssum) (syn. *Alyssum maritimum*) Tiny, white, 4-petalled flowers in dense fragrant clusters, up to 5 cm (2 in) across, are borne in profusion throughout summer. The short, multi-branched stems are thickly clothed with greyish green, lance-shaped leaves, up to 1.5 cm (½ in) long. This annual or short-lived perennial is widely used in summer bedding schemes, often as edging. HEIGHT & SPREAD 10×20 cm (4×8 in).

The profuse variety **'Carpet of Snow'** has pure white flowers. **'Golf Rose'** has deep pink flowers, while those of **'Little Dorrit'** are white. **'Oriental Night'** bears rich purple flowers. **'Violet Queen'** has

▼ *Lobularia maritima* 'Carpet of Snow'

▲ *Lobularia maritima* 'Oriental Night'

violet flowers, while the flowers of **'Wonderland'** are deep purplish pink.

CULTIVATION Plant in late spring in well-drained soil in a sunny situation. Do not incorporate organic material into the soil before planting because it encourages soft growth that can be susceptible to powdery mildew. Keep well watered and treat with a high-potash fertiliser, such as liquid tomato feed, when flowering has started. Remove faded blossoms and dead or withered leaves regularly.

PROPAGATION Sow seed in late winter or early spring in boxes or trays in a greenhouse or coldframe.

PESTS AND DISEASES Flea beetles may attack, especially when plants are young.

London pride see *Saxifrage* × *urbium*

Lonicera

Honeysuckle

Caprifoliaceae

Lonicera periclymenum 'Serotina'

Wafts of intensely sweet perfume and distinctive, delicate-looking flowers help to secure honeysuckle a special place in British gardens. Not all the blooms are fragrant, but careful selection from the 180 or so species can guarantee a succession of flowers throughout the year. Honeysuckles have tubular or bell-shaped flowers, up to 5cm (2in) long, with five lobes. In many plants the upper four lobes are fused, with the lower lobe curving back to reveal the stamens. The leaves, usually 3-10cm (1¼-4in) long, can be oval, or oblong to lance-shaped, or round. The fleshy berries, which are not poisonous, are ball or egg-shaped. They attract birds, hedgehogs and other wildlife, while the flowers are a good source of nectar for bees and moths – hence lonicera's common name.

Native to most of the Northern Hemisphere, lonicera offers deciduous, evergreen and semi-evergreen plants. All the recommended species and varieties are hardy. They prefer moist, but well-drained, loam-rich soil but will grow in most soil. Some prefer sun, others shade. However, plants on hot, dry sites are more vulnerable to aphids.

RECOMMENDED SPECIES AND VARIETIES

Honeysuckles are either bushy shrubs or woody climbers and the recommended plants are listed separately here.

SHRUBS

These honeysuckles are ideal for mixed and shrub borders. They include the richly scented, winter-flowering *Lonicera fragrantissima* and *L.* × *purpusii*. A low-growing plant, such as *L. pileata,* makes good ground cover, while *L. nitida* is suitable for formal hedges. These are some of the hardiest shrubs, and *L. maackii* tolerates especially severe conditions. Nonetheless, all shrub honeysuckles flower most freely in the sun. The flowers, 1.5-4cm (½-1½in) long, are borne in pairs where the leaves join the stem.

L. chaetocarpa Nodding, slightly scented, primrose-yellow flowers appear from late spring to early summer on this upright, deciduous plant. The long flowers, clasped in bracts, give way to bright red berries in mid summer. The leaves are bristly. HEIGHT & SPREAD 1.2×1.2m (4×4ft) after 5 years, ultimately 2.4m (8ft) tall.

L. fragrantissima The powerful fragrance of the creamy yellow blooms fills the air throughout winter. Dull red berries follow in spring. The leathery leaves are semi-evergreen in exposed positions and fully evergreen if the plant is sheltered from cold winds. HEIGHT & SPREAD 1.5×1.5m (5×5ft) after 5 years, ultimately 2.7m (9ft) tall.

L. involucrata (twinberry, Californian honeysuckle) Small, yellow or red-tinged flowers surrounded by heart-shaped bracts appear on this robust, deciduous plant in spring and are followed by shiny, black berries. The narrow, slightly hairy leaves are about 12.5cm (5in) long. HEIGHT & SPREAD 1.2×1.2m (4×4ft) after 5 years, ultimately 2.4m (8ft) tall.

▲ *Lonicera involucrata*

Deep orange-yellow flowers held by purple-tinged, heart-shaped bracts distinguish var. ***ledebourii*** which is slightly larger than *L. involucrata*.

L. korolkowii This graceful, deciduous shrub has pale rose-coloured blooms in late spring and early summer, followed by red berries. The young hollow twigs and the leaves are downy. HEIGHT & SPREAD 1.5×1.5m (5×5ft) after 5 years, ultimately 3m (10ft) tall.

L. maackii Fragrant white flowers turn yellow before fading on this vigorous, deciduous plant. In bloom from late spring to mid summer, the flowers give way to dark red or black berries. The leaf stems are purple with dense hairs. Although very hardy, this plant prefers rich soil and a sunny position. HEIGHT & SPREAD 3×3m (10×10ft) after 5 years, ultimately 4.5m (15ft) tall.

White blooms distinguish f. ***podocarpa*** which is slightly smaller than *L. maackii*.

▲ *Lonicera nitida*

L. nitida (box-leaved honeysuckle) With its small, dark green shiny leaves and rounded habit, this fast-growing, dense evergreen makes excellent formal hedging. Provided that it is not pruned into a hedge, creamy white fragrant flowers in spring are followed by shiny, transparent blue-purple berries. HEIGHT & SPREAD 1.5×1.8m (5×6ft) after 5 years, ultimately 2.4m (8ft) tall.

'Baggesen's Gold'♀ is grown for its dense, nodding branches of small, golden

Lonicera nitida 'Baggesen's Gold'

▲ *Lonicera pileata*

leaves that turn sulphur-green in winter.

L. pileata Ideal for ground cover, underplanting and rockeries, this evergreen or semi-evergreen shrub has a low, neat, spreading habit and tolerates partial shade. Yellowish white flowers in late spring are followed by transparent amethyst coloured berries. The young twigs are purple and covered with soft hairs, while the leaves are dark and shiny with prominent mid veins. HEIGHT & SPREAD 1×1.5m (3×5ft) after 5 years, ultimately 1.5m (5ft) tall.

'Moss Green' is a compact cultivar with bright green leaves.

L.* × *purpusii🏆 Cream-coloured flowers, heavy with perfume, appear on the bare twigs of this semi-evergreen from late winter to mid spring. This honeysuckle has dense branches, bristly leaves and red berries. HEIGHT & SPREAD 1.5×1.5m (5×5ft) after 5 years, ultimately 3m (10ft) tall.

1

'Winter Beauty'🏆 is an exceptionally fragrant winter-flowering plant with creamy white flowers.

L. rupicola* var. *syringantha This graceful, deciduous shrub has lilac-pink sweetly scented flowers in spring and early summer and small grey-green leaves. HEIGHT & SPREAD 1×1m (3×3ft) after 5 years, ultimately 1.8m (6ft) tall.

▲ *Lonicera rupicola* var. *syringantha*

L. standishii Fragrant creamy white flowers, sometimes tinted pale pink, appear in winter and early spring followed by red, heart-shaped berries. This deciduous or semi-evergreen plant is very hardy. HEIGHT & SPREAD 1.8×1.8m (6×6ft) after 5 years, ultimately 2.4m (8ft) tall.

L. tatarica This easy-to-grow deciduous plant thrives untamed. Hardy and drought-tolerant, it has white to pinkish flowers in late spring and early summer followed by scarlet or orange berries. HEIGHT & SPREAD 2×2m (6½×6½ft) after 5 years, ultimately 3m (10ft) tall.

'Arnold's Red' is a vigorous plant with very deep red fragrant flowers and blue tinted leaves. **'Hack's Red'** has rose-pink flowers.

L.* × *xylosteum (fly honeysuckle) This deciduous plant, naturalised in some parts of Britain, has yellowish white flowers, often tinted red, in summer. The berries are red, occasionally yellow. HEIGHT & SPREAD 1.5×1.5m (5×5ft) after 5 years, ultimately 3m (10ft) tall.

CLIMBERS

These plants, which climb by twining their stems around supports, may be trained over formal arches or left to scramble up trees, through bushes or over garden eyesores, such as a featureless wall. Evergreen species, such as *Lonicera henryi*, make excellent screens supported by trellis. The flowers, 4-5cm (1½-2in) long, are borne either in pairs, or in whorls of six, in a cluster or a spike. Some plants have perfoliate leaves. This means that two opposite leaves fuse around the stem, like a small ruff under the blooms. Most climbers prefer their roots in shade and their shoots in the sun.

L.* × *americana hort. see *L.* × *italica*

L.* × *americana🏆 Fragrant pink and cream blooms appear from mid summer to mid autumn shielded by oblong-elliptic perfoliate leaves. This evergreen needs a sheltered position in either sun or shade. HEIGHT & SPREAD 1.2×1.2m (4×4ft) after 5 years, ultimately 3m (10ft) tall.

▲ *Lonicera* × *americana*

***L.* × *brownii* 'Dropmore Scarlet'** (scarlet trumpet honeysuckle) Spikes of showy, orange-scarlet flowers perch above round, perfoliate leaves from early summer to early autumn, sometimes followed by orange-red berries. The elliptical lower leaves are slightly downy. This very hardy, deciduous hybrid needs part shade to reduce attack by aphids. HEIGHT & SPREAD 1.5×1.5m (5×5ft) after 5 years, ultimately 3.5m (12ft) tall.

▲ *Lonicera* × *brownii* 'Dropmore Scarlet'

L. caprifolium🏆 (early cream honeysuckle, perfoliate honeysuckle) Cup-like, greyish green leaves cradle the cream-flushed, pink flowers of this vigorous deciduous plant. Whorls of heavily scented flowers open from mid to late spring and are followed by clusters of bright orange-red berries. HEIGHT & SPREAD 1.8×1.8m (6×6ft) after 5 years, ultimately 4m (13ft) tall.

'Anna Fletcher' has lemon-yellow flowers.

L. etrusca This vigorous deciduous or semi-evergreen climber has creamy yellow fragrant flowers, often tinted red, from early summer to early autumn. Red berries follow. The upper leaves are perfoliate. HEIGHT & SPREAD 1.5×1m (5×3ft) after 5 years, ultimately 2.4m (8ft) tall.

'Donald Waterer' has striking red and cream fragrant flowers in mid summer followed by abundant red berries in autumn. This upright deciduous plant with red stems prefers a sunny position, and can be grown in a container. **'Michael Rosse'** has soft grey-green leaves that complement the slender, mid summer, cream flowers. In bloom at the same time, **'Superba'** has large trusses of fragrant yellow flowers flushed with pink emerging from a collar of grey-green, perfoliate, upper leaves. Red berries appear in autumn. This vigorous semi-evergreen, which prefers full sun, grows to about 3.5m (12ft) tall.

▲ *Lonicera etrusca* 'Superba'

L. giraldii Conspicuous yellow stamens decorate the red flowers of this evergreen with hairy leaves and stems. Clusters of early summer flowers give way to small blue-black berries. This hardy plant needs shelter from the wind in a position that is not too wet in winter. HEIGHT & SPREAD 1.2×1.2m (4×4ft) after 5 years, ultimately 3m (10ft) tall.

L.* × *heckrottii This compact, free-flowering, deciduous hybrid has a shrub-like habit and can be grown in a container in part shade. Long spikes of fragrant pink and orange flowers appear above perfoliate leaves from early to late summer. HEIGHT & SPREAD1.5×1.2m (5×4ft) after 5 years, ultimately 1.8m (6ft) tall.

'Goldflame' has rounded clusters of fragrant deep pink and yellow flowers.

L. henryi This vigorous evergreen with hairy shoots and dark green leaves has small yellow-orange flowers flushed pink in early and mid summer. Blue-black berries appear in autumn. HEIGHT & SPREAD 2.4×2.4m (8×8ft) after 5 years, ultimately 5m (16ft) tall.

L.* × *italica (syn. *L.* × *americana* hort.) Exceptionally fragrant flowers smother this vigorous deciduous plant from late spring to mid summer. Maroon in bud, the blooms open to reveal pink and yellow petals. The young stems are purple with obovate leaves. The late-summer berries are orange-red. HEIGHT & SPREAD 2×2m (6½×6½ft) after 5 years, ultimately 4m (13ft) tall.

L. japonica This evergreen or semi-evergreen plant is very vigorous and can become invasive. The fragrant white flowers appear from early summer to early autumn, ageing to yellow. Black berries follow. HEIGHT & SPREAD 2.4×2.4m (8×8ft) after 5 years, ultimately 4.5m (15ft) tall.

'Aureoreticulata' has leaves with yellow and green veins. Best in part shade, this prostrate semi-evergreen has insignificant, but fragrant white flowers, and can be used as ground cover. Fast-growing **'Halliana'** is a semi-evergreen suitable for pergolas and screens in sun or shade. Heavily scented white and yellow flowers are borne from mid summer to early autumn. The young leaves are hairy. **'Hall's Prolific'**, also a fast-growing semi-evergreen, flowers profusely.

Crimson and white fragrant flowers and purple-tinted leaves distinguish var. ***repens***, a vigorous semi-evergreen.

L. periclymenum (woodbine) Scrambling vigorously, this deciduous plant, which is native to Britain, Europe and W Asia, has sweetly scented creamy white flowers with purple to yellow undersides from early summer to early autumn. HEIGHT & SPREAD 1.8×1.8m (6×6ft) after 5 years, ultimately 3.5m (12ft) tall.

'Belgica' (early Dutch woodbine) has dense heads of heavily scented pink-and-red flowers in mid summer. Large bunches of orange berries in late summer turn red in autumn. This plant benefits from part shade. The vigorous **'Graham Thomas'**♀, originally a native wild plant, has profuse, fragrant, cream-white flowers from mid summer to early autumn. The berries are orange-red. This plant ultimately grows to 4m (13ft) tall. **'Serotina'**♀ (late Dutch honeysuckle) has abundant richly scented, purple, red and white flowers from mid

▲ *Lonicera* × *italica*

▲ *Lonicera periclymenum* 'Belgica'

▲ *Lonicera periclymenum* 'Graham Thomas'

▼ *Lonicera japonica* 'Halliana' (flowers)

▼ *Lonicera japonica* 'Halliana'

▼ *Lonicera periclymenum* 'Serotina'

1

▲ *Lonicera sempervirens*

▲ *Lonicera sempervirens f. sulphurea*

1

▲ *Lonicera similis var. delavayi*

summer to early autumn. Bronze-tinted leaves complement the purple-red autumn berries. This plant prefers partial shade.

L. sempervirens♀ (trumpet honeysuckle) Flowering from spring to early autumn, this semi-evergreen has spikes of scarlet blooms emphasised by perfoliate leaves. Large clusters of scarlet berries appear from late summer. This plant needs partial shade to reduce attack by aphids. HEIGHT & SPREAD 1.5×1.5 m (5×5 ft) after 5 years, ultimately 3 m (10 ft) tall.

The more vigorous f. ***sulphurea*** has bright yellow flowers and yellow berries that turn red. It needs a sheltered position.

L. similis* var. *delavayi A vigorous evergreen that excels on pergolas and archways, this plant has pairs of large, fragrant, white-and-yellow flowers, about 7 cm (2¾ in) long, in mid summer. The leaves are slightly hairy and the small berries are black. HEIGHT & SPREAD 2.4×2.4 m (8×8 ft) after 5 years, ultimately 4.5 m (15 ft) tall.

L. × tellmanniana♀ Bold displays of red-flushed, coppery yellow flowers perch in large clusters above oval, perfoliate leaves in late spring and early summer on this deciduous plant. HEIGHT & SPREAD 1.5×1.5 m (5×5 ft) after 5 years, ultimately 3.5 m (12 ft) tall.

L. tragophylla♀ Bright golden flowerheads appear in early summer on this vigorous, deciduous climber with slightly hairy, bronze-tinted young leaves. Not always easy to grow, but dramatic when established, this plant needs a moist shady position. HEIGHT & SPREAD 1.8×1.5 m (6×5 ft) after 5 years, ultimately 5 m (16 ft) tall.

CULTIVATION Plant in a shallow hole in moist, but well-drained, humus-rich soil if possible, although honeysuckles will grow in any soil. For shrubs, plant deciduous species and varieties in their dormant season, ideally in a sunny position for profuse flowering. Plant evergreen shrubs in spring. Plant bare-rooted plants of *L. nitida* from late autumn to early spring about 30 cm (1 ft) apart.

For climbers, plant pot-grown species and varieties at any time, bearing in mind that it is easier to establish deciduous climbers between autumn and spring in dry areas and in spring elsewhere. For evergreen climbers, try to plant in spring. If possible, position climbers with their roots in shade and their shoots in the sun. Water and feed in the growing season.

PROPAGATION For shrubs, take semi-ripe cuttings in late summer and plant in sandy compost in a coldframe, or take hardwood cuttings in early to mid autumn. Plant out the following spring. Alternatively, layer the outer shoots. Sow seed in autumn or spring.

For climbers, take ripewood cuttings of evergreens and *L. caprifolium*, *L. periclymenum*, *L. japonica* and their varieties and cultivars in late autumn and plant them in a coldframe. For plants that take some time to root, such as *L. × americana*, *L. etrusca*, *L. giraldii*, *L. sempervirens* and *L. tragophylla*, take softwood cuttings in spring or early summer and grow in a propagator.

PRUNING For evergreen and deciduous shrubs, thin and cut back after flowering. Cut back hedging plants by half their height in their first spring and again in summer to encourage bushiness. In subsequent years cut back by about a half until the hedge reaches the desired size.

For climbers, pruning is not necessary. However, cut back any straggly plants to encourage new growth, and prune vigorous plants to control their size. Autumn is the best time to do this in mild areas and spring is best in cold areas. Cut out any old or diseased wood in winter and encourage new growth by reducing the main stems by a about a third.

PESTS AND DISEASES Aphids can make flowering shoots unsightly. Leaf spot can affect *L. caprifolium* and mildew can be a problem for *L. japonica* 'Aureoreticulata'.

Loosestrife, purple
see *Lythrum salicaria*
Loosestrife, yellow
see *Lysimachia vulgaris*
Loquat see *Eriobotrya japonica*
Lords and ladies see *Arum maculatum*

Lotus

Leguminosae

Lotus plants are best grown where their long stems can trail and show off the fine silvery foliage and spectacular flowers.

RECOMMENDED SPECIES AND VARIETIES

L. berthelotii♀ (parrot's beak) This tender sub-shrub makes a good choice for a container or hanging basket in a sunny, sheltered spot in the garden provided it is overwintered under glass. It has trailing mats of semi-evergreen, silvery leaves and bears a mass of brilliant red and yellow, curved, beak-like flowers, up to 4 cm (1½ in) long, throughout summer. Each leaf, up to 2 cm (¾ in) long, is divided into 5 narrow segments. Native to the Canary Isles. HEIGHT & SPREAD 20 cm × 1 m (8 in × 3 ft).

▲ *Lotus berthelotii*

CULTIVATION Plant in early spring in a well-drained soil in a position in full sun. Alternatively, grow in containers of well-drained, soil-based compost in a frost-free greenhouse or conservatory. Plants can be brought outside once the danger of frost has passed.

PROPAGATION Take softwood cuttings in early summer.

PESTS AND DISEASES Usually trouble free.

Lovage (culinary herb) see HERBS p. 331
Love-in-a-mist see *Nigella damascena*
Love-lies-bleeding
see *Amaranthus caudatus*
Lungwort see *Pulmonaria*

Luma
Myrtaceae

These shrubs or small trees are grown for their glossy evergreen leaves and mottled bark. Lumas are not completely hardy and in Britain will thrive outdoors only in warm coastal regions, or in the shelter of a warm wall in mild inland areas.

RECOMMENDED SPECIES

***L. apiculata*♀** (syn. *Myrtus apiculata, M. luma*) This small, rounded, often many-stemmed tree is grown mainly for its cinnamon-coloured bark, which peels off after 5 years leaving light, dark and golden brown patches. White flowers, up to 2.5cm (1in) across, are followed in early autumn by red berries that turn black. The dark green oval leaves are about 2.5cm (1in) long. Native to Chile. HEIGHT & SPREAD 2.4×1.2m (8×4ft) after 10 years, ultimately 6m (20ft) tall.

▲ *Luma apiculata*

CULTIVATION In mild areas, plant outdoors in spring, in a well-drained soil in full sun. Alternatively, grow in a cool greenhouse in pots of multipurpose compost; move outside once the danger of frost has passed and return to the greenhouse before the first frosts return. Feed established pot plants with a weak liquid feed every fortnight from late spring to early summer. Water liberally during spring and summer but keep the compost just moist in winter.

PROPAGATION Sow seed under glass in spring or take semi-ripe cuttings in summer.

PRUNING Not normally required but, if wished, trim plants into shape in spring.

PESTS AND DISEASES Usually trouble free.

Lunaria
Honesty
Cruciferae

Purple or white flowers that bloom in late spring and early summer are followed by rounded, flat, silvery seedpods. Each flower has four petals and is up to 2cm (¾in) across. The seedpods are often used dried in flower arrangements: cut in late summer to avoid damage by autumn weather. These biennials or herbaceous perennials are hardy natives of central and southern Europe.

RECOMMENDED SPECIES AND VARIETIES

L. annua (syn. *L. biennis*) Clusters of purple or white flowers are borne on stiff upright stems. The translucent oval seedpods are 3-7.5cm (1¼-3in) long. Heart-shaped leaves, up to 15cm (6in) long, usually have coarsely toothed edges. A biennial plant, this will do well in dry shade. HEIGHT & SPREAD 1m×60cm (3×2ft).

'Alba Variegata' has white flowers and leaves edged in creamy white; var. ***albiflora*♀** also has white flowers.

L. biennis see *L. annua*

L. rediviva This short-lived perennial bears fragrant, pale purple flowers in branching clusters up to 30cm (12in) across. The pointed oval seedpods are 5-8cm (2-3¼in) long. Deep green oval leaves with toothed edges are up to 12.5cm (5in) long. HEIGHT & SPREAD 1m×60cm (3×2ft).

▲ *Lunaria rediviva*

CULTIVATION Plant in autumn or spring in a partly shaded site. *L. annua* needs a light soil and *L. rediviva* does best in moist soil.

PROPAGATION Sow seed where the plants are to grow – sow *L. annua* in late spring or early summer and *L. rediviva* in spring. Divide *L. rediviva* in autumn or spring.

PESTS AND DISEASES White blister may attack leaves; roots are liable to club root.

Lupinus
Leguminosae

The imposing flower spikes of lupins provide some of the brightest colours to be seen in an early-summer garden. Though few of the 250 species of annuals, herbaceous perennials and shrubs are commonly cultivated in Britain, extensive breeding has produced many garden hybrids to choose from. The sweet-pea-shaped flowers (with horizontal keel and reflexed standard) come in yellows, oranges, reds and blues – something for every colour scheme. Sometimes scented, lupins are valued for cutting.

Lupinus arboreus

Unless otherwise stated, all the lupins described below are hardy, and all have palmate leaves. The shrubby species are good for the wild garden; the herbaceous perennials suit more formal borders. The annuals with their smaller and more open flower spikes achieve maximum impact when planted in clumps. All lupins can be harmful if eaten.

RECOMMENDED SPECIES AND VARIETIES

***L. arboreus*♀** This fast-growing evergreen shrub has a sprawling habit, bearing its small spikes of pale yellow, scented flowers (sometimes suffused with white or purple) above pale green foliage from early to late summer. The leaves are about 5cm (2in) long and hairy underneath. The plant grows well in coastal areas and is useful for gardens exposed to sea breezes where it will shelter less wind-tolerant subjects. The seed is set freely which can cause the plant to spread over a wider area than desired – but makes it ideal for naturalising on a sunny bank with a light sandy soil where nothing much else will survive. The shrub is short-lived, lasting less than 5 years – and best replaced sooner. HEIGHT & SPREAD 2.4×2m (8×6½ft).

1

The flowers of **'Golden Spire'** are a deeper yellow. The plant is not completely hardy, except in mild, coastal areas.

L. chamissonis This shrubby evergreen ground-hugging perennial is formed of a mass of silvery grey leaves from which the flowers rise in late summer. The spikes carry

▼ *Lupinus chamissonis*

blue and white flowers, blotched yellow at the base. HEIGHT & SPREAD 1×1.5m (3×5ft).
L. hartwegii This hairy annual bears pale blue flowers from mid summer to early autumn. It is the largest annual species commonly cultivated. HEIGHT & SPREAD 1m×50cm (3ft×20in).

'Sunrise' has blue and gold flowers.
L. luteus Bright yellow, highly fragrant flowers bloom from early to late summer. Like *L. hartwegii*, this is a hairy annual with 5cm (2in) long leaves. HEIGHT & SPREAD 60×30cm (2×1ft).
L. nanus The most widely grown annual bears blue flowers mid summer to early autumn. Its leaves are about 4cm (1½in) long. HEIGHT & SPREAD 40×20cm (16×8in).

'Pixie Delight' has a mixture of blue, pink, white and bicoloured flowers.

GARDEN HYBRIDS

These herbaceous perennials are generally up to 1m (3ft) tall with a spread of 45cm (18in). The divided leaves are up to 20cm (8in) long. They flower in early summer, some producing bicoloured blooms where the keel is one colour (noted first) and the standard another. All the varieties below, except the Band of Nobles Series and Gallery Series, and the 'Lulu' mixture must be propagated by cuttings to come true.

Band of Nobles Series♀ (a range of colours, including yellow, pink, red, blue and violet); **'Chandelier'** (soft yellow); **'Deborah Woodfield'**♀ (cream pink); **'Esmerelder'**♀ (lilac); **'Helen Sharman'**♀ (orange and yellow); **'Kayleigh Ann Savage'**♀ (dusky pink flushed with cream). **'My Castle'** (red); **'Noble Maiden'** (creamy white); **'Olive Tolley'**♀ (pale rose); **'Pope John Paul'**♀ (white); **'Royal Wedding'**♀ (white). **'The Chatelaine'** (pink and white); **'The Governor'** (deep blue and white); **'The Page'** (carmine red). The **Gallery Series** and the **'Lulu'** mixture have been bred to meet the demand for perennial lupins which can be raised successfully from seed. These strains will flower in the first season from sowing. Shorter than most hybrids, to 45cm (18in) tall, both have a wide colour range.

▼ *Lupinus* 'Kayleigh Ann Savage'

CULTIVATION Grow lupins in sun or partial shade in neutral or slightly acid light sandy soil. Rich soils encourage soft growth. Plant out rooted cuttings of perennial species in spring. Taller lupins may need staking. Sow annuals in their final flowering position in early spring. In mild areas sow seed in early autumn for an earlier show. Deadhead plants to prolong flowering and prevent self-seeding.

PROPAGATION Take basal cuttings of the garden hybrids early to mid spring, ideally with a small piece of rootstock attached. For other perennial species, and for extra early flowering of annuals, sow seed in early spring in a coldframe, prick out into 10cm (4in) pots when large enough to handle and plant out in early summer. Soak seed for 24 hours in water before sowing to soften hard coats and accelerate germination.

PESTS AND DISEASES Aphids are troublesome. Powdery mildew infects leaves, as do viruses and fungal leaf spot. The stems can rot, especially if the soil is too rich.

Luzula see GRASSES p.303

Lychnis

Catchfly
Caryophyllaceae

With their bright summer flowers, often vivid pink or red and attractive to butterflies, catchflies give a splash of colour to borders and are suitable for cutting. The smaller kinds are useful for rock gardens or raised beds and *Lychnis flos-cuculi* is a pretty plant for moist places such as pool margins. Many species possess sticky nodes which trap, but do not digest, small insects. All the plants listed are herbaceous perennials.

RECOMMENDED SPECIES AND VARIETIES

L. alpina (syn. *L. viscaria* var. *alpina*) (Alpine catchfly) Rose-purple flowers, about 1cm (⅜in) across with neatly notched petals, are borne in head-like clusters from late spring to summer. The dark green linear to spoon-shaped leaves are mostly crowded at the base of the plant. This small, tufted perennial is short-lived, but will readily self-seed. HEIGHT & SPREAD 15×10cm (6×4in).

'Alba' has white flowers; **'Rosea'**, pink.
L. × arkwrightii Scarlet flowers up to 4cm (1½in) across appear in summer. The plant, hardy to about -20°C (-4°F), is especially useful for its dark red-flushed foliage. HEIGHT & SPREAD 40×20cm (16×8in).

'Vesuvius' has vivid scarlet flowers 5cm (2in) across.

▲ *Lychnis* x *arkwrightii* 'Vesuvius'

L. chalcedonica♀ An old cottage-garden favourite, the scarlet flowers, 3cm (1¼in) across, with cleft petals, bloom in clusters in early to mid summer. The pale green lance-shaped to oval leaves are paired along stiff stems. It dislikes very dry situations. HEIGHT & SPREAD 1m×40cm (36×16in).

The flowers of var. ***albiflora*** are white; **'Flore Pleno'** has double red blooms; and those of **'Rosea'** are pink.
L. coronaria (dusty miller, rose campion) Bold reddish purple flowers, up to 3cm (1¼in) across, bloom in branched clusters throughout summer. Handsome grey-felted ovate to lance-shaped leaves are arranged in pairs up the erect stems. HEIGHT & SPREAD 60×45cm (2×1½ft).

'Abbotswood Rose' see *L.* × *walkeri* 'Abbotswood Rose'. **Alba Group**♀ has white flowers. The large white flowers of **'Angel's Blush'** are flushed with pink. **Atrosanguinea Group** has deep pink flowers and pale grey foliage. **Oculata Group** has white flowers with a bright pink eye.
L. flos-cuculi (ragged robin) The bright pink flowers, up to 4cm (1½in) across and with deeply cut narrow-lobed petals, appear in laxly branched clusters in summer and early autumn. This rather delicate, spreading perennial has pairs of pointed deep green leaves. Native to Europe and Siberia. HEIGHT & SPREAD 60×40cm (2ft×16in).

'Alba Plena' has double white flowers while var. ***albiflora*** has white flowers. **'Nana'**, a dwarf plant only 15cm (6in) tall and most suitable for a rock garden has deep pink flowers.

L. flos-jovis Bold purple to pink or white flowers, up to 2cm (¾in) across, are borne in dense clusters in summer on the erect stems of this tufted, downy plant. HEIGHT & SPREAD 45×45cm (18×18in).

▲ *Lychnis flos-jovis* 'Hort's Variety'

'Hort's Variety' carries dense heads of rose-pink flowers. **'Nana'** (syn. 'Minor') has red flowers and reaches only 25cm (10in).

L. × haageana Scarlet or orange-red flowers, about 5cm (2in) across, are carried in clusters of just a few flowers in summer. Oval mid green leaves may be flushed purple. A short-lived perennial, hardy to -20°C (-4°F), it flowers readily in the first year from seed and can be grown as an annual. HEIGHT & SPREAD 45×30cm (18×12in).

'Grandiflora' produces red flowers up to 7cm (2¾in) across. **'Salmonea'** has salmon-pink flowers.

L. viscaria (sticky catchfly) Clusters of reddish purple flowers, 2cm (¾in) across, with purple-flushed calyxes, bloom in summer. The stiff stems of this tufted plant are very sticky at the upper nodes, and carry elliptical dark green leaves. HEIGHT & SPREAD 45×30cm (18×12in).

The flowers of var. *alba* are white; var. *alpina* see *L. alpina*. **'Plena'** has purplish

▼ *Lychnis viscaria*

▲ *Lychnis viscaria* 'Splendens Plena'

pink double flowers and **'Splendens Plena'**♀ has bright magenta double blooms.

***L. × walkeri* 'Abbotswood Rose'**♀ (syn. *L. coronaria* 'Abbotswood Rose') A tufted perennial with grey-green downy leaves and clusters of rose-pink flowers in summer. HEIGHT & SPREAD 40×30cm (16×12in).

L. yunnanensis White to pale pink flowers, up to 2cm (¾in) across, with cleft petals, bloom in lax clusters from late spring to summer. A useful rock garden species, this hairy perennial has slender stems and narrow, oval, bright green leaves. HEIGHT & SPREAD 20×15cm (8×6in).

CULTIVATION All plants are hardy to at least -25°C (-13°F) unless otherwise stated. Apart from *L. flos-cuculi* which needs moist ground, catchflies thrive in most well-drained garden soils in sun or partial shade. The smaller alpines like a gritty compost in full sun. *L. × arkwrightii* and *L. × haageana* can be grown as annuals, flowering readily within the year when sown in late winter or early spring. *L. coronaria*, *L. flos-jovis* and *L. viscaria* will all self-sow in the garden. Young plants can easily be moved.

PROPAGATION Sow seed in autumn or early spring in pots in a coldframe, pricking out seedlings as soon as they are large enough to handle. These will generally flower in their second season. The white-flowered cultivars cross readily so plant away from the coloured forms.

PESTS AND DISEASES Slugs and snails may eat the young shoots as they emerge in spring. The grey-felted leaves of some species, especially of *L. coronaria*, may be shredded by birds in winter. The foliage is sometimes susceptible to attacks of powdery mildew, with *L. coronaria* being the most vulnerable, especially in late summer.

▼ *Lychnis × haageana*

Lysichiton

Skunk cabbage, bog arum

Araceae

Massive, gleaming leaves make these hardy herbaceous perennials impressive features beside a garden pond or in boggy areas. Even more spectacular are the giant yellow or white spathes – leaf-like, open-ended tubes – that appear in spring. Inside the spathe is the spadix, a stiffly erect spike that carries the insignificant flowers. Lysichitons can be very slow to establish themselves and usually do not flower until they are four to six years of age, so it is best to buy plants at least two or three years old. They have stout rhizomes that develop large deep root systems to anchor the heavy plants.

RECOMMENDED SPECIES

L. americanus♀ (yellow skunk cabbage) The oblong, ribbed leaves are 30cm-1.2m (1-4ft) long and 30cm (1ft) wide. Bright green at first, they darken a little with age. The yellow spathe, about 30cm (1ft) long, sheaths a green spadix that turns yellow. Native to the west coast of N America. HEIGHT & SPREAD 1.2×1.5m (4×5ft).

L. camtschatcensis♀ (white skunk cabbage) A white spathe, about 30cm (1ft) long, encloses a pale green spadix bearing sweetly scented flowers. The oblong, strongly ribbed leaves are up to 1.2m (4ft) long and 30cm (1ft) wide. Native to coastal regions of NE Asia. HEIGHT & SPREAD 1×1m (3×3ft).

CULTIVATION Plant in spring or autumn in deep, humus-rich, wet or boggy soils, choosing a site in full sun or partial shade.

PROPAGATION Divide the thick clumps or sow seed in spring. Move and replant self-seeded plants in spring.

PESTS AND DISEASES Usually trouble free.

▼ *Lysichiton americanus*

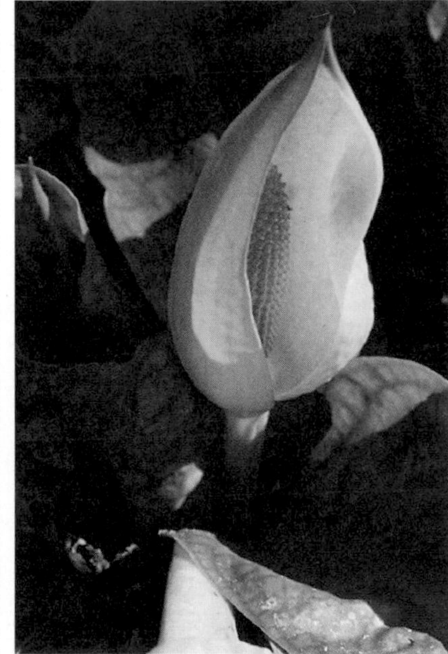

1

Lysimachia

Loosestrife

Primulaceae

Lysimachia punctata

Tall plants with elegant floral spires and also creeping, ground-cover specimens are included in this varied genus of hardy perennials. They prefer moist soil, whether in a border or at the water's edge, although they will grow in any fertile soil.

Lysimachias are native to N America, Europe and Asia. Of the recommended plants, *Lysimachia nummularia* is evergreen, while the others die down in winter.

RECOMMENDED SPECIES AND VARIETIES

L. ciliata Yellow star-shaped flowers, about 2.5cm (1in) wide, each on its own stem, nod from mid to late summer above this graceful plant's 15cm (6in) ovate leaves. HEIGHT & SPREAD 1.2m×45cm (4×1½ft).

L. clethroides ♀ (gooseneck loosestrife) Small white flowers, up to 1cm (⅜in) wide, grow as dense arched spikes in late summer, resembling the necks of geese. The oval to lance-shaped leaves are 13cm (5¼in) long. HEIGHT & SPREAD 1m×60cm (3×2ft).

L. ephemerum Pearly white flowers, 1cm (⅜in) wide, grow in arched spikes from mid to late summer complemented by grey-green leaves, up to 15cm (6in) long. HEIGHT & SPREAD 1m×60cm (3×2ft).

L. henryi Trailing stems carry heads of small yellow flowers from mid to late summer and 6cm (2½in) long oval to lance-shaped leaves. HEIGHT & SPREAD 15×45cm (6×18in).

L. nummularia (creeping Jenny, moneywort) Tiny black glands dot the shiny yellow cup-shaped flowers – 2cm (¾in) across – in early summer. This low-growing, vigorous, evergreen creeper has bright green, oval to round leaves, 2cm (¾in) long. HEIGHT & SPREAD 2.5cm×1m (1×36in).

'Aurea' ♀ makes an attractive carpet of golden leaves.

L. punctata (dotted loosestrife) Thriving near water, this plant also does well in broad swathes in a wild garden where its rampant habit is unlikely to cause problems. Clusters of upright spikes with bright yellow cup-shaped flowers, 1.5cm (½in) across, appear in summer. The leaves, 7cm (2¾in) long, are carried in pairs or whorls, and are elliptic and pointed with hairy edges. HEIGHT & SPREAD 1m×60cm (3×2ft).

L. thyrsiflora (tufted loosestrife) Tuft-like, open clusters of yellow flowers, 5mm (¼in) wide, appear from late spring to early summer from the middle leaf axils. Leaves are lance-shaped and up to 10cm (3½in) long. HEIGHT & SPREAD 60×60cm (2×2ft).

L. vulgaris (yellow loosestrife) Loose spikes of star-shaped, pale yellow flowers appear in mid summer. The oval to lance-shaped leaves, up to 9cm (3½in) long, are opposite or in whorls. This plant spreads by runners. HEIGHT & SPREAD 1×1m (3×3ft).

CULTIVATION Plant from autumn to spring in any fertile, preferably moisture-retaining soil. Mulch dry soils thoroughly in late winter or early spring. On open sites, support tall plants with stakes. Divide and replant yearly or every other year to control the spread of plants at water margins.

PROPAGATION Sow seed when ripe, or in early spring in a coldframe. Plant out in autumn. Divide plants from autumn to spring. Take stem cuttings from *L. nummularia* in spring.

PESTS AND DISEASES Usually trouble free.

▼ *Lysimachia ephemerum*

▲ *Lysimachia nummularia*

▲ *Lysimachia punctata*

Lythrum

Loosestrife

Lythraceae

Slender wands of flowers in shades of purplish pink appear in mid summer on these upright, hardy perennials that thrive on boggy ground. The small, tubular-based flowers, up to 2cm (¾in) wide, have four to eight petals. They open on tapering spikes on square stems. The leaves, up to 10cm (4in) long, are lance-shaped and carried in opposite pairs. They sometimes turn yellow in autumn. Although lythrums flourish at water margins, they grow elsewhere on rich, moisture-retentive soils. Native to Europe, Asia and N America.

RECOMMENDED SPECIES AND VARIETIES

L. salicaria (purple loosestrife) Suited to boggy ground, reddish purple flowers distinguish this species. It often has branched stems, each bearing 3 or 4 flower spikes. HEIGHT & SPREAD 1.2m×45cm (4×1½ft).

Lythrum salicaria

'Feuerkerze' ♀ ('Firecandle') has rose-pink flowers, while the flowers of **'Robert'** are bright pink and **'The Beacon'** has intense, rose-pink flowers.

L. virgatum Deep purple-red flowers are borne in pairs or clusters on leafy spikes. HEIGHT & SPREAD 1m×45cm (3×1½ft).

'Rosy Gem' has pink-flushed, purple flowers while **'The Rocket'** has bright, rose-pink flowers.

CULTIVATION Plant from autumn to spring ideally in moisture-retentive soil. Remove the flowerheads after flowering to prevent the spread of self-sown seed.

PROPAGATION Sow seed for the species in spring. Divide overcrowded clumps of the cultivars in autumn or spring. Alternatively, take softwood cuttings in spring and plant out later in the year.

PESTS AND DISEASES Usually trouble free.

▲ *Lythrum salicaria* 'Feuerkerze'

Lythrum salicaria 'Robert' ▲

▼ *Lythrum salicaria*

Macleaya

Plume poppy
Papaveraceae

Rising majestically above most other plants, macleaya's feathery flower plumes and shiny decorative leaves make it an ideal choice for a bold display at the back of a border. The small flowers appear in frothy panicles up to 60 cm (2 ft) long in mid summer. The grey-green rounded or heart-shaped leaves, 20 cm (8 in) wide, have serrated lobes with white downy undersides. Although these hardy herbaceous perennials grow to about 2 m (6½ ft), they rarely need to be staked. Native to China, they like full sun but will tolerate shade. The plants may take two years to establish, but, unless controlled, can then become invasive, spreading by rhizomes. Low-growing plants allow macleaya to be seen in its full splendour; plant *Macleaya microcarpa* 'Kelway's Coral Plume' with phloxes for colour and height contrast.

▼ *Macleaya cordata* 'Flamingo'

▼ *Macleaya cordata*

RECOMMENDED SPECIES AND VARIETIES

M. cordata♀ (plume poppy, tree celandine) Numerous, creamy white flowers form large plumes on this compact plant. HEIGHT & SPREAD 2 m×60 cm (6½×2 ft).

'Flamingo' has buff-pink flowers.

M. microcarpa Creamy white buds open as fluffy white flowers. If dead flowers are not removed, papery capsules appear, each containing one orange seed. Can be invasive. HEIGHT & SPREAD 2 m×60 cm (6½×2 ft).

'Kelway's Coral Plume'♀ has deep, coral-pink flowers in late summer.

CULTIVATION Plant autumn to spring in deep, moist, well-drained soil. In autumn, control *M. microcarpa* by removing any runners that have grown beyond the clump.

PROPAGATION Divide in spring, or take basal root cuttings and plant out in autumn.

PESTS AND DISEASES Usually trouble free.

Maclura

Moraceae

Orange-like but inedible fruit make these deciduous N American trees curiosities in any garden. They bear either male or female flowers, so both types need to be planted to ensure that fruit is produced. Alternatively, buy a female with a male branch grafted on to it. The trees are hardy to -10°C (14°F) and will flourish in any soil. There is only one species in the genus.

▲ *Maclura pomifera*

Maclura pomifera (Osage orange, bow wood) Insignificant yellow-green flowers appear in summer and are followed by orange-yellow globe-like fruit up to 14 cm (5½ in) across, consisting of numerous seeds in a rubbery pulp. The trees have vicious 2 cm (¾ in) long thorns and russet-brown fissured bark. Mid green leaves, 10 cm (4 in) long, taper to a point at both ends and have wavy edges. They turn yellow in autumn. HEIGHT & SPREAD 10×5 m (33×16 ft) after 20 years, ultimately growing to 16 m (52 ft) tall.

CULTIVATION Plant in late spring in any garden soil, choosing a position in full sun.

PROPAGATION Sow under glass in early spring and plant out late spring the next year; or take semi-ripe cuttings in summer.

PRUNING Trim to tidy up in late winter.

PESTS AND DISEASES Usually trouble free.

Magnolia

Magnoliaceae

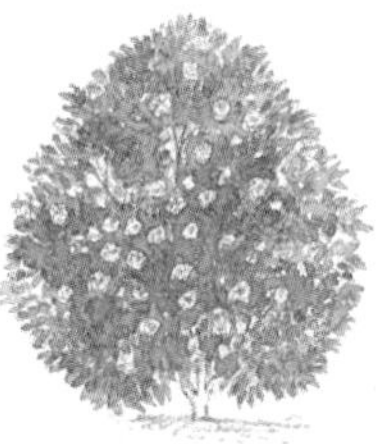

Magnolia grandiflora

Among the first plants to bloom in spring are the elegant magnolias, whose abundant, large and often deliciously scented flowers frequently open before the leaves, making a dramatic show against the bare branches. Ranging in colour from white, through pink to purple, the flowers vary in form from upright and vase-shaped to open and star-like. Instead of having an outer layer of sepals and an inner layer of petals, magnolia flowers have just one layer of petal-like structures called tepals. The leaves, usually 7.5-28 cm (3-11 in) long, are oval to obovate. Some magnolias produce attractive pinky brown cones with bright red seeds.

Varying from compact shrubs to large trees, these densely branched deciduous and evergreen plants are grown as freestanding specimens and trained as wall shrubs. They are hardy, although cold winds and late frosts can be damaging to early-flowering plants. When buying a magnolia, pick one no more than five years old and, since some varieties can take many years to bloom, it may be worth choosing a plant of about this age, especially if flowers are not evident at time of purchase. There are both slow and fast-growing magnolias but all are long-lived and produce more and more flowers as they get older.

RECOMMENDED SPECIES AND VARIETIES

***M.* 'Charles Raffill'**♀ Rose-pink in bud, the cup-and-saucer-shaped flowers are carmine-pink outside and white stained pink inside. The blooms, up to 25cm (10in) across, appear on leafless branches in early to mid spring. This fast-growing, pyramidal deciduous tree flowers at 7-10 years old. HEIGHT & SPREAD 6×4m (20×13ft) after 10 years, ultimately 18m (60ft) tall.

M. denudata♀ (syn. *M. heptapeta*) (yulan, lily tree) Lemon-scented, white blooms, tinged pink at the base, appear before the leaves in early to mid-spring. They open to cup-shaped and 15cm (6in) across. This broad-spreading deciduous shrub or small tree flowers when 3-5 years old. HEIGHT & SPREAD 3x3m (10x10ft) after 10 years, ultimately 4.5m (15ft) tall.

***M.* 'Elizabeth'**♀ Pale primrose-yellow, slightly scented, vase-shaped flowers, 10cm (4in) long, appear on bare branches in mid spring. Copper-coloured on unfurling, the foliage emerges in late spring with the last flowers. A broad-spreading deciduous shrub or small tree that flowers when 2-3 years old. HEIGHT & SPREAD 4.5x3m (15×10ft) after 10 years, ultimately 9m (30ft) tall.

***M.* 'Galaxy'**♀ Rose-pink flowers appear before the leaves in mid to late spring. They open to cup-shaped and 20cm (8in) across. A free-flowering deciduous, conical tree that flowers when 3-4 years old. HEIGHT & SPREAD 6×2.4m (20×8ft) after 10 years, ultimately 15m (50ft) tall.

***M.* 'George Henry Kern'** Pink, vase-shaped flowers, paler on the inside and 7.5cm (3in) across, appear in mid to late spring and sometimes into early summer. A free-flowering, deciduous shrub with small leaves, this shrub flowers when 2-3 years old. HEIGHT & SPREAD 1.2×1.5m (4×5ft) after 10 years, ultimately 2.4m (8ft) tall.

M. grandiflora (southern magnolia, bull bay) This evergreen can be trained against a wall or grown as a freestanding, rounded or pyramidal shrub or tree. The intensely fragrant, white or creamy white, cup-shaped flowers, up to 25cm (10in) across, appear from mid summer to mid autumn. The glossy green leaves sometimes have reddish-brown hairs underneath when young. Plants flower when 5-7 years old if raised vegetatively but after 30 years if grown from seed. HEIGHT & SPREAD 3x3m (10x10ft) after 10 years, ultimately 15m (50ft) tall.

'Exmouth'♀ has rich cream-coloured, heavily scented flowers. **'Samuel Sommer'** has large blooms, up to 30cm (12in) across.

***M.* 'Heaven Scent'**♀ Deep pink outside and paler within, vase-shaped flowers 12.5cm (5in) long appear in profusion on bare stems in mid to late spring. An upright, deciduous tree that flowers after 5 years. HEIGHT & SPREAD 5.5×3.5m (18×12ft) after 10 years, ultimately 13.5m (45ft) tall.

M. heptapeta see *M. denudata*

***M.* 'Iolanthe'**♀ Abundant, clear pink cup-and-saucer-shaped flowers, creamy white inside, appear on bare branches in early to mid spring. Measuring 25cm (10in) across, they are held sideways. A broad-spreading deciduous shrub or small tree that flowers when 5 years old. HEIGHT & SPREAD 3.5×3.5m (12×12ft) after 10 years, ultimately 12m (40ft) tall.

***M.* 'Jane'**♀ Upright dark pink buds, 10cm (4in) long, open to cup-shaped, fragrant flowers, deep pink outside and very pale pink within. They appear before the leaves in mid to late spring. A rounded to upright,

▲ *Magnolia* 'Heaven Scent'

▲ *Magnolia denudata*

▲ *Magnolia* 'Galaxy'

▲ *Magnolia grandiflora*

▲ *Magnolia* 'Iolanthe'

▲ *Magnolia* 'Jane'

deciduous shrub that will flower in its first year. HEIGHT & SPREAD 2.1×1.5m (7×5ft) after 10 years, ultimately 4.5m (15ft) tall.

***M.* × *kewensis* 'Wada's Memory'**♀ Profuse white, slightly fragrant flowers are borne on bare branches in mid spring. The tepals droop to one side until the flowers measure about 18cm (7in) across. The leaves are mahogany red on unfurling. A conical, deciduous tree that is free-flowering from 5 years old. HEIGHT & SPREAD 3×1.8m (10×6ft) in 10 years, ultimately 10m (33ft) tall.

M. kobus White flowers appear in early spring before the leaves. Measuring 10cm (4in) in length, they are vase-shaped at first before splaying open. A deciduous, many-branched shrub or medium-sized, pyramidal tree. It flowers after 10 years if raised from seed and 5 years if raised vegetatively. HEIGHT & SPREAD 2.4×1.8m (8×6ft) after 10 years, ultimately 9m (30ft) tall.

▲ *Magnolia liliiflora* 'Nigra'

***M. liliiflora* 'Nigra'**♀ (syn. *M.* × *soulangeana* 'Nigra') Tulip-shaped slightly scented, deep purple flowers, 12.5cm (5in) long, are white stained purple within. They appear in mid or late spring with the unfurling leaves and continue into early summer. A dense, slow-growing deciduous shrub that first flowers at 5-10 years old. HEIGHT & SPREAD 1.5×1.5m (5×5ft) after 10 years, ultimately 3m (10ft) tall.

***M.* × *loebneri* 'Leonard Messel'**♀ Deep pink tepals, paler within, open out to star-like blooms, 12.5cm (5in) across. They are slightly scented and borne profusely in mid-spring before the leaves appear. Plants first flower when 5 years old. This many-branched, deciduous plant is the most frost hardy of shrubby magnolias. HEIGHT & SPREAD 2.4×1.8m (8×6ft) after 10 years, ultimately 4.5m (15ft) tall.

***M.* × *loebneri* 'Merrill'**♀ Pure white, slightly scented flowers open to 15cm (6in) across and are seen during mid spring, before the leaves appear. Pyramidal at first, then broad-spreading, this small deciduous tree flowers when 5 years old. HEIGHT & SPREAD 4.5×3m (15×10ft) after 10 years, ultimately 12m (40ft) tall.

***M.* 'Pinkie'**♀ Dark pink buds opening to pale pink flowers, 18cm (7in) across, appear with the new leaves in mid to late spring. This spreading deciduous shrub flowers when 5 years old. HEIGHT & SPREAD 2.4×2.4m (8×8ft) after 10 years, ultimately 4.5m (15ft) tall.

M. salicifolia♀ Pure white, slightly fragrant flowers, opening to 12.5cm (5in) across, appear in mid spring before the leaves. The narrow, willow-like leaves are downy beneath and, like the bark and wood, have a lemony aniseed smell when crushed. A

▲ *Magnolia salicifolia*

▲ *Magnolia* x *loebneri* 'Leonard Messel'

▲ *Magnolia* x *loebneri* 'Merrill'

deciduous, upright shrub or pyramidal tree that first flowers when 5 years old. HEIGHT & SPREAD 4.5×3m (15×10ft) in 10 years, ultimately 15m (50ft) tall.

M. sargentiana* var. *robusta Cup-shaped, rose-pink flowers, 30cm (12in) across, are seen in early and mid spring on leafless stems. A wide-spreading deciduous tree that flowers after 10 years when raised vegetatively, but 30 years if raised from seed. HEIGHT & SPREAD 4×3.5m (13×12ft) after 10 years, ultimately 21.5m (70ft) tall.

***M.* 'Sayonara'**♀ White, scented, vase-shaped flowers appear in mid spring before the leaves and open to a cup-and-saucer shape, 15-20cm (6-8in) across. This deciduous plant flowers after 5 years and forms a broad-spreading shrub or tree. HEIGHT & SPREAD 4.5×3.5m (15×12ft) after 10 years, ultimately 9m (30ft) tall.

M. sieboldii♀ Intensely fragrant, pure white flowers with distinctive magenta stamens are seen in late spring and early summer and again in late summer and early autumn. The nodding saucer-shaped flowers are 10cm (4in) across and first appear on this broad-spreading deciduous shrub when it's 5 years old, if raised vegetatively, and 10 years old, when grown from seed. HEIGHT & SPREAD 2.4×2.4m (8×8ft) after 10 years, ultimately 6m (20ft) tall.

The pendent flowers of ssp. ***sinensis***♀ are lemon-scented and up to 12.5cm (5in) across. The underside of its leaves bear a silvery down. Plants reach a height and spread of 3m (10ft) after 10 years.

M. x soulangeana Goblet to tulip-shaped flowers, up to 10cm (4in) long, appear in mid spring before the leaves, with a second flush sometimes in late summer. They vary in colour from white to intense pink outside and from white to white tinged pink inside. This deciduous, broad-spreading shrub or tree first flowers at 5 years old. HEIGHT & SPREAD 4.5x3m (15x10ft) after 10 years, ultimately 9m (30ft) tall.

'Brozzonii'♀ has large, white flowers, flushed pink at the base, which splay open to 25cm (10in) across and appear in late spring. The goblet-shaped flowers of **'Lennei'**♀, pinky purple outside and white within, appear in mid to late spring. **'Nigra'** see *M. liliiflora* 'Nigra'. **'Picture'** has white tulip-shaped flowers heavily stained with purple outside, 15cm (6in) tall and seen in mid to late spring. **'Rustica Rubra'**♀ (syn. 'Rubra') has goblet-shaped, reddish purple flowers in mid to late spring that open to 20cm (8in) across. **'San Jose'** has deep pink flowers, white inside, that are 10-15cm (4-6in) long and seen in early to mid spring.

M. stellata♀ (star magnolia) Slightly fragrant, star-like white flowers, sometimes faintly flushed with pink, bloom in profusion in early to mid spring before the leaves. Made up of many ribbon-like tepals, the flowers open to 7.5-10cm (3-4in) across. A slow-growing, dense, deciduous shrub good for small gardens or growing in a tub. It will flower in its first season. HEIGHT & SPREAD 1.2x1.5m (4x5ft) after 10 years, ultimately 3.5m (12ft) tall.

'Royal Star' has pink-tinged buds, opening to white flowers. **'Waterlily'**♀ has ivory white flowers, 10cm (4in) across.

▲ *Magnolia x soulangeana* 'Rustica Rubra'

▲ *Magnolia stellata*

▲ *Magnolia stellata* 'Waterlily'

▲ *Magnolia* 'Susan'

M. 'Susan'♀ Deep pink, vase-shaped, fragrant flowers open out to 10-15cm (4-6in) across, revealing a paler pink inside. This upright, deciduous shrub flowers in profusion during mid to late spring, before the leaves appear. Plants bloom in their first year. HEIGHT & SPREAD 2.1x1.5m (7x5ft) after 10 years, ultimately 4.5m (15ft) tall.

M. wilsonii♀ Cup-shaped, highly fragrant, pendulous, white flowers, 10cm (4in) across, with red stamens appear with the foliage in late spring and early summer. This many-branched deciduous shrub has leaves with cinnamon-brown hairs underneath. Plants flower at 5 years old if raised vegetatively, at 5-10 years when grown from seed HEIGHT & SPREAD 3x3m (10x10ft) after 10 years, ultimately 6m (20ft) tall.

CULTIVATION Plant in autumn and spring in any humus-rich, moist but well-drained soil, except chalky. Buy a pot-grown plant and place in its permanent site to avoid any need for transplantation that might damage the tender fleshy roots. Most deciduous species and the evergreen, *M. grandiflora*, tolerate some sun but all, and in particular, *M. sieboldii*, *M. s.* ssp. *sinensis* and *M. wilsonii*, benefit from light shade. Shelter from cold winds. Shake snow from the branches of evergreens or its weight might break the leaves. Mulch plants with organic matter in drought conditions. It is better not to underplant magnolias since hoeing or forking around the base might damage the roots. Suppress weeds with bark chips.

PROPAGATION Sow ripe seed in spring although plants raised this way may take about 30 years to flower. Take greenwood cuttings of deciduous varieties and semi-ripe cuttings of evergreens. Layer plants that produce strong shoots, close to the ground.

PRUNING Cut back untidy plants and remove dead wood in late summer or after flowering for deciduous species and in spring for evergreens. Hard prune only mature specimens; do this in spring. If training *M. grandiflora* against a wall, spur prune to within 30-45cm (12-18in) of the framework in spring.

PESTS AND DISEASES Usually trouble free but sooty mould and bacterial leaf spot affect *M. grandiflora*.

Mahonia

Berberidaceae

Clusters of yellow flowers and glossy evergreen foliage help to brighten any winter or spring garden. These architectural shrubs make fine specimen plants, with some of the smaller species being useful as ground cover if left to spread. The tiny globular or bell-shaped flowers are often sweetly scented and are followed by small grape-like berries. The alternate pinnate leaves have a spiny edge. All mahonias are hardy, with the exception of *M. lomariifolia* which will only grow in milder regions. Native to Asia, Japan and Central and N America.

RECOMMENDED SPECIES AND VARIETIES

M. aquifolium (Oregon grape) The glossy dark green leaves, up to 30cm (1ft) long with 5 to 9 leaflets, are purplish in winter. Golden yellow flowers in dense clusters up to 7.5cm (3in) long, appear as early as late winter, but the main flowering period is in mid to late spring. This rounded, spreading

▲ *Mahonia aquifolium*

shrub will grow in shade and full sun. Native to western N America. HEIGHT & SPREAD 1m×60cm (3×2ft) after 5 years, ultimately 1.8m (6ft) tall.

'Apollo'♀ is a vigorous, low-growing plant with flower clusters up to 10cm (4in) long. The leaves have a reddish stem. **'Atropurpurea'** has reddish purple leaves in winter. **'Smaragd'** has bronze young leaves and flower clusters up to 10cm (4in) long.

M. bealei *see M. japonica* Bealei Group

M. japonica♀ The glossy dark green leaves of this upright shrub grow to 40cm (16in) long and have 13 to 19 leathery leaflets, each with a coarsely spined margin. The fragrant lemon-yellow flowers are carried in pendulous clusters, up to 20cm (8in) long, from mid winter to early spring. Native to China. HEIGHT & SPREAD 1.5×1m (5×3ft) after 5 years, ultimately 3m (10ft) tall.

▲ *Mahonia japonica*

Bealei Group (syn. *M. bealei*) has shorter, more upright flower clusters and the leaflets sometimes overlap.

M. lomariifolia♀ Thick leathery leaves, up to 60cm (2ft) long, have 19 to 40 leaflets. Bright yellow, slightly fragrant flowers, in dense erect clusters up to 25cm (10in) long, appear in winter. This upright shrub is not fully hardy and will only survive in the mildest areas. Native to Burma and China. HEIGHT & SPREAD 1.2m×30cm (4×1ft) after 5 years, ultimately 4m (13ft) tall.

M.* x *media An upright shrub with deep green leathery leaves about 60cm (2ft) long and varying numbers of leaflets. The yellow flowers are produced in clusters up to 25cm (10in) long and are at their best in winter. HEIGHT & SPREAD 1m×30cm (3×1ft) after 5

▲ *Mahonia aquifolium* 'Apollo'

▲ *Mahonia* x *media* 'Buckland'

▲ *Mahonia* x *media* 'Charity'

years, ultimately 3m (10ft) tall.

'Buckland'♀ has leaves sometimes tinged red in autumn and winter. The yellow flower clusters are long and spreading. **'Charity'**♀ has fragrant yellow flowers in erect clusters, at their best in late autumn to mid winter. **'Lionel Fortescue'**♀ has bright yellow, slightly fragrant flowers in upright clusters. **'Underway'**♀ is more compact with bright yellow flowers in upright clusters. **'Winter Sun'**♀ has fragrant yellow flowers in dense, erect clusters.

M. nervosa Leathery, deep green leaves, 38cm (15in) long, with 11 to 15 leaflets, often turn red in winter. Erect yellow flower clusters, 20cm (8in) long, appear in spring. Native to western N America. HEIGHT & SPREAD 40cm×1m (16in×3ft) after 5 years, also the ultimate size.

M. pinnata A spreading shrub with leaves up to 12cm (4¾in) long, that are bronze when young, turning bright green. They have 5 to 9, generally overlapping, leaflets. The bright yellow flowers, borne in clusters

▲ *Mahonia* x *media* 'Winter Sun'

up to 10cm (4in) long, appear from early to mid spring. The plant is only moderately frost hardy and will grow only in a sheltered position. Native to southern N America. HEIGHT & SPREAD 60×30cm (2×1ft) after 5 years, ultimately 1m (3ft) tall.

M. repens The dull green leaves are 20cm (8in) long with 3 to 7 leaflets. Golden yellow flowers open in mid to late spring in dense clusters, up to 7.5cm (3in) long, that appear on the end of the previous years' growth. A low-spreading, suckering shrub, native to western N America. HEIGHT & SPREAD 40cm×1m (16in×3ft) after 5 years, also the ultimate size.

***M.* x *wagneri* 'Pinnacle'**♀ The bright green leaves of this upright shrub are bronze at first. Dense clusters of bright yellow flowers, up to 10cm (4in) long, appear in late spring. HEIGHT & SPREAD 1m×60cm (3×2ft) after 5 years, ultimately 1.8m (6ft) tall.

***M.* x *wagneri* 'Undulata'**♀ The dark green leaves, up to 20cm (8in) long, have wavy edges and are bronze at first. Yellow flowers are carried in dense clusters about 10cm (4in) long in spring. A vigorous, erect shrub. HEIGHT & SPREAD 1m×60cm (3×2ft) after 5 years, ultimately 1.8m (6ft) tall.

CULTIVATION Mahonias thrive under a wide range of conditions but, as a general rule, plant *M.* x *wagneri* and species native to the Americas (and their cultivars) in drier soils in a sunny position. Plant *M.* x *media* and Asian species and their cultivars in a shady part of the garden. *M. nervosa* does not grow well in chalk soils.

PROPAGATION Sow seed in early to mid spring or take semi-ripe cuttings in early to mid summer. Any suckers can be dug up and replanted, immediately.

PRUNING Not normally required, but suckers may need to be cut or pulled out in late autumn to early spring.

PESTS AND DISEASES Usually trouble free.

Maianthemum

May lily
Convallariaceae

This herbaceous perennial has white flower spikes and glossy green kidney to heart-shaped leaves. Bright red, rounded berries about 6mm (¼in) across appear in summer. This ground-cover plant is suited to a shady

▲ *Maianthemum bifolium var. kamtschaticum*

spot and can be invasive. Native to W Europe, Asia and N America, it is hardy.

RECOMMENDED SPECIES AND VARIETIES

M. bifolium Cream, star-shaped, 4-petalled flowers about 3mm (⅛in) across appear from mid to late spring. The leaves, up to 7.5cm (3in) long, have wavy edges. HEIGHT & SPREAD 20cm×1m (8in×3ft).

The leaves of var. ***kamtschaticum*** (syn. *M. dilatatum*) are up to 20cm (8in) long. It can reach 35cm (14in) in height.

M. dilatatum see *M. bifolium var. kamtschaticum*

CULTIVATION Plant in moist but well-drained humus-rich soil in dappled shade. Protect from bright sunshine and droughts.

PROPAGATION Divide in early spring or summer. Sow seed under glass in winter. Young plants are slow to establish.

PESTS AND DISEASES Slugs and snails may attack foliage, especially when it is young.

Maidenhair tree see *Ginkgo biloba*

Malcolmia

Cruciferae

Malcolmia maritima

Drifts of pastel flowers grace cottage gardens and informal borders in summer. The plants are very fast growing, usually flowering four weeks after sowing and with successive sowings the flowering season can be extended throughout summer. They self-seed readily in undisturbed soil.

RECOMMENDED SPECIES

M. maritima (Virginian stock) Sweetly scented flowers, about 2cm (¾in) across, in red, lilac, rose or white, are carried in loose clusters on slender, branching stems. This hardy annual from the Mediterranean is low-growing, bearing elliptic grey-green leaves, up to 4cm (1½in) long. HEIGHT & SPREAD 20×36cm (8×14in).

CULTIVATION Plant in preferably neutral-to-alkaline, well-drained soil in a sunny position.

PROPAGATION Sow seed in situ successively throughout spring. Sow in the autumn for flowers the following spring.

PESTS AND DISEASES Usually trouble free.

Mallow see *Malva*
Mallow tree see *Lavatera*

Malope

Malvaceae

The easily grown and free-flowering hardy annual, *Malope trifida,* is the only member of this genus usually cultivated. An attractive addition to a sunny border, it is a stout-stemmed, upright plant. The showy trumpet-shaped flowers are produced over a long period and are suitable for cutting.

RECOMMENDED SPECIES AND VARIETIES

M. trifida Rose-purple, darker veined flowers are freely produced on long stalks from mid summer to mid autumn. Each flower has 5 petals and flares open to 8cm (3¼in) across. The bright green leaves have 3 or 5 pointed lobes. HEIGHT & SPREAD 1m×30cm (3×1ft).

▲ *Malope trifida*

'Pink Queen' has shell-pink flowers with centres and veins of a deeper shade. **'Vulcan'** has brilliant red flowers with an almost metallic sheen. **'White Queen'** has white silky-looking flowers. Seed of mixed colours is also available and will produce pink, purple, red and white flowers.

CULTIVATION Plant in late spring in full sun in any ordinary garden soil. Deadhead regularly to prolong the flower display.

PROPAGATION Sow clusters of seed 30cm (1ft) apart in mid spring where the plants are to grow. Once the seedlings are established, thin out to leave just one in each position. Alternatively, for earlier flowering, sow seed in early spring in a greenhouse or a coldframe and hardened off.

PESTS AND DISEASES Aphids and hollyhock rust may attack plants.

Malus

Crab apple
Rosaceae

Malus hupehensis

Clouds of spring blossom, colourful fruits and autumn colour make crab apples worthy of garden space. They are hardy, deciduous trees that are easily grown and being generally small are not difficult to place in an average garden. The bowl-shaped flowers with golden stamens are five-petalled and borne in clusters; some are fragrant. Flower colour ranges from white through pink and deep red. The apple-like fruits, 2.5-5cm (1-2in) long, ripen in early autumn and can be yellow, red or green flushed with red or purple. All fruits are attractive to birds. The leaves are generally small, less than 7.5cm (3in) long and about half as wide. The genus includes the culinary apple; the plants recommended below are all ornamental trees.

RECOMMENDED SPECIES AND VARIETIES

***M.* 'American Beauty'** Deep red, double flowers, to 4cm (1½in) across, are borne in spring on this vigorous upright tree. The leaves emerge bronze red but become more bronze green. Fruit is rather sparsely produced. HEIGHT & SPREAD 1.5×1m (5×3ft) after 5 years, ultimately 7m (23ft) tall.

***M. coronaria* var. *dasycalyx* 'Charlottae'** A small upright tree whose large, 3-lobed leaves, up to 10cm (4in) long, give a rich red display of colour in the autumn. The light pink, semi-double flowers, to 4cm (1½in) across, are very prolific in late spring and have a good fragrance. Fruit is yellowish green. HEIGHT & SPREAD 1.5×1m (5×3ft)

▼ *Malus* 'Evereste'

m

after 5 years, ultimately 6m (20ft) tall.

***M.* 'Evereste'**♀ A profusion of large flowers, 5cm (2in) across, are pink in bud but open to white. Autumn fruits, to 2.5cm (1in) across, are an attractive orange or red. This is a small conical tree. Its dark green leaves are sometimes lobed. HEIGHT & SPREAD 1.5×1m (5×3ft) after 5 years, ultimately 6m (20ft) tall.

M. floribunda♀ (Japanese crab) One of the most prolific flowering crab apples, the branches are covered in crimson buds in mid spring that open to white or pale pink flowers. Once the flowers are over they are followed by small yellow fruits. The leaves are fresh green. A small tree, in maturity it has a rounded crown often as broad as it is tall. Native to Japan. HEIGHT & SPREAD 1.5×1.2m (5×4ft) after 5 years, ultimately 7m (23ft) tall.

***M.* 'Golden Hornet'** see *M.* × *zumi* 'Golden Hornet'

***M.* × *hartwigii* 'Katherine'**♀ Large flowers, up to 5cm (2in) across, are deep pink in bud and open to semi-double pink flowers which gradually fade to pure white. The fruits although not conspicuous are red flushed with yellow. It is a small upright tree with a spreading crown. HEIGHT & SPREAD 1m×60cm (3×2ft) after 5 years, ultimately 4m (13ft) tall.

***M.* 'Hillieri'** see *M. schiedeckeri* 'Hillieri'

▲ *Malus* × *hartwigii* 'Katherine'

Malus hupehensis ▲

M. hupehensis♀ In late spring, every branch of this spreading tree is covered in a profusion of slightly scented, pure white flowers, to 4cm (1½in) across. These give way to hundreds of fruits, 1.5cm (½in) across, that ripen in early to mid autumn to a beautiful translucent red. As an added bonus the bright green leaves give a good display of autumn colour making this a truly multiseasonal plant. Native to W China. HEIGHT & SPREAD 1.5×1m (5×3ft) after 5 years, ultimately 10m (33ft) tall.

'Rosea' has rosy pink flowers.

***M.* 'John Downie'**♀ A small tree grown for its outstanding fruit colour of bright orange and red which makes a striking sight in autumn when the branches are laden. The fruits, 2.5cm (1in) across, are slightly longer than they are broad and can be made into a jelly. The late spring flowers are white. HEIGHT & SPREAD 1.5×1m (5×3ft) after 5 years, ultimately 6m (20ft) tall.

▲ *Malus* 'John Downie'

▲ *Malus* × *moerlandsii* 'Liset'

***M.* × *moerlandsii* 'Liset'** Late spring flowers are dark crimson in bud and emerge rose-red, followed by deep crimson fruits. The small rounded tree has new leaves that are purplish when they emerge but turn shiny deep green as they age. HEIGHT & SPREAD 1.2×1m (4×3ft) after 5 years, ultimately 4m (13ft) tall.

Another selection from this hybrid is **'Profusion'**. It is very similar to 'Liset' in size and foliage but holds the purple colour for longer. The fragrant flowers are more prolific and a carmine red. These are followed by deep red fruits, up to 1.5cm (½in) across, on long stalks.

M.* × *purpurea The leaves of this small spreading tree or large shrub are purplish green as are the new shoots. These become green as the season progresses. The mid spring flowers are dark purple at first but fade quickly and are followed by purple-red fruits. HEIGHT & SPREAD 1.2×1m (4×3ft) after 5 years, ultimately 4m (13ft) tall.

'Eleyi' is similar but has darker foliage and flowers which hold their colour better. The fruits persist well into late autumn. **'Lemoinei'** is also similar and makes a fine small erect tree with slightly double, more reddish flowers. The leaves of **'Neville Copeman'**♀ are more green in colour with just a hint of purple. This colour is kept well throughout the year. The flowers are light purple and are followed by clusters of striking orange red fruits.

▲ *Malus* × *moerlandsii* 'Profusion'

▲ *Malus* × *purpurea*

▲ *Malus* × *purpurea* 'Eleyi'

Malus × *purpurea* 'Neville Copeman' ▲

Malus x purpurea

M.* × *robusta A small, upright tree with white or pinkish flowers in mid or late spring. Red fruits generally follow in autumn but the colour can vary, so if a particular fruit colour is required it is best to choose one of the varieties. HEIGHT & SPREAD 1.5×1m (5×3ft) after 5 years, ultimately 6m (20ft) tall.

'Red Sentinel'♀ is grown for its outstanding display of autumn fruits that are up to 2.5cm (1in) across and are a deep glossy red in colour. The fruits are produced in great numbers and stay on the tree throughout most of the winter. The flowers, borne in mid to late spring, are white. **'Red Siberian'**♀ is another good selection for fruit colour and quantity. The cherry-like fruits are bright red flushed with yellow and also stay on the tree well into winter.

▲ *Malus* x *robusta*

▲ *Malus* x *robusta* 'Yellow Siberian'
Malus x *robusta* 'Red Sentinel' ▲

'Yellow Siberian'♀ is similar to 'Red Siberian' but has yellow fruits.
***M.* 'Royal Beauty'**♀ This is a small tree of weeping habit and rounded appearance. The leaves and stems are a reddish purple at first but most of this is lost as the season progresses. Deep red-purple flowers give way to dark red fruits in autumn. HEIGHT & SPREAD 1m×60cm (3×2ft) after 5 years, ultimately 3m (10ft) tall.
***M.* 'Royalty'** The leaves of this small upright tree emerge dark purple and lighten as the season progresses, giving a good display of red colour in autumn. Large purple-carmine flowers are followed in autumn by small, dark red fruits. HEIGHT & SPREAD 1.2m×60cm (4×2ft) after 5 years, ultimately 4m (13ft).

▲ *Malus* 'Royalty'

M. sargentii see *M. toringo* ssp. *sargentii*
***M.* x *schiedeckeri* 'Hillieri'** Semidouble flowers, borne in late spring, are deep pink or crimson in bud but open to light pink. These are followed in autumn by yellow fruits flushed with red. A medium-sized rounded shrub or sometimes a small tree. HEIGHT & SPREAD 1m×60cm (3×2ft) after 5 years, ultimately 3m (10ft) tall.

Decorative, cherry-sized red fruits are the main reason for choosing **'Red Jade'**. White flowers emerge from pink buds in late spring. A variable plant, it makes a small tree or medium-sized shrub and has long, slender, weeping branches.
M. toringo ssp. ***sargentii*** (syn. *M. sargentii)* Profuse pure white flowers in spring give way to abundant bright red autumn fruits. The leaves are often 3-lobed on this rounded, medium-sized shrub. Native to Japan. HEIGHT & SPREAD 1m×60cm (3×2ft) after 5 years, ultimately 2m (6½ft) tall.
M. toringoides Slightly fragrant, creamy white flowers open in late spring and give way to pear-shaped, red-yellow fruits in autumn, among red-yellow autumn foliage. The decorative fruits stay on the tree well into winter. An upright tree when young, it becomes more spreading in old age with large, lobed leaves up to 9cm (3½in) long and 5cm (2in) wide. Native to W China. HEIGHT & SPREAD 1.2m×60cm (4×2ft) after 5 years, ultimately 9m (30ft) tall.
M. transitoria♀ A very good tree for yellow and red autumn colour with small, narrowly lobed leaves. The white flowers give way to light yellow fruits in the autumn. An upright tree, it becomes spreading with age. Native to NW China. HEIGHT & SPREAD 1.2m×60cm (4×2ft) after 5 years, ultimately 7m (23ft) tall.

▲ *Malus* x *schiedeckeri* 'Red Jade'

▲ *Malus transitoria*

M. trilobata The large lobed leaves, up to 10cm (4in) long, give a rich display of reds in autumn. Clusters of 6 to 8 white flowers open in late spring on this upright tree. The small fruits in autumn are yellow-ochre. Native to the S Mediterranean. HEIGHT & SPREAD 1.5×1m (5×3ft) after 5 years, ultimately 12m (40ft) tall.

▲ *Malus trilobata*

M. tschonoskii♀ One of the most outstanding crab apples for autumn colour. The large leaves, up to 12.5cm (5in) long, have a silvery appearance when they emerge that is lost as the season progresses. In autumn they give a brilliant display, turning a mixture of reds, oranges, purples and yellows. A small upright tree, it becomes more spreading

▲ *Malus* 'Van Eseltine'

with age. White flowers flushed with pink give way to yellow-green fruits tinged with purple. Native to Japan. HEIGHT & SPREAD 1.5×1m (5×3ft) after 5 years, ultimately 12m (40ft) tall.

***M.* 'Van Eseltine'** Large double flowers, up to 5cm (2in) across, are borne prolifically on this small, columnar tree. The flowers emerge pink on opening from darker buds and give way to yellow fruits sometimes with a red flush on one side. It is a good plant for a small space. HEIGHT & SPREAD 1.2m×60cm (4×2ft) after 5 years, ultimately 4m (13ft) tall.

***M.* 'Winter Gold'** Flowers that are pink in bud open out to become white. In autumn, the flowers are followed by yellow fruits which persist on this malus well into early winter. This plant can form a medium-sized shrub or a small tree. HEIGHT & SPREAD 1m×60cm (3×2ft) after 5 years, ultimately 3m (10ft) tall.

***M.* 'Wisley'** Slightly scented, large flowers, to 5cm (2in) across, are a rich deep pink in colour. Large, purple-red fruits follow in autumn. The young leaves of the small tree emerge a good bronze red which becomes dark green as the season progresses. HEIGHT & SPREAD 1.2m×60cm (4×2ft) after 5 years, ultimately 4m (13ft) tall.

▲ *Malus* 'Wisley'

***M. yunnanensis* 'Veitch's Scarlet'** White flowers open in late spring from pink buds and give way to large fruits, up to 5cm (2in) across. These are scarlet in colour sometimes turning to crimson on one side. The plant can be a large shrub or small tree. HEIGHT & SPREAD 1m×60cm (3×2ft) after 5 years, ultimately 4m (13ft) tall.

***M.* x *zumi* 'Golden Hornet'**♀ A small tree offering an outstanding display of yellow autumn fruits. Produced in abundance, they are a clear bright yellow and persist on the tree into the new year. The flowers are white. HEIGHT & SPREAD 1.2×1m (4×3ft) after 5 years, ultimately 4m (13ft) tall.

Malus x zumi 'Golden Hornet'

▲ *Malus* x *zumi* 'Golden Hornet'

CULTIVATION Plant in any reasonably good soil which is not too wet. Choose a site preferably in full sun, although they will tolerate some shade.

PROPAGATION Species will grow readily from seed but it can take up to 10 years for plants to flower. Cultivated varieties can be raised by budding or grafting, therefore it is probably advisable to buy a healthy young tree from a reputable supplier.

PRUNING Remove dead wood in winter when plants are dormant.

PESTS AND DISEASES Malus are susceptible to a large number of diseases but on the whole are trouble free. Honey fungus and fireblight can be a particular problem.

Malva

Mallow

Malvaceaea

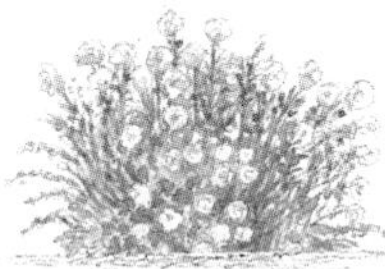

Malva moschata var. alba

Leafy spires of pink or white flowers appear throughout summer on these upright plants that can flourish on even the poorest soil if they are in full sun. The flowers are bowl or saucer-shaped and about 5cm (2in) wide. The palmate, lobed leaves, 10cm (4in), are often hairy. The recommended species, which are herbaceous perennials and biennials, are native to Britain and Europe and sometimes grow on waste land alongside roads. They are excellent for a wild or informal garden as well as looking good in a border. However, they tend to be short lived on heavy, damp soil where they do not flower profusely.

RECOMMENDED SPECIES AND VARIETIES

M. alcea var. ***fastigiata*** (cut leaved mallow) Saucer-shaped, bright pink flowers are carried where the leaves join the stem. This herbaceous perennial has pale green leaves and a narrow habit. HEIGHT & SPREAD 1.5m×50cm (5ft×20in).

M. moschata (musk mallow) A musk-like fragrance escapes from the flowers of this herbaceous perennial. The pink and white flowers are saucer-shaped and the pale green leaves are kidney-shaped. HEIGHT & SPREAD 1.5m×50cm (5ft×20in).

The flowers of var. ***alba***♀ are white with a strong, musky perfume; var. ***rosea*** has purple-tinted, rose-coloured flowers.

M. sylvestris (common mallow, tall mallow) Clusters of pale pink, saucer-shaped flowers complement the toothed leaves of this biennial. HEIGHT & SPREAD 1.2m×50cm (4ft×20in).

▲ *Malva moschata*

Malva sylvestris 'Primley Blue' ▲

▲ *Malva sylvestris* 'Mauritiana'

'Mauritiana' has magenta, deeply veined, flowers throughout summer to the first frosts. **'Primley Blue'** has veined flowers of delicate blue and grows up to 20cm (8in) high, while the flowers of **'Zebrina'** are glistening white with purple veins.

CULTIVATION Plant in autumn or spring on an open, sunny site on any well-drained soil. On exposed sites support young plants with pea sticks.

PROPAGATION Sow the seed of species under glass in early spring and plant out in autumn. Take basal stem cuttings from cultivars in spring and plant out in summer.

PESTS AND DISEASES Rust can be a problem with these plants.

m

Malvastrum

False mallow

Malvaceae

Saucer-shaped flowers are produced in strong terminal spires during summer and early autumn. The coarse, dull green leaves are heart-shaped or lobed. The recommended species, native to S America, benefits from an open, free-draining position.

RECOMMENDED SPECIES

M. lateritium Saucer-shaped, peach-coloured petals with a yellow base and a rose pink zone, 2.5-4 cm (1-1½ in) across. A sprawling late summer and early autumn flowering plant which is good for ground cover. The coarse lobed leaves are dull green and up to 8 cm (3¼ in) long. HEIGHT & SPREAD 30×60 cm (1×2 ft).

▲ *Malvastrum lateritium*

CULTIVATION Grow in borders in an open position. Plant in spring and trim any untidy stems as necessary during summer. Water freely in very dry weather and apply a slow-release general fertiliser in spring.

PROPAGATION Sow seeds of the species under glass in spring. Root softwood cuttings in a coldframe during summer.

PESTS AND DISEASES Usually trouble free.

Mammilaria see CACTI p. 107

Mandevilla

Apocynaceae

These evergreen climbers from S America are grown for their showy flowers, some of which are fragrant. They do well in a conservatory or well-lit position indoors. Train

▲ *Mandevilla splendens* 'Rosacea'

plants in conservatories up trelliswork, or around a circular support or up a miniature trellis in the house.

RECOMMENDED VARIETY

***M. splendens* 'Rosacea'** Clusters of pink trumpet-shaped flowers are borne in late summer. The 5 ruffled petals open to make a 10 cm (4 in) wide bloom, deepening in colour towards the throat. The oval leaves, glossy green with a tinge of bronze, are up to 20 cm (8 in) long. HEIGHT 3 m (10 ft).

CULTIVATION Place in good light with several hours of direct sunlight a day. Keep above 15°C (59°F) during active growth; a winter minimum of 7°C (45°F) is acceptable. Reasonable humidity is needed. Keep the compost moist during summer, but water more sparingly in winter, with minimal watering if the temperature falls below 10°C (50°F). Only repot if you want a large plant, otherwise keep in a 10 cm (4 cm) pot and top-dress in spring or feed once a week.

PROPAGATION Take semi-ripe cuttings in early summer.

PRUNING Prune the plant whenever it gets too big. Wear gloves, or wash hands well afterwards, as the white sap that oozes from cut stems may irritate the skin.

PESTS AND DISEASES Mealy bug can be a problem and aphids can damage young growth.

Manettia

Firecracker vine

Rubiaceae

The twining stems of these evergreen climbers from tropical regions of S America carry small but vivid flowers in spring and summer. They will twist around a trellis or wire loop and do best in a conservatory or well-lit position in the home.

RECOMMENDED SPECIES

M. luteorubra (syn. *M. inflata*) (firecracker vine) Bright orange-scarlet tubular flowers with bright yellow tips appear on and off throughout spring and summer. Each bloom is 2 cm (¾ in) long. The bright green leaves are broadly oval. HEIGHT 3 m (10 ft).

▲ *Manettia luteorubra*

CULTIVATION Place in good light, with direct sun for several hours a day. Keep at a minimum temperature of 10°C (50°F) in winter and provide with reasonable humidity at all times. Keep compost slightly moist during the growing season, and allow it to dry out between waterings in winter. Feed once a week in the growing season. If the plant outgrows its pot, repot in spring.

PROPAGATION Take semi-ripe cuttings in early summer.

PRUNING Hard pruning in spring may restore old, unattractively leggy plants.

PESTS AND DISEASES Whitefly can be troublesome.

Maple see *Acer*

Maranta

Marantaceae

Admired for their patterned foliage, these evergreen perennials provide eye-catching colour for a shady corner of the house. The insignificant flowers, produced in summer, may be removed as they detract from the foliage. Native to forest floors in tropical regions of Central and S America, marantas do best in humid conditions away from direct sunlight at a minimum temperature of 13°C (55°F). They are suitable for growing in a terrarium or bottle garden.

RECOMMENDED SPECIES AND VARIETIES

M. bicolor This plant's oval to oblong leaves are pale green, spotted with brown along a paler central zone, purple beneath, and up to 25 cm (10 in) long and 10 cm (4 in) wide. HEIGHT & SPREAD 30×30 cm (1×1 ft).

M. leuconeura (prayer plant) Dark green oblong to oval leaves, up to 15 cm (6 in) long and 7.5 cm (3 in) wide, may have grey or maroon veins with red or purple zoning on the upper surface and grey-green or maroon beneath. The species is not widely grown, though its colourful varieties are popular. HEIGHT & SPREAD 30×30 cm (1×1 ft).

The leaves of var. *erythroneura* (herringbone plant, also sold as *M. tricolor*) have

▲ *Maranta leuconeura* var. *kerchoveana*

m

bright red veins which contrast with the dark velvety green background and pale green zoning along the midrib. The grey-green leaves of var. *kerchoveana*♀ (rabbit's foot) have purple-brown or olive-green blotches like a rabbit's tracks on either side of the midrib. The blackish green foliage of var. *massangeana* has silvery central midrib zoning and prominent silver veins.

CULTIVATION Grow out of direct sunlight in one of the standard potting composts. Mist leaves often and feed regularly during the summer months. Keep out of draughts.

PROPAGATION Divide every 2 or 3 years in spring or summer, and keep humidity high. Alternatively, take stem cuttings in summer.

PESTS AND DISEASES Greenfly can be a nuisance.

Marguerite see *Argyranthemum*
Marguerite, blue see *Felicia amelloides*
Marguerite, golden see *Anthemis tinctoria*
Marigold, African see *Tagetes*
Marigold, French see *Tagetes*
Marigold, marsh see *Caltha palustris*
Marigold, pot see *Calendula*
Marigold, sun see *Dimorphotheca*
Marjoram see HERBS p. 332
Marjoram see *Origanum*
Marrow see p. 740

Marrubium

Labiatae

Showy or aromatic foliage makes the hardy perennial plants in this genus valuable in a planting scheme. The small tubular-lipped flowers that appear for much of the summer are unremarkable and often removed to retain the quality of the foliage, which provides a decorative backdrop in a summer flower border. The plants are native to temperate Eurasia and N America.

RECOMMENDED SPECIES AND VARIETIES

M. cylleneum Downy, grey-green, oval to rounded leaves, up to 5 cm (2 in) long, with shallowly toothed margins cover this plant. Yellow flowers open from leafy spikes, 25 cm (10 in) long, borne on tall hairy stems. HEIGHT & SPREAD 45×45 cm (1½×1½ ft).

M. incanum The grey-green, downy, oval leaves, up to 5 cm (2 in) long, have distinctly lobed or toothed margins. Tall, hairy white stems carry leafy spikes, 25 cm (10 in) long, dotted with white flowers. HEIGHT & SPREAD 45×60 cm (1½×2 ft).

M. vulgare (white horehound) Strongly scented rounded or oval leaves, up to 4 cm (1½ in) long, are further distinguished by scalloped and crimped edges. The white flowers open from leafy spikes, 25 cm (10 in) long, at the top of tall, downy white stems. HEIGHT & SPREAD 45× 60 cm (1½×2 ft).

CULTIVATION Plant in spring in well-drained soil in a sunny position.

PROPAGATION In spring, divide established crowns or sow seeds in a coldframe.

PESTS AND DISEASES Usually trouble free.

Marshmallow see *Althaea officinalis*
Marvel of Peru see *Mirabilis jalapa*
Masdevallia see ORCHIDS p. 466
Mask flower see *Alonsoa*

Matricaria

Mayweed

Compositae

White daisies with a yellow conical, button-like, centre are produced by these pleasantly aromatic annual plants. They have a filigree of finely dissected bright green leaves, with slender pointed segments. Despite often being considered weeds they are useful in the herb garden. The recommended species has a similar fragrance and medicinal uses to the true camomile, *Chamaemelum nobile.* It is also used in preparations to condition and lighten the hair. The genus is native to Europe and central Asia.

RECOMMENDED SPECIES

M. chamomilla see *M. recutita*

M. parthenium see *Tanacetum parthenium*

M. recutita (syn. *M. chamomilla*) (false or wild camomile, scented mayweed) Flowers about 2.5 cm (1 in) across, appear in branched clusters from late spring to late summer. In Britain this hardy plant is a common weed of meadows and is suited to a wild garden where it mixes well with other arable annuals such as cornflowers and poppies. It often colonises disturbed soil. HEIGHT & SPREAD 50×30 cm (20×12 in).

▲ *Matricaria recutita*

CULTIVATION Grow in any well-drained soil, in full or partial sun, sowing seed where it is to flower. Deadhead to prolong flowering.

PROPAGATION Sow seed, which is usually produced in abundance, during spring or summer. The plants usually self-sow in the garden.

PESTS AND DISEASES Occasionally infested with aphids.

Matteuccia see FERNS p. 264

Matthiola

Stock

Cruciferae

Matthiola incana

Grown for their fragrance and their spikes of spring and summer blooms in soft pastel shades, these plants flourish in sun or partial shade outdoors or as flowering pot plants in a cool greenhouse. While the shorter-stemmed types are good for bedding, those with longer stems are suitable as cut flowers. Stocks can be annuals, biennials or herbaceous perennials and are either hardy or half-hardy.

RECOMMENDED SPECIES AND VARIETIES

M. bicornis see *M. longipetala*

M. incana This species is usually biennial, but annual forms and the original herbaceous perennial are available. Single or double flowers are borne, in shades of crimson, lavender, lilac, mauve, pink, violet and white. The narrow, grey-green leaves are hairy and up to 15 cm (6 in) long. HEIGHT & SPREAD 75×45 cm (2½×1½ ft).

There are many cultivars and hybrids of *M. incana*. The annuals are half-hardy and have double or single blooms in the same range of colours as the species which appear in early or mid summer. The plants of **'Beauty of Nice'** are branched and grow to 60 cm (2 ft) tall, spreading to 40 cm (16 in). **Column stocks** are unbranched, and each

▼ *Matthiola* Column stocks var. 'Giant Excelsior'

m

▲ *Matthiola* Ten Week stocks var. 'Cinderella'

plant produces one large flower spike, 25cm (10in) long. The variety **'Giant Excelsior'** reaches a height of 75cm (2½ft) and a spread of 30cm (1ft). **Ten Week stocks** are branching plants which may flower in as few as 10 weeks after their seed is sown in a greenhouse. They grow to a height of 45cm (1½ft) and a spread of 30cm (1ft). **'Cinderella'** is a dwarf variety, reaching a height of 25cm (10in) and a spread of 10cm (4in). **Trisomic Seven Week stocks** are even faster growing. These plants attain a height of 45cm (1½ft) and a spread of 30cm (1ft).

The biennial forms of *M. incana* are upright bushy plants which are not quite fully hardy. They produce a mixture of single and double flowers in the same range of colours as the species, blooming in late spring and early summer. **Brompton stocks** grow to a height of 50cm (20in) and a spread of 30cm (1ft). **East Lothian stocks** reach a height and spread of 30 cm (1 ft).

The herbaceous perennials are sold as seed or as plants under the name **White perennial form.** White, 4-petalled, single flowers, each about 5cm (2in) across, are borne in spikes 15-23cm (6-9in) long from late spring to mid summer. This hardy plant forms a branching, shrubby clump with a stout, woody basal stem. Its height is 50cm (20in) and its spread 30cm (1ft).

M. longipetala (syn. *M. bicornis*) (night-scented stock) The single lilac flowers, in spikes 20cm (8in) long, appear in mid and late summer. They stay closed during the day but open in the evening, when their strong scent is evident. The narrow, grey-green leaves are hairy and up to 8cm (3¼in) long; the lower leaves are lobed. This hardy annual has a branching habit. HEIGHT & SPREAD 30×25cm (1ft×10in).

CULTIVATION Plant in fairly rich, moist soil in either full sun or partial shade. Improve sandy soil with compost or leaf-mould. Provide some support for taller varieties.

PROPAGATION Sow the seed of the annual stocks in a greenhouse in early spring and plant out the seedlings in late spring. Alternatively, sow seed outdoors in late spring, and where the plants are to grow.

Annual stocks of the Ten Week and Column types can be selected for double flowers. As soon as the seedlings have emerged, move them to an environment, indoors or outdoors, where the temperature does not exceed 8°C (46°F). After a week or so, the first leaves of some seedlings become noticeably paler than others – these will grow into double-flowered plants. Prick these out and grow on in a cool greenhouse; discard the dark green seedlings.

To select Trisomic Seven Week stocks for double flowers, prick out all seedlings. Once they have about 4 leaves, almost half the seedlings will be noticeably weaker in growth than the rest: discard these.

As a pot plant for late winter and very early spring flowering, sow the seed of 'Beauty of Nice' in early or mid summer in a cool greenhouse and grow on in boxes of general-purpose potting compost. In mid autumn move the young plants to pots 13-15cm (5-6in) in diameter.

Sow the seed of biennials and perennials in early or mid summer in an outdoor seedbed, or sow very thinly in a tray in a greenhouse. When the seedlings are large enough to handle, plant them 10cm (4in) apart, in 10cm (4in) deep boxes, filled with general-purpose potting compost. Plant out in early autumn if the climate is mild and the soil is well drained. Elsewhere, overwinter seedlings in a coldframe or cool greenhouse and plant out in mid spring the following year.

PESTS AND DISEASES Aphids, downy mildew and club root disease may be problems.

Maytenus

Celastraceae

Maytenus boaria

Most of these deciduous and evergreen trees and shrubs are sub-tropical or tropical and are too tender to be grown in British gardens. However, *Maytenus boaria*, with its graceful, weeping habit and handsome foliage, is reasonably hardy and easy to grow in this country.

This large genus, of over 200 species, is native to North or South America and the West Indies.

RECOMMENDED SPECIES

M. boaria This elegant frost-hardy tree has a conical habit when young, becoming

more rounded with age. The narrow evergreen leaves, up to 5cm (2in) long, are dark glossy green with a few very fine teeth. The drooping branches are slender and give the tree a weeping appearance. The very small yellow-green flowers appear in early spring and are of no real beauty, but the tree sometimes produces red fruit. Native to Chile. HEIGHT & SPREAD 1.2m×60cm (4×2ft) after 5 years, ultimately 10m (33ft) tall.
CULTIVATION Hardy in milder areas and undemanding, *M. boaria* can be grown in any well-drained soil.
PROPAGATION Take semi-ripe cuttings in summer, or sow seed in early to mid spring.
PRUNING None is necessary.
PESTS AND DISEASES Usually trouble free.

Mazus

Scrophulariaceae

The foliage of these creeping perennials is scattered with charming two-lipped flowers in late spring and summer. These low, mat-forming plants are useful for pockets in the rock garden, for gaps in paving or for naturalising in moist gravel.
RECOMMENDED SPECIES AND VARIETY
M. radicans Solitary white flowers with pink or purple in the throat are 2cm (¾in) long and appear throughout summer. The robust, creeping stems root down at intervals and carry pairs of small deep green or brownish green elliptical leaves that usually have darker, stitch-like markings around the edge. Native to damp places in New Zealand. HEIGHT & SPREAD 5×50cm (2×20in).
M. reptans The two-lipped flowers, up to 2cm (¾in) long, are pale to deep purple-blue and appear from late spring throughout the summer. The lower lips are neatly spotted with yellow or reddish yellow. A vigorous creeping plant, its prostrate stems root down at intervals and bear small mid to deep green leaves that are narrow and slightly toothed. Native to moist mountain grassland in the Himalayas and W China. HEIGHT & SPREAD 5×50cm (2×20in).
'Albus' has white flowers.

▲ *Mazus reptans*

CULTIVATION Grow plants in any moist soil in sun or partial shade. Plant out in spring or early summer and ensure that the plants receive adequate watering until they are well established. Avoid exposure to drying winds that will scorch the foliage.
PROPAGATION Remove rooted pieces from the parent plant and grow in a shaded coldframe until established.
PESTS AND DISEASES Usually trouble free.

Mazzard see *Prunus avium*
Meadowsweet see *Filipendula ulmaria*

Meconopsis

Papaveraceae

A member of the poppy family, this genus of hardy perennials includes plants to suit every gardener's palette – from white, yellow, red, pink and purple flowered species, to those whose blooms are various beautiful shades of blue.

Meconopsis flowers usually have between four and nine petals surrounding a central boss of many stamens. All meconopsis prefer cool conditions and, particularly in warmer regions, need some shade. They tend to do best in the cooler climates of the north and west where they can be grown in sunnier positions. Shelter is advisable to prevent winds from damaging the flowers and flattening taller species.

Some meconopsis excel in north-facing herbaceous borders; others thrive in informal areas of a woodland garden; while the smaller species are at home in a rock garden or in humus-rich soils provided they have a moist, cool root run and are in good light, but out of direct sun.

With the exception of the Welsh poppy, *Meconopsis cambrica*, the genus is native to the Himalayas and W China. Some meconopsis flower each year but others are monocarpic – they flower and fruit just once, then die. For the first three to four years, the monocarpic species consist of a single, but very attractive and decorative rosette of leaves. Some of these rosettes are evergreen, turning russet, orange-brown or gold in autumn. Others are herbaceous and the foliage dies to a large, resting bud in winter. The seed capsules are oblong to oval and may be hairy, bristly or smooth.
RECOMMENDED SPECIES AND VARIETIES
M. betonicifolia♡ (syn. *M. baileyi*) (Himalayan blue poppy, blue poppy) Bright sky-blue to lavender-pink flowers, up to 10cm (4in) across, are borne on stiff, bristly stalks from early to mid summer. The leaves, held in a whorl below the flowers, are oblong and hairy with a rather heart-shaped base. Bristly, elliptical seed capsules follow. In its preferred growing conditions, this plant usually flowers each year, especially in cooler, moister regions. Otherwise, it is monocarpic. It is usually easy to grow and often self-sows. HEIGHT & SPREAD 1.2m×60cm (4×2ft).

White flowers distinguish var. ***alba***.
M. cambrica (Welsh poppy) In bloom from spring to mid autumn, this yellow-flowered European species flourishes even in shaded, moist parts of the garden, and can become invasive. The flowers, about 6cm (2½in) across, are held almost upright on long stalks. The stems carry several dissected, pale green, almost hairless leaves. The seedpods are smooth, narrow and pointed. HEIGHT & SPREAD 45×30cm (1½×1ft).

Orange flowers distinguish var. ***aurantiaca***. **'Flore Pleno'** can have double orange or yellow flowers, while **'Frances Perry'** has scarlet flowers.

▼ *Meconopsis cambrica* var. *aurantiaca*

▼ *Meconopsis cambrica* 'Flore Pleno'

▼ *Meconopsis cambrica* 'Frances Perry'

M. grandis ♀ Magnificent flowers ranging from rich blue to a wine-like reddish purple adorn this stout herbaceous perennial. The cup-shaped flowers, 7.5-12.5cm (3-5in) across, open in early and mid summer. The rough hairy leaves are lance-shaped to elliptical with a tapered base. The upper 3-5 leaves are held in a whorl beneath the flowers. The seed capsules are somewhat bristly. HEIGHT & SPREAD 1.2m×80cm (4ft×32in).

M. horridula With its blue, lilac, lavender, or occasionally reddish blue flowers, this plant is at home in a shady rock garden or peat bed. The flowers, up to 7.5cm (3in) across, are borne in a distinct spike in cultivation and appear from late spring to mid summer. This monocarpic plant has roughly elliptical, bristly leaves with dark purplish blotches. The plant sometimes self-sows. HEIGHT & SPREAD 80×30cm (32×12in).

M. integrifolia Bowl-shaped, upright, deep primrose yellow flowers, about 23cm (9in) across, appear from late spring to mid summer. Tinged russet or pink when young, the leaves are lance-shaped to elliptical, with 3 veins and stiff hairs. The upper 3-7 leaves are held in a whorl beneath the flowers. The bristly seed capsules are topped by a stigma shaped like a cartwheel. This is a herbaceous monocarpic species. HEIGHT & SPREAD 30-90× 30cm (1-3×1ft).

M.. napaulensis Panicles of pink to red, occasionally purplish, flowers form loose spires on tall stout stems. The bowl-shaped flowers, up to 8cm (3¼in) across, appear from early to mid summer. This monocarpic species has magnificent rosettes of finely divided, hairy, evergreen leaves that are often russet in autumn, and bristly seed capsules. HEIGHT & SPREAD 2.5m×60cm (8×2ft).

M. paniculata This is like a yellow-flowered *M. napaulensis*, also blooming from early to mid summer. The pale green hairy leaves are lobed and toothed and held in large handsome evergreen rosettes that turn russet over winter. HEIGHT & SPREAD 2.5m×60cm (8×2ft).

▲ *Meconopsis paniculata*

M. quintuplinervia ♀ (harebell poppy) Solitary pale lavender flowers, about 3cm (1¼in) across, nod on slender stems throughout summer. Elliptical leaves covered with rust coloured hairs form a loose clump. This plant needs acid, humus-rich soil and does well in a rock garden. HEIGHT & SPREAD 45×45cm (1½×1½ft).

M. regia Large oblong panicles of deeply cupped, pale yellow flowers, up to 12.5cm (5in) across, appear in early to mid summer. A monocarpic species, its striking grey or silver leaf rosettes turn gold in autumn. The hairy leaves are lance-shaped to elliptical with fine edges; the seed capsules are bristly. HEIGHT & SPREAD 2m×80cm (6½ft×32in).

M. x sheldonii ♀ The large, blue flowers of this magnificent hybrid are flushed with green, like shot silk. This long-lived, vigorous plant forms substantial clumps. HEIGHT & SPREAD 1.2m×80cm (4ft×32in).

Crewdson hybrids have mid blue, slightly transparent petals. **'Slieve Donard'** ♀ has rich, deep blue flowers on plants about 75cm (2½ft) tall.

M. villosa see *Cathcartia villosa*

M. wallichii (syn. *M. napaulensis* 'Wallich's form', *M. napaulensis* 'Blue form') Flowers of pale blue to purplish blue or lavender appear from mid summer to early autumn. The evergreen rosettes of bristly leaves are finely lobed and the seed capsules have spreading bristles. HEIGHT & SPREAD 2m×80cm (6½ft×32in).

▲ *Meconopsis wallichii*

CULTIVATION Plant in spring or summer in well-drained, moist, slightly acid to neutral, humus-rich soil. If planting in chalky soil, add plenty of humus. Choose a cool, sheltered site, preferably in the shade or partial shade. Mulch with well-rotted manure or compost, and dress with bone meal in spring and summer.

Protect plants with hairy winter green rosettes from excessive winter wet with a cloche or pane of glass.

PROPAGATION Sow seed as soon as it is ripe or in early spring. Prick out seedlings as soon as they are large enough to handle and plant them out by mid to late summer. Otherwise, leave them until the following spring. Divide perennial species after flowering or in early spring.

PESTS AND DISEASES Slugs and snails may attack young shoots, and aphids may also infest young leaves and flower buds. Crown rot can kill plants in waterlogged soils and seedlings are prone to various fungal diseases.

Medlar see *Mespilus germanica*

Melaleuca

Myrtaceae

Suitable for a greenhouse or conservatory, these evergreen shrubs are grown for their bottlebrush flowerheads – the effect is produced by numerous, tiny, closely packed flowers made up of just a spray of stamens.

Native to Australasia, melaleucas are too tender to be grown outdoors in Britain, although most species can be brought out onto a patio for the summer – but keep them well-watered. They require a minimum temperature of 5°C (41°F).

RECOMMENDED SPECIES

M. gibbosa Purple flowerheads, in dense 3cm (1¼in) spikes, bloom from mid to late summer. The branches of this wiry shrub are crowded with light green, oval leaves about 5mm (¼in) long. HEIGHT & SPREAD 3×1.5m (10×5ft).

▲ *Melaleuca gibbosa*

M. hypericifolia Crimson flower spikes, up to 8cm (3¼in) long, appear from spring to late summer on this large graceful shrub. Mid green lance-shaped leaves, up to 4cm (1½in) long, cover the branches. HEIGHT & SPREAD 3×2m (10×6½ft).

M. squamea Purple, pink or mauve flowers, in spikes up to 2cm (¾in) long, are borne in early summer by this erect shrub. Narrow, mid green leaves, up to 1cm (⅜in) long, densely cover its branches. HEIGHT & SPREAD 1.5×1.2m (5×4ft).

▲ *Melaleuca squamea*

M. squarrosa Cream to yellow scented flowers, in spikes up to 5cm (2in) long, are borne from early to mid summer. This erect shrub has deep green oval leaves, up to 1.5cm (½in) long. HEIGHT & SPREAD 3×1.5m (10×5ft).
CULTIVATION Grow in neutral potting compost; keep moist during summer – less so in winter. Feed once a month in summer using a low-nitrogen fertiliser.
PROPAGATION Sow seed under glass in spring or take semi-ripe cuttings in summer.
PRUNING Cut back after flowering to keep within the bounds of the greenhouse.
PESTS AND DISEASES Red spider mite can be a nuisance.

Melandrium see *Silene*

Melianthus

Melianthaceae

Large, blue-green, serrated leaves give these tall plants their dramatic architectural grandeur. Curving down on slender grey and green stems, the deeply cut foliage is formed by up to 13 serrated leaflets. The leaves are about 50cm (20in) long. Native to southern Africa, melianthus can produce plumes of red flowers, but only during very hot British summers. Although a shrub, it is treated as a herbaceous perennial in Britain and the two recommended species are not reliably hardy. However, they will survive in a warm position in most parts of the country if protected in winter. Alternatively, melianthus can be grown in a conservatory.

RECOMMENDED SPECIES

M. major♀ (honey locust) About 11 oblong leaflets, each up to 13cm (5¼in) long, make this one of the most decorative foliage plants. It may bear brown-red flower plumes in late summer on 80cm (32in) stems. HEIGHT & SPREAD 2.4×2m (8×6½ft).
M. minor The leaves have up to 13 leaflets, each about 5cm (2in) long. Bright, brick-red flowers can appear on 40cm (16in) stems. HEIGHT & SPREAD 2×1m (6½×3ft).
CULTIVATION Plant in spring in fertile soil in a warm position. To encourage flowers, choose poor soil in full sun and do not feed. Plant at least 1m (3ft) apart to allow for

▲ *Melianthus major*

rapid root spread. Protect in winter with bracken, branches, coarse compost, or spun nylon netting. For conservatory plants, use a loam-based compost and 20cm (8in) pots.
PROPAGATION Remove and replant sections of rhizomatous root in spring or sow seed under glass in late winter.
PESTS AND DISEASES Usually trouble free, although red spider mite may attack conservatory plants.

Melissa

Bee balm, lemon balm
Labiatae

A delicious lemon scent is given off by the distinctive leaves of these hardy herbaceous perennials when they are crushed between the fingers. Although the white tubular flowers are insignificant, they crown the foliage with a light haze in summer and early autumn and are attractive to bees. The plant has a place in the garden both as a herb and as a decorative foliage plant, especially billowing out beside a path where the aroma of the leaves can be enjoyed.

Lemon balm does well in any type of soil and in any situation, including dry shade. An invasive habit in all but an acid soil in wet northern gardens makes it unsuitable for growing in small beds. The three species in the genus are natives of Europe. Only one is commonly grown.

RECOMMENDED SPECIES AND VARIETY

***M. officinalis* 'Aurea'** Gold-splashed, strongly veined and tooth-edged, the hairy,

▲ *Melissa officinalis* 'Aurea'

aromatic leaves, up to 5cm (2 in) long and broadly oval, are equally ornamental in a herbaceous border and in a herb garden. Numerous hairy upright and branched square stems are thrown up from slowly extending woody roots. As the flower stems develop, the variegation of the leaves starts to fade. The tiny white tubular flowers appear in whorls on spikes from mid summer to early autumn. HEIGHT & SPREAD 60-90×45cm (2-3×1½ft).
CULTIVATION Plant in spring or autumn in any ordinary garden soil in a dry sunny site or in partial shade. Plants flourish in limestone areas. Unless the flowers are wanted to attract bees to the garden, cut off flowering stems to about 15cm (6in) above ground level in mid summer to promote fresh growth, maintain variegation and prevent self-seeding.
PROPAGATION Divide the roots in spring or autumn. Take softwood cuttings and sow seeds in spring.
PESTS AND DISEASES Usually trouble free.

Melittis

Bastard balm
Labiatae

Tubular two-lipped flowers in shades of white, pink and purple, and often bicoloured, are borne by this herbaceous perennial. It is useful for the front of a border or a herb garden and effective in pockets on larger rock gardens. The sole species is native to W and central Europe and hardy to -25°C (-13°F).

M. melissophyllum Clusters of 2-6 flowers, each 3-4cm (1¼-1½in) long, appear at the upper leaf axils in late spring and early

▼ *Melittis melissophyllum*

summer. Bees are attracted to this aromatic plant which forms erect tufts of simple stems bearing pairs of oval, toothed, mid green and slightly shiny leaves. HEIGHT & SPREAD 30×20 cm (1 ft×8 in).

Selected forms include pink and white-flowered kinds.

CULTIVATION Plant in sun or part shade in well-drained soil that does not dry out rapidly.

PROPAGATION Sow seed in pots in a cold-frame during winter or early spring. Prick out seedlings once they are large enough to handle. Divide parent plants carefully in early spring or after flowering; they may take time to re-establish.

PESTS AND DISEASES Usually trouble free.

Mentha

Mint

Labiatae

A popular group of herbs grown for their decorative aromatic foliage. They can be invasive so plant them where their vigorous root systems do not swamp adjacent plants. (For culinary species, see HERBS p. 332.)

RECOMMENDED SPECIES AND VARIETIES

M. aquatica (water mint) An erect to spreading marginal aquatic plant. Oval or lance-shaped, aromatic mid or grey-green leaves are up to 6 cm (2½ in) long. Whorls of pinkish or lilac fluffy flowers are produced from late summer to autumn. HEIGHT & SPREAD 30×45 cm (1×1½ ft), or more.

M. × gracilis (syn. *M. × gentilis*) (ginger mint) Oval to lance-shaped aromatic leaves, up to 6 cm (2½ in) long are produced on erect reddish stems which during mid summer terminate in uninteresting tiny lilac flowers. HEIGHT & SPREAD 30×30cm (1×1 ft) or more.

'Variegata' has leaves flecked with gold and a scent that is reminiscent of ginger.

▲ *Mentha × gracilis* 'Variegata'

M. longifolia (horsemint) Strongly scented lance-shaped leaves are 8 cm (3¼ in) long. Terminal groups of insignificant white, lilac or mauve flowers are borne in summer. HEIGHT & SPREAD 60×30 cm (2×1 ft).

'Variegata' has hairy leaves splashed with yellow.

CULTIVATION Plant in a sunny, free-draining position. Lift and divide every third year to reduce the chances of mint rust.

PROPAGATION Divide roots in spring.

PESTS AND DISEASES Mint rust is the most likely problem.

Menyanthes

Bog bean

Menyanthaceae

A creeping, deciduous, aquatic marginal perennial is the only species in this genus. Hardiness and delightful flowers in spring recommend it for inclusion at the edge of a large pond – it is too vigorous for small ponds – where it tolerates up to 15 cm (6 in) of water and disguises the transition from the pond to the surrounding area throughout summer. At other times, creeping stems fulfil this role, but to a lesser extent. The plant is native to the Northern Hemisphere.

▲ *Menyanthes trifoliata*

M. trifoliata (buck bean) Up to 20 fringed, star-like flowers form loose spikes, 7.5 cm (3 in) long, on the prominent stems of this aquatic marginal throughout spring. The petals are white with a pinkish flush in bud. Leaves divided into 3 separate bluish green, broadly lance-shaped leaflets, up to 8 cm (3¼ in) long and 4 cm (1½ in) wide, grow upright from fleshy scrambling stems. HEIGHT & SPREAD 25×60 cm (10 in×2 ft), or spreading much farther in rich mud.

CULTIVATION Plant at the pond margin in spring or early summer in a latticework container, filled with heavy loam soil or aquatic plant compost. Cover the soil surface with pea gravel to prevent fish disturbing the plants. Remove faded flowerheads.

PROPAGATION Divide overgrown clumps in spring. Take stem cuttings in late spring or summer and root them in a pot of mud.

PESTS AND DISEASES Usually trouble free.

Menziesia

Ericaceae

Nodding clusters of tubular, urn or bell-shaped flowers appear at the end of stems beneath deciduous leaves. The flowers are borne in late spring and early summer and are purple, pink to nearly white or sometimes bicolour. These compact, slow-growing small to medium-sized shrubs must have acid soil and are suited to a woodland garden. They are hardy, and native to N America and Japan.

RECOMMENDED SPECIES AND VARIETIES

M. ciliicalyx var. ***purpurea*** Flowers about 1.5 cm (½ in) long with a yellowish green base and purplish lobes are freely produced on this long-lived, rounded variety. It has a tidy habit and egg-shaped leaves, up to 5 cm (2 in) long, with fine hairs on the margins. HEIGHT & SPREAD 30×30 cm (1×1 ft) after 5 years, ultimately 60×60 cm (2×2 ft).

Var. ***multiflora*** has a slightly shorter flower which is often paler in colour.

M. taxifolia see *Phyllodoce caerulia*

▲ *Menziesia ciliicalyx* var. *multiflora*

CULTIVATION Plant in an open part of the garden in moist, well-drained acid soil that is rich in organic matter. Menziesia will remain compact in a sunny situation.

PROPAGATION This is an extremely difficult shrub to propagate. The most reliable method is division in early spring.

PRUNING Not necessary but cut back straggly shoots to improve habit.

PESTS AND DISEASES Usually trouble free.

Merrywort see *Ulvaria*

Mertensia

Boraginaceae

Clusters of pendent tubular or bell-like blue flowers, complemented by bluish green or grey foliage, crowd the stems of these hardy herbaceous and semi-evergreen perennials in spring and early summer. They embellish a shady part of a flower border or brighten dappled shade beneath deciduous trees, apart from *Mertensia maritima,* which needs an open sunny position. Grow the small species in a rock garden.

RECOMMENDED SPECIES

M. ciliata In early summer, pale pink buds, borne in lax clusters, open into pale blue flowers, up to 1cm (⅜in) long, on this herbaceous perennial. The bluish green leaves, up to 8cm (3¼in) long, are narrow, elliptical and tapering. Native to open woodlands in the Rocky Mountains, USA. HEIGHT & SPREAD 60×30cm (2×1ft).

M. maritima (oyster plant) Small clusters of bright blue flowers, about 1cm (⅜in) long, open from pink buds in late spring and early summer. This semi-evergreen has trailing stems and beautiful fleshy elliptical or oval grey-blue leaves, up to 8cm (3¼in) long. It does not mix well with other plants. Native to coastal habitats in E Asia, Europe and USA. HEIGHT & SPREAD 15×50cm (6×20in).

M. pulmonarioides♀, syn. *M. virginica* (Virginian cowslip) Deep blue flowers, about 2cm (¾in) long, appear in drooping

▲ *Mertensia maritima*

▲ *Mertensia pulmonarioides*

clusters from mid to late spring and contrast with narrow, tapering to oval, bluish green leaves, up to 7.5cm (3in) long. The stems of this herbaceous perennial die back in mid summer. Native to USA. HEIGHT & SPREAD 50×40 cm (20×16in).

M. sibirica Clusters of 1cm (⅜in) long bluish purple flowers highlight the rounded or heart-shaped leaves, up to 8cm (3¼in) long. Native to Siberia. HEIGHT & SPREAD 45×30cm (1½×1ft).

CULTIVATION Plant all species in autumn or early spring in moist humus-rich soil in dappled shade, except *M. maritima*, which thrives in poor, dry, gravelly soil in full sun.

PROPAGATION Sow seeds in pots as soon as they are ripe. Put in a coldframe and prick out the seedlings as soon as they are large enough to handle. Divide herbaceous plants in early spring or straight after flowering.

PESTS AND DISEASES Aphids may infest young shoots. *M. maritima* is easily damaged by slugs and snails.

Mesembryanthemum see *Dorotheanthus*

Mespilus

Medlar
Rosaceae

Mespilus germanica 'Nottingham'

Sweet fruit – which can be eaten raw when overripe or, more often, used to make jelly – is borne by this undemanding deciduous shrub, a single-species member of the rose family. It is fully hardy and makes a large, wide-spreading ornamental shrub that is good as a specimen plant, for example, on a lawn. Medlars are native to SE Europe and central Asia.

Mespilus germanica Solitary white flowers, up to 4cm (1½in) across, appear in late spring and early summer, often in small numbers. Oblong leaves, dull green above and hairy beneath, grow to 10cm (4in) long and can provide good autumn colour, depending on the individual. Stout spines arm the branches and the marble-shaped hard green fruits, which appear in autumn, grow to about 2.5cm (1in) across. They are best eaten at the end of the year when, after storing for about 3 weeks, they turn soft and brown and the overripe flesh very sweet. HEIGHT & SPREAD 2.4×1.8m (8×6ft) after 10 years, ultimately 5×3m (16×10ft).

▲ *Mespilus germanica*

'Nottingham' has bigger fruits, flowers and leaves, and there are almost no spines.

CULTIVATION Grow anywhere, in any soil. Plant between late autumn and mid spring, avoiding frosty periods.

PROPAGATION Sow seed in early to mid spring. Cultivars must be grafted.

PRUNING None is required.

PESTS AND DISEASES Usually trouble free.

Metasequoia

Dawn redwood
Taxodiaceae

Metasequoia glyptostroboides

The sole, superb species of this genus grows into a majestic forest tree which, in a large garden, makes a striking, stand-alone specimen. The deciduous hardy conifer is well suited to acid soil in damp, dark corners, river banks or pond edges. It soon forms a neat, conical shape round a trunk that is buttressed at ground level. The cinnamon-brown bark flakes in long bootlace shreds.

Metasequoia glyptostroboides♀ The foliage resembles feathers, with pairs of opposite shoots close set with opposite rows of blunt-tipped needles some 2.5cm (1in) long and very soft to the touch. The leaves are bright light green when they open, then turn pink, gold and deep orange before dropping when there are hard winter frosts. Late spring frosts can damage the new leaves.

Yellow male flowers appear in large clusters with greener female flowers in small clusters close to them. The females develop into round, occasionally cylindrical, green cones up to 2cm (¾in) across; these hang on long stalks and ripen to dark brown. Native to China. HEIGHT & SPREAD 7×2m (23×6½ft) after 10 years, ultimately 40m (130ft) tall.

CULTIVATION Grow in fertile, moist, but not waterlogged soil. The tree grows much more slowly in alkaline soil than in its preferred acid conditions.

PROPAGATION Seed is the best method of propagation but is in short supply. Cuttings taken in mid to late autumn root easily with bottom heat.

PRUNING None is necessary, but the canopy can be raised by removing whole branches to clear the required length of trunk.

PESTS AND DISEASES Metasequoias are susceptible to root rot and butt rot if damaged round the base by mowing. Honey fungus can also strike.

Metrosideros

Myrtacae

These tender evergreen trees, shrubs and climbing plants are grown for their very showy flowers. The species listed below have flowers with only tiny, inconspicuous red petals, but their numerous crimson stamens give a fiery display in mid summer.

The branches and short leaf stalks on young plants grown from seed are glossy green and hairless. Older plants, together with younger plants grown from cuttings, have branches and leaf stalks covered with short white hairs. The oval leaves are thick and leathery, dark green above but densely felted and near white beneath.

The species in cultivation are best grown as shrubs. Native to Malaysia, Polynesia, Australia and New Zealand, they can only survive outside in Britain in frost-free gardens and are usually grown in pots and overwintered under glass.

RECOMMENDED SPECIES AND VARIETIES

M. excelsa (New Zealand Christmas tree) The flowers, with stamens as long as 4cm (1½in), are borne in broad, branched clusters up to 10cm (4in) across. The leaves are about 7cm (2¾in) long. HEIGHT & SPREAD 1×1m (3×3ft) after 5 years, ultimately 15m (50ft) tall.

M. kermadecensis Flowers in broad branched clusters up to 10cm (4in) wide display stamens about 1.5cm (½in) long. The leaves are as long as 5cm (2in). HEIGHT & SPREAD 1×1m (3×3ft) after 5 years, ultimately 15m (50ft) tall.

Metrosideros kermadecensis 'Variegata'

'Variegata' is very showy, with dark green leaves broadly and irregularly edged with yellow. Flowers are often produced by young plants only 50cm (20in) tall. This cultivar grows to a height and spread of about 60cm (2ft) after 5 years.

CULTIVATION Grow in pots of a well-drained, general purpose compost and overwinter in a frost-free greenhouse. Move outside once the danger of frost has passed. Give an occasional extra feed with a good general fertiliser. Plant outside only in a very well-drained, frost-free site.

PROPAGATION Sow seed in spring under glass. Take semi-ripe cuttings in early autumn. They may take all winter to root.

PRUNING Cut back after flowering to maintain a compact shape.

PESTS AND DISEASES Usually trouble free.

Meum

Spignel

Umbelliferae

Feathery foliage and bold white flowerheads in summer secure a place in a wild garden for this hardy and aromatic herbaceous perennial. It is particularly successful when established with other wild-garden plants in well-drained soil and in an open, sunny position, such as in a grassy sward. There is only one species in the genus.

Meum athamanticum

Meum athamanticum Prominent white flowerheads, 7.5cm (3in) across, consist of many tiny blossoms that are often tinged yellow and purple. They bloom from early to mid summer. The leaves are divided into 3 or 4 groups of thread-like bright green leaflets. Native to Europe. HEIGHT & SPREAD 60×30 cm (24×12in).

CULTIVATION Plant in spring in well-drained soil. Grow in close association with other plants in a sunny spot in a wild garden. Remove the faded flowerheads, unless fresh seedlings are required for natural colonising.

PROPAGATION Sow seeds in open ground in permanent growing positions immediately they ripen or in early spring. Seedlings do not transplant well.

PESTS AND DISEASES Usually trouble free.

Mezereon see *Daphne mezereum*

Microbiota

Cupressaceae

Microbiota decussata

This prostrate evergreen shrub provides excellent ground cover. The plant is native to SE Siberia and extremely hardy – it will thrive almost anywhere in the garden, including cold dark places where many other plants may not grow. The genus has only one species. It is closely related to juniperus, the main difference being that the berries are more woody than fleshy.

Microbiota decussata

Microbiota decussata Flattened sprays of trailing, dark green, scale-like foliage turn bronze in winter. The leaves sometimes go so brown in low temperatures that the plant could be mistaken as dead until the leaves recover their colour. Insignificant flowers in spring are followed by woody brown berries, 3mm (⅛in) across, in autumn. HEIGHT & SPREAD 10×30cm (4×12in) after 5 years, ultimately 30cm×1.2m (1×4ft).

CULTIVATION Plant in spring in any well-drained soil in sun or shade.

PROPAGATION Ripewood cuttings taken in winter, early spring or early autumn will root easily. Use rooting hormone on autumn cuttings.

PRUNING None required.

PESTS AND DISEASES Usually trouble free. Avoid growing microbiota close to paths or other areas frequented by dogs and cats, because their urine can poison the plant.

Milium see GRASSES p.301
Milkwort see *Polygala*
Miltoniopsis see ORCHIDS p.466
Mimosa see *Acacia dealbata*

Mimosa

Leguminosae

Mimosa pudica

Fluffy heads of summer flowers are borne by plants belonging to this large genus of tropical, thorny, shrubby plants. The only species in general cultivation in Britain is a tender greenhouse pot plant usually raised as an annual. This plant is something of a curiosity, as its much divided foliage collapses temporarily if touched in daylight. Plants belonging to the genus *Mimosa* should not be confused with *Acacia dealbata*, which has the common name mimosa.

RECOMMENDED SPECIES

M. pudica (sensitive plant) Ball-like lilac-pink to mauve flowers up to 2cm (¾in) across appear throughout summer. The tiny, bright to greyish green, lance-shaped leaflets are borne in ranks of 25 or more, each arrangement making up divisions of a larger leaf up to10cm (4in) long. This small shrub's prickly stems are generally erect, but can become loosely climbing unless pinched back from time to time, or supported. The plant is short-lived and is best replaced each spring. HEIGHT & SPREAD 60×60cm (24×24in).

▲ *Mimosa pudica*

CULTIVATION Grow in pots in a soil-based compost such as John Innes No.2. Choose a warm humid place out of direct sunlight, with a temperature of at least 13°C (55°F). Keep plants moist at all times. Feed once a month in summer with a general liquid houseplant fertiliser. Provide support or pinch out wayward shoots to shape.

PROPAGATION Sow seed in a propagator in spring. Take semi-ripe cuttings in summer.

PESTS AND DISEASES Red spider mite can be a problem.

Mimulus

Monkey flower

Scrophulariaceae

Mimulus 'Whitecroft Scarlet'

Dark patterns on the flowers of many of these plants give them a cheerful appearance that has been likened to the grinning face of a monkey. The flowers, borne from summer to early autumn, have two lips and a pouch and are particularly good at attracting bees and other insects to the garden. The pale green or grey-green leaves, 2–6cm (¾–2½in) long, held in pairs, may be oval, oblong or lance-shaped, with toothed edges.

Most species and varieties prefer moist, humus-rich, slightly acid soil, although alkaline soil will do. Bog gardens, the margins of ponds and streams, and damp, open woodland provide the best conditions. The larger varieties do well in informal borders, but can become invasive and smother less vigorous plants. Smaller varieties are ideal for moist, semi-shaded parts of a rock garden or for naturalising around ponds or streams. The more compact species – *Mimulus cardinalis* and *M. lewisii* – can grow in any moist garden soil, but really thrive in deep, fertile soil. *M cardinalis*, *M. cupreus* and *M. guttatus* also do well in containers provided they are well watered.

The genus includes annuals, herbaceous perennials and small shrubs. Native to N and S America, most plants are hardy in Britain. They mix especially well with water margin irises, hostas and rodgersias.

RECOMMENDED SPECIES AND VARIETIES

***M.* 'Andean Nymph'**♀ Cream flowers, about 4cm (1½in) long, are flushed with rose-pink and spotted with a deeper pink on the throat and lower lip. They are produced throughout summer. This spreading perennial is not frost-hardy. HEIGHT & SPREAD 20×30cm (8×12in).

M. aurantiacus♀ (syn. *M. glutinosus*, *Diplacus aurantiacus*, *D. glutinosus*) (bush monkey flower) Orange or deep yellow, unmarked flowers, about 4mm (⅛in) long, with widely spread petal-lobes, are borne in pairs in late spring and summer. This shrub has a much-branched woody base and sticky stems and leaves. It is not frost-hardy. HEIGHT & SPREAD 1×1m (3×3ft).

Reddish purple flowers distinguish var. ***puniceus*** (syn. *M. atrosanguineus*).

M. cardinalis♀ (scarlet monkey flower) The flowers of this herbaceous perennial are brilliant scarlet with yellow in the throat and about 5cm (2in) long. They are borne in long spikes in summer on erect stems. HEIGHT & SPREAD 1m×60cm (3×2ft).

▲ *Mimulus aurantiacus* var. *puniceus*

M. cupreus Numerous small, golden yellow flowers with some patterning in the throat change to bright copper as they age. They are about 3cm (1¼in) long and are borne in short spikes. Impatiens make good planting companions for this hardy annual. HEIGHT & SPREAD 30×20cm (12×8in).

M. glutinosus see *M. aurantiacus*

M. guttatus (common monkey flower) Brilliant golden yellow flowers, about 4cm (1½in) long, with red to purple-brown blotches on the lower lip appear in profusion in late spring and summer. This clump-forming herbaceous perennial has bright green, obovate to rounded, toothed leaves and thick, erect to spreading stems. HEIGHT & SPREAD 60×60cm (24×24in).

M. lewisii♀ (great purple monkey flower) This handsome plant has magenta-purple or deep rose-pink flowers, up to 5cm (2in) long, carried in tall spikes. A downy, rather sticky-stemmed, clump-forming herbaceous perennial, it is not frost-hardy. HEIGHT & SPREAD 60×45cm (24×18in).

▲ *Mimulus lewisii*

M. longiflorus (salmon bush monkey flower) Salmon-flushed yellow or cream flowers give this sticky shrub its common name. Pairs of funnel-shaped flowers, about 6 cm (2½ in) long, appear in summer. This much branched, woody-stemmed plant is not frost-hardy. HEIGHT & SPREAD 70×70 cm (28×28 in).
M. luteus (monkey flower) Masses of small bright yellow flowers, about 4 cm (1½ in) long, appear throughout summer on this spreading herbaceous perennial, which is widely naturalised in Britain. HEIGHT & SPREAD 30×40 cm (12×16 in).
M. moschatus (musk or musk flower) Small, pale yellow, musk-scented flowers, about 2.5 cm (1 in) long, are produced by a spreading, mat-forming, herbaceous perennial all summer long. HEIGHT & SPREAD 20×30 cm (8×12 in).

▲ *Mimulus primuloides*

M. primuloides This hairy, spreading, herbaceous perennial has most of its elliptical or oval leaves in basal rosettes. Small yellow flowers, up to 2 cm (¾ in) long, appear all through summer. HEIGHT & SPREAD 10×50 cm (4×20 in).
M. ringens (Allegheny monkey flower) Violet-blue flowers, about 3 cm (1¼ in) long, are borne in long erect clusters throughout summer. This is a herbaceous perennial with erect, leafy stems. HEIGHT & SPREAD 1 m×60 cm (3×2 ft).
M. tilingii (larger mountain monkey flower) Bright yellow flowers, about 3 cm (1¼ in) long, with brown patterns on the lower lip cover this dense, mat-forming, herbaceous perennial in summer. The spreading stems carry bright green, oval, toothed leaves, up to 3 cm (1¼ in) long. HEIGHT & SPREAD 20×40 cm (8×16 in).

More compact is var. ***caespitosus***, which is no taller than 10 cm (4 in), and has smaller, elliptical leaves.

RECOMMENDED HYBRIDS

Some of the most showy and easy-to-grow monkey flowers are of hybrid origin. The following hybrids are perennials, although often short-lived, and hardy to -5°C (23°F). The flowers are usually 2-3 cm (¾-1¼ in) long. Plants grow to a height of about 30 cm (12 in) and spread to 40 cm (16 in).

▲ *Mimulus* 'Highland Orange'

'Bees' Scarlet' has bright scarlet flowers. **'Highland Orange'** bears bright orange flowers. Those of **'Highland Pink'** are rich pink. **'Highland Red'**♀ has deep red blooms. **'Highland Yellow'** produces flowers of bright yellow. The soft tan flowers of **'Hose in Hose'** have a double corolla, one sitting inside the other. **'Inca Sunset'** carries orange-red blossoms. The flowers of **'Inshriach Crimson'** are deep crimson. Those of **'Whitecroft Scarlet'**♀ are red to reddish orange. **'Wisley Red'** produces velvety, blood-red flowers and grows to a height of not more than 15 cm (6 in).

▲ *Mimulus* 'Whitecroft Scarlet'

CULTIVATION Plant in a moist, humus-rich soil, ideally slightly acid, that does not dry out. Plant hardy perennials in autumn or spring, and annuals in late spring or early summer. Thin larger varieties to prevent them becoming invasive.

PROPAGATION Sow seed in winter or early spring in pots under glass. Alternatively, sow annual varieties in their flowering position in early spring, or in a cool greenhouse in late summer or early winter for early spring displays of flowers.

Divide perennials in autumn or early spring. Take semi-ripe cuttings from shrubby species in late summer. Take softwood cuttings of the hybrid perennials in early summer.

PESTS AND DISEASES Usually trouble free. Some systemic sprays used against slugs, snails and aphids will turn leaves yellow.

Mint (culinary herb) see HERBS p. 332
Mint see *Mentha*
Mint bush see *Prostanthera rotundifolia*

Mirabilis

Nyctaginaceae

Clusters of narrow, trumpet-shaped flowers in a range of brilliant colours make this a decorative plant for a warm sunny position. Only one of the 45 species native to south-eastern N America and to S America is commonly grown in British gardens. This is *Mirabilis jalapa*, a long-lived but tender herbaceous perennial. It can be grown as a half-hardy annual for summer bedding in a sunny border, or in a greenhouse or conservatory.

RECOMMENDED SPECIES

M. jalapa (marvel of Peru, four o'clock plant) Fragrant flowers appear from mid to late summer, opening from mid to late afternoon and fading the next morning. The blooms, up to 5 cm (2 in) long, can be purple, crimson, light orange, yellow, of mixed colours or striped. The ovate leaves are bright green and up to 10 cm (4 in) long. The small green fruits contain one large seed which is black when ripe. The plant has a bushy, erect habit and develops a large tuber, weighing up to 20 kg (44 lb). Native to Peru. HEIGHT & SPREAD 1×1 m (3×3 ft).

▲ *Mirabilis jalapa*

CULTIVATION Plant in any fertile, well-drained soil in a sheltered sunny position in the garden, after all danger of frost has passed. Lift the tubers in late autumn and store them in a frost-free place.

Alternatively, plant in containers filled with a soil-based potting compost and keep in a cool greenhouse or conservatory, placing the containers outside during summer if desired.

PROPAGATION Sow seeds every year in a warm greenhouse during early spring.

PESTS AND DISEASES Generally trouble free but the leaves may become infested by glasshouse whitefly.

Miscanthus see GRASSES p.301
Miss Wilmott's ghost see *Eryngium giganteum*
Mistletoe see *Viscum album*
Mock orange see *Philadelphus*
Molinia see GRASSES p.302

Moltkia

Boraginaceae

Masses of pendent funnel-shaped blue or purple flowers cover these pretty evergreen shrubs or sub-shrubs in summer. They are particularly useful for a rock garden or for the top of a dry retaining wall. Although fully hardy, plants dislike prolonged cold winters and cold drying winds.

RECOMMENDED SPECIES AND VARIETIES

M.* x *intermedia The bright blue flowers, each about 1.5cm (½in) long, are borne in drooping clusters throughout summer. The numerous deep green narrow leaves, up to 10cm (4in) long, are covered underneath with whitish bristles. This is a shrub with an open dome-shaped habit of growth. HEIGHT & SPREAD 23x23cm (9x9in), ultimately 30cm (1ft) tall.

M. petraea Hanging clusters of violet or blue flowers, about 8mm (⅜in) long, appear in summer. The narrow deep green leaves, 1-5cm (⅜-2in) long, have undersides covered with whitish bristles. A semi-evergreen shrub native to the Balkans. HEIGHT & SPREAD 20x20cm (8x8in), ultimately 40cm (16in) tall.

▼ *Moltkia x intermedia*

▼ *Moltkia petraea*

CULTIVATION Plant during spring in full sun in well-drained gritty soil, preferably neutral or alkaline. Choose a site sheltered from cold winds.

PROPAGATION Take semi-ripe cuttings or layer plants in late summer. Alternatively, sow seed in pots in a coldframe in winter or early spring.

PRUNING Not normally required. Remove straggly or dead branches in spring.

PESTS AND DISEASES Usually trouble free.

Molucella

Labiatae

Molucella laevis

Of the four species in this genus, the half-hardy annual *Molucella laevis* is by far the most widely grown. Its numerous tall stems bearing tall white flowers surrounded by prominent green calyxes (made up of sepals) add interest to a border and are a favourite among flower arrangers, both as cut flowers and dried for winter decoration.

RECOMMENDED SPECIES

M. laevis (bells of Ireland, shellflower) The common name is derived from the whorls of green bell-like calyxes which clothe the uppermost regions of the tall, upright stems. In late summer to early autumn each lime-green calyx forms an upturned collar, up to 5cm (2in) across, around a tiny white flower. The stems also carry rounded, lime-green leaves which are toothed and about 6cm (2½in) long. Native to W Asia. HEIGHT & SPREAD 60x30cm (2x1ft).

CULTIVATION Plant in a light, rich soil in an open, sunny situation after the spring frosts.

PROPAGATION Sow seed under glass in any seed compost in early spring at a temperature of 15°C (59°F). Harden off and plant out after the spring frosts. In mild areas you can scatter seed in the plant's flowering position in mid spring and thin out later.

PESTS AND DISEASES Usually trouble free.

▼ *Molucella laevis*

Monarda

Bergamot

Labiatae

Monarda didyma

These showy flowers, set against a backdrop of aromatic foliage, add colour and interest to a mixed herbaceous border. Monardas are also suitable for planting along the edge of water. Rounded whorls of narrow, tubular, two-lipped flowers appear in mid summer and attract bees and butterflies. The simple, opposite leaves can be dried and used in potpourri. Native to woodlands and watersides of N America.

RECOMMENDED SPECIES AND VARIETIES

M. citriodora (lemon mint) This annual bears white to pink or purple flowers, spotted darker purple, 2cm (¾in) long. Erect stems, often branched, carry serrated, lance-shaped, mid green leaves, to 6cm (2½in) long. HEIGHT & SPREAD 60x30cm (2x1ft).

▲ *Monarda citriodora*

M. didyma (Oswego tea, sweet bergamot, bee balm) Red flowers with red or purple bracts are carried in dense heads 4cm (1½in) across. This herbaceous perennial carries pairs of mid green leaves, about 10cm (4in) long, on erect stems. HEIGHT & SPREAD up to 1.2mx45cm (4x1½ft).

'Alba' has white flowers.

▼ *Monarda didyma*

Monarda fistulosa

Monarda 'Croftway Pink'

Monstera deliciosa

M. fistulosa (wild bergamot, purple bee balm) The lavender, lilac or pink narrow-lipped and tubular flowers are carried in crowded heads, about 4cm (1½in) across, over a long season, lasting all summer. This is a herbaceous perennial, with triangular or lance-shaped mid green leaves, which are about 10cm (4in) long. HEIGHT & SPREAD 1m×40cm (3ft×16in).

M. menthifolia (mint-leaved bergamot) Pale pink flowers are borne in crowded heads 2.5cm (1in) across. The lance-shaped mid green leaves of this herbaceous perennial are 8cm (3¼in) long and often have serrated edges. HEIGHT & SPREAD up to 75×40cm (30×16in).

M. punctata (horsemint) The yellowish purple dotted flowers are carried in whorls up to 2.5cm (1in) across at the apex of the stem. Under each flower there are yellowish or purple bracts. This biennial or short-lived perennial has lance-shaped mid green leaves that are 1.5-10cm (½-4in) long. HEIGHT & SPREAD 1m×40cm (3ft×16in).

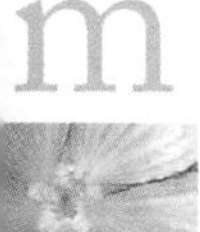

RECOMMENDED CULTIVARS

These cultivars usually bloom for a long period in summer. They grow to a height of 1-1.2m (3-4ft).

'Aquarius' has light mauve flowers with dark green foliage. **'Beauty of Cobham'**♀ bears pale pink flowers with a dark purplish calyx. **'Blaustrumpf'** ('Blue Stocking') with dark lilac flowers, is very vigorous. **'Cambridge Scarlet'**♀ has red flowers with a plum-red calyx. **'Capricorn'** has purple flowers. **'Croftway Pink'**♀ carries salmon-pink flowers. **'Fishes'** ('Pisces') has strong pink flowers with a green calyx. **'Kardinal'** has purple-tinted red flowers. **'Mahogany'** bears deep wine-red flowers. **'Prärienacht'** ('Prairie Night') carries dark lilac flowers. **'Schneewittchen'** ('Snow Maiden') is less robust, with small white flowers. **'Squaw'** is a vigorous grower with vermilion flowers.

CULTIVATION Plant in autumn or spring in sun or partial shade. Monardas prefer moist spots, but will grow in most soils if given adequate bulky organic manure or compost. The more vigorous cultivars can be invasive in wetter soils. Remove dead flowerheads as the flowers fade. Mulch each year and replant every 3 years. Annual species should be sown directly into the flowering position in spring. Staking is not usually required.

PROPAGATION Divide species and cultivars in spring. Species can also be raised from seed sown under glass in spring and planted out later in the year.

PESTS AND DISEASES Usually trouble free.

Moneywort see *Lysimachia nummularia*
Monkey flower see *Mimulus*
Monkey puzzle see *Araucaria araucana*
Monkshood see *Aconitum*

Monstera

Araceae

The Swiss cheese plant is the only species of these evergreen scrambling plants to be widely grown in this country, as a house and greenhouse plant. *Monstera deliciosa* is grown for its very large, glossy leathery leaves, which have deeply cut margins and irregular holes. The arum-like flowers are rarely produced under domestic conditions, because plants do not achieve sufficient size and maturity. Plants need a warm environment out of direct sunlight with a minimum temperature of 15°C (59°F). Given the right conditions, Swiss cheese plants are easily cared for and can grow very rapidly.

RECOMMENDED SPECIES

M. deliciosa (Swiss cheese plant) A robust, woody-stemmed, scrambling plant with large rounded or heart-shaped leaves up to 30cm (12in) long and as much across carried on long stalks. The leaves have either regular or irregular perforations according to the maturity of a particular part of the plant. Older leaves have the most pronounced incisions and holes, while young leaves are heart-shaped and often unbroken. The leaves densely clothe the scrambling stem, which is generally grown attached to a moss-covered pole or framework. Apart from the usual compost roots the plant also produces trailing aerial roots up to 60cm (24in) long. These should be left alone unless they become unsightly and must never be pushed into the compost. Native to tropical Central America. HEIGHT & SPREAD 3m×75cm (10×2½ft) under ordinary domestic conditions.

'Variegata' has leaves irregularly splashed with cream and yellow patches.

CULTIVATION Grow in a richly organic potting compost, such as John Innes No 3, plus as much as a third by volume of composted bark. Keep the soil moist but not waterlogged, and mist the foliage with clear water every day. If the plant is growing on a moss pole, ensure that the moss remains damp. Remove faded leaves and trim back wayward growths to maintain the desired shape.

PROPAGATION Take leaf-bud or stem-tip cuttings in summer. Air layering in summer is also successful.

PESTS AND DISEASES Scale insects and mealy bugs can be a nuisance.

Montbretia see *Crocosmia*

Monstera deliciosa 'Variegata'

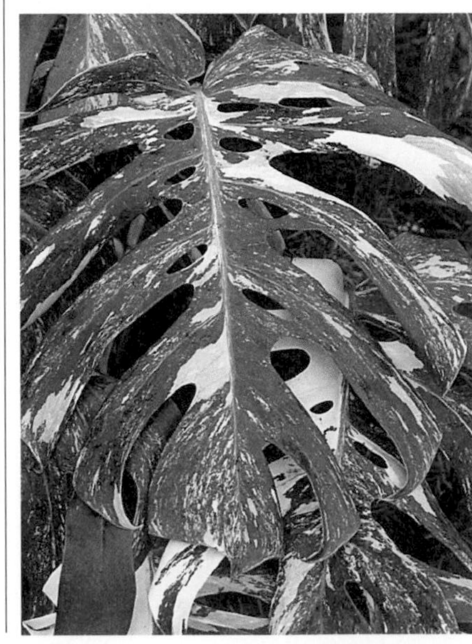

Morina

Whorlflower

Morinaceae

Prominent whorls of small tubular flowers spring from the axils of short, spiny bracts on this hardy perennial in summer. The elegantly arching, prickly, evergreen foliage forms a rosette at the base of the plant. Grow in a herbaceous border or as a single specimen in a bed of smaller plants. Plants are short-lived and require well-drained soil and protection from cold winds. Of the numerous European and central Asian species, only one species, native to the Himalayas, is commonly grown in British gardens.

RECOMMENDED SPECIES

M. longifolia Tubular flowers, up to 2.5 cm (1 in) long, each with 5 widely expanded petals, arch down from a circlet of 15-20 opening buds from early to mid summer. They are white on opening, then turn pink and deepen to crimson on fading. The dark green, narrowly oblong basal leaves, up to 30 cm (12 in) long, have wavy, spiny edges and a strong central vein. Shorter leaves are borne on the stems. HEIGHT & SPREAD 60-90 x 30-45 cm (24-36 x 12-18 in).

CULTIVATION Plant in spring in a sheltered sunny or partially shaded spot and in well-drained, moisture-retentive soil. In cold areas, protect plants in winter.

PROPAGATION Sow seeds as soon as they are ripe or in spring. Plants dislike disturbance, but young plants with multiple crowns may be carefully divided immediately after flowering. Or detach lateral growth with a narrow, pointed trowel or knife. Take root cuttings in spring.

PESTS AND DISEASES Poor drainage may cause plants to rot, otherwise trouble free.

▼ *Morina longifolia*

Morisia

Cruciferae

Bright and cheerful yellow flowers are clustered posy-like on this low-growing, hardy, evergreen perennial from the coastal sands of Corsica and Sardinia. It does well in a trough, a rock garden or in any sharply drained soil. It also makes an excellent pot specimen for an unheated, well-ventilated greenhouse. There is only one species.

Morisia monanthos (syn. *M. hypogaea*) Each plant bears many bright yellow, 4-petalled flowers, 1.5 cm (½ in) across, carried on short erect stalks in spring and early summer. Numerous radiating, deep green and shiny, pinnate leaves up to 8 cm (3¼ in) long form neat rosettes. HEIGHT & SPREAD 5 x 10 cm (2 x 4 in).

'Fred Hemingway' has flowers of a deeper yellow, that are also slightly larger.

▲ *Morisia monanthos* 'Fred Hemingway'

CULTIVATION Plant morisias in very well-drained, gritty soil or compost in full sunshine. Protect plants growing outdoors from excessive winter wet with a cloche or sheet of glass placed overhead.

PROPAGATION Sow seed in winter or early spring in a coldframe, or take root cuttings in early spring.

PESTS AND DISEASES Aphids may infest plants indoors. Red spider mite may be a problem when plants are grown under glass.

Morning glory see *Ipomoea purpurea*

Morus

Mulberry

Moraceae

There are few more permanent features in a garden than a mulberry tree, which may live for several hundred years. Hardy, deciduous and slow-growing, these trees form shapely, dense, spreading canopies of large, toothed leaves. They carry edible raspberry-like fruits in summer and autumn. After fast early growth, the bark becomes attractively knarled. Mulberries are self-fertile, with inconspicuous male and female flowers forming separate yellow-green catkins in spring. Both the white and black mulberry grow best in Britain in the south. In colder areas, plant mulberries against a south-facing wall. The black mulberry is the easier to grow and has sweeter fruit. If space is limited *Morus alba* 'Pendula' is best.

RECOMMENDED SPECIES AND VARIETIES

M. alba (white mulberry) The shiny, heart-shaped, light green leaves are about 12 cm (5 in) long and the fruits are white changing to light red. Native to China. HEIGHT & SPREAD 4 x 3 m (13 x 10 ft) in 20 years, ultimately 9 x 10 m (30 x 33 ft).

The weeping cultivar **'Pendula'**♀ is a smaller neater tree. The largest known specimen measures 4 x 4 m (13 x 13 ft).

▲ *Morus alba* 'Pendula'

M. nigra♀ (black mulberry) This picturesque, often leaning tree has coarse dark green leaves, heart-shaped, 15 cm (6 in) long, which turn golden yellow in autumn. The abundant red-black fruits, up to 2.5 cm (1 in) long, are delicious. Native to W Asia. HEIGHT & SPREAD 5 x 4 m (16 x 13 ft) after 20 years, ultimately 9 m (30 ft) tall.

CULTIVATION Cool well-drained soil and a sunny spot should produce robust mulberry

▼ *Morus nigra*

trees. They need protection from cold winds in exposed areas.
PROPAGATION Take care when planting not to damage or expose the fleshy roots. Hardwood cuttings taken in mid winter do well; use quite long shoots of the previous season's growth and dig them well in.
PRUNING Avoid pruning. If necessary for shaping or controlling size, prune between late autumn and late winter to prevent sap from bleeding.
PESTS AND DISEASES Die-back, often associated with nectria canker, can infect pruning wounds or storm-damaged branches.

Mother-in-law's tongue see *Sansevieria trifasciata*
Mountain avens see *Dryas octapetala*
Mouse plant see *Arisarum proboscideum*

Muehlenbeckia

Polygonaceae

Clusters of tiny flowers are borne by these twiggy shrubs in summer. Both species included here are evergreen and hardy. *Muehlenbeckia axillaris* is a useful ground-cover plant and *M. complexa* forms a bushy shrub or twining climber. The flowers are followed by white, succulent fruits, which enclose small, three-sided, black nuts. Some plants bear flowers of only one sex, others of both. Native to New Zealand.
RECOMMENDED SPECIES
M. axillaris The slender wiry branches of this prostrate shrub are clothed with small, rounded leaves 5mm (¼in) across. In mid summer, racemes of yellowish to white flowers are borne on short stalks. HEIGHT & SPREAD 5cm×1m (2in×3ft) after 5 years, ultimately 30cm (1ft) tall.
M. complexa Greenish yellow flowers are carried on spikes up to 4cm (1½in) long in early and mid summer. Leaves are rounded and 1.5cm (½in) across. Plants vary: some are dense, tangled shrubs with stiff, wiry branches and leathery leaves, others have long, slender, trailing or twining branchlets and softer leaves. HEIGHT & SPREAD of the climber, 6×6m (20×20ft) after 5 years and ultimately; of the shrub, 1×1.5m (3×5ft) after 5 years, ultimately 1.8m (6ft) tall.
CULTIVATION Plant in well-drained soil in sun or partial shade. Provide support for the climbing form of *M. complexa*.
PROPAGATION Sow seed when ripe or in late winter. Layer or take semi-ripe cuttings in summer.

▼ *Muehlenbeckia axillaris*

PRUNING Cut back in spring or summer if the plants become rampant.
PESTS AND DISEASES Usually trouble free.

Mugwort, white see *Artemisia lactiflora*
Mulberry see *Morus*
Mullein see *Verbascum*

Musa

Banana
Musaceae

Grown for the exotic appearance of their foliage, flowers and fruit, these tender evergreen perennials create a lush, tropical atmosphere in conservatories and large, brightly sunlit rooms. The fresh green leaves are up to 1.2m (4ft) long. Each oblong leaf has a stiff midrib with the rest of the leaf hanging slightly away from it as it arches out from the top of the 'trunk'.
RECOMMENDED SPECIES AND VARIETIES
***M. acuminata* 'Dwarf Cavendish'**♀ (syn. *M. cavendishii*) Yellow flower spikes are borne in summer, with red or purple bracts on a drooping stem. Small yellow bananas follow, which may be eaten. HEIGHT & SPREAD 2.4×3m (8×10ft).
M. basjoo Flowerheads with brown bracts and yellow flowers appear in summer. As a conservatory plant, its eventual height may cause problems, so cut it back to encourage shooting from the base. HEIGHT & SPREAD 2.4×1.5m (8×5ft).
M. cavendishii see *M. acuminata* 'Dwarf Cavendish'
CULTIVATION Grow in a 60cm (24in) pot in full sunlight. Keep *M. acuminata* at a temperature of around 21°C (70°F) during active growth and above 10°C (50°F) in winter. *M. basjoo* does best at slightly lower temperatures. Ensure good humidity and avoid draughts. Water generously in summer and sparingly in winter. Apply a high-potash feed weekly during the growing season. Repot young plants in spring, but fully grown plants just require regular feeding. Cut back to the base after flowering to stimulate new shoots.
PROPAGATION Divide plants with multiple crowns or sow seed (available from exotic-seed merchants) in spring. The seed is very hard and should be filed and soaked in warm water for 2 days before sowing.
PESTS AND DISEASES Red spider mite, the only serious pest, is aggravated by dry air.

▲ *Musa acuminata* 'Dwarf Cavendish'

Muscari

Grape hyacinth
Hyacinthaceae

Muscari armeniacum

These spring-flowering bulbs produce dense spikes of fragrant, globular, blue flowers. Most are very hardy and easy to grow. Grape hyacinths make ideal companion plants for all other bulbs that flower at the same time, particularly daffodils and tulips. The narrow, strap-shaped, mid green leaves are up to 30cm (12in) long.

Muscaris are best grown in a sunny well-drained position in a rockery or border; they tolerate light shade, but too shady a spot prevents flowering. Some multiply rapidly and some species, including *Muscari neglectum*, can be invasive. Native to the Mediterranean and SW Asia.
RECOMMENDED SPECIES AND VARIETIES
M. ambrosiacum see *M. muscarimi*
M. armeniacum♀ Densely packed, purple-blue flowers are borne in long unbranched clusters in mid spring among narrow semi-erect leaves. HEIGHT 15-20cm (6-8in).

'Blue Spike' is a double form with large heads of minute dark blue flowers tipped with greenish yellow. **'Cantab'** has light blue flowers with a white rim and **'Saffier'** has dark blue flowers with a white rim.
M. aucheri♀ (syn. *M. tubergenianum*) The bright blue, early spring flowers have white rimmed mouths and are almost spherical; they are paler at the top of the long, dense spikes. HEIGHT 20cm (8in).
M. azureum♀ Compact, bell-shaped flowers, pale to bright blue with a darker narrow

m

Muscari azureum 'Album'

stripe on the lobes, are carried on short dense spikes in early spring. The plant tolerates light shade and thrives in borders as well as rockeries. HEIGHT 10-15 cm (4-6 in).

'Album' has pure white flowers, which are sweetly scented.

M. botryoides Dense spikes of bright blue flowers with a white rim appear from early to mid spring; the leaves are narrow and erect. HEIGHT 20 cm (8 in).

'Album' has narrow clusters of pure white flowers.

M. comosum (tassel hyacinth) The lower flowers are brownish green and those at the top of the spike, on longer stalks, are bright violet to mauve. They are carried in loose clusters in late spring to early summer. HEIGHT 10-30 cm (4-12 in).

'Plumosum' bears a large open cluster of thread-like, mauve-blue, sterile florets.

Muscari latifolium

M. latifolium The fragrant flowers are dark violet-blue at the bottom, paler at the top. They are carried in long clusters in mid to late spring. Each plant has one strap-shaped, grey-green leaf. HEIGHT 15-30 cm (6-12 in).

M. macrocarpum (syn. *M. muscarimi* var. *flavum*, *Muscarimia macrocarpum*) Clusters of sweetly scented bright yellow flowers appear in late spring among the broad

Muscari muscarimi

grey-green leaves. The plant requires a hot, sunny site. HEIGHT 15-20 cm (6-8 in).

M. muscarimi (syn. *M. ambrosiacum*, *M. moschatum*, *Muscarimia ambrosiacum*) The musky scented flowers, purplish at first, fading to yellowish green then ivory, are borne on lax racemes in late spring. Plant in a sunny position. The leaves, which emerge in autumn, are almost evergreen. HEIGHT 15 cm (6 in).

M. neglectum (syn. *M. racemosum*) This is the most common species. It grows freely and so is useful for naturalising in shrub borders. Fragrant flowers, in dense spikes in early and mid spring are dark blue with a white rim at the mouth; they are paler at the top of the spike. HEIGHT 30 cm (12 in).

M. tubergenianum see *M. aucheri*

CULTIVATION Grape hyacinths grow in almost any reasonably well-drained soil in sun or light shade. Plant the bulbs 5-8 cm (2-3¼ in) deep, between late summer and late autumn. Most species can be grown in pots, tubs or window boxes.

PROPAGATION Lift and divide the bulbs every 3-4 years during summer, when they are dormant. Sow from seed from mid summer onwards in a frame or outdoors. They should flower in 3-4 years.

PESTS AND DISEASES Usually trouble free.

Musk see *Mimulus moschatus*

Mutisia

Compositae

Showy daisy-like flowers are borne by these exuberant evergreen perennial climbers in summer and autumn. The plants cling and climb by means of tendrils. They are not fully hardy – grow them outdoors in a sheltered position, with their roots in well-drained soil in the shade and their heads in the sun, or under the protection of a greenhouse or conservatory, where they will thrive more reliably. Native to S America.

RECOMMENDED SPECIES

M. decurrens Vivid orange flowers, up to 10 cm (4 in) across, bloom throughout summer. Lance-shaped mid green leaves, up to 12.5 cm (5 in) long, grow on untidy, multibranched stems. The plant is difficult to establish outdoors, where it needs the protection of a south or west-facing wall. HEIGHT & SPREAD 2×1 m (6½×3 ft).

M. ilicifolia Flowers up to 7.5 cm (3 in) across, with lilac pink petals raying from yellow discs, are produced throughout summer and into early autumn. Mid green oval leaves, up to 5 cm (2 in) long, cover vigorous scrambling stems. HEIGHT & SPREAD 3×1 m (10×3 ft).

CULTIVATION In spring plant in well-drained soil in a sheltered place outside or in a greenhouse border. If pot-grown, use a soil-based medium, such as John Innes No.3. In a conservatory provide shade; outdoors plant beneath an established shrub, which acts as a climbing frame. Trim back untidy growth in spring.

PROPAGATION Sow seeds under glass in spring or plant stem cuttings in summer. Layer semi-ripe stems in late summer or early autumn.

PESTS AND DISEASES Greenfly can often be a nuisance.

Myosotidium

Chatham Island forget-me-not
Boraginaceae

Myosotidium hortensia

Blue forget-me-not flowers and large, deep-veined shiny green leaves characterise this rare evergreen herbaceous perennial from Chatham Island, east of New Zealand. It is not reliably hardy, except in very sheltered gardens, but can be cultivated in a greenhouse or conservatory. There is only one species in the genus.

Myosotidium hortensia (syn. *M. nobile*) Dense heads of flowers up to 15 cm (6 in) across appear in early summer, carried high above the 30 cm (12 in) long oval to kidney-shaped leaves. This is not an easy plant to establish so, once growing, do not move. The plant needs protection from strong cold winds, which would damage the large leaves, and suits a cool, moist site, perhaps close to a water feature or under the light shade of trees or shrubs to offer protection from the midday sun. HEIGHT & SPREAD 45×60 cm (18×24 in).

Myosotidium hortensia

CULTIVATION Plant in fertile moist soil in spring, in a sheltered site. Top-dress annually in spring with seaweed, if possible. During severe weather, protect with branches and coarse leaves and bracken.

In pots, plant in peat-based compost in spring as seedlings come into growth.

PROPAGATION Divide with care in spring. Sow seed under glass, as soon as it is ripe, or in autumn, and plant out the following spring, after the last frosts.

PESTS AND DISEASES Usually trouble free.

m

Myosotis

Forget-me-not

Boraginaceae

Carpets of these blue flowers are a favourite sight in late spring. The species described are short-lived perennials or biennials and make dwarf-tufted clumps or mats suitable for growing in beds or borders, in rock gardens or under glass. *Myosotis scorpioides* is a moisture-loving plant and thrives at the water's edge. The flowers, each about 1 cm (⅜ in) across, are carried in flat-topped clusters and the simple leaves are arranged alternately. The cultivars of *M. alpestris* and *M. sylvatica* are grown as biennials. Forget-me-nots thrive in any well-drained soil, in full sun or – preferably – in light shade.

RECOMMENDED SPECIES AND VARIETIES

M. alpestris (syn. *M. rupicola*) Azure-blue fragrant flowers with distinctive yellow eye are borne in dense sprays from mid to late spring. This tufted hardy perennial with oval to oblong leaves is suitable for a rock garden. Native to Europe. HEIGHT & SPREAD 10-20×20 cm (4-8×8 in).

'Ruth Fischer' has light blue flowers.

M. australis Small white or yellow flowers appear in early summer. The upright plant carries tufts of greenish brown hairy leaves. This native of Australia and New Zealand is usually grown in a rock garden. HEIGHT & SPREAD 25×20 cm (10×8 in).

M. colensoi (syn. *M. decora*) White flowers are carried either singly or in clusters in early summer. This is a mat-forming perennial with narrowly oval to lance-shaped hairy leaves. It requires well-drained but not dry soil with adequate humus. Plant in a rock garden, a scree or an unheated well-ventilated greenhouse. Native to New Zealand. HEIGHT & SPREAD 5×20 cm (2×8 in).

M. decora see *M. colensoi*

M. palustris see *M. scorpioides*

M. rupicola see *M. alpestris*

M. scorpioides (syn. *M. palustris*) (water forget-me-not) Sky-blue flowers with yellow eyes are borne throughout summer. This perennial is for moist areas of the garden, especially pond margins. It is a loose-growing evergreen that spreads by rhizomes. The elongated spoon-shaped leaves are hairy. Native to Europe. HEIGHT & SPREAD 15-30×25 cm (6-12×10 in).

'Mermaid' produces small bright blue flowers on branching stems from tufts of shiny green leaves.

M. sylvatica Fragrant blue flowers are carried in open sprays from late spring to early summer. This tufted biennial has narrowly oblong to lance-shaped, mid green, hairy leaves. Native to Europe. HEIGHT & SPREAD 30×15 cm (12×6 in).

Myosotis scorpioides

Myosotis scorpioides 'Mermaid'

'Blue Ball' is compact with blue flowers, growing to 15 cm (6 in) tall. **'Carmine King'**, with carmine flowers, has an upright habit and grows to a height of 20 cm (8 in). **'Indigo'** and **'Royal Blue'** both have very deep blue flowers and are about 30 cm (12 in) tall. **'Spring Symphony Mixed'** is 20 cm (8 in) tall and **'Victoria Mixed'** reaches a height of 15 cm (6 in); blue, pink and white shades are available.

CULTIVATION Forget-me-nots are very hardy and will thrive in most situations, though they do best in light shade. Plant in early or mid autumn in any reasonable well-drained garden soil. Plant *M. scorpioides* in heavy fertile loam at water level or covered by up to 3 cm (1¼ in) of water. Position in sun or partial shade.

PROPAGATION Sow seed outdoors in early summer. Thin seedlings to 8 cm (3¼ in) apart once established. *M. scorpioides* can be divided in spring.

PESTS AND DISEASES Aphids may be troublesome. Powdery mildew can be very damaging in a dry spring.

Myrica

Myricaceae

The leaves of these plants release a delightful aroma when crushed. Male and female flowers, in the form of catkins, produced either on the same plant or on different plants, are borne in profusion in spring or summer. Most of the evergreen or deciduous plants in the genus are shrubs but some are small trees. They are very undemanding plants and will thrive under a wide range of conditions. The species described below tolerates extremely exposed sites and boggy conditions. Australia is the only place where the genus is not represented.

RECOMMENDED SPECIES

M. gale (sweet gale, bog myrtle) Sweetly fragrant, narrow, glossy, dark green leaves, up to 5 cm (2 in) long, are the chief feature of this hardy, deciduous, multistemmed, upright shrub. They are preceded by dense clusters of small golden brown catkins – up to 10 in a cluster – in late spring or early summer. Male and female catkins are most frequently on separate plants. Female catkins are the slightly fatter of the two. Native to Europe, N America and N Asia. HEIGHT & SPREAD 1 m×60 cm (3×2 ft) after 5 years, ultimately 1.5×2-3 m (5×6½-10 ft).

CULTIVATION Plant from late autumn to early spring in lime-free garden soil. Do not allow the plant to dry out immediately after planting. It thrives in very wet conditions and in full sun but will stand some shade.
PROPAGATION Sow seed in early to mid spring. Layer plants in autumn for planting the following autumn.
PESTS AND DISEASES Usually trouble free.

Myrrhis
Sweet cicely
Umbelliferae

Myrrhis odorata

Fern-like leaves surrounding umbrellas of white flowers are a pleasing spectacle near a pond or stream and in a wild garden. Prominent black seed heads, which provide a dramatic contrast to the pale green leaves, can be added to salads, when still green, and make excellent dried foliage once ripe. The leaves are also of culinary use. The scent of aniseed distinguishes this hardy perennial, which is native to the mountains of S Europe and prefers damp but not waterlogged conditions. There is only one species in the genus.
Myrrhis odorata A mass of tiny flowers with unequal petals open in tight clusters 5-7.5 cm (2-3 in) across from late spring to mid summer. They are supported on tall, hollow, branched stems with prominent basal sheaths. Long-stalked leaves up to 30 cm (12 in) high are produced in a clump at the base of the plant. Each has 2 or 3 soft green leaflets, usually blotched white at the bottom, with deeply cut lobes. HEIGHT & SPREAD 60-100×60-100 cm (2-3×2-3 ft).
CULTIVATION Plant between autumn and spring in moist but well-drained soil in sun or partial shade. Remove seeds to prevent self-seeding.
PROPAGATION Sow seed where required in spring, or when ripe. The main roots are difficult to divide so use any small plants that have self-sown.
PESTS AND DISEASES Watch for aphids, slugs and snails. Carrot flies are attracted by the aromatic foliage.

▼ *Myrrhis odorata*

Myrtle see *Myrtus*
Myrtle, bog see *Myrica gale*

Myrtus
Myrtle
Myrtaceae

These evergreen shrubs are grown for their fragrant summer flowers and glossy foliage, which is aromatic when crushed. Each saucer-shaped, five-petalled flower has a prominent boss of slender stamens. Myrtus will not withstand prolonged periods of frost and flourishes in British gardens only in milder areas. It often does well in gardens close to the sea. In cooler regions, grow plants in pots in a frost-free greenhouse and take them outside for the summer.
RECOMMENDED SPECIES AND VARIETIES
M. apiculata see *Luma apiculata*

▼ *Myrtus communis*

▲ *Myrtus communis* ssp. *tarentina*

M. communis♀ (common myrtle) This rounded many-stemmed shrub bears abundant white flowers in mid and late summer. The flowers measure up to 2 cm (¾ in) across. Small dark purple berries often follow in autumn. The deep green oval leaves grow to about 2.5 cm (1 in) long. Native to the Mediterranean and SE Europe. HEIGHT & SPREAD 1 m×60 cm (3×2 ft) after 5 years, ultimately 3 m (10 ft) tall.

A more compact plant, ssp. ***tarentina***♀ (syn. 'Jenny Reitenbach', 'Microphylla', 'Nana') has smaller leaves, pink-tinged flowers and white berries. Its cultivar **'Microphylla Variegata'** has leaves that are variegated in colour.

'Variegata' is a cultivar of the species that has grey-green leaves edged with a narrow white band.
M. luma see *Luma apiculata*
CULTIVATION In milder regions, plant outdoors in late spring in any well-drained soil, choosing a sheltered position in full sun.

Alternatively, grow plants in pots of multipurpose compost in a cool greenhouse. Keep the compost just moist in winter, but in summer water more freely and provide plenty of ventilation. Plants grown in containers can be moved outside from late spring to early autumn, avoiding any periods of frost.
PRUNING Not normally required, but plants can be trimmed into shape in spring when frosts have passed.
PROPAGATION Sow seed under glass in early or mid spring or take semi-ripe cuttings in early or mid summer. Variegated varieties should be raised from cuttings if they are to come true to type.
PESTS AND DISEASES Usually trouble free.

Nandina

Sacred bamboo

Berberidaceae

Nandina domestica 'Firepower'

Grown chiefly for its beautiful and elegant foliage and autumn and winter colour, the one species in this genus also has attractive flowers and fruits. It is native to warm-temperate Asia.

Although the shrub is frost hardy, nandina needs a sheltered position in the garden. Somewhat similar to bamboo in appearance, nandina is actually closely related to berberis.

***Nandina domestica*♀** This evergreen or semi-evergreen shrub forms a clump of erect leafy stems. The leaves are divided into several narrow lance-shaped leaflets, up to 7 cm (2¾ in) long. They are green in summer, but reddish purple when young, turning a similar or brighter hue in the autumn and winter. In mid summer, large branched sprays of starry, creamy white flowers, each 1 cm (⅜ in) wide, appear at the tips of the stems. After a hot summer they are often followed by showy, spherical, bright red berries, 5 mm (¼ in) across. HEIGHT & SPREAD 1 m×75 cm (3×2½ ft) after 5 years, ultimately 2 m (6½ft).

'Firepower' is a smaller plant, growing to 1.2 m (4 ft) high and 60 cm (2 ft) wide. It has broader leaflets that colour more brightly in autumn.

'Richmond' is a large, vigorous, free-fruiting form with showy scarlet berries. It reaches a height of 2.4 m (8 ft) and spreads to 1.5 m (5 ft) wide.

CULTIVATION Plant in early spring, in fertile, well-drained, fairly moist soil in a sunny, sheltered position.

PROPAGATION Sow seed in early spring or take semi-ripe cuttings in summer.

PRUNING Cut out old and weak shoots to soil level in early spring.

PESTS AND DISEASES Nandina is usually trouble free.

Narcissus

Daffodil

Amaryllidaceae

These bold, cheerful harbingers of spring dance in informal swathes in rough grass, brighten banks and hedgerows, or stand sentinel in formal borders

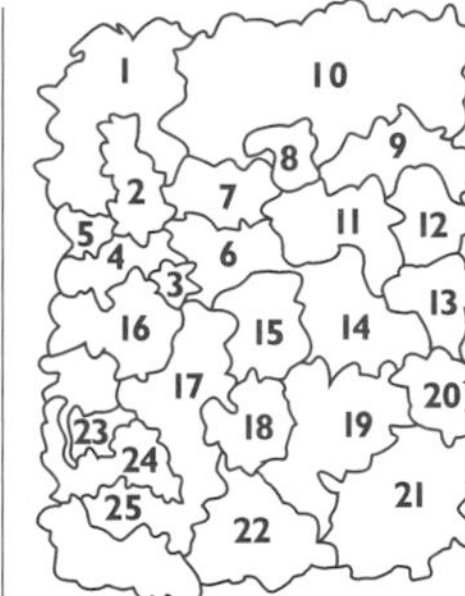

1 'Dutch Master'
2 'Little Beauty'
3 'Bravoure'
4 'Salome'
5 'Rainbow'
6 'Carlton'
7 'Ipi Tombi'
8 'Saint Keverne'
9 'Sabine Hay'
10 'Double Fashion'
11 'Tahiti'
12 'Sir Winston Churchill'
13 'Acropolis'
14 'Unique'
15 'Ice Wings'
16 'Thalia'
17 'February Gold'
18 'Quail'
19 'Geranium'
20 'Soleil d'Or'
21 *N. pseudonarcissus* ssp. *obvallaris*
22 'Mondragon'
23 'Cassata'
24 'Orangery'
25 'Tête-à-Tête'

Golden heads of daffodils among fresh green strap-like leaves are the epitome of spring. Although white daffodils are popularly referred to as narcissi, daffodil is the common name for all members of this genus. Almost all flower in late winter or early spring. Each bulb produces one or more flower stems, each with one or more blooms. Flowers range from 2.5-10cm (1-4in) across, with a central cup (corona) surrounded by six petals (perianth segments), which may be narrow and twisted or broad and flat. Colour varies from white to shades of yellow and orange-red or pink; daffodils are often bicoloured. In 'reversed bicolours', the cup is paler than the petals.

INDEX OF SPECIES & VARIETIES

In order to classify the many daffodil varieties they are grouped into 12 divisions.

(1) Trumpet daffodils
(2) Large-cupped daffodils
(3) Small-cupped daffodils
(4) Double daffodils
(5) Triandrus daffodils
(6) Cyclamineus daffodils
(7) Jonquilla daffodils
(8) Tazetta daffodils
(9) Poeticus daffodils
(10) Species and wild variants
(11) Split-corona daffodils
(12) Miscellaneous

The following lists the daffodils covered in the book; the division appears in brackets.

'Acropolis' (4)
'Actaea' (9)
'Arctic Gold' (1)
'Arish Mell' (5)
'Bantam' (2)
'Bell Song' (7)
'Biscayne' (1)
'Bravoure' (1)
bulbocodium (10)
'Canaliculatus' (8)
'Cantabile' (9)
'Carlton' (2)
'Cassata' (11)
'Chanterelle' (11)
'Charity May' (6)
'Cheerfulness' (4)
cyclamineus (10)
'Daydream' (2)
'Dolly Mollinger' (11)
'Double Fashion' (4)
'Dove Wings' (6)
'Dutch Master' (1)
'Empress of Ireland' (1)
'February Gold' (6)
'February Silver' (6)
'Feeling Lucky' (2)
'Foundling' (6)
'Geranium' (8)
'Golden Aura' (2)
'Golden Rapture' (1)
'Hawera' (5)
'Ice Follies' (2)
'Ice Wings' (5)
'Ipi Tombi' (2)
'Irish Minstrel' (2)
'Jack Snipe' (6)
'Jenny' (6)
'Jetfire' (6)
jonquilla (10)
'Jumblie' (12)
'Kingscourt' (1)
'Liberty Bells' (5)
'Little Beauty' (1)
'Little Gem' (1)
'Little Witch' (6)
Loch Owskeich' (2)
'Merlin' (3)
'Minnow' (8)
'Mondragon' (11)
'Mount Hood' (1)
'Orangery' (11)
'Paper White' (8)
'Papillon Blanc' (11)
papyraceus (8)
'Passionale' (2)
'Peeping Tom' (6)
'Pencrebar' (4)
'Petrel' (5)
'Pinza' (2)
'Pipit' (7)
poeticus var. *recurvus* (10)
pseudonarcissus (10)
ssp. *obvallaris* (10)
'Quail' (7)
'Rainbow' (2)
'Rijnveld's Early Sensation' (1)
'Rippling Waters' (5)
'Rip van Winkle' (4)
'Sabine Hay' (3)
'Saint Keverne' (2)
'Salome' (2)
'Segovia' (3)
'Sir Winston Churchill' (4)
'Soleil d'Or' (8)
'Spellbinder' (1)
'Sun Disc' (7)
'Sundial' (7)
'Suzy' (7)
'Sweetness' (7)
'Tahiti' (4)
'Telamonius Plenus' ('Van Sion') (4)
'Tête-à-Tête' (12)
'Thalia' (5)
'Trena' (6)
'Trevithian' (7)
triandrus (10)
'Tripartite' (11)
'Tuesday's Child' (5)
'Ulster Prince' (1)
'Unique' (4)
'Verona' (3)
'Vulcan' (2)
'W.P. Milner' (1)
'White Lion' (4)
'Xit' (3)
'Yellow Cheerfulness' (4)

▲ *Narcissus* 'Arctic Gold'

Though mostly 40-60cm (16-24in) tall, there are shorter varieties and dwarf forms just 10-20cm (4-8in) high. The basal leaves appear at the same time as the flowers and are more or less strap-shaped. They elongate as the flowers fade and should not be removed until they begin to die back, to encourage the formation of a mature bulb for the following year. Most daffodils are suitable for massing under trees or shrubs; smaller varieties are ideal for the front of a border or a rock garden. The more vigorous varieties can be naturalised in grass.

With the exception of tazettas and some jonquils, most daffodils are hardy. Some, especially the smaller varieties, are suitable for containers. Do not, however, allow the pots to freeze right through.

(1) TRUMPET DAFFODILS

One flower is produced per stem with a trumpet that is as long or longer than the petals. HEIGHT 40-60cm (16-24in).

'Arctic Gold'♀ has well-shaped, clear yellow flowers with broad overlapping petals. **'Biscayne'**♀ has yellow flowers. **'Bravoure'**♀ is tall with white petals and a yellow trumpet. **'Dutch Master'**♀ is a reliable golden hybrid with broad, smooth petals. **'Empress of Ireland'**♀ has exceptionally large white flowers. **'Golden Rapture'**♀ has large, well-shaped, golden-yellow flowers. **'Kingscourt'**♀ is an excellent robust variety with rich golden yellow flowers. **'Little Beauty'** is a perfect miniature, reaching just 15cm (6in) tall, with cream petals around a pale yellow trumpet. **'Little Gem'**♀ is an early-flowering dwarf hybrid, reaching just 15cm (6in) tall with small yellow flowers. **'Mount Hood'**♀ is vigorous with large, creamy white flowers.

'Rijnveld's Early Sensation'♀ is exceptionally early flowering (usually in mid or late winter). It has large yellow flowers on 30cm (12in) stems. **'Spellbinder'**♀ bears flowers that open sulphur yellow, though the trumpet gradually fades to cream. **'Ulster Prince'**♀ has golden yellow flowers. **'W.P. Milner'** has very pale creamy yellow nodding flowers on 30cm (12in) stems and is excellent for naturalising.

(2) LARGE-CUPPED DAFFODILS

One flower is carried per stem with a cup that is more than one-third, but less than the whole length of the petals. HEIGHT is typically 40-60cm (16-24in).

'Bantam'♀, just 30cm (12in) tall, has well-rounded brilliant yellow flowers with an almost flat, bright red cup. **'Carlton'**♀, vigorous and free flowering, has pale yellow flowers with a frilled cup. **'Daydream'**♀ has white petals and a dark lemon yellow cup. **'Feeling Lucky'**♀ is a striking hybrid with a bright red cup and yellow petals.

'Golden Aura'♀ bears well shaped golden flowers. The vigorous **'Ice Follies'**♀ has creamy white petals around a widely flaring lemon yellow cup that gradually fades to cream. **'Ipi Tombi'** is a large-flowered hybrid with yellow petals and a frilled orange cup. **'Irish Minstrel'**♀ has white petals and a yellow cup.

'Loch Owskeich'♀ has large flowers with yellow petals and a clear orange cup. **'Passionale'**♀ has broad, pointed white petals and a long, pale pink cup. **'Pinza'**♀ has yellow petals and a deep orange-red cup. **'Rainbow'**♀ has pure white petals and a pink-rimmed cup. **'Saint Keverne'**♀ has golden yellow flowers and is resistant to basal rot. **'Salome'**♀ has pure white petals and a pinkish orange cup. **'Vulcan'**♀ has vivid yellow petals with an orange cup.

▲ *Narcissus* 'White Lion'

(3) SMALL-CUPPED DAFFODILS

One flower is carried per stem with a cup that is not more than one-third the length of the petals. HEIGHT 40-60cm (16-24in).

'Merlin'♀ has pure white petals and a red-rimmed yellow cup. **'Sabine Hay'** has golden petals around a neat orange cup. **'Segovia'** is a vigorous dwarf hybrid – just 20cm (8in) tall – with white petals and a lemon yellow cup. **'Verona'**♀ has white flowers. **'Xit'**, a dwarf hybrid 18cm (7in) tall, has tiny 4cm (1½in) glistening white flowers. It is slightly tender.

(4) DOUBLE DAFFODILS

One or more flowers are carried on a stem. The petals, the cup or both may be double. HEIGHT 40-60cm (16in-2ft).

'Acropolis' bears flowers whose broad outer petals are pure white while the inner petals are a mixture of white and orange-red. **'Cheerfulness'**♀ bears 1-3 small, fully double, fragrant flowers of cream and pale yellow. **'Double Fashion'** has large, well-shaped flowers with pale yellow outer petals and ruffled orange inner petals.

'Pencrebar' is a dwarf hybrid, reaching only 18cm (7in) tall, with 1-2 small double yellow flowers. **'Rip van Winkle'** is an old cultivar valued for its ability to naturalise and its early flowering. It is 30cm (12in) tall and has rather uneven greenish yellow double flowers. **'Sir Winston Churchill'**♀ bears multiple rounded blooms of white and pale yellow. **'Tahiti'**♀ has strong stems of large, rounded, rich gold and orangey red blooms, good for cutting. **'Telamonius Plenus'** (**'Van Sion'**) is the common, early double yellow daffodil. Either the trumpet or the whole flower may be double.

'Unique'♀ has large rounded flowers with white outer petals and yellow inner ones. **'White Lion'**♀ is a vigorous hybrid

▼ *Narcissus* 'Bantam'

Narcissus 'Ice Follies' ▼

Narcissus 'Cheerfulness' ▼

▼ *Narcissus* 'Pinza'

Narcissus 'Salome' ▼

Narcissus 'Vulcan' ▼

with pointed white petals interspersed with pale yellow ones. **'Yellow Cheerfulness'♀** is a yellow version of 'Cheerfulness'.

(5) TRIANDRUS DAFFODILS

Resembling the parent species, *N. triandrus*, daffodils in this group usually have two or more pendent flowers, with reflexed petals, to a stem. HEIGHT 40-60 cm (16-24 in).

'Arish Mell' has up to 4 white flowers. **'Hawera'♀** has 3-5 small, pale yellow nodding flowers. Each bulb produces a succession of 18 cm (7 in) stems. **'Ice Wings'♀** bears 2-3 medium-sized white flowers with rather long trumpets. **'Liberty Bells'** has well-shaped lemon yellow flowers. **'Petrel'** has 3-7 small white nodding flowers on 30 cm (12 in) stems. **'Rippling Waters'♀** has up to 3 white flowers and grey foliage. **'Thalia'** has rather star-like white flowers; it is good for naturalising. **'Tuesday's Child'♀** has 1 or 2 well-shaped flowers with white petals around a yellow cup.

(6) CYCLAMINEUS DAFFODILS

The varieties in this group have the characteristics of *N. cyclamineus*, the parent species. There is usually one flower to a stem. The flower has a short pedicel (neck), is held at an acute angle to the stem, and its petals are strongly reflexed. Many of these hybrids are early flowering and are useful for growing under shrubs or for naturalising in grass. HEIGHT 30-60 cm (12-24 in).

'Charity May'♀ has early pale yellow flowers. **'Dove Wings'♀** has white petals around a lemon yellow trumpet. **'February Gold'♀** is early flowering with deep yellow flowers. **'February Silver'** has exceptionally long-lasting, large flowers with almost flat white petals around a yellow trumpet.

'Foundling'♀ has white petals and a salmon-pink cup. **'Jack Snipe'♀** has white petals and short yellow cup. It is excellent for naturalising. **'Jenny'♀** has pointed creamy white petals around a flared lemon trumpet that fades to cream. **'Jetfire'♀** is a sturdy hybrid with yellow flowers. The trumpets gradually turn bright orange. **'Little Witch'** reaches 30 cm (12 in) tall at most, with small golden flowers. It is good in grass. Early-flowering **'Peeping Tom'♀** has a long, golden yellow trumpet with a flared tip, surrounded by strongly reflexed petals. **'Trena'** has strongly reflexed white petals around a lemon yellow trumpet.

Narcissus 'Hawera'

▲ *Narcissus* 'Tuesday's Child'

(7) JONQUILLA DAFFODILS

Resembling *N. jonquilla*, these daffodils carry 1-3, often fragrant, flowers per stem. The petals are spreading, but not reflexed. Daffodils within this group require full sun. HEIGHT 30-40 cm (12-16 in).

▲ *Narcissus* 'Pipit'

'Bell Song' bears up to 3 white flowers with small pink cups; **'Pipit'♀**, 1 or 2 reversed bicolour flowers in lemon yellow with paler cups; **'Quail'♀**, 2-3 scented yellow flowers, with rather long cups; **'Sun Disc'♀**, a tiny solitary yellow flower, which fades to cream, on a 20 cm (8 in) stem; **'Sundial'♀,** 1 or 2 small early yellow flowers on a 20 cm (8 in) stem; **'Suzy'♀**, 1-4 deep yellow flowers with orange cups; **'Sweetness'♀**, single, small, golden and very fragrant flowers; and **'Trevithian'♀**, which has pale lemon yellow flowers.

(8) TAZETTA DAFFODILS

Daffodils in this group resemble *N. tazetta.* There are 3-20 flowers to each stout stem, depending on the variety. The petals are spreading and the flowers are mostly fragrant. The leaves are broad. These daffodils are less hardy than most and are prone to frost damage. HEIGHT 40 cm (16 in).

'Canaliculatus' has grey leaves and up to 7 tiny pure-white flowers with yellow cups to each 25 cm (10 in) stem. **'Geranium'♀** is a vigorous hybrid with 3-4 pure-white, broad flowers with orange cups. **'Minnow'** has 2-4 tiny creamy yellow flowers on a 25 cm (10 in) stem. **'Paper White'** (syn. *N. papyraceus*) is a well-known early tazetta, usually forced for early winter flowering. Each stem carries up to

▲ *Narcissus* 'Suzy'

Narcissus 'Sweetness' ▲

10 tiny, pure white, highly scented flowers. The fragrant but tender **'Soleil d'Or'** has many small, golden yellow flowers with orange cups.

(9) POETICUS DAFFODILS

These daffodils clearly show the characteristics of the *N. poeticus* group without admixture from any other. There is usually one fragrant flower to a stem with pure white petals and a flat, disc-shaped cup. This group is usually late flowering, and care must be taken to provide sufficient moisture. HEIGHT 30-40 cm (12-16 in).

'Actaea'♀ has an early large, round flower with white petals and small red-rimmed cup. **'Cantabile'♀** has a small, perfectly round white flower with a red-rimmed cup and green eye.

(10) SPECIES AND WILD VARIANTS

This group covers all species and wild or reputedly wild variants and hybrids, including those with double flowers. All differ greatly in their cultural requirements, most being unsuitable for general garden use. They make excellent pot plants for an alpine house. Most are increased by seed.

***N. bulbocodium*♀** (hoop petticoat) The flowers of this variable species have round, expanded trumpets and tiny, narrow yellow petals. The leaves are grass like. The plant needs a moist acid soil that dries out in summer. HEIGHT 10-25 cm (4-10 in).

***N. cyclamineus*♀** has narrow, deep yellow trumpets and long, completely reflexed yellow petals. It self-seeds freely in a cool, acid soil. HEIGHT 25-30 cm (10-12 in).

***N. jonquilla*♀** Up to 4 tiny golden yellow flowers appear rather later than most in mid

▲ *Narcissus* 'Geranium'

▲ *Narcissus bulbocodium*

to late spring. This strongly fragrant species is easy to grow in well-drained, limy soils in full sun. HEIGHT 30-40 cm (12-16 in).
N. poeticus var. ***recurvus***♀ (pheasant's eye narcissus) White, strongly scented flowers with slightly reflexed petals and tiny red-rimmed, green-eyed cups appear later than most in late spring. Bulbs may take a while to establish. Lack of moisture in late spring can cause blindness. HEIGHT 36 cm (14 in).
N. pseudonarcissus♀ (Lent lily) Narrow, twisted, sulphur-yellow petals almost clasp the creamy trumpets. It needs soil that is not too dry and can take years to become established. Once settled, it can self-sow to cover large areas. HEIGHT 25-36 cm (10-14 in).

The vigorous ssp. ***obvallaris***♀ (Tenby daffodil) is early-flowering, up to 30 cm (12 in) tall, and ideal for naturalising in grass. The clone in cultivation is sterile.
N. triandrus♀ Up to 4 flowers are carried per stem, each with a rounded cup and fully reflexed petals. This species can be naturalised in dry, acid soils or grown in a pot in an alpine house. HEIGHT 10-20 cm (4-8 in).

n

(11) SPLIT-CORONA DAFFODILS
Sometimes referred to as collar, orchid or papillon daffodils, the cup is split, forming an inner coloured layer.

'Cassata' has flat flowers with yellow inner petals laid evenly over white outer ones. **'Chanterelle'** has white flowers with yellow centres. **'Dolly Mollinger'** has white petals and orange centres.

'Mondragon' has golden cups and pale yellow petals; **'Orangery'**, white petals and orange cups; **'Papillon Blanc'**, white flowers; and **'Tripartite'**, 2-3 yellow flowers.

(12) MISCELLANEOUS
Daffodils not falling into any other division are grouped here.

'Jumblie'♀ is a vigorous dwarf hybrid with up to 3 flowers per 18 cm (7 in) stem and many stems per bulb. A deep gold trumpet is surrounded by paler, narrow, fully reflexed petals. **'Tête-à-Tête'**♀ is a dwarf hybrid with 1-3 small yellow flowers per 15 cm (6 in) stem.
CULTIVATION Plant bulbs in autumn. Most grow in any soil but will not tolerate waterlogged conditions. While in growth, they need sun for at least part of the day, and late-flowering varieties should be watered in dry periods. Plant species narcissi, that naturally increase by self-seeding, singly, and hybrids in groups of one variety.

Deadhead hybrids as soon as the flowers fade, both for appearance and to encourage a larger bulb to form, but leave the seed heads of species to ripen.
PROPAGATION Remove offsets of hybrid daffodils in autumn or lift and divide the clumps as the leaves turn yellow after flowering. Increase species by sowing seed as soon as it is ripe in early summer. Seedlings can take up to 7 years to flower.
PESTS AND DISEASES Waterlogged soils can cause fungal attacks. Narcissus fly and stem and bulb eelworm can attack bulbs.

Nasturtium see *Tropaeolum*
Navelwort see *Umbilicus rupestris*
Nectarine see p. 727

Nectaroscordum

Alliaceae

Bell-shaped flowers flushed flesh pink and dark red, with a greenish tinge towards the base, are borne in loose arrangements of up to 40 florets. These easily grown spring-flowering bulbs, hardy to -12°C (10°F), can become invasive. They have a pungent onion smell and the strap-shaped leaves give off a similar odour when crushed. After flowering, the stalks bend upwards to hold the off-white to brownish seedpods erect. Pods are 1 cm (⅜ in) long and diamond-shaped. The genus, formerly included in allium, is native to the E Mediterranean.
RECOMMENDED SPECIES AND VARIETIES
N. siculum (syn. *Allium siculum)* (Sicilian honey garlic) Pale greenish cream flowers, suffused with greenish red, appear from mid to late spring in rounded clusters 7.5 cm (3 in) across. HEIGHT 1 m (3 ft).
N. siculum bulgaricum Up to 30 flowers, larger and with less red than *N. siculum*, are carried in each cluster during late spring and early summer. HEIGHT 1 m (3 ft).
CULTIVATION Grow in any good garden soil in sun or partial shade. Plant between late summer and late autumn, 5 cm (2 in) deep and 25-40 cm (10-16 in) apart.
PROPAGATION Sow seed in sandy soil in late summer and plant out after two seasons.
PESTS AND DISEASES Can suffer from white onion rot.

▼ *Nectaroscordum siculum*

Nemesia

Scrophulariaceae

Grown for their abundant, brightly coloured, trumpet-shaped flowers, this genus includes half-hardy annuals and herbaceous perennials. The annuals make good summer bedding plants; the perennial species can be grown in a cool greenhouse and moved outside in summer. Some will survive outdoors over winter in mild areas. All species have narrow, toothed, opposite leaves, that are usually pale green.
RECOMMENDED SPECIES AND VARIETIES
N. caerulea (syn. *N. foetens*, *N. fruticans* hort.) Yellow-centred lilac flowers, 1.5 cm (½ in) across, bloom from early summer to early autumn on this dwarf, half-hardy perennial. The leaves are up to 4 cm (1½ in) long. HEIGHT & SPREAD 30×75 cm (1×2½ ft).

'Joan Wilder' has deep lavender blue flowers; **'Innocence'** has white flowers and **'Woodcote'**, purple flowers.
N. denticulata The scented, pinky-purple flowers of this perennial – which can survive winter outdoors – are about 1 cm (⅜ in) across; its leaves are up to 4 cm (1½ in) long. HEIGHT & SPREAD 25×30 cm (10×12 in).
N. foetens see *N. caerulea*
N. fruticans hort. see *N. caerulea*
N. strumosa Profuse yellow, white or

▼ *Nemesia caerulea* 'Joan Wilder'

purple flowers with yellow throats, about 2.5 cm (1 in) across, appear in summer. The leaves of this annual are up to 7.5 cm (3 in) long. HEIGHT & SPREAD 30×20 cm (12×8 in).

Varieties tend to be slightly smaller than the species: **'Blue Gem'** has brilliant blue flowers with prominent white stamens; the mixed colours of **Carnival Series** include cream, orange, pink, purple and yellow; **'KLM'** has blue and white flowers, and **'Mello Red & White'** is also bicoloured.

CULTIVATION Plant in late spring or early summer, after the risk of frost, in moisture-retentive soil in a sunny, sheltered position. Water frequently in dry weather. Cut back hard after first flowering for repeat flowering. Lift perennials in early autumn and overwinter in pots in a cool greenhouse. If *N. denticulata* is left to winter outdoors, do not cut the old flowering stems until spring.

PROPAGATION Sow seeds under glass in early spring. Take softwood cuttings of perennials in early spring or semi-hardwood cuttings in late summer.

PESTS AND DISEASES Poor greenhouse hygiene may cause foot rot.

Nemophila

Hydrophyllaceae

Distinctively marked flowers characterise this Californian genus of hardy annuals. The two species described flower from summer into autumn – most profusely in cool wet weather. Their low-growing habit makes nemophilas suitable for the edges of borders, rock gardens and containers.

▲ *Nemophila maculata*

Nemophila menziesii ▲

RECOMMENDED SPECIES AND VARIETIES

N. insignis see *N. menziesii*

N. maculata (five spot) White flowers, up to 4 cm (1½ in) across, appear from early summer to mid autumn. Each of the 5 petals bears purple veins and a deep violet blotch at the tip. The spreading, semi-prostrate plant has pale green, deeply lobed leaves. HEIGHT & SPREAD 15×20 cm (6×8 in).

N. menziesii (syn. *N. insignis*) (baby blue eyes) Sky-blue, white-centred, 5-petalled flowers, up to 4 cm (1½ in) across, grow on the long succulent stems of this spreading plant from early summer to mid autumn. The pale green, downy leaves are deeply lobed. HEIGHT & SPREAD 20×30 cm (8×12 in).

'Pennie Black' has deep purple-petalled flowers with white edges. **'Snowstorm'** is finely spotted with black on the innermost two-thirds of each white petal.

CULTIVATION Nemophilas thrive in moisture-retentive soil, in sun or partial shade. Shelter the fragile, succulent stems from wind and support them with short twigs. Water generously in dry weather.

PROPAGATION Sow seed in mid spring where plants are to grow. Early autumn sowings – successful in all but the coldest areas of the country – result in larger plants which are early to flower.

PESTS AND DISEASES Attacked by aphids.

Neoregelia

Bromeliaceae

The shiny, strap-like foliage of these evergreen, rosette-forming, tropical plants changes colour when the flowers appear. The centre of the leaf rosette forms an urn-like hollow that holds water and from which the flowerheads emerge. These bromeliads can be grown as houseplants but are best cultivated in a heated greenhouse.

RECOMMENDED SPECIES AND VARIETIES

N. carolinae (blushing bromeliad) Arching, bright green, finely toothed leaves are about 45 cm (1½ ft) long. The centre of the rosette turns red in mid summer when the flowers are produced. These are purple-blue and tubular with 3 petals, up to 3 cm (1¼ in) long, and borne in a compact cluster among bright red bracts. HEIGHT & SPREAD 30×45 cm (1×1½ ft).

▲ *Neoregelia carolinae* Meyendorffii Group 'Flandria'

Meyendorffii Group 'Flandria' (syn. *Nidularium flandria*) has narrow leaves, up to 35 cm (14 in) long, radiating from the central urn. Each is striped green and cream ending with cream edges. The base of the leaf rosette turns crimson when the flowers appear. Bright blue-mauve flowers with red bracts are 2.5 cm (1 in) long and only just emerge from the central urn. The most widely grown variety, f. *tricolor*♀, has yellow and green striped leaves.

CULTIVATION Plant in pots of equal parts loam-based compost and bark chips, or in soil-less compost. Place in a warm room or heated greenhouse with a minimum temperature of 10°C (50°F), high humidity, and plenty of light, but not full sun. Water by filling the central urn in the leaf rosette with soft water. Mist daily. Feed monthly from spring to late summer with a liquid houseplant feed. Remove faded flowers.

PROPAGATION Remove and replant offsets during spring and early summer.

PESTS AND DISEASES Usually trouble free.

Nepeta

Labiatae

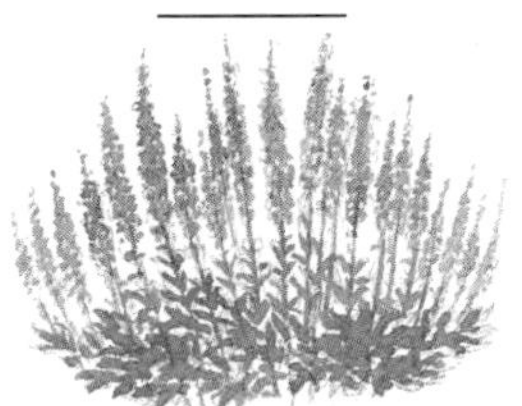

Nepeta x faassenii 'Six Hills Giant'

Tiny flowers in shades of blue, purple, yellow and white are borne in summer in delicate, hazy spikes above often silvery foliage. These are formed of clusters of blooms along the upper part of the stems.

Individual flowers are tubular or funnel-shaped with two lips: the upper lip is upright, the lower lip more spreading, and both lips are prominently lobed. The leaves are often hairy with toothed edges and, in some species, are aromatic. Cats are particularly attracted to *Nepeta cataria*. The herbaceous perennials have a loose, spreading habit. Native to Europe, N Africa and Asia, most are hardy, but *N. nepetella* may need winter protection in colder districts.

RECOMMENDED SPECIES AND VARIETIES

N. 'Blue Beauty' see *N. sibirica* 'Souvenir d'Andre Chaudron'

N. cataria (catnip, catmint) White flowers are dotted with violet. Both the upright stems and aromatic foliage are hairy and greyish green with leaves up to 4 cm (1½ in) long. HEIGHT & SPREAD 1 m×60 cm (3×2 ft).

'Citriodora' has light blue flowers and is lemon-scented.

N. x faassenii This plant has pale lavender flowers and hairy, silver-grey, aromatic leaves about 3 cm (1¼ in) long. HEIGHT & SPREAD 60×60 cm (2×2 ft).

'Six Hills Giant' grows up to 1 m (3 ft) and has darker lavender flowers.

N. glechoma see *Glechoma hederacea*

N. govaniana Pale yellow flowers are borne in loose spikes. Pointed, mid green leaves are up to 10 cm (4 in) long. A more upright

▲ *Nepeta* x *faassenii* 'Six Hills Giant'

plant, it prefers cool, moist conditions. HEIGHT & SPREAD 1m×60cm (3×2ft).
N. hederacea see *Glechoma hederacea*
N. lanceolata see *N. nepetella*
N. macrantha see *N. sibirica*
N. mussinii see *N. racemosa*
N. nepetella (syn. *N. lanceolata*) This compact plant has abundant pinkish white flowers and narrow grey-green leaves. HEIGHT & SPREAD 60×60cm (2×2ft).
N. nervosa This species has dense spikes of pale blue flowers and aromatic, narrow, mid green leaves up to 10cm (4in) long. HEIGHT & SPREAD 35×60cm (14in×2ft).
N. racemosa (syn. *N. mussinii*, *N. reichenbachiana*) A spreading plant with violet to lilac-blue flowers. The grey-green, aromatic leaves are about 3cm (1¼in) long. HEIGHT & SPREAD 30×60cm (1×2ft).

'Snowflake' has white flowers. **'Little Titch'** is just 15cm (6in) tall.
N. sibirica (syn. *N. macrantha*) Large lavender blue flowers are borne in loose spikes on this upright plant. The aromatic, narrow, dark green leaves, are about 7cm (2¾in) long. HEIGHT & SPREAD 1m×60cm (3×2ft).

'Souvenir d'Andre Chaudron' (syn. *N.* 'Blue Beauty') reaches 50cm (20in) in height and spreads vigorously. It has grey-green leaves and soft blue flowers.

▲ *Nepeta nervosa*

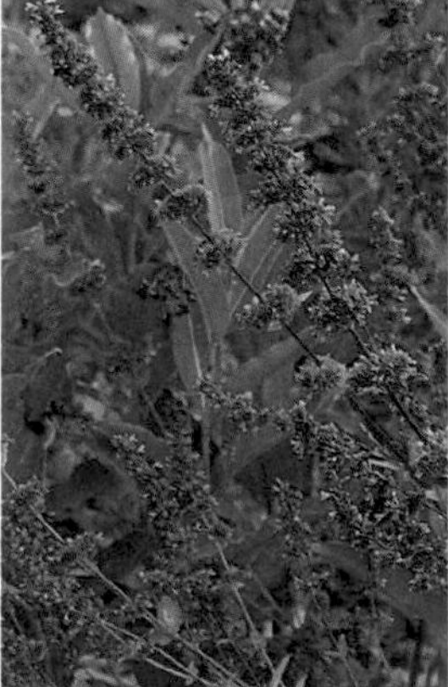

Nepeta racemosa ▲

CULTIVATION Plant in early spring in any well-drained soil in full sun, although *N. govaniana* prefers moist soil and part shade. Deadhead to prolong flowering. Clip back plants used for edging after flowering.
PROPAGATION Divide in early spring or take softwood cuttings in late spring. Sow fresh seed in late summer or early autumn.
PESTS AND DISEASES Powdery mildew can be troublesome in hot, dry summers.

Nephrolepis see FERNS p.264

Nerine
Amaryllidaceae

Airy pink nerine trumpets adding a bright splash to a border in autumn are likely to be those of *Nerine bowdenii*. This is the hardiest species of this genus of autumn-flowering, bulbous perennials from southern Africa: most are frost tender and need greenhouse protection in Britain. The wavy petalled trumpets are carried in 7.5-13cm (3-5in) clusters on graceful stems. They are bright red, pink or white and bloom for several weeks. The strap-shaped, mid green leaves, 30-45cm (1-1½ft) long, usually appear after the flowers.
RECOMMENDED SPECIES AND VARIETIES
N. bowdenii♀ Stout stems bear umbels (umbrella-like clusters) of up to 8 pink to deep rose flowers. HEIGHT 45cm (1½ft).

▲ *Nerine bowdenii*

'Mark Fenwick' is taller and more vigorous with soft pink flowers. **'Pink Triumph'** has deep pink flowers.
CULTIVATION Grow most nerines in frost-free conditions in a cool greenhouse.

The hardier *N. bowdenii* can be planted outdoors in early to mid spring or late autumn in any free-draining garden soil, preferably near a warm wall. Plant bulbs with their tips just below the soil surface; bury deeper in colder areas. Feed in early spring with a light dressing of fertiliser. Take bulbs grown in tubs indoors in winter.
PROPAGATION Nerines do best when left undisturbed, but if the bulbs become overcrowded, lift and divide in summer when the foliage dies down. Sow seeds in a sandy, well-drained soil. They will reach flowering size in 2-3 years depending on the species.
PESTS AND DISEASES Protect nerines from slugs and snails.

Nerium
Apocynaceae

Showy blossoms are produced throughout summer and into autumn on these tender evergreen shrubs. *Nerium oleander* is the only species in the genus, although there are many cultivated varieties. All parts of the plant are toxic; keep sap away from eyes.

▲ *Nerium oleander*

Nerium oleander (oleander) Papery pink or white flowers, up to 5cm (2in) across, and sometimes scented are usually borne in clusters on this upright shrub. The mid to deep green leaves are lance-shaped and up to 15cm (6in) long. HEIGHT & SPREAD 2×1m (6½×3ft) after 5 years, ultimately 6m (20ft).

'Géant des Batailles' has deep red double flowers; **'Luteum Plenum'**, large double yellow flowers; **'Peach Blossom'**, soft pink flowers; **'Professeur Granel'**; semidouble orange-red flowers; **'Roseum Plenum'**, fully double rose-pink flowers; and **'Variegatum'**, cream-yellow and green variegated foliage with soft pink flowers.
CULTIVATION Grow in large pots of soil-based compost in a well-ventilated greenhouse and ensure a minimum temperature of 10°C (50°F). Move plants outside in summer and keep well watered. Feed with a liquid tomato feed from late spring until late summer. Remove any faded flowers.
PROPAGATION Take semi-ripe cuttings during summer.
PRUNING Trim out any unwanted shoots as they appear and cut back hard to the woody framework in spring so that the plant can be completely reclothed in fresh growth.
PESTS AND DISEASES Greenfly, mealy bugs and scale insects can cause problems.

Nertera

Bead plant
Rubiaceae

Freely produced, rounded or pear-shaped red or orange fruits can completely cover these creeping and readily rooting alpines or pot plants between late summer and mid autumn. Little yellow funnel-shaped flowers open in late spring but are stemless, and so small that they are hidden among the mats of tiny evergreen leaves. Not all the species are hardy and only three are commonly cultivated in Britain. These have an almost limitless spread once established but are not easy to grow: they are very shallow rooted and must be kept moist. The genus is native to Australia, New Zealand, Chile, the Pacific islands and central S America.

RECOMMENDED SPECIES AND VARIETIES

N. balfouriana Tiny bright green leaves form a compact mat. Pear-shaped orange berries are about 8mm (⅜in) long. Usually cultivated as an alpine house plant, it can be grown outdoors if kept constantly moist. HEIGHT & SPREAD 5mm×25cm (¼×10in).

N. depressa Open mats of small spade-shaped shiny leaves have an offensive smell when crushed. This fast-growing species, which has rounded red berries about 4mm (⅛in) across, can be grown outside but is best moved to an alpine house in winter. HEIGHT & SPREAD 1×30cm (⅜in×1ft).

▲ *Nertera granadensis*

N. granadensis Rounded, matt, light green leaves, and 8mm (⅜in) orange berries characterise this compact species which is often incorrectly sold as *N. depressa*. It is not fully hardy and is usually grown as a pot plant. HEIGHT & SPREAD 1×30cm (⅜in×1ft).

CULTIVATION Plant in spring and summer in rich soil and keep moist to prevent the shallow roots from drying out. Move to a cool, well-ventilated greenhouse in winter.

PROPAGATION Divide in spring or sow ripe berries on the surface of the soil. Keep moist at all times.

PESTS AND DISEASES Slugs and snails may cause damage.

Nettle, flame see *Solenostemon*
Nettle, painted see *Solenostemon*
Nettle tree see *Celtis*
New Zealand bur see *Acaena*

Nicandra

Shoo fly plant
Solanaceae

Bell-shaped flowers open for a single day from summer to autumn on this showy hardy annual, followed by spherical green fruits, enclosed in a yellow winged calyx. The Peruvian genus consists of a single species, whose common name results from a reputation for repelling flies.

▲ *Nicandra physaloides*

N. physaloides Violet-blue, white-throated flowers, 4cm (1½in) across, appear singly from mid summer to early autumn among mid green foliage. This fast-growing hardy annual has branching stems and elliptical or lance-shaped leaves up to 10cm (4in) long. Spherical green fruits, known as apples of Peru, up to 5cm (2in) across, follow the flowers. HEIGHT & SPREAD 90×30cm (3×1ft).

CULTIVATION Grow in a sunny spot in rich, well-drained soil where plants are to flower. Water freely in dry spells and feed occasionally with liquid tomato fertiliser.

PROPAGATION Sow seeds into open ground in spring. Thin crowded seedlings.

PESTS AND DISEASES Usually trouble free.

Nicotiana

Tobacco plant
Solanaceae

Profuse clusters of tubular, five-petalled flowers are borne for long periods during summer and autumn. The blooms of flowering tobacco, *Nicotiana alata*, only open in the evening to release their powerful scent. Modern hybrids have a less intense fragrance but their flowers open throughout the day. Most nicotianas have large, oval, mid green leaves. The plants recommended below are herbaceous perennials but are mostly grown as half-hardy annuals. All parts of these S American natives are toxic.

RECOMMENDED SPECIES AND VARIETIES

N. alata (syn. *N. affinis*) (flowering tobacco) White flowers, 10cm (4in) long, are borne on this sticky plant from mid summer to mid autumn. HEIGHT & SPREAD 1m×40cm (3ft×16in), or more.

'Lime green' has yellow-green flowers.

N. langsdorffii♀ Pale green, scentless flow-

▲ *Nicotiana langsdorffii*

ers, 5cm (1in) long, are carried in drooping sprays from mid summer to mid autumn. HEIGHT & SPREAD 1.5m×40cm (5ft×16in).

N. × sanderae Slightly fragrant flowers, 7.5cm (3in) long, bloom in loose clusters from early summer until the first autumn frost. HEIGHT & SPREAD 60×30cm (2×1ft).

Domino Series comes in mixed colours or separately – in crimson, lime, salmon-pink and white. The flowers tilt upwards. Plants reach 30cm (1ft) tall. **'Havana Apple Blossom'**, 35cm (14in) tall, has flowers that are rose-pink outside and very pale pink inside. The flowers of **'Havana Lime Rose'**, 35cm (14in) tall, are yellow-green outside and rose-pink inside. **Merlin Series** seed is available in mixed colours only. Plants are 25cm (10in) high. **Nicki Series**, 40cm (16in) tall, is available as mixed colours or in pink. The **Sensation Series** is available in mixed colours only. The plants can reach 1m (3ft) in height.

N. sylvestris♀ Pendulous, slender, fragrant white flowers, 9cm (3½in) long, are borne in clusters in late summer. They close in full sun. The leaves are fiddle-shaped. HEIGHT & SPREAD 1.5m×75cm (5×2½ft).

CULTIVATION Plant in spring, in moist, fertile soil, in a sheltered site in full sun or light shade, after the danger of frost has passed. Deadhead regularly. If treating plants as perennials, cut stems to just above ground level after the first hard autumn frosts and protect with a dry mulch.

PROPAGATION Sow seed in early spring in a heated greenhouse.

PESTS AND DISEASES Young plants are liable to attacks from aphids and slugs.

▲ *Nicotiana sylvestris*

Nidularium

Bromeliaceae

The foliage of these evergreen, rosette-forming, tropical bromeliads changes colour when plants are in flower. The leaves around the central urn-like hollow turn red. Within the hollow, small tubular flowers are borne from time to time, mostly in summer. Plants may be grown in the home, but the best results are obtained in humid conditions in a heated greenhouse or conservatory. Native to Brazil.

RECOMMENDED SPECIES AND VARIETIES

N. flandria see *Neoregelia carolinae* Meyendorffii Group 'Flandria'

N. innocentii (bird's nest bromeliad) The strap-shaped, finely toothed, mid green leaves, with purple or blood-red undersides, are up to 30cm (1ft) long. Papery red bracts encircle the white flowers. HEIGHT & SPREAD 30×45cm (1×1½ft).

'Striatum' has several narrow, yellow stripes down the length of each green leaf.

N. regelioides The mid green leaves are mottled with purple. Each leaf is strap-shaped, finely toothed and up to 35cm (14in) long. They surround a central rosette of shorter leaves that colour red when the plant bears its red flowers. HEIGHT & SPREAD 30×60cm (1×2ft).

Nidularium regelioides

CULTIVATION Grow in pots of soil-less compost and feed twice during the growing season. Alternatively, grow in bark chips and feed monthly between late spring and late summer with a liquid houseplant feed. Keep in a heated greenhouse or conservatory or a warm room at a minimum temperature of 10°C (50°F). Nidulariums enjoy high humidity. Provide plenty of light but protect from exposure to full sun. Water freely into the centre of the rosettes, using soft water. Remove faded flowers.

PROPAGATION Remove and replant offsets during spring and early summer.

PESTS AND DISEASES Usually trouble free.

Nierembergia

Cupflower

Solanaceae

Nierembergia repens

Cup-shaped blooms, in shades of blue, violet or white, bring charm to a sunny border for many weeks in summer. The herbaceous perennials described below will grow in any garden soil, generally preferring a moist but sunny situation. All can be grown in containers to make colourful edging to a patio or terrace. Two species – *Nierembergia caerulea* and *N. scoparia* – are tender and usually treated as annuals, grown each year from seed or from overwintered cuttings. Native to S America.

Nierembergia caerulea

RECOMMENDED SPECIES AND VARIETIES

N. caerulea♀ (syn. *N. hippomanica*) This woody-based perennial bears a long succession of 2cm (¾in) wide, lilac-blue to pale violet flowers with a yellow throat from early summer to early autumn. Slender, branching stems also carry small, pointed, paddle-shaped, mid green leaves up to 8cm (3¼in) long. It is a very floriferous plant for a rock garden or border front. HEIGHT & SPREAD 30×20cm (12×8in).

N. frutescens see *N. scoparia*

N. hippomanica see *N. caerulea*

N. repens (syn. *N. rivularis*) This plant forms a low carpet of light green, spatular-shaped leaves up to 3cm (1¼in) long. From early to mid summer 3cm (1¼in) wide, white, cup-shaped flowers with yellow eyes are in bloom. The plant is hardy to -10°C (14°F). HEIGHT & SPREAD 5×60cm (2×24in).

'Violet Queen' has a similar habit, but the flowers are a deep violet.

N. rivularis see *N. repens*

N. scoparia (syn. *N. frutescens*) This bushy plant has a similar habit to *N. caerulea*, but is a little taller with narrower leaves and pale to deep violet flowers. HEIGHT & SPREAD 36×20cm (14×8in).

CULTIVATION Plant in spring in well-drained soil in a warm, sunny place. Propagate the tender species regularly or lift them for the winter. *N. repens* grows best in dry sandy soils and can spread excessively.

PROPAGATION The tender perennials are easily raised either from cuttings taken at any time during summer or from seed sown under glass in spring. Divide *N. repens* in spring.

PESTS AND DISEASES Aphids and whitefly cause problems under glass; slugs and snails damage plants out in the open.

Nigella

Ranunculaceae

Abundant, dainty, summer flowers are set against the feathery, deep green leaves of these hardy annuals. They also have inflated seed heads that are an attractive feature for some weeks after flowering has ended. Nigellas are easy to grow and self-seed readily. The flowers last well when cut and the seed heads can be used fresh or dried in floral arrangements. Each flower has a prominent cluster of stamens and styles at the centre. The leaves are finely divided.

RECOMMENDED SPECIES AND VARIETIES

N. damascena (love-in-a-mist) Blue, pink or white flowers, about 4cm (1½in) across, bloom on upright stems in early or mid summer. A ring of small, finely divided bracts extends, ruff-like, around the petals. HEIGHT & SPREAD 50×25cm (20×10in).

All the cultivars listed below have semi-double flowers. **'Dwarf Moody Blue'** has sky-blue flowers. It reaches a height of 20cm (8in) and a spread of 15cm (6in). **'Miss Jekyll'** has sky-blue flowers. **'Mulberry Rose'** has pale pink flowers, darkening as they age. **'Persian Jewels'** come in mixed colours. **'Shorty Blue'** has dark violet-blue flowers. It reaches 20cm (8in) in height and a spread of 15cm (6in).

Nigella damascena

Nigella damascena 'Persian Jewels'

N. hispanica (fennel flower) Blue, pink or white flowers, up to 6cm (2½in) across, appear on erect stems in early summer. HEIGHT & SPREAD 50×25cm (20×10in).

'Curiosity' has deep blue flowers with maroon stamens.

N. nigellastrum Star-shaped green-white flowers, tinged with red and about 1.5cm (½in) across, bloom in early summer. HEIGHT & SPREAD 40×20cm (16×8in).

'Summer Stars' has sky-blue flowers.

CULTIVATION Plant in spring in any garden soil in full sun. Deadhead to prolong the flower display.

PROPAGATION Sow seed where the plants are to grow in spring. In southern Britain and sheltered gardens elsewhere, sow seed in late summer where the plants are to grow. Thin the seedlings to 20cm (8in) apart. Move self-sown seedlings in spring. To grow *N. damascena* 'Dwarf Moody Blue' and *N. d.* 'Shorty Blue' as spring-flowering pot plants, sow seed in a cool greenhouse in early autumn.

PESTS AND DISEASES Usually trouble free.

Ninebark see *Physocarpus opulifolius*

Nomocharis

Liliaceae

Nomocharis aperta

Very showy lily-like flowers are borne by these hardy bulbous plants in mid summer. They can be a little tricky to grow, preferring partial shade and a rich organic soil which is damp but free draining. They grow best in areas of Britain where the climate is predominantly cool and moist. Allow plants to become well established and avoid disturbing them. Plants in this genus are native to the Himalayas and W China.

RECOMMENDED SPECIES

N. aperta Pink flowers of a flattened star-shape, with red spotting on the petals and maroon blotches at the base, are up to 10cm (4in) across. There are as many as 6 on each stem, Lance-shaped leaves, up to 10cm (4in) long, clothe the elegant flower stems. HEIGHT & SPREAD 60×15cm (24×6in).

Nomocharis aperta

N. farreri Soft pink saucer-shaped flowers with maroon spots and blotches towards the centre are up to 10cm (4in) across. The flowers are borne up to 10 each stem and start from a pendent position then turn upwards once fully open. The dark green lance-shaped leaves are 4cm (1½in) long and are produced in whorls up the flower stems. HEIGHT & SPREAD 90×15cm (36×6in).

Nomocharis farreri

N. pardanthina Nodding star-like flowers, up to 10cm (4in) across, have fringed petals which vary from white to pink and are blotched with maroon or dark purple at the base. There are up to 10 flowers on each stem. The dark green, lance-shaped leaves are up to 10cm (4in) long and are carried in whorls around the flower stems. HEIGHT & SPREAD 90×15cm (36×6in).

N. saluenensis This is the easiest species to grow. Up to 6 horizontal or star-like blooms are produced on each stem. The flowers are rose to pale rose-pink with dark central patches of maroon accompanied by small maroon spots. Dark green, lance-shaped leaves, up to 4cm (1½in) long, clothe the elegant flower stems. HEIGHT & SPREAD 75×15cm (30×6in).

CULTIVATION Plant bulbs 7.5–10cm (3–4in) deep in late autumn or spring in a richly organic moist soil with good drainage, in a semi-shaded area. Do not allow bulbs to dry out during the summer growing period. Apply a slow-release fertiliser in spring. Remove faded flowers.

PROPAGATION Sow seed in a coldframe in autumn and prick out into trays in late spring with the minimum of disturbance.

PESTS AND DISEASES Slugs and snails are the greatest problem, although greenfly can also be a nuisance. Lily beetle can be a problem in southern Britain.

Nothofagus

Southern beech

Fagaceae

Nothofagus obliqua

These deciduous or evergreen trees make fast-growing specimens suitable for a large lawn. The leaves are generally small. Insignificant flowers are produced in spring. The species listed here are from Argentina and Chile, except for *Nothofagus solandri*, from New Zealand. None of them are fully hardy in areas of prolonged or late frost.

RECOMMENDED SPECIES AND VARIETIES

N. alpina see *N. nervosa*

N. antarctica (Antarctic beech) The glossy green leaves of this upright, deciduous tree turn yellow in autumn. Just 2.5cm (1in) long, they are tightly clustered on the stems and have a very crinkled appearance. HEIGHT & SPREAD 5×2.4m (16×8ft) after 20 years, ultimately 15m (50ft) tall.

Nothofagus dombeyi

N. dombeyi This upright, conical, semi-evergreen tree has small, dark green leaves, up to 2.5cm (1in) long. HEIGHT & SPREAD 10×4m (33×13ft) after 20 years, ultimately 20m (66ft) tall.

N. nervosa (syn. *N. procera*, *N. alpina*) (Rauli beech) This handsome, deciduous tree of upright habit has pale green leaves,

Nothofagus antarctica

4-10 cm (1½-4 in) long, with prominent veins and a rather crinkled appearance. They turn pale gold and crimson in autumn. HEIGHT & SPREAD 8×3 m (26×10 ft) after 20 years, ultimately 20 m (66 ft) tall.

N. obliqua (Roble beech) The leaves of this upright, deciduous tree are pale green above, blue-green beneath, to 8 cm (3¼ in) long. HEIGHT & SPREAD 6×3 m (20×10 ft) after 20 years, ultimately 25 m (80 ft) tall.

N. procera see *N. nervosa*

N. pumilio This evergreen tree has a narrow, conical appearance with very open branches. The leaves, to 3 cm (1¼ in) long, are dark green, edged with small blunt teeth. HEIGHT & SPREAD 5.5×2.4 m (18×8 ft) in 20 years, ultimately 15 m (50 ft) tall.

N. solandri var. ***cliffortioides*** This evergreen tree bears small leaves, 1.5 cm (½ in) long, light green with a wavy edge. HEIGHT & SPREAD 4.5×2 m (15×6½ ft) after 20 years, ultimately 12 m (40 ft) tall.

CULTIVATION Plant in open ground from mid autumn to mid spring, avoiding frost or dry conditions. Do not plant in chalky soils.

PROPAGATION Sow seed in either early or mid spring.

PRUNING Not normally required.

PESTS AND DISEASES Usually trouble free.

n

Nuphar

Nymphaeaceae

Globular flowers, scattered over leathery floating foliage, highlight these hardy, deciduous deep-water aquatic perennials in summer. Versatility is a strong point – in addition to flourishing in full sun and still water, plants in this genus will also tolerate shade and moving water, unlike water lilies, their more showy relatives. A large wildlife pond is a suitable setting. The ideal water depth is 2 m (6½ ft) but plants can be grown in 1 m (3 ft) of water.

RECOMMENDED SPECIES

N. lutea (yellow water lily) Yellow waxy flowers, to 5 cm (2 in) across, with a strong alcoholic aroma bloom just above the water throughout summer. The leathery, mid green, floating leaves are oval to heart-shaped and up to 30 cm (12 in) long and 20 cm (8 in) wide. Translucent pale green leaves are produced under water in early spring before the floating foliage appears. The rootstock is vigorous and invasive unless restricted by container cultivation. Native to Eurasia, N America, West Indies, N Africa. Plant in water 2 m (6½ ft) deep. SPREAD 2 m (6½ ft). If the plant is grown in shallower water the spread will be less.

Nuphar lutea

CULTIVATION Plant in an open-sided aquatic planting basket in either a heavy loam soil or an aquatic planting compost. Cover the surface with pea gravel to prevent fish disturbing the soil. Use an aquatic plant fertiliser in early spring. Divide the plants when they become crowded.

PROPAGATION Divide established crowns in spring and early summer.

PESTS AND DISEASES Water-lily aphids can be troublesome.

Nymphaea

Water lily
Nymphaeaceae

Nymphaea alba

Grown for their waxy, star or cup-shaped summer flowers and floating foliage, water lilies are deciduous, perennial aquatic plants. There are tender, night-blooming water lilies available but those recommended below are hardy and flower during the day.

The flowers are often pure white but they also range in colour from pastel pink to rich crimson or from pale yellow to deep orange. The flowers of some varieties, such as *Nymphaea* 'Aurora', change colour as they age; this particular variety turns from yellow to blood-red. Nearly all flowers have prominent yellow or orange stamens. The blooms float among oval, rounded or heart-shaped leaves that are green, purplish green or green splashed with purple or maroon. If plants become crowded, the flowers rise above the leaves. The leaves shade the surface of the water and so help to reduce the amount of algae in a pond.

There are water lilies to suit every pond size. Those with a planting depth greater than 1.2 m (4 ft) are best for large ponds and those with a planting depth of less than 45 cm (1½ ft) are better in small pools or water tubs. The planting depths given below are the optimum for successful growth and the spreads given are what plants are likely to achieve if planted at the ideal depth.

RECOMMENDED SPECIES AND VARIETIES

N. alba (common white water lily) Snow-white, cup-shaped blossoms, up to 20 cm (8 in) across, float among circular mid green leaves, up to 30 cm (12 in) across. The ideal planting depth for this water lily is 3 m (10 ft). SPREAD 2 m (6½ ft).

N. **'Albatros'** White, star-shaped flowers grow up to 20 cm (8 in) across and float among deep green, circular leaves, also 20 cm (8 in) across. Young leaves are a purplish colour when they first appear. Plant at a depth of 1 m (3 ft). SPREAD 1 m (3 ft).

N. **'Amabilis'** Star-like, salmon-pink flowers, up to 25 cm (10 in) across, deepen to soft rose-pink with age. The yellow stamens become fiery orange. Deeply cleft, dark green, rounded leaves grow up to 25 cm (10 in) across. Plant this water lily at a depth of 1 m (3 ft). SPREAD 1 m (3 ft).

N. **'Andreana'** Deep brick-red, cup-shaped blossoms, up to 20 cm (8 in) across, are streaked with cream and yellow. The glossy green leaves, up to 25 cm (10 in) across, are blotched with maroon. The ideal planting depth is 60 cm (2 ft). SPREAD 60 cm (2 ft).

N. **'Apple Blossom Pink'** see *N.* 'Marliacea Carnea'

N. **'Atropurpurea'** Deep crimson-purple blooms, with a satiny sheen, float amid dark green rounded leaves up to 25 cm (10 in) across. Each cup-shaped flower is up to 15 cm (6 in) across with distinctive incurving petals. Plant at a depth of 60 cm (2 ft). SPREAD 1 m (3 ft).

N. **'Attraction'** Garnet-red flowers, flecked with white and up to 25 cm (10 in) across, have rich, mahogany-coloured stamens tipped with yellow and sepals that are off-white infused with rose-pink. They change from cup-shaped to star-shaped. The mid green oval leaves with overlapping lobes grow up to 30 cm (12 in) across. Plant at a depth of 1.2 m (4 ft). SPREAD 1.2 m (4 ft).

N. **'Aurora'** Cup-shaped flowers, up to 7.5 cm (3 in) across, start cream in bud, opening to yellow, then deepen through orange to blood red. The rounded leaves, up to 10 cm (4 in) across, are dark green mottled purple. The planting depth for this variety is 45 cm (1½ ft). SPREAD 60 cm (2 ft).

N. **'Brakeleyi Rosea'** Sweetly scented, star-shaped flowers, up to 15 cm (6 in) across, open rose-pink but age to flesh-pink or almost white. The deep green, rounded leaves are up to 25 cm (10 in) across. Plant at a depth of 75 cm (2½ ft). SPREAD 1 m (3 ft).

N. **'Caroliniana Nivea'** The star-shaped, white, fragrant blossoms are up to 15 cm (6 in) across and the mid green rounded leaves are as wide as 20 cm (8 in). Plant at a depth of 75 cm (2½ ft). SPREAD 1 m (3 ft).

N. **'Charles de Meurville'** Cup-shaped flowers, up to 25 cm (10 in) across, become star-shaped and the colour changes from plum, tipped and streaked with white, to deep wine red. The oval, olive-green leaves grow up to 30 cm (12 in) long. Plant at a depth of 1.2 m (4 ft). SPREAD 1.5 m (5 ft).

Nymphaea 'Colonel A.J. Welch'

N. **'Colonel A.J. Welch'** The lemon yellow, star-shaped flowers, up to 15 cm (6 in) across, have a slight fragrance. The rounded, olive-green leaves grow up to 25 cm (10 in) across. The blossoms of this variety often transform into new plantlets. Plant this water lily at a depth of 75 cm (2½ ft). SPREAD 1 m (3 ft).

N. **'Colossea'** Fragrant, cup-shaped, flesh-pink blossoms, up to 25 cm (10 in) across, sit among dull green, rounded leaves up to 30 cm (12 in) across. This is a vigorous, free-flowering variety and needs to be planted at a depth of 1.2 m (4 ft). SPREAD 1.2 m (4 ft).

N. **'Comanche'** Cup-shaped, deep apricot to orange blossoms, up to 10 cm (4 in) across, fade to bronze with age. The rounded leaves, up to 15 cm (6 in) across, are purplish when young but change to mid green as they unfurl, occasionally with purple spots. Plant this water lily at a depth of 60 cm (2 ft). SPREAD 1 m (3 ft).

Nymphaea 'Escarboucle'

N. **'Ellisiana'** Small, wine-red, star-shaped flowers are up to 10 cm (4 in) across, with orange stamens. The oval, dark green leaves grow up to 15 cm (6 in) across. This free-flowering water lily needs to be planted at a depth of 45 cm (1½ ft). SPREAD 60 cm (2 ft).

N. **'Escarboucle'**♀ Scented, crimson, cup-shaped, becoming star-shaped, flowers grow up to 30 cm (12 in) across in a large open pond. The rounded mid green leaves, up to 30 cm (12 in) across, are often tinged with bronze or brown. Plant at a depth of 1.5 m (5 ft). SPREAD 1.5 m (5 ft).

N. **'Firecrest'** Star-shaped, deep pink flowers, up to 10 cm (4 in) across, sport red-tipped stamens. The rounded leaves, up to 20 cm (8 in) across, are purplish when young, turning mid green with age. Plant at a depth of 60 cm (2 ft). SPREAD 1 m (3 ft).

Nymphaea 'Froebelii'

N. **'Froebelii'** The deep blood-red, cup-like flowers, which become star-shaped, are up to 10 cm (4 in) across and are produced among dull, purplish green rounded leaves, up to 15 cm (6 in) across. Plant this water lily in 60 cm (2 ft) of water. SPREAD 1 m (3 ft).

N. **'Gloriosa'** Star-shaped, fragrant, currant-red blooms, up to 15 cm (6 in) across, with bright orange stamens, float on the surface of the water. The dull bronze-green leaves are rounded and up to 15 cm (6 in) across. Plant at a depth of 60 cm (2 ft). SPREAD 1 m (3 ft).

N. **'Gonnère'**♀ The fully double, cup-shaped, white flowers, with conspicuous apple-green sepals, are up to 15 cm (6 in) across. Rounded bright green leaves grow up to 20 cm (8 in) across. The best planting depth is 60 cm (2 ft). SPREAD 1 m (3 ft).

N. **'Graziella'** Orange-red, cup-shaped flowers, rarely more than 5 cm (2 in) across, are produced freely throughout summer. The olive-green rounded leaves, up to 10 cm (4 in) across, are heavily blotched with brown and purple. Plant at a depth of 30 cm (1 ft). SPREAD 45 cm (1½ ft).

N. x ***helvola***♀ (syn. *N.* x *pygmaea* 'Helvola') Star-like yellow flowers, up to 5 cm (2 in) across, are freely produced by this plant.

Nymphaea 'Gonnère'

The olive-green, oval to heart-shaped leaves, up to 6 cm (2½ in) long, are splashed with purple and brown. Plant at a depth of 20 cm (8 in). SPREAD 30 cm (12 in).

N. **'Indiana'** Orange-red, cup-shaped flowers, up to 7.5 cm (3 in) across, age to deep red. The rounded leaves are dark green, up to 10 cm (4 in) across, and heavily blotched with purple. Plant at a depth of 60 cm (2 ft). SPREAD 75 cm (2½ ft).

N. **'James Brydon'**♀ The deep crimson, cup-shaped blossoms, up to 15 cm (6 in) across, smell of ripe apples. The dark purplish green, rounded leaves, up to 25 cm (10 in) across, are often flecked with maroon. This water lily should be planted at a depth of 1 m (3 ft). SPREAD 1 m (3 ft).

Nymphaea x *helvola*

Nymphaea 'James Brydon'

N. **'Laydekeri Fulgens'** The bright crimson, scented, cup-shaped flowers, with reddish stamens, are up to 8cm (3¼in) across. Leaves are rounded, dark green with purple undersides, as wide as 15cm (6in). Plant at a depth of 45cm (1½ft). SPREAD 60cm (2ft).
N. **'Laydekeri Lilacea'** Soft pink flowers, up to 8cm (3¼in) across, age to deep rosy crimson. Glossy green leaves, up to 15cm (6in) across, are sparsely blotched with brown. Plant this water lily at a depth of 45cm (1½ft). SPREAD 60cm (2ft).
N. **'Laydekeri Purpurata'** Cup-shaped wine-red flowers, up to 8cm (3in) across, have bright orange stamens. The dark green leaves, up to 15cm (6in) across, are purple beneath and often marked on the upper surface with maroon or black splashes. Plant at a depth of 45cm (1½ft). SPREAD 60cm (2ft).
N. **'Madame Wilfon Gonnère'** The cup-shaped, almost double, white blossoms, up to 15cm (6in) across, are flushed and spotted with deep rose-pink and are soft pink at the centre. The rounded mid green leaves, up to 25cm (10in) across, have distinctive overlapping lobes. Plant at a depth of 75cm (2½ft). SPREAD 1m (3ft).
N. **'Marliacea Albida'** Scented, white flowers, up to 15cm (6in) across, are flushed with soft pink on the undersides of the petals. The rounded, deep green leaves, up to 20cm (8in) across have red or purplish undersides. Plant at a depth of 1m (3ft). SPREAD 1.2m (4ft).
N. **'Marliacea Carnea'** (syn. *N.* 'Apple Blossom Pink') Flesh-pink blossoms, up to 20cm (8in) across, become star-like when fully open. This variety has a vanilla fragrance. It is the best hardy water lily for cut flowers. The oval, deep green leaves, up to 20cm (8in) across, are purplish when young. Plant this water lily at a depth of 1m (3ft). SPREAD 1.2m (4ft).

Nymphaea 'Marliacea Carnea'

N. **'Marliacea Chromatella'** ♀ Rich canary-yellow flowers, up to 15cm (6in) across, float among olive green leaves, to 20cm (8in) across, splashed with maroon and bronze. Plant this variety at a depth of 1m (3ft). SPREAD 1.2m (4ft).
N. **'Masaniello'** Fragrant, rose-pink, cup-shaped flowers, up to 12.5cm (5in) across, are flecked with crimson and age to deep carmine. The leaves are mid green, rounded and to 20cm (8in) across. Plant at a depth of 75cm (2½ft). SPREAD 1m (3ft).
N. **'Moorei'** Soft yellow, star-like blossoms, up to 15cm (6in) across, are slightly scented. The pale green, rounded leaves, up to 25cm (10in) across, are sometimes splashed with purple spots. Plant at a depth of 45cm (1½ft). SPREAD 75cm (2½ft).
N. **'Mrs Richmond'** The cup-shaped, pale rose-pink flowers, up to 10cm (4in) across, are bright red at the base of the petals. The flowers age to crimson. Rounded, mid green leaves grow up to 15cm (6in) across. Plant at a depth of 75cm (2½ft). SPREAD 1m (3ft).

Nymphaea 'Marliacea Albida'
Nymphaea 'Madame Wilfon Gonnère'
Nymphaea 'Marliacea Chromatella'

Nymphaea 'Masaniello'

Nymphaea 'Moorei'

Nymphaea 'Mrs Richmond'

N. ***odorata*** (sweet-scented water lily) The fragrant, white flowers, up to 15cm (6in) across, are star-like. The bright green leaves are rounded and up to 25cm (10in) across. Plant 1m (3ft) deep. SPREAD 1.2m (4ft).

The white flowers of var. ***minor*** (mill-pond lily), up to 8cm (3¼in) across, float among soft green leaves as wide as 10cm (4in). Plant at a depth of 30cm (12in). This variety will spread to 45cm (18in). **'Sulphurea Grandiflora'** has canary-yellow blooms, to 12.5cm (5in) across, held slightly above olive-green leaves, mottled with purple, up to 20cm (8in) across. Plant at a depth of 60cm (2ft). This plant spreads to 1m (3ft). **'Turicensis'** has soft rose-pink flowers, up to 13cm (5in) across. The mid green leaves are up to 20cm (8in) across. Plant this water lily at a depth of 45cm (18in). It will spread to 60cm (2ft).
N. × *pygmaea* **'Alba'** see *N. tetragona*
N. × *pygmaea* **'Helvola'** see *N.* × *helvola*
N. × *pygmaea* **'Rubra'** The blood-red, star-like flowers, up to 2.5cm (1in) across, have orange stamens. Rounded to heart-shaped, purplish green leaves, with distinctive reddish undersides, are up to 8cm (3¼in) long. This variety needs planting at a depth of 20cm (8in). SPREAD 30cm (12in).
N. **'Rose Arey'** Star-like, rose-pink flowers, up to 20cm (8in) across, smell of aniseed. The rounded leaves, up to 25cm (10in) across, are red when young and age to mid green tinged with red. Plant at a depth of 60cm (2ft). SPREAD 1m (3 ft).
N. **'Sioux'** Star-shaped flowers, up to 10cm (4in) across, start yellow, then turn orange, then crimson. The rounded leaves are 15cm (6in) across, dull green and mottled purple. Plant this variety at a depth of 60cm (2ft). SPREAD 1m (3ft).
N. ***tetragona*** (syn. *N.* × *pygmaea* 'Alba') White flowers no more than 5cm (2in) across float among oval or heart-shaped, dark green leaves, up to 8cm (3¼in) long. Plant this species in only 15cm (6in) of water. SPREAD 25cm (10in).
N. ***tuberosa*** (magnolia water lily) Cup-shaped, white flowers, 15–25cm (6–10in) across, rest among apple-green, rounded leaves, up to 40cm (16in) across. Plant at a depth of 1m (3ft). SPREAD 1.2m (4ft).

'Rosea' has pink flowers.

Nymphaea 'Rose Arey'

Nymphaea 'Sioux'

***N.* 'William Falconer'** Blood-red, cup-shaped flowers, to 10cm (4in) across, float among rounded leaves, to 15cm (6in) wide. The red-veined leaves start purplish green, then turn deep olive-green. Plant at a depth of 60cm (2ft). SPREAD 1m (3ft).

CULTIVATION Plant during spring and early summer, in aquatic planting compost or heavy loam soil in a plastic mesh basket. Cover the compost or soil with a layer of pea gravel to prevent fish from stirring it up. Apply slow-release aquatic fertiliser annually. To avoid congestion, divide water lilies every 3-5 years.

PROPAGATION Lift and divide the rootstock in spring every 3-5 years, apart from *N. tetragona*, which is propagated from ripe seed in summer. Alternatively, remove 'eyes', small growths on the creeping rootstock, during spring and early summer and grow on in small pots in a tank of water.

PESTS AND DISEASES Water lily aphids and, in southern Britain, water lily beetle can attack plants. Crown and root rot may cause stems and leaves to blacken and become slimy. Remove affected plants from the water at once and destroy.

Nymphoides

Menyanthaceae

Bright yellow, saucer-shaped blossoms with delicately fringed petals are produced all summer long on these deep-water aquatic plants. There are tender tropical species in this genus but it is the hardy deciduous perennials that are commonly grown in British garden ponds.

RECOMMENDED SPECIES AND VARIETIES

N. peltata (syn. *Villarsia nymphoides*) (water fringe) The flowers of this adaptable plant are up to 2.5cm (1in) across. Heart-shaped,

Nymphoides peltata

bright green leaves up to 10cm (4in) across are produced on numerous stringy stems, which grow up from the creeping, tangled rootstock. In ponds with a mud bottom, this plant can be very invasive. HEIGHT & SPREAD 5×60cm (2×24in).

'Bennettii' (syn. *Villarsia bennettii*) has leaves which are spotted with brown.

CULTIVATION Grow in an open sunny position in the deeper part of a pool, away from the planting shelf at the pond edge. Plant at a depth of 15-60cm (6-24in), in spring or early summer, in an open lattice-work container in heavy loam soil or an aquatic planting compost. Cover the surface of the container with pea gravel to prevent fish from disturbing the soil. Feed annually with a slow-release aquatic fertiliser. Divide plants to retain vigour, when the container becomes congested.

PROPAGATION Divide established plants during spring and early summer.

PESTS AND DISEASES Water lily aphids can be a problem.

Nyssa

Cornaceae

Nyssa sylvatica

These hardy deciduous trees are remarkable for the brilliant scarlet colour of their leaves in autumn. They look particularly effective planted in a group, beside water or against a background of evergreens. The lustrous, pointed, oval leaves, arranged alternately on the stem, are up to 15cm (6in) long. Small, insignificant flowers in spring and early summer are followed by fleshy blue-black berries in autumn.

RECOMMENDED SPECIES

N. sinensis The leaves on this large shrub or small tree turn every shade of red in autumn. Green flowers appear in

Nyssa sinensis

rounded heads 1.5cm (½in) across. Plant in a sheltered position, as the species is only moderately frost-hardy. Native to central China. HEIGHT & SPREAD 2.4×1.2m (8×4ft) after 10 years, ultimately 9m (30ft) tall.

N. sylvatica (tupelo) This tree has an upright, conical habit, which spreads with age. Leaves change to glorious shades of red, gold and yellow in mid or late autumn.

Nyssa sylvatica

The yellow-green flowers are borne in rounded clusters 1.5cm (½in) wide. Native to N and Central America. HEIGHT & SPREAD 4.5×2.4m (15×8ft) after 20 years, ultimately 15m (50ft) tall.

CULTIVATION Grow in a damp, lime-free soil, in sun or partial shade, but preferably sun. Plant specimens between late autumn and mid spring. Place them in their permanent positions while they are still small, because they may suffer if moved later on.

PROPAGATION Specimens are normally acquired as young plants, because they are not that easy to propagate. Sow seed in early or mid spring. Layer in autumn, and move rooted sections about 18 months later.

PRUNING No pruning required.

PESTS AND DISEASES Usually trouble free.

O

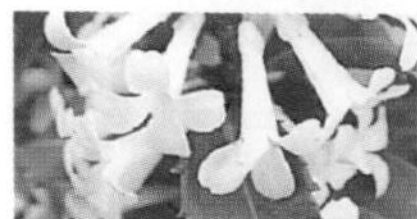

Oenanthe

Umbelliferae

This genus is characterised by fern-like foliage. It is seldom cultivated, apart from the colourful Japanese subspecies, *Oenanthe javanica* 'Flamingo'. A damp open setting, such as an informal bog garden, suits it best.

▲ *Oenanthe javanica* 'Flamingo'

RECOMMENDED SPECIES

***O. javanica* 'Flamingo'** (syn. *O. japonica*) Pink, cream and white splashes decorate the narrow oval toothed or lobed leaflets, many of which form compound leaves up to 15 cm (6 in) long. Dense heads of tiny white flowers appear throughout the summer. HEIGHT & SPREAD 30×25 cm (12×10 in).

CULTIVATION Plant in damp soil in spring. Remove flowerheads either as soon as they appear or immediately after flowering to retain the quality of the foliage.

PROPAGATION Divide carefully in spring.

PESTS AND DISEASES Slugs and snails may be troublesome.

Oenothera

Evening primrose

Onagraceae

Profuse, short-lived, showy flowers, often fragrant, distinguish this genus of annuals, biennials and perennials. Many bear flowers that open at twilight and fade by sunrise – to be replaced by new blooms the next evening; some have flowers that remain open all day. Evening primroses are not good as cut flowers, but they attract butterflies to the garden. Plant larger varieties in borders or a wild garden, and smaller ones in a rock garden. Most seed prolifically, and many self-sow. Native to the Americas.

Oenothera speciosa

RECOMMENDED SPECIES AND VARIETIES

O. acaulis (syn. *O. taraxacifolia*) White cup-shaped flowers that age to pink, up to 7.5 cm (3 in) wide, appear on this perennial throughout summer. The lance-shaped, 20 cm (8 in) long, grey-green leaves are lobed or deeply toothed. It is ideal in a rock garden. HEIGHT & SPREAD 15×20 cm (6×8 in).

'Aurea' has yellow flowers.

O. biennis (common evening primrose) A hardy biennial that self-sows easily and can become a nuisance, its seeds are the source of evening primrose oil. Fragrant yellow flowers, up to 7.5 cm (3 in) wide, appear from early summer to mid autumn. Rosettes of narrow oval to oblong leaves, up to 30 cm (1 ft) long, form at stem bases. Leaves farther up the stem are half as long. HEIGHT & SPREAD 1 m×40 cm (3 ft×16 in).

O. childsii see *O. speciosa*

O. fruticosa (syn. *O. linearis*) (sundrops) Fragrant yellow flowers, 5 cm (2 in) wide, borne on leafy spikes, open during the day from mid to late summer. This biennial or perennial has reddish upright stems and oval to lance-shaped green leaves, sometimes edged with red, up to 12.5 cm (5 in) long. HEIGHT & SPREAD 60×40 cm (2 ft×16 in).

'Fyrverkeri'♀ ('Fireworks') has red buds on red stems that open to yellow flowers. This perennial grows to about 40 cm (16 in) tall.

The toothed leaves of ssp. **glauca**♀ are broader and more or less grey-green.

O. linearis see *O. fruticosa*

O. macrocarpa♀ (syn. *O. missouriensis*) (Ozark's sundrops) Yellow flowers, 10 cm (4 in) across, are borne close to the dark green foliage on this almost prostrate plant. The oval to lance-shaped leaves, 2.5-7.5 cm (1-3 in) long, have a silvery mid rib. HEIGHT & SPREAD 12.5×18 cm (5×7 in).

O. odorata see *O. stricta*

O. perennis (syn. *O. pumila*) (sundrops) Fragrant yellow blooms, about 1.5 cm (½ in) wide, flower in loose spikes during the day in summer and early autumn. A perennial, it has slender upright stems and narrow spoon-shaped leaves, about 4 cm (1½ in) long. HEIGHT & SPREAD 40×30 cm (16×12 in).

▼ *Oenothera macrocarpa*

▲ *Oenothera perennis*

O. speciosa (syn. *O. childsii*, *O. speciosa* var. *childsii*) (white evening primrose) Fragrant summer flowers, 5 cm (2 in) wide, fade to delicate rose pink as they age. This perennial has creeping rhizomes and mid-green elliptical leaves, 5 cm (2 in) long. HEIGHT & SPREAD 30×45 cm (1×1½ ft).

'Pink Petticoats' has pale pink flowers, delicately veined and slightly frilled. **'Rosea'** also has pale pink flowers and grows to no more than 30 cm (1 ft) tall.

O. stricta (syn. *O. odorata*) This sprawling plant has rich yellow tubular flowers, about 4 cm (1½ in) across, sparsely spread along the stems. The pale green leaves are lance shaped, up to 10 cm (4 in) long. HEIGHT & SPREAD 1 m×40 cm (3 ft×16 in).

▲ *Oenothera fruticosa* 'Fyrverkeri'

Oenothera speciosa 'Rosea' ▲

'Sulphurea' has pastel yellow flowers that fade to peach.

O. taraxacifolia see *O. acaulis*

CULTIVATION Plant in autumn or spring in well-drained, sandy soil in a sunny position. Water generously during the growing season. Stake plants if required.

PROPAGATION Sow evening primrose seed in pots in a light sandy compost in early spring; or sow annuals and biennials in their growing position.

Divide perennials and replant in early spring, or take softwood cuttings in spring or early summer, grow under glass and plant

out the following spring. Remove and replant rooted rhizomes of *O. speciosa* in late summer and keep in a cold frame over winter if necessary.
PESTS AND DISEASES Usually trouble free.

Old woman see *Artemisia stelleriana*

Olea
Olive
Oleaceae

Olea europaea

These half-hardy evergreen trees and shrubs have attractive silvery foliage. *Olea europaea* is hardy enough to survive outdoors in mild areas of Britain. Olives make excellent outdoor tub plants for the summer but rarely thrive unless grown under glass. In Britain, fruit is not borne on outdoor trees and is rarely edible on those grown under glass.
RECOMMENDED SPECIES AND VARIETIES
O. europaea♀ (wild olive) The grey-green, lance-shaped leaves, about 7cm (3¼in) long, have silvery undersides. Clusters of tiny white flowers appear in mid summer, followed by red or purple oval fruits up to 4cm (1½in) long. This Mediterranean tree has an upright freely-branching habit. HEIGHT & SPREAD 2×1m (6½×3ft) after 10 years, ultimately 5m (16ft) tall.

▲ *Olea europaea*

The fruits of var. *europaea* **'El Greco'** are larger with small stones.
CULTIVATION Grow in a greenhouse, a border or in a soil-based compost in large tubs; water regularly in summer and feed with a general-purpose liquid feed in early spring and again in mid summer.
PROPAGATION Take semi-ripe cuttings in summer.
PRUNING Cut out weak shoots and trim to shape in spring.
PESTS AND DISEASES Scale insects and mealy bugs may trouble plants under glass.

Oleander see *Nerium oleander*

Olearia
Daisy bush
Compositae

Olearia macrodonta

Cheerful, daisy flowers and evergreen leathery leaves give summer and winter value in this genus of fast-growing shrubs or small trees. The small flowers are usually white and may be solitary or borne in clusters up to 10cm (4in) across.

Mainly from Australia and New Zealand, olearias are sun-loving and many are resistant to strong winds and salt spray, making them ideal coastal hedging plants. Most of the plants listed are hardy in warmer areas, provided that they are planted in well-drained soil. *Olearia* × *haastii* tolerates pollution, making it useful for town hedging.
RECOMMENDED SPECIES AND VARIETIES
O.* × *haastii Numerous fragrant, daisy-like white flowers appear in mid to late summer on this dense, rounded bush. Alternate oval leaves grow to 2.5cm (1in) and open dark, shiny green above, ageing to a dull grey-green. HEIGHT & SPREAD 1×1m (3×3ft) after 5 years, ultimately 1.8m (6ft) tall.
***O.* 'Henry Travers'**♀ (syn. *O. semidentata*) Only really suitable for gardens with little or no frost, the rounded bush bears large lilac flowers with a purple centre from early to mid summer. Slightly toothed lance-shaped dark green leaves grow to 6cm (2½in) long. HEIGHT & SPREAD 1.5×1m (5×3ft) after 5 years, ultimately 3m (10ft) tall.
O. macrodonta♀ A large, vigorous, upright shrub with peeling, papery bark, its numerous, tiny white flowers have a musky scent and appear in early summer in clusters up to 12cm (4¾in) across. The holly-like leaves are toothed and wavy and grow to 7.5cm (3in). Standing up well to salt winds it makes useful hedging in seaside gardens. HEIGHT & SPREAD 1×1m (3×3ft) after 5 years, ultimately up to 6m (20ft) tall.

▼ *Olearia macrodonta*

O.* × *mollis This compact, rounded, hardy shrub has white-felted branchlets, clusters of small white flowers in spring and pale green oval alternate leaves, 12mm (½in) long. HEIGHT & SPREAD 30×30cm (1×1ft) after 5 years, ultimately 2m (6½ft) tall.

'Zennorensis'♀ has dark green, sharply toothed leaves up to 10cm (4in) long, and pale brown-felted branches. It is a fine plant for warm coastal areas.
O. nummularifolia Small, solitary fragrant white flowers appear in mid summer on this dense, rounded hardy shrub. Its alternate leathery leaves are 5mm (¼in) long. HEIGHT & SPREAD 1×1m (3×3ft) after 5 years, ultimately 3m (10ft) tall.

The dwarf variety *cymbifolia* has slightly longer grey-green leaves, erect branches and solitary white flowers.
O. oleifolia see *O.* 'Waikariensis'
O. semidentata see *O.* 'Henry Travers'
O. stellulata♀ Large clusters of white flowers appear in spring or early summer. The 8cm (3¼in) toothed leaves have sunken veins. HEIGHT & SPREAD 3×2m (10×6½ft) after 5 years, ultimately 5m (16ft) tall.
***O.* 'Waikariensis'** (syn. *O. oleifolia*) White-felted angular branchlets carry grey-green alternate leaves, 5cm (2in) long. White flowers are borne in panicles on this freely flowering compact shrub in mid to late summer. HEIGHT & SPREAD 1×1m (3×3ft) after 5 years, ultimately 1.8m (6ft) tall.
CULTIVATION Grow in any well-drained soil. Most olearias thrive on chalk.
PROPAGATION Take semi-ripe cuttings

▲ *Olearia* 'Waikariensis'

Olearia × *mollis* 'Zennorensis' ▼

from late summer to late autumn.
PRUNING Prune after flowering, if necessary, to maintain a good shape.
PESTS AND DISEASES Usually trouble free.

Oleaster see *Eleagnus angustifolia*
Olive see *Olea*

Omphalodes

Navelwort
Boraginaceae

Omphalodes cappadocica

Sprays of blue or white flowers liven up the low clumps of foliage in spring or summer. Similar to forget-me-not blooms, each one opens to just 1cm (3/8in) across. *Omphalodes cappadocica* and *O. verna* are good spring-flowering plants for moist shady conditions. Their spreading habit makes them useful ground cover. Of some 25 species, only one annual and three herbaceous perennials and their varieties are widely grown.

RECOMMENDED SPECIES AND VARIETIES

O. cappadocica ♀ Branching sprays of bright blue flowers with whitish eyes are carried well above the leaves in spring. Glossy oval to heart-shaped leaves, up to 10cm (4in) long, rise in dense clumps from spreading rhizomes. Native to Asia Minor. HEIGHT & SPREAD 25×40cm (10×16in).

'Cherry Ingram' is more robust with larger deeper blue flowers. The blue petals of **'Starry Eyes'** have broad white margins.

O. linifolia ♀ White or very pale blue flowers are borne in erect branching sprays by this annual from early to mid summer. The grey-green lance-shaped leaves are up to 10cm (4in) long. The plant self-seeds freely in mild gardens. Native to SW Europe. HEIGHT & SPREAD 30 × 20cm (12 × 8in).

O

Omphalodes linifolia

Omphalodes luciliae

O. luciliae Loose sprays of powder blue flowers, often pink in bud, are carried in summer above pale grey-blue fleshy elliptic leaves up to 10cm (4in) long. Native to Turkish cliffs, it is difficult to establish except in scree, tufa, or in an alpine house. HEIGHT & SPREAD 10 ×15cm (4×6in).

O. verna (blue-eyed Mary) Lax clusters of pale blue flowers are produced in spring on stems up to 30cm (12in) tall. Dark green oval leaves are up to 15cm (6in) long. It spreads quickly by runners. Native to S European mountain woodland. HEIGHT & SPREAD 20×30cm (8×12in).

'Alba' has pure white flowers.

CULTIVATION Sow seed of *O. linifolia* thinly in its flowering position in spring. Plant *O. luciliae* in a very gritty alkaline compost or tufa under glass or in a trough. The other perennials thrive in moist humus-rich soils in full or partial shade.
PROPAGATION Sow seed of species in pots in autumn and keep in a cold frame. Divide named varieties of *O. cappadocica* in spring, or in late summer after flowering.
PESTS AND DISEASES Plants are particularly prone to slug and snail damage.

Oncidium see ORCHIDS p.467
Onion, edible see p.741
Onion, ornamental see *Allium*
Onoclea see FERNS p.264

Ononis

Rest harrow
Leguminosae

Showy heads of pink or white blooms are borne on these summer-flowering plants. The flowers have a characteristic pea shape, and the simple or trifolate leaves are abundant on tangled stems. The genus consists of annuals, herbaceous perennials and sub-shrubs. Those listed here are all sub-shrubs.

RECOMMENDED SPECIES

O. repens Rose-pink flowers, up to 1.5cm (½in) long, appear in small spikes in mid summer. The scrambling plant has tiny, mid green, oval, hairy leaflets on soft spiny stems. HEIGHT & SPREAD 30×60cm (1×2ft).

O. rotundifolia Pink or white flowers up to 1.5cm (½in) long are borne in loose spikes in summer. Erect stems are densely clothed with toothed, elliptical, mid green leaflets. HEIGHT & SPREAD 60×45cm (2×1½ft).

Ononis spinosa

O. spinosa (spiny rest harrow) Reddish pink flowers up to 1.5cm (½in) long appear in small spikes at mid summer on this dwarf sub-shrub. The spiny stems are clothed with small, mid green leaflets of variable length. HEIGHT & SPREAD 45×60cm (1½×2ft).
CULTIVATION Plant in spring in a sunny, open situation in any free-draining soil.
PRUNING Trim untidy growth in spring.
PROPAGATION Sow seed directly in the open ground in spring, or sow under glass in late summer and plant out in spring.
PESTS AND DISEASES Usually trouble free.

Onopordum

Compositae

These tall, vigorous silver-leaved plants are grown for their dramatic appearance and look best near the back of wide borders when planted against a darker background of tall shrubs or a high hedge. They are also ideal for semi-wild areas of larger gardens. The two species commonly grown are biennials and, although they self-seed, the removal of young unwanted plants is easy as they are very conspicuous and any roots left behind in the soil die off once the foliage has been removed. *Onopordum acanthium* is native to Britain and is hardy, while *O. nervosum*, native to Spain and Portugal, is only reliably hardy in milder areas of Britain.

Onopordum acanthium

RECOMMENDED SPECIES

O. acanthium (Scotch thistle, cotton thistle) Pinkish purple flowerheads, about 5cm (2in) across, often solitary but sometimes in small clusters, are borne in summer. Silvery grey hairy lobed leaves, up to 35cm (14in) long, first form a rosette at ground level from which the upright branching stems develop. Both the leaves and the wings along the length of each stem are spiny. HEIGHT & SPREAD 2.5×1m (8×3ft).

O. nervosum ♀ (syn. *O. arabicum*) Purple-red flowerheads, often solitary but sometimes in small clusters and up to 5cm (2in) across, are borne in summer. Silvery green leaves, up to 50cm (20in) long, are smooth above and patterned by a network of pale veins. The wings formed by the leaf bases and the under surfaces of the leaves are spiny. HEIGHT & SPREAD 2.5×1m (8×3ft).

Onopordum nervosum

CULTIVATION Plant in early autumn or very early spring in any good garden soil. *O. acanthium* thrives in sun or partial shade while *O. nervosum* prefers full sun. Deadhead to prevent self-seeding.

PROPAGATION Sow seed in small clusters where the plants are to grow and reduce the young plants to one at each position.

PESTS AND DISEASES Slugs and snails eat young plants, and aphids may be a problem.

Onosma

Boraginaceae

Dense nodding clusters of tubular flowers in yellow, white, pink or purple cover the small evergreen sub-shrubs in summer. They require a sunny, well-drained site and thrive on a hot bank or wall, where they can be planted on their sides so that their pendent flowers can be admired, while excessive moisture can quickly drain from their roots.

The narrow tubular flowers are 2cm (¾in) long, carried on woody, branching plants with numerous bristly leaves up to 10cm (4in) long. The species listed below are native to the Mediterranean and Asia Minor. They are hardy to -10°C (14°F) if protected from winter wet by planting them on their sides, or covering them with a cloche. In wetter regions, however, onosmas are better off in an alpine house.

RECOMMENDED SPECIES AND VARIETIES

O. alborosea Clusters of white, pink-tipped flowers appear amid a mound of branching hairy stems with lance-shaped to oblong leaves. The flowers age to pinkish purple. This is one of the hardiest of the genus. HEIGHT & SPREAD 25×40cm (10×16in).

Onosma alborosea

O. nana This is a neat rock garden plant with clusters of pale yellow flowers and narrow lance-shaped leaves. It is often short-lived, but usually self-sows. HEIGHT & SPREAD 20×20cm (8×8in).

Onosma taurica

O. taurica ♀ This vigorous species has bright yellow flowers up to 3cm (1¼in) long, which sometimes fade to white. HEIGHT & SPREAD 30×50cm (12×20in).

CULTIVATION Plant in very gritty well-drained compost in full sun. The plants also do well in a gritty compost in pots in an alpine house if watered sparingly in winter.

PROPAGATION Sow seed in pots in autumn, or take greenwood cuttings in summer.

PESTS AND DISEASES Usually trouble free in the garden, but in a greenhouse the plants may suffer infestations of aphids or whitefly.

Ophiopogon

Lily turf

Convallariaceae

Tiny white or purple bell-shaped flowers nestle among tufted clumps of handsome grass-like leaves in summer, later followed by blue, purple or black berries. These evergreen perennials make interesting ground cover plants for the front of a border, especially on dry soils. The flowers are often concealed by the foliage.

The species listed here are reasonably hardy, with the exception of *Ophiopogon jaburan* which is used for summer bedding or as a conservatory plant. Native to E Asia.

O. jaburan Dense spikes of white flowers, about 10cm (4in) long, appear in late summer; berries are violet-blue. The lustrous deep green leaves grow to 60cm (2ft) long. HEIGHT & SPREAD 60×30cm (2×1ft).

'Vittatus' has cream-striped leaves.

O. japonicus Loose 8cm (3in) spikes of white or pale purple flowers are followed by blue-black berries. The flowers are often hidden by the glossy dark green leaves that grow to about 30cm (12in) long. This species, suitable for moister sites, spreads by underground stolons and is good for carpeting. It may also be grown as an aquatic foliage plant, when it produces fewer flowers. HEIGHT & SPREAD 30×45cm (1×1½ft).

Ophiopogon planiscapus

O. planiscapus White flowers, sometimes tinted purple, appear crowded together on a more or less erect 8cm (3in) spike in late summer. The berries are blue-black and the deep green leaves grow to 30cm (12in) long. HEIGHT & SPREAD 25×30cm (10×12in).

Ophiopogon planiscapus 'Nigrescens'

'Nigrescens' ♀ has distinctive purple-black leaves, darker flowers and black fruits.

CULTIVATION All plants thrive in well-drained soil in sun or partial shade, except for *O. japonicus* which requires more moisture. Top-dress with compost and in colder gardens protect with conifer branches or horticultural fleece in winter. Replant every 3 or 4 years.

PROPAGATION Divide in spring or early autumn; or sow seed under glass in autumn or spring.

PESTS AND DISEASES Usually trouble free.

ORCHIDS

THE EASIEST TYPES TO GROW

THESE ORNAMENTAL PLANTS PRODUCE SHOWY OR DELICATE BLOOMS YEAR AFTER YEAR, AS LONG AS THEIR BASIC NEEDS ARE MET

Intense colours, delicate markings and unusually shaped petals make orchids ideal display plants. There is a huge diversity of flowers, from the dainty white blooms of *Phalaenopsis amabilis* to the large waxy ones of *Stanhopea tigrina*. Typically, each orchid flower has three petal-like sepals and three petals. The third, usually the lower, petal is called the lip and is often differently shaped from the other petals. It is usually more flamboyant and more intensely marked. Some are inflated and form a pouch or slipper, as in *Cypripedium*.

The family Orchidaceae is one of the largest plant families and includes more than 20 000 different species. The plants are evergreen or herbaceous perennials and are native to every continent except Antarctica. Some readily interbreed and orchid growers frequently produce new hybrids.

Cultivated orchids do best in environments that imitate their native habitats. Hardy orchids such as *Bletilla*, *Dactylorhiza* and *Epipactis* (see separate genus entries) can be grown in the garden. But most orchids grown in Britain must be kept indoors. Some will thrive only if grown in a cool greenhouse, with a minimum temperature of 4°C (39°F); a warm greenhouse, heated to at least 10°C (50°F); or a hot greenhouse which has a minimum temperature of 15°C (59°F). Others can be kept in a conservatory or grown as houseplants. Many greenhouse orchids will not suffer if they are brought into the house for a few weeks while they are in flower.

RECOMMENDED PLANTS

Roughly a third of all orchid species are terrestrial, growing on the ground. The remainder are epiphytic and live on the branches of trees or on rocks. In the tropics, the majority of orchids are epiphytes, while in temperate regions almost all the orchids are terrestrial.

TERRESTRIAL ORCHIDS

Terrestrial orchids usually have either rhizomes or underground tubers. Herbaceous species have an annual dormant period, when they die down, enabling them to survive periods when the climate is inhospitable. In general, herbaceous species with rhizomes become dormant in winter and herbaceous species with tubers become dormant in summer. Evergreens may have a dormant period when growth slows down. This is often in winter, but may occur after flowering.

FASCINATING FLOWERS Paphiopedilum, Oncidium *and* Vuylstekeara *show the variable but unmistakable blooms of exotic orchids.*

Cypripedium

The flamboyant blooms of these temperate slipper orchids have inflated lower petals.

C. formosanum (syn. *C. japonicum* var. *formosanum*) One or two pinkish white flowers, with red markings, are held on each stem. The lower, slipper-shaped petal is 7 cm (2¾ in) wide and spotted more densely than the other petals. The rhizomatous plant blooms in late spring. Its green, ribbed, fan-shaped leaves are 15 cm (6 in) long. Grow the plant in a cold or cool, well-ventilated greenhouse. Pot in a shallow clay container at the end of winter, in compost made up of 2 parts grit, 1 part orchid bark, 1 part loam and 1 part leaf-mould. The growing bud of the rhizome should just protrude from the compost. Keep the compost moist, and each winter remove the top 3 cm (1¼ in) and replace with a mix of equal parts grit, bark and leaf-mould. Add bonemeal in early spring. Repot only if the plant outgrows its container. Native to Taiwan. HEIGHT & SPREAD 30×30 cm (12×12 in) after 5 years.

▲ *Cypripedium formosanum*

C. insigne see *Paphiopedilum insigne*

Disa

Brightly coloured flowers are borne singly or in groups on these tuberous orchids.

▲ ***Disa uniflora***

D. uniflora Spectacular scarlet (occasionally orange) flowers, 5 cm (2 in) across, appear in groups of up to 5 in summer. A veined upper petal, paler than the others, partially encloses a small inner petal, which is often splashed yellow and red. The plant has 10-20 cm (4-8 in) long, shiny, evergreen, lance-shaped leaves arranged in a basal rosette, or sheathing the 30-60 cm (12-24 in) stem.

Keep the plant in a plastic container, in a cool greenhouse. Choose a peat compost with added sphagnum moss. The compost must remain moist at all times. Use water that is not alkaline – rainwater if necessary. Native to South Africa. HEIGHT & SPREAD 45×40 cm (18×16 in) after 5 years.

Ophrys

Plants in this genus are collectively known as bee orchids because of the close resemblance of their flowers to bees, as well as other insects.

▼ ***Ophrys tenthredinifera***

O. tenthredinifera (sawfly orchid) Six or more flowers, which are predominantly pink and 2cm (¾in) across, are produced in mid and late spring. They are carried on an erect central stem up to 30cm (12in) tall. The upper and side petals are spread open and flat. The fleshy lip is greenish yellow to pinkish brown, lobed and velvety, with a white-edged marking at the base. The pale green, lance-shaped leaves, which grow up to 8cm (3¼in) long, form a basal rosette round the 30cm (12in) tall central stem. The plant is tuberous.

Grow it in a shallow plastic pot in a cool greenhouse. Pot the tubers about 2.5cm (1in) deep in a compost made up of 3 parts grit, 2 parts loam, 1 part leaf-mould, and 1 part fine orchid bark. Repot the plant annually in late summer, when it is resting. Incorporate roughly a third of the old compost with the new compost.

Gradually increase watering as the plant grows in autumn and winter, keeping the compost moist but not wet – and allowing it to dry out to a depth of 2.5cm (1in) before each watering. Slowly reduce watering once flower buds have formed in spring. Water occasionally in summer. The plant does not need feeding. Native to Europe. HEIGHT & SPREAD 30×15cm (12×6in) after 3 years.

Orchis

Plants in this genus are tuberous and have single stems that bear many delicate flowers.

O. morio (green-winged orchid) Variably coloured flowers, in purple to white and 2.5cm (1in) wide, appear in mid and late spring. The pink to purple lip is broad, 3-lobed and white at the base. A central spike, which reaches 30cm (12in) tall, with up to 12 flowers, rises above a basal rosette of pale green, lance-shaped leaves, 8cm (3¼in) long.

▼ *Orchis morio*

Cultivate this species in the way described for *Ophrys tenthredinifera*. Native to Europe. HEIGHT & SPREAD 30×15cm (12×6in) after 3 years.

Paphiopedilum

These Asiatic slipper orchids are evergreen and have showy blooms that are long-lasting.

P. insigne♀ (syn. *Cypripedium insigne)* Each waxy flower has upper and lower petals that are spotted golden brown, oblong and pinched at the tip, and 2 narrow, golden brown side petals. The slipper-shaped lip is also golden brown, with a golden interior, speckled with brown. The flowers appear from autumn to spring. One or, occasionally, two blooms, 10cm (4in) long and 5cm (2in) wide, are carried on a 30cm (12in) tall stalk that rises from a clump of lax, dark green, strap-shaped leaves, which are up to 20-30cm (8-12in) long.

▲ *Paphiopedilum insigne*

Grow in a warm greenhouse or conservatory, in a pot or plastic-coated hanging basket. Maintain high humidity and keep the compost moist. Plant in a compost made up of 2 parts coarse bark, 1 part fine bark and half a part finely chopped sphagnum moss. Repot annually to maintain the plant's health. Native to NE India and Nepal. HEIGHT & SPREAD 30×50cm (12×20in) after 3 years.

Phragmipedium

Originating from S America, these evergreen slipper orchids often bear several striking blooms on a stem.

P. besseae Vivid scarlet flowers have pouched lips with yellow markings. The blooms are softly hairy and 6cm (2½in) across. They are held in groups of 1-4 on a 30cm (12in) tall spike between spring and autumn, and occasionally in winter. The 10-20cm (4-8in) long leaves are pale green and strap-shaped. The plant has a creeping rhizome from which it produces several leafy growths.

▲ *Phragmipedium besseae*

Keep the plant in a hot greenhouse, in the compost described for *Paphiopedilum insigne*. Pot in a shallow plastic pan to accommodate the rhizome. Native to Ecuador and Peru. HEIGHT & SPREAD 30×30cm (12×12in) after 3 years.

Growing terrestrial orchids

CULTIVATION See the individual entries for each plant's cultivation requirements. In general, do not allow the potting compost to become waterlogged and water orchids less often when they are dormant.

PROPAGATION Divide established rhizomatous plants when they are dormant. Take care with cypripediums, which dislike being disturbed. Tuberous orchids may produce extra tubers which can be potted separately. Raising the plants from seed is not recommended.

PESTS AND DISEASES Aphids and whitefly can affect plants that are grown in a cool or warm greenhouse; red spider mite, scale insect and mealy bug can affect orchids grown in a hot greenhouse. Fungal diseases may result from overwatering or lack of air movement.

Epiphytic orchids

These orchids use other plants, rocks and fallen trees for anchorage. They have specialised aerial roots that absorb moisture and nutrients from the air, rainwater and decayed plant matter.

Typically, an epiphytic orchid has a rhizome from which grow vertical swollen organs, called pseudobulbs. These are storage vessels for food and water. They are usually oval and are up to 10cm (4in) long. Some orchids, such as *Dendrobium chrysotoxum*, produce elongated cane-like pseudobulbs, which form the stems of the plant. New pseudobulbs are produced each year.

Vanda does not have a rhizome or pseudobulbs. Instead, it has an elongated, ever-lengthening stem. The leaves are fleshy to prevent water loss.

All the recommended epiphytic orchids described below are evergreens. Most epiphytic orchids have a dormant period when growth either slows down or stops altogether. This may occur in winter when there is not much daylight.

Cattleya

Spectacular, brightly coloured flowers are borne in groups on these tropical orchids.

C. bowringiana (syn. *C. skinneri* var. *bowringiana)* Lilac and purple flowers, 10cm (4in) across, are carried in groups of 10 or more in autumn on 20cm (8in) long spikes. Each 6cm (2½in) long, oblong pseudobulb is sheathed by a pair of stiff, oblong, pale green leaves, up to 20cm (8in) long. The plant forms a clump, which should be divided in winter or spring after 5 years. Grow it in a warm greenhouse in good light. Native to Central America. HEIGHT & SPREAD 40×40cm (16×16in) after 5 years.

▼ *Cattleya bowringiana*

Coelogyne

These orchids have glossy green leaves and their blooms are often highly scented.

C. cristata Showy white, fragrant flowers, boldly marked with yellow, are borne during winter and spring on arching, 20cm (8in) long stems. A stem

▲ *Coelogyne cristata*

bears 3–10 flowers, each of which is 8cm (3¼in) long by 5cm (2in) wide. The plant has green, rounded, wrinkled pseudobulbs, each with 2 dark green lance-shaped leaves, up to 30cm (12in) long. It is scrambling and can be grown in a pot or wooden-slatted basket.

Grow the plant in a warm greenhouse. It can also be kept indoors, on a windowsill, or in a conservatory, if humid enough. Native to the Himalayas. HEIGHT & SPREAD 10×30cm (4×12in) after 3 years.

Cymbidium

These orchids, which are popular houseplants, bear many flowers on their stems.

C. lowianum (syn. *C. giganteum* var. *lowianum*) Greenish sepals and petals surround a yellow flower centre and wide lip, which is splashed with red and white. The flowers are 8cm

▼ *Cymbidium lowianum*

(3¼in) long and wide, and appear in groups of up to 20 in late winter and throughout spring. They are carried on one or more arching spikes that can grow up to 1m (3ft) long. The plant forms large clumps and has clusters of green, strap-like leaves, up to 1m (3ft) long, arising from oval pseudobulbs.

Keep the plant in a warm greenhouse or conservatory in good indirect light. In summer, it can be moved into the garden and placed in dappled sunshine. Plant in a mixture of medium and fine bark. Divide in spring. This orchid is native to SW China, Burma and Thailand. HEIGHT & SPREAD 60×30cm (24×12in) after 3 years.

Dendrobium

Plants in this large genus vary greatly in appearance but they generally have showy and sometimes fragrant flowers.

D. chrysotoxum (syn. *D. suavissimum*) Yellow scented flowers, 5cm (2in) wide, have frilly lower petals partly coloured an

▲ *Dendrobium chrysotoxum*

intense orange-red. Flowers are borne in winter and spring on cane-like pseudobulbs. Bright green, leathery, oblong leaves are 10–15cm (4–6in) long. Grow the plant in a hot greenhouse. Native to Indochina. HEIGHT & SPREAD 20×20cm (8×8in) after 5 years.

Laelia

These plants have colourful and elegant blooms which are borne on one or more flower spikes.

L. anceps Lilac sepals and petals surround a tubular rose-pink lip with a yellow interior. Each arched flower spike, 75cm (30in) long, bears up to 6 flowers, 10cm (4in) across, in winter. The pseudobulbs, 7cm

▲ *Laelia anceps*

(3in) long, each produce one or two leathery green, oblong leaves, 20cm (8in) long. Grow in a hot or warm greenhouse in good light. Native to Mexico. HEIGHT & SPREAD 40×20cm (16×8in) after 3–4 years.

Masdevallia

Curiously shaped flowers are produced by these orchids which have no pseudobulbs.

M. coccinea (syn. *M. harryana, M. lindeni*) Brilliant white, yellow, orange, red or purple flowers are borne singly on one or more upright stalks in spring and early summer. Two or three flowers may be in bloom at a time. The flower is 2cm

▲ *Masdevallia coccinea*

(¾in) across and includes several partially fused, oval petals and a thread-like upper petal that arches behind the rest of the flower. The base of the flower is rolled into a tube which holds the tiny inner petals, including the lip. Glossy green, oblong leaves, 20cm (8in) long, grow from the top of the stems, which are 6cm (2½in) long. Grow the plant in a warm greenhouse. Native to Peru and Colombia. HEIGHT & SPREAD 18×15cm (7×6in) after 3 years.

Miltoniopsis

These orchids have pansy-like flowers and are native to South and Central America.

***M.* Anjou 'St Patrick'** The fragrant flowers, 8cm (3¼in) wide, have deep red petals splashed with white, and orange and yellow centres. They are carried in clusters on spikes,

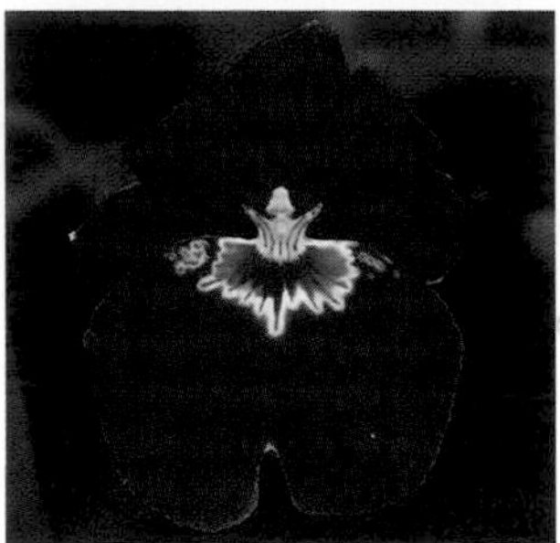

▲ *Miltoniopsis* Anjou 'St Patrick'

20cm (8in) long, in summer. Small pseudobulbs each bear 2 narrow, tapered pale green leaves, 40cm (16in) long. Grow in good indirect light in a warm greenhouse or as a houseplant. HEIGHT & SPREAD 30×20cm (12×8in) after 3 years.

Odontoglossum

The plants produce numerous star-shaped flowers on attractively arching stalks.

O. crispum Showy, white, blooms cluster on 50cm (20in) long stalks. Several spikes may be produced over autumn and winter. The flowers are 10cm (4in) long and 8cm (3¼in) wide. Narrow, green leaves are 40cm (16in) long, and egg-shaped pseudobulbs reach 10cm (4in). This is an easy orchid to grow in a warm greenhouse. Native to Colombia. HEIGHT & SPREAD 30×30cm (12×12in) after 3–4 years.

▼ *Odontoglossum crispum*

▲ *Oncidium sphacelatum*

Oncidium

Plants in this large genus usually produce sprays of small, sometimes fragrant blooms.

O. sphacelatum Each flower has petals that are yellow or reddish brown and yellow. The broad yellow lip has a red-brown, white and orange-red centre. Flowers measure 3cm (1¼in) across and are carried in branched clusters on arched stalks up to 1.5m (5ft) long, from winter until early summer. The plant has flattened pseudobulbs, and rigid linear leaves, 60cm (2ft) long. Grow in a hot greenhouse in good light. Native to Central America. HEIGHT & SPREAD 60×30cm (2×1ft) after 3-4 years.

Phalaenopsis

Striking moth-like flowers give the plants, which have no pseudobulbs, the common name of moth orchids.

P. amabilis ♀ The white flowers, 8cm (3¼in) across, are held on a slender, arching spike up to 1m (3ft) long. They are produced in winter. The plant has 3-5 leathery, oblong, mid green leaves, which are naturally drooping, and may be as long as 50cm (20in). Grow this plant in the shade, in a hot greenhouse, or on a draught-free windowsill in a house or conservatory, maintaining a high level of humidity. Native to Indonesia, New Guinea and NE Australia. HEIGHT & SPREAD 45×20cm (18×8in) after 4-5 years.

▲ *Phalaenopsis amabilis*

Stanhopea

The extraordinary blooms are waxy, heavily perfumed and hang below the plant.

S. tigrina ♀ Up to 4 cream, red-splashed flowers, 12cm (4¾in) long, are held on each 5cm (2in) long stalk. They appear in summer and last only a few days. The plant has clusters of small, oval pseudobulbs and deep green lance-shaped leaves, 30cm (12in) long. Grow it in a shady part of a hot greenhouse, in a wooden-slatted or plastic-mesh hanging basket, lined with moss. This allows the flower stalks to grow between the roots and hang down below the rest of the plant. Native to Mexico. HEIGHT & SPREAD 40×30cm (16×12in) after 3 years.

▲ *Stanhopea tigrina*

Vanda

These Asian climbing plants produce numerous spikes of flowers that are often fragrant.

***V.* Rothschildiana** ♀ This orchid flowers profusely, producing long spikes of spectacular purple and white marbled flowers in summer. Five large oval petals surround a small purple lip. Each 40cm (16in) long spike holds as many as 12 flowers, each measuring about 8cm (3¼in) across. The strap-shaped green leaves, which grow up to 35cm (14in) long, are arranged alternately on a constantly elongating stem that grows upwards. The stem produces occasional side growths and both stem and shoots have whitish aerial roots that are tipped with green or purple when the orchid is in active growth.

Grow the plant in a wooden-slatted or plastic-mesh basket to enable the long aerial roots to grow through the container and hang below the plant. Support the main stem with a stake, and hang the container from wires attached to both container and stake. Keep it in a hot greenhouse. Mist the plant daily. HEIGHT & SPREAD 1m×50cm (36×20in) after 3-4 years.

Vuylstekeara

These plants are hybrids. They produce spikes of showy, colourful flowers.

***V.* Cambria 'Plush'** Pretty, star-shaped, crimson, white and yellow flowers, up to 8cm (3¼in) wide, last for 4 weeks or more. There are as many as 6 flowers on each 40cm (16in) long spike. The bi-lobed lip is wider than the other petals. The pseudobulbs are small and oval, and the leaves are dull green, oblong and up to 20-30cm (8-12in) long. The plant blooms after the current year's pseudobulb has finished growing, often in autumn. Keep the plant in a warm greenhouse, or grow it on a warm windowsill, where it will be slightly smaller. HEIGHT & SPREAD 40×30cm (16×12in) after 3 years.

▼ *Vuylstekeara* Cambria 'Plush'

▲ *Vanda* Rothschildiana

Growing epiphytic orchids

CULTIVATION Epiphytic orchids need a humid environment. Damp down the floors and benches or use a humidifier to maintain an air humidity of 90-95 per cent at night and 80-85 per cent during the day.

Maintain humidity for any orchids grown on windowsills in the house or in a conservatory by placing their containers on a tray of moist pebbles. Keep the plants out of direct sunlight and cold draughts.

Grow small, young plants in a compost made up of 5 parts fine grade orchid bark to 1 part perlite. For established plants, use a mixture of 5 parts medium grade orchid bark and 1 part perlag. Repot plants in late winter or early spring. Unless otherwise stated in the individual plant descriptions, water epiphytic orchids liberally when they are in active growth and apply a liquid fertiliser once a fortnight. Reduce waterings and do not feed during the plant's resting period.

PROPAGATION Divide well-established plants during their resting periods. For orchids that have an ever-increasing stem, such as *Vanda*, remove any new growths from the base when repotting, and pot them up separately. Remove offshoots from orchids that have cane-like stems, such as *Dendrobium*, and pot them up separately. Raising orchids from seed is not recommended.

PESTS AND DISEASES Thrips, mealy bugs, red spider mites, and scale insects may all affect epiphytic orchids.

Ophrys see ORCHIDS p. 464
Opuntia see CACTI p. 108
Orache see *Atriplex*
Orange see *Citrus*
Orange, Mexican see *Choisya*
Orange, mock see *Philadelphus*
Orange, Osage see *Maclura pomifera*
Orange ball tree see *Buddleja globosa*
Orchid see p. 464
Orchid, poor man's see *Schizanthus*
Orchis see ORCHIDS p. 465
Oregano see *Origanum*

Origanum

Marjoram, oregano

Labiatae

Origanum rotundifolium

This popular genus of aromatic herbaceous perennials and deciduous sub-shrubs includes small plants for the rock garden, taller border perennials and the culinary herbs, *Origanum majorana*, *O. onites*, and *O. vulgare*. Origanum plants have upright or spreading wiry stems. The flowers are borne from mid summer to autumn. They are sometimes insignificant amid the conspicuous pale green, pink or reddish purple bracts, which usually deepen in colour with age and remain attractive for weeks. The stalkless, aromatic leaves have conspicuous veins. Origanums are native to open mountainous areas of the Mediterranean and Asia.

▲ *Origanum amanum*

RECOMMENDED SPECIES AND VARIETIES

O. amanum ♀ This small, tufted sub-shrub has bright green oval leaves up to 1.5 cm (½ in) long. Long-tubed pink flowers, up to 3.5 cm (1⅜ in) long, with small spreading lobes are borne among small green bracts which become flushed with pink as they age. It is an excellent plant for a sunny rock garden, an unheated greenhouse or conservatory. HEIGHT & SPREAD 8×30 cm (3¼×12 in).

***O.* 'Barbara Tingey'** Pink flowers, 1.5 cm (½ in) long, are borne among nodding clusters of large green bracts which gradually turn deep pink. The blue-green hairy leaves are up to 1.5 cm (½ in) long. The plants form a dense, spreading mound. HEIGHT & SPREAD 10×20 cm (4×8 in).

***O.* 'Buckland'** This semi-upright plant has very hairy grey-green leaves 1 cm (⅜ in) long. The bracts are pink early on. HEIGHT & SPREAD 20×15 cm (8×6 in).

O. calcaratum (syn. *O. tournefortii*) Tiny pink flowers are held amid narrow clusters of green bracts which rapidly become deep pink. This small clump-forming plant has hairy greyish green leaves up to 1 cm (⅜ in) long. HEIGHT & SPREAD 10×20 cm (4×8 in).

▲ *Origanum dictamnus*

O. dictamnus Small pink flowers appear amid small reddish purple bracts. A dome of branching stems bears rounded white-felted leaves up to 2 cm (¾ in) long. This foliage plant is best grown in an unheated well-ventilated greenhouse or conservatory, or in a rock garden but protected from winter wet. HEIGHT & SPREAD 10×20 cm (4×8 in)

O. × hybridum A small creeping sub-shrub with slightly hairy grey-green leaves up to 1.5 cm (½ in) long. Upright clusters of pinkish bracts become deeper pink with age. The pink flowers are 1 cm (⅜ in) in length. HEIGHT & SPREAD 30×30 cm (12×12 in).

***O.* 'Kent Beauty'** This low mound-forming hybrid is ideal for a rock garden. It has hairy grey-green rounded leaves up to 1.5 cm (½ in) long that are hidden in mid to late summer by pendent clusters of bracts up to 5 cm (2 in) long. These are pale green at first but quickly turn deep rose-pink. Small pink flowers are partly hidden among the bracts. HEIGHT & SPREAD 10×20 cm (4×8 in).

O. laevigatum ♀ This species makes a clump of stiff upright stems with blue-green leaves up to 2 cm (¾ in) long. It bears diffuse branching clusters of many small deep purple flowers with small purple bracts that are less conspicuous than in other species. HEIGHT & SPREAD 70×30 cm (28×12 in).

'Herrenhausen' ♀ has a purple tinge to the young leaves and larger, paler flower clusters. In **'Hopley's'** the whorls of purplish pink flowers are more widely spaced.

O. majorana (sweet marjoram) A perennial culinary herb, sometimes grown as an annual. It makes an upright clump with reddish stems, small grey hairy leaves and dense clusters of grey-green bracts. The white or pale pink flowers are insignificant. HEIGHT & SPREAD 60×30 cm (2×1 ft).

O. microphyllum Loose spikes of small pink flowers are borne amid deep purplish bracts in summer. This domed sub-shrub has tiny grey leaves on thin, branching stems. It is hardy to -8°C (18°F) in very well-drained soil. HEIGHT & SPREAD 25×30 cm (10×12 in).

***O.* 'Norton Gold'** A clump of stiff upright stems with yellow leaves and pink flowers. HEIGHT & SPREAD 70×50 cm (28×20 in).

***O.* 'Nymphenburg'** Deep pink flowers and large deep purple bracts crown a clump of stiff upright stems. The purple-tinged leaves are up to 2 cm (¾ in) long. HEIGHT & SPREAD 70×30 cm (28×12 in).

O. onites (pot marjoram) A culinary herb of shrubby habit with green leaves, 2 cm (¾ in) long, and insignificant flowers and bracts. HEIGHT & SPREAD 60×60 cm (2×2 ft).

O. pulchellum see *O. × hybridum*

***O.* 'Rosenkuppel'** A clump-forming plant with stiff upright stems bearing very deep pink flowers and deep purple bracts. The purple-tinged leaves are up to 2 cm (¾ in) long. HEIGHT & SPREAD 60×30 cm (2×1 ft).

O. rotundifolium ♀ Insignificant pink flowers are held amid cone-like clusters of large conspicuous pale apple-green bracts. The leaves are bright green and up to 1.5 cm (½ in) long. This prostrate sub-shrub needs sharp drainage and protection from winter wet. HEIGHT & SPREAD 10×30 cm (4×12 in).

O. tournefortii see *O. calcaratum*

O. vulgare (oregano, common marjoram, wild marjoram) A spreading culinary herb with stiff upright stems and clusters of pale lilac flowers amid small dark purple bracts. The rounded to oval leaves are 3 cm (1¼ in) long. HEIGHT & SPREAD 30 cm×1 m (1×3 ft).

'Aureum' ♀ (golden wild marjoram) has aromatic golden leaves which become greener in late summer, and a few insignificant lilac flowers. It is less invasive than the species. **'Aureum Crispum'** is similar but with wavy-edged leaves. **'Compactum'** has dark green leaves and many dark purple flower clusters. It reaches a height of 15 cm (6 in) and a spread of 30 cm (1 ft). **'Gold Tip'** has gold tips to the leaves.

CULTIVATION Plant the smaller perennials in spring in very well-drained soil in full sun. Plant culinary herbs and taller species in spring in full sun in any reasonably well-drained soil. Cut back after flowering.

PROPAGATION Sow the seed of species in autumn. Species and named varieties can be grown from softwood cuttings taken in late spring. The more robust clump-formers can be divided in early spring.

PESTS AND DISEASES Usually trouble free in the garden but may be affected by aphids and red spider mite under glass.

Ornithogalum

Hyacinthaceae

Ornithogalum nutans

These bulbous perennials enliven spring and summer beds with flowers which are usually star-shaped and white or green-and-white. The smaller species are ideal for a rock garden, raised bed or alpine house. The leaves are usually narrow and strap-shaped, and grow at the base of the plant. Unless otherwise stated, the plants listed below are hardy. Native to Asia, Africa and Mediterranean regions.

RECOMMENDED SPECIES AND VARIETIES

O. arabicum Clusters of white or creamy white scented blooms appear in late spring to early summer. Each flower is up to 3 cm (1¼ in) across with prominent black ovaries. It is not a hardy plant. HEIGHT 40 cm (16 in).

O. balansae see *O. oligophyllum*

O. longibracteatum (sea onion, false sea onion, German onion) Unscented white flowers, up to 1 cm (⅜ in) across and with a green stripe on the outer tepals are borne in spikes in early summer. This plant is not fully hardy; mulch in winter. It is evergreen in frost-free conditions. HEIGHT 1.5 m (5 ft).

▲ *Ornithogalum nutans*

O. nutans ♀ In mid to late spring this species bears unscented white flowers with a pronounced green midrib on the outside of the petals. Each flower measures up to 3 cm (1¼ in) across. HEIGHT 45 cm (1½ ft).

O. oligophyllum (syn. *O. balansae*) Unscented white blooms, up to 1.5 cm (½ in) across and green on the outside, bloom in early to mid spring from a rosette of broad prostrate leaves. HEIGHT 10 cm (4 in).

O. thyrsoides (chincherinchee) Dense conical spikes of unscented ivory white, cup-shaped flowers, up to 2 cm (¾ in) across, are borne in mid to late summer. Lift this tender species in autumn and plant out in mid to late spring. HEIGHT 45 cm (1½ ft).

▲ *Ornithogalum umbellatum*

O. umbellatum (star of Bethlehem) Spikes of unscented, 2.5 cm (1 in) wide, pure white flowers with green stripes on the reverse, are borne in mid to late spring. This species can become invasive. HEIGHT 30 cm (1 ft).

CULTIVATION Plant bulbs in spring in any well-drained soil about 8 cm (3¼ in) deep and 5-8 cm (2-3¼ in) apart, in full sun or semi-shade. *O. thyrsoides* can be grown in pots; plant bulbs 5 cm (2 in) deep in well-drained compost. Overwinter in a frost-free greenhouse and put outside in summer.

PROPAGATION Lift and divide bulblets in late summer. Sow ripe seed under glass and keep in a coldframe; plant out 2 years later.

PESTS AND DISEASES Usually trouble free.

Orontium

Golden club

Araceae

Strange but showy flower spikes in spring and summer distinguish this hardy deciduous perennial aquatic. It is a deep-water plant but will grow in variable depths, with a minimum of 10 cm (4 in). A sunny position is needed. The single species in the genus is native to eastern USA.

Orontium aquaticum Pencil-like flower spikes, bright yellow at the top, paling to white below, and up to 20 cm (8 in) long, are held above the water from spring to early summer. Oval to oblong blue-green leaves, up to 25 cm (10 in) long and 8 cm (3¼ in) wide, float on the surface of the water if the depth is at least 25 cm (10 in). When the plants grow in shallower water the leaves are erect and usually smaller. HEIGHT & SPREAD 20×60 cm (8×24 in). The height given is that visible above water.

CULTIVATION Plant in spring in a heavy loam soil or an aquatic planting compost in an open-sided aquatic planting basket.

▲ *Orontium aquaticum*

Cover the surface with pea gravel to prevent fish from disturbing the soil. Use an aquatic plant fertiliser in early spring.

PROPAGATION Divide in early spring or sow ripe seeds in a tray of mud in summer.

PESTS AND DISEASES Occasionally troubled by water-lily aphids.

Osmanthus

Oleaceae

Osmanthus delavayi

Clusters of small, usually fragrant, tubular flowers with four lobes that spread or curve back appear in spring or autumn on these evergreen shrubs. All the listed species produce white flowers in clusters 1.5-4 cm (½-1½ in) across. Although the blooms are not showy, the plants are valued for their fragrance and attractive leathery foliage. The small olive-like fruits, mostly black or purplish, are not edible.

Either sun or shade and most fertile soils, including chalk, suit these shrubs which are native to SE United States, much of Asia and some Pacific islands. Some can be trained into unusual and effective hedges. Those described are hardy to -15°C (5°F).

RECOMMENDED SPECIES AND VARIETIES

O. armatus Fragrant flowers 6 mm (¼ in) across appear during early autumn on this dense, bushy species whose light grey shoots bear stiff, dark green, glossy, oblong leaves, 8-15 cm (3¼-6 in) long and usually sharply toothed. Egg-shaped, 2 cm (¾ in) long, dark blackish purple fruits appear in early winter. HEIGHT & SPREAD 1 m×60 cm (3×2 ft) after 5 years, ultimately 4×4 m (13×13 ft).

▲ Osmanthus x burkwoodii

O. × burkwoodii♀ (syn. × *Osmarea burkwoodii*) Small groups of short-tubed scented flowers, about 1 cm (⅜ in) across, appear in mid spring. This hybrid between *O. decorus* and *O. delavayi* grows slowly into a dense shrub with neat 2.5-5 cm (1-2 in) long ovate leaves that are finely toothed and dark glossy green. HEIGHT & SPREAD 1 m×60 cm (3×2 ft) after 5 years, ultimately 3×3 m (10×10 ft).

O. decorus (syn. *Phillyrea decora*) Sweetly scented flowers are borne in mid spring by this rounded species of dense, upright habit. Its glossy, dark green, narrowly elliptic leaves are yellowish green beneath and 5-12 cm (2-4¾ in) long. The blackish purple oval fruits are 1.5 cm (½ in) long and appear in summer. HEIGHT & SPREAD 1×1 m (3×3 ft) after 5 years, ultimately 3×4 m (10×13 ft).

▲ Osmanthus delavayi

O. delavayi♀ Fragrant flowers 1.5 cm (½ in) long with reflexed lobes appear in mid and late spring. Broadly egg-shaped, 1 cm (⅜ in) long, blue-black fruits ripen in autumn on this usually compact, bushy species. It has neat, rounded or broadly ovate, dark green leaves that are stiff and glossy, up to 2.5 cm (1 in) long with a few small sharp teeth. HEIGHT & SPREAD 60×60 cm (2×2 ft) after 5 years, ultimately 1.8×2.4 m (6×8 ft).

O. forrestii see *O. yunnanensis*

O. heterophyllus (syn. *O. ilicifolius*) Fragrant flowers 6 mm (¼ in) wide with a short tube and recurved lobes are borne in early and mid autumn. They are followed

▲ Osmanthus heterophyllus

in early winter by oblong, 1.5 cm (½ in) long, purple-black fruits, which are seldom abundant. This holly-like species of compact, bushy habit has 4-6 cm (1½-2½ in) long, stiff, ovate leaves that are glossy dark green, paler beneath and usually with a few large, spine-tipped teeth. HEIGHT & SPREAD 1×1 m (3×3 ft) after 5 years, ultimately 3-6×3-6 m (10-20×10-20 ft).

'Argenteomarginatus' see **'Variegatus'**; **'Aureomarginatus'** (**'Aureus'**) leaves with golden yellow margins; **'Aureus'** see **'Aureomarginatus'**; **'Goshiki'** (**'Tricolor'**) bronze young growth and strongly spined, heavily mottled leaves splashed with creamy yellow and green; **'Gulftide'**♀ compact, to 2.4 m (8 ft) tall, with boldly spine-toothed, dark green leaves; **'Purpureus'** glossy, deep blackish purple young leaves and shoots become green tinged with purple by summer; **'Tricolor'** see **'Goshiki'**; **'Variegatus'**♀ (**'Argenteomarginatus'**) popular compact variety grows to 3 m (10 ft) tall and 3 m (10 ft) wide, leaves broadly edged with creamy white.

O. ilicifolius see *O. heterophyllus*

O. yunnanensis (syn. *O. forrestii*) Creamy white flowers, 1 cm (⅜ in) across, with spreading lobes appear in mid and late spring. This large species has 8-15 cm (3¼-6 in) long dull, olive-green, narrowly oblong or lance-shaped leaves. Young growth is flushed with bronze and the margins smooth-edged or wavy with many spiny teeth. The 1.5 cm (½ in) long fruit is bloomy dark purple, borne in summer but not freely produced. HEIGHT & SPREAD 1.2×1 m (4×3 ft) after 5 years, ultimately 10×10 m (33×33 ft).

CULTIVATION Plant in autumn or winter in any fertile, well-drained soil in sun or shade. *O. yunnanensis* needs some shelter.

PROPAGATION Take semi-ripe cuttings in summer. Sow seeds of species in spring.

PRUNING Not normally needed but shorten excess growth in mid to late spring.

PESTS AND DISEASES Usually trouble free.

× Osmarea see *Osmanthus*

Osmunda see FERNS p. 264

Osteospermum

Compositae

The centres of these daisy-like flowers contrast strikingly with the colours of the petals. Each flowerhead, up to 5 cm (2 in) wide, has a centre, which is properly called a disc floret, surrounded by linear petals called ray florets. They make an eye-catching summer display in an open border, as ground cover, or in containers. The soft leaves mix well with plants with strong leaf outlines, such as phormium and yucca. Unless stated otherwise, the recommended plants have a spreading habit and linear to lance-shaped or reverse lance-shaped leaves, some with slightly serrated edges, about 8 cm (3¼ in) long. There are about 70 species of this semi-woody, evergreen from South Africa. They are not reliably frost hardy and survive best in free-draining soils in mild areas. Dry sunny conditions suit them best. The plants can tolerate dry conditions in shade but may flower sparsely as a result.

RECOMMENDED SPECIES AND VARIETIES

O. 'Blackthorn Seedling'♀ The dark brown centres of this plant contrast with the rose-magenta petals. HEIGHT & SPREAD 30×60 cm (12×24 in).

▲ Osteospermum 'Buttermilk'

O. 'Buttermilk'♀ Pale primrose and white petals with dark brown centres appear among the grey-green, egg-shaped leaves of this upright plant. HEIGHT & SPREAD 60×30 cm (2×1 ft).

O. 'Cannington John' Pink, spoon-shaped petals offset white centres in this prostrate plant. HEIGHT & SPREAD 30×60 cm (1×2 ft).

O. caulescens (syn. *O. ecklonis* var. *prostratum*)

O. ecklonis (syn. *Dimorphotheca ecklonis*) The petals are soft white above and striped, slate-blue underneath, while the centre is a

O

▲ *Osteospermum ecklonis* var. *prostratum*

dark, metallic blue. This plant is upright. HEIGHT & SPREAD 60×60cm (2×2ft).

The recumbent form, var. ***prostratum***♀ (syn. *O. caulescens*), creeps along the ground to a height of 30cm (12in).

***O.* 'Gold Sparkler'** Gold-splashed, green leaves earn this upright plant its place in the garden. The flowers have pale pink petals and dark brown centres. HEIGHT & SPREAD 40×60cm (16×24in).

***O.* 'Hopleys'**♀ The yellow centres stand out against the mauvish pink petals with white bases and purple undersides. HEIGHT & SPREAD 30×60cm (1×2ft).

***O.* 'Jacarandum'**♀ The light purple petals have undersides streaked with yellow. HEIGHT & SPREAD 30×60cm (1×2ft).

O. jucundum♀ Black-purple centres are surrounded by petals that are mauve to rich purple above and dark purple underneath. The shiny, greyish green leaves are spoon-shaped. HEIGHT & SPREAD 20×60cm (8×24in).

***O.* 'Lady Leitrim'**♀ (syn. *O.* 'Pale Face') White petals shaded pink at the base and mauve underneath are set off by big, yellow centres. HEIGHT & SPREAD 30×60cm (1×2ft).

***O.* 'Langtrees'**♀ Yellow and blue centres contrast with pink petals that are bronze-coloured underneath. HEIGHT & SPREAD 30×60cm (1×2ft).

***O.* 'Merriments Joy'**♀ Yellowish green, lance to spoon-shaped leaves set off vivid reddish purple petals with pale, silvery purple undersides. HEIGHT & SPREAD 35×60cm (14×24in).

***O.* 'Pink Whirls'**♀ The spoon-shaped, pink petals have mauve undersides, while the centres are also mauve. This plant is upright. HEIGHT & SPREAD 60×60cm (2×2ft).

▲ *Osteospermum* 'Pink Whirls'

***O.* 'Silver Sparkler'**♀ Variegated cream and green leaves are complemented by flowers with white petals and purple centres. This plant is upright. HEIGHT & SPREAD 60×60cm (2×2ft).

▲ *Osteospermum* 'Silver Sparkler'

***O.* 'Stardust'**♀ Dark purplish red petals with mauve undersides contrast with the yellow to green flower centres. The hairy leaves are olive-green. HEIGHT & SPREAD 45×60cm (18×24in).

***O.* 'Weetwood'**♀ The white flower petals are deep mauve underneath and have yellow-white centres. The leaves are soft green. This is one of the hardiest cultivars. HEIGHT & SPREAD 60×60cm (2×2ft).

▲ *Osteospermum* 'Weetwood'

***O.* 'Whirligig'**♀ Grey-green leaves complement white, rippled, paddle-shaped petals with mauve undersides. The centres of this upright plant are powder-blue. HEIGHT & SPREAD 60×60cm (2×2ft).

CULTIVATION Plant in well-drained soil and in a sunny position in late spring. Staking is not necessary.

PROPAGATION Take semi-ripe stem cuttings in late summer for rooting under glass. Grow on in pots and plant out in spring. Sow the seed of species in late winter for early summer flowering plants.

PESTS AND DISEASES Usually trouble free.

Ostrya

Hop hornbeam

Betulaceae

Ostryas are deciduous trees with good yellow foliage in autumn and moderately slow growth. They bear male and female flowers on the same plant, followed by curious hop-like fruits which are a large part of their appeal. Those listed below cast a pleasant amount of dappled shade which allows grass to grow underneath reasonably well.

▲ *Ostrya carpinifolia*

RECOMMENDED SPECIES AND VARIETIES

O. carpinifolia (hop hornbeam) This shapely broad-headed tree makes an ideal specimen for a large garden in sheltered parts of Britain. Male flowers are in 7.5cm (3in) long, hanging yellow catkins, usually in threes. Females are smaller at 5cm (2in) long and green and reddish at first. They develop into clusters of light brown nuts measuring 5mm (¼in), enclosed in a flat, papery husk. The alternate leaves, up to 8cm (3¼in) long, are broadly oval with a pointed tip, regularly toothed edges and distinct parallel veins. Native to lime-rich valleys and mountain slopes of W Asia and S Europe. HEIGHT & SPREAD 6×4m (20×13ft) after 20 years, ultimately 20m (66ft) tall.

O. virginiana (American hop hornbeam) This sun-loving woodland tree is remarkably tolerant of a range of soils and is also very hardy. It has brown scaly bark and

▲ *Ostrya virginiana*

pointed oval leaves up to 10cm (4in) long with toothed edges. Native to eastern N America. HEIGHT & SPREAD 6×4m (20×13ft) in 20 years, ultimately 18m (60ft) tall.

CULTIVATION Plant out in spring, taking especial care not to disturb the roots. Young plants need protection from strong sunlight, but established trees respond well to good light.

PROPAGATION Sow seed in sandy compost outside in autumn. They may take 18 months to germinate.

PRUNING Pruning is only necessary to tidy damaged branches. Do it in early autumn.

PESTS AND DISEASES Usually trouble free.

Ourisia

Scrophulariaceae

Ourisia coccinea

Graceful flowers appear in summer above the foliage of these creeping evergreen perennials. The flowers, in shades of red, pink or white, are tubular or bell-shaped with five spreading lobes. The recommended plants are all evergreen. Ourisias are hardy and grow best in moist but well-drained, humus-rich soil, especially in the cooler conditions of northern gardens.

RECOMMENDED SPECIES AND VARIETIES

O. coccinea (syn. *O. elegans*) Loose spikes of nodding, scarlet flowers, each 3cm (1¼in) long, with protruding cream stamens, are carried on branched stalks above light green foliage. Oval, heavily veined and toothed leaves form rosettes 6-12.5cm (2½-5in) across. HEIGHT & SPREAD 20×40cm (8×16in).

***O.* 'Loch Ewe'** The clear pale pink flowers of this hybrid form lax whorls up the stem. Light green, oval-leaved rosettes, 6-12.5cm (2½-5in) across, spread to form clumps. HEIGHT & SPREAD 20×30cm (8×12in).

▲ *Ourisia coccinea*

***O.* 'Snowflake'**♀ Single or paired white flowers, 2cm (¾in) long, are borne above a low carpet of small, glossy, oval leaves. HEIGHT & SPREAD 10×15cm (4×6in).

▲ *Ourisia* 'Snowflake'

CULTIVATION Plant in light shade in moist, humus-rich soil. Divide and replant clumps into fresh soil every 3-4 years to maintain vigour. Alternatively, grow in an unheated well-ventilated greenhouse, ensuring plants are kept cool and shaded in summer.

PROPAGATION Divide plants or take small rooted pieces from the edge of a clump of plants in spring, or take greenwood cuttings in early summer. Sow seed of *O. coccinea* in early spring.

PESTS AND DISEASES Slugs and snails are a problem in the open garden.

Our Lady's milk thistle
see *Silybum marianum*

Oxalis

Oxalidaceae

Oxalis acetosella

Most garden species of these low-growing, spreading perennial plants are suitable for a sunny, well-drained spot in a rock garden or at the front of a mixed border. *Oxalis acetosella*, *O. magellanica* and *O. oregana* like damp, shady conditions, such as in woodland or under shrubs, where they naturalise and may spread widely. Many make excellent container plants for a cold greenhouse or conservatory. All species have compound leaves, consisting of three or more leaflets, and flat or cup-shaped five-petalled flowers, which generally open only in sunlight. Most species are moderately hardy, to -5°C (23°F), some are hardy to -15°C (5°F). *O. hirta* and *O. versicolor* are tender.

RECOMMENDED SPECIES AND VARIETIES

O. acetosella (wood sorrel) This hardy, shade-loving British native has clover-like, pale green leaves. It bears white or pale pink flowers, 2cm (¾in) across, in late spring. HEIGHT & SPREAD 5cm×1m (2in×3ft).

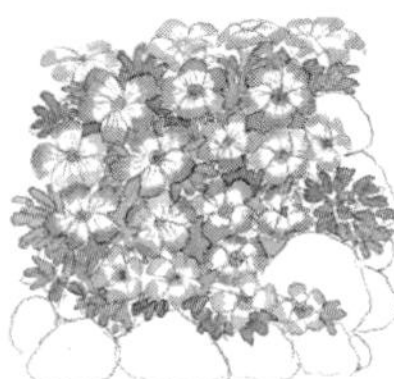

Oxalis adenophylla

O. adenophylla♀ Pink flowers, 2.5cm (1in) across, with a deeper pink centre are borne in early summer by this densely clump-forming, hardy species. Its attractive grey-blue leaves consist of up to 12 radiating leaflets. HEIGHT & SPREAD 10×15cm (4×6in).

***O.* 'Beatrice Anderson'** Pale violet-blue flowers, up to 3cm (1¼in) across, conspicuously veined with dark purple, are borne in early summer above grey-blue leaves with 8-10 umbrella-like, folding leaflets. Moderately hardy. HEIGHT & SPREAD 8×8cm (3¼×3¼in).

O. chrysantha Bright yellow flowers, 1.2cm (½in) across, appear from early to mid summer above glossy, pale green, trefoil leaves. Moderately hardy. HEIGHT & SPREAD 5×30cm (2×12in).

O. deppei see *O. tetraphylla*

O. depressa (syn. *O. inops*) Deep rose, pale-eyed flowers, up to 2cm (¾in) across, are borne in mid summer by this moderately hardy plant. Its grey-green, trefoil leaves make a dense, low-spreading mat. HEIGHT & SPREAD 5×30cm (2×12in).

O. enneaphylla♀ Funnel-shaped flowers, up to 3cm (1¼in) across, varying in colour from white to deep pink, appear in late spring and early summer above tufts of grey-blue leaves with around 9 umbrella-like, folding leaflets. One of the hardy species. HEIGHT & SPREAD 8×15cm (3¼×6in).

'Alba' has pure white flowers. **'Minutifolia'** is similar to the type but this plant is much more compact, with smaller leaves and white flowers. **'Rosea'** has pale purple-pink flowers. **'Rubra'** has deep pinkish red flowers.

O. hirta This tender species produces its light green, clover-like, hairy leaves up the full length of its upright stems. The flowers, deep reddish pink, occasionally white or purple, 2cm (¾in) across, appear from late autumn to mid winter. HEIGHT & SPREAD 30×10cm (12×4in).

O. inops see *O. depressa*

▲ *Oxalis* 'Ione Hecker'

O. 'Ione Hecker'♀ Large, pale violet-blue flowers, up to 3cm (1¼in) across, conspicuously veined with dark purple, appear from late spring to early summer above tufts of grey-blue leaves with around 9 umbrella-like, folding leaflets. Moderately hardy. HEIGHT & SPREAD 8×10cm (3¼×4in).

O. laciniata Flowers 2cm (¾in) across, ranging in colour from pinkish blue to deep blue, are borne in early summer above grey-blue leaves, each consisting of around 10 narrow, folding leaflets. It is a hardy plant but tricky, requiring cool conditions. HEIGHT & SPREAD 5×10cm (2×4in).

O. lactea double form
see *O. magellanica* 'Nelson'

O. lobata Small tufts of pale green leaves with 3-5 leaflets appear in spring, quickly die down for several months, before reappearing in early autumn at the same time as bright yellow, funnel-shaped flowers, 1.5-2cm (½-¾in) across. Moderately hardy. HEIGHT & SPREAD 10×10cm (4×4in).

▲ *Oxalis lobata*

O. magellanica Small white flowers, 1cm (⅜in) across, appear from late spring to late summer above small, clover-like leaves tinged with bronze. This hardy shade-lover can be invasive in moist soils. HEIGHT & SPREAD 5×30cm (2×12in).

'Nelson' (syn. *O. lactea* double form, 'Flore Pleno') is a double flowered cultivar.

O. obtusa In late spring and early summer rose-pink flowers with darker veining, up to 3cm (1¼in) across, are borne above short-stemmed, grey-green, clover-like, hairy leaves. This moderately hardy species does not always flower freely. HEIGHT & SPREAD 5×20cm (2×8in).

O. oregana This hardy shade-lover has green, hairy, clover-like leaves with a central greyish patch on each leaflet. White or pale pink flowers, usually with darker veining, 2cm (¾in) across, appear from late spring to mid summer HEIGHT & SPREAD 15×50cm (6×20in).

O. patagonica Flowers ranging in colour from red to pinkish blue, up to 2.5cm (1in) across, are carried from late spring to mid summer above hairy, grey-blue leaves with around 12 folded leaflets. Moderately hardy. HEIGHT & SPREAD 5×20cm (2×8in).

O. purpurea **'Ken Aslet'** From mid autumn to late winter bright yellow flowers, 2cm (¾in) across, are produced by this moderately hardy plant. Its green leaves, with 3-5 leaflets, are covered in white silky hairs. HEIGHT & SPREAD 10×20cm (4×8in).

O. regnellii
see *O. triangularis* ssp. *papilionacea*

O. tetraphylla (syn. *O. deppei*) (good luck plant) Clusters of 4-10 reddish purple flowers appear from early to late summer. The large leaves, composed of 4 triangular leaflets up to 5cm (2in) long, often have a horizontal purple band near the base of each leaflet. Moderately hardy. HEIGHT & SPREAD 15×15cm (6×6in).

▲ *Oxalis purpurea* 'Ken Aslet'

▲ *Oxalis tetraphylla* 'Iron Cross'

The leaflets of **'Iron Cross'** have a dark purple band, forming a cross on the leaf.

O. triangularis Clusters of pale pink flowers appear in mid summer above reddish purple, clover-like leaves with a darker blotch at the leaflet bases. Moderately hardy. HEIGHT & SPREAD 15×15cm (6×6in).

'Cupido' has very dark purple leaves and lilac-pink flowers. The flowers of ssp. *papilionacea* (syn. *O. regnellii*) are white, the leaves mid green.

O. versicolor The funnel-shaped, 2cm (¾in) wide flowers of this tender species are white with crimson margins on the underside, so that in bud they look striped. They appear from mid summer to early autumn. The leaves are composed of 3 narrow leaflets. HEIGHT & SPREAD 8×20cm (3¼×8in).

CULTIVATION Plant *O. acetosella*, *O. magellanica* and *O. oregana* in moist humus-rich soil in full or partial shade. Plant the other species in full sun in well-drained soil in the garden or under glass. Grow the moderately hardy species in a sheltered, sunny position or in a cold greenhouse or alpine house. The tender species need nearly frost-free conditions and do best in a cold greenhouse or an alpine house. Keep container-grown plants almost dry in winter.

PROPAGATION Divide in spring. Some species are rhizomatous and portions of rhizome can be removed and planted. The following are rhizomatous: *O. acetosella*, *O.* 'Beatrice Anderson', *O. enneaphylla*, *O.* 'Ione Hecker', *O. laciniata*, *O. magellanica*, *O. oregana*, *O. patagonica*, and *O. triangularis*. Some species set seed, which should be sown in late winter or spring.

PESTS AND DISEASES Slugs and snails.

Ox eye see *Buphthalmum*
Oxlip see *Primula elatior*

Oxydendrum

Sorrel tree, sourwood
Ericaceae

Oxydendrum arboreum

Vivid autumnal foliage in shades of red follows the slender, drooping flowerheads of this deciduous shrub or small tree. There is only one species in this genus. Although hardy, the plant needs summer heat to thrive and does best in warmer regions. It prefers an acid soil and produces the best leaf colour when planted in an open site.

▲ *Oxydendrum arboreum*

Oxydendrum arboreum Drooping clusters of tubular white flowers appear in late summer. The plant is at its best in early autumn, when its leaves turn red. The lanceolate leaves have elongated tapering points and reach up to 20cm (8in) long. They sometimes have finely serrated edges. Clothed in deeply furrowed bark, this species usually forms a tree-like shrub, but occasionally develops into a tree 18m (60ft) tall. Native to eastern USA. HEIGHT & SPREAD 1.8×1.5m (6×5ft) after 10 years, ultimately 6m (20ft) tall.

CULTIVATION Plant in autumn or spring in loose, friable acid soil that is moist but well drained. Position in full sun or partial shade.

PROPAGATION Sow shop-bought seed in mid to late winter under glass in peat or sphagnum. Protect from strong sunlight and keep the growing medium moist. Plant out when 3 or 4 years old, keeping root disturbance to a minimum. Alternatively, take softwood cuttings in summer.

PRUNING Not usually necessary, but plants can be shaped or unwanted lower branches removed in winter or early spring.

PESTS AND DISEASES Usually trouble free.

Oxypetalum see *Tweedia*

O

Ozothamnus

Compositae

Ozothamnus ledifolius

The shrubs of this genus are valued for their dense, evergreen foliage. There are smaller species, which suit a rock garden, and larger species to grow in a sunny border. Natives of mountain and heathland in Australia and New Zealand, the plants vary somewhat in hardiness. The species listed below used to belong to *Helichrysum*.

RECOMMENDED SPECIES AND VARIETIES

O. coralloides ♀ Erect, stout branchlets are covered with tiny, scale-like, shiny green leaves. The leaves' white, woolly undersurface shows at the margins and produces a coral-like effect. The flowers, infrequently produced in cultivation, are borne in 6mm (¼in) wide heads composed of tiny yellow florets. This compact shrub is hardy, but it requires perfect drainage. HEIGHT & SPREAD 30×40cm (12×16in) after 5 years, ultimately 40cm (16in) tall.

▲ *Ozothamnus ledifolius*

O. ledifolius ♀ (kerosene bush) The flowers of this small, dense shrub are borne in clusters about 3cm (1¼in) across. In late spring the flower buds are brick-red, opening to white in early summer. The yellow branchlets have narrow, shiny, dark green, leathery leaves about 1cm (⅜in) long with the margins turned under. The uppermost leaves of the plant are erect, showing their yellow felted undersurface and giving the plant a golden effect. Hardy in the southern counties and often successful farther north. HEIGHT & SPREAD 50×40cm (20×16in) after 5 years, ultimately 80cm (32in) tall.

O. rosmarinifolius This is an erect shrub whose slender branchlets, white with woolly hairs, are densely clothed with

▲ *Ozothamnus rosmarinifolius*

needle-like leaves up to 3cm (1¼in) long. The leaves' rough or warty upper surface is bright green and hairless in some forms of the species; greyish and hairy in others. The leaf margins are rolled under and the underside is white. The numerous flower clusters, up to 5cm (2in) across, are purplish or pinkish in bud opening to white, and appear from early to mid summer. The plant is reasonably hardy in southern counties. HEIGHT & SPREAD 1.8×1.2m (6×4ft) after 5 years, ultimately 3m (10ft) tall.

▲ *Ozothamnus rosmarinifolius* 'Silver Jubilee'

'Silver Jubilee' ♀ has white felted branchlets and 2.5cm (1in) long silvery leaves. The flowerheads are pinkish in bud opening to white.

O. selago This hardy rock-garden plant has erect branchlets clothed with small, scale-like, shiny green leaves, pressed flat against the twigs. The flowerheads, 6mm (¼in) across, are composed of numerous creamy white florets, and appear from late spring to early summer. HEIGHT & SPREAD 30×40cm (12×16in) after 5 years, ultimately 40cm (16in) tall.

CULTIVATION Plant in well-drained soil in an open, sunny situation.

PROPAGATION Take small cuttings of one-year-old wood, preferably with a heel, in early or mid spring.

PRUNING No pruning is necessary.

PESTS AND DISEASES Usually trouble free.

p-q

Pachyphragma

Cruciferae

The tiny white flowers begin to appear as winter yields to spring and continue until early summer. New leaves emerge almost as early from the mat formed by overwintering rosettes and the whole plant looks fresh and green by mid spring. This herbaceous perennial, with creeping rhizomes, provides excellent ground cover in shady parts of the garden. *Pachyphragma macrophyllum*, the only species in the genus, is hardy and will even tolerate heavy clay soils.

▲ *Pachyphragma macrophyllum*

Pachyphragma macrophyllum (syn. *Cardamine asarifolia*) Dense clusters of pure white, 4-petalled, 1.5cm (½in) wide flowers, are borne on erect stems. At close range the flowers emit a slightly unpleasant smell. The glossy, overlapping dark green leaves grow from the base. These are kidney-shaped with a scalloped edge and up to 10cm (4in) wide; 4 or 5 similar but smaller leaves grow from the flower stems. When ripe, the flattened pods, up to 12cm (4¾in) long, split open to release smooth brown seeds. HEIGHT & SPREAD 40×80cm (16×32in).

CULTIVATION Plant in autumn or spring in moist ground in partial to deep shade. Plants will thrive in clay or limy soils provided they are not allowed to dry out.

PROPAGATION Divide or take softwood cuttings in late spring. Sow seed in autumn.

PESTS AND DISEASES Usually trouble free.

Pachysandra

Buxaceae

A carpet of rich green or variegated leathery leaves, enlivened by small white flowers in late spring or early summer, provides excellent, weed-suppressing ground cover for shady places. These hardy, evergreen subshrubs are easily grown and particularly useful for the foot of shade-loving shrubs, such as rhododendrons and camellias. Native to E Asia and eastern USA.

▲ *Pachysandra terminalis*

RECOMMENDED SPECIES AND VARIETIES

P. terminalis♀ Creeping, rooting stems produce short erect branches bearing clusters of deep green, coarsely toothed, oval or oblong leaves up to 10cm (4in) long. In early spring white flowers appear in 4cm (1½in) long spikes at the ends of the previous year's shoots. Each spike contains several male flowers with prominent stamens, 1cm (⅜in) long, and a few smaller female flowers at the base. These may be followed by fleshy, oval, white fruits, 1.5cm (½in) long. HEIGHT & SPREAD 20×40cm (8×16in).

▲ *Pachysandra terminalis* 'Variegata'

'Green Carpet' is more compact, with smaller leaves and a height and spread of 10×20cm (4×8in). **'Variegata'**♀ has green leaves edged in creamy white, with a height and spread of 15×40cm (6×16in).

CULTIVATION Plant in early autumn or spring in a fairly moist yet well-drained, leafy soil in partial or full shade. Do not plant on shallow, chalky soils.

PROPAGATION Divide established plants in early autumn or early spring.

PESTS AND DISEASES Usually trouble free.

Pachystachys

Acanthaceae

Tropical, evergreen shrubs from the Americas, these house or greenhouse plants are grown for their striking flowering spikes. They are usually raised from cuttings every year, although it is possible to grow one plant for several years.

▲ *Pachystachys lutea*

RECOMMENDED SPECIES

P. lutea♀ (lollipop plant) Soft mid to deep green, lance-shaped leaves, up to 7.5cm (3in) long, are borne on upright stems. At the end of each stem is a 10cm (4in) spike of bright yellow bracts, from which emerge tubular, 2-lipped white flowers. HEIGHT & SPREAD 45×30cm (18×12in).

CULTIVATION Grow in the home or conservatory at a minimum temperature of 13°C (55°F) and in good but indirect sunlight. Use a soil-based compost, such as John Innes No. 2. Water freely in spring and summer, supplying a high potash liquid feed every 6 weeks. Water sparingly in winter.

PROPAGATION Take softwood cuttings in spring and early summer, then discard the old plant if you wish. Cuttings come into flower after about 3 months.

PRUNING In late winter or early spring cut back hard to encourage the development of vigorous young shoots suitable for cuttings.

PESTS AND DISEASES Red spider mite and whitefly may be troublesome.

Paeonia

Paeony, peony
Paeoniaceae

Paeonia delavayi var. lutea

The showy flowers of peonies are a striking sight in a mixed border and are often gloriously fragrant as well. The genus includes upright deciduous shrubs, also known as tree peonies, and herbaceous perennials which form compact clumps.

The blooms, which make excellent cut flowers, are borne in late spring and early summer. In the species they are single and globe-shaped, with up to ten petals and numerous stamens. The cultivars may be semidouble, with two or three rows of petals around a central boss of stamens; double, with a large number of petals, the inner ones usually smaller and obscuring the stamens; or anemone form, with one or two rows of outer petals and a centre of numerous densely arranged narrow petals derived from the stamens. Most of the cultivars are scented, and tend to flower more profusely than many of the species. The leaves are compound or lobed, some colouring to shades of yellow and red in the autumn, when the seedpods of a few species reveal brightly coloured seeds.

Peonies are tuberous-rooted plants and may take a year or two to become established. They should be allowed to remain where they are for many years as they resent disturbance. They do well in full sun on any fertile soil with plenty of organic material added at planting time. Although most peonies are hardy the shrubs can be caught by spring frost, and if they are planted in a location where early morning sun reaches them, the young growth may be damaged. Native to Europe, temperate Asia, China and NW America. The shrubs included below reach their full size in about five years.

RECOMMENDED SPECIES AND VARIETIES

P. arietina see *P. mascula* ssp. *arietina*

P. cambessedesii ♀ (Majorcan peony) This herbaceous perennial has single deep rose-pink flowers, 10cm (4in) across, with red filaments and purple stigmas. The flowers appear in late spring. The glossy dark green leaves have purple-red veins, stalks and undersurfaces. Each leaf is 25cm (10in) across, made up of lance-shaped leaflets 10cm (4in) long. This species is not reliably hardy, so plant it in a warm part of the garden such as at the base of a south-facing wall. HEIGHT & SPREAD 45×45cm (18×18in).

▲ *Paeonia cambessedesii*

P. corallina see *P. mascula*

***P.* 'Defender'** ♀ The single red blooms of this herbaceous perennial appear in late spring. The flowers are up to 15cm (6in) across with a central mass of yellow stamens. The glossy bright green leaves are 20cm (8in) wide, composed of elliptic to oblong leaflets up to 8cm (3¼in) long. HEIGHT & SPREAD 75×75cm (2½×2½ft).

▲ *Paeonia delavayi*

P. delavayi ♀ This shrubby tree peony bears deep maroon-red single flowers, 8cm (3¼in) across, with yellow anthers in late spring. The stiff stems bear deeply cut shiny leaves, up to 30cm (12in) across, dark green above and blue-green beneath. Each leaflet is up to 10cm (4in) long. HEIGHT & SPREAD 1.8×1m (6×3ft).

The golden yellow flowers of var. ***ludlowii*** ♀ (syn. *P. lutea* var. *ludlowii*) (Tibetan peony) are up to 12cm (4¾in) in diameter. They are unscented. The yellow flowers of var. ***lutea*** (syn. *P. lutea*) are unscented, up to 7.5cm (3in) across and carried in small clusters. The leaves are mid green.

P. emodi Fragrant, single white flowers, 12cm (4¾in) across with a central boss of golden yellow stamens, are borne in late spring. The glossy fresh green dissected foliage, up to 15cm (6in) wide, has 9 or more leaflets, each 17cm (6¾in) long. In cold gardens this herbaceous perennial needs winter protection. It tolerates light shade. HEIGHT & SPREAD 1×1m (3×3ft).

P. lactiflora This erect herbaceous perennial bears fragrant single white flowers, 6–10cm (2½–4in) across, in early summer. It has divided leaves up to 15cm (6in) wide with three stalks each carrying three leaflets up to 10cm (4in) long. HEIGHT & SPREAD 60×60cm (2×2ft).

'Adolphe Rousseau' has deep red double flowers, while those of **'Alexander Fleming'** are bright rose-pink. **'Bowl of Beauty'** ♀ bears semidouble, soft pink flowers with conspicuous golden yellow stamens which look like narrow petals. **'Duchesse de Nemours'** ♀ (syn. 'Mrs Gwyn Lewis') has strongly scented, double flowers with very large incurving outer petals, tinged with palest green and fading to white, and creamy yellow inner petals with irregular edges. The very fragrant double flowers of **'Félix Crousse'** ♀ (syn. 'Victor Hugo') are rich carmine with dark red centres, and ruffled, often white-tipped petals. **'Festiva Maxima'** ♀ produces scented, double flowers, composed of pure white outer petals, while the inner petals are white with a basal crimson blotch.

▲ *Paeonia lactiflora* 'Bowl of Beauty'

'Lady Alexandra Duff' ♀ has scented, soft pink, double blooms. The flowers of **'Laura Dessert'** ♀ are scented and double, the outer petals a creamy blush white, the incurving inner petals a rich lemon-yellow, often with deeply cut edges. **'Monsieur Jules Elie'** ♀ has silvery rose, large and fully double blooms. **'Sarah Bernhardt'** ♀ has double, scented flowers with apple-blossom pink petals, ruffled at the edges. **'White**

▲ *Paeonia lactiflora* 'Sarah Bernhardt'

▲ *Paeonia lactiflora* 'White Wings'

Wings' has single, scented, white blooms with prominent yellow stamens. The foliage of **'Whitleyi Major'**♀ (syn. 'The Bride') colours well in autumn. The single, ivory-white flowers have yellow anthers.
P. lutea see *P. delavayi* var. *lutea*.
P. lutea var. ***ludlowii*** see *P. delavayi* var. *ludlowii*

▲ *Paeonia mascula*

P. mascula (syn. *P. corallina*) Red, pink or occasionally white, single flowers are seen on this hardy herbaceous perennial from late spring to early summer. The flowers are 12cm (4¾in) across and have a central mass of yellow stamens. The glossy bright green leaves have 9-15 oval leaflets and are up to 25cm (10in) across. Position in full sun. HEIGHT & SPREAD 60cm×1m (2×3ft).

▼ *Paeonia mascula* ssp. *arietina*

The leaves of ssp. ***arietina*** (syn. *P. arietina*) are glossy dark green with hairy undersides. The single pinky red flowers are borne in late spring. Its cultivar **'Northern Glory'** has grey-green leaves and deep magenta flowers.

▲ *Paeonia mascula* ssp. *arietina* 'Northern Glory'

P. mlokosewitschii♀ Soft bluish green foliage is topped by single lemon-yellow flowers, 12cm (4¾in) across, in mid to late spring. This herbaceous perennial is a dwarf plant suitable for the front of the border. The leaves, up to 12cm (4¾in) across, are composed of broadly oval leaflets 6cm (2½in) across, and often have good autumn tints. HEIGHT & SPREAD 75×75cm (2½×2½ft).
P. obovata♀ Rose-pink flowers, 7cm (2¾in) in diameter, are borne in late spring. The shiny dark green leaves, about 20cm (8in) across, are composed of leaflets 15cm (6in) long. This herbaceous perennial is better suited to semi-shade than full sun. HEIGHT & SPREAD 60×60cm (2×2ft).

The flowers of var. ***alba***♀ have white petals with crimson bases and a central circle of golden stamens.
P. officinalis This herbaceous perennial is the parent of the traditional cottage-garden peonies. The fragrant single flowers are crimson, 15cm (6in) across, with yellow stamens. The glossy bright green leaves, 15cm (6in) across, are composed of elliptic to oblong leaflets up to 11cm (4¼in) long. HEIGHT & SPREAD 60×60cm (2×2ft).

Paeonia officinalis 'Rubra Plena'

'Anemoniflora Rosea'♀ has deep pink flowers with yellow stamens like small petals. **'Rosea Plena'**♀ has deep pink flowers. **'Rubra Plena'**♀ has crimson blooms.
P. peregrina **'Otto Froebel'**♀ In early summer, this herbaceous perennial has vermilion single flowers 12cm (4¾in) across.

▲ *Paeonia officinalis* 'Rosea Plena'

Its shiny green leaves, up to 12cm (4¾in) across, are composed of up to 17 segments, each 2cm (¾in) wide. This is generally a rather difficult plant to establish in gardens. It does best in a warm spot such as the base of a south-facing wall. HEIGHT & SPREAD 1m×60cm (3×2ft).
P. suffruticosa (Moutan peony, tree peony) This species, the authentic tree peony, makes a stately plant for a shrub border. Bowl-shaped flowers, 15cm (6in) across, open in late spring. Colour varies but flowers are usually white with a magenta or pink blotch at the base of each petal; pink and red forms also occur. The deeply cut leaves, 30cm (12in) across, are glossy dark green above and blue-green beneath. Each of the lobed leaflets is up to 10cm (4in) long. HEIGHT & SPREAD 2×1.5m (6½×5ft).

▲ *Paeonia suffruticosa*

'Rock's Variety' has large white flowers with a maroon blotch on the inner petals. There are also many double-flowered cultivars available in a range of colours.
P. veitchii A profusion of single crimson-purple flowers appear in late spring. Each flower is up to 10cm (4in) in diameter. With fresh green dissected leaves, about 12cm (4¾in) across, this herbaceous perennial makes a compact clump. Bluish seeds

▲ *Paeonia veitchii*

follow the flowers in autumn. HEIGHT & SPREAD 60×60cm (2×2ft).

The flowers of var. ***woodwardii*** are paler, in varying shades of pink.

CULTIVATION Plant herbaceous perennials from autumn to spring and shrubby peonies in autumn. All prefer a fertile, well-drained soil and a position in full sun.

Set the young plants of the herbaceous species so that the buds are about 2.5cm (1in) below the soil. Provide some support for the plants. Remove dead flowers as they fade. Cut down herbaceous perennials after the foliage has died in autumn.

PROPAGATION Sow ripe seed of species in pots of loam-based compost in a coldframe in autumn. Plant out in autumn if the seedlings are large enough, or grow on for another year.

Propagate cultivars of herbaceous perennials by careful division of existing clumps in autumn, cutting with a knife to ensure that the tuberous roots are not damaged too much in the process. Cultivars of shrubby species are propagated by grafting, usually carried out by specialists.

PRUNING Prune shrubby species after flowering occasionally to keep the shape and size required. Annual pruning is not necessary.

PESTS AND DISEASES Peonies can be attacked by chrysanthemum eelworms as well as swift moth caterpillars. The most widespread problem is peony wilt. Peony blotch produces grey-brown spots with reddish margins on the leaves and stems. Grey mould and viruses also afflict peonies.

Paeony see *Paeonia*
Pagoda tree see *Sophora japonica*
Painted lady see *Gladiolus carneus*
Painted tongue see *Salpiglossis sinuata*
Palm, Canary Island date see *Phoenix canariensis*
Palm, Chusan see *Trachycarpus fortunei*
Palm, date see *Phoenix*
Palm, kentia see *Howea fosteriana*
Palm, parlour see *Chamaedorea elegans*
Palm, sentry see *Howea*
Panicum see GRASSES p.300
Pansy see *Viola*

Papaver

Poppy

Papaveraceae

Papaver alpinum

Bright-flowering favourites of cottage and rock gardens, poppies range from quick-growing annuals to robust herbaceous and evergreen perennials. They are mostly sun-loving, preferring a well-drained site, and are ideally suited to wildflower gardens or for filling gaps in herbaceous borders.

The flowers – usually with four petals but sometimes more – come in a large range of colours, including white, yellow, pink, purple, violet, orange, red and almost black. The pods, containing numerous seeds, vary in shape from globular to oval, with a distinctive ring of pores at the top. They are not particularly decorative except for those of *Papaver somniferum*, which can be dried and used in floral arrangements. When cut, most species exude an orange or yellowish latex which can irritate the skin.

RECOMMENDED SPECIES AND VARIETIES

P. alpinum hort. (alpine poppy) White, yellow, orange or occasionally salmon-pink flowers, up to 4cm (1½in) across, appear in late spring and until mid summer if deadheaded. These dainty little tufted evergreen perennials are short-lived and are often grown as annuals as they self-sow readily in the garden. They have grey or grey-green finely divided leaves. The pods are small, barrel-shaped and bristly. HEIGHT & SPREAD 20×20 cm (8×8in).

'Alba' (syn. f. *album*) has white flowers with a boss of yellow stamens. **'Summer Breeze'** provides a fine selection of F_1 hybrids with flowers in shades of red, orange, yellow and white above a mound of grey foliage.

P. atlanticum (Moroccan poppy) Dull orange, saucer-shaped flowers, about 6cm (2½in) across, are borne on wiry branched stems in late spring and throughout summer. An evergreen perennial, it has deeply divided, rough leaves mostly crowded into a basal rosette. The seedpod is club-shaped and smooth. The plant self-sows in the garden. HEIGHT & SPREAD 50×50cm (20×20in).

'Flore Pleno' has semidouble flowers. **'Double Orange'** has semidouble and double, brick-red to tangerine blooms.

P. bracteatum see *P. orientale*

P. commutatum♀ In mid summer this annual species bears vivid scarlet flowers 6-9cm (2½-3½in) across with a large black blotch in the centre of each petal. The fleshy, bristly leaves are deeply divided. The seed capsule is smooth and almost spherical. HEIGHT & SPREAD 45×45cm (1½×1½ft).

▲ *Papaver commutatum* 'Ladybird'

'Ladybird' is a particularly large-flowered form with a big black blotch in the middle of each petal.

P. heldreichii see *P. spicatum*

P. lateritium Small fiery orange flowers, up to 5cm (2in) across, appear in late spring and early summer. A rhizomatous patch-forming herbaceous perennial, this species has lance-shaped, coarsely toothed leaves. HEIGHT & SPREAD 50×50 cm (20×20 in).

The species is quite rare in gardens and is generally represented by the following cultivar. **'Fireball'** (syn. 'Nanum', *P. orientale* 'Flore Pleno') is smaller, at only 30cm (1ft) tall, and has double orange flowers.

P. miyabeanum Pale yellow flowers up to 4cm (1½in) across are held on bristly stems in late spring and throughout summer. A delightful, little short-lived, evergreen perennial poppy, it has tufts of greyish, rough, deeply divided leaves and bristly round seedpods. It self-sows easily. HEIGHT & SPREAD 10×10cm (4×4in).

P. nudicaule (Iceland poppy) Bowl-shaped, bright yellow to orange or red flowers, 4-6cm (1½-2½in) across, appear in late spring and early summer if sown in autumn, or from mid to late summer if sown in spring. This annual or short-lived evergreen perennial forms basal tufts of yellowish or greyish green, deeply divided leaves. The seed capsule is club-shaped to oblong and covered with bristles. HEIGHT & SPREAD 45×45cm (1½×1½ft).

The cultivars mostly have large flowers, up to 12.5cm (5in) across. **'Aurora Borealis'** has large flowers in a wide range of colours from white to yellow, orange, salmon and red. **Champagne Bubbles Group**, to 40cm (16in) tall, has large flowers in various shades from yellow to red. **Garden Gnome (Gartenwerg) Group**, a dwarf strain to 30cm (12in) only, has flowers in the full range of colours from white and yellow through salmon and orange to red. **'Kelmscott Giant'** is about 80cm (32in) tall with flowers in pastel colours.

pq

'Oregon Rainbows' has single or semi-double blooms, up to 18cm (7in) wide, in the full colour range from white and yellow through to red, including bicolors and picotees with a darker or paler rim. **'San Remo'** produces single flowers which are mostly in yellows, oranges and reds. **'Unwins Giant Coonara'** is up to 50cm (20in) tall, with flowers in yellow, orange and red. **Wonderland Hybrids** provide dwarf plants in the full colour range.

Papaver orientale

P. orientale (oriental poppy) The deep red flowers, 10-15cm (4-6in) across, usually have a violet-black blotch at the base of the 4-6 petals. They appear from early to mid summer. This robust, bristly, herbaceous perennial forms large clumps, generally spreading by underground runners and with bristly, deep green, oblong to lance-shaped, deeply divided leaves up to 30cm (12in) long. The seed pod is round and smooth. HEIGHT & SPREAD 90×70cm (36×28in).

The cultivars of *P. orientale* listed here are 60-75cm (24-30in) tall unless stated otherwise. **'Allegro'** has bright scarlet petals with bold black blotches at their base. **'Beauty of Livermere'**♀ is 1.2m (4ft) tall with scarlet flowers with a large black

▲ *Papaver orientale*

Papaver orientale 'Allegro' ▼

▲ *Papaver orientale* 'Curlilocks'

blotch at the base of each petal. **'Black and White'**♀ has white petals with black blotches. **'Blue Moon'** is 1m (3ft) tall with flowers up to 25cm (10in) across that are mauve-pink with black at the base of each petal and maroon veins on their reverse. **'Cedric's Pink'** (syn. 'Cedric Morris') has soft pink petals with black blotches and is 1m (3ft) tall. **'Curlilocks'** has orange-red petals with a black blotch at their base and distinctive lacerated edges. **'Doubloon'** is 1m (3ft) tall with orange-red, unblotched double flowers. **'Indian Chief'** has mahogany-red unblotched flowers. **'Ladybird'** is 60cm (2ft) tall and its flowers are vermilion with a black blotch at the base of each petal. **'Marcus Perry'** is a vigorous plant with orange-scarlet, unblotched blooms. **'Mrs Perry'**♀ has rich salmon-pink flowers, each petal with a black blotch at the base. **'Perry's White'**, 1m (3ft) tall, has pure white flowers with a dark centre and a boss of violet-black stamens. **'Picotee'** has frilled white petals with a distinctive orange edge.

▲ *Papaver orientale* 'Mrs Perry'

Papaver orientale 'Perry's White' ▼

'Prinzessin Victoria Louise' has salmon-rose flowers, each petal with a black basal blotch. **'Salmon Glow'** is 1m (3ft) tall, with double salmon-pink flowers; **'Scarlet King'** has blood-red double flowers on stems 1m (3ft) high. **'Türkenlouis'**♀ is 1m (3ft) tall. The petals are deep scarlet, with a black basal blotch and finely cut edges.

P. rhoeas (common poppy, corn poppy, Flander's poppy) The early to mid summer flowers of this annual species are rich scarlet, occasionally paler red, pink or white, up to 9cm (3½in) across, with broad, rounded, overlapping petals with or without a black basal blotch. The leaves are lobed, with narrow, toothed segments and the seed capsule is rounded and smooth. HEIGHT & SPREAD 60×30cm (2×1ft).

▲ *Papaver orientale* 'Picotee'

Papaver orientale 'Prinzessin Victoria Louise' ▲

'Mother of Pearl' has single flowers in pastel shades of pink, silvery white and white. **Shirley** poppies are single-flowered plants in shades of red, pink, mauve, lilac and white, including bicolors and picotees edged with a darker or lighter colour. **Double Shirley** poppies are also available.

P. rupifragum Brick-red flowers, up to 4.5cm (1¾in) across, appear on branched, leafy stems in late spring and summer. It is a herbaceous perennial with grey-green, more or less smooth, deeply divided leaves. HEIGHT & SPREAD 50×50cm (20×20in).

'Flore Pleno' has semidouble flowers.

P. somniferum♀ (opium poppy) This fleshy upright annual has cup-shaped flowers that are white to pink or purple, up to 12.5cm (5in) across, the base of each petal normally with a dark blotch. The flowers open in mid summer and are followed by large, smooth, rounded grey-green seedpods, widely used in dried flower arrangements. HEIGHT & SPREAD 1m×30cm (3×1ft).

Many of the fully double forms are referred to as **Peony-Flowered Group**, named according to flower colour. Forms with double flowers and fringed petals are referred to as the **Carnation-Flowered Group**. Other cultivars include **'Hen and Chickens'**, with single pink flowers and large seedpods surrounded by numerous minor pods, **'Pink Chiffon'**, with pale pink flowers, and **'White Cloud'**, with large double white flowers with lacerated petals.

▲ *Papaver somniferum*

P. spicatum (syn. *P. heldreichii*) From early to mid summer spikes of flattish pale brick-red flowers are borne on stiff stems which rise out of a basal tuft of grey-green leaves. The flowers of this stout herbaceous perennial are up to 4.5cm (1¾in) across. HEIGHT & SPREAD 70×40cm (28×16in).

CULTIVATION Plant in a sunny well-drained site, though *P. atlanticum* and *P. rupifragum* will tolerate partial shade. Sow the annual species thinly where they are required to flower and provide some support when they come into bloom. With the exception of *P. nudicaule*, annuals dislike transplanting.

Plant the perennials in early spring. Dress the larger species with bone meal or mulch with well-rotted manure. Apart from *P. lateritium* and *P. orientale*, perennials resent disturbance once established.

PROPAGATION Sow seed in late autumn or early spring in pots in a coldframe. Divide *P. orientale* or take root cuttings after flowering in mid to late summer.

PESTS AND DISEASES Slugs and snails may attack seedlings. Aphids may attack plants in bud. *P. miyabeanum* and *P. spicatum* suffer from neck rot.

Paphiopedilum see ORCHIDS p. 465

Paradisea

Asphodelaceae

Fragrant white flowers adorn the slender stems of the two species in this genus in summer. Grey-green foliage offsets the almost translucent petals. These herbaceous perennials are suitable for growing in borders or at the edges of wooded areas and around shrubs.

RECOMMENDED SPECIES AND VARIETIES

P. liliastrum (paradise lily, St Bruno's lily) From 3-10 fragrant, funnel-shaped flowers, up to 5cm (2in) long and as wide at the mouth, bloom in loose, one-sided spikes from early to mid summer. Each of the 6 petal-like tepals (modified leaves fused with petals) has a green spot at the tip. The 4-7 linear leaves, up to 25cm (10in) long, arise from the base and tend to wither when flowering is over. Clusters of short, fleshy rhizomes with fibrous roots form distinct clumps. The fruits have 3 compartments filled with plentiful, small, ridged seeds. Native to S Europe. HEIGHT & SPREAD 60×45cm (2×1½ft).

▲ *Paradisea liliastrum*

'Major'♀ is a strong-growing plant with slightly larger flowers than the species.

P. lusitanica Sweet-smelling, bell-shaped flowers, 4cm (1½in) across, are carried in 2 layers of loose clusters in early summer. Each stem bears 20-25 flowers. The leaves are up to 25cm (10in) long. This species can be grown in dappled shade as ground cover. Native to Portugal and Spain. HEIGHT & SPREAD 75cm×1m (2½×3ft).

CULTIVATION Plant in early spring in well-drained, fertile soil that does not dry out and in a sunny or partially shaded spot.

PROPAGATION Divide in spring or after flowering. Sow seed when ripe or in spring.

PESTS AND DISEASES Slugs and snails may attack young plants.

Parahebe

Scrophulariaceae

Parahebe catarractae

Pretty white, pink or blue flowers bloom profusely all through summer and into autumn on these evergreen sub-shrubs. Plants are low-growing and bushy, with soft stems and woody bases. The hardy species are ideal for the rock garden and for edging borders and beds, and can also be grown in containers. The four-petalled flowers, up to 2cm (¾in) across, differ in shape from species to species, as do the leaves. All the species listed here are hardy. They all come from New Zealand, except *Parahebe perfoliata*, which is native to Australia.

RECOMMENDED SPECIES AND VARIETIES

***P. × bidwillii* 'Kea'** White flowers with purple-red veining are borne in racemes up to 25cm (10in) long. The green leaves, about 6mm (¼in) long, are oval, with incised edges. The prostrate branches with upturned ends often root at the nodes. HEIGHT & SPREAD 15×15cm (6×6in).

P. catarractae♀ White, pink or blue flowers are borne among leaves that are green or bronze, oval to lance-shaped, toothed and up to 7cm (2¾in) long. This is a variable species, ranging from prostrate to bushy and erect in growing habit. HEIGHT & SPREAD 6-50×50cm (2½-20×20in).

'Delight'♀ carries 20cm (8in) long clusters of violet-blue flowers with reddish purple centres and veining. The leaves are slightly bronzed and about 2.5cm (1in) long. This cultivar grows up to 25cm (10in) tall. The flowers of ssp. ***diffusa*** are white, pink or blue, and the plant has a prostrate habit. The white form of *P. catarractae* is similar to 'Delight', its white flowers with reddish purple centres and veins.

▲ *Parahebe catarractae* 'Delight'

P. decora Widely spaced white flowers, decorated with pink veins, grow in stiffly erect racemes up to 15cm (6in) tall. The leaves of this tiny, creeping, rooting species are green to purplish and only 3mm (⅛in) long. HEIGHT & SPREAD 15×30cm (6×12in).

P. lyallii The most common form has cup-shaped, white flowers with red centres and veins. Racemes up to 7cm (2¾in) long carry as many as 20 flowers. The leaves are broad, toothed and up to 1.5cm (½in) long. HEIGHT & SPREAD 15×60cm (6×24in).

'Clarence' bears lilac flowers.

P. 'Mervyn' Violet-blue flowers grow in racemes up to 10cm (4in) long, among green to purplish, rounded, toothed leaves. HEIGHT & SPREAD 10×25cm (4×10in).

▲ *Parahebe perfoliata*

P. perfoliata ♀ (digger's speedwell) The violet-blue flowers are widely spaced on the 10cm (4in) long racemes. Sprawling, wiry branches, 1m (3ft) or more in length, bear rounded, glaucous, blue-green leaves, sometimes toothed, up to 3cm (1¼in) wide. HEIGHT & SPREAD 1×1.5m (3×5ft).
CULTIVATION Plant in any soil that is well drained but not too dry at any time of year. Choose an open situation, in the sun or half shade. Cut back straggling growth after flowering and shear off old seed capsules.
PROPAGATION Small softwood cuttings taken at any time will root easily.
PESTS AND DISEASES Aphids may occasionally attack. Downy mildew can be troublesome in early autumn or spring.

Paris

Herb Paris
Trilliaceae

These shade-loving, hardy, herbaceous, woodland perennials are grown for their unusual flowers and prominent seed capsules. A single flower is borne at the top of each upright, unbranched stem which arises from the underground rhizomes. The flowers have green, leaf-like sepals, narrow petals and long stamens, and bloom in early summer. Immediately below each flower is a symmetrical whorl of leaves. A rounded, green or purple seed capsule, 2cm (¾in) wide, develops at the centre of each flower. The capsule turns brown and splits in late summer, revealing fleshy, black or red (poisonous) seeds. Plants suit a mixed or shrub border, perhaps within a woodland edge.
RECOMMENDED SPECIES AND VARIETIES
P. polyphylla (syn. *Daiswa polyphylla*) Green flowers, 15cm (6in) wide, are composed of 4-6 green sepals, equally long yellow petals and about 20 shorter greenish stamens. At the base of each flower is a whorl of deep green lance-shaped to oval leaves up to 15cm (6in) long. The seeds are bright red. Native to China and the Himalayas. HEIGHT & SPREAD 30-90×30cm (12-36×12in).

P. thibetica (syn. *Daiswa thibetica*) This plant has flowers slightly smaller than those of *P. polyphylla*, with yellowish green sepals, 5 linear petals and about 10 conspicuous creamy yellow stamens elongated into threads. The leaves are ovate, mid green and about 5cm (2in) long. The seeds are red. Native to the Himalayas. HEIGHT & SPREAD 20×15cm (8×6in).

▲ *Paris quadrifolia*

P. quadrifolia Each flower, about 6cm (2½in) wide, has 4 lance-shaped green sepals, up to 3cm (1¼in) long, and 4 petals. The mid green ovate leaves are up to 8cm (3¼in) long. The seed capsule is also green and the seeds are black. Native to Europe. HEIGHT & SPREAD 30×15cm (12×6in).
CULTIVATION Plant in partial shade in humus-rich soil, keeping plants moist at all times. Mark their position well, as they only come into growth in late spring.
PROPAGATION Divide clumps in spring. Sow seed in autumn and keep cool. If grown from seed, top growth may not appear until the second spring after sowing and flowering takes 5 years or more.
PESTS AND DISEASES Slugs and snails may attack young growth.

Parodia see CACTI p.106

Parrotia

Persian ironwood
Hamamelidaceae

Parrotia persica

There is just one species in this genus, a hardy deciduous tree, which brings spectacular autumn colour to the garden with its amber, crimson and gold foliage. Then, in mid winter, the bare, spreading branches become studded with tiny red flowers. An additional bonus is the attractive flaking bark seen on older trees.

▲ *Parrotia persica*

Parrotia persica ♀ The tree has a rounded habit, being almost as broad as it is tall. The flowers, consisting of red stamens only, emerge in dense clusters 1.5cm (½in) across, one cluster from each chocolate-brown bud case, in mid to late winter. The leaves are ovate with wavy edges and up to 12.5cm (5in) long. As the smooth, grey bark flakes away, an attractive pink and creamy yellow pattern develops on the trunk, shown to best advantage if the lower branches are removed. Native to N Iran and the Caucasus. HEIGHT & SPREAD 4×3m (13×10ft) after 20 years, ultimately 12m (40ft) tall.

▲ *Parrotia persica* 'Pendula'

'Pendula', with a domed habit and pendulous branches, is a smaller tree.
CULTIVATION Plant in well-drained, loamy soil between late autumn and mid spring. Site in sun, preferably, or light shade.
PROPAGATION Layer in autumn, digging up and transplanting rooted sections to new sites about 18 months later. Alternatively, sow seed in mid or late spring.
PRUNING No pruning is required, except to control the shape or size of the tree, best done between late autumn and early spring.
PESTS AND DISEASES Usually trouble free.

Parrot's bill see *Clianthus puniceus*
Parsley (culinary herb) see HERBS p.332
Parsnip see p.742
Pasqueflower see *Pulsatilla*
Passionflower see *Passiflora*

Parthenocissus

Vitaceae

Parthenocissus tricuspidata

Broad leaves that colour brilliantly before falling in autumn grace these vigorous deciduous climbers, which include virginia creeper. The foliage is cut into three to seven leaflets or is broadly lobed. Leaf tendrils which twine or adhere by adhesive pads make the plants suitable for walls or tree trunks. Species with twining tendrils may also be trained over hedges and large shrubs.

Small, often minute, greenish flowers with five petals appear in flattened compound clusters in late spring or summer. After a hot dry summer they may be followed by small blue-black or blue grapes. The genus is native to N America, E Asia and the Himalayas. The recommended plants are hardy to at least -5°C (23°F).

▲ *Parthenocissus henryana*

RECOMMENDED SPECIES AND VARIETIES

P. henryana♀ (syn. *Ampelopsis henryana*) A silvery white vein pattern, often tinted pink, enhances dark green velvety leaves, which turn red in autumn. The leaves have 3-5 toothed, oval, radiating leaflets, 4-12.5cm (1½-5in) long. Smooth, angled stems have sucker-tipped tendrils. North or east walls are best for cultivation and colouring. HEIGHT & SPREAD 3.5×2.4m (12×8ft) after 5 years, ultimately 10×6m (33×20ft).

P. quinquefolia♀ (virginia creeper) Matt green leaves turn stunning shades of crimson in autumn. The leaves, 2.5-10cm (1-4in) long, have 3 or 5 slender-tipped, coarsely serrated, radiating leaflets with paler undersides. Flowers in forked pompom-like arrangements, 6cm (2½in) across, open in late spring or early summer followed by tiny blue-black grapes. This vigorous, branching plant is best grown to the tops of trees. However, it may be prudent to cut plants

▲ *Parthenocissus tricuspidata*

back to limit their spread on walls or fences. HEIGHT & SPREAD 4.5×3m (15×10ft) after 5 years, ultimately 15×9m (50×30ft).

Smaller leaflets distinguish var. ***englemannii***.

P. tricuspidata♀ (Boston ivy) Maple-like deep green leaves, 5-20cm (2-8in) wide, turn rich crimson and scarlet in autumn. They are usually 3-lobed but sometimes comprise 3 leaflets. This species has pads at the tips of tendrils and, once established, is a rapid, branching grower, especially up trees where it can reach 18m (60ft) on maturity. In early to mid summer, yellow-green flowers appear on short sideshoots in arching clusters up to 5cm (2in) wide. The dark blue fruit is 1cm (⅜in) wide with a waxy patina. It is hardy to -15°C (5°F). HEIGHT & SPREAD 4.5×3m (15×10ft) in 5 years, ultimately 12×10m (40×33ft).

'Beverley Brook' is less vigorous with smaller leaves. **'Green Spring'** has bright green, glossy leaves 15-25cm (6-10in) wide, which turn reddish purple in autumn. **'Lowii'** is a vigorous, deciduous, woody-stemmed tendril climber with deeply cut crinkled leaves that turn crimson in autumn. **'Veitchii'** (syn. *Ampelopsis tricuspidata* 'Veitchii', *A. veitchii*) has purple-flushed leaves when young which take on spectacular reddish purple hues in autumn.

CULTIVATION Plant container-grown stock at any time, but ideally between mid autumn and early spring. Dig a pit 60cm (2ft) square and 45cm (18in) deep close to the base of a wall or large tree. Fill with a mixture of well-rotted manure or garden compost and loamy soil. Support young growth until self-clinging. Pinch out the growing points to encourage horizontal branching.

PROPAGATION Take semi-ripe cuttings in late summer or early autumn and grow one to a pot in sandy soil in a propagating frame at 13-16°C (55-61°F). Take hardwood cuttings 25-30cm (10-12in) long in late autumn and insert them to about half their length in a sheltered outside border. Layer long shoots in mid to late autumn and sever after one year.

PRUNING Remove unwanted or overcrowded growth during summer.

PESTS AND DISEASES Scale insects, weevils and red spider mites may be a problem. Aphids can infest young growth.

Pasqueflower see *Pulsatilla*

Passiflora

Passion flower

Passifloraceae

Passiflora caerulea

Extraordinary intricately formed flowers distinguish this intriguing genus of mainly evergreen climbing plants, native to warm regions of the Americas. The flowers consist of ten brightly coloured petals – strictly speaking, five outer sepals and five petals proper – surrounding a distinctive central 'crown' (corona) of thread-like filaments. These filaments are often in several rows and in bands of different colours. Within the corona is a stalk carrying the five pollen-bearing stamens and the three styles. Many species produce edible, egg-shaped or rounded, fleshy fruit known as passion fruit or granadilla. These are mostly yellow or orange and ripen in the autumn. The plants climb by means of clinging tendrils and have oval or multilobed leaves.

The recommended plants, with the exception of *Passiflora caerulea* which is moderately hardy, need a heated greenhouse or conservatory. Although most are vigorous and can grow many metres tall, they are usually cut back hard in cultivation.

RECOMMENDED SPECIES AND VARIETIES

P. alata♀ Deep crimson fragrant flowers, up to 12.5cm (5in) across, appear in spring and summer. The prominent corona has filaments up to 4cm (1½in) long, which are banded with purple, red and white. The

▲ *Passiflora alata*

egg-shaped fruits, up to 10cm (4in) long, are yellow. The dark green, oval or lance-shaped leaves are up to 15cm (6in) long. This plant needs a minimum temperature of 13°C (55°F). HEIGHT & SPREAD 5×1m (16×3ft).

P. × ***alatocaerulea*** (syn. *P.* × *belotii*) The flowers, produced in summer, are 12.5cm (5in) across, pale rose to purple with white exteriors and violet-blue filaments up to 2.5cm (1in) long. This plant, with mainly 3-lobed leaves up to 15cm (6in) long, needs a minimum temperature of 6°C (43°F). HEIGHT & SPREAD 7×1m (23×3ft).

P. **'Allardii'** White flowers shaded with purplish pink, up to 12.5cm (5in) wide, appear in summer and autumn. The corona has deep cobalt-blue filaments. The leaves are usually divided into 3 lance-shaped leaflets, each up to 5cm (2in) long. This hybrid is on the borderline of hardiness and is best grown in a cool greenhouse or conservatory. HEIGHT & SPREAD 7×1m (23×3ft).

▲ *Passiflora alatocaerulea*

▲ *Passiflora* 'Allardii'

P. ***amethystina***♀ The blue flowers with dark purple filaments appear in autumn or on and off throughout a warm year. The flowers are rarely more than 10cm (4in) across. Yellowish oval fruits, up to 7.5cm (3in) long, are occasionally produced. This luxuriant climber has 3-lobed leaves up to

▲ *Passiflora antioquiensis*

10cm (4in) long. The minimum temperature needed is 5°C (41°F). HEIGHT & SPREAD 7×1m (23×3ft).

P. ***antioquiensis***♀ Rose-red flowers, up to 12.5cm (5in) across, with small violet coronas, appear in profusion on long, drooping stems throughout summer. The deeply lobed leaves are up to 15cm (6in) long. One of the easiest and most colourful passion flowers for a conservatory or cool greenhouse, it tolerates temperatures as low as 5°C (41°F). HEIGHT & SPREAD 7×1m (23×3ft).

P. × ***belotii*** see *P.* × *alatocaerulea*

P. ***caerulea***♀ (syn. *P. chinensis, P. mayana*) (common passion flower) The mildly fragrant flowers of this hardy species are white, flushed with pink or purple. The coronas are blue, white and purple-banded. The flowers measure up to 10cm (4in) across. Produced in summer and early autumn, they are often followed by yellow or orange oval fruits up to 7.5cm (3in) long. The 5 to 7-lobed leaves are up to 15cm (6in) across. HEIGHT & SPREAD 10×1m (33×3ft).

'Constance Elliott'♀ has distinctive ivory-white flowers and conspicuous deep red stigmas.

P. × ***caeruleoracemosa***♀ Deep violet flowers, up to 7.5cm (3in) across, with deep purple-violet filaments appear in summer and early autumn. The leaves, with 3-5 lobes, are up to 12.5cm (5in) across. This plant needs a

▲ *Passiflora caerulea*

▲ *Passiflora caerulea* 'Constance Elliott'

minimum temperature of 7°C (45°F). HEIGHT & SPREAD 10×1m (33×3ft).

P. ***chinensis*** see *P. caerulea*

P. ***edulis*** (granadilla) The summer flowers, up to 7.5cm (3in) across, have narrow white petals flushed with green. The curly filaments are white and purple. The yellow or dull purple egg-shaped fruits, which are grown commercially in tropical countries, are up to 5cm (2in) long. This plant has woody angular stems and 3-lobed leaves up to 15cm (6in) across. It needs a minimum temperature of 13°C (55°F). HEIGHT & SPREAD 10×1m (33×3ft).

'Crackerjack' bears abundant, large, deep purple fruits.

P. × ***exoniensis***♀ Pendulous, rose-pink summer flowers, up to 12.5cm (5in) across, have small white coronas. The soft, downy leaves are mostly 3-lobed and up to 10cm (4in) long. The minimum temperature required for this plant is 7°C (45°F). HEIGHT & SPREAD 7×1m (23×3ft).

P. ***incarnata*** (may apple) The pale lavender flowers, 7.5cm (3in) across, have strange horn-like projections at the tips of the sepals. The corona has purplish blue filaments. Yellow fruits are freely produced. The 3-lobed leaves are 7.5-15cm (3-6in) long. This plant, which has an untidy habit, requires a minimum temperature of 7°C (45°F). HEIGHT & SPREAD 7×1m (23×3ft).

P. **'Lavender Lady'** Lavender-coloured

▲ *Passiflora incarnata*

petals, which are distinctly separated and slightly swept-back, and a purplish corona distinguish this plant. The flowers, up to 10cm (4in) across, appear for much of the summer. The deeply lobed leaves are up to 15cm (6in) long. The minimum temperature needed for this plant is 7°C (45°F). HEIGHT & SPREAD 7×1m (23×3ft).

P. mayana see *P. caerulea*

P. mollissima♀ (banana passion fruit) Pendulous, soft pink, green-flushed flowers from mid summer to late autumn have knobbly coronas. The flowers are up to 7.5cm (3in) across and the deeply lobed leaves, borne on soft, downy stems, are 12.5cm (5in) wide. The oblong-oval fruits are yellow and up to 7.5cm (3in) long. This plant needs a minimum temperature of 7°C (45°F). HEIGHT & SPREAD 7×1m (23×3ft).

P. quadrangularis♀ (giant granadilla) Fragrant white, pink or red flowers, up to 10cm (4in) across, appear throughout summer. The prominent coronas have 5 ranks of twisted filaments banded with violet and white. The yellow egg-shaped fruits, up to 20cm (8in) long, have purple juice. This plant, which needs a minimum temperature of 10°C (50°F), has angled, woody stems and oval or narrowly heart-shaped leaves up to 20cm (8in) long. HEIGHT & SPREAD 5×8m (16×26ft).

P. racemosa♀ (red passion flower) Clusters of pendent crimson flowers, each up to 12.5cm (5in) across, appear in summer and autumn. The corona has outer filaments in purple with white tips and short, inner ones in bright red. The undulating, 3-lobed, leathery leaves are up to 10cm (4in) long. The minimum temperature needed for the survival of this plant is 15°C (59°F). HEIGHT & SPREAD 5×1m (16×3ft).

P. rubra Greenish white flowers, up to 7.5cm (3in) wide in late summer and autumn, have striking red-purple or lavender filaments. Small reddish, rounded fruits, up to 2.5cm (1in) long, sometimes appear. The downy leaves with 2-3 lobes are up to 10cm (4in) across. This plant needs a minimum temperature of 15°C (59°F) to thrive. HEIGHT & SPREAD 5×1m (16×3ft).

P. sanguinolenta Dull red or deep pink flowers up to 7.5cm (3in) across, with strap-like petals appear in summer. The small, mostly 2-lobed leaves are very downy. This plant requires a minimum temperature of 7°C (45°F). HEIGHT & SPREAD 5×1m (16×3ft).

P. vitifolia The distinctive scarlet to blood-red flowers appear in summer. Up to 15cm (6in) across, they have a corona with 2 inner rows of short pink or white filaments and an outer row of longer maroon or yellow ones. Vine-like, 3-lobed leaves, up to 15cm (6in) long, are held on stems covered with dense, rust-coloured down. The minimum temperature needed is 16°C (61°F). HEIGHT & SPREAD 5×1m (16×3ft).

▲ *Passiflora sanguinolenta*

CULTIVATION Except for *P. caerulea*, plant in a cool or warm greenhouse or conservatory in a border offering an unrestricted root run, to promote sturdy growth and free flowering. Alternatively, plant in large containers of John Innes No.3 potting compost. Train plants under the roof. Although passion flowers like sun, provide some shade from late spring to early summer. Water freely in summer and feed every month with a high-potash liquid fertiliser. Water sparingly in autumn and winter.

Plant *P. caerulea* in any free-draining garden soil in late spring against a south or west-facing wall or fence. Protect from cold winds. In severe winters frost may cut the growth to ground level, but new growth should sprout again from the base in spring.

PROPAGATION Sow seed of species in spring under glass. Take semi-ripe cuttings of species and cultivars in summer.

PRUNING Reduce excessive growth in early spring. Regularly pinch back during the growing period to restrict the size. Thin out all weak shoots.

PESTS AND DISEASES Greenfly and whitefly can be a nuisance, and red spider mite can be especially troublesome under glass.

▲ *Passiflora vitifolia*

Paulownia

Scrophulariaceae

Paulownia tomentosa

Spectacular erect sprays of fragrant tubular flowers are produced in late spring by these deciduous trees. Potentially very tall and large, the trees are valuable for shade. A clammy coating to the hairy foliage is effective for catching aphids. Native to E Asia, all paulownia are hardy to -5°C (23°F). They require a rich, damp soil.

RECOMMENDED SPECIES AND VARIETIES

P. fargesii (syn. *P. lilacina)* Pale lilac flowers, about 6cm (2in) long, with yellow throats are held in 38cm (15in) long spikes at the end of the stems. Dull green leaves are oval to heart-shaped, 25cm (10in) long and 15cm (6in) wide. Stiff sticky hairs clad the young shoots. HEIGHT & SPREAD 8×4m (26×13ft) after 20 years, ultimately 20m (66ft) tall.

P. tomentosa (foxglove tree) Mauve flowers, about 5cm (2in) across, are held in sprays up to 30cm (12in) long at the end of the stems. The flowerbuds, which set in autumn, can be spoiled by cold, wet or windy weather. This species, which has a rounded habit, has silvery grey smooth bark. Individual trees can vary greatly in size and leaf dimension. The leaves, which are sometimes shallowly lobed, are 12.5-25cm (5-10in) long and wide. Some trees achieve the size given below in 20 years and then do not grow much more. Others reach 20m (66ft) high with an 8m (26ft) spread in 80 years. HEIGHT & SPREAD 8×6m (26×20ft) after 20 years.

CULTIVATION Grow in rich damp soil on a sunny sheltered site. In early or mid spring cut down to the ground any young trees spoiled by frost or stunted in growth – the regrowth will be spectacular.

PROPAGATION Sow seed in spring under glass and protect young plants from frost.

PESTS AND DISEASES Honey fungus can be a problem.

Pea, edible see VEGETABLES p.743
Pea, everlasting see *Lathyrus latifolius*
Pea, perennial see *Lathyrus latifolius*
Pea, sweet see *Lathyrus odoratus*
Peach, edible see FRUIT p.727
Peach, ornamental see *Prunus*
Pear, edible see FRUIT p.728
Pear, ornamental see *Pyrus*
Pearlwort see *Sagina*
Pearly everlasting see Anaphalis

pq

Pelargonium

Geranium

Geraniaceae

It is hard to imagine balcony gardens, hanging baskets or bedding schemes without at least one type of pelargonium on display. Easy to grow and with a wide range of flower colours and shapes they impart a bright, cheerful note to any summer garden

Richly coloured flowers and handsome, often variegated or heavily fragrant foliage are the outstanding features of these popular garden plants. The flowers usually have five petals with the upper two petals often larger than the rest and contrastingly veined. This large genus, native to Africa, the Middle East, Turkey and Australia, contains mostly shrubby perennials requiring an open, sunny position and frost-free conditions. Although only a few of the species are widely available, when it comes to varieties gardeners have dozens to choose from.

There are four main groups: 'ivy-leaved', with attractive foliage and a trailing habit that is ideal for hanging baskets; 'regal', with large richly coloured flowers; 'scented-leaved', with pleasantly aromatic foliage; and 'zonal' in which the leaves are marked with a band, or zone, of contrasting colour. Zonal pelargoniums are commonly known as geraniums, but should not be confused with plants of the genus *Geranium*. There are also 'angel' varieties with small two-toned flowers, 'stellar' varieties with star-shaped blooms, and 'unique' varieties which are large-flowered and fragrant. In addition, there are dwarf or miniature plants which are ideal for urns and window boxes.

While all pelargoniums can be grown as pot plants, many are used for summer bedding. Most are in flower from early to late summer and sometimes into autumn, although the spectacular blooms of regal pelargoniums are seen for only a few weeks in mid summer.

RECOMMENDED SPECIES AND VARIETIES

P. acetosum Salmon-pink flowers, up to 4cm (1½in) wide, with darker veins on the upper petals, appear in spring and summer. The glaucous, rounded leaves, up to 4cm (1½in) across, have red, toothed edges. HEIGHT & SPREAD 60×60cm (2×2ft).

***P.* 'Amethyst'**♀ (ivy-leaved) Bold heads of pinkish purple semidouble flowers are freely produced on stems which trail up to 60cm (2ft). The scalloped rounded leaves are up to 5cm (2in) across. HEIGHT & SPREAD 30×25cm (12×10in).

***P.* 'Apple Blossom Rosebud'**♀ (zonal) The double flowers of this plant have greenish centres and white petals edged with pink. They appear in tight rounded heads up to 15cm (6in) across among rounded leaves up to 10cm (4in) across. This plant is usually grown in pots. HEIGHT & SPREAD 60×45cm (24×18in).

***P.* 'Atomic Snowflake'** (scented-leaved) Rounded, lobed leaves, with gold variegations, smell of lemon. Purple-pink flowers, up to 2.5cm (1in) wide, are carried in loose heads. HEIGHT & SPREAD 45×30cm (18×12in).

***P.* 'Attar of Roses'**♀ (scented-leaved) Rose-scented leaves with crimped edges, and pale pink flowers in loose heads, up to 10cm (4in) across, appear on this plant. HEIGHT & SPREAD 60×45cm (24×18in).

P. australe Small starry flowers appear for much of the spring and summer. The flowers are pale pink or white with the upper petals veined with deep pink. This plant is an untidy scrambler with downy, faintly

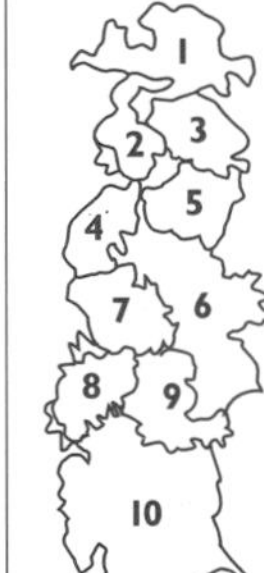

1 'Fragrans Variegatum'
2 'Catford Belle'
3 'Dolly Varden'
4 'Rote Mini-Cascade'
5 'Mrs Parker'
6 'Lady Plymouth'
7 'Mrs G.H. Smith'
8 'Bird Dancer'
9 'Graveolens'
10 'Lord Bute'

▲ *Pelargonium* 'Amethyst'

▲ *Pelargonium* 'Bird Dancer'

aromatic leaves up to 10cm (4in) across. HEIGHT & SPREAD 30×45cm (12×18in).

P. **'Bird Dancer'** (stellar) A profusion of delicately fringed, pink star-like flowers appear on this dwarf, bushy variety that is ideal for tubs and bedding. HEIGHT & SPREAD 25×20cm (10×8in).

P. **'Caroline Schmidt'**♀ (zonal) The leaves of this bedding plant are edged with silvery white. Double flowers of bright red are held in heads up to 12.5cm (5in) across. HEIGHT & SPREAD 45×30cm (18×12in).

P. **'Catford Belle'**♀ (angel) Semidouble mauve-pink flowers with deep maroon blotches are borne in dense heads, up to 10cm (4in) across. The leaves are mid green and deeply lobed. This compact plant is suitable for a window box. HEIGHT & SPREAD 45×45cm (18×18in).

P. **'Chelsea Gem'**♀ (zonal) This bedding plant has leaves edged with white. The pale pink double flowers are borne in heads up to 12.5cm (5in) across. HEIGHT & SPREAD 45×30cm (18×12in).

▼ *Pelargonium* 'Catford Belle'

▲ *Pelargonium* 'Chieko'

▲ *Pelargonium* 'Chocolate Peppermint'

P. **'Chieko'** (miniature) Double magenta flowers are carried in neat heads, about 7.5cm (3in) across. The leaves are up to 4cm (1½in) in width. HEIGHT & SPREAD 20×15cm (8×6in).

P. **'Chocolate Peppermint'** (scented-leaved) Soft green, peppermint-scented leaves have distinctive dark brown central zones. The pale mauve-pink flowers appear in small heads. HEIGHT & SPREAD 1m×75cm (36×30in).

P. **'Citriodorum'** (scented-leaved) The heart-shaped leaves of this plant are up to 5cm (2in) across with a rich lime scent. The 4cm (1½in) wide, mauve-pink, starry flowers appear in loose heads. HEIGHT & SPREAD 60×45cm (24×18in).

P. ***citronellum*** The lemon-scented leaves are pale green and downy. Pinkish flowers appear in loose clusters 7.5cm (3in) wide, on this shrubby plant with hairy stems and deeply lobed leaves, up to 7.5cm (3in) long. HEIGHT & SPREAD 2×1m (6½×3ft).

P. **'Clorinda'** (unique) Rose-pink flowers, up to 4cm (1½in) across, appear in loose clusters on this sturdy plant that is good in

▲ *Pelargonium* 'Clorinda'

▲ *Pelargonium crispum*

pots. Deeply lobed and toothed leaves, up to 7.5cm (3in) across, smell like cedar. HEIGHT & SPREAD 60×45cm (24×18in).

P. ***crispum*** (lemon geranium) The leaves, up to 5cm (2in) wide, with a strong lemon scent, are lobed with curly, crisped edges. The flowers, up to 2.5cm (1in) across, are usually soft pink marked with dark pink. HEIGHT & SPREAD 75×60cm (2½×2ft).

'Major' has slightly larger leaves. **'Variegatum'**♀ has cream-edged leaves.

P. **'Crystal Palace Gem'** (zonal) The heart-shaped leaves up to 7.5cm (3in) across of this bedding plant, are marked with yellow and lime green. Coral flowers appear in heads up to 10cm (4in) across. HEIGHT & SPREAD 45×30cm (18×12in).

P. **'Deacon Lilac Mist'** (zonal) The rounded leaves bear distinctive brown or maroon zones. The heads of double lilac-pink flowers are 12.5cm (5in) wide. This plant is suitable for bedding and pot cultivation. HEIGHT & SPREAD 45×30cm (18×12in).

P. **'Denticulatum Group'** (pine geranium) (scented-leaved) These shrubby plants have roughly triangular plain green leaves up to 7.5cm (3in) across. They are balsam-scented and deeply cut. Purple-pink flowers, up to 2cm (¾in) across, appear from late spring to late summer. HEIGHT & SPREAD 1.5×1m (5×3ft).

'Filicifolium' (fern-leaved geranium) has deeply divided, almost stringy foliage.

P. **'Distinction'** (zonal) Crinkly rounded leaves, up to 5cm (2in) across, have conspicuous dark zones. The small red flowers are held in clusters. HEIGHT & SPREAD 30×25cm (12×10in).

P. **'Dolly Varden'**♀ (zonal) The cream, green and red variegated foliage complements the scarlet flowers of this useful bedding plant. HEIGHT & SPREAD 45×30cm (18×12in).

P. × ***domesticum*** (regal) This complex group of hybrids has showy flowers, up to 5cm (2in) across, often two-toned or distinctively marked. The leaves are heart-shaped or lobed and frequently toothed or downy. HEIGHT & SPREAD 1m×60cm (3×2ft).

P. ***endlicherianum*** This scrambling species has distinctive purple-pink flowers, with upper petals up to 2.5cm (1in) long while the lower petals are very short or sometimes

▲ *Pelargonium* 'Distinction'

absent. The rounded leaves, up to 7.5cm (3in) wide, are shallowly lobed. Often grown in containers, this plant will survive in a sheltered, well-drained spot outside. HEIGHT & SPREAD 45×30cm (18×12in).

P. **'Fleurette'** (dwarf) Heads of double orange-salmon flowers, up to 10cm (4in) across, appear on this vigorously growing plant which has dark green leaves up to 5cm (2in) across. HEIGHT & SPREAD 30×25cm (12×10in).

P. **'Flower of Spring'**♀ (zonal) This popular bedding plant has shallowly lobed, rounded leaves with distinctive silver edges. The bright red flowers are held in heads up to 15cm (6in) across. HEIGHT & SPREAD 45×30cm (18×12in).

▲ *Pelargonium* 'Flower of Spring'

P. **'Fragrans Group'** (scented-leaved) Grey-green leaves with a spicy smell vary from roughly oval to heart-shaped, often toothed and crimped at the edges. Small heads of star-like white blossoms appear sporadically from spring until late summer. This small, somewhat wiry plant is normally grown on a windowsill. HEIGHT & SPREAD 45×30cm (18×12in).

'Fragrans Variegatum' has leaves edged with creamy yellow which age to green.

P. **'Freak of Nature'** (zonal) The white stems trail up to 60cm (2ft). The bright green leaves have conspicuous white central markings.

P. **'Friary Wood'** (zonal) This unusual bedding plant has golden leaves with chestnut-brown zoning. Pink double blossoms with a white eye appear in mid summer. HEIGHT & SPREAD 45×30cm (18×12in).

P. **'Friesdorf'** (dwarf) Deep pink star-like flowers, up to 2.5cm (1in) across, have narrow spatula-like petals. The rounded, irregularly edged leaves up to 7.5cm (3in) across, are deep green with almost black markings. This plant is suitable for bedding, pots or window boxes. HEIGHT & SPREAD 30×25cm (12×10in).

P. **'Fringed Aztec'**♀ (regal) The white petals of this plant have frilled edges and central mauve feathering. The flowers up to 5cm (2in) across, appear above lobed, cut, heart-shaped leaves. HEIGHT & SPREAD 45×30cm (18×12in).

P. **'Galilee'**♀ (ivy-leaved) Heads of double rose-pink flowers, up to 12.5cm (5in) wide, appear above smooth, sharply lobed foliage. This plant trails to 60cm (2ft).

P. **'Golden Brilliantissimum'** (zonal) The tricoloured foliage of this plant makes it ideal for bedding or pots. The rounded shallowly lobed leaves strikingly combine gold, red and green. Heads of double bright red flowers, up to 12.5cm (5in) wide, appear for most of the spring and summer. HEIGHT & SPREAD 45×30cm (18×12in).

P. **'Golden Ears'** (stellar) Orange-red, star-like double flowers, appear in tight heads up to 10cm (4in) wide. The sharply lobed, rounded leaves are up to 5cm (2in) across. They are gold with a deep bronze zoning. This plant is ideal for tubs and bedding. HEIGHT & SPREAD 25×20cm (10×8in).

P. **'Grand Slam'** (regal) One of the most widely grown regal pelargoniums, this plant has red satiny flowers up to 5cm (2in) across, with dark purple-red internal markings. The foliage of this excellent pot plant has toothed edges. HEIGHT & SPREAD 45×30cm (18×12in).

P. **'Graveolens'** (scented-leaved) Strong stems carry deeply cut, lobed leaves. Pink star-like flowers, 1.5cm (½in) across, appear in loose clusters. This vigorous, lemon-scented plant is the source of oil of geranium. HEIGHT & SPREAD 1m×60cm (3×2ft).

Pelargonium 'Graveolens'

▲ *Pelargonium* 'Graveolens'

P. **'Happy Thought'** (zonal) Star-like crimson flowers are held in heads up to 10cm (4in) across. The soft leaves are lightly scalloped and rounded, with light yellow centres. HEIGHT & SPREAD 30×25cm (12×10in).

P. **'Lady Plymouth'**♀ (scented-leaved) The variegated bluish green foliage edged in cream has a strong citrus fragrance. The pink star-like blossoms have narrow petals. HEIGHT & SPREAD 60×45cm (24×18in).

▲ *Pelargonium* 'Lady Plymouth'

P. **'Lass O' Gowrie'** (zonal) Grown for its sharply lobed, mid green, red and cream leaves and red, single star-like flowers, this plant is a favourite for patio tubs and urns. HEIGHT & SPREAD 30×25cm (12×10in).

P. **'L'Elégante'**♀ (ivy-leaved) This old-fashioned plant with bluish green leaves and yellow edges could almost be mistaken for an ivy. It trails to 60cm (2ft). In very hot or dry conditions the leaves develop a strong purplish flush. White star-like flowers, up to 7.5cm (3in) across, have broad somewhat reflexed petals marked with purple.

P. **'Lilac Gem'** (ivy-leaved) Lobed leaves with a distinctive purplish central zone appear on this plant, which trails to 60cm (2ft). Dense heads of double lilac flowers, up to 10cm (4in) across, appear from late spring until early autumn.

P. **'Lilian Pottinger'** (scented-leaved) A strong pine fragrance comes from the deeply cut, roughly heart-shaped leaves of this plant for a windowsill. The leaves are deeply cut with crisped edges. The white starry flowers, about 1.5cm (½in) across, appear in dense clusters. HEIGHT & SPREAD 45×30cm (1½×1ft).

P. **'Lord Bute'**♀ (regal) Dark crimson-

▲ *Pelargonium* 'L'Elégante'

▲ *Pelargonium* 'Mabel Grey'

purple flowers, up to 5cm (2in) across with pink edges, appear in mid summer. The leaves are slightly lobed and rounded. HEIGHT & SPREAD 45×30cm (18×12in).

P. **'Mabel Grey'**♀ (scented-leaved) This plant with lemon-scented foliage is ideal for a windowsill. Deeply divided, roughly heart-shaped leaves frame the small clusters of 1.5cm (½in) wide pink blossoms. HEIGHT & SPREAD 60×30cm (2×1ft).

P. **'Madam Layal'** (angel) Flowers, up to 2.5cm (1in) wide, have upper petals in dark violet-purple or rose and white, while the lower petals are white with violet-rose veins. HEIGHT & SPREAD 25×20cm (10×8in).

P. **'Morval'**♀ (dwarf) Double pink flowers, up to 12.5cm (5in) wide, contrast with the lightly scalloped, rounded golden green leaves. HEIGHT & SPREAD 45×30cm (18×12in).

P. **'Mr Henry Cox'** (zonal) Handsome rounded leaves with mid green centres are surrounded by deep purplish red and golden

Pelargonium 'Mr Henry Cox'

yellow zones. The flowers are blush-pink. HEIGHT & SPREAD 45×30cm (18×12in).

P. **'Mrs G.H. Smith'** (angel) White flowers, up to 4cm (1½in) wide, are conspicuously marked with pink centres. The heart-shaped leaves, up to 5cm (2in) wide, have crimped edges. This plant is excellent for

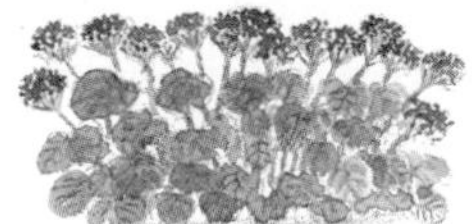

Pelargonium 'Mrs Parker'

pots, tubs or window boxes. HEIGHT & SPREAD 45×45cm (18×18in).

P. **'Mrs Parker'** (zonal) Bluish green leaves with broad irregular white margins, distinguish this traditional bedding plant. The double flowers are rose-pink in heads up to 12.5cm (5in) wide. HEIGHT & SPREAD 45×30cm (18×12in).

P. **'Mrs Pollock'** (zonal) The acutely lobed, heart-shaped leaves are dark green with broad, bright yellow edges. This bedding plant has red flower clusters up to 12.5cm (5in) across. HEIGHT & SPREAD 45×30cm (18×12in).

P. **'Mrs Quilter'** (zonal) Rounded mid green to gold leaves have strong bronze zoning. Pink flowers up to 2.5cm (1in) wide, appear in heads up to 10cm (4in) wide. This plant is usually used for bedding. HEIGHT & SPREAD 45×30cm (18×12in).

P. ***odoratissimum*** The apple-scented foliage has rounded leaves with lightly crimped and scalloped edges. The white flowers are just 1.5cm (½in) wide in loose clusters. HEIGHT & SPREAD 45×30cm (18×12in).

P. **'Orion'** (miniature) This free-flowering plant has rounded, lightly scalloped leaves up to 4cm (1½in) wide. It has clusters up to 7.5cm (3in) wide, of double flowers in bright orange-red. HEIGHT & SPREAD 20×20cm (8×8in).

P. **'Paton's Unique'**♀ (unique) This bedding plant has roughly triangular, lobed and cut leaves, up to 7.5cm (3in) wide. The flowers range from crimson to pink, veined with maroon. HEIGHT & SPREAD 60×60cm (2×2ft).

▲ *Pelargonium* 'Paton's Unique'

P. **'Paul Crampel'** (zonal) The rounded leaves of this bedding plant have purplish zoning. Scarlet flowers, up to 4cm (1½in) wide, appear in heads up to 12.5cm (5in) wide. HEIGHT & SPREAD 45×30cm (18×12in).

P. **'Prince of Orange'** (scented-leaved) This orange-scented plant has roughly triangular, much divided deeply cut leaves. The summer flowers, up to 4cm (1½in) wide, are light pink with delicate reddish markings in the throat. They are held in crowded groups up to 10cm (4in) wide. This plant is good for a windowsill. HEIGHT & SPREAD 45×30cm (18×12in).

P. ***quercifolium*** (oak-leaved geranium, almond geranium) A strong smell of balsam comes from this plant. The hairy leaves are more or less triangular, deeply cut and divided. Leaves and stems are sticky. Pale purple-pink flowers appear in small clusters. HEIGHT & SPREAD 60×30cm (24×18in).

▲ *Pelargonium quercifolium*

P. **Radula Group** (scented-leaved) Deeply cut leaves, up to 10cm (4in) wide, have a rose-lemon scent. Small pink and purple flowers appear in loose clusters. HEIGHT & SPREAD 1m×60cm (3×2ft).

P. **'Red Black Vesuvius'** (miniature) Dark green, almost black leaves up to 4cm (1½in) across, distinguish this plant which has bright red, single flowers in clusters up to 7.5cm (3in) wide. HEIGHT & SPREAD 20×20cm (8×8in).

P. **'Rigel'** (miniature) Rounded, dark green leaves are up to 4cm (1½in) across. Double scarlet flowers appear in clusters up to 7.5cm (3in) wide. HEIGHT & SPREAD 20×20cm (8×8in).

P. **'Rigi'** (ivy-leaved) This vigorous plant bears glossy, sharply lobed leaves, up to 5cm (2in) wide, and loose heads of deep cerise flowers, each up to 2.5cm (1in) across. HEIGHT & SPREAD 15×60cm (6×24in).

P. **'Rio Grande'** (ivy-leaved) Glossy, sharply lobed leaves, up to 5cm (2in) wide, cover the stems which trail to 60cm (2ft). Deep maroon, almost black flowers with white undersides appear freely in clusters up to 10cm (4in) across.

P. **'Rober's Lemon Rose'** (scented-leaved) This vigorous lemon-scented plant has narrow, roughly lance-shaped but deeply lobed blue-green leaves. Mauve and pink star-like flowers are held in loose clusters up to 7.5cm (3in) wide. HEIGHT & SPREAD 75×30cm (30×12in).

P. **'Rose Bengal'** (angel) Lobed leaves are up to 5cm (2in) across. The rose-purple flowers have 2 upper petals in a deeper purple with paler edges. HEIGHT & SPREAD 45×30cm (18×12in).

P. **'Rote Mini-Cascade'** (ivy-leaved) Deep red star-like blossoms, up to 2.5cm (1in) wide, are held in clusters above small, glossy, symmetrically lobed leaves, up to 5cm (2in) across. HEIGHT & SPREAD 10×45cm (4×18in).

P. **'Rouletta'** (ivy-leaved) Double flowers of deep magenta are held in heads up to 10cm (4in) across. The lobed leaves are up to 5cm (2in) wide and appear on stems

▲ *Pelargonium* 'Rober's Lemon Rose'

▲ *Pelargonium* 'Rouletta'

trailing to 60 cm (2 ft) long.

P. **'Royal Oak'** (scented-leaved) Lobed, balsam-scented leaves resemble those of an oak tree. The star-like flowers in clusters, have long narrow, mauve-pink petals conspicuously spotted with maroon. HEIGHT & SPREAD 75×45 cm (30×18 in).

P. **'Sancho Panza'**♀ (angel) The dark purple flowers, up to 4 cm (1½ in) across have a white edging. The heart-shaped leaves are about 5 cm (2 in) across. HEIGHT & SPREAD 45×45 cm (18×18 in).

P. **'Scarlet Unique'** (unique) This is one of the best bedding pelargoniums. The mid green leaves are roughly triangular, up to 7.5 cm (3 in) across, deeply lobed and cut. The scarlet flowers about 4 cm (1½ in) across, carry a darker blotch on each petal. HEIGHT & SPREAD 60×60 cm (2×2 ft).

▲ *Pelargonium* 'Sancho Panza'

P. **'Silver Kewense'** (dwarf) Rounded, shallowly lobed leaves, up to 4 cm (1½ in) across, are edged with white and occasionally tinged with violet. Heads of bright red flowers, growing to 10 cm (4 in) across, appear from late spring until early autumn. HEIGHT & SPREAD 30×25 cm (12×10 in).

P. **'Sugar Baby'** (ivy-leaved) Light pink flowers in 10 cm (4 in) clusters appear among the glossy, evenly lobed leaves up to 5 cm (2 in) wide. HEIGHT & SPREAD 15×60 cm (6×24 in).

P. **'Sussex Lace'** see *P.* 'White Mesh'

P. **'Sweet Mimosa'** (scented-leaved) Sweetly scented, deeply cut lobed leaves are around 7.5 cm (3 in) long. Pink flowers up to 2.5 cm (1 in) across are held in clusters. HEIGHT & SPREAD 45×30 cm (18×12 in).

P. **'Sybil Holmes'** (ivy-leaved) Double pink flowers in dense clusters, 12.5 cm (5 in) across, appear against symmetrically lobed, glossy green leaves up to 7.5 cm (3 in) across. The stems trail to 60 cm (2 ft).

P. **'Tavira'** (ivy-leaved) Double bright red flowers, held in clusters as wide as 10 cm (4 in) across, appear among glossy lobed leaves, about 7.5 cm (3 in) across. The trailing stems grow to 60 cm (2 ft) long.

P. **'The Crocodile'** (ivy-leaved) Heads of deep pink flowers up to 10 cm (4 in) wide, appear against conspicuously lobed, glossy leaves, 5 cm (2 in) wide, with golden veins. HEIGHT & SPREAD 15×60 cm (6×24 in).

P. **'Tip Top Duet'**♀ (angel) Flowers with deep wine-coloured upper petals and violet lower petals distinguish this plant with rounded leaves, up to 5 cm (2 in) wide and a neat upright habit. HEIGHT & SPREAD 45×30 cm (18×12 in).

▲ *Pelargonium* 'Tip Top Duet'

P. ***tomentosum***♀ (peppermint geranium) Peppermint-scented with large leaves, this species can be grown either as a shrubby pot plant or trained up a pillar or wall in the greenhouse. The spreading, softly downy leaves, 10 cm (4 in) across, clothe the scrambling stems. The tiny flowers are white with a pink flush and conspicuous red markings in the centre. They are borne freely in loose groups about 10 cm (4 in) wide. HEIGHT & SPREAD 90×60 cm (3×2 ft).

P. **'Vancouver Centennial'**♀ (stellar) Star-shaped brick-red flowers in neat heads up to 10 cm (4 in) across appear above bronze and gold symmetrically lobed foliage. This is an excellent plant for containers or beds. HEIGHT & SPREAD 30×25 cm (12×10 in).

P. **'White Mesh'** (syn. *P.* 'Sussex Lace') (ivy-leaved) Compact heads of soft pink flowers, 10 cm (4 in) across, are produced freely. The neatly lobed dark green leaves, about 7.5 cm (3 in) across, are conspicuously veined with yellow. They are held on stems which trail to 60 cm (2 ft).

P. **'Wood's Surprise'** (ivy-leaved) The rounded, symmetrically lobed foliage is 5 cm (2 in) across and marbled green and white. Double pale lilac flowers are freely produced in neat round groups 10 cm (4 in) across. The stems trail to 60 cm (2 ft).

CULTIVATION Grow in 15 cm (6 in) pots in a free-draining compost in a sunny, frost-free place. Water freely in summer and sparingly in winter. Feed every three weeks in summer. Repot in spring, replacing plants about every 2 years. Deadhead flowers and remove faded leaves regularly.

Plant bedding pelargoniums in fertile, neutral to alkaline, well-drained soil once all danger of frost has passed, then lift before the first sharp frosts. Replace bedding plants annually. Treat the ivy-leaved plants the same way when grown in hanging baskets.

PROPAGATION Take softwood cuttings during spring and summer.

PESTS AND DISEASES Usually trouble free.

Penstemon

Beard-tongue

Scrophulariaceae

Penstemon 'Papal Purple'

Flamboyant penstemons bring colour to the garden from early summer until the first autumn frosts. These profusely flowering plants are mainly evergreen perennials and sub-shrubs. They range from tiny alpine cushions, best suited to a rock garden, to large, upright, clump-forming plants for borders. The smallest species are best for raised beds and troughs. The more compact cultivars also do well in tubs. Alpine penstemons flower from early to mid summer, border penstemons from early summer to early autumn.

The tubular flowers, each about 2.5 cm (1 in) long, are predominantly blue, red or purple. They are borne in spikes or clusters. Each flower has five spreading lobes which

form two lips. There is often a bearded (hairy) throat. Leaves are mid green, generally lance-shaped, 2.5-15 cm (1-6 in) long and arranged opposite each other on the stem. Although evergreen penstemons can lose their leaves in cold winters. Some species are difficult and short-lived. Most cultivars are slightly tender and will probably be killed by frost: it is prudent to take cuttings as a precaution.

The genus is native to N and Central America. The recommended plants are divided into two groups:

1) Alpine penstemons
2) Border penstemons

RECOMMENDED SPECIES AND VARIETIES

ALPINE PENSTEMONS

P. alpinus Congested clusters of blue flowers, about 2.5 cm (1 in) long and usually tinged purple, appear on this hardy species. HEIGHT & SPREAD 15-60×20 cm (6-24×8 in).

P. campanulatus (syn. *P. kunthii*) This hardy species has loose clumps of long spikes of narrow flowers, usually reddish purple. HEIGHT & SPREAD 50×30 cm (20×12 in).

P. cardwellii Narrow, violet-purple flowers, up to 2.5 cm (1 in) long, are held in short spikes. The leaves are small, oval and finely toothed. This low-spreading shrub is one of the most reliable for a rock garden. HEIGHT & SPREAD 30×20 cm (12×8 in).

P. confertus This fairly hardy plant forms a compact clump with small cream-coloured flowers in dense whorls up the stem. HEIGHT & SPREAD 40×20 cm (16×8 in).

▲ *Penstemon confertus*

P. davidsonii Clusters of lilac to purple flowers bloom among the small glossy leaves of this sub-shrub. HEIGHT & SPREAD 20×30 cm (8×12 in).

The flowers of var. ***menziesii***♀ are pinkish lavender. **'Microphyllus'** is similar, but more compact.

P. fruticosus The bluish lavender flowers of this upright shrub are borne in clusters well above oval to broad leathery leaves. HEIGHT & SPREAD 15-40×30 cm (6-16×12 in).

The flowers of var. ***scouleri***♀ are either lavender or white and the leaves narrower and toothed. Profuse pure white flowers appear on var. ***scouleri albus***♀.

P. kunthii see *P. campanulatus*

▲ *Penstemon davidsonii var. menziesii*

▲ *Penstemon fruticosus var. scouleri albus*

P. laetus var. ***roezlii*** This hardy sub-shrub has spikes of violet-blue flowers and lance-shaped leaves. HEIGHT & SPREAD 50×30cm (20×12 in).

P. newberryi♀ Clusters of mid to deep rose-pink flowers appear in early summer on this shrub-like plant. HEIGHT & SPREAD 15-40×30 cm (6-16×12 in).

P. pinifolius♀ Loose spikes of narrow, vivid orange-red flowers appear on this low-growing shrub which bears light green, needle-like leaves. HEIGHT & SPREAD 25×30 cm (10×12 in).

'Mersea Yellow' has yellow flowers.

P. richardsonii Purplish pink to lavender flowers, 2.5 cm (1 in) long, appear in loose sprays in late summer. This hardy plant forms a low, spreading mound with prostrate or semi-upright stems. It looks particularly effective growing down a wall. HEIGHT & SPREAD 20×60 cm (8×24 in).

P. rupicola♀ Large pink to reddish purple flowers and glaucous, toothed leaves appear on this low-growing sub-shrub. HEIGHT & SPREAD 10×20 cm (4×8 in).

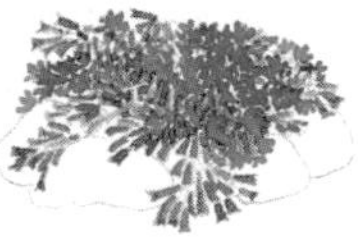

Penstemon rupicola

P. virens Flowers of vivid deep blue in dense domed heads, and dark green glossy, oval to lance-shaped leaves, make this one of the finest small species. HEIGHT & SPREAD 15-20×20 cm (6-8×8 in).

BORDER PENSTEMONS

Species and varieties

P. barbatus Loose spikes of pinkish red or rarely yellow flowers, are carried in mid summer on upright stems. HEIGHT & SPREAD 80×20 cm (32×8 in).

A more compact plant, var. ***praecox*** f. ***nanus***, is up to 50 cm (20 in) with pink or red flowers.

P. barbatus var. ***coccineus*** see ***P. wislizenii***

P. digitalis White flowers appear in loose spikes on this hardy plant for a sunny or partially shaded border. Leaves up to 8 cm (3¼ in) long are frequently tinged purple. HEIGHT & SPREAD 50-100×30 cm (20-40×12 in).

'Husker Red' (syn. *P. digitalis purpureus*) has leaves of a particularly dark purple.

P. glaber Deep blue to purple flowers are produced by this reliable plant, which forms an upright clump. HEIGHT & SPREAD 50×25 cm (20×10 in).

P. hartwegii♀ Spectacular spikes of red flowers up to 5 cm (2 in) long with white throats, appear among narrow glossy leaves on this plant, which is short-lived except in mild districts. HEIGHT & SPREAD 100×30 cm (40×12 in).

P. isophyllus♀ Long, narrow red flowers with cream throats and broad glossy leaves are carried by this upright species. HEIGHT & SPREAD 80×30 cm (32×12 in).

P. strictus Spikes of deep blue flowers appear on this upright plant with spoon to lance-shaped leaves. HEIGHT & SPREAD 60×20 cm (24×8 in).

P. wislizenii (syn. *P. barbatus* var. *coccineus*) Vivid scarlet flower spikes appear on erect stems in mid summer. HEIGHT & SPREAD 80×20 cm (32×8 in).

Cultivars

Large spikes of foxglove-like flowers appear on the following plants. Leaves are oval to lance-shaped, and up to 15 cm (6 in) long. The plants form bold clumps with stiff stems. Heights are 30-100 cm (12-40 in) and spreads average 30 cm (12 in).

The following are distinctly low-growing, reaching only 10-20 cm (4-8 in) tall. **'Edithiae'** has deep lilac flowers and a prostrate habit. **'Pink Dragon'** is a compact shrub with abundant small heads of clear

▼ *Penstemon* 'Catherine de la Mare'

pink flowers, while **'Six Hills'** has large, deep lavender flowers.

These plants grow 30-40cm (12-16in) tall. **'Catherine de la Mare'**♀ has bluish purple flowers, while **'Margery Fish'**♀ has flowers of deep to purplish blue. Both have a tendency to sprawl. **'Papal Purple'** has flowers in deep lavender with white throats.

The following plants grow to over 40cm (16in) tall, usually reaching a height of about 80cm (32in). On rich moist soils, the plants may reach 1m (3ft) tall. **'Alice Hindley'**♀ has flowers in pale mauve with white throats. The hardy **'Andenken an Friedrich Hahn'**♀ (syn. *P.* 'Garnet') has deep carmine flowers with a few white throat markings. **'Apple Blossom'**♀ has pale pink flowers with white throats and streaks. **'Beech Park'**♀ has white flowers with patches of pink, while those of **'Blackbird'** are deep rich burgundy, and **'Cherry Ripe'** has warm red flowers. **'Chester Scarlet'**♀ has very large bright red flowers, with deeper red throats. **'Countess of Dalkeith'** has deep purple and white flowers, while those of **'Evelyn'**, which is hardy, are pale pink. **'Hewell Pink Bedder'**♀ has reddish pink flowers and glaucous leaves. **'Hidcote Pink'**♀ has pink flowers with white and dark pink streaks.

▲ *Penstemon* 'Hewell Pink Bedder'

Penstemon 'Hidcote Pink' ▲

'Hidcote White' has similar, streaked white flowers. **'King George V'** has large scarlet flowers with red streaks on white throats. **'Midnight'** has deep reddish purple flowers. The white throats have a violet base. In **'Myddelton Gem'** the flowers are pinkish red with white throats, while **'Osprey'**♀ has large white flowers with pink margins. **'Peace'** has small pink-and-white flowers. **'Pink Endurance'** is like *P.* 'Evelyn' with flowers of a darker pink. **'Port Wine'**♀ and **'Raven'**♀ have deep reddish purple flowers, the latter with dark-veined white throats. **'Russian River'** has deep blue-mauve flowers, while those of the hardy **'Schoenholzeri'**♀ (*P.* 'Firebird') appear in pink-red compact spikes. **'Sour Grapes'** has flowers in bunches that are a

▲ *Penstemon* 'Schoenholzeri'

mixture of purple and blue. Hardy **'Stapleford Gem'**♀ has flowers in paler shades of purple and blue. **'White Bedder'**♀ has creamy white flowers, occasionally flushed with pink, with black anthers. It is moderately hardy.

CULTIVATION Plant in well-drained soil in full sun: alpine species need particularly well-drained gritty soil. Deadhead larger plants regularly and cut back smaller plants if they become straggly.

PROPAGATION Take cuttings of species in early summer and cuttings of border cultivars in late summer. Overwinter the rooted cuttings under glass and plant out in spring after the risk of frost is over. Sow the seed of species in late winter or early spring.

PESTS AND DISEASES Aphids, slugs and snails sometimes attack plants and eelworms are occasionally a problem.

Peperomia

Piperaceae

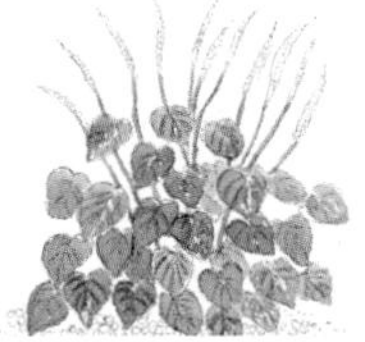

Peperomia caperata

Striking foliage and reddish stems make these tropical annuals and perennials popular as house or greenhouse plants. The foliage is fleshy or succulent, often with puckered or variegated markings. The slender flower spikes are insignificant, except on *Peperomia caperata* and *P. fraseri*. Native to the tropics, the plants require a minimum temperature of 10°C (50°F). Those listed are evergreen perennials.

RECOMMENDED SPECIES AND VARIETIES

P. argyreia♀ (syn. *P. sandersii*) (watermelon peperomia) This bushy plant has oval or rounded leaves, up to 12.5cm (5in) long, with broad silver bands. HEIGHT & SPREAD 25×25cm (10×10in).

P. caperata (emerald ripple peperomia) Tough, heart-shaped, crinkled leaves are up

▲ *Peperomia argyreia*

to 4cm (1½in) long. Dense, pencil-like, creamy white flowers, 7.5cm (3in) long, appear for most of the year. HEIGHT & SPREAD 15×15cm (6×6in).

'Variegata' has leaves splashed and edged with white. **'Little Fantasy'**♀ is up to 10cm (4in) tall and wide. It has deeply folded leaves with greyish undersides.

P. fraseri (flowering peperomia) Fragrant cream flower spikes, 5cm (2in) long, appear in summer. Heart-shaped leaves, up to 5cm (2in) long, have purple and red veins. HEIGHT & SPREAD 30×25cm (12×10in).

▲ *Peperomia fraseri*

P. obtusifolia Rounded leaves, up to 10cm (4in) long, often have a reddish margin. HEIGHT & SPREAD 25×25cm (10×10in).

In the **Magnoliifolia Group**, **'Golden Gate'** has leaves streaked with yellow and marked with green dots, while **'Greengold'** bears longer leaves with splashes of gold variegation and **'Tricolor'** has foliage with irregular splashes of cream and pale green.

***P. orba* 'Pixie'** Oval or elliptical leaves are rarely over 6mm (¼in) long. HEIGHT & SPREAD 10×10cm (4×4in).

'Pixie Variegata' has variegated foliage.

P. sandersii see *P. argyreia*

P. scandens♀ (cupid peperomia) Pinkish green stems trail up to 90cm (36in) on this scrambling plant with 5cm (2in) long, glossy oval leaves. HEIGHT & SPREAD 90×30cm (36×12in).

'Variegata' has yellow-edged leaves.

CULTIVATION Plant in pots in a proprietary potting compost, shaded from direct sun. Water moderately in summer and sparingly in winter. Feed monthly from spring to autumn. Remove faded leaves regularly.

PROPAGATION Divide in spring. Take stem or leaf cuttings in spring and summer.

PESTS AND DISEASES Mealy bug and vine weevil can be troublesome.

Pericallis

Compositae

Daisy-like flowers typify these herbaceous perennials and shrubs, which are mostly native to the Canary Islands. They are not hardy in Britain.

The pericallis recommended here has plenty of impact and brings a summery splash to late winter and early spring. It is short-lived and suitable only as a temporary conservatory plant or houseplant, but if kept cool and moist the flowering season can extend to several weeks.

▲ *Pericallis* x *hybrida*

RECOMMENDED SPECIES AND VARIETIES
P.* x *hybrida (syn. *Senecio hybridus, S. cruentus*) (cineraria) A mass of showy flowers each 2.5-5cm (1-2in) across are grouped into a tight, flattish or slightly domed head that almost hides the foliage. Blue, maroon, pink, purple, red or white petals contrast with the darker flower centres, which can be any of these colours. The triangular to heart-shaped fresh green leaves are up to 15cm (6in) long. This rough-textured foliage is shallowly lobed and toothed, with downy undersides. Although this is herbaceous it is grown as an annual. HEIGHT & SPREAD 25x10cm (10x4in).

Seed is available only in mixed colours. Established strains of compact growth habit include **Amigo Hybrids** (very dwarf), **Cindy Mixture, Mini-Starlet Mixture** and **'Spring Glory'** (syn. 'Dwarf British Beauty'). **Moll Hybrids** have flowers 4cm (1½in) wide and are taller and very spreading, reaching 40-45cm (16-18in) high and 50cm (20in) wide.
CULTIVATION Grow in pots of John Innes No.2 at a temperature of 7-15°C (45-59°F). Shade plants in spring and summer but provide full light in autumn and winter. Water regularly. Liquid feed once the final pot is filled with roots, but stop when the plant is in bud.
PROPAGATION Sow seed in spring for autumn flowering, and in mid to late summer for flowering in late winter and early spring. Ensure a temperature of around 15-20°C (59-68°F) for germination. Prick out seedlings 7cm (2¾in) apart. When they begin to crowd one another, move them to final pots in a cool, well-ventilated greenhouse, conservatory or light windowsill. Keep cool in winter and bring indoors when the flowers open if desired.
PESTS AND DISEASES Aphids can cause great damage, especially to young growth. Chrysanthemum leaf miners also attack.

Perilla

Labiatae

The striking, dark red-purple foliage of perillas provides a dramatic contrast to the floral display of many other summer bedding plants. These fast-growing, half-hardy annuals of branching, bushy habit look good as part of mixed plantings in large containers, as well as in beds and borders. The leaf colour complements pale pink flowers especially well.
RECOMMENDED SPECIES
P. frutescens var. ***crispa***♀ (syn. var. *nankinensis*) (beefsteak plant) The slightly curved leaves, reddish purple with a bronze sheen, are broadly oval and up to 12cm (4¾in) long. The margins of the leaves are very deeply cut. Short spikes of small, white or pale violet flowers appear in late summer and early autumn. HEIGHT & SPREAD 50x25cm (20x10in).
CULTIVATION Plant in late spring in fertile, moist soil in full sun with some shelter from wind. Pinch out the growing points of the strongest shoots during the first month after planting to encourage good plant shape.
PROPAGATION Sow seed in late winter under glass.
PESTS AND DISEASES Perillas attract aphids.

▲ *Perilla frutescens* var. *crispa*

Periwinkle see *Vinca*
Pernettya see *Gaultheria*

Perovskia

Russian sage
Labiatae

Prominent, grey stems in winter, aromatic leaves in spring and flowers that last from mid summer until autumn make Russian sage a plant for all seasons. Deeply cut, grey, narrowly oval leaves, up to 6cm (2½in) long, are covered in white hairs. Their aroma is similar to culinary sage. The stiff, upright stems give a strong, vertical shape. Widely grown in herbaceous and mixed borders, this hardy sub-shrub or herbaceous perennial needs full sun. The recommended plants have pale violet-blue, tubular, lipped flowers, each about 3mm (⅛in) wide.
RECOMMENDED SPECIES AND VARIETIES
P. atriplicifolia♀ The flowers are held in spires. HEIGHT & SPREAD 1.2x1m (4x3ft).
***P.* 'Blue Spire'**♀ Robust spikes of flowers appear on this plant. HEIGHT & SPREAD 1.2x1m (4x3ft).
CULTIVATION Plant in spring on well-drained soil in full sun.
PROPAGATION Divide and replant or take basal cuttings in spring.
PRUNING Cut back the previous year's stems to the ground in spring.
PESTS AND DISEASES Usually trouble free.

▲ *Perovskia* 'Blue Spire'

Persicaria

Knotweed

Polygonaceae

Persicaria bistorta 'Superba'

Flowers in shades of pink or white appear mostly late in the season on these hardy, herbaceous perennials. Excellent for the border or as ground cover, persicarias are easy to grow, although the taller species prefer slightly moist conditions. The low-growing plants will tolerate dry situations. They grow in full sun or partial shade but the best flower and leaf colour is obtained in a sunny position.

RECOMMENDED SPECIES AND VARIETIES

P. affinis (syn. *Polygonum affine*) Small pink or red flowers carried in dense, upright spikes about 8 cm (3¼ in) long appear in late summer. They often persist through autumn into winter, gradually fading in colour. The dark green, elliptic leaves, about 10 cm (4 in) long, turn to shades of red and bronze in autumn. A compact, low-growing plant, it can be grown in a rock garden or as edging to a path. It is native to the Himalayas. HEIGHT & SPREAD 60×60 cm (2×2 ft).

'Darjeeling Red'♀ has long-lasting pinky red flowers. Its lanceolate leaves turn russet brown as winter approaches. **'Donald Lowndes'**♀ is more compact and has salmon pink flowers which darken as the plant ages. **'Superba'**♀ (syn. 'Dimity') has pale pink flowers which turn crimson and striking rich brown leaves in autumn.

▲ *Persicaria affinis* 'Donald Lowndes'

P. amplexicaulis (syn. *Polygonum amplexicaule*) Small, pale pink or purple flowers in loose, tapering spikes up to 8 cm (3¼ in) long, appear in late summer to early autumn. Its dense habit and tall flowering stems make this a good plant for the herbaceous border. Native to the Himalayas. HEIGHT & SPREAD 1.2×1.2 m (4×4 ft).

'Firetail'♀ has bright crimson flowers.

P. bistorta (syn. *Polygonum bistorta*) (bistort, snakeweed, Easter ledges) Dense, cylindrical spikes, up to 9 cm (3½ in) long, consisting of a mass of small pale pink or white flowers appear in early summer and last for a long time. The ovate to oblong light green leaves, up to 20 cm (8 in) long, form thick, fast-growing ground cover. This plant does well in a mixed border or at the damp edges of a pond, although it can become invasive there. Native to Europe and W Asia. HEIGHT & SPREAD 75×60 cm (2½×2 ft).

▲ *Persicaria bistorta* 'Superba'

'Superba'♀ has clear pink flowers.

P. campanulata (lesser knotweed) A compact, mat-forming plant grown as much for its foliage as its tiny, bell-shaped, fragrant pale pink flowers. It has lance-shaped, ribbed, mid green leaves, 20 cm (8 in) long, with rounded ends and buff-coloured backs. The flowers are carried in branching clusters up to 8 cm (3¼ in) across which appear in late summer to early autumn. Native to the Himalayas. HEIGHT & SPREAD 1×1 m (3×3 ft).

There are 2 white-flowered selections, **Alba Group** and **'Southcombe White'**, which can be more invasive.

P. filiformis see *P. virginiana*

P. milletii Crimson flowers carried in dense round or cylindrical heads, 4 cm (1½ in) long, appear in mid to late summer. The slender, oblong, basal leaves are up to 30 cm (1 ft) long. A clump-forming species, it can be planted in a border or large rock garden and grows best in a rich, moist soil. Native to Nepal and China. HEIGHT & SPREAD 60×60 cm (2×2 ft).

P. mollis (syn. *Polygonum molle*) Very small, creamy white flowers are carried in dense clusters, up to 30 cm (1 ft) long, on branching stems in late summer. It is a tall-growing, bushy plant with dark green, wavy leaves up to 20 cm (8 in) long. It grows best in moist areas. Native to the Himalayas. HEIGHT & SPREAD 2.4 m×75 cm (8×2½ ft).

P. tenuicaulis Tiny white flowers are produced in loose spikes up to 10 cm (4 in) long in early spring. A low-growing plant used for ground cover or in a rock garden, it has ovate, mid green leaves up to 8 cm (3¼ in) long that are flushed with red underneath. This species is native to Japan. HEIGHT & SPREAD 15×20 cm (6×8 in).

P. vacciniifolia♀ Heather-pink flowers in spikes, 5 cm (2 in) long, appear from late summer to early autumn. The pointed, leathery leaves up to 2.5 cm (1 in) long change colour in autumn. The attractive trailing mats of foliage make this species good for ground cover, especially over rocks, walls or paved areas. This plant is native to the Himalayas. HEIGHT & SPREAD 20×60 cm (8 in×2 ft).

▲ *Persicaria milletii*

▲ *Persicaria virginiana* 'Painter's Palette'

P. virginiana (syn. *P. filiformis*) Creamy white and sometimes pink-tinged flowers, carried in spikes, 40 cm (16 in) long, appear in summer. The bright green, ovate leaves are 15 cm (6 in) long. This species is native to Japan and the Himalayas. HEIGHT & SPREAD 1.2 m×60 cm (4×2 ft).

'Painter's Palette' has variegated leaves with gold and pinky brown blotches.

CULTIVATION Plant from autumn to spring in any moist but well-drained soil, choosing a site in full sun or partial shade. Remove the faded flowerheads of taller species.
PROPAGATION Sow the seed of species under glass in spring and grow on until large enough to plant out in late summer or the following spring. Alternatively, divide from autumn to spring.
PESTS AND DISEASES Usually trouble free.

Persimmon see *Diospyros kaki*

Petasites

Butterbur, sweet coltsfoot
Compositae

If you have a boggy patch of garden to cover, these early-flowering perennials could be the answer. They thrive in damp, shady corners, where their small, daisy-like flowers are followed by large leaves. The edge of a pond or waterfall is another suitable location, but note that the roots can be invasive. Native to temperate regions of Europe, Russia and Asia.

RECOMMENDED SPECIES AND VARIETIES

P. fragrans (fragrant butterbur, winter heliotrope) Clusters of small, sweetly scented, daisy-like pale lilac or purple flowers appear in late winter or early spring. Each flower is 1 cm (⅜ in) across on a stem up to 30 cm (12 in) high. As the flowers fade the large, basal, rounded leaves, 12.5 cm (5 in) across, spring up with dark green upper surfaces and grey undersides. This plant covers the ground beautifully, but top growth can be killed back in bad winters. It can be invasive. HEIGHT & SPREAD 30 cm × 1.2 m (1 × 4 ft).

▲ *Petasites fragrans*

P. japonicus var. ***giganteus*** A tight bunch of yellowish white flowers, surrounded by a broad ruff of yellow-green bracts, is produced in late winter or early spring. Each flower is just 1 cm (⅜ in) across. This hardy plant has massive, rounded leaves, about 1 m (3 ft) across. They are shiny light green above and irregularly toothed. When these rough-surfaced leaves mass together, they form striking mounds which rival those made by the leaves of gunnera. HEIGHT & SPREAD 1 × 2.4 m (3 × 8 ft).

The leaves of **'Variegatus'** bear yellow streaks and blotches and the flowerheads are pale yellow.

CULTIVATION Plant in autumn or spring in moist, fertile soil, adding coarse compost at the time of planting. Deadhead flowers so that they do not detract from the foliage.
PROPAGATION Divide in either autumn or spring. Spring is better in cold gardens.
PESTS AND DISEASES Usually trouble free.

Petunia

Solanaceae

Colourful, trumpet-shaped flowers bloom from early summer until the first autumn frosts on these popular summer bedding plants. There are some 35 species, but almost all petunias now grown are the free-flowering F_1 hybrids, derived from just two species. Usually treated as half-hardy annuals, the F_1 hybrids are half-hardy perennials that flower the first year from seed. Grow petunias outdoors in window boxes, hanging baskets and other containers, as well as in borders, or as houseplants indoors. Allow the spreading varieties to hang over the edge of a container or use them as ground cover. Petunias thrive in coastal areas. Native to tropical S America.

RECOMMENDED SPECIES AND VARIETIES

P. × hybrida Flower colours, available as single colours and as mixtures, include white, cream, pale yellow, pink, red, mauve, purple and blue. The fluted petals may be edged or striped with white, or veined with darker colours, with the throats sometimes differently coloured. Some varieties have fringed petal edges, and others double flowers. Flowers are borne singly, on stems from which grow ovate, mid to dark green leaves as long as 5 cm (2 in). The entire plant is somewhat sticky and fleshy. The height range is 15-40 cm (6-16 in), and the habit of growth varies from compact to very spreading.

OTHER HYBRIDS

Varieties can be divided into three groups based on flower size.

MULTIFLORA GROUP

These bushy plants, 20-30 cm (8-12 in) tall, bear large numbers of flowers about 5 cm (2 in) across. This is the most widely grown and weatherproof group.

The following spread to 30 cm (12 in): **Carpet Series**♀, including the creamy yellow **'Buttercream'**; **Delight Series** and **Duo Series**, both with double flowers; **Mirage Series**♀, with larger flowers than the norm; and **Plum Pudding Series**, with deeper-coloured veining.

Some multiflora cultivars spread to 50 cm (20 in) or more, including **Cascadia Series**, the vigorous **'Purple Wave'**, **Solana Royal Series** and **Surfinia Series.**

GRANDIFLORA GROUP

The flowers of this group are fewer and larger, reaching up to 10 cm (4 in) across. However, they are more susceptible to wind and rain damage than the smaller blooms of the other groups. Plants grow to a height of 20-30 cm (8-12 in) and spread to 30 cm (12 in).

The **Cloud Series** and **Daddy Series** have marbled colours and dark veining. **'Lavender Storm'** has better weather resistance than most. **Pirouette Series** and **Super Fanfare Series** are double-flowered. Plants within the **Supercascade Series** are very spreading.

MILLIFLORA GROUP

This is the newest group, with the smallest flowers, 3 cm (1¼ in) or less across. The **Fantasy Series** is extremely free-flowering, with flowers about 3 cm (1¼ in) wide. It is characteristically dwarf and compact, growing to a height of 15 cm (6 in) and spreading to 20 cm (8 in). Much more spreading and with smaller tubular flowers are 2 similar series, **Carillon Series** and **Million Bells Series.** Their yellow-throated blooms are pink or blue and about 2 cm (¾ in) across, freely borne on plants 15 cm (6 in) tall, spreading to 30 cm (12 in).

▲ *Petunia* 'Lavender Storm'

▲ *Petunia* Fantasy Series

CULTIVATION Grow in light, well-drained soil in a site that is as sunny as possible. An over-rich soil, or excessive shade and moisture encourages leaf growth at the expense of flowers. Plant cultivars with large or double flowers in sheltered positions, since rain may mark their petals. Plant out after the last frosts. Deadhead as the flowers fade, and cut back straggly, spreading plants. Water container-grown plants regularly and frequently, and apply a liquid feed once a week, using a potash-rich fertiliser.
PROPAGATION Most of the listed plants can be propagated by seed or cuttings – seed is generally the chosen method. A few are only increased by taking cuttings. These are Cascadia Series, Solana Royal Series and Surfinia Series within the Multiflora Group, and the Carillon Series and Million Bells Series within the Milliflora Group.

Sow seed in early spring, at a temperature, if possible, of 20-25°C (68-77°F). Leave the seed uncovered, exposed to light, but do not let the surface dry out. Take stem cuttings in early spring from plants overwintered in a cool greenhouse which have been cut back in late winter. The cuttings will root quite easily if given bottom heat. Alternatively, buy seedlings or young plants in mid spring.
PESTS AND DISEASES Slugs and aphids are occasionally a problem. Losses due to soil-borne fungal infections may occur in badly drained soil. Plants may be affected by several viruses, including cucumber mosaic, tobacco mosaic and potato viruses. Plants raised from seed are normally virus free.

Phacelia

Hydrophyllaceae

In summer, the dense blue to mauve flowerheads of phacelias add colour to a rock garden, scree garden, alpine house or border. Of the two most commonly grown species, *Phacelia sericea* is a biennial or perennial and *P. tanacetifolia* is an annual that often self-seeds itself around the garden, even in poor soils. Both are hardy.
RECOMMENDED SPECIES
P. sericea Tiny, silvery blue, tubular flowers, about 5mm (¼in) long, with widely spreading lobes and prominent silver-blue stamens appear in late spring or early summer. They are borne in dense spikes that rise from a cluster of leaf rosettes. Each silver-haired leaf is up to 10cm (4in) long and is deeply divided. This short-lived, hardy perennial often grows as a biennial. It needs a sunny position and very sharp drainage and so is well suited to a scree bed or alpine house. Native to N America. HEIGHT & SPREAD 20×15cm (8×6in).

The leaves of ssp. ***ciliosa*** have broader segments and are less hairy.
P. tanacetifolia Bell-shaped, blue to mauve flowers, up to 1.5cm (½in) long, with

▲ *Phacelia tanacetifolia*

prominent stamens are borne in spikes in early to late summer. The blooms of this annual are particularly popular with bees. The hairy, deeply divided leaves grow up to 25cm (10in) long. This tall species makes an ideal border plant. Native to N America. HEIGHT & SPREAD 1m×30cm (3×1ft).
CULTIVATION Plant in spring in a sunny site in soil that is not too rich. *P. sericea* requires well-drained, gritty, lime-free soil. Protect *P. sericea* from winter wet. Alternatively, grow this species in pots of gritty compost and keep in an unheated greenhouse or alpine house.
PROPAGATION Sow the seed of *P. tanacetifolia* outdoors where they are to grow or under glass in spring. Replant self-sown seedlings if necessary in spring. Sow *P. sericea* in pots in autumn; they will not require protection during winter.
PESTS AND DISEASES *P. sericea* is susceptible to red spider mite if grown under glass.

Phalaenopsis see ORCHIDS p.467
Phalaris see GRASSES p.302
Pheasant's eye see *Adonis*
Pheasant's eye narcissus see *Narcissus poeticus* var. *recurvus*
Phegopteris see FERNS p.264

Phellodendron

Cork tree
Rutaceae

Phellodendron amurense

The pale yellow autumn colour and general lightness of the crown are delightful features of this deciduous tree. However, phellodendrons drain the goodness from the soil and require a lot of space. Rather insignificant yellow flowers are carried in clusters in mid summer, with male and female blooms

▲ *Phellodendron amurense*

on separate trees. Pea-sized, inedible black fruits – ripening in mid autumn – have five tiny stones and smell of turpentine if handled. The bark of the two species listed becomes distinctively fissured after about 20 or 30 years. Native to E Asia.
RECOMMENDED SPECIES
P. amurense (Amur cork tree) The bright green pinnate leaves are 25cm (10in) long and consist of 5-11 almost hairless lance-shaped leaflets, each 10cm (4in) long. This spreading tree develops corky, pale yellowish grey fissured bark which has a soft warm feel. The erect panicles of black berries on female trees contrast well with the pale yellow autumn leaves. This tree is very hardy in Britain, but unseasonal spring frost may cause stunted growth. HEIGHT & SPREAD 8×5m (26×16ft) after 20 years, ultimately 15m (50ft) tall.
P. chinensis The pinnate leaves, up to 40cm (16in) long, consist of 7 ovate pointed leaflets and are dark yellowish green above, paler and felted beneath. They often fold in half lengthways on hot sunny days. The bark is slightly corky, dark brownish grey and slightly fissured. The black berries contrast well with the pale yellow autumn colour. Some shelter is preferable. HEIGHT & SPREAD 8×5m (26×16ft) after 20 years, ultimately 18×12m (60×40ft).
CULTIVATION Grow in a moist and very fertile site. Planting is best done in spring with minimum root disturbance. Protection from late frost is essential. The best results are achieved if the tree is able to grow out of a sheltered environment into full sun.
PROPAGATION Plant softwood cuttings with bottom heat in mid summer or root cuttings in early winter.
PRUNING Not necessary.
PESTS AND DISEASES Usually trouble free.

Philadelphus

Mock orange
Philadelphaceae

White or cream flowers, heavy with the scent of orange blossom, smother these hardy deciduous shrubs in early and mid summer. The cup-shaped flowers have a conspicuous central boss of frothy yellow stamens or anthers. In most plants, the flowers are 2.5-5cm (1-2in) wide. The leaves, 2.5-10cm (1-4in) long, are generally ovate and prominently veined.

RECOMMENDED SPECIES AND VARIETIES

P. **'Avalanche'** Clusters of richly scented flowers appear on slender branches. HEIGHT & SPREAD 1×1m (3×3ft) after 5 years, ultimately 1.5m (5ft) tall.

P. **'Beauclerk'**♀ The sweetly scented, single flowers of this slightly arching shrub are up to 6cm (2½in) across. The fringed petals are flushed cerise at the base. HEIGHT & SPREAD 1.5×1.2m (5×4ft) after 5 years, ultimately 1.8m (6ft) tall.

▲ *Philadelphus* 'Beauclerk'

P. **'Belle Etoile'**♀ Clusters of heavily scented flowers with fringed petals, flushed pink at the base, appear on this compact shrub. HEIGHT & SPREAD 1.5×1.5m (5×5ft) after 5 years, ultimately 2.4m (8ft) tall.

P. **'Burfordensis'** Clusters of unscented flowers, each up to 7.5cm (3in) wide, appear against the toothed leaves of this vigorous shrub. HEIGHT & SPREAD 1.5×1.5m (5×5ft) after 5 years, ultimately 3m (10ft) tall.

P. ***coronarius***♀ The clusters of semidouble flowers have a rich, pervasive scent. The narrow, tapering leaves curl slightly at the edges. This bushy shrub is particularly suitable for very dry soils. HEIGHT & SPREAD 1.8×1.5m (6×5ft) after 5 years, ultimately 3m (10ft) tall.

▲ *Philadelphus coronarius*

▲ *Philadelphus coronarius* 'Variegatus'

'Aureus'♀ has bright golden yellow leaves in spring and early summer that turn greenish yellow later. Leaf colour is best when this upright shrub is grown in shade or semi-shade. The leaves of **'Variegatus'**♀ have irregular, broad, creamy white edges.

P. **'Erectus'** Masses of strongly scented flower clusters cover this upright, compact shrub with slightly hairy leaves. HEIGHT & SPREAD 1.5×1m (5×3ft) after 5 years, ultimately 1.8m (6ft) tall.

P. **'Innocence'** The leaves of this compact shrub are often variegated creamy white, while the fragrant flowers, borne singly, are pure white. HEIGHT & SPREAD 1.2×1m (4×3ft) after 5 years, ultimately 1.5m (5ft) tall.

P. × ***lemoinei*** Richly scented flowers are borne in clusters on this broad shrub. HEIGHT & SPREAD 1.2×1.2m (4×4ft) after 5 years, ultimately 1.8m (6ft) tall.

P. **'Manteau d'Hermine'**♀ Creamy white, sweetly scented, double flowers are borne in profuse clusters on this wiry bush. HEIGHT & SPREAD 45×45cm (1½×1½ft) after 5 years, ultimately 75cm (2½ft) tall.

P. ***microphyllus***♀ Dainty leaves and heavily scented flowers are carried on the chestnut-coloured wiry stems of this broad bushy shrub. HEIGHT & SPREAD 45×45cm (1½×1½ft) after 5 years, ultimately 75cm (2½ft) tall.

P. **'Silberregen'** ('Silver Showers') Abundant fragrant flowers appear one to a stem on this dense rounded shrub. HEIGHT & SPREAD 1×1m (3×3ft) after 5 years, ultimately 1.2m (4ft) tall.

P. **'Sybille'**♀ Fringed petals flushed pale pink at the base appear one to a stem or in small clusters on this graceful plant with sea-green leaves. HEIGHT & SPREAD 1×1m (3×3ft) after 5 years, ultimately 1.5m (5ft) tall.

▼ *Philadelphus microphyllus*

P. **'Virginal'**♀ The strongly scented, white flowers are double or semidouble and open wide to appear in large, branched clusters. This upright shrub is twiggy at the base and is best planted at the back of the border. HEIGHT & SPREAD 1.8×1.2m (6×4ft) after 5 years, ultimately 3m (10ft) tall.

CULTIVATION Plant between mid autumn and early spring in any fertile well-drained soil on a site that gets some sun.

PROPAGATION Take semi-ripe cuttings in mid or late summer and grow under glass. Plant out the following year.

PRUNING Cut back the flowering shoots immediately after flowering to where a new shoot is developing.

PESTS AND DISEASES Leaf spot and aphids can be troublesome.

Phillyrea

Jasmine box
Oleaceae

Cultivated for their fine evergeen foliage, these hardy, easy-to-grow trees and shrubs, reminiscent of the olive, make an excellent foil to border plants. Phillyreas tolerate hot dry conditions and even sea salt. The tough opposite leaves are short-stalked, simple or toothed, numerous and dense.

RECOMMENDED SPECIES AND VARIETIES

P. ***angustifolia*** A compact rounded shrub that is excellent near the sea, this plant has dark green or yellowish grey-green leaves, up to 6cm (2½in) long, which are narrow and lance-shaped. The minute fragrant cream flowers are borne in clusters in late spring and early summer. HEIGHT & SPREAD 2×2m (6½×6½ft) after 10 years, ultimately 3m (10ft) tall.

There is a compact narrow-leaved form, f. ***rosmarinifolia***, which seldom exceeds 2m (6½ft) tall.

P. ***latifolia*** This is a leafy, densely branched tree or large shrub that can also be clipped as a hedge. The leaves are variable, but always hard, thick, toothed and glossy. They are

▼ *Phillyrea latifolia*

generally deep green, ovate and 6cm (2½in) long. The small, dull white, spring flowers are fragrant. *P. latifolia* is very hardy in lowland Britain, but its blue-black one-seeded berries are rarely produced in this country. HEIGHT & SPREAD 5×4m (16×13ft) after 20 years, ultimately 10m (33ft).

'Rotundifolia' has ovate to rounded leaves.

CULTIVATION Grow in any soil in sunlight or partial shade.

PROPAGATION Take semi-ripe cuttings in late summer and keep moist at first. Alternatively, layer in autumn. The plants grow well from seed where it is available.

PRUNING None is necessary, but the shrubs may be clipped in summer to restrict size.

PESTS AND DISEASES Usually trouble free.

Philodendron

Araceae

Philodendron scandens

These tropical perennials make attractive houseplants or greenhouse specimens which are grown for their fine foliage. Flowers appear occasionally, but they are insignificant and are usually removed to prevent them from adversely affecting the development of the evergreen leaves. This diverse genus includes scrambling and upright plants that grow from a basal crown, as well as twiners and small shrubs. The climbing plants cling by means of aerial roots. Moss poles are the ideal support, although the roots may need some help in attaching themselves initially.

RECOMMENDED SPECIES AND VARIETIES

P. adreanum see *P. melanochrysum*

P. bipennifolium (syn. *P. panduriforme*) (fiddle-leaf philodendron) The leathery, mid-green, glossy leaves of this climbing or scrambling plant are about 30cm (1ft) long and have 5 lobes. The central lobe of mature leaves becomes extended. HEIGHT & SPREAD 2m×60cm (6½×2ft).

P. domesticum (spade-leaf philodendron) This climbing plant has glossy, swept-back, roughly triangular, bright green leaves up to 45cm (1½ft) long. HEIGHT & SPREAD 2×1m (6½×3ft).

P. erubescens♀ (blushing philodendron) Distinctive young reddish purple stems and leaves with coppery purple undersides and reddish edges, strongly tinged with purple, distinguish this plant. The oval to triangular, glossy dark green leaves are about 30cm (1ft) long. HEIGHT & SPREAD 3×1m (10×3ft).

'Burgundy'♀ has heart-shaped leaves flushed red with burgundy-coloured veins and claret-coloured stems. **'Imperial Red'** produces roughly triangular dark purple to red leaves. **'Red Emerald'** has elongated heart-shaped leaves with red ribs on their undersides, and shiny red leaf stalks.

P. laciniatum see *P. pedatum*

P. melanochrysum (syn. *P. andreanum*) (black-gold philodendron) This slow-growing climber has pendent, elongated, heart-shaped, black-green leaves about 25cm (10in) long. In dappled sunlight, the velvety coating on the upper leaf surfaces gives them a gold-tinged appearance. The leaf veins are pale green. HEIGHT & SPREAD 3×1m (10×3ft).

▲ *Philodendron melanochrysum*

***P.* 'New Red'** Arrow-shaped deep metallic red leaves, up to 20cm (8in) long, grow on this non-climbing plant. HEIGHT & SPREAD 1m×45cm (3×1½ft).

P. ornatum (syn. *P. sodiroi*) This climber has heart-shaped, rounded or triangular, dark green, glossy leaves up to 45cm (1½ft) long, often spotted grey with red veins beneath. HEIGHT & SPREAD 3×1m (10×3ft).

P. panduriforme see *P. bipennifolium*

P. pedatum (syn. *P. laciniatum*) This slow-growing climber has oval, glossy, deep green leaves, up to 60cm (2ft) long, divided into either 5 or 7 lobes. HEIGHT & SPREAD 2m×60cm (6½×2ft).

P. scandens (sweetheart plant) The heart-shaped, glossy, rich green leaves grow to 30cm (1ft) long on a mature plant. The smaller juvenile leaves are about 15cm (6in) long. This popular, fast-growing evergreen climber is often re-propagated to prevent it reaching its full size. HEIGHT & SPREAD 4m×60cm (13×2ft).

P. sodiroi see *P. ornatum*

***P. tuxtlanum* 'Royal Queen'** Leathery glossy leaves, up to 60cm (2ft) long, appear on this slow-growing, creeping or scrambling plant. The mature leaves are oblong, pointed or arrow-shaped. HEIGHT & SPREAD 2×1m (10×3ft).

CULTIVATION Grow in humid conditions out of direct sunlight at a minimum temperature of 15°C (59°F) in potting compost mixed with up to one-third of composted bark or perlite. Insert moss poles into the compost before planting. Water freely in summer and feed two or three times during the active growing period with a general liquid houseplant feed. Water sparingly in winter. Pinch back to encourage branching. Periodically wipe the foliage with a proprietary leaf-shine product or use a little warm milk and water dabbed on with cotton wool.

PROPAGATION Take leafbud or softwood cuttings during summer.

PESTS AND DISEASES Mealy bug and scale insect may be troublesome.

Phlomis

Labiatae

Phlomis fruticosa

Dense clusters of colourful, hooded, tubular flowers with two lips, and downy leaves which are often silvery grey appear throughout summer on these herbaceous perennials and evergreen shrubs. These plants are good for hot, dry spots and drought conditions. Phlomis is hardy if grown in free-draining soil in a sunny, open position. However, it is wise to overwinter a few cuttings in a cold frame, because adult plants may die in a very wet cold winter. The plants are evergreen except *Phlomis* ssp. *maroccana*, *P. cashmeriana* and *P. russeliana*. The height and spread measurements are the mature size reached within five years.

RECOMMENDED SPECIES AND VARIETIES

P. anatolica This upright bushy plant has downy stems and greyish green, lance-shaped leaves, up to 10cm (4in) long. The yellow flowers, up to 2.5cm (1in) long, are produced in whorls. HEIGHT & SPREAD 1m×60cm (3×2ft).

▼ *Phlomis anatolica*

'Lloyd's Variety' has densely hairy, grey, oval leaves, up to 12.5cm (5in) long. It does not flower, and spreads up to 75cm (2½ft).

P. bovei ssp. *maroccana* The flowers are purple-pink and up to 4cm (1½in) long. They are borne in whorls in loose spikes. The leaves are mid green, lance to heart-shaped and up to 7.5cm (3in) long. HEIGHT & SPREAD 1.5×1.5m (5×5ft).

▲ *Phlomis bovei* ssp. *maroccana*

P. cashmeriana The pale lilac flowers, up to 2.5cm (1in) long, are held in whorls. The narrow, oval, mid green leaves are up to 20cm (8in) in length. HEIGHT & SPREAD 60×45cm (2×1½ft).

P. chrysophylla♀ Golden yellow flowers, up to 5cm (2in) long, are borne in spikes or scattered in pairs along the stems. The oval leaves, up to 7.5cm (3in) long, are grey-green when young and take on a golden flush with age. HEIGHT & SPREAD 1×1m (3×3ft).

P. **'Edward Bowles'** Soft golden yellow flowers, up to 4cm (1½in) long, are produced in whorls. The coarse, lance-shaped, silvery green leaves are up to 15cm (6in) long. HEIGHT & SPREAD 1.2×1.2m (4×4ft).

P. fruticosa♀ (Jerusalem sage) Bright yellow flowers up to 4cm (½in) long, are borne in clusters. This is a sturdy low-growing shrub with dull green, oval or lance-shaped leaves, up to 10cm (4in) long. HEIGHT & SPREAD 1×1m (3×3ft).

▲ *Phlomis fruticosa* *Phlomis italica* ▲

P. italica Dull purple or pink flowers, up to 2.5cm (1in) long, are produced in small whorls at the ends of the branches. The rough, dull green, lance-shaped leaves are up to 10cm (4in) long. This is a stiff, upright, rather untidy-looking plant. HEIGHT & SPREAD 1m×60cm (3×2ft).

▲ *Phlomis longifolia*

P. lanata The orange-yellow flowers, up to 2.5cm (1in) long, appear in whorls on this dwarf shrub. The rounded, woolly, golden-green leaves, 2.5cm (1in) long, clothe stems that are conspicuously golden when young. HEIGHT & SPREAD 45×45cm (1½×1½ft).

P. longifolia Yellow flowers, up to 4cm (1½in) long, appear in clusters on this low-growing shrub. The lance-shaped, heart-shaped or oval leaves are up to 7.5cm (3in) long. Dull green above, the leaves are grey or yellowish beneath. HEIGHT & SPREAD 1.2×1.2m (4×4ft).

The basal leaves of var. *bailanica* are oval.

P. purpurea Flowers in shades of pink to purple or white, up to 2.5cm (1in) long, appear in whorls against the lance-shaped, mid green leaves, up to 10cm (4in) long. HEIGHT & SPREAD 60×60cm (2×2ft).

The flowers of var. *alba* are white.

P. russeliana♀ (syn. *P. samia, P. viscosa* hort.) Numerous stout upright stems bear clusters of golden yellow flowers, up to 4cm (1½in) long. The rough, heart-shaped greyish green leaves are up to 20cm (8in) long. HEIGHT & SPREAD 1m×60cm (3×2ft).

P. samia see *P. russeliana*

P. viscosa hort. see *P. russeliana*

CULTIVATION Plant in spring in well-drained soil in full sun.

PROPAGATION Take softwood cuttings in summer or semi-ripe cuttings in autumn.

PRUNING None is normally required.

PESTS AND DISEASES Usually trouble free.

Phlox

Polemoniaceae

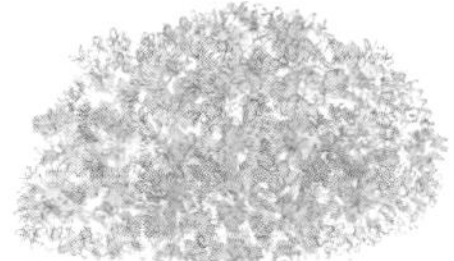

Phlox douglasii

Varying in size and habit, these annuals and hardy perennials from N America all have abundant and colourful flowers. Each flower has a narrow tube opening into five widely spreading petals, usually notched at their tips. There is often a contrasting colour in the throat. The recommended plants are divided into four groups: low-growing perennials, woodland perennials, border perennials and annuals.

RECOMMENDED SPECIES AND VARIETIES

LOW-GROWING PERENNIALS

A profusion of stemless or short-stemmed flowers, up to 2.5cm (1in) across, appears from early spring to early summer above evergreen, needle-like leaves, up to 2cm (¾in) long. These cushion-forming or low, mat-forming plants make a colourful carpet at the edge of a well-drained border or in a rock garden.

P. amoena hort. see *P.* × *procumbens*

P. bifida (sand phlox) Loose cushions of foliage bear clusters of flowers from white to deep lilac. There is also a blue-flowered form. This plant needs sharp drainage, and is best in a rock garden. HEIGHT & SPREAD 8×30cm (3¼×12in).

'Colvin's White' is a vigorous plant with pure white flowers, while **'Starbrite'** is compact with pale blue flowers.

P. caespitosa (cushion phlox) A tight cushion of foliage bears white or pale blue flowers, usually solitary but occasionally in small clusters. This plant needs to be grown in a greenhouse or on scree. HEIGHT & SPREAD 5×20cm (2×8in).

P. douglasii Flowers in white, lavender or pink appear singly, in pairs or in threes. HEIGHT & SPREAD 8×30cm (3¼×12in).

'Apollo' has good-sized violet-pink flowers, while **'Boothman's Variety'**♀ has lavender flowers with a deep blue centre. **'Crackerjack'**♀ is a compact plant bearing brilliant magenta blooms in great abundance. **'Eva'** is a compact plant with pinkish lavender flowers. **'Galaxy'** is also compact with darker violet flowers, while **'Iceberg'**♀ has white blooms flushed with the palest violet. **'Kelly's Eye'**♀ bears

▼ *Phlox douglasii* 'Crackerjack'

▲ *Phlox douglasii* 'Eva'

Phlox douglasii 'Iceberg' ▲

▲ *Phlox douglasii* 'Red Admiral'

masses of pale pink flowers with deeper coloured eyes, and **'Red Admiral'**♀ has flowers of deep crimson. **'Rose Cushion'** makes a very compact plant with rose-pink flowers, while **'Rosea'** has deep rose flowers. **'Violet Queen'** forms a very compact plant with flowers of darkest violet, and **'Waterloo'** bears purplish pink flowers.

P. ***kelseyi*** **'Rosette'** Abundant clusters of rounded deep pink flowers are borne by this plant, which forms a low shrubby mound. HEIGHT & SPREAD 5×20 cm (2×8 in).

P. ***nivalis*** (trailing phlox) Forming a small dense mat, this phlox has small clusters of purple to pink or white flowers. HEIGHT & SPREAD 5×20 cm (2×8 in).

'Camla' has pale pink flowers.

P. ***subulata*** (moss phlox) Clusters of red, purple, violet, lilac, pink or white flowers appear in late spring and early summer. HEIGHT & SPREAD 8×30 cm (3¼ in×1 ft).

'Alexander's Surprise' has large pinkish white flowers, while **'Amazing Grace'** has

▲ *Phlox subulata* 'Alexander's Surprise'

▲ *Phlox subulata* 'Amazing Grace'

pink flowers with a purple eye. **'Betty'** has large, deep pink flowers, and **'Bonita'** is a vigorous plant with large, purplish lilac flowers. **'Brightness'** has deep pink flowers with a crimson eye. **'Emerald Cushion Blue'** is a compact grower with lavender-

▲ *Phlox subulata* 'McDaniel's Cushion'

blue flowers, while the large flowers of **'G. F. Wilson'** are pale lavender. The flowers of **'Maischnee'** ('May Snow', 'Snow Queen') are pure white, while those of **'Marjorie'** are rose-pink. **'McDaniel's Cushion'**♀ is a vigorous plant with bright pink flowers. **'Oakington Blue Eyes'** bears lavender flowers, and **'Red Wings'**♀

▲ *Phlox subulata* 'Oakington Blue Eyes'

makes a vigorous plant bearing rose-red blooms with a darker eye. **'Samson'** has large, salmon-pink flowers with a red eye. **'Scarlet Flame'** has large, carmine blooms. **'Tamaongalei'** bears white blooms, streaked with reddish pink. **'Temiskaming'** is a very reliable plant with vivid deep magenta flowers. **'White Delight'** has pure white flowers.

WOODLAND PERENNIALS

These colourful, low carpeting or clump-forming, evergreen plants need a moist humus-rich soil in part shade, and are ideal between shrubs or taller plants, such as lilies, meconopsis, polygonatums and disporums. They have semi-prostrate stems, which root at the nodes, and oval or lance-shaped leaves, up to 3 cm (1¼ in) long. Loose flowerheads, each up to 2.5 cm (1 in) across, appear on upright stems in late spring and early summer. Height and spread measurements vary widely.

P. ***adsurgens***♀ Soft pink flowers have a pale eye and a dark central streak on each petal. The leaves are ovate. This temperamental plant requires perfect conditions to thrive. HEIGHT & SPREAD 25×60 cm (10 in×2 ft).

'Red Buttes' has pink and white flowers with deeper pink markings. Its overlapping petals give a rounded appearance. The narrow petalled flowers of **'Wagon Wheel'** are dark pink streaked with pale pink.

P. ***amoena*** hort. see *P.* × *procumbens*

P. **'Chattahoochee'** see *P. divaricata* ssp. *laphamii* 'Chattahoochee'

▲ *Phlox adsurgens* 'Red Buttes'

▲ *Phlox adsurgens* 'Wagon Wheel'

P. ***divaricata***♀ (blue phlox) This vigorous and spreading phlox bears clusters of flowers with notched petals, usually violet-blue with a darker eye. HEIGHT & SPREAD 20 cm×1 m (8 in×3 ft).

'Blue Dreams' has scented, lavender-blue flowers, and **'Charles Ricardo'** has fragrant, pale lavender flowers. **'Dirigo Ice'** bears large, very pale blue flowers. The flowers of ssp. ***laphamii*** are lilac with longer tubes and more rounded petals. Its cultivar, **'Chattahoochee'**♀, the most popular phlox, is very compact, bearing deep lilac flowers with a contrasting reddish purple eye. **'May Breeze'** is a vigorous plant with pale ice-blue flowers.

P. × ***procumbens*** (syn. *P. amoena* hort.) This plant, which forms a loose carpet, has purple flowers. HEIGHT & SPREAD 12×60 cm (4¾ in×2 ft).

'Millstream'♀ makes a dense mat bearing deep pink flowers with white centres

Phlox stolonifera

and reddish eyes. **'Variegata'** has green and cream variegated leaves and purple flowers.

P. stolonifera (creeping phlox) Flowers in either white or lavender to violet are carried in broad flat heads on stiffly upright stems. HEIGHT & SPREAD 25×60cm (10×24in).

'Ariane' has pure white, rounded flowers. **'Blue Ridge'**♀ has clear lavender-blue flowers. **'Mary Belle Frey'** has clear soft pink flowers, while those of **'Violet Vere'** are deep bluish violet.

BORDER PERENNIALS

These herbaceous perennials thrive in rich soils with adequate moisture. All do well in full sun or partial shade. The plants have glossy, oval or lanceolate leaves, up to 12cm (4¾in) long, and bear large clusters, up to 15cm (6in) wide, of often intensely fragrant flowers.

▼ *Phlox stolonifera* 'Mary Belle Frey'

▼ *Phlox carolina* 'Bill Baker'

P. carolina This plant has upright, spreading stems and bears pink to purple flowerheads in late spring and early summer. HEIGHT & SPREAD 50cm×1m (20in×3ft).

'Bill Baker' bears masses of soft pink, white-eyed flowers from late spring to mid summer. **'Miss Lingard'**♀ is similar, with white flowers.

P. maculata (meadow phlox) Long cylindrical clusters of pink, purple or white flowers are borne from mid to late summer. This plant is fairly resistant to mildew. HEIGHT & SPREAD 80cm×1m (32in×3ft).

Phlox maculata

'Alpha'♀ has deep pink flowers with a dark centre. **'Omega'**♀ bears white flowers with a small lilac eye.

P. paniculata Fine broad flowerheads in blue, purple, pink and white are borne from mid to late summer. This tall upright plant spreads to make large clumps. HEIGHT & SPREAD 60cm–1m×1m (2–3×3ft).

'Aida' is a shorter plant bearing soft purple flowers with a darker eye. **'Amethyst'**♀ has violet flowers, while **'Balmoral'** makes a tall, strong plant with pale pink flowers. **'Blue Boy'** is also tall, with bluish mauve blooms. **'Blue Ice'**♀ bears white blooms from pink buds. **'Border Gem'** is another tall variety with mauve-blue flowers. **'Brigadier'**♀ has deep pink flowers with an orange flush. **'Cecil Hanbury'** is a short-growing variety bearing orange-salmon flowers with red eyes. While **'Europe'** has white flowers with small pink eyes, **'Eventide'**♀ bears pale blue-mauve blooms. **'Fujiyama'**♀ has white flowers in long trusses, and **'Graf Zeppelin'** has white flowers with red eyes. **'Harlequin'** is a fairly vigorous plant with purple flowers and variegated foliage, while **'Mia Ruys'** is a low-growing plant with white flowers. **'Mies Copijn'** bears flowers that are clear pink throughout, and the flowers of **'Mother of Pearl'**♀ are white with a pink flush. **'Norah Leigh'** has variegated leaves and lilac flowers. **'Prince of Orange'**♀ is a strong-growing variety with orange-pink flowers, while **'Prospero'**♀ makes a tall plant with pale lilac flowers. **'Rembrandt'** has large white flowers, and those of **'Rijnstroom'** are deep rose-pink with paler eyes. **'San Antonio'** has dark blood-red flowers, while **'Sandringham'** has pale pink flowers with dark eyes. **'Skylight'** bears pinkish mauve flowers with white eyes. **'Starfire'** makes a tall plant with deep red flowers, while **'Tenor'** is a low-growing plant with ruby-red flowers. **'White Admiral'**♀ is another tall plant, but with pure white flowers. **'Windsor'**♀ has pinkish red flowers with darker red eyes.

P. pilosa (prairie phlox) Large loose heads of clear pink flowers with paler eyes are borne in late spring and early summer by this plant with spreading stems. HEIGHT & SPREAD 50cm×1m (20in×3ft).

ANNUALS

The recommended plants in this group are half hardy. Only one species is listed, but there are plenty of varieties and cultivars to choose from. They are excellent in bedding schemes or as fillers for a border.

P. drummondii Flower clusters in a range of pinks, purples, blues, white or three-coloured, sometimes with a contrasting centre, appear from mid summer to early autumn. Glossy lance-shaped to oval leaves set off the flowers. HEIGHT & SPREAD 10–45×25cm (4–18×10in).

'Carnival' lives up to its name with flowers, 2.5cm (1in) across, in a wide variety of colours, often with a centre in a contrasting colour. This plant grows up to 30cm (1ft) tall. Varieties in the **Grandiflora Group** have large flowers, purple above and white beneath. They also grow to 30cm (1ft) tall. The **Nana Compacta Group,** of which **'Beauty'** is a named cultivar, have large flowers mainly in dark shades of red, purple and lilac, less often white or yellow, and grow to 20cm (8in) tall. **'Twinkle'** in the **Stellaris Group** grows to only 15cm (6in) tall, bearing masses of 1.5cm (½in) wide starry flowers in a very wide range of colours.

CULTIVATION For the low-growing perennials, plant in well-drained soil in full sun. Clip them lightly to keep the plants tidy. For the woodland perennials, plant in humus-rich soil in partial shade. For the border perennials, plant in moisture-retentive soil in sun or partial shade. Support the taller plants. For the annuals, plant in full sun in good soil when the danger of frost is past.

PROPAGATION Take greenwood cuttings of the low-growing and woodland perennials in early to mid summer. Divide and replant the border perennials in fresh soil in early spring or autumn about every 3 years or, alternatively, take root cuttings in late winter to lessen the danger of eelworm attack. Sow seed of annuals under glass in early spring.

PESTS AND DISEASES The low-growing perennials are usually trouble free outside, but red spider mite may be troublesome under glass. Slugs and snails may damage the woodland perennials, while some of the border perennials are vulnerable to eelworm and mildew. The annuals are usually trouble free.

Phoenix

Date palm

Palmae

Phoenix canariensis

These tender tropical evergreen palms are grown for their handsome divided foliage. The leaves are feather-like, consisting of many lance-shaped leaflets. Their flowers and fruit are rarely produced in Britain. The trunks of all species are patterned to some extent by old leaf scars. They are sometimes placed in their pots outdoors in summer where they provide an interesting focal point. However, they are mostly grown in a conservatory or heated greenhouse.

RECOMMENDED SPECIES

P. canariensis♀ (Canary Island date palm) The leaves of this upright palm can grow up to 5m (16ft) long on mature plants. They consist of bright green leaflets up to 30cm (1ft) long. Large pendent sprays of tiny yellowish flowers may be produced in summer. Small yellowish fruits, up to 2.5cm (1in) long, may develop on mature plants in autumn and winter. The trunk is coarse and sturdy. Most gardeners keep this palm until it outgrows its allocated space, then replace it with a fresh specimen. HEIGHT & SPREAD 2×1m (6½×3ft) after 5 years, ultimately 18m (60ft) tall.

▲ *Phoenix canariensis*

P. dactylifera (date palm) This tree, grown commercially for its edible dates, is excellent under glass in Britain. The leaves are up to 3m (10ft) long, with leaflets, up to 30cm (1ft) long. The trunk is coarse and fibrous. The flowers, when produced, are small and yellowish. HEIGHT & SPREAD 3×1m (10×3ft) after 5 years, ultimately 30m (100ft) tall.

▲ *Phoenix roebelenii*

P. roebelenii♀ (pygmy date palm) The arching leaves of this palm are 1m (3ft) long. They consist of glossy dark green leaflets up to 20cm (8in) long. The coarse, fibrous trunk is slender. HEIGHT & SPREAD 1.5×1m (5×3ft) after 5 years, ultimately 3m (10ft) tall.

CULTIVATION Grow in pots of a soil-based potting compost, such as John Innes No. 2, in a greenhouse or conservatory, at a minimum temperature of 7°C (45°F), but with some shade. Water freely in summer and apply a liquid houseplant feed every month during the active growing period. Water sparingly in winter. Remove any faded leaves.

PROPAGATION Sow seed under glass at a minimum temperature of 24°C (75°F).

PESTS AND DISEASES Red spider mite and mealy bug can be a problem.

Phormium

Flax lily

Agavaceae

Phormium tenax Purpureum Group

The sword-shaped leaves of these evergreen perennials are used to full architectural effect in herbaceous and shrub borders. Native to New Zealand, the plants are normally grown outdoors in south and southwest Britain only. However, green-leaved species will survive cold winters with adequate shelter and protection. If grown in containers in a cool greenhouse or conservatory, the plants can be taken outside in summer. When positioning these plants, bear in mind that the pointed leaf-tips are sharp and could hurt young children.

RECOMMENDED SPECIES AND VARIETIES

P. cookianum♀ (syn. *P. colensoi*) (mountain flax) Arching, pale to dark green leaves, up to 1.2m (4ft) long, distinguish this species. In late summer slender flower stems are produced, carrying green and orange or yellow, tubular flowers up to 4cm (1½in) long. The slender nodding seed pods which twist and curve are a feature in autumn. HEIGHT & SPREAD 1.2m×30cm (4ft×12in).

The leaf colour of ssp. ***hookeri* 'Cream Delight'**♀ is reflected in its name. As with many cream variegated plants, this one is not as vigorous as the parent species. It may do better in a partially shaded spot. The drooping leaves of ssp. ***hookeri* 'Tricolor'**♀ have green centres and are striped yellow towards the red edges.

▲ *Phormium cookianum* ssp. *hookeri* 'Cream Delight'

P. tenax♀ (New Zealand flax) Perhaps the enormous size of this species precludes its use in smaller gardens, but it can make an outstanding feature where there is room. It can be used at the edge of a large pond as well as at the back of a border, and it thrives in coastal gardens. The tough leathery leaves are up to 3m (10ft) long. They are greyish green with red or orange edges and midrib. In late summer there are masses of dull reddish brown flowers, up to 5cm (2in) long, followed by erect seedpods. HEIGHT & SPREAD 4.5×1.2m (15×4ft).

'Nanum Purpureum'♀ has purple bronze-tinted leaves only 45cm (18in)

▲ *Phormium* 'Sundowner'

long. Plants in the **Purpureum Group**♀ have leaves in various shades of purple. **'Variegatum'**♀ has mid green leaves with creamy yellow stripes of varying widths on the edges, and plum-red flowering spikes.

GARDEN HYBRIDS

These plants have been selected for leaf colour as the flowers are not generally regarded as a feature. They reach a height of up to 3m (10ft) and spread to 1m (3ft).

The outer red-bonze leaves of **'Bronze Baby'** are arching. **'Duet'**♀ is a dwarf plant with bright green leaves with a creamy white stripe, up to 30cm (12in) long. **'Sundowner'**♀ has erect bronze leaves tipped purple and pink. **'Yellow Wave'**♀ has bright yellow-and-green leaves.

CULTIVATION Plant in any soil provided that it can be kept fairly moist throughout summer. Do not feed the plants as this encourages soft growth which may kill the plant in winter. If attempting to grow plants outdoors, protect them in winter with bracken, old branches of conifers or horticultural fleece. Deadhead in autumn to prevent winter rocking which can damage or even kill the plant. For container plants placed outside in spring and summer in a windy position or by the sea, consider trimming the leaves to a third of their length to diminish wind resistance.

PROPAGATION Divide in spring, making sure that each piece of root has 4-5 strong leaves. Alternatively, sow seed in spring under glass and grow on in individual pots under cover. Plant out, if appropriate, the following spring.

PESTS AND DISEASES Usually trouble free.

Photinia

Rosaceae

Photinia x fraseri 'Robusta'

Brilliant year-round leaf colour on the evergreens, and spectacular autumn fruit and foliage on the deciduous plants distinguish these hardy Asian shrubs. Clusters of white flowers in spring are followed by berries, 5-10mm (¼-⅜in) wide, in summer. The young evergreen leaves are red.

RECOMMENDED SPECIES AND VARIETIES

P. beauverdiana♀ Glorious bronze-red autumn leaves grace this deciduous shrub. The narrow oval leaves, up to 12.5cm (5in) long, have prominent veins underneath. Flower clusters, 5cm (2in) across, appear in late spring followed by dark red fruit. HEIGHT & SPREAD 1.5×2m (5×6½ft) after 5 years, ultimately 8m (26ft) tall.

▲ *Photinia beauverdiana*

P. davidiana (syn. *Stransvaesia davidiana*) This sprawling, semi-evergreen shrub has leathery, egg-shaped to pointed dark green leaves, up to 11cm (4¼in) long. They turn orange and red, and fall in early winter. The flower clusters, up to 10cm (4in) across, give way to red berries. HEIGHT & SPREAD 2.4×2.4m (8×8ft) after 5 years, ultimately 4m (13ft) tall.

P. x fraseri The bronze to red young leaves of this evergreen hybrid turn glossy green later. They are toothed, egg-shaped and up to 9cm (3½in) long. The flowers appear in clusters up to 12cm (4¾in) wide. HEIGHT & SPREAD 1.5×2m (5×6½ft) after 5 years, ultimately 4m (13ft) tall.

'Birmingham' has deep coppery red young leaves. **'Red Robin'**♀ has glossy, sharply toothed, bright red foliage at first.

▲ *Photinia x fraseri* 'Red Robin'

'Robusta'♀ displays thick, leathery, oblong leaves that are bright coppery red at first. It is one of the hardiest cultivars. **'Rubens'** (syn. *P. glabra* 'Rubens') has glossy bright red young foliage.

P. glabra **'Parfait'** (syn. *P.* 'Pink Lady', *P.* 'Variegata') This evergreen has smooth, bronze-red young leaves, up to 8cm (3in) long, initially edged in pink. The margins turn cream as the leaf becomes green flecked with grey-green. In a mild spring flower clusters, up to 10cm (4in) across, may appear, followed by red to black berries. HEIGHT & SPREAD 1.5×2m (5×6½ft) after 5 years, ultimately 3m (10ft) tall.

P. glabra **'Rubens'** (syn. *P. x fraseri* 'Rubens')

P. 'Pink Lady' see *P. glabra* 'Parfait'

P. **'Redstart'**♀ Red young leaves turn glossy green later on this vigorous evergreen. Clusters of white flowers on purplish red stalks in early summer are then followed by orangey red berries. HEIGHT & SPREAD 1.5×2m (5×6½ft) after 5 years, ultimately 5m (16ft) tall.

▲ *Photinia serratifolia*

P. serratifolia Leathery, toothed, mature leaves, up to 18cm (7in) long, are dark green above and yellowish below. The young growth is red tinted. Flower clusters are up to 18cm (7in) wide. HEIGHT & SPREAD 1.5×2m (5×6½ft) after 5 years, ultimately 5m (16ft) tall.

P. **'Variegata'** see *P. glabra* 'Parfait'

P. villosa♀ The leaves of this deciduous shrub turn orange and red in autumn. They are pointed, ovate to oblong and up to 3cm (1¼in) long. Flower clusters, 5cm (2in) across, are followed by egg-shaped fruits. HEIGHT & SPREAD 1.5×2m (5×6½ft) after 5 years, ultimately 5m (16ft) tall.

▲ *Photinia villosa*

CULTIVATION Plant on a sheltered site in well-drained fertile soil, except *P. davidiana* and *P. × fraseri* which prefer moist soil. Evergreens are lime tolerant, while deciduous plants prefer acid to neutral soil, although *P. beauverdiana* will withstand some lime.

PROPAGATION Sow ripe seed in autumn in a coldframe or take ripewood cuttings in mid to late autumn.

PRUNING None is necessary for deciduous plants. Cut back evergreens each year to encourage the growth of young red leaves.

PESTS AND DISEASES Fire blight may be a problem, especially in *P. davidiana*. Honey fungus may be troublesome and powdery mildew may appear on leaves in summer.

Phuopsis

Rubiaceae

A pink carpet of summer flowers attracts butterflies to this low-growing hardy perennial from the Caucasus Mountains. It is ideal for the front of a border, or beneath a wall or on a bank. The genus has only one species which usually dies back in winter, but might retain its leaves in a mild weather.

Phuopsis stylosa (syn. *Crucianella stylosa)* Pink, five-lobed, tubular flowers, about 2 cm (¾ in) across, form dense round heads. Pungent smelling, pale green leaves, up to 5 mm (¼ in) long, appear in whorls. HEIGHT & SPREAD 15×50 cm (6×20 in).

'Purpurea' has deeper purplish pink flowers.

▲ *Phuopsis stylosa* 'Purpurea'

CULTIVATION Plant plants in spring in any well-drained soil in full sun or light shade. Cut back after flowering to prevent the plant becoming too straggly.

PROPAGATION Divide plants in spring or take semi-ripe cuttings in early summer. Alternatively, sow the seed of the species in a coldframe in autumn.

PESTS AND DISEASES Usually trouble free.

Phygelius

Scrophulariaceae

Phygelius aequalis 'Yellow Trumpet'

Spikes of pendulous tubular flowers, up to 4 cm (1½ in) long, in yellow, orange, pink, red and scarlet adorn these short-lived shrubs for most of summer and early autumn. The plants can tolerate temperatures as low as -10°C (14°F), and in mild winters they are evergreen. However, in long periods of frost they lose their leaves and die back to the ground, although new growth usually emerges in spring. The toothed oval to pointed leaves, up to 10 cm (4 in) long, are deep to pale green. Native to South Africa, they are drought-tolerant but prefer free-draining soil and a sunny site. The recommended plants reach their ultimate size within the first year.

RECOMMENDED SPECIES AND VARIETIES

P. aequalis Dusky red-pink flowers form dense spikes on this compact bushy shrub. Each flower is flared at the mouth with an attractive yellow throat. HEIGHT & SPREAD 1 m×60 cm (3×2 ft).

'Yellow Trumpet' has yellow flowers.

P. capensis (Cape fuchsia, Cape figwort) Orange to deep-red flowers are carried in loose spikes on this sparsely branched shrub. HEIGHT & SPREAD 1 m×60 cm (3×2 ft).

P.* x *rectus Flowers of varying colours are arranged in loose spikes on this spreading, sparsely branched shrub. HEIGHT & SPREAD 1.5 m×75 cm (5×2½ ft).

'African Queen' has red flowers with orange and red lips, while the deep reddish pink flowers of **'Devil's Tears'** have yellow throats. **'Moonraker'** has pale yellow flowers, while those of **'Salmon Leap'** are orange. The dusky red-pink flowers of **'Winchester Fanfare'** have a scarlet tip.

CULTIVATION Plant in free-draining soil in a sunny but sheltered situation protected by a south or west-facing wall. Mulch the plants well. Remove early spikes after flowering to promote the growth of sideshoots.

PROPAGATION Take greenwood cuttings in mid to late summer or sow seed in spring.

PRUNING Cut dead stems to ground level in spring.

PESTS AND DISEASES Usually trouble free.

▲ *Phygelius* x *rectus* 'African Queen'

▲ *Phygelius aequalis* 'Yellow Trumpet'

X Phylliopsis

Ericaceae

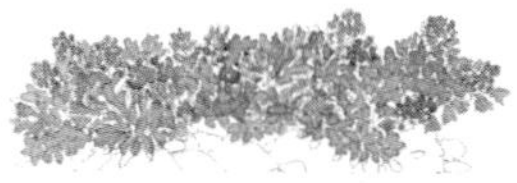

x *Phylliopsis hillieri* 'Pinocchio'

Loose spikes of many bell-shaped flowers appear above the foliage of this dwarf evergreen shrub. The leaves, up to 2 cm (¾ in) long, are a lustrous dark green. The plants do well in a peat bed or rock garden.

RECOMMENDED SPECIES AND VARIETIES

X *P.* 'Askival' Showy pink flowers appear in mid to late spring. HEIGHT & SPREAD 20×40 cm (8×16 in) after 5 years, ultimately 60 cm (2 ft) tall.

X *P.* 'Coppelia' Pink flowers appear in mid to late spring on this vigorous and easy to grow plant. HEIGHT & SPREAD 20×40 cm (8×16 in) after 5 years, ultimately 60 cm (2 ft) tall.

X *P. hillieri* 'Pinocchio' Elongated, upright spikes of rich pink flowers are open for a long period in mid to late spring. HEIGHT & SPREAD 20×40 cm (8×16 in) after 5 years, ultimately 60 cm (2 ft) tall.

CULTIVATION Grow in well-drained, acid, humus-rich soil in a sunny position.

PROPAGATION Take semi-ripe cuttings in late summer or early autumn.

PRUNING Remove any long shoots after flowering.

PESTS AND DISEASES Usually trouble free.

▲ x *Phylliopsis* 'Coppelia'

▲ x *Phylliopsis hillieri* 'Pinocchio'

Phyllodoce

Mountain heath, blue heather
Ericaceae

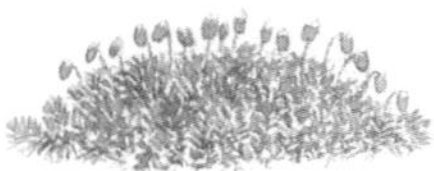

Phyllodoce caerulea

In mid spring and early summer, the pink, purple, red or white flowers of these hardy dwarf evergreen shrubs bring splashes of colour to the garden. The shrubs are particularly suitable for rockeries in areas with a high rainfall and they prefer acid soil. Although hardy, they need protection against frost when there is no snow cover, and against drying winds and strong sunlight, especially when covered in frost.

RECOMMENDED SPECIES

P. aleutica Nodding heads, up to 5 cm (2 in) wide, of rounded, yellowish white flowers appear in mid and late spring. The narrow, bright green leaves are up to 1 cm (⅜ in) long. A mat-forming species native to NE Asia and W Alaska. HEIGHT & SPREAD 20×30 cm (8×12 in) after 5 years, ultimately 25 cm (10 in) tall.

▲ *Phyllodoce aleutica*

P. breweri The purplish pink flowers of this prostrate shrub are dish-shaped and deeply split with conspicuous pink stamens. They form heads up to 7.5 cm (3 in) across that appear in late spring and early summer, and again, sometimes in autumn. Glossy dark green leaves, 1 cm (⅜ in) long, are narrow and densely arranged on the stem. Native to the Rocky Mountains of N America. HEIGHT & SPREAD 23×30 cm (9×12 in) after 5 years, ultimately 30 cm (12 in) tall.

P. caerulea♀ (syn. *Menziesia taxifolia*) Purplish pink, urn-shaped blooms which turn blue with age, appear from mid spring to early summer. They are held in flowerheads up to 5 cm (2 in) across. This bushy shrub has dense, glossy dark green foliage with narrow leaves up to 1 cm (⅜ in) long. Native to arctic and alpine Europe. HEIGHT & SPREAD 15×15 cm (6×6 in) after 5 years, ultimately 30 cm (12 in) tall.

▲ *Phyllodoce empetriformis*

P. empetriformis Bell-shaped, 5-lobed, rose-red flowers in heads up to 5 cm (2 in) wide, are borne on thin, nodding stalks between mid spring and mid summer. The narrow, bright green leaves of this small, spreading shrub are up to 1.5 cm (½ in) long. It is more tolerant of dry conditions than other species. Native to the Rocky Mountains of N America. HEIGHT & SPREAD 15×20 cm (6×8 in) after 5 years, ultimately 25 cm (10 in) tall.

P. nipponica♀ (syn. *P. caerulea* ssp. *japonica*) White, often pink-tinged flowers appear from mid spring to early summer, borne in spikes up to 5 cm (2 in) long. The narrow, dark green leaves, up to 1 cm (⅜ in) long, are grey beneath. A compact shrub native to Japan. HEIGHT & SPREAD 10×10 cm (4×4 in) after 5 years, ultimately 20 cm (8 in) tall.

▲ *Phyllodoce nipponica*

CULTIVATION Plant in spring or autumn in moist but well-drained, lime-free, humus-rich soil, choosing a spot in partial shade. Protect plants by covering with conifer twigs or sacking in winter.

PRUNING Not usually necessary but plants can be cut into shape after flowering.

PROPAGATION Take semi-ripe heeled cuttings in mid summer.

PESTS AND DISEASES Usually trouble free.

Phyllostachys see BAMBOOS p. 77

×Phyllothamnus

Ericaceae

This hardy evergreen shrub with clusters of spring flowers is the sole species in this hybrid genus. It is a cross between *Phyllodoce* and *Rhodothamnus*, and is suitable for semi-shaded sites on acid soil.

×*Phyllothamnus erectus* Bell-shaped, rosy purple flowers, up to 1.5 cm (½ in) long and wide, are borne in clusters of 8 or more at the ends of stems. The short, dark green, needle-like leaves are crowded together on tough, wiry stems to form a plant with a compact habit. HEIGHT & SPREAD 25×25 cm (10×10 in) ultimately after 5 years.

▲ × *Phyllothamnus erectus*

CULTIVATION Plant in spring in moisture-retentive, lime-free soil that is enriched with liberal quantities of organic matter. Feed established plants annually in spring with a slow-release fertiliser. Water regularly in dry weather and, once flowering is over, clip off the spent flowers.

PROPAGATION Take semi-ripe cuttings during late summer.

PESTS AND DISEASES Usually trouble free.

Physalis

Chinese lantern
Solanaceae

Physalis alkekengi

Bright orange, papery lanterns in late summer and early autumn are the main attraction of these plants. The genus contains hardy and tender annuals and herbaceous perennials but as the plants tend to be invasive only the two hardy perennials described are commonly cultivated. As well as adding colour to an informal border in autumn, the fruits retain their colour when dried for use in winter floral arrangements. The genus is widely distributed around the world, particularly in the Americas.

RECOMMENDED SPECIES AND VARIETIES

P. alkekengi ♀ (bladder cherry, winter cherry) A hardy plant with insignificant creamy white flowers which appear on rather floppy, unbranched stems in summer. They are carried in the upper leaf axils among pointed, lance-shaped, mid green leaves up to 12cm (4¾in) long. Bright red papery calyxes develop after the flowers, each one puffing out around an edible orange-red berry. Each lantern may be up to 5cm (2in) in diameter. For dried flower arrangements cut the stems as the calyxes begin to colour, and hang upside-down in an airy shed or attic to dry. HEIGHT & SPREAD 60×60cm (24×24in).

More pointed lanterns are seen on var. *franchetii*. The plant is larger than the parent species with mid green leaves and an intense orange-red calyx.

CULTIVATION Plant in any soil from autumn to spring, choosing a sunny site. To control the spreading roots, plant in a large pot and bury it in the ground. Alternatively, cut round the roots of the plant each autumn with a sharp spade to remove surplus material which can be used to increase the plant elsewhere in the garden.

PROPAGATION Divide in the dormant season, which is winter or early spring. Alternatively sow seed in a coldframe in early spring and plant out in early summer when the plants are large enough for the conditions in the particular garden.

PESTS AND DISEASES Usually trouble free.

▲ *Physalis alkekengi* var. *franchetii*

Physocarpus

Rosaceae

Physocarpus opulifolius 'Dart's Gold'

Abundant clusters of small white flowers appear in early summer on these hardy deciduous shrubs. Rounded and many-stemmed in habit, they are good plants for the back of the border. They do best in full sun and moist acid soil.

RECOMMENDED SPECIES AND VARIETIES

P. opulifolius (ninebark) Tiny white flowers, which may be tinged with pink, have 5 petals and numerous stamen. The flowers form clusters up to 5cm (2in) across. Small red berries follow in autumn. Mid green, ovate leaves have 3 lobes and are up to 6cm (2½in) long and wide with very serrated edges. The pale brown bark of the medium-sized deciduous shrub peels attractively after 5-10 years to reveal lighter shades of wood beneath. Native to N America. HEIGHT & SPREAD 1×1m (3×3ft) after 5 years, ultimately 3m (10ft) tall.

The leaves of **'Dart's Gold'** are bright yellow in mid spring, fading to dull green in the following 6-8 weeks. It is slightly smaller and denser than the species. **'Luteus'** does not keep its young yellow leaf colour for such a long time and leaves become olive green or tinged with bronze.

▲ *Physocarpus opulifolius* 'Luteus'
▼ *Physocarpus opulifolius* 'Dart's Gold'

CULTIVATION Plant between late autumn and mid spring in moist soil and a sunny position avoiding chalky ground.

PRUNING Little pruning is required, but plants can be trimmed between late autumn and early spring to keep them in shape and prevent straggling.

PROPAGATION Sow seed in late autumn or early spring in a coldframe. Position the coldframe in full sun and use a moist, fertile, acid soil. Alternatively, take semi-ripe cuttings in early or mid summer and plant them in a coldframe, or plant hardwood cuttings outdoors in late autumn.

PESTS AND DISEASES Usually trouble free.

Physoplexis

Campanulaceae

Unusual flask-shaped flowers in dense clusters are borne by this hardy tufted perennial from the SE Alps. A long stigma projects from the spiky top of the flower, where the petals are joined together at the tip. In the wild, the plant grows in rock crevices; in cultivation it can be grown outside in scree or tufa, a porous rock suited to lime-loving crevice plants. There is one species.

P. comosa ♀ (syn. *Phyteuma comosum*) Pale violet flowers with deep violet tips, 2cm (¾in) long, are borne in round, stemless clusters in early to mid summer. The dark green oval leaves are deeply toothed. HEIGHT & SPREAD 8×10cm (3¼×4in).

CULTIVATION Plant in very well-drained compost, preferably alkaline, in a pot in an alpine house, or outside in a trough, scree, or a hole in tufa.

PROPAGATION Sow seed in autumn or winter in a coldframe and keep cool through winter.

PESTS AND DISEASES Slugs, snails and aphids may prove troublesome.

Physostegia

Labiatae

Physostegia virginiana

Flower spikes crowded with dainty tubular flowers characterise these hardy herbaceous perennials. The species cultivated in British gardens makes a delightful show in the middle of a border in summer and autumn. Moist, rich soil and a position in sun or light shade suit the plant best and it may become

▲ *Physostegia virginiana*

invasive in its preferred growing site. In other soil types, the plant's vigour may be reduced. The genus is native to N America.

RECOMMENDED SPECIES AND VARIETIES

P. virginiana (obedient plant) (syn. *Dracocephalum virginicum*) Red, violet, rose or white tubular flowers, up to 2-3cm (¾-1¼in) long, cluster on spikes up to 20cm (8in) long, from late summer to early autumn. If the individual flowers are pushed to one side they remain in that position, hence the common name. Erect stems carry the flower spikes. The bright green leaves vary in shape but are generally narrow and tapering, up to 12.5cm (5in) long and have toothed edges. HEIGHT & SPREAD 1.2m×60cm (4×2ft).

'Alba' and **'Crown of Snow'** ('Schneekrone') have white flowers which are carried in compact spikes, up to 30cm (1ft) long. **'Summer Snow'**♀ also has white flowers and reaches a height of 1m (3ft). **'Vivid'**♀ has claret-pink flowers. The flowers of ssp. ***speciosa*** **'Bouquet Rose'** ('Rose Bouquet') are pale lilac-pink. **'Variegata'** has pale lavender-pink flowers amid grey leaves that are edged in cream.

▲ *Physostegia virginiana* 'Crown of Snow'

▲ *Physostegia virginiana* ssp. *speciosa* 'Bouquet Rose'

CULTIVATION Plant from autumn to spring in moist soil that has been enriched with organic matter and in a sunny or lightly shaded spot. Mulch during summer on light soils. The plants can be invasive so divide them every other year.

PROPAGATION Divide and replant in autumn to spring.

PESTS AND DISEASES Foot rot may attack damaged plant roots, especially on wet soils.

Phyteuma

Horned rampions
Campanulaceae

In summer, the blue to violet flowers of these upright, clump-forming, herbaceous perennials lend colour to the rock garden or the edge of a border. Narrow tubular flowers, that only open at the tips after the pollen is shed, form spikes or densely rounded heads within a ruff of leafy bracts. The mid green leaves at the base of the plants are often longer than those on the flower stems. These hardy plants are native to open situations and light woodland in Europe and western Asia.

RECOMMENDED SPECIES

P. comosum see *Physoplexis comosa*

P. hemisphaericum Round heads, up to 2.5cm (1in) wide, of deep blue flowers are held above clumps of grass-like leaves. Each leaf is 2.5-5cm (1-2in) long. HEIGHT & SPREAD 15×10cm (6×4in).

P. nigrum The dense spikes of deep purplish blue flowers are 3-5cm (1¼-2in) long. The oval leaves, up to 5cm (2in) long, form clumps. HEIGHT & SPREAD 60×20cm (24×8in).

P. orbiculare The dense globular heads of deep blue flowers are 4cm (1½in) wide. The clumps of this species are made up of rosettes of toothed leaves, each 4-6cm (1½-2½in) long and varying in shape from pointed to rounded. HEIGHT & SPREAD 30×20cm (12×8in).

▲ *Phyteuma orbiculare*

P. scheuchzeri Round heads, up to 2.5cm (1in) wide, of stalkless violet-blue flowers are borne in early summer. The plant forms vigorous clumps with strap-shaped or pointed mid green leaves, 2.5-5cm (1-2in) long. HEIGHT & SPREAD 40×30cm (16×12in).

CULTIVATION Plant in early spring in well-drained soil and full sun; although *P. nigrum* is tolerant of semi-shade. Cut the flowering stems back to the ground after flowering, unless seed is wanted.

PROPAGATION Sow seed in autumn in a coldframe and put in a shady place. Alternatively divide clumps in spring.

PESTS AND DISEASES Slugs and snails may prove troublesome.

Phytolacca

Phytolaccaceae

Phytolacca americana

A striking easily grown foliage plant that produces a mass of berries in autumn which look well against the autumnal tints of the leaves. The berries follow prominent spikes of tiny flowers in late summer. The recommended plants are best suited for growing in a wild or woodland setting in a garden. They are also striking specimens for a mixed border, although poisonous seeds and roots and a fetid smell make them less welcome there. These hardy plants tolerate moist soil and are invasive if left to self-seed.

▲ *Phytolacca americana*

RECOMMENDED SPECIES AND VARIETIES
P. americana (syn. *P. decandra*) (pokeweed) Nodding white or pink flower spikes, up to 15cm (6in) long, embellish this hardy perennial in late summer. The glossy green berries that follow the flower spikes turn maroon in autumn. Purple stems carry oblong mid green leaves, 30cm (2ft) across, that turn purple as they age. HEIGHT & SPREAD 1.5m×60cm (5×2ft).
P. clavigera see *P. polyandra*
P. decandra see *P. americana*
P. polyandra (syn. *P. clavigera*) Pink flowers, 1cm (⅜in) across, are borne in spikes, up to 30cm (12in) long on vivid red stems in late summer. The bright green leaves, up to 15cm (6in) across, turn yellow in autumn and show off the massed heads of blackish purple berries. HEIGHT & SPREAD 1.2m×60cm (4×2ft).

▼ *Phytolacca polyandra*

CULTIVATION Plant 60cm (2ft) apart from autumn to spring in any ordinary garden soil. Feeding is unnecessary. Stake the plants in windy areas to ensure that the fruits are visible. Cut the stems off before the berries drop to control the invasive nature of the plant by preventing self-seeding.
PROPAGATION Sow seeds in spring or autumn in open ground and transplant seedlings as soon as they are large enough. Divide large plants in spring.
PESTS AND DISEASES Usually trouble free.

Picea
Spruce
Pinaceae

Picea pungens 'Koster'

Spruces are hardy, evergreen, coniferous trees, mainly tall and narrowly conical, many with pendulous branches. Most species are too big for all but the largest gardens, but there are a number of smaller, more compact varieties available. It is best to be aware, however, that many 'dwarf' forms become, in time, quite large.

All spruces have single needles, irregularly arranged around the twigs and pointing forward. When the needles are shed, the small pegs from which they grow remain, leaving the twigs rough to the touch. Tiny, insignificant male and female flowers grow from the same young shoots, usually in clusters, in late winter and spring, before new foliage emerges. The female flowers develop into seed-bearing cones. These are ovoid or cylindrical, mainly pendulous, covered with pliable woody scales. They are generally green at first, ripening as the year progresses and fall from the tree one to three years later. Cones are not usually produced by dwarf cultivars.

Most trees do best in areas with high rainfall and mild winds, though if sites are chosen with care they will thrive almost anywhere except by the sea, where the wind is salt-laden. Dwarf trees may be planted in a rock garden or in tubs. Species are native to Europe, Asia and N America.

RECOMMENDED SPECIES AND VARIETIES
P. abies (Norway spruce) This is the traditional British Christmas tree. It has a strictly conical habit of growth, with an obvious leader at its tip and lower branches brushing right down to the ground. The sharply pointed needles, shiny dark green above, pale green underneath, are 2cm (¾in) long. Flowers are deep red. Cigar-shaped pendulous cones, 15cm (6in) long, ripen from green tinted purple to light brown within a year. The bark is smooth and a foxy brown colour. HEIGHT & SPREAD 6×3m (20×10ft) after 20 years, ultimately 50m (165ft) tall.

'Little Gem'♀ is a superb dwarf bush which forms a globe, with a slight depression on the top on older trees, on a short main stem. The short needles are dark green, with pale green new growth in spring. Height and spread are both 20cm (8in) after 20 years. **'Nidiformis'**♀ is a dense, compact, flat-topped bush, with short yellowish or light green needles, 50cm (20in) tall and 80cm (32in) wide after 20 years. Very slow-growing, the plant eventually – after 70 years or so – resembles a pile of cushions, one on top of another, each with a central nest-like depression.
P. breweriana♀ (Brewer's weeping spruce) Long, graceful, pendulous sideshoots are borne on slightly weeping main branches. The 2.5cm (1in) long, blue-green needles, each have 2 white stripes. Red flowers are followed in late spring by cigar-shaped cones, 12cm (4¾in) long. The cones are pointed at both ends, green at first ripening to dark purple in mid autumn. Plant this tree away from cold, dry winds and waterlogged soil. It makes a beautiful specimen tree. HEIGHT & SPREAD 4×2.4m (13×8ft) after 20 years, ultimately 25m (80ft) tall.
P. glauca var. ***albertiana*** **'Alberta Globe'** A slow-growing, rounded hardy dwarf bush of dense habit. The needles are grey-green and 1.5cm (½in) long. HEIGHT & SPREAD 1×1.2m (3×4ft) after 20 years, ultimately 1×1.5m (3×5ft).
P. glauca var. ***albertiana*** **'Conica'**♀ The

▲ *Picea breweriana*

Picea glauca var. albertiana 'Conica'

very hardy but slow-growing tree is perfectly conical, densely clothed with dusky green needles 1cm (⅜in) long. The new growth each spring is a bright, light green. HEIGHT & SPREAD 1.5×1.5m (5×5ft) after 20 years, ultimately 4×2m (13×6½ft).

***P. mariana* 'Nana'**♀ This cultivar forms a fine rounded, flattened, cushion. It has blunt, blue-green needles, 1.5cm (½in) long, on yellow-brown shoots. HEIGHT & SPREAD 60×40 cm (24×16in) after 20 years, ultimately 75cm×3m (2½×10ft).

P. omorika♀ (Serbian spruce) An almost columnar tree which grows to a tapering point, with pendulous branches turning up at the tips. Needles are glossy dark green above and blue-white beneath, 2cm (¾in) long. Red flowers produce narrow cones, 6cm (2½in) long, ultimately brown. This spruce is very hardy, tolerant of atmospheric pollution and one of the few that grow well in chalky soils. HEIGHT & SPREAD 7×2.4m (23×8ft), ultimately 30m (100ft) tall.

▲ *Picea omorika*

'Pendula'♀ has branches that hang nearly straight down from the trunk, their tips twisting upwards to reveal the silvery underside of the needles.

P. orientalis♀ (Oriental spruce) The tree has glossy, deep green, blunt needles lying tightly pressed along the shoots, only 8mm (⅜in) long. Many crimson flowers bloom in spring. The cylindrical cones which are purple ripening to rich brown, 10cm (4in) long, appear in autumn. HEIGHT & SPREAD 6×3m (20×10ft) after 20 years, ultimately 50m (165ft) tall.

The annual spring growth of **'Aurea'**♀ is bright yellow, ripening to pale green.

P. pungens (Colorado spruce) This very hardy tree with narrowly conical habit has sharp, stiff, grey-green needles, 3cm (1¼in) long. Flowers are red and green. The egg-shaped, pale brown cones are 10cm (4in) long. The aromatic and long-lasting foliage is good for decorations and flower arrangements. HEIGHT & SPREAD 3×1.5m (10×5ft) after 20 years, ultimately 35m (115ft) tall.

'Erich Frahm', with blue foliage, forms a regular cone, 6m (20ft) tall, spreading to 2m (6½ft), at 20 years old, ultimately reaching a height of 15m (50ft).

The following cultivars, with blue needles, all fall within the var. *glauca* group. All measurements are for plants after 20 years. The very hardy **'Glauca Prostrata'** has ground-creeping branches spreading to 1.5m (5ft), but is only 25cm (10in) high. **'Globosa'**♀ forms a vivid blue, flattened dome, 80cm (32in) high and wide.

▲ *Picea pugens* 'Globosa'

'Hoopsii'♀, bluish white, with dense branches forming a narrowly conical shape, is 5m (16ft) tall, spreading to 1.5m (5ft). **'Hoto'** has grey-blue needles and a regular, narrow, conical shape with dense branches and foliage. It is the same size as the species. **'Koster'**♀ is a slow-growing, narrowly conical tree with curving, silver-blue needles, 3m (10ft) tall and 1m (3ft) wide. **'Procumbens'**♀ is silver-grey and spreads irregularly, some branches drooping while others ascend. If ascending branches are removed, as is recommended, it reaches 1.5m (5ft) high and spreads to 3m (10ft).

P. smithiana♀ (West Himalayan spruce) This large tree has noticeably pendulous side branches, with dark green needles, 4cm (1½in) long. Flowers are green. Cigar-shaped cones, 20cm (8in) long, eventually glossy brown, appear in late autumn. This tree does not stand cold winds well, the needles soon becoming a sickly yellow brown. HEIGHT & SPREAD 3×2m (10×6½ft) after 20 years, ultimately 40m (130ft) tall.

CULTIVATION Plant in late spring in fertile, deep, neutral or acid soil that remains moist but is well drained. Choose a sunny site, sheltered from cold winds. Trees in general do not like shallow, chalky or dry soils. *P. abies* tolerates slightly more waterlogged soils. Late spring frosts can damage young trees and new growth.

PROPAGATION Sow seed of any species under glass in late winter, in pots or deep

▲ *Picea smithiana*

boxes of seed compost. Line out the seedlings in rows the following spring, and grow on for 2 or 3 years before planting out in their final positions.

Of the listed species, *P. abies*, *P. glauca*, *P. orientalis* and *P. pungens* can also be propagated by taking hardwood cuttings in early or mid autumn, and *P. breweriana*, *P. omorika* and *P. smithiana* can be propagated by grafting. For cultivars, the blue forms of *P. pungens* in particular, grafting is the only recommended method.

PRUNING Cutting back trees will disfigure rather than control the growth of most spruces. Confine pruning to removing dead twigs, branches that have reverted to green on coloured varieties and unwanted branches. Prune in winter as resin bleeding can occur attracting disease. Cut out branches growing the wrong way on prostrate varieties, or peg them out in the required direction.

PESTS AND DISEASES Red spider mite attacks most dwarf *P. abies* and *P. glauca* var. *albertiana* cultivars. Honey fungus and various root and butt rots also attack spruces, most commonly conifer root rot (*Phaeolus schwinitzii*) and conifer heart rot (*Fomes annosus*, syn. *Heterobasidion annosum*).

Pieris

Ericaceae

Pieris 'Forest Flame'

On acid soil pieris are among the most widely grown of evergreen shrubs, justly popular for their abundant flowers, the colourful new growth and the often attractive flower buds that form in autumn. The white to red flowers are pitcher-shaped and sometimes scented. Shrubs are generally long-lived and may be compact, upright or spreading in habit. Most are hardy but *P. formosa* and its varieties may be severely cut back or killed in the worst winters in cold areas and the young growth may be damaged by late frosts. They enjoy acid soil conditions similar to those required by rhododendrons, but are more tolerant of drought, dense shade and the presence of tree roots in the soil.

RECOMMENDED SPECIES AND VARIETIES

P. floribunda In early and mid spring, pure white flowers are produced in upright sprays up to 12.5cm (5in) long. The dull green leaves are oval with a pointed tip and about 7.5cm (3in) long. This is the hardiest species. It is compact in habit. Native to SE United States. HEIGHT & SPREAD 30×30cm (1×1ft) after 5 years, ultimately 1.5m (5ft) tall.

***P.* 'Forest Flame'**♀ The showy, red young growth on this compact, bushy plant fades to pink, cream or yellowish white, before gradually turning green. The rarely produced flowers are white, borne in large, spreading sprays, 15cm (6in) long, in mid to late spring. The lance-shaped leaves are about 12cm (4¾in) long. The first flush of new growth invariably gets frosted but this is a reliably hardy plant. HEIGHT & SPREAD 45×45cm (1½×1½ft) after 5 years, ultimately 2.1m (7ft) tall.

P. formosa The showy young growth is red at first before turning bronze and then deep green. The pointed, oval or spoon-shaped leaves are up to 18cm (7in) long. In late spring, pure white flowers are borne in upright or drooping sprays up to 15cm (6in) long. This is the least hardy of recommended species but if cut back by a harsh winter, it will usually regenerate. A dense shrub or small tree, native to W China and Burma. HEIGHT & SPREAD 60×60cm (2×2ft) after 5 years, ultimately 5m (16ft) tall.

The flowers of var. ***forrestii*** are lightly fragrant and the red young growth is particularly fine. Among the cultivars of this variety are **'Jermyns'**♀, with red winter buds that open white, and **'Wakehurst'**♀, which has bright red young growth, fading to pink and then to green. It tends to be early into growth and is therefore liable to have its new growth frosted.

▲ *Pieris japonica*

P. japonica (lily of the valley bush) White or occasionally pink or nearly red flowers are borne in upright or slightly drooping sprays, 15cm (6in) long, in early to mid spring. The glossy, mid green, oval to lance-shaped leaves are up to 6cm (2½in) long. A shrub of bushy habit, clothed to the ground with branches. Hardiness is variable. Native to Japan, E China, Taiwan. HEIGHT & SPREAD 60×60cm (2×2ft) after 5 years, ultimately 3m (10ft) tall.

Most cultivars come into growth late in the year and so are good for cold gardens. **'Blush'**♀ is of rather open habit, with pink flowers. **'Christmas Cheer'** (syn. 'Wada's Pink') has pink to white flowers, some of which open in winter. **'Debutante'**♀ has white flowers and is compact with bronzy new growth. The upright **'Dorothy Wyckoff'** has white flowers. **'Flamingo'** is tall and upright in habit, with deep pink flowers. The showy red young growth of **'Firecrest'**♀ fades to pink, cream or yellowish white, then gradually turns green. **'Grayswood'**♀ is dome-shaped, with long drooping sprays of white flowers. The non-flowering **'Little Heath'**♀ has yellowish green variegated leaves. **'Little Heath Green'**♀ is a dwarf spreading plant with bronzy red new growth. It rarely flowers. **'Mountain Fire'**♀ is one of the best cultivars for deep red new growth. The flowers are white. **'Pink Delight'**♀ has pink flowers fading to blush. **'Purity'**♀ is dense and compact, with bronzy new growth and abundant white flowers. **'Pygmaea'** (syn. 'Don') is slow-growing, with very narrow leaves that are bronzy when new. The white flowers are rarely produced. **'Red Mill'** is a hardy, tall-growing plant with dark red new growth. **'Sarabande'** is compact, with bronzy new growth and white flowers. **Taiwanensis Group** have upright or drooping white flowerheads. **'Tilford'** has white flowers. **'Valley Rose'** is tall and open-growing, with pink flowers fading to off-white. **'Valley Valentine'**♀ has deep rose to red flowers. **'Variegata'** is slow-growing and less vigorous with white variegated leaves. The flowers are white. **'White Pearl'** bears upright white flowerheads. **'White Rim'**♀ has showy creamy white variegation and white flowers.

▲ *Pieris japonica* 'Pink Delight'

CULTIVATION Plant in autumn or spring in a lime-free soil rich in organic matter. Plant those grown for their young foliage in partial shade. *P. japonica* needs a sunny site. Deadhead to encourage new flower buds.

PROPAGATION Take semi-ripe cuttings in late summer or layer low branches in early to late autumn. Alternatively, sow the seed of species under glass in spring or autumn.

PRUNING Cut back old straggly specimens in late winter. In late summer or autumn, cut off the dead wood on plants that have been frosted.

PESTS AND DISEASES Leaf spot may occur in wet seasons.

▲ *Pieris formosa* var. *forrestii* 'Wakehurst'

▲ *Pieris japonica* 'Valley Rose'

▲ *Pieris japonica* 'Valley Valentine'

Pilea

Urticaceae

The patterned foliage of these tropical evergreen perennials is their chief attraction. The species described here are popular as houseplants and for growing in a warm greenhouse or conservatory. The best-looking foliage is produced on young plants, which are easily raised from cuttings.

RECOMMENDED SPECIES AND VARIETIES

P. cadierei♀ (aluminium plant) The oval, glossy, dark green leaves, up to 4cm (1½in) long, are marked with many silver patches between the veins. Forms a bushy plant. HEIGHT & SPREAD 30×30cm (1×1ft).

'Minima' has pink stems and olive-green foliage with silvery markings. The leaves are small and scalloped. It reaches a height of 15cm (6in) and a spread of 20cm (8in).

P. involucrata (friendship plant) Oval, downy dark green leaves up to 6cm (2½in) long are marked bronze, silver or red around the veins. A loosely branching plant. HEIGHT & SPREAD 25×25cm (10×10in).

'Bronze' has strong-growing bronze-copper foliage. **'Moon Valley'** has leaves up to 10cm (4in) long tinged with bronze, dark bronze veins and scalloped edges.

▲ *Pilea involucrata* 'Moon Valley'

'Norfolk' is a smaller plant with a height of 20cm (8cm) and a spread of 15cm (6in). The oval leaves are bronze to black-green marked with prominent, raised silver bands.

P. microphylla (syn. *P. muscosa*) (artillery plant) Tiny, oval, mid green leaflets form compound, mossy-looking leaves. Myriad tiny flowers are heavily laden with pollen and if the plant is shaken or water droplets fall on it, clouds of pollen erupt like tiny explosions, hence the common name. This fleshy stemmed, densely branched species is treated as an annual and raised from cuttings. HEIGHT & SPREAD 25×25cm (10×10in).

P. peperomioides The fleshy, rounded mid green leaves, up to 10cm (4in) long, have prominent darker green veins. The leaf stalks are 10-15cm (4-6in) long. HEIGHT & SPREAD 30×30cm (1×1ft).

CULTIVATION Grow under glass or indoors at a minimum temperature of 10°C (50°F). Plant in well-drained, soil-based compost. Protect from direct sunlight and draughts. Water regularly in summer and feed with a liquid houseplant feed every 4-6 weeks. Water sparingly during winter. Pinch back plants as they develop in spring.

PROPAGATION Take softwood cuttings during spring and summer.

PESTS AND DISEASES Red spider mite can be troublesome.

Pimelea

Rice flower

Thymelaeaceae

Pimelea prostrata

Small, white or pink tubular flowers with four spreading petals are produced, usually in clusters, on these small evergreen shrubs. They are followed by white, pink, red or black berries, which are sometimes hard and nut-like. Male forms do not produce fruit. These plants can be bushy, erect or prostrate. All are native to Australia and New Zealand. The listed species is the only one widely available in Britain.

RECOMMENDED SPECIES

P. prostrata (syn. *P. coarctata*) White flowers with orange anthers are produced from mid spring to early summer in groups of about 10, forming a head 1cm (⅜in) across. This hardy alpine is very free flowering and prostrate, ideal for trailing over stones and walls in a rock garden. It has tiny grey-green leaves and forms patches. Conspicuous berry-like, fleshy white fruit appear in mid to late summer. Each bears one seed. HEIGHT & SPREAD 4×60cm (1½×24in).

▲ *Pimelea prostrata*

CULTIVATION Plant anytime from spring to autumn in well-drained gravelly, preferably lime-free soil in full sun.

PROPAGATION Sow seed in pots in autumn and leave outside to germinate in spring. Take semi-ripe cuttings in late summer.

PESTS AND DISEASES Usually trouble free.

Pimpernel see *Anagallis*

Pimpinella

Umbelliferae

Flat spreading heads of tiny creamy, white or pink summer flowers and delicate filigree foliage contribute an airy quality to any planting scheme that includes the hardy annuals and herbaceous perennials of this genus. The plants require an open, sunny position in a border or wild-flower garden and a free-draining soil. They are native to Eurasia and N Africa.

RECOMMENDED SPECIES AND VARIETIES

P. anisum (aniseed, anise) Myriad tiny creamy flowers on spreading heads, up to 10cm (4in) across, are produced from early to mid summer by this aromatic annual plant which is grown as a herb. Its delicate leaves are used as a culinary herb. Tiny, oval, greenish, aromatic fruits appear in late summer after the flowers have faded. The seeds are ripe and ready for culinary use when the tips of the fruits turn from green to grey. HEIGHT & SPREAD 45×25cm (18×10in).

P. major **'Rosea'** Spreading heads of minute pink flowers, up to 10cm (4in) across, crown the tall stems of this strong-growing perennial plant in early to mid summer. The divided fern-like leaves are mid green. HEIGHT & SPREAD 75-90×45cm (2½-3×1½ft).

▲ *Pimpinella major* 'Rosea'

CULTIVATION Grow in any well-drained soil and in an open, sunny situation. Remove faded flowerheads from perennial plants to prevent seeding.

PROPAGATION Sow seed directly into the open ground in spring where the plants are to grow. Thin the seedlings as soon as they are large enough to handle. The thinnings do not transplant successfully. Alternatively, sow seeds in pots in early spring and plant out seedlings in late spring. Divide *P. major* 'Rosea' in early spring.

PESTS AND DISEASES Usually trouble free.

Pincushion flower see *Scabiosa*
Pine see *Pinus*
Pineapple see *Ananas comosus*
Pineapple flower see *Eucomis*

Pinellia

Araceae

Hooded spathes, leaf-like open-sided tubes, wrap around upright pencil-like flower spikes, or spadices, to create an unusual effect in summer. These hardy, herbaceous, tuberous perennials thrive at the front of a partially shaded border.

▲ *Pinellia ternata*

RECOMMENDED SPECIES

P. ternata A leafless stem produces a small, hooded, tubular, green spathe, 5cm (2in) long, surrounding the spadix which is greenish with a purple base. The flat, oval, dull green leaflets up to 12.5cm (5in) long are borne in groups of 3 on erect stems. HEIGHT & SPREAD 20×15cm (8×6in).

CULTIVATION Plant tubers in spring 10cm (4in) deep in a rich organic soil in partial shade. Apply a slow-release fertiliser once yearly in spring when growth commences.

PROPAGATION Divide young tubers in the spring or collect bulbils from the leaf axils in late summer.

PESTS AND DISEASES Greenfly are sometimes troublesome.

Pinguicula

Butterwort

Lentiburiaceae

Pinguicula grandiflora

The broad, pale green, sticky leaves of these insectivorous plants trap small insects that alight on them. Handsome violet-like flowers appear in late spring and summer. Pinguiculas are small herbaceous evergreen perennials widespread in boggy areas of the Northern Hemisphere. The only species that is readily available is hardy and can be grown either outside in sunny, boggy conditions or in a cool greenhouse. Under glass, pinguiculas can be helpful in catching whitefly and aphids on their sticky leaves.

RECOMMENDED SPECIES

P. grandiflora The solitary funnel-shaped dark blue flowers, up to 4cm (1½in) across, have long slender spurs, white throats and spreading lobes. The pale green leaves, up to 4cm (1½in) long, form flattish rosettes. HEIGHT & SPREAD 15×10cm (6×4in).

CULTIVATION Plant outdoors in humus-rich, boggy soil and in sun or partial shade. Alternatively, grow under glass in pots of peat-based compost. Keep plants very wet in summer, but relatively drier in winter.

PROPAGATION Divide plants in late winter or sow ripe seed on sphagnum moss.

▲ *Pinguicula grandiflora*

PESTS AND DISEASES Liable to attack by slugs and snails. Birds may remove overwintering buds outdoors.

Pink see *Dianthus*

Pinus

Pine

Pinaceae

Pinus parviflora

These evergreen conifers range from semi-prostrate shrubs to tall forest trees 75m (245ft) high, but most are 15-50m (50-165ft) tall with stems up to 2m (6½ft) thick. These sizes are reached in 70-100 years, depending on the species and conditions. Young trees are conical, maturing to flat-topped specimens which can still be quite bushy. There are also many dwarf or slow-growing forms which are good for a rock garden or large landscaped area.

Some of these versatile trees are chosen for decorative purposes while others, particularly *Pinus sylvestris,* provide wind shelter. All have long, needle-like leaves in groups of two, three or five held on to the twigs by a sheath. The bark is an attractive feature on many, as are cones and flowers.

Male and female flowers appear in separate clusters on new shoots, usually in spring but in summer on *P. montezumae,* producing cones that ripen two years after setting. The male flowers, at the base of the new shoots, are generally catkin-like and 1.5-5cm (½-2in) long. The female flowers, on the growth tips, are immature cones, usually pea-sized.

The cones can be round, conical or even banana-like. They may crack open in strong sunshine, releasing winged seeds for wind dispersal, but some open only when forced to by the extreme heat of a forest fire.

Most pines prefer acid soils in a dry site; some tolerate poor, infertile soil and waterlogged conditions. They are native to temperate zones of the Northern Hemisphere, as far south as Central America and Indonesia. All those listed thrive in Britain but some are too tall to be suitable for anything but an extremely large garden.

Pinus bungeana

RECOMMENDED SPECIES AND VARIETIES

P. bungeana (lace bark pine, chequer bark pine) This large, slow-growing species has beautiful flaking bark, blotched with grey-green and creamy white when stems are 10cm (4in) thick. Mature trees have multiple stems, creating a broadly conical bush, devoid of branches to a height of 2m (6½ft). Rigid, sharply pointed, dark green needles are 7.5cm (3in) long in sparse groups of 3 and smell of turpentine when crushed. Male flowers are yellow and female flowers are green. The latter mature into yellow-brown, egg-shaped, stalkless cones 7cm (2¾in) long with a spine on each scale. They become foxy brown with age. This tree suits dry, stony soil. HEIGHT & SPREAD 2×1m (6½×3ft) after 10 years, ultimately 20×4m (66×13ft).

P. cembra ♀ (arolla pine) Very dark foliage adorns this tidy but austere, narrowly conical, sometimes columnar tree. This is a very hardy pine. Needles 5-9cm (2-3½in) long, in groups of 5, are dark glossy green on the outside, blue-grey on the inside. The male flowers are purple. The red female flowers ripen into 7.5cm (3in) long blue-purple to red-brown banana-shaped cones. They never fully open. This species is too large for many gardens. HEIGHT & SPREAD 1.5×1m (5×3ft) after 10 years, ultimately 20×2.4m (66×8ft).

P. coulteri♀ (big cone pine) Everything about this tree is large, but it is slow-growing in Britain and difficult to establish and propagate. Most trees are bushy although some are tall and slender with long, branchless stems. The cones, 30cm (12in) long and 20cm (8in) thick, weighing up to 3kg (6lb 8oz), are the largest borne by any pine, but only about 10 are produced by a tree in a lifetime. They are egg-shaped, more pointed at one end, with a slight curve in the longer axis. Each scale has a viciously pointed barb. The cones remain on the tree for many years, and stay closed. The seeds are up to 1.5cm (½in) across. Thumb-size purple male flowers and red female flowers the size of walnuts appear high up in the crown. The grey-green 30cm (12in) long needles are held in groups of 3. Young shoots, up to 2cm (¾in) thick, have an attractive dusting of grey. HEIGHT & SPREAD 2m×50cm (6½ft×20in) after 10 years, ultimately 25×12m (80×40ft).

P. densiflora **'Umbraculifera'** This is a very slow-growing, multistemmed form, with a dense head of branches resembling an umbrella. It is good for a rock garden but needs room with age. Salmon-pink young bark matures into fissured grey-red plates. Slender bright green needles up to 5cm (2in) long grow in pairs and point forwards. Male flowers are yellow-brown and female flowers are red. The ripe cones, often in bunches of 3 or more, are about 4cm (1½in) long, pale brown, stalkless and conical. They open in their second summer to release the winged seed. HEIGHT & SPREAD 2×1m (6½×3ft) after 10 years, ultimately 4×6m (13×20ft).

P. heldreichii var. *leucodermis*♀ A slow-growing two-needle pine, of narrow, conical habit, with closely clustered, prickly 8cm (3¼in) long stiff dark green needles. A shoot covered with needles resembles a series of bottle brushes. Female flowers are purple-red and the male flowers open yellow. Deep blue cones are pointed, egg-shaped, 10cm (4in) long, and produced in pairs. They turn yellow-brown, then pale brown with age. This variety is best on gravelly dry soils and will even grow on chalk. HEIGHT & SPREAD 2.4×2m (8×6½ft) after 10 years, ultimately 25×8m (80×26ft).

'Compact Gem' is a very slow-growing, dense, compact bush with a rounded habit that reaches its full size of 1m (3ft) tall, with a spread of 50cm (20in), in 40 years. It is suited to a rock garden. **'Satellit'** has steeply ascending branches, making a good narrow, columnar form that takes 50 years to reach

▲ *Pinus heldreichii* var. *leucodermis*

its full size of 15m (50ft) tall with a spread of 3m (10ft). Densely packed needles lie against the shoots when young, later spreading and becoming brush like. **'Schmidtii'**♀ is a very slow-growing dwarf form, taking 100 years to reach 3m (10ft) high and wide. This compact, very dense, mound-shaped bush is an excellent choice for a garden with dry or chalk-based soil.

P. montezumae Dramatic foliage distinguishes this tender species which has a broadly spreading crown over a 2m (6½ft) tall main stem. It needs a sheltered site to thrive and reach full size. Each branch is laden with numerous groups of 5 grey-green needles at least 30cm (12in) long and spread in flue-brush fashion on thick, smooth red-brown shoots. Serrated edges make the needles rough and sharp to the touch. Male flowers are purple and female flowers are red. The latter grow into 15cm (6in) long, prickly, blue-purple cones, ripening red to yellow-brown. Young trees have single cones; older trees bear clusters. HEIGHT & SPREAD 3×1.5m (10×5ft) after 10 years, ultimately 20×20m (66×66ft).

P. mugo (mountain pine) Plentiful red female flowers, in groups of 2 or 3, are the best feature of this very hardy, slow-growing, 2-needle species which can be a large shrubby bush or, more rarely, a small upright tree. Its many stems hug the ground then turn upwards from obvious knees. The green male flowers are often hidden by the pairs of densely packed 3-4cm (1¼-1½in) long dark green needles, which are curved and rigid, sometimes twisted. Blackish brown young cones ripen to yellow-brown. They are egg-shaped but very pointed, 6cm (2½in) long, stalkless and usually erect. They sometimes hang in groups of 3 or 4, but young trees always have single cones.

▲ *Pinus mugo*

This is a good maintenance-free plant for awkward places but will look untidy until very old. In tree form it reaches no more than 9m (30ft) with a bushy spread of 2-3m (6½-10ft). HEIGHT & SPREAD 1×1m (3×3ft) after 10 years, ultimately 3×9m (10×30ft).

'Gnom' is a compact, densely branched plant with tightly packed pairs of radially arranged 4.5cm (1¾in) long deep green needles. In 70 years it forms a dense rounded mound 2m (6½ft) high and wide. Older plants may be more conical. **'Humpy'** is a compact form suited to containers. It reaches 1m (3ft) in height and width in 40 years and is conical with 1.5cm (½in) long needles and noticeable red-brown winter buds. **'Mops'**♀ is a densely branched, dwarf, rounded bush similar to a mop head. It reaches 1m (3ft) in height and spread in 30 years and is suited to any situation. In winter it displays attractive resinous brown buds. **'Ophir'** is a flattened bun-

▲ *Pinus mugo* 'Mops'

shaped shrubby dwarf with pleasing golden yellow winter foliage, which reaches 60cm (2ft) high and 30cm (1ft) wide in 10 years. The slightly twisted 4-7cm (1½-2¾in) long needles are light green in summer. The

▲ *Pinus mugo* var. *pumilio*

shrubby, usually creeping, var. ***pumilio***♀ reaches perhaps 2m (6½ft) in height and 3m (10ft) in width in 100 years. Striking purple cones, which ripen dark brown, are more rounded than those of the species and only about 2.5cm (1in) long. Almost pure white winter buds coated with resin are conspicuous against very dark foliage. **'Winter Gold'** has 7cm (2¾in) long widely spread, twisted needles, with golden tips in winter. It is an open spreading dwarf bush, seldom exceeding 1m (3ft) in height and 2m (6½ft) in spread in over 50 years. Showy 1cm (⅜in) long, 4mm (⅛in) wide, resinous buds appear in winter.

▲ *Pinus mugo* 'Winter Gold'

P. parviflora♀ (Japanese white pine) Abundant soft green-blue foliage makes this tree an ideal centrepiece for a large lawn. The 6cm (2½in) needles, held in groups of 5, all have a vivid blue-white stripe on the inside. These groups stay closed for years, opening only when 4 or 5 years old. Male flowers are purple-red and female flowers start bright red. In early summer an 18cm (7in) long pale green, slightly upturned spiky candle of new growth protrudes from the pale yellow-brown spent male flowers, and the female blooms, purple by now, grace the tip of the 'candles'. The latter mature into blue-green, egg-shaped cones 3-4cm (1¼-1½in) long. The spreading branches are fairly horizontal, with short branchlets. The bark is smoother than that of other species. HEIGHT & SPREAD 3x2m (10x6½ft) after 10 years, ultimately 15x10m (50x33ft).

'Adcock's Dwarf'♀ is more of a compact bush than a conical tree, and slow-growing, reaching 2.4m (8ft) high and 1.2m (4ft) across in 30 years. Tightly packed bunches of greyish green needles up to 2.5cm (1in) long appear at the tips of young shoots. Smaller than the species, but similar in other ways, f. ***glauca*** reaches 12m

▲ *Pinus parviflora* 'Adcock's Dwarf'

(40ft) in 50 years. The foliage, blue-green rather than green-blue, is densely packed at the growth tips. Young trees have no branches but those on older trees can spread 3m (10ft) or more in all directions.

P. patula♀ (Jelecote pine) Only the south-west of Britain or very sheltered conditions suit this tender species, which has drooping needles, often in threes, sometimes fours or fives, that can be 30cm (12in) long on slightly grey shoots. This weeping shiny blue-green foliage, long, spreading branches and, frequently, multiple stems give the tree a graceful habit. It seldom flowers in Britain but when it does, clusters of 5 banana-shaped cones, each up to 9cm (3½in) long, are evenly spaced around the twigs. Tiny thorns can be seen on the larger cone scales. HEIGHT & SPREAD 2mx50cm (6½ftx20in) after 10 years, ultimately 20x9m (66x30ft).

P. pinea♀ (stone pine, umbrella pine) Gnarled and twisted heavy branches radiating from a 6m (20ft) clear main stem culminate in a dense umbrella-shaped canopy of needles on thin shoots and branches. The branches have orange-brown bark, while the main stem, which usually leans, shows regular ring bulges on deeply fissured dark grey to black bark. Stiff, 12cm (4¾in) long grey-green needles are smooth and in pairs. Male flowers are yellow and female flowers are green. The roundish 12cm (4¾in) long cones resemble a handful of green-brown pebbles glued together. Seeds, too, look and feel like small rounded stones. HEIGHT & SPREAD 2x2m (6½x6½ft) after 10 years, ultimately 10-15x10m (33-50x33ft).

***P. pumila* 'Glauca'**♀ This pine often lacks a main stem. All the branches are densely covered with grey-blue foliage and sweep upwards, unlike the species, which has lower branches that sometimes sprout roots where they touch the ground, causing the tree to spread widely. This very slow-growing pine has dark green 10cm (4in) long needles held in fives, sometimes more, each with a rich blue-green stripe on the inside. Only the red male flowers are visible. Rounded 3.5cm (1⅜in) cones ripen from purple-violet to dull brown and are held in delicate bunches that are easily shed. HEIGHT & SPREAD 1x1m (3x3ft) after 10 years, ultimately 2x6m (6½x20ft).

***P. strobus* 'Radiata'**♀ A compact, dwarf form that eventually makes a rounded, almost spherical, plant. It has the smooth and silver-grey bark of the species, which becomes fissured only when old. Crowded slender twigs are covered with 9cm (3½in) long blue needles pointing upwards at the branch tips. They are borne in fives and have a grey-white inner surface. Male flowers are yellow. The pink female flowers grow into green banana-shaped hanging cones 15cm (6in) long and 5cm (2in) thick, which ripen to brown. HEIGHT & SPREAD 30x30cm (1x1ft) after 10 years, ultimately 1.5x1.5m (5x5ft).

P. sylvestris♀ (Scots pine) This species, the only true British native pine, is very fast-growing when young but slows down with age, when it develops a rounded, flattened crown above a tall clean main stem which can be over 20m (66ft) tall before branching begins. With a mature trunk over 2m (6½ft) thick, this tall forest tree is not suited to an average garden. Needles in radially arranged pairs are stiff, somewhat twisted, 7cm (2¾in) long and blue-grey or blue-green. Beautiful salmon-pink papery bark peels from the upper stem of older trees, while much thicker bark at the stem base is fissured into regular plates that flake off, leaving deep pink or russet-red, scars. Male flowers are yellow and female flowers are red. Egg-shaped cones 7.5cm (3in) long ripen from green to brown. They crack open in late summer to release their seed.

▲ *Pinus sylvestris*

▲ *Pinus sylvestris* bark

HEIGHT & SPREAD 3×2m (10×6½ft) after 10 years, ultimately 35×4m (115×13ft).

'Aurea'♀ turns a rich golden yellow after the first hard frost. **'Beuvronensis'**♀ is covered with 1.5cm (½in) long bright blue-green needles. It makes a superb rock-garden plant, growing into a small, tidy dome seldom taller or wider than 1m (3ft) after 60 years. **'Chantry Blue'** is a slow-growing tree with blue needles. It is very conical in shape. In 30 years it reaches 4m (13ft) in height and is half as wide at ground level. Majestic **'Fastigiata'** resembles a tall, straight feather in silhouette. A medium to large garden is a suitable setting for this tree, which reaches 15m (50ft) in over 70 years but is never wider than 2m (6½ft). **'Gold Coin'** has striking bright yellow foliage. It is slow-growing, eventually reaching 2m (6½ft) in height and spread. **'Inverleith'** is identical to the large-growing species, apart from the distinction of creamy white variegations in the needles, and is suitable only for exceptionally large gardens. **'Lodge Hill'** is a compact dwarf plant with dense blue-grey foliage. Each branch ends with very dark terminal buds in winter. In 40 years it reaches 80cm (32in) in height with a spread of 60cm (2ft). **'Watereri'** is a dwarf form. An upright, conical tree when young, it becomes rounded with age, reaching 4m (13ft) high and almost as wide in over 100 years. The blue-grey needles are 3cm (1¼in) long, very stiff, somewhat twisted and borne in pairs. This pine is suited to a heather garden but will eventually outgrow the position.

▼ *Pinus sylvestris* 'Beuvronensis'

▲ *Pinus sylvestris* 'Watereri'

CULTIVATION Plant in the tree's final position, in good light, during mid to late autumn. Grow in well-drained acid soil, unless otherwise stated. Do not use strimmers or mowers near the tree base, as they can damage roots just under the surface.

PROPAGATION Sow seed in late winter under glass, or in late spring in the open. Plant out when 2 years old, or more. Graft cultivars in autumn with grafting scions about half the thickness of a pencil. Side grafting onto pencil-thick rootstocks is best.

PRUNING Seldom necessary. Remove any spindly lower branches. Pruning disfigures the conical shape of most pines.

PESTS AND DISEASES Plants are prone to infection by honey fungus, phytophthora and rusts. Adelgids, sawflies and pine shoot moth caterpillars can also cause damage. The caterpillars of the pine shoot moth, brown and about 2cm (¾in) long, can seriously damage young trees by boring into and killing shoots. Treat the problem with a contact insecticide.

Piptanthus

Leguminosae

Piptanthus nepalensis

Clusters of showy, bright yellow flowers above semi-evergreen foliage distinguish these slightly tender shrubs from the Himalayas and China. Only one of the two species is usually grown in Britain, and the plants benefit from the protection of a sunny wall in cold areas. In a hard winter, the erect stems may be killed, but established shrubs will usually make strong new growth from the base.

RECOMMENDED SPECIES

P. nepalensis (*P. forrestii*, *P. laburnifolius*) The flowers, like sweet peas, and about 3cm (1¼in) long, appear in spring at the tips of erect, dark green stems. The glossy dark green leaves have 3 elliptical leaflets, up to 10cm (4in) long, which usually last well into winter. Many conspicuous, flat, green or blackish seedpods appear in late summer. HEIGHT & SPREAD 1.2×1m (4×3ft) after 5 years, ultimately 2.4m (8ft) tall.

CULTIVATION Plant in early spring in a sheltered, sunny position in any well-drained, fairly fertile soil. Provide the protection of a south or west-facing wall in cold areas.

PROPAGATION Sow seeds under glass or in a coldframe in autumn or early spring.

PRUNING Cut out the oldest stems every 2 to 3 years and remove any frost-damaged stems in spring.

PESTS AND DISEASES Usually trouble free.

▲ *Piptanthus nepalensis*

Pittosporum

Pittosporaceae

Pittosporum tenuifolium 'Tom Thumb'

Often used as the backbone of borders or for hedging, these small trees and shrubs are admired for their evergreen foliage. Some are showy in flower. The tubular or bell-shaped blooms are up to 2cm (¾in) across, often with reflexed petals. They may be white, yellow or red, carried in clusters or singly and usually carry a pleasant honey fragrance. Many species carry male and female flowers on separate plants. If fertilised, the female plants go on to display globular or oval seed capsules which may be green, grey, yellow or red. The leaves are very variable in shape, ranging from linear to obovate. The foliage of *Pittosporum tenuifolium* is good for cutting.

Most of the species described below are reasonably hardy across Britain, but grow best in mild, southern areas. In more northerly regions improved vigour can be attained by providing a windbreak in the form of a hedge or wall. *P. anomalum*, *P. dallii* and *P. tenuifolium* are the hardiest species. *P. crassifolium* is particularly suited to mild, coastal areas since it is resistant to salt-laden winds. Native to Australasia.

RECOMMENDED SPECIES AND VARIETIES

P. anomalum Rigid, interlacing, near-black branches, sparsely clothed with tiny dark green toothed leaves, make the whole bush appear black. This shrub bears tiny solitary white or pale yellow flowers in spring. HEIGHT & SPREAD 60×60cm (2×2ft) after 5 years, ultimately 1m (3ft) tall.

P. crassifolium Leathery obovate leaves, 7.5cm (3in) long, are borne by this erect shrub or small tree. The leaves are grey-green above and densely white or brownish beneath. Clusters of red flowers appear in spring. Female and hermaphrodite plants go on to produce pale green seed capsules. HEIGHT & SPREAD 3×2m (10×6½ft) after 5 years, ultimately 10m (33ft) tall.

'Variegatum' has pale green leaves edged with creamy white. It bears female flowers and is slower growing than the species.

P. dallii This large shrub or small tree has dark green leathery leaves about 10cm (4in) long, distinctly toothed in the upper half. Clusters of white flowers in summer are only seen on mature plants. HEIGHT & SPREAD 1×1m (3×3ft) after 5 years, ultimately 3m (10ft) tall.

P. eugenioides (lemonwood) A near white trunk and branches clothed with glossy green, wavy-edged leaves, 12.5cm (5in)

▲ *Pittosporum eugenioides* 'Variegatum'

long, distinguish this tree. Mature plants produce numerous clusters of small yellow flowers in spring. When grown in a container it will reach up to 3m (10ft) tall, and makes a fine conservatory plant. HEIGHT & SPREAD 3×1m (10×3ft) after 5 years, ultimately 10m (33ft) tall.

'Variegatum'♀ bears male flowers and has broad cream edges to its leaves.

▲ *Pittosporum* 'Garnettii'

***P.* 'Garnettii'**♀ This large shrub or small tree with a conical habit has greyish green leaves about 6cm (2½in) long. The leaves have an irregular cream border and are tinted and spotted purplish pink in winter. Solitary dark red flowers are produced in spring. It is a hermaphrodite plant. HEIGHT & SPREAD 2×1m (6½×3ft) after 5 years, ultimately 4m (13ft) tall.

***P.* 'Margaret Turnbull'** Yellowish, slightly wavy leaves, about 4cm (1½in) long, have dark green margins while young, and become totally dark green with age. This female shrub produces dark red flowers from mid to late spring. HEIGHT & SPREAD 1.8×1m (6×3ft) after 5 years, ultimately 3m (10ft) tall.

▼ *Pittosporum tenuifolium*

P. tenuifolium♀ Dark young branches are clothed with thin wavy-edged leaves of various colours and sizes up to 7.5cm (3in) long, depending on the variety. The flowers are dark red, usually highly fragrant and borne singly in late spring. *P. tenuifolium* can be grown as a hedge or as a small tree and some of the colourful leaf forms make admirable tub plants for the patio. HEIGHT & SPREAD 5×1m (16×3ft) after 5 years, ultimately 10m (33ft) tall.

▲ *Pittosporum tenuifolium* 'Abbotsbury Gold'

'Abbotsbury Gold' is a reasonably hardy variety. Its leaves, about 4cm (1½in) long, are yellowish green with paler midribs and an irregular broad margin of darker green. Its female flowers are dark red and fragrant.

'Golden King' see 'Warnham Gold'.

'Irene Paterson'♀ is a popular variety with very pale green leaves usually heavily blotched and spotted white – as the leaves age they become greener. The dark red flowers are male. Although it is pleasing to the eye, it is slower growing than most other varieties and less hardy. **'Purpureum'** has pale green young leaves which become dark purple. The dark red flowers are male with yellow anthers. It is a less hardy cultivar than the others.

▲ *Pittosporum tenuifolium* 'Purpureum'

'Silver Queen'♀ is deservedly the most popular cultivar. A pyramidal tree with 3cm (1¼in) long, pale silvery green leaves with white wavy edges. Dark red flowers (mainly female) are produced in mid and

▲ *Pittosporum tenuifolium* 'Silver Queen'

late spring. This variety is hardy near London and worth trying farther north. **'Tom Thumb'**♀ is a dwarf, rounded shrub only reaching about 1m (3ft) tall. The young leaves are pale green becoming dark purple through winter. The dark red flowers have conspicuous yellow anthers.

'Warnham Gold' has a rather open habit. The leaves are about 4cm (1½in) long. They are pale green while young becoming bright yellow in autumn and winter. This beautiful large shrub is at its best in semi-shade – it can be scorched by the sun. The same or a very similar plant is sold under the name 'Golden King'. **'Wendle Channon'** is a bushy male variety with shiny green leaves, broadly and irregularly edged in yellow while young, the edges becoming creamy white later.
P. tobira♀ The 9cm (3½in) long, leathery mid green leaves of this bushy shrub are obovate with the base narrowed to a stout petiole. Clusters of creamy white, highly fragrant flowers in summer are followed by yellow seed capsules. Suitable for warmer gardens. HEIGHT & SPREAD 3×1m (10×3ft) after 5 years, ultimately 6m (20ft) tall.

▼ *Pittosporum tenuifolium* 'Wendle Channon'

▲ *Pittosporum tobira* 'Variegatum'

'Nanum' is a compact dwarf form, reaching a height of only 3m (10ft). **'Variegatum'**♀ has grey-green leaves with conspicuous creamy white edges.
CULTIVATION Plant in well-drained soils in spring or summer. Pittosporums do not object to lime. All benefit from a deep dry mulch applied around the base in winter to provide some protection. *P. crassifolium* makes an excellent windbreak in warm, coastal gardens. *P. tenuifolium* prefers semi-shade but usually does well in the open. Good ventilation is important for plants grown under glass.
PROPAGATION Sow seed in autumn or spring under glass. Grow on in pots in a coldframe for 2 years before planting out in late spring. The cultivars are best grown from semi-ripe cuttings taken in mid summer, overwintered in pots under glass and planted out the following spring.
PRUNING Prune as required to keep a good shape. Cut back *P. tenuifolium* in summer to keep it compact or to form a hedge.
PESTS AND DISEASES Scale insects and aphids are occasionally troublesome.

Plane see *Platanus*

Plantago
Plantain
Plantaginaceae

The neat rosettes of leaves, often covered in a silvery down, make useful additions to a rock garden or crevice. These hardy annual, biennial or perennial plants – some of which are persistent weeds – tolerate most soils and situations except dense shade. Spikes of tiny flowers appear in summer.

▲ *Plantago major* 'Rosularis'

▲ *Plantago major* 'Rubrifolia'

RECOMMENDED SPECIES AND VARIETIES
***P. asiatica* 'Variegata'** The lance-shaped, variegated leaves grow up to 10cm (4in) long. The insignificant flowers are borne on stout stems and are usually removed when they appear. This reliably perennial plant is suitable for planting in a damp, but free-draining sunny spot. HEIGHT & SPREAD 15×20cm (6×8in).
P. major Rosettes of oval or roughly heart-shaped leathery green leaves, up to 20cm (8in) long, appear on this hardy perennial. This plant is represented in the garden by the following cultivars. HEIGHT & SPREAD 25×25cm (10×10in).

'Atropurpurea' see 'Rubrifolia' **'Rosularis'** (syn. *P. rosea*) (rose plantain) has tufts of green leaves growing up to 7.5cm (3in) across. The cultivar **'Rubrifolia'** (syn. 'Atropurpurea') bears maroon leaves. The short spikes of greenish purple flowers are up to 25cm (10in) tall and have an architectural quality. **'Variegata'** produces green and cream variegated leaves.
P. nivalis The neat rosettes of lance-shaped leaves, up to 7cm (2¾in) long, are covered in silver hairs. The short spikes of insignificant grey summer flowers are best removed as they detract from the architectural quality of the leaves. This small perennial, suitable for a rock garden, requires a free-draining soil. HEIGHT & SPREAD 5×10cm (2×4in).
P. rosea see *P. major* 'Rosularis'

CULTIVATION Plant in spring in an open, sunny position. *P. nivalis* requires a top dressing of coarse grit in order to protect the hairy leaves from the soil. In very wet winters protect with a small square of glass resting on 2 bricks or 4 small stakes just above the foliage. Remove flower spikes of all varieties before seed sets.
PROPAGATION Sow seed or divide in spring.
PESTS AND DISEASES Usually trouble free.

Plantain see *Plantago*

Platanus

Plane tree
Platanaceae

Platanus orientalis

With their distinctively mottled bark and deciduous lobed leaves, planes are handsome trees, although few ordinary gardens are large enough to accommodate their monumental size. They are a familiar feature in parks and in streets and are tolerant of atmospheric pollution. However, little will grow under their spreading branches and their durable leaves can be a nuisance in autumn. The dappling on the trunks and branches occurs when irregular-sized plates of olive-green to light grey-brown bark are shed each spring to reveal pale gold inner layers. Insignificant spring flowers develop into conspicuous bristly globe-like clusters of nutlets, up to 6cm (2½in) across, borne on pendulous stalks that persist among bare branches all through winter. The species in cultivation are hardy in lowland Britain.

▲ *Platanus × hispanica*

RECOMMENDED SPECIES AND VARIETIES
P. × hispanica♀ (syn. *P. × acerifolia*) (London plane) The bright green, shallowly lobed leaves, with 3 or 7 segments, are about 20cm (8in) broad and long. This tree has a straight trunk and forms a rounded head. HEIGHT & SPREAD 10×6m (33×20ft) after 20 years, ultimately 45m (150ft) tall.
P. orientalis♀ (oriental plane) The deeply lobed, glossy dark green leaves are up to 20cm (8in) broad and long. This tree has a wide-spreading head of sinuous branches. HEIGHT & SPREAD 8×6m (26×20ft) after 20 years, ultimately 30m (100ft) tall.

▲ *Platanus orientalis*

The leaves of f. ***digitata*** (syn. 'Laciniata') have 3 or 5 exaggerated lobes.
CULTIVATION Plant from late autumn to early spring in sun or shade in any garden soil. Plane trees will even grow in poor soils or soils with restricted drainage.
PROPAGATION Take hardwood cuttings in early winter. After one year cut back the young plants to a strong bud and grow on for another 3-4 years before planting out.
PRUNING Plane trees can be pollarded in spring, by a professional tree surgeon.
PESTS AND DISEASES *P. × hispanica* can suffer from anthracnose die-back.

Platycerium see FERNS p.264
Platycladus see *Thuja*

Platycodon

Balloon flower
Campanulacea

Platycodon grandiflorus

Flower buds like small balloons develop into bells, making this tuberous rooted herbaceous perennial a fascinating plant for a large rock garden or a border. There is only one species in the genus, but the varieties and cultivars recommended increase the choice of flower colours.

▲ *Platycodon grandiflorus*

Platycodon grandiflorus The stiff, upright stems are flushed purple as they emerge in spring. From mid summer to autumn, they bear one or more blue flowers, up to 6cm (2½in) wide, with flared lobes. The bluish green, ovate to lance-shaped leaves, up to 10cm (4in) long, are held in whorls. HEIGHT & SPREAD 60×25cm (24×10in)

White flowers, sometimes faintly flushed with blue, appear on var. ***albus,*** while var. ***apoyama***♀ has large, blue flowers on a dwarf plant. The compact plant var. ***apoyama albus***, which is about 25cm (10in) high, has white flowers.

'Florist Rose' has rose-pink blooms, and **'Florist Snow'** has white flowers. The flowers of **'Fuji Pink'** are pale pink, while **'Fuji White'** has white blooms. **'Hakone'** has double, very deep blue flowers. The earlier flowering var. ***mariesii***♀, which is usually less than 40cm (16in) tall, has particularly dark blue flowers, while var.

▼ *Platycodon grandiflorus* 'Fuji Pink'

mariesii albus has pure white flowers. **'Parks Double Blue'** has double blue flowers. **'Perlemutterschale'** ('Mother of Pearl') is a vigorous plant with large, silvery pink flowers. The dwarf var. ***pumilus*** has blue flowers while var. ***roseus*** is pink flowered.
CULTIVATION Plant, ideally in spring, in any reasonably well-drained soil in a sunny or very lightly shaded position.
PROPAGATION Sow the seed of species in pots outside in autumn. Divide varieties and cultivars in spring or take softwood or semi-ripe cuttings in early summer.
PESTS AND DISEASES Usually trouble free, but may be attacked by slugs and snails.

Plectranthus

Swedish ivy
Labiatae

Trailing stems bearing soft evergreen foliage make these tender perennials a popular choice for growing in containers in warm conditions, where they tolerate dry air conditions successfully. *Plectranthus forsteri* is also frequently used in outdoor displays in summer as a ground-cover plant.
RECOMMENDED SPECIES AND VARIETIES
P. forsteri (syn. *P. coleoides* hort.) The oval, scallop-edged, dark green leaves are up to 5 cm (2 in) long and aromatic when rubbed. Tubular flowers, 3 cm (1¼ in) long, are white or light purple. The stems are prostrate and trailing. HEIGHT & SPREAD 20×60 cm (8×24 in).

'Marginatus' has dark green leaves with a white, cream or golden edge. The small tubular flowers are white, and are borne in upright sprays.

▲ *Plectranthus forsteri* 'Marginatus'

P. oertendahlii ♀ The leaves are rounded, attractively patterned by conspicuous white veins, dark green above and reddish below. The tiny flowers, white or pale mauve, are borne on erect spikes. The stems of this species have a trailing habit, although the tips curve upwards. HEIGHT & SPREAD 20×60 cm (8×24 in).
CULTIVATION Grow in hanging baskets or pots of potting compost and keep in a greenhouse, conservatory or on a warm windowsill. Maintain a minimum winter temperature of 10°C (50°F) and protect from exposure to direct sunlight. Plectranthus will tolerate dry air conditions. Alternatively, plant *P. forsteri* outdoors, once the danger of frost has passed, in any fertile, well-drained soil in a semi-shaded situation. Overwinter the plants under glass. Pinch out shoot tips if a bushy growth habit is required.
PROPAGATION Take stem cuttings in spring and summer; these will root very easily.
PESTS AND DISEASES Usually trouble free.

Pleioblastus see BAMBOOS p.78

Pleione

Orchidaceae

These Asian orchids with their big, showy flowers are easily grown in a frost-free greenhouse or on a cool, shaded windowsill. In warm parts of the country, some species will grow outdoors if they are given adequate winter protection.

These members of the orchid family have pseudobulbs – swollen basal stems which act as the plants' storage organs. Each year, a new stem emerges from the base of the previous season's pseudobulb. Both flowers and leaves are borne on this stem which then swells to become a new pseudobulb. Usually pear-shaped and purplish or green, the pseudobulbs are about 2.5 cm (1 in) long. The flowers, borne singly or in pairs, are made up of a central tube with a large lower lip, usually ridged and fringed and marked with coloured blotches, which is surrounded by five spreading tepals. Those plants described here flower in spring. Pleiones usually bear just one mid green, oval, pleated leaf, 7.5-15 cm (3-6 in) long, that emerges with or just after the flowers and continues to grow once the blooms have faded.
RECOMMENDED SPECIES AND VARIETIES
P. bulbocodioides This species has pale to deep rose flowers, 5-7 cm (2-2¾ in) across, with dark reddish purple spots and several ridges on the flower lip. *P. bulbocodioides* can be grown outdoors if protected. HEIGHT & SPREAD 10×10 cm (4×4 in).

Limprichtii Group ♀ has slightly smaller, generally deep pink to magenta flowers with 4 white ridges and deep red blotches on the lips. **Pricei Group** (see *P. formosana* Pricei Group).
P. × confusa Clear yellow flowers, 6-9 cm (2½-3½ in) across, have purple-blotched lips. HEIGHT & SPREAD 10×10 cm (4×4 in).
P. formosana The rose-pink or white flowers are 5-7 cm (2-2¾ in) across. On the lip there are abundant red or yellow markings and 2-5 ridges. The easiest species to grow, *P. formosana* can be grown outdoors in milder regions given adequate protection. HEIGHT & SPREAD 10×10 cm (4×4 in).

▲ *Pleione formosana* 'Alba'

'Alba' has white flowers with yellow lip markings. **'Avalanche'** has pure white flowers. **'Lilac Beauty'**, which flowers early in the season, has lilac-pink flowers with a paler lip, spotted with dark red. **'Oriental Grace'** has pinky violet flowers with a pale rose lip, spotted brown and yellow. The purplish pink flowers of **'Oriental Jewel'** have a very pale lip marked in yellowish brown. **'Oriental Splendour'** often bears 2 deep purplish rose flowers with a paler lip, marked with brown and yellow. The flowers of **Pricei Group** (syn. *P. bulbocodioides* Pricei Group) are similar to 'Oriental Splendour' but appear slightly earlier. **'Snow White'** bears white flowers with lemon-yellow markings on the lip that also appear early in the season.

▲ *Pleione formosana* 'Snow White'

P. forrestii This species carries large flowers 6-9 cm (2½-3½ in) across, varying in colour from pale to deep orange-yellow. The lip has deep red or brown blotches and several ridges. HEIGHT & SPREAD 10×10 cm (4×4 in).
P. speciosa (syn. *P. pogonioides* hort.) The rose-purple flowers, 5-7 cm (2-2¾ in) across, have lips with many reddish brown spots and 2-4 white or yellow ridges. HEIGHT & SPREAD 10×10 cm (4×4 in).

▲ *Pleione forrestii*

P. yunnanensis The rose-pink flowers, 5-7 cm (2-2¾ in) across, have lips with 5 ridges that are heavily blotched with purple. HEIGHT & SPREAD 10×10 cm (4×4 in).

OTHER HYBRIDS

There are many hybrids and hybrid groups available. The name grex is applied to a group of plants that may be difficult to separate individually. In most cases the flowers are 6-9 cm (2½-3½ in) across.

Alishan has pink flowers with white-tipped tepals and a white lip heavily spotted with reddish purple. **Eiger** has 2 white flowers to a stem and its tepals are very faintly flushed with pink. In **Hekla** the deep pinkish purple flowers have red markings on the lip.

▲ *Pleione* Hekla

Shantung has flowers in a range of colours from yellow to peach with lips usually fringed and spotted red. **'Muriel Harberd'**♀ is a cultivar of Shantung that has large peach-coloured flowers, up to 10 cm (4 in) across. Their lip is deep orange-red with conspicuous ridges. Another cultivar of Shantung is **'Ridgeway'**, a vigorous variety with pale apricot flowers whose deep yellow lip is heavily spotted orange-red.

Stromboli has deep reddish purple flowers. **Tolima** has deep rose-purple flowers with lips heavily spotted darker red and ridged in yellow or white. It often bears 2 flowers to a stem.

The vigorous **Versailles** is variable, but generally has very large rose-pink flowers up to 10 cm (4 in) across with a paler lip. Among the finest and most readily available cultivars of Versailles is **'Bucklebury'**♀. Its flowers are purple with a lip blotched brownish red.

▲ *Pleione* Shantung 'Ridgeway'

CULTIVATION Grow pleiones under glass or indoors in shallow containers of well-drained open compost, made up of chopped sphagnum moss, fine bark chips, a little loam and charcoal pieces, for example. Plant the pseudobulbs so that their bases are just covered by the compost. Keep in a cool greenhouse or alpine house. Pleiones can be grown indoors on a shady windowsill where summer temperatures do not exceed 25°C (77°F) but they need to be kept cool during their dormant period and are best overwintered in a cool greenhouse or alpine house. Do not water plants during their dormancy. Only begin watering when new growth appears, and then increase the amounts of water used gradually. During summer mist overhead daily and give a mild liquid feed weekly. Keep well-watered until leaf-fall when the dormant period begins.

▲ *Pleione* Versailles 'Bucklebury'

Alternatively, in milder regions plant *P. bulbocodioides* and *P. formosana* outdoors in mid to late spring, choosing a shady spot in free-draining soil to which leaf-mould and fine bark chips have been added. Ensure that the base of the pseudobulbs are just covered by the soil. Cover them with a cloche or pane of glass in winter to protect them from excessive winter wet.

PROPAGATION Divide plants in early spring before the new growth begins.

PESTS AND DISEASES Red spider mite, voles, slugs and aphids may be troublesome.

Plum see p. 728

Plum, ornamental see *Prunus*

Plumbago

Leadwort
Plumbaginaceae

Abundant sprays of pale, sky-blue flowers and a long flowering period earn *Plumbago auriculata* its place in conservatories, greenhouses and summer beds. This fast-growing, decorative shrub from South Africa is the only species commonly grown in Britain, although other species, with different coloured flowers, can sometimes be seen in warm greenhouses at botanical gardens. In the wild, plumbago plants support themselves by growing their whip-like shoots over and through other shrubs. In cultivation, they need support.

RECOMMENDED SPECIES AND VARIETIES

P. auriculata♀ (syn. *P. capensis*) Terminal clusters of slender-tubed sky-blue flowers, measuring 1.5 cm (½ in) across, appear from summer to early winter. The blooms have 5 spreading, rounded, lobes and are carried on slender, arching, creamy brown stems. The narrow, oblanceolate, thin-textured leaves are up to 8 cm (3¼ in) long. HEIGHT & SPREAD 1.5×1.5 m (5×5 ft) after 5 years, ultimately 3-4 m (10-13 ft) tall.

▲ *Plumbago auriculata*

Pure white flowers distinguish var. ***alba***.

P. larpentae see *Ceratostigma plumbaginoides*

CULTIVATION Plant in pots or in a greenhouse border in well-drained, fertile compost in sun or dappled shade. Tie selected main shoots to supports. If desired, move conservatory plants onto a patio in summer and return them in autumn. For summer bedding, move the plants outside after all danger of frost has passed. Reduce watering when the plants are not in active growth.

PROPAGATION Take semi-ripe cuttings in summer.

PRUNING Cut back shoots that flowered the previous year by two-thirds in early spring.

PESTS AND DISEASES Glasshouse whitefly may infest the foliage of plants under glass.

Plumbago, Chinese
see *Ceratostigma willmottianum*

Podocarpus
Podocarpaceae

Podocarpus salignus

This genus of evergreens includes shrubs suitable for a rock garden or for using as ground cover, as well as medium to large trees for larger gardens in warmer, southerly regions of Britain. These slow-growing plants are clothed with stiff, leathery, yew-like leaves, usually arranged spirally.

Where several plants are grown together – as ground cover, for example – fruits are produced if mainly female plants are used with an occasional male for pollination. Male and female plants can only be identified when in flower or fruit. From late spring to early summer, male plants bear erect catkin-like flowers and female plants have discreet cones. The cones, if pollinated, are followed by fleshy, red berries.

RECOMMENDED SPECIES AND VARIETIES

P. macrophyllus (Japanese yew, Buddhist pine) Commonly grown as a houseplant, this species grows up to 8m (26ft) tall in the wild, but makes a small, compactly conical shrub when grown in a container. The flat leaves, up to 10cm (4in) long, are bright green and bluish beneath. Their shape is needle-like, although broader and softer in appearance than pine needles. Native to Japan. HEIGHT & SPREAD 1.8×1m (6×3ft).

▼ *Podocarpus nivalis*

P. nivalis Foliage colour varies greatly between specimens of this generally low-growing, spreading shrub which is suitable for ground cover. The leathery leaves may be green, yellow, bluish or purple to bronze. It is hardy and variable in size. Native to New Zealand. HEIGHT & SPREAD 60×80cm (24×32in) after 5 years, ultimately 1-2m (3-6½ft) tall.

▲ *Podocarpus salignus*

P. salignus♀ Glossy, dark green, willow-like leaves are carried on the drooping branches of this slow-growing tree. The plant does best in sheltered situations in warmer regions of Britain. Native to Chile. HEIGHT & SPREAD 5.5×3m (18×10ft) after 25 years, ultimately 12m (40ft) tall.

CULTIVATION Plant *P. nivalis* in well-drained soil and an open situation in spring. *P. salignus* is not fussy about soil and grows in sun or shade. Both tolerate alkaline soils. Keep *P. macrophyllus* in good indirect sunlight at a temperature above 4°C (39°F). Repot in spring only when the plant has completely filled its pot with roots.

PROPAGATION Take semi-ripe cuttings in early autumn, root during winter, preferably under glass with bottom heat.

PRUNING Shear plants into shape between mid summer and autumn if necessary.

PESTS AND DISEASES Usually trouble free, but scale insects can sometimes infest plants.

Podophyllum
May apple
Berberidaceae

Used medicinally for centuries, this small genus is now of interest for the treatment of certain types of cancer. There are just five species in the genus, all rhizomatous perennials. With handsome leaves, simple flowers and colourful fruits, they give garden value for several months. The plants have a characteristic habit with erect stems bearing one or a few leaves at the top plus a single white or pink bowl-shaped flower in spring. Late summer brings forth a plum-like, fleshy but inedible fruit.

▲ *Podophyllum hexandrum*

Woodland plants in nature, the May apples do best in a moist, somewhat shaded position in the garden. Native to eastern N America and NE Asia.

RECOMMENDED SPECIES AND VARIETIES

P. emodi see *P. hexandrum*

P. hexandrum (syn. *P. emodi)* A solitary white flower, up to 6cm (2½in) wide, appears to sit on the unfolding leaves in mid spring, developing into a 4cm (1½in) long red fruit by late summer. The deeply lobed leaves, up to 25cm (10in) wide, are often mottled with purplish brown. HEIGHT & SPREAD 45×30cm (1½×1ft).

Light pink flowers are produced by var. ***chinense.***

P. peltatum (May apple, wild mandrake) A single, nodding white flower, up to 5cm (2in) across, is borne with the partly folded young leaves in mid spring. The shiny dark green leaves, up to 30cm (1ft) wide, are divided into several deep lobes which are often forked at the tips. An egg-shaped pale yellow fruit, 4cm (1½in) long, ripens in late summer or early autumn. HEIGHT & SPREAD 45×30cm (1½×1ft).

CULTIVATION Plant in a moist, leafy soil in autumn in a partially shaded spot. Strong sun or dry conditions may scorch the leaves.

PROPAGATION Sow seed in autumn and raise in a nursery bed, planting out in the spring of the second year, or carefully divide well-established clumps in late winter.

PESTS AND DISEASES Usually trouble free.

Poinsettia see *Euphorbia pulchemima*
Pokeweed see *Phytolacca americana*

Polemonium

Jacob's ladder
Polemoniaceae

Polemonium caeruleum

Clusters of cup-shaped summer flowers appear above distinctive basal rosettes that are composed of pairs of leaflets resembling the rungs of a ladder. Suitable for borders, rock gardens or the alpine house, these hardy perennials may be short-lived, but they self-seed readily. Native to Europe, Asia, Central and S America.

RECOMMENDED SPECIES AND VARIETIES

P. boreale The blue, purple or white flowers are about 1 cm (⅜ in) across. The plant is useful for a rock garden where it appreciates sandy or gravelly soil. HEIGHT & SPREAD 25×20 cm (10×8 in).

P. brandegeei Straw-yellow flowers, 2.5 cm (1 in) across, appear in terminal clusters of up to 12 in summer or early autumn. The leaves are sticky and have an unpleasant smell. The plant is best grown under glass but even there it is short-lived. HEIGHT & SPREAD 20×15 cm (8×6 in).

Sweetly scented white or yellow flowers are seen on ssp. ***mellitum***.

P. caeruleum Lavender-blue flowers, borne in early summer, have deep yellow stamens and are 2.5 cm (1 in) across. HEIGHT & SPREAD 60×60 cm (2×2 ft).

'Album' bears white flowers and **'Brise d'Anjou'** has clumps of yellow-edged, finely divided leaves and violet-blue flowers throughout summer.

P. carneum Clusters of salmon-pink, cup-shaped flowers, 2.5 cm (1 in) across, appear on this clump-former throughout summer. HEIGHT & SPREAD 45×45 cm (1½×1½ ft).

'Apricot Delight' has pinky apricot-coloured flowers.

▼ *Polemonium carneum* 'Apricot Delight'

▲ *Polemonium foliosissimum*

P. foliosissimum The lavender-blue or white flowers of this upright plant grow up to 2 cm (¾ in) wide and are enhanced by bright orange stamens. HEIGHT & SPREAD 75×60 cm (2½×2 ft).

***P.* 'Lambrook Mauve'**♀ This spreading plant bears pale mauve flowers that are about 2 cm (¾ in) across. HEIGHT & SPREAD 45×45 cm (1½×1½ ft).

P. pauciflorum Soft yellow tubular flowers, about 3 cm (1¼ in) long, are borne in loose clusters; some with a reddish tinge. This short-lived perennial is suitable for a rock garden and can also be used in the front of a herbaceous border in well-drained soil. HEIGHT & SPREAD 30×15 cm (12×6 in).

P. pulcherrimum Blue flowers, 1.5 cm (½ in) long, are borne in loose clusters and have a yellow or white eye. This plant is suitable for growing in a rock garden. HEIGHT & SPREAD 50×30 cm (20×12 in).

P. reptans This slightly woody-based plant carries pale blue pendulous tubular flowers about 1.5 cm (½ in) long. It does best in a shady, moist spot at the edge of woodland. HEIGHT & SPREAD 45×45 cm (1½×1½ ft).

CULTIVATION Plant from autumn to spring in sun or partial shade in any soil, but preferably moist. Deadhead to prevent too many seedlings arising and to encourage a possible second crop of flowers. Stake taller plants if necessary. Grow *P. brandegeei* in pots in a coldframe or in an alpine house in a gritty mixture with leaf-mould, and provide shade from summer sun.

PROPAGATION Divide plants in spring. Division every 2 or 3 years ensures vigorous growth. Sow seed in autumn and plant out the seedlings in spring.

PESTS AND DISEASES Usually trouble free.

▼ *Polemonium reptans*

Polyanthus
see *Primula* Polyanthus Group

Polygala

Milkwort
Polygalaceae

Polygala calcarea

Unusual flowers, with two wing-like sepals and a lip, adorn the milkworts in late spring and summer. The genus contains annuals, perennials and shrubs but it is mainly the small low-growing shrubs that are cultivated. *Polygala calcarea* is good for rock gardens and *P. chamaebuxus* is suitable for growing in partial shade among woodland bulbs or small ericaceous shrubs.

Polygala myrtifolia and *P.* × *dalmaisiana* are too tender for any but the mildest of British gardens, and are generally grown in containers in a cool greenhouse or conservatory and brought outside in summer. Native to Europe and South Africa.

RECOMMENDED SPECIES AND VARIETIES

P. calcarea Upright spikes of brilliant deep blue flowers with a white fringe on the lip pierce the low mat of deep green spatulate

▼ *Polygala calcarea*

▲ *Polygala calcarea* 'Lillet'

▲ *Polygala chamaebuxus* var. *grandiflora*

leaves in early summer. HEIGHT & SPREAD 5×20cm (2×8in) after 5 years, ultimately spreading to 60cm (2ft).

Bulley's form has larger flowers in a deeper shade of blue. **'Lillet'**♀ is more compact with flowers in a brighter blue.

P. ***chamaebuxus***♀ Clusters of flowers with yellow or white lips and bright yellow wings appear in late spring or early summer. The wings darken to brown with age. This hardy, suckering plant has glossy, dark green, oval leaves. HEIGHT & SPREAD 15×30cm (6×12in) after 5 years, ultimately spreading to 1m (3ft).

More colourful is var. ***grandiflora***♀ (syn. 'Purpurea', 'Rhodoptera'), bearing larger flowers with bright yellow lips and deep rosy purple wings. **'Loibl'** is a low-growing mat-former, reaching just 10cm (4in) high, and ultimately spreading to 60cm (2ft), with darker leaves than the species and deep purple-and-yellow flowers.

P. x ***dalmaisiana*** Similar in habit to *P. myrtifolia*, this tender shrub has lanceolate to ovate blue-green leaves and purplish red flowers. The flowers are borne from late spring to late summer. HEIGHT & SPREAD 1×1m (3×3ft) after 5 years, ultimately spreading to 2m (6½ft).

P. ***myrtifolia*** Greenish white flowers veined with purple, appear in clusters from late spring to late summer. This tender, branching shrub has blue-green, ovate leaves. HEIGHT & SPREAD Up to 1×1m (3×3ft) after 5 years, ultimately spreading to 2m (6½ft).

'Grandiflora' has larger deep violet-purple flowers with a white-crested lip. It flowers throughout the summer months.

CULTIVATION Plant in autumn or early spring. *P. calcarea* does best in gritty, limy soil with plenty of humus and in full sun. *P. chamaebuxus* does better in acid woodland soil, in partial shade.

Grow the tender species in ordinary well-drained compost in large containers in a cool greenhouse or conservatory.

PROPAGATION Take softwood heel cuttings of outdoor plants in early summer or sow seed of the species in autumn and keep cool through winter. Take cuttings from greenhouse species in mid spring.

PESTS AND DISEASES Aphid and whitefly are problems under glass.

Polygonatum

Solomon's seal

Liliaceae

Pendent, bell-like, and sometimes fragrant flowers appear in spring and early summer. These and glossy, architectural foliage characterise the herbaceous perennials in this genus. The plants described below are all hardy and rhizomatous. They look highly ornamental when planted among shrubs in a mixed border. Exceptionally among the recommended species, *Polygonatum hookeri* is suitable for growing in a rock garden and bears solitary, erect flowers. Plants generally grow best in partial shade and enjoy a moist, well-drained soil, rich in organic matter. Native to northern USA, Europe and Asia.

RECOMMENDED SPECIES AND VARIETIES

P. ***biflorum*** (syn. *P. canaliculatum*, *P. commutatum*) (great Solomon's seal) Greenish white drooping flowers, up to 1.5cm (½ in) long, are borne beneath bold, arching stems in pairs, and occasionally alone or in groups of 3 or 4, on this strong-growing plant in late spring. The stems are further clothed in bright, glossy, mid green, oval to elliptical leaves, up to 20cm (8in) long, with distinctive bluish undersides. HEIGHT & SPREAD 2m×60cm (6½×2ft).

P. ***canaliculatum*** see *P. biflorum*

P. ***commutatum*** see *P. biflorum*

P. ***falcatum*** Small white drooping blossoms, up to 1.5cm (½in) long, are liberally produced in early summer beneath upright stems, which arch at the ends. The stems bear narrow, lance or sickle-shaped mid green leaves, up to 23cm (9in) long. HEIGHT & SPREAD 1m×45cm (3×1½ft).

'Variegatum' has foliage variegated with creamy yellow at the margins.

P. ***hookeri*** Solitary pinkish or white flowers, up to 2cm (¾in) long, peep from crowded groups of lance-shaped, mid green leaves, up to 1.5cm (½in) long, during late spring to early summer. This small plant is suitable

▲ *Polygonatum hookeri*

for a damp, shady spot in a rock garden. HEIGHT & SPREAD 7.5×30cm (3×12in).

P. ***humile*** Solitary or paired, green-tipped, white, pendent flowers, up to 2cm (¾in) long, bloom in late spring. Lance-shaped or oval, mid green, downy leaves, up to 15cm (6in) long and 2.5cm (1in) wide, are arranged alternately on erect stems. HEIGHT & SPREAD 1m×60cm (3×2ft).

P. x ***hybridum***♀ (syn. *P. multiflorum*) In late spring clusters of tubular to bell-shaped white flowers with a greenish flush and up to 2cm (¾in) long, are produced from the leaf axils beneath this leafy plant's gently arching stems. The mid green, roughly oval and occasionally undulating leaves are up to 7.5cm (3in) long and 4cm (1½in) wide. HEIGHT & SPREAD 1.2×1m (4×3ft).

▲ *Polygonatum* x *hybridum*

'Striatum' (syn. 'Variegatum') has undulating leaves striped with cream. It reaches 60×30cm (2×1ft) in height and spread.

P. ***multiflorum*** see *P.* x *hybridum*

P. ***odoratum*** (angled Solomon's seal) Pendent, fragrant white flowers with greenish tips, up to 2cm (¾in) long, bloom in groups of 2 or 3 in the leaf axils in spring.

▲ *Polygonatum* x *hybridum* 'Striatum'

▲ *Polygonatum odoratum* 'Variegatum'

The mid green, lance-shaped or oval leaves, up to 12.5cm (5in) long, are borne on angular, arching stems. HEIGHT & SPREAD 60×30cm (2×1ft).

'Flore Pleno'♀ carries double flowers; **'Variegatum'** has leaves edged with cream and stems slightly flushed with red.

P. verticillatum (whorled Solomon's seal) Drooping, narrowly bell-shaped, greenish white flowers, about 1.5cm (½in) long, are produced in the upper leaf axils of this upright plant in early summer. The narrow leaves are mid green and up to 15cm (6in) long. HEIGHT & SPREAD 1m×45cm (3×1½ft).

'Rubrum' has pink-tinged shoots and dusky pink bell-shaped flowers.

CULTIVATION Plant from late autumn to early spring in a partially shaded position and in a well-drained soil that is rich in organic matter. Lift and divide in early spring every few years to maintain vigour.

PROPAGATION Divide during early spring.

PESTS AND DISEASES Solomon's seal sawfly can strip plants bare.

Polygonum see *Fallopia*, *Persicaria*
Polypodium see FERNS p.265
Polystichum see FERNS p.265

Poncirus

Japanese bitter orange
Rutaceae

Poncirus trifoliata

This slow-growing spiny shrub or very small tree, is the nearest thing to an orange tree that can be grown outdoors in Britain, if only in sheltered lowland areas. It bears edible, but sour, fruit and has been crossed with *Citrus* to produce a type of orange called citrange, and with *Fortunella* to create the kumquat.

The only species in its genus, this tough deciduous shrub is native to N China and Korea and hardy to -10°C (14°F). It forms a good thorn hedge and is long-lived, as records of an 80-year-old specimen testify.

Poncirus trifoliata White scented flowers, about 5cm (2in) across with 5 longish, often twisted petals, appear in early spring amid a tangle of thorns and smooth, vivid green, compressed branches. Each leaf consists of 3 leaflets: the terminal leaflet is obovate and up to 6cm (2½in) long, while the side pair are smaller and elliptic-ovate in shape. Small fruit up to 5cm (2in) across are produced in autumn and last throughout winter. HEIGHT & SPREAD 50×50cm (20×20in) after 5 years, ultimately 4m (13ft) tall.

CULTIVATION Plant during late spring in any well-drained soil, preferably in full sun.

PROPAGATION Cuttings are difficult and seed is unpredictable. It is best to buy the readily available plants.

PRUNING Seldom required and hazardous because of the spines.

PESTS AND DISEASES Usually trouble free.

Pondweed see *Potamogeton*
Pondweed, Canadian see *Elodea canadensis*
Pondweed, Cape see *Aponogeton distachyos*
Poplar see *Populus*

▼ *Poncirus trifoliata*

Poppy see *Papaver*
Poppy, blue see *Meconopsis betonicifolia*
Poppy, California see *Eschscholzia*
Poppy, Himalayan see *Meconopsis betonicifolia*
Poppy, horned see *Glaucium*
Poppy, Mexican see *Argemone mexicana*
Poppy, plume see *Macleaya*
Poppy, tree see *Romneya*
Poppy, Welsh see *Meconopsis cambrica*

Populus

Poplar
Salicaceae

Populus alba 'Raket'

These hardy, fast-growing, generally slender trees are grown for their deciduous foliage and pleasing habit. They are suitable only for larger gardens where they make effective windbreaks. They are tolerant of pollution and have the open head and pliable branches that withstand coastal winds. Be careful when choosing a tree, as many species grow very tall at an alarming rate and may become expensive to remove. For example, the Lombardy poplar, *Populus nigra* 'Italica', can grow to 35m (115ft) and the aspen, *P. tremula*, reaches 24m (79ft). The massive dimensions of these two trees have precluded them from this book.

All poplars have spreading roots that pull enormous amounts of water from the soil. They should never be planted near buildings, particularly those built on clay soil which shrinks as it dries, as they are likely to cause subsidence. Some species produce suckers when cut back or even cut down, which continue the demand for water.

Reddish male catkins appear on the bare shoots in early spring and grow to about 5cm (2in) long. The slender, greenish, female catkins are borne on separate trees;

▼ *Populus alba* 'Richardii'

pq

they are up to 10 cm (4 in) long and develop into strings of green capsules from which the tiny seeds disperse on cotton-like filaments, sometimes leading to unwelcome seedlings on neighbouring land.

RECOMMENDED SPECIES AND VARIETIES

P. alba **'Raket'** (syn. 'Rocket') Upright grey branches form a narrow, columnar tree. Glossy green leaves, 7 cm (2¾ in) long, are usually 5-lobed and have silvery white undersides that give a shimmering effect when they stir in summer breezes. Suckering can become a problem and on a windy site young trees need staking if they are to grow upright. HEIGHT & SPREAD 15×5 m (50×16 ft) after 20 years, ultimately 20 m (66 ft) tall.

P. alba **'Richardii'** The golden yellow leaves of this less vigorous poplar are 6-12 cm (2½-4¾ in) long and have silvery felted undersides. HEIGHT & SPREAD 10×6 m (33×20 ft) after 20 years, ultimately 15 m (50 ft) tall.

P. × *canadensis* **'Aurea'**♀ Clear yellow leaves turn golden in autumn. They are 8 cm (3¼ in) long and almost triangular. The tree is extremely vigorous. HEIGHT & SPREAD 16×12 m (52×40 ft) in 20 years, ultimately 20 m (66 ft) tall.

P. × *candicans* **'Aurora'** Cream, pink and green mingle on the variegated, broadly ovate leaves which can grow to 12 cm (4¾ in) long and are pine-scented. Canker usually causes die-back in middle age. HEIGHT & SPREAD 16×8 m (52×26 ft) in 20 years, ultimately 18 m (60 ft) tall.

▼ *Populus* × *canadensis* 'Aurea'

▼ *Populus tremula* 'Pendula'

P. nigra **'Lombardy Gold'** Triangular yellow leaves are up to 8 cm (3¼ in) long on this narrow, slow-growing tree. HEIGHT & SPREAD 5×1.5 m (16×5 ft) after 20 years, ultimately 8 m (26 ft) tall.

P. tremula **'Pendula'** This is one of the best and most robust weeping trees available in Britain, and more suitable for the average garden than its massive parent species. It tolerates a vast range of soil types and grows well in towns, though it does best on a moist, fertile site. Greyish purple catkins are borne in early spring before the balloon-shaped leaves. Suckers might appear so the planting position must be carefully chosen. HEIGHT & SPREAD 8×7 m (26×23 ft) after 20 years, ultimately 10 m (33 ft) tall.

CULTIVATION Poplars are easy to grow, but require ample space and moisture. Plant well away from buildings – twice as far away as the tree's ultimate height.

PROPAGATION Most poplars strike easily from mid winter hardwood cuttings planted outdoors or late summer semi-ripe cuttings reared under glass.

PRUNING Pruning is usually needed only if a tree becomes top heavy and unsafe. Many poplars react to pruning by suckering.

PESTS AND DISEASES Usually trouble free, except for *P.* × *candicans* 'Aurora' which is susceptible to canker.

Portulaca

Portulacaceae

Of the 40 species in this genus of mostly succulent annual plants, *Portulaca grandiflora* is by far the most popular. This brilliantly coloured and showy half-hardy annual adds a flourish to summer bedding schemes. It will thrive on a dry bank or as a filler in sunny spots in a rock garden. The flowers tend to close in shade or dull weather.

The other species described below, *P. oleracea*, is not showy but has edible leaves. Native to sub-tropical and tropical regions of the world.

RECOMMENDED SPECIES AND VARIETIES

P. grandiflora (rose moss, sun plant) A succession of saucer-shaped flowers, in shades of orange, pink, red, yellow or white, appear from mid summer to early autumn. The flowers have a silky sheen and are up to 5 cm (2 in) across. Reddish stems carry cylindrical leaves, up to 2.5 cm (1 in) long. HEIGHT & SPREAD 10-20×20 cm (4-8×8 in).

▼ *Portulaca grandiflora*

The following varieties, all with double blooms, have been bred so that their flowers close less readily in dull weather. **'Cloudbeater'** and **'Sundance'** have flowers in the same colour range as the species. **'Peppermint'** bears white flowers with pink stripes. **'Swan Lake'** bears white flowers.

P. oleracea (purslane) Small yellow flowers are produced on thick erect stems from mid summer to early autumn. The flat, spatula-shaped leaves are fleshy and up to 2.5 cm (1 in) across. They can be used in salads and soups. HEIGHT & SPREAD 30×20 cm (12×8 in).

CULTIVATION Plant in a sunny spot in well-drained, low-nutrient soil when all risk of frost has passed.

PROPAGATION Sow seed in a heated greenhouse in early spring. Prick out the seedlings into small pots or cellular trays. Alternatively, sow seed in mid to late spring in the flowering site.

PESTS AND DISEASES Aphids may be troublesome. Seedlings and young plants are susceptible to damping off.

Potamogeton

Pondweed

Potamogetonaceae

Potamogeton crispus

These hardy aquatic plants with submerged and floating leaves are often considered to be weedy and invasive, but at least one species (described below) is more restrained and has come to be highly regarded by pond-keepers. Though the flower spikes are decidedly unspectacular, the decorative foliage enhances any water garden and the plant will help to oxygenate the water.

RECOMMENDED SPECIES

P. crispus (curled pondweed) Brittle, branching stems are densely clothed with narrow, lance-shaped leaves up to 5 cm (2 in) long with crinkly edges. The dark green seaweed-like leaves are attractively flushed with copper. Tiny spikes of flowers appear above the surface of the water in summer but they have no decorative merit. The plant will grow in 60-100 cm (2-3 ft) of water. SPREAD 60 cm (2 ft).

CULTIVATION Plant in spring as bunches of cuttings fastened together at the base with narrow strips of lead. Push into a container of clean heavy garden soil or aquatic planting compost, being sure to bury the lead

strips. Top dress the container with pea gravel and place in water at least 60 cm (2 ft) deep. Remove decaying foliage in autumn and repot if necessary the following spring.
PROPAGATION Take softwood cuttings in summer and grow in a tray of mud placed in an unheated aquarium.
PESTS AND DISEASES Usually trouble free.

Potato see p. 744
Potato, duck see *Sagittaria latifolia*
Potato vine see *Solanum jasminoides*

Potentilla

Cinquefoil
Rosaceae

Potentilla 'Gibson's Scarlet'

Flowers resembling small wild roses, in yellow, orange, red, pink or white, bring an abundance of colour to the garden from late spring through summer and into autumn. The five-petalled flowers are usually about 2.5 cm (1 in) across and carried in loose clusters. There are species for the rock garden, shrubbery or border, all bearing vibrant blooms that contrast attractively with their green, greyish or silvery, divided leaves.

This widely distributed genus contains 500 species, including annuals, perennials and shrubs. The annuals are of little garden value, but several herbaceous to semi-evergreen perennials and one shrub (*P. fruticosa*) and its many varieties are popular additions to British gardens; these are described below. All are hardy and easy to grow if given a sunny spot.

RECOMMENDED SPECIES AND VARIETIES
P. alba White, yellow-eyed flowers appear in mid summer. The flowers are borne on 10 cm (4 in) stems above a mat of palmate leaves. The leaves are silver-grey beneath and dark green above. This low-growing perennial is a good ground-cover plant. HEIGHT & SPREAD 10×15 cm (4×6 in).
P. ambigua see *P. cuneata*
P. arbuscula see *P. fruticosa* 'Elizabeth'
P. atrosanguinea Loose clusters of flowers, each bloom up to 4 cm (1½ in) across, are produced throughout the summer by this upright perennial. The blooms vary in colour from yellow to orange and dark red. The dark green ternate leaves are silvery haired and toothed. HEIGHT & SPREAD 45×60 cm (1½×2 ft).

Yellow-orange flowers are borne by var. ***argyrophylla***.

P. aurea Bright yellow flowers, often with a darker centre, are carried in summer and early autumn above a compact mat of mid green, silky-edged leaves made up of 5 radiating leaflets. This low-growing plant is suited to a rock garden. HEIGHT & SPREAD 20×30 cm (8×12 in).

'Plena' has deep yellow, semidouble flowers.

P. cinerea (syn. *P. tommasiniana*) Light yellow flowers appear in late spring and early summer just above the palmate, grey-green leaves, which are composed of 3 or 5 narrow, toothed leaflets. The rooting stems of this perennial spread into a compact mat and it is well suited to a sunny rock garden. HEIGHT & SPREAD 10×40 cm (4×16 in).
P. crantzii (syn. *P. villosa*) Bright yellow, orange-eyed flowers appear in summer above the 3-5 fingered, dark green leaves. This plant forms a low mound with arching or prostrate stems coming up from a woody base and is suitable for a rock garden. It is more compact and free-flowering in poor soils, but may become lush and leafy in rich conditions, with few flowers. HEIGHT & SPREAD 20×40 cm (8×16 in).
P. cuneata♀ (syn. *P. ambigua*) Solitary bright yellow flowers are borne just above the low mat of foliage. Prostrate stems come up from a woody base clothed in small, mid green leaves, composed of 3 oval or wedge-shaped leaflets, coarsely toothed at the tip. This plant suits a rock garden. HEIGHT & SPREAD 10×20 cm (4×8 in).
P. eriocarpa Bright yellow, mostly solitary flowers in late summer are followed by attractive silky seed heads. The small, blue-green leaves are composed of 3 wedge-shaped leaflets and have reddish stalks. The plant forms a low mat and is suitable for a rock garden. HEIGHT & SPREAD 10×40 cm (4×16 in).

▼ *Potentilla atrosanguinea*

▲ *Potentilla atrosanguinea* var. *argyrophylla*

P. fragiformis see *P. megalantha*
P. fruticosa (shrubby cinquefoil) Yellow or white flowers, 2-5 cm (¾-2 in) wide, are borne freely in summer and often well into autumn, among small, pinnate, mid green, grey-green or sometimes silvery leaves. These compact, twiggy deciduous shrubs are useful in a sunny border. There are many varieties to choose from. HEIGHT & SPREAD 30-50×45 cm (12-20×18 in) after 5 years, but the ultimate size varies. Dwarf and spreading varieties reach up to 75 cm×1 m (2½×3 ft); the taller ones may grow to 1.8×1.5 m (6×5 ft).

'Abbotswood'♀ is low and spreading with dark foliage and white flowers appearing over a long period. **'Abbotswood Silver'** is similar, with white-edged leaves, but tends to revert to all-green foliage. **'Beesii'**♀ (syn. 'Argentea Nana') is dwarf with silvery leaves and large, bright yellow flowers. **'Daydawn'**♀ is a low-grower with small leaves and creamy peach-pink flowers. **'Elizabeth'**♀ (syn. *P. arbuscula*) makes a rounded bush ultimately 1×1.2 m (3×4 ft), with large, rich canary-yellow flowers.

'Goldfinger'♀ is dwarf with blue-green leaves and large, rich yellow flowers. **'Goldstar'** makes a dwarf, upright bush with large deep yellow flowers. **'Hopley's Orange'** is compact, with small leaves and dark-centred, orange flowers. **'Jackman's**

Variety' is vigorous and upright in growth, with large, light yellow flowers. **'Katherine Dykes'**♀ is similar in size and habit to 'Jackman's Variety', but has small primrose-yellow flowers. **'Klondike'**♀ is a compact, dwarf variety with golden yellow flowers.

'Longacre Variety'♀ forms a low mat with small leaves and vivid, light yellow flowers. **'Maanelys'**♀ (also sold as **'Moonlight'**) has light yellow flowers that are paler beneath. **'Manchu'** (syn. *P.* 'Mandshurica') is low and spreading with grey-green leaves and white flowers. The flowers are borne rather sparsely but over a long period. **'Mount Everest'** has narrow, yellowish green leaves and white flowers. It is an upright plant, up to 1m (3ft) tall.

'Pretty Polly' is low-growing, with pale pink flowers. **'Primrose Beauty'**♀ has grey-green leaves and pale primrose-yellow flowers on low, arching branches. **'Princess'** (also sold as **'Blink'** or **'Pink Panther'**) is low and spreading, with

▲ *Potentilla fruticosa* 'Princess'

▲ *Potentilla fruticosa* 'Red Ace'

yellow-centred, pale pink flowers. **'Red Ace'** is a low spreading bush with bright vermilion flowers that are pale creamy yellow on the back. The flowers fade in hot, dry weather. **'Royal Flush'** is almost prostrate, with rose-pink flowers, some with a few extra petals.

'Sunset' is low-growing with light to deep orange flowers. **'Tangerine'**♀ is low-growing, with large, light coppery yellow flowers. **'Tilford Cream'**♀ is a small, spreading shrub with large creamy white flowers. White flowers are seen on var. *veitchii*, carried on arching branches. The plant ultimately grows up to 1m (3ft) tall.

Potentilla 'Vilmoriniana'

'Vilmoriniana' is tall and upright with silvery leaves and cream blooms.

P. megalantha♀ (syn. *P. fragiformis*) Rich yellow flowers, up to 4cm (1½in) wide, appear in summer on stems up to 30cm (12in) long, above glossy mid green leaves composed of 3 broad, strongly toothed and heavily veined leaflets. This perennial is suitable for a rock garden. HEIGHT & SPREAD 30×60cm (1×2ft).

P. nepalensis Glowing red or orange flowers appear in early summer. The leaves are made up of 5 radiating, boldly toothed leaflets. This plant is good for borders. HEIGHT & SPREAD 45×60cm (1½×2ft).

'Miss Willmott'♀ bears rose-pink flowers with a darker centre and reaches just 35cm (14in) in height. **'Roxana'** has orange-scarlet blooms.

***P. neumanniana* 'Nana'** (syn. *P. verna* 'Pygmaea') Small, deep yellow flowers are borne from late spring to early summer. The bright green palmate leaves are composed of 5 or 7 sharply toothed leaflets. Spreading, woody-based stems form low mats well suited to a rock garden or dry wall. HEIGHT & SPREAD 10×30cm (4×12in).

P. nitida Almost stemless flowers in an unusual light rosy pink with a darker centre appear in mid to late summer. They contrast beautifully with the small, silvery leaves, which are made up of 3 wedge-shaped leaflets, toothed at the tips. This low mat-forming plant is suitable for a rock garden, alpine house, or unheated greenhouse. It flowers most freely in poor, gritty soil. HEIGHT & SPREAD 10×20cm (4×8in).

'Rubra' displays its deep rose-pink blooms more freely than the species.

P. recta Yellow flowers appear in mid summer. The plant makes a loose clump in borders with wiry stems that usually need staking. The shiny green palmate leaves are composed of 5 or 7 leaflets. HEIGHT & SPREAD 60×30cm (2×1ft).

▼ *Potentilla recta* 'Warrenii'

Pale yellow flowers are borne by var. ***pallida***♀ (syn. var. *sulphurea*). **'Warrenii'** (syn. 'Macrantha') has rich yellow blooms. Both plants flower throughout the summer as long as it is not too hot and dry.

P. rupestris White flowers are borne on erect or sprawling, sparsely leafy stems, above a rosette of pinnate leaves with 5 or 7 coarsely toothed, oval or rounded leaflets. Plant at the front of a perennial border. HEIGHT & SPREAD 45×30cm (1½×1ft).

P. tommasiniana see *P. cinerea*

P.* x *tonguei♀ Soft apricot-yellow flowers with a crimson centre are borne on spreading stems from mid to late summer. Dark green leaves composed of 3 or 5 oblong, toothed leaflets contrast well with the flowers. This plant suits a rock garden. HEIGHT & SPREAD 15×40cm (6×16in).

***P. verna* 'Pygmaea'** see *P. neumanniana* 'Nana'

P. villosa see *P. crantzii*

GARDEN VARIETIES

There are several plants for which the parentage cannot be exactly determined. These perennials flower throughout the summer, adding colour to a border, but they can also be grown in large blocks as ground-cover plants. Each flower is up to 4cm (1½in) across and held in a loose cluster. All have soft green leaves. HEIGHT & SPREAD 45×60cm (1½×2ft).

'Flamenco' bears scarlet flowers with frilled edges. **'Gibson's Scarlet'**♀ has bright scarlet flowers. **'Gloire de Nancy'** has orange-brown flowers flushed with deep coral-red. **'Helen Jane'** carries mid pink flowers. **'Melton'** has pinky red flowers. **'Monsieur Rouillard'** bears mahogany-red,

▼ *Potentilla* 'Flamenco'

pq

▲ *Potentilla* 'Gibson's Scarlet'

▲ *Potentilla* 'William Rollison'

semidouble flowers. It is one of the darkest varieties and looks best in light shade. **'William Rollison'**♀ bears orange-red, semidouble flowers with yellow reverse.

CULTIVATION Plant from autumn to spring in any moderately fertile and well-drained soil, except *P. crantzii*, *P. cuneata* and *P. nitida*, which need a gritty, poor soil if they are to produce a good display of flowers. All potentillas prefer a sunny situation. All, except the 3 species already mentioned, benefit from a spring mulch of organic material or compost.

Cut back flower stems (except those of *P. fruticosa*) as flowers fade.

PROPAGATION Sow seed of the species in a coldframe in spring and plant out seedlings in autumn. Divide and replant herbaceous perennials in early spring every 3-4 years, but this period can be extended if plants are given a good mulch each year. The woody-based perennials are increased by division or by cuttings taken in late spring or summer. Take cuttings of *P. fruticosa* and its varieties in late summer.

PRUNING The shrub *P. fruticosa* seldom requires pruning.

PESTS AND DISEASES Usually trouble free.

Pratia

Campanulaceae

Pratia pedunculata

Long-lasting carpets of small flowers cover the small leaves of these creeping evergreen perennials in summer. The flowers, up to 1.5cm (½in) across, are followed by fleshy berries. The plants are useful as rock plants, for ground cover, or even to make a lush, unusual lawn. Indeed, given favourable conditions of moist soil and shade, *Pratia angulata* and *P. pedunculata* can become invasive and so need a carefully chosen site.

RECOMMENDED SPECIES AND VARIETIES

P. angulata White flowers are produced over a long period in summer and followed by purplish red fleshy berries. Creeping branches carry rather fleshy leaves. Native to New Zealand. HEIGHT & SPREAD 5cm (2in) high with an indefinite spread.

'Treadwellii' is extremely vigorous, with long, trailing branches and larger leaves and larger white flowers than the species.

P. pedunculata Mats of creeping, small-leaved branches carry blue flowers on erect 3cm (1¼in) long stalks. Flowers appear throughout the summer. The species bears small green berries but these are not produced by most cultivated forms. Native to Australia. HEIGHT & SPREAD 10cm (4in) high with an indefinite spread.

'County Park' has violet-blue, fragrant flowers about 1.5cm (½in) across.

P. perpusilla This compact plant has small leaves and fragrant almost stemless white flowers followed by inconspicuous green berries. HEIGHT & SPREAD 1.5cm (½in) high with an indefinite spread.

CULTIVATION The plants grow best in a moist soil. Some forms can be invasive.

PROPAGATION Lift and divide during spring or summer.

PESTS AND DISEASES Slugs and snails may devour small plants in spring and autumn.

Prayer plant see *Maranta leuconeura*
Pride of India see *Koelreuteria paniculata*
Primrose see *Primula*
Primrose, Cape see *Streptocarpus*
Primrose, evening see *Oenothera*

▼ *Pratia angulata*

▼ *Pratia angulata* 'Treadwellii'

▼ *Pratia pedunculata*

▼ *Pratia pedunculata* 'County Park'

Primula

Primulaceae

The wild species of primula provide some of the loveliest plants for an informal garden. Selective breeding has discovered bedding plants of sparkling colour and specimens of gem-like perfection for growing under glass

A huge genus of perennial plants, primulas are widely distributed throughout the temperate regions of the Northern Hemisphere, in mountain and lowland, woodland and meadow. They vary in habit, from tiny cushions and low-growing mats to vigorous clump-forming plants up to 80cm (32in) high.

They all form rosettes of leaves at ground level and grow flowering stems (scapes) bearing one to many five-petalled flowers, often with a white or yellow eye. In some species the stem is so reduced that the flowers are borne above the foliage only by their individual stalks (pedicels). In other species, the 'candelabra' types, flowers are borne in several whorls up a strong stem.

One feature of the genus is the appearance of 'farina', a silvery, powdery wax, secreted by glands on the leaves, stems and even flowers of some species. It is also called paste or meal. Some people are allergic to it.

RECOMMENDED SPECIES AND VARIETIES

The plants are divided into five groups:
(1) Indoor species
(2) Alpine species
(3) Species for border and bog
(4) Primrose and polyanthus cultivars
(5) Auricula cultivars
All are hardy except the first group.

INDOOR SPECIES

These tender primulas are grown as annuals in pots for indoor decoration – to flower in a greenhouse or conservatory or in the house in winter and spring.

P. kewensis ♀ Fragrant, soft yellow, salver-shaped flowers, 2cm (¾in) wide, are closely borne on the stem in several whorls. The oval or spoon-shaped evergreen leaves have a light dusting of white farina. HEIGHT & SPREAD 30×25cm (12×10in).

P. malacoides (fairy primrose) Whorls of 4-6 small, single, or occasionally double, flowers are borne in shades of red, pink, purple or white with a small yellow eye. An easily grown species, generally grown as an annual, with oval, hairy, evergreen leaves, contact with which can cause an allergic skin reaction in some people. HEIGHT & SPREAD 30×20cm (12×8in).

'Bright Eyes' is a mixed selection covering the full range of colours. Each flower has a large, contrasting, dark eye, and sometimes a yellow throat. **'Carmine Pearl'** is a dwarf strain, 15-20cm (6-8in) tall, with carmine flowers. **'Fire Chief'** has brick-red flowers. **'Jubilee'** has cherry-red flowers. **'Lilac Queen'** has double flowers of soft lilac. **'Mars'** is a plant to 12cm (4¾in) high with deep lavender flowers. **'Ninette'** has deep crimson flowers. **'Rose Bouquet'** bears deep carmine blooms.

P. obconica Large clusters of 2.5cm (1in) wide flowers are borne in a range of colours, white, pink, red, pale lavender to deep purple, all with a greenish eye. Contact with the hairy, rounded, evergreen leaves can cause a severe skin allergy. HEIGHT & SPREAD 30×20cm (12×8in).

Giant-Flowered and **Juno** are mixed selections, but several excellent individual coloured varieties are available. **'Caerulea'** has purplish blue flowers. **'Giant White'** has large, pure white flowers. **'Salmon King'** bears reddish salmon-pink flowers. **'Snowstorm'** has pure white flowers.

ALPINE SPECIES

Suitable for growing in rock gardens or in an alpine house, these small clump-forming species grow to 15cm (6in) high. They have open-faced, salver-shaped, primrose-type, or occasionally more bell-shaped flowers, to 2cm (¾in) across, carried either singly, in trusses or in spikes in spring and early summer. European and Asiatic species have different cultural requirements.

P. allionii A dense cushion of evergreen foliage is smothered in early and mid spring with pink to reddish purple or white flowers with white eyes, 1.5 to 3cm (½-1¼in) wide. The sticky, fleshy, spoon-shaped to rounded leaves grow to 4cm (1½in) long.

▲ *Primula kewensis*

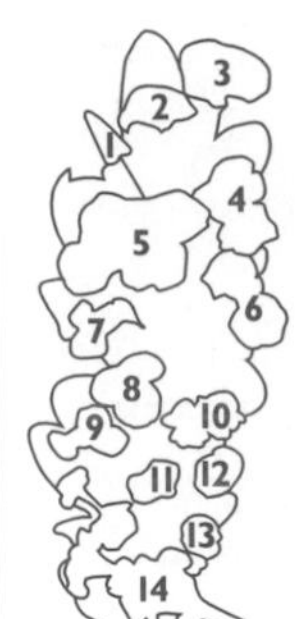

1 *Primula vialii*
2 *Primula denticulata* var. *alba*
3 *Primula denticulata*
4 *Primula auricula*
5 *Primula capitata*
6 *Primula auricula* 'Andrea Julie'
7 *Primula vulgaris* 'Lilacina Plena'
8 *Primula auricula* 'Lovebird'
9 *Primula auricula* 'Rolts'
10 *Primula marginata* 'Prichard's Variety'
11 *Primula* × *pubescens* 'Cream Viscosa'
12 *Primula* × *pubescens* 'Faldonside'
13 *Primula* × *pubescens* 'Boothman's Variety'
14 *Primula vulgaris*

This is one of the most popular alpine house plants, growing wild on shady cliffs in the Maritime Alps, with many varieties and hybrids. All need special care in cultivation, as they resent overhead water especially in winter, and are subject to botrytis unless dead leaves are removed meticulously. HEIGHT & SPREAD 5×20cm (2×8in) or more in many cultivars.

'Anna Griffith' is flat-growing and slow, and has pale lavender-pink petals with a fringed margin. **'Austen'** is purplish pink and slow-growing. **'Avalanche'** has large, creamy white flowers. **'Crowsley Variety'** has small leaves and very dark purplish red flowers with a white eye. **'Ken's Seedling'** (syn.'KRW') is vigorous, bearing large, violet-purple flowers with notched petals. **'Marion'** has large, pale pink flowers with a large white eye. **'Martin'** has pink to reddish purple or white flowers with white eyes. **'Mrs Dyas'** has small violet-pink flowers. **'Pennine Pink'** has purplish pink flowers. Easy to grow. **'Praecox'** is very early flowering, often in late autumn, with lilac-pink flowers. **'Snowflake'** is a superb alpine primula with large, pure white flowers. **'William Earle'** is vigorous, has dark purplish pink flowers with a white eye and very broad, wavy-edged petals.

P. auricula ♀ (bear's ear) Clusters of bright yellow, trumpet-shaped flowers with a white farinose eye appear from mid spring to early summer. The leathery, evergreen, pointed leaves grow to 12cm (4¾in) and may be with or without farina, toothed or untoothed. Growing in the wild from the French Alps to the Tatras, this is a good garden primula and the mother plant from which the auricula cultivars derive. HEIGHT & SPREAD 15×15cm (6×6in).

***P.* 'Beatrice Wooster'** This European hybrid has large clusters of deep rose-pink flowers with white eyes in mid spring and fleshy evergreen leaves to 15cm (6in) long. Fairly easy to grow and good in troughs. HEIGHT & SPREAD 10×20cm (4×8in).

P. capitata Dense, flat or conical heads of small, deep purplish blue flowers appear in mid and late summer. A native of the

pq

Himalayas, with rosettes of mealy, toothed, semi-evergreen leaves up to 15cm (6in) long, it is one of the more easily grown of the Asiatic species and self-seeds readily. HEIGHT & SPREAD 25×15cm (10×6in).

P. chionantha ♀ Fragrant, creamy white, yellow-eyed flowers are borne in whorls up the stem in early summer. With long, farinose deciduous leaves, this Chinese species is one of the easiest of the Asiatics to grow. HEIGHT & SPREAD 40×20cm (16×8in).

P. clarkei Clear rose-pink flowers, to 2cm (¾in) across, are borne in mid spring by this fine, very dwarf primula from Kashmir. With short, rounded, toothed, deciduous leaves, it is usually short-lived unless divided and replanted frequently. HEIGHT & SPREAD 5×10cm (2×4in).

P. concholoba Dense clusters of violet flowers, with exceptionally long tubes and farinose backs to the petals, appear in mid to late spring. This uncommon Himalayan species has toothed, lance-shaped, deciduous leaves up to 8cm (3in) long. HEIGHT & SPREAD 15×10cm (6×4in).

***P.* 'Ethel Barker'** Small, purplish pink flowers are borne in mid spring by this cushion-forming, evergreen European hybrid. HEIGHT & SPREAD 10×20cm (4×8in).

P. farinosa (bird's-eye primrose) Clusters of small lavender-pink, or occasionally white, flowers with a yellow eye appear in early spring. It has farinose rosettes of 2-10cm (¾-4in) long deciduous leaves with rolled edges. A British native, it needs the same treatment as the Asiatic species. It tends to be short-lived but is easily raised from seed. HEIGHT & SPREAD 10×8cm (4×3¼in).

P. flaccida ♀ (syn. *P. nutans*) Dense clusters of nodding, funnel-shaped, deep lilac-purple flowers are borne by this beautiful Chinese species in early summer. Its hairy deciduous leaves have waved margins and grow to 15cm (6in) long. It is usually short-lived but well worth maintaining from seed. HEIGHT & SPREAD 30×10cm (12×4in).

P. × forsteri (syn. *P. minima × hirsuta*) This variable hybrid of two European species forms cushions of rounded, glossy, evergreen leaves with toothed margins, and bears short-stalked deep pink flowers with a pale eye in mid and late spring. HEIGHT & SPREAD 10×20cm (4×8in).

'Bileckii' has deep rose flowers with a white eye and small rosettes of glossy triangular leaves with an irregular tip. **'Dianne'** has deep crimson flowers and larger rosettes of glossy leaves, toothed at the tip.

P. frondosa ♀ Large clusters of small, lilac-pink to red-purple flowers are borne in early spring by this Bulgarian species. The dark green, oval to spoon-shaped, toothed deciduous leaves are white and farinose on the underside and grow to 9cm (3½in) long. HEIGHT & SPREAD 12×10cm (4¾×4in).

P. glaucescens Small clusters of reddish purple flowers appear in late spring. This shy-flowering Italian evergreen alpine has short, glossy and leathery, finely-toothed leaves. HEIGHT & SPREAD 10×15cm (4×6in).

P. halleri Trusses of up to 19 small, lilac, yellow-eyed flowers appear in mid and late spring. The deciduous leaves have a dense covering of farina on the underside. Although native to SE Europe, it has the same cultural requirements as the Asiatic species. HEIGHT & SPREAD 15×20cm (6×8in).

P. juliae This parent of many of the modern primrose cultivars bears small, very short-stemmed trusses of deep magenta flowers with a yellow eye in mid and late spring. It is a creeping, stoloniferous plant, very easy to divide, with rounded and toothed semi-evergreen leaves. Native to the Caucasus. HEIGHT & SPREAD 15×20cm (6×8in).

P. marginata ♀ Flowerheads with as many as 20 shallow trumpet-shaped flowers, up to 2.5cm (1in) across, with a mealy white eye and varying in colour from pale to deep lilac, sometimes pinkish, are borne from early to late spring. A fine species from the Maritime Alps, it forms clusters of rosettes from gradually lengthening woody stems. The attractive evergreen leaves are covered with white farina and have jagged margins. HEIGHT & SPREAD 15×30cm (6×12in).

The flowers of var. ***alba*** are rather small and white or off-white. **'Beatrice Lascaris'** is a compact plant having clear blue flowers

▲ *Primula marginata* 'Beatrice Lascaris'

with a white eye and yellow-farinose, regularly toothed leaves. **'Caerulea'** has clear blue flowers and leaves covered with white farina. **'Clear's Variety'** has deeply toothed, yellow-farinose leaves, and small lilac flowers. **'Drake's Form'** is a strong-growing plant, with large, pale lilac flowers and handsome, white-farinose leaves. **'Holden Variety'** is very compact, with narrow, white-farinose leaves and small lilac-blue flowers. **'Hyacinthia'** is an easily grown, robust hybrid with toothed green leaves, only slightly farinose at their margins, and large, rounded, deep lilac flowers. **'Kesselring's Variety'** carries large clusters of deep lavender flowers and has leaves and stems covered with farina. **'Linda Pope'**♀ is the finest of all, with large, white-powdered, toothed leaves and exceptionally large, well-rounded, soft lilac-blue flowers with a white eye. **'Prichard's Variety'** has broad leaves edged with white farina, and large trusses of lilac-purple flowers.

P. minima Pink, occasionally white, flowers with a white eye and deeply notched, narrow petals appear singly or in pairs in late spring and early summer. The small, shiny, dark evergreen leaves are deeply toothed. Widely distributed from the E Alps to the Tatras, but not free-flowering. HEIGHT & SPREAD 5×15cm (2×6in).

P. minima* x *hirsuta see *P. ×forsteri*

***P.* 'Peter Klein'** Trusses of white-eyed pink flowers are borne in mid spring. A hybrid of two Asiatic primulas, it has finely toothed, narrow, semi-evergreen leaves. HEIGHT & SPREAD 15×15cm (6×6in).

P. petiolaris Dense trusses of pink flowers, with a yellow eye surrounded by a white ring, appear in early and mid spring. The spoon-shaped evergreen leaves of this Himalayan primula grow to 15cm (6in) long. Requires acid to neutral, humus-rich soil. HEIGHT & SPREAD 10×20cm (4×8in).

P.* x *pubescens♀ Large flattish heads of up to 15 flowers, possibly 2.5cm (1in) across, in various colours are borne from mid spring to early summer. This very variable European hybrid typically makes compact clumps of evergreen rosettes of thick, hairy, toothed, oval to lance-shaped leaves. An excellent free-flowering plant for the rock garden. HEIGHT & SPREAD 10×15cm (4×6in).

'Bewerley White' is a vigorous plant, with heads of creamy white flowers. **'Boothman's Variety'** (syn. 'Carmen') is a compact plant and easy to grow, with deep crimson, white-eyed flowers. **'Christine'** is a compact plant with yellowish green leaves and deep rose flowers with a white eye. **'Cream Viscosa'** is easy to grow, with loose clusters of slightly funnel-shaped cream flowers. **'Faldonside'** is a compact variety with white-eyed, pinkish red flowers. **'Freedom'** is very vigorous and tall, with large leaves and heads of deep purplish lilac flowers. **'Harlow Carr'** is vigorous with large creamy white flowers. **'Mrs J.H. Wilson'** is compact but vigorous with deep violet-purple flowers with white eyes. **'Rufus'** has very large, brick-red flowers with a yellow eye. **'The General'** is vigorous, with sparse trusses of yellow-eyed, velvety red flowers.

P. reidii Fragrant, creamy white flowers, nodding and broadly bell-shaped, are borne in clusters of up to 10 in late spring. An exquisite Himalayan species with hairy, oblong to lance-shaped, deciduous leaves up to 15cm (6in) long. HEIGHT & SPREAD 15×10cm (6×4in).

More robust than the species, var. ***williamsii*** has pale blue to white flowers.

P. scotica Clusters of up to 6 small dark purple flowers with white eyes are borne from late spring to early summer. This diminutive Scottish species has small, spoon-shaped deciduous leaves, thickly covered with farina on the underside. It needs rich but well-drained soil, like the Asiatic species, and is short-lived, but easy to propagate from seed. HEIGHT & SPREAD 8×5cm (3¼×2in).

P. vulgaris (primrose) The other parent of the modern primrose cultivars is our native primrose, widely distributed throughout Europe. From early to late spring it bears fragrant, pale yellow flowers with orange markings at the base of the petals, occasionally these may be white or pink. The semi-evergreen leaves are deeply veined. HEIGHT & SPREAD 12.5×25cm (5×10in).

The flowers of var. ***alba*** are pure white. **'Alba Plena'** is vigorous with double white flowers. **'Lilacina Plena'** (quaker's bonnet) is fairly vigorous with double lilac blue flowers. The flowers of ssp. ***sibthorpii***♀, a native of the E Balkans, are usually pink or purple, occasionally white, and the leaves are wedge shaped.

P. warshenewskiana Small bright pink flowers, with a yellow eye surrounded by a zone of white, are borne in trusses in late spring. A rhizomatous, creeping plant from central Asia and Afghanistan with short, toothed, deciduous leaves. HEIGHT & SPREAD 5×18cm (2×7in).

SPECIES FOR BORDER AND BOG

Most of these larger primulas are native to the Himalayas and E Asia, and grow into clumps 20cm (8in) or more wide. The leaves are 10-20cm (4-8in) long, and the flowers are borne in spikes or clusters or, in the candelabra species, in whorls up the stem. Some demand boggy conditions. The others thrive in humus-rich, moisture-retentive soil. They flower from late spring to mid summer, unless stated otherwise.

P. alpicola Fragrant, nodding, funnel-shaped flowers are borne in trusses. They are farinose and may be white, cream, yellow, or purple. The deciduous leaves are narrow oval. HEIGHT & SPREAD 15-40×20cm (6-16×8in).

In var. ***alba*** the flowers are white, in var. ***violacea*** pink to purple.

P. aurantiaca Deep brownish orange flowers are carried in whorls on dark purple stems. The oval, slightly farinose, dark green, deciduous leaves of this candelabra species often have a purple midrib. HEIGHT & SPREAD 30×20cm (12×8in).

P. beesiana Deep rose flowers with a yellow eye are borne in candelabra-type clusters covered with farina. The large semi-evergreen leaves are finely toothed. HEIGHT & SPREAD 30×20cm (12×8in).

P. bulleyana♀ In this candelabra species golden yellow flowers emerge from red buds. The semi-evergreen leaves have a purple midrib and the stems are coated with white farina. HEIGHT & SPREAD 50×20cm (20×8in).

P. burmanica The flowers of this deciduous candelabra type are purple with an orange eye. HEIGHT & SPREAD 30×20cm (12×8in).

P. chungensis This vigorous candelabra type has coarsely toothed deciduous leaves and produces small, fragrant, pale orange flowers from red buds. HEIGHT & SPREAD 60×20cm (24×8in).

P. cockburniana Bright orange-red flowers are carried in small whorls on white-farinose stems. A beautiful but very short-lived deciduous plant, easily kept going from seed. HEIGHT & SPREAD 25×15cm (10×8in).

P. denticulata♀ (drumstick primrose) The flowers are carried in dense, round clusters from early spring to early summer. They

▲ *Primula beesiana*

▲ *Primula bulleyana*

▲ *Primula denticulata*

come in shades of pink to purple, lavender and red, all with a yellow eye. The plant has finely toothed, slightly hairy deciduous leaves. Easily grown, it makes a colourful edging to a border or among shrubs. HEIGHT & SPREAD 40×20 cm (16×8 in).

The flowers of var. ***alba*** are pure white. **Ruby** has deep purplish red flowers

P. ***elatior*** (oxlip) One-sided clusters of up to 10 funnel-shaped, primrose-yellow flowers appear in mid and late spring. This British native has conspicuously veined, hairy, semi-evergreen leaves with toothed margins, and is a plant that establishes well in grass. HEIGHT & SPREAD 15×20 cm (6×8 in).

P. ***florindae*** (giant cowslip) Large trusses of nodding, bell-shaped, fragrant, yellow flowers are borne in summer on stout stems. It is a magnificent plant needing very wet conditions. Deciduous. HEIGHT & SPREAD 80×30 cm (32×12 in).

P. ***helodoxa*** see *P. prolifera*

P. **Inshriach Hybrids** Whorls of very bright flowers in shades of yellow, orange, pink and red are borne on plants of robust candelabra type. Deciduous. HEIGHT & SPREAD 50×20 cm (20×8 in).

P. **'Inverewe'** Bright orange-red flowers are borne by this strong-growing, semi-evergreen candelabra hybrid. HEIGHT & SPREAD 75×60 cm (2½×2 ft)

P. ***ioessa*** Nodding trusses of fragrant, large, cream or lilac, funnel-shaped flowers appear in early summer. Deciduous. HEIGHT & SPREAD 25×15 cm (10×6 in).

P. ***japonica*** Reddish purple, sometimes white or pink, flowers with a dark eye are carried in whorls on green or reddish stems. A candelabra type with pale green, coarsely toothed deciduous leaves, it is easily grown and does not need very damp conditions. HEIGHT & SPREAD 40×20 cm (16×8 in).

'Fuji' has white flowers. **'Miller's Crimson'** is vigorous with dark red flowers. **'Postford White'** has large white flowers with a yellow eye. An easily grown plant that comes true from seed.

P. ***littoniana*** see *P. vialii*

P. ***poissonii*** Deep purplish pink flowers with a yellow or white eye are carried in 2-6 whorls up the stem. An evergreen candelabra type primula with bluish green leaves. HEIGHT & SPREAD 40×20 cm (16×8 in).

P. ***polyneura*** Trusses of pale pink to crimson flowers, with a greenish yellow eye and notched petals, are borne in early summer. This deciduous primula has dark green, hairy lobed leaves and hairy stems, and grows well in woodland conditions. HEIGHT & SPREAD 40×20 cm (16×8 in).

P. ***prolifera*** (syn. *P. helodoxa*) Slightly pendent, short-stalked, bright yellow fragrant flowers are carried in whorls. A candelabra type with dark evergreen leaves. HEIGHT & SPREAD 60×20 cm (24×8 in).

P. ***pulverulenta*** Deep reddish purple flowers with a darker eye are carried in large whorls. The irregularly toothed deciduous leaves have a pale midrib. It is the most vigorous and long-lasting of the candelabras and is striking with its very white-farinose stems. HEIGHT & SPREAD 80×20 cm (32×8 in).

▲ *Primula pulverulenta*

Bartley Hybrids come in shades from pink to purple, with pale or dark eyes.

P. ***rosea*** The large flowers are vivid rose with a yellow eye, and borne in trusses in late spring. A bog-loving species, with glossy, oval, deciduous leaves, it is very good for pond margins, combining well with calthas, lysichitons and other bog plants. HEIGHT & SPREAD 15×20 cm (6×8 in).

'Grandiflora' is a large-flowered variety.

P. ***secundiflora*** Deep purple, funnel-shaped, pendent flowers are carried in a one-sided cluster, occasionally in 2-3 whorls. It is an easy species to grow, tolerating drier conditions than others in this group, and has smooth, narrow, evergreen or semi-evergreen leaves on white-farinose stalks. HEIGHT & SPREAD 40×20 cm (16×8 in).

P. ***sieboldii*** Large flowers in shades of pink and purple with a white eye, the petals usually notched or frilled, are carried in trusses. This spreading rhizomatous primula has pale green, hairy, oval deciduous leaves with wavy, blunt-toothed margins. The species and cultivars are excellent easily grown plants for moist borders, in the shade of rhododendrons and other woodland shrubs. HEIGHT & SPREAD 20×20 cm (8×8 in).

The flowers of var. ***alba*** are white. **'Dancing Ladies'** has pale pink or white flowers with a pink, occasionally blue, reverse. **'Manankoora'** has blue and white flowers. **'Mikado'** has lilac-blue flowers with a white eye. **'Pago-Pago'** has flowers in shades of red and pink. **'Snowflake'** has white flowers with unnotched petals.

P. ***sikkimensis*** (Himalayan cowslip) Narrow-tubular, cream or yellow flowers appear in large pendent clusters. A deciduous species that needs very damp ground. HEIGHT & SPREAD 40×20 cm (16×8 in).

P. ***veris*** (cowslip) Fragrant, deep yellow flowers, with an orange spot at the base of each petal, appear in one-sided trusses in late spring and early summer. A British semi-evergreen native, it is easily grown and can be established in grass. HEIGHT & SPREAD 25×20 cm (10×8 in).

P. ***vialii*** (syn. *P. littoniana*) Small, deep lavender flowers, opening from scarlet buds, form a dense cylindrical spike, vivid red above and blue below. An easily grown but short-lived plant, it is worth growing from seed as a biennial to replace any losses. Deciduous. HEIGHT & SPREAD 40×15 cm (16×6 in).

P. ***waltonii*** Deep purple, funnel-shaped flowers hang down in trusses. Deciduous. HEIGHT & SPREAD 50×20 cm (20×8 in).

P. ***wilsonii*** Purplish red flowers are carried in whorls by this evergreen, candelabra type. HEIGHT & SPREAD 60×20 cm (24×8 in).

PRIMROSE AND POLYANTHUS CULTIVARS

A large number of primrose cultivars has been developed as a result of selection and of crossing the European primrose, *P. vulgaris*, with the Caucasian primrose, *P. juliae*. Crossing *P. vulgaris* and the cowslip, *P. veris*, has produced the polyanthus cultivars. The primrose cultivars bear their flowers singly on elongated stalks. Many double-flowered varieties have been bred. The polyanthus cultivars carry their flowers in a cluster on stout upright stems.

Primrose and polyanthus cultivars are widely sold as mixed seed selections, including some for greenhouse use or for bedding that are more tender than those raised for garden use. There is a large range of vegetatively propagated cultivars, of which some of the best are described below.

Primrose

Flowering from early to mid spring. Semi-evergreen, ranging in height from 10-15 cm (4-6 in) and spreading about 25 cm (10 in).

'Alan Robb' has double pale apricot flowers. **'April Rose'** has double deep pink flowers. **'Captain Blood'** has double blood-red flowers. **'Chocolate Soldier'** has double flowers; the gold-edged petals are chocolate-brown becoming purple. **'Corporal Baxter'** has velvety crimson double flowers. **'Dawn Ansell'** is a 'jack-in-the-green' type: its double white flowers are surrounded by a ruff of large leaflets. **'Eugénie'** has double dark blue flowers, reddish purple towards the base of the petals. **'Freckles** has double dark red flowers dotted with white. **'Groeneken's Glory'** has bright bluish pink flowers with a green eye. **'Ken Dearman'** has double flowers, yellow at the base, shading to reddish orange towards the petal tips. **'Lilian Harvey'** has double purplish pink flowers. **'Marianne Davey'** has double pale yellow and cream flowers. **'Marie Crousse'** has violet double flowers, edged with white. **'Miss Indigo'** has double deep violet-blue flowers edged with white. **'Olive Wyatt'** has deep reddish pink double flowers. **'Rose O'Day'** has light rose-red double flowers. **'Roy Cope'** has red, scented, double flowers. **'Schneekissen'** (syn. 'Snow Cushion') has small, pure white flowers. **'Sue Jervis'** has double, soft salmon-pink flowers. **'Sunshine Susie'** has double, bright yellow flowers, partly flushed with pink. **'Val Horncastle'** has double, yellow and cream flowers. **'Wanda'**♀ has dark leaves and very deep reddish purple flowers; easy to grow. **'White Wanda'** has dark leaves and white flowers; easy to grow.

▲ *Primula* 'Dawn Ansell'

▲ *Primula* 'Groeneken's Glory'

Polyanthus

Flowering from early to late spring. Semi-evergreen, ranging in height from 15–20 cm (6–8 in) and spreading about 25 cm (10 in). **Cowichan** is a range of very dark reds, purples, and blues, with no central eye. The leaves are very dark green, tinged with purple. **Gold-laced Group** has very dark brownish purple flowers with a deep golden eye and each petal margined with gold. **'Guinevere'**♀ carries large heads of pink flowers on reddish stems. The leaves are bronze-tinged. **Hose-in-Hose** Two rows of petals give the appearance of one flower inside another. Plants may be of polyanthus or primrose habit, with flowers in shades of yellow, pink or red. **Jack-in-the-Green Group** Flowers in shades of yellow are each encircled by a ruff of small green leaves. Plants may be of primrose or polyanthus type. **'Kinlough Beauty'** has flowers of salmon-pink with a cream stripe down each petal. **'Lady Greer'**♀ has small, pale yellow flowers. **'McWatt's Claret'** has small, deep brownish red flowers. **'McWatt's Cream'** has small, pale cream flowers. **Silver-laced Group** has dark brownish purple flowers with a golden eye; the petals have a narrow white margin. **'Tawny Port'** is a compact plant with red-tinged foliage, bearing deep purplish red flowers.

AURICULA CULTIVARS

These highly bred, evergreen hardy plants are mostly grown under glass to protect the foliage and flowers from damage by rain. The rosettes of broad, fleshy, usually farinose, pointed leaves eventually form a dense clump if not divided. Growing to 15 cm (6 in) high, the flowers appear in mid spring in trusses of 2 to 20 on stout stems. They are mainly flat-faced or very slightly trumpet-shaped, with several concentric circles of colour. The colouring and amount of farina vary in the four different groups into which auriculas are divided: alpine, border, double and show.

Alpine auriculas

These have no farina on the leaves or flowers. Around the eye of the flower is a light-coloured (white or cream) or gold-coloured ring, surrounded by a deep colour which often turns paler towards the edge.

▲ *Primula* 'Kinlough Beauty'

▲ *Primula* 'Lady Greer'

▲ *Primula auricula* 'Argus'

'Andrea Julie' gold-centred, light red; easy to grow. **'Applecross'** gold-centred, rich crimson. **'Argus'** light-centred, deep plum shading to purplish red. **'Beatrice'** light-centred, blue. **'Blossom'** gold-centred, red. **'Bookham Firefly'** gold-centred, red. **'C.W. Needham'** light-centred, dark purple; with attractive toothed leaves. **'Elsie May'** light-centred, deep velvety plum. **'Jenny'** gold-centred, dull red. **'Joy'** light-centred, deep velvety crimson. **'Lisa'** light-centred, deep purple shading to lilac; a vigorous alpine auricula. **'Mark'** light-centred, bright pink; a vigorous plant. **'Prince John'** gold-centred, red. **'Rowena'** light-centred, purple shading to pale lilac. **'Sandra'** mauve with a small light centre. **'Sandwood Bay'** gold-centred, bright crimson. **'Sirius'** gold-centred, deep maroon shading to pale primrose. **'Valerie'** light-centred, dark mauve shading to light mauve. **'Winnifrid'** gold-centred, crimson shading to bright scarlet.

Border auriculas

These may have green leaves with little or no farina or they may be markedly farinose. The flowers also vary greatly, some with a farinose centre and some without, the latter usually also having leaves with no farina and flowers that are paler towards the edge. They make good border plants in rich but well-drained soil in partial shade.

'Blairside Yellow' is compact-growing with small, clear yellow flowers. **'Blue Velvet'** has purplish blue flowers with a cream centre fading to white. **'Broadwell Gold'** has farinose leaves and large, golden yellow flowers; a good increaser. **'Old Red Dusty Miller'** has farinose leaves and deep red flowers. **'Old Yellow Dusty Miller'** has very farinose leaves and bright yellow

▲ *Primula auricula* 'C.W. Needham'

▲ *Primula auricula* 'Prince John'

flowers; a vigorous border auricula. **'Paradise Yellow'** has large trusses of yellow flowers; a vigorous plant.

Double auriculas

These have 8 or more petals in a variety of colours – usually cream or yellow but also brown, crimson, lavender, pink or purple. The foliage is usually farinose.

'Camelot' has dark red flowers and is a vigorous and freely increasing plant. **'Catherine'** has lemon-yellow flowers and long, narrow leaves. **'Devon Cream'** has cream flowers with a deep yellow centre. **'Doublet'** is dark red and vigorous. **'Trouble'** includes mixed shades of yellow, pink, and green.

Show auriculas

The flowers have a ring of 'paste' (farina) round the central eye. The show auriculas are divided into three types. 'Selfs', where the petals are of only one colour, red, yellow or blue, apart from the paste. 'Edged' and 'fancy' show auriculas exhibit a mutation, where the outer edge of petal tissue is replaced with leaf tissue. Where there is no farina on the edge it is green. With a light covering of farina it is grey. With a heavy covering it is white. In the edged types, the petal colour (body colour) between the ring of paste and the outer edge of the petal is black. In the fancy types, it is a colour other than black.

'Alice Haysom' is a deep red self. **'Blue Nile'** is a good blue self. **'Brazil'** is a yellow self and increases well. **'C.G. Haysom'** is grey-edged. **'Chorister'** is a yellow self, fast-growing and prolific. **'Fanny Meerbeck'** is a red self. **Gildersome Green'** is green-edged. **'Gizabroon'** is a dark brownish red self. **'Gleam'** is a yellow self. **'Guinea'** is a bright yellow self and a vigorous plant. **'Lechistan'** is a strong-growing red self. **'Lovebird'** is grey-edged. **'Mojave'** is a red self. **'Moonglow'** is a creamy green self. **'Neat and Tidy'** is a dark red self. **'Nocturne'** is a dark red self. **'Orb'** is green-edged, an unusual shade of olive-green. **'Pot o' Gold'** is a yellow self with yellowish paste; freely increasing. **'Prague'** bears large trusses of green-edged flowers. **'Rajah'** is a green-edged fancy with bright scarlet body colour. **'Red Gauntlet'** is a scarlet self; freely increasing. **'Remus'** a dark blue self; freely increasing. **'Rolts'** is a green-edged fancy with red body colour. **'Stant's Blue'** is a bluish mauve self. **'Sweet Pastures'** is a green-edged fancy with yellow body colour.

CULTIVATION

INDOOR SPECIES Grow in peat-based or loam-based compost in 13cm (5in) pots. Feed regularly and shade from hot sun.

ALPINE SPECIES Plant the European alpines in a very well-drained bed with plenty of humus, or in a similar compost in pots, in a sunny position. Most of the Asiatic species need a richer and moister but still well-drained soil, with plenty of leaf mould or other humus, in partial shade. In pots, the Asiatic species do best in a peat-based or humus-rich compost, the European species in loam-based compost, both with good drainage. Apply liquid feed monthly in the growing season.

▲ *Primula auricula* 'Fanny Meerbeck'

SPECIES FOR BORDER AND BOG Plant in any moisture-retentive soil enriched with plenty of humus, leaf mould, compost or well-rotted manure. In dry areas grow in partial shade, but grow in full sun in damper ground. The candelabra species generally need more moisture than the others and should be watered in dry weather. Grow *P. florindae*, *P. rosea* and *P. sikkimensis* in very wet, even boggy, ground.

PRIMROSE AND POLYANTHUS CULTIVARS Plant in early spring in humus-rich soil, preferably with abundant, well-rotted manure, compost or leaf mould. In the south plants benefit from partial shade. Divide frequently, at least every two years, and replant in freshly treated soil. A rich, peat-based compost is ideal for plants grown indoors. A light, cool, airy windowsill suits them, and plenty of moisture.

▲ *Primula auricula* 'Lovebird'

AURICULA CULTIVARS Grow alpine, double and show auriculas in pots of soil-based compost with grit added to improve drainage. Water freely during the growing periods of autumn and spring and feed monthly, keeping water off the foliage and flowers. Repot in early summer. Keep partially shaded in hot weather. Grow border auriculas and the more robust alpine auriculas, such as 'Argus', 'Lisa' and 'Mark', in humus-rich, well-drained soil in full sun, partial sun in the south.

PROPAGATION

INDOOR SPECIES Sow seed in a peat-based compost, from early summer to autumn to give a succession of flowers. Transplant seedlings into separate small pots when 2 true leaves have appeared. Repot when full of roots into final 13cm (5in) pots and grow on in a cool, shaded frame. Bring into a cool greenhouse, minimum temperature 5-7°C (41-45°F), before the onset of frosts.

ALPINE SPECIES Sow species in autumn and keep cold through the winter. Remove offsets in spring and root them as cuttings.

SPECIES FOR BORDER AND BOG Sow seed in peat-based compost in autumn in a cold greenhouse or in heat in early spring. Divide strong plants in early spring.

PRIMROSE AND POLYANTHUS CULTIVARS Sow seed in peat-based compost in early spring at 15-18°C (59-64°F). Divide plants in early spring.

AURICULA CULTIVARS Remove offsets in early summer. Those with roots can go straight into individual 5cm (2in) pots. Treat those without roots as cuttings.

PESTS AND DISEASES Viruses and vine weevils are the main enemies of primulas. Grey mould, brown core, leaf spot, aphids (including root aphids), whitefly and red spider mite (especially under glass) and slugs and snails are problems too.

Prostanthera

Labiatae

Prostanthera cuneata

Peppermint-scented leaves and abundant flowers earn these evergreen shrubs their place in a garden. The short, tubular flowers have two lips. The upper lip is usually upright and may be lobed, while the lower lip is spreading and often divided into several lobes. Of the recommended plants, *Prostanthera cuneata* is hardy, except in the coldest gardens, whereas *P. rotundifolia* can be grown only in a frost-free garden or in pots that are overwintered under glass.

RECOMMENDED SPECIES AND VARIETIES

P. cuneata ♀ (alpine mint bush) White or pale violet flowers, about 2 cm (¾ in) across, with their throats heavily dotted in purple and orange-yellow, appear in summer. The short upper lip is slightly split and the lower lip is divided into 4 lobes. Highly aromatic, almost stalkless, dark green, rounded leaves, about 6 mm (¼ in) across, crowd the stems of these dense bushes, which may grow wider than they are high. HEIGHT & SPREAD 45×45 cm (1½×1½ ft) after 5 years, ultimately 60 cm (2 ft) tall.

▲ *Prostanthera cuneata*

Prostanthera rotundifolia ▲

'Alpine Gold' has yellowish leaves while **'Fastigiata'** has a more upright habit than other types of prostanthera.

P. rotundifolia (mint bush) Bell-shaped purple flowers, about 1.5 cm (½ in) wide, cover this upright shrub in early spring. Each flower has an upper lip with 2 lobes and a hairy lower lip with 3 lobes. The shiny, mid green, almost rounded, aromatic leaves, about 1 cm (⅜ in) across, usually have notched edges. This is a very showy plant for a frost-free garden or for a greenhouse or conservatory. HEIGHT & SPREAD 2×1 m (6½×3 ft) after 5 years, ultimately 2 m (6½ ft) tall.

CULTIVATION Plant *P. cuneata* in spring in well-drained, acid or neutral, humus-rich soil. Choose a site in full sun. Grow *P. rotundifolia* in pots of peaty compost and place in partial shade. During periods of frost keep the pots in a cool greenhouse or conservatory in a partly shaded position.

PROPAGATION Sow seed under glass in early spring. Alternatively, take semi-ripe cuttings in autumn.

PRUNING No pruning is normally required, but *P. rotundifolia* can be cut back hard immediately after flowering to encourage bushy growth.

PESTS AND DISEASES Usually trouble free.

Protea

Proteaceae

Striking bracted flowerheads, that are often brightly coloured, appear on these half-hardy evergreen trees and shrubs in spring and summer. Native to Africa, these are among the trickiest plants to grow in Britain. Proteas can be tried outside in a sheltered spot in the West Country, the Channel Islands and south-west Scotland, but they are generally more successful in a greenhouse or conservatory. Standard potting composts are rarely successful as proteas demand neutral to acid soil with low phosphate and nitrogen levels.

RECOMMENDED SPECIES AND VARIETIES

P. compacta The roughly egg-shaped flowerheads, up to 10 cm (4 in) across, have bright pink and white ribbon-like bracts in spring and early summer. This erect shrub has hard, somewhat leathery, elliptical leaves up to 12.5 cm (5 in) long. HEIGHT & SPREAD 3×2 m (10×6½ ft).

▲ *Protea compacta*

P. cynaroides (king protea) Goblet-like flowerheads roughly resembling a globe artichoke grow up to 20 cm (8 in) across in spring and early summer. They have many silky-haired, petal-like, pink to red bracts. The dark green oval leaves of this bushy, rounded shrub are up to 15 cm (6 in). HEIGHT & SPREAD 1.5×1.5 m (5×5 ft).

▲ *Protea cynaroides*

P. eximia The rounded, oblong flowerheads, up to 15cm (6in) long, have numerous pink bracts which are often flushed with red. This erect shrub or, rarely, small tree is clothed with oval or elongated, heart-shaped, bluish green leaves, up to 10 cm (4 in) long, that are tinged purple. HEIGHT & SPREAD 3×2 m (10×6½ ft).

CULTIVATION Plant in large pots in a mixture of equal parts of peat and acid, or neutral, loam. Place under glass at a minimum temperature of 5°C (41°F) in the coolest and brightest position possible. In summer stand the pots outside. During the active growing season water regularly and feed with a liquid tomato feed diluted to half strength.

PROPAGATION Sow seed under glass in spring or take semi-ripe cuttings in summer.

PRUNING No regular pruning is necessary, but remove any weak or unwanted shoots.

PESTS AND DISEASES Usually trouble free.

Prunella

Self heal

Labiatae

Prunella grandiflora 'Pink Loveliness'

The pink to purple or white flowers of these creeping herbaceous perennials provide a colourful and long-lasting display in summer. Prunellas are excellent for ground cover at the front of a border, or for splashes of colour among shrubs or under trees. The flowers, which are tubular with an upright upper lip and a spreading lower lip, are

▲ *Prunella grandiflora*

▲ *Prunella grandiflora* 'White Loveliness'

grouped in whorls amid conspicuous bracts. The plants are hardy and easy to grow in any soil, including poor types.

RECOMMENDED SPECIES AND VARIETIES

P. grandiflora (syn. *P.* × *webbiana)* Deep violet flowers, about 2.5 cm (1 in) long, are borne in dense spikes up to 4 cm (1½ in) long. The oval leaves, up to 10 cm (4 in) long, may be shallowly toothed. HEIGHT & SPREAD 30 cm × 1 m (1 × 3 ft).

Several named varieties have flower spikes up to 6 cm (2½ in) long. **'Alba'** has pure white flowers. **'Blue Loveliness'** has deep lilac-blue flowers while **'Loveliness'**♀ has pale violet-blue flowers. **'Pink Loveliness'** has soft pink flowers while those of **'Rotkäppchen'** (syn. *P.* 'Little Red Riding Hood') are deep carmine. The flowers of **'White Loveliness'** are white.

P. incisa see *P. vulgaris*

P. laciniata The cream flowers, sometimes flushed pink, are about 2.5 cm (1 in) long. The deeply cut leaves are about 5 cm (2 in) long. HEIGHT & SPREAD 30 cm × 1 m (1 × 3 ft).

P. vulgaris (syn. *P. incisa*) This plant has deep purple flowers about 2.5 cm (1 in) long. Deeply cut leaves, up to 5 cm (2 in)

▲ *Prunella vulgaris*

long, form a spreading carpet. HEIGHT & SPREAD 30 cm × 1 m (1 × 3 ft).

P. × webbiana see *P. grandiflora*

CULTIVATION Plant in early spring in any garden soil in sun or partial shade. Avoid rich soils which may encourage leafiness.

PROPAGATION Divide plants in autumn or during spring.

PESTS AND DISEASES Usually trouble free.

Prunus

Rosaceae

Dazzling displays of blossom enliven these well-loved trees in spring or summer. There are also species and varieties with good autumn leaf colour or attractive bark. Others are grown specifically for fruit, including almonds, apricots, plums, peaches and edible cherries. (See FRUIT p. 720.)

Ranging from pure white through pink to deep red, the profuse, five-petalled, cup-shaped flowers look particularly attractive in spring on bare branches. Some varieties bear semidouble or double flowers. Few are particularly fragrant. Unless stated otherwise, the leaves, 5-15 cm (2-6 in) long, are oval. Most have slightly serrated edges. This large genus is native mostly to temperate regions. All the recommended plants are frost-hardy, although their tolerance varies.

RECOMMENDED SPECIES AND VARIETIES

All the ornamental trees listed here are deciduous, except the cherry laurels, which are evergreen.

ORNAMENTAL ALMONDS

P. dulcis (common almond) Although it will produce almonds in Britain, this tree is grown mainly for its pink blossom in early to mid spring. The flowers, up to 5 cm (2 in) across, usually appear singly or in pairs. The fine-toothed leaves are lance-shaped. This tree is only moderately frost-hardy. HEIGHT & SPREAD 2.4 × 1.2 m (8 × 4 ft) after 10 years, ultimately 6 m (20 ft) tall.

'Roseoplena' has double pink flowers.

P. glandulosa (Chinese bush cherry) Abundant white or pink flowers, about 1.5 cm (½ in) across, appear singly or in pairs in mid spring. The pale green ovate leaves are about 6 cm (2½ in) long. This small rounded shrub prefers a sunny position. HEIGHT & SPREAD 1.5 × 1 m (5 × 3 ft) after 10 years and ultimately.

The cultivars produce an even better show of flowers than the species. **'Alba Plena'**♀ has double white flowers in late spring, while **'Sinensis'**♀ (syn. *P.* 'Rosea Plena') produces double pink flowers.

▲ *Prunus glandulosa* 'Alba Plena'

▲ *Prunus glandulosa* 'Sinensis'

P. tenella (dwarf Russian almond) Bright pink flowers, 2 cm (¾ in) across, wreath the branches in mid spring. The leaves are up to 9 cm (3½ in) long. This is the smallest prunus. It suckers freely and produces a good number of stems. HEIGHT & SPREAD 1 × 1 m (3 × 3 ft) after 10 years and ultimately.

'Fire Hill'♀ has pinkish red flowers.

P. triloba Pinkish white flowers, 2.5 cm (1 in) across, appear in profusion in early and mid spring on this small tree or large

▲ *Prunus tenella*

shrub of spreading habit. HEIGHT & SPREAD 2.4×1.2m (8×4ft) after 10 years, ultimately 4m (13ft) tall.

'Multiplex'♀ has large double flowers in peachy pink.

ORNAMENTAL PEACHES

P. persica (peach) Pale rose-pink flowers, about 4cm (1½in) wide, appear in mid spring. The rather pointed leaves of this small tree or large multistemmed shrub are up to 15cm (6in) long. HEIGHT & SPREAD 2.4×1.2m (8×4ft) after 10 years, ultimately 3m (10ft) tall.

This species needs the protection of a wall or unheated greenhouse if grown for its fruit (see PEACHES AND NECTARINES p.727). However, several cultivars have been developed for their flowers. **'Iceberg'** has pure white semidouble flowers and **'Klara Mayer'** has deep pink semidouble flowers. Both grow to medium-sized shrubs, with flowers up to 4cm (1½in) across.

ORNAMENTAL PLUMS

P. x blireana♀ Double pink, slightly fragrant flowers, about 2.5cm (1in) across, appear in mid spring on this large shrub or small, spreading tree. The ovate leaves, 7.5cm (3in) long, emerge a rich coppery purple and take on a more greeny tinge later. HEIGHT & SPREAD 2.4×1.2m (8×4ft) after 10 years, ultimately 4m (13ft) tall.

P. cerasifera A profusion of small white flowers appear in early spring followed, when pollination is good, by yellow or red fruits, up to 3cm (1¼in) long. The ovate leaves are up to 6cm (2½in) long. This large shrub or small tree has a spreading habit. HEIGHT & SPREAD 3×2m (10×6½ft) after 10 years, ultimately 6m (20ft) tall.

Plants in the **Myrobalan Group** have dark bronze, red or purple leaves. **'Nigra'**♀ has blackish purple leaves preceded by small pink flowers. The new leaves and stems of **'Pissardii'** are flushed dark red at first and deepen to dark purple later. The flowers are whitish. Both cultivars make good hedging.

P. x cistena♀ White flowers, 4cm (1½in) across, appear in late spring. Glossy leaves, 6cm (2½in) long, emerge red and deepen to reddish brown. HEIGHT & SPREAD 2×1.5m (6½×5ft) after 10 years and ultimately.

▲ *Prunus tenella* 'Fire Hill'

P. mume (Japanese apricot) Fragrant pink or white flowers, about 3cm (1¼in) wide, appear in late winter on this small upright tree. The broadly ovate leaves are 10cm (4in) long and tapering. HEIGHT & SPREAD 3×1.5m (10×5ft) after 10 years, ultimately 6m (20ft) tall.

'Beni-chidori' (syn. *P.* 'Beni-shidori') has deep pink, strongly scented, cup-shaped double flowers. The double white blooms of **'Omoi-no-mama'** are also very fragrant.

P. spinosa (blackthorn, sloe) Small, white, short-lived flowers appear in early spring followed in autumn by small blue-black fruits that can be used to make sloe gin. The leaves are up to 5cm (2in) long. This very hardy native shrub is armed with stout thorns. HEIGHT & SPREAD 3×2m (10×6½ft) after 10 years, ultimately 6m (20ft) tall.

'Plena' is double-flowered. **'Purpurea'** has purple leaves which fade to pale green.

ORNAMENTAL CHERRIES

***P.* 'Accolade'**♀ Semidouble rich pink flowers, up to 4cm (1½in) across, appear in clusters or singly in early spring. The dark green leaves, up to 10cm (4in) long, are deeply serrated. HEIGHT & SPREAD 2.4×1.2m (8×4ft) after 10 years, ultimately 6m (20ft) tall.

***P.* 'Amanogawa'**♀ The late-spring flowers are semidouble, pale pink and slightly fragrant, borne on upright branches. The toothed leaves, 10cm (4in) long, tapered at the tips, are flushed greenish bronze at first.

▲ *Prunus cerasifera* 'Nigra'

▲ *Prunus* 'Accolade'

They turn mid green later, then colour well in autumn. HEIGHT & SPREAD 2.4×1m (8×3ft) after 10 years, ultimately 4.5m (15ft) tall.

P. avium♀ (wild cherry) This vigorous upright tree bears profuse clusters of pendulous white flowers, about 2.5cm (1in) across, in mid spring. Small blackish red cherries sometimes appear in autumn. The leaves, 12.5cm (5in) long, are rather tapered at the tips and coarsely and irregularly toothed. They turn red and yellow in autumn. The bark is at first smooth but becomes fissured with age. HEIGHT & SPREAD 4×1.8m (13×6ft) after 10 years, ultimately 15m (50ft) tall.

'Plena'♀ blossoms even more freely in late spring.

P. cerasus (sour cherry) Dense clusters of white flowers, 2.5cm (1in) wide, in mid spring are often followed by black or red fruits in autumn. This plant makes a small bushy tree. HEIGHT & SPREAD 2.7×1.5m (9×5ft) after 10 years, ultimately 6m (20ft) tall.

The cultivars tend to produce bigger, more abundant flowers than the species. **'Rhexii'** has profuse double white flowers up to 4cm (1½in) across.

***P.* 'Cheal's Weeping'**
see *P.* 'Kiku-shidare-zakura'

***P.* 'Choshu-hizakura'**♀ Deep pink flowers are produced in profusion, one to a stem, in mid spring. The young leaves emerge coppery red and take on a green tinge later. HEIGHT & SPREAD 2.4×1.2m (8×4ft) after 10 years, ultimately 6m (20ft) tall.

▲ *Prunus avium* 'Plena'

***P.* 'Hillieri Spire'** see *P.* 'Spire'
P. incisa (Fuji cherry) This cherry tree flowers profusely in early spring before the leaves appear. The flowers, 2cm (¾in) wide, are white, flushed with pink. The leaves, up to 6cm (2½in) long, are double-toothed. Reddish at first, the leaves become green later in the season and turn shades of red and orange in autumn. This large shrub or small tree has an upright habit at first but becomes rounded with age. HEIGHT & SPREAD 3×1.8m (10×6ft) after 10 years, ultimately 6m (20ft) tall.

The flowers of **'Praecox'**♀ are more pink and open as early as mid winter if the weather is mild.
***P.* 'Kanzan'**♀ Masses of large, double, deep pink flowers, 5cm (2½in) across, appear in late spring. The leaves are up to 12.5cm (5in) long with tapering tips. When young, the leaves are flushed a coppery colour, but this is lost as the season progresses. In autumn they turn orange and yellow. The branches have an ascending habit, giving the tree a somewhat top-heavy appearance. HEIGHT & SPREAD 3×2m (10×6½ft) after 10 years, ultimately at least 6m (20ft) tall.

▲ *Prunus* 'Kanzan'

***P.* 'Kiku-shidare-zakura'**♀ (syn. *P.* 'Cheal's Weeping') The arching branches of this weeping tree are covered in deep pink, double flowers, 3cm (1¼in) across, in early spring. The leaves, about 7.5cm (3in) long, are flushed bronzy green at first and turn glossy green later. HEIGHT & SPREAD 2×1m (6½×3ft) after 10 years, ultimately 4m (13ft) tall.
***P.* 'Kursar'**♀ Clusters of 4cm (1½in) wide deep pink flowers appear in great profusion in mid to late spring. The leaves are up to 10cm (4in) long with pointed tips. When young they are bronzy in colour, turning green later in the summer. HEIGHT & SPREAD 2.4×1.2m (8×4ft) after 10 years, ultimately 5m (16ft) tall.
P. maackii (Manchurian cherry) Shiny bronzy gold bark is the outstanding feature of this hardy tree that becomes rounded with age. White flowers, 1.5cm (½in) wide, appear in spikes in mid spring. The ovate leaves are up to 10cm (4in) long. HEIGHT & SPREAD 3×1.5m (10×5ft) after 10 years, ultimately 9m (30ft) tall.
***P.* 'Okame'**♀ This decorative tree has abundant carmine coloured flowers, 2.5cm (1in) wide, in early spring. The leaves, 7.5cm (3in) long, turn red and orange in autumn. HEIGHT & SPREAD 2.4×1.2m (8×4ft) after 10 years, ultimately 5m (16ft) tall.

▲ *Prunus* 'Okame'

P. padus (bird cherry) Small, white, slightly almond-scented flowers appear on 15cm (6in) long spikes in late spring after the foliage has emerged. The leaves, which are up to 12.5cm (5in) long, are dark green above and bluish green beneath. HEIGHT & SPREAD 3×1.5m (10×5ft) after 10 years, ultimately 9m (30ft) tall.

The shoots of **'Colorata'**♀ are purple-brown and the leaves are at first coppery purple, fading to a dull green with purple veins. The flowers are pale pink. **'Watereri'**♀ has the same colour flowers as the species on spikes up to 20cm (8in) long.

▲ *Prunus padus*

***P.* 'Pandora'**♀ Ascending branches are covered in pale pink flowers, up to 2.5cm (1in) across, in early to mid spring. The leaves are up to 7.5cm (3in) long with tapering tips. Bronzy green as they emerge, they turn shades of red and yellow in autumn. HEIGHT & SPREAD 2.4×1.2m (8×4ft) after 10 years, ultimately 6m (20ft) tall.
P. pendula The weeping habit of this tree makes it look like the shape of an umbrella. Pale pink flowers, up to 1.5cm (½in) wide, appear in profusion in late spring. The leaves are up to 7.5cm (3in) wide. If a grafted plant, it will not grow much taller than the trunk. HEIGHT & SPREAD 2.4×1.8m (8×6ft) after 10 years, ultimately 4m (13ft).
***P.* 'Pink Perfection'**♀ Abundant double flowers, 4cm (1½in) wide, open deep pink but fade to white with age. The leaves, 10cm (4in) long and rather pointed, emerge pale bronze and gradually become green. The ascending branches give this tree a vase-shaped appearance. HEIGHT & SPREAD 2.7×1.8m (9×6ft) after 10 years, ultimately 6m (20ft) tall.
***P.* 'Pink Shell'**♀ The slender branches give this tree a delicate, slightly pendulous appearance, especially when it is in flower. The pale pink flowers, 2.5cm (1in) across, complement the pale green of the new foliage. The leaves, up to 11cm (4¼in) long, become darker green later. HEIGHT & SPREAD 2.4×1.5m (8×5ft) after 10 years, ultimately 5m (16ft) tall.
P. pumila* ssp. *depressa Small white flowers appear in abundance before the leaves emerge. Greyish green above and bluish white beneath, the leaves turn various shades of red in autumn. This small shrub makes good ground cover. HEIGHT & SPREAD 15cm×1m (6×36in) after 10 years, and ultimately.
P. sargentii♀ (Sargent's cherry) Pink flowers, 4cm (1½in) across, are freely borne in mid spring. The pointed leaves, about 10cm (4in) long, emerge bronzy green before turning plain green. In autumn, the leaves give a magnificent display of crimson and orange. The bark of this spreading tree

▲ *Prunus* 'Pink Shell'

is chestnut-brown. HEIGHT & SPREAD 3×1.8m (10×6ft) after 10 years, ultimately 15m (50ft) tall.

P. serrula ♀ This tree's outstanding feature is its shiny red-brown bark which peels off in strips that appear golden when they catch the light. The small white flowers are insignificant. The dull green leaves are narrowly lance-shaped and up to 10cm (4in) long. HEIGHT & SPREAD 2.4×1.2m (8×4ft) after 10 years, ultimately 5m (16ft) tall.

***P.* 'Shirofugen'** ♀ The abundant double flowers, 4cm (1½in) across, emerge white but turn purplish pink with age. This is one of the latest cherries to blossom and the flowers may not appear until early summer. The leaves are up to 9cm (3½in) long with pointed tips. Emerging an attractive bronze which persists into summer, the leaves turn mid green in late summer. HEIGHT & SPREAD 2.7×2m (9×6½ft) after 10 years, ultimately 10m (33ft) tall.

▲ *Prunus serrula*

***P.* 'Shirotae'** ♀ Semidouble pure white flowers, up to 5cm (2in) across, appear in abundance in mid spring. The large pale green leaves have long thread-like ends to their teeth, giving them a very feathery appearance. This small tree has a spreading, pendulous habit, and is often broader than it is tall. HEIGHT & SPREAD 1.8×1.8m (6×6ft) after 10 years, ultimately 4m (13ft) tall.

***P.* 'Shogetsu'** ♀ An abundance of white semidouble flowers, 5cm (2in) across, with frilled edges are borne during late spring. The leaves, which have attractive thread-like points to their teeth, emerge brown-green and turn pale green as they age. This small tree with spreading branches is often broader than it is tall. HEIGHT & SPREAD 2.4×1.8m (8×6ft) after 10 years, ultimately 6m (20ft) tall.

***P.* 'Spire'** ♀ (syn. *P.* 'Hillieri Spire') Pale pink flowers, 2.5cm (1in) across, are freely borne in mid spring. These are followed by a wonderful display of autumn tints as the pointed leaves, 9cm (3½in) long, turn orange and red. The tree's upright habit gives it a vase-like appearance. HEIGHT & SPREAD 2.7×1m (9×3ft) after 10 years, ultimately 10m (33ft) tall.

P.* × *subhirtella Pale pink flowers, about 2cm (¾in) across, appear before the pale green leaves in early or mid spring. The double-toothed leaves are 7.5cm (3in) long and taper to a point. This small upright tree and its cultivars provide a good display of autumn colour. HEIGHT & SPREAD 2.7×1.8m (9×6ft) after 10 years, ultimately 9m (30ft) tall.

'Autumnalis Rosea' ♀ has plentiful, small, pale pink flowers in late winter. The small white flowers of **'Autumnalis'** ♀ appear in early winter. **'Fukubana'** ♀ has abundant deep pink flowers in mid spring.

▲ *Prunus* 'Taihaku'

***P.* 'Taihaku'** ♀ (great white cherry) The large white flowers, 6cm (2½in) across, are produced in great clusters during mid spring. They provide an attractive contrast to the new foliage which emerges coppery green. The leaves, which gradually become plain mid green, are 15cm (6in) long and taper with thread-like ends to the serrated edges. This small tree has a spreading habit and is often as broad as it is tall. HEIGHT & SPREAD 2.7×1.5m (9×5ft) after 10 years, ultimately 10m (33ft) tall.

***P.* 'Ukon'** ♀ The abundant, semidouble, white flowers, 4cm (1½in) across, open with a green tinge that is lost as the season progresses. The leaves, 10cm (4in) long, are bronzy green when they emerge but mature to dark green. In autumn the leaves give an attractive display of reds and purples. HEIGHT & SPREAD 2.4×1.2m (8×4ft) after 10 years, ultimately 7m (23ft) tall.

▲ *Prunus* 'Ukon' in autumn

P.* × *verecunda (Korean hill cherry) White or pink flowers, 2.5cm (1in) across, appear in mid or late spring. The leaves emerge green-bronze, turn mid green later in the season and finally become red in autumn. HEIGHT & SPREAD 2.4×1.2m (8×4ft) after 10 years, ultimately 5m (16ft) tall.

***P. virginiana* 'Shubert'** Pendulous spikes of white flowers, 1cm (⅜in) across, are produced in mid spring. The broad leaves, 10cm (4in) long, are glossy green at first but quickly change to deep purple-red. This large shrub or small tree has a conical habit. HEIGHT & SPREAD 2.4×1.2m (8×4ft) after 10 years, ultimately 4m (13ft) tall.

P.* × *yedoensis ♀ A profusion of slightly almond-scented flowers, 2cm (¾in) across, is carried on arching branches in early spring. At first the flowers are flushed with pink but they turn pure white soon after opening. The double-toothed leaves, 11cm (4¼in) long, give a good display of autumn colour. HEIGHT & SPREAD 3×2.4m (10×8ft) after 10 years, ultimately 12m (40ft) tall.

The weeping branches of **'Shidare-Yoshino'**♀, covered in pink blossom in early spring, often brush the ground.

ORNAMENTAL CHERRY LAURELS

P. laurocerasus♀ (common or cherry laurel) The glossy mid green leaves of this vigorous large shrub or multistemmed small tree are up to 20cm (8in) long. White flowers, 1cm (⅜in) across, appear on upright spikes in mid spring followed by black fruits in early autumn. The berries, up 2cm (¾in) long, are often produced in great profusion. This species makes an excellent screen or windbreak. HEIGHT & SPREAD 3×2m (10×6½ft) after 10 years, ultimately 6m (20ft) tall.

'Camelliifolia', which reaches only 4m (13ft) tall, has leaves with a curled appearance. **'Castlewellan'** (syn. *P.* 'Marbled White') bears mid green leaves with grey-green patches and white marbling. It is a slow-growing plant which makes a dense shrub of rounded habit. The leaves of **'Otto Luyken'**♀ are deep glossy green and up to 10cm (4in) long. This dense shrub is about 1m (3ft) tall and broad. It is a good plant for a border of small shrubs or for hedging. The erect stems are covered in spikes of small white flowers in mid spring. **'Zabeliana'** makes good ground cover. It often spreads to 3m (10ft) but may grow only 1m (3ft) tall. It flowers freely in late spring. The shiny narrow leaves are 11cm (4¼in) long.

▲ *Prunus laurocerasus* 'Otto Luyken'

P. lusitanica♀ (Portugal laurel) Glossy green ovate to elliptic leaves, about 12cm (4¾in) long, appear on attractive red stalks. Cup-shaped, fragrant white flowers, 1.5cm (½in) wide, are borne in long, ascending spikes in early to mid summer. Small red fruits, ripening to black, may follow. A small, multistemmed tree of rounded habit, this is good for windbreaks and hedging. It grows better on shallow chalk soils than does *P. laurocerasus*. HEIGHT & SPREAD 2.7×2m (9×6½ft) after 10 years, ultimately 6m (20ft) tall.

The leaves of ssp. ***azorica***♀ are slightly larger than those of the species. They have a reddish tinge when young but turn dark green with age. It makes a tree about 4m (13ft) tall.

'Variegata' has white margins to its leaves. This plant is really a large shrub rather than a tree.

CULTIVATION Plant in moisture-retentive but well-drained fertile soil between late autumn and mid spring, avoiding frosty periods. Most prunus do best in a reasonably sunny position, but *P. laurocerasus*, which will not thrive on chalky soils, will be fine in shade.

PROPAGATION Sow the seed of species in a gritty compost in a coldframe in early spring. Alternatively, take greenwood cuttings of deciduous species in early summer and semi-ripe cuttings of evergreens in mid summer. Buy grafted cultivars.

PRUNING The deciduous trees rarely need pruning. However, they may be trimmed in mid summer to maintain their shape and size. When used as hedging, *P. lusitanica* and *P. laurocerasus* and their cultivars may be pruned to shape at any time, although late spring or early summer is best.

PESTS AND DISEASES Usually pest free, but susceptible to bacterial canker, silver leaf, wither tip and spur blight.

Pseudofumaria see *Corydalis*

Pseudolarix

Chinese golden larch

Pinaceae

Pseudolarix amabilis

These slow-growing but breathtakingly colourful trees from China come into their own in autumn, when the foliage steadily turns orange. Pseudolarix are hardy deciduous larches with beautiful cones that are pale green when they first appear and turn a yellowy orange later. Chinese golden larches make superb trees for any garden with acid soil. There is just one species in this genus.

▼ *Pseudolarix amabilis*

Pseudolarix amabilis♀ This conical tree has downward curving needles, 6cm (2½in) long, fanning out from a central bud. Male and female flowers appear together on the same tree in spring, long before the needles appear. The green female flowers look like tiny broccoli spears, while the male flowers are small and yellow about the size of a pea. Upright, stalkless cones, up to 3cm (1¼in) long, with fleshy scales appear in late autumn. The flowers and cones, however, are not produced until the tree is at least 40 years old. HEIGHT & SPREAD 2×1.5m (6½×5ft) after 20 years, ultimately 12m (40ft) tall.

CULTIVATION Plant in full sun or partial shade between mid autumn and early spring in moist but well-drained acid soil.

PROPAGATION Raising pseudolarix is difficult, and it is best to buy a young plant from a specialist nursery.

PRUNING Remove badly shaped branches in winter.

PESTS AND DISEASES Usually trouble free.

Pseudopanax

Araliaceae

The foliage of these hardy or half-hardy evergreen shrubs and trees is striking for its shapes and colours. The summer flowers are small, greenish and of no decorative merit. Male and female flowers are usually borne on separate plants and both need to be grown if the small rounded fruit are to appear. Native to Chile, New Zealand and Tasmania, some plants in the genus are used as conservatory plants. However, most will grow outdoors at the base of a wall with a south or west-facing aspect, provided they have a sunny position and free-draining soil.

RECOMMENDED SPECIES AND VARIETIES

***P.* Adiantifolius Group 'Cyril Watson'**♀ Tough, leathery, 3-lobed, spreading leaves,

▼ *Pseudopanax* Adiantifolius Group 'Cyril Watson'

up to 25cm (10in) long, are produced on this compact multistemmed shrub. They are mid green with pale conspicuous veins. This plant is usually grown in a pot or border in a greenhouse or conservatory and can only be grown outdoors in mild areas of Britain. HEIGHT & SPREAD 1.5×1m (5×3ft) after 5 years, also the ultimate size.

P. lessonii (houpara) The bright green leaves are divided into 3-5, coarsely toothed, lance-shaped leaflets, up to 10cm (4in) long. This plant can be grown both as a conservatory plant and in a sheltered spot outdoors. A small tree or large shrub, it will reach only about half its size if confined to a pot. HEIGHT & SPREAD 5×3m (16×10ft) after 5 years, also the ultimate size.

Leaves variegated with gold distinguish **'Gold Splash'**♀, while **'Purpureus'** has glossy bronze-green foliage in summer, turning purplish bronze in winter.

▲ *Pseudopanax lessonii* 'Gold Splash'

CULTIVATION Plant outdoors in a sheltered spot, preferably in full sun, in well-drained soil. Alternatively, grow in pots of free-draining potting compost, such as John Innes No.3, in a cool greenhouse or conservatory. Water freely during summer and sparingly in winter. Apply a slow-release fertiliser in spring.

PROPAGATION Take semi-ripe cuttings in summer.

PRUNING Remove any wayward shoots as they appear.

PESTS AND DISEASES Usually trouble free.

Pseudosasa see BAMBOOS p.78

Pseudotsuga

Pinaceae

Pseudotsuga menziesii

Given the right spot, these stately evergreen conifers with a broadly conical habit make handsome specimen trees. Only one of the four species is grown in Britain. *Pseudotsuga menziesii*, native to western N America, is a tall forest tree which grows quickly, so is suitable only for the largest gardens. However, the cultivars are smaller. The trees have a noticeable aroma of caramel in strong afternoon sunshine.

RECOMMENDED SPECIES AND VARIETIES

P. menziesii♀ (Douglas fir) The soft, dense, fragrant foliage is made up of needles, 2.5cm (1in) long, that are green above with 2 white bands underneath. Abundant cones, up to 10cm (4in) long, with protruding seed bracts, appear after about 10 years. HEIGHT & SPREAD 7×1.5m (23×5ft) after 20 years, ultimately 60m (200ft) tall.

'Fletcheri' will suit any garden with moist acid soil. As it grows only 2m (6½ft) tall, it is also suitable for small gardens. This is a flat-topped, rounded, bushy shrub with sweet-smelling, blue-green leaves.

The most hardy tree is var. ***glauca*** (blue Douglas fir), a narrow, conical variety with striking blue foliage. The needles grow to 5cm (2in) and the cones are up to 7cm (2¾in) long. This tree, which grows up to 40m (130ft) tall, does not tolerate lime.

'Glauca Pendula'♀ is a small, weeping tree with elegant silver-blue foliage that looks superb in winter and ultimately grows 10m (33ft) tall.

CULTIVATION Grow in moist but well-drained soil on a site in morning shade and afternoon sun to prevent frost damage to early new growth.

PROPAGATION Sow the seed of species in spring outdoors. Cultivars, which are normally grafted in late winter, are best bought ready grafted from a reputable nursery.

PRUNING Remove any broken branches right back to the main stem. If young plants have 2 leading shoots, remove one at the base. The remaining shoot will then straighten up quickly, even if it was quite crooked at first.

PESTS AND DISEASES Usually trouble free.

▲ *Pseudotsuga menziesii* 'Glauca Pendula'

Psylliostachys

Plumbaginaceae

Dainty summer flowers dot the slender spikes of these annuals. The plants are suitable for drying as everlasting flowers. Well-drained soil and a position in a sunny border meet their growing requirements. They are particularly suitable for growing in the salt-laden air of coastal areas.

RECOMMENDED SPECIES AND VARIETIES

P. suworowii (syn. *Limonium suworowii, Statice suworowii*) (pink poker, rat's tail statice) Tiny, tubular, pink to purple flowers appear from mid to late summer on erect spikes, up to 30cm (12in) long, that often curl at the top. The dull green lance-shaped leaves are up to 15cm (6in) long. This upright plant, native to W and central Asia, is half-hardy. HEIGHT & SPREAD 45×30cm (18×12in).

CULTIVATION Plant in well-drained soil once the risk of frost has passed. Choose a position in full sun. Weed and water regularly. Flower spikes intended for drying are best harvested when the tiny blossoms first open.

PROPAGATION Sow seeds in early spring in a propagator at 21°C (70°F) and plant outside in late spring to early summer.

PESTS AND DISEASES Aphids are often troublesome on young plants. Botrytis and powdery mildew sometimes affect plants establishing themselves outdoors.

▲ *Psylliostachys suworowii*

pq

Ptelea
Rutaceae

Just one species of this N American genus of deciduous shrubs or small trees is grown in British gardens. *Ptelea trifoliata* is a spreading shrub with aromatic leaves and winged fruit. Although hardy, it needs a sheltered position to thrive.

RECOMMENDED SPECIES AND VARIETIES
P. trifoliata♀ (hop tree) The yellowish green leaves are made up of 3-5, pointed oval leaflets, 10 cm (4 in) long. They are clammy to the touch because of the secretions from their glands. Rounded clusters of fragrant, greenish white, star-shaped flowers, each 1 cm (⅜ in) long, bloom in early summer and are followed by pale, lime-green fruits in late summer. Each fruit, about 2.5 cm (1 in) across, has 2 flattened seeds surrounded by an almost circular wing. The seeds are fertile in mid summer after warm summers. This large wide-spreading shrub has smooth red-brown stems. HEIGHT & SPREAD 1.5×1.5 m (5×5 ft) after 5 years, ultimately 4 m (13 ft) tall.

▲ *Ptelea trifoliata*

▲ *Ptelea trifoliata* 'Aurea'

'Aurea'♀ has soft yellow foliage that contrasts with the lime-green fruits.

CULTIVATION Plant in autumn or spring in any moist fertile soil, choosing a sheltered site in semi-shade.

PROPAGATION Sow the seed of species under glass as soon as it is ripe in mid to late autumn. Alternatively, take softwood cuttings from species and cultivars.

PRUNING Cut back lightly in early to mid spring to control unruly specimens.

PESTS AND DISEASES Usually trouble free.

Pterocarya
Wing-nut tree
Juglandaceae

Where there is light and space enough in the garden, these big, fast-growing deciduous trees offer a show of attractive feathery foliage. They develop a short thick trunk and a mass of heavy, spreading branches. Insignificant, greenish yellow, male and female flowers appear in drooping catkins in early summer on the previous year's growth. The pale green winged fruits follow in early autumn. The trees are hardy, but need a sheltered sunny site to thrive.

RECOMMENDED SPECIES AND VARIETIES
P. fraxinifolia♀ (Caucasian wing-nut) The glossy, bright green, pinnate leaves, 30-60 cm (1-2 ft) long, turn yellow in autumn. Each has 7-27, pointed, oblong leaflets up to 12 cm (4¾ in) long. The winged nuts dangle in distinctive pendulous strings up to 40 cm (16 in) long. Native to Iran and the Caucasus. HEIGHT & SPREAD 12×8 m (40×26 ft) after 20 years, ultimately 30 m (100 ft) tall.

▲ *Pterocarya fraxinifolia*

P. stenoptera (Chinese wing-nut) The pinnate leaves are 20-40 cm (8-16 in) long with 11-23 rounded oblong leaflets, each up to 10 cm (4 in) long. A glossy bright green in summer, the leaflets turn yellow in autumn. The winged nuts are borne in strings 20-30 cm (8-12 in) long. Native to China. HEIGHT & SPREAD 12×8 m (40×26 ft) after 20 years, ultimately 30 m (100 ft) tall.

▲ *Pterocarya stenoptera*

CULTIVATION Plant in spring in any moist but well-drained rich soil. Choose a site in full sun with shelter from the wind. Remove suckers as soon as they appear.

PROPAGATION Sow seed under glass in spring. Alternatively, either layer plants or take semi-ripe cuttings in late summer.

PESTS AND DISEASES Usually trouble free.

Pterocephalus
Dipsacaceae

In summer the pinkish purple flowers of these mat-forming plants bring colour to a rock garden. In its native Mediterranean and Asia, this genus includes annuals and perennials, but just one species of semi-evergreen plants is usually grown in British gardens.

RECOMMENDED SPECIES AND VARIETIES
P. perennis Pale pinkish purple flowers are held in rounded clusters, up to 4 cm (1½ in) across. The oval leaves are 4 cm (1½ in) long and covered with white downy hairs. HEIGHT & SPREAD 12×25 cm (4¾×10 in).

The leaves of ssp. ***belldifolius*** are green.

CULTIVATION Plant in spring in well-drained soil in a rock garden or sunny bed.

PROPAGATION Sow ripe seed in a cold-frame. Alternatively take softwood cuttings in early summer.

PESTS AND DISEASES Usually trouble free.

Pterostyrax

Styracaceae

Pterostyrax hispida

Between late spring and mid summer, fragrant five-lobed white flowers droop in abundant clusters from the gracefully spreading branches of these deciduous trees from E Asia. They have handsome, mid green, oval leaves that are edged with fine bristly teeth. Pterostyrax are quite hardy, and will grow anywhere except in shallow, chalky soils.

RECOMMENDED SPECIES

P. corymbosa♀ In late spring and early summer, small flowers in pendulous branched clusters, 8-15 cm (3¼-6 in) long, open beneath the branches. These are followed in late summer by downy, spindle-shaped fruits with 5 longitudinal ribs. The leaves are 7.5-18 cm (3-7 in) long. HEIGHT & SPREAD 3×3 m (10×10 ft) after 10 years, ultimately 8.5 m (28 ft).

Pterostyrax hispida

P. hispida♀ (epaulette tree) Drooping flower clusters, up to 23 cm (9 in) long, hang beneath the branches in early and mid summer. The spindle-shaped fruits are densely covered in stiff pale brown hairs. The leaves are 7.5-20 cm (3-8 in) long. HEIGHT & SPREAD 3×3 m (10×10 ft) after 10 years, ultimately 12 m (40 ft) tall.

CULTIVATION Plant in autumn or early spring in deep, fertile loamy soil choosing a position in full sun or part shade.

PROPAGATION Sow seed under glass in early spring or take softwood or semi-ripe cuttings in summer.

PRUNING Not usually required.

PESTS AND DISEASES Usually trouble free.

Pulmonaria

Lungwort

Boraginaceae

Pulmonaria officinalis

Distinctive foliage and long-lasting spring flowers make these low-growing, hardy herbaceous perennials ideal as ground cover. They are particularly useful in shady garden areas. The leaves, 15-30 cm (6-12 in) long, are deep green or spotted or marbled with silvery white and are covered in fine bristles. The funnel-shaped flowers, to 2 cm (¾ in) long with spreading lobes, appear from early to late spring. Colours range through shades of blue, pink to purple, and white. The plants grow best in humus-rich moist soil, in partial or full shade. Native to Europe and Asia.

RECOMMENDED SPECIES AND VARIETIES

P. angustifolia♀ Very deep blue flowers are borne in dense heads among long, narrow, unspotted dark green leaves. HEIGHT & SPREAD 30×45 cm (1×1½ ft).

The flowers of ssp. ***azurea*** are deeper blue and the plant is a little taller. **'Munstead Blue'** has reddish violet flowers turning to rich blue. **'Rubra'** see *P. rubra*

P. **'Beth's Blue'** Loose heads of deep blue flowers open from red buds. The leaves are mid green with white streaks and blotches. HEIGHT & SPREAD 30×45 cm (1×1½ ft).

P. **'Blue Ensign'** Dark violet-blue flowers in compact heads are carried among narrow, unmarked, dark green leaves. HEIGHT & SPREAD 30×45 cm (1×1½ ft).

P. **'Glacier'** Pale pink flowers eventually turn to white on this well-spreading plant. Long leaves are sparsely spotted with paler green. HEIGHT & SPREAD 30×45 cm (1×1½ ft).

P. **'Lewis Palmer'**♀ (syn. *P.* 'Highdown') Dark blue flowers are held in large dense heads. The long, narrow, dark green leaves are heavily blotched with greenish white. HEIGHT & SPREAD 30×45 cm (1×1½ ft).

P. longifolia A densely clump-forming plant with long narrow leaves that are dark green and vividly spotted with white. The bright blue flowers open from dark buds. HEIGHT & SPREAD 30×45 cm (1×1½ ft).

'Bertram Anderson' has especially well-marked leaves and brightly coloured flowers. It is more compact.

P. **'Mawson's Blue'** Deep blue flowers are borne among narrow dark green leaves. A low-growing plant, it spreads slowly. HEIGHT & SPREAD 30×45 cm (1×1½ ft).

P. mollis Large violet-blue flowers are carried in dense heads. The large, downy, unspotted leaves are deep green. HEIGHT & SPREAD 45×60 cm (1½×2 ft).

P. **'Mournful Purple'** Rich purple flowers are borne in drooping clusters. The dark green leaves are blotched with pale green. HEIGHT & SPREAD 30×45 cm (1×1½ ft).

P. officinalis The flowers, borne in compact clusters, are deep pink in bud, then pink and finally violet-blue when mature. Heart-shaped leaves are spotted pale green or white. HEIGHT & SPREAD 30×45 cm (1×1½ ft).

'Bowles' Blue' has pale blue flowers early in the season and leaves that are moderately marked with white and pale green. The flowers of **Cambridge Blue Group** are light blue and the leaves are variably spotted with silver. **'Sissinghurst White'**♀ is a very vigorous plant with flowers that open white from pale pink buds. The leaves are spotted with silver. For ssp. ***rubra*** see *P. rubra*. **'White Wings'** has white flowers with pink eyes. It is a more compact plant with sparsely pale-spotted leaves.

P. **'Roy Davidson'** The long, narrow leaves of this compact plant are heavily spotted with white. Pale blue to violet flowers are borne in dense heads. HEIGHT & SPREAD 30×45 cm (1×1½ ft).

P. rubra♀ (syn. *P. angustifolia* 'Rubra', *P. officinalis* ssp. *rubra*) The pinkish red flowers of this vigorous, ground-covering plant are carried in large open heads that bloom very early and keep their colour unchanged. The large, pale green leaves are unspotted and very hairy. HEIGHT & SPREAD 45 cm×1 m (1½×3 ft).

Pulmonaria rubra var. albocorollata

The leaves of the less vigorous var. ***albocorollata*** (syn. var. *alba*) are paler and the small white flowers are carried on shorter stems. **'Barfield Pink'** has white and pink-striped flowers and is less vigorous and floriferous. **'Bowles' Red'** has faintly spotted leaves and the flowers are orangey. The grey-green leaves of **'David Ward'** have cream edges and the flowers are pale coral. The large red flowers of the vigorous **'Redstart'** are carried on upright stems among soft green leaves.

P. saccharata (syn. 'Picta') The leaves of this strong-growing clump-former have variable white spots and blotches, sometimes almost completely covering the whole leaf. The flowers are pink in bud, changing to a

Pulmonaria saccharata Argentea Group

Pulmonaria saccharata 'Dora Bielefeld'

Pulmonaria saccharata 'Mrs Moon'

pale reddish violet. HEIGHT & SPREAD 30×60cm (1×2ft).

'Alba' has paler leaf spots, and white flowers from pink buds. The leaves of **Argentea Group**♀ are silvery white and narrow with mottled green edges. The strong-growing **'Dora Bielefeld'** is one of the best varieties for flower colour. Its blooms open clear pink and darken to violet among pale, sparsely spotted leaves. **'Frühlingshimmel'** has brightly spotted leaves and pale blue flowers with a darker eye. The leaves of **'Leopard'** are dark green, spotted and blotched with white. The reddish pink flowers are borne on upright stems. **'Mrs Moon'** has leaves spotted pale green, and pink to violet flowers. **'Pink Dawn'** is a compact plant with wavy-edged leaves blotched with pale whitish green. The large flowers are deep pink becoming violet.

P. vallarsae Violet flowers are borne amid wavy-edged, blotched, downy leaves. HEIGHT & SPREAD 25×60cm (10×24in).

'Margery Fish'♀ has whitish grey leaves with green spotted margins. The reddish pink flowers mature to violet.

CULTIVATION Plant from autumn to spring in any reasonably moist, humus-rich soil in partial or even full shade.

PROPAGATION Divide in late autumn.

PESTS AND DISEASES Liable to attack by slugs and snails, and some varieties may develop powdery mildew during summer.

Pulsatilla

Pasqueflower

Ranunculaceae

Pasqueflowers are some of the loveliest of all alpine plants. Their foliage is feathery and the large flowers are covered with soft down on the outside. The flowers are followed by long-lasting, decorative, silky seedheads. These clump-forming, hardy evergreen or herbaceous perennials grow best in the well-drained situation of a rock garden or raised bed, in full sun and well away from more vigorous and invasive rock plants. They can also be grown in pots in an unheated greenhouse or alpine house.

The solitary bell or goblet-shaped flowers vary from nodding to erect. Colours may be white or shades of yellow, pink, lavender, purple or red. There are usually six petal-like sepals which surround a boss of conspicuous golden stamens. The plants recommended below are herbaceous tuft-forming perennials except for the evergreen *Pulsatilla vernalis*. Height is given for plants in flower; most increase in height slightly when in fruit.

RECOMMENDED SPECIES AND VARIETIES

P. alpina (alpine pasqueflower) Erect bowl to saucer-shaped flowers, up to 6cm (2½in) across, are white with a bluish or lilac flush on the outside. They are borne from late spring to early summer among mid green, ferny leaves covered with silky hairs. The plant is slow to flower from seed, taking 8 or more years to build up to a good flowering clump. Native to central and S Europe. HEIGHT & SPREAD 45×45cm (18×18in).

The bell-shaped flowers of ssp. ***apiifolia***♀ (syn. ssp. *sulphurea*, syn. *Anemone sulphurea*) are primrose yellow.

Pulsatilla alpina ssp. apiifolia

P. halleri♀ Bell-shaped flowers, up to 9cm (3½in) across, are lavender to violet-purple and appear in spring before the leaves unfurl. The ferny leaves are densely silky. Native to central and E Europe. HEIGHT & SPREAD 20×20cm (8×8in).

The flowers of ssp. ***slavica***♀ are violet and the leaves are less finely divided.

P. pratensis Nodding bell-shaped flowers, 3-4cm (1¼-1½in) long, are dark purple to reddish purple and occasionally greenish yellow. They are borne in late spring and early summer above finely divided silky leaves. HEIGHT & SPREAD 15×15cm (6×6in).

Pulsatilla halleri ssp. slavica

P. vernalis♀ (syn. *Anemone vernalis*) (spring pasqueflower) Bell-shaped flowers up to 6cm (2½in) across, are white flushed with blue or lilac outside. The erect to semi-erect flowers appear in early to mid spring above leathery, deep green, divided leaves. An evergreen, it is excellent for an alpine house or unheated greenhouse. Outdoors, it needs protection from winter wet. Native to Europe and Siberia. HEIGHT & SPREAD 10×20cm (4×8in).

P. vulgaris♀ (syn. *Anemone pulsatilla*) (common pasqueflower) Slightly nodding, bell-shaped flowers borne in spring are up to 9cm (3½in) across and are pale to dark purple, red or white. The pale green leaves are very finely cut. Native to England, France and central Europe. HEIGHT & SPREAD 20×20cm (8×8in).

The flowers of ssp. ***alba***♀ are white. **'Barton's Pink'** has flowers of delicate rose. **'Eva Constance'** has deep reddish black flowers. **'Papageno'** has semidouble, cut-petal flowers ranging from white to pink, lavender and red shades. **'Rode Klokke'** ('Rote Glocke') has deep red flowers. The flowers of var. ***rubra*** are in shades of red.

CULTIVATION Plant in spring or autumn in gritty well-drained neutral to chalky soil in

Pulsatilla vulgaris

Pulsatilla vulgaris ssp. alba

full sun, although *P. alpina* ssp. *apiifolia* prefers acid soil. Remove dead leaves on herbaceous species in autumn. Avoid disturbance once plants are established.
PROPAGATION Sow seed when ripe or in autumn. Take root cuttings in winter or early spring.
PESTS AND DISEASES Usually trouble free.

Pumpkin see p. 741

Punica

Pomegranate
Lythraceae

Only one variety of this genus is commonly grown in Britain, *Punica granatum* var. *nana*, a summer-flowering, tender, semi-evergreen shrub. Native to western Asia, it can be grown in a greenhouse, conservatory or very sunny, warm room, where it makes a good specimen plant. Its fruits rarely ripen. Pot-grown plants can be moved outside once the danger of frost has passed.
RECOMMENDED VARIETY
P. granatum* var. *nana (dwarf pomegranate) Bright orangey scarlet flowers, up to 4 cm (1½ in) across, are produced throughout the summer by this bushy shrub. Round, pale orange fruits, about 3 cm (1¼ in) across, follow the flowers in early autumn. The fresh green, broadly lance-shaped leaves are 2-4 cm (¾-1½ in) long. HEIGHT & SPREAD 1×1 m (3×3 ft).

▲ *Punica granatum var. nana*

CULTIVATION Grow in pots of potting compost and place in direct sunlight in a warm greenhouse or conservatory or well-lit room. Provide a minimum winter temperature of 7°C (45°F). If wished, move plants outside in summer. Water regularly in summer, but only occasionally in winter. Feed fortnightly during the growing season. Pot on annually in spring until the plant reaches the desired size.
PROPAGATION Take semi-ripe cuttings during summer.
PRUNING Cut back in spring to reduce the size of the plant, if required.
PESTS AND DISEASES Usually trouble free.

Purslane see *Portulaca oleracea*

Puschkinia

Liliaceae

Dense spikes of flowers appear in spring on this hardy bulbous perennial. It is ideal for the rock garden, where it will spread freely, and is a good choice for naturalising in short grass. It can also be used in dry soil conditions around shrubs, although it does need full sun. There is only one species.
Puschkinia scilloides (striped squill) Star-shaped pale blue flowers with a darker blue stripe running down the centre of each petal are borne in spikes about 10 cm (4 in) long. The dark green strap-like leaves are up to 15 cm (6 in) long. HEIGHT 15 cm (6 in).

▲ *Puschkinia scilloides*

CULTIVATION Plant in autumn in an open position in any soil, provided it is not waterlogged. Apply a slow-release general fertiliser as the leaves start to emerge in spring. Remove faded foliage when it has died back completely.
PROPAGATION Divide and replant mature clumps in autumn or sow seed in late summer in a coldframe.
PESTS AND DISEASES Usually trouble free.

Pussy toes see *Antennaria*
Pygmaea see *Chionohebe*

Pyracantha

Firethorn
Rosaceae

Pyracantha rogersiana

Long-lasting berries in brilliant shades of red, orange, or yellow adorn these hardy evergreen shrubs. Generally lasting from late summer to autumn, they are up to 1 cm (⅜ in) in diameter and grow in dense clusters. Frothy clusters of tiny, white, five-petalled flowers appear in early summer. The oval leaves, up to 7.5 cm (3 in) long, have toothed edges. Generally mid to dark green, some varieties have variegated leaves. Pyracanthas are armed with sharp thorns and should be handled with care. They will grow in almost any well-drained fertile soil, although in chalky conditions the foliage may yellow. They may sometimes be defoliated in a severe winter, but usually recover quickly. Fire blight and pyracantha scab can be problems, but new disease-resistant strains are now available. Pyracanthas are effective when grown as freestanding specimen shrubs and also make excellent hedges. They are, however, mainly grown as wall shrubs and are invaluable for brightening up a shady site. With the exception of *P.* Alexander Pendula, heights and spreads given below refer to wall-grown plants. Freestanding shrubs are usually 10 to 15 per cent smaller. Native to E Europe and Asia.
RECOMMENDED SPECIES AND VARIETIES
***P.* Alexander Pendula** Sparse yellow berries turn red later on. If grown as a freestanding specimen, this shrub forms a dense hummock with weeping branches. Trained against a wall it forms a graceful cloak. HEIGHT & SPREAD 50 cm×1.5 m (20 in×5 ft) after 5 years, ultimately 60 cm (2 ft) tall.
P. atalantioides (syn. *P. gibbsii*) Crimson berries appear from summer until the following spring. Upright at first, the almost thornless stems arch over later on. It is very hardy but particularly susceptible to fire blight. HEIGHT & SPREAD 1.8×1.5 m (6×5 ft) after 5 years, ultimately 4.5 m (15 ft) tall.
'Aurea' (syn. *P. gibbsii* 'Flava') has large clusters of rich yellow berries.
P. coccinea This species bears bright red berries. The plant forms a dense shrub. HEIGHT & SPREAD 1.5×1.5 m (5×5 ft), ultimately 3.5 m (12 ft) tall.
'Red Column' has reddish shoots and masses of berries which ripen early. It is upright in habit. **'Red Cushion'** has vivid red berries. This densely leafy variety reaches a spread of 1.8 m (6 ft).
P. gibbsii see *P. atalantioides*
***P. gibbsii* 'Flava'** see *P. atalantioides* 'Aurea'
***P.* 'Golden Charmer'** Large clusters of yellowish orange berries ripen early. Upright at first, the branches arch over as the plant ages. HEIGHT & SPREAD 1.5×1.2 m (5×4 ft) after 5 years, ultimately 3 m (10 ft) tall.
***P.* 'Golden Sun'** see *P.* 'Soleil d'Or'
***P.* 'Harlequin'** The decorative foliage is variegated with cream and pink. It has small red berries. HEIGHT & SPREAD 1×1 m (3×3 ft) after 5 years, ultimately 1.8 m (6 ft) tall.

▼ *Pyracantha coccinea* 'Red Column'

▲ *Pyracantha* 'Golden Charmer'

P. **'Mohave'** The berries are reddish orange. This dense shrub is resistant to disease, and birds avoid the berries. HEIGHT & SPREAD 1.8×1.5m (6×5ft) after 5 years, ultimately 4.5m (15ft) tall.

'Mohave Silver' is a less vigorous sport of 'Mohave' with silver-edged leaves

P. **'Navaho'** Small reddish orange berries ripen slowly. The plant has a dense, spreading habit. It is particularly resistant to fire blight. HEIGHT & SPREAD 1×1.2m (3×4ft) after 5 years, ultimately 3.5m (12ft) tall.

P. **'Orange Glow'**♀ Red-orange berries ripen in early autumn and last into winter. A dense, upright shrub, resistant to scab disease. HEIGHT & SPREAD 1.8×1.8m (6×6ft) after 5 years, ultimately 4.5m (15ft) tall.

P. rogersiana♀ Masses of reddish orange berries appear in mid summer. Upright at first, the stems eventually arch over. HEIGHT & SPREAD 1.8×1.2m (6×4ft) after 5 years, ultimately 3m (10ft) tall.

'Flava'♀ has bright yellow berries.

P. **'Shawnee'** Yellow to light orange berries

▲ *Pyracantha* 'Navaho'

ripen in mid summer. This plant is densely branching, spreading at the base. It is fairly resistant to fire blight and scab. HEIGHT & SPREAD 1.8×1.2m (6×4ft) after 5 years, ultimately 3m (10ft) tall.

P. **'Soleil d'Or'** (syn. *P.* 'Golden Sun', *P.* 'Yellow Sun') This plant carries large clusters of deep golden yellow berries. The plant has reddish stems and a semi-spreading habit. HEIGHT & SPREAD 1.5×1.5m (5×5ft) after 5 years, ultimately 3m (10ft) tall.

P. **'Sparkler'** The white-mottled leaves become pink-tinged in autumn and winter. Not reliably hardy, this is best grown against a sheltered wall or in a cold greenhouse. HEIGHT & SPREAD 1.2×1.2m (4×4ft) after 5 years, ultimately 2.4m (8ft) tall.

P. **'Teton'** Yellowish orange berries are borne in profusion. A vigorous upright shrub with reddish shoots, resistant to fire blight. HEIGHT & SPREAD 1.8×1.2m (6×4ft) after 5 years, ultimately 3m (10ft) tall.

P. **'Yellow Sun'** see *P.* 'Soleil d'Or'

▼ *Pyracantha* 'Shawnee'

▲ *Pyracantha* 'Soleil d'Or'

CULTIVATION Plant in any fertile, well-drained soil that is not too chalky in sun or shade. If using as hedging, set young plants 50cm (20in) apart. Water all plants until established. Feed occasionally. Support wall-grown plants with trellis or wires and tie in vigorous shoots each year from early summer to autumn.

PROPAGATION Take semi-ripe cuttings in mid to late summer.

PRUNING Trim established plants to shape from early spring to mid summer. Prune before flowering for maximum berry production. For hedging plants, lightly trim sideshoots at time of planting, leaving leading shoots untouched. Cut back sideshoots of established plants from early spring to late summer. Only shorten leaders if few sideshoots are produced.

PESTS AND DISEASES Aphids may infest stems and leaves. Woolly aphids may be troublesome. Fire blight and pyracantha scab can be problems. Birds may eat the berries.

Pyrethrum see *Tanacetum coccineum*

Pyrus

Ornamental pear

Rosaceae

Pyrus salicifolia 'Pendula'

Ornamental pears are hardy deciduous trees valued for their habit, white blossom and decorative foliage. Individual flowers are 2-4cm (¾-1½in) across and are borne in clusters. The fruits have no ornamental value and most are not suitable for eating. (For fruiting pear trees, see p.728.)

RECOMMENDED SPECIES AND VARIETIES

P. callyerana **'Chanticleer'**♀ Clusters of flowers appear from early to mid spring and again, occasionally, in summer. The leathery, glossy green leaves, up to 10cm (4in) long, are roughly oval, with pointed tips. In autumn, they turn to shades of red and sometimes persist through winter. This tree is narrowly pyramidal. HEIGHT & SPREAD 5×2.4m (16×8ft) after 10 years, ultimately 15m (50ft) tall.

P. communis **'Beech Hill'** Bunches of flowers are carried from early to mid spring. The mid green leaves, about 10cm (4in) long, are oval with somewhat pointed tips and usually curled. The foliage sometimes takes on attractive autumn colouring. This tree forms a lofty spire that casts little shade. HEIGHT & SPREAD 4×2.4m (13×8ft) after 10 years, ultimately 10m (30ft) tall.

P. nivalis (snow pear) Clusters of white flowers appear in late spring. The roughly oval leaves, 7.5cm (3in) long, are white, with a felted texture when young. Older leaves are green above, remaining white and felted beneath. This forms a small tree with upright branches that become more spreading. HEIGHT & SPREAD 5×3m (16×10ft) after 10 years, ultimately 10m (30ft) tall.

▲ *Pyrus nivalis*

P. salicifolia **'Pendula'**♀ Dense clusters of creamy blossom appear in mid spring. The narrow leaves, up to 9cm (3½in) long, are white and felted until early summer, turning greyish green later. This tree forms a dense mound of weeping branches. HEIGHT & SPREAD 5×2.7m (16×9ft) after 10 years, ultimately 8m (26ft) tall.

CULTIVATION Plant from mid autumn to early spring in full sun or partial shade, preferably in heavy, but well-drained and well-cultivated soil.

PROPAGATION It is advisable to buy a healthy specimen from a reputable supplier.

PRUNING Not normally necessary, but trim trees lightly into shape in summer if desired.

PESTS AND DISEASES Usually trouble free.

Quamash see *Camassia*

Queen of the prairie see *Filipendula rubra*

Queen's tears see *Billbergia nutans*

Quercus
Oak
Fagaceae

Quercus canariensis

The foliage, size and shape of these long-lived deciduous and evergreen trees varies considerably. All oaks bear acorns, egg-shaped nuts held in basal cups covered with woody, sometimes fringed, scales. Oak trees have spreading tops and deep-spreading roots, making them unsuitable for smaller gardens. The trees below are hardy.

RECOMMENDED SPECIES AND VARIETIES

Q. borealis see *Q. rubra*

Q. canariensis♀ (Algerian oak) A round-headed tree with semi-evergreen leaves that persist in all but the hardest winters. The obovate leaves, 12.5cm (5in) long, have rounded lobes. The bark becomes fissured and brownish grey. Native to S Europe and N Africa. HEIGHT & SPREAD 8×5m (26×16ft) after 20 years, ultimately 30m (100ft) tall.

Q. castaneifolia **'Greenspire'**♀ A narrow tree with glossy oblong or oval deciduous leaves about 18cm (7in) long with coarse triangular teeth. HEIGHT & SPREAD 14×5m (46×16ft) after 20 years, ultimately 30m (100ft) tall.

Q. coccinea (scarlet oak) Deciduous dark green leaves, 15cm (6in) long, have pointed lobes and turn scarlet in autumn. Silvery grey-brown bark remains smooth for many years. Acorns seldom appear in Britain. Native to eastern USA and SE Canada. HEIGHT & SPREAD 10×8m (33×26ft) after 20 years, ultimately 25m (80ft) tall.

'Splendens'♀ has good autumn colour.

pq

▲ *Quercus coccinea*
▼ *Quercus coccinea* 'Splendens'

▲ *Quercus frainetto*

Q. frainetto (Hungarian oak) The multi-lobed, leathery deciduous leaves, up to 18cm (7in) long, are narrow at the base and widest at the tip. Native to E Europe. HEIGHT & SPREAD 8×5m (26×16ft) after 20 years, ultimately 30m (100ft) tall.

'Hungarian Crown'♀ is faster-growing and has a broad head of even branches.

Q. ilex♀ (holm oak) An evergreen round-topped tree with dark grey fissured bark. The leathery leaves, up to 6cm (2½in) long, are glossy dark green above and grey beneath. Small, fertile green acorns appear after a hot summer. Although hardy, this tree does best in mild districts and is particularly good near the sea. Native to S Europe. HEIGHT & SPREAD 6×5m (20×16ft) after 20 years, ultimately 25m (80ft) tall.

Quercus ilex

Q. palustris♀ (pin oak) A deciduous tree with a dense crown and silver-grey bark. The glossy green leaves, up to 12.5cm (5in) long, are deeply lobed. Red-brown foliage follows a hot summer. The short shoots on young trees are pin-like and angular. Native to N America, this species tolerates wet soil. HEIGHT & SPREAD 9×5m (30×16ft) after 20 years, ultimately 30m (100ft) tall.

Q. pedunculata see *Q. robur*

Q. petraea♀ (syn. *Q. sessiliflora*) (durmast oak, sessile oak) This deciduous tree grows well in coastal areas and has grey to black-brown bark and large ovate leaves, up to 17cm (6¾in) long, with round lobes. The acorn cups are stalkless. A long-lived British native. HEIGHT & SPREAD 6×4m (20×13ft) after 20 years, ultimately 35m (115ft) tall.

Q. phellos♀ (syn. *Q. pumila*) (willow oak) A rounded, semi-evergreen tree with glossy elliptic leaves, up to 15cm (6in) long, that turn yellow and orange in autumn. It requires a sheltered site and good moist soil. Acorns are seldom produced. Native to south-eastern USA. HEIGHT & SPREAD 4×3m (13×10ft) after 20 years, ultimately 8m (26ft) tall.

▲ *Quercus palustris*

Q. robur♀ (syn. *Q. pedunculata*) (English oak) This long-lived British native has a broad crown. The deciduous, mid to deep green leaves, up to 14cm (5½in) long, are obovate with rounded lobes. HEIGHT & SPREAD 6×4m (20×13ft) after 20 years, ultimately 32m (105ft) tall.

'Concordia' is a small, rounded slow-growing tree with upright golden foliage. A columnar tree with distinctly upright branches, f. *fastigiata* can reach an ultimate height of 28m (92ft). **'Fastigiata Koster'**♀ (Cypress oak) is a faster-growing columnar tree that also reaches 28m (92ft).

Q. rubra♀ (syn. *Q. borealis*) (red oak) A rounded deciduous tree with a large spreading head. The soft mid green leaves, up to 20cm (8in) long, have triangular to acute points and lobes. They turn dull red, brown and orange-yellow in autumn. The smooth trunk is silver-grey or pale brown. Fertile acorns are rare. Native to N America. HEIGHT & SPREAD 10×6m (33×20ft) after 20 years, ultimately 30m (100ft) tall.

Q. sessiliflora see *Q. petraea*

Q. x *turneri* (Turner's oak) The shallowly lobed dark green leaves, up to 8cm (3¼in) long, often remain on the tree all winter. The stems soon become fissured and dark brown. A rounded semi-evergreen tree. HEIGHT & SPREAD 8×4m (26×13ft) after 20 years, ultimately 18m (60ft) tall.

CULTIVATION Plant in any deep, well-drained soil. Established trees grow best in an open, sunny position, but will tolerate partial shade when young. Plant young specimens because a vigorous taproot is produced at an early age.

PROPAGATION Sow ripe acorns in autumn under glass or in open ground; seeds planted outdoors need protection from mice and other creatures. Graft or take ripewood cuttings of cultivars.

PRUNING Oaks need little pruning, but the removal of basal sideshoots will give a clear trunk. Singling double or multiple leading shoots on young plants can save money on tree surgery later on. All pruning is best done in winter.

PESTS AND DISEASES Many organisms live on oak trees, but healthy trees resist the majority of them.

Quince, edible see *Cydonia*
Quince, flowering see *Chaenomeles*
Quince, Japanese see *Chaenomeles*

Radish see p. 745
Ragged robin see *Lychnis flos-cuculi*

Ramonda
Gesneriaceae

Crevices in walls or between rocks are the spots for these evergreen rosettes which carry flat, rounded flowers on strong stems. Appearing in late spring to early summer, the blue to violet flowers, 2 cm (¾ in) across, are enhanced by clustered golden anthers. The thick, roughly oval leaves, up to 8 cm (3¼ in) long, are toothed and wrinkled.

Ramondas are hardy, perennial and long-lived. They favour vertical or very steeply inclined rock faces in partial or full shade. In times of drought the leaves shrivel, only to recover after rainfall. Hard frost produces a similar reaction and garden plants have survived temperatures of -20°C (-4°F) unscathed. Ramondas associate well with silver saxifrages.

RECOMMENDED SPECIES AND VARIETIES

R. myconi♀ (syn. *R. pyrenaica*) The dull, dark green leaves have dense russet hairs on their undersides. Branching stems carry 5-petalled mauve-blue flowers. Native to the Pyrenees. HEIGHT & SPREAD 10×15 cm (4×6 in).

'Rosea' has soft pink flowers.

R. nathaliae♀ Neat, flat rosettes have pale green, glossy leaves. The lavender-blue flowers have 4, occasionally 5, petals. Native to the northern Balkan Peninsula. HEIGHT & SPREAD 10×10 cm (4×4 in).

R. pyrenaica see *R. myconi*

R. serbica This differs from the other two species in having rather ragged leaf edges and longer leaf stalks. It can also be taller. The flowers are lilac-blue with purple anthers. It is not always easy to establish. Native to the northern Balkan Peninsula. HEIGHT & SPREAD 15×15 cm (6×6 in).

CULTIVATION Plant in early spring in well-drained, gritty soil away from direct sun. Choose lightly shaded crevices in walls or between rocks, where the plant can face outward rather than upward.

PROPAGATION Sow seed in spring on the surface of gritty compost. Don't let the seedlings dry out and protect from direct sun at all times. Prick out the seedlings in the second spring after germination. Alternatively, divide in early spring or take leaf cuttings in summer.

PESTS AND DISEASES Apart from slugs and snails they are usually trouble free.

▲ *Ramonda myconi*

▲ *Ramonda nathaliae*

Rampion see *Phyteuma*

Ranunculus
Buttercup, crowfoot
Ranunculaceae

Ranunculus aconitifolius 'Flore Pleno'

Cupped flowers with bold centres of crowded stamens appear in spring or summer. Many have an almost metallic sheen to their petals. The genus is native to N Africa, N America, Asia, Europe and New Zealand, and thrives in any habitat, from lowland marshes to mountains. As 'buttercups' they are better known to most gardeners as weeds, but the genus includes garden plants of merit, including alpines and taller herbaceous species.

The taller species are selections from the commoner lawn weeds and should be planted with care in case they become invasive. They are suited to moist spots in either sun or partial shade, especially next to water or moist woodland areas rather than in a formal border. The alpine species require moist but very well-drained soil and, except for *R. lyallii* which prefers shade, enjoy a sunny site. *R. glacialis* and *R. lyallii* require acid or neutral soil. All species flourish if other plants are not too close and are best given a place to themselves.

Those listed are perennials. All except *R. asiaticus* are hardy, and all but *R. lyallii* are herbaceous.

RECOMMENDED SPECIES AND VARIETIES

***R. aconitifolius* 'Flore Pleno'**♀ Loose clusters of double white buttons 1 cm (⅜ in) across open at the top of stems in late spring. Deeply cut and toothed dark green, palmate leaves grow to 3 cm (1¼ in) long. HEIGHT & SPREAD 60×40 cm (24×16 in).

***R. acris* 'Flore Pleno'** (bachelor's buttons) Golden yellow double flowers, 2.5 cm (1 in) across, appear in late spring as a cluster on top of stems. Wiry stalks bear sparse, dark green hairy leaves that are 4 cm (1½ in) wide and 3 cm (1¼ in) long. The palmate foliage is deeply divided, with 3-7 wedge-shaped segments. This non-invasive plant makes a compact clump. HEIGHT & SPREAD 1 m×30 cm (3×1 ft).

R. alpestris Between 1 and 3 white flowers 2 cm (¾ in) across appear in spring on stems that also carry a few small, linear leaves. Larger, rounded, basal leaves, 2.5 cm (1 in) across, are dark glossy green, deeply lobed and toothed. This tufted alpine usually lasts only around 3 years in cultivation, but is still worth a place in a sunny trough or raised bed. HEIGHT & SPREAD 5×10 cm (2×4 in).

Ranunculus asiaticus

R. asiaticus Single or semidouble flowers open on 30 cm (12 in) long slender, branched stems in late spring or early summer. This poppy-like, sun-loving alpine ranges from red, through orange and yellow, to pure white. It is a fairly tall, open plant with slim tuberous roots. Long-stalked, palmate leaves up to 6 cm (2½ in) across are further divided in the lobes, forming a rather sparse, 15 cm (6 in) wide basal ruff. HEIGHT & SPREAD 30×20 cm (12×8 in).

***R. bulbosus* 'Speciosus Plenus'** see *R. constantinopolitanus* 'Plenus'

R. calandrinioides♀ Pearly white flowers with a pink flush appear in late winter or early spring on 12 cm (4¾ in) long sparingly branched stems. The blooms are 5 cm (2 in) across, with delicate petals that can be damaged by harsh weather. Wavy-edged, tapering leaves, 10 cm (4 in) long with a blue-grey cast, emerge in early winter as a loose tuft. Growth dies down in mid summer. This alpine is long-lived but increases in size slowly. HEIGHT & SPREAD 12×15 cm (4¾×6 in).

***R. constantinopolitanus* 'Plenus'** (syn. *R. bulbosus* 'Speciosus Plenus') Double yellow flowers 3cm (1¼in) across appear in early summer. Dark green leaves, 3-lobed, toothed and up to 3cm (1in) across, make a compact clump. HEIGHT & SPREAD 30×30cm (12×12in).

R. crenatus Milky white, anemone-like flowers, 2cm (¾in) across with a yellow-rimmed gréen centre, open in early summer. They are carried singly or in pairs on 4-10cm (1½-4in) stems. This semi-evergreen alpine forms a mat of mid green, rounded 2cm (¾in) long leaves tipped with 3 lobes. It suits a well-watered scree bed. HEIGHT & SPREAD 4-10×10cm (1½-4×4in).

R. ficaria (lesser celandine) Flowers 2cm (¾in) across with about 8 oblong, glossy yellow petals open in early spring. Leathery heart-shaped leaves 2cm (¾in) long are carried on long stalks. This tuft-forming plant is ideal for the wild garden but can spread invasively. HEIGHT & SPREAD 10-20×30cm (4-8×12in).

The var. ***albus*** has white flowers; var. ***aurantiacus*** (syn. 'Cupreus') has copper coloured petals and stamens and **'Brazen Hussy'** has golden flowers and purple-bronze young foliage. **'Collarette'**, **'E.A. Bowles'** and ***flore-pleno*** are yellow; **'Double Mud'** (syn. double cream) is creamy yellow. All are double-flowered. **'Green Petal'**, ssp. ***major***, **'Primrose'**, **'Randall's White'** and **'Salmon's White'** are self-descriptive.

▼ *Ranunculus ficaria* 'Brazen Hussy'

▼ *Ranunculus ficaria* 'Primrose'

▼ *Ranunculus ficaria* 'Double Mud'

▼ *Ranunculus ficaria* 'Collarette'

▼ *Ranunculus ficaria* 'Green Petal'

▼ *Ranunculus ficaria* 'Randall's White'

R. glacialis The white, sometimes pale rose-pink flowers, 4cm (1½in) across have a cluster of golden stamens. Up to 3 appear on stout reddish stems in early summer. Smooth, 3-lobed, fleshy leaves grow to 3cm (1¼in) long. This low, clump-forming alpine can be difficult in cultivation. HEIGHT & SPREAD 15×20cm (6×8in).

R. gouanii Semidouble golden flowers 3cm (1¼in) across appear on branching stems in early summer. The mid green basal leaves, up to 7cm (2¾in) across, are deeply lobed into 3-5 oval, toothed fingers. This alpine is clump-forming. HEIGHT & SPREAD 30×15cm (12×6in).

R. gramineus♀ Loose sprays of bright yellow flowers 2cm (¾in) across appear on the branching stems of this alpine in early summer, just clear of the tips of erect, slender blades of blue-green foliage. HEIGHT & SPREAD 40×10cm (16×4in).

▼ *Ranunculus gouanii*

R. lyallii Multipetalled white flowers 5cm (2in) across appear in open sprays in early summer. Almost round, deep green leaves are 15cm (6in) across and leathery. This evergreen alpine has a tufted habit and is suited to a large rock garden. It is intolerant of dry, hot places and rarely flowers unless planted in a cool, moist site. HEIGHT & SPREAD 40×35cm (16×14in).

R. montanus Up to 3 bright yellow shiny flowers 3cm (1¼in) across appear in early summer, rising from a dense clump of deep green basal leaves, which are 2.5cm (1in) across and deeply cleft into 3-5 toothed lobes. Stem leaves are smaller and simpler. This alpine species dislikes dry sites. HEIGHT & SPREAD 10-30×25cm (4-12×10in).

'Molten Gold'♀ has a stockier habit and a richer flower colour.

R. parnassiifolius White goblet-like flowers, 2.5cm (1in) across and occasionally suffused with pink veining, are borne successively through late spring by this alpine. They are single or in open sprays of up to 5 or more and rise from a 10cm (4in) wide cluster of ground-hugging basal leaves. The stalked, conspicuously ribbed foliage is dark green, heart-shaped and 4cm (1½in) long. HEIGHT & SPREAD 10-25×15cm (4-10×6in).

R. repens var. ***pleniflorus*** Double, bright yellow flowers 3cm (1¼in) across appear in late spring and early summer. Dark green divided leaves are up to 3cm (1¼in) long. This invasive plant is ideal as ground cover in moister spots where it can be controlled. HEIGHT & SPREAD 30cm×1m (1×3ft).

CULTIVATION Plant from autumn to spring in moist soil in a sunny site. Tall herbaceous species also thrive in semi-shade. *R. lyallii* prefers a cool, shaded position. *R. asiaticus* enjoys a warm, sheltered spot and light, nutritious soil. *R. glacialis* and *R lyallii* need acid or neutral soil.

PROPAGATION Lift and divide all except *R. lyallii* after flowering and replant. Raise all species from seed, sown as soon as it is ripe. Prick out seedlings into individual pots. Plant out in mid spring the following year.

PESTS AND DISEASES Aphids can attack. Dry weather may cause powdery mildew.

Raoulia

Scab weed

Compositae

Mats or cushions of dense creeping growth, often silvery, provide year-round cover for rock gardens, and raised and scree beds. Small white or yellow flowers appear scattered amongst the rosettes of tiny leaves from late spring to early summer. Raoulias are reasonably hardy evergreen perennials, but thrive only in very well-drained soil. Native to New Zealand.

RECOMMENDED SPECIES AND VARIETIES

R. australis Loose rosettes of rounded leaves up to 5mm (¼in) long and covered in tiny hairs form a solid mat of silver-grey foliage. Lemon-yellow, starry flowers are 4mm (¼in) wide. Protect the plant from winter rain with a cloche or pane of glass. HEIGHT & SPREAD 1.5 x 30cm (½ x 12in).

▲ *Raoulia australis*

Lutescens Group (syn. *R. lutescens*) The minute, congested grey-green leaves resemble fine moss. The tiny flowers are pale yellow. Fully hardy in some gardens but not cooler, wetter parts of Britain, such as W Scotland. HEIGHT & SPREAD 1.5 x 30cm (½ x 12in).

R. glabra A carpet of 4mm (⅛in) long, oval green leaves produces a modest display of miniature, tubular white flowers, 5mm (¼in) across. This plant does not thrive in hot, dry weather and is best grown in cooler, wetter areas of Britain. HEIGHT & SPREAD 2 x 45cm (¾ x 18in).

R. haastii Densely crowded rosettes of tiny emerald-green oval leaves 1.5mm (1/16in) long make an irregularly mounded mat, with white, tufted, stemless flowers no more than 2mm (⅛in) across. In mid autumn the foliage turns chestnut brown, returning to green just before flowering. HEIGHT & SPREAD 5 x 30cm (2 x 12in).

R. hookeri This vigorous plant forms a silver-grey mat of 5mm (¼in) long oval

▼ *Raoulia haastii*

▲ *Raoulia hookeri*

leaves, with rounded, fluffy, straw-coloured flowers up to 6mm (¼in) wide. The plant is best grown in poor soil to curb its invasive tendencies. Cover the plant in winter in wet areas with a cloche or pane of glass. HEIGHT & SPREAD 2 x 30cm (¾ x 12in).

R. lutescens see *R. australis* Lutescens Group

R. monroi A loose, feathery, silver-green mat is composed of 3mm (⅛in) long leaves that are broadly linear. Cream daisy-like flowers, 5mm (¼in) wide, with narrow petals, are held in clusters just above the foliage. HEIGHT & SPREAD 2 x 30cm (¾ x 12in).

R. subsericea Closely overlapping 5mm (¼in) long oblong leaves form columnar rosettes crowded together in a carpet of silvery green. The white daisy-like flowers, about 2cm (¾in) wide, last until late autumn. This species will grow over limestone, unlike most other raoulias. It should live for 10 years or so. HEIGHT & SPREAD 2.5 x 60cm (1 x 24in).

▲ *Raoulia subsericea*

R. tenuicaulis The closely grouped leaves are oval with almost spiny tips, 5mm (¼in) long and bright green; they become silvery in a sunny situation. Honey-scented daisy-like flowers, with white petals and greenish yellow centres, are up to 6mm (¼in) across. HEIGHT & SPREAD 2.5cm x 1m (1in x 3ft).

CULTIVATION Plant in the garden in mid spring. Soil must be non-limy and well-drained, preferably with a surface layer of about 5cm (2in) sandy grit. Do not allow the soil to become parched. Open, sunny positions produce the best silvering of foliage and encourage flowering. All plants benefit from winter cover to protect them from excess wet, although in drier districts some can survive without it.

PROPAGATION Sow fresh seed in mid spring. Alternatively, detach rooted shoots and pot them in spring.

PESTS AND DISEASES Plants are prone to attack by fungal diseases in winter. Pluck or snip out affected rosettes, and maintain winter cover.

Raspberry, edible see p. 729
Raspberry, ornamental see *Rubus*
Rebutia see CACTI p. 108
Red-hot cat's tail see *Acalypha hispida*
Red-hot poker see *Kniphofia*
Redwood, dawn see *Metasequoia glyptostroboides*

Rehmannia

Scrophulariaceae

The brightly coloured funnel-shaped flowers appear in spring and summer on these half-hardy herbaceous perennials. The downy leaves are oval or lance-shaped. The species recommended here can only be grown outdoors in milder areas in well-drained soil. Elsewhere, they are best grown in a greenhouse or conservatory and moved outside during summer. Rehmannias require a free-draining loamy compost and sunny position, but with some shading from intense summer sun. Native to China.

RECOMMENDED SPECIES AND VARIETIES

R. angulata see *R. elata*.

R. elata (syn. *R. angulata*) The semi-pendent flowers, up to 10cm (4in) long, are bright rose-purple with a yellow throat liberally spotted red. They appear from late spring to mid summer. The branching stems carry mid-green, roughly heart-shaped leaves, up to 25cm (10in) long, that have lobed or toothed edges. It is often treated as a biennial. HEIGHT & SPREAD 75cm–1.5m x 60cm (2½–5 x 2ft).

CULTIVATION Outdoors in mild areas, plant in well-drained, humus-rich soil in a sunny, sheltered spot when the danger of frosts has passed. Elsewhere, grow under glass in pots of soil-based compost such as John Innes No.2. Plant outdoors or move pots to a sunny sheltered spot once the danger of frost has passed. Lift plants in autumn before the first frosts. Pinch back any wayward shoots and remove faded flowers and leaves.

PROPAGATION Sow seed under glass in autumn or spring. Alternatively, take root cuttings in winter.

PESTS AND DISEASES Greenfly can be troublesome.

▼ *Rehmannia elata*

r

Reseda

Mignonette
Resedaceae

The flowers of reseda plants are often sweetly fragrant and are most attractive to bees. The genus comprises hardy and half-hardy annuals, biennials and herbaceous perennials, native to the Mediterranean, E Africa and SW Asia. They are popular bedding and wild-garden plants and some make interesting cut flowers. All enjoy an open, sunny position in a free-draining soil.

RECOMMENDED SPECIES AND VARIETIES

R. lutea (wild mignonette) Short, slender spikes of tiny 6-petalled, almost scentless, yellowish green blossoms, each no more than 6mm (¼in) across, appear in mid to late summer. It is a sparingly branched plant with mid-green leaves, up to 15cm (6in) long, that are roughly lance-shaped and deeply divided. This is a short-lived perennial which often behaves as a biennial. HEIGHT & SPREAD 30×15cm (12×6in).

R. luteola (dyer's weld) The slender, upright, flower spikes of this species are up to 60cm (2ft) long, mostly unbranched, but occasionally producing sub-spikes. The flowers are tiny, only 5mm (¼in) in diameter, and are greenish yellow on white. They are produced from mid to late summer. This strong-growing biennial has lance-shaped, wavy-edged, mid-green leaves up to 10cm (4in) long. HEIGHT & SPREAD 1m×45cm (3×1½ft).

R. odorata (sweet mignonette) Conical heads of tiny buff or whitish green flowers, each with petals no more than 5mm (¼in) long surrounding conspicuous orange-brown stamens, are borne from mid-summer to autumn. They are intensely fragrant. The oval mid green leaves grow up to 10cm (4in) long. It is a fast-growing, erect-branching annual. HEIGHT & SPREAD 45×30cm (1½×1ft).

'Machet' is a traditional garden variety with large, dense whitish green flower spikes tinged with red.

CULTIVATION Plant in spring in an open sunny position in free-draining soil. Remove faded flowerheads. Dig up annual and biennial plants when the foliage starts to turn brown at the end of the summer. Retain true perennials, cutting back their foliage in autumn. *R. odorata* is also sometimes grown in a pot as a houseplant.

PROPAGATION Sow seed during the spring where the plants are to flower, except for *R. odorata* which is best started off in pots in a coldframe.

PESTS AND DISEASES Greenfly can be a problem.

▼ *Reseda lutea*

Rhamnus

Buckthorn
Rhamnaceae

Rhamnus alaternus 'Argenteovariegata'

Handsome foliage and abundant black berries in autumn provide the main features of these deciduous, sometimes evergreen, trees and shrubs. Small greenish white flowers are carried in clusters in summer. The berries are poisonous.

RECOMMENDED SPECIES AND VARIETIES

***R. alaternus* 'Argenteovariegata'**♀ The leaves, up to 5cm (2in) long, are variegated green and grey and have creamy margins. They are elliptic to ovate, finely toothed and have 3-5 pairs of veins. The black berries are 6mm (¼in) across. This evergreen shrub is one of the finest variegated plants for the medium to large-sized garden. Native to the Mediterranean. HEIGHT & SPREAD 1×1m (3×3ft) after 5 years, ultimately 4m (13ft) tall.

R. catharticus A deciduous spiny tree with ovate toothed leaves up to 8cm (3¼in) long. These have 3-5 pairs of veins and are bright green above, paler beneath. The numerous black berries are 6mm (¼in) across. The bark on the shoots has a pungent smell if scraped. This British native species is important to wildlife. HEIGHT & SPREAD 4×3m (13×10ft) after 20 years, ultimately 6m (20ft) tall.

R. frangula (syn. *Frangula alnus*) The alternate, lustrous deep green, untoothed leaves, no more than 6cm (2½in) long, are ovate and pointed and have 8-9 pairs of veins. The berries, about 6mm (¼in) across, are orange-red at first and then turn purple-black. This deciduous shrub is a British native. HEIGHT & SPREAD 2×1.5m (6½×5ft) after 5 years, ultimately 6m (20ft).

CULTIVATION Plant in spring or autumn in any soil in sun or partial shade. *R. catharticus* tolerates lime.

PROPAGATION Sow seed in spring.

PRUNING None required.

PESTS AND DISEASES Usually trouble free.

▼ *Rhamnus frangula*

Rheum

Ornamental rhubarb
Polygonaceae

Rheum palmatum 'Atrosanguineum'

Though they are best known for their large and handsome foliage, these hardy clump-forming herbaceous perennials are also sometimes grown for their unusual flower spikes. Particularly useful for waterside or bog garden plantings, ornamental rheums must have a damp, organic-rich soil, but will otherwise prosper in most situations except heavy shade. The genus also includes the culinary rhubarb, *R. × hybridum* and its cultivars, which are grown for their colourful, edible stems (see p. 730).

RECOMMENDED SPECIES AND VARIETIES

***R.* 'Ace of Hearts'** (syn. 'Ace of Spades') The roughly heart-shaped leaves are mid-green with a strong crimson flush and conspicuous crimson veins beneath. They reach up to 45cm (18in) long and 30cm (12in) across. Tall, slender sprays of tiny pink flowers appear in early to mid summer. HEIGHT & SPREAD 1.2×1.2m (4×4ft).

***R.* 'Ace of Spades'** see *R.* 'Ace of Hearts'.

R. alexandrae Slender flower stalks bearing sparse creamy yellow flowers and pendent, broadly lance-shaped, yellowish green bracts up to 10cm (4in) long appear in early and mid summer. The glossy, dark green, roughly heart-shaped leaves, up to 25cm (10in) long and 15cm (6in) wide, are neatly arranged in a rosette at the base. HEIGHT & SPREAD 1.5×1m (5×3ft).

R. australe (Himalayan rhubarb) The

▲ *Rheum palmatum* 'Atrosanguineum'

broadly heart-shaped, strongly veined leaves grow to 75cm (30in) long and 60cm (24in) across, mostly with wavy edges and distinct hairiness beneath. The red-tinged leaf stalks are up to 1m (3ft) long. The tiny flowers vary in colour from plant to plant and can be white or shades of pink through to burgundy. They are borne in dense, narrow spikes. HEIGHT & SPREAD 2x2m (6½x6½ft).

R. palmatum♀ The hairy or downy mid-green to bluish-green leaves are up to 60cm (24in) long and wide, deeply lobed and with coarsely toothed edges. They have strong green or reddish purple stems. Tall sprays of tiny flowers appear in early and mid summer. Most gardeners retain the flowers, although removing them results in larger leaves. HEIGHT & SPREAD 2.5x1.8m (8x6ft).

'Atrosanguineum' (syn. 'Atropurpureum') has leaves suffused with red, while **'Bowles' Crimson'** produces foliage with crimson undersides. The leaves of var. *rubrum* are strongly flushed with deep maroon-red, while var. *tanguticum* has leaves which are much more deeply incised and lobed.

CULTIVATION Plant from autumn to spring in a moist, humus-rich soil in full sun or partial shade. Water regularly in dry seasons. Remove faded flower spikes and any yellowing leaves immediately.

PROPAGATION Divide plants in autumn. Alternatively, sow the seed of species and natural varieties under glass in spring.

PESTS AND DISEASES Usually trouble free.

Rhipsalis see CACTI p.109

Rhodiola

Crassulaceae

Fleshy, succulent leaves and flat, clustered flower heads characterise these low, clump-forming herbaceous perennials which flower in early summer. Grow rhodiolas in rock gardens, raised beds or containers. They mingle well with small sedums.

The flowers are star-shaped, with five petals, and have especially prominent stamens that are often twice as long as the petals. In the past, rhodiolas were included in the genus *sedum*.

RECOMMENDED SPECIES AND VARIETIES

R. heterodonta This hardy plant produces an open tuft of slightly arching stems, sparingly clad in ovate, toothed leaves that are 1.5cm (½in) long and grey-green, with a bluish bloom. Yellow flowers in shallow rounded heads, 3cm (1¼in) across, are generously displayed at the shoot tips from late spring to early summer. Native to the Himalayas. HEIGHT & SPREAD 30x20cm (12x8in).

▲ *Rhodiola rosea*

R. rosea (rose root) This robust, erect, clump-forming species carries 2.5cm (1in) long, oblong leaves of glaucous green held alternately on sturdy stems. Terminal heads, 7cm (2¾in) across, of pale yellow flowers bloom in early and mid summer. The hardy plant is attractive to butterflies and bees. Native to Britain and Arctic regions. HEIGHT & SPREAD 30x30cm (12x12in).

CULTIVATION Grow in most medium-to-light soils, but add plenty of grit to heavy ground. Over-moist and heavy soils can cause the rootstock to rot. Sunny positions promote good leaf colour and bloom, whereas shade can result in lax growth and poor flowering. The best time to plant out is mid spring. Lengthy periods of drought will stress the foliage, turning it yellow or red, but full recovery usually follows a generous watering.

PROPAGATION Sow fresh seed in mid autumn in pots in a cold frame. Established plants can be divided. Alternatively, cuttings from non-flowering shoots can be taken in late spring. However, the root growth achieved may be insufficient for winter dormancy.

PESTS AND DISEASES Aphids can attack the plants.

Rhodochiton

Scrophulariaceae

These elegant climbers will cling with twining leaf-stalks to any suitable support. They produce striking tubular flowers surrounded by umbrella-like calyxes over a long period in summer and autumn. Although the plants are in fact rather tender perennials, they are usually grown as half-hardy annuals. The leaves are deciduous when the plant is in the garden, deciduous or semi-evergreen when the plant is grown indoors. The species described here makes a useful climber for a cool greenhouse or conservatory as well as for summer bedding. Native to Mexico.

RECOMMENDED SPECIES AND VARIETIES

R. atrosanguineus♀ (syn. *R. volubilis*) The maroon to purple tubular flowers are flared abruptly at the mouth and hang down from slender stems. Each flower, up to 6cm (2½in) long, hangs within a bowl-shaped, red-purple calyx. The dark green leaves grow to 7.5cm (3in) long and are ovate, sometimes slightly lobed. HEIGHT & SPREAD 3mx50cm (10ftx20in).

▲ *Rhodochiton atrosanguineus*

CULTIVATION Plant in well-drained soil in full sun in early summer. Support plants with wires against a wall or in a greenhouse, with a narrow pyramid of canes or with trimmed conifer thinnings. Alternatively, grow the plant through a shrub.

PROPAGATION Sow seed in early spring in a cool greenhouse and plant out in early summer, when the danger of frost is past.

PESTS AND DISEASES Usually trouble free.

Rhododendron

Rhododendron and Azalea

Ericaceae

For those who garden on acid soil, rhododendrons are among the most prized ornamental shrubs. Trusses of translucent flowers are borne in profusion in a vast range of delicate and striking colours, while the mostly evergreen foliage gives year-round form and texture to the garden. Plants can be grown en masse, as single specimens or in containers

INDEX OF SPECIES AND VARIETIES

The species and varieties have been divided into 12 groups:

Rhododendron Species, Large (RSL); Rhododendron Species, Medium (RSM); Rhododendron Species, Dwarf (RSD); Rhododendron Hybrids, Large (RHL); Rhododendron Hybrids, Medium (RHM); Rhododendron Hybrids, Dwarf (RHD); Azalea Species (AS); Azalea Hybrids, Ghent/Rustica (AHG/R); Azalea Hybrids, Knaphill/Exbury (AHK/E); Azalea Hybrids, Mollis (AHM); Azalea Hybrids, Occidentale (AHO); Azalea Hybrids, Japanese (AHJ)

A list of plants covered follows in alphabetical order with the relevant group in brackets.

r

'Addy Wery' (AHJ)
'Albert Schweitzer' (RHL)
albrechtii (AS)
'Alexander' (AHJ)
'Alice' (RHL)
'Alison Johnstone' (RHM)
'Amoenum' (AHJ)
anwheiense (RSM)
'Anna Baldsiefen' (RHD)
'Anna Rose Whitney' (RHL)
arboreum (RSL)
argyrophyllum ssp. *nankingense* (RSL)
augustinii (RSL)
'Beauty of Littleworth' (RHL)
'Beethoven' (AHJ)
'Bengal' (RHD)
'Berryrose' (AHK/E)
'Betty Wormald' (RHL)
'Blaauw's Pink' (AHJ)
Blandfordiiflorum Group (RSM)
'Blue Danube' (AHJ)
'Blue Diamond' (RHM)
'Blue Peter' (RHM)
'Bodnant Red' (RSD)
'Bo-peep' (RHM)
'Bow Bells' (RHM)
'Brocade' (RHM)
'Bruce Brechtbill' (RHM)
'Buccaneer' (AHJ)
bureaui (RSM)
bureavioides (RSM)
'Buttermint' (RHM)
calophytum (RSL)
calostrotum (RSD)
ssp. *calostrotum* (RSD)
ssp. *keleticum* (RSD)
campylogynum (RSD)
'Carmen' (RHD)
'Caroline Allbrook' (RHM)
'Cecile' (AHK/E)
Charopoeum Group (RSD)
'Cheer' (RHM)
'Chikor' (RHD)
'Chinese Silver' (RSL)
'Chippewa' (AHJ)
'Christmas Cheer' (RHM)
ciliatum (RSD)
'Cilpinense' (RHD)
cinnabarinum (RSM)
ssp. *xanthocodon* (RSM)
'Claret' (RSD)
'Coccineum Speciosum' (AHG/R)
Concatenans Group (RSM)
concinnum (RSM)
'Conroy' (RSM)
Cordifolia Group (RSD)
'Cornell Pink' (RSM)
'Countess of Haddington' (RHM)
'Cowslip' (RHM)
'Creamy Chiffon' (RHM)
Cremastum Group (RSD)
'Crest' (RHL)
Cubittii Group (RSM)
'Cunningham's White' (RHM)
'Curlew' (RHD)
'Cynthia' (RHL)
dauricum (RSM)
'David' (RHL)
davidsonianum (RSL)
'Daviesii' (AHG/R)
decorum (RSL)
degronianum (RSM)
'Delicatissimum' (AHO)
'Diamant' (AHJ)
dilatatum (AS)
'Doncaster' (RHM)
'Dopey' (RHM)
'Dora Amateis' (RHD)
'Dusty Miller' (RHM)

Forest giants 30 m (100 ft) tall, with leaves longer than a man's arm, are at one extreme of the diverse and outstandingly ornamental rhododendron genus. At the other extreme are alpine creepers only 5 cm (2 in) tall, with leaves smaller than a fingernail. There are hundreds of species and hybrids in between, including dramatic specimen plants, border shrubs, rock garden miniatures and houseplants, most needing acid, moist soil with an open structure. Where the soil is alkaline, containers or a raised bed of acid soil allow gardeners to grow rhododendrons.

Most rhododendrons are evergreen, but a few are semi or fully deciduous. Rhododendrons grow wild in much of the Northern Hemisphere, including the moister parts of arctic and temperate N America, the arctic and mountainous regions of Europe, Papua New Guinea and much of SE Asia. If eaten in large quantities, the leaves and flowers are poisonous.

Breeders have now produced virtually

◀ *Rhododendron* 'Percy Wiseman'

edgeworthii (RSM)
'Egret' (RHD)
'Electra' (RSL)
'Elisabeth Hobbie' (RHM)
'Elizabeth' (RHM)
'Exquisitum' (AHO)
'Fabia' (RHM)
falconeri (RSL)
fastigiatum (RSD)
'Fastuosum Flore Pleno' (RHL)
'Favorite' (AHJ)
'Fireball' (AHK/E)
flavum (AS)
'Florida' (AHJ)
formosum (RSM)
fortunei (RSL)
ssp. *discolor* (RSL)
'Fragrantissimum' (RHM)
'Fred Peste' (RHM)
fulvum (RSL)
'Furnivall's Daughter' (RHM)
'Geisha Orange' (AHJ)
'Gibraltar' (AHK/E)
'Gigha' (RSD)
'Ginny Gee' (RHD)
'Glowing Embers' (AHK/E)
'Golden Torch' (RHM)
'Goldsworth Orange' (RHM)
'Gomer Waterer' (RHM)
'Grace Seabrook' (RHL)
'Grumpy' (RHD)
'Haida Gold' (RHM)
'Halfdan Lem' (RHM)
'Harvest Moon' (RHM)
'Hatsugiri' (AHJ)
'Hino-crimson' (AHJ)
'Hinode-giri' (AHJ)
'Hino-mayo' (AHJ)
'Homebush' (AHG/R)
'Hoppy' (RHM)
'Hotei' (RHM)
'Hydon Dawn' (RHM)
'Idealist' (RHL)
'Irene Koster' (AHO)
'Irohayama' (AHJ)
'Jean Marie de Montague' (RHM)
'Johanna' (AHJ)
'John Cairns' (AHJ)
johnstoneanum (RSM)
keiskei (RSD)
'Kermesina' (AHJ)
'Kilimanjaro' (RHL)
'Kirin' (AHJ)
'Klondyke' (AHK/E)
'Kluis Sensation' (RHM)
'Kuri-no-Yuki' (AHJ)
'Lady Alice Fitzwilliam' (RHM)

every flower colour except a true blue. Two or more colours blend in the flowers of newer varieties, while spots and blotches of another colour, or flares of a deeper colour on the centre of the upper lobe widen the choice. Many white and pale pink flowers are scented. Flower shape varies from a narrow tube to almost flat; some are lobed, frilled or scalloped at the rim. The largest are trumpets 12.5cm (5in) long. Flowers are generally borne in clusters, some with up to 50 in a truss.

The usual flowering time in Britain is mid spring to early summer but the flowers of *R. moupinense* are borne in mid winter, 'Christmas Cheer' flowers in late winter to early spring, and 'Polar Bear' flowers at the end of summer. The foliage adds form and texture. Leaf shape is almost round to long and narrow, and young growth may be red, purple or grey as well as shades of green; red bud scales often give extra colour. Leaf surfaces may be shiny or may have hairs that form either a thick felt or a smooth, shiny mat, both known as indumentum. Several species have aromatic foliage.

RHODODENDRON SPECIES, LARGE
The largest-growing rhododendron species are most often seen in botanic gardens, and in large woodland gardens which have the soil and shelter plants need. Yet a smaller garden can use just one to spectacular effect as a specimen plant that is of interest all year.

The typical large species reaches 3m (10ft) or more in both height and spread in 15 years. Many are valued for their handsome foliage as well as for their flowers, with leaves that are on average 12.5×5cm (5×2in). In the plants listed, the flower size is given only when it is outside what is usual for this group; flowers described as small are 5cm (2in) long and all others are an average of 7.5cm (3in) long.

R. arboreum Only milder areas or sheltered sites are suitable for this plant, whose flowers are crimson-scarlet to pink and white, usually spotted, and borne in early to late spring. Scarlet-flowered plants tend to be the most tender. If growth is cut back by frost, it is often renewed from the trunk. The upright, narrow plant is 5m (16ft) or more tall with stiff leaves.

The clone **'Tony Schilling'**♀ has deep pink flowers.

Rhododendron arboreum

▲ *Rhododendron* 'Tony Schilling'

INDEX CONTINUED

▲ Rhododendron argyrophyllum 'Chinese Silver'

R. argyrophyllum ssp. ***nankingense*** The small, pink flowers are borne in late spring on a plant hardy enough for sheltered gardens. The dark green leaves are shiny on top with white indumentum beneath.

R. a. **'Chinese Silver'**♀ is a selection with rich, clear pink flowers.

Rhododendron augustinii

R. augustinii The bluest flowers of any rhododendron, varying from light to dark lavender-blue, are only 4cm (1½in) long and carried in plentiful trusses in late spring. The narrow, upright plant has pointed leaves, about 7.5×2.5cm (3×1in). It thrives in moderate climates but young growth can be damaged by late frosts.

'Electra'♀ has dark blooms.

R. calophytum♀ The large white to pink flowers, blotched with maroon, open in late winter to mid spring. The plant makes a rounded shape, often wider than it is high. One of the hardiest of the large species, it needs shelter for its early flowers and for the large leaves which are long and narrow, up to 30×8cm (12×3¼in).

R. davidsonianum♀ Pink flowers, 3cm (1¼in) long, with or without a deep pink blotch, are very freely produced from a young age in late spring. The plant is variable in flower colour and hardiness. It is fairly upright with long arching shoots and scaly leaves about 7.5×2.5cm (3×1in). It needs plenty of light to avoid becoming straggly, but responds well to pruning.

▼ Rhododendron augustinii

R. decorum Wide open, white to pale pink, fragrant flowers are borne in late spring to early summer. The easily grown, upright plant with a rough bark is one of the few species that has scented flowers and is hardy enough for most gardens.

▲ Rhododendron decorum

R. falconeri♀ Creamy white, long-lasting flowers are borne in large compact trusses in mid to late spring. Matt, veined leaves, up to 35×17cm (14×6¾in), have rust coloured indumentum on the lower surface. The plant forms a tree and does best in mild, well-sheltered gardens in the south and west; it takes 10-20 years to flower.

R. fortunei Scented white to pink flowers are borne in late spring to early summer amid leaves with purplish stalks. This is the hardiest of the scented species.

In ssp. ***discolor***♀ the flowers are later.

R. fulvum♀ Pink to white flowers, blotched or spotted with deep maroon, about 4cm (1½in) long, appear in mid to late spring. The rounded shrub or small tree has upright shoots bearing dark green leaves with cinnamon-coloured indumentum on the underside. It is hardy in all but the coldest gardens if sheltered from wind.

▲ Rhododendron macabeanum

R. macabeanum♀ Yellow flowers, usually with a reddish blotch, appear in early or late spring. The vigorous, upright plant has leaves that measure 38×20cm (15×8in) and have whitish woolly indumentum beneath. It does best in milder or sheltered gardens.

R. morii♀ The small, white (occasionally pink) flowers are blotched and spotted red or purple. They are borne from early to late spring. This is a free-flowering and easily grown species with narrow leaves. Grow in a sheltered position as new growth may be harmed by spring frosts.

R. oreodoxa Freely produced, frost-hardy flowers, usually pale pink, are 4cm (1½in) long and borne in early to mid spring. The upright but well-branched plant has leaves up to 9×4cm (3½×1½in).

The commoner var. ***fargesii***♀ is easily grown.

R. ponticum This is the very vigorous, common purple rhododendron, naturalised in numerous parts of Britain and invasive in many western areas. The flowers are pale to deep pinkish purple and spotted or blotched with a deeper shade and appear in late spring to mid summer. The leaves are up to 20×7.5cm (8×3in) on a plant that is compact in the open but straggly in shade. The plant tolerates severe winds but is not fully hardy in the coldest inland areas. It clips into a sturdy hedge.

'Variegatum' has white leaf markings.

R. rex White to pink flowers with a crimson blotch and spots are borne in early to late spring. The broad, large bush, hardy enough for any sheltered garden, has leaves measuring up to 38×14cm (15×5½in) that are dark green above with thick, woolly, fawn indumentum below.

▲ Rhododendron rubiginosum

R. rubiginosum Profuse pink to mauve-pink flowers up to 4cm (1½in) long are borne in early to mid spring. The leaves, measuring up to 11×5cm (4¼×2in), are dark green on top, brown and scaly beneath. The fast-growing, erect species is hardy in most areas and is suitable for growing as an informal hedge.

R. sinogrande♀ This has the largest leaves of any rhododendron species at 70×30cm (28×12in) or more; they are dark green and shiny on top with a thin fawn indumentum beneath. Large trusses of creamy white flowers with a crimson blotch are borne in mid to late spring. The plant is not reliably hardy away from the west or south coasts and needs a sheltered woodland site.

▲ *Rhododendron thomsonii*

R. thomsonii The fleshy, blood-red flowers open in loose trusses in early to late spring. An upright-growing plant, it has smooth or peeling reddish brown bark and rounded leaves that are often bluish grey when young. It is suitable for all but the coldest areas but is susceptible to mildew.

R. yunnanense The pink to white, late spring flowers, are variously blotched with deep pink, red, yellow or green. Flowers are only 3 cm (1¼ in) long but the trusses are very numerous and often open from multiple buds enhancing the display. Scaly leaves, up to 10×2.5 cm (4×1 in), may be semi-deciduous, especially after a hard winter. The plant does best in a fairly open site but is prone to bark split in the coldest areas.

'Openwood'♀ is a clone with mauve-lavender flowers speckled with red.

RHODODENDRON SPECIES, MEDIUM

These plants reach 1-2.4 m (3-8 ft) in both height and spread in 15 years. Many eventually grow much larger but, because they are fairly slow-growing, they are suitable for smaller gardens, where they make fine specimen plants. Most need a position sheltered from the wind and not in a frost pocket.

In the plants listed leaves are, on average, 7.5×4 cm (3×1½ in). Flowers average 4 cm (1½ in) long; those described as large are 5 cm (2 in) and any other sizes are given.

R. anwheiense♀ (syn. *R. maculiferum* ssp. *anwheiense*) Pink flowers in late spring are fairly frost-resistant on a very hardy, compact bush with mid green leaves.

R. bureaui♀ White to rose flowers are borne in late spring. The hardy plant is rounded and compact in an open site, more straggly in shade. It is renowned for its foliage: the leaves are a shiny dark green when mature with thick, rust-red, woolly indumentum underneath and on the stems.

The closely related ***R. bureavioides*** has shorter leaf stalks and larger flowers.

R. cinnabarinum This variable species has waxy, semi-pendent, tubular flowers that range from yellow through orange and pink to red and purple. They are borne in mid spring to mid summer. The plant varies from erect and sparse to dense and compact. Its scaly, usually evergreen leaves (often greyish-blue when young) are up to 11.5×5.5 cm (4½×2¼ in). Many of the plants are susceptible to mildew.

The most commonly grown are **Blandfordiiflorum Group** with bicoloured yellow and red flowers, **Concatenans Group** and **'Conroy'**♀, both with orange flowers, **Purpurellum Group** with purple flowers, **Roylei Group** with red flowers, and ssp. ***xanthocodon***♀ with yellow flowers.

R. concinnum The deep red, purplish red or pink flowers, only 2.5 cm (1 in) long, are borne in mid to late spring. The plant, with leaves that are dark green above and very scaly below, is hardy in a sheltered garden.

Pseudoyanthinum Group♀ has the richest flower colour.

R. dauricum The small, rosy purple or white flowers, in early winter to mid spring, often come from multiple buds. The plant is usually erect and rather narrow, but may be dwarf. It is hardy (although late frosts may damage young growth) and semi-evergreen with leaves 3×1.5 cm (1¼×½ in).

▲ *Rhododendron dauricum*

The tall **'Midwinter'**♀ is one of the earliest species to flower and the blooms are moderately frost-resistant.

R. degronianum see *R yakushimanum*

R. edgeworthii♀ The sweetly scented white flowers, often flushed rose, are up to 7.5 cm (3 in) long and are borne in late spring. The plant has a spreading to upright habit and is one of the few with both scales and fawn brown indumentum on its leaves which measure about 3×1.5 cm (1¼×½ in). The plant needs well-drained soil and a mild climate. Alternatively, it can be grown in a greenhouse or conservatory.

R. formosum♀ White flowers, up to 7.5 cm (3 in) long, are often flushed pink and may be scented. They open in late spring to early summer. The plant varies from fairly compact to more open, and has scaly leaves up to 12.5×5 cm (5×2 in). It does best in milder areas but may survive for years on a sheltered wall in moderately cold gardens.

R. johnstoneanum♀ The sometimes fragrant flowers are white to greenish yellow and are freely borne in mid to late spring. The fairly vigorous plant is rather an untidy grower, especially when young. It is an easy species for milder gardens.

R. maddenii♀ Fragrant flowers in white, often flushed pink or purple, and sometimes greenish yellow at the base appear in late spring to mid summer. Scaly, dark green leaves reach 20×7.5 cm (8×3 in) on a variable plant which may be compact, upright or sprawling; it needs a mild climate.

More tolerant of a harsher climate if grown in a sheltered spot is ssp. ***crassum***♀.

R. makinoi♀ Rose-pink flowers open in early summer on a compact plant. The dark green, narrow leaves, 18×2.5 cm (7×1 in), curve back at the edges. They often have whitish indumentum above, and thick, tawny indumentum below. The plant grows best in a neutral, near-alkaline soil.

R. moupinense♀ The white to pink flowers are among the earliest to open, in mild spells from mid winter to mid spring, and they are fairly frost hardy. The plant is upright or spreading with a cinnamon-brown, peeling bark and stiff, scaly leaves up to 5×2.5 cm (2×1 in). It needs good drainage and resists drought well.

R. mucronulatum Deep rosy purple to pink or occasionally white flowers are carried singly, but often from clustered buds. They open from mid winter to mid spring and are quite frost-resistant. The deciduous plant is upright with an open habit and has leaves up to 7.5×3 cm (3×1¼ in).

'Cornell Pink' has bright pink flowers. **'Winter Brightness'**♀ has purplish rose flowers. The lower growing var. ***chejuense*** has purple to pink flowers.

R. niveum♀ The tight trusses of large, smoky lilac to deep mauve flowers are borne in early to mid spring. The compact, rounded bush has leaves that are dark above with white to fawn wool known as indumentum on the under surface. It is hardy enough for most sheltered gardens.

R. orbiculare Large, rose-coloured bell-shaped flowers open in mid to late spring on a bush that is broad and domed, but can become straggly in a shady spot. The plant, which is hardy in most areas, has almost round, bright green leaves that measure up to 12.5×7.5 cm (5×3in).

R. oreotrephes The variable flowers in shades of pale pink to rose-purple are borne in mid to late spring. The plant is rounded to upright with scaly leaves that are glaucous green when young and sometimes semi-deciduous. It is hardy in most areas.

▼ *Rhododendron orbiculare*

R. pachysanthum ♀ Bell-shaped, white to pale rose-pink flowers are freely produced on mature plants in early to mid spring. Given some shelter, the dense, rounded shrub with upright growth is hardy enough for all parts of Britain. The leaves are just over 10×5 cm (4×2 in) with silvery to brown indumentum above and thick indumentum on the under surface that turns from white to brown.
R. pseudochrysanthum ♀ White to pale pink flowers spotted with red are freely borne in early to late spring. The plant is usually wider than high. It enjoys partial shade and is intolerant of fertiliser.

▲ *Rhododendron racemosum*

R. racemosum Flowers in shades of pink and white, just under 2.5 cm (1 in) long, are freely borne in early to late spring. The small, scaly leaves are up to 5×3 cm (2×1¼ in) and dark green above, milky-grey below. The plant varies from compact to upright and is often leggy. Variable in hardiness, it does best in a fairly open position.

'Rock Rose' ♀ is a tall plant with clear pink flowers.
R. veitchianum ♀ This greenhouse species has large white flowers, often blotched yellow, that open in late winter to mid summer. They are scented and often frilly. The plant varies from compact to somewhat straggly and may be taller than wide.

Cubittii Group ♀ has similar flowers but with a pink flush in mid to late spring. The plant is hardy enough to grow outside in the mildest western gardens.
R. wardii Saucer-shaped yellow flowers are borne in late spring to early summer. The leaves are up to 12.5×6 cm (5×2½ in) and often milky-green when young. This variable species makes a compact or open plant and often becomes leggy in shade. It is hardy enough for most sheltered gardens.
R. yakushimanum (syn. *R. degronianum* ssp. *yakushimanum*) Flowers that usually open pink and fade to white are borne in late spring. Recurved leaves have semi-persistent indumentum above lasting into their second year, and thick, tawny woolly indumentum below. The plant usually forms a very compact, broad dome. This very hardy species grows well in sun or shade. (See also Rhododendron hybrids, Medium.)

Rhododendron yakushimanum

RHODODENDRON SPECIES, DWARF

These plants typically reach up to 1 m (3 ft) in 15 years but spread wider, forming a low mass of growth. Most are alpine plants and do best in an open position in northern areas of Britain, and with only light shade in the south. The leaf size averages 2.5×1.5 cm (1×½ in) and the typical flower size is 2.5 cm (1 in) long; in the plants listed, flower size is given only when it differs from this.
R. calostrotum This variable species has an erect to creeping habit. In ssp. ***calostrotum***, which is usually mound-shaped with grey-green scaly leaves, the saucer-shaped flowers, about 4 cm (1½ in) across, are held up singly or in pairs. They are sometimes purple but in **'Gigha'** ♀ the flowers are rich rose-crimson and smother the plant in late spring. In ssp. ***keleticum*** ♀, which forms a lower mound with narrower, dark green leaves, the flowers are purplish crimson and bloom in late spring to early summer. **Radicans Group** is near-prostrate in habit with very small leaves.
R. campylogynum The bell-shaped, long-stalked flowers, 1–2.5 cm (⅜–1 in) long, appear in late spring and early summer. The scaly leaves are dark to medium green, and greyish white below (except in the Cremastum Group). Most of the variable but usually compact plants are hardy, but if they are to grow well they need a soil that does not dry out and coolish summers. **Charopoeum Group** is compact in habit with the largest rose-coloured flowers; **'Claret'** has dark shiny leaves and claret-coloured flowers; **Cremastum Group 'Bodnant Red'** is an upright grower with red flowers; **Leucanthum Group** has white flowers; **Myrtilloides Group** has the smallest leaves and purple flowers; in **'Patricia'** the flowers are plum red.
R. ciliatum ♀ White to pale pink, bell-shaped flowers, up to 5 cm (2 in) long, are borne in early to late spring. The hairy, scaly leaves are up to 9×3 cm (3½×1¼ in). The compact plant can sometimes become leggy when grown in a shady position; it is easy to grow but is slightly too tender for the coldest gardens.
R. fastigiatum Abundant purple to blue-purple flowers, up to 2 cm (¾ in) long, are borne in mid to late spring. Blue-grey, scaly leaves up to 15×6 mm (½×¼ in) clothe the compact, low, easily grown plant.
R. keiskei Pale yellow flowers are borne in early to late spring. The scaly leaves are about 5×2 cm (2×1 in) on a plant that varies from straggly to very low and compact. **Cordifolia Group**, usually sold under the name **'Yaku Fairy'** ♀, is the most dwarf form and is exceptionally free-flowering.

▲ *Rhododendron fastigiatum*

▲ *Rhododendron keiskei*

R. lepidostylum ♀ Yellow flowers, borne in early summer, tend to be lost amid the new growth. The scaly, bristly leaves are 4×2 cm (1½×¾ in) and are glaucous. The compact, broad plant prefers light sandy soil.
R. leucaspis Freely produced, flat-faced white flowers, 5 cm (2 in) across, are borne singly or in pairs in early to mid spring. Hairy, scaly, roundish leaves up to 6×3 cm (2½×1¼ in) clothe the compact plant, which is suited only to mild areas.
R. pemakoense Pinkish purple flowers, up to 4 cm (1½ in) long, are borne singly or in pairs with great abundance in early to late spring. The very compact plant is easily grown in most areas, but the swelling flower buds are often damaged by frost.
***R. polycladum* Scintillans Group** ♀ Dark purple-blue flowers, perhaps the nearest to true blue in dwarf species, appear in mid to

▲ *Rhododendron polycladum* 'Scintillans Group'

late spring in the most usual form of this plant. Flowers are 1.5cm (½in) long. Scaly, dark leaves up to 20×6mm (¾×¼in) clothe the very hardy but rather straggly plant, which is susceptible to mildew.

R. russatum♀ Flowers, to 2cm (¾in) long, in shades of reddish purple, deep indigo-blue or almost black-purple open in mid to late spring. The scaly leaves, up to 4×1.5cm (1½×½in), are dark green. The hardy, easily grown plant can vary from compact and spreading to upright and straggly.

R. saluenense Large, usually reddish purple flowers, about 4cm (1½in) across, are borne in mid spring to early summer. The dark, shiny leaves are up to 4×1.5cm (1½×½in) on a plant varying from compact and spreading to straggly.

The leaves of ssp. ***chameunum***♀ are coppery purple in winter and the hardy plant is more compact.

R. trichostomum♀ White to rose flowers, 1.5cm (½in) long, open in profuse trusses in late spring to early summer. The aromatic, narrow leaves, 3×1cm (1¼×⅜in), are dark green and scaly. The plant is erect but compact in the open, straggly in shade, and usually hardy enough for most areas.

▲ *Rhododendron williamsianum*

R. williamsianum♀ Rose to almost white, bell-shaped flowers, up to 4cm (1½in) long, are borne in mid to late spring. The almost round leaves are bronze-coloured when young and the new growth is susceptible to frost damage, although the plant is hardy. It forms a dense, spreading shrub, becoming dome-shaped with age.

r

RHODODENDRON HYBRIDS, LARGE

These plants reach 2.4-3m (8-10ft) high or more in 15 years. They vary in habit from upright with a bare trunk to domed and clothed to the ground with foliage. The leaf size averages 15×5cm (6×2in) and the flower size averages 6cm (2½in) long. Flowers are borne on plants five or more years old. Although plants are large for small gardens, a single one makes a specimen that gives interest all year round. The hardy plants are suitable for an open position in all but the severest climates. The woodland plants need shelter from wind and cold.

'Albert Schweitzer' Hardy. Flowers of rose-pink with a dark red blotch are borne in large, rounded trusses in late spring to early summer on a vigorous, upright plant.

'Alice'♀ Hardy. Large, deep pink flowers, lighter at the centre, fade to off-white in sun. They are borne in full, upright trusses in late spring on a tidy, upright plant.

▲ *Rhododendron* 'Alice'

'Anna Rose Whitney'♀ Hardy. Bright, deep rose-pink flowers in large, open-topped trusses appear in late spring. The upright shrub is vigorous and often untidy, needing pruning to control and shape it. It is susceptible to powdery mildew.

'Beauty of Littleworth'♀ Hardy. The huge, upright trusses of white flowers, speckled crimson, weigh down the branches of the upright, leggy, vigorous shrub in late spring.

'Betty Wormald'♀ Hardy. Rose-pink flowers with a paler centre are borne in conical trusses in late spring to early summer. The upright shrub is fairly tidy.

'Crest'♀ Woodland. Orange buds open to large trusses of long-lasting primrose flowers in late spring. The upright but fairly open shrub is rather slow to start flowering.

'Cynthia'♀ Hardy. Large, pyramidal trusses of deep rose-pink flowers spotted with crimson open in late spring to early summer. A leggy plant when young, the plant is fairly tidy when mature if grown in plenty of light. It is susceptible to mildew.

'David'♀ Woodland. Rounded trusses of frilly, blood-red flowers with deeper spots bloom in late spring. The very upright plant flowers when quite young – after 4-5 years.

'Fastuosum Flore Pleno'♀ Hardy. Light bluish mauve, semidouble flowers are borne in early to mid summer and are long-lasting. The plant is upright but compact.

'Grace Seabrook' Hardy. The blood-red flowers are in large full trusses in mid to late spring and can be damaged by late frosts. The broad shrub has upright growth bearing handsome, pointed, dark green leaves. It takes 4-5 years before it flowers.

'Idealist'♀ Woodland. Pink buds open into pale yellow, pink-tinged flowers with a small red blotch. Trusses appear in mid to late spring. The upright, vigorous bush with glossy leaves is easy to grow.

'Kilimanjaro'♀ Woodland. Large, compact trusses with luminous red flowers with crimson spotting are borne in late spring to early summer. They are beautiful but the upright plant has a straggly, sparse habit.

'Lady Clementine Mitford'♀ Hardy. Pinkish white flowers edged in peach-pink are borne in late spring to early summer. The vigorous, spreading but dense plant is easily grown. It is broader than tall with dark leaves that are silvery when young.

'Lady Eleanor Cathcart'♀ Hardy. Clear pink flowers with a maroon flare are borne in late spring to early summer. The vigorous and upright plant forms a domed bush with long, greyish green leaves. The plant resists cold and is heat resistant but does not flower freely when young.

'Lem's Monarch'♀ Woodland. Huge trusses of pale pink flowers ringed with deeper pink open in late spring to early summer. The strong-growing plant is often wider than it is high with large, thick leaves. It is hardy in most of Britain if given shelter.

'Loderi King George'♀ Woodland. The huge, scented, blush-pink flowers, fading to pure white, are in loose, tall trusses in late spring to early summer. This plant, which needs plenty of room in a sheltered spot, has a vigorous, open growth habit with large leaves that are sometimes prone to yellow veining. **'Loderi Venus'**♀ is similar but with slightly later, light pink flowers.

▲ *Rhododendron* 'Loderi King George'

'Loder's White'♀ Woodland or hardy. Mauve-pink buds open to white flowers in late spring. The well-branched and fairly compact plant, which grows as wide as it is high, can be damaged in very hard winters, but is capable of making a good recovery.

'Lord Roberts' Hardy. The dark red flowers with a small dark flare appear in early to mid summer on a dense upright plant.

'Markeeta's Prize'♀ Woodland or hardy. Large, bright scarlet flowers open in late spring. The stiff, upright shrub has thick, dark leaves and is hardy in most areas.

'Mrs A.T. de la Mare'♀ Hardy. The flowers open from pale pink buds to pure white with a green throat in late spring and early summer. The compact, upright plant has glossy leaves. It is hardy enough for cold areas, but the flowers are thin in texture so are prone to weather damage.

'Mrs Charles E. Pearson'♀ Hardy. Mauve-pink buds open to pale pinkish

▲ *Rhododendron* 'Mrs A.T. de la Mare'

mauve flowers with brown spots and are carried in tall trusses in late spring. The plant is strong and upright-growing but reasonably compact, and it is easy to grow.

'Mrs G.W. Leak' Hardy. Showy flowers, freely produced after a few years, are pink with a large brown and crimson flare in late spring. The upright, compact plant has dull green leaves that are prone to leaf spot.

'Pink Pearl' Hardy. Large pink flowers with brown speckling are borne in tall trusses in late spring and early summer. The vigorous shrub can become leggy and sparse, and tends to be straggly in shade.

'Polar Bear'♀ Woodland. Strongly scented, large white flowers are borne in loose trusses in mid to late summer. The plant is strong-growing and eventually very big, with large leaves that are often a rather pale green. It needs shelter to protect the flowers and the late growth.

'Taurus'♀ Hardy. The flowers are rich blood-red and appear in mid to late spring. The plant forms an upright, fairly rigid shrub with showy red buds that contrast with the deep green, pointed leaves. It is very hardy but needs shelter from late frosts.

'Virginia Richards' Hardy. Trusses of flowers open rosy pink and fade to soft apricot-cream with a darker centre. The rounded bush has glossy, dark green foliage but is susceptible to mildew.

RHODODENDRON HYBRIDS, MEDIUM

These plants reach a height of 1-2.4m (3-8ft) in 15 years and are often about as wide as they are high. On average the leaves measure 10×4cm (4×1½in) and the flowers are 4cm (1½in) long. Many of the plants are crosses of *R. yakushimanum* and are familiarly called 'yak' hybrids. These are compact, low-growing, free-flowering shrubs and are suitable for small gardens. The flower colour tends to fade a few days after opening in most varieties.

In the plants listed, those described as hardy or as 'yak' hybrids are hardy enough for most gardens; those described as woodland need shelter from wind and frosts; those described as small-leaved hybrids have scaly leaves and masses of small flowers. Tender hybrids are suitable only for growing in a greenhouse or the mildest gardens.

The plants in the category *forrestii* hybrids are hardy and have smallish leaves and red flowers on a fairly compact bush to 1-1.2×1m (3-4×3ft). Plants in *williamsianum* hybrid category are all hardy and form plants of a rounded shape with roundish leaves and abundant loose trusses of pink or cream flowers.

'Alison Johnstone' Woodland. The bell-shaped flowers are golden amber, flushed pink, and are borne in late spring. The plant makes a compact and rounded shrub in an open situation. The grey-green leaves may develop a yellow edge, especially in sun. It is easily grown but is susceptible to mildew.

▲ *Rhododendron* 'Alison Johnstone'

▲ *Rhododendron* 'Blue Diamond'

'Blue Diamond' Small-leaved hybrid. Fine violet-blue flowers bloom in large clusters of 4-5 in mid to late spring. The fairly compact plant is hardy in most of Britain but has leaves susceptible to chlorosis and leaf spot.

'Blue Peter'♀ Hardy. Pale lavender-blue flowers with a large purple flare are borne in late spring. The shrub is spreading, even sprawling, and grows wider than high.

'Bo-peep'♀ Small-leaved hybrid. Dainty, pale yellow flowers open in twos and threes, often from multiple buds, during early spring. The upright shrub makes a very pretty plant for milder gardens.

'Bow Bells'♀ *williamsianum* hybrid. Deep pink buds open to light pink flowers borne in lax trusses during late spring. The shrub is upright and compact when grown in the open, but may become leggy in shade. Its young foliage is reddish bronze.

'Brocade'♀ *williamsianum* hybrid. Frilly, peach-pink, bell-shaped flowers are borne in loose trusses in late spring. It forms a large plant but takes a few years to flower freely.

▲ *Rhododendron* 'Bruce Brechtbill'

'Bruce Brechtbill' Hardy. Compact trusses of pink flowers have yellow tinges. The very compact rounded plant, about as wide as high, has shiny, tough foliage.

'Buttermint' Hardy. Pink and yellow shades blend to give the flowers a good orange effect, which is rare in rhododendrons. The compact shrub, hardy in most of Britain, is wider than high, even when grown in shade. Young leaves are tinged bronze, but may scorch in strong sunlight. The growth may become rather congested.

'Caroline Allbrook'♀ 'yak' hybrid. Frilly, lavender-rose flowers are borne in late spring to early summer. The broad, compact shrub starts flowering at a young age.

'Cheer' Hardy. The shell-pink flowers have a prominent red blotch and are borne in abundant trusses in mid to late spring. The dense shrub is very hardy, and so is a useful rhododendron for cold gardens.

'Christmas Cheer' Hardy. The flowers, in small, conical trusses, open blush-pink and fade to near white. This rugged, free-flowering plant has frost-resistant buds that open during mild winter spells with a final flush in mid to late spring. The compact shrub, about as wide as high, has medium-green leaves with a thin brown indumentum below on the underside.

▲ *Rhododendron* 'Cheer'

Rhododendron 'Christmas Cheer' ▼

▲ *Rhododendron* 'Countess of Haddington'

'Countess of Haddington' ♀ Tender. White flowers, flushed rose, are slightly scented and open in mid spring. The compact plant, often wider than high, has hairy leaves. It is suitable only for mild gardens or indoors as its buds cannot withstand more than a few degrees of frost.
'Cowslip' *williamsianum* hybrid. Bell-shaped, hanging flowers, pale primrose-yellow to cream, are marked with pink or red. Flowers are borne in mid to late spring. The fairly compact plant with rounded leaves is hardy enough for most of Britain if given some protection.
'Creamy Chiffon' Hardy. Double, creamy yellow flowers are borne in long-lasting, compact trusses in late spring. The upright plant, usually taller than wide, is fairly hardy but tends to die off after a few years.
'Cunningham's White' ♀ Hardy. Pink buds open to white flowers with yellow to green or brown markings in late spring to early summer. Different clones of this hybrid exist, usually compact with dark foliage, but some forms are untidy. It is easy to grow and hardy enough for exposed sites; it makes an informal flowering hedge.
'Doncaster' Hardy. Flowers that are dark red, with a slight blue cast as they fade, have black spots and are borne in late spring to early summer. The compact and spreading shrub is usually wider than high.
'Dopey' ♀ 'yak' hybrid. Deep red flowers which may bleach a little on the lobes but do not fade, are long-lasting and open in late spring to early summer. The compact plant, as wide as it is high, is quite hardy and easy to grow.

r

▲ *Rhododendron* 'Dopey'

▲ *Rhododendron* 'Dusty Miller'

'Dusty Miller' 'yak' hybrid. The flowers open pale pink flushed red but soon fade out to cream. The compact, quite hardy plant has a silvery indumentum on both surfaces of the leaf.
'Elisabeth Hobbie' ♀ *forrestii* hybrid. Scarlet-red flowers open in mid to late spring. The rounded, tight bush which is best in full exposure is tough, reliable and suitable for severe climates.
'Elizabeth' *forrestii* hybrid. Large, bright red flowers are freely produced in mid spring, and sometimes in autumn. The dome-shaped plant, wider than high, has mid green leaves that are extremely susceptible to mildew, and the plant is not quite hardy in the coldest gardens.
'Fabia' ♀ Woodland. Freely produced, variable flowers are in various shades of pink through orange to red, usually giving an overall effect of orange. They are borne in late spring and early summer on a plant that is often wider than high, sometimes fairly compact in the open but invariably loose and floppy in shade. The leaves have a thin light fawn indumentum beneath. The plant is not hardy enough for colder gardens.
'Fragrantissimum' ♀ Tender. The large flowers are white tinged with pink and are strongly scented. They open in mid to late spring on a very straggly bush with small, hairy leaves. The plant is hardy enough only for mild coastal areas but can be grown in a container, pruned frequently to make a better shape, and moved under cover for the winter.

▲ *Rhododendron* 'Elizabeth'

Rhododendron 'Fabia' ▼

'Fred Peste' 'yak' hybrid. Strong red flowers, which do not fade much, are borne in a fairly lax truss in late spring to early summer. The compact plant, wider than tall, has dark foliage with brownish indumentum on the leaf's underside.
'Furnivall's Daughter' ♀ Hardy. Showy, bright pink flowers with a large strawberry-red flare are borne in late spring to early summer. The rounded plant is often wider than high, with rather rough leaves.
'Golden Torch' ♀ 'yak' hybrid. Pink buds open to very pale yellow flowers which fade to off-white. They are borne in compact trusses in early summer on a low and compact shrub, wider than high, which starts flowering when about 3 years old.
'Goldsworth Orange' Hardy. Salmon-pink flowers with orange shading and brown spots are borne in early summer. The upright shrub is compact in sun but can become open with age in the shade. It is a little slow to start flowering, at about 6 years old, but is hardy and easy to grow.
'Gomer Waterer' ♀ Hardy. Rosy lilac buds open to white flowers flushed with mauve-pink in early summer. The vigorous but dense and compact shrub has dark, leathery leaves. It is very free-flowering and hardy.
'Haida Gold' Woodland. Greenish yellow flowers open in late spring. This fairly compact, upright plant with bluish green foliage starts to flower quite young at 4–7 years old, but new growth comes early so is easily damaged by late frosts.
'Halfdan Lem' Hardy. Rich red flowers that tend to fade are borne in late spring in big trusses. Large, thick, deep green leaves and red buds enhance the vigorous plant, which is often wider than high and apt to sprawl with age. It needs a lot of room, but is hardy in most of Britain.
'Harvest Moon' Hardy. Full trusses of cream-coloured flowers with a small reddish brown flare open in late spring on a fairly compact plant with heavily veined leaves. It is hardy in most of Britain.

▲ *Rhododendron* 'Golden Torch'

'Hoppy' 'yak' hybrid. Plentiful, frilly flowers are pale lilac-pink fading to near white. They are borne in late spring to early summer on quite a tall plant with long, dark leaves. It starts flowering at 3 years old.
'Hotei'♀ Woodland. Heavy-textured flowers are deep yellow, each one encircled with a large yellow calyx. They are borne in mid to late spring on a well-branched plant which flowers when about 6 years old and requires some shade and good drainage. It is hardy enough for most of Britain.

▲ *Rhododendron* 'Hydon Dawn'

'Hydon Dawn'♀ 'yak' hybrid. Freely borne, frilled flowers of pale pink, deeper at the centre and fading to near white, open in late spring to early summer on a very compact bush. It is hardy and easy to grow.
'Jean Marie de Montague' (syn. 'The Hon. Jean Marie de Montague') Hardy. Bright red flowers open in late spring on an upright plant. It is hardy enough for all but the most severe conditions.
'Kluis Sensation'♀ Hardy. Dark red flowers spotted with crimson open in tight trusses in early summer. The slow-growing, fairly compact plant, as wide as it is high, is quite hardy but its dark crinkled foliage tends to turn yellowish.
'Lady Alice Fitzwilliam'♀ Tender. Scented flowers are pink in bud and open to white with some yellow in the throat. They are borne in mid to late spring on a fairly compact plant, about as wide as it is high. It is hardy enough for milder gardens and may do well on a sheltered wall in colder places.
'Lavender Girl'♀ Hardy. Lightly scented, lavender-pink flowers, paler in the centre, are borne in late spring. The vigorous, easily grown plant, as wide as it is high, is hardy throughout Britain.
'Linda'♀ *williamsianum* hybrid. Frilled, rose-pink flowers open in late spring. Pale green leaves do not appear early so are not vulnerable to frost damage. The very hardy plant is compact and as wide as it is high.
'Madame Masson' Hardy. Star-shaped, white flowers with a bold yellow flare are borne in tight, rounded trusses in early summer. The dense, spreading plant, which is easy to grow, has shiny leaves.
'May Day'♀ Woodland. Red to orange-red flowers are borne in mid to late spring.

▲ *Rhododendron* 'May Day'

The compact, rounded or flat-topped shrub is not suitable for the coldest gardens because it is vulnerable to bark-split.
'Mrs Furnival'♀ Hardy. Light rose-pink flowers with a bold, deeper flare open in late spring on a compact, rounded shrub.
'Mrs T.H. Lowinsky' Hardy. White flowers with a large orange-brown flare open from mauve pink buds in dense trusses in early summer. The compact, rounded plant is very hardy and easy to grow.
'Nancy Evans'♀ Woodland. Orange-red buds open to profuse, rounded trusses of deep yellow flowers in late spring. The neat, rounded plant with bronzy new growth needs good drainage and is then hardy in most gardens with a little shelter.
'Nobleanum' Hardy. This is usually the first rhododendron to open its flowers, at the end of autumn in mild areas, and in mid to late winter in cold areas. Several clones are available: **'Nobleanum'** and **'Nobleanum Coccineum'** have scarlet-rose flowers; **'Nobleanum Album'** has white flowers and **'Nobleanum Venustum'** produces white to pink flowers. The plant is hardy enough for most of Britain.
'Odee Wright' Woodland. Yellow flowers with pink tinges and light red spotting are borne in late spring. The slow-growing, neat plant with shiny, dark leaves is suitable for all but the coldest British gardens.
'Penheale Blue'♀ Small-leaved hybrid. Profuse, bright violet-blue flowers open in mid spring on a neat, rounded plant. The leaves seldom suffer from the leaf spot that afflicts many 'blue' hybrids. The plant is hardy but the flowers are borne early in the season and may be caught by frost.

▲ *Rhododendron* 'Nancy Evans'

▲ *Rhododendron* 'Penheale Blue'

'Percy Wiseman' 'yak' hybrid. The flowers, freely produced in late spring, are peach-pink and cream, fading to cream. The compact plant has pale green, rounded leaves. It is hardy anywhere in Britain.
'Pink Cherub'♀ 'yak' hybrid. Pale pink flowers that fade to near white open in late spring. The compact, rounded plant is free-flowering, hardy and easy to grow.
'Pink Pebble'♀ *williamsianum* hybrid. Bell-shaped, pink flowers open in mid to late spring on a plant with rounded leaves. It needs full light and is not hardy enough for the coldest gardens.
'Praecox'♀ Small-leaved hybrid. Rosy purple flowers are borne in clusters from multiple buds in early spring, but they are not frost resistant. The upright plant itself is hardy enough for any British garden.
'President Roosevelt' Hardy. Bright red flowers paling to near white in the centre are borne in rounded trusses in late spring. The leaves of this sprawling plant are variegated with yellow; leaves and branches that revert to green must be removed.
'Princess Alice'♀ Tender. Lightly lemon-scented, white flowers with a yellow flare open in mid spring. The plant is hardy enough to grow outside in mild areas and then keeps a neat shape, but if grown indoors it becomes straggly.
'St Breward'/'St Tudy'♀ Small-leaved hybrid. The two virtually indistinguishable sister seedlings bear masses of showy, violet-

▲ *Rhododendron* 'Pink Pebble'

▲ *Rhododendron* 'Scintillation'

▲ *Rhododendron* 'Surrey Heath'

▲ *Rhododendron* 'Temple Belle'

▲ *Rhododendron* 'Susan'

blue flowers in mid to late spring. The leaves, reddish when young, tend to suffer from leaf spot. These upright plants are hardy in all but the coldest British gardens.
'Scintillation'♀ Hardy. Pastel pink flowers with brown spotting are borne in early summer. The broad plant has glossy leaves and is hardy enough for any British garden.
'Sleepy' 'yak' hybrid. The pale purple flowers fading to off-white open in late spring. The plant tends to be untidy.
'Sneezy'♀ 'yak' hybrid. Pink flowers spotted with red and fading to pale pink open in late spring. This fairly neat, compact shrub is as wide as it is high.
'Snow Lady'♀ Small-leaved hybrid. Pure white flowers with black anthers open in clusters in early spring. The small, rounded plant is not hardy enough for the coldest gardens and is susceptible to mildew.
'Surrey Heath'♀ 'yak' hybrid. The pink flowers have paler centres that give a two-toned effect. They open in late spring on a compact, dense plant.
'Susan'♀ Hardy. Bluish mauve flowers, fading to pale lavender, open in late spring. Dark green leaves, with a thin layer of light fawn indumentum below, clothe a plant that is susceptible to mildew.
'Temple Belle'♀ *williamsianum* hybrid. Pendulous pink flowers are borne in mid to late spring. The neat, dense bush with rounded leaves is generally hardy, but its early growth may be caught by late frosts.
'The Hon Jean Marie de Montague' see 'Jean Marie de Montague'.
'Titian Beauty' 'yak' hybrid. Bright red flowers are freely produced in loose trusses in early summer and, unlike many other red 'yak' hybrids, these flowers do not fade out. The upright but neat and compact shrub is hardy in all but the coldest gardens.
'Tortoiseshell Orange'♀ has orange-red flowers and **'Tortoiseshell Wonder'**♀ has pale salmon-pink flowers. Woodland hybrids. A group of moderately hardy hybrids with a rather open habit and pastel-shaded flowers. These shrubs are not suitable for cold gardens.
'Unique'♀ Hardy hybrid. Pale ochre-yellow flowers, blushed pink fading to ivory white are borne in mid to late spring. It is a very tidy shrub with a dense habit and hardy enough for any British garden.
'Vanessa Pastel'♀ Woodland hybrid. The creamy pink and red flowers open in late spring to early summer. Suitable for moderately cold areas or a sheltered site, the beautiful hybrid has a fairly low habit and grows wider than its height. Its sister **'Vanessa'** has pinker flowers and a more sparse, upright habit. Not suitable for cold gardens.
'Venetian Chimes' 'yak' hybrid. Red flowers, borne in fairly compact trusses in late spring to early summer, fade to deep pink. The poor, rather thin foliage is easily damaged by sun and cold and the plant itself is not for very cold gardens.
'Vintage Rose'♀ 'yak' hybrid. Pale pink flowers in late spring to early summer are easily weather damaged. This compact plant with fine foliage grows wider than high. Not suitable for the coldest gardens.
'Vulcan'♀ Hardy hybrid. A vigorous plant bearing bright red flowers in domed trusses in early summer with narrow leaves. Hardy enough for any British garden, but its late growth can suffer frost damage in autumn.
'Wilgen's Ruby'♀ Hardy hybrid. Bright red flowers appear in late spring on this low, almost spreading bush. The red shade is not one of the best, however.
'Winsome'♀ Woodland hybrid. Bright pink flowers open in late spring. The compact plant has bronzy new growth and dark leaves. Not suitable for very cold gardens.

▲ *Rhododendron* 'Vanessa'

▲ *Rhododendron* 'Yellow Hammer'

'Yellow Hammer'♀ Small-leaved hybrid. Masses of tiny yellow flowers, some of which often open in autumn as well as in mid spring, combine with an abundance of tiny leaves. The straggly, upright hybrid benefits from pruning either when in flower or a few weeks later.

RHODODENDRON HYBRIDS, DWARF
This group of hybrids, reaching a height of up to 1m (3ft) in 10-15 years, includes the alpine types, generally with small leaves and a spreading habit. The flowers are about 2cm (¾in) long and the leaves grow up to 2.5cm (1in) long. Dwarf hybrids are at their best when planted in clumps.
'Anna Baldsiefen'♀ Small-leaved hybrid. Bright pink flowers open in early to mid spring on this neat, erect, columnar plant. Hardy, but rather early flowering for frost hollows and also subject to rust fungus.
'Bengal' *forrestii* hybrid. Bright red flowers open in mid to late spring. The low, dense, mounding hybrid, with smooth leaves, is very hardy and easy to please.
'Carmen'♀ *forrestii* hybrid. The deep red flowers are borne in mid to late spring. This popular and widely grown plant bears small, deep green leaves and has a tidy, compact habit. Not suitable for very cold gardens.
'Chikor' Small leaved hybrid. Masses of relatively large yellow flowers are borne in

▲ *Rhododendron* 'Bengal'

▲ *Rhododendron* 'Cilpinense'

late spring on this upright, but low-growing, twiggy plant with small leaves. It dislikes hot summers and resents fertiliser.

'Cilpinense'♀ Small leaved hybrid. Blush pink flowers cover the bush in early spring. The vigorous but fairly tidy grower has hairy leaves. Opening buds and flowers are very frost sensitive, so the plant is best suited to milder western areas.

'Curlew'♀ Small-leaved hybrid. Clear yellow flowers with red spotting are borne in mid to late spring on this dwarf hybrid. Not for the coldest gardens or frost pockets.

'Dora Amateis'♀ Small-leaved hybrid. Pure white flowers are borne in abundance in mid to late spring. The foliage of this semi-dwarf American hybrid can get rather yellowish, but the plant is very hardy and suitable for any British garden.

'Egret'♀ Small-leaved hybrid. Tiny, bell-shaped white flowers open in profusion in late spring amid small deep green leaves. The plant is hardy and easy to grow.

'Ginny Gee'♀ Small-leaved hybrid. Masses of pink and white flowers obscure the small leaves in mid to late spring. This very dense shrub, wider than it is tall, is hardy and easy to grow.

'Grumpy' 'yak' hybrid. Cream-coloured flowers, tinged pink at first, open in late

▲ *Rhododendron* 'Moerheim'

spring to early summer and contrast well with the handsome dark leaves. This is one of the lowest-growing 'yak' hybrids and is wider than it is high. The late second growth sometimes gets frosted.

'Merganser'♀ Small-leaved hybrid. Primrose-yellow, bell-shaped flowers are freely produced in late spring. The compact plant, wider than it is high, bears dark green, narrow leaves that are glaucous white below. Hardy and easy to grow in most of Britain.

'Moerheim'♀ Small-leaved hybrid. A low and compact shrub, wider than it is high, with small leaves and plentiful pale violet flowers in mid spring. The plant is a hardy and easy-to-grow hybrid.

'Patty Bee'♀ Small-leaved hybrid. The pale yellow flowers of this mound-forming plant are freely produced in mid to late spring. This shrub is one of the best hardy yellow-flowered dwarfs.

'Pink Drift' Small-leaved hybrid. A very dense-growing dwarf, usually wider than high, that bears an abundance of pinkish mauve flowers in late spring. The leaves are tiny. Hardy and easy to grow. The plant is susceptible to mildew.

'Princess Anne'♀ Small-leaved hybrid. Masses of pale yellow flowers appear in late spring. The hardy plant forms a compact spreading mound and the light green leaves are bronze when young.

'Ptarmigan'♀ Small-leaved hybrid. Plentiful pure white flowers, resembling a mantle of snow, are borne in early to mid spring. A little straggly when young, the plant soon forms a tight mound with tiny dark leaves. Although hardy, a favourable site is required to enjoy the early flowers.

'Ramapo'♀ Small-leaved hybrid. The pale violet flowers appear in mid to late spring. Fine grey-blue leaves cover this compact, vigorous plant that is wider than it is high. Exceptionally hardy.

'Razorbill'♀ Small-leaved hybrid. The long-lasting, bright pink tubular flowers open from multiple buds and are carried in

▲ *Rhododendron* 'Princess Anne'

▲ *Rhododendron* 'Ramapo'

upright clusters in mid to late spring. The attractive crinkled leaves cover a fairly vigorous, mound-forming plant. The shrub is sufficiently hardy for most of Britain.

'St Merryn'♀ Small-leaved hybrid. The plentiful rich violet-blue flowers open in mid to late spring. Growing wider than high, this is one of the smallest 'blue' hybrids and has dark foliage.

'Sapphire'♀ Small-leaved hybrid. A spreading, open shrub that produces light purple-blue flowers in mid spring and small leaves. Reasonably hardy.

'Sarled'♀ Small-leaved hybrid. Long-lasting tubular flowers open pale pink and fade to creamy white in late spring. This upright, neat, compact plant has tiny, narrow leaves. It is easy to grow and quite hardy.

'Scarlet Wonder'♀ *forrestii* hybrid. An abundance of bright red flowers are borne in late spring. This fairly compact and spreading shrub grows wider than high. One of the most popular dwarf red-flowered shrubs, it is very hardy.

'Snipe'♀ Small-leaved hybrid. Masses of lavender-pink flowers, fading to pale pink, open in early to mid spring and completely hide the foliage. The compact rounded plant grows as wide as it is high. The flowers are vulnerable to frost and the plant is

▲ *Rhododendron* 'Snipe'

rather susceptible to powdery mildew.
'Teal' Small-leaved hybrid. Relatively large yellow flowers appear in late spring on this upright but tidy shrub. The plant is not suitable for very cold gardens.
'Wee Bee' Small-leaved hybrid. Two-toned dark and light pink flowers are borne in abundance in mid to late spring. This very compact and low-growing plant is hardy, but the flowers may be frost-damaged in colder areas.
'Wren' Small-leaved hybrid. The yellow flowers, spotted red, are freely produced in late spring on this slow-growing, spreading, very dwarf hybrid. It is hardy enough for all but the coldest gardens, but needs good soil conditions with organic matter and must not be allowed to dry out.

Azaleas

AZALEA SPECIES
The deciduous azaleas are mostly very hardy, tolerate full sun or light shade and will stand cutting back hard after flowering (except in the rare cases when they are grafted). Their flowering season begins from late spring to mid summer, often with scented flowers. The plants reach a height and spread of 1-2.5×1-2.5 m (3-8×3-8 ft) in 10-15 years and have light green leaves which develop fine autumn colour in some species. Azalea mildew affects the leaves of some species and their hybrids.

r

R. albrechtii♀ Flat-faced flowers in bright rose-purple to deep rose are 4 cm (1½ in) across and are borne in mid to late spring. The upright, tidy, twiggy shrub has leaves 11 cm (4¼ in) long. Although very hardy, its flowers and growth are early so it does best sheltered by light woodland.
R. dilatatum see *R. reticulatum*
R. luteum♀ (syn. *A. ponticum, R. flavum*) (common yellow azalea, Pontic azalea). The bright yellow flowers, 5 cm (2 in) across, are strongly fragrant, and are borne in late spring to early summer. The upright, spreading, sometimes suckering plant is very hardy and has leaves 12.5 cm (5 in) long that colour brilliantly in autumn.
R. occidentale♀ Fragrant white flowers, 10 cm (4 in) across, are sometimes flushed pink and have a yellow blotch. The flowers are borne in mid to late summer on a tall plant which is hardy in most areas. The shiny leaves, 10 cm (4 in) long, need watching for mildew. (See also Azalea hybrids, Occidentale.)

▲ *Rhododendron luteum*

R. reticulatum♀ (syn. *R. dilatatum, R. wadanum*) Flowers, 5 cm (2 in) across, are borne singly or in pairs, in shades of purple or white in mid spring to early summer on a broad plant that has tiered branches. The leaves are 6 cm (2½ in) long, usually in groups of 3 and often turn purple in autumn. The plant is very hardy in areas with hot summers where wood is well-ripened, but it is less successful in the north.
R. schlippenbachii♀ (royal azalea) The almost flat flowers, 8 cm (3¼ in) across, vary from rose-pink to white and are borne in late spring. The symmetrical bush has leaves 12 cm (4¾ in) long. Although hardy, it needs shelter to protect its early growth.
R. vaseyi♀ (pink shell azalea) Flowers in shades of pink or white, 5 cm (2 in) across, appear in mid to late spring. The narrow, willow-like leaves, 12.5 cm (5 in) long, of this hardy broad plant turn red in autumn.

▲ *Rhododendron reticulatum*

R. viscosum♀ (swamp azalea) The flowers are usually white and sticky with a spicy fragrance. They are up to 4 cm (1½ in) across with a narrow tube and are borne in early to late summer. The leaves are 7.5 cm (3 in) long on a hardy, upright, suckering plant. It needs moist soil.
R. wadanum see *R. reticulatum*

Rhododendron schlippenbachii

AZALEA HYBRIDS, GHENT/RUSTICA
The flowers on these very hardy plants are 6 cm (2½ in) across with long tubes, and are carried in trusses in late spring to early summer. Most have no scent. The shrubs reach a height and spread of 2.4 m (8 ft).
'Coccineum Speciosum'♀ bears brilliant orange-red flowers. **'Daviesii'**♀ has white flowers with a yellow blotch. Two plants are sold by this name, one of them scented. In **'Homebush'**♀ the double, deep carmine flowers are in rounded trusses. **'Narcissiflorum'** has double flowers of pale yellow.
AZALEA HYBRIDS, KNAPHILL/EXBURY
The largest and brightest azalea flowers are found in this group of plants, and some are scented. They come into flower between late spring and early summer. Some have red or bronze-tinted foliage, some have fine autumn colour, and some have both. Seedlings are often sold unnamed, simply by colour. The plants listed are very hardy and in a favourable site reach a height and spread of 2.4 m (8 ft) in 15 years.
'Berryrose'♀ has deep pink flowers with a yellow blotch and coppery young leaves. **'Cecile'**♀ bears salmon-pink flowers with a deep blotch; it is not a strong grower. **'Fireball'** has deep orange-red flowers and bronzy foliage. **'Gibraltar'**♀ bears vivid

▲ *Rhododendron* 'Narcissiflorum'

▲ *Rhododendron* 'Gibraltar'

▲ *Rhododendron* 'Satan'

orange flowers. **'Glowing Embers'** has reddish orange flowers with an orange blotch. The flowers of **'Klondyke'**🏆 are scented, large and golden yellow, and the young foliage is coppery red. **'Persil'**🏆 has a yellow flare on the white flowers. In **'Satan'**🏆 the flowers are scarlet and there is good autumn colour. **'Silver Slipper'**🏆 has white flowers that are flushed pink and have a yellow blotch. **'Strawberry Ice'**🏆 bears pale pink flowers shaded with yellow. In **'Sun Chariot'**🏆 the buttercup-yellow flowers have a deep orange eye. **'Surprise'** has large, frilled flowers of orange-yellow.

AZALEA HYBRIDS, MOLLIS

These azaleas are selections or seedlings of the Japanese species *R. molle* ssp. *japonicum*. The unscented flowers in late spring are usually available in red, orange, salmon or yellow. Flowers are funnel-shaped, about 6cm (2½in) long and held in trusses. The plants are very hardy with an upright, bushy habit, and grow to about 1.4m (4½ft).

AZALEA HYBRIDS, OCCIDENTALE

All these plants, derived from the species *R. occidentale* (see Azalea species), are sweetly scented and flower very freely in late spring to early summer, bearing blooms up to 7.5cm (3in) across in trusses. They are

▲ *Rhododendron* 'Strawberry Ice'

hardy, reach a height of 2.1-2.4m (7-8ft), and usually spread wider than high. They need watching for mildew.

'Delicatissimum'🏆 has cream flowers tinged pink and with a yellow flare. **'Exquisitum'** is cream flushed pink and with an orange flare. **'Irene Koster'** is pale pink inside, fading to white, with a deeper pink outside.

AZALEA HYBRIDS, JAPANESE (EVERGREEN)

The name used to refer to these plants is not strictly accurate since they are not all from Japan and not all completely evergreen. These azaleas can generally stand hotter and drier sites than dwarf rhododendrons. They should be planted in full sun in the north and light shade in the south. There are numerous tender varieties grown as houseplants and frequently brought into flower for Christmas – *R. simsii* for example; they are seldom sold as named cultivars. Although evergreen azaleas are easy to grow, they need watching for the unsightly swellings caused by galls, which form on leaves and young shoots (also occasionally on flowers) soon after new growth unfurls.

▲ *Rhododendron* 'Exquisitum'

The average size of the plants listed is 60cm-1m (2-3ft) tall and the same in spread; those described as low or creeping seldom exceed 30cm (1ft). The plants have small, dark, glossy leaves and bear masses of wide funnel flowers, about 4cm (1½in) across, in shades of red, purplish pink, salmon and white, and held in trusses. Some have 'hose-in-hose' flowers with one flower inside another. Varieties described as 'early' flower in late spring, 'mid season' flower in late spring to early summer, and 'late' flower in early to mid summer.

'Addy Wery'🏆 is upright with vermilion flowers borne early. **'Alexander'** is creeping and bears its reddish orange blooms very late. **'Amoenum'** makes a low plant with rosy purple, hose-in-hose blooms in mid season. **'Beethoven'**🏆 is of medium height with large lilac-mauve flowers in mid season. **'Blaauw's Pink'**🏆 has salmon-pink hose-in-hose flowers early on a medium plant. **'Blue Danube'** has large bluish lilac flowers in early to mid season on a low plant. **'Buccaneer'** is an upright plant whose warm orange flowers are early. **'Chippewa'** has bright pink flowers late and is good in the north. **'Diamant'**, a range of very low, dense plants that do well in the north, has early blooms in white, pink, rosy red or lilac-purple. **'Favorite'** has deep rosy pink, early flowers on a medium shrub. **'Florida'**🏆 has deep red, hose-in-hose blooms in mid season on a medium plant. **'Geisha Orange'** is low with reddish orange early blooms and is good in the north. The low, spreading **'Hatsugiri'**🏆 has early, magenta flowers. **'Hino-crimson'**, a low to medium grower, bears strong red blooms in early to mid season. **'Hinodegiri'** carries bright crimson, early flowers on a low to medium plant. **'Hino-mayo'**🏆 is low and nearly deciduous, with bright pink, early to mid season flowers. **'Irohayama'**🏆 has mauve-pink, white-centred blooms in

▲ *Rhododendron* 'Hino-crimson'

▲ *Rhododendron* 'Hinode-giri'

▲ *Rhododendron* 'John Cairns'

mid season on a medium bush. **'Johanna'**, also medium, has carmine-red flowers in mid season and handsome foliage. The medium to tall **'John Cairns'**♀ has large scarlet flowers in mid season. **'Kermesina'** makes low, compact growth, thrives in the north and has mid season, deep pink blooms. **'Kirin'**♀ has hose-in-hose, mid season flowers in two shades of pink on a medium plant that is not very hardy. **Kure-no-Yuki'**♀ is low, with white flowers in mid season. **'Lemur'** does well in the north, with pink flowers in mid season. **'Leo'**♀ has orange-pink, mid season blooms on a low, spreading shrub. **'Mother's Day'**♀, also low and spreading, carries its large crimson flowers in early to mid season. ***R. nakaharae*** is a creeping plant that does well in the north and flowers late; the form sold as **'Mariko'** has scarlet flowers. **'Orange Beauty'**♀ flowers are early and salmon-orange on a medium shrub that is good in the north. **'Palestrina'**♀ has white, early to mid season flowers on an erect, medium plant. **'Panda'** does well in the north, with pure white blooms borne in mid season on a low plant. **'Pink Pancake'** is low, spreading and late to bear its blooms of strong pink. **'Purple Triumph'** has purple flowers in early to mid season on a low shrub. **'Rosebud'**♀ has double pink blooms in mid season on a medium shrub. **'Squirrel'** is low to medium and does well in the north, bearing its bright red blooms late. **'Stewartstonian'**♀ has large red flowers in early to mid season on a medium plant. **'Vida Brown'**, a low grower, has crimson, hose-in-hose blooms in mid to late season. **'Vuyk's Rosy Red'**♀ bears large reddish pink flowers in mid season on a low to medium shrub. **'Vuyk's Scarlet'**♀, of similar size, has early crimson flowers and does well in the north. **'Wombat'**, also good in the north, is low and spreading with pink flowers in mid season.

▲ *Rhododendron* 'Leo'

CULTIVATION Rhododendrons thrive only in an acid soil that is moist but well drained. Their fibrous root system appreciates a relatively loose, friable soil that the roots can easily penetrate. Open up clay soil by working in plenty of gritty sand and also organic matter such as oak or beech leaf-mould; or instead use conifer needles or a compost of bracken, bark, straw or garden and household waste. Alternatively, make a raised bed to lift the roots partly above the normal surface. Mix the original soil with lighter soil from elsewhere, or use new soil entirely.

If the soil is alkaline, build an isolated raised bed lined with permeable woven plastic and fill it with suitable soil or ericaceous (lime-free) compost. In very wet areas plant on a mound and in a dry area plant in a slight hollow.

Rhododendrons must be planted at the correct depth. The rootball needs covering with no more than 2-3cm (about 1in) of soil. Planting too deeply can stunt or kill the plant. Plants from open ground establish better and faster in a garden than those grown in containers. The usual age on sale is a 2 to 5-year-old plant. Plants 6-10 years old or more are sold but are much more expensive. Rhododendron planting can be

▲ *Rhododendron* 'Kirin'

▲ *Rhododendron* 'Rosebud'

▲ *Rhododendron* 'Vuyk's Scarlet'

done at any time, particularly from containers, but autumn planting is best. It gives the plant time to form new roots before growth starts in spring. Spring planting entails much more aftercare with watering, and even more care is needed by plants put in during the growing season.

If it is necessary to transplant a rhododendron, do it in autumn or early spring. The shallow root ball is easy to lift intact. Put the plant on a sheet of thick polythene and pull it to the new position.

Generally the larger the leaf of a plant, the more shade and shelter from wind the rhododendron needs. Shade from early morning sun helps to reduce frost damage to early flowering varieties. Young plants are especially vulnerable to frost and cold. To protect them, cover them overnight at risky periods with cloches, or with garden fleece or light sacking supported on canes to keep it clear of the plants. Remove covers in the morning once the frost has gone.

It is also worth giving longer protection to young plants in mid winter, especially over their first season. Make a wigwam from evergreen conifer branches pushed in the ground and tied at the top; or with a circle of wire netting, kept in place with canes and covered with branches, or filled with loose bracken fronds or conifer shoots.

Protection from wind and sun can be provided by widely spaced trees that have open crowns, and these do not take too much of the ground's moisture. A building gives shade but can produce harmful air turbulence. The best wind shelter is a permeable windbreak that filters wind and reduces its strength. Woven plastic netting makes a temporary windbreak but the best long-term solution is a hedge or a belt of trees.

Water rhododendrons in dry weather, especially in the first season after planting and when they are making new growth. Soak the soil well occasionally rather than watering little and often. Fine mist, small drops or water from a seep hose is best.

Keep the ground under and close to rhododendrons free of plants that compete for moisture and nutrients. Plants that like the same conditions as rhododendrons but will not compete include primulas, lilies, meconopsis, gentians, trilliums and erythroniums put in groups between the rhododendrons. Shrubs and smaller-leaved trees that are suitable include camellias, cornus, some maples, viburnums and cotoneasters.

Mulching helps to conserve moisture, reduce weed growth, moderate soil temperature and eventually add humus to the soil. Mulching with leaf-mould, garden compost or rotted bracken is best as they help provide nutrients that plants require and do not use up the soil's nitrogen, which other mulches such as pulverised bark and wood chips, often do as they break down. Many dwarf plants are intolerant of fertilisers and are easily scorched.

Apply 2.5 cm (1 in) of a fine mulch every year, or apply up to 7.5 cm (3 in) of a coarse mulch of bark or wood chips every 2-3 years. Do not build up a mulch too deep and bury the rhododendron roots. Do not use fresh grass mowings. They keep out water and a thick layer generates enough heat to kill rhododendron roots.

Deadheading faded flower trusses brings on better new growth and more flower buds for the next season. Young plants and those that have flowered very freely should have preference if time is limited. Take care not to break off or damage the buds or young shoots just below the flowers.

Growing in containers 'Yak' hybrids are perhaps the best choice for containers; they are hardy, free-flowering, leafy and fairly slow-growing. Evergreen azaleas are suitable for smaller pots if space is limited.

Use an acid, free-draining compost such as peat mixed with composted bark, good garden soil, leaf-mould or grit. Add slow-release fertiliser. Wrap the pot to protect the roots in cold weather, and shade it in hot weather.

Tender rhododendrons and azaleas can also be grown in containers to bring into the house when in flower and put outside in the shade for the summer. They need careful watering. When the pots are outside, plunge them into cool, moist soil if possible. Indoors, they cannot tolerate hot, dry air for long so keep them in a cool porch or unheated room as much as possible.

The plants can stay in containers for years. Repot smaller ones into a slightly larger pot every second year and give liquid or slow-release food in the growing season. Remove part of the roots of large plants every 2 to 3 years and put them back in the same pot with fresh compost added.

PROPAGATION For species, reliable seed collected in the wild or from hand-pollinated plants is available from rhododendron societies, but vegetative reproduction is easier. Always propagate hybrids vegetatively; seedlings from them vary greatly from the parent and are usually inferior.

If seed is used, sow it in spring or, if heat and artificial light are available, sow as soon as it is ripe when the capsules turn brown and start to split open. Sow in peat or sifted fresh sphagnum moss. Water from beneath to avoid botrytis. When large enough to handle, prick seedlings out into a tray of pure peat or an acidic humus-rich compost leaf-mould mixture. Keep seedlings in the protection of a greenhouse or frame for their first winter.

Rhododendrons vary in their readiness to root from cuttings. The easiest are cuttings of evergreen azaleas and dwarf rhododendrons, which root more quickly with bottom heat. If using bottom heat, keep the temperature at 21°C (70°F) or lower, as too high a temperature encourages rotting. Remove well-rooted cuttings from bottom heat. Take cuttings from mid summer onwards as shoots become springy when bent instead of breaking. Wound thicker cuttings on one or both sides to encourage rooting. Grafting is needed to raise those plants that are almost impossible to root, but this is better left to professionals.

Layering is an easy way to propagate a plant in the garden. Help layers of larger varieties to root by wounding the bark underneath. Keep the layer moist throughout the growing season. It takes a few years for an adequate root system to develop.

PRUNING Most rhododendrons need no pruning, but old or straggly specimens benefit from being cut back. The best times to prune are late winter, especially for late-flowering plants, or just after flowering.

As a rule, smooth-barked rhododendrons – mostly species – do not respond well to being cut back but the commoner hybrids do. Carry out severe pruning in two or three stages, leaving some foliage each time. Remove the thick branches first and, if these put out new growth, cut back or remove altogether the thinner branches.

Most small-leaved species and hybrids can be trimmed after flowering to maintain a compact shape, without loss of flowering. Most deciduous azaleas can be invigorated or reduced in size by pruning.

PESTS AND DISEASES Vine weevil larvae eat plants at and below soil level and are especially injurious to young plants in containers. Adult vine weevils, greenfly (aphids), caterpillars and slugs eat new leaves. Rabbits and deer feed on azaleas and dwarf rhododendrons.

Grey mould (botrytis) afflicts seedlings in autumn and winter. Powdery mildew may be troublesome on established plants. Honey fungus is the worst killer of rhododendrons. Phytophthora, root rot, mostly affects plants that have been kept too wet and too warm; plants grown in containers are especially at risk. Rust fungus attacks plants but is rarely fatal. Unsightly galls may occur on evergreen azaleas and some rhododendron hybrids.

Rhodohypoxis
Hypoxidaceae

Rhodohypoxis baurii 'Fred Broome'

These dwarf bulbs produce a continuous display of flowers from spring to the end of summer. The six-petalled flowers offer a range of pastel colours from warm white to dusky ruby, and each flower lasts for several weeks. The velvety petals are arranged in two sets of three, one set above the other. Although not fully hardy, they may be grown in warm spots where little frost occurs, or in a container that can be moved to a frost-free place. All put up tufts of grassy, linear to lance-shaped foliage, and have corm-like rootstocks. Plants are usually grouped together. Native to SE Africa.

RECOMMENDED SPECIES AND VARIETIES

R. baurii ♀ Flowers varying from white to red, 1.5-2cm (½-¾in) wide, rise singly on hairy stems, amid prominently hairy, dull green leaves that are about 5cm (2in) long. HEIGHT & SPREAD 10×5cm (4×2in).

'Alba' has white flowers. **'Albrighton'** bears flowers of a deep pink. Red or deep pink flowers are borne by var. *baurii*. **'Dawn'** produces large, pale pink flowers that fade to white. **'Douglas'** has flowers of a rich, deep red. **'Eva-Kate'** is a large form with deep pink flowers. **'Fred Broome'** produces rich, shell-pink flowers with firm, broad petals. **'Harlequin'** is a pink and white bi-coloured form. **'Margaret Rose'** has well-shaped, large pink flowers. **'Perle'** has clear white flowers. **'Picta'** bears large white flowers tipped with pink. **'Ruth'** is a large, white-flowered form. **'Stella'** has deep pink flowers. **'Susan Garnett-Botfield'** is very free-flowering, with pink blooms. **'Tetra Red'** has red flowers.

R. milloides Red to magenta, occasionally white or pink, flowers up to 4cm (1½in) across are borne singly on hairy stems. This is a taller, erect species with almost hairless bright green leaves up to 15cm (6in) across, spreading readily by stolons. HEIGHT & SPREAD 18×15cm (7×6in).

CULTIVATION Plant in a light, sandy, neutral to acid soil with added humus in early autumn. The soil must retain moisture without becoming clammy in summer. Grow in full sun in northern Britain, but in southern Britain plants benefit from light shade. Provide a warm, sheltered position with winter protection from excessive wetness, and guard against spring frosts. Water in warm, dry weather. Divide plants every 3-4 years, in late spring, to keep them healthy and flowering freely.

PROPAGATION Sow seed in early spring. Alternatively, divide clustered corms in late spring, during their growing season.

PESTS AND DISEASES Mice unearth and eat corms. Wireworms can also cause damage.

▲ *Rhodohypoxis baurii* 'Fred Broome'

▲ *Rhodohypoxis baurii* 'Picta'

r

Rhoeo see *Tradescantia*

Rhoicissus
Vitaceae

Rhoicissus capensis

These tender, evergreen, climbing shrubs produce lustrous large-leaved foliage, held on twining stems. They climb by means of tendrils. *R. capensis* is ideal for the house, conservatory or greenhouse. It is easily grown, not harmed by gas or oil fumes and may be set in a fairly shaded, but not dark, position. Grow in a pot, supported by canes or a moss stick, or in a border, allowing the plant to climb a trellis or screen. Native to tropical and southern Africa.

RECOMMENDED SPECIES AND VARIETIES

R. capensis ♀ This ornamental plant has shiny, dark green, tooth-edged leaves that grow to 20cm (8in) long and consist of 3-5 diamond-shaped leaflets. Pale reddish brown hairs cover the leaves and stems when young. HEIGHT & SPREAD 1m×50cm (3ft×20in) after 5 years, ultimately 2m×50cm (6½ft×20in) in a pot; ultimately 6×1m (20×3ft) in a greenhouse border.

CULTIVATION Grow plants in John Innes No.2 potting compost, or in a greenhouse border in a similar compost. Rhoicissus species require a minimum temperature of 7-10°C (45-50°F). Give plants plenty of light in winter, but move them to a lightly shaded spot in summer. Water carefully in summer and apply liquid feed every 2 weeks. Water sparingly in winter, never allowing a plant to become waterlogged. Mist plants occasionally in summer. Repot annually in mid spring.

PROPAGATION Take 10cm (4in) cuttings in mid or late spring.

PRUNING Pinch back growths 2 or 3 times in the first spring or summer to encourage bushy growth. If plants become too large, cut them back by up to two-thirds.

PESTS AND DISEASES Usually trouble free.

Rhubarb, edible see p.730
Rhubarb ornamental see *Rheum*

Rhus
Sumac
Anacardiaceae

Rhus typhina

Brilliant shades of red, orange and yellow colour these hardy deciduous shrubs or small trees in autumn. Grown for their large pinnate leaves, some sumacs produce unusual fruit in autumn. Insignificant green flowers appear in spring. The sap of some species can be an irritant. Sumacs will grow in any soil but may be invasive.

RECOMMENDED SPECIES AND VARIETIES

***R. glabra* 'Laciniata'** hort. see *R.* × *pulvinata* Autumn Lace Group

R. hirta see *R. typhina*

***R.* × *pulvinata* Autumn Lace Group** (syn. *R. glabra* 'Laciniata' hort.) The leaves, 45cm (1½ft) long, have 11-31, deeply cut, mid green leaflets that turn to orange or yellow in autumn. The plant has a suckering habit. HEIGHT & SPREAD 3×3m (10×10ft) after 10 years, ultimately 4m (13ft) tall.

'Red Autumn Lace' has dissected leaflets that turn a fiery red in autumn.

R. typhina ♀ (syn. *R. hirta*) (stags-horn sumac) The leaves, up to 45cm (1½ft) long, have 11-13, mid-green leaflets with toothed edges. These change to shades of yellow, orange, red and purple in autumn. Upright,

▲ *Rhus typhina* 'Dissecta'

furry crimson fruit, up to 20cm (8in) long, appear in autumn. It has a suckering habit and can spread widely. HEIGHT & SPREAD 3.5×5m (12×16ft) after 10 years, ultimately 8m (26ft) tall.

In autumn, the deeply cut leaves of **'Dissecta'**♀ (syn. 'Laciniata') turn to shades of yellow and red.

CULTIVATION Plant in spring in any well-drained garden soil, preferably in full sun.

PROPAGATION Dig up and transplant suckers in autumn or spring. Alternatively, take root cuttings in early winter.

PRUNING Cut plants back hard in winter, although this will have the disadvantage of stimulating those with a suckering habit.

PESTS AND DISEASES Verticillium wilt may be a problem.

Ribes

Ornamental currant
Grossulariaceae

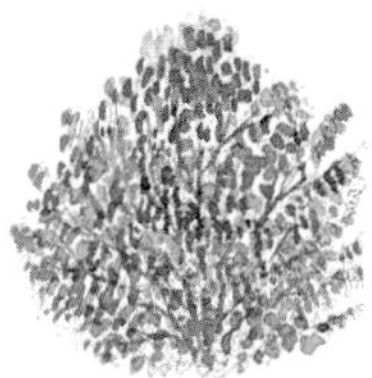

Ribes sanguineum 'Brocklebankii'

Clusters of spring flowers shaped like fuchsias, and lobed, green or gold leaves that may colour vividly in autumn give a long period of interest to the ornamental currant. The alternate leaves have three to five lobes and grow to 7.5cm (3in) long. The small, five-petalled flowers grow in racemes up to 10cm (4in) long and are very showy on some species. The plants sometimes bear small round black or red fruits in summer. Some are evergreens, all are hardy.

RECOMMENDED SPECIES AND VARIETIES

R. alpinum (mountain currant) The leaves of this tall shrub turn bright yellow in autumn. The small greenish yellow flowers appear in mid spring. Native to N Europe. HEIGHT & SPREAD 1×1m (3×3ft) after 5 years, ultimately 2m (6½ft) tall.

'Aureum' has golden leaves that blaze in full sun. It is smaller than the species, often broader than it is tall.

R. americanum Red, orange and yellow tints light up the autumn foliage. The leaves have a number of coarse teeth on their outer edge and emit a strong odour when crushed. The spring flowers are yellow. Native to eastern N America. HEIGHT & SPREAD 1×1m (3×3ft) after 5 years, ultimately 1.5m (5ft) tall.

'Variegatum' has cream and pale green streaks on the leaves. The autumn colour is not as bright as the species.

R. × gordonianum Long, drooping clusters of small red flowers with a yellow centre are carried on the rounded shrub in mid spring. HEIGHT & SPREAD 1×1m (3×3ft) after 5 years, ultimately 2m (6½ft) tall.

R. laurifolium This small evergreen shrub has greenish yellow flowers in late winter. The dark green leaves, lighter underneath, have small teeth rather than lobes and are up to 12.5cm (5in) long. Native to China. HEIGHT & SPREAD 50×50cm (20×20in) after 5 years, ultimately 1m (3ft) tall.

▲ *Ribes laurifolium*

R. odoratum (buffalo currant) Bright yellow, clove-scented flower clusters bloom in mid to late spring on the small, spreading shrub. Pale green leaves, usually deeply toothed, turn red and purple in autumn. Native to central USA. HEIGHT & SPREAD 1×1m (3×3ft) after 5 years, ultimately 2m (6½ft) tall.

▲ *Ribes odoratum*

R. sanguineum (flowering currant) Small rosy-red flowers appear in mid spring. They have a rather pungent smell. The shrub has a rounded, spreading habit and is the most commonly grown ornamental currant. Native to western N America. HEIGHT & SPREAD 1.2×1.2m (4×4ft) after 5 years, ultimately 2m (6½ft) tall.

▲ *Ribes sanguineum* 'King Edward VII'

'Brocklebankii'♀ has pale yellow leaves and pale pink flowers in mid spring. It does not grow as big as the species. **'King Edward VII'** has deep red flowers which appear in drooping bunches in early spring. It has a lower, more spreading habit than the species and is slower growing. **'Pulborough Scarlet'**♀ has a profusion of deep red flowers on drooping racemes in mid spring. It is the best of the red-flowered varieties. **'Tydeman's White'**♀ is the best white-flowering variety, producing clusters of white flowers in mid spring.

▲ *Ribes sanguineum* 'Brocklebankii'

R. speciosum♀ Profuse pendulous clusters of deep red flowers bloom in mid to late spring on the rounded shrub. The glossy green leaves are semi-evergreen. This Californian plant is only moderately frost hardy and usually needs the protection of a wall. HEIGHT & SPREAD 1×1m (3×3ft) after 5 years, ultimately 3m (10ft) tall.

CULTIVATION Ribes tolerate a wide range of soil types and growing conditions.

PROPAGATION Raise deciduous species from hardwood cuttings taken in autumn. Raise evergreen species from semi-ripe cuttings taken in autumn.

PRUNING Flowers are carried on the previous season's growth, so trim the plant immediately after flowering to maintain good shape. At the same time, cut back some of the older stems to ground level. This encourages new growth and better flowering, but any berries are lost.

PESTS AND DISEASES Usually trouble free.

Ricinus

Castor-oil plant
Euphorbiaceae

Ricinus communis

This fast-growing tropical shrub from Africa is grown as a half-hardy annual or as a conservatory plant for its striking foliage. Most varieties usually reach a height of 1.2-1.8m (4-6ft). The seed coats are extremely poisonous and are best removed as they ripen. *Ricimus communis* is the only species in the genus.

Ricinus communis This branching shrub carries long-stalked leaves that are 25cm (10in) or more across. The leaves are deeply lobed in 5-11 segments which are toothed, glossy and deep bronze when young. Insignificant green and red flowers are borne in clusters. Female plants bear clusters of spiny fruits which burst open to reveal hard black seeds. HEIGHT & SPREAD 1m×60cm (3×2ft) as an annual outdoors, 1.8×1.5m (6×5ft) in containers.

Heights given for cultivars are for plants in their first season's growth. **'Carmencita'** has shiny dark brown leaves and bright red flower buds and seed pods. It reaches 1.8m (6ft) tall. **'Gibsonii'** has dark purple-red foliage with a metallic sheen and grows to 1.5m (5ft) tall. The lower leaves of **'Impala'** are bronze-green and the upper leaves are bronze-carmine. Creamy yellow flowers are followed by maroon seed pods. It grows to 1.2m (4ft) tall. **'Zanzibarensis'** has large white-veined green to reddish purple leaves. It grows to 2.4m (8ft) tall.

CULTIVATION Plant in moist fertile soil in sun when all risk of frost has passed. Water and feed in dry weather. For conservatories plant in pots 20cm (8in) across, or in beds.

PROPAGATION Sow seeds individually in 10cm (4in) pots in early spring. Soak the seeds for 24 hours before sowing. Germinate in warm conditions and grow on in a heated greenhouse or conservatory.

PESTS AND DISEASES Young plants are susceptible to damping off and stem rot.

▼ *Ricinus communis* 'Carmencita'

Robinia

Leguminosae

Robinia pseudoacacia 'Frisia'

Hanging clusters of white or pink, often scented, sweetpea-like flowers add to the decorative value of the light and airy foliage of these small to medium deciduous trees and shrubs. The delicate leaves, made up of numerous small leaflets, are borne alternately on slender branches that tend to be of angular appearance and are often thorny; they can be quite brittle and are prone to break in heavy winds. A native of N America and Mexico.

RECOMMENDED SPECIES AND VARIETIES

R. hispida♀ (rose acacia) Small pink flowers appear in early to mid summer on pendulous racemes up to 7.5cm (3in) long. The dark green, pinnate leaves grow to 25cm (10in). The rounded shrub is moderately frost hardy, but needs protection from winds. HEIGHT & SPREAD 1×1m (3×3ft) after 5 years, ultimately about 2.4m (8ft) tall.

▲ *Robinia hispida*

R. × margaretta Pale pink flowers are produced on 15cm (6in) racemes in early summer on this frost-hardy large shrub or small tree. The pale green leaves grow to 25cm (10in) long and have rounded leaflets. HEIGHT & SPREAD 2×2m (6½×6½ft) after 5 years, ultimately about 4m (13ft) tall.

The cultivar **'Pink Cascade'** has larger flowers that are deeper in colour. It grows slightly larger than the species.

R. pseudoacacia♀ (false acacia) The elegant, upright tree has an open habit and 30cm (12in) long delicate leaves that are light green above and pale blue-green beneath. The shoots are well armed with thorns. The small white flowers in 20cm (8in) long racemes appear in early summer and are slightly scented. The plant is extremely hardy. HEIGHT & SPREAD 1.5×1m (5×3ft) after 5 years, ultimately 20m (66ft) tall.

▲ *Robinia pseudoacacia*

Robinia pseudoacacia 'Bessoniana' ▼

'Bessoniana' is smaller than the species and has a narrower crown. It is almost thornless, but does not flower as well as the species. **'Frisia'** is an elegant small tree reaching an ultimate height of only 9m (30ft). In spring the leaves emerge a bright yellow-gold. It retains its leaf colour better if planted in full sun.

R. × slavinii Pale pink flowers are borne in racemes 10cm (4in) long in early summer on this elegant small tree. It is a good choice for a small garden. HEIGHT & SPREAD 120×60cm (4×2ft) after 5 years, ultimately 6m (20ft) tall.

'Hillieri'♀ has small, slightly scented lilac-pink flowers.

CULTIVATION Robinias thrive under a wide range of conditions.
PROPAGATION Seed of the species can be sown in spring, but the cultivars need to be grafted. *R. pseudoacacia* suckers freely, and the suckers can be transplanted.
PRUNING Not generally necessary.
PESTS AND DISEASES Usually trouble free.

Rockcress see *Arabis*
Rock jasmine see *Androsace*

Rodgersia

Saxifragaceae

Large, divided leaves, held well above ground level on long stalks, give these hardy perennials architectural value in the garden, particularly beside ponds and in boggy ground. The foliage can be subtly coloured with bronze tints. Plumes of tiny star-like flowers appear in mid summer carried well above the foliage, though they are not always reliably produced. The plants are native to China, Japan and Korea.

RECOMMENDED SPECIES AND VARIETIES
R. aesculifolia♀ Green and bronze-tinged crinkled leaves, 5cm (10in) across, resemble large horse-chestnut leaves with coarsely toothed, deep lobes. Plumes of very small, fragrant flowers are white with a pink tinge. HEIGHT & SPREAD 1.2m×90cm (4×3ft).
R. pinnata Deep green leaves are arranged in pairs of leaflets with each leaflet 20cm

▼ *Rodgersia pinnata*

▲ *Rodgersia pinnata* 'Superba'

(8in) long. Tall plumes carry a mass of flowers in shades of white, yellow or pink.

'Elegans' has cream flowers with a pink tinge. The green leaves of **'Superba'**♀ are tinted bronze and the branched sprays of rose-pink flowers are over 50cm (20in) long. HEIGHT & SPREAD 1×1m (3×3ft).
R. podophylla♀ Deeply veined leaves are bronze when young, becoming green and fading to copper tints in autumn. They are palmate in shape with 5 large triangular leaflets divided and toothed at the ends. Plumes of small, creamy white flowers are 30cm (1ft) long and are carried well above the leaves. HEIGHT & SPREAD 1×1.2m (3×4ft).
R. sambucifolia The emerald-green, bronze-tinged pinnate leaves have distinct veining and are each up to 60cm (2ft) long. Creamy white flowers are borne in sprays with arching tips above the foliage in mid summer. HEIGHT & SPREAD 1×1m (3×3ft).
R. tabularis see *Astilboides tabularis*
CULTIVATION Rodgersias grow best in humus-rich, moist soil. In other soils add a generous mulch in spring and water freely in dry spells. They prefer a shaded site, protected from strong winds which can damage the leaves. Plant from autumn to spring in soil with added well-rotted compost or manure. Mulch in subsequent seasons.
PROPAGATION Divide rhizomes in spring or autumn. Sow seed of species in autumn and plant out seedlings the following year. The flower and leaf colour of resulting plants may be variable.
PESTS AND DISEASES Usually trouble free.

Romneya

Californian tree poppy
Papaveraceae

Huge white poppy heads with papery petals around central golden stamens, and backed by jagged grey leaves, make exotic additions to the garden from mid summer to early autumn. Despite their Californian origin, Romneyas are hardy in well-drained sunny borders or in a sheltered spot against a sunny wall in cold areas. They are perennial sub-shrubs which dislike disturbance or competition from nearby plants, but once established their roots can be invasive.

RECOMMENDED SPECIES AND VARIETIES
R. coulteri♀ The 6 almost round petals form 2 overlapping layers around golden stamens. Petals unfold crinkled and filmy from the smooth buds in mid summer to early autumn to become silken and almost translucent as the flowers open out to a width of 10-15cm (4-6in). The solitary flowers are slightly fragrant. Bristly ovoid pods, up to 3cm (1¼in) long and packed with brown seeds, form after flowering.

▲ *Romneya coulteri*

The large grey leaves have 5-9 lobes and are roughly hand-shaped. Native to California and Mexico. HEIGHT & SPREAD 2.5×2m (8×6½ft).

Growing to a height of 1.5m (5ft) var. *trichocalyx* has more finely divided leaves and somewhat thinner stems. **'White Cloud'** has bold flowers, very grey foliage and spreads vigorously.
CULTIVATION Plant in spring in a sunny well-drained site, with minimal root disturbance until established. Provide frost protection for young plants in cold areas. Flowering occurs on the current season's stems, so prune in spring, or in winter to prevent rocking.
PROPAGATION Take 7.5-10cm (3-4in) long root cuttings in early spring. Cover with soil to a depth of about 1.5cm (½in) and keep in a cold frame until growth begins. Alternatively, sow seeds when fresh or in spring at a temperature of 15°C (59°F), or take basal cuttings in early spring.
PESTS AND DISEASES Usually trouble free.

Rock Plants

Gems of form and colour

DELICATELY FORMED ALPINE PLANTS BRING THE FASCINATION OF THE MINIATURE TO GARDENS OF ALL SIZES

Small and usually slow-growing, rock plants offer a vast array of shape, colour and texture. Their carpets, rosettes or domes of foliage, and abundant and often brightly coloured flowers can transform a garden. Most produce their best displays in spring or summer but a careful choice of plants ensures a colourful show throughout the year.

Many rock plants are true alpines and originate from rocky slopes and mountain meadows above the tree line. Most thrive in full sun and require a free-draining and gritty soil. The term alpines is also often used for other plants that grow well in similar conditions, including many dwarf conifers, shrubs and bulbs. Some small woodland dwellers, such as *Erythronium*, *Hepatica* and *Trillium*, are also used as rock plants. However, these plants need a humus-rich soil and a shady site.

Given the right planting conditions, alpines are easy to grow and need minimal attention. Rock features require no hoeing or digging and little general maintenance other than regular weeding.

▼ CREATIVE CASCADE *Brightly coloured* Aurinia *and* Aubrieta *tumble down the rocks in spring.*

Rock features

The small size of rock plants means that they are best appreciated when grown in a self-contained site. The traditional rock garden, a sloping feature with outcrops of rocks, provides excellent conditions. Plants grow in pockets of soil between rocks, or in ledges and crevices. A peat bed or water feature can be incorporated to further extend the range of plants grown.

Alpines also grow well in a scree bed, an area with very gritty soil. It is constructed on a slope or as a slightly raised area, and may form part of a rock garden. A self-contained scree bed takes up less space than a traditional rock garden so can be a good choice for a smaller garden.

Raised beds too have naturally good drainage and display rock plants well. They are particularly useful in those gardens with poor drainage, or can be filled with ericaceous compost and used to grow lime-haters in gardens with limy soil.

Rock plants look equally attractive displayed in less formal settings. Gaps in paving or the top of a retaining wall are useful places. Containers, including old kitchen sinks and troughs, make excellent planting sites which suit the miniature scale of the plants and look highly attractive, particularly in a small garden or patio area.

Alpines also grow well in an unheated greenhouse or an alpine house, which provides cool, airy conditions.

The right place

Vigorous carpeting plants, such as *Acaena* (New Zealand bur) and some *Campanula* and *Thymus* (thyme) species, are best grown in a rock garden or scree bed, where they have plenty of space to spread. They also look good when planted on top of a wall and allowed to cascade over the bricks or stones, or grown in gaps left between slabs of paving.

Small alpines that form cushions, such as some *Saxifraga,* are better off in containers or raised beds, isolated from any strong-growing competitors. Larger cushion-forming plants grow well in scree beds or in vertical rock crevices, where water cannot collect in leaf rosettes and cause rotting.

Some alpines may rot and develop fungal diseases if they are exposed to prolonged rain. They include *Asperula* (woodruff), *Draba* (whitlow grass) and some species of *Primula*.

If possible, keep these plants under glass, where they produce their best displays. When grown outdoors, protect each plant from winter wet by

▲ MIX AND MATCH *Contrast shapes, textures and colours for interest throughout the year.*

▶ GROWING ON GRIT *Many alpines thrive in the free-draining conditions of a scree bed.*

placing a brick on either side of it and laying a sheet of glass on top to keep off rain.

Year-round colour

There are a host of alpines that provide colour in spring, making a rock feature a bright focal point in the garden. *Aurinia* (yellow alyssum), *Aubrieta, Daphne, Gentiana* (gentian), *Pulsatilla* (pasque flower) and *Primula* species are good choices and associate well with small spring-flowering bulbs, such as *Crocus* and *Narcissus*.

Follow on with the pinks of *Dianthus*, blues of *Campanula* and snowy white plumes of the silver saxifrages. *Armeria* (thrift), *Chiastophyllum* (lamb's tail), *Geranium* (cranesbill), *Helianthemum* (rock rose) and *Sedum* (stonecrop) all add to a blaze of summer colour.

Grow late-flowering *Carlina* (carline thistle) and *Gentiana* with autumn-flowering *Crocus*, *Cyclamen*, *Colchicum* (autumn crocus) and *Origanum* for elegant autumn displays. Include plants with interesting leaves that last through winter. Some sedums, silver saxifrages and *Sempervivum* (houseleek) provide valuable colour. Choose cushion saxifrages, which have pink, yellow or white blooms, and dwarf cyclamen, such as *Cyclamen coum*, for floral colour in late winter.

Intersperse different types of plants to provide longer seasons of interest in each area of the rock garden. For example, grow dwarf bulbs through carpeting plants that flower in summer, and place autumn crocuses and colchicums to distract the eye from faded summer leaves. Use plants with vivid winter foliage to hide any empty spaces left by the herbaceous species.

Conifers make excellent contrasts to low-growing plants and provide interest throughout the year. Some conifers do not stay dwarf when planted out so choose reliable miniature varieties. *Chamaecyparis pisifera* 'Nana Aureovariegata', *Juniperus communis* 'Compressa', *Picea abies* 'Little Gem' and *Pinus mugo* 'Gnom' are good choices for a rock feature.

▲ Lateral planting *Low-growing New Zealand bur and thyme spill across stone steps.*

▼ In proportion *An old sink is just the right size to show off a few favoured alpines.*

The right soil

Rock plants thrive in a well-draining and gritty soil, set on a drainage layer of rubble. Top dress plants with a layer of gravel, grit or stone chippings.

In a rock garden, use equal parts of soil and small stone chippings or gravel, and add an equal part of organic matter if the soil is sandy. Use three parts chippings or gravel and two parts soil for rock plants that prefer a stony ground, and three parts chippings or gravel with one part soil for a scree bed.

Use equal parts of good quality soil or John Innes No.2 compost and chippings or gravel in a raised bed. In a container, use the same mixture on a layer of broken crocks. Raise the pot on bricks to improve drainage.

Use a fibrous, humus-rich soil for a peat bed. Leafmould or equal parts of composted bark, coir and garden compost, with a little sand, are suitable alternatives to peat. Top dress with bark chips or coco shell.

Rock plants for every season

Spring

- ***Aurinia saxatilis*** Dense clusters of golden yellow flowers and silvery grey, oval leaves.
- ***Draba aizoides*** Lemon yellow flower clusters above dense tufts of deep green, bristly leaves.
- ***Gentiana acaulis*** Blue trumpet-shaped flowers and mats of dark green, oval, evergreen leaves.
- ***Primula marginata*** Lilac trumpet-shaped blooms and rosettes of grey-green scalloped leaves.
- ***Pulsatilla vulgaris*** Purple, pink or white, bell-shaped flowers and light green, feathery foliage.

Summer

- ***Armeria juniperifolia*** Dense heads of purple or pink blooms and mounds of deep green foliage.
- ***Chiastophyllum oppositifolium*** Bell-shaped, yellow flowers and bright green succulent leaves.
- ***Dianthus alpinus*** Rose to crimson single flowers and lance-shaped green leaves.
- ***Helianthemum* hybrids** Clusters of flowers in a wide range of colours and oval to lance-shaped green leaves.

Autumn

- ***Carlina acaulis*** Round, off-white or pale brown flowerheads and rosettes of spiny grey-green leaves.
- ***Gentiana septemfida*** Deep blue or purplish trumpet-shaped flowers and tufts of mid green pointed leaves.
- ***Origanum rotundifolium*** Large apple green bracts and low mounds of bright green leaves.

Winter

- ***Cyclamen coum*** Pink flowers with reflexed petals, and kidney-shaped, green or silvery, patterned leaves.
- ***Saxifraga* 'Cranbourne'** Shallow, cup-shaped, rose-purple flowers and cushions of dark green leaves.
- ***Sempervivum tectorum*** Rosettes of fleshy evergreen leaves tipped with rich red-brown.

Rosa

Rose

Rosaceae

Most beautiful and romantic of flowers, inspiring not only gardeners but also lovers and poets, roses have been cultivated for more than 4000 years – and remain the world's most popular garden shrubs

Whether they are massed in traditional formal beds, trained on a fence, trellis or tree, or combined with other plants in a mixed bed, there are roses for almost any garden. They can stand alone as billowing or weeping specimens in a lawn, or serve as an informal flowering hedge. Some roses make neat rock-garden plants, some spread low and wide for ground cover, while smaller types do well in containers.

Some 150 species of rose have been found in the wild – all in the Northern Hemisphere. There are some distinctions between the species native to Europe and the Middle East, to the Far East, and to North America. These distinctions, and the additional ones shown by hybrids that occurred naturally between species, have given plant breeders numerous features to blend and develop over the last 100 years or more. The result is several thousands of rose varieties for gardeners to choose from, with new ones being added every year.

r

• THE MAIN GROUPS •

Traditionally, roses were grouped according to the parent species or place of origin but as new varieties have been developed

1 *R.*'Arthur Bell'
2 *R.* Anna Livia
3 *R.*'Fountain'
4 *R.* Iceberg
5 *R.* Red Ace
6 *R.*'Fountain'
7 *R.* Bonica
8 *R.* Painted Moon
9 *R.* Polar Star
10 *R.*'Chanelle'
11 *R.*'Southampton'

the grouping has become complex. All roses recommended here are listed alphabetically in the index overleaf and the group that each belongs to is indicated in brackets after its name. Each one of these groups is then treated separately, with descriptions given for the roses belonging to them. The groups are:

- Species Roses and their hybrids
- Old Garden Roses (including Gallica, Damask, Alba, Centifolia, Moss, Bourbon, Portland, Hybrid Perpetual, and China Roses)
- Large-flowered Bush Roses (or Hybrid Tea Roses)
- Polyantha Roses
- Cluster-flowered Bush Roses (or Floribunda Roses)
- Modern Shrub Roses
- Rugosa Roses
- Patio Roses (or Dwarf Cluster-flowered Bush Roses)
- Miniature Roses (including Miniature Climbing Roses)
- Ground-cover Roses
- Climbing Roses
- Rambler Roses

The care of roses is treated on pp.599-601. Nearly all roses are hardy everywhere in Britain. They grow on almost any soil provided that it is not waterlogged and not virtually pure sand, chalk or blue clay. A few species and some old hybrids and sports developed from them do well on fairly poor soil, but most roses thrive on a rich soil containing plenty of organic matter. All flower better and are more vigorous with regular pruning, but the method, severity and timing vary according to type.

Roses holding the Award of Garden Merit of the Royal Horticultural Society and the Royal National Rose Society are indicated by the symbol ♀. *Roses awarded the RNRS Gold Medal are indicated by* +. *This award is based on three-year trials at the RNRS trial grounds, during which the roses are assessed by a panel of experts every week throughout the summer and autumn.*

SPECIES ROSES AND THEIR HYBRIDS

All roses are descended from the wild or species roses. These have long, arching shoots that bear along their entire length single, five-petalled flowers, often sweetly scented. Most species roses flower only in early summer, some in late spring, but several have decorative hips in autumn. In the plant descriptions here, the hips are mentioned only if they are particularly showy.

Species roses are vigorous deciduous shrubs whose pinnate leaves vary in the number of leaflets and range from light to mid green, sometimes with a purple tinge. The plants are hardy, often resistant to pests and diseases and not as demanding in their soil requirements as modern roses. They make superb specimen or border plants.

Original species are the only roses to come true from seed. Natural or cultivated hybrids, or selected named forms of wild roses retain most of the characteristics of a species but seedlings from them do not reproduce reliably the parents' features.

***R. californica* 'Plena'** see *R. nutkana* 'Plena'

R. 'Canary Bird' see *R. xanthina* 'Canary Bird'

▲ *Rosa* 'Dupontii'

R. 'Dupontii' The scented, white, single blooms, faintly flushed pink and with pale yellow stamens, are up to 10cm (4in) across. They are set off by grey-green leaves. HEIGHT & SPREAD 2.1×2.1m (7×7ft).

R. ecae Golden yellow, single flowers, about 3cm (1¼in) across, show well against the ferny foliage. This rose suits smaller gardens. HEIGHT & SPREAD 1.5×1.2m (5×4ft).

'Helen Knight' see *R.* 'Helen Knight'

R. fedtschenkoana Spasmodic blooms over the summer follow the first flush of single white flowers that are 5cm (2in) across. A sprawling, suckering plant with grey-green leaves. HEIGHT & SPREAD 2.1×2.1m (7×7ft).

***R. foetida* 'Bicolor'** Orange-red, single blooms with bright yellow on the back of the petals are 7.5cm (3in) across and have a musty smell. The leaves are glossy. This open-growing shrub is susceptible to black spot. HEIGHT & SPREAD 1.5×1.5m (5×5ft).

R. 'Geranium'♀ (syn. *R. moyesii* 'Geranium') Bright crimson, single flowers 5cm (2in) across are followed by long-lasting, flagon-shaped scarlet hips on tall, arching growth. The dainty leaves are rounded. HEIGHT & SPREAD 2.4×2.1m (8×7ft).

R. glauca♀ (syn. *R. rubrifolia*) The clusters of single, pink flowers 2cm (¾in) across are very fleeting but are followed by red hips that last up to 4 months. Long, arching, plum-red shoots, almost thornless when young, bear leaves with a purplish bloom. HEIGHT & SPREAD 2.1×1.8m (7×6ft).

***R. x harisonii* 'Harison's Yellow'**♀ (syn. *R. pimpinellifolia* 'Harisonii') Bright yellow, semidouble blooms, up to 7.5cm (3in) across, appear in mid to late spring on a plant of upright, rather uneven growth. HEIGHT & SPREAD 1.8×1.2m (6×4ft).

R. 'Helen Knight'♀ (syn. *R. ecae* 'Helen

Knight') The flowers are bright yellow. This hybrid is not completely hardy, but with the protection of a wall it thrives and climbs well. HEIGHT & SPREAD 2.4×2.4m (8×8ft).

***R.* 'Highdownensis'**♀ (syn. *R. moyesii* 'Highdownensis') Reddish pink, single flowers 5cm (2in) across bloom on this strong-growing, arching plant. In autumn it carries flagon-shaped, orange-red hips. HEIGHT & SPREAD 2.7×1.8m (9×6ft).

R. hugonis see *R. xanthina* f. *hugonis*

***R. macrophylla* 'Master Hugh'**♀ Cerise single flowers, 7.5cm (3in) across, and purplish green leaves distinguish this rose. Most striking are the very large, orange-red hips that last for several months. HEIGHT & SPREAD 4.5×2.4m (15×8ft).

***R. moyesii* 'Geranium'** see *R.* 'Geranium'

***R. moyesii* 'Highdownensis'** see *R.* 'Highdownensis'

***R. moyesii* 'Sealing Wax'** see *R.* 'Sealing Wax'

R. multibracteata♀ Bright pink, single flowers, 4cm (1½in) across, bloom against small, grey-green leaves on a shrub that makes a mound of twiggy growth. HEIGHT & SPREAD 2.1×2.1m (7×7ft).

R. nitida Bristly reddish stems carry vivid lilac-pink flowers, 5cm (2in) across, followed by hips. A low, compact shrub that suckers freely, spreading virtually as far as it is allowed. HEIGHT & SPREAD 1×1m (3×3ft).

***R. nutkana* 'Plena'**♀ (syn. *R. californica* 'Plena') Abundant, bright pink, semi-double flowers 4cm (1½in) across spangle the large mound of tangled growth in late spring. HEIGHT & SPREAD 1.8×1.8m (6×6ft).

R. omeinensis* f. *pteracantha see *R. sericea* ssp. *omeinensis* f. *pteracantha*

***R.* 'Paulii'** (syn. *R.* 'Paulii Alba') White, single flowers, 7.5cm (3in) across, and veined grey-green leaves are carried on strong, arching shoots. A wide-spreading bush. HEIGHT & SPREAD 1.2×1.5m (4×5ft).

R. pimpinellifolia♀ (syn. *R. spinosissima*) White, single flowers 5cm (2in) across are borne on a low, twiggy, dense plant that spreads by suckers and is very prickly. HEIGHT & SPREAD 60cm×1.2m (2×4ft).

'Harisonii' see *R.* × *harisonii* 'Harison's Yellow'

R. primula (incense rose) Pale primrose-yellow, single flowers 4cm (1½in) across bloom in small clusters on reddish stems. The small, glossy leaves have a sweet aroma, especially after rain. An arching, open plant. HEIGHT & SPREAD 1.8×1.8m (6×6ft).

R. roxburghii (burr rose, chestnut rose) Lilac-pink, single or double flowers, 5cm (2in) across, are borne on angular growth with grey, flaking bark. The flowers are followed by distinctive, prickly green hips that resemble chestnuts. HEIGHT & SPREAD 1.8×1.8m (6×6ft).

R. rubrifolia see *R. glauca*

***R.* 'Sealing Wax'** (syn. *R. moyesii* 'Sealing Wax') Single, bright pink flowers, 5cm (2in) across, are followed by long-lasting, flagon-shaped scarlet hips. Dainty, rather rounded leaves are borne on tall arching growth. HEIGHT & SPREAD 2.4×2.1m (8×7ft).

R. sericea* ssp. *omeinensis* f. *pteracantha (syn. *R. omeinensis* f. *pteracantha*) White 4-petalled blooms, borne in late spring, are 4cm (1½in) across. Large, flattened, translucent thorns are borne on reddish shoots. HEIGHT & SPREAD 2.4×2.4m (8×8ft).

▲ *Rosa primula*

R. spinosissima see *R. pimpinellifolia*

***R.* 'Stanwell Perpetual'** Blush-pink, double blooms, 7.5cm (3in) across, open out flat and are repeat-flowering on a thorny shrub with grey-green leaves that spreads widely by suckers. HEIGHT & SPREAD 1×1.2m (3×4ft).

R. virginiana♀ Single, bright pink flowers, 6cm (2½in) across, are followed by red hips. The shiny green leaves develop striking autumn colour. A bushy, rounded shrub that suckers freely. HEIGHT & SPREAD 1.2×1.5m (4×5ft).

***R. xanthina* 'Canary Bird'**♀ (syn. *R.* 'Canary Bird') Vivid yellow, single flowers,

INDEX OF PLANTS

The letters in brackets after each plant name indicate the section where the plant is described. (Cl)=Climbing Roses; (Flor)=Cluster-flowered Bush Roses; (GrC)=Ground Cover Roses; (HT)=Large-flowered Bush Roses (Hybrid Teas); (Min)=Miniature Roses; (MC)=Miniature Climber; (MS)=Modern Shrub Roses; (OGG)=Old Garden Roses – Gallicas; (OGD)=Old Garden Roses – Damasks; (OGA)=Old Garden Roses – Albas; (OGCe)=Old Garden Roses – Centifolias; (OGM)=Old Garden Roses – Moss; (OGB)=Old Garden Roses – Bourbons; (OGP)=Old Garden Roses – Portland; (OGHP) =Old Garden Roses – Hybrid Perpetuals; (OGCh)=Old Garden Roses – China; (Pat)=Patio Roses (Dwarf Cluster-flowered Bush Roses); (Poly)=Polyantha Roses; (Ra)=Rambler Roses; (Rug)=Rugosa Roses; (Sp)=Species Roses and their Hybrids.

▲ *Rosa* 'Stanwell Perpetual'

about 4cm (1½in) across, appear in late spring on arching shoots. This shrub is less rampant when grown as a weeping standard. HEIGHT & SPREAD 2.4×2.4m (8×8ft).

The pale yellow blooms of f. ***hugonis***♀ (syn. *R. hugonis*) (golden rose of China) are 5cm (2in) across and appear in late spring on a dense bush with dainty, ferny foliage. This rose spreads to 1.8m (6ft).

OLD GARDEN ROSES

Some very ancient Gallica, Damask and Alba roses are included in this group, but most are hybrids raised from the ancient roses in the 19th century. They vary widely in habit, some making arching shrubs up to 2.1m (7ft) tall, others twiggy, upright and no more than 1.2m (4ft), and a few growing into airy bushes less than 1m (3ft) tall.

Although both single and semidouble flowers are found among Old Garden Roses, double flowers are far more typical – indeed the blooms are packed with petals and often quartered, that is arranged in 4 whorls. Most are sweetly fragrant. Of the nine families, Gallicas, Damasks, Albas, Centifolias and Moss roses flower, almost without exception, only at mid summer. The China Roses, Bourbons, Portlands and Hybrid Perpetuals are generally repeat-flowering, though some varieties are a great deal more so than others.

The leaves of most Old Garden Roses are matt or semi-glossy, looking rather rough in comparison with the glossy foliage of modern varieties. The foliage of China Roses is rather different, always smooth and much more pointed. Whether smooth or rough, Old Garden Rose foliage is reasonably healthy and if affected by disease, most plants are vigorous enough to shrug it off.

Gallica Roses

All the listed Gallica Roses bear flowers 7.5-10cm (3-4in) across, unless stated otherwise. They bloom in mid summer only, have a sweet scent and are borne in small clusters, or occasionally singly, on bushes with few thorns and plenty of leaves.

***R.* 'Belle de Crécy'**♀ The double, quartered blooms that open flat are deep cerise-pink, fading to soft purple. The leaves are grey-green on a bushy plant. HEIGHT & SPREAD 1.2×1m (4×3ft).

***R.* 'Camaïeux'** A striking combination of crimson-purple and lilac-pink streaks the petals of the rather loosely formed, semi-double blooms. This rose bears grey-green leaves on its arching stems HEIGHT & SPREAD 1×1m (3×3ft).

***R.* 'Cardinal de Richelieu'**♀ The rich, warm purple, double blooms have petals that curve back rather loosely with age. The flowers are well set off by dark green leaves on a bushy, rather arching plant. HEIGHT & SPREAD 1×1.1m (3×3½ft).

▲ *Rosa* 'Charles de Mills'

***R.* 'Charles de Mills'**♀ Very full, double, quartered flowers, up to 11cm (4¼in) across, are a light beetroot-purple and bloom with great freedom. The twiggy bush sometimes gets top-heavy and needs support. HEIGHT & SPREAD 1.2×1m (4×3ft).

***R.* 'Complicata'**♀ (syn. *R. gallica* 'Complicata') The spectacular single, bright pink, white-eyed blooms with a boss of golden stamens open flat all along the arch-

Darling Flame (Min)
'Dawn Chorus' (HT)
'De Meaux' (OGCe)
'De Rescht' (OGP)
'Dicbar' (Flor)
Dortmund (Cl)
Doctor McAlpine (HT)
Dream Girl (Cl)
'Dreaming Spires' (Cl)
Drummer Boy (Flor)
'Du Maître d'Ecole' (OGG)
Dublin Bay (Cl)
'Duc de Guiche' (OGG)
'Duchesse de Montebello' (OGG)
'Duchess of Portland' (OGP)
'Dupontii' (Sp)
Dutch Gold (HT)
'Easter Morning' (Min)
R. ecae (Sp)
R. ecae 'Helen Knight' (Sp)
'E.H. Morse' (HT)
Edith Holden (Flor)
Elina (HT)
Elizabeth of Glamis (Flor)
'Emily Gray' (Ra)
'Empress Josephine' (OGG)
'Ena Harkness, Climbing' (Cl)
English Garden (MS)
'English Miss' (Flor)
'Ernest H. Morse' (HT)
Escapade (Flor)
Essex (GrC)
'Etoile de Hollande, Climbing' (Cl)
Evelyn (MS)
Eye Paint (Flor)
'F.E. Lester' (Ra)
'F.J. Grootendorst' (Rug)
R. fedtschenkoana (Sp)
Felicia (MS)
'Félicité Parmentier' (OGA)
'Félicité Perpétue' (Ra)
Fellowship (Flor)
Festival (Pat)
'Fimbriata' (Rug)
Flower Carpet (GrC)
R. foetida 'Bicolor' (Sp)
'Fountain' (MS)
Fragrant Cloud (HT)
Fragrant Delight (Flor)
Fragrant Dream (HT)
'Francesca' (MS)
'Francis E. Lester' (Ra)
R. × *francofurtana* (Sp)
'François Juranville' (Ra)
'Frau Karl Druschki' (OGHP)
'Fred Loads' (MS)
Freedom (HT)
'Fru Dagmar Hastrup' (Rug)
Frühlingsgold (MS)
'Frühlingsmorgen' (MS)
R. gallica var. *officinalis* (OGG)
R. gallica var. *officinalis* 'Complicata' (OGG)
R. gallica var. *officinalis* 'Versicolor' (OGG)
Galway Bay (Cl)
'Gaujard' (HT)
Gentle Touch (Pat)
'Geranium' (Sp)
Gertrude Jekyll (MS)
Gingernut (Pat)
'Gipsy Boy' (MS)
R. glauca (Sp)
'Glenfiddich' (Flor)
'Gloire de Dijon' (Cl)
'Gloire des Mousseuses' (OGM)
Golden Celebration (MS)
Golden Jubilee (HT)
Golden Showers (Cl)
Golden Wedding (Flor)
'Golden Wings' (MS)
Golden Years (Flor)
'Goldfinch' (Ra)
Graham Thomas (MS)
'Grandpa Dickson' (HT)
'Great Maiden's Blush' (OGA)
Greenall's Glory (Flor)
'Gruss an Aachen' (Flor)
'Guinée' (Cl)
Gwent (GrC)
'Gypsy Boy' (MS)
Hampshire (GrC)
Handel (Cl)
Hannah Gordon (Flor)
R. × *harisonii* 'Harison's Yellow' (Sp)
Harry Wheatcroft (HT)
Harvest Fayre (Flor)
'Helen Knight' (Sp)
'Henri Martin' (OGM)
Heritage (MS)
Hertfordshire (GrC)
'Highdownensis' (Sp)
Highfield (Cl)
High Hopes (Cl)
'Honey Bunch' (Pat)
Honeymoon (Flor)
'Honorine de Brabant' (OGB)
R. hugonis (Sp)
Iceberg (Flor)
'Iceberg, Climbing' (Cl)
Ice Cream (HT)
'Iced Ginger' (Flor)
Ingrid Bergman (HT)
Invincible (Flor)
'Irène Watts' (OGCh)
'Ispahan' (OGD)
Jacqueline du Pré (MS)
Jane Asher (Pat)
Jardins de Bagatelle (HT)
'Jenny Duval' (OGG)
'Judy Fischer' (Min)
Julia's Rose (HT)
Just Joey (HT)
Keepsake (HT)
Kent (GrC)
King's Ransom (HT)
'Königin von Dänemark' (OGA)
'Korresia' (Flor)
L.D. Braithwaite (MS)
'Lady Hillingdon, Climbing' (Cl)

ing shoots. Unlike other Gallicas, this large bush is thorny and has grey-green leaves. HEIGHT & SPREAD 2.1×2.4m (7×8ft).

R. 'Comtesse de Lacépède' see *R.* 'Du Maître d'Ecole'

R. 'Crimson Damask' see *R. gallica* var. *officinalis*

R. 'Duc de Guiche'♀ Crimson-purple, globular double blooms are slightly quartered, showing a green eye. The leaves are dark green. A shrubby, spreading plant. HEIGHT & SPREAD 1.2×1.2m (4×4ft).

R. 'Duchesse de Montebello'♀ Large, blush-pink, very double blooms flower early in summer. The leaves are grey-green. HEIGHT & SPREAD 1.5×1.2m (5×4ft).

R. 'Du Maître d'Ecole'♀ (syn. *R.* 'Comtesse de Lacépède', *R.* 'Rose du Maître d'Ecole') Quartered double flowers in a mixture of rose-pink and purple, fading to lilac, are 11cm (4¼in) across and show a green eye when they open flat. The leaves are greyish green on lax shoots that droop under the weight of bloom. HEIGHT & SPREAD 1×1.2m (3×4ft).

R. × *francofurtana* (syn. *R.* 'Empress Josephine') Deep pink petals with darker veining and wavy edges make up the semidouble cupped flowers, which are striking but loosely formed. The spreading bush has dark leaves and narrow autumn hips. HEIGHT & SPREAD 1.2×1.2m (4×4ft).

R. gallica* var. *officinalis♀ (syn. *R.* 'Crimson Damask', *R. officinalis*) (apothecary's rose, red rose of Lancaster) Deep pink, large, semidouble flowers cover this neat, upright plant with dark green leaves.

▲ *Rosa gallica* var. *officinalis*

HEIGHT & SPREAD 1×1m (3×3ft).

'Complicata' see *R.* 'Complicata'.

'Versicolor'♀ (syn. *R. mundi*, *R. m.* ssp. *versicolor*, *R. versicolor*) has pale blush-pink, semidouble flowers, striped and splashed with reddish pink and up to 11cm (4¼in) across. They are borne on a twiggy plant.

R. 'Jenny Duval' see *R.* 'Président de Sèze'

R. officinalis see *R. gallica* var. *officinalis*

R. mundi see *R. gallica* 'Versicolor'

R. mundi* ssp. *versicolor see *R. gallica* 'Versicolor'

R. 'Président de Sèze'♀ (syn. *R.* 'Jenny Duval') The double, quartered blooms in deep magenta-pink edged with lilac-pink make a vivid show. The bushy growth bears rich green leaves. HEIGHT & SPREAD 1.2×1m (4×3ft).

R. 'Rose du Maître d'Ecole' see *R.* 'Du Maître d'Ecole'

R. 'Scharlachglut'♀ (syn. *R.* 'Scarlet Fire', *R.* 'Scarlet Glow') Bright cherry-red, single blooms with golden stamens are large and borne abundantly in clusters or singly, but they have no scent. Large, pear-shaped orange hips hang on into winter on the sprawling growth, which makes a semi-climber. HEIGHT & SPREAD 3×1.8m (10×6ft).

▲ *Rosa* 'Tuscany Superb'

R. 'Tuscany Superb'♀ Velvety, maroon, double flowers, up to 8cm (3in) across, are often quartered and are lightly scented. Dark green leaves clothe the upright, bushy plant. HEIGHT & SPREAD 1×1m (3×3ft).

R. versicolor see *R. gallica* 'Versicolor'

Damask Roses

The plants listed have richly fragrant flowers, most about 7.5cm (3in) across, borne in loose clusters in mid summer only. The bushes are open-growing with small, rather rounded leaves on bristly stems. Some have hips but they are small and not showy.

R. 'Celsiana' (syn. *R.* 'Amélia') The pale pink, semidouble blooms with crinkled petals open wide to show golden stamens.

INDEX OF PLANTS CONTINUED

The grey-green leaves are aromatic. HEIGHT & SPREAD 1.5×1.2m (5×4ft).

***R.* 'Ispahan'**🏆 Large, blush-pink, double blooms are freely borne over a long period, giving good value from the single flowering. The tall, generally upright plant has comparatively large leaves with a blue tinge. HEIGHT & SPREAD 1.8×1.4m (6×4½ft).

***R.* 'La Ville de Bruxelles'**🏆 The wealth of petals gives a domed centre to the beautiful clear pink, double flowers. The upright but bushy plant carries luxuriant, fresh green leaves. HEIGHT & SPREAD 1.5×1m (5×3ft).

***R.* 'Madame Hardy'**🏆 Pure white, double blooms open flat from the palest pink buds, showing petals exquisitely arranged round a green eye. The well-branched, erect plant has plentiful mid green foliage. HEIGHT & SPREAD 1.5×1.5m (5×5ft).

***R.* 'Marie Louise'** The mauve-pink, double flowers are 10cm (4in) across and so full-petalled that they weigh down the dark-leaved, rather lax shoots. The outer petals curve back as the flower opens out flat. HEIGHT & SPREAD 1.2×1m (4×3ft).

Alba Roses

All the plants listed have fragrant flowers, borne in clusters only in mid summer. They vary in size, from 5-11cm (2-4¼in) across. The vigorous, upright plants, with few thorns and plenty of grey-tinged leaves, do well in poor soil and partial shade.

***R.* × *alba* 'Alba Maxima'**🏆 (syn. *R.* 'Maxima') Profuse double flowers are creamy white with a hint of buff in the bud. HEIGHT & SPREAD 2.1×1.5m (7×5ft).

'Alba Semiplena'🏆 (syn. *R.* 'Semiplena') has semidouble flowers.

***R.* 'Cuisse de Nymphe'** see *R.* 'Great Maiden's Blush'

***R.* 'Félicité Parmentier'**🏆 Rounded, pale yellow buds open into small, light pink flowers that are double and sometimes quartered. The plant puts out suckers if it is grown on its own roots instead of grafted. HEIGHT & SPREAD 1.2×1m (4×3ft).

***R.* 'Great Maiden's Blush'** (syn. *R.* 'Cuisse de Nymphe', *R.* 'Maiden's Blush, Great') The double flowers are open cups, blush-pink at the centre and creamy pink at the edge. They are rather loosely formed and are freely borne. HEIGHT & SPREAD 2.1×1.5m (7×5ft).

***R.* 'Königin von Dänemark'**🏆 (syn. *R.* 'Queen of Denmark') The soft pink of the double blooms deepens towards the centre. The flowers open flat and are quartered. The plant is less upright than other Albas. HEIGHT & SPREAD 1.5×1.2m (5×4ft).

***R.* 'Madame Legras de Saint Germain'** The large, white, double blooms look like powder-puffs on this large, arching shrub. HEIGHT & SPREAD 1.8×1.8m (6×6ft).

***R.* 'Maiden's Blush'** Open cup-shaped double flowers are pink at the centre, fading to creamy pink at the edge. HEIGHT & SPREAD 1.2×1m (4×3ft).

***R.* 'Maiden's Blush, Great'** see *R.* 'Great Maiden's Blush'

***R.* 'Maxima'** see *R.* × *alba* 'Alba Maxima'

***R.* 'Queen of Denmark'** see *R.* 'Königin von Dänemark'

***R.* 'Semiplena'** see *R.* × *alba* 'Alba Semiplena'

Centifolia Roses

The crowded petals of these double, globular blooms, which are often called cabbage roses, make the clusters so heavy that they tend to droop and the arching, thorny stems need some support. The plants listed bloom once only, are richly scented and do not produce hips.

R.* × *centifolia (Provence rose, cabbage rose) The numerous, rich pink, mid summer blooms are 10cm (4in) across on this lax shrub with drooping, grey-green leaves. HEIGHT & SPREAD 1.5×1.2m (5×4ft).

'Cristata'🏆 (syn. *R.* Chapeau de Napoléon, *R.* 'Cristata') has buds enclosed by an enlarged, bristly, crested green calyx. The rich pink mid summer blooms are 10cm (4in) across.

***R.* 'De Meaux'** (syn. *R.* 'Rose de Meaux') The rich pink blooms, paler round the edge, are little pompoms only about 4cm (1½in) across but abundant on the arching stems. They open in early summer. HEIGHT & SPREAD 1×1m (3×3ft).

Moss Roses

The buds and stems of these roses have a soft bristly green covering with a spicy aroma, known as moss. Full-petalled double flowers, usually fragrant and 7.5-10cm (3-4in) across, bloom in clusters in mid summer only, on arching plants with mid green leaves. There are no hips.

***R.* 'Capitaine John Ingram'**🏆 The dark crimson blooms are lighter on the back of the petals and fade to purple. The bristly moss is tinged red. HEIGHT & SPREAD 1.2×1.2m (4×4ft).

'Poulmuti' (GrC)
'Precious Platinum' (HT)
'Président de Sèze' (OGG)
Pretty Polly (Pat)
R. primula (Sp)
Princess Royal (HT)
Pristine (HT)
Purple Tiger (Flor)
Queen Elizabeth (Flor)
Queen Mother (Pat)
'Queen of Denmark' (OGA)
'Rambling Rector' (Ra)
Ray of Sunshine (Pat)
Red Ace (Min)
Redgold (Flor)
'Red Grootendorst' (Rug)
Red Rascal (Pat)
Red Sunblaze (Min)
'Reine des Violettes' (OGHP)
Remember Me (HT)
Remembrance (Flor)
Renaissance (HT)
Robin Redbreast (Pat)
Rob Roy (Flor)
'Rose de Meaux' (OGCe)
'Rose de Rescht' (OGP)
'Rose du Maître d'Ecole' (OGG)
Rose Gaujard (HT)
Rosemary Harkness (HT)
'Roseraie de l'Haÿ' (Rug)
'Rosy Cheeks' (HT)
'Rosy Mantle' (Cl)
R. roxburghii (Sp)
'Royal Gold' (Cl)
Royal William (HT)
R. rubrifolia (Sp)
'Ruby Wedding' (HT)
R. rugosa 'Alba' (Rug)
R. rugosa var. *rubra* (Rug)
R. rugosa 'Scabrosa' (Rug)
Saint Cecilia (MS)
Sally Holmes (MS)
'Sanders' White Rambler' (Ra)
Sarah (HT)
Savoy Hotel (HT)
'Scarlet Fire' (OGG)
'Scarlet Glow' (OGG)
Scarlet Queen Elizabeth (Flor)
'Scharlachglut' (OGG)
Schneewittchen (Flor)
'Schoolgirl' (Cl)
'Seagull' (Ra)
'Sealing Wax' (Sp)
'Semiplena' (OGA)
R. sericea ssp. *omeinensis* f. *pteracantha* (Sp)
Sexy Rexy (Flor)
'Shailer's White Moss' (OGM)
Sheila's Perfume (Flor)
Shine On (Pat)
Shocking Blue (Flor)
'Shot Silk, Climbing' (Cl)
Silver Jubilee (HT)
'Silver Lining' (HT)
'Silver Wedding' (HT)
Snow Carpet (GrC)
'Snow Queen' (OGHP)
Solitaire (HT)
'Southampton' (Flor)
'Souvenir de Claudius Denoyel' (Cl)
'Souvenir de la Malmaison' (OGB)
'Souvenir de Saint Anne's' (OGB)
'Souvenir du Docteur Jamain' (Cl)
'Spanish Beauty' (Cl)
Sparkling Scarlet (Cl)
R. spinosissima (Sp)
'Stacey Sue' (Min)
'Stanwell Perpetual' (Sp)
Starina (Min)
Strawberry Fayre (Pat)
Suffolk (GrC)
Suma (GrC)
Summer Wine (Cl)
Sunblest (HT)
Super Star (HT)
Surrey (GrC)
Sussex (GrC)
'Swan Lake' (Cl)
Swany (GrC)
Sweet Dream (Pat)
Sweet Juliet (MS)
Sweet Magic (Pat)
Sympathie (Cl)
Tall Story (Flor)
Tango (Flor)
Tear Drop (Pat)
Tequila Sunrise (HT)
The Countryman (MS)
'The Fairy' (Poly)
The McCartney Rose (HT)
'The New Dawn' (Cl)
The Pilgrim (MS)
The Prince (MS)
The Times Rose (Flor)
Topsi (Flor)
Troika (HT)
Trumpeter (Flor)
'Tuscany Superb' (OGG)
Uncle Walter (HT)
'Veilchenblau' (Ra)
Velvet Fragrance (HT)
Vidal Sassoon (HT)
R. virginiana (Sp)
'Viridiflora' (OGCh)
Warm Welcome (MC)
Warm Wishes (HT)
'Wee Jock' (Pat)
'Wendy Cussons' (HT)
'Whisky Mac' (HT)
'White Bath' (OGM)
'White Cockade' (Cl)
'White Pet' (Poly)
Wiltshire (GrC)
Wishing (Flor)
R. xanthina 'Canary Bird'
'Yellow Doll' (Min)
'Yesterday' (Poly)
'Yvonne Rabier' (Poly)
'Zéphirine Drouhin' (Cl)
'Zigeunerknabe' (MS)

R. × *centifolia* 'Muscosa'♀ (common moss rose) Clear pink blooms open from buds covered with a reddish moss. HEIGHT & SPREAD 1.5×1.2m (5×4ft).

R. 'Gloire des Mousseuses' The lilac-pink blooms, fading to pale pink, are mossy in bud. The leaves are bright green. The flowers have good scent. HEIGHT & SPREAD 1.2×1m (4×3ft).

R. 'Henri Martin'♀ Profuse crimson blooms open flat on a branching shrub with vivid green moss. This plant needs support. HEIGHT & SPREAD 1.5×1.2m (5×4ft).

▲ *Rosa* 'Nuits de Young'

R. 'Nuits de Young' Velvety, deep maroon-purple blooms that are globular at first, open into loose cups showing golden stamens. This wiry plant has sparse, dark leaves. HEIGHT & SPREAD 1.2×1m (4×3ft).

R. 'Shailer's White Moss'♀ (syn. *R.* 'White Bath') The white, urn-shaped blooms have plenty of moss. The drooping leaves are dark green. HEIGHT & SPREAD 1.2×1m (4×3ft).

R. 'White Bath' see *R.* 'Shailer's White Moss'

Bourbon Roses

The plants listed, mainly repeat-flowering, have well-scented, double, cupped blooms with incurved petals opening to 7.5-10cm (3-4in) across. The vigorous open growth bears dark green leaves. There are no hips.

R. 'Blairii Number Two'♀ Pale pink flowers, even paler at the petal edges, are borne only in mid summer. A vigorous plant that can be grown as a climber. HEIGHT & SPREAD 3.5×2.4m (12×8ft).

R. 'Boule de Neige' Small white flowers with just a touch of pink open from pink buds. The petal edges curve back, giving the blooms a globular shape. HEIGHT & SPREAD 1.5×1.2m (5×4ft).

R. 'Honorine de Brabant' Pale pink, quartered blooms are striped with deeper pink and mauve. They last from mid summer until the autumn frosts. There are large, leathery leaves and few thorns. HEIGHT & SPREAD 1.8×1.8m (6×6ft).

R. 'Madame Isaac Pereire'♀ Fragrant, deep pink blooms tinged with purple are 12.5cm (5in) across. They are rather loosely formed with some quartering. The autumn display is magnificent, but if the weather is cold at the first flush some flowers are malformed. HEIGHT & SPREAD 2.1×1.5m (7×5ft).

▲ *Rosa* 'Madame Isaac Pereire'

R. 'Madame Pierre Oger' The tightly cupped, rosy crimson blooms have thin, papery petals with a pearly sheen. There is a good repeat-flowering. A loose plant which needs some support. HEIGHT & SPREAD 1.8×1.1m (6×3½ft).

R. 'Souvenir de la Malmaison' Shell-pink flowers deepen to blush-pink at the raised, quartered centre. They reach 12.5cm (5in) across and weigh down the dark-leaved shrub in fine weather, but may fail to open properly during wet spells. HEIGHT & SPREAD 1.2×1.2m (4×4ft).

R. 'Souvenir de Saint Anne's'♀ Fragrant, semidouble, creamy white flowers, up to 10cm (4in) across, bloom with great freedom and good continuity on this sturdy plant. HEIGHT & SPREAD 1.2×1.2m (4×4ft).

Portland Roses

The compact, upright bushes with light green leaves have their main flowering in mid summer, with some repeat flowering until the autumn frosts. The blooms are in clusters and generally have good fragrance.

▼ *Rosa* 'Souvenir de Saint Anne's'

R. 'Comte de Chambord' see *R.* 'Madame Knorr'

R. 'De Rescht'♀ (syn. *R.* 'Rose de Rescht') Deep fuchsia-pink, pompom-shaped flowers, 6cm (2½in) across and packed with petals, are carried in numerous clusters on this short, upright-growing plant. HEIGHT & SPREAD 1m×60cm (3×2ft).

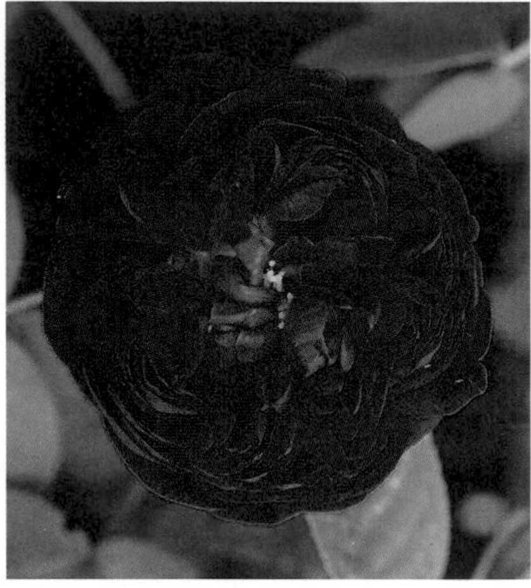

▲ *Rosa* 'De Rescht'

R. 'Duchess of Portland' see *R.* 'Portlandica'

R. 'Madame Knorr'♀ (syn. *R.* 'Comte de Chambord') Quartered, rich pink blooms, double and 10cm (4in) across, develop a hint of lilac as they fade. There is an abundant second flowering. The light green leaves are tinged with grey. HEIGHT & SPREAD 1.2×1m (4×3ft).

R. 'Portlandica' (syn. *R.* 'Duchess of Portland') The single to semidouble blooms are a deep pinky scarlet. They are up to 10cm (4in) across and make a good repeat display on this bushy, upright plant. HEIGHT & SPREAD 1.5×1m (5×3ft).

R. 'Rose de Rescht' see *R.* 'De Rescht'

Hybrid Perpetual Roses

These vigorous, upright, rather leggy plants with dark green leaves bear globular, shapely blooms about 9cm (3½in) across, which are the forerunners of the Large-flowered Bush Roses (Hybrid Teas). The flowers, borne singly or in small clusters from mid summer to autumn, include some with strong colours, except yellow, and these fade less if grown in some shade.

R. 'Baron Girod de l'Ain' The cupped, double blooms have bright crimson, waved petals edged with white. They are strongly fragrant and borne both in clusters and singly. A bushy plant. HEIGHT & SPREAD 1.2×1m (4×3ft).

R. 'Baronne Prévost'♀ Bright pink, quartered double blooms with a moderate scent open wide and flat on this freely branching plant with plentiful foliage. HEIGHT & SPREAD 1.2×1m (4×3ft).

R. **'Frau Karl Druschki'** (syn. *R.* 'Snow Queen') Dazzling white, double flowers open from pink-tinged buds on the arching stems. The blooms are not affected by rain. They have little scent. This leggy plant bears plentiful leathery foliage. HEIGHT & SPREAD 1.5×1m (5×3ft).
R. **'Mrs John Laing'** Beautifully formed, double, rosy lilac flowers with a rich scent are freely borne, singly and in clusters, on stout stems. An upright plant. HEIGHT & SPREAD 1.2×1m (4×3ft).

▲ *Rosa* 'Paul Neyron'

R. **'Paul Neyron'** Globular, 12.5cm (5in) wide flowers, mostly carried singly, are a deep raspberry-pink. They have only a slight scent. The leaves are dark green and leathery on a vigorous, upright plant. HEIGHT & SPREAD 1.5×1m (5×3ft).
R. **'Reine des Violettes'** The velvety, rosy violet flowers fade to lilac and are double, with quartering at the centre, and held in clusters. The plant has arching shoots and grey-green leaves. HEIGHT & SPREAD 1.5×1m (5×3ft).
R. **'Snow Queen'** see *R.* 'Frau Karl Druschki'

China Roses
The dainty flowers are varied in form and appear from early summer to autumn, but they have very little scent. They are carried in clusters of 3-4, with each flower opening to about 7.5cm (3in) across. These open-growing, airy shrubs have small dark leaves, almost always shiny.
R. **x *chinensis*** 'Mutabilis' see *R.* × *odorata* 'Mutabilis'
R. **'Irène Watts'**♀ Abundant ivory-white, double flowers, 8cm (3¼in) across, are shaded with pale orange-pink. There is a generous repeat on a plant that is small and bushy with matt leaves. HEIGHT & SPREAD 45×45cm (1½×1½ft).
R. **x *odorata* 'Mutabilis'** (syn. *R.* × *chinensis* 'Mutabilis', *R.* 'Mutabilis') Numerous, single blooms, 6cm (2½in) across, open from coppery buds to ochre-yellow flowers that turn pink, crimson and finally slate-purple as they age. All these colours can be seen at the same time. The plum-red stems and dark green leaves have a coppery tinge when new. The plant needs a warm spot to thrive. HEIGHT & SPREAD 1.2×1.2m (4×4ft).
'Viridiflora' (syn. *R.* 'Viridiflora') has unusual, green double flowers, 5cm (2in) across, sometimes with brownish tints. (The petals are actually modified leaves.) They turn purple as they age and become rather untidy. This rose reaches a height of 1m (3ft) and a spread of 75cm (2½ft).
R. **'Viridiflora'** see *R.* × *odorata* 'Viridiflora'

LARGE-FLOWERED BUSH ROSES (HYBRID TEA ROSES)
The flowers of the hundreds of Hybrid Teas available include all shades, except blue. Most hold their flower colour well, apart from a few that fade or discolour in hot sun or rain. Almost all varieties are double but some have fewer or thicker petals. These are less weighed down and damaged by rain, but they do tend to open fast and be over quickly.

The classic Hybrid Tea flower shape has a high, conical centre amid outer petals that reflex as they open. A fully opened flower is generally about 10cm (4in) across. Some varieties open to a more cupped shape. The first flowers appear in early summer and flowering continues well into autumn, with two main flushes and scattered blooms between. Most varieties have some scent and a number are richly fragrant. The blooms are on long, strong stems either singly or in small clusters. These plants need well-cultivated, moist soil and pruning, deadheading, and a careful watch for black spot, powdery mildew, rust and aphids.

Hybrid Teas are hardy and deciduous, generally with mid green leaves that have 5 ovate leaflets. They make upright growth and each variety's reliably uniform height makes them ideal for massing in formal beds. However, it is now common to mix varieties of different colours and heights, or to plant a group of Hybrid Teas in a mixed border that includes winter foliage to compensate for the bare rose bushes. Tall narrow varieties can make informal hedges.
R. **Abbeyfield Rose**♀ Freely borne deep rosy pink flowers with high centres are loosely formed and lightly scented. The foliage is dark and glossy on this low, bushy plant. HEIGHT & SPREAD 60×60cm (2×2ft).
R. **Alexander**♀+ The deep vermilion, lightly scented blooms are well shaped, and often have scalloped petals. A rose of upright growth with healthy, glossy foliage. HEIGHT & SPREAD 1.5m×60cm (5×2ft).
R. **Alpine Sunset** Soft yellow with a peachy flush, the blooms are full-petalled and sweetly scented. Plentiful light green, glossy leaves are borne on strong, upright stems. HEIGHT & SPREAD 60×60cm (2×2ft).
R. **Barkarole** Heavily perfumed and full-petalled, the deep red, large blooms are set off by dark, glossy foliage on a spreading bush. HEIGHT & SPREAD 1m×60cm (3×2ft).
R. **Big Purple** The flowers are a rich purple, full-petalled and sweetly scented. They are set off by dark, semi-glossy leaves. HEIGHT & SPREAD 1m×60cm (3×2ft).

▲ *Rosa* Blessings

R. **Blessings**♀ A long display of rosy, salmon-pink blooms are produced. The large, loosely formed flowers appear, often in clusters, on a sturdy, bushy plant. HEIGHT & SPREAD 1m×60cm (3×2ft).
R. **Blue Moon** The abundant lilac-mauve, fragrant flowers are elegantly formed. This rather narrow plant is short of leaves and often uneven in growth. HEIGHT & SPREAD 1m×60cm (3×2ft).
R. **Cherry Brandy** Scented blooms in blends of orange and salmon-pink make a fine display against glossy leaves on plants of an uneven growth. HEIGHT & SPREAD 75×60cm (2½×2ft).

▲ *Rosa* 'Cheshire Life'

R. **'Cheshire Life'** The profuse vermilion flowers are loosely formed. The growth is strong and well branched. HEIGHT & SPREAD 75×60cm (2½×2ft).

▲ *Rosa* Congratulations

▲ *Rosa* 'Dawn Chorus'

R. **Chicago Peace** Full yellow blooms, flushed orange and pink, are freely borne. The dark, glossy leaves are normally very healthy and the growth strong and bushy. HEIGHT & SPREAD 1.2m×60cm (4×2ft).
R. **Congratulations** Light pink, beautifully shaped blooms are carried profusely on long stems. The bush is rather lanky and has healthy, dark leaves. HEIGHT & SPREAD 1.5m×60cm (5×2ft).
R. **'Dawn Chorus'** Deep orange blooms are set off particularly well by red-tinged leaves. The flowers offer only moderate scent and size but the plant is vigorously bushy. HEIGHT & SPREAD 75×60cm (2½×2ft).
R. **Doctor McAlpine** Deep pink, well-scented blooms are borne singly and in clusters on a healthy plant that is spreading and bushy. HEIGHT & SPREAD 45×60cm (1½×2ft).
R. **Dutch Gold** Deep yellow blooms keep their colour well and show to advantage against handsome dark leaves. The scent is moderate, the plant bushy and the growth strong. HEIGHT & SPREAD 1m×60cm (3×2ft).
R. **Elina**♀ (syn. *R.* Peaudouce) Abundant shapely, creamy white blooms are borne one to a stem. They have a light scent, long stems and petals that withstand rain. A strong grower with dark leaves that may be affected by mildew in late summer. HEIGHT & SPREAD 1.2m×60cm (4×2ft).
R. **'Ernest H. Morse'+** (syn. *R.* 'E.H. Morse') Sweetly scented, rich crimson flowers, bloom with great freedom and a good repeat. Open-centred, they fade with age. This healthy, bushy plant has handsome, glossy leaves. HEIGHT & SPREAD 1m×60cm (3×2ft).

▲ *Rosa* Fragrant Cloud

R. **Fragrant Cloud+** Well-scented, dusky scarlet flowers are densely petalled but neatly formed, and carried in numerous trusses. The colour dulls a little in the sun. The dark leaves need watching for black spot. HEIGHT & SPREAD 75×60cm (2½×2ft).
R. **Fragrant Dream** The blend of apricot shades in the profuse, fragrant, full-petalled blooms is enhanced by abundant, healthy leaves. The plant is an upright grower. HEIGHT & SPREAD 75×60cm (2½×2ft).
R. **Freedom**♀**+** Shapely, deep butter-yellow flowers that keep their colour are freely borne but have only a slight scent. A bushy uniform plant with plenty of glossy leaves. HEIGHT & SPREAD 75×60cm (2½×2ft).
R. **'Gaujard'** see *R.* Rose Gaujard
R. **Golden Jubilee** Well-formed, lightly scented yellow blooms are flushed pink at the petal edges. The growth is bushy and the leaves large and glossy. HEIGHT & SPREAD 75×60cm (2½×2ft).
R. **'Grandpa Dickson'+** The well-formed, full-petalled, light yellow blooms pale and the rolled-back petal edges turn pink. An upright, very thorny plant. HEIGHT & SPREAD 75×60cm (2½×2ft).
R. **Harry Wheatcroft** Golden yellow in bud, these well-formed blooms have petals striped scarlet and yellow on their upper sides; the scent is light. The leaves on the bushy growth are dark and glossy. HEIGHT & SPREAD 75×60cm (2½×2ft).
R. **Ice Cream** Ivory-white blooms show well against dark, bronze-tinted foliage on a bushy plant. The full flowers are fragrant. HEIGHT & SPREAD 75×60cm (2½×2ft).
R. **Ingrid Bergman**♀ The abundant velvety blooms of dusky red have little scent. This sturdy plant has dark, leathery foliage and fairly even growth. HEIGHT & SPREAD 1m×60cm (3×2ft).
R. **Jardins de Bagatelle** see *R.* Sarah
R. **Julia's Rose** The loosely formed flowers are an unusual, light pinkish brown. They have little scent. This well-branched plant has rich green foliage but is not a robust grower. HEIGHT & SPREAD 60×60cm (2×2ft).

▲ *Rosa* Julia's Rose

R. **Just Joey**♀ Copper-pink blooms that fade to creamy orange have wavy-edged petals. The flowers are pleasantly scented but the foliage tends to be sparse. HEIGHT & SPREAD 75×60cm (2½×2ft).
R. **Keepsake** The immaculately formed, globular, cerise-pink flowers have a lighter shading at the base of the petals. This vigorous plant has healthy, dark foliage. HEIGHT & SPREAD 1m×60cm (3×2ft).
R. **King's Ransom** Plentiful, rich yellow, well-shaped blooms are held upright over glossy dark foliage on this vigorous, branching, healthy plant. The scent is light. HEIGHT & SPREAD 75×60cm (2½×2ft).

▲ *Rosa* 'La France'

R. **'La France'** Pleasantly scented, semi-double, silvery pink blooms appear profusely in clusters. This plant is vigorous. HEIGHT & SPREAD 75×60cm (2½×2ft).
R. **L'Oréal Trophy** The lightly scented, orange-salmon flowers hold their colour well. HEIGHT & SPREAD 1.2m×60cm (4×2ft).
R. **Lovely Lady**♀ The abundant well-formed blooms of pure, clear pink are moderate in fragrance. There is plenty of

▲ *Rosa* 'Lovers' Meeting'

healthy, dark foliage on this bushy plant. HEIGHT & SPREAD 1m×60cm (3×2ft).

***R.* 'Lovers' Meeting'** The shapely, warm orange blooms are lightly scented and appear in clusters. The bronze-tinted leaves are held on red shoots. This spreading plant is healthy but likely to suffer die-back from frost. HEIGHT & SPREAD 75×60cm (2½×2ft).

***R.* Loving Memory** The plentiful, vivid crimson-red blooms hold their colour well and are shapely with a light fragrance. The plant is vigorous, tall and upright. HEIGHT & SPREAD 1.1m×60cm (3½×2ft).

***R.* 'Madame Butterfly'** The very fragrant, pale pink flowers are soft yellow at the heart and fade to cream. They are dainty but full-petalled and numerous on a firm-stemmed, upright plant with small leaves. HEIGHT & SPREAD 60×60cm (2×2ft).

***R.* 'National Trust'** The bright red well-shaped blooms have little scent. There is plentiful, dark foliage. HEIGHT & SPREAD 60×60cm (2×2ft).

***R.* 'Ophelia'** Light pink flowers are especially profuse later in the season. The foliage is not too plentiful. HEIGHT & SPREAD 60×60cm (2×2ft).

***R.* Painted Moon** Flowers in blends of light yellow, crimson and pink, are carried in large clusters, but have little scent. The bushy plant has plentiful glossy foliage. HEIGHT & SPREAD 75×60cm (2½×2ft).

▲ *Rosa* 'National Trust'

***R.* Pascali** Shapely white flowers with a hint of buff at the centre and little scent are borne profusely, rarely in clusters. The leaves are dark on a very narrow, upright plant. HEIGHT & SPREAD 1m×60cm (3×2ft)

***R.* Paul McCartney** see *R.* The McCartney Rose

***R.* Paul Shirville**♀ Beautifully formed, soft pink blooms, tinged amber at the heart, are sweetly scented and carried with great freedom, sometimes in extra-large clusters. This well-branched bush has abundant dark leaves, though black spot may afflict them. HEIGHT & SPREAD 75×60cm (2½×2ft).

***R.* Peace**♀+ The superb, full blooms of pale yellow have waved petals, often tinged pink at the edge. The lightly scented flowers, usually borne one to a stem, are profuse in mid summer and in autumn. Glossy foliage clothes this vigorous, branching plant. HEIGHT & SPREAD 1.2m×60cm (4×2ft).

***R.* Peaudouce** see *R.* Elina

***R.* Peer Gynt** Bright yellow blooms with a reddish flush, deeper on the outer petals, are full, globular, and mostly in large clusters. The scent is light. A bushy plant. HEIGHT & SPREAD 75×60cm (2½×2ft).

***R.* Piccadilly** Scarlet petals with yellow on the outer side merge to orange as the profuse, shapely blooms open. They withstand rain well, but fade in the sun. There is little scent. The bushy plant has handsome, dark foliage, sometimes affected by black spot. HEIGHT & SPREAD 75×60cm (2½×2ft).

***R.* 'Pink Favourite'** Bright pink, full-petalled high-centred blooms are profusely borne with a good repeat. The colour fades slightly and the scent is light. Strong and branching growth bears plentiful glossy leaves. HEIGHT & SPREAD 1m×60cm (3×2ft).

▼ *Rosa* Painted Moon

▲ *Rosa* Polar Star

***R.* 'Pink Peace'** The deep pink, sweetly scented blooms are rather loosely formed. This plant flowers freely and is vigorous, with plenty of dark, leathery foliage. HEIGHT & SPREAD 1.1m×60cm (3½×2ft).

***R.* Polar Star** Beautifully formed, fragrant blooms are borne on strong, upright stems. The flowers are not easily spoiled by rain and the large dark leaves are usually healthy. HEIGHT & SPREAD 75×60cm (2½×2ft).

***R.* Pot o' Gold** The golden yellow, well-scented, full blooms have slightly scalloped petals. The abundant flowers appear singly and in sprays on a bushy plant with glossy leaves. HEIGHT & SPREAD 75×60cm (2½×2ft).

***R.* 'Precious Platinum'** The vibrant blood-red flowers are large, well-shaped, lightly scented and freely produced. The leaves are dark and glossy on a bushy. healthy plant. HEIGHT & SPREAD 75×60cm (2½×2ft).

▲ *Rosa* Rosemary Harkness

***R.* Princess Royal** Large, shapely blooms in deep golden yellow suffused with apricot are very profuse. The scent is slight. Healthy leaves clothe this strong, bushy plant. HEIGHT & SPREAD 75×60cm (2½×2ft).

▲ *Rosa* Pristine

***R.* Pristine** Strongly fragrant, large-petalled blooms in ivory-white shade to blush pink at the edges. Dark leaves are carried on the strong stems of this robust plant. HEIGHT & SPREAD 1.1m×60cm (3½×2ft).

***R.* Remember Me** Coppery orange flowers with some vivid red tints bloom singly and in clusters on the dense, upright growth that carries ample healthy, dark foliage. HEIGHT & SPREAD 75×60cm (2½×2ft).

***R.* Renaissance** The shapely, delicate, blush-pink blooms are very fragrant. They are carried with freedom and continuity. The bush is upright with plenty of foliage. HEIGHT & SPREAD 75×60cm (2½×2ft).

***R.* Rose Gaujard+** (syn. *R.* 'Gaujard') The numerous, bright cerise blooms with silvery-backed petals are full and, though shapely in bud, usually have a split, muddled centre as they open. They are borne singly among plentiful glossy dark leaves on a branching, vigorous, healthy plant. HEIGHT & SPREAD 1m×60cm (3×2ft).

***R.* Rosemary Harkness** Orange, salmon and yellow blend in well-formed, large, fragrant blooms, that pale as they age. This freely branching plant has glossy dark leaves. HEIGHT & SPREAD 75×60cm (2½×2ft).

***R.* 'Rosy Cheeks'** The large, well-scented, carmine-pink flowers are yellow on the petals' underside. This plant is bushy with bright, glossy leaves. HEIGHT & SPREAD 60×60cm (2×2ft).

***R.* Royal William**♀ Blood-red, fully fragrant, gracefully formed blooms are carried in great profusion on strong shoots. The leaves are dark on this healthy, vigorous plant. HEIGHT & SPREAD 1m×60cm (3×2ft).

***R.* 'Ruby Wedding'** The warm crimson, lightly scented blooms are full-petalled, shapely and held on strong stems. This well-branched plant has dainty foliage. HEIGHT & SPREAD 75×60cm (2½×2ft).

***R.* Sarah** (syn. *R.* Jardins de Bagatelle) Richly perfumed, cream blooms with blush-pink round the petal edges are borne on strong upright stems. The foliage is plentiful on a well-branched plant of even growth. HEIGHT & SPREAD 60×60cm (2×2ft).

***R.* Savoy Hotel**♀ Large, full-petalled blooms are light pink with deeper shading at the centre. They are lightly scented. The leaves are dark on the spreading plant. HEIGHT & SPREAD 60×60 cm (2×2ft).

***R.* Silver Jubilee**♀**+** Continuous and abundant large, shapely blooms have a pale pink centre tinged salmon at the base and set among deeper pink petals. The colour lasts well but there is little scent. The normally healthy plant is sturdy with a wealth of glossy dark leaves. HEIGHT & SPREAD 75×60cm (2½×2ft).

***R.* 'Silver Lining'+** Pale pink, strongly fragrant blooms are silvery white on the back of the very dense petals, which develop a deeper pink rim as they age. The plant is an upright grower with glossy leaves. HEIGHT & SPREAD 75×60cm (2½×2ft).

***R.* 'Silver Wedding'** Ivory blooms with a light scent are cream at the centre, neatly formed and borne in clusters. The dark-leaved plant is not a strong grower. HEIGHT & SPREAD 60×60cm (2×2ft).

***R.* Solitaire+** The clear yellow, pink-edged fragrant blooms are set off by dark bronze-tinted, glossy foliage. The plant is healthy and very vigorous but uneven in growth. HEIGHT & SPREAD 1.2m×60cm (4×2ft).

***R.* Sunblest** Golden yellow, moderately full blooms hold their colour in sun and rain. The bushy, healthy plant is an even grower with small, shiny, light green leaves. HEIGHT & SPREAD 75×60cm (2½×2ft).

***R.* Super Star+** The vivid vermilion blooms are well formed, full and borne abundantly in clusters. There is a light scent. The blooms withstand rain and do not fade. The upright plant grows robustly but its dark foliage is susceptible to mildew. HEIGHT & SPREAD 1m×60cm (3×2ft).

***R.* Tequila Sunrise**♀ Brilliant yellow petals edged with scarlet form full, well-shaped blooms. They are plentiful, lightly scented and retain their colour to make a striking

▲ *Rosa* Solitare

Rosa Tequila Sunrise ▼

r

▲ *Rosa* 'Wendy Cussons'

▲ *Rosa* 'Whisky Mac'

▲ *Rosa* 'Cécile Brunner'

show against dark, glossy leaves on a sturdy plant. HEIGHT & SPREAD 75×60cm (2½×2ft).

***R.* The McCartney Rose** (syn. *R.* Paul McCartney) Deep candy-pink, elegant flowers are richly perfumed and carried on a robust upright plant with gleaming, dark foliage. HEIGHT & SPREAD 1m×60cm (3×2ft).

***R.* Troika**♀ Scarlet buds open to shapely coppery orange flowers with golden centres; they age to creamy pink. They are almost rainproof but only lightly scented. This vigorous, normally healthy bush has plenty of glossy leaves. HEIGHT & SPREAD 1.1m×60cm (3½×2ft).

***R.* Uncle Walter** Bright scarlet flowers with the classic, high-centred shape, but little scent, are borne profusely in clusters. This plant is spindly and it needs support. It does well on a pillar. HEIGHT & SPREAD 1.5m×60cm (5×2ft).

***R.* Velvet Fragrance** The heavily scented, deep crimson-pink blooms are beautifully formed and set off by glossy, dark leaves. This plant is vigorous with upright growth. HEIGHT & SPREAD 1.1m×60cm (3½×2ft).

***R.* Vidal Sassoon** The large flowers are lavender-pink with brown overtones, and have a rich, slightly lemony scent. The leaves are glossy on a strong-stemmed plant. HEIGHT & SPREAD 75×60cm (2½×2ft)

***R.* Warm Wishes** Shapely, well-scented blooms of a pale orange-pink are borne over a long period on a well-branched bush with glossy leaves. HEIGHT & SPREAD 75×60cm (2½×2ft).

***R.* 'Wendy Cussons'**+ Very fragrant, elegantly formed, deep pink flowers are freely borne and withstand rain well. Leathery leaves are dark and glossy on this well-branched and wide-spreading plant. HEIGHT & SPREAD 1m×60cm (3×2ft).

***R.* 'Whisky Mac'** Profuse, richly scented, yellow blooms with an orange flush are full-petalled and finely formed. They show well against abundant dark leaves, bronze-tinged when young, on an upright-growing plant. This rose is marred by die-back from frost, and by susceptibility to rust and mildew. HEIGHT & SPREAD 75×60cm (2½×2ft).

POLYANTHA ROSES

One parent of Polyantha Roses was *R. multiflora*, a vigorous, cluster-flowered wild rose. The short, generally upright, early Polyanthas carried numerous flower clusters but tended to produce different-coloured sports and their health was suspect. Only a few of these early Polyantha plants are still available.

Most of the roses sold as Polyanthas now are the result of crossing true Polyanthas with Teas and other roses from China. They retain the bushy growth of the originals and make successful, free-flowering shrubs with two main flushes of clustered bloom, usually faintly scented. They are suitable for foreground planting and small gardens or patios.

***R.* 'Ballerina'**♀ Pale pink, single flowers, 2.5cm (1in) across, shading to a white centre, are borne in big, mop-head clusters on this spreading shrub. The generous repeat flowering is followed by an autumn crop of small hips. The mid green leaves are plentiful, small, narrow and shiny. HEIGHT & SPREAD 1×1m (3×3ft).

***R.* 'Cécile Brunner'**♀ (syn. *R.* 'Maltese Rose') Lightly scented, flesh-pink, double flowers, deepening in colour at the heart, are high-centred at first, then open loosely to 4cm (1½in) across. This airy plant has dark green, pointed healthy leaves. HEIGHT & SPREAD 1.1m×60cm (3½×2ft).

***R.* 'Little White Pet'** see *R.* 'White Pet'

***R.* 'Maltese Rose'** see *R.* 'Cécile Brunner'

***R.* 'Mevrouw Nathalie Nypels'**♀ (syn. *R.* 'Nathalie Nypels') Clear pink, semidouble, lightly scented blooms, 6cm (2½in) across, are borne in abundant clusters. The small, light green leaves are plentiful. HEIGHT & SPREAD 75×75cm (2½×2½ft).

***R.* 'The Fairy'**♀ Pale pink, double, rosette-shaped blooms, 5cm (2in) across, are in profuse clusters; they come into flower late but then make a continuous show on stiff but spreading shoots. The glossy leaves need watching for black spot. HEIGHT & SPREAD 76cm×1m (2½×3ft).

***R.* 'White Pet'**♀ (syn. *R.* 'Little White Pet') Clusters of creamy white, double pompom blooms, 5cm (2in) across, appear all summer. The dark leaves stay on the plant late. HEIGHT & SPREAD 45×45cm (1½×1½ft).

***R.* 'Yesterday'**♀ Deep rosy lilac flowers, white at the centre, bloom all summer in small trusses. They are scented, semidouble and 2.5cm (1in) across on an airy bush with small, shiny, mid-green leaves. HEIGHT & SPREAD 1.1×1.1m (3½×3½ft).

***R.* 'Yvonne Rabier'**♀ Sweetly scented, white, double, rosette-shaped, 5cm (2in) wide blooms, tinged yellow at the heart, flower all summer in small clusters. The deep green leaves stay on into winter. HEIGHT & SPREAD 45×45cm (1½×1½ft).

CLUSTER-FLOWERED BUSH ROSES (FLORIBUNDA ROSES)

Crosses between cluster-flowered Polyantha Roses and Hybrid Teas produced the Floribundas, which became popular during the 1930s – and the number of varieties still increases yearly. Because their parents had little scent, most Floribundas also lacked scent until recently, when more care has been taken to breed new varieties from the more fragrant strains.

In their size, habit of growth and uses in the garden the Floribundas do not differ from Hybrid Teas. The main difference between these two groups lies in the flowers and the way in which they are carried on the plant. The individual flowers of Floribundas are smaller and they are borne in large clusters or trusses, some having 20 or more blooms. Because the flowers in each truss do not all open at once, the flowering period is lengthened considerably – and as the old clusters fade, new ones are forming to continue the display. There is not the gap of a few weeks that occurs between the flushes of bloom in the case of many Hybrid Teas.

▼ *Rosa* 'Ballerina'

Since most Floribundas have fewer, and more substantial, petals than Hybrid Teas, water drains more easily from the flowers and they withstand wet weather better.

In the plants listed below, flower size is given only if it is very different from the average 6cm (2½in). The flowers are double, semidouble or single according to variety, and have a light scent unless stated otherwise. The spread is generally a little less than the height, and is given only when it differs markedly.

Rosa Allgold

R. **Allgold+** Shapely, bright yellow, double blooms hold their colour in sun and rain, making a vivid show all summer. The small, healthy leaves are bright green on this bushy plant. HEIGHT 60cm (2ft).

R. **Amber Queen**♀ Amber-yellow, fragrant double blooms, suffused with soft orange, are carried in large clusters with good continuity of flowering. This spreading, healthy plant has dark foliage, red-tinted when young. HEIGHT 60cm (2ft).

R. **Anna Livia**♀ Soft salmon-pink, double blooms in big clusters are rainproof and carried above bushy growth whose leathery, glossy foliage is among the healthiest of all roses. HEIGHT 75cm (2½ft).

R. **Anne Harkness** The huge heads of light apricot, rosette-shaped flowers appear later than other roses and continue well into autumn. A tall plant with dark, semi-glossy, healthy leaves. HEIGHT 1.2m (4ft).

R. **'Arthur Bell'**♀ Golden yellow, shapely double blooms that are larger than most floribundas and fade to cream. They are strongly scented. This plant is upright with healthy, shiny leaves. HEIGHT 1m (3ft).

R. **Bright Smile** Sparkling clear yellow, semidouble flowers in small clusters come into bloom early on a bushy, spreading plant whose glossy leaves are usually healthy. HEIGHT 60cm (2ft).

R. **Bucks Fizz** Light, warm orange, well-formed, double blooms on an upright plant are set off by healthy foliage that is red-tinged when young, then a glossy, dark green. HEIGHT 1m (3ft).

▲ *Rosa* Anne Harkness

▲ *Rosa* Anna Livia

▲ *Rosa* Champagne Cocktail

▼ *Rosa* Bright Smile

R. **By Appointment** The double flowers have creamy petals round the close-furled, deep apricot centre. They come in large, well-spaced trusses and are enhanced by the dark, shiny leaves. HEIGHT 75cm (2½ft).

R. **Champagne Cocktail** Large, fragrant, semidouble flowers of pale yellow are flecked with rich pink and are deeper pink on the back of the petals. They are abundant on this erect plant with dark, glossy, healthy leaves. HEIGHT 1m (3ft).

R. **'Chanelle'** Shapely and fragrant double blooms in creamy pink and apricot are freely borne and unspoiled by rain. The leaves are normally very healthy. HEIGHT 75cm (2½ft).

R. **Chinatown**♀+ The very large, sweetly scented, bright yellow, double flowers in medium-sized clusters are sometimes edged with pink. This tall plant has bright green, glossy leaves. HEIGHT 1.2m (4ft).

R. **City of London**♀ Blush-pink, fragrant, double blooms are borne in graceful sprays against bright green, glossy leaves. HEIGHT 1.1m (3½ft).

R. **Dame Wendy** The abundant, full, bright peach-pink, double flowers hold their colour well. A spreading plant with purplish young foliage that matures to dark

▲ *Rosa* Elizabeth of Glamis

grey-green. HEIGHT 75 cm (2½ ft).
R. **'Dicbar'** see *R.* Memento
R. **Drummer Boy** This short, spreading plant bears clusters of bright blood-red, semidouble blooms, displayed against abundant foliage. HEIGHT 45 cm (1½ ft).
R. **Edith Holden** Warm brownish gold, semidouble flowers open wide, showing a bright yellow eye. The blooms are numerous on a strong, bushy plant with dark green leaves. HEIGHT 75 cm (2½ ft).
R. **Elizabeth of Glamis+** Large, shapely, double blooms in salmon-pink with an orange tint are carried in well-spaced clusters and are strongly fragrant. The colour withstands rain but the plant does not thrive in heavy, cold soils. HEIGHT 75 cm (2½ ft).
R. **'English Miss'** The delicate, blush-pink, strongly scented blooms, shading to white, are cupped and full-petalled. The leaves are dark, purplish and semi-glossy. HEIGHT 75 cm (2½ ft).
R. **Escapade**♀ The fragrant, pale rosy violet, semidouble blooms, which open wide to show the white centre, hold their colour well and make a long, generous display. The vigorous plant has shiny, light green, very healthy leaves. HEIGHT 1 m (3 ft).
R. **Eye Paint** The showy, wide-open, single flowers are small and scarlet with a white eye, golden stamens and white backs to the petals. They are carried in huge clusters against dark, glossy leaves. The flowers have little scent. HEIGHT 1.4 m (4 ft).

▼ *Rosa* 'English Miss'

▼ *Rosa* Escapade

▲ *Rosa* Eye Paint

R. **Fellowship+** Scented, cupped, deep orange, double blooms are carried singly and in clusters with great freedom on an upright, well-branched plant with glossy, dark green leaves. HEIGHT 75 cm (2½ ft).
R. **Fragrant Delight**♀ The glowing, orange-tinted, salmon-pink, double flowers fade to a pale pink. They have a rich scent and are numerous, shapely and semi-double. The large open sprays show well against red stems and dark green, bronze-tinted leaves. HEIGHT 1 m (3 ft).
R. **'Glenfiddich'** The rich amber-yellow, double flowers are shapely and bloom with good continuity on this upright plant with dark, glossy leaves. HEIGHT 75 cm (2½ ft).
R. **Golden Wedding** Bright yellow, high-centred, full-petalled and shapely flowers bloom in small clusters on a vigorous, healthy plant with glossy, dark foliage. HEIGHT 75 cm (2½ ft).
R. **Golden Years** Golden yellow flowers open to wide, full-petalled cups and are carried in profusion on an upright plant with dark, glossy leaves. HEIGHT 75 cm (2½ ft).
R. **Greenall's Glory** The semidouble blooms are blush-pink at the centre and silvery white towards the edge. This low, spreading plant has bronze-tinged, glossy leaves. HEIGHT 45 cm (1½ ft).
R. **'Gruss an Aachen'** The very large, full-petalled blooms are creamy white to blush-pink. The sprays are shown off well by the dark, leathery foliage. HEIGHT 45 cm (1½ ft).
R. **Hannah Gordon** Freely borne, semi-double, shapely white blooms have their petals edged with cherry-pink. This tall, open-growing bush has healthy, glossy, dark leaves. HEIGHT 1 m (3 ft).
R. **Harvest Fayre** Large clusters of light golden orange, well-formed, double flowers glow against the light green leaves densely clothing the bushy, strong plant. HEIGHT 75 cm (2½ ft).
R. **Honeymoon** Full-petalled, canary-yellow, rosette-shaped blooms show beautifully against the semi-glossy leaves of this very vigorous plant. HEIGHT 1 m (3 ft).

▲ *Rosa* Iceberg

R. **Iceberg**♀**+** (syn. *R.* 'Schneewittchen') The double white blooms, which are sometimes stained pink by rain, are carried in large clusters on slender shoots. The pointed leaves are light green. Flowering often continues until Christmas on this vigorous, gracefully spreading, almost thornless plant. HEIGHT 1 m (3 ft).
R. **'Iced Ginger'** The flowers are ivory-buff at the centre and coppery pink towards the edge. They are double, profuse and stiff-stemmed on a strong-growing bush. HEIGHT 1 m (3 ft).
R. **Invincible** The nonstop, bright scarlet-crimson, double blooms, which hold their colour well in sun and rain, are shapely on a robust, upright plant with dark green, semi-glossy leaves. HEIGHT 75 cm (2½ ft).
R. **'Korresia'** The sparkling bright yellow, double flowers with wavy-edged petals hold their colour and are sweetly perfumed. They are ideal for bedding and bloom continuously in well-spaced trusses enhanced by bright green, shiny leaves on a tidy plant. HEIGHT 75 cm (2½ ft).
R. **Lilli Marlene** Deep scarlet, double blooms, opening wide and rather loose, hold their colour and are profusely borne in

▲ *Rosa* 'Korresia'

▲ *Rosa* Many Happy Returns

▲ *Rosa* Margaret Merril

large, stiff-stemmed trusses. They have very little scent. This dense, branching plant is well covered with glossy, mid green leaves. HEIGHT 75 cm (2½ ft).

***R.* 'Macrexy'** see *R.* Sexy Rexy

***R.* Many Happy Returns**♀ Abundant clusters of finely formed, blush-pink, large double blooms cover a dense, spreading plant, which has large, glossy, pointed leaves. HEIGHT 1 m (3 ft).

***R.* Margaret Merril**♀ Richly fragrant, pearly white, double blooms, with a faint blush at the centre and pinkish gold stamens, are exquisitely formed. They are abundantly borne in clusters. The dark leaves are glossy. HEIGHT 75 cm (2½ ft).

***R.* 'Masquerade'+** Small, semidouble blooms that change from yellow to flame to pink and then red as they age are borne in huge trusses that show all the colours at the same time and repeat well if assiduously deadheaded. This tall, freely branching bush has dark, glossy leaves. HEIGHT 1.1 m (3½ ft).

***R.* Matangi+** The orange-red, double blooms have a white eye and are silvery white on the back of the petals They are carried on a bushy plant with dark, glossy leaves. HEIGHT 1.1 m (3½ ft).

***R.* Melody Maker** Light vermilion, full-petalled blooms with a silvery sheen in the centre are held in large trusses on a bushy, dark-leaved plant. HEIGHT 75 cm (2½ ft).

***R.* Memento** (syn. *R.* 'Dicbar') Seldom out of flower, this rose bears its orange-red, double blooms in clusters. The flowers hold their colour well and open out wide against this bushy plant's plentiful dark leaves. HEIGHT 75 cm (2½ ft).

***R.* Mountbatten**♀ Sunny soft yellow, full-petalled flowers bloom in large clusters and singly on a tall plant with dark glossy leaves. HEIGHT 1.2 m (4 ft).

***R.* 'Oranges and Lemons'** Orange-yellow petals striped with scarlet make eye-catching large, double blooms that are well displayed in open clusters on this upright plant. New leaves have a coppery tinge. HEIGHT 1 m (3 ft).

***R.* Peppermint Ice** Pale green shades in the ivory-white petals make the full-petalled, shapely blooms unusual. They are profuse, and set off by the glossy leaves on this well-branched plant. HEIGHT 75 cm (2½ ft).

***R.* Perestroika** As the shapely, golden yellow, double flowers open, the petals roll back at the edges. The blooms shine out from this low, rounded plant clothed with dark, glossy, usually healthy foliage. The flowers are virtually unscented. HEIGHT 45 cm (1½ ft).

▼ *Rosa* Matangi

▼ *Rosa* Memento

▲ *Rosa* 'Oranges and Lemons'

***R.* 'Pink Parfait'+** The satin-pink, double blooms, rich cream at the petal base, are very shapely as they open and are held in profuse clusters. The open, rather slender growth has dark green foliage. HEIGHT 75 cm (2½ ft).

***R.* Purple Tiger** Very striking mauve blooms with variable purple striping and touches of ivory are full-petalled and open out wide. This plant has few thorns and is well filled out with dark leaves. HEIGHT 75 cm (2½ ft).

***R.* Queen Elizabeth**♀**+** Clear pink, cupped blooms that are well formed and double are held singly and in small clusters at the top of the bush on strong stems with few thorns. This tall, upright plant is rather narrow with an ample covering of very large, healthy leaves. HEIGHT 1.8 m (6 ft).

***R.* Redgold** Double blooms with a variable red edging merging with the bright gold centre are held in large sprays. They age to a pinky orange. The tall, strong shoots have rather sparse leaves. HEIGHT 1 m (3 ft).

***R.* Remembrance** Deep scarlet, double flowers are carried with abundance in large trusses and over a long season. This compact and bushy plant has glossy, dark leaves. HEIGHT 60 cm (2 ft).

***R.* Rob Roy** The rich crimson-scarlet, well-formed, double blooms are large and

▼ *Rosa* Purple Tiger

borne both singly and in small clusters. The growth is upright, with sparse, semi-glossy, dark green foliage. HEIGHT 1m (3ft).
R. Scarlet Queen Elizabeth Large, globular, deep scarlet blooms appear in great profusion on a stiff, upright plant with plenty of dark foliage. HEIGHT 1.2m (4ft).
R. Schneewittchen see *R.* Iceberg

▲ *Rosa* Sexy Rexy

Rosa Trumpeter ▲

R. Sexy Rexy♀ (syn. *R.* 'Macrexy') Palest coral-pink, small but full-petalled blooms with slightly frilled petals are borne in large clusters over a long period. They are shown off by plentiful dark, glossy leaves. HEIGHT 75cm (2½ft).
R. Sheila's Perfume Well-formed, golden yellow, double blooms, their large petals edged with pinky red, are richly fragrant. The foliage is glossy, dark green and healthy on a strong-stemmed, well-branched plant. HEIGHT 75cm (2½ft).
R. Shocking Blue The numerous and unusually coloured, vivid magenta-mauve, double blooms are carried in medium clusters. They are well formed and rich in fragrance. The leaves are a good dark green but the plant is not a strong grower. HEIGHT 75cm (2½ft).
R. 'Southampton'♀ Apricot, large, double blooms are fragrant and borne in big clusters on an upright bush with shiny, very healthy leaves. HEIGHT 1m (3ft).
R. Tall Story Soft yellow, semidouble flowers are carried among light green, semi-glossy leaves along arching branches, which make the plant so wide-spreading that it can

▼ *Rosa* Sheila's Perfume

▲ *Rosa* 'Southampton'

▲ *Rosa* Tango

be used for ground cover. The flowers give a good repeat display. HEIGHT & SPREAD 75cm×1.5m (2½×5ft).
R. Tango♀ In these unique orange-scarlet blooms, each petal has a fine white rim, a yellow base and a yellow back. The flowers are profuse and full-petalled, opening wide on an upright plant with glossy, dark leaves. HEIGHT 75cm (2½ft).
R. The Times Rose♀+ The continuous display has trusses of dark crimson-red, very full blooms that open to flat rosettes showing golden stamens. This sturdy, spreading plant is well clothed with healthy, coppery tinged, shiny leaves that turn dark green as they age. HEIGHT 75cm (2½ft).
R. Topsi+ Orange-scarlet, semidouble blooms that keep their colour flower with great profusion. Both flowers and leaves are large on the short but sturdy bush. It may be subject to die-back. HEIGHT 45cm (1½ft).
R. Trumpeter♀ Heavy trusses of orange-scarlet double blooms may make this plant rather sprawling. The flowers, which have little scent, are well shown off by plenty of glossy healthy leaves. HEIGHT 75cm (2½ft).
R. Wishing Peach and salmon shades blend in the shapely double blooms, which are borne in well-spaced clusters. They stand out against the gleaming leaves that fill out this bushy plant. HEIGHT 60cm (2ft).

▲ *Rosa* Wishing

MODERN SHRUB ROSES

Some of the most free-flowering of all roses are among the Modern Shrubs, whose branching stems bear generous clusters of blooms in a full palette of colours. The diversity of the plants reflects the variety of parents used to produce roses with the vigour and free growth of the old and the long flowering period and bright tints of the new. The flowers can be single, semi-double or double, and are mostly carried in clusters. There are sprawling growers that make mounds more than 3m (10ft) tall, upright shrubs resembling Floribunda bush roses, and spreading, freely branching ones like the sweetly scented Hybrid Musks. The English Roses combine the flower form and scent of old roses with a modern range of colour. Rugosa Roses belong here but are treated separately below.

The bigger Modern Shrubs make beautiful specimen plants, and most of the others are successful as hedging. These plants' informal habit of growth suits mixed borders better than carefully pruned bush roses. With few exceptions Modern Shrub Roses are repeat flowering, a later blooming being encouraged by diligent deadheading.
R. Abraham Darby Apricot-pink double blooms that are fragrant, cup-shaped and

▼ *Rosa* Abraham Darby

r

▲ *Rosa* 'Buff Beauty'

10 cm (4 in) across, are borne on this English Rose, which makes spreading growth. HEIGHT & SPREAD 1.5×1.5 m (5×5 ft).

***R.* 'Buff Beauty'**♀ Large clusters of buff to apricot, lightly scented, double flowers that fade to pale cream are 7.5 cm (3 in) across and extremely profuse. Dark, glossy foliage clothes this spreading Hybrid Musk shrub. HEIGHT & SPREAD 1.2×1.2 m (4×4 ft).

***R.* Constance Spry**♀ The outstanding, clear pink blooms are 10 cm (4 in) across, double, urn-shaped and richly perfumed. Although not repeat flowering, they are carried very freely over a long period in mid summer. The long, arched shoots need support and look well on a dome-shaped frame. HEIGHT & SPREAD 1.8×1.5 m (6×5 ft).

▲ *Rosa* 'Cornelia'

***R.* 'Cornelia'**♀ The apricot-pink, scented, double blooms are only 5 cm (2 in) across and are borne in large trusses. They are set off by the dark green leaves. This robust, arching Hybrid Musk has a generous repeat flowering in autumn. HEIGHT & SPREAD 1.5×1.5 m (5×5 ft).

***R.* English Garden** The ivory-white, quartered, double blooms, shading to yellow in the centre, are fragrant and open to 10 cm (4 in) across. A short, upright English Rose. HEIGHT & SPREAD 1 m×60 cm (3×2 ft).

▲ *Rosa* English Garden

***R.* Evelyn** Light apricot-pink, double blooms with a full fragrance are 9 cm (3½ in) across. This English Rose is fairly small but bushy. HEIGHT & SPREAD 1.1×1 m (3½×3 ft).

***R.* Felicia**♀ Many sprays of double, light pink flowers that open flat to 7.5 cm (3 in) across have the sweet Hybrid Musk scent. They show well against dark, shiny leaves on this spreading plant. HEIGHT & SPREAD 1.5×2.1 m (5×7 ft).

***R.* 'Fountain'** Small clusters of crimson double flowers are abundantly borne throughout the season on this upright shrub with dark green foliage. HEIGHT & SPREAD 1.5×1.5 m (5×5 ft).

***R.* 'Francesca'** Apricot-yellow, semidouble flowers with a light scent are 7.5 cm (3 in) across. There is plentiful dark, glossy foliage on the spreading Hybrid Musk bush. HEIGHT & SPREAD 1.2×1.2 m (4×4 ft).

***R.* 'Fred Loads'**♀+ Large trusses of bright orange-vermilion blooms 10 cm (4 in) across are borne on light green stems above bright green, glossy leaves. The flowers are semidouble and lightly scented, and the plant is a strong, upright grower. HEIGHT & SPREAD 1.8×1.1 m (6×3½ ft).

***R.* Frühlingsgold**♀ Very large and fragrant semidouble blooms of primrose-yellow cover the long, arching shoots – but in early summer only. The flowers open to 10 cm (4 in). The leaves are markedly small. HEIGHT & SPREAD 2.4×2.1 m (8×7 ft).

***R.* 'Frühlingsmorgen'** The glowing single blooms are pink with a primrose centre and amber stamens. They open to 10 cm (4 in) across, making a magnificent display in spring but without much of a repeat flowering. The arching shoots carry small, matt grey-green leaves. HEIGHT & SPREAD 1.8×1.8 m (6×6 ft).

▲ *Rosa* Felicia

***R.* Gertrude Jekyll**♀ Full-scented, rich pink blooms that are very double in form and up to 12.5 cm (5 in) across make a generous display on this rather open-growing English Rose shrub. HEIGHT & SPREAD 1.5×1.1 m (5×3½ ft).

***R.* 'Gipsy Boy'**♀ see *R.* 'Zigeunerknabe'

***R.* Golden Celebration** Huge, golden yellow, double flowers form cups some 12.5 cm (5 in) across and have a rich fragrance. There are dark, glossy leaves on this nicely rounded bush. HEIGHT & SPREAD 1.2×1.2 m (4×4 ft).

***R.* 'Golden Wings'**♀ Great quantities of single, pale yellow blooms with amber stamens are produced by this rose throughout the summer. The flowers are 10 cm (4 in)

▲ *Rosa* Gertrude Jekyll

Rosa 'Golden Wings' ▲

r

across and lightly scented. This spreading plant branches freely. HEIGHT & SPREAD 1.5×1.5m (5×5ft).

R. Graham Thomas♀ The fragrant, golden yellow, cupped flowers are 10cm (4in) across, very double and borne abundantly. Shown off against glossy, healthy leaves, they make an outstanding English Rose with tall, upright growth. HEIGHT & SPREAD 1.5×1.2m (5×4ft).

R. 'Gypsy Boy'♀ see *R.* 'Zigeunerknabe'

▲ *Rosa* Heritage

R. Heritage The clusters of very large, fragrant, light pink blooms are 12.5cm (5in) across and full-petalled, with petals curving in to form a globular flower. This fairly upright English Rose has dark green leaves. HEIGHT & SPREAD 1.2×1.2m (4×4ft).

R. Jacqueline du Pré♀ Blush-pink, semidouble flowers with scalloped petals show well against the dark, shiny leaves. The fragrant flowers, 10cm (4in) across, give an excellent repeat blooming. Branching growth fills out the vigorous shrub. HEIGHT & SPREAD 1.5×1.5m (5×5ft).

R. L.D. Braithwaite Cupped, full-petalled, crimson flowers bloom in profusion among greyish green leaves. They are fragrant, double and 10cm (4in) across. This quite short English Rose is upright but filled out with bushy growth. HEIGHT & SPREAD 1×1.1m (3×3½ft).

R. 'Lavender Lassie'♀ Enormous heads of double, bright pink flowers weigh the strong shoots down to the ground unless this plant is staked. These plentiful, well-scented, rosette-shaped blooms are 9cm (3½in) across and show well against the healthy, shiny leaves. HEIGHT & SPREAD 1.5×1.2m (5×4ft).

R. 'Marguerite Hilling'♀ The outstandingly profuse early summer show of semidouble, mid pink flowers is followed by a lesser display later in the season. The scented flowers, 7.5cm (3in) across, are borne on the arching shoots of a dense, spreading shrub with matt leaves. HEIGHT & SPREAD 2.1×2.1m (7×7ft).

R. Mary Rose Pink double flowers with a hint of lilac in them and a light scent are

▲ *Rosa* Mary Rose

carried on this short, shrubby English Rose. The flowers are 10cm (4in) across. HEIGHT & SPREAD 1.1×1.1m (3½×3½ft).

R. 'Nevada'♀ The huge and profuse creamy white flowers with golden stamens open to 12.5cm (5in) across. They are semidouble, lightly scented and smother the arching stems of this large, spreading shrub. HEIGHT & SPREAD 2.1×2.1m (7×7ft).

Rosa 'Nevada'

R. 'Penelope'♀+ Clusters of abundant, light peach-pink, semidouble flowers 7.5cm (3in) across fade to cream. This sweet-scented Hybrid Musk has broad, glossy, dark green leaves on a well-branched, bushy plant. HEIGHT & SPREAD 1.2×1.2m (4×4ft).

R. Saint Cecilia Double, full-scented blooms in blends of pink and orange eventually open out flat, reaching 10cm (4in) across. This English Rose makes a bushy plant. HEIGHT & SPREAD 1.1×1.1m (3½×3½ft).

R. Sally Holmes♀ Dense clusters of large, single, ivory-white flowers are almost too crowded to display themselves fully but make a spectacular display against the dark, glossy leaves. The scented blooms are 12.5cm (5in) across and borne on a strong-growing upright plant. HEIGHT & SPREAD 2×1m (6½×3ft).

R. Sweet Juliet Apricot blooms that are double and quartered with a rich fragrance open to 10cm (4in) across and are carried on arching stems on this English Rose. HEIGHT & SPREAD 1.2m×75cm (4×2½ft).

R. The Countryman Rich pink flowers with a full fragrance are carried on a spreading shrub. The double blooms are 7.5cm (3in) across and as well as an early summer show, make a generous second display in autumn. HEIGHT & SPREAD 1×1m (3×3ft).

R. The Pilgrim Double yellow blooms, the colour darkening in the centre, open to 7.5cm (3in) across and have a full scent. The plant is upright and bushy. HEIGHT & SPREAD 1×1m (3×3ft).

R. The Prince The crimson flowers open cupped and the outer petals reflex until they form a rosette. The colour darkens to purple as the blooms age. The fragrance is strong and the growth low and bushy with dark green leaves. HEIGHT & SPREAD 60×60cm (2×2ft).

R. 'Zigeunerknabe' (syn. *R.* 'Gipsy Boy', *R.* 'Gypsy Boy') The large clusters of double crimson blooms open to show golden stamens and are 9cm (3½in) across. They cover the very vigorous, tangled shrub at mid summer but there is no repeat flowering and the blooms have little scent. The leaves are rather coarse. HEIGHT & SPREAD 1.8×1.8m (6×6ft).

RUGOSA ROSES

The robust descendants of *R. rugosa* now grown in gardens were raised about 1900 – which classifies them as Modern Shrub Roses. They are, however, distinctive enough to justify a section on their own.

These roses do well in most soils, even poor ones. They are shrubby, upright, very spiny and generally well clothed to the ground with bright green, glossy, deeply veined and notably healthy foliage. As well as being vigorous, colourful border plants, they make excellent hedges.

Rugosa flowers, borne in early summer and then more or less continuously until early autumn, are usually about 8cm (3½in) across and purplish pink or white. They are mostly in clusters and are single, semidouble or double. Single and semidouble flowers are usually followed by round orange-red hips that can be very striking.

R. 'Agnes' The scented, pale amber blooms, paler at the edge, are double and have crinkled petals. The autumn flowering is only half-hearted. The foliage is rather dark. HEIGHT & SPREAD 1.8×1.5m (6×5ft).

▲ *Rosa* The Countryman

▲ *Rosa* 'Agnes'

▲ *Rosa rugosa* var. *rubra*

▲ *Rosa* Boys' Brigade

▲ *Rosa* 'Blanche Double de Coubert'

***R.* 'Blanche Double de Coubert'**♀ Pure white, very fragrant, semidouble blooms are 10cm (4in) across on an open plant and have papery petals that do not withstand rain. They do not produce hips. HEIGHT & SPREAD 1.5×1.2m (5×4ft).

***R.* 'F.J. Grootendorst'** (syn. *R.* 'Red Grootendorst') Fringed petals distinguish the bright crimson-red, double blooms, only 4cm (1½in) across. They are carried in large clusters but have no scent. HEIGHT & SPREAD 1.5×1.2m (5×4ft).

***R.* 'Fimbriata'** The pale blush-pink, semidouble blooms have prettily fringed petals and a moderate scent. HEIGHT & SPREAD 1.2×1m (4×3ft).

***R.* 'Fru Dagmar Hastrup'**♀ Fragrant, light pink single blooms with creamy yellow stamens are freely borne with good continuity. Large hips appear while the flowers are still on this spreading shrub. HEIGHT & SPREAD 1.2×1.2m (4×4ft).

***R.* 'Pink Grootendorst'**♀ The scentless double blooms are bright pink and held in clusters. HEIGHT & SPREAD 1.5×1.2m (5×4ft).

***R.* 'Red Grootendorst'** see *R.* 'F.J. Grootendorst'

***R.* 'Roseraie de l'Haÿ'**♀ Velvety, light purple-red blooms, 10cm (4in) across, are borne freely. They are fragrant and double, and open flat and rather loose on a plant well covered with healthy foliage that turns golden in autumn. There are no hips. HEIGHT & SPREAD 1.8×1.8m (6×6ft).

***R. rugosa* 'Alba'**♀ White, scented, silky single flowers are followed by orange-red hips, borne alongside late flowers. The bright green leaves turn gold in autumn. HEIGHT & SPREAD 1.8×1.8m (6×6ft).

The flowers of var. ***rubra***♀ are purple-red. **'Scabrosa'**♀ has single blooms, 14cm (5½in) across, with velvety, purplish pink petals and yellow stamens. There is a fine crop of hips. It reaches a height of 1.5m (5ft) and a spread of 1.2m (4ft).

PATIO ROSES (DWARF CLUSTER-FLOWERED BUSH ROSES)

Breeders have crossed Floribundas with Miniatures to create a group of roses halfway between the two – too big in flower and leaf to be Miniatures and too short for Floribundas. Patio roses have the upright bushy growth and clustered blooms of the Floribundas, a resemblance reflected in their alternative name, given in brackets above.

Patio roses tend to be more wide-spreading than the Floribundas, forming cushions of floral colour over a long season as the blooms in the early clusters open in succession and fresh flower clusters follow on. Their short stature suits cultivation in planters, tubs and other containers, but if pot-grown, these roses need extra feeding to keep up such enthusiastic flowering.

Unless stated otherwise, the patio roses included here have mid green leaves and clusters of double, slightly scented blooms, generally about 3cm (1¼in) across when fully open but with some larger ones opening to 5cm (2in).

***R.* Angela Rippon** The full-petalled, large, rosy salmon blooms are immaculately formed and set off by plenty of matt leaves HEIGHT & SPREAD 45×45cm (1½×1½ft).

***R.* Anna Ford**♀+ Deep orange-red blooms that fade to orange open wide and flat. They are semidouble, freely and continuously produced and set off by very shiny, bright green leaves. HEIGHT & SPREAD 45×45cm (1½×1½ft).

***R.* Boys' Brigade** Large clusters of small, crimson-red, white-eyed flowers with little scent are in bloom over a long period. The leaves are plentiful and glossy. HEIGHT & SPREAD 45×45cm (1½×1½ft).

***R.* Buttons** Clusters of well-spaced, salmon-red flowers make a bright display against the abundant, glossy foliage. HEIGHT & SPREAD 45×45cm (1½×1½ft).

***R.* Cider Cup**♀ The high-centred, beautifully formed, deep apricot-pink blooms are enhanced by glossy foliage. HEIGHT & SPREAD 45×45cm (1½×1½ft).

***R.* Festival** Large, shapely, bright crimson-scarlet flowers are made striking by silvery white on the back of the petals. They are semidouble and bloom with good continuity, against dark green, glossy foliage. HEIGHT & SPREAD 45×45cm (1½×1½ft).

▲ *Rosa* Gentle Touch

***R.* Gentle Touch**♀ Neatly furled buds, open flat into small, pale pink flowers, tinged acid-yellow in the middle. This plant has healthy dark green, semi-glossy leaves. HEIGHT & SPREAD 45×45cm (1½×1½ft).

***R.* Gingernut** Flowers in bronze-orange with a reddish back to the petals are well spaced in trusses that cover the plant evenly. There is plenty of glossy foliage. HEIGHT & SPREAD 45×45cm (1½×1½ft).

***R.* 'Honey Bunch'** The small but full-

petalled and shapely flowers are a muted soft yellow suffused with salmon-pink. They are sweet-scented, freely borne and held against healthy bright green, glossy leaves. HEIGHT & SPREAD 45×45 cm (1½×1½ ft).

***R.* Jane Asher** Small, bright scarlet blooms are freely produced over a long season on a small but very tough plant with glossy leaves. HEIGHT & SPREAD 40×45 cm (16×18 in).

***R.* Little Bo-Peep**♀+ Small, full-petalled, blush-pink buds, delicately formed and very numerous, open out flat to show the yellow stamens in the pale pink blooms. The spreading plant has tiny glossy leaves. HEIGHT & SPREAD 30×50 cm (12×20 in).

***R.* Minilights** Continuously flowering clusters of pale yellow, single blooms blend with the abundant light green leaves on this spreading plant. HEIGHT & SPREAD 25×50 cm (10×20 in).

***R.* Peek A Boo** Masses of apricot-pink blooms are borne in graceful sprays over a long period, making a cushion of bloom on a background of small, dark leaves. HEIGHT & SPREAD 45×45 cm (1½×1½ ft).

***R.* Pretty Polly+** The small, soft pink blooms are well formed, long-lasting and very freely borne. They show a deeper pink centre as they open. There is a dense covering of glossy foliage. HEIGHT & SPREAD 40×45 cm (16×18 in).

***R.* Queen Mother**♀ The numerous, light pink, semidouble flowers, which open flat, give a continuous display, enhanced by healthy dark, glossy leaves on a rather spreading plant. HEIGHT & SPREAD 45×45 cm (1½×1½ ft).

***R.* Ray of Sunshine** Golden yellow, semidouble flowers that hold their colour well are neatly furled at first, then open out flat. The leaves are small and glossy. HEIGHT & SPREAD 40×45 cm (16×18 in).

▼ *Rosa* Queen Mother

***R.* Red Rascal** Bright crimson-scarlet flowers that are full-petalled, shapely and unfading bloom abundantly, set off by dark, glossy foliage. HEIGHT & SPREAD 40×45 cm (16×18 in).

***R.* Robin Redbreast** Single blooms the colour of redcurrants and with a whitish eye are carried in large trusses on a dense plant with dark, glossy leaves. HEIGHT & SPREAD 45×45 cm (1½×1½ ft).

***R.* Shine On** Shapely full-petalled flowers in warm pinky orange shades bloom profusely and with good continuity on this neat plant with small, glossy leaves. HEIGHT & SPREAD 45×45 cm (1½×1½ ft).

***R.* Strawberry Fayre** The flowers are blood-red at the petal edges, striped and mingled red and white within. They are set off by dark green, glossy leaves. HEIGHT & SPREAD 45×45 cm (1½×1½ ft).

***R.* Sweet Dream**♀ The peachy pink blooms, tightly cupped and crammed with petals, appear in many clusters on a plant well covered with healthy glossy foliage. HEIGHT & SPREAD 45×45 cm (1½×1½ ft).

***R.* Sweet Magic**♀ Well-formed, orange flowers with gold highlights open out flat and flush pink as they age. They bloom profusely all season against glossy leaves. HEIGHT & SPREAD 45×45 cm (1½×1½ ft).

***R.* Tear Drop** Clusters of semidouble, blush-white blooms with yellow stamens give a continuous display. They are unmarked by rain and complemented by the tiny, glossy leaves. HEIGHT & SPREAD 30×45 cm (1×1½ ft).

***R.* 'Wee Jock'** Bright crimson-scarlet, neatly formed blooms are freely borne on a dense plant with glossy foliage. HEIGHT & SPREAD 45×45 cm (1½×1½ ft).

MINIATURE ROSES

Thin, twiggy shoots and tiny leaves and flowers distinguish true Miniature Roses from Patio Roses. Miniatures are about 38 cm (15 in) tall at most, some much smaller, and little more than half as wide. They are probably descended from *R. chinensis* 'Minima', a dwarf Chinese cultivated rose, introduced to the West in the 19th century. Most early Miniatures had flowers in shades of red and pink, or white but breeders have now raised hundreds of varieties and greatly extended the colour range.

Miniatures are often thought of as houseplants because they are so often sold in pots, but they are quite hardy outdoor plants that cannot survive long in a dry, indoor atmosphere. They need watching carefully for mildew and black spot, to which some are very susceptible. In a border they make the best effect in a group or as an edging. Their size suits pots, planters and window boxes but in such confinement, they must be fed and watered.

The flowers are borne in clusters with the blooms opening to about 2.5 cm (1 in) across, and rather less on the tiniest plants. Unless stated otherwise, the Miniatures listed below have mid green leaves, and double or semidouble flowers that are slightly scented and repeat flowering. Conscientious deadheading will encourage continuity of flowering.

▲ *Rosa* Baby Masquerade

▲ *Rosa* Shine On

Rosa 'Cinderella' ▲

***R.* Apricot Sunblaze** Cupped blooms of light orange-red appear over a long flowering period among glossy, dark leaves. HEIGHT 38 cm (15 in).

***R.* Baby Masquerade** The profuse flowers change from yellow to orange to pink to red as they age, with all colours on show together. The bush is dense with shiny, dark green leaves. HEIGHT 38 cm (15 in).

***R.* Benson and Hedges Special** Golden yellow blooms are borne prolifically and combine well with the light green, glossy leaves on a plant that bushes out more than most miniatures. HEIGHT 38 cm (15 in).

***R.* Bush Baby** Full and neatly formed, light salmon-pink blooms show amber at the heart as they open wide. The leaves are glossy. HEIGHT 25 cm (10 in).

***R.* 'Cinderella'** Exquisite, full-petalled, white blooms tinged with pink grace the tiny, thornless bush which has very healthy leaves. HEIGHT 23 cm (9 in).

***R.* Darling Flame** Vivid vermilion flowers with yellow shading and golden anthers are carried in numerous clusters on a plant with dark, glossy leaves. HEIGHT 38 cm (15 in).

▲ *Rosa* 'Judy Fischer'

***R.* 'Easter Morning'** Ivory-white blooms, up to 4cm (1½in) across, are unspoiled by rain. They are luminous against the dark, glossy foliage. HEIGHT 38cm (15in).

***R.* 'Judy Fischer'** Rich ruby-red blooms are well matched by the fine dark leaves. HEIGHT 38cm (15in).

▲ *Rosa* 'Little Buckaroo'

***R.* 'Little Buckaroo'** Blooms are scarlet with white centres and gold stamens. The leaves are dark green. HEIGHT 38cm (15in).

***R.* Magic Carrousel** Rosette-shaped, creamy white blooms are edged with warm pink and make a fine show against the glossy leaves. HEIGHT 38cm (15in).

***R.* 'Mr Bluebird'** Lavender-purple flowers are held against dark green leaves. HEIGHT 30cm (12in).

***R.* 'New Penny'** The abundant, coppery orange flowers open flat and become pinker as they age. The leaves are dark and glossy. HEIGHT 25cm (10in).

***R.* Peace Sunblaze** Tiny pink-and-white blooms are carried in numerous compact clusters. A leafy bush. HEIGHT 38cm (15in).

***R.* Peach Sunblaze** Peachy apricot, cupped blooms with abundant repeat flowering are enhanced by plenty of leaves on this bushy plant. HEIGHT 25cm (10in).

▲ *Rosa* Red Ace

***R.* Red Ace** The dark crimson-scarlet blooms are velvety and shapely. An upright plant. HEIGHT 30cm (12in).

***R.* Red Sunblaze** Bright blood-red flowers open wide but full and are quick to repeat. The matt leaves are a fresh green. HEIGHT 30cm (12in).

***R.* 'Stacey Sue'** This free-flowering plant bears prettily shaped, light pink, full-petalled blooms above glossy foliage. HEIGHT 25cm (10in).

***R.* Starina** Scarlet and gold blooms that are shapely and lasting make a fine show, set off to perfection by glossy, light green leaves. HEIGHT 38cm (15in).

***R.* 'Yellow Doll'** Tiny, light yellow blooms with narrow petals are freely borne on a bushy plant with glossy leaves. HEIGHT 30cm (12in).

MINIATURE CLIMBING ROSES

Some of these varieties are climbing sports of the Miniature bush roses. Others, which grow rather larger, have been specially developed as small climbers for confined spaces such as patios. They need a position in full sun and all do well in containers if well fed and watered.

***R.* Laura Ford**♀ Strong yellow flowers, even deeper in the late-summer blooms, take on a pink flush in hot sun. This vigorous plant has plenty of dark, shiny leaves. HEIGHT 2.1m (7ft).

***R.* Nice Day** Soft salmon-pink, full-petalled flowers with a sweet scent open wide to form loose rosettes, profusely borne. A freely branching plant with plenty of dark, glossy foliage. HEIGHT 2.1m (7ft).

***R.* Orange Sunblaze, Climbing** Bright vermilion blooms appear with good continuity on a short plant with glossy foliage. HEIGHT 1.5m (5ft).

***R.* Warm Welcome**♀+ Bold orange-vermilion blooms with yellow at the heart are fragrant and borne with great freedom, starting early and continuing until the frosts. The glossy leaves have a coppery tone when young. HEIGHT 2.1m (7ft).

▲ *Rosa* Warm Welcome

GROUND-COVER ROSES

Low-growing but spreading shrubs, each covering a lot of ground, make up the group known as Ground-cover Roses. However, despite the name, permanent, weed-smothering cover for the soil is not possible with roses. They give no leaf cover in winter so weeds can grow in the bare ground and, since roses are thorny, removing weeds from beneath them is not easy.

Ground-cover Roses vary in height and spread. Most branch much more freely than Hybrid Teas or Floribundas, and they are well clothed to the base with leafy shoots. They carry their flowers in clusters. A sunny position at the front of a border or lining a path or drive suits these plants, but their spreading habit lends itself to tumbling over a wall, drooping gracefully over the side of a tub, or sprawling down a sloping bank.

Unless stated otherwise, the plants listed are repeat-flowering with blooms that have little scent, and the leaves are mid green.

***R.* Avon** (syn. *R.* 'Poulmuti') Numerous pale pink buds open to pearly white, semi-double flowers, 2.5cm (1in) across, and show prominent golden stamens. The bushy growth bears glossy leaves. HEIGHT & SPREAD 30cm×1m (1×3ft).

***R.* Bonica**♀ Sprays of pink, cup-shaped, semidouble flowers are borne throughout summer on this bushy, hardy plant. The leaves are dark leathery green. HEIGHT & SPREAD 1×1.5m (3×5ft).

***R.* Essex** Single, rich pink blooms, 2.5cm (1in) across, with a white eye flower continuously in large clusters. The dense growth of trailing shoots bears glossy leaves. HEIGHT & SPREAD 60cm×1.2m (2×4ft).

***R.* Flower Carpet**♀ Glowing bright pink, double blooms, 4cm (1½in) across, appear in heavy trusses all summer. This plant is healthy with glossy leaves that stay on late. HEIGHT & SPREAD 1×1.2m (3×4ft).

***R.* Gwent** Bright lemon-yellow, cupped, semidouble blooms, 5cm (2in) across, are profusely borne over a long season. The leaves are dark and glossy. HEIGHT & SPREAD 45cm×1m (1½×3ft).

r

▲ *Rosa* Flower Carpet

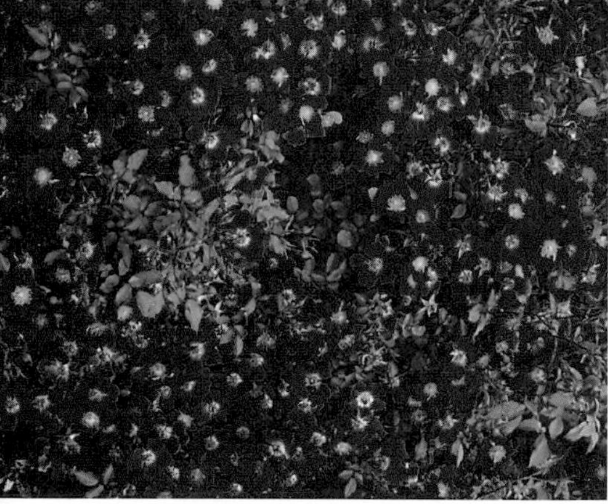
▲ *Rosa* Hampshire

R. Hampshire The deep scarlet, yellow-eyed, single blooms, up to 2.5cm (1in) across, are extremely showy. This plant produces small, glossy, bright green leaves that are usually healthy. HEIGHT & SPREAD 30×75cm (1×2½ft).

R. Hertfordshire The carmine-pink, single blooms, 2.5cm (1in) across and borne in large clusters, open wide showing vivid yellow stamens. There is an ample coverage of healthy bright green leaves. HEIGHT & SPREAD 45cm×1m (1½×3ft).

▲ *Rosa* Hertfordshire

R. Kent+ White semidouble flowers, 4cm (1½in) across, are borne in great profusion. They are not spoiled by rain and give a generous repeat flowering. The neat shrub has shiny leaves. HEIGHT & SPREAD 45×75cm (1½×2½ft).

R. Laura Ashley Light magenta-pink, single flowers, 4cm (1½in) across, with pale yellow centres are lightly scented. They are freely borne against small, glossy leaves. HEIGHT & SPREAD 60cm×1.2m (2×4ft).

R. Northamptonshire Pearly pink, semi-double flowers, 6cm (2½in) across, are held in large clusters. The dense leaves are shiny. HEIGHT & SPREAD 45cm×1.1m (1½×3½ft).

R. 'Nozomi'♀ Dainty, single, pearly pink flowers, 2cm (¾in) across and fading to white, are borne in huge clusters along the dense shoots. The leaves are small, shiny and dark. HEIGHT & SPREAD 1×1.8m (3×6ft).

R. Pearl Drift Elegant pink buds open to white, semidouble blooms with a pearly blush and golden stamens. They are 10cm (4in) across, freely and continuously borne, and shown off by the dark, glossy leaves. HEIGHT & SPREAD 1×1.2m (3×4ft).

R. Pheasant Full-petalled, deep pink, double flowers, 2.5cm (1in) across, hold their colour well and have a sweet scent. They are held in large trusses along the trailing shoots, but in early summer only. The leaves are small and glossy. HEIGHT & SPREAD 30cm×3m (1×10ft).

R. 'Poulmuti' see *R.* Avon

R. Snow Carpet♀ Dainty but very double, white pompom blooms, 2.5cm (1in) across, flower with good continuity over a very long season. The ground-hugging shoots bear little, dark green leaves. HEIGHT & SPREAD 15×45cm (6×18in).

R. Suffolk Bright scarlet, single flowers, 4cm (1½in) across, bloom profusely all summer. They open wide to show prominent golden stamens and are followed by orange-red hips in autumn. There are plenty of light green leaves. HEIGHT & SPREAD 45cm×1m (1½×3ft).

R. Suma♀ Massed ruby-red, very double blooms, 2.5cm (1in) across, open all along the spreading shoots. The small dark leaves turn red in autumn. HEIGHT & SPREAD 1×1.8m (3×6ft).

▲ *Rosa* Suffolk

R. Surrey♀**+** The frilly-edged, double blooms, 6cm (2½in) across, are deep pink at the centre, paler at the edge and moderately fragrant. They are borne in large trusses throughout the summer. This plant is generously clothed with glossy leaves. HEIGHT & SPREAD 1×1.2m (3×4ft).

R. Sussex The lightly scented, buff-apricot blooms, gradually fading, are 5cm (2in) across and flower all season. The dark bronzy green leaves are glossy. HEIGHT & SPREAD 60cm×1.2m (2×4ft).

▲ *Rosa* Swany

R. Swany♀ White, very full-petalled double blooms, 4cm (1½in) across, are held with great freedom on the sprawling flexible shoots. The leaves are dark, glossy and healthy. HEIGHT & SPREAD 1×1.2m (3×4ft).

R. Wiltshire Profuse, deep pink, double blooms, 6cm (2½in) across, flower early and go on well into autumn. This wide-spreading bush has tiny, dark, glossy leaves. HEIGHT & SPREAD 60cm×1.2m (2×4ft).

CLIMBING ROSES

The typical Climbing Rose sends out long shoots which either scramble up through shrubs or trees by hooking their thorns over twigs and branches, or have to be tied to a frame or to fixed wires. Climbing Roses generally have small clusters of quite large blooms, are repeat-flowering, and form a permanent framework of strong, fairly stiff shoots. But a few do not conform. There are some that flower only once a season and some that have flexible shoots bearing huge heads of small blooms – all typical features of Ramblers, for there is some confusion and overlap between the two.

Climbers grown on walls or fences need to have their shoots trained and tied in to grow as near to horizontal as possible. This encourages the production of flowering sideshoots. On pillars and obelisks, shoots can be spiralled round and tied to the support to achieve the same effect. Vigorous climbers grown through trees need training only in their early stages.

Deadheading helps Climbers to produce a better second flowering, although the task

may be difficult to carry out on the stronger growers. Lack of deadheading does not mean that there is no second blooming at all, but it will usually be less profuse.

In the varieties listed, those with the word 'Climbing' at the end of the name are climbing sports that first occurred spontaneously from bush varieties and have been reproduced by breeders. The flowers look like those on the bush versions, but the continuity of flowering is often not as good.

The blooms of Climbing Roses can be double, semidouble or single. Sometimes, especially in climbing sports, they are very large and shapely, reaching 10cm (4in) across. Those which are not sports of bush roses are generally 7.5-10cm (3-4in) across. The blooms of *R. banksiae* 'Lutea' and some of the other tree-climbers, however, are no more than 2.5cm (1in) across but make up for it by massing together, 100 or more to a single truss. Unless stated otherwise the flowers are lightly scented and the leaves, usually with 5 leaflets, are mid green.

***R.* Agatha Christie** Clear pink, double blooms show well against the dark, glossy leaves. The bushy grower is a convenient size for a pillar or obelisk. HEIGHT 3m (10ft).

▲ *Rosa* 'Alchymist'

***R.* 'Alchymist'** The well-scented, very full-petalled blooms are a light buff-yellow with orange shading; there is no second flowering. The growth is upright and the leaves are bronze-green when young. HEIGHT 2.4m (8ft).

***R.* 'Allgold, Climbing'** Unfading, bright yellow, double flowers appear in clusters. The stiff growth is covered with healthy, bright green leaves. HEIGHT 4.2m (14ft).

***R.* 'Aloha'** Very large, bright pink, double blooms have an orange flush at the heart and a sweet fragrance. The dark, bronzy foliage has been troubled by rust in some areas. The upright habit is suitable for growing up a pillar. HEIGHT 2.4m (8ft).

***R.* Altissimo**♀ Deep scarlet, single blooms with large petals open wide to reveal orange stamens. The dark, glossy leaves are held on stiff, upright growth. HEIGHT 3m (10ft).

***R. banksiae* 'Lutea'**♀ This plant does best in a site protected from frost and cold spring winds, such as a warm wall, which must be extensive to accommodate it. Even then it may be slow to become established. It bears sweetly scented, rounded, double blooms, 2.5cm (1in) across, that are light yellow and carried in large clusters, in early summer only. HEIGHT 6m (20ft).

***R.* Bantry Bay** Bright pink, semidouble blooms are generously borne over a long season and with a good repeat. The plant is freely branching with dark, glossy leaves. HEIGHT 3.5m (12ft).

***R.* 'Bobbie James'**♀ Huge, fragrant sprays of small, creamy white, semidouble blooms are borne in early summer only. The rampant grower has shiny, dark green leaves with copper tinges. HEIGHT 9m (30ft).

***R.* 'Céline Forestier'**♀ Fragrant, buff-yellow, double blooms with pink undertones that open out flat are carried in small clusters. The plant is moderately vigorous but not completely hardy and needs a sheltered position. HEIGHT 2.4m (8ft).

***R.* 'Compassion'**♀ Fragrant, pink, shapely flowers with apricot shading bloom with great continuity. Dark, shiny leaves are held on stiff, branching shoots. HEIGHT 3m (10ft).

▲ *Rosa* 'Compassion'

***R.* 'Crimson Glory, Climbing'** Strongly perfumed, dark crimson blooms that are large and double make a sumptuous display on this extensive plant, but the foliage is rather sparse and may be attacked by mildew. HEIGHT 4.5m (15ft).

***R.* Dortmund** Showy clusters of single, bright red blooms with a white eye are carried on an upright grower with healthy, dark green, glossy leaves. HEIGHT 3m (10ft).

***R.* Dream Girl**♀ The double, warm pink flowers have a fine scent and are abundant but appear only at mid summer with no repeat. They are well set off by glossy leaves. HEIGHT 2.7m (9ft).

***R.* 'Dreaming Spires'** Large, double, richly scented blooms are in a clear yellow which shows up well against the dark green, glossy foliage that covers the stiff, branching growth. HEIGHT 3m (10ft).

***R.* Dublin Bay**♀ Showy clusters of blood-red, double blooms are enhanced by the handsome, dark green, glossy leaves. The flowers are virtually scentless. This climber has bushy growth that makes it very like a shrub. HEIGHT 2.1m (7ft).

***R.* 'Ena Harkness, Climbing'** The bright crimson, double blooms are inclined to droop – an advantage since this large climber is seen mostly from below. The flowers are large, shapely and double, with a good repeat. The stiff, branching plant has glossy, healthy foliage. HEIGHT 4.5m (15ft).

***R.* 'Etoile de Hollande, Climbing'**♀ Large, dark crimson blooms with a rich, sweet scent are carried on the vigorous, well-branched grower whose foliage is dark green. HEIGHT 5m (16ft).

***R.* Galway Bay** Beautifully formed double blooms, with mid pink petals that are darker

▲ *Rosa* Dortmund

▲ *Rosa* Galway Bay

▲ *Rosa* Bantry Bay

Rosa Golden Showers ▲

on the back, are borne abundantly in medium-sized clusters. The growth is stiff and branching. HEIGHT 3m (10ft).

***R.* 'Gloire de Dijon'**♀ The buff-yellow, very double blooms are sometimes quartered and give a continuous display, but they are only lightly scented. The plant is well branched with dark green leaves. HEIGHT 4.5m (15ft).

***R.* Golden Showers**♀ Shapely yellow buds open to rather loosely formed, scented double flowers with large petals, the yellow coloration fading quite quickly to cream. Upright growth and moderate size makes this a successful plant for a pillar. HEIGHT 2.4m (8ft).

***R.* 'Guinée'** The darkest of dusky red blooms and a delicious perfume distinguish this rose. The flowers are well formed, large and double. They make a profuse first flowering but give only a slight repeat. The leaves, too, are dark on a well-branched plant, but they are susceptible to mildew. HEIGHT 4.5m (15ft).

***R.* Handel**♀ Cupped, double blooms of creamy white edged with cerise are carried in large clusters and have a good repeat. There is dark, shiny foliage on the vigorous, freely branching plant, which will spread well on a wall. HEIGHT 3m (10ft).

▼ *Rosa* Handel

***R.* High Hopes** Light pink, shapely, double blooms combine elegantly with the dark green, glossy foliage. The flowers have little scent. HEIGHT 3m (10ft).

***R.* Highfield** Light yellow, double blooms with a sweet fragrance are freely borne on this stiff, well-branched plant with big, glossy, dark green leaves. HEIGHT 3m (10ft).

***R.* 'Iceberg, Climbing'**♀ Profuse clusters of double white flowers with a reliably abundant repeat. Mildew sometimes affects the glossy leaves. HEIGHT 3m (10ft).

***R.* 'Lady Hillingdon, Climbing'**♀ The richly tea-scented, apricot-orange double blooms are beautifully shaped and carried on a well-branched plant. This rose performs at its best with some protection from a south or west-facing wall or fence. HEIGHT 4.5m (15ft).

***R.* 'Lady Sylvia, Climbing'** Light pink, large double blooms are carried singly and in small clusters on stiff growth. This climber rarely produces flowers after the first flush. HEIGHT 3.5m (12ft).

***R.* Lavinia**♀ Large and fragrant, mid pink, double blooms are enhanced by the background of fine dark leaves on a freely branching plant. HEIGHT 3.5m (12ft).

***R.* Leaping Salmon** Full-scented, salmon-pink blooms that are large and double stand out well against handsome, glossy leaves on a branching plant. HEIGHT 3m (10ft).

***R.* 'Leverkusen'** Pale yellow, long-stemmed, semidouble blooms, deepening in colour at the centre, are held in small clusters and give a good repeat. The dark, glossy leaves may develop mildew. HEIGHT 3m (10ft).

***R.* 'Madame Alfred Carrière'**♀ The clusters of white, blush-tinted, double blooms are very freely produced and have a good repeat. This is a rose of great vigour which easily covers the wall of a large house, and tolerates a shady wall. The pale green leaves may develop mildew. HEIGHT 5.5m (18ft).

***R.* 'Madame Grégoire Staechelin'**♀ (syn. *R.* 'Spanish Beauty') The first flowering, in late spring, is very early and spectacular with large, carmine-pink, semidouble blooms carried extraordinarily freely. The display extends over several weeks but there is no repeat flowering. HEIGHT 6m (20ft).

***R.* 'Maigold'**♀ Orange-yellow, fragrant, semidouble blooms are profuse and first appear in late spring, but there is only spasmodic blooming after that. The stiff, very thorny shoots are well covered with shiny, bronze-green leaves. HEIGHT 2.4m (8ft).

***R.* 'Masquerade, Climbing'** Showy, double flowers change from yellow to pink to a strong red, just as in the Floribunda bush version, and give a good display after the first flush. HEIGHT 3m (10ft).

***R.* 'Meg'** The clusters of very large, apricot-pink flowers have orange stamens and a strong fragrance. The blooms are semidouble and 10cm (4in) across but appear only spasmodically after the first flush in early summer. This sturdy grower forms hips in autumn, but they remain green. HEIGHT 3.5m (12ft).

▲ *Rosa* 'Leverkusen'

***R.* 'Mermaid'**♀+ Large, luminous light yellow blooms with amber stamens are borne in clusters on a branching, very thorny plant which, though vigorous, is a slow grower when first planted. It is not completely hardy, needing a sheltered situation, and the shiny leaves are not entirely resistant to mildew. HEIGHT 6m (20ft).

***R.* Morning Jewel**♀ Sparkling, bold pink, semidouble flowers cover the plant with early and late displays, making a bright contrast with the shiny, dark green leaves on the branching plant. HEIGHT 3.5m (12ft).

***R.* 'Mrs Sam McGredy, Climbing'**♀ The large, double blooms in a coppery red with a hint of salmon are unlike those of any other rose. There is rather sparse, dark green foliage but vigorous growth. HEIGHT 3.5m (12ft).

Rosa
'New Dawn'

R. 'New Dawn'♀ (syn. *R.* 'The New Dawn') Thriving anywhere, even on a north wall, this vigorous plant has its slender shoots laden with a tremendous profusion of strongly scented, light satin-pink, double blooms which are very shapely and borne in small sprays. The leaves are healthy and glossy. HEIGHT 3m (10ft).

R. Night Light Red-gold buds open to large, golden yellow, double flowers with little scent. The plant is stiff and branching with dark, glossy leaves. HEIGHT 3m (10ft).

▲ *Rosa* 'Parade'

r

R. 'Parade'♀ There is a continuous show of heavy flower clusters, whose carmine-pink, double blooms tend to droop. A reddish tinge warms the dark, glossy leaves. HEIGHT 3m (10ft).

R. Parkdirektor Riggers Bright red, semi-double, well-formed blooms with a touch of white at the heart are carried in numerous clusters and give a good repeat. The flowers show to advantage against the dark green, glossy leaves. HEIGHT 3.5m (12ft).

R. 'Paul's Scarlet Climber'+ Fairly small, bright red, double flowers give a reliably generous display, though at mid summer only. The well-branched plant has abundant foliage. HEIGHT 3m (10ft).

R. 'Phyllis Bide'♀+ A combination of fawn, pink and yellow distinguishes the

▲ *Rosa* 'Pink Perpétué'

small, double blooms, which are borne in clusters with great freedom. The growth is slender and branching with glossy leaves. HEIGHT 2.4m (8ft).

R. 'Pink Perpétué' Pink blooms with a deeper pink reverse are carried in large clusters and with great freedom. Deadheading is necessary to get a good second show. The plant has an abundance of glossy leaves. HEIGHT 2.7m (9ft).

R. 'Rosy Mantle' Rather loosely formed, double blooms in bright rose-pink with lighter shading are sweetly scented and freely borne over a long season. The open growth is clothed with glossy, dark foliage. HEIGHT 3m (10ft).

R. 'Royal Gold' Shapely, large, double blooms of deep golden yellow are borne singly or in small clusters and with a good repeat. The plant easily becomes gaunt and leggy and could do with its glossy leaves being more numerous. It is best grown as a pillar rose. HEIGHT 2.4m (8ft).

R. 'Schoolgirl' The light orange to apricot blooms are very large, double and beautifully formed. The plant is open-growing and leggy, and the glossy leaves, though large, are sparse. HEIGHT 3m (10ft).

R. 'Shot Silk, Climbing'♀ An abundant first flush produces strongly fragrant, large, double blooms of salmon-pink blended with yellow. They are rather loose when opened and the repeat flowering is unreliable. There are handsome, glossy leaves. HEIGHT 3m (10ft).

R. 'Souvenir de Claudius Denoyel'♀ Cupped, loosely formed, double flowers with a full fragrance make a great splash of bright crimson in early summer, and a more subdued show later. The plant is a vigorous grower. HEIGHT 5.5m (18ft).

R. 'Souvenir du Docteur Jamain' Velvety dark red, perfumed, double flowers bloom in profusion and make a continuous display set off by dark leaves. HEIGHT 3m (10ft).

R. 'Spanish Beauty' see *R.* 'Madame Grégoire Staechelin'

R. Sparkling Scarlet Small, semidouble scarlet flowers are carried in large trusses on a plant with stiff, well-branched growth. HEIGHT 3m (10ft).

R. Summer Wine♀ Single coral-pink flowers with orange stamens are borne in small clusters. This stiff, branching plant has large, glossy leaves. HEIGHT 3m (10ft).

▲ *Rosa* 'Swan Lake'

R. 'Swan Lake' The shapely, high-centred white blooms tinged with pink are double. This plant is well branched with shiny, dark green leaves that need watching for black spot. HEIGHT 3m (10ft).

R. Sympathie Clusters of blood-red, double blooms are carried on stiff, branching growth, well furnished with glossy leaves. This rose will easily cover a wall. HEIGHT 4.5m (15ft).

R. 'The New Dawn' see *R.* 'New Dawn'

▲ *Rosa* 'White Cockade'

R. 'White Cockade'♀ Sprays of white, double flowers are shown off against very dark green, glossy leaves. This short plant is useful for a patio, pillar or obelisk. HEIGHT 2.1m (7ft).

R. 'Zéphirine Drouhin'♀ Profuse clusters of well-scented, deep pink, double blooms are borne over a long period and with a good repeat. This almost thornless plant has

▲ *Rosa* 'Zéphirine Drouhin'

open growth but its leaves are susceptible to mildew. HEIGHT 2.4m (8ft).

RAMBLER ROSES

Ramblers bear large clusters of small blooms and come into flower only once a year, in early to mid summer. They have flexible shoots, and send up fresh ones from ground level each year; a number of the old shoots can be pruned away to maintain the plant's vigour. Like Climbing Roses, Ramblers have to be trained on supports but they are less suitable for growing against walls, where the air is frequently still and mildew is more likely to develop on the dense growth. Their very pliable shoots, however, are ideal for training round pillars, over arches and wherever curving shapes are needed. Ramblers' flexibility is also an advantage in weeping standards because the shoots hang down or 'weep' naturally.

The flowers can be double or semidouble and are carried in clusters that often contain as many as 20. The blooms are generally about 5cm (2in) across; in the plants listed, flower size is given only if it differs from this. Unless stated otherwise, the flowers are lightly scented and the leaves, with 5 or 7 leaflets, are mid green.

***R.* 'Adélaïde d'Orléans'**♀ Delicate blush-pink, semidouble blooms are set off by plenty of leaves and these stay on the bushy plant well into winter. HEIGHT 4.5m (15ft).

***R.* 'Albéric Barbier'**♀ The flowering comes in early summer and is exquisite, with small clusters of light orange buds opening to creamy white, double blooms. The plant is almost evergreen, with fine, glossy leaves and rampant growth. HEIGHT 4.5m (15ft).

▲ *Rosa* 'Albertine'

***R.* 'Albertine'**♀ Very fragrant, double flowers that are large for a Rambler, at 9cm (3½in) across, are a warm pink and shapely at first but they become loose as they open. The young shoots are plum-red, and the leaves dark green and prone to develop mildew. HEIGHT 4.5m (15ft).

***R.* 'Alexandre Girault'** Scarlet, double flowers with 'quilled' petals, each reflexed to form a point, have a white eye round a boss of yellow stamens. The scarlet deepens as the flower ages. There are few thorns on the long, whippy shoots which carry dark, glossy leaves. HEIGHT 6m (20ft).

***R.* 'Crimson Shower'**♀ The large flower clusters come after mid summer and, although not repeating, make a display over a long period. The flowers are crimson, small and double, and are borne on lax shoots with an abundance of little, shiny leaves. HEIGHT 2.4m (8ft).

***R.* 'Emily Gray'+** The buttery yellow blooms have a pleasing scent, are semidouble and open to 9cm (3½in) across, becoming loose as they do so. The bright green, shiny leaves stay on the plant for a long time. HEIGHT 4.5m (15ft),

***R.* 'Félicité Perpétue'**♀ (syn. *R.* 'Little White Pet, Climbing') Enormous heads of creamy white, very double pompom flowers sometimes have their petals tipped with red. Small, dark leaves cover stems that are plum-red when young. The vigorous plant sends up new shoots freely from the base. HEIGHT 4.5m (15ft).

***R.* 'Francis E. Lester'**♀ (syn. *R.* 'F.E. Lester') This free-flowering rose has no repeat but displays its large trusses of small, blush-pink, single blooms over a long period. The flowers have a rich fragrance. HEIGHT 4.5m (15ft).

***R.* 'François Juranville'**♀ Fragrant, warm salmon-pink, double blooms are numerous, well formed and full-petalled. They are large, opening up to 9cm (3½in) across and making a glowing display against the dark leaves. HEIGHT 5m (16ft).

***R.* 'Goldfinch'** Each creamy yellow, semidouble bloom has a cushion of bright orange-yellow stamens in the centre – the reason for the plant's nickname 'poached egg rose'. The dense, vigorous growth bears leaves that are a conspicuously bright, glossy green. HEIGHT 2.7m (9ft).

***R.* 'Little White Pet, Climbing'** see *R.* 'Félcité Perpétue'

***R.* 'Paul's Himalayan Musk'**♀ Lilac-pink, double blooms are carried in large sprays on long, enormously vigorous shoots that can swarm up a tree. The shoots bear large, greyish olive leaves that are rather drooping. HEIGHT 9m (30ft).

▲ *Rosa* 'Félicité Perpétue'

***R.* 'Paul Transon'**♀ Unusually among the Ramblers, the numerous blooms are mixed shades of coppery orange and salmon-pink. In a warm season the plant gives a limited second flowering. HEIGHT 3m (10ft).

***R.* 'Rambling Rector'**♀ This vigorous grower, suitable for training up a small tree, has very large trusses of creamy white, semidouble blooms. HEIGHT 6m (20ft)

***R.* 'Sanders' White Rambler'**♀ Sweetly scented, white, double blooms of rosette shape are carried in plentiful clusters. The glossy, bright green, outstandingly healthy foliage makes a superb, dense background for them. HEIGHT 3.5m (12ft).

***R.* 'Seagull'**♀ White, single and semidouble flowers are held in huge clusters. The very strong shoots are stiffer than in most Ramblers and carry leaves of a greyish green. HEIGHT 6m (20ft).

▲ *Rosa* 'Seagull'

***R.* 'Veilchenblau'**♀ Semidouble flowers of an unusual violet-blue are white at the centre. The clusters are carried on shoots that have few thorns and are well covered with bright green, shiny leaves. HEIGHT 4.5m (15ft).

CULTIVATION

Site and soil Roses need a position where they have plenty of sun – preferably for at least three-quarters of the day. They never do as well in a shady site; a position under a tree is worst of all, not only because of the shade, but because the tree's roots compete for nutrients. The only roses that put on any show without direct sunlight are climbers recommended for north walls, but even

▲ *Rosa* 'Veilchenblau'

these always do better on a south or west wall. An exposed, windy position is another to avoid. Wind rocks the plants and makes the roots loose in the soil so they cannot take up nutrients. Wind also makes the shoots whip about and damage the blooms.

Slightly acid soil, with a pH of 6.5, is best for roses. A medium loam retains the water they need but does not become waterlogged. The claim that roses prefer clay is not true where the clay does not let water drain away reasonably well. Roses do not like their roots to stand in water because this deprives them of the air they need to thrive. They do not like growing in chalk either; the only exceptions are some of the Old Garden Roses, for instance the Hybrid Perpetuals, which do tolerate chalk. There are also some roses, the Rugosas for example, that cope well with light, sandy soils. But light soils, whether chalky or sandy, are always made better for roses by adding as much humus-forming matter as possible.

Since roses like a moist soil, apply a mulch round them regularly. It reduces evaporation, suppresses weeds and can improve the soil and provide some nutrients if it is made up of well-rotted stable manure, garden compost, chipped bark, or some other organic matter. Put it on in late spring when the soil has begun to warm up, applying a layer about 7.5 cm (3 in) thick.

Unless roses are grown for exhibition, they require an application of a powdered or granular rose fertiliser only twice a year. Scatter a small handful round each plant in spring, immediately after pruning, and again soon after mid summer, when the first flush of bloom is over. Work it gently into the top 2.5 cm (1 in) of soil, taking care not to damage the roots. Do not make a later application; this would encourage the growth of late shoots that have no time to ripen before the first frost and would be destroyed. A fertiliser rich in potash used for the second application helps shoots to ripen.

Planting Before planting, cut out any damaged or diseased shoots from the top growth and trim back tough, not fibrous, roots by about a third. Make the planting hole wide enough for the roots to be spread out and deep enough for the budding union (the swelling at the base of the main stem) to be 2.5 cm (1 in) below the soil surface. Work a small handful of rose fertiliser into the soil at the bottom of the hole, then set the plant in the hole. Place a cane across the hole to check that the depth is right. Container-grown roses often have the budding union well above the soil because the pots are too small for them. Make sure that this is rectified in the actual planting. Work in soil round the roots so that there are no air pockets round them, then fill in the hole and tread the soil down firmly.

When planting roses in spring, cut the shoots hard back to about 3 or 4 buds immediately after firming the soil – except with climbing roses, whose shoots should be left just as they came from the nursery.

Plant Climbing Roses at least 45 cm (1½ ft) away from a wall or fence (and even farther from a tree), with the roots fanned outwards away from the support. Soil near a wall, fence or tree is liable to be very dry.

Training climbing roses Some of the more lax-growing shrub roses may be better displayed if trained on a frame, but for most gardeners the only roses that need training are Climbers and Ramblers. These are not true climbing plants because they do not have tendrils, suction pads, or other means of attaching themselves to supports – in nature they scramble up surrounding trees or shrubs by hooking their thorns over branches and twigs. On an artificial support such as a wall, arch, pillar, fence or pergola, there is little for the thorns to gain purchase on and the shoots always have to be tied to the support.

When growing a rose on a wall, tie the shoots to wires threaded through vine eyes driven into the brickwork and stretched horizontally about 45 cm (1½ ft) apart up the wall. Tie the shoots into positions as horizontal as possible; this encourages flower-bearing sideshoots to break into life along their entire length. If it is not done, the blooms come mainly at the top. Garden twine is satisfactory for tying-in, but plastic ties are stronger and last much longer. When training a Climber or Rambler up a pillar, spiral it round the support rather than letting it go straight up. The comparatively stiff shoots of a Climber are more difficult to train than the flexible shoots of Ramblers.

For training into trees, one of the loveliest ways of growing climbing roses, choose the Ramblers *R.* 'Paul's Himalayan Musk' or *R.* 'Rambling Rector', for example, or a vigorous Climber such as *R.* Sympathie or *R.* 'Souvenir de Claudius Denoyel'. Bear in mind, however, that the weight of such a rose when fully grown, to say nothing of the extra wind resistance of its leaves, means that only a large, strong tree in prime condition can support it. Do not be tempted to use an old and half decayed apple tree, which a gale may bring down. For growing up a full-grown, healthy apple tree, or something of similar size, choose a more modest size of rose, such as *R.* 'New Dawn'.

Plant the Climber or Rambler far enough out from the tree trunk to avoid the major tree roots, both for convenience in digging the hole and to reduce competition for water and nutrients. Set away from the tree trunk, the rose will not be completely deprived of rain by the tree's leaves.

Train the rose towards the tree along a stout cane or rope tied at an angle between the tree trunk and a long peg driven into the ground beside the rose. Tie the rose shoots to the support for a year or two until they make their way up through the lower branches, and then leave them to find their own way upwards. It is best to plant on the windward side of the tree so that the rose shoots tend to be blown into it rather than out. Pruning is not possible, but the roses used for this kind of planting get along very well without it, as they would in the wild; the old shoots are replaced by new, but much more slowly than they would be if the old were pruned out each year.

Rose hedges Many shrub roses make excellent hedges, but some take up a lot of space. Hybrid Musks such as *R.* 'Felicia' and *R.* 'Penelope' send out long flowering shoots at awkward angles, which is a nuisance if the hedge runs alongside a path. The answer is to train such spreading shrub roses either along horizontal wires strung between posts or on a chain-link fence. The Rugosas and upright-growing shrub roses such as *R.* 'Fred Loads', or Floribundas such as *R.* Chinatown and *R.* Queen Elizabeth, rarely need such training when used for hedges.

Deadheading The natural yearly cycle of a rose is to produce flowers in early summer which, once they have been pollinated, form hips containing the seeds from which new plants could grow. If hips are allowed to develop, much of a plant's energy goes into forming them and the seeds they contain, instead of into producing new flowers. Deadheading – the removal of spent blooms

before hips start to form – induces a repeat-flowering rose to try again to produce hips and seeds, starting the cycle off by producing more flowers. Do not deadhead species roses or any other roses you are growing for their decorative hips. Old Garden Roses need no deadheading unless blooms become waterlogged by rain and form soggy, unsightly balls that will not open but turn brown. Ramblers need deadheading only to clear the plant of spent blooms.

All other roses are generally repeat-flowering and deadheading stimulates the production of later blooms. It needs doing at least twice a season, that is after each main flush. In practice, however, it is best done whenever a faded flower is seen, simply by snipping off the spent flower. With Hybrid Teas and Floribundas it is best not just to snap off the flower but to cut back to 2 or 3 leaves below the old flowerhead. This can produce stronger new shoots with bigger flowers, though it may take longer for them to appear.

If individual blooms in a Floribunda truss shed their petals neatly as they are spent, wait for the whole cluster to be over before deadheading. If blooms become unsightly with withered petals, snip off the individual spent flowers and when the whole cluster is over, cut back the shoot.

Suckers Almost all the roses on sale are budded or grafted onto wild rose roots known as understocks or rootstocks. These give the cultivated variety extra vigour and, according to the type of stock, other desirable qualities such as a longer life, or greater ability to cope with heavy clay soils or light, sandy ones. Any shoot coming from below the budding union – the point where the cultivated rose was budded onto the stock – is a sucker that is coming from the stock itself and will have the features of the wild rose, not of the cultivated variety. If it is allowed to develop, other dormant buds at the base of the sucker are stimulated into growth, and gradually the stronger-growing stock will take over from the cultivated rose. A sucker must not simply be cut back; this would be the equivalent of pruning and make it grow more vigorously. Pull it away whole from the rootstock, clearing back the soil if necessary to see its point of origin; this removes its dormant buds as well.

A sucker is generally a lighter green than the other shoots with thorns of a different shape, and the leaves may have 7 leaflets rather than the 5 of most cultivated roses. But as some cultivated roses have 7 leaflets, the number of leaflets is not a reliable guide. To be certain that a suspect shoot is a sucker, scrape back a little soil at the base of the rose to find the spot from which the sucker originates; if it comes from below the budding union, remove it.

The stem of a standard rose is part of the rootstock; any shoots coming from below the head are suckers and must be pulled off.

PROPAGATION Seed is produced in the hips of species roses but it is not bound to come true because the flowers may have been cross-pollinated with other roses by visiting insects. Protecting and hand-pollinating plants may guarantee true seed but cuttings taken in autumn are an easier method of propagation. They take 3 or 4 years to make full-sized plants sturdy enough to be allowed to flower. In the first year, flower buds should be nipped out, energy being diverted to root growth. Budding or grafting onto rootstocks establishes plants more quickly but is best left to professionals.

The less highly bred a rose is, the more easily does it root, but actual species tend to make a great deal of leafy growth instead of flowering. Hybrid Teas do not always make such vigorous plants on their own roots as they do on selected rootstocks, but Floribundas are generally the most easily rooted. Miniatures, Ramblers and Modern Shrub Roses are generally the most successful. Shrubs are especially worth raising for an inexpensive flowering hedge as many may be needed.

PRUNING Rose shoots have a much more limited life span than those of many shrubs. They need renewing if worthwhile flowers are to be produced each year, especially on the more highly bred modern kinds such as Hybrid Teas and Floribundas. The pruning of roses is primarily to encourage new shoots to grow, but also to remove dead and diseased wood, to shape a nicely balanced bush and to open up its centre so as to improve air circulation, which helps the plant to remain healthy.

Pruning is not the exacting task it was once made to seem. Even a quick cut with a hedge trimmer promotes the production of essential new shoots, but diseased growth still has to be removed. Even using secateurs, roses should generally be pruned much less severely than traditional methods recommended.

Species Roses These need no pruning except for the removal of any dead wood as soon as it is noticed.

Old Garden Roses Most of these bloom only once each season and any pruning should be done in summer after the flowering to give time for plenty of new wood to develop and ripen before the frosts start. Ripe shoots are needed to carry the next year's blooms. Cut out any unhealthy growth, then cut back main shoots by about one-third and sideshoots by two-thirds. Some growers recommend only every other year or so, and others advocate no pruning at all. But regular attention to the bushes does maintain long-term vigour.

Large-flowered and Cluster-flowered Bush Roses (Hybrid Teas and Floribundas) Prune in spring. Cut out any unhealthy wood, then shorten the main shoots of Hybrid Teas to about 20 cm (8 in) and those of Floribundas to 25-38 cm (10-15 in). Treat Polyanthas in the same way as Floribundas.

Modern Shrub Roses and Rugosas Prune in spring, first removing any dead or diseased wood, then cutting back main shoots by about one-third and sideshoots by two-thirds. Shrubs with very upright growth, reflecting the habit of their Floribunda parentage, need the main shoots cutting back by about half to prevent them from becoming leggy.

Climbers Do not prune them during their first year. After that, prune in mid autumn when the blooming of the repeat-flowering types is over. Prune the sideshoots only, cutting each back by about two-thirds. Leave the main stems alone, but if one is exceeding its allotted space cut it back to size. The only other reason to cut main shoots is if the rose becomes very bare at the base. In that case, cut 1 or 2 main shoots hard back to about 1 m (3 ft) and new growth should come from low down.

Ramblers Do not prune in the first year. After that, remove 2 or 3 entire main stems each year after flowering. It is usually easier to remove them in sections. Cut back each remaining main stem by about one-quarter, and sideshoots by two-thirds.

Miniature and Patio Roses There are two methods. The first is to give the bushes a light trim to keep them shapely and balanced. The second is to treat them in the same way as Hybrid Teas and Floribundas, removing any unhealthy wood, then cutting back main shoots by a third on smaller plants and a half on larger ones.

Ground-cover Roses These need a minimum of pruning. Trim lightly to keep them tidy and cut back more strongly any vigorous shoots that may unbalance the shape of the bush.

PESTS AND DISEASES Good cultivation of roses is the best defence. Strong plants in the right situation, well tended and pruned to ensure a flow of air through them are better able to resist or recover from pests and diseases. An increasing number of roses are bred with healthy growth as one of their characteristics. Rugosas and many of the Species have always been healthy, and the Old Garden Roses manage to cope with disease better than many modern roses.

The main diseases that afflict roses, all of them passed from rose to rose by airborne spores, are black spot, powdery mildew and rose rust.

The most troublesome pests are greenfly (aphids), caterpillars including those of tortrix moths and lackey moths, and leaf-rolling sawflies. A number of other insects can damage roses, though fortunately they never seem to attack all at the same time, and they may not appear at all in some years. They include froghoppers, chafers and other beetles, leaf miners, rose slugworms, red spider mites, leafhoppers, thrips and capsid bugs.

Roscoea

Zingiberaceae

Roscoea cautleyoides

These handsome, hardy, herbaceous perennials are suitable for a rock garden or the front of a border. Most species bloom all summer, die down in autumn, then rest for an unusually long period, emerging only in late spring. The roots are tuberous. Native to China and the Himalayas.

RECOMMENDED SPECIES AND VARIETIES

R. alpina A single, somewhat floppy stem bears a succession of flowers, one at a time, from mid summer through to autumn. The flowers are deep rose to purple and up to 2.5cm (1in) long. Two to four unstalked, oval leaves, up to 10cm (4in) long, are arranged in a single tuft around the stem base. HEIGHT & SPREAD 15×15cm (6×6in).

R. auriculata A succession of purple flowers, 5cm (2in) long, appear on 6-10 erect stems. Each stem bears one flower at a time. Linear to lance-shaped leaves, about 25cm (10in) long, grow in sparse tufts. HEIGHT & SPREAD 40×30cm (16×12in).

'Beesiana' has flowers entirely yellow or yellow stained with purple.

▲ *Roscoea cautleyoides*

R. cautleyoides♀ Daffodil-yellow flowers 4cm (1½in) long grow in spikes on top of upright stems from mid to late summer. The plant has 2-3 stems. Four or so flowers are in bloom at any one time. The lance-shaped leaves are as long as 35cm (14in). HEIGHT & SPREAD 30×20cm (12×8in).

R. humeana♀ Two to five, or more, purple or lilac-pink flowers, about 5cm (2in) long, open simultaneously in late spring or early summer. The plant has a single, stout stem, which bears 5-7 ovate leaves 20cm (8in) long that often emerge after the flowers have begun to bloom. HEIGHT & SPREAD 30×20cm (12×8in).

▲ *Roscoea humeana*

R. purpurea Purple, purple-and-white or all white flowers are 6cm (2½in) long. They open one at a time on a strong stem, which bears 20cm (8in) long lance-shaped leaves. HEIGHT & SPREAD 30×20cm (12×8in).

▲ *Roscoea purpurea*

R. scillifolia A cluster of 2-5 lilac-pink or purple flowers grows at the top of a single, slender, erect stem. Each flower is about 2.5cm (1in) long. On the lower half of the stem are set the 12 cm (4¾in) long rectangular leaves. HEIGHT & SPREAD 40×30cm (16×12in).

CULTIVATION Plant tubers in autumn or early spring, no less than 15cm (6in) deep, in a humus-rich, well-drained soil, preferably neutral or slightly acid. Choose a position in good light. Remove faded flowers.

PROPAGATION Species will self-seed in favourable conditions, such as after a good summer. Sow seed any time in spring, or divide and replant the tubers as soon as the foliage has died down.

PESTS AND DISEASES Soil pests, including wireworms and vine weevil larvae, may cause root damage. Slugs eat young foliage. Wet, clammy soils encourage fungal diseases in the rootstock.

Rose, Christmas see *Helleborus niger*
Rose, guelder see *Viburnum opulus*
Rose, Lenten see *Helleborus orientalis*
Rose, rock see *Helianthemum*
Rose, sun see *Cistus*
Rosemary (culinary herb) see HERBS p.332
Rosemary see *Rosmarinus*
Rosemary, bog see *Andromeda*
Rose of Sharon see *Hypericum calycinum*

Rosmarinus

Rosemary
Labiatae

Rosmarinus officinalis

Grown for its dense, strongly aromatic, evergreen foliage, this native of dry coastal areas around the Mediterranean thrives in full sun and well-drained soil. Small clusters of flowers, in shades of mauve and blue, pink and white, appear on shoots of the previous year. Valued as a culinary herb, rosemaries range in height from a medium-sized shrub to a low-growing, trailing plant. They also make a fine, informal hedge. Some varieties are half-hardy and should be grown in containers that can be moved to a sheltered spot or under glass in winter. The rest are hardy to -5°C (23°F) or just below.

RECOMMENDED SPECIES AND VARIETIES

R. officinalis The blunt-ended, needle-like leaves are 2-5cm (¾-2in) long, dark green and rather glossy above, white felted below. Mauve and dark blue, tubular, 2-lipped flowers, up to 2cm (¾in) long, are borne from mid spring to early summer and spasmodically until early autumn. HEIGHT & SPREAD 75×75cm (2½×2½ft) after 5 years, ultimately 1.5m (5ft) tall.

▲ *Rosmarinus officinalis*

White-flowered var. ***albiflorus*** is sought after as a herb and for flower arranging. The half-hardy and fairly prostrate var. ***angustissimus*** **'Corsican Blue'** has blue flowers. **'Aureus'** (syn. 'Aureovariegatus', 'Gilded', 'Variegatus') has leaves with irregular yellow variegation. **'Benenden Blue'** (syn. 'Collingwood Ingram') is a smaller variety of dense, semi-erect then cascading habit, with gentian-blue flowers. It reaches a final height of 1m (3ft). **'Fota Blue'** is a half-hardy, free-flowering variety with very dark blue flowers. Semi-prostrate in habit, it has a mature height of 60cm (2ft).

'Jackman's Prostrate' has pale blue flowers from early spring onwards and reaches a final height of only 30cm (1ft).

'Lady in White' has white flowers. **'Majorca Pink'** is of columnar habit and has short, relatively broad, dull green leaves and lilac-pink flowers which open from early spring onwards. It is moderately hardy and reaches a final height of 1.2m (4ft). **'McConnell's Blue'** is a spreading and prostrate plant with broad leaves and blue flowers. Half-hardy, it has an ultimate height of 40cm (16in). **'Miss Jessopp's**

▲ *Rosmarinus officinalis* 'McConnell's Blue'

Upright'🏆 (syn. 'Fastigiatus', f. *pyramidalis*) is a vigorous, erect variety with narrowly oblong leaves and light mauve-blue flowers. Good for hedging, it may grow to a height of 1m (3ft) after 5 years, ultimately reaching a height of 1.8m (6ft).

'Primley Blue' (syn. 'Frimley Blue') is an upright, tidy variety with clear blue flowers. Mature height 1m (3ft). **Prostratus Group**🏆 (syn. *R. corsicus* 'Prostratus', *R.* × *lavandulaceus* hort., *R. officinalis* var. *lavandulaceus, R. o.* var. *repens, R. repens*) forms large, dense, trailing mats, up to 60cm (2ft) high, of fresh green leaves, studded with light blue flowers. Plants are half-hardy.

'Roseus' has lilac-pink flowers. **'Severn Sea'**🏆, a plant of spreading, arching habit, with violet-blue flowers, grows to 1m (3ft) tall. **'Sissinghurst Blue'**🏆 is of upright habit, very free-flowering with rich blue blossom, and reaches a height of 1.2m (4ft). **'Sudbury Blue'** is of upright habit, with dense, blue-green foliage and mid blue flowers. **'Tuscan Blue'** is a fast-growing, upright plant with reddish brown stems. The light green, rather broad leaves smell of nutmeg. The large blue flowers often appear in winter.

CULTIVATION Plant in mid spring, or late spring for the less hardy forms, in a sunny position in any ordinary, well-drained soil. For hedging, use 'Miss Jessopp's Upright', spacing the plants 60cm (2ft) apart.

PROPAGATION Take semi-ripe cuttings in mid to late summer and insert in a cold-frame. Pot up the rooted cuttings and over-winter in a frost-free frame or greenhouse.

PRUNING Cut out dead wood and shorten straggly shoots in early spring. Overgrown bushes may be cut by half in mid spring.

PESTS AND DISEASES Usually trouble free.

Rowan see *Sorbus aucuparia*
Rubber plant see *Ficus elastica*

Rubus

Rosaceae

Rubus arcticus

As well as producing raspberries, blackberries, loganberries and tayberries, this genus also includes plants grown for their ornamental value. These include hardy, erect or scrambling, evergreen and deciduous shrubs and climbers. Although some of them bear edible fruit, they are valued more for their flowers, foliage and attractive stems. (For fruiting species, see p.723.) In spring or summer, five-petalled flowers are borne either singly or in clusters.

RECOMMENDED SPECIES AND VARIETIES

The species here are divided into two groups – evergreen and deciduous. Unless otherwise stated, all the plants bear prickles.

EVERGREEN SPECIES AND VARIETIES

R. arcticus (crimson bramble) A semi-evergreen alpine creeper, useful for a rock garden or as ground cover. Pink or red flowers, up to 2.5cm (1in) wide, are borne singly on short thornless stems, from time to time through summer. Each mid green leaf has 3-5 serrated leaflets. Plant in lime-free soil. HEIGHT & SPREAD 2×25cm (¾×10in).

R. calycinoides see *R. pentalobus*

R. henryi var. ***bambusarum*** Grown for its foliage, this elegant climber has leaves, as long as 12.5cm (5in), with 3 distinct lance-shaped leaflets. Sprays of pink flowers, up to 7.5cm (3in) long, appear in early summer. Edible black fruit, about 1.5cm (½in) across, carried in clusters, are sometimes produced in autumn. HEIGHT & SPREAD 3.5×1.8m (12×6ft) after 5 years, ultimately 6m (20ft).

R. pentalobus (syn. *R. calycinoides*) Oval, 3-5 lobed leaves, to 4cm (1½in) long, form a mat of foliage over the stems of a spreading, prostrate shrub. Wrinkled leaves covered with grey down partially conceal white flowers, up to 2cm (¾in) wide, in early summer. Red berries may follow. The plant self-roots from branches along the ground. HEIGHT & SPREAD 5×20cm (2×8in) after 5 years, ultimately 60cm (2ft) or more across.

'Betty Ashburner' is a popular form.

R. tricolor This scrambling carpeter, with long trailing stems that self-root readily, will spread indefinitely unless curbed. The heart-shaped leaves, up to 10cm (4in) long, are dark green above and whitish beneath. White flowers, up to 2.5cm (1in) wide, carried in mid summer, are sometimes followed by red, raspberry-like, edible fruits. The stems are covered in red bristles. HEIGHT & SPREAD 60cm×3m (2×10ft) after 5 years.

DECIDUOUS SPECIES AND VARIETIES

***R.* 'Benenden'**🏆 (syn. *R.* Tridel 'Benenden') In late spring and early summer, this shrub carries saucer-shaped,

▲ *Rubus* 'Benenden'

pure white flowers, up to 6cm (2½in) across, with a tuft of golden stamens. The broadly oval, mid green, 3-5 lobed leaves are up to 8cm (3¼in) long. The upright thornless stems with peeling bark arch with age. HEIGHT & SPREAD 2×2m (6½×6½ft) after 5 years, ultimately 3m (10ft) tall.

R. cockburnianus🏆 Purple shoots overlaid with a white bloom make this arching shrub a spectacular feature in winter. Dark green leaves, up to 20cm (8in) long, have 5-9 oval leaflets and are white beneath. Sprays of purple flowers, up to 12cm (4¾in) long, are produced in early summer. Inedible black fruits follow the flowers. HEIGHT & SPREAD 1.8×1.2m (6×4ft) after 5 years, ultimately 2.4m (8ft).

The glowing yellow, fern-like foliage of **'Golden Vale'** mellows to lime-green as the season progresses. This plant reaches a maximum height of about 1.8m (6ft).

▼ *Rubus cockburnianus* 'Golden Vale'

R. phoenicolasius (Japanese wineberry) Spreading, biennial stems are densely covered with reddish bristles and a few prickles. Each mid green leaf, to 18cm (7in) long, is whitish beneath and has 3-5 toothed oval leaflets. Pale pink flowers appear in spikes up to 20cm (8in) long in mid summer. Edible, conical, red berries, to 2cm (¾in) long, follow in late summer; they will ripen better if the plant is grown against a wall. HEIGHT & SPREAD 1.5×1.5m (5×5ft) after 5 years, ultimately 3m (10ft) tall, if supported.

R. thibetanus🏆 This erect shrub has purple biennial stems which are white-bloomed in winter. Dark green pinnate leaves, up to 23cm (9in) long, with many leaflets, are covered with silky hairs and are white beneath. Purple flowers, up to 1.2cm (½in) wide, are followed by edible, round black fruits. HEIGHT & SPREAD 1.8×1m (6×3ft) after 5 years, ultimately 2.4m (8ft) tall.

R. Tridel 'Benenden' see *R.* 'Benenden'
CULTIVATION Plant in spring in any well-drained soil in sun or shade. Grow *R. phoenicolasius* against a sunny wall.
PROPAGATION Take semi-ripe cuttings of evergreens and semi-evergreens in mid to late summer. Take softwood cuttings of deciduous species in spring or hardwood cuttings in late autumn. Layer *R.* 'Benenden' in spring.
PRUNING Cut back the previous season's growth of *R. cockburnianus* and *R. thibetanus* to ground level in spring, as soon as new shoots appear. Alternatively, remove a proportion of the flowered shoots at ground level after flowering. Thin out the other species and varieties annually, as necessary.
PESTS AND DISEASES Usually trouble free.

Rudbeckia

Coneflower
Compositae

Rudbeckia 'Goldquelle'

These hardy herbaceous perennials and annuals are grown for their brightly coloured daisy-like flowers, which brighten the garden from late summer to early autumn. The blooms are in shades of yellow and orange and all have prominent cone-shaped centres in contrasting colours, surrounded by gracefully drooping petals. The erect stems of rudbeckias form sturdy clumps. Native to N America.

RECOMMENDED SPECIES AND VARIETIES

R. echinacea* var. *purpurea see *Echinacea purpurea*

R. fulgida This herbaceous perennial bears flowers up to 7cm (2¾in) across with yellow to orange petals and purplish brown centres. The mid green lance-shaped leaves reach a length of 12cm (4¾in). The original species is not usually grown in gardens, where selected varieties are preferred. HEIGHT & SPREAD 60×45cm (24×18in).

The narrow, deep yellow petals of var. ***deamii***♀ surround a black centre. The petals of var. ***sullivantii* 'Goldsturm'**♀ are golden, also around a black centre.

R. gloriosa see *R. hirta*

***R.* 'Goldquelle'**♀ Double flowers, up to 10cm (4in) across, have deep yellow petals surrounding green centres. The mid green leaves are divided, hairy beneath and up to 10cm (4in) long. The plant is a herbaceous perennial. HEIGHT & SPREAD 75×50cm (30×20in).

r

▲ *Rudbeckia fulgida* var. *deamii*

***R.* 'Herbstsonne'** ('Autumn Sun') Discs, up to 10cm (4in) across, of floppy golden yellow petals surround green centres. The oval, mid green leaves of this herbaceous perennial grow to 15cm (6in) long. Both flowers and leaves are borne on wavy stems. HEIGHT & SPREAD 2m×60cm (6½×2ft).

▲ *Rudbeckia* 'Herbstsonne'

R. hirta (syn. *R. gloriosa*) (black-eyed Susan) Pale yellow petals surround dark red centres. The blooms are up to 7.5cm (3in) across. The narrow, pointed, deep green, bristly leaves are ribbed and grow to 10cm (4in) in length.This short-lived herbaceous perennial is usually grown as an annual. The flowers last well in water when cut. HEIGHT & SPREAD 30-100×50cm (1-3ft×20in).

The double or semidouble flowers of the cultivar **'Goldilocks'** have deep golden petals and black centres. The petals of **'Marmalade'** are a rich gold and the small centres are jet-black.

R. laciniata The blooms, up to 10cm (4in) across, have bright yellow petals and yellowish green centres. The mid green pinnate leaves grow to 10cm (4in) long, with as many as 10 leaflets. This tall herbaceous perennial is ideal for the back of the border. HEIGHT & SPREAD 1.8m×60cm (6×2ft).

'Hortensia' (syn. 'Golden Glow') has bright golden yellow, double flowers on branching stems.

R. maxima The golden flowers, up to 5cm (2in) across, have black conical centres. The greyish green, oval to oblong leaves grow to 12cm (4¾in) in length. This herbaceous perennial enjoys slightly damper situations than most rudbeckias. HEIGHT & SPREAD 1.5m×60cm (5×2ft).

R. purpurea see *Echinacea purpurea*

R. subtomentosa Golden flowers, up to 10cm (4in) across, are produced by this herbaceous perennial. The flattish centres are purplish black. The soft oval leaves grow to 12.5cm (5in) long and have toothed edges and a covering of grey hairs. This species likes rather moister conditions than most other rudbeckias. HEIGHT & SPREAD 75×50cm (30×20in).

CULTIVATION Plant from autumn to mid spring in any reasonably fertile, moisture-retentive soil, choosing an open sunny situation. In drier conditions apply a moisture-retaining mulch in spring, to prevent the plants from wilting in hot sun when in flower. Deadhead faded flowers and stake taller plants.
PROPAGATION Divide established plants in spring or autumn. Alternatively, sow the seed of herbaceous perennials on open ground in spring. Sow the seed of *R. hirta* where they are to flower in early spring.
PESTS AND DISEASES Usually trouble free.

Rue see *Ruta graveolens*
Rue, meadow see *Thalictrum flavum*
Rue anemone
see *Anemonella thalictroides*

Ruscus

Butcher's broom
Ruscaceae

Ruscus aculeatus

Attractive foliage and showy red berries earn these tough evergreen perennials a place under a tree or in any dry shady area. The foliage is distinctive in that the true leaves are reduced to minute scales and the shoots are flattened into the shape of leaves, known as cladodes. Tiny greenish flowers are borne on the cladodes in spring or autumn, with male and female flowers usually on separate plants. When fertilised, the female flowers develop into bright red berries which last well into winter.

The listed species are all hardy and can be used to provide ground cover in dry, shady places. The cut foliage lasts well in water and is used by flower arrangers. Native to Europe, W Asia and the Azores.

▲ *Ruscus aculeatus*

RECOMMENDED SPECIES AND VARIETIES

R. aculeatus Wiry green stems bear stiff, spine-tipped, ovate or lance-shaped cladodes up to 2.5cm (1in) long. Starry pale green flowers are borne on the upper surface of the cladodes. Brilliant scarlet berries, 1cm (⅜in) across, may be abundant on female plants where both sexes are grown in proximity. The plant has a variable habit, but is often rather erect. HEIGHT & SPREAD 1×1m (3×3ft).

The compact, self-fertile clone **'Sparkler'** is free-fruiting.

R. hypoglossum Arching stems bear soft, ovate cladodes up to 10cm (4in) long. Starry light green flowers sit in the axil of a green bract on the upper surface of each cladode. Bright red globular berries, 1.5cm (½in) across, follow the flowers. HEIGHT & SPREAD 60cm×1m (2×3ft).

R. racemosus see *Danae racemosa*

▲ *Ruscus hypoglossum*

CULTIVATION Plant in autumn in any well-drained soil, in shade or sun. Butcher's brooms are very tolerant of dry, shady conditions. To encourage fruiting, plant a mixture of male and female plants, or a hermaphrodite variety if available.

PROPAGATION Divide in spring.

PESTS AND DISEASES Usually trouble free.

Rush, flowering
see *Butomus umbellatus*

Russelia

Scrophulariaceae

Clusters of brightly coloured blossoms embellish these tender evergreen shrubs and sub-shrubs in summer and autumn. They perform best when growing unrestricted in a conservatory or a greenhouse border, but display their lax habit well in hanging baskets. Plants need a minimum temperature of 10°C (50°F). The genus is native to Central and S America.

RECOMMENDED SPECIES

R. equisetiformis♀ (coral plant) Narrow, tubular red flowers, up to 2.5cm (1in) long, bloom in cascading clusters, from mid summer to early autumn on this branching evergreen shrub. It has strange, slender rush-like stems and tiny mid green scale-like leaves. HEIGHT & SPREAD 1×1m (3×3ft).

▲ *Russelia equisetiformis*

CULTIVATION Plant in spring in well-drained soil that has been enriched with organic matter. The plants require great cultural care if grown in the confined conditions of hanging baskets. Stake plants growing in a conservatory or greenhouse border. Cut out any untidy shoots as they appear. Deadhead the flowers when practicable. Water well in summer and keep much drier during autumn and winter. Apply a slow-release fertiliser in spring.

PROPAGATION Take stem cuttings during spring and summer.

PESTS AND DISEASES Mealy bugs can be a nuisance.

Russian vine see *Fallopia baldschuanica*

Ruta

Rue

Rutaceae

These hardy evergreen sub-shrubs are mainly grown for their aromatic leaves which are sometimes used as medicinal or culinary herbs. The S European species described below will grow happily in poor chalky soils in a sunny position.

RECOMMENDED SPECIES AND VARIETIES

R. graveolens (common rue) Deeply divided, blue-green leaves, about 4cm (1½in) long, clothe this compact, rounded bush. Terminal clusters of small, starry yellow flowers appear in mid summer. HEIGHT & SPREAD 45×30cm (1½×1ft).

▲ *Ruta graveolens*

▲ *Ruta* 'Jackman's Blue'

'Jackman's Blue'♀, more compact, bears distinctly glaucous leaves, but is rather more reluctant to flower.

CULTIVATION Plant in spring in an open, sunny site in free-draining soil. Trim back in spring to the old wood to maintain the shape of the plants. Some people are allergic to the foliage so wear gloves when pruning. Do not apply fertiliser as soft growth will be induced, leading to winter damage.

PROPAGATION Sow seed of species, including *R. graveolens*, in trays under glass as soon as it is available in late summer. Pot on seedlings and plant out in early summer of the following year. For cultivars, such as 'Jackman's Blue', take semi-ripe cuttings in summer and root in coarse, gritty compost in a coldframe. Pot on and keep in a coldframe over winter.

PESTS AND DISEASES Usually trouble free.

S

Sagina
Pearlwort
Caryophyllaceae

The low mound of *Sagina subulata* 'Aurea' and the glossy cushion of *S. boydii*, both evergreens, provide year-round interest. These decorative and slow-growing hardy perennials are worthy of a place in a trough or raised bed. 'Aurea' does well in the cracks in paving in the company of small thymes and other sun-loving crevice plants.

RECOMMENDED SPECIES AND VARIETIES

S. boydii The deep green, highly glossed foliage is made up of tight rosettes of narrow, pointed leaves, up to 1.5cm (½in) long, which form a dense hump. The white flowers in summer are tiny and sparse. HEIGHT & SPREAD 5×10cm (2×4in).

▲ *Sagina subulata* 'Aurea'

***S. subulata* 'Aurea'** Golden, linear leaves up to 2cm (¾in) long are carried in loose clusters and form soft mounds. A profusion of tiny, star-like, white flowers appears in early summer. It is hardy, but not usually long-lived in cultivation. HEIGHT & SPREAD 10 x 30cm (4 x 12in).

CULTIVATION Plant in well-drained gritty soil. *S. boydii* benefits from winter protection or from growing in an alpine house.

PROPAGATION Increase by cuttings or by careful division in spring. Use coarse sand to promote root growth with both cuttings and – in the initial stage – divisions.

PESTS AND DISEASES Moulds may attack pearlworts during winter. *S. boydii* is frequently infested with aphids.

Sagittaria
Arrowhead
Alismataceae

Elegant, arrow-shaped leaves and loose clusters of decorative flowers grace these submerged and emergent aquatic plants. Widely grown in ponds and aquaria, sagittarias require a well-lit position, preferably in still water. The species described are hardy marginals, and require a water depth of up to 15cm (6in), but will tolerate a little more. Both spread by underground runners and quickly form dense colonies. In winter they produce dormant buds, or turions, resembling small tubers, that detach themselves from the parent plant. Sagittarias are native to the USA.

RECOMMENDED SPECIES AND VARIETIES

S. japonica see *S. sagittifolia*

S. latifolia (duck potato) White 3-petalled flowers, up to 2.5cm (1in) across and with a conspicuous yellow centre, are borne in mid to late summer. The soft green leaves grow up to 60cm (24in) long. HEIGHT & SPREAD 1.2m×60cm (4×2ft).

▲ *Sagittaria sagittifolia*

S. sagittifolia (syn. *S. japonica*) (arrowhead, water archer) Loose spikes of white 3-petalled flowers, each up to 2.5cm (1in) across and with a purplish brown centre, are borne in mid to late summer. Upright mid green leaves grow to 45cm (18in) in length. HEIGHT & SPREAD 45×30cm (18×12in).

'Flore Pleno' is a fine double variety.

CULTIVATION Plant from late spring to mid summer in clean, heavy garden soil or a proprietary aquatic planting compost either in an aquatic planting basket or on the marginal shelf of a pool. Cover the soil with a layer of pea gravel to prevent fish from disturbing it. And if ducks are likely to be a nuisance, cover with fine wire-netting. Remove faded foliage in autumn.

PROPAGATION Divide in spring.

PESTS AND DISEASES Water-lily aphids are often troublesome.

Saintpaulia
African violet
Gesneriaceae

Saintpaulia ionantha

Brightly coloured, star-shaped flowers are produced almost all year round by these tender perennials, native to E Africa. They have soft, velvety, rounded leaves – those of the plants recommended here are up to 5cm (2in) across. They make ideal houseplants and greenhouse specimens for warm humid conditions out of direct sunlight.

RECOMMENDED SPECIES AND VARIETIES

***S.* 'Bright Eyes'**♀ A profusion of single deep violet flowers, up to 1.5cm (½in) across and with conspicuous yellow centres, are produced on short stalks. The leaves are dark green and form a compact rosette. HEIGHT & SPREAD 10×25cm (4×10in).

***S.* 'Colorado'**♀ The single magenta flowers are up to 2cm (¾in) across with neatly frilled edges and bright yellow centres. The plant forms a neat rosette of dark green leaves. HEIGHT & SPREAD 10×25cm (4×10in).

***S.* 'Garden News'**♀ Beautiful fully double white flowers up to 2cm (¾in) across are produced above rosettes of bright green leaves. HEIGHT & SPREAD 10×25cm (4×10in).

S. ionantha The main parent of the modern African violet cultivars bears single flowers, violet-blue or white with a violet throat. Up to 2.5cm (1in) across, they are produced just above the leaves in loose clusters of 2–8. The rather fleshy leaves are rounded or scalloped, usually hairy and dull green, often with reddish undersides. HEIGHT & SPREAD 10×25cm (4×10in).

***S.* 'Rococo Pink'**♀ Fully double iridescent

▼ *Saintpaulia* 'Bright Eyes'
Saintpaulia 'Garden News' ▼

▲ *Saintpaulia* 'Rococo Pink'

pink blooms, up to 2.5cm (1in) across, are produced on this tidy rosette-forming plant. The leaves are mid green. HEIGHT & SPREAD 10×25cm (4×10in).

S. **'Starry Trail'**♀ This trailing variety has blue flowers up to 2.5cm (1in) across with a distinctive white edge to the petals. Mid green leaves are borne on drooping stems. HEIGHT & SPREAD 10×30cm (4×12in).

S. **'Wonderland'**♀ This plant has semi-double, light blue, ruffled flowers up to 2cm (¾in) across, and mid-green leaves. HEIGHT & SPREAD 10×25cm (4×10in).

CULTIVATION Grow in pots of rich free-draining compost, preferably soil-less. Maintain a minimum temperature of 15°C (59°F). Place in a well-lit position protected from full sun. Allow the plants to become slightly pot-bound. Water sparingly and liquid feed in spring and summer, preferably from beneath; water occasionally in winter. Remove faded leaves and flowers.

PROPAGATION Leaf cuttings in summer.

PESTS AND DISEASES Whitefly and mealy bug can cause trouble.

Salal see *Gaultheria shallon*

Salix
Willow
Salicaceae

salix alba var. sericea

Fluffy catkins, slender shoots and coloured bark are among the many attractive features of these trees and shrubs. Willows are predominantly deciduous and totally hardy. Most are undemanding about site and soil and tolerate the British climate perfectly well, but excessive heat in southern gardens harms a few sub-alpines. In most species there are separate male and female trees, with showier catkins on the males.

The larger willows have wide-spreading, moisture-seeking roots, which can damage nearby buildings, walls or drains. For these, 40m (130ft) is the minimum recommended planting distance from a house.

The smallest willows are creeping shrubs no more than 2.5cm (1in) in height, while the largest trees reach 30m (100ft). The larger trees and coppice shoots may grow as much as 2.5cm (1in) a day in early summer.

RECOMMENDED SPECIES AND VARIETIES

In the garden, willows have five distinct uses, and they are grouped here as follows:
(1) Landscape, feature and shelter plants
(2) Willows grown for buds and catkins
(3) Willows grown for winter twig colour
(4) Summer-foliage feature plants
(5) Alpine and shrubby willows

LANDSCAPE, FEATURE AND SHELTER

Large willows create a leafy summer backdrop to other plants or to water. The flexible branches and twigs rapidly form a good windbreak.

S. alba (white willow) Slender branches droop slightly on this large spreading tree. The narrow, pointed, matt green leaves have blue-grey undersides covered with fine hairs, giving the tree a silvery appearance. Native to Britain. HEIGHT & SPREAD 6×3m (20×10ft) after 20 years, ultimately 20m (66ft) or more tall.

The smaller var. ***sericea***♀ has a brilliant silver crown and is slower growing. Final height is 10m (33ft), reached after 15 years.

S. caprea (goat willow) Although not suitable for a small garden, this woodland willow makes a good windbreak. It has broadly oval, fresh green leaves, finely toothed with a short point. Silvery green female catkins or bright yellow male catkins appear before the leaves. Native to Britain. HEIGHT & SPREAD 15×10m (50×33ft) – final size, reached in less than 20 years.

salix caprea 'Kilmarnock'

More suitable for small gardens are the small weeping cultivars. The male form is often sold as **'Kilmarnock'**♀ and the female form as **'Weeping Sally'**. They are elegant trees with a narrow head of weeping shoots, often no taller than 1.5m (5ft), and some 2m (6½ft) across, after 10-15 years. They require some pruning to keep their shape.

S. x ***pendulina*** **'Elegantissima'** Cascades of weeping shoots form a spectacular large specimen tree, especially beside a pond that catches its reflection. The narrow pendulous leaves are fresh green. Disease resistant. HEIGHT & SPREAD 8×6m (26×20ft) after 10-15 years, ultimately 25×25m (80×80ft).

WILLOWS FOR BUDS AND CATKINS

Pussy willow buds, held upright against the rather erect stems, last for several weeks in late winter and early spring. Then they open fully into powder-puff male catkins, 1-2cm (⅜-¾in) long and usually yellow, or female catkins, which are less fluffy and a silvery green. Some plants have coloured or textured stems.

S. aegyptiaca (musk willow) Long, yellow male catkins make this large rounded shrub or small tree a haze of colour in late winter before the broad, deep green leaves appear. Native to Turkey, Armenia and Iran. HEIGHT & SPREAD 6×4m (20×13ft) after 10-15 years, ultimately 12m (40ft) tall.

S. daphnoides **'Aglaia'**♀ Long, pearly grey pussy willow buds are borne on the plum-purple shoots of this male tree early in the year. The species, native to central Europe, is often short lived. HEIGHT & SPREAD 5×4m (16×13ft) after 10-15 years, ultimately 10m (33ft) tall.

S. gracilistyla♀ This ornamental spreading shrub has furry stems and silky pink catkins. Native to Japan, China and Korea. HEIGHT & SPREAD 80×80cm (32×32in) after 5 years, ultimately 2m (6½ft) tall.

'Melanostachys'♀, a male clone, has unusual black catkins in early spring, which turn brick-red and then gold. The stems are a rich plum-purple colour.

S. udensis **'Sekka'** (syn. *S. sachalinensis* 'Sekka') Numerous pearly buds develop into large, silky, pink male catkins in early spring on this sprawling shrub. The shoots are often flattened. Native to Japan and E Russia. HEIGHT & SPREAD 3×8m (10×26ft) after 10-15 years, ultimately 5m (16ft) tall.

WILLOWS FOR WINTER TWIG COLOUR

Brilliantly coloured young stems are obtained by regularly cutting back these willows to near ground level. If this is done at the end of winter in alternate years, good colour is combined with catkins on the yearling stems. Older shoots are not brightly coloured. Leaves are narrow and 5-15cm (2-6in) long. The plants listed grow to 1m (3ft) in one year and to 1.5-2m (5-6½ft) after two years. After 10-15 years a plant has a spread of about 3m (10ft) with some 50 stems. The roots spread widely even on plants that are cut back.

S. acutifolia **'Blue Streak'**♀ Shiny, deep purplish violet shoots are dusted with a silver-grey bloom. The young silvery buds make a striking contrast though the catkins are dull yellow.

S. alba var. ***vitellina***♀ (golden willow) The young shoots are a striking orange-yellow.

'Britzensis'♀ has orange-red stems.

S. x ***rubens*** **'Basfordiana'**♀ The yellow stems of this male plant bear slender yellow catkins with glossy leaves in spring. **'Sanguinea'** is a red-stemmed female variety.

ALPINE AND SHRUBBY WILLOWS

Several of these plants are suitable for beds or permanent containers. Some are spread-

▲ *Salix alba* var. *vitellina*
Salix alba var. *vitellina* 'Britzensis' ▲

ing but their roots are not invasive. The true alpines do not thrive in hot conditions nor in competition with other plants.

S. alpina (syn. *S.* 'Jacquinii') This is a low spreading shrub with glossy round leaves. Male plants have purplish catkins, which turn golden yellow, females have greenish catkins. Native to the Alps and Carpathians. HEIGHT & SPREAD 25×20cm (10×8in).

▲ *Salix exigua*

S. exigua (coyote willow) Very narrow, long, silvery, pale green leaves distinguish this open-growing shrub with its graceful, slender branches. Yellow male catkins appear in spring at the same time as the leaves; the green female catkins, on separate plants, are hidden by the leaves. Native to western N America and N Mexico. HEIGHT & SPREAD 4m (13ft) tall, spreading 30cm (1ft) a year by suckers.

***S. hastata* 'Wehrhahnii'**♀ White woolly catkins maturing to a brilliant yellow are borne on stout, dark reddish purple stems by this small multistemmed shrub. The rounded leaves are dark green. Native to Japan, China and Korea. HEIGHT & SPREAD 80×80cm (32×32in) after 5 years, ultimately 2m (6½ft) tall.

S. lindleyana A mat of tiny, glossy, pale green leaves trails over rocks and scree. Male catkins are browny green, female catkins reddish brown. Native to the Himalayas. HEIGHT & SPREAD 10×30cm (4×12in) after 5 years.

S. repens* var. *argentea♀ Silver leaves are borne on an ornamental, low and sprawling bush. Roundish silver catkins are small but often numerous. Native to Britain. HEIGHT & SPREAD up to 70×120cm (28×48in).

'Voorthuizen' is a completely prostrate cultivar of *S. repens*, with trailing stems and tiny silvery leaves.

S. reticulata♀ The summer catkins on this minute prostrate plant may be as tall as the whole plant at 4cm (1½in). They vary in colour from brown to purple and yellow. The stalked, round, deciduous leaves are leathery and heavily veined. Native to N Asia, N America and Europe. HEIGHT & SPREAD 4×20cm (1½×8in) after 15 years.

WILLOWS FOR SUMMER FOLIAGE

Curious or brightly coloured foliage is a feature of several medium-size willows that enliven a garden bed. Larger curiosities serve as dramatic specimen plants.

***S. babylonica* 'Crispa'** (syn. *S. babylonica* 'Annularis') Spiralling narrow leaves on this erect shrub often form complete rings. Shoots tend to die back. HEIGHT & SPREAD 1.5×1m (5×3ft) after 10-15 years.

▲ *Salix hastata* 'Wehrhahnii'

***S. babylonica* var. *pekinensis* 'Tortuosa'**♀ (syn. *S. matsudana* 'Tortuosa') This curiously twisted, fast-growing tree has contorted greenish twigs and leaves. Even large branches and trunks are bent and often they split because of it. Female catkins appear before the leaves. HEIGHT & SPREAD 10×7m (33×23ft) when mature at about 15 years.

S. elaeagnos♀ (hoary willow) Slender purple-brown shoots, bearing yellow catkins in spring, form a dense shrub. The very narrow, long, graceful leaves are grey-green above, silvery below. Native to S Europe and Turkey. HEIGHT & SPREAD 2×2m (6½×6½ft) after 6 years and ultimately.

S. fargesii Large glossy leaves and long erect catkins succeed the brilliant red winter buds. Glossy green new shoots mature to a polished red-brown in the second year. In cold areas the spectacular foliage sometimes suffers damage. Native to SE Asia. HEIGHT & SPREAD 1.5×1.5m (5×5ft) after 5 years, ultimately 5m (16ft) tall.

▲ *Salix integra* 'Hakuro-Nishiki'

S. helvetica♀ (Swiss willow) Glaucous, thickly woolly leaves make this small rounded bush into a bright blue-green ball of colour. In early spring the catkins are silvery green, the male flowers turning golden yellow with pollen. Native to the Alps, it relishes an exposed position. HEIGHT & SPREAD 1×1m (3×3ft) in 6 years.

***S. integra* 'Hakuro-Nishiki'** (syn. 'Albomaculata') Slender catkins are followed by the pink and white, variegated leaves of this graceful branched shrub. Prune in early spring to encourage new growth. A willow bred from a Japanese species, it is often grown as a 1m (3ft) high standard. HEIGHT & SPREAD 1.5×1.5m (5×5ft) as a shrub.

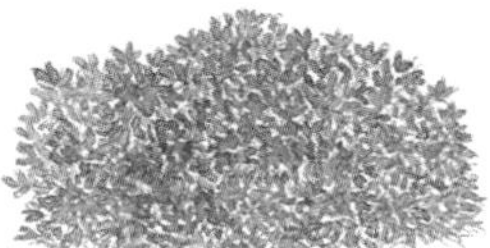

Salix lanata

S. lanata♀ (woolly willow) Grey-green, downy, rounded leaves form a low spreading bush suitable for a rock garden. The erect catkins become fluffy and turn yellow in summer. Native to Scotland. HEIGHT & SPREAD 30×30cm (1×1ft) after 5 years, ultimately 90cm×2m (3×6½ft).

CULTIVATION Though tolerant of a wide range of soils, willows generally prefer damp heavy soil and thrive least on shallow chalk. They do best in full light. Alpine types grow best in dry air, low temperatures and moist rocky ground.

PROPAGATION Semi-ripe or hardwood cuttings root readily. Grafting is needed to reproduce exactly the named varieties.

PRUNING Only plants grown for twig colour need hard pruning. Cut them down to the ground at the end of winter, cutting half the shoots in alternate years. Trim other willows sparingly, otherwise excessive growth is stimulated.

PESTS AND DISEASES Aphids, moths, beetles and weevils occasionally cause damage. Midges and mites cause galls but these are usually best left alone. *S. alba* sometimes suffers from watermark disease caused by the bacterium *Erwinia salicis*.

Salpiglossis

Solanaceae

Funnel-shaped, strikingly marked flowers are freely produced on these upright branching plants. Only one species, a half-hardy annual, is normally cultivated in Britain, and this has given rise to numerous hybrids. The plants thrive in a sunny sheltered position in mild dry areas. A bed or large container on a patio with a southerly aspect suits them well and they flower from mid summer to early autumn. In cooler regions, they can be grown as pot plants in a greenhouse or conservatory, flowering in spring and early summer. The flowers are ideal for cutting and last well in water.

RECOMMENDED SPECIES AND VARIETIES

S. sinuata (painted tongue) This Chilean species is rarely grown, but seed of dwarf hybrids in mixed colours is widely available. The flowers, up to 7cm (2¾in) long, range in colour from yellow to orange, red, rose, purple and blue. The petals are often overlaid by another colour, usually gold, though darker veins are also a feature. The slender stems are covered in sticky hairs. The narrow, lance-shaped, pale green leaves have wavy, toothed edges and grow to 10cm (4in) long.

Bolero grows to 60cm (2ft) tall. **Carnival** reaches a height of 45cm (1½ft). **Casino**♀, **Festival** and **Flamenco** reach a height of 35cm (14in).

CULTIVATION Plant after all risk of frost has passed in moist but well-drained soil, choosing a sheltered spot in full sun. Alternatively, grow in pots of general purpose or potting compost and keep in a greenhouse or conservatory; plants can be moved outside in summer. In winter, maintain a temperature of 10°C (50°F).

Provide support for taller varieties, and removed faded flowers on all varieties to prolong flowering.

PROPAGATION For plants grown outside, sow seed in late winter or early spring in a heated greenhouse. For pot plants, sow seed in a heated greenhouse in late summer for spring flowering, and in late winter for late spring and early summer flowering.

PESTS AND DISEASES Soil-borne fungal attack may cause wilt and die-back.

▲ *Salpiglossis sinuata*

▲ *Salpiglossis* Casino

Salvia

Sage

Labiatae

salvia argentea

The upright flower spikes of this large genus of annuals, perennials and shrubs provide some of the brightest colours for summer borders or for winter displays in a greenhouse or conservatory. Many salvias have soft hairy leaves and some species, including the herb sage (*Salvia officinalis*), are grown for their decorative and aromatic foliage. The individual flowers are tubular with two lips, the upper lip often elongated and pulled forward to form a hood. The flower spikes are formed by whorls of flowers along the stems. Most salvias prefer drier conditions in well-drained soil in full sun.

RECOMMENDED SPECIES AND VARIETIES

Salvias vary in hardiness and can be divided into 3 groups accordingly; there are hardy, half-hardy and tender species and varieties.

HARDY SPECIES AND VARIETIES

These can be grown outdoors all year round in Britain.

S. argentea♀ A mass of woolly, silver, oval to oblong leaves, up to 20cm (8in) long, form a basal rosette. White flowers, 1.5cm (½in) long, appear in branching spikes on strong upright stems in early summer. This herbaceous perennial or biennial often dies after the plant has flowered. It is mainly grown for its decorative leaf rosettes. Native to the Mediterranean. HEIGHT & SPREAD 60-90×45cm (2-3×1½ft).

S. haematodes
see *S. pratensis* Haematodes Group

S. horminum see *S. viridis*

S. nemorosa **'Ostfriesland'**♀ ('East Friesland') Dense upright spikes of purple flowers, each about 6mm (¼in) long, cover these bushy herbaceous perennials in mid summer. The rough, narrow oval leaves, 10cm (4in) long, are mid green. HEIGHT & SPREAD 45×45cm (1½×1½ft).

S. officinalis (common sage) This aromatic evergreen sub-shrub is widely cultivated for its ornamental foliage as well as for use as a culinary herb. The rough, grey-green, pointed oval to oblong leaves are up to 7.5cm (3in) long. Flowers in shades of blue and purple, 2cm (¾in) long, appear in short spikes intermittently throughout the summer. Native to the Mediterranean. HEIGHT & SPREAD 60cm×1m (2×3ft).

The leaves of **'Icterina'**♀ are marbled with primrose yellow and gold. **'Kew Gold'**♀ has bright golden yellow leaves but flowers sparsely. **Purpurascens Group**♀ has soft purple leaves that gradually darken through the summer. **'Tricolor'**♀ has white, deep pink and purple leaves which

▲ *Salvia nemorosa* 'Ostfriesland'

Salvia officinalis Purpurascens Group ▼

▼ *Salvia officinalis* 'Icterina'

▲ *Salvia przewalskii*

▲ *Salvia sclarea var turkestanica*

darken as summer progresses.

***S. pratensis* Haematodes Group**♀ (syn *S. haematodes*) Light lavender-blue flowers, 3cm (1¼in) long, are borne in loose panicles in early summer. The dark green, rough leaves, 15cm (6in) long, have wavy, toothed edges and form a basal rosette. *S. pratensis* (meadow clary) is a short-lived herbaceous perennial, native to Europe, including Britain. HEIGHT & SPREAD 1m×38cm (3ft×15in).

S. przewalskii Violet to purple or blue flowers, 2cm (¾in) long, appear on branching stems in late summer. The heart-shaped leaves, up to 10cm (4in) long, are mid-green above, beige beneath. They form a clump at the base of the plant. A herbaceous perennial, native to China, with tuberous roots. HEIGHT & SPREAD 1.2×1m (4×3ft).

S. sclarea* var. *turkestanica (clary sage) White and purple flowers, 3cm (1¼in) long, appear in mid summer on branching spikes. Prominent purple bracts persist after the flowers fade. The dark green, hairy, aromatic leaves are up to 23cm (9in) long and, if touched, their unpleasant smell can cling to clothing. A short-lived evergreen perennial or biennial that seeds itself freely. Native to central Asia. HEIGHT & SPREAD 1m×30cm (3×1ft).

S.* × *superba♀ Masses of violet-blue flowers, 1.5cm (½in) long, are borne on numerous branching spikes in mid summer. Crimson-purple bracts persist after the flowers have faded. The rough, narrow pointed leaves of this herbaceous perennial are mid-green and grow to 10cm (4in) long. HEIGHT & SPREAD 60-90×45cm (2-3×1½ft).

Salvia x superba

'Rubin' has pink flowers and claret-striped bracts. **'Superba'** has purple flowers.

***S.* × *sylvestris* 'Rose Queen'** Pale pink flowers, about 1.5cm (½in) long, with red bracts appear on branching spikes in early summer. The narrow pointed, dark green, veined leaves of this herbaceous perennial are up to 7cm (2¾in) long. HEIGHT & SPREAD 1.2m×60cm (4×2ft).

S. verticillata In late summer, long arching spikes carry tiny, vivid violet flowers with crimson-tinted bracts that persist after the flowers fade. The oval to oblong, mid-green leaves, 10cm (4in) long, form a large clump. A herbaceous perennial, native to Europe and W Asia. HEIGHT & SPREAD 75×45cm (2½×1½ft) or more.

The flowers of **'Alba'** are white.

S. viridis (syn. *H. horminum*) White or lilac flowers, 1.5cm (½in) long, appear in spikes in early summer and their colourful bracts last throughout summer. These can be blue, pink, purple or white, with darker veins. The flowerheads can be dried. The mid-green oval leaves are up to 5cm (2in) long. An annual, native to the Mediterranean, of very upright habit. HEIGHT & SPREAD 45×20cm (1½ft×8in).

The cultivar of *S. viridis*, **'Claryssa'**, has larger bracts of more intense colour, and grows to 40cm (16in).

HALF-HARDY SPECIES AND VARIETIES

These are half-hardy herbaceous perennials and sub-shrubs which can be grown outdoors in summer and overwintered under glass. These can also be treated as annuals by raising new plants from cuttings or seed each year. There are also half-hardy annuals available.

S. cacaliifolia♀ Bright blue flowers, 2cm (¾in) long, appear on loose spikes in late summer. The shiny mid green leaves grow to 10cm (4in) long. A herbaceous perennial of loose habit, native to Central America. HEIGHT & SPREAD 1m×45cm (3×1½ft).

S. candelabrum♀ Violet-blue flowers, 4cm (1½in) across and flecked with white, appear in mid summer on branching spikes. The dark grey-green, aromatic leaves grow to 9cm (3½in) long. This herbaceous perennial or sub-shrub, native to Spain, may survive outside in more protected gardens. HEIGHT & SPREAD 90×60cm (3×2ft).

S. cardinalis see *S. fulgens*

S. coccinea Long spikes of red flowers, each about 2cm (¾in) long, appear from early to mid summer. Dark green, downy, heart-shaped leaves, about 6cm (2½in) long, are also borne by this annual of graceful habit, native to tropical S America. HEIGHT & SPREAD 60-90×30cm (2-3×1ft).

'Coral Nymph' has pink and white flowers, **'Lady in Red'**♀ has scarlet.

S. confertiflora Deep red flowers, 12mm (½in) long, appear in spikes in late summer or autumn. The yellowy green, ovate leaves, 20cm (8in) long, are rough and densely woolly. They give off a foetid smell when crushed. A herbaceous perennial, native to Brazil. HEIGHT & SPREAD 1.2m×60cm (4×2ft).

S. discolor♀ Deep purple, almost black flowers, 3cm (1¼in) long and with hooded white calyxes, appear in late summer. The pointed, oval, grey to whitish green leaves are 10cm (4in) long. All parts of the plants are covered with white hairs. A herbaceous perennial, native to Peru. HEIGHT & SPREAD 45×30cm (1½×1ft).

S. farinacea (mealy sage) Tiny blue, lavender or purple flowers appear in slender spikes throughout summer. The narrow, mid or dark green leaves are up to 8cm (3in) long. The densely branched stems of this herbaceous perennial are covered with a white dust. A plant of upright habit usually raised from seed. Native to Texas and N Mexico. HEIGHT & SPREAD 50×25cm (20×10in).

'Strata' has clear blue flowers with contrasting silver calyxes, which are prominent when the flowers are in bud. It reaches 40cm (16in) in height. **'Victoria'**♀ has

▼ *Salvia farinacea*

deep purple-blue flowers and grows 50 cm (20 in) tall. **'White Victory'**🏆 has silvery white blooms and reaches 35 cm (14 in) tall.

S. fulgens🏆 (syn. *S. cardinalis*) Scarlet flowers, up to 3 cm (1¼ in) long, appear in branching spikes towards the end of summer. The pointed oval leaves, 12 cm (4¾ in) long, are bright green above and white-hairy underneath. A herbaceous perennial, native to Mexico, with upright stems which are woody at the base. HEIGHT & SPREAD 1.2 m×75 cm (4×2½ ft).

S. grahamii **hort.**
see *S. microphylla* var. *neurepia*

S. greggii (autumn sage) Flowers 1.5 cm (½ in) across, ranging in colour from red to purple, appear in clusters on thin wiry stems in late summer. The narrow oblong leaves, matt and deep green, grow to 3 cm (1¼ in) in length. An upright evergreen sub-shrub from Texas and Mexico. HEIGHT & SPREAD 1×1 m (3×3 ft).

The hybrid **x *lycioides*** (syn. *S. lycioides*) has deep purple flowers. **'Peach'** see *S.* × *jamensis* 'Pat Vlasto'.

S. guaranitica🏆 Dark gentian-blue flowers, 5 cm (2 in) long, appear in terminal spikes in late summer. The dark green, ovate leaves are 12.5 cm (5 in) long. This evergreen perennial, also grown as an annual, can survive outside in warmer gardens if protected with horticultural fleece or a dry mulch. Native to S America. HEIGHT & SPREAD 1.2 m×45 cm (4×1½ ft).

S. involucrata🏆 In late summer, pinky crimson flowers, 3-5 cm (1¼-2 in) long, are carried in compact spikes. The oval mid green leaves are 25 cm (10 in) long. A herbaceous perennial with woody-based stems, native to Mexico. HEIGHT & SPREAD 1.5 m×60 cm (5×2 ft).

'Bethellii' has larger, dark cerise blooms.

S. x jamensis **'Pat Vlasto'** (syn *S. greggii* 'Peach' hort.) Deep pink, tubular flowers, 2.5 cm (1 in) long, appear in spikes from mid summer onwards. The ovate leaves, 3 cm (1¼ in) long, are mid green. An evergreen sub-shrub. HEIGHT & SPREAD 75×45 cm (2½×1½ ft).

S. lycioides see. *S. greggii* × *lycioides*

S. microphylla var. ***neurepia***🏆 (syn *S. grahamii* hort., *S.* 'Kew Red') Vibrant scarlet flowers, 2.5 cm (1 in) long, are carried in spikes and last from early summer to the first frosts. The pale green, ovate leaves are up to 4 cm (1½ in) long. An upright-growing, evergreen sub-shrub of rounded habit, native to Mexico. HEIGHT & SPREAD 1.2 m×75 cm (4×2½ ft).

The flowers of **'Newby Hall'**🏆 are brighter scarlet.

S. patens🏆 (gentian sage) Pale or deep blue flowers, 2.5 cm (1 in) across, are borne on long slender spikes in late summer and autumn. The oval leaves, 10-20 cm (4-8 in) long, are pale green. An upright, branching herbaceous perennial which has tuberous roots that can be lifted and stored over the winter. In warm sheltered gardens with well-drained soil, the tubers will usually survive the winter outdoors if left undisturbed. Often raised from seed. Native to Mexico. HEIGHT & SPREAD 60-75×30 cm (2-2½×1 ft).

▲ *Salvia involucrata*

'Cambridge Blue'🏆 has pale blue flowers and is available as seed strain. **'Chilcombe'** has mauve-blue flowers.

S. splendens (scarlet sage) Scarlet flowers, each up to 5 cm (2 in) long, appear from early to mid summer on dense flower spikes. Conspicuous red bracts persist after the flowers fade. The pointed oval, mid to dark green leaves, up to 7 cm (2¾ in) long, have toothed edges. This is the bushy annual, native to Brazil, that is widely grown as a bedding plant. HEIGHT & SPREAD 30×25 cm (12×10 in).

'Blaze of Fire' has red flowers. **'Laser Purple'** and **'Phoenix Purple'** both produce purple blooms. **Sizzler Series** has flowers in shades of pink, red and purple as well as white. **'Vanguard'**🏆 has red flowers.

S. uliginosa🏆 Azure flowers, 1½ cm (½ in) across, open from purple buds in late summer and continue well into autumn. The shiny, narrow, mid green leaves are 9 cm (3½ in) long. This herbaceous perennial prefers moister conditions and may survive the winter outside in mild areas. It often breaks into growth late in spring, so it should not be presumed dead till then. Native to S America. HEIGHT & SPREAD 1.5-2.5 m×60 cm (5-8×2 ft).

TENDER SPECIES AND VARIETIES

These plants are best grown in a greenhouse or conservatory with a minimum temperature of 7°C (45°F). They flower so late in the year that, grown outside even in mild areas, they risk being killed by the first frosts before flowering has finished.

S. buchananii🏆 (syn. *S. bacheriana*) Spikes of purple flowers, up to 5 cm (2 in) long, appear from mid summer to mid autumn. The dark green lanceolate leaves, up to 6 cm (2½ in) long, have a leathery shiny surface. A herbaceous perennial with woody-based stems, native to Mexico. HEIGHT & SPREAD 60×30 cm (2×1 ft).

S. leucantha🏆 (Mexican sage bush) White flowers, 2 cm (¾ in) long with purple calyxes, appear from mid summer to mid autumn on spikes up to 50 cm (20 in) long. The mid green lanceolate leaves grow to 10 cm (4 in) long. Leaves, stems and flowers of this herbaceous perennial are covered in dense white wool. HEIGHT & SPREAD 1-1.5 m×45 cm (3-5×1½ ft).

▲ *Salvia uliginosa*

S. oppositiflora🏆 Spikes of brilliant red flowers, tinged with orange and up to 4 cm (1½ in) long, appear in mid summer. The heart-shaped hairy leaves, about 5 cm (2 in) long, are pale green above with dense white wool beneath. A herbaceous perennial, native to Peru. HEIGHT & SPREAD 60×45 cm (2×1½ ft).

CULTIVATION Plant hardy salvias from autumn to spring in any free-draining soil in full sun. Some staking will be needed for taller plants. Cut back the flowering stems of hardy herbaceous perennials after the first flowers fade to encourage a second crop of blooms later in the season.

Plant half-hardy salvias in late spring after danger of frosts has passed, choosing a warm, protected spot. Lift plants in autumn before the first hard frosts and overwinter in a cool greenhouse or conservatory. Alternatively, grow in containers of compost and move outside during the summer.

Grow tender salvias in pots of compost in a greenhouse or conservatory. Maintain a minimum winter temperature of 7°C (45°F). Water freely during the growing season and feed every 3 weeks.

PROPAGATION Divide hardy plants in autumn or spring, or sow the seed of species in open ground in spring.

Take softwood or tip cuttings of half-hardy and tender perennials in summer and grow on under glass through the winter. Alternatively, sow seed in early spring in a heated greenhouse – salvias for bedding out are always propagated in this way.

PRUNING If necessary, control the size of *S. officinalis* by cutting back in spring. Other shrubby salvias do not need pruning.

PESTS AND DISEASES Red spider mites and leafhoppers can be a problem under glass. Capsid bugs and powdery mildew may attack the leaves of plants grown outside.

Sambucus

Elder

Caprifoliaceae

Sambucus racemosa

Familiar residents of English hedgerows, elders have long been cultivated for their colourful foliage and scented flowers. Although they are not particularly showy, the flat creamy white clusters of starry flowers possess a delicate charm. The flowers are borne in early summer and can be used to make wine as can the small black berries which ripen in early autumn.

All elders bear pinnate leaves with 5-7 toothed, ovate leaflets, each up to 12.5cm (5in) long. When allowed to grow freely the plants develop an untidy habit. However, they can be cut back almost to ground level every 2 or 3 years, to which they respond by producing brightly coloured regrowth. There are 20 hardy species of elder but generally the cultivars of only two species – *Sambucus nigra* and *S. racemosa* – are grown in Britain. They make a colourful summer feature in a large, informal garden. Native to Europe.

RECOMMENDED SPECIES AND VARIETIES

S. nigra (European elder) This rampant, invasive species with mid green leaves has little appeal to most gardeners, but there are several cultivars that make attractive garden subjects. HEIGHT & SPREAD 6×4m (20×13ft) after 10 years, ultimately 8m (26ft) tall.

'Aurea'♀ (golden elder) is a very hardy variety. It needs full sun for its leaves to develop the best golden colour, which deepens as summer ends. It can be coppiced to good effect every 1-3 years. **'Aureomarginata'** has bright yellow-edged foliage and should be treated in the same way as 'Aurea'. **'Guincho Purple'**♀ bears green foliage to begin with, which develops into purple-black growth in summer, finally turning red in autumn. The flowers are pinkish in bud on purple stalks. If it is shaded or coppiced, it tends to stay quite green all year. Finely divided green leaflets distinguish f. ***laciniata***♀ (fern-leaved elder). It can be coppiced to resemble a clump of ferns, or allowed to grow into a small tree of 4×3m (13×10ft) in 20 years. **'Linearis'** has variably shaped leaflets often cut to the midrib. The plant seldom exceeds a height and spread of 2×2m (6½×6½ft). **'Marginata'** is a silver to white variegated variety. It is vigorous and produces coppice regrowth of around 1.5m (5ft) in the first year. The green leaves have creamy edges. Full sun is needed to produce good colour. **'Pulverulenta'** is a small slow-growing plant with white-mottled leaves.

▼ *Sambucus nigra* 'Marginata'

Sambucus nigra 'Pulverulenta' ▼

▲ *Sambucus nigra* 'Aurea'

S. racemosa (European red elder) Roughly conical heads of yellowish white flowers are borne by this spreading shrubby tree. The berries are bright, glossy scarlet. HEIGHT & SPREAD 3×3m (10×10ft) after 10 years, ultimately 4m (13ft) tall.

'Sutherland Gold'♀ is a deeply cut, golden variety with yellowish flowers. It needs full light to develop good foliage colour but often suffers from heat in southern Britain. **'Tenuifolia'**♀ is a slow-growing, cut-leaved variety that grows well on lime-rich soils. It seldom exceeds a height and spread of 1.5×1.5m (5×5ft).

CULTIVATION Plant in any well-drained soil, ensuring that the golden and variegated forms have plenty of sunlight.

PROPAGATION Plant hardwood cuttings outdoors in winter, or semi-ripe heel cuttings in late summer under glass.

PRUNING Left unpruned, elders tend to become untidy and unstable. They may be pruned to the ground in winter, losing flowers and fruit, or old wood may be cut out and young shoots reduced by a half.

PESTS AND DISEASES Aphids and mosaic virus may occasionally strike.

Sanguinaria

Bloodroot

Papaveraceae

There is just one species in this genus, a hardy herbaceous perennial bearing short-lived anemone-like flowers in spring. After the flowers have faded, the grey-green leaves open to their full extent forming a dense canopy. Bloodroot with its rhizomatous roots is a useful plant for naturalising in leafy woodland. It is also good for a shady spot in a rock garden or a peat border. The name of this woodland plant from N America refers to the crimson sap that oozes from its rhizomes when they are cut.

Sanguinaria canadensis Solitary white, 8-petalled flowers, 5cm (2in) across, are held at the top of stout upright stems, 10cm (4in) tall, in spring. The rounded, lobed and scalloped leaves, carried on stiff stalks, grow to 10cm (4in) across. HEIGHT & SPREAD 30×45cm (1×1½ft) after 3 or 4 years.

▲ *Sanguinaria canadensis* 'Plena'

'Plena'♀, the most widely grown cultivar, and the best for gardens, has double flowers. **'Rosea'** (also sold as **'Pink'**) has blooms flushed with rose pink.

CULTIVATION Plant in cool, humus-rich soil in light shade in spring or autumn.

PROPAGATION Lift and divide plants every few years in autumn.

PESTS AND DISEASES Usually trouble free, though wireworm or cutworm may damage the rhizomes.

Sanguisorba

Burnet

Rosaceae

Striking flowers and attractive foliage enhance the perennial border throughout the summer. The tiny flowers with protruding stamens are packed into spherical or oblong heads held at the top of slender stems, producing a bottlebrush effect. These hardy rhizomatous perennials have pinnate leaves, divided into several rounded or oblong, serrated leaflets. The genus is naturally distributed in Europe, Asia and N America.

RECOMMENDED SPECIES AND VARIETIES
S. albiflora (syn. *S. magnifica alba*) Nodding white flower heads, up to 6cm (2½in) long, are borne from mid summer to early autumn. The grey-green leaves are composed of 11-15 rounded, 5cm (2in) long, clearly stalked leaflets. HEIGHT & SPREAD 75×40cm (30×16in).
S. canadensis Creamy white flowers, carried in erect, narrowly cylindrical heads up to 20cm (8in) long, appear from mid summer to mid autumn. The pale green leaves have up to 8 pairs of narrow, 10cm (4in) long leaflets. HEIGHT & SPREAD 1.8m×60cm (6×2ft).
S. magnifica alba see *S. albiflora*
S. minor (salad burnet) Spherical green flowerheads, 1.5cm (½in) across, are borne in early summer and early autumn. The flowerheads are often tinged with purple and become reddish in fruit. The pinnate leaves have 9-25 rounded leaflets, about 2cm (¾in) long. HEIGHT & SPREAD 1m×45cm (3ft×18in).
S. obtusa Nodding, rich rose-pink flowerheads, up to 7.5cm (3in) long, appear from mid summer to early autumn. The grey-green leaves are composed of 13-17 thick-textured, 5cm (2in) long, rounded leaflets. HEIGHT & SPREAD 60×40cm (24×16in).
S. officinalis (great burnet) Oblong or globular, dull crimson flowerheads, up to 2cm (¾in) across, appear in early summer to early autumn on branched leafy stems. This erect plant bears leaves with up to 7 pairs of 5cm (2in) long, ovate leaflets. HEIGHT & SPREAD 1m×60cm (3×2ft).
CULTIVATION Plant in any moderately moist soil, in full sun or light shade, in autumn. Taller plants may need support from twigs pushed in around the clump.
PROPAGATION Lift and divide in early spring. Alternatively, sow seed in autumn or early spring.
PESTS AND DISEASES Usually trouble free.

▼ *Sanguisorba officinalis*

Sansevieria

Dracaenaceae

Sansevieria trifasciata 'Laurentii'

Erect, sword-like leaves, often patterned and variegated, make this tropical evergreen perennial one of the most popular house plants. Mature plants produce rather insignificant fragrant, lily-like flowers. These are creamy, white or greenish and may be removed when they first appear, though they are quite pleasing and may be followed by red berries. Sansevierias are extremely easy to grow, but avoid over-watering, especially in winter, and maintain a minimum temperature of 10°C (50°F).

RECOMMENDED SPECIES AND VARIETIES
S. trifasciata (mother-in-law's tongue) The stiff, upright, dull green leaves grow up to 75cm (30in) long. They are beautifully patterned and splashed with dark green and resemble a snakeskin. Native to W Africa. HEIGHT & SPREAD 25×15cm (10×6in).

'Gigantea' grows to a height of 75cm (2½ft) and has green-patterned leaves with yellow margins. **'Golden Hahnii'**♀ has rosettes of pale green foliage, marked and marbled with darker green and with bold yellow, informally banded edges. **'Hahnii'** is a dwarf plant that forms rosettes of broadly lance-shaped, leathery leaves, up to 15cm (6in) long. **'Laurentii'**♀ has erect, fleshy, sword-like, dark green leaves with gold edges and cross bands of dark green.

▼ *Sansevieria trifasciata* 'Golden Hahnii'

▲ *Sansevieria trifasciata* 'Laurentii'

CULTIVATION Grow sansevierias in free-draining gritty compost, preferably in a sunny position, though some shade is tolerated. Never overwater. Feed occasionally with a liquid house-plant fertiliser in summer. Keep the foliage free from dust, especially where light levels are low and in winter. Sansevierias are slow-growing, making only a few fresh leaves each year. They tolerate neglect but grow faster and better if their compost is replaced regularly.
PROPAGATION Take leaf cuttings in spring and summer. Divide variegated plants in spring and summer.
PESTS AND DISEASES Usually trouble free.

Santolina

Compositae

Santolina chamaecyparissus

These summer-flowering, dwarf evergreen shrubs are grown for their mounds of aromatic, finely divided foliage and pale button-like flowers. They are suitable for growing in large rock gardens, at the front of shrub borders or as low hedging. The species below bear 2cm (¾in) wide flowerheads, held singly on long stems. The plants are frost hardy but relatively short-lived and need replacing every 5-10 years. The measurements given below are for full-grown 5-year-old plants.

RECOMMENDED SPECIES AND VARIETIES
S. chamaecyparissus♀ (syn. *S. incana*) (cotton lavender) Silvery, finely dissected, woolly leaves, up to 4cm (1½in) long, form a clense leafy mass. Bright lemon-yellow flowers appear in mid summer. HEIGHT & SPREAD 60×60cm (2×2ft) or more.

The following cultivars are slightly smaller than the species. **'Lambrook Silver'** has silver, thread-like foliage and deep

▲ *Santolina chamaecyparissus* 'Lemon Queen'

yellow flowers. Its neat tight habit makes it good for hedging. **'Lemon Queen'** has grey-green foliage and, despite the name, cream flowers. With a height and spread of just 20×20cm (8×8in), var. ***nana***♀ is a good rock garden plant. **'Pretty Carol'** has greyish leaves.

S. pinnata The smooth, divided, mid green leaves grow up to 4cm (1½in) long. White flowers appear in mid to late summer. HEIGHT & SPREAD 60cm×1m (2×3ft).

The widely grown ssp. ***neapolitana***♀ has longer and more feathery leaves than the species and lemon-yellow flowers. Its cultivar **'Edward Bowles'** has greenish-grey leaves and pale primrose-yellow flowers. It reaches a height and spread of about 45×50cm (18×20in).

S. rosmarinifolia (syn. *S. virens*, *S. viridis*) Bright green, thread-like leaves grow up to 5cm (2in) long. Lemon-yellow flowers are borne in mid to late summer. HEIGHT & SPREAD 60cm×1m (2×3ft).

'Primrose Gem'♀ has feathery mid green foliage and pale primrose-yellow flowers.

CULTIVATION Plant in spring or early autumn in full sun in any well-drained soil. For hedges, plant about 30cm (1ft) apart.

PROPAGATION Take semi-ripe cuttings from mid to late summer. Pot on in spring and move outdoors. Plant out in early autumn or the following spring.

PRUNING Cut back by at least half every spring to maintain a bushy neat habit. Trim lightly after flowering. For hedges, shear to shape after flowering once a year.

PESTS AND DISEASES Usually trouble free.

S

Sanvitalia

Compositae

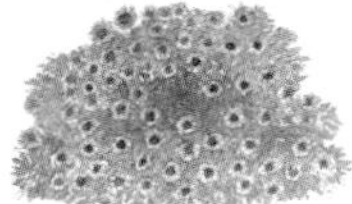

Sanvitalia procumbens

The bold flowers of *Sanvitalia procumbens* spread a bright cover over the ground from summer to autumn. The plant is a hardy annual, flourishing in well-drained soil in a sunny spot edging a bed or border or hugging a path, though its exuberant trailing habit is best displayed in a container, such as a hanging basket or a window box.

RECOMMENDED SPECIES AND VARIETIES

S. procumbens (creeping zinnia) The flowers, appearing from mid summer to early autumn, are 2.5cm (1in) across and made up of bright yellow ray florets (petals) and dark purple centres of flattened cone shape. The mid green leaves, up to 6cm (2½in) long, are borne in pairs. Native to Mexico. HEIGHT & SPREAD 15×40cm (6×16in).

'Mandarin Orange' has golden orange ray florets. **'Irish Eyes'** has ray florets of the same colour, but the centres are greenish.

CULTIVATION Grow in a sunny situation in well-drained, preferably light, soil.

PROPAGATION Sow seeds in mid spring where the plants are to grow, thinning the seedlings to 25-30cm (10-12in) apart. On light soils, early autumn sowing is also successful but defer the final thinning until mid spring to allow for winter losses. For container culture or for earlier flowering, sow seeds in early spring in a heated greenhouse. Prick out the seedlings into cell trays, to minimise root disturbance at planting.

PESTS AND DISEASES Usually trouble free.

Saponaria

Soapwort

Caryophyllaceae

This genus of hardy summer-flowering plants includes popular rock-garden species and plants for borders. The recommended species are low-growing evergreen perennials, except *Saponaria officinalis*, a herbaceous perennial, and the border annual, *S. vaccaria*. Soapwort's five-petalled flowers are pink, unless stated otherwise. The leaves are roughly lance-shaped. The plants thrive in dry, sunny, sheltered locations.

RECOMMENDED SPECIES AND VARIETIES

***S.* 'Bressingham'**♀ Almost stemless flowers smother the low, dense, foliage mounds of this dwarf plant. The flowers, about 1cm (⅜in) across, appear in early summer. Deep green, bunched leaves grow to 2cm (¾in) long. HEIGHT & SPREAD 5×15cm (2×6in).

S. caespitosa Pink to purple flowers, about 1.5cm (½in) across, bloom on slender, upright stems in early summer. The leaves are rather fleshy and about 2.5cm (1in) long. The plant may not be hardy in colder districts and benefits from winter protection. HEIGHT & SPREAD 12.5×15cm (5×6in).

▼ *Saponaria ocymoides*

▲ *Saponaria officinalis*

S. ocymoides♀ (tumbling Ted) Abundant loose clusters of pink flowers, about 1cm (⅜in) wide, smother the foliage mat in early summer. This robust, fairly vigorous, but short-lived plant has hairy leaves about 2cm (¾in) long and self-seeds readily. HEIGHT & SPREAD 10×45cm (4×18in).

'Rubra Compacta'♀ is a tight, slower-growing plant with profuse, rich carmine blooms. The white-flowered **'Alba'** is neither as robust nor as abundant in flower.

S. officinalis (bouncing Bet) Flowers about 2.5cm (1in) across are borne in small clusters from late summer to mid autumn. With leaves up to 8cm (3in) long, it is a robust hairless plant with erect stems. It self-seeds freely (not the double-flowered varieties, though) and spreads invasively by thick underground stolons. Native to Britain. HEIGHT & SPREAD 80×50cm (32×20in).

'Alba Plena', **'Rosea Plena'** and **'Rubra Plena'** are double-flowered forms, white, pink and red. **'Dazzler'** has leaves variegated gold to cream and pink flowers.

S. x olivana♀ A profusion of 2.5cm (1in) wide flowers are borne above tufts of leaves, about 2cm (¾in) long in early summer. HEIGHT & SPREAD 5×15cm (2×6in).

S. pumilio (syn. *S. pulvinaris*) Pale pink to carmine flowers, about 2.5cm (1in) across, appear in mid summer over a dense pad of foliage. The leaves are about about 2cm (¾in) long. Often a short-lived plant. HEIGHT & SPREAD 7.5×20cm (3×8in).

S. vaccaria (syn. *Vaccaria hispanica*) This hardy annual has graceful sprays of flowers, 1cm (⅜in) across, which appear from late spring to mid summer. HEIGHT & SPREAD 80×25cm (32×10in).

CULTIVATION Plant the low-growing alpine species in early spring in gritty, well-drained, lime-free soil or scree in a sheltered, sunny position. *S. ocymoides* is an easily grown plant for sunny walls and path edges. Plant *S. vaccaria* in a sunny position in a mixed border in spring or early autumn. Grow *S. officinalis* in full sun or partial shade in any well-drained soil.

PROPAGATION Take semi-ripe cuttings of the alpines. *S. ocymoides* may also be raised from seed, sown outdoors in early summer. Sow seed of *S. vaccaria* in early spring or early autumn where it is to flower. Divide *S. officinalis* in spring or sow seed in situ in early spring or early autumn.

PESTS AND DISEASES Slugs and aphids can be troublesome, so too can leaf spot.

Sarcococca

Christmas box, sweet box
Buxaceae

Sarcococca hookeriana var. digyna

Providing abundant fragrant flowers in winter and glossy evergreen foliage, these hardy, many stemmed, small shrubs are good for the front of the border. Most species spread by suckers and, although invasive, they make good edging plants. The cut stems are useful for winter flower arrangements, though the sweet heady scent can be overpowering when blooms are brought indoors. The tiny, cream or white flowers are petal-less but with prominent anthers and are gathered in tassel-like clusters, 1-2cm (⅜-¾in) long, where the leaves join the branches. All species bear attractive berries about 6mm (¼in) wide. These and all other parts of the plant are harmful if eaten. Sarcococcas are native to W China.

RECOMMENDED SPECIES AND VARIETIES

S. confusa♀ Clusters of cream flowers are borne on the new season's growth in mid winter, the same time that the berries of the previous year turn black and become noticeable. The pointed elliptic leaves, 3-5cm (1¼-2in) long, are mid-green above and lighter beneath. A non-suckering species, and therefore less invasive. HEIGHT & SPREAD 1×1m (3×3ft) after 5 years, ultimately 1.5m (5ft) tall.

S. hookeriana **var.** ***digyna***♀ White flowers with pink sepals are borne in clusters in mid to late winter. The black fruits appear in summer. Bright green and narrowly elliptic, the leaves are 6cm (2½in) long. HEIGHT & SPREAD 75×75cm (2½×2½ft) after 5 years, ultimately 1.2m (4ft) tall.

'Purple Stem' has reddish purple flower buds and young shoots.

S. hookeriana **var.** ***humilis*** Similar to *S. h.* var. *digyna*, this lower-growing variety makes an excellent ground-cover plant. HEIGHT & SPREAD 60×60cm (2×2ft) after 5 years, when it will have reached full size.

S. ruscifolia Clusters of ivory-white flowers appear in late winter and early spring, the blood-red berries in summer. The pointed ovate leaves, 2.5-6cm (1-2½in) long, are dark green above, paler beneath. HEIGHT & SPREAD 75×75cm (2½×2½ft) after 5 years, ultimately 1.2m (4ft) tall.

CULTIVATION Plant in early spring in moist but well-drained, loamy soil in partial shade. If plants become invasive, dig up suckers using a sharp spade.

PROPAGATION Transplant rooted suckers or take hardwood cuttings in autumn.

PRUNING Not necessary except to shape or restrict the spread of a plant.

PESTS AND DISEASES Usually trouble free.

▼ Sarcococca hookeriana var. humilis

Sasa see BAMBOOS p.76
Sasaella see BAMBOOS p.76

Sassafras

Lauraceae

Sassafras albidum

These handsome deciduous trees have aromatic distinctively shaped leaves and give fine autumn colour. Not completely hardy, they prefer a sheltered position and require lime-free soil.

RECOMMENDED SPECIES

S. albidum The aromatic, dark green leaves have paler undersides and turn brilliant shades of red and gold in autumn. The leaves are alternate and ovate and grow to 15cm (6in) long. Some are entire, some 2-lobed, some 3-lobed. Tiny yellow flowers are borne in 3-5cm (1¼-2in) long racemes in late spring, and in autumn blue-black, ovoid berries, 1cm (⅜in) long, are carried on bright red, fleshy stalks. The bark is deeply fissured and the twigs and branches zigzag. In Britain it often grows as a multi-stemmed shrub, but is still ornamental. Native to the USA. HEIGHT & SPREAD 2×1m (6½×3ft) after 5 years, ultimately up to 17m (56ft) tall.

CULTIVATION Grow in well-drained, lime-free soil in a position sheltered from late spring frosts, which can kill young growth.

PROPAGATION Sow fresh seed in autumn, take root cuttings in winter or transplant the suckers that are freely produced by sassafras.

PESTS AND DISEASES Usually trouble-free.

▼ Sassafras albidum

Satsuma see *Citrus reticulata*

Saururus

Lizard's tail
Saururaceae

Saururus cernuus

Remarkable tail-like spikes of flowers emerge in summer from the decorative foliage of the two species in this genus. These hardy herbaceous perennials require an open sunny position in a bog garden or at the edge of a pond, where they disguise the transition to the surrounding ground. The recommended species quickly colonises bare ground round taller and more vigorous, upright-growing marginal and bog-garden plants.

RECOMMENDED SPECIES

S. cernuus (swamp lily, water dragon) Tiny, fragrant, cream-coloured flowers appear from mid to late summer, massed on arching spikes, which look rather like white pipe cleaners. The mid green, heart-shaped leaves, up to 7.5cm (3in) long, turn copper or red in autumn if frost has not damaged them. A clump-forming species, native to eastern N America. HEIGHT & SPREAD 23×30cm (9×12in).

CULTIVATION Plant in spring or early summer directly into a bog garden or shelf at the margin of a pond. Preferably (because swamp lilies are so invasive) plant in heavy loam or aquatic planting compost in an aquatic planting basket and stand the basket on a marginal shelf. Do not submerge plants by more than 2.5cm (1in) of water. If planting at the margin of a pond, cover the soil with a layer of pea gravel to prevent fish stirring up the mud.

PROPAGATION Divide plants in spring.

PESTS AND DISEASES Water-lily aphids can be a nuisance.

Savory see HERBS p.332

Saxifraga

Saxifrage

Saxifragaceae

Saxifraga cebennensis

Complex cushions or mats of leaf rosettes are smothered in colour when saxifrages burst into flower. This large genus is the mainstay of a rock garden, offering a plant for almost every position and the choice of a succession of flowers from late winter to autumn. Many plants can also be grown in pots in an unheated, well-ventilated greenhouse or frame and the genus includes the trailing houseplant *Saxifraga stolonifera.*

Saxifrages usually have low-growing rosettes of leaves that may be stiff, fleshy or feathery. The shallow, cup or saucer-shaped flowers have five petals and come in all colours except blue. Native to mountainous and arctic areas of Europe, Asia and N and S America, saxifrages grow in a variety of soils.

The recommended plants are divided into four groups: silver saxifrages, cushion saxifrages, mossy saxifrages, and a group of miscellaneous plants. All are hardy evergreen perennials, except for *S. fortunei* 'Wada', which is semi-evergreen, and *S. granulata,* which dies back in winter.

RECOMMENDED SPECIES AND VARIETIES

SILVER SAXIFRAGES

Beads of lime decorate the silver-grey or green foliage of these plants. Most silver saxifrages prefer limy soil which increases this beading. The encrusted leaves, formed into flattish rosettes, are fleshy or leathery and usually narrow and roughly linear. Plumes of countless flowers – white unless stated otherwise – arch over mounds of leaf rosettes in late spring and early summer. The individual flowers are 1-1.5cm (⅜-½in) wide. Most can tolerate shade and dry conditions. Long-lived and vigorous, they make good companions for ramondas and haberleas but are unsuitable for planting with slower-growing saxifrages.

▼ *Saxifraga* x *burnatii*

S. aizoon see *S. paniculata*

S.* x *burnatii Upright flower clusters appear on reddish stems over neat rosettes. Each silver-green rosette is about 4cm (1½in) across. HEIGHT & SPREAD 20x15cm (8x6in).

S. callosa ♀ (syn. *S. lingulata)* Irregular grey-green rosettes, each up to 7.5cm (3in) across, give a tousled appearance to this plant. Flower clusters, 30-40cm (12-16in) long, appear on each arched stem. HEIGHT & SPREAD 30x40cm (12x16in).

S. cochlearis Silvery rosettes, each about 2.5cm (1in) wide, of outward-curving, spoon-shaped leaves form cushions. Open, arching spikes of flowers appear on pale brown or mahogany-red stems. HEIGHT & SPREAD 25x15cm (10x6in).

'Major' ♀ is a larger-leaved version of *S. cochlearis,* while **'Minor'** ♀ is a compact, dwarf version.

S. cotyledon A central rosette, to 12cm (4¾in) wide, of fleshy, toothed, dark green leaves is surrounded by smaller rosettes. The flowers, sometimes spotted pink or red, are carried in conical clusters. HEIGHT & SPREAD 30-60x20cm (12-24x8in).

***S.* 'Doctor Ramsay'** Rosettes, each about 5cm (2in) across, of spoon-shaped leaves distinguish this plant. HEIGHT & SPREAD 20x15cm (8x6in).

***S.* 'Esther'** Sprays of pale yellow flowers, which later fade to almost white, arch over leaf rosettes. The leaves, predominantly dark green, are about 2.5cm (1in) across. This plant is slow-growing. HEIGHT & SPREAD 30x20cm (12x8in).

***S.* 'Kathleen Pinsent'** Wands of pink flowers appear above silvery rosettes of spoon-shaped leaves. This is a short-lived plant. HEIGHT & SPREAD 40x10cm (16x4in).

▼ *Saxifraga* 'Esther'

▼ *Saxifraga paniculata*

▲ *Saxifraga* 'Southside Seedling'

S. paniculata (syn. *S. aizoon)* (lifelong saxifrage) This easy-to-grow plant has silver-green rosettes, each up to 2.5cm (1in) wide, with inward-curving leaves. The flowers appear in loose, upright sprays. HEIGHT & SPREAD 5-30x20cm (2-12x8in).

There are two dwarf varieties – var. ***baldensis*** and **'Munitifolia'**. The flowers of **'Lutea'** ♀ are pale yellow, while those borne by **'Rosea'** are shell-pink.

***S.* 'Southside Seedling'** ♀ Clusters of white flowers heavily spotted with crimson appear above bright green rosettes, each up to 10cm (4in) wide. HEIGHT & SPREAD 30x15cm (12x6in).

***S.* 'Tumbling Waters'** ♀ Arching spires of flowers appear above silvery green leaf rosettes, each up to 10cm (4in) across, on an easy-to-grow, hummock-forming plant. HEIGHT & SPREAD 75x30cm (30x12in).

***S.* 'Whitehill'** Violet tinted leaf rosettes, each about 3cm (1¼in) wide, have heavy beads of lime encrustation. The abundant flowers are creamy white. HEIGHT & SPREAD 30x40cm (12x16in).

CUSHION SAXIFRAGES

Flowering from late winter to mid spring, these slow-growing, dwarf plants form dense, rounded mounds of leaf rosettes. The foliage includes neat rosettes of densely packed, needle-like leaves, as well as more open rosettes with broader, blunter leaves, and uneven humps of fleshy leaves. The flowers, 5-25mm (¼-1in) wide, have rich yellow or orange centres and can sit almost stemless on the cushion or be raised on stalks up to 15cm (6in) high.

Cushion saxifrages are often grown in a greenhouse or frame, where they are easy to see, but will thrive in a scree garden, raised bed or trough as well as in a rock garden, provided they have good light and protection from hot sun.

S.* x *apiculata see *S.* 'Gregor Mendel'

S. 'Aretiastrum' (syn. *S.* 'Valerie Finnis') Elegant, pale yellow flowers appear over grey-green rosettes. HEIGHT & SPREAD 10×7.5cm (4×3in).
S. 'Boston Spa' Masses of yellow flowers appear above a bright green cushion. HEIGHT & SPREAD 4×20cm (1½×8in).
S. 'Bridget' This plant forms a loose hump of spiny, silvered rosettes. Pink-tinted stems bear pale mauve flowers. HEIGHT & SPREAD 10×7.5cm (4×3in).
S. 'Buttercup' Glossy rosettes and bright yellow flowers distinguish this slow-growing plant. HEIGHT & SPREAD 6×6cm (2×2in).
S. 'Carmen' (syn. *S.* × *elisabethae)* Abundant clusters of yellow flowers are carried over a low, dull green cushion on this vigorous plant. HEIGHT & SPREAD 5×15cm (2×6in).
S. 'Cranbourne'♀ (syn. *S.* 'Valborg', *S.* 'Valentine') Abundant, deep rose-pink flowers fade to a paler hue with age on this plant with a dome of dark green rosettes. HEIGHT & SPREAD 4×10cm (1½×4in).
S. 'Crenata' Scallop-edged, saucer-shaped, white flowers distinguish this plant. HEIGHT & SPREAD 10×7.5cm (4×3in).
S. x *elisabethae* see *S.* 'Carmen'

▼ *Saxifraga* 'Cranbourne'

▼ *Saxifraga federici-augusti*

S. 'Faldonside'♀ Rich yellow flowers appear in profusion over a hard, grey-green cushion. This plant is vulnerable to various moulds. HEIGHT & SPREAD 7.5×7.5cm (3×3in).
S. federici-augusti♀ (syn. *S. frederici-augusti*) This plant has striking claret coloured hairs on the stems, and bears purple-red flowers. Spoon-shaped, silver-grey leaves form a tight cluster of rosettes. HEIGHT & SPREAD 20×10cm (8×4in).
S. ferdinandi-coburgi♀ This tough, easy-to-grow plant has grey-green leaf rosettes with clusters of golden yellow flowers. HEIGHT & SPREAD 7.5×10cm (3×4in).
S. 'Gloria'♀ Many saucer-shaped, white flowers appear above a spiky-leafed cushion. HEIGHT & SPREAD 7.5×7.5cm (3×3in).
S. 'Gold Dust' Profuse clusters of golden flowers appear on this vigorous plant. HEIGHT & SPREAD 9×15cm (3½×6in).
S. 'Grace Farwell' Burgundy flowers appear over a dull green cushion. HEIGHT & SPREAD 6×10cm (2½×4in).
S. 'Gregor Mendel'♀ (syn. *S.* × *apiculata)* Abundant clusters of primrose-yellow flowers are borne over a bright green cushion. This is a vigorous, easy-to-grow plant. HEIGHT & SPREAD 15×30cm (6×12in).

▼ *Saxifraga ferdinandi-coburgi*

▼ *Saxifraga* 'Grace Farwell'

▲ *Saxifraga* 'Iris Prichard'

S. 'Haagii' Dark green rosettes set off the golden flowers on this tough hybrid. HEIGHT & SPREAD 10×15cm (4×6in).
S. 'Hindhead Seedling' From its grey-green cushion, this plant sends up yellow flowers early in the year. HEIGHT & SPREAD 5×7.5cm (2×3in).
S. 'Iris Prichard' Apricot coloured flowers rise above a hard cushion of silvery, spiny leaves. HEIGHT & SPREAD 10×10cm (4×4in).
S. x *irvingii* see *S.* 'Walter Irving'
S. 'Jenkinsiae'♀ Abundant lilac-pink flowers appear just above a hard, dark green cushion. HEIGHT & SPREAD 5×7cm (2×2¾in).
S. 'Johann Kellerer' (syn. *S.* × *kellereri)* One of the earliest to flower, in mid winter, the plant has lilac-pink flowers above a compact, grey-green cushion. HEIGHT & SPREAD 10×15cm (4×6in).
S. 'Joy' see *S.* 'Kaspar Maria Sternberg'
S. juniperifolia A very prickly, bright green cushion carries sparse, spindly stems of up to 10 yellow flowers. HEIGHT & SPREAD 7.5×10cm (3×4in).
S. x *kellereri* see *S.* 'Johann Kellerer'
S. 'Kaspar Maria Sternberg' (syn. *S.* 'Joy') Pure white flowers appear over a solid grey-green cushion. HEIGHT & SPREAD 7.5×6cm (3×2½in).
S. 'Maria Luisa' Dense clusters of white flowers appear early in the year above a grey-green cushion. HEIGHT & SPREAD 7.5×7.5cm (3×3in).
S. x *megasaeflora* see *S.* 'Robin Hood'
S. 'Moonlight' see *S.* 'Sulphurea'
S. 'Myra' Carmine flowers emerge above a dark green cushion of squat rosettes. HEIGHT & SPREAD 2×7.5cm (¾×3in).
S. 'Penelope' Amber blooms are accentuated by the green cushion. HEIGHT & SPREAD 5×7.5cm (2×3in).
S. poluniniana Almost stemless flowers, which open white and then age to pink, smother a strong-growing dark green cushion. HEIGHT & SPREAD 5×10cm (2×4in).
S. 'Primrose Dame' A hard, prickly cushion and clusters of lemon-yellow flowers

distinguish this plant. HEIGHT & SPREAD 10×10cm (4×4in).
S. **'Riverslea'**♀ Grey-green foliage complements rich claret flowers. HEIGHT & SPREAD 5×7.5cm (2×3in).
S. **'Robin Hood'** (syn. *S.* × *megasaeflora)* Unusual flowers with widely separated pink petals distinguish a plant of tousled appearance. HEIGHT & SPREAD 7×7.5cm (2¾×3in).
S. **'Salomonii'** Clusters of white flowers appear above a grey-green cushion. HEIGHT & SPREAD 5×7.5cm (2×3in).
S. sancta Clusters of yellow flowers sit on the light green cushion of this easy-to-grow plant. HEIGHT & SPREAD 10×15cm (4×6in).
S. sempervivum Stems bearing rosy purple hairs and rosy purple flowers rise above an uneven mound of silver-grey rosettes. HEIGHT & SPREAD 12×10cm (4¾×4in).

▼ *Saxifraga sempervivum*

S. **'Sulphurea'** (syn. *S.* 'Moonlight') Sulphur-yellow flowers nod over a firm mound of grey-green rosettes. HEIGHT & SPREAD 15×15cm (6×6in).
S. **'Valborg'** see *S.* 'Cranbourne'
S. **'Valentine'** see *S.* 'Cranbourne'
S. **'Valerie Finnis'** see *S.* 'Aretiastrum'
S. **'Vesna'** Dense, rounded cushions of dark green rosettes are topped by abundant clusters of pale yellow flowers. HEIGHT & SPREAD 5×6cm (2×2½in).
S. **'Walter Irving'** (syn. *S.* × *irvingii*) Dark-eyed, pale lilac flowers rise above a tight, grey-green cushion. HEIGHT & SPREAD 3×6cm (1¼×2½in).

MOSSY SAXIFRAGES

Most of these plants form spongy hummocks of soft, feathery foliage and have a mass of slender-stalked flowers in late spring and early summer.
S. cebennensis♀ Open, sticky, mid to dark green rosettes, about 2cm (¾in) wide, form tight domes. White flowers, about 1cm (⅜in) wide appear in abundance. This plant is best kept in a greenhouse. HEIGHT & SPREAD 10×15cm (4×6in).
S. exarata White, cream, yellow or occasionally red flowers appear above a compact cushion of dark green rosettes on this dwarf plant which survives best in a greenhouse. HEIGHT & SPREAD 15×15cm (6×6in).

The recommended hybrids are easy-to-grow plants with flowers 1.2-2.5cm (½-1in) wide, carried in small groups on upright stems, 3-15cm (1¼-6in) tall. Dwarf hybrids form a mound about 15cm (6in) wide. More vigorous plants reach about 30cm (12in) wide.

S. **'Bob Hawkins'** has variegated leaves in green, cream and pink with white flowers. *S.* **'Cloth of Gold'**, a slow-growing plant vulnerable to dry spells and hot sun, has mainly yellow foliage, arranged in rosettes, and white flowers. *S.* **'Dartington Double'** has double white flowers. *S.* **'Findling'** (syn. *S.* 'The Foundling') also has white flowers. The vigorous *S.* **'Four Winds'** has rich crimson flowers. *S.* **'Gaiety'** bears deep pink flowers. *S.* **'Hi-Ace'** is a slow-growing dwarf plant with rose-pink blooms over green and white variegated foliage. *S.* **'Pixie'** has cream and pink flowers. The vigorous, compact *S.* **'Silver Cushion'** bears variegated leaves in silver-grey and green that complement shell-pink flowers. Crimson blooms appear on *S.* **'Triumph'**. Pure white flowers give *S.* **'White Pixie'** its name.

OTHER SAXIFRAGES

The plants in this diverse group each have different growing requirements, which are given after the individual plant descriptions.
S. cuneifolia (spoon-leafed saxifrage) Open clusters of about 12 star-shaped, white flowers, with yellow and sometimes red spots, appear from late spring to mid

▼ *Saxifraga cebennensis*

▼ *Saxifraga* 'Cloth of Gold'

▼ *Saxifraga* 'Pixie'

▼ *Saxifraga* 'White Pixie'

S

summer. The long-stalked leaves, mid green, roughly wedge-shaped, with blunt teeth, form mats of flat rosettes, about 7cm (2¾in) wide. This plant requires fairly moist, neutral to acid, humus-rich soil and dappled shade. HEIGHT & SPREAD 10–25×30cm (4–10×12in)

'Variegata' has yellow and green foliage.

***S. fortunei* 'Wada'** Bright green, glossy leaves mature to bronze-red on a semi-evergreen plant that thrives in sheltered woodland conditions. The rounded, lobed leaves, to 8cm (3¼in) wide, form clumps. White flowers, about 2cm (¾in) across, appear in autumn. This plant needs lime-free soil and shade. It is not hardy in severe winters. HEIGHT & SPREAD 30×30cm (1×1ft).

S. granulata (meadow saxifrage) Long-stalked, grey-green kidney-shaped leaves, to 5cm (2in) wide, form a tuft. Branched stems carry a loose cluster of white flowers, each about 3cm (1¼in) wide, from mid spring to early summer. This easy-to-grow, herbaceous plant dislikes dry soil. It looks good naturalised in grass. HEIGHT & SPREAD 30×20cm (12×8in).

saxifraga granulata

'Plena' is a double-flowered plant.

S. oppositifolia (purple saxifrage) Rosy-purple flowers, to 2.5cm (1in) wide, borne singly, cover this exceptionally hardy plant in spring. A dense mat of creeping shoots is clad in tiny, congested, deep green leaves. Favouring a limy soil, this plant is ideal for a rich scree bed, a raised bed or a trough. HEIGHT & SPREAD 5cm×20cm (2×8in).

'Alba' has pure white flowers. **'Latina'** has rose-pink flowers and slightly encrusted foliage. **'Ruth Draper'** produces large blooms of rich crimson. The vigorous **'Splendens'**♀ bears deep pink flowers.

▼ *Saxifraga* 'Ruth Draper'

S. × primulaize Pale carmine flowers appear in late spring over mid green, fleshy, roughly oblong, lobed leaves. This plant prefers moist soil in partial shade. HEIGHT & SPREAD 20×20cm (8×8in).

S. stolonifera (syn. *S. sarmentosa*) (mother of thousands, strawberry geranium) The thin, reddish runners of this houseplant carry plantlets that root on contact with moist soil. The hairy leaves, to 10cm (4in) wide, are rounded and toothed. They are dark green with silver markings on the leaf surface and reddish beneath. White flowers appear in summer. The plant needs a temperature of at least 5°C (41°F). It spreads as wide as the pot. LENGTH 1m (3ft).

S. umbrosa Upright, branched stems carry clusters of tiny, white, star-shaped flowers with pink centres in early summer. This plant, which does best in moist soil in partial shade, forms a close mat of flat, leathery rosettes of bluntly elliptic, scalloped-edged, mid to dark green leaves, up to 3cm (1¼in) long. HEIGHT & SPREAD 25×30cm (10×12in).

The compact **'Clarence Elliott'**♀ has rose-pink flowers.

saxifraga umbrosa

S. × urbium♀ (London pride) From its long-lived mat of rather fleshy rosettes, each about 7.5cm (3in) across, the plant raises delicate, airy clusters of star-like, pinkish, white flowers in early summer. It is easy to grow in a damp soil, with some shade. This plant is good for edging paths. HEIGHT & SPREAD 25×60cm (10×24in).

Rich, yellow blotches decorate the fleshy-leaved rosettes of ***S. × 'Variegata'***.

***S.* 'Winifred Bevington'** Slender sprays of rose-centred, white flowers, each about 8mm (⅜in) wide, appear in early summer above a tight hump of leaf rosettes, each about 2.5cm (1in) wide. This plant thrives in light soil in partly shaded positions. HEIGHT & SPREAD 10×20cm (4×8in).

▲ *Saxifraga × urbium*

▼ *Saxifraga umbrosa*

CULTIVATION For silver saxifrages, with the exception of *S. cotyledon,* which needs lime-free soil, plant in well-drained, gritty, limy soil, ideally with partial shade in the middle of the day. For cushion saxifrages, plant in gritty, limy soil in good light but with protection from hot sun. For pot-grown plants, use a mixture of John Innes No.2 compost and about one-third sharp sand or stone chippings. For mossy saxifrages, plant in well-drained soil, ideally neutral to slightly acid, and protect from hot sun. Cover *S. cebennensis* and *S. exarata* with glass from autumn to early spring to protect them from winter wet.
PROPAGATION Separate young rosettes and root them as individual cuttings in sharp sand. The best times for this are from mid to late summer for silver saxifrages, throughout summer for cushion saxifrages, and from early to mid summer for mossy saxifrages. Sow the ripe seed of species under glass and plant out when the seedlings are large enough to handle.
PESTS AND DISEASES Vine weevil can damage silver saxifrages, especially pot-grown plants. Stem eelworm sometimes damages cushion saxifrages, while the roots of plants grown in wet conditions may rot. Aphids, red spider mite and botrytis can affect mossy saxifrages.

Saxifrage see *Saxifraga*

Scabiosa

Scabious, pincushion flower
Dipsacaceae

Showy flowerheads with centres resembling pincushions make these hardy annuals and perennials attractive components of summer beds and borders. *Scabiosa columbaria, S. graminifolia* and *S. lucida* are sufficiently dwarf for a rock garden. The plants attract bees and butterflies. They are native to Europe, Asia and Africa.
RECOMMENDED SPECIES AND VARIETIES
S. atropurpurea (sweet scabious) Dark crimson flowerheads 5 cm (2 in) across are held on slender stems from mid summer to early autumn. The mid green leaves of this erect annual are narrow, deeply lobed and held in a compact rosette. HEIGHT & SPREAD 1 m×23 cm (3 ft×9 in).
S. banatica see *S. columbaria*
S. caucasica Pale blue blooms, 7.5 cm (3 in) across, appear for a long period over the summer. They are good for cutting. The grey-green leaves of this herbaceous perennial form a tight cluster at the base of the plant. Each leaf is lance-shaped with tips cut into narrow segments. HEIGHT & SPREAD 60×60 cm (2×2 ft).
'Clive Greaves'♀ bears an abundance of lavender-blue flowerheads. **'Miss Willmott'**♀ has off-white flowerheads.

▲ *Scabiosa graminifolia*

S. columbaria (syn. *S. banatica*) Lilac-blue flowerheads, 4 cm (1½ in) across, are carried on tall, wiry, branched stems in summer. This evergreen perennial forms a mat of grey-green leaves beneath the flowerheads. HEIGHT & SPREAD 30×30 cm (1×1 ft).
'Nana' reaches just 15 cm (6 in) high.
S. graminifolia Lilac to pink flowerheads, 4 cm (1½ in) across, rise on 25 cm (10 in), branched stems, from late spring to early summer. This evergreen perennial has grassy silvery grey leaves. It is best grown in a rock garden or the front of a border. HEIGHT & SPREAD 25×30 cm (10 in×1 ft).
'Rosea' has rich pink flowerheads.
S. lucida The unbranched flower stems and flower colour of pale carmine to purple are the only differences between this species and *S. columbaria.* HEIGHT & SPREAD 30×30 cm (1×1 ft).
CULTIVATION Plant in spring in a light, well-drained soil in a sunny situation.
PROPAGATION Sow seed of the annuals in the flowering site in early autumn or late spring. Autumn-sown annuals need the protection of a cloche through winter. Lift and divide perennial species in early spring.
PESTS AND DISEASES Slugs damage young foliage. Powdery mildew can be a problem.

Scabious see *Scabiosa*
Scarlet pimpernel see *Anagallis arvensis*

Scaevola

Fan flower
Goodeniaceae

Large numbers of flowers are borne throughout summer on these tender evergreen perennials. *Scaevola aemula* is the only species commonly grown in Britain. It can only be grown outdoors all year round in the warmest districts. Elsewhere, it is best overwintered in a frost-free greenhouse or conservatory. Its naturally sprawling habit

▲ *Scaevola aemula* 'Blue Fan'

makes it particularly useful for containers, especially hanging baskets and window boxes. Native to Australia.
RECOMMENDED SPECIES AND VARIETIES
S. aemula Blue, purple-blue, lilac or white flowers, about 3 cm (1¼ in) across, each have 5 lobes, that radiate outwards on one side to form a fan shape. Sharply toothed, oblong, dark green leaves, up to 5 cm (2 in) long, are borne on thick, short-jointed stems. HEIGHT & SPREAD 30×60 cm (1×2 ft).
'Blue Fan' has purple-blue flowers with a white eye. **'Petite'** has smaller leaves and flowers than the species. **'Alba'** has white flowers and more slender stems.
CULTIVATION Plant out after the risk of frost has passed in any well-drained soil in full sun or light shade. Lift plants before first frosts and overwinter in a frost-free greenhouse or conservatory. Alternatively, grow in pots of general purpose or potting compost and keep in a cool greenhouse or conservatory. Plants can be moved outside in late spring and summer.
PROPAGATION Take softwood cuttings in late summer.
PESTS AND DISEASES Usually trouble free.

Schefflera

Umbrella tree
Araliaceae

These evergreen trees and shrubs are popular foliage plants in homes, conservatories and offices. Native mainly to tropical Australasia, scheffleras are fairly adaptable but rarely flower in cultivation. The dimensions are for a plant in a 20cm (8in) pot.

RECOMMENDED SPECIES AND VARIETIES

S. actinophylla ♀ (syn. *Brassaia actinophylla*) (umbrella tree) Five to seven leaflets fan out from each long stalk. The leathery textured mid green leaflets, up to 30cm (12in) long, are oval with pointed tips. HEIGHT & SPREAD 1.5-2×1m (5-6½×3ft) after 5 years, ultimately 2m (6½ft) tall.

Schefflera actinophylla

S. arboricola ♀ (syn. *Heptapleurum arboricola*) (parasol plant) Dark green glossy leaflets, 7-15 to a stalk, are held on a plant with largely upright habit. Young foliage is often slightly bronze. The elongated oval leaflets, to 15cm (6in) long, have pointed tips. HEIGHT & SPREAD 3×1.5m (10×5ft) after 10 years, ultimately 3m (10ft) tall.

The deep green leaves of **'Trinetta'** are splashed bright yellow.

S. elegantissima ♀ (syn. *Aralia elegantissima, Dizygotheca elegantissima*) (false aralia) Narrow, bronze, toothed leaflets distinguish this graceful plant. With age, the leaflets, to 18cm (7in) long, become wider with fewer teeth. The plant needs constant conditions. Overwatering, dryness, sudden changes in temperature or dry air can prompt leaf loss. HEIGHT & SPREAD 3m×70cm (10ft×28in) after 5 years, ultimately 3m (10ft) tall.

CULTIVATION Place *S. actinophylla* and *S. arboricola* in full sun or bright, indirect light. Position *S. elegantissima* in good indirect light or direct sun for half the day. Keep a plant at a minimum temperature of 10°C (50°F) if possible, although they will tolerate cooler temperatures for short periods. Water whenever the soil begins to dry out, decreasing watering in winter. Repot every year until the plant reaches the desired size. From then on, give an annual top dressing.

PROPAGATION Scheffleras are not easy to propagate at home. Try taking softwood cuttings in early summer and use rooting powder and bottom heat.

PRUNING Pinch out the tips or cut the top part of the main stem down to the lowest leaves to encourage branching.

PESTS AND DISEASES Scale insects can damage all plants, while red spider mites can affect *S. elegantissima*.

Schisandra

Schisandraceae

Schisandra rubriflora

These woody climbing plants are grown for their flowers and sometimes showy fruit. They climb by means of twining stems to a height of 4m (13ft) or more. Native to India and Burma, they are best grown on a south or west wall. In milder areas they can be trained on free-standing structures such as arches or pergolas.

RECOMMENDED SPECIES

S. rubriflora (syn. *S. grandiflora* var. *rubriflora*) Clusters of bright or dark red, bowl-shaped flowers are carried along the stems of this deciduous climber in early summer. The 2.5cm (1in) wide male and female flowers are carried on separate plants. Grow male and female plants together for a display of bright red berries in autumn. The pendulous clusters of berries are up to 12cm (4¾in) long. The narrowly oval leaves are mid green, up to 15cm (6in) long and 7cm (2¾in) wide. This species does well outside in a sheltered spot. HEIGHT 5-8m (16-26ft).

CULTIVATION Plant out in spring in any well-drained, moisture-retaining soil, out of direct sunlight. Avoid lime-rich soil. Mulch annually in spring. Water well in dry periods, especially wall-trained plants. Give plants a framework to climb over. They may need tying in until established. Prune only to retain desired shape, in late winter.

PROPAGATION Sow seed when ripe or propagate by layering. Semi-ripe cuttings taken in mid summer are less successful.

PESTS AND DISEASES Aphids can be a problem on leaves and young shoots.

Schizanthus

Poor man's orchid, butterfly flower
Solanaceae

Exotic flowers and handsome, bright green foliage make these tender annuals popular as pot plants. They can be grown outdoors as summer bedding in a warm sheltered spot or in a greenhouse or conservatory. The orchid-like flowers come in a mixture of rich colours often with contrasting markings inside. The leaves are deeply dissected and often feathery. Native to Chile.

RECOMMENDED SPECIES AND VARIETIES

S. pinnatus Pink flowers, up to 4cm (1½in) across, with a yellow throat and violet markings are produced in dense clusters from late summer to winter. The bright green leaves are up to 13cm (5in) long. HEIGHT & SPREAD 60×30cm (2×1ft).

The following varieties have a spread of 20-30cm (8-12in) and, unless otherwise stated, reach a height of 30-45cm (12-18in). **'Butterfly Mixture'** has a wide range of colours from deep red and purple with yellow or white throats marked with violet to orange and buff. It can reach a height of 60cm (2ft). **'Dwarf Bouquet'** has flowers in shades of pink, purple and yellow. It reaches a height of 30cm (12in) and a spread of 15cm (6in). Variously coloured, **'Giant Hybrids'** reach a height of 1.2m (4ft). **'Hit Parade'** has large, well-marked flowers in red, pink, lilac, violet, purple and white. **'Star Parade'** is a compact plant with large flowers in almost any combination of colours.

S. × wisetonensis The flowers vary in colour from lavender and white to pink and brown and are often flushed with yellow. They are up to 2.5cm (1in) across and are

Schizanthus 'Hit Parade'

Schizanthus 'Star Parade'

carried in bold clusters in late summer and autumn. The bright green leaves are as long as 15 cm (6 in). HEIGHT & SPREAD 45×30 cm (18×12 in).
CULTIVATION Grow in pots of John Innes No. 2 and keep in a greenhouse or conservatory with a minimum temperature of 5°C (41°F). Plants can be moved outside when the danger of frost has passed and planted in any moisture-retentive, well-drained soil in full sun. When the taller varieties reach a height of 15 cm (6 in) pinch out the growing points to encourage bushy growth. They may need support.
PROPAGATION Sow seed under glass in late spring for late summer and autumn flowering. Sow during late summer for winter and early spring flowering.
PESTS AND DISEASES Greenfly can be troublesome.

Schizophragma
Hydrangeaceae

Few climbers can match the elegant, creamy white flowerheads of these vigorous, deciduous plants. Large, flattened flower sprays like old-fashioned lace caps are formed from an outer ring of sterile flowers – each with an enlarged, petal-like sepal – and an inner circle of small, densely packed, fertile flowers. The plants are in bloom in mid summer. Clinging by their aerial roots, they can clamber high into a tree or up a tall wall, although they grow slowly at first. They are shade-tolerant and like a cool root run, but flower more freely in full sun. There are four species, all native to Asia, where they climb into deciduous trees and sometimes grow up cliffs. Two species, both hardy, are grown in Britain.
RECOMMENDED SPECIES
S. hydrangeoides Flowerheads about 25 cm (10 in) wide have sterile flowers with sepals about 3 cm (1¼ in) long. The coarsely toothed leaves, which turn yellow in autumn, are broadly oval or rounded and up to 12 cm (4¾ in) long. Native to Japan. HEIGHT & SPREAD 2×1 m (6½×3 ft) after 5 years, ultimately 10 m (33 ft) tall.
S. integrifolium♀ The flowerheads of this plant are about 30 cm (1 ft) wide, while the sepals of the sterile flowers are about 8 cm (3¼ in) long. The dark green, ovate leaves, 10–18 cm (4–7 in) long, have a rounded base and pointed apex. The leaf edges may have a few small teeth. This plant is native to central and W China. HEIGHT & SPREAD 2×1 m (6½×3 ft) after 5 years, ultimately 12 m (40 ft) tall.
CULTIVATION Plant in fertile, well-drained soil at the foot of a tall wall or large tree, preferably where the plants can have their heads in the sun. As they are slow starters, tie young plants to wires, canes or some other support until the aerial roots take hold of the tree or wall.

S

▲ *Schizophragma integrifolium*

PROPAGATION Take softwood or semi-ripe cuttings in summer.
PRUNING None usually necessary. Cut back some of the long shoots to a lateral shoot in winter to limit growth.
PESTS AND DISEASES Usually trouble free.

Schizostylis
Kaffir lily
Iridaceae

Schizostylis coccinea

Star-shaped, red, pink or white flowers appear above narrow, sword-shaped leaves from late summer to early autumn. This genus of hardy perennials likes an open, sunny position and moist soil. In cold districts plants may be short-lived, so protect their crowns in winter once flowering has finished. The flowers are good for cutting.
RECOMMENDED SPECIES AND VARIETIES
S. coccinea Between 4 and 10 bright red blossoms, about 2.5 cm (1 in) across, are carried on each slender stem. The leaves are light green, prominently ribbed and up to 40 cm (16 in) long. The plant has a fleshy root, which is vulnerable to drying out. Native to southern Africa. HEIGHT & SPREAD 60×25 cm (24×10 in).

'Alba' produces pretty white flowers, but tends to be short-lived and less hardy. **'Jennifer'**♀ has large pink flowers. **'Major'**♀ (syn. 'Gigantea', 'Grandiflora') is a very free-flowering, robust plant with bright red flowers. **'Mrs Hegarty'**, with pink blooms, is late flowering. **'Sunrise'**♀ bears large soft pink blossoms. **'Viscountess Byng'** has bright red flowers, which bloom later than other schizostylis, in mid autumn.
CULTIVATION Plant in spring or autumn in an open, sunny position in moist soil beside a pool or stream would be fine, provided that the soil does not become waterlogged for more than a month or two of the year. Remove flowers as they fade and rake off dead foliage in late autumn, after plants have died back. Lift and divide crowded clumps in spring every 3–4 years.
PROPAGATION Divide and replant established clumps in spring.
PESTS AND DISEASES Usually trouble free, but slugs and snails may damage shoots.

▲ *Schizostylis coccinea*

▲ *Schizostylis coccinea* 'Sunrise'

Schlumbergera see CACTI p. 109

Scilla

Hyacinthaceae

Small starry or bell-shaped flowers, usually in shades of blue or purple, decorate rock gardens or containers mainly in spring. The flowers are held on leafless stems among glossy mid green, strap-shaped leaves, 10-20cm (4-8in) long. This genus of dwarf bulbous perennials is distributed worldwide. All listed plants are hardy in Britain, except *Scilla peruviana* which only tolerates temperatures as low as -5°C (23°F).

RECOMMENDED SPECIES AND VARIETIES

S. amethystina see *S. litardierei*

S. autumnalis (autumn squill) Loose racemes of starry pale pinkish lilac flowers appear in late summer or early autumn. HEIGHT 25cm (10in).

S. bifolia♀ Fragrant bluish violet, starry flowers are borne in late winter and early spring. This species will grow in semi-shade. HEIGHT 15cm (6in).

'Rosea' has pink flowers.

S. campanulata see *Hyacinthoides hispanica*

S. litardierei (syn. *S. amethystina, S. pratensis*) Some 15 to 30 pale-lilac to lavender-blue, starry flowers appear in mid to late spring. HEIGHT 25cm (10in).

S. mischtschenkoana (syn. *S. tubergeniana*) Open bell-shaped flowers, 2cm (¾in) across, very pale blue with a darker blue stripe, appear in late winter. Each stem bears up to 6 flowers. Plant among other early-flowering bulbs, such as snowdrops. HEIGHT 10cm (4in).

S. non-scripta see *Hyacinthoides non-scripta*

S. nutans see *Hyacinthoides non-scripta*

S. pratensis see *S. litardierei*

S. peruviana Dense flowerheads of starry, violet-blue flowers appear in late spring and early summer. The broad deep green leaves are almost evergreen. HEIGHT 25cm (10in).

'Alba' has pure white flowers, blue-violet anthers and a blue ovary.

S. siberica♀ (siberian squill) Stems bearing bright azure-blue, bell-shaped flowers appear in early spring. HEIGHT 20cm (8in).

'Alba' has pure-white flowers. **'Spring Beauty'** is a deeper blue and very vigorous.

S. tubergeniana see *S. mischtschenkoana*

CULTIVATION Plant bulbs in late summer, in humus-rich, fast-draining soil, 5-7.5cm (2-3in) deep and 5-7.5cm (2-3in) apart for larger bulbs. Position in dappled shade. *S. peruviana* needs a dry sunny situation to flower and should be protected with a dry mulch in winter.

PROPAGATION Lift and divide every 4-5 years in late summer. Alternatively, sow seed in early summer in trays in a greenhouse. Plant out at the end of the second year and they should flower 2-3 years later.

PESTS AND DISEASES Stored bulbs can suffer from various moulds if not kept dry.

Scindapsus see *Epipremnum*

Scottish maple see *Acer pseudoplatanus*

▼ *Scilla peruviana*

▼ *Scilla siberica* 'Spring Beauty'

▲ *Scilla siberica*

Scrophularia

Scrophulariaceae

Striking foliage or unusual flowers in summer earn some of the hardy herbaceous or semi-evergreen plants in this genus a place in the garden. Most have strong-smelling leaves. The recommended species is best confined to a wild garden. Give the variety 'Variegata' a prominent position, allowing it to show off its remarkable leaves, in a bed or border, beside a pond or in a bog garden. Both plants flourish in damp, partially shaded places.

RECOMMENDED SPECIES AND VARIETIES

S. auriculata (syn. *S. aquatica*) (water figwort) Strong, vigorously growing, winged stems are clothed with coarse, dark green, lance-shaped leaves up to 25cm (10in) long. The leafy flowering stems die back in autumn and new leaf tufts develop, which overwinter. Strange pouch-like maroon flowers, up to 1cm (⅜in) long, are borne sparingly on branching flower spikes throughout summer. Native to W Europe. HEIGHT & SPREAD 90×60cm (36×24in).

▲ *Scrophularia auriculata* 'Variegata'

'Variegata' has decorative green and cream leaves that are at their best in spring and early summer. Remove the flower spikes as soon as they emerge to retain the quality of the foliage as long as possible.

CULTIVATION Plant at any time between autumn and early spring in moist soil and preferably in a little shade. Remove the flowering spikes either immediately they appear or as the blossoms fade – if they are retained, they will seed freely.

PROPAGATION Divide and replant at any time between autumn and spring.

PESTS AND DISEASES Usually trouble free.

Scutellaria

Skullcap
Labiatae

Scutellaria alpina

Colourful snapdragon-like flowers grace these shrubby plants in summer and autumn. They may be annuals, perennials or sub-shrubs, evergreen or deciduous and vary from hardy to tender. It is mainly species from mountain habitats that are of interest, since they are suitable for rock gardens. The listed plants are all hardy perennials and all, except *S. altissima, S. hastifolia* and *S. incana,* are evergreen. *S. hastifolia* and *S. scordiifolia,* too vigorous for association with slower-growing rock plants, are best placed on the fringes of the rockwork. The genus is distributed worldwide.

RECOMMENDED SPECIES AND VARIETIES

S. alpina Clusters of pale-lipped, purple flowers, 2.5cm (1in) long, are held on erect stems, 20cm (8in) tall, from early to late summer. The plant bears mid green oval, bluntly toothed, 2cm (¾in) long leaves. HEIGHT & SPREAD 20×30cm (8×12in).

▲ *Scutellaria alpina*

'Alba' has white flowers.

S. altissima Loose spikes of cream or pale lilac, 2cm (¾in) long flowers appear in mid summer. The erect plant has simple or branched stems bearing 15cm (6in) long, broadly spear-shaped, mid green leaves. HEIGHT & SPREAD 75×30cm (2½×1ft).

S. hastifolia (syn *S. hastata*) Violet flowers, sometimes pink, 2cm (¾in) long, decorate the 45cm (18in) tall stems in summer. The leaves are lance-shaped, moderately toothed and up to 5cm (2in) long. HEIGHT & SPREAD 45×45cm (18×18in).

S. incana Loose, flat-topped clusters of violet flowers tinged with blue appear in mid summer. The flowers are up to 2.5cm (1in) long. The upright, hairy stems also bear heart-shaped, dull green leaves, as long as 10cm (4in) with serrated edges. This plant is too big for a rock garden. HEIGHT & SPREAD 1m×60cm (3×2ft).

▲ *Scutellaria indica var. parvifolia*

S. indica var. *parvifolia* (syn. *S. i.* var. *japonica*) Pale purple flowers, about 2cm (¾in) long, are held in sprays during early summer. The plant has a spreading habit with its stems forming a low mound of shoots clad in 1cm (⅜in) wide, rounded, hairy leaves with bluntly toothed edges. HEIGHT & SPREAD 5×25cm (2×10in).

'Alba' has pure white flowers.

S. nana var. *sapphirina* Short, loose heads of 2cm (¾in) long, clear blue 'snapdragon' flowers are produced through the summer. The ascending stems bear ovate, toothed leaves, up to 3cm (1¼in) long. HEIGHT & SPREAD 10×20cm (4×8in).

S. orientalis Yellow flowers, occasionally spotted or stained red, to 3cm (1¼in) long, appear in summer. They can also be pure purple, pink or red. This variable plant makes a shrub-like clump of woody stems bearing rounded, 1.5cm (½in) broad leaves with deep narrow lobes. HEIGHT & SPREAD 30×30cm (12×12in).

The leaves of ssp. *pinnatifida* are even more deeply lobed than the species.

S. prostrata In late summer 1.5cm (½in) long flowers, yellow flushed with violet, decorate a mat of foliage. Tiny rounded leaves cover the creeping shoots. HEIGHT & SPREAD 7.5×30cm (3×12in).

S. scordiifolia Leafy spikes, up to 30cm (12in) tall, rise from tufts of 3cm (1¼in) long elliptical leaves to bear 2cm (¾in) long flowers in a range of blues, through summer. This robust plant is inclined to be invasive on good soils. HEIGHT & SPREAD 30×60cm (12×24in).

CULTIVATION Plant in a sunny but not too dry situation in early spring. A rich soil can produce rank, invasive growth in those species noted for vigour. To curb this spread and improve flowering, trim the stems back to about 10cm (4in) in late winter or after flowering.

PROPAGATION Divide clumps in early spring or sow seed in pots in a coldframe at a similar time, and plant out the following spring. Cuttings of lateral shoots, taken in late spring, root readily.

PESTS AND DISEASES Usually trouble free.

Sedum

Stonecrop
Crassulaceae

Sedum acre

These succulent plants bring pleasant variations of form and colour to less hospitable parts of the garden, where there is little shade and the soil is poor and tends to parch. They are for the most part very easy to grow. Sedums range from tiny mats or mounds to plants as tall as 1m (3ft). Grow smaller sedums in rock gardens, troughs and raised beds, tucked into the cracks between paving stones, or in containers. Larger sedums are often found in mixed borders.

Foliage varies from grey-green to deep purple. The star-like flowers, nearly always with five petals, are generally yellow, pink, purple or white. Some species bloom well into autumn. A few sedums are notorious for spreading excessively, but the majority need little curbing.

All the plants listed here are hardy perennials, except the half-hardy *Sedum sieboldii.*

RECOMMENDED SPECIES AND VARIETIES

S. acre (biting stonecrop) A creeping, pale green mat of crowded shoots distinguished by scaly, overlapping, triangular leaves, 4mm (⅛in) long, is covered with 1.5cm (½in) wide yellow flowers in early summer. The flowers are arranged in loose, flat clusters, each containing 3-5 blooms. The plant is an evergreen. It originates from the Balkans and is now naturalised in parts of Britain. HEIGHT & SPREAD 5×15cm (2×6in).

'Aureum' has a neater habit and a golden tint to its leaf tips in spring.

S. aizoon Several upright stems bear alternate, oblong to lance-shaped, toothed leaves, 5cm (2in) long, which are mid green and velvety. Pale yellow flowers, 1.5cm (½in) wide, appear in dense, terminal clusters in mid summer. This robust, herbaceous perennial is native to Siberia, China and Japan. HEIGHT & SPREAD 30×25cm (12×10in).

'Euphorbioides' has rich yellow flowers, borne in somewhat larger clusters.

***S. alboroseum* 'Mediovariegatum'** The pale green leaves have yellow centres on this striking herbaceous perennial. A strong, clumped growth of upright stems carries paired, oval leaves, 5cm (2in) long, smooth and velvety to the touch, and 3cm (1¼in) wide terminal clusters of white flowers in early autumn. Native to China and Japan. HEIGHT & SPREAD 30×12cm (12×4¾in).

S. album This vigorous and somewhat untidy plant has a sprawling tangle of shoots that easily spreads to 30cm (12in) in a single season, and will continue to spread year

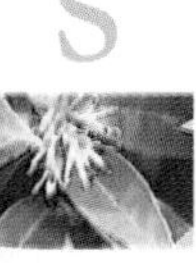

after year. The leaves are typically cigar-shaped, up to 1.5cm (½in) long, smooth and shiny, and arrayed 'bottle brush' fashion on 8cm (3¼in) long shoots. The white flowers, 1cm (⅜in) across, are carried in flattish heads on stems up to 15cm (6in) tall in mid summer. The plant is evergreen, but must be cut back hard every autumn. Found in Europe, Scandinavia and W Asia, *S. album* is firmly naturalised in Britain. HEIGHT & SPREAD 15×30cm (6×12in).

'Chloroticum' has very clear green foliage. **'Coral Carpet'** has leaves that turn red in hot, dry conditions. The leaves of ssp. ***teretifolium*** **'Murale'** take on a purple hue.

S. anacampseros Lax stems sprouting from creeping tubers form a vigorous mat. There is no real limit to its spread. Alternate leaves, 2cm (¾in) long, fleshy, broadly spatulate and blue-green, clothe the upper half of the stems. They are semi-deciduous. Purple flowers arranged in globular heads 4cm (1½in) wide top the stems from mid to late summer. Native to S Europe. HEIGHT & SPREAD 10×100cm (4×40in).

S. cauticolum♀ A herbaceous perennial of somewhat straggling habit, with creeping stems terminating in 2.5cm (1in) wide heads of purple flowers in early and mid autumn. The slightly toothed, fleshy leaves are rounded, 2.5cm (1in) long, bluish green rimmed purple-red. Native to Japan, HEIGHT & SPREAD 10×30cm (4×12in).

'Bertram Anderson' is more upright and branching, with purple-blue leaves and red flowers. **'Lidakense'** has a smaller, neater habit of growth.

S. dasyphyllum A dwarf evergreen perennial, whose foliage has year-round beauty. Little egg-shaped, polished leaves, 3mm (⅛in) long, clasp 4cm (1½in) long crowded shoots, producing a pale grey mound suffused with pink. The 6mm (¼in) wide flowers, white ridged with pink, spangle the plant in early and mid summer. Native to the Mediterranean. HEIGHT & SPREAD 7×15cm (2¾×6in).

S. ewersii The rounded leaves of this prostrate, herbaceous perennial are sparsely toothed, fleshy, 2cm (¾in) long, blue-green and in opposed pairs, on floppy stems that root down from their nodes. Branching heads, 4cm (1½in) wide, of rose-pink flowers bloom in late summer and early autumn. Widely distributed through the Himalayas, Mongolia and China. HEIGHT & SPREAD 10×30cm (4×12in).

S. forsterianum see *S. rupestre*

S. **'Herbstfreude'**♀ ('Autumn Joy') Stout, upright stems carry pale green, fleshy, oval, toothed leaves, about 5cm (2in) long, and terminal heads, up to 8cm (3¼in) across, of pink flowers that deepen to bronze-red. The flowers bloom in early and mid autumn. This herbaceous perennial is usually grown in flowerbeds, being too large for most rock gardens. HEIGHT & SPREAD 45×45cm (18×18in).

S. hispanicum var. ***minus*** This evergreen mat-forming plant has bunched, linear leaves, 6mm (¼in) long, at the tops of almost bare, 5cm (2in) stems, which crowd together to form a dense, spreading mat. Purplish pink flowers, 1cm (⅜in) across, are borne in loose heads in early and mid summer. The plant grows in the wild in S Europe and as far east as Iran, but not in Spain, despite its name. HEIGHT & SPREAD 5×30cm (2×12in).

'Aureum' is slow-growing, compact and has a yellow tinge to its foliage.

S. kamtschaticum♀ Lax, fleshy stems radiate from stumps of previous growth, bearing mid green, toothed, elliptic, widely spaced leaves, up to 6cm (2½in) long, and flattish, terminal clusters of deep yellow flowers, from early summer to early autumn. Each flower is about 1.5cm (½in) wide. This tough, vigorous, semi-evergreen perennial is usually planted in a border. Native to NE Siberia, China and Japan. HEIGHT & SPREAD 10×60cm (4×24in).

var. ***ellacombeanum***♀ has pale yellow flowers and neater, more compact growth. var. ***floriferum*** **'Weihenstephaner Gold'**♀ has extra flowering shoots, giving an extended display, until mid autumn. **'Variegatum'**♀ is eye-catching, with pale orange flowers and gold-rimmed leaves.

S. lydium Densely tufted, 5mm (¼in) long, linear leaves, bright green tinged with red and fleshy, borne at the tips of creeping stems, form an evergreen mat. Sparse, rounded, 2cm (¾in) wide clusters of white flowers appear on erect 2.5cm (1in) stalks from early to mid summer. This sedum prefers partial shade and moister, cooler conditions than most other species. It is native to Asia Minor. HEIGHT & SPREAD 2.5×15cm (1×6in).

S. middendorffianum A neat herbaceous perennial, forming a crowded clump of 15cm (6in) long stems carrying narrowly oblong, 2cm (¾in) long, sparsely toothed leaves that are a fresh green and fleshy. Bright yellow flowers bloom in 2cm (¾in) wide terminal clusters between mid and late summer. This vigorous plant is native to N Asia. HEIGHT & SPREAD 15×45cm (6×18in).

S. oppositifolium see *S. spurium* var. *album*

S. oreganum An evergreen with richly coloured, glossy foliage, the plant makes a moderately vigorous creeping hummock.

▼ *Sedum* 'Bertram Anderson'

▼ *Sedum* 'Herbstfreude'

▼ *Sedum kamtschaticum*

Sedum kamtschaticum 'Variegatum' ▼

▲ *Sedum middendorffianum*

S

Blunt, wedge-shaped leaves, 2 cm (¾ in) long, bright green suffused with deep red, clad creeping stems, with terminal heads, 2.5 cm (1 in) across, of rich yellow flowers, in mid summer. Native to NW America. HEIGHT & SPREAD 8×30 cm (3¼×12 in).

S. pachyclados (syn. *Rhodiola pachyclados*) The plant consists of packed rosettes of fresh green, rounded, fleshy 1 cm (⅜ in) long leaves. Creamy white flowers, 1 cm (⅜ in) across, sit almost stemless on the mat in mid and late summer. This plant dies back to resting buds in winter, when it can be damaged by excessive wet. Native to Afghanistan. HEIGHT & SPREAD 5×15 cm (2×6 in).

S. pilosum Spear-shaped, fleshy, 1 cm (⅜ in) long leaves form a single, squat, barrel-shaped rosette of grey-green, downy, overlapping leaves. From this, in late spring and early summer of the second year, rise pink flowers in dense heads up to 5 cm (2 in) across, on upright leafy stems some 10 cm (4 in) long. Although biennial, the plant is persistent due to self-sown seedlings. Several plants tend to grow together. Native to Asia Minor, the Caucasus and Iran. HEIGHT & SPREAD 10×4 cm (4×1½ in).

S. pluricaule Grey-green, oval leaves, 1 cm (⅜ in) long, clad the upper third of stems that creep then rise to hold domed clusters, 5 cm (2 in) wide, of crowded purple flowers in mid and late summer. This is a bushy semi-deciduous plant. Native to Siberia. HEIGHT & SPREAD 8×20 cm (3¼×8 in).

S. populifolium This open, bushy herbaceous perennial has stalked, pale green, heart-shaped leaves, unevenly edged in deep, blunt toothing and about 2.5 cm (1 in) long. Pink-tipped, white flowers, 1.5 cm (½ in) long, held in branched terminal clusters, appear all through summer. Native to Siberia. HEIGHT & SPREAD 20×30 cm (8×12 in).

S. reflexum see *S. rupestre*

S. 'Ruby Glow' ♀ Deep green leaves and ruby-red flowers suffused with purple appear on this upright plant. The fleshy, oval leaves, 5 cm (2 in) long, grow in pairs along the stems. The flowers 1.5 cm (½ in) across, are borne in globular heads about 7.5 cm (3 in) wide. The plant, a herbaceous perennial, blooms in early and mid autumn. HEIGHT & SPREAD 20×25 cm (8×10 in).

S. rupestre (syn. *S. forsterianum*, *S. reflexum*) A robust, evergreen mat-former of rather untidy habit, this plant is too invasive for most rock gardens. Wandering shoots carry massed, 1.5 cm (½ in) long, awl-shaped, fleshy, blue-grey leaves. Flower stems rise to 20 cm (8 in), with dense heads, 2.5 cm (1 in) across, of yellow blooms in mid summer. Native to W Europe. HEIGHT & SPREAD 20×60 cm (8×24 in).

S. sediforme This strong-growing evergreen makes an upright, 15 cm (6 in) tall clump of branching stems, with terminal spikes of 1.5 cm (½ in) long, oval, pale blue-green, fleshy leaves. In mid and late summer, blooming stems rise to 30 cm (12 in) or more, carrying white flowers, 1.5 cm (½ in) wide, in branching clusters. Native to S Mediterranean and N Africa. HEIGHT & SPREAD 30×30 cm (12×12 in).

S. sexangulare A vigorous, soft mat of slender, creeping stems is densely clad in fresh green, cylindrical, 4 mm (⅛ in) long leaves that are evergreen. Tall stems bear branched clusters, 3 cm (1¼ in) wide, of yellow flowers through summer. Native to E Europe. HEIGHT & SPREAD 7×60 cm (2¾×24 in).

S. sieboldii This straggling herbaceous perennial, almost prostrate has fresh green leaves rimmed with red. They are rounded, smooth, fleshy and 1.5 cm (½ in) long. Pale pink flowers appear in autumn, 4-6 together in loose, broadly conical clusters, about 3 cm (1¼ in) across. The plant is hardy only in mild areas. From Japan. HEIGHT & SPREAD 10×60 cm (4×24 in).

Sedum sieboldii 'Mediovarigatum'

'Mediovarigatum' ♀ has grey-green leaves with creamy centres; give the plant some protection in winter.

S. spathulifolium This evergreen perennial typically forms a spreading mound, 5 cm (2 in) tall, of crowded leaf rosettes 2 cm (¾ in) wide, on brittle stems, with leaves fleshy, grey-green, spoon-shaped and 1 cm (⅜ in) wide. Alternatively, foliage may be silvery, pale grey or purple dusted with grey. Bright yellow flowers, 1.5 cm (½ in) wide, are borne in branched heads on 10 cm (4 in) stems in early summer. Native to parts of western N America. HEIGHT & SPREAD 10×20 cm (4×8 in).

The foliage of **'Aureum'** turns yellow in summer. **'Cape Blanco'** ♀ is more compact, with leaves powdered silver-grey. **'Purpureum'** ♀ is a strong spreading plant, with leaves flushed plum-red in summer.

S. spectabile ♀ (ice plant) A profusion of pink flowers with purple centres, carried in dense, domed clusters 10 cm (4 in) across,

Sedum spectabile

top the stems of this robust, upright, clump-forming plant in early autumn. The oval, shallow-toothed leaves, 5 cm (2 in) long, pale blue-green, smooth and fleshy, grow in pairs. The plant is often found in a border. It dies down to resting buds over winter. Native to China. HEIGHT & SPREAD 40×40 cm (16×16 in).

▲ *Sedum spectabile* 'Brilliant'

▲ *Sedum spectabile* 'Iceberg'

'Brilliant' ♀ has flowers coloured deep rose; **'Carmen'** has carmine flowers; those of **'Iceberg'** are white; **'Meteor'** has flowers of deep carmine.

S. spurium A mass of partly naked, creeping stems hold tufts of dark green, broadly spatulate, toothed, smooth and fleshy leaves, 2.5 cm (1 in) long, which form a mat about 5 cm (2 in) high. Deep mauve flowers are borne in loose heads 6 cm (2½ in) across on 10 cm (4 in) tall flower stems in mid and late summer. Use this semi-deciduous plant as ground cover, because of its invasive spreading habit. Native to the Caucasus. HEIGHT & SPREAD 10×90 cm (4×36 in).

The flowers of var. ***album*** (syn. *S. oppositifolium*) are white; **'Atropurpureum'** has dark red leaves and red flowers; **'Coccineum'** has bright red flowers; **'Erdblut'** has green leaves edged with crimson and crimson flowers; **'Fuldaglut'** has dark red leaves and flowers; **'Purpurteppich'** ('Purple Carpet') has purple leaves and flowers; **'Schorbuser Blut'** ♀ ('Dragon's Blood') has older leaves tinged bronze and deep red flowers; **'Variegatum'** has leaves edged with pink and cream.

S. telephium A herbaceous perennial which is similar in many respects to *S. spectabile*.

▼ *Sedum spurium*

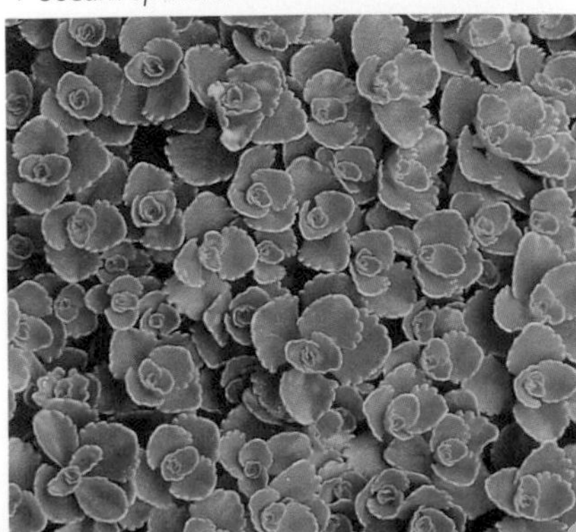

S

▲ *Sedum spurium* 'Fuldaglut'
Sedum spurium 'Purpurteppich' ▲

▲ *Sedum telephium*

Diamond-shaped leaves with blunt-toothed edges, bright green, waxy and 4 cm (1½in) long, grow alternately up the stems. Red-purple or whitish flower heads, 7.5cm (3in) across, bloom in late summer and early autumn. Native to Europe. HEIGHT & SPREAD 20×30cm (8×12in).

'Atropurpureum'♀ has all growth suffused with purple. **'Munstead Dark Red'** has dark red flowers. **'Variegatum'** has leaves coloured green, cream and pink.

S. **'Vera Jameson'**♀ This sprawling clump has rounded leaves, slightly toothed, fleshy, smooth, purple-hued, 3cm (1¼in) long. Pale, dusky pink flowers carried in 5cm (2in) wide panicles are borne in autumn, before the plant dies down for winter. HEIGHT & SPREAD 20×30cm (8×12in).

CULTIVATION Sedums accept a wide range of soil types, but not cold, heavy, wet soils. *S. lydium* and the telephium types require some moisture-retentive material at their roots; for other species quite dry soils are satisfactory. Most sedums require a sunny location. Some will thrive in sun or partial shade, including *S. alboroseum* 'Mediovariegatum', *S. cauticolum* and *S.* 'Herbstfreude'. *S. lydium* prefers partial shade. Leave dead growth of herbaceous species in place over winter, to be cleared away in early spring.

PROPAGATION Increase perennial species by division in late autumn, or by taking cuttings of non-flowering shoots in spring. Sow seed in early spring, grow on in pots and plant out in mid spring of the following year.

PESTS AND DISEASES Aphids and mealy bugs are the major pests. Over-wet soils promote rotting of the rootstock.

Sea buckthorn see *Hippophaë rhamnoides*
Sea kale see *Crambe maritima*
Sea lavender see *Limonium*
Sea pink see *Armeria*

Selaginella

Selaginellaceae

Though many look rather like mosses, selaginellas are related to ferns, and are flowerless. They are tender plants which thrive in shady, damp situations and make ideal plants for a bottle garden, terrarium or humid conservatory.

RECOMMENDED SPECIES AND VARIETIES

S. kraussiana♀ This ground-hugging perennial forms a moss-like mat up to 60cm (24in) across. The stems, which root as they spread, are covered with tiny bright green overlapping oval leaves. HEIGHT & SPREAD 5×60cm (2×24in).

'Aurea' has leaves that are golden green. **'Variegata'** has leaves splashed with cream.

S. martensii This species, less moss-like, has stems as long as 30cm (12in) long bearing bright green oval leaves up to 1cm (⅜in) long. The stems start off growing upright, and then arch over. Stiff roots grow vertically downwards into the compost. HEIGHT & SPREAD 30×80cm (12×32in).

CULTIVATION Site in shade or soft, indirect light in a humid atmosphere and at a minimum winter temperature of 7°C (45°F). Water to keep plants damp but not wet, using soft water if possible. Repot when plants reach the edge of the container.

PROPAGATION Take a cutting of a section of stem that has started to produce roots and pot on. Larger plants can also be carefully divided in spring.

PESTS AND DISEASES Usually trouble free.

Self-heal see *Prunella*

Selinum

Umbelliferae

Bold, spreading heads of tiny white or, occasionally, purplish flowers emerge from the decorative foliage of these strong-growing hardy perennials in summer. The plant described here brings height to a border and distinction to a wild-flower garden.

RECOMMENDED SPECIES

S. wallichianum (syn. *S. tenuifolium*) The finely divided, lacy green leaves of this vigorous hardy perennial are about 25cm (10in) long. Tiny white blossoms massed in flat, spreading heads, up to 20cm (8in) across, are carried on tall, greenish bronze stems in mid summer. HEIGHT & SPREAD 1.5×1m (5×3ft). Native to central Asia.

CULTIVATION Plant in early summer in free-draining soil and in a sunny or partially shaded position. Remove faded flowerheads and cut back dying foliage in autumn.

PROPAGATION Sow seeds in mid spring in the open ground where they are to grow or in small pots in early spring for careful transplanting in early summer. Plants do not transplant well unless they have a rootball.

PESTS AND DISEASES Usually trouble free.

▼ *Selinum wallichianum*

Semiaquilegia

Ranunculaceae

These elegant upright, hardy, herbaceous perennials mix well with alpine meadow plants. They are closely related to the genus aquilegia, but the nodding, bell-shaped flowers do not have the characteristic spurs of that genus. They can be short-lived, particularly when summers bring long periods of hot dry weather. Native to E Asia.

RECOMMENDED SPECIES AND VARIETIES

S. adoxoides Pink to purple flowers, up to 2.5cm (1in) wide, appear on widely branching stems in late spring to early summer. The narrow, mid green, lobed leaves are 3cm (1¼in) long. HEIGHT & SPREAD 20×15cm (8×6in).

S. ecalcarata Loose, pendulous clusters of chocolate-brown to purple-brown flowers, each about 2.5cm (1in) wide, appear in spring and early summer. This vigorous plant has grey-green leaves, made up of 3 leaflets, each 2.5cm (1in) long. HEIGHT & SPREAD 30×30cm (1×1ft).

'Flore Pleno' has double flowers.

CULTIVATION Plant in early spring or mid autumn in a light, well-drained soil in an open situation shaded from midday sun.

PROPAGATION Sow ripe seed in pots under glass in late summer and plant out the following autumn. Plants will self-sow freely in the garden and will hybridise readily with species of aquilegia.

PESTS AND DISEASES Usually trouble free, although aphids may be a problem.

Semiarundinaria see BAMBOOS p. 79

▼ *Semiaquilegia ecalcarata*

Sempervivum

Houseleek

Crassulaceae

These evergreen succulents are grown for their dense mats of fleshy foliage since most produce only a smattering of flowers in summer. The starry flowers, about 2.5cm (1in) across, are held in clusters well above the leaf rosettes at the top of fat, leafy stems. After flowering, the leaf rosettes at the base of the stems die, but the plant lives on, aided by offsets on rooting stolons. Native to Europe and N Africa, most are hardy in Britain, doing well in a rock garden, though a few need protection from winter wetness.

RECOMMENDED SPECIES AND VARIETIES

S. andreanum Rich green rosettes of brown-tipped leaves form a spreading mat. Each rosette is up to 4cm (1½in) across. The pink flowers are held on 15cm (6in) stems. HEIGHT & SPREAD 2.5×20cm (1×8in).

S. arachnoideum♀ (Cobweb houseleek) Light green, globular rosettes, up to 2cm (¾in) across, with their leaf tips criss-crossed by cobweb-like hairs, form a tight, shallow mound. The rose-red flowers are held on 12.5cm (5in) stems. Protect in winter. HEIGHT & SPREAD 2.5×20cm (1×8in).

'Stansfieldii' has a crimson flush to its leaves, while slightly larger rosettes are formed by ssp. ***tomentosum***♀ with the leaves more heavily covered in 'cobwebs'.

Sempervivum arachnoideum ssp. tomentosum

S. calcareum This variable species typically forms a flat clump of 7.5cm (3in) wide rosettes. The tips of the blue-green leaves have purple-brown blotches. Pale pink flowers grace stems up to 25cm (10in) tall. HEIGHT & SPREAD 5×30cm (2×12in).

'Greenii' forms rosettes no more than 4cm (1½in) wide.

S. ciliosum Prized for the symmetry of its globular rosettes, each up to 5cm (2in) across, this species forms a grey-green mound. The lemon-yellow flowers are carried on stems up to 10cm (4in) tall. HEIGHT & SPREAD 5×25cm (2×10in).

The leaves of var. ***borisii*** develop attractive red tints in full sun.

S. grandiflorum Fleshy, sticky, open rosettes, 2.5cm (1in) wide, form loose mats with offsets on long stolons. The large yellow flowers are held on 20cm (8in) stems. The plant does best in acid soils. HEIGHT & SPREAD 5×30cm (2×12in).

S. marmoreum This variable species forms mats of spiky-tipped, dark green rosettes, up to 6cm (2½in) across. The red flowers are carried on 20cm (8in) stems. HEIGHT & SPREAD 5×30cm (2×12in).

Sempervivum marmoreum

'Brunneifolium' has a denser habit, with brownish leaves that turn red in winter.

S. montanum Fleshy, semi-open, fresh green rosettes, up to 7.5cm (3in) wide, with long-stoloned offsets, make a broad mat. The large 'starfish' flowers are a deep claret held on 10cm (4in) stems. HEIGHT & SPREAD 6×36cm (2½×14in).

Smaller rosettes, up to 5cm (2in) across, tipped with reddish brown are formed by ssp. ***stiriacum***.

S. pittonii Grey-green, downy rosettes, up to 5cm (2in) across, form a spreading clump. The flowers are pale yellow and held on 12.5cm (5in) stems. This species benefits from winter cover. HEIGHT & SPREAD 5×15cm (2×6in).

S. tectorum♀ The rosettes of this variable species can be up to 18cm (7in) across, forming into large clumps. The flowers are among the most attractive of the genus with heads of up to 100 dusky pink blooms on stems as much as 50cm (20in) tall. HEIGHT & SPREAD 7.5×30cm (3×12in).

The densely packed ssp. ***alpinum*** has small rosettes. **'Atropurpureum'** has rich red-purple foliage. **'Atroviolaceum'** has purple-violet leaves. **'Nigrum'** has bright green foliage tipped with purple. The leaves of **'Sunset'** have orange-red tips in autumn.

S. thompsonianum Small, 2cm (¾in), globular rosettes, which turn reddish in full sun, make a dense mat. On rare occasions pink-and-yellow flowers are seen on 7.5cm (3in) stems. This species requires winter protection. HEIGHT & SPREAD 2.5×15cm (1×6in).

GARDEN HYBRIDS

These are grown for their rosette colouring: **'Alpha'**, green and crimson with hairy tips; **'Blood Tip'**, green and crimson; **'Commander Hay'**♀, green flushed with red; **'Director Jacobs'**, deep red with silvery hairs; **'Jubilee'**, hairy, light green flushed with maroon in summer; **'King George'**, like 'Jubilee' but with persistent colour; **'Mahogany'**, rich reddish brown; **'Rosie'**, flushed pink; **'Royal Ruby'**, deep red; **'Rubin'**, bronze-red.

Sempervivum 'Rosie'

Sempervivum 'Rubin'

CULTIVATION Plant in spring or early summer in a well-drained, light soil and sunny situation (they tolerate periods of drought). Some prefer acid soils and in wet regions the cobwebbed types need to be covered with a pane of glass or brought into an alpine house for the winter.

PROPAGATION Plant the ready-rooted offshoots in spring or summer or sow seed in trays in a coldframe in early spring and plant out the following year.

PESTS AND DISEASES Rust can be a problem. Plants may rot in cool, wet soils.

Senecio

Compositae

Senecio cineraria 'White Diamond'

The yellow-flowered weeds of this genus are well known, but it also contains excellent annuals, perennials, pot plants, sub-shrubs and climbers, that are suitable for a garden or conservatory. They range from the tender to the very hardy. Most have daisy flowers, usually bright yellow but sometimes purple or white. The genus is widely distributed, with species found in all continents except Antarctica.

RECOMMENDED SPECIES AND VARIETIES

S. cineraria (syn. *Cineraria maritima*) Egg-shaped, often deeply lobed, grey leaves are up to 15 cm (6 in) long and covered in greyish woolly hairs, as are the stems. This evergreen sub-shrub, which forms a mound of foliage, is best treated as a half-hardy annual but may survive winters in milder areas. It can be raised annually from seed. Yellow daisies to 2.5 cm (1 in) across appear in clusters in mid summer, but are best removed. HEIGHT & SPREAD 50×50 cm (20×20 in).

'White Diamond'♀ looks much whiter than the species.

S. compactus see *Brachyglottis compacta*

S. cruentus see *Pericallis × hybrida*

S. greyii hort. see *Brachyglottis* 'Sunshine'

S. × hybridus see *Pericallis × hybrida*

S. leucostachys see *S. viravira*

***S. macroglossus* 'Variegatus'**♀ (Cape ivy, waxvine) Triangular, slightly succulent leaves up to 7.5 cm (3 in) across are ivy-like with 3-5 lobes. Leaves are bright, deep green and glossy with an irregular creamy white margin; others are entirely cream. This tender evergreen climber is suited to a house or conservatory. Solitary pale creamy yellow daisies, 6 cm (2½ in) across with darker yellow centres, appear rarely, usually in winter. The purple-toned twining stems grow rapidly and need the support of wires or canes. They become woody with age. HEIGHT & SPREAD 1.8 m×50 cm (6 ft×20 in).

S. monroi see *Brachyglottis monroi*

S. pulcher Loose sprays of rich reddish purple daisies, up to 7.5 cm (3 in) across with a yellow centre, are produced in autumn. They are carried on erect stems above rosettes of elliptic, slightly toothed, dark green leaves, which taper to a narrow base. Grow this herbaceous perennial in a sheltered site outdoors, or in a conservatory. HEIGHT & SPREAD 60×45 cm (2×1½ ft).

S. rowleyanus (string of beads) Prostrate strings of tiny, succulent, spherical pale green leaves, each about 8 mm (⅜ in) across, are produced by this tender perennial. It grows best in a conservatory but may be situated in a well-lit window, cascading from a jardinière or hanging basket. Small, daisy-like white flowers up to 1.5 cm (½ in) across are produced intermittently throughout summer and into autumn. HEIGHT & SPREAD 5×30 cm (2×12 in).

S. scandens Large branched clusters of yellow daisies, each 1.5 cm (½ in) wide, open in winter. This robust, woody-based evergreen perennial produces long arching or trailing stems, clothed in thin-textured narrowly triangular, mid to bright green leaves, up to 10 cm (4 in) long. It needs to be grown in a conservatory and is best treated as a climber, given support on trellis or wires. HEIGHT & SPREAD 5×2 m (16×6½ ft).

S. smithii Large, rounded clusters of yellow-centred white daisies, up to 5 cm (2 in) wide, appear in summer at the end of erect, leafy stems. The long-stalked, oblong or oval basal leaves are dark greyish green and up to 25 cm (10 in) long. This hardy herbaceous perennial grows best in a moist situation. HEIGHT & SPREAD 1.2×1 m (4×3 ft).

***S.* 'Sunshine'** see *Brachyglottis* 'Sunshine'

S. viravira♀ (syn. *S. leucostachys*) Deeply divided greyish leaves, densely covered in white hairs, are the main feature of this semi-evergreen perennial. They are up to 7.5 cm (3 in) long, with several pairs of narrow segments. The plant is shrubby and often grown as a half-hardy annual for bedding but in sheltered gardens it survives most winters. It usually produces clusters of small, button-like, pale yellow flowers of little ornamental value. These appear from mid to late summer. HEIGHT & SPREAD 75×75 cm (2½×2½ ft).

CULTIVATION Treat *S. cineraria* and *S. viravira* as half-hardy annuals and plant out on well-drained soil in full sun after the spring frosts. *S. macroglossus* 'Variegatus', *S. rowleyanus* and *S. scandens* need to be grown in a greenhouse or conservatory and kept at a minimum temperature of 7°C (45°F). In cold areas grow *S. pulcher* under glass, too. *S. smithii* prefers moist peaty soil in a cool situation. Trim perennials each spring to maintain their shape.

PROPAGATION Sow seed in late winter or early spring. Tender species need to be raised in a greenhouse; *S. smithii* in a coldframe. Alternatively, take semi-ripe cuttings in late summer, root under a coldframe and grow on, under protection, for planting out the following spring. Divide herbaceous perennials in early spring.

PESTS AND DISEASES Slugs and snails.

Senna

Leguminosae

Senna corymbosa

These tropical and sub-tropical trees, shrubs and sub-shrubs are grown for their pleasing, much divided foliage, clusters of brightly coloured sweet-pea flowers and curious pod-like fruits. They are usually kept in a conservatory or greenhouse, in pots or tubs. They grow very quickly, so it is a good idea to propagate them regularly to ensure compact, well-formed plants. The listed plants are fully grown within five years.

RECOMMENDED SPECIES AND VARIETIES

S. artemisioides♀ (syn. *Cassia artemisioides*) (wormwood senna, feathery cassia) Grey-green, downy, narrowly linear leaflets arranged in pairs, make up the leaves, which are up to 6 cm (2½ in) long. Small, fragrant, rich yellow flowers, carried in unbranched clusters up to 7.5 cm (3 in) long, bloom from mid winter until early summer. The fruits are oblong, flattened pods, up to 10 cm (4 in) long, mid green but often burnished brown. Keep this erect to spreading evergreen shrub in a minimum temperature of 13°C (55°F). Native to Australia. HEIGHT & SPREAD 3×2 m (10×6½ ft).

S. corymbosa (syn. *Cassia corymbosa*) The leaves, up to 60 cm (2 ft) long, consist of many small, pointed, broadly lance-shaped,

Senecio macroglossus 'Variegatus'

Senecio viravira

Senna corymbosa

S

dull yellow-green leaflets. Golden yellow flowers are held in clusters up to 15cm (6in) long from mid summer to early autumn. The green, bean-like pods are straight or curved and up to 12.5cm (5in) long. This evergreen may grow into a small tree in the wild, but remains shrubby in a pot. Grow at a temperature of at least 10°C (50°F). Native to N and S America. HEIGHT & SPREAD 3×2m (10×6½ft).

S. marilandica (syn. *Cassia marilandica*) (wild senna) This is a shrubby and somewhat unruly plant with several stems that start erect, then tumble over. The stems are clothed with dull greenish yellow leaves up to 25cm (10in) long, made up of a number of pairs of small oval leaflets. Flowers are brown and yellow, in clusters as long as 7.5cm (3in), appearing between mid summer and mid autumn. The stiff, downy, green fruits are up to 10cm (4in) long. This deciduous plant requires a minimum temperature of 1°C (34°F). Native to N America. HEIGHT & SPREAD 1×1m (3×3ft).

CULTIVATION Grow in a well-ventilated greenhouse or conservatory, where plants will get plenty of sun, in pots of a soil-based compost such as John Innes No.3. Water freely throughout summer and apply a liquid houseplant feed regularly. Water sparingly in winter. Repot as necessary.

PROPAGATION Sow seed in spring or take semi-ripe heel cuttings during summer.

PRUNING Trim back regularly during the growing season to maintain an attractive shape. If a plant is allowed to become overgrown before trimming back, it will not provide satisfactory regrowth.

PESTS AND DISEASES Red spider mite is a nuisance and can cause rapid defoliation.

Sensitive plant see *Mimosa pudica*
Serviceberry see *Amelanchier*
Shallon see *Gaultheria shallon*
Shallot see p.741
Sheep's bit see *Jasione*
Shibataea see BAMBOOS p.79
Shoo fly see *Nicandra physalodes*
Shooting star see *Dodecatheon*

S

Shortia

Diapensiaceae

Shortia soldanelloides

Pink or white flowers appear in spring above glossy, bronze-tinted foliage. Spreading slowly, these deciduous, evergreen or semi-evergreen sub-shrubs form mats of long-stemmed, rounded leaves. Native to N America and E Asia, shortias grow best in the shade, thriving in cool, moist areas of NW England, Scotland and Ireland. The recommended plants are hardy provided they have humus-rich, acid soil and dappled shade – a position near trees is ideal. Dwarf rhododendrons and cassiopes make good planting companions. Shortias resent disturbance once established.

RECOMMENDED SPECIES AND VARIETIES

S. galacifolia Pure white or faintly pink-tinged flowers with delicately scalloped petals complement finely scalloped leaves, about 5cm (2in) wide. The flowers, 2cm (¾in) long, are almost bell-shaped. The plant dies down to resting buds in winter. HEIGHT & SPREAD 10×30cm (4×12in).

S. soldanelloides (fringebell) Deeply frilled, trumpet-shaped flowers stand above a low clump of bright green, broadly toothed leaves that are often stained mahogany red. Ranging from rich to pale pink and occasionally white, the flowers are about 2cm (¾in) long. The attractive evergreen leaves are about 3cm (1¼in) across. HEIGHT & SPREAD 5×20cm (2×8 in).

With fewer teeth on its leaves, var. ***ilicifolia*** is available in named forms including **'Askival Sunrise'** with pink flowers and **'Askival Iceberg'** with pure white flowers.

S. uniflora Pale pink, flared, bell-shaped flowers, about 3cm (1¼in) wide, are borne on this semi-evergreen plant. It has heavily veined leaves, about 2.5cm (1in) wide. HEIGHT & SPREAD 15×30cm (6×12in).

▲ *Shortia uniflora*

The flowers of **'Grandiflora'** are about 4cm (1½in) wide.

CULTIVATION Plant in late spring in moist but well-drained, peaty, acid soil in partial shade. In warm, dry regions ensure that the plants do not dry out.

PROPAGATION Sow seed in a coldframe or greenhouse in early spring and protect from frost. Plant out in the second spring after germination. Alternatively, take basal cuttings in early summer.

PESTS AND DISEASES Usually trouble free.

Shrimp plant see *Justicia brandeegeana*

Sidalcea

Prairie mallow, checker mallow

Malvaceae

Sidalcea 'Elsie Heugh'

Tall spires of long-lived silky flowers are borne by these hardy herbaceous perennials in mid summer. The open, funnel-shaped blooms are found in white and shades of pink, held on stems which rise above the rosettes of rounded, mid green leaves. The leaf rosettes are produced early in the season and are an effective weed suppressor.

These elegant plants often extend their garden value by producing a second flush of blooms in autumn. Sidalceas prefer fairly cool, moist conditions but may not survive very hard winters. Both the species listed below are native to N America.

RECOMMENDED SPECIES AND VARIETIES

S. candida The pure white flowers of this species are up to 2.5cm (1in) across. The leaves may reach 20cm (8in) across. HEIGHT & SPREAD 75×50cm (30×20in).

S. malviflora The pink blossoms are up to 5cm (2in) in diameter. The leaves grow to 6cm (2½in) across. HEIGHT & SPREAD 1m×50cm (36×20in).

GARDEN VARIETIES

The more commonly grown garden varieties have flowers up to 5cm (2in) across and leaves about 6cm (2½in) wide. Unless otherwise stated, they reach a height of 1m (3ft) and a spread of 50cm (20in).

The flowers of **'Croftway Red'** appear in early summer. **'Elsie Heugh'** has fringed,

▼ *Sidalcea* 'Elsie Heugh'

Sidalcea 'Rose Queen'

pale pink blossoms. It may reach a height of 60cm (2ft). **'Loveliness'** has pale pink petals and the plant has a compact habit. The blossoms of **'Party Girl'** are a delicate rose-pink. **'Puck'** has deep pink flowers and it grows to 60cm (2ft) high. The flowers of **'Rose Queen'** are deep rose-pink. It has a rather bushy appearance. **'Sussex Beauty'** has clear pale pink blooms. The petals of **'William Smith'**♀ are bright rose-pink, flushed with salmon.

CULTIVATION Plant from autumn to spring in any reasonably fertile soil. Choose a sunny spot, but in hot, dry gardens plant in light shade and apply a mulch of well-rotted compost to help to keep the roots cool and moist. Cut off faded flowering stems to encourage a second flush of blooms. Do not allow plants to set seed as this weakens them. Stake in windy, exposed spots.

PROPAGATION Divide named cultivars in spring or autumn. Sow seed of species in a coldframe in late winter or early spring. Plant out in early summer in their permanent positions.

PESTS AND DISEASES Usually trouble free.

Silene

Campion, catchfly
Caryophyllaceae

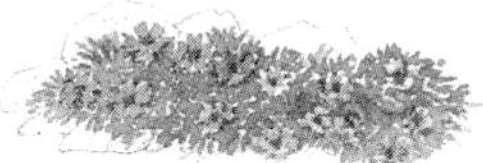

Silene acaulis

Salver-shaped flowers with a swollen calyx, which in some species is very pronounced, make an attractive addition to a rock garden, although *Silene dioica* and *S. fimbriata* are better suited to a woodland environment. The genus is native to much of the Northern Hemisphere and includes annuals, biennials and perennials. Those listed below are hardy perennials.

RECOMMENDED SPECIES AND VARIETIES

S. acaulis A mass of pale pink to deep rose flowers, up to 1.5cm (½in) across, appear on very short stems over a dense cushion of foliage in late spring. This species can, however, be reluctant to flower well. The evergreen rosetted leaves are linear, up to 1cm (⅜in) long, and bright green. HEIGHT & SPREAD 5×15cm (2×6in).

The flower stems of ssp. ***acaulis*** are up to 5cm (2in) tall. **'Alba'** has white flowers. **'Frances'** has yellow leaves. **'Mount Snowdon'** is very compact.

S. alpestris White flowers, up to 2cm (¾in) across, appear from early to mid summer with petals bearing several prominent blunt teeth. Sparse light green leaves are narrowly tapering and up to 5cm (2in) long. This herbaceous species makes an upright, airy clump of slender, branched stems. HEIGHT & SPREAD 30×20cm (12×8in).

'Flore Pleno'♀ is multipetalled.

S. dioica **'Flore Pleno'** Red double flowers, 2cm (¾in) across, open in early summer, held in lax, branched clusters. Long-stalked, egg-shaped leaves are bright green and up to 5cm (2in) long. HEIGHT & SPREAD 60×30cm (24×12in).

S. elisabethae In mid to late summer a single stem, normally holding a solitary flower, rises from a ruff of mid green leaves. The deep rose to pink bloom is 3cm (1¼in) wide. The plant is semi-evergreen. HEIGHT & SPREAD 15×20cm (6×8in).

S. fimbriata Clusters of white flowers, up to 4cm (1½in) across with heavily fringed petals, appear on the arched branches of this herbaceous plant in early summer. The attractive inflated calyx is exposed after the flower has perished. Hairy, dark green leaves are egg-shaped and up to 10cm (4in) long. Cut back after flowering to encourage a second crop of flowers later in the year. HEIGHT & SPREAD 60×60cm (2×2ft).

S. keiskei Pink flowers, 1.5cm (½in) wide, appear from mid summer to early autumn on the wiry, branched stems of this herbaceous species. Elliptic 2cm (¾in) long, mid green leaves make a delicate, rather tangled clump. HEIGHT & SPREAD 15×20cm (6×8in).

Smaller than the species, var. ***minor*** is just 5cm (2in) tall.

S. maritima see *S. uniflora*

S. schafta♀ Light pink flowers, 2cm (¾in) across, appear in a succession of open sprays from mid summer to mid autumn. This easy-to-please semi-evergreen produces a tuft of slender shoots bearing 2cm (¾in) long, narrowly oval, pale green leaves. HEIGHT & SPREAD 15×30cm (6×12in).

Silene schafta 'Shell Pink'

Silene uniflora 'Druett's Variegated'

Silene uniflora 'Robin Whitebreast'

'Abbotswood' (see *Lychnis × walkeri* 'Abbotswood Rose'); **'Shell Pink'** is as its name suggests.

S. uniflora (syn. *S. maritima*) (sea campion) White flowers, 2cm (¾in) wide with deeply notched petals, appear on this herbaceous species in late spring. They are held in a few clusters crowning a straggly mat of grey-green foliage. The sparse, oval leaves are up to 4cm (1½in) long. HEIGHT & SPREAD 10×15cm (4×6in).

'Druett's Variegated' has creamy leaf margins. **'Robin Whitebreast'** (syn. 'Flore Pleno') bears double flowers.

CULTIVATION Plant between autumn and spring in well-drained fertile soil. Most enjoy a sunny site, while *S. dioica* and *S. fimbriata* thrive in partial shade. *S. keiskei* needs a cool, moist site and acid soil. *S. uniflora* suits a seaside garden.

PROPAGATION Sow seed in early spring, and put out young plants in autumn. Take cuttings of single rosettes of *S. acaulis* in early to mid summer. Take basal cuttings of *S. dioica* 'Flore Pleno' and *S. fimbriata* in early summer, or divide in autumn.

PESTS AND DISEASES Usually trouble free.

Silk tassel bush see *Garrya elliptica*
Silver berry see *Elaeagnus angustifolia*
Silver bush see *Convolvulus cneorum*
Silver inch plant see *Tradescantia zebrina*

Silybum

Compositae

Flamboyant foliage characterises the hardy biennial described here, one of two species in this genus. The plant's decorative potential is best seen in an open sunny spot in a wild garden, where its extremely spiny leaf margins can do no harm. Purple flowers bloom on erect stems in spring and summer but emerging flower stems may be cut off to prolong the foliage display. The plant can be invasive unless seed heads are removed after flowering.

RECOMMENDED SPECIES AND VARIETIES

S. marianum (Our Lady's milk thistle, blessed thistle, holy thistle) White-marbled, dark green leaves, up to 50cm (20in) long and 25cm (10in) wide, with distinctive spiny margins form a decorative basal rosette. This striking biennial's faintly fragrant, thistle-like, purple flowers are up to 5cm (2in) across and bloom on erect stems from late spring to early summer. Native to the Mediterranean. HEIGHT & SPREAD 1.5×1m (5×3ft).

▲ *Silybum marianum*

S

CULTIVATION Plant in late spring in any fertile soil in an open sunny site. Feeding is unnecessary and induces soft growth which would succumb to frost damage.

PROPAGATION Sow seeds in late spring or early summer in a nursery bed and transplant seedlings as soon as they are large enough. Seeds sown earlier in the year produce plants that flower in the first year, preventing the development of the desirable basal rosette.

PESTS AND DISEASES Prone to slug and snail damage.

Sinningia

Gesneriaceae

Sinningia speciosa

Prized for their brightly coloured flowers and downy leaves, these tropical tender perennials are grown as houseplants in Britain. They need a minimum temperature of 13°C (55°F) and benefit from high humidity and indirect sunlight. Usually treated as summer-flowering pot plants, they can be kept after dying back and, with care, will flower again the following year.

RECOMMENDED SPECIES AND VARIETIES

S. cardinalis (syn. *Gesneria cardinalis*) The open, trumpet-shaped flowers, up to 5cm (2in) long, are bright red. The leaves are oval to heart-shaped, up to 15cm (6in) long. HEIGHT & SPREAD 30×30cm (1×1ft).

▼ *Sinningia cardinalis*

S. speciosa (gloxinia) The bell or trumpet-shaped flowers, up to 5cm (2in) long, appear throughout summer. They vary from white and purple to pink and red, they are often blotched or striped with a contrasting colour. The oval to oblong, soft downy leaves, up to 15cm (6in) long, are green to grey-green, often with reddish undersides or a reddish purple flush. HEIGHT & SPREAD 30×30cm (1×1ft).

▼ *Sinningia* 'Waterloo'

OTHER HYBRIDS

There are a number of hybrids available, all similar to *S. speciosa*.

'Blanche de Méru' has white flowers that are fringed pinkish white. **'Etoile de Feu'** has fiery red flowers. **'Hollywood'** has blue flowers darkening to deep purple. **'Kaiser Friederich'** has red flowers edged with white. Those of **'Kaiser Wilhelm'** are blue with white edges. **'Mont Blanc'** has large, pure white flowers. **'Violacea'** has deep violet flowers. **'Waterloo'** has rich, dark red flowers.

CULTIVATION Plant tubers in early spring in pots of soil-less or soil-based compost. Water freely in summer, but avoid getting water on the leaves because unsightly brown spots are likely to develop. Feed regularly with a liquid houseplant fertiliser. Shade from direct sunlight and keep the humidity high. Remove fading blossoms and yellowing leaves. Reduce watering in autumn, stopping completely when all the foliage has faded. Either store plants in their pots or place tubers in peat in a cool, dry, frost-free place until spring.

PROPAGATION For the species, surface sow the seed in spring under heated glass. Take soft stem cuttings of the hybrids in spring or early summer.

PESTS AND DISEASES Mealy bug and vine weevil can be troublesome.

Sisyrinchium

Iridaceae

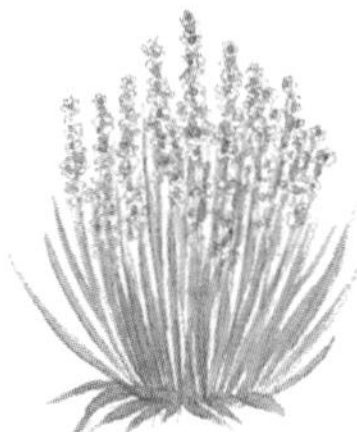

Sisyrinchium striatum

The small, starry or cup-shaped flowers of sisyrinchium are produced in succession in such profusion that although they are short-lived they create a display for much of the summer. Each flower is about 1cm (⅜in) across. The narrow, sword-like, grassy foliage forms handsome fans. Sisyrinchiums are hardy herbaceous perennials that demand a position in full sun. They prefer a very well-drained site and will not endure winter waterlogging. If left unattended sisyrinchiums can scatter seed freely, the seedlings sometimes becoming a nuisance. Native to the Americas.

RECOMMENDED SPECIES AND VARIETIES

S. album hort. see *S. idahoense* 'Album'

S. angustifolium (syn. *S.* × *anceps*, *S. bermudianum*) (blue-eyed grass) The bright blue, cup-shaped flowers have yellow centres and are borne on stiff stems. The mid green

▲ *Sisyrinchium angustifolium*

leaves are up to 30cm (12in) long. HEIGHT & SPREAD 30×25cm (12×10in).

S. atlanticum Branching winged stems bear clusters of violet-blue flowers with bright yellow centres during mid summer. The bluish green foliage is up to 45cm (18in) tall. HEIGHT & SPREAD 45×30cm (1½×1ft).

S. bellum hort. see *S. idahoense*

S. bermudianum see *S. angustifolium*

***S.* 'Biscutella'** In mid summer this hybrid produces small yellow flowers stained and veined with purple. It has clumps of mid green leaves up to 20cm (8in) long. HEIGHT & SPREAD 36×30cm (14×12in)

***S.* 'Blue Ice'** Large, pale blue, cup-shaped flowers appear from mid to late summer. The pale blue-green leaves are up to 20cm (8in) long. HEIGHT & SPREAD 30×20cm (12×8in).

S. boreale see *S. californicum*

S. brachypus see *S. californicum* Brachypus Group

S. californicum (syn. *S. boreale*) Broadly winged stems carry star-like, bright yellow blooms in late spring and summer. The clumps of grey-green leaves are up to 30cm (1ft) tall. HEIGHT & SPREAD 45×30cm (1½×1ft).

Brachypus Group (syn. *S. brachypus*) has profuse flowers on plants only 15cm (6in) in height and spread. The leaves are produced in tight clumps.

▼ *Sisyrinchium californicum* Brachypus Group

S. depauperatum This long-flowering species produces white, cup-shaped flowers with maroon centres from late summer until early autumn. It has mid green foliage, 30cm (12in) long. HEIGHT & SPREAD 40×40cm (16×16in).

***S.* 'E.K. Balls'** Mauve to violet, cup-shaped flowers are borne all summer on this small hybrid. The greyish green leaves are up to 15cm (6in) long. HEIGHT & SPREAD 25×15cm (10×6in).

***S.* 'Hemswell Sky'** This slow-growing hybrid has pale blue to bluish white, cup-shaped flowers borne in mid summer. The mid green leaves are 15cm (6in) long. HEIGHT & SPREAD 20×15cm (8×6in).

S. idahoense (syn. *S. bellum*, *S. macounii*) Pale to dark violet-blue, cup-shaped flowers with yellow centres are borne in mid summer. The mid green leaves are up to 30cm (12in) long. HEIGHT & SPREAD 40×30cm (16×12in).

'Album' (syn. *S. album* hort., *S.* 'May Snow') has pure white flowers with yellow centres.

S. macounii see *S. idahoense*

***S.* 'May Snow'** see *S. idahoense* 'Album'

S. montanum The narrow-winged flower stems bear bright violet-blue starry blooms with yellow centres in mid to late summer. The pale green leaves are up to 30cm (12in) long. HEIGHT & SPREAD 40×30cm (16×12in).

***S.* 'Mrs Spivey'** This free-flowering hybrid produces star-like white blossoms in early summer. It has fans of narrow, sword-like mid green leaves, up to 20cm (8in) long. HEIGHT & SPREAD 25×15cm (10×6in).

***S.* 'North Star'** see *S.* 'Pole Star'

S. nudicaule* × *montanum Purple and brown starry flowers are produced for much of the summer. The mid green leaves are up to 30cm (12in) long. HEIGHT & SPREAD 40×25cm (16×10in).

▼ *Sisyrinchium idahoense* 'Album'

S. patagonicum Star-like blossoms are produced throughout the summer. The buds and backs of the petals are brown, but open to bright yellow inside. It has deep green foliage, 20cm (8in) long. HEIGHT & SPREAD 30×15cm (12×6in).

***S.* 'Pole Star'** (syn. *S.* 'North Star') White cup-shaped flowers appear for much of the summer. It has clumps of mid green leaves, 15cm (6in) long. HEIGHT & SPREAD 15×15cm (6×6in).

***S.* 'Quaint and Queer'** Dull purple, cup-shaped flowers with bright yellow centres are produced on a small but vigorous plant. It has mid green leaves, up to 15cm (6in) long. HEIGHT & SPREAD 15×15cm (6×6in).

S. striatum Clumps of grey-green leaves, to 45cm (18in) long, produce strong stems with dense spikes of cup-shaped cream or pale yellow flowers, veined with purple-brown on the back, in mid to late summer. HEIGHT & SPREAD 60×30cm (2×1ft).

'Aunt May' (syn. 'Variegatum') has leaves striped with cream and grey-green. The blooms are produced on slender spikes.

CULTIVATION Grow in an open position in a soil which is not waterlogged in winter. Plant in spring and keep well watered until established. Remove discoloured foliage and fading blossoms.

PROPAGATION Sow seed in a coldframe in late winter or spring, or divide in spring.

PESTS AND DISEASES Usually trouble free.

▼ *Sisyrinchium striatum* 'Aunt May'

Skimmia

Rutaceae

Skimmia japonica 'Rubella'

Star-like, white or yellow flowers, sometimes tinged pink, appear in dense, oval sprays at the end of stems in spring. The small blooms have four or five petals. Aromatic leaves are closely set and semi-glossy. There are male and female forms of these mound-forming evergreen shrubs, with a male pollinating up to five females. The female forms bear berries, which often persist through winter.

Skimmias, which are native to the Himalayas and E Asia, prosper in seaside gardens and tolerate atmospheric pollution. All require moist soil and most need shade or semi-shade from trees as protection from sun and frost.

RECOMMENDED SPECIES AND VARIETIES

S. x *confusa* **'Kew Green'**♀ Sweet-scented off-white or cream flowers are borne in trusses up to 10cm (4in) long. Narrowly oblong to egg-shaped rich green leaves are 6-10cm (2½-4in) long and aromatic when crushed. This male plant tolerates full sun. HEIGHT & SPREAD 45x60cm (18x24in) after 5 years, ultimately 1m (3ft) tall.

▲ *Skimmia* x *confusa* 'Kew Green'

S. japonica. Sprays up to 7.5cm (3in) long of small white flowers appear into late spring. On female plants, these are followed by 8mm (⅜in) wide, bright red berries, if plants of both sex are planted close together. Dense foliage is pale to mid green or yellowish. Narrowly egg-shaped or oval leathery leaves are up to 10cm (4in) long. HEIGHT & SPREAD 50x50cm (20x20in) after 5 years, ultimately 1.2m (4ft) tall.

'Bowles Dwarf' has dark green, slender leaves, up to 4cm (1½in) long. There are male plants, that reach a height and spread of

▲ *Skimmia japonica*

30cm (1ft), and female plants, that reach 23cm (9in) tall and wide. The berries are up to 1.5cm (½in) across. **'Fragrans'**♀ is a dome-shaped male plant that grows to 1m (3ft) tall and wide. Its flowers are scented like lily-of-the-valley and borne in sprays up to 10cm (4in) long. **'Kew White'** is an open-growing female plant with a good show of white berries. It reaches a height and spread of 1m (3ft) tall and wide and does best in shade. **'Nymans'**♀ has off-white flowers and red-tinged stalks with bluntly pointed leaves up to 6cm (2½in) long. It is female and extremely free fruiting, with 1cm (⅜in) wide berries, and is of slender,

▲ *Skimmia japonica* 'Nymans'

open growth. **'Redruth'** is an hermaphrodite but is best pollinated by 'Fragrans' to give open sprays of berries. It reaches a height of 1m (3ft) and a spread of 75cm (2½ft), with upright shoots carrying broad, bright green leaves.

Clusters of creamy white flowers appear in sprays up to 7.5cm (3in) long on the hermaphrodite ssp. ***reevesiana*** in late spring. Dark green leaves, 7.5cm (3in) long and narrowly lance-shaped, often have a pale edge. Matt, deep red berries, which ripen in late summer, are oval or pear-shaped. This low, compact plant grows 75cm (2½ft) tall and wide. It dislikes chalky soils. Its cultivar **'Robert Fortune'**♀ is more widely grown.

'Rubella'♀ has coppery stalks bearing 7.5cm (3in) long open sprays of pink buds all winter. These open in early spring into richly scented male flowers with yellow anthers. Red-rimmed, bright green leaves are 10cm (4in) or more long. This dense, upright plant grows 1.5m (5ft) tall and wide.

▲ *Skimmia japonica* 'Rubella'

'Ruby King' is a male plant with large conical sprays of reddish flowers opening from deep red buds. Narrow taper-pointed leaves are dark green. **'Veitchii'** (syn. 'Foremanii') has fragrant, creamy white flowers in 5cm (2in) sprays into late spring. Large bunches of spherical fruits persist throughout winter. Rich green leaves are distinctly broad, oval to egg-shaped. This vigorous, upright plant of dense habit reaches 1.5m (5ft) tall and

▲ *Skimmia* 'Veitchii'

wide. **'Wakehurst White'** (syn. 'Fructu Albo') has pleasantly fragrant, pale creamy white flowers in clusters up to 3cm (1¼in) across. Up to 25 ivory white berries, each 6mm (¼in) long and 3mm (⅛in) wide, are held in groups. Leathery egg-shaped to elliptic leaves are 8cm (3¼in) long and dark yellow-green above, paler beneath. This low, spreading evergreen reaches 50cm (20in) tall and 1m (3ft) wide. **'Wisley Female'** has whitish flowers. Narrow, pointed berries show well below slender dull green leaves, which are 7.5cm (3in)

long and also pointed and narrow. It has a spread of 1 m (3 ft).

S. laureola Fragrant, hermaphrodite or unisexual greenish ochre flowers appear in 5-7.5 cm (2-3 in) sprays into late spring. The purplish black fruits are rarely seen in cultivation. This low compact species has very dark green leaves of variable shape up to 10 cm (4 in) long. HEIGHT & SPREAD 40×45 cm (16×18 in) after 5 years, ultimately 1×1 m (3×3 ft).

▲ *Skimmia laureola*

CULTIVATION Plant container-grown specimens any time, ideally in early autumn or spring. Choose well-drained soil in partial shade. *S. japonica* ssp. *reevesiana* prefers lime-free soil.

PROPAGATION Take semi-ripe or ripewood cuttings in late summer or early autumn.

PRUNING None required.

PESTS AND DISEASES Usually trouble free. Yellow leaves and shoot die-back are caused by heavy, poorly drained, cold soil or very limy soil. Whitened foliage is a sign of frost damage.

Skullcap see *Scutellaria*
Slipper flower, slipperwort see *Calceolaria*

Smilacina

False Solomon's seal

Convallariaceae

Sprays or clusters of small, star-shaped flowers are carried at the ends of the shoots of these elegant, herbaceous perennials, whose foliage resembles Solomon's seal. *Smilacina racemosa* is the only one of the 25 species native to the Himalayas, E Asia and N America recommended for British gardens. It is quite hardy and easily cultivated in any lime-free, fairly moist soil in light shade. The smaller *Smilacina stellata* may be invasive, particularly on light soils.

RECOMMENDED SPECIES

S. racemosa♀ Fluffy-looking, creamy white flowers in a densely packed cluster, up to 15 cm (6 in) long, appear from mid spring to mid summer, often becoming slightly pink as they age. Arching stems bear almost stalkless, elliptic, light green leaves, about 15 cm (6 in) long. The leaves, which turn yellow in autumn, are alternate with prominent parallel veins. The small berries are red or greenish red and finely speckled with dark red or purple. This rhizomatous plant forms clumps. HEIGHT & SPREAD 75×75 cm (2½×2½ ft).

▲ *Smilacina racemosa*

CULTIVATION Plant in autumn or spring in fairly moist, humus-rich, acid or neutral soil in partial shade.

PROPAGATION Divide in spring.

PESTS AND DISEASES Usually trouble free.

Smilax

Smilacaceae

Grown for their foliage and fruit, these evergreen or deciduous climbing perennials are useful for covering the walls of a greenhouse or conservatory. Those species most commonly grown are tender, requiring a minimum temperature of 3°C (37°F). Their tough, prickly stems, clothed in shiny, leathery green leaves, scramble up supports or wires. The pale yellowish green flowers are insignificant but are sweetly scented. Male and female flowers are borne on separate plants and both types need to be grown if the brightly coloured berries are to be seen at all, which is why the fruit is rare in Britain.

▲ *Smilax aspera*

RECOMMENDED SPECIES AND VARIETIES

S. aspera Spiny stems, growing in a zigzag pattern, are liberally clothed with lance or narrowly heart-shaped dark green leaves, up to 10 cm (4 in) long, with prickly edges and main veins. Fragrant flowers appear in late summer, followed by black or red berries. A vigorous, handsome evergreen climber. HEIGHT & SPREAD 3×1 m (10×3 ft).

S. china Rounded or oval, mid green leaves, up to 10 cm (4 in) long, often turn red in autumn. Flowers appear in late spring usually followed by bright red berries in autumn. A deciduous scrambling climber. HEIGHT & SPREAD 5×2 m (16×6½ ft).

CULTIVATION Plant in pots of a soil-based compost such as John Innes No. 2. Water freely throughout summer, but sparingly in winter. Feed with a liquid houseplant fertiliser during summer. Repot every 18 months. Plants can be grown outdoors in frost-free areas in well-drained soil against a warm wall.

PROPAGATION Sow seed in spring under glass or divide well-established plants in spring when repotting.

PRUNING Cut back excessive growth regularly throughout the growing season.

PESTS AND DISEASES Red spider mite and mealy bugs can cause problems.

Smoke tree, smoke bush see *Cotinus*
Snakeroot, black see *Cimicifuga racemosa*
Snakeroot, button see *Liatris spicata*
Snapdragon see *Antirrhinum*
Sneezeweed see *Helenium autumnale*
Snowbell see *Soldanella, Styrax*
Snowberry see *Symphoricarpus*
Snowdrop see *Galanthus*
Snowdrop tree see *Halesia*
Snowflake see *Leucojum*
Snow-in-summer see *Cerastium tomentosum*
Snowy mespilus see *Amelanchier*
Soapwort see *Saponaria*

Solandra

Chalice vine
Solanaceae

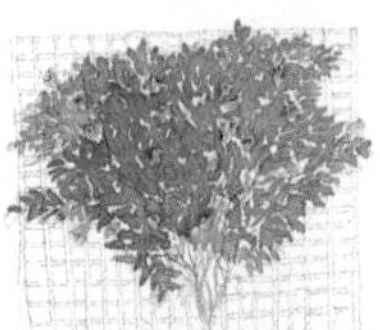

Solandra maxima

Richly fragrant at night, large flowers bloom freely among the handsome shiny foliage of these tender evergreen, woody-stemmed climbers. Grown as specimen plants in the conservatory or greenhouse they like a light position but need shading from intense sunlight.

RECOMMENDED SPECIES AND VARIETIES

S. hartwegii see *S. maxima*

S. maxima (syn. *S. hartwegii*) The large, tubular to funnel-shaped flowers are golden with purple veins, up to 20cm (8in) long, and with undulating petals. They bloom from late spring to mid summer. The mid green leaves, produced during winter and early spring, are shiny but downy beneath, elliptical and up to 10cm (4in) long. It requires a minimum temperature of 7°C (45°F). HEIGHT & SPREAD 12×5m (40×16ft).

▲ *Solandra maxima*

CULTIVATION Plant in spring in pots of soil-based compost such as John Innes No.2. Water freely during summer and sparingly in winter. Feed monthly with a high-potash liquid feed during the growing season. Tie in stems to supports. Regularly remove fading foliage and dead flowerheads.

PROPAGATION Take semi-ripe cuttings during summer.

PRUNING Cut out any wayward shoots as they appear and thin out crowded growth after flowering.

PESTS AND DISEASES Red spider mite and mealy bug can be troublesome.

S

Solanum

Solanaceae

Solanum jasminoides 'Album'

This wide-ranging genus includes annuals, perennials, trees, sub-shrubs and shrubs both hardy and tender, deciduous and evergreen. It contains plants that are poisonous, such as bittersweet (*Solanum dulcamara*), but also useful plants such as the aubergine (*S. melongena*, see p.733) and the potato (*S. tuberosum*, see p.744). The flowers have a prominent yellow centre and the leaves are lance or oval-shaped and sometimes downy.

RECOMMENDED SPECIES AND VARIETIES

S. crispum (Chilean potato tree) Fragrant lilac to violet flower clusters, 10cm (4in) across, appear from mid summer to early autumn. The dark green leaves, up to 15cm (6in) long, can be slightly downy. Round white fruits are flushed yellow. A semi-evergreen vine hardy in mild areas, it prefers shelter. HEIGHT & SPREAD 4×1m (13×3ft).

'Glasnevin'♀ has deep blue flowers.

S. jasminoides (potato vine) Star-like white and lilac-tinged blooms in clusters up to 10cm (4in) across, cover this half-hardy evergreen or semi-evergreen vine in summer. The deep green, 3-5 lobed leaves are up to 5cm (2in) long. It requires a minimum of 3°C (37°F) but may stand some frost. HEIGHT & SPREAD 3m×60cm (10×2ft).

'Album'♀ has white long-lasting flowers and darker leaves tinged with purple.

▼ *Solanum crispum*

▼ *Solanum crispum* 'Glasnevin'

▲ *Solanum jasminoides* 'Album'

S. pseudocapsicum (Jerusalem cherry, winter cherry) Bright orange-red, round fruits, up to 2cm (¾in) across, appear in autumn and winter on this tender, shrubby pot plant. White star-like flowers, up to 1.5cm (½in) across, bloom in summer. The dark to mid green leaves, up to 8cm (3¼in) long, can have undulating edges. This plant needs a minimum of 5°C (41°F). HEIGHT & SPREAD 45×45cm (1½×1½ft).

S. sisymbriifolium (viscid nightshade) Round orange berries, up to 2cm (¾in) wide, are enclosed in a papery covering. Stout, yellow spiny stems have divided leaves, up to 8cm (3¼in) long. The spiny, violet-blue or white, star-like, summer flowers are about 3cm (1¼in) across. A half-hardy annual. HEIGHT & SPREAD 1m×60cm (3×2ft).

S. wendlandii (giant potato creeper) Lilac-blue flowers in drooping clusters up to 15cm (6in) across, appear in summer on this tender, semi-evergreen vine. The stout woody stems have short hook-like spines and bright green leaves up to 25cm (10in) long. HEIGHT & SPREAD 5×1m (16×3ft).

CULTIVATION Plant hardy species and varieties in spring in an open sunny position in a free-draining soil. Plant tender solanums in pots of John Innes No.3, and keep in a greenhouse or conservatory with plenty of light but shaded from intense sunshine. Water freely in spring and summer, sparingly in winter. Feed monthly in summer with a liquid houseplant feed. Mist above the open flowers of species grown for their decorative fruits with water to aid setting.

PROPAGATION Sow seed in spring under glass or take semi-ripe cuttings in summer.

PRUNING Cut back wayward growths in summer. Prune climbing shrubs hard during spring if they become untidy.

PESTS AND DISEASES Indoor plants can suffer from red spider mite.

Soldanella

Snowbell

Primulaceae

Soldanella alpina

Delicate, fringed bell-shaped flowers about 1.5cm (½in) long, emerge in spring on upright, springy stems. The leaves of this hardy, evergreen perennial are generally 1-4cm (⅜-1½in) wide. Native to mountains of S Europe and the Balkans, snowbells spread by runners. They may be difficult to grow in warmer, drier regions of Britain, but do well in Northern Ireland and W Scotland where they need winter cover.

RECOMMENDED SPECIES AND VARIETIES

S. alpina Lilac to purple-blue flowers, are carried in clusters of 2-4 on abundant, upright stems. The leaves are dark green. HEIGHT & SPREAD 15×15cm (6×6in).

S. carpatica♀ The leaves of this plant have violet undersides. The flowers, carried up to 5 to a stem, are lilac to purple-blue. HEIGHT & SPREAD 15×20cm (6×8in).

S. cyanaster The pure blue, widely flared flowers have exceptionally deep fringing. Up to 4 flowers are carried on each stem. HEIGHT & SPREAD 15×20cm (6×8in).

S. hungarica Violet-blue flowers are carried 2-8 to a stem. The leaves can be smooth or crinkled and may be violet underneath. HEIGHT & SPREAD 15×30cm (6×12in).

▲ *Soldanella carpatica*

▲ *Soldanella hungarica*

S. minima Dainty, white flowers with violet markings in the throat appear over a carpet of dull green leaves. HEIGHT & SPREAD 8×20cm (3¼×8in).

'Alba' is white without throat colour.

S. montana Slightly flared, purple-blue flowers are held 3-4 to a stem. This vigorous plant develops a mat of distinctly veined, light green leaves, up to 6cm (2½in) wide, with a prominent notch at the tip. HEIGHT & SPREAD 20×30cm (8×12in).

S. pindicola The blue-grey underside of the leaves help to distinguish this plant, which has lilac to purple-blue flowers. HEIGHT & SPREAD 15×15cm (6×6in).

S. villosa Purple-blue flowers in clusters of 3-4 appear over prominently veined leaves, to 7cm (2¾in) wide. The leaves and flower stalks are very hairy. HEIGHT & SPREAD 25×45cm (10×18in).

CULTIVATION Plant in fairly rich, peaty, well-drained soil in spring in a position with some summer shade. *S. montana, S. pusilla* and *S. villosa* need neutral to acid soil. Water regularly to prevent the roots from drying out. In wet areas, cover resting plants with a cloche in winter to protect them from rotting.

PROPAGATION Divide or remove rooted runners after flowering and grow them on in pots. Plant out the following spring. Alternatively, sow seed in pots in spring.

PESTS AND DISEASES Slugs and aphids attack this plant. It is also vulnerable to rot.

Solenopsis see *Laurentia*

Solenostemon

Coleus, painted nettle

Labiatae

Grown for their brightly coloured, nettle-like foliage, the garden varieties of solenostemons are cultivars or hybrids of the tropical, evergreen perennial, *Solenostemon scutellarioides.* Their leaves are broadly lance-shaped, up to 10cm (4in) long, and variously crinkled and scalloped. The short spikes of insignificant, blue flowers are usually removed. For best results replace plants annually, except those grown as standards.

RECOMMENDED VARIETIES

The species is seldom grown and cultivated varieties are more readily available. Unless stated otherwise, plants reach a height of 60cm (2ft). They require a minimum temperature of 10°C (50°F).

'Autumn' has maroon and green leaves with scalloped edges. **'Beauty'** has crimped leaves, pinkish purple darkening towards the centre and with yellow edges. **'Black Prince'** has almost black leaves and is good for growing as a standard. **'Buttermilk'**♀, with a neat upright habit, has bright green leaves mottled and spotted with cream. **'Carnival'** has green and red leaves with brown marks. **'Crimson Ruffles'**♀ has rich beetroot-red leaves with purple veins and a faint green edge. **'Freckles'** has leaves of red and green in irregular patterns. **'Funfair'** has large, irregular-edged leaves of yellow dappled with pink and white. **'Kentish Fire'** bears small leaves, salmon-pink with a brown halo and green scalloped edges. It reaches a height of 45cm (1½ft). **'Kiwi Fern'** has finely cut leaves of dark maroon with a green and ivory edge. **'Picturatus'**♀ has crimson-red and brown leaves with a green margin. **'Pineapple Beauty'**♀ bears large leaves of lime-green to gold with a dark maroon centre. The leaves of **'Pineapplette'**♀ have a frilled edge and are yellow with red speckles.

▲ *Solenostemon* 'Pineapplette'

Rainbow Mixed is a seed-raised selection, producing a wide range of leaf shapes and colours. **'Royal Scot'**♀ has small, pointed leaves, orange-red with a bright golden edge. **Wizard Mixed** is a seed-raised selection, up to 25cm (10in) tall, branching freely from the base and with leaves combining pink, red, black and white.

CULTIVATION Grow in John Innes No.3. Remove faded foliage regularly and pinch out the growing points of leggy plants to encourage bushy development. Remove flowers as they appear.

PROPAGATION Sow seed of the mixed selections under glass in spring and summer. Take softwood cuttings of these and of the named varieties in spring and summer.

PRUNING To grow as a standard, choose a thick-stemmed plant and remove the side-

shoots. When the stem is 1m (3ft) high, pinch out the top to develop a bushy crown. Later, remove leaves on the stem.
PESTS AND DISEASES Red spider mite and mealy bugs can be troublesome.

Solidago
Golden rod
Compositae

Solidago 'Goldenmosa'

The bright yellow flowers of golden rod enliven a border from summer into autumn; the smaller members of the genus are ideal for a rock garden. Tiny, daisy-like flowers form frothy flowerheads on upright stems. The leaves are generally lance-shaped, mid green and 8-12.5cm (3¼-5in) long. The plants recommended here are hardy herbaceous perennials. Native to the Americas and Eurasia.
RECOMMENDED SPECIES AND VARIETIES
S. brachystachys see *S. cutleri*
S. caesia Clusters of small bright yellow flowers are borne from late summer to mid autumn. The flower stems are wiry. HEIGHT & SPREAD 1m×60cm (3×2ft).

▲ *Solidago caesia*

S. canadensis Tiny, bright yellow flowers are produced in massed clusters on strong stems in late summer and early autumn. HEIGHT & SPREAD 1.5×1m (5×3ft).
***S.* 'Cloth of Gold'** Bright yellow flowers are borne in profusion in late summer on this dwarf plant with strong upright stems. HEIGHT & SPREAD 45×25cm (18×10in).
S. cutleri (syn. *S. brachystachys*) Bright yellow flower clusters appear from late summer to autumn. The elliptical leaves, up to 15cm (6in) long, are sometimes toothed. HEIGHT & SPREAD 45×30cm (1½×1ft).
S. flexicaulis Short yellow flower clusters appear from late summer into early autumn. Strong, erect stems carry oval or elliptical, 15cm (6in) long leaves with toothed edges. HEIGHT & SPREAD 1.2m×60cm (4×2ft).

'Variegata' (syn. *S. latifolia*) has brown and gold stippled leaves and reaches a height of 60cm (2ft) and a spread of 30cm (1ft).
***S.* 'Golden Baby'** ('Gold Kind') Clusters of soft yellow flowers appear from late summer into autumn. HEIGHT & SPREAD 45×45cm (1½×1½ft).
***S.* 'Golden Dwarf'** ('Goldzwerg') Bright yellow flowerheads appear during late summer on strong stems. HEIGHT & SPREAD 30×30cm (1×1ft).
***S.* 'Golden Thumb'** see *S.* 'Queenie'
***S.* 'Goldenmosa'**♀ Deep golden-yellow flowerheads appear from late summer to autumn. The leaves are yellowish green. HEIGHT & SPREAD 75×45cm (2½×1½ft).
S. hybrida see × *Solidaster luteus*
S. latifolia see *S. flexicaulis* 'Variegata'
***S.* 'Lemore'** see × *Solidaster luteus* 'Lemore'
***S.* 'Queenie'** (syn. *S.* 'Golden Thumb') Dense, bright yellow flowerheads appear in late summer. The leaves are pale green and gold. HEIGHT & SPREAD 30×30cm (1×1ft).
S. virgaurea Loose heads of bright yellow flowers appear throughout late summer and into autumn on strong, erect stems. HEIGHT & SPREAD 1m×60cm (3×2ft).

A dwarf form, ssp. ***alpestris*** var. ***minutissima*** reaches 10cm (4in) in height and spread and has small leaves.
CULTIVATION Plant from autumn to spring in any moist but well-drained soil in sun or partial shade. Deadhead and cut back dying foliage in autumn. Lift and divide every 3 years, replanting the outside shoots.
PROPAGATION Divide in autumn or spring.
PESTS AND DISEASES Usually trouble free.

× Solidaster
Compositae

A profusion of small, yellow daisy-like flowers are borne in clusters on tall stems by this hardy herbaceous perennial in late summer. It thrives in well-drained soil, in an open sunny situation. There is only one species in this hybrid genus between aster and solidago.

▼ × *Solidaster luteus*

× *Solidaster luteus* (syn. × *S. hybridus*, *Solidago hybrida*) Canary-yellow flowers are held in rounded, branching clusters. The upright stems bear narrow mid green leaves, up to 15cm (6in) long. HEIGHT & SPREAD 1m×45cm (3×1½ft).

'Lemore'♀ (syn. *Solidago* 'Lemore') is shorter and has lemon-yellow blooms.

▲ × *Solidaster luteus* 'Lemore'

CULTIVATION Plant between autumn and spring in full sun in any well-drained soil. Remove faded flowerheads and cut back old foliage in autumn. Divide every 3 years.
PROPAGATION Divide and replant in autumn or spring.
PESTS AND DISEASES Usually trouble free.

Sollya
Pittosporaceae

Clusters of bell-shaped flowers nod on this frost-tender evergreen climber. Native to Australia, it is suitable for conservatories and sheltered positions in warm gardens.
RECOMMENDED SPECIES
S. heterophylla♀ (syn. *S. fusiformis*) (bluebell creeper, Australian bluebell) Sky-blue

▼ *Sollya heterophylla*

occasionally white or mauve flowers, about 1.5cm (½in) wide, are held in drooping clusters from mid summer to early autumn. The small cylindrical fruits have many seeds. The linear leaves are up to 7cm (2¾in) long. HEIGHT & SPREAD 1.8×1.8m (6×6ft) after 5 years, also the ultimate size.
CULTIVATION Plant in full sun in gritty soil in a conservatory, greenhouse or warm garden where there is little or no frost. Water generously in summer. Grow garden specimens on trellis or among shrubs.
PROPAGATION Take greenwood cuttings in summer or autumn.
PRUNING Cut out any dead wood in winter or early spring and prune to restrict growth.
PESTS AND DISEASES Usually trouble free.

Solomon's seal see *Polygonatum*

Sophora
Leguminosae

Sophora japonica

These hardy deciduous and evergreen trees and shrubs, with their handsome pinnate leaves, give an airy grace to the garden. After several years, they bear hanging clusters of unusual tubular yellow or white flowers. These are followed by long seedpods that resemble a string of beads. The leaves are composed of pairs of oval leaflets. All parts of the plants are poisonous.
RECOMMENDED SPECIES AND VARIETIES
S. japonica♀ (pagoda tree) Rich green leaves clothe this deciduous, round-headed tree. Creamy white flowers are borne during late summer and autumn on mature trees, 30 or more years old. Native to China. HEIGHT & SPREAD 4×3m (13×10ft) after 20 years, ultimately 15m (50ft) tall.
S. microphylla Striking yellow flowers borne in dangling clusters, appear on mature trees in late spring. The narrow evergreen leaves, up to 15cm (6in) long, are dark green. This shrub or small tree is native to New Zealand. HEIGHT & SPREAD 2.4×2.4m (8×8ft) after 10 years, ultimately 6m (20ft) tall.
S. tetraptera♀ Large bright yellow flowers appear before the new leaves in late spring. This deciduous shrub or small tree does best planted against a sunny sheltered wall. Native to New Zealand. HEIGHT & SPREAD 3×3m (10×10ft) after 10 years, ultimately 6m (20ft) tall.

▼ *Sophora japonica*

▼ *Sophora tetraptera*

CULTIVATION Plant in early or mid spring in any fertile, well-drained soil. Choose a site in full sun, sheltered from north and east winds. If training plants against a wall, tie in shoots to supports.
PROPAGATION Sow seed under glass in early or mid spring, or take semi-ripe cuttings in early autumn.
PRUNING None is required.
PESTS AND DISEASES Red spider mite may be a problem, especially on wall-trained plants. Scale insects attack occasionally.

Sorbaria
False spirea
Rosaceae

Sorbaria tomentosa var. angustifolia

Sorbarias are grown for their long, decorative clusters of tiny white flowers with prominent stamens, which appear during the summer. These deciduous, frost-hardy shrubs have a rounded, multistemmed habit. The handsome leaves are long, pinnate and alternate. They are native to E Asia and the Himalayas.
RECOMMENDED SPECIES AND VARIETIES
S. aitchisonii see *S. tomentosa* var. *angustifolia*
S. arborea see *S. kirilowii*
S. kirilowii (syn. *S. arborea*, *Spiraea arborea*) Flower clusters, up to 30cm (1ft) long, are produced in mid summer. Leaves consisting of 13-17 toothed leaflets grow up to 30cm (1ft) long. Native to central and W China. HEIGHT & SPREAD 1.5×1m (5×3ft) after 5 years, ultimately 4.5m (15ft) tall.
S. lindleyana see *S. tomentosa*
S. sorbifolia Tiny white flowers appear in clusters up to 25cm (10in) long in mid and late summer. The doubly serrated leaves with 13-25 leaflets grow up to 30cm (1ft) long. HEIGHT & SPREAD 1m×60cm (3×2ft) after 5 years, ultimately 1.8m (6ft) tall.

▼ *Sorbaria sorbifolia*

S. tomentosa♀ (syn. *S. lindleyana*) Clusters of flowers produced in mid and late summer reach up to 45cm (1½ft) in length. Heavily toothed leaves, comprising 11-23 leaflets, grow up to 45cm (1½ft) long. HEIGHT & SPREAD 1.5×1m (5×3ft) after 5 years, ultimately 4.5m (15ft) tall.

There are more flowers produced by var. ***angustifolia***♀ (syn. *S. aitchisonii*).

▼ *Sorbaria tomentosa* var. *angustifolia*

CULTIVATION Plant from mid autumn to mid spring, avoiding dry or frosty periods, in any good, fairly moist soil. They flower best in a sunny position.
PROPAGATION Divide plants, dig up suckers or take root cuttings in late autumn to early spring, avoiding frosty periods. Sow seed in early to mid spring.
PRUNING Remove dead wood in late winter or early spring or cut back plants at the same time to promote strong shoots and better flowering.
PESTS AND DISEASES Usually trouble free.

Sorbus

Rosaceae

Sorbus aria 'Majestica'

Autumn berries and graceful foliage earn a place for these easily grown, hardy deciduous shrubs or trees in many gardens. They range in size from *Sorbus reducta* at 60cm (2ft) tall to *S. thibetica* 'John Mitchell' at 20m (66ft). Many of the small trees have open foliage which casts little shade, making them well suited to small gardens. The foliage often displays outstanding autumn colour, and clusters of red, orange, yellow, pink or white berries, about 1cm (⅜in) across, add to the decorative effect. The berries do attract birds, although white and yellow berries are reputedly eaten less and so remain on the trees longer. The leaves are either pinnate (divided into many leaflets) or simple (undivided) in shape. The pinnate leaves are between 10-30cm (4-12in) long, while most simple leaves are 5-15cm (2-6in) long with a serrated edge. The flat-topped clusters of small flowers, between 5-20cm (2-8in) across, are usually white or cream, occasionally flushed with pink. They are borne in late spring or early summer and tend to be short-lived. The bark is usually smooth and grey, becoming rougher with age.

S

RECOMMENDED SPECIES AND VARIETIES
S. aria (whitebeam) Silver-white when young, the leaves become a glossy green above but remain silvery white beneath. The ovate, toothed, simple leaves turn brown and gold in autumn. The berries are deep crimson. A multistemmed, rounded tree. Native to Europe. HEIGHT & SPREAD 6×4m (20×13ft) after 20 years, ultimately 15m (50ft).

'Lutescens'♀ has a more conical habit than the species. The young leaves are covered with creamy white hairs. **'Majestica'**♀ (syn. 'Decaisneana') has larger leaves and fruits than the species. It is a vigorous grower particularly when young.
S. aucuparia (mountain ash, rowan) Large clusters of brilliant red berries are always plentiful. The pinnate leaves give rich coppery autumn tones. Clusters of creamy white flowers in late spring have a pervasive fragrance. This neat tree, often multistemmed, is open and graceful with an upright habit. Native to Europe. HEIGHT & SPREAD 5×2m (16×6½ft) in 20 years, ultimately 12m (40ft).

'Aspleniifolia' has more deeply cut and toothed leaflets. The ascending branches of **'Sheerwater Seedling'**♀ give this tree a narrow crown and make it a good choice where space is limited. The large clusters of fruits colour orange-red during autumn.

▲ *Sorbus aucuparia* 'Sheerwater Seedling'

▲ *Sorbus cashmiriana*

S. cashmiriana♀ (Kashmir rowan) The flowers of this small tree are flushed pale pink. The delicate, finely toothed pinnate leaves are rich green above, grey-green beneath. Drooping clusters of large white fruit stay on the tree after leaf-fall. A spreading tree of rounded habit, native to W Himalayas. HEIGHT & SPREAD 4×3m (13×10ft) in 20 years, ultimately 7m (23ft) tall.
S. intermedia (Swedish whitebeam) The large berries are shiny red and the white spring flowers have pale pink stamens.

▲ *Sorbus intermedia*

Simple, slightly lobed leaves are glossy dark green above and grey-green beneath. The stems are grey and scaly and the bark flakes on older trees. A small rounded tree of spreading habit. Native of NW Europe. HEIGHT & SPREAD 7×5m (23×16ft) after 20 years, ultimately 12m (40ft) tall.

▲ *Sorbus* 'Joseph Rock'

'Brouwers'♀ is more upright in habit.
***S.* 'Joseph Rock'**♀ The red, purple and orange autumn colour is outstanding on this small upright tree. The large clusters of berries are a creamy yellow ripening to pale orange-yellow. The pinnate leaves have sharply toothed, narrow leaflets, bright green above, dull green beneath. Native to China. HEIGHT & SPREAD 6×3m (20×10ft) after 20 years, ultimately 9m (30ft) tall.
S. x kewensis♀ Abundant brilliant red fruit hang in dense bunches. The pinnate leaves also give good autumn colour. This tree has an upright habit. HEIGHT & SPREAD 4×2m (13×6½ft) after 20 years, ultimately 6m (20ft) tall.
S. koehneana♀ Drooping clusters of berries

▼ *Sorbus* x *kewensis*

ripen to brilliant white on reddish stalks. The small pinnate leaves on this upright shrub are bright green. Native to W China. HEIGHT & SPREAD 1m×80cm (36×32in) after 5 years, ultimately 3m (10ft) tall.

S. reducta ♀ Clusters of small flowers in spring give way to rose-pink berries. The small pinnate leaves give strong red-bronze colouring in autumn. This dwarf multi-stemmed shrub makes a good rockery plant. Native of W China. HEIGHT & SPREAD 60×60cm (2×2ft) after 5 years, ultimately 60cm×1m (2×3ft).

S. sargentiana (Sargent's rowan) ♀ White spring flowers in wide clusters mature to abundant large bunches of small orange-scarlet fruits. This large tree of rounded habit has distinctive big sticky leaf buds in winter. Matt green, pinnate leaves, up to 30cm (1ft) long, turn a brilliant orange-red in autumn. Native to SW China. HEIGHT & SPREAD 5×4m (16×13ft) in 20 years, ultimately 10m (33ft) tall.

Sorbus sargentiana

***S. thibetica* 'John Mitchell'** ♀ (syn. *S. aria* 'Mitchellii') Green berries ripen to orange or yellow in late summer. The simple leaves, up to 20cm (8in) long, can be nearly circular. Lustrous dark green above with bright silver hairs beneath, the leaves turn yellow in autumn. This large tree has a rounded crown. Native to SW China. HEIGHT & SPREAD 6×3m (20×10ft) after 20 years, ultimately 20m (66ft) tall.

▲ *Sorbus thibetica* 'John Mitchell'

S. vilmorinii (Vilmorin's rowan) The delicate pinnate leaves have a fern-like appearance. They are rich red and purple in autumn. Fruits ripen through shades of carmine and pink to white flushed with pink. This large shrub or small tree is rounded and spreading with slender, arching branches and often grows as broad as it is tall. Native to W China. HEIGHT & SPREAD 3.5×2.4m (12×8ft) after 20 years, ultimately 4.5m (15ft) tall.

CULTIVATION Plant in any well-drained soil from autumn to spring in sun or part shade.

PROPAGATION Growing from seed can have varying results – buy a grafted plant if particular qualities are desired.

PRUNING None required.

PESTS AND DISEASES Usually trouble free, but fire blight can be a problem.

Sorrel (culinary herb)
see HERBS p.333

Sorrel, wood see *Oxalis acetosella*

Southernwood
see *Artemesia abrotanum*

Spanish dagger see *Yucca gloriosa*

Sparaxis

Iridaceae

Sparaxis tricolor

Brilliantly coloured, six-petalled flowers appear in early and mid summer. These tender, bulbous perennials need full sun and a well-drained soil. They can also be grown in pots and kept under glass or moved outdoors into a sunny spot in summer.

RECOMMENDED SPECIES AND VARIETIES

S. tricolor (harlequin flower) Wiry stems carry loose heads of star-like, multi-coloured flowers, up to 5cm (2in) wide, ranging from red, orange and yellow to white. Some have striking gold and red or black throats. The plants have narrow, strap-like leaves up to 25cm (10in) long. HEIGHT & SPREAD 30cm (1ft).

CULTIVATION Plant corms in spring in well-drained soil, covered to their own depth. A south-facing pocket on a rock garden is ideal. Lift after the first frost has blackened the leaves and store in a cool, frost-free place. In mild districts, it may be safe to plant in autumn and leave corms in the ground over winter if protected by straw. Alternatively, plant in pots of gritty, soil-based compost in late autumn or early spring. Keep under glass in a cool but frost-free position in plenty of light.

PROPAGATION Sow seed in spring for flowers appearing from mid summer, or sow in late autumn for flowers appearing from early to mid summer. Alternatively, separate and replant the corms in spring or autumn.

PESTS AND DISEASES Usually trouble free, although autumn-planted specimens are vulnerable to frost damage and soft rot.

Sparrmannia

Tiliaceae

Sculptural, pale green leaves earn *Sparrmannia africana* its place in cool conservatories and greenhouses. This vigorous South African tender evergreen shrub has white summer flowers with prominent red and yellow stamens. *S. africana* prefers cool conditions in winter, but freezing temperatures damage leaves and may kill the plant.

RECOMMENDED SPECIES

S. africana ♀ (African hemp) The distinctly veined leaves, about 15cm (6in) long, are roughly triangular with shallow lobes. They are hairy and almost coarse to the touch. HEIGHT & SPREAD 1.5×1.8m (5×6ft) after 5 years, ultimately 6m (20ft) tall.

▲ *Sparrmannia africana*

CULTIVATION Grow in soil-based compost in good light in a cool greenhouse or conservatory. Water regularly when in growth and feed every 2 weeks. Repot each year until the desired size is reached – use a 30cm (12in) pot to keep the plant about 1.5m (5ft) tall. Train on a trellis if desired.

PRUNING Cut back if necessary to maintain the desired size, but avoid summer pruning which may limit flowering. Pinch out the tips to encourage bushiness.

PROPAGATION Take semi-ripe cuttings in early summer.

PESTS AND DISEASES Prone to whitefly and red spider mite.

Spartium

Leguminosae

Spartium junceum

There is only one species in this genus, a hardy deciduous shrub with rush-like green stems. It grows best in sandy or alkaline soil, and is an especially good plant for coastal gardens. Its tall slender stems make it excellent for the back of a border.

Spartium junceum♀ (Spanish broom) A profusion of fragrant, yellow, hooded flowers cover this shrub from early summer through to early autumn. The flowers appear in loose sprays, up to 45 cm (1½ ft) long, on the current season's dark green shoots. The inconspicuous, mid green, linear leaves are up to 2 cm (¾ in) long. HEIGHT & SPREAD 1.5×1.5 m (5×5 ft) after 5 years, ultimately 3 m (10 ft) tall.

▲ *Spartium junceum*

CULTIVATION Plant in spring or early autumn, in an open sunny position in sandy soil. Deadhead to prevent self-seeding.
PROPAGATION Sow seed in early spring in sandy compost. Prick out singly into 10 cm (4 in) pots for the first growing season, then pot into 13 cm (5 in) pots. Transfer plants to their permanent sites after the second growing season.
PRUNING Cut out any weak growths and snip off the tips of the main shoots during the first season. In early spring of the second season, cut back last summer's shoots by a half. In subsequent seasons cut back all new shoots to about 2 buds annually. Trim shrubs lightly in autumn to encourage early flowering and trim in spring to encourage a compact habit.
PESTS AND DISEASES Usually trouble free.

Spathiphyllum

Peace lily

Araceae

White or greenish arum-like flowers and handsome leaves characterise these tropical, evergreen perennials, grown indoors or in a conservatory or greenhouse. Each sail-like spathe partially surrounds a spike made up of tiny flowers. Plants flower at intervals throughout the year. They do well in warm, humid conditions out of direct sunlight, and so make excellent houseplants for shady corners where many other plants will not thrive. Keep in a temperature of 15°C (59°F) or more.

▲ *Spathiphyllum* 'Mauna Loa'

RECOMMENDED SPECIES AND VARIETIES
S. **'Mauna Loa'** This robust, beautiful plant has leaves up to 30 cm (12 in) long. White, oval spathes, 8 cm (3¼ in) long, surround fragrant white flower spikes. HEIGHT & SPREAD 1 m×60 cm (3×2 ft).
S. wallisii A compact plant with wavy-edged, bright green leaves up to 30 cm (12 in) long, and white spathes and fragrant flowers. The spathes are up to 8 cm (3¼ in) tall. Native to Central America. HEIGHT & SPREAD 60×45 cm (2×1½ ft).
CULTIVATION Grow in a warm, humid atmosphere in a moist, soil-less potting compost. Repot about once a year. Water freely in summer and regularly apply a liquid houseplant feed. Water only sparingly in winter to keep compost moist. Regularly clean the leaves with a little warm milk applied with cotton wool and mist frequently with clear water, especially during summer.
PROPAGATION Divide plants in spring.
PESTS AND DISEASES Mealy bugs can be troublesome, and sometimes scale insects.

Speedwell see *Veronica*

Sphaeralcea

Malvaceae

These hardy and half-hardy perennials and sub-shrubs with an unruly habit bear profuse, colourful cup-shaped flowers. Well-drained, rich soil and an open, sunny site are necessities. Native to N and S America.

RECOMMENDED SPECIES AND VARIETIES
S. fendleri Pale red-orange flowers, up to 2.5 cm (1 in) across, bloom in clusters in late summer and early autumn. This half-hardy sub-shrub has roughly oval, deeply 3-lobed grey-green leaves up to 4 cm (1½ in) long. HEIGHT & SPREAD 1.2 m×50 cm (4 ft×20 in).
S. munroana Apricot-pink to pale red or orange flowers, up to 2.5 cm (1 in) across, are produced in summer. The heart-shaped grey-green leaves are up to 5 cm (2 in) long. Hardy in milder areas. HEIGHT & SPREAD 1 m×50 cm (3 ft×20 in).

▲ *Sphaeralcea munroana*

'Pale Pink' has pale pink flowers.
CULTIVATION Plant in spring in fertile, well-drained soil and in a warm, sunny spot. Remove growth with faded blooms. Cut back dead growth on *S. fendleri* in spring.
PROPAGATION Divide plants or sow the seed of species in spring.
PESTS AND DISEASES Usually trouble free.

Spider flower see *Cleome*
Spider plant see *Chlorophytum comosum*
Spike heath see *Bruckenthalia spiculifolia*
Spinach see p. 745
Spindle tree see *Euonymus*

Spiraea

Rosaceae

Spiraea 'Arguta'

These hardy deciduous shrubs are invaluable for their abundant heads of tiny, starry flowers. Spiraeas may be grown as specimen shrubs and because of their dense growth most also make attractive hedging plants. All are native to the Northern Hemisphere.

Spiraeas fall into two categories: early flowering varieties that flower in spring or early summer on the previous year's growth and late flowering varieties that flower from mid summer or later, on the current season's growth.

RECOMMENDED SPECIES AND VARIETIES
S. ***aborea*** see *Sorbaria kirilowii*
S. ***palmata*** ssp. ***elegans*** see *Filipendula palmata* 'Elegantissima'
S. ***ulmaria*** see *Filipendula ulmaria*
S. ***venusta*** **'Magnifica'** see *Filipendula rubra* 'Venusta'

EARLY-FLOWERING VARIETIES
S. **'Arguta'** (syn. *S.* × *arguta* 'Bridal Wreath') Tight clusters, up to 5 cm (2 in)

across, of dainty white-petalled flowers appear from mid to late spring. The tapering, pointed leaves, up to 4cm (1½in) long, are a bright, fresh green. A dense, rounded shrub with arching stems. It can produce suckers. HEIGHT & SPREAD 1.2×1m (4×3ft) after 5 years, ultimately 1.8m (6ft) tall.

***S.* × *arguta* 'Bridal Wreath'** see *S.* 'Arguta'

***S.* × *arguta* 'Compacta'** see *S.* × *cinerea*

***S.* × *arguta* 'Nana'** see *S.* × *cinerea*

S. betulifolia Dense white flowerheads, up to 7.5cm (3in) across, appear in mid summer. The grey-green leaves are broadly oval and grow to 4cm (1½in) in length. This shrub forms mounds of reddish brown stems. HEIGHT & SPREAD 50×50cm (20×20in) after 5 years, ultimately 85cm (34in) tall.

The leaves of var. ***aemiliana*** have rounded toothed edges and it reaches a height and spread of about 30cm (1ft).

S.* × *cinerea (syn. *S.* × *arguta* 'Compacta', *S.* × *arguta* 'Nana') Dense white flower clusters, up to 2.5cm (1in) across, appear in late spring. The narrow pale green leaves, up to 3cm (1¼in) long, have grey-green, downy upper surfaces when young. Downy, arching stems form a densely branched shrub. HEIGHT & SPREAD 1.2×1m (4×3ft) after 5 years, ultimately 1.5m (5ft) tall.

'Grefsheim'♀ blooms in mid spring. The leaves are about 4cm (1½in) long.

S. nipponica Clusters, up to 4cm (1½in) across, of white flowers with green centres appear in early summer. Grey-green leaves, up to 3cm (1¼in) in length, clothe long, arching stems. The plant forms a dense, bushy shrub. HEIGHT & SPREAD 1×1m (3×3ft) after 5 years, ultimately 1.8m (6ft) tall.

'Snowmound'♀ (syn. var. *tosaensis* hort.) has abundant, dense clusters of flowers. The leaves are dark green.

S. prunifolia Dense clusters, up to 6cm (2½in) across, of small double white flowers appear from mid to late spring. The 5cm (2in) long, mid green leaves, turn yellow in autumn. Arching stems form a graceful shrub. HEIGHT & SPREAD 1.2×1m (4×3ft) after 5 years, ultimately 1.8m (6ft) tall.

S. thunbergii♀ White flowerheads, up to 2.5cm (1in) across, are borne in early spring before the foliage. The narrow pale green leaves, up to 4cm (1½in) long, may persist until late autumn or even winter. A shrub with a twiggy habit and slender, arching branches. HEIGHT & SPREAD 1×1m (3×3ft) after 5 years, ultimately 1.5m (5ft) tall.

S.* × *vanhouttei♀ Flattish white flower clusters, up to 5cm (2in) across, appear in early summer. The coarsely toothed, diamond-shaped leaves, dark green above and greenish blue beneath, are up to 4cm (1½in) long. This shrub forms thickets of gracefully arching branches. HEIGHT & SPREAD 1.2×1.2m (4×4ft) after 5 years, ultimately 1.8m (6ft) tall.

Pink Ice has shrimp-pink new growths and flower buds in spring. The pale green leaves have cream variegation.

▲ *Spiraea* × *vanhouttei*

▲ *Spiraea japonica* 'Nana'

LATE-FLOWERING VARIETIES

S. albiflora see *S. japonica* var. *albiflora*

***S.* × *billiardii* 'Triumphans'** Crowded plumes, up to 20cm (8in) long, of purplish pink flowers are carried from mid to late summer. The oval mid green leaves are up to 5cm (2in) long, with finely toothed edges. HEIGHT & SPREAD 1.5×1m (5×3ft) after 5 years, ultimately 1.8m (6ft) tall.

***S. callosa* 'Alba'** see *S. japonica* var. *albiflora*

S. crispifolia see *S. japonica* 'Bullata'

S. japonica Flattish rosy pink flowerheads, up to 30cm (1ft) across, appear from mid to late summer. The coarsely toothed mid green leaves are up to 8cm (3¼in) long. HEIGHT & SPREAD 1.2×1m (4×3ft) after 5 years, ultimately 1.5m (5ft) tall.

The flowerheads of var. ***albiflora*** (syn. *S. albiflora*, *S. callosa* 'Alba', *S. japonica* 'Alba') are white. Slender, light green leaves grow to 4cm (1½in) long. This compact shrub reaches a height and spread of 80cm (32in). The dusky purple buds of **'Anthony Waterer'**♀ open to crimson flowers, produced until autumn. Some shoots and leaves are variegated pink and cream. It forms a low twiggy shrub spreading to 1.2m (4ft). **'Bullata'** (syn. *S. crispifolia*) has pinkish scarlet flowerheads up to 7.5cm (3in) across, which appear in mid summer. The oval, dark green leaves reach a length of 2.5cm (1in). This variety forms a compact shrub, with a height and spread of 45cm (1½ft). **'Crispa'** bears deep pink flowerheads in mid summer. The strongly toothed and twisted leaves, up to 10cm (4in) long, are reddish when young, turning to dark glossy green. This shrub has a height of 1.5m (5ft) and spread of 1.2m (4ft). **'Goldflame'**♀ bears reddish orange young foliage, turning yellow as it matures. Some of the leaves become variegated, others turn pale yellowish green. Slightly arching stems form a bushy shrub, reaching a height and spread of up to 1m (3ft). **'Gold Mound'**♀ has bright gold foliage and forms a compact shrub with a height and spread of 25cm (10in). **'Little Princess'** bears pinkish crimson flowerheads, up to 4cm (1½in) across, from mid summer to early autumn. The leaves, 3cm (1¼in) long, are bronze when young, turn mid green as they mature, and take on red tints in autumn. This variety forms a low compact mound, reaching a height of 60cm (2ft) and spread of 1m (3ft). **'Nana'**♀ (syn. 'Alpina', 'Nyewoods') produces masses of flowerheads, up to 4cm (1½in) across, from late spring to late summer. The oval leaves, 3cm (1¼in) long, are pale green, turning coppery red in autumn. The shrub forms a dense, compact mound, reaching a height of 45cm (1½ft) and spread of 1.2m (4ft). **'Shirobana'**♀ has flowerheads up to 5cm (2in) across, from mid to late summer. Most blooms are white, with some pink ones mixed in, sometimes on the same head. The leaves are pale green. This bushy shrub attains a height and spread of 1.2m (4ft).

CULTIVATION Plant from autumn to spring in any reasonably fertile soil with the exception of *S.* × *billiardii* 'Triumphans' which dislikes shallow, chalky soils. All spiraeas thrive in full sun but can tolerate light shade. For hedging, set plants at intervals a third of their ultimate height.

PROPAGATION Take semi-ripe cuttings in late summer. Plants with a suckering habit can be divided during the dormant season.

PRUNING Prune early-flowering spiraeas after flowering by cutting out any weak or old wood. Cut back all growth of late-flowering spiraeas hard in early spring. For hedging plants, cut back previous year's growth to 15cm (6in) above ground in the second season. Remove tips of all subsequent shoots when they are 7.5-10cm (3-4in) long. Thereafter, shear to shape annually, after flowering is over.

PESTS AND DISEASES Usually trouble free.

Spiraea, false see *Sorbaria*
Spring snowflake see *Leucojum vernum*
Spruce see *Picea*
Spurge see *Euphorbia*
Squash see p.741
Squill, autumn see *Scilla autumnalis*

Stachys

Labiatae

These clump or mat-forming perennials are valuable for their carpets of foliage and their spikes of flowers in summer. Plant them as ground cover, as edging, or in borders and rock gardens. Most species are best in well-drained soil in full sun. *Stachys coccinea* may not be fully hardy in cold exposed gardens. Native to temperate regions of the world.

RECOMMENDED SPECIES AND VARIETIES

S. byzantina (syn. *S. lanata*) (lamb's ears, lamb's tongue) Thick, woolly, grey leaves, up to 10cm (4in) long, form dense mats. Whorls of tiny mauve-pink flowers are carried in leafy spikes during summer. HEIGHT & SPREAD 40×50cm (16×20in).

'Cotton Ball' is a good carpeting foliage plant that produces spikes of round, silver-white bobbles. **'Silver Carpet'** has distinctive velvety silver leaves with no flowers.

S. coccinea Two lipped, scarlet flowers are borne in the leaf axils in slender spikes during summer. The heavily veined, oval, mid green leaves are up to 5cm (2in) long. HEIGHT & SPREAD 60×45cm (24×18in).

▼ *Stachys byzantina*

▼ *Stachys coccinea*

▲ *Stachys corsica*

S. corsica A hardy prostrate, creeping evergreen plant, suitable for the rock garden, with pale green, rounded leaves up to 1cm (⅜in) long. Pale purple to creamy white, almost stemless flowers, 1.5cm (½in) long, are borne in mid summer. HEIGHT & SPREAD 2.5×30cm (1×12in).

S. grandiflora see *S. macrantha*

S. lanata see *S. byzantina*

S. macrantha (syn. *S. grandiflora*) Mauve-pink, 2-lipped flowers, 3cm (1¼in) long, are carried in whorls in erect stems on this clump-forming plant in mid summer. It needs moisture-retentive soil to produce the green, scalloped-edged, crinkled, oval leaves, up to 5cm (2in) across. HEIGHT & SPREAD 60×25cm (24×10in).

'Robusta'♀ has deep mauve flowers on a compact spike.

S. officinalis (wood betony) Two-lipped, reddish purple, pink or white flowers, 2cm (¾in) long, are borne in mid summer. The plant forms a mat of foliage from which emerge erect flower spikes. The oval or oblong leaves with rounded teeth are up to 15cm (6in) long. HEIGHT & SPREAD 60×30cm (24×12in).

'Rosea Superba' has rose-pink flowers and corrugated leaves.

CULTIVATION Plant in autumn or early spring in any ordinary, well-drained garden soil and in a sunny spot, except for *S. corsica* which prefers moist soil and a lightly shaded position.

PROPAGATION Sow seed in early spring to produce plants to set out later in the year. Divide mature plants in autumn or spring. Take cuttings of non-flowering shoots of *S. corsica* in late summer and pot up the rooted cuttings to grow on for planting out the following spring. Provide protection from winter frosts. Remove rooted stems from *S. corsica* in mid spring and grow them on for autumn planting.

PESTS AND DISEASES Usually trouble free.

Stachyurus

Stachyuraceae

A graceful, arching habit and catkin-like drooping clusters of pale yellow flowers give these hardy shrubs or small trees, which can be trained as wall shrubs, their garden value. Yellow buds first appear in mid autumn and persist until opening in late winter or early spring. Native to E Asia.

RECOMMENDED SPECIES

S. praecox♀ Pendulous clusters, up to 10cm (4in) long, of pale yellow, urn-shaped flowers hang from shiny red-brown stems. Clusters of yellow globular berries follow. The glossy leaves are narrowly ovate and pointed, up to 14cm (5½in) long. HEIGHT & SPREAD 1.5×1.8m (5×6ft) after 5 years, ultimately 2.4m (8ft) tall.

CULTIVATION Plant in autumn in any well-drained, fertile soil in sun or partial shade. Plants do best in humus-rich acid soil, though some lime is tolerated. Provide shelter from cold winter winds.

PROPAGATION Take semi-ripe cuttings in mid summer with gentle bottom heat in a greenhouse. Layering is also successful.

PRUNING Cut weak shoots back to the ground after flowering.

PESTS AND DISEASES Usually trouble free.

Stanhopia see ORCHIDS p.467

Stapelia

Carrion flower

Asclepiadaceae

Large, malodorous flowers at the base of fleshy stems distinguish these greenhouse perennials. Native to the hot, arid climate of east, central and southern Africa, they must be grown in a warm greenhouse. The striking five-petalled flowers, in late summer and early autumn, look attractive but are pungent. The succulent, angled stems branch from the base to form a clump.

RECOMMENDED SPECIES AND VARIETIES

S. gettleffii Yellow flowers, up to 15cm (6in) across, have purple blotches in the centre and purple staining inside the spreading petals. Greyish green stems are toothed. HEIGHT & SPREAD 20×30cm (8×12in).

S. variegata (syn. *Orbea variegata*) Pale yellow flowers with brown blotches and bands inside, and maroon spotting on the

▲ *Stapelia variegata*

petals appear freely on this clump-forming plant. The particularly pungent flowers are 10cm (4in) across. The erect, grey-green toothed stems are sometimes tinged with purple. HEIGHT & SPREAD 10×20cm (4×8in).
CULTIVATION Plant in a free-draining compost in a greenhouse with a minimum winter temperature of 10°C (50°F). Feed fortnightly in spring and summer. Water sparingly in winter. Repot in mid spring.
PROPAGATION Sow seed shallowly in early to mid spring at 18-21°C (64-70°F). Take stem cuttings in summer, brush the cut surface with flowers of sulphur and leave to dry for a few days before potting. Divide established plants in spring.
PESTS AND DISEASES Mealy bugs and root mealy bugs may be troublesome.

Staphylea

Bladder nut
Staphyleaceae

Staphylea colchica

Loose clusters, up to 12.5cm (5in) long, of small white or pink flowers are borne on these deciduous shrubs or small trees from mid to late spring. In autumn the plant produces curious and decorative seedpods that when ripe look like an inflated bladder. These frost-hardy plants are native to temperate parts of the Northern Hemisphere.

RECOMMENDED SPECIES AND VARIETIES
S. colchica♡ Erect sprays, up to 12.5cm (5in) long, of small, fragrant, yellowish white tubular flowers are borne during mid to late spring. Flowers are followed by seedpods. The bright green leaves have 3 or 5 leaflets with shiny undersides and are up to

▲ *Staphylea colchica*

15cm (6in) long. The multistemmed shrub has a rounded, spreading habit. HEIGHT & SPREAD 1×1m (3×3ft) after 5 years, ultimately 3m (10ft) tall.
S. holocarpa Hanging clusters, up to 10cm (4in) long, of white flowers appear in profusion on this large shrub or small tree. Flowers sometimes take on a pinkish tinge. Blue-green leaves, up to 20cm (8in) long, have 3 leaflets. Seedpods are often not very numerous. HEIGHT & SPREAD 1.5×1m (5×3ft) after 5 years, ultimately 6m (20ft) tall.
'Rosea'♡ is very decorative with slightly larger pale pink flowers.
CULTIVATION Plant during mild damp spells from mid autumn to mid spring in moist, fertile soil, on a sunny site.
PROPAGATION Sow seed in compost from early to mid spring. Propagation from seed and cuttings is relatively easy but plants will be variable and if a particular feature is required take semi-ripe cuttings from early to mid summer.
PRUNING None usually required except to shape and remove any dead wood.
PESTS AND DISEASES Usually trouble free.

Star of Bethlehem see *Ornithogalum*
Statice see *Limonium sinuatum*

Stephanandra

Rosaceae

Stephanandra incisa

Admired for their elegant foliage and graceful spreading habit, these hardy deciduous shrubs have alternate toothed or lobed leaves that often give a colourful display in autumn. In early to mid summer, the plants bear tiny creamy or greenish white flowers in branched clusters which are followed by small seed capsules. Their beauty lies more in their foliage and general habit than in the flowers. Native to NE Asia.

RECOMMENDED SPECIES AND VARIETIES
S. incisa (syn. *S. flexuosa*) A graceful deciduous shrub forming a low, rounded bushy plant with a mass of thin zigzag branches whose reddish brown colour is conspicuous in winter. The leaves are up to 7.5cm (3in) long and turn orange-brown in autumn. HEIGHT & SPREAD 1×2m (3×6½ft) after 5 years, ultimately 1.5m (5ft) tall.
'Crispa' (syn. *S.* 'Prostrata') is low-growing, forming a wide mat of interlaced shoots. The leaves are smaller and more deeply cut. It reaches 60cm (2ft) high with an ultimate spread of about 3m (10ft).
S. tanakae A broad deciduous shrub with arching orange-brown branches. Leaves, up to 12.5cm (5in) long, have 3 pointed lobes and are deeply incised and turn orange in autumn. HEIGHT & SPREAD 1.5×2m (5×6½ft) after 5 years, ultimately 2.4m (8ft) tall.

▲ *Stephanandra tanakae*

CULTIVATION Plant in fairly moist, fertile, acid or neutral soil in sun or partial shade in autumn or early spring.
PROPAGATION Take softwood cuttings in summer, alternatively divide established plants in autumn.
PESTS AND DISEASES Usually trouble free.

Stephanotis

Asclepiadaceae

Stephanotis floribunda

Sweetly scented flowers and attractive glossy foliage make this climbing plant ideal for a warm conservatory. It flowers freely if its needs, regarding temperature, humidity and soil moisture, are met.

RECOMMENDED SPECIES

Stephanotis floribunda ♀ (Madagascar jasmine, wax flower) White waxy flowers, 4cm (1½in) long, have 5 petals flaring from a tubular base in summer. Dark green, glossy, evergreen leaves clothe the twining stems. HEIGHT & SPREAD 1-2m×50cm (3-6½ft×20in) in a 20cm (8in) pot.

CULTIVATION Place in good, indirect light, with a minimum growing temperature of 17°C (63°F) and 13°C (55°F) in winter. Keep the compost and air moist but reduce watering in winter. Regular feeding is important for bud formation. A potash-rich feed will stimulate flowers.

PROPAGATION Take softwood cuttings from non-flowering shoots in early summer. Bottom heat, humidity and rooting powder help rooting which may take months.

PRUNING Trim after flowering if needed.

PESTS AND DISEASES Scale insects, red spider mites and mealy bugs can cause problems.

Sternbergia

Amaryllidaceae

Sternbergia lutea

Crocus-like flowers characterise these bulbous perennials from the dry mountains of the eastern Mediterranean. In most cases the long, basal, strap-shaped leaves are produced at the same time as the flowers. Most species open their generally deep yellow flowers in mid to late autumn and although they are reasonably hardy in Britain, all need a warm summer dormancy to flower. Only *Sternbergia lutea* is reliable as a garden plant, doing best in a well-drained limy soil against a sunny wall. Others are best grown in an alpine house or unheated greenhouse.

▲ *Sternbergia candida*

RECOMMENDED SPECIES AND VARIETIES

S. candida Solitary white funnel-shaped flowers, up to 5cm (2in) long, stand on 20cm (8in) stems in late winter to early spring at the same time as the grey-green leaves appear. HEIGHT 10-20cm (4-8in).

S. clusiana (syn. *S. macrantha*) The 7cm (2¾in) long, rather pointed yellow flowers are almost stemless and appear before the leaves. HEIGHT 7.5cm (3in).

S. fischeriana Narrow, 4cm (1½in) long, funnel-shaped yellow flowers appear in early spring. The basal leaves are grey-green. HEIGHT 10cm (4in).

S. lutea The most easily grown plant with yellow funnel-shaped flowers, 5cm (2in) long, in early autumn among bright green leaves. HEIGHT 15cm (6in).

Angustifolia Group plants are similar to the species, but with narrower leaves.

S. macrantha see *S. clusiana*

S. sicula Star or funnel-shaped yellow flowers, up to 4cm (1½in) long, appear in autumn, with or just before the narrow leaves on this variable plant. HEIGHT up to 7.5cm (3in).

CULTIVATION Plant the bulbs in late summer. Plant *S. lutea* 10cm (4in) deep and 7.5cm (3in) apart in a free-draining soil in full sun – the sunny base of a wall is an ideal spot. *S. sicula* can also be grown outdoors in similar conditions.

Pot bulbs intended for an alpine house or unheated greenhouse in a gritty, loam-based compost. Water sparingly when in growth, taking care to avoid overwatering which can cause the bulbs to rot. Dry off completely when dormant.

PROPAGATION As leaves die back in spring, lift and divide overcrowded clumps. Do not disturb established plants unnecessarily.

PESTS AND DISEASES Usually trouble free but may suffer basal rot or narcissus fly.

Stewartia

Theaceae

Stewartia pseudocamellia

Long-lasting displays of white summer flowers and brightly coloured, smooth, flaking bark give these evergreen and deciduous trees interest for many months of the year. The foliage of deciduous species produce brilliant autumn colour. Native to SE Asia and SE United States.

RECOMMENDED SPECIES AND VARIETIES

S. pseudocamellia ♀ (Japanese stewartia) The bright green, finely toothed, elliptic leaves, up to 8cm (3¼in) long, turn yellow, red and purple in autumn. Solitary, 5-petalled white flowers, about 6cm (2½in) across, are cup-shaped and have orange-yellow anthers. As the bark matures it becomes dark red and brown and flakes off in irregular patches. This deciduous shrub or small tree is fairly hardy. HEIGHT & SPREAD 4.5×3m (15×10ft) after 20 years, ultimately 20m (66ft) tall.

▲ *Stewartia pseudocamellia*

Koreana Group ♀ has the best claret-red autumn colour.

S. sinensis ♀ (Chinese stewartia) A large shrub or small tree with bright green oval leaves, up to 10cm (4in) long, that turn red in autumn. The red-brown bark flakes to light grey or pale greenish cream. The fragrant white flowers are 5cm (2in) across, and have yellow anthers. HEIGHT & SPREAD 6×5m (20×16ft) after 20 years, ultimately 9m (30ft) tall.

CULTIVATION Grow in a neutral to acid, well-drained soil in semi-shade. Protect roots from the sun. Shelter from cold winds and frost. Avoid disturbance once planted.

PROPAGATION Sow seed in autumn or early spring or take semi-ripe cuttings of sideshoots, using bottom heat for both.
PRUNING None necessary.
PESTS AND DISEASES Usually trouble free.

Stipa see GRASSES p.302
Stock see *Matthiola*
Stock, Virginian see *Malcomia maritima*

Stokesia
Stokes' aster
Compositae

Fringed lavender, blue or white petals radiate from the disc florets of this hardy perennial, which is the only species in the genus. The flowers make a summer show in a sunny border and the narrow evergreen leaves form an overwintering rosette. A well-drained soil is necessary for the plant to flourish. Native to SE United States.
Stokesia laevis Blue, many-petalled flowers with white centres, 6–10cm (2½–4 in) across, are borne from mid to late summer. Strong branching stems are clothed with narrow, lance-shaped mid green leaves, up to 20cm (8in) long. HEIGHT & SPREAD 90×60cm (36×24in).
'Alba' has white flowers. **'Blue Star'** has deep blue flowers and reaches only 45×45cm (18×18in) in height and spread.

▲ *Stokesia laevis* 'Alba'

'Wyoming' has cornflower-blue flowers. It grows to just 35×35cm (14×14in). Varieties of *S. laevis* have whitish centres.
CULTIVATION Plant in autumn or spring in well-drained soil and in a sunny spot. Apply a slow-release fertiliser each spring.
PROPAGATION Divide plants in spring, alternatively raise from seed sown during late summer or early spring.
PESTS AND DISEASES Slugs and snails may damage the overwintering rosettes of leaves. Otherwise usually trouble free.

Stone cress see *Aethionema*
Stonecrop see *Sedum*
Storax see *Styrax*
Stork's bill see *Erodium*
Stransvaesia see *Photina*

Stratiotes
Water soldier
Hydrocharitaceae

Stratiotes aloides

This hardy, evergreen perennial is a free-floating aquatic plant with decorative spiky leaves. Large colonies of plants are produced on creeping runners. There is only one species in this genus. Native to Europe.
Stratiotes aloides The rosettes of distinctive spiky leaves are rather like those of a pineapple. They are narrow and lance-shaped and up to 45cm (18in) long with sharply toothed or spined edges. Small, white, 3-petalled flowers, up to 3cm (1¼in) long, appear in mid to late summer.
CULTIVATION Place in a pond in spring or summer, allowing plants to float freely, in water to a depth of 30cm (12in) or more. Thin overcrowded colonies. Older plants do not overwinter as well as young ones. In spring when plants reappear from their winter dormancy on the floor of the pond, discard those that are least attractive.
PROPAGATION Divide plantlets in summer.
PESTS AND DISEASES Usually trouble free.

Strawberry see p.730
Strawberry, Indian see *Duchesnea indica*
Strawberry tree see *Arbutus*

Strelitzia
Strelitziaceae

Grown for their brightly coloured, beak-like flowers, held within boat-shaped bracts, these tender evergreen perennials should be kept in a conservatory or greenhouse.
RECOMMENDED SPECIES
S. reginae♀ (bird of paradise) Each orange and blue flower emerges from a 12.5cm (5in) long, green, orange-bordered bract, which produces several flowers in succession, as spring progresses. The bracts are carried at the top of tall, erect stems. Leaves are somewhat bluish green and up to 75cm (2½ft) long. Native to South Africa. HEIGHT & SPREAD 1–1.8×1m (3–6×3ft).
CULTIVATION Grow plants in pots of John Innes No.3 compost, or in a greenhouse border with fertile soil. Ensure plenty of light, but give shade from full, direct summer sun. Keep plants in a temperature of at least 10°C (50°F). Water freely in spring and summer and feed regularly with a general liquid fertiliser. In winter, keep

▲ *Strelitzia reginae*

compost barely damp, especially if only the minimum temperature can be maintained. Remove faded flowers and dead leaves.
PROPAGATION Divide plants in spring. Sow seed in seed compost in early or mid spring at a temperature of 18–21°C (64–70°F).
PESTS AND DISEASES Mealy bugs and scale insects can be troublesome.

Streptocarpus
Cape primrose
Gesneriaceae

Streptocarpus 'Constant Nymph'

Clusters of elegant flowers in a wide range of colours are borne on these tender perennials. The funnel-shaped flowers on delicate stems have five flared lobes. Some have dark veins radiating outwards while others have contrasting white or yellow throats. In Britain, Cape primroses need to be grown in pots indoors or in a cool greenhouse or conservatory. Native to Africa.
RECOMMENDED SPECIES AND VARIETIES
The recommended plants are divided into 2 groups: rosette-forming and stemmed.
ROSETTE-FORMING PLANTS
Rosette-forming plants have basal rosettes of strap-shaped, wrinkled leaves. The flowers are held well above the foliage in clusters at the ends of bare stems. Unless otherwise stated, leaves are about 30cm (1ft) long.
S. candidus Fragrant white flowers, up to 4cm (1½in) across, are freely produced in summer. The leaves grow to 60cm (2ft) long. HEIGHT & SPREAD 25×50cm (10×20in).

S. cyaneus The pink flowers, borne in spring and summer, are 6cm (2½in) across. HEIGHT & SPREAD 25×50cm (10×20in).
S. primuliformis ssp. ***formosus*** Pale mauve flowers with a yellow throat grow to about 6cm (2½in) across in summer. HEIGHT & SPREAD 25×50cm (10×20in).
S. rexii This compact species produces pale violet or white flowers, about 7.5cm (3in) across, in summer. Each bloom has 7 distinct stripes in a deep shade of violet. HEIGHT & SPREAD 25×50cm (10×20in).

Hybrids

Many excellent hybrids are available with abundant blooms and a flowering season which may last from mid spring to early autumn. The following varieties have flowers up to 6cm (2½in) across.
'Albatross'♀ has white flowers, with a yellow throat. The blooms of **'Catrin'** are deep pink, with a white throat. The flowers of **'Constant Nymph'** are violet-blue, with darker veins and a creamy yellow throat. **'Cynthia'**♀ is a free-flowering variety with magenta flowers. **'Heidi'**♀ is a compact plant. Its blue flowers have deep purple markings on the lower lobes. **'Helen'**♀ has pale blue flowers. The shell-pink flowers of **'Lisa'**♀ have a white throat and are produced in abundance. The blooms of **'Paula'**♀ have reddish purple petals and a yellow throat. The flowers of **'Ruby'**♀ are a rich red. **'Sarah'**♀ has dark purple flowers. The petals of **'Stella'**♀ are pink, with red veining. **'Susan'**♀ has magenta flowers with golden yellow centres. **'Tina'**♀ is a vigorous, compact-growing variety. The pink blooms have darker lower petals.

▲ *Streptocarpus* 'Falling Stars'

▼ *Streptocarpus* 'Gloria'

▲ *Streptocarpus* 'Kim'

The following varieties have small flowers, up to 3cm (1¼in) across. The abundant sky-blue blooms of **'Falling Stars'**♀ have white throats and dark veining. This plant looks particularly delicate. **'Gloria'**♀ has masses of pale pink flowers, with slightly darker veining and a white throat. The blooms of **'Happy Snappy'** are deep magenta. **'Kim'**♀ has velvety, deep inky blue flowers with a white throat, and a compact habit. **'Laura'** is an extremely free-flowering variety with pale pink flowers with deep pink veining on the lower petals. The profuse, upturned blooms of **'Snow White'**♀ have yellow throats.

STEMMED PLANTS

These plants produce mostly round or oval leaves, which are attached to the long, slender, main stems in pairs. Unless otherwise stated, the blooms are borne in spring and summer. The sprawling habit of some stemmed species makes them ideal for hanging baskets or in pots on shelves.
S. caulescens Deep purple flowers, up to 2cm (¾in) across, are borne in profusion. The dark green, softly hairy leaves grow to 6cm (2½in) in length. This shrubby plant is upright in habit. HEIGHT & SPREAD 40×30cm (16×12in).
***S.* 'Concord Blue'**♀ Numerous blue flowers, about 3cm (1¼in) across, are produced. The leaves are small and round. This plant has a bushy habit. HEIGHT & SPREAD 30×30cm (1×1ft).
S. glandulosissimus This species bears violet-blue flowers, up to 3cm (1¼in) across. The oval leaves reach a length of 12.5cm (5in). This is a good plant for a hanging basket. HEIGHT & SPREAD 20×75cm (8×30in).

▲ *Streptocarpus saxorum*

S. saxorum♀ (false African violet) Mauve flowers, up to 4cm (1½in) across, with a white throat, appear from early spring to autumn. The round leaves, up to 3cm (1¼in) across, are blue-green, hairy and succulent. This almost prostrate plant is ideal for hanging baskets. HEIGHT & SPREAD 30×60cm (1×2ft).
CULTIVATION Grow in pots of houseplant or potting compost in a greenhouse or conservatory. Situate in good light but protect against strong, direct sunlight during spring and summer. Indoor plants do well in an east or west-facing window. Ventilate well on warm days to prevent temperatures rising above 21°C (70°F). Maintain a minimum winter temperature of at least 4°C (39°F) for rosette-forming types and 10°C (50°F) for stemmed kinds. Plants flower best if root-bound, so repot only when pots are full of roots. Water generously from spring to autumn, sparingly in winter. Avoid splashing leaves with water to avoid marking. Cut stems when flowering is finished. Snap off yellow leaf tips in autumn.
PROPAGATION Take leaf cuttings from established rosette-forming plants in spring or early summer. Take stem cuttings of stemmed plants, ideally in late spring. Sow seed under glass in early spring.
PESTS AND DISEASES Aphids, mealy bugs and vine weevil grubs may prove troublesome. Grey mould can affect plants in autumn and winter. Powdery mildew may be a problem.

Strobilanthes

Acanthaceae

A large group of hardy and tender perennials and sub-shrubs, a few of which are grown for their striking tubular flowers borne in summer above coarse, often hairy or downy leaves. The plants do best in a rich, well-drained soil and in an open or partially shaded situation. Plant in a mixed border, shrubbery or alongside a pond or stream. The genus is native to Asia.

RECOMMENDED SPECIES

S. atropurpureus The tubular flowers are indigo to deep purple and are up to 4cm

▲ *Strobilanthes atropurpureus*

(1½in) long. Flowers are borne in dense, branching clusters on this hardy perennial plant from mid to late summer. The erect, branching stems are clothed with oval to heart-shaped, coarse, mid green leaves with serrated edges. The leaves are up to 10cm (4in) long and 8cm (3¼in) across. HEIGHT & SPREAD 1.2m×60cm (4×2ft).

CULTIVATION Plant in spring in moisture-retentive, rich but free-draining soil and in an open or partially shaded position. Cut off faded blossoms. Apply a slow-release fertiliser in spring.

PROPAGATION Divide and replant in early spring. Alternatively take basal stem cuttings in late spring.

PESTS AND DISEASES Usually trouble free.

Stylophorum

Papaveraeae

Papery yellow petals unfold into saucer or cup-shaped flowers from spring to summer, showing the prominent styles from which this genus is named. These hardy perennial poppies need moist, well-drained, leafy soil and a shady site. The rosettes of lobed leaves may be scorched in sunny sites. *Stylophorum lasiocarpum* needs shelter from wind.

▼ *Stylophorum diphyllum*

RECOMMENDED SPECIES

S. diphyllum (celandine poppy) Four-petalled yellow flowers, up to 5cm (2in) across, open from late spring to early summer. Flowers may be solitary on the top of branched, erect stems or in small loose bunches, with leafy bracts below. The basal leaves are bluish green and grow on stalks up to 50cm (20in) long and form a loose rosette. They are up to 15cm (6in) across and cut into 5-7 deep, oblong lobes, irregularly scalloped round the edges. Hairy, seed cases, 2.5cm (1in) long, droop when ripe. Native to eastern N America. HEIGHT & SPREAD 30-45×45cm (12-18×18in).

S. lasiocarpum Clusters of pale yellow, cup-shaped flowers, up to 4cm (1½in) across, bloom on branched stems from late spring to early summer. The sharply lobed and toothed basal leaves are paired and are mid green and whitish on the undersides. The plant lives for only 2-4 years, often behaving as a biennial. Native to central and E China. HEIGHT & SPREAD 45×30cm (18×12in).

CULTIVATION Plant from spring to autumn in moist, well-drained, leafy soil and in a shady site.

PROPAGATION Sow seeds when ripe or in spring. Seeds may be sown where plants are to flower or seedlings can be transplanted. Divide *S. diphyllum* in spring.

PESTS AND DISEASES Usually trouble free.

Styrax

Snowbell

Styracaceae

Styrax obassia

Profuse clusters of dangling, white, bell-shaped flowers appear in early summer among fine glossy foliage on these graceful deciduous small trees or shrubs. Fairly slow-growing, they produce flowers after about 10-15 years. Rounded, pale green fruits often hang from the branches well into winter. The plants dislike lime and thrive on acid soil. They need a sheltered position.

RECOMMENDED SPECIES

S. hemsleyana♀ Long bunches of flowers, up to 15cm (6in), appear in early summer. The small flowers have conspicuous yellow anthers. The pale green leaves, about 15cm (6in) long, have fine serrated edges. The species is fairly tender, especially when young, and in colder areas needs a sheltered position such as a south or west-facing wall protected by other shrubs. HEIGHT & SPREAD 2.4×1.8m (8×6ft) after 10–15 years, ultimately 6m (20ft) tall.

S. japonica♀ The most reliable of the snowbells has wide-spreading, slightly drooping branches below which numerous clusters of flowers hang in early summer. White flowers have prominent yellow stamens and are seen to best advantage from below. The leaves are oval and glossy. HEIGHT & SPREAD 2.4×1.2m (8×4ft) after 10 years, ultimately 9m (30ft).

S. obassia♀ Large rounded leaves, up to 15cm (6in) long, are softly felted below. The lax clusters, up to 20cm (8in) long, of fragrant flowers appear in early summer. Though fairly hardy the plant needs shelter and should be protected from early morning sun. HEIGHT & SPREAD 4×2m (13×6½ft) after 10-15 years, ultimately 9m (30ft) tall.

▲ *Styrax obassia*

CULTIVATION Plant in lime free, moist but well-drained soil in a sheltered position.

PROPAGATION Sow seed or take semi-ripe cuttings in mid summer.

PESTS AND DISEASES Usually trouble free.

Sumach see *Rhus*
Sun drops see *Oenothera perennis*
Sunflower see *Helianthus*
Sun rose see *Cistus*
Swan river daisy see *Brachyscome*
Swede see p.746
Sweet cicely see *Myrrhis odorata*
Sweet cicely see HERBS p.333
Sweetcorn see p.746
Sweet flag see *Acorus calamus*
Sweet gale see *Myrica gale*
Sweet gum see *Liquidambar styraciflua*
Sweetheart plant see *Philodendron scandens*
Sweetheart vine see *Ceropegia linearis woodii*
Sweet pepper bush see *Clethra alnifolia*
Sweet william see *Dianthus barbatus*
Swiss cheese plant see *Monstera deliciosa*
Sycamore see *Acer pseudoplatanus*

Symphoricarpos

Snowberry

Caprifoliaceae

Symphoricarpos x chenaultii 'Hancock'

These hardy deciduous shrubs are grown chiefly for their graceful habit and long-lasting, ornamental berries. The inedible fruits are produced in white or in shades of pink or red. Appearing in mid autumn, the berries may last into winter. The insignificant summer flowers are rich in nectar and popular with bees. The oval leaves are up to 3cm (1¼in) long. Snowberries are easy to grow and thrive in sun or shade. They may be grown as specimen shrubs or used as hedging. The majority sucker freely. Most are native to N America.

RECOMMENDED SPECIES AND VARIETIES

***S. x chenaultii* 'Hancock'** The tiny, spherical berries are a deep lilac-pink. The young bronze leaves turn bright green as they age. This dense, sprawling shrub is suckering and useful as ground cover under trees. HEIGHT & SPREAD 60cm x 1.5m (2x5ft) after 5 years, ultimately 1m (3ft) tall.

S. orbiculatus (coralberry, Indian currant) Hanging clusters of white or pink flowers are followed by bunches of tiny, deep purplish red berries. After hot summers these may persist into late winter. This species forms a densely bushy shrub. HEIGHT & SPREAD 1.2x1.2m (4x4ft) after 5 years, ultimately up to 1.8m (6ft) high.

The leaves of **'Foliis Variegatis'** (syn. 'Variegatus') are bright green, edged with yellow. It spreads to 1.5m (5ft). **'Taff's Silver Edge'** (syn. 'Albovariegatus', 'Argenteovariegatus') has leaves with silvery white margins. It reaches a height and spread of 1.2m (4ft).

CULTIVATION Plant bare-rooted specimens between late autumn and early spring and container-grown specimens at any time. Plant in any ordinary, well-drained soil, choosing a sunny or shady situation.

PROPAGATION Detach large, rooted suckers between late autumn and early spring and replant in new situations. Take hardwood cuttings in late autumn.

PRUNING In late autumn and early spring, thin out overgrown specimens and occasionally remove unwanted suckers. Cut hedging plants back to 30cm (12in) above ground level after planting. When subsequent shoots reach a length of 15cm (6in), shear back to encourage bushiness. Trim established hedges 2 or 3 times during summer, to maintain a good shape. After about 4 years, cut a few older shoots down to the ground in late winter.

PESTS AND DISEASES Usually trouble free.

▲ *Symphoricarpos orbiculatus*

Symphyandra

Campanulaceae

Symphyandra wanneri

These sun-loving, hardy herbaceous perennials are native to E Europe. Nodding bell-shaped flowers, produced in late summer, are borne above loosely clumped or rosetted foliage. The plants are often short-lived in cultivation and several species behave as biennials, dying after their summer flowering, but they set plenty of viable seed, which germinates readily. Symphyandra need to be grown in very well-drained soil and are ideal for a sunny crevice in a rock garden or scree bed.

RECOMMENDED SPECIES

S. armena A succession of nodding, white flowers, 2cm (¾in) long and with blunt lobes, are held on leafy and rather floppy flowering stems. The 4cm (1½in) long leaves are heart-shaped, coarsely toothed and form a clump at the base of the plant. HEIGHT & SPREAD 30x30cm (1x1ft).

▲ *Symphyandra hofmannii*

S. hofmannii A strong-growing species that develops a large rosette of sharp-tipped, oval leaves, that are up to 15cm (6in) long and coarsely toothed. From the rosette of leaves rises usually one leafy, branching stem that bears pendent, creamy white flowers 3cm (1¼in) long. HEIGHT & SPREAD 60x30cm (2x1ft).

S. ossetica The pale blue flowers are up to 5cm (2in) long and hang from upright, leafy, branching stems. The rounded leaves are up to 6cm (2½in) long and have coarsely toothed edges. The leaves form lax rosettes at the base of the plant. It is reliably perennial in mild areas. HEIGHT & SPREAD 40x30cm (16x12in).

S. pendula Trusses of pendent, creamy white flowers, up to 5cm (2in) long, are held on branched, leafy stems. They have deep, pointed lobes at the mouth. The coarsely toothed, crinkled, narrowly heart-shaped leaves, up to 15cm (6in) long, form a basal clump. HEIGHT & SPREAD 45x30cm (18x12in).

S. wanneri The pendent, mid blue flowers, 2cm (¾in) long, are held in lax clusters on branching stems. The pointed, oval, toothed leaves, up to 10cm (4in) long, form a basal rosette. HEIGHT & SPREAD 30x20cm (12x8in).

S. zanzegura The nodding or pendent, violet flowers, up to 5cm (2in) long, are deeply lobed. They hang from slender, arching leafy stems. The rounded, deeply lobed leaves, about 6cm (2½in) long, form a basal clump. This plant is reliably perennial in milder districts. HEIGHT & SPREAD 15x30cm (6x12in).

CULTIVATION Plant in mid spring in a sunny site in a light, very well-drained soil.

PROPAGATION Sow seed in seed compost in winter or early spring. Alternatively, take cuttings of non-flowering shoots in late summer and place in sharp sand. Pot seedlings on in a potting compost mixed with an equal amount of grit.

PESTS AND DISEASES Slugs and aphids may be a problem.

S

Symphytum

Comfrey

Boraginaceae

These vigorous, coarse-leaved, hardy herbaceous perennials are grown for both their flowers and foliage. The individual blooms are tubular or bell-shaped. Comfrey is mostly cultivated in the wilder parts of the garden, although the variegated foliage varieties are excellent for general border decoration. They are tolerant of most soil conditions and situations.

RECOMMENDED SPECIES AND VARIETIES

S. asperum (prickly comfrey) Showy flowers, up to 1cm (⅜in) long, appear in early and mid summer, opening pink and then turning blue or lavender. This is an untidy branched plant with bristly stems clothed in coarse, mid green, oval or lance-shaped leaves up to 25cm (10in) long. HEIGHT & SPREAD 1-1.5×1m (3-5×3ft).

S. caucasicum A soft, hairy plant with oval or lance-shaped mid green leaves up to 20cm (8in) long. The arching spikes of reddish purple then blue flowers, up to 8cm (3¼in) long, appear in early summer. HEIGHT & SPREAD 60×60cm (2×2ft).

'Eminence' has velvety leaves which are mid green, tinted with grey and short branched spikes of rich blue flowers. It reaches 45cm (1½ft) in height and spread.

***S.* 'Goldsmith'** This hybrid is grown for its broadly lance-shaped leaves, up to 15-25cm (6-10in) long, which are dark green, edged and splashed with gold and cream. In early spring, pink and white or blue flowers, 1cm (⅜in) long, appear. HEIGHT & SPREAD 30×45cm (1×1½ft).

▼ *Symphytum* 'Goldsmith'

***S.* 'Hidcote Blue'** The soft blue flowers start red in bud and eventually turn white. They are produced in profusion during late spring and early summer. This vigorous plant has rough oval or lance-shaped leaves up to 20cm (8in) long. HEIGHT & SPREAD 45×45cm (1½×1½ft).

***S.* 'Langthorn's Pink'** Bright pink flowers, 1cm (⅜in) long, are produced in clusters all summer long on this tall plant. The coarse elliptical or lance-shaped mid green leaves are up to 20cm (8in) long. HEIGHT & SPREAD 1.2×1m (4×3ft).

S. officinale (common comfrey) The leaves of this plant can be added in layers to the compost heap rather like a compost activator. They are oval to broadly lance-shaped, coarse, mid green and up to 25cm (10in) long. The small, late spring and summer flowers are yellowish cream, pink or purple. HEIGHT & SPREAD 1.2×1m (4×3ft).

The flowers of var. ***ochroleucum*** are pale yellow.

S. orientale A profusion of white flowers, up to 2cm (¾in) long, are borne in forked clusters in late spring and summer. The oval or heart-shaped, dull green leaves are hairy and up to 15cm (6in) long. A resilient plant for difficult soil conditions. HEIGHT & SPREAD 60×60cm (2×2ft).

S. peregrinum see *S.* × *uplandicum*

***S.* 'Rubrum'** Small red flowers are produced freely throughout summer. The mid green leaves are broadly lance-shaped to oval and up to 20cm (8in) long. This coarse plant makes good ground cover. HEIGHT & SPREAD 60×45cm (2×1½ft).

S.* × *uplandicum (syn. *S. peregrinum*) Hairy, lance-shaped or oval, coarse mid green leaves, up to 30cm (12in) long, are carried on stout bristly stems. Flowers, 1cm (⅜in) long, are rose in bud and turn blue-purple. They appear in late spring and early summer. A tall, branching plant. HEIGHT & SPREAD 90-120×60cm (3-4×2ft).

▲ *Symphytum* x *uplandicum*

'Variegatum' has leaves boldly edged with cream-white. It reaches a height of 1m (3ft) and spread of 45cm (1½ft) or more.

CULTIVATION Plants are easily grown in any soil that retains moisture during summer. Plant at any time from autumn to spring in sun or partial shade. Remove faded flowers and foliage. Feed sparingly with a slow-release fertiliser each spring.

PROPAGATION Divide established plants in spring. Sow seed of the species in a cold-frame during late summer or spring.

PESTS AND DISEASES Usually trouble free.

Symplocos

Symplocaceae

This large, sub-tropical genus has only one reliably hardy species, *Symplocos paniculata*. A deciduous shrub or small tree, it is grown for its fragrant flowers and decorative fruits. Native to E Asia from the Himalayas to China and Japan.

RECOMMENDED SPECIES

S. paniculata Small, scented, 5-petalled, white flowers are borne in rounded clusters, 2.5-5cm (1-2in) wide, in late spring and early summer. The oval, bright blue or black berries, 6mm (¼in) long, ripen in autumn, but only occur where 2 or more bushes are planted together. Oval, slightly hairy, light yellowish green leaves, up to 9cm (3½in) long, have deeply marked veins and finely toothed margins. HEIGHT & SPREAD 1m×60cm (3×2ft) after 5 years, ultimately 3m (10ft) tall.

▲ *Symplocos paniculata*

CULTIVATION Plant in a warm, sheltered position in full sun in any fertile, deep soil.

PROPAGATION Sow seed in autumn; germination may be slow.

PRUNING None usually required.

PESTS AND DISEASES Usually trouble free.

Syngonium
Goosefoot plant
Araceae

These tropical, evergreen, scrambling and climbing plants are grown for their decorative foliage, as pot plants in a house, conservatory or greenhouse. They enjoy a position out of direct sunlight. A high level of humidity is desirable along with a minimum temperature of 15°C (59°F). Native to Central and S America.

RECOMMENDED SPECIES AND VARIETIES

S. podophyllum (syn. *Nephythytis triphylla*) A scrambling, woody stemmed climbing plant popularly grown as a houseplant on a mossed pole or trellis. The leaves are bright green with prominent pale green veins. They are arrow-shaped when young, becoming lobed as they mature, and can grow very large – as much as 30 cm (12 in) long and 20 cm (8 in) across or more. Plants occasionally produce greenish white to cream or rarely yellow arum-like flowers up to 11 cm (4¼ in) long, at which time the rest of the plant sometimes develops a reddish tinge. HEIGHT & SPREAD 2 m × 60 cm (6½ × 2 ft).

▲ *Syngonium podophyllum*

'Emerald Gem' has dark green, fleshy, shiny leaves that are strikingly arrow-shaped when young. **'Silver Knight'** has silvery green leaves. **'Variegatum'** has bright green leaves splashed with pale green.

CULTIVATION Grow in pots out of direct sunlight in a richly organic, soil-less compost. Repot in fresh compost at least every other year. Provide a support for the climbing stems. Mist plants regularly with clear water, especially in spring and summer. Clean the leaves regularly with a little warm milk and water applied with cotton wool. Water moderately in spring and summer, sparingly in autumn and winter. Feed during summer with a liquid houseplant fertiliser. Remove faded leaves.

PROPAGATION Take leaf-bud or stem-tip cuttings during summer.

PESTS AND DISEASES Mealy bugs and scale insects can be a nuisance, along with red spider mites, especially when growing conditions are too dry.

Synthyris
Kittentails
Scrophulariaceae

Synthyris stellata

Small bluish purple flowers crowded on the narrow spikes of these plants make a decorative impact in the spring garden. The genus is composed of alpines and woodland evergreen perennials and many are fairly easy to grow. The plants retain appealing basal rosettes of toothed and rounded leaves throughout the winter. The recommended species is a woodland plant that flourishes in well-drained, moist soil in partial shade at the edge of a shrub border, in a peat garden or in an open wooded area. The genus is native to western N America.

RECOMMENDED SPECIES

S. stellata Dense, narrow flower spikes, up to 15 cm (6 in) long, are carried on erect stems in mid spring. The small, bluish purple flowers form shallow bells on short tubes and the 4 deep lobes are irregularly and finely toothed round the edges, almost as if they had been gnawed by a tiny rodent. Two prominent stamens protrude beyond the tubular mouths of the flowers and stand out noticeably as they are whitish against the blue petals. The stems of the clump-forming plant are almost leafless, the few leaves that do grow are almost stalkless. Basal rosettes of heart or kidney-shaped, thick mid green leaves, up to 5 cm (2 in) across, are deeply and doubly toothed or shallowly divided and taper gradually towards the tip. The seed capsule, up to 8 mm (⅜ in) across, is almost round. In its native habitat it grows on stream banks and at the edges of woodland. HEIGHT & SPREAD 15-30 × 30 cm (6-12 × 12 in).

CULTIVATION Plant in spring in leafy soil that is moist and well drained. The addition of grit to the soil is beneficial. Woodland plants grow best in a partially shaded position, alpine plants do best in a rock garden in sun. Plants will grow in dry, poorish soil but are less robust and make less of a show.

PROPAGATION Divide the fibrous roots after flowering. Alternatively, sow seeds in spring or when ripe.

PESTS AND DISEASES Usually trouble free.

Syringa
Lilac
Oleaceae

Syringa microphylla 'Superba'

A glorious display of late-spring flowers is provided by these hardy deciduous shrubs and small trees. The small tubular flowers, borne in clusters, are available in a wide palette of colours and many are sweetly scented. All the species listed have mid to dark green leaves. Easy to grow in a sunny position and thriving in town gardens, lilacs make good specimen or border shrubs. Bushier species and varieties can also be grown as informal hedges and screens. Native to E Asia and SE Europe.

RECOMMENDED SPECIES AND VARIETIES

***S. meyeri* 'Palibin'**♀ The lavender-pink flowers of this rounded, compact shrub are borne in numerous small clusters, about 5 cm (2 in) across, in late spring to early summer. The elliptic leaves grow to 3 cm (1¼ in) long. This dense shrub is slow-growing and is suitable for any garden. HEIGHT & SPREAD 30 × 20 cm (12 × 8 in) after 5 years, ultimately 1.2 m (4 ft) tall.

***S. microphylla* 'Superba'**♀ A slender-branched bush that bears small, erect heads of deliciously fragrant, rosy pink flowers that are deeper in bud; these appear in late to early spring, then often again in early autumn. The mid green leaves, up to 5 cm (2 in) long, are oval and pointed. HEIGHT & SPREAD 1 × 1 m (3 × 3 ft) after 5 years, ultimately 1.8 m (6 ft) tall.

S.* x *persica♀ (Persian lilac) The fragrant, soft-lilac flowers are carried in small, erect

▼ *Syringa microphylla* 'Superba'

▲ *Syringa reflexa*

heads up to 7.5cm (3in) across in late spring and early summer. Tightly packed, narrow leaves, up to 5cm (2in) long, are often lobed. This rounded, slender-branched shrub is free-flowering and has a semi-arching habit. HEIGHT & SPREAD 1.2×1m (4×3ft) after 5 years, ultimately 1.8m (6ft) tall.

'Alba' has white flowers and the branches are more slender.

S. reflexa♀ The flowers are rich purplish pink outside, whitish within. These are borne in abundance in late spring to early summer in densely packed, drooping, cylindrical plumes up to 20cm (8in) long. This very free-flowering, upright shrub has oval to lance-shaped, dark green leaves, up to 20cm (8in) long, that have a rough texture. HEIGHT & SPREAD 1.5×1.2m (5×4ft) after 5 years, ultimately 3.5m (12ft) tall.

Syringa vulgaris

S. vulgaris (common lilac) Richly scented, lilac-coloured flowers are borne erect in dense, pyramidal panicles, between 15-25cm (6-10in) long, in late spring to early summer. The ovate to heart-shaped leaves grow to 12cm (4¾in) long. A large, upright shrub or small tree. This species and its cultivars are the most commonly grown members of the genus. HEIGHT & SPREAD 1.5×1.2m (5×4ft) after 5 years, ultimately 3.5m (12ft) tall.

'Andenken an Ludwig Späth'♀ (syn. 'Souvenir de Louis Spaeth') Deep wine-red, scented, single flowers are carried in large heads in mid to late spring. This shrub has a strong, spreading habit.

'Charles Joly'♀ Dark purplish red, double, scented flowers in mid to late spring. Dark green leaves and an erect habit.

'Congo' Dark lilac-red in bud opening to rich pink, single flowers that are strongly scented. The small, graceful heads are very freely produced. Mid to late spring. A rounded bush reaching an ultimate height of 1.8m (6ft).

'Esther Staley'♀ (× *hyacinthiflora*) Carmine-red buds open to single, fragrant, bright pink flowers in late spring. This large, free-flowering shrub has numerous slender, erect stems.

▼ *Syringa vulgaris*

▲ *Syringa* × *hyacinthiflora* 'Esther Staley'

'Firmament'♀ Pinkish mauve in bud opening to beautiful, fragrant lilac-blue single flowers. Mid spring. Compact habit.

'Katherine Havemeyer'♀ Highly fragrant, deep purple-lavender flowers fading to pale lilac-pink are borne in dense pyramidal heads. Late spring. Fairly open habit.

'Madame Lemoine'♀ Compact heads of creamy white buds opening to pure white, scented double flowers are carried in compact heads. Mid spring. A broad bush.

'Michel Buchner' Large heads of clear lilac, sweetly scented, double flowers. Late spring. Broad, open habit.

'Mrs Edward Harding'♀ Semidouble, lilac-red scented flowers. Mid to late spring. Very free-flowering and the best red in this group. Tall and rather loose habit.

'Primrose' Graceful, slightly scented heads of small, single, primrose-coloured flowers. Mid spring. Very free-flowering with a compact habit.

'Sensation' Narrow heads of purple-red, single flowers that are edged with white are

▼ *Syringa vulgaris* 'Madame Lemoine'

▲ *Syringa vulgaris* 'Primrose'

borne in mid spring. Fairly compact habit.

'Vestale'♀ Small, pure-white scented flowers are borne in long, rather loose broad heads in mid spring. Compact habit.

CANADIAN HYBRIDS

These are very hardy, vigorous, disease-free shrubs bearing fragrant, plume-like heads in late spring and early summer. The leaves are broadly ovate and pointed.

S. x*josiflexa* **'Bellicent'** Fragrant rose-pink flowers are carried in large plumes, up to 25cm (10in) long, amid dark green leaves. HEIGHT & SPREAD 1.5×1.2m (5×4ft) after 5 years, ultimately 4.5m (15ft) tall.

S. x *prestoniae* **'Elinor'**♀ Dark purplish red buds opening to pale lilac are borne in semi-erect, slender plumes, up to 20cm (8in) long, in late spring and early summer. HEIGHT & SPREAD 1.2×1m (4×3ft) after 5 years, ultimately 4.5m (15ft) tall.

▼ *Syringa vulgaris* 'Sensation'

▲ *Syringa vulgaris* 'Mrs Edward Harding'

CULTIVATION Grow in full sun in any reasonably fertile soil. Lilacs are particularly suitable for chalky clay. They benefit from an annual dressing of bone meal, then a mulch while the soil is still moist. Remove faded flowerheads in early summer. Bare-rooted plants are best planted in autumn. Container-grown lilacs may be planted at any time of the year, but always check that they are not pot-bound and that they have a well-balanced branch system. The cultivars of *S. vulgaris* need time to become fully established, so do not permit flowering in the first year, and only allow 1 or 2 flowers in the second year. This does not apply to Canadian hybrids.

PROPAGATION Take semi-ripe cuttings with a heel in mid summer. Insert cuttings into a sandy medium in a propagating frame with a bottom heat of 16°C (61°F). Alternatively, the cultivars of *S. vulgaris* may be grafted onto *Ligustrum ovalifolium* (privet). Greenwood cuttings of Canadian hybrids, taken in early summer, root readily in the same conditions.

▼ *Syringa* x *persica*

▲ *Syringa vulgaris* 'Charles Joly'

Pot rooted cuttings into 10cm (4in) pots of John Innes No.2 compost and grow them in a coldframe; plant out in a nursery bed in early spring of the following year. Grow on for 1 or 2 years before transplanting to their flowering position.

PRUNING Ideally, remove the flower clusters as soon as they fade to prevent seed from forming. Unwanted suckers must be wrenched off – rather than cut off – as close as possible to the roots or main stem to discourage further suckering. Do this from mid summer onwards. Thin out any crossing and weak branches from mid autumn onwards. Pinch and shape young shrubs.

Rejuvenate overgrown bushes by cutting to about 1m (3ft) above ground in early winter. Thin the resulting shoots. Flowers will appear on the new growth in 2-3 years. Varieties of rather lax habit may need their branches shortening by a third after flowering.

PESTS AND DISEASES Lilac leaf miners and scale insects, particularly willow scale, can attack the plant. Lilac blight and silver leaf may also be troublesome.

Frost damage kills the flowers and causes die-back of shoots. The damaged parts are frequently attacked by grey mould.

Tagetes

Compositae

Tagetes patula

Crisp flowers in a range of bright yellow, orange and red shades are borne in profusion throughout the summer. These popular half-hardy annuals have few rivals for ease of cultivation and length of flowering. Their value is greatly enhanced by the relative lack of other easy-to-grow, yellow-flowered bedding plants.

Tagetes blooms are borne singly on branched stems. The flowers of African marigolds are much larger than those of the French varieties. The dark green leaves, up to 15 cm (6 in) long in the African varieties and 5-10 cm (2-4 in) long in the smaller kinds, are deeply cut and have toothed margins. The leaves have a pungent aroma which is more noticeable when the plants are handled and the foliage bruised.

All tagetes have a rather stiffly upright habit of growth, but French marigolds tend to be more spreading than African varieties. African marigolds are taller than the French varieties. The species plants are all native to Mexico, and Central and S America.

RECOMMENDED SPECIES AND VARIETIES

T. erecta (African marigold) The fully double blooms, shaped like flattened spheres, grow to 12.5 cm (5 in) in diameter. Colours range from cream, through all shades of yellow, to orange. African marigolds are popular plants for central positions in beds and borders. When purchasing plants of African varieties, choose specimens that have not yet come into flower, if possible, as they may otherwise be rather slow to become established and reach their full height. HEIGHT & SPREAD 1.5 m × 50 cm (5 ft × 20 in).

The **Crackerjack Series** grows to 75 cm (30 in) and the **Discovery Series** reaches a height of 25 cm (10 in). Both have orange, gold and yellow blooms. The **Excel Series** reach 30 cm (12 in) and are in shades of yellow and orange. The **Inca Series** has orange or yellow flowers and grows to 30 cm (12 in) tall. **'Vanilla'** may reach a height of 35 cm (14 in) and is cream flowered. The spread of all these varieties is about 30 cm (12 in).

T. patula (French marigold) Masses of blooms, each up to 6 cm (2½ in) across, are produced in constant succession throughout the season. There are single and double-flowered varieties and many have blooms comprising more than one colour. French marigolds are popular plants for window-boxes, tubs and other containers, and are also often used as edging for borders. HEIGHT & SPREAD 25-45 × 25 cm (10-18 × 10 in).

The orange, yellow, or bicoloured flowers of the **Boy Series** are double, with crested centres. These varieties are up to 15 cm (6 in) tall. **'Orange Boy'** is the most popular. Varieties in the taller **Honeycomb Series** attain a height of 25 cm (10 in). They have rich mahogany petals, with gold edges. The double flowers of the **Jacket Series** are orange and yellow bicolours, with crested centres. These plants grow to about 15 cm (6 in) tall. **'Naughty Marietta'** has single gold blooms, with a maroon blotch at the base of each petal. It reaches a height of 30 cm (12 in). The **Safari Series** grows to 25 cm (10 in). The semidouble flowers are produced in shades of orange, scarlet, yellow and in some varieties are bicoloured. **'Safari Tangerine'** is an excellent variety. The **Sophia Series** has orange, red or yellow double flowers and reaches a height of 30 cm (12 in). **'Tiger Eyes'** has flowers with rich red outer petals and a golden crested centre. It grows to about 20 cm (8 in) in height.

▲ *Tagetes patula* 'Safari Tangerine'

▲ *Tagetes tenuifolia*

T. tenuifolia (syn. *T. signata*) Masses of small single flowers, up to 2.5 cm (1 in) across, are produced in a range of bright colours. This species is very bushy in habit and the blooms appear in such profusion that the plants can look like balls of flowers. They are often used to edge borders. HEIGHT & SPREAD 30 × 30 cm (12 × 12 in).

The **Gem Series** has orange or yellow flowers. **'Golden Gem'** and **'Lemon Gem'** are two popular varieties. The blooms of **'Starfire Mixed'** appear in a range of colours – red, yellow and bicoloured.

OTHER HYBRIDS

Afro-French marigolds are hybrids between varieties of *T. erecta* and *T. patula* and they include some of the most commonly grown of all tagetes. These plants are similar in habit to French marigolds, but are somewhat taller. The flowers grow to 7.5 cm (3 in) in diameter and are produced all through the season. The varieties included here reach a height of up to 35 cm (14 in) and spread of 30 cm (12 in).

The mahogany flowers of **'Red Seven Star'** are double. The **Solar Series** produce yellow or orange double flowers. The blooms of the **Zenith Series** are double, and are orange, yellow or bicoloured.

CULTIVATION Plant in early summer, when the risk of frosts has passed, in full sun in any ordinary garden soil. Overfeeding encourages foliage at the expense of the flowers.

Deadhead African varieties regularly to remove unsightly flowers and encourage continued flowering. Deadhead French varieties from time to time to ensure that the succession of blooms is carried on as long as possible. Water all varieties thoroughly in prolonged dry spells.

PROPAGATION Sow seed under glass: sow African varieties in mid spring and all other varieties from early spring onwards. Maintain a minimum temperature 20°C (68°F) to ensure rapid germination. Prick out seedlings 5 cm (2 in) apart in seed trays. Harden off in a coldframe or cloche and keep the seedlings well watered. Feed with any general purpose liquid feed.

PESTS AND DISEASES Tagetes are susceptible to slug and snail attack, especially during the period immediately after planting if the weather is wet. Aphids may infest the plants. In hot summers, red spider mite may become troublesome.

Grey mould may infect the centres of the flowers of African marigolds in prolonged wet weather, causing the flowerheads to decay and turn brown.

Taiwania

Taxodiaceae

Taiwania cryptomerioides

These conical to columnar, slow-growing evergreen conifers make ideal specimen trees. Their upward-curving branches bear drooping branchlets, covered in needles. Not fully hardy, taiwanias need a warm, humid sheltered site, such as at the foot of a slope or in a moist valley. There is only one species, native to Taiwan, in this genus.

T. cryptomerioides This very beautiful tree grows into a column of silver-grey foliage. The drooping whip-like branchlets are covered with sharp, pointed needles that curve forwards towards the branch tip. Male and female flowers are borne together on the same tree in spring. The male flowers are tiny, tight green clusters, often bunched together, while the female flowers are tiny single green clusters. The round cones rarely appear in Britain but if seen, they are 1.5cm (½in) across, green at first, ripening to brown in the autumn. The reddish brown bark peels off the trunk in loose strips. Long cold spells can kill the foliage but the tree will recover given time. HEIGHT & SPREAD 2.7×1.2m (9×4ft) after 20 years, ultimately 12m (40ft).

CULTIVATION Plant specimens that are at least 30cm (1ft) tall in late spring. The trees prefer soil that is acid and moist but well drained, although they will grow on the heaviest of clay soils.

Choose a site sheltered from the morning sun in winter but which is particularly warm and humid in summer. A position sheltered from cold winds is also necessary.

PROPAGATION Sow seed in a coldframe in spring. Alternatively take hardwood cuttings in autumn.

PRUNING None usually required except the removal of dead or frost-damaged wood.

PESTS AND DISEASES Usually trouble free.

▲ *Taiwania cryptomerioides*

Tamarix

Tamarisk

Tamaricaceae

Tamarix tetrandra

Tiny pink flowers in slender plume-like sprays cover these hardy, deciduous small trees and shrubs. Small, scale-like leaves are carried on fine, slender branches that bend easily in the wind. These plants are ideal for seaside locations as they tolerate salt and strong winds and can act as effective windbreaks. They are unsuitable for heavy soil but are tolerant of drought.

RECOMMENDED SPECIES AND VARIETIES

T. ramosissima (syn. *T. pentandra*) Feathery pink flowers in tresses 7.5cm (3in) long are borne on the current season's shoots in late summer. The tiny leaves are pale grey-green. Young branches are green but soon age to red-brown. Plants grow rapidly to their maximum height then spread sideways by arching outwards. They have a suckering habit. HEIGHT & SPREAD 5×6m (16×20ft) after 10 years, also the ultimate size.

'Pink Cascade' produces a spectacular display of pink flowers which can obscure all the mid green foliage in late summer.

'Rubra'♀ (syn. 'Summer Glow') produces a mass of deep pink flowers.

T. tetrandra♀ Numerous feathery sprays, 5cm (2in) long, of light pink flowers are borne on the previous season's wood during spring and early summer. The shrub forms a loose, open bush with arching branches, covered in tiny, pale green leaves. HEIGHT & SPREAD 4×4m (13×13ft) after 10 years, also the ultimate size.

▲ *Tamarix ramosissima*

CULTIVATION Plant between late autumn and early spring. The plants grow best in full sun in any well-drained soil.

PROPAGATION Take hardwood cuttings in autumn, preferably using a sandy rooting medium. Plant out the following spring.

PRUNING For use as a windbreak, cut back *T. ramosissima* hard in spring once new growth commences and cut back *T. tetrandra* after flowering. This will also encourage strong flowering shoots.

PESTS AND DISEASES Usually trouble free.

▲ *Tamarix tetrandra*

Tanacetum
Compositae

Yellow disc florets and white, pink, purple or red ray florets (petals) or button-like yellow flowers highlight the hardy annual and perennial plants in summer. Many have decorative and scented leaves. All the plants require well-drained soil and an open sunny position. Some, including invasive tansy, contribute character to a wild garden or herb garden, while the neat habit of others fits them for a place in a rock garden. The majority embellish a mixed border.

RECOMMENDED SPECIES AND VARIETIES

T. ***argenteum*** A mass of small, white, daisy-like flowers with yellow centres is produced from mid to late summer. This low-growing, mat-forming perennial has finely cut and crimped silvery grey leaves, up to 7.5cm (3in) long. HEIGHT & SPREAD 20×30cm (8×12in).

The finely cut, silvery foliage of ssp. ***canum*** forms tight, low mounds. The plant, ideal for a rock garden, grows to 15cm (6in) tall. Remove the flowers to retain the quality of the foliage.

T. ***balsamita*** (alecost, costmary) Tiny yellow disc flowers, surrounded by white ray florets, bloom in profusion in late summer on this aromatic herbaceous perennial, which is suitable for a herb garden. The elliptical mid green leaves, up to 25cm (10in) long, have rounded toothed edges. HEIGHT & SPREAD 75×45cm (30×18in).

The flowers of ssp. *balsamita* (syn. var. *tanacetoides*) look like tiny yellow buttons because there are no white ray florets round the yellow centres. The leaves and stems of ssp. *balsamitoides* (syn. *tomentosum*) are hairy. It has yellow, button-like flowers.

T. ***cinerariifolium*** (Dalmatian pyrethrum) White ray florets fan out from yellow centres on flowers, up to 2.5-4cm (1-1½in) across, that bloom from mid to late summer. This slender-stemmed herbaceous perennial has deeply cut, lance-shaped, pungent, grey-green leaves, up to 20cm (8in) long, with white downy undersides. HEIGHT & SPREAD 45×30cm (18×12in).

T. ***coccineum*** (syn. *Pyrethrum roseum*) (pyrethrum) Bold yellow centres contrast with white, pink, purple and red ray florets on single flowers, up to 7.5cm (3in) across, produced in late spring and early summer. Robust, erect stems carry finely divided, bright green, aromatic leaves, up to 10cm (4in) long, on this hardy herbaceous perennial. HEIGHT & SPREAD 75×60cm (30×24in).

▲ *Tanacetum coccineum* 'James Kelway'

'Brenda'♀ carries magenta-pink flowers; **'Bressingham Red'** has bright red flowers; **'Eileen May Robinson'**♀ produces pink flowers; **'James Kelway'**♀ displays deep scarlet flowers; **'Robinson's Pink'** has pink flowers; **'Robinson's Red'** has red flowers; **'Snow Cloud'** has white flowers. Apart from 'Eileen May Robinson', which grows to 75cm (30in) tall, all these varieties reach a height of 60cm (24in) tall.

T. ***corymbosum*** Groups of 3-15 yellow-centred white flowers, up to 1cm (⅜in) across, appear in mid summer on this herbaceous perennial. Much divided and sharply toothed, mid green leaves, up to 5cm (2in) long, are borne on erect branching stems. HEIGHT & SPREAD 60×45cm (24×18in).

▲ *Tanacetum densum*

T. ***densum*** Tiny, yellow, daisy-like flowers, bloom on heads, 7.5cm (3in) across, from mid to late summer. This shrubby, clump-forming perennial is evergreen in sheltered areas. The oval silvery grey-green leaves, up to 5cm (2in) long, are deeply cut. HEIGHT & SPREAD 30×30cm (18×18in).

The leaves of ssp. *amani* are grey and hairy. Remove the yellow flowers to retain the quality of the foliage. The plant reaches a height of 20cm (8in).

T. ***haradjanii*** Terminal clusters of small, bright yellow, button-like late-summer flowers are supported by broadly lance-shaped and much divided silvery grey leaves, up to 5cm (2in) long. A rock garden is a suitable place to grow this hardy, shrubby, mat-forming evergreen perennial. HEIGHT & SPREAD 30×30cm (12×12in).

T. ***macrophyllum*** Small white blossoms with a yellowish tinge appear in dense clusters in mid summer. This hardy herbaceous perennial, suitable for a wild garden, has coarsely toothed lance-shaped leaves, up to 20cm (8in) long, HEIGHT & SPREAD 90×60cm (36×24in).

T. ***parthenium*** **'Aureum'** (syn. *Chrysanthemum parthenium*) (golden feverfew) The profuse single, daisy-like white blossoms, up to 1cm (⅜in) across, are tinged with gold and appear throughout summer. Remove them to retain the quality of the bright golden, deeply cut, oval leaves, up to 7.5cm (3in) long. This shrubby perennial is short-lived. HEIGHT & SPREAD 45×30cm (18×12in).

▲ *Tanacetum parthenium* 'Plenum'

'Plenum' has white double flowers. **'White Bonnet'** has ivory white double flowers and grows to 30cm (12in) tall.

T. ***vulgare*** (tansy) Clusters of tiny button-like mustard-yellow flowers appear from late summer to autumn. This strongly aromatic hardy herbaceous perennial has much divided and deeply toothed, bright green, lance-shaped leaves, up to 15cm (6in) long. It spreads prettily in a wild garden, but needs careful placing in a herb garden. HEIGHT & SPREAD 1.2m×60cm (4×2ft).

Up to 60cm (24in) tall, var. ***crispum*** (crisp-leafed tansy) has crisp, fern-like leaves. **'Silver Lace'** has silvery variegated foliage that fades as summer progresses.

▲ *Tanacetum vulgare*

CULTIVATION Plant in spring in well-drained soil in an open, sunny spot. Overwinter the hairy or grey-leaved kinds as rooted cuttings in a coldframe or unheated greenhouse. Remove the flowers from plants grown for their decorative leaves. Remove faded blossoms from plants cultivated for their flowers. Apply a slow-release fertiliser sparingly in early spring.
PROPAGATION Sow seed of the species in spring. Raise *T. parthenium* 'Aureum' from seed in spring. Divide herbaceous perennials in spring. Take softwood cuttings of shrubby perennials in spring or summer.
PESTS AND DISEASES Usually trouble free.

Tangerine see *Citrus reticulata*
Tansy see *Tanacetum vulgare*
Tarragon see HERBS p.333

Taxodium

Swamp cypress
Taxodiaceae

These graceful deciduous trees that thrive in waterlogged conditions can surround their trunks with upright roots that have been likened to standing otters. The roots emerge from undisturbed ground or water and can grow up to 1m (3ft) tall over 40 years. The trees are the ideal conifer for wet conditions, but are too large for many private gardens. In autumn the foliage turns rusty orange or rich brown. Rounded, woody cones are sometimes produced. Native to SE North America.

RECOMMENDED SPECIES AND VARIETIES
T. ascendens (pond cypress) The foliage of this narrow, conical-shaped tree feels and looks rather like new grass. The tree is slightly tender in Britain and late frosts may check its growth without killing it. HEIGHT & SPREAD 2m×80cm (6½ft×32in) after 5 years, ultimately 25m (80ft) tall.

'Nutans' (syn. *T. distichum* 'Nutans') has upright, feathery foliage. The branchlets nod in mid summer.

T. distichum♀ (swamp cypress) This fast-growing tree with a broadly conical habit has reddish brown, fibrous bark. The trunk can be swollen and reinforced at the base. HEIGHT & SPREAD 5×2m (16×6½ft) after 10 years, ultimately 40m (130ft) tall.
CULTIVATION Grow in any lime-free, waterlogged soil, including heavy, sticky clays. Protect young trees from frost with straw, bracken or a floating cloche.
PROPAGATION Sow seed in mid to late spring in lime-free soil under glass. Plant outside in autumn of the following year. Alternatively, take hardwood cuttings in autumn. Use a rooting hormone and grow in a heated bed.
PRUNING None is required.
PESTS AND DISEASES Grey squirrels may strip the bark of young trees.

▼ *Taxodium distichum*

Taxus

Yew
Taxaceae

Taxus baccata 'Dovastoniana'

Evergreen trees and shrubs, yews range in habit from low-growing, ground-cover plants to large trees. They are fine plants for hedging or topiary. Their foliage may be green, yellow or variegated according to variety. Tolerant of most soil conditions, yews thrive in sun or shade, though most yellow cultivars scorch in hot sun. Yew plants are either male or female. After pollination the minute flowers of female plants develop a single seed, enclosed in a fleshy, berry-like aril. This decorative, scarlet fruit may be as large as 1cm (⅜in) across. Most parts of yews are poisonous.

RECOMMENDED SPECIES AND VARIETIES
T. baccata♀ (common yew, English yew) The leaves are flattened needles, 3cm (1¼in) long, ending in a fine point. They spread out from the twigs in 2 ranks. Each leaf is dark green above with 2 pale green bands beneath. The bark flakes off to show purple-brown scars. HEIGHT & SPREAD 1.5m×60cm (5×2ft) after 5 years, ultimately 20m (66ft) tall.

'Adpressa Variegata'♀ is a male plant (no berries) with leaves only 1cm (⅜in) long. The new shoots in spring are entirely golden. The ranked needles of the mature foliage are golden with a green line down the middle. **'Dovastoniana'**♀ (Westfelton yew) grows into an elegant, very widely spreading tree, having long branches with weeping sideshoots. The ranked needles are very dark green, almost black, and the tree is usually female. The berries are mostly borne on the pendulous sideshoots, making the whole tree very attractive in autumn. In 5 years it may grow to 50cm (20in) high and 2m (6½ft) wide, but it will reach an ultimate height of 7m (23ft) **'Dovastonii Aurea'**♀ is a superb male form. Its new pendulous growth in spring is golden yellow, and ripens eventually to pale green needles with bright yellow margins. The dense, ranked foliage of **'Elegantissima'**♀ is pale green; the young foliage is deep gold.

▲ *Taxus baccata* 'Dovastoniana'

▲ *Taxus baccata* 'Elegantissima'

In 5 years this tree may reach a height and spread of 2m (6½ft). There are male and female clones. **'Fastigiata'**♀ (syn. 'Hibernica') (Irish yew) has very dark green needles on steeply ascending, almost vertical branches. With age these branches tend to broaden out. Needles are radially arranged and the tree has male and female forms. In 5 years it grows to 1.5m (5ft) high and 50cm (20in) wide. **'Fastigiata Aureomarginata'**♀, a female clone, is upright-growing and has well-defined, golden margins on its younger needles. Older leaves, growing on the inside of the plant, are dark green with pale green margins. **'Repandens'**♀ is a low, spreading bush with dense foliage. Its branches droop at the ends. It is a good ground-cover plant. The ranked needles, 3cm (1¼in) long, have

a glossy dark green upper surface. This female cultivar reaches 30cm (1ft) high and 1m (3ft) across after 5 years. **'Semperaurea'**♀ is a dense, spreading shrubby bush. The branches sweep up, and each one is covered with radially arranged, deep golden leaves, which turn rusty yellow when mature. In 5 years this male cultivar reaches 50cm (20in) high and 1m (3ft) wide. **'Standishii'**♀ is a tightly packed golden column. The variety is always female. The needles are radially arranged and remain bright yellow throughout the year. It requires full sun and makes a good container plant. In 5 years it reaches a height of 1m (3ft) and a width of 18cm (7in). **'Summergold'** is a broad, flat shrub. The needles are ranked, and each one has a yellow border, the centre of the needle being a fine, green line. The new growth of this male clone is all yellow. In 5 years it will be 50cm (20in) high and 1.5m (5ft) wide. This is one of the few golden ground-cover plants that prefer full afternoon sun.

***T. × media* 'Hicksii'** This very vigorous semi-upright tree is excellent for hedging. It has glossy dark green, radially arranged leaves. HEIGHT & SPREAD 2×1m (6½×3ft) after 5 years, ultimately 8m (26ft) tall.

▼ *Taxus baccata* 'Fastigiata Aureomarginata'

CULTIVATION Plant in any soil that is not waterlogged. Green-leaved varieties may be planted in full sun or deep shade. Afternoon sun should be avoided for golden leaved varieties except 'Standishii' and 'Summergold', though heavy shade will make them more green than yellow. For hedging, plant *T. baccata* or *T. × media* 'Hicksii' 50-80cm (20-32in) apart. Deep planting will kill yews, so make sure that the root collar is at, or slightly above, ground level, even after mulching.

PROPAGATION Take hardwood cuttings in autumn or softwood cuttings in spring. Do not overwater, and disturb the roots as little as possible when potting on.

PRUNING Pruning of yews grown as trees or shrubs is not necessary, except to maintain shape and size. Clip hedges and topiary twice in a season: a heavy cut in late spring and a light cut in late summer. Larger yews can be pruned back almost to a stump even when quite old. Heavy pruning should only be carried out in mid spring.

PESTS AND DISEASES Phytophthora root rot and die-back affect yews.

Teasel see *Dipsacus*
Tea tree see *Leptospermum*

Tecoma

Bignoniaceae

This genus of tropical and sub-tropical trees and shrubs bears brightly coloured flowers. Grown in a conservatory or greenhouse, they need full light and a minimum temperature of 10°C (50°F).

RECOMMENDED SPECIES AND VARIETIES

T. capensis♀ (syn. *Tecomaria capensis*) (Cape honeysuckle) This evergreen scrambler produces orange-red tubular blooms 5cm (2in) long through spring and summer. It has glossy, dark green, pinnate leaves, comprising 5-9 leaflets 2-4cm (¾-1½in) long. HEIGHT & SPREAD 3×1m (10×3ft).

'Aurea' has golden yellow flowers.

CULTIVATION Grow in a greenhouse or conservatory in a large pot or in a border using John Innes No.2 compost. Water freely in spring and summer, sparingly in autumn and winter. Feed with a liquid general fertiliser in summer. Remove faded flowers and leaves regularly.

PROPAGATION Sow seed in spring or take semi-ripe cuttings in summer.

▲ *Tecoma capensis*

PRUNING Control growth by pinching back regularly in summer.

PESTS AND DISEASES Red spider mite can be troublesome.

Tecomaria see *Tecoma*

Telekia

Compositae

This hardy, coarse-growing herbaceous perennial produces shaggy heads of bright yellow or orange-yellow daisy-like flowers in late summer. The untidy habit makes it most suited to a larger herbaceous border or wild garden where there is plenty of space.

▲ *Telekia speciosa*

RECOMMENDED SPECIES

T. speciosa (syn. *Buphthalmum speciosum*) Golden yellow flowers, up to 5cm (2in) across, are borne in clusters during late summer. It has heart-shaped or oval leaves, up to 30cm (1ft) long, with toothed edges. HEIGHT & SPREAD 1.2-1.8×1m (4-6×3ft).

CULTIVATION Plant between autumn and spring in any type of soil and keep moist. It will grow in either sun or shade, but can flag badly in full sun. Apply a slow-release fertiliser in spring. Cut off dead flowers.

PROPAGATION Divide plants in autumn or spring or sow seed in a coldframe during late summer or spring.

PESTS AND DISEASES Usually trouble free.

Tellima

Fringe cup
Saxifragaceae

A hardy, herbaceous perennial, flowering in late spring and early summer, tellima is a woodland native of western N America, as far north as Alaska. Suited to cool, shady conditions, it associates well with hardy ferns. Easily grown and forming compact clumps, tellima plants can be massed to create good ground cover. The genus has only one species.

▲ *Tellima grandiflora*

Tellima grandiflora Upright stems are dotted with small, bell-shaped flowers, about 6mm (¼in) across, with fringed, yellow-green petals, which turn deep pink with age. The fruit is a small green capsule. The light green, hairy leaves at the base of the stems are rounded with several triangular lobes and grow to 10cm (4in) wide. Tellima is frost-hardy but may be damaged in cold northern gardens. HEIGHT & SPREAD 75×30cm (2½×1ft).

Odorata Group has flowers with a slight but distinct sweet scent. **Rubra Group** (syn.'Purpurea') contains forms in which the foliage is tinged with purplish red especially in winter.

CULTIVATION Plant in any well-drained soil in a cool, partially shaded position. Tellimas are fairly tolerant of dry soil but do better in slightly moist conditions. They tolerate fairly deep shade but produce fewer flowers.

PROPAGATION Divide plants in early autumn or spring.

PESTS AND DISEASES Usually trouble free.

t

Teucrium

Germander
Labiatae

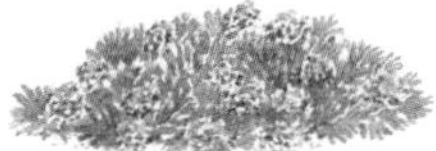

Teucrium polium

Noted for their aromatic foliage, these summer-flowering, evergreen shrubs or sub-shrubs have a neat habit. The flowers have a prominent five-lobed lower lip, but lack an upper lip. Small species make excellent rock-garden plants while taller plants make good hedging or specimen plants in a warm border. Not all species are reliably hardy and they thrive in the warmer parts of Britain. Most are native to the Mediterranean region.

RECOMMENDED SPECIES AND VARIETIES

T. aroanium The silver-grey leaves of this sub-shrub are up to 2.5cm (1in) long. Dull purple-blue flowers, up to 2cm (¾in) long, are borne in plentiful clusters at the leaf nodes. Frost hardy. HEIGHT & SPREAD 10×30cm (4×12in).

T. chamaedrys The lustrous green, holly-like leaves, 2cm (¾in) long, are grey-felted beneath. The rosy-purple flowers, up to 1.5cm (½in) long, are held in loose spikes. It is a hardy sub-shrub, with an upright habit. HEIGHT & SPREAD 30×30cm (1×1ft).

'Nanum' is a compact, dwarf plant. **'Rose Carpet'** has rich bluish rose flowers. **'Variegatum'** has yellow-blotched leaves.

T. fruticans Loose spikes of pale blue flowers, 2.5cm (1in) long, appear in summer. The aromatic grey-green leaves are up to 2.5cm (1in) long. Both the leaves and arching stems are covered in silver-grey down. This bushy shrub is not reliably hardy. HEIGHT & SPREAD 1.2×4m (4×13ft).

'Azureum'♀ has rich purple flowers.

▲ *Teucrium fruticans*

▼ *Teucrium fruticans* 'Compactum'

'Compactum' reaches a height of 45cm (1½ft) and a spread of 30cm (1ft).

T. hircanicum The stems of this hardy sub-shrub are clad in shaggy hairs, and hold greyish, broadly lanceolate leaves 2.5cm (1in) long. The reddish purple flowers, 2cm (¾in) long, in short dense spikes appear in late summer to early autumn. HEIGHT & SPREAD 60cm×1m (2×3ft).

▲ *Teucrium polium*

T. polium The deep green oak-like leaves of this low hummock-forming sub-shrub are about 2cm (¾in) long. The flowers are red-purple, yellow or white. They are about 6mm (¼in) long and borne in dense heads at the tips of the shoots. Not reliably hardy. HEIGHT & SPREAD 20×30cm (8×12in).

'Album' has white flowers.

T. pyrenaicum The almost circular, bristly and bluntly toothed dull green leaves of this semi-evergreen sub-shrub grow to 3cm (1¼in) across. Bicoloured purple and cream flowers 2cm (¾in) long are held in profuse dense terminal heads. This hardy plant has a creeping habit. HEIGHT & SPREAD 10×30cm (4×12in).

T. scorodonia The crinkled, triangular grey-green leaves are up to 7cm (2¾in) long. Greenish yellow, occasionally pure white flowers, up to 2cm (¾in) long, are held in one-sided spikes. This is one of the few species to favour acid soils and cool places, and spreads on woody rhizomes. It is only reliably hardy in mild areas. HEIGHT & SPREAD 30×45cm (1×1½ft).

'Crispum' has puckered leaf edges. In **'Crispum Marginatum'** these are coloured white to pink.

T. subspinosum Dark green leaves, 5mm (¼in) long, grow on spiny silver-grey branches. The clear pink flowers are 3mm (⅛in) long and are borne in pairs at the shoot tips. This congested, rounded bush is fully hardy, but shoot tips may die back in winter. HEIGHT & SPREAD 15×20cm (6×8in).

CULTIVATION Plant in autumn or spring in

▼ *Teucrium scorodonia* 'Crispum'

▲ *Teucrium subspinosum*

almost any reasonably light soil in a sunny position. Grow the smaller, less hardy species in pots of John Innes No. 2 in a cool greenhouse or alpine house.

PROPAGATION Take semi-ripe cuttings in mid to late summer. Alternatively, divide *T. scorodonia* in early spring or sow seed in late winter or early spring.

PRUNING Trim *T. fruticans* to shape in spring. Otherwise none is required.

PESTS AND DISEASES Usually trouble free.

Thalictrum

Ranunculaceae

Lacy grey-green summer foliage highlights these hardy herbaceous perennials. Airy clusters of flowers appear from early to mid summer. The stamens often form prominent tassels, which impart a charming fluffy aspect. Among the recommended species are tall plants for a mixed border or woodland edge, and small plants for a rock garden or trough.

The plants are slender and generally upright, with leaves made up of many small, lobed leaflets. Most do best in a well-drained soil and a sunny or lightly shaded site. *Thalictrum kiusianum* requires an acid soil and a cool spot. *T. minus* may become invasive in a rich, very fertile soil.

RECOMMENDED SPECIES AND VARIETIES

T. aquilegiifolium A mass of fluffy lilac-purple flowers, 20-30cm (8-12in) across, appear on stiff, erect stems. The coarsely divided grey-green leaves grow up to 30cm (12in) long. HEIGHT & SPREAD 1m×30cm (3×1ft).

The flowers of var. ***album*** are creamy white. **'Thundercloud'** (**'Purple Cloud'**)♀ has violet-purple flowers.

***T. chelidonii* dwarf form** The rose-lilac flowers, 2cm (¾in) across, are borne in branched clusters up to 5cm (2in) across. Mid green leaves, up to 45cm (18in) long, are composed of multitoothed leaflets. HEIGHT & SPREAD 30×20cm (12×8 in).

T. delavayi♀ (syn. *T. dipterocarpum*) Small, semi-pendulous purple flowers with protruding yellow stamens are borne in loose branched clusters. The thin stems of this plant are often grown over shrubs rather than supported by stakes. The grey-green leaves, up to 36cm (14in) long, consist of many 3-lobed leaflets. HEIGHT & SPREAD 1.5m×60cm (5×2ft).

'Hewitt's Double'♀ has masses of deep purple double flowers.

T. dipterocarpum see *T. delavayi*

T. diffusiflorum Large semi-pendent lilac flowers, 2cm (¾in) across, are borne on branched stems. This short-lived species does best in cool, moist northerly gardens. The grey leaves are deeply divided and up to 20cm (8in) long. HEIGHT & SPREAD 1m×30cm (3×1ft).

T. flavum (meadow rue) Tiny pale yellow flowers are held in fluffy clusters up to 5cm (2in) across. The glaucous blue-green leaves, up to 40cm (16in) long, are composed of lobed leaflets. HEIGHT & SPREAD 1.5m×60cm (5×2ft).

The leaves of ssp. ***glaucum***♀ (syn. *T. speciosissimum*) are more glaucous.

T. isopyroides Tiny brown and yellow flowers are held in loose spikes, about 7.5cm (3in) long, on this clump-forming species. The finely divided blue-green leaves grow up to 10cm (4in) long. HEIGHT & SPREAD 20×20cm (8×8in).

T. kiusianum Tiny fluffy pink-mauve flowers are borne in open clusters, up to 5cm (2in) across, on this dainty, low-growing plant. The mid green, 3-lobed leaflets form leaves up to 12.5cm (5in) long. The plant spreads slowly by stolons. HEIGHT & SPREAD 7×20cm (2¾×8in).

T. minus Small, nodding, creamy yellow, occasionally pale purple, flowers are carried in fluffy clusters, about 7.5cm (3in) across, on tall stems. The pale green leaves, up to 25cm (10in) long, are made up of many deeply lobed leaflets. HEIGHT & SPREAD 30×20cm (12×8in).

The var. ***adiantifolium*** has insignificant purple-green flowers on stems up to 1m (3ft) high and grey-green foliage.

T. speciosissimum see *T. flavum* ssp. *glaucum*

▼ *Thalictrum minus var. adiantifolium*

▲ *Thalictrum tuberosum*

T. tuberosum Distinctive creamy white flowers, 3cm (1¼in) across, form open clusters, up to 15cm (6in) long, on tall stems. Mid green, 3-lobed leaflets make up the 12.5cm (5in) long leaves. HEIGHT & SPREAD 30×20cm (12×8in).

CULTIVATION Plant from autumn to spring in reasonably fertile, well-drained soil, in a sunny or lightly shaded spot. *T. kiusianum* needs to be planted in fibrous, acid soil and in a cool, moist spot. Stake tall species.

PROPAGATION Divide clumps and replant in early spring; young plants may take 2 years to become established. Sow fresh seed in autumn in pots. Keep in a coldframe over winter and plant out in spring. Alternatively, sow seed in early spring and grow on the young plants in pots for the first year.

PESTS AND DISEASES Usually trouble free.

Thamnocalamus see BAMBOOS p. 79

Thermopsis

Leguminosae

The curious name comes from *thermos*, a Greek word meaning 'hot' which was also an ancient name for the lupin, to which thermopsis flowers bear some resemblance. All are tough and vigorous rhizomatous perennials with erect stems bearing mid green leaves about 6cm (2½in) long, divided into three leaflets, and yellow or purple, pea-type flowers. The species listed below produce 10-20cm (4-8in) spikes of 2.5cm (1in) long bright yellow flowers in summer. They are reliably hardy and easy to grow in a sunny herbaceous border. Native to temperate parts of N America and E Asia.

RECOMMENDED SPECIES AND VARIETIES

T. caroliniana see *T. villosa*

T. fabacea see *T. lupinoides*
T. lanceolata Dense spikes of flowers are carried at the top of erect, hairy stems from late spring to early summer. The flowers are followed by curved woolly pods. The leaves are almost stalkless and woolly beneath. HEIGHT & SPREAD 75×60cm (2½×2ft).

▲ *Thermopsis lupinoides*

T. lupinoides (syn. *T. fabacea*) Spikes of flowers are produced from early to mid summer, followed by straight pods. This plant spreads vigorously, producing stems that are hairy at first, later becoming smooth. The leaves are slightly hairy. HEIGHT & SPREAD 75cm×1.5m (2½×5ft).

▲ *Thermopsis montana*

T. montana Open flower spikes appear in mid summer. The flowers are followed by straight, hairy pods. The clumps of erect, hairless stems also bear leaves made up of ovate leaflets. HEIGHT & SPREAD 60×60cm (2×2ft).
T. villosa (syn. *T. caroliniana*) Dense spikes of flowers appear in early or mid summer, followed by hairy pods. The robust, erect stems also bear leaves with grey-green undersides. HEIGHT & SPREAD 1.5×1m (5×3ft).
CULTIVATION Plant in autumn in any fertile, well-drained soil in a sunny position.
PROPAGATION Divide in spring or sow seed in pots under a coldframe in spring and plant out when large enough to handle.
PESTS AND DISEASES Usually trouble free.

Thistle, carline see *Carlina acanthifolia*
Thistle, Scotch see *Onopordum acanthium*

Thlaspi
Pennycress
Cruciferae

Thlaspi cepaeifolium ssp. rotundifolium

Some of the scree-dwelling alpine species of this genus carry blooms which rival daphnes in the sweetness of their perfume. The four-petalled flowers appear from mid to late spring. In their natural habitat the plants are hardy, evergreen perennials, but they can be difficult to cultivate.
RECOMMENDED SPECIES AND VARIETIES
T. alpinum White flowers, 6mm (¼in) across, open successively in loose spikes. The stalked oval leaves, about 1.5cm (½in) long, are borne in basal rosettes. This tufted, mat-forming plant dislikes limy soils. Native to the central Alps. HEIGHT & SPREAD 10-15×20cm (4-6in×8in).
The ssp. ***brevicaule*** is more compact.
T. cepaeifolium ssp. ***rotundifolium*** Sweetly fragrant, rosy lilac flowers, 1cm (⅜in) across, are borne in flattened heads just above the foliage. This is a variable species, but it typically produces tufted rosettes of grey-green, paddle-shaped and fleshy leaves that are 2cm (¾in) long. The plant spreads by creeping shoots. Native to an area from the Alps to the Balkans. HEIGHT & SPREAD 5×15cm (2×6in).
CULTIVATION Plant in early spring in a raised bed in well-drained soil containing a mixture of two parts fine gravel to one part fibrous soil. Position in a sunny spot. *T. alpinum* does not perform well in limy soil.
PROPAGATION Sow seed in winter and grow the young plants on in pots for the first year.
PESTS AND DISEASES Aphids may attack.

Thorn apple see *Datura*
Thrift see *Armeria*

Thuja
Arbor vitae
Cupressaceae

Thuja occidentalis 'Rheingold'

Trees belonging to this small genus of evergreen conifers are clothed to the ground with densely covered slender branches. Juvenile foliage has a soft, feathery appearance, maturing into flattened sprays of scale-like leaves. The foliage is aromatic when crushed. The larger conical thujas are suitable only for a spacious garden or for hedging, while the dwarf, rounded varieties suit smaller gardens, rockeries or containers.

Native to temperate regions of the Northern Hemisphere, thujas prefer a sunny position in a moist, acid, well-drained soil. Although most withstand shade, particularly *Thuja plicata* and its varieties, the foliage tends to be less vibrant and will not be variegated. Prolonged drought can kill these trees, especially specimens 50-70 years old. All recommended plants are hardy, although *T. orientalis* and its cultivars do best in a sheltered position.
RECOMMENDED SPECIES AND VARIETIES
T. occidentalis (American arbor vitae, white cedar) Slender branches are covered with flattened sprays of small scale-like foliage, glossy yellowish green above and matt green below. Oblong, upright cones consist of 8-10 overlapping scales joined at the base and measuring 1cm (⅜in) long. Yellow-green at first, the cones turn brown in autumn. This is a tidy tree when young, taking on a more open, conical shape within 5 years. HEIGHT & SPREAD 2×1m (6½×3ft) after 20 years, ultimately 20m (66ft) tall.

'Danica'♀ quickly becomes an almost round, dwarf bush. After 20 years it is just 50cm (20in) high and wide. The branches are all vertically arranged, bearing erect sprays of bright green foliage. It is useful for rock gardens and containers. **'Ericoides'** has soft juvenile foliage which is a dull grey-green in summer and turns brown, sometimes purple, in winter. This is a good plant for adding subtle colour and texture variation to a rock garden, and it is very effective with heathers. It grows into a willowy rounded or conical bush, reaching a height of 1m (3ft) and spread of 50cm (20in) in 20 years. It is easily damaged by snow. **'Golden Globe'** forms a rounded dwarf bush bearing golden yellow foliage throughout the year. In 20 years it reaches a diameter of 50cm (20in). Probably the

▲ *Thuja occidentalis* 'Golden Globe'

smallest dwarf and rounded thuja of all is **'Hetz Midget'**, which reaches a height and spread of just 25cm (10in) in 20 years. Its bright green foliage is carried on stout shoots. **'Holmstrup'**♀ forms a pointed spire of rich green foliage, remaining glossy throughout the year. It is best grown in pots for at least 5 years to establish its shape before planting in its final position. In 20 years it reaches 2.4m (8ft) high and 50cm (20in) wide. **'Lutea Nana'**♀ produces

▲ *Thuja occidentalis* 'Holmstrup'

dense yellow foliage that bronzes in winter. It will reach 1m (3ft) high and 50cm (20in) wide in 20 years.

'Rheingold'♀ is a slow-growing bush that varies from egg-shaped to conical. In 20 years it attains a height and spread of 2×1.5m (6½×5ft). The colour is a deep gold with amber tints, giving good value in winter. **'Smaragd'** is very similar in size,

▼ *Thuja occidentalis* 'Smaragd'

shape and growth to 'Holmstrup' except that it has bright almost emerald-green foliage. **'Spiralis'** grows into a brilliant blue-green column with spirally arranged branches covered with twisted sprays of foliage. It reaches a height and spread of 3×1.5m (10×5ft) after 20 years. The dense foliage of **'Sunkist'** is golden yellow. In summer it has glowing yellow tips. After 20 years it achieves a height and spread of 2×1.5m (6½×5ft), eventually growing into a narrowly conical tree, 20m (66ft) high and 4m (13ft) across at ground level.

▲ *Thuja occidentalis* 'Sunkist'

T. orientalis (syn. *Platycladus orientalis*) (Chinese arbor vitae) This species grows into a large shrub or small tree with dense erect sprays of pale greeny yellow foliage on almost vertical branches. In mid autumn the plant bears the largest cones in the genus, measuring 2cm (¾in) long. They are generally egg-shaped and always upright, with a ring of hooked barbs pointing back around the top. The colour is silvery green ripening to brown. This species is the slowest growing of all the thujas. HEIGHT & SPREAD 1m×75cm (3×2½ft) after 20 years, ultimately 3m (10ft) tall.

▲ *Thuja orientalis* 'Aurea Nana'

'Aurea Nana'♀ forms a bright yellow-green, densely packed globe, reaching 30cm (12in) all round after 20 years. The foliage of **'Elegantissima'**♀ is golden yellow at first, then tinged with bronze and eventually greenish yellow in winter. It has a conical shape and reaches 75cm (2½ft) high and 50cm (20in) wide in 20 years. **'Meldensis'** is egg-shaped and densely clothed with sea-green foliage that turns a deep purple in winter. In 20 years it reaches only 30cm (12in) high and 20cm (8in) wide, making it suitable for containers. The foliage of **'Rosedalis'** is initially bright yellow, turning sea-green in mid summer and almost plum-purple in winter. It is a dense, slow-growing plant with soft juvenile foliage. In 20 years this egg-shaped bush will be 80cm (32in) high with a spread that is about half its height.

▲ *Thuja orientalis* 'Rosedalis'

T. plicata (western red cedar) If left unpruned this species rapidly grows into a large tree, but with regular trimming it makes an excellent, easily controlled, dense hedge. The bright green leaves are marked with a white cross beneath. The upright, egg-shaped cones are about 1.5cm (½in) long. HEIGHT & SPREAD 10×2m (33×6½ft) after 20 years, ultimately 30m (100ft) tall.

The foliage of **'Atrovirens'**♀ is the darkest and shiniest green of all *T. plicata* cultivars. This strictly conical tree is slightly slower growing than the species, but it can still reach a large size, attaining a height and spread of 8×2m (26×6½ft) after 20 years. It is very hardy and makes an excellent hedge. **'Aurea'**♀ has yellow-green foliage with an attractive scattering of pure yellow splashes. In 20 years it reaches 10m (33ft) high and 2m (6½ft) wide. **'Copper Kettle'** is similar to *T. orientalis* 'Aurea Nana' but slightly smaller and the tips of the branches turn

coppery in winter. **'Fastigiata'** is the best cultivar for hedging because of its tidy habit. In 20 years a height of 8m (26ft) can be attained with a spread of 2m (6½ft). However, if left unpruned the tree will eventually be 30m (100ft) high and 5m (16ft) wide at ground level, ably forming the centrepiece to a large lawn or lining a formal avenue. **'Rogersii'** has dense gold and bronze foliage, becoming more bronzed in winter. It grows into a low, compact and conical bush. In 20 years it will be 1m (3ft) high and 1m (3ft) wide. The straggly branched young **'Stoneham Gold'**♀ develops into a narrowly conical

Thuja plicata 'Stoneham Gold'

tree after 40 years. Broad sprays of foliage look heavier and coarser than those of the species. The tree is green with coppery gold young shoots. In 20 years it will be 3m (10ft) high and 1m (3ft) across. A good plant for rock gardens and containers.

The colour of **'Zebrina'** depends on the amount of sunlight it receives, but is typically an alternating pattern of green and golden stripes. The stripes are not as pronounced in the shade.

CULTIVATION Plant young trees between late autumn and early spring in a moist, well-drained acid soil in a sheltered position. For hedges, space the trees 60cm (2ft) apart and pinch out growing tips when the required height is reached.

PROPAGATION Take semi-ripe cuttings at any time from autumn to early summer. Insert them in a mixture of equal parts peat and sharp sand and keep them well watered.

PRUNING Older trees can spread by layering as the weight of the foliage causes the lower branches to bow down. If necessary, prune the lower branches right back to the main stem in early spring or mid autumn. Raise the crown by continuing this process to the desired height. If the tree gets too large it can be topped, with professional assistance, but it will continue to grow with an even heavier crown. *T. plicata* and its cultivars used as hedging need to be clipped once a year in early spring.

PESTS AND DISEASES Rabbits eat thujas, and dogs' urine turns the foliage rusty brown. Honey fungus and a newly recognised disease known as canker rot also damage thujas. Canker rot usually infects trees via wounds made by storm damage or pruning: the branches turn yellow and then brown. Remove and burn affected branches as they occur and sterilise all pruning tools.

t

Thujopsis

Cupressaceae

Thujopsis dolabrata

The branching foliage of this tidy-looking, hardy coniferous tree is highly distinctive, and so dense that the main stem cannot be seen, even in young plants. The tree is conical and is most suitable for large gardens as it will overwhelm anything near it. It can be trained to form a dense hedge. There is only one species in the genus. Native to Japan.

Thujopsis dolabrata♀ (hiba, false arbor vitae) The foliage is made up of tightly packed overlapping scales about 4mm (⅛in) across, forming flattened sprays. The upper surface is dark green to yellow, quite polished and waxy looking. Underneath each leaf scale is a pure white, comma-shaped mark. Cones are produced in autumn. HEIGHT & SPREAD 2×1m (6½×3ft) after 10 years, ultimately 15m (50ft) tall.

▲ *Thujopsis dolabrata*

'Aurea' usually has golden yellow variegated foliage, although some specimens have only slight variegation that can revert to green. **'Nana'** has smaller, more tightly packed leaf scales than the species. It reaches a height of 45cm (1½ft) and a spread of 2m (6½ft), and forms a flat-topped, ground-hugging dwarf plant. The foliage sprays spread outwards from the centre then curve sharply upwards towards the tips. It is a good plant for rock gardens or as ground cover. **'Variegata'** has creamy white variegation, but it often reverts to pure green.

CULTIVATION Plant in spring or autumn on any moist but well-drained soil. Site variegated plants in full sun, although the green varieties are shade tolerant.

PROPAGATION Take semi-ripe cuttings in late summer and early autumn.

PRUNING Little pruning is required. Topping should be avoided.

PESTS AND DISEASES Usually trouble free.

Thunbergia

Clock vine

Acanthaceae

These strongly growing annual and perennial climbers bear abundant, brightly coloured tubular flowers from spring to autumn. All are tender in Britain and, with the exception of *Thunbergia alata*, need to be grown in a greenhouse or conservatory all year round. Native to Africa and Asia.

RECOMMENDED SPECIES AND VARIETIES

T. alata (black-eyed Susan) Cream to orange flowers, up to 4cm (1½in) across and often with a dark purple-brown throat, appear from early summer to mid autumn. The dark green leaves grow up to 7.5cm (3in) long. Although perennial, the plant is usually treated as an annual. HEIGHT & SPREAD 2m×25cm (6½ft×10in).

▲ *Thunbergia alata*

***T. fragrans* 'Angel Wings'** Fragrant white flowers, up to 5cm (2in) across, are borne in succession throughout summer. The dark green leaves are triangular, sometimes toothed and up to 7.5cm (3in) long. HEIGHT & SPREAD 1.5m×25cm (5ft×10in).

T. grandiflorum♀ (blue trumpet vine, Bengal clock vine) This vigorous species has sprays of sky-blue, yellow-throated flowers, up to 7.5cm (3in) across, from summer to early autumn. The oval mid green leaves, up to 20cm (8in) long, have pointed tips. HEIGHT & SPREAD 6×4.5m (20×15ft).

'Alba' has white flowers.

T. mysorensis♀ Flowers in hanging sprays, up to 40cm (16in) long, appear from spring to autumn. The blooms of this very vigorous species are yellow, with reddish purple, backward-curving lobes. The deep green narrow leaves grow to 15cm (6in) long. HEIGHT & SPREAD 6×4.5m (20×15ft).

CULTIVATION Grow in pots of loam-based potting compost in a greenhouse or conservatory and provide a minimum winter temperature of 10°C (50°F). Place in full light. Water frequently in spring and summer. Feed weekly with a general-purpose liquid fertiliser. Keep plants dry in winter. Give them wires or canes to climb up. *T. alata* can be grown as a houseplant on a sunny windowsill. It can be moved outdoors in summer to a sunny, sheltered position.

PROPAGATION Sow seed of *T. alata* and *T. fragrans* under glass in early spring. Take softwood cuttings of other species and varieties in spring or early summer. Alternatively, layer them in mid summer.
PRUNING Prune lightly in late winter to early spring, before growth resumes.
PESTS AND DISEASES Aphids and red spider mite may attack plants.

Thyme (culinary herb) see HERBS p.333
Thyme see *Thymus*

Thymus
Thyme
Labiatae

Thymes are sun-loving evergreen perennials, grown for their aromatic and often colourful foliage and tiny blooms. All species have two-lipped, tubular flowers, flared at the mouth, and most bloom in mid summer. Thymes are widely used in pavement plantings, rock gardens and at the front of borders; they can also be grown in containers. The prostrate species look good planted where their creeping stems can drape over the edge of a trough or raised bed. *Thymus vulgaris*, *T. × citriodorus*, *T. herba-barona* and *T. pulegioides* are also grown as culinary herbs (see Herbs, p.333). Most thymes are hardy, but replacement is often necessary after three to four years when growth becomes excessive or straggly. They grow throughout the Northern Hemisphere, especially in hot, dry areas.

RECOMMENDED SPECIES AND VARIETIES

T. ***caespititius*** This spreading, prostrate plant is grown for its purple to pale pink flowers, borne in loose spikes, 2cm (¾in) tall. It has bright green, narrowly spoon-shaped leaves, up to 1cm (⅜in) long. HEIGHT & SPREAD 5×36 cm (2×14in).

'Aureus' has yellow-variegated foliage.

T. ***cilicicus*** Profuse lilac-pink to purple flowers are borne in rounded heads, 2cm (¾in) across. The narrow, mid green leaves are 6mm (¼in) long. This low, shrubby plant is only fully hardy in sheltered gardens. HEIGHT & SPREAD 10×30cm (4×12in).

T. **× *citriodorus*** (lemon thyme) This upright shrubby hybrid bears lance-shaped, mid green, lemon-scented leaves, 1cm (⅜in) long. Lilac flowers are borne in 2.5cm (1in) spikes. HEIGHT & SPREAD 15×15cm (6×6in).

▼ *Thymus cilicicus*

'Archer's Gold', **'Aureus'**♀, **'Bertram Anderson'**♀, **'Golden King'**, **'Golden Lemon'** and **'Golden Queen'** all have leaves suffused with yellow of differing shades. They may suffer from harsh frosts and cold winds. **'Fragrantissimus'** has lemon-scented leaves. **'Silver Queen'**♀ is variegated with grey and creamy white. **'Variegatus'** has green and cream foliage.

T. **'Doone Valley'** Dark green leaves, 3mm (⅛in) long and blotched with yellow, cover this shrubby plant. The flowers are purple-pink and borne in dense heads. HEIGHT & SPREAD 10×20cm (4×8in).

T. **'Hartington Silver'** The dark green leaves are 3mm (⅛in) long and blotched with cream. Purple-pink flowers are borne in dense heads. The plant has a bushy habit. HEIGHT & SPREAD 10×20cm (4×8in).

▲ *Thymus* 'Hartington Silver'

T. ***herba-barona*** (caraway thyme) Dark green leaves, up to 6mm (¼in) long and scented of caraway, cover this mat-forming, plant. The flowers are lilac-pink, in clusters 2cm (⅛in) across, on upright stems. HEIGHT & SPREAD 5×45cm (2×18in).

T. **'Porlock'** The dark, glossy leaves of this mat-forming, prostrate plant are narrowly lance-shaped, and about 1cm (⅜in) long. They are densely borne and very fragrant. Abundant mauve, purple or occasionally white flowers are borne in 1.5cm (½in) spikes. HEIGHT & SPREAD 5×30cm (2×12in).

T. ***pulegioides*** (broad-leaf thyme) This shrubby plant forms a low tussock covered with dark green oblong leaves about 1.5cm (½in) long. The flowers are purple to pink, in blunt spikes 5-25cm (2-10in) long. HEIGHT & SPREAD 7.5×20cm (3×8in).

T. ***serpyllum*** (creeping thyme, wild thyme) Dense, dark, narrowly lance-shaped leaves clothe this mat-forming species. Squat spikes of purple, mauve or, rarely, white

▼ *Thymus pulegioides*

▲ *Thymus serpyllum* var. *albus*

flowers are profusely borne. HEIGHT & SPREAD 5×30cm (2×12in).

The flowers of var. ***albus*** are white. **'Annie Hall'** has shell-pink blooms. Bright crimson flowers appear on var. ***coccineus***♀, of which there is a vigorous form, **'Major'**. The small and dense **'Elfin'** has emerald-green foliage, bearing only a few purple flowers. **'Goldstream'** has yellow-variegated foliage. **'Minimus'** and **'Minor'** (syn. 'Minus') are dwarf forms. **'Pink Chintz'**♀ has profuse pink flowers. **'Rainbow Falls'** and **'Russetings'** have bronzed foliage.

T. ***vulgaris*** (common thyme) This wiry-stemmed shrubby plant has very dark green leaves about 1.5cm (½in) long. Pink or white flowers are borne in oblong clusters. This species can be quite variable in size. HEIGHT & SPREAD 25×30cm (10×12in).

The flowers of var. ***albus*** are white. **'Erectus'** is an upright form. **'Silver Posy'** has pale grey foliage.

CULTIVATION Plant in spring or early summer in well-drained, light or gritty soil in a sunny, sheltered spot. Clip back the shrubby types lightly after flowering.

PROPAGATION Divide low-growing species in early spring. Take semi-ripe heeled cuttings from shrubby species in early summer and place in sharp sand. Seed can be sown in pots in autumn or early spring, in a coldframe.

PESTS AND DISEASES Usually trouble free.

Tiarella
Foam flower
Saxifragaceae

Tiarella cordifolia

These hardy evergreen perennials produce small, white or pink flowers in elegant, frothy spires. The foliage is useful as ground cover at the edge of a shady rock garden, shrub bed or rocky bank. The creeping tiarellas, such as *Tiarella cordifolia*, can be too vigorous for all but the largest of rock gardens. The species included here flower from late spring to early summer. Cultivars are valued mainly for variation of foliage.

RECOMMENDED SPECIES AND VARIETIES
T. collina see *T. wherryi*
T. cordifolia♀ Spires of white blooms, 23cm (9in) tall, rise from the distinctive foliage. The leaves of this mat-forming plant are shallowly lobed, about 7.5cm (3in) wide and pale green. They develop a bronze tint with the onset of winter. HEIGHT & SPREAD 23cm×1m (9×36in).
T. polyphylla Nodding spikes of creamy white flowers, 20cm (8in) tall, are held above the leaves. Each 3-lobed, mid green leaf is about 5cm (2in) wide with toothed edges. The plant spreads on rhizomatous roots to form a clump. HEIGHT & SPREAD 20×30cm (8×12in).
'Pink' has pale pink flowers.
T. trifoliata Spires of white blooms, 25cm (10in) tall, rise above a strong tuft of leaves. The clump-forming, mid green leaves are 3-lobed and about 4cm (1½in) long. HEIGHT & SPREAD 45×30cm (18×12in).

▲ *Tiarella wherryi*

T. wherryi♀ (syn. *T. collina*) Pink or white flowers are held in spires, 23cm (9in) tall, above the leaves. The clump-forming, palmate leaves are about 7.5cm (3in) long, and frequently bear handsome deep claret mottling. HEIGHT & SPREAD 15×30cm (6×12in).
'Bronze Beauty' has coppery foliage. **'Pink Foam'** has clear pink flowers.
CULTIVATION Plant during autumn or spring in any moisture-retentive, humus-rich garden soil. Tiarellas do best in a cool, shady situation.
PROPAGATION Divide plants in mid autumn or early spring. Alternatively, sow seed in a coldframe in early spring.
PESTS AND DISEASES Usually trouble free.

Tibouchina

Melastomataceae

Brightly coloured flowers highlight this shrub which needs to be grown in a conservatory or greenhouse. Well-drained soil-based compost, indirect sunlight and a minimum of 7°C (45°F) are all essential.
RECOMMENDED SPECIES
T. urvilleana (syn. *T. semidecandra*) (glory bush) Satiny, blue-purple, saucer-shaped flowers, up to 7.5cm (3in) across, are produced in clusters from mid summer to early winter. The slender-branched, evergreen shrub has oval, mid to deep green leaves, up to 10cm (4in) long. They are soft and velvety and have prominent veins. Native to Brazil. HEIGHT & SPREAD 5×2m (16×6½ft) after 5 years. Prune regularly, to restrict size to 2×1m (6½×3ft).

▲ *Tibouchina urvilleana*

CULTIVATION Plant tibouchinas at any time of the year except winter in a pot of John Innes No.3 compost, or directly into a conservatory or greenhouse border. Water freely in summer but sparingly in winter. Feed with a general liquid fertiliser during spring and summer. Remove faded flowers and foliage.
PROPAGATION Take softwood cuttings in spring or semi-ripe cuttings in summer.
PRUNING Cut back stems which have flowered to within 2 buds of the main branch each spring and remove any unwanted wood. Pinch out the tips of young growths in early summer to encourage branching.
PESTS AND DISEASES Mealy bugs and glasshouse red spider mites are troublesome.

Tickseed see *Bidens frulifolia, Coreopsis*
Tiger flower see *Tigridia pavonia*

Tigridia

Tiger flower

Iridaceae

These frost-tender bulbs produce a succession of short-lived but vividly coloured flowers in summer. Upright or slightly pendulous, the flowers have three large outer tepals that form a bowl, with three much smaller petals inside. Each plant has three to five, flattened, sword-shaped leaves. Native to Guatemala and Mexico.
RECOMMENDED SPECIES
T. pavonia Brightly coloured flowers, 10cm (4in) across, are produced in shades of yellow, orange, red, pink and white, with purplish spots and blotches on the bowl, from mid summer to early autumn. HEIGHT 50cm (20in).

▲ *Tigrida pavonia*

CULTIVATION Plant bulbs about 10cm (4in) deep and 15cm (6in) apart in any well-drained soil in a sunny spot when the danger of frost has passed. Dig well-rotted manure into the soil before planting, and keep moist during the growing season. Lift bulbs in autumn after the leaves have died down, and store them in dry sand in a well-ventilated place, with a minimum temperature of 10°C (50°F). Alternatively, plant in containers of well-drained compost. Keep well watered and in a very sunny position. Overwinter the pots in a frost-free place.
PROPAGATION Separate offsets from the bulbs when they are lifted in autumn. Offsets should flower in 2-3 years.
PESTS AND DISEASES Usually trouble free.

Tilia

Lime, linden

Tiliaceae

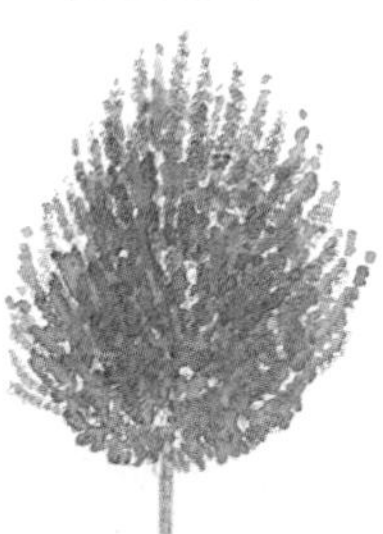

Tilia cordata

Limes are large, stately deciduous trees that are native throughout the temperate regions of the Northern Hemisphere. They are best suited to large gardens. The bright green leaves are generally heart-shaped with a serrated edge and turn pale yellow in autumn. The new shoots often grow in a characteristic zigzag pattern. Numerous small, fragrant pale yellow flowers hang in clusters in summer. Only a few seeds develop fully into hard-shelled grey-green round fruits about 8 mm (⅜ in) across.

RECOMMENDED SPECIES AND VARIETIES

T. cordata🏆 (small-leaved lime) This upright tree develops a rounded crown after many years. The heart-shaped leaves grow up to 7.5 cm (3 in) long, and are glossy dark green above, lighter beneath. HEIGHT & SPREAD 7×3m (23×10ft) after 20 years, ultimately 20 m (66 ft) tall.

'Greenspire'🏆 is a vigorous tree with a narrowly conical habit.

T. × ***euchlora***🏆 (Crimean lime) This is a semi-pendent tree with arching branches. The rounded leaves, 10 cm (4 in) long, are dark green above and paler blue-green beneath. They have toothed edges. HEIGHT & SPREAD 7.5×3m (25×10ft) after 20 years, ultimately 20 m (66 ft) tall.

T. × ***europaea*** (common lime) Much favoured in parks and avenues, this tree can be grown only in the largest gardens. The heart-shaped leaves grow up to 7.5 cm (3 in) long. HEIGHT & SPREAD 7.5×3m (25×10ft) after 20 years, ultimately 40 m (130 ft) tall.

'Wratislaviensis'🏆 is smaller, with pale yellow young leaves.

T. ***mongolica***🏆 (Mongolian lime) This compact, graceful tree of upright habit develops a rounded crown in old age. New leaves open coppery bronze before turning glossy green, then bright yellow in autumn. They are rounded, 7 cm (2¾ in) long and so coarsely toothed that when young they appear to be lobed. It requires a sheltered garden. HEIGHT & SPREAD 5×3m (16×10ft) after 20 years, ultimately 10 m (33 ft) tall.

T. **'Petiolaris'**🏆 (weeping silver lime) This large stately tree with a graceful weeping habit has long arching branches. The leaves, 6-12 cm (2½-4¾ in) long, are rounded, toothed and sometimes almost lobed. They are silvery underneath and are at their most attractive when ruffled by the wind. HEIGHT & SPREAD 14×8m (46×26ft) after 20 years, ultimately 32 m (105 ft) tall.

T. ***platyphyllos*** (large-leaved lime) This species grows into a monumental tree of rounded habit. The rounded leaves, up to 12 cm (4¾ in) long, are dark green above and slightly silvery beneath, with sharply toothed margins. They have soft bristly hairs above and below. HEIGHT & SPREAD 7.5×3m (25×10ft) after 20 years, ultimately 35 m (115 ft) tall.

▼ *Tilia platyphyllos*

'Fastigiata' has a very upright, rather conical habit and is smaller, reaching an ultimate height of about 13 m (43 ft). **'Rubra'**🏆 (red-twigged lime) bears bright red-brown new shoots that are very decorative in winter. The effect can be enhanced by frequent pollarding or annual clipping.

T. ***tomentosa*** (silver lime) This tree is upright at first and then develops a slightly weeping habit with a rounded crown in old age. The rounded, sharply toothed leaves, up to 10 cm (4 in) long, are dark green above and silvery felted beneath. HEIGHT & SPREAD 7.5×3m (25×10ft) after 20 years, ultimately 35 m (115 ft).

'Brabant'🏆 has a more upright habit and a dense conical head.

CULTIVATION Plant in late spring – or in autumn in mild gardens – in moist, fertile soil. Lime trees tolerate partial shade, but develop best in full sun.

PROPAGATION Take semi-ripe cuttings in summer or layer in winter.

PRUNING Not generally required, but hard pruning is tolerated in winter. Remove basal shoots from *T.* × *europaea.*

PESTS AND DISEASES Aphids are attracted to *T.* × *europaea* and *T. platyphyllos.* Caterpillars eat lime leaves and gall mites attack in late summer. Fungi and canker can cause die-back in older trees, and honey fungus can also occur. Leaf spot may cause trees to defoliate in warm, wet weather.

Tillandsia

Air plant
Bromeliaceae

These tropical evergreen perennials bear exotic flowers at intervals throughout summer. The plants listed are all epiphytes. With the exception of *Tillandsia usneoides,* they have long, narrow leaves that form single rosettes and bear tubular flowers with prominent bracts. Native to tropical and sub-tropical regions of N, Central and S America. Grow in a warm conservatory or greenhouse.

RECOMMENDED SPECIES AND VARIETIES

T. ***argentea*** The leaves, covered with white scales and up to 10 cm (4 in) long, form an almost spherical rosette, with a fleshy base. The bright red flowers, up to 2.5 cm (1 in) long, are enclosed by greenish red bracts. HEIGHT & SPREAD up to 25×20cm (10×8in).

T. ***balbisiana*** The plant forms a dense, bulbous rosette. The tough, whip-like leaves, up to 45 cm (18 in) long, are mid green and edged with purple. Bright red bracts surround violet flowers up to 4 cm (1½ in) long. HEIGHT & SPREAD 45×30cm (18×12in).

▲ *Tillandsia balbisiana*

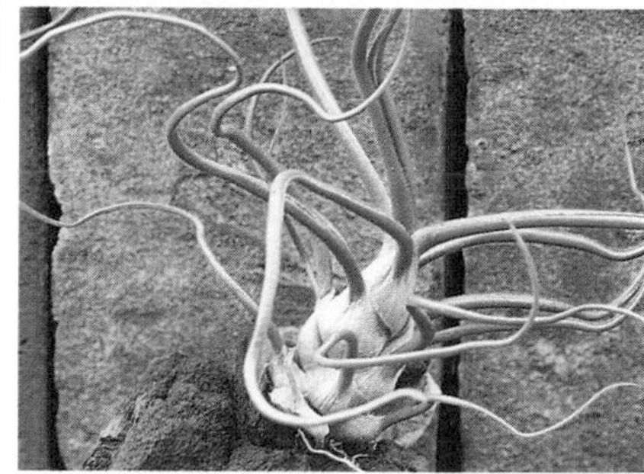

▲ *Tillandsia bulbosa*

T. ***bulbosa*** This is a rosette-forming plant with a swollen base and coarse, thread-like leaves, green flushed with dark red and up to 30 cm (12 in) long. Violet-blue flowers, about 4 cm (1½ in) long, partially enclosed by red bracts, are carried in an erect spike. HEIGHT & SPREAD 20×45cm (8×18in).

T. ***caput-medusae*** Twisted, rolled leaves arise from a hollow, bulb-like base on this bizarre, contorted, rosette-forming plant. The leaves, up to 15 cm (6 in) long, are dark green and covered in grey scales. The plant freely produces long spikes of violet-blue flowers, surrounded by papery red, pink or green bracts, each flower up to 4 cm (1½ in) long. HEIGHT & SPREAD 20×20cm (8×8in).

T. ***lindenii*** The pointed, arching leaves are mid green lined with reddish brown, grooved, have scaly undersides and are up to 40 cm (16 in) long. The flat, paddle-shaped flower spike, up to 30 cm (12 in) tall, largely consists of compressed, pinkish green leafy bracts from which emerge, 1 or 2 at a time, deep blue pansy-like flowers with white throats. HEIGHT & SPREAD 45×50cm (18×20in).

T. ***usneoides*** (Spanish moss) This pendulous plant has dense festoons of long, wiry, multibranched stems and linear leaves, about 3 cm (1¼ in) long. Both stems and leaves are covered with silvery white, moisture-retaining scales. The fragrant, greenish yellow or pale blue flowers, 1 cm (⅜ in) long, are borne singly in the leaf bracts. HEIGHT & SPREAD 1m×15cm (36×6in).

CULTIVATION Attach plants to a pad of moss wired to a piece of wood and hang them from the wall or roof of a warm greenhouse or conservatory. Alternatively, grow plants in pots filled with bark chippings. Suspend *T. usneoides* from a wire, without moss or wood. Plants require indirect sunlight, high humidity and a mini-

mum temperature of 10°C (50°F). Water throughout the year and mist regularly.
PROPAGATION Detach offsets in spring.
PESTS AND DISEASES Mealy bugs are sometimes troublesome.

Tithonia
Mexican sunflower
Compositae

Vivid flowers from summer to autumn and striking height are the main characteristics of the Mexican sunflower. This half-hardy annual makes most impact at the back or centre of a wide bed.

RECOMMENDED SPECIES AND VARIETIES
T. rotundifolia (syn. *T. speciosa*) Slightly scented orange flowers, up to 8cm (3¼in) across, appear from mid summer to mid autumn. The plant is strong-growing and erect with dark green hairy stems and mid green simple or 3-lobed leaves, up to 30cm (12in) long. Seeds of the species are not readily available and cultivars represent it in gardens. HEIGHT & SPREAD 3×1m (10×3ft).

'Goldfinger' has rich orange ray florets (petals) round a golden yellow centre. It reaches a height and spread of 75×50cm (30×20in). **'Torch'** has flame-red ray florets round a golden yellow centre. It reaches 120×50cm (48×20in) in height and spread.

▲ *Tithonia rotundifolia*

T. speciosa see *T. rotundifolia*
CULTIVATION Plant 50cm (20in) apart in well-drained soil in a sheltered site in full sun when all risk of frost has passed. Incorporate organic matter, such as garden compost, into very poor soil. In exposed situations, some support should be given to the plants, especially the taller variety 'Torch'. Deadhead regularly.
PROPAGATION Sow seed in early spring. Prick out the strong-growing seedlings individually into 8cm (3in) pots. Plant out in the garden when frosts are over.
PESTS AND DISEASES Slugs and aphids may be troublesome.

Ti tree see *Leptospermum scoparium*
Toadflax see *Linaria*
Toadflax, ivy-leaved see *Cymbalaria muralis*
Tobacco plant see *Nicotiana*

t

Tolmiea
Pickaback plant
Saxifragaceae

The single species of this genus is an easy-to-grow evergreen perennial for a shady corner of the garden. Useful for ground cover, it can also be grown indoors on a north-facing windowsill. Native of the cool coniferous forests of western N America.

▲ *Tolmiea menziesii*

Tolmiea menziesii Nodding, dull greenish brown, tubular flowers, about 1.5cm (½in) long, are borne in narrow racemes on erect stems from late spring to early summer. The mid green leaves, up to 10cm (4in) wide, often produce a small plantlet at the junction of the leafstalk and blade. HEIGHT & SPREAD 60×30cm (2×1ft).

'Taff's Gold'♀ (also sold as **'Variegata'**) bears leaves that are variably mottled and splashed with yellow and cream.
CULTIVATION Plant in a leafy, moist, acid or neutral soil in full or partial shade in autumn or early spring. Repot houseplants every 1-2 years in early spring. Water freely when actively growing, and feed monthly in spring and summer.
PROPAGATION Divide in spring or detach well-developed plantlets in summer.
PESTS AND DISEASES Usually trouble free.

Tomato see p. 747

Trachelium
Campanulaceae

Tiny tubular flowers mass into showy blossoms on these hardy and half-hardy perennials, enlivening a border or rock garden in spring and summer. *Trachelium caeruleum* is most successful when grown as an annual. Native of the Mediterranean area.

RECOMMENDED SPECIES AND VARIETIES
T. caeruleum♀ The pale blue or mauve flowers are produced in clusters as wide as 15cm (6in) from mid to late summer. The oval to broadly lance-shaped mid green leaves grow to 10cm (4in) long. It is good for an annual or mixed border. HEIGHT & SPREAD 90×30cm (36×12in).

▲ *Trachelium caeruleum*

T. jacquinii Dense, rounded heads of small, bluish lilac flowers, 10cm (4in) across, appear from mid to late summer. The mid green leaves of this woody based perennial grow up to 7.5cm (3in) long. This species is best for a crevice in a rock garden. HEIGHT & SPREAD 15×20cm (6×8in).
CULTIVATION Plant in late spring in well-drained soil and in a sunny, sheltered position. Remove faded flowers.
PROPAGATION Sow seed in early spring or take basal cuttings in late spring .
PESTS AND DISEASES Usually trouble free.

Trachelospermum
Apocynaceae

Trachelospermum asiaticum

Sprays of small, sweetly scented flowers make these vigorous, twining evergreen climbers a delight in summer. Although frost-hardy, they benefit from a warm, sheltered position against a south or west-facing wall if grown outdoors. In the coldest areas they can be grown in a cool greenhouse or conservatory, but they need space to spread.

RECOMMENDED SPECIES AND VARIETIES
T. asiaticum♀ The creamy white flowers have an orange throat and age to buff yellow. Each flower is 2cm (¾in) across with 5 spreading lobes. They are sometimes followed by pairs of slender pods up to 23cm (9in) long, containing silky plumed seeds. Some of the 2-5cm (¾-2in) long lance-shaped leaves turn red in winter. Native to Japan and Korea. HEIGHT & SPREAD 1.8×1.5m (6×5ft) after 5 years, ultimately 6m (20ft) tall.
T. jasminoides♀ (syn. *T. majus*) White, fragrant flowers 2.5cm (1in) wide open in mid to late summer and age to cream. Pods are produced occasionally. The lance-shaped leaves are up to 7.5cm (3in) long. Less hardy than *T. asiaticum*, it is best grown under glass in colder regions. Native to S China and Taiwan. HEIGHT & SPREAD 2×1.8m (6½×6ft) after 5 years, ultimately 8m (26ft) tall.

'Variegatum'♀ has leaves which are boldly splashed and edged with creamy

white, often tinged with coppery red in winter. The leaves of **'Wilsonii'** vary from lance-shaped to oval and are strongly tinged with deep coppery red in winter.
CULTIVATION Plant in early spring in well-drained soil against a sheltered, sunny south or west-facing wall. Tie in to horizontal wires. Alternatively, grow in pots of fertile, well-drained compost in a cool greenhouse or conservatory, positioned in partial shade and supported by wires or a trellis.
PROPAGATION Take semi-ripe cuttings in late summer.
PRUNING During winter tie in or prune out any long shoots that are growing away from the wall to keep the shrub tidy.
PESTS AND DISEASES Usually trouble free.

Trachycarpus

Chusan fan, windmill palm

Palmae

These slow-growing specimen evergreens have a distinctive habit. Large, fan-shaped leaves top a tall, single trunk that is covered in fibre. Large, downward-curving sprays of numerous small yellow flowers with many bracts at the base are borne among the foliage near the top of the stem. Although frost-hardy, these trees need full sun and a sheltered position. They are not suitable for gardens in the north-east of Britain.
RECOMMENDED SPECIES
T. fortunei♡ (syn. *Chamaerops excelsa* hort.) Dense sprays, up to 60 cm (2 ft) long, of small yellow flowers appear in early summer. Mid green, pleated leaves, up to 1.2 m (4 ft) wide, are carried on sharply toothed stalks, up to 1 m (3 ft) long. The leaves last for many years. Trees bear either male or female flowers and so it is necessary to grow plants of either sex for the small, spherical, blue-black fruits to be produced. HEIGHT & SPREAD 1×1 m (3×3 ft) after 5 years, ultimately to 4 m (13 ft) tall or more.
CULTIVATION Plant in mid to late spring in well-drained soil in a position sheltered from north and east winds. During the first 3 years, protect with a screen of matting or hessian and a deep mulch of bracken or straw in severe weather.
PROPAGATION Remove basal suckers with 2 or 3 leaves in mid to late spring and pot into 15 cm (6 in) pots of multipurpose potting compost. Place in a coldframe or greenhouse with a minimum temperature of 10°C (50°F). Grow on under glass for a year before hardening off and planting out.
PRUNING None required.
PESTS AND DISEASES Usually trouble free.

▼ *Trachycarpus fortunei*

Tradescantia

Spider lily, spiderwort

Commelinaceae

Tradescantia x andersoniana 'J.C. Weguelin'

With their leafy, wandering stems, tradescantias make good houseplants. Vigorous and easy to grow, they cascade out of pots and hanging baskets. There are also hardy, clump-forming plants for the mixed or herbaceous border. All have three-petalled triangular flowers, about 2.5 cm (1 in) across, which are usually short-lived.
RECOMMENDED SPECIES AND VARIETIES
OUTDOOR PLANTS
These hardy perennials suit the front of a border. *T. brevicaulis* is also useful for a rock garden. The linear-lanceolate, mid green leaves are up to 35 cm (14 in) long. The solitary flowers are short-lived, but new blooms appear as the old ones fade.
T. x andersoniana Clusters of blue, purple or white flowers, each up to 4 cm (1½ in) across, appear from early summer to early autumn. The lance-shaped leaves grow to 40 cm (16 in) long. HEIGHT & SPREAD 60×45 cm (24×18 in).
'Isis'♡ carries deep blue blooms. **'J.C. Weguelin'**♡ has lavender-blue flowers. **'Osprey'**♡ bears white flowers with purple-blue stamens.
T. brevicaulis Narrow, fleshy leaves cover the branched flower stems which carry rose-red flowers in early summer. HEIGHT & SPREAD 24×15 cm (9½×6 in).
T. virginiana From a compact clump of fleshy, grass-like foliage this species produces flowers throughout the summer. HEIGHT & SPREAD 60×45 cm (24×18 in).
'Caerulea Plena' produces double royal blue flowers.

▲ *Tradescantia x andersoniana 'Osprey'*

INDOOR PLANTS
There are several tradescantias, commonly known as wandering Jews, which thrive in average room temperatures and though they require good light, they do not need high humidity. The stems trail to about 60 cm (24 in) or more.
***T. fluminensis* 'Quicksilver'**♡ (inch plant) The pointed oval leaves, up to 7 cm (2¾ in) long, are evenly striped green and white. Pure white flowers are carried in clusters at the ends of the stems in mid summer.
***T. pallida* 'Purpurea'**♡ (purple heart) A robust plant with red-purple broadly lance-shaped leaves. The flowers in mid summer are bright magenta pink.
T. zebrina♡ (syn. *T. pendula, Zebrina pendula*) (silvery inch plant) A vigorous plant for hanging baskets or as ground cover for a conservatory border. The stems carry closely packed leaves on either side. The 5 cm (2 in) long leaves have a green central stripe with a glistening silvery band on either side. The undersides are purple. The mauve-pink flowers appear in mid summer.
'Purpusii'♡ (bronze inch plant) has olive-green leaves to 7 cm (2¾ in) long with a rich bronze-purple flush if grown in good light. The flowers are mauve-pink. **'Quadricolor'**♡ bears leaves with irregular longitudinal bands in pink, olive green, cream and silver. It is prone to leaf drop.
CULTIVATION Plant out garden species from autumn to spring in any fertile soil in full sun. Houseplants require full sunlight, especially the variegated types. Keep them above 17°C (63°F), although they will survive down to a few degrees above freezing in winter. Water generously in summer but more sparingly in winter. Repot small plants annually in spring, but large plants can be fed once a week instead. Pinch out regularly to promote bushy growth. Houseplants are best replaced after 2 or 3 years.
PROPAGATION Divide garden plants between autumn and spring. Take tip cuttings of houseplants at any time of the year.
PESTS AND DISEASES Slugs attack the young leaves of garden plants.

Treasure flower see *Gazania rigens*

Topiary: The art of garden sculpture

CREATE EYE-CATCHING FEATURES BY CLIPPING AND TRAINING PLANTS INTO FORMAL OR FANCIFUL SHAPES

Topiaries lend elegance, humour or rustic charm to gardens, patios, balconies and entrances. Ranging in shape from cubes and spirals to abstract designs and animals, these living sculptures can be created in lawns, containers and borders or from hedges.

BIRD LIFE *A whimsical topiary shape can add humour to a garden.*

A tree or shrub with dense, small-leaved foliage and pliable, thin stems is ideal for topiary. The evergreen *Buxus sempervirens* (box), *Taxus baccata* (yew) and *Ligustrum ovalifolium* (oval-leaved privet) are particularly suitable; the hollies *Ilex* × *altaclerensis* and *I. aquifolium* also make long-lived topiaries. Site them in a sheltered area in fertile and free-draining soil, to promote vigorous and even growth. In an exposed site or a heavy soil, use tough plants such as *Carpinus betulus* (hornbeam) or *Crataegus monogyna* (hawthorn). Like all deciduous plants, they are best used to fashion simple shapes.

The topiarist's tool kit includes sharp hand shears and secateurs. For large areas that lack detail, a powered hedge-trimmer saves time and heavy-duty loppers or a pruning saw are useful for renovating old topiaries. Most topiaries take five to ten years to form their shapes, but *Hedera helix* (ivy) can be trained over a framework to create a feature in two to four years. Green varieties are most effective; topiaries made from variegated ivies often lack definition because of the breaks in colour.

◄ WELCOMING ARCH *Two box trees create an abstract frame for a cottage doorway.*

Creating topiary

Simple shapes may be cut freehand, provided that you have a good eye. Clip a little at a time and stand back to view your work regularly. A framework is useful if accuracy is vital or the shapes are complicated. For example, pairs of cones are more likely to match and animals will look more convincing if they are cut to outlines.

Frames for simple shapes can be made with canes and galvanised wire. Otherwise, they can be bought from garden centres or made up by a blacksmith. Place the frame over the shrub. As the plant develops, prune any leaves and branches that grow outside the framework. This can be left in place or cut out once the shape has formed.

Simple styles

Cubes, cones and other geometric shapes introduce a formal note to their setting. They are especially effective in pairs, framing a view or gateway, or multiples of pairs, set along a pathway.

Spheres are simple to execute, either by eye or using a framework. Box is particularly suitable because its new shoots develop from the plant's centre, and yew and *Lonicera nitida* (box-leaved honeysuckle) also form dense rounded mounds. To create a standard – a sphere on a clear stem – train a single leader up a cane then pinch out the top growth regularly until it forms a rounded bush.

Trees that grow naturally in a conical pattern, such as yew and the cypress *Cupressus macrocarpa* 'Goldcrest', can be shaped easily into geometric cones. Make a template out of a wigwam of canes and place it over the plant to form an outline against which to cut.

A spiral can be created from an established cone (see facing page). Alternatively, train the leader shoot of a young plant round a cane, winding like a corkscrew as it develops.

To make a cube, place four young plants in a square; they will knit together to form a base. Mark the precise shape

▲ SHAPELY BOUNDARY *Regular columns enliven a hedge of* Chamaecyparis lawsoniana.

▼ SIMPLE SPHERES *A line of symmetrical box topiaries makes an unusual surround for a border.*

▶ GRAND SCALE *Angular lines and simple contours combine to create an imposing yew feature.*

with canes and string for accurate clipping. If possible, use four cuttings from the same plant to ensure even growth.

To create a pyramid or obelisk from the square base, clip the sides at oblique angles, allowing the inner shoots to form a central point.

Humorous shapes

An animal, train or freeform design adds a whimsical air to the garden. Use a framework to create the shape from a young plant, or exploit the natural form of a growing plant. For example, after two or three years' growth, a bushy yew will have several branches that can be coaxed into a new shape by trimming, bending or tying. To create a topiary pheasant or a squirrel, use upright branches to form a body and head, and peg a long, wispy branch to the ground to make a tail. A plant that is naturally conical, such as holly, often has evenly arranged branches which can be adapted into a tiered 'cakestand'.

Hedge-top topiary

Many topiary effects can be created on the top of a hedge. For a quick result, clip the top of a mature deciduous or evergreen hedge into a simple scalloped or castellated design. Use string to measure and mark out the pattern before you cut.

Columns, pilasters or buttresses fashioned on a long run of hedging create a pleasing architectural effect. Allow the sides of the hedge to grow out at regular intervals and trim to shape over three to five years, again using string to measure and mark out the pattern.

Windows can be cut into hedges to give peephole views into the landscape beyond. While the hedge is growing, train pliable young branches round an iron frame firmly staked into the ground.

Evergreen hedges are best for creating elaborate shapes, such as small animals. Allow some leader shoots to grow out of the hedge top, then shape them either freehand or to the outline of a framework.

Caring for topiaries

Feed topiaries with a slow-release fertiliser in spring, and water during dry spells until the plants are two or three years old. Topiaries in containers need watering all year round because the dense foliage prevents rainwater reaching the soil.

Clip once a year, in late summer or more often if the shrub is fast-growing. Privet and hawthorn shapes, for example, may need three trims in the growing season.

At the onset of winter, insulate the roots of pot-grown topiaries from frost by wrapping hessian sacking or bubble-wrap polythene round the container. The trunks of standards are vulnerable and also need to be insulated. Brush any heavy snow off topiary shapes.

Old, neglected topiaries can sometimes be renovated, particularly those created from yew which stands hard pruning. Clip in stages over three years, cutting one side of the plant at a time.

• Creating a spiral •

A cone-shaped topiary can be quickly adapted into an elegant, slender spiral by the following method. The best results are obtained from plants that are at least 1 m (3 ft) in height, and the spiral looks most effective when the central trunk is revealed as the pattern winds up to the top.

1 Tie a length of string to the apex of the plant and wind it in a loose spiral round the foliage. Secure the end of the string to the stem or a branch at the bottom of the shrub.

2 Carefully following the spiral marked by the string, cut away the outer branches of the plant with a pair of secateurs. Aim to keep the tiers even all the way round.

Tricyrtis

Toad lily

Liliaceae

Tricyrtis formosana

Spectacular flowers are produced by the hardy herbaceous perennials in this genus during summer and autumn. The flowers stand out well against light green foliage plants in a mixed border.

▲ *Tricyrtis formosana*

RECOMMENDED SPECIES AND VARIETIES

T. formosana ♀ (syn. *T. stolonifera*) Heavily spotted, purplish pink, spurred flowers with yellow-tinged throats appear in early autumn. They are up to 7.5cm (3in) across. The dark green, lance-shaped leaves, 10cm (4in) long, are sparingly produced. HEIGHT & SPREAD 60×45cm (24×18in).

▲ *Tricyrtis hirta*

T. hirta (Japanese toad lily) Bell-shaped flowers, up to 2.5cm (1in) across, bloom in clusters in late summer or early autumn. They are white, spotted with purple. Dark green, narrow leaves, up to 15cm (6in) long, are carried on strong stems densely clothed with white down. HEIGHT & SPREAD 90×45cm (36×18in).

'Alba' has white flowers flushed green.

T. latifolia Yellow or yellowish green, purple-spotted flowers, up to 5cm (2in) across, are produced sparingly in mid summer. The leaves are up to 15cm (6in) long and borne on an erect, hairy stem. HEIGHT & SPREAD 90×45cm (36×18in).

T. macrantha ssp. ***macranthopsis*** Bell-shaped, chocolate-spotted yellow flowers, up to 7.5cm (3in) across, are borne at the tips of arching stems in late summer or autumn. The dark green, oval leaves are up to 10cm (4in) long and 5cm (2in) wide. HEIGHT & SPREAD 90×45cm (36×18in).

T. macropoda Beautiful cup-shaped whitish purple flowers, up to 5cm (2in) across, are sprinkled with small purple spots. They appear in late summer, offset by dark green leaves, up to 12.5cm (5in) long. HEIGHT & SPREAD 75×45cm (30×18in).

T. ohsumiensis Faintly spotted, cup-shaped primrose-yellow flowers, up to 5cm (2in) across, are borne in late summer. The dark green leaves are up to 15cm (6in) long. HEIGHT & SPREAD 45×30cm (18×12in).

T. stolonifera see *T. formosana*

CULTIVATION Plant in spring in soil enriched with organic matter and in a sheltered place. Remove faded flowerheads.

PROPAGATION Sow seed in autumn or spring or divide plants in spring.

PESTS AND DISEASES Slugs and snails can be troublesome, especially in early spring. Powdery mildew may affect foliage.

Trifolium

Clover

Leguminosae

Rounded heads of tiny flowers in summer and leaves with three leaflets are the familiar features of these pretty plants. Occasionally a leaf may be composed of four or even up to seven leaflets. The genus includes hardy annuals, biennials and perennials, a few of which are evergreen. Clover makes good ground cover, but some species can become invasive. Native to all temperate and sub-tropical regions outside Australasia.

RECOMMENDED SPECIES AND VARIETIES

T. incarnatum (crimson clover) Tiny bright red flowers borne in heads up to 7.5cm (3in) long appear over mid summer. Slender erect stems carry dark green leaves, up to 4cm (1½in) across, with rounded leaflets. This annual is often grown for its value as a green manure. HEIGHT & SPREAD 30×30cm (12×12in).

T. ochroleucum (sulphur clover) Sulphur yellow, oval flowerheads, up to 3cm (1¼in) wide, bloom in early and mid summer. The brightly coloured flowers are complemented by mid green, oval to lance-shaped leaflets. These semi-evergreen leaves are up to 3cm (1¼in) long, on stalks up to 15cm (6in) long. As a short-lived perennial, the plant will last 3-4 years. HEIGHT & SPREAD 30×30cm (12×12in).

▲ *Trifolium ochroleucum*

T. pratense (purple clover) This is a bushy, short-lived, semi-evergreen perennial bearing reddish purple to pink, occasionally cream, flowerheads, up to 2.5cm (1in) across, in mid summer. The dark green, oval leaflets are up to 2.5cm (1in) long. The plant is commonly grown as a forage crop or for green manure. HEIGHT & SPREAD 30×60cm (12×24in).

▲ *Trifolium pratense*

'Green Ice' has cream flowers and two-toned green leaves. **'Susan Smith'** has dark pink flowers and leaflets with golden veins.

T. repens (white clover, shamrock) Tiny white blossoms, in fragrant heads up to 2.5cm (1in) across, are produced from late spring until early autumn. The plant, a semi-evergreen perennial, has dark green leaves on creeping stems, each rounded leaflet up to 2cm (¾in) long. HEIGHT & SPREAD 15×60cm (6×24in).

'Purpurascens' is a robust plant with reddish brown leaflets edged with green. **'Purpurascens Quadrifolium'** is similar but many leaves have 4 or more leaflets.

CULTIVATION Grow in an open, sunny position in a free-draining soil, although plants will tolerate most other conditions found in the garden, with the exception of

▲ *Trifolium repens* 'Purpurascens'

dense shade. Deadhead as required. To use clover as green manure, dig the plant into the soil in late summer or early autumn.
PROPAGATION Sow seed or divide plants in spring. Clover self-seeds freely.
PESTS AND DISEASES Usually trouble free.

Trillium

Wood lily
Trilliaceae

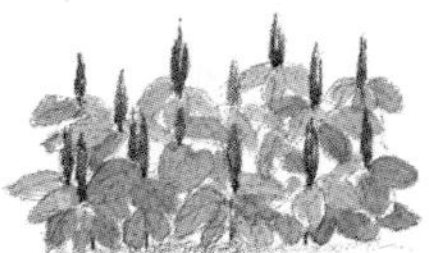

Trillium chloropetalum

Each stem of these herbaceous perennials is topped by a cluster of three leaves and a single three-petalled flower. Most trilliums are hardy but a few can be damaged by late frosts. Plants are sometimes slow to become established and once settled resent disturbance at the roots. As woodland dwellers in their native N America, trilliums are ideal for moist, shady sites.

RECOMMENDED SPECIES AND VARIETIES

T. catesbyi (syn. *T. stylosum*) (bashful wake-robin) Nodding flowers, up to 5cm (2in) across, appear from late spring to early summer. The pink petals are flushed with red and curl elegantly upwards. The leaves are up to 10cm (4in) long and have wavy edges. HEIGHT & SPREAD 20×10cm (8×4in).

T. cernuum (nodding trillium) Pendent white or pinkish flowers, 4cm (1½in) across, appear in mid spring. The petals curl up at the tips and the prominent anthers are purple. The leaves are up to 10cm (4in) long. HEIGHT & SPREAD 60×30cm (24×12in).

▲ *Trillium chloropetalum*

T. chloropetalum♀ The upright flowers, which appear from mid to late spring, can be white, white with a pink flush, greenish orange, brown or maroon. Narrow petals, 9cm (3½in) long, are set off by a ruff of bright green leaves, up to 20cm (8in) long. HEIGHT & SPREAD 45×45cm (18×18in).

T. cuneatum (toad trillium) Purple or brownish purple upright flowers are borne above round leaves from mid to late spring. The leaves are blotched with bronze and up to 10cm (4in) across. HEIGHT & SPREAD 40×30cm (16×12in).

T. erectum♀ (birthroot, lamb's quarters, wet-dog trillium) Slightly nodding, deep claret flowers, 5cm (2in) across, appear in mid spring. The pointed oval, pale green leaves are up to 15cm (6in) long. HEIGHT & SPREAD 40×30cm (16×12in).

▲ *Trillium erectum*

The flowers of f. ***albiflorum*** are white, tinged with green. The petals of f. ***luteum*** are a rich yellow, veined with deep red.

T. grandiflorum♀ (wake-robin) Showy, pure white, outward-facing flowers appear in late spring. The petals have wavy edges and are up to 7.5cm (3in) long. The flowers sometimes open pink. The leaves are 10cm (4in) long, with pointed tips. HEIGHT & SPREAD 45×45cm (18×18in).

▲ *Trillium grandiflorum*

Double flowers are seen on f. ***flore-pleno***.

T. luteum♀ (syn. *T. sessile* var. *luteum*) Greenish yellow upward-facing flowers, 5cm (2in) across, appear on upright stems in mid spring. The almost circular leaves are up to 12cm (4¾in) across. They are mid green, blotched with dark bronze-green. HEIGHT & SPREAD 40×30cm (16×12in).

T. ovatum var. ***hibbersonii*** Pinkish upward-facing flowers, about 5cm (2in) across, that turn white with age, are produced in spring. They are flanked by diamond-shaped mid green leaves, 7.5cm (3in) long. HEIGHT & SPREAD 20×45cm (8×18in).

T. recurvatum Reddish brown to purple-green, upright flowers, up to 6cm (2½in) across, appear in spring. The leaves are mottled in bronze and up to 12cm (4¾in) long. HEIGHT & SPREAD 40×30cm (16×12in).

T. rivale♀ Nodding white or pink flowers, spotted with purple and about 3cm (1¼in) across, appear from early to mid spring. The dark green leaves with carmine spots are 4cm (1½in) long. This species can be damaged by late frost and is best grown in pots so that it can be overwintered under glass. HEIGHT & SPREAD 15×10cm (6×4in).

T. sessile Upright, scented flowers appear in early spring. The dark reddish brown petals are about 5cm (2in) long. The leaves are marbled with grey and are 12cm (4¾in) long. HEIGHT & SPREAD 20×30cm (8×12in).

T. sessile var. ***luteum*** see *T. luteum*

T. stylosum see *T. catesbyi*

CULTIVATION Plant in autumn in moist, but well-drained, fibrous soil that is acid or neutral. Position in moderate shade.
PROPAGATION Sow seed in autumn in a coldframe or take root cuttings in autumn.
PESTS AND DISEASES Slugs and snails may be troublesome.

Triteleia

Alliaceae

A cluster of funnel-shaped flowers is held by a single stem in early summer. Long, narrow leaves grow from the base of the plant. Triteleias are useful for rock gardens or borders and can be grown in containers. The flowers are good for cutting. Native to western parts of the USA.

RECOMMENDED SPECIES AND VARIETIES

***T. laxa* 'Queen Fabiola'** ('Koningin Fabiola') As many as 20 violet-blue flowers,

▲ *Triteleia laxa* 'Queen Fabiola'

up to 5cm (2in) long, are carried in a loose umbel on a stout, upright flower spike that may attain a height of 50cm (20in). The plant produces only 1 or 2 narrow leaves, up to 30cm (12in) long. HEIGHT & SPREAD 50×15cm (20×6in).

CULTIVATION Plant the corms in early autumn, 7.5cm (3in) deep and 10cm (4in) apart, in a free-draining position in an open, sunny spot. In very cold weather cover with straw or a mulch. Supply a high potash liquid feed in early summer. Remove faded blossoms and allow foliage to die back.

For indoor pot plants, bury corms in four parts John Innes No.2 compost to one part sharp grit. Leave pots in sand inside a coldframe, cool but frost-free and with plenty of light, until shoots begin to appear, then bring them indoors.

PROPAGATION Remove offsets in autumn. It will be 2 or 3 years before they flower.

PESTS AND DISEASES Usually trouble free.

Tritonia

Iridaceae

These half-hardy, bulbous perennials are grown for their summer spikes of brightly coloured, funnel-shaped flowers. They can also be grown as pot plants. Native to tropical and southern Africa.

RECOMMENDED SPECIES AND VARIETIES

T. disticha **ssp.** ***rubrolucens*** (syn. *T. rosea*, *Crocosmia rosea*) Funnel-shaped, deep pink flowers, up to 4cm (1½in) long, appear in late summer or early autumn. The mid-green, grassy leaves grow to 30cm (1ft) long. HEIGHT 45cm (1½ft).

T. rosea see *T. disticha* ssp. *rubrolucens*

CULTIVATION Plant corms 5cm (2in) deep and 15cm (6in) apart during spring in free-draining soil in a warm, sunny position. In winter, cover with a mulch of bark chips, removing it when the danger of severe frost has passed. Remove faded flowerheads and old foliage in autumn.

Grow pot plants in four parts John Innes No.2 compost to one part sharp grit. Overwinter pots in a frost-free greenhouse or conservatory and keep the compost dry.

PROPAGATION Divide in autumn or spring.

PESTS AND DISEASES Usually trouble free.

Trochodendron

Trochodendraceae

The solitary species of this genus is an evergreen shrub or small tree grown for its striking, spirally arranged foliage and unusual green flowers. Native to E Asia.

T. aralioides The vivid green flowers, 2cm (¾in) across, are made up of numerous stamens radiating from green discs, giving a wheel-like appearance. Clusters of flowers are borne in late spring and early summer. The lustrous leaves, up to 12.5cm (5in)

Trochodendron aralioides

▲ *Trochodendron aralioides*

long, grow on long stalks. They are apple-green or yellowish green with scalloped margins. HEIGHT & SPREAD 1.2×1m (4×3ft) after 5 years, ultimately 8m (26ft) tall.

CULTIVATION Plant out container-grown stock in spring in moist, well-drained soil, choosing a sunny place sheltered from cold winds. Do not plant in dry or chalky soil.

PROPAGATION Take semi-ripe cuttings in late summer or sow seed in autumn.

PRUNING None required.

PESTS AND DISEASES Usually trouble free.

Trollius

Globeflower

Ranunculaceae

Trollius europaeus

The common name aptly describes the large rounded blooms of the majority of the species in this genus, although the flowers of *T. acaulis* and *T. pumilus* are flatter and more buttercup-like. The flower colours range from pale cream to orange, with varieties flowering from late spring to early summer. The flowers are generally about 5cm (2in) across. Deeply divided leaves provide lush ground cover.

Globeflowers are hardy clump-forming perennials. They are easy to grow, as long as the soil does not dry out during summer. They thrive around pond edges or along the banks of a stream and can also be grown successfully in a herbaceous border, given liberal watering and a mulch to prevent the soil drying out in hot weather. Small species, such as *T. acaulis* and *T. pumilus* suit rock gardens, troughs and peat beds. Native to Europe, Asia and N America.

RECOMMENDED SPECIES AND VARIETIES

T. acaulis Small and neat, this species has bright yellow flowers in early summer and 5cm (2in) wide leaves which grow on short stalks from the crown. HEIGHT & SPREAD 25×25cm (10×10in).

T. chinensis (syn. *T. ledebourii*) In early and mid summer showy, orange-yellow flowers bloom on tall stems. The leaves are up to 12cm (4¾in) long. HEIGHT & SPREAD 75×45cm (30×18in).

▲ *Trollius chinensis* 'Golden Queen'

'Golden Queen'♀ and **'Imperial Orange'** both have orange flowers.

T. × cultorum see Garden Varieties

T. europaeus (common globeflower) Pale yellow flowers, 4cm (1½in) across, show up well against bright green, deeply divided leaves, up to 12cm (4¾in) across. HEIGHT & SPREAD 75×45cm (30×18in).

▲ *Trollius europaeus*

'Superbus'♀ is more free-flowering with deeper yellow flowers.

T. ledebourii see *T. chinensis*

T. pumilus Yellow flowers, 4cm (1½in) across, appear from late spring to early summer on this neat, slow-growing small plant. HEIGHT & SPREAD 23×23cm (9×9in).

T. yunnanensis The neat clump of leaves is brightened by yellow flowers, 4cm (1½in) across, from early to mid summer. HEIGHT & SPREAD 75×45cm (30×18in).

▲ *Trollius* 'Orange Princess'

GARDEN VARIETIES

These plants are often listed under *T.* × *cultorum*. All flower from late spring to early summer. The figure given is the height, the spread is usually slightly less.

'Alabaster', pale creamy yellow, 60cm (2ft); **'Canary Bird'**, lemon yellow, 75cm (2½ft); **'Earliest of All'**, yellow, 75cm (2½ft); **'Etna'**, deep orange, 60cm (2ft); **'Golden Cup'**, golden yellow, 75cm (2½ft); **'Goldquelle'**♀, bright yellow, 60cm (2ft); **'Helios'**, pale yellow, 60cm (2ft); **'Lemon Queen'**, lemon yellow, 60cm (2ft); **'Orange Princess'**♀, orange yellow, vigorous in growth, 1m (3ft).

CULTIVATION Plant from autumn to early spring, but not in frosty weather. Best grown in rich, moist soil, trollius will thrive in sun or partial shade. Cut off old flowering stems to encourage a second flush.

PROPAGATION Lift and divide clumps in autumn if they have outgrown their space or are not flowering well.

PESTS AND DISEASES Usually trouble free, although mice and voles sometimes eat the leaves and buds in early summer.

Tropaeolum

Tropaeolaceae

Tropaeolum speciosum

These hardy and half-hardy herbaceous perennials or tender annuals are grown for their brightly coloured, trumpet-shaped flowers. They include climbers and scramblers that are ideal for training on walls or trelliswork or for growing through shrubs. Native to Central and S America.

RECOMMENDED SPECIES AND VARIETIES

T. canariense see *T. peregrinum*

T. majus (common nasturtium) These tender annuals are used in borders, for climbing up trelliswork and also in pots and hanging baskets. The yellow, orange or red flowers, up to 5cm (2in) across and with a distinctive long spur, appear in summer. The leaves, up to 7.5cm (3in) across, are circular, with wavy edges. HEIGHT & SPREAD 2×2.3m (6½×7½ft).

'Alaska' has cream and green variegated foliage and orange or red flowers. It reaches a height and spread of 25cm (10in). **'Empress of India'** has dark bluish green foliage and crimson-scarlet blossoms. It reaches 25cm (10in) in height and spread. **Gleam Series** have semi-double flowers in yellow, red and orange. They reach a height and spread of 35cm (14in). **'Hermine Grashoff'**♀ has double orange-scarlet blooms. It reaches a height and spread of 20cm (8in). **'Jewel Mixed'** is early flowering with semi-double blooms from yellow through orange to crimson. It reaches 30cm (1ft) in height and spread. **'Tom Thumb'** is compact with yellow, orange or red flowers. It reaches a height and spread of 25cm (10in). **'Whirlybird'** has yellow to red, single flowers without spurs. It reaches 25cm (10in) in height and spread.

T. peregrinum (syn. *T. canariense*) (canary creeper) Bright yellow, spurred flowers, up to 2.5cm (1in) across, appear in summer and autumn. The blue-green, lobed leaves are up to 7.5cm (3in) across. A fast-growing, tender annual climber. HEIGHT & SPREAD 4×1m (13×3ft).

T. polyphyllum (wreath nasturtium) This hardy, scrambling, herbaceous perennial produces yellow, spurred flowers, up to 2.5cm (1in) long, during early to mid summer. Grey-green leaves, up to 5cm (2in) long, are borne on fleshy stems. This species particularly dislikes winter wet. HEIGHT & SPREAD 10×60cm (4×24in).

T. speciosum♀ (Scottish flame flower, flame creeper) Bright red flowers, up to 2.5cm (1in) across, are produced from mid to late summer. Bright blue berries surrounded by purplish red, papery scales often appear in autumn. The plant's vibrant green leaves, up to 5cm (2in) long, have 5-7 lobes. A hardy, herbaceous perennial climber. HEIGHT & SPREAD 3m×60cm (10×2ft).

T. tuberosum Bright orange-scarlet flowers, up to 4cm (1½in) long and with a prominent spur, are borne from mid summer into autumn. Greyish green leaves, up to 4cm (1½in) long, are held on strong purplish stems. This half-hardy herbaceous perennial climber grows from a potato-like tuber. HEIGHT & SPREAD 3m×60cm (10×2ft).

The distinctive flowers of var. ***lineamaculatum* 'Ken Aslet'**♀ are red and orange.

CULTIVATION Plant in spring in a moisture-retentive but well-drained soil in full sun. *T. majus* and its cultivars prefer poor soil. Keep well watered in summer. Lift the tubers of *T. tuberosum* in winter and store them in peat in a cool, dry, frost-free place.

▲ *Tropaeolum speciosum*

▲ *Tropaeolum tuberosum*

PROPAGATION Sow seed under glass in autumn or spring or divide roots in early spring before any growth appears. Separate the tubers of *T. tuberosum* in autumn.

PESTS AND DISEASES Aphids may attack.

Trout lily see *Erythronium americanum*
Trumpet creeper see *Campsis*

Trees

A living framework for the garden

TAKE THE LONG VIEW AND GROW TREES TO BRING STRUCTURE AND A SENSE OF PERMANENCE TO A PLANTING SCHEME

Even when young, trees give a garden a feeling of maturity. Planted singly or in groups, they provide scale and structure, act as focal points and frame views. Their silhouettes, leaves, fruits, flowers and barks enrich all planting schemes. These tall, woody plants are often the most prominent and long-lived species in the garden. They are usually single-stemmed, though a few are multistemmed.

SPRING BORDER *Small* Cornus *and* Prunus *are attractive trees for beds.*

Apart from their aesthetic value, trees are of great practical benefit, providing shelter from cold winds and sun glare, giving privacy and hiding unsightly areas from view. Many trees, particularly *Quercus robur* (English oak) and other native species, benefit wildlife (see WILDLIFE GARDENS p.710).

Choose a tree that suits the particular conditions and requirements of your garden and site it where it has enough room to spread. Once a tree starts to outgrow its setting, it needs to be pruned regularly, which can destroy its natural form and grace.

Plant and stake a tree with care (see p.810). For the first three years after planting, water during dry spells, mulch and carry out any formative pruning and training. Keep a 1m (3ft) wide area round the tree free from weeds or other plants in these early years. Once the tree has established a good root system, it will usually require very little attention.

◀ FOLIAGE AND FLOWERS *Cherry blossom, maple leaves and rhododendron flowers mingle.*

Size and shape

The immense range of tree sizes means that there is a tree for most gardens. The genus *Acer* (maple), for example, includes *A. pseudoplatanus* (sycamore), which can reach 30m (100ft) in height, and *A. palmatum* (Japanese maple), which grows to only 4m (13ft) after 20 years.

There is a wide range of species under 15m (50ft) tall, which are suitable for many gardens. They include the colourful *Robinia pseudoacacia* 'Frisia' and *Cercis siliquastrum* (Judas tree). Crab apples, such as *Malus* × *zumi* 'Golden Hornet', or ornamental plums, such as *Prunus* × *blireana*, grow to a maximum height of 4m (13ft), which makes them ideal for small gardens.

When choosing a tree, consider the spread of its branches as well as its height. Although the weeping aspen, *Populus tremula* 'Pendula', reaches only 8m (26ft) in height, its spread of 7m (23ft) may obscure too much of the outlook and cast an excessive amount of shade in a small garden.

▲ SUNLIT GLADE *Light filters through the elegant divided leaves of* Sophora japonica.

Trees that have oval, rounded and weeping shapes generally take up more space than those that are columnar, conical or pyramidal. The weeping katsura, *Cercidiphyllum japonicum* f. *pendulum*, for example, is three times the width of the narrow Lawson cypress *Chamaecyparis lawsoniana* 'Grayswood Pillar'.

Decorative foliage

After size and shape, the foliage is often the most significant feature to consider when choosing a tree. Evergreens, which include the majority of conifers, give colour throughout the year. Deciduous trees, which include most broadleaved trees and a few conifers, such as *Larix* (larch) and *Metasequoia* (dawn redwood), burst into exhilarating life in spring and are often brightly tinted in autumn.

▶ GOLDEN ELDER *The bright leaves of* Sambucus nigra *'Aurea' lighten a dark corner.*

Trees with green leaves bring a restful air to the garden and provide foils to vividly coloured flowers. Green-leaved species growing at the end of a garden magnify its size, while species with coloured leaves tend to bring the background nearer. If planted in the foreground, these trees make strong features. Variegated foliage, such as that of the holly *Ilex* × *altaclerensis* 'Golden King', brightens up shady corners.

Many deciduous trees have foliage that offers a variety of beautiful colours. For example, the rowan *Sorbus thibetica* 'John Mitchell' emerges silvery white and then turns from green to yellow in autumn; and the bronze leaves of *Cercidiphyllum japonicum* turn blue-green and then pink, yellow and purple.

Autumn colour can be a major feature of trees, providing a bright display in the garden when many plants have finished flowering. *Nyssa sylvatica*, with its gold, scarlet and russet tones, and *Amelanchier lamarckii*, a snowy mespilus with brilliant yellow and red foliage, are good choices.

The shape of leaves also adds to the interest of some trees. The almost square leaves of *Liriodendron tulipifera* (tulip tree) are fine examples, as are the fan-shaped leaves of *Ginkgo biloba* (maidenhair tree). The frond-like foliage of *Gleditsia triacanthos* (honey locust) has a delicate appeal.

FLOWERS AND FRUITS

The flowering season of trees is often short-lived but the blooms can be outstandingly beautiful. Large pale *Magnolia* flowers are a magnificent sight after winter, and clouds of blossom make the ornamental fruit trees, *Malus* and *Pyrus,* real attractions in spring. *Cercis* is covered in clusters of pink flowers in late spring. The pendulous catkins of *Betula* (birch) and papery bracts of *Cornus* (dogwood) have their own distinctive charm.

Many trees produce fruits that are highly ornamental. Edible varieties, such as apples and pears, add their highlights to the garden in autumn. Striking fruits are also produced by *Sorbus* 'Joseph Rock', with its orange-yellow berries, and *S. vilmorinii*, which has pink-flushed white berries.

The fruits of some trees are poisonous, including those of laburnum and *Taxus baccata* (yew). These trees should not be planted in gardens where young children play.

▲ BURNISHED COPPER *The polished bark of* Prunus serrula *gives colour all year round.*

CHOOSING THE BEST-SHAPED TREE FOR YOUR GARDEN

The outline and branch structure of a tree adds form to a garden throughout the year and can affect the way it is used. Examples of the main shapes are given below.

COLUMNAR

Columnar trees provide distinct vertical emphasis and smooth outlines. Plant them as focal points, to frame views or in groups or avenues.

Acer rubrum Scanlon
Chamaecyparis lawsoniana 'Grayswood Pillar'
Cupressus sempervirens
Prunus 'Amanogawa'
Sorbus aucuparia 'Sheerwater Seedling'
Taxus baccata 'Fastigiata'

CONICAL

The ascending branches of conical trees form upswept outlines. They blend well in mixed designs, as well as making good screens or focal points.

Carpinus betulus 'Fastigiata'
Cupressus arizonica 'Pyramidalis'
Fagus sylvatica 'Dawyck'
Magnolia × *kewensis* 'Wada's Memory'
Prunus 'Spire'
Tilia cordata 'Greenspire'

OVAL

Taller than they are broad, these trees make attractive specimen plants, look good in mixed plantings and provide protection from wind and sun.

Fraxinus ornus
Ilex × *altaclerensis*
Laurus nobilis
Liriodendron tulipifera
Magnolia grandiflora
Quercus coccinea
Sorbus 'Joseph Rock'
Tilia cordata

PYRAMIDAL

The horizontal branches of these trees form pyramid shapes at maturity. Use them as single specimens, in mixed plantings or as screens.

Abies koreana
Alnus glutinosa 'Laciniata'
Chamaecyparis pisifera 'Boulevard'
Corylus colurna
Juniperus scopulorum 'Blue Heaven'
Ilex aquifolium 'Pyramidalis'

ROUNDED

Often spreading as broad as they are high, rounded trees make good specimens, focal points and screens, and provide shelter from wind and sun.

Amelanchier lamarckii
Arbutus × *andrachnoides*
Catalpa bignonioides
Eucryphia × *intermedia*
Malus × *zumi* 'Golden Hornet'
Paulownia tomentosa
Sorbus aria
Styrax japonica

WEEPING

Weeping trees have pendent main branches and side stems. Use them as specimens, particularly by water, or in mixed plantings.

Betula pendula 'Youngii'
Fagus sylvatica 'Pendula'
Morus alba 'Pendula'
Sophora japonica 'Pendula'
Picea breweriana
Pyrus salicifolia 'Pendula'
Salix caprea 'Kilmarnock'
Tsuga canadensis 'Pendula'

Barks and outlines

The bark of some trees cracks, flakes or peels as their trunks and branches grow, forming patterns, textures and colours which provide interest in winter after the leaves have fallen. *Prunus serrula* has a peeling, polished trunk. The trunk of *Acer rufinerve* (snake-bark maple) has distinctive lengthwise stripes and the new bark of *A. griseum* (paper-bark maple) is a rich cinnamon colour.

In winter, the skeletons of most deciduous trees make gauntly attractive features. The airy crown of a birch is particularly elegant, *Nyssa sylvatica* has a handsome conical shape and the contorted branches of *Salix babylonica* var. *pekinensis* 'Tortuosa' are best appreciated after the leaves fall.

Small gardens

In a small garden, choose a tree that has two or more seasons of interest. Look for a species or cultivar which is naturally small or takes a long time to reach a substantial height. Consider also the size of its leaves, flowers and fruits; if these are large the tree may look out of scale.

The slow-growing *Acer griseum*, *A. davidii* 'George Forrest', the hawthorn *Crataegus persimilis* 'Prunifolia' and *Betula utilis* var. *jacquemontii* are all good trees for confined areas. Many ornamental fruit trees also make excellent choices.

Provided there is enough light, a tree can thrive in even a tiny garden or on a patio or balcony. Grow it in a large tub and water and feed regularly. A small apple tree grafted onto dwarfing rootstock is ideal for growing in a container, and the narrowly columnar holly *Ilex aquifolium* 'Green Pillar' or cultivars of *Cupressus sempervirens* (Italian cypress), such as the golden-leaved 'Swane's Gold', will also do well.

Focal points

A tree makes a handsome specimen, particularly in the centre or at the edge of a lawn, where it provides a tall contrast to the even surface of the turf. Species that have spreading branches, including the round-headed *Morus nigra* (mulberry), or a weeping habit, such as *Fraxinus excelsior* 'Pendula' (weeping ash) or *Pyrus salicifolia* 'Pendula' (weeping pear), are particularly effective; their forms are often displayed to best advantage in open sites.

Specimen trees also look attractive planted beside a water garden. Weeping species are excellent because their pendent branches have a flowing appearance; the willow *Salix* × *pendulina* 'Elegantissima' and the beech *Fagus sylvatica* 'Pendula' make eye-catching features but need plenty of room.

Trees can make commanding features in borders, giving distinct vertical accents. A strong, narrow silhouette, such as that of *Acer rubrum* Scanlon, looks especially good here.

A pair of columnar or conical trees placed one either side of a gateway provides a natural framework for a view, and a tree can make an excellent focal point at the end of a hedge or a pathway.

Grouping trees

Where there is space, plant several trees in a group to create a strong feature or provide a backdrop of form, colour and texture. Plant an odd number of trees to create a natural-looking grouping and use both evergreen and deciduous trees. The evergreens provide a permanent show, while the deciduous trees offer a changing display.

▲ YEAR'S TURNING Nyssa sylvatica *glowing with autumn colour is a spectacular centrepiece.*

◀ PLANTING EFFECT *Shapely trees create a strong, contrasting backdrop to flowering plants.*

Use a combination of contrasting leaf shapes or foliage colours to add interest. A creamy variegated tree adds lightness to a group of dark-foliaged trees; for example, the silver-leaved weeping pear and the purple-foliaged *Acer palmatum* 'Bloodgood' make a striking combination. However, avoid using too many trees with differently coloured leaves as they may compete with each other for attention.

Groups of trees are central to the design of a woodland garden. The upright, round-headed *Prunus* × *subhirtella* 'Autumnalis' or the open *Cercidiphyllum japonicum* are well suited to informal schemes. Tall trees, such as ashes or oaks, add height to a group of smaller ones, including dogwoods, birches and hollies.

In a small garden use silver birches, snake-bark maples and *Arbutus* × *andrachnoides* (strawberry tree), underplanted with several shrubs, to create an attractive grouping.

In a large and formal setting a double line of neatly clipped columnar trees, such as *Taxus baccata* 'Fastigiata', makes an impressive avenue.

Windbreaks and screens

Trees are useful as windbreaks and screens and many species make excellent hedging when they are densely planted (see p.318). A line of beech or yew, for example, can provide a substantial boundary.

Use trees to create a screen which offers privacy, filters noise or hides ugly sights. Round-headed or pyramidal species, including the hazel *Corylus colurna* and *Catalpa bignonioides* (Indian bean tree), are particularly suitable because of their widths.

A row of trees can be used to create a shelterbelt, but in a small garden a single tree can be sufficient to break the force of the wind. Conifers with foliage that is not too dense, such as *Pinus sylvestris* (Scots pine), the false cypress *Chamaecyparis obtusa* and *Thuja plicata* 'Zebrina', are excellent choices for windbreaks. The deciduous *Crataegus monogyna*, *Laburnum* and *Sorbus thibetica* 'John Mitchell', will also provide shelter from harsh winds.

▼ Floral focus *This well-placed* Pyrus salicifolia *'Pendula' makes a delicate centrepiece.*

HOW FAR FROM THE HOUSE?

Before planting a tree, consider its impact on neighbouring plants, houses and walls. Make sure the mature branches will not shade windows, and do not plant the tree close to a building or underground pipes or cables.

Trees may damage the foundations of a nearby building by direct pressure or by absorbing water from soils that shrink as they dry out. Root damage by direct pressure is most likely to be caused by trees with very vigorous root systems, such as ash, willow, poplar and large species of oak. These trees may cause particular problems on a shrinkable clay or peat soil.

It is worth seeking professional advice before planting a tree. As a general guide, leave a distance between a tree and building of a third to a half of the tree's ultimate height. Where the spread will be greater than the height, leave a distance equal to the radius of the spread. If planting on shrinkable peat or clay, place the tree farther away, at least as far as its ultimate height.

If your soil is shrinkable and you have a thirsty tree growing in your garden, take specialist advice before attempting any work on it. Severe pruning may reduce the tree's uptake of water and cause the surrounding soil to swell which may affect nearby buildings.

TREES FOR ALL SEASONS IN SMALL AND LARGE GARDENS

Small gardens

- ***Abies koreana*** Wide-spreading pyramidal evergreen with glossy, dark green needles, silver-white underneath, and purple to blue cones in autumn.
- ***Acer davidii* 'George Forrest'** Rounded and deciduous with spreading branches and a purplish red, white-striped trunk. Red-gold foliage and winged seeds in autumn.
- ***Amelanchier lamarckii*** Rounded, deciduous and multistemmed with clusters of white flowers in spring and leaves that emerge copper-bronze and turn yellow and red in autumn.
- ***Crataegus persimilis* 'Prunifolia'** Rounded, spreading and deciduous with clusters of white flowers in early summer. Orange and scarlet-tinted foliage in autumn and dark red berries.
- ***Cryptomeria japonica* 'Elegans Aurea'** Columnar evergreen with yellow-green foliage, turning bronze in winter, and brownish red peeling bark.
- ***Malus coronaria* var. *dasycalyx* 'Charlottae'** Oval, upright and deciduous with pink, semidouble, scented flowers in late spring. Bright red leaves and yellow-green fruit in autumn.
- ***Picea pungens* 'Koster'** Narrowly conical evergreen with scaly grey bark and silver-blue needles.
- ***Pyrus salicifolia* 'Pendula'** Rounded and deciduous with grey-silver leaves on weeping branches, clusters of white flowers in spring and green to brown fruits in autumn.
- ***Salix daphnoides* 'Aglaia'** Oval and deciduous with purple shoots and long, grey, pussy-willow buds in winter and early spring, and dark green foliage.
- ***Sorbus vilmorinii*** Rounded and deciduous with small white flowers in spring, ferny foliage turning rich red and purple, and small pink fruit in autumn.

Large gardens

- ***Aesculus indica* 'Sydney Pearce'** Rounded and deciduous with bronze-tinged leaves turning yellow to orange in autumn. White or pink flower candles in summer and conkers in autumn.
- ***Betula albosinensis* var. *septentrionalis*** Oval and deciduous with peeling, pink, brown and copper bark. Catkins in early spring and yellow leaves in autumn.
- ***Betula pendula* 'Laciniata'** Narrowly conical and deciduous with silver-white bark and deeply cut foliage turning yellow in autumn.
- ***Carpinus betulus* 'Fastigiata'** Conical and deciduous with a grey trunk, and yellow-green catkins in spring. Dark green leaves turning gold and winged seeds in autumn.
- ***Ilex* × *altaclerensis* 'Camelliifolia'** Dense pyramidal evergreen with glossy dark green leaves and plentiful red berries.
- ***Picea breweriana*** Pyramidal evergreen with weeping branches, blue-green needles and green cones ripening to purple in autumn.
- ***Sophora japonica*** Rounded and deciduous with cream tubular flowers on mature trees in late summer and autumn, and divided leaves turning yellow in autumn.
- ***Sorbus aria* 'Lutescens'** Oval and deciduous with silver-white foliage in spring turning mid green then bright yellow in autumn. Small white flowers in late spring and red to brown fruits in autumn.
- ***Stewartia pseudocamellia*** Oval and deciduous with brown flaking bark. Large white flowers in summer and green leaves turning orange, red and purple in autumn.
- ***Tilia cordata* 'Greenspire'** Conical and deciduous with clusters of cream flowers in mid summer and shiny green heart-shaped leaves turning gold in autumn.

Tsuga
Hemlock
Pinaceae

The graceful, sweeping branches of these broadly conical evergreen conifers are densely clothed in drooping or arched branchlets. Needle-like leaves, arranged in ranks on the shoots, are short, blunt and flat, and often have pure white undersides which contrast well with the dark green, sometimes blue-green, upper surface. Small, pendulous cones ripen the same year in which they form and remain on the tree for two or three years. Male and female flowers appear in separate clusters on the same tree in spring. The trees listed here are hardy and make fine specimen trees or hedges. Native to the forests of N and E Asia and N America.

RECOMMENDED SPECIES AND VARIETIES
T. canadensis (eastern hemlock) The dark green leaves have white undersides. The egg-shaped cones are 2cm (¾in) long and hang gracefully from the tips of the shoots. This multi-stemmed, broad-crowned tree is rather too large for most gardens, but there are a number of smaller cultivars. HEIGHT & SPREAD 6×2m (20×6½ft) after 20 years, ultimately 15m (50ft).

'Cole's Prostrate' forms a dense blue-green carpet and is suitable for a rock garden. This spreading plant reaches a height of only 30cm (12in). **'Fantana'** is a small, slow-growing bushy plant with foliage and branches that radiate out like a fan. The plant, growing up to 2m (6½ft) tall, makes a good rock-garden plant and is also useful for containers. **'Jeddeloh'**♀ does well in any garden situation and grows into a dense complete umbrella, up to 1m (3ft) tall, with fresh light green foliage. **'Minuta'** is an extremely slow-growing, bun-forming dwarf conifer that seldom exceeds a height of 50cm (20in). It is suitable for the smallest of gardens, including window boxes. Best planted when it is at least 10 years old.

▲ *Tsuga canadensis* 'Cole's Prostrate'

Tsuga canadensis 'Pendula'

'Pendula'♀, up to 2m (6½ft) tall, displays a low, wide-spreading canopy of overlapping branches and leaves, and makes a superb centrepiece for a lawn or large rock garden. Plant when it is at least 20 years old.
T. heterophylla♀ (western hemlock) A broadly conical tree that bears dense, dark green foliage hanging from slightly ascending branches. Some needles twist upwards to display silvery white undersides. Flowers are bright red; the pendulous green cones are tinged purple. This makes a majestic specimen tree, but is too large for most gardens. HEIGHT & SPREAD 18×7m (60×23ft) after 20 years, ultimately 40m (130ft) tall.
T. mertensiana (mountain hemlock) A tight, densely branched conical tree with beautiful blue-grey foliage and large pendulous cigar-shaped cones up to 7cm (2¾in) long. The needles are radially arranged, rather than ranked. This superb garden tree can be clipped and pruned regularly if required. HEIGHT & SPREAD 6×1.5m (20×5ft) after 20 years, ultimately 15m (50ft).

Tsuga mertensiana

CULTIVATION Plant from mid autumn to mid spring in a moist, loamy soil. Shade and cold positions are tolerated and *T. canadensis* and its cultivars will also do well over chalk. *T. heterophylla* tolerates some waterlogging.
PROPAGATION Sow seed of the species in spring or take ripewood cuttings in autumn.
PRUNING Very little required, although specimens, especially *T. heterophylla,* can be clipped into handsome hedges. Remove branches back to the main stem if wide-spreading canopies need to be controlled.
PESTS AND DISEASES Prone to honey fungus and sensitive to sulphur dioxide.

Tulbaghia
Society garlic
Alliaceae

These hardy and half-hardy semi-evergreen perennials and bulbs are grown for their star-like summer flowers. They demand an open, sunny position in a free-draining soil and a mulch in winter in cold areas.

RECOMMENDED SPECIES AND VARIETIES
T. violacea This bulb produces lilac-pink to purplish pink, 6-petalled flowers, up to 2.5cm (1in) across, during late summer and early autumn. The strong flower spikes will remain upright even in adverse weather. This is a vigorous, clump-forming plant with long, narrow, mid green to bluish green leaves which often remain for much of the winter. HEIGHT 60cm (2ft).

▲ *Tulbaghia violacea*

'Silver Lace' has variegated foliage and larger flowers. It is not fully hardy.
CULTIVATION Plant in spring in full sun and in any well-drained soil that does not dry out totally. Remove faded flowerheads. Apply a slow-release fertiliser in spring.
PROPAGATION Divide plants in spring.
PESTS AND DISEASES Usually trouble free.

Tulip tree see *Liriodendron tulipifera*

▲ *Tulbaghia violacea* 'Silver Lace'

Tulipa

Tulip

Liliaceae

Jewel-coloured flowers burst into life in spring. Whether forming stately processions across a border or ornamenting a bed in vivid patches, the presence of tulips in the garden lifts the spirits

Since their introduction from Turkey 400 years ago, tulips have been one of the most popular and rewarding bulbs for late spring displays. They are grown for their elegant flowers which are available in nearly every conceivable colour except true blue.

The six-petalled flowers are generally cup or goblet-shaped – although some may be rather starry – and mature blooms tend to open so wide in the sun that they are almost flat. Each erect stem normally carries a single flower but some varieties bear two or three flowers per stem. There are usually two or more lance-shaped basal leaves and smaller stem leaves which are often greyish green. The bulbs, which vary greatly in size, have a pointed tip and a brownish skin.

The genus as a whole is very varied, from the tiny mountain species suitable for the rock garden or greenhouse, through to the gaudy modern hybrids that are planted in huge beds in public parks and gardens. Around 100 species of tulip are known, mostly from W and central Asia, and there are thousands of garden hybrids that have been developed over the years.

The small species tulips are best planted in clumps towards the front of a border and they make colourful rock garden residents.

1 'Don Quichotte'
2 'Yokohama'
3 'Casablanca'
4 'Arabian Mystery'
5 'Rococo'
6 'Golden Apeldoorn'
7 'Kees Nelis'
8 'Attila'
9 'Prinses Irene'

INDEX OF SPECIES AND VARIETIES

Tulips are grouped into 15 divisions, with the last division covering the species tulips:

(1) Single early tulips
(2) Double early tulips
(3) Triumph tulips
(4) Darwin hybrid tulips
(5) Single late tulips
(6) Lily-flowering tulips
(7) Fringed tulips
(8) Viridiflora tulips
(9) Rembrandt tulips
(10) Parrot tulips
(11) Double late tulips
(12) Kaufmanniana tulips
(13) Fosteriana tulips
(14) Greigii tulips
(15) Species tulips

A list of tulips covered in this book follows in alphabetical order with the relevant division in brackets.

The larger-flowered hybrids can be used for general garden display either in formal beds – planted with forget-me-nots (*Myosotis*) or wallflowers (*Erysimum*) – or in clumps planted among herbaceous plants. Tulips can also be grown in containers for display on a patio or terrace.

All require a heavy loam soil that is nevertheless free-draining and a warm, dry summer dormant period to ripen the bulb. It is normal practice to lift the bulbs of the modern hybrids as the leaves fade and store them until replanting in autumn. Species tulips can be left in the ground where they may spread to form large patches, particularly *T. saxatilis, T. sprengeri* and *T. sylvestris.* If the bulbs dwindle, new bulbs can be added annually to boost the display.

▲ *Tulipa* 'Apricot Beauty'

▲ *Tulipa* 'Bellona'

Tulipa 'Prinses Irene' ▲

RECOMMENDED SPECIES AND VARIETIES

Holland is traditionally associated with the tulip – the country's national flower – and hundreds of varieties, old and new, have been developed there. As early as 1600, faced with an ever-increasing choice of tulip hybrids, the Dutch introduced a system of classification according to flowering time. This is still in use today and has been expanded to include new groups containing hybrids with similar characteristics. The garden hybrids are currently grouped into 14 recognised divisions. The 15th division in this book covers the species tulips.

(1) SINGLE EARLY TULIPS

Tulips within this division are the earliest to flower and can therefore be lifted earlier than most other tulips, making room for early summer bedding schemes. They are in bloom from early spring and are viewed to full advantage among forget-me-nots (*Myosotis*) and early bulbs, such as scillas and puschkinnias. They will flower in late winter under glass and many are excellent for forcing. HEIGHT 20-35 cm (8-14 in).

'Apricot Beauty', salmon-rose with a

reddish flush. **'Bellona'**, scented with pure golden yellow flowers. **'Brilliant Star'**, scarlet. **'Christmas Marvel'**, cherry pink. **'Couleur Cardinal'**, plum with a scarlet interior. **'Diana'**, pure white. **'Flair'**, feathers of orange on a buttercup-yellow background. **'Generaal de Wet'**, bright orange. **'Grand Duc'** see 'Keizerskroon'. **'Keizerskroon'**♀, a red blaze on a yellow background. **'Prinses Irene'**♀, orange with purple feathering.

(2) DOUBLE EARLY TULIPS

These tulips generally flower just a little later than those in the single early division. The blooms are large, often up to 10cm (4in) across, and fully double. They are suitable for large bedding schemes where bold, vivid swathes of colour are required, such as those seen in public parks. The shorter Murillo types (marked M) can also be planted in pots, tubs and window boxes. HEIGHT 25–40cm (10–16in).

'Carlton', deep red. **'Electra'** (M), deep cherry red. **'Monte Carlo'**♀, sulphur yellow. **'Orange Princess'**, soft orange flamed with purple and green. **'Oranje Nassau'** (M), blood red flushed with fiery red. **'Peach Blossom'** (M), deep rose pink.

▲ *Tulipa* 'Peach Blossom'

'Schoonoord' (M), pure white. **'Stockholm'**♀, scarlet with a yellow base. **'Willemsoord'** (M), carmine and white.

(3) TRIUMPH TULIPS

This group usually flowers from mid to late spring. Many of the Mendel tulips, which had their own division before the reclassification by the Tulip Committee in 1981, are now included here. The division contains many cultivars that are excellent for forcing. Available in a wonderful selection of colours, the triumph tulips are most effective when interplanted with winter pansies (*Viola*) and polyanthus. HEIGHT 40–50cm (16–20in).

'Abu Hassan', glowing cardinal red with crimson stripes on buttercup yellow edges. **'African Queen'**, deep ruby red with feathery white edges. **'Arabian Mystery'**, deep bluish purple edged in white. **'Athleet'**, pure white. **'Attila'**, light purple-violet. **'Cassini'**, deep red; excellent for forcing. **'Don Quichotte'**, deep rose pink. **'Douglas Bader'**, deep rose pink on the outside; paler inside. **'Garden Party'**, glowing carmine edged in white; feathers of carmine against a white background inside. **'Golden Melody'**, buttercup yellow. **'Kees Nelis'**, blood red edged in orange-yellow. **'Merry Widow'** (syn. **'Lustige Witwe'**), deep glowing red edged in pure white; excellent for forcing. **'Negrita'**, doge purple with beetroot-purple veining and a bluish grey base. **'New Design'**, pale yellow fading to pinkish white with red edges. The leaves have pinkish white edges. **'Yokohama'** bears strong yellow, rather pointed flowers.

(4) DARWIN HYBRID TULIPS

This is a comparatively new division, the first cultivar being introduced in 1936. The tulips have large flowers at the top of tall, sturdy stems. They make excellent cut flowers. In the garden they flower from mid to late spring. They are stunning when planted in large drifts and equally effective planted among wallflowers (*Erysimum*). HEIGHT 50–60cm (20–24in).

'Apeldoorn', cherry red edged with scarlet. **'Apeldoorn's Elite'**♀, cherry red edged with buttercup yellow. **'Beauty of Apeldoorn'**, an exterior flushed with magenta and edged in golden yellow; golden yellow inside with a black base. **'Big Chief'**♀, a rose-pink exterior with an orange-red edge; the inner petals flamed cream. **'Elizabeth Arden'**, dark salmon pink flushed with violet and a yellow and white base. **'Golden Apeldoorn'**, golden yellow with black anthers. **'Gordon Cooper'**, deep reddish pink, edged with scarlet and a blue and yellow base. **'Gudoshnik'**, deep yellow spotted and flushed with shades of orange-red; the base and anthers are black. **'Holland's Glorie'**♀, deep carmine, edged in poppy-red with a yellow base; orange-red inside and a greenish black base. **'Jewel of Spring'**♀, sulphur yellow with a reddish edge. **'Oranjezon'** (**'Orange Sun'**), bright pure orange. **'Oxford'**♀, scarlet flushed with blood red; capsicum red inside. **'Parade'**♀, scarlet edged in yellow; black base and anthers. **'President Kennedy'**♀, buttercup yellow spotted red and a deep bronzy-green base.

(5) SINGLE LATE TULIPS

These tulips flower from mid to late spring. They are tall – up to 70cm (28in) – with classically shaped flowers in a wide range of colours, making them excellent for large spring bedding schemes and they are often used in parks. HEIGHT 50–70cm (20–28in).

'Aristocrat'♀, soft purplish violet edged with white. **'Bleu Aimable'**, bluish lilac. **'Clara Butt'**, salmon pink. **'Georgette'**, a multiflowered variety in red with yellow edges and just 45cm (18in) tall. **'Greuze'**, violet purple. **'Halcro'**♀, carmine-red with a yellow base and green edging. **'Landseadel's Supreme'**♀, glowing cherry red with a creamy yellow base.

▲ *Tulipa* 'Maureen'

'Maureen'♀, marble white. **'Mrs John T. Scheepers'**♀, yellow. **'Orange Bouquet'**♀ is a multiflowered variety bearing deep orange flowers with a pale yellow base and greenish yellow anthers. Just 40cm (16in) tall. **'Queen of Bartigons'**, salmon pink with a whitish base. **'Queen of Night'**, deep velvety maroon. **'Red Georgette'**♀ is a multiflowered variety in glowing scarlet and just 40cm (16in) tall. **'Shirley'**, ivory white with a fine purple edge, a white base spotted with pale purple and brownish violet anthers. **'Sorbet'**♀, rosy white flamed with carmine-red and a creamy white base. Up to 70cm (28in) tall. **'Sweet Harmony'**♀, lemon yellow edged in ivory white and yellow anthers. **'Temple of Beauty'**♀, lily-shaped salmon-rose flowers. The leaves are slightly mottled. **'Union Jack'**, raspberry red on an ivory white

▲ *Tulipa* 'Apeldoorn's Elite'

▲ *Tulipa* 'Big Chief'

Tulipa 'Oxford' ▲

background. The base is white edged in blue.

(6) LILY-FLOWERING TULIPS

The tall, stately flowers of this group have pointed and reflexed petals. Opening in late spring, they are excellent for bedding schemes or interplanting in herbaceous borders. HEIGHT 50-60 cm (20-24 in).

'Aladdin', scarlet edged in yellow. **'Ballade'**♀, reddish magenta edged in white and a yellow base. **'Ballerina'**, marigold-orange, slightly scented. **'China

▲ *Tulipa* 'China Pink'

Pink'**, pink with a white base. **'Mariette'**, deep satin rose with a white base. **'Marilyn'**, white with fuchsia-purple feathering; ivory white flamed with red inside. **'Maytime'**, reddish violet with narrow white edges and a yellow base. **'Queen of Sheba'**, bright red with a fine yellow edge. **'Red Shine'**, deep ruby red. **'West Point'**, primrose yellow. **'White Triumphator'**, pure white.

(7) FRINGED TULIPS

The petals of this charming group of tulips have fringed edges, often in a contrasting colour. The showy flowers, which appear in late spring, are excellent for cutting. Like the single early and Darwin tulips, they look good among wallflowers (*Erysimum*) and forget-me-nots (*Myosotis*). HEIGHT 45-60 cm (18-24 in).

'Blue Heron', violet purple with a purplish fringe. **'Burgundy Lace'**, fringed wine red flowers. **'Fancy Frills'**, ivory-white flame on a rich, deep pink with a whitish to rose-pink fringe. **'Fringed Beauty'**, vermilion with golden yellow fringed edges and just 25 cm (10 in) tall. **'Hamilton'**, rich buttercup yellow. **'Redwing'**, glowing cardinal red with a lighter red fringe.

(8) VIRIDIFLORA TULIPS

An interesting group of tulips, with slender, urn-shaped flowers striped or flamed with green. They were put in their own division in 1981. The subtle colour combinations are much sought after by flower arrangers.

▲ *Tulipa* 'Hamilton'

Blooming in late spring, they make an effective display when planted in clumps at the front of a herbaceous border. HEIGHT 35-45 cm (14-18 in).

'Artist', purplish and salmon rose; salmon rose and green inside. **'Esperanto'**, mid pink flamed with green, fading to reddish brown with a greenish-yellow base. Variegated leaves. **'Golden Artist'**, golden orange with broad green stripes through the petals. **'Groenland'** (syn. **'Greenland'**), green edged with rose. **'Hollywood'**, red tinged with green. **'Humming Bird'**, mimosa yellow feathered green on the outside; mimosa yellow and green inside. **'Pimpernel'**, purple-red and green. **'Spring Green'**♀, ivory white feathered green with light green anthers.

▲ *Tulipa* 'Spring Green'

(9) REMBRANDT TULIPS

Greatly prized by the tulip fanciers of old, these tulips are often depicted in paintings by the Dutch old masters. They display the characteristic mottled and flecked flowers in late spring. The distortion of the colours is caused by a virus which can be transmitted to other varieties by aphids. As a result, very few varieties are now cultivated and they are sold in mixtures only. The old Bizarre and Bijbloemen tulips belong to this group.

(10) PARROT TULIPS

Fringed and twisted petals in bright primary colours means that this division contains some of the showiest tulip blooms of all. The mid to late spring flowers are long lasting and can be up to 20 cm (8 in) across. HEIGHT 50-60 cm (20-24 in).

'Apricot Parrot'♀, pale apricot yellow tinged with creamy white and deep rose; purple anthers. **'Black Parrot'**, as its name suggests, a deep purple exterior and blackish purple interior. **'Blue Parrot'**, bright violet-blue tinged with bronze; purple inside. **'Estella Rijnveld'** (syn. **'Gay Presto'**), red flamed with white. **'Fantasy'**♀, salmon pink feathered and striped green. **'Flaming Parrot'**, deep,

▲ *Tulipa* 'Fantasy'

strong yellow, lightening to the edges, flamed with bright crimson; primrose yellow flamed with blood red inside. **'Orange Favourite'**, orange with green blotches and a yellow base. **'Rococo'**, red with a crinkled yellow-green edge. **'Texas Gold'**, deep yellow with a red feathering at the edges. **'White Parrot'**, pure white.

(11) DOUBLE LATE TULIPS

Tulips in this division flower in late spring or a little earlier in warmer districts. They have large, peony-like flowers, often up to 10 cm (4 in) across. Although they are prone to damage from heavy rain, they make up for it with a long flowering period. HEIGHT 40-45 cm (16-18 in).

'Allegretto', red edged in yellow.

▼ *Tulipa* 'White Parrot'

'Angélique', pale pink, lighter at the edges. **'Carnaval de Nice'**, white flamed and feathered deep red. The leaves have a fine white edge. **'Casablanca'**, ivory white with a dark yellow mark on outer petals. **'Maywonder'**, deep rose pink. **'Mount Tacoma'**, pure white. **'Uncle Tom'**, deep maroon red.

(12) KAUFMANNIANA TULIPS
These small tulips, often with bicoloured flowers, are ideal for early spring bedding displays. They are also useful for planting in rockeries, tubs, pots and window boxes. Some have attractively mottled foliage. HEIGHT 15-20cm (6-8in).

'Alfred Cortot'♀, carmine red; deep scarlet inside with a black base. Mottled foliage. **'Ancilla'**♀, soft pink flushed with red; a central red ring inside. **'Early Harvest'**♀, deep red with yellow edges and a yellow base. Mottled leaves. **'Giuseppe Verdi'**, carmine edged in yellow; golden yellow blotched red inside. **'Heart's Delight'**, carmine red edged in pale rose and a golden yellow base with red blotches. Mottled leaves. **'Jeantine'**♀, carmine edged in apricot with a golden yellow base. **'Johann Strauss'**, dark red edged in sulphur yellow; white inside with a golden yellow base. Mottled leaves. **'Love Song'**, orange-red flushed with carmine and a deep buttercup-yellow base with bronze green blotches. Mottled leaves. **'Showwinner'**♀, scarlet with a buttercup-yellow base. Mottled leaves. **'Shakespeare'**, carmine red edged in yellow; salmon flushed with scarlet inside and a golden-yellow base. Just 15cm (6in) tall. **'Stresa'**♀, currant red edged in yellow. Mottled leaves.

(13) FOSTERIANA TULIPS
Ideal for bedding schemes, the fosteriana tulips are generally taller and have much larger flowers than those in the kaufmanniana or greigii divisions. They flower in mid spring. HEIGHT 20-40cm (8-16in).

'Candela', pure yellow with black anthers. **'Cantata'**, vermilion red with a yellow-rimmed black basal blotch. **'Madame Lefeber'** (syn. **'Red Emperor'**), very large fiery red flowers. **'Orange Emperor'**, carrot orange with a pale buttercup-yellow base. **'Princeps'**, red with a greenish bronze base. Only 20cm (8in) tall. **'Purissima'** (syn. **'White Emperor'**), large creamy white flowers.

(14) GREIGII TULIPS
Perhaps these tulips offer the best value as their foliage is also a feature. The leaves are beautifully marked with maroon mottling. If the flowers are deadheaded as soon as they are finished they can be left in the ground until it is time to plant the summer bedding. The shorter varieties are ideal for pots and window boxes as well as borders, beds and rockeries, flowering from mid to late spring. HEIGHT 25cm (10in).

'Cape Cod', apricot edged in yellow with a black and red base. Only 20cm (8in) tall. **'China Lady'**, carmine rose edged in white; ivory white inside and a greenish-bronze base with red blotches. **'Corsage'**♀, pale rose-pink edged in yellow; inside deep pink with yellow feathering, bronze base and 35cm (14in) tall. **'Donna Bella'**♀, carmine edged in cream; creamy yellow inside and a black base with scarlet blotches. **'Oratorio'**, rose-pink; apricot pink inside with a black base. **'Oriental Splendour'**♀, carmine red edged in lemon yellow and a green-ringed red base. It is 35cm (14in) tall. **'Pandour'**, pale yellow flamed with carmine red. **'Plaisir'**♀, carmine red; vermilion red inside edged in pale sulphur yellow and a black and yellow base. Just 15cm (6in) tall. **'Red Riding Hood'**♀, carmine red with a black base. Just 20cm (8in) tall. **'Toronto'**♀, rose red tinged with vermilion, 2-3 blooms to a stem. **'United States'**, fiery red feathered to the edges on a buttercup-yellow background. **'Zampa'**♀, primrose yellow, flushed red, bronze-and-green base and just 15cm (6in) tall.

▲ *Tulipa* 'Angélique'

▲ *Tulipa* 'Princeps'

▲ *Tulipa* 'Purissima'

▲ *Tulipa aucheriana*

▲ *Tulipa* 'Zampa'

(15) SPECIES TULIPS
T. acuminata Spindly, twisted flowers in red or yellow, with red markings appear in mid spring. The leaves are grey-green. This species tends to be short lived. HEIGHT 30-40cm (12-16in).
T. aucheriana♀ A solitary, 5cm (2in) pink flower with a yellow centre arises from a basal rosette of leaves in mid spring. This species is easily grown on a well-drained, sunny rock garden. HEIGHT 7.5cm (3in).
T. biflora (syn. *T. polychroma*) This easy-to-grow bulb flowers in early spring, bearing 1-3 tiny, star-like flowers of white with a yellow eye, which are suffused with green on the outside. The narrow, upright leaves are grey-green. HEIGHT 8-10cm (3-4in).
T. clusiana* var. *chrysantha♀ Slender, 7.5cm (3in) yellow flowers with red marks on the outside, are carried on thin stems with narrow, grey-green leaves in mid spring. HEIGHT 20-30cm (8-12in).

T. c. **'Cynthia'** has paler, creamy yellow flowers.

T. eichleri see *T. undulatifolia*
***T. humilis* Violacea Group** Tulips within this very variable group are easy to grow, producing one, rarely 2 or 3, large, rounded flowers of rich violet pink with a black or yellow centre in late winter or early spring. The narrow, grey-green leaves form a rosette. HEIGHT 15cm (6in).
T. kolpakowskiana♀ Pointed yellow flowers, suffused with red, orange or green on the outside, are borne in mid spring. This slender tulip has narrow, grey-green leaves. HEIGHT 10-20cm (4-8in).
T. linifolia♀ Brilliant red open flowers, 7.5cm (3in) across, appear in late spring. The grey-green leaves are narrow. This species is easily grown in a sunny, well-drained soil. HEIGHT 12.5cm (5in).

Batalinii Group 'Bright Gem' is a vigorous and long-lived hybrid. The rounded, sulphur-yellow flowers have pointed tips. This tulip increases freely in a well-drained

▲ *Tulipa linifolia* Batalinii Group 'Bright Gem'

soil in full sun. HEIGHT 12.5-20cm (5-8in).

T. marjolettii This long-lived bulb produces 7.5cm (3in) flowers in late spring. The blooms are primrose yellow, flushed pink and purple on the outside. HEIGHT 40-50cm (16-20in).

T. montana (syn. *T. wilsoniana*) Deep red flowers with a small black basal mark appear in mid spring among narrow, wavy-edged, grey-green leaves. HEIGHT 15-20cm (6-8in).

T. orphanidea **Whittallii Group** This vigorous stoloniferous tulip flowers in late spring. The slender flowers – nodding in the bud – are orange, shaded with bronze. HEIGHT 15-20cm (6-8in).

T. praestans **'Fusilier'**♀ Vigorous and long-lived, this bulb produces 1-4 orange-red flowers in mid spring. It is ideal for the rock garden or front of border and can also be grown in thin grass under trees. The upright, rather broad leaves are pale grey-green. HEIGHT 30cm (12in).

'Unicum' has yellow variegated leaves.

T. saxatilis Up to 4 large, pink flowers with a yellow eye are borne in late spring among shiny green leaves. This stoloniferous bulb is best left undisturbed in a dry sunny position where it will slowly spread to form large patches. It may be naturalised in thin grass. HEIGHT 30-50cm (12-20in).

▲ *Tulipa saxatilis*

'Lilac Wonder' is not stoloniferous. It is shorter than the species and bears solitary purple-pink flowers.

T. sprengeri♀ Slender bright orange-red flowers flushed with yellow-green on the outside are borne in late spring among upright, shiny green leaves. It is easily grown in any well-drained soil and can seed to cover large areas. The seedlings flower after 3-4 years. HEIGHT 30cm (12in).

T. sylvestris Nodding, rather pointed flowers of yellow, flushed with green on the outside, are borne by this easy-to-grow bulb in mid spring. This species spreads freely by stolons but can be shy to flower. It is best grown in a shady bed with other woodland bulbs. HEIGHT 30cm (12in).

T. tarda♀ Up to 5 white, 6cm (2½in) flowers appear on 2cm (¾in) stems in mid spring. The flowers are flushed with green on the outside and open wide in the sun to display a large yellow central eye. The mid green leaves are semi-erect. This species is easily grown, long-lived and ideal for a rock garden or border front. HEIGHT 10cm (4in).

Tulipa tarda

T. turkestanica♀ Up to 10 small creamy white flowers are borne by this long-lived species. The flowers have a small yellow centre that contrasts attractively with their brownish purple anthers. The narrow leaves are grey-green. It is very early flowering, often in late winter, and is easily grown. HEIGHT 15-30cm (6-12in).

T. undulatifolia (syn. *T. eichleri*) Large, 7.5cm (3in), orange-red flowers with a black basal blotch are borne in mid spring. This robust species has grey-green, wavy-edged leaves. HEIGHT 30-40cm (12-16in).

T. urumiensis♀ Starry yellow flowers, flushed with lilac and up to 7.5cm (3in) across, are produced in early spring. The mid green, linear leaves are up to 12.5cm (5in) long. HEIGHT 15cm (6in).

T. wilsoniana see *T. montana*

CULTIVATION Tulips are completely hardy and most need a heavy loam soil, preferably alkaline, that is free-draining. Avoid waterlogged soils. Plant the bulbs from early to late autumn. It is beneficial to add organic matter to the soil but avoid using manure. Plant the bulbs 15-20cm (6-8in) deep (or deeper on light sandy soils) and 10-15cm (4-6in) apart. If bulbs are to be lifted after flowering, planting depth is less important.

Tulip bulbs easily bruise; plant only those that are firm and undamaged. Provide a potash-rich fertiliser in late winter and give plants plenty of water while they are in growth. Deadhead flowers as soon as they fade to encourage the growth of new bulbs.

If lifting the bulbs, do so as soon as the foliage fades. Then dry them off, clean off any soil and store them in a well-ventilated place until replanting in the autumn. Protect stored bulbs against mice. Only the larger bulbs will flower. The small bulbs can be grown on in a nursery bed or discarded.

Many of the species bulbs, especially those that increase by stolons, should be planted 10-15cm (4-6in) deep in a well-drained soil in full sun and left undisturbed. Tulips are good pot plants for an unheated greenhouse or conservatory. Use a loam-based compost for container-grown tulips.

PROPAGATION Remove offsets from the bulbs of larger hybrids after lifting. These are then grown on for some years until they reach flowering size. All species can be propagated by seed sown in sunny well-drained beds outside in autumn, but only *T. sprengeri* is usually raised this way. Seedlings take up to 7 years to flower. Some species spread by the production of stolons.

PESTS AND DISEASES Aphids spread the virus that causes the split colouring in the Rembrandt and parrot tulips. *T. greigii* hybrids are especially prone to slug damage. Mice can be a problem to tulips grown in containers. Various fungal diseases, especially tulip fire (*Botrytis tulipae*), may attack.

Turk's-cap see *Lilium martagon*
Turnip see p.748

Tweedia

Asclepiadaceae

The single species in this genus is a climbing shrub with more or less twining stems, grown for its flowers that are pale blue to start with, gradually turning purple and then mauve. Native to S Brazil and Uruguay, it is too tender to survive British winters, but is ideal for a cool greenhouse or conservatory. It can be grown as an annual in the garden, where its colourful flowers are useful components of summer bedding schemes.

▲ *Tweedia caerula*

Tweedia caerulea♀ (syn. *Oxypetalum caeruleum*) The 5-petalled flowers, up to 2.5cm (1in) across, are borne in summer among oblong or heart-shaped, mid green leaves up to 10cm (4in) long. HEIGHT & SPREAD 60-90×30cm (2-3×1ft).

CULTIVATION Plant outdoors after the last frosts in any reasonably fertile soil and in full sun. Pinch back young plants.

PROPAGATION Sow seed under glass at a temperature of 18-21°C (64-70°F) in spring. Pot up seedlings in a greenhouse. Harden off first if planting out as annuals.

PESTS AND DISEASES Usually trouble free.

Twin flower see *Linnaea borealis*
Twin-leaf see *Jeffersonia diphylla*
Typha see GRASSES p.303

U-V

Ulex

Leguminosae

Clusters of golden yellow flowers bloom from early to late spring, and intermittently throughout the year, emitting a honeyed fragrance on warm days. Although these shrubs are almost leafless, green shoots and spines qualify them for the description 'evergreen'. They require poor, well-drained soil and a position in full sun, such as on a dry, sunny bank. Plant them away from paths as the spines are sharp. The shrubs catch fire readily during a drought so should not be planted near a house or roadside. The recommended plants are hardy and native to Britain.

RECOMMENDED SPECIES AND VARIETIES

U. europaeus (European gorse, furze) Yellow flowers, up to 2.5cm (1in) long, are borne by this shrub. The small, spine-tipped leaves drop to reveal intricately branched, viciously spiny, mid to dark green shoots. HEIGHT & SPREAD 1m×85cm (3ft×2ft9in) after 5 years, ultimately 1.8m (6ft) tall.

'Flore Pleno'♀ (syn. 'Plenus') has yellow double flowers. It is more compact in habit and slower-growing than the species, reaching just 75×60cm (2½×2ft) after 5 years and ultimately 1m (3ft) tall.

U. gallii **'Mizen'** Golden yellow flowers, 1.5cm (½in) long, open from late summer to autumn. This prostrate shrub has stout, spiny branchlets. HEIGHT & SPREAD 30×30cm (1×1ft) after 5 years (also the ultimate size).

▼ *Ulex europaeus* 'Flore Pleno'

CULTIVATION Plant container-grown plants in spring or early autumn in well-drained, poor or ordinary soil and in a sunny site. Do not plant in shallow, chalky or rich soils.

PROPAGATION Sow 1 or 2 seeds in individual pots of John Innes No.1 compost in mid spring. Stand the pots in a coldframe or greenhouse. Thin out to single seedlings in mid summer and grow on in a coldframe. Plant out the following autumn. Take semi-ripe cuttings of 'Flore Pleno' in late summer and plant them out a year later.

PRUNING None usually required.

PESTS AND DISEASES Frost may cause die-back. Otherwise trouble free.

Ulmus

Elm

Ulmaceae

Shapes and sizes of elms vary, but no species is reliably resistant to Dutch elm disease. The trees and shrubs are mainly deciduous and all the species described below are hardy. They require well-drained, fertile soil and a place in the sun.

RECOMMENDED SPECIES AND VARIETIES

U. glabra **'Camperdownii'** The dull green, rough-textured leaves, which turn yellow in autumn, are up to 10cm (4in) long, egg-shaped and coarsely toothed. Dense stalkless clusters of flowers are borne in late winter. This compact tree with pendulous branches forms a dome. It is suitable for planting in exposed inland and coastal positions. HEIGHT & SPREAD 3.5×1.8m (12×6ft) after 10 years, ultimately 8m (26ft) tall.

U. x hollandica **'Jacqueline Hillier'** Oval, rough-textured and double-toothed dark green leaves that persist into winter are an endearing feature of this suckering, slow-growing shrub. It has a dense habit and makes a neat hedge. HEIGHT & SPREAD 1.2×1.2m (4×4ft) after 10 years, ultimately 1.8m (6ft) tall.

▼ *Ulmus* x *hollandica* 'Jacqueline Hillier'

U. **'Dampieri Aurea'** (syn. *U.* 'Wredei') This narrow, conical, deciduous tree has crowded broad leaves, up to 6cm (2½in) long, pleasingly suffused with golden yellow. HEIGHT & SPREAD 4×2m (13×6½ft) after 10 years, ultimately 10m (33ft) tall.

U. parvifolia **'Geisha'** The oval, toothed, dark green leaves are creamy when young. Insignificant flowers appear in early autumn. A low, spreading habit characterises this semi-evergreen dwarf shrub. HEIGHT & SPREAD 45cm×1m (1½×3ft) after 10 years, ultimately 60cm (2ft) tall.

▲ *Ulmus parvifolia* 'Geisha'

U. **'Wredei'** see *U.* 'Dampieri Aurea'

CULTIVATION Plant bare-rooted stock from late autumn to early spring and container-grown stock at any time of year. Choose a fertile soil and an open, sunny position.

PROPAGATION Remove suckers from 'Jacqueline Hillier' and grow in a nursery bed for at least 2 years before planting out in final positions. Otherwise, buy stock from a reputable nursery.

PRUNING None required.

PESTS AND DISEASES Leaves may be eaten by caterpillars or distorted by aphids. Gall mites produce blisters on the foliage. Elm bark beetles transmit Dutch elm disease, which kills branches and causes browning of the leaves, eventually killing the tree.

Umbilicus

Crassulaceae

The only species of this genus that is widely grown in Britain, *Umbilicus rupestris*, is characterised by orderly rosettes of shiny, round, succulent leaves which flatten themselves neatly against niches in a wall or rock garden. Upright spires of small, greenish white flowers in summer, resembling small foxgloves, add to the plant's unobtrusive charm. Gritty, well-drained, non-limy soil and sun or partial shade are the growing requirements of this evergreen perennial.

The plants are never a nuisance in the garden; although they may self-sow in crevices, the fine roots of any unwanted seedlings are easily removed. The genus is native to S Europe and SW Asia.

▲ *Umbilicus rupestris*

RECOMMENDED SPECIES

U. rupestris (navelwort, pennywort) Up to 50 small drooping flowers, in the shape of tubular bells and up to 1cm (⅜in) long, bloom from early to late summer on a tapered spire, 20-40cm (8-16in) tall. They have a toothed edge and are greenish white, sometimes flushed with pink. The circular, round-toothed, dark green fleshy leaves, up to 5cm (2in) across, are dimpled in the centres, accounting for one of the plant's common names. They form a basal rosette on pink-tinged, succulent stalks, from 2-10cm (¾-4in) long. The few smaller leaves along the flowering stem are more kidney-shaped than round. Narrow tubular seed capsules, enclosed within the flower bell, produce tiny brown seeds. Plants grow in the wild over rocks and banks. HEIGHT & SPREAD 30×15cm (12×6in).

CULTIVATION Plant in spring or autumn in moist, gritty, well-drained soil, in sun or partial shade. Limy soil is unsuitable.

PROPAGATION Sow seed as soon as it is ripe or in spring, preferably where you wish the plants to flower.

PESTS AND DISEASES Usually trouble free.

Umbrella plant see *Darmera peltata*
Umbrella tree see *Schefflera actinophylla*
Urn plant see *Aechmea fasciata*

Ursinia

Jewel of the Veldt
Compositae

Eye-catching daisy flowers bring sunshine colours to sunny beds and borders. Foiled by attractive lacy foliage, the vivid orange or yellow blooms can be seen through most of the summer, although they tend to close up during dull weather. The species of this South African genus grown in Britain are treated as half-hardy annuals. Those described below have a bushy habit, producing flowers up to 5cm (2in) across on wiry stems from mid to late summer.

RECOMMENDED SPECIES AND VARIETIES

U. anthemoides Orange 'petals' (ray florets) have a purple-brown base making a dark ring round the centre of the daisy. Pale green leaves are finely divided and scented. HEIGHT & SPREAD 30×20cm (12×8in).

▲ *Ursinia anthemoides*

'Solar Fire' has orange flowers without the dark ring.

U. calenduliflora This species differs from *U. anthemoides* in having yellow flowers and less finely divided foliage. HEIGHT & SPREAD 30×20cm (12×8in).

U. speciosa This species produces yellow or orange-yellow, purple-centred daisy flowers. HEIGHT & SPREAD 30×20cm (12×8in).

CULTIVATION Plant out in spring, once the risk of hard night frosts has passed, choosing a sunny, sheltered situation. Ursinias flower best in poor, dry soil – a dry, sunny bank is an ideal setting. Deadhead to prolong the flowering period.

Ursinia also makes an attractive summer-flowering pot plant for a cool greenhouse or a sunny position in a conservatory. Put 3 plants in a 15cm (6in) pot.

PROPAGATION Sow seed in early spring in trays in the greenhouse. Sowing directly into the flowering positions in mid spring is also successful, though plants will commence flowering later.

PESTS AND DISEASES Usually trouble free.

Uvularia

Bellwort
Convallariaceae

The fresh green foliage and nodding yellow flowers of these herbaceous perennials bring colour and grace to a cool shady site in spring and early summer. The flowers are narrowly bell-shaped, with six, usually twisted, petals. The leaves are borne on erect or arching stems.

These rhizomatous plants are native to deciduous woodland in N America and are best planted in a woodland edge or beside a pond. They also suit a shady situation in a large rock garden.

RECOMMENDED SPECIES AND VARIETIES

U. grandiflora♀ Nodding, bright yellow flowers adorn this species in late spring and early summer. Each flower is up to 5cm (2in) long, with narrow, twisted petals. The flowers hang down on slender stalks that emerge from the point where the upper leaves join the stems. The bright green leaves are ovate, 7.5-13cm (3-5¼in) long, and hairy beneath. They are fused together in pairs around the stem. The plant has a clump-forming habit. HEIGHT & SPREAD 75×45cm (2½×1½ft).

▲ *Uvularia grandiflora*

The flowers produced by var. ***pallida*** are pale yellow.

U. perfoliata Pale yellow, nodding flowers up to 3cm (1¼in) long, with twisted petals, appear in late spring and early summer. The thin flower stalks emerge where the upper leaves join the stems. The light greyish green elliptic to oval leaves are about 7.5cm (3in) long. The plant has a clump-forming habit. HEIGHT & SPREAD 60×30cm (2×1ft).

U. sessilifolia Nodding, creamy yellow flowers, about 2.5cm (1in) long, appear in late spring and early summer. They hang from the leaf axils near the arching tips of the upright leafy stems. The fresh green leaves are narrowly oblong and about 7.5cm (3in) in length. This species has a creeping habit. HEIGHT & SPREAD 40×40cm (16×16in).

CULTIVATION Plant in early autumn or early spring in a partially shaded situation in well-drained, fairly moist, humus-rich soil.

PROPAGATION Divide in autumn or early spring. Sow seed in pots in a coldframe as soon as it is ripe.

PESTS AND DISEASES Slugs and snails may attack young growth.

Vaccinium

Ericaceae

Vaccinium corymbosum

The decorative shrubs in this large genus are valuable in areas with acid soils. Most will grow in moist soil and can tolerate exceptionally acid, peaty or sandy soil. The genus includes deciduous plants, whose leaves turn colour before falling, and evergreens. The alternate leaves have smooth or serrated edges. Widespread throughout the Northern Hemisphere, the plants generally produce pretty but small urn-like, bell-shaped or tubular flowers. The many-seeded berries include blueberry and cranberry, but some of the other berries are insipid or sour. The recommended plants are fairly hardy, but *Vaccinium delavayi*, *V. floribundum*, *V. glaucoalbum* and *V. nummularia* are unsuitable for cold areas.

RECOMMENDED SPECIES AND VARIETIES

V. corymbosum♀ (blueberry) Deciduous ovate to lance-shaped leaves, up to 8cm (3¼in) long, turn orange to scarlet in autumn. The rounded, blue-black berries ripen in late summer and early autumn, attracting birds unless the shrub is protected by netting. This plant will grow in wet ground. HEIGHT & SPREAD 1m×60cm (3×2ft) after 5 years, ultimately 1.5m (5ft) tall.

V. delavayi Shiny, dark green, obovate leaves, about 1.5cm (½in) long, grow on this dwarf evergreen with a compact habit. HEIGHT & SPREAD 20×20cm (8×8in) after 5 years, ultimately up to 1m (3ft) tall.

V. floribundum (syn. *V. mortinia*) Red-tinted young growth helps to earn this low, spreading evergreen its place in the garden. The leaves, to 1.5cm (½in), partly hide the red berries. HEIGHT & SPREAD 50cm×1.2m (20in×4ft) after 5 years, ultimately up to 1.2m (4ft) tall.

V. glaucoalbum♀ Stiff, oval leaves, up to 8cm (3¼in) long, have attractive waxy white undersides. A profusion of black berries with a bluish white bloom appear in autumn on this compact, evergreen shrub. HEIGHT & SPREAD 1×1m (3×3ft) after 5 years, ultimately 1.2m (4ft) tall.

V. mortinia see *V. floribundum*

V. nummularia This dwarf evergreen is grown for its thick, shiny, oval leaves, up to 2.5cm (1in) long, that are bronzy when young. The shoots are hairy and the pinkish flowers appear in late spring and early summer. The berries are black. HEIGHT & SPREAD 20×20cm (8×8in) after 5 years, ultimately 40cm (16in) tall.

▼ *Vaccinium glaucoalbum*

▲ *Vaccinium nummularia*

V. ovatum The leathery, evergreen foliage of this bushy, erect shrub is a glossy, pinkish brown when young. The oval to oblong leaves are up to 3cm (1¼in) long. This plant thrives in woodland conditions and tolerates shade. Its size is rather variable. HEIGHT & SPREAD 60×45cm (2×1½ft) after 5 years, ultimately up to 4m (13ft) tall.

V. vitis-idaea (cowberry, mountain cranberry) Lustrous green, egg-shaped leaves, up to 2.5cm (1in) long, give excellent ground cover and make this dwarf, creeping evergreen the best choice for a small garden. Bright red, sharp-tasting berries follow the summer flowers. HEIGHT & SPREAD 15×20cm (6×8in) after 5 years, ultimately 30cm (12in) tall.

Plants in the vigorous **'Koralle Group'**♀ may be invasive, while ssp. ***minus*** is less so.

CULTIVATION Plant in autumn or spring in acid soil that does not dry out in summer. Provide shelter for *V. nummularia* and *V. glaucoalbum* in cold gardens.

▼ *Vaccinium vitis-idaea*

PROPAGATION Take softwood cuttings, including a heel of the old wood, in late summer and grow in a peat-sand mixture with bottom heat. Sow seed of species in moist peat in a coldframe in autumn. If using a propagator, sow seed in winter. Layer ground-hugging plants.

PRUNING Cut back the tips of vigorous shoots once a year in spring if necessary to keep the plant tidy.

PESTS AND DISEASES Usually trouble free, but rabbits and deer will eat unprotected plants and birds will eat unprotected berries of *V. corymbosum*.

Valerian, common see *Valeriana officinalis*

Valerian, red see *Centranthus ruber*

Valeriana

Valerian

Valerianaceae

Rounded clusters of tiny pink or white, tubular to flat flowers are borne above the foliage from spring to mid summer. The genus includes hardy herbaceous perennials, shrubs and sub-shrubs. Common valerian, *Valeriana officinalis*, has been cultivated for centuries for its medicinal properties. It is now more often grown as an ornamental. All the valerians described below are native to the Northern Hemisphere.

RECOMMENDED SPECIES AND VARIETIES

V. 'Alba' see *Centranthus ruber albus*

V. alliariifolia Tiny pink flowers, in clusters about 4cm (1½in) across, appear from early to mid summer. The bright green, heart-shaped leaves grow to 20cm (8in) across. Fluffy ornamental seed heads follow the flowers in autumn. This species is ideal for woodland gardens or other moist, shady areas. HEIGHT & SPREAD 1×1m (3×3ft).

V. 'Coccinea' see *Centranthus ruber*

V. officinalis (common valerian, garden heliotrope) Flower clusters, up to 4cm (1½in) across, are borne in mid summer. They may be white or shades of pink. The blooms rise above a mass of mid green, much divided foliage. The leaves may be up to 5cm (2in) long. The plant forms a clump. HEIGHT & SPREAD 1.2×1m (4×3ft).

▼ *Valeriana officinalis*

▲ *Valeriana phu* 'Aurea'

***V. phu* 'Aurea'** This hardy perennial is valued for its bright spring foliage. The divided leaves, up to 5cm (2in) long, are deep golden yellow at first, fading to mid green as spring turns to summer. Clusters of insignificant white flowers appear in summer. The plant makes a loose mound. HEIGHT & SPREAD 1.2×1m (4×3ft).

CULTIVATION Plant in autumn in any reasonably fertile, moist but well-drained soil, choosing a sunny situation. In drier gardens try to find a moist area in semi-shade. Select a sunny site for *V. phu* 'Aurea' to encourage the brightest spring foliage. Stake plants when necessary in windy situations.

PROPAGATION Sow seed in a coldframe in spring. Divide established plants in autumn.

PESTS AND DISEASES Cats are attracted to *V. officinalis* and may lie on the plant.

Vancouveria

Berberidaceae

Handsome divided foliage is enlivened in early summer by loose sprays of tiny white or yellow flowers. Vancouverias are hardy and easily grown in cool, moist, shady conditions. These graceful rhizomatous evergreen or herbaceous perennials form excellent ground cover between shrubs or among larger ferns. The two species below are native to moist woodland in western regions of the United States.

RECOMMENDED SPECIES

V. chrysantha Small, bright yellow flowers, about 1cm (⅜in) wide, are carried in airy sprays on dark stalks in late spring. The leaves form a dark, evergreen carpet. Each leaf, up to 23cm (9in) long, is composed of up to 9 oval or shallowly 3-lobed, rather leathery leaflets. The plant needs a sheltered and partly shaded position. HEIGHT & SPREAD 30cm×1m (1×3ft).

V. hexandra Pure white flowers, up to 1.5cm (½in) wide, are carried in sprays. They open in late spring from red-tinged buds. The leaves, up to 23cm (9in) long,

▲ *Vancouveria hexandra*

comprise up to 9 thin, roughly oval, shallowly 3-lobed, bright green leaflets. This herbaceous perennial is the hardiest species. HEIGHT & SPREAD 30cm×1m (1×3ft).

CULTIVATION Plant in early autumn or early spring in a well-drained, moist soil enriched with plenty of leaf-mould, choosing a spot in partial shade.

PROPAGATION Divide in autumn or spring.

PESTS AND DISEASES Usually trouble free, but the young foliage may be attacked by slugs. Vine weevils can also be a problem.

Vanda see ORCHIDS p.467

Veltheimia

Hyacinthaceae

Highly distinctive tubular flowers adorn the plants of this small South African genus. In winter and spring the flowers are produced in prominent spikes and last for several weeks. Even when the plants are not in flower the bold, broad, glossy foliage is a decorative feature for the house, conservatory or greenhouse. The plants are bulbous and have a minimum temperature requirement of 5°C (41°F).

RECOMMENDED SPECIES AND VARIETIES

V. bracteata♀ (syn. *V. viridifolia*) Tubular pink flowers with cream markings and up to 4cm (1½in) long, hang in a densely packed spike, up to 10cm (4in) long, at the top of a strong, thick, upright stem from mid winter to early spring. The flower stem emerges from the centre of a clump of glossy green, lance-shaped, wavy-edged leaves, up to 30cm (12in) long and 10cm (4in) wide, which grow, rosette-like, from the top of a scaly, pale brown bulb. HEIGHT & SPREAD 45×30cm (18×12in).

'Rosalba' produces white flowers spotted with pink.

V. viridifolia see *V. bracteata*

CULTIVATION Pot up bulbs individually in early autumn, using John Innes No.2 compost. Ensure that the tips of the bulbs are at or just beneath the surface of the compost and place the pots in a cool greenhouse or conservatory. Water only when the compost has dried out slightly. The flower spikes emerge as the days shorten. Water and feed well-established bulbs regularly once the flowers appear.

Cut off the flower stems as the flowers fade. Dry bulbs off from early to late summer. Repot annually in autumn to encourage the production of good-quality flower spikes and offsets, although repotting is not essential.

PROPAGATION Sow seed in spring or separate offsets at potting time.

PESTS AND DISEASES Usually trouble free.

▼ *Veltheimia bracteata*

Veratrum

False hellebore

Melanthiaceae

The species recommended here are robust, clump-forming perennials with handsome, pleated leaves from which arise tall, branching spires of small, star-shaped flowers. They are hardy and easily cultivated in moist, fertile soils in sun or partial shade. All parts of the plants are poisonous if eaten. Native to temperate regions throughout the Northern Hemisphere.

RECOMMENDED SPECIES

V. album Upright stems carry large, branched plumes of greenish white flowers about 2cm (¾in) wide in mid and late summer. At the base of the stems, the pointed, oval, mid green leaves are up to 30cm (1ft) long. Native to Europe and N Asia. HEIGHT & SPREAD 2m×60cm (6½×2ft).

▼ *Veratrum album*

▲ *Veratrum nigrum*

V. nigrum Long, narrow, spike-like plumes of blackish purple flowers make a striking display in late summer and early autumn. Dark green, oval leaves, up to 36 cm (14 in) long, form compact clumps. Native to S Europe and N Asia. HEIGHT & SPREAD 1.2 m×60 cm (4×2 ft).

V. viride Long narrow plumes with drooping lower branches bear pale or bright green flowers about 2 cm (¾ in) wide. The stems arise from clumps of oval mid green leaves, 30 cm (12 in) long. Native to N America. HEIGHT & SPREAD 1.8 m×60 cm (6×2 ft).

CULTIVATION Plant in autumn in a fairly moist, fertile soil in sun or partial shade.

PROPAGATION Sow seed in pots in a cold-frame. Alternatively, divide well-established plants in autumn.

PESTS AND DISEASES Usually trouble free although the leaves may be damaged by slugs and snails.

Verbascum

Mullein

Scrophulariaceae

Verbascum Cotswold Group 'Gainsborough'

Showy spires of saucer-shaped flowers are produced by these stately plants from early summer through to autumn. Most mulleins have yellow flowers, but some produce blooms in white or shades of pink and mauve. Individual flowers are generally 2-4 cm (¾-1½ in) across. Typically, mulleins produce a rosette of basal leaves, as well as smaller leaves growing up the stems. Some plants have striking white-felted foliage.

The genus consists of annuals, biennials and evergreen or semi-evergreen perennials and sub-shrubs. The majority of species grown in British gardens are natives of S Europe and most are hardy. They can be used at the back of a border. Although often short-lived, they are readily propagated to supply replacement plants.

RECOMMENDED SPECIES AND VARIETIES

***V.* 'Arctic Summer'** see *V. bombyciferum* 'Polarsommer'

V. blattaria (moth mullein) Pale yellow flowers are borne in loose spikes up to 10 cm (4 in) long. The individual flowers have contrasting purple stamens. The lance-shaped leaves are up to 30 cm (12 in) long. This biennial prefers to be planted in moister situations than most mulleins. HEIGHT & SPREAD 1.8 m×30 cm (6×1 ft).

The flowers of f. ***albiflorum*** are white.

▲ *Verbascum blattaria f. albiflorum*

▲ *Verbascum bombyciferum*

V. bombyciferum ♀ (syn. *V.* 'Broussa') A succession of sulphur-yellow flowers are borne on spikes up to 20 cm (8 in) long. The oval silvery leaves are up to 50 cm (20 in) long. All of this much-branched biennial or short-lived evergreen perennial, except the flowers, is covered in dense white hairs, giving the plant a silvery appearance. HEIGHT & SPREAD 1.8 m×75 cm (6×2½ ft).

'Polarsommer' (syn. *V.* 'Arctic Summer') has white flowers.

***V.* 'Broussa'** see *V. bombyciferum*

V. chaixii (nettle-leaved mullein) Much-branched spires, up to 20 cm (8 in) long, are crowded with yellow flowers. The individual flowers bear contrasting purple stamens. The tongue-shaped leaves, up to 30 cm (12 in) long, are covered with white wool. This plant is a semi-evergreen perennial. HEIGHT & SPREAD 1.2 m×45 cm (4×1½ ft).

'Album' produces white flowers with mauve centres.

▲ *Verbascum chaixii 'Album'*

V. dumulosum ♀ Yellow flowers, 1.5 cm (½ in) across, are held in spires up to 10 cm (4 in) long on this compact evergreen sub-shrub from Turkey. The grey, woolly leaves grow to about 5 cm (2 in) in length and are roughly oval or lance-shaped, varying from plant to plant. This species is suitable for a rock garden and is reasonably hardy if given a sheltered site. HEIGHT & SPREAD 25×15 cm (10×6 in).

V. phoeniceum (purple mullein) Delicate flower spires, up to 20 cm (8 in) long, bear blooms in shades of pink and purple, and occasionally in white. Slightly wavy, deep green leaves grow to about 15 cm (6 in) long. This biennial or short-lived evergreen perennial is often grown as an annual. Established plants may self-sow. HEIGHT & SPREAD 1 m×30 cm (3×1 ft).

V. thapsus (Aaron's rod, great mullein)

Dense woolly spires of yellow flowers, up to 25cm (10in) long, are produced by this biennial. The white or grey foliage is woolly. The roughly oval or oblong leaves are about 45cm (1½ft) long. HEIGHT & SPREAD 2m×45cm (6½×1½ft).

BORDER HYBRIDS

There are a number of evergreen or semi-evergreen perennials that are excellent for growing in a border. All those described have a spread of about 30cm (12in).

Among the **Cotswold Group** of hybrids are **'Cotswold Beauty'**♀, which has pale buff to amber flowers and is 1.2m (4ft) tall; **'Cotswold Queen'**, bearing yellow flowers flushed with apricot and growing to 1.5m (5ft) tall; **'Gainsborough'**♀, with primrose-yellow blooms and silver-grey leaves, reaching a height of 1.5m (5ft); **'Mont Blanc'**, a pure white form with silvery white leaves that grows to 1m (3ft) and **'Pink Domino'**♀, that reaches a height of 1.2m (4ft) and has rose-pink flowers with a darker pink eye.

'Helen Johnson'♀ has pink flowers and grows to 1.2m (4ft) tall. **'Vernale'** bears vivid yellow blooms with lilac anthers. Its leaves are dark green. This robust plant grows to a height of 1.8m (6ft).

ROCK GARDEN HYBRIDS

There are some smaller hybrids available, all evergreen sub-shrubs, which are suitable for growing in rock gardens or under glass. They have a height of 25cm (10in) and a spread of 15cm (6in).

Bright yellow flowers are carried by **'Golden Wings'**♀ in branching spires, up to 20cm (8in) long. Each bloom is about 1.5cm (½in) across and has orange anthers. The mid green leaves of this plant grow to 4cm (1½in) long. **'Letitia'**♀ has yellow flowers and blue-grey foliage.

CULTIVATION Plant in any reasonably fertile soil in spring or autumn, choosing a site in full sun. Stake taller plants in exposed positions. Remove faded flowerheads to encourage a second flowering.

▼ *Verbascum* 'Letitia'

Plant *V. dumulosum*, *V.* 'Golden Wings' and *V.* 'Letitia' in crevices, to provide maximum shelter. Protect them from winter damp with a cloche or sheet of glass or transparent plastic. Alternatively, grow them in a cold greenhouse or alpine house.

PROPAGATION Sow the seed of biennial species in early summer for planting out in autumn the following year. Sow seed of *V. phoeniceum* under glass in late winter and plant out in spring. Move and replant self-sown seedlings of *V. phoeniceum* in spring.

Take root cuttings of perennials, sub-shrubs and cultivars in late winter.

PESTS AND DISEASES Powdery mildew sometimes affects the foliage.

Verbena

Verbenaceae

Verbena 'Sissinghurst'

Dense terminal clusters of small primrose-like flowers in shades of blue, pink, red, violet and white are used to decorate sunny beds and borders in summer. They also make good container plants. There are two main types of plant: the hardy, summer-flowering perennials and the dwarf, half-hardy bedding plants grouped under *Verbena* × *hybrida* and *V. peruviana*. Some are trailing and used in containers. Mostly native to tropical and sub-tropical America.

▼ *Verbena bonariensis*

RECOMMENDED SPECIES AND VARIETIES

V. bonariensis (syn. *V. patagonica*) (South American vervain, tall verbena) Tiny lavender-blue flowers are carried in rounded clusters at the top of wiry stems from late summer to autumn. The stems are anchored by dark green, elliptic, often toothed, basal leaves, 12.5cm (5in) long. This herbaceous border perennial is only hardy in sheltered British gardens. In more exposed sites cover the roots in winter with a mulch of rough compost or bracken to protect from frost. HEIGHT & SPREAD 1.8m×50cm (6ft×20in)

V. chamaedrifolia see *V. peruviana*

▲ *Verbena corymbosa*

V. corymbosa Small heliotrope-blue flowers are carried in flattish, terminal clusters from early to mid summer. This border perennial is hardy in most British gardens. It has underground rhizomes from which the stems arise. The triangular mid green leaves have deep veins and are up to 6cm (2½in) long. In a damp site the plant can be invasive. HEIGHT & SPREAD 1.2×1m (4×3ft)

V. hastata (blue vervain) At the top of branched stems tiny blue flowers are held in candelabra-shaped heads, 12.5cm (5in) across. The blooms appear in mid summer and are long-lasting. This is a truly hardy herbaceous border perennial. The mid green serrated leaves are 15cm (6in) long. HEIGHT & SPREAD 1.2m×60cm (4×2ft).

V.* × *hybrida These half-hardy dwarf plants are useful for filling gaps at the front of a border and for edging stone paths. They can also be utilised in more formal bedding schemes or in containers.

Although strictly perennials, they are best treated as annuals in British gardens. Their habit varies from upright and compact to spreading and mat-forming. They have small ovate to lanceolate mid green leaves. The flowers are up to 2.5cm (1in) across, held in tight heads from mid summer

▲ *Verbena* 'Lawrence Johnston'

▲ *Verbena* 'Silver Anne'

until the first frosts. HEIGHT & SPREAD 20×30cm (8×12in).

The following varieties do not come true from seed and are propagated by cuttings: **'Lawrence Johnston'**♀ (brilliant scarlet); **'Silver Anne'**♀ (pink, vigorous); **'Sissinghurst'**♀ (bright pink); **'Tapien Purple'** and **'Tapien Rose'** (both with a cascading habit that is excellent for hanging baskets).

The following are usually raised annually from seed: **'Apple Blossom'** (pink); **'Blue Lagoon'**; **'Imagination'** (deep violet-blue, with a spreading habit); **'Peaches and Cream'** (coral pink, ageing to creamy yellow); **'Quartz Scarlet'** (scarlet with white eye, vigorous); and **'Sandy Scarlet'**.

Two worthwhile strains of mixed colours are **'Derby'**, which has an upright, compact habit, and **'Showtime'**, with a spreading habit. Both strains include some white-eyed flowers.

▼ *Verbena* 'Peaches and Cream'

V. officinalis (vervain) Long, slender spikes of small mauve flowers are produced from mid summer to early autumn by this hardy perennial. The square-sectioned stems bear pairs of deeply divided, mid green leaves, up to 7.5cm (3in) long. HEIGHT & SPREAD 45×30cm (1½×1ft).

V. patagonica see *V. bonariensis*

V. peruviana (syn. *V. chamaedrifolia*) A profusion of bright crimson or scarlet flowers like open stars, 1cm (⅜in) across, are borne in clusters from early summer to late autumn. This semi-evergreen prostrate perennial for the front of the border is used as a half-hardy filler for summer displays. The mid green leaves are oval with toothed edges and 5cm (2in) long. HEIGHT & SPREAD 7.5cm×1m (3in×3ft).

'Alba' has white flowers.

V. rigida♀ (syn. *V. venosa*) Purple flowers, 6mm (¼in) across, appear in tight clusters on the top of the branched stems from mid summer to early autumn. This stiffly erect, hardy herbaceous perennial for the late summer border has lance-shaped mid green leaves, 7.5cm (3in) long. HEIGHT & SPREAD 60×30cm (2×1ft).

V. venosa see *V. rigida*

CULTIVATION Verbenas do best in warm, sunny spots and fertile soil. Plant the hardy perennials in spring. *V. corymbosa* does best in moist soil. The taller ones will need staking. Plant out the half-hardy plants once the danger of frost has passed.

PROPAGATION Divide the hardy plants in spring. Take softwood cuttings of half-hardy plants that will not come true from seed in summer and overwinter under glass.

▼ *Verbena rigida*

Sow seed of other half-hardy hybrids in early spring under heated greenhouse conditions. Cover the seed shallowly with compost, and cover the pot or tray with black polythene until emergence begins. Pinch out the growing points of the young plants when they are 6cm (2½in) high, to encourage bushy growth.

PESTS AND DISEASES In hot, dry summers aphids, tarsonemid mites and powdery mildew can be troublesome.

Verbena, lemon-scented see *Aloysia triphylla*

Verbena, shrub see *Lantana*

Vernonia

Ironweed

Compositae

In summer and autumn, flat-topped clusters of rusty brown flowers crown *Vernonia crinata*, the most popular representative of this genus to be grown in British gardens. This hardy herbaceous perennial needs to be positioned in a large border where it can provide a stately backdrop for smaller, more colourful plants. Vernonias can be invasive and to prevent self-seeding remove the seed heads when they appear in autumn.

RECOMMENDED SPECIES

V. crinata Tall stems carry numerous small, rusty brown flowers in flat-topped clusters, 20cm (8in) across, from late summer to mid autumn. The seed heads turn to purple in autumn before the seeds drop. The narrow, tapering, dark green leaves are 18cm (7in) long and often toothed. Native to the southern United States. HEIGHT & SPREAD 1.8m×50cm (6ft×20in)

CULTIVATION Plant from autumn to spring in any moisture-retentive but well-drained soil in an open, sunny site. Plants may need some support.

PROPAGATION Divide from autumn to spring and move self-sown seedlings in spring. Alternatively, sow seed under glass or where the plants are to grow in spring.

PESTS AND DISEASES Usually trouble free.

▼ *Vernonia crinata*

Veronica

Speedwell
Scrophulariaceae

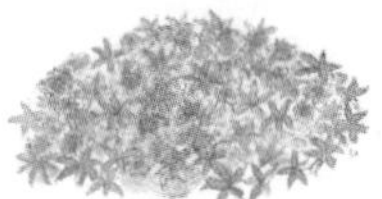

Veronica prostrata

Tiny, mostly blue flowers, carried in slender spikes or held singly, make these hardy perennials valuable for summer colour. A number of species make fine border plants while other species are suitable for the rock garden. There are ground-hugging plants and shrubby clump-formers, most growing best in sunny, well-drained soils, though *Veronica beccabunga* requires a moist soil. The four-petalled, saucer-shaped flowers are 6-20mm (¼-¾in) across. Pink and white flowered varieties are also available. The leaves are narrowly to broadly oval.

RECOMMENDED SPECIES AND VARIETIES

V. austriaca Loose spikes of clear blue flowers are borne from early to mid summer. This evergreen plant has a semi-upright, but rather floppy habit, vigorously forming a clump with downy, 2.5-5cm (1-2in) long, oval leaves. It can be grown in a rock garden but needs winter cover in cold wet areas. Native to E Europe. HEIGHT & SPREAD 20×60cm (8×24in).

Corfu Form and **'Ionian Skies'** have particularly bright blue flowers.

Loose spikes of clear blue flowers are borne by ssp. ***teucrium*** (syn. *V. teucrium*) in early to mid summer among rounded leaves that are up to 3cm (1¼in) long. **'Crater Lake Blue'**♀ has vivid sky-blue flowers, both **'Kapitän'** and **'Royal Blue'**♀ have deep blue flowers.

▼ *Veronica austriaca ssp. teucrium*

V. beccabunga (brooklime) Starry, blue flowers veined with violet are carried in slender spires in late spring and mid summer by this hardy perennial. Dark green oval leaves are up to 4cm (1½in) long. The plant is found in the wild, growing in or near water, but will grow on moist soils in the garden where its rather floppy habit can mask any unsightly low features round a pool. HEIGHT & SPREAD 60×60cm (2×2ft).

V. bombycina China-blue flowers are borne in short spikes during late spring above a loose mound of oval, almost white leaves with a dense, downy covering. This evergreen can be damaged by winter wet and cold and is best grown in an alpine house. Native to S Turkey and the Lebanon. HEIGHT & SPREAD 5×20cm (2×8in).

V. chamaedrys (germander speedwell) Narrow spikes of white-eyed, bright blue flowers sprout from upper leaf joints over a long period from early spring to mid summer. This rather untidy, sprawling plant is suitable for a rock garden. The oval to triangular evergreen leaves are unevenly toothed, 1-2.5cm (⅜-1in) long and dull green. Native to Britain. HEIGHT & SPREAD 15×30cm (6×12in).

V. cinerea♀ Unusual, ash-grey, broadly strap-shaped evergreen leaves, up to 2cm (¾in) long, set off the clusters of purplish blue or pink flowers in early summer on this tough and rather invasive carpeting plant. Flowering shoots rise over a broad mat of woody stems. It is hardy and suitable only for a large rock garden. Native to Turkey. HEIGHT & SPREAD 10×30cm (4×12in).

V. exaltata Spikes of tiny clear blue flowers are carried in mid summer. This hardy perennial will stand upright without the need for staking. The dark green, lance-shaped leaves, up to 10cm (4in) long, have jagged edges. Native to Europe. HEIGHT & SPREAD 1.2m×30cm (4×1ft).

▼ *Veronica chamaedrys*

V. fruticans (rock speedwell) Deep blue flowers are enhanced by a reddish eye, and rise in short, loose spikes during mid summer to early autumn. The hardy rock plant is of bushy growth with fine, partly woody stems and evergreen, 1cm (⅜in) long, oval leaves. Native to Europe. HEIGHT & SPREAD 15×30cm (6×12in).

V. gentianoides♀ A stately hardy perennial, suitable for a rock garden, this species has spires of flowers resembling small hollyhocks and is undemanding and generous with bloom. The 20cm (8in) spikes of powder-blue flowers are borne in early summer. The dark green, glossy, evergreen leaves, 2.5cm (1in) long, form a clump. Native to SE Europe. HEIGHT & SPREAD 30×40cm (12×16in).

Veronica gentianoides

'Nana' is more compact with pale blue flowers. **'Variegata'** is slightly less vigorous than the species with pale blue flowers and leaves marked with broad cream stripes.

V. incana see *V. spicata* ssp. *incana*

V. longifolia Bright blue, saucer-shaped flowers are carried in dense, slender spikes 25cm (10in) long. A hardy perennial, this rather floppy plant has stems with whorls of mid green leaves up to 8cm (3¼in) long. Native to Europe and Russia. HEIGHT & SPREAD 1m×30cm (3×1ft).

'Schneeriesin' bears deep blue flowers on longer spikes.

▼ *Veronica longifolia*

V. nummularia (Pyrenean speedwell) Dense clusters of blue or pink flowers are held at the tips of shoots which rise from bare stems along the ground. The shoots of this mat-forming hardy rock plant are packed with 1 cm (⅜ in) long, rounded, fleshy evergreen leaves. Native to the Pyrenees. HEIGHT & SPREAD 5×30 cm (2×12 in).

V. pectinata Profuse clusters of pale blue flowers cover a mass of velvety shoots and deeply toothed, small, rounded evergreen leaves during late spring to early summer. This hardy rock plant forms a mat of creeping stems. Native to Iran and Turkey. HEIGHT & SPREAD 10×30 cm (4×12 in).

'Rosea' has rose-lilac blooms.

V. peduncularis Small spikes of bright blue flowers with white eyes are borne in early spring and summer on this hardy perennial. It is a plant suitable for rock gardens and paving because of its mat-forming habit, its prostrate stems clothed with small, glossy evergreen leaves up to 2.5 cm (1 in) long. Native to Turkey and the Caucasus. HEIGHT & SPREAD 10×40 cm (4×16 in).

'Georgia Blue' is more spreading.

V. prostrata♀ Small dense spikes of bright blue flowers are borne in late spring to early summer on this mat-forming, hardy rock plant with small, dark green, evergreen leaves. Native to S Europe. HEIGHT & SPREAD 10×45 cm (4×18 in).

'Blue Sheen' has bright blue flowers. **'Lodden Blue'** has dusky blue flowers. **'Mrs Holt'** has deep pink flowers. **'Rosea'** has pink-lilac flowers. **'Spode Blue'** has china-blue flowers. **'Trehane'** has violet-blue flowers. The dwarf form **'Nana'** has deep blue flowers.

***V.* 'Shirley Blue'**♀ This is a reliable dwarf plant for growing at the front of a border. The bright blue flowers are carried on stiff stems among deep green leaves. HEIGHT & SPREAD 25×25 cm (10×10 in).

▼ *Veronica prostrata* 'Rosea'

V. spicata Profuse dense spikes of blue flowers are seen in mid to late summer on this hardy compact perennial. It is a good plant for the front of a mixed border with tussocks of mid green lance-shaped leaves up to 8 cm (3¼ in) long. Native to Europe, Turkey and central and E Asia. HEIGHT & SPREAD 45×45 cm (18×18 in).

'Erika' has pink flowers and grows to just 30 cm (12 in) tall.

V. spicata* ssp. *incana♀ (syn. *V. incana*) Dense spikes of mid blue flowers are borne in mid to late summer among the bright, silver-grey leaves of this hardy perennial. HEIGHT & SPREAD 45×45 cm (18×18 in).

'Nana' has starry, violet-blue flowers in mid summer that are crowded in narrow spires on upright shoots. A dwarf plant, the stems creep along the ground and bear greyish, oval leaves, 2 cm (¾ in) long, and bluntly toothed. Native to the Caucasus. HEIGHT & SPREAD 7.5×20 cm (3×8 in).

'Wendy'♀ has a looser habit with bright blue flowers and grey leaves. **'Romiley Purple'** has a bushy habit and dark blue flowers and **'Rotfuchs'** ('Red Fox') has deep pink flowers.

V. stelleri see *V. wormskjoldii*

V. teucrium see *V. austriaca* ssp. *teucrium*

V. wormskjoldii (syn. *V. stelleri*) Short spikes of violet-blue, cup-shaped flowers are borne in late summer on this easily grown, hardy perennial. A clump-forming plant for the rock garden or path edge, the semi-erect stems are clothed with oval, evergreen leaves up to 3 cm (1¼ in) long. Native to N America and Greenland. HEIGHT & SPREAD 20×40 cm (8×16 in).

CULTIVATION Plant from autumn to spring. Any reasonably light soil with some humus content will suffice. Choose locations for planting where there is plentiful sun but shelter from cold, harsh winds. Remove spent flowers to encourage compact habit and good flowering in the following year. Plants soon become weak because of the growth of too many stems, so split them up every 2 or 3 years. Many of the taller types will need staking. Feeding is not required.

PROPAGATION Divide clump or mat-forming species from autumn to early spring, replanting the offsets in the required places. Some species, for example *V. bombycina* and *V. chamaedrys*, are too slender and loose in habit for division. For these species take semi-ripe cuttings of non-flowering shoots in mid to late summer. Grow on in pots in the shelter of a coldframe, and plant them out in late spring.

Species can be raised from seed sown in early spring to produce plants for setting out later in the year.

PESTS AND DISEASES Powdery mildew may attack the foliage in summer.

Veronica, shrubby see *Hebe*
Vervain see *Verbena*
Vetch see *Vicia*
Vetch, kidney see *Anthyllis vulneraria*
Vetch, spring see *Lathyrus vernus*

Viburnum

Caprifoliaceae

Viburnum plicatum 'Mariesii'

These hardy evergreen and deciduous shrubs offer a tremendous diversity of foliage, flowers and fruit, providing year-round colour and interest. Seldom exceeding a height of 4.5 m (15 ft), viburnums are easy to grow and make handsome features in a mixed border or can be grown as individual specimens in a lawn. They are also useful hedging and ground-cover plants.

The flowers are mainly white or cream, but can be entirely pink or flushed pink. They are borne in dense round clusters or flat wide heads and are often deliciously scented. The leaves vary considerably from species to species, but all are opposite and toothed and between 5–18 cm (2–7 in) in length. Some species produce brilliantly coloured autumn foliage. Fleshy fruits, often seen in great profusion from late summer and lasting into late winter or early spring, are about 8 mm (⅜ in) across and can be red, orange, yellow, blue or black.

RECOMMENDED SPECIES AND VARIETIES

V. × bodnantense The clusters of sweetly scented pink to white flowers open continuously from early winter to early spring. This erect, twiggy deciduous shrub has dull green ovate leaves – the young foliage is tinged with bronze. HEIGHT & SPREAD 1.8×1.5m (6×5ft) after 5 years, ultimately 3m (10ft) tall.

'Charles Lamont'♀ carries flowers that are bright pink in bud, opening to a silvery pink. **'Dawn'** has rose-red flowers in bud, opening flushed pink. This is the most commonly seen variety. **'Deben'** has apple blossom pink buds that open to white.

V. × ***burkwoodii*** Sweetly scented pink buds open to white in mid to late spring. The leaves are a rich lustrous green above and covered with a pale brown down on the underside. This evergreen develops into a dense, twiggy, round-headed shrub. HEIGHT & SPREAD 1×1.2m (3×4ft) after 5 years, ultimately 2.4m (8ft) tall.

'Anne Russell'♀ is a more compact shrub with slightly larger clusters of fragrant flowers that are pink in bud, opening to pure white. **'Fulbrook'** flowers later and has larger, conical clusters of flowers that are pink in bud, opening to pure white. **'Park Farm Hybrid'**♀ has a more spreading habit and larger, pinker flower clusters.

V. × ***carlcephalum***♀ Large, dense clusters of intensely fragrant white flowers (that are pink in bud) appear in late spring on this fast-growing, upright deciduous shrub with a rather stiff appearance. The light green, broadly ovate leaves often have red tints in autumn. HEIGHT & SPREAD 1.5×1.2m (5×4ft) after 5 years, ultimately 3m (10ft) tall.

V. ***carlesii*** Rounded clusters of very fragrant, waxy white flowers, pink in bud, open in mid to late spring. This is a dense, round-headed deciduous shrub with mid green leaves that offer red tints in autumn. HEIGHT & SPREAD 1×1m (3×3ft) after 5 years, ultimately 2m (6½ft) tall.

'Aurora'♀ has intense red buds opening to pale pink. The leaves are bright green with a hint of copper on opening. **'Charis'** is a vigorous variety with red buds that open to pale pink and then white. **'Diana'** is purplish red in bud, opening to pink and fading to almost white.

V. ***cinnamomifolium***♀ This round-headed evergreen shrub is grown for its elegant oval

▼ *Viburnum cinnamomifolium*

▲ *Viburnum davidii*

leaves that are dark green and leathery. Small dull white flowers appear in mid summer and are followed by blue fruits. Plant in a sheltered position. HEIGHT & SPREAD 1×1m (3×3ft) after 5 years, ultimately 4.5m (15ft) tall.

V. ***davidii***♀ A low-growing, densely branched evergreen shrub grown primarily for its leathery, dark green leaves with 3 conspicuous veins. Small white flowers, borne in flat heads in early summer, are followed by iridescent blue fruits that last throughout winter. HEIGHT & SPREAD 30×40cm (12×16in) after 5 years, ultimately 1.5m (5ft) tall.

V. ***farreri***♀ This densely branched, upright deciduous shrub bears drooping clusters of pale pinkish white scented flowers from late autumn to early spring. The bright green leaves are bronze when young. HEIGHT & SPREAD 1m×75cm (3×2½ft) after 5 years, ultimately 2.4m (8ft) tall.

'Candidissimum' (syn. 'Album') is less densely branched with pure white fragrant flowers and lighter green leaves. **'Nanum'**, a compact, densely twiggy shrub, reaches an ultimate height of 1m (3ft). The pale pink scented flowers are less abundant.

▼ *Viburnum farreri* 'Candidissimum'

▲ *Viburnum opulus*

V. ***henryi*** Dull white, slightly fragrant flowers in early to mid summer are followed by rich red, oval fruits that turn black in winter. This stiffly branched evergreen shrub has dark green shiny leaves with paler undersides. HEIGHT & SPREAD 1×1m (3×3ft) after 5 years, ultimately 2.4m (8ft) tall.

V. × ***juddii***♀ Clusters of scented flowers in spring are pink and open to white. This bushy deciduous shrub has dark green oval leaves. HEIGHT & SPREAD 1×1m (3×3ft) after 5 years, ultimately 1.8m (6ft) tall.

V. ***opulus*** (guelder rose) A dense, multi-stemmed deciduous shrub grown primarily for its display of bright red oval fruits in early to mid autumn. Flattened clusters of small creamy white flowers are produced in early summer. The dark green maple-like leaves sometimes produce brilliant orange and red autumn colour, but this is quite variable. HEIGHT & SPREAD 1.5×1.5m (5×5ft) after 5 years, ultimately 4.5m (15ft) tall.

'Aureum' has bright yellow leaves that turn pale green. This plant requires a sheltered situation preferably in shade for part of the day otherwise leaf scorch occurs. **'Compactum'**♀ is a dense, twiggy shrub, growing to 1.5m (5ft) tall, that produces a

▼ *Viburnum opulus* 'Compactum'

▲ *Viburnum opulus* 'Notcutt's Variety'

▲ *Viburnum opulus* 'Roseum'

good display of flowers, bright red fruits and occasionally autumn colour. **'Notcutt's Variety'** is vigorous with large flowers and fruit and attractive red autumn colour. **'Roseum'**♀ (snowball tree) has pure white globular flowerheads that are apple green on opening and often fade to a dull pink. **'Xanthocarpum'**♀ produces a conspicuous display of translucent yellow fruits.

V. plicatum Grown for their spectacular flowers, these deciduous shrubs can be compact and upright in habit, or can have horizontal branches that create an elegant tiered effect. The flowerheads, borne in late spring and early summer, are made up of masses of creamy white flowers surrounded by white ray florets. Autumn colour is not predictable, but can be rich reddish purple. HEIGHT & SPREAD 1×1.2m (3×4ft) after 5 years, ultimately 3m (10ft) tall.

Large, globular flowerheads of white sterile flowers are seen on **'Grandiflorum'**♀, fading to pink as they age. Branches are horizontally arranged. **'Lanarth'** is a vigorous variety with large white flowerheads and both ascending and horizontal branches. **'Mariesii'**♀ attractively combines tiers of horizontal branches and abundant white flowers. **'Nanum Semperflorens'** is a compact, slow-growing shrub with ascending branches. It reaches a height of only 1.5m (5ft). Small white flowers are borne over a long period of time from early to late summer. **'Pink Beauty'**♀ is compact with ascending and horizontal branches. The white flowers turn pink with age. **'Shasta'** is a broad-spreading plant with horizontal branches that are covered in a profusion of large pure white flowers.

V. **'Pragense'**♀ This large, round-headed evergreen shrub is grown for its shiny dark green leaves that are felted beneath. Clusters of creamy white flowers are borne in late spring. HEIGHT & SPREAD 1×1m (3×3ft) after 5 years, ultimately 2.4m (8ft) tall.

▲ *Viburnum opulus* 'Xanthocarpum'

▲ *Viburnum plicatum* 'Lanarth'

V. rhytidophyllum A densely branched, round-headed evergreen shrub with shiny, dark green, wrinkled leaves that are felted beneath. Clusters of yellowish white flowers appear in late spring and early summer. The bright red fruits turn black in autumn and winter. HEIGHT & SPREAD 1×1m (3×3ft) after 5 years, ultimately 4.5m (15ft) tall.

V. sargentii This upright, multistemmed deciduous species has maple-like leaves that are bronze when young, turning rich yellow-green. Clusters of creamy white flowers in spring are followed by bright red translucent fruits that last from early autumn through to early winter. HEIGHT & SPREAD 1.2×1m (4×3ft) after 5 years, ultimately 4.5m (15ft) tall.

'Onondaga'♀ bears pink fertile flowers surrounded by white sterile flowers in late spring and early summer. The flowers contrast well with the dark purple-maroon young foliage. The plant is more upright in habit than the species.

V. tinus (laurustinus) This evergreen shrub has a dense, bushy, rounded habit and shiny dark green leaves. The flowers, carried in large flat heads, are pink to pure white, ageing to whitish pink or white fading to pink. Buds appear from mid autumn onwards and open progressively from mid winter. The fruits are deep blue turning black. HEIGHT & SPREAD 1.2×1.2m (4×4ft) after 5 years, ultimately 3.5m (12ft) tall.

Viburnum tinus

'Eve Price'♀ is a compact shrub with flowers that are pink in bud, opening to pale pink. The intensity of flower colour varies from year to year. **'French White'** is vigorous with large pure white flowers. **'Gwenllian'** has masses of pink flowers, deep pink in bud. **'Variegatum'** is a creamy yellow variegated form with small pink flower buds opening white.

CULTIVATION Viburnums do well in sun or light, dappled shade in most soils including those that are thin and chalky. The evergreen species tend to be more shade tolerant. *V. rhytidophyllum* and other large-leaved evergreens do not tolerate wind exposure, and deciduous winter flowerers require some frost protection. Viburnums flower well from an early age, generally between 1-3 years. Species grown for their decorative berries usually do best when planted in groups of 2 or 3.

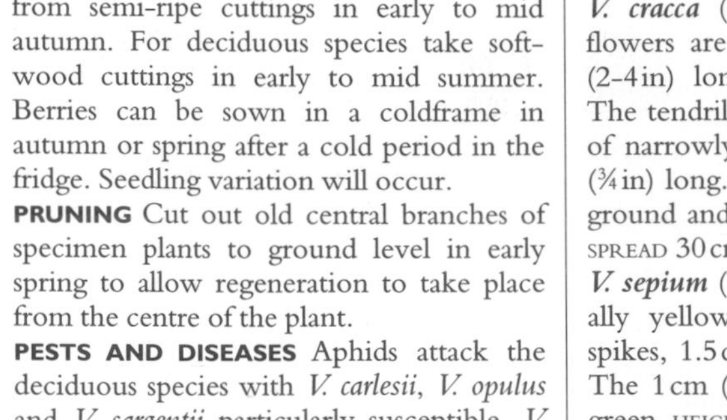

PROPAGATION Raise evergreen species from semi-ripe cuttings in early to mid autumn. For deciduous species take softwood cuttings in early to mid summer. Berries can be sown in a coldframe in autumn or spring after a cold period in the fridge. Seedling variation will occur.
PRUNING Cut out old central branches of specimen plants to ground level in early spring to allow regeneration to take place from the centre of the plant.
PESTS AND DISEASES Aphids attack the deciduous species with *V. carlesii*, *V. opulus* and *V. sargentii* particularly susceptible. *V. tinus* is affected by sooty mould after an attack of either aphids or whiteflies. Honey fungus may occur in older species.

Vicia
Vetch
Leguminosae

These hardy herbaceous perennials have small, brightly coloured, two-lipped flowers and fern-like foliage. They are best suited to informal or wild areas in a garden as their creeping, clambering habit can make them invasive. Native to the woods and hedgerows of the British countryside.

▼ *Vicia cracca*

RECOMMENDED SPECIES
V. cracca (tufted vetch) Small violet-blue flowers are carried in one-sided, 5-10cm (2-4in) long spikes throughout summer. The tendril-tipped shoots bear paired rows of narrowly oval, dark green leaflets 2cm (¾in) long. The shoots scramble across the ground and through other plants. HEIGHT & SPREAD 30cm×1m (1×3ft).
V. sepium (bush vetch) Purple, or occasionally yellow, flowers are borne in short spikes, 1.5cm (½in) long, in mid summer. The 1cm (⅜in) long, oval leaves are dark green. HEIGHT & SPREAD 45×60cm (1½×2ft).
V. sylvatica Loose spikes, 1.5cm (½in) long, of pale lilac flowers are borne by this vigorous species in mid summer. Leaves with 6-12 pairs of mid green, oblong leaflets are carried along the shoots. HEIGHT & SPREAD 1×2m (3×6½ft).
CULTIVATION Plant in autumn or early spring in any soil as long as it contains little clay. Choose a site in full sun or partial shade. Provide twiggy supports for the plants to scramble over.
PROPAGATION Sow seed in the garden where the plants are to grow from late autumn to early spring.
PESTS AND DISEASES Powdery mildew may affect the foliage during dry spells.

Vinca
Periwinkle
Apocynaceae

Vinca major

These vigorous trailing plants form extensive carpets of foliage and produce five-petalled, propeller-shaped flowers mainly in spring and early summer and intermittently throughout the growing season. The hardy sub-shrubs or perennials listed here make good ground-cover plants in shrubberies and mixed beds or in wild gardens. Periwinkles grow well in shade provided it is not too dry and are useful for growing under deciduous trees and shrubs. However, flower production is more profuse in full sun. The plants are poisonous. Native to N Africa, central Asia and Europe.

RECOMMENDED SPECIES AND VARIETIES
V. difformis The glossy dark green leaves are narrowly lance-shaped and grow up to 7cm (2¾in) long. The violet-blue or white saucer-shaped flowers are 2.5cm (1in) across. This sub-shrub requires a moister, more protected site than the other species, but given the right conditions it will grow well and flower throughout the later part of the year. The plant may be evergreen in more protected gardens. HEIGHT & SPREAD 30×60cm (1×2ft).
V. herbacea A herbaceous perennial that bears trailing shoots with mid green leaves up to 5cm (2in) long. The pale blue or white flowers, 3cm (1¼in) across, are well spaced along the stems. HEIGHT & SPREAD 30×60cm (1×2ft).
V. major An evergreen sub-shrub with long prostrate shoots covered with ovate to lance-shaped leaves that grow up to 9cm (3½in) long. The bright blue flowers are 3cm (1¼in) across. HEIGHT & SPREAD 36×36cm (14×14in).
'Aureomaculata' see 'Maculata'. Pure

▼ *Vinca minor f. alba*

▲ *Vinca major* var. *oxyloba*

▲ *Vinca major* 'Maculata'

white flowers are seen on var. **alba**, while ssp. ***hirsuta*** has hairy leaf stalks and violet-blue flowers with hairy sepals.

'Maculata' (syn. 'Aureomaculata') has pale blue flowers. The leaves are dark yellowish green in the centre and have light yellowish green margins. Dark green leaves and narrow, pointed dark violet flowers with narrow lobes distinguish var. ***oxyloba***.

▼ *Vinca minor* 'Alba Variegata'

▲ *Vinca minor* 'Burgundy'

'Variegata'♀ carries light green leaves with pale yellow margins and is decorated with rich lavender-blue flowers in early summer.

V. minor This is an evergreen sub-shrub with long trailing shoots and blue-pink or purplish flowers. The glossy dark green leaves, up to 5cm (2in) long, are lance-shaped or elliptic. The flowers are 3cm (1¼in) across. This plant is usually found in gardens as one of the following selections. HEIGHT & SPREAD 20×80cm (8×32in).

White flowers are seen on f. ***alba***. **'Alba Variegata'** has yellow variegation on its leaves and white flowers. **'Argenteo-variegata'**♀ produces violet-blue flowers and dull green leaves which have pale yellow-striped margins and midribs. **'Atropurpurea'**♀ carries dark green leaves and purple flowers. **'Aureovariegata'** has blue flowers and leaves that are striped and edged with yellow. **'Azurea Flore Pleno'**♀ bears dark green leaves and carries dark blue double flowers.

'Burgundy' has dark green leaves and reddish purple flowers. **'Gertrude Jekyll'**♀ produces medium green leaves and narrow creamy white flowers carried well above the foliage. **'La Grave'**♀ is a compact plant with dark green leaves and lavender-violet flowers. **'Multiplex'** has double purple flowers. **'Silver Service'** carries grey-green leaves with silver variegation and double mid blue flowers.

▼ *Vinca minor* 'Argenteovariegata'

▲ *Vinca minor* 'Multiplex'

CULTIVATION Plant from autumn to spring in any well-drained garden soil in a partially shaded or sunny spot. On dry soils mulch in spring to conserve moisture. Cut back in spring to control the size of the plants.

PROPAGATION Divide or remove trailing stems which have rooted into the ground from autumn to spring. Take softwood cuttings in summer and plant out at any time after they have rooted.

PESTS AND DISEASES Usually trouble free, but sometimes rust can appear on the leaves and reduce the plant's vigour.

▼ *Vinca major* 'Variegata'

Viola

Violaceae

Steeped in mythology and folklore, violas have an enduring place in British gardens for the cheerful splashes of colour they can bring throughout the year. Some have a sweet fragrance or can be used for culinary flavouring

Violas include the well-loved cottage-garden plants pansies and violets, as well as a wide range of cultivated varieties. They are all good at the front of borders and in rock gardens, often flowering throughout summer. *Viola* × *wittrockiana* and its varieties, known as the 'winter-flowering' pansies, are excellent in containers and can remain in flower during mild spells in winter and spring. Most violas are native to northern temperate areas. They are generally hardy evergreen perennials which are often treated as annuals or biennials. Most thrive in any soil and many do equally well in sun or partial shade. Only a few need special protection.

All have flat, roundish, five-petalled flowers, but these exhibit a diverse range of size, colour and patterning. Some have a tube or spur projecting from the back of the flower. Most violas have mid green, oval to heart-shaped leaves, 2-4 cm (¾-1½ in) long, sometimes with toothed edges.

RECOMMENDED SPECIES AND VARIETIES

V. alba (syn. *V. obliqua* ssp. *alba*) White flowers, 2 cm (¾ in) across, with violet veins appear in late spring and early summer. This plant will grow in shade. HEIGHT & SPREAD 10×30 cm (4×12 in).

V. bertolonii Patterned with violet and yellow, the spurred flowers, 2.5 cm (1 in) wide, appear from mid to late summer. HEIGHT & SPREAD 10×30 cm (4×12 in).

V. biflora (yellow wood violet) Bright yellow flowers, 2 cm (¾ in) across, are produced from mid to late spring. This plant tolerates some shade. HEIGHT & SPREAD 5×30 cm (2×12 in).

V. cornuta♀ (horned pansy) Fragrant white or lilac flowers, 2.5 cm (1 in) across, with pointed spurs appear from early to mid summer on this clump-forming plant. HEIGHT & SPREAD 15×30 cm (6×12 in).

Plants in the **Alba Group**♀ produce white flowers, as does the dwarf plant **'Alba Minor'**, while **'Belmont Blue'** has pale sky-blue flowers and those of the **Lilacina Group** are shades of lilac. **'Minor'**♀ is a compact lavender-blue variety. **'Rosea'** has pinkish violet flowers and **'Victoria Cawthorne'** has purplish pink flowers.

V. elatior Pale blue flowers, up to 3 cm (1¼ in) across, are borne from late spring to early summer. The leaves are lance-shaped. HEIGHT & SPREAD 30×30 cm (12×12 in).

V. gracilis Deep purple flowers, 2.5 cm (1 in) across, appear from mid to late spring above a low mound of tangled stems. HEIGHT & SPREAD 10×30 cm (4×12 in).

'Lutea' has yellow flowers.

V. hederacea (syn. *V. reniforme*) Twisted violet-blue flowers, 2 cm (¾ in) across, with white-tipped petals appear from summer to early autumn against kidney-shaped leaves. This plant is best grown under glass in equal quantities of compost and grit. HEIGHT & SPREAD 5×30 cm (2×12 in).

V. hirta (hairy violet) White or violet flowers, 1.5 cm (½ in) across, appear from spring to early summer. Loose bunches of leaves are held on hairy stems. HEIGHT & SPREAD 7×10 cm (2¾×4 in).

V. jooi Reddish purple flowers, 2 cm (¾ in)

1 Universal yellow
2 Universal hybrid
3 Universal violet blotch
4 Universal red blotch
5 Universal rose
6 Viola 'Sorbet Plum Velvet'
7 Universal apricot
8 Universal white blotch
9 Universal true blue
10 Universal yellow blotch

across, appear from mid to late spring. HEIGHT & SPREAD 5×15 cm (2×6 in).

V. labradorica hort. see *V. riviniana* Purpurea Group

V. obliqua ssp. *alba* see *V. alba*

V. odorata (sweet violet) Violet flowers, 1.5 cm (½ in) across, appear from early to late spring and again from late summer to early autumn. HEIGHT & SPREAD 7.5×15 cm (3×6 in).

V. pedata Flowers, 2.5 cm (1 in) across, appear from late spring to early autumn. The upper petals are purple, the lower ones pale lilac. The leaves are deeply divided. HEIGHT & SPREAD 15×15 cm (6×6 in).

V. pedatifida (prairie violet) Reddish violet flowers, 2 cm (¾ in) across, with dark veins appear in spring and summer. The leaves are deeply cut. HEIGHT & SPREAD 10×15 cm (4×6 in).

V. reniforme see *V. hederacea*

V. riviniana (dog violet) Spurred blue-violet flowers, 2 cm (¾ in) across, are borne from early spring to early autumn. This European native can be rather invasive. HEIGHT & SPREAD 10×30 cm (4×12 in).

The **Purpurea Group** (syn. *V. labradorica* hort.) have flowers of purple and violet. The leaves are often tinged purple.

V. septentrionalis (northern violet) Pale to deep violet flowers, up to 3 cm (1¼ in) across, appear from spring to early summer. HEIGHT & SPREAD 20×25 cm (8×10 in).

The flowers of f. ***alba*** are white.

V. tricolor (heartsease, wild pansy) Flowers, 1.5 cm (½ in) across, appear from spring to summer on this annual or biennial. Some flowers are yellow with white markings, while others are purple, marked with white. Colour combinations also occur. HEIGHT & SPREAD 10×30 cm (4×12 in).

V. × wittrockiana (pansy) Flowers, up to 10 cm (4 in) across, in a range of colours and often with a central blotch, appear from early summer to early autumn. These hybrids are grown as annuals or biennials. HEIGHT & SPREAD 15×20 cm (6×8 in).

The following plants produce flowers in spring and summer. A range of bright colours without a central blotch distinguish the flowers of **Clear Crystal Series**. The flowers of **'Joker Light Blue'** are pale blue with a white central blotch, while the **Joker Series**♀ has bicoloured flowers in a mixture

▲ *Viola cornuta*

of colours, all with central markings. **'Jolly Joker'** has rich purple flowers with vivid orange centres, while **'Padparadja'** has deep orange flowers without markings. **Super Chalon Giants** has ruffled flowers in deep red, yellow and purple with darker central blotches. **Swiss Giant Series** produces a range of brightly coloured flowers, all with purple-black central blotches.

The 'winter-flowering' pansies include the **Delta Series** with flowers in a range of colours, with or without central blotches. **Ultima Mixed**♀ has brightly coloured flowers that may be marked with contrasting colours, while those of the **Universal Series**♀ are available in single colours – red, orange, yellow, blue, purple and white – or in mixed colours, often with a central blotch.

OTHER HYBRIDS

VIOLAS

These plants have rounded flowers, 3-5 cm (1¼-2 in) across, with a central blotch. They are usually scented. The plants grow to 15 cm (6 in) tall and 33 cm (13 in) wide.

'Ardross Gem' has pale pink to dark mauve flowers with a golden central blotch. **'Huntercombe Purple'**♀ has spurred purple flowers. **'Irish Molly'** has yellowy bronze flowers. **'Jackanapes'**♀ has spurred flowers with brown upper petals and yellow lower petals, streaked brown. **'Julian'** has scented, pale lilac-blue flowers with yellow centres, while **'Maggie Mott'**♀ has silvery mauve blooms with cream centres. **'Martin'**♀ has rich, velvety purple flowers with a golden eye. **'Moonlight'**♀ has creamy yellow scented flowers, and **'Nellie Britton'**♀ has spurred mauve-pink flowers.

▼ *Viola* 'Maggie Mott'

VIOLETS

Nodding, spurred flowers, up to 2.5 cm (1 in) across, with narrowly oval petals distinguish these plants. This group includes the sweetly scented Parma violets that are not very hardy and need protection in winter. Violets have a height and spread of 30 cm (12 in).

'Coeur d'Alsace' has scented salmon-pink flowers. **'Comte de Brazza'** is a Parma violet with white double flowers, shaded with pale blue. **'Duchesse de Parme'** has double, mauve, scented flowers. **'Marie Louise'** is a Parma violet with double mauve flowers, while the flowers of **'Sulphurea'** are apricot-yellow with a cream centre.

VIOLETTAS

These plants have sweetly fragrant, oval flowers, up to 2 cm (¾ in) across, each with a central yellow blotch. They grow to 10 cm (4 in) tall and spread to 25 cm (10 in).

'Buttercup' has heavily scented, pale yellow flowers, while **'Dawn'** has primrose-yellow flowers. The scented flowers of **'Little David'**♀ are cream with frilled petals, and **'Rebecca'** has heavily scented white flowers with purple streaked edges.

▼ *Viola gracilis* 'Lutea'

Viola 'Huntercombe Purple' ▼

▼ *Viola* 'Jackanapes'

Viola 'Little David' ▼

CULTIVATION Plant in spring in any reasonably fertile well-drained soil, ideally on a sunny site. Deadhead regularly.
PROPAGATION Take basal cuttings in mid summer. Alternatively, sow seed in spring.
PESTS AND DISEASES Mosaic virus, pansy sickness and rust can cause problems.

Violet see *Viola*
Violet, African see *Saintpaulia*
Violet, dog's tooth see *Erythronium dens-canis*
Violet, water see *Hottonia palustris*
Viper's bugloss see *Echium vulgare*
Virginia creeper see *Parthenocissus quinquefolia*
Virgin's bower see *Clematis*

Viscum
Viscaceae

This evergreen shrub that is mentioned in folklore is parasitic, growing on the branches of host trees such as *Malus*, *Populus* and *Tilia*. It is easy to grow the native species, *Viscum album*, although it takes seven years to fruit.

RECOMMENDED SPECIES
V. album (mistletoe) Branching yellowy green stems form a globular hanging bush. The stems carry pairs of pale green oblong-shaped leaves, up to 10cm (4in) long. Male and female flowers are borne on separate plants, and both are needed to produce the pearly berries from autumn to mid winter.
PROPAGATION In late winter or early spring remove mature berries and rub the seed into bark crevices or under a sliced flap of bark. Choose a healthy, mature host and a branch of at least 10cm (4in) diameter, and at least 1.5m (5ft) off the ground. The tree should ideally be the same species as the host of the parent plant.
PRUNING None is required.
PESTS AND DISEASES Usually trouble free.

▲ *Viscum album*

Vitaliana
Primulaceae

In spring primrose-like flowers stud the dense cushions or mats of this native of the Alps, Apennines and mountains of Spain. It is excellent in a rock garden, scree bed or trough. Although frost-hardy, this plant needs some protection from winter wet. The genus contains only one species.
V. primuliflora (syn. *Androsoce vitalliana*, *Douglasia vitaliana*) Bright lemon-yellow, stemless flowers, up to 2cm (¾in) across, appear above greyish green needle-like leaves, up to 1cm (⅜in) long, which often form rosettes. HEIGHT & SPREAD 5×25cm (2×10in).

The oblong leaves of ssp. ***praetutiana*** are white underneath.

▲ *Vitaliana primuliflora* ssp. *praetutiana*

CULTIVATION Plant in early spring in well-drained neutral or acid soil, ideally in full sun. Improve heavy soil with coarse grit or stone chippings, but avoid limestone. Protect from winter wet with a cloche, or sheet of glass or transparent plastic. Alternatively, grow in pots of gritty compost in an unheated greenhouse.
PROPAGATION Detach rooted shoots from the parent plant in summer and grow in 7.5cm (3in) pots in an unshaded coldframe. Water well during warm dry spells.
PESTS AND DISEASES Aphids sometimes infest young leaves.

Vitex
Verbenaceae

Grown for its scented blossoms and handsome foliage, this genus includes evergreen and deciduous shrubs and trees.

RECOMMENDED SPECIES
V. agnus-castus (chaste tree) Clusters of fragrant, tubular, violet or lilac-coloured flowers, up to 15cm (6in) long, cover this spreading shrub in autumn. The dark green leaves, borne on grey downy shoots, are divided into oval or lance-shaped leaflets, about 12.5cm (5in) long. HEIGHT & SPREAD 2.4×2.4m (8×8ft) after 5 years, also the ultimate size.

▲ *Vitex agnus-castus*

CULTIVATION Plant in spring in free-draining soil in a warm, sheltered spot, preferably against a wall. Water well in summer and apply a slow-release fertiliser in spring.
PROPAGATION Take semi-ripe cuttings in summer or sow seed under glass in spring.
PRUNING If necessary, trim back the previous year's growth in spring. Remove any weak, crossing or damaged shoots.
PESTS AND DISEASES Usually trouble free.

Vitis
Grapevine
Vitaceae

Vitis coignetiae

Covering pergolas and trellises with colourful leaves and fruit, ornamental grapevines are at their best in autumn. The leaves are rounded, often with pointed lobes, and turn brilliant shades of orange, red and yellow in autumn. Inconspicuous greenish flowers appear in early or mid summer followed, after a good summer, by bunches of small grapes. (For plants grown for their fruit, see p.726.)

The plants are native to the Northern Hemisphere. Most are hardy and deciduous, climbing by means of twining tendrils. The vines grow straight up before branching, but will spread nearer to the ground if cut back at planting time.

Only heights are given for the recommended plants as spread depends on the way the plant is trained.

▲ *Vitis vinifera* 'Purpurea'

RECOMMENDED SPECIES AND VARIETIES
V. amurensis (Amur grape) Red, downy, young growth in spring gives way to dark green leaves, up to 30cm (12in) long with 5-7 lobes, that turn purple and red in autumn. Small black grapes appear in early or mid autumn. HEIGHT 3m (10ft) after 5 years, ultimately 6m (20ft) tall.
V. coignetiae♀ (crimson glory vine) Smooth, rounded, dark green leaves, up to 30cm (12in) long, with rust-red hairs underneath thickly cover the stems of this vigorous species. Heart-shaped at the base, the leaves have 3 or 5 short, pointed, coarsely toothed lobes. In autumn they turn spectacular shades of yellow, orange-red and purple-crimson, especially when grown on poor soil. The inedible, 1.5cm (½in) wide black grapes have a purple bloom. Perhaps the finest of the ornamental vines, this species is best grown over trees or old buildings. HEIGHT 3.5-4.5m (12-15ft) after 5 years, ultimately 25m (80ft) tall.
***V.* 'Brant'**♀ has palmate, deeply lobed, mid green leaves, turning deep bronze-red, pink and orange in autumn, although the veins remain green. Purple-black fruits are borne in cylindrical bunches in mid or late autumn. HEIGHT 3m (10ft) after 5 years, ultimately 9m (30ft) tall.
V. vinifera (grape vine, wine grape) The 3 or 5-lobed leaves are up to 15cm (6in) long and wide with woolly undersides. Panicles of small flowers appear in late spring, followed by edible fruit. HEIGHT 3m (10ft) after 5 years, ultimately 9m (30ft) tall.

Ornamental varieties include the following plants. **'Incana'** (dusty miller grape) bears 3-lobed or unlobed pale green leaves covered in pale down, especially when young. Black fruits appear in mid or late autumn. **'Purpurea'**♀ (Teinturier grape) has ovate to round leaves with 3 or 5 coarsely serrated lobes. Young leaves are pale and downy, turning claret-red and eventually rich purple in autumn. Purple-black fruits with a blue bloom are borne in early or mid autumn.
CULTIVATION Plant in mild weather from late autumn to early spring. For autumn colour, choose a poor soil (which will also restrict growth) and a site facing south or west. Trim plants to within 25cm (10in) of the ground, and tie in the young growths.
PROPAGATION Sow seed in late autumn in trays of seed compost kept in a coldframe or greenhouse. Except for *V. coignetiae*, take cuttings of single buds of the previous summer's shoots in late winter and grow under glass. Alternatively, take 30cm (12in) hardwood cuttings in late autumn and plant out when rooted. Layer one-year-old growths of *V. coignetiae* in mid autumn.
PRUNING Thin out old growth and shorten young growth in late summer.
PESTS AND DISEASES Scale insects, especially brown scale, may infest stems and foliage, and weevils and caterpillars may eat the leaves.

Vriesea

Bromeliaceae

With eye-catching flowerheads and attractive leaf rosettes, these tropical perennials make bold, colourful houseplants and conservatory specimens. Vibrant spikes of flowers rise above funnel-shaped rosettes formed by plain or patterned, sword-shaped evergreen leaves. Native to S America, these epiphytic plants need high humidity, warmth and shade from direct sunlight.
RECOMMENDED SPECIES AND VARIETIES
V. carinata (lobster claws) In summer or autumn, yellow tubular flowers, up to 5cm (2in) long, enclosed by shorter red bracts, are held in short spikes above pale green leaves, up to 20cm (8in) long. HEIGHT & SPREAD 30×45cm (12×18in).

▲ *Vriesea fosteriana*

V. fosteriana Mid green leaves, up to 45cm (18in) long, have maroon bands on the undersides. A bold spike of flowers, up to 1m (3ft) tall, is produced in late summer or autumn. The flower spike has yellow leathery bracts, about 4cm (1½in) long, embracing yellow petals tipped with reddish brown. HEIGHT & SPREAD 1m×60cm (3×2ft).
V. hieroglyphica (king of the bromeliads) Broad strap-shaped leaves, up to 80cm (32in) long, are yellowish green, cross-banded and chequered with dark brownish green. Summer spikes of tubular yellow flowers, each up to 4cm (1½in) long, are enclosed by yellow-green papery bracts. HEIGHT & SPREAD 60×75cm (24×30in).
V. saundersii♀ Ash-grey, scaly, strap-like leaves blotched with maroon, up to 30cm (1ft) long, form neat rosettes. Sword-shaped flower spikes appear from late summer to autumn carrying 5-7 sulphur-yellow flowers, up to 5cm (2in) long, enclosed by pale green or yellow-green bracts. HEIGHT & SPREAD 70×45cm (28×18in).
V. splendens♀ (flaming sword) Arching, strap-shaped leaves, up to 60cm (2ft) long, are olive-green with purple-brown cross-bands. A bold orange-red, sword-like flower spike appears from late summer to late autumn. It has flattened red bracts, up to 7.5cm (3in) long, embracing smaller yellow tubular flowers. HEIGHT & SPREAD 90×45cm (36×18in).

▲ *Vriesea splendens*

CULTIVATION Grow indoors or under glass in semi-shade at 15-18°C (59-64°F) during active growth, and at a minimum winter temperature of 15°C (59°F). Plant in 10cm (4in) pots in John Innes No.2 compost mixed in equal parts with bark chips or perlite. Pour water, ideally soft water, into the centre of the rosette. Water freely in spring and summer but sparingly in winter. Feed monthly from spring to autumn with a general liquid fertiliser. Repot as necessary in spring.
PROPAGATION Separate suckering rosettes in spring and leave to dry off for 2 days before potting on.
PESTS AND DISEASES Mealy bug and scale insects can be troublesome.

Vuylstekeara see ORCHIDS p.467

Wahlenbergia

Campanulaceae

Wahlenbergia saxicola

Single, upturned bell-shaped flowers on slender stalks appear in summer on these annuals or perennials. The plants listed here can be grown in a cold greenhouse or, given the right conditions, in a rock garden.

RECOMMENDED SPECIES AND VARIETIES

W. albomarginata White or pale blue flowers, 2 cm (¾ in) across, rise above a creeping mat of rosetted, spoon-shaped leaves up to 4 cm (1½ in) long. Although hardy, this evergreen perennial benefits from winter cover. Native to New Zealand. HEIGHT & SPREAD 5×15 cm (2×6 in).

▲ *Wahlenbergia albomarginata*

'Blue Mist' has pale blue flowers with deeper blue veining.

W. congesta Pale blue, delicate cupped flowers, 1.5 cm (½ in) across, are held on frail stalks in summer. This little rambling perennial evergreen sends up from creeping stems densely tufted rosettes of 2.5 cm (1 in) long, rounded leaves. Native to Australasia. HEIGHT & SPREAD 2.5×20 cm (1×8 in).

W. gloriosa Purple bell-shaped flowers, 4 cm (1½ in) across, are held on wiry upright stems from mid summer to early autumn. This evergreen perennial forms a low clump with crowded tufts of 3 cm (1¼ in) long strap-shaped leaves. Native to Australia. HEIGHT & SPREAD 15×20 cm (6×8 in).

▲ *Wahlenbergia gloriosa*

W. pumilio see *Edrianthus pumilo*

W. saxicola Pale blue flowers, about 2 cm (¾ in) wide, appear on erect stalks in early summer. Spoon-shaped leaves, up to 2.5 cm (1 in) long, are borne in loose, flat mat-forming clusters. This evergreen perennial is easy to grow and hardy in all but the coldest of gardens. Native to Tasmania. HEIGHT & SPREAD 10×25 cm (4×10 in).

W. serpyllifolia see *Edrianthus serpyllifolius*

CULTIVATION Plant in a sheltered sunny position in a light, humus-rich, non-limy well-drained soil. Add plenty of coarse grit if the soil is inclined to heaviness.

PROPAGATION Sow seed or take softwood cuttings in late spring. Alternatively, take rooted tufts from the main growth after flowering and grow in a cold frame.

PESTS AND DISEASES Slugs can cause serious damage to young leaves.

Wake robin see *Trillium*

Waldsteinia

Rosaceae

Waldsteinia ternata

The creeping habit of this evergreen perennial makes it useful as ground cover planted with shrubs, or underplanted with bulbs. Wide-open, broad-petalled, potentilla-like flowers have a mass of golden stamens.

RECOMMENDED SPECIES

W. ternata Lax clusters of 2-4 upward-facing yellow flowers, 2 cm (¾ in) across, appear in early summer. A hardy, evergreen perennial, it spreads by rooted runners. The tufted, 3-lobed leaves, up to 7.5 cm (3 in) wide, have jagged, toothed edges and form dense cover. Found wild from S Alps to Japan. HEIGHT & SPREAD 15×45 cm (6×18 in).

CULTIVATION Plant in spring or autumn in fertile, well-drained soil. Position in partial shade in hotter, drier parts of the country.

PROPAGATION Snip off rooted shoots in late summer for growing on in pots.

PESTS AND DISEASES Usually trouble free.

Wallflower see *Erysimum cheiri*
Walnut see *Juglans*
Wandering Jew see *Tradescantia fluminensis*
Wand flower see *Dierama*
Wandflower see *Galax urceolata*
Water arum see *Calla palustris*
Water hawthorn see *Aponogeton distachyos*
Water lily see *Nymphaea*
Water soldier see *Stratiotes aloides*

Watsonia

Iridaceae

The elegant, upright spikes of flowers produced by these half-hardy perennials in mid to late summer make them good border plants. They look very effective when associated with grey-leafed plants. Each stem carries a branching spike of tubular flowers that have six lobes spreading out into a star shape. The leaves along the stems and at the base of the plant are narrow, upright and sword-like. Native to southern Africa, they like a sunny position in free-draining soil.

RECOMMENDED SPECIES

W. beatricis see *W. pillansii*

W. borbonica (syn. *W. pyramidata*) Rich pink flowers grow up to 4 cm (1½ in) long. The mid green leaves grow up to 60 cm (2 ft) long. HEIGHT 1 m (3 ft).

The flowers of ssp. *ardernei* are normally white but may, rarely, be pink.

W. meriana Flowers may be orange, pinky-red, purple and, rarely, yellow, depending on the variety. The blooms, each up to 5 cm (2 in) long, branch irregularly from strong

▼ *Watsonia meriana*

spikes. The mid green leaves are about 45cm (18in) long. HEIGHT 1m (3ft).

W. pillansii (syn. *W. beatricis*) Orange or orange-red flowers grow up to 5cm (2in) long. The mid green leaves grow up to 60cm (2ft) long. HEIGHT 1m (3ft).

W. pyramidata see *W. borbonica*

CULTIVATION Plant corms 10cm (4in) deep and 20cm (8in) apart in well-drained soil in a sunny position. In cold areas, plant in spring and after flowering gently lift and store for the winter. In mild areas, plant in autumn or spring and overwinter in the ground, under a generous layer of bark-chip mulch. Remove the mulch in early spring before the shoots appear.

Apply a slow-release fertiliser in spring. Remove faded flowerheads and rake off dead foliage at the end of the season.

PROPAGATION Sow seed in spring under glass. Although the corms do not like to be disturbed, they can occasionally be divided.

PESTS AND DISEASES Apart from occasional damage from earwigs and thrips, they are usually trouble free.

Wattle see *Acacia*
Waxberry see *Gaultheria hispida*
Wax flower see *Stephanotis floribunda*

Weigela

Caprifoliaceae

Weigela florida

Clusters of funnel-shaped flowers – mostly in shades of red, pink or white – are borne in late spring and early summer by these long-lived, deciduous plants. Among the easiest and most popular of all summer-flowering shrubs, weigelas are stalwarts of the shrubbery and are also suitable for a mixed border. The foxglove-like flowers are borne on the previous season's wood, so for the best display weigelas should be pruned straight after flowering. They are mostly native to E Asia, and are hardy in all parts of Britain, thriving in any fertile soil.

RECOMMENDED SPECIES AND VARIETIES

W. florida Rose-pink flowers, paler inside and 2.5cm (1in) long, are borne in clusters along arching branches. The light green, ovate leaves are up to 10cm (4in) long. They are wrinkled and prominently veined. HEIGHT & SPREAD 1x1m (3x3ft) after 5 years, ultimately 2.1m (7ft) tall.

'Aureovariegata' has cream-edged leaves and rose-pink flowers. **'Bristol Snowflake'** has white flowers. **'Foliis Purpureis'**♀ (also sold as **'Purpurea'**) is a slow-growing, compact variety with purplish leaves and dark pink flowers.

W. japonica Dense down covers the undersides of the mid green oval, tapering leaves, that are up to 10cm (4in) long. It is mainly grown in the guise of the cultivar **'Dart's Colourdream'**♀, which bears both pink and cream blooms. HEIGHT & SPREAD 1x1m (3x3ft) after 5 years, ultimately growing to 2.4m (8ft) tall.

W. maximowiczii Pale yellow or greenish yellow flowers, up to 4cm (1½in) long, appear in small clusters in mid spring. The narrow mid green leaves are up to 10cm (4in) long. HEIGHT & SPREAD 1x1m (3x3ft) after 5 years, ultimately 1.5m (5ft) tall.

W. middendorffiana Pale yellow bell-shaped flowers with orange blotches in the centre appear in mid to late spring. The blooms are up to 4cm (1½in) long, held in small clusters at the end of the branches. The bright green, ovate leaves are wrinkled and rather narrow. This species is hardy but starts into growth early and may be frost-damaged unless given a sheltered position. HEIGHT & SPREAD 1x1m (3x3ft) after 5 years, ultimately 1.5m (5ft) tall.

▲ *Weigela middendorffiana*

GARDEN HYBRIDS

The garden hybrids are mostly derived from and have superseded *W. florida*, and are sometimes listed with it. They are generally showy and free flowering. Most have mid green ovate leaves with a slender tip and prominent veins. The clusters of 2.5cm (1in) long flowers cover the branches. HEIGHT & SPREAD 1x1m (3x3ft) after 5 years, ultimately 1.8m (6ft) tall.

'Abel Carriere'♀ has large rose-carmine flowers, fading later, with a gold flare. **'Briant Rubidor'** (also sold as **'Olympiade'** or **'Rubidor'**) has soft yellow leaves and red flowers. **'Bristol Ruby'** has an upright habit and crimson flowers. **'Candida'** is a compact variety with white flowers.

'Eva Rathke' is slow-growing with crimson flowers. **'Evita'** is dense and broad, bearing red flowers. **'Fiesta'** is vigorous with an open habit and red flowers. **'Looymansii Aurea'** has yellow-green young leaves and does best in light shade. It bears pink flowers.

'Minuet' has small, rounded leaves. It bears fragrant pink flowers and is compact and very hardy. **'Mont Blanc'**♀ bears large white fragrant flowers which age to pink. **'Nana Variegata'** is a dwarf, rounded shrub with cream-edged leaves and pale pink flowers. **'Newport Red'** has dark red flowers. **'Praecox Variegata'**♀ has smooth, yellow-variegated leaves that turn white in summer. Its crimson buds open into pink flowers. **'Snowflake'** is compact with white flowers often tinged with pink. **'Victoria'** has purple-flushed leaves and red flowers.

▲ *Weigela* 'Newport Red'

Weigela 'Praecox Variegata' ▼

CULTIVATION Plant from mid autumn to early spring in any well-drained fertile soil that does not dry out. Choose a sunny or partially shaded site. Mulch generously and feed in spring.

PROPAGATION Take softwood cuttings in early summer, or semi-ripe cuttings in mid summer and root in a coldframe. Alternatively, grow from hardwood cuttings taken after late autumn.

PRUNING Trim back just after flowering to maintain vigour. Thin out a few old shoots to the ground and shorten the strongest new shoots to a few buds above old wood.

PESTS AND DISEASES Usually trouble free.

Whitebeam see *Sorbus*
Whitlow grass see *Draba*
Wild angelica see *Angelica sylvestris*
Wild ginger see *Asarum*
Willow see *Salix*
Willow bell see *Campanula persicifolia*
Willowherb see *Epilobium*
Windflower see *Anemone*
Winged spindle see *Euonymus alatus*
Wintergreen see *Gaultheria procumbens*
Winter's bark see *Drimys winteri*
Wintersweet see *Chimonanthus praecox*
Wire netting bush see *Corokia cotoneaster*

WATER GARDENS PROVIDE CONDITIONS THAT SUIT A WEALTH OF BEAUTIFUL PLANTS, AND MAKE ARRESTING FOCAL POINTS

A water feature introduces a unique play of movement and light into the garden and enables the gardener to grow a wide range of plants which thrive in water or in the moist soil at the water's edge.

The smallest space can accommodate a trough filled with miniature plants, such as *Acorus gramineus* 'Variegatus' and the water lily *Nymphaea* × *pygmaea* 'Rubra'. In a larger garden, a pond provides a unique focus, and can set the garden's style. It may incorporate a moving-water feature, such as a fountain or waterfall, for added interest.

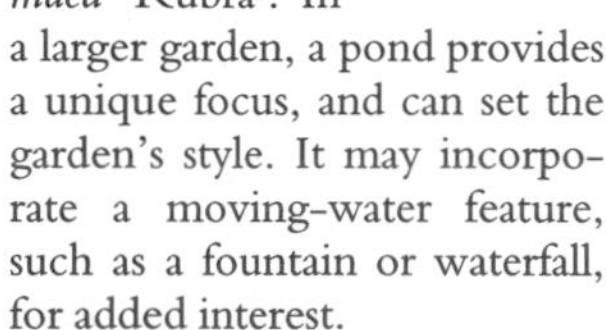

FLOATING GRACE *Exquisite water lilies suit every pond.*

Site a pond in a flat sunny area of the garden, away from overhanging trees. For a formal pond, choose a design with a geometric shape, defined edges and a neat surround of stone or brickwork. Select plants with simple architectural outlines, such as the stiffly upright *Typha minima*, and be restrained in your planting.

A pond with an irregular, curving shape looks good in an informal garden, and also provides a valuable habitat for wildlife. See WILDLIFE GARDENS (p.710). Soften its edges with turf or stones and incorporate a bog garden to provide a visual link between the pond and the rest of the garden. Water plants with relatively loose habits, such as *Mimulus* (monkey flower), *Caltha* (marsh marigold) and *Myosotis scorpioides* (water forget-me-not) are particularly well suited to an informal pond. Allow their foliage to entwine for a natural effect.

▶ EYE-CATCHING *Upright* Iris ensata *makes a bold display of purple beside a tranquil pool.*

NATURAL BALANCE

For a balanced and healthy ecology in a pond, include plants that grow at different levels. Submerged plants, such as *Potamogeton crispus* (curled pondweed) and *Hottonia palustris* (water violet) are essential because they produce oxygen and absorb nutrients that encourage algae.

Plants whose foliage floats on the water surface are also necessary because they reduce the amount of light reaching lower levels and so discourage algae. They include plants which are entirely floating, such as *Eichhornia crassipes* (water hyacinth), and deep-water aquatics, including water lilies, which have floating leaves and flowers but whose roots are below the surface of the water. Use these plants to cover between a third and a half of the pond and leave the rest clear.

Marginal plants, which grow in shallow water at the pond's edges, do not greatly affect the clarity and balance of the water. However, along with bog plants, they provide shelter for wildlife and help to create a lush effect.

COLOURFUL SCHEMES

The waxy star-like flowers and softly rounded or heart-shaped leaves of water lilies make these plants central to any water planting scheme.

Plain green-leaved varieties with single-colour flowers, such as the pure white *Nymphaea* 'Albatros' and the bright red *N.* 'Froebelii', are good choices and there are many attractive varieties which have

◀ HARMONIOUS GROUPING *A lavish mix of water plants results in a soothing scene.*

PLANTING UP A WATER GARDEN

Plant up a water garden in late spring or early summer. Slide floating plants carefully onto the water surface and dig bog-garden plants directly into the soil. Use fine-mesh aquatic baskets for any other water plants, to contain growth.

Fill the basket with clean, heavy garden soil, free from weeds, sticks and stones, or use an aquatic-planting compost. Insert the plant then soak the soil to expel any air. Top up the basket and cover the surface with pea gravel.

Lower the basket carefully into place. Plant marginals so that the roots are covered by 2.5-15 cm (1-6 in) of water, and deep-water aquatics in a depth of 25-90 cm (10-36 in), depending on the plant. Place young deep-water aquatics in a depth of 25-30 cm (10-12 in) at first and move to the correct planting depth once they are established. Submerged plants grow in any depth of water. Keep deep-water and floating plants away from moving water.

Water gardens need little maintenance. During the growing season, thin out vigorous plants and divide rhizomes when necessary. Use a hooked stick to pull out blanket weed. Remove dead foliage in autumn.

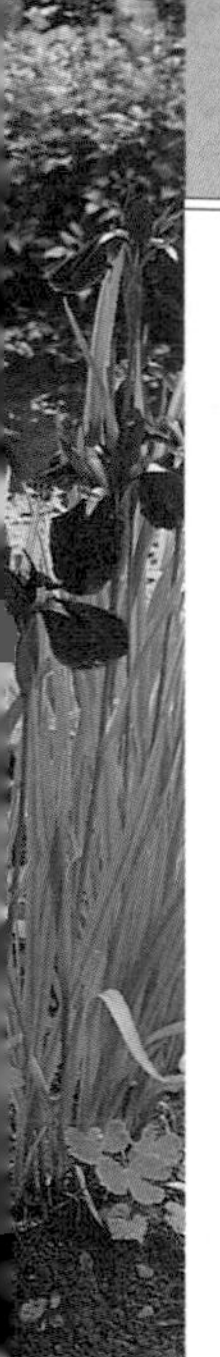

▶ SHADES OF GREEN *Arching foliage of ferns and grasses leads the eye to the water in a stream.*

blotched or marked foliage, including *N.* 'Indiana'. The forked flowers of *Aponogeton distachyos* (water hawthorn), the fringed blooms of *Nymphoides peltata* and the upright flower spikes of *Orontium aquaticum* also make striking and colourful displays in deep water.

Round the margins, include flowering species and plants with architectural foliage or outlines. The flowering rush *Butomus umbellatus*, for example, has unusual twisted narrow leaves, and also produces pink blooms from mid summer to autumn. The sword-like cream and green *Acorus calamus* 'Variegatus' is an excellent choice and combines well with the blue-flowered *Myosotis scorpioides*; the upright *Iris laevigata* (water iris) makes a fine match with the creeping, green-leaved *Lysimachia nummularia*.

Integrate the pond margins with a bog garden by growing plants that thrive in both sites; the yellow-flowered *Mimulus guttatus* and *Lythrum salicaria* (purple loosestrife), with its slender purple spires, make an impressive display. Alternatively, adopt a single-colour scheme using, for example, a mass planting of white *Iris laevigata* 'Alba' to complement a show of *Zantedeschia aethiopica* (arum lily).

LONGER SEASON

Create strong drifts of colour in a bog garden by grouping together several plants of the same species. Include *Caltha palustris* (kingcup) and *Primula denticulata* for spring colour, followed by the waterside irises *Iris ensata* and *I. pseudacorus*, and candelabra primulas, such as *Primula bulleyana*.

Many flowering water plants produce their best displays in summer, so include foliage plants that have extended seasons of interest. The umbrella plant *Darmera peltata*, whose main feature is large, dark green leaves that turn a soft pinky bronze in autumn, is a good choice. The ornamental rhubarb *Rheum palmatum* 'Bowles' Crimson', with its colourful leaves, and the feathery *Athyrium felix-femina* (lady fern) are also useful, making fine backdrops and providing textured interest.

▼ PAIRED UP Lysichiton *(bog arum) and marsh marigolds combine well in a bog garden.*

▼ STATELY FOCUS *Creamy white arum lilies stand out among other bog-loving plants.*

PLANTS IN AND AROUND THE POND

DEEP-WATER AQUATICS

- ***Aponogeton distachyos*** Spikes of white forked flowers from late spring to autumn and dark green, strap-like leaves.
- ***Nymphaea* 'Froebelii'** Deep red, starry flowers in summer and purple-green rounded leaves.
- ***Nymphaea* 'Marliacea Chromatella'** Yellow flowers in summer and olive-green, streaked, rounded leaves.
- ***Nymphoides peltata* 'Bennettii'** Fringed yellow flowers in summer and spotted heart-shaped leaves.

FLOATERS

- ***Eichhornia crassipes*** Spikes of lavender-blue flowers in summer and dark green, rounded leaves.
- ***Stratiotes aloides*** Spiky rosettes of dark green leaves.

MARGINALS

- ***Butomus umbellatus*** Clusters of pale pink flowers in mid summer and early autumn, and twisted bronze to mid green leaves.
- ***Iris laevigata*** Mid blue flowers in early summer and green sword-like leaves.
- ***Lythrum salicaria*** Spires of purple flowers from mid to late summer and mid green, lance-shaped foliage.
- ***Mimulus guttatus*** Hooded yellow blooms, dotted red, all summer and bright green, toothed, oval leaves.
- ***Myosotis scorpioides*** Sky-blue clusters in summer and spoon-shaped green leaves.

BOG-GARDEN PLANTS

- ***Caltha palustris*** Deep yellow, cup-shaped flowers in spring and dark green, rounded foliage.
- ***Darmera peltata*** White or pink clusters in spring and parasol-like, dark green leaves which turn bronze.
- ***Primula japonica* 'Postford White'** White flowers in early summer and pale green, toothed leaves.
- ***Rheum palmatum* 'Bowles' Crimson'** Tall red spikes in summer and green leaves with red undersides.

Wisteria

Leguminosae

Wisteria sinensis

Though their flowering season is of short duration, wisterias are among the most beautiful of all climbers for walls, fences, pergolas, arches and old trees. Their violet-blue, purple, pink or white flowers – all in the typical pea-family shape, and often beautifully scented – hang in long, elegant trails in late spring and early summer before the attractive feathery foliage is fully expanded. The bean-like seedpods that follow the flowers are distinctive. The pinnate leaves are divided into seven to nineteen narrow leaflets. All wisteria species are twining, woody, deciduous climbers. Given something for the stems to twine around – those of some species twine clockwise, others anticlockwise – wisterias climb vigorously to a considerable height and need plenty of room to look at their best. They can live to be 100 years old and a mature plant will be very heavy so careful thought is required when positioning a young plant.

Wisterias can be trained as self-supporting, tree-like standards when they are supported during training (perhaps for 20 years) after which the supports are taken away to leave a free-standing specimen. They can be grown in large containers and can also be forced into early flower under glass.

Most wisterias are hardy throughout the British Isles, but will flourish best in a sunny, sheltered spot facing south or west. Buy a grafted or layered plant, or one grown from a cutting; a seed-raised plant may take 15 to 20 years to flower.

For a good flowering display, careful pruning and training is essential.

RECOMMENDED SPECIES AND VARIETIES

W. floribunda (Japanese wisteria) Fragrant violet-blue flowers appear with the early leaves in hanging trails 25-30 cm (10-12 in) or more long. Flowers open in sequence from the base of the cluster to the tip. Each leaf has 11-19 light to mid green leaflets. Native to Japan. HEIGHT up to 9 m (30 ft).

'Alba'♀ (syn. *W. multijuga* 'Alba') has white flowers tinged with lilac. **'Burford'** has strongly scented lilac-blue flowers in pendent clusters that reach 60 cm (2 ft) or more long. The flowers of **'Kuchi-beni'** ('Peaches and Cream') are pink and white. **'Multijuga'**♀ (syn. 'Macrobotrys') has long flower trails, 60 cm (2 ft) or more, of purple and violet flowers. The flowers of **'Purple Patches'** are violet-purple. **'Rosea'**♀ has pale pink flowers with a rose pink throat. The flowers of **'Snow Showers'** are pure white. **'Violacea Plena'** has violet-blue, double flowers.

W.* x *formosa The strongly fragrant pale violet flowers hang in 25-30 cm (10-12 in) trails and nearly the whole length of cluster opens at one time as the leaves are emerging. Each leaf usually has 13 leaflets. HEIGHT up to 9 m (30 ft).

▲ *Wisteria floribunda* 'Alba'

▼ *Wisteria floribunda* 'Rosea'

▲ *Wisteria floribunda* 'Multijuga'

W

▲ *Wisteria x formosa* 'Kokkuryu'

▲ *Wisteria sinensis*

▲ *Wisteria sinensis* 'Alba'

▲ *Wisteria sinensis* 'Caroline'

▲ *Wisteria venusta*

More commonly grown than the hybrid are the varieties **'Issai'**, which flowers as a young plant, producing lilac-blue flowers, and **'Kokkuryu'** ('Black Dragon'), which has double purple flowers.

W. sinensis♀ (Chinese wisteria) This fast-growing and vigorous climber bears dense trails, 15-30cm (6-12in) long, of slightly fragrant blue-violet flowers, all of which open together, before the leaves unfurl. Each leaf has 7-13 dark to mid green leaflets. Native to China. HEIGHT 10-15m (33-50ft) or more.

'Alba'♀ ('Shiro-capital) has white flowers. **'Caroline'** is a free-flowering climber with strongly scented, deep blue-purple flowers. **'Prolific'** is very free-flowering with blue-lilac flowers.

W. venusta (silky wisteria) Fragrant white flowers in hanging clusters, 10-15cm (4-6in) long, have a yellow blotch at the base of the upright petals. The flowers open all at once as the leaves unfurl. The silky-haired leaves are divided into 9-13 leaflets. Native to Japan. HEIGHT up to 9m (30ft).

The wild form, f. ***violacea,*** has violet-purple flowers.

CULTIVATION Most soils are suitable, but planting in a rich, moist loam will give the best results. Position the plant out of cold winds and early morning sun to avoid frost and wind damage to flower buds. Mature plants can become heavy so it is essential to provide strong trellis or wires for support. Thread new shoots behind the wires and do not try to twine them as the shoots snap easily. Do not tie them tightly. Feed plants with high potash fertiliser and mulch them in spring if the soil is not very fertile. Foliage will be produced at the expense of flowers if wisterias are overfed.

To force a tub-grown plant into early flower, move it under glass in mid to late winter at a minimum temperature of 10°C (50°F). Spray the plant twice daily with water, and keep it indoors until all danger of frost has passed.

PROPAGATION Wisteria is a very difficult plant to propagate, though it can be attempted in the following ways. To raise one or two new plants, layer low-growing lateral shoots between mid autumn and late spring. Alternatively, take 7.5-10cm (3-4in) semi-ripe heel or nodal cuttings in late summer and root in a propagating frame, preferably with bottom heat.

PRUNING For the first few years, train new growth to form a main stem and several horizontal side branches. After that cut back most of the long shoots not needed as new main branches to about 5 or 6 buds in mid summer. Prune all sideshoots back to 2 or 3 buds from the previous year's growth in late winter to form flowering spurs.

PESTS AND DISEASES Birds may attack the buds and flowers. Aphids may infest young growths and also spread a virus disease that causes leaf mottling. Thrips may damage the foliage. In warm conditions, red spider mites may attack the leaves, causing fine mottling. Drought or low night temperatures may cause bud-drop, and very alkaline soil can cause chlorosis. Fungal infections can cause brown or black leaf spots – rarely serious – but honey fungus can kill wisterias, particularly old plants.

Witch hazel see *Hamamelis*
Woad see *Isatis*
Wood anemone see *Anemone nemorosa*
Woodbine see *Lonicera*
Woodruff see *Asperula*
Woodwardia see FERNS p.265
Wormwood see *Artemisia*

ENTICE A HOST OF BIRDS, BUTTERFLIES AND OTHER CREATURES INTO THE GARDEN BY OFFERING THE FOOD AND SHELTER THEY NEED

Creating a welcoming area for wildlife is possible in any garden, no matter where it is sited or what its size. Given appropriate conditions, a wide range of creatures will soon appear, providing an endless source of fascination and entertainment for the gardener. In addition, a wildlife garden can play a valuable role in conservation, supporting native plants and creatures that may no longer easily survive in the countryside.

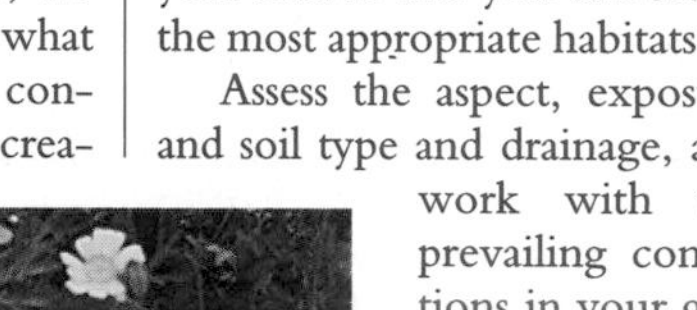

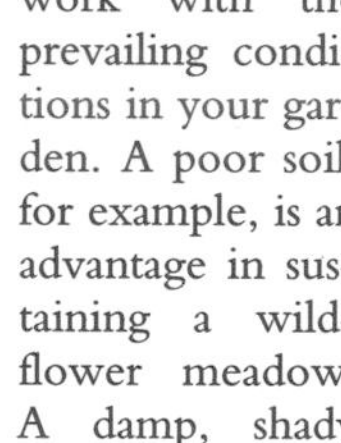

SUMMER SCARLET *Corn poppies complement a meadow or flowerbed.*

Ideally a wildlife garden should contain a woodland area, wild-flower meadow and a pond – features which can be adapted to suit a small garden. Find out about the wildlife in your area so that you can create the most appropriate habitats.

Assess the aspect, exposure and soil type and drainage, and work with the prevailing conditions in your garden. A poor soil, for example, is an advantage in sustaining a wildflower meadow. A damp, shady spot suits many woodland plants, including *Euphorbia amygdaloides* (wood spurge), *Oxalis acetosella* (wood sorrel) and *Sorbus aucuparia* (rowan tree).

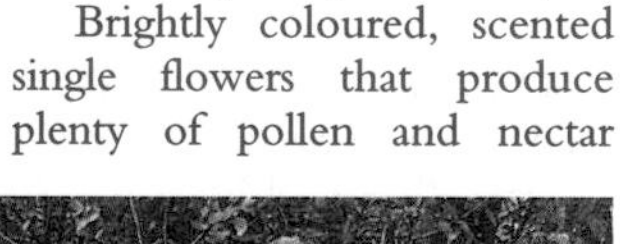

Brightly coloured, scented single flowers that produce plenty of pollen and nectar attract a wide range of insects, which encourages insect-eating birds, such as wrens, to visit the garden. Night-flowering nectar plants, including *Nicotiana alata* (flowering tobacco) and *Matthiola longipetala* (night-scented stock), are a valuable source of food for night-flying insects, which may in turn attract bats.

Whirligig beetles and pond skaters quickly turn up in a new pond, followed by dragonflies, diving beetles and frogs and toads. Hedges and nesting boxes will encourage wrens, finches, blackbirds, dunnocks, song thrushes and the tit family to make their homes in your garden. A woodland area may attract hedgehogs, bats and a range of other creatures.

Do not use chemical sprays as they disrupt the natural food chain and create an imbalance. A garden that is wildlife friendly will encourage natural predators and help to keep down pests and diseases. See ALLIES IN THE GARDENER'S WORLD (p.32).

NATIVE PLANTS

Growing native plants helps to conserve species that are now rarely found in the wild. Many native plants look attractive combined with cultivated flowers in beds and borders. For example, red-flowered *Papaver rhoeas* (corn poppy) and the deep pink *Agrostemma githago* (corn cockle) make pretty additions to an annual flowerbed.

Although native plants such as *Digitalis purpurea* (foxglove), *Viola tricolor* (heartsease) and some *Geranium* (cranesbill) species may earn a place in the garden by appearance alone, many are also rich sources of seeds, nectar and pollen, and support a range of creatures.

Bees, butterflies and hoverflies, for example, depend on nectar-rich flowers, such as those of the attractive herb *Origanum vulgare* (marjoram). Pollen-rich plants, including *Achillea millefolium* (yarrow) and *Taraxacum officinale* (dandelion), are also much appreciated by insects. Once the creamy white flowers of *Filipendula ulmaria* (meadowsweet) set their seed, they attract many birds, including siskins, as will *Rumex* (dock) and *Cirsium* (plume thistle). Goldfinches find *Dipsacus fullonum* (teasel) irresistible and yellowhammers eat the seeds of most large grasses.

◄ SECLUDED SPOT *A thicket of plants including (from front) cowslips, heartsease and foxgloves creates an informal attraction in the garden and provides a sheltered retreat for wildlife.*

▲ BIRD SANCTUARY *Roses and honeysuckle surround a nesting box on a wooden fence.*

Native plants can be bought from a mail-order supplier, garden centre or nursery.

WILD-FLOWER MEADOWS

A grassy meadow that is studded with a variety of native flowering plants not only looks beautiful, but also provides a haven for insects, and thus their predators. In addition, many grasses provide food for butterflies, caterpillars and bees.

Choose either a spring-flowering meadow or a late summer-flowering meadow as they are mowed at different times of the year.

A spring-flowering meadow may include plants such as *Cardamine pratensis* (cuckoo flower) and *Primula veris* (cowslip) as well as bulbs, including *Narcissus pseudonarcissus* (Lent lily) and *Leucojum aestivum* (summer snowflake).

For a summer-flowering meadow, select plants such as *Centaurea scabiosa* (greater knapweed), *Knautia arvensis* (field scabious) and *Rumex acetosa* (sorrel), which provide a bright show and combine well with *Colchicum autumnale* (meadow saffron) which provides some later colour.

To achieve a successful meadow, you first need to reduce the fertility of the soil. This ensures that grasses grow at a slower rate, which allows flowering plants to thrive.

If you are starting with bare soil, remove the richer topsoil and sow onto the less fertile subsoil, preferably in autumn. Use a mixture of fine grasses and native plants. Make up your own mixture, or buy one ready-made from a garden centre, nursery or a specialist supplier. These mixtures usually consist of 80 per cent grasses with 20 per cent flowering plants and are available to suit different soils and situations. Check to make sure that the seed is of native origin and the grasses are non-invasive and low-growing.

To convert a lawn into a meadow, strip off the turf then remove the topsoil and sow. Alternatively, mow the grass very closely and at frequent intervals for at least two seasons, removing all the grass clippings, which would otherwise add nutrients to the soil. Then introduce the flowering plants, either raised from seed or bought as plants from a garden centre or nursery.

The simplest way to create a meadow, however, is to leave a section of the lawn unmowed. A whole range of lawn weeds, including yarrow, *Bellis perennis* (daisy) and *Ranunculus* (buttercup), look attractive when they are left to flower. However, you may need to introduce more flowering plants to achieve a good balance between flowers and grasses.

Delay cutting a spring-flowering meadow until mid summer. This gives the flowers time to set seed. Mow a summer-flowering meadow in late spring, then leave it uncut until mid autumn. Always remove the mowings.

Each year, leave a different section of a summer-flowering meadow uncut in autumn. This will provide valuable shelter for insects and small mammals throughout the winter.

▲ NECTAR SOURCE *Small tortoiseshell butterflies feed on the nectar of* Sedum spectabile.

BUTTERFLY BORDERS

As butterflies like to bask in sunny sheltered spots, make sure there are clumps of nectar-rich plants in sunny parts of the garden that are protected from winds. Have a succession of plants in flower to provide food for butterflies from the spring through to the autumn. Late summer is a very active time for butterflies so include plenty of plants that bloom then.

In a perennial border, grow *Aubrieta* to attract the painted lady, red admiral, brimstone and small tortoiseshell. The same butterflies use *Lavandula* (lavender) as a nectar source, as do the small copper, common blue, meadow brown and small skipper. *Aster* (Michaelmas daisy), *Centranthus* (valerian), *Phlox*, and *Sedum* also attract a wide range of butterflies.

Shrubs, such as *Cornus alba* (red-barked dogwood) and *Escallonia*, are useful additions to a mixed border, while *Buddleja davidii* (butterfly bush) is a favourite in summer.

◀ WILD CORNER Calendula *and* Verbascum *combine with lilies and lupins in a natural area.*

Annuals that provide nectar include *Centaurea cyanus* (cornflower), *Helichrysum bracteatum* (strawflower), *Iberis umbellata* (candytuft), *Lobularia maritima* (sweet alyssum) and *Reseda odorata* (sweet mignonette).

Food plants for the next generation must also be provided as butterflies lay their eggs on plants that the emerging caterpillars will eat. Establish a patch of nettles in an out-of-the-way spot to provide food for the caterpillars of many butterflies, including the small tortoiseshell, red admiral, peacock, comma and painted lady. Cut some of the nettles down to the ground at different times of the year so that there are young leaves available.

Other useful food plants include cuckoo flowers, which support the caterpillars of the orange tip butterfly, and the common holly, *Ilex aquifolium*.

WOODLAND EDGE

A woodland edge provides a rich natural habitat for wildlife. Re-creating this environment, even on a small scale, will bring rewards in the diversity of creatures that it attracts.

The woodland area consists of various layers of vegetation – tall trees, smaller trees, a lower canopy of shrubs, and ground-cover plants and early bulbs. If there is insufficient room to grow tall trees, such as *Salix caprea* (goat willow) and

Quercus robur (English oak), choose a mixture of smaller trees and large shrubs to create the top layer. *Corylus avellana* (hazel), *Crataegus monogyna* (hawthorn), *Prunus padus* (bird cherry) and *Viburnum opulus* (guelder rose) are all of value in supporting wildlife.

In a smaller garden, use a mixed hedge as the top layer, or substitute climbing plants, including *Lonicera periclymenum* (woodbine) and *Hedera helix* (ivy), grown up a trellis. Do not trim hedges during the nesting season.

For the next layer down, select several small shrubs, especially those that produce berries. These include *Berberis* (barberry), *Cotoneaster*, *Pyracantha* (firethorn), *Euonymus* (spindle tree) and *Ligustrum vulgare* (privet).

Excellent ground cover for the woodland edge is provided by the shade-tolerant *Vinca* (periwinkle), *Ajuga* (bugle) and *Galium odoratum* (sweet woodruff). Some spring-flowering bulbs, such as *Galanthus* (snowdrop) and *Hyacinthoides non-scripta* (bluebell), also grow well here. Other useful plants include *Angelica sylvestris* (wild angelica), *Arum maculatum* (lords-and-ladies), *Ranunculus ficaria* (lesser celandine) and wood spurge.

A thick mulch of shreddings, bark, wood chippings or leaf-mould will complete the woodland habitat. Do not be too tidy in this area – leave dead stems and flowerheads to create a litter layer similar to that in a natural wood. This layer provides food and shelter for hundreds of tiny creatures, which all play a part in creating a balanced food chain. However, remove any diseased matter.

Supplementing habitats

A woodland edge, or a quiet and secluded area of the garden, is the ideal place to encourage hedgehogs to take up residence and reduce the slug population.

A pile of logs covered with long grass and dead twigs or leaves makes a good place for them to hibernate and attracts many insects too. Alternatively, buy or make a wooden box to house hedgehogs. Provide a tunnel, 10cm (4in) high and 30cm (12in) long, as the entrance to prevent foxes from gaining access. Cover the box with a layer of polythene to keep it dry and use a heap of dry leaves and sticks to provide some camouflage.

▼ Town garden *Pink* Lavatera *and purple* Buddleja *frame an overgrown path.*

▶ Wetland *An informal pond surrounded by plants provides water and shelter for wildlife.*

Encourage birds to nest in your garden by providing artificial nesting boxes. These are best put up in autumn or mid winter so that the birds can explore them thoroughly before the nest-building season begins.

The larger the entrance hole, the wider the range of birds that can make use of the nesting box, but you will probably find that the largest species become the most successful occupants. A diameter of 3cm (1¼in) allows smaller birds like tits, nuthatches and tree sparrows to use it. The entrance hole should be near the top to prevent cats or squirrels from reaching in. An open-fronted box or a simple platform, such as half a coconut shell, provides a nesting site for other birds, such as spotted flycatchers.

Position a nesting box in a place where it has shelter from wind, rain and strong sunlight, and away from bird tables. If fixing the box to a house, choose a wall facing north, north-east, east or south-east. Keep the box well away from branches to prevent predators from gaining easy access.

A bird table will attract many birds but food must be put out regularly. Seeds will bring finches, nuts attract tits and siskins, and fruit will be eaten by thrushes, fieldfares and blackbirds. You can also put out fat for tits and nuthatches.

Bats will take up residence in a nesting box. As these creatures are particularly susceptible to pesticides, boxes should be made from untreated wood and left unpainted and unvarnished. Rough-sawn timber is best because it allows the bats to get a good grip when they land. A bat box is similar in shape to a bird box, but smaller and with an entrance slit in the base. Make sure that there are no branches or other obstructions within 1 m (3 ft) of the box.

A WILDLIFE POND

A pond is one of the most important features that you can provide for wildlife. Many water-living species make their homes there, small mammals, bees, butterflies and other insects come to drink and birds use the shallow water for drinking and bathing.

Site a pond in an open, sunny position away from trees. Use a flexible sheet liner to make it as the sides of preformed plastic ponds are too steep and slippery for many creatures. The pond should include some sloping sides and areas of shallow water round the edges so that wildlife has easy access. Make sure that one area is at least 60 cm (2 ft) deep to prevent the water from freezing solid in winter.

Create a border of plants round part of the pond edge. A marsh or bog garden, which provides ideal conditions for a range of moisture-loving plants, is easily formed by extending the pond liner at one end. Many bog-garden plants are attractive to bees and butterflies. For example, the red-barked dogwood, *Primula* and *Lobelia* produce nectar and will also provide shelter for amphibians and other creatures.

Pond-side features, such as rocks, a grassed area and a gentle slope covered with sand or gravel, are useful to a variety of different creatures – and a paved area is helpful for access and maintenance.

To colonise the new habitat, obtain a few buckets of water and pond sludge from an existing pond to introduce hundreds of creatures. You can also buy water snails and water fleas from garden centres to help to keep the water clear of algae.

Many other creatures will turn up of their own accord. Expect to see damselflies, pond-skaters, water boatmen and diving beetles. Frogs, toads and newts may also appear. If you want amphibians to use the pond, it is inadvisable to stock fish – especially goldfish.

Plants grow at different levels within a pond and together create a balanced ecology. Submerged aquatic plants, such as *Potamogeton crispus* (curled pondweed) and *Hottonia palustris* (water violet), are oxygenators. Floating plants or plants with floating leaves, such as the native *Nymphaea alba* (white water lily), help to shade the lower levels from light and thus discourage algae. Marginal plants, which include *Iris pseudacorus* (yellow water flag) and *Carex* (sedge), provide useful hiding places for wildlife. See also WATER PLANTS (p. 706).

In a small garden where there is no space for a pond, substitute a birdbath. A stone one is best – plastic birdbaths are too slippery, although adding a layer of stones or wood provides a foothold. Break any ice that forms daily.

WALLS, ROCKS AND PAVING

Bare walls, fences and paved surfaces can be adapted to benefit wildlife. Fix a trellis 8-10 cm (3¼-4 in) in front of a wall or fence. Build ledges behind the trellis to create nesting sites for robins, wrens and other birds.

Grow climbers or wall shrubs over the trellis. Common ivy is particularly useful. It is often used for cover and nest sites by birds, and camouflage by moths and butterflies, which may also hibernate there. In addition, its flowers provide late pollen and nectar and its fruit is a source of food for birds in late winter and spring. *Cotoneaster franchetii* is another good choice because it produces orange-red berries in autumn, which attract birds.

Use the tops or cracks and crevices in walls as sites for plants like the stonecrop *Sedum acre*, or *Aubrieta* and *Aurinia*. On a patio or in a small town garden, plant up containers and hanging baskets with plants that are rich in nectar and pollen or produce seeds and berries, and include some evergreens, such as ivy, to provide winter shelter.

When laying paving slabs, leave large gaps between them and sow wild-flower seed there. Omit some slabs altogether, to create sites for plants that thrive in hot, dry conditions. These include *Thymus serpyllum* (wild thyme), *Linum perenne* (perennial flax) and *Dianthus deltoides* (maiden pink).

◀ WALL PLANTS Aubrieta *and* Aurinia *tumble down a wall above* Symphytum *(comfrey).*

PLANTS TO ATTRACT WILDLIFE

PLANTS FOR BIRDS

- ***Berberis*** spp. Shrubs with yellow or orange flowers in late spring and blue-black or red fruit in autumn.
- ***Cotoneaster*** spp. Shrubs with white flowers in late spring and early summer and red berries in autumn.
- ***Dipsacus fullonum*** (teasel) Biennial with large purple summer flowerheads which ripen to spiky seed heads.
- ***Helianthus annuus*** (sunflower) Annual bearing large yellow flowers with edible seeds in late summer.
- ***Ligustrum vulgare*** (privet) Semi-evergreen shrub with white clusters in summer and black fruits in autumn.
- ***Lonicera periclymenum*** (woodbine) Deciduous climber with cream flowers in summer and autumn, followed by red berries.
- ***Pyracantha*** spp. (firethorn) Evergreen shrubs with white flower clusters in summer and bright autumn berries.

PLANTS FOR BEES

- ***Achillea millefolium*** (yarrow) Perennial with white flat-topped clusters in late summer and autumn.
- ***Filipendula ulmaria*** (meadowsweet) Perennial with large creamy white flowers in mid summer.
- ***Thymus*** spp. Evergreen perennials with tiny pink or purple flowers in summer.

PLANTS FOR BUTTERFLIES

- ***Aster*** (Michaelmas daisy) Perennials with mauve, pink or white flowers in late summer and autumn.
- ***Aubrieta deltoidea*** Evergreen perennial with violet to mauve, starry flowers in spring.
- ***Buddleja davidii*** (butterfly bush) Deciduous shrub with purple spikes in summer.
- ***Centranthus ruber*** (red valerian) Perennial with clusters of star-shaped red flowers in summer.
- ***Sedum spectabile*** (ice plant) Perennial with pink clusters in early autumn.

X-Z

Xanthoceras

Sapindaceae

Xanthoceras sorbifolium

There is only one species in this genus, a large deciduous shrub or small tree grown for its upright spikes of fragrant flowers. Moderately frost hardy, it grows best in southern Britain, where warmer weather will ripen the wood and encourage abundant flowering. This is an excellent plant for chalky soils.

Xanthoceras sorbifolium ♀ White flowers with a carmine centre, up to 3 cm (1¼ in) across, are produced in mid spring. The flower spikes at the ends of branches can be up to 20 cm (8 in) long, while the rest are about half that length. The compound leaves have 9-17 leaflets and grow to around 20 cm (8 in) long. They are pale green at first but darken with age. The plant has a rather upright habit of growth and can make a small tree in milder parts of Britain. Native to N China. HEIGHT & SPREAD 1.8×1 m (6×3 ft) in 10 years, ultimately 5 m (16 ft) tall.

CULTIVATION Plant from mid autumn to mid spring, avoiding dry or frosty periods, in any fertile soil, preferably chalky. Choose a sheltered position in full sun.

PROPAGATION Sow seed in pots in early to mid spring.

PRUNING Remove any dead wood in early spring before leaves emerge.

PESTS AND DISEASES Usually trouble free, but coral spot fungus can be a problem.

▲ *Xanthoceras sorbifolium*

Xanthorhiza

Ranunculaceae

Xanthorhiza simplicissima

This deciduous frost-hardy shrub is grown for its impressive autumn colour. It is also a good ground cover plant. There is only one species in the genus.

Xanthorhiza simplicissima (yellow root) Bright green leaves, up to 30 cm (12 in) long, with 3-5 deeply cut leaflets, turn to shades of purple, red and yellow during autumn. Tiny, deep purple, five-part flowers appear in early to mid spring. These are produced in abundance on drooping plumes up to 20 cm (8 in) long. This multistemmed shrub produces many suckers from underground roots. When cut, the stems and roots are a brilliant yellow, which gives the plant its common name. A suckering habit makes propagation easy. Native to E United States. HEIGHT & SPREAD 1 m×60 cm (3×2 ft) after 5 years and ultimately.

CULTIVATION Plant from early autumn to late spring in any good, relatively moist soil, avoiding thin soils over chalk. Choose a shady position.

PROPAGATION Divide the plants in early spring.

PESTS AND DISEASES Usually trouble free.

▲ *Xanthorhiza simplicissima*

Yarrow see *Achillea*
Yesterday-today-and-tomorrow see *Brunfelsia pauciflora*
Yew see *Taxus*
Yew, plum see *Cephalotaxus*
Youth and old age see *Zinnia*

Yucca

Agavaceae

Yucca gloriosa

These striking evergreen shrubs are grown for the architectural value of their long, sword-like, often rigid leaves. The leaves are held in clumps or rosettes from which tall, exotic-looking flower stems rise in mid to late summer, bearing numerous 10 cm (4 in) wide, bell-shaped flowers.

Native to S United States and Central America, most species are hardy enough for hot sunny sites in British gardens. *Yucca aloifolia* and *Y. elephantipes* are too tender to be grown outside, but make excellent container plants for a conservatory or house.

RECOMMENDED SPECIES AND VARIETIES

Y. aloifolia (Spanish bayonet) A strong erect stem bears a crown of rigid, 45 cm (1½ ft) long leaves. The leaves have finely toothed edges and end in a sharp point. The flowers are white, sometimes flushed with purple and held in 60 cm (2 ft) high panicles, but are rarely seen on containerised plants. HEIGHT & SPREAD 75×75 cm (2½×2½ ft) after 5 years, ultimately 3 m (10 ft) tall or more.

'Variegata' has yellow-edged leaves.

Y. elephantipes ♀ Strong stems bear bright green spineless leaves up to 1.2 m (4 ft) long. White, pendent, cup-shaped flowers are carried in erect, branched clusters in mid and late summer. Flowers are rarely seen, however, on plants grown indoors. This

▲ *Yucca filamentosa*

▲ *Yucca flaccida* 'Golden Sword'

▲ *Yucca gloriosa* 'Variegata'

species makes a small tree in its native Mexico, but is much smaller when grown in a container as a houseplant, as it is in Britain. HEIGHT & SPREAD 100×30cm (3×1ft) after 5 years, ultimately 1.8m (6ft) tall.

'Variegata' has bright green leaves with creamy white edges.

Y. filamentosa♀ (Adam's needle) Narrow mid green leaves form rosettes. The stiffly erect leaves, up to 75cm (2½ft) long, are adorned with numerous wavy white threads. Creamy white, tulip-shaped flowers are carried in plumes up to 1.8m (6ft) high that stand above the foliage. HEIGHT & SPREAD 60×75cm (2×2½ft) after 5 years, ultimately 1m (3ft) tall.

'Bright Edge'♀ has leaves that are emerald green with wide yellow edges. **'Garland's Gold'** has broad leaves with edges striped creamy yellow. The smaller **'Variegata'**♀ has cream streaks and pink-tinged edges to its glaucous green leaves.

Y. flaccida Mid green or glaucous leaves, curving downwards at the tips, form low clumps. The leaves are up to 60cm (2ft) long with many short white threads along the edges. Creamy white flowers are carried in erect panicles up to 1.5m (5ft) tall. This species spreads by short basal side growths. HEIGHT & SPREAD 60×75cm (2×2½ft) after 5 years, ultimately 75cm (2½ft) tall.

'Golden Sword'♀ has leaves banded with creamy yellow. **'Ivory'**♀ is a free-flowering variety bearing creamy white, green-stained flowers.

Y. glauca This low-growing, short-stemmed evergreen species forms rounded heads of spiky greyish leaves, up to 60cm (2ft) long, with white edges and some hanging threads. Well-established plants bear nodding greenish white flowers in erect panicles up to 1.5m (5ft) tall. HEIGHT & SPREAD 60×75 (2×2½ft) after 5 years, ultimately 1m (3ft) tall.

Y. gloriosa♀ (Adam's needle, Spanish dagger) Stout semi-woody stems are topped by a cluster of straight, fiercely spiny, glaucous green leaves, up to 60cm (2ft) long. Creamy white flowers sometimes tinged with red are carried in panicles up to 2.1m (7ft) tall. The species may not flower for 5 or more years. HEIGHT & SPREAD 60×60cm (2×2ft) or more after 5 years, ultimately 1.5m (5ft) or more tall.

'Variegata'♀ has leaves edged and striped with creamy yellow.

▲ *Yucca gloriosa*

Y. recurvifolia♀ Spiky leaves, up to 75cm (2½ft) long, rise from a short stem that eventually branches. All but the upper central leaves are recurved. Creamy flowers are borne in dense, erect panicles up to 2.1m (7ft) high. HEIGHT & SPREAD 1×1m (3×3ft) after 5 years, ultimately 2.4m (8ft) tall.

'Marginata' has leaves edged with pale yellow. **'Variegata'** bears leaves with a yellowish green band down the centre.

Y. whipplei Long, narrow, rigid, spine-tipped leaves form a dense, almost globular cluster. The leaves are grey-green, glaucous and finely toothed. Tall plumes of large milky green, purple-edged, scented bells are held in densely packed panicles on long stout stems. Plant this slightly tender garden plant in a sunny, well-drained site, where temperatures remain above -5°C (23°F). HEIGHT & SPREAD 40×40cm (16×16in) after 5 years, ultimately 1m (3ft) tall.

CULTIVATION Plant hardy species in spring in any well-drained garden soil in full sun. Plant the tender *Y. aloifolia* and *Y. elephantipes* in a 25cm (10in) pot of John Innes compost No. 2 or 3 in spring and maintain a minimum night-time temperature of 7°C (45°F). Place in a sunny position. Repot as necessary in spring.

PROPAGATION Remove well-rooted suckers in early or mid spring and replant in permanent positions. Alternatively, lift the plants in late spring and remove small buds from the base of the stem. Dip in dry wood ashes to stop excessive bleeding. Line out in sandy soil, 1.5cm (½in) below the surface, in a coldframe; the buds slowly grow into young plants.

PRUNING None required.

PESTS AND DISEASES Leaf spot can damage the foliage.

Yulan see *Magnolia denudata*
Yushania see BAMBOOS p.79

Zantedeschia

Arum lily, calla lily
Araceae

A petal-like, modified leaf called a spathe enfolds a fleshy spike of tiny flowers (called a spadix) at the top of a long stem on these stately plants. Blooming in late spring and early summer these lilies are much prized as cut flowers. Plants have arrow-shaped leaves and large rhizomes. Native to South Africa, the genus zantedeschia includes both hardy and tender plants. All species and varieties prefer damp or wet soil and so may be grown at the side of a pond. Some plants can be grown in water.

RECOMMENDED SPECIES AND VARIETIES

Z. aethiopica ♀ A creamy white spathe, up to 25cm (10in) long, surrounds a yellow spadix. This plant is the hardiest zantedeschia, being able to withstand several degrees of frost. It can be grown in water as an aquatic plant, provided that the water does not freeze solid. HEIGHT & SPREAD 1m×50cm (3ft×20in).

▼ *Zantedeschia aethiopica*

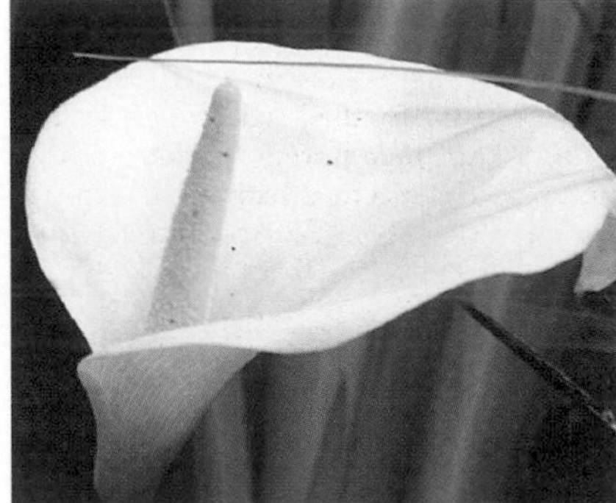

▲ *Zantedeschia aethiopica* 'Crowborough'

▲ *Zantedeschia aethiopica* 'Green Goddess'

'Crowborough' is even hardier than the species. **'Green Goddess'** ♀ has a white spathe heavily marked with green.

Z. elliottiana ♀ The broad leaves, up to 28cm (11in) long, of this tender plant have translucent white spots. The spathe and spadix are yellow. The plant should be brought indoors for winter. There are many named, coloured forms available. HEIGHT & SPREAD 75×30cm (2½×1ft).

Z. rehmannii ♀ Pink to maroon spathes with whitish flowers distinguish this plant which should be brought indoors for winter. The leaves are up to 20cm (8in) long. HEIGHT & SPREAD 80×30cm (32×12in).

CULTIVATION Plant the rhizomes of *Z. aethiopica* and its cultivars 10cm (4in) deep and about 40cm (16in) apart in moist or wet, fertile soil. If treating as an aquatic plant, place in a planting basket at a depth of 15-30cm (6-12in).

Plant *Z. elliottiana* and *Z. rehmannii* in 20-25cm (8-10in) pots, in John Innes No. 2 or No. 3 or in a moist, peat-based compost. Keep in a greenhouse over winter, then in late spring or early summer plant outside or place the pots outside. Feed regularly and reduce watering in late summer before bringing the plants inside once more.

PROPAGATION Best done by dividing the rhizomes in late summer.

PESTS AND DISEASES Leaf spot can mark and damage the leaves.

Zauschneria

Onagraceae

The abundance of flowers produced by these evergreen perennials will brighten the front of a border in late summer and early autumn. The funnel-shaped flowers grow in clusters on the ends of slender stems. The lance-shaped, rich green or grey-green leaves are mostly downy. Zauschnerias need a sunny position in order to thrive and are hardy when grown on a free-draining soil; the greatest threat to their survival is winter wet. Native to California and Mexico.

RECOMMENDED SPECIES AND VARIETIES

Z. californica (syn. *Epilobium californicum* hort.) (Californian fuchsia, humming-bird flower) The rich scarlet flowers are about 3cm (1¼in) long. The lance-shaped, greyish green leaves, up to 4cm (1½in) long, have a downy texture. HEIGHT & SPREAD 45×45cm (1½×1½ft) or more.

The flowers of ssp. ***cana*** (syn. *Epilobium canum, E. microphyllum*) are vermilion to scarlet. Its cultivars **'Albiflora'** and **'Dublin'** ♀ (syn. 'Glasnevin') have white flowers and slightly longer, bright orange-red flowers respectively. 'Dublin' rarely exceeds 30cm (1ft) in height or spread.

The flowers of ssp. ***latifolia*** have more prominent stamens than the species and the leaves are smaller.

The flowers of ssp. ***mexicana*** (syn. *Epilobium villosum, Z. cana* ssp. *villosa*) are red. Its cultivar **'Solidarity Pink'** has pale pink flowers.

Z. cana ssp. ***villosa*** see *Z. californica* ssp. *mexicana*

CULTIVATION Plant in late spring in an open sunny position in very well-drained soil. In cold areas a site at the foot of a south or west-facing wall is best. When

▲ *Zauschneria californica* ssp. *cana* 'Dublin'

established, apply a slow-release fertiliser during early spring. To protect plants from winter weather, do not cut back the foliage until late spring.
PROPAGATION Take softwood cuttings in summer, sow seed under glass in early spring, or divide in late spring.
PESTS AND DISEASES Usually trouble free.

Zea see GRASSES p.302
Zebra plant see *Aphelandra squarrosa*
Zebra plant see *Calathea zebrina*
Zebrina see *Tradescantia*

Zelkova
Ulmaceae

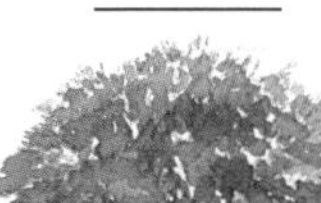

Zelkova serrata

These stately trees with upswept branches make an impressive focal point in a large garden. They are particularly valued for their distinctive goblet-like outline and splendid autumn colour. Fairly hardy and shade tolerant, they will grow in any soil and can live for over 100 years. The recommended trees have insignificant flowers.
RECOMMENDED SPECIES
Z. carpinifolia (Caucasian elm) A dense aerial forest of upright branches develops above a short, thick trunk, which is as much as 1m (3ft) across and often reinforced by buttress-like thickened sections at the base. The bark is pale grey. The pointed, elliptic-oblong leaves, 4–7.5cm (1½–3in) long, have rough, toothed edges. They turn yellow and then warm orange-brown in autumn. The species is native to mountainous forests of the Caucasus and N Iran. HEIGHT & SPREAD 6×4m (20×13ft) after 20 years, ultimately 30m (100ft) tall.
Z. serrata ♀ (Japanese zelkova, saw leaf zelkova) Toothed, ovate-oblong leaves, about 5cm (2in) long, turn yellow, orange and red in autumn. The smooth, flaky, brownish grey bark sometimes reveals small patches of pale orange. This tree is often pruned as a bonsai. Native to SE Asia. HEIGHT & SPREAD 6×4m (20×13ft) after 20 years, ultimately 30m (100ft) tall.

▲ *Zelkova carpinifolia*

▲ *Zelkova serrata*

CULTIVATION Plant in spring in any soil, ideally fertile, in partial shade. If you wish to restrict the growth rate, plant in poor soil and do not feed.
PROPAGATION Store seed in a paper bag in a refrigerator in winter and sow under glass in spring. Harden the seedlings outside in summer.
PESTS AND DISEASES Dutch elm disease is sometimes a problem. Otherwise, these trees are usually trouble free.

Zenobia
Ericaceae

Aniseed-scented, bell-like flowers hang from the long stalks of this bushy deciduous or semi-evergreen shrub for acid soils. There is one species in the genus.
Zenobia pulverulenta White flowers, up to 1cm (⅜in) long, arranged in unbranched clusters, open from early to mid summer. The alternate, ovate-oblong to broadly elliptic leaves, 2–7cm (¾–2¾in) long, have a blue-white bloom when young. The plant spreads by suckers. It is hardy, but young growth is occasionally damaged by frost. Native to eastern N America. HEIGHT & SPREAD 1.2m×60cm (4×2ft) after 5 years, ultimately 1.8m (6ft) tall.
CULTIVATION Plant out in autumn or spring, if possible, in a moist, acid soil in sun or partial shade. Remove the developing seed heads if desired.

▲ *Zenobia pulverulenta*

PROPAGATION Take semi-ripe cuttings in summer. Alternatively, sow the seed under glass in late winter.
PRUNING Cut back after flowering to near ground level about every 5 years, or more frequently if the plant becomes straggly.
PESTS AND DISEASES Usually trouble free.

Zephyranthes
Amaryllidaceae

Beautiful erect, cup-shaped blossoms crown the stems of the hardy to half-hardy bulbs in this genus in spring or autumn. It is essential to grow these clump-forming plants in a well-drained soil and in an open sunny position, such as the edge of a border or at the base of a south or west-facing wall. Cloche protection from the worst of the winter rain is necessary for most species and beneficial for the recommended plant. The bulbs are also easily grown in pots in an unheated greenhouse or conservatory. Native to N and S America.

▲ *Zephyranthes candida*

RECOMMENDED SPECIES
Z. candida (zephyr flower) Pure white or, occasionally, rose-tinged petals open into starry flowers, up to 5cm (2in) across, in late summer and autumn. They are carried on individual leafless stems up to 15cm (6in) long. The dark green leaves, virtually evergreen, are narrow and rush-like and up to 25cm (10in) long. HEIGHT & SPREAD 25×10cm (10×4in).
CULTIVATION Plant *Z. candida* in spring in very well-drained soil and in a sunny spot, or pot in John Innes No.3 compost with up to 25 per cent of sharp grit added. Plunge the pot in sand in a coldframe. Dry off pot-grown plants in late spring and repot or top-dress them with fresh compost. Water well in late summer.
PROPAGATION Divide bulbs of *Z. candida* in late spring. Alternatively, sow seed in early spring in a coldframe.
PESTS AND DISEASES Usually trouble free.

Zephyr flower see *Zephyranthes candida*

Zigadenus
Melanthiaceae

Small, star-like blossoms highlight the hardy bulbs and rhizomes in this genus in summer. They require well-drained, rich soil and an open position, but one that is not baked by the sun. A place in a mixed border or a shrub border is suitable. The plants, which are poisonous, are native to N America and N Asia.
RECOMMENDED SPECIES
Z. elegans (white camass) Spikes of greenish white star-like, 6-petalled blossoms, up to 2cm (¾in) across, each with a distinctive yellowish green basal nectary, are produced throughout summer. The grey-green, semi-erect leaves of this clump-forming plant are narrow and strap-like and grow up to 30cm (12in) long. HEIGHT & SPREAD 45×15cm (18×6in).
CULTIVATION Plant in spring in cool, moist, well-drained soil that has been enriched with organic matter and in an open position. Water freely throughout spring and summer. Apply a slow-release fertiliser in early spring.
PROPAGATION Divide in early spring or sow seeds in a coldframe in autumn.
PESTS AND DISEASES Usually trouble free.

▲ *Zigadenus elegans*

Zinnia
Youth and old age
Compositae

Zinnia elegans

Showy dahlia-like flowers, available in a wide range of brilliant colours, appear from mid summer until the first frosts. The longer-stemmed plants make very good cut flowers, while the smaller varieties are suitable for planting at bed and border edges and in containers. Zinnias perform best in hot, dry summers and tend to be disappointing when grown in cool, wet climates.

The plants described below are half-hardy annuals of erect habit. They have more or less stalkless leaves, undivided and smooth-edged, arranged in pairs along the stems. Native to S United States and Mexico, the plants are not frost hardy.
RECOMMENDED SPECIES AND VARIETIES
Z. angustifolia This short, small-flowered species makes an excellent summer groundcover plant and is also useful as a filler for a sunny position in a rock garden. The single, star-shaped flowers are about 4cm (1in) across and in favourable conditions are borne in great abundance. HEIGHT & SPREAD 25-35×30cm (10-14×12in).

'Starbright Mixed' has gold, orange and white flowers. **'Tropical Snow'** carries white flowers.
Z. elegans Purple flowers, about 6cm (2½in) across, appear on coarse, upright stems in summer. The ovate or lance-shaped leaves, about 8cm (3¼in) long, are light to mid green. HEIGHT & SPREAD 100×30cm (40×12in).
Z. haageana (syn. *Z. mexicana*) Upright stems bear light green lance-shaped leaves, about 4cm (1½in) long, that are lightly covered in hairs. The single flowers grow to 4cm (1½in) across and are bright orange. HEIGHT & SPREAD 60×30cm (24×12in).

▲ *Zinnia haageana*

OTHER VARIETIES
Z. elegans and *Z. haageana* are the parent species of almost all the most commonly grown varieties. The flower colour range, unless otherwise stated, includes orange, pink, purple, red, white and yellow.

'Chippendale' has single deep red flowers with golden tips on the ray florets and grows as tall as 60cm (2ft). **Dahlia-Flowered Mixed** and **Giant Double Mixed** both have semidouble flowers up to 12cm (4¾in) across and grow to a height of about 60cm (2ft). **'Envy'** produces lime-green flowers, grows to 60cm (2ft) tall and will tolerate some shade.

'Persian Carpet' has semidouble flowers, about 5cm (2in) across, which are bicoloured in chocolate, cream, gold, maroon, purple and yellow, and grows to a height of about 40cm (16in). This variety performs better than the larger-flowered ones in cooler, wetter summers. **Sun Bow Mixed** has fully double, almost spherical flowers about 3cm (1¼in) across, which resemble pompon dahlias. The plant grows up to 50cm (20 in) tall.

'Thumbelina' is a very compact dwarf plant growing to 10-15cm (4-6in) tall with double and semidouble flowers about 4cm (1½in) across. Of all zinnias, this performs best in wet summers. **'Whirligig Mixed'**, about 50cm (20in) tall, has large single flowers about 8cm (3in) across with the ray florets tipped with a contrasting colour.
CULTIVATION Plant in full sun in a fertile, well-drained soil after all risk of frost has passed. Water in after planting, but avoid any further watering. Deadhead throughout the flowering period.
PROPAGATION Zinnias resent root disturbance, and if treated as half-hardy annuals they should be raised in pots. Sow seed in a greenhouse in mid spring about six weeks before planting out. Alternatively, sow in late spring in the final planting position and thin out the seedlings to the required spacing as soon as they are well established.
PESTS AND DISEASES Aphids, capsid bugs, chrysanthemum eelworms and earwigs may attack the plants. Seedlings are susceptible to damping off, and in wet conditions fungal foot and root rots may cause subsequent losses. Grey mould may infect the flowers in wet seasons.

Zinnia, creeping
see *Sanvitalia procumbens*

Food from the garden

Even in a small garden, fruit will grow against a sunny wall and vegetables can be sown among flowering plants. With a larger space, a kitchen garden can make a real contribution to both your eating enjoyment and the household budget

The Fruit Garden

Fruit trees and bushes can be as rewarding as any ornamental plant. Trees trace decorative shapes against a sunny wall – as well as giving fruit. And strawberries, raspberries and currants provide delicious summer tastes

Tree fruit and soft fruit

The fruits that grow in British gardens are divided into 'tree fruit' and 'soft fruit', which mostly grow on bushes. Soft fruit can be more rewarding as they produce their fruit more quickly after planting and also need no cross-pollination, which can result in more reliable cropping. Most varieties of tree fruit must be pollinated by another variety growing in your own or a neighbour's garden. Trees can be grown in a variety of shapes, including bush trees, pyramids, cordons, espaliers and fans. The choice depends on whether the tree will be grown against a wall or fence (a restricted form) or if it will be free-standing (unrestricted). The charts of varieties on the following pages will help you to choose the varieties of fruit that are most suitable to your garden – and to your palate.

Planting a young fruit tree

The best time to plant a fruit tree is on a fine day in autumn, when the soil is not wet and sticky. Free-standing trees need to be staked for four years. Free-standing trees on dwarfing rootstocks, which have a small root system, need a permanent stake. First, drive the stake into position and then dig the hole next to it. For the full method of planting a tree, see page 808.

Restricted trees require a supporting framework – either horizontal wires or trellis – which may be fixed to a wall or fence or may stand alone. Wires are spaced 15 cm (6 in) apart for fan trees, with the lowest wire 38 cm (15 in) above the soil. Espaliers need stronger wire spaced 38-45 cm (15-18 in) apart and coinciding with the 'arms' of the tree, with the lowest wire 45 cm (18 in) above the soil. The wires for cordons are spaced 60 cm (24 in) apart, with the bottom wire 60 cm (24 in) above the soil. Plant fruit trees no more than 15 cm (6 in) from a wall or fence so that they benefit from the extra warmth.

How to train and prune a new tree

Fruit trees are pruned for two reasons – in the early years to form the desired shape, in later years to allow maximum light to get in and to maintain the balance between growth of new wood and fruit production.

Winter pruning directs energy to the growth buds at the expense of flower buds, and should be kept to the minimum in the early years so as not to delay cropping. Early fruiting of unrestricted forms can be encouraged by bending new shoots outwards and tying them down, as horizontal shoots will produce more flower buds.

Summer pruning is less stimulating to growth and also removes unwanted shoots. Stone fruits, such as plums and peaches, are usually pruned in summer because silver leaf disease may occur at other times.

Starting with a feathered maiden – a one-year-old tree with laterals (or feathers) – it is possible to train any shape. But two-year-old trees can be bought partly trained.

Unrestricted trees can be trained as 'bush' trees, which have an open centre, or as 'spindlebush' or 'pyramid' trees which have a central trunk and tiers of horizontal branches. Restricted trees can be trained as cordons, espaliers, step-overs or fans. The eventual size of each shape depends on the type of rootstock it is grown on (see the chart of varieties for each type of fruit).

Spur-forming and tip-bearing varieties

Most varieties of fruit trees develop fruiting spurs which carry the flower buds each year. However, some types develop a flower bud at the end of each year's new growth, and are called 'tip bearers'. The different types are identified in the charts.

Always ensure that sufficient flower buds are left after pruning.

Good hygiene with fruit pruning

After pruning a fruit tree – especially if diseased wood has been removed – clean the tools with a sterilant by spraying them with a small hand sprayer or by dipping them into a bucket of sterilant solution.

There is no need to paint cuts unless there is a high incidence of canker and silver leaf diseases in the neighbourhood, in which case paint the wounds with pruning paint within 30 minutes of making the cut.

When cutting wood out of a tree, unless cutting to a bud or shoot, always leave the basal 5 mm ($^1/_4$ in) intact. This will ensure that the tree's natural protection mechanism is able to shut out diseases.

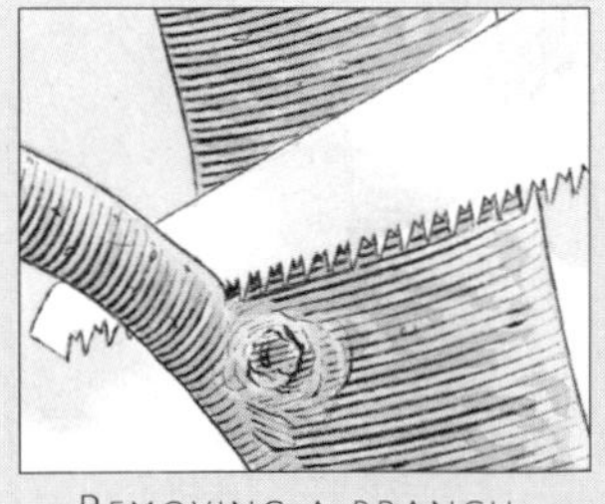

Removing a branch

• Training a bush tree •

A 'bush' has a stem 75 cm (30 in) high. A higher stem gives a 'standard' which is too large for small gardens. A bush is easy to grow but can have poor light penetration.

1 First winter After planting a feathered maiden (a one-year-old tree with laterals), cut back the main stem to 75 cm (30 in) above soil level to leave four laterals. These laterals provide the basic framework of the adult tree. Shorten them by two-thirds of their length, each to a bud pointing away from the centre of the tree.

Remove any laterals on the main stem lower than the selected laterals. During spring and summer, the four laterals will grow longer and sub-laterals will sprout from them.

2 **FIRST SUMMER** In August on apples and pears remove all upright sub-lateral shoots longer than 23 cm (9 in).

Similar shoots on plum and cherry trees are shortened to 10 cm (4 in) by breaking them off between your finger and thumb (see left). Leave all the other sub-lateral shoots intact.

3 **SECOND WINTER** Shorten the leading laterals by half of their new growth to an outward facing vegetative bud (one that is flat and pointed and will produce a new shoot).

• TRAINING A SPINDLEBUSH TREE •

A spindlebush has one central stem with side branches growing from it, so that the tree looks like a capital 'A'. It takes up less space and is more light-efficient than a bush.

1 **FIRST WINTER** After planting a feathered maiden (a one-year-old tree with laterals), cut the main stem back to a bud 25 cm (10 in) above the top lateral. Then remove the top lateral so that it does not compete with the main stem for leadership. Remove all laterals on the main stem lower than 45 cm (18 in) above soil level. In spring the main stem will extend and more laterals will grow below the cut.

2 **FIRST SUMMER** In August on apples and pears remove all upright sub-lateral shoots longer than 23 cm (9 in). Similar shoots on plums and cherries are shortened to 10 cm (4 in) by breaking them off between finger and thumb.

Tie or weigh down to the horizontal all laterals that are growing upwards (see right). Laterals at the top of the tree are likely to be too vigorous and should be weighed down below the horizontal. The overall tree shape now resembles a capital 'A' and is very efficient at intercepting sunlight.

▶ Tie down upright laterals so that the tree looks like a capital 'A'.

3 **SECOND WINTER** Prune the tree in the same way as in the first winter.

• TRAINING A PYRAMID •

Like a spindlebush, a pyramid tree has a central stem. But the laterals of a pyramid are tied down less severely – to about 30 degrees above the horizontal.

1 **FIRST WINTER** After planting a feathered maiden (a one-year-old tree with laterals), prune as for a spindlebush but also shorten all the laterals by half. For stone fruits, wait until April before pruning.

2 **FIRST SUMMER** In August, cut back the current season's extension growth on laterals to 20 cm (8 in) and sublaterals to 15 cm (6 in). Tie or weigh down laterals to 30 degrees above the horizontal. Remove the ties in the autumn.

3 **SECOND WINTER** Cut back the extension growth on the main stem by two-thirds. For stone fruits (plums and cherries), wait until April before pruning.

• CORDON •

A single stem bears fruit all along it on short spurs. Double or triple-stemmed cordons can also be grown. Cordons take the least space.

1 **FIRST WINTER** After planting a feathered maiden (a one-year-old tree with laterals), cut back the main stem between the topmost lateral and its tip by half.

Tie the main stem to a cane along its entire length and then tie the cane to the support wires at an angle of 45 degrees (see right). Shorten all laterals to a length of 7.5-10 cm (3-4 in).

If you wish to cover an archway, train the stem vertically instead of at 45 degrees in order to release its full vigour.

2 **FIRST SUMMER** In August, shorten all new laterals longer than 23 cm (9 in) to 5 cm (2 in). Then shorten to 2.5 cm (1 in) all the sub-laterals that have grown from the laterals that were pruned in the first winter (see right).

3 **SECOND WINTER** Cut the leader as in the first winter.

4 **SECOND SUMMER** Prune the tree in the same way as in the first summer. Once the required height has been reached, cut the top of the stem back to a lateral in June.

• TRAINING AN ESPALIER •

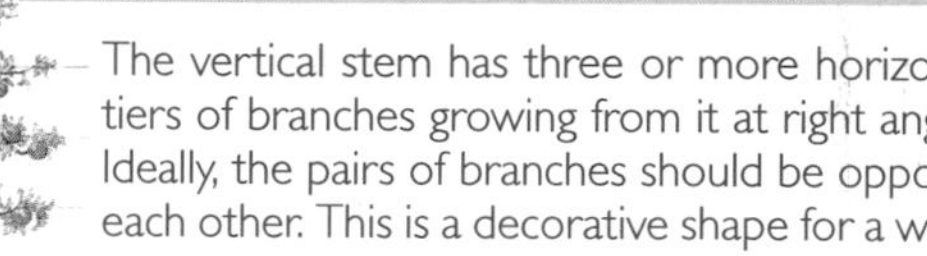

The vertical stem has three or more horizontal tiers of branches growing from it at right angles. Ideally, the pairs of branches should be opposite each other. This is a decorative shape for a wall.

1 **FIRST WINTER** After planting a feathered maiden (a one-year-old tree with laterals), select two of the laterals that are growing at the height of the bottom support wire – 45 cm (18 in) above soil level. They will form the first tier of branches.

Shorten these laterals by half their length, each to an upward facing bud (see left).

Tie the laterals to bamboo canes and then tie the canes to the horizontal support wires.

Cut off the main stem to three. buds immediately above the second wire. This will cause the leader to extend and two new laterals to grow to coincide with the wire.

Remove any laterals on the main stem that are lower than the first tier.

2 FIRST SUMMER In August, shorten all sub-laterals to 5 cm (2 in) long. Select the second tier of laterals to coincide with the second support wire. Tie them to bamboo canes and then tie the canes to the wire at right angles to the main stem. At this time of year the wood is still pliable and will bend to the horizontal easily. Cut back any remaining laterals to 5 cm (2 in).

3 SECOND WINTER On the second tier, prune as for the first tier in the first winter. Prune the extension growth on the first tier to half its length. (When each tier has grown to the required length, prune any extension growth back to its point of origin in June to minimise regrowth.)

Cut the main stem three buds above the third wire.

4 SECOND SUMMER In August, cut back all the sub-laterals to a length of 5 cm (2 in).

Select shoots that have grown from the pruning cuts made to the sub-laterals in the first summer, and shorten them to 2.5 cm (1 in) (see right).

Select the third tier and fix the laterals on canes to the wire.

• TRAINING A STEP-OVER •

FIRST WINTER AND SECOND SUMMER A step-over can be used to edge a border or pathway. It is a single-tier espalier, so train and prune the tree as an espalier for the first two seasons.

• TRAINING A FAN •

Branches fan out from a short stem, producing a large fruiting area. Peaches, nectarines and plums are the most common fans – grown against a wall.

1 FIRST WINTER After planting a feathered maiden (a one-year-old tree with laterals), cut back the main stem to leave two laterals at the bottom wire. Cut the laterals back by two-thirds of their length to upward-facing buds. Prune stone-fruits in April to avoid disease.

2 FIRST SUMMER As shoots grow, select and tie four shoots from each lateral to canes, and tie the canes to the support wires, copying the spread-out fingers of a hand. Avoid tying shoots in a vertical position.

Rub out any shoots growing towards the wall or fence. Pinch back all other shoots to two leaves.

3 SECOND WINTER Cut each of the eight selected sub-laterals by half their length. Leave the pruning of stone fruits until April.

4 SECOND SUMMER Pinch out any flowers. Select and tie four shoots from each sub-lateral as in the first summer, but when they are 45 cm (18 in) long pinch out their tips.

Growths that are produced by these shoots in the third summer on acid cherries, peaches and nectarines will fruit in the fourth summer and will need to be replaced immediately after the fruit is picked. Apples, pears, plums and sweet cherries will fruit in the third summer on spurs that have developed because of the pinching back of shoots since planting.

Avoid tying shoots vertically. Rub off shoots growing towards the fence or wall, and pinch back excess shoots to two leaves.

Pruning established trees

As trees get older their most important requirement is light. It will power the leaves to produce food, initiate flower buds, ripen wood and keep the tree dry, reducing the incidence of wet diseases.

BUSH Do not allow branches to become too vertical; they will stop light entering the centre, and fruiting will only occur on the outside of the canopy.

Sub-laterals growing off the branches should be renewed when six years old by cutting them off at the branch (three years old for peaches, nectarines and acid cherries). Upright new shoots can be tied or weighted down to take their place.

Excess vertical shoots on spur bearers can be removed in summer by pulling them off with a gloved hand when they are 15-20 cm (6-8 in) long. Less regrowth occurs than if they are removed in the winter. With tip bearers, remove vertical shoots longer than 23 cm (9 in) in winter to leave shorter shoots with flower buds.

▲ Pull off excess vertical shoots on spur bearers with a gloved hand.

SPINDLEBUSH Stop cutting the top of the main stem in winter when the tree has reached the required height – usually as high as you can reach with outstretched arms. Instead, cut in June to a weak-growing lateral.

Renew laterals when six years old by cutting them out at the main stem with an angled cut which leaves a sloping stub. The stub should have a long underside, and although no buds are visible shoots will grow out horizontally.

Summer-prune apples and pears by removing upright shoots longer than 23 cm (9 in) growing from the laterals – particularly if they are close to fruit to allow light to colour the fruit. Similar shoots on plums and cherries are shortened to 10 cm (4 in) by breaking them off between finger and thumb.

▲ Renew laterals when 6 years old by cutting them out with an angled cut which leaves a sloping stub.

PYRAMID Once the desired height has been reached – as high as you can reach with outstretched arms – prune the main stem in June to a weak lateral. Remove any upright vigorous shoots in the top of the tree.

In August, shorten the current season's growth on laterals to 20 cm (8 in) and sub-laterals to 15 cm (6 in).

CORDON, ESPALIER AND STEP-OVER Once the height of the tree has been established, continue to summer prune. As the spurs become too numerous, cut some out and reduce complicated spur systems.

FAN For apples, pears, plums and sweet cherries, once the basic shape has been formed, pruning is aimed at promoting spurs. Each summer rub off shoots growing towards the wall or fence. Keep pinching back new shoots to six leaves, and shorten them to three leaves once the fruits have been picked. Tie in shoots to fill gaps where necessary. Each winter (April for stone fruits), cut out dead, diseased and bare wood. Remove any thick vertical wood as it will cause lower parts to stop growing.

▲ Vertical cordons can be curved at the top to form an archway.

For peaches, nectarines and acid cherries, once the basic shape has been formed pruning is aimed at encouraging replacement shoots because the best fruit is on one-year-old wood.

Each summer rub out shoots growing towards the wall.

Select replacement shoots – with a back-up shoot in each case – for shoots currently fruiting. Pinch back all others to two leaves. After picking, cut out shoots that have fruited and tie in their replacements. Any unwanted shoots can be cut back to two leaves.

▲ On peaches and acid cherries, select replacement shoots.

Apples

Malus x domestica
Rosaceae

Apples are the most widely grown tree fruit in Britain because they are hardy and there is a large choice of varieties. Different types can be harvested from August to November.

CULTIVATION

If possible, maintain the soil at pH 6.5 (see p. 803).

Each February, apply a compound fertiliser following the maker's recommendations.

Lay an organic mulch in April to conserve moisture and control weeds, or anchor black plastic sheeting to the soil.

During dry periods in spring and summer, water trees with 25 litres per m^2 (4½ gal per sq yd) every ten days. Apply the water to the soil under the canopy of the tree. While the fruit is growing – from July to September – be more generous with water to ensure good fruit size and flower buds for the following year. Trees against walls may need even more water.

In the first growing season after planting, remove any flowers or young fruit to avoid weakening the tree's growth.

In subsequent years thin the young fruit – ideally within four weeks of petal-fall but up to early July – to leave only one or two on each cluster. Always remove the central fruit; it will be malformed at harvest time.

RECOMMENDED VARIETIES OF APPLES

Apples are classified as either dessert (to be eaten without cooking), or culinary (which need cooking). Cross-pollination is necessary to ensure a crop and will only occur when two varieties growing close together flower at the same time. So when buying trees choose them from the same pollination group. Crab apples will pollinate other apple trees. Quality is out of a maximum of 5.

VARIETY	SEASON OF USE	POLLINATION GROUP	FRUIT QUALITY	FRUITING HABIT	COMMENTS
Dessert apples					
Discovery	Pick mid August; eat soon.	3	4	Tip-bearing	Resistance to scab disease.
Worcester Pearmain	Pick early-mid Sept; eat Sept-Oct.	3	4	Tip-bearing	Resistant to mildew but prone to scab. Reliable.
Egremont Russet	Pick late Sept; eat Oct-Dec.	2	5	Spur-forming	Scab resistant but prone to bitter pit.
Sunset	Pick late Sept; eat Oct-Dec.	3	5	Spur-forming	Cox-like flavour but small fruits – thin out to obtain bigger ones.
Red pippin	Pick late Sept; eat Oct-Feb.	3	4	Spur-forming	Pendulous habit. Cox-like flavour.
Falstaff	Pick early Oct; eat Oct-Jan.	3	4	Spur-forming	Fairly hardy.
Jonagold	Pick mid Oct; eat Nov-Feb.	4	5	Spur-forming	Large fruits and heavy cropper. Poor donor of pollen.
Ashmead's Kernel	Pick mid Oct; eat Dec-Feb.	4	5	Spur-forming	Russet variety. Erratic cropper.
Idared	Pick mid Oct; eat Nov-April.	2	3	Spur-forming	For eating raw or cooking.
Culinary					
Grenadier	Pick mid Aug; eat Aug-Oct.	3	4	Spur-forming	Scab resistant. High acidity.
George Neal	Pick late Aug/ early Sept; eat Aug-Oct.	2	5	Spur-forming	Low acidity. Juicy.
Bramley's Seedling	Pick mid Oct; eat Nov-March.	3	5	Tip-bearing/ spur-forming	High acidity. Poor donor of pollen. Dwarf rootstock needed to control tree size.

CHOOSING THE RIGHT ROOTSTOCK

When buying a new tree choose one with the most suitable rootstock. It will decide the eventual size of the tree, when and how heavily it will crop, and the shape into which it can be trained.

ROOTSTOCK	1ST FRUIT YEAR	FULL-CROP YEAR	SIZE OF CROP	AFTER 10 YEARS HEIGHT	SPREAD	POSSIBLE SHAPE OF TREE
MM 106	3-5	7-8	41-50kg (90-110lb)	4-5.5m (13-18ft)	5m (16ft)	Cordon, fan, spindlebush, espalier, bush, pyramid.
M 26	3-4	5-6	30-34kg (65-75lb)	3-3.5m (10-12ft)	3.5m (12ft)	Cordon, fan, spindlebush, espalier, bush, pyramid.
M 9	3-4	5-6	16-20kg (35-45lb)	2.4-3m (8-10ft)	3m (10ft)	Step-over, cordon, fan, spindlebush, bush, pyramid.
M 27	2-3	4-5	7-11kg (15-25lb)	1.5-1.8m (5-6ft)	1.8m (6ft)	Spindlebush, bush, cordon, step-over, tub, limited area.

HARVESTING AND STORAGE

Allow the apples to ripen on the tree and pick them when they detach easily. Don't allow them to over-ripen; it will affect the number of flowers next year.

On a free-standing tree, ripening starts on the south side which receives the most sun.

Fruit for storing needs to be slightly under-ripe. You can judge the correct degree of ripeness by painting iodine on a cut cross-section of one of the apples. If 50-60 per cent of the surface turns blue-black, the fruit should store safely until Christmas at least. If the fruit is not ripe enough, the stain will cover a greater area; if it is over-ripe the stain will be smaller.

For storage, put unblemished fruit in clear polythene bags – a maximum of 2kg (4½lb) per bag for easy handling. Tie the bags at the top and use a knitting needle to puncture each bag – two holes for every kilogram of fruit (one hole per pound). This will allow the fruit to breathe and ripen without rotting.

Place the bags in a dark, cool but frost-free place such as a cellar or garage. The bags will ensure that the apples do not shrivel through loss of water. Inspect the fruit occasionally and remove any rotting ones.

PESTS AND DISEASES

The main pests of apple trees are apple sawfly and codling moth (see Pests, p.824). Nest boxes put out close to fruit trees will encourage birds which will eat the caterpillars. Pheromone traps placed in the tree in early May kill some of the male codling moths, reducing the next generation. The increase in trapped moths also indicates the best time to spray.

You can provide a hibernation site for overwintering caterpillars by wrapping sacking or corrugated cardboard around the tree trunk in July. After the fruit has been picked, caterpillars in these traps can be destroyed by boiling the sacking or burning the cardboard.

The main diseases of apple trees are canker, brown rot, powdery mildew and apple scab (see Diseases and Disorders, p.838). To avoid them, clear up dead leaves and other plant material in autumn, remove any mummified fruit during winter pruning and water regularly during dry spells.

Blackberries see *Raspberries and Blackberries* p.729

Cherries

***Prunus avium* (Sweet cherry)**
***Prunus cerasus* (Acid cherry)**
Rosaceae

Cherry growing has entered a new phase with the introduction of dwarfing rootstocks which allow free-standing (unrestricted) trees to be netted against birds when the fruit is ripening. Previously, cherry trees were too large. They can also now be grown as restricted forms such as espaliers and fans.

CULTIVATION

Cherries will grow in most soils that have good drainage. In cool areas they are best trained as fans on a south-to-west-facing wall or fence for extra warmth. The acid variety 'Morello' is more hardy than sweet cherries and is often grown on a north-facing wall.

Buds may need to be netted against finches in winter.

Feed sweet cherries in February, using a compound fertiliser at the rate recommended on the label (the same as for apples). Acid cherries may need higher rates because of the amount of pruning.

Ripening fruit should be sheltered from the rain to prevent splitting. Apply netting against birds as the fruit starts to colour.

Water cherry trees in the same way as apples.

PROTECTION AGAINST WIND AND FROST

Cherries flower in April, so the blossom needs to be protected from cold winds and frost. Grow hedging to keep out cold winds, or put up open-mesh fencing. Avoid frost pockets,

RECOMMENDED VARIETIES OF CHERRY TREES

Old varieties need pollination from a variety in a different incompatibility group, but the same flowering group. Universal donors (UD) can pollinate any other variety, provided it is in the same flowering group. Self-fertile varieties will grow alone.

VARIETY	SEASON OF USE (PICK AND USE)	INCOMPATIBILITY GROUP	FLOWERING GROUP
Sweet Cherry			
Early Rivers	Mid to late June	1	1
Merchant	Early July	UD	3
Vega	Mid July	UD	3
Stella	Late July	UD. Self-fertile	4
Sunburst	Late July	UD. Self-fertile	4
Noir de Guben	Late July	UD	1
Van	Late July	2	3
Lapins	Early August	UD. Self-fertile	4
Acid cherry			
Morello	August	Self-fertile	5

CHERRY ROOTSTOCKS

The vigour of the rootstock will decide the size of the tree and the shapes in which it can be trained. Both Colt and Inmil rootstocks can be used for bush, espalier, pyramid, spindlebush and fan trees.

ROOTSTOCK	1ST FRUIT YEAR	FULL CROP YEAR	AFTER 10 YEARS YIELD	HEIGHT	SPREAD
Colt	3	7	9-16kg (20-35lb)	5m (16ft)	5m (16ft)
Inmil	3	6	5-11kg (11-25lb)	3.5m (12ft)	3.5m (12ft)

which are areas of low-lying ground or places where cool air flowing downhill becomes trapped by a solid fence. Draping the tree with hessian, supported off the flowers, will give protection against frost, but allow access for insects to pollinate the flowers during the day.

HARVESTING AND STORAGE

Pick cherries when they are ripe, with the stalk attached. Eat them as soon as possible, although they can be frozen.

If they are picked slightly under-ripe, cherries can be stored in a refrigerator for up to two weeks, but they must be picked with the stalk attached. Tie them up in a polythene bag and puncture the bag with a knitting needle – two holes per kilogram of fruit (one hole per pound).

PESTS AND DISEASES

Slugworms graze away the leaf surface to leave a skeleton. The damage is seen in May-June and July-August. Spray with derris, fenitrothion, permethrin or malathion. Cherry blackflies can attack young leaves (see Pests, p. 824).

Cherry trees can also suffer from bacterial canker and silver leaf (see Diseases and Disorders, p. 838).

Currants and Gooseberries

Ribes nigrum **(Blackcurrant)**
Ribes sativum
(Redcurrant/white currant)
Ribes grossularia
(Gooseberry)

Blackcurrants, redcurrants, white currants and gooseberries are cultivated in a similar way. Blackcurrant bushes have the stems growing from soil level; the other currants and gooseberries have a clean stem, called a 'leg', below the branches. Red and white currants and gooseberries are usually grown as bushes, but can also be cordons or fans. Currants are eaten fresh; gooseberries include both dessert and culinary varieties.

CULTIVATION

Currants and gooseberries will grow on most soils, provided a pH level of 6.5 is maintained. All of them, particularly gooseberries, need good drainage.

RECOMMENDED VARIETIES OF CURRANTS AND GOOSEBERRIES

Most of the new varieties have considerable resistance to frost, either through later flowering or resistance bred into the plants. The season for currants and gooseberries is from late June to August.

SEASON OF USE	VARIETY	CHARACTERISTICS
Blackcurrants Pick/use mid-late July	Ben Sarek	Small, compact bush. Heavy crops of large berries. Resistant to mildew. Tolerant of frost at flowering time.
	Ben Lomond	Good crops of large berries. Flavour good but acidic. Some frost and mildew resistance.
	Wellington	Heavy crops of sweet, medium-sized berries. Vigorous but spreading bush.
	Ben Nevis	Thick-skinned, medium-sized berries. Heavy cropping. Flavour fair. Some mildew resistance.
	Ben More	Heavy cropping. Large fruit with sharp flavour. Some mildew resistance.
Pick/use early August	Baldwin (Hilltop strain)	Medium-sized berries which hang well without splitting. Acid flavour. Good cropper and fairly compact bush.
Redcurrants Pick early July	Jonkheer van Tets	Heavy cropper. Long to very long bunches of good-flavoured fruit. Vigorous, upright growth; often damaged by wind.
Pick/use mid July	Laxton's No. 1	Good-quality, bright-red fruit of good flavour and small seeds.
Pick late July	Red Lake	Heavy crops of very large, bright-red fruit. Good flavour.
	Stanza	Heavy crops of firm, dark-red fruit borne on a short bunch. Good flavour. Vigorous growth.
Pick/use August	Redstart	High-yielding, reliable cropper. Rather acid flavour. Ripe fruit will hang on the bush for some time.
White currants Pick mid July	White Grape	Excellent sweet flavour. Medium yield and fruit size.
	White Versailles	Large, sweet fruit. Heavy cropper.
Gooseberries Pick/use late June	Early Sulphur	Good flavour. Heavy cropper. Makes excellent jam.
Pick mid July	Careless	Moderately vigorous and spreading bush. Green berries with fair flavour. Culinary.
	Jubilee	Heavier cropping selection of 'Careless'. Dual-purpose fruit.
	Greenfinch	Vigorous, upright bush. Resistant to mildew and leaf spot. Fair flavour. Only suitable for cooking.
Pick late July	Invicta	Well-flavoured pale-green berries. Vigorous, spreading and thorny. Resistant to mildew. Train as a fan-shape because of weak joints between branches and stem. Dual-purpose.
	Whitesmith	Very heavy crops of large, very well-flavoured white berries. Vigorous upright bush but spreading with age. Dual-purpose.
	Leveller	Very large, yellow-green berries. Good flavour. Weak on poor soils and needs good drainage. Dessert.
	Whinham's Industry	Heavy crops of red berries. Excellent flavour. Very vigorous; tolerates poor soils but susceptible to mildew. Dual-purpose.

Protect the buds of gooseberries and red and white currants from finches in winter, using nets. Blackcurrants are not usually attacked.

Blackcurrants need more fertiliser and water than other bush fruits. Feed them in February with a compound fertiliser at the rate recommended on the label.

Between May and August blackcurrants need up to 50 litres per m^2 (9 gal per sq yd) of water possibly every five to seven days. The other bush fruits need only 25 litres per m^2 (4½ gal per sq yd). Apply fertilisers and water within a circle 45 cm (18 in) around each plant.

Protect flower buds from frost (see Cherries).

• ***Blackcurrants***

Plant in October or November while the soil is still warm and gaining moisture. Two-year-old bushes can be bought from garden centres, and hardwood cuttings root easily (see p. 819), particularly if pushed through a black plastic sheet anchored to the soil.

Plant bushes with the base of the stems buried to encourage new shoots to emerge from below soil level. On normal soil, cut off the stems to leave stubs 2.5 cm (1 in) long. On good soil which will give quick growth, half of the stems can be left intact.

Each year, in November/December, cut back some of the stems to a stub 2.5 cm (1 in) long to encourage new growth. Count the stems and divide by four, then cut out that number. Remove diseased, old and low-lying stems first.

• ***Red and white currants and gooseberries***

The plants are usually grown on a clean stem 20 cm (8 in) long.

After planting, cut off half of the one-year-old wood on the leading laterals to encourage new extension growth and sideshoots.

In later years, prune out whole branches to let in light that will ripen the remaining wood and deter disease.

In July cut back all sideshoots to 5 cm (2 in) to form fruiting spurs and avoid overcrowding. Gooseberries can be cut back immediately before picking to allow easier access past the spines to reach the fruit.

In later years when the crop decreases, cut out whole spurs to make way for new shoots.

Red and white currants and gooseberries can also be grown as single-stem or multi-stem cordons and fans on wires.

HARVESTING AND STORAGE

As currants ripen, they change colour from green to black, red or white. Pick entire stalks when fully ripe.

Culinary gooseberries will lighten in colour and dessert varieties will turn yellow-gold or red when ready to pick.

All fruits can be kept in the salad tray of a refrigerator for up to two weeks.

PESTS AND DISEASES

Gooseberry sawfly caterpillars may attack in April (see Pests, p. 824). Gall mites can cause blackcurrant buds to swell in spring and lead to a disease called reversion. Other possible diseases include botrytis, leaf spot, gooseberry mildew and coral spot (see Diseases and Disorders, p. 838).

Gooseberries see *Currants and Gooseberries*

Grapes

Vitis vinifera

Vitaceae

With the increased popularity of conservatories, grapevines can now be grown for dessert fruit throughout Britain. Grapes grown outdoors north of the Midlands are only suitable for wine-making, and then only if grown on a south or west-facing wall. In the Midlands and the South, grapes can be grown outdoors for both eating and wine-making.

CULTIVATION

In November/December plant the vine in the greenhouse soil. Alternatively, plant it outside so that the roots can grow unhindered, and train the stem through the wall.

For outdoor growing, plant vines against a south or west-facing wall. Good soil drainage is needed, so clay soils will need the addition of sand and organic material. Chalk soil usually drains well, but the pH may be too high, so add organic material to the planting hole. Avoid making the soil too rich – the plant will produce too much growth at the expense of flowers. Plant 15 cm (6 in) away from the wall and mulch indoor vines to conserve moisture.

Each March apply a compound fertiliser according to the instructions on the label. A high-potash liquid feed should be applied every two weeks from when the flower buds start to open until the fruit is picked.

Vines can be grown in pots, which will restrict the roots and produce smaller plants. Indoor and potted vines need up to 50 litres of water per m^2 (9 gal per sq yd) weekly. After the first year, vines growing in a garden can find enough water as long as the roots are not restricted.

Indoors, flower pollination can be encouraged by gently shaking the stem at midday. Alternatively, if you have the time, hand pollinate by using a ball of cotton wool or a soft-bristled brush daily.

Shade the glass of a greenhouse from June to late August. When dessert grapes reach pea-size, they should be thinned if the bunches are tightly packed with little room to grow. Use long-bladed scissors in one hand and a small forked stick in the other. Never touch the fruit with your fingers.

On several occasions over about ten days, remove some of the fruit from within the bunch, plus any small fruits, leaving a 1.5 cm (½ in) gap between

▲ A greenhouse can be insulated with bubble plastic until late spring.

RECOMMENDED VARIETIES OF GRAPES

SEASON OF USE	VARIETY	CHARACTERISTICS
Greenhouse types		
Pick in May	Black Hamburgh	Large dark red/purple fruit. Good flavour. Ripens freely without heat.
Pick in July	Muscat Hamburgh	Large dark red/purple fruit. Excellent flavour. Needs heat, and another variety that flowers at the same time to cross-pollinate.
	Muscat of Alexandria	Requires heat to crop well. Superb quality amber-coloured fruit.
Outdoor types		
Pick in September	Siegerrebe	Excellent muscat flavour. Highly recommended for dessert and wine. Protect from wasps. White.
	Mueller-Thurgau	Grow against south-facing wall for best performance. White.
	Madeleine Sylvaner	Consistent cropper. Reasonably hardy. Only fair flavour. White.
Pick in October	Madeleine Angevine	Heavy-cropping wine grape. Vigorous. Only fair quality. White.
	Seyval Blanc	Vigorous and resistant to mildew. Heavy cropper. Some frost resistance. White.
Pick in late October	Brandt	Masses of small red grapes for eating and wine. Resistant to mildew.

▲ Using long-bladed scissors and a forked stick, thin out grape clusters.

fruits. Remove diseased fruits as the bunches ripen.

Ripening fruit outdoors will need to be netted against birds.

PRUNING VINES

Grapevines grown indoors or outdoors on a wall are trained by the cordon system, which consists of a main stem (the rod) with fruiting laterals (spurs) 30 cm (12 in) apart along it.

After planting, shorten the stem by two-thirds, to a bud.

First spring and summer On indoor vines, select a strong shoot to become the rod and tie it to the underside of horizontal wires fixed 38 cm (15 in) from the glass and 30 cm (12 in) apart.

Outdoors, select two shoots and tie them to wires or trellis to create a double cordon.

Pinch back any laterals as they grow to five leaves, and sub-laterals to one leaf. Remove flowers and tendrils.

Second winter By the end of January, cut back last season's stem growth by two-thirds, and all laterals to one bud.

Second summer Indoors, train rods as in the first summer and select only one lateral every 30 cm (12 in) on last season's wood. Rub off unwanted laterals. Pinch back laterals as before.

Outdoors, train rods horizontally left and right. Select one lateral every 30 cm (12 in) on last season's wood. Rub off unwanted laterals. Pinch back laterals as before.

Both indoors and outdoors, allow three or four laterals to produce a bunch of flowers each and pinch them back to two leaves beyond the flowers.

Later seasons Prune last season's stem growth by two-thirds until long enough, and then back to one bud of last season's growth each winter. Treat laterals and sub-laterals as before. Increase fruiting laterals by four to six each year.

To stimulate laterals to grow along the full length of the rod as it grows longer, detach the rod from the wires in late January and lay it on the floor. When growth has started again, reattach it.

If the vine is creating a lot of work by growing too vigorously, select a lateral low down and train it as an extra rod.

Warning Vines become heavy, so monitor the greenhouse or conservatory roof for possible collapse.

HARVESTING AND STORAGE

Taste rather than colour is the only reliable way to decide when to pick grapes, both dessert and wine-making types. Dessert grapes are cut from the vine with a 'handle' of 5 cm (2 in) of stem both sides of the bunch. Treat bunches gently.

PESTS AND DISEASES

Birds will eat outdoor grapes before they are ripe. Netting is the only protection. Wasps are attracted to early outdoor fruit when it becomes ripe and sweet. Pick the fruit as it ripens.

Vines can be attacked by grey mould and powdery mildew (see Diseases and Disorders, p. 838). Powdery mildew is a particular problem of cold greenhouses. Outdoor vines are only affected in a dry place. Use resistant varieties and prune the canopy to aid ventilation.

Peaches and Nectarines

Prunus persica

Rosaceae

Peaches and nectarines will fruit successfully in Britain outdoors but only in a warm, sheltered position. Leaves must be kept clean from peach leaf curl to ensure survival of the tree. The late-ripening varieties must be grown in a greenhouse.

CULTIVATION

Peaches and nectarines will grow in most soils. They flower early so need protection from cold winds and frosts (see Cherries). Nectarines are less hardy than peaches and should only be grown on a south-to-west-facing wall or fence.

Hand pollination is necessary both outdoors and in a greenhouse. Dab the flowers with a ball of cotton wool or a soft brush every two days from flower-opening to petal-fall.

Fertiliser rates are higher than most other tree fruit as a lot of wood is cut out each year. Use a compound fertiliser in February at the rate recommended on the label. Water as for apples if grown outdoors. In a greenhouse, give 25–50 litres of water per m^2 (4½–9 gal per sq yd) during the growing season, depending on the heat of the sun and whether the roots are inside or outside.

A fan-trained tree is easier to maintain than a free-standing tree. Whether growing a tree from a one-year-old or from a

RECOMMENDED VARIETIES OF PEACHES AND NECTARINES

SEASON OF USE	VARIETY	CHARACTERISTICS
Peaches		
Pick/use mid July	Duke of York	Large fruit size. Juicy and refreshing flavour. Heavy cropper.
Pick/use mid July	Garden Lady	Compact habit. Ideal for growing in pots on a patio.
Pick/use mid to late July	Hale's Early	Heavy cropper but usually needs thinning. Average flavour but melting flesh.
Pick/use early August	Peregrine	Large fruit size. Juicy with excellent flavour. Reliable and high yielding.
Pick/use mid August	Rochester	Flowers late, misses early frosts. Reliable cropper outdoors. Juicy and good flavour.
Pick/use early to mid September	Bellegarde	Large to very large fruit size. Extremely good flavour. Must be grown in greenhouse.
Nectarines		
Pick/use late July	Early Rivers	Large fruit size. Juicy and good flavour.
Pick/use mid August	Lord Napier	Large fruit size. Regular and heavy cropper for outdoor growing. White aromatic flesh.
Pick/use mid August	Garden Delight	Compact habit. Ideal for growing in pots on a patio.
Pick/use early September	Pine Apple	Medium to large fruit. Grow in greenhouse. Outstandingly rich flavour and melting flesh.

ROOTSTOCKS FOR PEACHES AND NECTARINES

The rootstock of a tree decides the size of the tree and the shapes in which it can be trained. Both St Julien A and Pixy rootstocks can be used to train bush and fan-shape trees.

ROOTSTOCK	1ST FRUIT YEAR	FULL CROP YEAR	AFTER 10 YEARS YIELD	HEIGHT	SPREAD
St Julien A	4	7	22 kg (40 lb) Fan: 11 kg (25 lb)	5 m (16 ft)	5 m (16 ft)
Pixy	2	4	11 kg (25 lb) Fan: 5 kg (11 lb)	2.4 m (8 ft)	2.4 m (8 ft)

▲ A fan-trained peach tree grown against a wall or fence.

ready-trained fan, remove all blossoms in the first year.

The fruit is borne on wood of the previous year's growth, so wood that has borne fruit should be cut off after fruiting and new growths tied in. Select the strongest new growths as they grow, and pinch out all other unwanted shoots.

Within four weeks of petal-fall, thin the fruit to leave one per 15-20cm (6-8in). In a dry summer, more thinning may be needed as the fruit ripens.

HARVESTING AND STORAGE

The flesh around the stalk softens as it ripens and the skin takes on a reddish flush. Lift the fruit in your palm and twist it gently; ripe fruit will detach easily. Store in a cool place for up to a week, but fruit fresh from the tree tastes best.

PESTS AND DISEASES

Brown scale are sap-sucking insects protected by dark brown shells up to 6mm (¼in) long. In large numbers they will affect the vigour of the tree, and are most serious on greenhouse trees. Spray with tar oil in December, or use malathion or pirimiphos-methyl in early July.

The main diseases of peach trees are bacterial canker, peach leaf curl and silver leaf (see Diseases and Disorders, p.838).

A physiological disorder called split stone rots the kernel. Acid soil and drought cause a deep crack to show at the stalk end of the fruit. Correct the pH and mulch over moist soil – but not before April or May.

Pears

Pyrus communis
Rosaceae

Pears require more sun and warmth than apples but will grow well in various conditions. In colder areas, grow cordons, espaliers or fans against a south or west-facing wall or fence. Young leaves are easily damaged by wind, so trees need to be in a sheltered position.

Pear trees must be cross-pollinated so there has to be a nearby variety which flowers at the same time.

CULTIVATION

Pears will grow in most soils, but need protection from frosts and wind in April and May (see Cherries). The protection will increase temperatures and encourage pollinating insects.

Feed and water as for apples. During a drought pears can develop drooping yellow leaves, early leaf-drop and poor growth, so watering is critical.

Thin out the fruitlets to one per cluster as they swell and turn downwards.

On all forms of tree, lateral branches should not descend lower than the horizontal to ensure a balance between growth and fruiting.

In winter, remove very thin new shoots. Thicker shoots will produce flower buds in their second year on spur-bearing varieties and can be pruned back to these flower buds in winter. Prune restricted forms in summer (see pp.721-2).

Old wood can be a site for pear scab to overwinter, so wood should be removed every five to six years and replaced with new shoots.

RECOMMENDED PEAR VARIETIES

Most varieties are dessert fruit for eating raw. Choose varieties from the same pollination group. Quality is out of a maximum of 5.

PICKING TIME	EATING TIME	VARIETY	POLLINATION GROUP	FRUIT QUALITY
Dessert pears				
Pick late August	Sept	Beth	4	4
	Sept	Williams' Bon Chretien	3	5
Pick mid-late September	Oct	Beurre Hardy	3	4
	Sept	Onward	4	5
	Oct	Conference	3	4
Pick October	Oct	Concorde	4	4
	Dec	Josephine de Malines	3 Tip bearer (see p. 720)	4
	Oct	Doyenne du Comice	4	5
Culinary pears				
Pick late October	Feb-Apr	Catillac	4	Hard flesh

ROOTSTOCKS FOR DIFFERENT PURPOSES

Rootstocks control the size of the tree and the shapes in which it can be trained. Both Quince A and C rootstocks can be used to train bush, pyramid, spindlebush, espalier, fan and cordon trees.

ROOT-STOCK	1ST FRUIT YEAR	FULL CROP YEAR	AFTER 10 YEARS YIELD	HEIGHT	SPREAD
Quince A	4	7	16-40kg (35-88lb)	3.5m (12ft)	3.5m (12ft)
Quince C	3	5	11-35kg (24-77lb)	3m (10ft)	3m (10ft)

HARVESTING AND STORAGE

Early varieties, except Concorde which is yellow when unripe, are picked when the background colour changes from green to almost yellow, and its stalk comes away from the tree. Varieties harvested from September onwards are picked under-ripe and stored in a cool dark place in polythene bags (see Apples). They should not ripen on the tree as this will reduce next year's blossom.

PESTS AND DISEASES

Pear leaf blister mite, codling moth and pear midge are all major pests of pears (see Pests, p.824). Slugworms graze away the leaf surface in May-June and July-August. Spray with derris, fenitrothion, permethrin or malathion.

Canker, fireblight, pear scab, brown rot and honey fungus can all attack pear trees (see Diseases and Disorders, p.838).

Plums

Prunus domestica
Rosaceae

Plums include gages, damsons and bullaces. Dried plums are known as prunes. In small gardens plum trees can be grown as espaliers, cordons or fans on dwarfing rootstocks that keep the tree to a small size.

CULTIVATION

Plums will grow in most soil, provided it has good drainage. The flowers must be protected from cold winds and frosts in April (see Cherries). In colder areas, grow the trees as cordons, espaliers or fans on a south-to-west-facing wall. Feed and water as for apples.

Plum trees often produce root suckers which should be cut off or burnt off in summer with glyphosate weedkiller when 20cm (8in) high.

Like apples and pears, plums need to be thinned to improve the fruit and to encourage flower buds next year. Before late June, thin out the fruitlets to leave one every 5cm (2in).

Do not allow the soil to dry out as the stone may split inside the fruit. Water in dry spells and mulch when the weather warms up in late spring.

Summer prune (see pp.721-2) in July, earlier than apples, by

RECOMMENDED PLUM VARIETIES

Some varieties are self-fertile – another variety is not needed for pollination. In practice, another variety flowering at the same time will ensure a crop in difficult seasons. Two varieties can be relied on to flower regularly and act as pollen donors – 'Denniston's Superb' for early flowerers and 'Oullins Gage' for late flowerers.

SEASON OF USE	VARIETY	POLLINATION GROUP
Dessert plums		
Late July	Opal	3 Self-fertile
Early to mid August	Blue Tit	5 Self-fertile
	Oullins Gage	4 Self-fertile
Late August	Denniston's Superb	2 Self-fertile
	Victoria	3 Self-fertile
Early September	Reeves Seedling	3
	Jefferson	1 Denniston's Superb will donate pollen
Culinary plums		
Early August	Czar	3 Self-fertile
Mid August	Pershore	3 Self-fertile
Late September	Marjorie's Seedling	5 Self-fertile
	Shropshire Prune (A damson that can be eaten fresh)	5

ROOTSTOCKS FOR DIFFERENT PURPOSES

Rootstocks control the size of the tree and the shapes in which the tree can be trained. St Julien A and Pixy rootstocks can be used to train bush, cordon, espalier, fan, spindlebush and pyramid trees.

ROOT-STOCK	1ST CROP YEAR	FULL CROP YEAR	AFTER 10 YEARS YIELD	HEIGHT	SPREAD
St Julien A	4	7	11-25kg (24-55lb)	5m (16ft)	5m (16ft)
Pixy	2	4	7-11kg (15-24lb)	2.4m (8ft)	2.4m (8ft)

snapping the unwanted shoots between finger and thumb to avoid disease infection. Spurs will then develop.

HARVESTING AND STORAGE

When the plums part easily from the tree they are ripe. Pick over the tree three to five times to collect the fruit as it ripens.

If plums are picked slightly under-ripe, with the stalk on the fruit, they will keep for up to four weeks in a refrigerator. Put them in a polythene bag tied at the neck and punctured with a knitting needle – two holes for every kilogram of fruit (one hole per pound). Take them out of the refrigerator and allow them to develop colour for 24 hours before eating.

PESTS AND DISEASES

Caterpillars of plum fruit moth tunnel into fruit, often causing premature ripening. Pheromone traps reduce the caterpillars and also act as a guide to the best spraying time. Spray in late June with fenitrothion, pirimiphos-methyl or permethrin. A second spray two or three weeks later kills late hatchings.

The main diseases of plum trees are bacterial canker, brown rot and silver leaf (see Diseases and Disorders, p.838).

Raspberries and Blackberries

***Rubus idaeas* (Raspberry), *Rubus fruticosus* (Blackberry)**

Rosaceae

Raspberries are the most widely grown cane fruit , but blackberries and the hybrids – such as tayberries and loganberries – are planted for their flowers, leaves and autumn colours as well as for fruit. They make an attractive display on an archway.

Canes are cut out each year after fruiting, and the new canes grow on to fruit next year. The new canes should be limited to 10 per metre of raspberries and 6–8 per plant of blackberries and hybrid berries.

However, the new canes can provide a home for diseases that overwinter in them. Two-yearly cropping will avoid the disease problem and eliminates the need to spray. Cutting off all canes after fruiting also makes pruning and training easier. Tie in new canes as they grow.

Cane fruit can be grown in a greenhouse or conservatory to extend fruiting at the start and the end of the season, but as raspberries are woodland plants their roots should be kept cool by growing them in white pots and watering regularly.

CULTIVATION

Cane fruits will grow on most soil. However, growth is hampered by poorly drained clay soil (especially raspberries) and by sandy soil where watering in the growing season is essential.

Each March apply a compound fertiliser according to the instructions on the label.

Water the canes throughout summer, especially as the berries start to colour, and again after picking. Always water at soil level rather than overhead to lessen the risk of infection.

The usual method of training is between pairs of wires 30cm (12in) apart, starting 90cm (36in) above the soil and spaced to a height of 1.8m (6ft).

• ***Raspberries***

Most raspberries fruit in July and August, and their production of cane and fruit follows a two-year cycle. Each autumn after the fruit has been picked, the cane that has borne the fruit is cut off at soil level. The new cane is then tied to the wires to fruit next year. Tops of canes can be bent over and tied to the top wire. If you cut them off you will lose fruiting spurs.

Autumn-fruiting varieties grow and fruit in the same season. All canes are cut off at soil level each February, and a greater number of new canes are allowed to grow than for summer raspberries. The row is usually 45cm (18in) wide.

Raspberries will not tolerate even temporary waterlogging. In wet places they can be planted on a ridge of soil.

▲ The tops of raspberry canes can be wound around the top wire.

• ***Blackberries and hybrid berries***

Growth and fruiting follows a two-year cycle, so canes that have finished fruiting are cut out at soil level.

The canes need to be tied to the wire supports either in the shape of a fan or woven between the top wire and the bottom wire. Alternatively, tie the cane vertically and then horizontally along each wire to the left and right of the plant.

HARVESTING AND STORAGE

Raspberries and blackberries are usually picked without stalks, but most of the hybrid berries are picked with the stalk intact.

The fruit can be frozen, but warm fruit fresh from the plant has the best flavour.

PESTS AND DISEASES

The main pests of cane fruit are raspberry beetles, raspberry cane midges and aphids (see Pests, p.824). Nets or a fruit cage will deter birds.

Possible diseases include cane blight, cane spot and spur blight (see Diseases and Disorders, p.838). They can be avoided by cropping all cane fruit only once every two years, and cutting out all the canes after fruiting.

VARIETIES OF RASPBERRIES AND OTHER CANE FRUIT

SEASON OF USE	VARIETY	CHARACTERISTICS
Raspberries		
SUMMER-FRUITING		
Pick early to mid July	Glen Moy	Spine-free canes. Some resistance to aphids. Avoid planting with 'Malling Promise' or 'Malling Jewel' to reduce virus infection.
	Glen Clova	Heavy cropper. Vigorous cane growth. Avoid planting with 'Malling Promise' or 'Malling Jewel'.
	Malling Delight	Large orange-red fruits. Some aphid resistance. Heavy cropper.
Pick mid July to mid August	Malling Admiral	Good cropper. Vigorous canes. Some resistance to spur blight, mildew, cane botrytis.
	Malling Jewel	Good cropper. Sparse cane production. Tolerant of virus.
	Glen Prosen	Spine-free canes. Susceptible to spur blight and cane botrytis. Good crops.
Pick late July to late August	Leo	Large bright orange-red fruit. Very vigorous. Good resistance to spur blight, cane botrytis and aphids. Susceptible to cane spot. Some frost resistance.
AUTUMN-FRUITING		
Pick mid August to October	Autumn Bliss	Very good crops. Prolific canes requiring minimal support. Good resistance to aphids.
Blackberries		
Pick/use late July	Bedford Giant	Large, sweet fruit. Thorny. Plant 4.5 m (15 ft) apart.
Pick/use mid August	Ashton Cross	Good crops. Excellent flavour. Moderate vigour. Very spiny. Plant 3 m (10 ft) apart.
Pick late August to September	Loch Ness	Thornless. Well-flavoured. Plant 2.4 m (8 ft) apart. Fairly hardy.
	Fantasia	Vigorous canes; strong thorns. Heavy crops; good flavour.
	Oregon Thornless	Thornless. Mild flavour. Ornamental parsley-leaved blackberry. Fairly disease-free.
Hybrid berries		
Pick mid July to August	Tayberry	Heavy crops of long conical fruit. Excellent for jam.
	Loganberry LY59	Good crops of long berries. Plant 2.7 m (9 ft) apart.
	Loganberry LY654	Thornless. Otherwise as LY59.

Rhubarb

Rheum x hybridum
Polygonaceae

The stems of rhubarb are long, succulent and red with an acid taste, and must be cooked. Established plants can be forced into early growth to give sweeter stems for harvesting from early March. A range of varieties will produce suitable stems until September.

CULTIVATION

Rhubarb will grow in most soil, but not poorly drained clay. It prefers full sun but will tolerate shade for 25 per cent of the day. Each March, apply a compound fertiliser following the instructions on the label. First-year plants need watering in early summer, but rainfall normally gives enough water for established plants.

Rhubarb is grown from 'setts' which should be the size of a person's fist and have at least one prominent bud. Plant setts from late autumn to late March with the crown slightly above soil level. Space them 90 cm (3 ft) apart each way.

Rhubarb responds well to annual dressings of rotted compost applied in May.

Do not harvest any stems in the first year, and keep the soil weed-free to allow plants to become established. In the second year, harvest only two or three stems from each plant. In subsequent years stems can be removed when they are big enough. Any flower stems should be cut out.

To maintain vigour, lift plants every three years and divide them into 'setts' before replanting. Healthy established plants can be cut up with a spade or knife.

Rhubarb plants die down in winter. Established plants can be 'forced' into early growth the following spring. Cover selected plants in December or January with either wooden boxes or plastic bins. Specially made terracotta forcers which have lids to give access to the stems can also be used. Start harvesting stems in early March.

After being forced, plants need to be grown in the normal way for a year before being forced again.

Plants will crop well for six or seven years.

HARVESTING AND STORAGE

Pull the stems from the plant by holding them towards the base and twisting outwards and upwards. Ideally the stems should be cooked immediately, but they can be stored in a refrigerator for up to three days wrapped in a plastic bag to avoid loss of moisture.

PESTS AND DISEASES

Rhubarb is not usually attacked by pests. The crown of the plant may rot because of cold wet weather, poor drainage or being planted too deep.

Strawberries

Fragaria x ananassa
Rosaceae

Strawberries are the quickest fruit to produce a harvest after planting. They can be grown in a small garden and will do well in a patio container, growing bag or even a hanging basket. Their season of fruiting can be extended from March through to November by using different varieties, together with protection from rain and cold weather in the spring and autumn.

To ensure good crops, buy plants from a reputable source, and where possible plants that have been 'certified' by the Ministry of Agriculture, Fisheries and Food (MAFF).

RECOMMENDED VARIETIES OF RHUBARB

SEASON OF USE	VARIETY
April/May (suitable for forcing)	Early Victoria Timperly Early
May/June (main crop)	Cawood Delight
July/Sept	The Sutton Strawberry rhubarb

WHERE AND HOW TO PLANT

Strawberries will grow on most soil, but sandy soil needs watering in summer and clay needs good drainage – perhaps by building a raised bed or a ridge of soil. Chalky soil can cause deficiency of iron and manganese which can be rectified by using a chelated-iron compound. Strawberry plants need full sun, except for alpines which tolerate some shade.

Before planting, ensure a pH level of 6.5 (see p.803). Apply 35g of sulphate of potash per m^2 (1oz per sq yd) and 17g of superphosphate per m^2 (½oz per sq yd). Alternatively, use well-rotted farmyard manure at one barrowload to $5m^2$ (6 sq yd). Every February apply 17g of sulphate of potash per m^2 (½oz per sq yd).

Bare-root and container-grown plants are both available. Bare-root plants need a period of establishment after planting before they are able to carry a crop successfully. If you plant them between July and September, a full crop can be picked the following year; but if they are planted at any other time the first flush of flowers has to be removed. Early planting with cold-stored runners in May gives the earliest crop. Plants sold in containers can be planted all year round, even when carrying flowers and fruit. Replace plants after four years, or sooner if growing poorly.

Roots of bare-root plants should be soaked in water before planting. The roots must point downwards in the hole and the 'crown' buried to half its depth. If planted too deep it will rot and if too shallow new roots will not grow.

Rows should be 30-36in (75-90cm) apart. Depending on the vigour of the variety, place the plants 15-24in (38-60cm) apart in each row.

▲ Planting a bare-root strawberry plant, roots downwards.

Planting through a polythene sheet reduces weeds and keeps the fruit clean. And if you build up a ridge or wide bed of soil beneath the polythene, it will improve soil drainage, improve root growth and cause water to run off the sheet, reducing rotting of the fruit.

CULTIVATION

After planting, water through the holes in the polythene. As the flowers open, more water is needed but avoid wetting the flowers – it will encourage grey mould. In order for the water to get to the soil, spike some holes in the polythene. Low-pressure trickle irrigation is particularly useful beneath polythene.

On frosty nights in spring, protect the flowers with straw or sheets of perforated polythene, hessian or fleece.

As the fruits grow, protect them from soil splash by tucking straw or strawberry mats under them. To maintain fruit size remove runners (sideshoots) as they appear.

After picking, cut back the foliage to 10cm (4in) from the crown. Remove it, together with straw and debris, and burn it to kill pests and diseases. Add a general fertiliser to the soil and fork it in. Liquid feed plants growing through polythene. Water the plants if the soil is dry to encourage new leaves.

To maintain good fruit size, reduce the number of 'crowns' in each plant (where the leaves and flowers grow) to two or three. Pull the excess away from the edge of the plant.

HARVESTING

Pick the fruit only when dry by pinching the stalk between thumb and fingernails. Handle the fruit by the stalk to avoid bruising. Fruit for jam can be picked without a stalk.

Strawberries can be stored cool for up to two days, but warm strawberries fresh from the plant have the most flavour.

PROPAGATING STRAWBERRIES

The easiest method of producing new plants is to encourage the runners to root into pots of compost sunk into the soil around the parent plant.

A quicker method is to cut off the tips of the runners, complete with a 2.5cm (1in) piece of stem, when roots start to show. Insert them into small pots of compost and keep them under a polythene tent or in a propagator until fully rooted in about six weeks.

PESTS AND DISEASES

The main pests of strawberries are aphids, slugs, glasshouse red spider mite and strawberry beetles (see Pests, p.824). The most common diseases are grey mould and powdery mildew (see Diseases and Disorders, p.834).

RECOMMENDED VARIETIES OF STRAWBERRIES

Summer-fruiting varieties are most popular because they used to be the only varieties available to amateur growers. Perpetual (or remontant) varieties fruit later and extend the season into autumn. The table shows flavour, cropping and fruit size of each variety with scores out of 5.

SEASON OF USE	VARIETY	FLAVOUR	CROPPING	FRUIT SIZE	COMMENTS
Summer fruiting					
Pick early June	Honeoye	5	4	3	Some resistance to botrytis.
	Tamella	3	5	5	Very heavy cropper. Big fruit size. Moderate flavour.
	Elvira	4	5	4	Susceptible to mildew.
	Cambridge Vigour	4	4	3	Cropping and size better in first year.
	Royal Sovereign	5	3	4	Susceptible to diseases.
Pick mid June	Redgauntlet	1	5	5	Possible second crop in autumn. Disease resistant.
	Cambridge Favourite	3	4	3	Disease resistant but buy plants free of June Yellows disease.
	Elsanta	5	4	5	Vigorous. Poor disease resistance except mildew.
	Hapil	4	4	5	Vigorous. Crops well on all soils and dry conditions.
Pick mid July	Bogota	3	4	4	Fruit freezes well. Moderate disease resistance.
Perpetuals (Remontants)					
Pick late July	Rapella	4	5	4	Freeze well. Prone to mildew.
Alpines					
Pick mid summer to autumn	Baron Solemacher	–	–	–	Small fruit but excellent flavour.

The Vegetable Garden

In a large garden, enough vegetables can be grown to support a household through the year. Even a small patch can provide special treats

Artichoke, Globe

Cynara cardunculus Scolymus Group
Compositae

Globe artichokes are large perennial plants growing to 1.2-1.5m (4-5 ft) tall and highly suitable for the back of a herbaceous border where the striking thistle-like green leaves make a good backdrop for contrasting flowers. The base of the scales around the flower and the base of the flower itself (called the fond) are the edible parts of the plant.

TYPES AND VARIETIES

Globe artichokes are usually grown from offsets (rooted suckers). They may also be raised from seeds, but the results are more variable and less predictable.

GRAND CAMUS DE BRETAGNE Large heads of good flavour; southern counties only.

GREEN GLOBE IMPROVED Reduced spines and consistent quality. Widely available.

PURPLE GLOBE Hardier with purple flowerheads. Offsets obtained from a garden centre may give better results than seeds.

VERT DE LAON The best for flavour, but suitable for southern counties only.

CULTIVATION AND HARVESTING

Globe artichokes need a sunny and sheltered position in fertile, well-drained soil. In April, plant offsets 1m (3ft) apart and about 5cm (2in) deep. Protect them from full sun in the early stages. Keep them watered and mulch well with manure or compost once established. In the first year, remove flowerheads or harvest them small to encourage growth.

In the second and third years, allow 4-6 stems to develop and harvest the king head (on the leading stem) first when it is still green and tightly folded; harvest the lateral heads in June and July.

▲ Harvest the king head when it is still green.

Plants will need protection over winter. Cut down the stems and cover the rootstock with straw to protect from frost. Remove the straw in spring.

Plants should be renewed every three years by taking root offsets. In November or April, select a strong shoot and cut down into the rootstock with a spade or knife. If growing from seed, sow the seeds indoors in February or outdoors in March, thin to 23×30cm (9×12in), and plant out in May. Transplant the following year and use the best plants for division for later crops.

PESTS AND DISEASES

Aphids and slugs may cause trouble.

Why rotate crops of vegetables?

If the same vegetables are grown in the same place year after year, the soil will become exhausted of its fertility and pests and diseases will increase. If space is available, divide the garden into three plots, growing different crops on each plot in consecutive years. For a three-year rotation, the crops could be grown as follows – although the order is not essential.

	FIRST PLOT	SECOND PLOT	THIRD PLOT
First year	Brassicas	Potatoes	Peas, beans, salad crops
Second year	Potatoes	Peas, beans, salad crops	Brassicas
Third year	Peas, beans, salad crops	Brassicas	Potatoes

Some plants provide benefits for those that follow them. Leguminous vegetables (peas, beans) enrich the soil with nitrogen, leaving it ideal for nitrogen-dependent brassicas the following year. Similarly, the earthing up of potatoes and their dense foliage, which help to keep weeds down, can benefit onions and carrots that struggle to survive in weedy ground. At the very least, try to avoid planting the same crop in the same place for at least two years.

Asparagus

Asparagus officinalis
Asparagaceae

Asparagus is a hardy perennial plant with tall, wispy, fern-like shoots and leaves. During spring tender spears emerge from beneath the soil and it is these that are eaten. Once established, asparagus is simple to grow, requiring very little attention except for feeding and weeding. However, an asparagus bed takes up a lot of room for only six weeks of harvesting each year.

TYPES AND VARIETIES

Asparagus may be grown from seed or from one-year-old crowns. Newer varieties are 'all male'; they give higher yields since their energy is not spent in producing seed.

CONNOVER'S COLOSSAL A traditional variety which has thick stalks and crops early.

FRANKLIM F_1 All male, heavy crops of thick spears.

LUCULLUS F_1 All male with long slim spears.

CULTIVATION

Take care over preparing an asparagus bed, as it may be productive for up to 20 years. Sandy soils are most suitable but heavier soils can be used if the drainage can be improved by, say, creating a raised bed. The bed should be dug and well manured. Remove all perennial weeds. The site should preferably be open and sheltered from strong winds.

Seed may be sown under glass in February-March, hardened off and transplanted into the prepared bed in June. Alternatively, sow in the open in April for transplanting the following year. Crowns (preferably one-year-old roots) must be kept moist and handled carefully.

Asparagus may be grown in a trench and earthed up, or on the flat. Earthing up produces a longer blanched stem; on the flat – which is easier – the stems are shorter.

▲ When planting asparagus, spread out the roots.

Plant them out in April – 10 cm (4 in) deep at 38 cm (15 in) intervals, spreading the roots out from the crown.

The spears may be harvested from the second year after planting. In late April cut with a knife below the soil surface when the spears are about 15 cm (6 in) above ground.

The traditional date for the end of the season is June 21. After that, fern must be allowed to grow to develop the crown for the next year.

A mulch of chopped straw put on in early spring will help to suppress weeds and conserve moisture. Apply a top dressing of fertiliser in summer and add compost or manure in autumn to maintain fertility. Keep asparagus weed-free, taking care to avoid damaging the shallow roots.

PESTS AND DISEASES

Asparagus beetle and slugs may be a problem; violet root rot and rust are the only likely diseases.

Aubergines

Solanum melongena

Solanaceae

Aubergines are shrubby sub-tropical plants related to tomatoes and potatoes and more distantly to sweet peppers. They became known as eggplants in Britain because the first types grown here had oval white fruits. Modern varieties generally have large, dark and shiny purple fruits, which may be 15-20 cm (6-8 in) long and around 450 g (1 lb) in weight, depending on variety. These follow small, mauve, potato-like flowers.

TYPES AND VARIETIES

A few varieties are available, offering a choice of size and colour.

EASTER EGG AND OVA Novelty varieties with many small, white fruits.

LONG PURPLE Medium sized, elongated fruits.

MONEYMAKER F_1 Elongated, purple-black fruits. Early and prolific.

SLICE RITE F_1 Large, almost black fruits weighing up to 450 g (1 lb) each.

CULTIVATION

Aubergines are best grown in a greenhouse like tomatoes. Raise seed under glass in March at not lower than 20°C (68°F). Eventually move the plants into 20 cm or 23 cm (8 in or 9 in) pots, or into growing bags. Alternatively, plant them in well-drained and manured soil in the border, 60 cm (24 in) apart each way.

For large fruits, pinch out the growing point when 30 cm (12 in) tall and limit each plant to 5 or 6 fruits, or fewer. They will need supporting.

Mist plants with water frequently to discourage red spider mite, and water a little and often, applying a liquid tomato feed regularly once the fruits start to develop.

Cut the fruits from the stem with secateurs when they are fully grown and while the skin is still shiny and smooth. Overripe fruits have a dull skin and are bitter. Aubergines may be kept for a few days in the salad drawer of a refrigerator, but keep them apart from tomatoes and apples, which will cause the aubergines to overripen.

PESTS AND DISEASES

Red spider mite and aphids are likely to be found on aubergines; also whitefly in greenhouse crops. They may suffer from grey mould and damping-off diseases.

Beans, Broad

Vicia faba

Leguminosae

Broad beans are easy to grow, needing little attention other than providing support for the plants – most varieties reach 1-1.4 m (3-4½ ft) tall. The white-and-black flowers have a heavy sweet scent and develop into long green pods, with a 'furry' lining, that are filled with white or green beans.

TYPES AND VARIETIES

There are two types of broad bean: Longpods and Windsors. Longpods are the hardier, early to mature and high yielding, having 8-10 kidney-shaped beans in pods up to 40 cm (16 in) long. Windsor varieties – considered to have better flavour – are generally later to mature, with shorter and broader pods containing 4-7 flat, circular beans in each.

• *Longpods*

AQUADULCE CLAUDIA Reliable longpod variety for sowing in autumn or early spring, growing to 1.3 m (4½ ft). Good flavour.

EXPRESS An early maturing and prolific longpod, good flavour. For early sowing.

IMPERIAL GREEN LONGPOD Tall growing, extra long pods with large green seeds of fine flavour, good for freezing.

RELON Tall, vigorous, late. Has very long pods with green seeds of fine flavour, good for freezing.

THE SUTTON Sturdy longpod dwarf variety, 30 cm (12 in) tall. It can be sown in autumn and grown under cloches, or in the open February-July.

• *Windsors*

JUBILEE HYSOR Late Windsor variety, pods packed with 6 or more large white beans.

RED EPICURE Red flowers followed by green pods with red seeds. Unique flavour.

CULTIVATION

Autumn-sown broad beans require a light soil that will drain well over the winter; spring-sown crops may be grown in heavier clay soils. Certain varieties only, such as Aquadulce Claudia or The Sutton, can be sown in warmer areas in November. Do not add fertiliser to these crops until spring, to avoid soft growth. In colder areas, sowing can start in the early spring, under protection in February, or in the open in March. Sow again at monthly intervals to give a succession of supplies.

Broad beans, especially low-growing varieties, can be grown in blocks or double rows, with seed sown 7.5 cm (3 in) deep, 23 cm (9 in) apart each way, and 60 cm (2 ft) between each pair of double rows. For tall varieties, it is easier to support single rows, 45 cm (18 in) apart, with the seeds 12 cm (4¾ in) apart. Once the plants are growing, support them with string around the rows. Keep the beans well watered once flowering. When they are in full flower and the first pods are swelling, pinch out the tops of the growing shoots to promote growth of the seeds and to discourage blackfly.

HARVESTING AND STORAGE

Harvesting begins in late May and June, depending on sowing time. Pods can be picked very young for cooking whole. Otherwise pick when the beans can be seen swelling inside the pods. When shelled the beans should be tender and the scar where the bean was attached to the pod white or green, not black. Old beans are tough and have poor flavour. Once picked, use as soon as possible, or keep the beans unshelled in a cool place for a few days only.

PESTS AND DISEASES

Black bean aphid is the main problem, especially on later sown crops. Chocolate spot disease may also occur.

Beans, French or Dwarf

Phaseolus vulgaris

Leguminosae

Most types of french beans are dwarf and bushy in habit, but climbing types (pole beans) are grown on canes or strings like runner beans. French bean pods may be round like a pencil – the slenderest types are called 'filet' or fine beans – or flattened like a runner bean. The colour is usually green, but yellow and purple varieties are also available. The young pods of french beans freeze well, and can be cooked whole or sliced. Older pods are shelled and the fresh green beans (flageolets) are cooked. The beans may also be left to mature fully on the plant and then dried for later use (haricots).

TYPES AND VARIETIES

French beans are half-hardy annuals and in a hot summer will be more successful than the other beans or peas. Most types are dwarf, bushy plants which mature earlier than the climbers. Climbing beans give heavier crops than dwarf varieties and need supporting in the same way as runner beans.

• *Dwarf french beans*

ARAMIS Fine filet-type pods, 13-15 cm (5¼-6 in) long and stringless. Good flavour.

MONT D'OR (GOLDEN BUTTER) Yellow, waxy pods, stringless and flat, black seeds within. Good flavour. Upright or semi-climbing habit.

PURPLE QUEEN Dark purple pods easy to see when harvesting. They have excellent flavour and turn dark green on cooking.

TENDERGREEN Heavy crops of stringless, medium length round pods 15-17 cm (6-6¾ in). Recommended for freezing.

THE PRINCE Good crops of long, slender, flat pods, dark green.

• *Climbing french beans*

BLUE LAKE Tender, round, green stringless pods if harvested for fresh beans. Or leave to mature for haricots.

HUNTER Straight, flat pods, 25 cm (10 in) or more. Stringless. Crop well over a long period.

CULTIVATION

The cultivation of french beans is largely the same as for runner beans, except that dwarf varieties can be grown in tubs or growing bags, or entirely under glass or cloches, sowing in April for an early crop. Outdoor sowings can begin in May, but be prepared to sow again if seedlings are caught by frost. Sow again in June – and in July if cloches are available to cover the crop when the nights grow cool in late summer.

Sow dwarf beans in blocks 23 cm (9 in) apart each way for the highest yields, or in rows 45 cm (18 in) apart at 10 cm (4 in) centres for easier picking. Support climbing beans as for runner beans. They may not grow as tall and a closer spacing may be used, rows 45 cm (18 in) apart, the poles or strings 10 cm (4 in) apart within the row.

HARVESTING

Begin picking as soon as the first pods develop – about 7-8 weeks after sowing. Pick young for fresh beans, before they can be seen swelling within the pod. For flageolet beans, allow the seeds to develop on the plant, and pick, shell and cook the beans green. For haricots, leave the pods on the plant until yellow, then harvest the whole plant and hang up to dry. Shell the beans and dry fully before storing in jars.

PESTS AND DISEASES

Slugs, black bean aphid, bean seed fly and red spider mite are all potential pests. Grey mould disease is a possible problem. Brown spots on leaves indicate halo blight. Burn diseased plants and spray the others with copper compound before the first pods develop.

Beans, Runner

Phaseolus coccineus
Leguminosae

The plants are tender climbing perennials that are grown as annuals, because they are cut down by the first frost of autumn. Runner beans were originally grown for their flowers alone, hence their alternative name, scarlet runners.

TYPES AND VARIETIES

Most runner bean varieties have red flowers, a few have white or white and red flowers. Plant breeders have aimed to produce stringless beans. Some dwarf varieties which do not need supports are also available; other varieties can be grown as dwarf plants by 'pinching out' the growing point.

• *Stringless runner beans*

DESIREE White flowers, pods 25 cm (10 in) or more. Good yields.

PICKWICK Dwarf and bushy; short stringless pods. Red flowers.

POLESTAR Red flowers; early and heavy crop of smooth, fleshy pods 25-30 cm (10-12 in) long.

• *Traditional varieties*

ACHIEVEMENT Long, straight beans, for table or exhibition. Freeze well.

ENORMA Very good crop of long, smooth beans 35-38 cm (14-15 in) long. Popular with exhibitors.

KELVEDON MARVEL First to crop, prolific. Can be grown as a pinched crop, in the open or under cloches. Beans 20-25 cm (8-10 in) long.

CULTIVATION

For soil preparation, see Broad beans.

Runner beans are climbing plants and need rigid support for all but dwarf or pinched crops. A double line of canes or poles is ideal if there is space. In a small garden use a wigwam or maypole structure. Netting attached to a south-facing fence is suitable, provided there is easy access for picking later.

Erect the support structure before sowing or planting. For a double row, push a pair of 2.4 m (8 ft) canes firmly into the ground 60 cm (2 ft) apart and tie them together at the top. Place the other pairs at 30 cm (12 in) intervals, and fix a horizontal cane across the tops to give rigidity.

As the plants start to grow, twist the shoots gently anticlockwise around the supports; thereafter they will find their own way. Nip out the top shoot when it reaches the top of the supports. For wigwams (four or five poles tied together) or maypoles (one central pole with strings coming from it), aim for one support at each corner of a square 60×60 cm (2×2 ft).

Runner beans must not be put out until all danger of frost is passed – towards the end of May, depending on the area. Seed can be sown indoors for transplanting, or sown outside, 3 seeds to the inside of each support 5 cm (2 in) deep. Water in transplants. Once the plants are in flower and beans are developing, water freely.

TWO WAYS TO SUPPORT RUNNER BEANS

WIGWAM

DOUBLE ROW OF CANES

Runner beans can be grown without supports by using dwarf varieties, growing 30 cm (12 in) high, or by pinching out the growing tips of standard varieties.

HARVESTING AND STORAGE

Begin picking beans as soon as the first ones reach a reasonable length and before they can be seen swelling and the pods become tough and stringy – the younger they are, the better. Well-grown plants will crop from late July up to the first frosts.

PESTS AND DISEASES

Slugs, black bean aphid, bean seed fly and red spider mite are all potential pests. Grey mould is a possible disease. Brown spots on leaves indicate halo blight; burn diseased plants and spray the others with copper compound before the first pods develop.

Beetroot

Beta vulgaris
Chenopodiaceae

Beetroots are biennial plants grown as annuals. They thrive in most garden soils and, if space is limited, are not out of place in a flowerbed. The upright growth – up to 25 cm (10 in) high – of deep red stems and glossy green leaves is most attractive. The roots are usually deep red, but pink, yellow and white varieties are also available.

TYPES AND VARIETIES

Most beetroots are the familiar globe shape but longer cylindrical varieties are also available, particularly useful for slicing and good for storing for winter use. Beetroot 'seed' is a dried fruit containing several true seeds. Breeders have produced monogerm varieties which have only one seed per fruit, reducing the need for thinning. These all have 'mono' in the variety name.

BOLTARDY Bolt resistant, medium-sized globe variety for sowing from March to July. Good texture, colour and flavour.

BURPEES GOLDEN Golden-rooted variety with distinctive, succulent flavour. Bolt resistant and stores well. Sow March-July.
CHELTENHAM MONO Long-rooted monogerm variety. Stores well, bolt resistant.
DETROIT 2 LITTLE BALL Baby beet with small, round, deep red roots, ideal for bottling, pickling and freezing. Good for late sowing in July.
FORONO Medium-length cylindrical variety with good colour and flavour. Sow from May onwards. Stores well.
MONOGRAM Globe-shaped monogerm variety. Rich, deep red colour with smooth skin and good flavour. Vigorous and uniform. Sow March-July.

CULTIVATION

Beetroot for exhibition is best grown in deep, well-drained, sandy soil which has been manured the previous autumn, but a satisfactory crop can be grown in a sunny position in most garden soils. Excessively acid soils will need to be limed.

Soak the seed in warm water for an hour before sowing to aid germination. Sow thinly along the row or in groups of 2 or 3 seeds at intervals along the row, about 2 cm (¾ in) deep. The spacing will depend upon how large you wish the beets to grow – for most uses, space globe varieties in rows 18 cm (7 in) apart and at intervals of 10 cm (4 in). For larger maincrop beets, sow rows at 30 cm (12 in) apart, thinning to 7.5-10 cm (3-4 in) in the rows.

Start sowing outdoors in March when the soil begins to warm up. Continue until July, sowing at 3-4 weekly intervals to give a continuous supply. Earlier sowing can be made under cloches in late February or under glass in cellular trays for planting out. The main crop is sown in May and June when any variety can be used. For spring sowings, and late ones in July, use bolt-resistant varieties only – these are less likely to run to seed before being ready to use. Beetroot can be harvested from about 12 weeks after sowing. It should be kept weed-free and watered gently in dry periods.

HARVESTING AND STORAGE

Globe beetroot can be pulled out of the soil when it is between the size of a golf ball and a cricket ball – roots left in the ground too long become woody. After lifting, twist off the leaves so that 5 cm (2 in) of stalk remains. Cylindrical varieties need to be lifted carefully with a fork. For storing in the autumn, shake the soil off roots and place them in almost dry peat or sand in a cool, frost-free place where they will keep through to the following March. Late globe beetroot, sown in July and ready in October, can be left in the ground in milder areas and covered with straw or leaf-mould.

PESTS AND DISEASES

Beetroot is largely trouble free, but may be attacked by black fly. Damping off may affect seedlings, and mineral deficiencies in the soil will show up in the leaves.

Brassicas

***Brassica* species**

Cruciferae

Many of the vegetables which are called brassicas – broccoli, brussels sprouts, cabbage and cauliflower – are closely related. All are rich in vitamins and minerals, provide dietary fibre and form a major part of the produce grown in vegetable gardens and allotments. They share many cultural requirements and pest and disease problems.

SOILS FOR BRASSICA CROPS

A major problem with growing brassicas of all types (including turnip, swede and kohlrabi) is a soil-borne fungal disease called club root, which can cause huge swellings to grow on the roots, preventing them from functioning properly. To avoid this developing, do not grow brassicas in the same ground more often than once in three years, and add lime to acid soil to bring it up to a pH of 6.5-7.5.

Brassicas grow best in well-drained, fertile soil that has been manured for the previous year's crop. Shallow and sandy soils are not generally suitable.

CULTIVATION OF LEAFY BRASSICA CROPS

Leafy brassicas are usually grown by sowing in a seedbed first and then transplanting to the permanent site. This means the seedbed area can be specially prepared for sowing, leaving the main site free for another crop – legumes (peas and beans) are ideal, as they leave good levels of nitrogen in the soil for brassicas to follow.

Sow thinly in drills 15 cm (6 in) apart and up to 2.5 cm (1 in) deep. Transplant when the seedlings are about 10-15 cm (4-6 in) tall and with 3 or 4 true leaves, using only the strongest and healthiest plants. Ensure that the plants are firm in the ground after planting, and then water in.

Measures will need to be taken against cabbage root fly. Fit a disc of carpet or thick plastic, 7.5 cm (3 in) across, around the base of the plants when they are transplanted.

A general fertiliser or liquid feed can be applied in the growing season to promote growth, especially in the quicker-growing crops, such as summer cauliflower and calabrese (broccoli). Nitrogen should not be applied in autumn to overwintering crops, such as spring cabbage, brussels sprouts and winter cauliflower; fertilise these in spring.

PESTS AND DISEASES OF BRASSICA CROPS

All brassicas are prone to attack by cabbage root fly and cabbage whitefly caterpillars. Aphids, flea beetle, whitefly, pigeons and slugs and snails may be a problem. Club root and downy mildew are the main diseases.

TIMETABLE FOR GROWING BRASSICAS

VARIETY	SOWING	PLANTING OUT	SPACING	HARVEST
Broccoli Calabrese	Feb-Apr	Apr-July	45×20 cm (18×8 in)	June-Nov
Sprouting	May	June-July	60×75 cm (24×30 in)	Feb-Mar
Brussels sprouts	Feb-Apr	Apr-May	60×75 cm (24×30 in)	Sep-Mar
Cabbage Spring greens	Aug	Sep	30 × 10 cm (12×4 in)	Mar-May
Spring hearts	Aug	Sep	30×30 cm (12×12 in)	Apr-May
Early summer	Feb Under glass	Apr	40×30 cm (16×12 in)	June-July
Summer	Mar-Apr	May-June	40×30 cm (16×12 in)	July-Sep
Autumn/ winter	Mar-May	Apr-July	60×40 cm (24×16 in)	September onwards
Cauliflower Summer	Oct-Feb Under glass	Feb-May	60×45 cm (24×18 in)	June-Aug
Autumn/ winter	Mar-June	May-July	60×60 cm (24×24 in)	September onwards
Mini	Mar-May in situ		15×15 cm (6×6 in)	July onwards

Broccoli

Brassica oleracea Cymosa Group

Broccoli is particularly rich in vitamins A, B and C. It falls into two groups – calabrese and sprouting broccoli. Calabrese is fast-growing, maturing in summer and autumn with a large, dense, central head of flower buds on a single stem. Once this central head has been harvested, most varieties will produce smaller secondary heads. Sprouting broccoli is an extremely hardy vegetable producing several spears of purple or creamy yellow flower buds in early spring. These provide a welcome crop at a time of year when little else is available and can be grown in cold areas and heavy soils where many other vegetables would fail.

For details of cultivation, see Brassicas.

TYPES AND VARIETIES

A good choice of varieties is available to suit a range of garden conditions and to crop between February and November.

• *Calabrese*

CORVET F_1 Mid season variety with big, round, grey-green heads, good for freezing. Good crop of sideshoots. Suitable for growing in northern areas.

GREEN COMET F_1 Tight, deep green central heads, 15-18 cm (6-7 in) across, followed by small secondary spears. Early.

MERCEDES F_1 Early variety with dark, medium-sized heads on short plants. Reliable.

SHOGUN F_1 Late variety with good-quality heads, 15 cm (6 in) across, followed by secondary spears. It will grow in a range of soil types.

TRIXIE F_1 Clubroot resistant, compact plants. Deep rounded heads followed by several secondary spears.

ROMANESCO (Italian broccoli) Unique variety with pyramid-shaped head made up of many tightly packed pointed spears, yellow-green in colour. May also be listed as 'green cauliflower'. Harvest in October-November.

• *Sprouting broccoli*

PURPLE SPROUTING Comes in early and late strains. Masses of small purple spears, packed with flavour and vitamins, throughout spring. Colour turns to dark green on cooking. Very hardy.

WHITE SPROUTING Similar to purple, but with white spears and more delicate flavour; early and late strains available.

Brussels sprouts

Brassica oleracea Gemmifera Group
Cruciferae

Brussels sprouts are hardy biennial plants which mature during autumn and winter. The sprouts should be harvested as required while still tightly closed, starting at the bottom of the stem and working upwards. A selection of varieties will give a long cropping period, with the tops used as greens after the sprouts have been picked.

For details of cultivation, see Brassicas.

TYPES AND VARIETIES

Plant breeders have developed many new hybrid varieties of sprouts, which produce high yields of good-quality, tight button sprouts on each plant, good for freezing. The following selection is listed in order of their maturity.

OLIVER High yields of pale sprouts; very early. September-October.

PEER GYNT Early crops on compact plants. September onwards.

ROGER Tall plants, giving high yields of large sprouts. November onwards.

RAMPART Mid season; tall plants giving firm sprouts which hold well on the plant. Late November onwards.

FORTRESS Late hardy variety, compact with firm, dark green sprouts. January-March.

Cabbages

Brassica oleracea var. *capitata*
Cruciferae

Cabbages come in a wide range of types and varieties and with careful planning, they can be available throughout the year.

For details of cultivation, see Brassicas.

TYPES AND VARIETIES

The cabbage plant is a biennial which is cultivated as an annual. The varieties that follow are grouped according to the time of harvesting.

• *Spring cabbage*

Sow in August in a row closely spaced – 10 cm (4 in) apart – for fresh greens – or use thinnings for greens and leave others to develop a heart later in the season.

▲ A cut in the stump produces a crop of greens.

Cut a deep cross into the stumps and leave them to grow a second crop of greens.

DURHAM EARLY Dark green leaves for greens; medium-sized conical heart. April-May.

DUNCAN F_1 Compact and early. A dark green, pointed-heart cabbage, ideal for spring. Or sow in spring for use in summer and autumn.

PIXIE Early and compact variety for close spacing. Small, solid, pointed hearts.

SPRING HERO F_1 Large, round hearts in May and June.

• *Summer cabbage*

Solid, round or pointed heads, for cutting between June and September. For the earliest crops, raise young plants under glass and then transplant them. Some varieties 'stand well' – they may be left in the ground for a while once they are ready for harvesting, without deteriorating.

In order of maturity:

HISPI F_1 Large, pointed hearts, dark green; early.

SPITFIRE F_1 A dark green cabbage with pointed head, ready in July from an outdoor sowing.

DERBY DAY Small round heads, or use as greens. June-July.

STONEHEAD F_1 The heads are small, solid, heavy and round. The variety stands well. August-September.

MINICOLE F_1 Small, solid, oval heads, which will stand for up to three months. May be grown at close spacing, 25×25 cm (10 x 10 in). August-September.

RUBY BALL F_1 Solid red cabbage with good flavour. Ready in August, will stand through to winter.

• *Autumn and winter cabbages*

A selection of different types can be grown for use in autumn and winter, either from stored crops or direct from the garden.

CELTIC F_1 Blue-green leaves and dense winter-white type heart, but more frost hardy. November-January.

HOLLAND WINTER WHITE EXTRA LATE Dense heads of white cabbage for cooking, salads or coleslaw. Plant in June, cut in October-November before severe frosts and store until required.

JANUARY KING HARDY LATE STOCK 3 Blue-green leaves, medium-sized firm hearts tinged with red. Very hardy. Plant in June; ready October-November and standing well into the winter.

SAVOY KING F_1 Early savoy variety with green, crinkled leaves and solid hearts with good flavour. Plant early July, harvest September-October.

TUNDRA F_1 Savoy cross with green leaves and white heart, good for cooking or salads. Very hardy. December-February.

WIVOY F_1 Late savoy variety with small heads, ready in December and standing through to March.

Carrots

Daucus carota ssp. *sativa*
Umbelliferae

Carrots are hardy vegetables and can be grown for harvesting throughout the year. They are biennial plants which are grown as annuals. As they are quick to mature, they can be grown in the space between other plants in a mixed bed, or as part of a crop rotation system.

CARROTS: VARIETIES AND TIMING

TYPE/VARIETY	DESCRIPTION	SOWING	HARVEST
Amsterdam Forcing Amsterdam Forcing -Amstel, Amsterdam Forcing -Sweetheart	Small to medium, succulent roots. Early	Jan-Apr under cloches	June-Sep
Nantes Nantes-Express, Nantes-Tiptop, Tamino F_1	Medium, cylindrical stump roots. Early	Jan-Apr under cloches	July-Sep
Paris Market Parmex, Rondo	Round. Early	Late Apr-May	July-Sep
Chantenay Chantenay Red Cored, Chantenay Red Cored Supreme, Chantenay Royal	Short, stump-rooted. Maincrop	Late Apr-early May	Oct-Nov
Berlicum Berlicum 2 Berjo Camberley	Large roots. Late maincrop	Mid May	Dec
Autumn King Autumn King, Autumn King-Vita Longa	Large roots. Late maincrop	Mid May	Dec

CULTIVATION

Carrots may follow a 'hungry' crop, such as leafy brassicas, in a crop rotation plan since their need for nitrogen is low. Also, fresh manure in the soil will make the roots fork. Ideally, the soil should be deep, well cultivated with good drainage and free of stones. Shorter wedge varieties can be used for shallower soils.

Choose a sunny or lightly shaded spot for growing carrots. The use of cloches or plastic mulches early in the season and successional sowing times can make carrots available throughout the year. Remove cloches or covers in April.

The soil must not be allowed to dry out and then watered heavily; this can result in the roots splitting. Keep the soil just moist.

The seeds can be sown in shallow drills, with rows 15 cm (6 in) apart and thinned to a spacing of 8-10 cm (3¼-4 in). A closer spacing will give a greater number of smaller carrots. Later thinnings can be used as young carrots.

HARVESTING AND STORAGE

Young carrots can be pulled as soon as they are large enough for eating. Small roots of Amsterdam Forcing may be frozen whole and larger roots sliced and frozen. Maincrop roots for keeping through the winter can be left in the ground, with a layer of soil or straw as protection against frost, and lifted as required. Otherwise, lift them in autumn. Loosen them carefully with a fork and shake off the soil, but do not wash the carrots. Remove any damaged roots – either use them immediately or destroy them – and cut the foliage to leave 2 cm (¾ in) of stalk. Place the carrots separately in a box of sand or dry peat, store them in a cool building and use them through to March.

PESTS AND DISEASES

Carrot fly is a major problem. Aphids can weaken the plants and also bring disease. Sclerotina rot and violet root rot can spoil the plants in the ground or in storage.

Cauliflowers

***Brassica oleracea* Botrytis Group**
Cruciferae

Cauliflowers are available from the garden during three seasons of the year and come in various colours – white, green and purple. Mini-cauliflowers with heads of only 10 cm (4 in) across are useful where space is limited.

For details of cultivation, see Brassicas.

TYPES AND VARIETIES

Summer cauliflowers grow quickly and generally have smaller heads than later, more slow-growing types. Winter cauliflowers are vulnerable to frosts and can only be grown in frost-free areas.

• *Summer varieties*

DOK ELGON Deep, well-protected heads. Harvest August-September.

DOMINANT More tolerant of drier conditions. May also be used for mini-cauliflowers. Harvest late June-July.

GARANT Mini-cauliflower, quick growing for successional sowing, making heads in summer.

MONTANO F_1 Matures about 12 weeks after transplanting. Knobbly, white curds. Harvest in June.

PLANA F_1 Vigorous growth, deep heavy heads. Harvest in August.

VIOLET QUEEN F_1 Deep purple heads, up to 20 cm (8 in), cooking to green. Attractive in salads. Harvest August-September.

• *Autumn and winter*

BARRIER REEF Australian-bred variety with vigorous growth protecting large white heads. Harvest in October.

PURPLE CAPE Red-purple curds, cooking green. Matures February-March.

WALCHEREN WINTER SELECTIONS Hardy Dutch-bred selections with firm, white heads. One type is Armado April which matures in April. Another variety, Maystar, matures in May.

CULTIVATION

Cauliflowers are the most difficult of the brassica crops to grow, and they need careful feeding, watering and pest control to be successful.

Mini-cauliflowers may be sown where they are to grow and can be harvested after only a few weeks. All other cauliflowers are usually transplanted after the seeds have been sown and raised in coldframes or in a sheltered seedbed outdoors. A good supply of water to the plants is needed throughout the season.

Summer crops may need protection from the sun by snapping some of the outer leaves to shade the curd – the cauliflower itself.

Crops which are to be grown through the winter need to be planted in a position which is well drained and sheltered from the frost.

Cauliflowers are harvested when the curds are well developed, but before they begin to open out and divide.

Celery

Apium graveolens
Umbelliferae

Celery is a biennial plant, growing 30-60 cm (1-2 ft) tall. Traditional varieties, which have to be planted in a trench to encourage long white stems, can be difficult to grow. But modern self-blanching and green-stemmed varieties are much easier. Whichever type is grown, celery is still a crop needing good, well-manured soil and frequent watering and feeding. It is also susceptible to pests.

TYPES AND VARIETIES

There are two types of celery. Trench celery is grown in rows in a trench and earthed up to make the stems tall and pale. Self-blanching and green-stemmed varieties are grown in square blocks.

CELEBRITY Self-blanching. Long sticks, crisp, early and vigorous.

GOLDEN SELF-BLANCHING Dwarf variety with crisp, creamy stalks of fine flavour; yellow foliage.

HOPKINS FENLANDER – Hardy trench variety grown for its flavour. Has pale green stems if not earthed up.

LATHOM SELF-BLANCHING Compact plants with crisp stems of good flavour. Resistant to bolting.

VICTORIA F_1 A pale, green-stemmed variety with an excellent flavour. Grow it as self-blanching.

CULTIVATION

Celery needs a sunny site and good, well-manured soil. Seed is sown under glass in March or April and hardened off for planting out in May or June. A check to growth, such as planting out too soon or dryness at the roots, may induce bolting – running to seed – before being ready to eat.

Self-blanching and green-stemmed varieties are not hardy, unlike trench varieties, and must not be planted out until the danger of frost has passed. Seedlings may be transplanted into a coldframe – with lights removed – from late May onwards, 23 cm (9 in) apart or planted out in square blocks, preferably with straw placed around the edges of the block. The plants will shield each other within the block and encourage creamy yellow or pale green stems, depending on the variety.

▲ Plant self-blanching types in blocks.

For trenching celery, plant out in May or June, either in a single row in a 38 cm (15 in) wide trench, or in two rows 30 cm (12 in) apart. When the plants are 30 cm (12 in) high – about early August – pile earth up around the stalks to blanch them. As the plant grows, keep earthing up to the bottom of the leaves.

Celery must always have a plentiful supply of water – dryness around the roots can lead to stringy growth, splitting along the stems or bolting. Feeding with a liquid or nitrogenous fertiliser is also required throughout the season.

HARVESTING AND STORAGE

Harvest with a knife from August onwards, replacing the straw around the edge of the block. The stems will keep for a short time in the salad section of the refrigerator.

Self-blanching varieties must be lifted before the first frosts; trench-grown types can be left in the ground well into the winter, depending on the variety.

PESTS AND DISEASES

Celery can be prone to attack by celery leaf miner and celery leaf spot. It is also attractive to slugs and snails.

Courgettes see Marrows and Courgettes

Cucumbers and Gherkins

Cucumis sativus

Cucurbitaceae

Two types of cucumber are available: those for growing under glass (in a greenhouse or coldframe), sometimes known as frame cucumbers; and those for growing outdoors, called ridge cucumbers, which include gherkins for pickling. Apple varieties with small, round, yellow fruits which are tasty and juicy can also be found. Outdoor varieties are the easiest to grow in most gardens where there is shelter from the wind and a sunny spot. They are also less prone to pests and diseases than those grown under glass, which are more demanding in the conditions and attention they require.

CULTIVATION

Cucumber seeds require a temperature of 21-25°C (70-75°F) to germinate. Seed which has been 'chitted' – placed on a wet kitchen towel for one or two days before sowing – will be more successful.

Growing in a greenhouse

Sow seeds singly in pots or cellular trays in late February for planting in a heated greenhouse in late April to early May. Sow in late April for planting in an unheated greenhouse in late May. Transplant the seedlings carefully, into large pots of proprietary compost 60 cm (2 ft) apart, or two plants to a growing bag. Cordon cucumbers are traditionally grown by training the main stem up a stake and pinching out the growing point when it reaches the ridge of the roof.

▲ Sideshoots from the main stem are cut off two leaves beyond a young fruit.

The sideshoots are then tied to horizontal wires, 30 cm (12 in) apart, and cut off two leaves beyond a developing fruit or when about 60 cm (2 ft) long.

All-female varieties can be grown more simply by gently winding a string tied to the base of the stem and to the roof around the main stem. Sideshoots are removed altogether because all the fruit forms on the main stem.

Ordinary varieties, and occasionally all-female varieties, will produce male flowers which have only a stalk behind the flower

CUCUMBERS: VARIETIES AND TIMING

VARIETY	WHERE GROWN	NOTES
Burpless Tasty Green F_1	Outdoors	Slender, smooth skin. Easy to digest. Pick at 23 cm (9 in)
Bush Champion F_1	Outdoors	Compact bush habit. Resistant to cucumber mosaic virus
Conda F_1	Outdoors	Gherkin, heavy crop. Pickle or eat fresh
Crystal Apple	Outdoors	Round, pale fruits. Good flavour, quick growing
Femspot F_1	Heated greenhouse	All-female, disease-resistant
Petita F_1	Greenhouse	Mini-cucumbers 20 cm (8 in). All-female
Pepinex 69 F_1	Greenhouse	Large fruits. All-female
Telegraph Improved	Greenhouse	Long, straight, dark green fruits

and no tiny cucumber. They should be pinched out as they appear.

Cucumbers need to be kept well watered and fed regularly with a liquid fertiliser. Keep the humidity high by wetting the floor, and cool on hot days by shading.

Growing outdoors

Growing cucumbers outdoors is simpler than under glass, although the season is shorter. Grow them in large pots of proprietary compost, or in growing bags, in a sheltered, sunny spot. Or grow them in a garden bed. They can be left to scramble over the ground or trained on wires or netting, as in a greenhouse.

Seed can be raised indoors in late April for planting out in early June, or else sown directly into the compost in late May or early June. Cucumbers grown in garden soil need a high humus content, so prepare planting holes 45 cm (18 in) apart enriched with manure or garden compost.

Pinch out the growing point after six or seven leaves have developed on both the main shoot and on sideshoots that have not developed fruits. Leave sideshoots with flowers unpinched. Keep the plants well watered and feed once the cucumbers start to form. Do not pinch out male flowers on outdoor cucumbers as fertilisation is necessary for the fruits to form.

HARVESTING

Cut cucumbers and gherkins from the plant when young for best flavour. Do not allow fruits to mature fully on the plant and turn yellow; this will stop the plant flowering.

PESTS AND DISEASES

Red spider mite and whitefly are likely to be found on greenhouse crops, and slugs and snails will attack outdoors. Aphids may bring cucumber mosaic virus. Many soil-borne diseases can be avoided by using proprietary compost or growing bags.

Gherkins see Cucumbers and Gherkins

Leeks

Allium porrum
Alliaceae

The versatile leek is the easiest member of the onion family to grow. Late varieties are very hardy and will succeed further north than many other crops.

Most garden soils are suitable and pest and disease problems are generally less than with other onion crops. The leek is a biennial plant which is grown as an annual for its long shank of tightly wrapped leaves. Leeks can grow as tall as 45 cm (18 in), depending on variety.

Sometimes only the white shank is used in the kitchen after the coarsest outer leaves have been removed, but both white and green parts can be chopped for use in soups and casseroles. Young thinnings may be used as baby vegetables or 'mini-leeks' – used raw like salad onions or lightly cooked for a delicate flavour. Leeks are one of the most useful of winter vegetables.

TYPES AND VARIETIES

Leeks are classified according to when they are ready for harvest. A wide range of varieties is available, with many seed merchants offering their own selections.

• ***Early season***

(Ready in late summer and early autumn)

KING RICHARD Very early. Long, narrow shank with mild flavour; good for mini-leeks and exhibition. Not winter hardy.

LYON PRIZETAKER Long, thick, white shanks popular with exhibitors and cooks. For harvesting throughout autumn.

SWISS GIANT-ALBINSTAR Long and slender white shanks, good for exhibition. Autumn and early winter.

• ***Mid-season maincrop***

(Harvest from October to early spring)

AUTUMN MAMMOTH 2-ARGENTA and AUTUMN MAMMOTH-GOLIATH Thick, heavy stems with mild flavour. Long harvest period.

MUSSELBURGH Hardy, reliable and popular; short and thick.

• ***Late season***

(Harvest from New Year until spring)

GIANT WINTER 3 AND WINTRA Long stems, January-March.

LONGBOW Long shank, topped with dark green foliage. Harvest through winter to spring.

CULTIVATION

Leeks will grow in most garden soils that have been cultivated and manured and have reasonable drainage. Seed can be sown where the leeks are to grow or in a seedbed for transplanting when the permanent bed is available. Leeks need a long season to mature, but once ready they will remain in good condition for a long time.

Sow leeks outdoors in early spring. Put the seed thinly in shallow drills, in rows 30 cm (12 in) apart. Thin the seedlings to 15 cm (6 in) apart.

If transplanting, lift when 15-20 cm (6-8 in) tall, trim the ends of the leaves and roots and transplant into holes made with a dibber 15-20 cm (6-8 in) deep at the same spacing as for sown crops. Drop the plant into the hole so that the roots reach the soil at the bottom and water in without pushing back the soil.

▲ Trim the leaves and roots of young leeks.

For a very early crop – summer and early autumn – sow an early variety under glass in January-February and transplant in April. For a spring crop, sow a late variety in June and transplant in July.

Once established, leeks should be watered only in long dry periods and kept weed free. They can be grown on the flat or gradually earthed up by drawing soil around the plants as they grow, to gain a longer length of blanched stem.

For mini-leeks grow a long-stemmed variety such as King Richard, only 1 cm (½ in) apart.

HARVESTING AND STORAGE

Leeks may be used young or left in the ground to mature. Once ready, they will stand for a long time. Lift them carefully with a fork. The hardier varieties may be left in the ground throughout the winter.

PESTS AND DISEASES

Leeks are less susceptible to pests and diseases than other members of the onion family, but may suffer from leek rust, stem and bulb eelworm, onion fly and white rot.

Lettuces

Lactuca sativa
Compositae

Lettuces can be grown in almost any garden. For a few plants in the summer, a packet of mixed seed can be sown in short rows every 2-3 weeks between other plants in the flower border or in tubs.

For a spring crop in cold areas, sow a hardy variety in mid October under cloches and cut them in April. In milder areas, sow outdoors in late August-early September, thin in spring and cut in May.

For summer-autumn crops, sow outdoors from late March to July for harvesting from June to October.

For an early winter crop, sow outdoors in early August and protect with cloches from late September.

TYPES AND VARIETIES

There are four main types of lettuce – butterhead, crisphead, cos and loose-leaf. Butterhead are cabbage-shaped hearting lettuces growing to about 30 cm (12 in) across, with soft round leaves. Crispheads have crinkly, crunchy leaves and tight hearts, and are sometimes sold in the shops as 'Iceberg'. Cos are taller, more upright – reaching up to 25 cm (10 in) high – and have crisp, well-flavoured leaves. Loose-leaf types have crinkly, curly leaves that can be cut as needed, leaving the stump to grow again.

• ***Butterhead***

Spacing: outdoors – 30×30-35 cm (12×12-14 in); under glass – 23×23 cm (9×9 in) apart.

ALL THE YEAR ROUND Hardy; sow spring, summer and autumn. Slow to bolt.

AVONDEFIANCE For summer sowing, resistant to mildew and root aphid.
BUTTERCRUNCH (Sometimes listed as Crisphead) Sweet, dark green, compact, long standing. Sow spring and summer.
MAY KING Hardy. Sow spring and summer outdoors; in autumn sow either uncovered or under cold glass or cloche.
MUSETTE Summer and autumn crop. Good disease resistance. Sow late March to early August.
TOM THUMB Sow Mar-May 15×15cm (6×6in) apart. Very compact. Good for small areas, tubs, window boxes.

• *Crisphead*

Spacing: 30×30-35cm (12×12-14in) in the open; 23×23cm (9×9in) under glass.
AVONCRISP Good for summer sowings. Resistant to mildew and root aphid.
GREAT LAKES 659 For spring sowing. Large and spreading. Slow to bolt. Keeps well.
KELLY'S Crisp, bright green leaves. Sow November-January in cold greenhouse or frame.
LAKELAND Reliable, mildew and root-aphid resistant. For use in spring, summer and autumn. Sow late March–early August.
SALADIN Solid iceberg-type head, crisp and sweet. Dark green outer leaves. Stands well. Sow mid February until late July.
WARPATH Sow spring and summer at 23×23cm (9×9in) spacing. Compact heads of good flavour.
WEBB'S WONDERFUL Large, solid, crisp heads; dark green crumpled leaves. Long standing. Sow late March to early August.

• *Cos type*

Spacing: 30×30-35cm (12×12-14in) apart.
LITTLE GEM Small growing, tight hearts, good flavour. Sow 15×15cm (6×6in), spring to autumn.
LOBJOITS GREEN COS Large, tall and upright. Dark green, crisp, sweet leaves. Sow spring and autumn outside.
VALDOR Sow August-September outdoors or under glass. Firm heads in early spring.
VALMAINE Large and crisp. For loose-leaf use or for hearting. Mildew resistance. Sow summer and autumn.
WINTER DENSITY Hardy for autumn sowing outdoors, or spring to summer. Small growing; dense, crisp hearts with good flavour.

• *Loose-leaf*

Spacing: 30×30cm (12×12in). Loose-leaf varieties can also be grown close together and harvested as separate leaves. Sow early spring to summer.
LOLLO BIONDA Pale green, very indented leaves.
LOLLO ROSSA Pretty, crisp, frilly, red-tinged leaves.
RED SALAD BOWL Very attractive, oak-shaped leaves tinged with red.
SALAD BOWL Green oak-leaf lettuce. Rarely bolts.

CULTIVATION AND HARVESTING

Lettuces need an open site with a well-draining and humus-rich soil. Acid soils are not suitable – a pH of 6.5-7.5 is required. Slight shading is possible for summer varieties; but avoid cold, wet and exposed sites for winter crops.

As the time from sowing to harvest is short at the height of the season, lettuces can be sown in between rows of slower plants, such as parsnips, or in a spare corner of the flowerbed. The attractive loose-leaf varieties, for instance, can be used as edging plants or grown in tubs.

Lettuces are best sown very thinly in shallow drills where they are to grow. If raising seed to transplant, use pots or peat blocks and ensure the plants are well watered before and after planting. For summer crops, sow outdoors in short rows every 2-3 weeks to give a continual supply that does not all mature at once. For best results, sow at the time of year recommended on the packet.

The seedlings of hearted lettuces must be thinned before they become crowded.

Loose-leaf varieties may be grown close together or at 30cm (12in) spacings. Cut the leaves as required or else cut each plant at the base after 6 weeks and leave the stump to regrow.

Cos varieties can also be grown this way for a continual supply of fresh leaves. Summer lettuce must be kept well watered especially in hot, dry periods to prevent the plants bolting (running to seed before being ready to eat).

▲ Loose-leaf types can be cut and left to regrow.

LETTUCES: GETTING THE TIMING RIGHT

WHEN TO SOW	WHERE TO SOW	WHEN TO HARVEST
Early Feb-Mar	Sow under glass; plant out under cloches	Mid May-June
Late Mar-July	Outdoors	June-Oct
Early Aug	Outdoors. Cover with cloches in late September	Nov-Dec
Aug-Sep	Outdoors in mild areas	May
Sep-Oct	Heated glass, 7°C (45°F)	Jan-Mar
Mid Oct	Outdoors, under cloches	Apr

For hearted lettuce, pull up as soon as the heart is formed. Left longer, a flower stalk will grow and the plant will become bitter and unusable. Once lifted, use immediately or store for a few days in the refrigerator in a polythene bag.

PESTS AND DISEASES

Birds and slugs are troublesome. Root aphid and cutworm attack roots and stems at ground level, especially during summer. Greenfly can make the leaves unusable and transmit viruses. Damping off is a problem with seedlings. Downy mildew and grey mould are worse in cold, wet conditions.

Lesser known salad crops

CORN SALAD Also known as lamb's lettuce, corn salad is a hardy annual forming a rosette of small, flat leaves with a flavour between that of lettuce and dandelion. It is most usefully sown in August and September as a winter crop. Thin to 10cm (4in) apart. Keep well watered in dry periods and free of weeds. Harvest like spinach.
ROCKET Salad rocket is a hardy annual which forms a rosette of deeply lobed leaves with a sharp spicy flavour. Older leaves may be cooked like spinach. Sow in succession from early spring outdoors and again in early autumn in mild areas; otherwise sow under glass in September for a winter seedling crop. Pick the leaves when about 5-8cm (2-3¼in) long, and allow the stump to regrow.
CHINESE LETTUCE Chinese stem lettuce (also known as Celtuce) grows on a stem up to 30cm (12in) high. Cultivate it like lettuce.

Marrows and Courgettes

Cucurbita pepo

Cucurbitaceae

Marrows and courgettes (marrow fruits cut young) are tender annuals originating in the Americas and easy to grow in a border or growing bags on a sunny patio. Courgettes

Pumpkins and squashes

Unusual types of marrow, pumpkins and squash are grown in the same way as marrows. The types for use during the summer mostly have soft skins, like courgettes, and can be treated the same way; those for use during winter have hard skins and can be successfully stored. Edible gourds may be listed in catalogues as squash.

can be cut from each plant throughout the summer; indeed, cutting is important to encourage new fruits to form. Courgettes is the French name, zucchini the Italian.

The plants are quick growing with large indented, slightly prickly leaves and stems and large edible yellow flowers. A bush variety will grow to about 1 m (3 ft) across while trailing types can reach several metres long. Two or three plants are enough to supply a family with courgettes all summer.

TYPES AND VARIETIES

Varieties sold as courgettes are strains of bush marrow that will produce a succession of small fruits, as long as they are harvested regularly. All will produce larger fruits as well if left to develop.

ALL GREEN BUSH An all-rounder. A heavy crop of green courgettes or marrows.

AMBASSADOR F_1 Bush type with long fruiting season.

EARLY GEM (STORR'S GREEN F_1) Early bush variety with bright green fruits; marrows or courgettes.

GOLD RUSH F_1 Compact bush type with golden yellow fruits, best for courgettes.

LONG GREEN TRAILING Variety for the larger garden. Has distinctive dark green fruits with pale green stripes. Long Green Bush also available.

TIGER CROSS F_1 – Attractive striped fruits for marrows or courgettes. Resistant to cucumber mosaic virus.

CULTIVATION

Marrows are a tender crop and need a sunny site – and crops will be heavier during a hot summer. Plants grown in a border will do best in humus-rich soil with good drainage. Prepare planting holes 30 cm (12 in) wide, with garden compost or manure dug in.

Trailing varieties can be grown on strong supports or along the ground; bush varieties are more compact.

If cloches are available, seed can be sown indoors in mid April, two to a pot or cellular tray, growing on the stronger seedling for 5-6 weeks until it has three or four true leaves. Chitting will improve germination – place the seed on moist kitchen paper in a warm place for a day or two before sowing. Plant the seedlings out at a spacing of 1 m (3 ft) apart for bush varieties or 1.5 m (5 ft) for trailing types. Growing bags are particularly suitable for marrows and courgettes – two plants to a bag.

Where no protection from frost is available, sowing must be delayed until early or mid May. Seeds can be sown directly in the planting position in a growing bag or in pots for transplanting.

Young plants will need protection from slugs and snails. Once established, they grow quickly and thrive in sunshine, but mulch them to conserve moisture. The plants must be kept well watered but do not require feeding until the fruits begin to form. A liquid tomato fertiliser is suitable.

Deep yellow male and female flowers appear, the female having a small, unformed fruit behind it. They will be pollinated by insects. Cut the fruits throughout the season

▲ Flowers may be male (left) or female (right).

to keep the plants flowering. Courgettes should be cut when 10-15 cm (4-6 in) long; marrows will have the best flavour if cut when 20-25 cm (8-10 in) long.

HARVESTING AND STORAGE

Harvest courgettes and marrows by cutting the stalk behind the fruits, taking care not to cut leaves or flowers. Courgettes should be used within a few days, or frozen. Marrows will keep longer in a cool but frost-free place. If they are allowed to mature on the plant and are brought in before the frosts, they can be stored up to Christmas.

PESTS AND DISEASES

Slugs and snails can destroy young plants and spoil the fruits. Cucumber mosaic virus causes stunted, twisted growth with a yellow mottling on leaves and fruits.

Onions and Shallots

Allium cepa
Alliaceae

Onions can be grown easily if the soil is fertile and the drainage is good, although some pests and diseases may be a problem. Shallots are also easy to grow and have extremely good keeping qualities.

TYPES AND VARIETIES

Onions are biennials grown as annuals. They can be grown from seed or from 'sets' – small bulbs from the previous year. Growing from sets is quicker, easier and reliable, but more expensive.

• ***Spring-sown bulb onions***

Grown from seed sown in spring, and harvested in September-October.

AILSA CRAIG Exhibitors' favourite. Large, good colour and flavour.

ALBION F_1 Large, white-skinned globes.

BEDFORDSHIRE CHAMPION Large, brown skin.

BRUNSWICK Red skin, mild flavour. Good for salads.

HYGRO F_1 High quality, mild, yellow-skinned and round.

RED BARON Dark red skin, strong flavour.

RIJNSBURGER Several strains available, firm, good quality.

• ***Autumn sown bulb onions***

The onions are grown from seed sown in autumn and are overwintered for harvest the following June-July. They generally do not store for as long as spring-sown bulbs. In order of maturity: 'Express Yellow F_1'; 'Buffalo F_1'; 'Imai Yellow'; 'Senshyu Semi Globe Yellow'.

• ***Bulb onions grown from sets***

Only a few varieties are available as sets, but they will give a reliable crop of good-quality bulbs which will store well. Sets are useful where the growing season is shorter. Some sets are sold after heat treatment to reduce the chance of bolting. Examples are 'Centurion F_1', 'Sturon', 'Stuttgart Giant', 'Turbo'. A few varieties often grown from seed may also be offered as sets.

• ***Shallots***

Shallots are perennial onions with distinctive flavour, usually sold as sets. They can be used fresh in salads, in cooking or for pickling. They store well.

ATLANTIC Early and high yielding. Crisp and crunchy.

CREATION F_1 New hybrid grown from seed.

HATIVE DE NIORT Large, brown skinned. Exhibitors' choice.

PIKANT Strong flavoured. Bolt resistant.

• ***Pickling and mini-onions***

A few varieties are sold specifically for pickling or as mini-onions. Use fresh as salad onions or pickle in vinegar.

BARLETTA White skins for pickling or mini-onions.

GIANT ZITTAU Brown skinned. Grow at close spacing for pickling.

PARIS SILVERSKIN Tiny, white cocktail onions. Quick growing. Will succeed in poor soils.

PURPLETTE Multipurpose, red-skinned onion. Grow as mini-onions for salad or pickling, or grow for bulb onions.

• ***Salad and bunching onions***

Salad onions come in two types – the familiar spring onions, which are pulled as the bulb starts to swell, and Japanese bunching onions, which grow long and straight. Japanese types may be earthed up for a longer blanched length and can be left in the ground for use as required. Use both for salads or oriental cooking.

HIKARI For harvest late summer. Not winter hardy.

ISHIKURA Long straight white stems.

NORTH HOLLAND BLOODRED-REDMATE Red, crisp and mild. Can also be grown to maturity for bulb onions.
WHITE LISBON Familiar spring onion variety. Mild flavoured and quick growing.
WHITE LISBON WINTER HARDY Very hardy. First to harvest from an autumn sowing.

• *Welsh onions*

Welsh onions grow in large clumps and are very hardy, remaining green all year. The hollow leaves up to 45-60cm (18-24in) tall can be cut and used like chives, although they have a stronger flavour. Alternatively, divide the plants and use them as salad onions, raw or in oriental dishes. Sow in spring and thin until clumps are 30×23cm (12×9in) apart. Divide every 2-3 years and replant the outer sections.

CULTIVATION

Onions need a sunny position in fertile and cultivated ground with good drainage. Manure should be dug in the previous autumn and a firm, fine seedbed prepared if using seed. Add lime if necessary. Sow seed thinly in shallow drills; germination may be slow.

▲ Sow onion seeds thinly in a sunny bed.

Onions should be grown as part of a rotation system wherever possible to reduce the build-up of soil-borne diseases.

The main crop of bulb onions is harvested in early autumn, and most varieties will store well into the winter. The spacing given will provide a good crop of medium-sized onions; use a wider spacing for larger ones. For earlier crops, raise seed under glass in January and transplant in April, or sow under cloches.

Bulb onions need to be kept weed free and watered only in dry periods. In late summer, the foliage turns yellow and falls over. Ensure that the tops of the bulbs are exposed and leave them in the ground for a fortnight to ripen.

▲ Leave the bulbs exposed to ripen.

For autumn-sown bulb onions, look at the back of the seed packet for the precise sowing time for your area of the country. Thin the seedlings in early spring and apply a top dressing of general fertiliser.

Sets should be planted so that the tops are just at ground level. Plant shallot sets in a drill 15cm (6in) apart in rows 20cm (8in) apart, so that only the tips protrude – in both cases push them back into the ground if they are lifted by birds or frost.

Sow shallots from seed as for spring-sown bulb onions, with seedlings at 5cm (2in) centres. Pickling onions should be left unthinned to encourage a crop of small bulbs. Salad onions can be obtained from the thinnings of other types, or from successional sowings from spring through to late summer. Sow them in close rows or broadcast thinly.

Harvesting can begin 6-8 weeks after sowing. Cloches will make the first crops available sooner from sowings made in August or spring.

HARVESTING

Bulb onions need to be dried fully before storage. Lift with a fork and dry them on the surface in good weather, or under cover. Store only sound bulbs; use any imperfect or large-necked bulbs first. Store in trays, nets, old tights or in onion ropes in a cool, dry place. Salad onions may be lifted as needed, at 1-2cm (up to 1in) across for bulbing types. Japanese varieties may be harvested when pencil thick or left until the size of small leeks.

PESTS AND DISEASES

Bulb onions are the type that are most susceptible to pests and diseases, but other onion crops may be affected as well. Onion fly and stem and bulb eelworm are common pests; downy mildew and white rot may also occur.

ONIONS: GETTING THE TIMING AND SPACING RIGHT

VARIETY	SOWING	SPACING	HARVEST
Bulb onions (spring sown)	Feb-Apr	23-30×4cm (9-12×1½in)	Sep-Oct
Bulb onions (autumn sown)	Aug	23-30×4cm (9-12×1½in)	June-July
Bulb onion sets	Plant in Mar-Apr	25×5cm (10×2in)	Aug
Shallots	Plant in mid Feb/mid Mar	20×15cm (8×6in)	July
Pickling onions	Apr	30×1cm (12×⅜in)	July-Aug
Salad onions (spring sown)	Feb-June	10×2.5cm (4×1in)	June-Nov
Salad onions (autumn sown)	Aug-Sep	10×2.5cm (4×1in)	Apr-June

Growing garlic

A hardy perennial of the onion family, garlic needs a long growing season, so should be planted either in late autumn or early spring.

▲ Plant cloves in late autumn or early spring.

Plant single cloves 15cm (6in) apart each way with only the tips protruding. Lift in July-August and dry thoroughly. Garlic can be stored for several months.

Parsnips

Pastinacea sativa
Umbelliferae

Parsnips can be slow to germinate but from then on they are easy crops to grow. They are biennials grown as annuals. They thrive in most garden soils which can offer a sunny or lightly shaded site. The choice of canker-resistant varieties and use of crop rotation will help to avoid disease.

TYPES AND VARIETIES
Varieties can be selected for their flavour and according to their length – choose shorter varieties for shallower soils and canker resistance.

AVONRESISTER Small, bulbous-shaped roots with good canker resistance. Creamy, sweet flesh.

COBHAM IMPROVED MARROW Medium-sized, wedge-shaped, white roots of fine flavour. Good resistance to canker.

GLADIATOR F_1 A high-yielding, high-quality, sweet-flavoured variety with good canker resistance. Wedge-shaped.

LANCER A bayonet-shaped variety with excellent flavour and canker resistance.

TENDER AND TRUE Long, smooth, white, fleshy roots of very good flavour. Good for the kitchen or exhibition. High canker resistance.

WHITE GEM Early maturing, large, wedge-shaped roots with smooth skin and white flesh of excellent flavour. Good canker resistance.

CULTIVATION
The best results will be obtained in deep, cultivated sandy loam soil, with good drainage. Parsnips can be grown in a sunny position or light shade. Lime very acid soils. Parsnips should ideally follow a well-manured crop in a rotation system; fresh manure can cause the roots to fork.

Sow the seeds from mid February to April in shallow drills 40cm (16in) apart, and thin to 15cm (6in) apart. Or sow 2 or 3 seeds to a station and thin to the strongest seedling.

Germination takes up to 28 days. Put a few radish seeds in with the parsnips to come up early and show where the row is. Water during dry spells. Quicker crops, such as lettuce and radish, can be sown between rows while the parsnips develop.

HARVESTING AND STORAGE
Parsnips can be lifted with a fork once the leaves have died down. Parsnips are very hardy and can be left in the ground until needed; indeed, frost is said to improve the flavour by turning the starch in the roots to sugar. Some may be lifted in autumn for use when the ground is too hard for harvesting – keep these cool in sand or damp peat.

PESTS AND DISEASES
Parsnips may be attacked by carrot fly, celery leaf miner and sometimes aphids. Parsnip canker can be avoided by the choice of resistant varieties, by using a crop rotation system, by liming and by using good general cultural practice.

Peas

Pisum sativum
Leguminosae

Young peas picked straight from the vine are among the sweetest tastes of summer, superior to anything that can be bought in the shops. Once peas have been picked, their eating quality deteriorates rapidly.

TYPES AND VARIETIES

• ***Round-seeded***
Hardy varieties of pea that can be sown in the open – or under protection in late autumn or early spring for an early crop.

• ***Wrinkle-seeded***
Less hardy varieties that cannot be sown until the soil warms up in the spring. They are sweeter than round-seeded types. There are three groups of wrinkle-seeded peas – first earlies which can be picked 11-12 weeks after sowing, second earlies after 13-14 weeks, and maincrop after 15-18 weeks. A single sowing of different types will give a short succession of crop, and a series of sowings will give the longest season. Mildew-resistant varieties are recommended for mid summer sowings.

Leafless peas are new wrinkle-seeded varieties with more clinging tendrils than leaves, able to cling to supports without being tied. The pods grow on the top of the plants away from slugs and are easy to pick.

• ***Petis pois***
Sweet dwarf varieties of garden peas that are picked when they are young and tender.

• ***Mangetout***
The pods and seeds are eaten whole, and are generally the easiest to grow. There are two types – flat podded, with tiny undeveloped seeds (also called sugar peas or snow peas); and snap peas, with full, fleshy pods which snap if broken. When fully mature, snap peas may be used whole or podded like garden peas.

• ***Asparagus pea***
A half-hardy bushy plant unrelated to the pea. It grows 15-30cm (6-12in) high and up to 60cm (2ft) across. It has red flowers which develop into green-winged pods, best harvested when 2.5cm (1in) long. The pods have the flavour of asparagus and are cooked like mangetout.

CULTIVATION
Mangetout varieties are the easiest to grow. To sow peas, use a hoe or spade to draw out a flat drill 15cm (6in) wide and 5cm (2in) deep. Space the seeds 5-8cm (2-3¼in) apart each way along the drill – losses can be expected in overwintered sowings. Make the next drill 60cm (2ft) away, or as far away as the expected height of the plants. Cover the seed and protect from birds.

▲ Pea plants can be supported by twigs or nets.

Support is necessary for all but the leafless kinds – use twiggy sticks stuck in the ground or a line of plastic netting held up on canes.

Crops will be disappointing on poor or wet soils, and in hot, dry summers.

Asparagus peas need a warm, sunny site in light, fertile soil. Sow in May at 20cm (8in) intervals and 40cm (16in) between rows and water well; in colder areas sow under glass and plant out in June. A second sowing will give a longer cropping period. Pick regularly during August.

PEAS: VARIETIES AND TIMING

VARIETY	TYPE	SOWING	HARVEST
Feltham First Douce Provence Meteor	Round-seeded hardy	Oct-Nov or Jan-Mar	May-June
Early Onward Kelvedon Wonder Little Marvel Hurst Beagle	Round, or first early wrinkled	Mar	June-July
Hurst Green Shaft Onward Cavalier Senator Leafless vars.	Second early and maincrop wrinkled	Mar-June	June-Sep
Kelvedon Wonder Cavalier Senator	Mildew-resistant varieties for mid summer sowing	June-July	Sep-Oct
Wavereux Oregon Sugar Pod Sugar Snap	Petis pois and mangetout	Mar-June	July-Sep

HARVESTING AND STORAGE

First earlies can be picked 11-12 weeks after sowing; second earlies after 13-14 weeks; maincrop after 15-16 weeks. For the most succulent peas and mangetout, begin picking as soon as the first pods are ready, and use or freeze immediately. Peas may also be dried, by leaving them on the plant until fully mature and hanging the whole plant in a shed at the end of the season.

PESTS AND DISEASES

Peas must be protected from birds, slugs and possibly mice. Pea moth larvae and thrips may be troublesome in mid summer.

Peppers, Sweet and Hot

Capsicum annuum

Solanaceae

Sweet peppers (also known as capsicums) are hollow with the seeds held on a central core inside the thick fleshy skins. They are green ripening to red, sometimes to white, yellow or deep purple. The flesh is crunchy and juicy; fully ripe fruits are the sweetest. Hot peppers (cayenne and chilli) have much smaller, pointed fruits, 2.5-5cm (1-2in) long or more, depending on variety.

TYPES AND VARIETIES

• ***Sweet peppers***

ARIANNE F_1 Thick-walled variety ripening to orange. Compact plants.

CANAPE F_1 High yielding and early. May be grown outdoors.

GYPSY F_1 Early, light green, tapered fruits, ripening to deep red. Good yields under glass. Resistant to tobacco mosaic virus.

LUTEUS F_1 Quick growing, large, thick-walled fruits, green, turning to a mild, sweet yellow. Resistant to tobacco mosaic virus.

NEW ACE F_1 Reliable and early to crop. Green fruits, turning to red, thin walled, square shape. Best grown under glass.

REDSKIN F_1 Compact plants around 38cm (15in) tall, ideal for containers outside or even a large windowsill. Early fruiting, green to red.

SLIM PIM F_1 Japanese type, 10cm (4in) slim fruits, green to red, for cooking whole in oriental dishes.

Seed companies offer mixed colours.

• ***Hot peppers***

APACHE F_1 Compact plants bearing good crop of medium-hot chillis. Green to red.

CHILLI SERRANO Prolific variety with small, very hot fruits. Green to red.

HUNGARIAN WAX Tapered fruits 10cm (4in) long, sweet in flavour when picked young, maturing to hot. Green, ripening through yellow and orange to red.

CULTIVATION

Both sweet and hot peppers are best grown in a greenhouse or under polythene. Sweet peppers may also be grown outdoors in a sheltered and sunny spot; and compact varieties can be raised on a warm windowsill.

Sow seed under heated glass in March and pot seedlings on in stages. Plant in 20 or 23cm (8 or 9in) pots, or growing bags, or in the greenhouse soil 45cm (18in) apart.

If growing sweet peppers outdoors, plant out in May under cloches or June in the open. Support will be needed.

▲ Outdoor plants need support with stakes.

Keep plants moist. Once the fruits have started to form, feed regularly with liquid tomato fertiliser. Mist with water to discourage red spider mite. High temperatures may induce flowers to drop in sweet peppers, but will improve flavour in hot types.

The fruits of both sweet and hot peppers may be used at any time between green and red (colour depending on variety) once grown to full size. For fullest flavour allow them to mature on the plant. Pick while the skin is smooth and shiny. They keep in the refrigerator for up to two weeks. Peppers freeze well and hot types may also be dried.

PESTS AND DISEASES

Peppers are susceptible to red spider mite, aphids and whitefly. Blossom end rot may also be a problem.

Potatoes

Solanum tuberosum

Solanaceae

Potatoes are easy to grow, tolerant of most soils and can also be grown successfully in large pots or tubs. Some diseases can be a problem and potatoes are not frost-hardy.

Potatoes consist of three groups – first earlies, second earlies and maincrop. Maincrop are the 'old' potatoes that are stored and used through winter. In most gardens it is impracticable to grow enough for all your needs, but an early variety is worth growing for its flavour. The plants grow about 60cm (2ft) high and wide.

Potatoes are members of the nightshade family, and all green parts – shoots, tubers exposed to the light which turn green, and any green tomato-like fruits which form – are poisonous.

TYPES AND VARIETIES

A wide range of varieties is available. Some are less susceptible to disease than others. A few of the freely available varieties are as follows:

• ***First earlies***

ARRAN PILOT Heavy cropper with resistance to scab and drought. White skin and flesh of good flavour.

MARIS BARD Very early with heavy yield. White skin and creamy flesh.

PENTLAND JAVELIN Very white, waxy flesh. Resistant to eelworm and scab.

• ***Second earlies***

ESTIMA A heavy crop of white-skinned tubers with yellow flesh. Cooks and keeps well. Resistant to blight, slugs and drought.

NADINE A new variety with exhibition looks, white skin and cream flesh. Stays moist and firm on cooking. Resistant to eelworm.

WILJA Dutch-bred variety with light yellow skin and flesh. High yielding and resistant to blight.

• ***Maincrop***

CARA High yield of pink tubers, good for baking. Resistant to blight and eelworm.

DESIREE High yield of red-skinned tubers with yellow flesh, good for chips or baking. Succeeds in most soil types and in drought.

MARIS PIPER High yields of white-skinned tubers with cream flesh, especially good for baking or chips. Eelworm resistant.

CULTIVATION

Potatoes are susceptible to soil pests and virus diseases, so ensure that these problems do not build up in the garden. Potatoes should be grown in a different part of the garden each year in as long a rotation as possible. Only 'seed' potatoes which are certified as being virus free should be used for planting. Early varieties require 'chitting' – keeping the seed in a well-lit, frost-free place so that the eyes can develop into short shoots before planting out.

A first early crop can be grown in warmer areas of the country; second earlies and maincrops can be grown everywhere, avoiding frost pockets or heavy shade. The soil should be fertile but most soil types are suitable. The seed tubers should be planted in furrows 7.5-15cm (3-6in) deep and then covered with soil.

As shoots reach 23cm (9in), loosen the soil between rows and pull it up around the leaves to ensure that tubers are not exposed to light – a process called earthing up.

▲ Draw soil around plants to cover the tubers.

POTATOES: GETTING THE TIMING RIGHT

TYPE	PLANTING DISTANCE	HARVEST
First earlies Arran Pilot Maris Bard Pentland Javelin	End March 30×60cm (12×24in)	June-July When flowers fully open
Second earlies Estima Nadine Wilja	First half of April 30×60cm (12 × 24in)	July-Aug When flowers fully open
Maincrop Cara Desiree Maris Piper	Second half of April 38×75cm (15×30in)	Sept-Oct When top growth dies down

▲ When harvesting, lift all tubers from soil.

Water regularly once the tubers begin to form. You can lift a plant gently with a fork to see them.

HARVESTING AND STORAGE

Potatoes should be lifted carefully with a fork to limit damage. Leave them to dry on the surface for a few hours. All the tubers must be removed from the soil to prevent disease being carried over to next year. Store healthy potatoes in the dark, in an airy, frost-free place. Maincrop tubers will store for several months if allowed to mature and provided the skins do not come off when rubbed with the fingers.

PESTS AND DISEASES

Aphids may carry virus disease. Potato cyst eelworm, slugs and wireworms may cause damage. Potato blight can ruin crops.

Pumpkins and Squashes see Marrows and Courgettes

Radishes

Raphanus sativus
Cruciferae

Radishes are quick and easy to grow and are an ideal crop for small areas. As well as the familiar red roots, there are two other main types – white Japanese mooli varieties and winter radishes, such as Black Spanish Round which grows to around 450g (1lb) in weight. Small salad varieties have leaves 13cm (5¼in) high but the larger types may reach 60cm (24in) high with a spread of 45cm (18in). All are grown as annuals.

TYPES AND VARIETIES

• *Summer salad varieties*

Varieties may be red, red and white, or all white – and either globe-shaped or cylindrical. Sow January-February under cloches, March to mid summer outdoors, at fortnightly intervals for a continual supply. Space the plants 2.5cm (1in) apart, in rows 15cm (6in) apart.

CHERRY BELLE Round scarlet roots with crisp white flesh, especially good for early sowings.

FRENCH BREAKFAST Cylindrical red roots with white tip. Mild, sweet and crisp when harvested young.

LONG WHITE ICICLE Use when 7-15cm (3-6in) long. Has an excellent flavour; crisp and mild.

SCARLET GLOBE A quick-maturing variety for sowing from January to August. Has a pungent taste.

• *Japanese radish – Mooli*

White-skinned, up to 30cm (12in) long. Use fresh or cooked. Sow 5-10cm (2-4in) apart in rows 15cm (6in) apart.

APRIL CROSS F_1 For spring or late summer sowing. Stays in good condition in the ground, slow to bolt.

MINO EARLY A crisp, tender and mild variety. Sow June-September for use in autumn-winter.

MINOWASE SUMMER F_1 Sow in summer. Harvest from when roots are 15cm (6in). Late to bolt.

• *Winter radishes*

Sow late July and August. Thin to 15cm (6in) apart, in rows 23cm (9in) apart. Harvest after 10-12 weeks.

BLACK SPANISH ROUND Black skin, crisp white flesh of good flavour. Hardy.

CHINA ROSE Deep pink skin, white flesh, 12cm (4¾in) long.

MANTANGHONG F_1 Tennis-ball-sized Chinese radish. Light green skin and magenta flesh. For salads or stir fries.

CULTIVATION

Radishes are easy to grow. Choose a sunny site, except for summer sowings which do better in slight shade. Larger varieties need an open, stone-free soil. Ground which has been manured for a previous crop is ideal.

▲ Harvest summer radishes when young.

Radishes are quick to germinate – the small salad varieties requiring very little space – and are ready in only 3-6 weeks. Sow in shallow drills 1cm (⅜ in) deep, very thinly – or broadcast them – and rake over lightly. Thin if necessary as soon as the seedlings emerge. Water when dry to keep the plants growing quickly.

Winter radish is sown in July and August and is ready for use after 10-12 weeks.

HARVESTING AND STORAGE

Summer radish is at its best when grown quickly and used young. If left too long, roots become strong flavoured and woody. Japanese varieties can be used when about 15cm (6in) long, or left in the ground longer if wanted for cooking.

Once pulled, use summer radish as soon as possible. In mild areas, winter radishes can be left in the ground until required, with a covering of soil or straw to protect them from frost. In colder areas, lift in October and store in a cool, frost-free place.

PESTS AND DISEASES

Radishes are largely untroubled by disease but may need protection from birds, slugs, flea beetle and cabbage root fly.

Spinach

Spinacia oleracea
Chenopodiaceae

Spinach, a hardy and quick-growing annual, is grown as a cut-and-come-again crop. The young leaves are picked as required and used in salads or cooked – young, raw spinach leaves have the flavour of pea pods. Successional sowings can make spinach available throughout the year.

TYPES AND VARIETIES

Spinach is usually divided into winter and summer varieties, but many newer strains can be used in either season.

BROAD-LEAVED PRICKLY Very hardy winter variety with prickly coated seeds.

Spinach beet and seakale beet

Spinach beet (also known as perpetual spinach) and seakale beet (also known as chard or Swiss chard) are both hardy biennials and easy to grow. Although they are closely related to beetroot they are grown for their leaves, which can be used like spinach.

Spinach beet looks similar to spinach, but the leaves are larger and thicker and the plant withstands dry summer weather much better. The stems are green and a supply of leaves can be picked throughout the year. Seakale beet is taller, with leaves up to 45cm (18in) long.

Both these forms of leaf beet will grow in most soils. Sow seed in a sunny position in April by placing 3 or 4 seeds together at 23cm (9in) intervals along shallow drills, 38cm (15in) apart.

Thin to the strongest seedling, then water well in dry weather and apply liquid feed if taking leaves frequently. A second sowing can be made in July to give a supply through to the next spring.

As with spinach, leaf beet should be picked regularly to keep it growing, and used straight from the garden. Covering the plants with cloches or with straw will help to protect them over winter. Leaf beet is not commonly troubled by pests and diseases.

WILD SEAKALE – A LUXURY VEGETABLE

Seakale is a perennial plant with coarse, rhubarb-like leaves that grows wild on the southern coast of Britain. Once common in gardens, it is now an unusual luxury vegetable. It grows easily on well-drained limy soil. In spring, the young shoots are blanched under large pots. Grow it from seeds or crowns planted in spring.

MEDANIA Vigorous and versatile with distinctive red stems and thick, smooth leaves. Can be sown from spring through to autumn. Slow to bolt and resistant to mildew.

MONNOPA Strong-growing plants with thick, round, medium green leaves of good flavour. Lower in oxalic acid than other varieties and thus thought to be more suitable for children to eat. Sow the seeds in spring or autumn.

CULTIVATION

Spinach grows best in fertile soil which ideally has been manured the previous year. Sow summer crops thinly in shallow drills, 30cm (12in) apart, from March onwards every 2-3 weeks to give a continuous supply. Early sowings should be made in full sun, but in late spring and summer, spinach can be sown as a catch crop between other, taller vegetables, such as peas and beans, which will lend some shade.

The seedlings should be thinned as soon as they emerge to grow 15cm (6in) apart, using the later thinnings in the kitchen.

Regular picking is necessary to keep the plants growing. Spinach needs a good supply of water, especially in hot weather, but in prolonged hot spells, plants may bolt rapidly.

Autumn sowings are made in late August and September using a winter-hardy or bolt-resistant variety in a sunny position. Crops in cold areas will benefit from being covered with cloches in October or November and can be used from mid October through to April.

HARVESTING

Summer spinach is harvested by breaking off the young, outside leaves from each plant. Up to half of the leaves can be picked at a time.

When growth is vigorous in the summer, plants may be cropped several times within a month or so, before the leaves become more bitter as the plant starts to flower.

Alternatively, cut the whole plant at the base of the leaves while still young and leave the stump to regrow.

Pick leaves from autumn crops more sparingly.

▲ Instead of removing separate leaves, you can cut off the whole plant and leave it to regrow.

PESTS AND DISEASES

Spinach is largely untroubled by pests. Seedlings are susceptible to damping off and downy mildew, and spinach blight – a form of cucumber mosaic virus – can occur.

Swedes

Brassica napus
Cruciferae

Swedes are biennial plants, grown as annuals and are among the hardiest of all the root crops. They produce globe-shaped roots about 10cm (4in) in diameter. The leaves grow to about 25cm (10in) with a spread of 40cm (16in).

VARIETIES

Only a few cultivars are available.

BEST OF ALL Hardy variety which stores well or can be left in the ground until required. Yellow flesh under purple skin.

LIZZY Bred for its soft, buttery texture and sweet taste.

MARIAN High yielding with some resistance to club root and mildew. Purple skinned with fine flavour and texture.

CULTIVATION

For details of the soil requirement and pests and diseases, see Brassicas.

Sow swedes where they are to grow, in drills 38cm (15in) apart and thin to 23cm (9in) apart within the rows. The main sowing period is from mid May in northern areas to June farther south. Beyond thinning, weeding and watering in dry periods and checking for pests, swedes require little attention.

▲ Harvesting swedes after 16 weeks.

HARVESTING AND STORAGE

Swedes can be harvested in early autumn, before fully grown, or left in the ground until required, up to the following March.

For storage, lift in late autumn with a fork, twist off the tops and store in outdoor clamps or boxes of sand or dry soil in a frost-free shed.

Sweetcorn

Zea mays
Graminae

Sweetcorn is a half-hardy annual, most likely to succeed in the south where it needs a sunny and sheltered site, good soil and plenty of water. Space is also necessary, as many varieties reach 1.5m (5ft) tall, and sweetcorn needs to be grown together in square blocks to aid pollination.

TYPES AND VARIETIES

Modern F_1 hybrids make sweetcorn a more reliable crop in Britain than formerly, and early maturing varieties may be tried in northerly areas. Supersweet varieties are genetically different from standard varieties, with higher sugar levels.

• ***Standard varieties***

EARLIKING F_1/EARLIBELLE F_1 Reliable early varieties, cropping late July-August.

JUBILEE F_1 Late vigorous variety cropping in August-September. Good-quality cobs 19cm (7½in) long.

KELVEDON GLORY F_1 Popular variety giving good yields of well-filled 18 cm (7in) cobs in mid August-September.

SUNDANCE F_1 Mid season variety for September cropping. Vigorous even in poor summers and in northern districts.

• *Supersweet varieties*
Most seed companies offer their own varieties. For example:
CONQUEST F_1 Early maturity in mid August. Good for short growing seasons. Cobs 18-20 cm long (7-8 in).
HONEY AND CREAM F_1 Supersweet variety with cobs which are mostly yellow, but with some white ones among them. Very attractive. Ready to harvest 80 days after sowing.
SWEET 77 Moderate yields of large cobs.

CULTIVATION

Sweetcorn grows best in deep, humus-rich and well-drained soil, but more important is the need for a sunny and sheltered site. Seed may be sown outside where it is to grow from mid May onwards, or as soon as the soil is warm: 10°C (50°F) is required for good germination and establishment. Cloches or plastic mulches are ideal for warming up the soil.

Seed may also be started indoors in April, one seed to a pot or cellular tray, for planting out in May or early June.

▲ Sweetcorn must be grown in square blocks.

Sweetcorn must be grown in blocks to aid wind pollination – rows 60 cm (2 ft) apart, plants 25 cm (10 in) apart.

Supersweet varieties must be grown well away from standard varieties to avoid cross-pollination, which will cause a loss of sweetness.

HARVESTING AND STORAGE

Each plant will produce one or two cobs. When the tassels have shrivelled, peel back the outer sheath and squeeze one or two kernels. The juice should be like clotted cream – if it is watery it is under ripe, too thick and it is over ripe. Pull off the cob and use immediately for best results. Supersweet varieties retain their sweetness better after picking than standard varieties, which quickly become starchy.

PESTS AND DISEASES

Frit fly maggot is the main pest of sweetcorn. Spray plants with fenitrothion as the shoots appear. By raising seeds under glass and planting out in late May, you will avoid the worst infection period. Or sow outdoors in early June.

Birds can also be a problem.

Tomatoes

Lycopersicum lycopersicum
Solanaceae

Tomatoes are a rewarding crop to grow, although disease and disorders can damage plants, both in the garden and greenhouse. Numerous varieties are available, from giant beef tomatoes to tiny red or yellow cherry types. The two main types are cordon varieties, which are grown as a single stem, and bush varieties, which may be grown without staking or removal of sideshoots.

Some tomatoes grow best in a heated greenhouse; others do well in the garden, or in growing bags outdoors – or even in a window box. The plants must have maximum light and shelter if grown outside, and need careful watering and feeding.

CULTIVATION

Tomatoes grown in a greenhouse need good ventilation and shading in mid summer. Outdoor tomatoes require a sheltered position which will catch as much sun as possible. The proven outdoor varieties will fruit every summer, but crops will be heavier in more favourable years. Using cloches, tomatoes can be planted out earlier and the fruits left to ripen longer. A black plastic mulch, into which the seedlings are planted, will help to retain warmth and moisture in the soil and suppress weeds.

▲ Cordon tomatoes can be fixed to a cane.

• *Cordon varieties*
Most tomatoes are of the cordon type. The plants are supported with a cane and tied in loosely at about 30 cm (1 ft) intervals, or are grown winding up a loose string.

TOMATOES: A SELECTION OF GOOD VARIETIES

NAME	PLANTING	FRUIT	NOTES
Ailsa Craig	Cordon. Greenhouse or outdoors	Medium size	Good flavour
Alicante	Cordon. Greenhouse or outdoors	Medium size	Very good flavour. Reliable
Dombito F_1	Cordon. Greenhouse only	Beefsteak	Allow four fruits per truss
Gardener's Delight	Cordon. Greenhouse or outdoors	Cherry type	Abundant sweet fruits
Golden Sunrise	Cordon. Greenhouse or outdoors	Medium	Yellow fruit
Red Alert	Bush. Outdoors	Small cherry type	Easy to grow, good flavour. Early
Shirley F_1	Cordon. Greenhouse only	Large red	Heavy crop. Disease resistant
Sweet 100 F_1	Cordon. Greenhouse or outdoors	Small	Sweet and abundant
Tomato Tumbler F_1	Small bush. Outdoors	Small	For hanging baskets, window boxes and pots

TIMINGS

Heated greenhouse	Sow Dec-Jan	Plant Feb-Mar	Pick from June
Cool greenhouse	Sow Feb-Mar	Plant Apr-May	Pick from July
Outdoors	Sow Mar-Apr	Plant May-June	Pick from Aug

▲ Pinching out sideshoots on a tomato cordon.

Remove sideshoots growing from the leaf axils to concentrate the plant's resources into producing fruit.

Remove the leaves below the first truss of yellow flowers and any yellowing or diseased leaves.

Stop the plant's growth by pinching out the growing point after 7 trusses have formed on plants grown in a heated greenhouse, or 6 trusses on plants grown in a cool greenhouse or outdoors.

• *Bush varieties*

Bush tomatoes are smaller than cordon types and suitable for growing outdoors. They do not require staking and the sideshoots do not have to be removed. Place straw beneath the plants to help to protect the fruits.

The plants can be raised from seed under glass or bought from a nursery in pots for planting out. If buying plants, choose those which are stocky and dark green in colour, 15-23 cm (6-9 in) tall. Thin, spindly or pale plants will never catch up.

Plant 45 cm (18 in) apart. Alternatively, grow in 23 cm (9 in) pots or two plants to a growing bag. Apply a proprietary tomato fertiliser, following the instructions on the label. Plants should be watered regularly, to ensure a continual supply of water to the roots without flooding or drying out.

HARVESTING AND STORAGE

Tomatoes can be picked once they have developed an even orange colour – greenish yellow on yellow varieties – or left a little longer to mature. They must be used promptly if they have been left to ripen fully on the plant. They can be stored in a polythene bag in the bottom of the refrigerator for a week or so.

At the end of the season the stems of outdoor crops can be laid on straw under cloches to ripen. Otherwise, pick the green fruits and ripen a few at a time on a sunny windowsill or put them in a drawer with a couple of apples – the apples give off ethylene, which helps the ripening process. Check regularly and remove any ripe or spoiling fruits.

PESTS AND DISEASES

Whitefly, red spider mite and eelworm may attack tomatoes, especially when grown under glass. Disease can be caused by viruses, moulds and rots, and potato blight can wipe out a crop in a bad year. Magnesium deficiency can occur in fast-growing plants. Diseases will also arise if tomatoes are grown in the same soil for several years in succession.

Growing crops in bags

In a greenhouse, tomatoes and other crops can be grown in growing bags without diseases building up in the soil. The bags, which contain compost, can also be used on a patio to grow tomatoes, courgettes or runner beans.

▲ Make an X-shaped cut and plant a seedling.

▲ Sink a plastic pot next to the plant.

Make two X-shaped cuts in the top of the bag and plant two seedlings. Sink an empty 8 cm (3 in) flowerpot in the compost next to each seedling and water into the pots.

Keep refilling the pots until the bag swells. Add liquid feed the same way. Plants with a large leaf area such as courgettes and tomatoes will need a lot of water on a hot, sunny day.

Turnips

Brassica rapa
Cruciferae

Turnips are biennials grown as annuals, with leaves growing to about 23 cm (9 in) high and as much across. Turnip tops can be harvested in the early spring and are a nutritious alternative to spinach.

TYPES AND VARIETIES

Turnips are divided into early and maincrop varieties. Earlies are quick to mature and are used young and straight from the garden. Maincrop varieties are larger, slower growing and can be stored through the winter.

• *Early varieties*

PURPLE TOP MILAN White, flat roots with purple top. Very good flavour. Quick to mature from early sowings.

SNOWBALL Early, quick growing. Very white and tender flesh. Best eaten young, either in salads or cooked.

TOKYO CROSS F_1 Fast growing and ready in six weeks. Good flavour.

• *Maincrop varieties*

GOLDEN BALL Compact, with yellow skin and flesh. Good for late sowing; stores well.

MANCHESTER MARKET (includes GREEN TOP STONE) Large, white globe roots with green tops and white flesh. Tops can be used for spring greens. Hardy.

CULTIVATION

For details of the soil requirement and pests and diseases, see Brassicas.

Sow early crops under cloches from February or in the open from March to June, at two or three week intervals.

▲ Sow 2 or 3 turnip seeds together at intervals.

Sow 2 or 3 seeds together 13 cm (5¼ in) apart each way and thin to the strongest seedling. Alternatively, sow thinly in rows 25 cm (9 in) apart and thin to 10 cm (4 in) apart in the row.

Turnips can be grown as an intercrop between rows of other crops. Early crops need a fertile soil and watering in dry periods to ensure rapid growth.

Sow maincrop turnips in July-August and thin to a spacing of 15 cm (6 in) in rows 30 cm (12 in) apart. For turnip tops, sow a maincrop variety thinly in autumn, in rows 7.5 cm (3 in) apart. Leave the seedlings over winter without thinning and harvest the tops in March and April when they are about 10-15 cm (4-6 in) high. The roots may be left in the ground to resprout for a fresh crop.

HARVESTING AND STORAGE

Early turnips should be lifted when they are between the size of golf and tennis balls – from about 6 weeks after sowing depending on the time of year. Use them soon after they have been lifted.

Maincrop turnips are ready 6-12 weeks after sowing, or they can be left in the ground until they are needed. In cold and wet areas, lift the roots in late autumn and store them in a clamp (a mound of soil and straw). Or put them in boxes of dry soil or sand in a cool, frost-free place.

What plant is that?

When faced with an eye-catching but unknown plant in a park or garden, you can discover its name by using The Plant Identifier. And when you are seeking the right plant for a particular use in your garden, turn to Plants for Special Purposes

The Plant Identifier

Faced with an unfamiliar flowering plant, you can discover its name by following the visual pathway on these pages

Visiting a public park or a friend's garden, you may see a plant so colourful, striking or unusual that you yearn to add it to your own garden. But what is its name? It probably has no label, or your friend has forgotten. The Plant Identifier provides the answer by taking you along a visual pathway until you reach a list of possible candidates. Photographs that accompany the lists may give you the answer immediately, but if you are still in doubt turn to the main entries on each of the listed plants to make a final identification.

To use The Plant Identifier start by turning to the time of year when you are making the identification – Spring, Early Summer, Late Summer, Autumn or Winter. Then locate the type of plant according to three major categories – 'Trees and Shrubs', 'Climbing and Rambling Plants' and 'Soft-stemmed Plants' (which include all herbaceous plants, bulbs and annuals). Then move on to the colour of the flower, and then to the shape. If necessary, The Plant Identifier will lead you through more plant characteristics, such as height, in a series of logical diagnostic steps.

The most frequent terms used for the shapes of flowers are: 'Trumpet or bell shaped', 'Bowl or plate shaped', 'Pompom shaped', 'Daisy-like', 'Pea-like' and 'Arum-like' (see below).The shapes relate to single flowers, not to a cluster.

Where possible, lists give full names of varieties, but if several plants in a genus flower at the same time, you will be referred to the main part of the book; for example, '*Enkianthus* species & cultivars'.

Spring

As the days lengthen the first flowers open in late February and March, and build up to a climax of rhododendrons in May

TREES AND SHRUBS

WHITE OR CREAM FLOWERS

Trumpet or bell shaped

Arbutus menziesii
Buddleja asiatica
Daphne species

▲ *Daphne blagyana*

Enkianthus species & cultivars
Erica species & cultivars
Gaultheria species & cultivars
Halesia species
Lonicera species & cultivars
Pieris formosa

▲ *Pieris formosa*

Pieris japonica
Rhododendron species & cultivars
Stephanandra tanakae
Vaccinium corymbosum
Vaccinium glaucoalbum
Vaccinium praestans

Bowl or plate shaped, borne singly

Clematis marmoraria
Cotoneaster microphyllus
Ilex aquifolium & cultivars
Magnolia species & cultivars

▲ *Magnolia* × *loebneri* 'Merrill'

Paeonia suffruticosa
Pittosporum tobira
Poncirus trifoliata
Prunus species & cultivars

Bowl or plate shaped, borne in groups on trees

Amelanchier 'Ballerina'
Amelanchier canadensis
Amelanchier laevis
Amelanchier lamarckii
Crataegus monogyna & cultivars
Drimys lanceolata
Malus species & cultivars

▲ *Malus toringo* ssp. *sargentii*

Prunus species & cultivars
Pyrus calleryana 'Chanticleer'
Pyrus nivalis
Pyrus salicifolia 'Pendula'
Sambucus nigra f. *laciniata*
Sorbus species

Bowl or plate shaped, borne in groups on shrubs more than 60cm (2ft) tall

Chaenomeles speciosa 'Nivalis'
Clematis x *cartmanii* 'Joe'
Choisya species & cultivars
Cornus species & cultivars
Deutzia species & cultivars
Drimys winteri
Exochorda species & cultivars
Phillyrea latifolia
Photinia species
Pyracantha species & cultivars
Skimmia species
Spiraea species
Staphylea colchica
Symplocos paniculata
Viburnum species

▲ *Staphylea colchica*

Bowl or plate shaped, borne in groups on shrubs less than 60cm (2ft) tall

Hebe macrantha
Hebe ochracea
Iberis sempervirens & cultivars

▲ *Iberis sempervirens*

Pompom shaped

Crataegus laevigata 'Plena'

▲ *Crataegus laevigata* 'Plena'

Daisy-like

Helichrysum frigidum
Illicium anisatum

▲ *Helichrysum frigidum*

Pea-like

Cercis siliquastrum f. *albida*
Cytisus multiflorus
Robinia pseudoacacia & cultivars

▲ *Robinia pseudoacacia*

RED OR PINK FLOWERS

Trumpet or bell shaped

Crinodendron hookerianum
Daphne species

▲ *Daphne cneorum*

Embothrium coccineum & cultivars
Enkianthus species & cultivars
Lonicera tatarica 'Arnold's Red'
Malus species & cultivars
x *Phylliopsis* species & cultivars
Rhododendron species & cultivars
Ribes sanguineum & cultivars
Ribes speciosum
Syringa reflexa
Vaccinium species

Bowl or plate shaped

Camellia x *williamsii*

▲ *Camellia* x *williamsii*

Chaenomeles x *superba* 'Knap Hill Scarlet'
Cornus florida 'Cherokee Chief'
Crataegus x *lavallei* 'Carrierei'
Cydonia oblonga & cultivars
Magnolia species & cultivars
Malus species & cultivars
Prunus species & cultivars
Rhododendron species & cultivars
Rubus spectabilis
Sorbus cashmiriana

Pompom shaped

Crataegus laevigata 'Paul's Scarlet'

▲ *Crataegus laevigata* 'Paul's Scarlet'

Pea-like

Caragana arborescens 'Lorbergii'
Cercis canadensis 'Forest Pansy'
Cercis siliquastrum
Indigofera heterantha
Robinia hispida

▲ *Cercis siliquastrum*

Flowers in small, tight clusters

Parrotia persica & cultivars

▲ *Parrotia persica*

ORANGE FLOWERS

Trumpet or bell shaped

Rhododendron cinnabarinum 'Conroy'
Rhododendron cultivars

▲ *Rhododendron* 'Fireball'

YELLOW FLOWERS

Trumpet or bell shaped

Corokia buddlejoides
Enkianthus chinensis
Forsythia species & cultivars

▲ *Forsythia viridissima* 'Bronxensis'

Lonicera involucrata
Mahonia species & cultivars
Rhamnus catharticus
Rhododendron species & cultivars
Ribes americanum
Ribes odoratum
Stachyurus praecox

Bowl or plate shaped, borne singly

Halimium lasianthum & cultivars

▲ *Halimium lasianthum* ssp. *formosum*

Helianthemum lunulatum
Hypericum aegypticum
Kerria species & cultivars
Magnolia 'Elizabeth'
Rosa 'Canary Bird'
Rosa ecae
Rosa 'Helen Knight'

Bowl or plate shaped, borne in groups

Cornus mas

▲ *Cornus mas*

Corokia x *virgata*
Corylopsis species & cultivars
Euonymus europaeus 'Red Cascade'
Lindera species
Paeonia delavayi var. *ludlowii*
Rhamnus frangula
Rhododendron wardii
Sassafras albidum
Stephanandra incisa

Pompom shaped

Acacia species
Aurinia saxatilis & cultivars
Azara lanceolata
Azara petiolaris
Buxus sempervirens & cultivars

▲ *Buxus sempervirens* 'Latifolia'

Daisy-like

Euryops acraeus

▲ *Euryops acraeus*

Pea-like

Caragana arborescens & cultivars
Coronilla valentina

▲ *Coronilla valentina*

Cytisus species & cultivars
Genista species & cultivars
Sophora species & cultivars

▲ *Cytisus* × *praecox* 'Warminster'

PURPLE OR VIOLET FLOWERS

Trumpet or bell shaped

Clematis addisonii
Lonicera rupicola var. *syringantha*
Paulownia tomentosa
Penstemon davidsonii
Rhododendron species & cultivars

▲ *Rhododendron polycladum* Scintillans Group

Ribes divaricatum
Syringa species & cultivars
Thymus caespititius

▲ *Syringa vulgaris* 'Charles Joly'

Bowl or plate shaped

Akebia species
Brunfelsia pauciflora & cultivars
Hebe 'Caledonia'

▲ *Hebe* 'Caledonia'

Hebe 'Wingletye'
Magnolia liliiflora 'Nigra'
Magnolia x *soulangeana* 'Picture'
Malus species & cultivars

GREEN FLOWERS

Bowl or plate shaped

Aucuba japonica & cultivars
Azara microphylla
Daphne pontica

▲ *Azara microphylla*

TREES AND SHRUBS WITH CATKINS

Alnus species & cultivars
Betula species & cultivars
Carpinus betulus & cultivars
Corylopsis species
Corylus species & cultivars

▲ *Corylus avellana*

▲ *Garrya elliptica*

Garrya elliptica
Ostrya species
Myrica gale
Salix species & cultivars

TREES AND SHRUBS WITH COLOURFUL NEW FOLIAGE

Acer species & cultivars
Aesculus indica & cultivars
Aesculus x *neglecta* 'Erythroblastos'
Alnus x *spaethii*
Catalpa x *erubescens* 'Purpurea'
Corylopsis sinensis var. *sinensis* 'Spring Purple'
Fagus sylvatica 'Zlatia'
Gymnocladus dioica
Gleditsia triacanthos 'Sunburst'
Osmanthus heterophyllus 'Goshiki'
Osmanthus yunnanensis
Picea orientalis 'Aurea'
Pieris species & cultivars
Tilia mongolica

▲ *Picea orientalis* 'Aurea'

▲ *Pieris formosa* var. *forestii* 'Wakehurst'

SHRUBS WITH STRIKING NEW FOLIAGE

Abelia × *grandiflora*
Cornus alba 'Spaethii'
Corylopsis sinensis var. *sinensis* 'Spring Purple'
Koelreuteria paniculata
Ligustrum lucidum 'Tricolor'
Lonicera nitida 'Baggesen's Gold'
Mahonia × *wagneri* cultivars
Osmanthus heterophyllus cultivars

▲ *Pieris* 'Forest Flame'

Pieris species & cultivars
Pittosporum tenuifolium 'Purpureum'

CLIMBING PLANTS

WHITE OR CREAM FLOWERS

Bowl or plate shaped

Clematis – Early Large-Flowered Group
Clematis armandii & cultivars

▼ *Clematis armandii*

Trumpet or bell shaped

Clematis cirrhosa & cultivars
Clematis montana & cultivars

RED OR PINK FLOWERS

Trumpet or bell shaped

Clematis alpina 'Willy'
Clematis macropetala 'Markham's Pink'
Clematis 'Rosie O' Grady'

▲ *Clematis macropetala* 'Markham's Pink'

Bowl or plate shaped

Clematis – Early Large-Flowered Group
Clematis armandii 'Apple Blossom'
Clematis 'Broughton Star'
Clematis montana cultivars

▼ *Clematis* 'Sealand Gem'

YELLOW FLOWERS

Trumpet or bell shaped

Clematis cirrhosa
Clematis 'Helios'
Clematis napaulensis
Lonicera species & cultivars

▲ *Lonicera* × *tellmanniana*

Bowl or plate shaped

Clematis – Early Large-Flowered Group
Jasminum mesnyi
Jasminum nudiflorum
Smilax china

▲ *Jasminum nudiflorum*

BLUE FLOWERS

Trumpet or bell shaped

Clematis alpina 'Frances Rivis'
Clematis macropetala

▼ *Clematis alpina* 'Frances Rivis'

Bowl or plate shaped

Clematis – Early Large-Flowered Group

▲ *Clematis* 'Daniel Deronda'

PURPLE FLOWERS

Trumpet or bell shaped

Clematis alpina cultivars
Clematis macropetala cultivars
Clematis simsii

▲ *Clematis macropetala*

Bowl or plate shaped

Clematis – Early Large-Flowered Group
Akebia × *pentaphylla*
Akebia quinata
Akebia trifoliata

▲ *Akebia quinata*

Pea-like

Vicia sepium
Wisteria sinensis

▲ *Wisteria sinensis*

SOFT-STEMMED PLANTS

WHITE OR CREAM FLOWERS

Trumpet or bell shaped, on plants less than 30cm (12in) tall, flowers borne singly

Fritillaria meleagris alba
Galanthus species & cultivars
Ipheion uniflorum 'Album'
Narcissus cantabricus
Narcissus 'Jenny'

▼ *Galanthus plicatus*

Pleione species & cultivars
Raoulia tenuicaulis
Shortia species
Silene uniflora
Soldanella minima
Vinca major alba

Trumpet or bell shaped, on plants less than 30cm (12in) tall, flowers borne in groups

Ajuga reptans 'Alba'
Allium triquetrum
Convallaria majalis & cultivars
Corydalis caucasica var. *alba*
Dodecatheon dentatum
Epimedium diphyllum
Haberlea rhodopensis 'Virginalis'

▲ *Haberlea rhodopensis* 'Virginalis'

Hyacinthus orientalis 'L'Innocence'
Hymenocallis × *festalis*
Muscari azureum album
Narcissus 'Rippling Waters'
Ourisia 'Snowflake'
Puschkinia scilloides var. *libanotica* 'Alba'

Trumpet or bell shaped, on plants 30cm–1m (1–3ft) tall

Disporum species & cultivars
Dodecatheon meadia f. *album*
Fritillaria verticillata
Geum rivale 'Album'
Gladiolus 'The Bride'
Leucojum aestivum 'Gravetye Giant'

▼ *Geum rivale* 'Album'

Leucojum nicaeense
Narcissus 'Empress of Ireland'
Narcissus 'Mount Hood'
Nectaroscordum siculum
Symphytum species

Bowl or plate shaped, on plants less than 30cm (12in) tall, flowers borne singly

Anemone species & cultivars
Arenaria balearica
Caltha leptosepala
Erythronium californicum 'White Beauty'
Helleborus niger & cultivars
Hepatica nobilis 'White'
Podophyllum species
Ranunculus species
Rhodohypoxis 'Ruth'
Sanguinaria canadensis
Saxifraga poluniniana
Tulipa species
Trillium species
Vinca minor f. *alba*
Viola species & cultivars

▲ *Vinca minor* f. *alba*

Bowl or plate shaped, on plants less than 30cm (12in) tall, flowers borne in groups

Aponogeton distachyos
Arabis alpina ssp. *caucasica* 'Schneehaube' ('Snowcap')
Asphodelus albus
Cardamine pratensis 'Edith'
Epimedium grandiflorum 'White Queen'
Libertia formosa
Maianthemum bifolium
Menyanthes trifoliata
Omphalodes verna 'Alba'
Ornithogalum arabicum
Pachyphragma macrophyllum
Polemonium brandegeei ssp. *mellitum*
Primula species & cultivars
Ranunculus species
Saxifraga species
Tulipa tarda

▲ *Saxifraga cebennensis*

Bowl or plate shaped, on plants 30cm–1m (1–3ft), flowers borne singly

Anemone coronaria De Caen Group 'Die Braut'
Aquilegia flabellata var. *pumila* f. *alba*
Caltha palustris var. *alba*

▲ *Caltha palustris* var. *alba*

Eomecon chionantha
Geranium sanguineum 'Album'
Glaucidium palmatum 'Album'
Helleborus orientalis
Paeonia emodi
Trillium cernuum
Trillium grandiflorum
Tulipa marjolettii

Bowl or plate shaped, on plants 30cm–1m (1–3ft) tall, flowers borne in groups

Allium neapolitanum
Allium ursinum
Camassia leichtlinii 'Alba Group'

▲ *Camassia leichtlinii* 'Alba Group'

Crambe maritima
Lunaria species & cultivars
Matthiola incana & cultivars
Pelargonium 'Fragrans Group'
Vancouveria hexandra

Bowl or plate shaped, on plants more than 1m (3ft) tall

Crambe cordifolia
Eremurus himalaicus
Verbascum blattaria f. *albiflorum*

▲ *Verbascum blattaria* f. *albiflorum*

Pompom shaped

Pachysandra terminalis

▲ *Pachysandra terminalis*

Daisy-like

Anemone blanda cultivars
Helichrysum bellidioides
Petasites fragrans

▲ *Anemone blanda* 'White Splendour'

Arum-like

Lysichiton camtschatcensis

▲ *Lysichiton camtschatcensis*

Heart shaped

Dicentra cucullaria
Dicentra spectabilis 'Alba'

▲ *Dicentra spectabilis* 'Alba'

RED OR PINK FLOWERS

Trumpet or bell shaped, on plants less than 30cm (12in) tall, flowers borne singly

Asarum caudatum
Fritillaria acmopetala
Pleione species & cultivars
Pulsatilla rubra
Semiaquilegia adoxoides

▲ *Pleione* 'Versailles'

Trumpet or bell shaped, on plants less than 30cm (12in) tall, flowers borne in groups

Corydalis solida & cultivars
Epimedium × *youngianum* 'Roseum'
Hyacinthus orientalis cultivars
Ourisia coccinea

▲ *Ourisia coccinea*

Ourisia 'Loch Ewe'
Shortia soldanelloides

Trumpet or bell shaped, on plants 30cm–1m (1–3ft) tall

Allium unifolium
Bergenia species & cultivars
Calamintha grandiflora
Dodecatheon pulchellum 'Red Wings'
Gladiolus communis ssp. *byzantinus*
Hippeastrum 'Bestseller'
Nectaroscordum siculum

▲ *Calamintha grandiflora*

Bowl or plate shaped, on plants less than 30cm (12in) tall, flowers borne singly

Anemone nemorosa & hybrids
Erythronium dens-canis

▼ *Anenome nemorosa* 'Robinsoniana'

Geranium sanguineum cultivars
Oxalis enneaphylla cultivars
Primula species & cultivars
Pulsatilla vulgaris cultivars
Rhodohypoxis species
Silene acaulis
Tulipa species

Bowl or plate shaped, on plants less than 30cm (12in) tall, flowers borne in groups

Allium karataviense
Allium oreophilum 'Zwanenburg'
Aubrieta species & cultivars
Epimedium grandiflorum 'Rose Queen'
Geranium cinereum 'Ballerina'
Geranium cinereum subcaulescens
Geranium sanguineum 'Cedric Morris'
Iberis umbellata cultivars
Oxalis species & cultivars
Primula species & cultivars
Trillium species

▲ *Primula vulgaris* ssp. *sibthorpii*

Bowl or plate shaped, on plants 30cm–1m (1–3ft) tall

Cardamine species
Helleborus orientalis pink form
Helleborus × *sternii* 'Boughton Beauty'

▲ *Helleborus* × *sternii* 'Boughton Beauty'

Matthiola incana & cultivars
Paeonia species

▲ *Paeonia delavayi*

Papaver rupifragum
Pelargonium acetosum
Persicaria milletii
Podophyllum hexandrum var. *chinense*
Tulipa species

Daisy-like

Anemone blanda cultivars

▲ *Anemone blanda* 'Radar'

Pea-like

Lathyrus vernus

▲ *Lathyrus vernus*

Heart shaped

Dicentra species & cultivars

▲ *Dicentra* 'Bountiful'

Cyclamen flowers

Cyclamen trochopteranthum

▲ *Cyclamen trochopteranthum*

Iris flowers

Iris 'Banbury Melody'
Iris 'Raspberry Blush'

▲ *Iris* 'Raspberry Blush'

ORANGE FLOWERS

Trumpet or bell shaped, on plants less than 30cm (12in) tall

Geum rivale 'Leonard's Variety'
Hyacinthus orientalis 'Gipsy Queen'

▲ *Hyacinthus orientalis* 'Gipsy Queen'

Trumpet or bell shaped, on plants 30cm–1m (1–3ft) tall

Hippeastrum 'Orange Sovereign'

▲ *Hippeastrum* 'Orange Sovereign'

Trumpet or bell shaped, on plants more than 1m (3ft) tall

Fritillaria imperialis

▲ *Fritillaria imperialis*

YELLOW FLOWERS

Trumpet or bell shaped, on plants less than 30 cm (12 in) tall

Chiastophyllum oppositifolium
Corydalis cheilanthifolia
Corydalis wilsonii
Crocus flavus
Crocus × *luteus* 'Golden Yellow'
Dionysia aretioides & cultivars

▲ *Dionysia aretioides* 'Phyllis Carter'

Geum rivale 'Lionel Cox'
Hyacinthus orientalis 'City of Haarlem'
Narcissus species & cultivars
Pleione × *confusa*
Pleione forrestii
Vitaliana primuliflora

Trumpet or bell shaped, on plants 30 cm–1 m (1–3 ft) tall

Anigozanthos flavidus
Fritillaria pallidiflora
Mimulus guttatus
Narcissus cultivars
Tulipa acuminata
Uvularia species

▲ *Uvularia perfoliata*

Bowl or plate shaped, on plants less than 30 cm (12 in) tall; flowers borne singly

Anemone species
Eranthis species
Erythronium species & cultivars
Hacquetia epipactis
Papaver miyabeanum
Primula kewensis
Primula vulgaris
Ranunculus species & cultivars
Raoulia species
Tulipa species
Viola species & cultivars

▲ *Viola* 'Buttercup'

Bowl or plate shaped, on plants less than 30 cm (12 in) tall; flowers in groups

▲ *Draba aizoides*

Aurinia saxatilis
Draba species
Duchesnea indica
Epimedium alpinum
Epimedium perralderianum
Epimedium pinnatum ssp. *colchicum*
Epimedium × *versicolor* 'Sulphureum'
Narcissus jonquilla
Narcissus 'Sundial'
Polemonium brandegeei
Primula species & cultivars
Trillium erectum f. *luteum*
Trillium luteum
Tulipa sylvestris
Vancouveria chrysantha
Viola biflora

Bowl or plate shaped, on plants 30 cm–1 m (1–3 ft) tall; flowers borne singly

Caltha palustris
Helleborus foetidus Wester Flisk Group
Helleborus orientalis Kochii Group
Pulsatilla alpina ssp. *apiifolia*
Trillium chloropetalum

▲ *Caltha palustris*

Bowl or plate shaped, on plants 30 cm–1 m (1–3 ft) tall; flowers borne in groups

Astelia species
Epimedium × *perralchicum*

▲ *Epimedium* × *perralchicum*

Narcissus 'Yellow Cheerfulness'
Sisyrinchium californicum
Stylophorum diphyllum

Bowl or plate shaped, on plants more than 1 m (3 ft) tall

Asphodeline lutea
Paeonia mlokosewitschii
Verbascum blattaria
Verbascum bombyciferum

▼ *Paeonia mlokosewitschii*

Daisy-like

Doronicum 'Frühlingspracht'
Doronicum orientale
Doronicum pardalianches

▲ *Doronicum pardalianches*

Pea-like

Sophora microphylla
Sophora tetraptera
Thermopsis lanceolata
Thermopsis villosa

▲ *Thermopsis villosa*

Arum-like

Arum creticum
Lysichiton americanus
Orontium aquaticum

▼ *Arum creticum*

HEART-SHAPED

Dicentra macrantha

▲ *Dicentra macrantha*

IRIS FLOWERS

Iris species & cultivars

▲ *Iris winogradowii*

BLUE FLOWERS

TRUMPET OR BELL SHAPED, ON PLANTS LESS THAN 30CM (12IN) TALL

Ajuga reptans cultivars
Campanula cashmeriana
Corydalis flexuosa & cultivars
Crocus tommasinianus
Gentiana acaulis cultivars
Gentiana verna ssp. *balcanica*
Hyacinthus orientalis & cultivars
Mertensia species
Muscari species & cultivars
Scilla bifolia
Scilla siberica
Soldanella cyanaster
Synthyris stellata

▼ *Ajuga reptans* 'Atropurpurea'

TRUMPET OR BELL SHAPED, ON PLANTS 30CM–1M (1–3FT) TALL

Hyacinthoides hispanica
Hyacinthoides non-scripta

▲ *Hyacinthoides non-scripta*

TRUMPET OR BELL SHAPED, PLANTS MORE THAN 1M (3FT) TALL

Amsonia orientalis
Anchusa azurea
Symphytum × uplandicum

▲ *Symphytum × uplandicum*

BOWL OR PLATE SHAPED, ON PLANTS LESS THAN 30CM (12IN) TALL

Anemone apennina & cultivars
Chionodoxa species
Hepatica × media 'Ballardii'
Myosotis alpestris
Omphalodes species
Primula marginata cultivars
Primula obconica 'Caerulea'
Primula vulgaris 'Lilacina Plena'
Scilla species
Veronica species
Vinca species
Viola elatior

▲ *Viola elatior*

BOWL OR PLATE SHAPED, ON PLANTS 30CM–1M (1–3FT) TALL

Anemone coronaria De Caen Group 'Mister Fokker'
Brunnera macrophylla cultivars
Camassia cusickii
Camassia leichtlinii 'Caerulea Group'
Malva sylvestris
Myosotis species & cultivars
Polemonium caeruleum cultivars
Polemonium reptans

▼ *Brunnera macrophylla*

DAISY-LIKE

Anemone blanda & cultivars

▲ *Anemone blanda*

PURPLE FLOWERS

TRUMPET OR BELL SHAPED, ON PLANTS LESS THAN 30CM (12IN) TALL; FLOWERS BORNE SINGLY

Asarum hartwegii
Crocus tommasinianus
Fritillaria meleagris
Ipheion uniflorum 'Froyle Mill'
Pleione formosana 'Oriental Grace'
Pleione 'Hekla'
Pleione 'Tolima'
Pulsatilla species
Soldanella species

▼ *Ipheion uniflorum* 'Froyle Mill'

Trumpet or bell shaped, on plants less than 30cm (12in) tall; flowers borne in groups

Allium oreophilum
Aquilegia bertolonii
Haberlea species

▲ *Haberlea rhodopensis* var. *ferdinandi-coburgii*

Hyacinthus orientalis
Muscari latifolium
Primula concholoba
Ramonda serbica
Soldanella species

Trumpet or bell shaped, on plants 30cm–1m (1–3ft) tall

Calamintha nepeta
Cardamine pentaphyllos
Dodecatheon jeffreyi
Fritillaria persica
Mertensia species
Muscari neglectum

▼ *Fritillaria persica*

Bowl or plate shaped, on plants less than 30cm (12in) tall

Anemone apennina 'Purpurea'
Anemone nemorosa 'Bowles' Purple'
Cardamine pratensis 'Flore Pleno'
Helleborus purpurascens
Hepatica americana
Lobularia maritima 'Oriental Night'
Oxalis species & cultivars

▲ *Oxalis* 'Ione Hecker'

Phlox subulata cultivars
Primula species & cultivars
Ramonda serbica
Saxifraga oppositifolia
Soldanella montana
Trillium species
Vinca species
Viola species

Bowl or plate shaped, on plants 30cm–1m (1–3ft) tall

Allium hollandicum 'Purple Sensation'
Cortusa matthioli
Helleborus orientalis cultivars
Helleborus torquatus
Lunaria annua

▼ *Lunaria annua*

Lunaria rediviva
Matthiola incana & cultivars
Pulsatilla alpina
Ruscus hypoglossum

Pompom shaped

Allium giganteum
Dipsacus sativus

▲ *Allium giganteum*

Daisy-like

Anemone hortensis
Aster tongolensis 'Napsbury'

▲ *Anemone hortensis*

Iris-like

Iris species & cultivars
Roscoea humeana

▼ *Roscoea humeana*

Flowers in pyramidal groups

Dactylorhiza elata
Dactylorhiza majalis

▲ *Dactylorhiza majalis*

GREEN OR GREEN-YELLOW FLOWERS

Bowl or plate shaped

Helleborus species & cultivars
Paris quadrifolia
Rhodiola rosea
Trillium chloropetalum
Trillium luteum

▲ *Helleborus argutifolius*

EARLY SUMMER

From late May to mid July, masses of strongly coloured flowers include the hardy and half-hardy annuals

TREES AND SHRUBS

WHITE OR CREAM FLOWERS

TRUMPET OR BELL SHAPED

Abelia species & cultivars

▲ *Abelia* 'Edward Goucher'

Arbutus menziesii
Buddleja davidii 'White Profusion'
Calluna species & cultivars
Daphne acutiloba
Enkianthus campanulatus 'Albiflorus'
Enkianthus cernuus
Fuchsia species & cultivars
Gaultheria species & cultivars
Lavandula angustifolia 'Alba'
Lavandula stoechas f. *leucantha*
Leucothoe davisiae
Leucothoe fontanesiana
Penstemon confertus
Penstemon fruticosus ssp. *scouleri* f. *albus*
Penstemon virens var. *albus*
Pterostyrax hispida

▼ *Pterostyrax hispida*

Rhododendron species & cultivars
Rosmarinus officinalis var. *albiflorus*
Stephanandra tanakae
Styrax hemsleyanus
Styrax japonicus
Styrax obassia
Thymus species
Weigela 'Bristol Snowflake'

▲ *Thymus serpyllum* var. *albus*

BOWL OR PLATE SHAPED, BORNE SINGLY

Cistus × *aguilarii* & cultivars
Clematis species & cultivars
Cotoneaster species & cultivars
Eucryphia species & cultivars

▲ *Eucryphia milliganii*

Leptospermum lanigerum
Myrtus species & cultivars
Philadelphus × *lemoinei*
Philadelphus microphyllus
Romneya coulteri
Rosa species & cultivars
Rubus species
Stewartia species & cultivars

TREES WITH BOWL OR PLATE-SHAPED FLOWERS, BORNE IN GROUPS

Aralia species & cultivars
Clethra delavayi
Drimys winteri

▲ *Drimys winteri*

Olea europaea & cultivars
Prunus lusitanica & cultivars
Ptelea trifoliata & cultivars
Sambucus nigra 'Laciniata'
Sorbus species
Symplocos paniculata

BOWL OR PLATE SHAPED, ON SHRUBS LESS THAN 60CM (2FT) TALL; FLOWERS BORNE IN GROUPS

Cotoneaster × *suecicus* 'Coral Beauty'
Hebe albicans
Hebe buchananii

▲ *Hebe albicans*

Hebe ochracea & cultivars
Hebe 'Pewter Dome'
Helianthemum 'Double Cream'
Helianthemum 'Wisley White'
Iberis species & cultivars
Potentilla cultivars

BOWL OR PLATE SHAPED, ON SHRUBS OVER 60CM (2FT) TALL; FLOWERS BORNE IN GROUPS

Aralia species & cultivars
Cistus species & cultivars
Cornus species & cultivars
Cotoneaster species & cultivars
Deutzia species & cultivars
Drimys winteri
Escallonia cultivars
Exochorda species & cultivars
× *Halimiocistus sahucii*
Hebe species & cultivars
Hydrangea species & cultivars

▲ *Hydrangea macrophylla* 'Lanarth White'

Nandina domestica & cultivars
Osmanthus × *burkwoodii*
Philadelphus coronarius
Pyracantha species & cultivars
Rosa cultivars
Rubus species
Sorbaria sorbifolia
Spiraea species & cultivars
Symplocos paniculata
Viburnum species

DAISY-LIKE

Helichrysum frigidum
Olearia species & cultivars

▼ *Olearia* 'Waikariensis'

Pea-like
Gymnocladus dioica
Ononis rotundifolia

Fringed flowers
Chionanthus species

▲ *Chionanthus retusus*

GREEN-WHITE FLOWERS

Trumpet or bell shaped
Lavandula viridis

▲ *Lavandula viridis*

WHITE & RED FLOWERS

Trumpet or bell shaped
Fuchsia 'Alice Hoffman'
Fuchsia 'Cascade'
Fuchsia 'Lady Thumb'
Fuchsia 'Madame Cornelissen'
Fuchsia magellanica var. *molinae*
Fuchsia 'Pink Marshmallow'
Fuchsia 'Swingtime'

▲ *Fuchsia* 'Lady Thumb'

RED OR PINK FLOWERS

Trumpet or bell shaped, flowers borne singly
Abelia schumannii
Gaultheria procumbens
Hibiscus rosa-sinensis & cultivars
Lavatera maritima
Russelia equisetiformis

▲ *Russelia equisetiformis*

Trumpet or bell shaped, on shrubs less than 60cm (2ft) tall; flowers in groups
Calluna vulgaris cultivars

▲ *Calluna vulgaris* 'Sister Anne'

Lavandula stoechas ssp. *pedunculata*
Origanum species & cultivars
Penstemon species & cultivars
Teucrium subspinosum
Thymus species
Vaccinium vitis-idaea

▲ *Origanum amanum*

Trumpet or bell shaped, on shrubs more than 60cm (2ft) tall; flowers in groups
Abelia floribunda
Buddleja davidii 'Royal Red'
Cestrum 'Newellii'
Clerodendrum bungei
Embothrium coccineum & cultivars
Enkianthus species & cultivars
Kolkwitzia amabilis

▲ *Kolkwitzia amabilis*

Lonicera korolkowii
Melianthus major
Rhododendron cultivars
Syringa reflexa
Weigela florida & cultivars

Bowl or plate shaped, flowers borne singly
Cistus species & cultivars

▲ *Cistus crispus*

Cydonia oblonga
Deutzia species & cultivars
Helianthemum cultivars
Potentilla nitida
Rosa species & cultivars

Bowl or plate shaped, flowers borne in groups
Cistus species & cultivars
Cotoneaster splendens
Deutzia species & cultivars
Escallonia species & cultivars
Hebe species & cultivars
Helianthemum cultivars
Jasminum beesianum
Kalmia species & cultivars
Lantana camara 'Brasier'
Parahebe catarractae ssp. *diffusa*

▲ *Potentilla* 'Gibson's Scarlet'

Potentilla cultivars
Rosa cultivars
Spiraea betulifolia var. *aemiliana*
Spiraea japonica

Pompom shaped
Crataegus laevigata 'Paul's Scarlet'
Hydrangea species & cultivars
Metrosideros excelsa

▲ *Metrosideros kermadecensis* 'Sunninghill'

Metrosideros kermadecensis & cultivars
Rosa cultivars

Pea-like
Erythrina crista-galli
Hedysarum multijugum
Indigofera amblyantha

▲ *Indigofera amblyantha*

Ononis repens
Ononis rotundifolia
Polygala × *dalmaisiana*
Robinia × *margaretta*

Bottle brush shaped

Callistemon species & cultivars

▲ *Callistemon citrinus* 'Splendens'

RED & PURPLE FLOWERS

Trumpet or bell shaped

Fuchsia 'Eva Boerg'
Fuchsia 'Lena'
Fuchsia magellanica & cultivars
Fuchsia 'Mrs Popple'
Fuchsia riccartonii
Fuchsia 'Royal Velvet'

▲ *Fuchsia* 'Royal Velvet'

ORANGE FLOWERS

Trumpet or bell shaped

Campsis × *tagliabuana* 'Madame Galen'

▲ *Campsis* × *tagliabuana* 'Mme Galen'

Fuchsia 'Thalia'
Hedychium densiflorum 'Assam Orange'
Hibiscus rosa-sinensis 'Weekend'
Mimulus aurantiacus

Bowl or plate shaped

Helianthemum 'Ben Afflick'
Helianthemum 'Ben Dearg'
Helianthemum 'Fire Dragon'

▲ *Helianthemum* 'Fire Dragon'

Potentilla 'Hopleys Orange'
Potentilla 'Tangerine'
Rosa cultivars

Pompom shaped

Buddleja globosa
Rosa cultivars

▲ *Buddleja globosa*

YELLOW FLOWERS

Trumpet or bell shaped

Cestrum parqui
Diervilla sessilifolia
Diervilla × *splendens*
Enkianthus chinensis
Hibiscus rosa-sinensis 'Lemon Chiffon'
Phlomis fruticosa
Phlomis longifolia var. *bailanica*
Teucrium scorodonia
Weigela middendorffiana

▼ *Weigela middendorffiana*

Bowl or plate shaped

Fremontodendron species & cultivars
Helianthemum species & cultivars
Hypericum species & cultivars

▲ *Hypericum coris*

Lantana camara 'Drap d'Or'
Linum arboreum
Liriodendron species & cultivars
Paeonia delavayi var. *lutea*
Pittosporum species & cultivars
Potentilla species & cultivars
Rosa cultivars
Sorbaria tomentosa
Stephanandra incisa

Pompom shaped

Artemisia abrotanum
Buddleja × *weyeriana* & cultivars

▲ *Buddleja* × *weyeriana*

Eucalyptus globulus
Rosa species & cultivars

Daisy-like

Brachyglottis species & cultivars
Euryops acraeus

▼ *Euryops acraeus*

Small tight clusters

Helichrysum italicum
Helichrysum splendidum
Santolina species

Pea-like

Caragana arborescens 'Lorbergii'
Colutea arborescens
Coronilla minima
Coronilla valentina ssp. *glauca*
Genista species & cultivars
Laburnum alpinum 'Pendulum'
Laburnum × *watereri* 'Vossii'

▲ *Laburnum* × *watereri* 'Vossii'

Lupinus arboreus
Piptanthus nepalensis
Senna marilandica

PINK, YELLOW OR WHITE FLOWERS WITH DARK BLOTCH IN THE CENTRE

Bowl or plate shaped

Cistus species & cultivars
Halimium species & cultivars
× *Halimiocistus wintonensis*
Paeonia suffruticosa

▼ × *Halimiocistus wintonensis*

BLUE FLOWERS

Trumpet or bell shaped, flowers borne in groups

Buddleja alternifolia
Buddleja davidii cultivars

▲ *Buddleja davidii* 'Nanho Blue'

Buddleja lindleyana
Caliuna vulgaris 'Spring Torch'
Calluna vulgaris 'Winter Chocolate'
Cestrum elegans
Lavandula species & cultivars
Penstemon species
Rhododendron ponticum
Syringa × *persica*
Teucrium fruticans
Thymus species

▲ *Teucrium fruticans*

Bowl or plate shaped

Hebe cupressoides & cultivars
Hebe 'Mrs Winder'
Hebe pimeleoides 'Quicksilver'
Hydrangea 'Blue Deckle'
Hydrangea involucrata
Hydrangea macrophylla & cultivars
Hydrangea serrata & cultivars

▲ *Hydrangea serrata* 'Bluebird'

PURPLE FLOWERS

Trumpet or bell shaped, flowers borne singly

Clematis addisonii
Clematis simsii
Lavatera arborea 'Variegata'
Lavatera maritima

▲ *Lavatera arborea* 'Variegata'

Bowl or plate shaped, flowers borne singly

Cistus × *pulverulentus* & cultivars
Paeonia delavayi
Rubus thibetanus

▲ *Cistus* × *pulverulentus* 'Sunset'

Bowl or plate shaped, flowers borne in groups

Deutzia compacta 'Lavender Time'
Fuchsia 'Mantilla'
Hebe 'Caledonia'
Hebe × *franciscana* 'Blue Gem'
Hebe × *franciscana* 'Variegata'
Hebe 'Wingletye'
Hebe 'Youngii'

▲ *Hebe franciscana* 'Variegata'

Hydrangea aspera & cultivars
Lantana montevidensis
Pittosporum crassifolium
Rubus cockburnianus
Solanum laciniatum

▲ *Solanum laciniatum*

Pompom shaped

Hydrangea species & cultivars
Melaleuca gibbosa
Rosa cultivars

▲ *Hydrangea macrophylla*

Pea-like

+ *Laburnocytisus adamii*
Ononis repens

CLIMBING AND RAMBLING PLANTS

WHITE OR CREAM FLOWERS

Trumpet or bell shaped

Billardiera longiflora
Clematis macropetala 'Snowbird'
Codonopsis convolvulacea 'Alba'
Jasminum species & cultivars
Lonicera caprifolium
Lonicera etrusca 'Superba'
Lonicera japonica 'Halliana'

▲ *Lonicera japonica* 'Halliana'

Lonicera japonica 'Hall's Prolific'
Lonicera periclymenum 'Graham Thomas'

Bowl or plate shaped

Clematis species & cultivars
Hydrangea anomala ssp. *petiolaris*
Hydrangea serratifolia
Rosa cultivars
Schizophragma hydrangeoides
Schizophragma integrifolium
Trachelospermum asiaticum
Trachelospermum jasminoides

▲ *Trachelospermum jasminoides*

Pea-like

Lathyrus odoratus & cultivars
Lathyrus sativus
Wisteria venusta

▲ *Wisteria venusta*

WHITE & RED FLOWERS

Trumpet or bell shaped

Lonicera etrusca 'Donald Waterer'

▲ *Lonicera etrusca* 'Donald Waterer'

RED OR PINK FLOWERS

Trumpet or bell shaped

Clematis 'Duchess of Albany'
Clematis 'Gravetye Beauty'
Clematis macropetala 'Markham's Pink'
Clerodendrum splendens
Lonicera × *americana*
Lonicera × *brownii* 'Dropmore Scarlet'
Lonicera giraldii
Lonicera periclymenum 'Belgica'

▲ *Lonicera* × *heckrottii*

Lonicera × *heckrottii*
Rhodochiton atrosanguineus
Tropaeolum species

Bowl or plate shaped

Clematis species & cultivars
Jasminum × *stephanense*
Passiflora × *exoniensis*
Passiflora sanguinolenta
Rosa cultivars
Rubus henryi
Rubus odoratus

▲ *Rubus odoratus*

Schisandra rubrifolia
Tropaeolum species

Pompom shaped

Rosa cultivars

▲ *Rosa* 'Zepherine Drouhin'

Pea-like

Lathyrus grandiflorus
Lathyrus latifolius
Lathyrus odoratus & cultivars

▲ *Lathyrus latifolius*

ORANGE FLOWERS

Trumpet or bell shaped

Campsis grandiflora
Campsis radicans
Eccremocarpus scaber
Lonicera etrusca 'Superba'

▲ *Lonicera etrusca* 'Superba'

Lonicera sempervirens
Thunbergia alata

▼ *Lonicera sempervirens*

Pompom shaped

Rosa 'Mrs Sam McGredy, Climbing'
Rosa 'Orange Sunblaze, Climbing'

▲ *Rosa* 'Orange Sunblaze, Climbing'

Daisy-like

Mutisia decurrens

▲ *Mutisia decurrens*

YELLOW FLOWERS

TRUMPET OR BELL SHAPED

Jasminum species & cultivars

▲ *Jasminum mesnyi*

Lonicera species & cultivars
Tropaeolum majus

BOWL OR PLATE SHAPED

Clematis species & cultivars
Rosa cultivars
Smilax china
Thunbergia alata

▲ *Thunbergia alata*

BLUE FLOWERS

TRUMPET OR BELL SHAPED

Clematis 'Arabella'
Clematis macropetala

▲ *Codonopsis clematidea*

Codonopsis clematidea
Codonopsis convolvulacea
Codonopsis forrestii

BOWL OR PLATE SHAPED

Clematis cultivars
Solanum crispum

▲ *Solanum crispum*

PEA-LIKE

Lathyrus nervosus

▲ *Lathyrus nervosus*

PURPLE FLOWERS

TRUMPET OR BELL SHAPED

Clematis species & cultivars
Lonicera henryi

▲ *Clematis* 'Kermesina'

PEA-LIKE

Lathyrus grandiflorus
Lathyrus odoratus & cultivars
Vicia cracca

▲ *Vicia cracca*

Vicia sepium
Vicia sylvatica
Wisteria sinensis

SOFT-STEMMED PLANTS

WHITE OR CREAM FLOWERS

TRUMPET OR BELL SHAPED, ON PLANTS LESS THAN 30CM (12IN) TALL

Ajuga reptans 'Alba'
Campanula species & cultivars
Cymbalaria muralis 'Nana Alba'

▲ *Cymbalaria muralis* 'Nana Alba'

Freesia 'Ballerina'
Lamium species & cultivars
Nemesia caerulea 'Innocence'
Nicotiana x *sanderae* cultivars
Ourisia 'Snowflake'
Petunia x *hybrida* cultivars
Prunella species & cultivars
Wahlenbergia albomarginata

TRUMPET OR BELL SHAPED, ON PLANTS 30CM–1M (1–3FT) TALL WITH OVAL-SHAPED LEAVES

Antirrhinum majus cultivars
Campanula species & cultivars

▲ *Campanula alliariifolia*

Lilium species & cultivars
Lindelofia longiflora 'Alba'
Marrubium species & cultivars
Mentha longifolia & cultivars
Mirabilis jalapa
Monarda species
Nepeta cataria
Nicotiana x *sanderae* cultivars
Penstemon cultivars
Penstemon digitalis
Plectranthus oertendahlii
Polygonatum species & cultivars
Salvia argentea
Symphytum species

TRUMPET OR BELL SHAPED, ON PLANTS 30CM–1M (1–3FT) TALL WITH LONG, NARROW LEAVES

Allium unifolium
Gypsophila species & cultivars
Hemerocallis cultivars

▲ *Hemerocallis* 'Pandora's Box'

Lilium species & cultivars
Linaria purpurea 'Springside White'
Paradisea liliastrum
Polygonatum species & cultivars

Trumpet or bell shaped, on plants 30cm–1m (1–3ft) tall with lobed leaves

Acanthus species & cultivars
Heuchera Bressingham Hybrids

▲ *Heuchera micrantha* var. *diversifolia* 'Palace Purple'

Heuchera micrantha var. *diversifolia* 'Palace Purple'
Linanthus liniflorus

Trumpet or bell shaped, on plants more than 1m (3ft) tall

Agapanthus species & cultivars

▲ *Agapanthus campanulatus albidus*

Campanula species & cultivars
Cardiocrinum giganteum
Digitalis purpurea f. *albiflora*
Lilium species & cultivars
Morina longifolia
Polygonatum biflorum

Bowl or plate shaped, on plants less than 30cm (12in) tall; flowers borne singly

Arenaria species
Dianthus species & cultivars
Lychnis yunnanensis
Nymphaea species
Oenothera acaulis
Oxalis species & cultivars
Pratia species

▲ *Dianthus* 'Musgrave's Pink'

Pulsatilla alpina
Pulsatilla vulgaris & cultivars
Ranunculus species
Rhodohypoxis 'Ruth'
Sagina boydii
Silene alpestris
Viola hederacea

Bowl or plate shaped, on plants less than 30cm (12in) tall; flowers borne in groups; leaves oval shaped

Arabis alpina ssp. *caucasica* 'Schneehaube' ('Snowcap')
Begonia semperflorens & cultivars
Houttuynia cordata & cultivars
Lobularia maritima cultivars
Lychnis alpina 'Alba'
Myosotis species
Primula japonica cultivars
Saxifraga × *urbium*
Sedum species & cultivars

▲ *Saxifraga* × *urbium*

Bowl or plate shaped, on plants less than 30cm (12in) tall; flowers borne in groups; leaves long and narrow

Arthropodium cirratum
Dianthus barbatus
Dianthus squarrosus
Libertia pulchella

▼ *Dianthus squarrosus*

Bowl or plate shaped, on plants less than 30cm (12in) tall; flowers borne in groups; leaves feather-like or lobed

Geranium sessiliflorum ssp. *novae-zelandiae* 'Nigricans'
Oxalis triangularis ssp. *papilionacea*
Pelargonium species & cultivars
Polemonium brandegeei ssp. *mellitum*
Thalictrum kiusianum
Tiarella species

▲ *Tiarella cordifolia*

Bowl or plate shaped, on plants 30cm–1m (1–3ft) tall; flowers borne singly

Aquilegia flabellata var. *pumila* f. *alba*
Asparagus species & cultivars
Dianthus anatolicus
Diplarrhena moraea
Geranium sanguineum 'Album'
Impatiens species & cultivars
Malva moschata
Nigella nigellastrum
Oenothera speciosa
Paeonia lactiflora
Paeonia obovata
Papaver orientale 'Perry's White'
Verbascum phoeniceum

▼ *Papaver orientale* 'Perry's White'

Bowl or plate shaped, on plants 30cm–1m (1–3ft) tall; flowers borne in groups; leaves oval shaped

Linum perenne album

▲ *Linum perenne album*

Lysimachia clethroides
Matthiola incana
Primula denticulata var. *alba*
Smilacina racemosa

Bowl or plate shaped, on plants 30cm–1m (1–3ft) tall; flowers borne in groups; leaves long and narrow

Allium carinatum ssp. *pulchellum* f. *album*
Anthericum species
Asphodelus albus
Camassia leichtlinii 'Alba'
Libertia species

▲ *Libertia grandiflora*

Linum perenne album
Lychnis viscaria f. *album*
Ornithogallum thyrsoides
Zigadenus elegans

Bowl or plate shaped, on plants 30cm–1m (1–3ft) tall; flowers borne in groups; leaves rounded or with lobes

Anemone virginiana
Aquilegia fragrans
Galax urceolata
Menyanthes trifoliata

continued on next page

▲ *Pelargonium* 'L'Elegante'

Pelargonium species & cultivars
Tellima grandiflora

Bowl or plate shaped, on plants 30cm–1m (1–3ft) tall; flowers borne in groups; leaves feather-like

Consolida ajacis
Dictamnus albus

▲ *Dictamnus albus*

Filipendula species & cultivars
Myrrhis odorata
Polemonium caeruleum var. *album*
Thalictrum tuberosum

Bowl or plate shaped, on plants 30cm–1m (1–3ft) tall; flowers in groups; leaves resembling an arrowhead

Sagittaria sagittifolia

▼ *Sagittaria sagittifolia*

Bowl or plate shaped, on plants more than 1m (3ft) tall

Alcea species & cultivars
Angelica archangelica
Asparagus setaceus
Clematis recta 'Purpurea'
Delphinium cultivars
Eremurus himalaicus
Filipendula species & cultivars
Gillenia trifoliata
Papaver somniferum 'White Cloud'
Sagittaria latifolia
Saururus cernuus
Verbascum blattaria f. *albiflorum*
Xerophyllum tenax

▲ *Alcea rosea*

Pompom shaped

Achillea ptarmica & cultivars
Haemanthus albiflos
Leucanthemum × *superbum* cultivars

▲ *Leucanthemum* × *superbum* 'Wirral Supreme'

Meum athamanticum
Paeonia cultivars
Valeriana officinalis

Daisy-like

Achillea & cultivars
Anthemis tinctoria 'Alba'
Argyranthemum frutescens
Argyranthemum gracile
Aster alpinus var. *albus*
Celmisia semicordata
Chamaemelum nobile
Helichrysum bellidioides
Leucanthemum × *superbum*
Osteospermum cultivars

▲ *Osteospermum* 'Weetwood'

Stokesia laevis
Tanacetum species

Pea-like

Galega × *hartlandii* 'Alba'
Galega officinalis 'Alba'

Arum-like

Calla palustris
Zantedeschia aethiopica 'Crowborough'

▲ *Zantedeschia aethiopica* 'Crowborough'

Flowers in feathery plumes

Artemisia lactiflora
Aruncus species
Rodgersia species

▲ *Aruncus dioicus*

Bottlebrush shaped

Sanguisorba canadensis

▲ *Sanguisorba canadensis*

Flowers in dense, flattened clusters

Achillea clavennae
Achillea grandifolia
Achillea millefolium

▲ *Achillea grandifolia*

RED OR PINK FLOWERS

Trumpet or bell shaped, on plants less than 30cm (12in) tall

Anomatheca laxa
Asarum caudatum
Geranium cinereum var. *subcaulescens* 'Splendens'

▲ *Petunia* 'Fantasy mixed'

Heuchera cultivars
Incarvillea mairei 'Frank Ludlow'
Mimulus species & cultivars
Nemesia denticulata
Nicotiana × *sanderae* cultivars
Ophiopogon planiscapus 'Nigrescens'
Ourisia species & cultivars
Oxalis enneaphylla
Petunia × *hybrida* cultivars
Pulsatilla vulgaris var. *rubra*
Salvia splendens 'Sizzler'
Salvia splendens 'Vanguard'

Trumpet or bell shaped, on plants 30cm–1m (1–3ft) tall with oval-shaped leaves

Antirrhinum majus cultivars
Clematis integrifolia cultivars
Clintonia andrewsiana
Lamium species
Mimulus lewisii
Mirabilis jalapa
Monarda species & cultivars
Morina longifolia
Nepeta nepetella
Origanum laevigatum species & cultivars
Penstemon species & cultivars

▲ *Penstemon* 'Cherry Ripe'

Prunella grandiflora cultivars
Psyllostachys suworowii

Trumpet or bell shaped, on plants 30cm–1m (1–3ft) tall with long, narrow leaves

Allium species
Anigozanthos flavidus red
Crocosmia 'Emberglow'
Dierama dracomontanum
Hemerocallis cultivars

▲ *Dierama dracomontanum*

Lilium species & cultivars
Penstemon species & cultivars
Tritonia disticha ssp. *rubrolucens*

Trumpet or bell shaped, on plants 30cm–1m (1–3ft) tall with feather-like or lobed leaves

Corydalis sempervirens
Heuchera species & cultivars
Teucrium chamaedrys

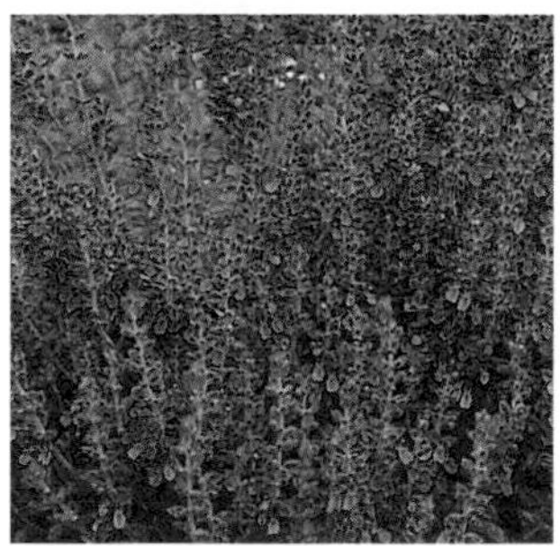

▲ *Teucrium chamaedrys*

Trumpet or bell shaped, on plants more than 1m (3ft) tall

Acanthus hungariacus
Crocosmia 'Lucifer'
Cyrtanthus elatus
Dierama pendulum
Digitalis species & cultivars
Lilium chalcedonicum
Lilium 'Cote d'Azur'
Lilium davidii
Lilium martagon
Lilium 'Pink Perfection Group'
Lilium speciosum var. *rubrum*
Monarda species
Symphytum species

▼ *Crocosmia* 'Lucifer'

Bowl or plate shaped, on plants less than 30cm (12in) tall; flowers borne singly

Dianthus species & cultivars

▲ *Dianthus* 'Lemsii'

Geranium sanguineum cultivars
Oenothera speciosa 'Rosea'
Rhodohypoxis species & cultivars
Saponaria species

Bowl or plate shaped, on plants less than 30cm (12in) tall; flowers in groups

Allium oreophilum 'Zwanenburg'
Begonia semperflorens & cultivars
Gypsophila species & cultivars
Iberis umbellata cultivars
Impatiens species & cultivars
Lobularia maritima 'Wonderland'
Lychnis species & cultivars
Malcomia maritima
Oxalis triangularis
Pelargonium species & cultivars
Potentilla nepalensis & cultivars

▲ *Potentilla nepalensis* 'Roxana'

Primula species & cultivars
Saponaria species & cultivars
Saxifraga × *primulaize*
Sempervivum species & cultivars
Thalictrum isopyroides

Bowl or plate shaped, on plants 30cm–1m (1–3ft) tall; flowers borne singly

Dianthus species & cultivars
Glaucidium palmatum
Malva species & cultivars

▲ *Malva sylvestris* 'Mauritania'

Nomocharis species
Impatiens balsamina
Paeonia species & cultivars
Papaver species & cultivars
Primula japonica 'Miller's Crimson'
Tradescantia pallida 'Purpurea'
Tradescantia zebrina 'Purpusii'
Verbascum phoeniceum

Bowl or plate shaped, on plants 30cm–1m (1–3ft) tall; flowers borne in groups

Allium cernuum
Astrantia species & cultivars
Begonia × *tuberhybrida* cultivars
Consolida ajacis
Dianthus armeria
Dianthus barbatus & cultivars
Dictamnus albus var. *purpureus*
Filipendula palmata cultivars
Geum chiloense 'Mrs J Bradshaw'
Hemerocallis cultivars
Impatiens species & cultivars
Lychnis species & cultivars
Lythrum species & cultivars
Matthiola incana
Pelargonium species & cultivars
Persicaria milletii
Rodgersia pinnata
Saponaria vaccaria & cultivars
Verbascum phoeniceum

▼ *Lychnis flos-jovis* 'Hort's Variety'

Bowl or plate shaped, on plants more than 1m (3ft) tall; flowers in groups

Althaea officinalis
Butomus umbellatus
Delphinium species & cultivars
Eremurus robustus
Filipendula species & cultivars
Rodgersia sambucifolia

▲ *Butomus umbellatus*

Daisy-like

Centaurea montana 'Carnea'
Centaurea simplicicaulis
Cosmos species & cultivars
Crepis incana
Felicia petiolata
Gaillardia species & cultivars
Lampranthus species & cultivars
Osteospermum jucundum
Osteospermum 'Hopleys'
Osteospermum 'Langtrees'
Osteospermum 'Pink Whirls'

▲ *Osteospermum* 'Langtrees'

Pea-like

Lotus berthelotii
Lupinus cultivars
Polygala species

▼ *Lotus berthelotii*

Flowers in feathery plumes

Astilbe glaberrima var. *saxatilis*
Rheum palmatum & cultivars

▲ *Astilbe glaberrima* var. *saxatilis*

Heart shaped

Dicentra species & cultivars

▲ *Dicentra* 'Spring Morning'

Iris-like

Iris species & cultivars
Roscoea scillifolia

▼ *Iris ensata* 'Rose Queen'

Bottlebrush shaped

Sanguisorba officinalis

▲ *Sanguisorba officinalis*

Thistle-like

Onopordum nervosum

▲ *Onopordum nervosum*

Flowers in dense, flattened clusters

Achillea species & cultivars

▼ *Achillea* 'Lachsschönheit'

ORANGE FLOWERS

Trumpet or bell shaped

Crocosmia species & cultivars
Hemerocallis cultivars
Lilium species & cultivars
Mimulus 'Highland Orange'

▲ *Mimulus* 'Highland Orange'

Bowl or plate shaped

Begonia sutherlandii
Begonia × *tuberhybrida* cultivars
Euphorbia species
Geum species & cultivars

▲ *Geum chiloense* 'Dolly North'

Glaucium corniculatum
Impatiens species & cultivars
Papaver species & cultivars
Potentilla species & cultivars
Primula chungensis
Primula cockburniana

Pompom shaped

Tagetes species & cultivars

▼ *Tagetes* 'Excel Orange'

Daisy-like

Cosmos sulphureus
Lampranthus aurantiacus
Lampranthus brownii
Tagetes species & cultivars

▲ *Lampranthus aurantiacus*

YELLOW FLOWERS

Trumpet or bell shaped, on plants less than 30cm (12in) tall

Allium flavum
Freesia cultivars
Hemerocallis 'Stella de Oro'
Mimulus species & cultivars
Petunia x *hybrida* cultivars
Primula elatior
Sisyrinchium patagonicum

▲ *Mimulus primuloides*

Trumpet or bell shaped, on plants 30cm–1m (1–3ft) tall

Anigozanthos species & cultivars

▲ *Campanula thyrsoides*

Campanula thyrsoides
Hemerocallis cultivars
Lysimachia punctata
Mimulus guttatus
Nemesia species & cultivars
Penstemon pinifolius 'Mersea Yellow'
Primula florindae
Primula sikkimensis

Trumpet or bell shaped, on plants more than 1m (3ft) tall

Cautleya spicata
Lilium cultivars

▲ *Lilium* 'African Queen'

Bowl or plate shaped, on plants less than 30cm (12in) tall

Alchemilla species
Azorella trifurcata & cultivars
Delphinium nudicaule 'Luteum'
Dianthus cultivars
Hypericum trichocaulon
Lysimachia species & cultivars
Myosotis australis
Oenothera species & cultivars

▼ *Oenothera macrocarpa*

Papaver miyabeanum
Paris thibetica
Polemonium brandegeei
Ranunculus species & cultivars
Sedum species & cultivars
Sempervivum species
Trollius species
Verbascum dumulosum

Bowl or plate shaped, on plants 30cm–1m (1–3ft) tall

Allium moly
Asphodeline species
Begonia x *tuberhybrida* cultivars
Chelidonium majus
Euphorbia species
Geum species & cultivars
Glaucium species
Hemerocallis cultivars
Hypericum species
Lysimachia species & cultivars
Meconopsis villosa
Oenothera species & cultivars
Polemonium pauciflorum
Potentilla recta
Primula species
Pulsatilla alpina ssp. *apiifolia*
Ranunculus acris 'Flore Pleno'
Sisyrinchium californicum
Stylophorum diphyllum
Trollius species

▲ *Allium moly*

Bowl or plate shaped, on plants more than 1m (3ft) tall

Asphodeline lutea
Eremurus stenophyllus
Paeonia mlokosewitschii
Thalictrum flavum
Verbascum blattaria
Verbascum bombyciferum
Verbascum thapsus

▼ *Paeonia mlokosewitschii*

Daisy-like, on plants less than 1m (3ft) tall

Achillea species & cultivars
Anthemis species & cultivars
Argyranthemum maderense
Asteriscus maritimus
Coreopsis species & cultivars
Hieracium species
Leucanthemum x *superbum* 'Sonnenschein'
Matricaria recutita
Osteospermum 'Buttermilk'
X *Solidaster luteus*
Tagetes species & cultivars
Tanacetum densum
Ursinia species

▲ *Anthemis tinctoria* 'E.C. Buxton'

Daisy-like, on plants more than 1m (3ft) tall

Buphthalmum salicifolium
Tanacetum vulgare

▼ *Buphthalmum salicifolium*

Pea-like

Lathyrus aureus
Lupinus species & cultivars
Thermopsis species

▲ *Thermopsis villosa*

Arum-like

Zantedeschia elliottiana

▲ *Zantedeschia elliottiana*

Iris-like

Iris species & cultivars
Roscoea cautleoides

▼ *Roscoea cautleoides*

Flowers in dense, flattened clusters

Achillea millefolium 'Hoffnung'
Achillea x *lewisii* 'King Edward'
Achillea 'Moonshine'
Achillea 'Taygetea'

▲ *Achillea* 'Taygetea'

YELLOW FLOWERS SPOTTED CRIMSON OR BROWN

Bowl or plate shaped

Tigridia pavonia

▲ *Tigridia pavonia*

GREEN FLOWERS

Trumpet or bell shaped

Ballota 'All Hallows Green'
Heuchera americana
Heuchera cylindrica 'Greenfinch'
Nicotiana x *sanderae* cultivars

▼ *Nicotiana* x *sanderae*

Bowl or plate shaped

Euphorbia species
Paris quadrifolia
Paris thibetica

▲ *Euphorbia amygdaloides* var. *robbiae*

GREEN-WHITE FLOWERS

Trumpet or bell shaped

Heuchera 'Green Ivory'
Polygonatum verticillatum

▲ *Heuchera* 'Green Ivory'

Bottlebrush shaped

Sanguisorba minor

▼ *Sanguisorba minor*

GREEN FLOWERS VEINED PURPLE WITH PINK-TINGED PETALS

Trumpet or bell shaped

Epipactis gigantea

▲ *Epipactis gigantea*

BLUE FLOWERS

Trumpet or bell shaped, on plants less than 30cm (12in) tall

Ajuga pyramidalis
Ajuga reptans & cultivars
Campanula species
Corydalis cashmeriana
Echium vulgare 'Blue Bedder'
Freesia 'Royal Blue'
Gentiana species & cultivars

▲ *Gentiana gracilipes*

Laurentia axillaris
Lobelia erinus & cultivars
Myosotidium hortensia
Nemesia caerulea
Penstemon species & cultivars
Petunia x *hybrida* cultivars
Prunella grandiflora 'Blue Loveliness'
Scutellaria scordiifolia
Synthyris stellata
Wahlenbergia species

Trumpet or bell shaped, on plants 30cm-1m (1-3ft) tall; flowers borne singly; leaves oval shaped

Clematis species & cultivars
Codonopsis ovata

▲ *Codonopsis ovata*

Trumpet or bell shaped, on plants 30cm-1m (1-3ft) tall; flowers in groups; leaves oval shaped

Brunnera macrophylla cultivars
Campanula species & cultivars
Lobelia valida
Mertensia ciliata
Nepeta species
Penstemon species & cultivars
Plectranthus forsteri & cultivars
Salvia candelabrum
Salvia farinacea 'Strata'
Symphytum caucasicum

▼ *Nepeta nervosa*

Trumpet or bell shaped, on plants 30cm-1m (1-3ft) tall with narrow leaves

Amsonia tabernaemontana var. *salicifolia*
Dracocephalum ruyschianum
Penstemon species & cultivars

▲ *Amsonia tabernaemontana* var. *salicifolia*

Trumpet or bell shaped, on plants more than 1m (3ft) tall

Amsonia orientalis
Anchusa azurea
Symphytum × *uplandicum*

▲ *Amsonia orientalis*

Bowl or plate shaped, on plants less than 30cm (12in) tall

Anchusa caespitosa
Delphinium cashmerianum
Maranta leuconeura var. *kerchoveana*
Myosotis alpestris

▼ *Myosotis scorpioides* 'Mermaid'

Myosotis scorpioides 'Mermaid'
Myosotis sylvatica & cultivars
Nemesia strumosa 'Blue Gem'
Nemophila menziesii
Polemonium boreale
Veronica species

Bowl or plate shaped, on plants 30cm-1m (1-3ft) tall

Aphyllanthes monspeliensis
Camassia leichtlinii Caerulea Group
Consolida ajacis
Cynoglossum nervosum
Delphinium species & cultivars
Linum species

▲ *Delphinium grandiflorum*

Nigella nigellastrum 'Summer Stars'
Phacelia species
Polemonium species & cultivars
Primula vialii
Tradescantia virginiana 'Isis'
Veronica species

Bowl or plate shaped, on plants more than 1m (3ft) tall

Delphinium species & cultivars
Meconopsis betonicifolia
Meconopsis grandis
Meconopsis × *sheldonii* & cultivars

▼ *Delphinium* 'Spindrift'

Daisy-like

Felicia species & cultivars
Osteospermum cultivars
Stokesia laevis

▲ *Felicia amelloides* 'Santa Anita'

Pea-like

Polygala calcarea Bulley's form
Polygala calcarea 'Lillet'

▲ *Polygala calcarea* 'Lillet'

Iris-like

Iris species & cultivars

▼ *Iris* 'Gerald Darby'

Hood or helmet shaped

Aconitum napellus

▲ *Aconitum napellus*

PURPLE FLOWERS

Trumpet or bell shaped, on plants less than 30cm (12in) tall with oval-shaped leaves

Ajuga reptans & cultivars
Asarum hartwegii
Campanula species
Cymbalaria hepaticifolia
Horminum pyrenaicum
Hosta venusta
Lamium species & cultivars
Nemesia caerulea cultivars

▲ *Nemesia caerulea* 'Joan Wilder'

Nemesia denticulata
Nepeta × *faassenii*
Penstemon glaber

▲ *Nepeta* × *faassenii*

Petunia × *hybrida* cultivars
Primula species & cultivars
Prunella grandiflora
Salvia splendens & cultivars
Scutellaria alpina
Teucrium species

Trumpet or bell shaped, on plants less than 30cm (12in) tall with long, narrow leaves

Allium species
Penstemon species
Polygonatum hookeri

▲ *Polygonatum hookeri*

Trumpet or bell shaped, on plants less than 30cm (12in) tall with feather-like or lobed leaves

Aquilegia bertolonii
Delphinium brunonianum

▲ *Aquilegia bertolonii*

Pulsatilla species & cultivars
Teucrium species

Trumpet or bell shaped, on plants 30cm–1m (1–3ft) tall, with oval-shaped leaves

Campanula species & cultivars

▲ *Campanula latifolia*

Cynoglossum officinale
Hosta species & cultivars
Mentha longifolia & cultivars
Mertensia sibirica
Monarda species & cultivars
Nepeta species & cultivars
Penstemon species & cultivars
Phlomis purpurea
Primula secundiflora
Salvia species & cultivars

Trumpet or bell shaped, on plants 30cm–1m (1–3ft) tall with long, narrow leaves

Allium species
Bletilla striata
Echium vulgare
Hemerocallis cultivars
Penstemon species & cultivars

▲ *Penstemon* 'Catherine de la Mare'

Trumpet or bell shaped, on plants 30cm–1m (1–3ft) tall with feather-like or lobed leaves

Delphinium cashmerianum
Delphinium requienii
Salvia species & cultivars
Semiaquilegia ecalcarata
Verbena species & cultivars

▲ *Semiaquilegia ecalcarata*

Trumpet or bell shaped, on plants more than 1m (3ft) tall

Ballota nigra
Lilium martagon var. *cattaniae*
Malva sylvestris
Nicandra physalodes
Strobilanthes atropurpureus

▲ *Strobilanthes atropurpureus*

Symphytum officinale
Symphytum × *uplandicum*
Verbena hastata

Bowl or plate shaped, on plants less than 30cm (12in) tall with oval-shaped leaves

Lychnis species & cultivars
Nemesia versicolor

Primula × *pubescens* cultivars
Veronica cinerea
Viola species

▲ *Viola* × *wittrockiana* 'Universal'

Bowl or plate shaped, on plants with long, narrow leaves

Allium senescens
Sisyrinchium idahoense

▲ *Allium senescens*

Bowl or plate shaped, on plants less than 30cm (12in) tall with feather-like or lobed leaves

Cortusa matthioli
Erodium glandulosum
Erodium manescaui
Geranium species & cultivars
Oxalis species & cultivars
Pelargonium species & cultivars
Pulsatilla vulgaris
Thalictrum chelidonii
Viola species & cultivars

▲ *Geranium himalayense* 'Gravetye'

Bowl or plate shaped, on plants 30cm–1m (1–3ft) tall with oval-shaped leaves

Impatiens species & cultivars
Mathiola incana
Nemesia strumosa
Primula pulverulenta
Verbascum phoeniceum

▲ *Verbascum phoeniceum*

Bowl or plate shaped, on plants 30cm–1m (1–3ft) tall with long, narrow leaves

Allium species & cultivars
Tradescantia × *andersoniana* & cultivars

▲ *Tradescantia* × *andersoniana* 'Karminglut'

Bowl or plate shaped, on plants 30cm–1m (1–3ft) tall with lobed or feather-like leaves

Delphinium species & cultivars
Pelargonium species & cultivars
Solanum sisymbriifolium
Thalictrum diffusiflorum

▼ *Delphinium* 'Spindrift'

Bowl or plate shaped, on plants more than 1m (3ft) tall

Delphinium cultivars
Lythrum salicaria

▲ *Lythrum salicaria*

Malva sylvestris
Thalictrum minus adiantifolium

Pompom shaped

Dipsacus fullonum
Dipsacus sativus
Globularia cordifolia

▲ *Globularia cordifolia*

Daisy-like

Catananche caerulea

▲ *Catananche caerulea*

Felicia petiolata
Lampranthus spectabilis
Osteospermum jucundum
Stokesia laevis

Pea-like

Galega officinalis
Hedysarum coronarium
Lupinus albifrons
Polygala species & cultivars

▲ *Galega officinalis*

Iris-like

Iris species & cultivars
Roscoea alpina
Roscoea purpurea

▲ *Roscoea purpurea*

Thistle-like

Cynara cardunculus
Onopordum acanthium

▲ *Cynara cardunculus*

Late Summer

Late-flowering annuals and shrubs come into flower, and berries form on the shrubs and climbers that bloomed earlier

TREES AND SHRUBS

WHITE OR CREAM FLOWERS

Trumpet or bell shaped

Abelia chinensis
Abelia × grandiflora
Buddleja davidii 'White Profusion'
Calluna vulgaris cultivars
Hibiscus syriacus & cultivars
Lavandula angustifolia 'Alba'
Ligustrum species
Nerium oleander
Oxydendrum arboreum
Rosmarinus officinalis var. *albiflorus*

▲ *Oxydendrum arboreum*

Bowl or plate shaped, borne singly

Asparagus verticillatus
Cistus × aguilarii & cultivars

▲ *Cistus × aguilarii* 'Maculatus'

Clematis species & cultivars
Cotoneaster species & cultivars
Eucryphia species & cultivars
Myrtus communis & cultivars
Philadelphus species
Potentilla cultivars
Rosa species & cultivars
Rubus pentalobus

Bowl or plate shaped, borne in groups

Aralia species & cultivars
Clematis flammula
Clethra species
Cotoneaster species & cultivars
Escallonia cultivars
× *Halimiocistus sahucii*
Holodiscus discolor

▲ *Holodiscus discolor*

Hydrangea species & cultivars
Iberis species & cultivars
Philadelphus coronarius
Rosa cultivars
Sorbaria sorbifolia
Spiraea species & cultivars

Daisy-like

Olearia species & cultivars

▲ *Olearia* 'Waikariensis'

Pea-like

Gymnocladus dioica
Ononis rotundifolia
Sophora species

▲ *Sophora japonica*

Catkin-like

Itea ilicifolia
Itea virginiana

▲ *Itea ilicifolia*

WHITE-AND-RED FLOWERS

Trumpet or bell shaped

Fuchsia 'Alice Hoffman'
Fuchsia 'Lady Thumb'

▲ *Fuchsia* 'Lady Thumb'

Fuchsia 'Madame Cornelissen'
Fuchsia magellanica var. *molinae*
Fuchsia 'Snowcap'
Fuchsia 'Swingtime'

RED OR PINK FLOWERS

Trumpet or bell shaped on shrubs less than 60cm (2ft) tall

Calluna vulgaris cultivars

▲ *Calluna vulgaris* 'Silver Queen'

Lavandula angustifolia cultivars
Teucrium species
Thymus species & cultivars

▲ *Teucrium subspinosium*

Trumpet or bell shaped on shrubs more than 60cm (2ft) tall

Abelia floribunda
Abelia schumannii
Bouvardia cultivars
Buddleja davidii 'Royal Red'
Clerodendrum bungei
Hibiscus rosa-sinensis & cultivars
Hibiscus syriacus & cultivars
Jasminum beesianum

▲ *Abelia floribunda*

Lantana camara 'Brasier'
Melianthus major
Nerium oleander
Russelia equisetiformis
Salvia officinalis
Teucrium species

Bowl or plate shaped, borne singly

Cistus species & cultivars
Potentilla nitida & cultivars
Rosa species & cultivars

▲ *Cistus crispus*

Bowl or plate shaped, borne in groups

Callicarpa bodinieri var. *giraldii*
Cotoneaster splendens
Escallonia species & cultivars
Hydrangea species & cultivars
Parahebe catarractae ssp. *diffusa*
Potentilla cultivars
Rosa species & cultivars
Rubus odoratus
Spiraea species

▼ *Potentilla nepalensis* 'Miss Willmott'

Pompom shaped

Metrosideros excelsa
Metrosideros kermadecensis & cultivars
Rosa species & cultivars

▲ *Metrosideros kermadecensis* 'Variegata'

Pea-like

Erythrina crista-galli
Hedysarum multijugum
Indigofera amblyantha
Polygala × *dalmaisiana*

▲ *Indigofera amblyantha*

RED AND PINK/PURPLE FLOWERS

Trumpet or bell shaped

Fuchsia 'Eva Boerg'
Fuchsia 'Lena'
Fuchsia magellanica & cultivars

▲ *Fuchsia* 'Eva Boerg'

Fuchsia 'Mrs Popple'
Fuchsia riccartonii
Fuchsia 'Royal Velvet'

ORANGE FLOWERS

Bowl or plate shaped

Helianthemum 'Ben Afflick'
Helianthemum 'Ben Dearg'
Potentilla 'Hopleys Orange'

▲ *Potentilla* 'Hopleys Orange'

Potentilla 'Tangerine'
Rosa cultivars

Pompom shaped

Buddleja × *weyeriana* & cultivars
Rosa cultivars

▲ *Buddleja* × *weyeriana* 'Golden Glow'

YELLOW FLOWERS

Trumpet or bell shaped

Cestrum parqui
Diervilla sessilifolia
Diervilla × *splendens*
Hibiscus rosa-sinensis 'Lemon Chiffon'
Koelreuteria paniculata
Linum arboreum
Phlomis fruiticosa
Phlomis longifolia var. bailanica

▲ *Diervilla sessilifolia*

Teucrium scorodonia
Weigela middendorffiana

Bowl or plate shaped

Fremontodendron species & cultivars
Helianthemum species
Hypericum species & cultivars
Jasminum fruticans
Jasminum parkeri
Lantana camara 'Drap d'Or'

▲ *Hypericum kouytchense*

Potentilla species & cultivars
Rosa cultivars
Sorbaria tomentosa

Pompom shaped

Artemisia abrotanum
Buddleja globosa
Rosa species & cultivars

▼ *Buddleja globosa*

Daisy-like

Brachyglottis compacta
Brachyglottis monroi
Brachyglottis 'Sunshine'

▲ *Brachyglottis* 'Sunshine'

Euryops acraeus
Helichrysum italicum
Helichrysum splendidum

Pea-like

Colutea arborescens
Lupinus arboreus
Piptanthus nepalensis

▼ *Lupinus arboreus*

BLUE FLOWERS

Trumpet or bell shaped

Buddleja davidii 'Nanho Blue'
Buddleja 'Lochinch'
Caryopteris × *clandonensis* & cultivars

▲ *Caryopteris* × *clandonensis* 'Heavenly Blue'

Hibiscus syriacus & cultivars
Lavandula angustifolia 'Munstead'
Rosmarinus officinalis

▲ *Rosmarinus officinalis*

Bowl or plate shaped

Hebe cupressoides & cultivars
Hebe 'Mrs Winder'
Hydrangea species & cultivars

▼ *Hydrangea serrata*

PURPLE FLOWERS

Trumpet or bell shaped

Buddleja species
Calluna vulgaris cultivars
Caryopteris × *clandonensis* 'Ferndown'
Cestrum elegans
Clematis addisonii
Fuchsia 'Mantilla'
Lantana montevidensis
Lavandula species & cultivars
Phlomis purpurea
Teucrium fruticans
Thymus species & cultivars
Vitex agnus-castus

▲ *Vitex agnus-castus*

Bowl or plate shaped

Cistus × *pulverulentus*
Hebe species & cultivars
Hydrangea aspera & cultivars

▼ *Hydrangea aspera* Villosa Group

TREES AND SHRUBS WITH WINGED SEEDPODS

Acer species & cultivars
Fraxinus angustifolia 'Raywood'
Fraxinus excelsior 'Westhof's Glorie'
Fraxinus ornus

▲ *Fraxinus ornus*

TREES AND SHRUBS WITH COLOURFUL FRUIT, BERRIES AND SEEDPODS

Smaller than pea-size

Azara microphylla & cultivars
Berberis species & cultivars
Daphne species & cultivars
Lonicera nitida 'Baggesen's Gold'
Lonicera pileata
Osmanthus decorus
Ribes sanguineum & cultivars

▼ *Ribes sanguineum*

Pea-size, red or pink

Aucuba japonica & cultivars
Crataegus laevigata 'Paul's Scarlet'
Crataegus laevigata 'Plena'
Crataegus monogyna & cultivars
Daphne acutiloba
Lindera species
Lonicera species
Malus hupehensis

▲ *Malus hupehensis*

▲ *Malus* × *moerlandsii* 'Liset'

Malus x *moerlandsii* 'Liset'
Photinia villosa
Prunus pumila var. *depressa*
Skimmia japonica reevesiana
Viburnum species & cultivars

Pea-size, yellow

Azara dentata
Celastrus species
Daphne cneorum
Malus floribunda
Malus x *hartwigii* 'Katherine'
Pyracantha 'Soleil d'Or'

▼ *Pyracantha* 'Soleil d'Or'

Pea-size, blue/purple/violet/black

Amelanchier species
Azara petiolaris
Azara serrata
Berberis candidula
Lindera obtusiloba
Lonicera species & cultivars

▲ *Lonicera henryi*

Phillyrea latifolia
Prunus laurocerasus & cultivars
Prunus padus & cultivars
Prunus spinosa
Prunus x *yedoensis* & cultivars
Ribes species & cultivars
Rosa x *harrisonii*
Sambucus nigra

Cherry-size, blue/purple/violet/black

Amelanchier laevis
Azara lanceolata
Morus nigra
Osmanthus species
Prunus avium 'Plena'
Prunus x *cistena*
Prunus virginiana 'Shubert'
Rubus cockburnianus
Rubus thibetanus

▼ *Morus nigra*

Cherry-size, brown

Illicium anisatum
Illicium floridanum
Lindera praecox
Platanus x *hispanica*

▲ *Platanus orientalis*

Platanus orientalis
Rosa xanthina 'Canary Bird'

Cherry-size, green

Alnus glutinosa & cultivars

▲ *Alnus glutinosa*

Alnus incana & cultivars
Betula costata
Betula 'Jermyns'
Betula pendula & cultivars

Cherry-size, orange

Crataegus x *lavallei* 'Carrierei'

▼ *Crataegus* × *lavallei* 'Carrierei'

Malus x *purpurea* 'Neville Copeman'

▲ *Malus* × *purpurea* 'Neville Copeman'

Rosa fedtschenkoana
Rosa sericea ssp. *omeinensis* f. *pteracantha*
Rubus spectabilis

Cherry-size, red

Daphne retusa
Malus species & cultivars

▲ *Malus* 'Evereste'

Morus alba
Prunus species & cultivars
Rosa x *alba* 'Alba Semiplena'
Rosa 'Fru Dagmar Hastrup'
Rosa 'Geranium'
Rosa 'Maiden's Blush'
Rosa rugosa cultivars
Rosa xanthina hugonis
Rubus species

Cherry-size, yellow

Malus x *robusta* 'Yellow Siberian'
Prunus tenella & cultivars
Rubus biflorus

▼ *Malus* × *robusta* 'Yellow Siberian'

Cherry-size, white

Cornus alba 'Sibirica'
Gaultheria species & cultivars
Sorbus cashmeriana
Symphoricarpos albus & cultivars

▲ *Symphoricarpos albus*

More than cherry-size, brown

Aesculus × *carnea*
Alnus cordata

▲ *Alnus cordata*

More than cherry-size, green

Aesculus indica & cultivars
Aesculus × *neglecta* 'Erythroblastos'
Aesculus parviflora
Aesculus pavia
Alnus glutinosa & cultivars
Pyrus nivalis
Pyrus salicifolia 'Pendula'

▼ *Pyrus salicifolia* 'Pendula'

More than cherry-size, red

Arbutus species
Cornus kousa
Malus species & cultivars

▲ *Malus* 'Veitch's Scarlet'

More than cherry-size, yellow

Malus × *zumi* 'Golden Hornet'
Poncirus trifoliata
Prunus mume & cultivars

▲ *Malus* × *zumi* 'Golden Hornet'

CLIMBING AND RAMBLING PLANTS

WHITE OR CREAM FLOWERS

Trumpet or bell shaped

Clematis campaniflora
Codonopsis convolvulacea 'Alba'
Jasminum officinale
Thunbergia alata & cultivars

▼ *Jasminum officinale*

Bowl or plate shaped

Clematis fargesii
Clematis – Early Large-Flowered Group (second flowering)
Clematis – Late Large-Flowered Group

▲ *Clematis* 'John Huxtable'

Clematis × *triternata* 'Rubromarginata'
Clematis – Viticella Group
Jasminum azoricum
Trachelospermum species

Hydrangea-like flowers

Hydrangea anomala ssp. *petiolaris*

▲ *Hydrangea anomala* ssp. *petiolaris*

Hydrangea serratifolia
Schizophragma hydrangeoides
Schizophragma integrifolium

▼ *Schizophragma integrifolium*

WHITE-AND-BLUE FLOWERS

Trumpet or bell shaped

Ipomoea tricolor 'Flying Saucers'
Ipomoea tricolor 'Heavenly Blue'

▲ *Ipomoea tricolor* 'Heavenly Blue'

RED OR PINK FLOWERS

Trumpet or bell shaped

Clematis 'Comtesse de Bouchaud'
Clematis 'Duchess of Albany'
Clematis 'Gravetye Beauty'

▲ *Clematis* 'Gravetye Beauty'

Bowl or plate shaped

Clematis 'Edward Prichard'
Clematis – Early Large-Flowered Group (second flowering)
Clematis – Late Large-Flowered Group
Clematis – Viticella Group
Clerodendrum splendens
Jasminum × *stephanense*
Passiflora × *exoniensis*
Rubus henryi
Tropaeolum speciosum
Tropaeolum tuberosum

▲ *Clematis* 'Rouge Cardinale'

ORANGE FLOWERS

Trumpet or bell shaped

Campsis grandiflora
Campsis radicans
Eccremocarpus scaber
Thunbergia alata & cultivars

▲ *Eccremocarpus scaber*

Daisy-like

Mutisia decurrens

▲ *Mutisia decurrens*

YELLOW FLOWERS

Trumpet or bell shaped

Campsis radicans f. *flava*
Clematis 'Aureolin'
Clematis 'Bill Mackenzie'
Clematis 'Burford'
Clematis 'Corry'
Clematis 'Helios'
Clematis rehderiana
Clematis tangutica
Thunbergia alata 'Susie Hybrids'

▼ *Clematis* 'Helios'

Bowl or plate shaped

Clematis akebioides
Clematis 'Gravetye'

▲ *Clematis* 'Moonlight'

Clematis ladakhiana
Clematis 'Moonlight'
Clematis petriei
Clematis 'Wada's Primrose'
Smilax china
Smilax discotis
Tropaeolum majus & cultivars

Fan shaped

Tropaeolum peregrinum

▲ *Tropaeolum peregrinum*

BLUE FLOWERS

Trumpet or bell shaped

Clematis 'Arabella'
Codonopsis clematidea
Codonopsis convolvulacea
Codonopsis forrestii
Convolvulus tricolor & cultivars
Ipomoea indica
Ipomoea nil

▼ *Codonopsis clematidea*

Bowl or plate shaped

Clematis – Early Large-Flowered Group (second flowering)
Clematis – Late Large-Flowered Group

▲ *Solanum crispum*

Clematis – Viticella Group
Solanum crispum

PURPLE FLOWERS

Trumpet or bell shaped

Clematis 'Arabella'
Clematis 'Etoile Violette'
Clematis 'Petit Faucon'
Ipomoea indica
Ipomoea purpurea

▲ *Ipomoea purpurea*

Bowl or plate shaped

Clematis patens
Clematis – Early Large-Flowered Group (second flowering)
Clematis – Late Large-Flowered Group
Clematis – Viticella Group
Clematis 'Vyvyan Pennell'
Passiflora × *caeruleoracemosa*

▲ *Clematis* 'Vyvyan Pennell'

▲ *Passiflora* × *caeruleoracemosa*

Pea-like

Lathyrus odoratus
Vicia species

▲ *Lathyrus odoratus*

SOFT-STEMMED PLANTS

WHITE OR CREAM FLOWERS

Trumpet or bell shaped, on plants less than 30cm (12in) tall

Cymbalaria muralis 'Nana Alba'
Gypsophila species & cultivars
Liriope spicata 'Alba'
Lobelia erinus & cultivars
Nemesia caerulea 'Innocence'
Petunia × *hybrida* cultivars
Prunella grandiflora cultivars

▲ *Liriope spicata* 'Alba'

Trumpet or bell shaped, on plants 30cm–1m (1–3ft) tall

Agapanthus species & cultivars
Antirrhinum majus cultivars
Gypsophila species & cultivars
Hibiscus moscheutus 'Disco Belle Mixed'
Hibiscus trionum
Hosta species & cultivars
Limonium sinuatum
Lobelia siphilitica 'Alba'
Malope trifida 'White Queen'
Mentha longifolia & cultivars
Nepeta species & cultivars
Nicotiana alata
Nicotiana × *sanderae* & cultivars
Penstemon digitalis

▼ *Hibiscus trionum*

Trumpet or bell shaped, on plants more than 1m (3ft) tall

Acanthus mollis
Acanthus spinosus
Crinum × *powellii* 'Album'
Hemerocallis cultivars
Hibiscus manihot & cultivars
Hibiscus moscheutus
Lilium species & cultivars
Nicotiana species & cultivars

▲ *Nicotiana sylvestris*

Bowl or plate shaped, on plants less than 30cm (12in) tall with oval-shaped leaves

Begonia semperflorens & cultivars
Houttuynia cordata & cultivars
Lychnis species & cultivars
Pratia species
Rhodohypoxis cultivars

▲ *Houttuynia cordata*

Bowl or plate shaped, on plants less than 30cm (12in) tall with long, narrow leaves

Dianthus species & cultivars
Libertia pulchella
Sisyrinchium 'Pole Star'

▼ *Dianthus* 'Dewdrop'

Bowl or plate shaped, on plants less than 30cm (12in) tall with feather-like or lobed leaves

Oenothera acaulis
Pelargonium species & cultivars
Potentilla alba
Thalictrum kiusianum

▲ *Potentilla alba*

Bowl or plate shaped, on plants less than 30cm (12in) tall with succulent leaves

Sedum species & cultivars

▲ *Sedum forsterianum*

Bowl or plate shaped, on plants 30cm–1m (1–3ft) tall with oval-shaped leaves

Begonia grandis ssp. *evansiana* 'Alba'
Begonia × *tuberhybrida* cultivars

▼ *Begonia* × *tuberhybrida* 'Non-Stop'

Lychnis species & cultivars
Polemonium caeruleum var. *album*
Saponaria officinalis 'Alba Plena'

Bowl or plate shaped, on plants 30cm–1m (1–3ft) tall with long, narrow leaves

Allium carinatum ssp. *pulchellum* f. *album*
Libertia species
Schizostylis coccinea var. *alba*
Xerophyllum tenax

▲ *Schizostylis coccinea* var. *alba*

Bowl or plate shaped, on plants 30cm–1m (1–3ft) tall with feather-like or lobed leaves

Anemone vitifolia
Astrantia major ssp. *involucrata* 'Shaggy'

▲ *Astrantia major* ssp. *involucrata* 'Shaggy'

Delphinium grandiflorum
Malva moschata var. *alba*
Nigella species
Oenothera speciosa
Papaver orientale 'Perry's White'
Pelargonium species & cultivars
Thalictrum tuberosum

Bowl or plate shaped, on plants more than 1m (3ft) tall

Anemone × *hybrida* & cultivars
Clematis recta 'Purpurea'
Liatris spicata 'Alba'
Papaver somniferum 'White Cloud'
Romneya coulteri
Selinum wallichianum
Yucca species & cultivars

▲ *Romneya coulteri*

Pompom shaped

Achillea ptarmica The Pearl Group
Artemisia schmidtiana & cultivars
Callistephus chinensis cultivars
Dahlia 'Hillcrest Albino'
Dahlia 'Kenora Challenger'
Dahlia 'My Love'
Dahlia 'Omo'
Dahlia 'Small World'
Dendranthema species & cultivars
Dianthus cultivars

▼ *Dahlia* 'Hillcrest Albino'

Daisy-like on plants less than 30cm (12in) tall

Achillea species & cultivars
Aster species
Gazania 'Cream Beauty'
Tanacetum species
Zinnia species & cultivars

▲ *Achillea clavennae*

Daisy-like on plants 30cm–1m (1–3ft) tall

Achillea species & cultivars
Argyranthemum species
Aster species
Echinacea purpurea 'White Lustre'
Erigeron cultivars
Osteospermum 'Silver Sparkler'
Stokesia laevis
Tanacetum species

▲ *Osteospermum* 'Silver Sparkler'

Daisy-like on plants more than 1m (3ft) tall

Achillea species & cultivars
Aster species & cultivars
Dahlia merckii 'Alba'
Eupatorium species
Senecio smithii

▼ *Aster novae-angliae* 'Herbstschnee'

Arum-like

Arisaema candidissimum
Calla palustris

▲ *Arisaema candidissimum*

Flowers in feathery plumes

Artemisia lactiflora
Aruncus species & cultivars
Astilbe species & cultivars
Astilboides tabularis
Filipendula purpurea f. *alba*
Filipendula ulmaria

▲ *Aruncus dioicus*

Bottlebrush shaped

Sanguisorba albiflora

▼ *Sanguisorba albiflora*

Flowers in dense, flattened clusters

Achillea millefolium
Lychnis chalcedonica 'Alba'

▲ *Achillea millefolium*

WHITE FLOWERS WITH PURPLE SPOTS

Trumpet or bell shaped, on plants 30cm–1m (1–3ft) tall

Tricyrtis hirta
Tricyrtis macropoda

▲ *Tricyrtis hirta*

RED OR PINK FLOWERS

Trumpet or bell shaped, on plants less than 30cm (12in) tall

Lobelia erinus 'Rosamund'
Nemesia denticulata
Nicotiana × *sanderae*

continued on next page

▼ *Nicotiana* × *sanderae*

Origanum species & cultivars
Petunia x *hybrida* cultivars
Silene schafta

Trumpet or bell shaped, on plants 30cm–1m (1–3ft) tall with oval-shaped leaves

Antirrhinum majus cultivars
Clematis integrifolia cultivars
Diascia species & cultivars
Hibiscus moscheutus 'Disco Belle Mixed'
Lobelia species & cultivars
Origanum x *hybridum*
Origanum majorana
Penstemon species & cultivars
Platycodon grandiflorus cultivars
Prunella grandiflora
Salpiglossis sinuata & cultivars
Salvia greggii

▲ *Salpiglossis sinuata* 'Splash'

Trumpet or bell shaped, on plants 30cm–1m (1–3ft) tall with long, slender leaves

Amaryllis belladonna
Anigozanthos flavidus red
Crocosmia cultivars
Hemerocallis cultivars
Lilium species & cultivars
Nerine bowdenii & cultivars
Tritonia disticha ssp. *rubrolucens*

▼ *Amaryllis belladonna*

Trumpet or bell shaped, on plants 30cm–1m (1–3ft) tall with feather-like or lobed leaves

Ipomopsis aggregata
Lavatera trimestris & cultivars
Limonium sinuatum
Malope trifida & cultivars

▲ *Lavatera trimestris* 'Silver Cup'

Trumpet or bell shaped, on plants more than 1m (3ft) tall

Canna cultivars
Crinum x *powellii*
Crocosmia 'Lucifer'
Hibiscus moscheutus
Ipomoea coccinea
Ipomopsis rubra
Lavatera species & cultivars
Lilium martagon
Lilium Pink Perfection Group
Lilium speciosum var. *rubrum*
Lobelia 'Pink Flamingo'
Physostegia virginiana
Salvia species

▼ *Lilium* Pink Perfection Group

Bowl or plate shaped, on plants less than 30cm (12in) tall

Begonia semperflorens & cultivars
Dianthus erinaceus
Dianthus petraeus
Dianthus superbus
Geranium sanguineum var. *striatum*
Lobularia maritima 'Wonderland'
Lychnis alpina 'Rosea'
Lychnis flos-cuculi 'Nana'

▲ *Lychnis flos-cuculi* 'Nana'

Malvastrum lateritum
Oenothera speciosa 'Rosea'
Oxalis triangularis
Pelargonium species & cultivars
Portulaca grandiflora & cultivars
Rhodohypoxis species & cultivars
Silene keiskei
Verbena x *hybrida* cultivars

Bowl or plate shaped, on plants 30cm–1m (1–3ft) tall with oval-shaped leaves

Alonsoa warscewiczii
Begonia grandis ssp. *evansiana*

▼ Begonia x tuberhybrida

Begonia x *tuberhybrida* cultivars
Catharanthus roseus
Impatiens species & cultivars
Lychnis species & cultivars
Nomocharis species
Saponaria officinalis
Tradescantia cultivars

Bowl or plate shaped, on plants 30cm–1m (1–3ft) tall with long, narrow leaves

Hemerocallis cultivars
Nomocharis species

▲ *Hemerocallis* 'Luxury Lace'

Bowl or plate shaped, on plants 30cm–1m (1–3ft) tall with feather-like or lobed leaves

Anemone hupehensis & cultivars
Anemone tomentosa
Astrantia species & cultivars
Dianthus caryophyllus & cultivars
Glaucium corniculatum
Ipomopsis aggregata
Papaver species & cultivars
Pelargonium species & cultivars
Potentilla atrosanguinea

▼ *Potentilla atrosanguinea*

Bowl or plate shaped, on plants more than 1m (3ft) tall

Anemone × *hybrida* & cultivars
Butomus umbellatus
Delphinium cardinale

▲ *Delphinium cardinale*

Eremurus robustus
Ipomopsis rubra
Malva moschata
Papaver somniferum 'Pink Chiffon'

Pompom shaped

Dahlia cultivars

▲ *Dahlia* 'Ellen Houston'

Daisy-like

Cosmos atrosanguineus

▼ *Cosmos atrosanguineus*

Cosmos bipinnatus & cultivars
Crepis incana
Dahlia coccinea
Dahlia 'Bishop of Llandaff'
Eupatorium species & cultivars
Gazania 'Christopher'
Helipterum 'Goliath'
Lampranthus species
Osteospermum 'Hopleys'
Osteospermum 'Langtrees'
Osteospermum 'Pink Whirls'
Zinnia 'Chippendale'

Pea-like

Clianthus species
Lathyrus latifolius 'Red Pearl'
Lotus bertholetti
Lupinus cultivars

▲ *Lupinus* 'Chelsea Pensioner'

Flowers in feathery plumes

Astilbe species & cultivars
Filipendula camtschatica
Filipendula purpurea
Filipendula rubra & cultivars

▼ *Filipendula rubra*

Filipendula ulmaria 'Rosea'
Sanguisorba obtusa

▲ *Sanguisorba obtusa*

Thistle-like

Silybum marianum

▲ *Silybum marianum*

Flowers in dense, flattened clusters

Achillea 'Apfelblüte'
Achillea 'Fanal'
Achillea 'Lachsschönheit'
Achillea millefolium 'Cerise Queen'
Lychnis chalcedonica & cultivars

▼ *Achillea* 'Fanal'

RED-AND-WHITE FLOWERS

Pompom shaped

Dahlia 'Barbarry Snowball'
Dahlia 'Kyoto'
Dahlia 'Wootton Cupid'

▲ *Dahlia* 'Wootton Cupid'

RED-AND-YELLOW FLOWERS

Trumpet or bell shaped

Abutilon megapotamicum

▲ *Kniphofia uvaria*

Kniphofia species & cultivars
Lobelia laxiflora

▼ *Lobelia laxiflora*

PINK, PURPLE AND YELLOW FLOWERS

Bowl or plate shaped, on plants 30 cm–1 m (1–3 ft) tall

Schizanthus pinnatus

▲ *Schizanthus pinnatus*

ORANGE FLOWERS

Trumpet or bell shaped

Crocosmia cultivars
Hemerocallis cultivars
Lilium species & cultivars
Salpiglossis sinuata & cultivars

▲ *Hemerocallis* 'Hornby Castle'

Bowl or plate shaped

Begonia sutherlandii
Begonia x *tuberhybrida* cultivars
Geum cultivars
Impatiens walleriana
Malvastrum lateritium
Papaver species & cultivars
Pelargonium cultivars
Portulaca grandiflora & cultivars

▲ *Begonia sutherlandii*

Pompom shaped

Dahlia cultivars
Dendranthema cultivars
Tagetes species & cultivars

▲ *Dahlia* 'David Howard'

Daisy-like

Cosmos sulphureus
Gazania rigens
Gazania 'Sundance'
Lampranthus aurantiacus

▲ *Lampranthus aurantiacus*

Lampranthus brownii
Ligularia dentata 'Desdemona'
Sanvitalia procumbens cultivars
Tagetes species & cultivars
Ursinia anthemoides
Zinnia cultivars

YELLOW FLOWERS

Trumpet or bell shaped, on plants less than 30 cm (12 in) tall

Allium flavum
Epilobium glabellum 'Sulphureum'
Mimulus moschatus
Penstemon confertus
Petunia x *hybrida* cultivars
Teucrium polium

▼ *Penstemon confertus*

Trumpet or bell shaped, on plants 30 cm–1 m (1–3 ft) tall

Anigozanthos flavidus 'yellow'
Antirrhinum majus cultivars
Cautleya spicata

▲ *Cautleya spicata*

Crocosmia 'Canary Bird'
Crocosmia 'Citronella'
Hemerocallis 'Stella de Oro'
Hibiscus trionum & cultivars
Limonium sinuatum
Linaria dalmatica
Linaria vulgaris
Monarda punctata
Nicotiana x *sanderae*
Penstemon pinifolius 'Mersea Yellow'
Polemonium pauciflorum
Salpiglossis sinuata & cultivars
Sisyrinchium striatum
Tricyrtis species

Trumpet or bell shaped, on plants more than 1 m (3 ft) tall

Canna cultivars
Clematis aethusifolia
Lilium Citronella Group
Lilium 'Limelight'
Monarda punctata
Teucrium polium

▲ *Lilium* Citronella Group

Bowl or plate shaped, on plants less than 30 cm (12 in) tall

Azorella trifurcata & cultivars
Oenothera species & cultivars
Papaver miyabeanum

▲ *Oenothera macrocarpa*

Polemonium species
Portulaca grandiflora & cultivars
Portulaca oleracea
Potentilla species & cultivars
Sedum species & cultivars
Trollius acaulis
Trollius pumilus

Bowl or plate shaped, on plants 30 cm–1 m (1–3 ft) tall

Begonia x *tuberhybrida* cultivars
Chelidonium majus & cultivars
Eremurus stenophyllus ssp. *stenophyllus*
Eschscholtzia species
Glaucium flavum
Oenothera species & cultivars
Papaver species
Polemonium species
Potentilla species

▲ *Glaucium flavum*

Bowl or plate shaped, on plants more than 1m (3ft) tall

Verbascum species & cultivars

▲ *Verbascum* 'Gainsborough'

Pompom shaped

Artemisia species
Dahlia cultivars
Dendranthema cultivars
Tagetes species & cultivars

▲ *Dahlia* 'Hamari Gold'

Daisy-like, on plants less than 30cm (12in) tall

Achillea x *lewisii*
Anthemis tinctoria & cultivars
Asteriscus maritimus
Chamaemelum nobile
Gazania cultivars
Sanvitalia procumbens
Tagetes species & cultivars

▲ *Asteriscus maritimus*

Daisy-like, on plants 30cm–1m (1–3ft) tall

Achillea species & cultivars
Anthemis species & cultivars
Argyranthemum maderense
Buphthalmum salicifolium
Helichrysum bracteatum
Lindheimera texana
Matricaria recutita
Osteospermum 'Buttermilk'
Rudbeckia fulgida & cultivars

▲ *Rudbeckia fulgida* var. *deamii*

Solidago species & cultivars
x *Solidaster luteus*
Ursinia species

Daisy-like, on plants more than 1m (3ft) tall

Helianthus species & cultivars
Inula species
Ligularia species & cultivars
Rudbeckia species & cultivars
Telekia speciosa

▲ *Telekia speciosa*

Pea-like

Lupinus species & cultivars
Scutellaria prostrata
Thermopsis lupinoides
Thermopsis montana

▼ *Thermopsis lupinoides*

Flowers in dense, flattened clusters

Achillea 'Coronation Gold'
Achillea filipendulina 'Gold Plate'
Achillea 'Hoffnung'
Achillea x *lewisii* 'King Edward'
Achillea 'Moonshine'
Achillea 'Taygetea'

▲ *Achillea* 'Coronation Gold'

Slipper shaped

Calceolaria integrifolia & cultivars

▲ *Calceolaria integrifolia* 'Sunshine'

YELLOW OR RED FLOWERS SPOTTED CRIMSON OR BROWN

Bowl or plate shaped

Tigridia pavonia & cultivars

▲ *Tigridia pavonia*

GREEN FLOWERS

Trumpet or bell shaped

Ballota 'All Hallows Green'
Epipactis gigantea

▲ *Ballota* 'All Hallows Green'

Eucomis bicolor
Galtonia princeps
Galtonia viridiflora
Heuchera cylindrica 'Greenfinch'
Nicotiana langsdorffii
Nicotiana x *sanderae* cultivars

▲ *Nicotiana* x *sanderae* 'Lime Green'

Bowl or plate shaped

Molucella laevis

▲ *Molucella laevis*

FLOWERS IN LONG, DROOPING TASSELS

Amaranthus caudatus 'Viridis'

▼ *Amaranthus caudatus* 'Viridis'

BLUE FLOWERS

Trumpet or bell shaped, on plants less than 30cm (12in) tall

Codonopsis ovata
Corydalis cashmeriana
Limonium species & cultivars
Lobelia erinus & cultivars
Lobelia tenuior & cultivars
Petunia x *hybrida* cultivars
Phacelia sericea
Prunella grandiflora

▲ *Petunia* 'Fantasy Blue'

Trumpet or bell shaped, on plants more than 30cm (12in) tall

Agapanthus species & cultivars
Clematis integrifolia cultivars
Echium plantagineum 'Blue Bedder'
Gentiana species & cultivars
Gilia species
Limonium species & cultivars
Nepeta species & cultivars
Penstemon cultivars
Penstemon glaber
Penstemon strictus
Phacelia tanacetifolia
Platycodon grandiflorus & cultivars
Salvia species & cultivars

▼ *Platycodon grandiflorus*

Bowl or plate shaped, on plants less than 30cm (12in) tall

Myosotis scorpioides 'Mermaid'
Nemophila menziesii
Polemonium boreale
Verbena x *hybrida* 'Imagination'

▲ *Myosotis scorpioides* 'Mermaid'

Bowl or plate shaped, on plants 30cm–1m (1–3ft) tall

Delphinium grandiflorum
Linum species
Lobelia species & cultivars
Malva sylvestris 'Cottenham Blue'
Matthiola longipetala
Nemesia versicolor
Nigella species & cultivars

▲ *Nigella damascena* 'Persian Jewels'

Phacelia sericea ssp. *ciliosa*
Phacelia tanacetifolia
Polemonium species
Tradescantia virginiana 'Zwanenburg Blue'

Daisy-like

Aster species & cultivars
Dahlia merckii
Osteospermum 'Whirligig'
Stokesia laevis & cultivars

▼ *Stokesia laevis* 'Blue Star'

Pompom shaped

Ageratum houstonianum
Gilia capitata

▲ *Gilia capitata*

Hood or helmet shaped

Aconitum carmichaelii
Aconitum napellus

▲ *Aconitum carmichaelii* Wilsonii Group

Fan shaped

Scaevola aemula

▲ *Scaevola aemula*

Thistle-like

Eryngium species

▼ *Eryngium* x *tripartitum*

BLUE AND WHITE FLOWERS

Trumpet or bell shaped

Ipomoea cultivars
Lobelia erinus
Nemesia strumosa 'K.L.M.'

▲ *Lobelia erinus* (mixed)

PURPLE FLOWERS

Trumpet or bell shaped, on plants less than 30cm (12in) tall

Campanula poscharskyana
Clintonia andrewsiana
Cyananthus lobatus
Cymbalaria hepaticifolia
Hemerocallis cultivars
Liriope spicata
Lobelia erinus cultivars
Mentha x *gracilis* & cultivars
Penstemon cultivars
Salpiglossis sinuata & cultivars
Teucrium species
Thymus species & cultivars

▲ *Cyananthus lobatus*

Trumpet or bell shaped, on plants 30cm–1m (1–3ft) tall with oval-shaped leaves

Ballota nigra 'Archer's Variegated'
Clematis integrifolia 'Tapestry'
Cuphea hyssopifolia
Echium vulgare
Hosta species & cultivars
Lobelia cultivars
Lychnis flos-cuculi
Mentha longifolia & cultivars
Origanum vulgare
Penstemon species & cultivars

▲ *Penstemon* 'Catherine de la Mare'

Salvia species & cultivars
Tulbaghia violacea

Trumpet or bell shaped, on plants more than 1m (3ft) tall

Lilium martagon var. *cattaniae*
Nicandra physalodes
Salvia przewalskii
Strobilanthes atropurpureus
Verbena hastata

▲ *Salvia przewalskii*

Bowl or plate shaped, on plants less than 30cm (12in) tall

Allium senescens
Dianthus cultivars
Erodium glandulosum

▲ *Erodium manescaui*

Erodium manescaui
Lobularia maritima 'Violet Queen'
Lychnis species & cultivars
Nemesia species & cultivars
Oxalis species & cultivars
Pelargonium species & cultivars
Sedum species & cultivars
Thalictrum species
Verbena x *hybrida* 'Tapien Purple'
Viola odorata
Viola pedata

Bowl or plate shaped, on plants 30cm–1m (1–3ft) tall

Allium species
Anemone hupehensis & cultivars
Delphinium grandiflorum
Epilobium fleischeri
Impatiens balsamina & cultivars
Lychnis viscaria
Malva sylvestris
Pelargonium species & cultivars
Potentilla nepalensis
Thalictrum diffusiflorum
Tradescantia virginiana 'Purple Dome'
Tulbaghia violacea

▼ *Tulbaghia violacea*

Pompom shaped

Dahlia cultivars
Echinops species & cultivars
Liatris spicata & cultivars
Thalictrum aquilegifolium & cultivars

▲ *Echinops ritro* 'Veitch's Blue'

Daisy-like

Aster amellus 'Framfieldii'
Aster x *frikartii* 'Flora's Delight'
Centaurea cineraria
Dahlia merckii
Eupatorium purpureum
Lampranthus species & cultivars
Osteospermum jucundum
Stokesia laevis
Zinnia elegans

▼ *Lampranthus blandus*

Pea-like

Hedysarum coronarium
Lupinus species & cultivars
Polygala myrtifolia

▲ *Lupinus* Band of Nobles Series

Hood or helmet shaped

Aconitum carmichaelii

▲ *Aconitum carmichaelii*

Thistle-like

Cynara cardunculus

▼ *Cynara cardunculus*

AUTUMN

Through late September, October and November, dahlias and asters bloom and trees take on rich leaf colours

TREES AND SHRUBS

WHITE OR CREAM FLOWERS

TRUMPET OR BELL SHAPED

Abelia × grandiflora & cultivars
Arbutus unedo

▲ *Arbutus unedo*

Calluna vulgaris cultivars
Elaeagnus x ebbingei & cultivars
Elaeagnus pungens cultivars
Hibiscus syriacus & cultivars

BOWL OR PLATE SHAPED

Clethra barbinervis

▲ *Clethra barbinervis*

× *Fatshedera lizei*
Magnolia grandiflora & cultivars
Viburnum tinus

POMPOM SHAPED

Fatsia japonica & cultivars

▲ *Fatsia japonica*

RED OR PINK FLOWERS

TRUMPET OR BELL SHAPED

Arbutus unedo f. rubra
Calluna vulgaris cultivars
Hibiscus syriacus & cultivars

▲ *Hibiscus syriacus* 'Mauve Queen'

BOWL OR PLATE SHAPED

Hebe 'Eveline'

▲ *Hebe* 'Eveline'

Hebe 'Simon Delaux'
Parahebe catarractae ssp. *diffusa*

YELLOW FLOWERS

TRUMPET OR BELL SHAPED

Mahonia lomariifolia
Mahonia × media cultivars

▲ *Mahonia lomariifolia*

BOWL OR PLATE SHAPED

Hypericum × moserianum & cultivars

▲ *Hypericum × moserianum*

BLUE FLOWERS

TRUMPET OR BELL SHAPED

Caryopteris × clandonensis & cultivars
Hibiscus syriacus & cultivars

▲ *Hibiscus syriacus*

PURPLE FLOWERS

TRUMPET OR BELL SHAPED

Calluna vulgaris cultivars

▲ *Calluna vulgaris* 'Silver Queen'

Caryopteris × clandonensis 'Ferndown'
Origanum amanum

BOWL OR PLATE SHAPED

Hebe species & cultivars

▲ *Hebe* 'Autumn Glory'

TREES AND SHRUBS WITH COLOURFUL FOLIAGE

LEAVES OVAL

Amelanchier laevis
Cotinus species & cultivars
Enkianthus species & cultivars
Fothergilla species & cultivars

▲ *Fothergilla major*

Hamamelis species & cultivars
Maclura pomifera
Nyssa species & cultivars
Oxydendrum arboreum
Parrotia persica & cultivars
Pyrus species & cultivars
Zelkova serrata

LEAVES LOBED

Acer species & cultivars
Fagus sylvatica heterophylla 'Aspleniifolia'
Ginkgo biloba
Lindera obtusiloba
Liquidambar styraciflua & cultivars
Quercus coccinea
Quercus rubra
Sassafras albidum

▼ *Ginkgo biloba*

Leaves feather shaped

Metasequoia glyptostroboides
Rhus species & cultivars

▲ *Metasequoia glyptostroboides*

Leaves round

Disanthus cercidifolius

▲ *Disanthus cercidifolius*

Leaves needle-like

Larix decidua

▲ *Larix decidua*

Pseudolarix amabilis
Taxodium distichum

Trees and shrubs with berries or seedpods

WHITE

Gaultheria cuneata
Gaultheria miquelliana
Gaultheria mucronata cultivars

▼ *Gaultheria mucronata* 'Alba'

Sorbus koehneana
Symphoricarpos species & cultivars

RED OR PINK

Ampelopsis brevipedunculata
Berberis species & cultivars
Cotoneaster species & cultivars
Daphne tangutica
Euonymus species & cultivars
Gaultheria species & cultivars
Lonicera x *purpusii* & cultivars
Pyracantha species & cultivars
Ricinus species & cultivars
Rosa species
Skimmia japonica

▲ *Skimmia japonica*

Sorbus species & cultivars
Taxus baccata
Vaccinium species & cultivars
Viburnum opulus
Viburnum rhytidophyllum

ORANGE

Corokia x *virgata*
Cotoneaster franchetii
Euonymus europaeus 'Red Cascade'
Hippophae rhamnoides
Pyracantha species & cultivars
Sorbus species & cultivars

▲ *Cotoneaster franchetii*

YELLOW

Cotoneaster species & cultivars
Pyracantha species & cultivars

▲ *Pyracantha* 'Soleil d'Or'

PURPLE OR BLACK

Aralia species & cultivars
Asparagus verticillatus
Berberis species & cultivars
Billardiera longiflora
Cestrum parqui
Clerodendrum trichotomum
Gaultheria mucronata
Gaultheria shallon
Leycesteria formosa

▲ *Leycesteria formosa*

Liriope species & cultivars
Myrtus communis & cultivars
Phellodendron species
Rhamnus species
Symplocos paniculata
Vaccinium corymbosum
Vaccinium cylindraceum

Trees and shrubs with winged seedpods

Acer capillipes
Acer circinatum
Acer platanoides
Carpinus betulus & cultivars
Fraxinus excelsior & cultivars
Halesia monticola

▲ *Halesia tetraptera*

Halesia tetraptera
Ptelea trifoliata
Pterocarya fraxinifolia
Pterocarya stenoptera

CLIMBING OR RAMBLING PLANTS

WHITE OR CREAM FLOWERS

Bowl or plate shaped

Clematis 'Alba Luxurians'
Clematis flammula
Clematis 'Huldine'
Passiflora species & cultivars

▲ *Passiflora caerulea* 'Constance Elliot'

RED OR PINK FLOWERS

Bowl or plate shaped

Clematis 'Abundance'

▲ *Clematis* 'Abundance'

Clematis 'Ernest Markham'
Clematis 'Kermesina'
Clematis 'Madame Grange'
Clematis 'Madame Julia Correvon'
Clematis 'Margaret Hunt'
Clematis 'Mrs Spencer Castle'
Clematis 'Voluceau'

YELLOW FLOWERS

Bowl or plate shaped

Clematis tibetana ssp. *vernayi*

▲ *Clematis tibetana* ssp. *vernayi*

BLUE FLOWERS

Bowl or plate shaped

Clematis 'Ascotiensis'
Clematis 'Lady Betty Balfour'

▲ *Clematis* 'Ascotiensis'

PURPLE FLOWERS

Trumpet or bell shaped

Clematis 'Etoile Rose'
Clematis 'Etoile Violette'
Passiflora amethystina

▲ *Clematis* 'Etoile Violette'

Bowl or plate shaped

Clematis 'Blue Belle'
Clematis × *eriostemon* 'Hendersonii'
Clematis 'Polish Spirit'
Clematis 'Prince Charles'
Clematis 'Royal Velours'
Clematis viticella

▲ *Clematis* 'Prince Charles'

SOFT-STEMMED PLANTS

WHITE OR CREAM FLOWERS

Trumpet or bell shaped

Colchicum autumnale f. *album*
Colchicum speciosum 'Album'
Crocus boryi
Gentiana sino-ornata 'Alba'
Hibiscus species & cultivars
Kniphofia species & cultivars
Leucojum autumnale
Lilium formosanum

▲ *Colchicum autumnale* f. *album*

Bowl or plate shaped

Anemone vitifolia
Liriope cultivars
Lobularia maritima cultivars
Schizostylis coccinea var. *alba*
Sedum species & cultivars

▼ *Schizostylis coccinea* var. *alba*

Daisy-like

Aster species & cultivars
Dahlia merkii 'Alba'
Dendranthema species
Echinacea purpurea 'White Lustre'
Eupatorium altissimum
Eupatorium perfoliatum
Tanacetum balsamita

▲ *Aster* 'Albanian'

Cyclamen flowers

Cyclamen hederifolium 'Album'

▲ *Cyclamen hederifolium* 'Album'

WHITE FLOWERS WITH PURPLE OR BROWN SPOTS

Bowl or plate shaped

Tricyrtis species

▲ *Tricyrtis formosana*

RED OR PINK FLOWERS

Trumpet or bell shaped

Colchicum species & cultivars
Diascia vigilis
Hibiscus moscheutus & cultivars
Origanum species & cultivars

▲ *Silene schafta* 'Shell Pink'

Physostegia virginiana
Salvia confertiflora
Salvia fulgens
Salvia involucrata
Silene schafta & cultivars
Teucrium chamaedrys

Bowl or plate shaped

Alonsoa warscewiczii
Anemone tomentosa
Lobularia maritima 'Wonderland Rose'
Persicaria campanulata
Persicaria vacciniifolia
Schizostylis coccinea
Sedum species & cultivars
Verbena × *hybrida* cultivars

▲ *Alonsoa warscewiczii*

Daisy-like

Aster cultivars
Dahlia coccinea
Dahlia 'Bishop of Llandaff'
Senecio pulcher

▲ *Dahlia* 'Bishop of Llandaff'

Cyclamen flowers

Cyclamen species

▼ *Cyclamen cilicium*

Flowers in feathery plumes

Astilbe cultivars

▲ *Astilbe* 'Jo Ophorst'

Pink, purple and yellow flowers

Bowl or plate shaped

Schizanthus pinnatus

▲ *Schizanthus pinnatus*

Orange flowers

Trumpet or bell shaped

Hedychium coccineum 'Tara'

▲ *Hedychium coccineum* 'Tara'

Bowl or plate shaped

Malvastrum lateritium

▼ *Malvastrum lateritium*

Daisy-like

Lampranthus aurantiacus
Lampranthus brownii
Zinnia haageana

▲ *Lampranthus aurantiacus*

Yellow flowers

Trumpet or bell shaped

▲ *Epilobium glabellum* 'Sulphureum'

Epilobium glabellum 'Sulphureum'
Hibiscus manihot
Hibiscus trionum & cultivars
Monarda punctata
Sternbergia lutea
Tricyrtis macrantha ssp. *macranthopsis*
Tricyrtis ohsumiensis

Bowl or plate shaped

Oxalis purpurea 'Ken Aslet'

▲ *Oxalis purpurea* 'Ken Aslet'

Daisy-like

Bidens ferulifolia 'Sunshine'
Rudbeckia fulgida var. *deamii*

▲ *Rudbeckia fulgida* var. *deamii*

Rudbeckia maxima
X *Solidaster luteus*

Blue flowers

Trumpet or bell shaped

Crocus pulchellus
Cyananthus lobatus
Gentiana asclepiadea
Gentiana x *macaulayi* cultivars
Gentiana sino-ornata & cultivars
Salvia patens
Salvia uliginosa

▲ *Salvia uliginosa*

Daisy-like

Aster species & cultivars

▲ *Aster novi-belgii* 'Audrey'

Purple flowers

Trumpet or bell shaped

Colchicum 'Lilac Wonder'
Crocus banaticus

▲ *Crocus medius*

Crocus medius
Cyananthus microphyllus
Origanum vulgare
Salvia buchananii
Strobilanthes atropurpureus

Bowl or plate shaped

Epilobium fleischeri
Liriope species & cultivars
Oxalis oregana
Sedum cauticola & cultivars
Sedum telephium
Verbena x *hybrida* 'Tapien Purple'

▲ *Sedum cauticola* 'Bertram Anderson'

Daisy-like

Aster species & cultivars
Dahlia merckii
Senecio pulcher
Zinnia elegans

▲ *Aster novi-belgii* 'Remembrance'

Iris-like

Iris unguicularis & cultivars
Roscoea auriculata
Roscoea purpurea

▼ *Roscoea purpurea*

Winter

In the darkest days of the year winter-flowering shrubs, cyclamens and the earliest irises bring interest to the garden

Trees and Shrubs

White or Cream Flowers

Trumpet or Bell Shaped

Buddleja asiatica
Daphne mezereum f. *alba*
Elaeagnus × *ebbingei* & cultivars
Lonicera fragrantissima
Lonicera × *purpusii* & cultivars
Lonicera standishii
Pieris japonica
Rhododendron 'Nobleanum Album'
Rhododendron mucronulatum 'Winter Brightness'
Viburnum farreri

▲ *Pieris japonica*

Bowl or Plate Shaped

Crataegus monogyna 'Biflora'
Prunus incisa 'Praecox'
Prunus × *subhirtella* 'Autumnalis'
Viburnum tinus

▲ *Prunus* × *subhirtella* 'Autumnalis'

Tassel-like

Sarcococca confusa
Sarcococca ruscifolia

▼ *Sarcococca confusa*

Red or Pink Flowers

Trumpet or Bell Shaped

Daphne mezereum var. *rubra*
Erica species & cultivars
Rhododendron 'Nobleanum'
Rhododendron sutchuenense
Salvia oppositiflora

▲ *Erica carnea* 'Challenger'

Bowl or Plate Shaped

Prunus × *subhirtella* 'Autumnalis Rosea'
Viburnum × *bodnantense*

▲ *Viburnum* × *bodnantense* 'Deben'

Flowers Similar to Honeysuckle

Grevillea rosmarinifolia

▼ *Grevillea rosmarinifolia*

Tassel-like

Hamamelis × *intermedia* & cultivars
Sarcococca hookeriana var. *digyna*
Sarcococca hookeriana var. *humilis*

▲ *Sarcococca hookeriana* var. *digyna*

Yellow Flowers

Trumpet or Bell Shaped

Mahonia species & cultivars

▲ *Mahonia* × *media* 'Charity'

Bowl or Plate Shaped

Chimonanthus praecox 'Grandiflorus'
Chimonanthus praecox 'Luteus'
Cornus mas

▼ *Chimonanthus praecox* 'Grandiflorus'

Pompom Shaped

Acacia dealbata

▲ *Acacia dealbata*

Tassel-like

Hamamelis japonica
Hamamelis mollis
Hamamelis vernalis

▲ *Hamamelis mollis* 'Pallida'

Yellow-Green Flowers

Trumpet or Bell Shaped

Daphne laureola

▲ *Daphne laureola*

Purple Flowers

Bowl or Plate Shaped

Rhododendron dauricum 'Midwinter'

▼ *Rhododendron dauricum* 'Midwinter'

TREES AND SHRUBS WITH CATKINS

Betula species & cultivars
Corylus species & cultivars
Garrya elliptica & cultivars
Populus tremula
Salix aegyptiaca

▲ *Garrya elliptica*

CLIMBING PLANTS

YELLOW FLOWERS

Bowl or plate shaped

Jasminum nudiflorum

▲ *Jasminum nudiflorum*

SOFT-STEMMED PLANTS

WHITE OR CREAM FLOWERS

Trumpet or bell shaped

Galanthus cultivars
Crocus species & cultivars
Salvia leucantha

▼ *Crocus chrysanthus* 'Cream Beauty'

Bowl or plate shaped

Helleborus niger & cultivars
Helleborus orientalis & cultivars
Hepatica nobilis white form
Ranunculus calandrinioides

▲ *Helleborus niger* 'Sunset'

Cyclamen flowers

Cyclamen coum & cultivars
Cyclamen hederifolium album

▲ *Cyclamen hederifolium album*

Iris flowers

Iris 'Natascha'
Iris unguicularis 'Alba'

▲ *Iris* 'Natascha'

RED OR PINK FLOWERS

Bowl or plate shaped

Helleborus orientalis pink form
Helleborus × *sternii* 'Boughton Beauty'

▼ *Helleborus orientalis* pink form

Cyclamen flowers

Cyclamen species & cultivars

▲ *Cyclamen libanoticum*

YELLOW FLOWERS

Trumpet or bell shaped

Crocus ancyrensis
Crocus chrysanthus & cultivars
Narcissus species & cultivars

▲ *Crocus* 'Goldilocks'

Bowl or plate shaped

Hacquetia epipactis
Helleborus orientalis Kochii Group

▲ *Hacquetia epipactis*

Iris flowers

Iris danfordiae

▼ *Iris danfordiae*

GREEN FLOWERS

Bowl or plate shaped

Helleborus species & cultivars

▲ *Helleborus foetidus*

PURPLE FLOWERS

Bowl or plate shaped

Helleborus orientalis cultivars
Helleborus purpurascens
Helleborus torquatus
Hepatica americana

▲ *Helleborus purpurascens*

Iris flowers

Iris 'George'
Iris 'Pauline'
Iris unguicularis & cultivars

▼ *Iris unguicularis*

Plants for Special Purposes

These lists will help you to choose the best plants for particular areas, aspects and soil types. The lists should be used in conjunction with the detailed information in individual genus entries as not all species in a genus may be suitable for a particular purpose

• PLANTS FOR MOIST SHADE •

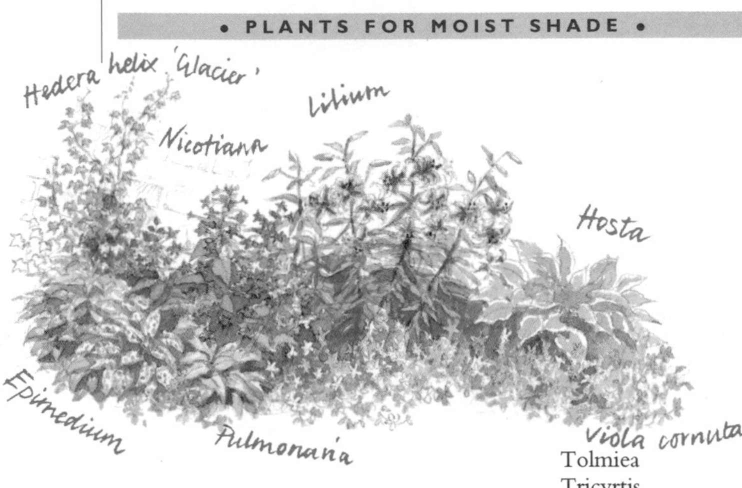

ANNUALS AND BIENNIALS
Digitalis
Impatiens
Lobelia
Mimulus
Nicotiana

BULBS
Arisaema
Arum
Eranthis
Erythronium
Galanthus
Leucojum
Lilium

CLIMBERS
Hedera
Hydrangea

FERNS
Athyrium
Cyathea
Dryopteris
Matteuccia
Onoclea
Woodwardia

PERENNIALS
Actaea
Aquilegia
Aruncus
Astilbe
Astrantia
Cimicifuga
Convallaria
Digitalis
Dodecatheon
Epimedium
Gentiana
Glaucidium
Haberlea
Helleborus
Heuchera
Hosta
Hylomecon
Kirengeshoma
Lysimachia
Meconopsis
Omphalodes
Pachysandra
Podophyllum
Polygonatum
Primula
Pulmonaria
Ramonda
Rodgersia
Smilacina
Thalictrum
Tiarella
Tolmiea
Tricyrtis
Trillium
Trollius
Uvularia
Veratrum
Vinca
Viola

SHRUBS
Acer
Aucuba
× Fatshedera
Fatsia
Hamamelis
Hydrangea
Kalmia
Mahonia
Sarcococca
Stewartia
Vaccinium

TREES
Acer
Hamamelis
Stewartia

PLANTS FOR • NORTH AND EAST-FACING WALLS •

CLIMBERS
Actinidia
Akebia
Celastus
Fallopia
Hedera
Hydrangea
Jasminum
Lathyrus
Lonicera
Muehlenbeckia
Parthenocissus
Schizophragma
Tropaeolum
  speciosum

SHRUBS
Chaenomeles
Pyracantha

PLANTS FOR • SOUTH AND WEST-FACING WALLS •

CLIMBERS
Abutilon
Aristolochia
Campsis
Celastrus
Clematis
Clianthus
Eccremocarpus
Embothrium
Hedera (particularly
  variegated forms)
Humulus
Ipomoea
Jasminum
Lapageria
Lonicera
Mutisia
Passiflora
Plumbago
Rosa
Sollya
Thunbergia
Trachelospermum
Tweedia
Vitis
Wisteria

SHRUBS
Abelia
Carpenteria
Ceanothus
Chimonanthus
Clerodendrum
Clianthus
Fremontodendron
Magnolia
Pyracantha
Solanum

TREES
Acacia

• PLANTS FOR DRY SHADE •

ANNUALS AND BIENNIALS
Lunaria

BULBS
Cyclamen

CLIMBERS
Hedera

FERNS
Asplenium
Polypodium

PERENNIALS
Anemone
Lamium
Ramonda
Saxifraga umbrosa

SHRUBS
Buxus
Elaeagnus
Hypericum
Kerria
Ribes
Ruscus
Sarcococca
Symphoricarpos
Vinca

• PLANTS FOR DRY SUNNY SITES •

ANNUALS AND BIENNIALS
Calandrinia
Calendula
Cleome
Cosmos
Crepis
Dorotheanthus
Eschscholzia
Helianthus
Iberis
Limnanthes
Linaria
Oenothera
Onopordum
Papaver
Portulaca
Salvia
Tagetes

BULBS
Allium
Crocus
Ixia
Nerine
Sternbergia
Tulipa

PERENNIALS
Acantholimon
Achillea
Aethionema
Agave
Alyssum
Anthemis
Arabis
Arenaria
Armeria
Artemisia
Aubrieta
Aurinia
Ballota
Calandrinia
Centaurea
Centranthus
Cerastium
Coreopsis
Cosmos
Dianthus
Dictamnus
Echium
Eryngium
Euphorbia
Gaillardia
Gypsophila
Helichrysum
Iberis
Kniphofia
Limonium
Linaria
Liriope
Lychnis
Malva
Nepeta
Osteospermum
Papaver
Perovskia
Salvia
Sedum
Sempervivum
Stachys
Tanacetum
Verbascum
Verbena
Yucca
Zauschneria

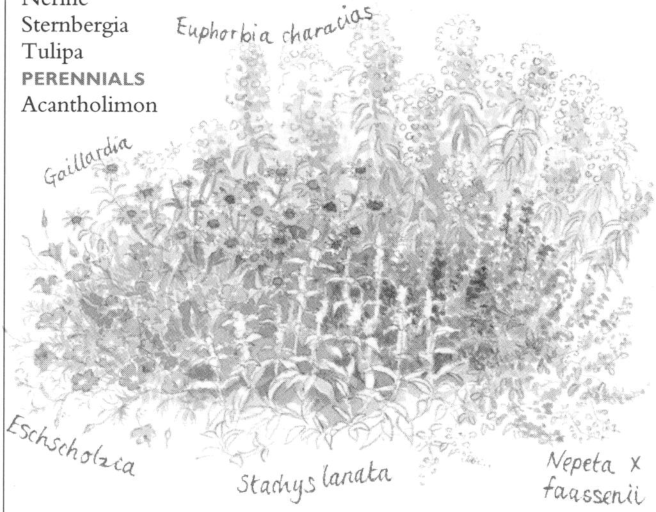

SHRUBS
Artemisia
Brachyglottis
Buddleja
Caragana
Ceanothus
Cistus
Clianthus
Corokia
Cytisus
Genista
× Halimiocistus
Halimum
Helianthemum
Hibiscus
Lavandula
Lavatera
Olearia
Phlomis
Phormium
Piptanthus
Potentilla
Rosmarinus
Ruta
Salvia
Santolina
Spartium
Tamarix
Teucrium
Thymus

TREES
Cercis
Gleditsia
Juniperus
Pinus
Thuja

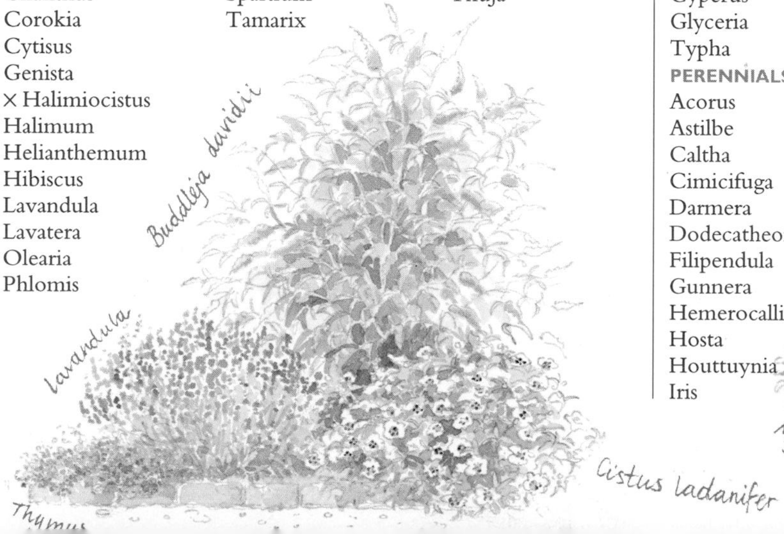

• PLANTS FOR COLD WINDY SITES •

BULBS
Allium

GRASSES
Miscanthus
Stipa

PERENNIALS
Acaena
Achillea
Ajuga
Armeria
Bergenia
Cimicifuga
Coreopsis
Dryas
Hesperis
Iris
Persicaria
Primula
Pulmonaria
Sempervivum
Tanacetum

SHRUBS
Acer
Berberis
Buddleja
Calluna
Caragana
Corylus
Crataegus
Erica
Euonymus (deciduous species)
Gaultheria
Hippophae
Ilex
Kalmia
Leucothoe
Pachysandra
Prunus
Ruscus
Salix
Sambucus
Spartium
Tamarix

TREES
Acer
Carpinus
Chamaecyparis
Crataegus
× Cupressocyparis
Cupressus
Fagus
Fraxinus
Juniperus
Pinus
Populus
Prunus
Salix
Sorbus
Thuja
Tsuga

• PLANTS FOR PERMANENTLY MOIST OR BOGGY SITES •

ANNUALS AND BIENNIALS
Myosotis

FERNS
Matteuccia
Onoclea
Osmunda

GRASSES
Carex
Cyperus
Glyceria
Typha

PERENNIALS
Acorus
Astilbe
Caltha
Cimicifuga
Darmera
Dodecatheon
Filipendula
Gunnera
Hemerocallis
Hosta
Houttuynia
Iris
Ligularia
Lobelia
Lysichiton
Lysimachia
Lythrum
Mimulus
Myosotis
Persicaria
Petasites
Primula
Ranunculus
Rodgersia
Salix
Symphytum
Trollius
Zantedeschia

SHRUBS
Andromeda
Gaultheria
Myrica

TREES
Alnus
Betula nigra
Metasequoia
Populus
Taxodium

• PLANTS THAT DO BEST IN ACID SOIL •

Most of the plants listed below will also grow successfully in neutral soil.

BULBS
Lilium
Nomocharis
CLIMBERS
Lapageria
PERENNIALS
Begonia
Cassiope
Celmisia
Corydalis
Gentiana (autumn-flowering)
Iris
Kirengeshoma
Lewisia
Maianthemum
Meconopsis
Phlox
Rhodohypoxis
Shortia
Tricyrtis
SHRUBS
Agapetes
Andromeda
Arbutus
Arctostaphylos
Callistemon
Calluna
Camellia
Clethra
Corylopsis
Crinodendron
Daboecia
Embothrium
Enkianthus
Erica
Fothergilla
Gaultheria
Halesia
Hamamelis
Kalmia
Kalmiopsis
Leptospermum
Leucothoe
Magnolia
Menziesia
Myrica
Photinia
Phyllodoce
Pieris
Rhododendron
Ulex
Vaccinium
Zenobia
TREES
Abies
Arbutus
Embothrium
Eucryphia
Hamamelis
Magnolia
Nyssa
Picea
Pinus
Pseudolarix
Stewartia

• PLANTS FOR CHALKY SOIL •

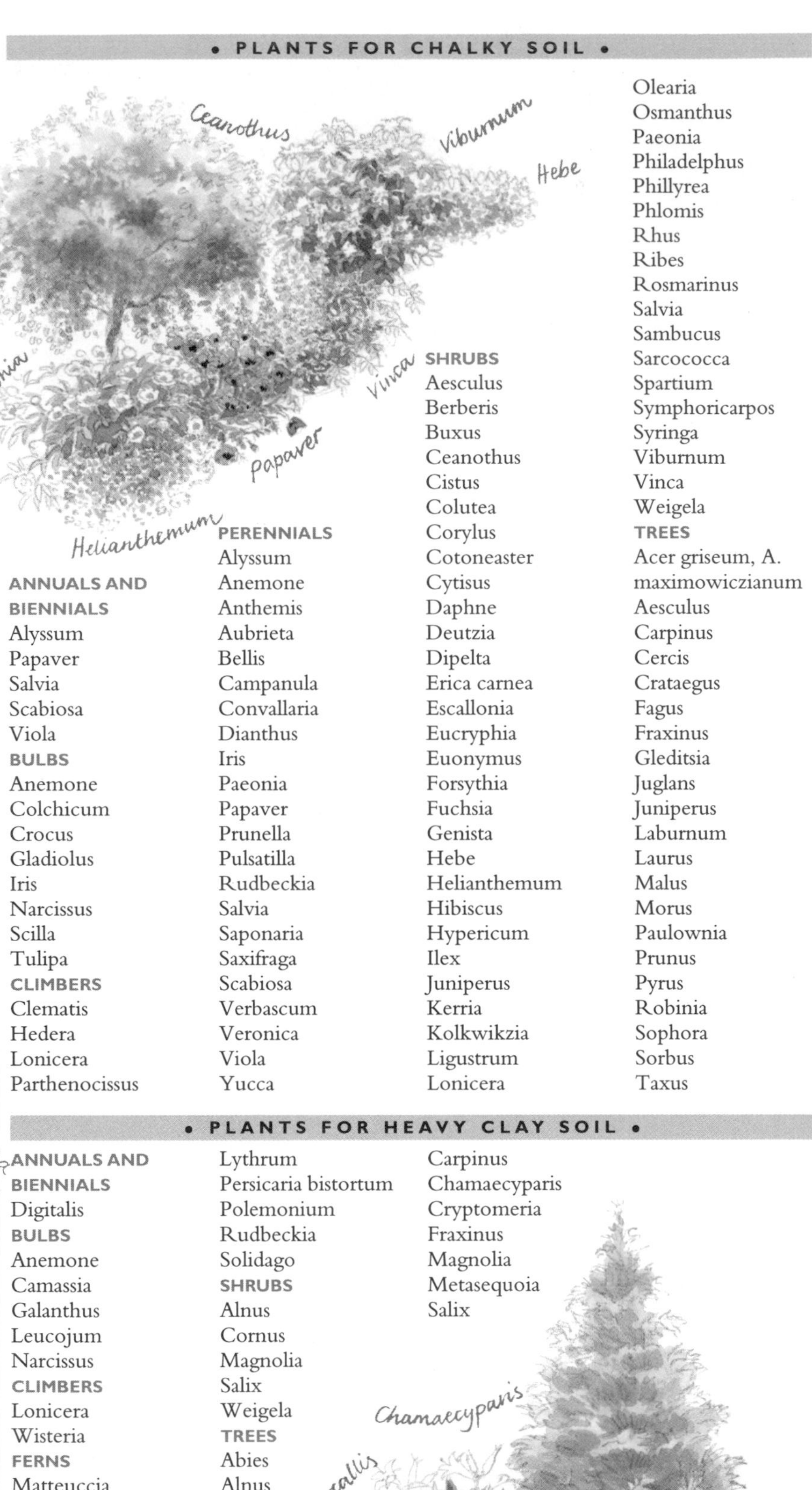

ANNUALS AND BIENNIALS
Alyssum
Papaver
Salvia
Scabiosa
Viola
BULBS
Anemone
Colchicum
Crocus
Gladiolus
Iris
Narcissus
Scilla
Tulipa
CLIMBERS
Clematis
Hedera
Lonicera
Parthenocissus
PERENNIALS
Alyssum
Anemone
Anthemis
Aubrieta
Bellis
Campanula
Convallaria
Dianthus
Iris
Paeonia
Papaver
Prunella
Pulsatilla
Rudbeckia
Salvia
Saponaria
Saxifraga
Scabiosa
Verbascum
Veronica
Viola
Yucca
SHRUBS
Aesculus
Berberis
Buxus
Ceanothus
Cistus
Colutea
Corylus
Cotoneaster
Cytisus
Daphne
Deutzia
Dipelta
Erica carnea
Escallonia
Eucryphia
Euonymus
Forsythia
Fuchsia
Genista
Hebe
Helianthemum
Hibiscus
Hypericum
Ilex
Juniperus
Kerria
Kolkwikzia
Ligustrum
Lonicera
Olearia
Osmanthus
Paeonia
Philadelphus
Phillyrea
Phlomis
Rhus
Ribes
Rosmarinus
Salvia
Sambucus
Sarcococca
Spartium
Symphoricarpos
Syringa
Viburnum
Vinca
Weigela
TREES
Acer griseum, A. maximowiczianum
Aesculus
Carpinus
Cercis
Crataegus
Fagus
Fraxinus
Gleditsia
Juglans
Juniperus
Laburnum
Laurus
Malus
Morus
Paulownia
Prunus
Pyrus
Robinia
Sophora
Sorbus
Taxus

• PLANTS FOR HEAVY CLAY SOIL •

ANNUALS AND BIENNIALS
Digitalis
BULBS
Anemone
Camassia
Galanthus
Leucojum
Narcissus
CLIMBERS
Lonicera
Wisteria
FERNS
Matteuccia
Osmunda
Woodwardia
GRASSES
Cyperus
PERENNIALS
Aconitum
Helenium
Hemerocallis
Lysimachia
Lythrum
Persicaria bistortum
Polemonium
Rudbeckia
Solidago
SHRUBS
Alnus
Cornus
Magnolia
Salix
Weigela
TREES
Abies
Alnus
Carpinus
Chamaecyparis
Cryptomeria
Fraxinus
Magnolia
Metasequoia
Salix

• PLANTS FOR SEASIDE GARDENS •

ANNUALS AND BIENNIALS
Antirrhinum
Arctotis
Dimorphotheca
Dorotheanthus
Gypsophila
Iberis
Linaria
Linum
Matthiola
Penstemon
Phacelia
Senecio

BULBS
Canna
Chionodoxa
Crocosmia
Crocus
Narcissus
Scilla
Zantedeschia

CLIMBERS
Fallopia
Wisteria

PERENNIALS
Achillea
Agapanthus
Anaphalis
Anthemis
Argyranthemum
Armeria
Artemisia
Aubrieta
Centaurea
Convolvulus
Cordyline
Dianthus
Dimorphotheca
Eryngium
Euphorbia
Geranium
Gypsophila
Iberis
Limonium
Linaria
Linum
Nepeta
Papaver
Penstemon
Phlomis
Phormium
Sedum
Sempervivum
Senecio
Stachys
Veronica
Yucca

SHRUBS
Arbutus
Brachyglottis
Calluna
Caryopteris
Ceanothus
Cistus
Corokia
Cotoneaster
Cytisus
Elaeagnus
Erica
Escallonia
Euonymus
Euphorbia
Fuchsia
Genista
Griselinia
Halimium
Hebe
Helianthemum
Hippophae
Hydrangea
Ilex
Lavandula
Lupinus arboreus
Olearia
Parahebe
Phlomis
Pittosporum
Potentilla
Rosmarinus
Santolina
Spartium
Spiraea
Tamarix
Ulex

TREES
Acer
Chamaecyparis
Cupressocyparis
Elaeagnus
Pinus
Trachycarpus

PLANTS FOR • OUTSTANDING AUTUMN COLOUR •

E = Evergreen

CLIMBERS
Parthenocissus
Vitis

FERNS
Osmunda

GRASSES
Hakonechloa

PERENNIALS
Bergenia (E)
Epimedium
Paeonia
Tiarella

SHRUBS
Acer
Berberis
Calluna (E)
Cercidiphyllum
Cornus
Cotinus
Cotoneaster
Crataegus
Enkianthus
Erica (E)
Hamamelis
Paeonia
Parrotia
Photinia
Prunus
Rhus
Sorbus
Vaccinium
Viburnum

TREES
Acer
Crataegus
Cryptomeria (E)
Eucryphia
Euonymus
Fothergilla
Ginkgo
Hamamelis
Larix
Liquidambar
Liriodendron
Nyssa
Parrotia
Populus
Prunus
Quercus
Sorbus
Stewartia
Taxodium

• PLANTS WITH FRAGRANT FLOWERS •

ANNUALS AND BIENNIALS
Erysimum
Heliotropium
Lathyrus
Matthiola
Nicotiana
Oenothera
Reseda
Verbena
Viola

BULBS
Crinum
Crocus
Freesia
Gladiolus
Hyacinthus
Lilium
Narcissus

CLIMBERS
Clematis
Hoya
Jasminum
Lathyrus
Lonicera
Stephanotis
Wisteria

GREENHOUSE
Brugmansia
Gardenia
Genista
Hoya
Stephanotis

PERENNIALS
Aponogeton
Asphodeline
Centaurea
Convallaria
Crambe
Dianthus
Dictamnus
Erysimum
Hesperis
Lathyrus
Matthiola
Phlox
Primula
Romneya
Viola

SHRUBS
Abelia
Azara
Brugmansia
Buddleja
Chimonanthus
Choisya
Colletia
Cytisus
Daphne
Elaeagnus
Erica
Gardenia
Genista
Hamamelis
Heliotropium
Lavandula
Lonicera
Magnolia
Mahonia
Myrtus
Osmanthus
Philadelphus
Rhododendron
Ribes
Rosa
Sarcococca
Skimmia
Syringa
Viburnum
Zenobia

TREES
Drimys
Eucryphia
Hamamelis
Magnolia
Robinia
Tilia

• WINTER-FLOWERING PLANTS •

BULBS
Anemone
Chionodoxa
Crocus
Cyclamen
Eranthis
Galanthus
Iris
Leucojum vernum
Narcissus
Scilla

CLIMBERS
Clematis
Jasminum

PERENNIALS
Bergenia
Helleborus
Hepatica
Iris
Pulmonaria
Viola

SHRUBS
Camellia
Chimonanthus
Cornus
Daphne
Erica
Garrya
Hamamelis
Lonicera
Mahonia
Rhododendron 'Christmas cheer'
R. moupinense
Sarcococca
Viburnum

TREES
Corylus
Hamamelis
Parrotia
Prunus × subhirtella 'Autumnalis'

• PLANTS WITH GREY OR SILVER FOLIAGE •

E = Evergreen

ANNUALS AND BIENNIALS
Eschscholzia
Papaver
Salvia
Senecio

BULBS
Allium
Cyclamen

GRASSES
Cortaderia
Festuca

PERENNIALS
Achillea
Anaphalis (E)
Androsace
Anthemis (E)
Arctotis (E)
Argyranthemum
Centaurea
Cerastium
Cynara
Dianthus (E)
Eryngium
Euphorbia
Helichrysum (E)
Leontopodium
Lychnis
Nepeta
Onopordum
Perovskia
Pulsatilla
Salvia
Saxifraga (E)
Sedum (E)
Sempervivum (E)
Senecio
Stachys
Tanacetum
Verbascum

SHRUBS
Artemisia (E)
Ballota (E)
Brachyglottis (E)
Buddleja
Calluna (E)
Convolvulus (E)
Hebe (E)
Helianthemum (E)
Hippophae (E)
Lavendula (E)
Phlomis (E)
Rosa glauca
Ruta (E)
Salix
Salvia
Santolina (E)

TREES
Cedrus (E)
Chamaecyparis (E)
Cupressus (E)
Eucalyptus (E)
Juniperus (E)
Picea (E)
Populus
Pyrus
Salix

• PLANTS FOR CUT FLOWERS •

* = Suitable for drying

ANNUALS AND PERENNIALS
Anthemis
Antirrhinum
Calendula
Callistephus
Catananche
Clarkia
Coreopsis
Cosmos
Dahlia
Delphinium
Dianthus
Digitalis
Gaillardia
Gomphrena
Gypsophila
Helianthus
Helichrysum
Iberis
Lathyrus
Matthiola
Moluccella*
Nigella*
Reseda*
Silene
Verbascum
Verbena
Zinnia

BULBS
Allium
Crocosmia
Freesia
Gladiolus
Iris
Lilium
Narcissus
Nerine
Ornithogalum
Sparaxis
Tulipa
Zantedeschia

GRASSES
Briza
Cortaderia
Lagurus
Pennisetum
Stipa

PERENNIALS
Achillea*
Agapanthus
Alstroemeria
Anaphalis
Anemone
Antirrhinum
Aquilegia
Aster
Astilbe*
Catananche*
Centaurea*
Coreopsis
Dahlia
Delphinium
Dendranthema
Dianthus
Digitalis
Doronicum
Echinops*
Erigeron
Eryngium*
Erysium
Euphorbia
Gaillardia
Geum
Gypsophila
Helenium
Helianthus
Helichrysum*
Heuchera*
Iberis
Iris
Liatrus
Limonium*
Lupinus
Lychnis
Monarda
Paeonia
Phlox
Physostegia
Rudbeckia
Scabiosa
Schizostylis
Silene
Solidago*
Tanacetum
Trollius
Valeriana
Verbascum
Verbena

SHRUBS
Camellia
Forsythia
Philadelphus
Rosa
Syringa

TREES
Acacia

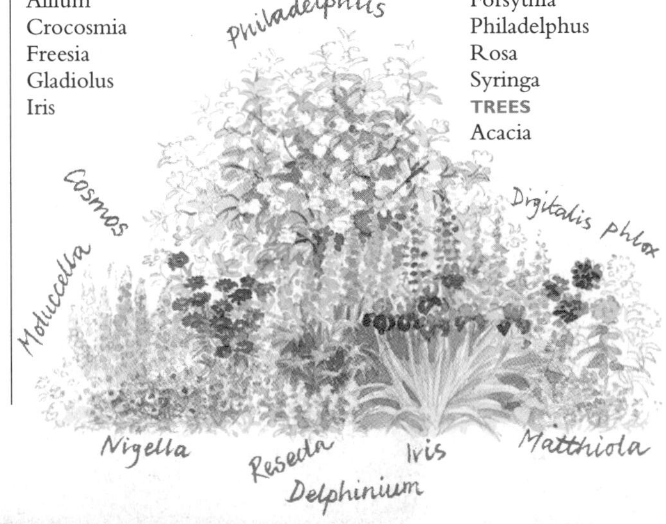

How to grow and increase your plants

The health of plants in a garden depends on the condition of the soil, together with proper feeding and appropriate pruning. Healthy plants can then be propagated to increase your stock

Getting the Best from Plants

To make a successful garden, you need to buy healthy plants, know your soil, apply the right feeds and carry out correct planting and staking

What to look for when buying new plants

The best time of the year for buying plants is spring, when the widest selection is available from garden centres and nurseries. But wait until the spring is well and truly established – the first few days of sunny weather after a hard winter can be deceptive, and a sudden return of frosts and bitter winds could kill delicate plants.

Container-grown plants, which have been raised in pots or trays, are easy to establish since they have well-developed root systems. But don't confuse container-grown plants with *containerised* plants, which have been potted up just prior to sale. These have immature root systems so do not establish themselves as quickly.

Bare-rooted shrubs or trees are those which have been grown in the open, then lifted from the ground and sold without soil around their roots.

Container-grown plants

Reject any plants that have scorched, withered or distorted leaves. A good plant will have well-coloured healthy foliage.

Check also that the soil is neither too dry nor too wet, that the surface of the potting compost is free of weeds and algae, and that the crown of the plant is firm and undamaged.

▲ The roots should reach the outside of the rootball.

Lift the plant up carefully by its stem. If it comes out of the pot easily, it may mean it is not yet established or that the compost is not adequately settled.

Reject a plant if its roots have grown through the bottom of the container and into the standing area – it will have been standing in the container too long. A few small roots emerging from the holes in the bottom of the pot are acceptable – a sign that the plant is well established.

Do not buy a container plant if the flowers are in full bloom; they will fade rapidly when transferred to the garden. Instead, choose one with plenty of buds – just a few flowers are enough to confirm that the plant is what it claims to be.

Check that there are no signs of any pests or diseases on the plant.

When buying a shrub, select a bushy plant with three or more young branches in its lower third. A thinly branched plant may be only a recently rooted cutting which could take a long time to increase size and produce a mature display.

Look for a well-balanced crown that is in the right proportion to the pot in which it is growing. It should have evenly spread branches, with none that are spindly.

▲ The crown should be well balanced and in proportion to the pot.

Shrubs and trees with bare roots

Bare-rooted shrubs and trees are plants which have been grown in the open ground, then lifted from the nursery just before dispatch or collection, having been ordered in advance. Avoid any with shrivelled or discoloured stems, or buds that are beginning to grow, or that have white hair-roots appearing.

Distorted stems could also indicate a diseased or badly grown plant. Bare-rooted plants should be planted only in the dormant season – between November and March.

Rootballed plants

The soil around the roots of a rootballed tree or shrub is held together with hessian or netting. To check a plant's condition, squeeze the rootball between your hands. It should be both firm and moist. If the mesh is damaged or too wide, or if the soil is too loosely packed, the roots may have started to dry out.

▲ The rootball, held together with mesh, should be firm and moist.

Buying seeds

When buying packets of seeds, choose those which are displayed in a cool, dry setting. Seeds exposed to hot sun deteriorate rapidly. Check their sell-by date to ensure they are not old stock.

Seeds are also available in other forms which, although more expensive, are easier to handle and more accurate to sow than those in packets. Pelleted seeds have a coating of material which disintegrates when it gets wet. Another form has seeds attached to strips of paper or tape. Cut to the desired length, it is placed in a shallow furrow 1.5cm (½in) deep and covered with soil. Seeds that have been partially pregerminated are quicker to grow, but they are much more expensive and are available for only a limited range of plants.

A plant that doesn't grow

If a plant dies soon after you plant it, or if it fails to grow in the way you hoped, return it to the place where you bought it. A garden centre or nursery will often replace the plant or advise you where you may have gone wrong in caring for it.

Analysing the soil in your garden

Soil consists of ground-down rock mixed with organic matter such as animal and vegetable remains. Micro-organisms break down the organic material to form humus which helps to hold particles together, and retains moisture and nutrients. Humus itself is also a source of nutrients. Dark soil is often rich in organic matter; pale grey soil contains little.

THE SIX MAIN TYPES OF SOIL STRUCTURE

CHALKY SOIL

CHALK Self-draining, strongly alkaline and fairly fertile, chalky soil can be difficult to garden, with many of the drawbacks of clay and sand. However, it is ideal for many alpine plants. It is usually dark, with stony subsoil below, and soft and sticky when wet.

PEAT Found in areas of high rainfall and boggy conditions, peat retains moisture and is rich in organic matter – but has few nutrients. Not many plants thrive in it because of its high acidity. It is dark brown or grey, with a spongy texture.

PEATY SOIL

CLAY SOIL

CLAY Dense, heavy and sticky when wet, clay can become waterlogged in winter. It can also shrink and crack in hot weather, damaging plant roots in the process. But clay contains plenty of plant foods and when its texture is improved it can be a fertile soil. Smooth to the touch, it clings to the hand and can be moulded into a ball.

SAND A dry, light and 'hungry' soil, sand drains rapidly and soluble fertilisers are swiftly lost. If irrigation is available, sand can – when fortified with lime, fertilisers and plenty of organic matter – be good for growing vegetables. It feels gritty when handled, and the grains do not stick together.

SANDY SOIL

LOAM SOIL

LOAM A combination of clay, silt and sand, loam is the ideal soil because of its light texture. A sandy loam is easier to work than a medium loam, but is slightly less fertile because nutrients are more easily washed out by rain; a clay loam can be more fertile but difficult to manage. Loamy soil feels gritty, will crumble slightly and stains the skin.

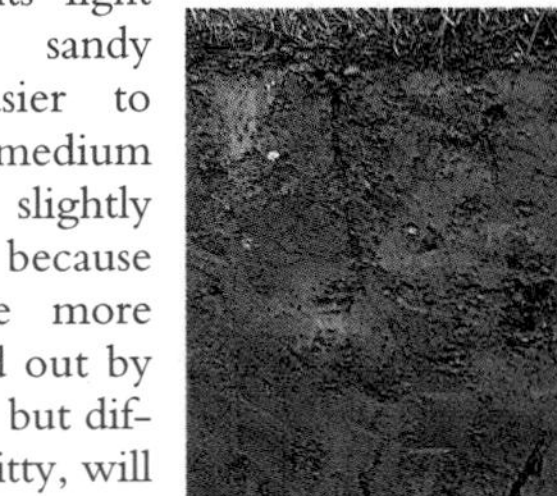

SILTY SOIL

SILT Similar to clay but with larger particles. As a result, fertilisers are steadily leached away by rain, leaving a soil which is less rich and rather acid. Silt is smooth and silky but cannot be moulded to shape.

CHECKING THE PH LEVEL OF SOIL

The pH (potential of hydrogen) is a method of measuring the alkalinity or acidity of a soil, and is expressed as a number from 0 to 14. Neutral soil measures pH 7 – a higher figure means the soil is alkaline, a lower figure indicates acidity. Most garden plants grow best in a slightly acid soil of pH 6-7.

To reduce the acid level in soil – to 'sweeten' it – add a dressing of lime or a lime-rich material such as mushroom compost. For example, vegetables – particularly members of the cabbage family – need soil with a pH level of 7 or 8. To increase the pH of the soil by 0.5, add 180 g of hydrated lime per square metre (5 oz per square yard). To maintain the right level, repeat this treatment every three years or so.

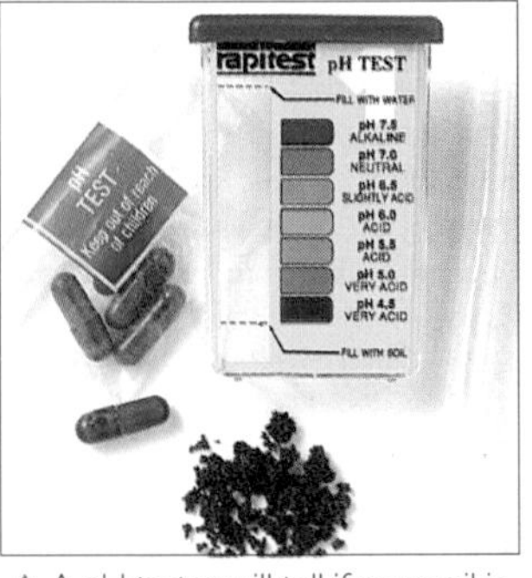

▲ A pH tester will tell if your soil is suitable for acid-lovers like azaleas or lime-lovers like cabbages.

To increase the acid level of the soil, dig in plentiful quantities of leaf-mould, composted bark, rotted garden compost or rotted manure. Alternatively, add sulphate of ammonia at a rate of 50 g per m² (1½ oz per sq yd).

Use a simple pH soil-test kit or an electronic pH meter, available from garden centres, to check the acidity level before deciding what plants to grow.

How to improve clay soil

▲ Remedy poor drainage by adding organic material.

To overcome poor drainage in a garden consisting of clay soil, dig in a mixture of organic and inorganic material.

The organic matter can be partly-rotted manure, garden compost, leaf-mould or composted bark. Apply about a bucketful to each 0.8 m² (1 sq yd).

Also apply two bucketfuls of sharp sand (not builder's sand), grit, weathered ashes or gypsum. Use only gypsum from garden suppliers (builder's gypsum contains chalk), and apply about 1.4 kg per 0.8 m² (3 lb per sq yd).

For a very acid clay soil, also apply hydrated lime at 0.25 kg per 0.8 m² (½ lb per sq yd). However, it is always best to choose plants that will grow well in your soil rather than try to change the soil significantly.

Testing how quickly your soil drains

To test the quality of the soil drainage in a new garden, dig a hole about 60 cm (2 ft) deep and fill it with water. If the water drains away within 24 hours the drainage is good; if it remains for 48 hours or more, the drainage needs to be improved (see *How to improve clay soil*, above).

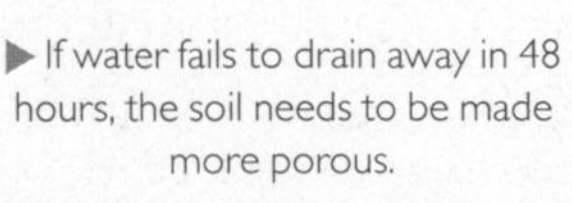

▶ If water fails to drain away in 48 hours, the soil needs to be made more porous.

Manures, mulches and fertilisers

The addition of organic material helps to create a well-balanced soil and increase its fertility. Organic materials are those derived from animal matter or plant debris. Generally, materials regarded as manures are those having an organic origin, such as dung, garden compost and leaf-mould, which break down into humus. They must be well rotted.

Mulches are materials applied to the surface of soil in order to enrich it, suppress annual weeds and help to keep the soil warm and moist. Well-rotted organic material used as a mulch, rather than being dug into the soil, breaks down more slowly and reduces the speed of nutrients being leached.

Fertilisers provide little or no humus, but have concentrated salts – for example, superphosphate of lime, sulphate of ammonia and sulphate of potash – which supplement the soil's own nutrients.

Types of fertiliser

Both artificial and organic fertilisers supplement the three principal nutrients that are essential to the growth of healthy plants – nitrogen, phosphorus and potassium. These chemicals can be bought separately or combined in a general-purpose fertiliser. Growmore, for example, consists of equal amounts of nitrogen, phosphorus and potassium, in the form of sulphate of ammonia, superphosphate of lime and sulphate of potash.

Nitrogen produces growth. Too much of it creates lush, leafy soft growth; too little results in small yellow leaves and lack of vigour. Phosphorus is important to seedlings and in the formation of seeds. Too little turns leaves dull purple and slows down growth; too much causes premature ripening. Potassium enhances flower colour; it also improves resistance to pests and diseases and hardens the tissues. Other nutrients, called trace elements, are also necessary for healthy growth, but in tiny quantities. They are present in a number of fertiliser formulations, including those based on seaweed. Trace-element deficiencies can often be remedied with a foliar feed (see below). Slow-release formulas, such as Osmacote and Vitex Q4, also contain trace elements, and are ideal on permanent plantings.

As well as being sold as powder, pellets or granules (for slow release), fertilisers are available in liquid form which can be applied to the roots of a plant for rapid absorption. Alternatively, they are sold as foliar feeds, applied with a watering can and rapidly absorbed through the leaves. Liquid fertilisers are available as a balanced feed for general purposes, or as mixtures for specific plants, such as roses, tomatoes and carnations.

Fertilisers must be applied according to the manufacturer's instruction or the result may be counterproductive. Always wear gloves when handling fertilisers in dry form.

How to make a compost heap

The decomposed remains of garden waste and kitchen peelings, combined with a limited amount of shredded paper, coffee grounds and tea bags, provide a useful soil improver and source of humus. If quantities are small, they need to be mixed with other organic material brought in from elsewhere, such as straw and animal manure. Do not put fallen leaves on a compost heap; they take longer to decompose so rot them down separately in a wire-mesh bin to make leaf-mould.

To make a heap that rots quickly, use only soft material. Grass cuttings can be used if they are well mixed with other material. Never use cooked food, diseased plants, weeds carrying seeds, or the roots of perennial weeds such as couch grass, oxalis or bindweed. Woody material, such as prunings, need to be shredded before being added to the heap.

Build a container (preferably two) of slats and posts plus a lid, or buy ready-made ones.

• FIVE STEPS TO GOOD COMPOST •

1 The compost heap should be at least 1 m (3 ft) square and about 1 m high, but if possible make it larger. The bigger the heap the hotter and more efficient the result. Start with a 15 cm (6 in) layer of woody stems and prunings to allow air to penetrate the heap.

2 Mix together enough soft vegetable material to form a layer 15 cm (6 in) deep.

A layer of animal manure can be placed on top of the vegetable matter to aid decomposition.

If possible, build up the heap in 15 cm (6 in) layers. If you have no manure, add to each layer a proprietary compost starter or other source of nitrogen such as sulphate of ammonia or dried blood.

3 To keep in the heat produced by decomposition, cover the heap with perforated plastic sheeting, topped by an old carpet, or by the compost-bin lid. The covering will also prevent the heap from drying out or becoming too wet.

4 The heap should not need watering. If it becomes soggy, mix in dry material, such as straw; if it seems too dry, add soft leafy material or grass mowings. Turn the heap twice to aerate it.

5 When the heap becomes dark and crumbly – in three to six months, but longer in winter – it can be forked into the soil or spread round plants as a mulch, but first make sure the soil is moist.

The uses of foliar feeding

Foliar feeds enter a plant's sap stream slightly quicker than fertiliser applied to the soil, but by only a day or two. However, foliar feeding is useful for giving a boost to plants growing in containers, as the leaves will absorb nutrients even though the roots are restricted.

Foliar feeds are often used to apply trace elements, such as iron for plants that are growing on alkaline soil, or to rectify other mineral deficiencies.

To make a foliar feed, mix a normal-strength solution of liquid fertiliser, following the instructions on the packet. Spray it on the plants – the finer the droplets the more readily they are absorbed.

Organic manures and fertilisers

MATERIAL	CHARACTERISTICS	SOURCE	APPLICATION
BARK (COMPOSTED)	Bark increases the soil's humus content, protects roots, suppresses weeds and retains moisture. It also increases the acidity of the soil. Softwood bark is more acidic and contains fewer nutrients than hardwood bark.	Garden centres and mail-order companies. Use only commercially bagged supplies which have been detoxified. Avoid cheap bulk supplies.	Surface mulch and soil-texture improver. Use with a nitrogen-rich fertiliser. As a surface mulch, spread it 5cm (2in) thick. As a soil conditioner dig in 4-8kg per m^2 (7-14lb per sq yd).
BONEMEAL	Has 20-25% phosphorus and 3-6% nitrogen. A good slow-release fertiliser.	Garden centres and mail-order companies, in bags.	Good for use in autumn and winter. Use 140-200g per m^2 (4-6oz per sq yd). To apply as a liquid manure, add to water, stir well and apply at once.
COIR/ COCONUT FIBRE	Good moisture-holding capacity but tends to dry out quickly on the surface. Little nutrient value.	Garden centres and by mail order.	Use as an alternative to peat when making up composts for potting and propagation. For ecological reasons coir is not recommended for large-scale use as a soil conditioner or mulch.
DRIED BLOOD	Has about 12% nitrogen content. One of the fastest-acting fertilisers. Good for spring and summer.	Sold in bags at garden centres and by mail order.	Before sowing or planting in spring or summer and to plants in growth. Apply 35-100g per m^2 (1-3oz per sq yd). It is not fully soluble but it can be used as a liquid manure if stirred well and applied at once at a rate of 15-30g per 4.5 litres (½-1oz per gallon) of water.
FARMYARD MANURE	Well-balanced plant food, containing nitrogen, phosphorus and potassium. Avoid on acid soils. Horse manure is richer, dryer and more open-textured than pig or cattle manure. When mixed with straw and rotted, it is a soil improver, source of organic matter and protective, weed-suppressing mulch.	Farms, stables (when it is often mixed with straw) and garden centres. Quality varies according to the animals' diet and how manure is stored. Ideally, buy it fresh from a farm and add it to the compost heap to rot. Proprietary brands are an acceptable substitute, but are concentrated and expensive.	Use decayed or composted manure as a top dressing – either neat or mixed with an equal measure of soil. Apply it only in spring or summer – one wheelbarrowful of well-rotted manure to each 10m^2 (12 sq yd) per year.
FISH, BLOOD AND BONE	About 3% nitrogen and 8% phosphorus.	Garden centres and by mail order.	In late winter or early spring, use as a general-purpose soil dressing before putting plants in a bed or sowing seeds. Apply 140g per m^2 (4oz per sq yd).
GARDEN COMPOST	Soil improver and source of organic matter. As a mulch, it retains moisture and protects roots from frost. Dug in, it improves soil texture.	See facing page.	Spread it 5cm (2in) thick as a mulch. To improve the soil dig in generously, as with farmyard manure.
GREEN MANURE	Organic material rich in nitrogen, such as mustard, rape and clover. Dug in it improves soil fertility; as a mulch it retains moisture and protects roots from frost. Use it to supplement manure or fertiliser. Also grow it as a winter ground cover to prevent nutrients from being washed through the soil.	Sow your own where it is to be used, following the instructions on the seed packet.	Sow in autumn. Cut down to ground when 20cm (8in) high, and dig into the soil two days later while still green. As a mulch, cut and lay it 5cm (2in) thick over the soil.
HOOF AND HORN MEAL	Contains 12-14% nitrogen. Coarse-ground meal is slower acting than fine-ground.	Garden centres and by mail order, but expensive.	Apply in spring and summer at 90g per m^2 (2½oz per sq yd).

MATERIAL	CHARACTERISTICS	SOURCE	APPLICATION
LEAF-MOULD	A nutritious mulch, but needs anchoring with sand, bark or netting. Also good as a soil-texture improver. Compost separately from other organic material for at least a year.	Garden centres or homemade.	Use leaf-mould with a nitrogen-rich fertiliser, which will help to break it down. As a mulch spread a layer 2.5cm (1in) thick. As a soil improver, dig in 2.5kg per m^2 (5lb per sq yd).
MUSHROOM COMPOST	Has nitrogen, phosphorus and potassium, according to nature of compost. Good improver of soil texture. Contains lime, so do not use it on alkaline soil or on lime-hating plants.	Garden centres or mushroom growers.	As a surface mulch at any time. Or dig in up to 11kg per m^2 (20lb per sq yd). Good way of raising pH if the soil is acid.
PEAT	Peat has little value as plant food, but for several decades has been a valuable ingredient in composts used for propagation. It can also be used to bulk up soil-based compost when it is used in large containers or small raised beds. Difficult to re-wet once it has dried out.	Garden centres and by mail order.	To make your own compost for raising cuttings, mix 50% peat with 50% horticultural sand (measured by volume). Large-scale use of peat is not recommended because its extraction destroys unique wildlife habitats. Alternatives include coir and composted bark.
SEAWEED MEAL	Contains about 2% nitrogen, 2% phosphorus, and is rich in trace elements. Acts as a soil conditioner and encourages plant growth. Particularly useful on poor soil.	Garden centres and by mail order.	Use in autumn as a general-purpose fertiliser/soil conditioner, or three months before planting, at 140g per m^2 (4oz per sq yd).
WOOD ASH	An alkaline material and good source of potassium. Amount of potassium varies between 15% and 4%. Keep it dry to prevent nutrients from being washed out, or add it to the compost heap.	Bonfires or wood-burning stoves.	Use wood ash to reduce acidity of soil. May be used at any time of the year. Apply up to 140g per m^2 (4oz per sq yd). As a liquid 15g per 4.5 litres (½oz per gallon) of water.

Inorganic fertilisers

MATERIAL	CHARACTERISTICS	SOURCE	APPLICATION
PHOSPHATE OF POTASH	Roughly 50% phosphorus, 35% potassium. Soluble fertiliser and highly concentrated. Good liquid fertiliser during growth.	Garden centres but expensive.	At any time of year. As a liquid fertiliser use up to 15g per 4.5 litres (½oz per gallon) of water. Or dig in 140g per m^2 (4oz per sq yd).
ROCK PHOSPHATE	Contains about 3% nitrogen and 20% phosphorus. It is a slow-acting fertiliser which is used as an alternative to bone meal.	Garden centres.	Use in the same way as bone meal. Apply in autumn or winter – either before planting or raked into the soil as a top dressing – at 120g per m^2 (3½oz per sq yd).
SULPHATE OF AMMONIA	Contains 20% nitrogen and is used in many compound fertilisers. Fairly rapid action. Good on limy soils but increases the acidity of acid soils. Must be stored in a dry place.	Garden centres.	Use in spring or early summer. Never mix it with lime as ammonia gas will be released, wasting nitrogen. Apply up to 75g per m^2 (2oz per sq yd) of soil. As a liquid manure, use 15g per 4.5 litres (½oz per gallon) of water.
SULPHATE OF MAGNESIUM (EPSOM SALTS)	Has 10% magnesium, is soluble and quick-acting, so best used as a foliar feed. Less a fertiliser than a supplement of magnesium.	Garden centres.	Use in spring and summer. Apply up to 75g per m^2 (2oz per sq yd). As a liquid spray use 15g per 4.5 litres (½oz per gallon) of water.
SULPHATE OF POTASH	Contains 48% potassium. Holds well in the soil.	Garden centres.	Use at any time of the year. Apply up to 140g per m^2 (4oz per sq yd). As a liquid, use 15g per 4.5 litres (½oz per gallon) of water.
SUPERPHOSPHATE OF LIME	Contains 12–18% phosphoric acid. Quick-acting, reasonably soluble fertiliser. Despite its name, it will not increase soil alkalinity as the lime is a form of gypsum.	Garden centres.	Use alone or mixed with other fertilisers in spring or early summer. Apply up to 140g per m^2 (4oz per sq yd). As a liquid, mix 30g per 4.5 litres (1oz per gallon) of water.

Gardening the organic way

Organic gardening is gardening with the wider environment in mind. It relies on natural methods to control pests and to build up the fertility of the soil. Organic gardening recycles farm and garden wastes rather than disposing of them in ways that would pollute the environment

Enriching the soil

The starting point for effective organic gardening is to create soil that holds moisture but drains well and encourages extensive root growth. It will provide plants with a balanced, slow-release diet to promote steady growth. The plants will then be less prone to attack by pests and diseases than chemically fed plants.

The ground should be cultivated as little as possible. Don't walk on the soil when it is wet, and keep it covered with growing plants or a mulch wherever possible.

SOIL IMPROVERS To improve the soil, use garden compost and leaf-mould – made by recycling kitchen and garden waste – augmented with brought-in ingredients such as animal manure and extra autumn leaves. Do not use manures derived from intensive farming systems because of the higher levels of food additives, antibiotics and other chemicals.

Garden compost, well-rotted manure, mushroom compost, hay, seaweed, cocoa shells and grass cuttings are all rich in nutrients. Use them only during the spring or summer. If they are applied when plants are not actively growing, their goodness will be leached from the soil and wasted.

Low-nutrient materials, such as straw, leaf-mould, composted bark and prunings chopped up in a shredder, may be applied at any time of the year and in any quantity.

If possible, use one wheelbarrow load of well-rotted farmyard manure or two barrow loads of garden compost to each $10m^2$ (12sq yd) of ground each year.

Organic soil improvers can be used either as a surface mulch or mixed with the top 15cm (6in) layer of soil. A mulch acts as an insulating layer and should be applied to warm, wet soil only.

Unrotted soil improvers, such as hay, straw, seaweed and grass cuttings, can be composted first or added straight to the garden. If they are not composted, use them as a mulch.

GREEN MANURES Plants grown specifically to benefit the soil's fertility and structure are called green manures. They may be dug into the soil or cut and used as a mulch, and are especially useful in the vegetable garden. Grazing rye, for example, can be grown in winter as a soil cover to prevent plant nutrients being washed out. It also improves the structure of the soil and prevents weeds. Other plants used as green manures are clover, *Phacelia tanacetifolia*, mustard, fenugreek and winter tares. All can be bought as seeds.

SLOW-RELEASE FERTILISERS AND MINERAL SUPPLEMENTS Fertilisers of natural origin – plant, animal and rock – release their nutrients slowly. They can be used to adjust a major deficiency, or where compost and other materials are not available in sufficient quantities. They include hoof and horn, fish blood and bone meal, rock phosphate, dolomite limestone (to raise alkalinity), vinash (a by-product of the wine industry), seaweed meal, calcified seaweed, crab shells, gypsum and sulphur.

Making organic liquid manure

In organic gardening the aim is to feed the soil, which feeds the plants. Although liquid feeds do not strictly comply with this aim because they supply the plant more or less directly, their use can be essential when plants are grown in pots, tubs and other containers. And you can make your own.

NETTLE LIQUID Soak 1kg of nettle tops in 10 litres of water (2lb to 2 gallons) for two weeks. Strain the mixture and use one part of the nettle liquid in ten parts of water. Be prepared – this is a smelly process.

▲ Soak nettles in water for two weeks to make liquid manure.

COMFREY LIQUID Find a bucket or barrel with a small hole in the bottom and stuff it with comfrey (*Symphytum*) leaves. Place a container beneath the hole to catch the black liquid which will seep out as the leaves decay – after about two weeks. Dilute this 10 to 20 times with water before using.

Controlling pests and diseases

A great deal of pest control occurs naturally – ladybirds eating greenfly, beetles eating weevils, frogs eating slugs, and so on. And there are many things that can be done to encourage these gardener's allies (see page 32). Plants are

PREVENTATIVE METHODS OF PLANT PROTECTION

Barriers, traps and scaring devices are available to protect plants from pests, and from the diseases that they can introduce.

NETTING

Netting is used to exclude birds, rabbits, cats and other large pests. Fleece and other fine-mesh crop covers can be used to keep out smaller pests, such as greenfly, cabbage caterpillars, cabbage and carrot root fly, flea beetles and weevils. Lightweight covers can be laid directly over plants, or supported on canes or wire hoops.

PLASTIC BOTTLES

Cut the bottom off plastic bottles and stand them over young plants to protect them from slugs, snails and other pests. The larger the bottle the more growing space for the plant, but take care not to trap a slug inside. The bottles also act as cloches, protecting plants against the weather.

STICKY TRAPS AND BARRIERS

Cards covered with a non-drying glue, available from garden centres, can trap greenhouse pests, including whitefly. Protect fruit trees and shrubs from climbing pests, such as winter moth and ants, with grease bands or with fruit-tree grease applied to the trunks. Apply the bands above any supporting stakes or to the stakes as well.

PHEROMONE-BAITED TRAPS

Use traps baited with synthetic pheromones (female sex hormones) to catch codling moths and plum moths. The male moths are lured away from the females which remain unfertilised, and so the population is reduced.

capable of withstanding low concentrations of pests, which provide useful feeding grounds for the pests' predators.

Helping plants to help themselves

Choosing the right plant for the right place is essential. A sun-loving plant will not thrive in shade; roses will always be more prone to powdery mildew in dry soils – especially in a small dry bed against a house; and hostas will be eaten by slugs in moist conditions.

Buy plants that look healthy and are not pot-bound. When buying fruit trees and bushes, choose plants that are certified as being virus-free. Consider planting resistant varieties if you know that a problem is likely to occur, and when transplanting, choose sturdy plants that will grow quickly.

The importance of timing

Avoid sowing too early, before the soil has warmed up. Slow-growing seedlings are much more likely to succumb to pests or diseases.

In the greenhouse, a heated bench is an effective remedy against 'damping off' early in the season. Outdoors, if an early start is required, soil can be warmed with cloches or a sheet of clear plastic for a couple of weeks before planting. And cloches can be left on after planting until the weather improves.

By carefully sowing at the right time, and avoiding periods when plants are particularly at risk, some pests and diseases, such as pea moth, pea mildew and potato-cyst eelworms, can be avoided (see 'Directory of Pests', p. 824).

Crop rotation

Vegetable growers rotate crops every year, only returning to the original site after three or four years. Perennials, shrubs and trees are not suitable for regular rotation, but the same principles apply. Never replace a rose with another rose, for example. Likewise, new fruit trees and bushes are best planted in a fresh position where the same type of fruit has not been grown for several years.

Dealing with an attack

When a problem arises, first identify the cause (see 'Pests' p. 824 and 'Diseases and Disorders' p. 838). Fruitless hours can be wasted trying to eliminate a pest when, for example, the cause may be a disease, mineral deficiency or virus.

BIOLOGICAL CONTROL

The section 'Allies in the Gardener's World' (p. 32) illustrates the wide range of creatures that are on the gardener's side, helping to keep pests and diseases under control.

A major drawback is that they are not always present in large enough numbers when you want them. One solution is to purchase suitable creatures in quantity to release when a particular pest occurs.

Predators and parasites that are commercially produced – and are usually known as biological control agents – are available from some garden centres and mail-order catalogues. They can be used to deal with a range of pests occurring in both the greenhouse and the open garden, including glasshouse whitefly, red spider mite, mealy bug, aphids, vine weevil and slugs.

HAND PICKING

An effective way of dealing with a small outbreak of pests or diseases is to pick, squash or cut out the problem area. Regular 'health' checks can prevent problems getting out of hand.

SPRAYING

In an organic garden try to avoid the use of any pesticide sprays. If spraying is essential, use a non-persistent pesticide such as derris, pyrethrum, insecticidal soap or sulphur. Follow the instructions on the label, and treat only those plants that are infected.

▲ If a plant is badly infested, spray with insecticidal soap.

Controlling weeds

Organic gardeners control weeds by digging, hoeing, mulching and hand weeding; there are no organic weed-killers. In some cases, weeds can be useful. For example, clover in a lawn extracts nitrogen from the air and feeds the grass. Other weeds provide food and shelter for garden allies.

USING A MULCH

Since weeds cannot grow in the dark, covering the soil with a mulch will inhibit or prevent their growth. The ultimate effect, however, will depend on how much light the mulch keeps out.

LIVING MULCHES

Close-growing plants help to keep the soil free of weeds as they compete with them for light and space.

BIODEGRADABLE MULCHES

Organic material that gradually decays in the soil is more appropriate in a 'green' garden than sheets of black polythene. The choice of material depends on the appearance you want to achieve. Bark chips, for example, may be more pleasing to the eye than grass cuttings in an ornamental border.

▲ Bark chips make an attractive mulch in an organic garden.

For the effective control of weeds, use a minimum 10 cm (4 in) layer of mulch. A thinner layer may be used over a skin of cardboard, newspaper or a synthetic membrane. The following are all effective mulches: leaf-mould, shredded prunings, cocoa shells, straw, hay, wood chips (from garden centres), bark chips and grass cuttings.

Planting new perennials, shrubs and trees

Whether a new plant comes in a container or with bare roots, the correct planting technique is essential if it is to get off to a rapid and healthy start.

ESTABLISHING A NEW • CONTAINER-GROWN PLANT •

Container-grown shrubs are sold in plastic pots of compost. They can be planted at any time of the year, but if you plant them in summer make sure to keep the soil moist until the autumn.

1 Remove all weeds from the bed, and dig over the soil to a spade's depth. Then firm the soil with your feet.

2 Dig a hole as deep as, and slightly wider than, the plant's container. The surface of the compost in the container should be level with the surrounding soil.

3 Break up the soil at the bottom of the hole with a fork and incorporate some organic material. Separately, mix some soil with more of the organic material.

4 Water the plant thoroughly. Then remove the container and check the extent of the root system (right). If the roots are wound around the outside of the rootball, gently tease out some of the outer roots so they will establish more quickly in the surrounding soil.

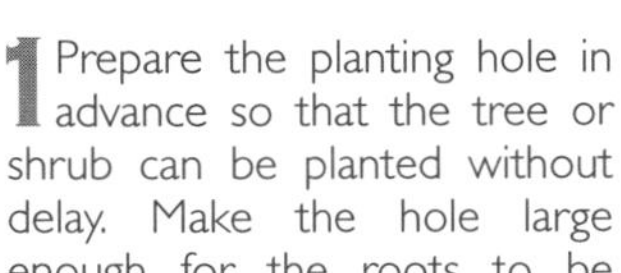

5 Holding the plant by the stem, and with one hand supporting the ball of soil, place it in the hole (left). Fill the hole to the top with the planting mixture and tread it down firmly. Top up with more of the mixture, tread down again and water thoroughly. Finally mulch the soil around the plant.

PLANTING BARE-ROOT TREES • AND SHRUBS •

Bare-rooted trees and shrubs are ordered from a nursery in advance and delivered between November and March. They should be planted as soon as possible after delivery, but not when the ground is frozen.

1 Prepare the planting hole in advance so that the tree or shrub can be planted without delay. Make the hole large enough for the roots to be spread out completely. Fork over the base of the hole and incorporate some organic matter such as garden compost.

2 Before planting the tree or shrub, soak the roots in water for two hours and trim off any broken or damaged roots.

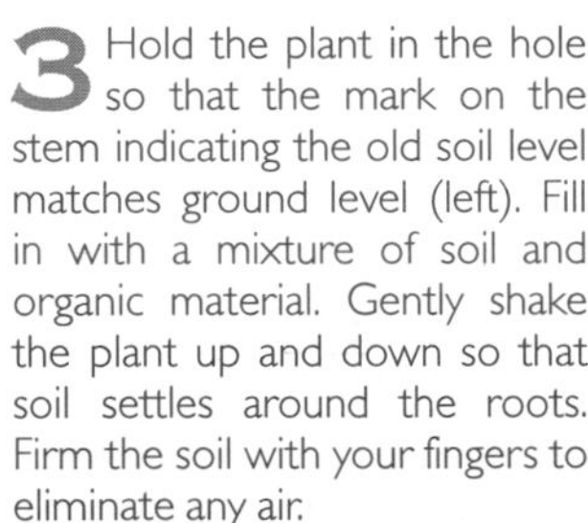

3 Hold the plant in the hole so that the mark on the stem indicating the old soil level matches ground level (left). Fill in with a mixture of soil and organic material. Gently shake the plant up and down so that soil settles around the roots. Firm the soil with your fingers to eliminate any air.

4 Check the finished planting level; it should coincide with the soil mark on the stem. Finally, firm the soil with your heel. Water thoroughly and mulch the soil around the plant, leaving a gap of 10 cm (4 in) around the base of the stem.

PLANTING A CLIMBING SHRUB • AGAINST A WALL OR FENCE •

Climbers of borderline hardiness need a warm and sheltered spot, facing south or west. North and east-facing borders receive less sunshine and are exposed to the coldest winds. East-facing borders tend to be very dry because they are sheltered from the rain-bearing winds, which mostly come from the west.

1 The soil at the foot of a wall or fence is usually dry, so before planting dig in plenty of organic matter, such as garden compost, and give it a soaking. Make sure the soil is kept moist in future. Plant a climber 30 cm (12 in) away from the fence so it benefits from rain.

2 Ivy, Virginia creeper and climbing hydrangea fasten themselves to a fence and need no assistance once they have become established, but most other climbers need support throughout their lives. Put up trellis, horizontal wires or rigid plastic netting with a mesh size of 10-15 cm (4-6 in). Fix it on battens 2.5 cm (1 in) away from the wall. Fasten shoots with string or a wire plant ring.

HOW TO TRANSPLANT • ESTABLISHED SHRUBS •

Shrubs – either deciduous or evergreen – can be moved to a new part of the garden in autumn or spring, but not when the soil is frozen or waterlogged. Small, young shrubs transplant most easily.

1 Dig a trench around the shrub – beneath the outer edge of the canopy. Then dig under and lever it out. Crumble away loose soil to lighten the plant and limit the size of its new hole. Slip a tarpaulin or strong plastic sheet under the shrub and get someone to help you to move it. Trim off any diseased or damaged roots.

2 Dig the planting hole as deep as, and wider than, the rootball. Mix two parts of soil from the hole with one part of well-rotted compost, manure or composted bark. Hold the plant in place so that the top of the rootball is flush with the new ground level, and fill in around the plant with the prepared soil mixture.

3 Tread the soil down firmly and top up with more of the planting mixture. Water the soil thoroughly and apply a feed.

STAKING A YOUNG • TREE •

Until a young tree has established a root system – which takes from two to three years – it is vulnerable to wind damage and unable to support its own weight. Stout wooden stakes impregnated with preservative, and various ties for restraining trees to the stakes, can be bought from most garden centres.

1 Drive the stake in 60 cm (2 ft) before planting, so that the roots do not get damaged.

2 The top of the stake should reach about one-third of the way up the trunk.

3 After planting the tree, secure it as close as possible to the top of the stake in order to reduce the danger of rubbing. Use a plastic strap-and-buckle that has a rubber buffer. Loop the strap around the tree and thread it through the buffer. Pull the strap tight, then buckle it around the stake.

4 Check the tie at least twice a year, loosening or tightening as necessary so as not to chafe or strangle the trunk. The tree should be independent of the stake after three years.

Giving support to perennials and annuals

TWIGGY FRAMEWORK Most tall perennials and annuals need supporting during the growing season. Twiggy branches pruned from your own trees make good supports, and they will soon become invisible as the plants grow. Push each branch into the soil between the plants. Bend the tops over and interlock them to form a framework that the plants will grow through.

SUPPORT BY TWIGS

BAMBOO CANES AND STRING A cheap but time-consuming method is to use canes and garden string, fillis or raffia – not wire or nylon cord, which will cut into the plant stems. Place three or four canes in the soil around a plant, and link them at two or three levels – not above the plant – with the string. Add new layers of string as the plants grow taller.

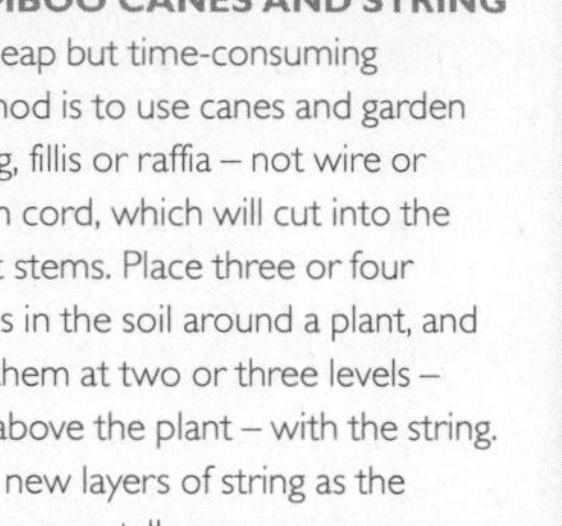

CANE-AND-STRING FRAME

HEAVY CANES OR NETTING Thick-stemmed plants can be tied to canes. As the plant grows, the canes may need to be replaced with thicker, longer ones. Nylon netting or chicken wire stretched horizontally between wooden stakes can make an effective support for plants in an herbaceous border.

METAL 'SCAFFOLDING'

PURPOSE-MADE SYSTEMS Many plant-support systems are available from garden centres. Some consist of interlocking metal stakes which can be linked together to create miniature scaffolding; others have adjustable ring supports through which the plants grow. They vary in cost and finish, and are reusable for several years.

Four ways of staking a tree

SHORT VERTICAL STAKE
A short stake allows the upper part of a tree to move in the wind, strengthening the trunk as it develops. The tie is made a third of the way up the trunk – usually about 50 cm (20 in) high on a normal tree. Loosen the tie once or twice a year as the tree grows.

SHORT DIAGONAL STAKE
As the stake is placed on an angle, the bottom end is well away from the tree's roots. So this is a good way of staking a container-grown tree. The stake should lean into the prevailing wind, and the tie should still be 50 cm (20 in) high.

TWO STAKES AND A CROSSBAR
Two stakes are used to give greater support in an exposed situation. The tree is tied to the centre of a crossbar 50 cm (20 in) from the ground. This sturdy frame is suitable for a fairly large tree. As with all methods, remove the stakes after three or four years.

GUY-ROPE STAKING
To hold large trees while they establish themselves, three stakes can be driven into the ground at an angle, with guy ropes attached to the trunk. Proprietary systems can be bought which include guy ropes with rubber anti-friction tubes.

Planting and caring for bulbs and corms

Most bulbs perform best in a sunny position, but cyclamens, endymions, erythroniums and eranthis (winter aconites) grow well in shade. Crocus, galanthus (snowdrops) and eranthis thrive under trees and shrubs. Gladioli, amaryllis, nerines and sparaxis are sensitive to cold and are best planted at the foot of a south-facing wall where they will get plenty of sun and protection from cold wind. Plant spring-flowering bulbs between September and November. Plant summer-flowering bulbs in March – or April/May for the less-hardy types. Plant autumn-flowering bulbs in July/August.

• PREPARING THE SOIL •

1 Several days before planting, dig the ground and remove weeds and stones. Good drainage is essential so add gravel to heavy soil.

2 Mix plenty of well-rotted garden compost, leaf-mould or composted bark into the soil – a bucketful to the square metre – and leave it to settle for a few days.

3 A slow-release fertiliser such as bone meal or seaweed meal, can also be added, but is not essential.

• PUTTING IN THE BULBS •

1 Using a narrow trowel, or a bulb planter (shown below), dig holes about twice as deep as the bulbs. In clay or loam soil, put a little sharp sand or grit in the bottom of the hole. Insert each bulb point upwards. Gently press and twist the bulb so that it makes firm contact with the earth. Then cover it with the excavated soil.

If new bedding plants or herbaceous perennials are to be planted at the same time, put them in before the bulbs.

2 Mark and label the position of each group of bulbs so that you do not disturb them before the shoots appear.

PLANTING BULBS AMONG MAT-FORMING PLANTS

Loosen the surface slightly with a hand fork, then use a blunt dibber to make holes for the bulbs. Under plants that have only a single root, such as *Gypsophila repens,* roll the matted stems to one side and plant the bulbs with a narrow trowel.

• LIFTING AND STORING BULBS•

Bulbs may need to be lifted to survive the winter, or to make room for other plants, or because they are too congested.

Ideally, spring-flowering bulbs, including hyacinths, narcissi and tulips, should not be touched until the foliage has died down. Then they can be split up and replanted straight away. But the demands on space for summer bedding plants may mean that the bulbs need to be moved to another position where they can die down naturally.

1 With a garden fork, ease the bulbs from the ground, complete with the leaves, stems and soil. Then crumble off the soil without damaging the skins. Throw away any bulbs that are pulpy or rotting, and move the remaining ones to a spare bed in an area of the garden that is lightly shaded.

2 Dig a trench 30 cm (12 in) deep and wide. Lay a length of fine-mesh wire netting or plastic netting along the bottom of the trench so that it protrudes a little at each end.

3 Place the bulbs along the netting – almost but not quite touching each other – with at least half their stems and leaves clear of the trench. Fill in the trench to cover the bulbs and water them in. This will allow the bulbs to build up their reserves to produce flowers the following growing season.

When the leaves and stems have shrivelled, pull the netting at each end of the trench to lift the bulbs clear. Lay them in deep trays of moist compost or coir, with the leaves uncovered, and leave them in a lightly shaded place to finish drying out. When the leaves have withered completely, clean off the dead leaves, roots and shrivelled skins. Use any bulblets attached to the mother bulb for propagation, or discard them. Place the bulbs in shallow boxes, in single layers and uncovered, and store them in a cool dry place until replanting time.

• LIFTING AND STORING CORMS IN WINTER •

In areas where the weather is mild, gladioli, ixias and sparaxis corms may be left in the ground throughout the year. Elsewhere, when the leaves begin to brown in October, the corms should be lifted.

1 Carefully lift the corms with a fork. Cut off the top stems and leaves to within about 2.5 cm (1 in) of the corm. Place the corms in trays and leave uncovered for seven to ten days in a cool airy shed to dry.

2 Break away old shrivelled corms and put aside any small cormlets for increasing stock. Remove the tough outer skins from the large corms and burn any that appear to have lesions or that are rotting.

Dust the corms with pirimiphos-methyl to control thrips. To prevent dry rot and gladiolus scab, dust with sulphur or dip in a solution of carbendazim. Store in trays in a cool but frost-free place until spring.

Forcing bulbs for indoor display

In early autumn, plant bulbs in pots of compost – or if the container has no drainage hole, use bulb fibre. Daffodils, tulips and crocuses can be planted alternately in two layers, but keep hyacinths in a single layer. Moisten the compost, wrap the bowl in newspaper and put it in the dark in a shed. After six or eight weeks check for growth. Then move the container into a light, cool room. When buds are visible, put the container on display.

Pruning Shrubs and Climbers

Pruning is a way of controlling a plant's growth. It may encourage its vigour, alter its size and shape, or improve its flowers and foliage. Not all shrubs need annual pruning; many need only occasional tidying up

Six main methods of pruning

Pruning tools

Three types of tool will cope with all normal pruning needs for shrubs and small trees.

Anvil secateurs

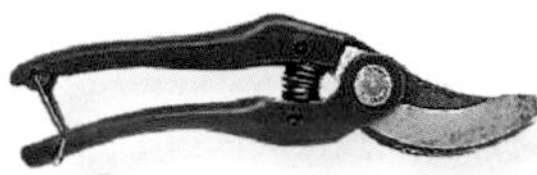

Bypass secateurs

- Secateurs (either anvil or bypass types) are used for pruning most shrubs and evergreen hedging plants.

Long-handled loppers

- A pair of long-handled loppers are needed for cutting thick shoots and branchlets on shrubs and small trees.

Pruning saw

- A pruning saw is necessary for cutting off large branches.

Keep all your pruning tools clean and sharp so that they work efficiently. To avoid the danger of spreading diseases, it is advisble to clean secateurs with a garden sterilant after use.

• METHOD 1 •

Shrubs which flower on previous year's wood

Some shrubs produce their flowers on shoots that developed the previous year. They can be pruned immediately after they finish flowering. This encourages fewer but larger flowers and keeps the shrub's growth within bounds.

WHEN TO PRUNE

Just as soon as the flowers have died down.

HOW TO PRUNE

▲ Pruning *Buddleja alternifolia* after flowering.

Cut back each shoot that has borne flowers to two or three shoots or buds from its junction with the main stem. This will reduce the shrub to its main framework. The new shoots that then grow in the coming months will produce flowers the following season.

WHICH SHRUBS TO PRUNE

Buddleja alternifolia, Cytisus (all species except *C.* 'Porlock'), *Deutzia, Kerria, Mahonia aquifolium* (when it is used as ground cover), *Prunus glandulosa, P. triloba, Rubus, Spiraea* 'Arguta', *Weigela.*

• METHOD 2 •

Shrubs which flower on the new shoots

Some shrubs flower on the new shoots that grow each year. They can be pruned in the spring as the shoots start to grow. The method of pruning is used to restrict a shrub's size or to encourage larger but fewer flowers.

WHEN TO PRUNE

In early spring, when the severe weather is over and new shoots are beginning to grow.

HOW TO PRUNE

Cut back last year's flowered shoots to two or three buds or green shoots before the old shoots meet a main branch. Unless you need to remove a branch altogether, avoid cutting back into the older wood because new shoots might not grow. After pruning, mulch with a 5 cm (2 in) layer of rotted manure or garden compost, and feed with a general fertiliser at 75 g per m^2 (2 oz per sq yd).

WHICH SHRUBS TO PRUNE

Buddleja davidii, Caryopteris, Ceanothus (deciduous types), *Ceratostigma, Colutea, Cytisus* 'Porlock', *Fuchsia, Indigofera, Lippia, Passiflora, Santolina, Solanum crispum, Spartium, Spiraea japonica* 'Bullata', *S. x bumalda, S. douglasii, S. japonica, S. salicifolia, Tamarix ramosissima.*

▼ Pruning a caryopteris in spring.

• METHOD 3 •

Clearing out old growth from the centre

Some shrubs, including the common forsythia and *Hydrangea macrophylla* and its cultivars, are improved by having some of the oldest growth taken out low down on the bush every year. The technique is used to reduce overcrowding and allow sunlight to penetrate into the centre of the shrub.

WHEN TO PRUNE

Spring.

HOW TO PRUNE

▲ Pruning a Forsythia shrub in spring.

Cut out the oldest stems almost to the ground. These are rough-looking and have sub-laterals as well as laterals. Two-year-old stems – which have laterals only – may be removed if you wish.

WHICH SHRUBS TO PRUNE
Hydrangea macrophylla, and overgrown specimens of *Berberis, Clethra, Corylopsis, Cotoneaster, Forsythia, Genista, Kolkwitzia, Potentilla, Ribes sanguineum, Symphoricarpos.*

• METHOD 4 •

Cutting out dead and straggly growth

Most shrubs at some time become straggly or damaged, or a branch may have died. This is the technique to use for a general tidying up.

WHEN TO PRUNE
At any time of the year, as required.

HOW TO PRUNE
Cut out diseased shoots to clean, healthy wood about 12.5 cm (5 in) below the diseased area. Cut back any dead or damaged branches to a healthy shoot or bud, facing outwards, near the ground. Any particularly weak shoots can be cut right back to the main branch. Prune straggly or unsightly branches by half, to a strong shoot or bud facing outwards. Do not remove well-shaped, healthy wood, as you will only remove buds that will produce flowers later.

How to make a pruning cut

Cut the stem just above an outward-facing shoot or bud, slanting the secateurs in the same direction as the shoot or bud. Avoid leaving a stump of the stem above the cut – it will be vulnerable to die-back or disease.

▲ Outward-facing shoot.

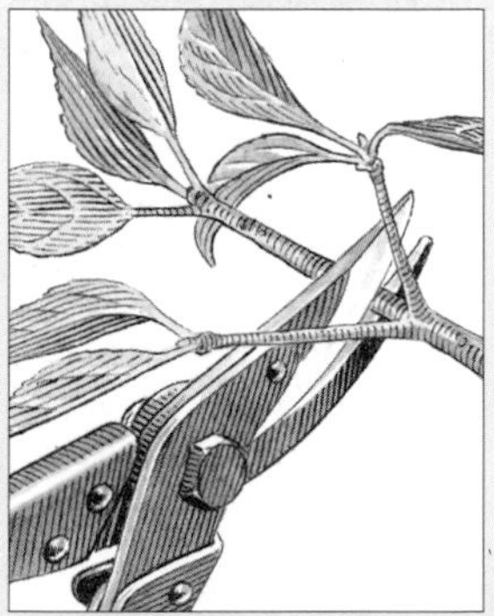

▲ Opposite shoots.

On a plant where the shoots or buds appear opposite each other, cut straight across the stem, just above them.

▲ Removing a damaged stem of *Viburnum opulus.*

WHICH SHRUBS TO PRUNE
Just a few of the most popular shrubs that can be pruned this way are *Camellia, Cistus, Daphne, Euonymus, Hebe, Potentilla* and *Viburnum.*

• METHOD 5 •

Rejuvenating large overgrown evergreens

Evergreens do not usually need routine pruning, apart from cutting out damaged stems or untidy growth. However, after several years they can become overgrown or bare at the base, and may then be given a very hard pruning. But, they will not flower the following year.

WHEN TO PRUNE
Early spring.

HOW TO PRUNE
Begin by using long-handled loppers to remove the top growth. Then, using a saw, cut off all the main branches down almost to ground level.

Mulch the ground around the shrub with well-rotted manure or garden compost, and apply a general-purpose fertiliser at the rate of 75 g per m² (2 oz per sq yd).

▲ Cutting back an old specimen of *Pieris japonica.*

WHICH SHRUBS TO PRUNE
Aucuba (spotted laurel), *Olearia* (daisy bush), *Pernettya, Philadelphus* (mock orange), *Pieris, Prunus laurocerasus* and *P. lusitanica* (cherry laurels).

• METHOD 6 •

Restricting the size of climbing plants

Most climbing plants can be left unpruned until they have overrun their space. Then they may be pruned when the flowers have faded. For the pruning of *Clematis* and *Wisteria,* see the individual genus entries.

WHEN TO PRUNE
For flowering climbers, prune after the flowers have faded. For non-flowering climbers, prune in spring or summer.

HOW TO PRUNE
Cut back self-clinging climbers, such as ivy, as far as necessary on the wall. Detach others from their supports first. Then prune all lateral growths, leaving the main stems, which can be shortened. Remove any very old stems, but keep younger ones that are growing from ground level or low down on the plant.

Finally, retie the remaining stems to the supports, spacing them evenly. Flowering climbers should bear blooms again the following year.

WHICH SHRUBS TO PRUNE
Actinidia, Campsis, Fallopia baldschuanica (Russian vine) *Hedera* (ivy), *Hydrangea anomala* ssp. *petiolaris* (climbing hydrangea), *Lonicera japonica* and *L. periclymenum* (honeysuckles), *Parthenocissus* (Virginia creeper), *Vitis* (grape vine).

Preventing reversion

Shrubs with variegated foliage may develop shoots with all-green foliage. These will grow more vigorously than the variegated shoots and will eventually take over the plant. Cut them out completely as soon as you notice them, right back to variegated growth.

All-gold or all-cream shoots may also appear and should be removed, although they tend to grow less vigorously than the variegated shoots.

Variegated shrubs which can show reversion include cultivars of *Elaeagnus, Euonymus* and *Ilex* (holly).

▲ Cutting back *Actinidia kolomikta* after flowering.

How to Propagate Plants

You can multiply the plants in your garden at almost no cost by sowing seed or by taking pieces from your existing stock and growing them into young plants

Growing plants from seed

Raising seedlings under cover

Plants which cannot survive in the open during frosty weather, such as half-hardy annuals, are first sown in containers under cover – either in a greenhouse or indoors. The technique can also be used to bring on early blooms or crops. Sow the seeds between February and early April. You can buy them from a garden centre or collect them from your own plants. Use plastic containers, as they are strong and easy to clean. Small seed trays or 13 cm (5 in) pots are usually most suitable. Scrub containers that have been used before in warm soapy water.

• SOWING THE SEEDS •

1 Fill the container with slightly moist seed compost. When sowing very fine seeds, first sprinkle a little fine-sieved compost on the surface. Using the bottom of another pot, gently firm down the compost.

2 Sow seeds thinly and evenly. For easier control, fold the open flap to form a spout and carefully tap them out of the packet. Fine seed can be distributed more evenly if first mixed with a little silver sand.

3 Cover the seeds with a thin layer of sifted compost or vermiculite – a layer of about the seeds' own depth is enough. Some seeds should be left uncovered – very fine ones, such as begonias, lobelias and calceolarias, and those that need light to germinate, such as sinningias, streptocarpus and saintpaulias.

4 Identify the contents with a plastic label. Stand the container in water to half its depth until the compost is wet.

5 Ideally, put the container in a heated frame or propagator at a temperature of 12-18°C (54-64°F).

Alternatively, cover the container with a polythene bag and fold it underneath. Stand the container in a warm shady place, such as a shaded windowsill. For extra warmth put it in an airing cupboard, but check daily for germination and then immediately move it into the light.

6 Once the seeds have germinated, turn the bag inside out each day to prevent drips. When growth is established, take off the cover and move the container into good light, but not direct sun.

• PRICKING OUT •

1 Seedlings are ready to be 'pricked out' when the first true leaves appear above the seed leaves. Fill a standard seed tray – about 33x20 cm (13x8 in) – with moist potting compost and mark out plant holes about 4 cm (1½ in) apart with a pointed stick or pencil.

2 Gently prise up a small clump of seedlings, complete with the compost clinging to the roots. Hold a seedling by a seed leaf – not the stem, which is easily damaged – and gently tease it from the other seedlings with the stick.

3 Lower the seedling into a hole and gently firm the soil down around it so that it will not yield if gently tugged. When the tray is full, label it and water the seedlings with a fine-rosed can.

4 Put the trays in a greenhouse or coldframe, or on a shaded windowsill. Three days later, move them to a sunnier, but lightly shaded, position. Keep the compost moist.

The danger of damping off

Seedlings planted too closely or overwatered may contract damping-off disease which causes rot at soil level. Remove and destroy dead seedlings or leaves and spray the rest with copper fungicide or Cheshunt compound. Next time, give your seedlings more space, and always use fresh compost and clean containers.

DAMPING OFF

Hardening off half-hardy annuals

In early May, or April in mild areas, move the seedlings of half-hardy annuals to an unshaded coldframe, cloche or polythene tunnel. For the first few days open the frame or raise the sides of the tunnel slightly. Gradually increase ventilation until – by mid May at the earliest (the end of May in northern England and frosty areas) – the coverings are completely open. Delay opening fully if the weather is cold, wet or windy. Close all openings at night until the danger of frost has passed.

PUT SEEDLINGS IN A COLDFRAME

GRADUALLY INCREASE VENTILATION

Growing seedlings outdoors

An outdoor seedbed needs careful preparation if the plants are to germinate successfully. It must be firm, moist and consist of a fine tilth. Dig heavy soil in autumn or winter to allow it to settle before the frost arrives. Light, sandy soils can be left until spring. There is no need to add organic matter; if the soil is poor, rake in a balanced fertiliser.

Hardy annuals are usually sown in March and April, but some can be sown in autumn to give the young plants a quick start in spring. Seed packets advise on the best times for sowing. Perennials are treated in the same way as hardy annuals, but if you collect seeds from your own plants sow them as soon as possible. The viability of seed decreases with time, so sow old seed more thickly than fresh. Discard any seed that is more than two years old.

Pelleted seeds, coated with clay or other material, are easier to handle but need to be kept moist until the seedlings appear. Primed, also called pregerminated, seed is available for plants that need high germination temperatures.

• PREPARING THE SEEDBED •

1 In warm weather, when the soil is dry enough to walk on without sticking to your boots, hoe or lightly fork it over to a depth of 7.5 cm (3 in). When the soil has dried out, tread it down firmly to break up lumps, then rake the surface to create a fine tilth (the particles should be small and evenly sized).

2 Prepare rows in the soil for sowing – running from north to south if possible so that the seedlings will receive the greatest amount of sunshine when they germinate. Space the rows according to the advice on the seed packet. Use the edge of a draw hoe to make shallow 'drills' about 1.5 cm (1/2 in) deep.

• SOWING THE SEED •

If the weather is dry, water the seedbed the day before sowing – not after sowing. Sow thinly to simplify thinning later. Or sow pinches of seeds at regular intervals according to the advice on the packet.

1 Mix very small seeds with fine sand to help to distribute them evenly. To control the seeds, dribble them from your hand between the folds in the skin.

2 To close the drills, use the back of a rake to pull the raised earth back over the seeds – working along the length of the rows, not across them.

3 Tamp soil down gently with the back of the rake. Be careful not to bury the seeds too deeply or to press the soil down too hard. As a rule of thumb, cover seeds with soil to about twice their size. Sow some surplus seeds at the end of rows to fill gaps later.

• THINNING OUT THE SEEDLINGS •

Seedlings are ready to be thinned out when they have two or three 'true leaves', above the first pair of 'seed leaves'. If the weather is particularly dry, thin in the evening and water the bed afterwards.

1 Lift the unwanted seedlings from the soil with one hand while holding down the soil around nearby seedlings with the other. Remove weak or malformed seedlings first.

2 Thin the rest so they are spaced at half the distance required. Do not leave discarded seedlings on the ground; they will attract pests, so put them on the compost heap.

3 When the leaves of adjacent plants touch, remove alternate seedlings to leave the row at the full spacing. Fill any gaps with the surplus seedlings that were sown at the end of the rows.

Growing new plants from cuttings

Cuttings can be taken from most parts of a plant, but the techniques vary according to the time of year. Different plants respond better to different methods. Take cuttings only from healthy, well-established plants. In general, the younger and softer the material, the faster it will root.

WHICH TECHNIQUE TO USE, AND WHEN

ROOT CUTTINGS
During late autumn or winter, pieces of root are removed and replanted. The method is suitable for perennials and shrubs that have fleshy roots, including bergenias, romneyas and oriental poppies. Do not take root cuttings from grafted plants; only the rootstock will grow.

LEAF CUTTINGS
Some houseplants are commonly propagated from leaf cuttings, which can be taken at any time of the year. There are three methods.
Leaf petiole A healthy leaf is taken from the parent plant and the stem (petiole) is inserted into compost. Suitable for peperomias and saintpaulias.
Leaf section A leaf is cut into pieces, each containing a portion of the main vein. The pieces are pushed vertically into the soil or laid across it. Suitable for sansevieria and streptocarpus.

▲ Plantlets from peperomia leaf-petiole cuttings.

Leaf slashing The underside of a leaf is slit across the main veins and the whole leaf laid flat on compost. New plants emerge from the slits. Most commonly used on rex-type begonias.

STEM CUTTINGS
Six types of cutting can be taken from a stem or shoot of a plant. The type of cutting that is used depends on the time of year and the state of development of the stem.

▲ Hypericum growing from softwood cuttings.

Basal cuttings are taken of soft new growth from herbaceous perennials, just as it emerges from the soil. The technique is used for plants which become hollow-stemmed later in the season, such as dahlias, delphiniums and dendranthemas (chrysanthemums).
Softwood cuttings are taken in spring. The entire cutting consists of soft growth with no woodiness. Suitable for fuchsias and hydrangeas.
Greenwood cuttings are taken in early summer when the bottom end of the cutting is just beginning to ripen. Greenwood cuttings are slightly slower to root than softwood cuttings, but are less prone to wilt. Suitable for dendranthemas and pelargoniums (geraniums).
Semi-ripe cuttings are taken in July or August when most of the stem is fresh and green but the bottom end is turning ripe and brown. Suitable for forsythias, philadelphus and weigelas.
Ripewood cuttings are usually used for evergreens. The cuttings are taken in late summer or early autumn and left in a coldframe to root. Suitable for aucuba, escallonia and hebe.
Hardwood cuttings are taken in autumn – usually from deciduous shrubs – after the leaves have fallen and the stems have become woody. This is an easy method of propagation but the cuttings take the longest time to root.

• ROOT CUTTINGS FOR PERENNIALS •

Herbaceous perennials are often propagated by division (see p.820), but root cuttings are an excellent alternative.

1 During autumn or winter, lift the plant, wash off the soil and remove a root. Then replant the parent plant.

2 Cut thick or fleshy roots, as found on dicentras, oriental poppies and romneyas, into pieces 5-7.5 cm (2-3 in) long. Trim off any excess fibrous roots. Cut the upper end – nearest the plant – straight across and cut the lower end at a slant. This is in order to distinguish the top from the bottom when you put the cutting in the compost. Cut thin-rooted plants, such as phlox and verbascums, into 5 cm (2 in) pieces.

3 Fill a large pot with equal parts of peat and horticultural sand. For thick cuttings, make planting holes 5 cm (2 in) apart, and about 5-7.5 cm (2-3 in) deep. Insert each cutting, slanted end down, until the flat top is flush with the surface of the compost. Cover with 5 mm (1/4 in) of sand. Leave the pot of cuttings in a closed coldframe during winter.

With thin cuttings, lay them flat on the surface of a seed tray filled with cuttings compost and cover with a layer of compost. Leave them in a closed coldframe throughout winter.

4 Pot the rooted cuttings individually in spring, when they have developed three or four pairs of leaves and also some roots which develop after the leaves. Up to this point water sparingly, if at all. Put each one in an 8 cm (3 in) pot of John Innes No.1 compost or a soilless equivalent and return them to the coldframe. Stand them outdoors through the summer, and plant them in their flowering positions in autumn.

LEAF-PETIOLE CUTTINGS FOR • SOME HOUSEPLANTS •

The easiest way of producing new plants from leaves is with leaf-petiole cuttings. The method is used for saintpaulias and peperomias. Clean equipment and fresh compost are essential as the cuttings are susceptible to rotting and disease. Cuttings can be taken at any time, as long as the leaves are new and fully developed, but they root faster in summer.

▶ Saintpaulia and peperomia plants.

1 Use a craft knife or garden knife to slice through a leaf stalk about 5 cm (2 in) from the leaf itself. Fill a seed tray with an equal mix of peat and perlite, or cuttings compost for African violets, and firm the surface until the compost is within 1 cm (3/8 in) of the rim.

2 Use a dibber or pencil to make a shallow hole in the compost. Insert the leaf at an angle so that it is almost lying flat in the compost but is firmly held by it. Press the compost down around the stalk. When all cuttings are planted, water them carefully with a fine spray.

3 Put the cuttings in a lightly shaded, bottom-heated propagator at a temperature of about 20°C (68°F).

4 As new plantlets start to appear, usually within five or six weeks, feed them with a liquid houseplant fertiliser. When they are large enough to be handled, put them into individual pots to harden off in a greenhouse or on a windowsill.

LEAF CUTTINGS FOR • MOTHER-IN-LAW'S TONGUE •

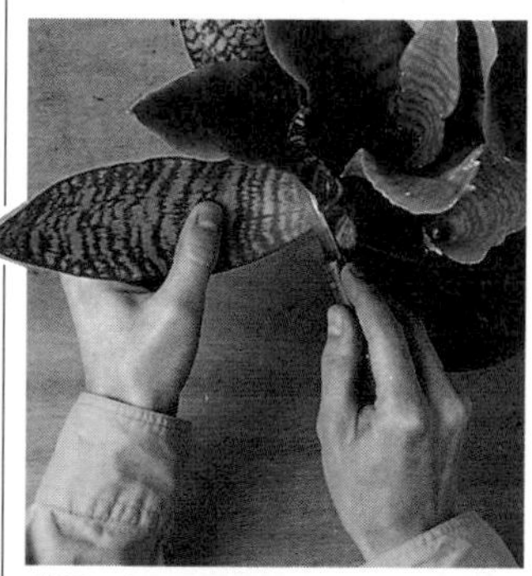

1 During spring or summer, use a craft knife or garden knife to cut a healthy and fully expanded leaf from the plant, close to the crown. Cut the leaf at right angles to the midrib into a series of 2.5 cm (1 in) long sections. This is easiest to do on a hard, clean surface.

2 Fill a 13 cm (5 in) pot with moist cuttings compost. Press the leaf sections into the compost for half their depth, with the end nearest the leaf tip uppermost. Firm the compost and spray with water. Cover the pot with a polythene bag or put it in a heated propagator. Keep the cuttings out of direct sunlight in a constant temperature of 20°C (68°F).

3 In about six weeks, when the sections start to produce plantlets (left), remove the cover. Pot the plantlets singly in 8 cm (3 in) pots of John Innes No.1 compost or in a soilless potting compost.

LEAF SLASHING FOR • LARGE-LEAVED BEGONIAS •

A single leaf, provided it is large enough, can be used to produce several new plants – a method commonly used for large-leaved begonias such as *Begonia masoniana* and *B. rex*.

1 At any time between June and September, select a mature healthy leaf that is fully expanded and cut it about 2.5 cm (1 in) from the base with a sharp knife. Make a series of fine cuts, about 2 cm (3/4 in) long, on the underside of the leaf across the major veins. This is easiest on a hard, clean surface.

2 Fill a seed tray with moist John Innes No.1 compost or cuttings compost. Lay the leaf, cut side down, on the compost and secure it with a few pebbles or wire staples. Cover with polythene. Keep the tray where it will receive light – but not direct sunlight – with a temperature of 20°C (68°F).

3 Little plantlets will start to sprout from the cuts in the veins within three or four weeks. Remove the polythene cover and leave the young plants to grow on in a warm and shady position for another two or three weeks.

4 Carefully separate the rooted cuttings and pot them individually in 8 cm (3 in) pots of potting compost.

• BASAL CUTTINGS FOR PERENNIALS •

As well as being propagated by division, many clump-forming perennials, such as dendranthemas (chrysanthemums), delphiniums and lupins, can be propagated from young basal shoots.

1 In spring, when the young shoots which appear at the base of the plant are about 10 cm (4 in) long, cut them off at crown level or just below.

2 Plant them individually in 8 cm (3 in) pots, filled with cuttings compost or equal parts of horticultural sand and peat and put them in a coldframe.

3 Keep the cuttings well watered by spraying from overhead, and keep the frame closed. About six weeks later, pot the cuttings singly in 8 cm (3 in) pots of John Innes No.1 compost or soilless potting compost. Keep them in the coldframe until frosts have finished. Plant them in their flowering positions in autumn.

Using rooting compound on cuttings

Stem cuttings can be dipped in a rooting hormone to increase the speed with which they take root. The compounds are available as powder, gel or liquid. Buy the right type for the cuttings you are taking, and follow the instructions given on the packet.

Treat only the cut base of the stem and any other wounded area that has been made to encourage rooting. Tap off any excess.

Most healthy plants will root if taken at the right time, so rooting hormones are not essential. For example, cuttings of impatiens (busy lizzie), *Tradescantia zebrina*, hedera (ivy), pelargonium and salix (willow) all root quickly without artificial help.

• SOFTWOOD CUTTINGS FOR PERENNIALS •

Softwood cuttings are immature, soft shoot tips in the first flush of growth, taken in April or May. The method is commonly used for hardy herbaceous perennials and greenhouse plants, as well as fuchsias and hydrangeas. Cuttings will root best in a warm propagating case with heating cables in the bottom.

Softwood cuttings wilt quickly; get all the materials ready before taking the cuttings so that they can be inserted into the compost immediately. Take the cuttings in the morning and put them straight into a polythene bag.

1 Softwood cuttings should be young and non-flowering, just firm but not hard, and about 7.5cm (3in) long. Remove a shoot that has four or five pairs of leaves.

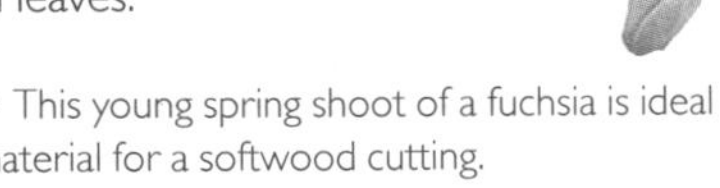

▶ This young spring shoot of a fuchsia is ideal material for a softwood cutting.

2 Using a craft knife or garden knife, slice the bottom off the shoot, just below the lowest pair of leaves. Without damaging the stem, pull off the bottom two pairs of leaves. Then dip the base of the cutting in hormone rooting powder – preferably one that contains a fungicide.

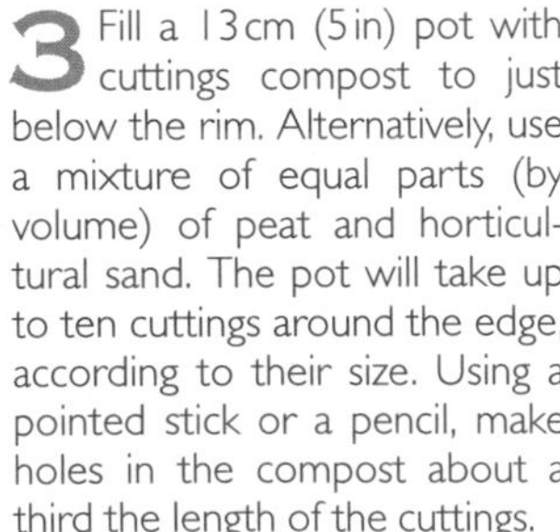

3 Fill a 13cm (5in) pot with cuttings compost to just below the rim. Alternatively, use a mixture of equal parts (by volume) of peat and horticultural sand. The pot will take up to ten cuttings around the edge, according to their size. Using a pointed stick or a pencil, make holes in the compost about a third the length of the cuttings.

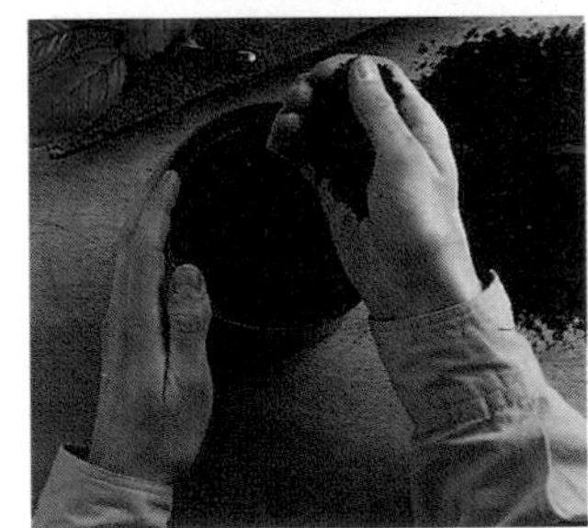

4 Insert each cutting in a hole and press it in place. Water them in, using a fungicidal solution to prevent rot. Keep the cuttings in a propagator (preferably with bottom heat), covered and shaded.

5 When the cuttings have rooted – after about a month – pot them individually in 8cm (3in) pots of potting compost. Keep them watered and shaded until they have become established. Plant them in their flowering positions the following spring.

GREENWOOD CUTTINGS FOR • SHRUBS AND SUB-SHRUBS •

Greenwood cuttings are taken from the soft tip of a stem when spring growth has started to slow – about the beginning of June. The lower stem is firm but not hard. The technique is used for ericas, lantanas, pelargoniums and dendranthemas (chrysanthemums).

1 Take the cuttings early in the morning and put them in a plastic bag – if they start to dry out they may not root.

2 Use a craft knife or garden knife to trim the cuttings to about 7.5-10cm (3-4in) long. Cut the leaves from the lower half of the cutting. Dip the cut end in a hormone rooting powder of softwood strength, preferably containing a fungicide.

3 Almost fill a 13cm (5in) pot with cuttings compost. Make small holes in the compost around the edge of the pot, and insert the cuttings up to the leaves. Then firm them in.

4 Put the pot in a covered propagating case, preferably with bottom heat, or beneath a polythene tent to prevent dehydration. Ensure the cuttings have plenty of light, but shade them from direct sunlight.

5 Repot the young plants individually in 8cm (3in) pots of potting compost. Plant them in their flowering positions the following spring.

6 After five to eight weeks the cuttings should have rooted and they can be gradually hardened off by increasing the ventilation.

• SEMI-RIPE CUTTINGS FOR SHRUBS •

Many shrubs root well from semi-ripe material taken from mid July to the end of August – earlier in very hot summers. Some examples are actinidia, choisya, lavandula, philadelphus and weigela.

Semi-ripe cuttings need to be rooted in warm conditions in a coldframe or propagating case. Bottom heat helps, but is not essential.

1 The cuttings are taken from the current year's growth – the tips of the shoots are soft but the lower stem is firm. Remove 15-20cm (6-8in) long, non-flowering sideshoots with leaves growing on them. Take off the leaves from the lower part of the shoot and sever it just below a leaf joint. Cut off the soft tip above a leaf to leave a cutting 5-10cm (2-4in) long.

2 Use an 8cm (3in) pot for up to five cuttings, a 13cm (5in) pot for from five to ten. Almost fill with cuttings compost. Dip the base of the cutting in a hormone rooting agent. Make holes in the compost around the edge of the pot, but make sure the leaves will not touch. Insert each cutting to a third of its length and firm the compost. Water well, preferably using a fungicidal solution.

3 To prevent the cuttings drying out, a humid atmosphere is essential. Fit a plastic bag over the pot, supported by two hoops of galvanised wire. Water the cuttings and put them in a draught-free, warm and shaded place such as a coldframe or propagator. Rooting is faster with bottom heat.

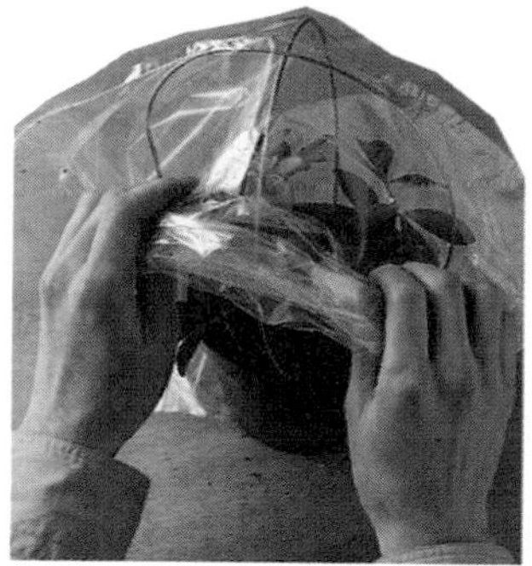

4 Once the cuttings have rooted, harden them off by making a few holes in the plastic bag to let air in. Slit the bag a week later, and a week after that remove the cover completely.

5 Remove the rooted cuttings and carefully separate them with a plant label or pencil. Then pot each young plant in an 8cm (3in) pot of potting compost. Water them in, and do not allow the compost to dry out.

Keep the pots under cover and harden off in spring when the young plants can be planted out or transferred to larger pots.

Taking heeled cuttings

Some semi-ripe cuttings will root more strongly if they are removed from the shrub with a heel-like sliver of the previous year's wood attached. This heel helps roots to form because it surrounds the base of the new growth, an area rich in the plant's growth hormones. Cut off a main shoot that has several sideshoots – preferably without flowers. Pull off a sideshoot, or make a slanting cut into the main stem below the junction with the sideshoot; then cut in the opposite direction to remove the shoot.

• RIPEWOOD CUTTINGS FOR EVERGREENS •

Evergreen shrubs are often propagated from ripewood cuttings which are taken in late summer or early autumn. The cuttings are planted in a coldframe or heated propagator and left over winter. Aucuba, escallonia and hebe can be reproduced in this way.

1 Take heel cuttings (see box, above) in late summer from a stem of the current season's growth. Trim the leaves off the bottom third and pinch out the tip.

With plants that are difficult to root – such as daphne and eleagnus – cut a 2.5cm (1in) long shallow vertical groove in the stem. Dip the cut end in a rooting hormone powder of ripewood strength and cover the groove with the powder.

2 Dig the soil in a coldframe thoroughly and add a mixture of peat and sand. Plant each cutting up to its leaves. Be sure that the leaves of adjacent cuttings are not touching or they may rot. Close the lid securely and keep the plants shaded. Remove the shading as the days grow shorter. In cold weather, cover the frame with insulation – such as old carpet, blanket or newspapers.

3 Grow the shrubs on for another year in individual pots. Then plant them out in spring.

Helping evergreens to stay moist

Cuttings of evergreen shrubs and trees may dry out as they lose moisture through their leaves. And this will cause them to fail. To prevent evaporation, you can put the cuttings in a coldframe and spray them with an antidesiccant spray. such as a Christmas-tree spray. But best of all, if you have a greenhouse, install a mist propagating unit which maintains the moisture level automatically.

HARDWOOD CUTTINGS FOR • TREES AND SHRUBS •

The easiest way of growing new deciduous shrubs or trees is to take hardwood cuttings in late autumn or early winter – ideally in October or early November. After the cuttings have been planted, little attention is needed for the next 12 months when the new young plants are moved to their permanent positions. Before taking the cuttings, choose a patch of soil sheltered from north and east winds, and dig it thoroughly – if the soil is clay dig in horticultural sand or grit and organic matter to help drainage.

1 Choose a shoot that has just completed its first season's growth. Use a sharp knife or secateurs to cut it from the plant close to the main stem. Trim the cutting just below a bud at the base and just above a bud at the top so that it is about 25cm (10in) long.

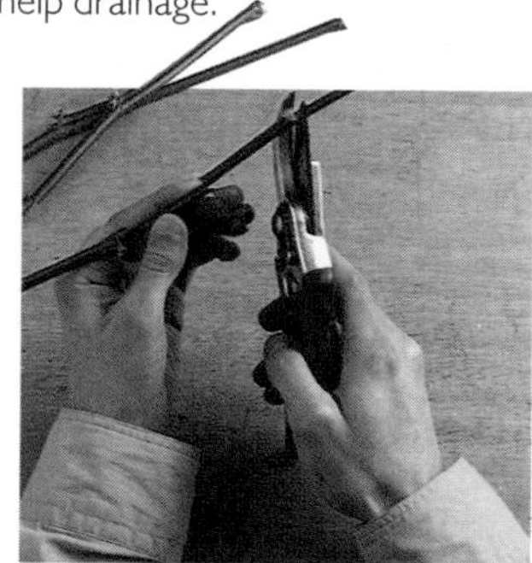

2 To encourage the cutting to root, remove a thin sliver of bark near the base on one or both sides, using a sharp knife. Lightly dip the base and the wounded strips into hormone rooting compound.

3 Make a narrow V-shaped trench in the prepared soil by pushing in a spade to its full depth and pulling it forwards. Spread horticultural sand 2.5cm (1in) deep in the bottom of the trench and stand the cuttings on it, 10cm (4in) apart, so that half or two-thirds of each cutting is below ground. Fill the trench with soil and tread it firm.

4 In early spring tread the soil firm if it has been lifted by frost. Keep the area free of weeds, and water during dry spells throughout spring and summer. Some plants, including populus, salix, cornus and ribes, will be ready to be moved to their permanent sites, or potted up, the following autumn. But if little growth has been made, leave the cuttings for another year.

Increasing perennials by division

The easiest way of propagating herbaceous perennials is by division, which involves lifting a plant from the soil and separating it into two or more pieces. Each piece when replanted will grow as an identical plant to the parent. Division is not only used to increase the number of plants, but also to perpetuate existing stocks which are beginning to deteriorate or become overcrowded.

Division is done between October and April, but not when the soil is frozen or sticky. Perennials that flower early in the year are best divided in autumn.

• FIBROUS-ROOTED PLANTS •

Fibrous-rooted perennials, such as heleniums, phlox and Michaelmas daisies (*Aster novi-belgii*), need to be pulled apart into separate pieces. Young ones can often be separated by hand, but old, overgrown plants can be difficult to divide because the roots and crowns form a solid mass. Two garden forks make the job easier.

1 Once the plant has been lifted, force the prongs of two garden forks into the clump, back to back. Separate the clump by first pushing the handles of the forks together.

2 Then pull them wide apart. Repeat until you have two halves, then separate the halves. Alternatively, cut the clump into pieces with an old knife or a sharpened spade.

3 Cut away and discard the central woody part of each piece. Then divide the remainder into pieces, each containing about six buds or shoots. Discard unhealthy growth and plant the divisions in their flowering positions. Water well in dry weather.

• RHIZOMATOUS-ROOTED PLANTS •

Plants that grow from rhizomes, which lie just below the surface, are easily lifted – ideally in early spring when new growth buds are sprouting. Examples of rhizomatous plants are bergenias, monardas, physalis and polygonatums.

1 Lift the rootstock with a garden fork and prise off the soil to reveal the main rhizome and the younger stems coming from it. If necessary, wash the clump under a tap or in a bucket of water. Choose side growths about 7.5 cm (3 in) long which have healthy roots and two or three vigorous growth buds. Cut them off with a knife.

2 Discard the old rhizome and trim the cut pieces to just below a cluster of fine healthy roots, removing any dead material. Plant the cut pieces, with the root cluster downwards, at about the same depth as the original plant. Fill in the soil and press it firmly into place around the new plant.

• FLESHY AND TUBEROUS ROOTS •

Some herbaceous perennials grow from tubers, which are thickened, fleshy rootstocks or crowns.

The small tubers of liatris and spring-flowering anemones can be easily pulled apart by hand (see left).

However, the large, fleshy roots of hemerocallis and peonies have to be cut into pieces with a knife, as follows.

1 Lift a clump of plants – in autumn for peonies – and carefully clean off the soil. Wash them in a bucket of water, if necessary. This will reveal growth buds, as with these hemerocallis tubers (right).

2 Divide the rootstock into several pieces, cutting through the crown from the top downwards. Then plant them immediately in their flowering positions. A piece with only one bud will take longer to establish itself than a section of three or four tubers and buds.

Peonies, which often resent disturbance, may take a season or longer to recover.

Dividing bearded irises

Lift the plants and cut off the younger rhizomes from around the edge of the clump. Each portion of rhizome should have one or two strong, healthy leaves. Peel off withered leaves and trim the remainder to a fan shape to reduce wind rock. Then plant in the flowering position.

A TRIMMED RHIZOME

Increasing shrubs, climbers and houseplants by layering

Layering is a simple way of inducing the stem of a healthy plant to take root while still attached to the plant. Some trees and shrubs, such as willows and hazels, do this naturally when their stems touch the ground. Layering is a method that can succeed where cuttings fail.

Carnations and pinks are examples of herbaceous plants that respond to layering. Suitable shrubs include magnolia, viburnum, cassiope, corylopsis, heathers and many climbers, including wisteria and clematis. Deciduous plants are best layered in autumn or winter; evergreens in autumn or spring.

• ORDINARY LAYERING •

1 Fork over the soil near the plant – beneath the branch to be layered – and enrich it with well-rotted compost or manure. Lighten heavy soil with horticultural sand.

2 Select a vigorous, young and flexible shoot, like the one on this willow (right) and bend it down to soil level, about 25cm (10in) from its tip. Strip the leaves where the shoot touches the soil and snick the underside with a knife, cutting towards the growing tip.

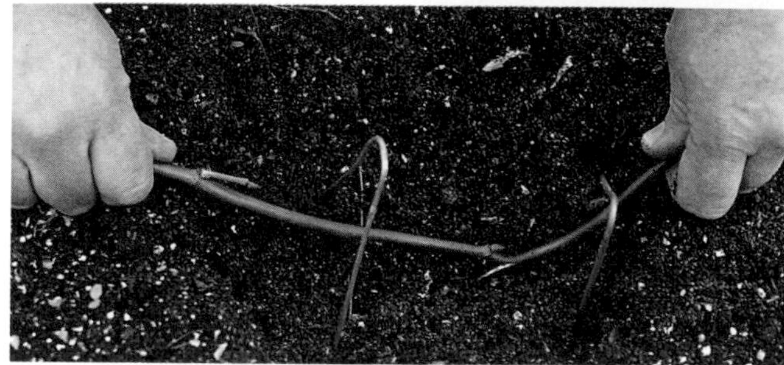

3 Dig a hole 7.5-10cm (3-4in) deep beneath the wound and partly-fill it with seed compost or a mixture of peat and horticultural sand. Bend a piece of galvanised wire into a hairpin and peg the wounded stem into the hole. Cover it with compost and water thoroughly. Ensure that the compost never dries out.

4 A year later, check that the shoot has taken root by carefully scraping away the soil. If it has, sever the new plant from the parent with its rootball, and replant in its flowering position. If the roots are not yet established, replace the soil and leave for a few more months.

• SERPENTINE LAYERING •

Climbers with long flexible stems, such as honeysuckle and jasmine, may produce three or four new plants from a single stem.

1 In autumn, choose a trailing shoot that has grown during the current year. Bend it down to the ground and make a small hole. Then wound the shoot by cutting a shallow tongue in the underside (cutting towards the growing tip) or twisting it sharply. Pin the shoot into the hole with bent wire and cover it with seed compost.

2 Leave the next two pairs of leaves above ground and repeat the process along the length of the shoot.

3 Firm the compost and water well. Keep the soil moist until the following autumn, when the young plants that have developed can be severed from the stem and transplanted.

Increasing heathers by 'dropping'

Heaths and heathers can be propagated by a form of layering called 'dropping'. The plant is transplanted into a deeper hole so that the branches are almost buried, with only the tips exposed. Roots develop on the branches, which can then be used as separate plants. The same technique can also be used for dwarf rhododendrons.

In late autumn or spring, dig a bowl-shaped hole deep enough to take the plant with only the tops of the branches above ground. On heavy soil, dig in sand and organic material in the bottom of the hole to improve drainage.

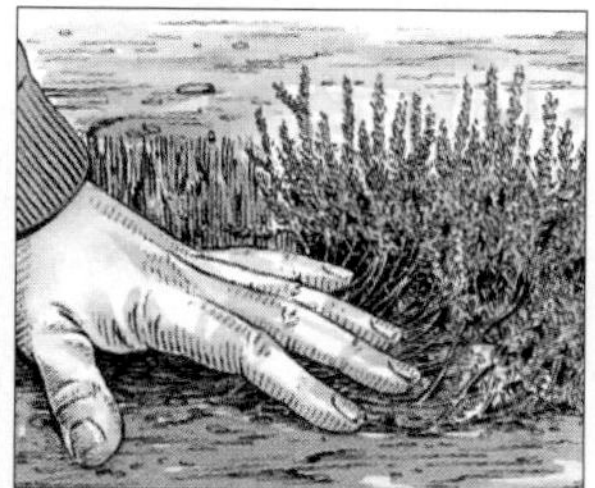

Lift the plant and put it in the hole, spreading the stems in a circle so that only 2.5cm (1in) is exposed.

Then fill in the centre with a mixture of soil, sand and organic matter, working it well around each stem.

Keep the soil moist and free of weeds until the following autumn. Then lift the plant, cut off those stems that have developed shoots and plant them out. Discard the parent plant.

• TIP LAYERING •

Blackberries and loganberries will produce roots from the tip of a cane if it touches the ground. This habit can be used to increase your stock of plants, including the ornamental berry *Rubus* 'Benenden'.

1 In summer, bend a new shoot down to the ground and tie it to a bamboo cane. Then bury the tip 12cm (5in) deep. Alternatively, tie the shoot down and plant the tip in a pot of seed compost that has been buried in the ground (right). Water the soil and keep it moist. A new plant should develop in the pot within a few weeks.

2 To check that roots are growing on the young plant, scrape away some of the compost (right).

In the autumn, sever the new plant from the parent and move it to its permanent growing position.

• AIR LAYERING •

Branches that are too stiff to bend for normal layering can be 'layered in the air'. The method is used for rubber plants indoors and rhododendrons and magnolias outdoors. It is done from May to July.

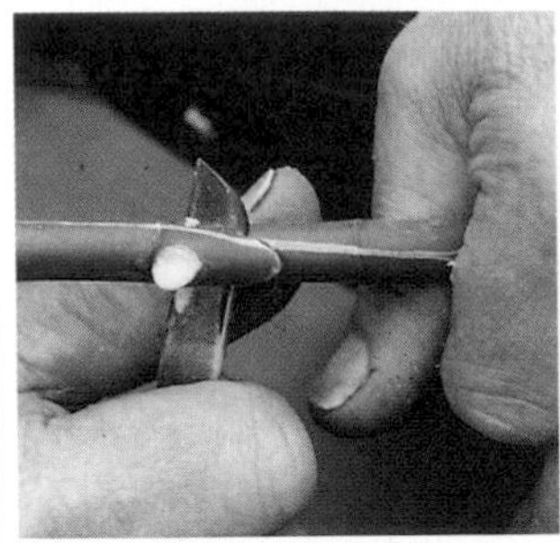

1 From the current year's growth, select a branch and strip off the leaves from the middle. Using a sharp knife, make a shallow cut into the stem, slicing upwards, and dust the wound with hormone rooting powder.

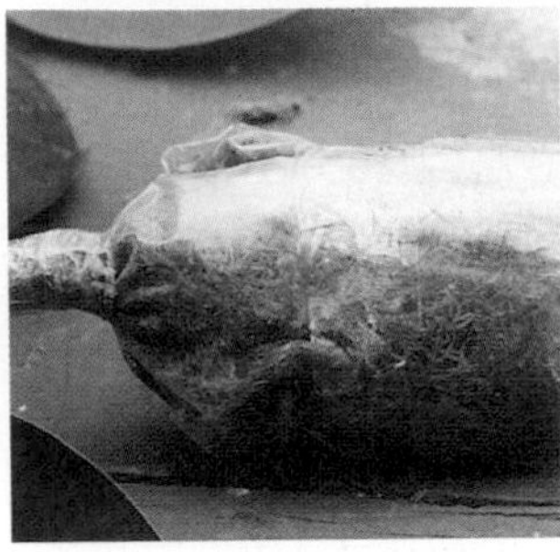

2 Wrap a piece of polythene around the stem below the cut to make a tube, and secure it with sticky tape or string. Pack the tube tightly with an equal mixture of moist peat, horticultural sand and sphagnum moss, and secure the top of the tube.

3 Between three and six months later, when the stem has rooted, cut off the stem below the roots at a leaf joint (left) and remove the polythene. Cut off the stump (above) and put the new plant in a 13cm (5in) pot of potting compost. Keep a hardy shrub moist in a closed coldframe for two weeks and then harden off. Plant out in spring.

Growing shrubs from suckers

Some plants produce shoots, or 'suckers', which arise from below ground level next to the plant. To produce a new plant, expose the base of a sucker in autumn or winter to establish that roots have formed. If they have, cut off the sucker close to where it originated from a root or stem of the parent plant and replant in a permanent site.

Increasing your stock of bulbs and corms

Plants that grow from bulbs, such as narcissi and tulips, or corms, such as crocuses and gladioli, can be increased by removing the young bulblets and cormlets (called offsets) that develop on the parent each year.

• GROWING NEW PLANTS FROM OFFSETS •

When the plant has finished flowering and the foliage has faded, dig it up and pull off the offsets. Throw away the smallest. Half-hardy bulbs and corms such as gladioli should be stored in a frost-free place until late the following spring.

Choose a piece of ground in a sunny or lightly shaded part of the garden that will not be needed for the next two years.

1 Dig out a shallow trench about 12cm (5in) deep for large bulblets or 5cm (2in) deep for cormlets.

2 Put a 1cm (3/8in) layer of horticultural sand or grit in the trench, and plant the offsets twice as far apart as their width.

3 Cover them with another layer of sand about 2.5cm (1in) deep and fill in the trench with soil.

4 When the young plants reach flowering size two or three years later, move them to their final positions.

Budding and grafting

Budding and grafting are propagation methods used for plants which are difficult or slow to increase from seed or by other methods. The plant to be increased, known as the scion, is united with a chosen root system, known as the stock, so that the two become a single unit. The result is a plant that has the best of both plants – the vigour of the stock and the flowering or fruiting quality of the scion. Budding and grafting are specialised methods of propagation that are best left to professionals.

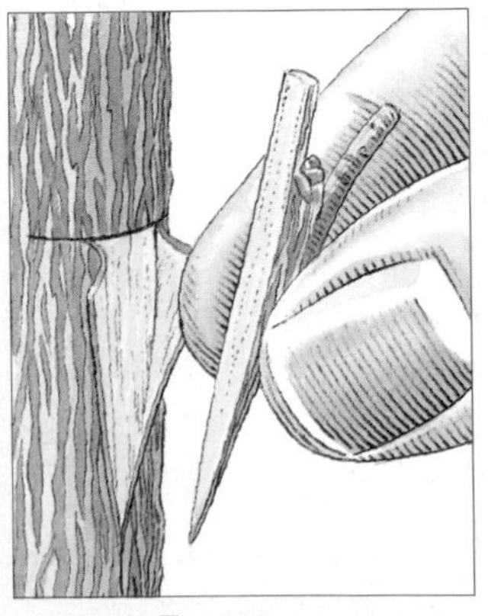

T-BUDDING

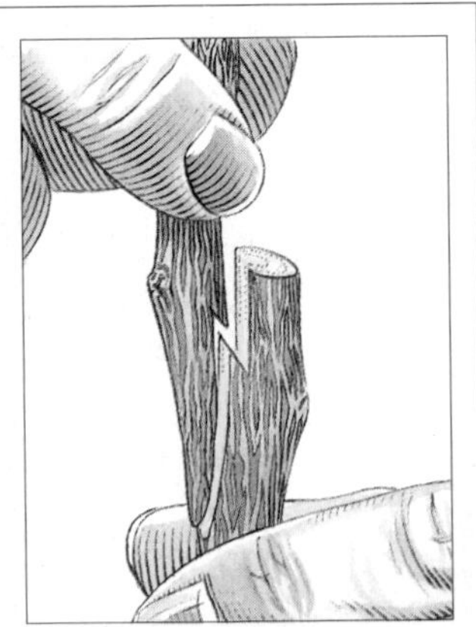

WHIP-AND-TONGUE GRAFT

Trouble-shooting in the garden

Pests, diseases and various plant disorders may affect your garden from time to time, but in most cases the trouble can be controlled with good growing techniques and by using chemical sprays only on those plants that are most seriously affected

Directory of Pests

GARDEN CHEMICALS

All garden sprays and powders recommended in these pages are listed under their chemical names. They are sold by various trade names, but the chemical contents are always given on the labels

PROBLEM	PLANTS AT RISK	RECOGNITION	DANGER PERIOD	TREATMENT
ADELGIDS	Many conifers, such as larch, pine, spruce and fir.	Small dark insects, related to aphids, suck the sap of the leaves and stems. They excrete a sticky honeydew on which sooty moulds develop. In early summer, colonies cluster beneath white waxy wool.	April and May.	Spray thoroughly once with malathion from early March through to May, and again about three weeks later.
APHIDS	Most cultivated plants growing in the open, under glass or indoors.	Colonies of small round-bodied insects suck the sap from leaves and distort plant growth. They excrete honeydew on which sooty mould grows, and can also spread viruses. Aphids, which are mostly wingless, may be black, green, pink, red, yellow or variously coloured.	Spring and early summer in the open, but any time of the year under glass or indoors.	Outdoors or in a greenhouse, spray thoroughly with systemic insecticide such as heptenophos, or with non-systemic insecticides such as malathion, pirimicarb, fenitrothion or derris. Inside the house, use derris only. See also WATER LILY APHIDS. **Organic advice** Encourage predators – ladybirds, bluetits, hoverflies, beetles (p. 32).
APPLE BLOSSOM WEEVILS See WEEVILS				
APPLE CAPSIDS See CAPSID BUGS				
APPLE SAWFLIES	Apples and plums.	Small ant-like flies lay their eggs in the blossom. The newly hatched caterpillars burrow through to the cores of the young fruit which either fall prematurely or develop scars as they grow.	May and June.	Spray thoroughly at weekly intervals when the petals start to fall, using malathion, pirimiphos-methyl or fenitrothion. **Organic advice** If the level of attack warrants it, spray with derris liquid – usually at petal-fall.
ASPARAGUS BEETLES	Asparagus.	Yellow-and-black beetles and their humpbacked larvae feed on the foliage and shoots. A severe infestation of the beetles can strip plants.	May and early June.	Spray with derris or malathion as soon as damage is seen. **Organic advice** Pick off and destroy beetles as they are seen. Clean up plant debris at all times, but especially in late autumn to prevent overwintering.
BEAN SEED FLIES	Beans, peas, sweetcorn and other vegetable crops.	Seedlings fail to emerge. Small maggots eat germinating seeds and the stems of young seedlings.	Seed-sowing time and as seedlings emerge.	Apply pirimiphos-methyl dust to the seed drill before sowing, and dust along the drill when the seedlings emerge. **Organic advice** Raise plants indoors or cover newly sown seed with horticultural fleece or polythene to encourage quick growth.

PROBLEM	PLANTS AT RISK	RECOGNITION	DANGER PERIOD	TREATMENT
BIRDS	Plums, pears, gooseberries, flowering cherries and forsythia damaged by bullfinches; ripening apples and pears by blackbirds and tits; many plants attacked by sparrows; brassica seedlings and fruit by wood pigeons.	Flower buds, ripening fruit and seedlings eaten.	November to May.	Cover plants with netting. Use bird scarers such as black cotton or string stretched between canes above plants, strips of foil hung from lines or canes, and small windmills, preferably with a rattle device. Change the scarer at least once a week.
BLACKCURRANT GALL MITES See GALL MITES				
BLACKFLIES See APHIDS				
BOX SUCKERS	Box shrubs and trees.	The tips of leaves curve inwards and form tight clusters. Caused by tiny yellowish or green nymphs which suck the sap.	Spring.	Control the nymphs by spraying in spring with a systemic insecticide, such as heptenophos & permethrin. Kill the adults in mid summer with malathion spray. Cut out damaged shoots and destroy them before April.
BRYOBIA MITES	Apples, gooseberries, ivies.	The leaves develop a light freckling on the upper surface, and later turn bronze and wither. Unlike red spider mites, bryobia mites feed on the top of the leaf and do not produce silk webbing.	March onwards throughout the growing season.	Spray with heptenophos & permethrin, fenitrothion or malathion during the growing season. In winter, spray thoroughly with tar-oil wash to destroy the overwintering eggs.
BULB EELWORMS See STEM AND BULB EELWORMS				
BULB MITES	Bulbs of narcissi, hyacinths, tulips, lilies, gladioli, dahlias and freesias.	Small, pearl-white mites invade damaged tissue of the bulbs, whether the damage is caused by other pests, a disease or by garden tools.	Depends on the time of the damage.	Take control measures against the primary problem.
BULB SCALE MITES	Narcissi and hippeastrums.	The foliage of narcissi becomes slightly distorted. Cutting the bulb in half reveals brown marks. On hippeastrums, the leaves are malformed and stained with russet-brown scars.	January to April on narcissi, especially if forced; any time on hippe-astrums under glass.	Destroy badly affected plants – no chemical is really effective although powdered sulphur may relieve the symptoms. Maintain good hygiene in a greenhouse, and do not handle healthy bulbs after diseased ones. Expose dormant bulbs to frost for several nights before planting.
CABBAGE ROOT FLIES	Recently transplanted brassicas, especially cabbages, cauliflowers and brussels sprouts. Radishes, turnips, swedes and wallflowers.	Outer leaves wilt and develop a purple/blue/red tinge. Young plants wilt and are easily pulled out of the ground. Established plants may survive but give a smaller yield. Small white maggots feed on the roots.	April to August.	Protect transplants with pirimiphos-methyl dust in the soil, or water with spray-strength pirimiphos-methyl when established. **Organic advice** Protect transplants with a 13 cm (5 in) square of rubbery carpet underlay, slit to the centre. Place it on the soil around the stem. Cover crop with horticultural fleece.

PROBLEM	PLANTS AT RISK	RECOGNITION	DANGER PERIOD	TREATMENT
CABBAGE WHITEFLIES	Cabbages, brussels sprouts and other brassicas.	Leaves may be sticky and covered with sooty mould. Clouds of small white flies rise up when plants are disturbed.	Growing season.	Spray the underside of the leaves regularly with malathion, pirimiphos-methyl or pyrethrum, or a systemic spray such as heptenophos & permethrin. Do not spray within a week of harvest. Remove and burn infected plants after harvest. **Organic advice** Pick off leaves infested with young whitefly scales (usually the lower leaves). Spray with insecticidal soap, preferably on a cold day when the whiteflies are less active.
CAPSID BUGS	Apples, beans, currants, buddleja, dahlias, forsythias, hydrangeas and many other plants.	Tattered holes appear in younger leaves as adult bugs and nymphs feed on the sap. Flower buds and shoots may be killed or deformed. On apples, raised brown patches occur on buds, fruit and leaves.	April to August.	Bugs have usually left before symptoms are seen. Spray plants with heptenophos, permethrin, fenitrothion or malathion in spring, summer and early autumn. In winter, clear up all garden debris.
CARNATION FLIES (Carnation leaf miner)	Carnations and pinks.	Maggots tunnel into the leaves and stems causing infected shoots to wilt and die.	Throughout the year.	Not easily eradicated. Spray with heptenophos, permethrin or malathion as soon as the mines appear on the foliage in September.
CARROT FLIES	Carrots, parsnips, parsley and celery.	Reddening of foliage and sometimes stunted growth. Roots riddled with tunnels made by fly maggots.	June to October.	In areas where the pest is prevalent, sow thinly in May. Protect plants by watering the soil with a spray-strength solution of pirimiphos-methyl. Alternatively, dust rows with pirimiphos-methyl when sowing. Grow carrots under very fine netting or horticultural fleece. Early or late sowings will avoid the worst periods of attack. If possible, grow the crop in a windy spot. Intercrop with onions – four rows of onions for every row of carrots.
CATERPILLARS	Many different species.	Foliage with irregularly shaped edges and holes. Caterpillars present.	From March onwards in the open but any time under glass.	Crush small outbreaks by hand, including eggs. Spray large infestations with fenitrothion, malathion, permethrin, heptenophos & permethrin, or derris as soon as the buds open. Wrap a grease band around trees in mid autumn to trap wingless female moths. See also TORTRIX CATERPILLARS. **Organic advice** Encourage wasps and birds. A biological control in spray form, *Bacillius thuringiensis,* can be used outside and under glass.
CATS	Seedlings in newly cultivated soil.	Holes dug in fresh soil. Seedlings scattered.	Any time.	Spray soil with cat repellent.

PROBLEM	PLANTS AT RISK	RECOGNITION	DANGER PERIOD	TREATMENT
CELERY LEAF MINERS (Celery flies)	Celery, carrots and parsnips.	Brown blotches on foliage caused by small white maggots tunnelling through the leaves, which shrivel and die. Severe outbreaks can destroy plants.	From May to autumn.	Spray plants with heptenophos & permethrin or malathion when symptoms are first seen, or cut off and burn affected leaflets. **Organic advice** Pick off infected leaves, or squash the larvae within them. If the pest is a regular problem, grow celery under fine netting or horticultural fleece.
CHAFER BEETLES	Many annuals and perennials, tubers and stems of fruit and vegetables.	Top growth wilts and dies as the fat, white, C-shaped larvae, 4 cm (1½ in) long, with three pairs of legs and a brown head, eat the roots.	May/June.	Before planting, treat the soil with pirimiphos-methyl dust, or work it in around the roots of existing plants. **Organic advice** Mainly a problem of newly cultivated land. Numbers are quickly reduced by cultivation and weed control.
CHERRY BLACKFLIES	Flowering and fruiting cherries.	Young leaves curl and twist as black aphids feed on them. Sticky honeydew and sooty mould often present.	May to July.	Immediately after flowering, spray with a systemic insecticide, such as heptenophos & permethrin. In late December/early January treat with a tar-oil winter wash. **Organic advice** Encourage the aphids' natural enemies – ladybirds, spiders, earwigs, hoverflies, ground beetles, parasitic wasps and bluetits (p. 32).
CHRYSANTHEMUM EELWORMS (Leaf and bud eelworms)	Primarily dendranthemas (chrysanthemums), but also callistephus, calceolarias, peonies and other ornamentals.	Buds damaged, blooms distorted and stems scarred. Caused by microscopic worms. Severe infestation can kill plants.	July to September.	There is no safe treatment for chrysanthemum eelworms. Dig up and burn all infected plants.
CHRYSANTHEMUM LEAF MINERS	Mainly dendranthemas (chrysanthemums), but also cinerarias and other pot plants.	White meandering tracks left by maggots tunnelling inside the leaves.	Any time under glass; late spring or summer outdoors.	Immediately symptoms are seen spray with heptenophos & permethrin or pirimiphos-methyl. Repeat fortnightly if infestation is severe. If only a few leaves affected, pick and destroy them. Eliminate sow thistle and groundsel to prevent overwintering.
CHRYSANTHEMUM STOOL MINERS	Dendranthemas (chrysanthemums).	The growth of shoots is inhibited by maggots – light yellow in colour – which tunnel into the stools of the plant and cause damage to the roots.	September to May.	Dust stools with pirimiphos-methyl. After lifting stools to take cuttings, water them with a spray-strength solution of fenitrothion.

PROBLEM	PLANTS AT RISK	RECOGNITION	DANGER PERIOD	TREATMENT
CODLING MOTHS	Mainly apples but also pears.	Entry tunnels through the eye end of fruit where caterpillars eat their way to the core. Damage is rarely noticed until the fruit is cut open.	June to August.	Spray in mid June with fenitrothion, permethrin, heptenophos & permethrin, or malathion, and repeat three weeks later to kill young caterpillars before they enter the fruit. **Organic advice** Encourage bluetits into the garden, especially in winter; they are very effective predators of codling moths. Hang pheromone traps in the trees from late spring to late summer.
CRANE-FLY LARVAE See LEATHERJACKETS				
CUTWORMS	Lettuces, other vegetables and young ornamental annuals.	Stems often eaten at soil level by fat green or grey-brown caterpillars which curl up into a C shape when picked up.	Dry spells from early spring to late summer.	Eliminate weeds, which attract cutworms. Protect plants at sowing time by working a little pirimiphos-methyl dust into the soil. **Organic advice** Fork over soil in winter to expose the pests to predators, particularly blackbirds. Protect young plants with collars made from toilet rolls, cans or drainpipe. Push the collar into the soil around the plant. At the first sign of damage, search in the soil and destroy any caterpillars.
EARWIGS	Dendranthemas (chrysanthemums), clematis, dahlias and other ornamentals.	Petals and leaves left tattered by feeding insects.	May to October.	Spray or dust with pirimiphos-methyl or malathion. Trap earwigs in rolls of corrugated cardboard, old sacking or flowerpots filled with straw, and then destroy them. **Organic advice** Control earwigs only if they are causing harm. They eat greenfly and are valuable pest controllers in their own right.
EELWORMS • See also CHRYSANTHEMUM EELWORMS, POTATO-CYST EELWORMS, STEM AND BULB EELWORMS	Many herbaceous plants, vegetable crops and strawberries.	Deformed and discoloured leaves or flowers caused by microscopic worms tunnelling through plant tissue. They multiply at alarming speed.	Growing season.	None. Destroy all infested plants. Remove all weeds, especially over winter. Remove all plant debris in autumn. Do not plant soft bulbs.
FLEA BEETLES	Cabbages, radishes, turnips, wallflowers and related plants. Young seedlings are particularly at risk, especially in dry weather.	Young leaves pitted with minute holes by tiny shiny black beetles which jump when disturbed.	Sunny spells in April and May or when soil is dry.	Dust vulnerable seedlings with pirimiphos-methyl. Good garden hygiene will help to reduce the risk of attack. **Organic advice** Encourage quick early growth of plants. Water regularly in hot, dry weather. Grow highly susceptible plants under fine net or horticultural fleece.
FROGHOPPERS	Dendranthemas, lavenders, roses, solidagos, perennial asters and many other plants.	Frothy masses of cuckoo spit on stems and leaves. Small sap-feeding insects are concealed beneath the froth.	May to July.	Spray forcefully with malathion or heptenophos & permethrin. **Organic advice** Damage is seldom severe enough to warrant control. Spray with a strong jet of water to dislodge the creatures.

PROBLEM	PLANTS AT RISK	RECOGNITION	DANGER PERIOD	TREATMENT
FRUIT-TREE RED SPIDER MITES	Apples, plums, pears, damsons, cotoneasters, hawthorns, sorbus.	Leaves turn bronze and wither. In a bad attack, they fall off in July. The mites are invisible to the naked eye. Tiny red spiders that run over leaves are called brick spiders and do no harm.	April to September.	Spray with tar-oil wash to kill overwintering eggs, or spray immediately after flowering with heptenophos & permethrin, fenitrothion or malathion. **Organic advice** Mulch trees, and water in dry weather. Predators usually keep the pest under control. If attack is severe, spray with derris or insecticidal soap.
GALL MIDGES	Many cultivated species.	Disfiguring galls on stems, leaves and flowers caused by tiny red, white or yellow maggots.	Late winter, early spring.	Remove and burn infected buds in early spring. When the first flowers open, spray with carbendazim and again after about three weeks.
GALL MITES	Many deciduous trees, including elm, lime, maple and sycamore. Also blackcurrants.	Small galls on the leaves' upper surface are caused by mites feeding. The galls are harmless to trees. On blackcurrants the buds are greatly enlarged, and the mites transmit reversion virus.	Spring. From February and March on black-currants.	None for trees but remove and burn affected buds on blackcurrants in early March. When the first flowers open, spray with lime sulphur and repeat about three weeks later. Use carbendazim on sulphur-shy varieties.
GALL WASPS	Oaks, and some species of roses and willows.	Solitary or numerous outbreaks of galls – similar to peas, cherries, silk buttons and spangles – grow out of leaves. Caused by tiny wasps living in plant tissues.	May to October.	Remove and destroy the galls if possible; however, damage to the plant is rarely serious, so gall wasps are not a real cause for concern.
GLADIOLUS THRIPS See THRIPS				
GLASSHOUSE LEAFHOPPERS See LEAFHOPPERS				
GLASSHOUSE RED SPIDER MITES	Mainly plants in a greenhouse, but also peaches, nectarines, vines, fuchsias, impatiens and primulas. Strawberries and runner beans can be affected outdoors in a hot, dry season.	Fine, light mottling of the leaves, and later a bronze discoloration. Fine cobwebbing over the plant indicates a severe attack; throw the plant away.	Any time under glass; soft fruits from June to September.	Spray with heptenophos & permethrin, pirimiphos-methyl or insecticidal soap. **Organic advice** Keep plants growing strongly. Do not allow them to dry out or become pot bound. Keep atmosphere moist. Introduce *Phytoseiulus persimilis,* a predatory mite. In autumn remove debris from the greenhouse and scrub down the fittings with hot soapy water.
GLASSHOUSE WHITEFLIES	In a greenhouse: tomatoes, cucumbers, fuchsias, abutilons, dendranthemas (chrysanthemums). In the house: pelargoniums and coleus.	Whiteflies often seen on underside of leaves, which become soiled with honeydew and sooty mould.	All year.	In a greenhouse, spray regularly with malathion, heptenophos & permethrin or permethrin. Fumigate with pirimiphos-methyl smokes. In the house, use derris. **Organic advice** Gently suck up the flies with a vacuum cleaner. Hang up sticky traps. Introduce *Encarsia formosa,* a parasitic wasp, as soon as the first pests are seen. Spray with insecticidal soap.
GOLDEN NEMATODE See POTATO-CYST EELWORMS				

PROBLEM	PLANTS AT RISK	RECOGNITION	DANGER PERIOD	TREATMENT
GOOSEBERRY SAWFLIES	Gooseberries.	Leaf tissue stripped down to skeleton of veins by green, black-spotted caterpillars.	April to August.	Spray early in May, or when symptoms first appear, with fenitrothion, malathion, pyrethrins or derris. **Organic advice** Frequently inspect the underside of the leaves at the centre of the bush, and pick off sawfly eggs and caterpillars. Cordons or espaliers are easier to treat.
GREENFLIES See APHIDS				
HOLLY LEAF MINERS	Holly.	White blotches on the leaves caused by maggots tunnelling through them. The leaves may fall from young trees.	Late May to July.	Spray regularly with heptenophos & permethrin, following manufacturer's instructions.
LEAF AND BUD EELWORMS See CHRYSANTHEMUM EELWORMS				
LEAF-CURLING APHIDS	Apples, damsons, pears, peaches and plums.	Immature leaves pucker and curl as aphids feed on plant tissue.	Mid spring to mid summer.	Spray with a systemic insecticide such as heptenophos & permethrin before the trees blossom and again, if necessary, after blossom appears. Also spray with tar-oil wash in winter. **Organic advice** See APHIDS.
LEAF EELWORMS	Particularly troublesome in greenhouses with begonias, coleus, gloxinias, ferns and other foliage plants. Outdoors: mint, strawberries and other soft fruit.	Brown or black blotches between leaf veins, and distortion of buds and young growth, caused by tiny pests.	Winter.	No cure; severely infested plants should be burnt. Maintain good hygiene and grow plants in dry conditions.
LEAFHOPPERS • See also RHODODENDRON LEAFHOPPERS	Roses, pelargoniums, primulas and others, both under glass and in the open.	Coarse white flecks on leaves and – often on the underside – the cast-off skins of the insects.	April to October, but any time under glass.	Spray with fenitrothion, malathion or heptenophos & permethrin, repeating if necessary at fortnightly intervals.
LEAF MINERS See CELERY LEAF MINERS, CHRYSANTHEMUM LEAF MINERS, HOLLY LEAF MINERS, LILAC LEAF MINERS				
LEAF-ROLLING ROSE SAWFLIES	Bush and climbing roses.	Leaves become tightly rolled up along their length. The sawflies are unlikely to damage the plant.	May, June and July.	Pick off and burn affected leaves. Alternatively, spray every fortnight in May with heptenophos & permethrin, fenitrothion or liquid derris. **Organic advice** Clear away mulches in autumn and lightly fork over the soil to expose the pupae to predators.

PROBLEM	PLANTS AT RISK	RECOGNITION	DANGER PERIOD	TREATMENT
LEATHERJACKETS (Crane-fly larvae)	Brassicas, other vegetables and various ornamental plants. Young plants and lawns are particularly susceptible.	Plants turn yellow, wilt and sometimes die as the roots are attacked by fat, grey-brown, legless grubs. Large numbers of grubs on a lawn will cause yellow patches in dry spells.	April to June.	Incorporate pirimiphos-methyl dust in the soil around established plants. **Organic advice** Fork over infested soil thoroughly and frequently to expose pests to birds. On lawns, water the grass well then cover it with sacking or thick cardboard overnight. The leatherjackets will come to the surface and can be swept up or left for the birds. On cultivated land, put grass mowings under the cover, leave for two days, then uncover.
LILAC LEAF MINERS	Lilac *(Syringa)* and privet *(Ligustrum)*.	The caterpillars of a species of moth burrow into lilac leaves. They also cause leaf-mine blotches on privet leaves.	June onwards.	Spray large infestations with malathion, pirimiphos-methyl or heptenophos & permethrin. On small outbreaks pick off and burn affected leaves.
LILY BEETLES	Lilies, fritillaria, nomocharis and polygonatum.	Scarlet beetles with black heads and legs feed on the leaves and other aerial parts of plants. Primarily found in parts of Surrey and adjoining counties.	May onwards.	Spray with malathion, fenitrothion, permethrin, or heptenophos & permethrin. **Organic advice** Check plants frequently in spring and remove any beetles. Spray plants with derris.
MEALY BUGS	Many greenhouse and houseplants, especially succulents, hippeastrums, vines, camellias, citrus, coleus and orchids.	Patches on leaves and stems of tiny sap-eating pink insects, covered with tufts of woolly or mealy white wax.	Any time.	Spray with systemic insecticide such as heptenophos & permethrin or with non-systemic insecticides such as malathion. **Organic advice** Introduce the biological control agent *Cryptolaemus montrouzieri* – a beetle which eats mealy bugs.
MICE AND VOLES	Bulbs and corms, including crocus, lily, narcissus and tulip, in open ground or in storage. Peas and beans at sowing time.	Damage and droppings.	Any time between autumn and spring, especially with bulbs recently planted where the soil is still soft.	Before planting, dust bulbs and corms with a proprietary animal repellent. Rodent traps should be covered to avoid endangering birds and pets. In storerooms lay bait containing coumatetralyl or difenacoum.
MILLIPEDES	Root vegetables, bulbs, tubers and corms.	Grey-black worm-like insects, similar to centipedes but slower in movement and with more legs, feed inside the rootstock of plants.	Late summer to autumn.	Improve garden hygiene and dig deeply. Protect seeds, bulbs and corms with pirimiphos-methyl dust.

PROBLEM	PLANTS AT RISK	RECOGNITION	DANGER PERIOD	TREATMENT
MUSTARD BEETLES	Mustard, watercress, cabbages, swedes and turnips.	Stems and leaves attacked by metallic-blue beetle and brown-yellow larvae.	May to August.	Dust or spray with malathion, but not on watercress, to avoid killing fish. Raise the water level of watercress beds to drown beetles and larvae. **Organic advice** See FLEA BEETLES.
NARCISSUS FLIES	Amaryllis, narcissi and snowdrops.	Softening and rotting of bulbs as grubs burrow into them, particularly in dry soil. Affected bulbs fail to flower, just producing narrow grass-like leaves.	Late spring to early summer. Bulbs planted in sunny sites are more vulnerable than those planted in shade.	Lift and burn affected bulbs and any grubs still in the soil. Apply pirimiphos-methyl dust to the soil before or soon after planting. **Organic advice** As foliage dies down, holes are left in the soil which allow narcissus flies to lay eggs near the bulbs. Rake soil into the holes. Alternatively, cover bulbs with horticultural fleece as the leaves die.
OAK-APPLE GALL See GALL WASPS				
ONION FLIES	Young plants of onions, shallots and leeks.	Adult flies lay eggs on the leaves from which white maggots hatch to tunnel into the plant tissues. The leaves yellow and wither, and the stems and bulbs rot. Small white maggots are found in roots and bulbs.	Most damage occurs in June/July, but plants can be attacked at other times in the growing season.	Burn infested plants and dig over the ground to expose insects' dormant pupae to the winter cold and to birds. Treat the soil with pirimiphos-methyl before sowing or planting.
PEA AND BEAN WEEVILS	Young garden peas and beans; older plants are unaffected.	Leaf edges are scalloped where eaten by the small beetle-like insects and their larvae.	March to July.	Apply pirimiphos-methyl dust or fenitrothion spray as soon as the symptoms appear. **Organic advice** Spray with derris dust.
PEA MOTHS	Garden peas.	Small maggot-like caterpillars of a moth feed on the peas inside the ripening pods.	May to August.	Spray when flowers first open, and again two weeks later, with fenitrothion or permethrin. Alternatively, grow early-maturing varieties of peas. **Organic advice** Sow peas early (February) or late (May) so that they are not in flower in June/July.
PEAR-LEAF BLISTER MITES	Pears, sorbus, cotoneasters and other related trees.	Clusters of dark brown pustules on the upper surface of the leaves where mites burrow into plant tissue. Young shoots may also be damaged.	April to August.	Pick off and burn infested leaves. If the attack is severe, spray at the end of March with lime-sulphur (available from some garden centres) or with fenitrothion. A difficult pest to eliminate.

PROBLEM	PLANTS AT RISK	RECOGNITION	DANGER PERIOD	TREATMENT
PEAR MIDGES	Pears.	Young fruits swell rapidly, then fail to develop. Black cavities contain small yellowish white larvae. Affected fruit falls in May/June.	April to May.	Spray with fenitrothion just before the blossoms open. **Organic advice** Pick off affected fruitlets when first seen and burn them. Fork over the soil under the trees in summer and remove old leaves or fruit in autumn.
PEA THRIPS See THRIPS				
PLUM SAWFLIES See APPLE SAWFLIES				
POPLAR BEETLES	Poplar trees.	The leaves are shredded to a skeleton of veins by beetles and their larvae.	May to September.	Spray young trees with malathion when symptoms are first seen or in early spring. Repeat if necessary.
POTATO-CYST EELWORMS (Golden nematode, Yellow potato-cyst eelworms)	Potatoes and tomatoes.	Plants grow poorly. If infection is severe, they may wilt and die. Roots reveal tiny white, yellow or brown cysts which can only be seen through a magnifying glass.	May to August.	Dig up and burn affected plants and avoid planting potatoes or tomatoes on the same site for five years. **Organic advice** Build up the organic level in the soil by applying leaf-mould, compost or well-rotted manure. Grow early potatoes which may crop before eelworm levels build up. Choose varieties that are resistant to eelworm.
RABBITS	Many plants, particularly lettuces.	Chewed or damaged plants. On young trees, bark can be stripped just above soil level.	Growing season.	Protect plants with high wire-mesh fencing, buried 30 cm (12 in) below soil level to prevent burrowing.
RASPBERRY BEETLES	Raspberries, loganberries and blackberries.	The tiny larvae of the raspberry beetle feed on the ripening fruit.	June to August.	Spray thoroughly with fenitrothion, derris or malathion as soon as flowering ceases. **Organic advice** In autumn lightly fork over the soil around raspberries. Remove any mulch and replace it with fresh material in spring.
RASPBERRY CANE MIDGES See GALL MIDGES				
REDCURRANT BLISTER APHIDS	Red, white and black currants.	Irregular red or green blisters raised on leaves. Aphids may be seen underneath leaves, but symptoms will persist after the pests have flown.	May and June.	Spray in January with tar-oil wash to kill overwintering eggs. Repeat a fortnight later and again immediately after leaf-fall. Rake up any leaves from under plants and destroy them. **Organic advice** Encourage natural predators of aphids (p. 32).
RED SPIDER MITES See FRUIT-TREE RED SPIDER MITES, GLASSHOUSE RED SPIDER MITES				

PROBLEM	PLANTS AT RISK	RECOGNITION	DANGER PERIOD	TREATMENT
RHODODENDRON LACEBUGS	Young and adult rhododendrons.	Fine mottling on the upper surface of leaves, with a rusty-brown or chocolate spotting on the underside.	May and June.	Cut out and burn infested branches in May. Spray in late May with fenitrothion or permethrin, and again in mid June. **Organic advice** Don't grow rhododendrons in exposed, dry or sunny sites. Some species and hybrids are less vulnerable than others; grow them if the pest is known to be a problem.
RHODODENDRON LEAFHOPPERS	Rhododendrons.	Dark green insects with red stripes lay their eggs in the flower buds. Leafhoppers are harmless but leave entry sites for rhododendron bud blast (p. 854).	Late July to October.	Spray with heptenophos & permethrin or fenitrothion two or three times in August and September.
ROOT APHIDS AND ROOT MEALY BUGS	Cacti and succulents, primulas and other pot plants, lettuces and some outdoor ornamentals.	Colonies of white, wax-covered aphids or mealy bugs infest the roots of plants. Growth is checked, and the plants may turn yellow and wilt.	Outdoors: late summer and autumn. Under glass: any time.	Water the affected plant roots with a spray-strength solution of pirimiphos-methyl. **Organic advice** Grow resistant varieties of lettuce. Mealy bugs are worse in dry conditions, so keep the soil or compost moist.
ROOT-KNOT EELWORMS	Cucumbers and tomatoes under glass, as well as other greenhouse and pot plants. Also some outdoor plants.	Roots develop lumpy galls where eelworms are present which check and affect growth.	Any time.	No chemical cure. Burn infested plants and wash contaminated pots in garden disinfectant.

ROOT MEALY BUGS See ROOT APHIDS AND ROOT MEALY BUGS

SAWFLIES See APPLE (AND PLUM) SAWFLIES, GOOSEBERRY SAWFLIES, SOLOMON'S-SEAL SAWFLIES.

PROBLEM	PLANTS AT RISK	RECOGNITION	DANGER PERIOD	TREATMENT
SCALE INSECTS	Particularly troublesome on greenhouse and houseplants, but also ornamental shrubs, trees and fruit grown outside.	Brown, yellow or white scales – flat or oval – mainly on the underside of leaves and clustered alongside the veins and on the stems.	Late spring or early summer outdoors, but at any time of the year when under glass.	Spray with pirimiphos-methyl, heptenophos & permethrin, or malathion three times at two-week intervals. **Organic advice** A parasitic wasp, *Metaphycus helvolus,* can be bought for use in a greenhouse. Alternatively, gently remove scales by hand or with a soft toothbrush, or spray with insecticidal soap.
SLUGS AND SNAILS	Many garden plants, including their roots, tubers, bulbs and corms.	Irregularly shaped holes eaten in bulbs, roots, stems, leaves and flowers. Slime trails reveal their active presence. Slugs and snails usually feed at night, hiding by day.	Warm and humid weather in spring and autumn.	Remove decaying plant material and scatter metaldehyde or methiocarb pellets, or a slug killer based on aluminium-sulphate. **Organic advice** Avoid heavy dressings of manure or mulch around young plants. Never transplant seedlings into cold wet soil. Protect young plants with individual cloches made from plastic water bottles. Encourage predators (p. 32).

PROBLEM	PLANTS AT RISK	RECOGNITION	DANGER PERIOD	TREATMENT
SOLOMON'S-SEAL SAWFLIES	Solomon's seal and other polygonatums.	Grey-blue larvae with black heads strip the foliage.	Summer.	Spray with heptenophos & permethrin or malathion when the larvae are first seen. **Organic advice** Pick off the larvae when they begin to appear in late spring.
SPANGLE GALL See GALL WASPS				
SQUIRRELS	Many shrubs and trees, including ripe fruits. Also bulbs and corms.	Bark stripped from trees, fruits damaged and bulbs and corms dug up.	Between autumn and spring, particularly where gardens adjoin woodland.	Dust bulbs and corms with proprietary rodent repellent before planting. Protect valuable crops with a covering of netting.
STEM AND BULB EELWORMS	Daffodils, tulips, hyacinths, onions, phlox and many other plants.	Leaves become swollen and distorted; bulbs crack and rot; plants die.	Dormant bulbs in late summer and autumn; growing plants usually in spring.	Destroy affected plants and avoid replanting in the same soil for at least three years. Maintain good hygiene in the garden.
STRAWBERRY BEETLES	Strawberries.	Glossy-black ground beetles, 2 cm (¾ in) long eat pieces of the fruit as it ripens, causing damage similar to that made by birds. The pest may be found under the plants.	Early summer.	Remove any debris and garden litter, remove weeds and maintain good hygiene. Use methiocarb slug pellets to kill the pest, but follow the harvest-interval details on the packaging. **Organic advice** In winter, remove debris and litter.
STRAWBERRY EELWORMS See LEAF EELWORMS				
SUCKING INSECTS • See also BOX SUCKERS	Apples and pears.	Plants fouled by sap-sucking insects, leaving sticky excretions which together distort young growth. Also infest blossom trusses causing symptoms similar to frost damage.	April to July.	Spray fruit trees with heptenophos & permethrin, or malathion soon after petal-fall. As an alternative for apple trees, apply a winter spray of tar oil.
SWIFT MOTHS	Carrots, parsnips and various herbaceous perennials.	The caterpillars of the swift moth are dirty-white with brown heads. They live in the soil and feed on roots, tubers, corms and rhizomes, and may eat up into the stems.	During the growing season.	Protect susceptible plants by incorporating pirimiphos-methyl dust in the soil. **Organic advice** Usually a problem only on newly cleared land. Thorough winter digging will expose caterpillars and kill them. Good weed control and regular cultivation reduce the risk.

PROBLEM	PLANTS AT RISK	RECOGNITION	DANGER PERIOD	TREATMENT
TARSONEMID MITES	Begonias, dahlias, fuchsias, gerberas, pot cyclamens, ferns and other greenhouse plants. Outdoors, similar mites attack strawberries and Michaelmas daisies (*Aster*).	Tiny mites feed on the concealed parts of plants causing leaf distortion and discoloration. The mites may also infest the flowers, which then do not open properly.	Any time of the year under glass.	There is no effective chemical control, but the symptoms may be relieved with the application of powdered sulphur. Maintain good hygiene in the greenhouse at all times.
THRIPS	Roses, carnations, privets, gladioli and some other species. Also peas and onions.	Fine silvery flecks on infected petals and foliage are caused by tiny thrips. Severe infestation can discolour and kill the flowers.	Early summer to early autumn, particularly in hot, dry weather.	Treat corms before storage – and again before planting – with pirimiphos-methyl dust. If symptoms appear, spray the plants with malathion or heptenophos & permethrin. **Organic advice** Keep the plants growing strongly by giving them good conditions. Do not let the soil dry out.
TORTRIX CATERPILLARS	Shrubs, trees and herbaceous perennials especially dendranthemas (chrysanthemums), heleniums and perennial phlox. Various greenhouse and house plants are also at risk.	Leaves and stems are drawn together by silken webs which are spun by the caterpillars to create protective coverings while they feed.	May and June outdoors; any time under glass.	Remove and destroy the caterpillars by hand. Alternatively, spray the plants with fenitrothion or derris.
VINE WEEVILS	Many, especially those grown in containers. Cyclamen, primulas and begonias are particularly susceptible.	Plants wilt and collapse suddenly. Fat, white, brown-headed larvae are found in the soil around the roots. Adult weevils eat notches out of the leaves. Most damage is done under glass.	Most of the year.	Spray heavily with pirimiphos-methyl. **Organic advice** Check the compost of newly bought plants. Protect pots and greenhouse staging with a band of non-drying glue, which can be bought at some garden centres. Adult vine weevils cannot fly; they must walk up the side of pots. Use a parasitic nematode *Heterorhabditis megedis.*
VOLES See MICE AND VOLES				
WASPS	The ripening fruits of apples, pears and plums.	The wasps enlarge the damage already caused to fruit by birds.	Late summer to early autumn.	Trace the nest and spray an anti-wasp insecticide at the entrance at dusk, when most of the wasps will be inside. **Organic advice** Wasps are excellent natural predators, controlling caterpillars and other pests. They should only be killed if really necessary.

PROBLEM	PLANTS AT RISK	RECOGNITION	DANGER PERIOD	TREATMENT
WATER LILY APHIDS	Water lilies *(Nymphea* and *Nuphar)* and pondside plants.	Colonies of aphids disfigure the leaves and stems and discolour the flowers.	Growing season.	Spray plants frequently with a strong jet of water to dislodge the aphids; fish will eat them. Alternatively, submerge the foliage with sacking or weighted netting for several hours.
WATER LILY BEETLES	Water lilies, especially *Nuphar.*	Holes are eaten in the upper surface of the leaves by the brown adult beetles and their dark brown or black larvae. The flowers may also be eaten.	Early to late summer.	Spray plants often with a strong jet of water to dislodge the aphids; fish will eat them. Alternatively, submerge the foliage with sacking or weighted netting for several hours.
WEEVILS • See also VINE WEEVILS	Various species of cultivated plants.	Adult weevils are small or medium-sized, usually dark coloured and with a long snout; larvae are white legless grubs with a discernible head. Both feed on roots, tubers, corms, stems, leaves, flowers and fruit, but damage is seldom severe.	Late spring, early summer.	Dust or spray foliage, soil or potting composts with pirimiphos-methyl.
WHITEFLIES See CABBAGE WHITEFLIES, GLASSHOUSE WHITEFLIES				
WIREWORMS	Potatoes, lettuces, tomatoes and dendranthemas (chrysanthemums).	Yellow-brown larvae live in the soil to feed on the roots of potato tubers, and also on the stems of other plants.	The early years of newly cultivated land.	Use pirimiphos-methyl dust when planting. Reduce the colonies of wireworms by frequent cultivation of the soil.
WOOLLY APHIDS	Apple trees and related ornamental trees and shrubs, including crab apples, cotoneasters and pyracanthas.	Tufts of waxy white wool on trunks, branches and twigs produced by aphids. Galls can also occur and may split, allowing diseases to enter the plant.	April to September.	Immediately wool appears, spray with a high volume of malathion or heptenophos & permethrin. In winter, spray trees with tar-oil wash. A difficult pest to control. **Organic advice** Encourage natural aphid predators (p. 32). Cut out severely galled branches. Spray with insecticidal soap under high pressure.
YELLOW POTATO-CYST EELWORMS See POTATO-CYST EELWORMS				

Directory of Diseases and Disorders

Garden Chemicals

All garden sprays and powders recommended in these pages are listed under their chemical names. They are sold by various trade names, but the chemical contents are always given on the labels.

PROBLEM	PLANTS AT RISK	RECOGNITION	DANGER PERIOD	TREATMENT
ANTHRACNOSE OF BEANS	Dwarf and climbing french beans and sometimes runner beans.	Sunken, dark brown patches occur on pods, and brown spots appear on the leaves. They are caused by fungus.	Growing season, particularly during cool wet weather.	Destroy all diseased plants and grow fresh plants from new seeds in a new position. Do not save seed from plants that may have the disease. If a serious outbreak reappears, spray before flowering with carbendazim or mancozeb.
ANTHRACNOSE OF CUCUMBERS	Cucumbers, melons and vegetable marrows grown under glass.	Leaves often very pale with transparent spots which become dry and brown in the centre.	Growing season.	Burn all infected leaves. Spray or dust with sulphur during the growing season. Reduce humidity in the greenhouse and provide adequate ventilation. At the end of the season disinfect with cresylic acid or other sterilant.
ANTHRACNOSE OF TREES	Weeping willows and London planes.	Leaves curl, become discoloured and fall prematurely. Severe outbreaks can denude trees by August, followed by die-back.	Spring or during mild wet summers.	Cut out infected shoots and burn, together with any fallen leaves. As leaves unfold spray small trees with copper fungicide, such as Bordeaux mixture, and repeat twice during the summer.
APPLE CANKER See CANKER				
APPLE SCAB	Only trees of the genus *Malus*.	Small blister-like pimples on young shoots and fallen leaves. The blisters later burst the bark and form ring-like cracks or scabs.	Growing season, but particularly after a wet May.	Cut out and burn diseased shoots in winter. Spray regularly, following the maker's instructions, with myclobutanil or carbendazim (except on sulphur-shy varieties). **Organic advice** Pick up fallen apple leaves in autumn, or run a mower over them. Worms will take the pieces into the soil, burying the spores. Grow resistant varieties.
APRICOT DIE-BACK	Apricots.	Branches exude large amounts of gum, and die. Often caused by fungi entering the branches through a wound.	Through-out the year.	Cut out and burn all the dead wood. Avoid pruning in winter. If appropriate, improve cultural conditions, as the disease can be caused by malnutrition of the plant.
ARABIS MOSAIC VIRUS	Herbaceous, bulbous and woody plants; fruit crops such as strawberries; vegetables such as celery and lettuce.	Mottling of the leaves and plant distortion caused by a virus in the soil and transmitted by a type of eelworm.	Growing season.	No chemical control – destroy diseased plants. Avoid growing plants susceptible to infection. Remove plant debris in autumn.

PROBLEM	PLANTS AT RISK	RECOGNITION	DANGER PERIOD	TREATMENT
ARMILLARIA See HONEY FUNGUS				
ASH CANKER See CANKER				
ASTER WILT	Primarily asters of the *novi-belgii* species.	The leaves turn yellow and wilt, then die. The disease is caused by a microscopic fungus that inhabits the rootstock, transmitting a poison through the sap.	Growing season.	Destroy infected plants and – since the disease is soil-borne – propagate from healthy stock on a fresh site.
AZALEA GALL	Small-leaved rhododendrons, including pot-grown *R. simsii* and Kurume azaleas.	Leaves and flowers are replaced by red or pale green fleshy galls, which later produce a white floury coating of fungus spore. The disease is spread by air or by insect-borne spores which enter the plant tissue.	Growing season.	Remove and burn the galls before they turn white and produce fresh spores. In the greenhouse control spore-bearing insects, such as aphids. Spray severe attacks before the leaves curl, using Bordeaux mixture or other copper fungicide.
BACTERIAL CANKER	Primarily plums (particularly 'Victoria'), but also peaches, damsons and cherries, as well as ornamental prunus.	In late spring, small brown spots appear on leaves. The spots later drop out to give a 'shot hole' appearance. Elongated lesions exude amber-coloured gum on dying shoots.	Autumn and winter, although symptoms do not appear until the following year.	Cut out and burn all infected areas. Spray foliage with Bordeaux mixture in mid August, mid September and mid October. Prune during summer. **Organic advice** Take care not to wound trees when staking, tying up or strimming.
BARK SPLITTING	Many species, including fruit trees.	The tree's bark splits and fissures open up.	Any time.	Cut out dead wood and remove loose bark to reveal a clean wound. Feed, mulch and water the tree properly and the wound should heal naturally.
BASAL ROT	Crocuses, narcissi and onions.	Bulbs usually do not grow in spring, and the roots start to rot. If a corm or bulb is sliced downwards, it shows dark strands spreading from the chocolate-brown rot at the base, up through the inner scales.	Any time, including storage of narcissi bulbs.	Destroy rotten corms and bulbs. **Organic advice** Grow resistant varieties of the bulbs.
BASAL (or fusarium) ROT OF LILIES	Lilies.	Growth either fails to appear above ground or is yellow and weak. Bulbs quickly rot and disintegrate.	Any time.	Examine bulbs carefully before planting. Burn affected bulbs. Do not plant new lily bulbs in the same bed for several years.

PROBLEM	PLANTS AT RISK	RECOGNITION	DANGER PERIOD	TREATMENT
BEECH BARK DISEASE	Young and mature beech trees.	Insect feeding holes in the bark create wounds through which fungus enters. Wounds weep at first, followed by yellowing of foliage and red-black bumps on the bark. Branches die back and the tree eventually dies.	Late spring.	In the early stages, insect attacks can be prevented by using a tar-oil wash in winter or spraying with malathion during the growing season.
BIRCH POLYPORE	Birch trees.	Die-back caused by grey-brown horseshoe-shaped bracket fungus, up to 15 cm (6 in) across. The fungus attacks dead wood and rapidly spreads decay.	Any time.	Cut out and destroy dead wood. Mulch trees regularly with well-decayed manure.
BITTER PIT	Apples.	Sunken brown spots develop beneath the skin of the fruit and throughout the flesh.	Particularly in hot dry summers with acute water shortages. Not apparent until harvesting or in storage.	Feed, mulch and prevent the soil from drying out. In mid June spray with calcium nitrate – 8 rounded tablespoons to 23 litres (5 gallons) of water – and repeat three times at three-weekly intervals. **Organic advice** Avoid high applications of nitrogen-rich manures.
BLACKLEG	Pelargoniums and potatoes.	Affected tissues become soft, the leaves turn yellow and the cutting or plant dies – the result of a black rot developing at the base of the stem. The rot is caused by fungi or bacteria.	Soon after pelargonium cuttings are taken. In June for potatoes. A problem on cold wet soil.	Destroy severely affected plants. No treatment for potatoes other than to plant healthy seed tubers and to choose less susceptible varieties. Protect pelargoniums with sterilised compost. Maintain strict greenhouse hygiene and water carefully with mains water.
BLACK SPOT See ROSE BLACK SPOT				
BLIGHT	Tomatoes and potatoes.	In damp conditions, leaves develop yellow-brown blotches and a white furry coating underneath. They turn brown and rot. On tomato fruits, a dry brown rot develops which may not be obvious till after picking. Potatoes may rot in store.	Any time between May and August.	Spray every 10-14 days, particularly in a wet season, with mancozeb or carbendazim. Spray potatoes before the leaves touch other plants, and tomatoes when the first fruits set. **Organic advice** Grow resistant potatoes. Earthing up or mulching helps. As symptoms spread, cut off all foliage, and wait three weeks before harvesting.
BLINDNESS	Narcissi and tulips, especially those grown in containers.	Shoots fail to develop flower buds – or those which do turn brown and wither – due to waterlogged or excessively dry roots.	Hot summers.	The cause may be waterlogged or very dry roots, or BASAL ROT. Blindness can also be caused by shallow planting. If so, allow container plants to die down, then store the bulbs in a well-lit cool shed over summer and replant at the correct depth in autumn.
BLOSSOM END ROT	Tomatoes, peppers and aubergines.	Circular brown or black patch at the blossom end of the fruit, which gradually enlarges to penetrate the flesh. Caused by a calcium shortage and dehydration.	As fruit develops.	Prevent the soil from drying out and maintain even growth. This disease is particularly a problem with plants that are grown in pots or growing bags, where they may need to be watered several times a day.

PROBLEM	PLANTS AT RISK	RECOGNITION	DANGER PERIOD	TREATMENT
BLOTCHY RIPENING •See also GREENBACK	Tomatoes.	Hard green or yellow patches on the fruit, most often on lower trusses.	Growing season.	The problem may occur if plants have poor soil, are growing too fast under poor light, or are overwatered or too dry. A high temperature can also be a factor. Take appropriate action. A potash feed may help. Grow resistant varieties such as 'Alicante', 'Eurocross', 'Grenadier' and 'Shirley'.
BLUE MOULD	Stored vegetables, corms and bulbs.	Blue or blue-green spores of fungus, encouraged by a moist atmosphere, appear on plant material.	Any time.	Ensure dry and cool conditions and that all plant material is healthy when stored. Dust bulbs – not vegetables – with carbendazim before storing.
BOOTLACE FUNGUS See HONEY FUNGUS				
BORON DEFICIENCY	Beetroots, swedes and celery.	Edible roots turn brown inside; celery stalks develop brown cracks.	May to August.	Mix 30g (1oz) of borax with 10 litres (2 gallons) of water and spread it over 10m² (12sq yd) of soil.
BOTRYTIS See GREY MOULD				
BRACKET FUNGUS	All trees, especially alder, ash, beech, oak, poplar and – particularly vulnerable – birch.	Fungi, up to 30cm (12in) across, sprout from trunks and branches of trees. The spores spread through dead or damaged tissues and may cause die-back.	July to October, but fungi may appear months after infection.	Bracket fungus can be a symptom of many different diseases. Seek professional advice.
BROWN CORE	Primulas.	Plants wilt and can easily be lifted due to the roots rotting back from the tips.	Growing season.	The disease only affects plants that are set too deeply in the soil or are overcrowded. Burn affected plants and avoid growing primulas on the infected site for several years.
BROWN ROT	All tree fruit.	Concentrically ringed browny white fungus appears on fruits originally injured by insects and birds.	Summer, and in store.	Destroy infected fruit and cut out dead shoots. Spray fruit with carbendazim before picking to protect in storage. Do not store diseased or damaged fruit. **Organic advice** At end of season remove remaining fruit from the tree. Remove and destroy all plant debris.
BUD BLAST See RHODODENDRON BUD BLAST				
BUD-DROP	Camellias, sweet peas, wisterias and many houseplants.	Buds drop before flowering.	Growing season.	Nothing can save falling buds. Prevent bud-drop by mulching with organic matter. Water well in dry periods – for camellias particularly June-September. Bud-drop is caused by a shortage of water, sometimes in autumn when you may not think of watering.

PROBLEM	PLANTS AT RISK	RECOGNITION	DANGER PERIOD	TREATMENT
CALLISTEPHUS WILT • See also FUSARIUM WILT	Callistephus.	Blackened stems with white or pink fungus outgrowths. Prevalent on wet, badly drained soils.	Growing season.	Remove and burn infected plants. Improve drainage by adding coarse grit to soil or installing a drainage system.
CANE BLIGHT	Raspberries.	Leaves on fruiting canes wilt and wither in summer, and canes may snap in the wind. The canes have dark patches at ground level and the bark splits or cracks.	Growing season.	Cut out all diseased canes to below soil level and burn. Disinfect knife immediately. Spray new canes with Bordeaux mixture. Handle canes with care to prevent damage. Do not transplant infected canes to a new site. **Organic advice** Tie in canes well to prevent wind-rock, which can cause damage that is then a source of entry for the disease.
CANE SPOT	Raspberries, loganberries and hybrid berries.	Round purple spots which later form cankers on canes, spots with a whitish centre on leaves and misshapen fruits – the result of bacterial infection.	May to October.	Cut out and burn badly infected canes. Spray with carbendazim fortnightly from bud-burst to petal-fall.
CANKER • See also BACTERIAL CANKER, PARSNIP CANKER, STEM CANKER	Many trees and shrubs, including apple, ash and poplar.	Brown, cracked and sunken patches appear on the bark. Slime oozes from the area. Encirclement of a shoot or trunk causes die-back.	Any time.	Cut out and burn infected areas and small branches. Spray with Bordeaux mixture or copper fungicide, following the instructions on the label. If a tree is badly affected, destroy it. **Organic advice** Do not grow apple trees on wet, badly drained soil. *Populus nigra* is resistant to canker.
CARNATION RINGSPOT	Two carnation species – *Dianthus barbatus* and *D. caryophyllus.*	Circular grey spots develop on foliage, stems and occasionally on the flowers. Foliage may shrivel under damp conditions. Grey fungus may appear in the centre of the spots.	Growing season.	Remove diseased leaves and spray at regular intervals with Bordeaux mixture, following the instructions on the label.
CARNATION STEM-ROT AND DIE-BACK	All species.	Rotting caused by soil-borne fungus which enters the stems through wounds.	During wet periods and on poorly drained soil.	Spray stock plants with carbendazim. Use only sterilised composts for potting.
CELERY HEART ROT	Celery.	When celery is lifted the centres have a wet, slimy brown rot, often extending up the stalk. Bacteria are believed to enter through wounds caused by slugs, or severe frost injury.	Growing season.	Ensure good cultivation on well-drained soil and use a balanced fertiliser. Choose a fresh site for new celery to avoid a build-up of bacteria in the soil. Control slugs and give winter protection in cold districts. Carry out crop rotation.

PROBLEM	PLANTS AT RISK	RECOGNITION	DANGER PERIOD	TREATMENT
CELERY LEAF SPOT	Celery and celeriac – mature plants and seedlings.	Small brown spots on leaves and stems develop to become black fruiting bodies of fungus.	Wet weather.	Spray seedlings and plants with Bordeaux mixture or mancozeb, repeating at weekly intervals if necessary. Feed established plants with high-potash fertiliser to avoid soft growth. **Organic advice** Clear up all crop debris. Do not overuse nitrogen-rich feeds. Destroy any infected plants at the end of the season.
CHLOROSIS (Mineral)	Many plants, especially hydrangeas, peaches, ceanothus, raspberries and acid-loving plants, such as camellias and rhododendrons, on alkaline soil.	Leaves lose their rich green colour to become pale yellow or white.	Growing season.	Dig peat, pulverised bark or crushed bracken into the soil and use only fertilisers sold as lime-free. For iron deficiency (the commonest form of chlorosis) use a chelated-iron compound.
CHLOROSIS (Viral)	Vast range of garden plants.	The foliage turns yellow, either across the whole leaf, on the margins or just on the veins. The yellowing may occur in patterns of lines or rings.	Growing season.	Control aphids (see p. 824) which spread infection. Destroy badly infected plants, and buy virus-free plants where they exist.
CHOCOLATE SPOT	Broad beans.	Beans, foliage and sometimes the stems become covered with chocolate-coloured spots caused by a fungal disease. The whole plant may die.	June or July, or after severe winter frosts. Over-wintered crops are most at risk in a wet spring.	Spray with Bordeaux mixture or carbendazim as foliage appears. Encourage strong growth by liming the soil if necessary, using a potash fertiliser, ensuring good drainage and sowing seeds thinly. **Organic advice** Don't sow autumn or early spring crops on wet soils. Don't sow or plant too close together.
CHRYSANTHEMUM VIRUS DISEASES	Most varieties of dendranthema (chrysanthemum), both plants grown outdoors and those under glass.	Distorted blooms, break-up or greening of the flower colour, leaf mottling or stunted growth – the result of viruses transmitted by pests, including aphids.	Growing season.	Destroy all the affected plants. Prevent further infection by thoroughly washing your hands in hot soapy water and sterilising any equipment that has been used in tri-sodium orthophosphate.
CLEMATIS WILT	Clematis, especially large-flowered varieties.	Upper parts of shoot wilt, with young leaves wilting first and leaf stalks blackening where they join the blade. Caused by fungus.	Early spring and through the growing season.	Cut wilted shoots back to below soil level. Drench shoots with carbendazim when first damage is seen and again in spring. **Organic advice** Plant new clematis 15 cm (6 in) deeper than their level in the pot. Avoid wounding stems when planting, and tie stems to their support in the growing season to prevent damage. Clear up all diseased material and burn it.
CLUB ROOT	Brassicas, wallflowers, stocks, turnips and radishes.	Leaves of brassicas wilt and turn red, purple or yellow; roots become swollen and distorted. Plants wilt on hot days, but may recover if watered.	Throughout the growing season.	Once soil is infected, little can be done. Prevent the disease by liming the soil in winter to keep pH at 7-7.5. On badly drained soil make raised beds. Never bring in plants that may have the disease; raise your own from seed in sterilised compost. Kale, winter broccoli and spring cabbage grow better in infected soil than other brassicas. There are a few resistant types.

PROBLEM	PLANTS AT RISK	RECOGNITION	DANGER PERIOD	TREATMENT
COLLAR ROT	Plants grown in greenhouses.	Plants collapse at or just above soil level due to organisms rotting the tissue.	Any time.	Remove all dead and decaying tissues, and dust with Bordeaux powder. Repot plants in a lighter, sterilised compost and water carefully.
COMMON SCAB	Potatoes, beetroots, radishes, swedes and turnips.	Ragged-edged scabs develop on potato tubers due to organisms related to bacteria. The scabs do not render the potatoes inedible, but they should be removed before the potatoes are cooked.	Growing season.	Burn peelings or severely infected tubers. Avoid liming the soil before sowing or planting; instead, add humus – such as green manure – and maintain even growth by keeping the soil moist and by mulching. Grow resistant varieties, such as 'Arran Pilot', 'King Edward' and 'Pentland Crown'. Put a layer of grass mowings in the bottom of the trench when planting.
CORAL SPOT	Many trees and shrubs, including acers, maples, magnolias and redcurrants.	Rashes of pink or coral-red spots on dead twigs. Coral spot is a fungus that can kill trees or shrubs if it is able to enter living shoots. Affected plants may recently have been transplanted or suffered from drought or waterlogging.	Any time in plants under stress.	Cut out and burn all dead wood and prune 10-15 cm (4-6 in) below the diseased area. **Organic advice** Identify and rectify any cultural problems. Avoid injury to bark which would allow the disease to enter.
CORE ROT	Freesia and gladiolus corms.	Rotting spreads from the centre outwards, as the corm becomes spongy and turns brown or black.	During storage.	Burn infected corms. After lifting corms, dust them with sulphur or soak them in carbendazim, and store them in a dry atmosphere at 7-10°C (45-50°F).
CORKY SCAB OF CACTI	Cacti, especially epiphyllums and opuntias.	Sunken patches of irregular rusty or corky scabs.	Growing season.	Destroy badly affected plants and improve cultural conditions.
CORTICIUM See RED THREAD				
COX SPOT	'Cox's Orange Pippins' and (less so) some other apple varieties.	Small, round tan-coloured spots on leaves due to an unknown PHYSIOLOGICAL DISORDER	Usually after drought.	Try watering during dry spells and mulching the trees.
CRACKING	All types of root vegetables, especially carrots and parsnips. Also apples, pears, plums, gages and tomatoes.	Roots split lengthways; no symptoms appear above soil level. Fruit skins split to expose inner flesh.	Growing season – dry periods followed by heavy rain.	Avoid irregular growth by mulching heavily and maintaining even watering to prevent the soil from drying out.

PROBLEM	PLANTS AT RISK	RECOGNITION	DANGER PERIOD	TREATMENT
CRINKLE	Strawberries.	Yellow spots appear on the leaves, the centre of which may become red or purple. When these spots multiply and turn brown and the leaves pucker, the outbreak is severe. The cause is an aphid-borne virus which stunts growth.	Growing season.	Burn diseased plants and protect remainder by controlling aphids.
CROWN GALL	Many species, including soft and tree fruit, vegetables, shrubs and herbaceous perennials.	Hard or soft galls, sometimes in a chain along a root or shoot and often occurring in wet soil, are the result of bacteria entering through wounds.	Growing season.	Destroy infected plants and provide suitable drainage to prevent soil from becoming waterlogged. Avoid damage when planting and during cultivation.
CROWN ROT OF RHUBARB	Rhubarb.	Leaves become spindly and discoloured and die early. The main bud rots, followed by the whole of the crown, due to bacterial disease. Most common in wet soil.	Growing season.	Dig up and burn entire plant and never plant rhubarb on the same site again.
CUCUMBER MOSAIC VIRUS	Cucumbers and many other plants.	Leaves and fruit become mottled and puckered, and growth is stunted. Caused by an aphid-borne virus.	Growing season.	Burn affected plants immediately and control aphids. If the disease is a regular problem, grow resistant varieties.
DAMPING-OFF	Seedlings sown under glass in crowded and wet conditions.	Seedlings rot at ground level, topple over and die – killed by a parasitic fungus.	From seed-sowing to emergence of third pair of true leaves.	Remove and destroy dead seedlings. Water seed boxes with copper or Cheshunt compound. To prevent future trouble, sow thinly, use a sterilised seed compost, water carefully and ensure good ventilation. Always use clean containers, and never use rainwater from a butt unless the butt is cleaned regularly.
DIANTHUS LEAF SPOT	*Dianthus barbatus, D. caryophyllus* and occasionally *D. chinensis.*	Leaves develop circular or oval spots with tiny black spores, surrounded by a purple border, or small, round purple spots which gradually increase and coalesce. Infected leaves wither and die off at the tips. Caused by several fungi.	During damp periods of the growing season.	Remove infected leaves and spray plants with Bordeaux mixture or carbendazim.
DIE-BACK	Mainly fruit trees and shrubs.	Shoots die back from the tips, often killing larger branches. Foliage turns brown or yellow and withers. Damage may be due to frost, fungal infection or PHYSIOLOGICAL DISORDERS.	Any time.	Cut out all infected areas back to healthy wood and burn the cuttings. Treat identifiable disease appropriately; if unidentifiable, improve cultural conditions.

PROBLEM	PLANTS AT RISK	RECOGNITION	DANGER PERIOD	TREATMENT
DOWNY MILDEW	Brassica seedlings, marrows, courgettes and onions.	Plants develop a grey or whitish furry covering on the underside of the leaves, with blotches of yellow on the upper side, the result of being overcrowded, poorly watered and inadequately ventilated. Onion bulbs may rot in store.	During growing season, and on onions in store.	Thin out plants and spray with carbendazim or mancozeb (wait 14 days before eating). **Organic advice** Rotate future crops. Grow resistant varieties where available. Always sow seeds in fresh sterilised compost, and improve ventilation when raising plants under glass.
DROPSY See OEDEMA				
DRY ROT	Potatoes and some other tubers; also crocuses, freesias and gladioli.	Exposed growth turns yellow-brown and then collapses as leaf sheaths rot. Tubers (or corms) develop small dark lesions which enlarge and merge as the tubers shrivel and die. The cause is a soil-borne fungus.	From January onwards and during storage.	Destroy all infected tubers or corms as soon as the first symptoms appear. Before storing or replanting healthy ones, dust them with sulphur or dip them in a solution of carbendazim. Store them in a dry, cool, frostproof place. Plant tubers or corms in a fresh site each year.
FAIRY RINGS	Lawns.	Inner and outer rings of lush, dark green grass appear in the lawn, with brown or dead turf between them. In summer and autumn – especially during wet weather – small brown-capped toadstools flourish between the rings.	Any time.	Remove diseased turf to a depth of 30 cm (12 in) and water the soil with a solution of carbendazim. Alternatively, fork over the area to a depth of 8 cm (3 in) and water with carbendazim solution. **Organic advice** Improving the growing conditions might help, together with applications of sulphate of iron.
FIRE BLIGHT	Cotoneasters, hawthorns, sorbus species, apples, pears and other related ornamentals.	Flowers turn black, leaves turn brown and wither. Golden or white slime may exude from the stems. The symptoms can appear suddenly, giving the plant the appearance of having been scorched by fire.	Flowering time.	Remove and destroy the diseased shoots when the symptoms are identified, cutting back beyond the damage by at least 30 cm (12 in). If the whole plant shows symptoms, dig it up and remove it. Plant a resistant variety, such as *Sorbus intermedia, Malus* × *moerlandsii* 'Liset' or *Pyrus calleryana* 'Bradford'.
FOOT ROT	Tomatoes, bedding plants, sweet peas, peas and beans.	Stem bases turn black and rot, and the roots usually die due to various fungi.	Growing season.	Rotate vegetable and bedding plants, and always use sterile compost for pot plants. Water bedding plants in seed boxes with Cheshunt compound when they are put in their planting holes. If necessary, repeat at weekly intervals.
FROST DAMAGE	Young leaves and shoots on most species of flowering plants, shrubs and trees.	Cracking of tree trunks, blackening and shrivelling of leaves, and blackened flower centres and buds.	Mid winter and spring.	Cut out frostbitten shoots to prevent entry of fungi. Protect plants from further damage by covering them with paper, straw or sacking. Harden off tender plants before planting out.
FRUIT-DROP	All tree fruit.	Fruits drop prematurely while still immature.	Flowering time and just after.	Ensure that suitable pollinators are in the garden, and feed, mulch and water the tree. In cold seasons, fruit-drop is due to poor pollination and nothing can be done.

PROBLEM	PLANTS AT RISK	RECOGNITION	DANGER PERIOD	TREATMENT
FUSARIUM WILT • See also CALLISTEPHUS WILT	Carnations, dianthus species, dwarf and runner beans, garden peas and sweet peas.	Leaves become discoloured and plants wilt due to several species of fungus. Stems may also become discoloured.	Growing season.	Remove and burn the infected plants. Sterilise the soil or grow susceptible plants on a fresh site each year. Propagate carnations and dianthus species from healthy plants only. Drench with carbendazim, according to the instructions on the label.
GLADIOLUS DRY ROT	See DRY ROT			
GLADIOLUS SCAB	Gladioli.	Reddish specks appear on the leaves, which enlarge and darken. Leaf tips shrivel. Craters develop at the base of the corms with raised rims and glossy coating. Yellow spots on the corms exude gum.	Scab strikes in summer but may not reveal itself until corms are lifted and stored.	As for DRY ROT.
GLADIOLUS YELLOWS	Gladioli.	Yellow stripes appear on the leaves, which gradually turn completely yellow and then die back. The flower stems may be crooked and greener than normal.	During the growing season, but the disease develops in storage.	Burn the infected plants immediately symptoms appear. Grow gladioli corms on a fresh site each year, and avoid nitrogen-rich fertilisers and manures.
GOOSEBERRY MILDEW (AMERICAN)	Gooseberries.	White mealy powder, caused by a fungal disease, covers leaves, shoots and fruits which later turn brown. Shoots may become distorted. The fruits are small and tasteless.	April onwards.	Remove diseased shoots and burn them immediately. Spray with carbendazim or bupirimate & triforine. **Organic advice** A problem when soil is dry and the weather is humid. Mulch plants and keep them well pruned to allow air to circulate. Grow resistant varieties. Do not overfeed with nitrogen-rich fertilisers.
GOOSEBERRY MILDEW (EUROPEAN)	Gooseberries, blackcurrants and occasionally redcurrants.	A light, powdery white covering develops on the upper leaf surface and sometimes on the underside and berries. Widespread on old bushes, but not as damaging as American gooseberry mildew.	Late April on goose-berries; late May to September on currants.	As for GOOSEBERRY MILDEW (AMERICAN).
GREENBACK • See also BLOTCHY RIPENING	Tomatoes.	As fruit starts to ripen, a ring (partial or complete) of hard leathery tissue is left around the stalk end. This area does not turn red – see PHYSIOLOGICAL DISORDERS.	As fruit develops.	The major cause is thought to be exposure to heat, so even fruits shaded from the sun in a greenhouse can succumb. In hot weather, ventilate the greenhouse and provide shade. Maintain even growth by ensuring that the soil does not dry out. Alternatively, grow resistant varieties.
GREY BULB ROT	Tulips, hyacinths and other bulbous plants.	Young shoots do not appear in spring. A dry grey rot at the neck of the bulbs gradually spreads to develop clusters of black fungi, and then the bulbs disintegrate.	Soon after planting.	Remove and burn all debris from infected plants; replace surrounding soil with sterilised compost. Dust bulbs and corms with carbendazim before planting. Preferably avoid planting bulbs in infected areas for several years.

PROBLEM	PLANTS AT RISK	RECOGNITION	DANGER PERIOD	TREATMENT
GREY MOULD (Botrytis)	Many types, both outdoors and under glass.	A grey velvety mould, caused by a fungal disease, forms on leaves, flowers and soft fruits. The disease is encouraged by damp, overcrowded conditions and poor ventilation in a greenhouse.	Growing season. Worst in winter for lettuces.	If possible destroy infected plants. Pick off dying flowers and buds. Spray herbaceous plants with carbendazim. Destroy diseased bulbs; dust healthy ones with carbendazim. Cut out infected areas on trees or shrubs. Spray soft fruit with carbendazim when flowers appear, and until just before fruits ripen. Under glass, spray with carbendazim or propiconazole as symptoms appear.
GUMMING	Cherries and other prunus species.	Gum, exuding on the surface of branches and trunks, gradually hardens – the result of unsuitable soil conditions or malnutrition.	Any time, but at its worst in summer.	Gumming should stop with good feeding, mulching and watering. Gum may have to be removed in order to cut out dead wood beneath. Do this in October.
GUMMOSIS OF CUCUMBER	Cucumbers, melons, vegetable marrows and courgettes that are grown in a greenhouse or coldframe.	Small grey sunken spots exude sticky liquid. This develops into a velvety dark green mould, and the fruits crack. The symptoms sometimes appear on the leaves and stems as brownish patches.	Inadequate ventilation and heat under cool damp conditions.	Burn all diseased fruits. Disinfect greenhouse or coldframe with phenolic compound or a garden disinfectant before planting another crop.
HARD ROT	Chiefly gladiolus corms, but also the corms of crocus and freesia.	Sharply defined tiny brown spots on leaves which develop infectious fungi in diseased tissue; black-brown sunken spots on corms. More common in the south of Britain than the north.	Fungus spreads fast in wet weather in poor soils. Symptoms may appear in storage.	Destroy all diseased bulbs and corms, and burn the foliage at the end of the season as the disease may overwinter on dead plant debris. Dip healthy corms in a solution of carbendazim before storing.
HEATHER DIE-BACK	Calluna and erica.	The foliage develops a greyish tinge, then wilts, turns brown and dies.	Throughout the growing season in badly drained soil.	No cure. Dig up and burn infected plants. Keep remaining plants healthy by applying an acid-formulation fertiliser in April, and mulching with leaf-mould, shredded bark or woodchips. Improve drainage.
HONEY FUNGUS (Bootlace fungus)	Most trees and shrubs. Common among rotting tree stumps, some herbaceous perennials and some bulbs.	Toadstools at soil level at the base of the trunk. White fan-shaped growths of fungus occur beneath the bark of roots and at soil level. Black 'bootlace' threads on diseased roots spread infection.	Autumn.	Destroy dead or dying plants and as many roots as possible. Sterilise the soil with a phenolic compound such as Armillatox. The 'bootlaces' do not necessarily mean disaster. Many species of the fungus are not invasive.
HORMONE WEEDKILLER DAMAGE	All types, but tomatoes and vines particularly susceptible.	Leaves become narrow, often yellow, fan-shaped and frequently cupped.	Growing season.	Plants usually recover without treatment. To avoid future damage, do not use weedkiller spray on a windy or hot day, or use weedkiller equipment for any other jobs. Mowings from a freshly treated lawn can be put on a compost heap, provided they are not spread on the garden for at least six months and are well decomposed.

PROBLEM	PLANTS AT RISK	RECOGNITION	DANGER PERIOD	TREATMENT
INK DISEASE	Bulbous irises, lachenalias, tritonias and crocosmias.	As the young leaves show through the ground, they have yellow streaks which become black blotches. If the leaves develop, they may turn red and wither. Diseased bulbs have black crusty patches on their outer scales.	Wet season.	Remove and burn all infected bulbs.
INTERNAL RUST SPOT	Potatoes.	Brown spots and blotches in the flesh of potato tubers, possibly due to dry soil.	Growing season.	Incorporate plenty of well-rotted manure or compost into the soil before planting, and water regularly.
IRIS MOSAIC VIRUS	Bulbous and bearded irises.	Yellow streaks and spots occur on young leaves. Plants may be stunted. The flowers often show darker streaks on the normal ground colour.	Growing season.	Destroy all infected plants. Control aphids which spread the virus (see p. 824).
LEAF MOULD	Tomatoes that are being grown under glass. Rare on outdoor plants.	Purple-brown mould on the underside of leaves, with yellow blotches on the upper side. The plant's growth is checked and fruit develops poorly.	Summer. Sometimes as early as April, but not usually until June.	Improve the cultural conditions and maintain a maximum temperature in the greenhouse of 21°C (70°F) with good ventilation. Do not let high temperature coincide with high humidity. Remove and destroy lower foliage if it shows signs of attack. Check the disease by spraying with carbendazim or copper fungicide. Grow resistant varieties.
LEAF ROT	Dianthus species, including garden pinks.	Leaves and stems develop white or brownish water-soaked spots with dark margins, or grey spots. Flower buds may also be affected.	Growing season.	Remove and burn all diseased tissues and spray plant with Bordeaux mixture.
LEAF SPOT	Blackcurrants and gooseberries, celery and spinach, plus a wide range of ornamental plants.	The leaves and stems develop round or oval brown spots – sometimes with a black pinpoint – and the leaves then fall prematurely.	Late spring onwards.	Remove and burn all diseased leaves. Spray plants with mancozeb, carbendazim or Bordeaux mixture, following the instructions on the label.
LEAFY GALL	Many species, but in particular sweet peas, dahlias, pelargoniums, chrysanthemums, carnations, gladioli and strawberries.	Abortive shoots, often flattened with thickened distorted leaves, develop at soil level due to bacterial infection.	During propagation and the growing season.	Remove and burn all infected plants. Wash tools in tri-sodium orthophosphate and wash your hands after handling infected material. When replanting, choose a non-susceptible plant. Always grow susceptible plants in clean containers and sterilised compost.

PROBLEM	PLANTS AT RISK	RECOGNITION	DANGER PERIOD	TREATMENT
LEEK RUST	Leeks.	Shoots become twisted or malformed and covered with an orange powder.	Summer and early autumn, or in spring on over-wintered crops.	If rust attacks late varieties of leeks, spray with mancozeb. **Organic advice** On leeks, symptoms often disappear when autumn arrives, so no treatment is necessary. Leek rust is more likely where potash is low, nitrogen is high and drainage is poor.
LETTUCE VIRUS DISEASES See ARABIS MOSAIC VIRUS, CUCUMBER MOSAIC VIRUS				
LICHENS	Grass, trees and shrubs.	Grass: overlapping leaf structures which grow horizontally in the turf – deep green-black when moist, and grey-green or brown when dry. Trees and shrubs: thin crusts of grey or orange tissue, or leafy-looking plants, growing on the bark.	Grass: at any time; trees and shrubs: harmless.	Grass: rake out the growths and treat affected areas with dichlorophen. Drain if possible and spike the surface. Brush in lime-free sand, top-dress and feed. Trees and shrubs: lichen on these are harmless and should be left. Encourage vigorous growth of the host by feeding in spring and summer.
LILAC BLIGHT	Syringas.	Brown angular spots develop on the leaves, followed by young shoots turning black and withering.	Spring.	Cut the infected shoots back to healthy buds and spray with Bordeaux mixture. Spray again the following spring when the leaves start to appear.
LILY DISEASE	Lilies – particularly *Lilium candidum*.	Leaves develop small red-brown oval-shaped, water-saturated spots of fungus which spread rapidly. In humid conditions, leaves may turn brown, flowers rot and stems collapse.	Wet seasons.	Cut off and burn infected growths. When new leaves appear in spring, spray all plants with carbendazim or Bordeaux mixture. Repeat at fortnightly intervals until flowering begins and, during a wet season, again after flowering. Destroy all infected material at the end of the season, as the fungus can overwinter in the soil.
LIME-INDUCED CHLOROSIS See CHLOROSIS				
MAGNESIUM DEFICIENCY	All types of plants, particularly tomatoes and apples.	Leaves turn yellow (sometimes orange-brown) between the veins, giving a marbled effect; they then fall prematurely. Symptoms appear first on older leaves. In light, acid, sandy soil the problem is worse in a wet season as magnesium is easily leached.	During the growing season, or following the use of a high-potash fertiliser.	Spray the plants with a solution of magnesium sulphate – 8 tablespoons to 11 litres (2½ gallons) of water – plus a few drops of liquid detergent. **Organic advice** If lime is needed, use dolomitic (magnesian) limestone.
MANGANESE DEFICIENCY	Many species.	Yellowing occurs between the veins of older leaves. Dead patches may appear among the yellow areas. The disorder occurs mainly in poorly drained sandy soil, highly organic soil and wet areas of low acidity.	Growing season.	Spray the plants with a solution of manganese sulphate – 2 tablespoons to 11 litres (2½ gallons) of water plus a few drops of liquid detergent – or apply chelated or fritted compounds.
MILDEW See DOWNY MILDEW, GOOSEBERRY MILDEW (AMERICAN), GOOSEBERRY MILDEW (EUROPEAN), POWDERY MILDEW				

PROBLEM	PLANTS AT RISK	RECOGNITION	DANGER PERIOD	TREATMENT
MINERAL DEFICIENCIES See BORON DEFICIENCY, CHLOROSIS (Mineral), MAGNESIUM DEFICIENCY, MANGANESE DEFICIENCY, NITROGEN DEFICIENCY, POTASSIUM DEFICIENCY, WHIPTAIL				
MINT RUST	Mint.	Thickened and distorted shoots bear orange-coloured fungal spores.	Symptoms appear in spring; affected plants are permanently diseased.	Cut out and burn affected shoots, and spray the soil with propiconazole. Burn off withered top growth of the mint bed in autumn or early winter.
MOSAIC VIRUS See ARABIS MOSAIC VIRUS, CUCUMBER MOSAIC VIRUS, IRIS MOSAIC VIRUS				
MOULD See BLUE MOULD, GREY MOULD, LEAF MOULD, SNOW MOULD, SOOTY MOULD				
NARCISSUS FIRE	Narcissi – particularly in the West Country.	Rotting flowerheads caused by fungal disease, together with GREY MOULD spreading to the leaves.	Wet seasons.	Burn infected leaves to stop fungus overwintering. Remove plants showing infection in spring. Spray remainder when 2.5 cm (1 in) high with bupirimate & triforine, or thiram. Repeat at 10 day intervals until the flower buds emerge from the leaf sheaths.
NECK ROT	Onions.	A grey velvety mould develops near the neck of stored onions causing them to rot rapidly.	Growing season, but symptoms do not appear until storage.	Destroy diseased onions as they appear. Store only those onions which are well ripened and hard in a dry, airy place. Use a 3 or 4 year rotation system. Do not overfeed with nitrogen-rich manures or fertilisers as large bulbs are more prone to neck rot than smaller ones.
NITROGEN DEFICIENCY	All types, but most commonly fruit trees and vegetables.	The young leaves turn pale yellow-green, and later develop yellow, red or purple tints. The plants are small, stunted and lack vigour.	Growing season.	Use nitrogenous fertiliser such as blood, fish and bone or sulphate of ammonia in spring. Improve soil structure and fertility generally. For a quick result, water with a liquid feed or apply a nitrogen-rich foliar feed. A temporary deficiency can arise in cold weather, but it will disapper as the soil warms up.
OEDEMA (Dropsy)	Many species, but frequently on succulents, semi-succulents, camellias and ivy-leaved pelargoniums.	Small bumps on the leaves are caused by too much water inside the plant. This can be due to a saturated soil or to a wet atmosphere. Leaves sometimes fall off.	Any time.	Reduce watering. Increase greenhouse ventilation to reduce humidity. The infected leaves will not recover but they should be left; they will help the plant to lose its excess water.
ONION NECK ROT See NECK ROT				
PANSY SICKNESS 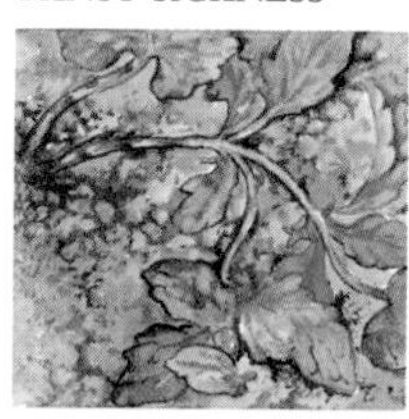	Violas.	Roots and stems are attacked by soil-borne organisms causing plants to collapse.	Growing season.	Remove and destroy diseased plants and their roots. Water seedlings and established plants with Cheshunt compound, repeating at weekly intervals if necessary. Choose a new site every year.

PROBLEM	PLANTS AT RISK	RECOGNITION	DANGER PERIOD	TREATMENT
PARSNIP CANKER	Parsnips.	Reddish brown cankers may form on the shoulder of a root, with the leaves developing small black spots with green halos. The disease is caused by fungus.	June onwards.	Avoid disease by sowing seeds early in deep loamy soil, enriched with balanced fertiliser, and lime if needed. Improve drainage and rotate crops. Control carrot fly (see p. 826). If trouble persists, grow resistant varieties. **Organic advice** Small roots, produced by growing parsnips at a spacing of 7.5-10 cm (3-4 in), are less prone to canker. Earthing up may help.
PEACH LEAF CURL	Almonds, apricots, nectarines, peaches and related ornamental prunus species.	Leaves develop large red blisters, turn white, then brown and finally fall prematurely due to fungus.	Before bud-burst.	Remove and burn infected leaves. Spray with mancozeb or Bordeaux mixture in January/early February. Repeat a fortnight later and just before leaf-fall. **Organic advice** Wall-trained trees can be protected from rain with a small roof of polythene. It should be in place before bud-burst, and may be removed once all foliage is expanded. The sides should be left open.
PEAR SCAB	Pears.	Leaves and fruit form dark brown velvety blotches, and the fruit becomes distorted. The symptoms are caused by a fungus disease that overwinters on fallen leaves and also on the tree, so young shoots in spring may be blistered and cracked.	Growing season, but most severe after a wet May.	See APPLE SCAB.
PEONY WILT (Peony blight)	Peonies.	GREY MOULD forms on the stems at soil level, causing them to collapse. It then spreads to form brown blotches on the leaves of neighbouring plants.	Growing season.	Cut out all affected shoots to below soil level, and burn them. Dust the crowns of the plants with dry Bordeaux powder. Spray with carbendazim or mancozeb soon after the leaves appear.
PETUNIA WILT	Petunias, zinnias, salpiglossis and other bedding plants.	Plants wilt, often as they are about to flower, and the base of the stems may become discoloured.	Growing season.	Burn all diseased plants. Rotate bedding plants so that vulnerable types are grown on a fresh site each year.
PHYTOPHTHORA ROOT ROT	Trees and shrubs. Most common on Lawson cypress, rhododendrons and azaleas, beech, heathers, limes, apples, prunus and yews.	Small, sparse yellow foliage, with partial die-back often up one side of the plant. The whole plant may die. Sometimes only recognised when new growth fails to appear in spring.	Warm wet periods.	None. Only obtain plants from a reputable nursery. Avoid waterlogging or poorly drained soil. Never transplant from an infected area onto clean soil.

PROBLEM	PLANTS AT RISK	RECOGNITION	DANGER PERIOD	TREATMENT

• PHYSIOLOGICAL DISORDERS •

Healthy plants depend on a combination of essentials – water, mineral salts, air, temperature and light. If any of these essentials is lacking or the balance is wrong, the result may produce a physiological disorder.

Correct watering must be available at each stage of a plant's growth. Too much, too little or sporadic watering can create problems from which a plant may never recover.

Mineral salts should be present in the soil in the correct quantities and form. Some plants need more or less nutrients than others, according to the nature of the soil, the growing conditions and the care they are given. Symptoms of plant problems often indicate MINERAL DEFICIENCIES.

An atmosphere that is too humid can lead to the growth of fungal diseases, while one that is too dry may cause poor growth and induce flower buds to drop. Fluctuating temperatures which are either too high or too low can cause similar problems, while a lack of light leads to thin, weak and colourless plants, with the flowering reduced or non-existent.

Physiological disorders can usually be rectified by careful cultivation – feeding, mulching, watering, drainage and correct spacing.

PROBLEM	PLANTS AT RISK	RECOGNITION	DANGER PERIOD	TREATMENT
POTASSIUM DEFICIENCY 	Plants in clay, chalky soil or peat, particularly those that need extra potash – potatoes, beans, tomatoes, apples, pears, currants.	Stunted growth and reduced leaf size. The leaves turn a dull blue-green, and turn brown at the tips or margins, or curl downwards. Shoots, and sometimes whole branches, die back. Fruit are sparse, small, highly coloured.	Any time.	For fruit, apply sulphate of potash every March at 100-140g per m^2 (3-4oz per sq yd). To improve flowering or berrying on trees and shrubs, apply sulphate of potash at 18g per m^2 (½ oz per sq yd) in early spring or late summer.

POTATO BLACKLEG See BLACKLEG

POTATO BLIGHT See BLIGHT

PROBLEM	PLANTS AT RISK	RECOGNITION	DANGER PERIOD	TREATMENT
POWDERY SCAB 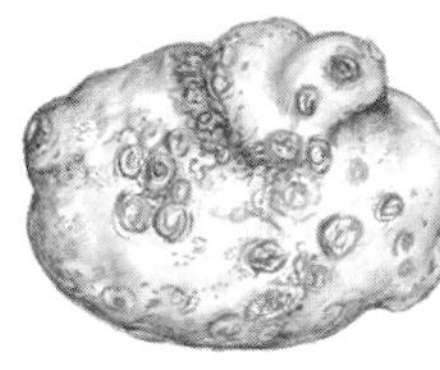	Potatoes.	Raised round scabs which subsequently burst to release a powdery mass of spores. Tubers may be deformed by a soil-inhabiting fungus and have an earthy taste.	In heavy soils, during cool damp weather through the growing season.	Destroy diseased tubers. Avoid planting potatoes on the same site for several years. Improve drainage and grow resistant varieties.
POWDERY MILDEW 	A wide range of plants including strawberries, roses and apples.	A white mildew, caused by a fungus, appears on leaves, shoots and flowers, and weakens the plant. Warm dry weather encourages the disease.	Growing season.	Remove and burn infected growth. Water well and mulch with garden compost, leaf-mould or well-rotted manure. Avoid overuse of nitrogenous fertiliser. Spray with dinocap or triforine, following the instructions on the label. Sulphur can be applied as a dust. Buy resistant varieties of rose, apple and strawberry plants.
PYRACANTHA SCAB 	Pyracanthas.	Leaves and berries acquire a thick, felt-like, olive-brown or black coating – a fungal disease resembling soot – and scabby lesions form on the shoots. Leaves may drop early and berries become disfigured and shrivelled.	During wet periods.	Cut out and burn all diseased shoots. Spray with carbendazim at fortnightly intervals as soon as the disease is seen. **Organic advice** Don't grow pyracanthas in damp places. Grow resistant varieties.
RASPBERRY VIRUS 	Raspberries.	Leaves develop yellow blotches and become distorted. Canes are stunted and the crop is poor.	Growing season.	Dig up and burn all affected plants. Plant new canes on a fresh site and control aphids, which spread the virus disease. Only buy raspberry canes which are certified free from virus.

PROBLEM	PLANTS AT RISK	RECOGNITION	DANGER PERIOD	TREATMENT
RAY BLIGHT	Dendranthemas in the greenhouse.	Dark, water-soaked spots or blotches on petals cause flowers to rot.	Spreads rapidly in humid conditions when the temperature reaches 16°C (61°F).	Reduce humidity and remove all infected plants. Sterilise or change the soil.
RED THREAD (Corticium)	Grass.	Dead patches of turf with outbreaks of red fungus.	Autumn, after rain.	Spray with dichlorophen and, if necessary, alternate treatment with carbendazim, according to manufacturer's instructions. Aerate the soil and apply a nitrogenous fertiliser in spring.
REVERSION	Blackcurrants.	Flower buds are hairless and a bright magenta instead of the normal dull grey. Despite vigorous shoots, the leaves are also smaller and have fewer lobes than normal. The disease is caused by a virus.	Early summer.	Control the gall mites which spread the virus (see p. 829). Destroy badly diseased bushes and replace with plants which are certified as free of virus disease.
RHIZOME ROT	Rhizomatous irises.	Leaf fan collapses at soil level due to the soft, yellow and evil-smelling rot at its growing point.	Any time, but mostly in wet weather.	Destroy badly infected plants. On less severe outbreaks, cut out the rotting parts and dust the wounds with Bordeaux mixture.
RHODODENDRON BUD BLAST	Evergreen rhododendron species and hybrids.	Buds turn grey or brown. In spring, black, bristle-like structures appear on the infected buds, bearing a pinhead of fungus spores which are transmitted by rhododendron leafhoppers.	Between October and December.	Control the rhododendron leafhoppers (see p. 834). Destroy all affected buds and spray with Bordeaux mixture just before flowering and at monthly intervals.
ROSE BLACK SPOT	Roses.	Leaves develop sooty irregular spots on both surfaces which, when severe, can lead to yellowing and leaf-fall. Caused by a fungal disease.	Growing season.	Spray with carbendazim, myclobutanil or mancozeb in February and then at two-weekly intervals. **Organic advice** Grow resistant varieties. Do not overfeed with nitrogen-rich fertilisers. Remove dead leaves from the soil in autumn. In spring, cut out infected shoots before bud-burst, remove old leaves and apply mulch.
RUSSETING	Apples, pears and other fruits.	Roughening of the skin – a natural characteristic, but sometimes a symptom of disease, such as powdery mildew, frost damage, or chemical damage.	Any time.	Control mildew, use chemicals carefully and ensure good cultivation. See FROST DAMAGE and POWDERY MILDEW.

PROBLEM	PLANTS AT RISK	RECOGNITION	DANGER PERIOD	TREATMENT
RUST • See also LEEK RUST, MINT RUST, WHITE RUST	Many decorative plants, including rose bushes, fuchsias and hollyhocks.	Shoots become malformed and covered with orange-coloured fungal spores.	Growing season.	Remove all the affected stems. Spray plants with myclobutanil or mancozeb at the first sign of an attack, following the instructions on the label.
SALIX WATERMARK	Willows – most common on *Salix alba* varieties.	Leaves turn red and wilt, then die but remain on the tree. Infection can be confirmed by cutting through an affected branch. A watery reddish brown or brown-black stain will be found on the wood.	Growing season.	Remove and burn all infected plants. Sterilise tools that have been used with tri-sodium orthophosphate.
SCAB See APPLE SCAB, COMMON SCAB, CORKY SCAB OF CACTI, GLADIOLUS SCAB, PEAR SCAB, POWDERY SCAB, PYRACANTHA SCAB				
SCALD	Plums, apples and soft fruit – particularly tomatoes and grapes under glass.	Plums have red sunken patches; apples have discoloured patches on the skin encircled by a halo; tomatoes have creamy white wrinkled patches; grapes have discoloured patches.	Long hot summers.	Remove affected fruits – even if the flesh beneath is undamaged – before GREY MOULD develops. Damp down the greenhouse early in the day so that any moisture on the fruit dries out before the sun is too strong. Shade greenhouse crops during bright periods.
SCLEROTINIA DISEASE	Herbaceous perennials, bulbs, corms, tubers – including stored root crops, especially carrots and parsnips.	Plants may wilt suddenly, develop yellow basal leaves and collapse where the disease entered. Diseased tissue has a white fluffy mass containing large black fungal growth. The roots eventually soften and decay.	During growing season and when crops are in store.	Burn all diseased plants to prevent risk of the infection spreading. **Organic advice** Use a minimum 4 year rotation. Control weeds in the garden, on which the disease may overwinter.
SCORCHING (Scorch)	Most types of greenhouse and indoor plants, plus acers and beeches.	Affected leaves develop pale brown spots or become papery, either due to cold drying winds or – often when in a greenhouse – scorching by the sun.	Spring for trees and shrubs; summer for greenhouse and indoor plants.	Shade the greenhouse or remove vulnerable plants, especially if the panes are damaged. Ensure that plants are adequately watered, but avoid wetting the leaves during bright warm periods. Water indoor plants from the base to avoid wetting the leaves.
SEEDLING BLIGHT	Zinnias.	Leaves develop red-brown spots with grey centres; the stems develop brown canker-like areas; and the seedlings collapse and die – all due to a fungal disease.	While the plant is small.	Once the symptoms have appeared, the affected plants must be burnt. Protect seedlings in boxes with a copper-containing fungicidal spray.
SHOTHOLE	Cherries, plums, peaches and ornamental prunus species.	Leaves develop brown patches which become irregularly shaped holes, either due to leaf-spotting fungi or BACTERIAL CANKER.	Growing season.	Feed trees annually. Mulch and water well in spring, and give small trees a foliar feed. If symptoms appear next season, spray with carbendazim during summer, and at leaf-fall.

PROBLEM	PLANTS AT RISK	RECOGNITION	DANGER PERIOD	TREATMENT
SILVER LEAF	Peaches, plums, cherries and other prunus species; apples, pears and lilacs; and other trees and shrubs.	Some leaves become silvered and later turn brown, while infected branches die back. A flat purple fungus develops on dead wood.	September to May.	Cut a branch, at least 2.5 cm (1 in) thick, and moisten the wound. If it is diseased a brown or purple stain will appear. Cut out the affected branches to a point 15 cm (6 in) below the fungus. Sterilise tools with tri-sodium orthophosphate. Prune plums and cherries only in June–August. Try biological control with trichoderma pellets.
SMOULDER	Narcissi.	Leaves develop grey velvety mould and rot, and bulbs decay – the result of a fungal disease. More severe in a cold, wet season.	Foliage symptoms in the spring; bulbs during storage.	Destroy infected bulbs and store remainder in a cool, dry place. Remove and burn affected plants during the growing season as soon as symptoms are seen. Spray the rest with mancozeb at 10 day intervals.
SMUTS	Herbaceous perennials, bulbs, corms, tubers, onions, sweetcorn.	Blister-like swellings form on leaves and stalks, then burst to discharge masses of sooty spores. Caused by a fungal disease. Looks similar to SOOTY MOULD.	Long hot summers.	Burn diseased plants and plant new ones on a different site. Protect healthy plants by spraying with Bordeaux mixture or bupirimate & triforine. Disinfect coldframes or greenhouse.
SNOW MOULD	Grass.	Most obvious after a snow thaw or during moist weather when patches of turf turn brown and die, and are covered with a white, cotton-like growth of fungus.	Any time, but most severe in October.	Treat as for RED THREAD. After August, apply an autumn lawn fertiliser only, which is low in nitrogen but high in phosphate and potash.
SOFT ROT	Root vegetables and stored roots.	A bacterial disease which reduces plants to a soft, slimy and foul-smelling rot. The disease enters the plant through damaged tissues.	Any time.	Destroy infected plants and vegetables. Improve your cultural methods and storage conditions.
SOOTY MOULD	Very wide range of plants, both outdoors and under glass.	Dark brown or black sooty fungus appears on the top side of the leaves. It is always associated with sap-feeding insects such as aphids, adelgids, scale insects, whiteflies and mealy bugs.	Throughout the year.	Wipe off the mould with a damp cloth, then apply a systemic insecticide, such as heptenophos & permethrin, to control the pest that is feeding on the plant.
SPLITTING See CRACKING				
SPUR BLIGHT	Raspberries and loganberries.	Canes develop purple to silver blotches, spotted with black, caused by a fungal disease. The spores spread the disease to healthy plants.	Spring and summer.	After fruiting, cut out and destroy infected canes. When new canes are a few centimetres high, spray with carbendozim or bupirimate & triforine, and repeat 3 or 4 times at fortnightly intervals.

PROBLEM	PLANTS AT RISK	RECOGNITION	DANGER PERIOD	TREATMENT
STEM CANKER	Conifers.	The red fruiting bodies of a fungal disease appear on dead bark. The fungus enters through wounds caused by frost, damage or injury to cause DIE-BACK of shoots.	After frost.	Cut out all infected shoots right back to healthy wood.
STEM ROT	Tomatoes, godetias, lobelias and carnations, each of which is affected by a different disease.	Rotting of stems – but no obvious fungal growth – is visible on the affected areas.	Growing season.	Where possible, cut out and burn all diseased tissue, and spray plants with carbendazim. Alternatively, destroy diseased plants.
STONY PIT VIRUS	Old pear trees.	Fruit pitted and deformed, with patches of dead, stony cells in the flesh making it inedible. The virus appears first on one branch and then over the years spreads throughout the whole tree until all the fruit is affected.	Any time.	Cut down and burn diseased trees.
STRAWBERRY VIRUS DISEASES	Strawberries.	Virus diseases that are spread by aphids are ARABIS MOSAIC VIRUS and CRINKLE.	Any time.	Control the aphids (see p. 824). Destroy all diseased plants and replenish the stock with certified virus-free plants.
TAR SPOT	Acers, especially sycamores.	Fruiting bodies of fungi appear as yellow patches on the upper surface of leaves, developing into large black blotches, or red-brown to yellowish blotches.	When the tree is in leaf.	Burn diseased leaves as they fall. Spray small trees in spring, when the leaves unfold, with copper-containing fungicide or bupirimate & triforine. **Organic advice** The effect of the disease is mainly on appearance. No treatment is needed other than for cosmetic reasons.
TOBACCO MOSAIC VIRUS	Primarily tomatoes, but also some cacti, orchids and herbaceous species.	Various strains produce varied symptoms – dark and light green mottling on the leaves; bright yellow spots and patches on leaves and fruit stalks; and fruits blotched with brown.	Growing season.	None. Burn all diseased plants and their roots, including debris in the soil. Eradicate greenhouse pests. Sow only tomato seeds that are certified to be free of virus infection.
TOMATO SPOTTED WILT VIRUS	Tomatoes under glass, houseplants and herbaceous species outdoors.	A mosaic or mottling of the foliage, which may be distorted, due to a virus transmitted by thrips.	Growing season.	Destroy all infected plants and control thrips (see p. 836).

PROBLEM	PLANTS AT RISK	RECOGNITION	DANGER PERIOD	TREATMENT
TOMATO VIRUS DISEASES See ARABIS MOSAIC VIRUS, CUCUMBER MOSAIC VIRUS, TOBACCO MOSAIC VIRUS, TOMATO SPOTTED WILT VIRUS				
TREE RUST 	Mainly birch, plum, poplar and willow.	Masses of brown, orange or yellow spores, caused by fungi developing on the underside of leaves and stems. Serious outbreaks can kill plants.	Summer.	Destroy severely infected plants. Remove affected leaves on mild outbreaks and spray with propiconazole, bupirimate & triforine, or mancozeb when symptoms are first seen. Encourage vigorous growth by good cultural treatment.
TULIP FIRE 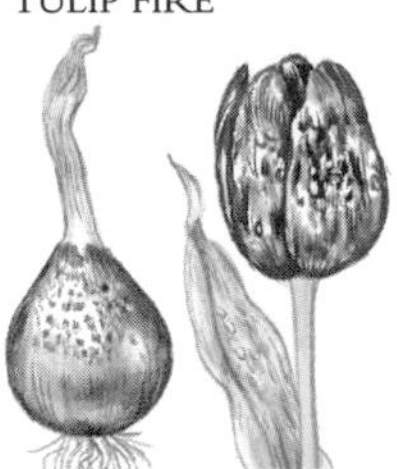	Tulips.	Small brown spots on the petals, which later become covered in GREY MOULD. Caused by a fungal disease. Bulbs rot and bear small black fungal growths.	Flowering time – particularly in cold wet weather; bulbs shortly before or after planting.	Destroy all diseased plants and rotting or fungus-bearing bulbs. If possible, choose a fresh site each year, especially after the disease has appeared. Spray with carbendazim or mancozeb when leaves are about 5 cm (2 in) high and repeat at 10 day intervals until flowering.
VERTICILLIUM WILT 	Cotinus, rhus and acer, tomatoes and carnations in greenhouses, Michaelmas daisies.	The leaves of one or two shoots wilt, and affected branches eventually die back. The disease is caused by a soil-borne fungus entering wounds. On tomatoes all leaves wilt, but recover overnight.	Growing season.	On trees and shrubs cut back affected branches to living tissue. If trouble recurs, lift and burn the plant. Destroy diseased greenhouse plants, and sterilise the greenhouse at the end of the season. Take tip cuttings of diseased Michaelmas daisies, and burn old plants. Carbendazim gives some control.
VIOLET ROOT ROT 	Primarily carrots, parsnips and asparagus, but also some ornamentals and fruit crops.	Leaves turn yellow and die as purple-violet threads of fungus attack the roots.	Growing season.	Lift and burn diseased plants. Isolate the infected area by sinking pieces of rigid polythene or corrugated iron 30 cm (12 in) deep for the rest of the life of the bed. Avoid growing vulnerable plants there for several years. **Organic advice** Avoid planting crops in wet, acid soils.

• VIRUS DISEASES •

Viruses are microscopic particles, capable of causing disease in living cells, and can enter plant tissues only through wounds.

Viruses may be transmitted to other plants through the air, soil, fungi, seeds, vegetative grafting, propagation and by handling. Most viruses, however, are spread by insects, such as aphids, eelworms, leafhoppers, mites, thrips and whiteflies. Symptoms of a virus disease vary. There may be colour variation in the leaves, stems, flowers and tubers, or there may be plant distortion, wilting, stunted growth and tissue decay.

A plant may suffer from one or many viruses, with a different combination of viruses producing a number of different symptoms.

There is no chemical treatment for virus-infected plants, and any that are severely diseased should be destroyed. Use only healthy plants for propagation and where possible buy only new stock certified as being free of viruses. Good garden hygiene and the control of the insects that carry the viruses both help to prevent virus diseases from entering the garden.

PROBLEM	PLANTS AT RISK	RECOGNITION	DANGER PERIOD	TREATMENT
WART DISEASE 	Potatoes.	Developing tubers produce large warty outgrowths, and subsequently disintegrate, due to a soil-borne fungus.	Growing season.	This is a Notifiable Disease and must be reported to the local plant health inspector or the Ministry of Agriculture, Fisheries and Food. All new potato varieties are immune to the disease, but some older ones are not. All diseased potatoes must be destroyed.

PROBLEM	PLANTS AT RISK	RECOGNITION	DANGER PERIOD	TREATMENT
WHIPTAIL	Broccoli and cauliflowers.	Leaves become distorted – ruffled, thin and strap-like – due to a lack of molybdenum.	During the growing period in acid soils.	Water with a solution of molybdate – 1 rounded tablespoon in 9 litres (2 gallons) of water for every 8 m² (10 sq yd) of soil. **Organic advice** As molybdenum is not available to plants on acid soils, lime the soil, if necessary, to bring pH to 6.5.
WHITE BLISTER	Brassicas and related ornamental plants, including honesty (lunaria).	Leaves and stems develop white glistening pustules filled with powdery spores. The disease is caused by a fungus. Severely affected foliage may be very distorted.	Growing season.	Remove and burn all diseased leaves and stems from the plant.
WHITE ROT	Mainly salad onions, and occasionally leeks, shallots and garlic.	Bulbs develop a white fungus at their base and rot.	Growing season.	Burn the affected plants. Grow onions on a new site each year – once the disease has struck, the soil remains contaminated for up to 20 years. No chemical treatment is available to amateur gardeners.
WHITE RUST	Dendranthemas (chrysanthemums).	The upper leaf surface develops yellow to pale green spots. The underside has buff or white spots. The spots may turn brown and die in the centre.	Growing season.	A Notifiable Disease which must be reported to the local plant health inspector or the Ministry of Agriculture, Fisheries and Food. Destroy diseased plants immediately.
WINTER KILLING	Mainly wallflowers.	Sideshoots either die back or the plant dies. Caused by FROST DAMAGE and GREY MOULD.	Late winter to late spring.	Set out plants early so that they are fully established before winter and carry out good cultivation.
WIRE STEM	Brassicas and other seedlings.	The base of the stems turns brown and shrinks, and easily breaks. Seedlings die or become stunted, both due to a fungal disease.	During early growth.	Destroy diseased plants. Raise seedlings in sterilised compost.
WITCHES' BROOMS	Prunus species and birches.	Clusters of erect shoots, growing abnormally from a single point, on infected branches. The condition is caused by a fungal disease.	Throughout the life of the tree.	Cut off the affected branch to a point 15 cm (6 in) below the broom.

Glossary

Technical terms have been avoided wherever possible in this book, but sometimes they are unavoidable. The following definitions will make them clear

a

ALPINE
Strictly speaking, any plant that is native to mountainous regions, growing between the tree line and permanent snow line. 'Alpine' is also loosely applied to any small plant suitable for growing in a rock garden.

ALPINE HOUSE
A greenhouse that has continuous ventilation along the eaves, vents at bench level and, ideally, a door at each end. No heat is necessary; however, as alpine plants dislike cold wet conditions, some growers maintain their alpine houses at 1°C (34°F).

ANNUAL
A plant that completes its life cycle in a single growing season – from seed to flowering, to setting seed and dying.

b

BASAL LEAVES
Leaves arising directly from the crown of a plant or on a very short stem.

BIENNIAL
A plant which takes two seasons to complete its life cycle – for example, the foxglove. In year one it forms leaves; in year two it forms flowers and seeds, then dies.

BRACT
A modified leaf which is sometimes brightly coloured and conspicuous to attract pollinating insects, such as the scarlet bracts of poinsettia *(Euphorbia pulcherrima)*.

BULB FRAME
A coldframe in which bulbs in pots can be plunged in sand, soil or gravel for winter to protect them from frost. A bulb frame can be used instead of an alpine house.

c

CAPSULE
The dry or nearly dry fruit containing loose seeds. When the capsule is ripe the seeds may be shaken out by the action of the wind or passing animals, or it may split, forcibly ejecting the seeds.

CATKIN see FLOWER FORMATIONS, p. 861

CHITTING
Sprouting tubers, particularly potatoes and dahlias, before planting. Also applied to seeds germinated before sowing.

CHLOROSIS
The loss or insufficiency of chlorophyll – the green pigment in the cells of leaves and young stems. The lack of chlorophyll causes the leaves to appear bleached or yellowish. Chlorosis is usually due to mineral deficiency, but viruses may be a cause.

CLOCHE
Sheets of clear glass, rigid plastic or plastic film that are used for raising early crops in open ground, and for protecting plants from bad weather – alpines, for example.

CLONE
A group of identical plants raised from a single parent plant by cuttings or division rather than by seed.

COMPOST
A mixture of loam, sand, peat, leaf-mould or other materials used for growing plants in containers. The term also refers to organic material obtained by stacking plant remains such as vegetable trimmings, straw and grass mowings until they decompose.

COMPOUND
Leaves, flowers or fruits having two or more similar units.

CONIFER
Tree or shrub, usually evergreen and having linear or needle-like leaves, and which usually bears its seeds in cones.

COPPICING
The cutting back of trees and shrubs close to the ground, often annually, to produce vigorous young shoots. In gardens it is usually done for decorative purposes – to encourage brightly coloured stems or the formation of large leaves.

CORM
The underground storage organ of some plants, including crocuses and gladioli. Similar to a bulb, it consists of a swollen stem with a bud at the top which produces shoots and a new corm.

COROLLA see FLOWER

CORONA
The trumpet or cup-like flower part of such genera as *Narcissus* and *Hymenocallis*.

CORYMB see FLOWER FORMATIONS, p. 861

COTYLEDON
The first leaf or pair of leaves to appear when a seed germinates. They are also called seed leaves because they are formed within the seed. In some cases, such as the broad bean, the seed leaves remain underground – the first shoot to appear bears the true leaves. Seed leaves frequently differ in shape from true or adult leaves.

CROWN
The part of an herbaceous perennial at soil level from which roots and shoots grow.

CULTIVAR
Cultivated variety: a variant of a plant produced in cultivation as opposed to one that occurs in the wild (see also GENUS).

CUTTINGS see p. 816

CYME see FLOWER FORMATIONS, p. 861

d

DAMPING DOWN
Watering the floor and benches of a greenhouse to create a humid atmosphere.

DEADHEADING
Nipping off dead or faded flowerheads from a plant to prevent seeding and to encourage new flowers. Roses and many bedding plants need regular deadheading.

DICOTYLEDON
All flowering plants are botanically classified into two main groups by the number of cotyledons (seed leaves) present in the seed at maturity. Monocotyledons have one seed leaf, dicotyledons have two.

DIOECIOUS
Plants having male and female flowers on separate plants, such as willow and holly.

DISC
The flattened or domed centre of a daisy flower, composed of tiny tubular florets.

DOT PLANT
An isolated or specimen plant – usually tall – in a formal flowerbed, selected to emphasise contrast in height, colour and texture.

DRILL
A straight, usually narrow, furrow in which seeds are sown outdoors.

e

EPIPHYTE
A plant, such as an orchid or bromeliad, which has adapted to living above the soil, adhering to tree branches or rocks.

ERICACEOUS
A term used for plants that grow best in acid soil, such as ericas (heather). Also used to refer to lime-free compost used for growing ericaceous plants.

ETIOLATED
Growth which has become long, thin and pallid because of lack of light or as a result of blanching – as in forcing rhubarb.

EYE
Immature growth bud, such as the eyes of potato or dahlia tubers. The term is also used to describe the centre of a flower if it is different in colour from the petals.

f

F$_1$ HYBRID
Seeds obtained by crossing two pure bred closely related varieties which have been inbred for several generations. The plants produced tend to have an increased level of vigour and uniformity.

FASTIGIATE
Erect habit of growth developed by some trees and shrubs, such as Lombardy poplars.

FEATHERED
Lateral shoots on the main stem of a young tree. They are left on the tree until the trunk is fully established – about a year or two – when they must be removed.

FERTILISERS see p. 804

FLORET
A small individual flower which is part of a large head or cluster.

FLOWER
The part of a plant concerned with sexual reproduction. The essential parts are the female ovaries (or carpels), which eventually bear the seeds, and the anthers which produce pollen, the male sex cells. The carpels and anthers are usually surrounded by an inner ring of coloured leaves, known as petals, and an outer ring of protecting sepals, usually green. There are, however, a great many variations to this basic pattern. The great majority of plants bear flowers with both male and female organs (monoecious), but others have single-sex flowers on separate plants (dioecious).

Petals and sepals are usually clearly differentiated in shape, size and colour, but sometimes – with the tulip, for example, they are similar. Petals and sepals may be separate, as in buttercups, or fused, as in primroses or convolvulus. They may both be absent, as in hazel or poplar, or the petals may be missing (pachysandra and parrotia).

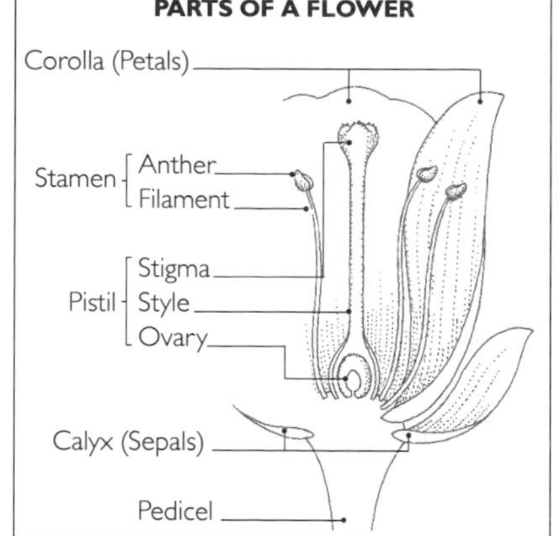

FRUITING BODY
The reproductive organ of a fungus, such as a mushroom or toadstool. Also the pin-head-like growth on bread mould.

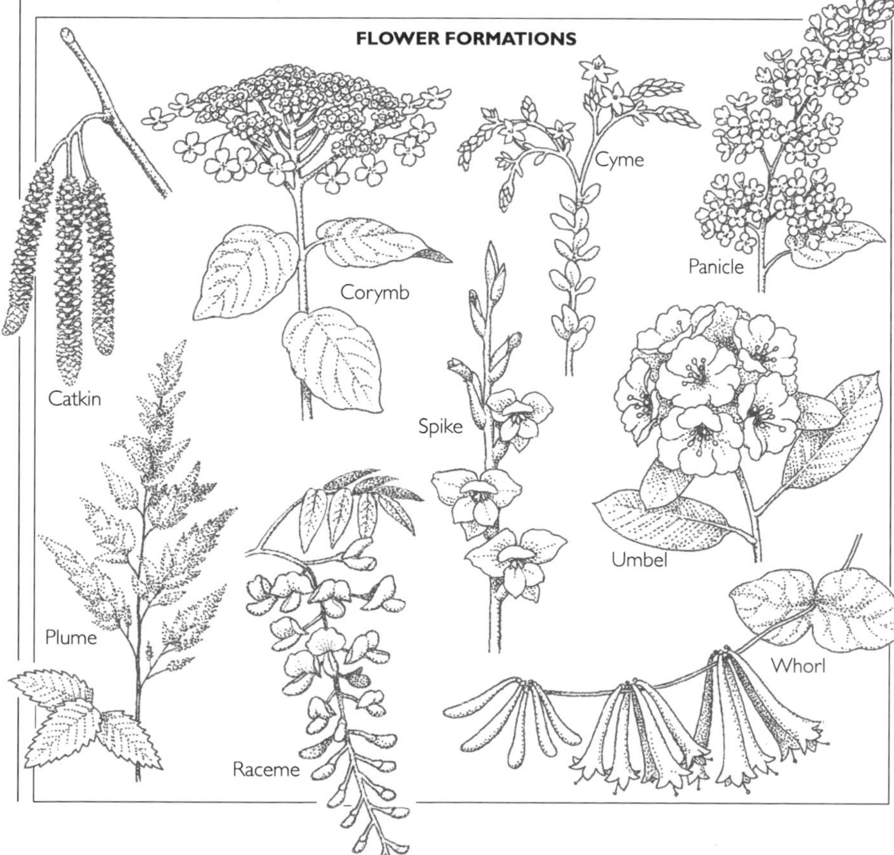

FUMIGATE
A system of destroying pests and diseases in a greenhouse or coldframe with poisonous fumes. Canisters or pellets are ignited to produce a dense smoke.

g

GENUS (plural: genera)
The category in botanical classification below family. A genus is a group of closely related plants known as species. All the species of beech trees, for example, are grouped under the genus *Fagus*. Related genera are grouped in turn into a family, in this case Fagaceae. The common beech is identified by a genus and a species name, *Fagus sylvatica*. A natural variety is identified by a third name in italics, such as *Fagus sylvatica* var. *heterophylla*, and a cultivated variety (or cultivar) by quotation marks, as *Fagus sylvatica* 'Dawyck'. A cross (or hybrid) between two species is identified by a multiplication sign: for example, the hybrid willow *Salix* × *rubens*.

GERMINATION
The initial stage of a plant's development from a seed. Germination periods vary: given the right conditions of temperature, moisture, light and oxygen, it may occur within days or take many weeks or months.

GLABROUS
Smooth or bare – used to describe a part of a plant that is hairless.

GLAUCOUS
Describing the grey-blue colour of some plants, or the grey or white waxy bloom on them. An example is the white bloom on the leaves of some brassicas, particularly cabbages, and succulents such as sedums.

GRAFTING
Propagating plants by joining a stem or bud of one plant to the root of another so they unite to form a new individual. It is widely used in cultivating fruit trees and roses.

h

HABIT
The characteristic shape and growth form of a plant.

HALF-HARDY
Frost-tender species of plants that can only be grown in the open reliably during summer – for example, canna and French and African marigolds. See also TENDER.

HALF-STANDARD
A tree or shrub, usually with a single stem growing 75 cm–1.2 m (2½–4 ft) high before the head branches.

HARDENING OFF
The gradual acclimatisation of tender and half-hardy plants, grown under heated glass or other forms of protection, to outside conditions. Plants are usually placed in a coldframe in late spring, with air gradually admitted until the lights of the frame are left off entirely.

HARDY
Plants which survive frosts in the open, year by year, anywhere in Great Britain.

HERBACEOUS
Any plant that does not form a persistent woody stem. Botanically, the term applies to annuals, biennials and perennials – but by common usage is chiefly associated with perennials which die down in autumn and reappear the following spring.

HOSE-IN-HOSE
An abnormal floral mutation in which flowers appear to grow in pairs, one arising from the centre of another. Primrose and polyanthus are examples.

HUMUS
The dark brown residue from the final breakdown of dead vegetable matter. The term is often used to describe partly decayed matter that is brown and crumbly, such as well-made compost or leaf-mould.

HYBRID
The result of crossing two distinct varieties or, occasionally, genera. Hybrids may either show a blending of characteristics from each parent or favour one more than the other.

INCISED
The margins of a leaf, stipule or bract that is deeply and sharply toothed or lobed.

INFLORESCENCE
The arrangement of flowers on a stem, often referred to as a flowerhead.

INORGANIC
A chemical compound or fertiliser that does not contain carbon. The term is applied to synthetically produced fertilisers, although some naturally occurring plant nutrients have inorganic origins, as, for example, the mineral fertiliser rock phosphate.

JOINT see NODE

JUVENILE
Plants which have a distinct early phase, when either the habit, leaf shape or some other characteristic differs from those of the adult. Eucalyptus trees commonly bear juvenile and adult leaves.

LATERAL
A stem or shoot that branches off from a bud in the leaf axil of a larger stem.

LEADER
The main stem (or stems) of a tree or shrub that extends the existing branch system.

LEAF see box, below

LEAF-MOULD
Partially decayed dead leaves which have broken down to a brown, flaky condition resembling peat. Oak and beech leaves are the most suitable materials.

LIME
Calcium, a chemical used in horticulture, particularly to neutralise acid soils.

LOAM
A reasonably fertile soil that is neither wet and sticky, nor dry and sandy. It is moisture-retentive and contains a blend of clay, silt, sand and humus, and is rich in minerals.

LOBE
Descriptive of leaves, stipules, bracts or petals that are cleft into separate areas that are still united by part of the surface.

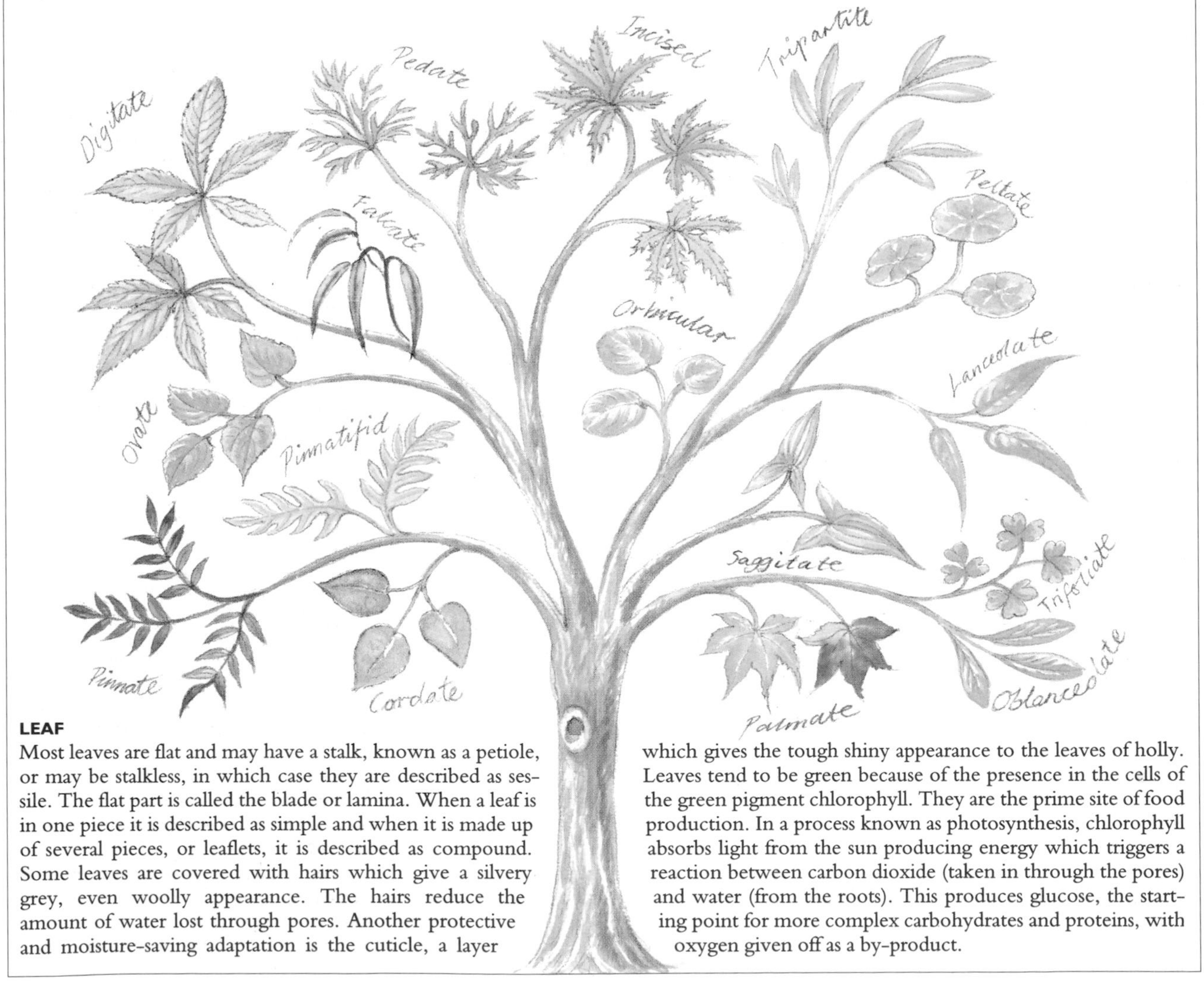

LEAF
Most leaves are flat and may have a stalk, known as a petiole, or may be stalkless, in which case they are described as sessile. The flat part is called the blade or lamina. When a leaf is in one piece it is described as simple and when it is made up of several pieces, or leaflets, it is described as compound. Some leaves are covered with hairs which give a silvery grey, even woolly appearance. The hairs reduce the amount of water lost through pores. Another protective and moisture-saving adaptation is the cuticle, a layer which gives the tough shiny appearance to the leaves of holly. Leaves tend to be green because of the presence in the cells of the green pigment chlorophyll. They are the prime site of food production. In a process known as photosynthesis, chlorophyll absorbs light from the sun producing energy which triggers a reaction between carbon dioxide (taken in through the pores) and water (from the roots). This produces glucose, the starting point for more complex carbohydrates and proteins, with oxygen given off as a by-product.

m

MAIDEN
A nursery term for a young grafted tree in the process of being trained. Applied particularly to one-year-old fruit trees.
MANURE see p. 804
MONOCARPIC
A plant which dies after flowering and seeding. Annuals and biennials are true monocarpic plants, but the term is also applied to perennial plants which grow for a number of years before flowering and then dying.
MONOCOTYLEDON
A group of flowering plants that have only one seed leaf in each mature seed. See also COTYLEDON and DICOTYLEDON.
MONOECIOUS
A plant that bears bisexual flowers or separate male and female flowers on the same plant; for example, corylus (hazel) and juglans (walnut).
MULCH
A layer of organic matter, such as decayed manure, leaf-mould, garden compost, straw or composted bark, which is spread on the soil around plants. A mulch conserves moisture in the soil, adds nutrients and suppresses weeds. The term is also used for inorganic material including gravel and black polythene sheeting.

n

NATURALISING
Growing plants, particularly bulbs, in simulated natural environments, such as grass or woodland conditions.
NODE
A stem joint, which is sometimes slightly swollen, from where young leaves and side-shoots arise.

o

OFFSET
A young plant that arises naturally on the parent, as with many sorts of bulbs, or on short lateral stems, as with sempervivum (right).

OPPOSITE
The arrangement of leaves in alternate opposite pairs, as on ligustrum and syringa. See also LEAF.
ORGANIC
Any chemical compound containing carbon. The term is applied to substances derived from the decay of living organisms, such as garden compost. It is also applied to a style of gardening that rejects the use of synthetic chemicals and products.

p

PANICLE see FLOWER FORMATIONS
PEDICEL
The stalk of an individual flower – applied particularly to branched flowers.
PEDUNCLE
The stem that supports a flowerhead.
PERENNIAL
Any plant that lives for three or more years; usually applied to a non-woody plant.
PERIANTH
A term used when sepals and petals are indistinguishable from each other. The combined sepals and petals of a tulip or hyacinth flower are known as the perianth.
PERLITE
Lightweight expanded volcanic rock in granular form, used in place of sand or grit to open up or lighten composts used for potting or cuttings.
PETAL see FLOWER FORMATIONS, p. 861
PETIOLE
The stalk that attaches a leaf to the stem.
pH see p. 803
PINCHING OUT see STOPPING
PISTIL see PARTS OF A FLOWER, p. 861
PLUNGE
To set a pot or any other plant container up to the rim in the soil, or in a special bed of ashes, peat, grit or sand.
POLLARD
A tree cut back to the main trunk and maintained in a bushy state by regular pruning at intervals of between one and a few years.
POLLEN
The male cells of a plant contained in the anthers or pollen sacs.
POLLINATION
The transference of pollen grains onto the stigma of a flower. This may occur naturally by gravity, wind or insects, or can be done artificially by hand.
PRICKING OUT
The first planting out of seedlings or small-rooted cuttings. The resulting plantlets are later moved into larger pots, pans or trays, or set out into a nursery bed or into their growing position.
PROPAGATION see p. 814
PROVENANCE
The place where seed originated in the wild. Knowing the provenance will have a bearing on the conditions under which the progeny will thrive in cultivation.

r

RACEME see FLOWER FORMATIONS, p. 861
RADICAL
Usually used to describe the basal leaves of biennials or perennials. The leaves arise at the base of the plant or near to soil level.
RAY FLORET
Small flower with long strap-shaped petals. Typical of the daisy family where a ring of ray florets surrounds the central boss of disc florets to form the flowerhead.
REMONTANT
Flowering at intervals throughout the growing season, as in repeat-flowering roses.
RESTING PERIOD
The period when a plant is either dormant or making little or no extension growth.
RHIZOME
A horizontal, creeping underground stem, which acts as a storage organ.
ROOTSTOCK
A propagation term for a plant upon which another is grafted. The term also applies to the crown and root system of herbaceous perennials and suckering shrubs.
ROSETTE
Ring of leaves that all arise at more or less the same point on the stem, often basal.
RUNNER Prostrate stems, such as those produced by strawberry plants, which root at the nodes to form new plantlets.

s

SAND PLUNGE see PLUNGE
SCION
A shoot, part of a shoot, or bud of one plant that is joined to a rootstock of another as a propagation technique. Scions and rootstocks are the means of propagating fruit trees by grafting, and roses by budding.
SCREE
A heap or a slope of rocky detritus eroded from mountainsides or cliffs. Since some types of plants require these conditions in a garden, a scree bed can be created by mixing coarse gravel or stone chippings with soil.
SELECTION
A particular variation of an existing variety or species that is selected for its desirable characteristics. It is always raised from seed. Also incorrectly referred to as a 'strain'.
SELF-COLOURED
A flower having a single uniform colour.
SELF-FERTILE
A plant, particularly a fruit tree, that does not need pollen from another plant to set seed and produce fruit.
SELF-STERILE
Fruit trees, especially sweet cherries, that need pollen from another plant to set fruit.
SEPAL see FLOWER
SERIES
A selection or colour mixture of a plant variety (usually an annual, bedding plant or vegetable variety) raised from seed. A particular named series or mixture raised by two or more seedsmen may vary slightly.
SERRATED
The sharply cut indentations in the margin of a leaf – like the teeth of a saw.
SESSILE
Stalkless – a leaf or flower that arises straight from the stem.
SHRUB
A branched perennial plant with persistent woody stems.

SPADIX
A fleshy flower spike with small flowers embedded in shallow pits. It is primarily found in members of the Araceae, or aroid family, such as anthurium and zantedeschia, where it is surrounded and protected by a white or coloured bract called a spathe. In some cases, the spadix terminates in a naked club or spindle-shaped organ which may heat up, giving off a fetid smell that attracts pollinating insects.

SPATHE
A modified leaf or large bract, sometimes coloured, which surrounds the flower spike (spadix) in members of the Araceae, or aroid family.

SPECIES
A unit of classification applied to an individual, or a group of closely allied plants, within a genus. Species have unique characters, which consistently breed true to type from seed. The type species refers to the original plant collected and described.

SPECIMEN PLANT
Any plant, but usually a tree or shrub, which is grown where it can be viewed from all angles, as when planted in a lawn.

SPHAGNUM (MOSS)
The generic name for bog mosses. They have unique water-holding, aerating and cleansing properties, and are frequently used as a growing medium for orchids.

SPIKE see FLOWER FORMATIONS, p. 861

SPIT
The depth to which soil is dug with a spade or a fork – about 25-30 cm (10-12 in).

SPORE
A minute dust-like body composed of a single cell, by which lower plants – such as ferns, fungi and mosses – reproduce. A spore gives rise to an intermediate generation upon which the sex organs appear and which eventually produce plantlets.

SPUR
1: A short lateral branchlet of a tree – particularly on apple and pear trees – which bears flower buds.
2: A tubular outgrowth of a sepal or petal that produces nectar.

STAMEN see FLOWER

STAMINODE
A non-functional, rudimentary male reproductive organ, sometimes similar to a narrow petal, as in pulsatillas.

STERILE
Plants that rarely or never set seed. Many double-flowered varieties are sterile, as the reproductive organs have become petals.

STIPULE
One of the pair of leaf-like outgrowths at the base of a leaf-stalk, for example, as in rose and potentilla.

STOLON
A stem which, on contact with moist soil, roots at the tip and forms a new plant – for example, the cane of a blackberry. The term is sometimes incorrectly used to mean RUNNER.

STOOL
Often describing a tree or shrub which is maintained as a clump of young stems by annual pruning close to ground level. Stooling is carried out to provide young growth for propagation purposes, or to maintain a foliage effect, such as the juvenile state of some eucalyptus. Also called 'coppicing'. The term also applies to crowns and rootstock of some herbaceous plants – dendranthema (chrysanthemum), for example.

STOPPING
Removing or pinching out the growing point of a stem, either to promote a branching habit or to induce flower buds.

STRAIN see SELECTION

STRATIFICATION
A method of breaking the dormancy of seeds born in fleshy fruits of many hardy plants. The seeds are exposed to a period of low temperature prior to sowing.

SUB-ALPINE
A plant native to mountain regions just below the alpine zone.

SUB-SHRUB
A low-growing shrub, or one with soft stems and a woody base, such as argyranthemums and many pelargoniums.

SUCCULENT
Plants with thick fleshy leaves or stems adapted to life under arid conditions. Cacti, with leafless stems swollen with water storage tissue, are examples.

SUCKER
A shoot which arises from below ground, usually from the roots of a plant.

SYNONYM
An alternative name for a plant. Sometimes a plant has been named by more than one botanist or has been reclassified in the light of further knowledge. In such cases, the oldest or most taxonomically accurate name takes priority.

t

TAP ROOT
The main anchoring root of a plant, particularly applied to trees.

TENDER
A term to describe any plant vulnerable to frost damage. See also HALF-HARDY.

TENDRIL
A modified stem or leaf that twines around supports, enabling certain plants, such as sweet peas, grapes, hops and passionflowers, to climb.

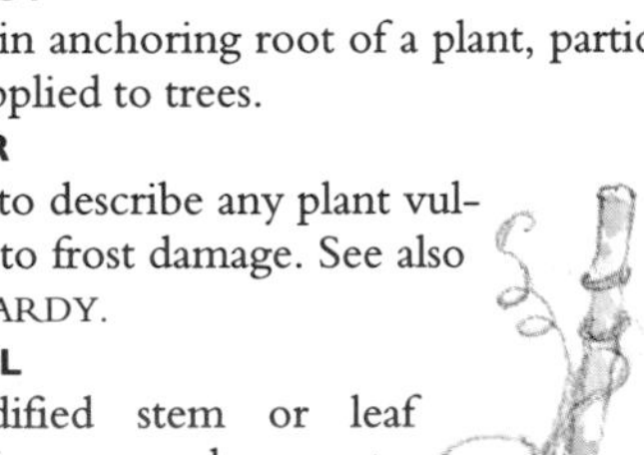

TEPAL
A term used to describe petals and sepals where they are indistinguishable, as in lilies and tulips.

TERNATE
In groups of three. Trillium has leaves and floral organs in groups of three, and laburnum leaves have three leaflets.

TERRESTRIAL
Used in reference to plants, such as some bromeliads and orchids which are primarily epiphytic, that have become adapted to living in the soil.

TESSELLATED
A term that describes petals which have a distinct chequered pattern of a contrasting shade or colour – as, for example, *Fritillaria meleagris*.

TOOTHED
Teeth-like indentations, usually along the margins of leaves, also described as dentate. See also SERRATED.

TRUSS
A popular term used to describe a cluster of flowers or fruits.

TUBER
A thickened fleshy root, as on a dahlia, or an underground stem, such as a potato, which serves as a storage organ, and as a means of surviving periods of cold or drought.

TUFA
Soft limestone which, because of its ability to absorb and retain moisture, is often used in rock gardens or troughs, where small alpine plants are able to grow on it.

TUFT
Bristly, sometimes mat-like, habit of growth, found particularly in alpine plants.

u

UNDERPLANT
To surround and interplant larger plants with smaller ones.

UNDULATE
Leaf, sepal or petal margins that are waved or crimped.

v

VARIEGATED
Leaves – and sometimes petals – that are marked, spotted or otherwise decoratively patterned with a contrasting colour, most commonly cream or gold.

VEGETATIVE
Propagation by cuttings, division, layering or grafting, as distinct from propagation with seeds.

w

WEEPING
Applied to a tree or shrub of pendulous habit, either natural, as in some species of salix, or artificially induced, as in weeping standard roses.

WHORL see FLOWER FORMATIONS, p. 861

Acknowledgments

Production credits

BOOK PRODUCTION MANAGER
Chris Reynolds

ASSISTANT BOOK PRODUCTION MANAGER
Tony Ashe

ASSISTANT BOOK PRODUCTION CONTROLLER
Dean Russell

PRE-PRESS PRODUCTION MANAGER
Martin Hendrick

PRE-PRESS SUPPORT
Jim Lindsay, Howard Reynolds, Tony Rilett

Picture Credits

Below is a list of the images used in *New Encyclopedia of Garden Plants & Flowers* supplied by photograph libraries and specialist sources. Some abbreviations have been used: GPL = The Garden Picture Library, HSC = The Harry Smith Collection and PHPL = Photos Horticultural Picture Library. B = Bottom. T = Top. C = Centre. L = Left. R = Right. Where given, the names of gardens and designers are shown in brackets.

21 BR PHPL. 27 BC HSC. 28 BL GPL/John Glover. 32 CL PHPL, BL GPL/Geoff Dann. 32-33 B GPL/Steven Wooster. 33 TR GPL/Alan Bedding. 38 BR GPL/Mel Watson. 43 C GPL/Christopher Fairweather. 47 C PHPL. 51 BL GPL/Jerry Pavia, BC GPL/Clive Boursnell. 53 BR GPL/John Glover. 55 C PHPL. 61 BR GPL/Densey Clyne. 76 C GPL/Morley Read, BL John Glover, BR David Crampton, Drysdale Garden Exotics, Fordingbridge. 77 TL PHPL/MJK, C PHPL, BL GPL/Brigitte Thomas, BC PHPL. 78 CR GPL/Brian Carter (Trebah Gardens, Cornwall), BR Beckett Picture Library. 79 TL HSC, TR David Crampton, Drysdale Garden Exotics, Fordingbridge, C BC PHPL, BL Beckett Picture Library, BR David Crampton, Drysdale Garden Exotics, Fordingbridge. 84 BL Jerry Harpur/RHS Garden Wisley. 84-85 T John Glover, B Photon Photo Library. 85 TR John Glover (Nash's Garden, Shrops), BR GPL/Howard Rice (Clare College, Cambs). 86 TL Jerry Harpur/CG Carey-Parker, BL Clive Nichols (Designer: Jill Billington). 86-87 T Jerry Harpur/Peter Ottaway, B Clive Nichols/Graham Strong. 87 BL Clive Nichols (Keukenhof Gardens, Holland). 92 TC PHPL. 96 BR GPL/Marianne Majerus. 100 TR GPL/John Glover. 104 CR GPL/Chris Burrows. 106 TC T.M. Hewitt, Holly Gate Nursery, Ashington, BL Eric Crichton. 109 TR BR HSC, C CL Beckett Picture Library, BL T.M. Hewitt, Holly Gate Nursery, Ashington. 110 TC Pat Brindley, BL Plant Portraits Worldwide. 113 TC HSC. 125 TR John Glover. 150 TR HSC. 162 BL GPL/Howard Rice, BR Eric Crichton. 162-3 T John Glover. 163 T Eric Crichton, B John Glover. 164 BR(inset) Ardea, London/Bob Gibbons, BR NHPA/David Woodfall. 165 BL PHPL. 166 CR BR HSC. 181 CR GPL/Howard Rice. 182 C GPL/JS Sira, BC GPL/John Glover. 189 TC GPL/John Glover. 192 BL HSC. 207 TL GPL/Juliette Wade. 210 ('Heide') GPL/Chris Burrows, BR GPL/John Glover. 211 ('Yellow Heide') GPL/Chris Burrows. 224 TL GPL/Brigitte Thomas. 226 BL PHPL. 227 TR Beckett Picture Library. 238 TR BL PHPL. 262 BL Clive Nichols (Spinner Nursery, Hampshire). 263 TL GPL/Howard Rice, TC Beckett Picture Library. 264 TR PHPL. 265 CL Andrew Lawson, BR Clive Nichols (Designer: J. Billington). 267 BR HSC. 269 CL, 271 BL, 280 BR PHPL. 286 TC GPL/Kathy Charlton, BC PHPL. 289 TC GPL/Henk Dijkman. 292 CL GPL/Neil Holmes. 294 TR GPL/Neil Holmes, CL GPL/Brian Carter, BL GPL/Paul Windsor. 295 T B GPL/John Glover. 299 TL GPL/Howard Rice. 300 TR GPL/David Russell, BL Sheila & Oliver Mathews, BR PHPL. 301 CL GPL/David Askham, C (*Hordeum*) Andrew Lawson, CR HSC, BR Eric Crichton. 302 TL Andrew Lawson, BR A-Z Botanical Collection. 303 CR GPL/Sunniva Harte, BR Jonathan Buckley. 306 TR GPL/Jerry Pavia, CL GPL/Ron Sutherland, BL GPL/JS Sira. 306-7 B Eric Crichton, T GPL/John Miller. 310 TR Holt Studios Ltd/Bob Gibbons, CL GPL/Neil Holmes, BL John Glover. 310-11 Eric Crichton. 311 T B John Glover. 318 CL Sheila & Oliver Mathews, BL Clive Nichols (Stourton House, Wiltshire). 318-19 T GPL/Didier Willery, B GPL/Densey Clyne. 319 TR Clive Nichols (Designer: Jill Billington). 330 BR Jerry Harpur. 337 C HSC. 341 BR Biofotos/Heather Angel. 342 C GPL/Lamontagne, B GPL/Lynne Brotchie. 342-3 T Eric Crichton, B GPL/Steven Wooster. 343 T GPL/JS Sira, B Eric Crichton. 344 T GPL/Zara McCalmont, B Elizabeth Whiting/Dennis Stone. 345 T Arcaid/Richard Bryant (Designer: David Falla), B Eric Crichton. 346 CR PHPL. 347 CL HSC. 353 TR GPL/Chris Burrows, C GPL/David Russell. 362 L Beckett Picture Library. 363 BC HSC. 374 BL PHPL. 377 BL GPL/Sunniva Harte. 382 BL GPL/David Russell. 383 TL GPL/John Glover. 386 BC PHPL. 387 CL John Sutton. 390-1 T Jerry Harpur (Designer: Christopher Masson), B John Glover (Nash's Garden, Shrops). 391 TR Holt Studios Ltd/Nigel Cattlin, CR Eric Crichton. 392 BR HSC. 393 BR PHPL. 398-9 Sheila & Oliver Mathews. 403 TL GPL/Howard Rice. 408 BR NHPA/Anthony Bannister. 410 BR PHPL. 414 R Beckett Picture Library. 419 TR PHPL. 420 T GPL/John Glover. 424 TL GPL/Howard Rice. 428 T PHPL. 429 C Bruce Coleman Ltd/Eckart Pott, BR PHPL. 430 PHPL. 431 L GPL/Jerry Pavia. 433 TL Beckett Picture Library, BC GPL/Howard Rice, BR Ardea, London/John Mason. 434 C Eric Crichton. 439 BC GPL/Howard Rice. 444 TL PHPL. 451 BL GPL/Howard Rice, BL (*Nemophila menziesii*) GPL/Marijke Heuff. 452 BC GPL/Philippe Bonduel. 454 L NHPA, C PHPL. 455 TL, 460 CL, 461 L, 463 TC, C PHPL. 464 TR PHPL. 465 TC HSC, C John Glover, BR Eric Crichton. 466 TL TC CL Eric Crichton, CR PHPL, BR HSC. 467 TL Beckett Picture Library, TR John Glover, C PHPL, BL Ardea, London/Ian Beames, BR PHPL. 491 CR, 494 L, 495 TC, 496 BR PHPL. 497 C HSC. 504 CR PHPL. 511 L Plant Portraits Worldwide, C HSC. 520 TR Eric Crichton. 540 BR Plant Portraits Worldwide. 542 L PHPL. 552-3 GPL/Lamontagne. 555 BL GPL/Lamontagne. 558 TC GPL/Brian Carter, CR GPL/David Askham. 559 BR GPL/Christopher Fairweather. 560 BR GPL/Michael Howes. 561 TC GPL/Lamontagne, BC GPL/Christopher Fairweather. 562 TL GPL/Brian Carter. 565 TL GPL/Christopher Fairweather, TC GPL/John Glover, BC GPL/Brian Carter. 566 TC GPL/Brian Carter, CL GPL/John Glover, BL GPL/Clive Boursnell. 572 BL Eric Crichton. 572-3 T Eric Crichton, B John Glover. 573 T Jerry Harpur (Home Farm, Royle), B Eric Crichton. 575, 580 B, 583 TL BR, 585 BR, 586 CR, 587 BL Michael Gibson. 589 BR David Austin Roses Limited. 590 TC David Austin Roses Limited, TR BL BR Michael Gibson. 591 L BR David Austin Roses Limited. 600 Michael Gibson. 606 L PHPL. 614 BC GPL/John Glover. 619 BL, 627 BC PHPL. 630 C GPL/Kathy Charlton. 632 BC PHPL. 636 L HSC. 638 TR Beckett Picture Library. 641 R GPL/Rex Butcher. 646 T GPL/Howard Rice. 651 R PHPL. 659 TR GPL/Philippe Bonduel. 667 TR CR PHPL. 670 T Eric Crichton, CL GPL/John Glover, BL GPL/Gary Rogers. 670-1 B GPL/Jerry Pavia. 671 T GPL/David Secombe. 673 BR GPL/Lamontagne. 676 CL Jerry Harpur (Eastgrove Cottage), BL Sheila & Oliver Mathews. 677 TC Jerry Harpur (Iden Croft), CR Jonathan Buckley. 678 Eric Crichton. 678-9 T Jonathan Buckley, B John Glover (The Anchorage, Kent). 682 BL PHPL/MJK. 684 L GPL/Rex Butcher, TR PHPL/ACM. 685 TL TR GPL/Brian Carter. 686 BL GPL/Howard Rice. 688 TC HSC. 690 TL PHPL, TC Plant Portraits Worldwide. 693 BR HSC. 694 BL GPL/John Glover, BC GPL/Brian Carter, BR GPL/Didier Willery. 695 GPL/John Glover. 702 BL GPL/Brian Carter. 704 BR PHPL. 706 B Jerry Harpur (Designer: Chris Grey-Wilson). 706-7 T PHPL, B GPL/JS Sira. 707 T Jonathan Buckley, B GPL/Ron Sutherland. 708 BL PHPL. 709 TL C PHPL, TC GPL/John Glover. 710 CL GPL/Marijke Heuff, B GPL/Steven Wooster. 710-11 HSC. 711 T Andrew Lawson, B GPL/Gary Rogers. 712 GPL/Lynne Brotchie. 712-13 Clive Nichols. 713 Andrew Lawson. 714 BL, 717 BL GPL/John Glover. 718 TR GPL/JS Sira. 726, 727 HSC. 728 GPL/Jane Legate. 729 GPL/Michael Howes. 731 HSC. 733 PHPL. 738 HSC. 745 L GPL/Mel Watson. 746 R HSC. 751 TR PHPL. 753 BL GPL/Neil Holmes. 754 CR GPL/Howard Rice, BR GPL/JS Sira. 756 TC(R) BC(L) GPL/Howard Rice. 757 TR GPL/Brian Carter, C(L) GPL/John Glover, CR PHPL, BC(R) Andrew Lawson, BR GPL/JS Sira. 758 TC(R) GPL/Morley Read. 759 TL HSC. 760 TC(R) GPL/Brigitte Thomas, C Beckett Picture Library. 761 BL GPL/Brigitte Thomas. 762 TL GPL/Jerry Pavia. 763 CL Andrew Lawson, C(R) PHPL. 764 TL PHPL. 765 CL PHPL, CR HSC. 766 TL PHPL, C GPL/John Glover. 768 CR Andrew Lawson, BL HSC. 769 C GPL/Jerry Pavia. 770 C(R) HSC. 772 CL GPL/Neil Holmes C(L) GPL/Howard Rice, BL PHPL, BR HSC. 774 BC(L) HSC. 776 TC(R) GPL/Brian Carter. 778 TR PHPL, C(L) GPL/John Glover, BR PHPL. 779 TC(L) PHPL, TC(R) TR HSC, BC(L) GPL/Michel Viard. 780 TC(L) HSC, TR GPL/John Glover, CL A-Z Botanical Collection/Maurice Nimmo. 781 TC(L) CL HSC, C Clive Nichols, BL GPL/Howard Rice. 782 C(R) HSC, BL PHPL, BC(R) A-Z Botanical Collection/Dan Sams. 783 TC(L) PHPL, TR GPL/Marijke Heuff, C GPL/John Glover, BC(R) GPL/Brian Carter. 784 TL A-Z Botanical Collection/Mike Danson, TC(L) GPL/Joanne Pavia. 785 TR GPL/Chris Burrows, BC(R) PHPL, BR GPL/John Glover. 786 TL GPL/David Russell, CL HSC. 787 TC(R) Clive Nichols, CR(lower) GPL/Chris Burrows, BL GPL/Rex Butcher, BR PHPL. 788 TR PHPL, (*Scaevola*) BC(L) HSC. 789 CR A-Z Botanical Collection. 790 TC(L) CR BL John Glover, C(L) HSC. 792 TL HSC, BL Clive Nichols. 793 TL A-Z Botanical Collection, TR A-Z Botanical Collection/Margaret Higginson, CL(upper) A-Z Botanical Collection/Andy Williams, CL(lower) BL HSC, C(L) Beckett Picture Library, BC(R) PHPL. 794 CL CR Clive Nichols, BL BR John Glover, BC PHPL. 795 TC(L) BC(L) John Glover, (*Iris* 'Natascha') PHPL. 805 (all) Cranfield University Soil Survey and Land Research Centre. 811 T B, 820 TL TC PHPL. 821 TL CL Eric Crichton, CR BR PHPL. 822 TL TC CL C HSC, CR BR Eric Crichton. 840 CL John Glover.

ORIGINATION: Opus Graphics Ltd and Rodney Howe Ltd, London, England
PAPER: Townsend Hook Ltd, Snodland, England
PRINTING: Maury Imprimeur SA, Malesherbes, France
BINDING: Reliures Brun SA, Malesherbes, France

40–499–01